FINANCIAL TIMES

WORLD DESK REFERENCE

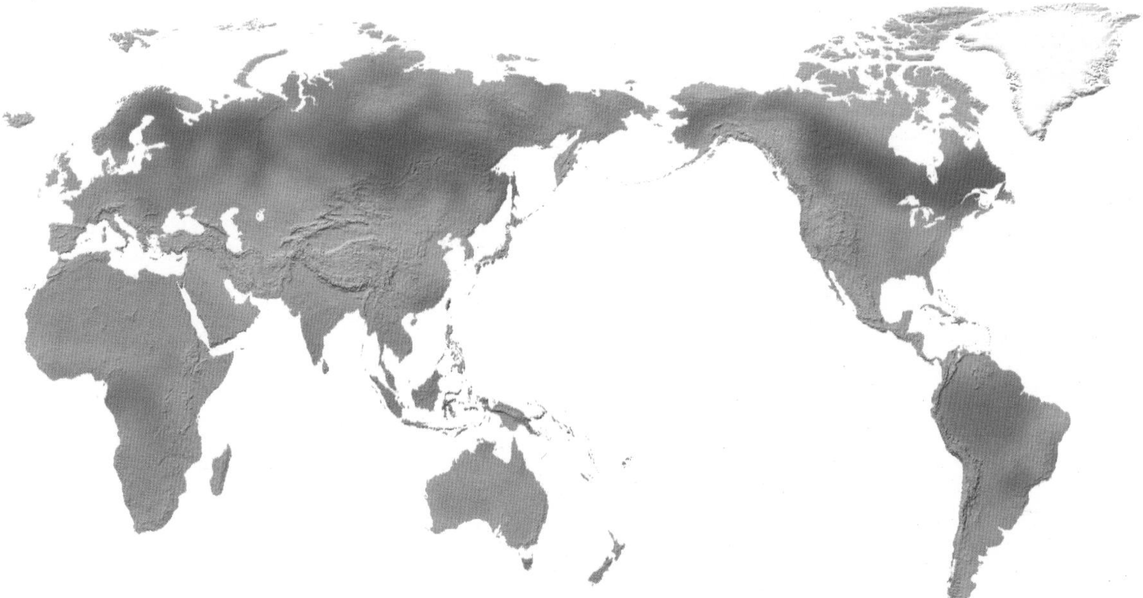

DORLING KINDERSLEY PUBLISHING, INC.
LONDON • NEW YORK • MUNICH • MELBOURNE • DELHI

This book has its own web site. For the very latest update information, visit
www.dk.com/world-desk-reference

A DORLING KINDERSLEY PUBLISHING BOOK
www.dk.com

FOR THE FOURTH EDITION

EDITOR-IN-CHIEF
Andrew Heritage

SENIOR MANAGING ART EDITOR
Philip Lord

SENIOR CARTOGRAPHIC MANAGER
David Roberts

SENIOR CARTOGRAPHIC EDITOR
Simon Mumford

FOURTH EDITION UPDATED AND EDITED BY
Cambridge International Reference on Current Affairs (CIRCA)

PROJECT MANAGER
Catherine Jagger

EDITORIAL SUPERVISION
Roger East

DATABASE AND GRAPHICS
Carolyn Postgate, Elizabeth Postgate, Rosemary Payne

EDITORIAL AND RESEARCH
Philippa Youngman, Farzana Shaikh, Joceline Bury, Lawrence Joffe, Richard Thomas, John Coggins, Harry Drost, Clive Leatherdale

MAP CORRECTIONS
Encompass Graphics, Brighton

PICTURE RESEARCH
Louise Thomas, ilumi

DORLING KINDERSLEY CARTOGRAPHY

EDITORIAL DIRECTION
Andrew Heritage

MANAGING EDITORS
Ian Castello-Cortes, Wim Jenkins

PROJECT EDITORS
Debra Clapson, Catherine Day, Jo Edwards, Jane Oliver

EDITORS
Alastair Dougall, Ailsa Heritage, Nicholas Kynaston, Lisa Thomas, Susan Turner, Chris Whitwell, Elizabeth Wyse

ADDITIONAL EDITORIAL ASSISTANCE
Sam Atkinson, Louise Keane, Zoë Ellinson, Caroline Lucas, Sophie Park, Laura Porter, Jo Russ, Crispian Martin St. Valery, Sally Wood, Ulrike Fritz-Weltz

READERS
Jane Bruton, Reg Grant, Ann Kramer, Lesley Riley

ART DIRECTION
Chez Picthall, Philip Lord

PROJECT DESIGNERS
Martin Biddulph, Scott David, Carol Ann Davis, David Douglas, Yahya El-Droubie, Karen Gregory

DESIGNERS
Tony Cutting, Rhonda Fisher, Nicola Liddiard, Katy Wall

ADDITIONAL DESIGN ASSISTANCE
Paul Bayliss, Carol Ann Davis, Adam Dobney, Kenny Laurenson, Paul Williams

SYSTEMS COORDINATOR
Phil Rowles

PRODUCTION
Michelle Thomas

PROJECT CARTOGRAPHERS
Caroline Bowie, Ruth Duxbury, James Mills-Hicks, John Plumer, Julie Turner

CARTOGRAPHERS
James Anderson, Dale Buckton, Roger Bullen, Tony Chambers, Jan Clark, Tom Coulson, Martin Darlison, Claire Ellam, Julia Lunn, Michael Martin, Alka Ranger, Peter Winfield, Claudine Zante

PICTURE RESEARCH
Alison McKittrick, Sarah Moule, Christine Rista, Louise Thomas

DATABASE MANAGER
Simon Lewis

INDEX GAZETTEER
Margaret Hynes, Julia Lynch, Barbara Nash, Jayne Parsons, Janet Smy

Printed and bound by Graficas Estella, Spain

Published in the United States
by Dorling Kindersley Publishing Inc.
95 Madison Avenue, New York, New York 10016
A Penguin Company

Previously published as the DK World Reference Atlas

First American Edition 1994
10 9 8 7 6 5 4

Second Edition 1996. Revised 1998. Third Edition (revised) 2000. Fourth Edition (revised) 2002.

A catalog record for this book is available from the Library of Congress.

ISBN: 0-7894-8356-4

FOREWORD

THIS DESK REFERENCE is presented to the public in the full knowledge that the world is in a state of continual flux. Political fashions and personalities come and go, while the ebb and flow of peoples and ideas across the face of the planet creates constant shifts in the cultural landscape. All the material assembled for this book has been researched from the most up-to-date and authoritative sources; our team of consultants and contributors, designers, editors, and cartographers have endeavored not only to explain the meaning of this material, to place it in a useful and clear context, but also to present it in a way that has a lasting value and relevance, regardless of the turmoil of daily events. This new edition, bearing the imprimatur of the *Financial Times*, has been completely revised and updated, to reflect the global changes of the past few years. It includes the latest statistical data, and over 60 new photographs.

The publishers would like to thank the many consultants and contributors whose diligence, perseverance, and attention to detail made this book possible.

GENERAL CONSULTANTS

Anthony Goldstone, Senior Editor Asia-Pacific, *The Economist* Intelligence Unit, London
Professor Jack Spence, Director of Studies, The Royal Institute of International Affairs, London

REGIONAL CONSULTANTS

ASIA
Anthony Goldstone, London

AFRICA
James Hammill, Lecturer in African Politics, University of Leicester
Kaye Whiteman, Editor-in-Chief, *West Africa Magazine*, London

RUSSIA AND CIS
Martin McCauley, Senior Lecturer, School of Slavonic and East European Studies, University of London

CENTRAL AND SOUTH AMERICA
Nick Caistor, Producer, Latin American Section, BBC World Service

USA
Michael Elliot, Diplomatic Editor, *Newsweek*, Washington DC

EUROPE
John Ardagh, London
Rory Clarke, Senior Editor Europe, *The Economist* Intelligence Unit, London
Charles Powell, Centre for European Studies, St Antony's College, Oxford

MIDDLE EAST
John Whelan, Ex Editor-in-Chief, *Middle East Economic Digest*

PACIFIC
Jim Boutilier, Professor in History, Royal Roads Military College, Victoria, Canada

CARIBBEAN
Canute James, *Financial Times*, Kingston, Jamaica

CONTRIBUTORS

Janice Bell, School of Slavonic and East European Studies, University of London
Gerry Bourke, Asia Correspondent, *The Guardian*, Islamabad
Vincent Cable, Director, International Economics Programme
P K Clark, MA, Former Chief Map Research Officer, Ministry of Defence
Ken Davies, Senior Editor, *The Economist* Intelligence Unit, London
Roger Dunn, Analyst, Control Risks Group, London
Aidan Foster-Carter, Senior Lecturer in Sociology, University of Leeds
Professor Murray Forsyth, Centre for Federal Studies, University of Leicester
Natasha Franklin, School of Slavonic and East European Studies, London
Adam Hannestad, *Blomberg Business News*, Copenhagen
Peter Holden, *The Economist* Research Department, London
Tim Jones, Knight Ritter, Brussels
Angella Johnstone, Home Affairs Correspondent, *The Guardian*, London
Oliver Keserü, International Chamber of Commerce, Paris
Robert Macdonald, *The Economist* Intelligence Unit
William Mader, Former Europe Bureau Chief, *Time Magazine*, Washington DC
Professor Brian Matthews, Institute of Commonwealth Studies, London
Nick Middleton, Oriel College, Oxford
Professor Mya Maung, Department of Finance, Boston College, Massachusetts
Judith Nordby, Leeds University
Simon Orme, London
Professor Richard Overy, Department of History, King's College, London
Steve Percy, East Asia Service, BBC World Service
Douglas Rimmer, Honorary Senior Research Fellow, Centre for West African Studies, University of Birmingham
Donna Rispoli, Linacre College, Oxford
Ian Rodger, *The Financial Times*, Zürich
The Royal Institute of International Affairs, London
Struan Simpson, St. James Research, London
Julie Smith, Brasenose College, Oxford
Elizabeth Spencer, London
Michiel Van Kuyen, Erasmus University, Rotterdam
Steven Whitefield, Pembroke College, Oxford
Georgina Wilde, Regional Director, Asia-Pacific, *The Economist* Intelligence Unit, London
H P Willmott, Visiting Professor, Dept. of Military Strategy & Operations, The National War College, Washington DC
Andrew Wilson, Sydney Sussex College, Cambridge
Tom Wingfield, *Reuters*, Bangkok
The World Conservation Monitoring Centre, Cambridge
Cambridge International Reference on Current Affairs (CIRCA)

CONTENTS

FOREWORD 3
THE CONTRIBUTORS 3
CONTENTS 4–5
ICON & CHART KEY 6–7
(see also flaps on front and back cover)
DATA SOURCES 8

1
WORLD FACTFILE

THE PHYSICAL WORLD 10–11
THE POLITICAL WORLD 12–13
THE SOLAR SYSTEM 14–15
CLIMATE 16–17
ENVIRONMENT 18–19
NORTH AMERICA 20–21
SOUTH AMERICA 22–23
EUROPE 24–25
AFRICA 26–27
WEST ASIA 28–29
NORTH ASIA 30–31
SOUTH ASIA 32–33
AUSTRALASIA AND OCEANIA 34–35
TIMELINE OF GLOBAL HISTORY 36–39
THE FORMATION OF THE MODERN WORLD 40–41
THE WORLD IN 1492 42–43
THE AGE OF DISCOVERY 1492–1648 44–45
THE AGE OF EXPANSION 1648–1789 46–47
THE AGE OF REVOLUTION 1789–1830 48–49
THE AGE OF EMPIRE 1830–1914 50–51
THE AGE OF GLOBAL WAR 1914–1945 52–53
THE MODERN AGE 1945–1996 54–55
POPULATION 56–57
THE WORLD ECONOMY 58–61
GLOBAL TOURISM 62–63
GLOBAL SECURITY 64–65
TIME ZONES 66–67
WORLD CHRONOLOGY OF 2000–2001 68–69
INTERNATIONAL ORGANIZATIONS 70–73

2
THE NATIONS OF THE WORLD

AFGHANISTAN 76–79
ALBANIA 80–81
ALGERIA 82–85
ANDORRA 86–87
ANGOLA 88–89
ANTARCTICA 90–91
ANTIGUA & BARBUDA 92–93
ARGENTINA 94–97
ARMENIA 98–99
AUSTRALIA 100–105
AUSTRIA 106–109
AZERBAIJAN 110–111

BAHAMAS 112–113
BAHRAIN 114–115
BANGLADESH 116–119
BARBADOS 120–121
BELARUS 122–125
BELGIUM 126–129
BELIZE 130–131
BENIN 132–133
BHUTAN 134–135
BOLIVIA 136–139
BOSNIA & HERZEGOVINA 140–141
BOTSWANA 142–143
BRAZIL 144–149
BRUNEI 150–151
BULGARIA 152–155
BURKINA 156–157
BURMA (MYANMAR) 158–161
BURUNDI 162–163

CAMBODIA 164–167
CAMEROON 168–169
CANADA 170–175
CAPE VERDE 176–177
CENTRAL AFRICAN REPUBLIC 178–179
CHAD 180–181
CHILE 182–185
CHINA 186–193
COLOMBIA 194–197
COMOROS 198–199
CONGO 200–201
CONGO, DEM. REP. (ZAIRE)..... 202–205
COSTA RICA 206–207
CÔTE D'IVOIRE .... see IVORY COAST
CROATIA 208–209
CUBA 210–213
CYPRUS 214–215
CZECH REPUBLIC 216–217

DENMARK 218–221
DJIBOUTI 222–223
DOMINICA 224–225
DOMINICAN REPUBLIC 226–227

EAST TIMOR .... see INDONESIA
ECUADOR 228–229
EGYPT 230–233
EL SALVADOR 234–235
EQUATORIAL GUINEA 236–237
ERITREA 238–239
ESTONIA 240–241
ETHIOPIA 242–245

FIJI 246–247
FINLAND 248–251
FRANCE 252–257

GABON 258–259
GAMBIA 260–261
GEORGIA 262–263
GERMANY 264–269
GHANA 270–271
GREECE 272–275
GRENADA 276–277
GUATEMALA 278–279
GUINEA 280–281
GUINEA-BISSAU 282–283
GUYANA 284–285

HAITI 286–287
HONDURAS 288–289
HUNGARY 290–293

ICELAND 294–295
INDIA 296–301
INDONESIA 302–305
EAST TIMOR 305
IRAN 306–309
IRAQ 310–313
IRELAND, REPUBLIC OF 314–315
ISRAEL 316–319
ITALY 320–325
IVORY COAST (CÔTE D'IVOIRE)........ 326–327

JAMAICA 328–329
JAPAN 330–335
JORDAN 336–337

KAZAKHSTAN 338–341
KENYA 342–345
KIRIBATI 346–347
KOREA, NORTH 348–349
KOREA, SOUTH 350–353
KUWAIT 354–355
KYRGYZSTAN 356–357

LAOS 358–361
LATVIA 362–363
LEBANON 364–365
LESOTHO 366–367
LIBERIA 368–369
LIBYA 370–373
LIECHTENSTEIN 374–375
LITHUANIA 376–377
LUXEMBOURG 378–379

MACEDONIA 380–381
MADAGASCAR 382–383
MALAWI 384–385
MALAYSIA 386–389
MALDIVES 390–391
MALI 392–393
MALTA 394–395
MARSHALL ISLANDS 396–397
MAURITANIA 398–399
MAURITIUS 400–401
MEXICO 402–405
MICRONESIA 406–407
MOLDOVA 408–409
MONACO 410–411
MONGOLIA 412–413
MOROCCO 414–417
MOZAMBIQUE 418–421
MYANMAR see BURMA

NAMIBIA 422–423
NAURU 424–425
NEPAL 426–427
NETHERLANDS 428–431
NEW ZEALAND 432–435
NICARAGUA 436–437
NIGER 438–439
NIGERIA 440–443
NORWAY 444–447

OMAN 448–449

PAKISTAN 450–453
PALAU 454–455
PANAMA 456–457
PAPUA NEW GUINEA 458–459
PARAGUAY 460–461
PERU 462–465
PHILIPPINES 466–469
POLAND 470–473
PORTUGAL 474–477

QATAR 478–479

ROMANIA 480–483
RUSSIAN FEDERATION 484–491
RWANDA 492–493

ST. KITTS & NEVIS 494–495
ST. LUCIA 496–497
ST. VINCENT & THE GRENADINES 498–499
SAMOA 500–501
SAN MARINO 502–503
SÃO TOMÉ & PRÍNCIPE 504–505
SAUDI ARABIA 506–509
SENEGAL 510–511
SERBIA see YUGOSLAVIA
SEYCHELLES 512–513
SIERRA LEONE 514–515
SINGAPORE 516–517
SLOVAKIA 518–519
SLOVENIA 520–521
SOLOMON ISLANDS 522–523
SOMALIA 524–525
SOUTH AFRICA 526–529
SPAIN 530–533
SRI LANKA 534–535
SUDAN 536–537
SURINAME 538–539
SWAZILAND 540–541
SWEDEN 542–545
SWITZERLAND 546–549
SYRIA 550–553

TAIWAN 554–557
TAJIKISTAN 558–559
TANZANIA 560–561
THAILAND 562–565
TOGO 566–567
TONGA 568–569
TRINIDAD & TOBAGO 570–571
TUNISIA 572–575
TURKEY 576–579
TURKMENISTAN 580–581
TUVALU 582–583

UGANDA 584–585
UKRAINE 586–589
UNITED ARAB EMIRATES 590–591
UNITED KINGDOM 592–597
UNITED STATES 598–605
URUGUAY 606–609
UZBEKISTAN 610–613

VANUATU 614–615
VATICAN CITY 616–617
VENEZUELA 618–621
VIETNAM 622–625

YEMEN 626–629
YUGOSLAVIA (SERBIA & MONTENEGRO) 630–633

ZAMBIA 634–635
ZIMBABWE 636–639

OVERSEAS TERRITORIES & DEPENDENCIES

WORLD MAP 640-641
AMERICAN SAMOA, ANGUILLA, ARUBA, BERMUDA, BRITISH INDIAN OCEAN TERRITORY, BRITISH VIRGIN ISLANDS 642-643
CAYMAN ISLANDS, CHRISTMAS ISLAND, COCOS (KEELING) ISLANDS, COOK ISLANDS, FAEROE ISLANDS, FALKLAND ISLANDS, FRENCH GUIANA 644-645
FRENCH POLYNESIA, GIBRALTAR, GREENLAND, GUADELOUPE, GUAM, GUERNSEY, ISLE OF MAN 646-647
JERSEY, JOHNSTON ATOLL, MARTINIQUE, MAYOTTE, MIDWAY ISLANDS, MONTSERRAT, NETHERLANDS ANTILLES 648-649
NEW CALEDONIA, NIUE, NORFOLK ISLAND, NORTHERN MARIANA ISLANDS, PARACEL ISLANDS, PITCAIRN ISLANDS, PUERTO RICO 650-651
REUNION, ST. HELENA & DEPENDENCIES, ST. PIERRE & MIQUELON, SPRATLY ISLANDS, SVALBARD, TOKELAU, TURKS & CAICOS ISLANDS (US), VIRGIN ISLANDS, WAKE ISLAND, WALLIS & FUTUNA 652-653

3
INDEX ~ GAZETTEER

GLOSSARY OF GEOGRAPHICAL TERMS 654–655
GLOSSARY OF ABBREVIATIONS 656
GEOGRAPHICAL PLACE NAMES 657
A–Z INDEX ~ GAZETTEER 659–729
ACKNOWLEDGEMENTS AND PICTURE CREDITS 730

COVER FLAPS
KEY TO SYMBOLS, ICONS, AND ABBREVIATIONS USED IN THE ATLAS

Key to Charts and Icons

Icons and trend indicators vary. Not all variations are shown in the key below, but where they do occur the symbols have been "stacked."

COUNTRY PROFILES

1952 — Date of country's independence, or formation.

1847 — Date when the country's current borders were established.

Aug 2 — National Day

GB — Vehicle country identifying code

+3 — Time zone(s) of country (hours plus or minus from GMT)

+44 — International telephone Dialling Code

.de — Internet country identifying code

CLIMATE

Indication of the climatic types and zones found in each country.

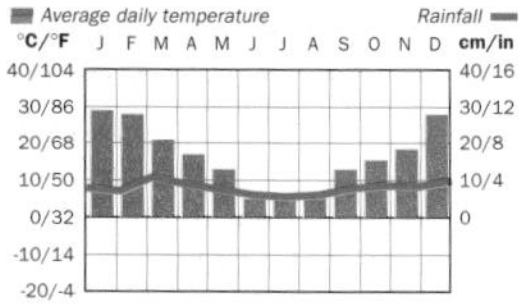

Average daily temperature
Rainfall
°C/°F J F M A M J J A S O N D cm/in
40/104 30/86 20/68 10/50 0/32 -10/14 -20/-4
40/16 30/12 20/8 10/4 0

Statistics are given for the national capital. They represent maximum summer and minimum winter averages.

TRANSPORTATION

Indicates on which side of the road vehicles are driven in each country.

The country's principal international airport with annual passenger numbers.

Total size of national merchant or cargo fleet.

THE TRANSPORTATION NETWORK

National communications infrastructure given in kilometers and miles.

Extent of national paved road network

Extent of expressways, freeways or major highways

Extent of commercial rail network

Extent of inland waterways navigable by commercial craft

TOURISM

The ratio of foreign visitors to population.

Number of visitors per year, including business travelers.

Indicators showing trend in recent visitor numbers (up/level/down).

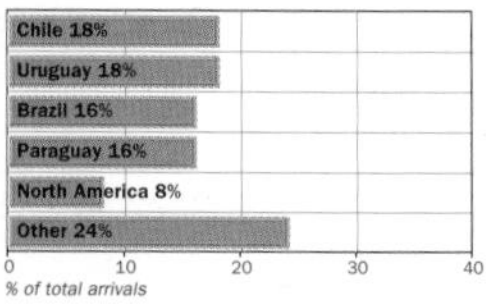

Chile 18%
Uruguay 18%
Brazil 16%
Paraguay 16%
North America 8%
Other 24%
0 10 20 30 40
% of total arrivals

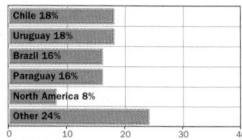

The state of each nation's tourism is explained, with reasons given when there is no significant tourist industry. The chart shows the percentage of total visitors by country of origin.

PEOPLE

An easy indication of the population density in each country (high/medium/low).

Main languages spoken, including official languages.

Population density. This is an average over the whole country.

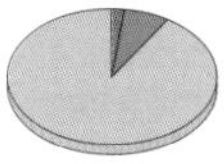

The pie chart proportions show the religious affiliations of those who profess a belief.

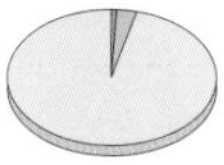

This pie chart illustrates the ethnic origin of the country's population.

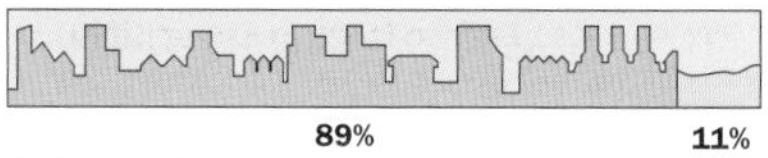

89%
11%

This graph represents the proportion of the population living in urban areas (grey) and rural areas (green).

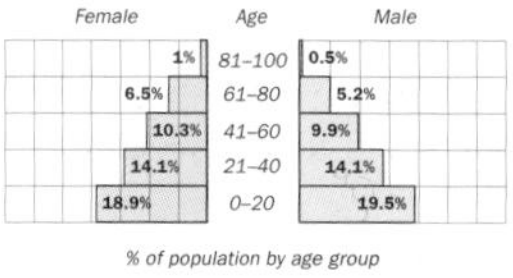

Female
Age
Male
1% 81–100 0.5%
6.5% 61–80 5.2%
10.3% 41–60 9.9%
14.1% 21–40 14.1%
18.9% 0–20 19.5%
% of population by age group

This chart shows the breakdown of the population by age groupings, providing an interesting insight into the country's demography.

POLITICS

Indicates the existence of full multiparty, democratic elections.

Dates of last and next legislative elections for Upper (U.) and Lower (L.) Houses.

Name of head of state. In many cases this is a nominal position and does not indicate that this is the country's most powerful person.

A graphic representation of the political makeup of the country's government, based on each party's showing at the last election. Where there are two houses, the more important elected body is shown first.

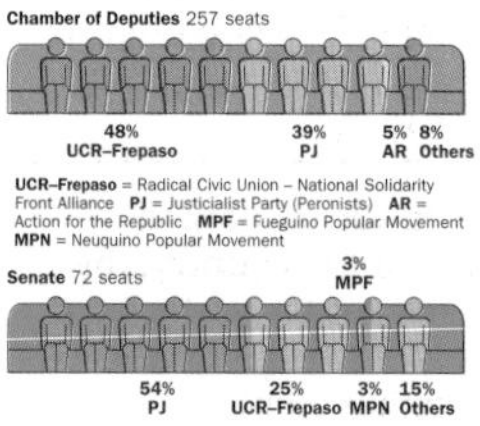

Chamber of Deputies 257 seats
48% UCR–Frepaso
39% PJ
5% AR
8% Others
UCR–Frepaso = Radical Civic Union – National Solidarity Front Alliance PJ = Justicialist Party (Peronists) AR = Action for the Republic MPF = Fueguino Popular Movement MPN = Neuquino Popular Movement
Senate 72 seats
3% MPF
54% PJ
25% UCR–Frepaso
3% MPN
15% Others

WORLD AFFAIRS

Indication of membership of the UN (United Nations), and date of entry.

Comm — Abbreviations indicate membership of international organizations.

Non-membership of additional international organizations.

AID

Indication as to which countries are aid givers (donors), or aid recipients.

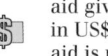

The amount of net international aid given or received is shown in US$. Undisclosed military aid is not included.

Symbols indicate whether aid payments or receipts are rising, level, or declining.

DEFENSE

An indication of the status of conscription and mandatory military service.

The defense budget, the country's annual expenditure (in US$) on arms and military personnel.

Symbols indicate if the trend in defense spending is rising, level, or declining.

THE ARMED FORCES

Icons represent the main branches of the national armed forces.

Army: equipment and personnel

Navy: equipment and personnel

Air force: equipment and personnel

Nuclear capability: armaments

ECONOMICS

An indication of the average rate of inflation per annum, over the past decade.

Gross National Product (GNP) – the total value of goods and services produced by a country.

Exchange rates against the US$ at the start and end of the last year.

❑ World GNP Ranking	24th
❑ GNP per Capita	$24,388
❑ Balance of Payments	$2.2bn
❑ Inflation	5.6%
❑ Unemployment	10.6%

The score cards are intended to give a broad picture of the country's economy. Gross National Product (GNP), unlike GDP, includes income from investments and businesses held abroad. Balance of payments is the difference between a country's payments to and receipts from abroad.

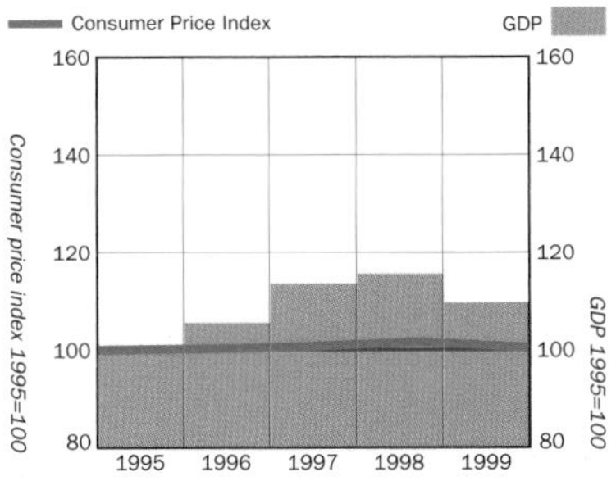

Consumer Price Index
GDP
Consumer price index 1995=100
GDP 1995=100
160
140
120
100
80
1995
1996
1997
1998
1999

This graph shows year-on-year variations in GDP and consumer prices.

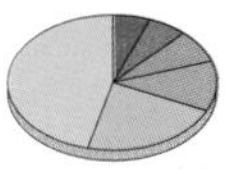

This pie chart gives a broad picture of the country's principal import trading partners.

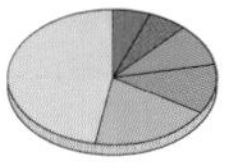

This pie chart gives a broad picture of the country's principal export trading partners.

RESOURCES

▷ Indicates the capacity of the combined national electricity generating sources (in kilowatts).

Oil produced in barrels per day (b/d). Refining capacity, oil reserves, and other fossil fuels are given where applicable.

Estimated livestock resources.

Main mineral reserves are listed in descending order of economic importance.

Fish catch per year (where fishing is a major industry).

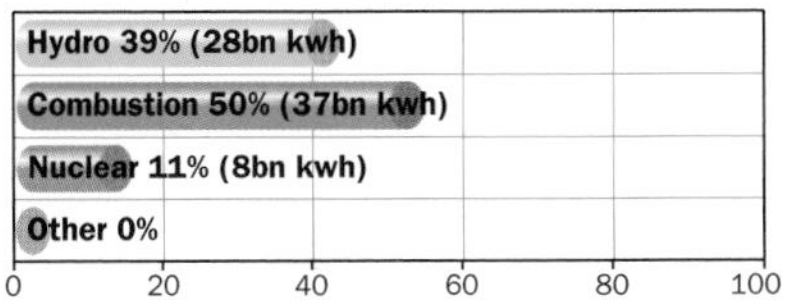

Hydro 39% (28bn kwh)
Combustion 50% (37bn kwh)
Nuclear 11% (8bn kwh)
Other 0%
0
20
40
60
80
100

% of total generation by type

Percentages of the different energy sources used for the generation of electricity are represented graphically ("Combustion" indicates the burning of fossil fuels, wood etc.). An account of the country's resource base is given in the text.

ENVIRONMENT

▷ The 2001 Index of progress toward environmental sustainability, based on 22 core indicators. Compiled by the World Economic Forum taskforce.

Percentage of land which is protected or conserved by law. Protection is often only theoretical.

Trend in total CO_2 emissions since 1990 (up/level/down) and current emissions per capita.

ENVIRONMENTAL TREATIES

National parties to international environmental treaties.

Ramsar: (wetlands)

Montreal Protocol: (CFC emissions)

CITES: (endangered species)

CBD: (biological diversity)

Basel: (hazardous wastes)

Kyoto: (greenhouse gases)

MEDIA

▷ Indicates the average rates of television ownership across the country.

Media free to express critical views.

Partial controls or constraints on media freedom.

Severe restrictions on media freedom.

PUBLISHING AND BROADCAST MEDIA

National broadcast and print media, by size and ownership.

Main national newspapers

Television stations: state-owned/independent

Radio: state-owned/ independent

CRIME

▷ An indication of the status of capital punishment and the death penalty; either used, or not used.

Prison population statistics

Symbols show general trend in crime figures.

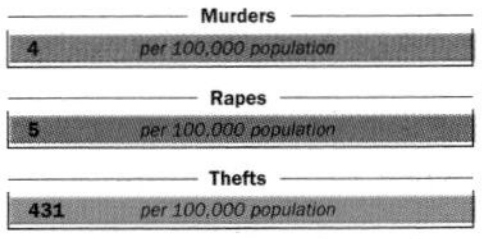

Murders
4
per 100,000 population
Rapes
5
per 100,000 population
Thefts
431
per 100,000 population

This section records official crime figures only. Reported statistics are normally lower than the actual figures.

CHRONOLOGY

Beginning at a significant date in the recent history of the country, the outline chronology continues through to the present day, and highlights key dates and turning points.

EDUCATION

▷ Displays the age until which children are legally required to attend school.

Literacy rate. UNESCO defines as literate anyone who can read and write a short statement.

The number of students in all forms of tertiary education within that country.

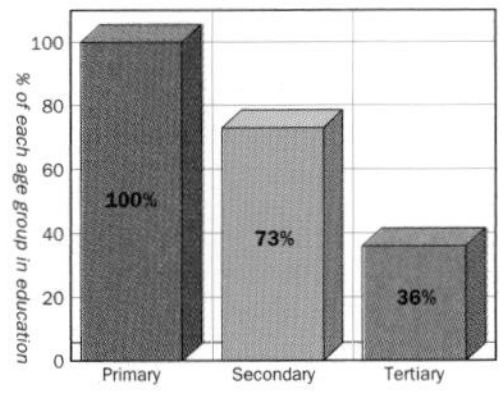

% of each age group in education
100
80
60
40
20
0
100%
73%
36%
Primary
Secondary
Tertiary

This graph shows the percentages of each age group in education. Primary is up to age 11; secondary is age 11–16/18; tertiary is expressed as a percentage of 20–24-year-olds.

HEALTH

▷ An indication of the existence of health services and benefits provided by the state.

Ratio of the number of people per doctor is given as a national average.

Major causes of death are listed.

SPENDING

▷ Indicates the trend in GDP per capita over the previous decade – either showing an increase, or decrease.

Levels of car ownership (per 1000 head of population)

Rates of telephone connectivity (per 1000 head of population)

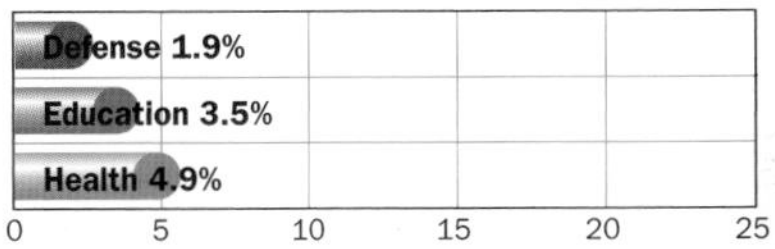

Defense 1.9%
Education 3.5%
Health 4.9%
0
5
10
15
20
25

Defense, Health, Education spending as % of GDP

Percentage of the country's GDP that is spent on defense, education, and health.

WORLD RANKING

Schooling, educational attainment, and human development rankings are based on the UN Human Development Index (which covers 161 countries and Hong Kong).

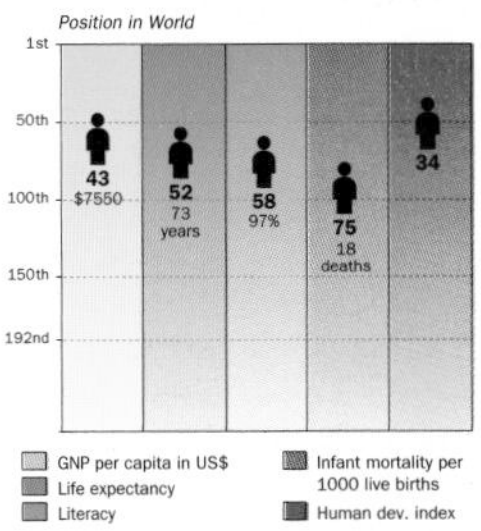

Position in World
1st
50th
100th
150th
192nd
43
$7550
52
73 years
58
97%
75
18 deaths
34
GNP per capita in US$
Life expectancy
Literacy
Infant mortality per 1000 live births
Human dev. index

Sources of Statistical Data Used in This Book

Airports Council International

Amnesty International

Automobile Association (AA)

British Petroleum:
World Energy Data

Cambridge International Reference on Current Affairs (CIRCA)

Commonwealth Secretariat:
Small States Economic Review and Basic Statistics

Convention on International Trade in Endangered Species (CITES)

Dorling Kindersley

Europa World Yearbook

European Bank for Reconstruction and Development (EBRD)

Financial Times

Fischer Weltalmanach

Food and Agriculture Organization (FAO)

International Atomic Energy Agency (IAEA)

International Institute for Strategic Studies (IISS):
The Military Balance

International Labor Organization (ILO):
World Labor Report

International Monetary Fund (IMF):
Balance of Payments Statistics Yearbook,
Direction of Trade Statistics Yearbook,
Government Financial Statistics Yearbook,
International Financial Statistics,
World Economic Outlook

International Road Federation

International Union for Conservation of Nature (IUCN)

International Union of Railways

INTERPOL International Crime Statistics

Lloyd's Register of Shipping

Organization for Economic Cooperation Development (OECD):
Economic surveys

OECD Development Assistance Committee (DAC):
Development Cooperation

Organization of Petroleum Exporting Countries (OPEC)

Royal Automobile Club (RAC)

United Nations Demographic Yearbook

United Nations Energy Statistics Yearbook

United Nations Industrial Commodity Statistics Yearbook

United Nations International Trade Statistics Yearbook

United Nations Statistical Yearbook

United Nations Statistical Yearbook of Asia and the Pacific

United Nations Children's Fund (UNICEF)

United Nations Development Program (UNDP):
Human Development Report

United Nations Educational, Scientific, and Cultural Organization (UNESCO): Statistical Yearbook

United Nations Environment Program (UNEP)

United Nations Framework Convention on Climate Change

United Nations Population Fund (UNFPA):
The State of World Population

United States Central Intelligence Agency (CIA)

World Bank: World Development Indicators,
World Development Report, World Bank Atlas

World Conservation Monitoring Center (WCMC):
Biodiversity Data Sourcebook

World Economic Forum

World Health Organization (WHO)

World Tourist Organization (WTO)

Worldwide Fund for Nature (WWF)

1

WORLD FACTFILE

The Physical World

THE EARTH'S SURFACE IS constantly being transformed: it is uplifted, folded, and faulted by tectonic forces; weathered and eroded by wind, water, and ice. Sometimes change is dramatic, the spectacular results of earthquakes or floods. More often it is a slow process lasting millions of years. A physical map of the world represents a snapshot of the ever-evolving architecture of the Earth. This terrain map shows the whole surface of the Earth, both above and below the sea. The size of the Earth can be measured in different ways. When taken from the Equator, the diameter of the Earth measures 12,756 km (7927 miles); when taken from pole to pole, the diameter measures 12,714 km (7900 miles). Two-thirds of the Earth's surface is covered by oceans. The landscape of the ocean floor, like the surface of the land, has been shaped by movements of the Earth's crust over millions of years to form volcanic mountain ranges, deep trenches, basins, and plateaux. Ocean currents constantly redistribute warm and cold water around the world. The largest ocean in the world is the Pacific, which covers an area of over 181 million square km (70 million square miles).

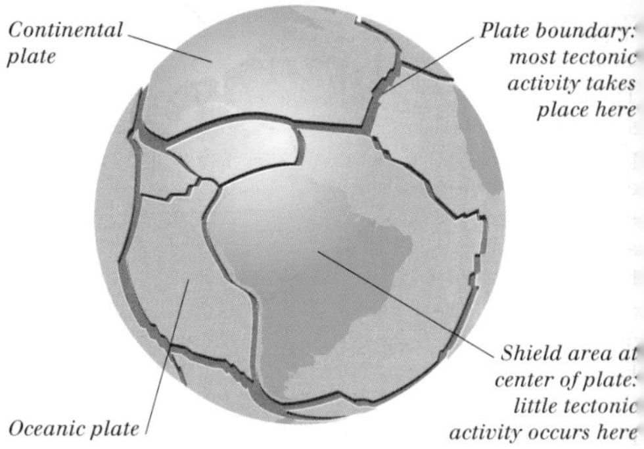

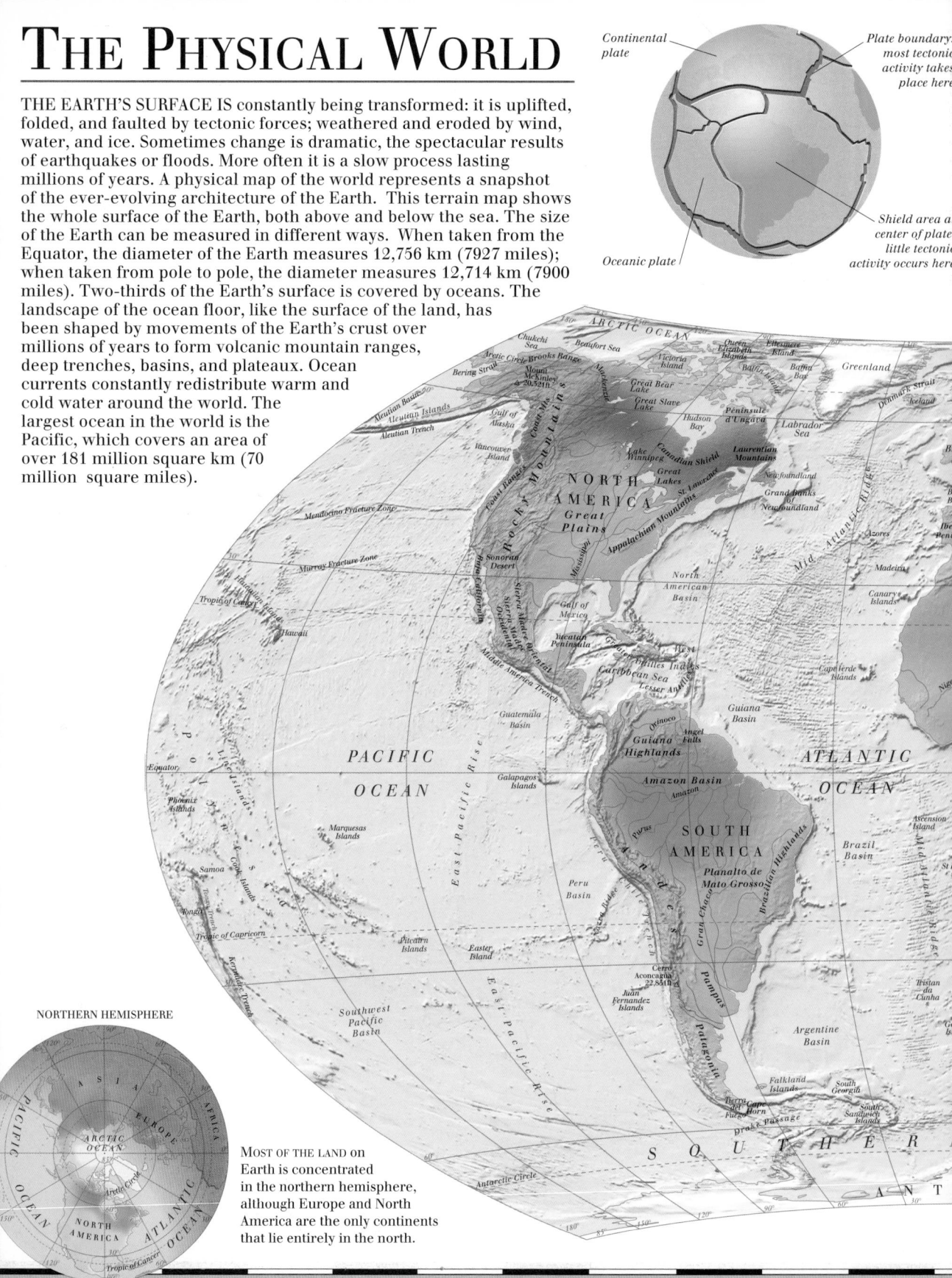

Continental plate
Plate boundary: most tectonic activity takes place here
Shield area at center of plate: little tectonic activity occurs here
Oceanic plate

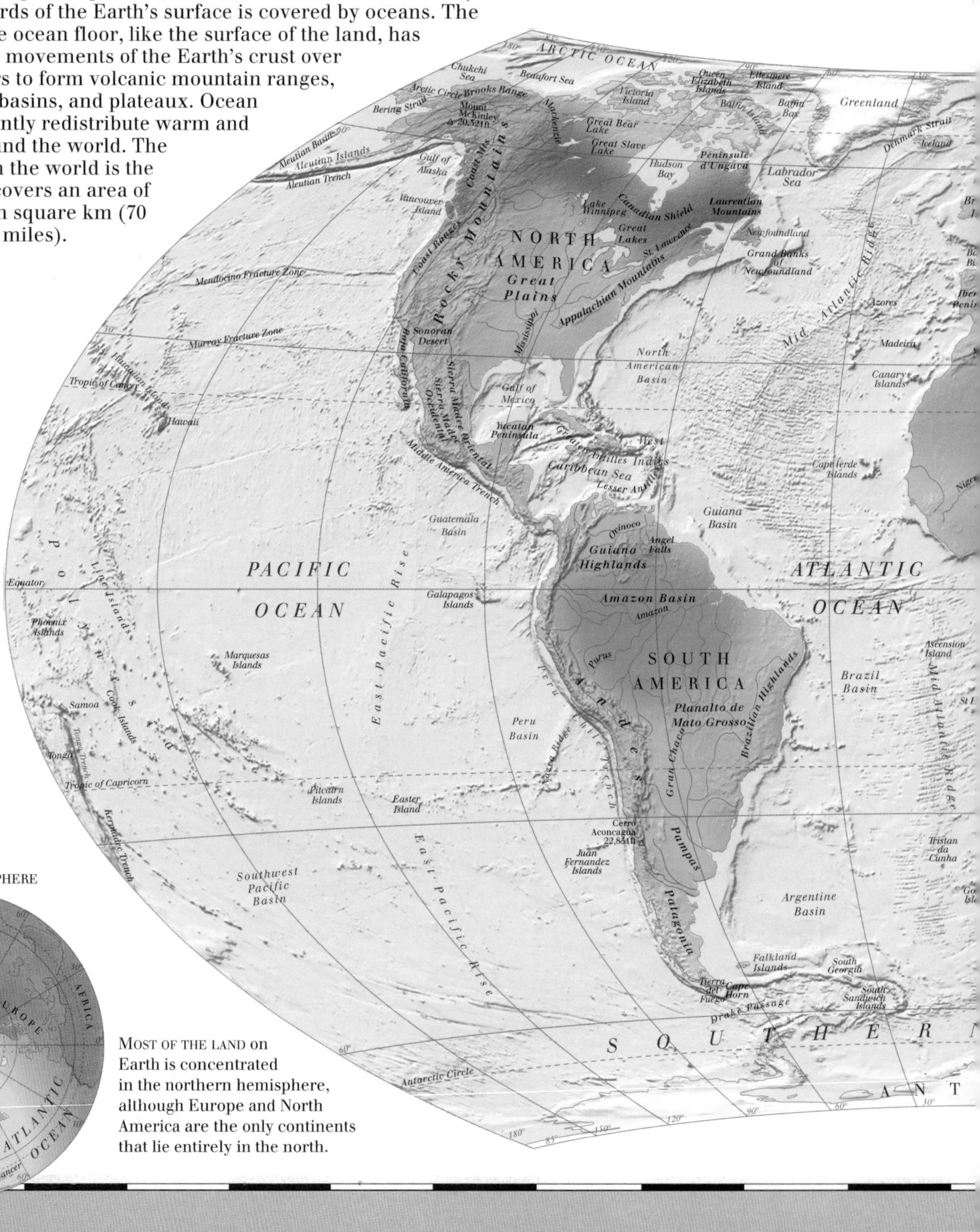

ARCTIC OCEAN
Chukchi Sea
Beaufort Sea
Arctic Circle
Brooks Range
Bering Strait
Mount McKinley 20,321ft
Victoria Island
Queen Elizabeth Islands
Ellesmere Island
Baffin Island
Baffin Bay
Greenland
Great Bear Lake
Great Slave Lake
Mackenzie
Aleutian Basin
Aleutian Islands
Aleutian Trench
Gulf of Alaska
Coast Mts
Hudson Bay
Peninsule d'Ungava
Labrador Sea
Denmark Strait
Iceland
Vancouver Island
Lake Winnipeg
Canadian Shield
Laurentian Mountains
Great Lakes
St. Lawrence
Newfoundland
Grand Banks of Newfoundland
Coast Ranges
Rocky Mountains
NORTH AMERICA
Great Plains
Appalachian Mountains
Mendocino Fracture Zone
Azores
Mid-Atlantic Ridge
Murray Fracture Zone
Sonoran Desert
Baja California
Mississippi
Madeira
North American Basin
Canary Islands
Tropic of Cancer
Hawaiian Islands
Hawaii
Sierra Madre Occidental
Sierra Madre Oriental
Gulf of Mexico
Yucatan Peninsula
Greater Antilles
West Indies
Caribbean Sea
Lesser Antilles
Middle America Trench
Cape Verde Islands
Guatemala Basin
Orinoco
Angel Falls
Guiana Basin
Guiana Highlands
PACIFIC OCEAN
ATLANTIC OCEAN
Equator
Line Islands
Galapagos Islands
Amazon Basin
Amazon
Phoenix Islands
Polynesia
Marquesas Islands
East Pacific Rise
Purus
SOUTH AMERICA
Ascension Island
Samoa
Cook Islands
Peru
Peru Basin
Planalto de Mato Grosso
Brazilian Highlands
Brazil Basin
Tonga
Tonga Trench
Nazca Ridge
Peru-Chile Trench
Andes
Gran Chaco
Tropic of Capricorn
Pitcairn Islands
Easter Island
Cerro Aconcagua 22,831ft
Juan Fernandez Islands
Pampas
Tristan da Cunha
Kermadec Trench
Southwest Pacific Basin
Patagonia
Argentine Basin
Falkland Islands
South Georgia
Tierra del Fuego
Cape Horn
Drake Passage
South Sandwich Islands
SOUTHERN
Antarctic Circle
ANT

NORTHERN HEMISPHERE

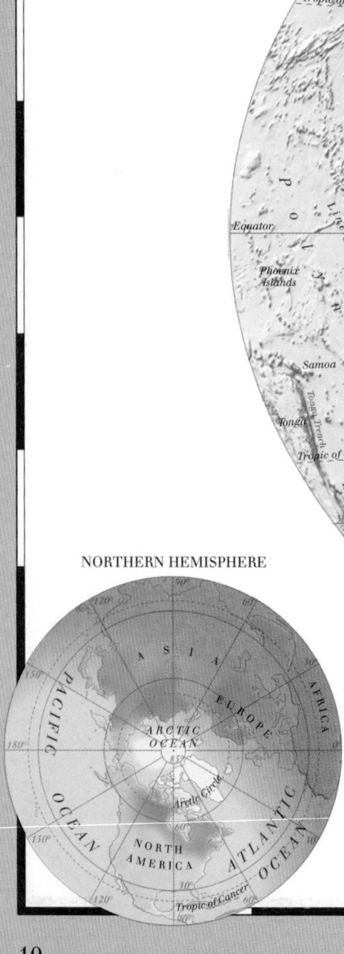

ASIA
EUROPE
AFRICA
PACIFIC OCEAN
ARCTIC OCEAN
Arctic Circle
NORTH AMERICA
ATLANTIC OCEAN
Tropic of Cancer

MOST OF THE LAND on Earth is concentrated in the northern hemisphere, although Europe and North America are the only continents that lie entirely in the north.

THE DYNAMIC EARTH

THE EARTH'S CRUST is made up of eight major (and several minor) rigid continental and oceanic tectonic plates, which constantly move relative to one another. It is this movement which causes volcanic eruptions, earthquakes, and sometimes tsunamis along the plate boundaries. The largest volcanoes formed by this process are Aconcagua in Argentina at 6959 m (22,831 ft) and Kilimanjaro in Tanzania at 5895 m (19,340 ft), both of which are now extinct. Plate tectonics are responsible for the formation of the Himalayas – which were created by two colliding plates – and the Hawaiian Islands, created by the Pacific plate's movement over a "hot spot" of magma.

GEOGRAPHICAL REGIONS

- ice
- tundra
- needleleaf forest
- broadleaf forest
- cultivated land
- hot desert
- cold desert
- tropical grassland
- tropical rainforest
- mountain
- submarine regions

PHYSICAL WORLD FACTFILE

HIGHEST MOUNTAINS

1 **Everest**	8848 m	(29,028 ft)
2 **K2**	8611 m	(28,251 ft)
3 **Kangchenjunga I**	8590 m	(28,169 ft)
4 **Makalu I**	8463 m	(27,766 ft)
5 **Cho Oyu**	8201 m	(26,906 ft)

LONGEST RIVERS

1 **Nile**	6695 km	(4160 mi)
2 **Amazon**	6516 km	(4048 mi)
3 **Yangtze**	6380 km	(3964 mi)
4 **Mississippi /Missouri**	6019 km	(3740 mi)
5 **Ob'-Irtysh**	5570 km	(3461 mi)

LARGEST DESERTS

1 **Sahara**	9,065,000 km²	(3,263,400 mi²)
2 **Australian**	3,750,000 km²	(1,350,000 mi²)
3 **Gobi**	1,295,000 km²	(466,200 mi²)
4 **Arabian**	750,000 km²	(270,000 mi²)
5 **Sonoran**	311,000 km²	(111,960 mi²)

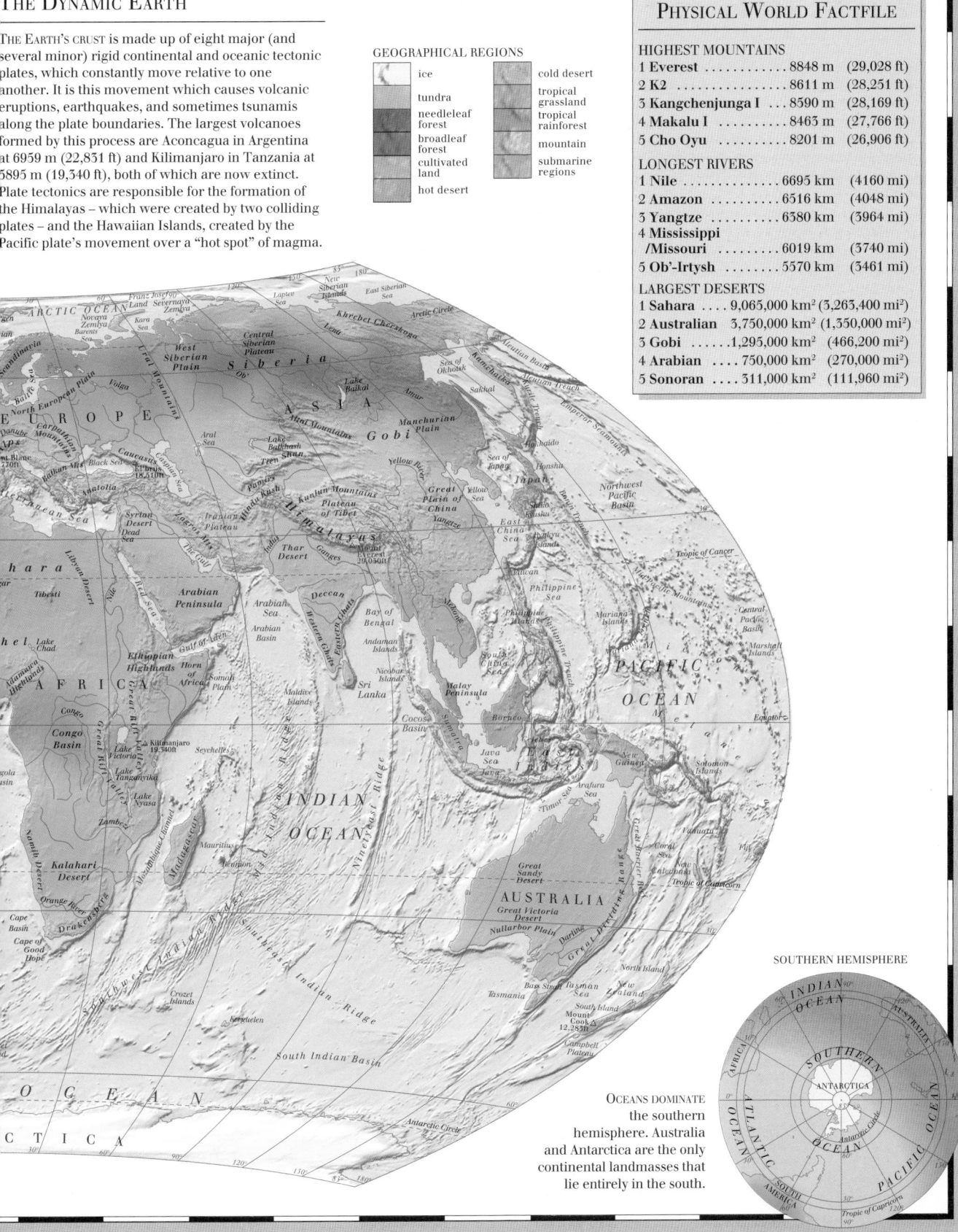

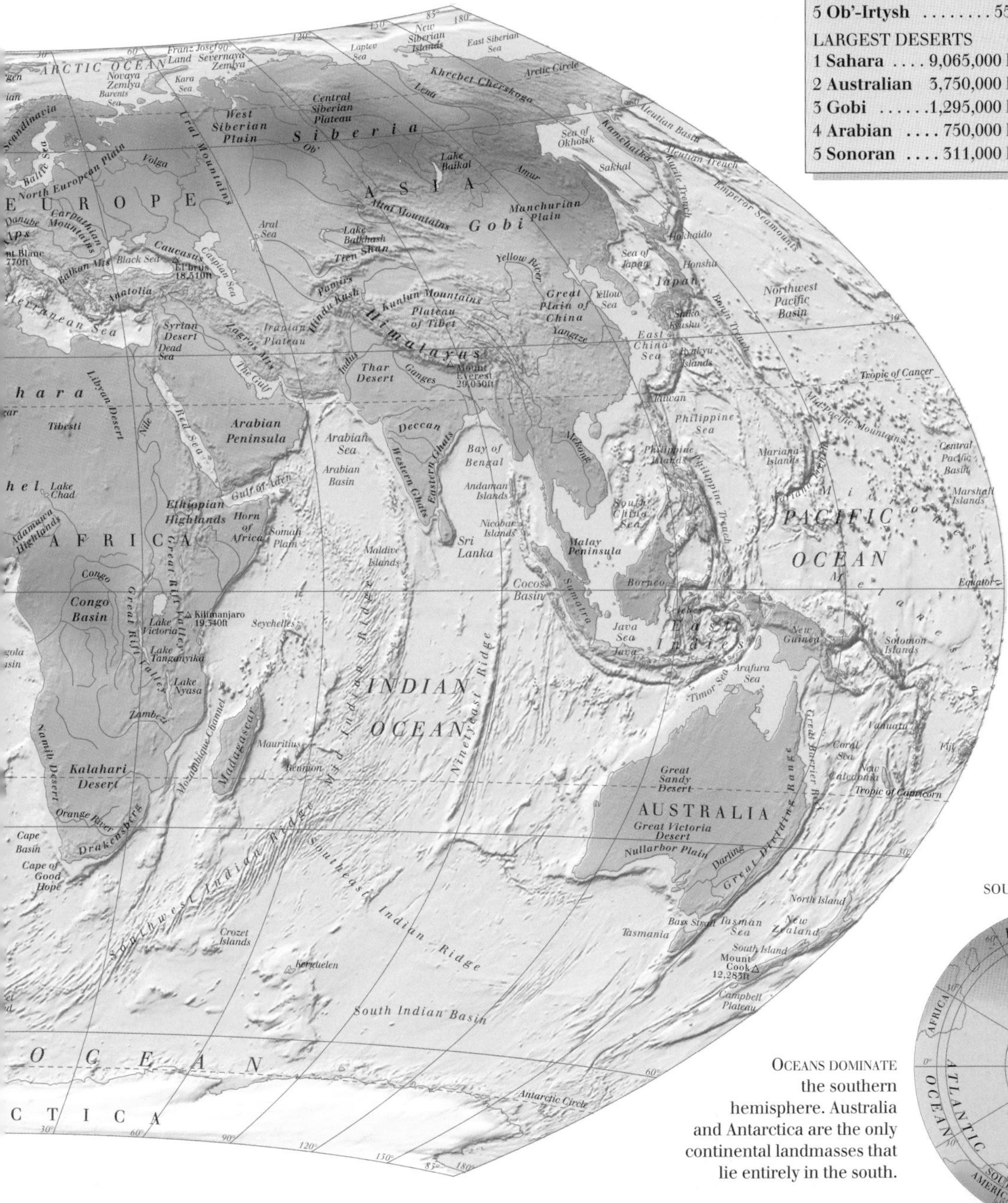
ARCTIC OCEAN
Novaya Zemlya
Barents Sea
Kara Sea
Laptev Sea
New Siberian Islands
East Siberian Sea
Arctic Circle
Khrebet Cherskogo
Lena
Central Siberian Plateau
West Siberian Plain
Siberia
Ural Mountains
Sea of Okhotsk
Kamchatka
Aleutian Basin
Aleutian Trench
Sakhal
Lake Baikal
Amur
ASIA
EUROPE
North European Plain
Volga
Baltic
Scandinavia
Altai Mountains
Gobi
Manchurian Plain
Emperor Seamounts
Aral Sea
Lake Balkhash
Tien Shan
Caucasus
Caspian Sea
Black Sea
Elbrus 18,510ft
Carpathian Mountains
Danube
Balkan Mts
Anatolia
Mediterranean Sea
Yellow River
Sea of Japan
Hokkaido
Honshu
Japan
Northwest Pacific Basin
Pamirs
Hindu Kush
Kunlun Mountains
Plateau of Tibet
Himalayas
Great Plain of China
Yellow Sea
Yangtze
Shiko
Kyushu
East China Sea
Ryukyu Islands
Syrian Desert
Dead Sea
Iranian Plateau
Zagros Mts
The Gulf
Indus
Thar Desert
Ganges
Mount Everest 29,030ft
Tropic of Cancer
Sahara
Libyan Desert
Tibesti
Nile
Red Sea
Arabian Peninsula
Arabian Sea
Arabian Basin
Deccan
Western Ghats
Eastern Ghats
Bay of Bengal
Mekong
Taiwan
Philippine Sea
Philippine Islands
Philippine Trench
Mariana Islands
Mariana Trench
Central Pacific Basin
Marshall Islands
Lake Chad
Gulf of Aden
Ethiopian Highlands
Horn of Africa
Somali Plain
Andaman Islands
Nicobar Islands
Sri Lanka
Maldive Islands
Malay Peninsula
South China Sea
PACIFIC OCEAN
AFRICA
Great Rift Valley
Congo
Congo Basin
Kilimanjaro 19,340ft
Lake Victoria
Lake Tanganyika
Lake Nyasa
Seychelles
Cocos Basin
Sumatra
Borneo
Java Sea
Java
East Indies
New Guinea
Solomon Islands
Equator
Arafura Sea
Timor Sea
INDIAN OCEAN
Ninetyeast Ridge
Zambezi
Mozambique Channel
Madagascar
Mauritius
Réunion
Namib Desert
Kalahari Desert
Orange River
Drakensberg
Cape Basin
Cape of Good Hope
Vanuatu
Fiji
Coral Sea
New Caledonia
Tropic of Capricorn
Great Barrier Reef
Great Sandy Desert
AUSTRALIA
Great Victoria Desert
Nullarbor Plain
Darling
Great Dividing Range
Southwest Indian Ridge
Southeast Indian Ridge
Crozet Islands
Kerguelen
North Island
New Zealand
Bass Strait
Tasmania
Tasman Sea
South Island
Mount Cook 12,283ft
Campbell Plateau
South Indian Basin
OCEAN
Antarctic Circle
ANTARCTICA

SOUTHERN HEMISPHERE

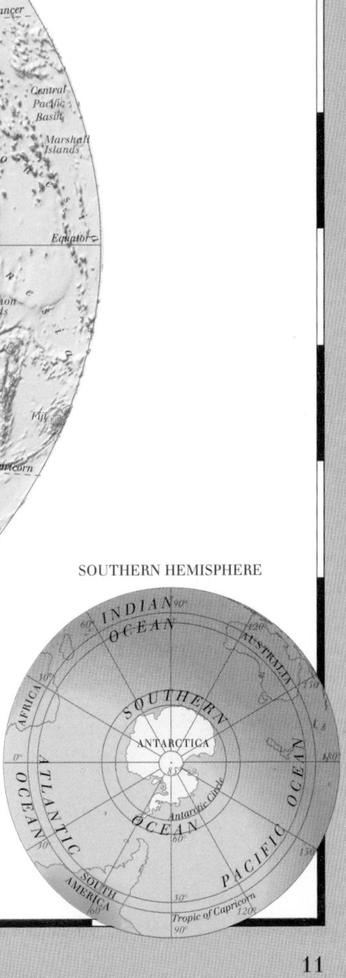
INDIAN OCEAN
AUSTRALIA
AFRICA
SOUTHERN OCEAN
ANTARCTICA
Antarctic Circle
ATLANTIC OCEAN
PACIFIC OCEAN
SOUTH AMERICA
Tropic of Capricorn

OCEANS DOMINATE the southern hemisphere. Australia and Antarctica are the only continental landmasses that lie entirely in the south.

THE POLITICAL WORLD

THERE WERE 192 INDEPENDENT COUNTRIES in the world at the beginning of the 21st century, with East Timor on the way to becoming the 193rd. In 1950 there were only 82. With the exception of Antarctica, where territorial claims have been deferred by international treaty, every land area of the Earth's surface either belongs to, or is claimed by, one country or another. Some 60 overseas dependent territories remain, administered variously by France, Australia, Denmark, New Zealand, Norway, the UK, the USA, and the Netherlands. Over the last half-century, national self-determination has been a driving force for many states with a history of colonialism and oppression. In many cases, where the impetus toward independence has been religious or ethnic in origin, disputes with minority groups have also caused violent internal conflict. Many newly formed states have moved peacefully toward independence, successfully establishing democracy. Dictatorship by military regime or individual despot is often the result of the internal power struggles which characterize the early stages in the lives of new nations.

ARCTIC OCEAN
Alaska (part of US)
Bering Sea
Aleutian Is (part of US)
CANADA
Hudson Bay
Baffin Bay
Greenland (to Denmark)
ICELAND
Faeroe Islands (to Denmark)
REPUBLIC OF IRELAND
Isle of Man (to UK)
Channel Islands (to UK)
St Pierre & Miquelon (to France)
UNITED STATES OF AMERICA
PACIFIC OCEAN
Midway Islands (to US)
Tropic of Cancer
Hawaii (part of US)
Johnston Atoll (to US)
Guadalupe (part of Mexico)
Revillagigedo Islands (part of Mexico)
MEXICO
Gulf of Mexico
Bermuda (to UK)
ATLANTIC OCEAN
Azores (part of Portugal)
PORTUGAL
Gibraltar (to UK)
Ceuta (part of Spain)
Melilla (part of Spain)
Madeira (part of Portugal)
Canary Islands (part of Spain)
WESTERN SAHARA (disputed)
BAHAMAS
Turks & Caicos Is (to UK)
Puerto Rico (to US)
Virgin Is (to US)
British Virgin Is (to UK)
Anguilla (to UK)
ANTIGUA & BARBUDA
ST KITTS & NEVIS
Guadeloupe (to France)
DOMINICA
Martinique (to France)
ST LUCIA
ST VINCENT & THE GRENADINES
BARBADOS
GRENADA
TRINIDAD & TOBAGO
CUBA
Cayman Is (to UK)
JAMAICA
HAITI
DOM. REP.
BELIZE
Navassa I. (to US)
Montserrat (to UK)
GUATEMALA
HONDURAS
Caribbean Sea
Netherlands Antilles (to Neth.)
Aruba (to Neth.)
EL SALVADOR
NICARAGUA
COSTA RICA
PANAMA
Clipperton Island (to French Polynesia)
CAPE VERDE
SENEGAL
GAMBIA
GUINEA-BISSAU
GUINEA
SIERRA LEONE
LIBERIA
VENEZUELA
GUYANA
SURINAME
French Guiana (to France)
COLOMBIA
ECUADOR
Galapagos Is (part of Ecuador)
Kingman Reef (to US)
Palmyra Atoll (to US)
Baker & Howland Is (to US)
Jarvis I (to US)
Equator
KIRIBATI
Tokelau (to NZ)
SAMOA
Wallis & Futuna (to France)
American Samoa (to US)
Cook Islands (to NZ)
TONGA
Niue (to NZ)
French Polynesia (to France)
Tropic of Capricorn
Pitcairn Islands (to UK)
PERU
BRAZIL
Fernando de Noronha (part of Brazil)
Ascension (to St Helena)
BOLIVIA
Lake Titicaca
PARAGUAY
Trindade (part of Brazil)
CHILE
ARGENTINA
URUGUAY
Easter Island (part of Chile)
Sala y Gomez (part of Chile)
San Felix Island (part of Chile)
San Ambrosio Island (part of Chile)
Juan Fernandez Islands (part of Chile)
Kermadec Islands (part of NZ)
Tristan da Cunha (to St Helena)
Chatham Islands (part of NZ)
Falkland Islands (to UK)
South Georgia & South Sandwich Islands (to UK)
South Shetland Islands
South Orkney Islands
SOUTHE
Peter I Island (to Norway)
Antarctic Circle
Arctic Circle

OLDEST COUNTRIES

San Marino
301 CE

France
486 CE

Thailand
1238 CE

Denmark
950 CE

Andorra
1278 CE

KEY

———	Full borders
....	Disputed borders
- - - - - -	Undefined borders
— — — —	Extent of dependent island territories
—— —— ——	Extent of country boundaries for island territories
Tristan da Cunha (to St Helena)	Dependent territory with self-government
Gough Island (part of Tristan da Cunha)	Territory without self-government (the state it belongs to is given in brackets)

INTERNATIONAL BORDERS

THERE ARE THREE main types of boundary between states. Full borders represent internationally recognized territorial boundaries. Undefined borders exist where no fixed boundary has been demarcated. A disputed border is where a *de facto* territorial boundary exists, which is not agreed upon or is subject to arbitration. Disputed borders exist throughout the world, including the borders between India and Pakistan, between the UK and Ireland, and within Israel.

COUNTRIES WITH THE MOST LAND BORDERS

1 **China** *14*: (Afghanistan, Bhutan, Burma, India, Kazakhstan, Kyrgyzstan, Laos, Mongolia, Nepal, North Korea, Pakistan, Russian Federation, Tajikistan, Vietnam)

Russian Federation *14*: (Azerbaijan, Belarus, China, Estonia, Finland, Georgia, Kazakhstan, Latvia, Lithuania, Mongolia, North Korea, Norway, Poland, Ukraine)

2 **Brazil** *10*: (Argentina, Bolivia, Colombia, French Guiana, Guyana, Paraguay, Peru, Suriname, Uruguay, Venezuela)

ARCTIC OCEAN
Barents Sea
Arctic Circle
RUSSIAN FEDERATION
NORWAY
SWEDEN
FINLAND
EST.
LAT.
LITH.
RUSS. FED.
POLAND
BELARUS
GERMANY
LUX
CZECH REP.
SLOVAK
UKRAINE
MOLDOVA
AUSTRIA
HUNGARY
ROMANIA
CROATIA
B-H
BULGARIA
Black Sea
GEORGIA
ARMENIA
MACEDONIA
ALBANIA
GREECE
TURKEY
AZERBAIJAN
VATICAN CITY
TUNISIA
MALTA
Mediterranean Sea
CYPRUS
LEBANON
ISRAEL
SYRIA
IRAQ
JORDAN
IRAN
KUWAIT
BAHRAIN
QATAR
UAE
The Gulf
SAUDI ARABIA
OMAN
YEMEN
Red Sea
LIBYA
EGYPT
NIGER
CHAD
SUDAN
ERITREA
DJIBOUTI
NIGERIA
ETHIOPIA
SOMALIA
CENTRAL AFRICAN REPUBLIC
CAMEROON
GABON
CONGO
DEM. REP. CONGO (ZAIRE)
UGANDA
KENYA
RWANDA
BURUNDI
TANZANIA
Cabinda
SEYCHELLES
ANGOLA
ZAMBIA
MALAWI
MOZAMBIQUE
COMOROS
Mayotte (to France)
MADAGASCAR
NAMIBIA
BOTSWANA
ZIMBABWE
SWAZILAND
LESOTHO
SOUTH AFRICA
Réunion (to France)
MAURITIUS
Tromelin (part of Réunion)
Rodrigues (part of Mauritius)
Agalega Islands (part of
KAZAKHSTAN
Caspian Sea
Aral Sea
Lake Balkhash
UZBEKISTAN
TURKMENISTAN
KYRGYZSTAN
TAJIKISTAN
AFGHANISTAN
PAKISTAN
MONGOLIA
Lake Baikal
CHINA
NEPAL
BHUTAN
BANGLADESH
INDIA
Arabian Sea
Socotra (part of Yemen)
Laccadive Is (part of India)
MALDIVES
SRI LANKA
Bay of Bengal
Andaman Is (part of India)
Nicobar Is (part of India)
BURMA (MYANMAR)
LAOS
THAILAND
VIETNAM
CAMBODIA
British Indian Ocean Territory (to UK)
INDIAN OCEAN
Cocos (Keeling) Islands (to Australia)
Christmas Island (to Australia)
Sea of Okhotsk
Kurile Is (part of Russian Fed.)
Aleutian Is. (part of US)
NORTH KOREA
SOUTH KOREA
Sea of Japan
JAPAN
PACIFIC OCEAN
Ryukyu Is (part of Japan)
Tropic of Cancer
TAIWAN
Paracel Is (disputed)
South China Sea
Spratly Is (disputed)
PHILIPPINES
BRUNEI
MALAYSIA
SINGAPORE
INDONESIA
Java Sea
EAST TIMOR (under UN transitional authority from Feb 2000)
Ashmore & Cartier Islands (to Australia)
Northern Mariana Is (to US)
Wake Island (to US)
Guam (to US)
MARSHALL ISLANDS
PALAU
MICRONESIA
Equator
NAURU
KIRIBATI
PAPUA NEW GUINEA
SOLOMON ISLANDS
TUVALU
Coral Sea Islands (to Australia)
VANUATU
New Caledonia (to France)
FIJI
Tropic of Capricorn
AUSTRALIA
Norfolk Island (to Australia)
Lord Howe Island (part of Australia)
NEW ZEALAND
Amsterdam Island
St Paul Island
Prince Edward Islands (part of South Africa)
Crozet Islands
French Southern & Antarctic Territories (to France)
Kerguelen
Heard & McDonald Islands
Bouvet Island (to Norway)
Bounty Islands (part of NZ)
Antipodes Islands (part of NZ)
Auckland Islands (part of NZ)
Campbell Island (part of NZ)
Macquarie Island (part of Australia)
OCEAN
ANTARCTICA
(all territorial claims are held in abeyance under the 1959 Antarctic Treaty)
Antarctic Circle

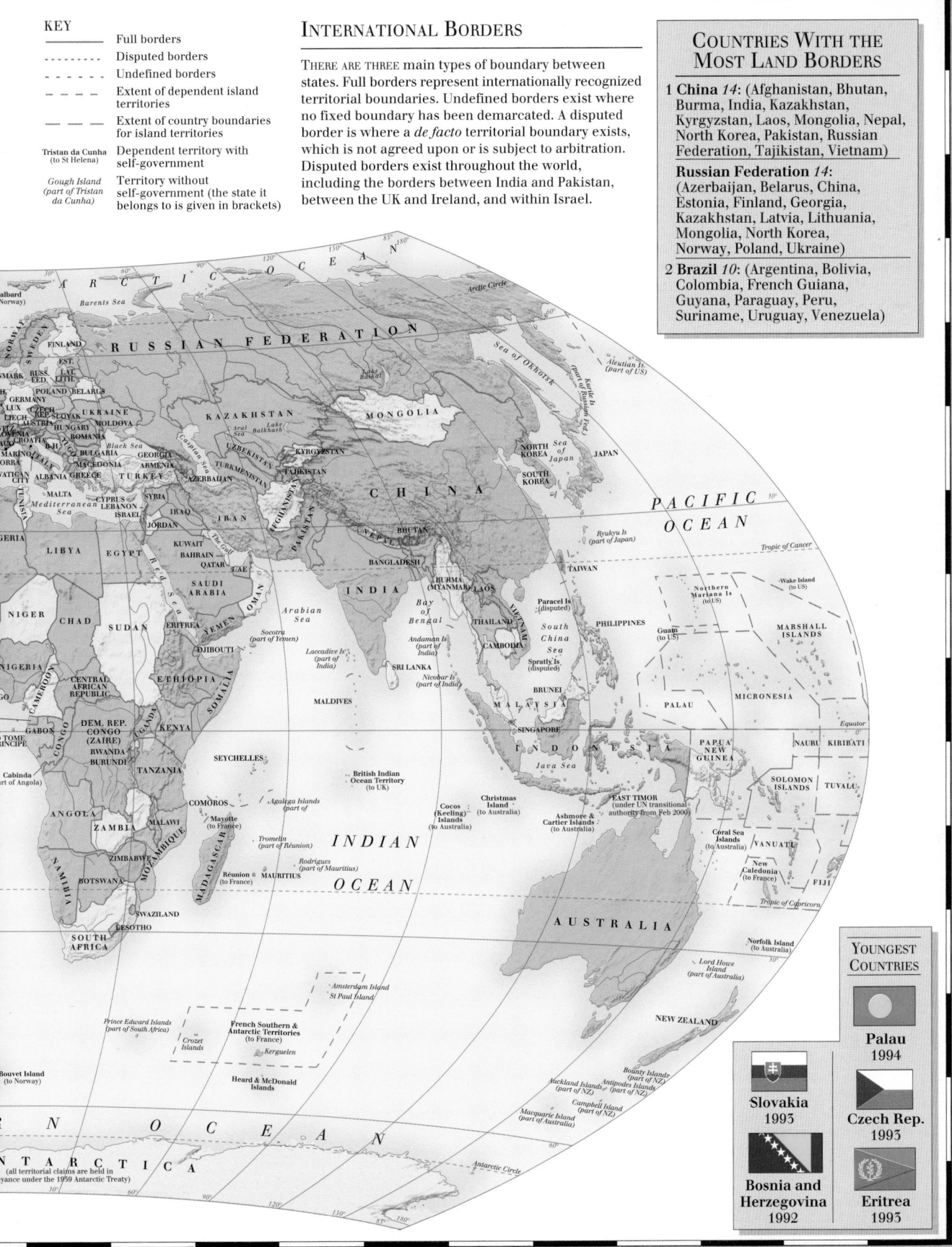

YOUNGEST COUNTRIES

Palau
1994

Slovakia
1993

Czech Rep.
1993

Bosnia and Herzegovina
1992

Eritrea
1993

Mars

Diameter: 6786 km
Mass: 642 m million million tons
Temperature: –137 to 37°C
Distance from Sun: 228 million km
Length of year: 1.88 years
Surface gravity: 1 kg = 0.38 kg

Earth

Diameter: 12,756 km
Mass: 5976 m million million tons
Temperature: –70 to 55°C
Distance from Sun: 150 million km
Length of year: 365.25 days
Surface gravity: 1kg = 1 kg

Venus

Diameter: 12,102 km
Mass: 4870 m million million tons
Temperature: 457°C
Distance from Sun: 108 million km
Length of year: 224.7 days
Surface gravity: 1 kg = 0.88 kg

Mercury

Diameter: 4878 km
Mass: 330 m million million tons
Temperature: –173 to 427°C
Distance from Sun: 58 million km
Length of year: 87.97 days
Surface gravity: 1 kg = 0.38 kg

The Earth

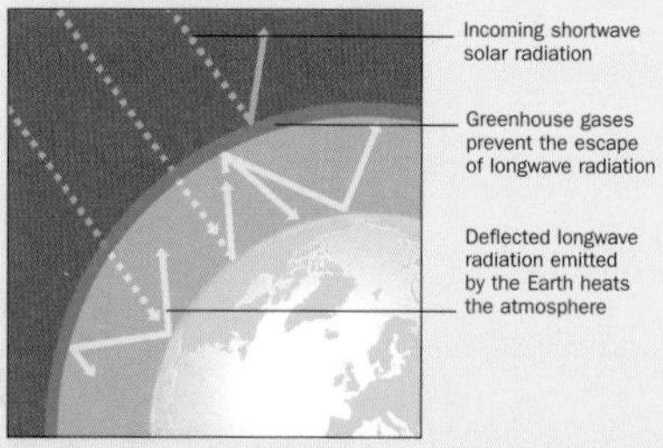
Incoming shortwave solar radiation
Greenhouse gases prevent the escape of longwave radiation
Deflected longwave radiation emitted by the Earth heats the atmosphere

GASES SUCH AS CARBON dioxide are known as "greenhouse gases" because they allow shortwave solar radiation to enter the Earth's atmosphere, but help to stop longwave radiation from escaping. This traps heat, raising the Earth's temperature. An excess of these gases helps trap more heat and can lead to global warming.

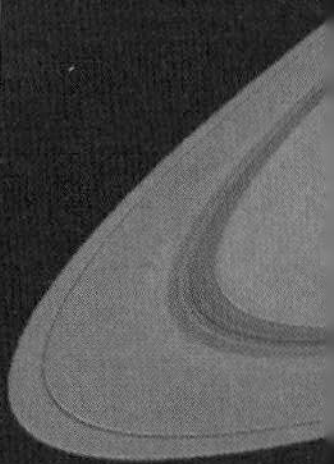

The Solar System

THE SOLAR SYSTEM CONSISTS of the nine major planets, their moons, the asteroids, and the comets that orbit around the Sun. The Sun itself is composed of 70% hydrogen and 30% helium, and at its core nuclear fusion reactions turning hydrogen into helium produce the heat and light which make life possible on Earth. Of the planets, the inner four (Mercury, Venus, Earth, and Mars) are termed terrestrial, while the next four (Jupiter, Saturn, Uranus, and Neptune) are termed gas giants. Pluto, at the edge of the solar system, is much smaller, and made of rock. The largest natural satellite in the Solar System is Ganymede (5262 km – 3270 miles – in diameter), which orbits around Jupiter, the largest planet. Halley's comet is the brightest comet when seen from Earth, and orbits the Sun once every 76 years. The largest asteroid is named Ceres (940 km – 584 miles – in diameter), which is found in the asteroid belt between Mars and Jupiter. The planet Earth is unique within the solar system (and possibly the universe), being the only planet capable of sustaining life.

Jupiter

Diameter: 142,984 km
Mass: 1,900,000,000 million million million tons
Temperature: -153°C
Distance from Sun: 778 million km
Length of year: 11.86 years
Surface gravity: 1 kg = 2.53 kg

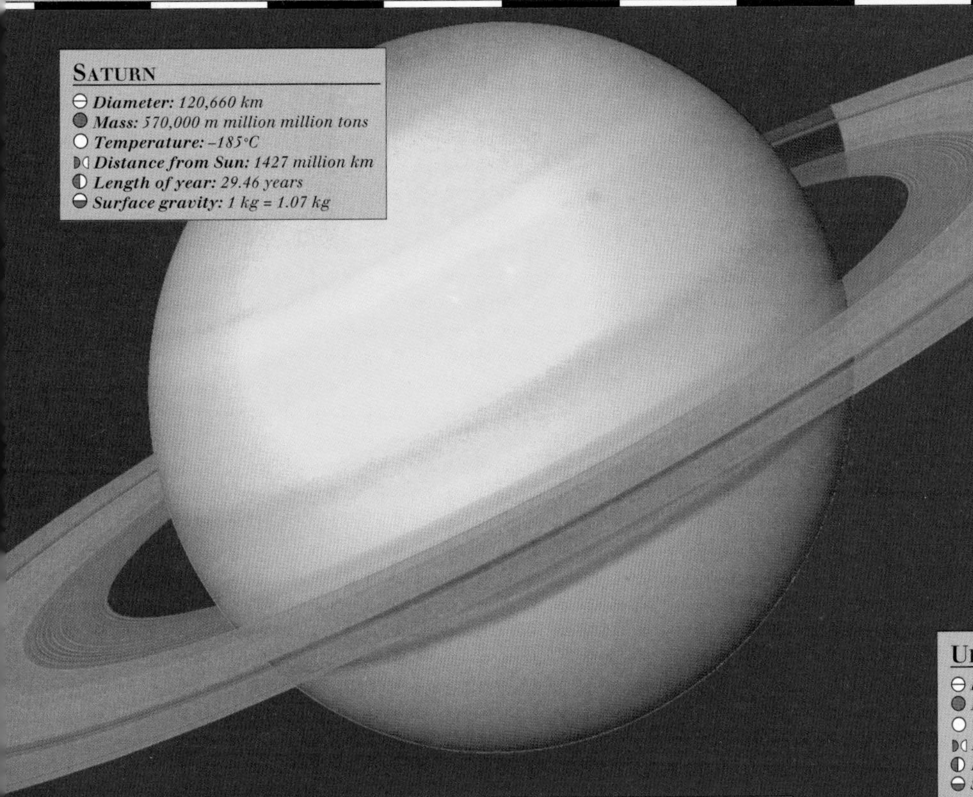

SATURN

- Diameter: 120,660 km
- Mass: 570,000 m million million tons
- Temperature: –185°C
- Distance from Sun: 1427 million km
- Length of year: 29.46 years
- Surface gravity: 1 kg = 1.07 kg

URANUS

- Diameter: 51,118 km
- Mass: 102,000 m million million tons
- Temperature: –214°C
- Distance from Sun: 2870 million km
- Length of year: 84.01 years
- Surface gravity: 1 kg = 0.92 kg

MOON AND TIDES

NEAR SIDE OF THE MOON

TIDES ARE CREATED by the pull of the Sun and the Moon's gravity on the surface of the oceans. Waves are formed by wind blowing over the surface of the oceans. The highest tides occur when the Earth, the Moon, and the Sun are aligned (*below left*). The lowest tides are experienced when the Sun and Moon align at right angles to one another (*below right*).

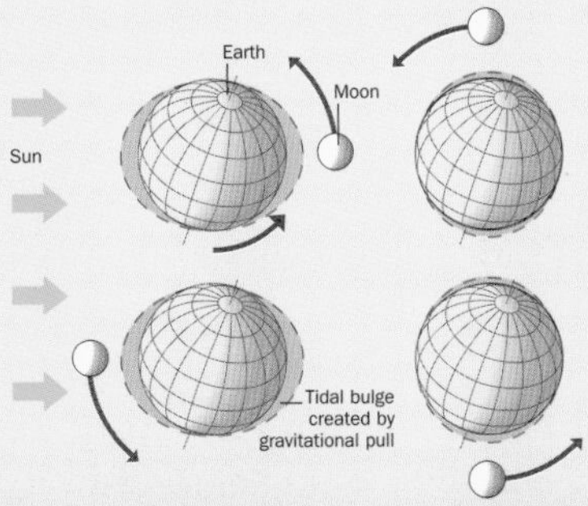

HIGHEST HIGH TIDES
LOWEST HIGH TIDES
Earth
Moon
Sun
Tidal bulge created by gravitational pull

FAR SIDE OF THE MOON

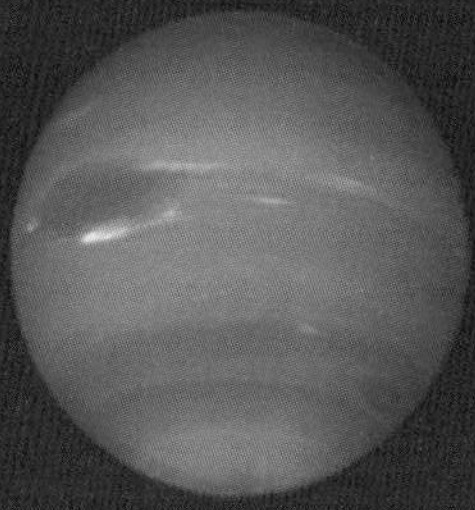

NEPTUNE

- Diameter: 49,528 km
- Mass: 13 m million million tons
- Temperature: –225°C
- Distance from Sun: 4497 million km
- Length of year: 164.79 days
- Surface gravity: 1 kg = 1.18 kg

PLUTO

- Diameter: 2300 km
- Mass: 13 m million million tons
- Temperature: –236°C
- Distance from Sun: 5900 million km
- Length of year: 248.54 years
- Surface gravity: 1 kg = 0.30 kg

Timeline of Space Exploration

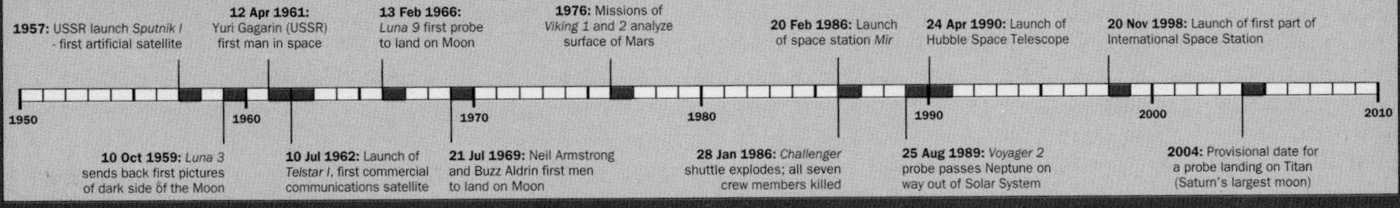

1957: USSR launch Sputnik I - first artificial satellite
12 Apr 1961: Yuri Gagarin (USSR) first man in space
13 Feb 1966: Luna 9 first probe to land on Moon
1976: Missions of Viking 1 and 2 analyze surface of Mars
20 Feb 1986: Launch of space station Mir
24 Apr 1990: Launch of Hubble Space Telescope
20 Nov 1998: Launch of first part of International Space Station
1950
1960
1970
1980
1990
2000
2010
10 Oct 1959: Luna 3 sends back first pictures of dark side of the Moon
10 Jul 1962: Launch of Telstar I, first commercial communications satellite
21 Jul 1969: Neil Armstrong and Buzz Aldrin first men to land on Moon
28 Jan 1986: Challenger shuttle explodes; all seven crew members killed
25 Aug 1989: Voyager 2 probe passes Neptune on way out of Solar System
2004: Provisional date for a probe landing on Titan (Saturn's largest moon)

The Climate

THE EARTH'S CLIMATIC REGIONS consist of stable patterns of weather conditions averaged out over a long period of time. Different climates are categorized according to particular combinations of temperature and humidity. By contrast, weather consists of short-term fluctuations in wind, temperature, and humidity conditions. Different climates are determined by latitude, altitude, the prevailing wind, and circulation of ocean currents. Longer-term changes in climate, such as global warming or the onset of ice ages, are punctuated by shorter-term events which comprise the day-to-day weather of a region, such as frontal depressions, hurricanes, and blizzards.

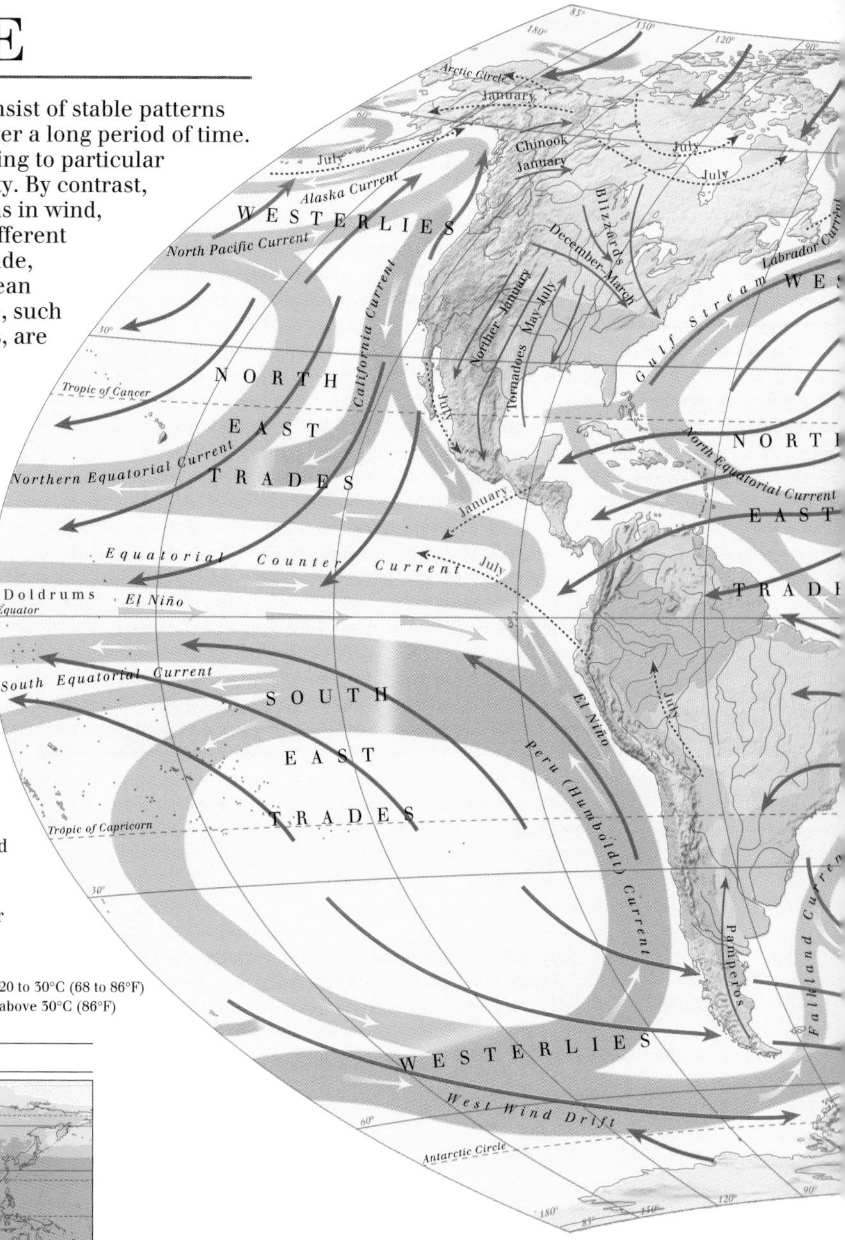
Arctic Circle
January
July
Chinook
January
July
July
Alaska Current
WESTERLIES
North Pacific Current
Blizzards
December–March
Labrador Current
WES
Norther January
Tornadoes May–July
California Current
Gulf Stream
NORTH
EAST
TRADES
Tropic of Cancer
July
North Equatorial Current
NORTH
EAST
Northern Equatorial Current
January
Equatorial Counter Current
July
TRADES
Doldrums
El Niño
Equator
South Equatorial Current
SOUTH
EAST
TRADES
El Niño
July
Peru (Humboldt) Current
Tropic of Capricorn
Pamperos
Falkland Current
WESTERLIES
West Wind Drift
Antarctic Circle

CLIMATE ZONES
- Ice cap
- Tundra
- Subarctic
- Cool continental
- Warm humid
- Mediterranean
- Semi-arid
- Arid
- Tropical
- Humid equatorial

OCEAN CURRENTS
- Warm
- Cold

PREVAILING WINDS
- Warm
- Cold

LOCAL WINDS
- Warm
- Cold
- June Seasonal*

* (seasonal winds which can either be warm or cold)

TEMPERATURE

THE WORLD CAN BE DIVIDED into three major climatic zones, stretching like large belts across the latitudes: the tropics which are warm, the cold polar regions, and the temperate zones which lie between them. Temperature is also controlled by altitude: mountainous regions are typically colder than those at sea level.

- below - 30°C (-22°F)
- -30 to - 20°C (-22 to -4°F)
- -20 to - 10°C (-4 to 14°F)
- -10 to 0°C (14 to 32°F)
- 0 to 10°C (32 to 50°F)
- 10 to 20°C (50 to 68°F)
- 20 to 30°C (68 to 86°F)
- above 30°C (86°F)

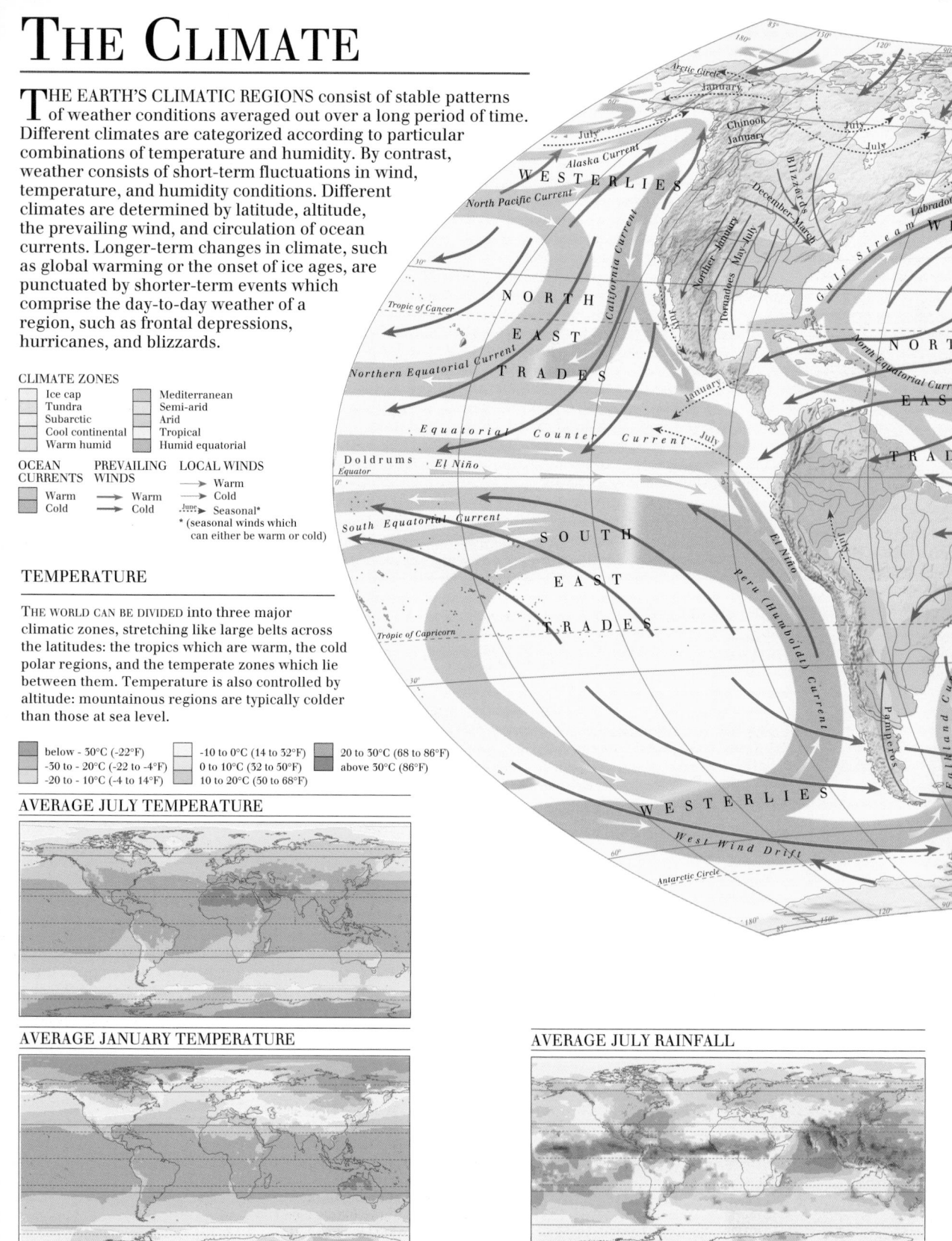

AVERAGE JULY TEMPERATURE

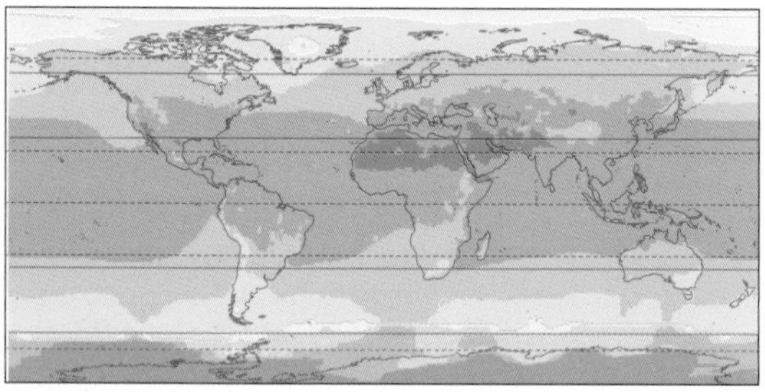

AVERAGE JANUARY TEMPERATURE

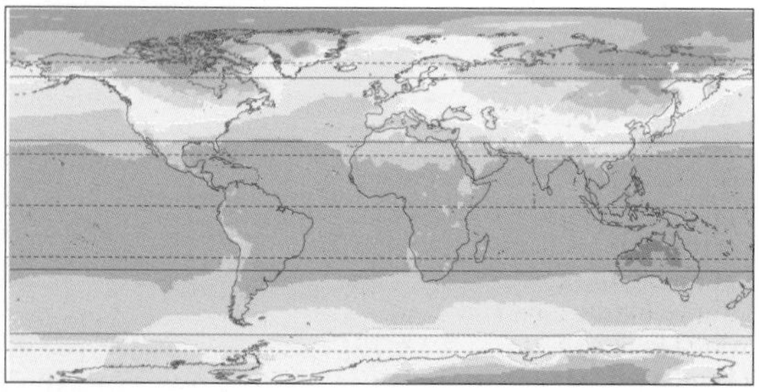

AVERAGE JULY RAINFALL

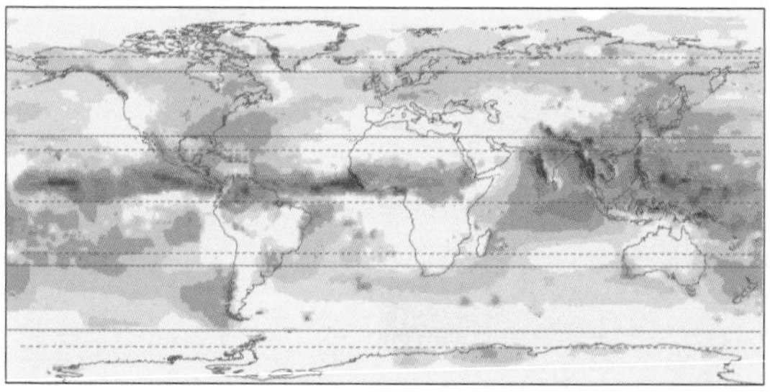

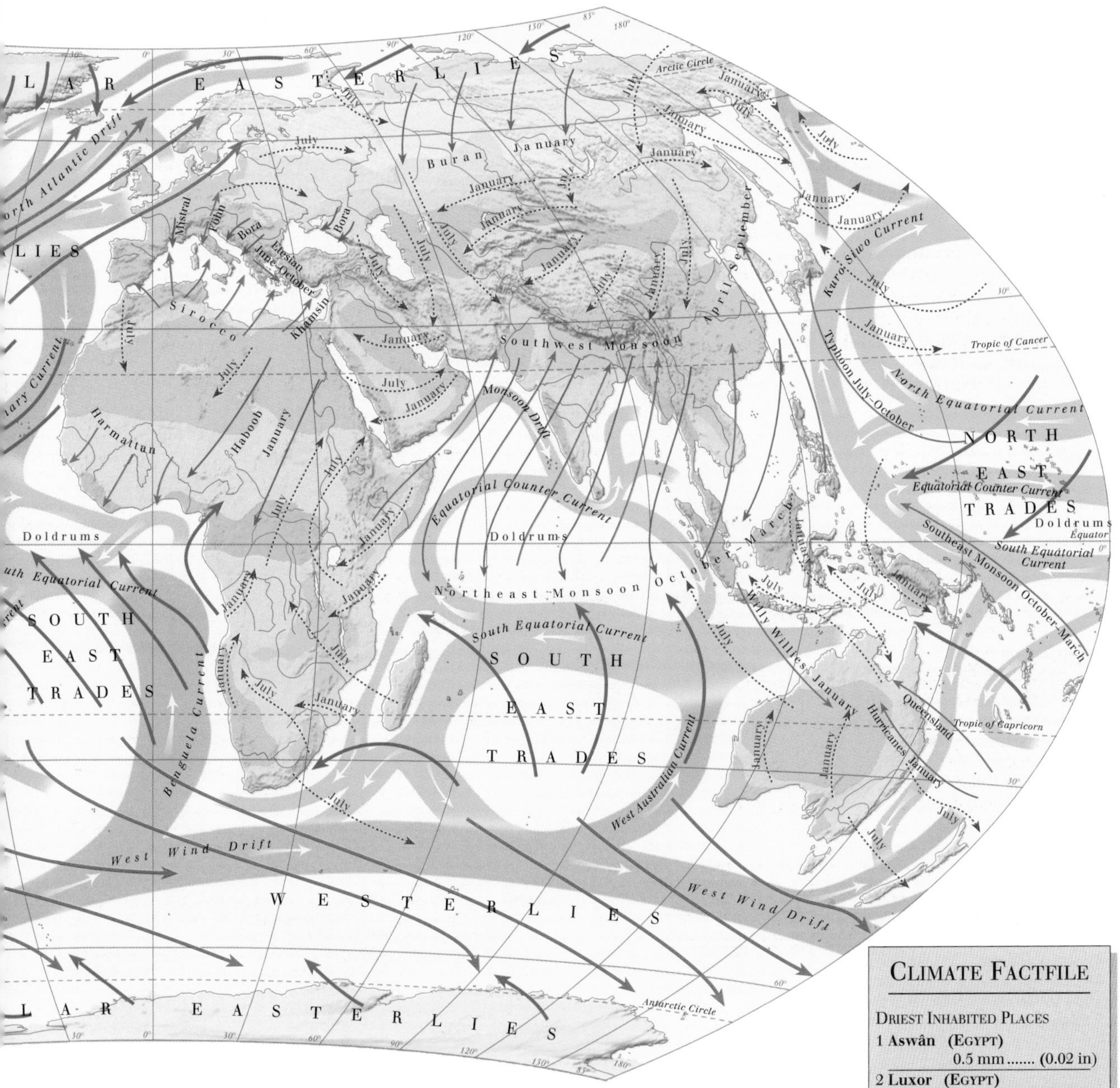
EASTERLIES
North Atlantic Drift
Buran
January
July
Mistral
Föhn
Bora
Etesian June–October
Sirocco
Khamsin
Southwest Monsoon
Monsoon Drift
Harmattan
Haboob
Arctic Circle
Kuro Siwo Current
April–September
Typhoon July–October
Tropic of Cancer
North Equatorial Current
NORTH EAST TRADES
Equatorial Counter Current
Doldrums
Equator
South Equatorial Current
Southeast Monsoon October–March
Northeast Monsoon October–March
Willy Willies January
Queensland
Hurricanes January
Tropic of Capricorn
SOUTH EAST TRADES
Benguela Current
West Australian Current
West Wind Drift
WESTERLIES
Antarctic Circle

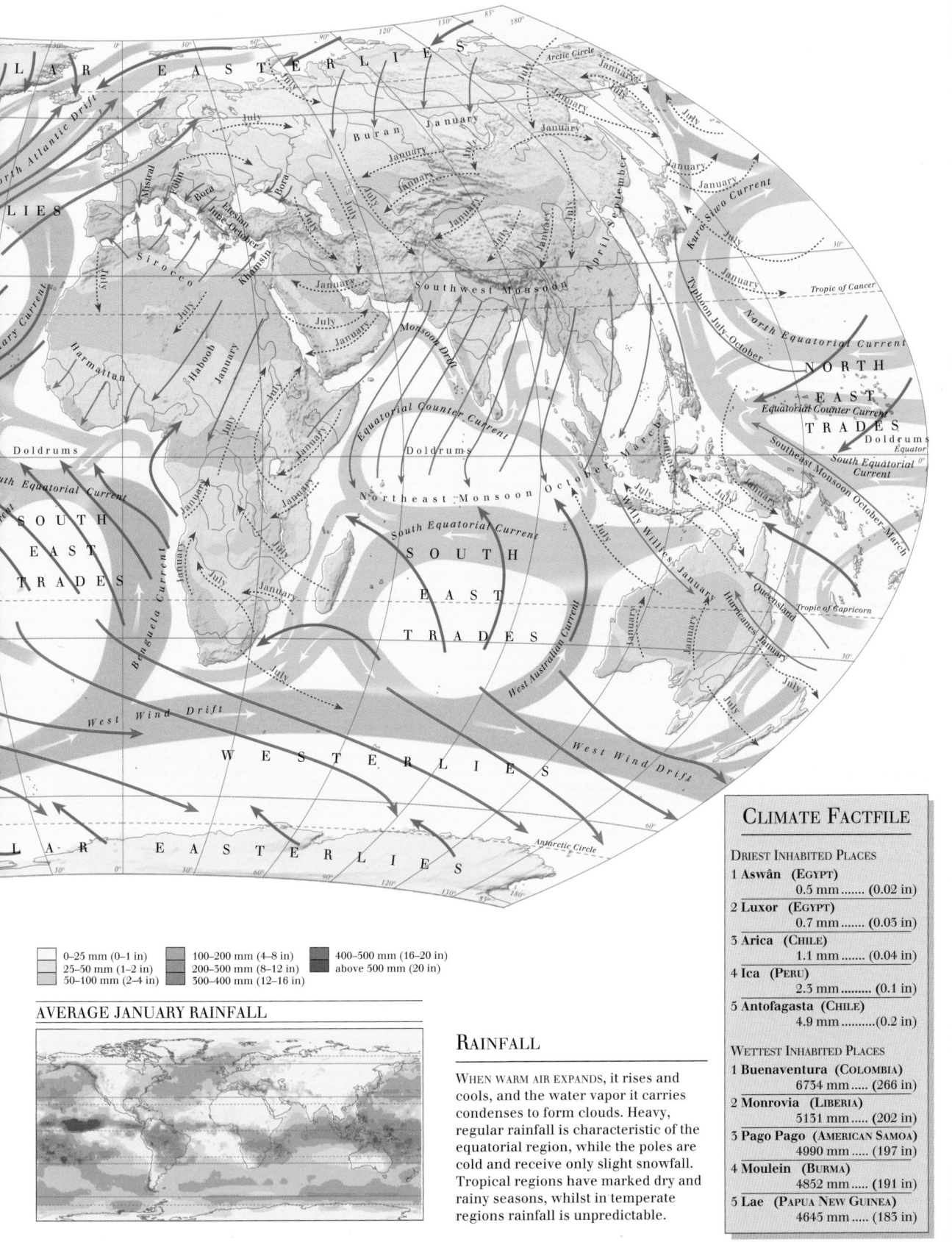

0–25 mm (0–1 in)
25–50 mm (1–2 in)
50–100 mm (2–4 in)
100–200 mm (4–8 in)
200–300 mm (8–12 in)
300–400 mm (12–16 in)
400–500 mm (16–20 in)
above 500 mm (20 in)

AVERAGE JANUARY RAINFALL

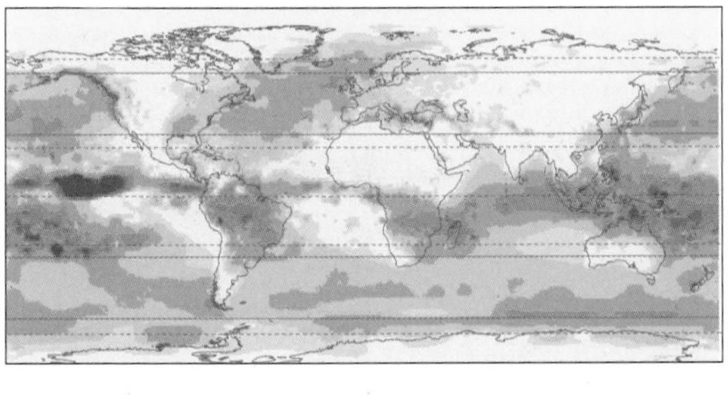

RAINFALL

WHEN WARM AIR EXPANDS, it rises and cools, and the water vapor it carries condenses to form clouds. Heavy, regular rainfall is characteristic of the equatorial region, while the poles are cold and receive only slight snowfall. Tropical regions have marked dry and rainy seasons, whilst in temperate regions rainfall is unpredictable.

CLIMATE FACTFILE

DRIEST INHABITED PLACES

1 **Aswân** (EGYPT)
0.5 mm .... (0.02 in)

2 **Luxor** (EGYPT)
0.7 mm .... (0.03 in)

3 **Arica** (CHILE)
1.1 mm .... (0.04 in)

4 **Ica** (PERU)
2.3 mm .... (0.1 in)

5 **Antofagasta** (CHILE)
4.9 mm ....(0.2 in)

WETTEST INHABITED PLACES

1 **Buenaventura** (COLOMBIA)
6734 mm ..... (266 in)

2 **Monrovia** (LIBERIA)
5131 mm ..... (202 in)

3 **Pago Pago** (AMERICAN SAMOA)
4990 mm ..... (197 in)

4 **Moulein** (BURMA)
4852 mm ..... (191 in)

5 **Lae** (PAPUA NEW GUINEA)
4645 mm ..... (183 in)

The Environment

THE EARTH CAN BE DIVIDED into a series of biogeographical regions, or biomes – ecological communities where certain species of plant and animal co-exist within particular climatic conditions. Within these broad classifications, other factors affect the local distribution of species in each biome, such as soil richness, altitude, and human activities such as urbanization, intensive agriculture, and deforestation. Apart from the polar ice caps, there are few areas which have not been colonized by animals or plants over the course of the Earth's history. Because of all animals' reliance on plants for survival, plants are known as primary producers. The availability of nutrients and temperature of an area is defined as its primary productivity, which affects the quantity and type of animals which are able to live there, although cold and aridity restrict the quantity of life.

Biodiversity

THE NUMBER OF PLANT AND ANIMAL SPECIES, and the range of genetic diversity within the populations of each species, make up the Earth's biodiversity. The plants and animals which are endemic to a region – that is, those which are found nowhere else in the world – are also important in determining levels of biodiversity. Human settlement and intervention have encroached on many areas of the world once rich in endemic plant and animal species. Increasing international efforts are being made to monitor and conserve the biodiversity of the Earth's remaining wild places.

Arctic Circle
Rocky Mountains
Great Plains
Canadian Shield
North European Plain
Mediterranean Sea
ATLANTIC OCEAN
Tropic of Cancer
Sahara
Caribbean Sea
Sahel
PACIFIC OCEAN
Equator
Amazon Basin
Congo Basin
ATLANTIC OCEAN
Gran Chaco
Tropic of Capricorn
Kalahari Desert
Pampas
SOUTHERN OCE
Antarctic Circle
ANTARCT

ANIMALS

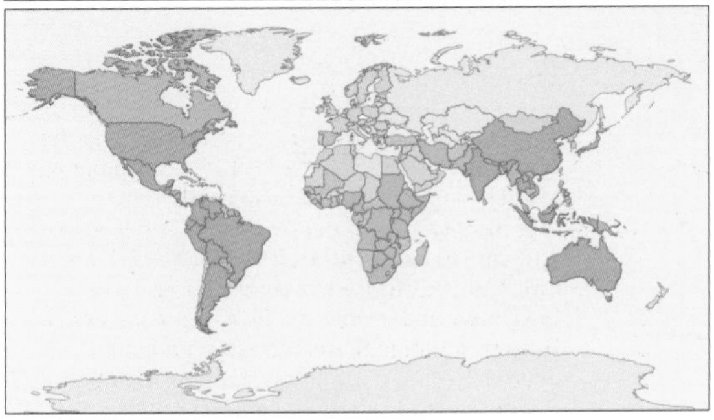

Number of animal species per country

- More than 2000
- 1000–1999
- 700–999
- 400–699
- 200–399
- 100–199
- 0–99
- Data not available

ANIMAL ADAPTION

THE DEGREE OF AN ANIMAL'S ADAPTABILITY to different climates and conditions is extremely important in ensuring its success as a species. Many animals, particularly the largest mammals, are becoming restricted to ever-smaller regions as human development and modern agricultural practices reduce their natural habitats. In contrast, humans have been responsible – both deliberately and accidentally – for the spread of some of the world's most successful species. Many of these introduced species are now more numerous than the indigenous animal populations.

PLANTS

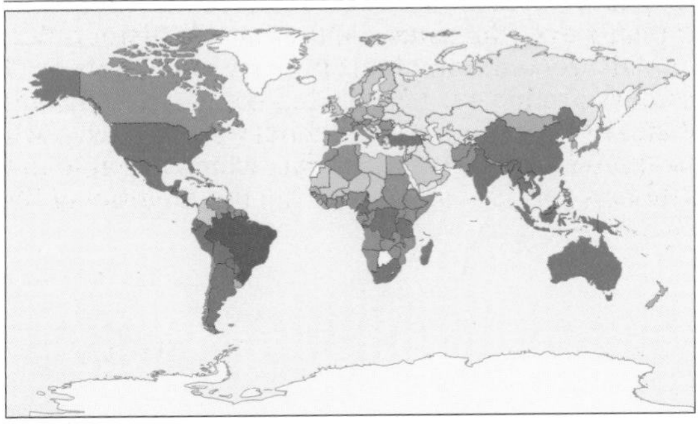

Number of plant species per country

- More than 50,000
- 7000–49,999
- 3000–6999
- 2000–2999
- 1000–1999
- 600–999
- 0–599
- Data not available

PLANT ADAPTION

ENVIRONMENTAL CONDITIONS, such as climate, soil type and the competition with other organisms, influence the development of plants into distinctive forms. Similar conditions in different parts of the world create similar adaptions in the plants, which may then be modified by other, local, factors specific to the region.

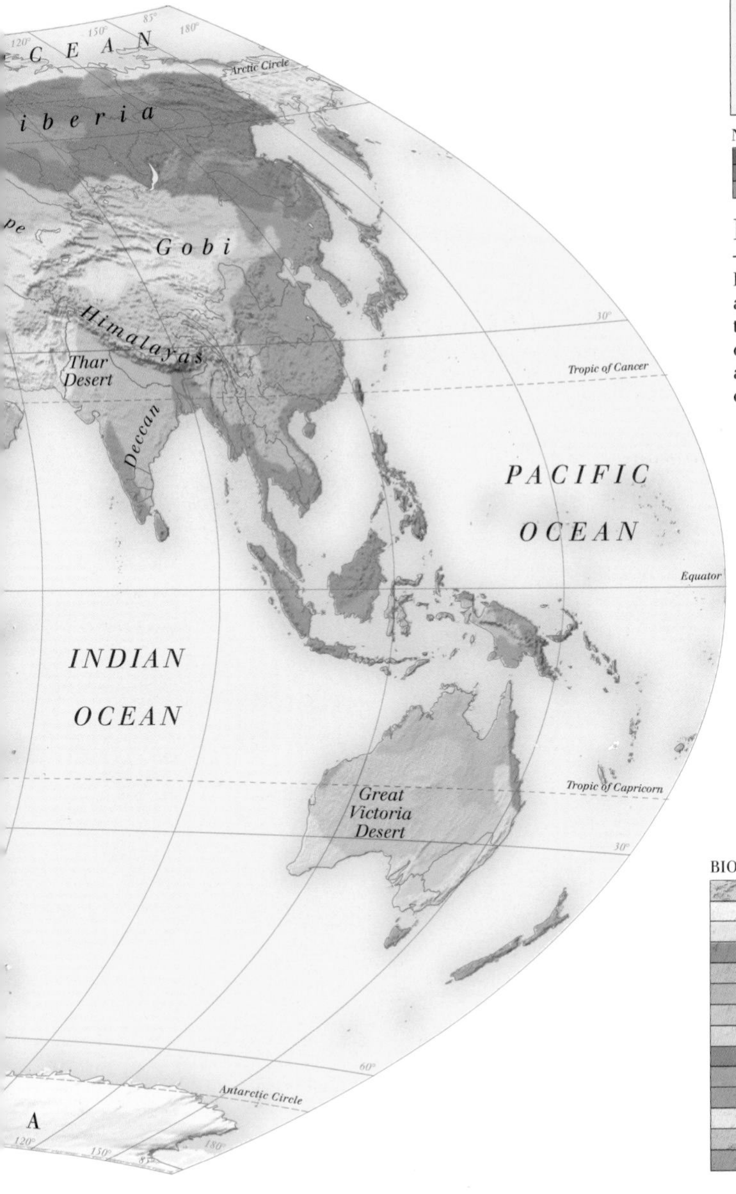
C E A N
Arctic Circle
i b e r i a
G o b i
Himalayas
Thar Desert
Deccan
Tropic of Cancer
PACIFIC OCEAN
Equator
INDIAN OCEAN
Tropic of Capricorn
Great Victoria Desert
Antarctic Circle
A

BIOME TYPES

- Mountains
- Polar regions
- Tundra
- Tropical rain forests
- Dry woodlands
- Savanna
- Temperate grasslands
- Mediterranean
- Coniferous forests
- Temperate rain forests
- Broadleaf forests
- Cold deserts
- Hot deserts
- Wetlands

ENVIRONMENT FACTFILE

LARGEST PROTECTED AREAS

Seychelles	95%
Ecuador	43%
Kiribati	39%
Venezuela	36%
Denmark	32%

HIGHEST ANNUAL DEFORESTATION

Brazil	23,090 km²	(8936 mi²)
Indonesia	13,120 km²	(5077 mi²)
Sudan	9590 km²	(3711 mi²)
Zambia	8510 km²	(3293 mi²)
Mexico	6310 km²	(2442 mi²)

IDENTIFIED SPECIES

Micro-organisms	5800
Invertebrates	1,021,000
Plants	322,500
Fish	19,100
Reptiles & amphibians	12,000
Mammals	4000

ENDANGERED SPECIES

Mammals	484
Birds	403
Reptiles	100
Amphibians	49
Fish	291
Invertebrates	763

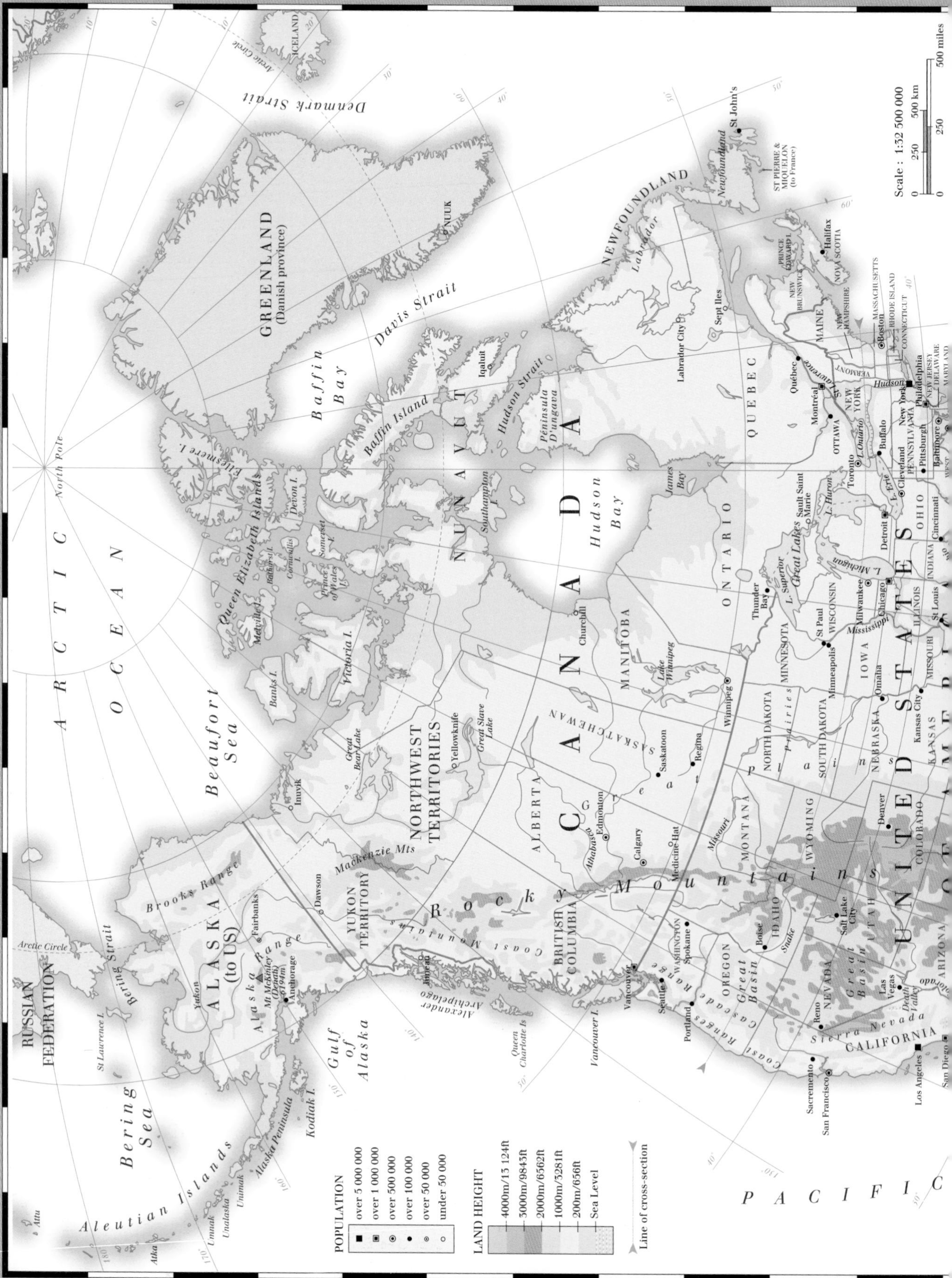
ARCTIC OCEAN
North Pole
Arctic Circle
Denmark Strait
ICELAND
GREENLAND
(Danish province)
NUUK
Davis Strait
Baffin Bay
Baffin Island
Iqaluit
Hudson Strait
Péninsula D'ungava
Ellesmere I.
Queen Elizabeth Islands
Devon I.
Somerset I.
Cornwallis I.
Bathurst I.
Melville I.
Prince of Wales I.
Banks I.
Victoria I.
Southampton I.
NUNAVUT
Hudson Bay
James Bay
CANADA
Beaufort Sea
Inuvik
Great Bear Lake
NORTHWEST TERRITORIES
Yellowknife
Great Slave Lake
Mackenzie Mts
YUKON TERRITORY
Dawson
Brooks Range
ALASKA (to US)
Fairbanks
Alaska Range
Mt McKinley (Denali) 6194m
Anchorage
Yukon
Arctic Circle
Bering Strait
RUSSIAN FEDERATION
St Lawrence I.
Bering Sea
Aleutian Islands
Attu
Atka
Umnak
Unalaska
Unimak
Alaska Peninsula
Kodiak I.
Gulf of Alaska
Coast Mountains
Juneau
Alexander Archipelago
Queen Charlotte Is
Vancouver I.
BRITISH COLUMBIA
Vancouver
Rocky Mountains
ALBERTA
Edmonton
Athabasca
Calgary
Medicine Hat
SASKATCHEWAN
Saskatoon
Regina
MANITOBA
Churchill
Lake Winnipeg
Winnipeg
ONTARIO
Thunder Bay
Sault Saint Marie
Toronto
OTTAWA
QUEBEC
Québec
Montréal
Labrador City
Sept Iles
NEWFOUNDLAND
Labrador
Newfoundland
St John's
ST PIERRE & MIQUELON (to France)
PRINCE EDWARD I.
NEW BRUNSWICK
NOVA SCOTIA
Halifax
St Lawrence
Great Plains
Great Lakes
L. Superior
L. Michigan
L. Huron
L. Erie
L. Ontario
MAINE
NEW HAMPSHIRE
VERMONT
MASSACHUSETTS
RHODE ISLAND
CONNECTICUT
Boston
NEW YORK
New York
Hudson
NEW JERSEY
DELAWARE
MARYLAND
Philadelphia
Baltimore
PENNSYLVANIA
Pittsburgh
Buffalo
Cleveland
OHIO
Cincinnati
Detroit
INDIANA
ILLINOIS
Chicago
Milwaukee
WISCONSIN
St Paul
Minneapolis
MINNESOTA
IOWA
MISSOURI
St Louis
Mississippi
Kansas City
KANSAS
NEBRASKA
Omaha
SOUTH DAKOTA
NORTH DAKOTA
MONTANA
Missouri
WYOMING
COLORADO
Denver
UTAH
Salt Lake City
IDAHO
Boise
Snake
WASHINGTON
Spokane
Seattle
Cascade Range
OREGON
Portland
Great Basin
NEVADA
Reno
Las Vegas
Death Valley
Sierra Nevada
CALIFORNIA
Sacramento
San Francisco
Los Angeles
San Diego
ARIZONA
Coast Ranges
UNITED STATES
PACIFIC
Scale : 1:32 500 000
0 250 500 km
0 250 500 miles
POPULATION
over 5 000 000
over 1 000 000
over 500 000
over 100 000
over 50 000
under 50 000
LAND HEIGHT
4000m/13 124ft
3000m/9845ft
2000m/6562ft
1000m/3281ft
200m/656ft
Sea Level
Line of cross-section

NORTH AMERICA

A T L A N T I C
O C E A N
Gulf of Mexico
Caribbean Sea
MEXICO
TEXAS
LOUISIANA
MISSISSIPPI
ALABAMA
GEORGIA
SOUTH CAROLINA
FLORIDA
ARKANSAS
BAHAMAS
CUBA
JAMAICA
HAITI
DOMINICAN REPUBLIC
GUATEMALA
BELIZE
HONDURAS
EL SALVADOR
NICARAGUA
COSTA RICA
PANAMA
COLOMBIA
VENEZUELA
El Paso
Ciudad Juárez
Hermosillo
Chihuahua
Culiacán
Torreón
Monterrey
Dallas
San Antonio
Houston
Baton Rouge
New Orleans
Mobile
Birmingham
Atlanta
Charlotte
Charleston
Jacksonville
Tampa
Miami
NASSAU
Aguascalientes
León
Guadalajara
Morelia
MEXICO CITY
Puebla
Acapulco
Tampico
Mérida
Campeche
Peninsula de Yucatán
Bahía de Campeche
Golfo de California
Sierra Madre Occidental
Sierra Madre Oriental
Altiplano de Mexicana
Rio Grande
Mississippi
Appalachian
Tropic of Cancer
Equator
Islas Revillagigedo (to Mexico)
Guadalupe (to Mexico)
Galapagos (to Ecuador)
BERMUDA (to UK)
HAVANA (La Habana)
CAYMAN ISLANDS (to UK)
TURKS & CAICOS ISLANDS (to UK)
NAVASSA I. (to US)
KINGSTON
PORT-AU-PRINCE
SANTO DOMINGO
PUERTO RICO (to US)
SAN JUAN
VIRGIN IS (to US)
BRITISH VIRGIN IS (to UK)
ANGUILLA (to UK)
ANTIGUA & BARBUDA
ST KITTS & NEVIS
MONTSERRAT (to UK)
GUADELOUPE (to France)
DOMINICA
MARTINIQUE (to France)
ST LUCIA
BARBADOS
ST VINCENT & THE GRENADINES
GRENADA
TRINIDAD & TOBAGO
ARUBA (to Neth.)
NETHERLANDS ANTILLES (to Neth.)
Greater Antilles
Lesser Antilles
BELMOPAN
GUATEMALA CITY
SAN SALVADOR
TEGUCIGALPA
MANAGUA
SAN JOSÉ
PANAMA CITY

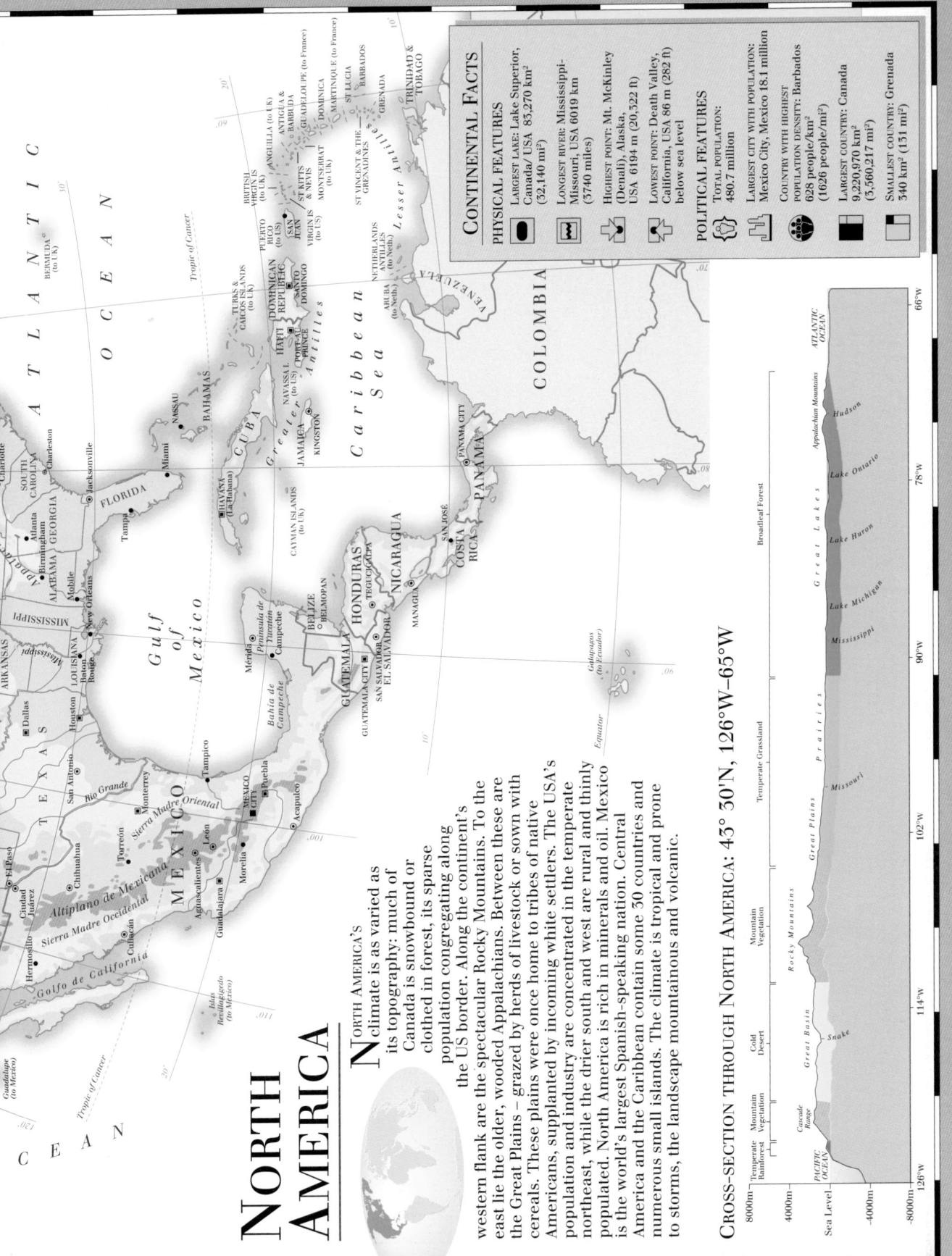

NORTH AMERICA'S climate is as varied as its topography: much of Canada is snowbound or clothed in forest, its sparse population congregating along the US border. Along the continent's western flank are the spectacular Rocky Mountains. To the east lie the older, wooded Appalachians. Between these are the Great Plains – grazed by herds of livestock or sown with cereals. These plains were once home to tribes of native Americans, supplanted by incoming white settlers. The USA's population and industry are concentrated in the temperate northeast, while the drier south and west are rural and thinly populated. North America is rich in minerals and oil. Mexico is the world's largest Spanish-speaking nation. Central America and the Caribbean contain some 30 countries and numerous small islands. The climate is tropical and prone to storms, the landscape mountainous and volcanic.

CROSS-SECTION THROUGH NORTH AMERICA: 43° 30'N, 126°W–65°W

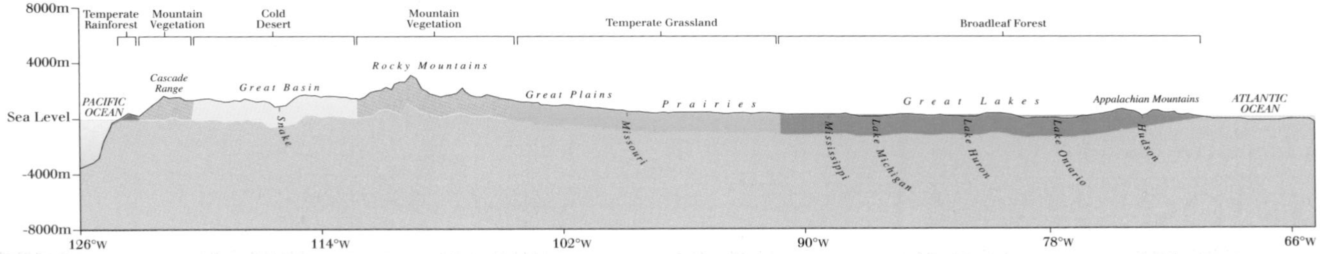

8000m
4000m
Sea Level
-4000m
-8000m
Temperate Rainforest
Mountain Vegetation
Cold Desert
Mountain Vegetation
Temperate Grassland
Broadleaf Forest
PACIFIC OCEAN
Cascade Range
Great Basin
Snake
Rocky Mountains
Great Plains
Missouri
Prairies
Mississippi
Lake Michigan
Great Lakes
Lake Huron
Lake Ontario
Appalachian Mountains
Hudson
ATLANTIC OCEAN
126°W
114°W
102°W
90°W
78°W
66°W

CONTINENTAL FACTS

PHYSICAL FEATURES

- LARGEST LAKE: Lake Superior, Canada/ USA 83,270 km² (32,140 mi²)
- LONGEST RIVER: Mississippi-Missouri, USA 6019 km (3740 miles)
- HIGHEST POINT: Mt. McKinley (Denali), Alaska, USA 6194 m (20,322 ft)
- LOWEST POINT: Death Valley, California, USA 86 m (282 ft) below sea level

POLITICAL FEATURES

- TOTAL POPULATION: 480.7 million
- LARGEST CITY WITH POPULATION: Mexico City, Mexico 18.1 million
- COUNTRY WITH HIGHEST POPULATION DENSITY: Barbados 628 people/km² (1626 people/mi²)
- LARGEST COUNTRY: Canada 9,220,970 km² (3,560,217 mi²)
- SMALLEST COUNTRY: Grenada 340 km² (131 mi²)

SOUTH AMERICA

THE WORLD'S fourth-largest continent includes one of its most important resources – the Amazonian rainforest. It is a major source of oxygen and includes half of all known living species, while the Amazon – the world's second longest river – contains one fifth of the world's fresh water. The Andes mountain chain reaches down South America's western flank, sheltering the prairies of the Gran Chaco, the Pampas, and the wastes of the far south. Most South Americans are *mestizo* – of mixed European and Amerindian descent – and live in the coastal regions. Spanish is the most widely spoken language, and over 90% of South Americans are Roman Catholic. South America has massive mineral resources, many exploited by US and European multinationals.

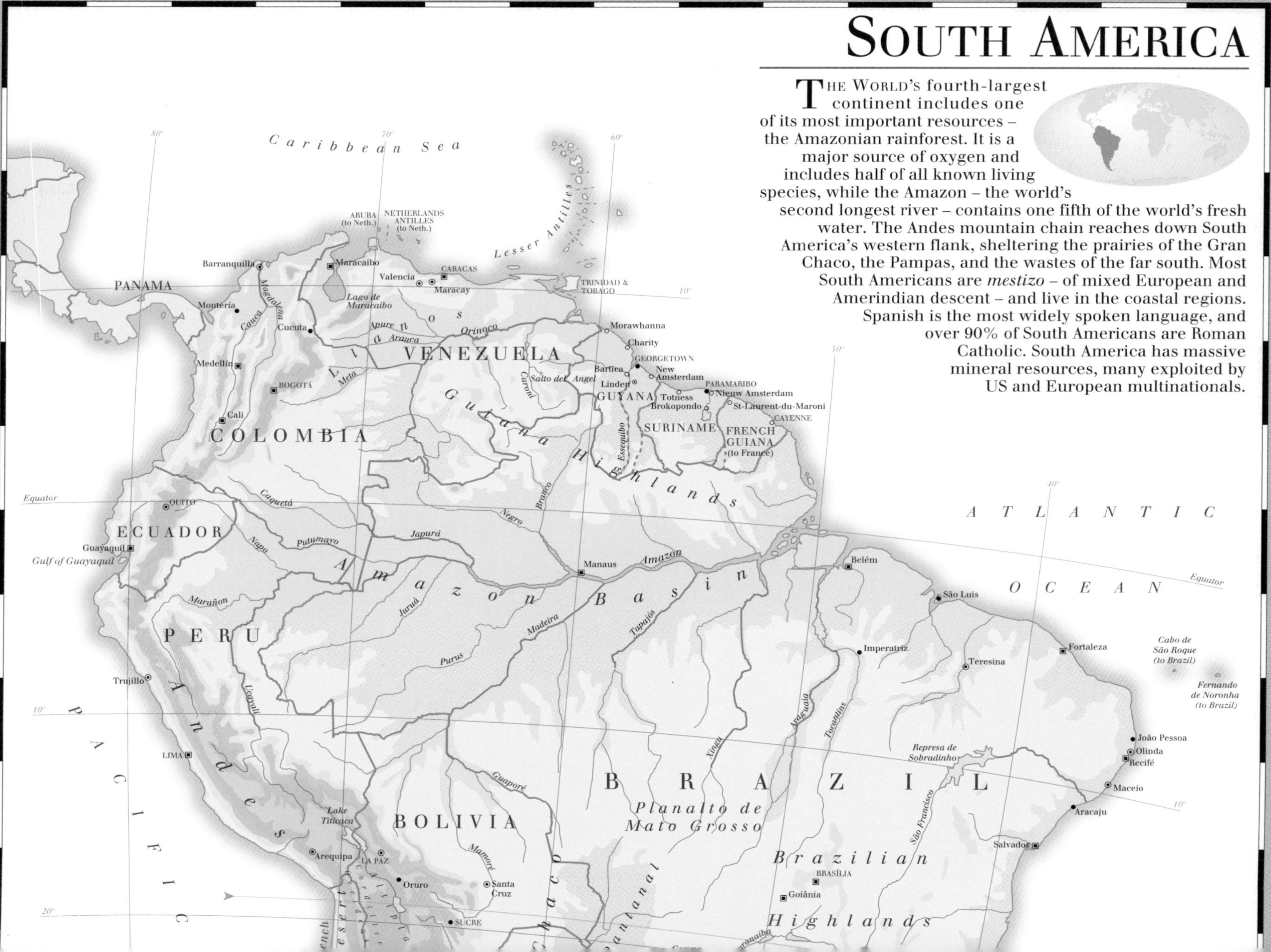
Caribbean Sea
Lesser Antilles
ARUBA (to Neth.)
NETHERLANDS ANTILLES (to Neth.)
TRINIDAD & TOBAGO
PANAMA
Barranquilla
Maracaibo
Lago de Maracaibo
Valencia
CARACAS
Maracay
Montería
Cucuta
Medellín
BOGOTÁ
Cali
COLOMBIA
VENEZUELA
Llanos
Orinoco
Apure
Arauca
Meta
Caroní
Salto del Angel
Guiana Highlands
Morawhanna
Charity
GEORGETOWN
New Amsterdam
Bartica
Linden
GUYANA
Totness
Brokopondo
PARAMARIBO
Nieuw Amsterdam
St-Laurent-du-Maroni
CAYENNE
SURINAME
FRENCH GUIANA (to France)
Essequibo
Equator
QUITO
ECUADOR
Guayaquil
Gulf of Guayaquil
Caquetá
Putumayo
Napo
Japurá
Negro
Branco
Manaus
Amazon
Amazon Basin
Marañon
Juruá
Purus
Madeira
Tapajós
PERU
Trujillo
LIMA
Ucayali
Andes
PACIFIC
ATLANTIC OCEAN
Belém
São Luis
Imperatriz
Fortaleza
Teresina
Cabo de São Roque (to Brazil)
Fernando de Noronha (to Brazil)
João Pessoa
Olinda
Recifé
Maceio
Aracaju
Salvador
Represa de Sobradinho
São Francisco
Xingu
Araguaia
Tocantins
BRAZIL
Planalto de Mato Grosso
Brazilian Highlands
BRASÍLIA
Goiânia
Guaporé
Mamoré
BOLIVIA
Lake Titicaca
Arequipa
LA PAZ
Oruro
Santa Cruz
SUCRE
80°
70°
60°
50°
40°
10°
20°

PARAGUAY
URUGUAY
ARGENTINA
CHILE
Andes
Atacama
Pampas
Patagonia
PACIFIC OCEAN
ATLANTIC OCEAN
Islas de los Desventurados (to Chile)
Islas Juan Fernández (to Chile)
FALKLAND ISLANDS (to UK)
ASUNCIÓN
Fernando de la Mora
Lambaré
Campinas
Juiz de Fora
São Paulo
Nova Iguaçu
Rio de Janeiro
Sorocaba
Santos
Curitiba
Tropic of Capricorn
Porto Alegre
Salto
Paysandú
Rosario
Córdoba
L. Mar Chiquita
Cerro Aconcagua 6959m
Valparaiso
SANTIAGO
BUENOS AIRES
La Plate
Las Piedras
MONTEVIDEO
La Plata
Concepción
Salado
Paraná
Uruguay
Colorado
Negro
Bahía Blanca
Puerto Montt
Golfo San Matías
Península Valdés
Isla de Chiloé
Chubut
Golfo San Jorge
Deseado
Isla Wellington
Bahía Grande
Str. of Magellan
Tierra del Fuego
Beagle Channel
Cape Horn
Scale : 1:26 500 000
0 250 500 km
0 250 500 miles

POPULATION

- over 5 000 000
- over 1 000 000
- over 500 000
- over 100 000
- over 50 000
- under 50 000

LAND HEIGHT

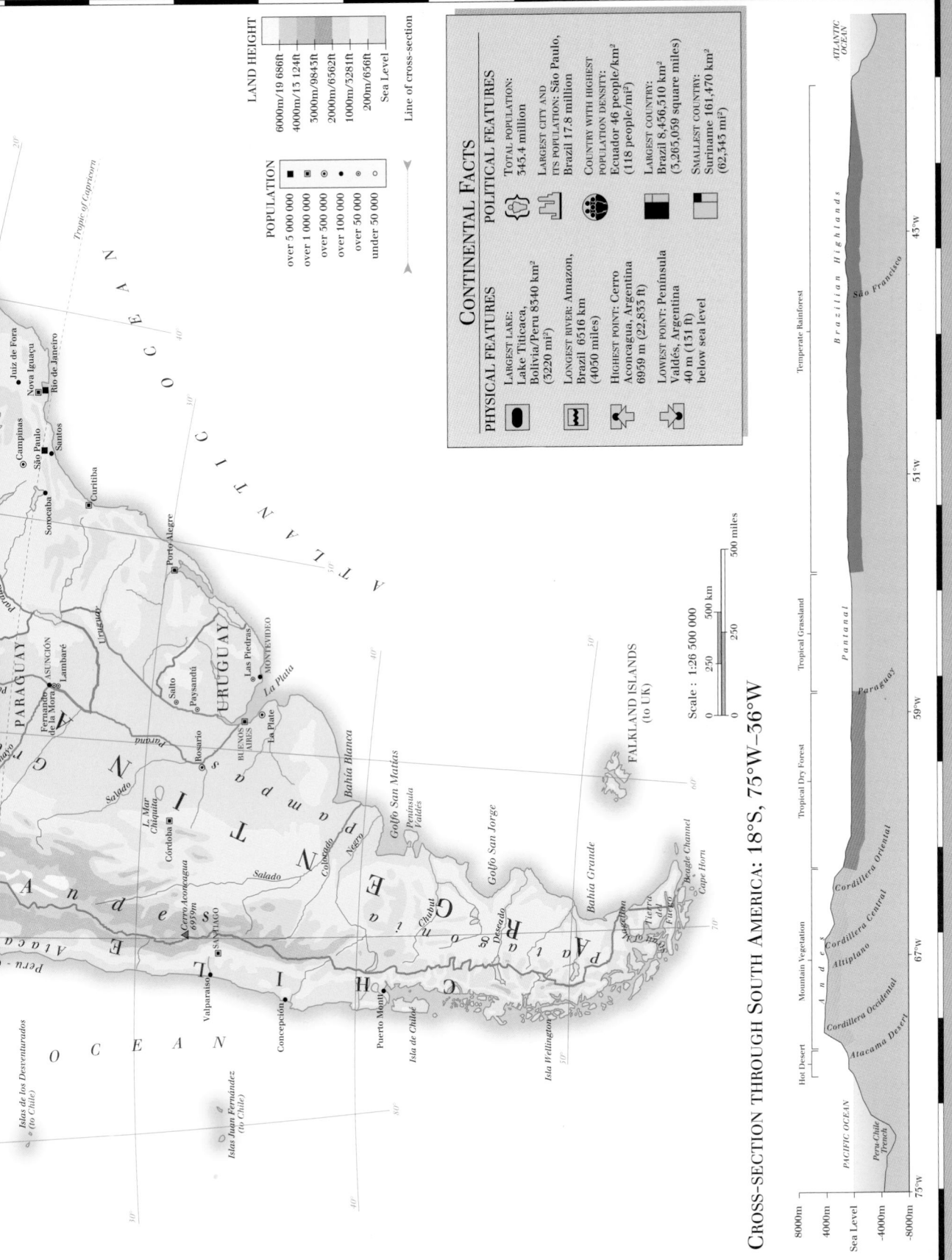

- 6000m/19 686ft
- 4000m/13 124ft
- 3000m/9843ft
- 2000m/6562ft
- 1000m/3281ft
- 200m/656ft
- Sea Level

Line of cross-section

CONTINENTAL FACTS

PHYSICAL FEATURES

LARGEST LAKE: Lake Titicaca, Bolivia/Peru 8340 km² (3220 mi²)

LONGEST RIVER: Amazon, Brazil 6516 km (4050 miles)

HIGHEST POINT: Cerro Aconcagua, Argentina 6959 m (22,833 ft)

LOWEST POINT: Península Valdés, Argentina 40 m (131 ft) below sea level

POLITICAL FEATURES

TOTAL POPULATION: 345.4 million

LARGEST CITY AND ITS POPULATION: São Paulo, Brazil 17.8 million

COUNTRY WITH HIGHEST POPULATION DENSITY: Ecuador 46 people/km² (118 people/mi²)

LARGEST COUNTRY: Brazil 8,456,510 km² (3,265,059 square miles)

SMALLEST COUNTRY: Suriname 161,470 km² (62,343 mi²)

CROSS-SECTION THROUGH SOUTH AMERICA: 18°S, 75°W–36°W

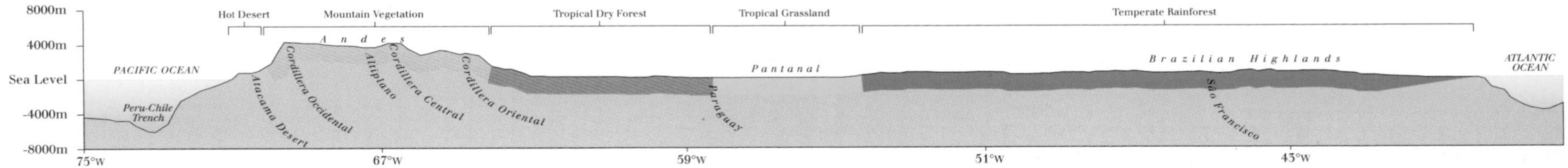
8000m
4000m
Sea Level
-4000m
-8000m
Hot Desert
Mountain Vegetation
Tropical Dry Forest
Tropical Grassland
Temperate Rainforest
PACIFIC OCEAN
Peru-Chile Trench
Atacama Desert
Cordillera Occidental
Altiplano
Cordillera Central
Cordillera Oriental
Andes
Pantanal
Paraguay
Brazilian Highlands
São Francisco
ATLANTIC OCEAN
75°W
67°W
59°W
51°W
43°W

EUROPE

THE SMALLEST CONTINENT AFTER AUSTRALIA, Europe has a wide variety of climates and landscapes. The tundra of the far north gives way to a cool, wet, heavily forested region. The North European Plain is well-drained, fertile, and rich in oil, coal, and natural gas. The shores of the Mediterranean are generally warm, dry, and hilly, ideal for cultivating olives, citrus fruits, and grapes. A great curve of mountain ranges, including the Pyrenees, Alps, and Carpathians, divides north from south. To the east, the rolling plains of European Russia and the Ukraine, clothed in coniferous forests or cultivated for wheat, run up to the Ural Mountains. Europeans are mainly Christian – Catholic or Protestant – and speak a variety of languages, most of which spring from Latin (Romance), Germanic, or Slavic roots.

GREENLAND
(Danish province)
Arctic Circle
JAN MAYEN
(to Norway)
Denmark Strait
REYKJAVÍK
Akureyri
ICELAND
Norwegian
Sea
FAEROE IS
(to Denmark)
Shetland Is
Orkney Is
Outer Hebrides
Edinburgh
Belfast
REPUBLIC OF IRELAND
ISLE OF MAN (to UK)
DUBLIN
UNITED KINGDOM
Manchester
Cork
Birmingham
Cardiff
LONDON
NETHER
AMSTERD
Rotterdam
BRUSSELS
English Channel
GUERNSEY (to UK)
JERSEY (to UK)
Seine
PARIS
Nantes
Loire
FRANCE
Bay of Biscay
Bordeaux
Massif Central
Rhône
Toulouse
Pyrenees
ANDORRA
Marse
A Coruña
Porto
PORTUGAL
Tagus
LISBON
SPAIN
Zaragoza
Ebro
Barcelona
MADRID
Valencia
Mallorca
Palma
Balearic Is
Eivissa
Sevilla
Málaga
GIBRALTAR (to UK)
Ceuta (to Spain)
Melilla (to Spain)
MOROCCO
ALGERI
ATLANTIC OCEAN
Azores
(to Portugal)
POPULATION
over 5 000 000
over 1 000 000
over 500 000
over 100 000
over 50 000
under 50 000
LAND HEIGHT
3000m/9843ft
2000m/6562ft
1000m/3281ft
200m/656ft
Sea Level
Line of cross-section
Scale : 1:22 500 000
0
250
500 km
0
250
500 miles

CROSS-SECTION THROUGH EUROPE: 46°N, 5°W–48°E

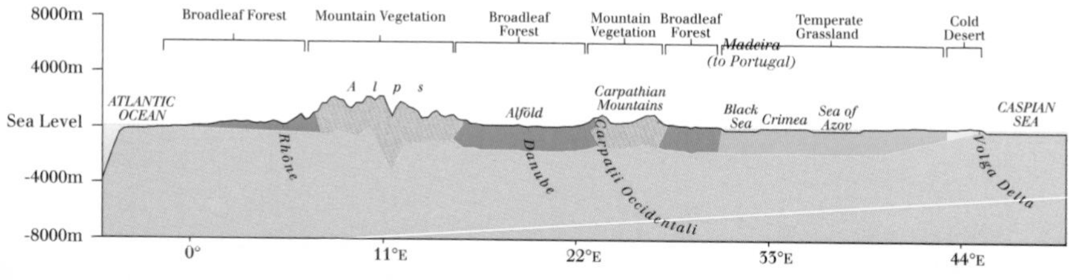
8000m
4000m
Sea Level
-4000m
-8000m
Broadleaf Forest
Mountain Vegetation
Broadleaf Forest
Mountain Vegetation
Broadleaf Forest
Temperate Grassland
Cold Desert
Madeira
(to Portugal)
ATLANTIC OCEAN
Alps
Rhône
Alföld
Danube
Carpathian Mountains
Carpatii Occidentali
Black Sea
Crimea
Sea of Azov
CASPIAN SEA
Volga Delta
0°
11°E
22°E
33°E
44°E

CONTINENTAL FACTS

PHYSICAL FEATURES

LARGEST LAKE: Ladoga, European Russia 18,390 km² (7100 mi²)

LONGEST RIVER: Volga, European Russia 3688 km (2290 miles)

HIGHEST POINT: El' brus, Caucasus Mts, European Russia 5642 m (18,510 ft)

LOWEST POINT: Volga Delta, Caspian Sea, European Russia 28 m (92 ft) below sea level

POLITICAL FEATURES

TOTAL POPULATION: 704.9 million

COUNTRY WITH HIGHEST POPULATION DENSITY: Monaco 16,410 people/km² (42,503 people/mi²)

LARGEST CITY AND ITS POPULATION: Moscow, European Russia 9.3 million

LARGEST COUNTRY: European Russia 3,955,818 km² (1,527,341 mi²)

SMALLEST COUNTRY: Vatican City, Italy 0.44 km² (0.17 mi²)

SVALBARD (to Norway)
Novaya Zemlya
Karskoye More
Barents Sea
Arctic Circle
Pechora
Murmansk
Tromsø
Arkhangel'sk
Severnaya Dvina
Kemi
NORWAY
SWEDEN
FINLAND
Gulf of Bothnia
Vaasa
Onezhskoye Ozero
Ladozhskoye Ozero
Trondheim
Tampere
Turku
HELSINKI
Åland
St Petersburg
RUSSIAN FEDERATION
Kazan'
Ufa
Ural
Yaroslavl'
Nizhniy Novgorod
Orenburg
Samara
Uppsala
OSLO
Örebro
STOCKHOLM
Vänern
Vättern
TALLINN
Tartu
ESTONIA
MOSCOW
Kristiansand
Göteborg
Gotland
RIGA
LATVIA
Baltic Sea
European Plain
EUROPEAN RUSSIA
Volga
Saratov
Tula
KAZAKHSTAN
DENMARK
Malmö
COPENHAGEN
Šiauliai
LITHUANIA
Daugavpils
Orsha
KALININGRAD (to Russian Fed.)
VILNIUS
MINSK
BELARUS
Voronezh
Gdańsk
North
Hamburg
Elbe
BERLIN
Wisla
WARSAW
Łódź
POLAND
Homyel'
Don
Volgograd
Astrakhan'
Volga Delta
Kharkiv
KIEV
Dnieper
Donets'k
Dnipropetrovs'k
Rostov-na-Donu
UKRAINE
Caspian Sea
GERMANY
Frankfurt am Main
PRAGUE
Kraków
CZECH REPUBLIC
SLOVAKIA
Dniester
MOLDOVA
CHIŞINĂU
Odesa
Sea of Azov
Crimea
Krasnodar
Makhachkala
Caucasus
El'brus 5642m
GEORGIA
TBILISI
AZERBAIJAN
ARMENIA
AZERB.
Danube
Strasbourg
München
VIENNA
BRATISLAVA
Miskolc
Iaşi
Carpathian Mts
Salzburg
BUDAPEST
Carpaţii Occidentali
AUSTRIA
HUNGARY
Alföld
ROMANIA
Braşov
Black Sea
LJUBLJANA
SLOVENIA
ZAGREB
CROATIA
Timişoara
Novi Sad
BUCHAREST
Trabzon
Milano
Po
BELGRADE
Danube
Varna
ITALY
SAN MARINO
BOSNIA & HERZEGOVINA
SARAJEVO
YUGOSLAVIA
BULGARIA
SOFIA
MONACO
Split
Adriatic Sea
Podgorica
SKOPJE
Plovdiv
Istanbul
ANKARA
Irmak
IRAN
Appennino
ROME
VATICAN CITY
MACEDONIA
TIRANA
ALBANIA
Thessaloníki
Bursa
TURKEY
Napoli
Gaziantep
Konya
Adana
Tyrrhenian Sea
Lárisa
GREECE
İzmir
SYRIA
IRAQ
Sardinia
Cágliari
ATHENS
Pátra
Aegean Sea
Palermo
Sicily
Ionian Sea
NICOSIA
CYPRUS
LEBANON
ISRAEL
Mediterranean Sea
MALTA
Iráklelo
Crete
TUNISIA
LIBYA
EGYPT

ST HELENA (to UK)
OCEAN
Namibe
Lubango
NAMIBIA
Walvis Bay
WINDHOEK
Kalahari Desert
BOTSWANA
GABORONE
Francistown
ZIMBABWE
HARARE
Bulawayo
LUSAKA
LILONGWE
Zambezi
Blantyre
Nampula
Quelimane
Beira
MOZAMBIQUE
Mozambique Channel
Limpopo
PRETORIA
Johannesburg
MAPUTO
MBABANE
SWAZILAND
Bloemfontein
MASERU
LESOTHO
Orange
SOUTH AFRICA
Durban
Drakensberg
East London
Port Elizabeth
Cape Town
Cape of Good Hope
MADAGASCAR
Mahajanga
ANTANANARIVO
Fianarantsoa
Farafangana
MAURITIUS
PORT LOUIS
RÉUNION (to France)
Tropic of Capricorn
Scale : 1:36 000 000
0 500 1000 km
0 500 1000 miles
POPULATION
over 5 000 000
over 1 000 000
over 500 000
over 100 000
over 50 000
under 50 000
LAND HEIGHT
4000m/13 124ft
3000m/9843ft
2000m/6562ft
1000m/3281ft
200m/656ft
Sea Level
Line of cross-section

AFRICA

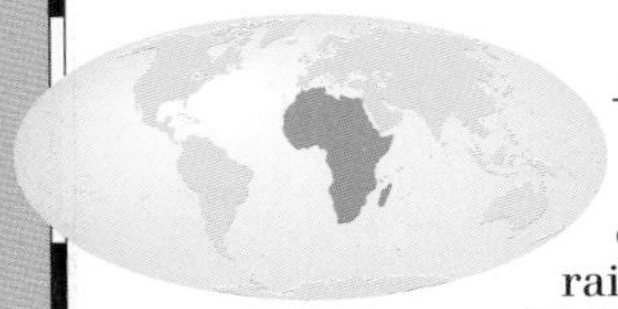

AFRICA IS THE SECOND-LARGEST CONTINENT after Asia. It is dominated by the Sahara in the north and the Great Rift Valley in the east. The Mediterranean climate of the extreme north and south enables cultivation of grapes and other fruit. A belt of tropical rainforest lies along the Equator, while Africa's great tropical grasslands provide grazing for herds of wild animals and domestic livestock. A narrow strip of Egypt is watered by the world's longest river, the Nile, which sustained prehistoric communities. The center and south of the continent are rich in minerals. Almost one-tenth of the world's population lives in Africa – a wide variety of peoples with their own distinctive languages and cultures. Although Islam and Christianity are widespread, many Africans adhere to their own local customs and religious beliefs.

CONTINENTAL FACTS

PHYSICAL FEATURES

LARGEST LAKE: Lake Victoria 68,880 sq km (26,560 square miles)

LONGEST RIVER: Nile, Uganda/ Sudan/ Egypt 6695 km (4160 miles)

HIGHEST POINT: Kilimanjaro, Tanzania 5895 m (19,341 ft)

LOWEST POINT: Lac' Assal, Djibouti 156 m (512 ft) below sea level

POLITICAL FEATURES

TOTAL POPULATION: 783.8 million

LARGEST CITY AND POPULATION: Lagos, Nigeria, 13.4 million

COUNTRY WITH HIGHEST POPULATION DENSITY: Mauritius 645 people/km² (1671 people/mi²)

LARGEST COUNTRY: Sudan 2,376,000 sq km (917,374 square miles)

SMALLEST COUNTRY: Seychelles 270 sq km (104 square miles)

CROSS-SECTION THROUGH AFRICA 7°N, 15°W–55°E

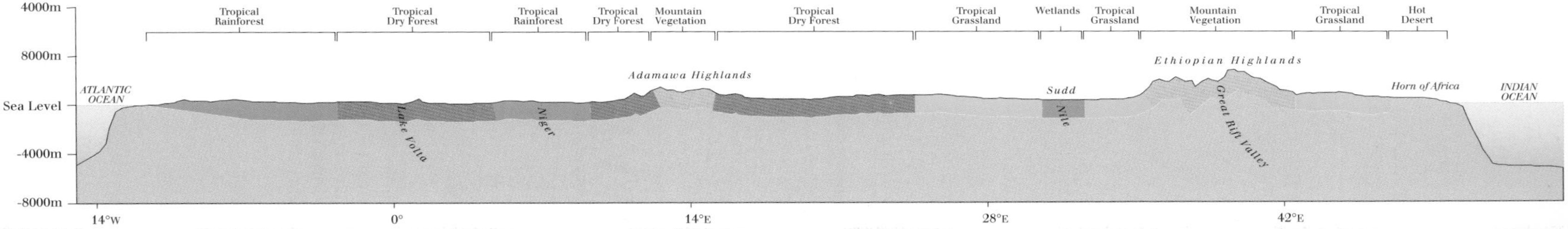
4000m
8000m
Sea Level
-4000m
-8000m
Tropical Rainforest
Tropical Dry Forest
Tropical Rainforest
Tropical Dry Forest
Mountain Vegetation
Tropical Dry Forest
Tropical Grassland
Wetlands
Tropical Grassland
Mountain Vegetation
Tropical Grassland
Hot Desert
ATLANTIC OCEAN
Lake Volta
Niger
Adamawa Highlands
Sudd
Nile
Ethiopian Highlands
Great Rift Valley
Horn of Africa
INDIAN OCEAN
14°W
0°
14°E
28°E
42°E

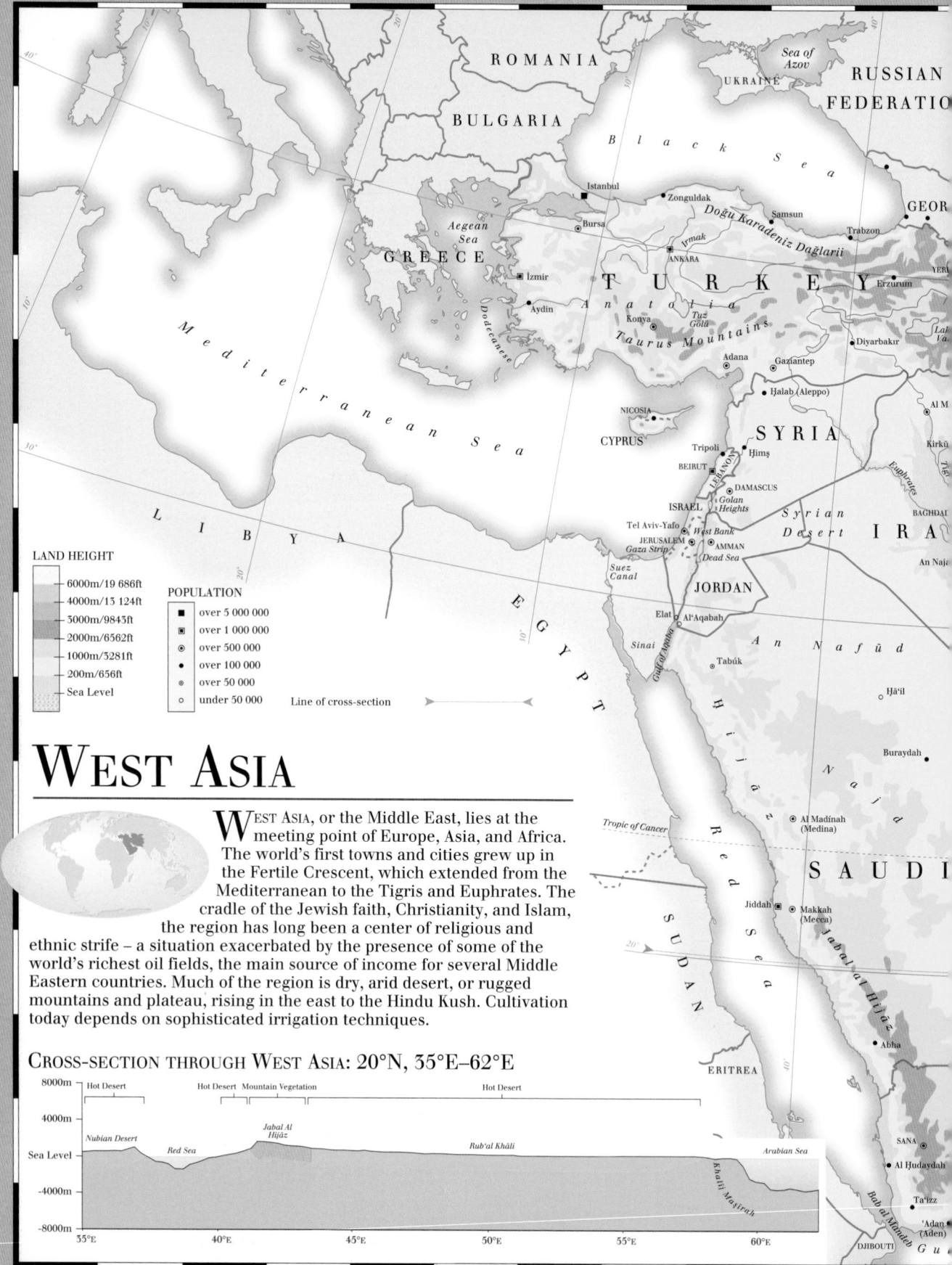

ROMANIA
Sea of Azov
UKRAINE
RUSSIAN FEDERATIO
BULGARIA
Black Sea
Istanbul
Zonguldak
Samsun
GEOR
Doğu Karadeniz Dağlarii
Trabzon
Bursa
Aegean Sea
Irmak
ANKARA
GREECE
İzmir
TURKEY
Erzurum
Aydin
Anatolia
Konya
Tuz Gölü
Taurus Mountains
Dodecanese
Diyarbakır
Mediterranean Sea
Adana
Gaziantep
Halab (Aleppo)
NICOSIA
CYPRUS
SYRIA
Tripoli
Hims
BEIRUT
LEBANON
DAMASCUS
Golan Heights
ISRAEL
Syrian Desert
IRA
Tel Aviv-Yafo
West Bank
JERUSALEM
AMMAN
Gaza Strip
Dead Sea
LIBYA
Suez Canal
JORDAN
EGYPT
Elat
Al'Aqabah
Sinai
Gulf of Aqaba
An Nafūd
Tabūk
LAND HEIGHT
6000m/19 686ft
4000m/13 124ft
3000m/9843ft
2000m/6562ft
1000m/3281ft
200m/656ft
Sea Level
POPULATION
over 5 000 000
over 1 000 000
over 500 000
over 100 000
over 50 000
under 50 000
Line of cross-section

West Asia

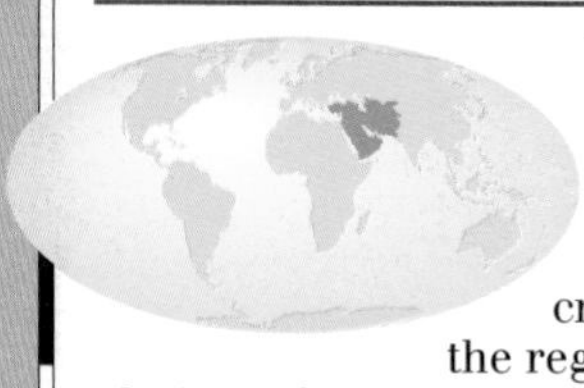

West Asia, or the Middle East, lies at the meeting point of Europe, Asia, and Africa. The world's first towns and cities grew up in the Fertile Crescent, which extended from the Mediterranean to the Tigris and Euphrates. The cradle of the Jewish faith, Christianity, and Islam, the region has long been a center of religious and ethnic strife – a situation exacerbated by the presence of some of the world's richest oil fields, the main source of income for several Middle Eastern countries. Much of the region is dry, arid desert, or rugged mountains and plateau, rising in the east to the Hindu Kush. Cultivation today depends on sophisticated irrigation techniques.

Cross-section through West Asia: 20°N, 35°E–62°E

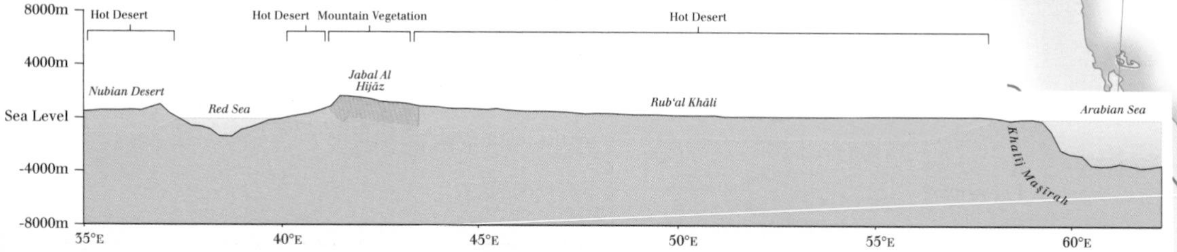
8000m
4000m
Sea Level
-4000m
-8000m
Hot Desert
Hot Desert
Mountain Vegetation
Hot Desert
Nubian Desert
Red Sea
Jabal Al Hijâz
Rub'al Khâli
Arabian Sea
35°E
40°E
45°E
50°E
55°E
60°E

KAZAKHSTAN
Aral Sea
UZBEKISTAN
Kyzyl Kum
Ozero Aydarkul'
Dashkhovuz
Urganch
TASHKENT
Namangan
Osh
Khŭjand
BISHKEK
Karakol
Ozero Issyk-Kul'
Kirghiz Range
Naryn
KYRGYZSTAN
Tien Shan
CHINA
Caspian Sea
AZERBAIJAN
BAKU
Gäncä
Länkäran
Krasnovodsk
Nebitdag
Karakumy
TURKMENISTAN
Khrebet Kopetdag
ASHGABAT
Chardzhev
Amu
Mary
Samarqand
Qarshi
TAJIKISTAN
DUSHANBE
Kŭlob
Khorugh
Kurgan-Tyube
Pamirs
Karakoram Range
K2 8611m
Indus
Mazār-e-Sharīf
Baghlān
Hindu Kush
Jalālābād
KĀBUL
Peshāwar
ISLĀMĀBĀD
Rāwalpindi
Tabriz
Rasht
Gorgān
Mashhad
Reshteh-ye Kuhhā ye Alborz
TEHRĀN
Hamadān
Qom
Dasht-e-Kavīr
Bākhtarān
Herāt
AFGHANISTAN
Gujrānwāla
Lahore
Chenab
Faisalābād
IRAN
Eşfahān
Plateau of Iran
Hāmūn-e Şāberī
Helmand
Kandahār
Multān
Ahvāz
Zagros Mountains
Quetta
Başrah
Ābādān
Kermān
Zāhedān
Thar Desert
KUWAIT CITY
KUWAIT
Shīrāz
Sukkur
Indus
PAKISTAN
INDIA
Persian Gulf
Bandar-e 'Abbās
Strait of Hormuz
BAHRAIN
MANAMA
DOHA
QATAR
Hyderābād
Karāchi
Tropic of Cancer
RIYADH
Al Hufūf
Dubai
Sharjah
ABU DHABI
Şuḩār
Gulf of Oman
Arabian Sea
Ḩaraḑ
UNITED ARAB EMIRATES
MUSCAT
Ar Rustāq
Nazwá
Şūr
ARABIA
Scale : 1:17 000 000
0 200 400 km
0 200 400 miles
Rub' al Khāli
OMAN
Khalīj Maşīrah
INDIAN OCEAN
Şalālah
YEMEN
Hadhramaut
Al Mukallā
Socotra (to Yemen)
Aden

CONTINENTAL FACTS

PHYSICAL FEATURES

LARGEST LAKE: Caspian Sea 371,000 km² (143,205 mi²)

LONGEST RIVER: Euphrates, Syria/Iraq 2815 km (1750 miles)

HIGHEST POINT: K2, Kashmir, India/Pakistan 8611m (28,252 ft)

LOWEST POINT: Dead Sea, Israel/Jordan 392 m (1286 ft) below sea level

POLITICAL FEATURES

TOTAL POPULATION: 467.7 million

LARGEST CITY AND ITS POPULATION: Istanbul, Turkey 9.5 million

COUNTRY WITH HIGHEST POPULATION DENSITY: Bahrain 907 people/km² (2350 people/mi²)

LARGEST COUNTRY: Saudi Arabia 2,114,690 km² (816,480 mi²)

SMALLEST COUNTRY: Bahrain 680 km² (263 mi²)

UKRAINE
EUROPEAN
RUSSIA
Arctic Circle
Karskoye
More
Ostrov
Komsomolets
Ostrov Oktyabr'skoy
Revolyutsii
Ostrov
Bol'shevik
Severnaya Zem
Poluostrov Yamal
Poluostrov Taymyr
Gydanskiy
Poluostrov
Ozero
Taymyr
Severo-Sibirskaya Nizmen
Salekhard
Nadym
Noril'sk
Ob'
Ural Mountains
Serov
Ural'sk
Ural
Yekaterinburg
Khanty-Mansiyk
Chelyabinsk
Tyumen'
Zapadno-
Sibirskaya
Ravnina
Nizhnevartovsk
RUSSIAN
ASIATIC
FEDERATION
Sredne
Sibirsko
Ploskogor
Nizhnyaya Tunguska
Podkamennaya Tunguska
Yenisey
Atyrau
Aktyubinsk
Kostanay
Caspian Sea
Aktau
Ustyurt
Plateau
KAZAKHSTAN
Ishim
Irtysh
Omsk
Aral Sea
Aral'sk
Syr Darya
ASTANA
Tomsk
Novosibirsk
Zhezkazgan
Karaganda
Barnaul
Krasnoyarsk
Bratsk
Boday
TURKMENISTAN
UZBEKISTAN
Kyzylorda
Rubtsovsk
Semipalatinsk
Abakan
Lena
Ozero
Baykal
Ozero
Balkhash
Shymkent
Taraz
Ili
Taldykorgan
Almaty
Ozero
Zaysan
Uvs
Nuur
Kyzyl
Irkutsk
Ulan-Ude
Chita
Yablonovyy
Ölgiy
Hovd
Hyargas
Nuur
Altai Mountains
Hövsgöl
Nuur
AFGHANISTAN
KYRGYZSTAN
TAJIKISTAN
Yining
Erdenet
Darhan
ULAN BATOR
Choybalsan
Kerulen
Kashi
Tien Shan
Ürümqi
Altay
MONGOLIA
Tarim He
Turpan
Hami
Hami
Bayanhongor
PAKISTAN
Taklimakan
Shamo
Hotan
Saynshand
Gobi
Aksai
Chin
Kunlun Shan
Altun Shan
Yumen
Qilian Shan
Qaidam Pendi
Baotou
Datong
BEIJING
(PEKING)
Huang He
Qing Zang
Gaoyuan
Golmud
Qinghai Hu
Xining
Tianjin
INDIA
Himalayas
TIBET
Lanzhou
Taiyuan
Shijiazhuan
CHINA
Huang He (Yellow R.)
Xi'an
Zhengzhou
NEPAL
Brahmaputra
Xixabangma Feng
8012m
Lhasa
Salween
Mekong
Tropic of Cancer
BHUTAN
INDIA
Chengdu
Chang Jiang (Yangtze)
Wuhan
Chongqing
Dongting
Hu
Changsha
Guiyang
Kunming
Xi Jiang
BURMA
(MYANMAR)
VIETNAM
LAOS
Nanning
Guangzhou
Shantou
Hong Kong
(Xianggang)
Macao
(Aomen)
Gulf of
Tongking
Haikou
Hainan Dao
South
China
Sea

Continental Facts

PHYSICAL FEATURES

LARGEST LAKE: Aral Sea, Kazakhstan/Uzbekistan 66,500 km² (25,700 mi²)

LONGEST RIVER: Chang Jiang (Yangtze), China 6380 km (3965 miles)

HIGHEST POINT: Xixabangma Feng, China 8012 m (26,286 ft)

LOWEST POINT: Turpan Hami (Turfan Basin), China 154 m (505 ft) below sea level

POLITICAL FEATURES

TOTAL POPULATION: 1546 million

LARGEST CITY AND ITS POPULATION: Tokyo, Japan 26.4 million

COUNTRY WITH HIGHEST POPULATION DENSITY: Taiwan 688 people/km² (1782 people/mi²)

LARGEST COUNTRY: Asiatic Russia 13,119,582 km² (5,065,471 mi²)

SMALLEST COUNTRY: Taiwan 32,260 km² (12,455 mi²)

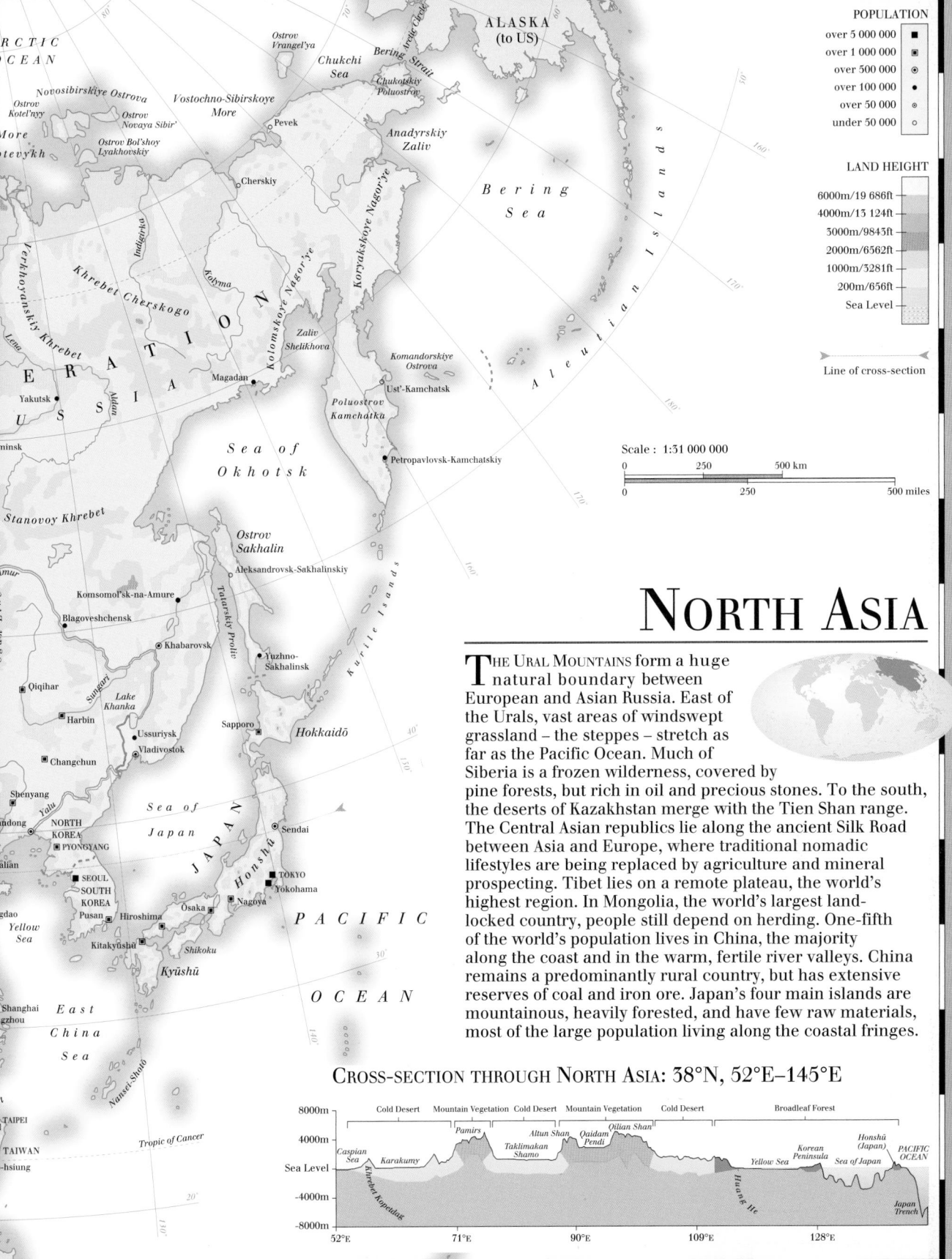

POPULATION
over 5 000 000
over 1 000 000
over 500 000
over 100 000
over 50 000
under 50 000
LAND HEIGHT
6000m/19 686ft
4000m/13 124ft
3000m/9843ft
2000m/6562ft
1000m/3281ft
200m/656ft
Sea Level
Line of cross-section
Scale : 1:31 000 000
0
250
500 km
0
250
500 miles
ALASKA (to US)
Ostrov Vrangel'ya
Chukchi Sea
Bering Strait
Arctic Circle
Chukotskiy Poluostrov
Novosibirskiye Ostrova
Ostrov Kotel'nyy
Ostrov Novaya Sibir'
Ostrov Bol'shoy Lyakhovskiy
Vostochno-Sibirskoye More
Pevek
Anadyrskiy Zaliv
Cherskiy
Bering Sea
Aleutian Islands
Koryakskoye Nagor'ye
Kolomskoye Nagor'ye
Indigirka
Kolyma
Khrebet Cherskogo
Verkhoyanskiy Khrebet
Lena
Aldan
Zaliv Shelikhova
Komandorskiye Ostrova
Ust'-Kamchatsk
Magadan
Yakutsk
Poluostrov Kamchatka
Sea of Okhotsk
Petropavlovsk-Kamchatskiy
Stanovoy Khrebet
Ostrov Sakhalin
Aleksandrovsk-Sakhalinskiy
Amur
Komsomol'sk-na-Amure
Blagoveshchensk
Tatarskiy Proliv
Kurile Islands
Khabarovsk
Yuzhno-Sakhalinsk
Qiqihar
Sungari
Lake Khanka
Harbin
Ussuriysk
Vladivostok
Sapporo
Hokkaidō
Changchun
Shenyang
Yalu
Sea of Japan
JAPAN
NORTH KOREA
PYONGYANG
Sendai
Honshū
SEOUL
SOUTH KOREA
TOKYO
Yokohama
Nagoya
Pusan
Hiroshima
Ōsaka
PACIFIC OCEAN
Yellow Sea
Kitakyūshū
Shikoku
Kyūshū
Shanghai
East China Sea
Nansei-Shotō
TAIPEI
TAIWAN
Tropic of Cancer

NORTH ASIA

THE URAL MOUNTAINS form a huge natural boundary between European and Asian Russia. East of the Urals, vast areas of windswept grassland – the steppes – stretch as far as the Pacific Ocean. Much of Siberia is a frozen wilderness, covered by pine forests, but rich in oil and precious stones. To the south, the deserts of Kazakhstan merge with the Tien Shan range. The Central Asian republics lie along the ancient Silk Road between Asia and Europe, where traditional nomadic lifestyles are being replaced by agriculture and mineral prospecting. Tibet lies on a remote plateau, the world's highest region. In Mongolia, the world's largest land-locked country, people still depend on herding. One-fifth of the world's population lives in China, the majority along the coast and in the warm, fertile river valleys. China remains a predominantly rural country, but has extensive reserves of coal and iron ore. Japan's four main islands are mountainous, heavily forested, and have few raw materials, most of the large population living along the coastal fringes.

CROSS-SECTION THROUGH NORTH ASIA: 38°N, 52°E–145°E

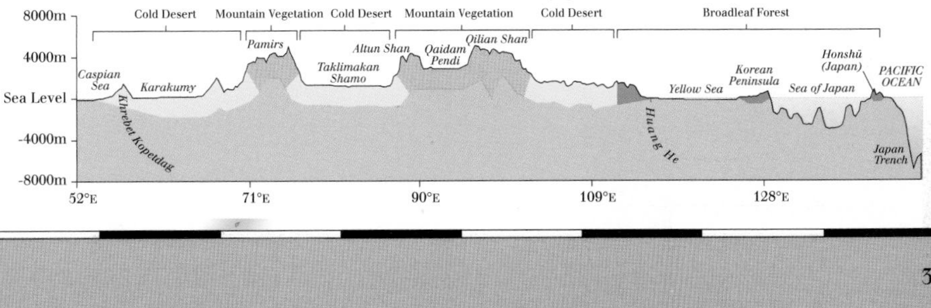
8000m
4000m
Sea Level
-4000m
-8000m
52°E
71°E
90°E
109°E
128°E
Cold Desert
Mountain Vegetation
Cold Desert
Mountain Vegetation
Cold Desert
Broadleaf Forest
Caspian Sea
Khrebet Kopetdag
Karakumy
Pamirs
Taklimakan Shamo
Altun Shan
Qaidam Pendi
Qilian Shan
Huang He
Yellow Sea
Korean Peninsula
Sea of Japan
Honshū (Japan)
PACIFIC OCEAN
Japan Trench

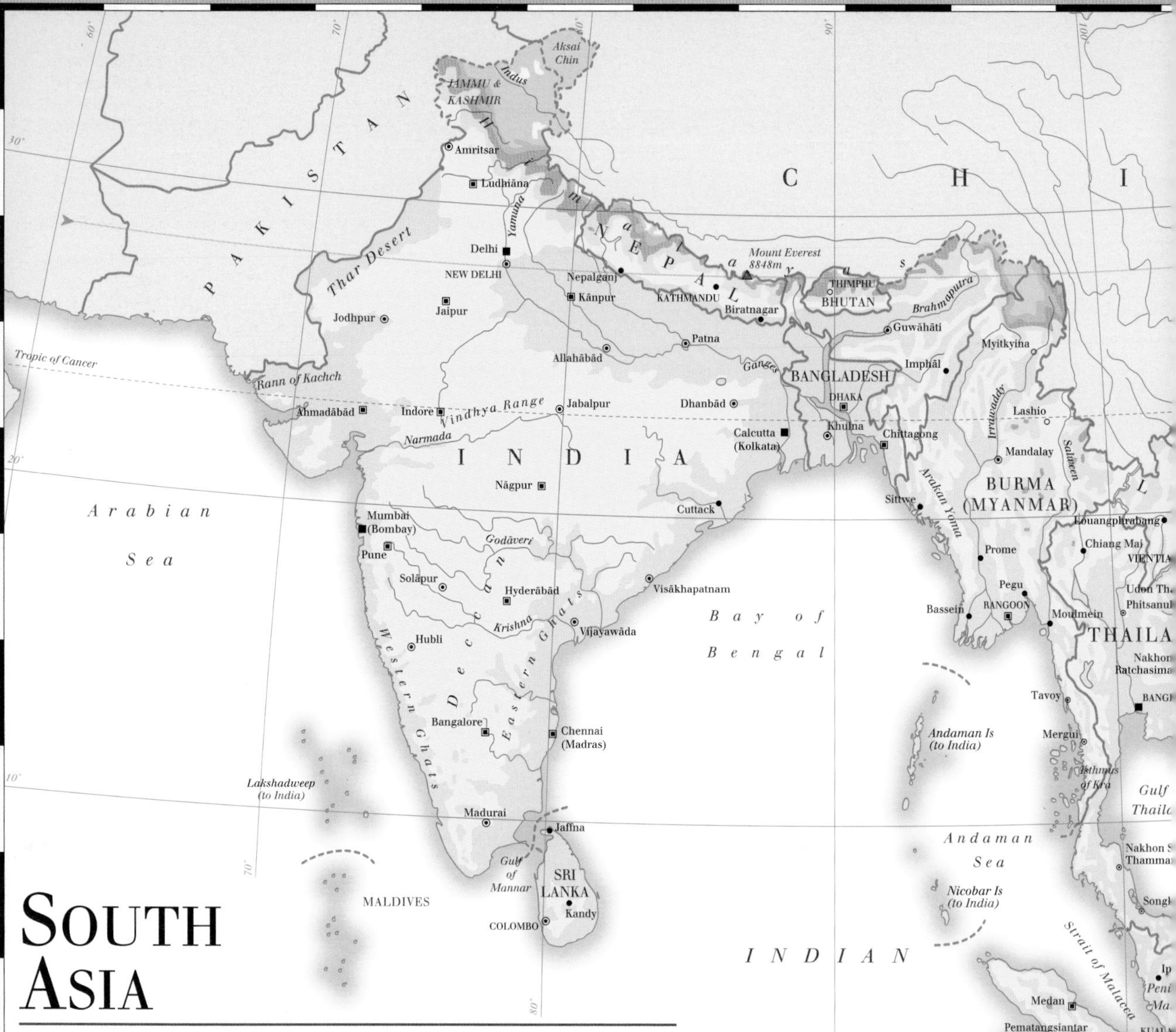
Aksai Chin
JAMMU & KASHMIR
Indus
Amritsar
Ludhiāna
P A K I S T A N
C H I
H i m a l a y a s
Yamuna
Thar Desert
Delhi
NEW DELHI
Nepalganj
N E P A L
Mount Everest 8848m
THIMPHU
BHUTAN
Kānpur
KATHMANDU
Biratnagar
Brahmaputra
Guwāhāti
Jodhpur
Jaipur
Patna
Tropic of Cancer
Allahābād
Myitkyina
Rann of Kachch
Ganges
BANGLADESH
Imphāl
Ahmadābād
Indore
Vindhya Range
Jabalpur
Dhanbād
DHAKA
Lashio
Narmada
Calcutta (Kolkata)
Khulna
Chittagong
Irrawaddy
I N D I A
Mandalay
Salween
Nāgpur
Arakan Yoma
BURMA (MYANMAR)
Sittwe
A r a b i a n
S e a
Mumbai (Bombay)
Cuttack
Louangphrabang
Godāvari
Pune
Prome
Chiang Mai
VIENTIA
Solāpur
Hyderābād
Visākhapatnam
Pegu
Udon Th
Phitsanul
Krishna
Bassein
RANGOON
Moulmein
Hubli
Vijayawāda
B a y o f
B e n g a l
THAILA
Western Ghats
Deccan
Eastern Ghats
Nakhon Ratchasima
Tavoy
BANGK
Bangalore
Chennai (Madras)
Andaman Is (to India)
Mergui
Lakshadweep (to India)
Isthmus of Kra
Gulf of Thaila
Madurai
Jaffna
A n d a m a n
S e a
Gulf of Mannar
SRI LANKA
Nakhon S Thamma
MALDIVES
Kandy
Nicobar Is (to India)
Songk
COLOMBO
Strait of Malacca
I N D I A N
Medan
Pematangsiantar
Danau Toba
KUALA LUMPUR
O C E A N
Pakambaru
Equator
Pada

SOUTH ASIA

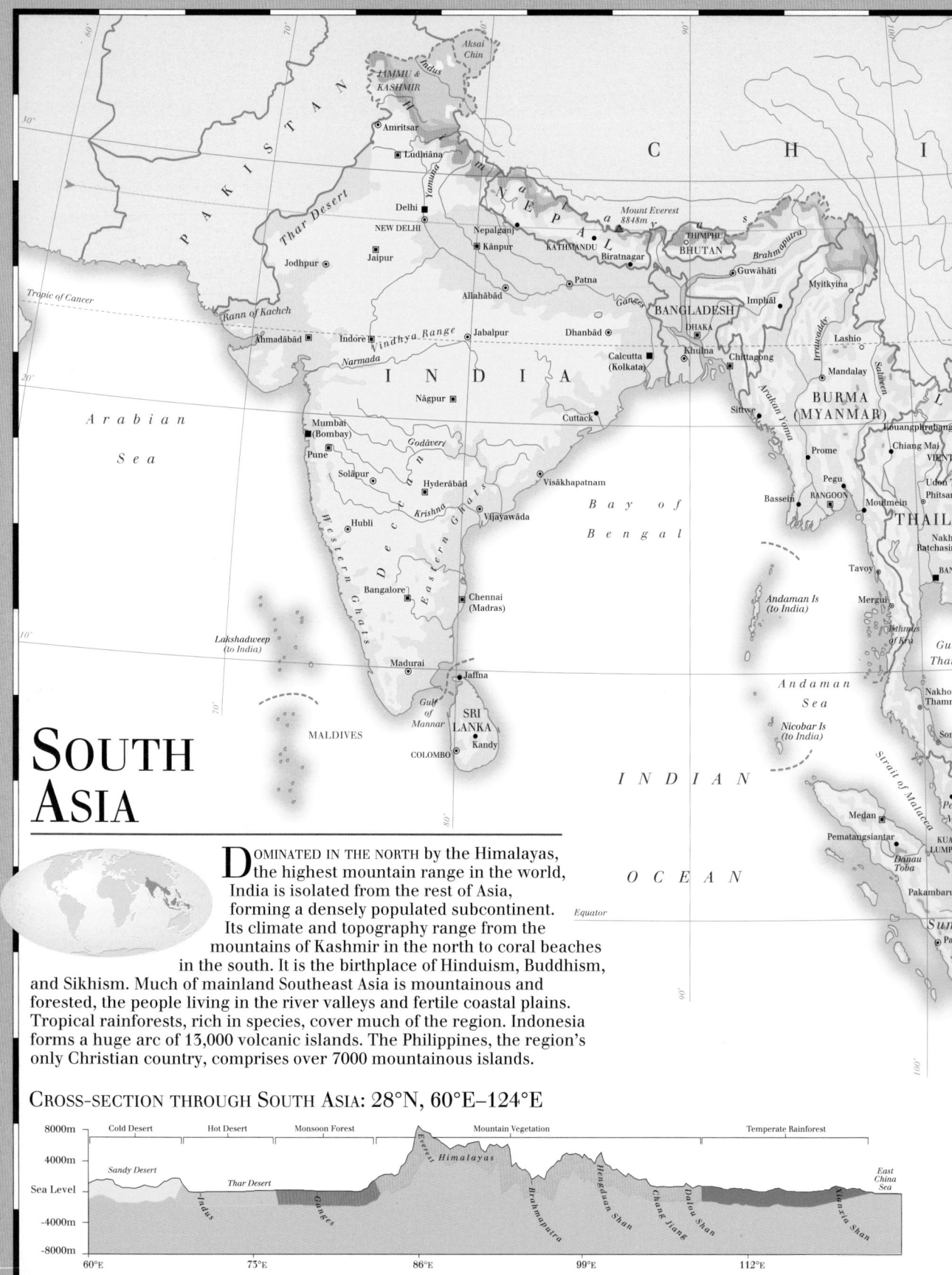

DOMINATED IN THE NORTH by the Himalayas, the highest mountain range in the world, India is isolated from the rest of Asia, forming a densely populated subcontinent. Its climate and topography range from the mountains of Kashmir in the north to coral beaches in the south. It is the birthplace of Hinduism, Buddhism, and Sikhism. Much of mainland Southeast Asia is mountainous and forested, the people living in the river valleys and fertile coastal plains. Tropical rainforests, rich in species, cover much of the region. Indonesia forms a huge arc of 13,000 volcanic islands. The Philippines, the region's only Christian country, comprises over 7000 mountainous islands.

CROSS-SECTION THROUGH SOUTH ASIA: 28°N, 60°E–124°E

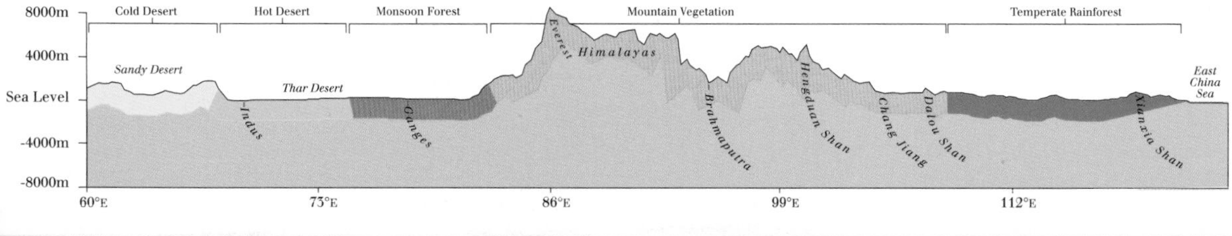
8000m
4000m
Sea Level
-4000m
-8000m
Cold Desert
Hot Desert
Monsoon Forest
Mountain Vegetation
Temperate Rainforest
Sandy Desert
Thar Desert
Indus
Ganges
Everest
Himalayas
Brahmaputra
Hengduan Shan
Chang Jiang
Dalou Shan
Xianxia Shan
East China Sea
60°E
73°E
86°E
99°E
112°E

Continental Facts

PHYSICAL FEATURES

Largest lake: Tônlé Sap, Cambodia 2850 km² (1000 mi²)

Longest river: Mekong, China/Vietnam 4425 km (2750 miles)

Highest point: Mount Everest, Nepal 8848 m (29,030 ft)

Lowest point: About half of Bangladesh lies between sea level and 8 m (25 ft)

POLITICAL FEATURES

Total population: 1706 million

Largest city and its population: Mumbai, India 18.1 million

Country with highest population density: Singapore 5902 people/km² (15,285 people/mi²)

Largest country: India 2,973,190 km² (1,147,949 mi²)

Smallest country: Maldives 300 km² (116 mi²)

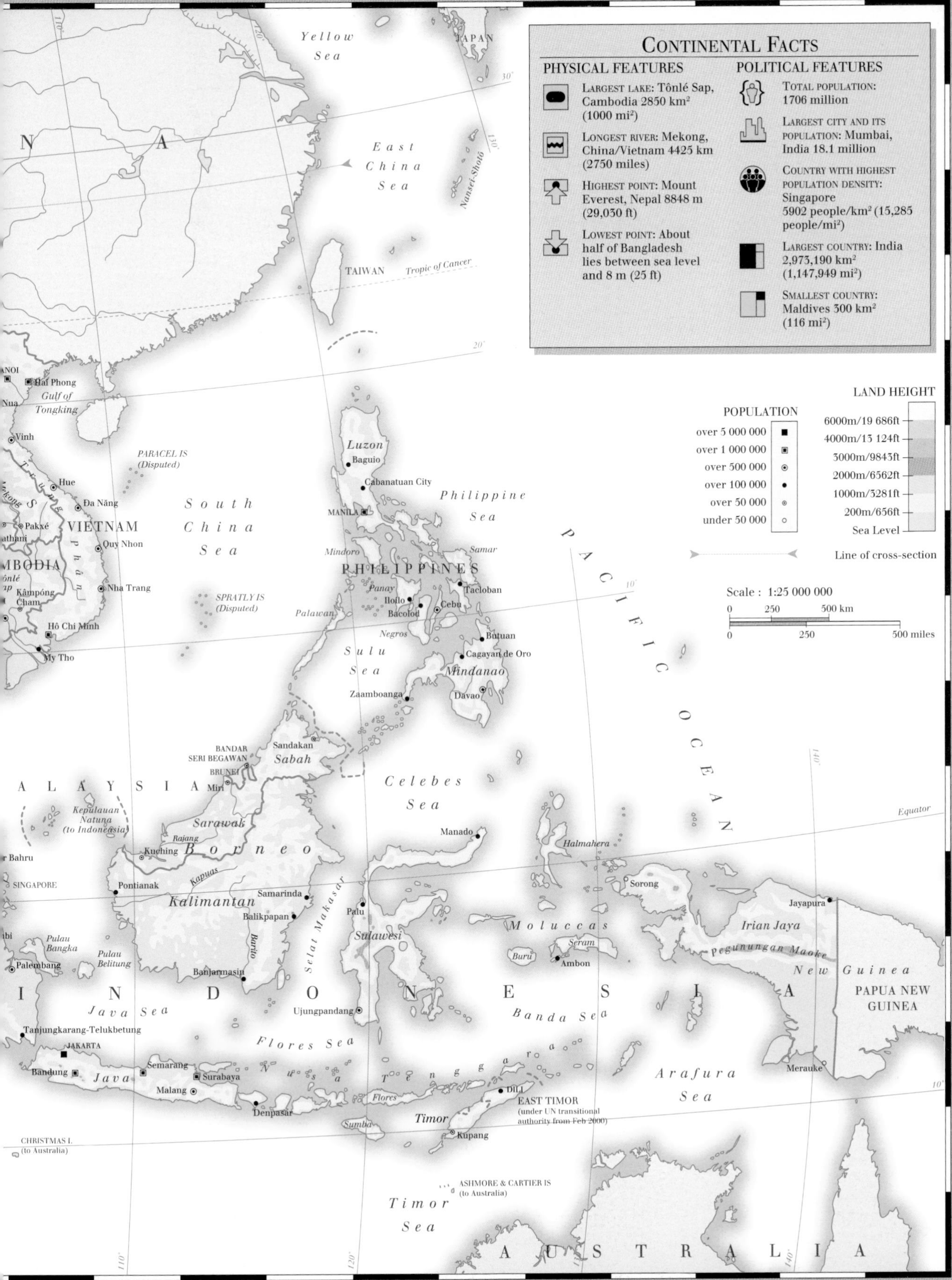
Yellow Sea
JAPAN
East China Sea
Nansei-Shotō
TAIWAN
Tropic of Cancer
Hai Phong
Gulf of Tongking
Vinh
Hue
Đa Năng
Pakxé
VIETNAM
Quy Nhon
Nha Trang
Kâmpóng Cham
Hô Chi Minh
My Tho
PARACEL IS (Disputed)
SPRATLY IS (Disputed)
South China Sea
Luzon
Baguio
Cabanatuan City
MANILA
Mindoro
PHILIPPINES
Philippine Sea
Samar
Panay
Iloilo
Bacolod
Cebu
Tacloban
Palawan
Negros
Butuan
Cagayan de Oro
Sulu Sea
Mindanao
Zaamboanga
Davao
PACIFIC OCEAN
BANDAR SERI BEGAWAN
BRUNEI
Sandakan
Sabah
Miri
MALAYSIA
Kepulauan Natuna (to Indonesia)
Sarawak
Rajang
Kuching
Borneo
SINGAPORE
Pontianak
Kapuas
Kalimantan
Samarinda
Balikpapan
Barito
Banjarmasin
Celebes Sea
Manado
Halmahera
Equator
Sorong
Jayapura
Palu
Selat Makasar
Sulawesi
Moluccas
Irian Jaya
Seram
Buru
Ambon
Pegunungan Maoke
New Guinea
PAPUA NEW GUINEA
Pulau Bangka
Pulau Belitung
Palembang
INDONESIA
Java Sea
Ujungpandang
Banda Sea
Tanjungkarang-Telukbetung
JAKARTA
Flores Sea
Bandung
Java
Semarang
Surabaya
Malang
Nusa Tenggara
Dili
Denpasar
Flores
EAST TIMOR (under UN transitional authority from Feb 2000)
Arafura Sea
Merauke
Sumba
Timor
Kupang
CHRISTMAS I. (to Australia)
ASHMORE & CARTIER IS (to Australia)
Timor Sea
AUSTRALIA
LAND HEIGHT
6000m/19 686ft
4000m/13 124ft
3000m/9843ft
2000m/6562ft
1000m/3281ft
200m/656ft
Sea Level
POPULATION
over 5 000 000
over 1 000 000
over 500 000
over 100 000
over 50 000
under 50 000
Line of cross-section
Scale : 1:25 000 000
0 250 500 km
0 250 500 miles

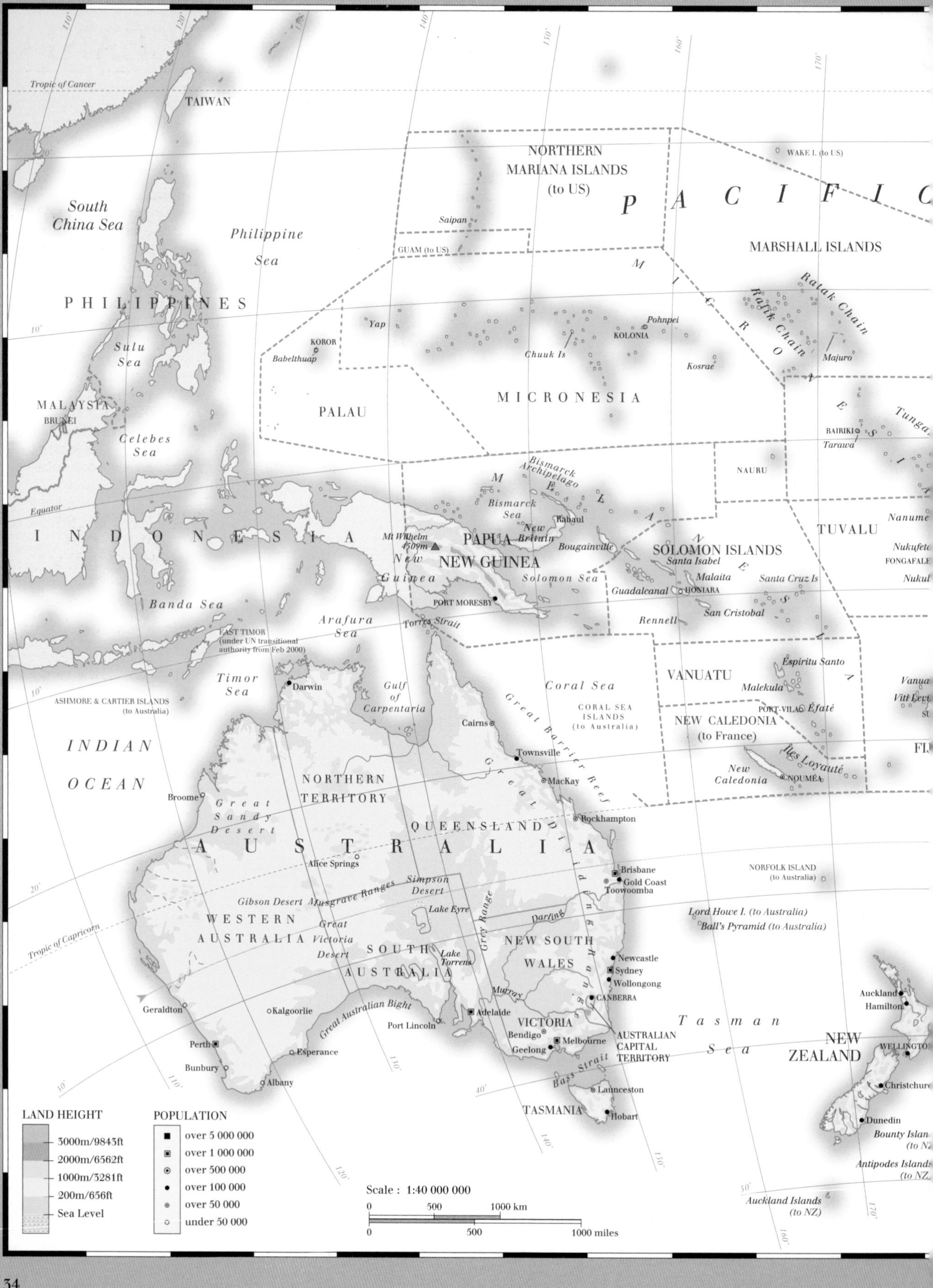
Tropic of Cancer
TAIWAN
NORTHERN MARIANA ISLANDS (to US)
WAKE I. (to US)
P A C I F I C
South China Sea
Philippine Sea
Saipan
GUAM (to US)
MARSHALL ISLANDS
Ratak Chain
Ralik Chain
M I C R O N E S I A
PHILIPPINES
Yap
Pohnpei
KOLONIA
KOROR
Babelthuap
Chuuk Is
Kosrae
Majuro
Sulu Sea
MALAYSIA
BRUNEI
PALAU
MICRONESIA
Tungaru
BAIRIKI
Tarawa
Celebes Sea
Bismarck Archipelago
NAURU
Equator
Bismarck Sea
Rabaul
New Britain
TUVALU
Nanumea
INDONESIA
Mt Wilhelm 4509m
PAPUA NEW GUINEA
New Guinea
Bougainville
SOLOMON ISLANDS
Santa Isabel
Malaita
Nukufetau
FONGAFALE
Nukulaelae
Solomon Sea
Guadalcanal
HONIARA
Santa Cruz Is
Banda Sea
PORT MORESBY
San Cristobal
Arafura Sea
Torres Strait
Rennell
EAST TIMOR (under UN transitional authority from Feb 2000)
Espiritu Santo
VANUATU
Timor Sea
Darwin
Gulf of Carpentaria
Coral Sea
Malekula
Vanua Levu
Viti Levu
ASHMORE & CARTIER ISLANDS (to Australia)
CORAL SEA ISLANDS (to Australia)
PORT-VILA
Éfaté
NEW CALEDONIA (to France)
Cairns
Great Barrier Reef
INDIAN OCEAN
Townsville
Îles Loyauté
FIJI
New Caledonia
NOUMÉA
MacKay
NORTHERN TERRITORY
Broome
Great Sandy Desert
Rockhampton
QUEENSLAND
AUSTRALIA
Great Dividing Range
Alice Springs
Brisbane
Gold Coast
Toowoomba
NORFOLK ISLAND (to Australia)
Simpson Desert
Gibson Desert
Musgrave Ranges
Lake Eyre
Lord Howe I. (to Australia)
Ball's Pyramid (to Australia)
Darling
WESTERN AUSTRALIA
Great Victoria Desert
Grey Range
Tropic of Capricorn
SOUTH AUSTRALIA
NEW SOUTH WALES
Lake Torrens
Newcastle
Sydney
Wollongong
Murray
CANBERRA
Auckland
Hamilton
Geraldton
Kalgoorlie
Great Australian Bight
Adelaide
VICTORIA
Tasman Sea
Port Lincoln
Bendigo
Melbourne
AUSTRALIAN CAPITAL TERRITORY
NEW ZEALAND
WELLINGTON
Perth
Geelong
Esperance
Bunbury
Bass Strait
Albany
Launceston
Christchurch
TASMANIA
Hobart
Dunedin
Bounty Islands (to NZ)
Antipodes Islands (to NZ)
Auckland Islands (to NZ)
LAND HEIGHT
3000m/9843ft
2000m/6562ft
1000m/3281ft
200m/656ft
Sea Level
POPULATION
over 5 000 000
over 1 000 000
over 500 000
over 100 000
over 50 000
under 50 000
Scale : 1:40 000 000
0 500 1000 km
0 500 1000 miles

AUSTRALASIA & OCEANIA

OCEANIA, A CONTINENT OF ISLANDS stretching across a vast area of the Pacific Ocean, is home to less than half of one per cent of the world's population. Dominated by Australia, it includes few other countries with significant land mass apart from New Zealand, Papua New Guinea, and Fiji, but a myriad volcanic and coral islands in three main groups, Micronesia, Melanesia, and Polynesia. Australia, flat and dry, is sparsely populated, most people living along the coastal lowlands, especially in the southeast. Its first inhabitants, the Aboriginal peoples, retain some of their original lands in the interior, but the European and Asian settlers of recent centuries form most of the population. Australia is rich in minerals, such as gold, uranium and iron ore, which are the basis of its prosperity. Mountainous Papua New Guinea is covered in tropical rainforest, while New Zealand is temperate, rugged, and volcanic in the north. Owing to their isolation, these countries' flora and fauna have evolved many unique species. The peoples of Oceania colonized the Pacific by 1500CE, and the many insular farming and fishing communities have developed distinctive cultures, the Maoris of New Zealand being among the most notable.

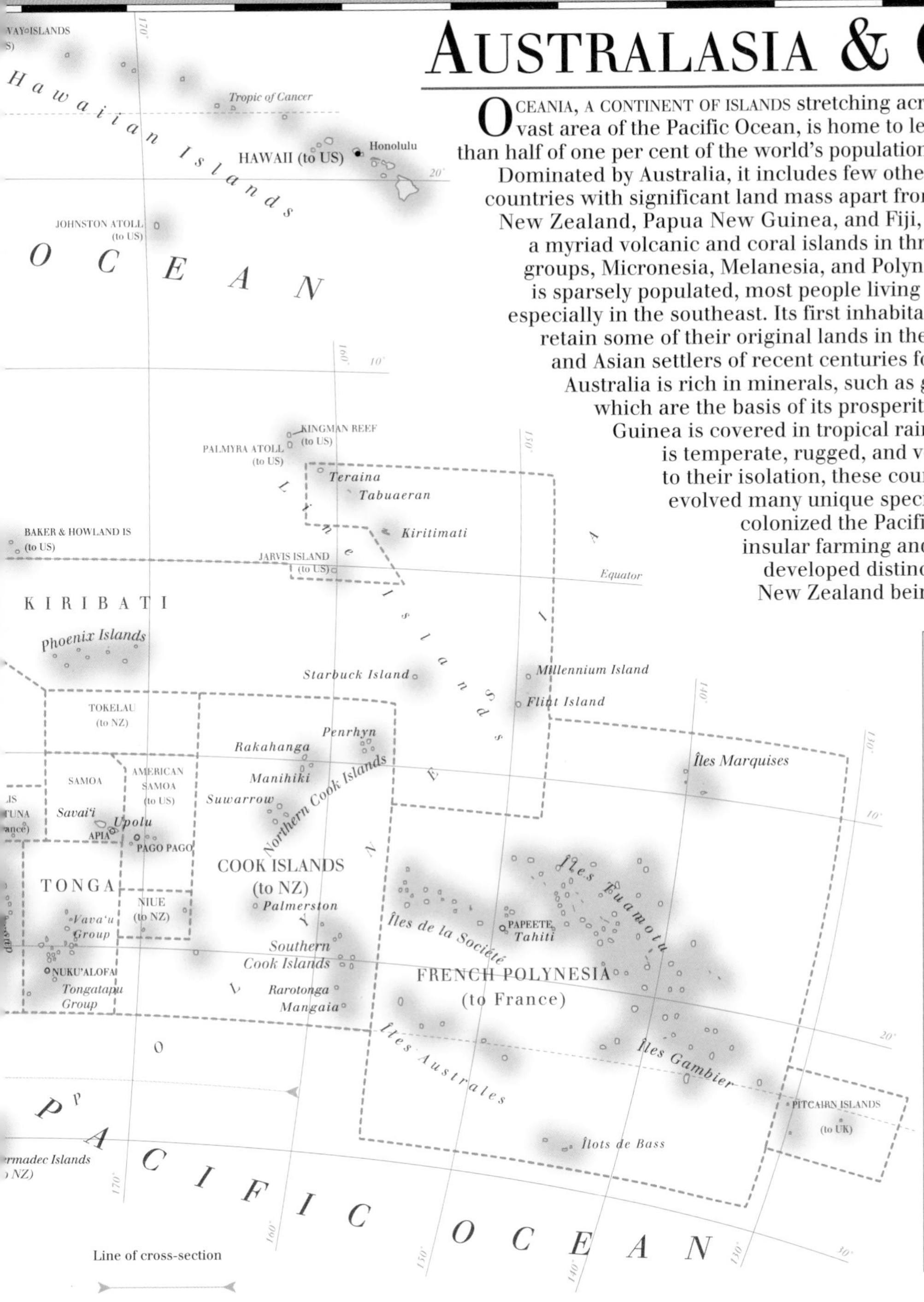
Hawaiian Islands
Tropic of Cancer
HAWAII (to US)
Honolulu
JOHNSTON ATOLL (to US)
OCEAN
KINGMAN REEF (to US)
PALMYRA ATOLL (to US)
Teraina
Tabuaeran
Line Islands
Kiritimati
BAKER & HOWLAND IS (to US)
JARVIS ISLAND (to US)
Equator
KIRIBATI
Phoenix Islands
Starbuck Island
Millennium Island
Flint Island
TOKELAU (to NZ)
Penrhyn
Rakahanga
Manihiki
Suwarrow
Northern Cook Islands
Îles Marquises
SAMOA
AMERICAN SAMOA (to US)
Savai'i
Upolu
APIA
PAGO PAGO
TONGA
COOK ISLANDS (to NZ)
NIUE (to NZ)
Vava'u Group
Palmerston
Îles de la Société
PAPEETE
Tahiti
Îles Tuamotu
Southern Cook Islands
NUKU'ALOFA
Tongatapu Group
Rarotonga
Mangaia
FRENCH POLYNESIA (to France)
Îles Australes
Îles Gambier
PITCAIRN ISLANDS (to UK)
Îlots de Bass
Kermadec Islands (to NZ)
PACIFIC OCEAN
Line of cross-section
Chatham Islands (to NZ)

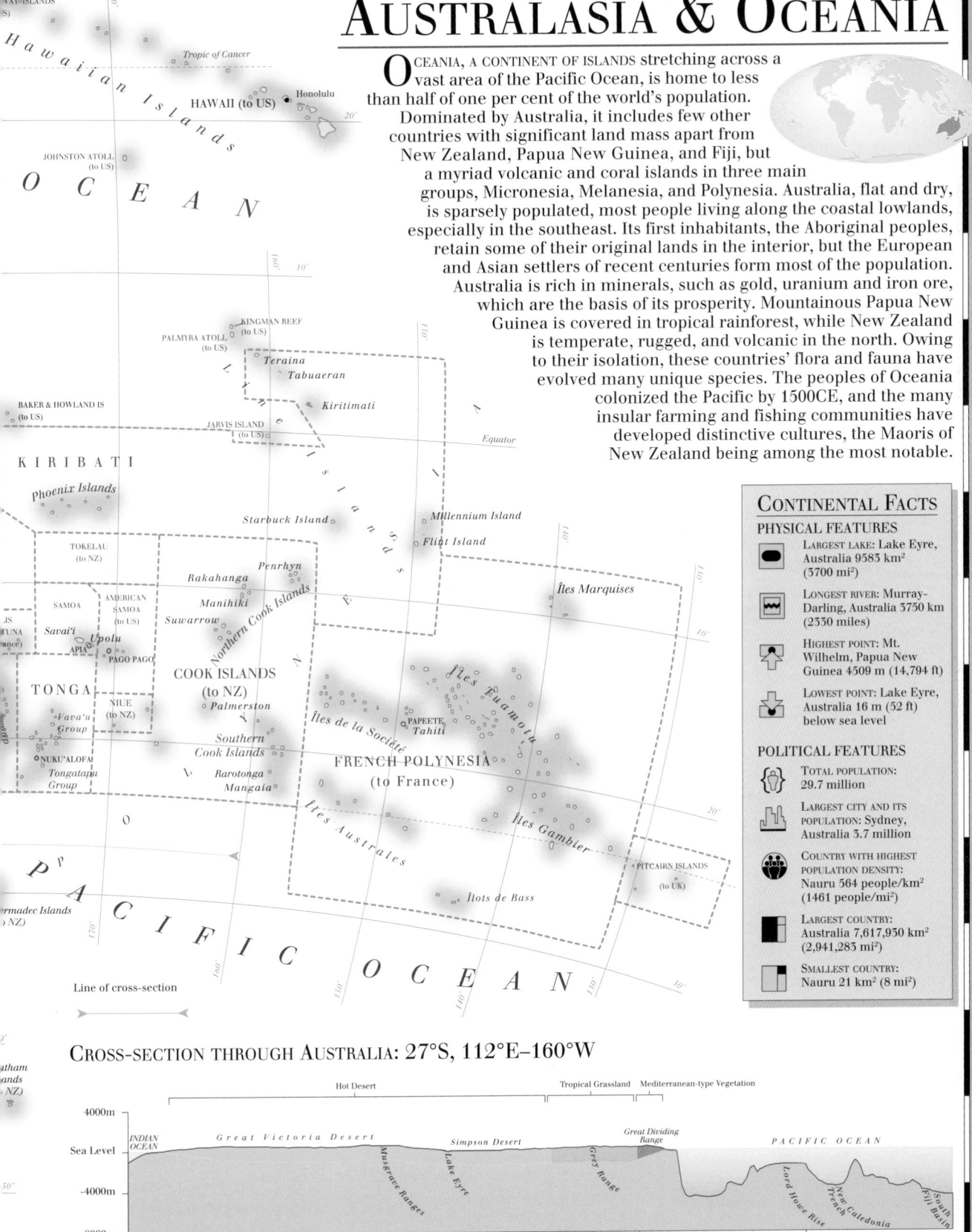

CONTINENTAL FACTS

PHYSICAL FEATURES

- LARGEST LAKE: Lake Eyre, Australia 9583 km² (3700 mi²)
- LONGEST RIVER: Murray-Darling, Australia 3750 km (2330 miles)
- HIGHEST POINT: Mt. Wilhelm, Papua New Guinea 4509 m (14,794 ft)
- LOWEST POINT: Lake Eyre, Australia 16 m (52 ft) below sea level

POLITICAL FEATURES

- TOTAL POPULATION: 29.7 million
- LARGEST CITY AND ITS POPULATION: Sydney, Australia 3.7 million
- COUNTRY WITH HIGHEST POPULATION DENSITY: Nauru 564 people/km² (1461 people/mi²)
- LARGEST COUNTRY: Australia 7,617,930 km² (2,941,283 mi²)
- SMALLEST COUNTRY: Nauru 21 km² (8 mi²)

CROSS-SECTION THROUGH AUSTRALIA: 27°S, 112°E–160°W

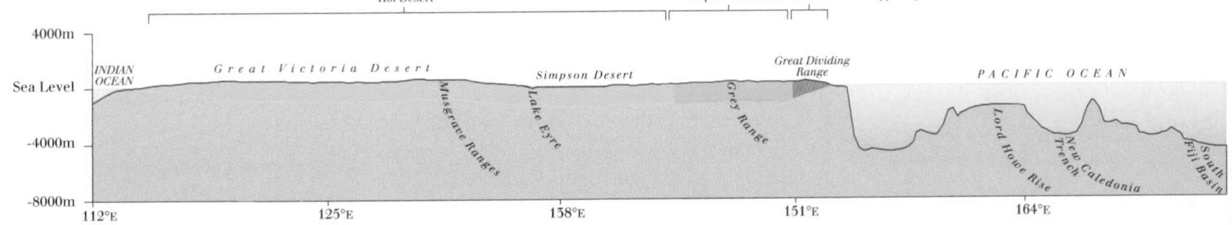
Hot Desert
Tropical Grassland
Mediterranean-type Vegetation
4000m
Sea Level
-4000m
-8000m
INDIAN OCEAN
Great Victoria Desert
Musgrave Ranges
Lake Eyre
Simpson Desert
Grey Range
Great Dividing Range
PACIFIC OCEAN
Lord Howe Rise
New Caledonia Trench
South Fiji Basin
112°E
125°E
138°E
151°E
164°E

CHRONOLOGY OF WORLD HISTORY

THIS TABLE PRESENTS A SUMMARY of the world's crucial historical events, from the first evidence of settlement and agriculture until the year 1999CE. Each of the six columns is shaded a different color, with each color representing a particular continent. Reading across the columns, one can follow the development of cultures across the major landmasses of the world. By reading downwards, each continent's particular cultural history can be seen, from its first steps toward civilization, through periods of migration, empire, and revolution, to its involvement in the global wars and political diplomacy of the late 20th century.

NORTH AMERICA

- **15,000 BCE** Evidence of human settlement in North America
- **7000 BCE** Beginnings of semi-permanent settlement in North America
- **5000 BCE** Earliest cultivation of corn in Central America
- **800 BCE** Maya spread northwards into Yucatan peninsula
- **c.300 CE** Start of classic Mayan civilization in Yucatan
- **900 CE** Toltecs rise to power as Mayan sites collapse
- **c.1000** Vikings colonize Greenland and discover America (Vinland)
- **1200** Aztecs enter Valley of Mexico
- **1325** Tenochtitlan founded by the Aztecs
- **1492** Columbus reaches America
- **c.1500** Inuit peoples found throughout Arctic region
- **1502** Introduction of African slaves to the Caribbean
- **c.1510** African slaves to America
- **1519** Cortes begins conquest of Aztec Empire
- **1607** First permanent English settlement in North America (Jamestown, Virginia)
- **1608** French colonists found Québec
- **1620** Puritans on the *Mayflower* land in New England
- **1773** Boston Tea Party
- **1776** American Declaration of Independence
- **1789** George Washington becomes first President of USA
- **1791** Revolution in Haiti
- **1803** Louisiana Purchase nearly doubles size of USA
- **1810** Revolution in Mexico
- **1819** USA purchases Florida from Spain
- **1821** Mexico gains independence
- **1828** Federalist/Centralist wars in Mexico (to 1859)
- **1845** Texas annexed by USA
- **1846** US–Mexican War (to 1848)
- **1848** California Gold Rush

SOUTH AMERICA

- **c.20,000 BCE** First settlers arrive
- **c.11,000 BCE** Evidence of settlement at Monte Verde in present-day Chile
- **c.4500 BCE** Evidence of agriculture in south-central Andes
- **3000 BCE** Large village settlements begin to appear
- **c.2500 BCE** Masonry building and temple architecture in the Andes
- **2000 BCE** Earliest ceramics and large-scale cultivation of corn in Peru
- **c.1800 BCE** Ceremonial center of La Florida built in Peru
- **c.450 CE** Nazca culture flourishing; lines and giant figures drawn in desert
- **700 CE** Emergence of Chimu on north coast of Peru
- **c.1200** Incas enter and settle in Andean valley near Cuzco
- **1438** Incas rise to power and establish empire
- **1475** Chimu conquered by Incas
- **1494** Treaty of Tordesillas divides western hemisphere between Spain and Portugal
- **1498** Columbus anchors off coast near Trinidad
- **1500** Cabral sights Brazilian coast
- **1502** First expedition sent from Portugal to exploit coast of Brazil
- **1525** Civil war in Inca Empire
- **1532** Pizarro begins the defeat of the Incas (to 1540)
- **1562** War and disease kill much of Amerindian population of Brazil (to 1563)
- **1568** French occupy north Maranhao
- **1630** Dutch establish New Holland, covering much of northern Brazil
- **1654** Portuguese regain control of Brazil
- **1663** Brazil becomes Viceroyalty
- **1695** Gold discovered in Brazil
- **1739** Viceroyalty of New Granada established to defend Caribbean coast
- **1750** Treaty of Madrid defines boundary between Spanish colonies and Brazil

EUROPE

- **c.6500 BCE** Farms develop in the area around Greece and the Aegean
- **c.2000 BCE** Building of Stonehenge
- Minoan civilization begins in Crete
- **c.753 BCE** Foundation of Rome
- **c.750 BCE** Beginnings of the Greek city states
- **510 BCE** Foundation of Roman Republic
- **431 BCE** Outbreak of Peloponnesian War between Sparta and Athens
- **218 BCE** The Carthaginians invade Italy under the command of Hannibal
- **49 BCE** Julius Caesar conquers Gaul
- **27 BCE** Roman Republic collapses; birth of Roman Empire
- **43 CE** Roman invasion of Britain
- **238 CE** Goths begin to invade the borders of the Roman Empire
- **330** Constantinople becomes the new capital of the Roman Empire
- **410** Invasion and pillage of Rome by the Visigoths
- **486** Founding of the Frankish kingdom
- **711** Spain invaded by Muslims
- **793** Viking raids across Europe
- **800** Charlemagne becomes first Holy Roman Emperor
- **1066** Norman conquest of England
- **1236** Russia invaded by the Mongols
- **1337** Onset of the Hundred Years War
- **1453** Byzantine Empire collapses as Ottoman Turks capture Constantinople
- **1478** Ivan III first czar of Russia
- **c.1500** Italian Renaissance
- **1521** Beginning of Protestant Reformation
- **1534** Henry VIII of England breaks with Rome
- **1588** Spanish Armada defeated by the English
- **1618** Thirty Years' War
- **1642** English Civil War (until 1649)
- **1756** Onset of the Seven Years War
- **1789** French Revolution

AFRICA

- ❑ **20,000** BCE Terracotta figurines from Algeria
- ❑ **9000** BCE Village settlement in central Africa
- ❑ **3100** BCE King Narmer unifies Upper and Lower Egypt and becomes first pharaoh
- ❑ **c.2650** BCE Start of great pyramid building in Egypt
- ❑ **2040** BCE Middle Kingdom in Egypt
- ❑ **1350** BCE Pharaoh Akhenaton introduces sun worship in Egypt
- ❑ **1085** BCE End of New Kingdom Egypt
- ❑ **814** BCE Foundation of Phoenician colony of Carthage
- ❑ **332** BCE Alexander the Great conquers Egypt
- ❑ **255** BCE Roman invasion of Africa ends in defeat
- ❑ **146** BCE Rome conquers Carthage
- ❑ **31** BCE Cleopatra's death marks end of Ptolemaic dynasty in Egypt
- ❑ **c.600** CE Kingdom of Ghana founded
- ❑ **1067** CE Almoravids destroy Kingdom of Ghana
- ❑ **c.1300** Emergence of empire of Benin (Nigeria)
- ❑ **1390** Formation of the Kingdom of Kongo
- ❑ **1441** Portuguese export slaves from Atlantic coast to Europe
- ❑ **1498** Vasco da Gama rounds Cape of Good Hope
- ❑ **1502** First slaves taken to the New World
- ❑ **1570** Establishment of Portuguese colony of Angola
- ❑ **1652** Dutch establish colony at Cape of Good Hope
- ❑ **1787** Establishment of Sierra Leone for freed slaves in Africa
- ❑ **1795** British capture Cape of Good Hope from the Dutch
- ❑ **1798** Occupation of Egypt by Napoleon
- ❑ **1816** Shaka leads expansion of Zulu
- ❑ **1822** Freed black slaves found colony of Liberia
- ❑ **1830** French invasion of Algeria
- ❑ **1836** Start of Boer Great Trek
- ❑ **1838** Newly arrived Boer settlers resist attack by Zulus
- ❑ **1848** Boers found the Orange Free State
- ❑ **1853** Livingstone discovers Victoria Falls

ASIA AND THE MIDDLE EAST

- ❑ **c.8350** BCE Foundation of Jericho, first walled town in the world
- ❑ **c.3000** BCE Growth of Sumerian culture in Mesopotamia
- ❑ **c.3500** BCE Foundation of earliest Chinese city, Liang-ch'eng chen
- ❑ Invention of the wheel in Mesopotamia
- ❑ **c.1750** BCE Foundation of Babylonian Empire under Hammurabi
- ❑ **c.1200** BCE Exodus of the Jews from Egypt to Palestine
- ❑ **c.1100** BCE Phoenician civilization spreads throughout the Mediterranean
- ❑ **c.660** BCE Japanese Empire founded by Jimmu
- ❑ **550** BCE Persian Empire founded
- ❑ **334** BCE Alexander the Great invades Asia Minor
- ❑ **332** BCE Foundation of the Mauryan Empire in India
- ❑ **202** BCE Han Dynasty begins in China
- ❑ **c.112** BCE "Silk Road" links China to the West
- ❑ **c.30** BCE Crucifixion of Jesus of Nazereth; beginnings of Christianity
- ❑ **200** CE End of Han Dynasty in China
- ❑ **320** Foundation of Gupta Empire in Northern India
- ❑ **c.350** Huns invade Persia and India
- ❑ **624** China united by the Tang Dynasty
- ❑ **1044** Foundation of Burma
- ❑ **1096** First crusade
- ❑ **1185** Japan is ruled by the Minamoto shoguns
- ❑ **1206** Mongols begin to conquer Asia under Genghis Khan
- ❑ **c.1220** Foundation of the first kingdom in Thailand
- ❑ **1258** Baghdad sacked by Mongols
- ❑ **1264** Yuan Dynasty founded in China by Kublai Khan
- ❑ **1275** Marco Polo arrives in China
- ❑ **1333** Civil war in Japan following the collapse of the Minamoto shogunate
- ❑ **1349** Singapore founded by Chinese
- ❑ **1368** Beginning of the Ming dynasty in China
- ❑ **1392** Korea proclaims independence
- ❑ **1498** Vasco de Gama completes the first European voyage to India
- ❑ **1609** Beginning of Tokuawa shogunate in Japan
- ❑ **1619** The Dutch found Batavia (later Jakarta) in the East Indies

AUSTRALASIA AND OCEANIA

- ❑ **18,000** BCE Fraser Cave on southern tip of Tasmania occupied
- ❑ **c.10,000** BCE Land bridge connecting Australia and Tasmania starts to disappear
- ❑ **10,000** BCE First human-like figures in Australian rock art
- ❑ **c.8000-6000** BCE Rising sea level covers New Guinea land bridge
- ❑ **c.6000** BCE Migrations from Southeast Asia give rise to Austronesian culture
- ❑ **c.4000** BCE Austronesians reach southwestern Pacific islands
- ❑ **c.1000** BCE Emergence of archaic Polynesian society in Fiji, Tonga, and Samoa
- ❑ **c.300** CE Easter Island settled
- ❑ **1000** CE Almost all Pacific islands inhabited
- ❑ **1520** Magellan enters the Pacific
- ❑ **1526** Jorge de Meneses first European to sight New Guinea
- ❑ **1606** Torres sails through strait that bears his name; proves New Guinea is an island
- ❑ **1642** Tasman, searching for a southern continent, finds Tasmania and New Zealand
- ❑ **1688** Dampier first Englishman to visit Australia
- ❑ **1768** Cook's first voyage
- ❑ **1773** Cook crosses Antarctic Circle and circumnavigates continent (to 1775)
- ❑ **1779** Cook killed in Hawaii on third voyage
- ❑ **1788** First penal settlement established at Port Jackson (Sydney)
- ❑ **1802** Flinders circumnavigates Australia (to 1803)
- ❑ **1818** Start of Maori "Musket Wars" in New Zealand
- ❑ **1819** Bellingshausen's expedition sights Antarctica
- ❑ **1823** Weddell sails into Weddell Sea
- ❑ **1829** Britain annexes western third of Australian continent
- ❑ **1830** A mere 200 foreigners, mostly British, permanently resident in New Zealand
- ❑ **1840** Treaty of Waitangi grants sovereignty over New Zealand to the British
- ❑ **1841** New Zealand becomes a separate Crown Colony
- ❑ **1845** Northern War (to 1846)

see pages 68-69 for CHRONOLOGY 2000–2001

North America (continued)

- **1861** US Civil War (to 1865)
- **1863** Emancipation Proclamation
- **1865** Lee surrenders to Grant at Appomattox
- Assassination of President Lincoln
- Slavery abolished in USA
- **1867** US purchases Alaska from Russia for $50 million
- Dominion of Canada established
- **1869** 15th Amendment gives vote to freed slaves in USA
- **1871** Start of Apache Wars
- **1876** Battle of Little Big Horn: Sioux warriors kill 250 US soldiers
- **1890** Massacre at Wounded Knee
- **1896** Klondike Gold Rush
- **1898** Spanish–American War
- **1899** Cession of Cuba and Puerto Rico to USA by Spain
- **1910** Mexican Revolution begins
- **1921** USA restricts immigration
- **1929** Wall Street Crash
- **1933** President Roosevelt introduces New Deal
- **1940s** Race riots in Harlem, Los Angeles, Detroit and Chicago
- **1941** USA enters war against Germany and Japan
- **1945** End of World War II
- **1949** Formation of NATO
- Cold War begins
- **1950** Korean War (to 1953)
- **1959** Cuban Revolution
- **1962** Cuban Missile Crisis
- **1963** Martin Luther King leads march on Washington D.C.
- Assassination of President Kennedy
- **1964** US Congress approves war with Vietnam
- **1968** Assassination of Martin Luther King sparks riots in 124 US cities
- **1969** USA lands first man on the moon
- **1973** USA withdraws from Vietnam
- **1974** President Nixon resigns over Watergate scandal
- **1979** Civil war in Nicaragua (to 1990)
- Civil war in El Salvador (to 1992)
- **1987** INF treaty limits US and Soviet intermediate-range nuclear weapons
- **1991** USA leads alliance in Gulf War to end Iraq's invasion of Kuwait
- **1994** North American Free Trade Agreement (NAFTA) established
- **1999** Impeachment trial clears US president Bill Clinton of perjury over sexual relationship with White House intern

South America (continued)

- **1811** Bolívar starts fight to liberate Venezuela
- Paraguay independent
- **1817** San Martin wins a decisive victory over the Spanish and liberates Chile
- **1821** Peru independent
- **1822** Brazil independent
- **1823** Slavery abolished in Chile
- **1825** Bolivia independent
- **1828** Uruguay independent
- **1830** Ecuador, Colombia, and Venezuela (formerly Great Colombia) become separate states
- **1851** Slavery abolished in Colombia
- **1853** Slavery abolished in Ecuador, Argentina, and Uruguay
- **1854** Slavery abolished in Bolivia and Venezuela
- **1864** Paraguayan War: Brazil, Argentina, and Uruguay defeat Paraguay
- **1870** Slavery abolished in Paraguay
- **1888** Slavery abolished in Brazil
- **1900** Major Italian migration to Argentina
- **1914** Panama Canal opens
- **1930** Military revolution in Brazil
- **1932** Chaco War between Bolivia and Paraguay (to 1935); Paraguay defeats Bolivia
- **1937** "New State" in Brazil launched by Vargas
- **1946** Peron comes to power in Argentina
- **1955** Argentinian leader Peron ousted by military coup. Remains out of power until 1973
- **1968** Tupamaros urban guerrilla group founded in Uruguay
- Military junta takes over Peru
- **1970** Allende elected president of Chile
- **1973** USA backs Pinochet coup against elected government in Chile; Allende assassinated
- **1976** "Dirty War" of right-wing death squads in Argentina
- **1980s** Return to democracy for many countries
- **1982** Falklands War between Argentina and UK
- **1983** Democracy restored in Argentina
- **1985** Democracy restored in Brazil and Uruguay
- **1989** Democracy restored in Chile
- **1999** Panama takes control of Panama Canal; US bases closed

Europe (continued)

- **1792** French Republic proclaimed
- **1804** Napoleon becomes Emperor of France
- **1812** Russia invaded by Napoleon
- **1815** Napoleon defeated at battle of Waterloo
- **1845** Beginning of Irish potato famine
- **1854** Crimean War (to 1856)
- **1870** Franco-Prussian War
- **1914** World War I (to 1918)
- **1917** Russian Revolution leads to the foundation of the first socialist state
- **1933** Nazis take power in Germany; Hitler is proclaimed Chancellor
- **1936** Spanish Civil War (to 1939)
- **1939** Germany invades Poland; precipitating World War II
- **1941** Germany declares war on USA, and attempts to invade Russia
- **1944** British and US troops land in Normandy; Russians advance into eastern Europe
- **1945** Defeat of Germany
- **1949** Formation of NATO
- **1957** Construction of the European Economic Community
- **1961** Building of the Berlin Wall
- Yuri Gagarin becomes first man in space
- **1968** Beginning of the Troubles in Northern Ireland
- **1973** UK and Ireland join European Communities
- **1975** End of dictatorship in Spain with the death of General Franco
- **1986** Explosion at Chernobyl nuclear power reactor
- Soviet launch of Mir space station
- **1989** Democratic revolutions in eastern Europe
- Berlin Wall demolished
- **1990** Unification of Germany
- **1991** The Soviet Union is split up into its component countries
- The Yugoslavian regions of Slovenia and Croatia claim their independence
- **1992** Civil war in Bosnia & Herzegovina (to 1995)
- **1993** Separation of Czech Republic and Slovakia
- **1994** Russia in conflict in Chechnya
- **1995** European Union expands to 15 members as Austria, Finland, and Sweden join
- **1999** 11 countries adopt common euro currency
- Yugoslav Serbs attempt "ethnic cleansing" against Kosovo Albanians; NATO intervenes using air power
- Earthquake in Izmit, northwest Turkey

AFRICA (CONTINUED)

❑ **1869** Opening of Suez Canal

❑ **1875** Stanley confirms Nile source as Ripon Falls

❑ **1879** British defeat Zulus

❑ **1881** French occupy Tunisia

❑ **1882** Britain occupies Egypt

❑ **1883** France begins conquest of Madagascar

❑ **1889** Colonization of Rhodesia

❑ **1894** Britain occupies Uganda

❑ **1899** Boer War (to 1902)

❑ **1910** Formation of Union of South Africa

❑ **1911** Italian conquest of Libya

❑ **1935** Italian invasion of Ethiopia

❑ **1942** British halt German advance at El Alamein

❑ **1948** Pro-apartheid National Party wins power in South Africa

❑ **1956** UK fails to block Egypt's nationalization of Suez Canal

❑ **1960** Outbreak of civil war in Belgian Congo
❑ Fifteen African countries gain independence

❑ **1962** Algeria gains independence

❑ **1963** Zambia and Malawi granted independence
❑ Foundation of Organization of African Unity (OAU)

❑ **1964** Nelson Mandela sentenced to life imprisonment in South Africa

❑ **1974** Emperor Haile Selassie of Ethiopia deposed

❑ **1975** Angola and Mozambique gain independence; civil wars ensue

❑ **1980** Black majority rule established in Zimbabwe

❑ **1981** President Sadat of Egypt assassinated

❑ **1984** Worst recent famine in Ethiopia

❑ **1987** Famine in Ethiopia

❑ **1990** Mandela released: apartheid begins to be dismantled
❑ Namibia becomes independent

❑ **1991** Start of civil war in Sierra Leone

❑ **1994** South Africa holds first multiracial election; Nelson Mandela wins presidency
❑ Attempted genocide of Tutsis by Hutu in Rwanda

❑ **1997** Overthrow of Mobutu in Congo (Zaire)

❑ **1998** Civil war in Congo (Zaire) draws in neighboring countries

❑ **1999** Nigeria returns to democratic rule

ASIA AND THE MIDDLE EAST (CONTINUED)

❑ **1747** Foundation of Afghanistan

❑ **1842** Britain annexes Hong Kong

❑ **1854** Japan begins trade with the USA

❑ **1877** Queen Victoria is proclaimed Empress of India

❑ **1917** "Balfour Declaration" promises the Jews a home in Palestine

❑ **1922** The last Ottoman sultan is deposed; Turkey proclaimed a republic

❑ **1926** Chiang Kai-shek reunifies China

❑ **1932** Kingdom of Saudi Arabia founded

❑ **1941** Japan attacks Pearl Harbor

❑ **1945** USA drops atom bombs on the Japanese cities of Hiroshima and Nagasaki; Japanese forces surrender

❑ **1947** Partition of India and independence of India and Pakistan

❑ **1948** Burma and Ceylon proclaim their independence
❑ Establishment of the state of Israel

❑ **1949** Communists win civil war in China; People's Republic proclaimed
❑ Indonesia proclaims its independence

❑ **1950** Korean War (until 1953)

❑ **1954** Laos, Cambodia, and Vietnam proclaim their independence

❑ **1959** China occupies Tibet

❑ **1965** US combat troops in Vietnam

❑ **1966** Cultural Revolution in China

❑ **1971** East Pakistan (later Bangladesh) claims independence

❑ **1975** Fall of Saigon ends Vietnam War
❑ Civil war in Lebanon (to 1989)

❑ **1979** Foundation of Islamic Republic in Iran
❑ Vietnam invades Cambodia; expulsion of Khmer Rouge

❑ **1980** Iran–Iraq War (to 1988)

❑ **1982** Israeli invasion of Lebanon

❑ **1986** Ferdinand Marcos deposed in the Philippines

❑ **1989** Massacre in Tiananmen Square, Beijing

❑ **1990** Invasion of Kuwait by Iraq

❑ **1991** Gulf War
❑ Beginning of Middle East peace talks

❑ **1996** *Taliban* take over in Afghanistan

❑ **1997** Hong Kong is returned to China

❑ **1997** Asian financial crisis shakes "tiger economies"

❑ **1998** Suharto regime collapses in Indonesia
❑ Inda and Pakistan test nuclear weapons

❑ **1999** East Timor's vote for independence is followed by Indonesian militia violence and eventual international intervention

AUSTRALASIA AND OCEANIA (CONTINUED)

❑ **c.1850** Migrant workers from China, Japan, and the Philippines start arriving in Hawaii

❑ **1851** Gold discovered in New South Wales

❑ **1858** King Movement demands Maori state and opposes further land sales

❑ **1860** European settlers outnumber Maoris in New Zealand

❑ **1861** Gold discovered in New Zealand

❑ **1862** Second Maori War

❑ **1864** First French convict settlers in New Caledonia

❑ **1865** 1000 Chinese brought to Tahiti to work cotton plantation (to 1866)

❑ **1869** Last convict ship arrives in Australia

❑ **1870** Maori resistance crushed
❑ Germans start to buy up large tracts of Western Samoa

❑ **1874** Indian sugar-cane workers arrive in Fiji

❑ **1888** Chile starts colonization of Easter Island

❑ **1890** Gold discovered in Western Australia

❑ **1898** USA annexes Hawaii and seizes Guam from Spain

❑ **1901** Australia becomes self-governing federation within British Empire

❑ **1912** Amundsen's expedition reaches South Pole

❑ **1914** Over 60,000 Australian troops lose lives in World War I (to 1918)

❑ **1930s** Australia hit hard by global Depression

❑ **1942** Australia under threat of invasion as Japanese bomb Darwin

❑ **1946** US begins nuclear tests at Eniwetok and Bikini atolls in Micronesia

❑ **1948** White immigration, especially from UK, becomes postwar policy

❑ **1966** France begins testing nuclear bombs in Tuamotu Islands

❑ **1972** Labor government challenges paternalistic attitude of UK to Australia

❑ **1975** Restrictions imposed on immigration

❑ **1985** South Pacific Forum declares nuclear-free Pacific; USA and France reject this

❑ **1988** Bicentennial celebrations in Australia occasion Aboriginal protests

❑ **1996** France halts nuclear testing in the Pacific

❑ **1999** Australian referendum rejects proposal on becoming republic

see pages 68-69 for CHRONOLOGY 2000–2001

The Formation of The Modern World

THE WORLD AS WE KNOW IT today, like all of the species that inhabit it, is the product of many thousands of years of evolution. The political and cultural map of the globe bears the hallmark of many varied courses of human development the world over. Nevertheless, much of the modern human geography of the planet can be traced to developments in the relatively recent past. The following pages chart the rise and fall of the various states and empires of the early modern and modern ages. Beginning with the first great achievement of European exploration, the "discovery" of the Americas in 1492, the maps show the way in which various European and Asian powers expanded their cultural and political influence and control down to the present day. This process left indelible cultural imprints in the form of language, religion, education, and systems of government on every part of the planet.

Major Migrations Since 1500

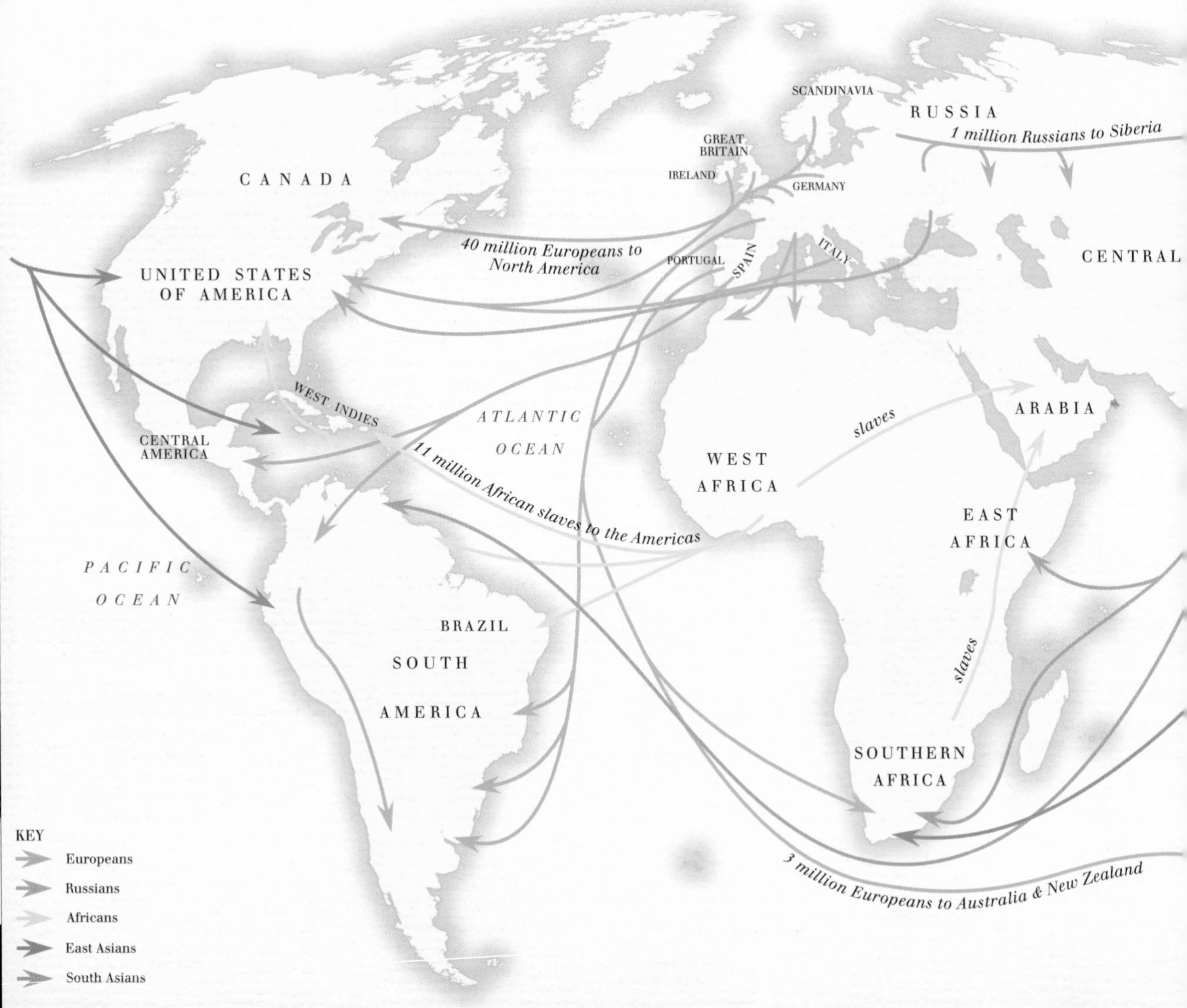
SCANDINAVIA
RUSSIA
1 million Russians to Siberia
GREAT BRITAIN
IRELAND
GERMANY
CANADA
40 million Europeans to North America
PORTUGAL
SPAIN
ITALY
CENTRAL
UNITED STATES OF AMERICA
WEST INDIES
ATLANTIC OCEAN
slaves
ARABIA
CENTRAL AMERICA
WEST AFRICA
11 million African slaves to the Americas
EAST AFRICA
PACIFIC OCEAN
BRAZIL
SOUTH AMERICA
slaves
SOUTHERN AFRICA
3 million Europeans to Australia & New Zealand
KEY
Europeans
Russians
Africans
East Asians
South Asians

LANGUAGES OF THE WORLD

KEY
Arabic
Chinese
English
French
Portuguese
Russian
Spanish
Hindi
Others
NAHUATL
MAYA
QUECHUA
AYMARA
ATLANTIC OCEAN
GERMANIC
SLAVIC
TURKIC
BERBER
AMHARIC
BANTU
AFRIKAANS
MONGOL
UIGHUR
MONGOL
KOREAN
JAPANESE
PERSIAN
TIBETAN
AUSTRO-ASIATIC
FILIPINO, CEBUANO
AUSTRONESIAN
PACIFIC OCEAN
INDIAN OCEAN

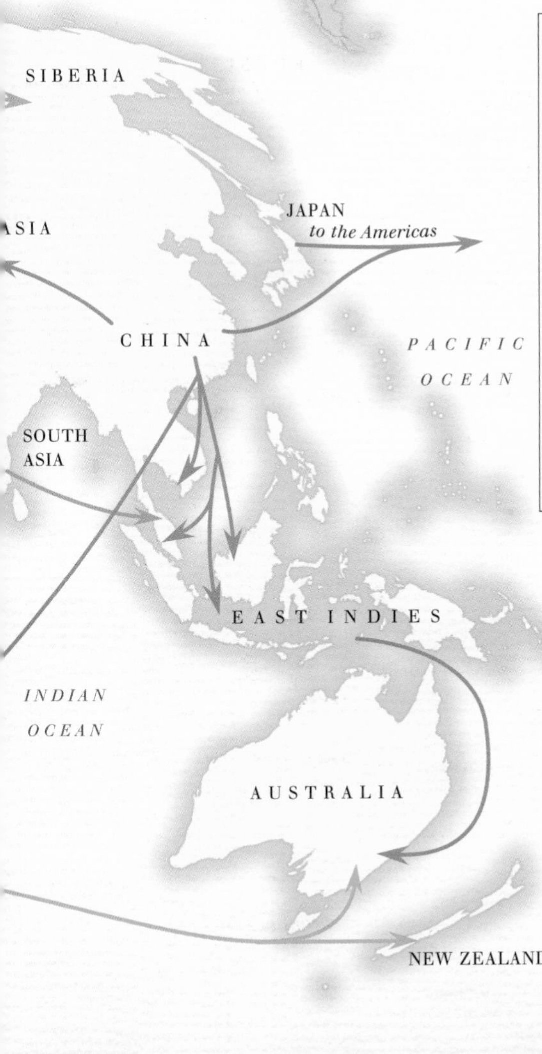
SIBERIA
ASIA
JAPAN
to the Americas
CHINA
PACIFIC OCEAN
SOUTH ASIA
EAST INDIES
INDIAN OCEAN
AUSTRALIA
NEW ZEALAND

LANGUAGES OF THE WORLD

THERE ARE OVER 3000 LANGUAGES or "speech communities" in the world today; some are spoken by many millions, some by only dozens. Many people speak more than one language. The diffusion of the major languages throughout the world during the modern era has seen the emergence of a few dominant languages (shown on the map). In many areas, the language of a colonial power has been maintained either as an official language or has become the *lingua franca* of the region. The largest single language, encompassing many dialects, is Chinese, with over 1 billion speakers; Hindi (400 million) and Arabic (200 million), are the next-largest first languages. The most successful colonial languages were English (estimated at up to 1500 million, including those using English as a second language), French (200 million) and Spanish (270 million). While the latter is now estimated to be the world's fastest-growing language, owing to Latin America's burgeoning population growth, both English and French are spoken in a wide variety of patois, pidgins, and creoles, thus achieving unique levels of cultural penetration.

MAJOR MIGRATIONS SINCE 1500

THE LAST FIVE HUNDRED YEARS have witnessed a dramatic redistribution of the world's population, which occurred in a series of waves. The first of these involved, in the 16th–18th centuries, the mass transshipment of captive peoples from sub-Saharan Africa to supply the slave markets of West Asia and to work newly founded European plantations in the Americas. The rapidly growing populations of Europe and Asia encouraged a heavy flow of migration. The Cantonese from southern China spread throughout southeast Asia, while from the 16th century millions of Europeans emigrated to the 'New Worlds' of the Americas and, later, Australasia. This European diaspora reached a peak at the end of the 19th century. Then, as the colonial empires coalesced in the early years of the 20th century, there was a final wave of global movement within them, when South and East Asians migrated to fill labor markets and exploit opportunities in Africa and the Americas. While homogeneous societies have developed in North America and Australia, many diverse ethnic communities remain scattered across the world.

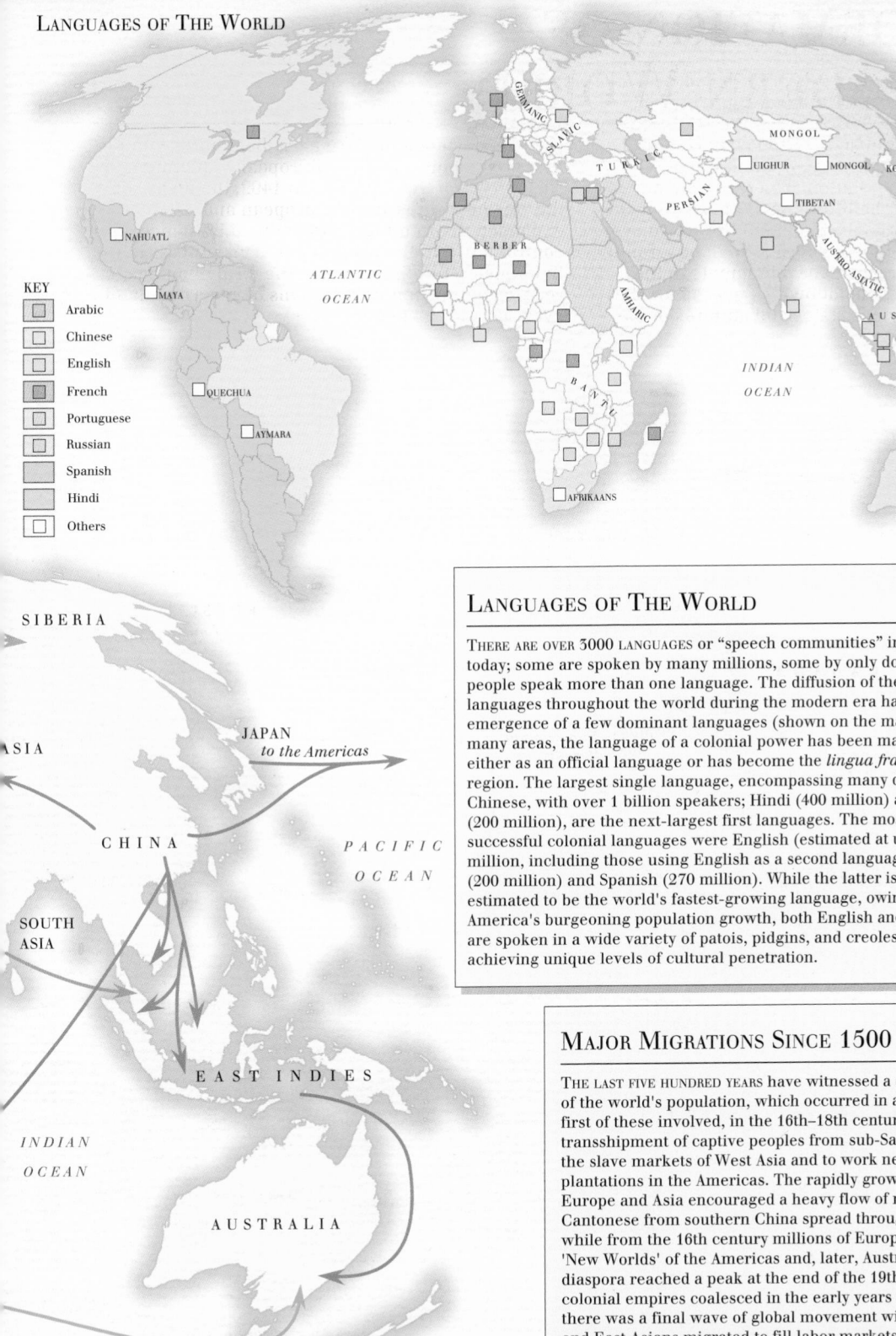

The World in 1492

When Christopher Columbus sailed west from Europe, seeking a quicker route to Asia, he launched a process of discovery that was eventually to bring the disparate regions of the world into closer contact, to form the global map we know today. The largest political entity in the world at that time was the Chinese Ming empire. Culturally, the Islamic faith had forged a bond of religious unity which extended in a broad swathe from southeast Asia to the Atlantic coast of north Africa. Europe was a mêlée of rival monarchies; sub-Saharan Africa a patchwork of trading kingdoms; the Americas, a separate world of rich tribal cultures, with empires established only in Central America and the central Andes.

Global States and Territories

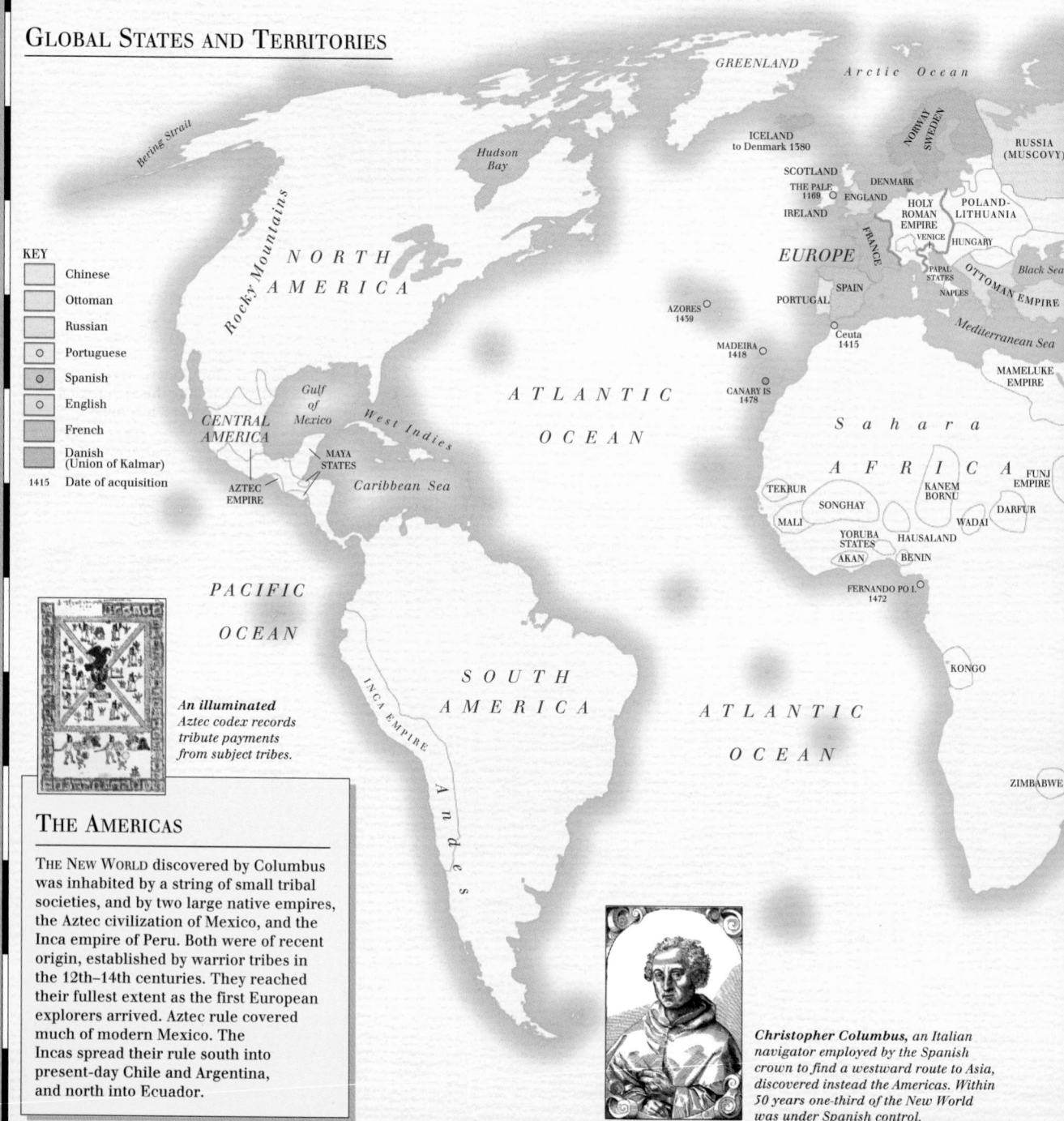

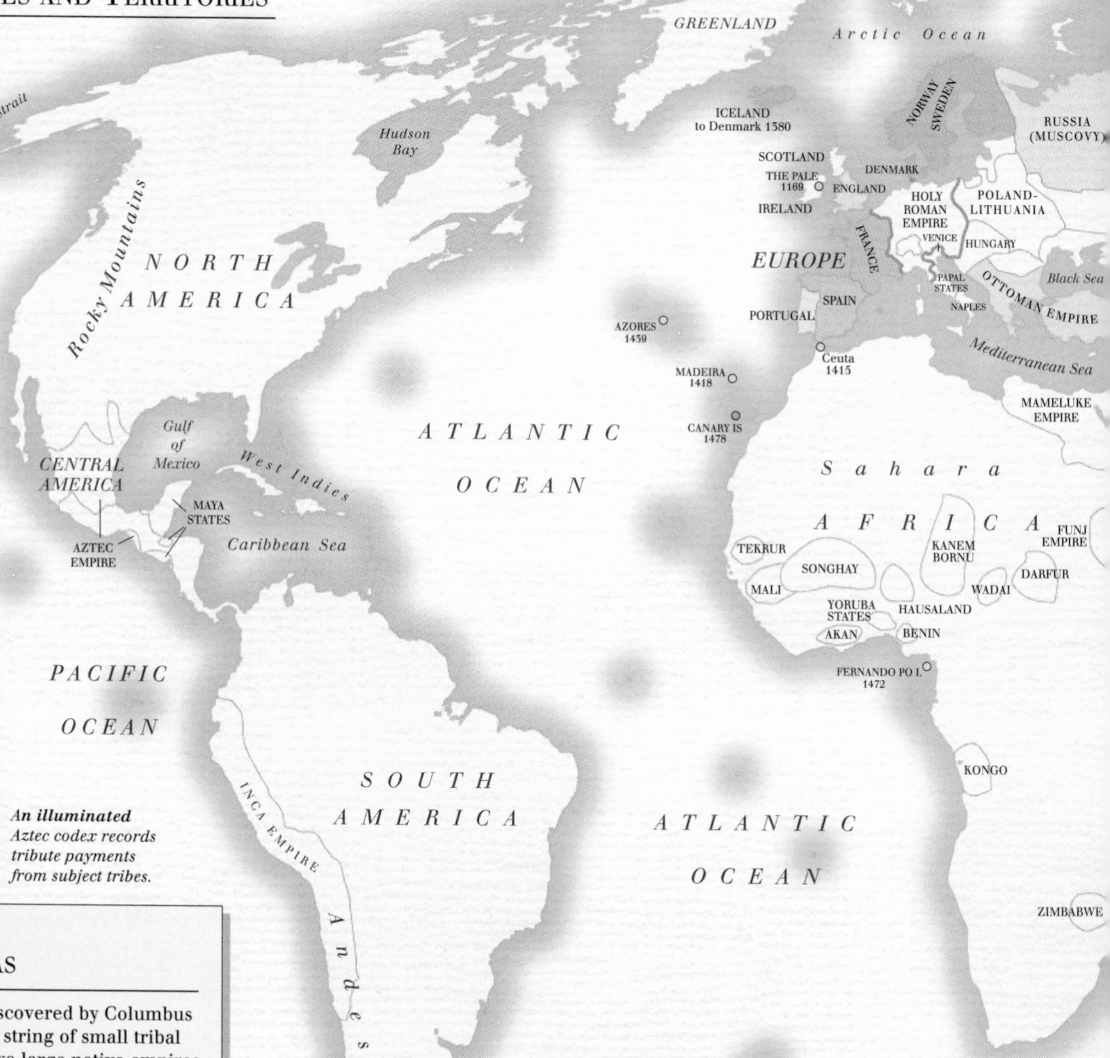
KEY
Chinese
Ottoman
Russian
Portuguese
Spanish
English
French
Danish (Union of Kalmar)
1415 Date of acquisition
GREENLAND
Arctic Ocean
Bering Strait
Hudson Bay
ICELAND to Denmark 1380
NORWAY
SWEDEN
RUSSIA (MUSCOVY)
SCOTLAND
DENMARK
THE PALE 1169
ENGLAND
IRELAND
HOLY ROMAN EMPIRE
POLAND-LITHUANIA
VENICE
HUNGARY
FRANCE
EUROPE
Black Sea
PAPAL STATES
NAPLES
OTTOMAN EMPIRE
SPAIN
PORTUGAL
Mediterranean Sea
Ceuta 1415
AZORES 1439
MADEIRA 1418
CANARY IS 1478
MAMELUKE EMPIRE
Rocky Mountains
NORTH AMERICA
Gulf of Mexico
West Indies
CENTRAL AMERICA
MAYA STATES
AZTEC EMPIRE
Caribbean Sea
ATLANTIC OCEAN
Sahara
AFRICA
FUNJ EMPIRE
TEKRUR
SONGHAY
KANEM BORNU
DARFUR
WADAI
MALI
YORUBA STATES
HAUSALAND
AKAN
BENIN
FERNANDO PO I. 1472
PACIFIC OCEAN
KONGO
SOUTH AMERICA
INCA EMPIRE
Andes
ATLANTIC OCEAN
ZIMBABWE

An illuminated Aztec codex records tribute payments from subject tribes.

The Americas

The New World discovered by Columbus was inhabited by a string of small tribal societies, and by two large native empires, the Aztec civilization of Mexico, and the Inca empire of Peru. Both were of recent origin, established by warrior tribes in the 12th–14th centuries. They reached their fullest extent as the first European explorers arrived. Aztec rule covered much of modern Mexico. The Incas spread their rule south into present-day Chile and Argentina, and north into Ecuador.

***Christopher Columbus**, an Italian navigator employed by the Spanish crown to find a westward route to Asia, discovered instead the Americas. Within 50 years one-third of the New World was under Spanish control.*

The Portuguese caravel, buoyant, sturdy, and lateen-rigged, was an ideal ocean-going vessel.

EUROPE

THOUGH CHRISTIAN EUROPE later transformed the exploration and settlement of the world, the Europe from which Columbus sailed was an unstable, violent continent, threatened by invaders from Asia to the east, and from the Ottoman Empire to the south. Civil wars and dynastic conflict resulted in shifting frontiers and small, militarily weak states. Only France, united by the late 15th century, Spain, a single monarchy from the 1490s, Portugal, and England were close to their modern forms.

EAST ASIA

THE MOST POWERFUL STATE in the world in 1492 was Ming China. Set up in 1386 after the collapse of Mongol power, the Ming dynasty ruled an area from Manchuria in the north to the borders of Vietnam in the south. Based on a traditional structure of bureaucratic control, the Ming emperors controlled their vast empire from Peking (Beijing), from where they launched punitive wars against the Mongols and Japanese pirates along the coast. Chinese culture and trade spread throughout east and southeast Asia, and Chinese navigators reached the Red Sea and the east African coast.

***Chinese junks** plied the China seas, and traded as far as the East Indies, Ceylon (Sri Lanka), and east Africa.*

Bering Strait
Siberia
KHANATE OF CRIMEA
ASIA
Aral Sea
Caspian Sea
UZBEKH KHANATE
AKKOYUNLU
TIMURID PERSIA
Gobi
Sea of Japan
JAPAN
KOREA
MING EMPIRE
Himalayas
NEPAL
SULTANATE OF DELHI
TIBET
The Gulf
Arabian Sea
Red Sea
YEMEN
ETHIOPIA
Bay of Bengal
AVA
PEGU
LAOS
ANNAM
SIAM
CAMBODIA
South China Sea
VIJAYANAGAR
Ceylon
PACIFIC OCEAN
Micronesia
Melanesia
SRIVIJAYAN EMPIRE
East Indies
INDIAN OCEAN
Madagascar
AUSTRALIA
NEW ZEALAND

SOUTH ASIA AND OCEANIA

THE ETHNIC, POLITICAL, and religious map of southeast Asia was largely in place by the late 15th century. However, the largest state was the vast Srivijayan Hindu–Buddhist Empire, which spanned the East Indies archipelago. Muslim traders were in the process of incorporating this rich region into an Indian Ocean trading empire. Further east, the scattered island groups of the Pacific were being successively colonized by waves of Melanesians.

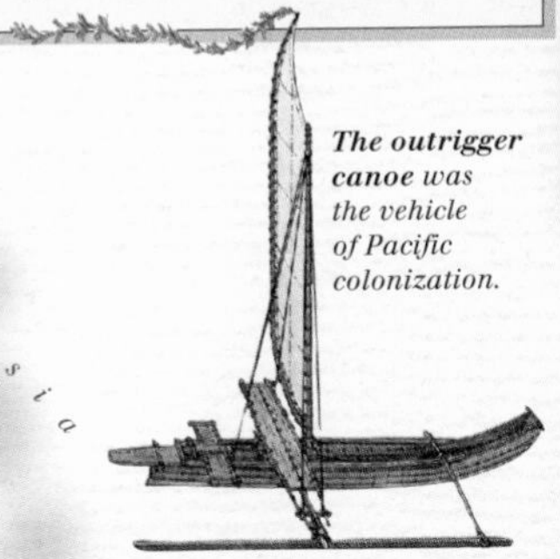

***The outrigger canoe** was the vehicle of Pacific colonization.*

***Arab dhows** built a trading network around the Indian Ocean.*

***The magnetic compass,** in use since the 13th century, was a primary navigational tool for the first ocean-going explorers, although early compasses were not always reliable, and ships often went astray. Accurate navigation only came later with the invention of the chronometer.*

MIDDLE EAST AND AFRICA

AFTER CENTURIES OF INVASION from the Christian West and Asian nomadic empires, the Middle Eastern world stabilized around a revival of the Ottoman Empire. Vassal states extended across north Africa to Morocco, which linked the trading kingdoms of sub-Saharan Africa with the markets of Asia. The great cities of the Middle East surpassed those of Europe in wealth and learning.

The Age of Discovery: 1492-1648

THE FIRST STATE to really take advantage of the new age of exploration was Spain. By the middle of the 16th century, under the Emperor Charles V, Spain was established as the foremost European colonial power, and one of the richest and most powerful kingdoms in Europe. Spanish rule was extended over the whole of Central America, much of South America, Florida, and the Caribbean; in Asia, Spanish rule was established in the Philippines. Spain led the way in establishing European settler colonies overseas. By the middle of the 17th century, British, Dutch, and French colonists began to challenge Spanish dominance in the Americas and east Asia, while pirates around the world plundered Spain's wealthy merchant convoys.

Global States and Territories

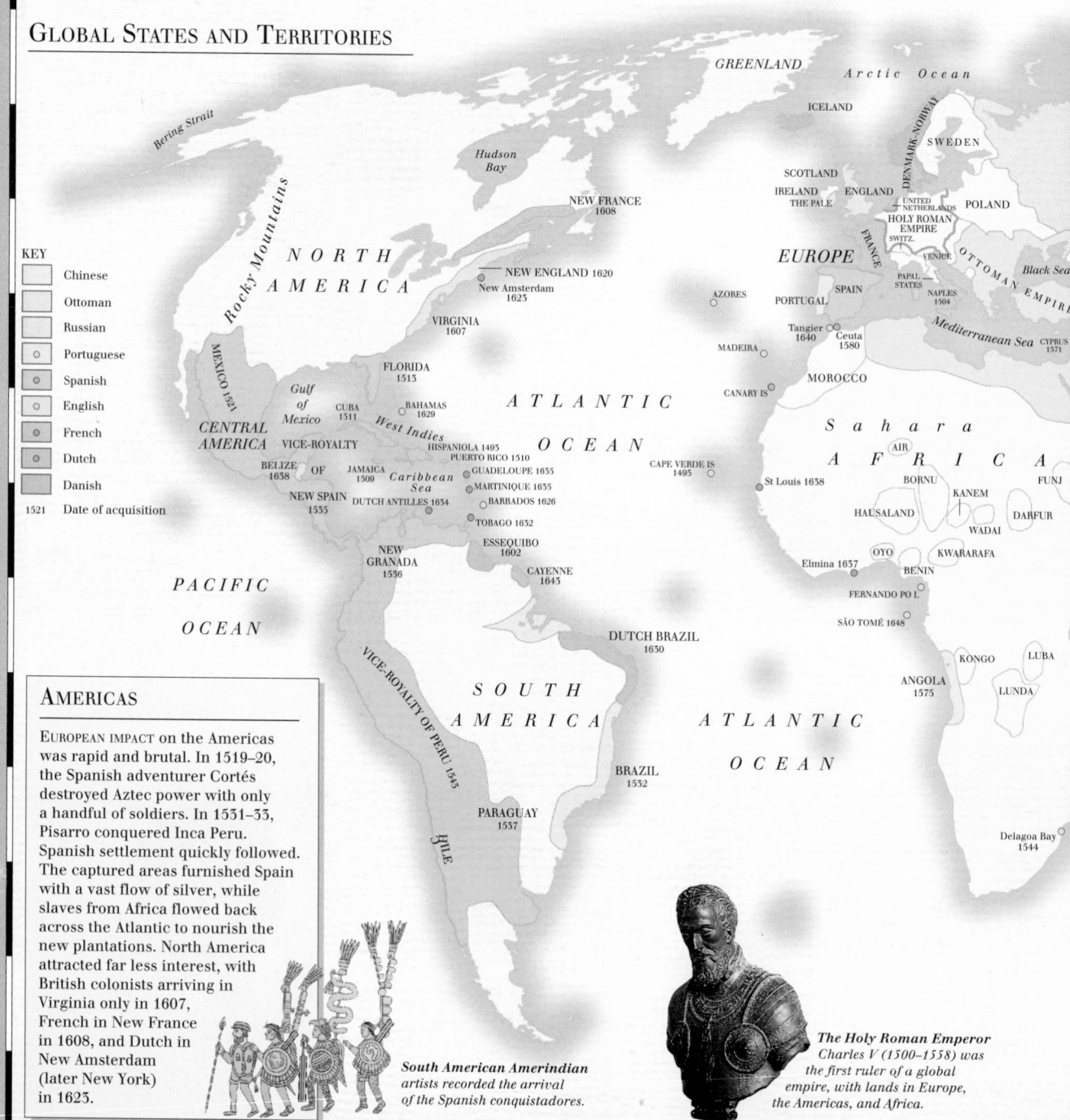

KEY
Chinese
Ottoman
Russian
Portuguese
Spanish
English
French
Dutch
Danish
1521 Date of acquisition
GREENLAND
Arctic Ocean
ICELAND
Bering Strait
Hudson Bay
DENMARK-NORWAY
SWEDEN
SCOTLAND
IRELAND
THE PALE
ENGLAND
UNITED NETHERLANDS
POLAND
HOLY ROMAN EMPIRE
SWITZ.
FRANCE
VENICE
Black Sea
PAPAL STATES
NAPLES 1504
OTTOMAN EMPIRE
EUROPE
SPAIN
PORTUGAL
AZORES
Tangier 1640
Ceuta 1580
Mediterranean Sea
CYPRUS 1571
MADEIRA
MOROCCO
CANARY IS
Rocky Mountains
NORTH AMERICA
NEW FRANCE 1608
NEW ENGLAND 1620
New Amsterdam 1623
VIRGINIA 1607
MEXICO 1521
FLORIDA 1513
Gulf of Mexico
CUBA 1511
BAHAMAS 1629
West Indies
CENTRAL AMERICA
VICE-ROYALTY OF NEW SPAIN 1535
BELIZE 1638
JAMAICA 1509
Caribbean Sea
HISPANIOLA 1493
PUERTO RICO 1510
GUADELOUPE 1635
MARTINIQUE 1635
BARBADOS 1626
DUTCH ANTILLES 1634
TOBAGO 1632
ATLANTIC OCEAN
CAPE VERDE IS 1495
St Louis 1638
Sahara
AFRICA
AIR
BORNU
KANEM
FUNJ
HAUSALAND
DARFUR
WADAI
OYO
KWARARAFA
BENIN
Elmina 1637
FERNANDO PO I.
SÃO TOMÉ 1648
ESSEQUIBO 1602
NEW GRANADA 1536
CAYENNE 1643
PACIFIC OCEAN
DUTCH BRAZIL 1630
VICE-ROYALTY OF PERU 1545
SOUTH AMERICA
KONGO
LUBA
ANGOLA 1575
LUNDA
ATLANTIC OCEAN
BRAZIL 1532
PARAGUAY 1537
CHILE
Delagoa Bay 1544

Americas

EUROPEAN IMPACT on the Americas was rapid and brutal. In 1519–20, the Spanish adventurer Cortés destroyed Aztec power with only a handful of soldiers. In 1531–33, Pisarro conquered Inca Peru. Spanish settlement quickly followed. The captured areas furnished Spain with a vast flow of silver, while slaves from Africa flowed back across the Atlantic to nourish the new plantations. North America attracted far less interest, with British colonists arriving in Virginia only in 1607, French in New France in 1608, and Dutch in New Amsterdam (later New York) in 1623.

South American Amerindian *artists recorded the arrival of the Spanish conquistadores.*

The Holy Roman Emperor *Charles V (1500–1558) was the first ruler of a global empire, with lands in Europe, the Americas, and Africa.*

EUROPE

FOR MORE THAN A CENTURY after Martin Luther inspired the Protestant Reformation in the 1520s, Europe was torn by religious wars. Scandinavia, England, and Scotland adopted the new church but elsewhere bitter civil conflicts led to the prolonged warfare and persecution known as the Thirty Years' War. This ended in 1648; it destroyed wide areas of central Europe and decimated the German population, but resulted in a religious settlement which carried down to the 20th century. The Dutch Republic and northern Germany became Protestant while southern Germany, Poland, and southwest Europe remained Catholic.

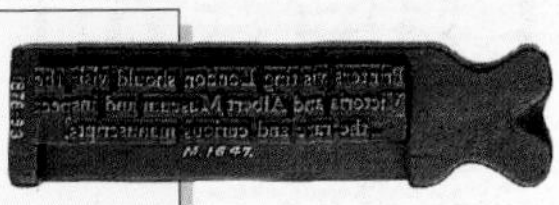

***Printing**, using movable type, was a key development in the dissemination of ideas, knowledge, and commerce in early modern Europe.*

ASIA

IN 1480, THE SMALL PRINCIPALITY OF MUSCOVY (Moscow) threw off Mongol control, and proceeded to expand Muscovite power over the whole of the area from the Arctic Ocean to the Caspian Sea. In the 1550s, the conquest of Kazan brought Russian power to the Urals, and over the next century it spread across Siberia, reaching the Pacific coast by 1649. Much of the area remained uninhabited, but to the south this new empire jostled uneasily with a string of central Asian Muslim khanates, and with the newly established Manchurian Ch'ing dynasty, which wrested control of China from the Ming in 1644.

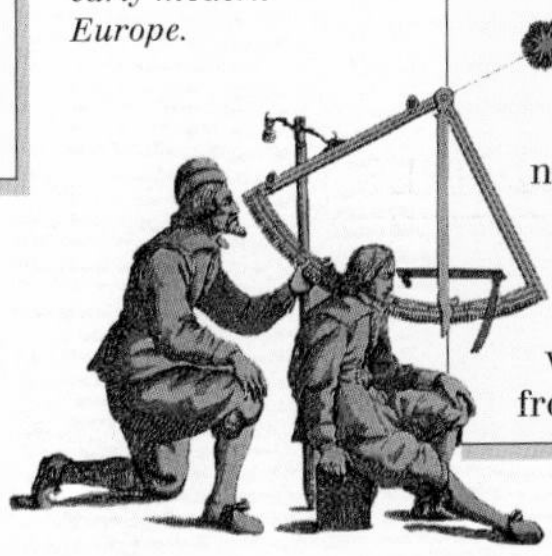

***European navigators** and surveyors produced accurate maps and charts of their voyages.*

RUSSIAN EMPIRE
Siberia
Bering Strait
KAZAKHSTAN
ASIA
Aral Sea
KHWARIZM
KHOKAND KHANATE
KASHGAR KHANATE
UZBEKISTAN
Caspian Sea
SAFAVID PERSIA
The Gulf
Himalayas
TIBET
NEPAL
MUGHAL EMPIRE
MANCHU (CH'ING) EMPIRE
Sea of Japan
JAPAN
KOREA
Deshima 1641
OMAN 1508
Diu 1535
Surat 1608
Daman 1559
Bombay 1534
Hooghly 1640
ARAKAN
BURMA
Arabian Sea
Bay of Bengal
Goa 1510
Masulipatam 1611
Madras 1639
LAOS
ANNAM
SIAM
Macao 1557
FORMOSA 1624
PHILIPPINES from 1565
South China Sea
PACIFIC OCEAN
CEYLON 1505
Galle 1640
ETHIOPIA
Malacca 1641
Micronesia
MOLUCCAS from 1605
Melanesia
PORTUGUESE EAST AFRICA from 1505
INDIAN OCEAN
Makassar 1607
Batavia 1619
East Indies
1610 TIMOR 1618
Madagascar
AUSTRALIA
NEW ZEALAND

***The Indian Mughal** ruler Shahjahan (1592–1648), builder of the Taj Mahal.*

SOUTH ASIA AND OCEANIA

THE PORTUGUESE and the Spanish were the first European powers to open trade with the powerful Asian states of Mughal India and Ch'ing China. The Spanish opened trans-Pacific routes between Central America, the Philippines, and China. But the establishment of the Dutch and British East India companies in the early 17th century announced the advent of two new maritime powers.

***West African** trading kingdoms produced artifacts such as this bronze Portuguese soldier from Benin.*

AFRICA AND THE MIDDLE EAST

WHILE EUROPE WAS DIVIDED by the Reformation, Islam experienced a remarkable resurgence in the 16th century. The revival of the Ottoman Empire brought Islamic rule over much of southeast Europe. Islam spread along trade routes to sub-Saharan Africa. In east Africa, it spread south along the coast. Further east, Muslim rulers established new imperial states in Persia (Iran) and India.

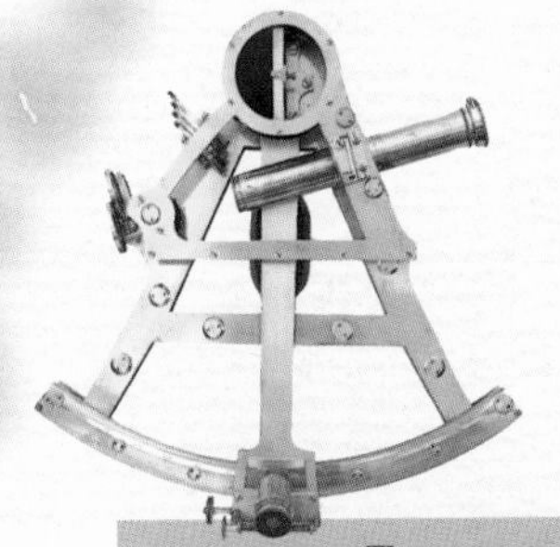

***The sextant** allowed navigators to take accurate measurements of heavenly bodies in relation to the horizon, thus allowing latitude to be calculated correctly. Early sextants had to be hand-held and were often used on shore rather than on board ship.*

The Age of Expansion: 1648-1789

THE YEARS FROM the middle of the 17th century to the end of the 18th century saw a massive consolidation of European discovery and exploration, which took the form of colonial settlement and political expansion. This period also witnessed the beginning of a sharp rise in European population and in its economic strength, accompanied by rapid developments in the arts and sciences. All these factors powered European expansion – a process that would bring European culture to every part of the globe, gradually filling in the world map, and bringing it into often fatal contact with less robust indigenous cultures. By the last quarter of the 18th century, with Europe poised on the brink of political turmoil, only Africa and Australasia remained largely unmolested by European attentions.

Global States and Territories

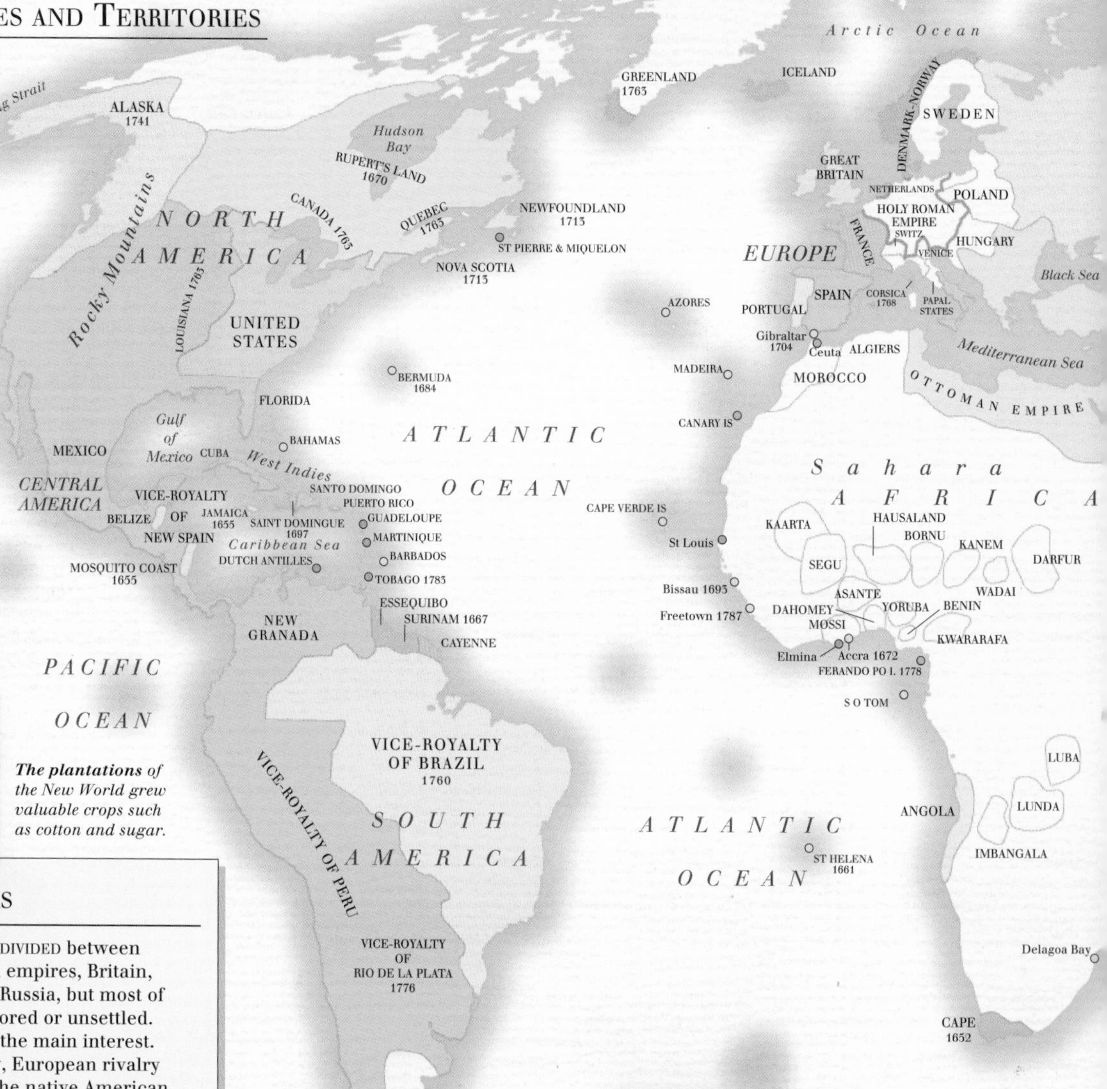

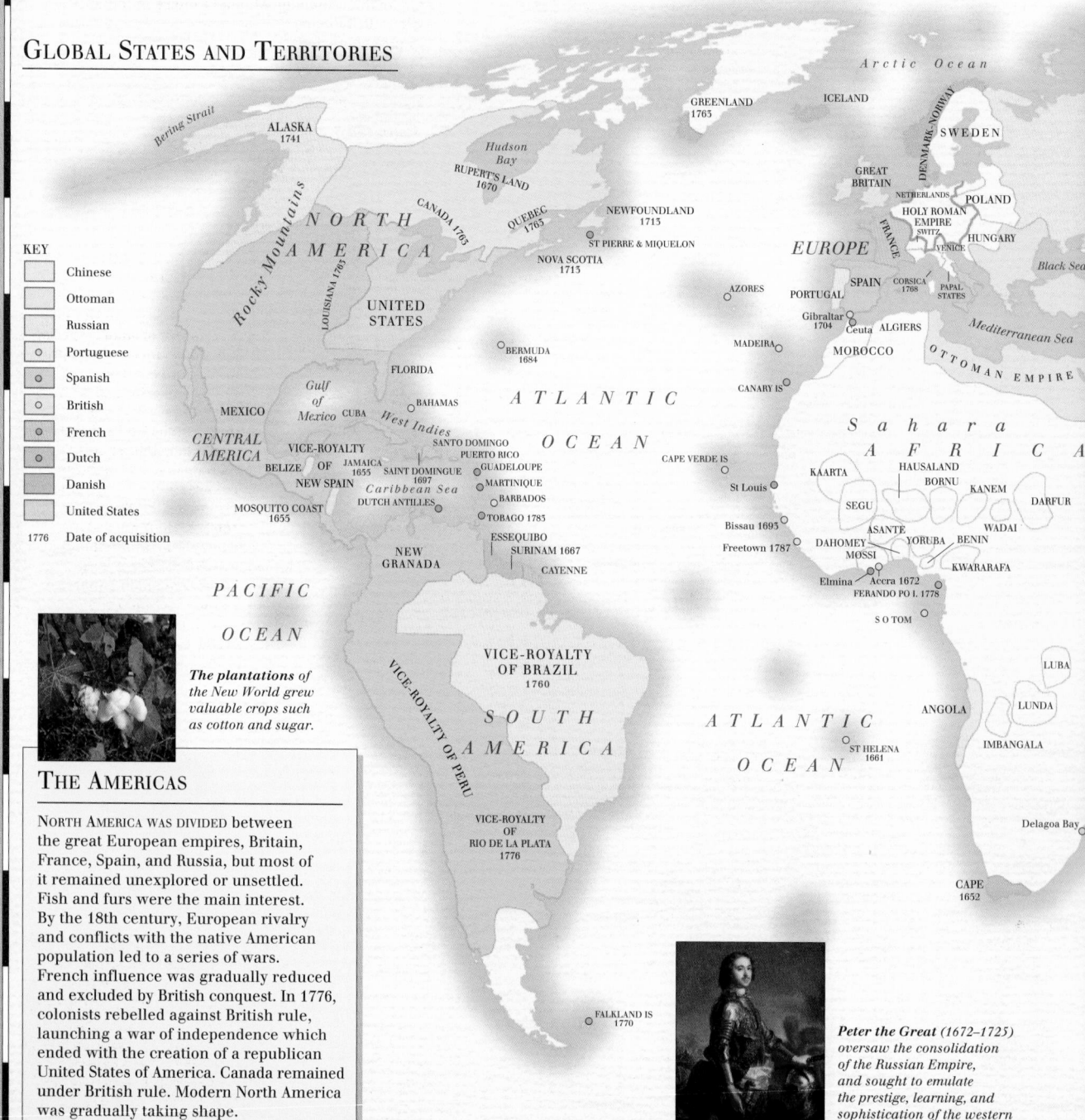

KEY
Chinese
Ottoman
Russian
Portuguese
Spanish
British
French
Dutch
Danish
United States
1776 Date of acquisition
Arctic Ocean
Bering Strait
ALASKA 1741
Hudson Bay
RUPERT'S LAND 1670
CANADA 1763
QUEBEC 1763
NEWFOUNDLAND 1713
ST PIERRE & MIQUELON
NOVA SCOTIA 1713
GREENLAND 1763
ICELAND
DENMARK-NORWAY
SWEDEN
GREAT BRITAIN
NETHERLANDS
POLAND
HOLY ROMAN EMPIRE
SWITZ.
HUNGARY
VENICE
FRANCE
EUROPE
Black Sea
SPAIN
CORSICA 1768
PAPAL STATES
PORTUGAL
AZORES
Gibraltar 1704
Ceuta
ALGIERS
Mediterranean Sea
MADEIRA
MOROCCO
OTTOMAN EMPIRE
CANARY IS
NORTH AMERICA
Rocky Mountains
LOUISIANA 1763
UNITED STATES
BERMUDA 1684
FLORIDA
Gulf of Mexico
MEXICO
CUBA
BAHAMAS
West Indies
ATLANTIC OCEAN
CENTRAL AMERICA
VICE-ROYALTY OF NEW SPAIN
BELIZE
JAMAICA 1655
SANTO DOMINGO
PUERTO RICO
SAINT DOMINGUE 1697
GUADELOUPE
MARTINIQUE
Caribbean Sea
DUTCH ANTILLES
BARBADOS
TOBAGO 1783
MOSQUITO COAST 1655
ESSEQUIBO
SURINAM 1667
CAYENNE
NEW GRANADA
CAPE VERDE IS
St Louis
Bissau 1693
Freetown 1787
Sahara
AFRICA
KAARTA
HAUSALAND
BORNU
KANEM
DARFUR
SEGU
WADAI
ASANTE
DAHOMEY
YORUBA
BENIN
MOSSI
KWARARAFA
Elmina
Accra 1672
FERANDO PO I. 1778
S O TOM
PACIFIC OCEAN
VICE-ROYALTY OF BRAZIL 1760
VICE-ROYALTY OF PERU
SOUTH AMERICA
LUBA
LUNDA
ANGOLA
IMBANGALA
ATLANTIC OCEAN
ST HELENA 1661
VICE-ROYALTY OF RIO DE LA PLATA 1776
Delagoa Bay
CAPE 1652
FALKLAND IS 1770

***The plantations** of the New World grew valuable crops such as cotton and sugar.*

The Americas

North America was divided between the great European empires, Britain, France, Spain, and Russia, but most of it remained unexplored or unsettled. Fish and furs were the main interest. By the 18th century, European rivalry and conflicts with the native American population led to a series of wars. French influence was gradually reduced and excluded by British conquest. In 1776, colonists rebelled against British rule, launching a war of independence which ended with the creation of a republican United States of America. Canada remained under British rule. Modern North America was gradually taking shape.

***Peter the Great** (1672–1725) oversaw the consolidation of the Russian Empire, and sought to emulate the prestige, learning, and sophistication of the western European monarchies.*

EUROPE

AFTER THE CRISIS of the Thirty Years' War, Europe began to develop a more settled state system as successful dynastic houses imposed more centralized rule. The Habsburgs acquired control over Hungary and much of central Europe. Russia's frontiers pushed into Poland and the Ukraine. The French Bourbon monarchy became the most powerful in Europe. Its material wealth and culture made it a rival to the older empires of Asia. French became the common language of educated Europeans, and French philosophy led to the intellectual "Enlightenment."

Isaac Newton *(1642–1727), the leading scientist of Europe's Age of Reason.*

ASIA

THE CH'ING DYNASTY forged the shape of modern China. By 1658 the whole of southern China was under Manchu control. Formosa (Taiwan) was occupied in 1683, outer Mongolia in 1697. A protectorate was established over Tibet in 1751. Over the course of this expansion, the population of China tripled and the economy boomed through trade in tea, porcelain, and silk with Russia and the West. Manchu China was powerful enough to resist incursions by the European empires, avoiding the fate of the crumbling Mughal Empire in India, where Britain and France competed for trade and territory.

Dutch and British *East Indiamen carried the vast European trade with Asia.*

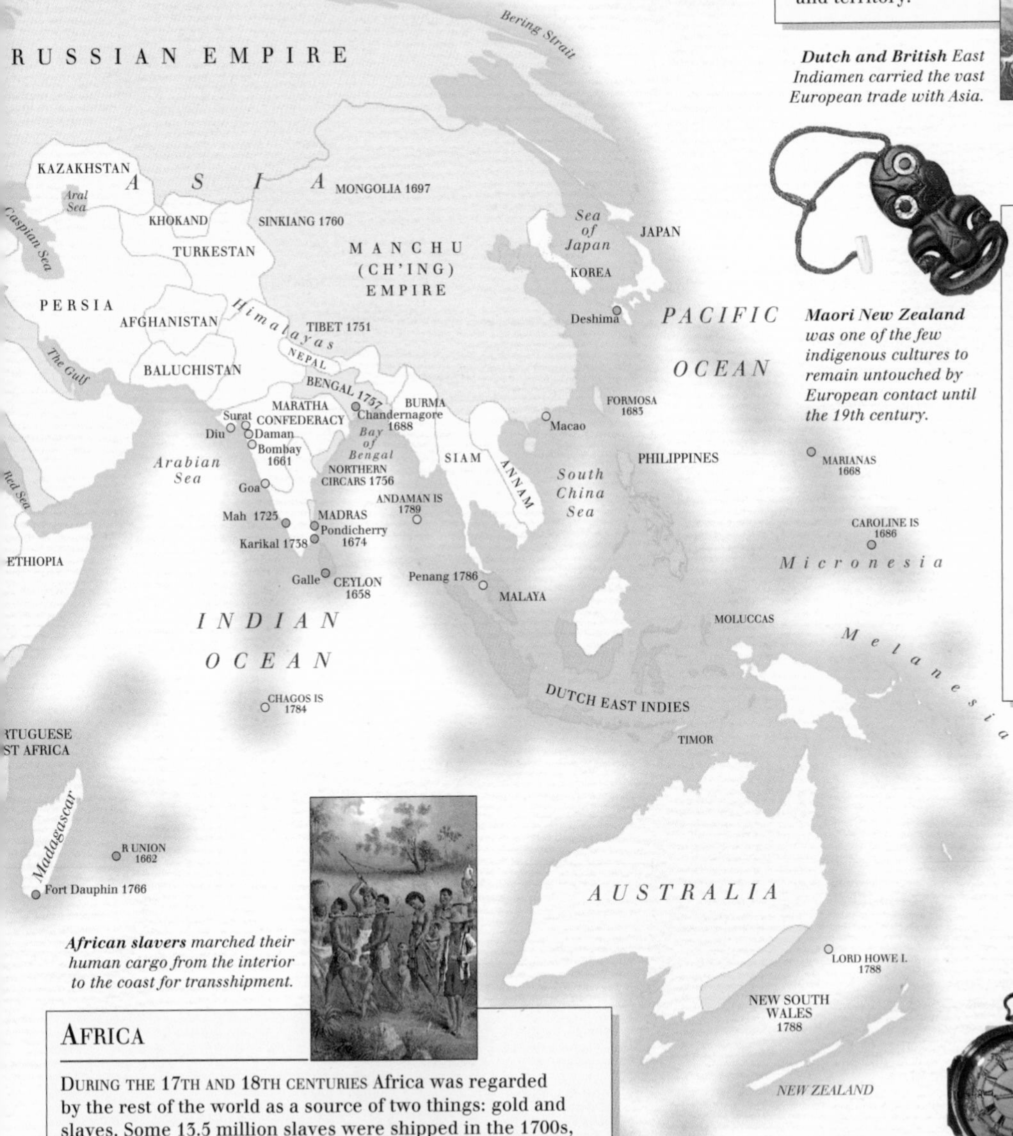
RUSSIAN EMPIRE
Bering Strait
KAZAKHSTAN
ASIA
MONGOLIA 1697
Aral Sea
Caspian Sea
KHOKAND
SINKIANG 1760
TURKESTAN
MANCHU (CH'ING) EMPIRE
Sea of Japan
JAPAN
KOREA
PERSIA
AFGHANISTAN
Himalayas
TIBET 1751
Deshima
PACIFIC OCEAN
The Gulf
NEPAL
BALUCHISTAN
BENGAL 1757
MARATHA CONFEDERACY
BURMA
Chandernagore 1688
FORMOSA 1683
Surat
Diu
Daman
Bombay 1661
Macao
Bay of Bengal
SIAM
PHILIPPINES
MARIANAS 1668
Arabian Sea
NORTHERN CIRCARS 1756
ANNAM
South China Sea
Red Sea
Goa
ANDAMAN IS 1789
Mah 1725
MADRAS
Pondicherry 1674
Karikal 1738
CAROLINE IS 1686
ETHIOPIA
Micronesia
Galle
CEYLON 1658
Penang 1786
MALAYA
MOLUCCAS
INDIAN OCEAN
Melanesia
DUTCH EAST INDIES
CHAGOS IS 1784
TIMOR
RTUGUESE
ST AFRICA
Madagascar
R UNION 1662
Fort Dauphin 1766
AUSTRALIA
LORD HOWE I. 1788
NEW SOUTH WALES 1788
NEW ZEALAND

Maori New Zealand *was one of the few indigenous cultures to remain untouched by European contact until the 19th century.*

OCEANIA

SOUTHEAST ASIA AND OCEANIA were areas of small, warring kingdoms, increasingly prey to the ambitions of European traders, first Spanish and Portuguese, then Dutch and British. Yet, by the late 18th century, there was still little formal colonization. Though first discovered by Tasman in 1692, most of Australasia was still unexplored and unsettled, except for a number of small penal colonies set up by the British in New South Wales (1788) and Tasmania (1804).

African slavers *marched their human cargo from the interior to the coast for transshipment.*

AFRICA

DURING THE 17TH AND 18TH CENTURIES Africa was regarded by the rest of the world as a source of two things: gold and slaves. Some 13.5 million slaves were shipped in the 1700s, from the west coast and from Portuguese Angola. African dealers sold to European middlemen, who in turn sold on the surviving slaves. In northern and northeastern Africa, Arab slavers traded with the Ottoman Empire. But the rest of Africa remained isolated from the outside world.

Harrison's chronometer, *invented in 1762, allowed navigators to measure time accurately, and thus calculate longitude correctly. This greatly reduced the risk of shipwreck and heralded the beginning of accurate mapping of the world.*

THE AGE OF REVOLUTION: 1789-1830

IN 1789 ROYAL POWER was shattered by the French Revolution. The collapse of the most powerful monarchy in Europe reverberated worldwide. The revolutions in France and America ushered in the idea of the modern nation state, and of popular representative government. Revolutionary outbreaks occurred elsewhere in Europe, and overseas colonies in Latin America won their independence. At the same time, an industrial revolution was taking place in Europe, transforming the old trading economy into a manufacturing base which would require a global supply of raw materials and a global market to fuel it. The revolutionary years thus marked the beginning of the modern political and economic world order.

GLOBAL STATES AND TERRITORIES

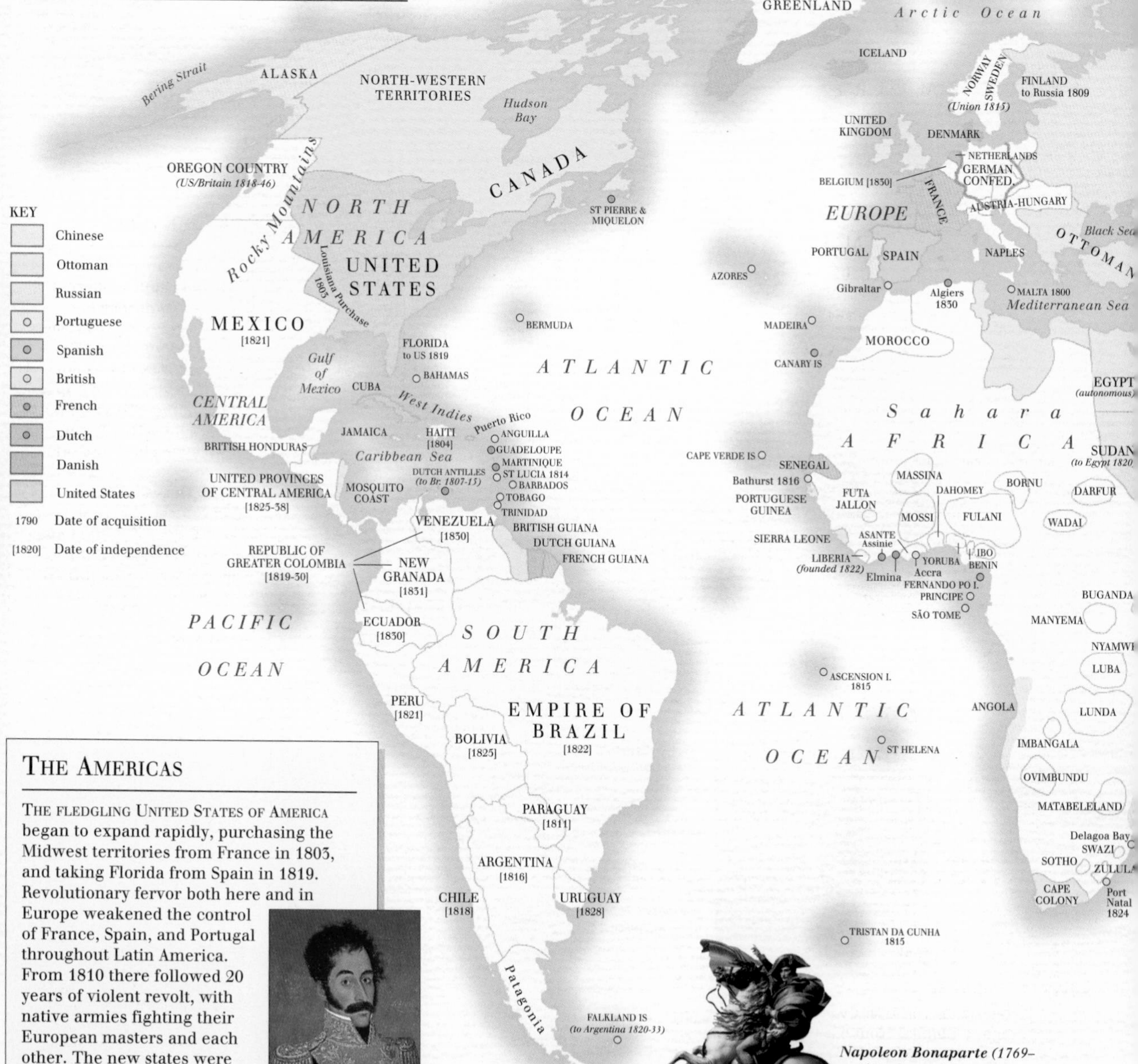
KEY
Chinese
Ottoman
Russian
Portuguese
Spanish
British
French
Dutch
Danish
United States
1790 Date of acquisition
[1820] Date of independence
GREENLAND
Arctic Ocean
ICELAND
Bering Strait
ALASKA
NORTH-WESTERN TERRITORIES
Hudson Bay
NORWAY
SWEDEN
(Union 1815)
FINLAND to Russia 1809
UNITED KINGDOM
DENMARK
NETHERLANDS
GERMAN CONFED.
BELGIUM [1830]
FRANCE
AUSTRIA-HUNGARY
OREGON COUNTRY (US/Britain 1818-46)
Rocky Mountains
CANADA
NORTH AMERICA
UNITED STATES
Louisiana Purchase 1803
ST PIERRE & MIQUELON
EUROPE
Black Sea
OTTOMAN
PORTUGAL
SPAIN
NAPLES
AZORES
Gibraltar
Algiers 1830
MALTA 1800
Mediterranean Sea
MEXICO [1821]
BERMUDA
MADEIRA
FLORIDA to US 1819
MOROCCO
Gulf of Mexico
CUBA
BAHAMAS
ATLANTIC OCEAN
CANARY IS
EGYPT (autonomous)
CENTRAL AMERICA
West Indies
Puerto Rico
Sahara
AFRICA
JAMAICA
HAITI [1804]
ANGUILLA
GUADELOUPE
MARTINIQUE
ST LUCIA 1814
BARBADOS
TOBAGO
TRINIDAD
Caribbean Sea
DUTCH ANTILLES (to Br. 1807-15)
BRITISH HONDURAS
CAPE VERDE IS
SENEGAL
SUDAN (to Egypt 1820)
UNITED PROVINCES OF CENTRAL AMERICA [1825-38]
MOSQUITO COAST
Bathurst 1816
MASSINA
DAHOMEY
BORNU
DARFUR
PORTUGUESE GUINEA
FUTA JALLON
MOSSI
FULANI
WADAI
VENEZUELA [1830]
BRITISH GUIANA
DUTCH GUIANA
FRENCH GUIANA
SIERRA LEONE
ASANTE
Assinie
LIBERIA (founded 1822)
Elmina
YORUBA
Accra
IBO
BENIN
FERNANDO PO I.
PRINCIPE
SÃO TOME
REPUBLIC OF GREATER COLOMBIA [1819-30]
NEW GRANADA [1831]
BUGANDA
MANYEMA
ECUADOR [1830]
PACIFIC OCEAN
SOUTH AMERICA
NYAMWE
LUBA
ASCENSION I. 1815
PERU [1821]
EMPIRE OF BRAZIL [1822]
ATLANTIC OCEAN
ANGOLA
LUNDA
BOLIVIA [1825]
ST HELENA
IMBANGALA
OVIMBUNDU
MATABELELAND
PARAGUAY [1811]
Delagoa Bay
SWAZI
ARGENTINA [1816]
SOTHO
ZULUL
CHILE [1818]
URUGUAY [1828]
CAPE COLONY
Port Natal 1824
TRISTAN DA CUNHA 1815
Patagonia
FALKLAND IS (to Argentina 1820-33)

THE AMERICAS

THE FLEDGLING UNITED STATES OF AMERICA began to expand rapidly, purchasing the Midwest territories from France in 1803, and taking Florida from Spain in 1819. Revolutionary fervor both here and in Europe weakened the control of France, Spain, and Portugal throughout Latin America. From 1810 there followed 20 years of violent revolt, with native armies fighting their European masters and each other. The new states were prey to political violence and instability, but they never again came under European rule.

***Simón Bolívar** (1783–1830) led armies of liberation in Peru, Bolivia, and Venezuela.*

***Napoleon Bonaparte** (1769–1821) began his career as a commander in the French Revolutionary wars. By 1804 he had become emperor of France, which dominated much of western Europe.*

EUROPE

UNDER NAPOLEON BONAPARTE, France subordinated a large part of Europe and destroyed the old feudal order. Napoleon helped to shape the new nation states that emerged in 19th-century Europe – Belgium, Italy, and Germany. He gave much of Europe its modern legal code and systems of education and local government.

Steam-powered engines *transformed the European industrial economy.*

ASIA

THE PRINCIPAL COLONIAL POWER in Asia was Russia, whose consolidation of its empire in northern and central Asia continued throughout the 19th century. But now the Dutch began to extend their control of the East Indies, while a bitter struggle between the British and the French was conducted in and around the Indian Ocean. France was gradually forced to concede many of its footholds in India, where the British East India Company rapidly extended its interests by a mixture of diplomacy and military force. But the elusive key to Asia's largest markets remained the slumbering giant of Ch'ing China, whose Manchu rulers, like those of Japan, remained unimpressed by European overtures.

The spices of the East Indies, *such as pepper, were among the most highly valued traded commodities from Asia.*

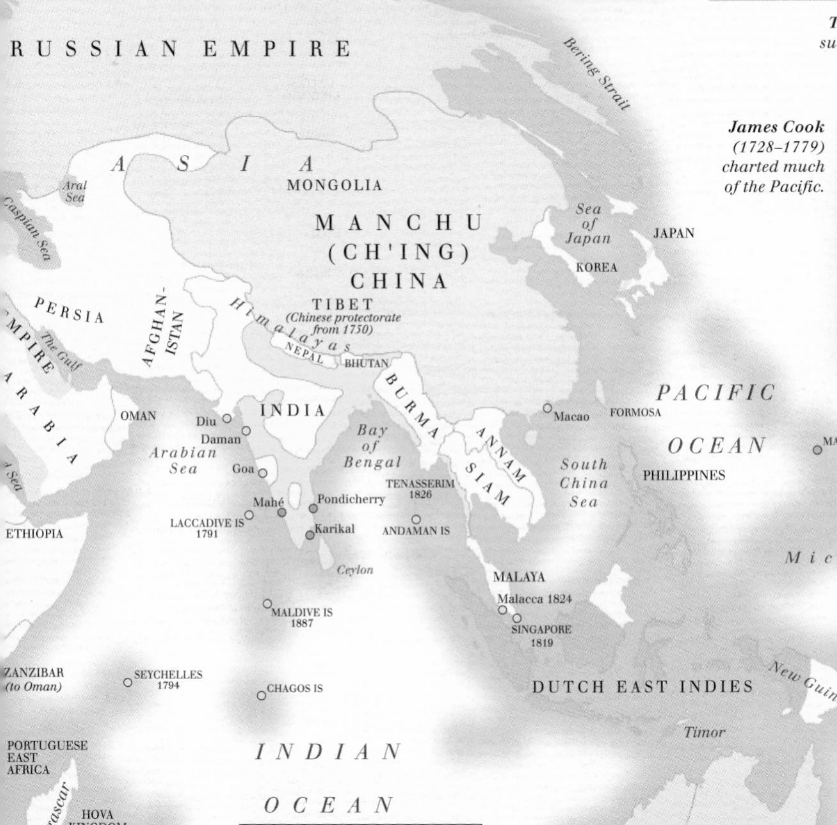
RUSSIAN EMPIRE
Bering Strait
ASIA
Aral Sea
Caspian Sea
MONGOLIA
MANCHU (CH'ING) CHINA
Sea of Japan
JAPAN
KOREA
PERSIA
EMPIRE
The Gulf
AFGHAN-ISTAN
TIBET
(Chinese protectorate from 1750)
Himalayas
NEPAL
BHUTAN
ARABIA
OMAN
Diu
Daman
INDIA
Bay of Bengal
BURMA
ANNAM
SIAM
Macao
FORMOSA
PACIFIC OCEAN
Arabian Sea
Goa
TENASSERIM 1826
South China Sea
PHILIPPINES
MARIANAS
Mahé
Pondicherry
LACCADIVE IS 1791
Karikal
ANDAMAN IS
ETHIOPIA
CAROLINE IS
Ceylon
Micronesia
MALAYA
Malacca 1824
MALDIVE IS 1887
SINGAPORE 1819
Melanesia
New Guinea
ZANZIBAR (to Oman)
SEYCHELLES 1794
CHAGOS IS
DUTCH EAST INDIES
Timor
PORTUGUESE EAST AFRICA
INDIAN OCEAN
Madagascar
HOVA KINGDOM
MAURITIUS 1810
RÉUNION
WESTERN AUSTRALIA 1829
NEW SOUTH WALES
AUSTRALIA
LORD HOWE I.
NEW ZEALAND
CHATHAM IS 1791
TASMANIA (Van Diemen's Land)
AUCKLAND IS 1806
MACQUARIE IS 1811

James Cook *(1728–1779) charted much of the Pacific.*

OCEANIA

THOUGH PORTUGUESE and Dutch explorers had confirmed the existence of Australasia in the 16th and 17th centuries, it was not until the voyages of Captain Cook in the 1770s that the geography of the Pacific was established, and the fertile eastern coast of Australia was explored and charted. Over the next 30 years, small settlements were established around the coast; by 1829, Britain had brought the whole continent under the British flag.

The first European *migrants to Africa settled in Cape Colony.*

AFRICA

THE NORTHERN REGIONS OF AFRICA were part of the vast Islamic Ottoman Empire; from here Islam spread south to west Africa and the Horn of Africa. Holy wars (or *jihads*) in the late 18th and early 19th centuries completed the conversion to Islam of much of Saharan and sub-Saharan Africa. Large tribal kingdoms flourished in the Congo basin and southern Africa.

The development *during the European industrial revolution of mechanized manufacturing plant and machinery, such as power looms, gave Europe effective control of a booming global trade in raw materials and mass-manufactured commodities.*

THE AGE OF EMPIRE: 1830-1914

THE 19TH CENTURY was dominated by the spread of modern industry and transportation, and the expansion of European trade and influence worldwide. Industry made Europe rich and powerful; its capital cities were monuments to the self-confidence of the new European age. Railroads and steam ships revolutionized communications, bringing a stream of industrial goods, technical know-how, and European settlers across America, Africa, and Asia. Modern industry and weapons brought Europe to the summit of global influence. In these developments lay the origins of the division of the world into rich and poor regions; a developed, prosperous north and an under-developed, dependent south.

GLOBAL STATES AND TERRITORIES

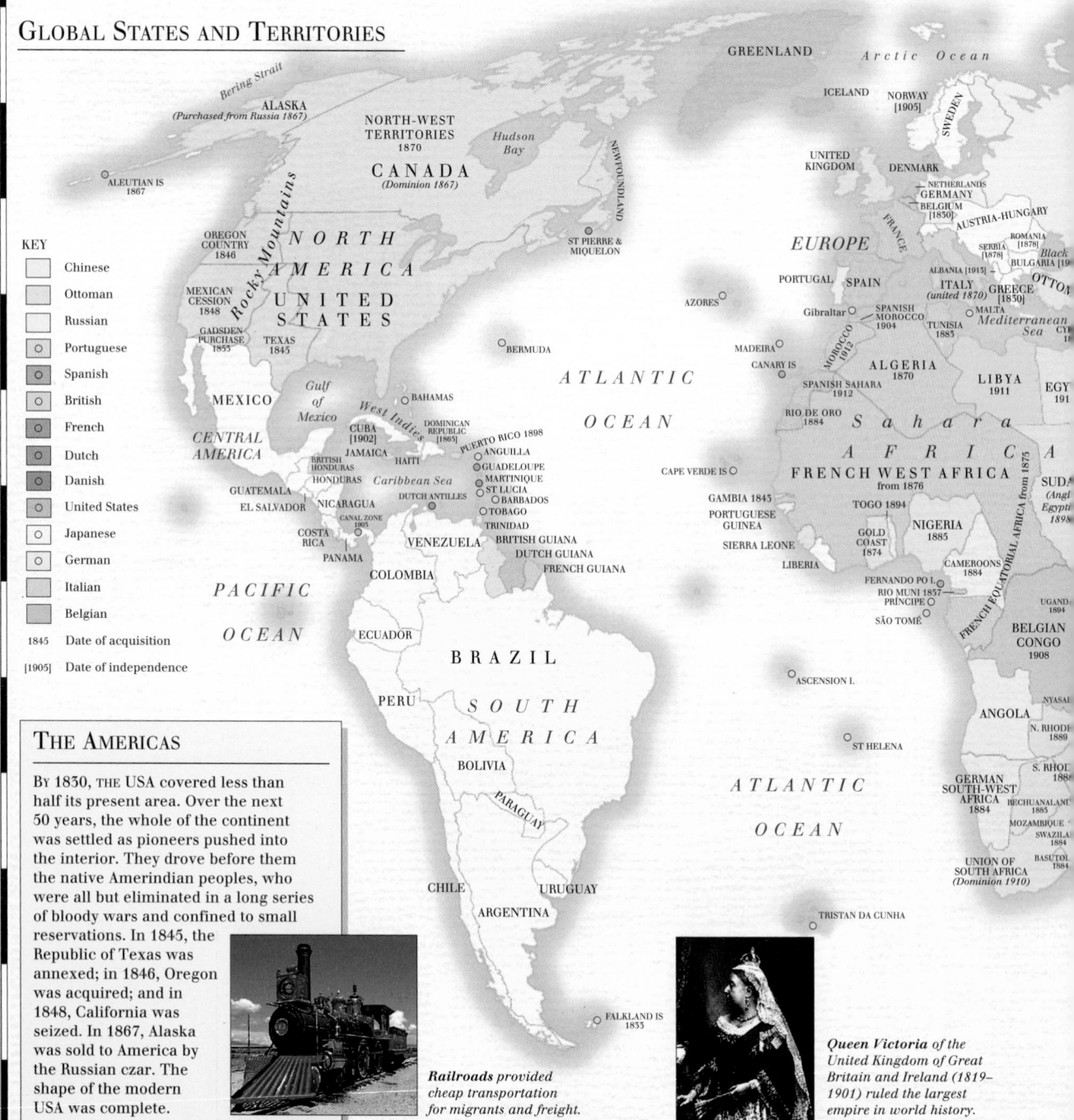

KEY
Chinese
Ottoman
Russian
Portuguese
Spanish
British
French
Dutch
Danish
United States
Japanese
German
Italian
Belgian
1845 Date of acquisition
[1905] Date of independence
Bering Strait
ALASKA
(Purchased from Russia 1867)
ALEUTIAN IS 1867
NORTH-WEST TERRITORIES 1870
CANADA
(Dominion 1867)
Hudson Bay
NEWFOUNDLAND
GREENLAND
Arctic Ocean
ICELAND
NORWAY [1905]
SWEDEN
UNITED KINGDOM
DENMARK
NETHERLANDS
GERMANY
BELGIUM [1830]
AUSTRIA-HUNGARY
ROMANIA [1878]
SERBIA [1878]
BULGARIA
ALBANIA [1913]
EUROPE
FRANCE
PORTUGAL
SPAIN
ITALY (united 1870)
GREECE [1830]
MALTA
Gibraltar
SPANISH MOROCCO 1904
TUNISIA 1883
Mediterranean Sea
MOROCCO 1912
OREGON COUNTRY 1846
Rocky Mountains
NORTH AMERICA
UNITED STATES
MEXICAN CESSION 1848
GADSDEN PURCHASE 1853
TEXAS 1845
ST PIERRE & MIQUELON
AZORES
BERMUDA
MADEIRA
CANARY IS
ALGERIA 1870
LIBYA 1911
SPANISH SAHARA 1912
RIO DE ORO 1884
Sahara
ATLANTIC OCEAN
MEXICO
Gulf of Mexico
West Indies
BAHAMAS
CUBA [1902]
DOMINICAN REPUBLIC [1865]
PUERTO RICO 1898
JAMAICA
HAITI
ANGUILLA
GUADELOUPE
MARTINIQUE
ST LUCIA
BARBADOS
TOBAGO
TRINIDAD
CENTRAL AMERICA
BRITISH HONDURAS
HONDURAS
Caribbean Sea
GUATEMALA
EL SALVADOR
NICARAGUA
DUTCH ANTILLES
CANAL ZONE 1903
COSTA RICA
PANAMA
VENEZUELA
BRITISH GUIANA
DUTCH GUIANA
FRENCH GUIANA
COLOMBIA
CAPE VERDE IS
AFRICA
FRENCH WEST AFRICA from 1876
GAMBIA 1843
PORTUGUESE GUINEA
SIERRA LEONE
LIBERIA
TOGO 1894
GOLD COAST 1874
NIGERIA 1885
CAMEROONS 1884
FERNANDO PO I.
RIO MUNI 1857
PRÍNCIPE
SÃO TOMÉ
FRENCH EQUATORIAL AFRICA from 1875
BELGIAN CONGO 1908
PACIFIC OCEAN
ECUADOR
BRAZIL
PERU
SOUTH AMERICA
BOLIVIA
PARAGUAY
CHILE
URUGUAY
ARGENTINA
FALKLAND IS 1833
ASCENSION I.
ST HELENA
ATLANTIC OCEAN
ANGOLA
GERMAN SOUTH-WEST AFRICA 1884
UNION OF SOUTH AFRICA (Dominion 1910)
TRISTAN DA CUNHA

THE AMERICAS

BY 1830, THE USA covered less than half its present area. Over the next 50 years, the whole of the continent was settled as pioneers pushed into the interior. They drove before them the native Amerindian peoples, who were all but eliminated in a long series of bloody wars and confined to small reservations. In 1845, the Republic of Texas was annexed; in 1846, Oregon was acquired; and in 1848, California was seized. In 1867, Alaska was sold to America by the Russian czar. The shape of the modern USA was complete.

***Railroads** provided cheap transportation for migrants and freight.*

***Queen Victoria** of the United Kingdom of Great Britain and Ireland (1819–1901) ruled the largest empire in world history.*

EUROPE

IN THE 19TH CENTURY, Europe was transformed into an industrial economy. In the new industrial cities, pressure developed for liberal reforms and parliamentary politics. Nationalists created new states in Germany, Italy, Greece, Serbia, and Belgium. While the modern map of Europe gradually began to take shape, European imperialists brought still more areas of the world under their control.

***Sailing ships** carried most oceanic trade until 1900.*

ASIA

BUILDING ON COLONIAL INTERESTS that stretched back into the 18th century, Britain and France transformed the political world of south Asia. Britain extended its rule in India and, in 1885, Burma was brought under British control. The Vietnamese and Chinese Empires were pressured by Europeans anxious to trade and to spread Christianity: the Ch'ing Empire conceded areas of influence; the Vietnamese Empire resisted and was brought under French domination by force. By the 1890s the whole of southern Asia except for Siam was dominated by Europe, which created the modern state structure of the region.

***The Japanese emperor Meiji** (1852–1912) opened Japan to Western trade and influence.*

***The colonization** of Australia and New Zealand was based on sheep farming.*

OCEANIA

DURING THE 19TH century, Australia and New Zealand remained closely tied to the British homeland. British settlers came to farm and later to prospect for gold and other valuable minerals. In 1840, New Zealand came under British rule and the native Maoris were forced off the land. Not until 1872 was the continent of Australia traversed, and not until 1901 was a single state, the Commonwealth of Australia, proclaimed.

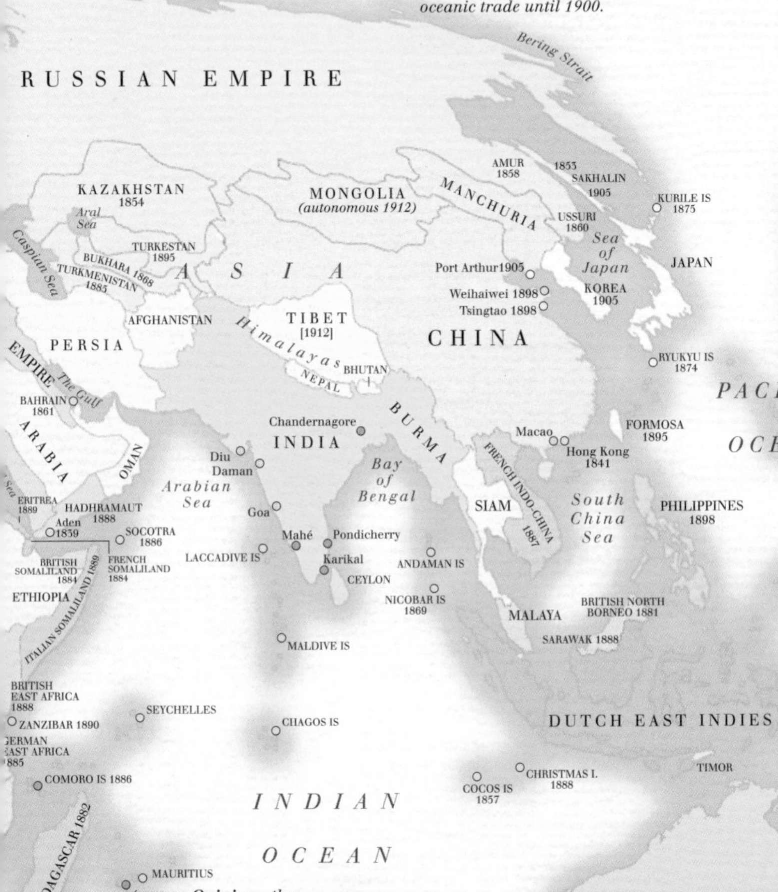

RUSSIAN EMPIRE
Bering Strait
KAZAKHSTAN 1854
Aral Sea
Caspian Sea
MONGOLIA (autonomous 1912)
MANCHURIA
AMUR 1858
1855 SAKHALIN 1905
KURILE IS 1875
USSURI 1860
Sea of Japan
JAPAN
TURKESTAN 1895
BUKHARA 1868
TURKMENISTAN 1885
ASIA
Port Arthur1905
Weihaiwei 1898
Tsingtao 1898
KOREA 1905
AFGHANISTAN
TIBET [1912]
Himalayas
CHINA
PERSIA
EMPIRE
NEPAL
BHUTAN
RYUKYU IS 1874
The Gulf
BAHRAIN 1861
ARABIA
OMAN
Chandernagore
INDIA
BURMA
Macao
FORMOSA 1895
Hong Kong 1841
PACIFIC OCEAN
Diu
Daman
Arabian Sea
Bay of Bengal
FRENCH INDO-CHINA 1887
SIAM
South China Sea
PHILIPPINES 1898
MARIANAS 1899
ERITREA 1889
HADHRAMAUT 1888
Aden 1839
SOCOTRA 1886
Goa
Mahé
Pondicherry
Karikal
GUAM 1898
BRITISH SOMALILAND 1884
FRENCH SOMALILAND 1884
LACCADIVE IS
ANDAMAN IS
CEYLON
CAROLINE IS 1899
Micronesia
ETHIOPIA
ITALIAN SOMALILAND 1889
NICOBAR IS 1869
MALAYA
BRITISH NORTH BORNEO 1881
SARAWAK 1888
MALDIVE IS
BISMARCK ARCHIPELAGO 1884
NAURU 1888
BRITISH EAST AFRICA 1888
SEYCHELLES
ZANZIBAR 1890
GERMAN EAST AFRICA 1885
CHAGOS IS
DUTCH EAST INDIES
NEW GUINEA
Melanesia
PAPUA 1906
SOLOMON IS 1893
COMORO IS 1886
CHRISTMAS I. 1888
COCOS IS 1857
TIMOR
INDIAN OCEAN
MADAGASCAR 1882
MAURITIUS
RÉUNION
NEW CALEDONIA 1853
AUSTRALIA (Commonwealth 1901)
NORFOLK ISLAND
NEW ZEALAND 1840 (Dominion 1907)
CHATHAM IS.
TASMANIA
AUCKLAND IS
MACQUARIE IS

***Quinine** – the cure for malaria.*

***New medicines** made the colonization of Africa possible.*

AFRICA

THE POLITICAL STRUCTURE of independent Africa was torn up by encroaching European empires. As native societies reacted violently to European intrusion, so European military and political power was increased to secure European interests. In 1884, in Berlin, the European powers divided Africa between them. The "Partition of Africa" established the modern frontiers of many states.

***The European** imperial powers maintained control of their often far-flung colonies by military superiority. Native forces were rarely a match for the large, highly trained armies, powerful navies, and technically advanced weaponry which the Europeans had at their disposal.*

***The Gatling gun,** the most successful of the hand-driven machine guns of the 19th century.*

THE AGE OF GLOBAL WAR: 1914-1945

IN 1914, IMPERIAL AND MILITARY rivalry in Europe provoked the first of two world wars, the largest and most destructive wars in human history. At the end of the first war, in 1918, the old international order was dead. The Russian Empire collapsed in revolution and was transformed by a communist minority into the Soviet Union. The German, Habsburg, and Ottoman empires were dismembered. A fragile peace ensued but the old equilibrium was gone. The rise of strident nationalism in Germany, Japan, and Italy destroyed the peace once again in 1939. The second war cost the lives of 50 million people and ravaged Europe and Asia. At its end, in 1945, the USA and the Soviet Union had emerged as the new superpowers.

GLOBAL STATES AND TERRITORIES

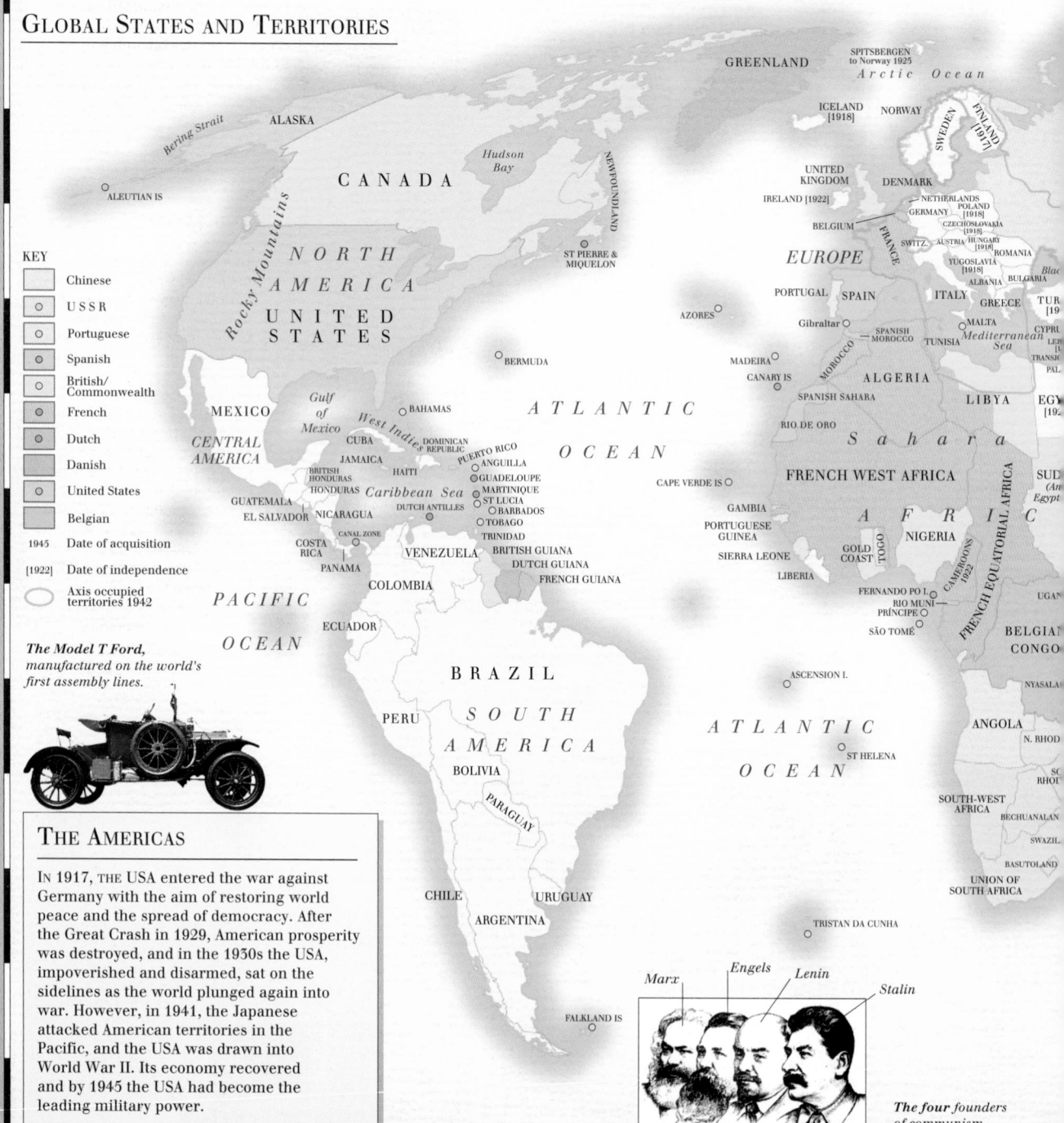

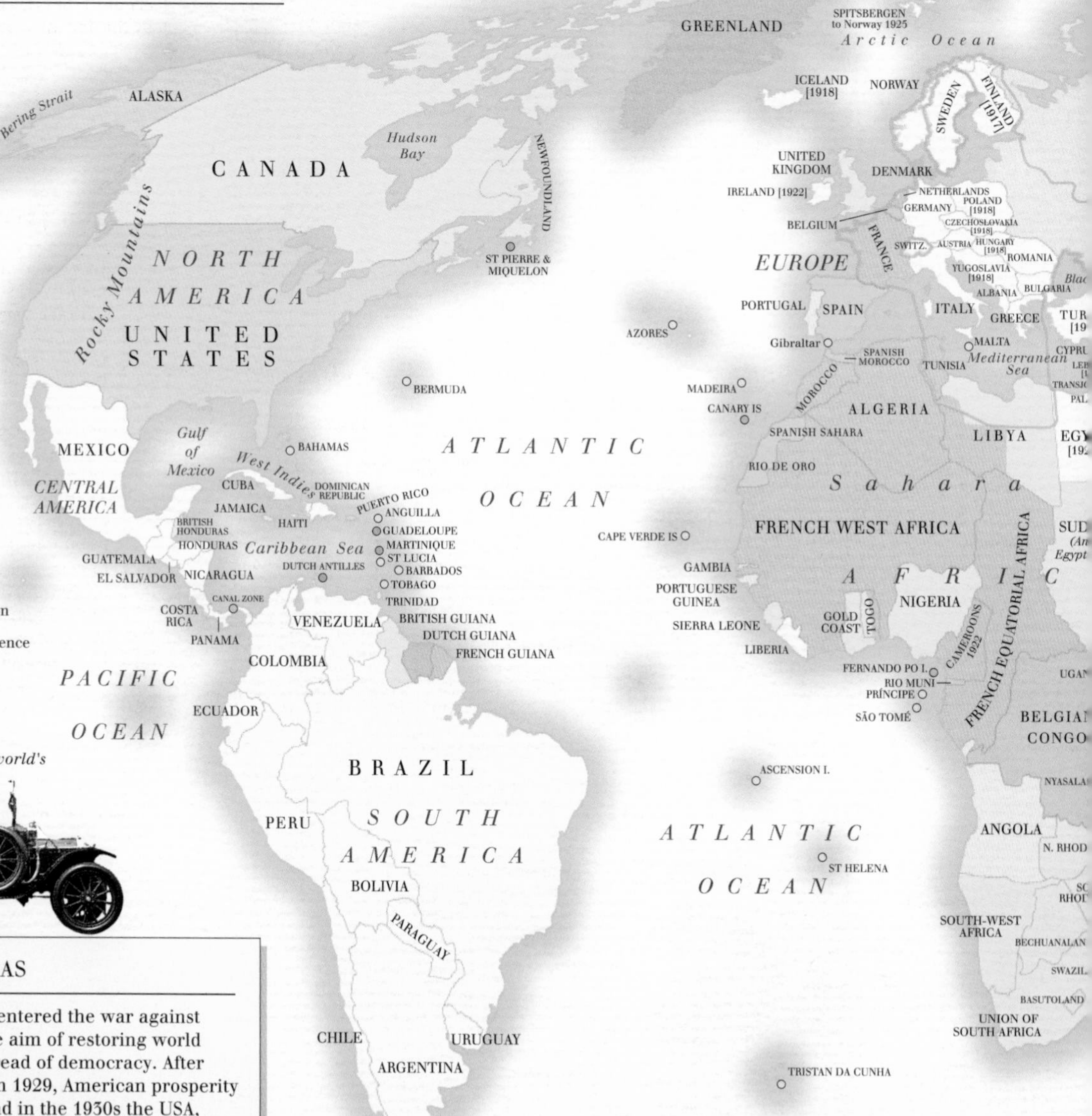
GREENLAND
SPITSBERGEN to Norway 1925
Arctic Ocean
ICELAND [1918]
NORWAY
SWEDEN
FINLAND [1917]
Bering Strait
ALASKA
Hudson Bay
NEWFOUNDLAND
CANADA
ALEUTIAN IS
UNITED KINGDOM
DENMARK
IRELAND [1922]
NETHERLANDS
POLAND [1918]
GERMANY
CZECHOSLOVAKIA [1918]
BELGIUM
FRANCE
SWITZ.
AUSTRIA
HUNGARY [1918]
ROMANIA
YUGOSLAVIA [1918]
ALBANIA
BULGARIA
Rocky Mountains
NORTH AMERICA
UNITED STATES
ST PIERRE & MIQUELON
EUROPE
PORTUGAL
SPAIN
ITALY
GREECE
AZORES
Gibraltar
SPANISH MOROCCO
MALTA
TUNISIA
Mediterranean Sea
BERMUDA
MADEIRA
MOROCCO
CANARY IS
ALGERIA
SPANISH SAHARA
LIBYA
MEXICO
Gulf of Mexico
BAHAMAS
ATLANTIC OCEAN
West Indies
CENTRAL AMERICA
CUBA
DOMINICAN REPUBLIC
PUERTO RICO
RIO DE ORO
Sahara
JAMAICA
ANGUILLA
BRITISH HONDURAS
HAITI
GUADELOUPE
HONDURAS
Caribbean Sea
MARTINIQUE
ST LUCIA
GUATEMALA
CAPE VERDE IS
FRENCH WEST AFRICA
EL SALVADOR
NICARAGUA
DUTCH ANTILLES
BARBADOS
TOBAGO
TRINIDAD
GAMBIA
CANAL ZONE
COSTA RICA
PANAMA
VENEZUELA
BRITISH GUIANA
DUTCH GUIANA
FRENCH GUIANA
PORTUGUESE GUINEA
AFRICA
NIGERIA
SIERRA LEONE
GOLD COAST
TOGO
LIBERIA
CAMEROONS 1922
FRENCH EQUATORIAL AFRICA
COLOMBIA
PACIFIC OCEAN
ECUADOR
FERNANDO PO I.
RIO MUNI
PRÍNCIPE
SÃO TOMÉ
BELGIAN CONGO
ASCENSION I.
BRAZIL
PERU
SOUTH AMERICA
BOLIVIA
PARAGUAY
ATLANTIC OCEAN
ST HELENA
ANGOLA
SOUTH-WEST AFRICA
BECHUANALAND
BASUTOLAND
UNION OF SOUTH AFRICA
CHILE
URUGUAY
ARGENTINA
TRISTAN DA CUNHA
FALKLAND IS
KEY
Chinese
USSR
Portuguese
Spanish
British/ Commonwealth
French
Dutch
Danish
United States
Belgian
1945 Date of acquisition
[1922] Date of independence
Axis occupied territories 1942

The Model T Ford, manufactured on the world's first assembly lines.

THE AMERICAS

IN 1917, THE USA entered the war against Germany with the aim of restoring world peace and the spread of democracy. After the Great Crash in 1929, American prosperity was destroyed, and in the 1930s the USA, impoverished and disarmed, sat on the sidelines as the world plunged again into war. However, in 1941, the Japanese attacked American territories in the Pacific, and the USA was drawn into World War II. Its economy recovered and by 1945 the USA had become the leading military power.

Marx
Engels
Lenin
Stalin

The four founders of communism.

EUROPE

BOTH WORLD WARS had their origins in Europe. In 1914. Germany invaded Belgium; Britain, France, and Russia combined to defeat it, with US help. In 1918 new nation states were established in eastern Europe. But, by 1939, revived German nationalism started a second world war; much of western Europe came under a German "New Order" until the Soviet Union, Britain, and the USA developed sufficient military strength to reconquer Europe and defeat Germany.

World War II *was decided by mechanical and industrial superiority.*

ASIA

THE COLLAPSE OF THE CHINESE EMPIRE in 1911, followed in 1917 by the disappearance of the Russian Empire, produced instability across Asia. Full-scale war broke out between Japan and China in 1937, with Japan trying to conquer China. The Soviet Union was the victim of German aggression from 1941. Both Japan and Germany were held at bay by communist forces which eventually succeeded in imposing stable politics on Asia. By 1945, the Soviet Union had reconquered its lost territories and dominated eastern Europe. In China, communist armies filled the vacuum left by the Japanese defeat.

Mahatma Gandhi *(1868–1948) led India to independence through peaceful noncooperation and protest.*

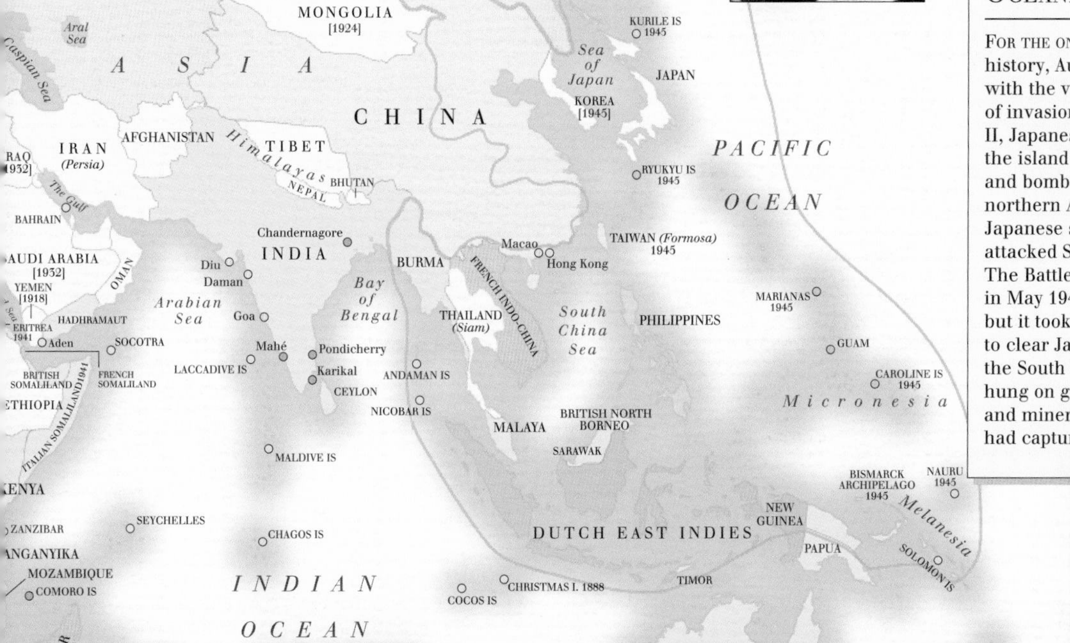

U S S R
Bering Strait
SAKHALIN 1945
MONGOLIA [1924]
Aral Sea
Caspian Sea
A S I A
KURILE IS 1945
Sea of Japan
JAPAN
KOREA [1945]
C H I N A
IRAQ [1932]
IRAN (Persia)
AFGHANISTAN
Himalayas
TIBET
BHUTAN
NEPAL
PACIFIC
RYUKYU IS 1945
OCEAN
The Gulf
BAHRAIN
Chandernagore
INDIA
SAUDI ARABIA [1932]
OMAN
YEMEN [1918]
Diu
Daman
Arabian Sea
Bay of Bengal
BURMA
FRENCH INDO-CHINA
Macao
Hong Kong
TAIWAN (Formosa) 1945
ERITREA 1941
HADHRAMAUT
Goa
THAILAND (Siam)
South China Sea
PHILIPPINES
MARIANAS 1945
Aden
SOCOTRA
Mahé
Pondicherry
Karikal
GUAM
BRITISH SOMALILAND
FRENCH SOMALILAND
LACCADIVE IS
ANDAMAN IS
CEYLON
CAROLINE IS 1945
ETHIOPIA
ITALIAN SOMALILAND 1941
NICOBAR IS
MALAYA
BRITISH NORTH BORNEO
Micronesia
SARAWAK
MALDIVE IS
KENYA
BISMARCK ARCHIPELAGO 1945
NAURU 1945
SEYCHELLES
NEW GUINEA
Melanesia
ZANZIBAR
CHAGOS IS
DUTCH EAST INDIES
TANGANYIKA
PAPUA
SOLOMON IS
MOZAMBIQUE
COMORO IS
INDIAN
CHRISTMAS I. 1888
TIMOR
COCOS IS
OCEAN
MADAGASCAR
MAURITIUS
RÉUNION
NEW CALEDONIA
AUSTRALIA
(Dominion 1926)
LORD HOWE I.
NEW ZEALAND
CHATHAM IS
TASMANIA
AUCKLAND IS
MACQUARIE IS

OCEANIA

FOR THE ONLY TIME in its history, Australia was faced with the very real prospect of invasion. In World War II, Japanese armies reached the island of New Guinea, and bombed towns in northern Australia. Japanese submarines attacked Sydney harbor. The Battle of the Coral Sea, in May 1942, saved Australia, but it took almost three years to clear Japanese forces from the South Pacific, where they hung on grimly to the rich oil and mineral resources they had captured.

RISE OF ASIA

Japan promoted *itself as the liberator of Asia from the chains of European colonialism.*

Haile Selassie *(1892–1975), ruler of Ethiopia, the only independent empire in Africa.*

MIDDLE EAST

IN 1918, THE TURKISH EMPIRE disappeared after 400 years of Ottoman rule. The modern map of north Africa and the Middle East was carved out of its ruins by the victors of World War I. World War II accelerated the foundation of a new state of Israel following the genocide of Europe's Jews by Nazi Germany. This led to conflict between native Arabs and Jewish migrants.

The conquest *of the air was the most important technological achievement of the period. It added a devastating dimension to warfare, in the form of aerial bombing, while transforming civil transportation.*

A German Zeppelin *airship of the 1930s.*

The Modern Age: 1945–Present Day

The wartime alliance between the USA and the Soviet Union turned sour in efforts to reconstruct Europe and the Far East. The world became divided into two hostile camps: liberal capitalism was on one side, communism on the other. The two sides fought a "Cold War," each trying to contain and subvert the other. The main conflicts of the war occurred over small issues – Korea (1950–1953), Cuba (1962), Vietnam (1954–1975). Larger wars were avoided because of the nuclear deterrent. With the crumbling of communist power in Russia and Eastern Europe, the stalemate of the Cold War was replaced by a less stable international order, dominated by economic uncertainty and revived nationalism.

Global States and Territories

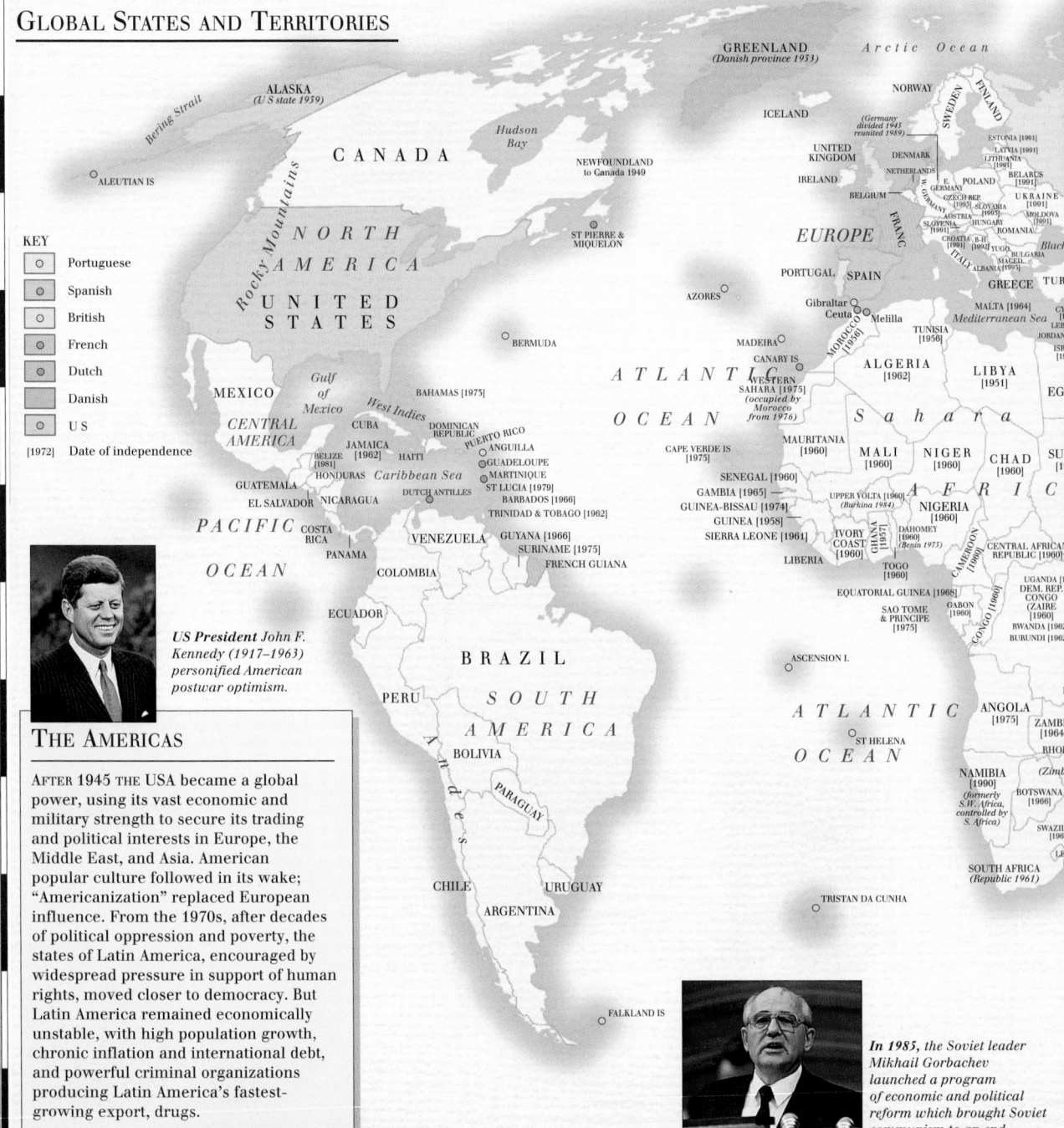

KEY
Portuguese
Spanish
British
French
Dutch
Danish
US
[1972] Date of independence
GREENLAND
(Danish province 1953)
Arctic Ocean
ALASKA
(US state 1959)
Bering Strait
ALEUTIAN IS
CANADA
Hudson Bay
Rocky Mountains
NORTH AMERICA
UNITED STATES
NEWFOUNDLAND to Canada 1949
ST PIERRE & MIQUELON
ICELAND
NORWAY
SWEDEN
FINLAND
(Germany divided 1945 reunited 1989)
UNITED KINGDOM
IRELAND
DENMARK
NETHERLANDS
BELGIUM
FRANCE
EUROPE
PORTUGAL
SPAIN
ITALY
GREECE
AZORES
BERMUDA
MEXICO
Gulf of Mexico
West Indies
CENTRAL AMERICA
CUBA
BAHAMAS [1975]
DOMINICAN REPUBLIC
PUERTO RICO
JAMAICA [1962]
HAITI
BELIZE [1981]
HONDURAS
Caribbean Sea
ANGUILLA
GUADELOUPE
MARTINIQUE
ST LUCIA [1979]
BARBADOS [1966]
TRINIDAD & TOBAGO [1962]
DUTCH ANTILLES
GUATEMALA
EL SALVADOR
NICARAGUA
COSTA RICA
PANAMA
PACIFIC OCEAN
VENEZUELA
GUYANA [1966]
SURINAME [1975]
FRENCH GUIANA
COLOMBIA
ECUADOR
PERU
BRAZIL
SOUTH AMERICA
BOLIVIA
PARAGUAY
Andes
CHILE
URUGUAY
ARGENTINA
FALKLAND IS
ATLANTIC OCEAN
MADEIRA
CANARY IS
WESTERN SAHARA [1975] (occupied by Morocco from 1976)
CAPE VERDE IS [1975]
Gibraltar
Ceuta
Melilla
MOROCCO [1956]
ALGERIA [1962]
TUNISIA [1956]
LIBYA [1951]
Sahara
MAURITANIA [1960]
MALI [1960]
NIGER [1960]
CHAD [1960]
SENEGAL [1960]
GAMBIA [1965]
GUINEA-BISSAU [1974]
GUINEA [1958]
SIERRA LEONE [1961]
LIBERIA
IVORY COAST [1960]
GHANA [1957]
UPPER VOLTA [1960] (Burkina 1984)
DAHOMEY [1960] (Benin 1975)
TOGO [1960]
NIGERIA [1960]
CAMEROON [1960]
CENTRAL AFRICAN REPUBLIC [1960]
AFRICA
EQUATORIAL GUINEA [1968]
SAO TOME & PRINCIPE [1975]
GABON [1960]
CONGO [1960]
DEM. REP. CONGO (ZAIRE [1960]
RWANDA [1962]
BURUNDI [1962]
ASCENSION I.
ST HELENA
ANGOLA [1975]
NAMIBIA [1990] (formerly S.W. Africa, controlled by S. Africa)
BOTSWANA [1966]
SOUTH AFRICA (Republic 1961)
TRISTAN DA CUNHA
ESTONIA [1991]
LATVIA [1991]
LITHUANIA [1991]
BELARUS [1991]
POLAND
E. GERMANY
W. GERMANY
CZECH REP. [1993]
SLOVAKIA [1993]
AUSTRIA
HUNGARY
UKRAINE [1991]
MOLDOVA [1991]
ROMANIA
SLOVENIA [1991]
CROATIA [1991]
B-H [1992]
YUGO.
BULGARIA
MACED. [1993]
ALBANIA
MALTA [1964]
Mediterranean Sea

US President John F. Kennedy (1917–1963) personified American postwar optimism.

The Americas

After 1945 the USA became a global power, using its vast economic and military strength to secure its trading and political interests in Europe, the Middle East, and Asia. American popular culture followed in its wake; "Americanization" replaced European influence. From the 1970s, after decades of political oppression and poverty, the states of Latin America, encouraged by widespread pressure in support of human rights, moved closer to democracy. But Latin America remained economically unstable, with high population growth, chronic inflation and international debt, and powerful criminal organizations producing Latin America's fastest-growing export, drugs.

In 1985, *the Soviet leader Mikhail Gorbachev launched a program of economic and political reform which brought Soviet communism to an end.*

The Berlin Wall, symbol of the Cold War division of Europe, was demolished in 1989.

EUROPE

IN 1945, EUROPE LAY IN RUINS, but during the next 30 years, Western Europe experienced a long economic boom, restoring widespread prosperity and political stability. It progressed towards economic and political unity under the EU. In Eastern Europe development was overshadowed by Soviet communism until its collapse. As democracies, many new countries now face an uncertain future.

ASIA

IN SOUTHERN ASIA, popular nationalist movements came to power in India, Burma, Malaya, and Indonesia; in China and Indo-China, power passed to native communist movements whose roots went back to the 1920s. After 1949, China under Mao Zedong became, with its vast population and large military forces, a second communist superpower. Japan, meanwhile, was Asia's capitalist "miracle." Its economy and cities laid waste by bombing in 1945, it rebuilt with US aid so successfully that by the 1980s, it was the world's second-largest economy. China's potential economic growth, however, could put Japan's past achievements in the shade.

兵民是胜利之本

Chinese communism, based on the mobilization of peasants and workers, has nevertheless recognized the need for economic reforms.

RUSSIAN FEDERATION
Bering Strait
KAZAKHSTAN [1991]
Aral Sea
ASIA
MONGOLIA
UZBEKISTAN [1991]
KYRGYZSTAN [1991]
TURKMENISTAN [1991]
TAJIKISTAN [1991]
Sea of Japan
JAPAN
CHINA
S. KOREA [1948]
IRAN
AFGHANISTAN
Himalayas
BHUTAN
NEPAL
The Gulf
QATAR [1971]
BANGLADESH [1971] (formerly E. Pakistan)
SAUDI ARABIA
OMAN
INDIA [1947]
Arabian Sea
Bay of Bengal
(Vietnam united 1976)
PACIFIC OCEAN
MARIANAS
THAILAND
South China Sea
GUAM
(Yemen united 1990)
DJIBOUTI [1977]
ETHIOPIA
MICRONESIA [1991]
BRUNEI [1984]
PALAU [1995]
INDONESIA [1949]
Melanesia
SEYCHELLES [1976]
CHAGOS IS
SOLOMON IS [1978]
E. TIMOR (under UN transitional authority from Feb 2000)
INDIAN OCEAN
MADAGASCAR [1960]
RÉUNION
NEW CALEDONIA
AUSTRALIA
NEW ZEALAND
AUCKLAND IS (to N Z)
MACQUARIE IS (to Australia)

A treaty banning the testing of nuclear bombs in the Pacific was signed in 1986.

OCEANIA

THE POSTWAR economies of Japan, the USA, and Australia had by the 1990s created a new industrial and trading network around the Pacific Rim. Cheap labor and low overheads drew younger states – South Korea, Taiwan, Singapore, Malaysia, Indonesia – into the system and much of the world's manufacturing is now concentrated there, creating a consequent shift in the balance of the global economy.

Gamal Abd al-Nasser (1918–1970) of Egypt, galvanized the Arab states to resist the West.

AFRICA AND THE MIDDLE EAST

THE COLONIAL POWERS, weakened by war, faced an irresistible wave of demands for self-determination. Between 1958 and 1975, 41 African countries gained independence. In north Africa and throughout the Middle East a new form of anti-imperialism emerged in the 1970s in the form of Islamic fundamentalism. In South Africa, white rule and the apartheid system ended in 1994.

From the 1950s to the 1970s, superpower rivalry focused on space exploration. The Soviets put the first man in space in 1961, and the Americans landed on the moon in 1969. Since then, both manned and unmanned missions have become almost everyday events.

Population

THE WORLD'S POPULATION – 6.2 billion in 2001 – is likely to reach nearly 10 billion by 2050. Better nutrition, health care, and sanitation mean fewer infant deaths and longer life expectancy, although around 800 million people in the developing world are malnourished and over one billion live in extreme poverty. In much of Africa in particular, the AIDS epidemic is so severe that the population is set to fall significantly. Elsewhere it is lower birth rates, already familiar in most industrialized countries, that have slowed the rate of growth. The result is a rapidly aging population: by 2050 it is thought that there will be around two billion people over the age of 60. The distribution of population is very uneven, dependent on climate, terrain, natural resources, and economic factors. The great majority of people live in coastal zones and along river valleys. Urbanization is on the increase, and by 2001 just under half of the world's population lived in cities – most of them in Asia. The mass migration of people from rural areas in search of work has resulted in the growth of huge sprawling squatter camps on the edge of many Third World cities.

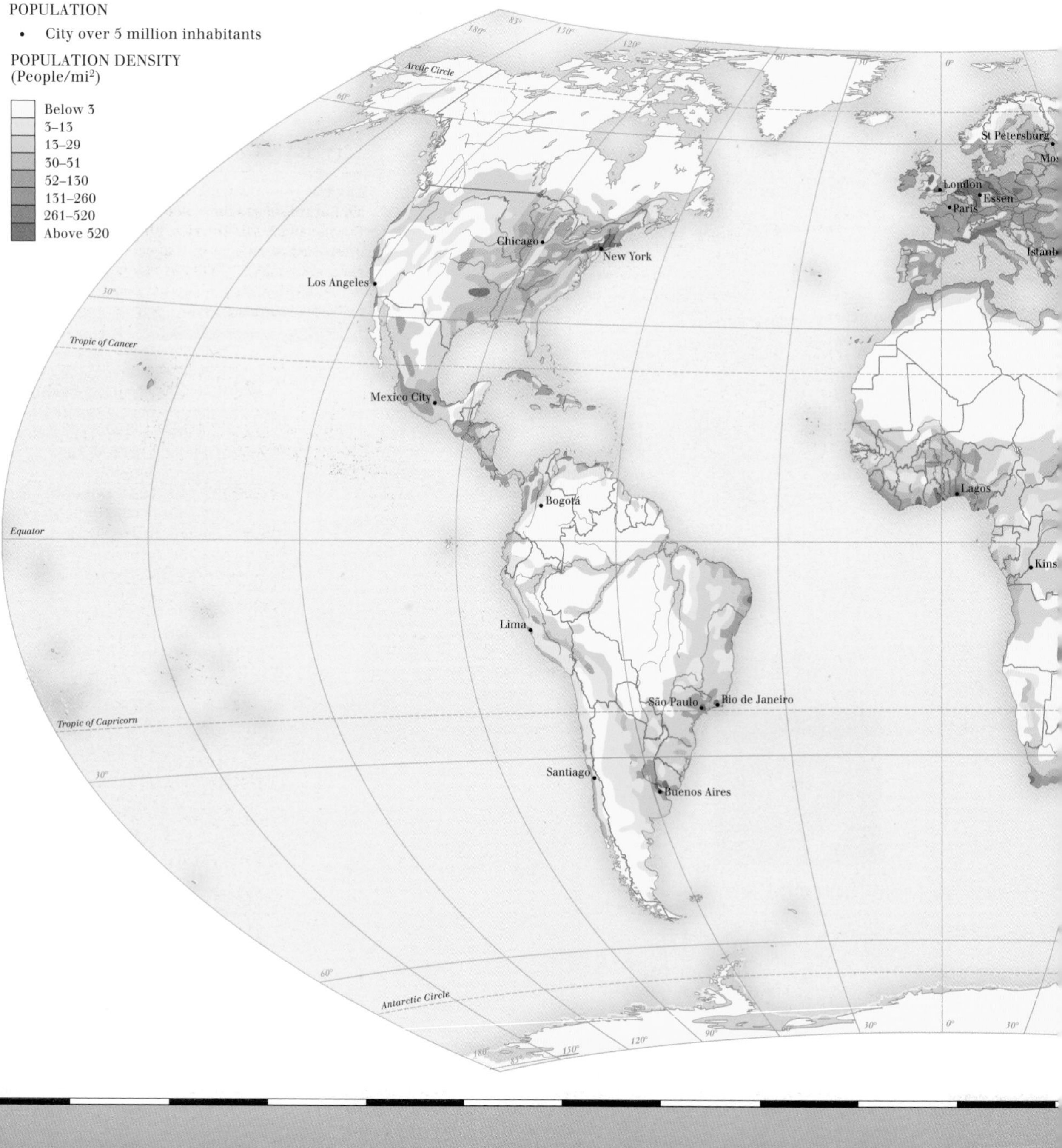
POPULATION
City over 5 million inhabitants
POPULATION DENSITY (People/mi²)
Below 3
3–13
13–29
30–51
52–130
131–260
261–520
Above 520
Arctic Circle
Tropic of Cancer
Equator
Tropic of Capricorn
Antarctic Circle
St Petersburg
London
Essen
Paris
Chicago
New York
Los Angeles
Mexico City
Bogotá
Lagos
Lima
São Paulo
Rio de Janeiro
Santiago
Buenos Aires

INFANT MORTALITY

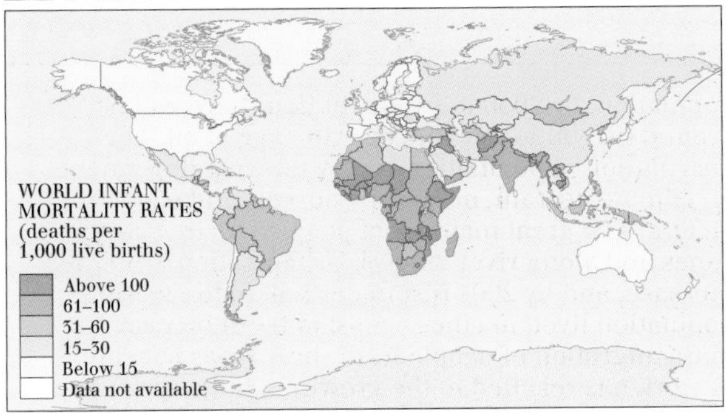
WORLD INFANT MORTALITY RATES (deaths per 1,000 live births)
Above 100
61–100
31–60
15–30
Below 15
Data not available

INFANT MORTALITY

INFANT MORTALITY RATES are highest in Africa, South America, and south Asia, where poverty and disease are rife, and where the standards of health care are not as high as in North America or Europe. The country with the highest infant mortality rate is Sierra Leone, where the recent civil war has devastated communities.

LIFE EXPECTANCY

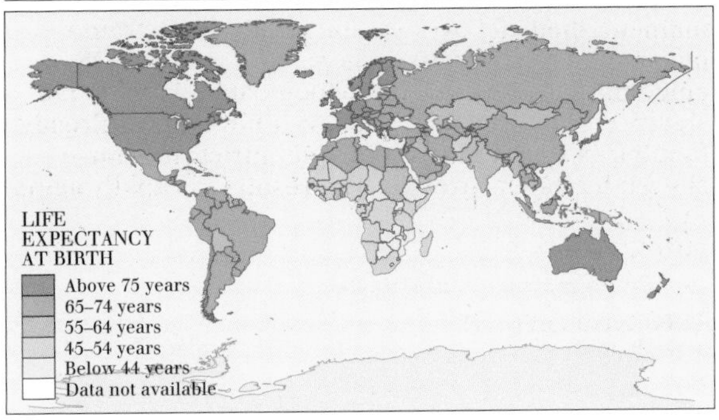
LIFE EXPECTANCY AT BIRTH
Above 75 years
65–74 years
55–64 years
45–54 years
Below 44 years
Data not available

Arctic Circle
Beijing
Tianjin
Seoul
Tokyo
Osaka
Tehran
Lahore
Wuhan
Shanghai
Chongqing
Delhi
Karachi
Dhaka
Calcutta (Kolkata)
Hong Kong
Mumbai (Bombay)
Hyderabad
Bangkok
Manilla
Bangalore
Chennai (Madras)
Tropic of Cancer
Equator
Jakarta
Tropic of Capricorn
Antarctic Circle

LIFE EXPECTANCY

LIFE EXPECTANCY IS also poorest in Africa, for similar reasons to those noted above. In western Europe and North America, life expectancy is increasing at such a rate that each successive generation may expect to live longer than the last. In the developed world, people can now expect to live twice as long as they did a century ago.

POPULATION FACTFILE

LARGEST POPULATIONS

1 **China**	1277 million people
2 **India**	1014 million people
3 **USA**	281 million people

LARGEST COUNTRIES BY AREA

1 **Russian Federation**	16,995,800 km^2 (6,562,100 mi^2)
2 **China**	9,326,410 km^2 (3,600,927 mi^2)
3 **Canada**	9,220,970 km^2 (3,560,217 mi^2)

MOST DENSELY POPULATED COUNTRIES

1 **Monaco**	16,253 people/km^2 (42,095 people/mi^2)
2 **Singapore**	5902 people/km^2 (15,285 people/mi^2)
3 **Vatican City**	2273 people/km^2 (5886 people/mi^2)

MOST SPARSELY POPULATED COUNTRIES

1 **Mongolia**	2 people/km^2 (5 people/mi^2)
2 **Namibia**	2 people/km^2 (5 people/mi^2)
3 **Australia**	2 people/km^2 (5 people/mi^2)

World Economy

THE WEALTHY COUNTRIES of the developed world, with their aggressive, market-led economies and their access to productive new technologies and international markets, dominate the world economic system. At the other extreme, many of the countries of the developing world are locked in a cycle of unpayable debt, rising populations, and unemployment. The state-managed economies of the former communist bloc began to be dismantled during the 1990s, and China is emerging as a major economic power following decades of isolation. Since the late 1980s, technological advances have enabled transactions between financial centers to occur at even greater speed, and new markets have sprung up throughout the world.

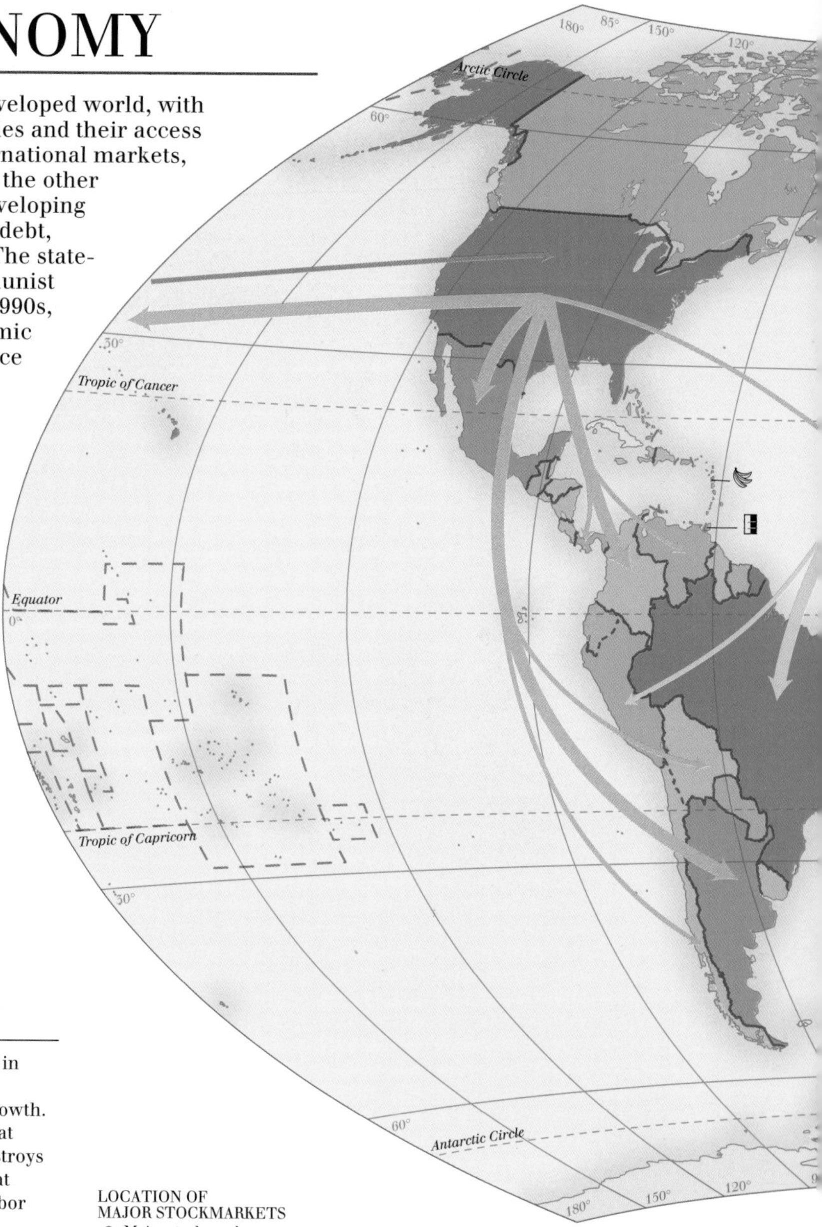
180°
85°
150°
120°
Arctic Circle
60°
30°
Tropic of Cancer
Equator
0°
Tropic of Capricorn
30°
60°
Antarctic Circle
180°
150°
120°

BALANCE OF TRADE
(MILLIONS US $)

Surplus:
- over 30,000
- 10,000–29,999
- 1000–9999
- 0-999

Deficit:
- 0–999
- 1000-9999
- 10,000–29,999
- below 30,000

data unavailable

DIRECT INVESTMENT
- from USA
- from Europe
- from Japan

COUNTRIES RELIANT ON A SINGLE EXPORT
- bananas
- coffee
- oil/petroleum
- copper

World Trade and Globalization

A basic tenet of liberal economics, now embodied in the World Trade Organization, is that free trade stimulates national economies and encourages growth. Its increasingly vocal critics contend, however, that "globalization" undermines local cultures and destroys local economies. It is multinational companies that benefit, they say, by producing goods wherever labor costs and environmental standards are lowest.

LOCATION OF MAJOR STOCKMARKETS
● Major stock markets

INTERNATIONAL TRADE

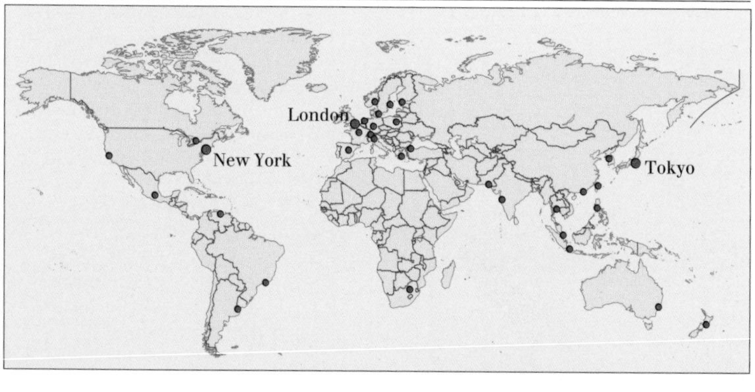
London
New York
Tokyo

World Economies

HIGHEST GNP PER CAPITA

1 Luxembourg	$42,930
2 Liechenstein	$40,000
3 Switzerland	$38,380
4 Norway	$33,470
5 Denmark	$32,050

LOWEST GNP PER CAPITA

1 Somalia and Ethiopia	$100
2 Congo (Zaire)	$110
3 Burundi	$120
4 Sierra Leone	$130
5 Guinea-Bissau	$160

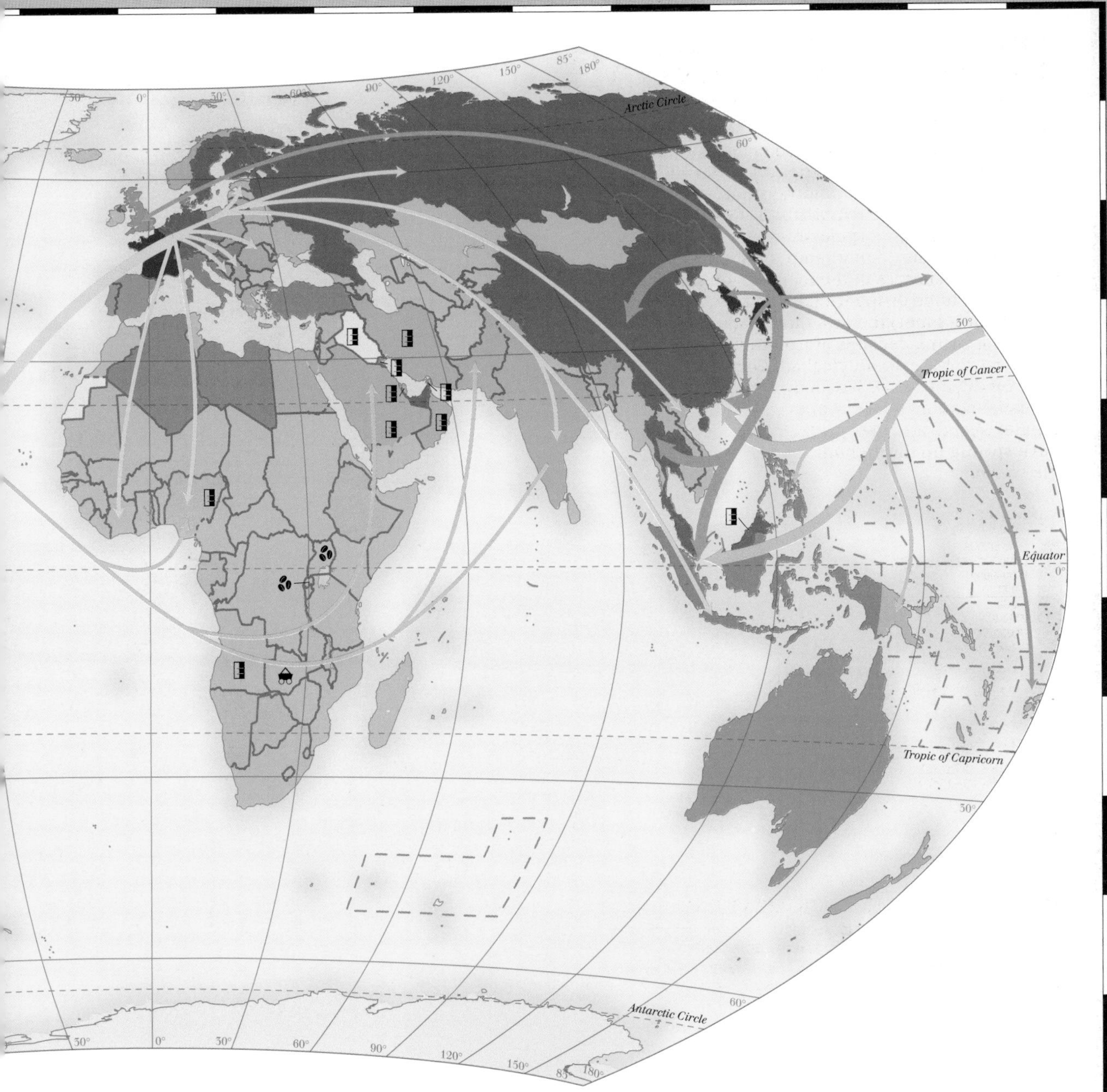
Arctic Circle
Tropic of Cancer
Equator
Tropic of Capricorn
Antarctic Circle
0°
30°
60°
90°
120°
150°
180°

Trade Blocs

INTERNATIONAL TRADE BLOCS are formed when groups of countries, often already enjoying close military and political ties, join together to offer mutually preferential terms of trade for both imports and exports. Increasingly, global trade is dominated by three main blocs: the EU, NAFTA, and ASEAN. They are supplanting older trade blocs such as the Commonwealth, a legacy of colonialism.

TRADE BLOCS

- EU
- ASEAN
- NAFTA
- SADC
- MERCOSUR
- ECOWAS

TRADE BLOCS

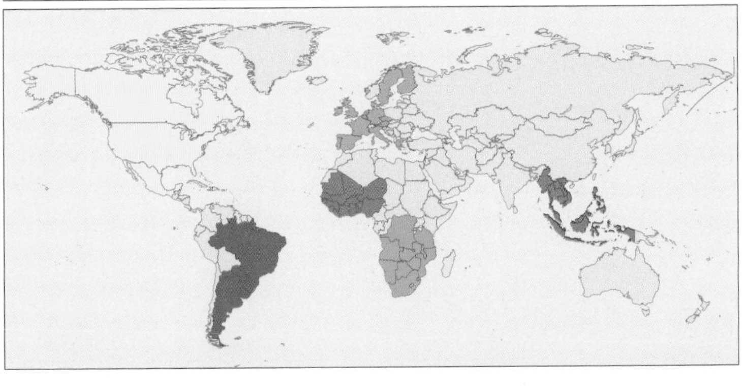

World Economy

THE SIZE OF A COUNTRY'S economy does not relate directly to its population or even its resources. Japan, for example, has a much "bigger" economy than China, India, Russia, or Latin America as a whole. Such imbalances usually occur because countries differ enormously in their living standards, the education and skills of their workforces, the productivity of their agriculture, and the value of their markets. A country's economic performance can be evaluated by calculating its gross national product (GNP). This is the total value of both the goods and the services (including so-called "invisible exports" – financial services, tourism, and so on) that it produces. Most trade (62% of the global total by value) is in manufactured goods, but during the last three decades the most rapidly growing sector has been services – banking, insurance, tourism, consultancy, accountancy, films, music and other cultural services, airlines, and shipping. Accounting for 20% of the total, services now exceed the value of trade in food and raw materials.

Comparative World Wealth

A global assessment of gross domestic product (GDP) by country reveals great disparities. The developed world, with only a quarter of the world's population, has 80% of the world's manufacturing income. This imbalance is maintained as war and political instability undermine poor countries' prospects.

***Mass-market tourism** is now an all-important source of revenue in many countries.*

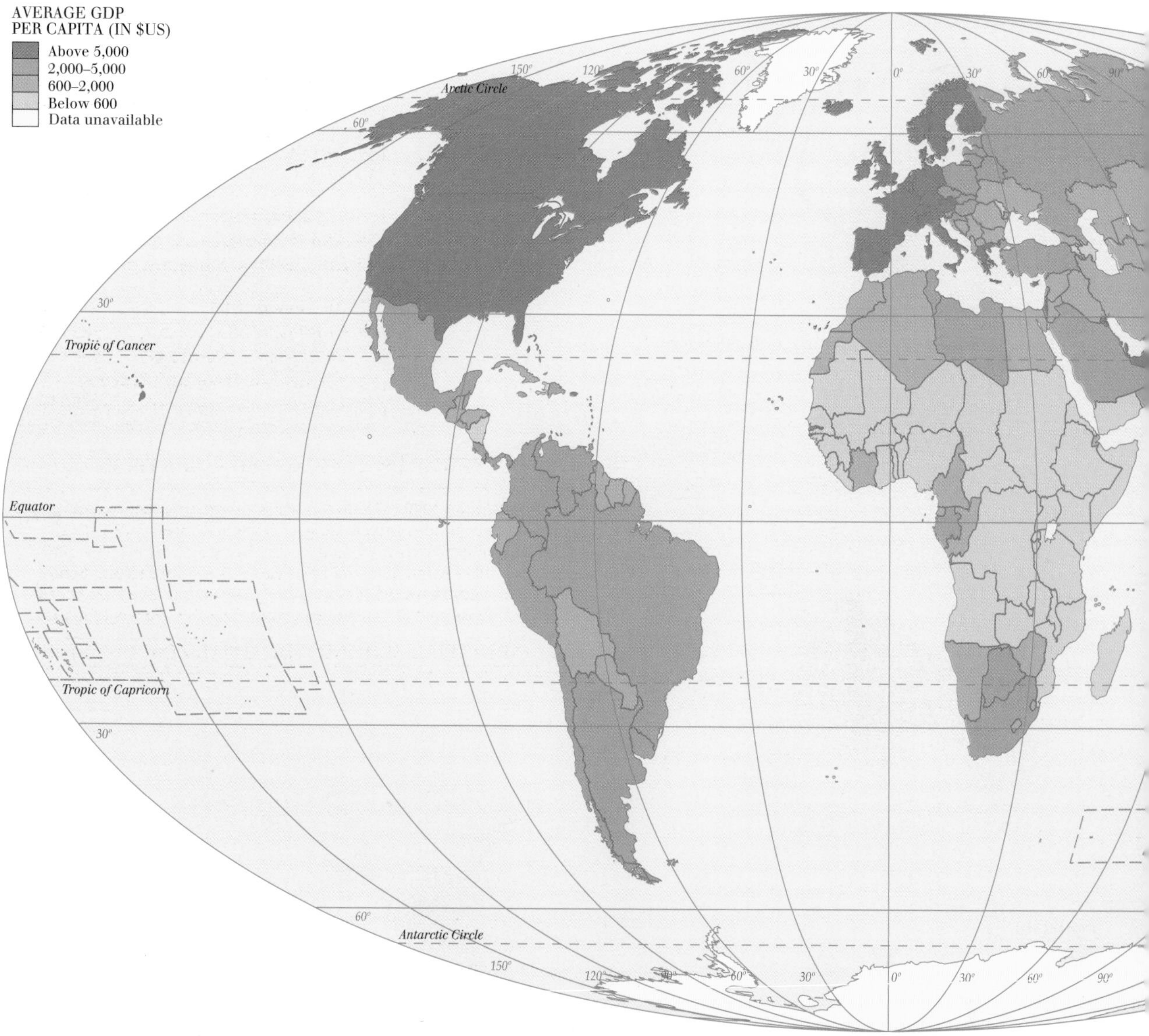
AVERAGE GDP
PER CAPITA (IN $US)
Above 5,000
2,000–5,000
600–2,000
Below 600
Data unavailable
Arctic Circle
Tropic of Cancer
Equator
Tropic of Capricorn
Antarctic Circle
150°
120°
60°
30°
0°
90°

INTERNATIONAL DEBT

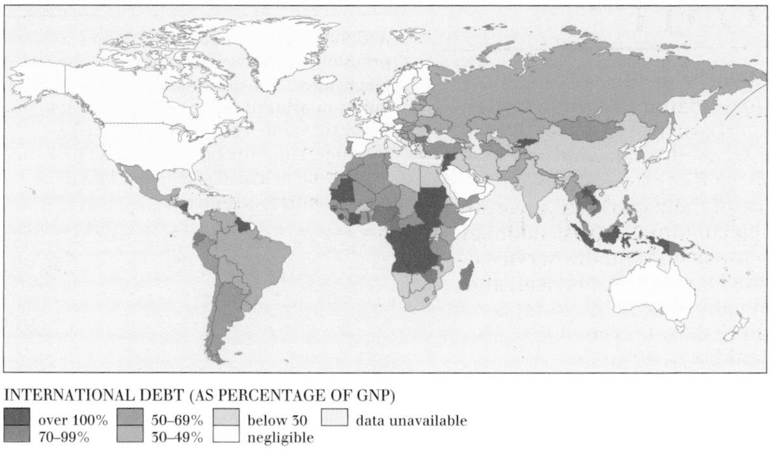
INTERNATIONAL DEBT (AS PERCENTAGE OF GNP)
over 100%
70–99%
50–69%
30–49%
below 30
negligible
data unavailable

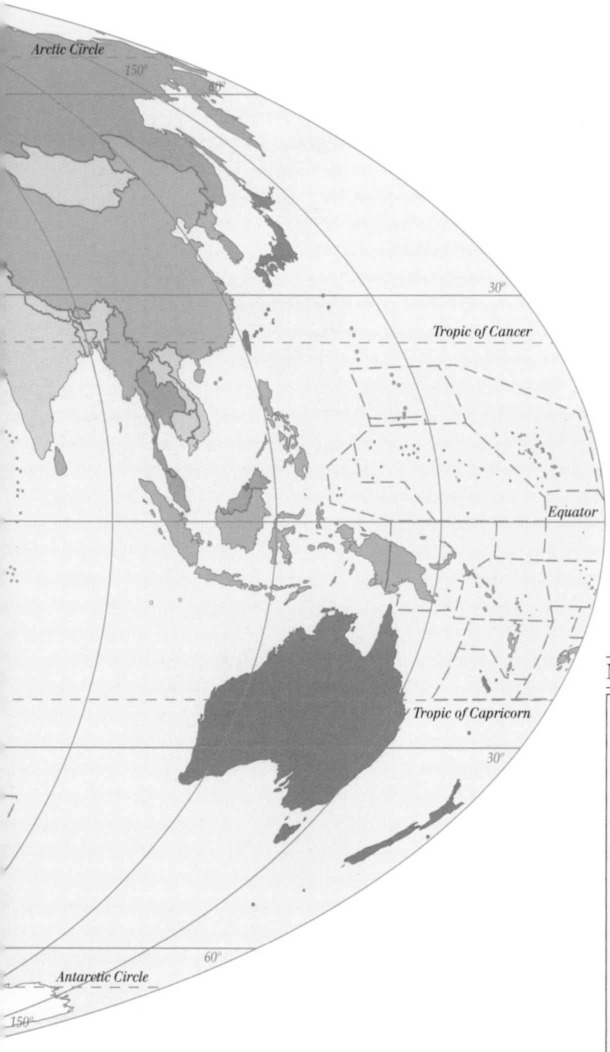
Arctic Circle
150°
60°
30°
Tropic of Cancer
Equator
Tropic of Capricorn
30°
60°
Antarctic Circle
150°

International Debt

In response to unsustainable levels of debt in the developing world, the IMF and World Bank have introduced a program to help heavily indebted poor countries (HIPCs) manage their repayments. The Jubilee 2000 campaign, advocating debt cancellation, has won some qualified support among creditor countries.

World's 20 Largest Corporations

		$ millions
1	**General Motors (USA)**	$176,558
2	**Wal-Mart Stores (USA)**	$166,809
3	**Exxon Mobil (USA)**	$163,881
4	**Ford Motor Company (USA)**	$162,558
5	**DaimlerChrysler (USA/Germany)**	$159,986
6	**Mitsui (Japan)**	$118,555
7	**Mitsubishi (Japan)**	$117,766
8	**Toyota Motor Company (Japan)**	$115,671
9	**General Electric (USA)**	$111,630
10	**Itochu (Japan)**	$109,069
11	**Royal Dutch/Shell Group (UK/Neth.)**	$105,366
12	**Sumitomo (Japan)**	$95,702
13	**Nippon Telegraph and Telephone (Japan)**	$93,592
14	**Marubeni (Japan)**	$91,807
15	**AXA (France)**	$87,646
16	**Intl. Business Machines (USA)**	$87,548
17	**BP Amoco (UK)**	$83,566
18	**Citigroup (USA)**	$82,005
19	**Volkswagen (Germany)**	$80,073
20	**Nippon Life Insurance (Japan)**	$78,515

Newly Industrialized Countries

In the 1990s, the fast-growing export-oriented "Asian tiger" economies such as Singapore, South Korea, and Taiwan offered exciting prospects for foreign investors. The 1997–1998 Asian financial crisis came as a severe shock. Some countries quickly returned to growth, but investors became more cautious about their exposure in NICs around the world.

NEWLY INDUSTRIALIZED AND INDUSTRIALIZING COUNTRIES

MEXICO
VENEZUELA
COLUMBIA
BRAZIL
CHILE
ARGENTINA
SOUTH AFRICA
THAILAND
MALAYSIA
SINGAPORE
INDONESIA
SOUTH KOREA
TAIWAN
PHILIPPINES

Global Tourism

Tourism is the world's biggest industry. In 2000 there were a record 698 million tourists worldwide, a number expected to rise to over one billion by 2010. France is the world's most popular destination country, with 75 million visitors annually, but with improved transportation, cheaper flights, and increased leisure time, many of the countries of the developing world are rapidly becoming tourist meccas. Since the 1960s, mass tourism has become increasingly specialized, encompassing sporting and adventure holidays as well as ecological tours. Tourism employs 200 million people worldwide – 8% of the working population. However, the benefits of tourism are not always felt at a local level, where jobs are often low-paid and menial.

TOURIST ARRIVALS
Data not available
Less than 50,000
50,000 - 99,999
100,000 - 399,999
400,000 - 1 million
1 million - 2.5 million
2.5 million - 10 million
More than 10 million
CARIBBEAN
BARBADOS
GRENADA
ST LUCIA
TRINIDAD & TOBAGO
DOMINICA
ANTIGUA & BARBUDA
GUADELOUPE (Fr.)
ST KITTS & NEVIS
BERMUDA (U K)
MARTINIQUE (Fr.)
ST VINCENT & THE GRENADINES
BAHAMAS
EUROPE
MONACO
SAN MARINO
LIECHTENSTEIN
GIBRALTAR (to UK)
LUXEMBOURG
MALTA
ANDORRA
AFRICA
CAPE VERDE
SAO TOME & PRINCIPE
GREENLAND (to Denmark)
Faeroe Islands (to Denmark)
ICELAND
United States of America
CANADA
UNITED STATES OF AMERICA
MEXICO
Bermuda (to UK)
BAHAMAS
CUBA
DOMINICAN REPUBLIC
Puerto Rico (to USA)
JAMAICA
HAITI
BELIZE
HONDURAS
GUATEMALA
EL SALVADOR
NICARAGUA
COSTA RICA
PANAMA
ST KITTS & NEVIS
ANTIGUA & BARBUDA
Guadeloupe (to Fr.)
DOMINICA
Martinique (to Fr.)
ST LUCIA
BARBADOS
GRENADA
ST VINCENT & THE GRENADINES
TRINIDAD & TOBAGO
VENEZUELA
GUYANA
SURINAME
French Guiana (to France)
COLOMBIA
ECUADOR
PERU
BRAZIL
BOLIVIA
PARAGUAY
CHILE
ARGENTINA
URUGUAY
PACIFIC OCEAN
ATLANTIC OCEAN
NORWAY
SWEDEN
UNITED KINGDOM
REP. OF IRELAND
DENMARK
NETH.
BELG.
GERMANY
LUX.
POL.
CZECH REP.
FRANCE
SWITZ.
AUSTRIA
SLOVENIA
CRO.
SAN MARINO
PORTUGAL
SPAIN
Gibraltar (to UK)
MOROCCO
ALGERIA
TUNISIA
WESTERN SAHARA
MAURITANIA
MALI
NIGER
CAPE VERDE
SENEGAL
GAMBIA
GUINEA-BISSAU
GUINEA
BURKINA
SIERRA LEONE
LIBERIA
IVORY COAST (CÔTE D'IVOIRE)
GHANA
TOGO
BENIN
NIGERIA
CAMEROON
EQUATORIAL GUINEA
SAO TOME & PRINCIPE
GABON

Even in the remote Himalayas, rubbish discarded by trekkers and mountaineers pollutes the landscape.

"Eco-tourism"

Spectacular and ecologically fascinating natural features such as tropical rainforests and coral reefs are becoming increasingly popular as tourist attractions. Holidays in such destinations can put serious pressure on the very ecological systems that bring in the visitors in the first place. Strenuous efforts are being made to limit the environmental impact of this so-called "eco-tourism."

The beautiful island of Phuket, Thailand, has been taken over by tourist developments.

A TOURIST PARADISE?

THE MOST REMOTE CORNERS of the world are now being penetrated by tourists in their quest for the exotic. In many parts of the developing world, tourism can be described as a form of "neo-colonialism;" hotels and beaches are owned by multinational companies, and most of the profits are taken outside the country. Tourism frequently alienates local people from their own land, and has a negative impact on the local culture and environment.

RUSSIAN FEDERATION
KAZAKHSTAN
MONGOLIA
GEORGIA
ARM.
AZERB.
UZBEKISTAN
TURKMENISTAN
KYRGYZSTAN
TAJIKISTAN
URKEY
SYRIA
IRAQ
IRAN
ISRAEL
JORDAN
KUWAIT
AFGHANISTAN
PAKISTAN
CHINA
NORTH KOREA
SOUTH KOREA
JAPAN
NEPAL
BHUTAN
BAHRAIN
QATAR
UAE
GYPT
SAUDI ARABIA
OMAN
BANGLADESH
INDIA
BURMA (MYANMAR)
LAOS
TAIWAN
PACIFIC OCEAN
ERITREA
YEMEN
UDAN
DJIBOUTI
ETHIOPIA
SOMALIA
THAILAND
VIETNAM
CAMBODIA
PHILIPPINES
Guam (to USA)
MALDIVES
SRI LANKA
UGANDA
KENYA
MALAYSIA
SINGAPORE
TANZANIA
SEYCHELLES
INDONESIA
PAPUA NEW GUINEA
EAST TIMOR (under UN transitional authority from Feb 2000)
COMOROS
MALAWI
MOZAMBIQUE
MADAGASCAR
INDIAN OCEAN
MAURITIUS
SWAZILAND
LESOTHO
AUSTRALIA
NEW ZEALAND
PACIFIC OCEAN
FIJI
MICRONESIA
NAURU
SOLOMON ISLANDS
VANUATU
SAMOA
TONGA
KIRIBATI
MIDDLE EAST
BAHRAIN
INDIAN OCEAN
COMOROS
MALDIVES
MAURITIUS
SEYCHELLES
ASIA
SINGAPORE

Eco-tourists *travel to the distant Antarctic, where they observe its rich wildlife.*

Global Security

THE ENDING OF THE COLD WAR in 1989 greatly reduced the risk of another global (and possibly nuclear) war, but did little to end localized tensions and conflicts. Since then territorial disputes, and particularly ethnic tensions, have undermined peace and security around the world. Conflict is now more frequent within states than between them. The first post-Cold War international war, following the invasion of Kuwait by Iraq in 1990, set the tone for joint action by more powerful states to punish apparent injustices elsewhere. Economic sanctions are usually employed as the first stage of punitive measures. The UN, with its laborious decision-making process, has tried to fill the role of global peacemaker wherever possible, without becoming involved in military action. On the other hand, regional organizations such as NATO (with the USA and the UK to the fore), the Russian-dominated Commonwealth of Independent States, or ECOWAS in west Africa, have taken direct action against the forces of the supposed aggressor. Attacks on the USA in 2001 underlined that ideological fanaticism is the greatest threat to global security.

ICELAN
Rockall
UNITE
KINGD
Northern Ireland
REP. OF IRELAND
UNITED STATES OF AMERICA
Gibraltar
SPA
Ceuta
MOROCCO
WESTERN SAHARA
CUBA
Guantanamo Bay
HAITI
BELIZE
GUATEMALA
EL SALVADOR
NICARAGUA
VENEZUELA
GUYANA
SURINAME
French Guiana
COLOMBIA
GHANA
TC
BOLIVIA
CHILE
ARGENTINA
Falkland Islands
DISPUTED TERRITORIES AND BORDERS
Countries involved in active territorial or border disputes
Disputed borders
Undefined borders
Disputed territories

USA

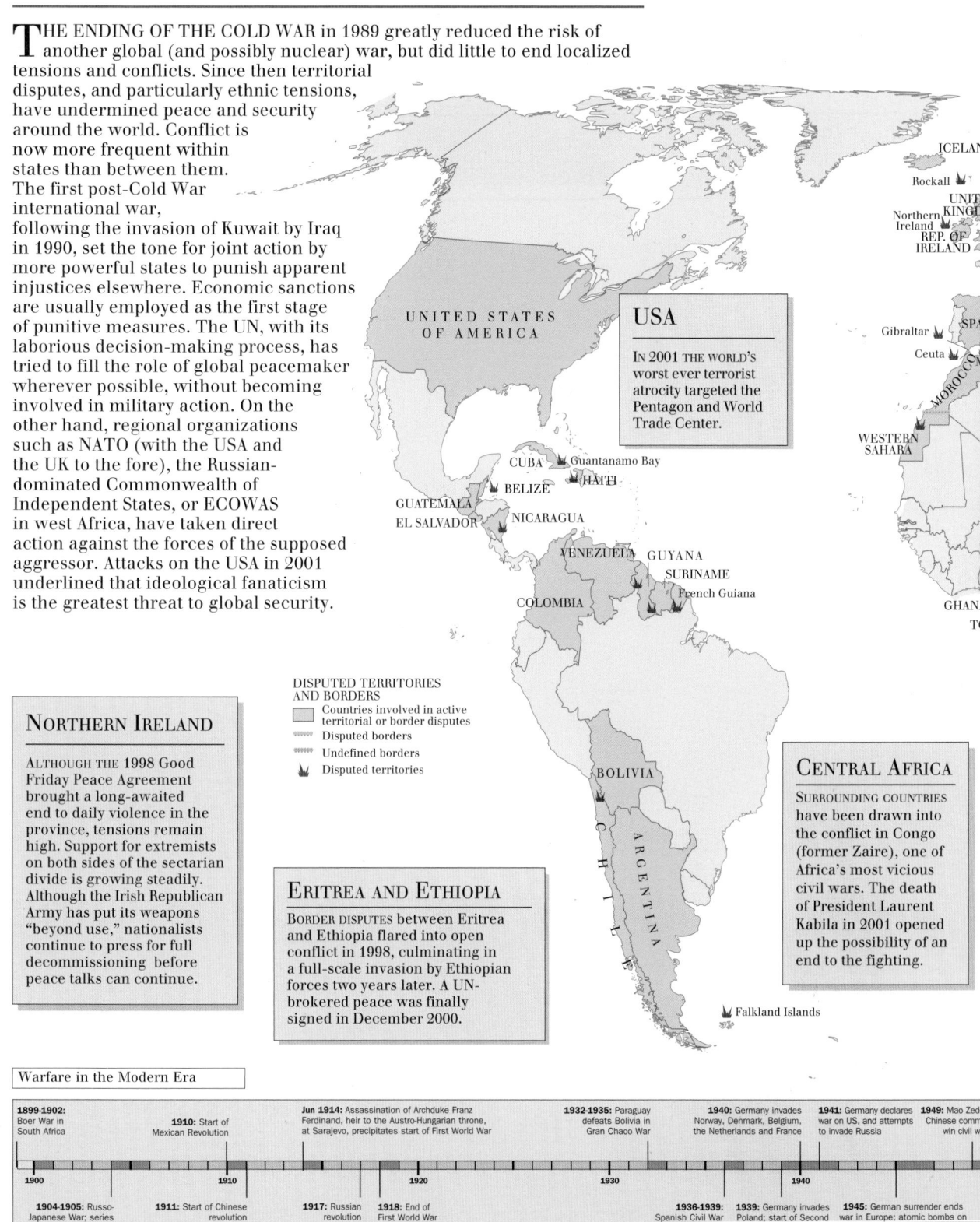

IN 2001 THE WORLD'S worst ever terrorist atrocity targeted the Pentagon and World Trade Center.

Northern Ireland

ALTHOUGH THE 1998 Good Friday Peace Agreement brought a long-awaited end to daily violence in the province, tensions remain high. Support for extremists on both sides of the sectarian divide is growing steadily. Although the Irish Republican Army has put its weapons "beyond use," nationalists continue to press for full decommissioning before peace talks can continue.

Eritrea and Ethiopia

BORDER DISPUTES between Eritrea and Ethiopia flared into open conflict in 1998, culminating in a full-scale invasion by Ethiopian forces two years later. A UN-brokered peace was finally signed in December 2000.

Central Africa

SURROUNDING COUNTRIES have been drawn into the conflict in Congo (former Zaire), one of Africa's most vicious civil wars. The death of President Laurent Kabila in 2001 opened up the possibility of an end to the fighting.

Warfare in the Modern Era

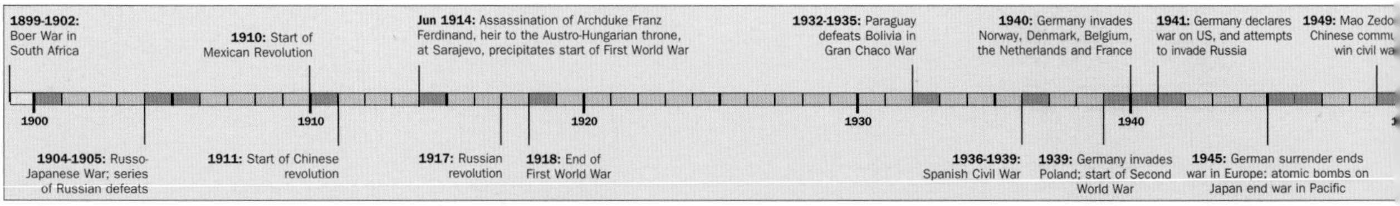
1899-1902: Boer War in South Africa
1910: Start of Mexican Revolution
Jun 1914: Assassination of Archduke Franz Ferdinand, heir to the Austro-Hungarian throne, at Sarajevo, precipitates start of First World War
1932-1935: Paraguay defeats Bolivia in Gran Chaco War
1940: Germany invades Norway, Denmark, Belgium, the Netherlands and France
1941: Germany declares war on US, and attempts to invade Russia
1949: Mao Zedo Chinese commu win civil wa
1900
1910
1920
1930
1940
1904-1905: Russo-Japanese War; series of Russian defeats
1911: Start of Chinese revolution
1917: Russian revolution
1918: End of First World War
1936-1939: Spanish Civil War
1939: Germany invades Poland; start of Second World War
1945: German surrender ends war in Europe; atomic bombs on Japan end war in Pacific

FORMER YUGOSLAVIA

THE COLLAPSE OF THE SOCIALIST YUGOSLAV STATE in 1991 led to fierce fighting across the successor states. Bosnia was plunged into a civil war which lasted until 1995. Four years later, Kosovo's Albanians were targeted by Serb "ethnic cleansing" until NATO intervened.

CHECHNYA

ATTEMPTS TO CRUSH ISLAMIC separatists in Chechnya since 1994 have drawn Russia into a protracted and extremely bloody guerrilla war. Although Russian forces are deployed throughout the republic, Muslim separatists continue their struggle with attacks across the region.

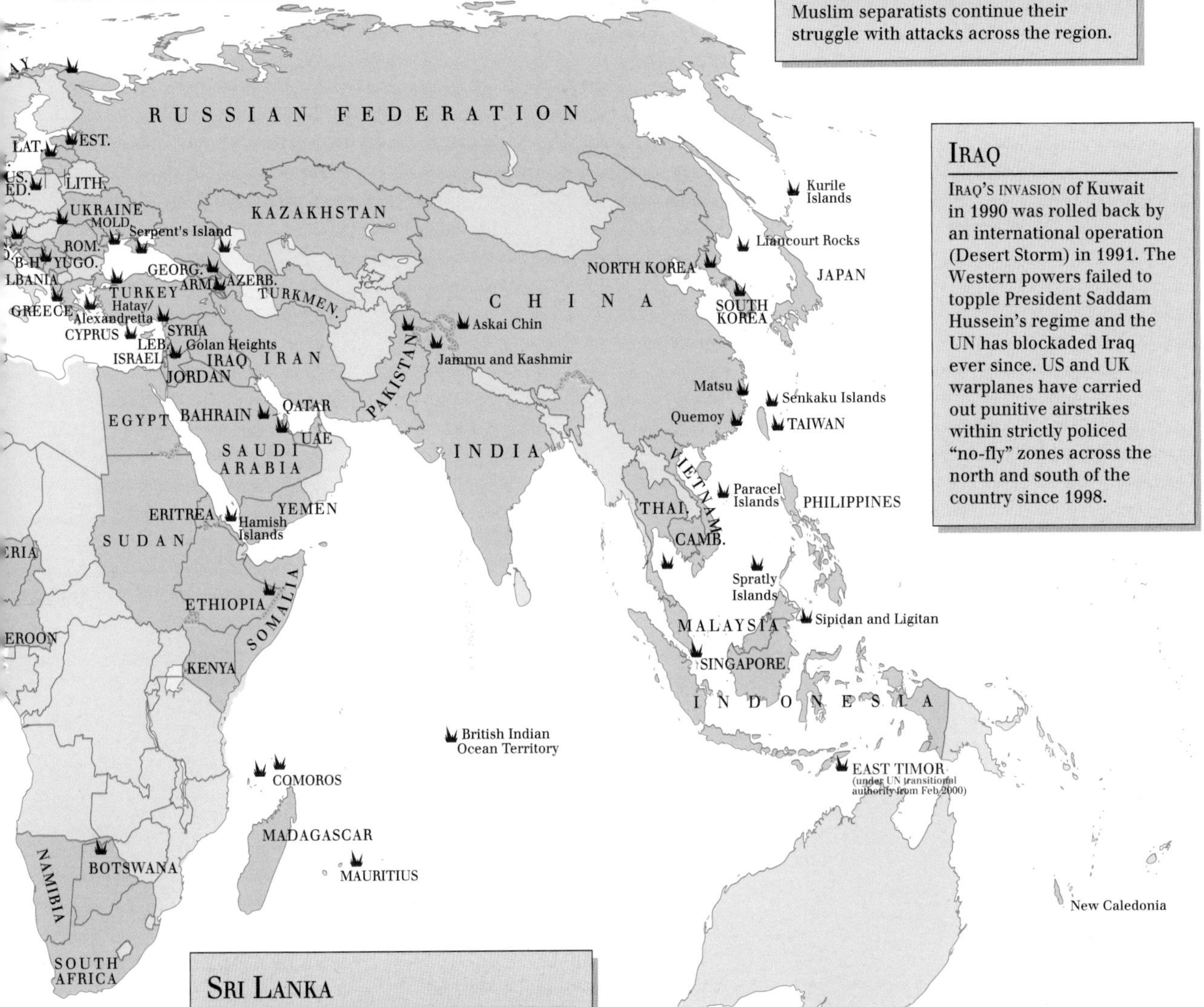
RUSSIAN FEDERATION
LAT.
EST.
LITH.
UKRAINE
MOLD.
Serpent's Island
ROM.
B-H
YUGO.
LBANIA
GREECE
TURKEY
Hatay/
Alexandretta
CYPRUS
GEORG.
ARM.
AZERB.
TURKMEN.
KAZAKHSTAN
SYRIA
LEB.
Golan Heights
ISRAEL
JORDAN
IRAQ
IRAN
EGYPT
BAHRAIN
QATAR
UAE
SAUDI ARABIA
YEMEN
ERITREA
Hamish Islands
SUDAN
ETHIOPIA
SOMALIA
KENYA
EROON
RIA
PAKISTAN
Askai Chin
Jammu and Kashmir
CHINA
INDIA
NORTH KOREA
SOUTH KOREA
JAPAN
Kurile Islands
Liancourt Rocks
Matsu
Quemoy
Senkaku Islands
TAIWAN
VIETNAM
THAI.
CAMB.
Paracel Islands
PHILIPPINES
Spratly Islands
MALAYSIA
Sipidan and Ligitan
SINGAPORE
INDONESIA
EAST TIMOR
(under UN transitional authority from Feb 2000)
British Indian Ocean Territory
COMOROS
MADAGASCAR
MAURITIUS
NAMIBIA
BOTSWANA
SOUTH AFRICA
New Caledonia

IRAQ

IRAQ'S INVASION of Kuwait in 1990 was rolled back by an international operation (Desert Storm) in 1991. The Western powers failed to topple President Saddam Hussein's regime and the UN has blockaded Iraq ever since. US and UK warplanes have carried out punitive airstrikes within strictly policed "no-fly" zones across the north and south of the country since 1998.

SRI LANKA

SINCE 1983 ETHNIC TAMIL militants, known as the Tamil Tiger rebels (LTTE), have been pursuing armed conflict in the north and east of the island, seeking their own state. Their war with government forces has cost more than 60,000 lives. After years of relative calm fighting intensified in 2000.

950-1953: Korean War
1954: Algerian war of independence begins
1960: Outbreak of civil war in Belgian Congo
1964: US Congress approves war with Vietnam
1965: India-Pakistan War over sovereignty of Kashmir
1968: Troubles begin in Northern Ireland
1975: USA withdraws from Vietnam
1975: Angola and Mozambique gain independence; civil wars ensue
1979-1992: Civil war in El Salvador
1979-1990: Civil war in Nicaragua
1980-1988: Iran-Iraq War
1982: Falklands War between UK and Argentina
1990-1991: Iraqi invasion of Kuwait and Gulf War
1992: Civil war in Bosnia-Herzegovina
1994: Massacre of Tutsis in Rwanda
1996: Start of conflict in Congo (former Zaire)
1999: 'Ethnic cleansing' of Albanians in Kosovo by Serbs. Russian offensive in Chechnya
2001: Terror attacks on USA

0 1960 1970 1980 1990 2000

TIME ZONES

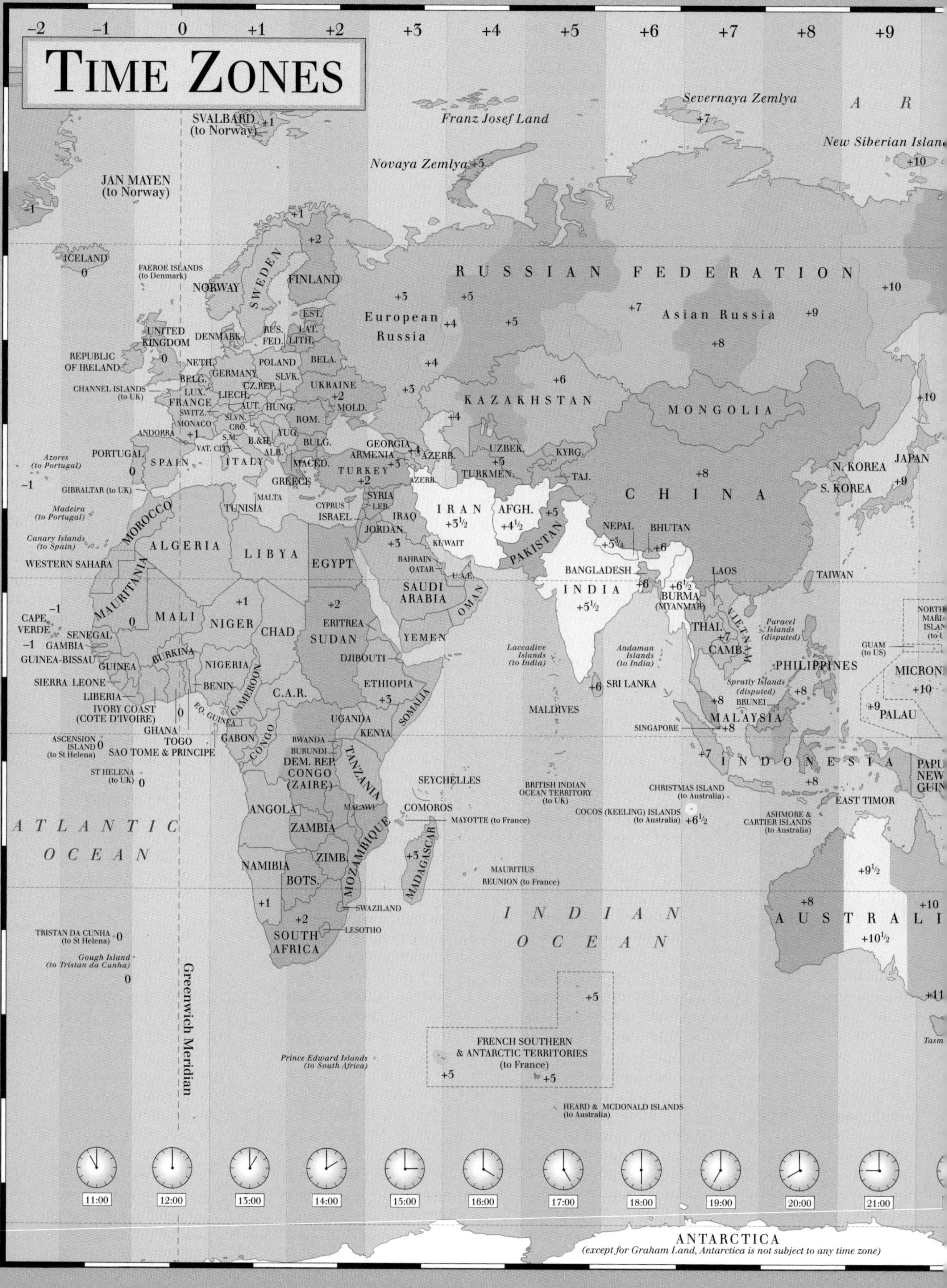

–2
–1
0
+1
+2
+3
+4
+5
+6
+7
+8
+9
SVALBARD (to Norway) +1
Franz Josef Land
Severnaya Zemlya +7
New Siberian Islands +10
Novaya Zemlya +5
JAN MAYEN (to Norway)
–1
ICELAND 0
FAEROE ISLANDS (to Denmark)
NORWAY
SWEDEN
FINLAND
+2
RUSSIAN FEDERATION
European Russia
Asian Russia
+3
+4
+5
+6
+7
+8
+9
+10
EST.
LAT.
LITH.
RUS. FED.
UNITED KINGDOM
DENMARK
REPUBLIC OF IRELAND
NETH.
BELG.
LUX.
GERMANY
POLAND
BELA.
CZ.REP.
SLVK.
UKRAINE
MOLD.
CHANNEL ISLANDS (to UK)
FRANCE
LIECH.
SWITZ.
AUT.
HUNG.
ROM.
MONACO
SLVN.
CRO.
ANDORRA
S.M.
B.&H.
YUG.
BULG.
VAT. CITY
ALB.
MACED.
ITALY
GREECE
PORTUGAL
SPAIN
Azores (to Portugal)
GIBRALTAR (to UK)
MALTA
TUNISIA
GEORGIA
ARMENIA
AZERB.
TURKEY
CYPRUS
SYRIA
LEB.
ISRAEL
IRAQ
JORDAN
KUWAIT
BAHRAIN
QATAR
U.A.E.
SAUDI ARABIA
OMAN
YEMEN
IRAN +3½
AFGH. +4½
PAKISTAN
TURKMEN.
UZBEK.
KYRG.
TAJ.
KAZAKHSTAN
MONGOLIA
CHINA
N. KOREA
S. KOREA
JAPAN
NEPAL +5¾
BHUTAN
BANGLADESH
INDIA +5½
BURMA (MYANMAR) +6½
LAOS
THAI.
VIETNAM
CAMB.
TAIWAN
Paracel Islands (disputed)
PHILIPPINES
GUAM (to US)
Spratly Islands (disputed)
BRUNEI
MALAYSIA
SINGAPORE
PALAU
INDONESIA
EAST TIMOR
PAPUA NEW GUINEA
Laccadive Islands (to India)
Andaman Islands (to India)
SRI LANKA
MALDIVES
BRITISH INDIAN OCEAN TERRITORY (to UK)
CHRISTMAS ISLAND (to Australia)
COCOS (KEELING) ISLANDS (to Australia) +6½
ASHMORE & CARTIER ISLANDS (to Australia)
AUSTRALIA
+9½
+10½
+11
Madeira (to Portugal)
Canary Islands (to Spain)
MOROCCO
WESTERN SAHARA
ALGERIA
LIBYA
EGYPT
MAURITANIA
MALI
NIGER
CHAD
SUDAN
ERITREA
DJIBOUTI
ETHIOPIA
SOMALIA
CAPE VERDE
SENEGAL
GAMBIA
GUINEA-BISSAU
GUINEA
BURKINA
NIGERIA
BENIN
SIERRA LEONE
LIBERIA
IVORY COAST (COTE D'IVOIRE)
GHANA
TOGO
EQ. GUINEA
CAMEROON
C.A.R.
UGANDA
KENYA
ASCENSION ISLAND (to St Helena)
SAO TOME & PRINCIPE
GABON
CONGO
RWANDA
BURUNDI
DEM. REP. CONGO (ZAIRE)
TANZANIA
ST HELENA (to UK)
SEYCHELLES
ANGOLA
MALAWI
COMOROS
MAYOTTE (to France)
ZAMBIA
ZIMB.
MOZAMBIQUE
MADAGASCAR
NAMIBIA
BOTS.
MAURITIUS
REUNION (to France)
SWAZILAND
LESOTHO
SOUTH AFRICA
TRISTAN DA CUNHA (to St Helena)
Gough Island (to Tristan da Cunha)
ATLANTIC OCEAN
INDIAN OCEAN
Greenwich Meridian
Prince Edward Islands (to South Africa)
FRENCH SOUTHERN & ANTARCTIC TERRITORIES (to France)
HEARD & MCDONALD ISLANDS (to Australia)
11:00
12:00
13:00
14:00
15:00
16:00
17:00
18:00
19:00
20:00
21:00
ANTARCTICA
(except for Graham Land, Antarctica is not subject to any time zone)

+11
+12
–12
–11
–10
–9
–8
–7
–6
–5
–4
–3
–2
International Dateline
I C O C E A N
Queen Elizabeth Islands
GREENLAND
(to Denmark)
Baffin Island
Arctic Circle
Alaska
(to US)
CANADA
Newfoundland
–3½
ST PIERRE & MIQUELON
(to France)
Kurile Islands
(to Rus. Fed.)
PACIFIC OCEAN
UNITED STATES OF AMERICA
ATLANTIC OCEAN
BERMUDA
(to UK)
PUERTO RICO (to US)
BRITISH VIRGIN ISLANDS (to UK)
VIRGIN ISLANDS (to US)
ANGUILLA (to UK)
ST KITTS & NEVIS
ANTIGUA & BARBUDA
MONTSERRAT (to UK)
GUADELOUPE (to France)
DOMINICA
MARTINIQUE (to France)
ST LUCIA
BARBADOS
ST VINCENT & THE GRENADINES
GRENADA
TRINIDAD & TOBAGO
DOM. REP.
TURKS & CAICOS ISLANDS
(to UK)
CAYMAN ISLANDS
(to UK)
BAHAMAS
HONDURAS
BELIZE
CUBA
JAMAICA
NAVASSA I.
(to US)
HAITI
NETH. ANT.
(to Neth.)
ARUBA
(to Neth.)
MEXICO
Tropic of Cancer
MIDWAY ISLANDS
(to US)
Hawaii
(to US)
WAKE ISLAND
(to US)
JOHNSTON ATOLL (to US)
MARSHALL ISLANDS
GUATEMALA
EL SALVADOR
NICARAGUA
COSTA RICA
PANAMA
Clipperton Island
(to France)
VENEZUELA
COLOMBIA
FRENCH GUIANA
(to France)
Equator
GUYANA
SURINAME
ECUADOR
Galápagos Islands
(to Ecuador)
WALLIS & FUTUNA
(to France)
KINGMAN REEF (to US)
PALMYRA ATOLL (to US)
BAKER & HOWLAND ISLANDS (to US)
JARVIS ISLAND
(to US)
NAURU
KIRIBATI
TUVALU
TOKELAU
(to NZ)
SOLOMON ISLANDS
Îles Marquises
–9½
PERU
BRAZIL
VANUATU
COOK ISLANDS
(to NZ)
FRENCH POLYNESIA
(to France)
BOLIVIA
NEW CALEDONIA
(to France)
FIJI
PARAGUAY
Tropic of Capricorn
CORAL SEA ISLANDS
(to Australia)
TONGA
SAMOA
NIUE (to NZ)
AMERICAN SAMOA
(to US)
–8½
PITCAIRN ISLANDS
(to UK)
San Felix Island
(to Chile)
San Ambrosia Island
(to Chile)
Easter Island
(to Chile)
CHILE
–11½
NORFOLK ISLAND
(to Australia)
Kermadec Island
(to NZ)
Juan Fernandez Island
(to Chile)
URUGUAY
ARGENTINA
NEW ZEALAND
+12¾
Chatham Island
(to NZ)
PACIFIC OCEAN
Bounty Island
(to NZ)
Campbell Island
(to NZ)
Macquarie Island (to Australia)
FALKLAND ISLANDS
(to UK)
CHILE
23:00
24:00
01:00
02:00
03:00
04:00
05:00
06:00
07:00
08:00
09:00
10:00
Antarctic Circle
ANTARCTICA
Graham Land

Chronology 2000–2001

THE NEW MILLENNIUM (whether it began in 2000 or 2001) has been characterized by volatile politics. Decades of rule by seemingly durable regimes crumbled across the world. Entrenched parties were ousted in Mexico and Taiwan and unpopular leaders were toppled by popular uprisings in Ivory Coast and Yugoslavia. In the USA a new presidential term, born amid debates about pregnant chads and the popular vote, was overshadowed within the year by the world's worst ever terrorist attack. Ethnic tensions continued to cause instability from the Pacific through the Indian subcontinent, to the Balkans and the heart of Africa.

North America

❑ **15th February 2000** US prison population passes two million.

❑ **4th May 2000** The "Love Bug" virus deletes over two million computer files in the USA and another million worldwide.

❑ **28th June 2000** Child refugee Elian Gonzalez returns to Cuba after an international custody battle.

❑ **2nd July 2000** Seventy years of rule by the Institutional Revolutionary Party in Mexico is ended by the election victory of Vicente Fox.

❑ **27th September 2000** An IMF/World Bank summit in Prague ends early because of anti-globalization protests.

❑ **13th December 2000** US Vice President Al Gore finally concedes defeat in the presidential election. George W. Bush goes on to become the first president in 112 years elected without a majority of votes.

❑ **17th January 2001** Power shortages in California lead to major blackouts across the state.

❑ **12th February 2001** The human genome is mapped by a team of international scientists.

❑ **28th April 2001** Dennis Tito from the USA becomes the first space tourist, aboard the International Space Station.

❑ **1st May 2001** President Bush declares the 1972 anti-ballistic missile (ABM) treaty a thing of the past, opening the way for development of the controversial missile defense shield.

❑ **11th June 2001** "Oklahoma bomber" Timothy McVeigh is executed.

❑ **23rd July 2001** The USA is the only industrialized country not to sign up to a new global environmental treaty on "greenhouse gas" emissions.

❑ **11th September 2001** Thousands die when hijacked aircraft are flown into the World Trade Center and the Pentagon in a concerted terrorist onslaught against the USA.

Central and South America

❑ **21st January 2000** President Mahuad of Ecuador is ousted by an Amerindian-led coup. Schoolteacher-turned-vice-president Gustavo Noboa is appointed in his place.

❑ **3rd March 2000** Former dictator Gen. Augusto Pinochet returns to Chile after being released from house arrest in UK. His arrival prompts a drawn-out campaign to bring him to trial in Chile.

❑ **16th July 2000** An enormous oil spill – Brazil's worst for 25 years – pollutes the Iguazu River. The state oil company Petrobras goes on to pay large fines for a series of disasters.

❑ **19th November 2000** President Fujimori of Peru announces his surprise resignation and self-exile in Japan amid a mushrooming corruption scandal. His secret police chief, Vladimiro Montesinos, flees into hiding.

❑ **13th January–16th February 2001** Massive earthquakes kill over 1000 people in El Salvador.

Europe

❑ **30th January 2000** A cyanide spill from a mine in Romania goes on to kill virtually all wildlife in the Tisza River downstream in Hungary.

❑ **3rd February 2000** The inclusion of the extreme right-wing Freedom Party in a governing coalition in Austria prompts the EU to impose diplomatic sanctions for seven months.

❑ **12th March 2000** Pope John Paul II makes an unprecedented apology for 2000 years of religious persecution by the Church.

❑ **26th March 2000** Vladimir Putin wins presidential elections in Russia on the back of a hugely popular military action in Chechnya.

❑ **21st June 2000** Fifty-eight Chinese illegal immigrants are found dead in the back of a lorry in Dover, UK. The deaths are part of an ongoing story of immigrants risking their lives to enter western Europe.

❑ **25th July 2000** The supersonic plane Concorde crashes on takeoff in Paris, killing 113 people.

❑ **21st August 2000** The *Kursk* nuclear submarine sinks off northern Russia with the loss of all 118 sailors aboard.

❑ **5th October 2000** Dictatorial Yugoslav president Slobodan Milošević is ousted in a popular revolution. Vojislav Kostunica is appointed in his place.

❑ **10th December 2000** European leaders agree at an EU summit in Nice on arrangements for the Union's eastward expansion.

❑ **15th December 2000** Ukraine's Chernobyl nuclear power plant, the scene of the world's worst ever nuclear accident in 1986, is finally closed down.

❑ **1st January 2001** Greece becomes the 12th country to adopt the euro as its official currency.

❑ **22nd January 2001** The UK's House of Lords votes in favor of allowing research on human cloning.

❑ **21st February 2001** The first registered case of foot-and-mouth precipitates an epidemic which devastates livestock across the UK and severely damages the country's rural economy.

❑ **26th February 2001** Ethnic Albanian rebels begin an insurrection in the north of Macedonia, leading to the arrival of NATO peacekeepers later in the year.

❑ **10th April 2001** The Netherlands becomes the first country in the world to legalize euthanasia.

❑ **13th May 2001** Right-wing businessman Silvio Berlusconi returns as prime minister of Italy, bringing "post-fascists" and northern separatists back into government.

❑ **12th July 2001** A movement led by ex-king Simeon II wins elections in Bulgaria. He becomes prime minister taking the name Saxecoburggotski.

AFRICA

❑ **22nd February 2000** Hundreds die in Kaduna, Nigeria, in religious clashes after proposals to introduce Islamic *sharia* law. The Muslim code is introduced into several northern states in the course of the year.

❑ **28th February 2000** Occupations of white-owned farms in Zimbabwe begin, leading to prolonged political insecurity and economic ruin.

❑ **1st March 2000** Baby Rositha Pedro is born in a tree after floods ravage Mozambique leaving hundreds of thousands homeless.

❑ **19th March 2000** Abdoulaye Wade is elected president of Senegal ending 40 years of Socialist Party rule.

❑ **12th May 2000** Ethiopian troops begin an invasion of Eritrea.

❑ **13th August 2000** A "national" parliament, Somalia's first for ten years, is established at a conference in neighboring Djibouti.

❑ **25th October 2000** A popular revolution ousts the military government in Ivory Coast but prompts violent clashes between supporters of rival political parties.

❑ **23rd December 2000** John Kufuor is elected president in Ghana's first democratic handover of power since independence in 1957.

❑ **16th January 2001** President Laurent Kabila of the Democratic Republic of Congo (DRC) is assassinated by his bodyguard. He is succeeded by his son Joseph, a change which improve the prospects of peace.

❑ **31st January 2001** Abdelbaset al-Megrahi of Libya is convicted of the 1988 "Lockerbie" bombing of a PanAm airplane over Scotland.

❑ **18th April 2001** Violence breaks out in the ethnic Berber-dominated region of Kabylia in northeastern Algeria.

WEST ASIA/MIDDLE EAST

❑ **18th February 2000** Reformists win a majority of seats in Iran's Consultative Council, but still face a determined conservative opposition.

❑ **24th May 2000** The last Israeli soldiers withdraw from southern Lebanon, ending 22 years of occupation.

❑ **10th June 2000** President Hafez al-Assad of Syria dies and is hastily succeeded by his son Bashar.

❑ **22nd September 2000** French doctors and human rights activists charter a plane to Iraq in contravention of continuing UN sanctions.

❑ **28th September 2000** New Palestinian uprising (*intifada*) begins after a controversial visit to the holy Haram al-Sharif/Temple Mount site by future Israeli prime minister Ariel Sharon.

❑ **2nd March 2001** The Afghan *Taliban* regime begins the demolition of ancient Buddhist statues near Bamian.

❑ **6th May 2001** Pope John Paul II becomes the first pope to pray in a mosque during visit to Syria.

❑ **27th August 2001** Abu Ali Mustafa of the Popular Front for the Liberation of Palestine is killed by an Israeli rocket strike.

❑ **7th October 2001** US coalition forces open "war against terrorism" with strikes against Afghanistan.

NORTH ASIA

❑ **1st March 2000** Extremely severe winter weather comes toward an end having killed 1.4 million livestock across Mongolia. Conditions are even worse the following year.

❑ **18th March 2000** Fifty years of rule by the nationalist Kuomintang is overturned in Taiwan with the election of democrat Chen Shui-bian as president.

❑ **1st April 2000** Japanese prime minister Keizo Obuchi falls into a coma and later dies. His replacement, Yoshiro Mori, turns out to be one of the least popular premiers of all time.

❑ **13th–15th June 2000** North Korean leader Kim Jong Il meets his South Korean counterpart Kim Dae Jung at a historic summit in Pyongyang – the first of its kind for 50 years.

❑ **21st March 2001** Human rights group Amnesty International points out that China executes more people than the rest of the world put together, with up to 40 people a week killed as part of the anticorruption "Strike Hard" campaign against .

❑ **1st April 2001** A US reconnaissance plane collides with a Chinese fighter near Hainan leading to a major diplomatic crisis.

❑ **16th July 2001** China and Russia sign their first friendship treaty since the Sino-Soviet split of the early 1960s, finding common ground in opposition to the proposed US missile defense system.

❑ **31st August 2001** New populist Japanese prime minister Junichiro Koizumi inflames regional tensions by visiting the controversial Yasakuni war shrine, where those commemorated include noted war criminals from Japan's occupation of east Asia before and during World War II.

SOUTH ASIA

❑ **11th May 2000** India's population officially passes one billion.

❑ **10th October 2000** Former Sri Lankan prime minister Sirimavo Bandaranaike, the world's first female elected head of government, dies.

❑ **19th January 2001** Philippines president, and former film star, Joseph Estrada is ousted in a popular uprising led by his vice president, and successor, Gloria Arroyo.

❑ **26th January 2001** A powerful earthquake in Gujarat, India, (measuring 7.9 on the Richter scale) kills an estimated 30,000 people and obliterates infrastructure.

❑ **1st June 2001** King Birendra of Nepal, and nine other members of the royal family, are murdered by Crown Prince Dipendra in a drunken rage. Dipendra kills himself in the attack and his uncle Gyanendra becomes king.

❑ **23rd July 2001** President Wahid of Indonesia is ousted by parliament and replaced by his deputy Megawati Sukarnoputri.

❑ **29th August 2001** East Timorese begin voting in elections ahead of expected independence.

AUSTRALIA AND OCEANIA

❑ **1st January 2000** Dawn of the new "millennium." Anticipated millennium bug in computers does not materialize.

❑ **17th March 2000** The UN votes to make Tuvalu its 189th member.

❑ **19th May 2000** Mahendra Chaudhry, Fiji's first ever ethnic I ndian prime minister, is ousted in a coup led by nationalist businessman George Speight.

❑ **20th October 2000** A peace treaty in the Solomon Islands ends two years of ethnic violence on Guadalcanal, although tensions persist.

❑ **23rd March 2001** The 15-year-old Mir space station, the last remnant of the Cold War era of space exploration, is brought crashing into the Pacific.

International Organizations

This listing gives the full names of all international organizations referred to, often by acronym, in the World Desk Reference. (Political parties are to be found under the Politics heading within each national entry.) The full names are followed by the date of the establishment or foundation, an indication of membership, where appropriate, and a summary of the organization's aims and functions.

ACC
Arab Cooperation Council
established 1989
members – Egypt, Iraq, Jordan, Yemen
Promotes Arab economic cooperation

ACP
African, Caribbean and Pacific Countries
established 1976
members – 78 developing countries and territories
Preferential economic and aid relationship with the EU under the Lomé Convention

ACS
Association of Caribbean States
established 1994
members – 25 Caribbean countries
Promotes economic, scientific, and cultural cooperation in the region

ADB
Asian Development Bank
established 1966
members – 43 Asian–Pacific countries and territories, 16 non-regional countries
Encourages regional development

AfDB
African Development Bank
established 1964
members – 53 African countries, 24 non-African countries
Encourages African economic and social development

AFESD
Arab Fund for Economic and Social Development
established 1968
members – 21 Arab countries (including Palestine)
Promotes social and economic development in Arab states

AL
League of Arab States (Arab League)
established 1945
members – 22 Arab countries (including Palestine)
Forum to promote Arab cooperation on social, political, and military issues

ALADI
Latin American Integration Association
established 1960
members – 12 Central and South American countries
Promotes trade and regional integration

AmCC
Amazonian Cooperation Council
established 1978
members – Bolivia, Brazil, Colombia, Ecuador, Guyana, Peru, Suriname, Venezuela
Promotes the harmonious development of the Amazon region

AMF
Arab Monetary Fund
established 1977
members – 22 Arab countries (including Palestine)
Promotes monetary and economic cooperation

AMU
Arab Maghreb Union
established 1989
members – Algeria, Libya, Mauritania, Morocco, Tunisia
Promotes integration and economic cooperation among north African Arab states

ANZUS
Australia–New Zealand–United States Security Treaty
established 1951
members – Australia, New Zealand, United States
Trilateral security agreement. Security relations between the USA and New Zealand were suspended in 1984 over the issue of US nuclear-powered or potentially nuclear-armed naval vessels visiting New Zealand ports. High-level contacts between the USA and New Zealand were resumed in 1994.

AP
Andean Pact (Acuerdo de Cartegena) – also known as Andean Community
established 1969
members – Bolivia, Colombia, Ecuador, Peru, Venezuela
Promotes development through integration

APEC
Asia-Pacific Economic Cooperation
established 1989
members – 20 Pacific Rim countries
Promotes regional economic cooperation

ASEAN
Association of Southeast Asian Nations
established 1967
members – Brunei, Burma, Cambodia, Indonesia, Laos, Malaysia, Philippines, Singapore, Thailand, Vietnam
Promotes economic, social, and cultural cooperation

BADEA
Arab Bank for Economic Development in Africa
established 1973
members – 18 Arab countries (including Palestine)
Established as an agency of the Arab League to promote economic development in Africa

BDEAC
Central African States Development Bank
established 1975
members – Cameroon, Central African Republic, Chad, Congo, Equatorial Guinea, France, Gabon, Germany, Kuwait
Furthers economic development

Benelux
Benelux Economic Union
established 1960
members – Belgium, Luxembourg, Netherlands
Develops economic ties between member countries

BOAD
West African Development Bank
established 1973
members – Benin, Burkina, Guinea-Bissau, Ivory Coast, Mali, Niger, Senegal, Togo
Promotes economic development and integration in West Africa

BSEC
Black Sea Economic Cooperation Group
established 1992
members – Albania, Armenia, Azerbaijan, Bulgaria, Georgia, Greece, Moldova, Romania, Russia, Turkey, Ukraine
Furthers regional stability through economic cooperation

CAEU
Council of Arab Economic Unity
established 1957
members – 12 Arab countries (including Palestine)
Encourages economic integration

Caricom
Caribbean Community and Common Market
established 1973
members – 13 Caribbean countries and Montserrat
Fosters economic ties

CBSS
Council of the Baltic Sea States
established 1992
members – Denmark, Estonia, Finland, Germany, Iceland, Latvia, Lithuania, Norway, Poland, Russia, Sweden
Promotes regional cooperation

CDB
Caribbean Development Bank
established 1969
members – 17 Caribbean countries/dependencies, 8 non-Caribbean countries
Promotes regional development

CE
Council of Europe
established 1949
members – 43 European countries
Promotes unity and quality of life in Europe

CEFTA
Central European Free Trade Agreement
established 1992
members – Bulgaria, Czech Republic, Hungary, Poland, Romania, Slovakia, Slovenia
Promotes trade and cooperation

CEI
Central European Initiative
established 1989
members – 17 eastern and central European countries: Albania, Austria, Belarus, Bosnia & Herzegovina, Bulgaria, Croatia, Czech Republic, Hungary, Italy, Macedonia, Moldova, Poland, Romania, Slovakia, Slovenia, Ukraine, Yugoslavia
Evolved from the Hexagonal Group; promotes economic and political cooperation, within the OSCE

CEMAC
Central African Economic and Monetary Community
established 1994
members – Cameroon, Central African Republic, Chad, Congo, Equatorial Guinea, Gabon
Aims to promote subregional integration, by economic and monetary union (replaced UDEAC)

CEPGL
Economic Community of the Great Lakes Countries
established 1976
members – Burundi, Congo (Zaire), Rwanda
Promotes regional economic cooperation

CERN
European Organization for Nuclear Research
established 1954
members – 20 European countries
Provides for collaboration in nuclear research for peaceful purposes

CILSS
Permanent Interstate Committee for Drought Control in the Sahel
established 1973
members – 9 African countries in the Sahel region
Promotes prevention of drought and crop failure in the region

CIS
Commonwealth of Independent States
established 1991
members – Armenia, Azerbaijan, Belarus, Georgia, Kazakhstan, Kyrgyzstan, Moldova, Russia, Tajikistan, Turkmenistan, Ukraine, Uzbekistan
Promotes interstate relationships among former republics of the Soviet Union

CMCA
Central American Monetary Council
established 1960
members – Costa Rica, El Salvador, Guatemala, Honduras, Nicaragua
Now a subsystem of SICA; furthers economic ties between members; one of its institutions is the BCIE – Central American Bank for Economic Integration

COI
Indian Ocean Commission
established 1982
members – Comoros, France (representing Réunion), Madagascar, Mauritius, Seychelles
Promotes regional cooperation

COMESA
Common Market for Eastern and Southern Africa
established 1993
members – 20 African countries
Promotes economic development and cooperation (replaced PTA)

Comm
Commonwealth
established 1931
members – 54 countries (although Fiji and Pakistan are currently suspended). Members are chiefly former members of the British Empire.
Develops relationships and contacts between members

CP
Colombo Plan
established 1950
members – Four donor countries: Australia, Japan, New Zealand, USA; and 20 Asia–Pacific countries
Encourages economic and social development in Asia–Pacific region

CPLP
Community of Portuguese-speaking Countries
established 1996
members – Portugal, Brazil, and five Portuguese-speaking African countries – Angola, Cape Verde, Guinea-Bissau, Mozambique, São Tomé & Príncipe
To promote political and diplomatic links between member states, and cooperation on economic, social, cultural, judicial, and scientific development among Portuguese-speaking countries

Damasc
Damascus Declaration
established 1991
members – Bahrain, Egypt, Kuwait, Oman, Qatar, Saudi Arabia, Syria, United Arab Emirates
A loose association, formed after the Gulf War, which aims to secure the stability of the region

EAC
East African Community
established 2001
members – Kenya, Tanzania, Uganda
Promotes economic cooperation

EAPC
Euro-Atlantic Partnership Council
established 1991
members – The 19 members of NATO plus 27 eastern European countries
Forum for cooperation on political and security issues (successor to the NACC, North Atlantic Cooperation Council)

EBRD
European Bank for Reconstruction and Development
established 1991
members – 60 countries
Helps transition of former communist European states to market economies

ECO
Economic Cooperation Organization
established 1985
members – Afghanistan, Azerbaijan, Iran, Kazakhstan, Kyrgyzstan, Pakistan, Tajikistan, Turkey, Turkmenistan, Uzbekistan
Aims at cooperation in economic, social, and cultural affairs

ECOWAS
Economic Community of West African States
established 1975
members – 15 west African countries
Promotes regional economic cooperation

EEA
European Economic Area
established 1994
members – The 15 members of the EU, and Iceland, Liechtenstein, and Norway
Aims to include EFTA members in the EU single market

EEC
Eurasian Economic Community
established 2001
members – Belarus, Kazakhstan, Kyrgyzstan, Russia, Tajikistan
Coordinates regional trade

EFTA
European Free Trade Association
established 1960
members – Iceland, Norway, Liechtenstein, Switzerland
Promotes economic cooperation

ESA
European Space Agency
established 1973
members – 15 European countries
Promotes cooperation in space research for peaceful purposes

EU
European Union
established 1992
members – 15 European countries
Aims to integrate the economies of member states and promote cooperation and coordination of policies

FZ
Franc zone
established Not applicable
members – France (including overseas departments and territories), Monaco, and 15 African states
Aims to form monetary union based on the linking of member country currencies to French franc (or, since 1999, to euro)

G10
Group of 10
established 1962
members – 11 members: G7 members, plus Belgium, the Netherlands, Sweden and Switzerland
Ministers meet to discuss monetary issues

G15
Group of 15
established 1989
members – 19 developing countries
Meets annually to further cooperation among developing countries

G24
Group of 24
established Not applicable
members – 24 countries within IMF representing the interests of developing countries

G3
Group of 3
established 1987
members – Colombia, Mexico, Venezuela
Aims to remove trade restrictions

G5
Group of 5
established Not applicable
members – Finance ministers of France, Germany, Japan, UK, USA
Meet informally to establish agenda of G7

G7
Group of 7
established 1975
members – The seven major industrialized countries: Canada, France, Germany, Italy, Japan, UK, USA
Summit meetings of the seven major industrialized countries, originally for economic purposes, but more recently for political purposes as well

G8
Group of 8
established 1994
members – Members of the G7 (Canada, France, Germany, Italy, Japan, UK, USA) and Russia
To include Russia in discussions of the G7 on international affairs

GCC
Gulf Cooperation Council
established 1981
members – Bahrain, Kuwait, Oman, Qatar, Saudi Arabia, UAE
Promotes cooperation in economic, political, and social affairs

GEPLACEA
Latin American and Caribbean Sugar Exporting Countries
established 1974
members – 23 countries
A forum for consultation on the production and sale of sugar

GGC
Gulf of Guinea Commission
established 2001
members – Congo, Gabon, Nigeria, São Tomé and Príncipe
Promotes regional cooperation

IAEA
International Atomic Energy Agency
established 1957
members – 132 countries
Promotes and monitors peaceful use of atomic energy

IBRD
International Bank for Reconstruction and Development
(also known as the World Bank)
established 1945
members – 183 countries
UN agency providing economic development loans

ICRC
International Committee of the Red Cross
established 1863
members – Up to 25 Swiss nationals form the international committee. Red Cross or Red Crescent societies exist in 175 countries
Coordinates all international humanitarian activities of the International Red Cross and Red Crescent Movement, giving legal and practical assistance to the victims of wars and disasters. It works through national committees of Red Cross or Red Crescent societies

IDB
Inter-American Development Bank
established 1959
members – 28 American countries and 18 non-regional countries
Promotes development in Latin America and the Caribbean through the financing of economic and social development projects and the provision of technical assistance

IGAD
Intergovernmental Authority on Development
established 1996
members – Djibouti, Eritrea, Ethiopia, Kenya, Somalia, Sudan, Uganda
Promotes cooperation on food security, infrastructure, and other development issues (supersedes IGADD, founded 1986, to promote cooperation on drought-related matters)

IMF
International Monetary Fund
established 1945
members – 183 countries. The voting rights of Congo (former Zaire) are currently suspended.
Promotes international monetary cooperation, the balanced growth of trade, and exchange rate stability; provides credit resources to members experiencing balance-of-trade difficulties.

IsDB
Islamic Development Bank
established 1975
members – 53 countries (including Palestine)
Promotes economic development on Islamic principles among Muslim communities
(agency of the OIC)

IWC
International Whaling Commission
established 1946
members – 43 countries
Reviews conduct of whaling throughout world; coordinates and funds whale research

LCBC
Lake Chad Basin Commission
established 1964
members – Cameroon, Central African Republic, Chad, Niger, Nigeria
Encourages economic and environmental development in Lake Chad region

Mekong River
Mekong River Commission
established 1995
members – Cambodia, Laos, Thailand, Vietnam
Accord on the sustainable development of Mekong River basin (replacing the 1958 interim Mekong Secretariat)

MERCOSUR
Southern Common Market
established 1991
members – Argentina, Brazil, Paraguay, Uruguay
Promotes economic integration, free trade, and common external tariffs

MRU
Mano River Union
established 1973
members – Guinea, Liberia, Sierra Leone
Aims to create customs and economic union in order to promote development

NAFTA
North American Free Trade Agreement
established 1994
members – Canada, Mexico, USA
Free-trade zone

NAM
Non-Aligned Movement
established 1961
members – 113 countries (including Palestine)
Fosters political and military cooperation away from traditional Eastern or Western blocs

NATO
North Atlantic Treaty Organization
established 1949
members – 19 countries
Promotes mutual defense cooperation. Since January 1994, NATO's Partnerships for Peace program has provided a loose framework for cooperation with former members of the Warsaw Pact and the ex-Soviet republics. A historic Founding Act signed between Russia and NATO in May 1997 allowed for the organization's eastward expansion, under which the Czech Republic, Hungary, and Poland were the first three countries to join.

NC
Nordic Council
established 1952
members – Denmark, Finland, Iceland, Norway, Sweden
Promotes cultural and environmental cooperation

OAPEC
Organization of Arab Petroleum Exporting Countries
established 1968
members – 10 Arab countries: Algeria, Bahrain, Egypt, Iraq, Kuwait, Libya, Qatar, Saudi Arabia, Syria, UAE
Aims to promote the interests of member countries and increase cooperation in the petroleum industry

OAS
Organization of American States
established 1948
members – 35 American countries (although Cuba has been suspended since 1962)
Promotes security, economic, and social development in the Americas

OAU
Organization of African Unity
established 1963
members – 51 African countries and Western Sahara
Promotes unity and cooperation in Africa. (The OAU is in the process of being transformed into the African Union.)

OECD
Organization for Economic Cooperation and Development
established 1961
members – 30 industrialized democracies
Forum for coordinating economic policies among industrialized countries

OECS
Organization of Eastern Caribbean States
established 1981
members – 7 Caribbean countries/dependencies: Antigua & Barbuda, Dominica, Grenada, Montserrat, St. Kitts & Nevis, St. Lucia, St. Vincent & the Grenadines
Promotes political, economic, and defense cooperation

OIC
Organization of the Islamic Conference
established 1971
members – 57 countries (including Palestine)
Furthers Islamic solidarity and cooperation

OIF
International Organization of Francophony
established 1970
members – 48 countries and the governments of Québec, New Brunswick, and the French Community of Belgium were represented at the summit in 1999 in New Brunswick, Canada. The Intergovernmental Agency of Francophony has 49 members.
To promote cooperation and cultural and technical links among French-speaking countries and communities.

OMVG
Gambia River Development Organization
established 1978
members – Gambia, Guinea, Guinea-Bissau, Senegal
Promotes integrated development of the Gambia River basin

Opanal
Agency for the Prohibition of Nuclear Weapons in Latin America and the Caribbean
established 1969
members – 32 countries (not including Cuba, who has signed but not ratified the Treaty of Tlatelolco)
Aims to ensure compliance with the Treaty of Tlatelolco (banning nuclear weapons from South America and the Caribbean)

OPEC
Organization of the Petroleum Exporting Countries
established 1960
members – 11 oil producers: Algeria, Indonesia, Iran, Iraq, Kuwait, Libya, Nigeria, Qatar, Saudi Arabia, United Arab Emirates, Venezuela
Aims to coordinate oil policies to ensure fair and stable prices

OSCE
Organization for Security and Cooperation in Europe
established 1972
members – 55 countries
Aims to strengthen democracy and human rights, and settle disputes peacefully (formerly CSCE; renamed 1994)

PARTNERSHIPS FOR PEACE (PfP)
see NATO
established Not applicable
members – 27 members: eastern European and former Soviet countries, Sweden, Finland, Malta, Austria, and Switzerland

PC
Pacific Community (formerly South Pacific Commission)
established 1948
members – 27 countries and territories
A forum for dialogue between Pacific countries and powers administering Pacific territories

PIF
Pacific Islands Forum (formerly the South Pacific Forum)
established 1971
members – 16 countries and self-governing territories
Develops regional political cooperation

RG
Rio Group
established 1987
members – 18 Latin American and Caribbean countries
Forum for Latin American and Caribbean issues (evolved from Contadora Group, established 1948)

SAARC
South Asian Association for Regional Cooperation
established 1985
members – Bangladesh, Bhutan, India, Maldives, Nepal, Pakistan, Sri Lanka
Encourages economic, social, and cultural cooperation

SACU
Southern African Customs Union
established 1969
members – 5 southern African countries: Botswana, Lesotho, Namibia, South Africa, Swaziland
Promotes cooperation in trade and customs matters among southern African states

SADC
Southern African Development Community
established 1992
members – 14 southern African countries
Promotes economic integration

San José
San José Group
established 1988
members – Costa Rica, El Salvador, Guatemala, Honduras, Nicaragua, Panama
A 'complementary, voluntary, and gradual' economic union

SCO
Shanghai Cooperation Organization (formerly Shanghai Five)
established 1996
members – China, Kazakhstan, Kyrgyzstan, Russia, Tajikistan, Uzbekistan
Promotes regional security and cooperation

SELA
Latin American Economic System
established 1975
members – 28 countries
Promotes economic and social development through regional cooperation

SICA
Central American Integration System
established 1991
members – 6 countries: Costa Rica, El Salvador, Guatemala, Honduras, Nicaragua, Panama
Coordinates the political, economic, social, and environmental integration of the region

UEMOA
West African Economic and Monetary Union
established 1994
members – 8 West African countries
Aims for convergence of monetary policies and economic union

UN
United Nations
established 1945
members – 189 countries; permanent members of the Security Council – China, France, Russia, UK, USA
Aims to maintain international peace and security and to promote cooperation over economic, social, cultural, and humanitarian problems.

Agencies include the regional commissions of the UN's Economic and Social Council: ECA (Economic Commission for Africa – established 1958); ECE (Economic Commission for Europe – established 1947); ECLAC (Economic Commission for Latin America and the Caribbean – established 1948); ESCAP (Economic and Social Commission for Asia and the Pacific – established 1947); ESCWA (Economic and Social Commission for Western Asia – established 1973).

Other bodies of the UN, in which most members participate, include UNICEF (the UN Children's Fund); UNCTAD (the UN Conference on Trade and Development); UNDP (the UN Development Program); UNHCR (the UN High Commissioner for Refugees); UNFPA (the UN Population Fund); IDA (the International Development Association).

Switzerland, Taiwan, and Vatican City do not belong to the UN.

WEU
Western European Union
established 1955
members – 10 countries
A forum for European military cooperation

WTO
World Trade Organization
established 1995
members – 141 countries (including Hong Kong and Macao) and the EU
Aims to liberalize trade through multilateral trade agreements (as the successor to GATT (the General Agreement on Tariffs and Trade))

2

THE NATIONS OF THE WORLD

THE NATIONS OF THE WORLD

• AFGHANISTAN ~ ZIMBABWE

OVERSEAS TERRITORIES & DEPENDENCIES

A

AFGHANISTAN

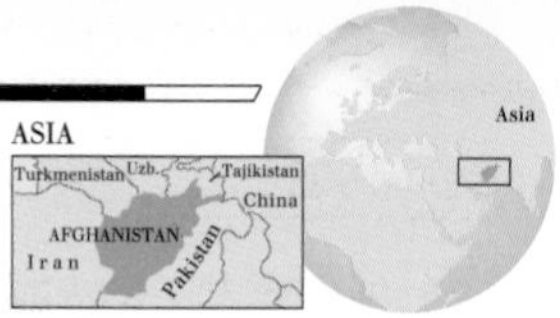
Asia
ASIA
Turkmenistan
Uzb.
Tajikistan
China
AFGHANISTAN
Iran
Pakistan

OFFICIAL NAME: Islamic State of Afghanistan **CAPITAL:** Kābul
POPULATION: 22.7 million **CURRENCY:** Afghani **OFFICIAL LANGUAGES:** Persian and Pashtu

1919 | 1919 | Aug 19 | AFG | +4.5 | +93 | .af

LANDLOCKED in central Asia, Afghanistan has borders with Iran, Pakistan, China, Tajikistan, Turkmenistan, and Uzbekistan. Three-quarters of its territory is inaccessible terrain. Agriculture is the main activity, but the country has been torn by armed conflict for decades. In the 1980s Islamic *mujahideen* factions defeated the communist regime, but rivalries undermined their fragile power-sharing agreement and the hard-line *taliban* militia swept to power. Islamic dress codes and behavior are vigorously enforced; women have few rights or opportunities. The *taliban* regime is notorious for harboring extremists.

***The Band-i-Amir River,** in the Hindu Kush. Afghanistan is mountainous and arid. Many Afghans are nomadic sheep farmers.*

CLIMATE

Mountain/cold desert

WEATHER CHART

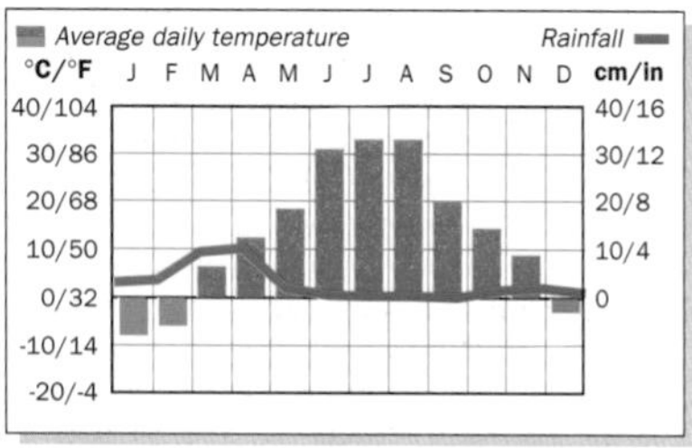
Average daily temperature
Rainfall
°C/°F
J F M A M J J A S O N D
cm/in
40/104
30/86
20/68
10/50
0/32
-10/14
-20/-4
40/16
30/12
20/8
10/4
0

Afghanistan has the world's widest temperature range, with lows of –50°C (–58°F) and highs of 53°C (127°F). Severe drought, a frequent problem, affected half the population in 2000.

TRANSPORTATION

Drive on right

Kābul International

Has no fleet

THE TRANSPORTATION NETWORK

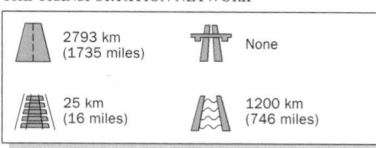

2793 km (1735 miles)

None

25 km (16 miles)

1200 km (746 miles)

The repair and reconstruction of the roads, severely damaged in the civil war, and the modernization of the air traffic control system are the most urgent priorities. Road rebuilding is usually carried out by local communities. However, neighboring Pakistan has undertaken to rebuild a number of key routes, including the Kabul–Peshawar link, which will benefit its own trade with central Asia.

Securing key supply routes was a crucial factor in intra-*mujahideen* feuding. It remains vital to the *taliban* in their efforts to gain control over the whole country, as well as to anti-*taliban* forces still active, especially in the north. Much of Afghanistan's outlying territory is sown with land mines.

TOURISM

Visitors : Population 1:5675

4000 visitors

No change in 1995–1998

MAIN TOURIST ARRIVALS

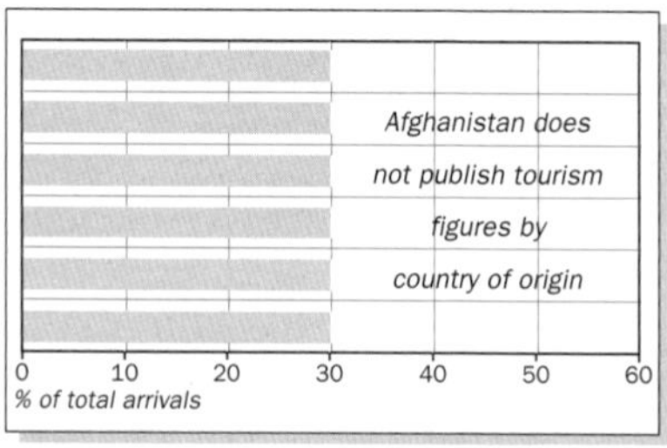
Afghanistan does not publish tourism figures by country of origin
0
10
20
30
40
50
60
% of total arrivals

Afghanistan is a war zone. There are virtually no visitors, while UN and aid agency personnel have frequently been withdrawn because of government restrictions on their activities. Few hotels are open in Kabul and travel is extremely dangerous. Air Ariana, the Afghan national airline, no longer flies from Kabul, but from Dushanbe in neighboring Tajikistan.

The lack of a formal economy means that Afghanistan gets few visits from businessmen, and any expatriates who were previously in Kabul have left.

PEOPLE

Pop. density low

Persian, Pashtu, Dari, Uzbek, Turkmen

35/km² (90/mi²)

THE URBAN/RURAL POPULATION SPLIT

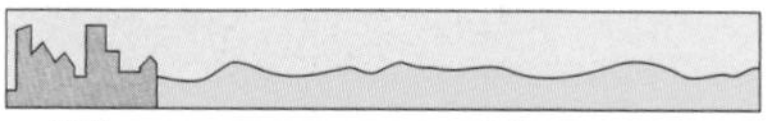
20%
80%

RELIGIOUS PERSUASION

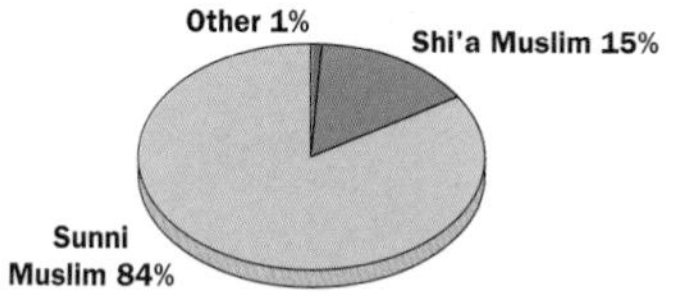
Other 1%
Shi'a Muslim 15%
Sunni Muslim 84%

ETHNIC MAKEUP

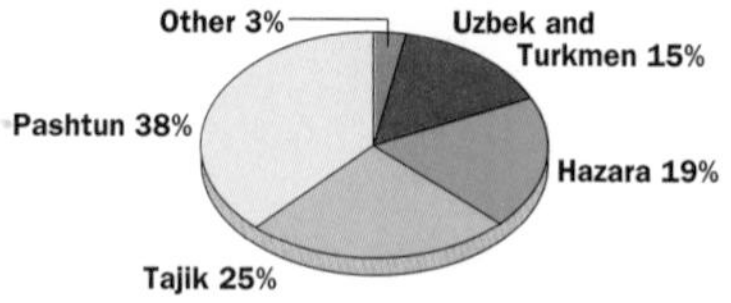
Other 3%
Uzbek and Turkmen 15%
Pashtun 38%
Hazara 19%
Tajik 25%

Ethnic Pashtuns form the largest group in Afghanistan and have been its traditional rulers; the main minorities are Tajiks, Hazaras, Uzbeks, and Turkmen. These ethnic divisions have largely determined intra-*mujahideen* feuding since 1992. The predominantly Pashtun *taliban*, who took power in 1996, wrested control from a Tajik–Uzbek alliance. Differences between Sunnis and Shi'as have become acute under the *taliban* regime, which is accused of encouraging discrimination against Shi'as.

Some two million of the country's population were killed in the ten-year conflict which followed the invasion by Soviet Union forces in 1979 and in the post-1992 civil war. As many people again were maimed. A further six million people were forced to flee to neighboring Pakistan and Iran; many have returned, but a substantial minority remain in exile. An estimated million are internally displaced.

Women enjoy few rights under the rigid Islamic regime of the *taliban*. They have no access to health care and very little to education. They are strictly banned from seeking public employment.

POPULATION AGE BREAKDOWN

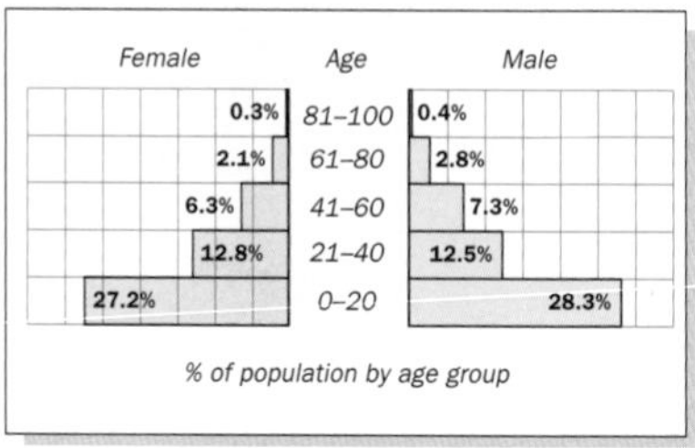
Female
Age
Male
0.3%
81–100
0.4%
2.1%
61–80
2.8%
6.3%
41–60
7.3%
12.8%
21–40
12.5%
27.2%
0–20
28.3%
% of population by age group

POLITICS

No multiparty elections

1988/Uncertain

Leader of the Taliban Mohammad Omar

AT THE LAST ELECTION

House of Representatives

Following the downfall of Najibullah's regime in April 1992, both houses were dissolved and an interim *mujahideen* legislature formed.

Senate

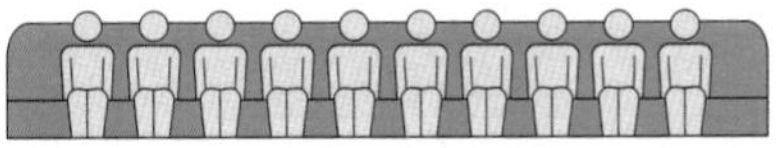

The *taliban* face opposition from the Northern Alliance, with which they have refused to share power.

Main Political Issues

Elections

According to the 7 March 1993 Islamabad peace accord, elections were to be held by the end of the year. However, they are still awaited.

Control of Kabul

Kabul remains under the control of the *taliban*, who captured the city in 1996. An opposition alliance headed by the former president, Burhanuddin Rabbani of the *Jamiat-i-Islami*, has failed to reverse the position.

Profile

The political system had virtually collapsed in Afghanistan prior to the *taliban* takeover. Rival *mujahideen* factions had been in control since April 1992, when President Najibullah was forced to step down.

In March 1993 *mujahideen* leaders agreed to a framework for an interim government, pending elections. In January 1994 the agreement collapsed amid differences between opposing factions in government. Fighting escalated with the involvement in early 1995 of the *taliban*, who eventually laid siege to Kabul. In September 1996 they ousted the government of President Burhanuddin Rabbani and imposed a strict Islamic regime.

By mid-1998 the *taliban* had extended their control over most northern regions. A UN-sponsored power-sharing arrangement in 1999 collapsed within months. In September 2001 the prospect of US-led intervention revived the hopes of anti-*taliban* groups.

Burhanuddin Rabbani, *president from 1992 until 1996.*

WORLD AFFAIRS

Joined UN in 1946

CP | ECO | IBRD | NAM | OIC

Afghanistan has been a pariah state under the *taliban* government, recognized only by Pakistan, Saudi Arabia, and the United Arab Emirates. The regime defied international opinion, and UN sanctions, by harboring Saudi extremist Osama bin Laden, the head of an anti-US terrorist network. It was also condemned over human rights and the destruction of ancient Buddhist statues in Bamian. When a worldwide "war on terrorism" became the top US priority after the New York and Washington attacks of September 2001, Afghanistan was threatened with imminent US-led military action, backing up demands that it hand bin Laden over for trial.

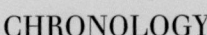

TAJIKISTAN
UZBEKISTAN
TURKMENISTAN
CHINA
IRAN
PAKISTAN
HINDU KUSH
KŪH-E VĀKHĀN
Sad Istragh 7037m
Feyzābād
Tāloqān
Zībāk
Kunduz
Khānābād
Andkhvoy
Āqchah
Balkh
Kholm
Sheberghān
Mazār-e Sharīf
Āybak
Shūlgareh
Baghlān
Meymaneh
Pol-e-Khomri
Bālā Morghāb
BAND-E TORKESTĀN
Bāmīān
Barikowt
Mahmūd-e-Rāqī
Asadābād
Mehtarlām
Towraghondī
Qal'eh-ye Now
Chārīkār
KĀBUL
Kowt-e 'Ashrow
Jalālābād
Barakī Barak
Khyber Pass
Herāt
SAFID KŪH
Harīrūd
Chaghcharān
KŪH-E BĀBĀ
Helmand
Ghūrīān
SĪĀH KŪH
Ghaznī
Gardēz
Khowst
Shīndand
CHALAP DALAM
Tarīn Kowt
Moqor
Zarghūn Shahr
Farāh
Delārām
KĀFAR JAR GHAR
Kalāt
Hāmūn-e-Şāberī
Gereshk
Lashkar Gāh
Kandahār
Zaranj
DASHT-E-MĀRGOW
Kūchnay Darvīshān
Spīn Būldak
Chahārborjak
RĪGESTĀN
Bahrām Chāh
AFGHANISTAN
Total Land Area : 652 090 sq. km (251 770 sq. miles)
LAND HEIGHT
3000m/9843ft
2000m/6562ft
1000m/3281ft
500m/1640ft
200m/656ft
POPULATION
over 1 000 000
over 100 000
over 50 000
over 10 000
under 10 000
0 100 km
0 100 miles
N

CHRONOLOGY

The foundations of an Afghan state of Pashtun peoples were laid in the mid-18th century, when Durrani Ahmad Shah became paramount chief of the Abdali Pashtun peoples.

- **1838–1842** First Anglo-Afghan war.
- **1878** Second British invasion of Afghan territory.
- **1879** Under Treaty of Gandmak signed with Amir Yaqub Ali Khan, various Afghan areas annexed by Britain. Yaqub Ali Khan later exiled. New treaty signed with Amir Abdul Rahman, establishing the Durand line, a contentious boundary between Afghanistan and Pakistan.
- **1919** Declaration of Afghan independence.
- **1933** Muhammed Zahir Shar takes power.
- **1953** Mohammed Daud Khan is named prime minister.
- **1963** Daud resigns after king

CHRONOLOGY *continued*

rejects his proposals for democratic reforms.

- **1965** Elections held, but monarchy retains power. Marxist Party of Afghanistan (PDPA) formed and banned. PDPA splits into the Parcham and Khalq factions.
- **1973** Daud mounts a coup, abolishes monarchy, and declares republic. *Mujahideen* rebellion begins. Refugees flee to Pakistan.
- **1978** Opposition to Daud from PDPA culminates in Saur revolution. Revolutionary Council under Mohammad Taraki takes power. Daud assassinated.
- **1979** Taraki ousted. Hafizullah Amin takes power. Amin killed in December coup backed by USSR. 80,000 Soviet Army troops invade Afghanistan. *Mujahideen* rebellion stepped up into full-scale guerrilla war, with US backing.
- **1980** Babrak Karmal, leader of Parcham PDPA, installed as head of Marxist regime.
- **1986** Najibullah replaces Karmal as head of government.
- **1989** Soviet Army withdraws. Najibullah remains in office.
- **1992** Najibullah hands over power to *mujahideen* factions.
- **1993** *Mujahideen* agree on formation of government.
- **1994** Power struggle between Rabbani and Hekmatyar.
- **1995** Anti-government *taliban* militia advance toward Kabul.
- **1996** *Taliban* take power and impose strict Islamic regime.
- **1998** Earthquake in northern regions kills thousands.
- **1999** Power-sharing agreement between *Taliban* and Northern Alliance breaks down.
- **2000** Country suffers worst drought in 30 years. UN imposes sanctions in response to *Taliban* support for Osama bin Laden.
- **2001** March. Ancient Buddhist statues in Bamain destroyed. September. Ahmed Shah Masood leader of opposition Northern Alliance assassinated. October. US coalition forces attack selected targets.

AID

Recipient

$142m (receipts) — Down 8% in 1999

The UN is the main source of aid. However, relations between foreign aid agencies and the *taliban* authorities are fraught, and working conditions for aid personnel are extremely hazardous. Humanitarian assistance for women and the work of Christian-based agencies create particular friction.

DEFENSE

Compulsory military service

$265m — Up 4% in 1999

AFGHAN ARMED FORCES

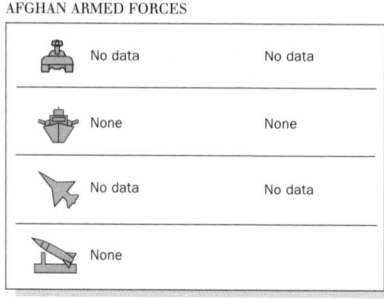

No data	No data
None	None
No data	No data
None	

In 1991, the US–Russian agreement to suspend military supplies to rival Afghan groups marked the end of the superpowers' active involvement. The Kabul communists had been almost totally dependent on Moscow for arms, even after the Soviet withdrawal in 1989.

Afghanistan has no formal defense arrangements, although there is a covert arms trade which has expanded with the activity of Islamic militants from abroad. The bulk of these arms originate in eastern Europe and the former Soviet Union. The movement of Islamist militants and weapons between Tajikistan and Afghanistan is tackled by CIS troops.

Afghanistan continues to hold hundreds of *Stinger* missiles given by the USA to the *mujahideen* in the 1980s. The USA, which was worried that they might be used against civilian airliners, offered to buy them back, but none have so far been returned.

In 1998 it was reported that the *taliban*, by then in control of most of the country, had started preliminary work to establish a national army, involving the dispatch of young men to military centers for training.

ECONOMICS

Inflation 46% p.a. (1985–1991)

$5.9bn — 4679–4750 afghanis

SCORE CARD

- World GNP Ranking........................106th
- GNP per Capita..............................$270
- Balance of Payments...................$-143m
- Inflation.....................................56.7%
- Unemployment....................................8%

EXPORTS

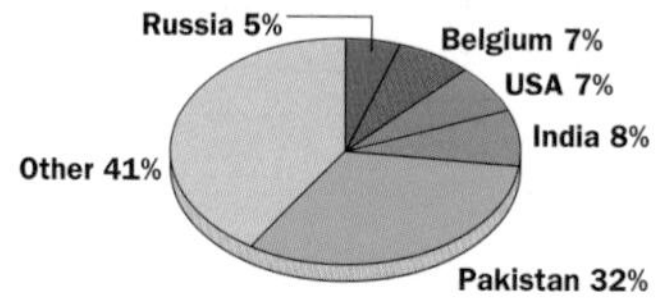
Russia 5%
Belgium 7%
USA 7%
India 8%
Other 41%
Pakistan 32%

IMPORTS

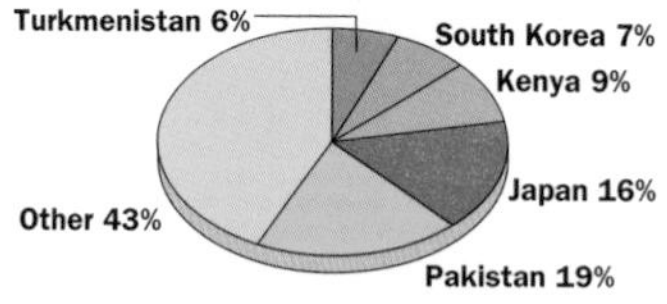
Turkmenistan 6%
South Korea 7%
Kenya 9%
Japan 16%
Other 43%
Pakistan 19%

Strengths

Very few, apart from illicit opium trade. Agriculture still the largest sector.

Weaknesses

Protracted fighting since 1979 has devastated the economy; agriculture and industry in ruins. Communication links damaged by 1998 earthquakes.

Profile

The protracted fighting has left Afghanistan one of the poorest and least developed countries in the world. Estimates suggest that $4 billion is needed to rebuild the country and that 80% of its infrastructure has been destroyed. Agricultural activity has fallen back from pre-1979 levels; the Soviets' "scorched earth" policy laid waste large areas, and much of the rural population fled to the cities. Many farmers turned back to growing poppies for opium production, but see little profit from the trade. The *taliban* have declared the production of opium to be anti-Islamic, and urge farmers to plant other crops instead, under a program funded by the UN, which considers Afghanistan to be the world's largest opium producer.

ECONOMIC PERFORMANCE INDICATOR

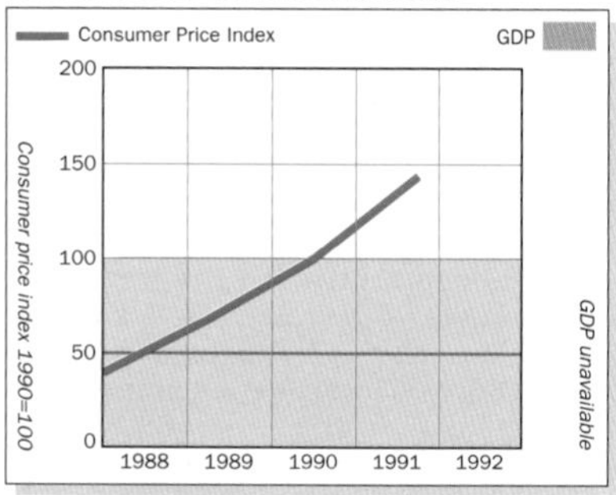
Consumer Price Index
GDP
200
150
100
50
0
Consumer price index 1990=100
1988
1989
1990
1991
1992
GDP unavailable

Mujahideen *guerrillas,* *members of just one of the many factions vying for power in Afghanistan, prepare to launch a rocket attack.*

RESOURCES

Electric power 494,000 kw

1250 tonnes

14.3m sheep, 1.5m cattle, 2.2m goats, 7.2m chickens

Not an oil producer and has no refineries

Natural gas, salt, coal, copper, lapis lazuli, barytes, talc

ELECTRICITY GENERATION

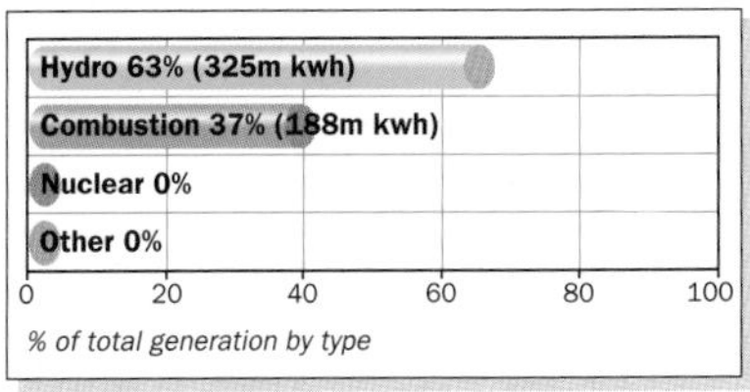
Hydro 63% (325m kwh)
Combustion 37% (188m kwh)
Nuclear 0%
Other 0%
0
20
40
60
80
100
% of total generation by type

Natural gas and coal are Afghanistan's most important strategic resources. Restoring the power generation system, which has suffered widespread deterioration and destruction, is a government priority. The construction of dams on the Kunar and Laghman rivers is being considered. Coal production has fallen from prewar levels and mines are also in urgent need of rehabilitation. Western technology is needed to rebuild the gas industry.

AFGHANISTAN : LAND USE

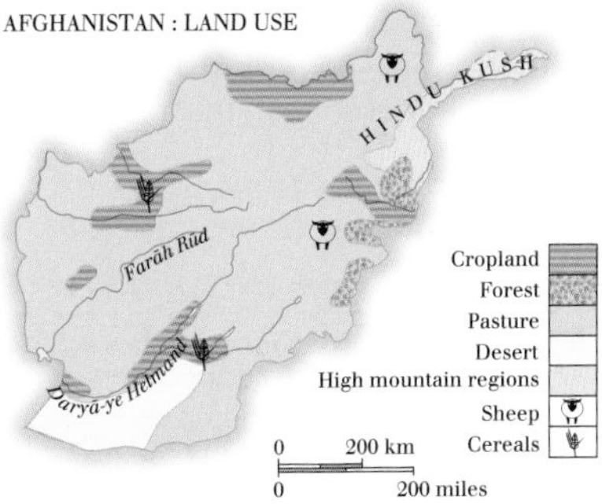
HINDU KUSH
Farāh Rūd
Daryā-ye Helmand
Cropland
Forest
Pasture
Desert
High mountain regions
Sheep
Cereals
0
200 km
0
200 miles

ENVIRONMENT

Not available

0.3% (0.2% partially protected)

0.05 tonnes per capita

ENVIRONMENTAL TREATIES

No | Yes | No

No | No | No

Environmental priorities are low, given Afghanistan's anarchic civil war conditions. However, the country's relative lack of industry, even in Kabul, means that industrial pollution is minimal. The biggest problem facing Afghanistan is land mines: over ten million have been laid, and the UN estimates that it will take 100 years to make the country safe for civilians.

MEDIA

TV ownership low

Daily newspaper circulation 6 per 1000 people

PUBLISHING AND BROADCAST MEDIA

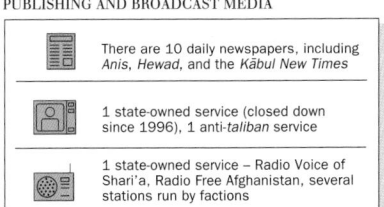

There are 10 daily newspapers, including *Anis, Hewad,* and the *Kābul New Times*

1 state-owned service (closed down since 1996), 1 anti-*taliban* service

1 state-owned service – Radio Voice of Shari'a, Radio Free Afghanistan, several stations run by factions

Most of the *mujahideen* factions run newspapers and radio stations, which follow the party line and denigrate rivals. Television and the Internet are banned, as are video cassette recorders and satellite dishes. The BBC, which broadcasts in Pashtu and Dari, is more popular than Radio Free Afghanistan, especially for its soap operas, which convey information on welfare issues.

CRIME

Death penalty used

Afghanistan does not publish prison figures

Levels of all crimes remain very high

CRIME RATES

No statistics for murders, rapes, and thefts are published due to the war situation

Fear of looting in Kabul stifled economic activity prior to the *taliban* takeover. Gun law operates widely; Herat, which had once been an exception, also experienced violence after falling to *taliban* forces.

EDUCATION

School leaving age: 13

37%

12,800 students

THE EDUCATION SYSTEM

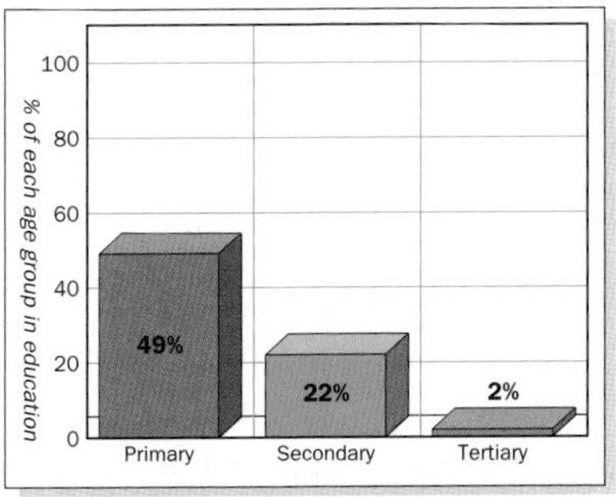
100
80
60
40
20
0
% of each age group in education
49%
22%
2%
Primary
Secondary
Tertiary

The education system is effectively male-only and based on rigid Islamic precepts. Education for girls up to 12 in a few schools in and around Kabul has been officially sanctioned since 1999, but higher education for women is strictly limited and segregation rigidly enforced; the literacy rate for women is the lowest in the world. Kabul University has been closed since 1992.

HEALTH

No welfare state health benefits

1 per 7001 people

Infectious, parasitic, respiratory, and digestive diseases

The health service has collapsed completely and almost all medical professionals have left the country. In mid-1996 only four regional hospitals were functioning. Infant and maternal mortality rates are among the highest in the world, and life expectancy is very low. Parasitic diseases and infections are a particular problem. The UN organized a program for the chlorination of well water, following an outbreak of cholera in Kabul.

The majority of women in Afghanistan are denied access to health care; their admission to hospital is strongly discouraged, as is the employment of female medical staff.

SPENDING

GDP/cap. decrease

CONSUMPTION AND SPENDING

1 per 1000 population

1 per 1000 population

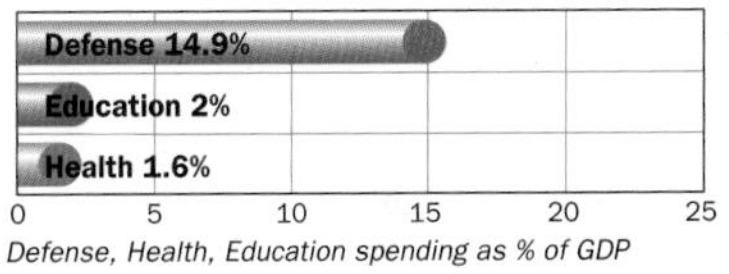
Defense 14.9%
Education 2%
Health 1.6%
0
5
10
15
20
25
Defense, Health, Education spending as % of GDP

The vast majority of Afghans live in conditions of extreme poverty. The country does not have the resources to feed its people at present – a situation exacerbated by the severe drought of 2000. The return of the remaining two to three million refugees from neighboring Pakistan and Iran would make Afghanistan even more dependent on outside assistance for its rehabilitation.

A number of *mujahideen* leaders accumulated personal fortunes during the civil war. These derive in part from the substantial foreign aid that was once available and, in some cases, from the trafficking of opium.

WORLD RANKING

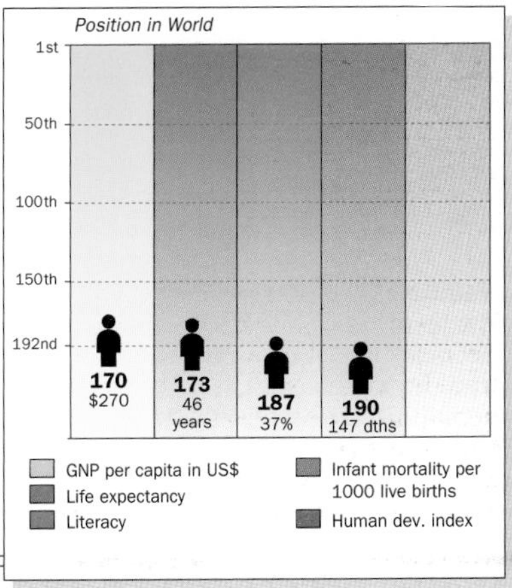
Position in World
1st
50th
100th
150th
192nd
170
$270
173
46 years
187
37%
190
147 dths
GNP per capita in US$
Life expectancy
Literacy
Infant mortality per 1000 live births
Human dev. index

A

ALBANIA

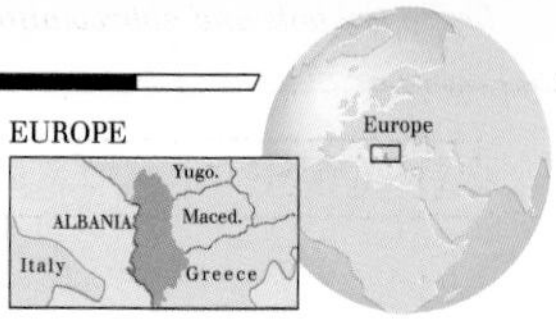
EUROPE
Europe
Yugo.
ALBANIA
Maced.
Italy
Greece

OFFICIAL NAME: Republic of Albania **CAPITAL:** Tirana
POPULATION: 3.1 million **CURRENCY:** Lek **OFFICIAL LANGUAGE:** Albanian

1912 | 1921 | Nov 28 | AL | +1 | +355 | .al

LYING AT THE southeastern end of the Adriatic Sea, opposite the heel of Italy, Albania is a mountainous country which became a one-party communist state in 1944. It held multiparty elections in 1991, but economic collapse provoked uprisings in 1997, which were only stabilized by OSCE troops. Still poverty-stricken, Albania has been more stable since the return home of the ethnic Albanian refugees who flooded in from war-torn Kosovo in 1999.

CLIMATE

Mediterranean/ continental

WEATHER CHART

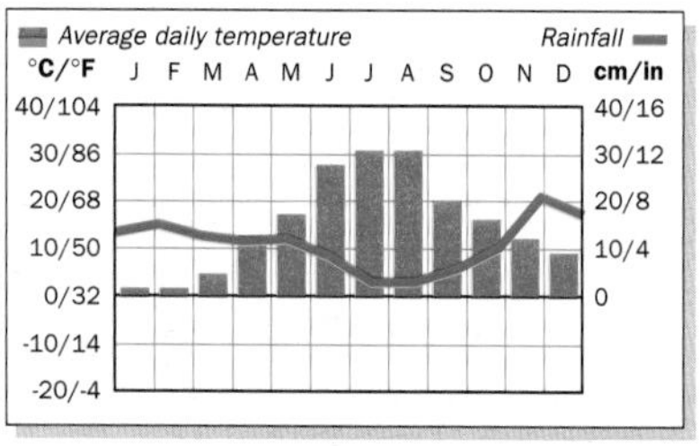
Average daily temperature
Rainfall
°C/°F
J F M A M J J A S O N D
cm/in
40/104
30/86
20/68
10/50
0/32
-10/14
-20/-4
40/16
30/12
20/8
10/4
0

The coastal climate is Mediterranean, but rather wet in winter. Heavy rain or snow falls in winter in the mountains.

TRANSPORTATION

Drive on right

Tiranë (Rinas)

25 ships 28,671 grt

THE TRANSPORTATION NETWORK

5400 km (3355 miles)	None
440 km (273 miles)	43 km (27 miles)

The transportation infrastructure is poor. The rail network is limited and roads are in disrepair. Private cars were first allowed in 1991. Buses and private vans are the main means of transportation.

TOURISM

Visitors : Population 1:79

39,000 visitors

Up 39% in 1999

MAIN TOURIST ARRIVALS

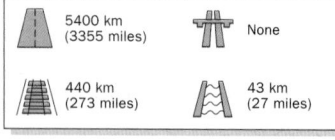

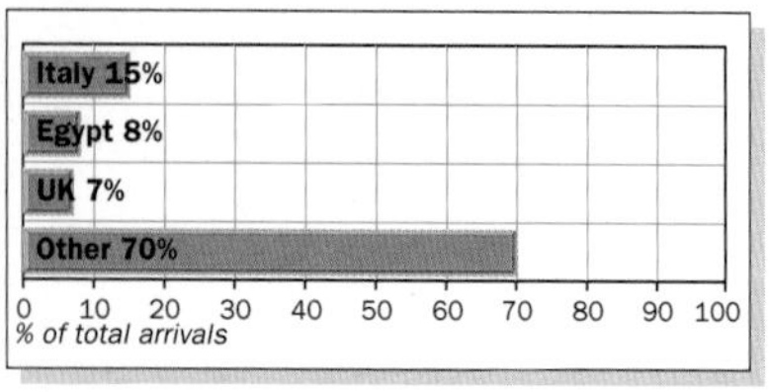
Italy 15%
Egypt 8%
UK 7%
Other 70%
0 10 20 30 40 50 60 70 80 90 100
% of total arrivals

Instability and then the war in Kosovo stalled plans to exploit Albania's scenic beauty. Facilities remain very limited, especially outside Tirana.

PEOPLE

Pop. density medium

Albanian, Greek

113/km² (293/mi²)

THE URBAN/RURAL POPULATION SPLIT

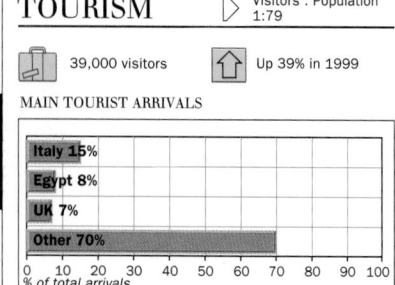

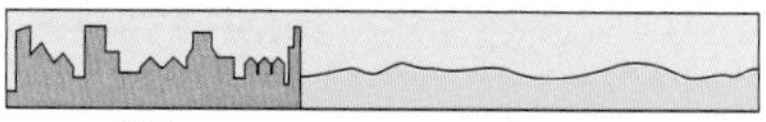
39%
61%

RELIGIOUS PERSUASION

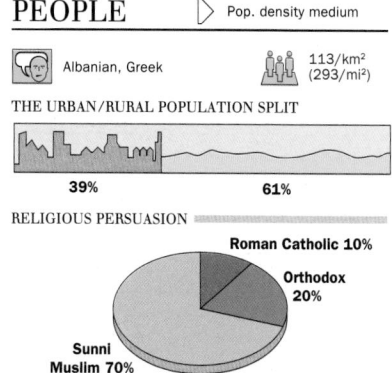

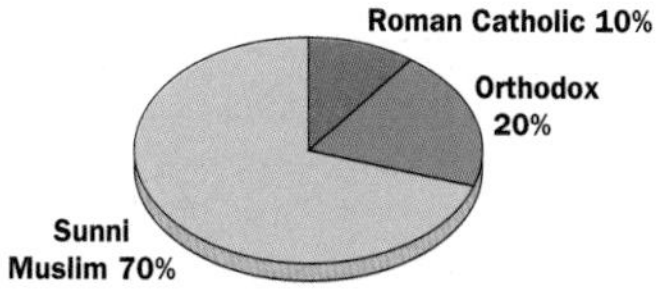
Roman Catholic 10%
Orthodox 20%
Sunni Muslim 70%

Official statistics admitted the existence of ethnic minorities in Albania only in 1989. The Greek minority strongly contests these statistics, which state that 98% of the population are Albanian. Located mainly in the south and identifying with Athens rather than Tirana, the Greeks claim to make up 10% of the population. They suffer considerable discrimination.

Under communism, Albania was the only officially atheist state in the world. Many Albanians maintained their beliefs in private – 70% are Muslim. Religious worship is now permitted and mosques have reopened. Society is traditional and male-dominated. The extended family remains strong.

In 1999 the country temporarily sheltered nearly half a million ethnic Albanian refugees fleeing "ethnic cleansing" in neighboring Kosovo.

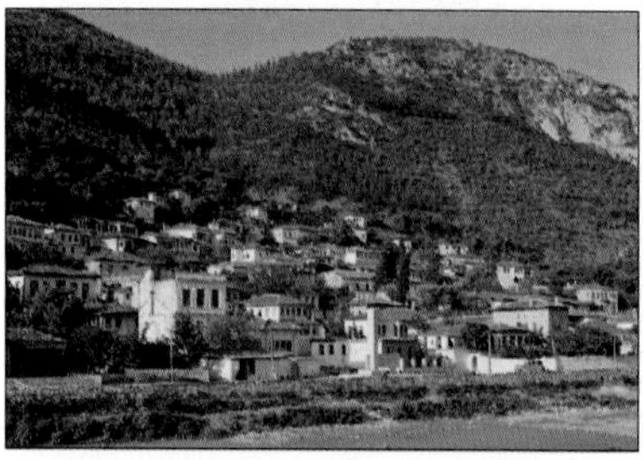

***City of a thousand windows.** Berat was preserved as a museum city while a new town was built further down the valley.*

POLITICS

Multiparty elections

2001/2005

President Rexhep Mejdani

AT THE LAST ELECTION

People's Assembly 140 seats

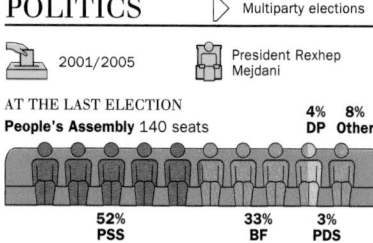

4% DP
8% Other
52% PSS
33% BF
3% PDS

PSS = Socialist Party of Albania **BF** = Union for Victory (led by the Democratic Party – **PD**) **DP** = Democrat Party (splinter from PD) **PDS** = Social Democratic Party

Albania was dominated for more than 40 years by communist ruler Enver Hoxha, who died in 1985. Then party reformers gradually gained the upper hand. An exodus of Albanians in 1991 finally persuaded the succeeding regime to call multiparty elections. The resulting center-right coalition failed, however, to create a Western-style liberal state.

Many people were ruined by investing in "pyramid" savings schemes which collapsed in 1997, prompting a rebellion in the south and forcing the government to resign. It was replaced by a new coalition led by the socialist PSS, victors in elections held that year. They won a further term in the mid-2001 elections, as socialist leader Ilir Meta claimed credit for restoring a measure of security and hope. The poll, though disputed by the PD, was praised internationally as the fairest yet.

WORLD AFFAIRS

Joined UN in 1955

WTO | CE | OSCE | OIC | PfP

Foreign policy in the late 1990s was dominated by the fate of Kosovo, the predominately ethnic Albanian region in neighboring Yugoslavia. Ethnic Albanian separatism also erupted in Macedonia in 2001, although Albania's own influence is small. Membership of NATO and the EU is a long-term goal. In 2001 an interim EU "stabilization and association agreement" was offered.

AID

Recipient

$480m (receipts)

Up 86% in 1999

Since 1991 the West has provided aid. Food aid was stepped up in 1997, when anarchy swept the country, and again in 1999 to help cope with the hundreds of thousands of refugees arriving from Kosovo, in neighboring Yugoslavia. EU aid now focuses on helping structural reforms.

DEFENSE

Compulsory military service

$140m

Up 37% in 1999

The armed forces reestablished officer ranks in 1991, and in 2000 were in the process of being reconstructed. Military service of 18 months is mandatory. The Kosovo crisis prompted Albania in 1999 to make its airspace available to NATO.

ECONOMICS

Inflation 44.7% p.a. (1990–1999)

$3.1bn

134.05–142.75 lekë

SCORE CARD

❑ WORLD GNP RANKING	131st
❑ GNP PER CAPITA	$930
❑ BALANCE OF PAYMENTS	$-155m
❑ INFLATION	0.4%
❑ UNEMPLOYMENT	14%

STRENGTHS

Oil and gas reserves. Significant economic growth achieved since 1997 collapse. Progress with privatization.

WEAKNESSES

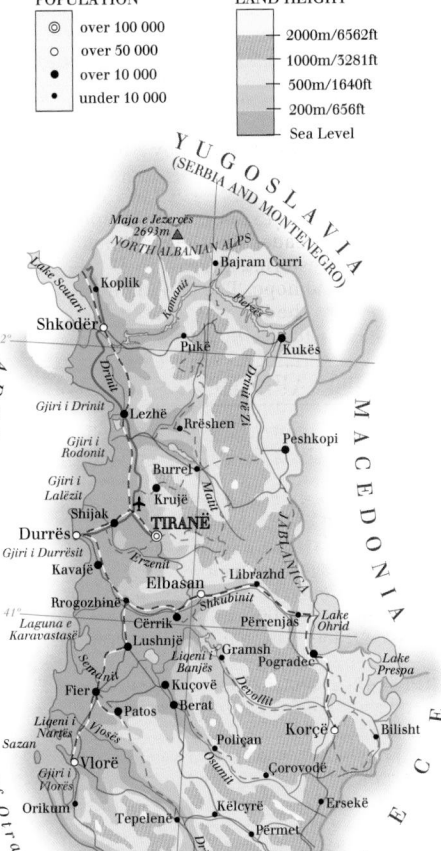

Rudimentary public services and energy, transportation, and water networks. Pyramid schemes wiped out savings.

EXPORTS

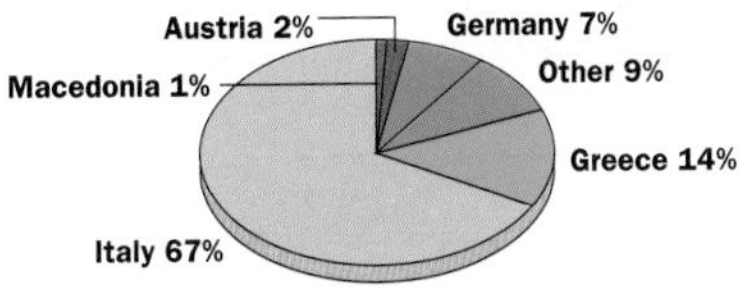
Austria 2%
Germany 7%
Macedonia 1%
Other 9%
Greece 14%
Italy 67%

IMPORTS

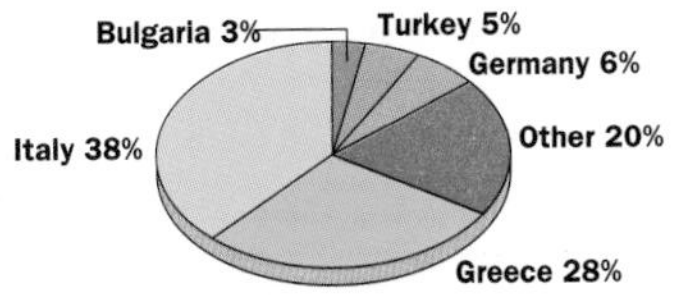
Bulgaria 3%
Turkey 5%
Germany 6%
Italy 38%
Other 20%
Greece 28%

ALBANIA

Total Land Area : 27 400 sq. km (10 579 sq. miles)

POPULATION
- over 100 000
- over 50 000
- over 10 000
- under 10 000

LAND HEIGHT
- 2000m/6562ft
- 1000m/3281ft
- 500m/1640ft
- 200m/656ft
- Sea Level

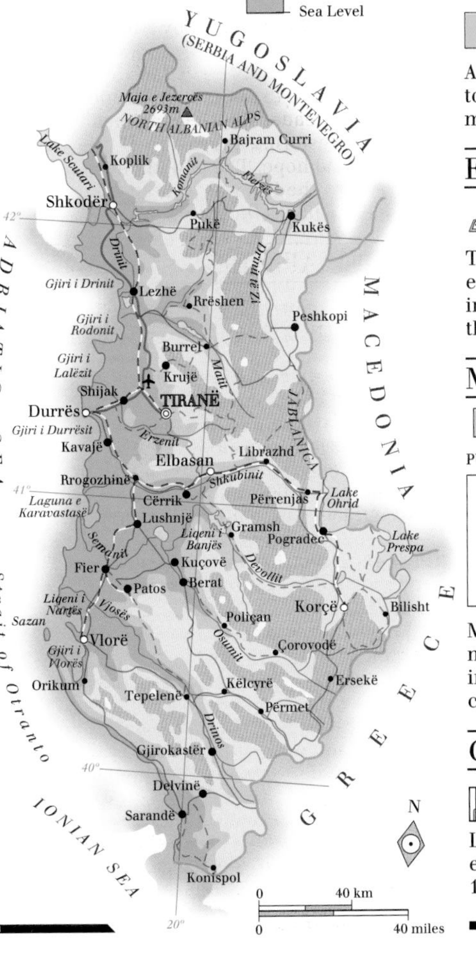
YUGOSLAVIA (SERBIA AND MONTENEGRO)
Maja e Jezercës 2693m
NORTH ALBANIAN ALPS
Bajram Curri
Lake Scutari
Koplik
Shkodër
Pukë
Kukës
Drinit
Gjiri i Drinit
Lezhë
Rrëshen
Peshkopi
Gjiri i Rodonit
Burrel
Gjiri i Lalëzit
Krujë
Shijak
TIRANË
Durrës
Gjiri i Durrësit
Kavajë
Elbasan
Librazhd
Rrogozhinë
Shkumbinit
Laguna e Karavastasë
Cërrik
Përrenjas
Lake Ohrid
Lushnjë
Gramsh
Pogradec
Lake Prespa
Fier
Kuçovë
Patos
Berat
Sazan
Vlorë
Poliçan
Korçë
Bilisht
Çorovodë
Orikum
Tepelenë
Këlcyrë
Ersekë
Përmet
Gjirokastër
Delvinë
Sarandë
Konispol
MACEDONIA
GREECE
ADRIATIC SEA
Strait of Otranto
IONIAN SEA
N
0 40 km
0 40 miles

RESOURCES

Electric power 1.9m kw

1110 tonnes

7218 b/d (reserves 181,828,800 bbl)

1.94m sheep, 1.12m goats, 4m chickens

Chromium, oil, coal, natural gas, copper, nickel

Albania needs huge capital investment to develop its minerals and to create a modern electricity supply system.

ENVIRONMENT

Sustainability rank: 78th

3% (0.8% partially protected)

0.5 tonnes per capita

Toxic waste pollution from communist-era heavy industry is among the worst in Europe. Years of shortages mean that most materials are recycled.

MEDIA

TV ownership medium

Daily newspaper circulation 37 per 1000 people

PUBLISHING AND BROADCAST MEDIA

There are 4 daily newspapers, including *Rilindja Demokratike*, *Zëri i Popullit*, and *Koha Jonë*, the best-selling newspaper

1 state-owned service, 75 private stations

1 state-owned service, 30 private stations

Media freedom has improved, but newspaper sales are in decline; the independent *Koha Jonë* has the largest circulation. Fewer dailies are party-run.

CRIME

Death penalty not used

1640 prisoners

Down 22% 1990–1998

Lawlessness is widespread; guns are easily available after the anarchy of 1997. Cannabis is widely grown.

CHRONOLOGY

Albania gained independence in 1912 for the first time in its history.

- ❑ **1924–1939** Ahmet Zogu, crowned King Zog in 1928, in power.
- ❑ **1939–1943** Occupied by Italy.
- ❑ **1944** Communist state; led by Enver Hoxha until 1985.
- ❑ **1991** First multiparty elections.
- ❑ **1997** Economic chaos as failure of pyramid schemes causes revolt.
- ❑ **1999** Refugee influx from Kosovo.
- ❑ **2001** PSS wins second term.

EDUCATION

School leaving age: 14

85%

34,257 students

The system is derived from the Soviet, Chinese, and Italian models. Albania has four universities.

HEALTH

Welfare state health benefits

1 per 714 people

Heart, respiratory, and digestive diseases, cancers

The health service is rudimentary, and dependent on Western aid for most drugs and medical supplies.

SPENDING

GDP/cap. increase

CONSUMPTION AND SPENDING

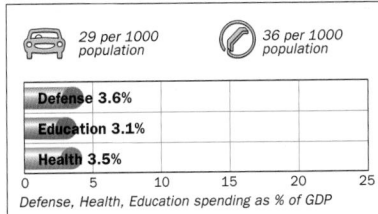

29 per 1000 population

36 per 1000 population

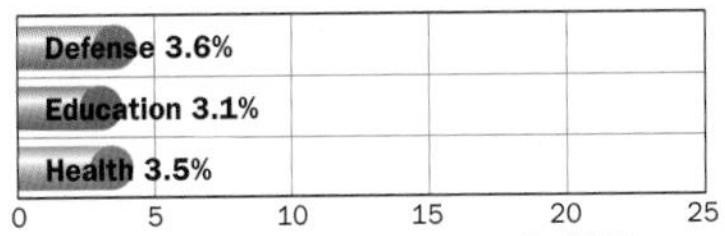
Defense 3.6%
Education 3.1%
Health 3.5%
0
5
10
15
20
25

Defense, Health, Education spending as % of GDP

Wealth is limited to a few private-sector entrepreneurs. Poverty is worst in northern rural areas but also acute in slum settlements around Tirana and other cities.

WORLD RANKING

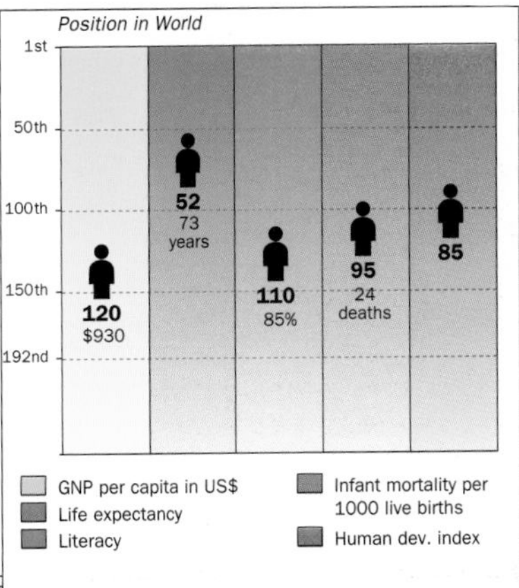
Position in World
1st
50th
100th
150th
192nd
120
$930
52
73 years
110
85%
95
24 deaths
85
GNP per capita in US$
Life expectancy
Literacy
Infant mortality per 1000 live births
Human dev. index

ALGERIA

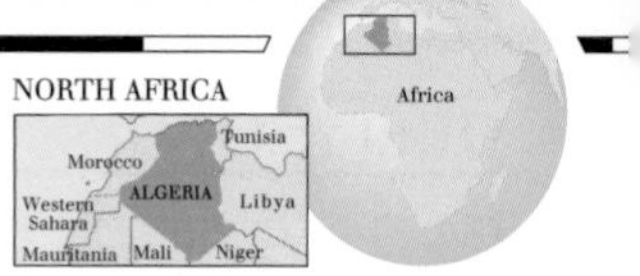
NORTH AFRICA
Africa
Morocco
Tunisia
Western Sahara
ALGERIA
Libya
Mauritania
Mali
Niger

OFFICIAL NAME: Democratic and Popular Republic of Algeria **CAPITAL:** Algiers
POPULATION: 31.5 million **CURRENCY:** Algerian dinar **OFFICIAL LANGUAGE:** Arabic

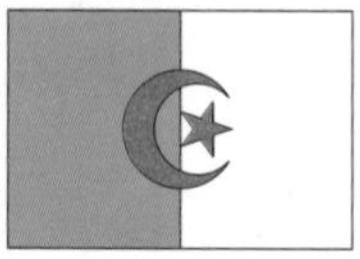

1962 | 1962 | Nov 1 | DZ | +1 | +213 | .dz

AFRICA'S SECOND-LARGEST COUNTRY, Algeria has borders with Morocco, Mauritania, Mali, Niger, Libya, and Tunisia. Algeria won independence from France in 1962. The military blocked Islamist militants from taking power after winning elections in 1991, setting up a new civilian regime and throughout the 1990s fighting a bloody terrorist conflict. Algeria has one of the youngest populations, and highest birthrates, in the region.

CLIMATE

Hot desert/ Mediterranean

WEATHER CHART

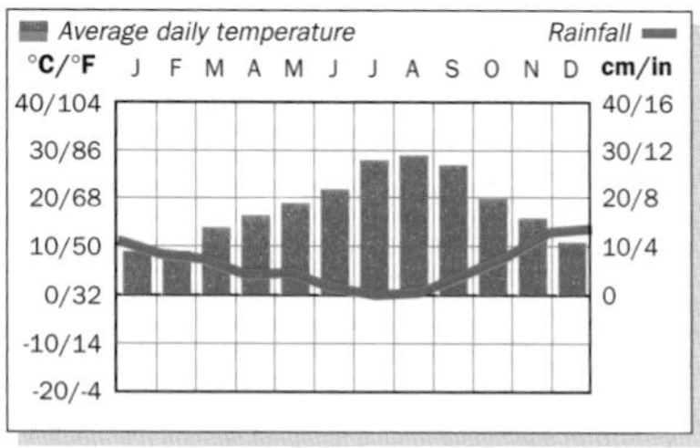
Average daily temperature
Rainfall
°C/°F
J F M A M J J A S O N D
cm/in
40/104
30/86
20/68
10/50
0/32
-10/14
-20/-4
40/16
30/12
20/8
10/4
0

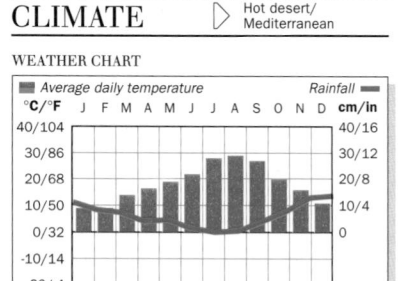

Coastal areas have a warm, temperate climate. The area to the south of the Atlas Mountains is hot desert.

TRANSPORTATION

Drive on right

Dar-el-Beida, Algiers 2.63m passengers

144 ships 964,186 grt

THE TRANSPORTATION NETWORK

71,656 km (44,525 miles)

640 km (398 miles)

3973 km (2469 miles)

None

There are five international airports. Rail is the quickest way to travel between the main urban centers.

TOURISM

Visitors : Population 1:37

859,000 visitors

Up 15% in 2000

MAIN TOURIST ARRIVALS

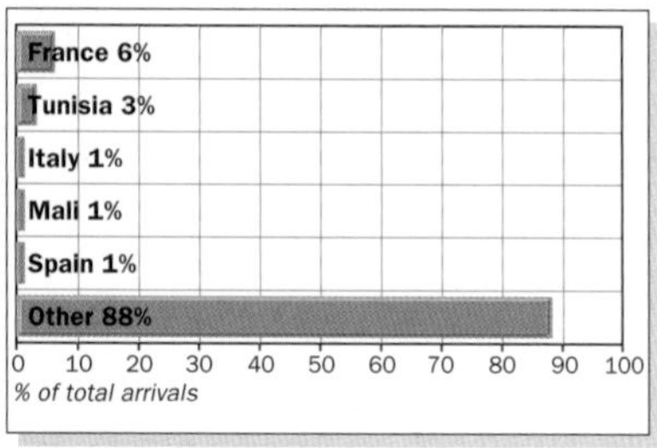
France 6%
Tunisia 3%
Italy 1%
Mali 1%
Spain 1%
Other 88%
0 10 20 30 40 50 60 70 80 90 100
% of total arrivals

The once-popular desert safaris are now rare. Tourists are a target for militant Islamist groups.

PEOPLE

Pop. density low

Arabic, Berber (Kabyle, Shawia, Tamashek), French

13/km² (34/mi²)

THE URBAN/RURAL POPULATION SPLIT

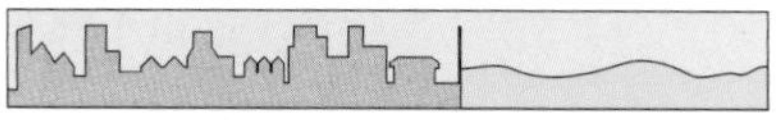
60%
40%

RELIGIOUS PERSUASION

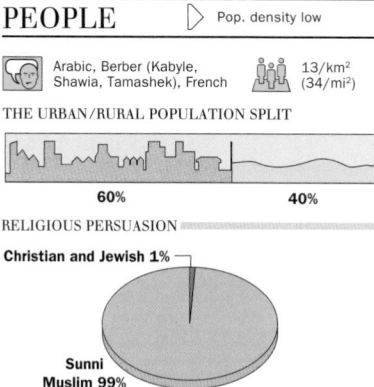

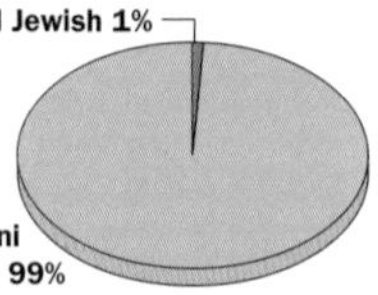
Christian and Jewish 1%
Sunni Muslim 99%

ETHNIC MAKEUP

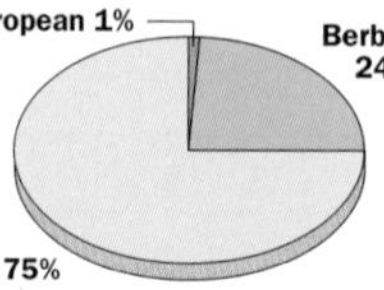
European 1%
Berber 24%
Arab 75%

Algeria's population is predominantly Arab, under 30 years of age, and urban; around a quarter are Berber. More than 85% speak Arabic, the official language, and 99% are Sunni Muslim. Of the million or so French who settled in Algeria before independence, only about 6000 remain. Most Berbers consider the mountainous Kabylia region their homeland. Demonstrations there have met with violent police crackdowns, particularly in the Berber Spring of 1980, and on its anniversary in 2001. As in the rest of north Africa, the mosque is an important provider of social and medical services.

POPULATION AGE BREAKDOWN

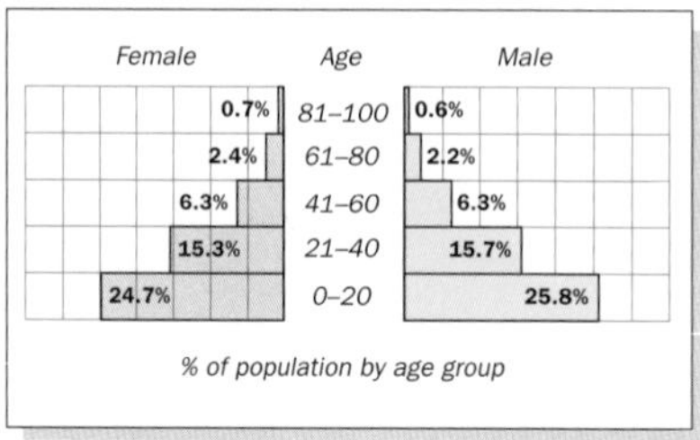
Female
Age
Male
0.7%
81–100
0.6%
2.4%
61–80
2.2%
6.3%
41–60
6.3%
15.3%
21–40
15.7%
24.7%
0–20
25.8%
% of population by age group

POLITICS

Multiparty elections

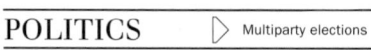

L. House 1997/2002
U. House 2000/2003

President Abdelaziz Bouteflika

AT THE LAST ELECTION

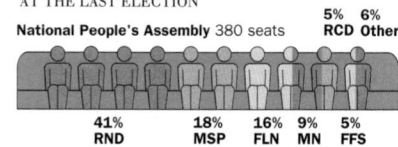

National People's Assembly 380 seats

5% RCD
6% Other
41% RND
18% MSP
16% FLN
9% MN
5% FFS

RND = National Democratic Rally **MSP** = Movement for a Peaceful Society **FLN** = National Liberation Front **MN** = en-Nahda Movement **FFS** = Front of Socialist Forces **RCD** = Rally for Culture and Democracy **App** = Appointed **Other** = Workers' Party, Progressive Republican Party, Union for Democracy and Liberty, Social Liberal Party, Independents

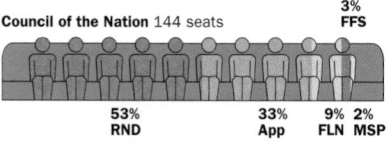

Council of the Nation 144 seats

3% FFS
53% RND
33% App
9% FLN
2% MSP

96 seats are elected, 48 are appointed by the president

Military rule was imposed in 1992. Elections were held in 1997, but Abdelaziz Bouteflika's presidential election victory in 1999 was marred by the withdrawal of all other candidates.

MAIN POLITICAL ISSUES

Islamic fundamentalism

Algeria has been scarred by appalling violence since 1992, as Islamist militants struggle to establish a theocracy. Its foremost proponent, the Islamic Salvation Front (FIS) won elections in 1991, but was prevented from taking power by a military clampdown, unleashing violence spearheaded by the extremist Armed Islamic Group (GIA).

The market economy

The FIS's strong showing in the 1991 polls was in part due to popular reaction against economic reforms first launched in 1988. After a brief suspension following the army takeover in 1992, the liberalization program was revived under pressure from the IMF and the World Bank.

PROFILE

Until 1988, Algeria was a Soviet-style regime. The aging ruling elite adopted privatization policies which were strongly opposed by Islamist militants, who were prevented from taking power by the army. Since 1992 tens of thousands of people have been killed in a terrorist campaign and ruthless state counter-terrorist action. Hopes for peace rose when Bouteflika became president in 1999, but some 3000 people, mainly civilians, were killed in 2000 alone.

WORLD AFFAIRS

Joined UN in 1962

AL | AMU | OIC | NAM | OPEC

Algeria's struggle for independence from France lasted from 1954 until 1962. Throughout the 1960s and 1970s, Algeria's success in rejecting a colonial power made it a champion for the developing world. It had a leading voice within the UN, the Arab League, and the Organization of African Unity. However, relations with the West remained essentially stable. Algeria was increasingly seen by the diplomatic community as a useful bridge between the West and Iran. In 1981, Algerian diplomats helped to secure the release of US hostages being held in Tehran. Algeria also attempted to act in a mediating role during the 1980–1988 Iran–Iraq War.

Algeria's influence overseas has diminished as the country has become increasingly unstable politically. A victory for the fundamentalist FIS in Algeria would greatly encourage Islamist militants in neighboring Morocco and Tunisia, and further undermine Egypt's embattled government.

France fears the spill-over of terrorism and has been shocked by the killings, especially those of seven French priests and of the French Roman Catholic bishop of Oran.

European governments are anxious to help stabilize the regime to avoid refugees seeking entry into France, Spain, and Italy.

***Saharan town,** showing the wide range of Algeria's scenery, from lush, irrigated gardens near water sources to barren sand dunes beyond. 80% of Algeria is desert.*

AID

Recipient

$89m (receipts)

Down 77% in 1999

As a major oil producer, Algeria receives relatively small quantities of aid. During the 1980s, its economy became dependent on eastern European manufactures, which were swapped for oil. The collapse of this trade in the 1990s led Algeria to turn to the West for loans. The growing weight of Western economic involvement in turn fortified the regime against criticism of its hardline methods against Islamic opponents. The IMF has provided loans to help Algeria meet payments on its debt, on condition that it move toward a market-oriented economy.

ALGERIA

Total Land Area : 2 381 740 sq. km (919 590 sq. miles)

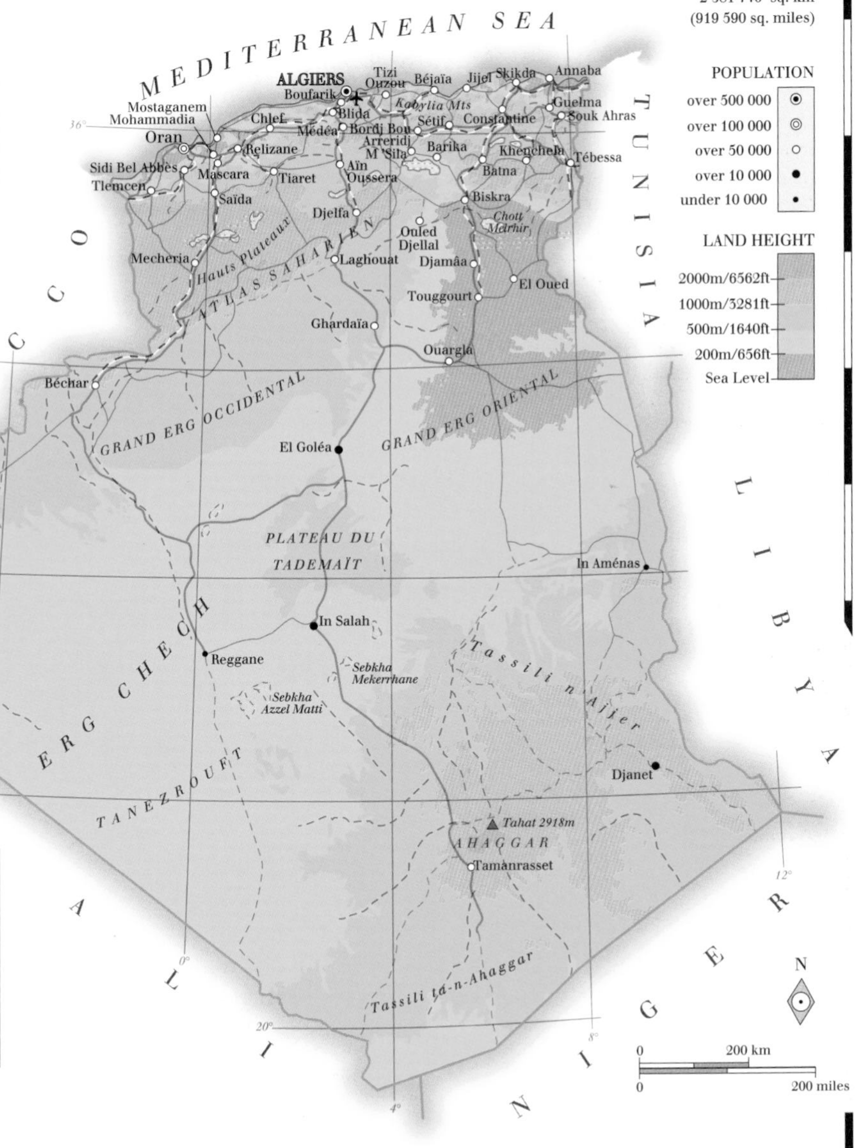
POPULATION
over 500 000
over 100 000
over 50 000
over 10 000
under 10 000
LAND HEIGHT
2000m/6562ft
1000m/3281ft
500m/1640ft
200m/656ft
Sea Level
MEDITERRANEAN SEA
ALGIERS
Boufarik
Tizi Ouzou
Béjaïa
Jijel
Skikda
Annaba
Guelma
Souk Ahras
Mostaganem
Mohammadia
Oran
Chlef
Blida
Médéa
Kabylia Mts
Sétif
Constantine
Bordj Bou Arreridj
M'Sila
Barika
Khenchela
Tébessa
Relizane
Sidi Bel Abbès
Tlemcen
Mascara
Tiaret
Aïn Oussera
Batna
Saïda
Djelfa
Biskra
Chott Melrhir
Ouled Djellal
Mecheria
Hauts Plateaux
ATLAS SAHARIEN
Laghouat
Djamâa
El Oued
Touggourt
Ghardaïa
Ouargla
Béchar
GRAND ERG OCCIDENTAL
GRAND ERG ORIENTAL
El Goléa
MOROCCO
TUNISIA
LIBYA
HAMADA DU DRA
PLATEAU DU TADEMAÏT
In Aménas
Tindouf
WESTERN SAHARA
MAURITANIA
In Salah
Reggane
ERG CHECH
Sebkha Mekerrhane
Sebkha Azzel Matti
Tassili n Ajjer
Djanet
TANEZROUFT
Tahat 2918m
AHAGGAR
Tamanrasset
Tassili ta-n-Ahaggar
MALI
NIGER
N
0
200 km
200 miles

***Abdelaziz Bouteflika,** who was elected president in 1999.*

***Abassi Madani,** leader of the Islamic Salvation Front (FIS).*

A

CHRONOLOGY

The conquest of Algeria by France began in 1830. By 1900, French settlers occupied most of the best land. In 1954, war was declared on the colonial administration by the National Liberation Front (FLN).

- **1962** Cease-fire agreed, followed by independence of Algerian republic.
- **1965** Military junta topples government of Ahmed Ben Bella. Revolutionary council set up.
- **1966** Judiciary "Algerianized." Tribunals try "economic crimes."
- **1971** Oil industry nationalized. President Boumedienne continues with land reform, a national health service, and "socialist" management.
- **1976** National Charter establishes a socialist state.
- **1980** Ben Bella released after 15 years' detention. Agreement with France whereby latter gives incentives for return home of 800,000 Algerian immigrants.
- **1981** Algeria helps to negotiate release of hostages from US embassy in Tehran, Iran.
- **1985** Two most popular Kabyle (Berber) singers given three-year jail sentences for opposing regime.
- **1987** Limited economic liberalization. Cooperation agreement with Soviet Union.
- **1988** Anti-FLN violence; state of emergency. Algeria negotiates release of Kuwaiti hostages from aircraft; Shi'a hijackers escape.
- **1989** Constitutional reforms diminish power of FLN. New political parties founded, including Islamic Salvation Front (FIS). AMU established.
- **1990** Political exiles permitted to return. FIS is victorious in municipal elections.
- **1991** FIS leaders Abassi Madani and Ali Belhadj arrested. FIS wins most seats in National People's Assembly.
- **1992** President Chadli overthrown by military. President Boudiaf assassinated. Madani and Belhadj given 12 years in jail.
- **1994** Political violence led by GIA.
- **1995** Democratic presidential elections won by Liamine Zéroual.
- **1996** Murders continue, notably of Catholic clergy and GIA leader.
- **1997** Madani released from jail but debarred from active politics.
- **1999** Abdelaziz Bouteflika elected president in poll boycotted by opposition candidates.
- **2000** Economic reforms announced.
- **2001** Fresh investment in oil and gas benefits economy. Civil strife continues; many thousands have now been killed. Resurgence of Berber protests.

DEFENSE

Compulsory military service

$3.1bn

Down 1% in 1999

The National Liberation Army (NLA), equipped with Russian weapons, is the dominant power in politics. There have been fears that parts of the army would forge an alliance with Muslim militants; the extreme rebel Armed Islamic Group, which has split from the FIS, is led by former army officers. However, the military are also suspected of taking part in reprisal killings of large numbers of Islamists.

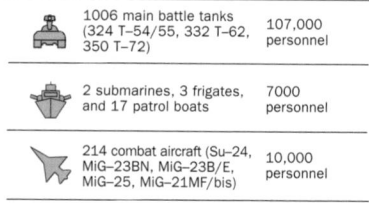

ALGERIAN ARMED FORCES

1006 main battle tanks (324 T–54/55, 332 T–62, 350 T–72)	107,000 personnel
2 submarines, 3 frigates, and 17 patrol boats	7000 personnel
214 combat aircraft (Su–24, MiG–23BN, MiG–23B/E, MiG–25, MiG–21MF/bis)	10,000 personnel
None	

ECONOMICS

Inflation 19.1% p.a. (1990–1999)

$46.5bn

68.16–73.42 dinars

SCORE CARD

World GNP Ranking	52nd
GNP per Capita	$1550
Balance of Payments	$2.4bn
Inflation	2.5%
Unemployment	30%

EXPORTS

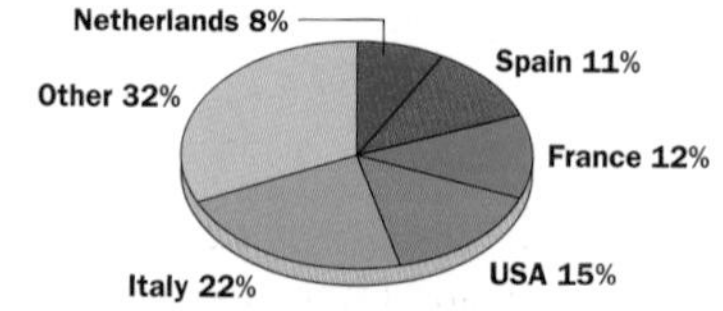
Netherlands 8%
Spain 11%
Other 32%
France 12%
USA 15%
Italy 22%

IMPORTS

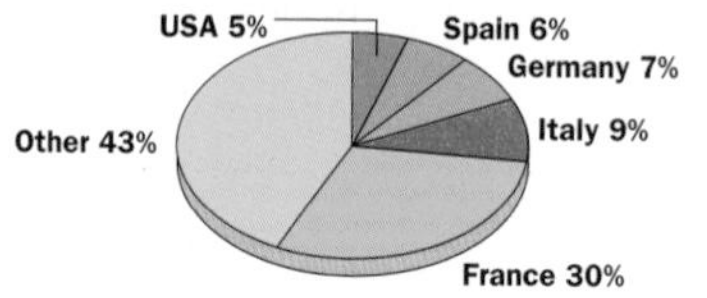
USA 5%
Spain 6%
Germany 7%
Other 43%
Italy 9%
France 30%

ECONOMIC PERFORMANCE INDICATOR

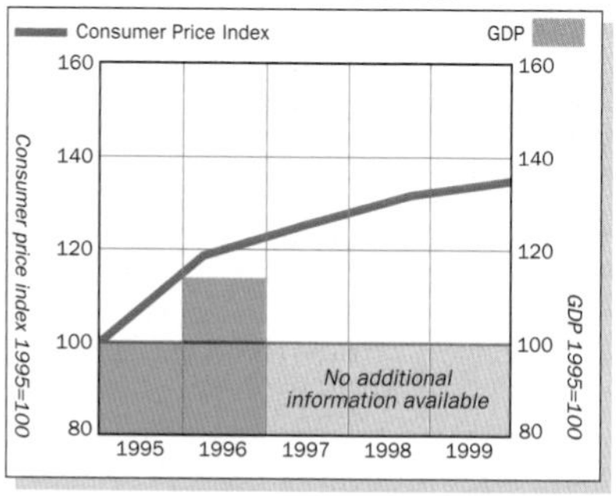
Consumer Price Index
GDP
160
140
120
100
80
Consumer price index 1995=100
GDP 1995=100
No additional information available
1995
1996
1997
1998
1999

Strengths

Oil and gas. Recent collaboration with Western oil companies should see improvements in productivity. Natural gas is supplied to Europe, with plans in hand for a third sub-sea pipeline to be built in 2001–2002.

Weaknesses

Political turmoil threatens many new projects and has led to an exodus of European and other expatriate workers important to the economy. Lack of skilled labor coupled with high unemployment. Limited agriculture. Shortages of basic foodstuffs. A thriving black market.

Profile

Under the pro-Soviet National Liberation Front, centralized socialist planning dominated the Algerian economy. In the late 1980s, the economic collapse of the Soviet Union led to a change in policy, and Algeria began moving toward a market economy. However, these reforms were frozen following the military takeover in 1992, although many have since been resumed under pressure from the IMF and the World Bank. The majority of the economy's most productive sectors remain under state control, although private investment is encouraged in the oil industry and, since early 2001, in telecommunications. A number of Western oil companies have signed exploration contracts with Algeria since it has accepted more competitive production-sharing agreements. However, Western investment levels are likely to remain small as long as the political situation is unstable.

ALGERIA : MAJOR BUSINESSES

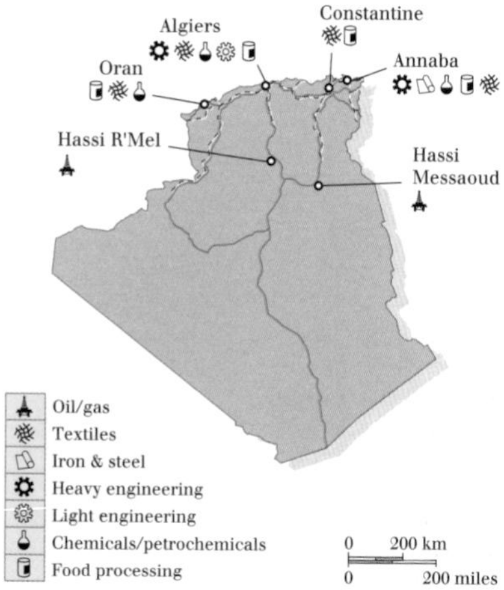
Algiers
Constantine
Oran
Annaba
Hassi R'Mel
Hassi Messaoud
Oil/gas
Textiles
Iron & steel
Heavy engineering
Light engineering
Chemicals/petrochemicals
Food processing
0 200 km
0 200 miles

RESOURCES

Electric power 6m kw

99,332 tonnes

1.6m b/d (reserves 9,200,000,000 bbl)

18.2m sheep, 3.4m goats, 1.7m cattle, 110m chickens

Oil, natural gas, iron, phosphates, lead, zinc, silver, copper, gold

ELECTRICITY GENERATION

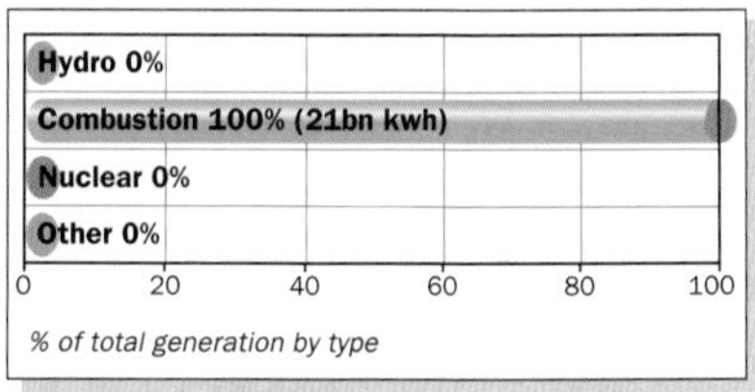
Hydro 0%
Combustion 100% (21bn kwh)
Nuclear 0%
Other 0%
0
20
40
60
80
100
% of total generation by type

Crude oil and natural gas, Algeria's main resources, have been produced since the 1950s. Algeria also has diverse minerals, including iron ore, zinc, silver, copper ore, lead, gold, and phosphates. In the 1960s and 1970s, Algeria sought to become a major manufacturer, with investments in building materials, refined products, and steel; none of these sectors is competitive on world markets. Agriculture employs one-quarter of Algeria's workforce, but its importance to the economy is diminishing. State forests cover some 2% of Algeria's land. Most are brushwood, but some areas include cork oak trees, Aleppo pine, evergreen oak, and cedar. Algeria has a large fishing fleet. Sardines, anchovies, tuna, and shellfish are the major species caught commercially.

ENVIRONMENT

Sustainability rank: 102nd

3% (0.1% partially protected)

3.4 tonnes per capita

ENVIRONMENTAL TREATIES

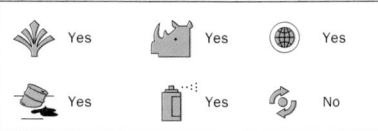

Yes	Yes	Yes
Yes	Yes	No

Since most of Algeria is desert or semidesert, over 90% of the population is forced to live on what remains – some 20% of the land. The desert is moving northward. Vegetation has been stripped for use as firewood and animal fodder, leaving fragile soils exposed which then require expensive specialist care to conserve them. Techniques for water purification are substandard, and rivers are being increasingly contaminated by untreated sewage, industrial effluent, and wastes from petroleum refining.

MEDIA

TV ownership medium

Daily newspaper circulation 38 per 1000 people

PUBLISHING AND BROADCAST MEDIA

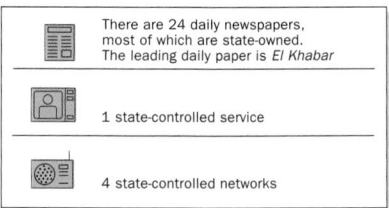

There are 24 daily newspapers, most of which are state-owned. The leading daily paper is *El Khabar*

1 state-controlled service

4 state-controlled networks

Newspapers, TV, and radio are state-controlled and permit no criticism of government actions. TV is broadcast in Arabic, French, and Kabyle (Berber), received by about two million sets. The five main daily newspapers have a combined circulation of 1.3 million. However, distribution is limited outside the major cities.

CRIME

Death penalty used

Algeria does not publish prison figures

Crime levels are rising sharply

CRIME RATES

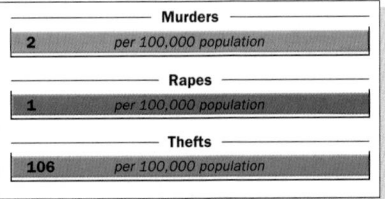

Murders
2 *per 100,000 population*

Rapes
1 *per 100,000 population*

Thefts
106 *per 100,000 population*

Thousands of people have been killed by radical Islamists since 1992, while human rights groups have accused pro-government death squads of brutal reprisal killings and of persecuting suspected Islamist militants.

EDUCATION

School leaving age: 15

68%

347,410 students

THE EDUCATION SYSTEM

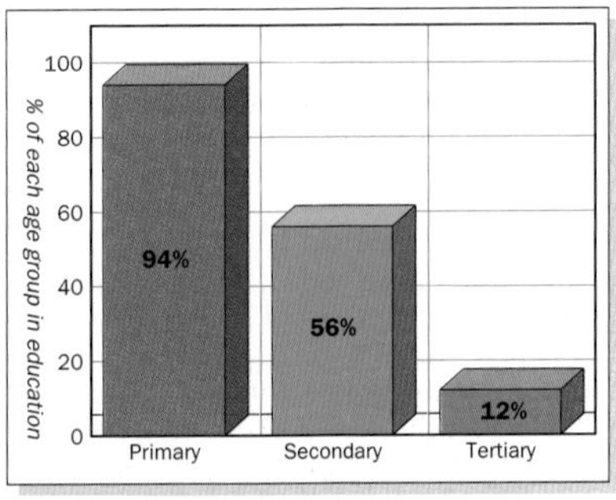
100
80
60
40
20
0
% of each age group in education
94%
56%
12%
Primary
Secondary
Tertiary

Over three-quarters of the school-age population receive a formal education, and the literacy rate is rising.

Since 1973, the curriculum has been Arabicized and the teaching of French has been restricted. New legislation in 1996 enforced the use of Arabic in public life, including for teaching.

Ten universities, seven polytechnics, and several technical colleges provide higher education.

ALGERIA : LAND USE

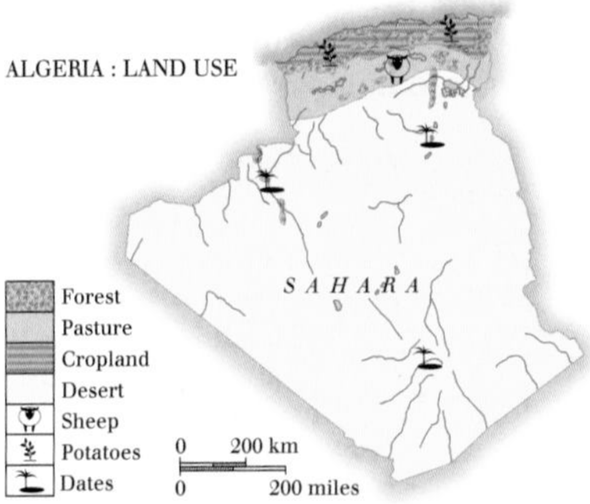
SAHARA
Forest
Pasture
Cropland
Desert
Sheep
Potatoes
Dates
0 200 km
0 200 miles

HEALTH

Welfare state health benefits

1 per 1000 people

Respiratory, heart, and cerebrovascular diseases, malaria

Since 1974 all Algerians have had the right to free health care. Primary health care is rudimentary outside main cities. Because the formal health care system is overburdened, many people turn to alternative forms of medicine. The infant mortality rate is well below the average for north Africa, and life expectancy is just above the regional average.

SPENDING

GDP/cap increase

CONSUMPTION AND SPENDING

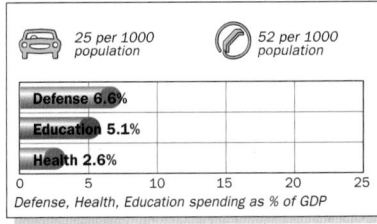

25 per 1000 population

52 per 1000 population

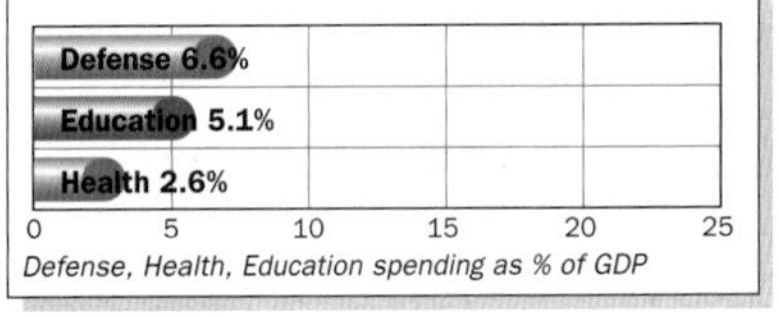
Defense 6.6%
Education 5.1%
Health 2.6%
0
5
10
15
20
25
Defense, Health, Education spending as % of GDP

There is great disparity in wealth between the political elite and the rest of the population. Those with connections in the military are the wealthiest group. Most Algerians have had to contend with soaring prices for basic necessities.

WORLD RANKING

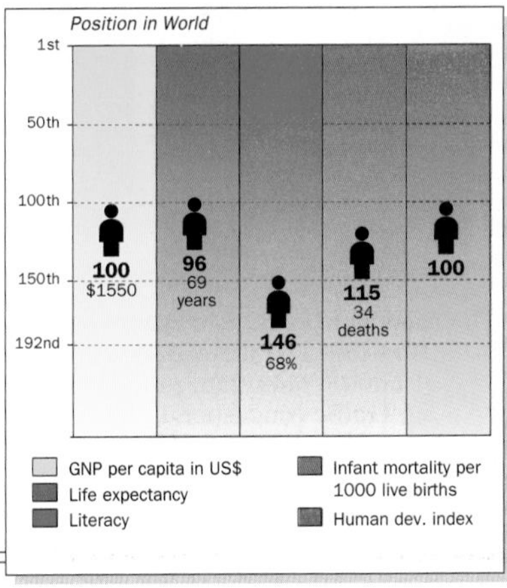
Position in World
1st
50th
100th
150th
192nd
100
$1550
96
69
years
146
68%
115
34
deaths
100
GNP per capita in US$
Life expectancy
Literacy
Infant mortality per 1000 live births
Human dev. index

ARGENTINA

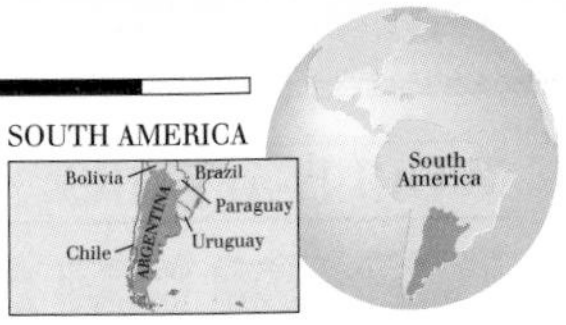
SOUTH AMERICA
Bolivia
Brazil
Paraguay
Uruguay
Chile
ARGENTINA
South America

OFFICIAL NAME: Argentine Republic **CAPITAL:** Buenos Aires
POPULATION: 37 million **CURRENCY:** Argentine peso **OFFICIAL LANGUAGE:** Spanish

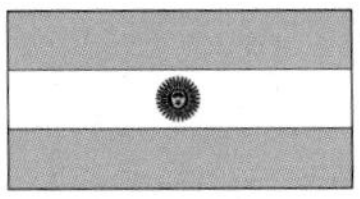

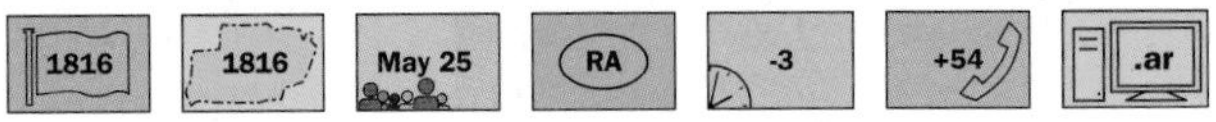
1816
1816
May 25
RA
-3
+54
.ar

OCCUPYING MOST OF THE southern half of South America, Argentina extends 3460 km (2150 miles) from Bolivia to Cape Horn. The Andes mountains in the west run north–south, forming a natural border with Chile. To the east they slope down to the fertile central pampas, the region known as Entre Ríos. Agriculture, especially beef, wheat, and fruit, and energy resources are Argentina's main sources of wealth. Politics in Argentina was characterized in the past by periods of military rule, but in 1983, Argentina returned to a system of multiparty democracy.

***Herding cattle** in the northeast, near Corrientes. Beef, Argentina's first source of wealth, remains a major export.*

CLIMATE

Mountain/steppe/ subtropical

WEATHER CHART

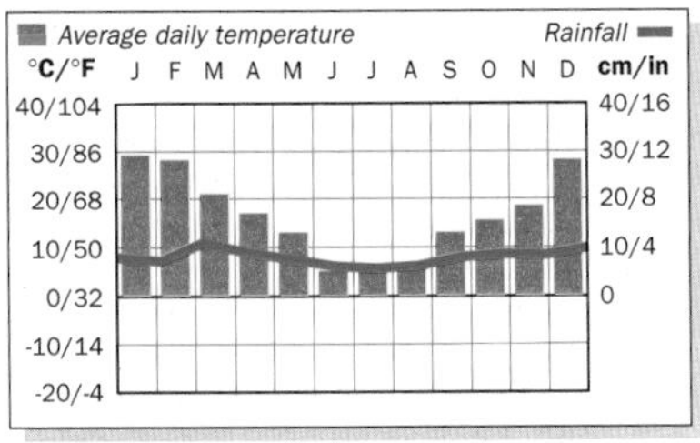
Average daily temperature
Rainfall
°C/°F
J F M A M J J A S O N D
cm/in
40/104
30/86
20/68
10/50
0/32
-10/14
-20/-4
40/16
30/12
20/8
10/4
0

The northeast is near-tropical. The Andes are semiarid in the north and snowy in the south. The western lowlands are desert, while the pampas have a mild climate with heavy summer rains.

TRANSPORTATION

Drive on right

Ezeiza International, Buenos Aires
7.3m passengers

501 ships
498,715 grt

THE TRANSPORTATION NETWORK

63,553 km (39,490 miles)	734 km (456 miles)
33,000 km (20,506 miles)	11,000 km (6835 miles)

Air travel is expensive, and inadequate connections between provinces frustrate business and tourism. The national airline, Aerolineas Argentinas, was privatized in 1990 but in 2000 was the object of a rescue plan; the 37 airports are privately operated. The privatized railroad, one of the largest in the world, is primarily used for freight, but Buenos Aires' subway and commuter lines have attracted strong investment and heavy use. Some 10,000 km (6000 miles) of roads are privatized, and tolls are among the highest worldwide. The six main terminals in the port of Buenos Aires are privately run. The government decreed in 2001 the implementation of a $20 billion national infrastructure program.

TOURISM

Visitors : Population 1:12

3m visitors

Up 3% in 2000

MAIN TOURIST ARRIVALS

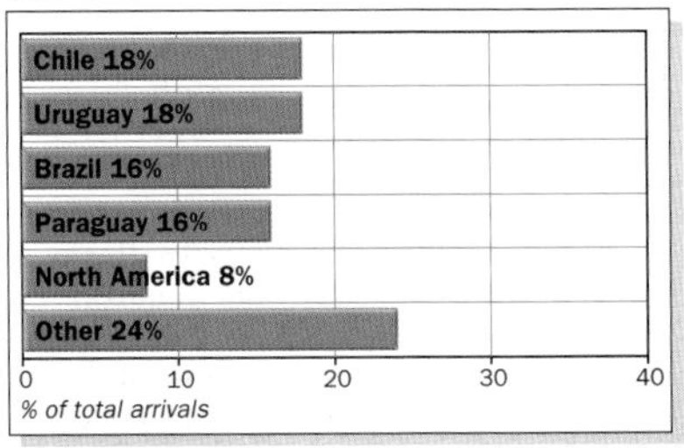
Chile 18%
Uruguay 18%
Brazil 16%
Paraguay 16%
North America 8%
Other 24%
0
10
20
30
40
% of total arrivals

Tourism has been undersold, and the government, working with business, has launched a massive international marketing campaign. Visitors, still mostly from neighboring countries, are attracted by Buenos Aires' rich city life, the fashionable Atlantic coastal resort of Mar del Plata, ski stations such as Bariloche and Las Leñas in the Andes, and wineries around Mendoza. Other major attractions are the Iguazú National Park, Antarctic cruises, and the renowned whale-watching hot-spot off Peninsula Valdés.

PEOPLE

Pop. density low

Spanish, Italian, Amerindian languages

14/km² (35/mi²)

THE URBAN/RURAL POPULATION SPLIT

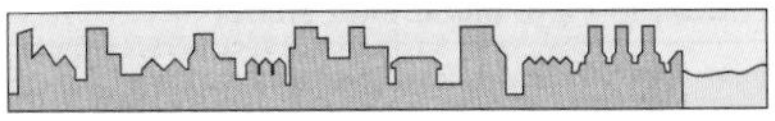
89%
11%

RELIGIOUS PERSUASION

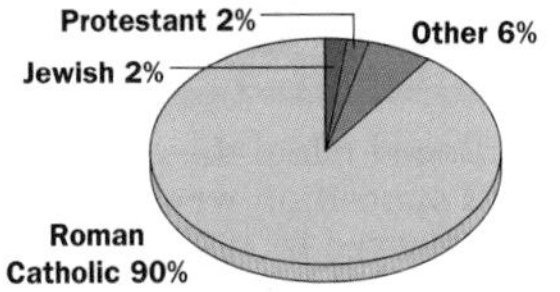
Protestant 2%
Other 6%
Jewish 2%
Roman Catholic 90%

ETHNIC MAKEUP

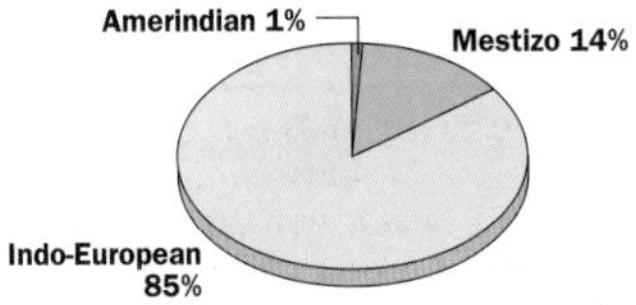
Amerindian 1%
Mestizo 14%
Indo-European 85%

Most Argentinians of European descent are from recent 20th-century migrations; over one-third are of Italian origin. Indigenous peoples are now a small minority, living mainly in Andean regions or in the *Gran Chaco*. Argentina also has communities of Lebanese, Syrians, Armenians, Japanese, and Koreans. In general, there is little ethnic tension.

POPULATION AGE BREAKDOWN

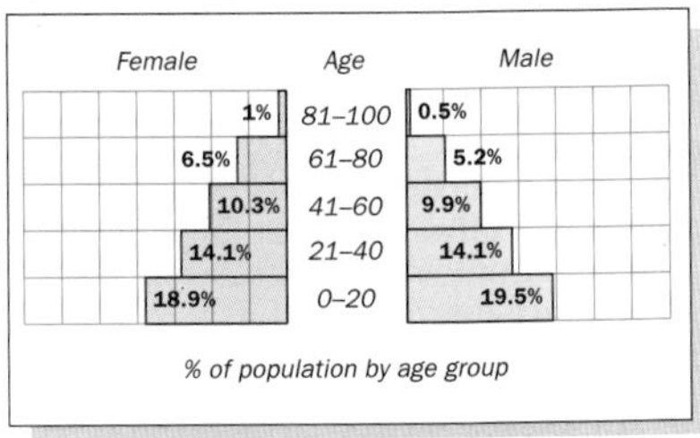
Female
Age
Male
1%
81–100
0.5%
6.5%
61–80
5.2%
10.3%
41–60
9.9%
14.1%
21–40
14.1%
18.9%
0–20
19.5%
% of population by age group

The vast majority of Argentinians are urban dwellers, with some 40% of the population living in Buenos Aires, one of the largest cities in Central and South America.

Catholicism and the extended family remain strong in Argentina. In addition, the family forms the basis of many successful businesses.

Women have a higher profile than in most Latin American states, and were enfranchised in 1947. Today, many enter the professions and rise to positions of influence in service businesses such as the media. The exception is party politics. Eva Perón, who inspired the musical *Evita*, did help to push women into a more active political role in the 1940s and 1950s, but this trend was reversed under military rule.

POLITICS

Multiparty elections

L. House 1999/2001
U. House 1998/2001

President Fernando de la Rua

Argentina is now a multiparty democracy; the president is head of state and government.

MAIN POLITICAL ISSUES

Economic growth

Austerity budgets, higher taxes, and reduced public spending earned the center-left de la Rua government few friends after taking office in late 1999. A major IMF-backed rescue package announced in 2001 – including the freezing of primary public expenditure until 2005, the part-privatization of pensions, and health insurance reform – was the government's bid to restore international and domestic confidence in the economy, the fundamentals of which, it argues, remain strong.

Convertibility

The system of convertibility, which keeps the peso pegged to the dollar, has been blamed for prolonging economic recession. Most Argentinians, however, haunted by hyperinflation in the 1980s and early 1990s, strongly support it.

Corruption

Alleged bribery of opposition senators over a key labor reform challenges the government's claim to be a clean alternative to the previous Menem administration.

Human rights

Amnesty laws conferring immunity on military officers accused of gross human rights abuses were ruled unconstitutional in early 2001, offering the prospect that more soldiers will face trial for crimes committed during the period of military rule (1976–1983).

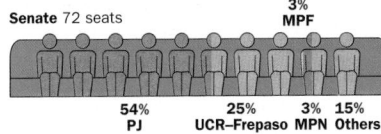

AT THE LAST ELECTION

Chamber of Deputies 257 seats

48%
UCR–Frepaso
39%
PJ
5%
AR
8%
Others

UCR–Frepaso = Radical Civic Union – National Solidarity Front Alliance **PJ** = Justicialist Party (Peronists) **AR** = Action for the Republic **MPF** = Fueguino Popular Movement **MPN** = Neuquino Popular Movement

Senate 72 seats

3%
MPF
54%
PJ
25%
UCR–Frepaso
3%
MPN
15%
Others

PROFILE

The Peronists dominated politics from the 1940s. The party, founded on mass working-class and left-wing intellectual support, was inimical to the military, and coups were staged in 1955, 1966, and 1976. President Menem won elections in 1989 on a populist platform but quickly steered the Peronists toward a right-wing free-market agenda. The UCR has tended to stay in opposition, only winning when the electorate wished to register a protest vote, as in 1983, but in 1999 it captured the presidency as part of a center-left alliance with FREPASO.

Fernando de la Rua, former mayor of Buenos Aires and president since 1999.

Domingo Cavallo, master of privatization, returned as economy minister in 2001.

BOLIVIA
PARAGUAY
GRAN CHACO
BRAZIL
URUGUAY
ANDES
PAMPAS
PATAGONIA
CHILE
ATLANTIC OCEAN
San Salvador de Jujuy
Salta
Tafí Viejo
San Miguel de Tucumán
Santiago del Estero
San Fernando del Valle de Catamarca
La Rioja
Formosa
Resistencia
Corrientes
Posadas
Reconquista
Goya
Mercedes
Córdoba
Cruz del Eje
San Juan
Rivadavia
Cerro Aconcagua 6959m
Villa Dolores
Las Heras
Mendoza
Villa Nueva
Godoy Cruz
San Luis
Luján
Río Cuarto
Rafaela
San Francisco
Santa Fe
Paraná
Concordia
Rosario
Gualeguaychú
Casilda
Villa Mercedes
Pergamino
San Nicolás de los Arroyos
Zárate
Campana
BUENOS AIRES
La Plata
Lomas de Zamora
Morón
Bragado
Junín
San Rafael
Santa Rosa
Olavarría
Azul
Tandil
Balcarce
Mar del Plata
Necochea
Tres Arroyos
Bahía Blanca
Neuquén
Viedma
Golfo San Matías
San Carlos de Bariloche
Esquel
Trelew
Rawson
Comodoro Rivadavia
Golfo San Jorge
Caleta Olivia
Lago Buenos Aires
Río Gallegos
Bahía Grande
Falkland Islands (UK)
Strait of Magellan
Tierra del Fuego
Ushuaia
Isla de los Estados
Cape Horn
Lago Mar Chiquita
Pilcomayo
Río de la Plata

ARGENTINA

Total Land Area : 2 736 690 sq. km (1 056 636 sq. miles)

POPULATION	LAND HEIGHT
over 1 000 000	4000m/13124ft
over 500 000	2000m/6562ft
over 100 000	1000m/3281ft
over 50 000	200m/656ft
over 10 000	Sea Level

0 200 km
0 200 miles

WORLD AFFAIRS

Joined UN in 1945

SELA | Mercsr | OAS | RG | G15

Argentina takes a pro-Western stance and has deployed its armed forces in a series of UN actions. Solid relations with the USA have not prevented successive governments resisting both US pressure for an open-skies agreement, which Argentine airlines fear would destroy them, and demands for royalty payments if domestic firms manufacture foreign-patented drugs.

Friction with Brazil over trade rules complicates Argentina's membership of MERCOSUR, which also links it with Uruguay and Paraguay. It wants MERCOSUR to be strengthened, and widened to include Chile as a full member.

The normalizing of relations with the UK in 1998 sidelined Argentina's claim to sovereignty over the nearby Falklands Islands (known locally as Las Malvinas), the focus of the 1982 war between the two countries.

In 1996 a criminal investigation was opened in Spain into the torture, disappearance, and killing of several hundred Spanish citizens in Argentina during the 1976–1983 period of military rule, and by late 1999 a reported 192 Argentines had been indicted.

A

AID

Recipient

$91m (receipts)

Up 18% in 1999

A $39.7 billion "financial shield" rescue package was agreed in 2001 with the IMF, the World Bank, the IDB, Spain, and domestic banks and pension funds.

CHRONOLOGY

The Spanish first established settlements in the Andean foothills in 1543. The indigenous Amerindians, who had stopped any Inca advance into their territory, also prevented the Spaniards from settling in the east until the 1590s.

- **1816** United Provinces of Río de la Plata declare independence; 70 years of civil war follow.
- **1835–1852** Dictatorship of Juan Manuel Rosas.
- **1853** Federal system set up.
- **1857** Europeans start settling the pampas; six million by 1930.
- **1877** First refrigerated ship starts frozen beef trade to Europe.
- **1878–1883** War against pampas Amerindians (almost exterminated).
- **1916** Hipólito Yrigoyen wins first democratic presidential elections.
- **1930** Military coup.
- **1943** New military coup. General Juan Perón organizes trade unions.
- **1946** Perón elected president, with military and labor backing.
- **1952** Eva Perón, charismatic wife of Juan Perón, dies of leukemia.
- **1955** Military coup ousts Perón. Inflation, strikes, unemployment.
- **1973** Perón returns from exile in Madrid and is reelected president.
- **1974** Perón dies; succeeded by his third wife "Isabelita," who is unable to exercise control.
- **1976** Military junta seizes power. Political parties are banned. Brutal repression during "dirty war" sees "disappearance" of over 10,000 "left-wing suspects."
- **1981** General Galtieri president.
- **1982** Galtieri orders invasion of Falkland Islands. UK retakes them.
- **1983** Pro-human rights candidate Raúl Alfonsín (UCR) win presidency in free multiparty elections. Hyperinflation.
- **1989–1992** Carlos Menem (Peronist) president; inflation down to 18%.
- **1995** Economy enters recession.
- **1998–1999** Argentina weathers financial crisis in Brazil.
- **1999** Fernando de la Rua elected president, leading center-left UCR–FREPASO alliance.
- **2000** Vice President and FREPASO leader, Carlos "Chaco" Alvarez, resigns over Senate bribes-for-votes scandal.

DEFENSE

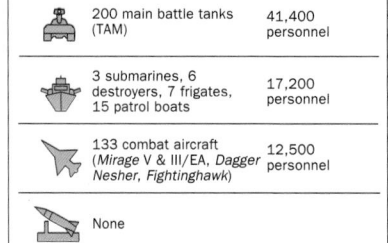

No compulsory military service

$5.4bn

Up 1% in 1999

The end of dictatorship led to trials and prison for the top brass, but subsequent immunity laws were meant to placate the military and close the chapter on the "dirty war" (1975–1983), during which some 15,000 to 30,000 were killed or "disappeared." The military made public admissions of guilt in 1995. A 2001 ruling in a kidnap and murder case, however, said that such immunity was unconstitutional and cleared the way for the trial of many more military personnel for human rights crimes. The armed forces now see themselves as modernized, participating in UN peacekeeping and cooperating on defense within the framework of the MERCOSUR trade bloc (Brazil, Argentina, Uruguay, and Paraguay). Argentina is a signatory of the Nuclear Non-Proliferation Treaty.

ARGENTINIAN ARMED FORCES

200 main battle tanks (TAM)	41,400 personnel
3 submarines, 6 destroyers, 7 frigates, 15 patrol boats	17,200 personnel
133 combat aircraft (*Mirage* V & III/EA, *Dagger Nesher, Fightinghawk*)	12,500 personnel
None	

ECONOMICS

Inflation 6.2% p.a. (1990–1999)

$276bn

0.9999–0.9984 Argentine pesos

SCORE CARD

- World GNP Ranking 18th
- GNP per Capita $7550
- Balance of Payments ....$-12.2bn
- Inflation ....–1.2%
- Unemployment 14%

EXPORTS

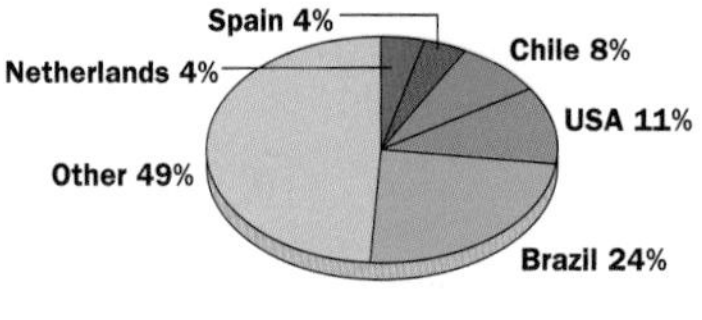

Spain 4%
Netherlands 4%
Chile 8%
USA 11%
Other 49%
Brazil 24%

IMPORTS

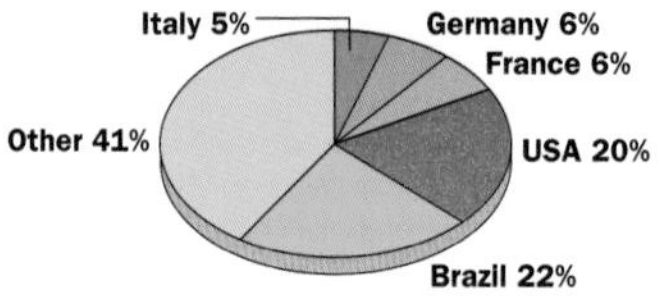

Italy 5%
Germany 6%
France 6%
Other 41%
USA 20%
Brazil 22%

Strengths

Rich and varied agricultural base. Powerful agribusiness (mainly beef, soya, wheat, fruit, and wine) and wealth of energy resources. Net exporter of oil. Currency stability: system backed by foreign exchange, peso pegged to dollar and euro. Low inflation.

Weaknesses

Vulnerability to external shocks and downturns in Brazil (largest export market). Investors scared by changes in assessment of country risk in emerging markets. Heavy debts, public and private, to refinance. Few banks extend loans. Global fluctuations in prices of vital non-oil commodities. High unemployment and risk of unrest. Endemic tax evasion. Subsidies and trade barriers bar agricultural produce from USA and EU.

ECONOMIC PERFORMANCE INDICATOR

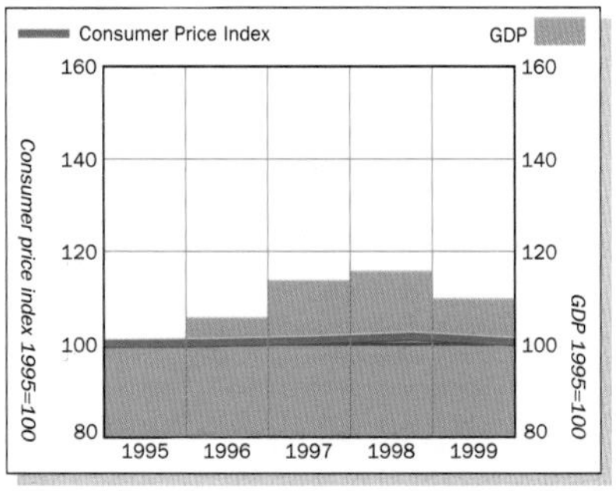

Consumer Price Index
GDP
160
140
120
100
80
Consumer price index 1995=100
GDP 1995=100
1995
1996
1997
1998
1999

Profile

The "miracle" recovery of the 1990s was based on stabilizing the peso (by pegging it to the US dollar) and on a combination of austerity and neoliberal reforms accompanied by privatization. Argentina rode out the Mexican crisis of 1995, but was hit by damage to foreign investor confidence and a shrinking Brazilian market in 1998–1999. Regional recession brought economic crisis by 2001, blamed by some on an overvalued peso.

ARGENTINA : MAJOR BUSINESSES

Salta
San Salvador de Jujuy
Corrientes
Córdoba
Santa Fé
Mendoza
Buenos Aires
Viedma
Wine
Textiles
Agribusiness
Metals
Oranges
Tobacco
Vehicle assembly
Light engineering
Cattle/Meat packing
Heavy engineering
0 400 km
0 400 miles
* significant multinational ownership

RESOURCES

Electric power 21.8m kw

1.35m tonnes

820,000 b/d (reserves 3,100,000,000 bbl)

55m cattle, 14m sheep, 3.4m goats, 60m chickens

Oil, natural gas, coal, iron, zinc, lead, uranium, tin, silver, copper, gold

ELECTRICITY GENERATION

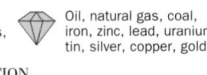

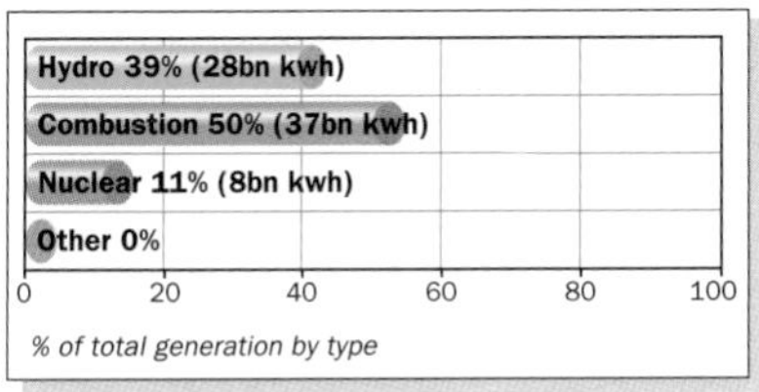
Hydro 39% (28bn kwh)
Combustion 50% (37bn kwh)
Nuclear 11% (8bn kwh)
Other 0%
0
20
40
60
80
100
% of total generation by type

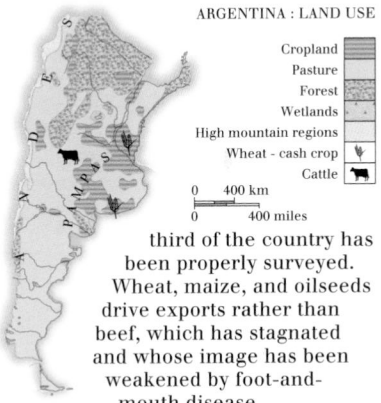

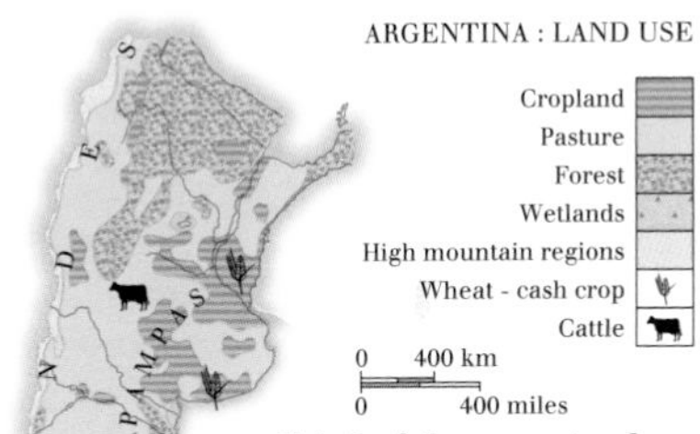
ARGENTINA : LAND USE
Cropland
Pasture
Forest
Wetlands
High mountain regions
Wheat - cash crop
Cattle
0 400 km
0 400 miles
PAMPAS
ANDES

Known oil and gas reserves are still underexploited, and copper and gold mining are just taking off; only one-third of the country has been properly surveyed. Wheat, maize, and oilseeds drive exports rather than beef, which has stagnated and whose image has been weakened by foot-and-mouth disease.

ENVIRONMENT

Sustainability rank: 19th

2% (2% partially protected)

3.9 tonnes per capita

ENVIRONMENTAL TREATIES

Yes Yes Yes

Yes Yes Yes

Environmental protection has low governmental priority. Legislation is weak and largely ignored by states which retain a good deal of autonomy. Political parties typically shy away from the level of public spending needed to tackle major environmental problems, and a corrupt judiciary had meant poor enforcement of existing laws. Key problems are hazardous waste, poor urban water and air quality and inadequate sewers, pesticide contamination due to agribusiness, deforestation, and illegal hunting.

MEDIA

TV ownership high

Daily newspaper circulation 123 per 1000 people

PUBLISHING AND BROADCAST MEDIA

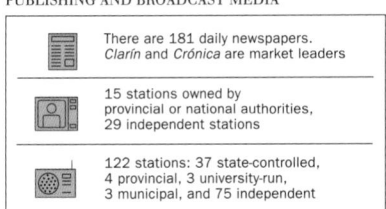

There are 181 daily newspapers. *Clarín* and *Crónica* are market leaders

15 stations owned by provincial or national authorities, 29 independent stations

122 stations: 37 state-controlled, 4 provincial, 3 university-run, 3 municipal, and 75 independent

Many journalists were murdered by the military in the 1970s, but the press was liberated under the UCR (1983–1989) and harries governments, especially on corruption. Investigative journalists, however, still face intimidation. Argentina boasts some 325,000 Internet domains, globally the fifth-highest.

CRIME

Death penalty not used

27,720 prisoners

Down 87% 1996–1998

CRIME RATES

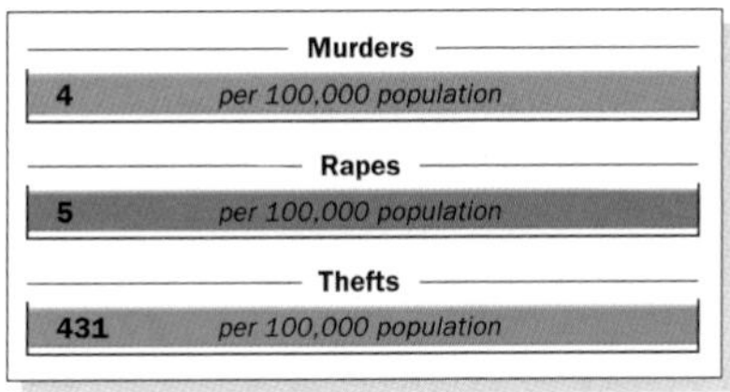
Murders
4 per 100,000 population
Rapes
5 per 100,000 population
Thefts
431 per 100,000 population

Half of Buenos Aires households own a gun for fear of violent crime. Law enforcement in the interior is weak. The judiciary and the police command little respect. Overcrowded prisons lead to frequent riots and criminal cases can take over a year to reach court.

EDUCATION

School leaving age: 14

97%

1.07m students

THE EDUCATION SYSTEM

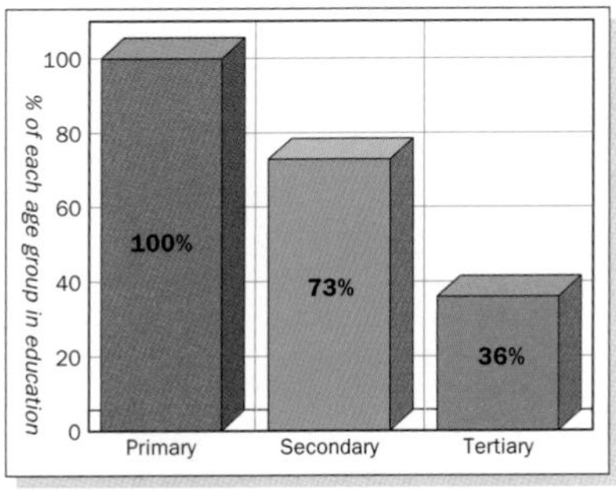
100
80
60
40
20
0
% of each age group in education
100%
73%
36%
Primary
Secondary
Tertiary

Public schooling is free and compulsory to the age of 14. Huge numbers of poor students drop out of the education system near or after this age, and 60–70% of middle-class students drop out by the close of five-year courses at cash-strapped free state universities. A fifth of government spending on education finds its way to private institutions.

HEALTH

Welfare state health benefits

1 per 370 people

Heart diseases, cancers, accidents

Buenos Aires has 33 hospitals, but free state provision suffers from underfunding, poorly paid staff, and long queues. Government-sponsored vaccination, mother-and-child schemes, feeding programs, and rural health projects barely tackle problems in the poorest provinces such as malnutrition, lack of decent water and sewers, and threadbare medical cover. A health care deregulation bill decreed in 2001 aims to dismantle trade unions' monopoly of health insurance schemes.

SPENDING

GDP/cap. increase

CONSUMPTION AND SPENDING

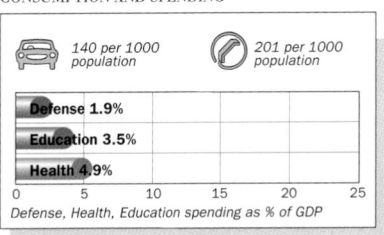

140 per 1000 population

201 per 1000 population

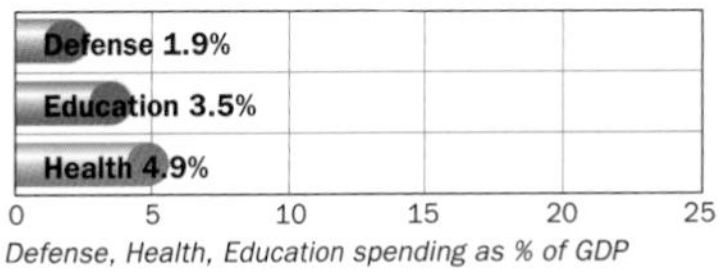
Defense 1.9%
Education 3.5%
Health 4.9%
0
5
10
15
20
25
Defense, Health, Education spending as % of GDP

A wealthy elite travels in private jets to their *estancias* (country estates), and vacation in Europe and the USA. Middle-income groups, squeezed after years of free-market reforms, complain of a lack of a "feel-good" factor. Some 40% of workers are in the black economy typified by temporary and low-paid jobs; in the provinces many rely on government work schemes. Unemployment remains in double digits. The World Bank in 2000 stated that 29% of the population, including 43% of children, live in poverty, some 7% of these too poor to buy basic necessities. Official figures for Buenos Aires and surrounding province show that in 2000 the richest tenth of people took 36% of total income, and the poorest three-tenths 8.2%.

WORLD RANKING

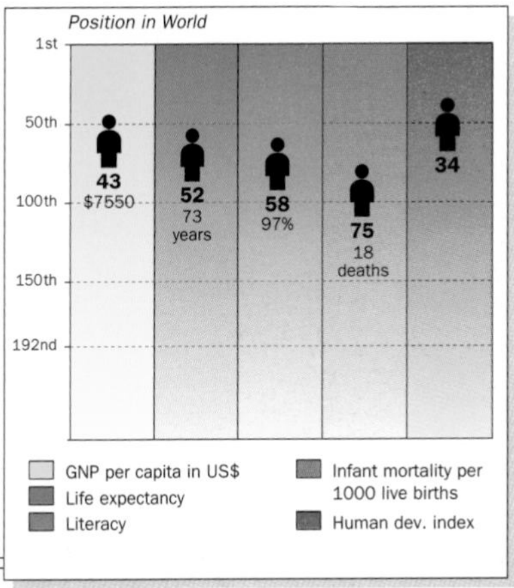
Position in World
1st
50th
100th
150th
192nd
43
$7550
52
73 years
58
97%
75
18 deaths
34
GNP per capita in US$
Life expectancy
Literacy
Infant mortality per 1000 live births
Human dev. index

A

ARMENIA

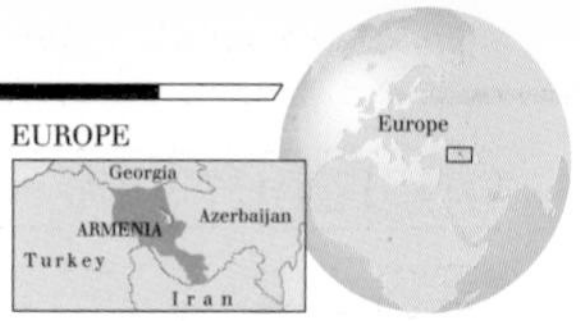
Europe
EUROPE
Georgia
ARMENIA
Azerbaijan
Turkey
Iran

OFFICIAL NAME: Republic of Armenia **CAPITAL:** Yerevan
POPULATION: 3.5 million **CURRENCY:** Dram **OFFICIAL LANGUAGE:** Armenian

1991 | 1991 | Sept 21 | ARM | +4 | +374 | .am

LANDLOCKED IN THE Lesser Caucasus Mountains, Armenia is the smallest of the former Soviet Union's republics and was the first to adopt Christianity as its state religion. It is bordered by Muslim states to the south, east, and west. Keen to develop links with the CIS, Armenia has kept to a path of radical economic reform, including privatization. The confrontation with Azerbaijan over the enclave of Nagorno Karabakh has dominated national life since 1988.

Landscape near Yerevan. Armenia's very dry climate results in expanses of semi-desert. Its famous vineyards flourish in sheltered areas.

CLIMATE

Mountain

WEATHER CHART

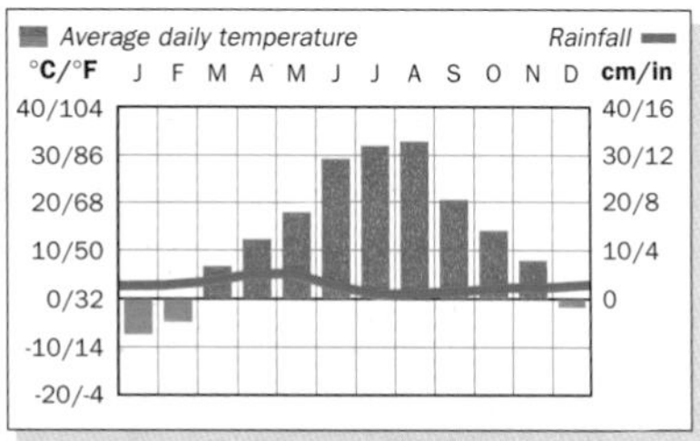
Average daily temperature
Rainfall
°C/°F
J F M A M J J A S O N D
cm/in
40/104
30/86
20/68
10/50
0/32
-10/14
-20/4
40/16
30/12
20/8
10/4
0

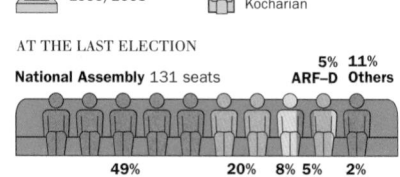

Armenia has a continental climate, with little rainfall in the lowlands. Winters can be very cold.

TRANSPORTATION

Drive on right

Yerevan International — Has no fleet

THE TRANSPORTATION NETWORK

15,998 km (9941 miles) — 7567 km (4702 miles)

796 km (495 miles) — None

Public transportation was badly hit by a war-induced fuel crisis. Road and rail links with Georgia, connecting with the main east–west corridor, need upgrading.

TOURISM

Visitors : Population 1:117

30,000 visitors — Down 27% in 2000

MAIN TOURIST ARRIVALS

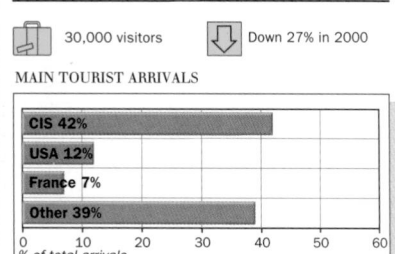

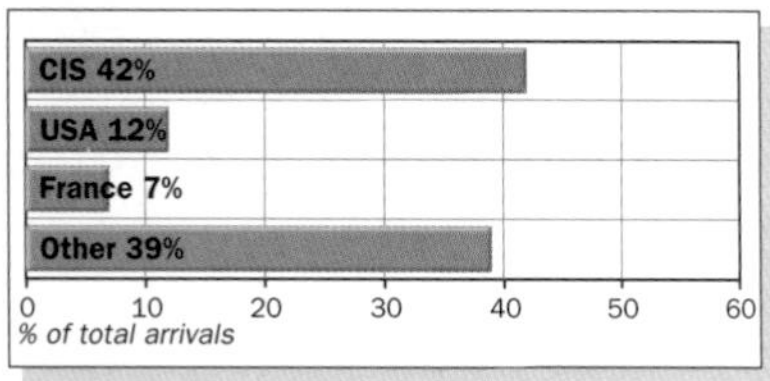
CIS 42%
USA 12%
France 7%
Other 39%
0
10
20
30
40
50
60
% of total arrivals

The 1700th anniversary of Armenian Christianity in 2001 boosted the war-damaged tourist industry. Most visitors are diaspora Armenians.

PEOPLE

Pop. density medium

Armenian, Russian — 117/km² (304/mi²)

THE URBAN/RURAL POPULATION SPLIT

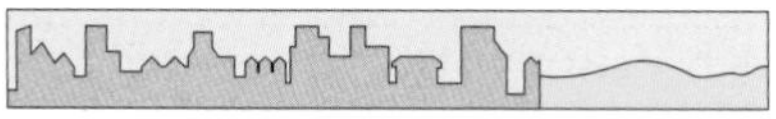
70%
30%

ETHNIC MAKEUP

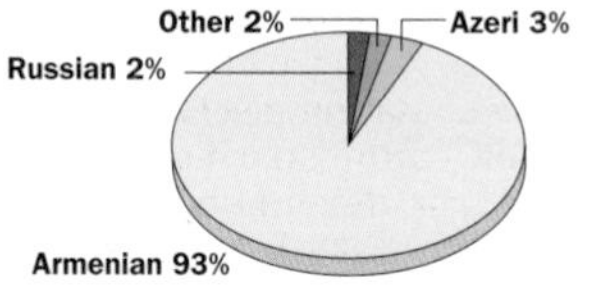
Other 2%
Azeri 3%
Russian 2%
Armenian 93%

Minority nationalities are well integrated in Armenia. There are strong contacts with the many Armenian emigrants, numbering nine million in the USA, France, and Syria.

Conflict with Azerbaijan has forced 350,000 Armenians in Azerbaijan to return to Armenia and 190,000 Azeris in Armenia to return to Azerbaijan.

POLITICS

Multiparty elections

1999/2003 — President Robert Kocharian

AT THE LAST ELECTION

National Assembly 131 seats

5% ARF–D
11% Others
49% UB
20% Ind
8% CP
5% LUB
2% Vacant

UB = Unity Bloc **Ind** = Independents
CP = Communist Party **LUB** = Law and Unity Bloc
ARF–D = Armenian Revolutionary Federation–Dashnaktsutyun
The Unity Bloc is an alliance of the Republican Party of Armenia (**RPA**) and the People's Party of Armenia (**PPA**)

Armenia became an independent multiparty democracy in 1991 and held its first parliamentary elections in July 1995. A new constitution approved by referendum set up a presidential republic, and in 1996 President Ter-Petrossian was reelected for a five-year term. The war with Azerbaijan, over the issue of whether the Armenian enclave of Nagorno Karabakh inside Azerbaijan should become part of Armenia, has simmered since a 1994 cease-fire. Ter-Petrossian resigned in 1998, after parliament opposed his softer line in search of peace. He was succeeded by Robert Kocharian, a former premier and ex-governor of Nagorno Karabakh. In 1999 the prime minister, RPA leader Vazgen Sarkissian, was shot dead in a dramatic attack on parliament. He was succeeded first by his brother Aram, then in 2000 by Andranik Markarian.

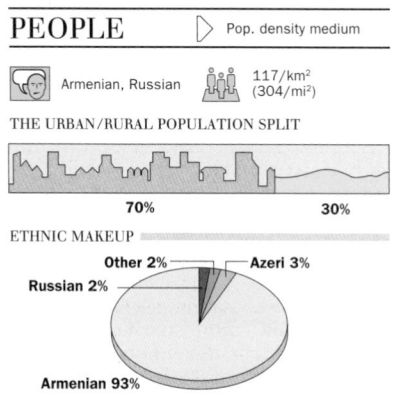

GEORGIA
TURKEY
AZERBAIJAN
IRAN
Noyemberyan
AZERBAIJAN ENCLAVES
Tashir
Alaverdi
Ashots'k'
Step'anavan
Amasia
Vanadzor
Ijevan
Berd
Gyumri
Spitak
Akhuryan
Dilijan
Artsvashen
Maralik
Art'ik
Aparan
Sevan
Aragats Lerr 4090m
Hrazdan
T'alin
Ch'arents'avan
Sevana Lich
SHAKH-DAG
Kamo
Tsaghkahovit
Ashtarak
Abovyan
Baghramyan
Ejmiadzin
Nor Hachn
GEGHAMA LERR
Vardenis
YEREVAN
Martuni
Hoktemberyan
Aras
Masis
Artashat
Vedi
Ararat
Yeghegnadzor
Jermuk
VARDENIS'HGHTA
Vayk'
Arp'a
Sisian
Goris
Vorotan
ZANGEZUR RANGE
K'ajaran
Kapan
Meghri
ARMENIA
Total Land Area : 29 800 sq. km (11 506 sq. miles)
POPULATION
over 1 000 000
over 100 000
over 50 000
over 10 000
under 10 000
LAND HEIGHT
3000m/9843ft
2000m/6562ft
1000m/3281ft
500m/1640ft
N
0
50 km
0
50 mi

WORLD AFFAIRS

Joined UN in 1992

BSEC | CIS | CE | EAPC | OSCE

Armenia joined the Council of Europe in 2001. Its continuing rivalry with Azerbaijan is diplomatically damaging.

A Turkish trade embargo has been in place since 1988. Russia signed a treaty of friendship in 1997 but has been less pro-Armenian since the Azeris rejoined the CIS. Work began on a gas pipeline between Iran and Armenia in 1998.

AID

Recipient

$208m (receipts) — Up 51% in 1999

The EBRD and the World Bank back infrastructure projects. Expatriate Armenians such as US billionaire Kirk Kerkorian are a major source of funds.

DEFENSE

Compulsory military service

$159m — Up 5% in 1999

Successes in the fighting over Nagorno Karabakh have increased the profile and autonomy of the army, which includes conscripts on 24-month national service. A cease-fire has broadly held since 1994, but peace talks, revived in 1999–2000, remain inconclusive.

ECONOMICS

Inflation 269.2% p.a. (1990–1999)

$1.9bn — 519.0–551.4 drams

SCORE CARD

❑ World GNP Ranking	141st
❑ GNP per Capita	$490
❑ Balance of Payments	$-319m
❑ Inflation	0.7%
❑ Unemployment	9%

STRENGTHS

Strong ties with Armenian emigrants. Deposits of rare metals, currently unexploited. Machine-building and manufacturing – includes textiles and bottling of mineral water.

WEAKNESSES

Dependent on imported energy, raw materials, and semi-finished goods. High inflation, unemployment, and stagnation. Widespread corruption.

EXPORTS

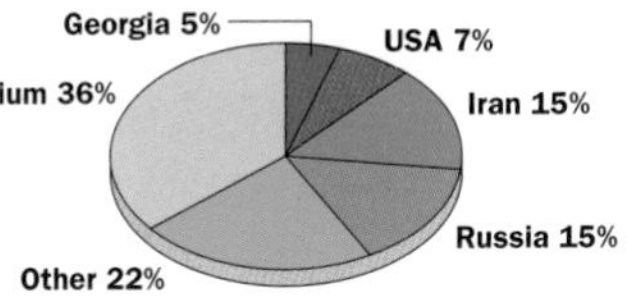
Georgia 5%
USA 7%
Belgium 36%
Iran 15%
Russia 15%
Other 22%

IMPORTS

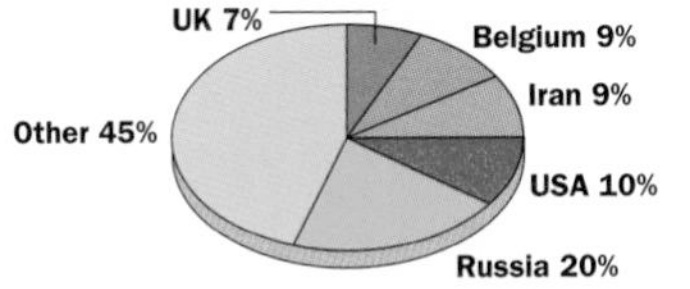
UK 7%
Belgium 9%
Iran 9%
Other 45%
USA 10%
Russia 20%

RESOURCES

Electric power 3m kw

3050 tonnes — Minimal oil production

536,000 sheep, 478,700 cattle, 5.2m chickens — Coal, oil, natural gas, rare metals

Energy resources are negligible, and mismanagement of the energy industry was deemed to have cost the country $200 million in the 1990s. Vegetables and fruit are grown in fertile lowlands, and grains in the hills; agriculture accounts for as much as a third of GDP.

ENVIRONMENT

Sustainability rank: 48th

7% — 0.8 tonnes per capita

Environmental groups, backed by the EU, demand the closure of the Medzamor nuclear power station, declared unsafe after the 1988 earthquake, but restarted in 1995 owing to the energy crisis. HEP generation near Lake Sevan has seriously lowered its water level.

MEDIA

TV ownership medium

Daily newspaper circulation 24 per 1000 people

PUBLISHING AND BROADCAST MEDIA

There are 11 daily newspapers, including *Azg*, *Yerkirn*, and *Ankakhutiun*

1 state-controlled service, several independent stations — 1 state-controlled service, several independent stations

Numerous TV and broadcasting stations assist media freedom. Independent journals and newspapers depend on the government-controlled paper industry.

CRIME

Death penalty used

Armenia does not publish prison figures — Down 14% 1996–1998

Reforms to the legal system introduced in 1999 included the replacement of the Supreme Court by an appeals court. Assassinations of political figures are common.

EDUCATION

School leaving age: 17

98% — 35,517 students

The education system, previously conforming to that of the USSR, now emphasizes Armenian history and culture; 12% of the population have received higher education.

CHRONOLOGY

Armenia lost its autonomy in the 14th century. In 1639, Turkey took the west and Persia the east; Persia ceded its part to Russia in 1828.

- ❑ **1877–1878** Massacre of Armenians during Russo-Turkish war.
- ❑ **1915** Ottomans exile 1.75 million Turkish Armenians; most die.
- ❑ **1920** Independence.
- ❑ **1922** Becomes a Soviet republic.
- ❑ **1988** Earthquake kills 25,000. Conflict with Azerbaijan over Nagorno Karabakh begins.
- ❑ **1991** Independence from USSR.
- ❑ **1994** Cease-fire with Azerbaijan.
- ❑ **1995** First parliamentary elections.
- ❑ **1998** Kocharian elected president.
- ❑ **1999** Shooting of prime minister in attack on parliament.

HEALTH

No welfare state health benefits

1 per 333 people — Circulatory diseases, cancers, accidents, violence

Hospitals suffer from the erratic electricity supply. Poor sewerage and other services have led to a rise in hepatitis, tuberculosis, and cholera.

SPENDING

GDP/cap. decrease

CONSUMPTION AND SPENDING

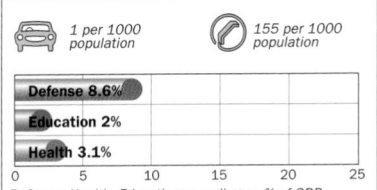

1 per 1000 population — *155 per 1000 population*

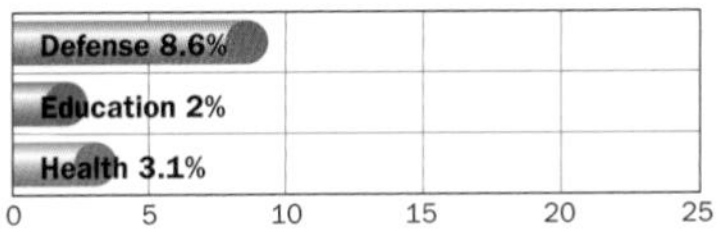
Defense 8.6%
Education 2%
Health 3.1%
0
5
10
15
20
25

Defense, Health, Education spending as % of GDP

The richest Armenian people are those living away from Armenia itself, particularly in the USA and France. The many refugees from Baku, Azerbaijan, are the poorest.

WORLD RANKING

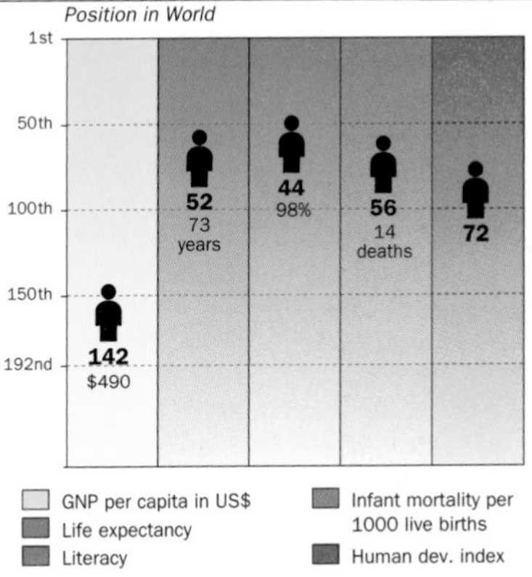
Position in World
1st
50th
100th
150th
192nd
142
$490
52
73 years
44
98%
56
14 deaths
72
GNP per capita in US$
Life expectancy
Literacy
Infant mortality per 1000 live births
Human dev. index

A

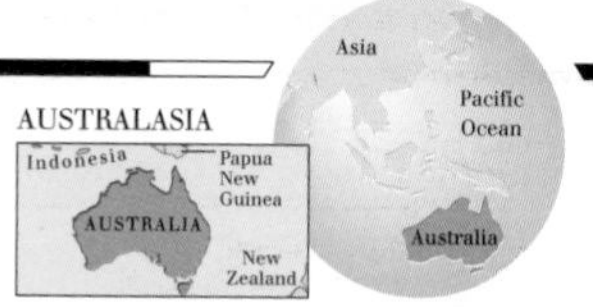
AUSTRALASIA
Asia
Pacific Ocean
Indonesia
Papua New Guinea
AUSTRALIA
New Zealand
Australia

AUSTRALIA

OFFICIAL NAME: Commonwealth of Australia **CAPITAL:** Canberra
POPULATION: 18.9 million **CURRENCY:** Australian dollar **OFFICIAL LANGUAGE:** English

1901 | 1901 | Jan 26 | AUS | +8 to +11 | +61 | .au

THE WORLD'S SIXTH-LARGEST COUNTRY, Australia is an island continent located between the Indian and Pacific Oceans. Its varied landscapes include tropical rainforests, the deserts of the arid "red center," snow-capped mountains, rolling tracts of pastoral land, and magnificent beaches. Famous natural features include Uluru (Ayers Rock) and the Great Barrier Reef. Most Australians live on the coast, and all the state capitals, including Sydney, host of the 2000 Olympics, are coastal cities. Only Canberra, the national capital, lies inland. The vast interior is dotted with large reserves, sparsely inhabited by communities from the small Aboriginal population.

Uluru (Ayers Rock), Northern Territory. *The renaming of Ayers Rock reflects growing Aboriginal influence in Australia.*

CLIMATE

Hot desert/steppe/tropical/Mediterranean

WEATHER CHART

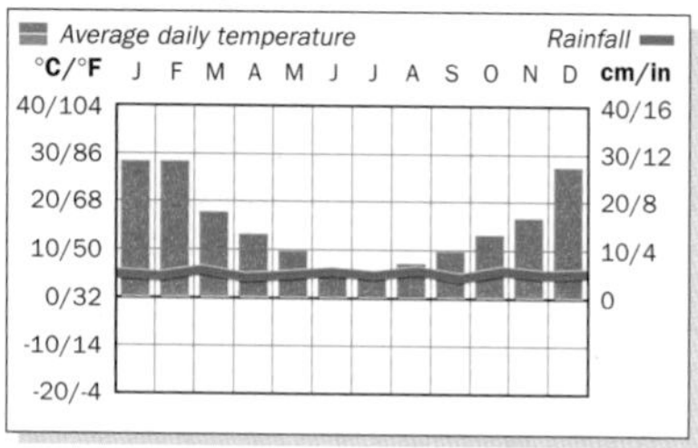
Average daily temperature
Rainfall
°C/°F
J F M A M J J A S O N D
cm/in
40/104
30/86
20/68
10/50
0/32
-10/14
-20/-4
40/16
30/12
20/8
10/4
0

The interior, west, and south are arid or semiarid and very hot in summer; central desert temperatures can reach 50°C (122°F). The north, around Darwin and Cape York Peninsula, is hot all year and humid during the summer monsoon. Only the east and southeast, within 400 km (250 miles) of the coast, and the southwest, around Perth, are temperate. Most Australians live in these areas.

TRANSPORTATION

Drive on left

Kingsford Smith, Sydney 21.6m passengers

617 ships 2.19m grt

THE TRANSPORTATION NETWORK

353,331 km (219,549 miles)	13,630 km (8469 miles)
36,026 km (22,387 miles)	8368 km (5200 miles)

Air transportation is well developed and vital to Australia's sparsely populated center and west. Sydney suffers from air congestion, but proposals for a new West Sydney airport remain controversial. Work has started on a high-speed train linking Sydney and Canberra, due to run from 2003. Most long-distance freight in Australia travels in massive trucks known as "road trains." Improvements in urban transportation are a priority and gained impetus in Sydney from the 2000 Olympic Games.

TOURISM

Visitors : Population 1:3.9

4.9m visitors

Up 10% in 2000

MAIN TOURIST ARRIVALS

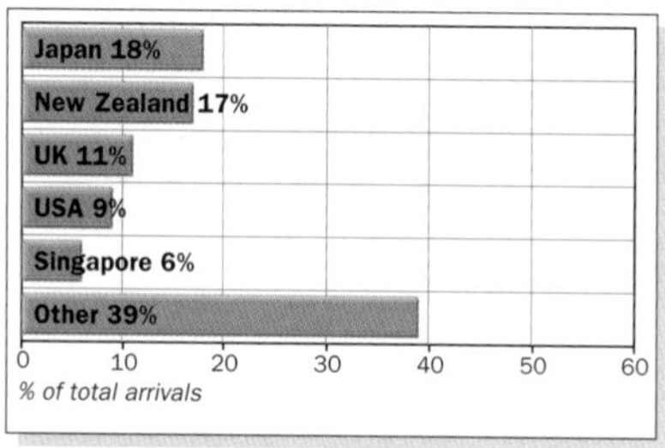
Japan 18%
New Zealand 17%
UK 11%
USA 9%
Singapore 6%
Other 39%
0
10
20
30
40
50
60
% of total arrivals

Tourism is now Australia's largest single foreign exchange earner. Faster, cheaper air travel and highly successful government marketing campaigns, both on a national and a state level, attract tourists in increasing numbers. The focus during the 1990s on drawing tourists from nearby Asian countries left the Australian tourist industry vulnerable after the Asian financial crisis of 1997. The Japanese form the largest single group of visitors to Australia, while many tourists also come from Europe, North America, and New Zealand.

The country's many attractions include wildlife, swimming and surfing off Pacific and Indian Ocean beaches, skin diving along the Great Barrier Reef, and skiing in the Australian Alps. Aboriginal culture and the town of Alice Springs are among the outback's attractions. The far north has tropical resorts, the northwest, pearl fishing. The vineyards of the south and southeast attract many visitors, as do the cultural life of Melbourne and Sydney and the arts festivals held in state capitals. Sydney's famous landmarks and cosmopolitan feel, as well as the world-renowned Bondi Beach, make it a favorite.

The mid-1980s saw a phenomenal boom; tourist arrivals rose almost 200% in five years to reach two million in 1990. Even though growth slowed during the early 1990s, by 2000 the number of visitors reached almost five million, boosted greatly by the celebrated Olympic Games.

INDIAN OCEAN
Bonaparte Archipelago
Derby
Broome
Port Hedland
GREAT SANDY DESERT
Onslow
Hamersley Range
Newman
Paraburdoo
Lake Disappointment
WESTERN AUSTRALIA
Lake Macleod
Carnarvon
Shark Bay
Dirk Hartog Island
Meekatharra
Lake Carnegie
Mount Magnet
Geraldton
Kalgoorlie
Moora
Perth
Fremantle
Northam
Merredin
Norseman
Rockingham
Bunbury
Collie
Wagin
Ravensthorpe
Esperance
Bridgetown
Cape Leeuwin
Manjimup
Albany

AUSTRALIA

Total Land Area : 7 617 930 sq. km (2 941 283 sq. miles)

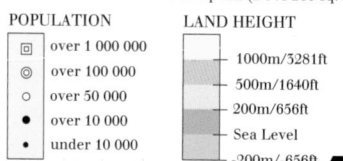

POPULATION	
⊡	over 1 000 000
◎	over 100 000
○	over 50 000
●	over 10 000
•	under 10 000

LAND HEIGHT

1000m/3281ft
500m/1640ft
200m/656ft
Sea Level
-200m/-656ft

PEOPLE

Pop. density low

English, Greek, Italian, Vietnamese, Aboriginal languages

2/km² (6/mi²)

THE URBAN/RURAL POPULATION SPLIT

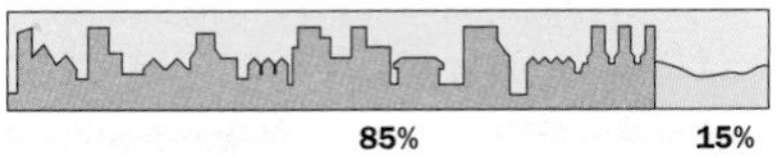
85%
15%

The first settlers arrived in Australia at least 100,000 years ago. Their modern descendants, the Aborigines, today make up less than 1% of the population. European settlement began in 1788 and was dominated by British and Irish immigrants – some of whom were convicts – until the gold rushes of the 1850s. Immigrants of other nationalities – including many Chinese – arrived to prospect for gold, then settled in the cities, especially Melbourne and Sydney. When the new federal government was installed in 1901, one of its first acts was to prevent further Chinese immigration. The act set out the "White Australia" policy, which conditioned attitudes to immigration for almost 70 years.

A massive immigration drive after World War II brought many more British settlers to Australia in the 1950s. Further government initiatives to "populate or perish" saw the arrival of large numbers of Italians and Greeks.

From the late 1960s, the "White Australia" policy was progressively wound down. It was officially ended during the 1972–1975 Whitlam administration. Ever since, up to 50% of immigrants each year have come from Asia, transforming Australia from an almost exclusively European enclave into a multicultural society in which immigrant groups are encouraged to maintain connections with their own cultures and languages.

Aborigines, the exception in an otherwise integrated society, number around 250,000. Economically and socially marginalized, they face considerable discrimination. Until the mid-1960s, they were denied the vote and full social benefits. Their land had been occupied as *terra nullius* – belonging to no one. Since the 1970s, Aborigines have made a more organized stand on land and civil rights. Native title to land was recognized in 1993, although controversies continue over the extent of its application. Civil rights campaigns have moved on from the initial phase of anti-racist protests to demand greater equality in areas such as health, housing, and education. Life expectancy is still 20 years lower than the rest of the population. Alcoholism is a pervasive problem both in towns and rural areas. Aborigines in urban areas may be relatively better housed but face particular problems in asserting their cultural identity.

During the 1950s and 1960s, Catholic–Protestant differences were sufficient to cause a rift in the ALP. However, a subsequent policy encouraging mixed denomination schooling, coupled with a decline in religious observance, has largely neutralized the issue.

RELIGIOUS PERSUASION

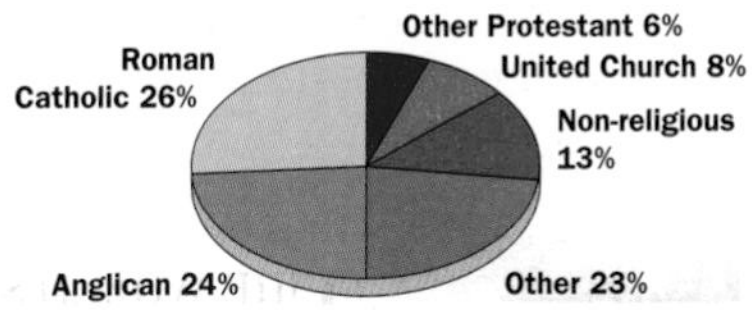
Other Protestant 6%
United Church 8%
Non-religious 13%
Other 23%
Anglican 24%
Roman Catholic 26%

ETHNIC MAKEUP

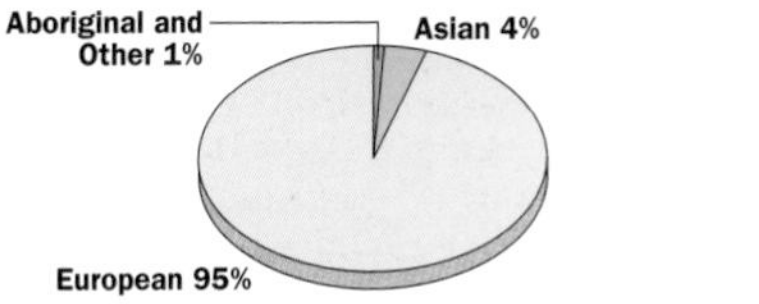
Aboriginal and Other 1%
Asian 4%
European 95%

PAPUA NEW GUINEA
ARAFURA SEA
Torres Strait
Bamaga
Cape York
Melville Island
Bathurst Island
Wessel Islands
Darwin
Arnham Land
Gulf of Carpentaria
Groote Eylandt
Cape York Peninsula
Katherine
Sir Edward Pellew Group
Wyndham
Wellesley Islands
Cooktown
Cairns
Karumba
Barkly Tableland
TANAMI DESERT
Tennant Creek
NORTHERN TERRITORY
Townsville
Mount Isa
Cloncurry
Hughenden
Winton
Mackay
GREAT BARRIER REEF
CORAL SEA
GREAT DIVIDING RANGE
Macdonnell Ranges
Alice Springs
Longreach
Emerald
Rockhampton
QUEENSLAND
Great Artesian Basin
SIMPSON DESERT
Uluru (Ayers Rock)
Birdsville
Bundaberg
Fraser I.
Maryborough
Gympie
Charleville
Cooper Creek
SOUTH AUSTRALIA
Lake Eyre
Cunnamulla
Toowoomba
Brisbane
Gold Coast
Ipswich
Surfers Paradise
Lismore
VICTORIA DESERT
Lake Torrens
Lake Frome
Grey Range
Bourke
Moree
Grafton
Armidale
Coffs Harbour
Tamworth
Port Macquarie
Broken Hill
NEW SOUTH WALES
Lake Gairdner
Port Augusta
Flinders Ranges
Dubbo
Taree
Whyalla
Maitland
Newcastle
Gosford
Port Pirie
Orange
Great Australian Bight
Eyre Peninsula
Elizabeth
Adelaide
Mildura
Bathurst
Lithgow
Sydney
Griffith
Goulburn
Wollongong
Port Lincoln
Spencer Gulf
Wagga Wagga
Queanbeyan
CANBERRA
Kangaroo I.
VICTORIA
Shepparton
Albury
Mount Kosciuszko 2228m
AUST. CAPITAL TERRITORY
Horsham
Bendigo
Wangaratta
Australian Alps
Mount Gambier
Ballarat
Melbourne
Traralgon
Cape Howe
TASMAN SEA
Warrnambool
Geelong
Moe
Morwell
Sale
Bass Strait
King I.
Flinders I.
Furneaux Group
Burnie
Ulverstone
Devonport
Launceston
TASMANIA
Hobart
SOUTH PACIFIC OCEAN
N
0 400 km
0 400 miles

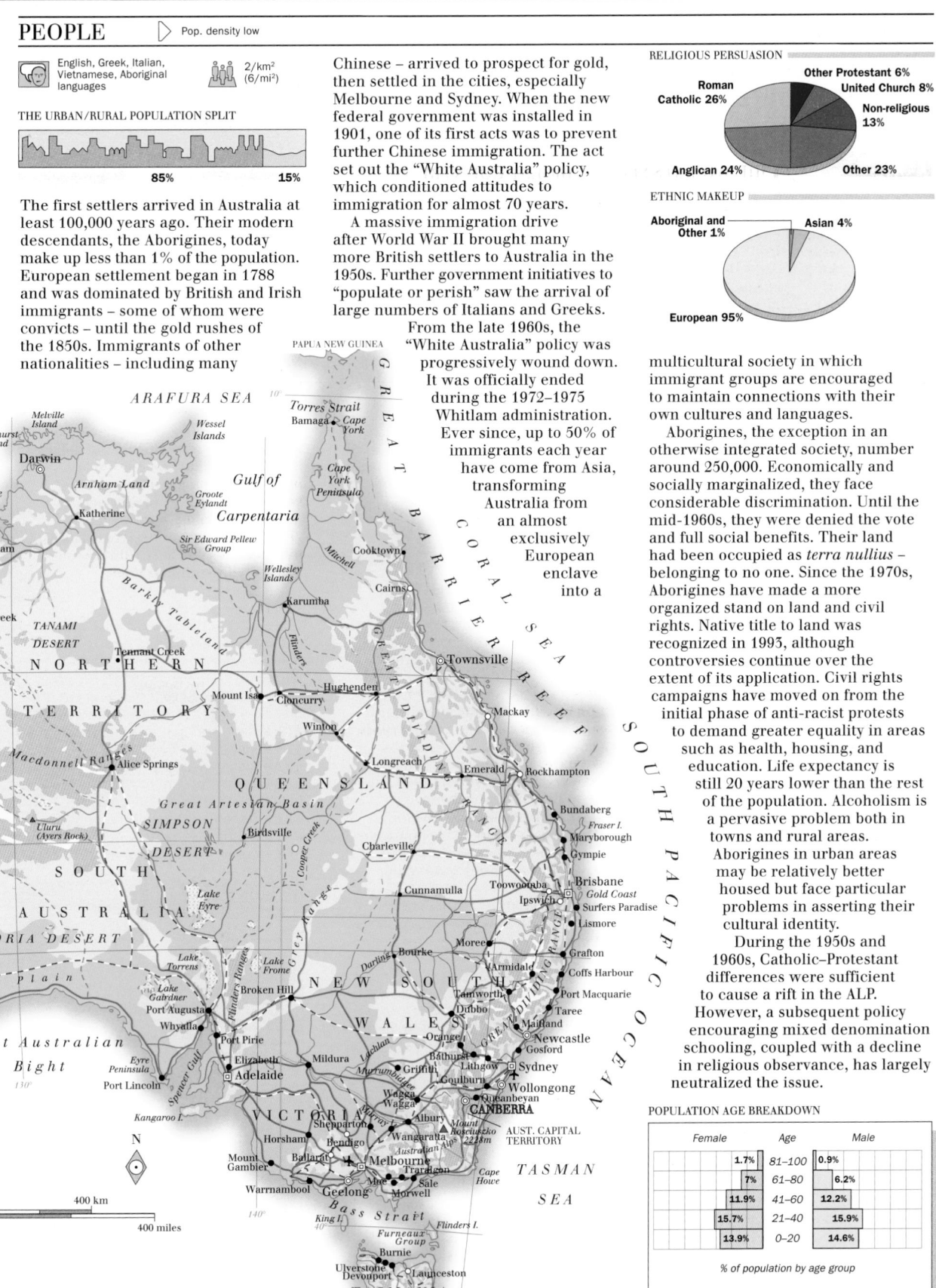

POPULATION AGE BREAKDOWN

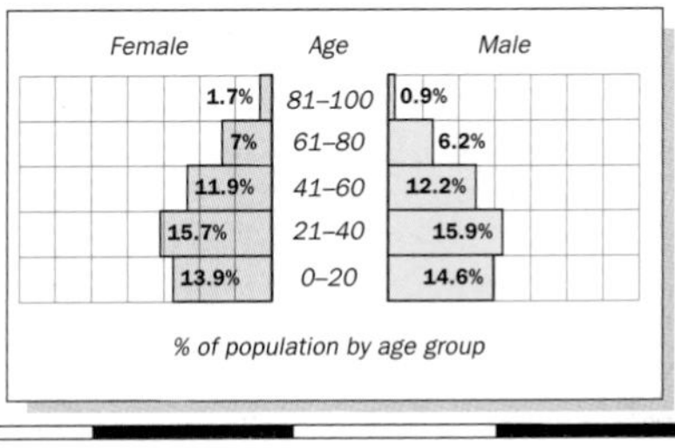
Female
Age
Male
1.7%
81–100
0.9%
7%
61–80
6.2%
11.9%
41–60
12.2%
15.7%
21–40
15.9%
13.9%
0–20
14.6%
% of population by age group

CHRONOLOGY

Dutch, Portuguese, French, and – decisively – British incursions throughout the 17th and 18th centuries signaled the end of a millennia of Aboriginal isolation. Governor Arthur Philip raised the Union Flag at Sydney Cove on January 26, 1788.

- ❑ **1901** Inauguration of the Commonwealth of Australia.
- ❑ **1915** Australian troops suffer heavy casualties at Gallipoli.
- ❑ **1929** Industrial upheaval and financial collapse caused by the Great Depression.
- ❑ **1939** Prime Minister Menzies announces Australia will follow Britain into war with Germany.
- ❑ **1942** Fall of Singapore to Japanese army. Japanese invasion of Australia seems imminent. Government turns to USA for help.
- ❑ **1950** Australian troops committed to UN–US Korean War against North Korean communists.
- ❑ **1962** Menzies government commits Australian aid to war in Vietnam.
- ❑ **1966** Adopts decimal currency.
- ❑ **1972** Whitlam government elected. Aid to South Vietnam ceases.
- ❑ **1975** Whitlam government dismissed by Governor-General Sir John Kerr. Malcolm Fraser forms coalition government.
- ❑ **1983** Bob Hawke becomes prime minister at the head of an ALP administration.
- ❑ **1985** Corporate boom followed by deepening recession.
- ❑ **1992** Paul Keating defeats Hawke in leadership vote, becomes prime minister; announces "Turning toward Asia" policy. High Court's "Mabo Judgment" recognizes Aboriginal land rights.
- ❑ **1993** Against most predictions, Keating's ALP government reelected. Native Title Act provides compensation for Aboriginal rights extinguished by existing land title.
- ❑ **1996** Defeat of Keating government. Liberal John Howard becomes Prime Minister. Shooting of 35 people by gunman in Port Arthur, Tasmania, prompts tightening of gun control laws. First death under Northern Territory's controversial euthanasia legislation; legislation later overruled at federal level.
- ❑ **1998** Elections: Howard's Liberal and National coalition retains power with reduced majority; fears of right-wing One Nation party breakthrough prove unfounded.
- ❑ **1999** Referendum rejects proposals to replace Queen as head of state by indirectly elected president.
- ❑ **2000** Olympic Games in Sydney.

POLITICS

Multiparty elections

L. House 1998/2001
U. House 1998/2001

HM Queen Elizabeth II

AT THE LAST ELECTION

House of Representatives 148 seats

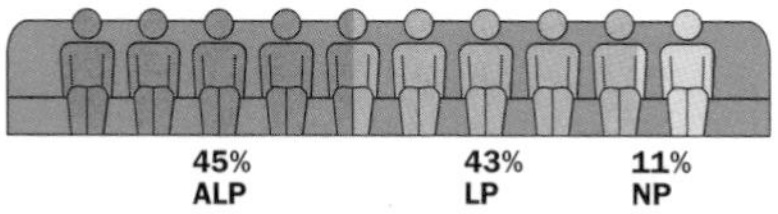
1% Ind
45% ALP
43% LP
11% NP

ALP = Australian Labor Party **LP** = Liberal Party
NP = National Party **Ind** = Independents
AD = Australian Democrats **G** = Greens

Senate 76 seats

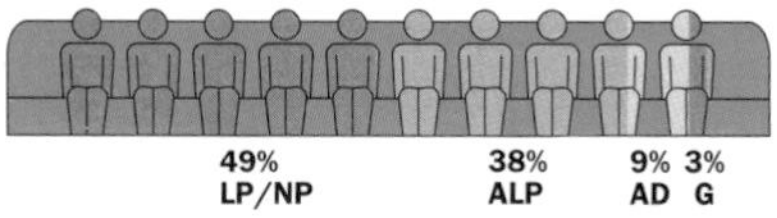
1% Others
49% LP/NP
38% ALP
9% AD
3% G

12 seats in the Senate are apportioned to each of the country's constituent states and two each to the Northern Territory and the Australian Capital Territory

Australia is a parliamentary democracy on the British model. There are six state governments, all but one (Queensland) bicameral. The Northern Territory became self-governing in 1978.

Main Political Issues

Aboriginal rights

Land rights (the subject of controversial court rulings) and demands for an apology for the past treatment of Aborigines are the basis for persistently tense and emotive ethnic relations. A government "statement of regret" in 1999 for the "stolen generation" – Aboriginal children forcibly raised by white families until the 1960s – only served to increase criticism of Prime Minister John Howard's refusal to give a full apology.

The right-wing fringe One Nation party has sought to capitalize on resentment of Aboriginal welfare dependency and policies of positive discrimination. Reports of racism in rural communities have risen.

Unemployment

The rise in unemployment to around 10% in the early 1990s was expected to sink Paul Keating's ALP government; surviving in 1993 thanks to a skillful campaign, it was swept out of office three years later. A short-lived economic boom had ended by 1998, and the much hyped possibility of global slowdown in 2001 raised fresh fears about the depth of possible recession. Unemployment was thought to be a big factor in the rise of Pauline Hanson's right-wing, anti-immigrant One Nation party. Although her initial breakthrough in Queensland was not sustained in the October 1998 general election, the party picked up renewed local support in 2001.

The Republic

Despite international press coverage, the republican issue is not of major importance to most Australians. The former ALP government played down the debate in order to avoid inflaming monarchist groups. In his 1996 oath of office, Prime Minister Howard swore allegiance to Queen Elizabeth II, but not her successors. His government's Constitutional Convention of February 1998 brought together a wide range of people, chosen by popular election, to debate the issue. Various models, including the popular election of the head of state, were rejected in favor of a model giving the power of selection to a two-thirds majority of parliament, but this was rejected by the people in a 1999 referendum.

Vineyards in South Australia. *Wine-making has been one of Australia's greatest agricultural success stories in recent years.*

Profile

The ALP and the Liberal and National parties have dominated Australian politics since 1945. The latter two, politically to the right, work together in coalition and broadly represent big business and agricultural interests. The ALP gained some of this support in the 1980s, adopting free-market policies and blurring the differences between parties, but 13 years of ALP rule ended in 1996, when a Liberal–National coalition took office. It held on with a much reduced majority in the 1998 poll and faced declining support in 2001.

Paul Keating, *resigned as leader of the ALP after his 1996 election defeat.*

John Howard, *leader of the LP, was elected prime minister in 1996.*

Aden Ridgeway, *Aboriginal senator and deputy leader of the AD.*

WORLD AFFAIRS

Joined UN in 1945

APEC | PC | Comm | OECD | PIF

Australia's international focus has shifted from Europe and the USA toward Asia. Geopolitically it is in an ambiguous position. It lost its place as a major UK trading partner after the UK joined the EU, but was still regarded as a European outsider by the Asian nations with which it wanted closer links. Australia took practical steps to redefine its role, backing the 1989 Asia Pacific Economic Cooperation forum (APEC) to create a multilateral regional trading bloc similar to the EU and NAFTA. The USA was a strong supporter, seeing APEC as a means of promoting free-market economics in Asia. Australia's ambition is for APEC to become the leading association in the region. However, the move toward market liberalization slowed following the 1997 Asian financial crisis.

Relations with the USA are tense on questions of trade. Australia objects to subsidized US wheat undercutting its own exports, particularly in the key Chinese market. It sees the EU and the USA as its main competitors in selling to southeast Asia.

On security issues Australia still supports the West. Against much public opposition, it sent troops to the 1991 Gulf War. Its commitment to the Pacific region also remains strong. In the post-Cold War era this is expressed mainly through development aid rather than defense arrangements, but Australian troops led the UN force in East Timor in 1999.

Within the Pacific region, fishing is a major issue. There have been a number of minor skirmishes with Indonesian and Japanese long-line fishing boats. Australia objects to this form of fishing, which kills large numbers of dolphins, and employs submarine patrols in an effort to regulate the industry.

In mid-2000 Australia was strongly criticized by the UN for its treatment of asylum seekers and the indigenous Aboriginal population.

AID

Donor

US$982m (donations) | Up 2% in 1999

Australia spends only 0.25% of its GNP on aid programs. Most is spent in the Asia–Pacific region. Particular areas of focus are those of HIV/AIDS programs and non-governmental organizations. The recipient of by far the greatest amount is Papua New Guinea, where Australian companies such as Broken Hill Proprietary have major mining operations.

DEFENSE

No compulsory military service

US$7.8bn | Up 1% in 1999

Strategic ties with the USA remain an important element of defense policy. Australia has defense arrangements with the Philippines, Brunei, and Thailand among others. Always aiming for self-reliance, Australia dramatically increased expenditure since 2000 to promote its position as a regional power. Updating military equipment and exploiting information technologies are priorities.

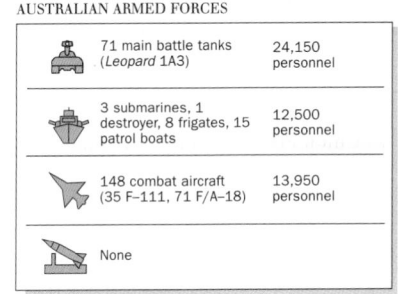

AUSTRALIAN ARMED FORCES

71 main battle tanks (*Leopard* 1A3)	24,150 personnel
3 submarines, 1 destroyer, 8 frigates, 15 patrol boats	12,500 personnel
148 combat aircraft (35 F-111, 71 F/A-18)	13,950 personnel
None	

ECONOMICS

Inflation 1.3% p.a. (1990–1999)

US$397.3bn | 1.5282–1.7997 Australian dollars

SCORE CARD

❑ World GNP Ranking	15th
❑ GNP per Capita	US$20,950
❑ Balance of Payments	US$–22.53bn
❑ Inflation	1.5%
❑ Unemployment	8%

EXPORTS

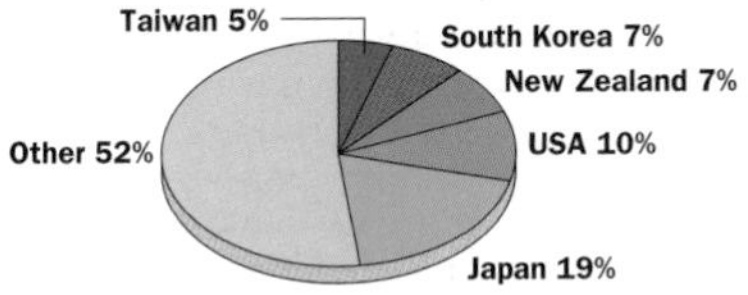
Taiwan 5%
South Korea 7%
New Zealand 7%
USA 10%
Other 52%
Japan 19%

IMPORTS

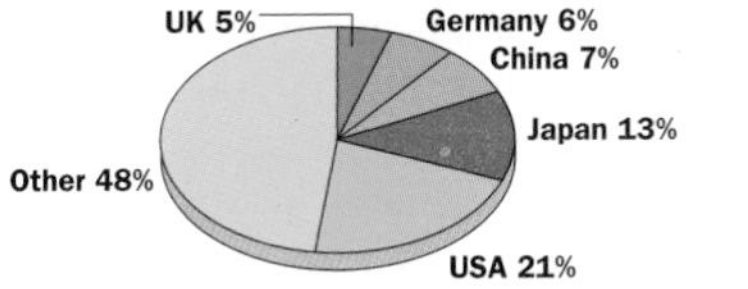
UK 5%
Germany 6%
China 7%
Japan 13%
Other 48%
USA 21%

Strengths

Efficient agricultural and mining industries. Vast mineral deposits. Highly profitable tourist industry with record of dramatic growth. Australia has a good history regarding both eonomic growth and inflation.

ECONOMIC PERFORMANCE INDICATOR

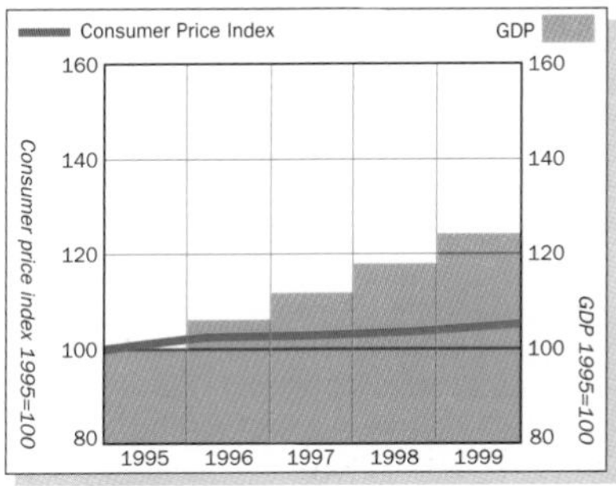
Consumer Price Index
GDP
160
140
120
100
80
Consumer price index 1995=100
GDP 1995=100
1995
1996
1997
1998
1999

Weaknesses

May suffer from EU and NAFTA protectionist policies. Political and financial instability in export markets in southeast Asia. Competition from Asian economies with lower wage rates and poorer working conditions. Unemployment likely to remain high. Balance of payments deficit.

Profile

Australian companies concentrated during the 1990s on the Asian market, which grew to represent 60% of Australia's trade. They were hit hard when the 1997 Asian financial crisis tipped the region into recession. Japan remains Australia's most important trading partner. In order to compete in Asia, Australia's economy has been undergoing massive structural adjustment. The Howard government, like its ALP predecessor until 1996, has been dismantling the tariffs that had made Australia one of the most protected economies within the OECD. Higher unemployment and the collapse of a number of businesses accompanied this change. It was further hit by global economic slowdown in 2001.

AUSTRALIA : MAJOR BUSINESSES

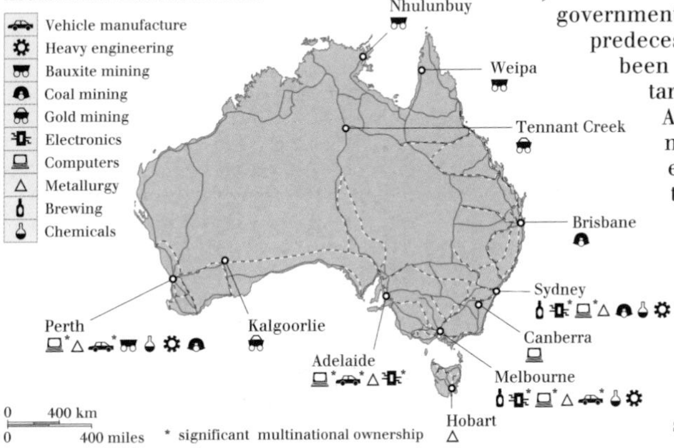
Vehicle manufacture
Heavy engineering
Bauxite mining
Coal mining
Gold mining
Electronics
Computers
Metallurgy
Brewing
Chemicals
Nhulunbuy
Weipa
Tennant Creek
Brisbane
Sydney
Canberra
Melbourne
Hobart
Adelaide
Kalgoorlie
Perth
0 400 km
0 400 miles
* significant multinational ownership

RESOURCES

Electric power 39.7m kw

214,227 tonnes

815,000 b/d (reserves 2,900,000,000 bbl)

117m sheep, 25.6m cattle, 92m chickens

Coal, iron, bauxite, zinc, lead, copper, nickel, opals, gold, uranium

ELECTRICITY GENERATION

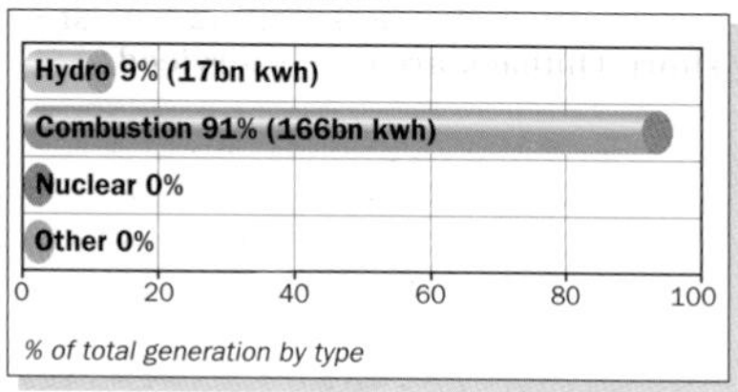
Hydro 9% (17bn kwh)
Combustion 91% (166bn kwh)
Nuclear 0%
Other 0%
0
20
40
60
80
100
% of total generation by type

Australia has one of the world's most important mining industries. It is a world leader in exports of coal, iron ore, gold, bauxite, and copper. Minerals account for a tenth of Australia's GDP and over half of its merchandise export earnings. Since the first discoveries of coal in 1798, mineral production in Australia has risen every year; in the decade to 1992 it doubled. Growth slowed but continued during the 1990s: many new projects are planned. The share of minerals in the total economy is expected to continue growing, but, having benefited from Australia's location close to the markets of southeast Asia, it was left vulnerable following the regional crisis of 1997.

While minerals underpin much of Australia's wealth, there is growing concern at the environmental cost of extraction. There is also ongoing uncertainty over the possibility of Aboriginal claims to land holding valuable minerals. The 1992 "Mabo Judgment" recognized Aboriginal land rights predating European settlement. The 1993 Native Title Act confirmed these rights and in 1996 the High Court's historic "Wik decision" enabled claims to be made over land which was subject to a "pastoral" lease. But legislation passed in 1998 cut back Aborigines' rights to make such claims.

AUSTRALIA : LAND USE

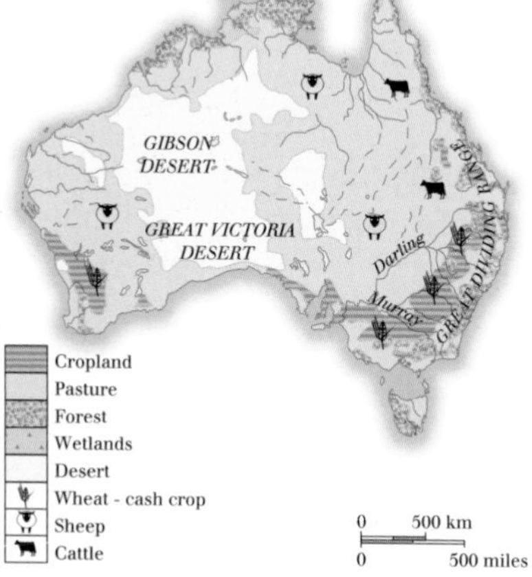
GIBSON DESERT
GREAT VICTORIA DESERT
Darling
Murray
GREAT DIVIDING RANGE
Cropland
Pasture
Forest
Wetlands
Desert
Wheat - cash crop
Sheep
Cattle
0 500 km
0 500 miles

Green Island in the far north of Queensland. It is part of the Great Barrier Reef which stretches 1995 km (1240 miles) down the coast.

ENVIRONMENT

Sustainability rank: 7th

7% (2% partially protected)

17.2 tonnes per capita

ENVIRONMENTAL TREATIES

Yes — Yes — Yes

Yes — Yes — Yes

Australia's voters are among the most environmentally conscious in the world, but the country's government has strongly resisted any commitment to cutting "greenhouse gas" emissions to help limit global warming. The 1997 Kyoto climate change conference agreed to allow Australia to increase greenhouse emissions by up to 8% until 2010, whereas most industrialized countries had to commit to cuts.

Green issues are dominated by the Australian Conservation Foundation (ACF) and the more radical Greenpeace organization. The ACF has concentrated on developing industry links and cooperative programs.

MEDIA

TV ownership high

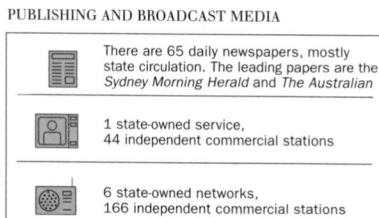

Daily newspaper circulation 296 per 1000 people

PUBLISHING AND BROADCAST MEDIA

There are 65 daily newspapers, mostly state circulation. The leading papers are the *Sydney Morning Herald* and *The Australian*

1 state-owned service, 44 independent commercial stations

6 state-owned networks, 166 independent commercial stations

The Australian press is firmly in the grip of press "barons" such as Rupert Murdoch and Kerry Packer, although cross-media rules prevent the ownership of newspapers and TV channels in the same city. Public-sector broadcasting remains dominated by the politically neutral Australian Broadcasting Corporation (ABC), which receives complaints about its coverage from all main parties.

CRIME

Death penalty not used

16,860 prisoners

Up 8% 1996–1998

CRIME RATES

Murders	4	per 100,000 population
Rapes	199	per 100,000 population
Thefts	6206	per 100,000 population

Crime is on the increase. Each state has its own police force and court system. The High Court and Family Court both have national jurisdiction. Since the 1970s, the legal system has been placing greater emphasis on individual rights. The disproportionate number of Aboriginal deaths in custody is of concern, as are rising narcotics-related offenses. Australia is active in drug control throughout southeast Asia. Gun control laws were strengthened following the 1996 Port Arthur shooting, when a lone gunman killed 35 people. In 1997 the Wood inquiry uncovered widespread police corruption in New South Wales and led to major reforms.

EDUCATION

School leaving age : 15

99%

1m students

THE EDUCATION SYSTEM

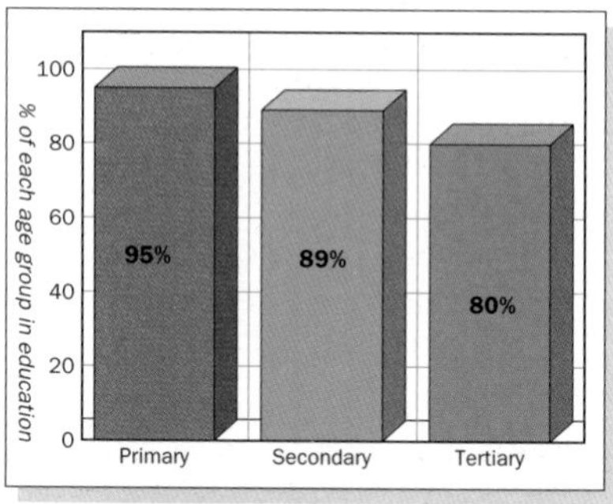
100
80
60
40
20
0
% of each age group in education
95%
89%
80%
Primary
Secondary
Tertiary

Education in Australia is a state responsibility, except in Canberra (where it is funded by the federal government). State education departments run the government schools and set the policies for educational practice and standards for all schools. Non-government schools, run by religious and other groups, exist in all states. Special provision is made for inaccessible outback areas, with recent moves to bring new technologies to the bush.

Schooling is compulsory from age 5–6 to age 15–16 in all states. After their final year at school, students sit for the Higher School Certificate. Universities are independent of state control and are funded by the federal government.

ABORIGINAL RIGHTS

CENTRAL TO THE ABORIGINAL cultural and spiritual framework is the relationship with tribal lands. The Aborigines' land rights campaign, like their civil rights campaign, began gathering momentum in the 1960s, when they were first included in the census and won the right to vote. Now a key political issue, it has far-reaching implications for national identity, for the country's most disadvantaged people, and for powerful mining and farming interests.

BACKGROUND

In the millennia before the arrival of Europeans, Aboriginal peoples ranged widely over their land. The indigenous population was then greatly reduced by exposure to disease and by conflict. Settlers acquired land without reference to any pre-existing rights of tribal peoples, based on the legal doctrine that before 1788 the land was *terra nullius* – belonging to no-one. Those Aborigines still living a traditional lifestyle were largely confined to reserves.

Land rights campaigns won an initial breakthrough when land councils were set up, first in the Northern Territory in 1976, then in other states. These provided a structure for holding freehold title to land in trust for its tribal inhabitants. However, in the absence of a uniform national land rights policy conservative states such as Queensland – which has the largest Aboriginal population – resisted moves to consolidate Aboriginal ownership. Particular flashpoints arose when mining companies were granted concessions to exploit sacred sites.

NATIVE TITLE ACTS IN THE 1990S

The first nationwide Native Title Act was introduced by the ALP federal government in 1993. It recognized the new situation created by a crucial 1992 court ruling. The so-called Mabo Judgment established that rights to land ownership did indeed exist in common law based on native title. This effectively reversed the old concept of *terra nullius* and recognized the pre-1788 Aboriginal occupancy.

Native dancers from Kuranda, northern Queensland, perform a traditional dance in front of protesters marching for increased Aboriginal land rights.

***An Aboriginal elder** surveys his native land in Western Australia.*

The 1993 law specified that native title existed for all Crown land, held by federal or by state government, unless it had specifically been extinguished. Native title met powerful resistance from mining companies, especially in Western Australia. In 1996, a court case brought by the Wik people of the Cape York peninsula in Queensland took the matter further. The Wik ruling said that native title still coexisted with the rights of farmers who had long leases from the Crown on huge tracts of grazing land, granted earlier in the century. Changes of use on such land (to allow mining, cash crops, and tourist developments) would therefore require consultation with Aborigines.

The government, by now a Liberal–National coalition, responded with a plan to protect leaseholders. Its own Native Title Amendment Bill, tightly restricting Aborigine land claims, split the country and was blocked in the Senate until July 1998.

Court battles continue over mining developments on sensitive tribal sites. Meanwhile, Liberal Prime Minister John Howard resisted making a formal government apology for the way in which white settlers mistreated Aboriginal people. Campaigners for such an apology see it as central to a national reconciliation agreement, especially after the recent controversy over the "stolen generation" – Aboriginal children forcibly removed from their families and brought up by whites under an assimilation policy which continued until the late 1960s.

HEALTH

Welfare state health benefits

1 per 400 people

Heart, cerebrovascular, and respiratory diseases, cancers

Australia's extensive public health service has among the highest standards in the world. Hospital waiting lists are short. Outback areas are serviced by the efficient Royal Flying Doctor Service. While vigilance continues in the areas of hygiene, nutrition, and general living standards, health authorities have targeted heart disease, injury prevention, personal fitness, Aboriginal health, and the prevention of cancers – particularly lung, cervical, breast, and skin cancers – as current priorities. Incentives to encourage private health insurance, introduced during the 1990s, sparked fears over public health funding and quality.

SPENDING

GDP/cap. increase

CONSUMPTION AND SPENDING

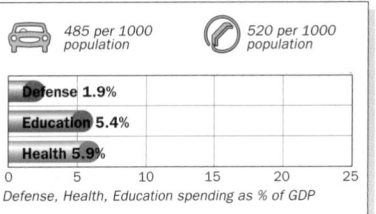

485 per 1000 population

520 per 1000 population

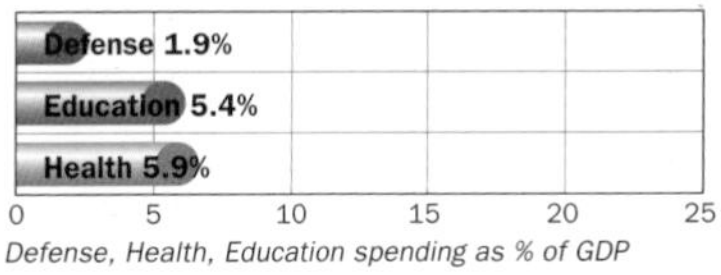
Defense 1.9%
Education 5.4%
Health 5.9%
0
5
10
15
20
25
Defense, Health, Education spending as % of GDP

Australians traditionally enjoyed reasonable equality of wealth distribution. A large proportion of families own two cars and have relatively high disposable incomes, and a benign climate helps most people to live comfortably. However, high unemployment during the 1990s recession widened the gap between rich and poor, and Australia slipped down the world standard of living list for a few years. The incidence of homelessness, critical poverty, and child neglect due to poverty have increased in recent years.

WORLD RANKING

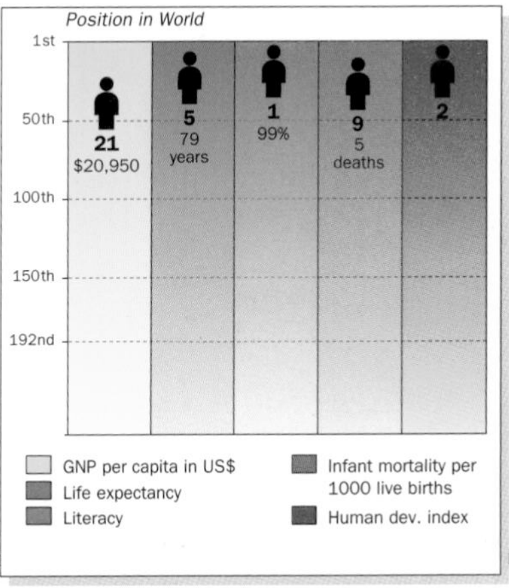
Position in World
1st
50th
100th
150th
192nd
21
$20,950
5
79
years
1
99%
9
5
deaths
2
GNP per capita in US$
Life expectancy
Literacy
Infant mortality per 1000 live births
Human dev. index

A

AUSTRIA

EUROPE
Europe
Germany
Czech Rep.
AUSTRIA
Hungary
Switz.
Italy
Slovenia

OFFICIAL NAME: Republic of Austria **CAPITAL:** Vienna **POPULATION:** 8.2 million
CURRENCY: Euro (Schilling until 2002) **OFFICIAL LANGUAGE:** German

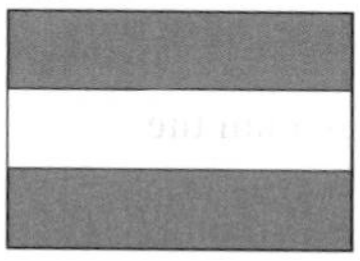

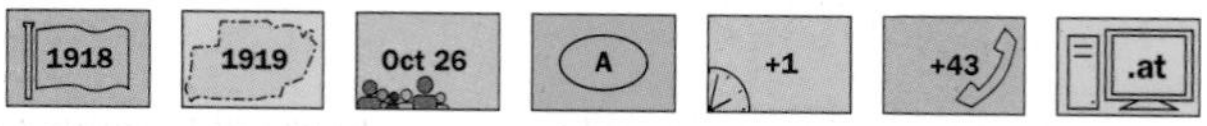
1918
1919
Oct 26
A
+1
+43
.at

LYING IN THE HEART OF EUROPE, Austria is dominated by the Alps in the west of the country, while fertile plains make up the east and north. Created in 1918, after the collapse of the Habsburg empire, Austria was absorbed into Hitler's Germany in 1938. It regained independence in 1955 after the departure of the last Soviet troops from the Allied Occupation Force. Its economy encompasses successful high-tech sectors, a tourist industry which attracts wealthier visitors, and a strong agricultural base. Joining the EU in 1995, in 2002 it was one of the first 12 EU states to adopt the Euro.

CLIMATE

Mountain/continental

WEATHER CHART

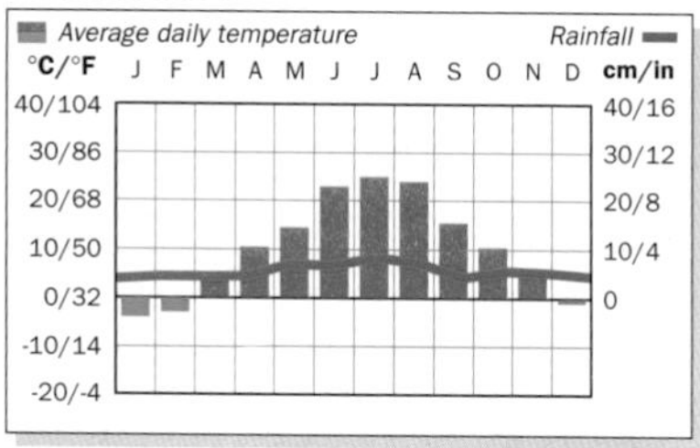
Average daily temperature
Rainfall
°C/°F
J F M A M J J A S O N D
cm/in
40/104
30/86
20/68
10/50
0/32
-10/14
-20/-4
40/16
30/12
20/8
10/4
0

Austria has a temperate continental climate. Alpine areas experience colder temperatures and higher precipitation.

TRANSPORTATION

Drive on right

Wien–Schwechat, Vienna 11.20m passengers

22 ships 68,000 grt

THE TRANSPORTATION NETWORK

200,000 km (124,274 miles)

1613 km (1002 miles)

5740 km (3567 miles)

358 km (222 miles)

Austria's central geographical position has encouraged the development of a sophisticated communications and transportation network.

The Tirol is situated in the heart of Austria's Alps. It is the most mountainous region of all and attracts both winter and summer visitors.

TOURISM

Visitors : Population 2.2:1

18m visitors

Up 3% in 2000

MAIN TOURIST ARRIVALS

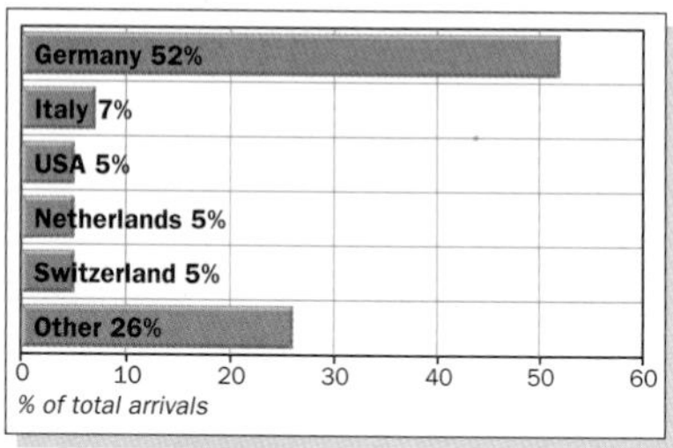
Germany 52%
Italy 7%
USA 5%
Netherlands 5%
Switzerland 5%
Other 26%
0
10
20
30
40
50
60
% of total arrivals

Well-developed Alpine skiing and winter sports resorts account for almost one-third of the country's total tourist earnings. Many resorts, such as St. Anton and Kitzbühel, cater for the top end of the market. In the summer season, which peaks in July and August, tourists visit the scenic Tirol and the lakes around Bad Ischl. Year-round major attractions are Vienna, with its coffee houses and the Prater park (whose Ferris wheel was immortalized in *The Third Man*), and Salzburg, Austria's second city. The latter is internationally famous for its summer music festival and as the birthplace of Mozart.

AUSTRIA

Total Land Area : 82 730 sq. km (31 942 sq. miles)

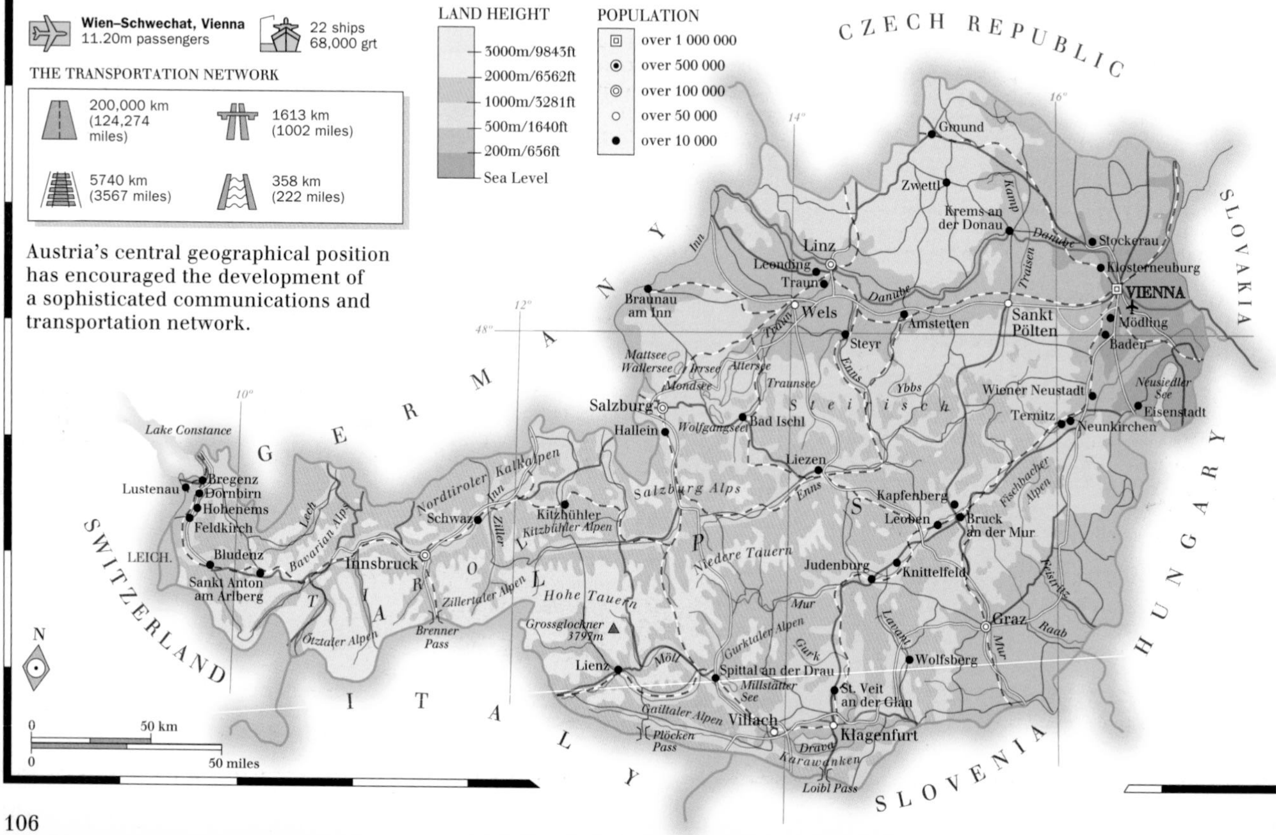
LAND HEIGHT
3000m/9843ft
2000m/6562ft
1000m/3281ft
500m/1640ft
200m/656ft
Sea Level
POPULATION
over 1 000 000
over 500 000
over 100 000
over 50 000
over 10 000
CZECH REPUBLIC
SLOVAKIA
HUNGARY
SLOVENIA
ITALY
SWITZERLAND
GERMANY
LEICH.
Lake Constance
Lustenau
Bregenz
Dornbirn
Hohenems
Feldkirch
Bludenz
Sankt Anton am Arlberg
Lech
Bavarian Alps
Innsbruck
Ötztaler Alpen
Brenner Pass
Zillertaler Alpen
Ziller
Inn
Schwaz
Nordtiroler Kalkalpen
Kitzbühler
Kitzbühler Alpen
Hohe Tauern
Grossglockner 3797m
Lienz
Möll
Gailtaler Alpen
Plöcken Pass
Villach
Drava
Karawanken
Loibl Pass
Klagenfurt
St. Veit an der Glan
Spittal an der Drau
Millstätter See
Gurktaler Alpen
Gurk
Mur
Lavant
Wolfsberg
Graz
Raab
Knittelfeld
Judenburg
Niedere Tauern
Salzburg Alps
Salzburg
Hallein
Wolfgangsee
Bad Ischl
Liezen
Enns
Kapfenberg
Leoben
Bruck an der Mur
Fischbacher Alpen
Rabnitz
Mattsee
Wallersee
Irrsee
Attersee
Mondsee
Traunsee
Steirisch
Braunau am Inn
Inn
Leonding
Linz
Traun
Wels
Traune
Steyr
Enns
Ybbs
Danube
Amstetten
Sankt Pölten
Traisen
Kamp
Gmund
Zwettl
Krems an der Donau
Stockerau
Klosterneuburg
VIENNA
Mödling
Baden
Wiener Neustadt
Ternitz
Neunkirchen
Eisenstadt
Neusiedler See
N
50 km
50 miles
0
10°
12°
14°
16°
48°

PEOPLE

Pop. density medium

German, Croat, Slovene

99/km² (257/mi²)

THE URBAN/RURAL POPULATION SPLIT

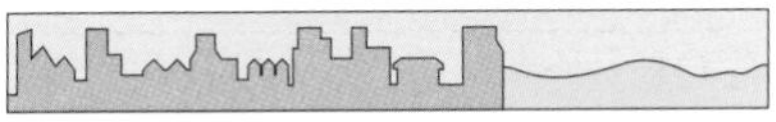
65%
35%

RELIGIOUS PERSUASION

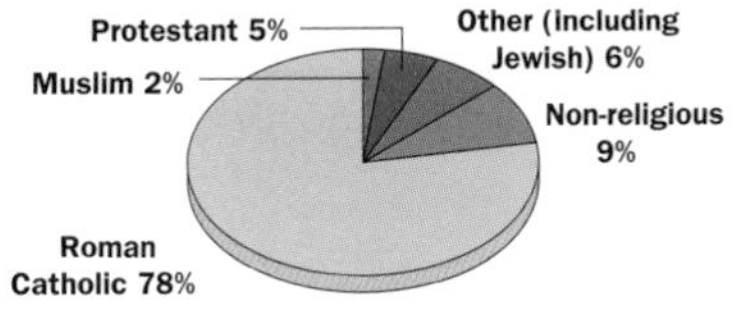
Protestant 5%
Other (including Jewish) 6%
Muslim 2%
Non-religious 9%
Roman Catholic 78%

ETHNIC MAKEUP

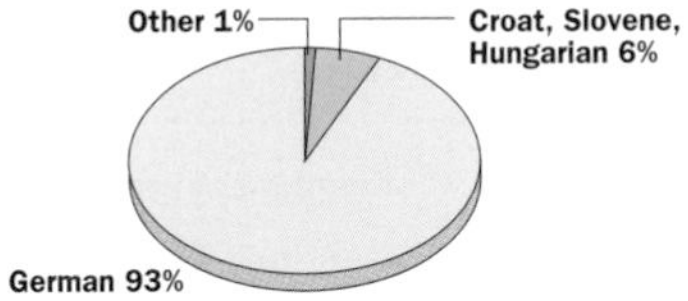
Other 1%
Croat, Slovene, Hungarian 6%
German 93%

Austrian society is homogeneous. Almost all Austrians are German speakers. However, Austrians like to consider themselves ethnically distinct from Germans. Minorities are few; there are some ethnic Slovenes, Croats, and Hungarians in the south and east, as well as some Romany communities. These minorities have been augmented by large numbers of immigrants from eastern Europe and refugees from the conflict in former Yugoslavia. The result has been a perceptible increase in ethnic tension, particularly as the far right claims that migrants are taking jobs from the local population.

The nuclear family is the norm in Austria. It is common for both parents to work. While gender equality is enshrined in the constitution, in practice society is still strongly patriarchal. Compared with the rest of Europe, few women enter politics.

Young Austrians tend to live in their parental home until they marry. This practice reflects the long time taken to complete university degrees, for which students do not receive maintenance grants. Austrians marry at a younger age than the European average. Nominally a Catholic country, Austria is socially less conservative than some German states.

POPULATION AGE BREAKDOWN

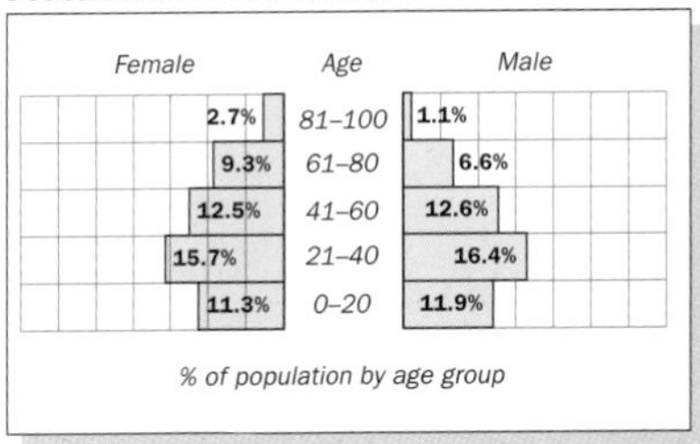
Female
Age
Male
2.7%
81–100
1.1%
9.3%
61–80
6.6%
12.5%
41–60
12.6%
15.7%
21–40
16.4%
11.3%
0–20
11.9%
% of population by age group

POLITICS

Multiparty elections

L. House 1999/2003
U. House varies by province

President Thomas Klestil

AT THE LAST ELECTION

National Council 183 seats

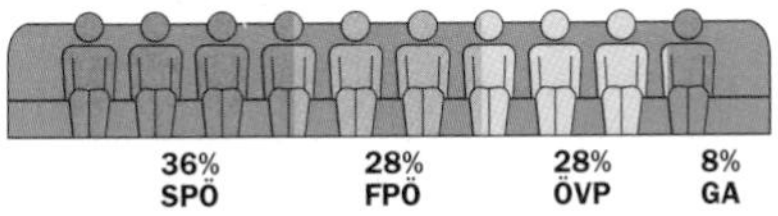
36% SPÖ
28% FPÖ
28% ÖVP
8% GA

SPÖ = Social Democratic Party of Austria **FPÖ** = Freedom Party of Austria **ÖVP** = Austrian People's Party **GA** = Green Alternative

Federal Council 64 seats

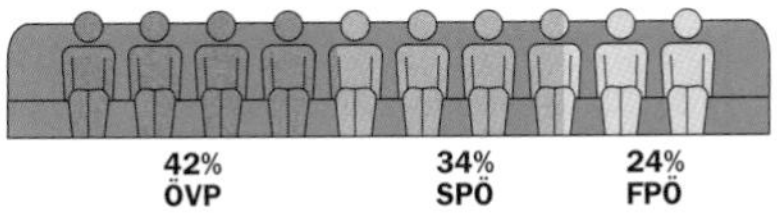
42% ÖVP
34% SPÖ
24% FPÖ

Austria is a federal, multiparty democracy. The chancellor (premier) holds real executive power. The long-established "grand coalition" between the socialist SPÖ and the conservative ÖVP was overturned in October 1999 by the formation of a coalition between the ÖVP and the far-right FPÖ.

MAIN POLITICAL ISSUE
Relations with EU partners

Austria's population is divided over the merits of EU membership. While the farming lobby remains apprehensive of EU agricultural policies, the country as a whole has benefited from lower food prices and greater consumer choice. Fears that membership is eroding national identity, as well as encouraging an influx of cheap east European labor, provided an electoral basis for the nationalist FPÖ. The party's inclusion in government in early 2000 provoked temporary diplomatic sanctions from the EU.

PROFILE

A coalition headed by the SPÖ, with the ÖVP as the junior partner, governed Austria almost without interruption from the 1950s until 1999. Their hold on power, with no real alternative, reached into all areas of public life. The FPÖ achieved a breakthrough in elections in 1999, when it came equal second with the ÖVP. A new right-wing coalition of the ÖVP and the FPÖ drew strong regional criticism. However, diplomatic sanctions were lifted in September 2000 after an EU report accepted that human rights had not been adversely affected by the FPÖ's presence in government. FPÖ leader Jörg Haider drew strong condemnation, having openly expressed admiration for some of Hitler's policies. He is still the driving force behind the party despite resigning formal leadership in May 2000. Later in the year, local elections showed dwindling support for the FPÖ, prompting talk of Haider's return to the forefront of Austrian politics.

The nine provincial assemblies and governments have considerable powers. Vienna, with provincial status, has long been dominated by the SPÖ.

***Dr. Thomas Klestil**, the ÖVP candidate, was elected president in 1992.*

***Wolfgang Schüssel**, ÖVP chancellor since 2000, in coalition with the far-right.*

WORLD AFFAIRS

Joined UN in 1955

EU | CE | PfP | OECD | OSCE

Despite the importance of relations with Germany, Austria's powerful northern neighbor and main trading partner, there has been a conscious policy of stressing Austria's independence and creating some diplomatic distance. Austria is keen to maintain its relationship with the USA, which is reinforced by Austria's role as supplier of small arms to the US Army. The inclusion of the far right in the Austrian government in 2000 provoked the imposition of of diplomatic sanctions by EU states for seven months.

Austria's status as a neutral state has begun to be questioned since Austria joined the EU, although in 1998 the SPÖ ruled out NATO membership. Austria is part of the Schengen Convention, ending border controls with other participating EU members. Its geopolitical position gives it considerable influence in eastern Europe; exports to the region trebled in the 1990s, while Austrian governments (until 2000) strongly supported the eastward enlargement of the EU.

AID

Donor

$527m (donations)

Up 16% in 1999

New projects are now assessed for their impact on the environment and on gender issues. Austria is a major donor of aid to eastern Europe. Poland is the largest recipient of official aid and Bosnia-Herzegovina the second. A major exporter to former Yugoslavia before the war, Austria has a key role in its reconstruction.

A

CHRONOLOGY

Austria came under the control of the Habsburgs in 1273. In 1867, the Dual Monarchy of Austria-Hungary was formed under Habsburg rule. Defeat in World War I in 1918 led to the breakup of the Habsburg empire and the formation of the Republic of Austria.

- **1934** Chancellor Dollfuss dismisses parliament and starts imprisoning social democrats, communists, and National Socialist (Nazi) Party members. Nazis attempt coup.
- **1938** The Anschluss – Austria incorporated into Germany by Hitler.
- **1945** Austria occupied by Soviet, British, US, and French forces. Elections result in ÖVP–SPÖ coalition.
- **1950** Attempted coup by Communist Party fails. Marshall Aid helps economic recovery.
- **1955** Occupying troops withdrawn. Austria recognized as a neutral sovereign state.
- **1971** SPÖ government formed under Chancellor Bruno Kreisky who dominates Austrian politics for 12 years.
- **1983** Socialists and the FPÖ form a coalition government under Fred Sinowatz.
- **1986** Kurt Waldheim, former UN secretary-general, elected president, despite war crimes allegations. Franz Vranitzky replaces Sinowatz as federal chancellor. Nationalist Jörg Haider becomes FPÖ leader, prompting the SPÖ to pull out of government. Elections produce stalemate. Return to "grand coalition" of SPÖ–ÖVP.
- **1990** ÖVP loses 17 seats in parliamentary elections.
- **1992** Thomas Klestil (ÖVP) elected president. Elections confirm some traditional ÖVP supporters defecting to FPÖ.
- **1995** Austria joins EU. Elections after coalition disagreement over budget; SPÖ and ÖVP increase representation; "grand coalition" re-forms in early 1996.
- **1997** Vranitzky resigns; replaced by Viktor Klima.
- **1998** Klestil reelected president.
- **1999** Haider's FPÖ wins 40% of votes in Carinthia regional poll, is equal second with ÖVP in general election in October; SPÖ remains as largest party.
- **2000** ÖVP accepts FPÖ into coalition, with Wolfgang Schüssel as chancellor; political crisis. EU imposes diplomatic sanctions, lifted after seven months.

DEFENSE

▷ Compulsory military service

$1.7bn

Down 7% in 1999

Under the 1955 State Treaty, which granted Austria its full independence, Austria is neutral, although it has participated in NATO's Partnerships for Peace program since 1995.

Despite the small size of its own forces, the Austrian arms industry is strong. It not only meets most of the hardware needs of its own army, but also exports arms to the USA and other countries.

AUSTRIAN ARMED FORCES

283 main battle tanks (169 M–60A3, 114 *Leopard* 2A4)	35,500 personnel
None	
52 combat aircraft (23 SAAB J-350e)	6500 personnel
None	

ECONOMICS

▷ Inflation 2.2% p.a. (1990–1999)

$205.7bn

13.73–14.66 schillings

SCORE CARD

❑ WORLD GNP RANKING	22nd
❑ GNP PER CAPITA	$25,430
❑ BALANCE OF PAYMENTS	$–5.7bn
❑ INFLATION	0.6%
❑ UNEMPLOYMENT	7%

EXPORTS

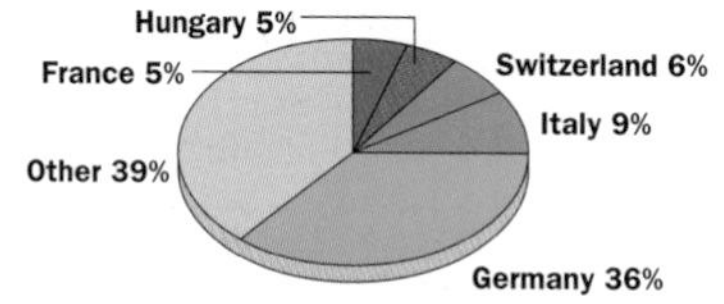
Hungary 5%
France 5%
Switzerland 6%
Italy 9%
Other 39%
Germany 36%

IMPORTS

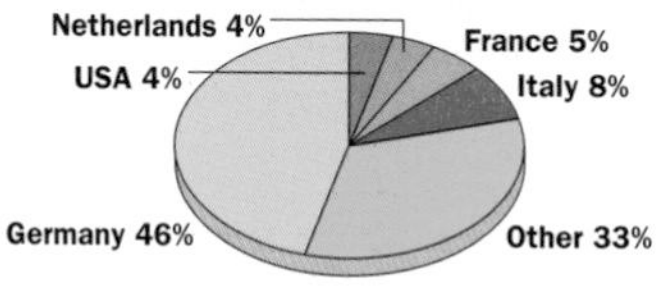
Netherlands 4%
USA 4%
France 5%
Italy 8%
Germany 46%
Other 33%

ECONOMIC PERFORMANCE INDICATOR

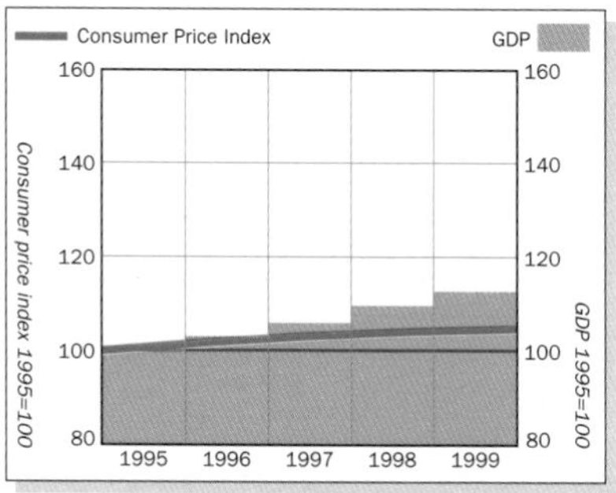
Consumer Price Index
GDP
160
140
120
100
80
1995
1996
1997
1998
1999
Consumer price index 1995=100
GDP 1995=100

STRENGTHS

Large manufacturing base. Strong chemical and petrochemical industries. Electrical engineering sector, textiles, and wood processing industries. Highly skilled labor force. Tourism is an important foreign currency earner.

WEAKNESSES

Lacks natural resources. Reliant on imported raw materials, particularly oil and gas. Process of introducing greater competition and deregulation has been slow.

PROFILE

Austria's industrial and high-tech sector is highly developed and contributes over a quarter of GDP. Some services, notably tourism, are highly sophisticated and profitable, although tourism receipts have been down in recent years.

A recession in the early 1990s was reversed by a rapid increase in exports to eastern Europe and Germany and by increased domestic demand.

There have been benefits from EU membership since 1995. Prices for many products, particularly food and books, have fallen. The Austrian labor market has also seen an influx of migrant labor more willing to accept flexible working arrangements and lower wages. Foreign investment has increased, as more multinationals locate their headquarters for east European operations in Austria. A far-reaching fiscal stabilization program instituted after accession enabled Austria to meet the economic convergence criteria necessary for it to join the final stage of economic and monetary union, introducing the euro in January 1999.

AUSTRIA : MAJOR BUSINESSES

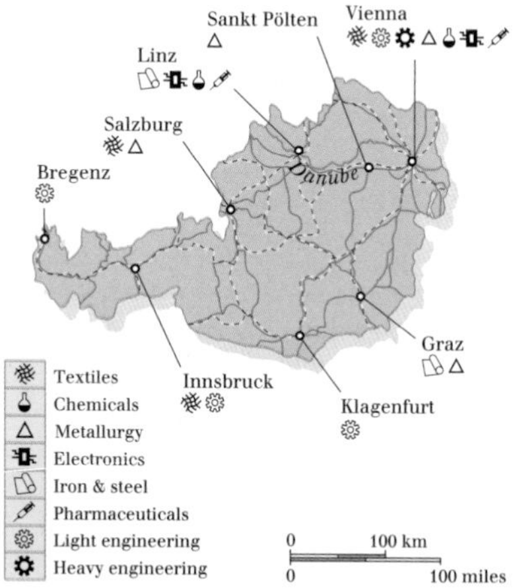
Sankt Pölten
Vienna
Linz
Salzburg
Bregenz
Danube
Graz
Innsbruck
Klagenfurt
Textiles
Chemicals
Metallurgy
Electronics
Iron & steel
Pharmaceuticals
Light engineering
Heavy engineering
0
100 km
0
100 miles

RESOURCES

Electric power 17.5m kw

3486 tonnes

19,489 b/d (reserves 78,265,440 bbl)

3.79m pigs, 2.15m cattle, 13.5m chickens

Iron, coal, magnesite, zinc, lead

ELECTRICITY GENERATION

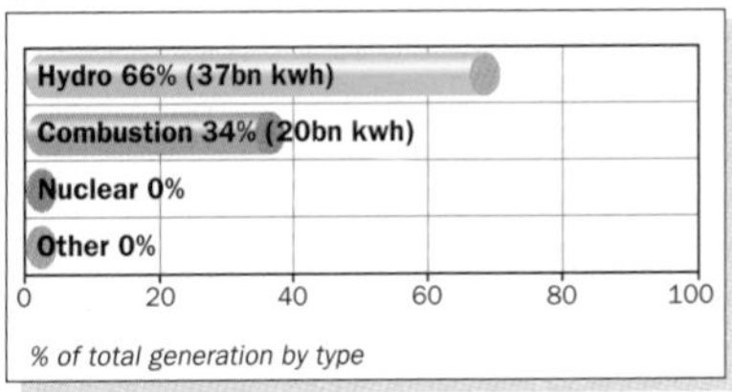
Hydro 66% (37bn kwh)
Combustion 34% (20bn kwh)
Nuclear 0%
Other 0%
0
20
40
60
80
100
% of total generation by type

AUSTRIA : LAND USE

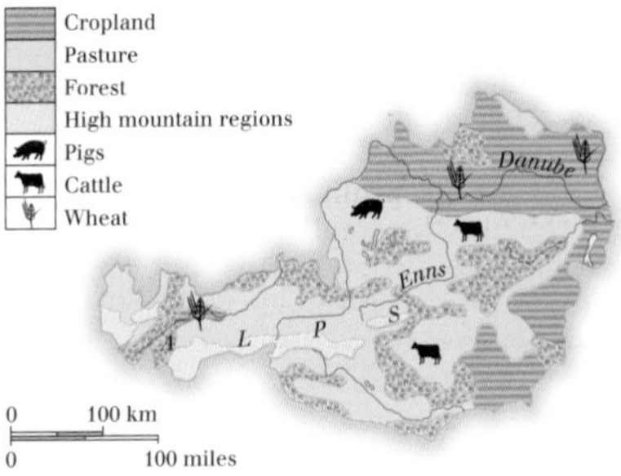
Cropland
Pasture
Forest
High mountain regions
Pigs
Cattle
Wheat
Danube
Enns
L
P
S
0
100 km
0
100 miles

Austria has few resources. It lacks significant oil, coal, and gas deposits and has to import a large amount of its energy. Russia is a key energy supplier, and gas is provided via pipelines running through the Czech and Slovak republics. Oil is imported up the Danube. Russia and Germany are the major suppliers of iron ore and raw steel for Austria's industry.

ENVIRONMENT

Sustainability rank: 8th

28% (24% partially protected)

7.8 tonnes per capita

ENVIRONMENTAL TREATIES

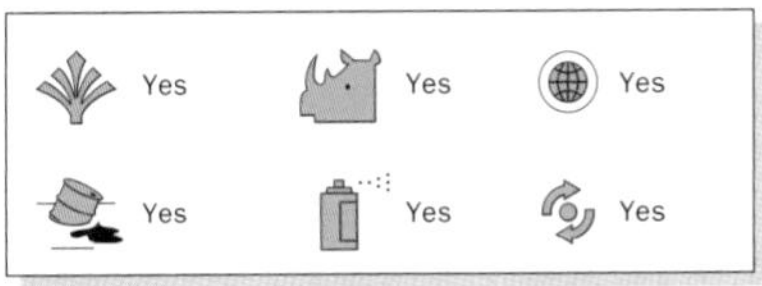
Yes
Yes
Yes
Yes
Yes
Yes

Environmental awareness is high. Domestic waste is separated for recycling, with heavy fines for failing to observe regulations. In 1999–2000 Austria recycled over 50% of domestic waste, including over 80% of glass. The safety of nuclear reactors in the neighboring Czech Republic, Slovakia, and Slovenia is a major concern.

MEDIA

TV ownership high

Daily newspaper circulation 296 per 1000 people

PUBLISHING AND BROADCAST MEDIA

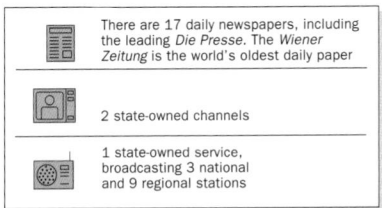

There are 17 daily newspapers, including the leading *Die Presse*. The *Wiener Zeitung* is the world's oldest daily paper

2 state-owned channels

1 state-owned service, broadcasting 3 national and 9 regional stations

TV and radio are controlled by the Austrian Broadcasting Company (ÖRF), which has a politically appointed general director. Cable TV is licensed by ÖRF to prevent it taking viewers from existing stations. A satellite program run jointly with German and Swiss TV provides German-language programs to counterbalance those available in English and French.

CRIME

Death penalty not used

7137 prisoners

Down 2% 1996–1998

CRIME RATES

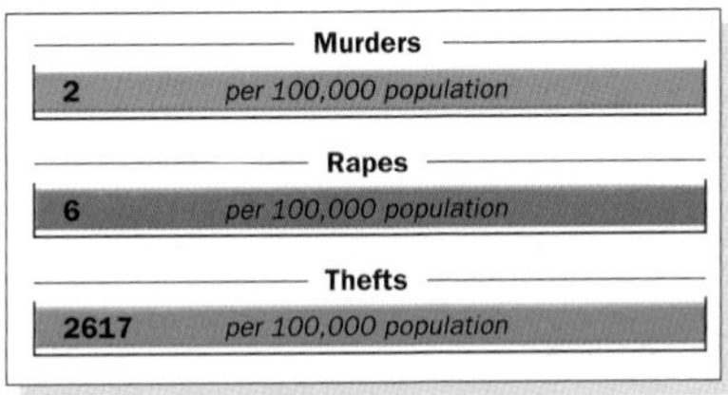
Murders
2 per 100,000 population
Rapes
6 per 100,000 population
Thefts
2617 per 100,000 population

Austria's crime rate is below Europe's average. However, the number of burglaries is rising. The arrival of the Russian mafia in Vienna has led to an increase in money laundering.

EDUCATION

School leaving age: 15

99%

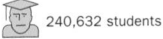

240,632 students

THE EDUCATION SYSTEM

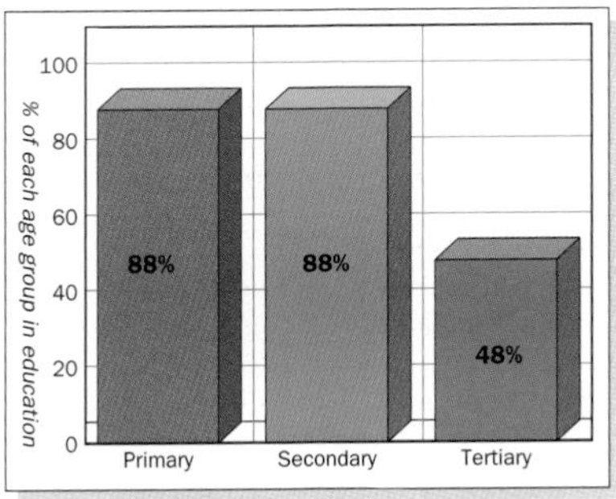
100
80
60
40
20
0
% of each age group in education
88%
88%
48%
Primary
Secondary
Tertiary

Of total government expenditure some 10% is spent on education. Children are streamed into two types of secondary school according to their academic ability. Those in a *Gymnasium* (11–18) take the *Reifeprüfung* or *Matura* which determines entry to university, but children in a *Hauptschule* (11–15) do not. The universities are oversubscribed, with students taking six years or more to finish their first degrees.

HEALTH

Welfare state health benefits

1 per 333 people

Heart and cerebrovascular diseases, cancers

Austria has relatively high levels of spending on health, accounting for 13% of total government expenditure. However, private spending on health is increasing and accounts for nearly one-third of the total, the highest proportion of any EU state, as patients increasingly choose to use the private health sector to avoid waiting lists for operations.

SPENDING

GDP/cap. increase

CONSUMPTION AND SPENDING

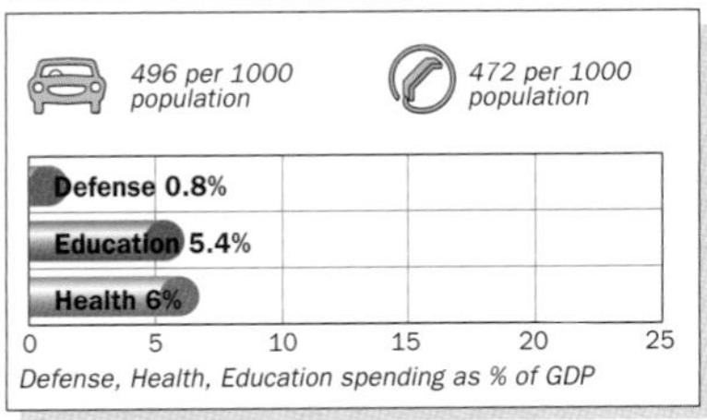
496 per 1000 population
472 per 1000 population
Defense 0.8%
Education 5.4%
Health 6%
0
5
10
15
20
25
Defense, Health, Education spending as % of GDP

Despite having had a left-of-center government for most of the last four decades, Austria has retained many of its traditional social divisions. Inherited wealth is still respected above earned wealth, and social mobility is somewhat less than in neighboring Germany. Austrians have the highest savings rate of any country in the OECD. Relatively few Austrians own stocks and shares, and limited amounts are invested in property. Legislation in 2000 banned anonymous savings accounts, a system unique in the EU to Austria which, it had been argued, encouraged money laundering and insider dealing. Government bonds offer low rates of interest and the property market is weak; many people, particularly in Vienna, tend to rent rather than buy their apartments. Refugees from the conflict in the former Yugoslavia form the poorest group in Austrian society.

WORLD RANKING

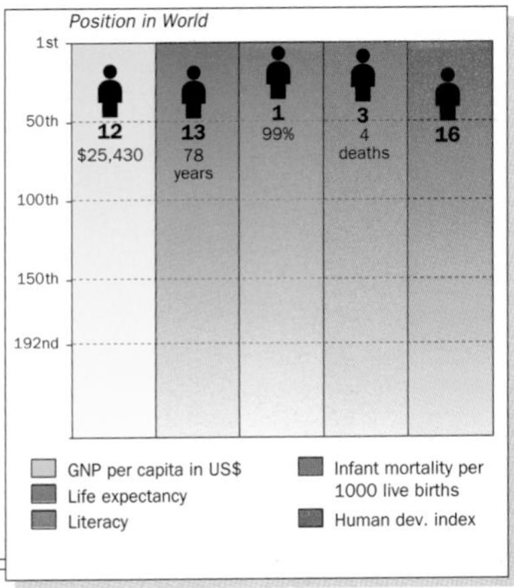
Position in World
1st
50th
100th
150th
192nd
12
$25,430
13
78
years
1
99%
3
4
deaths
16
GNP per capita in US$
Life expectancy
Literacy
Infant mortality per 1000 live births
Human dev. index

A

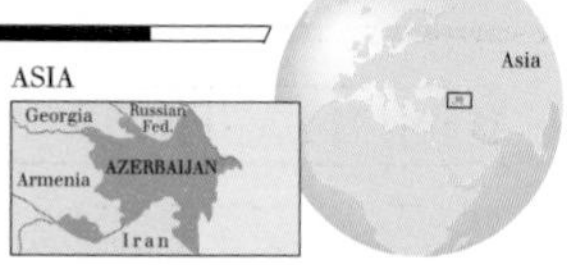
ASIA
Georgia
Russian Fed.
Armenia
AZERBAIJAN
Iran
Asia

AZERBAIJAN

OFFICIAL NAME: Republic of Azerbaijan **CAPITAL:** Baku
POPULATION: 7.7 million **CURRENCY:** Manat **OFFICIAL LANGUAGE:** Azerbaijani

1991 | 1991 | May 28 | AZ | +4 | +994 | .az

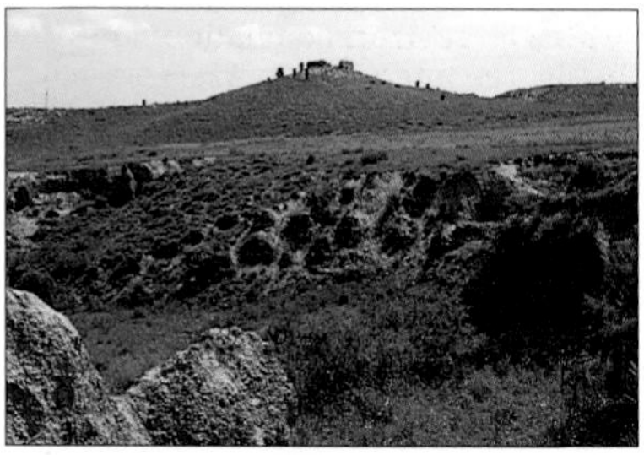

Landscape typical of the Lesser Caucasus mountains near Qazax in the extreme northwest of Azerbaijan.

SITUATED ON THE WESTERN COAST of the Caspian Sea, Azerbaijan was the first Soviet republic to declare independence. The issue of the disputed enclave of Nagorno Karabakh, which Armenia seeks to annex, led to full-scale war until 1994 and is still a dominant concern. Over 200,000 refugees and more than twice as many internally displaced added to the problems of the troubled economy. Azerbaijan's oil wealth, however, gives it long-term potential.

CLIMATE

Mountain/steppe

WEATHER CHART

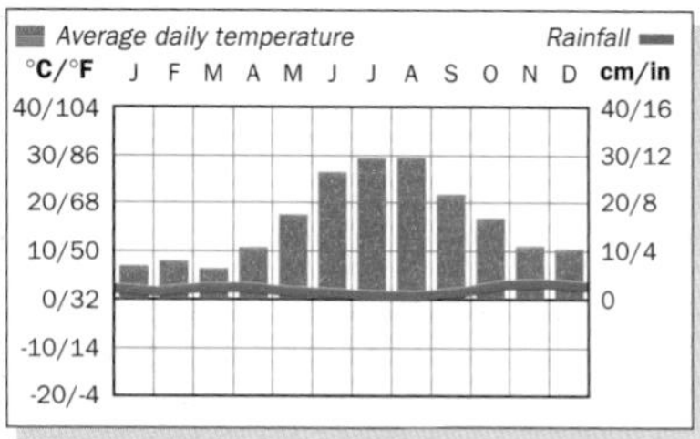
Average daily temperature
Rainfall
°C/°F
J F M A M J J A S O N D
cm/in
40/104
30/86
20/68
10/50
0/32
-10/14
-20/-4
40/16
30/12
20/8
10/4
0

Coastal areas are subtropical, but bitter winters inland have become a life-or-death issue for thousands of refugees.

TRANSPORTATION

Drive on right

Baku

287 ships 650,933 grt

THE TRANSPORTATION NETWORK

23,057 km (14,327 miles)	None
2116 km (1315 miles)	None

Links to the south via Iran and Turkey, rather than the north via Russia, are the focus of transportation spending.

TOURISM

Visitors : Population 1:13

602,000 visitors

Up 25% in 1999

MAIN TOURIST ARRIVALS

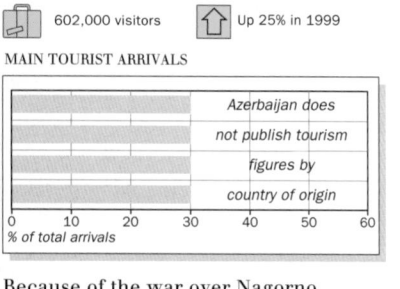

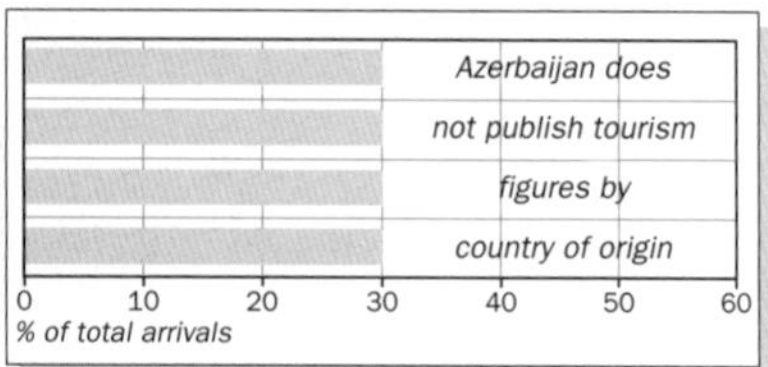
Azerbaijan does
not publish tourism
figures by
country of origin
0
10
20
30
40
50
60
% of total arrivals

Because of the war over Nagorno Karabakh, and strong anti-Western feelings (Azerbaijan perceives the West as taking the Armenian side in the conflict), there are few visitors, most of them on business.

PEOPLE

Pop. density medium

Azerbaijani, Russian

89/km² (230/mi²)

THE URBAN/RURAL POPULATION SPLIT

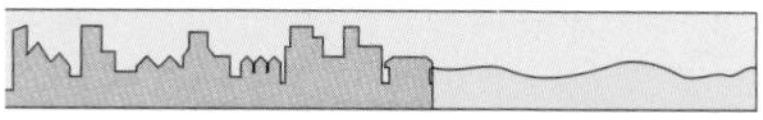
57%
43%

ETHNIC MAKEUP

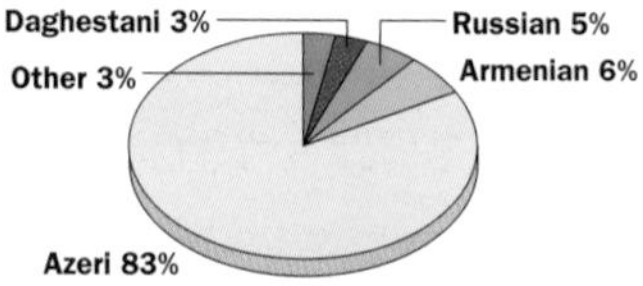
Daghestani 3%
Russian 5%
Other 3%
Armenian 6%
Azeri 83%

At the last census, held in 1989, Azeris made up 83% of the population. The proportion today is even greater – thousands of Armenians, Jews, and Russians have left as a result of rising Azeri nationalism. Racial hostility against those who remain is increasing.

Women, once prominent in the ruling party, have lost their political status and their general status is declining.

The once effective social security system is under great strain.

POLITICS

Multiparty elections

2000/2005

President Heydar Aliyev

AT THE LAST ELECTION

National Assembly 125 seats

2% CSP
1% Vacant
61% NA
21% Ind
5% APF
10% Others

NA = New Azerbaijan **Ind** = Independents **APF** = Azerbaijan Popular Front **CSP** = Civic Solidarity Party **Vacant** = Seat reserved for member from Nagorno Karabakh

The determination of the Nagorno Karabakh enclave to unite with Armenia led to war until 1994, with Armenia gaining control over 20% of Azeri territory. Peace talks have yet to reach an accord.

NA replaced the communists in 1995 and again dominated elections in 2000, which observers criticized as seriously flawed. NA supports septuagenarian President Heydar Aliyev, first elected in 1993 and reelected in 1998.

AZERBAIJAN

Total Land Area : 86 600 sq. km (33 436 sq. miles)

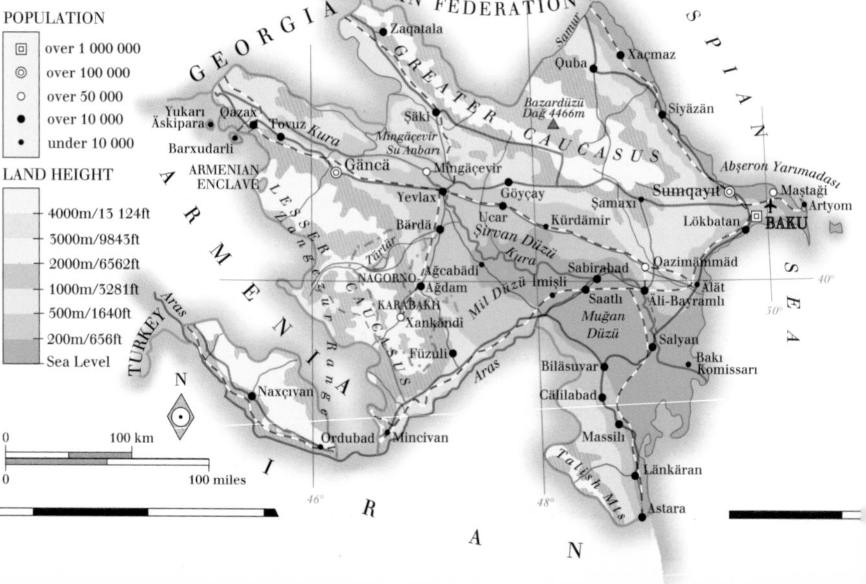
POPULATION
over 1 000 000
over 100 000
over 50 000
over 10 000
under 10 000
LAND HEIGHT
4000m/13 124ft
3000m/9843ft
2000m/6562ft
1000m/3281ft
500m/1640ft
200m/656ft
Sea Level
0 100 km
0 100 miles
RUSSIAN FEDERATION
CASPIAN SEA
GEORGIA
ARMENIA
IRAN
TURKEY
Zaqatala
Xaçmaz
Quba
Siyäzän
Bazardüzü Dağ 4466m
GREATER CAUCASUS
Şäki
Yukarı Äskipara
Qazax
Tovuz
Barxudarli
Kura
Mingäçevir Su Anbarı
Gäncä
Mingäçevir
ARMENIAN ENCLAVE
Abşeron Yarımadası
Sumqayıt
Maştağı
Artyom
BAKU
Lökbatan
Göyçay
Şamaxı
Yevlax
Bärdä
Ucar
Kürdämir
Şirvan Düzü
Tärtär
LESSER CAUCASUS
Zangezur Range
NAGORNO KARABAKH
Ağcabädi
Ağdam
Xankändi
Füzuli
Mil Düzü
İmişli
Sabirabad
Qazimämmäd
Älät
Äli-Bayramlı
Saatlı
Muğan Düzü
Salyan
Baki Komissarı
Biläsuvar
Cälilabad
Massili
Länkäran
Astara
Talış Mts
Aras
Naxçıvan
Ordubad
Mincivan
N
42°
40°
46°
48°
50°

WORLD AFFAIRS

Joined UN in 1992

CIS | CE | EAPC | OIC | OSCE

The West, as well as neighboring Iran (with a large Azeri population) and Russia, are interested in Azeri oilfields in the Caspian Sea. Relations with Russia under President Putin have improved. Turkey – with its common history and culture – is a natural ally. Azerbaijan joined the Council of Europe in 2001.

AID

Recipient

$162m (receipts)

Up 82% in 1999

World Bank aid has grown steadily. A pro-Armenian US Congress banned all but limited humanitarian aid from 1992.

DEFENSE

Compulsory military service

$203m

Up 3% in 1999

Azerbaijan has been a member of NATO's Partnership for Peace program since 1994. Its naval forces operate under CIS control.

ECONOMICS

Inflation 250% p.a. (1990–1999)

$3.7bn

4375–4456 manats

SCORE CARD

❑ WORLD GNP RANKING	121st
❑ GNP PER CAPITA	$460
❑ BALANCE OF PAYMENTS	$-600m
❑ INFLATION	–8.6%
❑ UNEMPLOYMENT	1%

STRENGTHS

Extensive oil and natural gas reserves starting to come on stream. Iron, copper, lead, and salt deposits. Cotton and silk.

WEAKNESSES

Antiquated Soviet-era industry. Poor infrastructure and corruption threaten development. Oil pipeline to Turkey not yet built. Fallout from war in Nagorno Karabakh still drains state resources.

EXPORTS

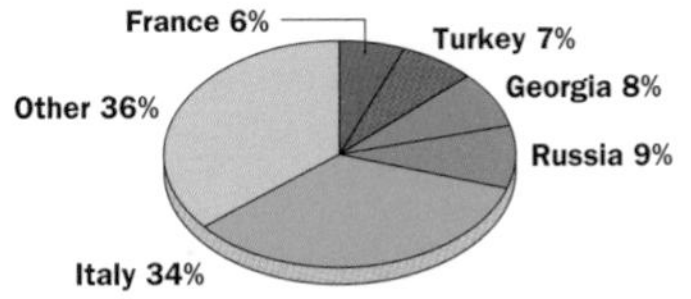

France 6%
Turkey 7%
Georgia 8%
Other 36%
Russia 9%
Italy 34%

IMPORTS

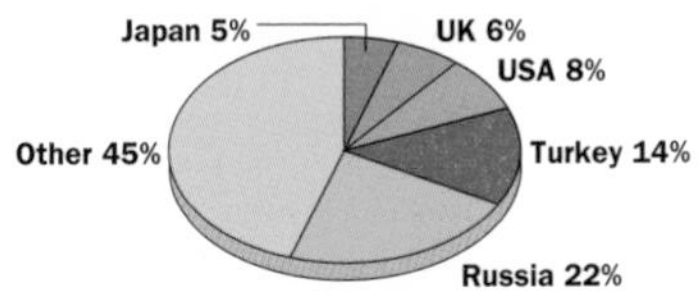

Japan 5%
UK 6%
USA 8%
Other 45%
Turkey 14%
Russia 22%

RESOURCES

Electric power 5.2m kw

8488 tonnes

300,000 b/d (reserves 6,900,000,000 bbl)

5.39m sheep, 1.95m cattle, 13.9m chickens

Iron, bauxite, copper, lead, zinc, limestone, salt, oil, gas

Relatively neglected in the Soviet period, Azerbaijan's Caspian Sea oilfields have attracted international interest. The shallow-water Guneshli field alone has over four million barrels of reserves. Offshore natural gas is plentiful.

ENVIRONMENT

Sustainability rank: 69th

6%

4.1 tonnes per capita

Under the Soviet regime oil pollution devastated the Caspian Sea, and pesticides were massively overused in agriculture. Major rivers suffer heavy pollution from Georgia and Armenia. Lack of funds restricts action.

MEDIA

TV ownership high

Daily newspaper circulation 28 per 1000 people

PUBLISHING AND BROADCAST MEDIA

There are 6 daily newspapers, including *Bakinskii Rabochii*, *Khalg Gazeti*, and *Respublika*

1 state-controlled service, 1 independent station

1 state-controlled service

A 1998 decree abolished censorship, but freedom is limited by newsprint controls, license restrictions, and intimidation.

CRIME

Death penalty not used

Azerbaijan does not publish prison figures

Down 19% 1996–1998

The judicial system returned to political control in 1993. Criminality is a particular problem in camps for those displaced in the Nagorno Karabakh conflict. Elsewhere, there is a low rate of violent crime, but assaults in the streets have become less rare.

EDUCATION

School leaving age: 17

96%

115,116 students

When it came to power in the mid-1990s NA began to reverse communist control over education policy, which had been particularly noticeable in the teaching of history. Baku, the main university, specializes in Oriental studies.

HEALTH

Welfare state health benefits

1 per 263 people

Heart, cerebrovascular and respiratory diseases, cancers

The already poor health care system effectively collapsed as a result of war and the transition to a market economy.

CHRONOLOGY

Under consecutive Persian, Ottoman, and Russian influences, Azerbaijan, one of the world's major oil producers in 1900, attained independence in 1918.

- ❑ **1920** Red Army invades. Soviet republic established.
- ❑ **1922** Incorporated in Transcaucasian Soviet Federative Socialist Republic (TSFSR).
- ❑ **1930** Forced collectivization of agriculture.
- ❑ **1936** TSFSR disbanded; Azerbaijan a full union republic (ASSR).
- ❑ **1945** Attempted annexation of Azeri region of Iran.
- ❑ **1985** Gorbachev tackles corruption in Communist Party of Azerbaijan.
- ❑ **1988** Nagorno Karabakh seeks unification with Armenia.
- ❑ **1990** Nagorno Karabakh attempts secession. Soviet troops move in.
- ❑ **1991** Independence.
- ❑ **1993** Aliyev president; reelected in 1998.
- ❑ **1994** Cease-fire in war with Armenia over Nagorno Karabakh.
- ❑ **1995–1999** General elections. Non-communist NA in power.

SPENDING

GDP/cap. decrease

CONSUMPTION AND SPENDING

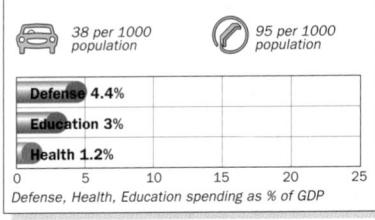

38 per 1000 population

95 per 1000 population

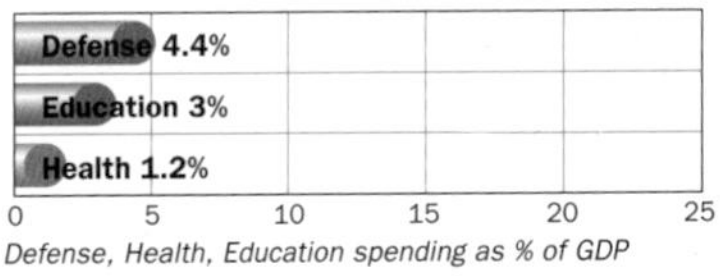

Defense 4.4%
Education 3%
Health 1.2%
0
5
10
15
20
25
Defense, Health, Education spending as % of GDP

New oil revenues are threatening to create a nouveau riche elite without reaching the 60% of Azerbaijan's population currently living in poverty.

WORLD RANKING

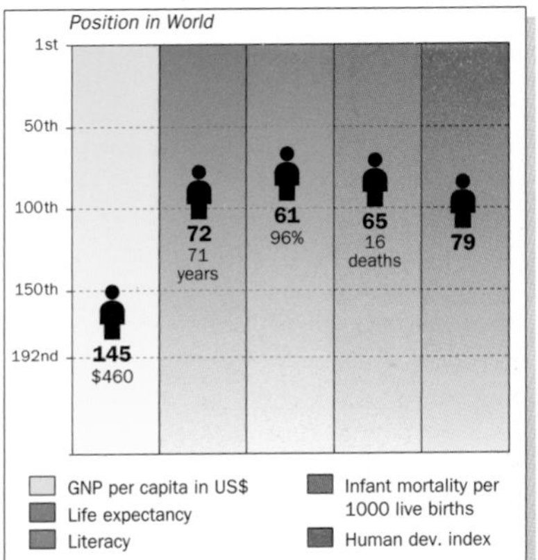

Position in World
1st
50th
100th
150th
192nd
145
$460
72
71 years
61
96%
65
16 deaths
79
GNP per capita in US$
Life expectancy
Literacy
Infant mortality per 1000 live births
Human dev. index

BAHAMAS

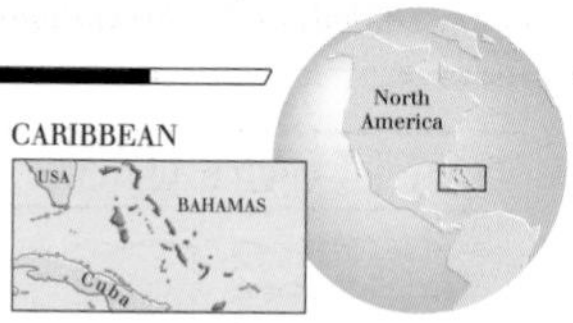
North America
CARIBBEAN
USA
BAHAMAS
Cuba

OFFICIAL NAME: The Commonwealth of the Bahamas **CAPITAL:** Nassau
POPULATION: 307,000 **CURRENCY:** Bahamian dollar **OFFICIAL LANGUAGE:** English

1973 | 1973 | July 10 | BS | -5 | +1242 | .bs

LOCATED OFF THE FLORIDA coast in the western Atlantic, the Bahamas comprises an archipelago of some 700 islands and 2400 cays, of which 30 are inhabited. One of the first transatlantic tourist destinations, the Bahamas today is also a major offshore financial center. It has one of the world's largest open-registry fleets, although only a tiny fraction is owned by Bahamian nationals.

CLIMATE

Tropical oceanic

WEATHER CHART

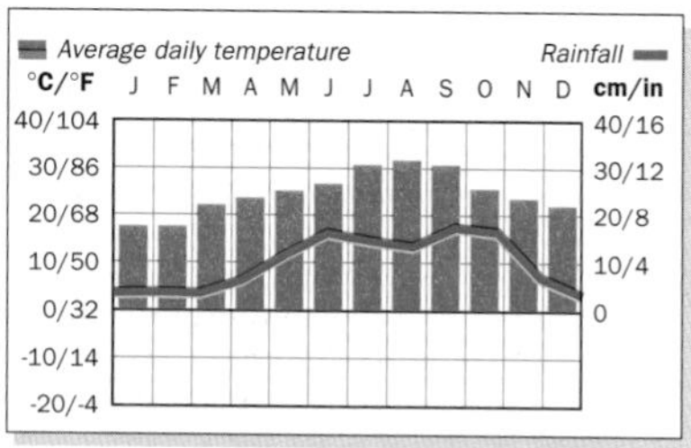
Average daily temperature
Rainfall
°C/°F
J F M A M J J A S O N D
cm/in
40/104
30/86
20/68
10/50
0/32
-10/14
-20/4
40/16
30/12
20/8
10/4
0

The whole of the Bahamas chain has a typically subtropical climate with consistently mild winters. Hurricanes may occur from July to December.

TRANSPORTATION

Drive on left

Freeport International 1.23m passengers

27.7m grt

THE TRANSPORTATION NETWORK

1546 km (961 miles)

None

None

None

While traveling around and between the major islands is relatively easy, transportation links for the many "Out Islands" are greatly restricted.

TOURISM

Visitors : Population 5.1:1

1.6m visitors

Up 3% in 1999

MAIN TOURIST ARRIVALS

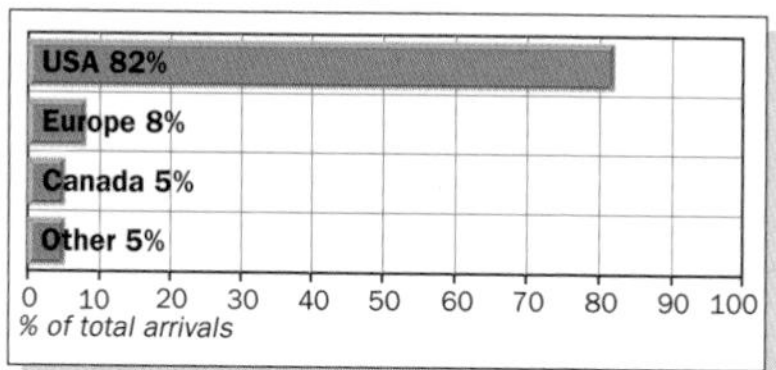
USA 82%
Europe 8%
Canada 5%
Other 5%
0 10 20 30 40 50 60 70 80 90 100
% of total arrivals

Casinos and beaches attract US visitors especially. The Bahamas is a major Caribbean cruise ship center. Larger hotel complexes on the main islands compete with small, family-run guesthouses in the outlying destinations.

PEOPLE

Pop. density low

English, English Creole, French Creole

31/km² (79/mi²)

THE URBAN/RURAL POPULATION SPLIT

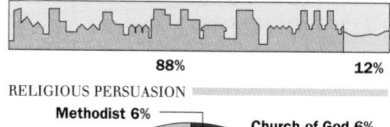

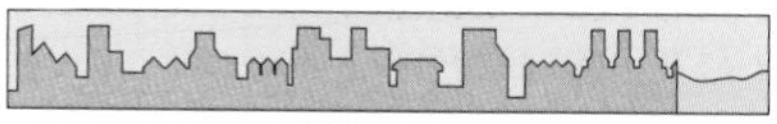
88%
12%

RELIGIOUS PERSUASION

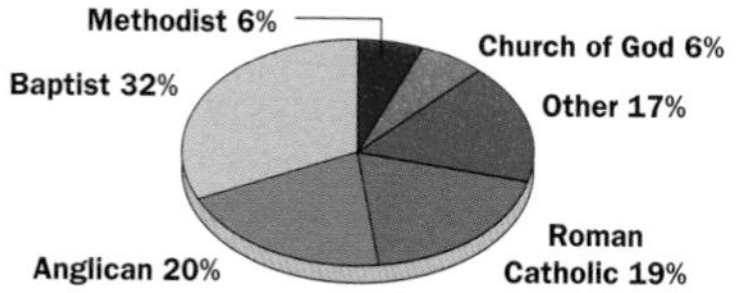
Methodist 6%
Church of God 6%
Baptist 32%
Other 17%
Roman Catholic 19%
Anglican 20%

Africans first arrived as slaves in the 16th century; their descendants constitute most of the population, alongside a rich white minority. Small families are the norm. Absentee fathers are fairly common, especially in outlying fishing communities. More women are now entering the professions.

POLITICS

Multiparty elections

L. House 1997/2002
U. House 1997/2002

HM Queen Elizabeth II

AT THE LAST ELECTION

House of Assembly 40 seats

85% FNM
15% PLP

FNM = Free National Movement
PLP = Progressive Liberal Party

Senate 16 seats

The members of the Senate are appointed by the governor-general on the recommendation of the prime minister and the leader of the opposition

The 1992 election defeat of Lynden Pindling, following drug-related corruption allegations, ended 25 years of continuous rule by his PLP. Pindling was instrumental in steering the Bahamas to independence, ending the domination of the white elite in Bahamian politics and bringing blacks into the political process for the first time. Prime Minister Hubert Ingraham has concentrated on tightening up ministerial accountability, and in October 1995 legislation was introduced to counter money laundering. Economic successes ensured his reelection in 1997. He faced protests in 1999 over the privatization of telecommunications.

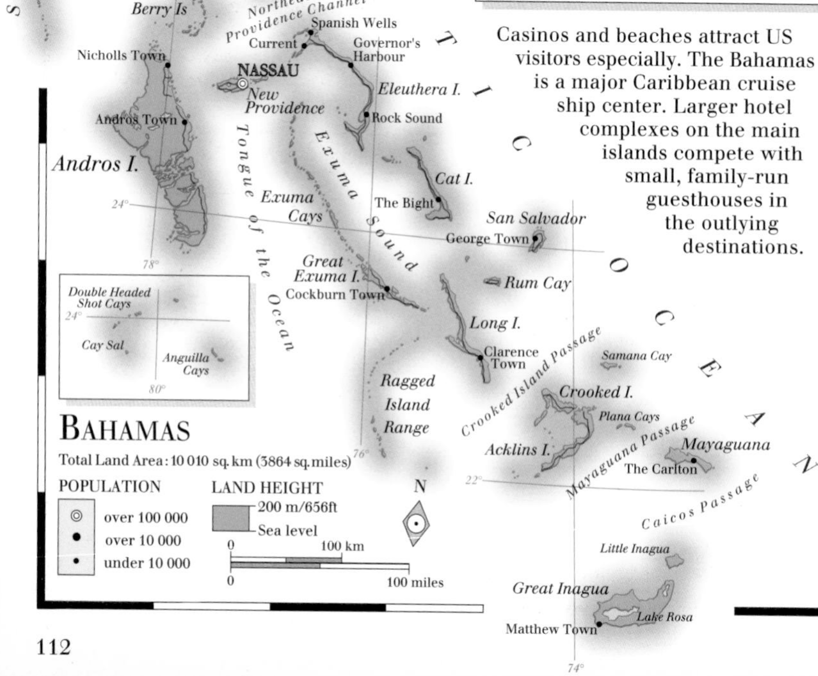
Straits of Florida
ATLANTIC OCEAN
West End
Freeport
Grand Bahama I.
Little Abaco
Abaco I.
Marsh Harbour
Hope Town
Northwest Providence Channel
Great Abaco
Bimini Is
Berry Is
Northeast Providence Channel
Spanish Wells
Current
Governor's Harbour
Nicholls Town
NASSAU
New Providence
Eleuthera I.
Rock Sound
Andros Town
Andros I.
Tongue of the Ocean
Exuma Sound
Cat I.
Exuma Cays
The Bight
San Salvador
George Town
Great Exuma I.
Cockburn Town
Rum Cay
Long I.
Clarence Town
Crooked Island Passage
Samana Cay
Ragged Island Range
Crooked I.
Plana Cays
Acklins I.
Mayaguana Passage
Mayaguana
The Carlton
Caicos Passage
Little Inagua
Great Inagua
Lake Rosa
Matthew Town
Double Headed Shot Cays
Cay Sal
Anguilla Cays
BAHAMAS
Total Land Area: 10 010 sq. km (3864 sq. miles)
POPULATION
over 100 000
over 10 000
under 10 000
LAND HEIGHT
200 m/656ft
Sea level
0 100 km
0 100 miles
N

WORLD AFFAIRS

Joined UN in 1973

ACS | Caricom | Comm | NAM | OAS

The Bahamas is seen as a center for transshipping narcotics and a money-laundering risk, for which G7 blacklisted the country for a year in 2000. The return of unauthorized immigrants to Haiti and Cuba dominates regional relations.

AID

Recipient

US$12m (receipts)

Up 300% 1997–1999

Aid is modest. The IDB and the USA provide soft development loans. China in 1998 loaned Nassau US$17 million for a convention and theater complex.

DEFENSE

No compulsory military service

US$26m

No change in 1999

The UK is the main trainer of and supplier for the small naval defense force. The interception of narcotics and illegal immigrants is the force's main activity. There is no land army.

ECONOMICS

Inflation 2.6% p.a. (1990–1999)

US$9.4bn

1 Bahamian dollar

SCORE CARD

❑ World GNP Ranking	87th
❑ GNP per Capita	US$13,990
❑ Balance of Payments	US$–672m
❑ Inflation	1.3%
❑ Unemployment	9%

STRENGTHS

Major international financial services sector, including banking, insurance, and business trade center. Major tourism and cruise ship destination. Growing container port. International ship registration.

WEAKNESSES

Growing competition in financial services and tourism from the rest of the Caribbean.

EXPORTS

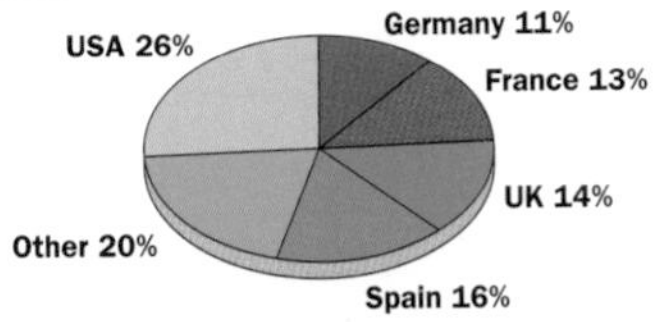
USA 26%
Germany 11%
France 13%
UK 14%
Spain 16%
Other 20%

IMPORTS

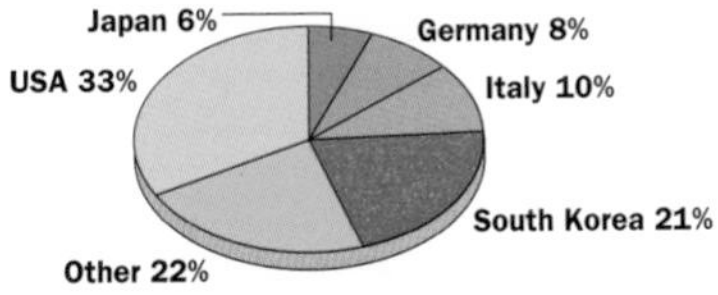
Japan 6%
Germany 8%
USA 33%
Italy 10%
South Korea 21%
Other 22%

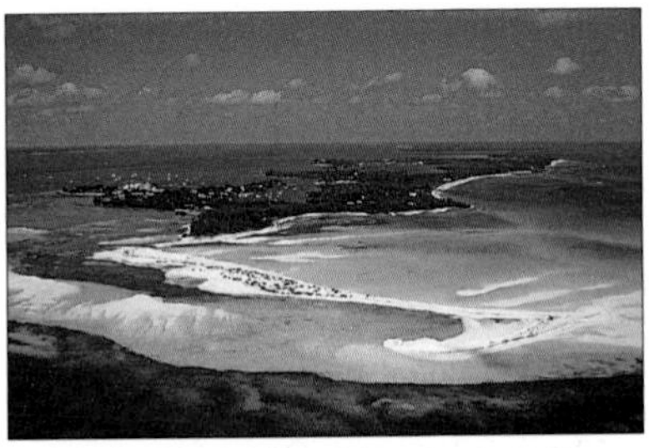

Archetypal island paradise. *Its natural beauty attracts more than five tourists per inhabitant to the Bahamas every year.*

RESOURCES

Electric power 401,000 kw

10,440 tonnes

Not an oil producer

14,500 goats, 5,900 pigs, 5,700 sheep, 5m chickens

Salt, aragonite

The Bahamas has no strategic resources. A 13.5 MW electricity generating plant was opened in 1998.

ENVIRONMENT

Not available

9%

6 tonnes per capita

As in other Caribbean states, hotel overdevelopment is a major cause for concern. Environmental groups have also pointed out the potential for accidents posed by the Bahamas' enormous oil storage depots.

MEDIA

TV ownership medium

Daily newspaper circulation 99 per 1000 people

PUBLISHING AND BROADCAST MEDIA

There are 4 daily newspapers, the *Nassau Guardian*, the *Tribune*, the *Bahama Journal*, and the *Freeport News*

1 state-owned service

5 services: 1 state-owned, 4 independent

The state-owned TV channel faces very stiff competition from Florida-based US broadcasters.

CRIME

Death penalty used

3789 prisoners

Gradually rising in the 1990s

The death penalty remains in force. Violent crime, ranging from narcotics-related murders to serious vandalism, is on the increase. Tourists can be targets for petty thefts. Illegal weapons are readily available.

EDUCATION

School leaving age: 14

96%

5305 students

As in much of the Caribbean, education follows the former British selective system. Students attend the University of the West Indies or go to the USA.

CHRONOLOGY

Once an English pirate base, the Bahamas, which gained its first parliament in 1729, formally became a British colony in 1783.

- ❑ **1920–1933** US prohibition laws turn Bahamas into prosperous bootlegging center.
- ❑ **1959–1962** Introduction of male suffrage; women gain the vote.
- ❑ **1973** Independence.
- ❑ **1983** Narcotics-smuggling scandals involving the government.
- ❑ **1997** Elections return Prime Minister Hubert Ingraham to office with increased majority.

HEALTH

Welfare state health benefits

1 per 658 people

Obstetric causes, heart diseases, cancers, crime, accidents

The Bahamian health service combines state and private systems. In the outlying islands access to care relies on the Flying Doctor Service and around 50 local health centers. There are two private clinics on New Providence.

SPENDING

GDP/cap. increase

CONSUMPTION AND SPENDING

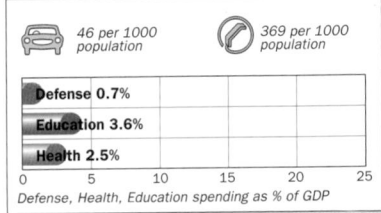

46 per 1000 population

369 per 1000 population

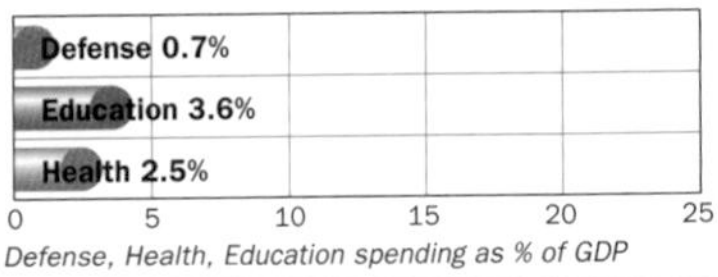
Defense 0.7%
Education 3.6%
Health 2.5%
0
5
10
15
20
25
Defense, Health, Education spending as % of GDP

There are marked wealth disparities. Urban professionals who work in the financial sector are at one end of the scale, and the poor fishermen from the outlying islands at the other. Cuban and Haitian refugees, who have no legal status, are the poorest group of all.

WORLD RANKING

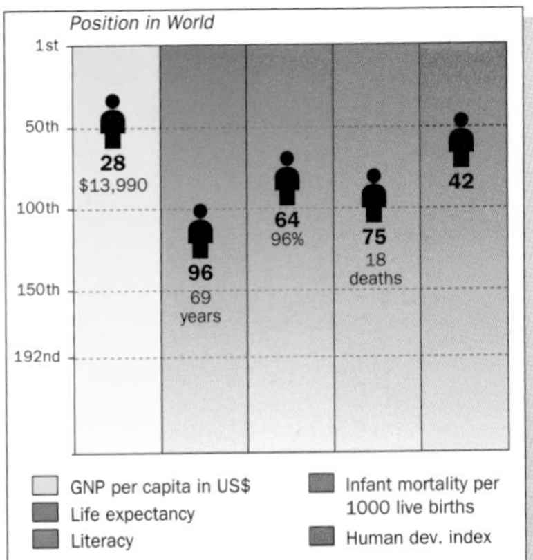
Position in World
1st
50th
100th
150th
192nd
28
$13,990
96
69 years
64
96%
75
18 deaths
42
GNP per capita in US$
Life expectancy
Literacy
Infant mortality per 1000 live births
Human dev. index

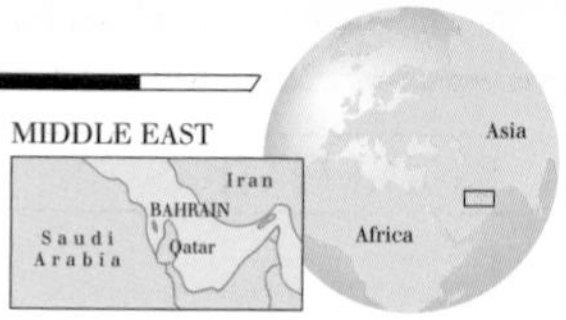
MIDDLE EAST
Asia
Iran
BAHRAIN
Saudi Arabia
Qatar
Africa

BAHRAIN

OFFICIAL NAME: State of Bahrain **CAPITAL:** Manama
POPULATION: 617,000 **CURRENCY:** Bahrain dinar **OFFICIAL LANGUAGE:** Arabic

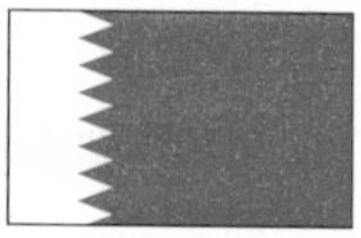

1971 | 1971 | Dec 16 | BRN | +3 | +973 | .bh

BAHRAIN IS AN ARCHIPELAGO of 33 islands situated between the Qatar peninsula and the Saudi Arabian mainland. Only three of the islands are inhabited. Bahrain Island is connected to Saudi Arabia's eastern province by a causeway opened in 1986. Bahrain was the first Gulf emirate to export oil; its reserves are now almost depleted. Services such as offshore banking, insurance, and tourism are major employment sectors for skilled Bahrainis.

CLIMATE

Hot desert

WEATHER CHART

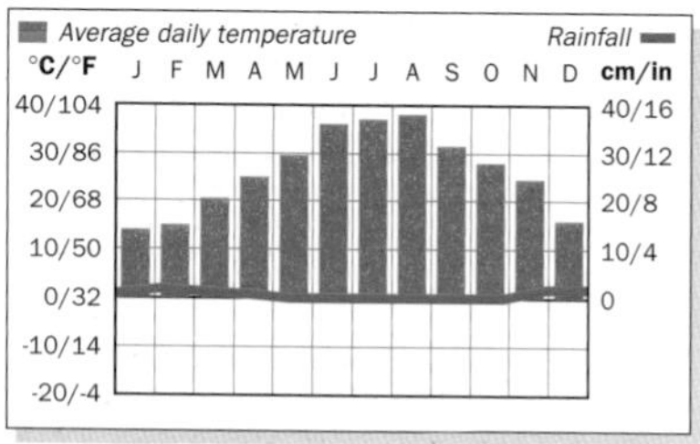
Average daily temperature
Rainfall
°C/°F
J F M A M J J A S O N D
cm/in
40/104
30/86
20/68
10/50
0/32
-10/14
-20/-4
40/16
30/12
20/8
10/4
0

Temperatures soar to 40°C (104°F) in June–September. In December–March the weather is pleasantly warm.

TRANSPORTATION

Drive on right

Bahrain International, Muharraq
3.42m passengers

110 ships
283,704 grt

THE TRANSPORTATION NETWORK

2433 km (1512 miles)

None

None

None

Saudi Arabia paid for a 25-km (16-mile) causeway linking it with Bahrain; the four-lane road was completed in 1986.

TOURISM

Visitors : Population 3.2:1

2m visitors

Up 14% in 1999

MAIN TOURIST ARRIVALS

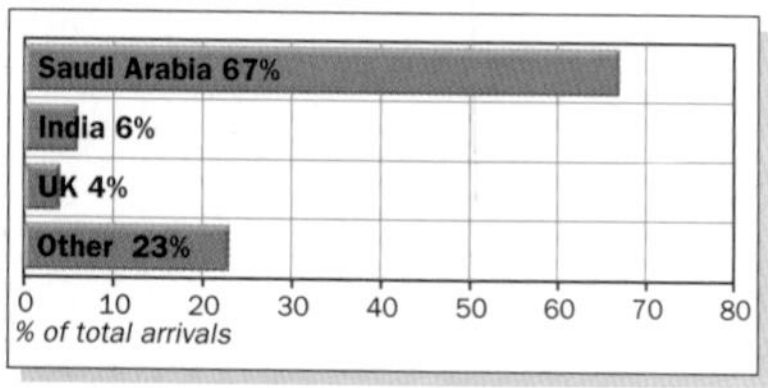
Saudi Arabia 67%
India 6%
UK 4%
Other 23%
0
10
20
30
40
50
60
70
80
% of total arrivals

Bahrain's liberal lifestyle and the opening of the causeway in 1986 has led to a boom in visitors from neighboring Gulf states. Bahrain has a modern airport and is a center for business conventions.

PEOPLE

Pop. density high

Arabic

907/km² (2350/mi²)

THE URBAN/RURAL POPULATION SPLIT

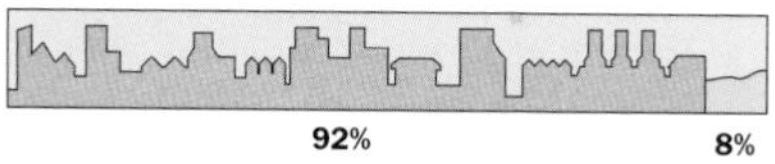
92%
8%

ETHNIC MAKEUP

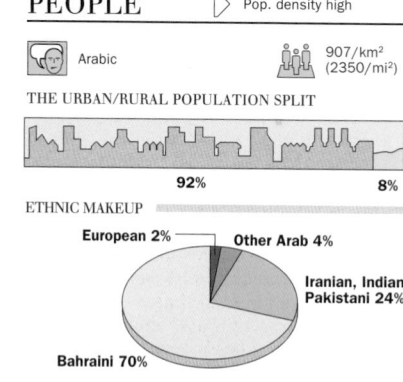

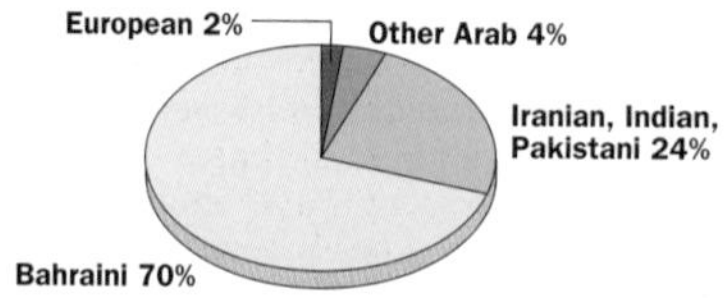
European 2%
Other Arab 4%
Iranian, Indian, Pakistani 24%
Bahraini 70%

Bahrain is the smallest and most densely populated Arab state. The key division is between Sunni and Shi'a Muslims, about 30% and 70% of the population respectively. Sunnis hold the best jobs in business and government. Shi'a Muslims tend to do menial work and have a lower standard of living. The most impoverished Shi'a Muslims tend to be of Iranian descent.

Bahrain has a smaller expatriate population than many other Arab countries. The ruling al-Khalifa family has responded to declining oil reserves by diversifying the economy to provide service industry jobs for Bahrainis.

Bahrain is the most liberal of the Gulf states. Alcohol is freely available. Women have access to education and are not obliged to wear the veil. Since 2000 they have been entitled to participate in the Consultative Council.

***The Grand Mosque, Manama.** It is the largest building in Bahrain and can accommodate 7000 people.*

POLITICS

No multiparty elections

Not applicable

Amir Shaikh Hamad bin Isa al-Khalifa

LEGISLATIVE OR ADVISORY BODIES

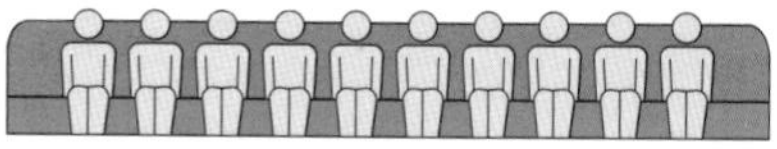

Bahrain is an absolute monarchy. A 30-member National Assembly was elected in 1973, but dissolved in 1975. An advisory Consultative Council was formed in 1993. Its 40 members are to be elected from 2001. A referendum in 2001 approved the resurrection of a legislative body.

The al-Khalifa family has dominated politics since 1783 by means of an effectively autocratic system, although the amir has been advised since 1993 by an appointed Consultative Council. In 2000 the council approved a national charter proposing a transition to a democratic kingdom, with the amir as king and a partially elected assembly, and with the council itself to be elected from 2001. The charter was approved by referendum in 2001.

Shaikh Hamad bin Isa al-Khalifa, who succeeded as amir in 1999, supports the policy of economic liberalization initiated by his late father. The repeal of the State Security Law in 2001 promised an end to the detention of political dissidents. Many were Shi'a opponents of the regime, who are traditionally backed by Iran.

WORLD AFFAIRS

Joined UN in 1971

AL | Damasc | GCC | OIC | OAPEC

Bahrain has good relations with the UK and the USA, but is keen to restore relations with Iraq. There is tension with Iran, but a dispute with Qatar over the Hawar islands was resolved in Bahrain's favor in 2001.

AID

Recipient

$4m (receipts)

Down 91% in 1999

Bahrain receives low levels of aid, but takes the lion's share from the offshore oilfield shared with Saudi Arabia, effectively a subsidy from the latter.

DEFENSE

No compulsory military service

$441m

Up 8% in 1999

The emirate's strong defense force includes a small but well-equipped air force. US air bases on Bahrain were used in the 1990–1991 Gulf War. The small navy is hard-pressed to patrol the 33-island archipelago.

ECONOMICS

Inflation –0.2% p.a. (1990–1998)

$4.9bn

0.3771–0.3770 Bahrain dinars

SCORE CARD

- ❑ WORLD GNP RANKING........................110th
- ❑ GNP PER CAPITA $7640
- ❑ BALANCE OF PAYMENTS....................$–420m
- ❑ INFLATION ....–0.4%
- ❑ UNEMPLOYMENT..................................15%

STRENGTHS

Oil. Arab world's major offshore banking sector following conflict with Lebanon. Inward investment. Tourism. Aluminum production.

WEAKNESSES

Depleted oil reserves and insufficient diversification. High unemployment. High levels of government borrowing.

EXPORTS

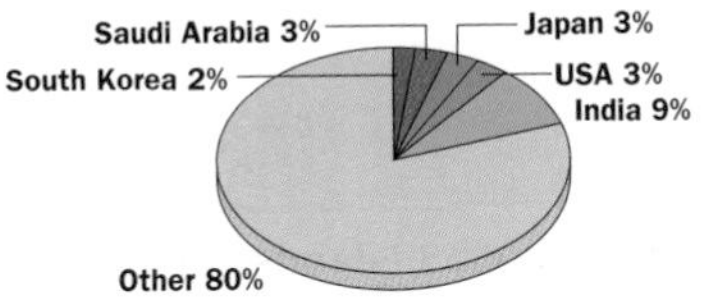
Saudi Arabia 3%
Japan 3%
South Korea 2%
USA 3%
India 9%
Other 80%

IMPORTS

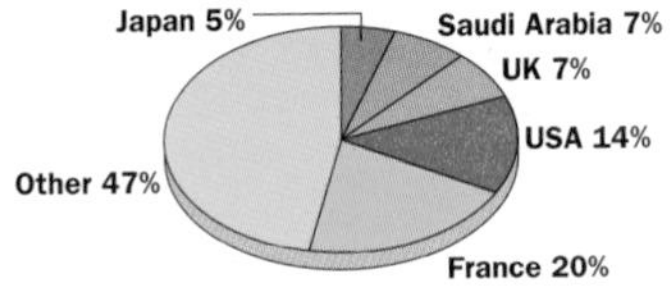
Japan 5%
Saudi Arabia 7%
UK 7%
USA 14%
Other 47%
France 20%

BAHRAIN

Total Land Area : 680 sq. km (263 sq. miles)

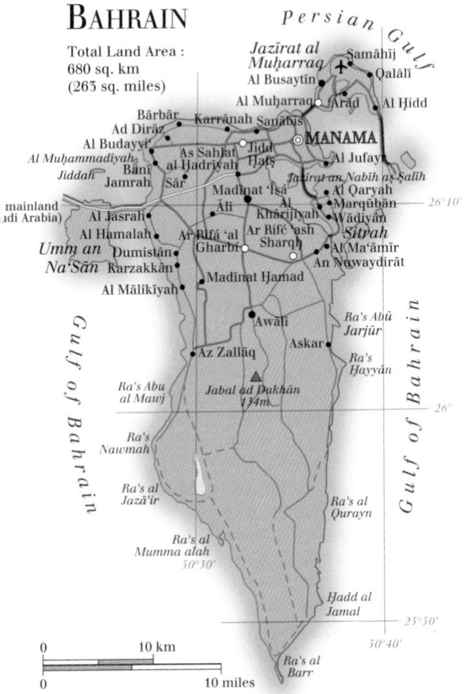
Persian Gulf
Jazīrat al Muḥarraq
Samāhij
Qalālī
Al Busaytīn
Al Muḥarraq
'Arad
Al Ḥidd
Bārbār
Karrānah
Sanābis
Ad Dirāz
MANAMA
Al Budayyi'
As Sahlat
Jidd Ḥafṣ
Al Jufayr
Al Muḥammadīyah
al Hadrīyah
Bānī Jamrah
Sār
Jiddah
Jazīrat an Nabīh aṣ Ṣāliḥ
Madīnat 'Īsá
Al Qaryah
mainland (Saudi Arabia)
'Alī
Marqūbān
Al Jasrah
Kharijīyah
Wādiyān
Al Hamalah
Ar Rifá 'al Gharbī
Ar Rifá 'ash Sharqī
Sitrah
Umm an Na'Sān
Dumistān
Al Ma'āmīr
Karzakkān
An Nuwaydirāt
Madīnat Ḥamad
Al Mālikīyah
Awālī
Ra's Abū Jarjūr
Askar
Az Zallāq
Ra's Ḥayyān
Gulf of Bahrain
Ra's Abu al Mawj
Jabal ad Dukhān 134m
Ra's Nawmah
Ra's al Jazā'ir
Ra's al Qurayn
Ra's al Mumma alah
Ḥadd al Jamal
Ra's al Barr
26°10'
26°
25°50'
50°30'
50°40'
0 10 km
0 10 miles
N
POPULATION
over 100 000
over 50 000
over 10 000
under 10 000
LAND HEIGHT
100m/328ft
Sea Level

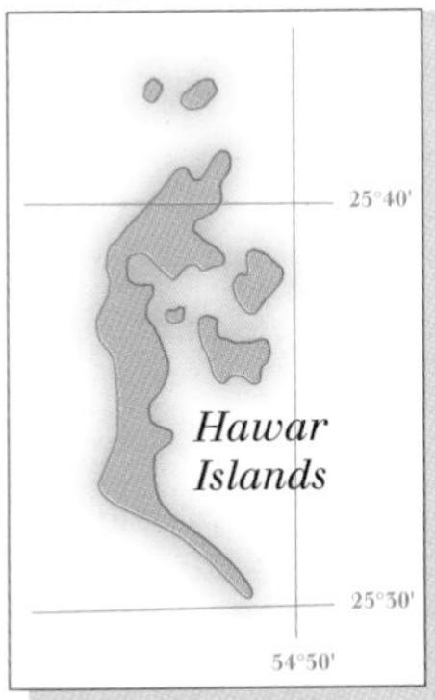
Hawar Islands
25°40'
25°30'
54°50'

RESOURCES

Electric power 1.1m kw

10,050 tonnes

34,927 b/d (reserves 165,768,720 bbl)

17,500 sheep, 16,300 goats, 465,000 chickens

Oil, natural gas

Bahrain remains dependent on its oil and gas production. Production of crude oil has declined sharply since the 1970s, and there are fears that reserves may run out by 2010. As oil has declined, so gas has assumed greater importance. Most is used to supply local industries, particularly the aluminum plant, which was established in 1972.

ENVIRONMENT

Not available

None

24.1 tonnes per capita

Local marine life, particularly the dugong, is vulnerable to upstream oil pollution from the Gulf. In 2000 Bahrain and Abu Dhabi signed an agreement on environmental concerns.

MEDIA

TV ownership high

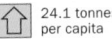

Daily newspaper circulation 117 per 1000 people

PUBLISHING AND BROADCAST MEDIA

There are 5 daily newspapers, *Akhbar al-Khalij, Gulf Daily News, Khaleej Times, Bahrain Tribune*, and *Al-Ayam*

1 state-owned service

2 services: 1 state-owned, 1 independent

Bahrain has a less authoritarian media regime than most of the Gulf. CNN and BBC satellite TV are freely available.

CRIME

Death penalty used

Bahrain does not publish prison figures

Down 62% 1996–1998

Crime is minimal, and theft and muggings are rare. Suspected political dissidents are monitored by the police. There was a spate of bombings in the mid-1990s.

CHRONOLOGY

Bahrain has been ruled since 1783 by the al-Khalifa family.

- ❑ **1971** Independence from Britain.
- ❑ **1981** Founder member of GCC.
- ❑ **1990–1991** Bahrain supports UN action expelling Iraq from Kuwait.
- ❑ **1994–1996** Shi'a unrest.
- ❑ **1999** Accession to throne of Shaikh Hamad bin Isa al-Khalifa.
- ❑ **2001** Referendum approves transition to democracy.

EDUCATION

School leaving age: 15

88%

7676 students

Female literacy rates are well above the Gulf average. Lack of funding has held up plans for a university.

HEALTH

Welfare state health benefits

1 per 1000 people

Circulatory diseases, perinatal deaths, injury, poisonings

The high-quality health service is free to Bahraini nationals. Some go abroad for advanced care. The Muharraq Health Center was upgraded in 2001.

SPENDING

GDP/cap. increase

CONSUMPTION AND SPENDING

243 per 1000 population

249 per 1000 population

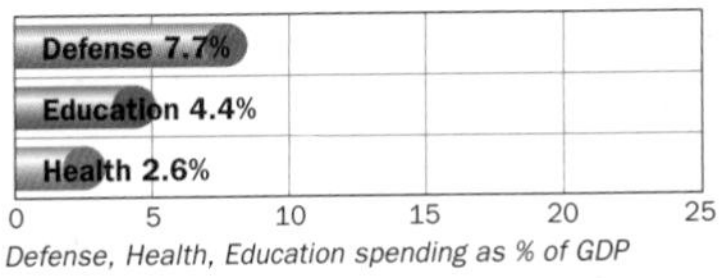
Defense 7.7%
Education 4.4%
Health 2.6%
0
5
10
15
20
25
Defense, Health, Education spending as % of GDP

Beneficiaries of the amir's extensive patronage form the wealthiest group in society. The country's largest religious community, the Shi'a Muslims, is also the poorest.

WORLD RANKING

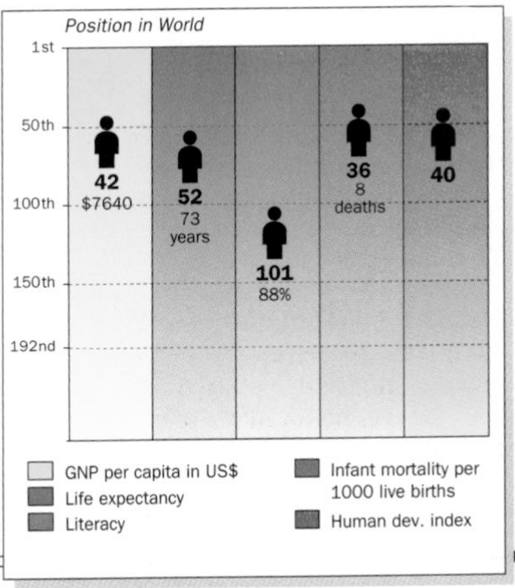
Position in World
1st
50th
100th
150th
192nd
42
$7640
52
73 years
101
88%
36
8 deaths
40
GNP per capita in US$
Life expectancy
Literacy
Infant mortality per 1000 live births
Human dev. index

BANGLADESH

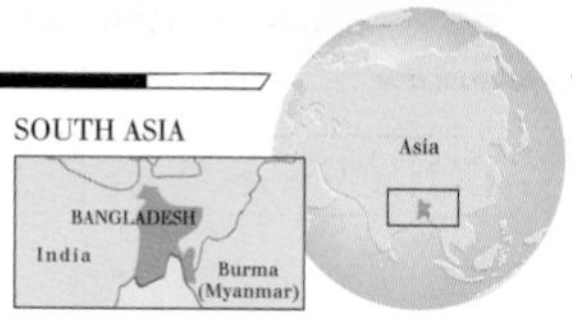
SOUTH ASIA
BANGLADESH
India
Burma
(Myanmar)
Asia

OFFICIAL NAME: People's Republic of Bangladesh **CAPITAL:** Dhaka
POPULATION: 129 million **CURRENCY:** Taka **OFFICIAL LANGUAGE:** Bengali

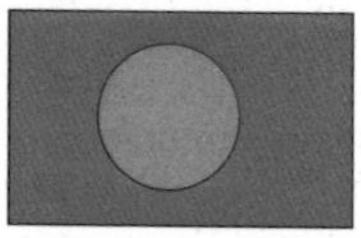

1971 | 1971 | March 26 | BD | +6 | +880 | .bd

BANGLADESH LIES at the north of the Bay of Bengal and shares borders with India and Burma. Most of the country is composed of fertile alluvial plains; the north and northeast are mountainous, as is the Chittagong region in the southeast. After its secession from Pakistan in 1971, Bangladesh had a troubled history of political instability, with periods of emergency rule. Effective democracy was restored in 1991. Bangladesh's major economic sectors are jute production, textiles, and agriculture. Its climate can wreak havoc – in 1991 a massive cyclone killed more than 140,000 people.

CLIMATE

Tropical/subtropical

WEATHER CHART

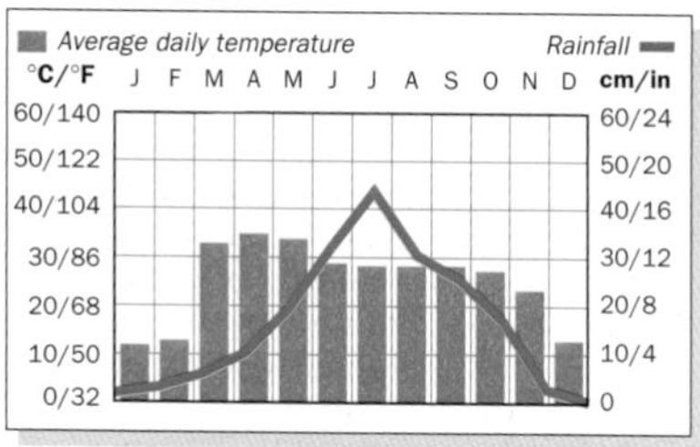
Average daily temperature
Rainfall
°C/°F
J F M A M J J A S O N D
cm/in
60/140
50/122
40/104
30/86
20/68
10/50
0/32
60/24
50/20
40/16
30/12
20/8
10/4
0

During the monsoon, the water level normally rises 6 m (20 feet) above sea level, flooding up to two-thirds of the country. The floods are made much worse when the Ganges, Jamuna, and Meghna rivers, which converge in a huge delta in Bangladesh, are swollen by the melting of the Himalayan snows and heavy rain in India. Cyclones build up regularly in the Bay of Bengal, with sometimes devastating effects on the flat coastal region.

TRANSPORTATION

Drive on left

Zia International, Dhaka 1.19m passengers

309 ships 413,800 grt

THE TRANSPORTATION NETWORK

19,112 km (11,876 miles)

None

2705 km (1681 miles)

8433 km (5240 miles)

Most transportation in Bangladesh is by water, although government policy is now concentrating on developing road and rail links, including the reopening of a passenger rail service into India in mid-2000. The Bangabandhu bridge across the Jamuna River, which bisects Bangladesh from north to south, was inaugurated in June 1998, after numerous delays. Bangladesh's two major ports, Mungla and Chittagong, are being upgraded to take advanced container ships.

Begum Khaleda Zia, *prime minister from 1991 until 1996.*

Sheikh Hasina Wajed, *Awami League leader, came to power in 1996.*

TOURISM

Visitors : Population 1:646

200,000 visitors

Up 16% in 2000

MAIN TOURIST ARRIVALS

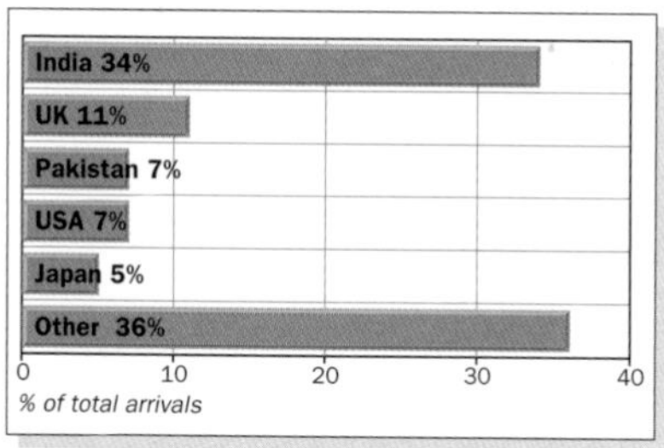
India 34%
UK 11%
Pakistan 7%
USA 7%
Japan 5%
Other 36%
0
10
20
30
40
% of total arrivals

After rising in the mid-1990s, tourist earnings began to fall again. Most visitors are Indian businessmen or Bangladeshis living overseas who return to visit relatives. The mogul architecture in Dhaka and the Pala dynasty (7th–10th centuries) city of Sonargaon are major attractions.

Traders on the Meghna River. *Life is governed by the vast network of rivers. The floodplains are among the most fertile in the world.*

PEOPLE

Pop. density high

Bengali, Urdu, Chakma, Marma (Magh), Garo, Khasi, Santhali, Tripuri, Mro

965/km² (2499/mi²)

THE URBAN/RURAL POPULATION SPLIT

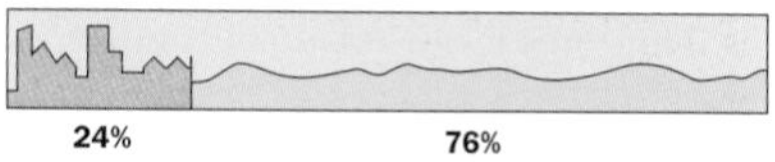
24%
76%

RELIGIOUS PERSUASION

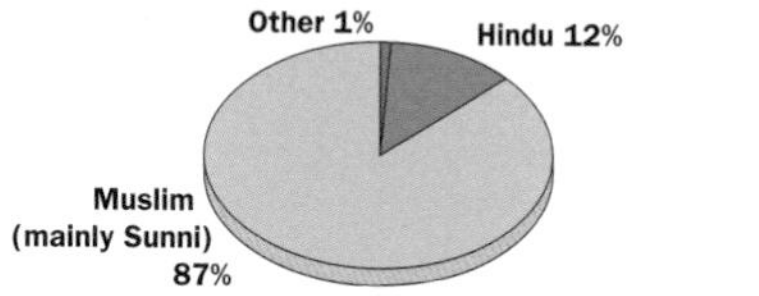
Other 1%
Hindu 12%
Muslim
(mainly Sunni)
87%

ETHNIC MAKEUP

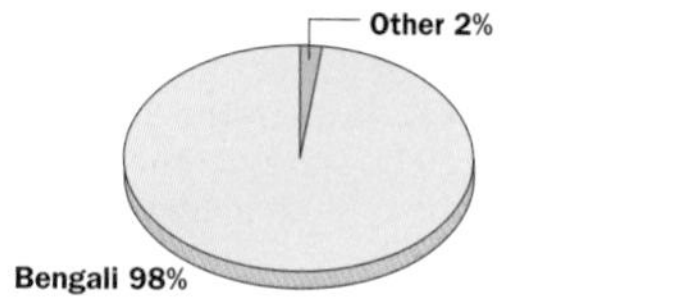
Other 2%
Bengali 98%

Bangladesh is one of the most densely populated countries in the world, despite the fact that three-quarters of the population is rural. As in India, there is considerable Muslim–Hindu tension; in 1992 the destruction of the Ayodhya mosque in northern India triggered violence in Bangladesh.

Although more than 50% of Bangladeshis, rural and urban, still live below the poverty line, there has been an improvement in living standards over the past decade.

The textile trade, by providing them with an independent income, has been one factor in the growing emancipation of Bangladeshi women. They are now included in official employment statistics and are the main customers of the most successful rural bank. Women have led both the government and the opposition. However, Bangladesh was criticized by Amnesty International in 2000 for insufficiently protecting women's rights, and a UN report later that year revealed that almost 50% of Bangladeshi women are victims of domestic violence.

POPULATION AGE BREAKDOWN

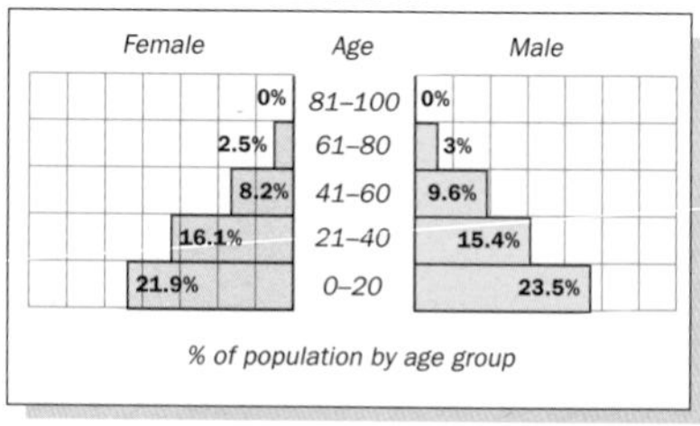
Female
Age
Male
0%
81–100
0%
2.5%
61–80
3%
8.2%
41–60
9.6%
16.1%
21–40
15.4%
21.9%
0–20
23.5%
% of population by age group

POLITICS

Multiparty elections

1996/2001

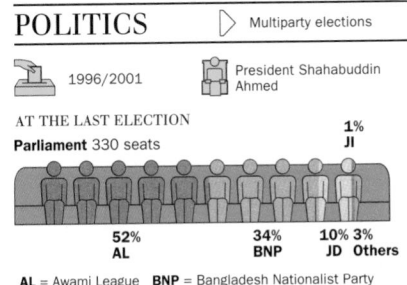

President Shahabuddin Ahmed

AT THE LAST ELECTION

Parliament 330 seats

1%
JI
52%
AL
34%
BNP
10%
JD
3%
Others

AL = Awami League **BNP** = Bangladesh Nationalist Party
JD = Jatiya Dal **JI** = Jamaat-e-Islami

Elections held in February 1996 were boycotted by opposition parties. 30 seats are reserved for women, of which 27 are held by the Awami League.

Bangladesh returned to multiparty democracy in 1991, following a period of military rule.

MAIN POLITICAL ISSUES

The state sector

Bangladesh is coming under mounting pressure from multilateral lending institutions, which account for the vast majority of the country's capital inflows, to cut costs in the state sector. Simultaneously, state-sector workers are demanding wage increases in line with inflation.

Autonomy for Chittagong Hill Tracts

Buddhist Mongol groups – the Chakma – continue to demand greater autonomy, although the low-level guerrilla war they have waged since 1974 has been contained. Many Chakmas fear persecution by Bengali Muslim settlers, despite a peace treaty signed in 1997 which provides for local autonomy, amnesty, and the return of refugees from India.

PROFILE

Between 1975 and 1990 the military was in power in Bangladesh. The overthrow of President Ershad in 1990 saw a return to multiparty politics; the army remains poised, however, to intervene in the event of a breakdown in law and order. Bangladesh's first woman prime minister, Begum Khaleda Zia, head of the BNP, was elected in 1991. A change from a presidential to a prime-ministerial system of government followed. The AL, which had steered Bangladesh to independence in 1971, mounted a sustained campaign against her regime, rejecting a February 1996 election as invalid and forcing fresh polls. The AL won the largest number of seats in the rerun election in June 1996. Its leader, Sheikh Hasina Wajed, in 2001 became the first prime minister to complete a full term, before handing over responsibility to a caretaker government for the period preceding legislative elections.

BANGLADESH

Total Land Area : 133 910 sq. km (51 703 sq. miles)

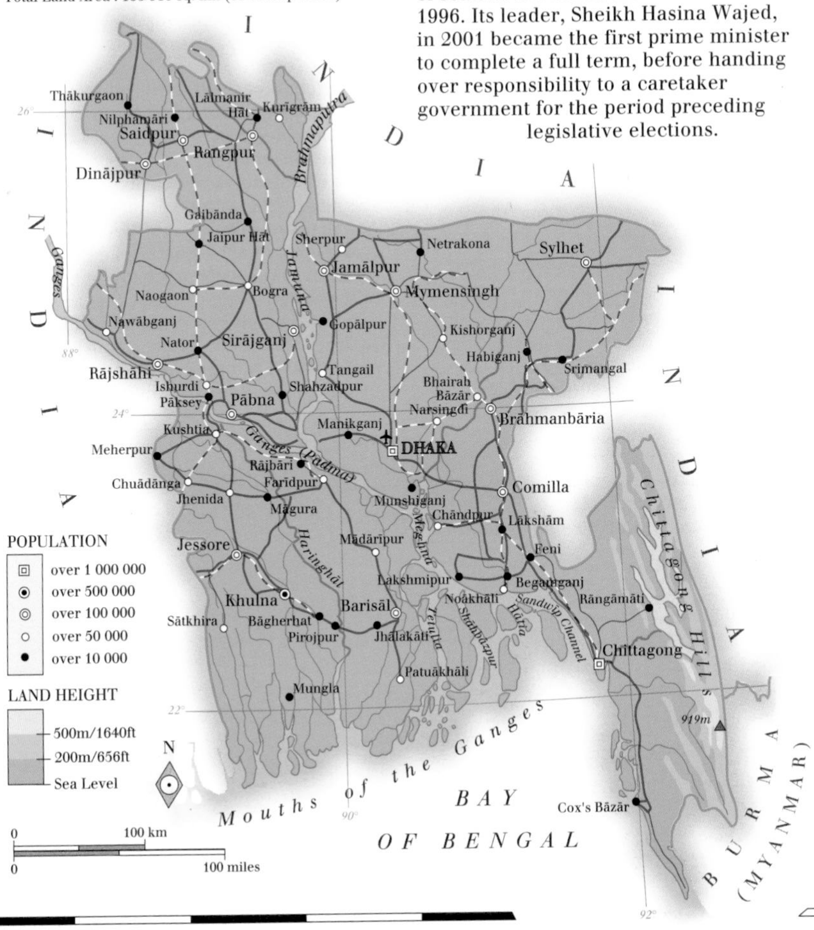
INDIA
BURMA (MYANMAR)
BAY OF BENGAL
Mouths of the Ganges
Thākurgaon
Nilphāmāri
Saidpur
Lālmanir Hāt
Kurigrām
Rangpur
Dinājpur
Brahmaputra
Gaibānda
Jaipur Hāt
Sherpur
Jamālpur
Netrakona
Sylhet
Mymensingh
Naogaon
Bogra
Jamuna
Gopālpur
Nawābganj
Nator
Sirājganj
Kishorganj
Habiganj
Srimangal
Rājshāhi
Ishurdi
Pāksey
Pābna
Tangail
Shahzadpur
Bhairab Bāzār
Narsingdi
Brāhmanbāria
Kushtia
Manikganj
DHAKA
Meherpur
Rājbāri
Faridpur
Ganges (Padma)
Chuādānga
Jhenida
Māgura
Munshiganj
Comilla
Chāndpur
Lākshām
Meghna
Jessore
Mādāripur
Haringhāta
Feni
Lakshmipur
Begamganj
Noākhāli
Rāngāmāti
Khulna
Barisāl
Sandwip Channel
Sātkhira
Bāgherhat
Pirojpur
Jhālakāti
Tetulia
Shahbazpur
Hatia
Chittagong
Chittagong Hills
Patuākhāli
Mungla
919m
Cox's Bāzār
POPULATION
over 1 000 000
over 500 000
over 100 000
over 50 000
over 10 000
LAND HEIGHT
500m/1640ft
200m/656ft
Sea Level
N
0
100 km
100 miles

WORLD AFFAIRS

Joined UN in 1974

Comm | NAM | OIC | SAARC | WTO

Good relations with the West, the main source of essential aid, are a priority. Relations with Pakistan have slowly improved since Pakistan's agreement in 1991 to accept the 250,000 pro-Pakistan Bihari Muslims in Bangladeshi refugee camps since 1971. Relations with India are improving. The damaging effects of the construction of the Farakka Dam on the Ganges, which deprived Bangladesh of irrigation water, have been alleviated by a 30-year agreement signed in 1996 guaranteeing the right of both parties to share the Ganges water. Bilateral relations eased further with the 1997 Chittagong Hill Tracts treaty; India had been accused of fomenting unrest.

AID

Recipient

$1.2bn (receipts)

Down 4% in 1999

Aid disbursements to Bangladesh each year are substantially greater than the annual value of foreign investment in the country. Aid also finances the bulk of state capital spending. The Bangladesh Development Aid Consortium meets annually to discuss aid spending under the auspices of the World Bank. One result of the level of aid is that Bangladesh has fallen into one of the traps of an aid-dependent economy: the large middle class has a vested interest in perpetuating a system which provides its members with lucrative contracts and access to external resources.

CHRONOLOGY

British rule in India began in Bengal in 1765, following the defeat of the ruler of Bengal at Plassey by Robert Clive, army head of the East India Company, in 1757.

- **1905** Muslims persuade British rulers to partition state of Bengal, to create a Muslim-dominated East Bengal.
- **1906** Muslim League established in Dhaka.
- **1912** Partition of 1905 reversed.
- **1947** British withdrawal from India. Partition plans establish a largely Muslim state of East (present-day Bangladesh) and West Pakistan, separated by 1600 km (1000 miles) of Indian, and largely Hindu, territory.
- **1949** Awami League founded to campaign for autonomy from West Pakistan.
- **1968** Gen. Yahya Khan heads government in Islamabad.

B

CHRONOLOGY *continued*

- **1970** Elections give Awami League, under Sheikh Mujibur Rahman, clear majority. Rioting and guerrilla warfare following Yahya Khan's refusal to convene assembly. The year ends with the worst recorded storms in Bangladesh's history – between 200,000 and 500,000 dead.
- **1971** Civil war, as Sheikh Mujib and Awami League declare unilateral independence. Ten million Bangladeshis flee to India. Pakistani troops defeated in 12 days by Mukhti Bahini – the Bengal Liberation Army.
- **1972** Sheikh Mujib elected prime minister. Nationalization of key industries, including jute and textile. Bangladesh achieves international recognition and joins Commonwealth. Pakistan withdraws in protest.
- **1974** Severe floods damage rice crop.
- **1975** Sheikh Mujib assassinated. Military coups end with General Zia ur-Rahman taking power. Institution of single-party state.
- **1976** Banning of trade union federations.
- **1977** Gen. Zia assumes presidency. Islam adopted as first principle of the constitution.
- **1981** Gen. Zia assassinated.
- **1982** Gen. Ershad takes over.
- **1983** Democratic elections restored by Ershad. Ershad assumes presidency.
- **1986** Elections. Awami League and BNP fail to unseat Ershad.
- **1987** Ershad announces state of emergency.
- **1988** Islam becomes constitutional state religion.
- **1990** Ershad resigns following demonstrations.
- **1991** Elections won by BNP. Khaleda Zia becomes prime minister. Ershad imprisoned. Role of the president reduced to ceremonial functions. Floods kill 150,000 people.
- **1994** Author Taslima Nasreen, who is accused of blasphemy, escapes to Sweden.
- **1996** General election, boycotted by opposition parties, returns BNP to power. Opposition parties reject February poll result and force fresh elections. Sheikh Hasina Wajed of the AL takes power.
- **2001** Supreme Court declares issuing of religious decrees (*fatwas*) to be a criminal offense.

DEFENSE

No compulsory military service

$667m

Up 6% in 1999

The military, which dominated politics between 1975 and 1990, still wields considerable influence, despite the restoration of civilian government. Although there is greater emphasis on poverty alleviation programs, spending on defense is disproportionately high, and is increasing. Plans to improve security by constructing a 4000-km (2500-mile) road along the border with India were announced in mid-2000.

BANGLADESHI ARMED FORCES

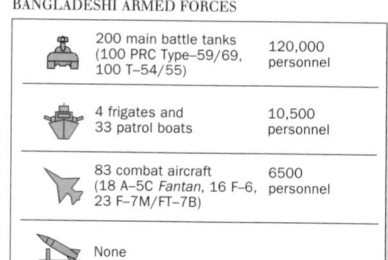

200 main battle tanks (100 PRC Type–59/69, 100 T–54/55)	120,000 personnel
4 frigates and 33 patrol boats	10,500 personnel
83 combat aircraft (18 A–5C *Fantan*, 16 F–6, 23 F–7M/FT–7B)	6500 personnel
None	

ECONOMICS

Inflation 4.1% p.a. (1990–1999)

$47.1bn

51.0–54.1 taka

SCORE CARD

- World GNP Ranking.......................50th
- GNP per Capita.............................$370
- Balance of Payments....................$–292m
- Inflation.......................................6.3%
- Unemployment.................................35%

EXPORTS

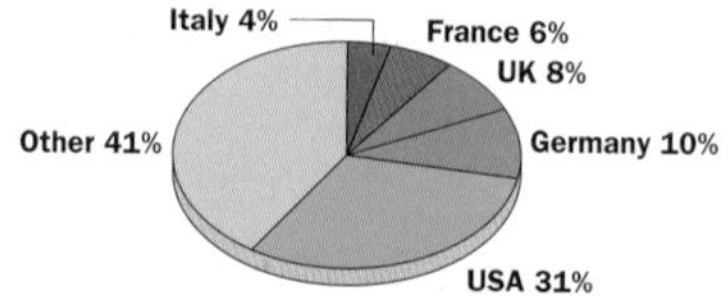
Italy 4%
France 6%
UK 8%
Germany 10%
USA 31%
Other 41%

IMPORTS

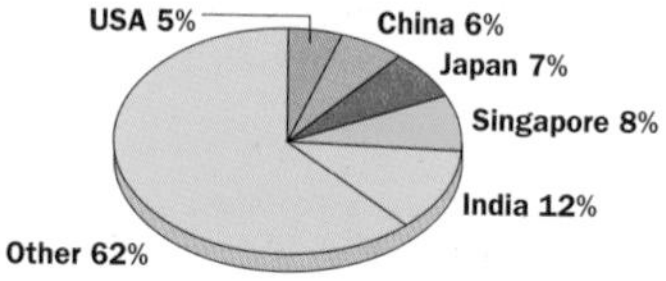
USA 5%
China 6%
Japan 7%
Singapore 8%
India 12%
Other 62%

Strengths

80% of the world's jute fiber exports come from Bangladesh. Low wages ensure a competitive and expanding textile industry, which provides over three-quarters of manufacturing export earnings.

Weaknesses

The agricultural sector, employing the majority of Bangladeshis, is vulnerable to the violent and unpredictable climate.

Profile

Government ministers like to portray Bangladesh as an emerging NIC, but its economy is still overwhelmingly dependent on agriculture and large aid inflows. Agriculture, which provides jute and tobacco, is productive; Bangladesh's soils, fed by the Ganges, Jamuna, and Meghna rivers, are highly fertile. However, the effects of the weather can be devastating, frequently destroying a whole year's crop. Agricultural wages are among the lowest in the world.

ECONOMIC PERFORMANCE INDICATOR

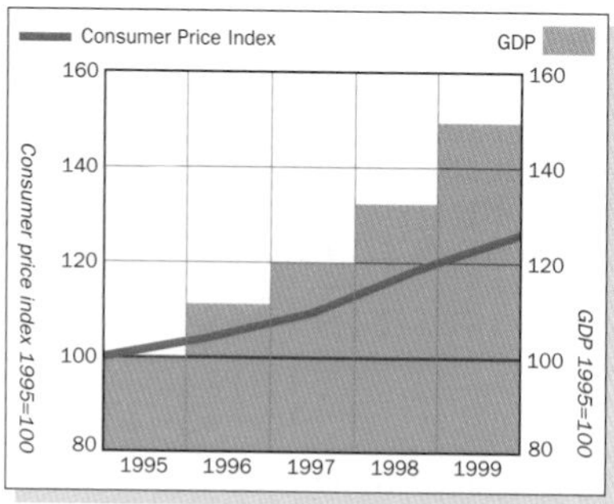
Consumer Price Index
GDP
Consumer price index 1995=100
GDP 1995=100
160
140
120
100
80
1995
1996
1997
1998
1999

The state sector, which owns large, inefficient and massively loss-making companies (such as the Bangladesh Jute Mills Corporation), is in difficulty. The World Bank, the source of most aid to the country, wishes to see loss-making concerns cut their workforces or else close down.

Textiles and garments are currently the healthiest sectors. Economic zones (export processing zones) with special concessions have attracted foreign investment, as well as helped to promote a small indigenous electronics industry. Bangladesh receives generous textile import quotas from the EU and NAFTA but fails to reach them.

BANGLADESH : MAJOR BUSINESSES

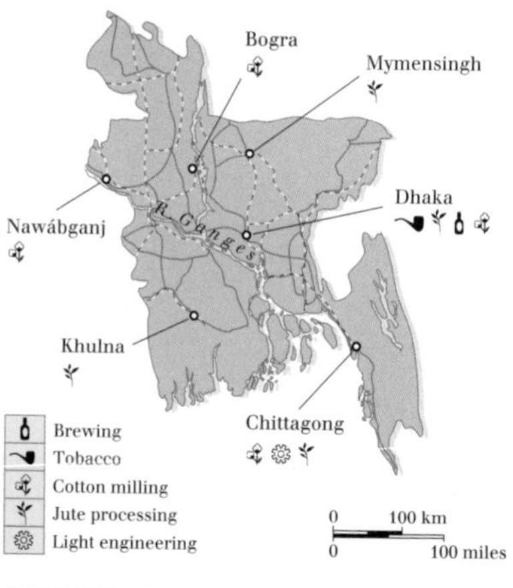
Bogra
Mymensingh
Dhaka
Nawábganj
R. Ganges
Khulna
Chittagong
Brewing
Tobacco
Cotton milling
Jute processing
Light engineering
0 100 km
0 100 miles

RESOURCES

Electric power 3.3m kw

1.34m tonnes

Reserves of 87,800 bbl

33.5m goats, 23.4m cattle, 138m chickens

Salt, oil, natural gas, limestone

ELECTRICITY GENERATION

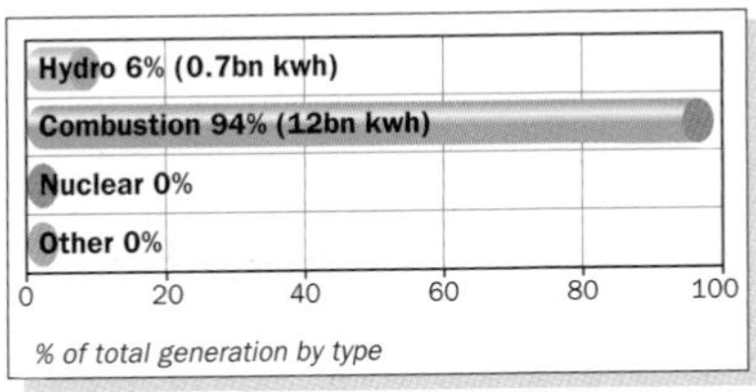
Hydro 6% (0.7bn kwh)
Combustion 94% (12bn kwh)
Nuclear 0%
Other 0%
0
20
40
60
80
100
% of total generation by type

BANGLADESH : LAND USE

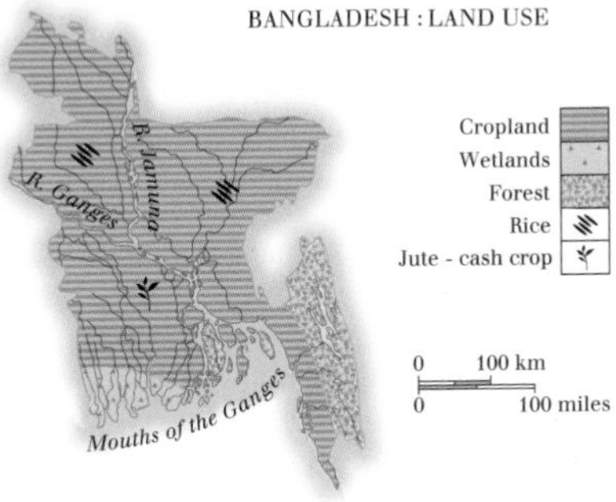
R. Ganges
R. Jamuna
Mouths of the Ganges
Cropland
Wetlands
Forest
Rice
Jute - cash crop
0 100 km
0 100 miles

Bangladesh is the world's major jute producer, accounting for 80% of world jute fiber exports and about 50% of world jute manufactures exports.

Bangladesh holds world-class gas reserves, estimated to last as much as 200 years at the present extraction rate. Natural gas from the Bay of Bengal, exploited by the state-owned Bangladesh Oil, Gas, and Minerals Corporation, came on stream in 1988.

ENVIRONMENT

Sustainability rank: 99th

1% (0.7% partially protected)

0.2 tonnes per capita

ENVIRONMENTAL TREATIES

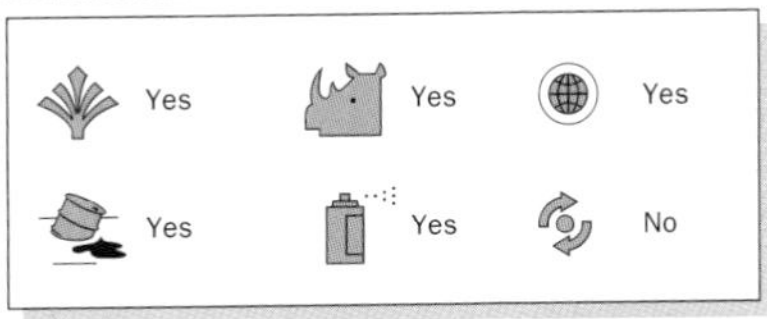
Yes
Yes
Yes
Yes
Yes
No

Bangladesh's climate gives rise to devastating floods and cyclones, with consequent huge death tolls and substantial damage to crops. The country is too poor to finance environmental initiatives.

MEDIA

TV ownership low

Daily newspaper circulation 9 per 1000 people

PUBLISHING AND BROADCAST MEDIA

There are 37 daily newspapers. *Dainik Ittefaq, Dainik Inquilab,* and *Dainik Janakantha* have the highest circulations

1 state-controlled service

1 state-controlled service

Press freedom, which emerged after the fall of President Ershad in 1990, has been gradually eroded under successive civilian governments. Of the daily newspapers, the ten English-language titles appeal mainly to the urban elite. Among political weeklies, the most prominent is *Holiday*. The vast majority – over 70% – of TV programs are produced locally by the state-run services, but foreign satellite channels are increasingly available.

CRIME

Death penalty used

44,111 prisoners

Up 17% 1996–1998

CRIME RATES

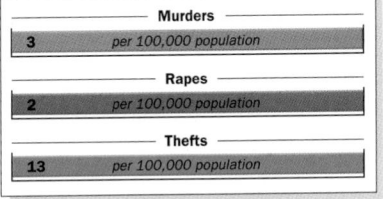

Murders
3 per 100,000 population

Rapes
2 per 100,000 population

Thefts
13 per 100,000 population

Rising levels of political and religious violence have led to the enforcement of antiterrorism legislation, containing provisions for summary justice and heavy penalties, including death. There has been a recent sharp rise in crimes against women, including murder, rape, abduction, and acid attacks. Deaths in Bangladeshi prisons are common, and in addition the human rights record of the security forces, especially the paramilitary Bangladesh Rifles, has been attacked by Amnesty International.

EDUCATION

School leaving age: 10

41%

434,309 students

THE EDUCATION SYSTEM

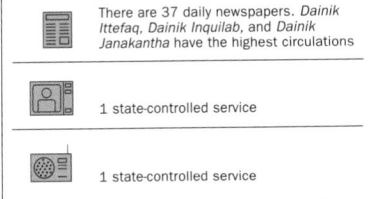

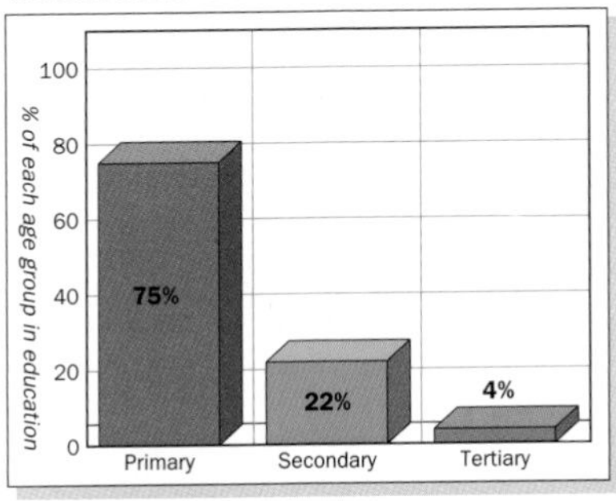
100
80
60
40
20
0
% of each age group in education
75%
22%
4%
Primary
Secondary
Tertiary

Education issues in Bangladeshi society have been poorly addressed, although successive governments have promised to improve literacy levels by increasing spending. A dramatic reduction in the 1990s in the number of child workers meant an accompanying rise in school attendance. Exam cheating is a serious problem. The seven universities are frequently beset by political violence.

HEALTH

Welfare state health benefits

1 per 5000 people

Parasitic, diarrheal, and communicable diseases

More resources are needed to boost health care in rural areas. Although primary health care in these areas improved in the 1990s, Bangladesh's health problems remain severe and are exacerbated by a shortage of medical staff and facilities. Priority for birth control programs has helped reduce the population growth rate by more than 20% over the last 15 years. Half the population is exposed to high levels of arsenic in drinking water.

SPENDING

GDP/cap. increase

CONSUMPTION AND SPENDING

1 per 1000 population

3 per 1000 population

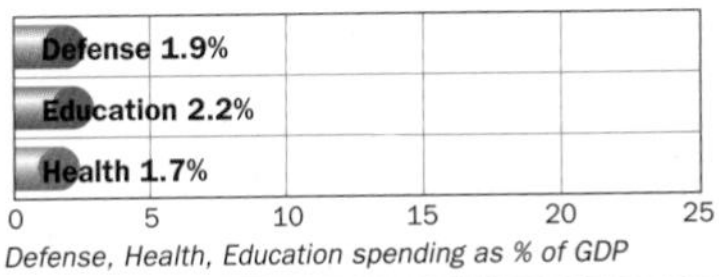
Defense 1.9%
Education 2.2%
Health 1.7%
0
5
10
15
20
25
Defense, Health, Education spending as % of GDP

Average incomes in Bangladesh remain very low, but wealth disparities are not quite as marked as in India or Pakistan. State officials tend to be among the better-off sector of society.

WORLD RANKING

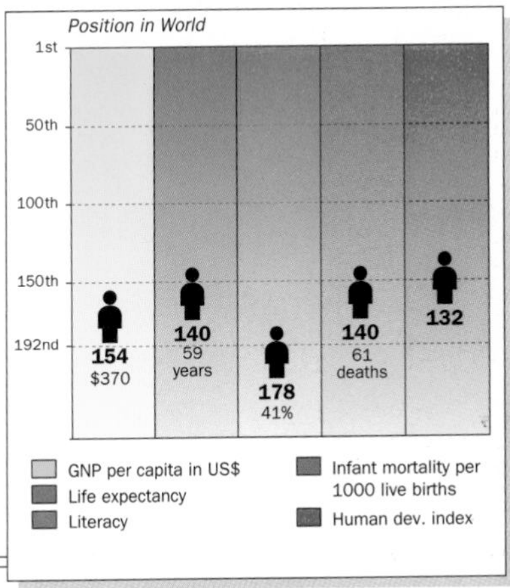
Position in World
1st
50th
100th
150th
192nd
154
$370
140
59
years
178
41%
140
61
deaths
132
GNP per capita in US$
Life expectancy
Literacy
Infant mortality per 1000 live births
Human dev. index

BARBADOS

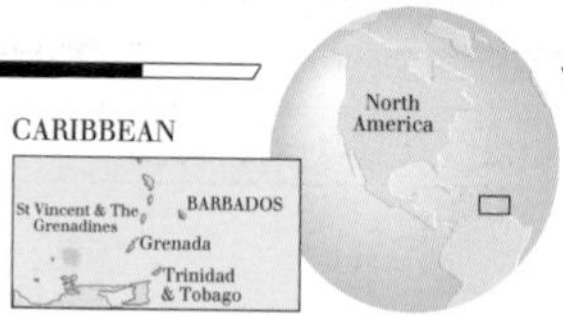
CARIBBEAN
North America
St Vincent & The Grenadines
BARBADOS
Grenada
Trinidad & Tobago

OFFICIAL NAME: Barbados **CAPITAL:** Bridgetown
POPULATION: 270,000 **CURRENCY:** Barbados dollar **OFFICIAL LANGUAGE:** English

1966 | 1966 | Nov 30 | BDS | -4 | +1246 | .bb

SITUATED TO THE NORTHEAST of Trinidad, Barbados is the most easterly of the West Indian Windward Islands. In the 16th century, the Portuguese were the first Europeans to reach the island, then inhabited by Arawak Indians. However, Barbados was not colonized until the 1620s, when British settlers arrived. Popularly referred to by its neighbors as "little England," Barbados now seeks to forge a new national identity for itself.

CLIMATE

Tropical oceanic

WEATHER CHART

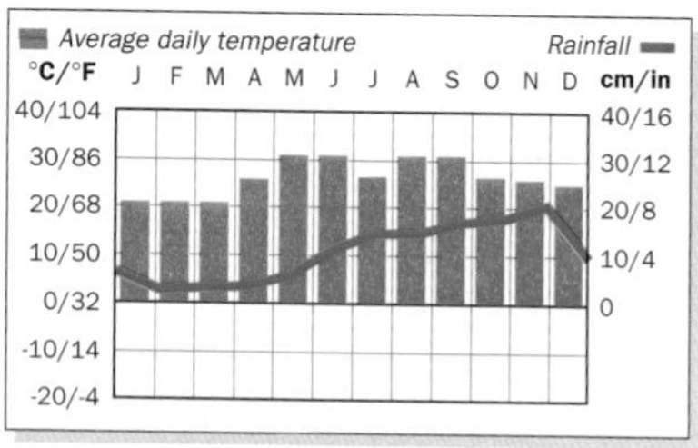
Average daily temperature
Rainfall
°C/°F J F M A M J J A S O N D cm/in
40/104
30/86
20/68
10/50
0/32
-10/14
-20/4
40/16
30/12
20/8
10/4
0

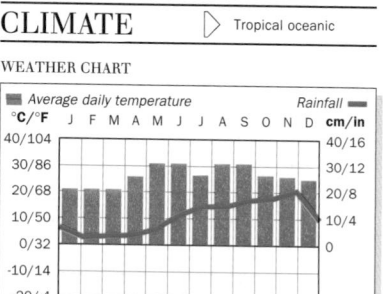

Barbados has a moderate tropical climate and is sunnier and drier than its more mountainous Caribbean neighbors. Hurricanes may occur in the rainy season.

TRANSPORTATION

Drive on left

Grantley Adams International, Bridgetown 1.21m passengers

69 ships 687,586 grt

THE TRANSPORTATION NETWORK

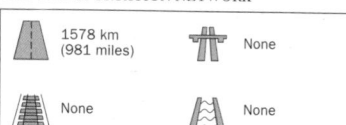

1578 km (981 miles)

None

None

None

A multi-million dollar expansion program has upgraded facilities at the international airport. Piers at Bridgetown's port have been improved with foreign aid, as have the island's paved roads. There are bus routes over most of the island.

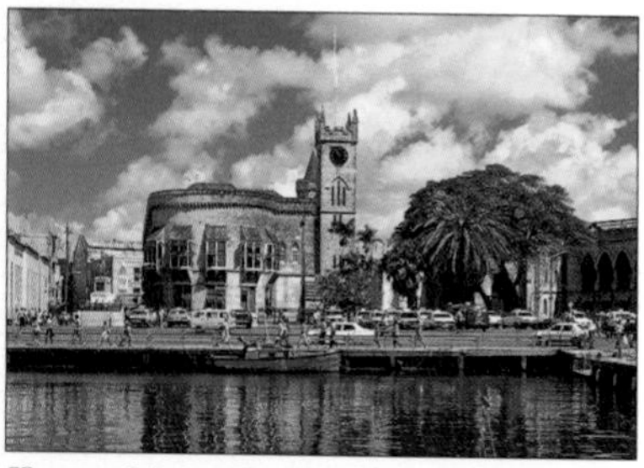

House of Assembly, Trafalgar Square, Bridgetown. *Barbados's parliament, the third oldest in the Commonwealth, dates from 1639.*

TOURISM

Visitors : Population 2.1:1

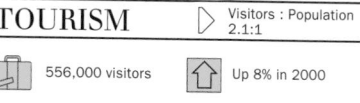

556,000 visitors

Up 8% in 2000

MAIN TOURIST ARRIVALS

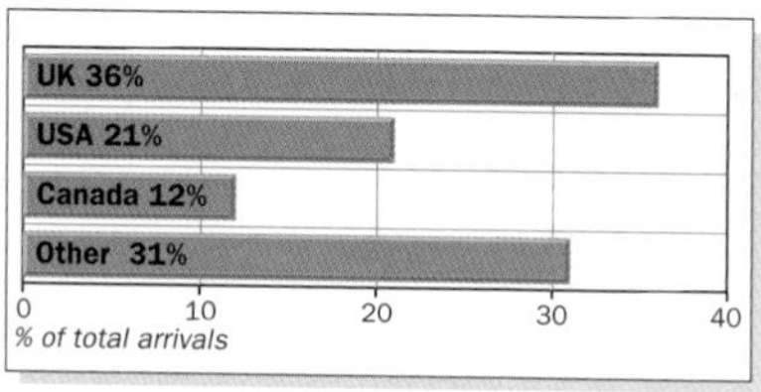
UK 36%
USA 21%
Canada 12%
Other 31%
0
10
20
30
40
% of total arrivals

Tourism has continued to grow steadily since an upsurge in 1997. The greatest proportion of visitors come from the UK, with sizable numbers also from the rest of Europe and North America.

PEOPLE

Pop. density high

Bajan (Barbadian English), English

628/km² (1626/mi²)

THE URBAN/RURAL POPULATION SPLIT

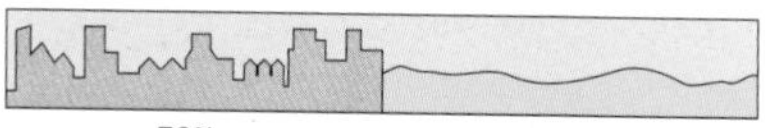
50%
50%

RELIGIOUS PERSUASION

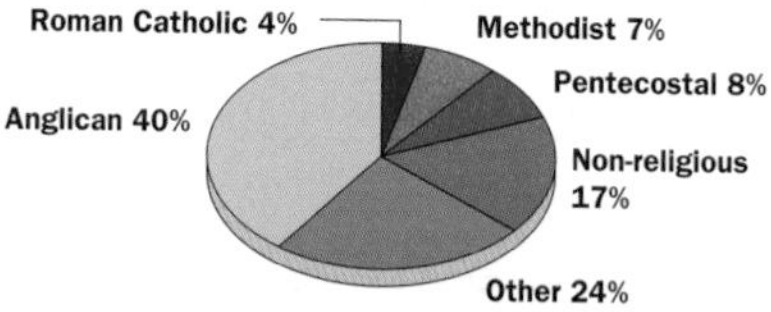
Roman Catholic 4%
Methodist 7%
Pentecostal 8%
Anglican 40%
Non-religious 17%
Other 24%

Most Bajans are the descendants of Africans brought to the island between the 16th and 19th centuries; there are also small groups of south Asians and Europeans, mainly expatriate Britons, many of whom take up residence on retirement. There is some latent tension between the white community, which controls most of the economy, and the majority black population, although this rarely spills over into violence. Increasing social mobility has allowed many black Bajans to move into the professions and the civil service. Barbados enjoys a higher standard of living than most Caribbean countries.

POLITICS

Multiparty elections

L. House 1999/2004
U. House 1999/2004

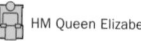

HM Queen Elizabeth II

AT THE LAST ELECTION

House of Assembly 28 seats

93% BLP
7% DLP

BLP = Barbados Labour Party
DLP = Democratic Labour Party

Senate 21 seats

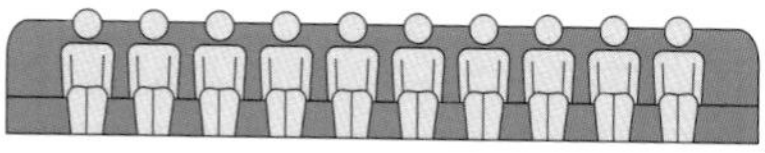

The members of the Senate are appointed. Twelve are chosen by the prime minister, 2 by the leader of the opposition, and 7 independents by the governor-general.

Barbados is a multiparty democracy. A primarily European, affluent elite finances the parties and has an indirect influence on government policy. The BLP swept to power in 1994 and won a further landslide in 1999. Owen Arthur, BLP leader and prime minister, prioritizes economic growth and international competitiveness. He has pledged to transform Barbados into a republic, while remaining a member of the Commonwealth.

WORLD AFFAIRS

Joined UN in 1966

ACS | Comm | Caricom | NAM | OAS

Considered to be an international tax haven, Barbados has been under pressure to implement reforms.

AID

Recipient

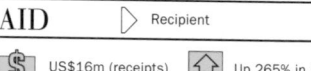

US$16m (receipts)

Up 265% in 1998

Most aid comes from the USA, the EU, and the UK, mainly in the form of development project loans and balance of payments support.

DEFENSE

No compulsory military service

US$12m

Down 8% in 1999

The small Barbadian army and the constabulary benefit from financial support and training from the US and UK governments, which also supply equipment. Barbados is the headquarters of the Regional Security System, established in 1982 by the Windward and Leeward Islands, a body which acts as a multinational security force for its members.

ECONOMICS

Inflation 3.1% p.a. (1990–1999)

US$2.3bn

1.98–1.99 Barbados dollars

SCORE CARD

- World GNP Ranking........136th
- GNP per Capita........US$8600
- Balance of Payments........US$–57m
- Inflation........1.6%
- Unemployment........12%

Strengths

Well-developed tourism based on climate and accessibility. Sugar industry. Information processing and financial services are important new growth sectors.

Weaknesses

Narrow economic base, vulnerable to downturns in tourism, failures of sugar harvest, and the sector's dependency on loans and secure markets. Relatively high manufacturing costs.

EXPORTS

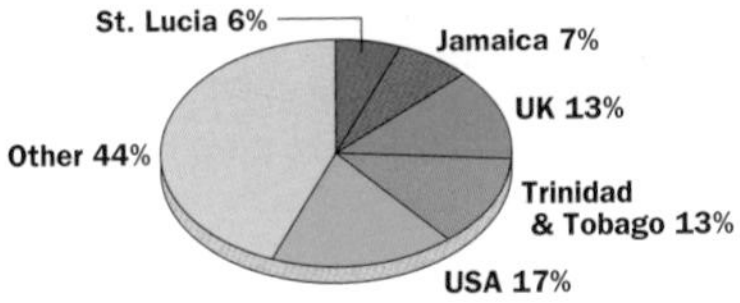
St. Lucia 6%
Jamaica 7%
UK 13%
Other 44%
Trinidad & Tobago 13%
USA 17%

IMPORTS

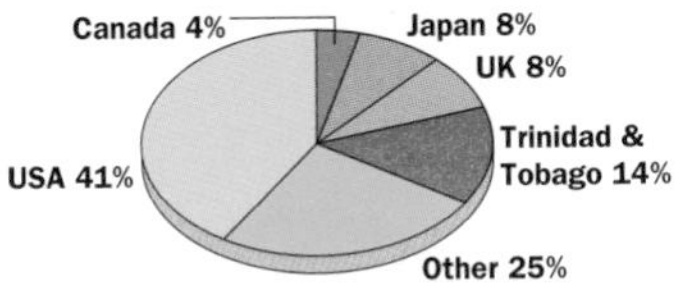
Canada 4%
Japan 8%
UK 8%
Trinidad & Tobago 14%
USA 41%
Other 25%

BARBADOS

Total Land Area : 430 sq. km (166 sq. miles)

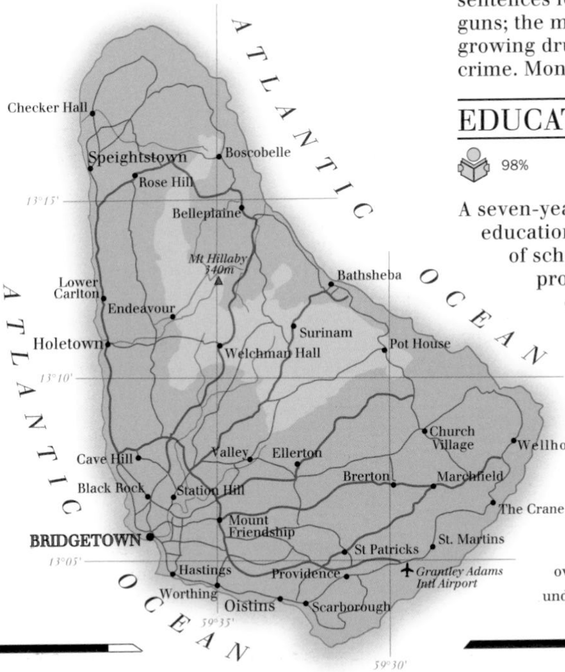
ATLANTIC OCEAN
ATLANTIC OCEAN
Checker Hall
Speightstown
Boscobelle
Rose Hill
Belleplaine
Mt Hillaby 340m
Bathsheba
Lower Carlton
Endeavour
Holetown
Surinam
Welchman Hall
Pot House
Church Village
Wellhouse
Cave Hill
Valley
Ellerton
Black Rock
Station Hill
Brerton
Marchfield
The Crane
Mount Friendship
BRIDGETOWN
St Patricks
St. Martins
Hastings
Providence
Grantley Adams Intl Airport
Worthing
Oistins
Scarborough
13°15'
13°10'
13°05'
59°35'
59°30'

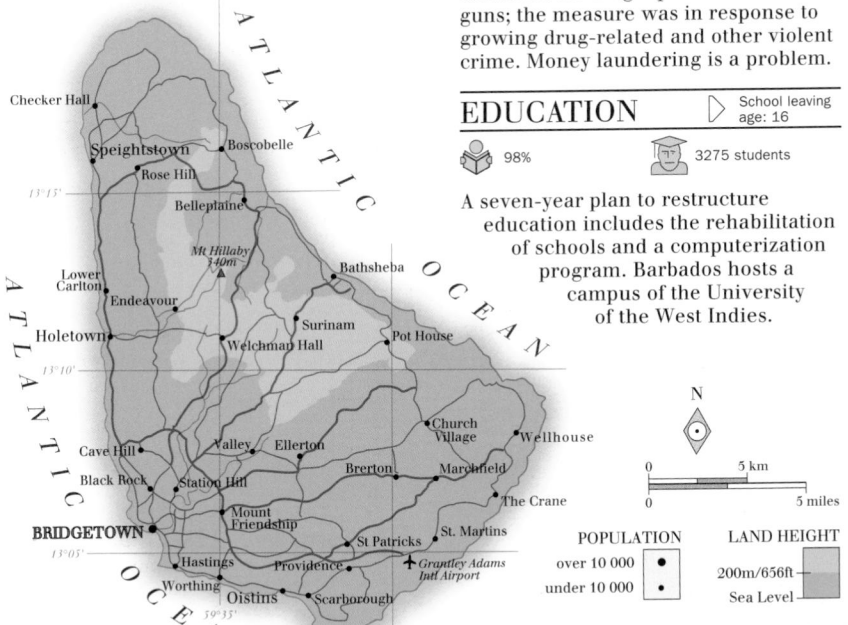

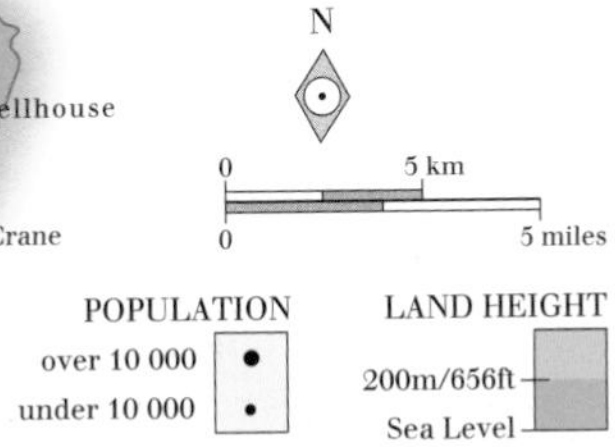
N
0
5 km
0
5 miles
POPULATION
over 10 000
under 10 000
LAND HEIGHT
200m/656ft
Sea Level

RESOURCES

Electric power 142,000 kw

2764 tonnes

902 b/d (reserves 7,246,800 bbl)

41,000 sheep, 33,000 pigs, 3.6m chickens

Oil, natural gas

Barbados has few strategic resources. The domestic petroleum industry provides about one-third of the country's energy requirements.

ENVIRONMENT

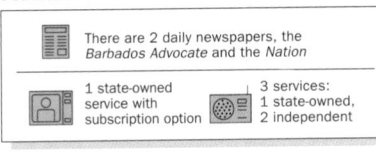

Not available

1%

3.7 tonnes per capita

Oil slicks created by waste dumped from passing ships are polluting the encircling reef and adversely affecting the life cycle of the flying fish, Barbados's main fish stock.

MEDIA

TV ownership high

Daily newspaper circulation 199 per 1000 people

PUBLISHING AND BROADCAST MEDIA

There are 2 daily newspapers, the *Barbados Advocate* and the *Nation*

1 state-owned service with subscription option

3 services: 1 state-owned, 2 independent

There is no political interference in the media. Two daily newspapers are privately owned. Multi-channel TV is available on subscription.

CRIME

Death penalty used

260 prisoners

Down 24% 1991–1998

A firearms amnesty announced in 1998 proposed heavy fines and prison sentences for illegal possession of guns; the measure was in response to growing drug-related and other violent crime. Money laundering is a problem.

EDUCATION

School leaving age: 16

98%

3275 students

A seven-year plan to restructure education includes the rehabilitation of schools and a computerization program. Barbados hosts a campus of the University of the West Indies.

CHRONOLOGY

Colonized by the British in 1627, Barbados grew rich in the 18th century from sugar produced using slave labor.

- **1951** Universal adult suffrage introduced.
- **1961–1966** Full internal self-government. Full independence from Britain.
- **1983** Supports and provides a base for the US invasion of Grenada.
- **1994–1999** The BLP wins two successive general elections.

HEALTH

Welfare state health benefits

1 per 800 people

Heart and cerebrovascular diseases, cancers

The health system is based on subsidized government-run clinics and hospitals, supplemented by more expensive private clinics and private doctors. Facilities are within easy reach of all Bajans.

SPENDING

GDP/cap. increase

CONSUMPTION AND SPENDING

168 per 1000 population

427 per 1000 population

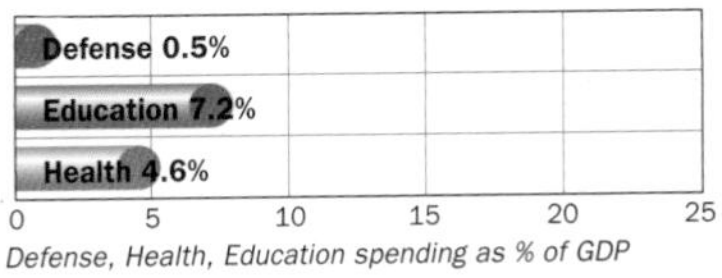
Defense 0.5%
Education 7.2%
Health 4.6%
0
5
10
15
20
25
Defense, Health, Education spending as % of GDP

A significant disparity exists between most Bajans and a small affluent group, its members usually of European origin, which owns and controls business and industry, and parades status symbols such as yachts. Prime Minister Arthur stated in 1998 that "abject poverty" existed in the country.

WORLD RANKING

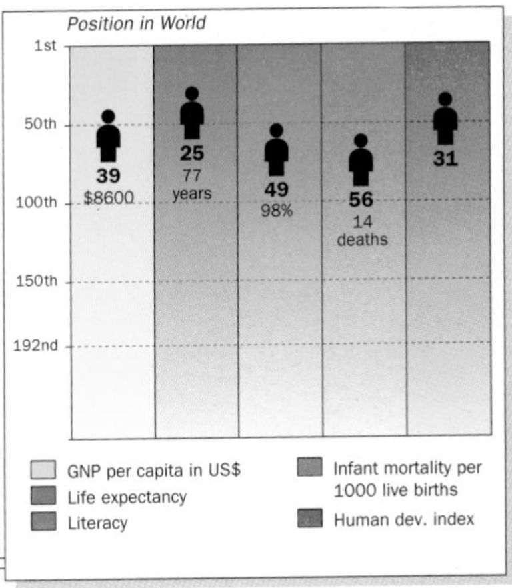
Position in World
1st
50th
100th
150th
192nd
39
$8600
25
77 years
49
98%
56
14 deaths
31
GNP per capita in US$
Life expectancy
Literacy
Infant mortality per 1000 live births
Human dev. index

B

BELARUS

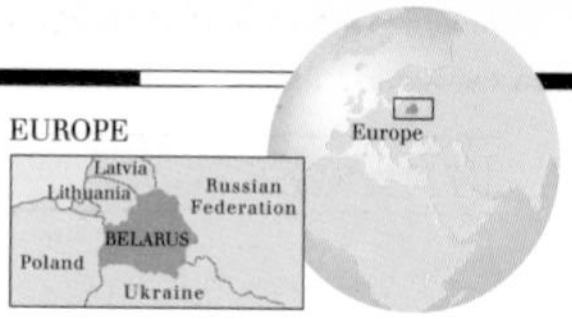
EUROPE
Europe
Latvia
Lithuania
Russian Federation
BELARUS
Poland
Ukraine

OFFICIAL NAME: Republic of Belarus **CAPITAL:** Minsk **POPULATION:** 10.2 million
CURRENCY: Belarussian rouble **OFFICIAL LANGUAGE:** Belarussian and Russian

1991 | 1991 | July 3 | BY | +2 | +375 | .by

FORMERLY KNOWN AS Belorussia (literally white Russia), Belarus is bordered by Lithuania and Latvia in the northwest, Ukraine in the south, and Poland and Russia in the west and east. Devastated in World War II, and with few resources other than agriculture, Belarus only reluctantly became independent of Moscow in 1991, and President Lukashenka has maintained close links with Russia. The Chernobyl nuclear disaster in Ukraine in 1986 has had lasting effects on the health of Belarussians and the environment.

CLIMATE

Continental

WEATHER CHART

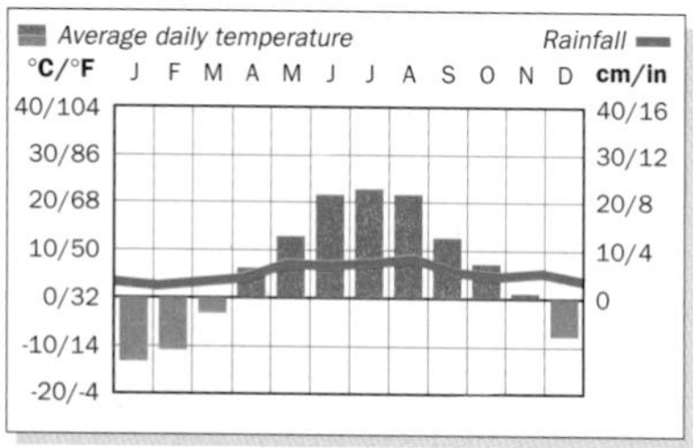
Average daily temperature
Rainfall
°C/°F
J F M A M J J A S O N D
cm/in
40/104
30/86
20/68
10/50
0/32
-10/14
-20/-4
40/16
30/12
20/8
10/4
0

Belarus has a continental climate somewhat moderated by the influence of the Baltic Sea. Temperatures in winter still drop well below freezing, however, while summers can be hot and humid. Summer is also the main season for rainfall.

Much of southern Belarus is marshy and sparsely populated. It includes the vast Pripet Marshes and the Dnieper lowlands.

TRANSPORTATION

Drive on right

Minsk International

Has no fleet

THE TRANSPORTATION NETWORK

60,567 km (37,635 miles)

None

5523 km (3432 miles)

Extensive canal and river systems

Belarus has no direct access to the sea, but is close to the Baltic ports. Railroad communications are good.

TOURISM

Visitors : Population 1:29

355,000 visitors

Up 42% in 1998

MAIN OVERSEAS ARRIVALS

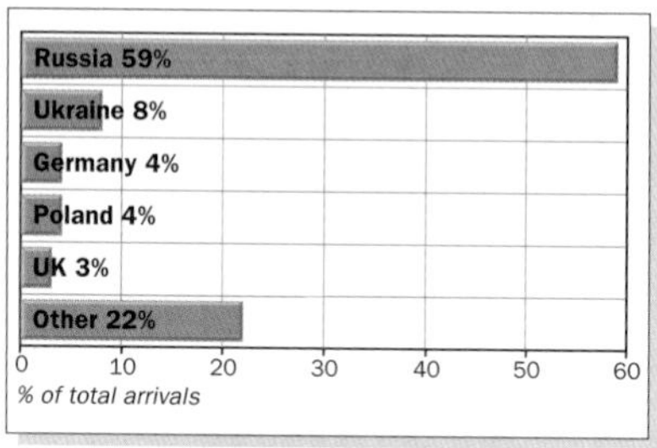
Russia 59%
Ukraine 8%
Germany 4%
Poland 4%
UK 3%
Other 22%
0
10
20
30
40
50
60
% of total arrivals

Belarus has fewer tourists than its neighbors. Many of its historic buildings were destroyed during World War II. Minsk was totally flattened, and is now characterized by Stalinist and high-rise buildings. There are few assets on which to build a tourist industry.

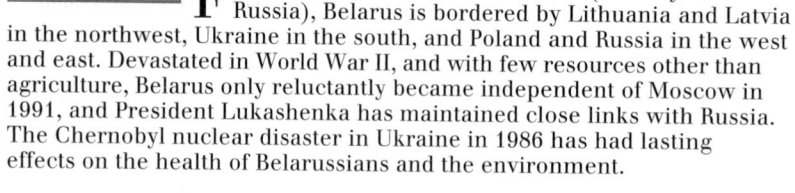

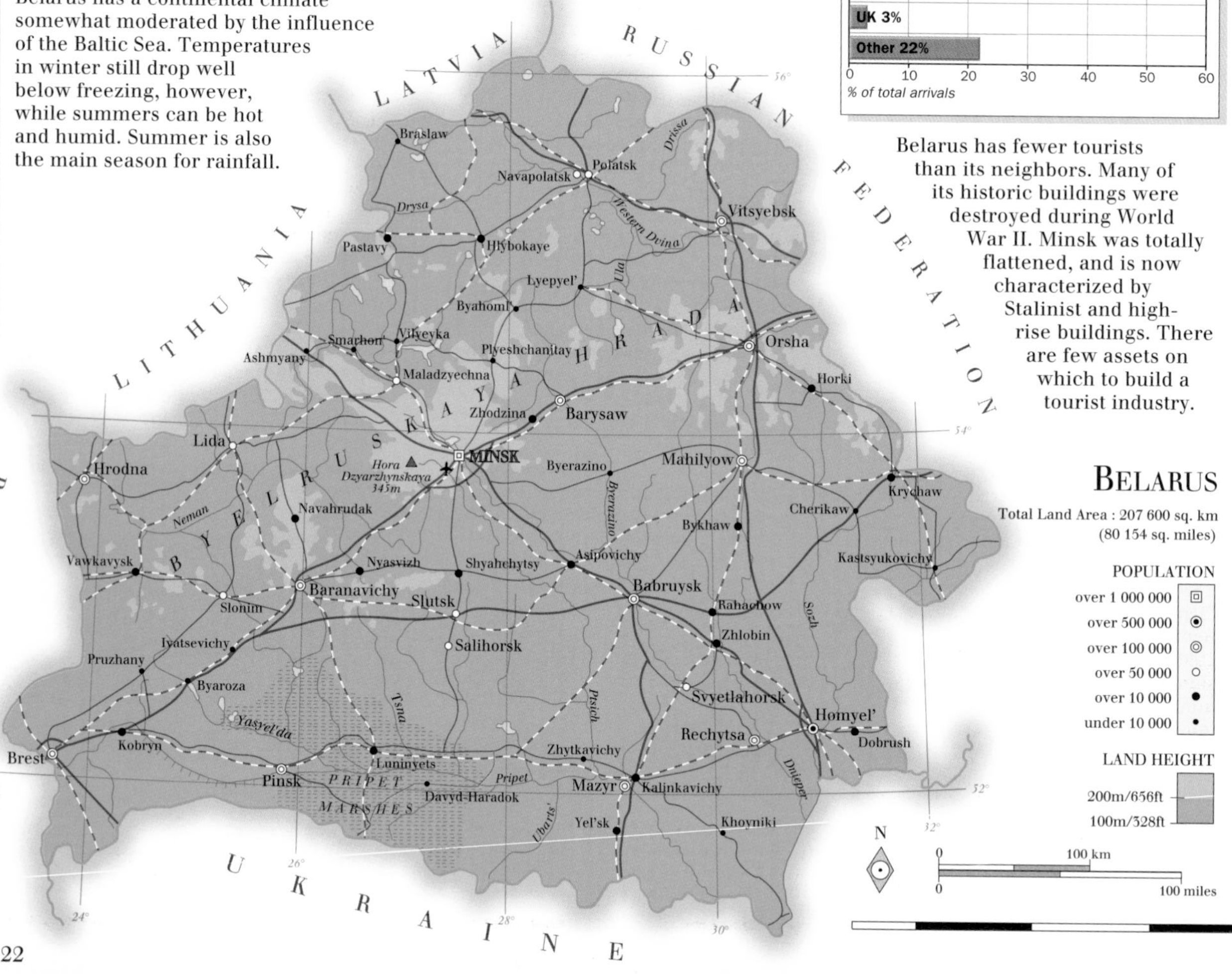
LATVIA
RUSSIAN FEDERATION
LITHUANIA
POLAND
UKRAINE
BYELARUSKAYA HRADA
Braslaw
Navapolatsk
Polatsk
Drissa
Drysa
Western Dvina
Vitsyebsk
Pastavy
Hlybokaye
Lyepyel'
Ula
Byahoml'
Smarhon'
Vilyeyka
Ashmyany
Pleshchanitsy
Orsha
Maladzyechna
Horki
Barysaw
Zhodzina
Lida
MINSK
Hora Dzyarzhynskaya 345m
Byerazino
Mahilyow
Hrodna
Neman
Navahrudak
Byerazino
Krychaw
Cherikaw
Bykhaw
Vawkavysk
Nyasvizh
Shyahchytsy
Asipovichy
Kastsyukovichy
Baranavichy
Slonim
Slutsk
Babruysk
Rahachow
Sozh
Salihorsk
Zhlobin
Ivatsevichy
Pruzhany
Byaroza
Svyetlahorsk
Yasyel'da
Tsna
Ptsich
Homyel'
Kobryn
Rechytsa
Dobrush
Brest
Luninyets
Zhytkavichy
Pinsk
PRIPET MARSHES
Pripet
Davyd-Haradok
Mazyr
Kalinkavichy
Dnieper
Ubarts'
Yel'sk
Khoyniki
N
BELARUS
Total Land Area : 207 600 sq. km (80 154 sq. miles)
POPULATION
over 1 000 000
over 500 000
over 100 000
over 50 000
over 10 000
under 10 000
LAND HEIGHT
200m/656ft
100m/328ft
0
100 km
0
100 miles

B

PEOPLE

Pop. density low

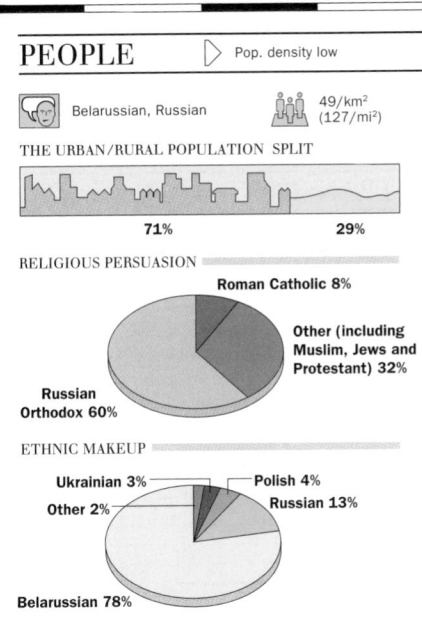

Belarussian, Russian

49/km² (127/mi²)

THE URBAN/RURAL POPULATION SPLIT

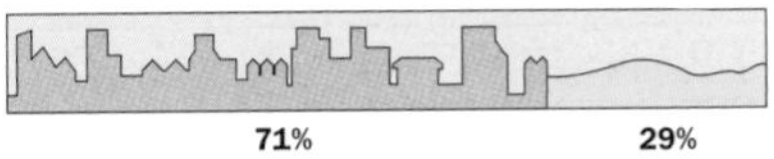
71%
29%

RELIGIOUS PERSUASION

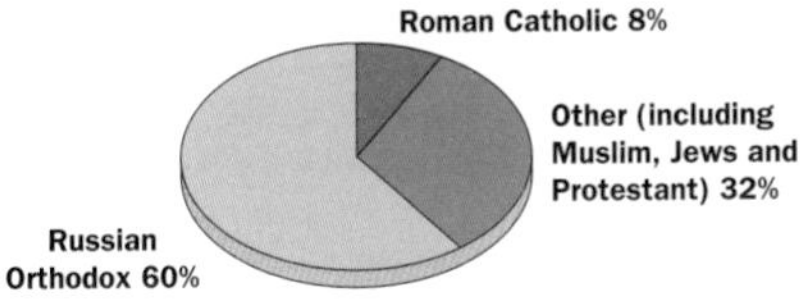
Roman Catholic 8%
Other (including Muslim, Jews and Protestant) 32%
Russian Orthodox 60%

ETHNIC MAKEUP

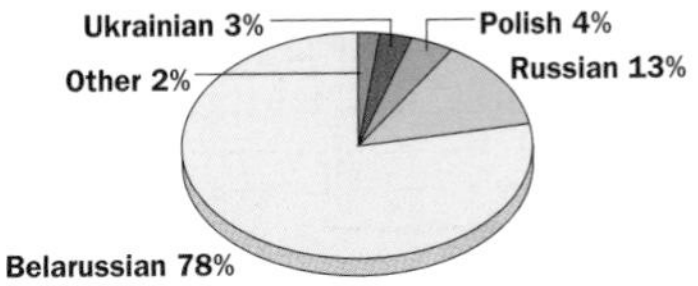
Ukrainian 3%
Polish 4%
Other 2%
Russian 13%
Belarussian 78%

Only 2% of the population is non-Slav and there is little ethnic tension. Under a law passed in 1992, the entire population has an automatic right to Belarussian citizenship. Most people speak Russian, and only 11% of the population are fluent in Belarussian, which is used mainly in rural areas. A 1995 referendum and 1998 legislation declared that both languages have equal status.

POPULATION AGE BREAKDOWN

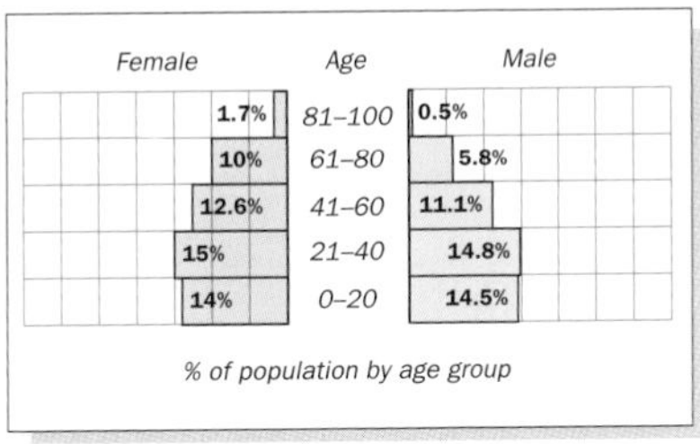
Female
Age
Male
1.7%
81–100
0.5%
10%
61–80
5.8%
12.6%
41–60
11.1%
15%
21–40
14.8%
14%
0–20
14.5%
% of population by age group

WORLD AFFAIRS

Joined UN in 1945

EAPC | CIS | IAEA | CEI | OSCE

Relations with Russia are paramount. Numerous bilateral agreements were signed after independence in 1991. Ties have been strengthened further by the pro-Russian president Aleksandr Lukashenka, although many in Russia fear that closer links will drain Moscow's resources for little strategic gain.

In mid-1998 diplomats were evicted from many official residences. The USA, the EU, and others temporarily withdrew their ambassadors in protest. The March 2001 clampdown on political opponents ended moves to relax EU sanctions, introduced in 1997 over authoritarian changes in the constitution.

AID

Recipient

$24m (receipts)

Down 44% 1997–1999

Although both the World Bank and the IMF provided loans for Belarus in the early 1990s, the lack of structural reforms since Lukashenka's administration came to power in 1994 has meant that further aid has been stalled. Some US bilateral aid continued, but the EU in particular has made it clear that support will depend on human rights improvements and the reversal of authoritarian threats to democracy.

Both the USA and the EU extended credits to Belarus to assist in the conversion of the defense industry to non-military production. Belarus also still requires aid to combat the effects of radiation pollution in the wake of the Chernobyl nuclear accident of 1986.

POLITICS

Multiparty elections

L. House 2000/2004
U. House 2000/2004

President Aleksandr Lukashenka

AT THE LAST ELECTION

House of Representatives 110 seats

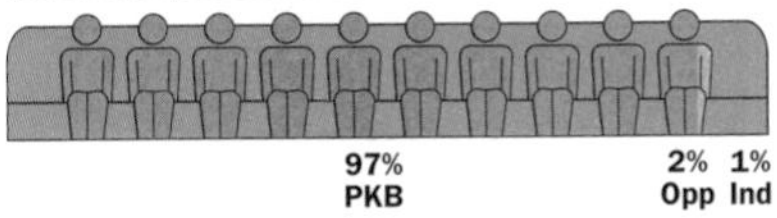
97% PKB
2% Opp
1% Ind

PKB = Party of Communists of Belarus and Government Supporters **Opp** = Minor Opposition Parties **Ind** = Independents

Council of the Republic 64 seats

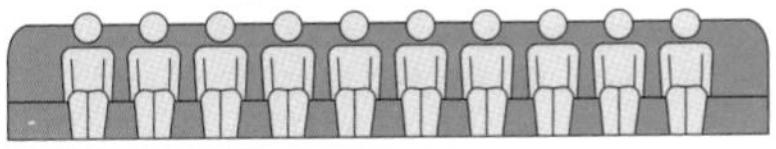

The Council of the Republic is indirectly elected

Under the 1994 constitution, amended in 1996, Belarus has a bicameral parliament and a directly elected president.

MAIN POLITICAL ISSUES

Relationship with Russia

In 1994 an accord (reinforced in 1999 and 2000) was signed on future monetary union with Russia. President Aleksandr Lukashenka has sought ever closer relations leading toward a joint presidency. A union treaty, forming the Community of Sovereign Republics (CSR), was concluded in 1996 but watered down before it was signed a year later. Belarus wants a union parliament as well as more joint economic programs.

The environment

The 1986 Chernobyl nuclear disaster continues to cast a shadow. The cleanup operation is slow and laborious and will take decades. It is a major drain on state finances, accounting for 25% of spending. A "Chernobyl tax" on businesses is still levied.

PROFILE

Belarus, by far the slowest of the former Soviet states to implement political reform, has struggled to find an identity since 1991. A post-Soviet constitution was not adopted until 1994, and only in 1995 was the first fully fledged post-Soviet parliament elected, dominated by the PKB and its Agrarian Party ally. There is no strong pluralist culture to check authoritarian moves by the president.

Aleksandr Lukashenka was unexpectedly elected as Belarus's first president in 1994. A referendum in 1996 approved a new constitution significantly strengthening his powers. Pro-Lukashenka deputies then voted to replace the Supreme Council with a new House of Representatives. Lukashenka has also extended his own term of office. The opposition contests the legitimacy of this, as does the EU. Parliamentary elections held in late 2000 and early 2001 were effectively invalidated by a clampdown on political opponents.

***President Aleksandr Lukashenka** seeks closer ties with the Russian Federation.*

***Vladimir Goncharik,** opposition candidate for presidential elections in 2001.*

CHRONOLOGY

After forming part of medieval Kievan Rus, Belarus experienced rule by three of its neighbors – Poland, Lithuania, and Russia – before incorporation into the USSR.

- **1918** Belarussian Bolsheviks stage coup. Independence as Belorussian Soviet Socialist Republic (BSSR).
- **1919** Invaded by Poland.
- **1920** Minsk retaken by Red Army. Eastern Belorussia reestablished as Soviet Socialist Republic.
- **1921** Treaty of Riga – Western Belorussia incorporated into Poland.
- **1922** BSSR merges with Russian Federation to form USSR.
- **1929** Stalin implements collectivization of agriculture.
- **1939** Western Belorussia reincorporated into USSR when Soviet Red Army invades Poland. ➪

B

CHRONOLOGY *continued*

- ❑ **1941–1944** Occupied by Germany during World War II.
- ❑ **1945** Founding member of UN (with Ukraine and USSR).
- ❑ **1965** K. T. Mazurau, Communist Party of Belorussia (PKB) leader, becomes first deputy chair of Soviet government.
- ❑ **1986** Radioactive fallout after Chernobyl accident affects 70% of country.
- ❑ **1988** Evidence revealed of mass executions (over 300,000) by Soviet military between 1937 and 1941 near Minsk. Popular outrage fuels formation of nationalist Belorussian Popular Front (BPF), with Zyanon Paznyak as president. PKB authorities crush demonstration.
- ❑ **1989** Belarussian adopted as republic's official language.
- ❑ **1990** PKB prevents BPF participating in elections to Supreme Soviet. BPF members join other opposition groups in Belorussian Democratic Bloc (BDB). BDB wins 25% of seats. PKB bows to opposition pressure and issues Declaration of the State Sovereignty of BSSR.
- ❑ **1991** March, 83% vote in referendum to preserve union with USSR. April, strikes against PKB and its economic policies. August, independence declared. Republic of Belarus adopted as official name. Stanislau Shushkevich elected chair of Supreme Soviet. December, Belarus, Russia, and Ukraine establish CIS.
- ❑ **1992** Supreme Soviet announces that Soviet nuclear weapons must be cleared from Belarus by 1999. Help promised from USA.
- ❑ **1993** Belarussian parliament ratifies START-I and nuclear nonproliferation treaties.
- ❑ **1994** New presidential constitution approved; Aleksandr Lukashenka defeats conservative prime minister Vyacheslav Kebich in elections. Monetary union (reentry into rouble zone) agreed with Russia.
- ❑ **1995** First fully fledged post-Soviet parliament elected.
- ❑ **1996** Union treaty with Russia. Referendum approves constitutional changes, thereby strengthening Lukashenka's powers.
- ❑ **1997** Belarus and Russia ratify union treaty and Charter.
- ❑ **1998** Western ambassadors withdrawn over eviction from embassies.
- ❑ **1999–2001** Further moves on union with Russia.
- ❑ **2000–2001** Disputed parliamentary elections; clampdown on PKB's political opponents.

DEFENSE

Compulsory military service

$466m

Down 1% in 1999

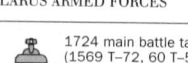

BELARUS ARMED FORCES

1724 main battle tanks (1569 T–72, 60 T–55, 95 T–80)	43,500 personnel
None	
230 combat aircraft (Su–24, Su–25, Su–27, MiG–23, MiG–29)	22,500 personnel
None	

After the breakup of the Soviet Union in 1991, Belarus briefly adopted a policy of neutrality. It also committed itself to disposing of its inherited nuclear capability. Tactical nuclear weapons were removed by 1993 and strategic nuclear weapons by 1996.

Despite joining the CIS collective security agreement in 1993, Belarus joined NATO's Partnerships for Peace program in 1995. Lukashenka has not developed NATO ties further, preferring to establish stronger military links with Moscow. Belarus now bears some of the costs of Russian troops stationed on its territory. Its union treaty with Russia was reinforced by a December 1997 Treaty on Military Cooperation and a 1999 agreement on joint procedures for arms exports.

ECONOMICS

Inflation 393.5% p.a. (1990–1999)

$26.3bn

900,000–1218 Belarussian roubles

SCORE CARD

❑ World GNP Ranking	60th
❑ GNP per Capita	$2620
❑ Balance of Payments	$–257m
❑ Inflation	293.7%
❑ Unemployment	2%

EXPORTS

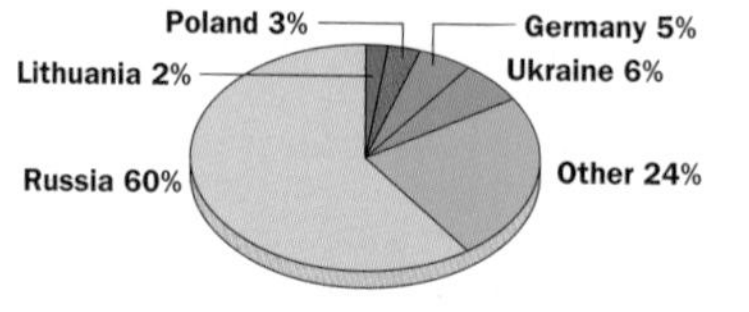
Poland 3%
Germany 5%
Lithuania 2%
Ukraine 6%
Russia 60%
Other 24%

IMPORTS

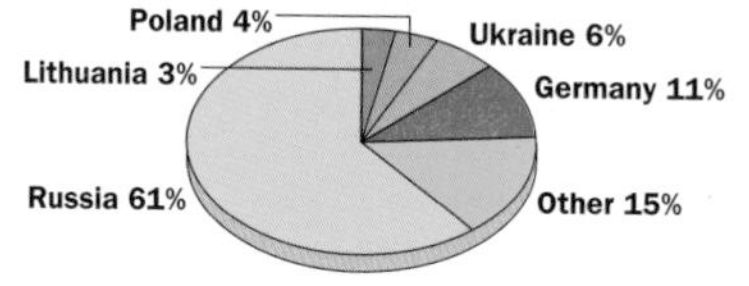
Poland 4%
Ukraine 6%
Lithuania 3%
Germany 11%
Russia 61%
Other 15%

Strengths

Low unemployment combined with relative social stability. Potential of forestry and agriculture.

Weaknesses

Lack of economic restructuring; support for outmoded businesses. High inflation. Few natural resources. Dependence on Russia for energy and raw materials. Cleanup costs of Chernobyl.

Profile

After 1991, Belarus adopted a slower pace of economic reform than other former Soviet states. Attempts to move more quickly to a market economy were thwarted by the largely conservative parliament. Upon election in 1994, Lukashenka suspended privatization moves, resuming them only half-heartedly in 1995, under a policy of "market socialism." Traditional industries continued to receive big subsidies, as the government printed money to increase production. A currency crisis in 1998, and rampant inflation, combined with two successive bad harvests in 1998–1999. Subsidized food had to be rationed. Claims of impressive economic growth are hard to substantiate.

ECONOMIC PERFORMANCE INDICATOR

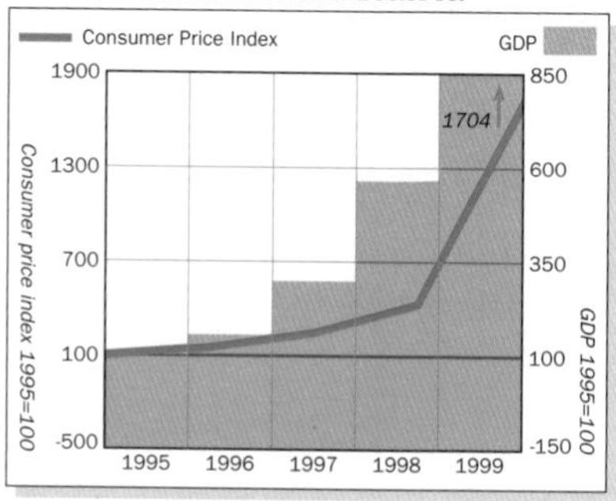
Consumer Price Index
GDP
1900
1300
700
100
-500
850
600
350
100
-150
1704
Consumer price index 1995=100
GDP 1995=100
1995
1996
1997
1998
1999

BELARUS : MAJOR BUSINESSES

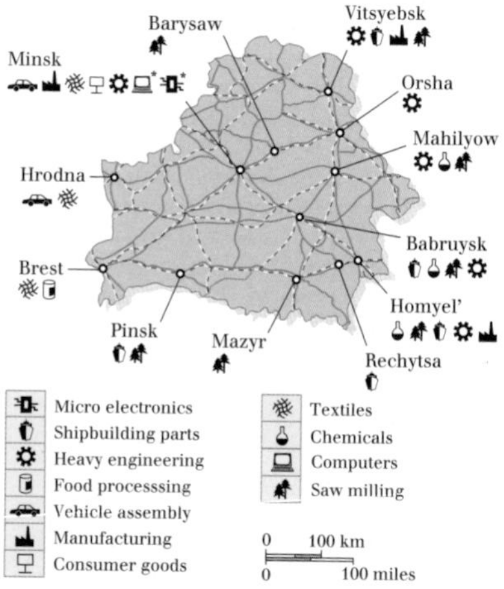
Barysaw
Vitsyebsk
Minsk
Orsha
Mahilyow
Hrodna
Babruysk
Brest
Homyel'
Pinsk
Mazyr
Rechytsa
Micro electronics
Shipbuilding parts
Heavy engineering
Food processsing
Vehicle assembly
Manufacturing
Consumer goods
Textiles
Chemicals
Computers
Saw milling
0 100 km
0 100 miles

* significant multinational ownership

RESOURCES

Electric power 7.4m kw

4805 tonnes

36,531 b/d (reserves 200,055,600 bbl)

4.33m cattle, 3.57m pigs, 30m chickens

Oil, natural gas, coal, rock salt

ELECTRICITY GENERATION

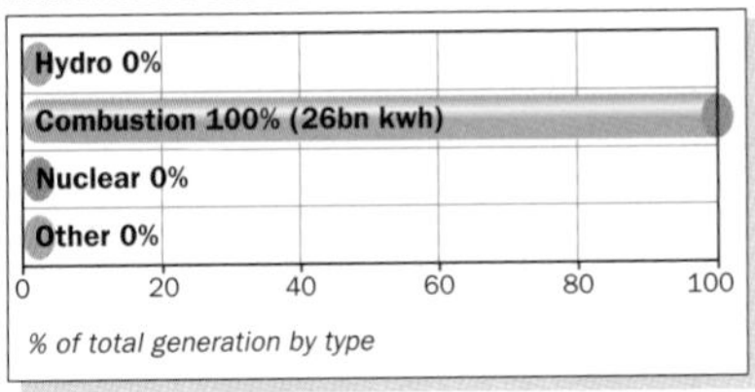
Hydro 0%
Combustion 100% (26bn kwh)
Nuclear 0%
Other 0%
0
20
40
60
80
100
% of total generation by type

Belarus has no significant strategic resources and is heavily dependent on the Russian Federation for fuel and energy supplies. Small quantities of oil and natural gas exist close to the Polish border.

BELARUS : LAND USE

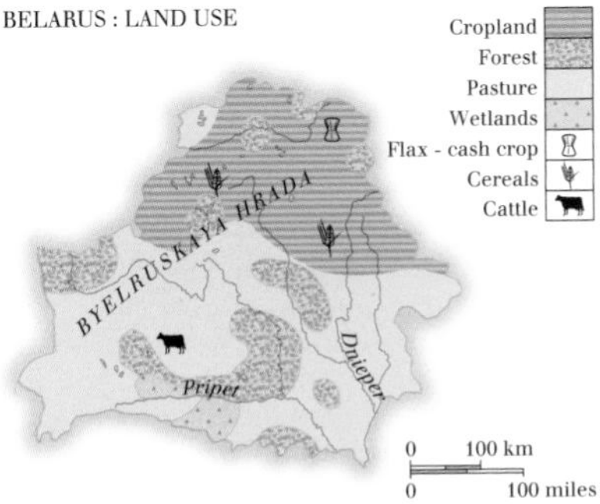
Cropland
Forest
Pasture
Wetlands
Flax - cash crop
Cereals
Cattle
BYELRUSKAYA HRADA
Pripet
Dnieper
0
100 km
0
100 miles

ENVIRONMENT

Sustainability rank: 57th

4%

6.1 tonnes per capita

ENVIRONMENTAL TREATIES

Yes

Yes

Yes

Yes

No

No

The massive leak from Ukraine's Chernobyl nuclear reactor in 1986 released a huge cloud of radiation. 70% of the fallout fell on Belarus, including the capital Minsk; 2.3 million people were immediately affected, and cases of leukemia and cancer continue to emerge. Farmland, forests, and water were all contaminated, including underwater streams feeding rivers in eastern Poland. Some areas in the fallout zone are still being farmed. The cleanup program swallows 25% of government finances, despite substantial Western aid.

The Belovezhskaya primeval forest, on the border with Poland, is Europe's largest nature reserve. It is also the home of the European bison or wisent.

MEDIA

TV ownership high

Daily newspaper circulation 173 per 1000 people

PUBLISHING AND BROADCAST MEDIA

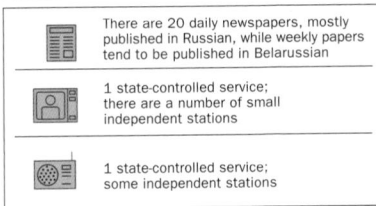

There are 20 daily newspapers, mostly published in Russian, while weekly papers tend to be published in Belarussian

1 state-controlled service; there are a number of small independent stations

1 state-controlled service; some independent stations

There is some independent TV, but critics of the government face harassment. Press freedom is curbed; state-backed publications predominate.

CRIME

Death penalty used

52,033 prisoners

Up 2% 1996–1998

CRIME RATES

Murders

10 *per 100,000 population*

Rapes

4 *per 100,000 population*

Thefts

529 *per 100,000 population*

As elsewhere in the former Soviet Union, economic hardship and a general breakdown in law and order have resulted in a significant rise in crime. The prison population exceeds the intended capacity of 40,000. Belarus has become a transshipment point for illegal narcotics destined for western Europe, while locally produced opium supplies the internal market.

EDUCATION

School leaving age: 15

99%

328,746 students

THE EDUCATION SYSTEM

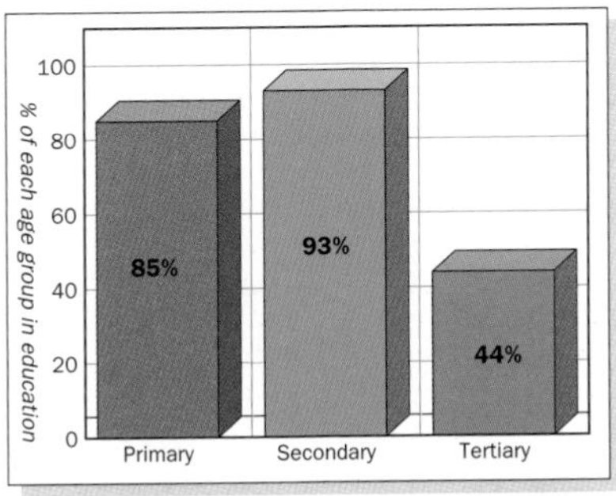
100
80
60
40
20
0
% of each age group in education
85%
93%
44%
Primary
Secondary
Tertiary

Education is officially compulsory for nine years, and teaching is mainly in Russian. The government began to make greater provision in the early 1990s for education in Belarussian – now used to teach nearly a third of all pupils. University education – taught in Russian – is of a fairly high standard.

HEALTH

Welfare state health benefits

1 per 233 people

Heart attacks, cancers, accidents, violence

Belarus's good health service, hitherto adequate, was placed under enormous strain after the Chernobyl nuclear disaster. A Chernobyl tax funds assistance for victims of the accident. The number of cancer and leukemia cases has soared, and extra wards and specialist units have had to be built. Many Belarussian doctors are being trained in the latest bone-marrow techniques in Europe and the USA.

By the end of 2000 there were 3158 people in Belarus registered as HIV-positive, mainly from drug use; 2700 were aged 15–29.

SPENDING

GDP/cap. decrease

CONSUMPTION AND SPENDING

135 per 1000 population

257 per 1000 population

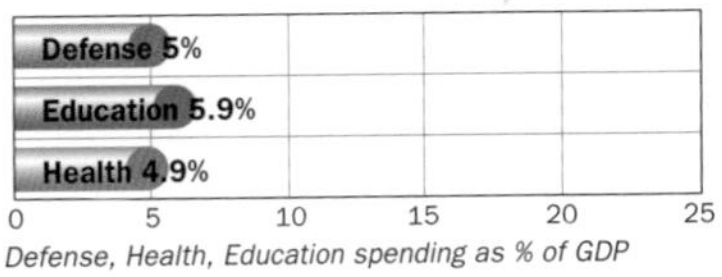
Defense 5%
Education 5.9%
Health 4.9%
0
5
10
15
20
25
Defense, Health, Education spending as % of GDP

The deteriorating economic situation has resulted in an overall drop in living standards. Rampant inflation particularly affects people on fixed incomes. Wealth is concentrated among a small, communist elite opposed to market mechanisms. Now they have the upper hand, they have strengthened their grip on the state's resources. Thus far Belarus has not seen the expansion of entrepreneurial activity found in Poland or Russia. Continued subsidies on foodstuffs have resulted in prices 200–300% lower than in Russia and Ukraine, spawning widespread smuggling across the border and the government's introduction of food rationing in 1998.

WORLD RANKING

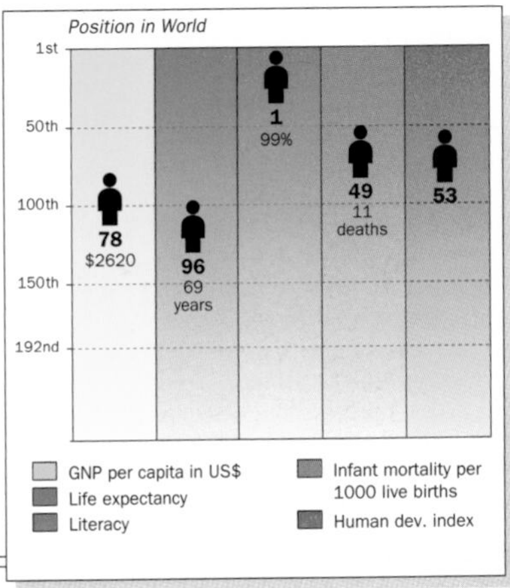
Position in World
1st
50th
100th
150th
192nd
78
$2620
96
69
years
1
99%
49
11
deaths
53
GNP per capita in US$
Life expectancy
Literacy
Infant mortality per 1000 live births
Human dev. index

BELGIUM

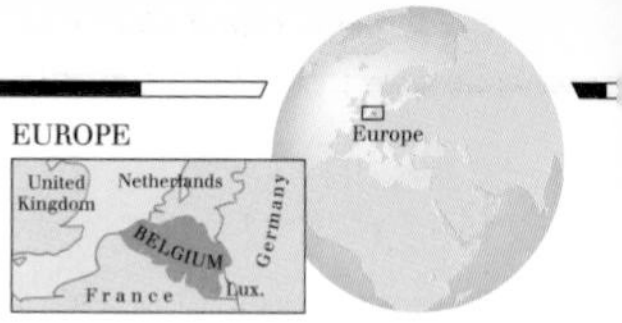
EUROPE
Europe
United Kingdom
Netherlands
Germany
BELGIUM
France
Lux.

OFFICIAL NAME: Kingdom of Belgium **CAPITAL:** Brussels **POPULATION:** 10.2 million
CURRENCY: Euro (Belgian franc until 2002) **OFFICIAL LANGUAGES:** Dutch, French, and German

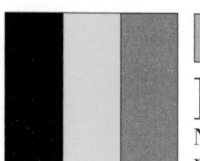

1830 | 1919 | July 21 | B | +1 | +32 | .be

LOCATED BETWEEN GERMANY, France, and the Netherlands, Belgium has a short coastline on the North Sea. The south includes the forested Ardennes region, while the north is crisscrossed by canals. Belgium has been fought over many times in its history; it was occupied by Germany in both world wars. Tensions have existed between the Dutch-speaking Flemings and French-speaking Walloons since the 1830s. These have been somewhat defused by Belgium's move to a federal political structure and the national consensus on the benefits of EU membership.

CLIMATE

Maritime

WEATHER CHART

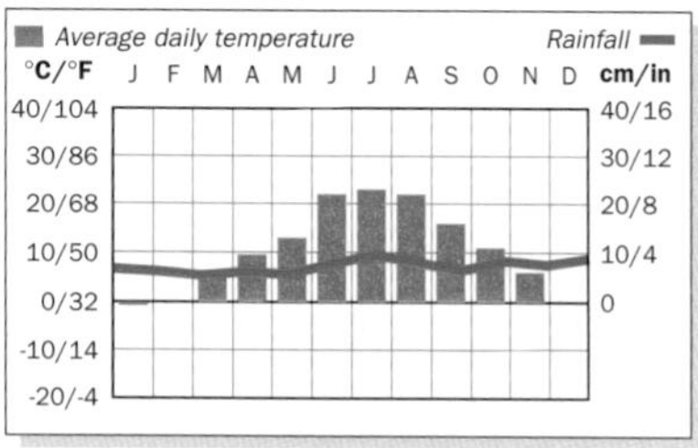
Average daily temperature
Rainfall
°C/°F
J F M A M J J A S O N D
cm/in
40/104
30/86
20/68
10/50
0/32
-10/14
-20/-4
40/16
30/12
20/8
10/4
0

Belgium has a typical maritime climate and is influenced by the Gulf Stream. Temperatures are mild with heavy cloud cover and much rain. The west coast climate can be disrupted by widely fluctuating weather conditions, caused by cyclonic disturbances. Summers tend to be short.

TRANSPORTATION

Drive on right

Zaventem International, Brussels 20m passengers

15 ships 340,800 grt

THE TRANSPORTATION NETWORK

117,701 km (73,136 miles)

1682 km (1045 miles)

3472 km (2158 miles)

2043 km (1269 miles)

Belgium can be crossed within four hours by car or train, and access to France, Germany, the Netherlands, and beyond is easy. The expressway network is extensive and so well lit that, along with the Great Wall of China, it is the most distinctive sight from orbit. The railroad system has been reduced since 1970, but it is still one of the world's densest networks. Using high-speed TGV lines, it is possible to reach Paris from Brussels in 1 hour 20 minutes and London via the Channel Tunnel in 2 hours 40 minutes. Antwerp is Europe's second-largest port. Brussels airport is to be expanded by a new concourse, due for completion in 2002.

TOURISM

Visitors : Population 1:1.6

6.4m visitors

Up 3% in 1999

MAIN TOURIST ARRIVALS

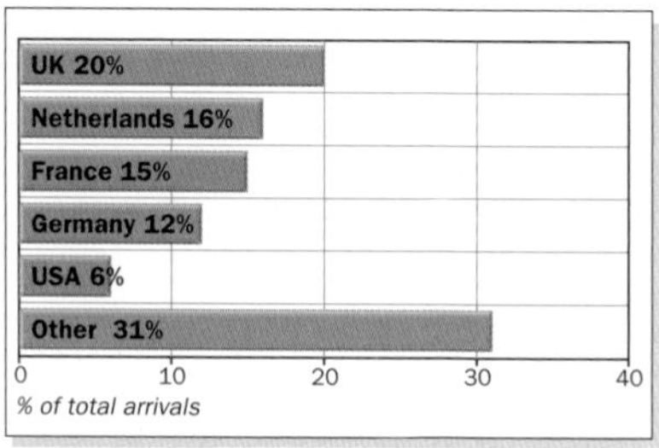
UK 20%
Netherlands 16%
France 15%
Germany 12%
USA 6%
Other 31%
0
10
20
30
40
% of total arrivals

Belgium's main attractions are its historic cities and the museums of Flemish art. Bruges, the capital of West Flanders, is often referred to as the "Venice of the North." With Gothic and Renaissance architecture and a complex canal system, it has become a favored destination for British weekend trippers and Japanese honeymooners. In Brussels, the famous "Grand Place," a cluster of Gothic, Renaissance, and Baroque buildings in a cobbled square, survived bombing during World War II. Much of the rest of the old city center, however, was destroyed. Belgium has 15 resorts on its 62-km (38-mile) coastline, with a single tramline running its entire length. Forests in the Ardennes to the south attract hikers.

The Ardennes, in the southeast, are famous for their forests, cuisine, and lakes. Rivers, such as the Meuse and Semois, dissect the region.

PEOPLE

Pop. density high

Dutch, French, German

311/km² (805/mi²)

THE URBAN/RURAL POPULATION SPLIT

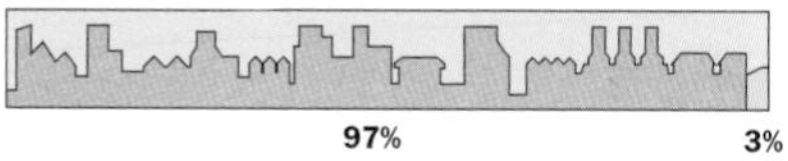
97%
3%

RELIGIOUS PERSUASION

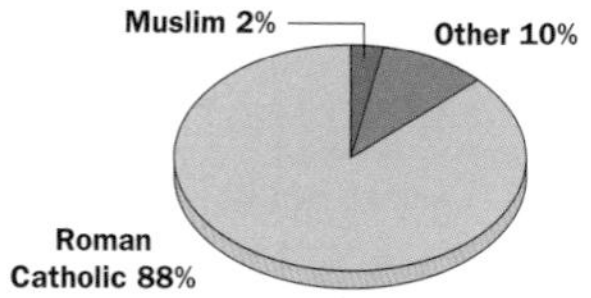
Muslim 2%
Other 10%
Roman Catholic 88%

ETHNIC MAKEUP

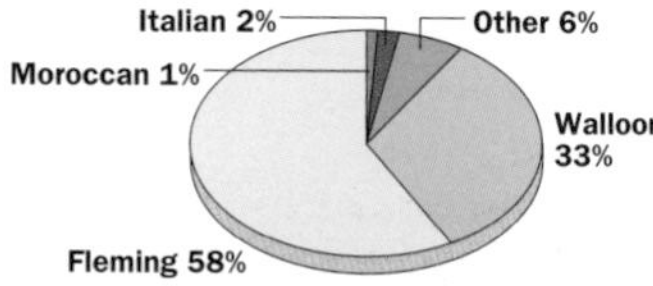
Italian 2%
Other 6%
Moroccan 1%
Walloon 33%
Fleming 58%

Belgium has been marked by the divisions between its Flemish and Walloon communities. The majority Dutch-speaking Flemings are concentrated in Flanders. Wallonia is French-speaking and Brussels is 85% francophone. French-speakers were in the ascendancy for many years, their greater economic wealth reinforced by a constitution giving them political control; tensions between Walloons and Flemings occasionally erupted into violence. In the past three decades, however, the situation has been reversed: Wallonia's industries have declined and Flanders is now the wealthier region. To defuse tensions, Belgium began in 1980 to change from being the most centralist to the most federal state in Europe; each community now controls most of its affairs and has its own government. A small German-speaking community in the east has extensive autonomy in educational and cultural matters.

Belgium has a sizeable immigrant population. Women account for 40% of the workforce and 19% of administrators and managers.

POPULATION AGE BREAKDOWN

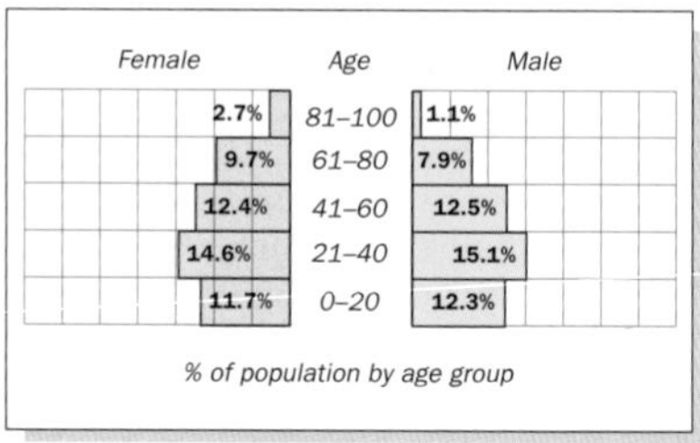
Female
Age
Male
2.7% 81–100 1.1%
9.7% 61–80 7.9%
12.4% 41–60 12.5%
14.6% 21–40 15.1%
11.7% 0–20 12.3%
% of population by age group

BELGIUM

Total Land Area : 32 820 sq. km (12 672 sq. miles)

POPULATION

- over 1 000 000
- over 100 000
- over 50 000
- over 10 000

LAND HEIGHT

- 500m/1640ft
- 200m/656ft
- Sea Level

0 40 km

0 40 miles

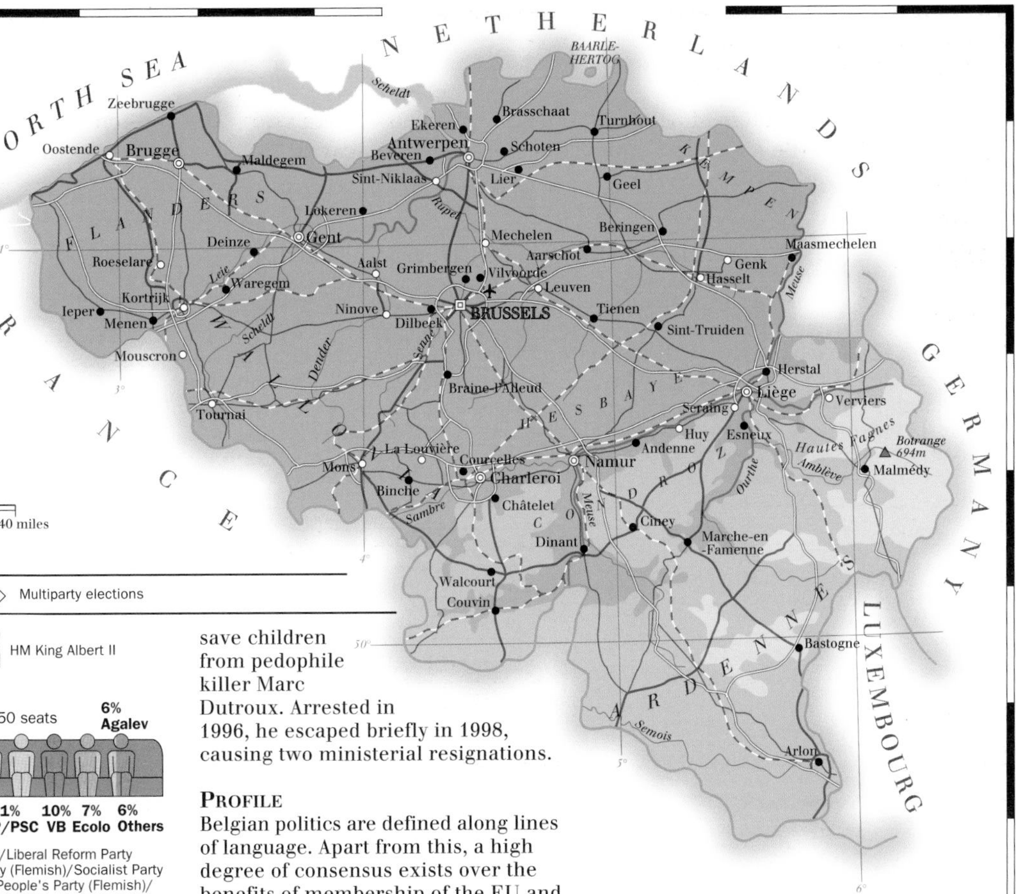
NORTH SEA
NETHERLANDS
GERMANY
LUXEMBOURG
FRANCE
FLANDERS
WALLONIA
KEMPEN
HESBAYE
CONDROZ
ARDENNES
Hautes Fagnes
Botrange 694m
BAARLE-HERTOG
Scheldt
Zeebrugge
Oostende
Brugge
Maldegem
Eeklo
Ekeren
Brasschaat
Turnhout
Antwerpen
Beveren
Schoten
Sint-Niklaas
Lier
Geel
Lokeren
Rupel
Mechelen
Beringen
Deinze
Gent
Aarschot
Maasmechelen
Roeselare
Aalst
Grimbergen
Vilvoorde
Genk
Hasselt
Leie
Waregem
Leuven
Kortrijk
Ninove
BRUSSELS
Tienen
Ieper
Menen
Dilbeek
Sint-Truiden
Mouscron
Dender
Senne
Herstal
Braine-l'Alleud
Liège
Verviers
Seraing
Tournai
Huy
Esneux
La Louvière
Andenne
Courcelles
Namur
Malmédy
Mons
Charleroi
Ambleve
Binche
Châtelet
Ourthe
Sambre
Meuse
Ciney
Dinant
Marche-en-Famenne
Walcourt
Couvin
Bastogne
Semois
Arlon

POLITICS

Multiparty elections

L. House 1999/2003
U. House 1999/2003

HM King Albert II

AT THE LAST ELECTION

Chamber of Representatives 150 seats

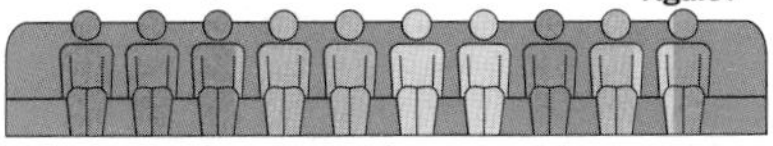
6% Agalev
28% VLD/PRL
22% SP/PS
21% CVP/PSC
10% VB
7% Ecolo
6% Others

VLD/PRL = Flemish Liberals Party/Liberal Reform Party (Walloon) **SP/PS** = Socialist Party (Flemish)/Socialist Party (Walloon) **CVP/PSC** = Christian People's Party (Flemish)/ Christian Social Party (Walloon) **VB** = Vlaams Blok **Ecolo** = French Greens **Agalev** = Flemish Ecologists **Co-op** = Co-opted members

Senate 71 seats

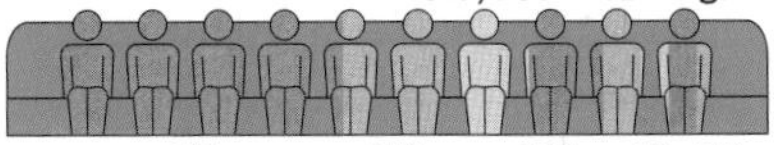
13% CVP/PSC
6% VB
4% Agalev
44% Co-op
15% VLD/PRL
11% SP/PS
4% Ecolo
3% Others

The Senate has 40 directly elected members and 31 co-opted members.

Until 1970, Belgium was a unitary state. Tensions between language groups led to four waves of federalist reforms from 1980, which culminated in the St. Michel Accords of 1993, confirming the state as a federal monarchy.

MAIN POLITICAL ISSUES

Language

Tensions between the two language groups are receding. However, the divisions remain strong. Each community has a right–liberal party (the VLD in Flanders, the PRL in Wallonia), a socialist party (SP/PS), a Christian democratic party (CVP/PSC), and a green party (Agalev/Ecolo).

Police handling of pedophile case

Apparent police incompetence, cover-ups, and corruption in combating the activities of pedophile rings has provoked public anger and protest, focusing in particular on failure to save children from pedophile killer Marc Dutroux. Arrested in 1996, he escaped briefly in 1998, causing two ministerial resignations.

PROFILE

Belgian politics are defined along lines of language. Apart from this, a high degree of consensus exists over the benefits of membership of the EU and monetary union. In recent years, support has increased for the racist VB, which objects to Belgium's Turkish, Moroccan, and African minorities. VB captured 28% of the vote in local elections in Antwerp in 1994 and 33% in 2000.

The ruling centrist coalition of the Socialist and Christian Democrat parties of the Flemish and Walloon communities had a parliamentary majority, but had difficulty in securing the necessary majority for the constitutional reforms enacted in the St. Michel Accords. These gave the regional governments – Flanders, Wallonia, and Brussels – significant powers under a federal government. The Dehaene government was defeated in the 1999 election, and a new coalition composed of the Liberals, Socialists, and Greens was formed by the VLD's Guy Verhofstadt.

King Albert II, *succeeded his brother King Baudouin who died in 1993.*

Guy Verhofstadt, *youthful leader of the VLD/PRL and prime minister since 1999.*

WORLD AFFAIRS

Joined UN in 1945

Benelux | CE | EU | OECD | NATO

Belgium's key concern is its role in the EU. It is a keen supporter of economic and monetary union. As a frequent victim of wars between France and Germany, Belgium sees the EU as a guarantor of western European peace. It is also perceived as an important foundation for Belgium's own federalist structure, without which many fear that Belgium could split into two.

Belgium has little in the way of an independent foreign policy, but does frequently contribute troops to the UN's operations. Belgian soldiers have served in Bosnia and Somalia in recent years and a number were killed in Rwanda in 1994.

AID

Donor

$760m (donations) Down 14% in 1999

Some 0.3% of GNP goes in overseas development aid. Belgian aid focuses on education and agricultural projects in Africa. The major beneficiaries are the former Belgian colonies of Burundi, Rwanda, and the Democratic Republic of Congo former Zaire).

B

CHRONOLOGY

Formerly ruled by the French dukes of Burgundy, Belgium became a Habsburg possession in 1477. It passed to the Austrian Habsburgs in 1713. Napoleon ended Austrian rule of the Low Countries in 1797.

- ❑ **1814–1815** Congress of Vienna; European powers decide to merge Belgium with the Netherlands under King William I of Orange.
- ❑ **1830** Revolt against Dutch; declaration of independence.
- ❑ **1831** European powers place Leopold Saxe Coburg as king.
- ❑ **1865** Leopold II crowned king.
- ❑ **1885** Berlin Conference gives Leopold Congo basin as colony.
- ❑ **1914** German armies invade. Belgium occupied until 1918.
- ❑ **1921** Belgo-Luxembourg Economic Union formed. Belgian and Luxembourg currencies locked.
- ❑ **1932** Dutch language accorded equal official status with French.
- ❑ **1936** Belgium declares neutrality.
- ❑ **1940** Leopold III capitulates to Hitler. Belgium occupied till 1944.
- ❑ **1948** Customs union with Netherlands and Luxembourg (Benelux) formed.
- ❑ **1950** King wins referendum but rumors over his wartime collaboration persist. Abdicates in favor of his son, Baudouin.
- ❑ **1957** Signs Treaty of Rome as one of six founding members of EEC.
- ❑ **1992** Christian Democrat and Socialist government led by Jean-Luc Dehaene takes over federal government.
- ❑ **1993** Culmination of reforms creating federal state. Greater powers for regions and city governments. Death of Baudouin. Succeeded by Albert II.
- ❑ **1995** Allegations of corruption and murder involving French-speaking PS force resignations of Walloon premier, federal deputy premier, and Willy Claes as NATO secretary-general.
- ❑ **1996** The murder and disappearance of young girls arouse fears of an international pedophile ring. Accusations of incompetence, even collusion, of authorities.
- ❑ **1998** Claes and 11 others found guilty of bribery.
- ❑ **1999** Belgium among first 11 countries to introduce euro. June, VLD/PRL wins general election. New coalition formed, including Greens for first time.

DEFENSE

No compulsory military service

$3.45bn

Down 2% in 1999

BELGIAN ARMED FORCES

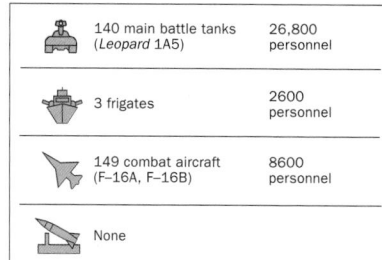

140 main battle tanks (*Leopard* 1A5)	26,800 personnel
3 frigates	2600 personnel
149 combat aircraft (F-16A, F-16B)	8600 personnel
None	

Belgium spends less on defense than the NATO average of 2.2% of GDP.

In 1994, as part of Belgium's program to reduce government debt, all three military services were targeted for cuts. The government abolished conscription and undertook to cut troop levels to 40,000. The defense budget was frozen for five years.

However, spending on paratroopers and transport planes has increased. The aim is to allow Belgian forces to fulfill their role in NATO's new rapid reaction forces. It will also make Belgian forces more useful to the UN's worldwide operations. In 1996, the Belgian and Netherlands navies were brought together under a joint operational command based at Den Helder, the Netherlands.

ECONOMICS

Inflation 2.2% p.a. (1990–1999)

$252bn

40.25–42.97 Belgian francs

SCORE CARD

❑ World GNP Ranking	20th
❑ GNP per Capita	$24,650
❑ Balance of Payments	$12bn
❑ Inflation	1.1%
❑ Unemployment	12%

EXPORTS

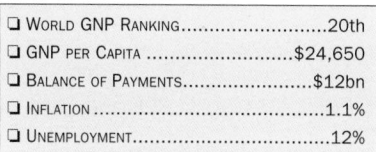

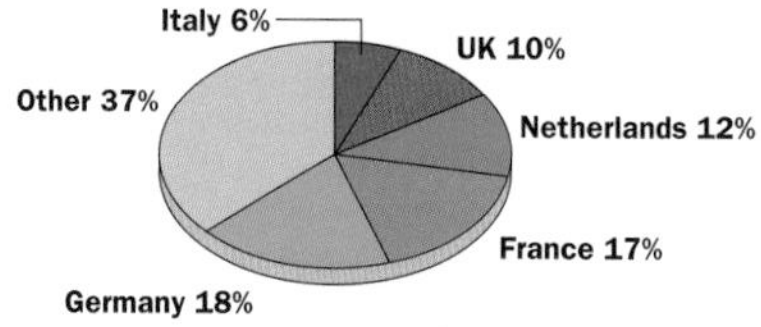
Italy 6%
UK 10%
Other 37%
Netherlands 12%
France 17%
Germany 18%

IMPORTS

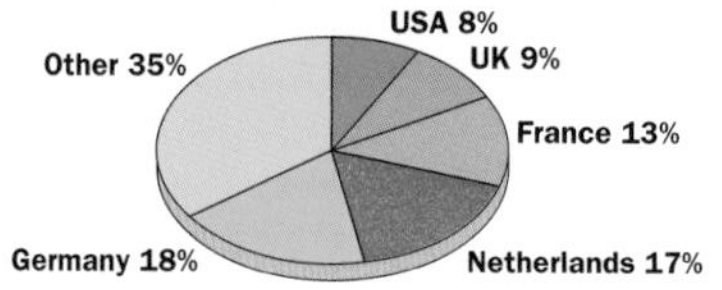
USA 8%
UK 9%
Other 35%
France 13%
Germany 18%
Netherlands 17%

Strengths

One of world's most efficient producers of metal products and textiles. Flanders is a world leader in new high-tech industries. Successful chemicals industry. Highly educated and motivated multilingual workforce: estimates suggest productivity is 20% above that of Germany. Location makes Belgium an attractive location for US multinationals. Good sea outlets and access to Rhine inland waterway from Antwerp and Ghent.

Weaknesses

Public debt of around 110% of GDP, well over EU target of 60%. High long-term and low-skill joblessness with sharp local variations. Large numbers of workers retire early, resulting in high state pension bill. Bureaucracy larger than European average.

ECONOMIC PERFORMANCE INDICATOR

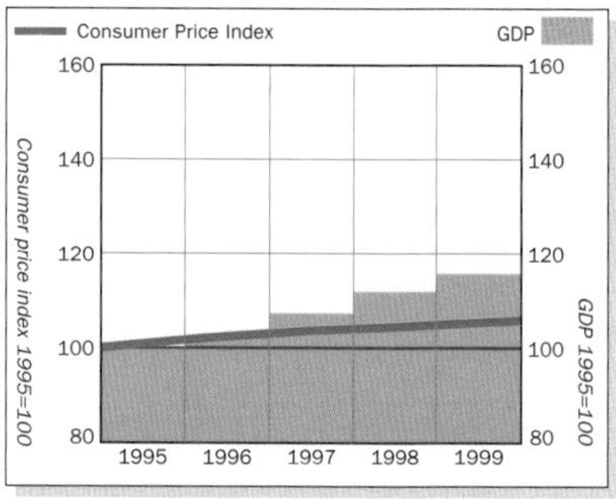
Consumer Price Index
GDP
160
140
120
100
80
1995
1996
1997
1998
1999
Consumer price index 1995=100
GDP 1995=100

Profile

Recession and rising unemployment in the early 1990s prompted the introduction of work-sharing schemes, benefit reforms, and a 1998 two-year, sectorally differentiated pay accord. Unemployment has now begun to fall. Progress in reducing Belgium's massive public debt allowed the country to join the euro from 1999, but it remains almost double the EU target of 60% of GDP.

BELGIUM : MAJOR BUSINESSES

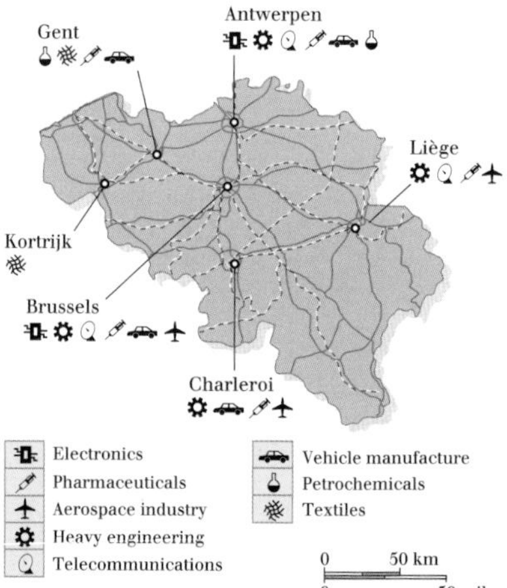
Gent
Antwerpen
Liège
Kortrijk
Brussels
Charleroi
Electronics
Pharmaceuticals
Aerospace industry
Heavy engineering
Telecommunications
Vehicle manufacture
Petrochemicals
Textiles
0
50 km
0
50 miles

B

RESOURCES

Electric power 14.9m kw

31,346 tonnes

Not an oil producer; refines 607,000 b/d

7.32m pigs, 3.16m cattle, 38m chickens

Coal, natural gas, shale, marble, sandstone, dolomite

ELECTRICITY GENERATION

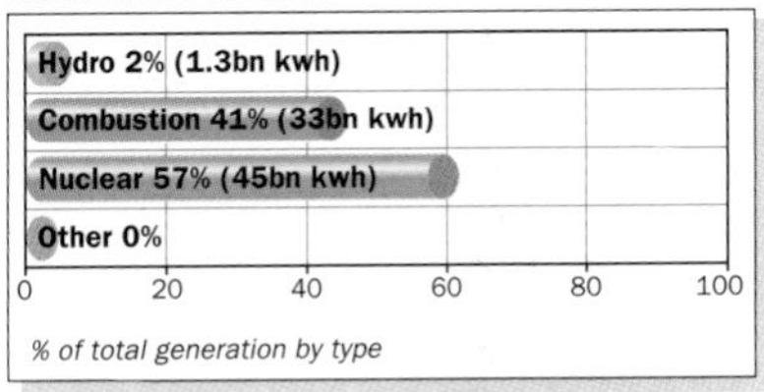

Hydro 2% (1.3bn kwh)
Combustion 41% (33bn kwh)
Nuclear 57% (45bn kwh)
Other 0%
0
20
40
60
80
100
% of total generation by type

Belgium has few natural resources and depends largely on the export of goods and services. The once-rich coal mines of Wallonia are almost depleted. There is some deciduous and conifer forestry in the Ardennes region.

BELGIUM : LAND USE

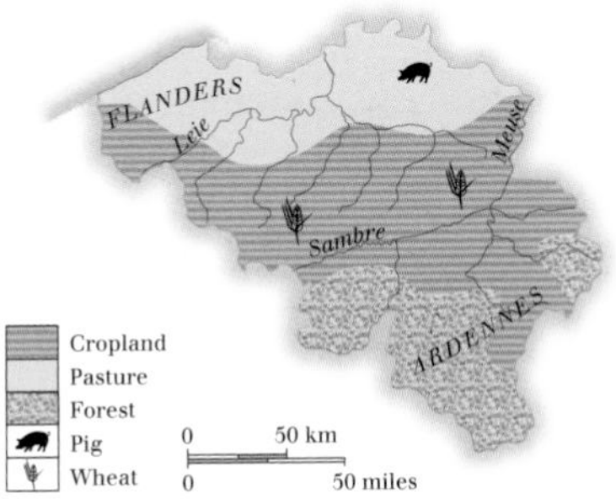

FLANDERS
Lys
Meuse
Sambre
ARDENNES
Cropland
Pasture
Forest
Pig
Wheat
0
50 km
0
50 miles

ENVIRONMENT

Sustainability rank: 79th

3%

10.5 tonnes per capita

ENVIRONMENTAL TREATIES

Yes Yes Yes

Yes Yes Yes

Flanders is concerned about the pollution of groundwater supplies through acid rain, heavy metals, fertilizers, and pesticides. Its government operates an environmental management plan to raise standards. Wallonia has strict laws against illegal tipping of waste, and regulations on air quality and emissions. Awareness of environmental issues is reflected in the rise of the two green parties, which entered government for the first time in the coalition formed in 1999.

MEDIA

TV ownership high

Daily newspaper circulation 161 per 1000 people

PUBLISHING AND BROADCAST MEDIA

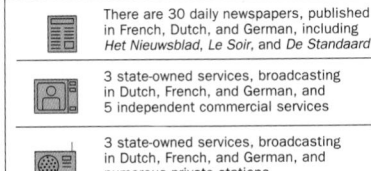

There are 30 daily newspapers, published in French, Dutch, and German, including *Het Nieuwsblad*, *Le Soir*, and *De Standaard*

3 state-owned services, broadcasting in Dutch, French, and German, and 5 independent commercial services

3 state-owned services, broadcasting in Dutch, French, and German, and numerous private stations

Newspapers tend to be regional and divided by language. Circulation is low, with the most widely read newspaper having a circulation of only 370,000. Over 80% of Belgians have cable TV, receiving as many as 30 channels from all over Europe. Commercial TV only began in 1989, with the Flemish station VTM showing mainly imported English-language programs and game shows.

CRIME

Death penalty not used

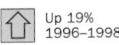

7410 prisoners

Up 19% 1996–1998

CRIME RATES

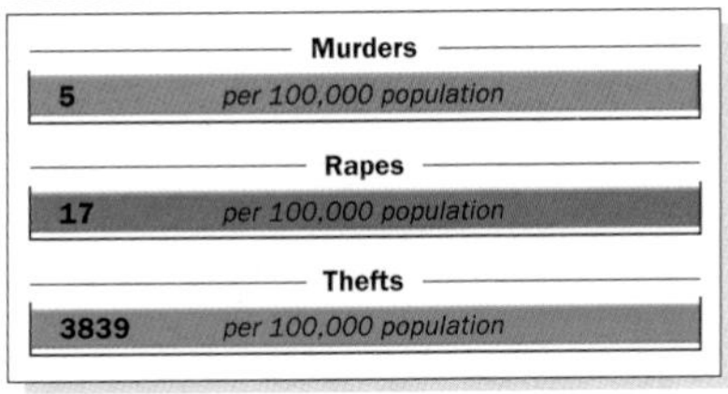

Murders
5 per 100,000 population
Rapes
17 per 100,000 population
Thefts
3839 per 100,000 population

Brussels has one of the lowest murder rates for any capital city. In urban areas pickpocketing is rising and car theft is a problem. Penalties for illegal drugs use are strict.

EDUCATION

School leaving age: 18

99%

358,214 students

THE EDUCATION SYSTEM

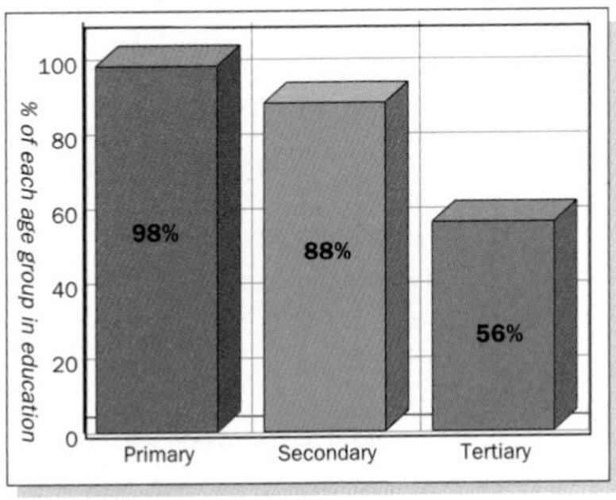

100
80
60
40
20
0
% of each age group in education
98%
88%
56%
Primary
Secondary
Tertiary

In Belgium parents can choose between schooling provided by the two language communities, by public authorities, or by private interests. Roman Catholic schools constitute the greatest number of "free" (privately organized) establishments. Since 1989 the system has been administered by the governments of the two main language groups. All universities are split by language.

HEALTH

Welfare state health benefits

1 per 294 people

Heart and respiratory diseases, cancers, accidents

The quality of health care, to which the government allocates just over 12% of total expenditure, is among the best in the world. Belgium is a world leader in fertility treatment and heart and lung transplants. Treatment is not free, but Belgians hold insurance enabling them to claim up to 75% of their costs.

Only heart disease and cancer rank before car accidents as a cause of death; over 70,000 accidents resulted in personal injury or death in 1997. There were nearly 8000 people living with HIV/AIDS in 1999.

SPENDING

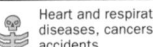

GDP/cap. increase

CONSUMPTION AND SPENDING

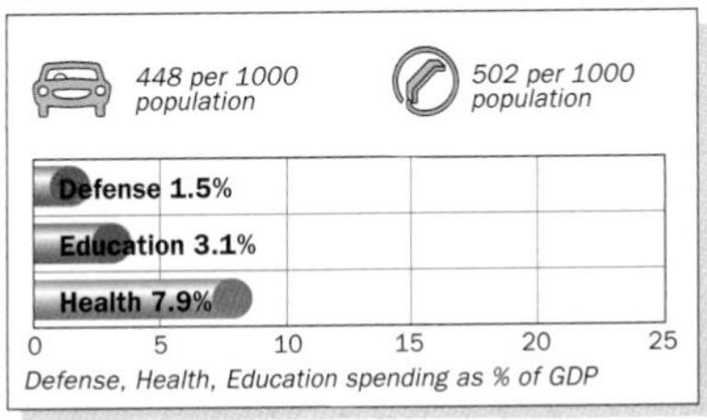

448 per 1000 population
502 per 1000 population
Defense 1.5%
Education 3.1%
Health 7.9%
0
5
10
15
20
25
Defense, Health, Education spending as % of GDP

Despite high levels of state debt and failing traditional industries, Belgium is one of Europe's richest countries. GDP per capita is lower than for Germany but higher than for Italy or the UK.

This statistic masks considerable regional differences. In Flanders, with its many high-tech businesses, only 8% are unemployed, while in Wallonia 17% are out of work.

The presence of highly paid EU officials and international company employees and bankers has made Brussels a distinctly wealthy, and expensive, city. The recession of the early 1990s prompted Belgians to save a higher proportion of their income, but the level of savings has fallen since then as consumer confidence has recovered.

WORLD RANKING

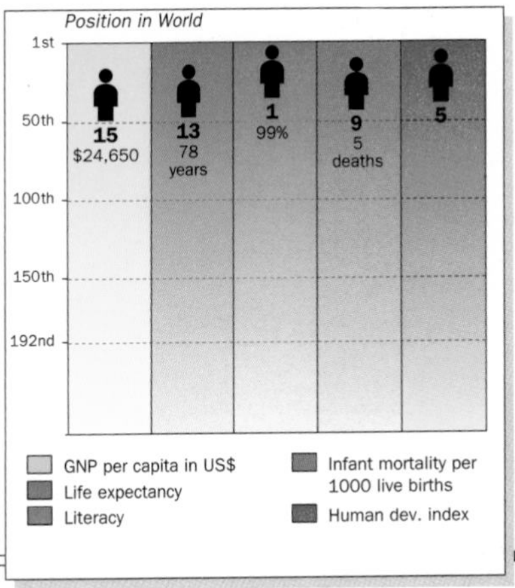

Position in World
1st
50th
100th
150th
192nd
15
$24,650
13
78
years
1
99%
9
5
deaths
5
GNP per capita in US$
Life expectancy
Literacy
Infant mortality per 1000 live births
Human dev. index

B

BELIZE

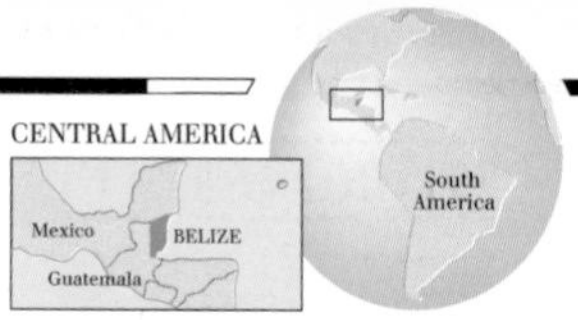
CENTRAL AMERICA
Mexico
BELIZE
Guatemala
South America

OFFICIAL NAME: Belize **CAPITAL:** Belmopan
POPULATION: 200,000 **CURRENCY:** Belizean dollar **OFFICIAL LANGUAGE:** English

1981 | 1981 | Sept 21 | BZ | -6 | +501 | .bz

FORMERLY BRITISH HONDURAS, Belize was the last Central American country to gain its independence, in 1981. It lies on the eastern shore of the Yucatan peninsula and shares a border with Mexico along the River Hondo. Belize is Central America's least populous country, and almost half of its land area is still forested. Its swampy coastal plains are protected from flooding by the world's second-largest barrier reef.

***Small fishing village near Belize City.** More than 500 tonnes of Caribbean spiny lobster, the main inshore species, are caught every year.*

CLIMATE

Tropical equatorial

WEATHER CHART

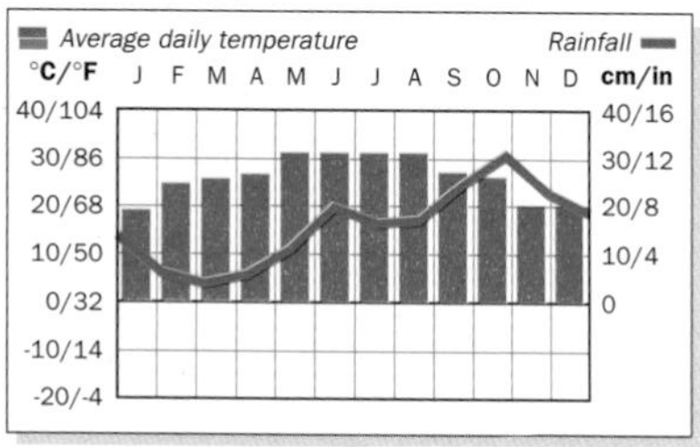
Average daily temperature
Rainfall
°C/°F
J F M A M J J A S O N D
cm/in
40/104
30/86
20/68
10/50
0/32
-10/14
-20/-4
40/16
30/12
20/8
10/4
0

Conditions are hot and humid for most of the year. Coastal regions are affected by hurricanes.

TRANSPORTATION

Drive on right

Philip S. W. Goldson, Belize City 272,000 passengers

1308 ships 2.4m grt

THE TRANSPORTATION NETWORK

488 km (303 miles)	None
None	825 km (513 miles)

A US$16 million IDB loan in 1998 helped improve the country's road network and its feeder roads. A terminal and runway extension have been completed at the international airport near Belize City.

TOURISM

Visitors : Population 1:1.1

181,000 visitors

Up 2% in 1999

MAIN TOURIST ARRIVALS

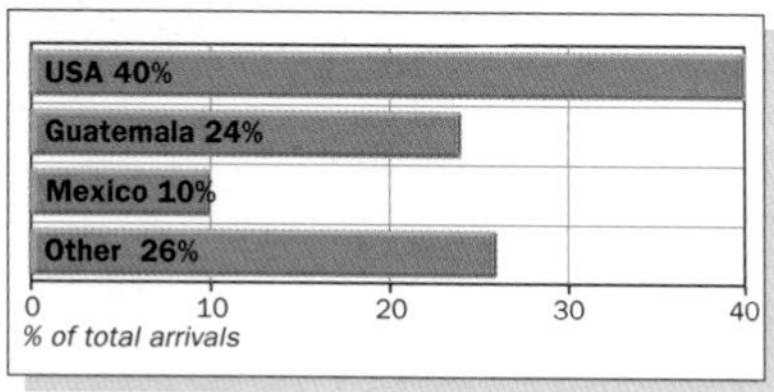
USA 40%
Guatemala 24%
Mexico 10%
Other 26%
0
10
20
30
40
% of total arrivals

The barrier reef, good beaches, and Mayan ruins draw visitors. Ecotourism is strongly promoted.

PEOPLE

Pop. density low

English Creole, Spanish, English, Maya, Garifuna (Carib)

9/km² (23/mi²)

THE URBAN/RURAL POPULATION SPLIT

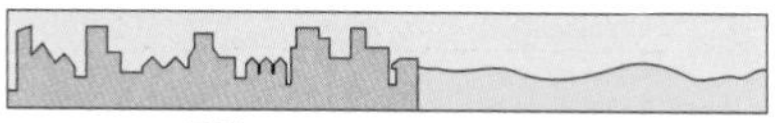
54%
46%

ETHNIC MAKEUP

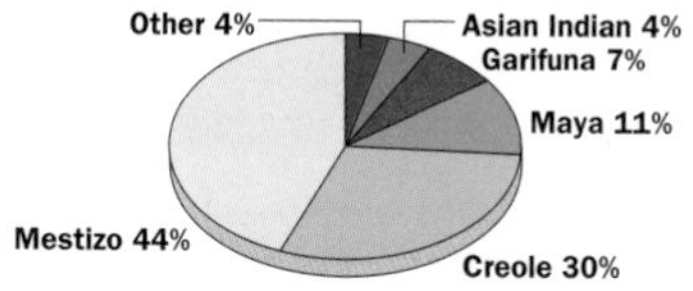
Other 4%
Asian Indian 4%
Garifuna 7%
Maya 11%
Creole 30%
Mestizo 44%

Over 80% of Belizeans are of mixed descent involving African, Amerindian, and European strands. Along with the *mestizo* and Creole populations there are the Afro-Carib *garifuna*. Christianity is dominant, and the Roman Catholic, Anglican, and Methodist churches run most of the schools.

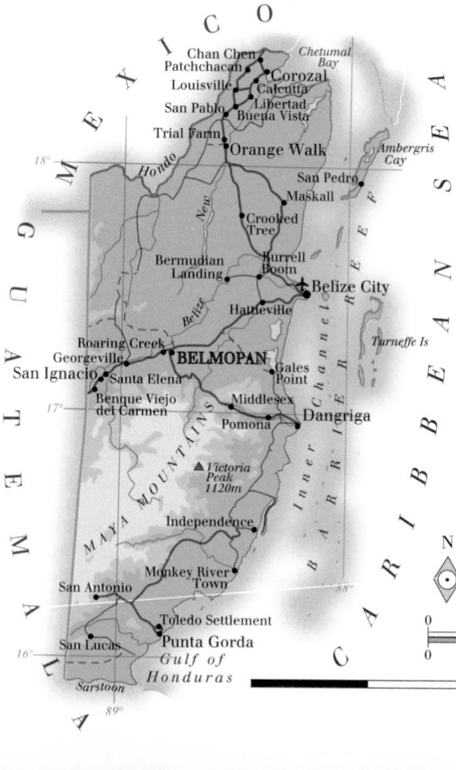
MEXICO
GUATEMALA
CARIBBEAN SEA
Chan Chen
Patchchacan
Louisville
San Pablo
Trial Farm
Chetumal Bay
Corozal
Calcutta
Libertad
Buena Vista
Orange Walk
Hondo
New
Ambergris Cay
San Pedro
Maskall
Crooked Tree
Bermudian Landing
Burrell Boom
Belize City
Hattieville
Belize
Turneffe Is
Roaring Creek
Georgeville
San Ignacio
Santa Elena
BELMOPAN
Gales Point
Benque Viejo del Carmen
Middlesex
Pomona
Dangriga
Inner Channel
BARRIER REEF
MAYA MOUNTAINS
Victoria Peak 1120m
Independence
Monkey River Town
San Antonio
Toledo Settlement
San Lucas
Punta Gorda
Gulf of Honduras
Sarstoon
18°
17°
16°
88°
89°

POLITICS

Multiparty elections

L. House 1998/2003
U. House 1998/2003

HM Queen Elizabeth II

AT THE LAST ELECTION

House of Representatives 29 seats

90% PUP
10% UDP

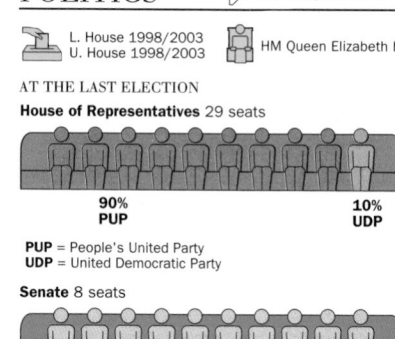

PUP = People's United Party
UDP = United Democratic Party

Senate 8 seats

The members of the Senate are appointed by the governor-general

The desire for independence dominated politics until the 1980s. The PUP, under George Price, negotiated this with the British in 1981. During the 1984–1989 UDP administration, the main concerns were to maintain a pro-US line and the fear of communism in the region. In the absence of any major ideological or policy distinctions, the UDP lost power to the PUP in 1989, winning it back in 1993; the pendulum swung back to the PUP again in 1998. Growth, job creation, "economic citizenship" for foreigners, and border tension with Guatemala are key issues, along with political reform.

BELIZE

Total Land Area : 22 800 sq. km (8803 sq. miles)

POPULATION
- over 10 000
- under 10 000

LAND HEIGHT
- 1000m/3281ft
- 500m/1640ft
- 200m/656ft
- Sea Level

N

0 — 50 km
0 — 50 miles

WORLD AFFAIRS

Joined UN in 1981

ACS | Comm | Caricom | NAM | OAS

The major concern is Guatemala's historic claim to over half of Belize. Suspended in 1986, the claim was revived in early 2000 as border tension rose.

AID

Recipient

US$46m (receipts) | Up 207% in 1999

In 1999 the IDB, the Commonwealth Development Corporation, the European Investment Bank, and the CDB invested in citrus farms. Belize is one of the highest per capita recipients of US aid.

DEFENSE

No compulsory military service

US$17m | No change in 1999

The small Belize Defense Force (BDF) took over full responsibility from the UK in 1994 for the country's defense. The UK withdrew its garrison in the same year, but maintains a jungle training school.

ECONOMICS

Inflation 2.9% p.a. (1990–1999)

US$673m | 1.99–1.97 Belizean dollars

SCORE CARD

- ❑ WORLD GNP RANKING.......................162nd
- ❑ GNP PER CAPITA.........................US$2730
- ❑ BALANCE OF PAYMENTS.................US$–77m
- ❑ INFLATION.......................................–1.2%
- ❑ UNEMPLOYMENT.................................14%

STRENGTHS

Sugar, textile manufacture, citrus fruits, bananas, shellfish, forestry, and considerable tourist potential. Sustainable public debt; fair access to concessionary foreign finance.

WEAKNESSES

Narrow export base dependent on preferential market access; reliance on imports of processed foods. Poor fiscal management in late 1990s.

EXPORTS

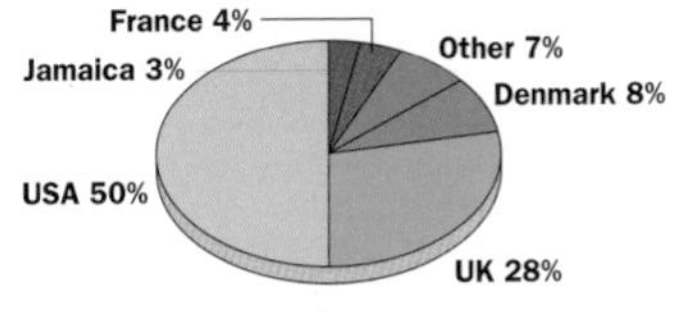
France 4%
Jamaica 3%
Other 7%
Denmark 8%
USA 50%
UK 28%

IMPORTS

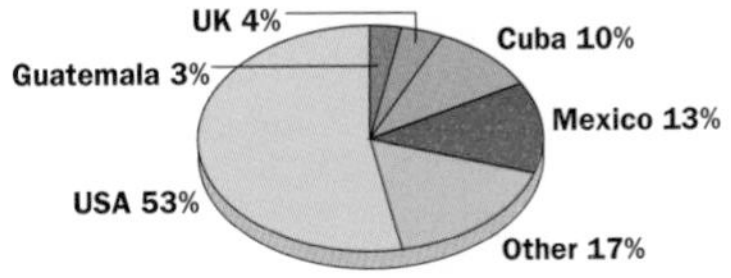
UK 4%
Guatemala 3%
Cuba 10%
Mexico 13%
USA 53%
Other 17%

RESOURCES

Electric power 52,000 kw

2620 tonnes | Not an oil producer

59,000 cattle, 24,000 pigs, 1.4m chickens | None

Hopes of finding significant oil and gas deposits in the north of the country have so far proved fruitless.

ENVIRONMENT

Not available

5% partially protected | 1.7 tonnes per capita

Tourism development and uncontrolled logging threaten the dense tropical forests and the habitats of mammals and birds. Mahogany was listed internationally as endangered in November 1995, meaning that all exports and transshipments now require a certificate of origin.

MEDIA

TV ownership medium

There are no daily newspapers

PUBLISHING AND BROADCAST MEDIA

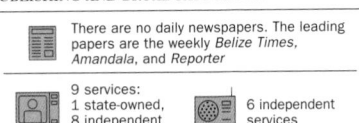

There are no daily newspapers. The leading papers are the weekly *Belize Times*, *Amandala*, and *Reporter*

9 services: 1 state-owned, 8 independent | 6 independent services

Belize has not suffered the degree of press interference experienced in neighboring states, but successive governments have remained sensitive to even minor criticisms. The two radio stations of the public Broadcasting Corporation of Belize were sold in 1998 to two local stations, but the government has retained ownership of the transmitters. Two official newspapers compete with party-political and independent publications.

CRIME

Death penalty used

89 prisoners | Increase in gun-related crime

Belize is a major transit point to the USA for cocaine, despite being decertified in 1997 for its anti-narcotics efforts. Drug-related crime is high. Armed robberies by criminal gangs based in neighboring Guatemala are also a major concern. A government ombudsman was appointed in June 2000 to investigate police brutality and corruption.

EDUCATION

School leaving age: 14

93% | 9457 students

Although most schools are run by the different churches, a handful are funded by the government, particularly those catering for special needs. The University College of Belize provides for higher education.

CHRONOLOGY

Originally part of the Maya heartland, between 1798 and 1981 Belize was effectively a British colony.

- ❑ **1919** Demands for more political rights by black Belizeans returning from World War I.
- ❑ **1936** New constitution with limited franchise.
- ❑ **1950** PUP formed. Voting age qualification for women reduced from 30 to 21.
- ❑ **1954** Full adult suffrage.
- ❑ **1972** Guatemala threatens invasion. Britain sends troops.
- ❑ **1981** Full independence.
- ❑ **1998** PUP wins crushing general election victory.

B

HEALTH

Welfare state health benefits

1 per 1818 people | Respiratory, heart, and cerebrovascular diseases

The health service provided by the government includes seven hospitals, more than 30 regional health centers, and numerous mobile clinics. Water supplies and sanitation have been improved; most homes in Belmopan now have both.

SPENDING

GDP/cap. increase

CONSUMPTION AND SPENDING

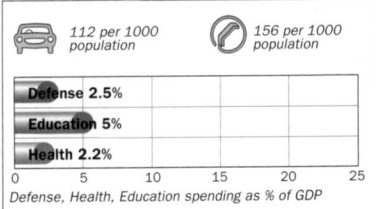

112 per 1000 population | *156 per 1000 population*

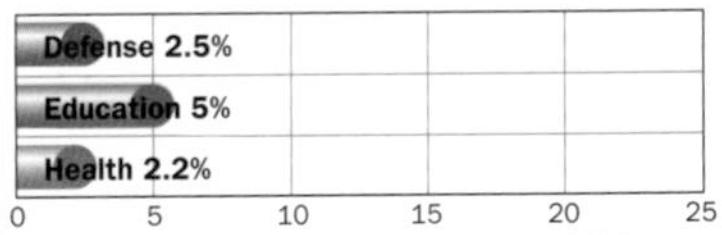
Defense 2.5%
Education 5%
Health 2.2%
0
5
10
15
20
25

Defense, Health, Education spending as % of GDP

The European Development Fund in 1999 granted 3.5 million Belizean dollars toward the reduction of rural poverty. Narcotics trading remains a source of wealth.

WORLD RANKING

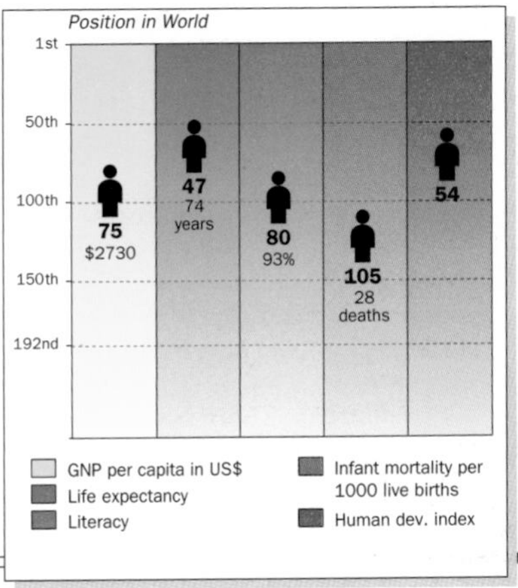
Position in World
1st
50th
100th
150th
192nd
75
$2730
47
74 years
80
93%
105
28 deaths
54
GNP per capita in US$
Life expectancy
Literacy
Infant mortality per 1000 live births
Human dev. index

B

BENIN

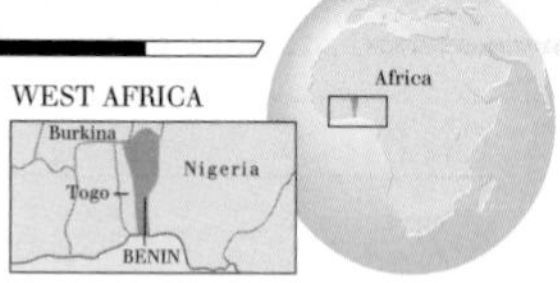
WEST AFRICA
Africa
Burkina
Togo
Nigeria
BENIN

OFFICIAL NAME: Republic of Benin **CAPITAL:** Porto-Novo
POPULATION: 6.1 million **CURRENCY:** CFA franc **OFFICIAL LANGUAGE:** French

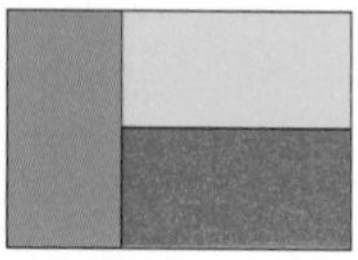

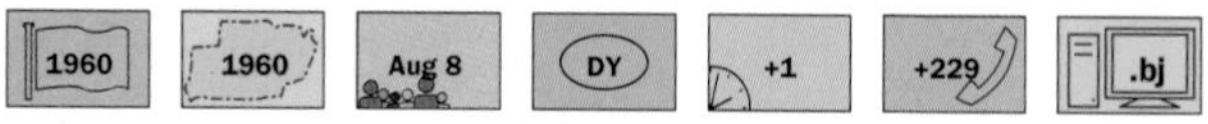
1960
1960
Aug 8
DY
+1
+229
.bj

BENIN STRETCHES NORTH from the west African coast, with a 100-km (60-mile) shoreline on the Bight of Benin. Formerly the kingdom of Dahomey, Benin was under French colonial rule, becoming part of French West Africa, until independence in 1960. In 1990 Benin was a pioneer of multipartyism in Africa, ending 17 years of one-party Marxist-Leninist rule. Benin's economy is based on well-diversified agriculture.

CLIMATE

Tropical wet & dry

WEATHER CHART

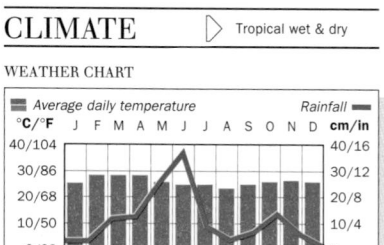

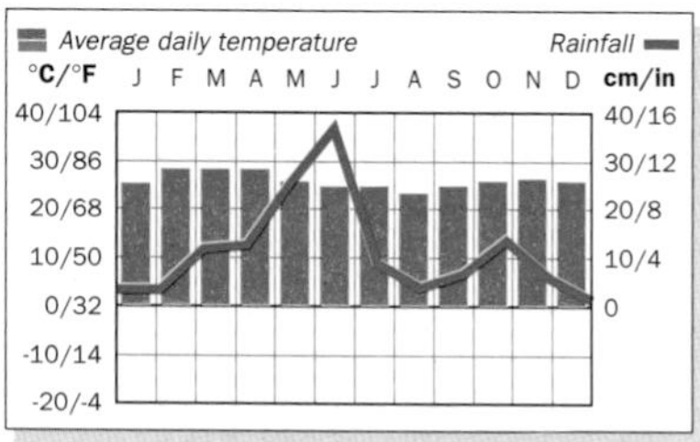
Average daily temperature
Rainfall
°C/°F
J F M A M J J A S O N D
cm/in
40/104
30/86
20/68
10/50
0/32
-10/14
-20/-4
40/16
30/12
20/8
10/4
0

There are two rainy seasons. The hot, dusty *harmattan* wind characterizes the December to February dry season.

TRANSPORTATION

Drive on right

Cotonou (Cadjehoun) 335,643 passengers

6 ships 900 grt

THE TRANSPORTATION NETWORK

1357 km (843 miles)

10 km (6 miles)

458 km (285 miles)

None

The joint Benin–Niger railroad runs only as far as Parakou. The Cotonou–Porto-Novo line reopened in 1999.

TOURISM

Visitors : Population 1:40

152,000 visitors

Up 1% in 1998

MAIN TOURIST ARRIVALS

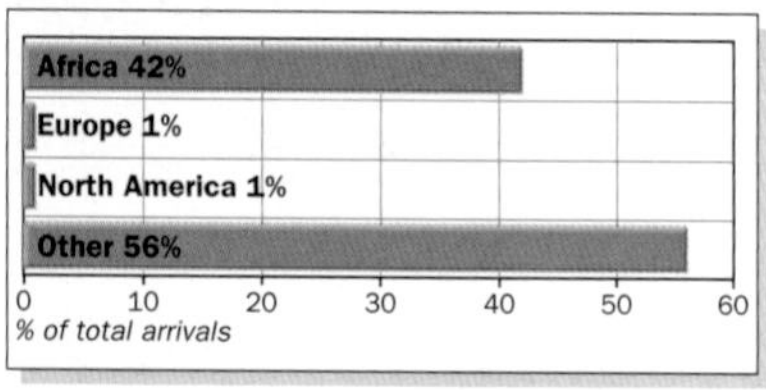
Africa 42%
Europe 1%
North America 1%
Other 56%
0
10
20
30
40
50
60
% of total arrivals

Tourism is not well developed, although there are plans to develop package tourism. There is some safari tourism in the north, particularly in the Atakora Mountains. Benin is popular for weekend breaks for visitors to Nigeria.

PEOPLE

Pop. density medium

Fon, Bariba, Yoruba, Adja, Houeda, Somba, French

55/km² (143/mi²)

THE URBAN/RURAL POPULATION SPLIT

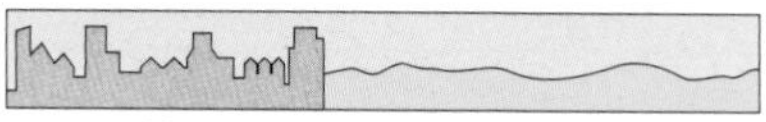
42%
58%

RELIGIOUS PERSUASION

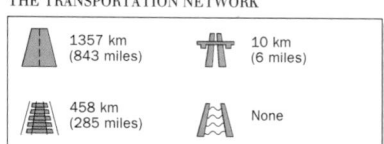

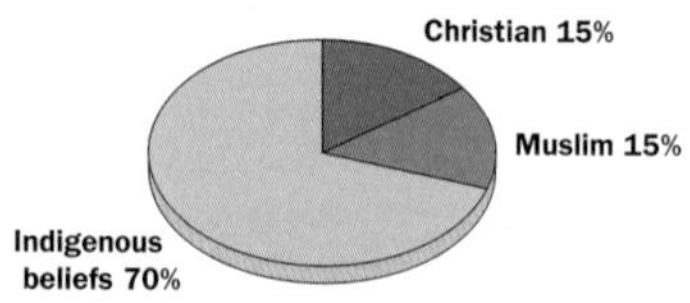
Christian 15%
Muslim 15%
Indigenous beliefs 70%

Benin is politically dominated by the southern Fon people. There is some north–south tension, partly because the south is more developed, and partly reflecting a Muslim–Christian divide. Women tend to wield power and influence in the retail trade.

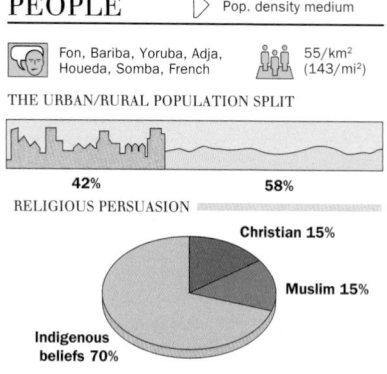

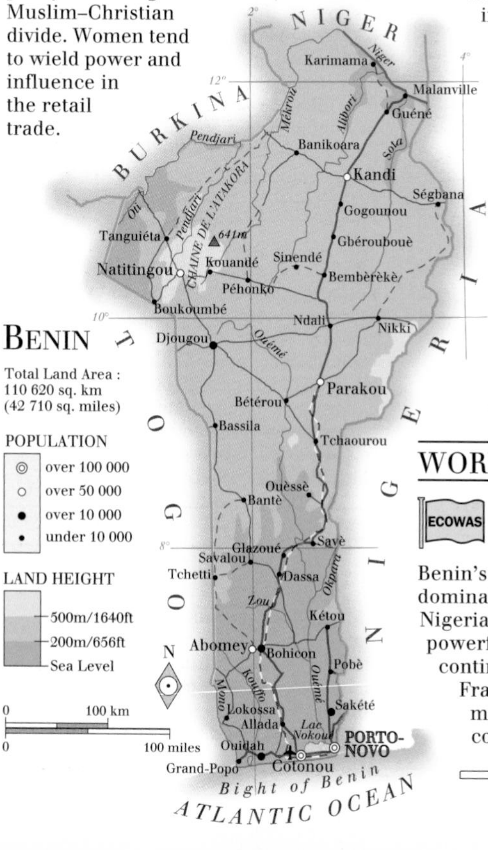
NIGER
BURKINA
TOGO
NIGERIA
Karimama
Niger
Malanville
Guéné
Mékrou
Alibori
Sota
Pendjari
Banikoara
Kandi
Ségbana
Oti
CHAINE DE L'ATAKORA
Gogounou
Tanguiéta
641m
Gbéroubouè
Natitingou
Kouandé
Sinendé
Bembèrèkè
Péhonko
Boukoumbé
Ndali
Nikki
Djougou
Ouémé
Parakou
Bétérou
Bassila
Tchaourou
Ouèssè
Bante
Glazoué
Savè
Savalou
Tchetti
Dassa
Okpara
Zou
Kétou
Abomey
Bohicon
Pobè
Couffo
Ouémé
Mono
Lokossa
Sakété
Allada
Lac Nokoué
PORTO-NOVO
Ouidah
Cotonou
Grand-Popo
Bight of Benin
ATLANTIC OCEAN
BENIN
Total Land Area : 110 620 sq. km (42 710 sq. miles)
POPULATION
over 100 000
over 50 000
over 10 000
under 10 000
LAND HEIGHT
500m/1640ft
200m/656ft
Sea Level
0
100 km
0
100 miles

POLITICS

Multiparty elections

1999/2003

President Mathieu Kérékou

AT THE LAST ELECTION

National Assembly 83 seats

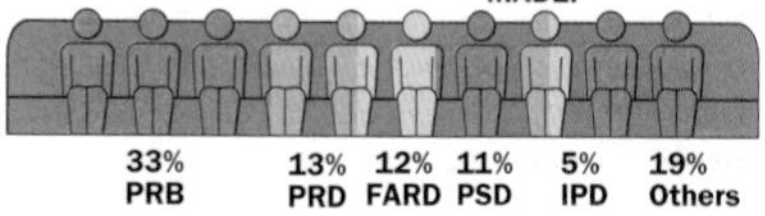
7% MADEP
33% PRB
13% PRD
12% FARD
11% PSD
5% IPD
19% Others

PRB = Benin Renaissance Party **PRD** = Party of Democratic Renewal **FARD** = Action Front for Renewal and Development **PSD** = Social Democrat Party **MADEP** = African Movement for Democracy and Progress **IPD** = Impetus for Progress and Democracy

Benin's image as a leader in African democratization was tarnished by allegations of fraud over the 2001 presidential election. Democratization had begun at the National Conference of 1990, when Mathieu Kérékou agreed to hold multiparty elections after years of military one-party rule. The main political parties in Benin tend to be regionally based and depend on the leadership of individuals influential in local communities. There are constantly changing alliances. Kérékou became the first of the African one-party leaders to hand over power peacefully, to Nicéphore Soglo, a former World Bank official, after elections in 1991. Soglo did not have an automatic majority in the National Assembly, and was forced to include members of the opposition parties in his government. The main political issue became his World Bank-style deregulation of the economy. He was defeated in a controversial election in 1996 which brought Kérékou back to power as president. Kérékou dismissed claims of vote-rigging in the presidential election in 2001, saying that democracy was "alive and kicking." He easily won reelection following Soglo's withdrawal from the race.

WORLD AFFAIRS

Joined UN in 1960

ECOWAS | OAU | OIC | FZ | UEMOA

Benin's foreign relations are largely dominated by its giant neighbor, Nigeria, which is by far the most powerful state in the region. The continuation of good relations with France, which is currently the main source of financial aid, is considered to be critical.

AID

Recipient

$211m (receipts)

No change in 1999

Benin's poverty is such that the maintenance of aid is at the top of the political agenda. France, the main protector of Benin since independence in 1960, is the major aid donor. Other donors include the World Bank, the IMF, the EU, Germany, Belgium, the Netherlands, Spain, and the USA. Almost all development finance comes from aid, and some has been used to finance debt-servicing. There is the usual problem of finding suitable projects, although Benin has a large, well-educated (if top-heavy) civil service, making implementation easier than in many parts of Africa.

DEFENSE

Compulsory military service

$34m

Up 3% in 1999

The 4500-strong army is actively involved in the attempt to curb smuggling on the Nigerian border. In 1989 the army was employed internally against rioters.

ECONOMICS

Inflation 9.3% p.a. (1990–1999)

$2.3bn

654.4–698.7 CFA francs

SCORE CARD

❑ World GNP Ranking	135th
❑ GNP per Capita	$380
❑ Balance of Payments	$–157m
❑ Inflation	0.3%
❑ Unemployment	Widespread underemployment

Strengths

Agriculture-based economy, with good product diversification. Long-overdue devaluation of the CFA franc in January 1994 made exports more competitive.

Weaknesses

Large-scale smuggling. Power failures caused by drought brought major economic problems in 1998, and resultant slowdown in GDP growth. Top-heavy civil service.

EXPORTS

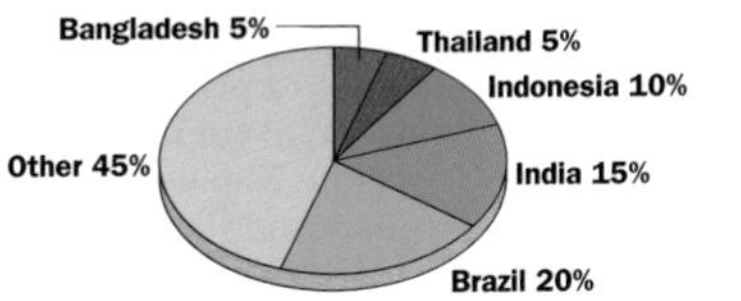
Bangladesh 5%
Thailand 5%
Indonesia 10%
India 15%
Brazil 20%
Other 45%

IMPORTS

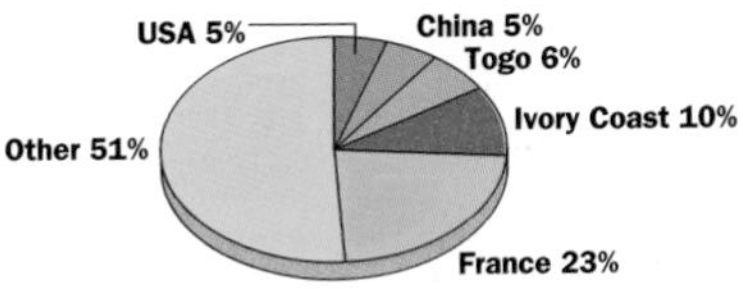
USA 5%
China 5%
Togo 6%
Ivory Coast 10%
France 23%
Other 51%

***Flat landscape near Cotonou,** characteristic of Benin's coastal region. Numerous lagoons lie behind its short 100-km (60-mile) coastline.*

RESOURCES

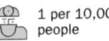

Electric power 15,000 kw

43,771 tonnes

1243 b/d (reserves 29,499,600 bbl)

1.44m cattle, 1.18m goats, 29m chickens

Oil, limestone, marble, gold

Since 1988 most electricity – which previously had to be imported from Ghana – is generated by the Nangbeto Dam on the River Mono.

ENVIRONMENT

Sustainability rank: 103rd

7%

0.2 tonnes per capita

Desertification in the north is the major problem. Benin has been used in the past as a dumping ground for toxic waste.

MEDIA

TV ownership low

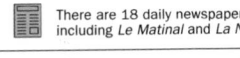

Daily newspaper circulation 2 per 1000 people

PUBLISHING AND BROADCAST MEDIA

There are 18 daily newspapers, including *Le Matinal* and *La Nation*

5 services: 1 state-owned, 4 independent

19 services: 1 state-owned, 18 independent

Benin publishes 65 newspapers and periodicals. The press has considerable freedom, and a media code of practice was introduced in 1999.

CRIME

Death penalty used

Benin does not publish prison figures

Up 219% 1996–1998

There has been a serious upsurge in armed crime since 1995, despite the reintroduction of the death penalty. Smuggling is a major problem along the border with Nigeria.

EDUCATION

School leaving age: 11

40%

14,055 students

More is spent on education than on defense, and this is reinforced by Benin's active intellectual community, the "Latin Quarter of Africa." The university at Abomey-Calavi is rated highly in medicine and law.

CHRONOLOGY

In 1625 the Fon, indigenous slave traders, founded the kingdom of Dahomey. Dahomey in turn conquered the neighboring kingdoms of Dan, Allada, and the coast around Porto-Novo.

- ❑ 1857 French establish trading post at Grand-Popo.
- ❑ 1889 French defeat King Behanzin.
- ❑ 1892 French protectorate.
- ❑ 1904 Part of French West Africa.
- ❑ 1960 Full independence.
- ❑ 1975 Renamed Benin.
- ❑ 1989 Marxism–Leninism abandoned as official ideology.
- ❑ 1996 Former ruler Kérékou defeats Soglo in controversial election.
- ❑ 2001 Kérékou reelected to presidency amid claims of electoral fraud.

HEALTH

No welfare state health benefits

1 per 10,000 people

Communicable and diarrheal diseases, malaria

Outside the major towns, health services and doctors are scarce. It is forecast that by 2030, one million people will have died of AIDS.

SPENDING

GDP/cap. increase

CONSUMPTION AND SPENDING

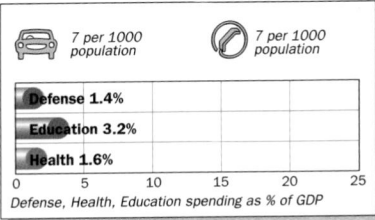

7 per 1000 population

7 per 1000 population

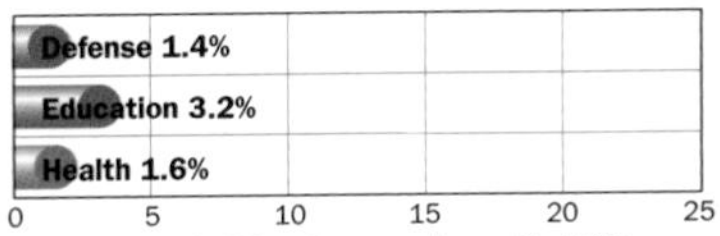
Defense 1.4%
Education 3.2%
Health 1.6%
0
5
10
15
20
25

Defense, Health, Education spending as % of GDP

Substantial differences in wealth reflect the strongly hierarchical nature of society, especially in the south. French cars are considered to be status symbols.

WORLD RANKING

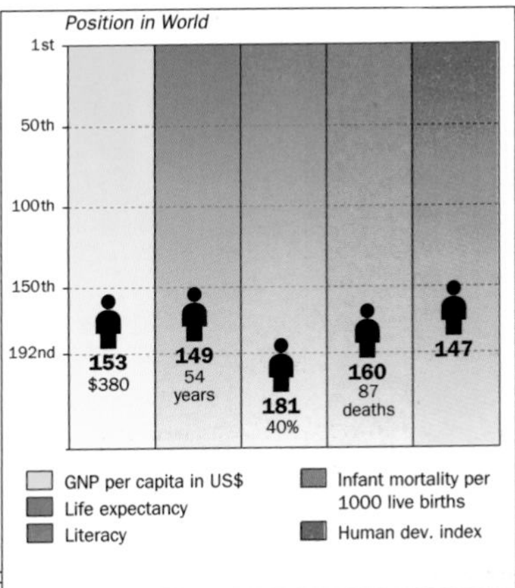
Position in World
1st
50th
100th
150th
192nd
153
$380
149
54
years
181
40%
160
87
deaths
147
GNP per capita in US$
Life expectancy
Literacy
Infant mortality per 1000 live births
Human dev. index

B

BOLIVIA

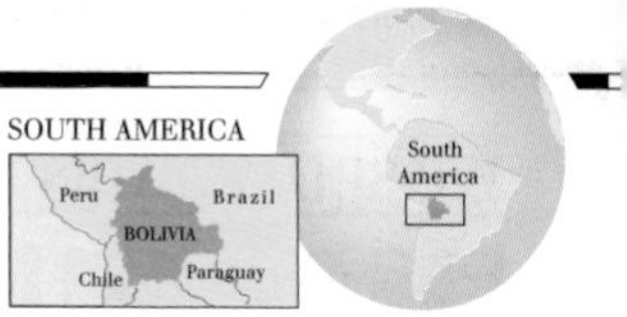
SOUTH AMERICA
Peru
Brazil
BOLIVIA
Chile
Paraguay
South America

OFFICIAL NAME: Republic of Bolivia **CAPITALS:** La Paz (administrative); Sucre (judicial)
POPULATION: 8.3 million **CURRENCY:** Boliviano **OFFICIAL LANGUAGES:** Spanish, Quechua, and Aymara

1825
1938
Aug 6
BOL
-4
+591
.bo

BOLIVIA LIES LANDLOCKED high in central South America and is one of the continent's poorest nations. Over half of the population lives on the *altiplano*, the windswept plateau between two ranges of the Andes, 3500 m (11,500 feet) above sea level. La Paz, the highest capital in the world, has spawned a neighboring large twin, El Alto. Bolivia has the world's highest golf course, ski run, and soccer stadium. The eastern lowland regions are tropical and underdeveloped but are rapidly being colonized.

CLIMATE

Tropical/mountain

WEATHER CHART

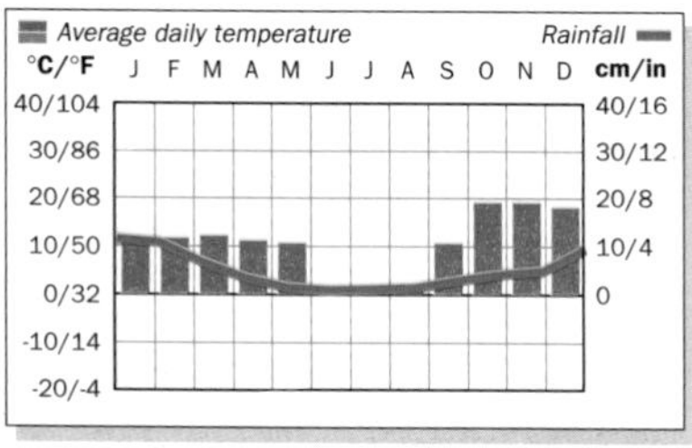
Average daily temperature
Rainfall
°C/°F J F M A M J J A S O N D cm/in
40/104
30/86
20/68
10/50
0/32
-10/14
-20/-4
40/16
30/12
20/8
10/4
0

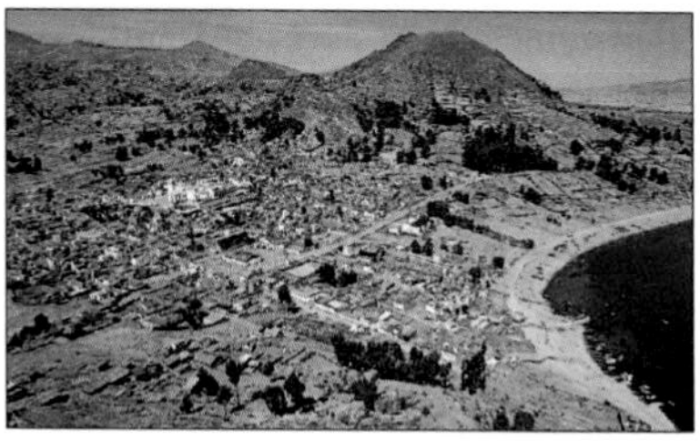

Copacabana on the shores of Lake Titicaca. It lies on a large headland owned by Bolivia on the Peruvian side of the lake.

The Andean *altiplano* has an extreme tropical highland climate with winter night frosts. Annual rainfall in the west is only 25 cm (10 in). The hot eastern lowlands receive most rain in summer.

TRANSPORTATION

Drive on right

El Alto, La Paz

1 ship 15,800 dwt

THE TRANSPORTATION NETWORK

2872 km (1785 miles)	27 km (17 miles)
3698 km (2297 miles)	14,000 km (8699 miles)

Obtaining more port access to the Pacific coast for landlocked Bolivia is important. Only 4% of roads are paved. The national railroad was privatized in 1996. Domestic airlines are generally reliable.

***Potato harvest** on the* altiplano. *Migration to the more fertile lands in the east has been encouraged.*

TOURISM

Visitors : Population 1:24

342,000 visitors

Down 21% in 1999

MAIN TOURIST ARRIVALS

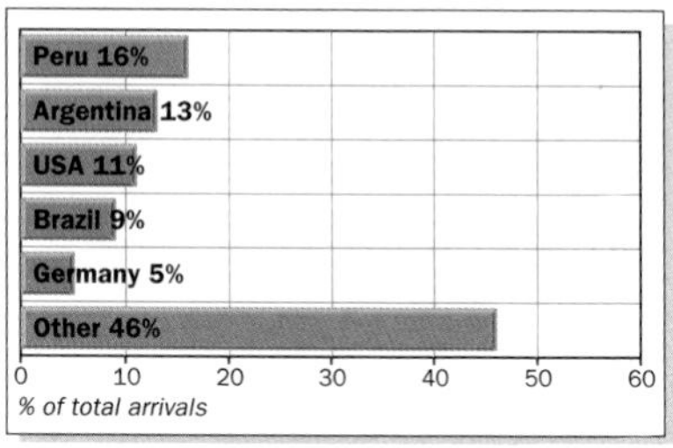
Peru 16%
Argentina 13%
USA 11%
Brazil 9%
Germany 5%
Other 46%
0 10 20 30 40 50 60
% of total arrivals

Foreign tourists are drawn by the traditional festivals, especially carnivals in February or March, the variety of Bolivia's scenery, and its Spanish colonial architecture. Major attractions include the Silver Mountain at Potosí, and Lake Titicaca, the highest navigable lake in the world, covering an area of 8970 square km (3463 square miles). Recent political stability encouraged some growth in tourism in the 1990s, but potential is limited by Bolivia's isolation, the rugged, inaccessible terrain, and the limited infrastructure.

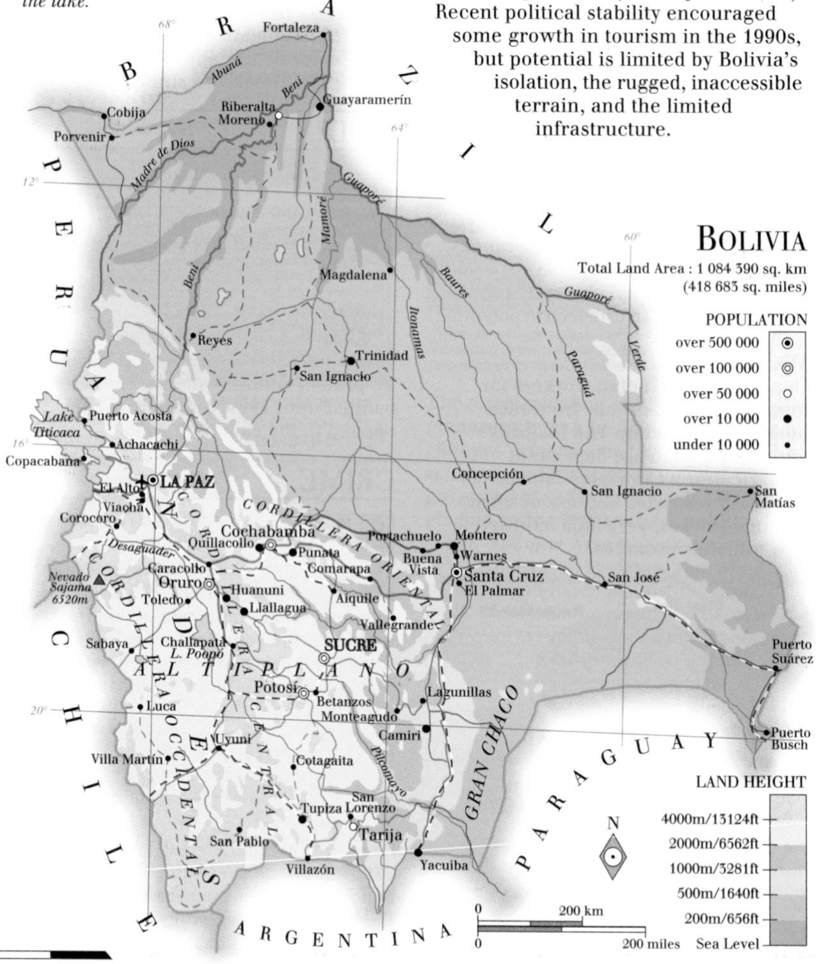
BOLIVIA
Total Land Area : 1 084 390 sq. km (418 683 sq. miles)
POPULATION
over 500 000
over 100 000
over 50 000
over 10 000
under 10 000
LAND HEIGHT
4000m/13124ft
2000m/6562ft
1000m/3281ft
500m/1640ft
200m/656ft
Sea Level
0 200 km
0 200 miles
BRAZIL
PERU
CHILE
ARGENTINA
PARAGUAY
LA PAZ
SUCRE
Cochabamba
Santa Cruz
Oruro
Potosí
Tarija
Trinidad
Cobija
Fortaleza
Riberalta
Guayaramerín
Magdalena
Reyes
San Ignacio
Concepción
San Matías
San José
Puerto Suárez
Puerto Busch
Camiri
Yacuiba
Villazón
Tupiza
Uyuni
Lake Titicaca
Copacabana
El Alto
CORDILLERA ORIENTAL
CORDILLERA OCCIDENTAL
ALTIPLANO
GRAN CHACO

PEOPLE

Pop. density low

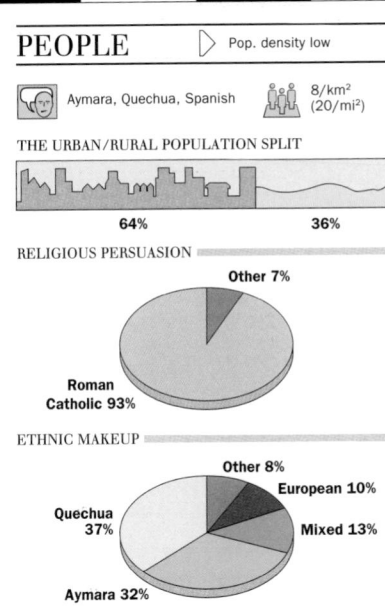

Aymara, Quechua, Spanish

8/km² (20/mi²)

THE URBAN/RURAL POPULATION SPLIT

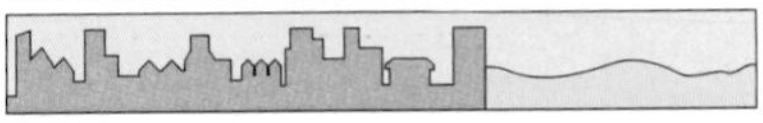
64%
36%

RELIGIOUS PERSUASION

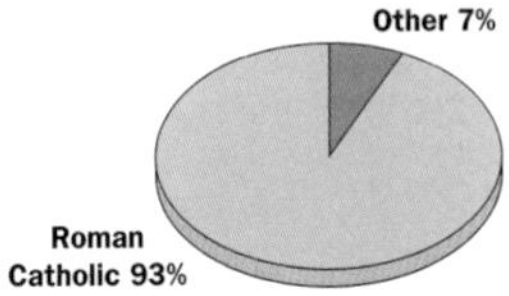
Other 7%
Roman Catholic 93%

ETHNIC MAKEUP

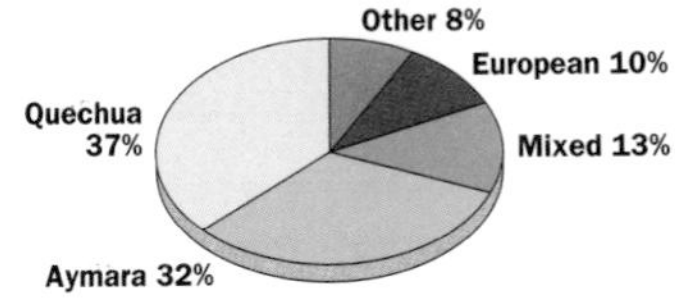
Other 8%
European 10%
Mixed 13%
Quechua 37%
Aymara 32%

Two-thirds of Bolivians are Aymara and Quechua Amerindians who historically have been marginalized. In recent years, however, they have played a more active role in politics by supporting new populist parties.

Wealthy city elites, dating back to Spanish colonial rule, retain great influence, but new entrepreneurs with political ambitions have appeared. Most Bolivians are subsistence farmers, miners, small traders, or artisans earning low incomes. Government schemes, spontaneous colonization, and the collapse of tin mining have led to large-scale migration from the Andes to lowland eastern regions in the last few decades.

Family life tends to be close-knit; Amerindians practice Roman Catholicism mixed with their own traditions and culture. Women have low status. There are some 130,000 lowland Amerindians in western regions.

POPULATION AGE BREAKDOWN

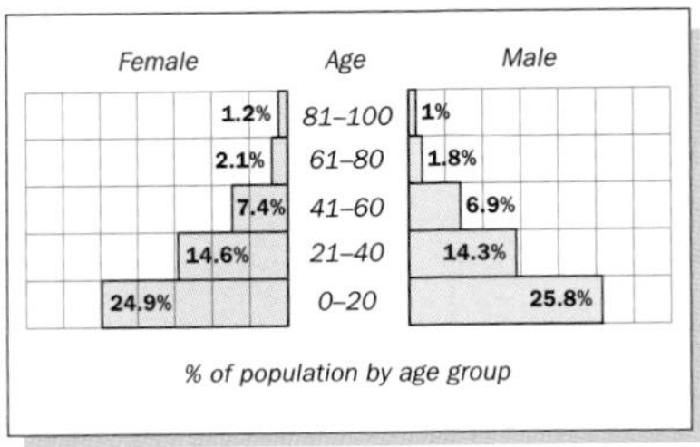
Female
Age
Male
1.2%
81–100
1%
2.1%
61–80
1.8%
7.4%
41–60
6.9%
14.6%
21–40
14.3%
24.9%
0–20
25.8%
% of population by age group

POLITICS

Multiparty elections

L. House 1997/2002
U. House 1997/2002

President Jorge Quiroga Ramirez

AT THE LAST ELECTION

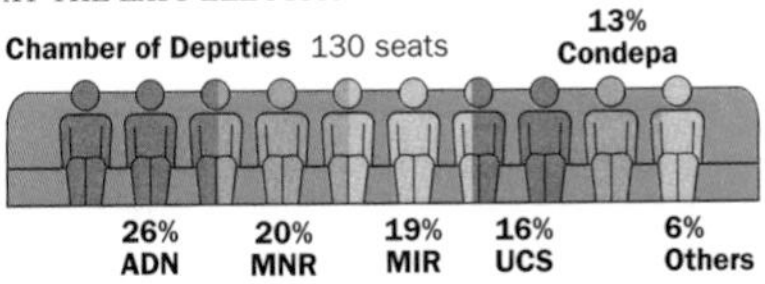
Chamber of Deputies 130 seats
13% Condepa
26% ADN
20% MNR
19% MIR
16% UCS
6% Others

ADN = Nationalist Democratic Action **MNR** = Nationalist Revolutionary Movement **MIR** = Revolutionary Leftist Movement **UCS** = Civic Solidarity Union **Condepa** = Conscience of the Fatherland

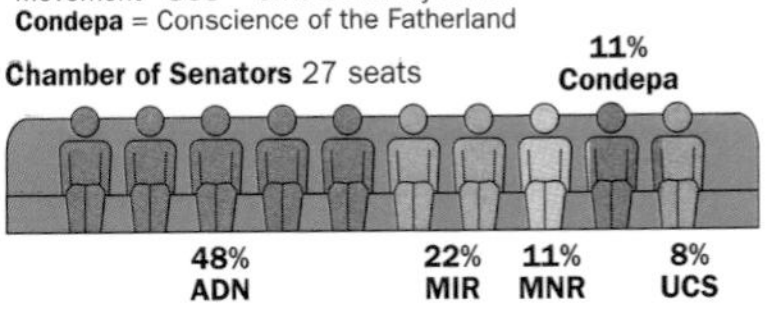
Chamber of Senators 27 seats
11% Condepa
48% ADN
22% MIR
11% MNR
8% UCS

Bolivia is a multiparty democracy.

MAIN POLITICAL ISSUES

Political stability

The current government is an uneasy "megacoalition" of parties who are jockeying for position in advance of the 2002 presidential elections. None will want to be associated with unpopular policies as polling approaches.

Cocaine

Poor farmers, denied alternatives, are opposed to the government's forced eradication of coca crops to ensure more US aid. Their leaders warn that serious domestic conflict will occur unless troops are withdrawn from coca-growing regions. The government's proposals to eradicate 35,000 hectares by 2002, when its term ends, provoked widespread unrest in 2000 and 2001.

PROFILE

From independence in 1825 to the early 1980s, Bolivia experienced, on average, more than one armed coup a year, punctuated by a national revolution in 1952 which delivered important reforms. The fragmented and drug-tainted military finally stepped down in 1982, but full elections were delayed until 1985.

More new populist parties have emerged to challenge traditional politics, although not the drift to free-market economic development. The pattern of politics remains one of parties competing for power in unstable coalitions. Nepotism remains rife, and narcotics, whose profits underpin the economy, are frequently implicated in political corruption scandals. The main trade union federation COB was the traditional focus of opposition, but coca growers and other popular groups have now assumed this role.

The right-wing MNR was defeated in the 1997 elections, but the coalition government under President Hugo Banzer, a former dictator, continued its economic austerity policies. He tried to suppress "uprisings" by peasant unions and coca growers in 2000, but was forced to make concessions. Diagnosed with cancer, he stepped down in July 2001.

WORLD AFFAIRS

Joined UN in 1945

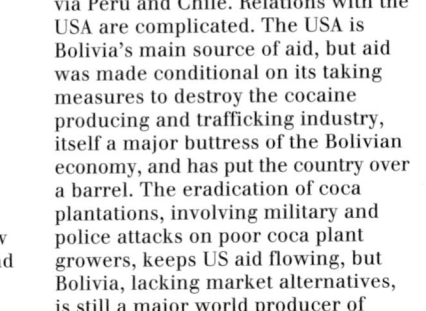

AP | AmCC | NAM | OAS | RG

Bolivia's main foreign policy concern is agreeing improved access to the Pacific via Peru and Chile. Relations with the USA are complicated. The USA is Bolivia's main source of aid, but aid was made conditional on its taking measures to destroy the cocaine producing and trafficking industry, itself a major buttress of the Bolivian economy, and has put the country over a barrel. The eradication of coca plantations, involving military and police attacks on poor coca plant growers, keeps US aid flowing, but Bolivia, lacking market alternatives, is still a major world producer of refined cocaine.

Bolivia, along with Chile, is an associate member of the South American common market MERCOSUR. As the most isolated and poorest economy in South America, it would be the major beneficiary of a tariff-free zone in the Andean region.

***Hugo Banzer Suárez**, elected president in 1997, resigned due to ill health in 2001.*

***Jorge Quiroga Ramirez**, stepped in to complete Banzer's term as president.*

CHRONOLOGY

The Aymara civilization was conquered by the Incas in the late 1400s. Fifty years later, the Incas were defeated by the *conquistadores* and Upper Peru, as it became, was governed by Spain from Lima.

- **1545** Cerro Rico, the Silver Mountain, discovered at Potosí. Provides Spain with vast wealth.
- **1776** Upper Peru becomes part of Viceroyalty of Río de la Plata centered on Buenos Aires.
- **1809** Simón Bolívar inspires first revolutionary uprisings in Latin America at Chuquisaca (Sucre), La Paz, and Cochabamba, but they fail.
- **1824** Spaniards suffer final defeat by Bolívar's general, José de Sucre.
- **1825** Independence.
- **1836–1839** Union with Peru fails. Internal disorder.
- **1864–1871** Ruthless rule of Mariano Melgarejo. Three Amerindian revolts over seizure of ancestral lands.

B

CHRONOLOGY *continued*

- **1879–1883** War of the Pacific, won by Chile. Bolivia left landlocked.
- **1880–1930** Period of stable governments. Exports from revived mining industry bring prosperity.
- **1903** Acre province ceded to Brazil.
- **1914** Republican Party founded.
- **1920** Amerindian rebellion.
- **1923** Miners bloodily suppressed.
- **1932–1935** Chaco War with Paraguay. Bolivia loses three-quarters of Chaco. Rise of radicalism and labor movement.
- **1951** Víctor Paz Estenssoro of MNR elected president. Military coup.
- **1952** Revolution. Paz Estenssoro and MNR brought back. Land reforms improve Amerindians' status. Education reforms, universal suffrage, tin mines nationalized.
- **1964** Military takes over in coup.
- **1967** Che Guevara killed while trying to mobilize Bolivian workers.
- **1969–1979** Military regimes rule with increasing severity. 1979 coup fails. Interim civilian rule.
- **1980** Military takes over again.
- **1982** President-elect Siles Zuazo finally heads leftist civilian MIR government. Inflation 24,000%.
- **1985** Paz Estenssoro's MNR wins elections. Austerity measures. Annual inflation down to 20%.
- **1986** Tin market collapses. 21,000 miners sacked.
- **1989** MIR takes power after close-run elections. President Paz Zamora makes pact with 1970s dictator General Hugo Banzer, leader of ADN.
- **1990** 1.6 million hectares (4 million acres) of rainforest recognized as Amerindian territory.
- **1993** MNR voted back to power.
- **1997** Banzer wins largest proportion of vote in presidential elections.
- **1999** Opposition demands inquiry into Banzer's role in regional military repression in 1970s.
- **2000** Government's water supply privatization plans and coca eradication provoke uprisings by peasants and coca growers.
- **2001** Banzer resigns due to ill-health.

AID

Recipient

$569m (receipts) | Down 9% in 1999

Most aid comes from the USA and depends on progress in coca crop eradication. Smaller amounts come from western European countries. Poor rural areas get project aid from Western NGOs, charities, and religious organizations. The plan, supported by the World Bank, to privatize the water supply led to an uprising in Cochabamba in 2000.

DEFENSE

Compulsory military service

$149m | Down 29% in 1999

BOLIVIAN ARMED FORCES

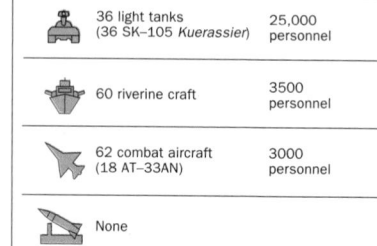

36 light tanks (36 SK–105 *Kuerassier*)	25,000 personnel
60 riverine craft	3500 personnel
62 combat aircraft (18 AT–33AN)	3000 personnel
None	

The military has not actively interfered in politics for nearly two decades. However, it is frequently used to quell internal dissent. The army is the main focus of defense spending, with weaponry bought almost entirely from the USA. The Bolivian navy consists mainly of gunboats on Lake Titicaca, which borders Peru, and on the Pilcomayo River. The army has worked with US forces against the cocaine business, although its integrity is questioned due to its past associations with narcotics trafficking. The main ambition of the military, apart from protecting its own interests and privileges, is the unrealizable aim of recapturing territory that would allow Bolivia access to the Pacific. Military service lasts for one year.

ECONOMICS

Inflation 9.1% p.a. (1990–1999)

$8.1bn | 5.92–6.36 bolivianos

SCORE CARD

World GNP Ranking	95th
GNP per Capita	$990
Balance of Payments	$-556m
Inflation	2.2%
Unemployment	4%

EXPORTS

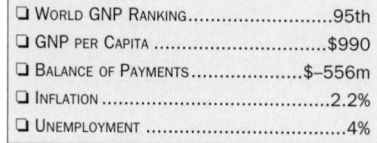

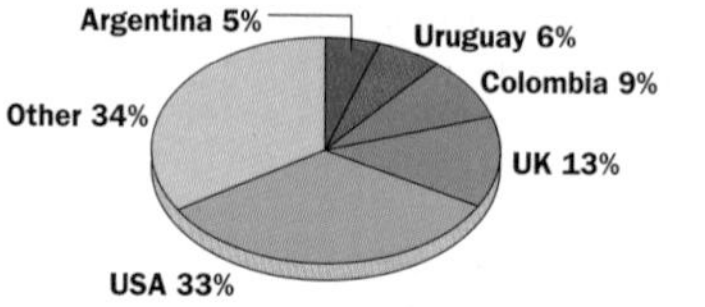
Argentina 5%
Uruguay 6%
Colombia 9%
UK 13%
USA 33%
Other 34%

IMPORTS

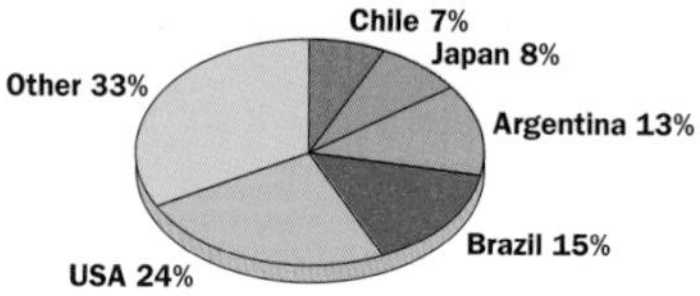
Chile 7%
Japan 8%
Argentina 13%
Brazil 15%
USA 24%
Other 33%

ECONOMIC PERFORMANCE INDICATOR

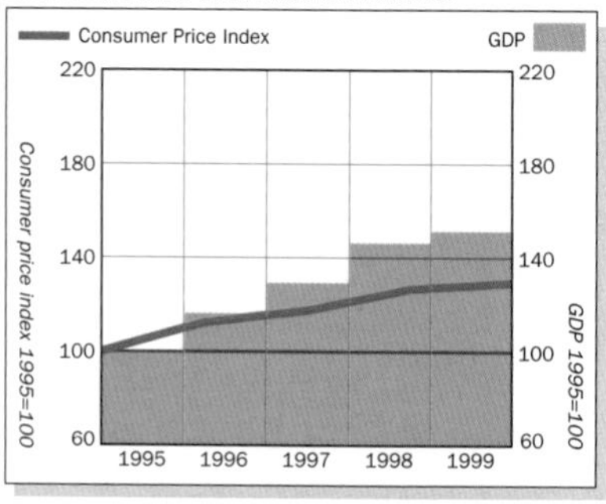
Consumer Price Index
GDP
Consumer price index 1995=100
GDP 1995=100
220
180
140
100
60
1995
1996
1997
1998
1999

Strengths

Mineral riches: gold, silver, zinc, lead, tin. Newly discovered oil and natural gas deposits attracting foreign investment.

Weaknesses

Raw materials vulnerable to fluctuating world prices. Lack of processed or manufactured exports with higher added value. Lack of integration between economic sectors and regions. Poor infrastructure.

Profile

Traditionally, the state used earnings from the publicly owned state mining sector to control the economy. Years of deep recession in the 1980s, accompanied by accelerating inflation and a collapsing currency, saw the introduction of severe, IMF-approved, austerity policies. These, along with the introduction of a new currency and tax reform, succeeded in curbing inflation, reducing public spending, and restoring international loans, but at the price of great social unrest. Growth was restored in the 1990s and a controversial "capitalization" program was launched which allowed for the 50/50 sell-off of shares in all six state companies on attractive terms to investors and employees. Narcotic revenues remain important for the economy.

BOLIVIA : MAJOR BUSINESSES

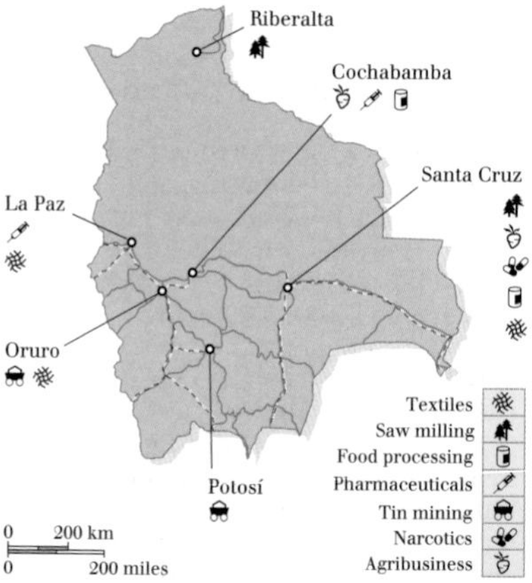
Riberalta
Cochabamba
Santa Cruz
La Paz
Oruro
Potosí
Textiles
Saw milling
Food processing
Pharmaceuticals
Tin mining
Narcotics
Agribusiness
0 200 km
0 200 miles

RESOURCES

Electric power 971,000 kw

6425 tonnes

29,975 b/d (reserves 87,547,200 bbl)

9m sheep, 6.9m cattle, 73.9m chickens

Tin, natural gas, oil, zinc, tungsten, gold, antimony, silver, lead

ELECTRICITY GENERATION

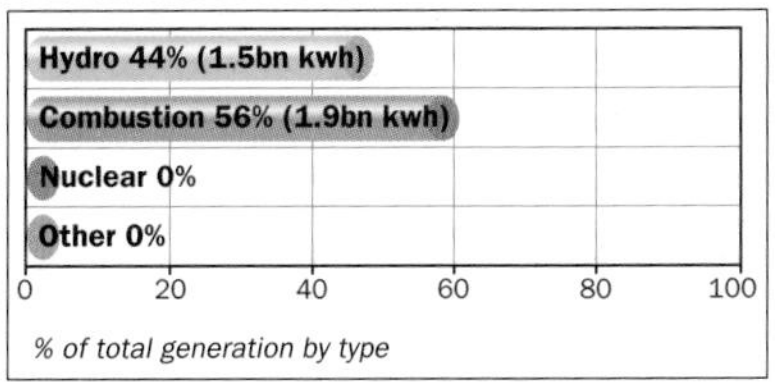
Hydro 44% (1.5bn kwh)
Combustion 56% (1.9bn kwh)
Nuclear 0%
Other 0%
0
20
40
60
80
100
% of total generation by type

Bolivia is the world's largest tin producer. The government is allowing foreign companies to prospect for more oil, and to increase sales of natural gas to Brazil and Argentina.

BOLIVIA : LAND USE

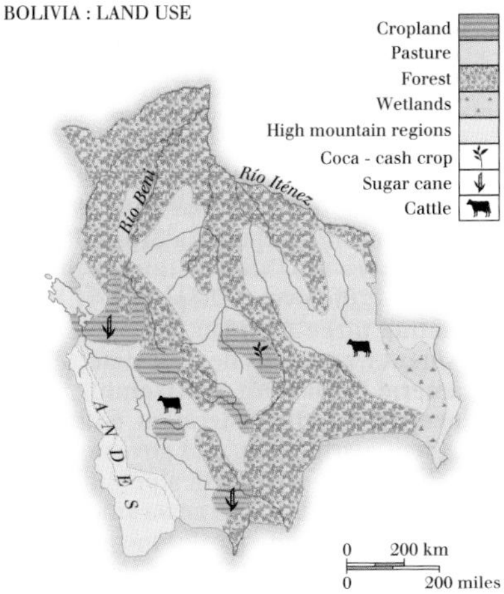
Cropland
Pasture
Forest
Wetlands
High mountain regions
Coca - cash crop
Sugar cane
Cattle
Rio Beni
Rio Iténez
ANDES
0 200 km
0 200 miles

ENVIRONMENT

Sustainability rank: 30th

14% (5% partially protected)

1.4 tonnes per capita

ENVIRONMENTAL TREATIES

Yes Yes Yes

Yes Yes Yes

Deforestation is Bolivia's major ecological problem, as throughout the Amazon region. Land clearances are running at 164,000 hectares (398,000 acres) a year. Much of the cleared land is turned over to cattle ranching or the growing of coca. Pesticide and fertilizer overuse in the coca business is a concern. The industry is effectively uncontrolled and rivers in Amazonia have high pollution levels.

Pollution problems are compounded by waste chemicals used in minerals industries. Mercury, used in the extraction of silver, has been found in dangerous quantities in river systems.

MEDIA

TV ownership medium

Daily newspaper circulation 55 per 1000 people

PUBLISHING AND BROADCAST MEDIA

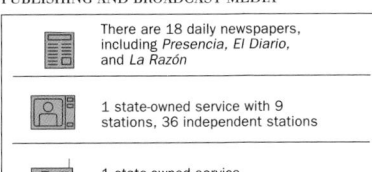

There are 18 daily newspapers, including *Presencia, El Diario,* and *La Razón*

1 state-owned service with 9 stations, 36 independent stations

1 state-owned service, 145 independent stations

Bolivia has strict defamation laws and considerable self-censorship. One of the TV stations is university-run, broadcasting mainly educational programs.

CRIME

Death penalty not used

Bolivia does not publish prison figures

Crime is rising in narcotics-trafficking centers

CRIME RATES

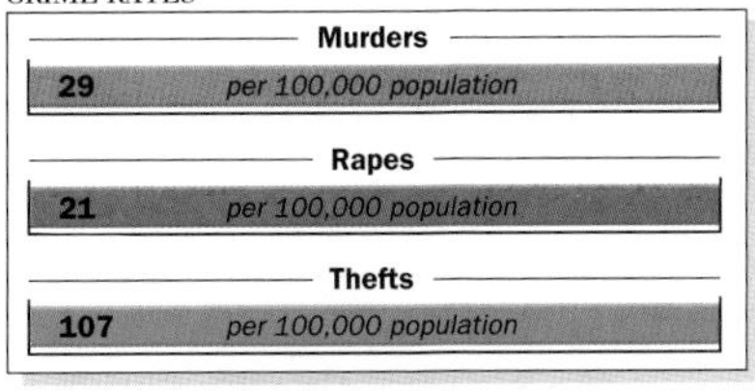
Murders
29 per 100,000 population
Rapes
21 per 100,000 population
Thefts
107 per 100,000 population

Violent crime is centered on narcotics-trafficking towns in the eastern lowlands, particularly Santa Cruz. Main cities are much safer for tourists, and have lower crime rates than cities in neighboring Peru. The police and army have a history of mistreating poor farmers and miners.

EDUCATION

School leaving age: 14

86%

109,503 students

THE EDUCATION SYSTEM

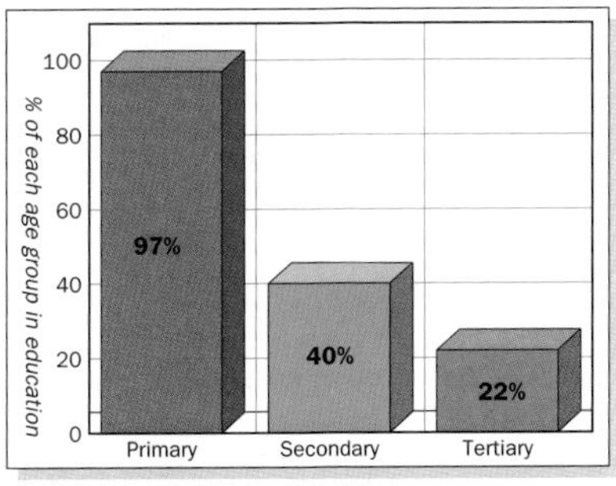
% of each age group in education
100
80
60
40
20
0
97%
40%
22%
Primary
Secondary
Tertiary

IMF targets for increased school attendance are being met, but education, based on a combination of the French and US systems, is seriously underfunded.

Although the majority of people speak indigenous languages, most teaching is in Spanish. Bolivia has one of the lowest literacy rates in South America. Reform and multilateral aid have led to some improvements.

HEALTH

No welfare state health benefits

1 per 769 people

Influenza, tuberculosis, other communicable diseases, malaria

Bolivia has one of the highest child mortality rates in the western hemisphere. Nearly 40% of children up to three years of age suffer from chronic malnutrition, and fewer than half the children under one year are immunized; diseases preventable by vaccination are a major cause of death. Bolivia has one of the lowest numbers of doctors per capita in Latin America, and formal health services are costly, so that over half the population does not use them. Some 60% of births take place at home with no trained assistant present. High maternal mortality was targeted in a Unicef-backed initiative in the 1990s. Official figures at the end of 1999 showed that 4100 people were living with HIV/AIDS.

SPENDING

GDP/cap. increase

CONSUMPTION AND SPENDING

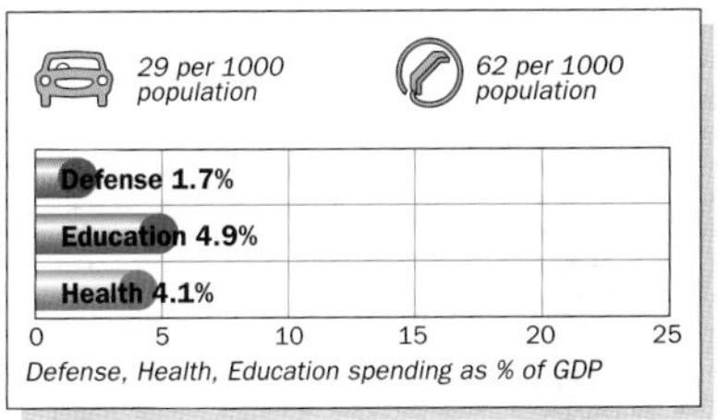
29 per 1000 population
62 per 1000 population
Defense 1.7%
Education 4.9%
Health 4.1%
0
5
10
15
20
25
Defense, Health, Education spending as % of GDP

Havoc created by economic reforms has widened the already huge gap between rich and poor. Generally, the indigenous population who form the rural poor are the worst off. The Andean highlands suffer from grinding poverty that has hardly changed in generations. Migrants to more prosperous eastern regions have faired better, but skewed land ownership remains a big problem. Poor housing, and lack of utilities and regular income are common to urban poverty. Only some 5% of people have bank accounts.

WORLD RANKING

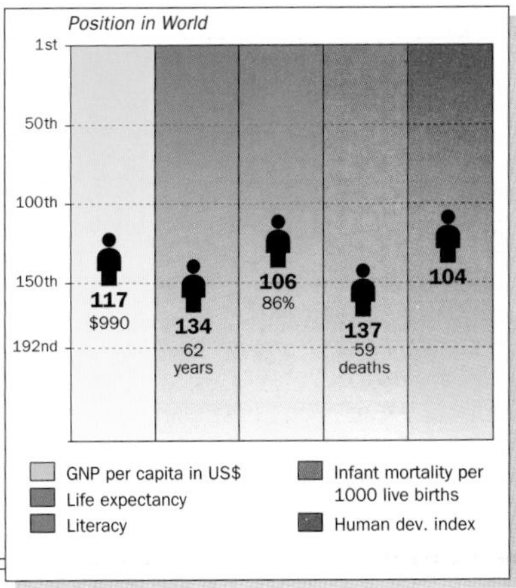
Position in World
1st
50th
100th
150th
192nd
117
$990
134
62
years
106
86%
137
59
deaths
104
GNP per capita in US$
Life expectancy
Literacy
Infant mortality per 1000 live births
Human dev. index

B

Botswana

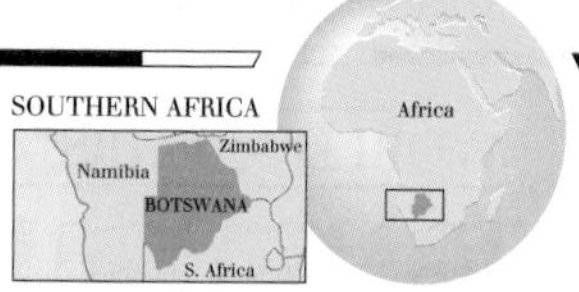
SOUTHERN AFRICA
Africa
Zimbabwe
Namibia
BOTSWANA
S. Africa

Official Name: Republic of Botswana **Capital:** Gaborone
Population: 1.6 million **Currency:** Pula **Official Language:** English

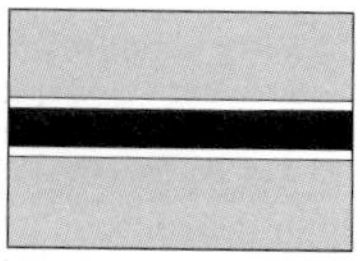

1966 | 1966 | Sept 30 | RB | +2 | +267 | .bw

Arid and landlocked, Botswana's central plateau separates the populous eastern grasslands from the Kalahari desert and the swamps of the Okavango delta in the west. Although Botswana is a multiparty democracy, the Botswana Democratic Party has won every election since independence. Diamonds provide Botswana with a prosperous economy, but rain is an even more precious resource, honored in the name of the currency, the pula.

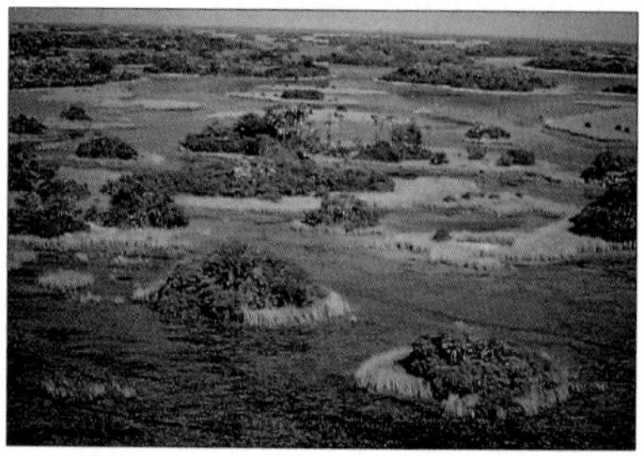

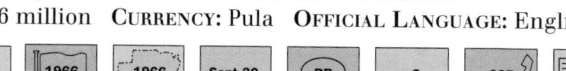

The Okavango Delta, "jewel of the Kalahari," is the largest inland river delta in the world and home to a rich variety of wildlife.

CLIMATE

Steppe/hot desert

WEATHER CHART

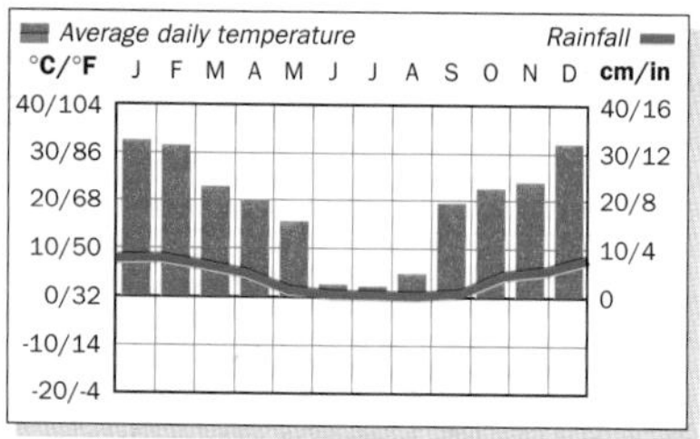
Average daily temperature
Rainfall
°C/°F
J F M A M J J A S O N D
cm/in
40/104
30/86
20/68
10/50
0/32
-10/14
-20/-4
40/16
30/12
20/8
10/4
0

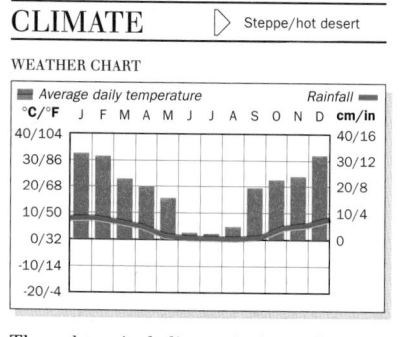

The subtropical climate is dry and prone to drought. Rainfall declines from 64 cm (25 in) in the north to under 10 cm (4 in) in the Kalahari desert in the west.

TRANSPORTATION

Drive on left

Sir Seretse Khama International, Gaborone
168,000 passengers

Has no fleet

THE TRANSPORTATION NETWORK

4343 km (2699 miles)	None
888 km (552 miles)	None

The opening of the trans-Kalahari road to Namibia in 1998 has reduced Botswana's dependence on South African ports. Upgrading existing rail and road networks is a priority.

TOURISM

Visitors : Population 1:2.1

750,000 visitors

Up 3% in 1998

MAIN TOURIST ARRIVALS

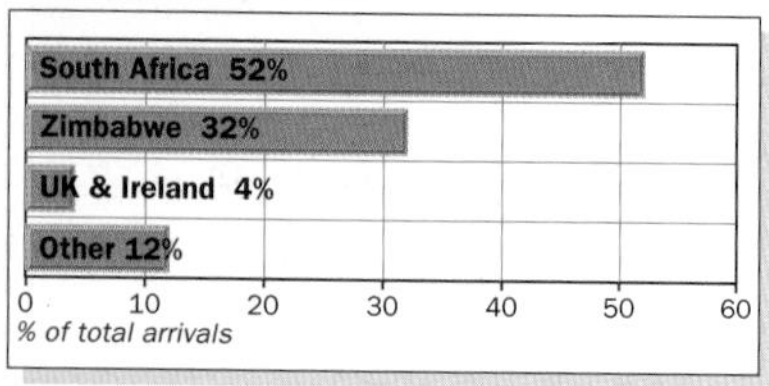
South Africa 52%
Zimbabwe 32%
UK & Ireland 4%
Other 12%
0
10
20
30
40
50
60
% of total arrivals

Tourism is aimed at wealthy wildlife enthusiasts and focuses on safaris, especially to the Okavango delta.

PEOPLE

Pop. density low

Tswana, English, Shona, San, Khoikhoi, Ndebele

3/km² (7/mi)²

THE URBAN/RURAL POPULATION SPLIT

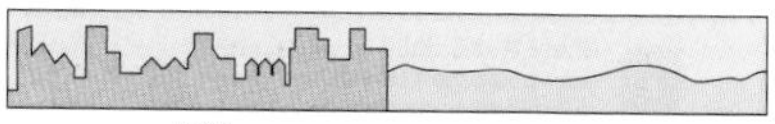

50% 50%

ETHNIC MAKEUP

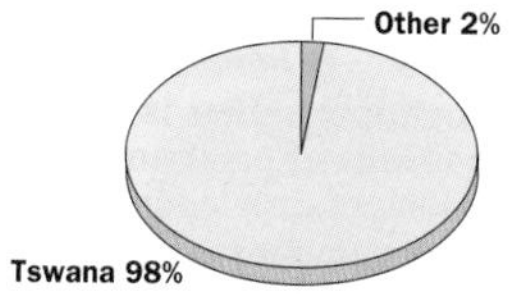
Other 2%
Tswana 98%

Botswana's stability reflects its ethnic homogeneity and the power of traditional authorities, notably the village *kgotla*, or parliament. Almost the whole population is Tswana, with the Bamangwato forming the largest Tswana group. Botswana's first inhabitants, the San (sometimes called Bushmen), have been marginalized. Whites continue to dominate the professions.

POLITICS

Multiparty elections

1999/2004

President Festus Mogae

AT THE LAST ELECTION

National Assembly 46 seats

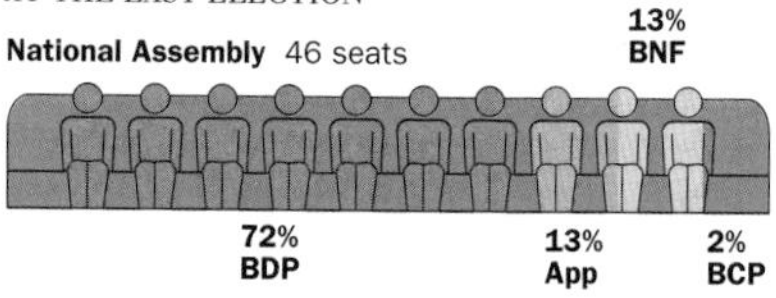
13%
BNF
72%
BDP
13%
App
2%
BCP

BDP = Botswana Democratic Party **BNF** = Botswana National Front **App** = Appointed **BCP** = Botswana Congress Party

In addition to 40 elected members, 4 are co-opted and the president and the attorney general are ex-officio members.

Although Botswana is formally a multiparty democracy, it has been ruled by the BDP since independence. In 1994, however, economic problems, corruption scandals, and increasing urbanization led to the mainly town-based BNF gaining seats at the expense of the BDP, which nevertheless retained its absolute parliamentary majority. Power transferred smoothly from President Masire to Festus Mogae in 1998. The opposition BNF split in two, and the 1999 elections confirmed the BDP's hold on power.

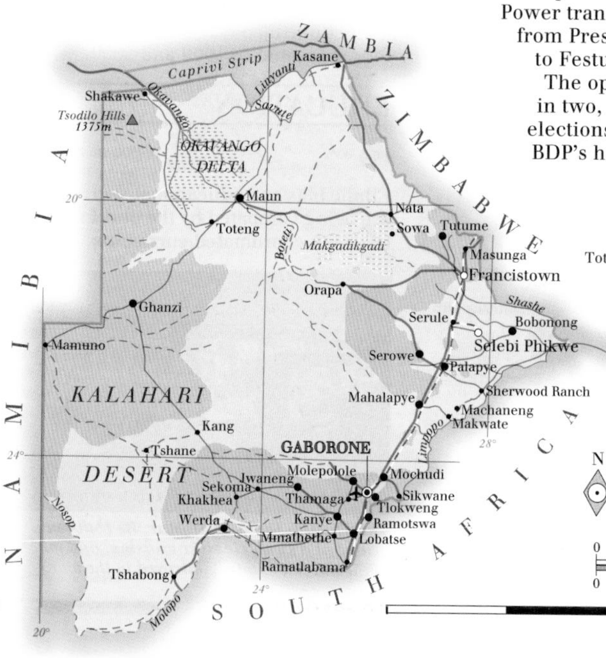
ZAMBIA
ZIMBABWE
NAMIBIA
SOUTH AFRICA
Caprivi Strip
Kasane
Shakawe
Tsodilo Hills 1375m
Okavango
OKAVANGO DELTA
Maun
Toteng
Nata
Sowa
Tutume
Makgadikgadi
Masunga
Francistown
Orapa
Ghanzi
Mamuno
Shashe
Serule
Bobonong
Selebi Phikwe
Serowe
Palapye
Sherwood Ranch
Mahalapye
Machaneng
Makwate
KALAHARI
DESERT
Kang
Tshane
GABORONE
Molepolole
Mochudi
Jwaneng
Sekoma
Khakhea
Thamaga
Sikwane
Tlokweng
Kanye
Ramotswa
Werda
Mmathethe
Lobatse
Tshabong
Ramatlabama
Nossob
Molopo
Limpopo
20°
24°
28°

Botswana

Total Land Area : 566 730 sq. km (218 814 sq. miles)

POPULATION

over 500 000
over 50 000
over 10 000
under 10 000

LAND HEIGHT

1000m/3281ft
500m/1640ft

N

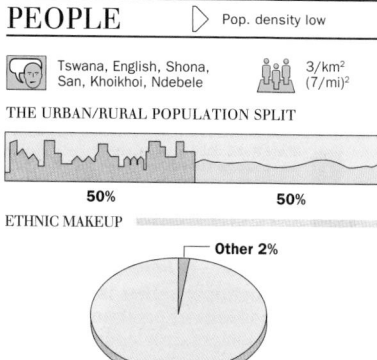

0 200 km
0 200 miles

B

WORLD AFFAIRS

Joined UN in 1966

Comm | NAM | OAU | SADC | WTO

Botswana has strongly backed a politically and economically stable postapartheid South Africa, and in 1994 appointed its first ambassador to Pretoria since 1966. Potential South African domination of the SADC is a concern. Traditionally pro-Western in orientation, Botswana cherishes its relations with the UK and the USA.

AID

Recipient

$61m (receipts)

Down 42% in 1999

Botswana's political and economic record has made it a favored aid recipient, notably from the EU, the UK, the USA, and the World Bank. Some 90% of EU aid goes to projects which try to balance wildlife needs with rural development. Aid is also targeted at transportation projects.

DEFENSE

No compulsory military service

$259m

Down 1% in 1999

Reforms of the armed forces in mid-2000 aimed at improving morale included the raising of the compulsory retirement age and the enlistment of women.

ECONOMICS

Inflation 10% p.a. (1990–1999)

$5.1bn

4.632–5.365 pula

SCORE CARD

WORLD GNP RANKING	109th
GNP PER CAPITA	$3240
BALANCE OF PAYMENTS	$170m
INFLATION	7.1%
UNEMPLOYMENT	40%

STRENGTHS

Diamonds: world's third-largest producer. Economic growth among the highest in the world, averaging 8.5% between 1980 and 1998. Prudent management, large financial reserves, and exchange control liberalization. Lucrative exports of assembly-produced vehicles, copper, nickel, beef.

WEAKNESSES

Overdependence on diamonds. Weak agriculture and industry. Small population, water shortages, and drought. Impact of beef industry on environment. High transportation costs to coast. Widespread unemployment.

EXPORTS

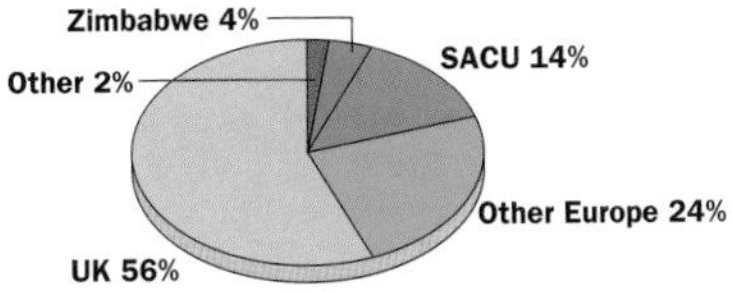
Zimbabwe 4%
Other 2%
SACU 14%
Other Europe 24%
UK 56%

IMPORTS

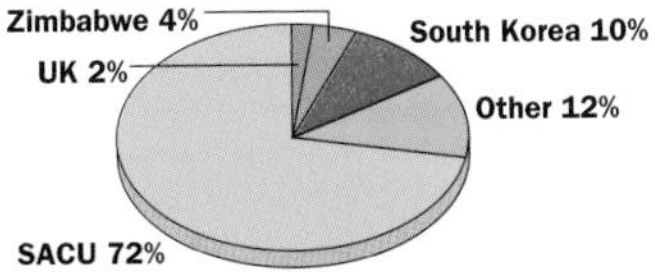
Zimbabwe 4%
UK 2%
South Korea 10%
Other 12%
SACU 72%

RESOURCES

Not available

2000 tonnes

Not an oil producer and has no refineries

2.38m cattle, 1.85m goats, 4m chickens

Diamonds, copper, coal, nickel, soda ash, gold

The Orapa 2000 diamond mining project began in May 2000. Large coal deposits are the basis of power grid expansion. Water is Botswana's scarcest resource.

ENVIRONMENT

Sustainability rank: 40th

19% (2% partially protected)

2.2 tonnes per capita

Botswana is trying to help communities to earn a living from wildlife protection. A campaign has been launched to curb the use of agrochemicals.

MEDIA

TV ownership low

Daily newspaper circulation 27 per 1000 people

PUBLISHING AND BROADCAST MEDIA

There is 1 daily newspaper, *Dikgang Tsa Gompieno*, published by the government

1 state-owned service

3 services: 1 state-owned, 2 independent

A government-funded TV service began broadcasting in 2000. The government bias of radio and the one daily paper is offset in the many journals.

CRIME

Death penalty used

Botswana does not publish prison figures

Down 11% 1992–1996

President Mogae warned of a "crime wave" in 1999. Official corruption and diamond smuggling stay major concerns. Human rights are generally respected.

EDUCATION

Schooling is not compulsory

77%

8850 students

Under the National Service Scheme, school-leavers work for 12 months in government departments and/or parastatal institutions.

CHRONOLOGY

From 1600, Tswana migrations slowly displaced San people. In 1895, at local request, the UK set up the Bechuanaland Protectorate to preempt annexation by South Africa.

- **1965** BDP, led by Sir Seretse Khama, wins first general election and all subsequent general elections.
- **1966** Independence declared
- **1980** Vice President Quett (later Ketumile) Masire succeeds the late Sir Seretse as president.
- **1985–1986** South African raids.
- **1992–1993** Strikes and corruption scandals prompt resignations of senior BDP figures.
- **1994** BDP support eroded in general election.
- **1998** Vice President Festus Mogae succeeds Masire as president.

HEALTH

Welfare state health benefits

1 per 5000 people

Tuberculosis, heart diseases, pneumonia

Primary health care remains a priority. The scourge of AIDS is particularly alarming, with one in three adult Bostwanans thought to be HIV positive, the highest rate of infection in the world.

SPENDING

GDP/cap. increase

CONSUMPTION AND SPENDING

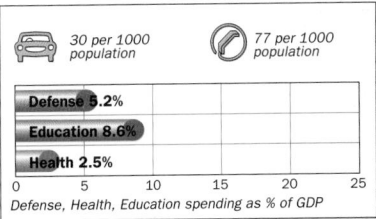

30 per 1000 population

77 per 1000 population

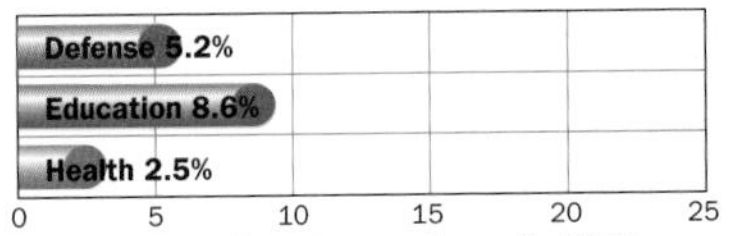
Defense 5.2%
Education 8.6%
Health 2.5%
0
5
10
15
20
25

Defense, Health, Education spending as % of GDP

GNP per capita is among Africa's highest, but most people are poor. Economic growth has exacerbated wealth inequalities.

WORLD RANKING

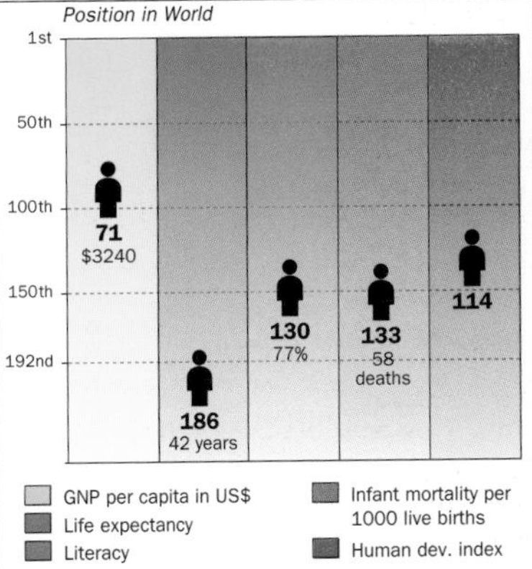
Position in World
1st
50th
100th
150th
192nd
71
$3240
186
42 years
130
77%
133
58
deaths
114
GNP per capita in US$
Life expectancy
Literacy
Infant mortality per 1000 live births
Human dev. index

B

BRAZIL

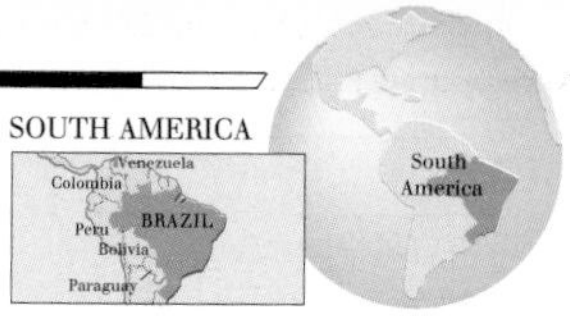
SOUTH AMERICA
Venezuela
Colombia
Peru
BRAZIL
Bolivia
Paraguay
South America

OFFICIAL NAME: Federative Republic of Brazil **CAPITAL:** Brasília
POPULATION: 170 million **CURRENCY:** Real **OFFICIAL LANGUAGE:** Portuguese

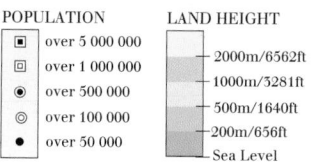

1822
1889
Sept 7
BR
-3
+55
.br

THE LARGEST COUNTRY in South America, Brazil became independent of Portugal in 1822. Today, it is renowned as the site of the world's largest tropical rainforest, the threat to which led to the UN's first international environment conference, held in Rio de Janeiro in 1992. Covering one-third of Brazil's total land area, the rainforest grows around the massive Amazon River and its delta. Apart from the basin of the River Plate to the south, the rest of the country consists of highlands. The mountainous northeast is part forested and part desert. Brazil is the world's leading coffee producer and also has rich reserves of gold, diamonds, oil, and iron ore. Cattle-ranching is an expanding industry. The city of São Paulo is the world's fourth-biggest conurbation, with 18 million inhabitants.

CLIMATE

Tropical equatorial/wet & dry/subtropical/steppe

WEATHER CHART

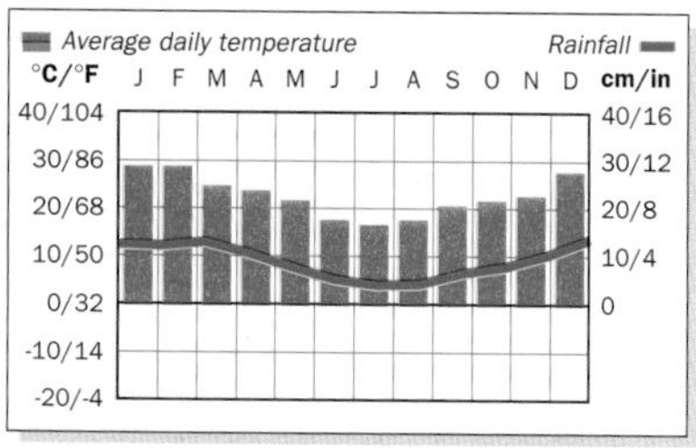
Average daily temperature
Rainfall
°C/°F
J F M A M J J A S O N D
cm/in
40/104
30/86
20/68
10/50
0/32
-10/14
-20/-4
40/16
30/12
20/8
10/4
0

Brazil's share of the Amazon basin, occupying half of the country, has a model equatorial climate. Its 150–200 cm (59–79 in) of rain are spread throughout the year. Temperatures are high, with almost no seasonal variation, but scarcely ever rise above 38°C (100°F).

The Brazilian plateau, occupying most of the rest of the country, has far greater temperature ranges. Rain falls mainly between October and April. The northeast, the least productive region of Brazil, is very dry and in recent years has been prone to severe drought. However, torrential rains hit Pernambuco and Alagoas in mid-2000, causing the worst flooding for 25 years. The southern states have hot summers and cool winters, when frost may occur.

TRANSPORTATION

Drive on right

Guarulhos International, São Paulo
14.6m passengers

504 ships
4.2m grt

THE TRANSPORTATION NETWORK

184,140 km (114,419 miles)	5000 km (3107 miles)
20,500 km (12,739 miles)	50,000 km (31,069 miles)

Air travel is expensive, while roads are clogged in cities and poor outside.

Proposed cross-border projects include a railroad, an inter-continental highway, and a 3442-km (2140-mile) waterway.

Parati, in Rio state, was one of Brazil's major gold exporting ports in the 17th century. Its colonial architecture is well preserved.

BRAZIL

Total Land Area : 8 456 510 sq. km (3 265 059 sq. miles)

POPULATION	LAND HEIGHT
over 5 000 000	2000m/6562ft
over 1 000 000	1000m/3281ft
over 500 000	500m/1640ft
over 100 000	200m/656ft
over 50 000	Sea Level

VENEZUELA
COLOMBIA
SERRA PACARAIMA
Serra Parima
Boa Vista
RORAIMA
GUY
Pico da Neblina 3014m
G U I A N A
Negro
Branco
Japurá
Içá
Represa Balbina
Mana
Solimões (Amazon)
A M A Z O N A S
Amazon Basin
Javari
Juruá
Madeira
Purus
Aripuanã
Juruena
ACRE
Porto Velho
Rio Branco
Roosevelt
RONDÔNIA
Chapada dos Parecis
Guaporé
PERU
BOLIVIA
70°
60°
N
0
500 km
500 miles

PARAGU
ARGEN

TOURISM

Visitors : Population 1:32

5.3m visitors

Up 4% in 2000

MAIN TOURIST ARRIVALS

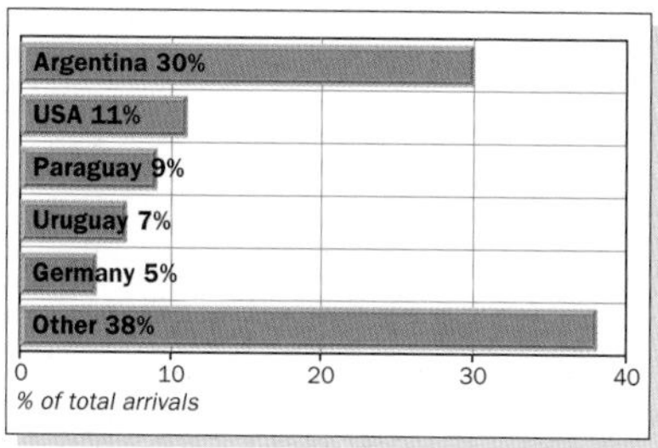
Argentina 30%
USA 11%
Paraguay 9%
Uruguay 7%
Germany 5%
Other 38%
0
10
20
30
40
% of total arrivals

Brazil is under-performing in tourism, with revenues equivalent to 2.5% of GDP in 1996, compared with a world average of around 10%. The situation is slowly improving.

Such attractions as Atlantic beaches stretching 2000 km (1200 miles), the Amazon river basin, the Pantanal – the vast wetland region in the west, and world famous carnivals are offset by the limited availability of medium- to low-cost travel and budget hotels, which deters domestic and foreign travelers.

In the virtual absence of low-cost charter flights domestic air travel is expensive. This is blamed on high airport charges and inertia in Brazil's aviation department, which is controlled by the air force.

Average overnight hotel rates are higher than in Europe and the USA, and the quality of service is generally poor. Basic infrastructure, such as sanitation and water supply, is also deficient.

***Rio de Janeiro** and Sugar Loaf Mountain seen from Corcovado (Hunchback) Peak. With a population of 11 million, the Rio conurbation is Brazil's largest after São Paulo.*

PEOPLE

Pop. density low

Portuguese, German, Italian, Spanish, Polish, Japanese, Amerindian languages

20/km² (52/mi²)

THE URBAN/RURAL POPULATION SPLIT

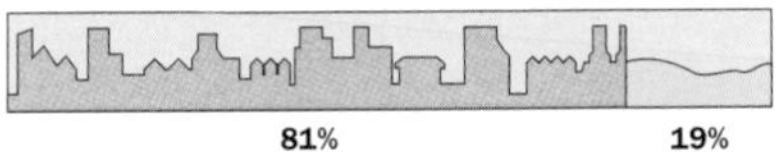
81%
19%

RELIGIOUS PERSUASION

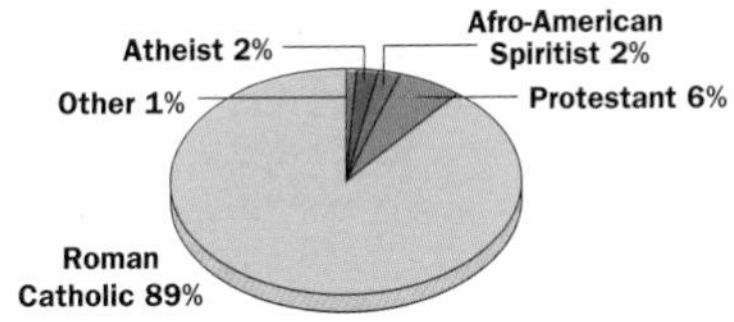
Atheist 2%
Afro-American Spiritist 2%
Other 1%
Protestant 6%
Roman Catholic 89%

ETHNIC MAKEUP

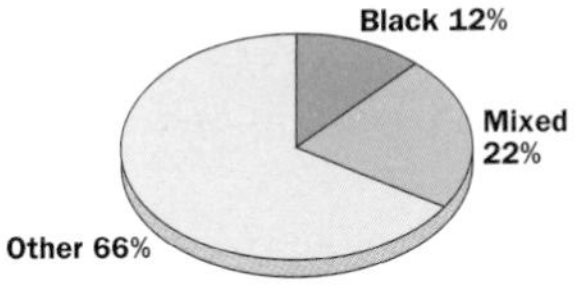
Black 12%
Mixed 22%
Other 66%

POPULATION AGE BREAKDOWN

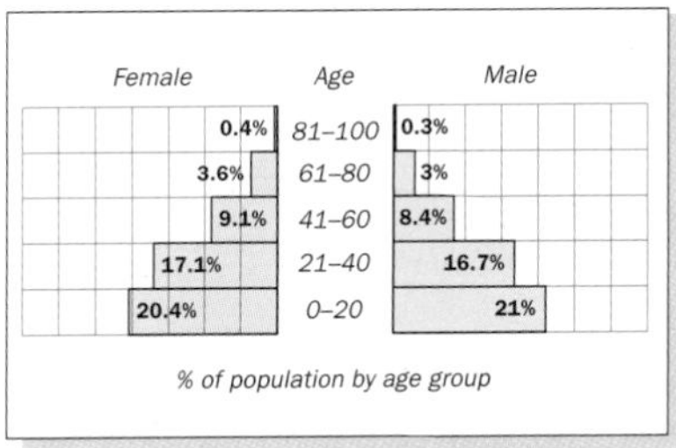
Female
Age
Male
0.4%
81–100
0.3%
3.6%
61–80
3%
9.1%
41–60
8.4%
17.1%
21–40
16.7%
20.4%
0–20
21%
% of population by age group

Brazil's population is highly diverse. It includes indigenous Amerindian groups, as well as the descendants of its Portuguese colonizers and the Africans brought to work the sugar plantations in the 17th century. More recent immigrant groups include both Italians and Japanese. Extremes of social disadvantage challenge the notion that Brazil is a "racial democracy." Poor, mixed-race migrants are treated as outcasts in cities, and Afro-Brazilians suffer higher infant mortality and poverty and more racial and job discrimination than other groups. Amerindians also experience widespread prejudice, and of the estimated 1000 groups present at the time of the arrival of the first Portuguese, about 210 remain, speaking some 180 different languages – a total population of about 220,000, who struggle to secure land rights and keep out encroachers.

Brazil is strongly Catholic, but other religions also flourish. The traditional emphasis on the family is under pressure in urban areas: migrants in particular often have to leave their families behind.

Women gained the vote in 1934, but are still discriminated against in jobs and politics.

ATLANTIC OCEAN
ATLANTIC
FRENCH GUIANA
AMAPÁ
Macapá
Ilha Caviana de Fora
Ilha Mexiana
Baía de Marajó
Equator
Ilha de Marajó
Belém
Amazon
Santarém
Baía de São Marcos
São Luís
Fortaleza
TERRITÓRIO DE FERNANDO DE NORONHA
Atol das Rochas
Fernando de Noronha
PARÁ
Marabá
Imperatriz
Teresina
MARANHÃO
CEARÁ
Mossoró
RIO GRANDE DO NORTE
Natal
Juazeiro do Norte
PARAÍBA
João Pessoa
Campina Grande
Olinda
Recife
PERNAMBUCO
Jaboatão
PIAUÍ
TOCANTINS
Maceió
ALAGOAS
Aracaju
SERGIPE
Taguatinga
Feira de Santana
BAHIA
Salvador
Baía de Todos os Santos
GOIÁS
DISTRITO FEDERAL
BRASÍLIA
Itabuna
Vitória da Conquista
Anápolis
Goiânia
Montes Claros
MINAS GERAIS
Uberlândia
Governador Valadares
Uberaba
Contagem
Belo Horizonte
ESPÍRITO SANTO
Vitória
SÃO PAULO
Ribeirão Preto
Juiz de Fora
Campos
Campinas
Volta Redonda
Petrópolis
RIO DE JANEIRO
Duque de Caxias
Niterói
Rio de Janeiro
Nova Iguaçu
São José dos Campos
Santo André
Santos
São Bernardo do Campo
São Paulo
Sorocaba
Londrina
Maringá
PARANÁ
Ponta Grossa
Curitiba
SANTA CATARINA
Joinville
Blumenau
Florianópolis
Lages
Passo Fundo
Caxias do Sul
Canoas
Porto Alegre
Lagoa dos Patos
Pelotas
Rio Grande
Lake Mirim

CHRONOLOGY

The first Portuguese, Pedro Alvares Cabral, arrived in Brazil in 1500. By the time Portugal took control of the region, in 1580, it was a thriving colony drawing its wealth from sugar plantations in the northeast, worked by imported Africans, or Amerindians captured from further and further inland.

- ❑ **1637–1654** Dutch control sugar-growing areas.
- ❑ **1763** Rio becomes capital.
- ❑ **1788** *Inconfidência* rebellion, led by Tiradentes, fails.
- ❑ **1807** French invade Portugal. King João VI flees to Brazil with British naval escort. In return, Brazil's ports opened to foreign trade.
- ❑ **1821** King returns to Portugal. Son Pedro made regent of Brazil.
- ❑ **1822** Pedro I declares independence and is made Emperor of Brazil.
- ❑ **1828** Brazil loses Uruguay.
- ❑ **1831** Military revolt after war with Argentina (1825–1828). Emperor abdicates. Five-year-old son succeeds him as Pedro II.
- ❑ **1835–1845** Rio Grande secedes.
- ❑ **1865–1870** Brazil wins war of Triple Alliance with Argentina and Uruguay against Paraguay.
- ❑ **1888** Pedro II abolishes slavery; landowners and military turn against him.
- ❑ **1889** First Republic established. Emperor goes into exile in Paris. Increasing prosperity as result of international demand for coffee.
- ❑ **1891** Federal constitution established.
- ❑ **1914–1918** World War I causes coffee exports to slump.
- ❑ **1920s** Working-class and intellectual movements call for end to oligarchic rule.
- ❑ **1930** Coffee prices collapse. Revolt led by Dr. Getúlio Vargas, the "Father of the Poor," who becomes president. Fast industrial growth.
- ❑ **1937** Vargas's position as benevolent dictator formalized in "New State," based on fascist model.
- ❑ **1942** Declares war on Germany. ➪

B

CHRONOLOGY *continued*

- ❑ **1945** Vargas forced out by military.
- ❑ **1950** Vargas reelected president.
- ❑ **1954** USA opposes Vargas's socialist policies. The right, backed by the military, demand his resignation. Commits suicide.
- ❑ **1956–1960** President Juscelino Kubitschek, backed by Brazilian Labor Party (PTB), attracts foreign investment for new industries, especially from USA.
- ❑ **1960–1961** Conservative Jânio da Silva Quadros president. Tries to break dependence on US trade.
- ❑ **1961** Brasília, built in three years, becomes new capital. PTB leader, João Goulart, elected president.
- ❑ **1961–1964** President's powers briefly curtailed as right wing reacts to presidential policies.
- ❑ **1964** Bloodless military coup under army chief Gen. Castelo Branco.
- ❑ **1965** Branco assumes dictatorship; bans existing political parties, but creates two official new ones. He is followed by a succession of military rulers. Fast-track economic development, the Brazilian Miracle, is counterbalanced by ruthless suppression of left-wing activists.
- ❑ **1974** World oil crisis marks end of economic boom. Brazil's foreign debt now largest in world.
- ❑ **1979** More political parties allowed.
- ❑ **1980** Huge migrations into Rondônia state begin.
- ❑ **1985** Civilian senator Tancredo Neves wins presidential elections as candidate of new liberal alliance, but dies before taking office. Illiterate adults get the vote.
- ❑ **1987** Gold found on Yanomami lands in Roraima state; illegal diggers rush in by the thousand.
- ❑ **1988** New constitution promises massive social spending but fails to address land reform. Chico Mendes, rubber-tappers' union leader and environmentalist, murdered.
- ❑ **1989** Brazil's first environmental protection plan drawn up. Yearly inflation reaches 1000%. Fernando Collor de Mello wins first fully democratic presidential elections.
- ❑ **1992** Earth Summit in Rio. Collor de Mello resigns and is impeached for corruption.
- ❑ **1994–1995** Plan Real ends hyperinflation. Congress resists constitutional reforms, but passes key privatizations of state monopolies.
- ❑ **1998–1999** Fernando Henrique Cardoso, in power since 1995, reelected president. Real devalued in economic crisis.
- ❑ **2000** Economy recovers. Ruling parties divide over elections of the heads of Congress.

POLITICS

Multiparty elections

L. House 1998/2002
U. House 1998/2002

President Fernando Henrique Cardoso

AT THE LAST ELECTION

Chamber of Deputies 513 seats

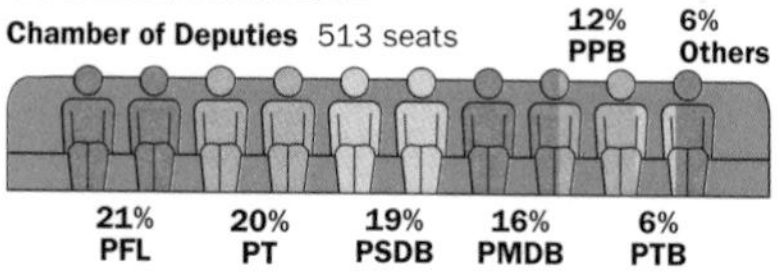
12% PPB
6% Others
21% PFL
20% PT
19% PSDB
16% PMDB
6% PTB

PFL = Liberal Front Party **PT** = PT–leftist coalition (includes the Workers' Party – **PT**, the Democratic Labor Party – **PDT**, and the Brazilian Socialist Party – **PSB**)
PSDB = Brazilian Social Democratic Party **PMDB** = Brazilian Democratic Movement Party **PPB** = Brazilian Progressive Party **PTB** = Brazilian Labor Party
Others include the Popular Socialist Party (PPS)

Federal Senate 81 seats

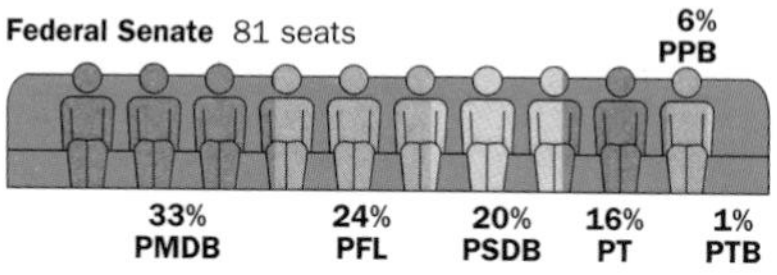
6% PPB
33% PMDB
24% PFL
20% PSDB
16% PT
1% PTB

Brazil is a democratic federal republic with 27 regional parliaments and a national Congress. In 1993, Brazilians voted to retain directly elected presidents.

Main Political Issues

Political stability
Conflict within and between the PSDB, PFL, and PMDB parties in the ruling center-right coalition threatens to intensify in the run-up to the 2002 presidential elections. Allegations of corruption and acrimonious campaigns for the leadership of the Congress bode ill for an agreement on an appropriate successor to President Cardoso who is constitutionally barred from seeking a third term. Meanwhile the prospect of a historic coalition of left-leaning parties is strengthening.

Sustainable growth
Falling interest rates, rising output, strong tax revenues, reduced debt, and tight fiscal and monetary polices are proof of the rapid recovery from the 1999 currency crisis. The debate now centers on how fast the economy can grow over the coming years. Doubts remain about inflation, the large current-account deficit, the spending plans of a new government, and the degree of Brazil's vulnerability to external shocks.

New diplomatic role
Brazil is conducting a more assertive foreign policy. In 2000 it hosted a meeting of South American presidents to promote greater geopolitical unity and strengthened trade links. Closer South American unity poses a potential challenge to US influence in the region.

Profile

Military rule between 1964 and 1985 led to gross human rights abuses, against Amazon Amerindians in particular, and to economic mismanagement, which left Brazil with a legacy of huge debts and inefficient state industries.

Brazil's young democracy is characterized by a weak party system, centered around personalities. Parties do not have set ideological programs, but form shaky coalitions and engage in horsetrading to get legislation through the Congress. The preponderance of small parties and corruption adds to the problems. Former President Collor de Mello was impeached in 1992 on fraud charges.

Dissatisfaction with the center-right provided a boost for the left, led by the influential Luís da Silva, when he came second to Collor de Mello in the 1989 presidential elections. However, his failure to beat Cardoso in 1994, and again in 1998, revealed a lack of fresh ideas and direction in his Workers' Party. Cardoso, the father of the successful anti-inflation plan for the real, held his shaky coalition together and emergency fiscal adjustments saved Brazil from a return to persistent economic crisis. A new administration elected in 2002 is unlikely to deviate much from his policy mix.

President Fernando Cardoso, *who took office in January 1995.*

Luís Ignacio da Silva, "Lula," *former leader of the left-wing Workers' Party.*

Getúlio Vargas, *the socialist president (1930–1954) who was known as "the Father of the Poor."*

Coffee plantation, *São Paulo state. Coffee was introduced into Brazil in the early 18th century. It is declining in importance and now accounts for less than 4% of export revenues.*

B

WORLD AFFAIRS

Joined UN in 1945

AmCC | G24 | Mercosr | OAS | RG

Brazil's hosting of a summit of South American presidents in 2000 to discuss transportation and energy links was widely viewed as a sign that it was seeking greater South American unity in advance of talks with the USA on a Free Trade Area of the Americas. Trade talks between MERCOSUR and the EU have also raised Brazil's leadership profile. Brazilian pressure recently helped to abort coups in Paraguay and end one in Ecuador, settle a border dispute between Peru and Ecuador, and ease relations between Hugo Chávez, Venezuela's left-leaning president, and the USA. Brazil rejected US calls for sanctions on Peru after fraudulent elections, and it has expressed concern that US aid could escalate conflict in Colombia.

AID

Recipient

$184m (receipts) — Down 44% in 1999

Recent main aid donors are the EU, the World Bank, and Japan for environmental, basic sanitation, road building, and antipoverty projects. As well as official aid, much comes from NGOs, mainly for environmental and housing projects.

DEFENSE

Compulsory military service

$15.98bn — Down 15% in 1999

BRAZILIAN ARMED FORCES

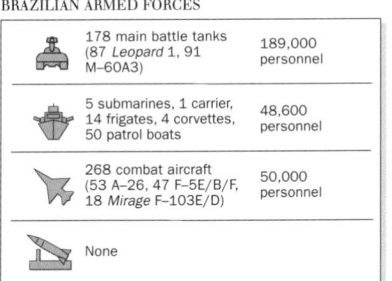

178 main battle tanks (87 *Leopard* 1, 91 M-60A3)	189,000 personnel
5 submarines, 1 carrier, 14 frigates, 4 corvettes, 50 patrol boats	48,600 personnel
268 combat aircraft (53 A-26, 47 F-5E/B/F, 18 *Mirage* F-103E/D)	50,000 personnel
None	

Brazil's dictatorship ended in 1985, but the military still has an important internal security role, for instance controlling vast regions of the north. The arms industry is large, but Brazil states that it has no intention of using its nuclear energy for military purposes: the Comprehensive Test Ban and Nuclear Non-Proliferation Treaties were signed in 1998.

Membership of the MERCOSUR trade bloc has led to increased military cooperation with Argentina, Paraguay, and Uruguay. Brazilian troops have participated in UN peacekeeping, most recently in East Timor.

ECONOMICS

Inflation 263.9% p.a. (1990–1999)

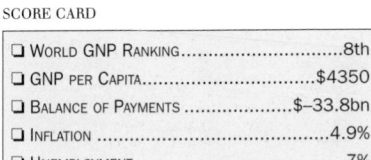

$730bn — 1.794–1.950 real

SCORE CARD

❑ WORLD GNP RANKING	8th
❑ GNP PER CAPITA	$4350
❑ BALANCE OF PAYMENTS	$-33.8bn
❑ INFLATION	4.9%
❑ UNEMPLOYMENT	7%

EXPORTS

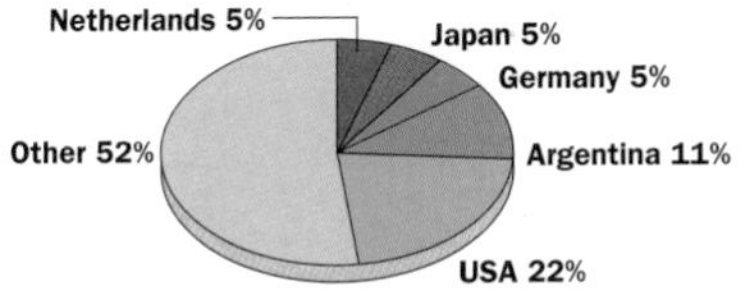
Netherlands 5%
Japan 5%
Germany 5%
Argentina 11%
USA 22%
Other 52%

IMPORTS

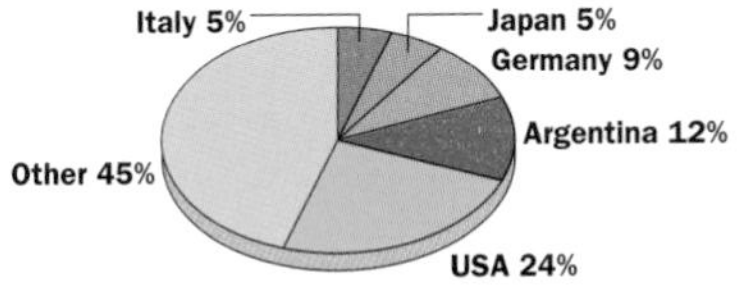
Italy 5%
Japan 5%
Germany 9%
Argentina 12%
USA 24%
Other 45%

STRENGTHS

Dominant economy in region. Strong foreign direct investment flows. Huge growth potential: immense natural resources; major producer of coffee, soy, sugar, oranges; large deposits of gold, silver, and iron; major steel producer; developing oil industry. Development aided by cross-border infrastructural projects and modernization of telecoms.

WEAKNESSES

Expensive domestic borrowing. Weak local capital markets. Vulnerability to external shocks and commodity price fluctuations. Modest productivity. Heavy debt burden. Great social inequalities threaten social unrest. Potential of political in-fighting at state and federal level to impact negatively on policy.

PROFILE

Brazil is the world's eighth-largest economy. Average growth from the start of the 20th century to the early 1970s was over 5%, second only to Japan over a comparable period. Diversification and industrialization transformed Brazil into a producer of cars, computers, and aircraft, but profligate spending produced heavy debts in the 1980s. International lenders demanded belt tightening in return for rescheduling and a steep recession followed in 1990–1992.

The launching of the new currency, the real, in 1994, was the fifth attempt at monetary stabilization since 1986; it contributed to a dramatic fall in inflation. Economic growth in 1994 boosted regional confidence and facilitated the launch of MERCOSUR.

ECONOMIC PERFORMANCE INDICATOR

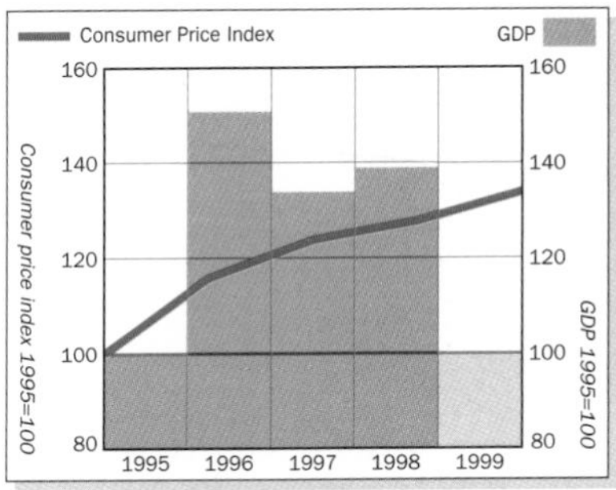
Consumer Price Index
GDP
160
140
120
100
80
1995
1996
1997
1998
1999
Consumer price index 1995=100
GDP 1995=100

In 1995 a fractious Congress blocked reforms of the tax and social security systems, but finally agreed to end state monopolies in such sectors as telecommunications and oil, thus reviving the privatization program.

The economy grew strongly through 1996 and 1997, but was seriously threatened by an international financial crisis in 1998. A $41.5 billion rescue package was arranged by the IMF, but foreign currency reserves were seriously drained in a bid to support the real which was devalued in January 1999 due to speculative pressures. A deep recession was avoided, however, by the successful application over 18 months of tight fiscal and monetary policies which restored domestic and international confidence.

By 2001, the government and most economists expected steady growth over the medium term, although a large current-account deficit (then covered by strong inflows of foreign direct investment), and inflationary blips, led others to worry that Brazil remained vulnerable to a large external shock. Sustainable growth was also linked to reform of the tax system, costly public pensions, and labor laws.

BRAZIL : MAJOR BUSINESSES

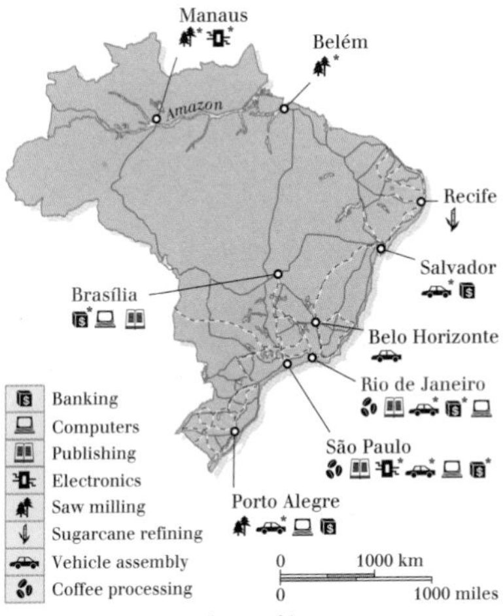
Manaus
Belém
Amazon
Recife
Salvador
Brasília
Belo Horizonte
Rio de Janeiro
São Paulo
Porto Alegre
Banking
Computers
Publishing
Electronics
Saw milling
Sugarcane refining
Vehicle assembly
Coffee processing
0
1000 km
0
1000 miles

* significant multinational ownership

B

RESOURCES

Electric power 63.3m kw

820,480 tonnes

1.3m b/d (reserves 8,100,000,000 bbl)

167m cattle, 27.3m pigs, 18.3m sheep, 950m chickens

Iron, manganese, coal, bauxite, nickel, oil, tin, silver, diamonds, gold

ELECTRICITY GENERATION

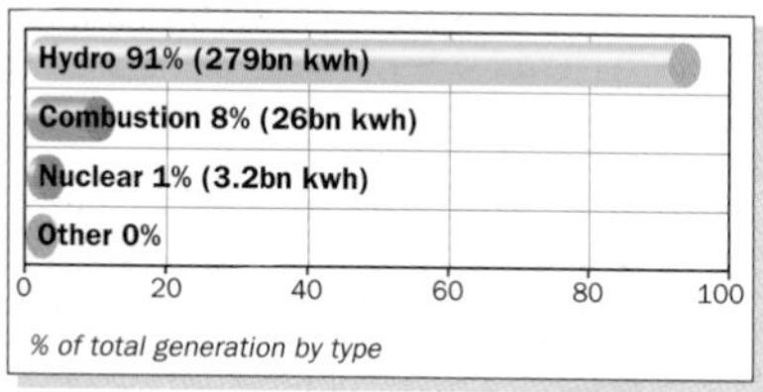
Hydro 91% (279bn kwh)
Combustion 8% (26bn kwh)
Nuclear 1% (3.2bn kwh)
Other 0%
0
20
40
60
80
100
% of total generation by type

Brazil pumps in gas from Argentina and Bolivia, and has similar plans with Venezuela and Uruguay. Nuclear power has been dogged by controversy and high costs. Hydropower, which already accounts for over 90% of electricity generation, is being expanded further, although output is vulnerable to drought. Producing ethanol from sugar represents an attempt to reduce gasoline imports, and the welcoming of foreign companies in areas of exploration and production is set to increase oil and natural gas reserves. Exploration of the Amazon's biodiversity was brought under government control in mid-2000, with all new ventures involving any living thing requiring official approval.

Amazon
AMAZON BASIN
BRAZIL : LAND USE
Cropland
Forest
Pasture
Cattle
Coffee – cash crop
Oranges
0 1000 km
0 1000 miles

***Equatorial vegetation near Manaus** in the center of Amazonas state. The brown waters of the Rio Solimões and the black waters of the Rio Negro meet near Manaus.*

ENVIRONMENT

Sustainability rank: 28th

4% (1% partially protected)

1.9 tonnes per capita

ENVIRONMENTAL TREATIES

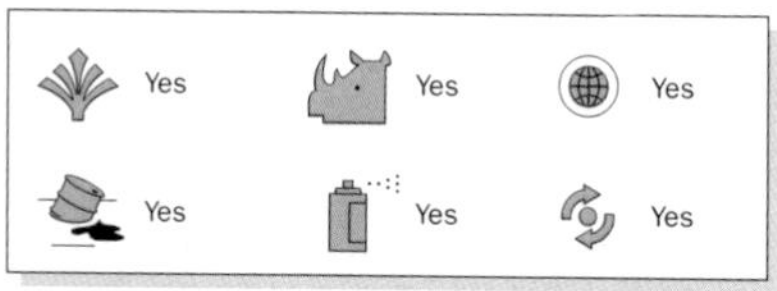
Yes
Yes
Yes
Yes
Yes
Yes

Federal agencies charged with protecting the Amazon rainforest are underfunded, understaffed, and accused of corruption.

The forest contains an estimated 90% of all the world's plant and animal species, but the demands of agriculture are leading to its destruction at a rate of 23,090 sq km (8936 sq miles) per year. As a result of such massive clearances, usually for cattle pasture and logging, vital genetic diversity is being lost. The government's latest and biggest campaign to stop illegal logging and burning was announced in 2000.

Opencast bauxite mines pollute rivers and threaten indigenous Amerindians, while in 2000 the worst oil spill in 25 years devastated the Iguaçu River. Urban industrial pollution and untreated sewage are major problems.

MEDIA

TV ownership high

Daily newspaper circulation 40 per 1000 people

PUBLISHING AND BROADCAST MEDIA

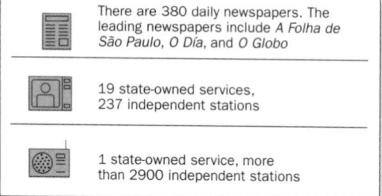

There are 380 daily newspapers. The leading newspapers include *A Folha de São Paulo*, *O Dia*, and *O Globo*

19 state-owned services, 237 independent stations

1 state-owned service, more than 2900 independent stations

TV and radio licenses are notoriously awarded as political favors. The huge Globo group dominates the home market, with radio, press, and online interests: its TV network is the fifth-largest in the world. However, it is being challenged by the Internet and the growth of new media companies, involving foreign multinationals. A constitutional amendment before the Congress allows foreign groups to take 30% stakes in TV, radio, and the press.

CRIME

Death penalty not used

87,053 prisoners

Up 1068% 1996–1998

CRIME RATES

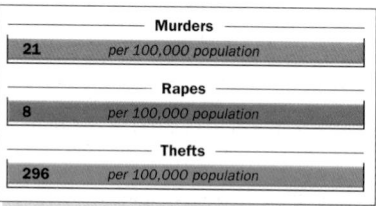

Murders
21 per 100,000 population

Rapes
8 per 100,000 population

Thefts
296 per 100,000 population

Crime levels are among the world's highest, especially in cities, with armed robbery and narcotics-related crime uppermost. Badly paid police are frequently accused of extortion, violence and the murder of citizens. Death squads, thought to be linked to the police, have targeted street children in major cities. A combination of atrocious conditions and overcrowding mean that violent disturbances in prisons are common. In 2000 the government announced a 120-point plan to crack down on crime.

In the countryside, landless squatters and indigenous peoples have been wounded and murdered in the process of being driven off land by gunmen funded by large landowners. In Roraima state, the discovery of large gold deposits has led to the homelands of Brazil's largest tribe, the Yanomami, being invaded by thousands of gun-toting prospectors, *garimpeiros*.

EDUCATION

School leaving age: 14

85%

1.87m students

THE EDUCATION SYSTEM

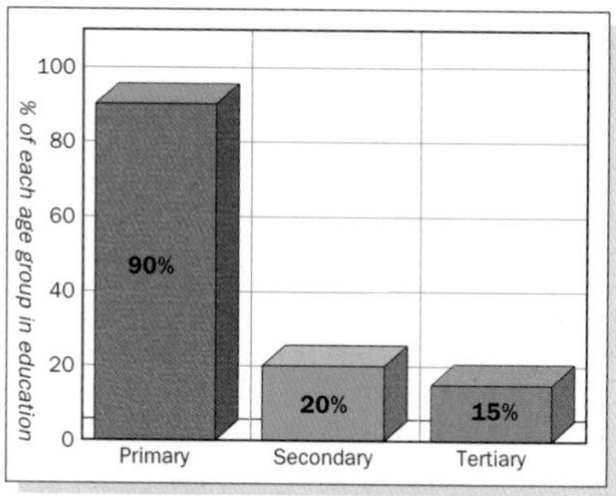
100
80
60
40
20
0
% of each age group in education
90%
20%
15%
Primary
Secondary
Tertiary

The average time spent at school is less than that in other Latin American countries. The portion of GDP spent on education is comparable to that of European countries, but it is misapplied, so that basic primary education remains weak, while many children of wealthy families receive excellent tuition at free public universities. Of Brazil's 95 universities, 55 are administered by the state. Nearly three million children do not attend school at all, especially those living in the northeast and in Amazonia, and the urban poor, including street children. However, the number of seven- to 14-year-olds in school has increased during the last decade. Despite an anti-illiteracy campaign, begun in 1971, the adult illiteracy rate is 15%.

— EXPLOITATION VERSUS PROTECTION IN AMAZONIA —

THE VAST AMAZON RIVER basin, extending across northern Brazil, contains one of the world's last great remaining virgin rainforests. Road-building projects, especially the construction of the Trans-Amazonian and Perimetral North highways to link with the Pan-American Highway, mean that it no longer enjoys the protection of inaccessibility. Since 1970, when it was still 99% intact, 600,000 sq km (over 230,000 sq miles) of Amazonia, more than 15% of the total, have been deforested. US and Brazilian researchers warned in January 2001 that the government's massive "Advance Brazil" road- and dam-

building project would by 2020 leave at best 28% of the forest untouched. Some of the damage is done by mining, particularly for gold, and the associated pollution of soil and water. Land clearance for ranching may also occur wherever the forest is opened up to exploitation by the building of access roads. It is logging, however, which poses the greatest threat. Amazonian tropical hardwoods are highly attractive to the timber industry. A score of foreign-owned multinational companies dominate the timber export business, and some 2500 logging companies and sawmills operate in the Brazilian Amazon. Brazilian mahogany is now protected by a moratorium on exploitation, but illegal logging is widespread; the government estimates that it accounts for 80% of all timber being extracted from the Amazon today.

ENVIRONMENTAL CONSEQUENCES

The rainforest typically has poor and shallow soil. Its ecology depends on the recycling of minerals in the leaf litter on the forest floor. In a damp environment, the leaf litter is broken down rapidly by soil organisms. Once exposed by the loss of tree cover, however, it dries out rapidly and can easily be washed away by the next rain. The forest cannot regenerate growth where substantial areas have been cleared. The deforestation has far-reaching implications. Forests act as "carbon sinks," fixing carbon dioxide produced by the burning of fuel, and thus helping to counteract the buildup of the "greenhouse gases" linked with global warming. Amazonia is also immensely rich in native plant and animal species. Its resource value, taking account of the potential significance of its genetic pool, for example in medicine or agriculture, was estimated in 2001 by a government research project as $2000 billion. This biodiversity, including much as yet undiscovered by the international scientific community, is dependent on proper protection of rainforest habitat.

INDIGENOUS PEOPLES

The gradual colonization of the Amazon region has brought violence and devastating disease epidemics to its indigenous peoples, along with the loss of their lands, forced removal, confinement to reservations, and the destruction of their lifestyle and culture. Although many of them have suffered extinction in the last half century, there remain nearly 200 distinct known forest-dwelling indigenous peoples. Under the 1988 constitution, forest peoples have the right to inhabit their ancestral lands, but they do not have legal title to them. In 1991, land along the Venezuela border inhabited by the Yanomami, one of the best-known hunter–gatherer groups, was designated an indigenous park by presidential decree. However, the National Indian Foundation (FUNAI), a government agency responsible for the demarcation of indigenous reserves, has come under heavy international criticism for failing to provide adequate protection.

HEALTH

Welfare state health benefits

1 per 769 people

Heart diseases, cancers, accidents, violence

Federal health is underfunded. Fewer than 20% of hospitals are state-run, but they need modernization. Private care is beyond the majority. On average only 15% of the health budget goes to child health, immunization, and other preventive programs. However, infant mortality, at 95 per 1000 children in 1970, had dropped to one-third of that level by 2000; access to potable water increased from 74% of the population in 1992 to 79% in 1998. In 2001 international drug companies and the USA dropped patent infringement claims against Brazil for distributing anti-AIDS drugs free to more than 100,000 HIV patients.

SPENDING

GDP/cap. increase

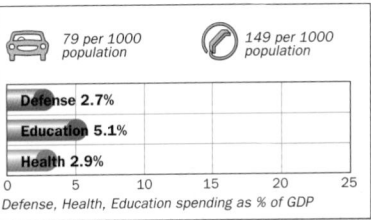

CONSUMPTION AND SPENDING

79 per 1000 population

149 per 1000 population

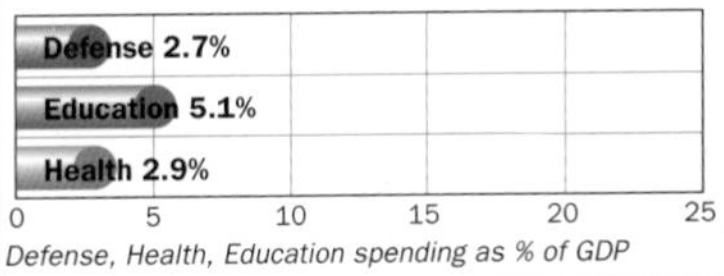
Defense 2.7%
Education 5.1%
Health 2.9%
0
5
10
15
20
25
Defense, Health, Education spending as % of GDP

Brazil's income distribution is among the most skewed in the world. IDB figures in 1999 showed that the richest 10% of the population take 50% of the income and the poorest 50% only 10%. Governments have failed to tackle the problem of homelessness and street children in large cities. An estimated one to five million families remain landless, while nearly 80% of farmland is owned by 10% of landowners. In July 2000 the government announced a substantial aid package for landless workers, declaring that vast tracts of land of unproven ownership would be redistributed among them.

WORLD RANKING

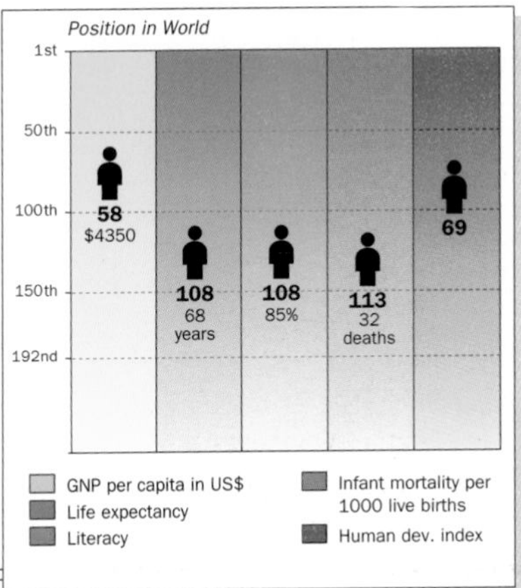
Position in World
1st
50th
100th
150th
192nd
58
$4350
108
68
years
108
85%
113
32
deaths
69
GNP per capita in US$
Life expectancy
Literacy
Infant mortality per 1000 live births
Human dev. index

BRUNEI

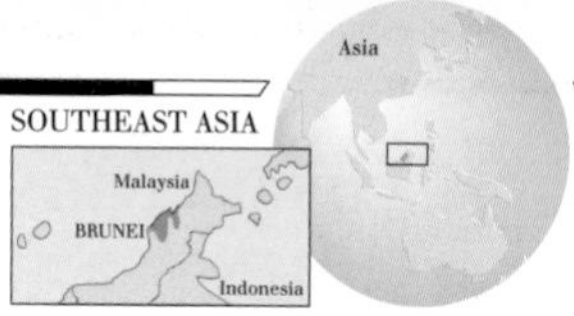
SOUTHEAST ASIA
Asia
Malaysia
BRUNEI
Indonesia

OFFICIAL NAME: Sultanate of Brunei **CAPITAL:** Bandar Seri Begawan
POPULATION: 328,000 **CURRENCY:** Brunei dollar **OFFICIAL LANGUAGE:** Malay

1984 | 1984 | Feb 23 | BRU | +8 | +673 | .bn

LYING ON THE NORTHWESTERN coast of the island of Borneo, Brunei is divided in two by a strip of the surrounding Malaysian state of Sarawak. The interior is mostly rainforest. Independent from the UK since 1984, Brunei is ruled by decree of the sultan. It is undergoing increasing Islamicization. Oil and gas reserves have brought one of the world's highest standards of living.

CLIMATE

Tropical equatorial

WEATHER CHART

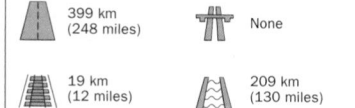

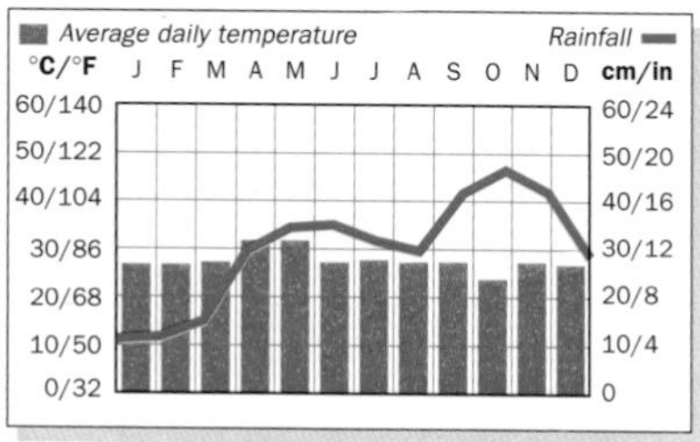
Average daily temperature
Rainfall
°C/°F
J F M A M J J A S O N D
cm/in
60/140
50/122
40/104
30/86
20/68
10/50
0/32
60/24
50/20
40/16
30/12
20/8
10/4
0

Just 480 km (300 miles) north of the equator, Brunei has a long rainy season with extremely high humidity.

TRANSPORTATION

Drive on left

Brunei International, Bandar Seri Begawan

97 ships 361,900 grt

THE TRANSPORTATION NETWORK

399 km (248 miles)	None
19 km (12 miles)	209 km (130 miles)

Interest-free loans for civil servants, subsidized gasoline, and limited public transportation account for the high rates of car ownership.

TOURISM

Visitors : Population 2.9:1

964,000 visitors

Up 13% in 1998

MAIN TOURIST ARRIVALS

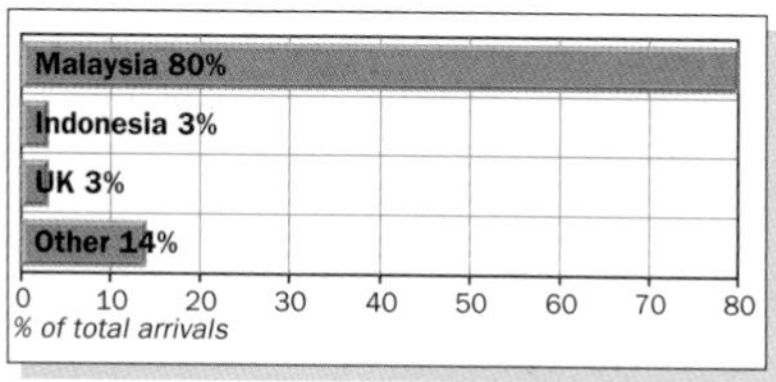
Malaysia 80%
Indonesia 3%
UK 3%
Other 14%
0
10
20
30
40
50
60
70
80
% of total arrivals

Although the goverment is keen to protect Bruneians from Western influence, it wants to develop quality tourism as part of its diversification program. Promoted as the "Gateway to Borneo," Brunei's rainforests could be developed for tourism. A former attraction was the Churchill Museum, founded by the late sultan. This has now been superseded by the Museum of Royal Regalia.

PEOPLE

Pop. density medium

Malay, English, Chinese

62/km² (161/mi²)

THE URBAN/RURAL POPULATION SPLIT

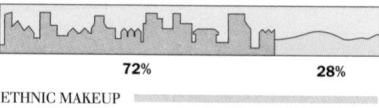

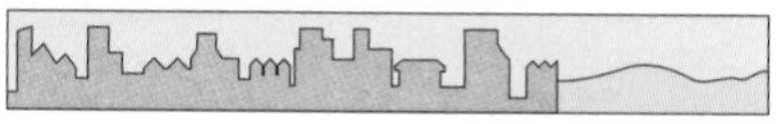
72%
28%

ETHNIC MAKEUP

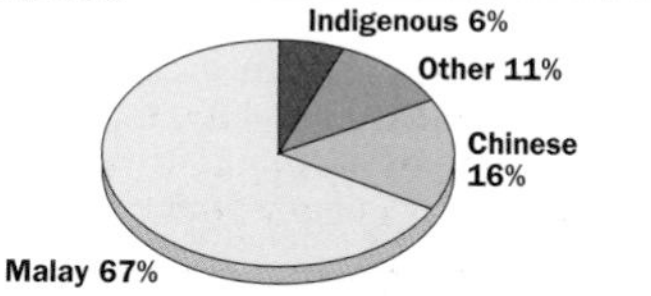
Indigenous 6%
Other 11%
Chinese 16%
Malay 67%

Malays are the beneficiaries of positive discrimination; many in the Chinese community are either stateless or hold British protected person passports. Among indigenous groups, the Murut and Dusuns are favored over the Ibans. Women, less restricted than in some Muslim states, are obliged to wear headscarves but not the veil. Many hold influential posts in the civil service.

POLITICS

No multiparty elections

Not applicable

HM Sultan Haji Sir Hassanal Bolkiah Mu'izzadin Waddaulah

LEGISLATIVE OR ADVISORY BODIES

Brunei is an absolute monarchy; the sultan consults four advisory councils: Religious Council, Privy Council, Council of Cabinet Ministers, and Council of Succession, which he appoints. Political parties have been banned since 1988.

Since a failed rebellion in 1962, a state of emergency has been in force and the sultan has ruled by decree. Hopes for democracy were dashed when political parties were banned in 1988. In 1990, "Malay Muslim Monarchy" was introduced, promoting Islamic values as the state ideology. This further alienated the large Chinese and expatriate communities. Power is closely tied to the royal family. One of the sultan's brothers holds the foreign affairs portfolio and the sultan himself looks after defense and finance.

WORLD AFFAIRS

Joined UN in 1984

APEC | ASEAN | Comm | OIC | WTO

Brunei claims part of the Spratly Islands. Political exiles opposed to the government and based in Malaysia are a main concern. Relations with the UK, the ex-colonial power, are good.

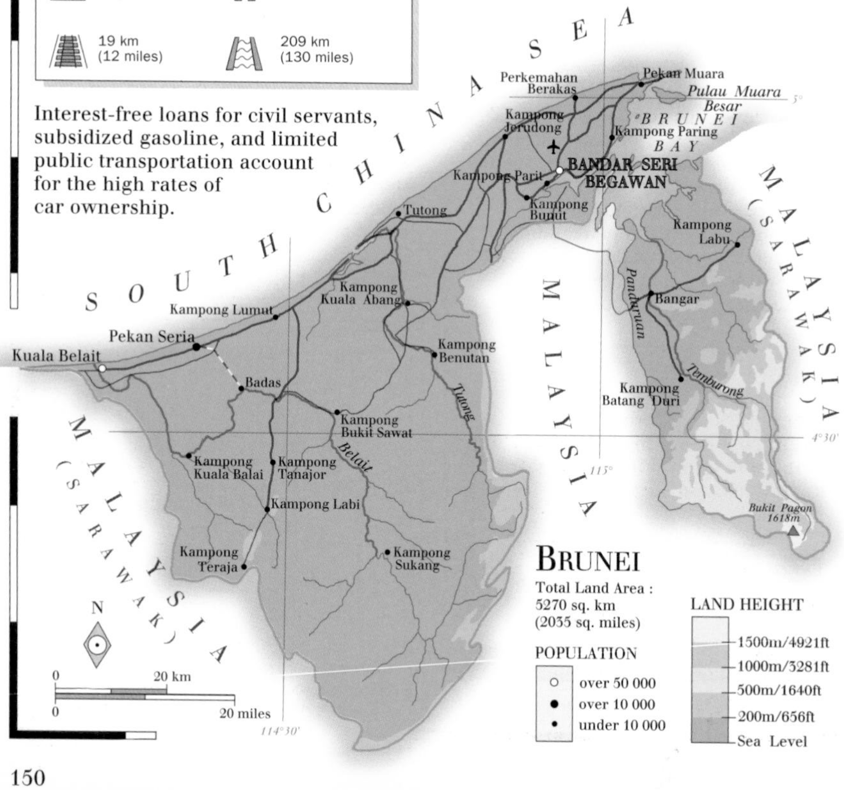
SOUTH CHINA SEA
MALAYSIA (SARAWAK)
MALAYSIA
Perkemahan Berakas
Pekan Muara
Pulau Muara Besar
BRUNEI BAY
Kampong Jerudong
Kampong Paring
BANDAR SERI BEGAWAN
Kampong Parit
Kampong Bunut
Tutong
Kampong Labu
Pandaruan
Bangar
Kampong Kuala Abang
Kampong Lumut
Pekan Seria
Kuala Belait
Kampong Benutan
Badas
Kampong Bukit Sawat
Kampong Batang Duri
Temburong
Kampong Kuala Balai
Kampong Tanajor
Belait
Tutong
Kampong Labi
Kampong Teraja
Kampong Sukang
Bukit Pagon 1618m
N
0 20 km
0 20 miles
BRUNEI
Total Land Area : 5270 sq. km (2035 sq. miles)
POPULATION
over 50 000
over 10 000
under 10 000
LAND HEIGHT
1500m/4921ft
1000m/3281ft
500m/1640ft
200m/656ft
Sea Level

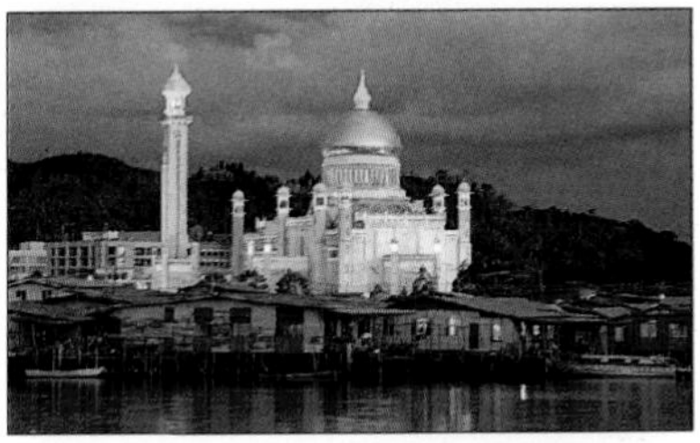

The magnificent Omar Ali Saifuddin mosque is surrounded by an artificial lagoon.

AID

Donor

Ad hoc handouts from the sultan

Not applicable

Aid spending is largely ad hoc. It has included donations to the Contras in Nicaragua, the Bosnian Muslims, and the homeless of New York.

DEFENSE

No compulsory military service

US$402m

Up 4% in 1999

As well as being head of the 5000-strong armed forces, the sultan has a personal bodyguard of 2000 UK-trained Gurkhas. The UK and Singapore are close defense allies.

ECONOMICS

Inflation 1.1% p.a. (1990–1998)

US$8.5bn

1.666–1.734 Brunei dollars

SCORE CARD

❑ World GNP Ranking	92nd
❑ GNP per Capita	US$26,286
❑ Balance of Payments	US$2.09bn
❑ Inflation	1%
❑ Unemployment	5%

Strengths

Twenty-five years of known oil reserves; 40 years of gas. Earnings from massive overseas investments, mainly in the USA and Europe, now exceed oil and gas revenues.

Weaknesses

Single-product economy. Failure of diversification programs could lead to problems in the future.

EXPORTS

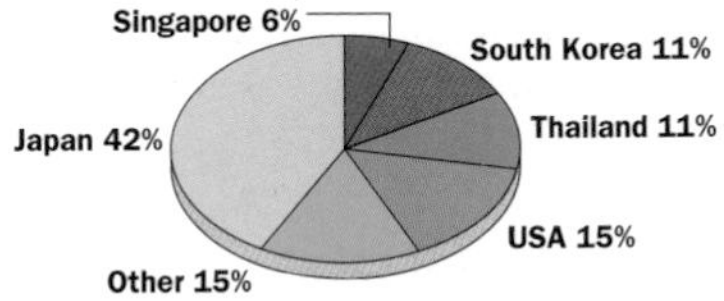
Singapore 6%
South Korea 11%
Japan 42%
Thailand 11%
USA 15%
Other 15%

IMPORTS

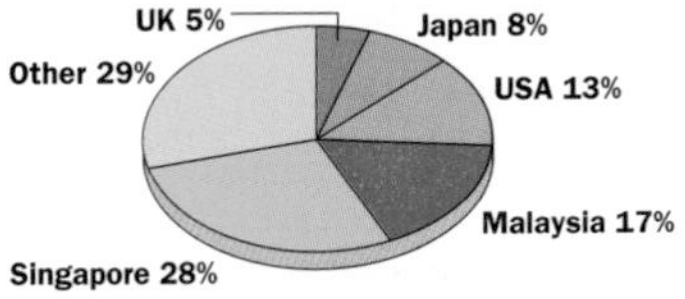
UK 5%
Japan 8%
Other 29%
USA 13%
Malaysia 17%
Singapore 28%

RESOURCES

Electric power 477,000 kw

4677 tonnes

195,000 b/d (reserves 1,400,000,000 bbl)

40,000 ducks, 6000 buffaloes, 5.5m chickens

Oil, natural gas

Oil and gas are the major resources. Energy policy is now focused on regulating output in order to conserve stocks, since reserves are of limited duration. Almost all food is imported.

ENVIRONMENT

Not available

14% (5% partially protected)

17.7 tonnes per capita

The Forestry Strategic Plan aims to protect Brunei's forests (which take up 80% of its land area). It has allocated 64% of their area for protection and recreation and the prevention of soil erosion. However, Brunei's mangrove swamps, the largest on the island of Borneo, remain unprotected.

MEDIA

TV ownership medium

Daily newspaper circulation 69 per 1000 people

PUBLISHING AND BROADCAST MEDIA

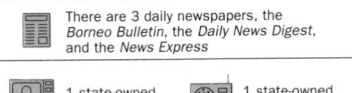

There are 3 daily newspapers, the *Borneo Bulletin*, the *Daily News Digest*, and the *News Express*

1 state-owned service

1 state-owned service

The state effectively controls all media. Brunei's television service now has a heavy religious content.

CRIME

Death penalty not used

312 prisoners

Down 30% 1996–1998

Crime levels are low. Most crime involves petty theft or is linked to alcohol and narcotics (both banned). A stolen car often makes TV news headlines. The state of emergency enables the government to detain without charge or trial for indefinitely renewable two-year periods.

EDUCATION

School leaving age: 16

92%

1878 students

Free schooling is available to the entire population, with the exception of the stateless Chinese, who do not qualify. The University of Brunei Darussalam was opened in 1985.

HEALTH

Welfare state health benefits

1 per 988 people

Heart diseases, cancers

The health service is free, although for major surgery many Bruneians tend to travel to Singapore.

CHRONOLOGY

Under British control since 1841, Brunei became a formal British Protectorate in 1888.

- ❑ **1929** Oil extraction begins.
- ❑ **1959** First constitution enshrines Islam as state religion. Internal self-government.
- ❑ **1962** Prodemocracy rebellion. State of emergency; sultan rules by decree.
- ❑ **1984** Independence from Britain. Brunei joins ASEAN.
- ❑ **1990** Ideology of "Malay Muslim Monarchy" introduced.
- ❑ **1991** Imports of alcohol banned.
- ❑ **1992** Joins Non-Aligned Movement.
- ❑ **1998** Sultan's son, Prince Al-Muhtadee Billah, made crown prince.

SPENDING

GDP/cap. increase

CONSUMPTION AND SPENDING

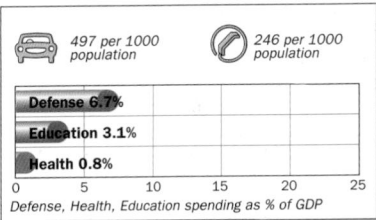

497 per 1000 population

246 per 1000 population

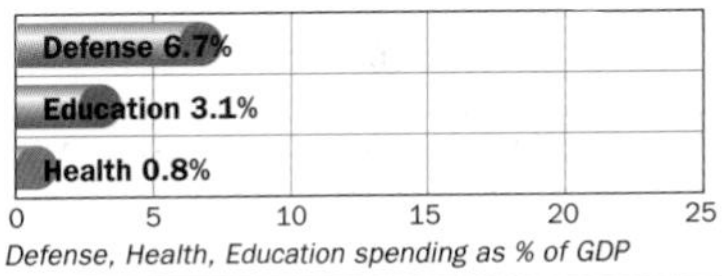
Defense 6.7%
Education 3.1%
Health 0.8%
0
5
10
15
20
25
Defense, Health, Education spending as % of GDP

The wealthiest people in Brunei are those close to the sultan, one of the world's richest men. A generally high standard of living, along with a degree of social mobility among Malays, keeps discontent to a minimum. Bruneians are major consumers of high-tech hi-fi and video equipment, designer-label watches, and Western designer clothes. The sultan's younger brother, Prince Jefri, in 2001 auctioned his possessions, ranging from fire engines to marble baths, after the failure of his business left him with debts of US$3 billion.

WORLD RANKING

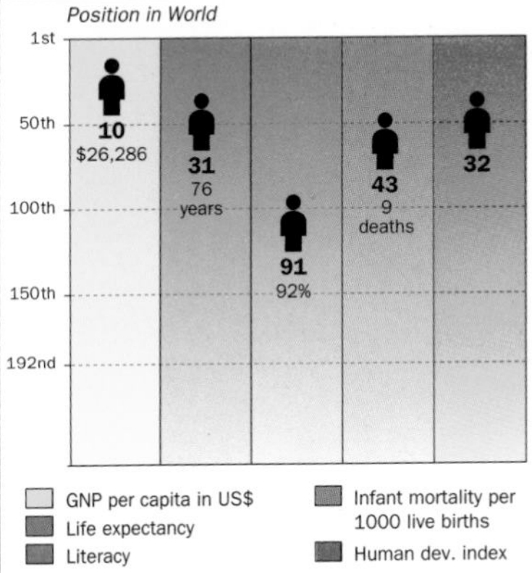
Position in World
1st
50th
100th
150th
192nd
10
$26,286
31
76 years
91
92%
43
9 deaths
32
GNP per capita in US$
Life expectancy
Literacy
Infant mortality per 1000 live births
Human dev. index

BULGARIA

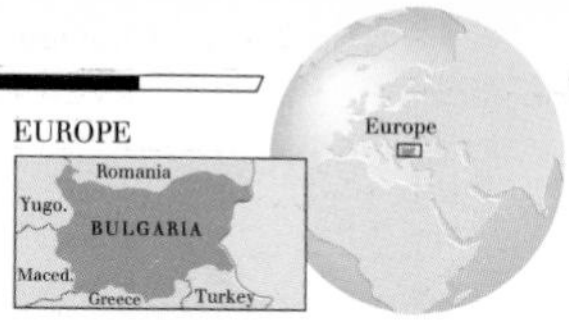
EUROPE
Europe
Romania
Yugo.
BULGARIA
Maced.
Greece
Turkey

OFFICIAL NAME: Republic of Bulgaria **CAPITAL:** Sofia
POPULATION: 8.2 million **CURRENCY:** Lev **OFFICIAL LANGUAGE:** Bulgarian

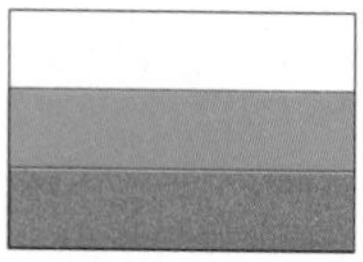

1908 | 1947 | March 3 | BG | +2 | +359 | .bg

LOCATED IN SOUTHEASTERN EUROPE, Bulgaria is a mainly mountainous country. The River Danube forms the northern border, while the popular resorts of the Black Sea lie to the east. The most populated areas are around Sofia in the west, Plovdiv in the south, and along the Danube plain. Bulgaria was ruled by the Turks from 1396 until 1878. In 1908, it became an independent kingdom and was under communist rule from 1947, with Todor Zhivkov in power from 1954 to 1989. The 1990s brought political instability as the country adjusted to democracy and economic reconstruction.

Rila Monastery *in the Rila Mountains. It is famous for its 1200 National Revival Period frescoes dating from the mid-19th century.*

CLIMATE

Mediterranean/continental

WEATHER CHART

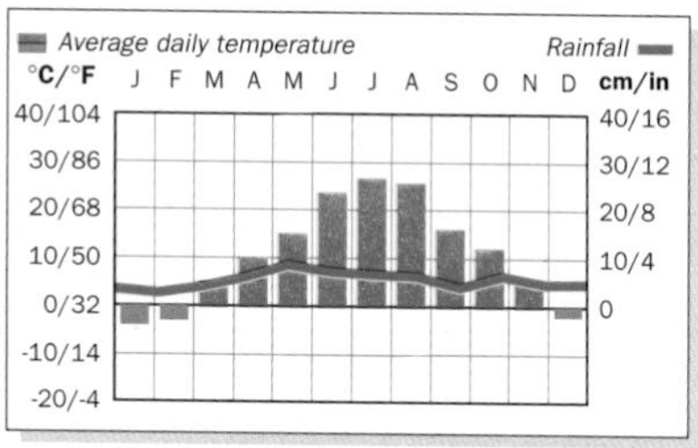
Average daily temperature
Rainfall
°C/°F
J F M A M J J A S O N D
cm/in
40/104
30/86
20/68
10/50
0/32
-10/14
-20/-4
40/16
30/12
20/8
10/4
0

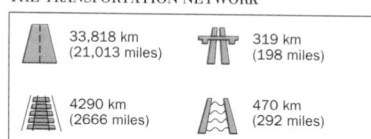

The central valley and the lowlands have warm summers and cold, snowy winters, but hot or cold winds from Russia can bring spells of more extreme weather. The hotter summers on the Black Sea coast have encouraged the growth of tourist resorts. Snow may lie on the high mountain peaks until June.

TRANSPORTATION

Drive on right

Sofia International 1.24m passengers

181 ships 1.1m grt

THE TRANSPORTATION NETWORK

33,818 km (21,013 miles)

319 km (198 miles)

4290 km (2666 miles)

470 km (292 miles)

At the crossroads between Europe and Asia, Bulgarian railroads and expressways were underfunded under Zhivkov (when north–south routes were deliberately left undeveloped) and in the economic uncertainty of the 1990s. Funding for modernizing key routes is now in place. Ferries are used for most cross-Danube traffic. In 2000 agreement was reached with Romania on building a second bridge across the river.

TOURISM

Visitors : Population 1:2.9

2.8m visitors

Up 13% in 2000

MAIN TOURIST ARRIVALS

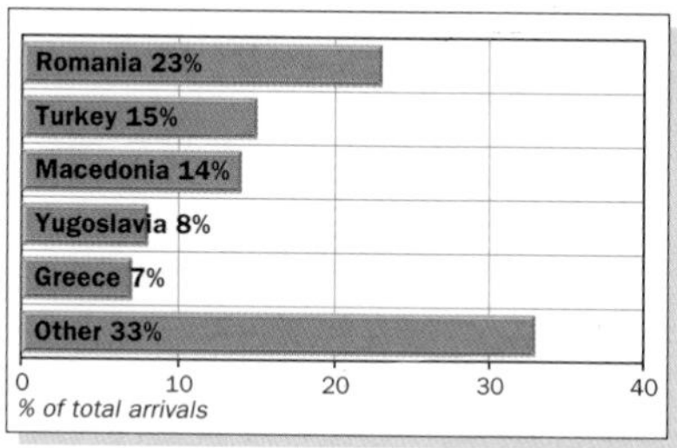
Romania 23%
Turkey 15%
Macedonia 14%
Yugoslavia 8%
Greece 7%
Other 33%
0
10
20
30
40
% of total arrivals

The tourist industry formerly catered for the east European mass-market. Western tourists are attracted by low prices for ski resorts and beach holidays. Bulgaria is now privatizing the industry and seeks to move it upmarket by stressing its heritage. Since the mid-1990s a slump in earnings has been reversed: Russians are returning in larger numbers and there is a growth in tours from western Europe, especially from Germany.

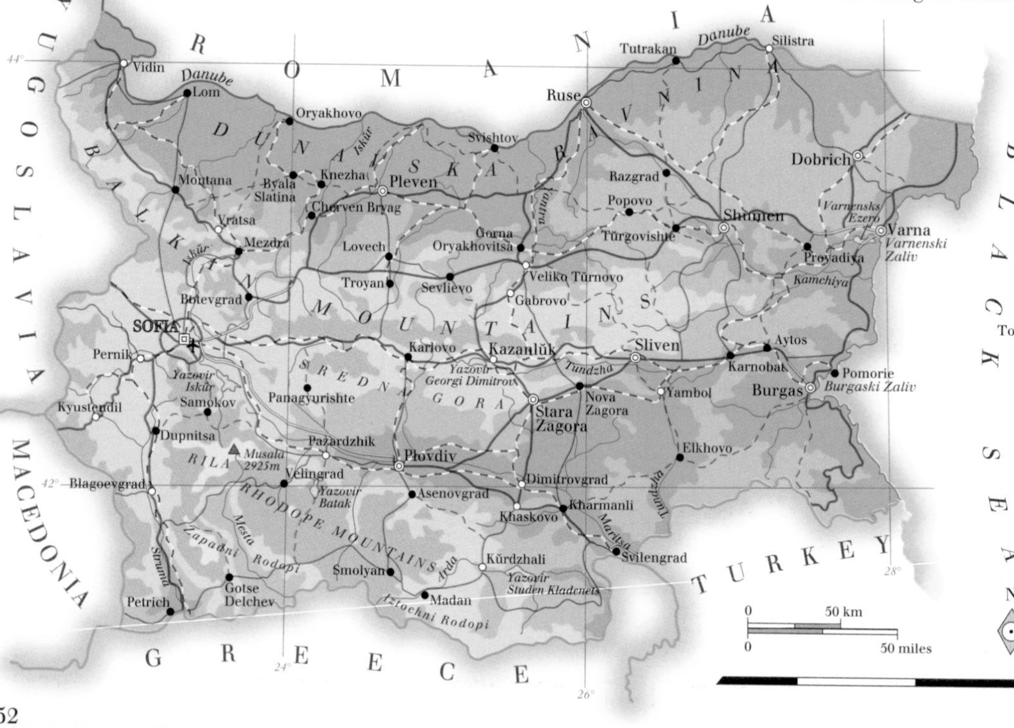
ROMANIA
YUGOSLAVIA
MACEDONIA
GREECE
TURKEY
BLACK SEA
Danube
Vidin
Lom
Oryakhovo
Svishtov
Ruse
Tutrakan
Silistra
Dobrich
Montana
Byala Slatina
Knezha
Pleven
Cherven Bryag
Razgrad
Popovo
Shumen
Targovishte
Varna
Varnenski Zaliv
Varnensko Ezero
Provadiya
Kamchiya
Vratsa
Mezdra
Lovech
Gorna Oryakhovitsa
Veliko Tŭrnovo
Troyan
Sevlievo
Gabrovo
Botevgrad
SOFIA
Pernik
DUNAVSKA RAVNINA
BALKAN MOUNTAINS
SREDNA GORA
Karlovo
Kazanlŭk
Sliven
Aytos
Karnobat
Pomorie
Burgas
Burgaski Zaliv
Yazovir Georgi Dimitrov
Tundzha
Stara Zagora
Nova Zagora
Yambol
Yazovir Iskŭr
Samokov
Panagyurishte
Kyustendil
Dupnitsa
Musala 2925m
RILA
Pazardzhik
Plovdiv
Elkhovo
Blagoevgrad
Velingrad
Yazovir Batak
Asenovgrad
Dimitrovgrad
Khaskovo
Kharmanli
Maritsa
Svilengrad
RHODOPE MOUNTAINS
Zapadni Rodopi
Mesta
Struma
Arda
Smolyan
Kŭrdzhali
Yazovir Studen Kladenets
Gotse Delchev
Petrich
Madan
Iztochni Rodopi
44°
42°
24°
26°
28°
0 50 km
0 50 miles
N

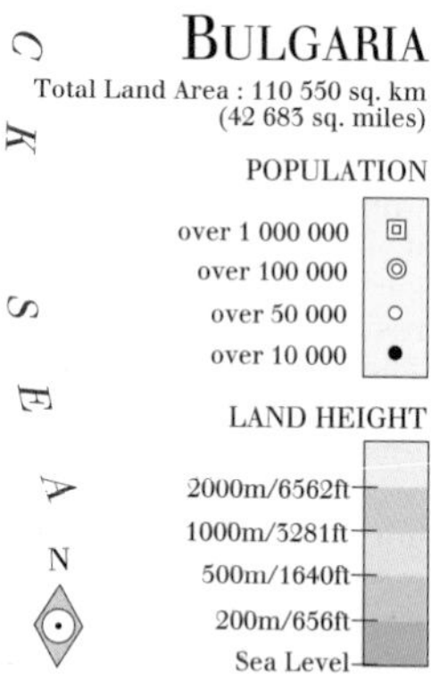
BULGARIA
Total Land Area : 110 550 sq. km (42 683 sq. miles)
POPULATION
over 1 000 000
over 100 000
over 50 000
over 10 000
LAND HEIGHT
2000m/6562ft
1000m/3281ft
500m/1640ft
200m/656ft
Sea Level

B

PEOPLE

Pop. density medium

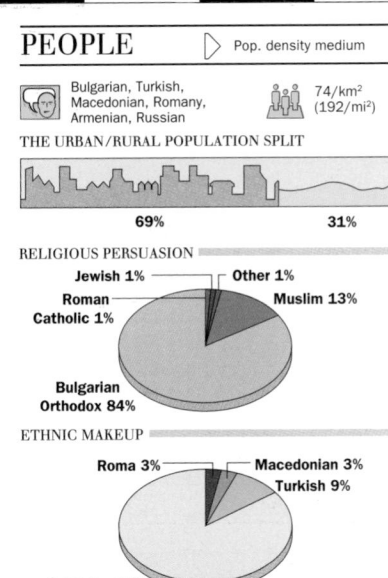

Bulgarian, Turkish, Macedonian, Romany, Armenian, Russian

74/km² (192/mi²)

THE URBAN/RURAL POPULATION SPLIT

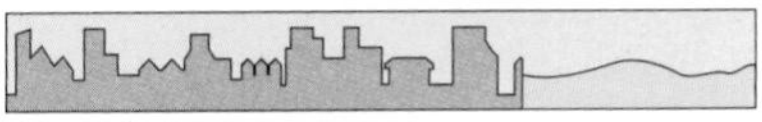
69%
31%

RELIGIOUS PERSUASION

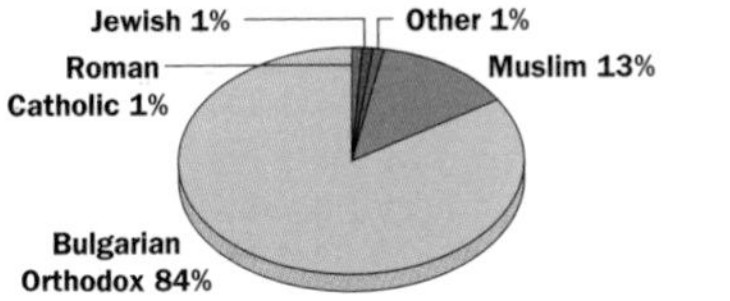
Jewish 1%
Other 1%
Roman Catholic 1%
Muslim 13%
Bulgarian Orthodox 84%

ETHNIC MAKEUP

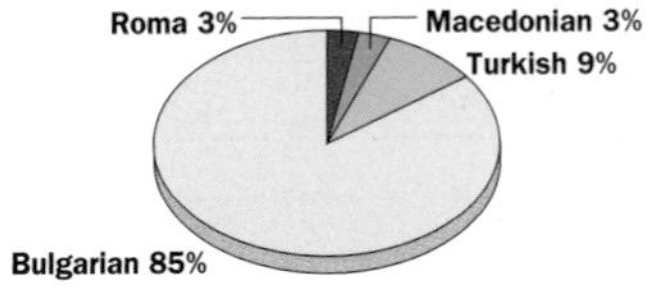
Roma 3%
Macedonian 3%
Turkish 9%
Bulgarian 85%

The government has sought the assimilation of separate ethnic groups, thereby suppressing cultural identities. In the 1970s, Bulgarian Muslims, or *Pomaks*, were forced to change Muslim names to Bulgarian ones. Bulgarian Turks were particularly targeted in the 1980s. Linguistic and religious freedom was granted in 1989, but 300,000 ethnic Turks, or 40%, still left for Turkey. Their farming skills have traditionally been important to agriculture. Recent privatizations have left many Turks landless and have provoked new emigration. The MRF, supported mainly by ethnic Turks, is a minority party whose influence can be strong within a balanced parliament.

Macedonians and Roma each account for 3% of the population. The latter minority has no protection and suffers discrimination at all levels. Women, especially Turkish women, have equal rights in theory, but society remains patriarchal.

POPULATION AGE BREAKDOWN

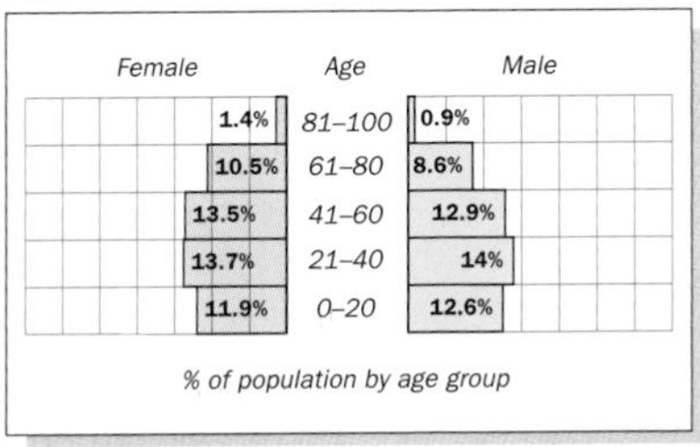
Female
Age
Male
1.4%
81–100
0.9%
10.5%
61–80
8.6%
13.5%
41–60
12.9%
13.7%
21–40
14%
11.9%
0–20
12.6%
% of population by age group

POLITICS

Multiparty elections

2001/2005

President Peter Stoyanov

AT THE LAST ELECTION

National Assembly 240 seats

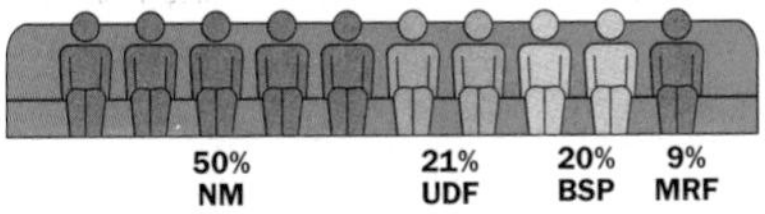
50% NM
21% UDF
20% BSP
9% MRF

NM = National Movement Simeon II
UDF = Union of Democratic Forces
BSP = Socialist Party
MRF = Movement for Rights and Freedoms

Bulgaria is a multiparty democracy.

PROFILE

Having moved falteringly to a pluralist democratic system after the fall of the communist Zhivkov regime in 1989, Bulgaria suffered during the 1990s from successive weak governments, each brought down by no-confidence votes. The UDF, a broad anticommunist alliance, fell from office in 1992, and by the time of the 1994 general election the former communist BSP appeared to be firmly in the ascendant, winning an overall majority. The BSP government resisted political and economic change. The result was one of the slowest privatization programs in eastern Europe, with the old communist web of patronage still intact. A new UDF government in 1997 launched free-market reforms backed up by the IMF. Its considerable success, and reorientation of policy toward the goals of EU and NATO membership, allowed the UDF to approach the June 2001 elections with some confidence, despite a surge in support for a monarchist party launched by ex-king Simeon II (who had left Bulgaria as a small child in 1946). The poll, however, left the UDF with less than a quarter of the National Assembly seats, exactly half of which went to the NM. Uncertainty over whether the ex-king himself would take on the role of prime minister ended when he formed a coalition with the MRF (representing mainly the ethnic Turkish minority) and was sworn in in July. He took the oath to the republic (although he had not formally given up his claim to the throne) as Simeon Saxecoburggotski, promising "spiritual and economic revival," clean government, tax cuts, and more privatization, with integration with the EU and NATO his top priorities.

Ex-king Simeon II *(Saxecoburggotski) returned as prime minister in 2001.*

Peter Stoyanov *of the UDF, became president in 1996.*

WORLD AFFAIRS

Joined UN in 1955

BSEC | CE | EAPC | CEFTA | OSCE

Bulgaria is among six "second wave" candidates for EU membership which began negotiations in March 2000. It hopes to join NATO in 2002.

Bulgaria conscientiously adhered to UN sanctions against former Yugoslavia, despite the costs of lost trade. Relations with Russia are no longer close, but are maintained carefully because of heavy Bulgarian dependence on Russia for oil and gas. Relations with Turkey have greatly improved since the tensions of the final years of communist rule.

AID

Recipient

$265m (receipts)

Up 29% 1997–1999

IMF, World Bank, and EBRD loans are mainly intended for infrastructure improvements. Large-scale EU assistance toward reforms, in preparation for Bulgaria's eventual EU membership, is estimated at 2% of GDP. Humanitarian aid focuses mainly on medical provision and children's homes.

CHRONOLOGY

Bulgaria was part of the Ottoman empire for five centuries until its independence in 1908. Under King Ferdinand, it sided with Germany during World War I, and subsequently lost valuable territory to Greece and Serbia. Under King Boris, Bulgaria once again sided with Germany in World War II.

- **1943** Child king Simeon II accedes.
- **1944** Allies firebomb Sofia. Soviet army invades. Antifascist Fatherland Front coalition, including Agrarian Party and Bulgarian Communist Party (BCP), takes power in bloodless coup. Kimon Georgiev prime minister.
- **1946** September, referendum abolishes monarchy. Republic proclaimed. October, general election results in BCP majority.
- **1947** Prime Minister Georgi Dmitrov discredits Agrarian Party leader Nikola Petkov. Petkov arrested and sentenced to death. International recognition of Dmitrov government. Soviet-style constitution adopted; one-party state established. Country renamed People's Republic of Bulgaria. Nationalization of economy begins.
- **1949** Dmitrov dies, succeeded as prime minister by Vasil Kolarov.
- **1950** Kolarov dies. "Little Stalin" Vulko Chervenkov replaces him

B

CHRONOLOGY *continued*

and begins BCP purge and collectivization.

- **1953** Stalin dies; Chervenkov's power begins to wane.
- **1954** Chervenkov yields power to Todor Zhivkov. Zhivkov sets out to make Bulgaria an inseparable part of the Soviet system.
- **1955–1960** Zhivkov exonerates victims of Chervenkov's purges.
- **1965** Plot to overthrow Zhivkov discovered by Soviet agents.
- **1968** Bulgarian troops aid Soviet army in invasion of Czechoslovakia.
- **1971** New constitution. Zhivkov becomes president of State Council and resigns as premier.
- **1978** Purge of BCP: 30,000 members expelled.
- **1984** Turkish minority forced to take Slavic names.
- **1989** June–August, exodus of 300,000 Bulgarian Turks. November, Zhivkov ousted as BCP leader and head of state. Replaced by Petur Mladenov. Mass protest in Sofia for democratic reform. December, Union of Democratic Forces (UDF) formed.
- **1990** Economic collapse. Zhivkov arrested. BCP loses constitutional role as leading political party, changes name to Bulgarian Socialist Party (BSP). June, election produces no overall result. August, Zhelyu Zhelev, UDF leader, becomes president. BSP in government. Country renamed Republic of Bulgaria; communist symbols removed from national flag.
- **1991** February, price controls abolished; steep price rises. July, new constitution adopted. October, UDF wins elections.
- **1992** Continued political and social unrest. October, UDF resigns after losing vote of confidence. December, Movement for Rights and Freedoms (MRF) forms government. Zhivkov convicted of corruption and human rights abuses.
- **1993** Ambitious privatization program begins.
- **1994** General elections return BSP to power.
- **1995** BSP leader, Zhan Videnov, heads coalition government.
- **1996** Financial crisis and collapse of lev. Presidential elections won by opposition UDF candidate, Peter Stoyanov.
- **1997** General election won by UDF, whose leader Ivan Kostov becomes prime minister.
- **2001** Despite economic upturn, voters turn to new party headed by ex-king, who becomes prime minister under name of Simeon Saxecoburggotski.

DEFENSE

Compulsory military service

$392m

Down 3% in 1999

BULGARIAN ARMED FORCES

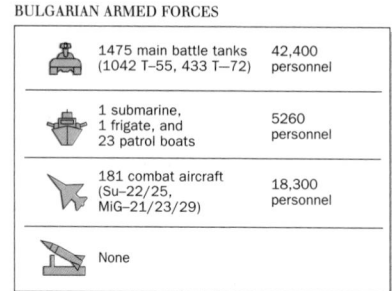

1475 main battle tanks (1042 T-55, 433 T–72)	42,400 personnel
1 submarine, 1 frigate, and 23 patrol boats	5260 personnel
181 combat aircraft (Su–22/25, MiG–21/23/29)	18,300 personnel
None	

Defense spending fell from 14% of GDP in 1985 to 3.3% in 1999. Plans to join NATO, which were announced in 1997, with the hope of joining in 2002, involved a major reorientation in defense thinking.

In late 1999 the government adopted "Plan 2004," which embodied a radical acceleration of its previous plans to restructure the armed forces. The new plan envisaged downsizing to only 45,000 personnel by 2004, and moving to an emphasis on rapid reaction capabilities. It was considered that this smaller but combat-ready force would be less costly to maintain in the long run.

In 1999 the Kosovo crisis prompted Bulgaria to make its airspace available to NATO.

ECONOMICS

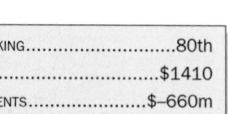

Inflation 112% p.a. (1990–1999)

$11.6bn

1.945–2.084 leva

SCORE CARD

World GNP Ranking	80th
GNP per Capita	$1410
Balance of Payments	$–660m
Inflation	2.6%
Unemployment	15%

EXPORTS

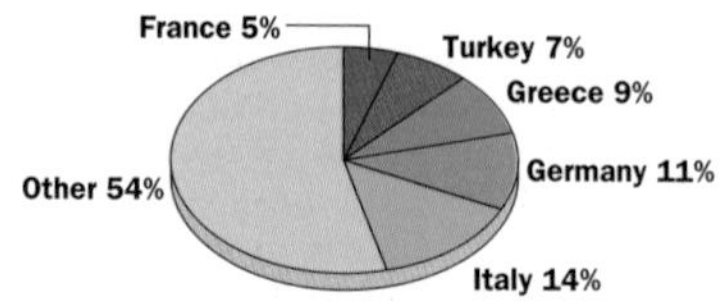
France 5%
Turkey 7%
Greece 9%
Germany 11%
Italy 14%
Other 54%

IMPORTS

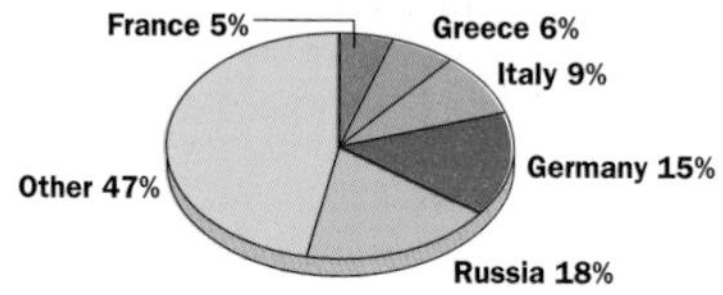
France 5%
Greece 6%
Italy 9%
Germany 15%
Russia 18%
Other 47%

ECONOMIC PERFORMANCE INDICATOR

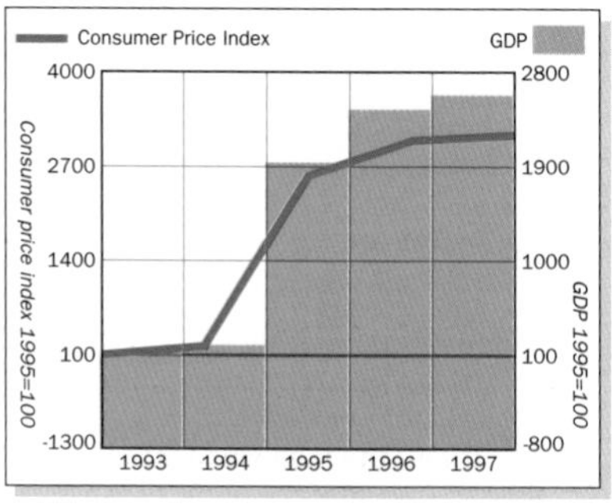
Consumer Price Index
GDP
Consumer price index 1995=100
GDP 1995=100
4000
2700
1400
100
-1300
2800
1900
1000
100
-800
1993
1994
1995
1996
1997

Strengths

Coal and natural gas. Good agricultural production, especially grapes for well-developed wine industry, and tobacco. Strong expertise in computer software.

Weaknesses

Outdated infrastructure and equipment, and outstanding debt throughout industry. Slow privatization and structural reform until 1998.

Profile

Restructuring the economy is linked to privatization – a process delayed for political and technical reasons until the late 1990s. A financial crisis in 1996 triggered the collapse of the national currency, the lev. Foreign investment is still low, despite laws that since 1992 have allowed foreign firms to own companies outright. Trade has shifted toward the EU, while trade with the former Soviet Union has fallen sharply. The UDF government, returned in 1997, followed IMF advice, with free-market reforms, backed by foreign loans, successfully bringing inflation under control. After a setback in 1999, attributed to the regional impact of the crisis over Kosovo, economic growth of 5% in 2000 confirmed Bulgaria's recovery.

BULGARIA : MAJOR BUSINESSES

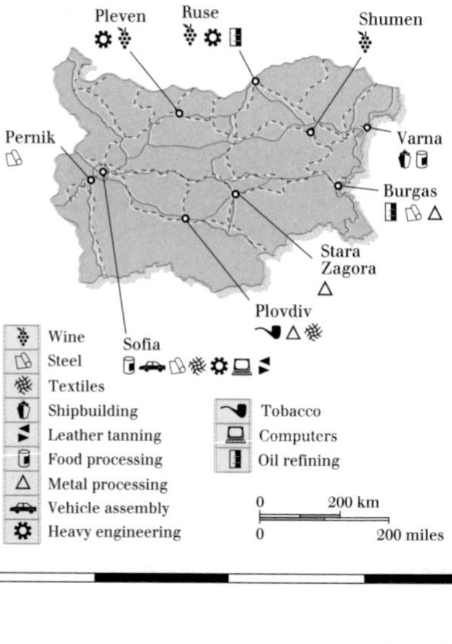
Pleven
Ruse
Shumen
Varna
Pernik
Burgas
Stara Zagora
Plovdiv
Sofia
Wine
Steel
Textiles
Shipbuilding
Leather tanning
Food processing
Metal processing
Vehicle assembly
Heavy engineering
Tobacco
Computers
Oil refining
0
200 km
0
200 miles

B

RESOURCES

Electric power 12.1m kw

16,674 tonnes

561 b/d (reserves 14,552,160 bbl)

2.55m sheep, 1.51m pigs, 13.9m chickens

Coal, iron, copper, lead, zinc, oil, natural gas

ELECTRICITY GENERATION

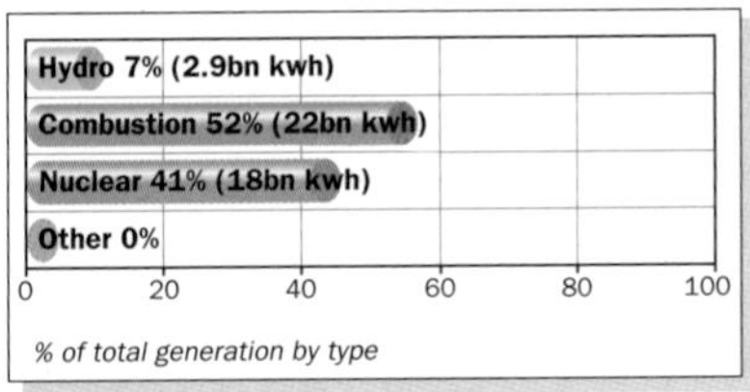
Hydro 7% (2.9bn kwh)
Combustion 52% (22bn kwh)
Nuclear 41% (18bn kwh)
Other 0%
0
20
40
60
80
100
% of total generation by type

Bulgaria has modest oil reserves and rather larger ones of coal and natural gas, but still has to import about 70% of its primary energy needs, much of it from the CIS. Unreliable supplies in the past led to frequent winter power cuts. These have largely disappeared since the mid-1990s, as reduced production in heavy industry and improved domestic supply have lowered import demand. Bulgaria is partly reliant on nuclear power. The EU is providing aid to upgrade two reactors at Kozloduy in return for the promised closure of other reactors there which pose particular safety risks. The government also plans to extend the controversial Chaira Dam, which began generating hydropower in 1993. Bulgaria has the northern hemisphere's largest manganese mine.

BULGARIA : LAND USE

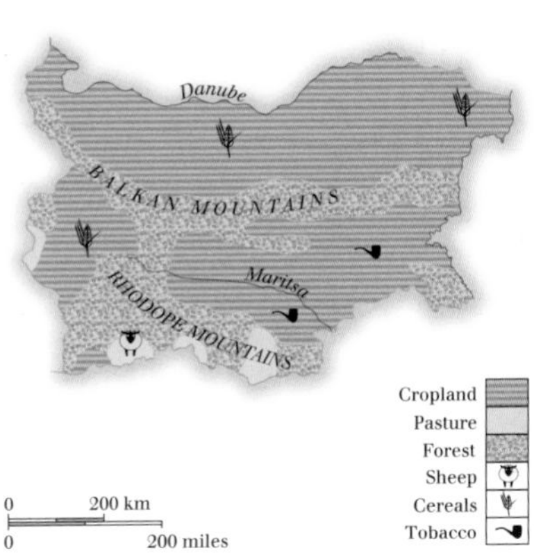
Danube
BALKAN MOUNTAINS
Maritsa
RHODOPE MOUNTAINS
Cropland
Pasture
Forest
Sheep
Cereals
Tobacco
0
200 km
0
200 miles

ENVIRONMENT

Sustainability rank: 60th

4%

6.1 tonnes per capita

ENVIRONMENTAL TREATIES

Yes Yes Yes

Yes Yes Yes

Environmental degradation led to the foundation in 1989 of the *Ecoglasnost* party. It circulated information on pollution and nuclear waste dump locations, and brought polluters to court. The Kozloduy nuclear complex, east of Lom, restarted in 1995 despite safety concerns, is under pressure to close its oldest reactors. Air pollution has diminished, but problems remain. NATO bombing of Serbian chemical and oil refineries on the Danube in 1999 has led to downriver pollution in Bulgaria.

MEDIA

TV ownership high

Daily newspaper circulation 254 per 1000 people

PUBLISHING AND BROADCAST MEDIA

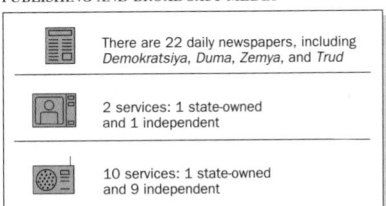

There are 22 daily newspapers, including *Demokratsiya, Duma, Zemya,* and *Trud*

2 services: 1 state-owned and 1 independent

10 services: 1 state-owned and 9 independent

Although it was liberalized in 1989, media freedom remains relative, and under new electronic media laws in 1998 state-run broadcasters retain an effective news monopoly. One group dominates the newspaper market, and of the others most are party-owned. Internet providers are regulated. Journalists also complain of the tough libel laws.

CRIME

Death penalty not used

9684 prisoners

Down 15% 1996–1998

CRIME RATES

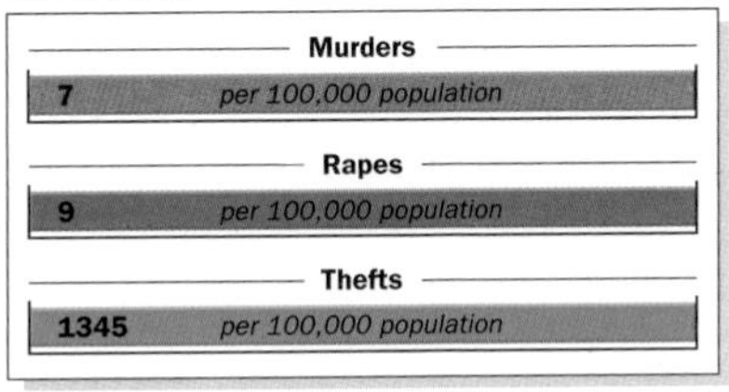
Murders
7 per 100,000 population
Rapes
9 per 100,000 population
Thefts
1345 per 100,000 population

In the 1990s Bulgaria became a key narcotics trafficking route to western Europe. Former security agents, party officials, and prestigious ex-athletes have moved into protection rackets, counterfeiting, and similar activities. Violations of minority rights are a sensitive political issue.

EDUCATION

School leaving age: 16

98%

262,757 students

THE EDUCATION SYSTEM

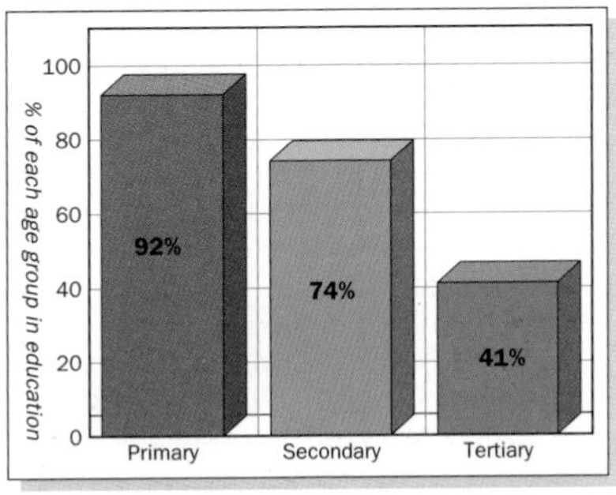
% of each age group in education
100
80
60
40
20
0
92%
74%
41%
Primary
Secondary
Tertiary

Education is free and compulsory between the ages of seven and 16. The system has been changed from a Soviet-inspired to a west European-style model. Government spending on education fell sharply until the 1999 budget. Teaching standards continue to be lowest in the rural and Turkish communities.

HEALTH

No welfare state health benefits

1 per 286 people

Heart and cerebrovascular diseases, cancers

Hospital facilities have kept pace with population growth, but the 1997 economic crisis brought the health service to the brink of collapse. A new health policy was formulated in 1999. The plan of action emphasizes primary care. The Bulgarian Red Cross assists in health administration.

SPENDING

GDP/cap. decrease

CONSUMPTION AND SPENDING

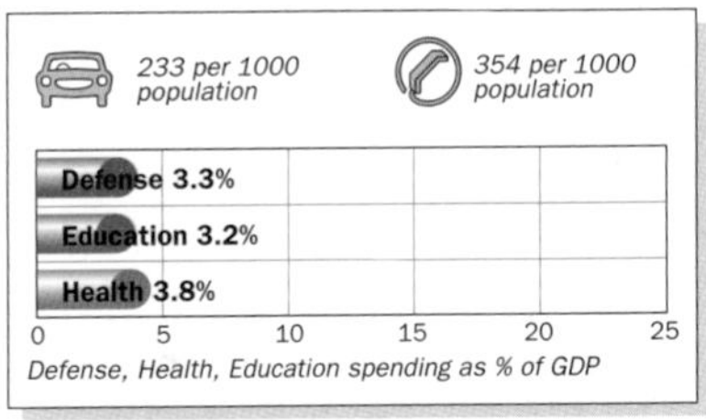
233 per 1000 population
354 per 1000 population
Defense 3.3%
Education 3.2%
Health 3.8%
0
5
10
15
20
25
Defense, Health, Education spending as % of GDP

Conquering the hyperinflation of 1995–1997 has remedied the most acute crisis, and associated hardship has been reduced. Turks and Roma remain the poorest people.

WORLD RANKING

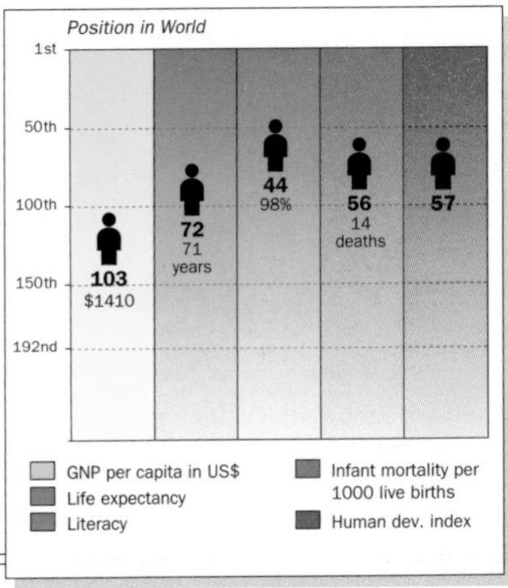
Position in World
1st
50th
100th
150th
192nd
103
$1410
72
71 years
44
98%
56
14 deaths
57
GNP per capita in US$
Life expectancy
Literacy
Infant mortality per 1000 live births
Human dev. index

B

BURKINA

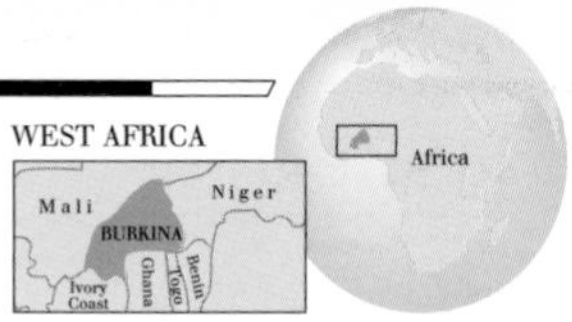
WEST AFRICA
Africa
Mali
Niger
BURKINA
Ivory Coast
Ghana
Togo
Benin

OFFICIAL NAME: Burkina Faso **CAPITAL:** Ouagadougou
POPULATION: 11.6 million **CURRENCY:** CFA franc **OFFICIAL LANGUAGE:** French

1960 | 1960 | Dec 11 | BF | 0 | +226 | .bf

LANDLOCKED IN WEST AFRICA, Burkina (formerly Upper Volta) gained independence from France in 1960. The majority of Burkina lies in the arid fringe of the Sahara known as the Sahel. Ruled by military dictators for much of its postindependence history, Burkina became a multiparty state in 1991. However, much power still rests with President Blaise Compaoré. Burkina's economy remains largely based on agriculture.

CLIMATE

Tropical/steppe

WEATHER CHART

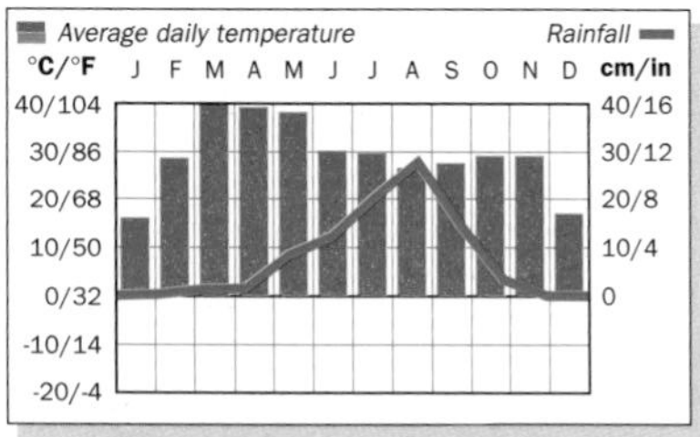
Average daily temperature
Rainfall
°C/°F
J F M A M J J A S O N D
cm/in
40/104
30/86
20/68
10/50
0/32
-10/14
-20/-4
40/16
30/12
20/8
10/4
0

The tropical climate comprises two seasons – unreliable rains from June to October, and a long dry season.

TRANSPORTATION

Drive on right

Ouagadougou International 186,673 passengers

Has no fleet

THE TRANSPORTATION NETWORK

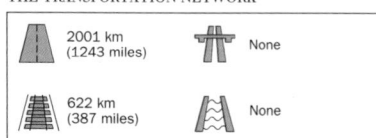

2001 km (1243 miles)

None

622 km (387 miles)

None

The railroad to the port of Abidjan in Ivory Coast provides the main commercial route to the sea. Roads through Benin, Togo, and Ghana provide alternative access.

TOURISM

Visitors : Population 1:55

218,000 visitors

Up 36% in 1999

MAIN TOURIST ARRIVALS

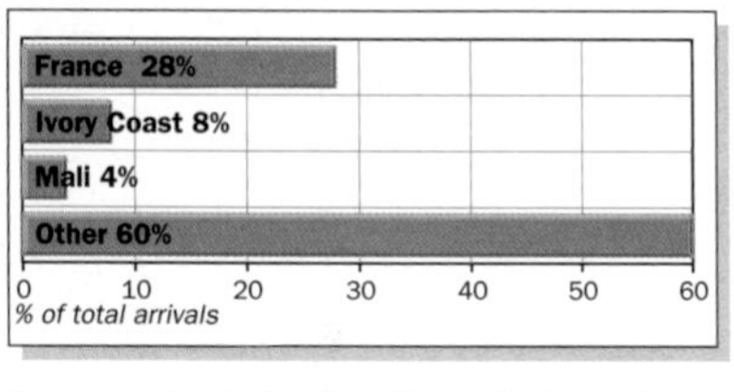
France 28%
Ivory Coast 8%
Mali 4%
Other 60%
0
10
20
30
40
50
60
% of total arrivals

Some potential exists for safari tourism, and the cities offer an attractive mix of colonial and African architecture. Big game hunting is allowed in some areas.

PEOPLE

Pop. density low

Mossi, Fulani, French, Tuareg, Dyula, Songhai

43/km² (113/mi²)

THE URBAN/RURAL POPULATION SPLIT

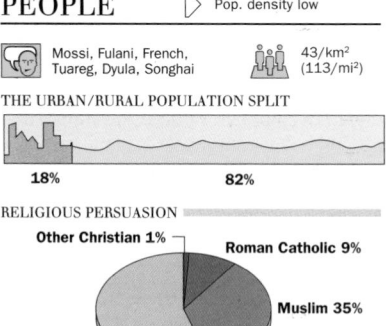

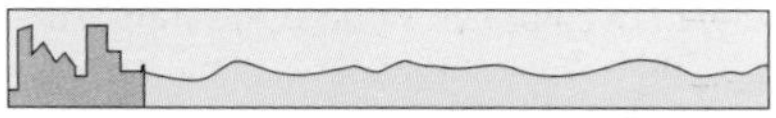
18%
82%

RELIGIOUS PERSUASION

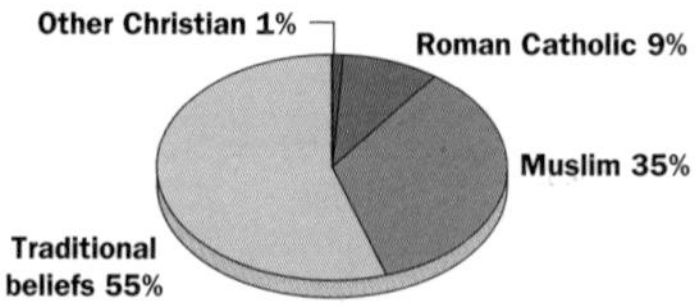
Other Christian 1%
Roman Catholic 9%
Muslim 35%
Traditional beliefs 55%

No ethnic group is dominant in Burkina, although the Mossi people who live in the area of their old empire around Ouagadougou have always played an important role in government. Burkina's first president, Maurice Yameogo, and Blaise Compaoré, leader since 1987, are both Mossi. The people from the west are much more ethnically mixed.

The extended family is important and reaches from the villages into the towns and cities. Extreme poverty has led to a strong sense of egalitarianism within society. The absence of women in public life belies their real power and influence, particularly within the traditional framework of the extended family. However, most women are still denied access to education and senior professional positions.

__Camel plowing.__ Burkina's poor soils and frequent droughts lead many young men to emigrate seasonally in search of work.

POLITICS

Multiparty elections

L. House 1997/2002

President Blaise Compaoré

AT THE LAST ELECTION

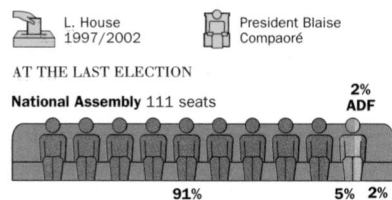

National Assembly 111 seats

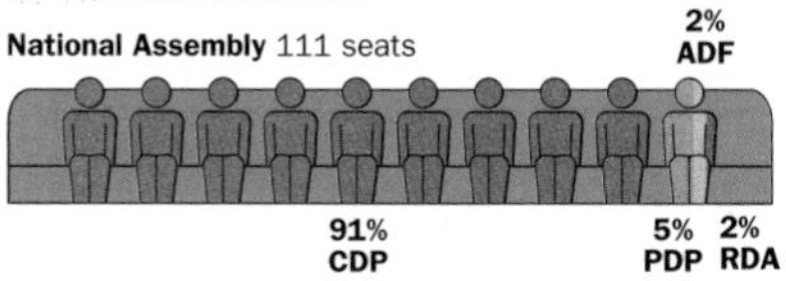
2% ADF
91% CDP
5% PDP
2% RDA

CDP = Congress for Democracy and Progress **PDP** = Party for Democracy and Progress **RDA** = African Democratic Rally **ADF** = Alliance for Democracy and Federation

House of Representatives 178 seats

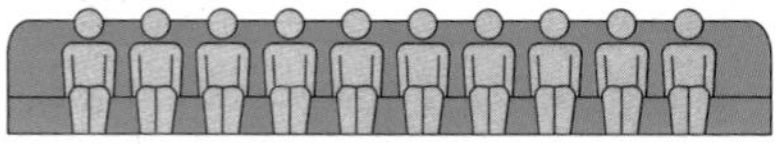

Members of the House of Representatives are appointed or indirectly elected on a nonparty basis by provincial councils and various communities

A multiparty democracy in theory, Burkina is still dominated in practice by former military dictator Blaise Compaoré, and the army remains influential behind the scenes. Compaoré has been in power since the assassination in 1987 of Capt. Thomas Sankara, his former superior. Several of Compaoré's close military colleagues have been murdered. His grip on power in Burkina appears to be solid, and he was reelected president in 1998 with almost 90% of the vote. Most opposition leaders are still living in exile, and opposition within Burkina remains underground.

The CDP and the government came under unexpected pressure in 1998 and 1999 after the assassination of a popular newspaper editor, Norbert Zongo, in which leading establishment figures were implicated.

WORLD AFFAIRS

Joined UN in 1960

CILSS | ECOWAS | OAU | OIC | FZ

Burkina's landlocked position means that good relations with countries to the south are a major foreign policy concern. Compaoré's relationship with other ECOWAS states was damaged by his support for rebellion in Liberia.

AID

Recipient

$398m (receipts)

No change in 1999

External aid, mostly from France and the EU, is important to the economy. The large number of NGOs has caused organizational problems; there is often difficulty in finding suitable projects for all the prospective donors.

BURKINA

Total Land Area : 273 800 sq. km
(105 714 sq. miles)

POPULATION
- ◎ over 100 000
- ○ over 50 000
- ● over 10 000
- • under 10 000

LAND HEIGHT
- 500m/1640ft
- 200m/656ft
- Sea Level

N

0 100 km
0 100 miles

MALI
NIGER
BENIN
TOGO
GHANA
IVORY COAST (CÔTE D'IVOIRE)
SUDAN
GOURMA
Djibo
Dori
Titao
Ouahigouya
Séguénéga
Barsalogo
Kongoussi
Tougan
Gourcy
Pissila
Yako
Kaya
Bogandé
Nouna
Toma
Boussé
Boussouma
Dédougou
Ziniaré
Réo
OUAGADOUGOU
Ténado
Koudougou
Koupéla
Tapoa
Diapaga
Kombissiri
Sapone
Manga
Garango
Fada-N'gourma
Boromo
Tenkodogo
Bobo-Dioulasso
Orodara
Houndé
Léo
Pô
Zabré
Tiébélé
Diébougou
Téna Kourou 747m
Banfora
Gaoua
Black Volta
Red Volta
White Volta
Bougouriba
Léraba
Pendjari
Mékrou
12°
4°
0°

DEFENSE

No compulsory military service

$75m

Down 7% in 1999

The main role of the 5600-strong army has been maintaining internal security. Burkina is reliant on France for most equipment and training.

ECONOMICS

Inflation 6% p.a. (1990–1999)

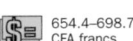

$2.6bn

654.4–698.7 CFA francs

SCORE CARD

❑ World GNP Ranking	133rd
❑ GNP per Capita	$240
❑ Balance of Payments	$-312m
❑ Inflation	-1.1%
❑ Unemployment	Not available

STRENGTHS
Remittances from plantation workers in Ghana and the Ivory Coast. Strongly improved economic management. Low debt burden. Ability to attract foreign aid. Cotton growing.

WEAKNESSES
Landlocked. Natural resources not in the main economically viable. Donors' fears over political instability. Food crop fluctuations. Prone to drought. Migrants' remittances have halved to about $80 million since 1988.

EXPORTS

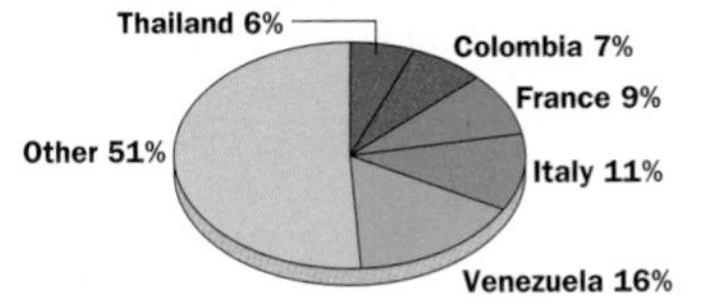
Thailand 6%
Colombia 7%
France 9%
Other 51%
Italy 11%
Venezuela 16%

IMPORTS

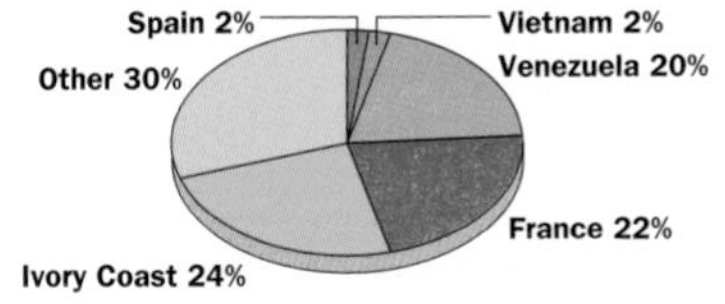
Spain 2%
Vietnam 2%
Venezuela 20%
Other 30%
France 22%
Ivory Coast 24%

RESOURCES

Electric power 78,000 kw

8045 tonnes

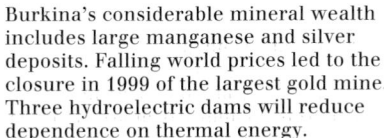

Not an oil producer and has no refineries

7.95m goats, 6.35m sheep, 21m chickens

Gold, antimony, marble, manganese, silver, zinc

Burkina's considerable mineral wealth includes large manganese and silver deposits. Falling world prices led to the closure in 1999 of the largest gold mine. Three hydroelectric dams will reduce dependence on thermal energy.

ENVIRONMENT

Sustainability rank: 104th

11% (8% partially protected)

0.1 tonnes per capita

Like other countries on the southern rim of the Sahara, desertification is the major ecological issue. The rate of tree cutting for fuel is on the increase.

MEDIA

TV ownership low

Daily newspaper circulation 1 per 1000 people

PUBLISHING AND BROADCAST MEDIA

There are 6 daily newspapers, including *Sidwaya, Le Pays, Le Journal de Soir,* and *L'Observateur Paalga*

3 services: 1 state-owned, 2 independent

1 state-owned service, 30 independent stations

There are a number of small independent newspapers funded by opposition groups. A code of practice was introduced in 1999.

CRIME

Death penalty not used

Burkina does not publish prison figures

Down 19% 1996–1998

Crime levels have traditionally been low. However, the urbanization of society and the increase in political violence have seen levels increase.

EDUCATION

School leaving age: 14

24%

8911 students

Education is based on the French system. Recently, practical subjects have received more emphasis.

CHRONOLOGY

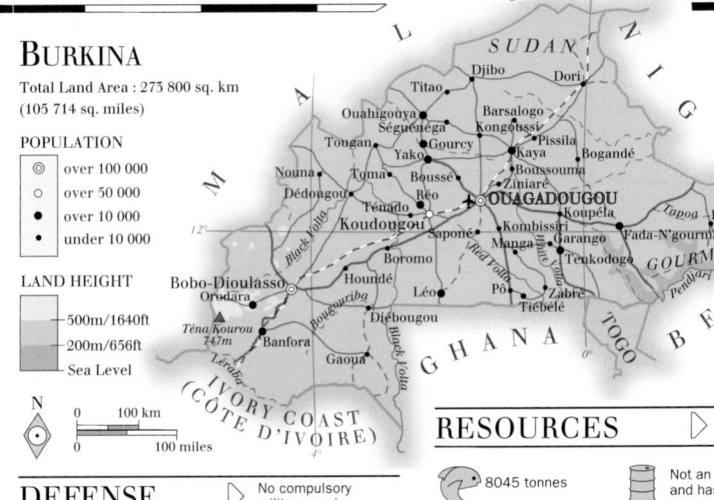

Ruled by Mossi kings from the 16th century, Burkina became an outpost of the French empire in the late 19th century. It was renamed Upper Volta at independence in 1960.

- ❑ **1980** Ousting of military ruler; Col. Saye Zerbo becomes president.
- ❑ **1982** Capt. Thomas Sankara takes power. People's Salvation Council (PSC) begins radical reforms.
- ❑ **1984** Renamed Burkina.
- ❑ **1987** Sankara assassinated, Capt. Blaise Compaoré takes power.
- ❑ **1991** New constitution. Compaoré elected president.
- ❑ **1997** CDP landslide election victory.
- ❑ **1999** General strike.
- ❑ **2001** Ex-presidential guard head accused of 1998 killing of journalist Norbert Zongo. Meningitis outbreak.

HEALTH

No welfare state health benefits

1 per 20,000 people

Malaria, diarrheal and respiratory diseases

Health spending focuses on primary health care and vaccination. AIDS had caused 43,000 deaths by 1999.

SPENDING

GDP/cap. increase

CONSUMPTION AND SPENDING

4 per 1000 population

4 per 1000 population

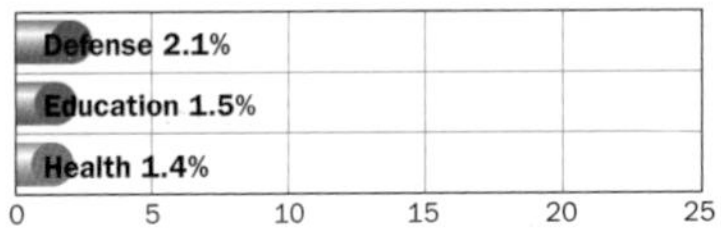
Defense 2.1%
Education 1.5%
Health 1.4%
0
5
10
15
20
25

Defense, Health, Education spending as % of GDP

Burkina is a country of extreme, almost universal, poverty. Displays of wealth are rare and ownership of high-tech items is limited to a small elite.

WORLD RANKING

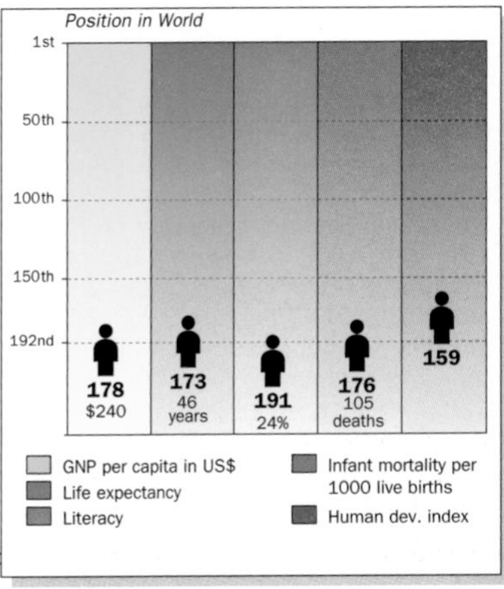
Position in World
1st
50th
100th
150th
192nd
178
$240
173
46 years
191
24%
176
105 deaths
159
GNP per capita in US$
Life expectancy
Literacy
Infant mortality per 1000 live births
Human dev. index

BURMA (MYANMAR)

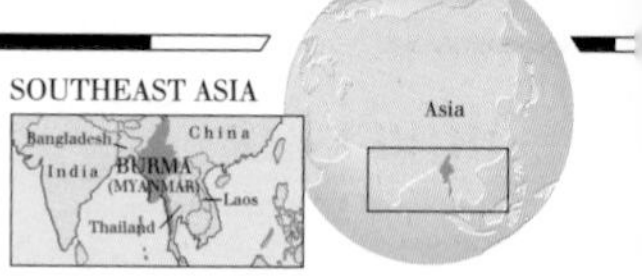
SOUTHEAST ASIA
Bangladesh
China
India
BURMA (MYANMAR)
Laos
Thailand
Asia

OFFICIAL NAME: Union of Myanmar **CAPITAL:** Rangoon (Yangon)
POPULATION: 45.6 million **CURRENCY:** Kyat **OFFICIAL LANGUAGE:** Burmese (Myanmar)

1948
1948
Jan 4
BUR
+6.5
+95
.mm

FORMING THE EASTERN SHORES of the Bay of Bengal and the Andaman Sea in southeast Asia, Burma is mountainous in the north, while the once-forested, fertile Irrawaddy basin occupies most of the country. Burma gained independence from British colonial control in 1948 and has recently suffered widespread political repression and ethnic conflict. In 1990, the National League for Democracy (NLD) gained a majority in free elections but was prevented from taking power by the military. Rich in natural resources, which include fisheries and teak forests, Burma's economy remains mostly agricultural.

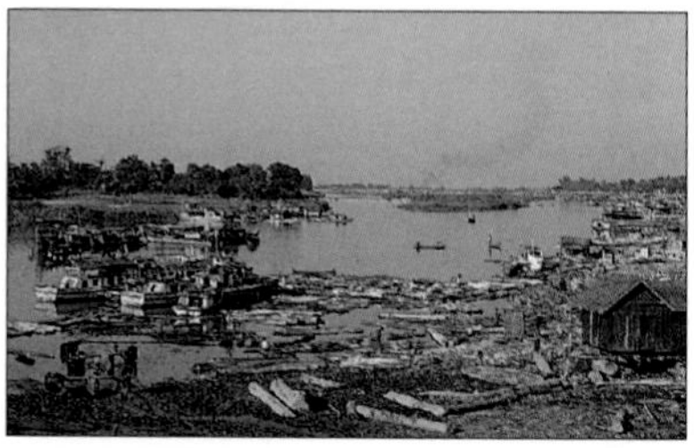

***Transporting timber** on the Irrawaddy River near Mandalay. Burma once had the world's largest reserves of teak.*

CLIMATE

Tropical/mountain

WEATHER CHART

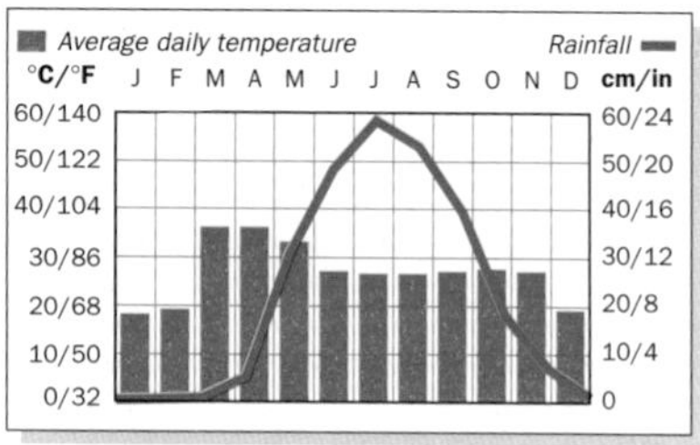
Average daily temperature
Rainfall
°C/°F
J F M A M J J A S O N D
cm/in
60/140
50/122
40/104
30/86
20/68
10/50
0/32
60/24
50/20
40/16
30/12
20/8
10/4
0

There are three seasons: the wet season, when rainfall in the far south Tenasserim region and Irrawaddy delta can reach 500 cm (197 in); summer, when northern Burma experiences 50°C (122°F) and 100% humidity; and winter, when it is rarely cooler than 15°C (59°F) except in the northern mountains.

TRANSPORTATION

Drive on right

Mingaladon, Rangoon 580,000 passengers

124 ships 492,306 grt

THE TRANSPORTATION NETWORK

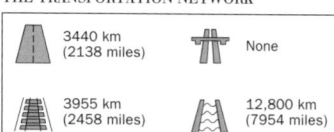

3440 km (2138 miles)

None

3955 km (2458 miles)

12,800 km (7954 miles)

Most current construction projects are linked to the booming China–Burma border trade, the majority of which was legalized in 1989. Old bridges and roads (including the famous Burma, Ledo, and Silk Roads, all key routes into China) are being renewed, and new ones built with Chinese aid. Although it will be easier to distribute key products, including opium, the motives for their construction are military as well as commercial. The state has relaxed its monopoly on transportation: since 1988, private bus companies have been given licenses to operate. Air and rail routes, however, remain under government control.

TOURISM

Visitors : Population 1:219

208,000 visitors

Up 5% in 2000

MAIN TOURIST ARRIVALS

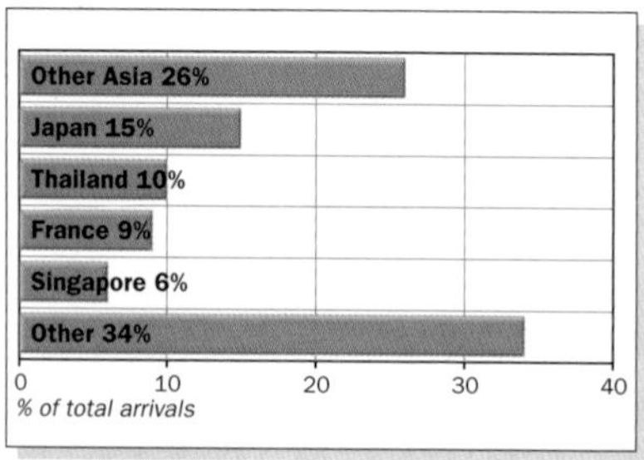
Other Asia 26%
Japan 15%
Thailand 10%
France 9%
Singapore 6%
Other 34%
0
10
20
30
40
% of total arrivals

From 1962 until 1988, tourists visiting Burma's palaces, Buddhist temples, and shrines were limited to one-week stays. However, Burma now has an open-door policy, designed to attract foreign exchange. Old hotels are being renovated and new ones built in joint ventures with private companies. Much of the finance comes from Singapore, Japan, and South Korea. China is also helping to build an international airport at Mandalay. There were widespread claims that the junta had used forced labor to restore historic landmarks before "visit Burma" year in 1996.

PEOPLE

Pop. density medium

Burmese, Karen, Shan, Chin, Kachin, Mon, Palaung, Wa

69/km² (180/mi²)

THE URBAN/RURAL POPULATION SPLIT

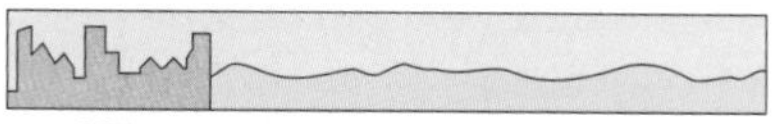
27%
73%

RELIGIOUS PERSUASION

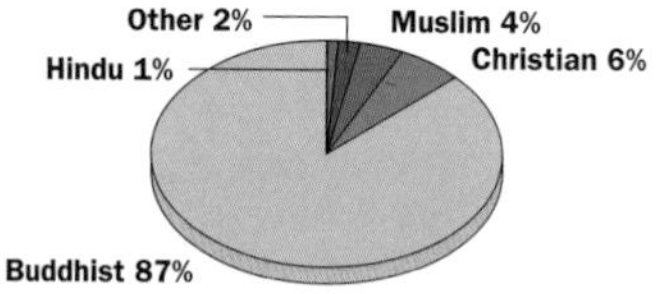
Other 2%
Muslim 4%
Hindu 1%
Christian 6%
Buddhist 87%

ETHNIC MAKEUP

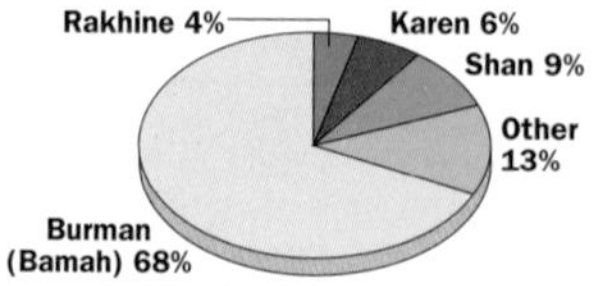
Rakhine 4%
Karen 6%
Shan 9%
Other 13%
Burman (Bamah) 68%

There is considerable ethnic tension between the Burman majority and the smaller ethnic groups. At independence the Shan, Karen, Kachin, Mon, Karenni, and Chin all unsuccessfully demanded their own state within a federation. They kept their demands alive with guerrilla activity against the state; in 1988 they united in common cause against the military dictatorship. Almost all factions had signed peace treaties with the junta by early 1996; the Shan agreed to a cease-fire in 2000, but fighting broke out again a few months later.

A savage history, mainly of Burman repression of smaller groups, still plays a large part in the mistrust felt by the minorities for the Burman. Each group maintains a distinct cultural identity. While the Burman claim racial purity, in fact many of them are of mixed blood or ethnically Chinese.

Family life in Burma is still based around the extended family. Women have a prominent role, and access to education. Many run or own businesses in their own right. However, top jobs in government are still held almost exclusively by men.

POPULATION AGE BREAKDOWN

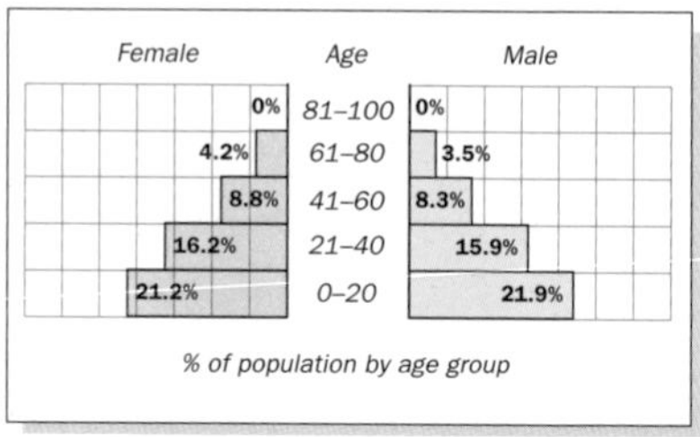
Female
Age
Male
0%
81–100
0%
4.2%
61–80
3.5%
8.8%
41–60
8.3%
16.2%
21–40
15.9%
21.2%
0–20
21.9%
% of population by age group

POLITICS

No multiparty elections

1990/suspended

Chairman Than Shwe

AT THE LAST ELECTION

Constituent Assembly 485 seats

2% NUP
1% MNDF
1% NDP
81% NLD
5% SNLD
2% RDL
8% Others

NLD = National League for Democracy
SNLD = Shan National League for Democracy
NUP = National Unity Party
RDL = Rakhine Democracy League
MNDF = Mon National Democratic Front
NDP = National Democratic Party for Human Rights

A Constituent Assembly, responsible for the drafting of a new constitution and with no legislative power, was elected in 1990, but prevented from convening by the SLORC.

Burma is ruled by the military-backed State Peace and Development Council (SPDC), under General Than Shwe.

MAIN POLITICAL ISSUES

Restoring democracy
Burma is ruled by the military with little regard to human rights. Opposition is not tolerated, and torture and killings are commonplace. Most of the ethnic rebel groups have agreed cease-fire terms with the regime. The focal point of opposition is Aung San Suu Kyi. She has been in and out of house arrest since 1995, although the junta is wary of an outright clampdown. Moves toward official dialogue in early 2001 raised hopes for a break in the deadlock.

Refugees
One million people have been displaced since 1988 to Burma's border regions. They include Rohingya Muslims who were repatriated from Bangladesh.

PROFILE

The military seized power in 1988 at the height of mass protests calling for the restoration of democracy, and the State Law and Order Restoration Council (SLORC) was formed soon afterwards. Elections won in 1990 by the NLD were disregarded, and the SLORC suppressed the prodemocracy opposition. The replacement of the SLORC by the SPDC in 1997 brought no major changes. Ethnic rebellion in border regions was effectively quelled in 1996, but low levels of fighting continued.

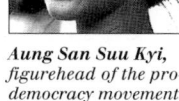

Aung San Suu Kyi, figurehead of the prodemocracy movement.

Gen. Than Shwe, leader of the military junta since 1992.

BURMA

Total Land Area : 657 540 sq. km (253 876 sq. miles)

Hkakabo Razi 5881m
CHINA
INDIA
BANGLADESH
LAOS
THAILAND
Myitkyina
Bhamo
Katha
Mawlaik
Falam
Shwebo
Lashio
Monywa
Mandalay
Maymyo
Sagaing
Amarapura
Myingyan
Kyaukse
Pakokku
Pagan
SHAN PLATEAU
Chauk
Meiktila
Taunggyi
Yenangyaung
Magwe
Yamethin
Minbu
Sittwe
Oyster I.
Taungdwingyi
Pyinmana
Loikaw
Kyaukpyu
Ramree I.
Thayetmyo
Allanmyo
Cheduba I.
Sandoway
Prome
Toungoo
Paungde
Pyu
Myanaung
Nyaunglebin
Letpadan
Pyuntaza
Henzada
Tharrawaddy
Pegu
Thonze
Kyaikto
Bassein
Insein
Kayan
Syriam
Thaton
Myaungmya
Twante
RANGOON
Martaban
Moulmeingyun
Kyaiklat
Moulmein
Labutta
Bogale
Pyapon
Mudon
Kyaikkami
Mouths of the Irrawaddy
Ye
Preparis I.
Great Coco I.
Little Coco I.
North Andaman (to INDIA)
Tavoy
BILAUKTAUNG RANGE
Kadan I.
Mergui
MERGUI ARCHIPELAGO
Saganthit I.
Letsok-Aw I.
Kanmaw I.
Lanbi I.
Isthmus of Kra
BAY OF BENGAL
ANDAMAN SEA
INDIAN OCEAN
Irrawaddy
Chindwin
Mali Hka
Nmai Hka
Shweli
Myitnge
Mekong
Salween
Sittang
Thaungyin
ARAKAN YOMA
25°
20°
15°
10°
95°
100°
N
0 200 km
0 200 miles
POPULATION
over 1 000 000
over 500 000
over 100 000
over 50 000
over 10 000
under 10 000
LAND HEIGHT
4000m/13 124ft
2000m/6562ft
1000m/3281ft
500m/1640ft
200m/656ft
Sea Level

WORLD AFFAIRS

Joined UN in 1948

CP | IAEA | ASEAN | NAM | WTO

Burma's key relationship is with China, which backs the SPDC military regime and is a major supplier of weapons to the Burmese army. The relationship allows China access to the Indian Ocean and gives it influence over a regime dependent on its support. While Burma's neighbors fear that the arrangement could destabilize the whole of the Asia–Pacific region, many favor a policy of "constructive engagement" with the SPDC. In July 1997, Burma was admitted to ASEAN, despite continuing concerns about its human rights record. The EU and western members of the UN have strongly condemned the human rights violations in Burma and threatened to impose economic sanctions in response to the regime's policies. In practice, however, the West maintains an ambivalent position. Economic ties are expanding, particularly between SPDC-owned state enterprises and Western multinationals which have an interest in Burmese offshore oil and gas drilling sectors.

CHRONOLOGY

From the 11th century, Burma's many ethnic groups came under the rule of three Tibeto-Burman dynasties, interspersed with periods of rule by the Mongols and the Mon. The Third Dynasty came into conflict with the British in India, sparking the Anglo-Burmese wars of 1824, 1852, and 1885.

- **1886** Burma becomes a province of British India.
- **1930–1931** Economic depression triggers unrest.
- **1937** Separation from India.
- **1942** Japan invades.
- **1945** Antifascist People's Freedom League (AFPFL), led by Aung San, helps Allies reoccupy country.
- **1947** UK agrees to Burmese independence. Aung San wins elections, but is assassinated.
- **1948** Independence under new prime minister, U Nu, who initiates socialist policies. Revolts by ethnic separatists, notably Karen liberation struggle.
- **1958** Ruling AFPFL splits into two. Shan liberation struggle begins.
- **1960** U Nu's faction wins elections.
- **1961** Kachin rebellion begins.

B

CHRONOLOGY *continued*

- **1962** Gen. Ne Win stages military coup. "New Order" policy of "Buddhist Socialism" deepens international isolation. Mining and other industries nationalized. Free trade prohibited.
- **1964** Socialist Program Party declared sole legal party.
- **1976** Social unrest. Attempted military coup. Ethnic liberation groups gain control of 40% of country.
- **1982** Nonindigenous people barred from public office.
- **1988** Thousands die in student riots. Ne Win resigns. Martial law. Aung San Suu Kyi, daughter of Aung San, and others form NLD. Gen. Saw Maung leads military coup. State Law and Order Restoration Council (SLORC) takes power. Ethnic resistance groups form Democratic Alliance of Burma.
- **1989** Army arrests NLD leaders and steps up antirebel activity. Officially renamed Union of Myanmar.
- **1990** Elections permitted. NLD wins landslide. SLORC remains in power, however. More NLD leaders arrested.
- **1991** Aung San Suu Kyi awarded Nobel Peace Prize.
- **1992** Gen. Than Shwe takes over as SLORC leader.
- **1995** Aung San Suu Kyi released from house arrest.
- **1996** Demonstrations against approval of Burma's membership of ASEAN.
- **1997** Ruling SLORC renamed State Peace and Development Council (SPDC). US imposes sanctions and bans further investment in Burma.
- **1998** NLD sets deadline for convening parliament; junta refuses.
- **1999** Aung San Suu Kyi rejects conditions set by SPDC for visiting the UK to see her husband, Michael Aris, who dies of cancer.
- **2000** Negotiations between junta and NLD begin.

AID

Recipient

$73m (receipts) — Up 24% in 1999

In 1988, Western countries, the World Bank, and certain UN agencies such as the UNDP halted bilateral aid. The UN has, however, continued funding some development projects through its Drug Control Program and the World Health Organization. The largest bilateral donor is China. Since 1997 the USA has tightened economic sanctions to force the regime to negotiate with the NLD.

DEFENSE

No compulsory military service

$2bn — Down 7% in 1999

BURMESE ARMED FORCES

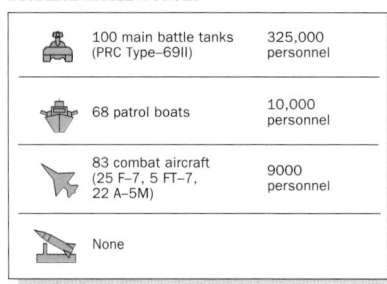

100 main battle tanks (PRC Type–69II)	325,000 personnel
68 patrol boats	10,000 personnel
83 combat aircraft (25 F-7, 5 FT-7, 22 A-5M)	9000 personnel
None	

The SPDC has steadily obtained modern weapons and military technology from around the world, primarily from China but also from France, Germany, Sweden, and the former Yugoslavia. Since 1989, China alone has delivered over $1 billion worth of arms to Burma, including tanks and jet fighters.

Burma's growing military capability is used mainly to control internal dissent, and the army has suppressed most ethnic insurgent campaigns by utilizing its military superiority and cutting numerous deals with rebel leaders. In early 1996 troops took control of the headquarters of the notorious Shan "drug warlord," Khun Sa, in what was widely seen as a "negotiated takeover."

ECONOMICS

Inflation 27.1% p.a. (1990–1999)

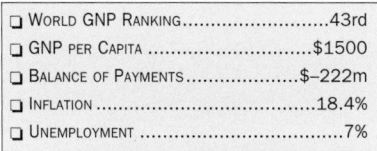

$73.9bn — 6.250–6.526 kyats

SCORE CARD

World GNP Ranking	43rd
GNP per Capita	$1500
Balance of Payments	$-222m
Inflation	18.4%
Unemployment	7%

EXPORTS

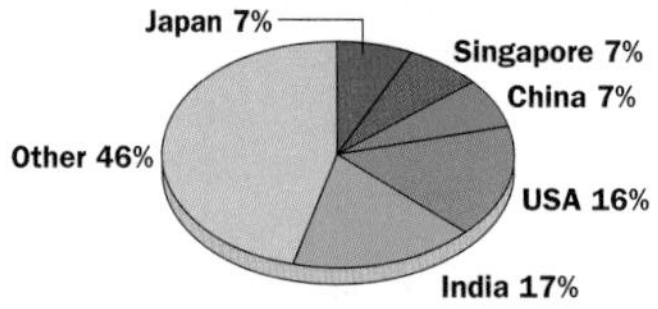
Japan 7%
Singapore 7%
China 7%
Other 46%
USA 16%
India 17%

IMPORTS

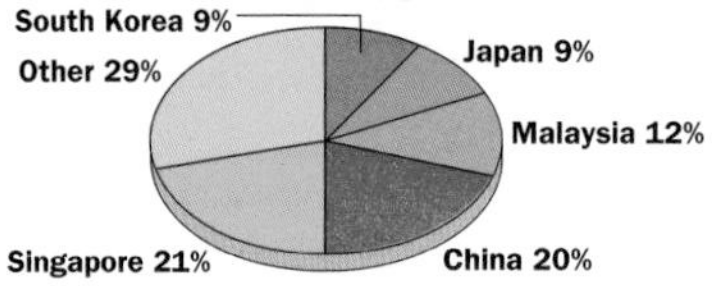
South Korea 9%
Other 29%
Japan 9%
Malaysia 12%
Singapore 21%
China 20%

Strengths

Very rich in natural resources: fertile soil, rich fisheries, timber including diminishing teak reserves, gems, offshore natural gas, and oil.

Weaknesses

Shortage of skilled labor, managers, and technicians. Rudimentary financial systems and institutions. Nationwide black market. Huge external debt. Dependence on imported manufactures.

Profile

Burma's economy is agriculture-based and functions mainly on a cash and barter system. Its key industries are controlled by military-run state enterprises. Every aspect of economic life is permeated by a black market, where prices are rocketing – a reaction to official price controls.

ECONOMIC PERFORMANCE INDICATOR

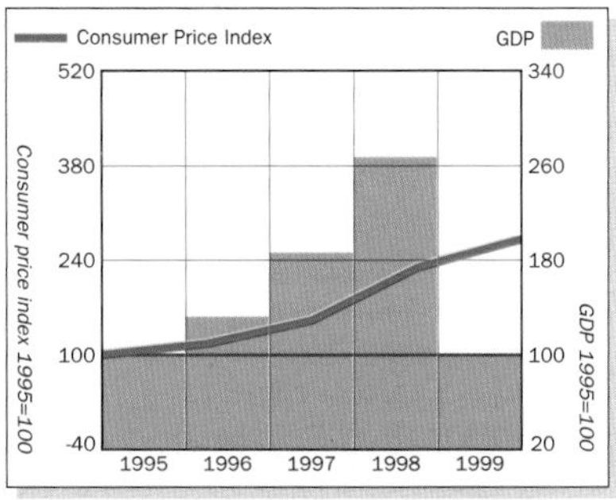
Consumer Price Index
GDP
520
380
240
100
-40
340
260
180
100
20
1995
1996
1997
1998
1999
Consumer price index 1995=100
GDP 1995=100

Since 1989, the SPDC's open-door market-economy policy has brought a flood of foreign investment in oil and gas (by Western companies), and forestry, tourism, and mining (by Asian companies). The recent boom in trade with China has turned less developed Upper Burma into a thriving business center. A narcotics-eradication program has been initiated in the northeastern border states, which account for about 60% of the world's heroin, by encouraging farmers to grow food crops instead of poppy. Few plans exist for the manufacturing sector, however, and dependence on imports continues.

BURMA : MAJOR BUSINESSES

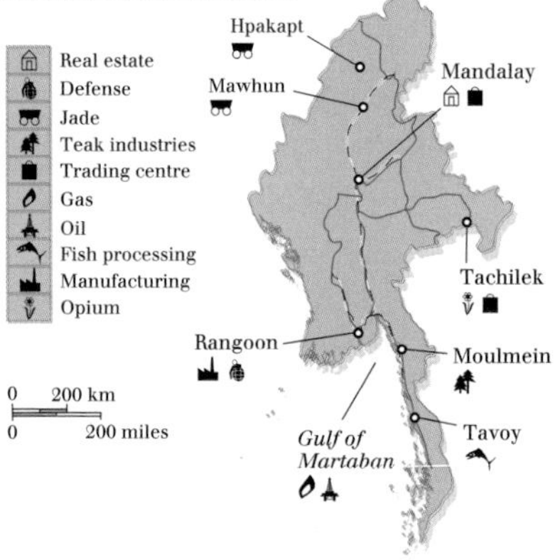
Real estate
Defense
Jade
Teak industries
Trading centre
Gas
Oil
Fish processing
Manufacturing
Opium
Hpakant
Mandalay
Mawhun
Tachilek
Rangoon
Moulmein
Tavoy
Gulf of Martaban
0 200 km
0 200 miles

B

RESOURCES

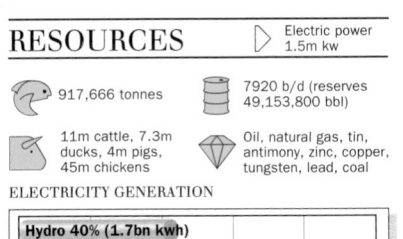

Electric power 1.5m kw

917,666 tonnes

7920 b/d (reserves 49,153,800 bbl)

11m cattle, 7.3m ducks, 4m pigs, 45m chickens

Oil, natural gas, tin, antimony, zinc, copper, tungsten, lead, coal

ELECTRICITY GENERATION

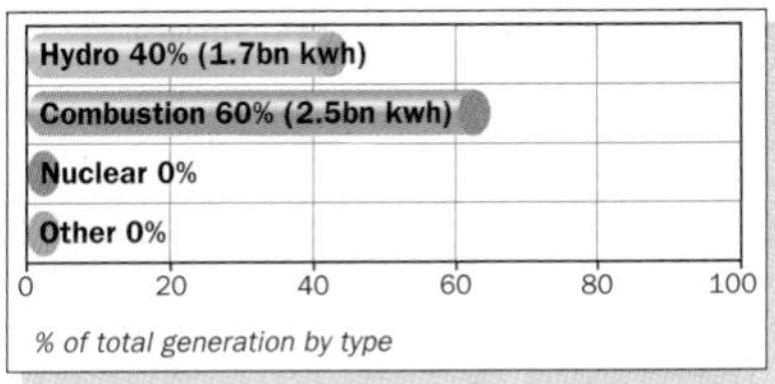
Hydro 40% (1.7bn kwh)
Combustion 60% (2.5bn kwh)
Nuclear 0%
Other 0%
0
20
40
60
80
100
% of total generation by type

Burma is the world's largest teak exporter. It is also a producer of pearls, rubies, and other gems. Foreign capital is funding exploration for natural gas and oil in the Tenasserim strip. Burma suffers from energy shortages, however.

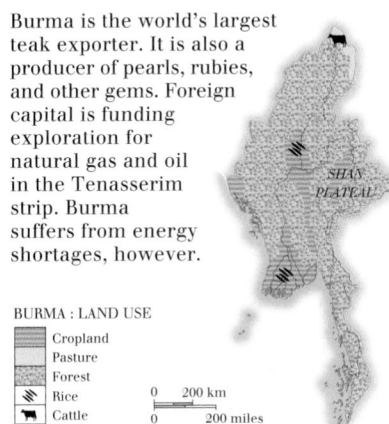

SHAN PLATEAU

BURMA : LAND USE

Cropland
Pasture
Forest
Rice
Cattle

0 200 km
0 200 miles

ENVIRONMENT

Not available

1%

0.2 tonnes per capita

ENVIRONMENTAL TREATIES

No	Yes	Yes
No	No	No

Deforestation is a major problem, and it has increased since the 1988 coup. Chinese companies have been given unrestricted logging concessions.

MEDIA

TV ownership low

Daily newspaper circulation 10 per 1000 people

PUBLISHING AND BROADCAST MEDIA

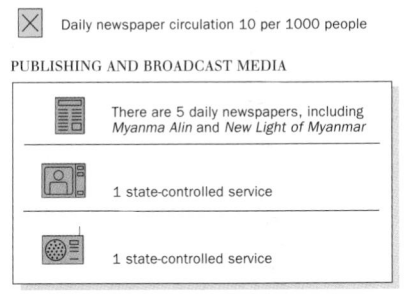

There are 5 daily newspapers, including *Myanma Alin* and *New Light of Myanmar*

1 state-controlled service

1 state-controlled service

Political dissent of any kind is a criminal offense. An underground prodemocracy press produces antigovernment material.

CRIME

Death penalty used

Burma does not publish prison figures

Up 1% 1996–1998

CRIME RATES

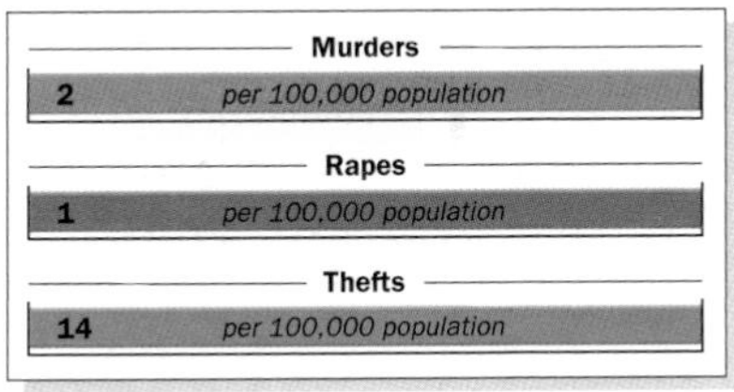
Murders
2 per 100,000 population
Rapes
1 per 100,000 population
Thefts
14 per 100,000 population

Levels of robbery, murder, bribery, corruption, embezzlement, and black marketeering are high, compared with similar totalitarian regimes. The state is guilty of illegal activity. The UN reports regularly on human rights abuses against civilians, and the murder of innocent civilians including children, women, Buddhist monks, students, minorities, and political dissidents.

There is a nominal civilian judicial system in Burma, but in practice all judges and lawyers are appointed by the junta and all legal functions are executed by the SPDC. The most common charge is that of sedition against the state or the army under the 1975 "Law to Protect the State from Destructionists." Among the SPDC's frequent arbitrary "notices" is Order 2/88, prohibiting assemblies of more than five persons. Most detainees have no legal rights of representation and are either jailed, used as forced labor or put under house arrest without public trial. Amnesty International is banned.

EDUCATION

School leaving age: 10

85%

385,300 students

THE EDUCATION SYSTEM

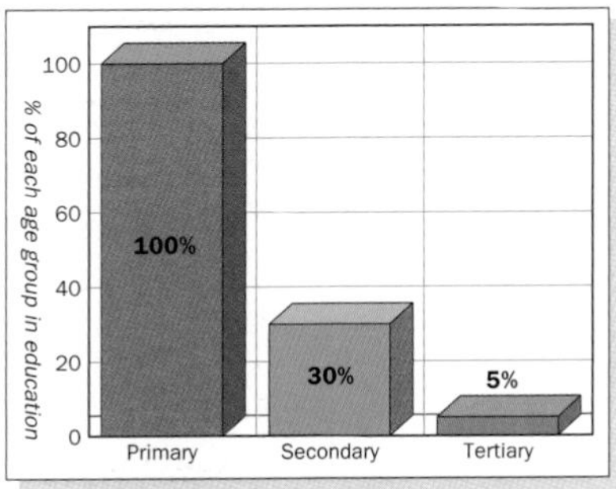
100
80
60
40
20
0
% of each age group in education
100%
30%
5%
Primary
Secondary
Tertiary

The education system provides ten years of schooling. Ethnic-language schools are discouraged. A shortage of teachers, many of whom have left or are in jail, has disrupted education. All but two universities were closed in the late 1990s by the regime, but quietly reopened in 2000. The NLD has criticized the shortened and "sanitized" courses on offer.

HEALTH

Welfare state health benefits

1 per 3333 people

Malaria, fevers, heart and diarrheal diseases

Leprosy, although it affects relatively few people compared with other diseases, has a higher prevalence in Burma than in the rest of Asia. In the last few years Burma has seen an increase in the incidence of malaria.

The growing number of AIDS cases is largely due to migrant prostitution across the Thai–Burmese border. They put an additional strain on health facilities, which are well developed but not comprehensive.

SPENDING

GDP/cap. increase

CONSUMPTION AND SPENDING

1 per 1000 population

6 per 1000 population

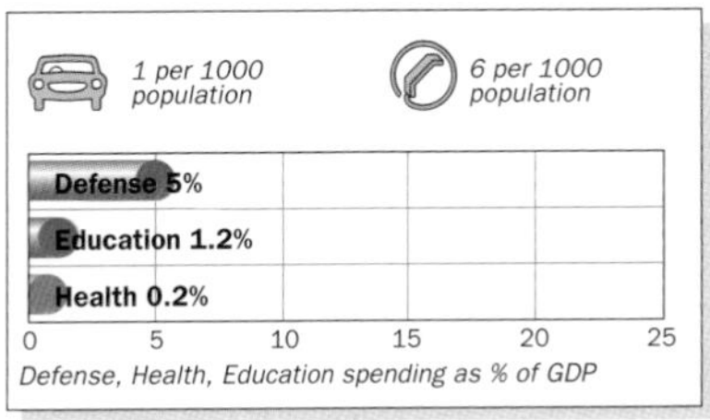
Defense 5%
Education 1.2%
Health 0.2%
0
5
10
15
20
25
Defense, Health, Education spending as % of GDP

The state monopoly of the production and distribution of goods by rationing under Gen. Ne Win's administration led to an increase in corruption and the rise of a nationwide black market, with huge disparities between official and unofficial prices. Only the military elite and their supporters could afford to live well. The situation has not changed significantly since 1988. Giant military enterprises grouped under a Defense Services holding company, whose capital amounts to 10% of GDP, now reap wealth and distribute privileges for a minority. Nevertheless, traditional social and economic mobility still exists. Climbing the socioeconomic ladder is mainly a matter of loyalty to the military. Dissidents forced out of their jobs and hill tribes form the poorest groups.

WORLD RANKING

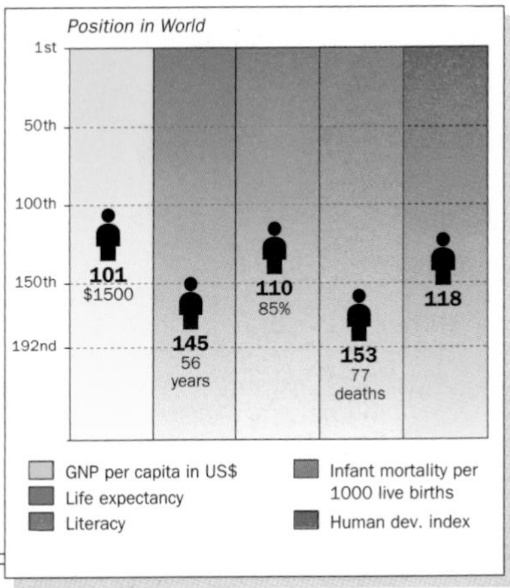
Position in World
1st
50th
100th
150th
192nd
101
$1500
145
56
years
110
85%
153
77
deaths
118
GNP per capita in US$
Life expectancy
Literacy
Infant mortality per 1000 live births
Human dev. index

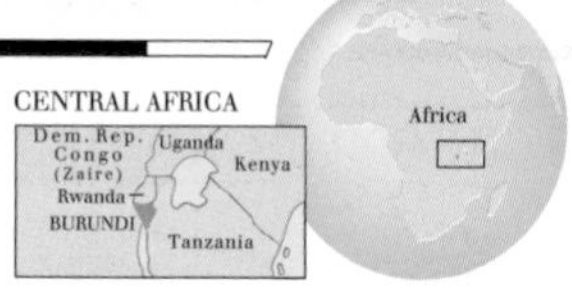
CENTRAL AFRICA
Dem. Rep. Congo (Zaire)
Uganda
Kenya
Rwanda
BURUNDI
Tanzania
Africa

BURUNDI

OFFICIAL NAME: Republic of Burundi **CAPITAL:** Bujumbura
POPULATION: 6.7 million **CURRENCY:** Burundi franc **OFFICIAL LANGUAGES:** French and Kirundi

1962 | 1962 | July 1 | RU | +2 | +257 | .bi

LANDLOCKED BURUNDI lies just south of the equator on the Nile–Congo watershed. Lake Tanganyika forms part of its border with Congo (former Zaire). Tension between the Hutu majority and the dominant Tutsi minority remains the main factor in politics. The current political unrest dates from the assassination of the first-ever Hutu president in a coup by the Tutsi-dominated army in October 1993, which sparked terrible violence.

Pig farming and fish ponds. The majority of Burundi's population depends on subsistence farming.

CLIMATE

Tropical wet & dry

WEATHER CHART

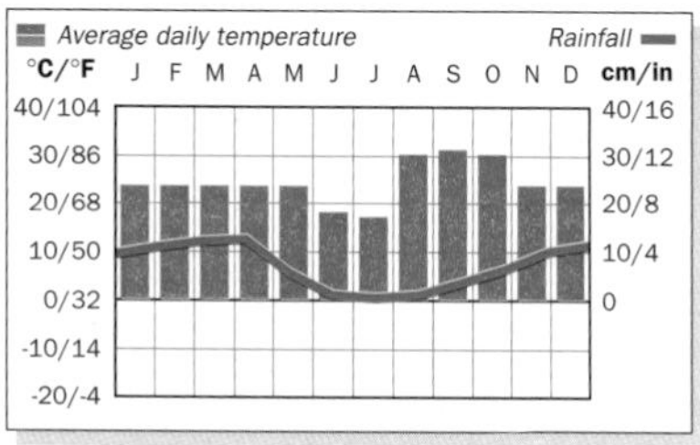
Average daily temperature
Rainfall
°C/°F
J F M A M J J A S O N D
cm/in
40/104
30/86
20/68
10/50
0/32
-10/14
-20/-4
40/16
30/12
20/8
10/4
0

Burundi is temperate with high humidity, much cloud, and frequent heavy rain. The highlands have frost.

TRANSPORTATION

Drive on right

Bujumbura International 57,934 passengers

Has no fleet

THE TRANSPORTATION NETWORK

1028 km (639 miles)

None

None

Lake Tanganyika is navigable

The dense road network has been rehabilitated. There are plans for a railroad to link Burundi with Rwanda, Uganda, and Tanzania.

TOURISM

Visitors : Population 1:223

30,000 visitors

Up 15% in 2000

MAIN TOURIST ARRIVALS

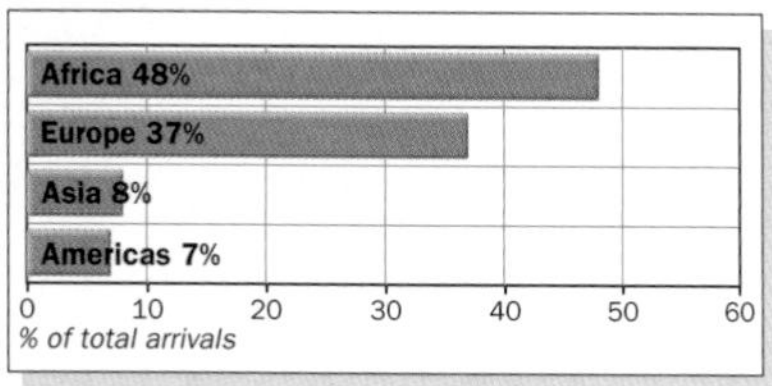
Africa 48%
Europe 37%
Asia 8%
Americas 7%
0
10
20
30
40
50
60
% of total arrivals

A lack of basic infrastructure and violent political strife deter tourists. The industry has limited potential, since Burundi lacks its neighbors' spectacular scenery and game parks.

PEOPLE

Pop. density high

Kirundi, French, Swahili

261/km² (677/mi²)

THE URBAN/RURAL POPULATION SPLIT

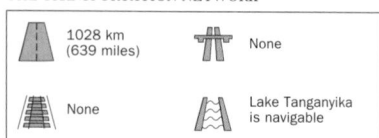

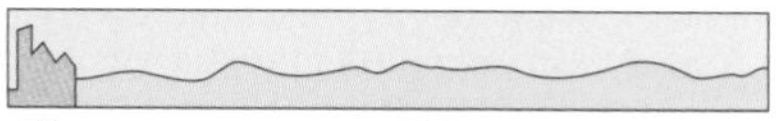
9%
91%

ETHNIC MAKEUP

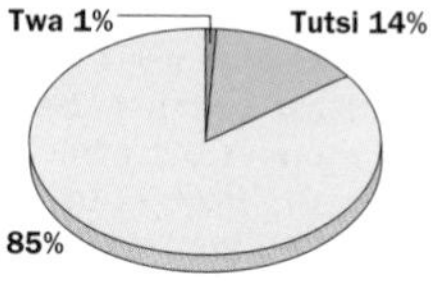
Twa 1%
Tutsi 14%
Hutu 85%

Burundi's history has been marked by violent conflict between the majority Hutu and the Tutsi, formerly the political elite, who still control the army. Large-scale massacres have occurred repeatedly over the past two decades. Hundreds of thousands of people, mostly Hutu, have been killed in political and ethnic conflict since October 1993. However, the Twa pygmies have not been greatly affected. Most Burundians are subsistence farmers; the vast majority are Roman Catholic.

POLITICS

No multiparty elections

1998/uncertain

President Pierre Buyoya

AT THE LAST ELECTION

Transitional National Assembly 117 seats

56% Frodebu
14% UPRONA
30% Others

Frodebu = Front for Democracy in Burundi
UPRONA = Union for National Progress

The Transitional National Assembly, inaugurated in July 1998, consisted of the members of the previous Assembly (or their replacements from the same party), single members of parties not formerly represented, and members of "civil society."

From 1966, the Tutsi dominated the only legal political party UPRONA, as well as the civil service, the judiciary, and the army. Tutsi President Buyoya attempted to promote greater racial integration. This backfired in a bloody coup in 1993 when the first Hutu president, Melchior Ndadaye of Frodebu, was assassinated four months after his election, and hundreds of thousands of Hutu were killed by the army or fled to neighboring countries. The situation worsened in 1994 as the country plunged into a vicious civil war between the Tutsi-dominated army and Hutu militias. Buyoya returned to power in a military coup in mid-1996, but despite his efforts to regain international acceptance, an economic boycott by neighboring countries caused serious damage. Attempts to organize a cease-fire in October 2000 failed amid renewed violence, but talks began again in January 2001 and a peace agreement was forged in July.

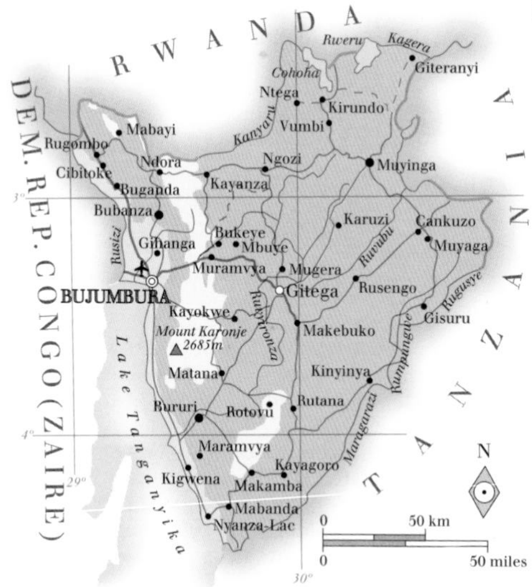
RWANDA
DEM. REP. CONGO (ZAIRE)
TANZANIA
Rweru
Kagera
Giteranyi
Cohoha
Ntega
Kirundo
Vumbi
Kanyaru
Mabayi
Rugombo
Cibitoke
Ndora
Bugarda
Kayanza
Ngozi
Muyinga
Bubanza
Karuzi
Cankuzo
Muyaga
Rusizi
Gihanga
Bukeye
Mbuye
Ruvubu
Muramvya
Mugera
BUJUMBURA
Gitega
Rusengo
Ruvuvu
Kayokwe
Ruvyironza
Gisuru
Mount Karonje 2685m
Makebuko
Lake Tanganyika
Matana
Kinyinya
Rumpungwe
Bururi
Rotovu
Rutana
Maramvya
Malagarazi
Kigwena
Kayagoro
Makamba
Mabanda
Nyanza-Lac
N
0 50 km
0 50 miles
29°
30°
3°
4°

BURUNDI

Total Land Area : 25 650 sq. km (9 903 sq. miles)

LAND HEIGHT
2000m/6562ft
1000m/3281ft
500m/1640ft

POPULATION
over 100 000
over 50 000
over 10 000
under 10 000

WORLD AFFAIRS

Joined UN in 1962

ACP | CEPGL | COMESA | OIF | OAU

Since 1995 Burundi has resisted proposals for UN/OAU intervention to prevent further bloodshed.

AID

Recipient

$74m (receipts)

Down 4% in 1999

The flight of hundreds of thousands of people since 1993 has disrupted agriculture, and large numbers remain dependent on UN food aid.

DEFENSE

No compulsory military service

$69m

Down 16% in 1999

The 40,000-strong army is run by Tutsi. The attempt to bring Hutu into officer ranks was a major factor behind the 1993 coup. The army seized power again in 1996, and a state of virtual civil war has existed between it and rebel Hutu militias. The miltary includes an air wing and a marine police force.

ECONOMICS

Inflation 11.8% p.a. (1990–1999)

$823m

631.2–780.4 Burundi francs

SCORE CARD

- World GNP Ranking........159th
- GNP per Capita........$120
- Balance of Payments........$–27m
- Inflation........3.4%
- Unemployment.......Widespread underemployment

STRENGTHS
Small quantities of gold and tungsten. Potential of massive nickel reserves and oil in Lake Tanganyika.

WEAKNESSES
Harsh regional sanctions since 1996 coup. Overwhelmingly agricultural economy (91% of labor force) under pressure from high birthrate. Little prospect of lasting political stability.

EXPORTS

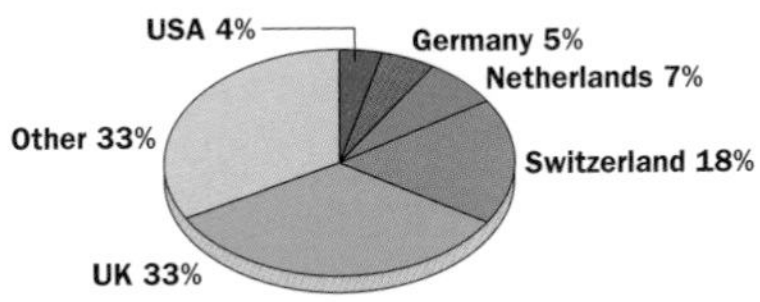
USA 4%
Germany 5%
Netherlands 7%
Switzerland 18%
Other 33%
UK 33%

IMPORTS

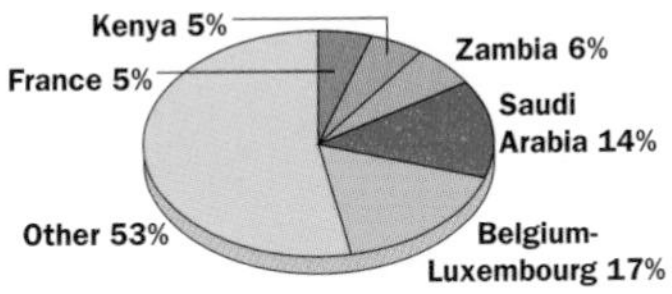
Kenya 5%
Zambia 6%
France 5%
Saudi Arabia 14%
Other 53%
Belgium-Luxembourg 17%

RESOURCES

Electric power 43,000 kw

20,306 tonnes

Not an oil producer and has no refineries

550,000 goats, 320,000 cattle, 4m chickens

Gold, tungsten, nickel, vanadium, uranium

Burundi has around 5% of the world's nickel reserves. Extraction, however, is not economically viable. There are also deposits of gold and vanadium. Surveys in the 1980s detected oil reserves below Lake Tanganyika, but production has yet to begin. Burundi imports gasoline from Iran and electricity from Congo (former Zaire). New HEP plants at Mugera and Rwegura, in the far north, are intended to meet most domestic electricity requirements.

ENVIRONMENT

Sustainability rank: 120th

6%

0.03 tonnes per capita

Only 2% of Burundi is forest and even this is now under pressure from one of Africa's highest birthrates. Burundi suffers from the problems associated with deforestation, particularly soil erosion. Some soils are also being exhausted from overuse. Several tree-planting programs have been introduced. UNESCO is also running ecological education initiatives at village level, aimed at women farmers.

MEDIA

TV ownership low

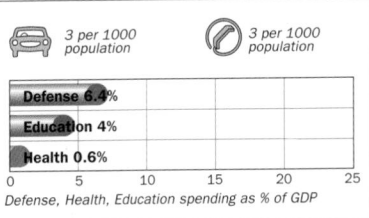

Daily newspaper circulation 3 per 1000 people

PUBLISHING AND BROADCAST MEDIA

There is 1 daily newspaper, *Le Renouveau du Burundi*, published by the government

1 state-controlled service

1 state-owned service, independent stations

Pro-Hutu/anti-Tutsi radio stations have been broadcasting since 1994. Radio Hope, an EU-funded station promoting peace, was launched in 1996.

CRIME

Death penalty used

Burundi does not publish prison figures

Up 78% 1990–1998

Burundi has an appalling human rights record. There have been frequent massacres of Hutu by the army. The worst pogroms occurred in 1972, 1988, 1993, and 1994.

EDUCATION

School leaving age: 13

48%

4256 students

Elementary schooling begins at seven, and is compulsory, though further schooling is not. There are around 70 elementary schoolchildren per teacher. There is one university.

CHRONOLOGY

From the 16th century, Burundi (formerly Urundi) was ruled by the minority Tutsi with the majority Hutu as their serfs. Merged with Rwanda, Burundi was controlled by Germany from 1884 and by Belgium from 1919.

- **1946** UN trust territory.
- **1959** Split from Rwanda.
- **1962** Independence.
- **1966** Army overthrows monarchy.
- **1972** 150,000 Hutu massacred.
- **1993** Ndadaye wins first free elections; killed four months later.
- **1996** Buyoya retakes power.
- **1999** Talks between warring groups.
- **2000** Renewed violence.
- **2001** Power-sharing agreement between Tutsis and Hutus.

HEALTH

No welfare state health benefits

1 per 10,000 people

Communicable infections, parasitic diseases

2.1 million people have no access to health services. By 1999 11% of the population were living with HIV/AIDS. Women have an average of seven children; very few use contraception.

SPENDING

GDP/cap. decrease

CONSUMPTION AND SPENDING

3 per 1000 population

3 per 1000 population

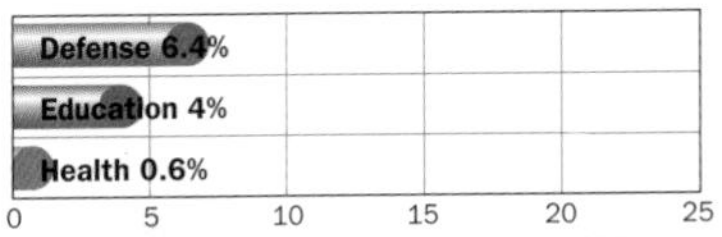
Defense 6.4%
Education 4%
Health 0.6%
0
5
10
15
20
25

Defense, Health, Education spending as % of GDP

Wealth is concentrated within the Tutsi political and business elite. Most of Burundi's people live at the level of subsistence farming.

WORLD RANKING

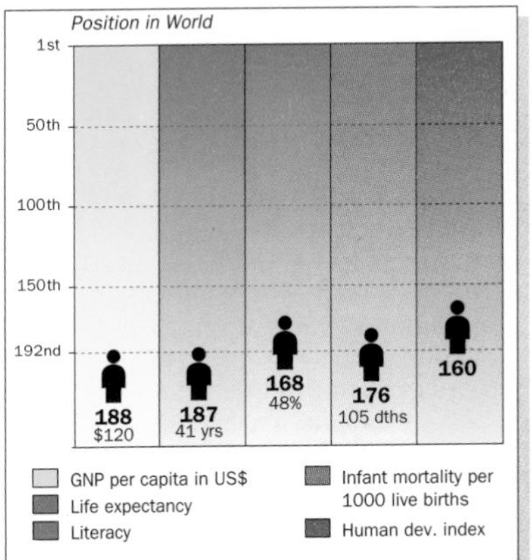
Position in World
1st
50th
100th
150th
192nd
188
$120
187
41 yrs
168
48%
176
105 dths
160
GNP per capita in US$
Life expectancy
Literacy
Infant mortality per 1000 live births
Human dev. index

CAMBODIA

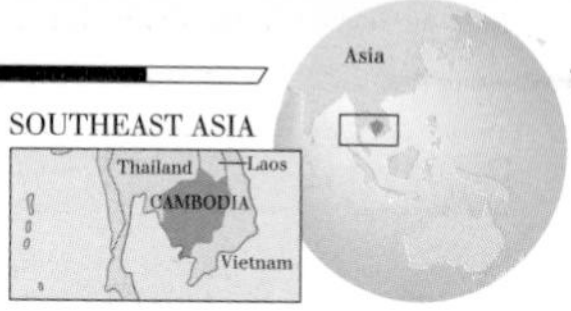
Asia
SOUTHEAST ASIA
Thailand
Laos
CAMBODIA
Vietnam

OFFICIAL NAME: Kingdom of Cambodia **CAPITAL:** Phnom Penh
POPULATION: 11.2 million **CURRENCY:** Riel **OFFICIAL LANGUAGE:** Khmer

C

1953 | 1953 | Nov 11 | K | +7 | +855 | .kh

LOCATED IN THE INDO-CHINESE peninsula in southeast Asia, Cambodia has a coastline on the Gulf of Thailand and shares borders with Thailand, Laos, and Vietnam. Its main topographical feature is the Tônlé Sap, or Great Lake, which drains into the Mekong River. Over three-quarters of Cambodia are forested, with mangroves lining the coast. Rice is the principal crop. Cambodia has emerged from two decades of civil war and invasion from Vietnam. The UN's biggest peacekeeping operation since its creation culminated in elections in 1993.

CLIMATE

Tropical monsoon

WEATHER CHART

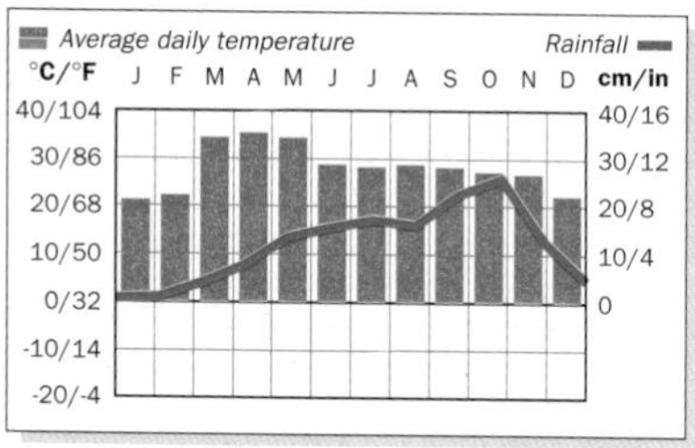
Average daily temperature
Rainfall
°C/°F J F M A M J J A S O N D cm/in
40/104 40/16
30/86 30/12
20/68 20/8
10/50 10/4
0/32 0
-10/14
-20/-4

Cambodia has a varied climate. Low-lying regions have moderate rainfall and the most consistent year-round temperatures. The dry season from December to April is characterized by high temperatures and an average of eight hours of sunshine a day. From May to September, winds are southeasterly, while from October to April they are north or northeasterly. During the rainy season, Cambodia is sultry and humid. The monsoons in 2000 caused severe flooding of the Mekong River which inundated Phnom Penh.

TRANSPORTATION

Drive on right

Pochentong, Phnom Penh
738,258 passengers

195 ships
616,400 grt

THE TRANSPORTATION NETWORK

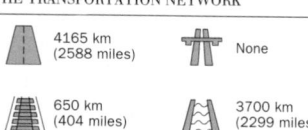

4165 km (2588 miles)
None
650 km (404 miles)
3700 km (2299 miles)

Long years of war led to a near-collapse of Cambodia's rail and road systems, which remain appalling. International aid has helped to begin rehabilitating key routes, such as Highways 3 and 5, and to rebuild the Chruoy Changvar Bridge out of Phnom Penh. The taxi-moped, bicycle, and rickshaw are the main forms of urban transportation.

Angkor Wat stands in the ruins of the ancient city of Angkor, once the capital of the Khmer empire. It is now one of Cambodia's leading tourist attractions.

TOURISM

Visitors : Population 1:42

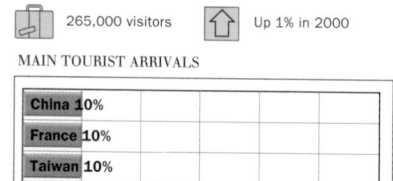

265,000 visitors
Up 1% in 2000

MAIN TOURIST ARRIVALS

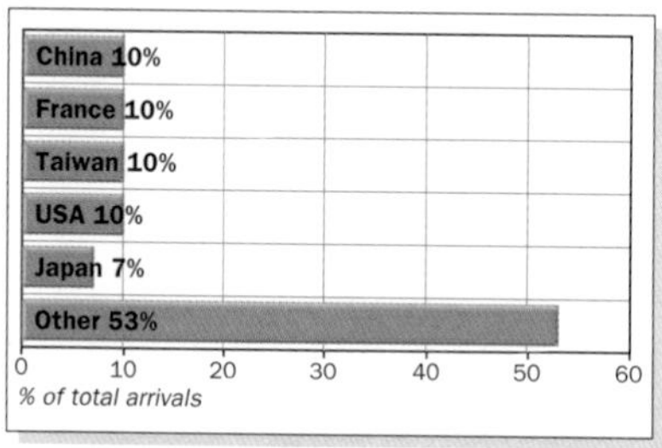
China 10%
France 10%
Taiwan 10%
USA 10%
Japan 7%
Other 53%
0 10 20 30 40 50 60
% of total arrivals

Cambodia, the center of the Khmer empire between 800 and 1400 AD, has some of the most impressive temples in southeast Asia. The most famous is at Angkor Wat, near Siemreab, which is being made safe for tourists after the Khmer Rouge relinquished control of the area in mid-1998. Kidnappings and murders of tourists by the Khmer Rouge kept Cambodia off the backpacker circuit in the mid-1990s. Once the political situation is fully stabilized, there is considerable potential, not only for adventurous independent travelers. Earnings from tourism rose in 2000.

PEOPLE

Pop. density medium

Khmer, French, Chinese, Vietnamese, Cham

63/km² (164/mi²)

THE URBAN/RURAL POPULATION SPLIT

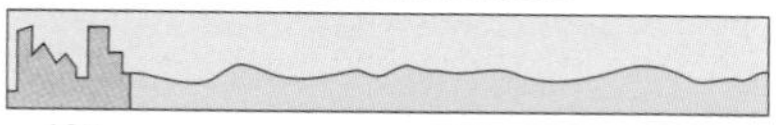
16%
84%

RELIGIOUS PERSUASION

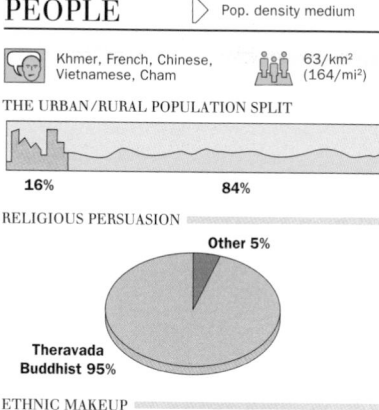

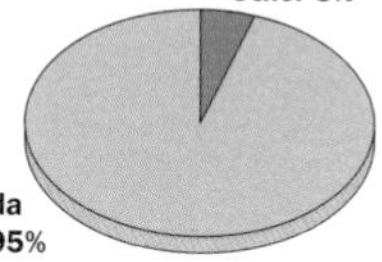
Other 5%
Theravada Buddhist 95%

ETHNIC MAKEUP

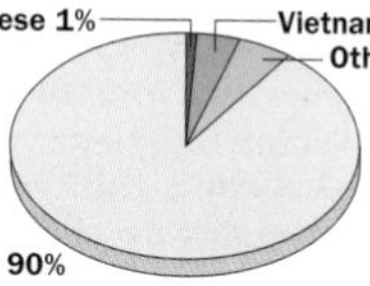
Chinese 1%
Vietnamese 4%
Other 5%
Khmer 90%

Cambodian society underwent one of the 20th century's most horrific experiments in social transformation between 1975 and 1979 under Pol Pot's Khmer Rouge regime. One in eight of the population died from warfare, starvation, overwork, or execution. Half a million more fled to Thailand. The Pol Pot regime's extreme radical beliefs led to the scrapping of money, possessions, and hierarchy. "Bourgeois" learning was despised, whereas peasants, soldiers of the revolution, and some industrial workers were officially given higher status. Boys and girls of 13 and 14 were taken from their homes, indoctrinated in the tenets of revolution, and allowed to kill those held guilty of bourgeois crimes. Violence at all levels was sanctioned in the name of revolution.

Pol Pot's regime ended with the Vietnamese invasion of 1979. Most professionals who had survived emigrated. The effects of revolution and subsequent civil war are still felt, and are reflected in the world's highest rate of orphans and widows.

POPULATION AGE BREAKDOWN

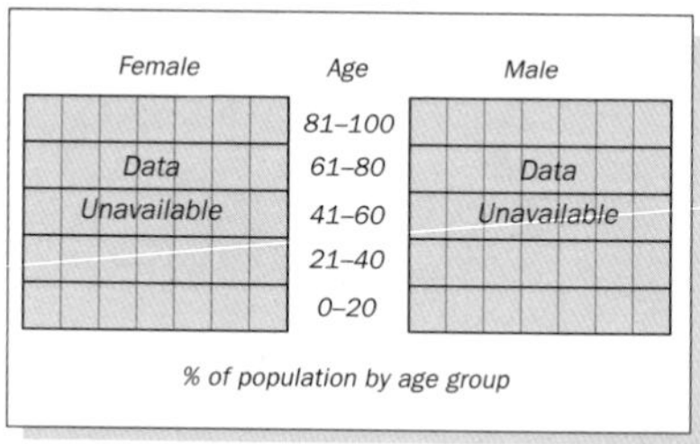
Female
Age
Male
81–100
61–80
41–60
21–40
0–20
Data Unavailable
Data Unavailable
% of population by age group

C

POLITICS

Multiparty elections

L. House 1998/2003
U. House 1999/2004

HM King Norodom Sihanouk

AT THE LAST ELECTION

National Assembly 122 seats

53%
CPP
35%
Funcinpec
12%
SRP

CPP = Cambodian People's Party
Funcinpec = United National Front for an Independent Neutral Peaceful and Cooperative Cambodia
SRP = Sam Rainsy Party

Senate 61 seats

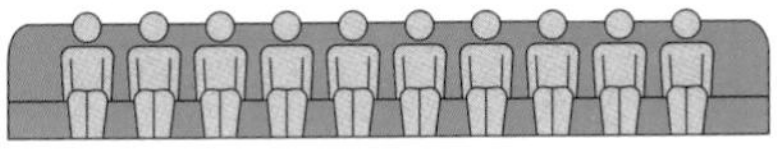

The membership of the Senate, first established in March 1999, is determined in proportion to the results of the 1998 legislative elections

Cambodia is a constitutional monarchy.

MAIN POLITICAL ISSUES

Royalist–CPP rivalry

Power struggles between the Funcinpec and the CPP came to a head with CPP leader Hun Sen's mid-1997 coup. After inconclusive elections in July 1998, the two parties re-formed their uneasy coalition in November.

Settling accounts with Khmer Rouge

The Khmer Rouge, which had resumed its armed struggle in 1993, surrendered in 1998. Mass defections and the death of Pol Pot earlier that year had weakened the group. The legislature in 2001 approved plans for a tribunal to try the surviving leaders for crimes against humanity.

PROFILE

In 1975, a US-installed government was overthrown by the Maoist Khmer Rouge under Pol Pot. That extremist and murderous regime was ousted in 1979 thanks to a Vietnamese invasion. The Khmer Rouge then joined a Western-backed anti-Vietnamese exile coalition with the supporters of the then Prince Sihanouk and the Khmer People's National Liberation Front (KPNLF), gaining UN recognition against the Vietnam-backed regime in Phnom Penh. In 1989 Vietnam withdrew its forces, paving the way for UN-supervised elections in 1993. The royalist Funcinpec emerged as the main winners and King Sihanouk formed a coalition government of national reconciliation, but the Khmer Rouge remained outside this coalition and resumed armed resistance until its surrender in June 1998. The strife-torn coalition meanwhile degenerated into open hostility in mid-1997, when Hun Sen of the communist CPP ousted his co-prime minister Prince Ranariddh. A year later the CPP failed to win elections outright, forcing it to seek a new coalition agreement with Funcinpec. Against expectations, that compromise proved a durable one.

Prime Minister Hun Sen, *who ousted his co-prime minister in 1997.*

King Norodom Sihanouk, *the pivotal figure in Cambodian society and politics.*

WORLD AFFAIRS

Joined UN in 1955

ASEAN | IAEA | OIF | Mekong River | NAM

During the civil war that followed the Vietnamese invasion of 1979, the Phnom Penh government (along with Vietnam), was reduced to an international pariah. It was recognized by few countries outside the Soviet bloc, and its seat at the UN was allotted to the exiled resistance coalition, despite one of its components being the Khmer Rouge, which had inflicted appalling violence and suffering on Cambodians.

Although Cambodia's 1993 constitution aims to make the country a nonaligned "island of peace," a neutral foreign policy was difficult to pursue so long as China continued to advocate the political rehabilitation of the Khmer Rouge. Cambodia's relations with Vietnam also remained problematic, fueled in part by the historic animosity between the two countries. The situation has improved since the late 1990s, and Cambodia's membership of ASEAN, which had been on hold pending the consolidation of full democratic government in Cambodia, was confirmed in April 1999.

AID

Recipient

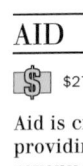

$279m (receipts)

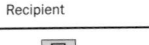

Down 17% in 1999

Aid is crucial to Cambodia's economy, providing the bulk of government revenues. Widespread corruption and political instability prompted some countries to withhold assistance in the late 1990s, but NGOs continued working in the country, and Western donors made fresh pledges in 2000.

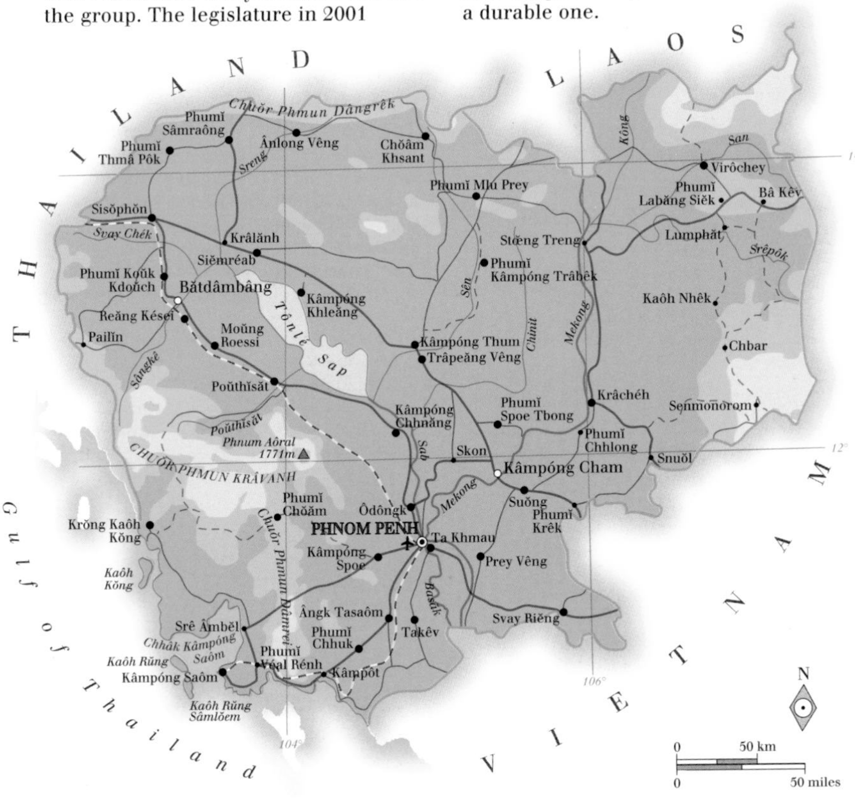

THAILAND
LAOS
VIETNAM
Gulf of Thailand
Chuŏr Phnum Dângrêk
Phumĭ Sâmraông
Phumĭ Thmâ Pŏk
Ânlong Vêng
Chŏâm Khsant
Sisŏphŏn
Svay Chék
Krâlănh
Siĕmréab
Phumĭ Mlu Prey
Stœng Treng
Virôchey
Phumĭ Labăng Siĕk
Bâ Kêv
Lumphăt
Srêpŏk
San
Kông
Phumĭ Koŭk Kdoŭch
Bătdâmbâng
Kâmpóng Khleăng
Phumĭ Kâmpóng Trâbêk
Kaôh Nhêk
Reăng Kései
Pailĭn
Moŭng Roessei
Tônlé Sap
Kâmpóng Thum
Trâpeăng Vêng
Chbar
Pouthĭsăt
Kâmpóng Chhnăng
Phumĭ Spoe Tbong
Krâchéh
Senmonorom
Phumĭ Chhlong
Snuŏl
Phnum Aôral 1771m
CHUŎR PHNUM KRÂVANH
Skon
Kâmpóng Cham
Phumĭ Chŏâm
Ŏdŏngk
Suŏng
Phumĭ Krêk
Krŏng Kaôh Kŏng
PHNOM PENH
Ta Khmau
Kâmpóng Spoe
Prey Vêng
Kaôh Kŏng
Chuŏr Phnum Dâmrei
Ângk Tasaôm
Svay Riĕng
Srê Âmběl
Phumĭ Chhuk
Takêv
Chhâk Kâmpóng Saôm
Kaôh Rŭng
Phumĭ Veal Rénh
Kâmpóng Saôm
Kâmpôt
Kaôh Rŭng Sâmlœm
Mekong
Sab
Sên
Chĭnit
Sângkê
Bassac
Sreng
N
0 50 km
0 50 miles

CAMBODIA

Total Land Area : 176 520 sq. km (68 154 sq. miles)

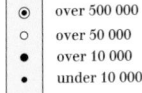

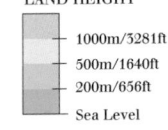

POPULATION		LAND HEIGHT
◉	over 500 000	1000m/3281ft
○	over 50 000	500m/1640ft
●	over 10 000	200m/656ft
•	under 10 000	Sea Level

C

CHRONOLOGY

A former French protectorate, Cambodia gained independence in 1953 as a constitutional monarchy with Norodom Sihanouk as king.

- ❑ **1955** Sihanouk abdicates to pursue political career; takes title "Prince."
- ❑ **1970** Right-wing coup led by Prime Minister Lon Nol deposes Sihanouk. Exiled Sihanouk forms Royal Government of National Union of Cambodia (GRUNC), backed by communist Khmer Rouge. Lon Nol proclaims Khmer Republic.
- ❑ **1975** GRUNC troops capture Phnom Penh. Prince Sihanouk head of state, Khmer Rouge assumes power. Huge numbers die under radical extremist regime.
- ❑ **1976** Country renamed Democratic Kampuchea. Elections. Sihanouk resigns; GRUNC dissolved. Khieu Samphan head of state; Pol Pot prime minister.
- ❑ **1978** December, Vietnam invades, supported by Cambodian communists opposed to Pol Pot.
- ❑ **1979** Vietnamese capture Phnom Penh. Khmer Rouge ousted by Kampuchean People's Revolutionary Party (KPRP), led by Pen Sovan. Khmer Rouge starts guerrilla war. Pol Pot held responsible for genocide and sentenced to death in absentia.
- ❑ **1982** Government-in-exile including Khmer Rouge and Khmer People's National Liberation Front, headed by Prince Sihanouk, is recognized by UN.
- ❑ **1989** Withdrawal of Vietnamese troops.
- ❑ **1990** UN Security Council approves plan for UN-monitored cease-fire and elections.
- ❑ **1991** Signing of Paris peace accords. Sihanouk reinstated as head of state of Cambodia.
- ❑ **1993** UN-supervised elections won by royalist Funcinpec. Sihanouk takes title of "King."
- ❑ **1994** Khmer Rouge refuses to join peace process.
- ❑ **1995** Former finance minister Sam Rainsy forms opposition party.
- ❑ **1996** Leading Khmer Rouge member Ieng Sary defects.
- ❑ **1997** Joint prime minister Hun Sen mounts coup against royalist co-premier Prince Ranariddh.
- ❑ **1998** April, death of Pol Pot; June, Khmer Rouge surrender; July, parliamentary elections; November, Hun Sen heads coalition government including Funcinpec.
- ❑ **1999** Cambodia admitted to ASEAN.
- ❑ **2001** Law approved on trials of Khmer Rouge leaders for atrocities committed by regime.

DEFENSE

No compulsory military service

$176m

Up 14% in 1999

CAMBODIAN ARMED FORCES

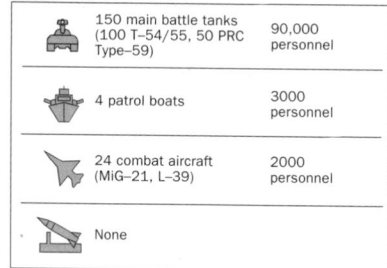

150 main battle tanks (100 T–54/55, 50 PRC Type–59)	90,000 personnel
4 patrol boats	3000 personnel
24 combat aircraft (MiG–21, L–39)	2000 personnel
None	

The coalition government's initial defense priority was to unify the command structures of armies under the control of diverse parties. The surrender of Khmer Rouge forces in mid-1998 and the disintegration of remaining pockets of Khmer resistance later that year, improved the prospects for a unified national army. Plans for the demobilization of 30,000 soldiers over a three-year period began in May 2000.

Under the nominal overall structure of the Royal Cambodian Armed Forces, there remain in existence three main armies – the CPP's Cambodian People's Armed Forces, Funcinpec's Armée Nationale Sihanoukiste, and the KPNLF's Khmer People's National Liberation Armed Forces. The rivalries between them remain intense, with the two first-named in open conflict as recently as 1997–1998. Although well equipped, their soldiers are poorly paid.

A system of conscription for five years between the ages of 18 and 35, has not been implemented since 1993.

ECONOMICS

Inflation 28.7% p.a. (1990–1999)

$3.02bn

3747–3835 riel

SCORE CARD

❑ World GNP Ranking	132nd
❑ GNP per Capita	$260
❑ Balance of Payments	$–96m
❑ Inflation	4%
❑ Unemployment	3%

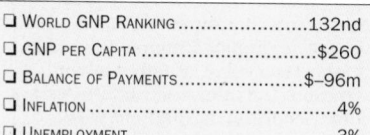

EXPORTS

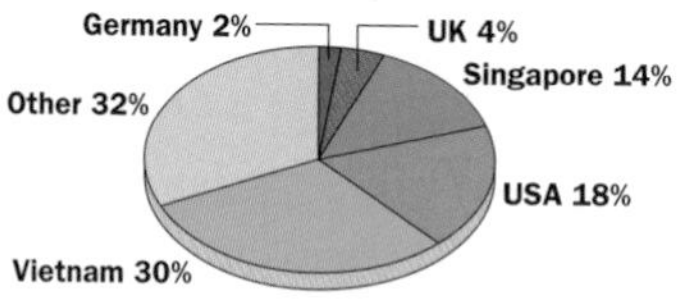
Germany 2%
UK 4%
Singapore 14%
Other 32%
USA 18%
Vietnam 30%

IMPORTS

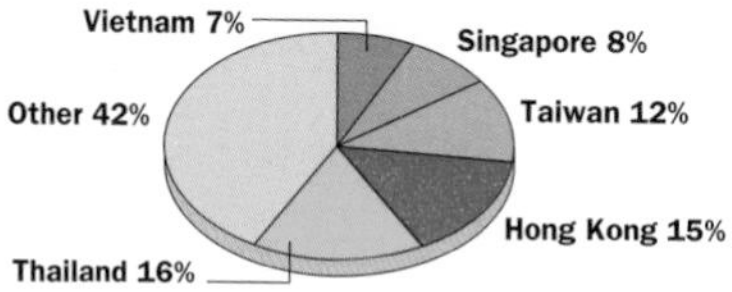
Vietnam 7%
Singapore 8%
Other 42%
Taiwan 12%
Hong Kong 15%
Thailand 16%

Strengths

Currently very few, as economy needs time and investment to recover from long-running conflicts. Considerable future potential. Relatively unbureaucratic mentality. Self-sufficiency in rice achieved by 1999. Gems, especially sapphires. Possible offshore oil wealth. Export-oriented garment industry.

Weaknesses

Tiny tax base makes economic reform hard to implement. Dependence on overseas aid; corruption at most levels of government limits its effectiveness. Disputes over land ownership rights.

ECONOMIC PERFORMANCE INDICATOR

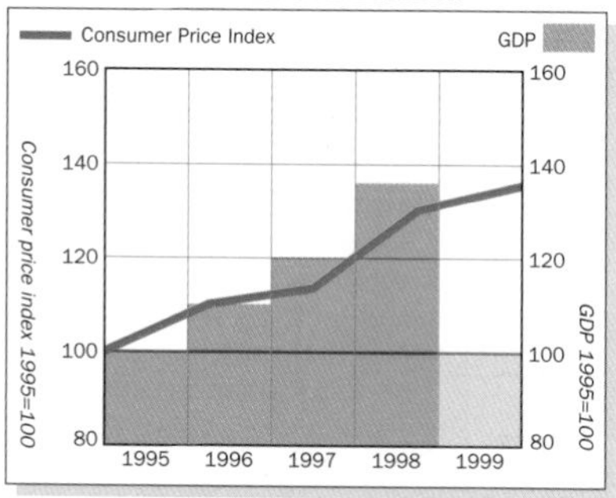
Consumer Price Index
GDP
160
140
120
100
80
Consumer price index 1995=100
GDP 1995=100
1995
1996
1997
1998
1999

Profile

The economy was devastated during the Pol Pot years. The Vietnamese attempted some reconstruction based on central planning, then switched to encouraging the private sector. Investment in the 1990s was heavily aid-dependent. The Asian financial crisis and internal turmoil affected funding after mid-1997.

CAMBODIA : MAJOR BUSINESSES

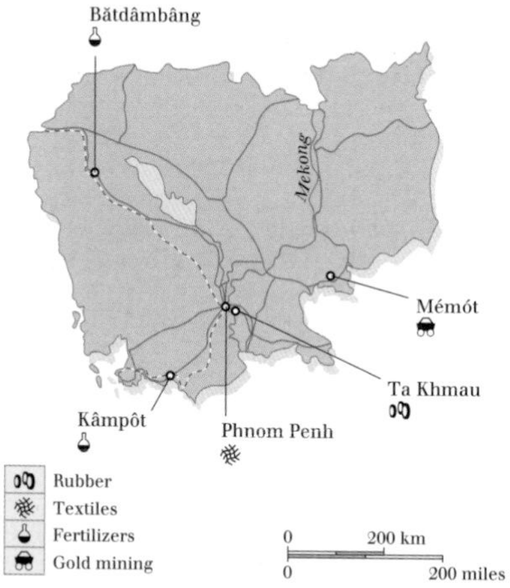
Bătdâmbâng
Mekong
Mémót
Ta Khmau
Kâmpôt
Phnom Penh
Rubber
Textiles
Fertilizers
Gold mining
0
200 km
0
200 miles

RESOURCES

Electric power 35,000 kw

114,600 tonnes

Not an oil producer

4.6m ducks, 3m cattle, 2.6m pigs, 13.2m chickens

Salt, phosphates, gemstones

Few currently exploited, apart from tropical rainforest timber, particularly teak and rosewood, much of which is felled illegally.

ELECTRICITY GENERATION

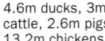

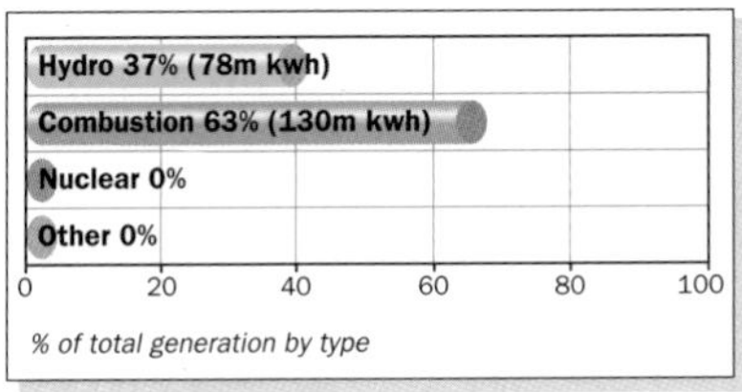
Hydro 37% (78m kwh)
Combustion 63% (130m kwh)
Nuclear 0%
Other 0%
0
20
40
60
80
100
% of total generation by type

CAMBODIA : LAND USE

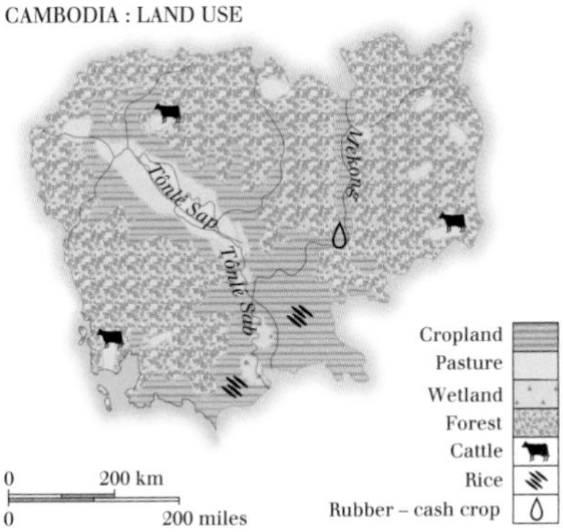
Tonle Sap
Mekong
Tonle Sab
Cropland
Pasture
Wetland
Forest
Cattle
Rice
Rubber – cash crop
0
200 km
0
200 miles

ENVIRONMENT

Not available

16%

0.05 tonnes per capita

ENVIRONMENTAL TREATIES

Yes	Yes	Yes
Yes	No	No

Deforestation is one of the most serious problems facing Cambodia. Illegal logging is the main culprit. Timber, one of the country's most valuable assets, was sold in huge quantities by all Cambodian factions to finance their war efforts. A moratorium on logging was declared at the end of 1992, but was largely ignored. Despite international pressure and efforts from 2000 to tighten controls, in many parts of the country logging is impossible to police. Tropical hardwoods extracted illegally from Cambodia find lucrative outlets through Thailand in particular. The environmental consequences – topsoil erosion and increased risk of flooding – are enormous and will hold back Cambodia's reconstruction.

MEDIA

TV ownership low

Daily newspaper circulation 2 per 1000 people

Phnom Penh has several independent TV stations in addition to the national network which broadcasts for ten hours a day.

The government has used a 1995 press law to prosecute numerous newspapers for defamation and disinformation.

CRIME

Death penalty not used

2490 prisoners

Civilian crime rates are now fairly stable

CRIME RATES

Detailed crime figures are not available

There are allegations that Cambodia is becoming Asia's new "narco-state." It is claimed that there has been a proliferation of narcotics trading, money laundering, and illegal banking operations. Mob killings go largely unremarked. Corruption in business is a major issue. Phnom Penh witnessed an increase in violent crime in the aftermath of the 1997 Hun Sen coup, owing to the spread of illegally owned firearms. Until the surrender of the Khmer Rouge in 1998, areas under its command, especially in the west around Pailin and Battambang, were particularly dangerous. Banditry was rife and policing virtually non-existent.

EDUCATION

School leaving age: 12

37%

8901 students

THE EDUCATION SYSTEM

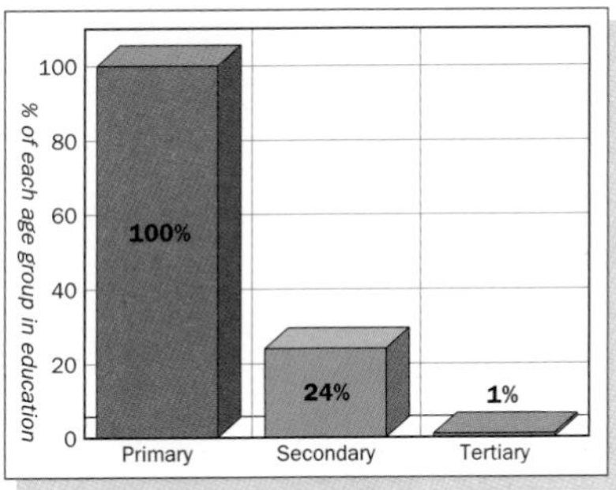
100
80
60
40
20
0
% of each age group in education
100%
24%
1%
Primary
Secondary
Tertiary

The government aims to put in place a nine-year period of education. Currently primary education is compulsory, and lasts for six years between the ages of six and 12. Only 5000 of Cambodia's 20,000 teachers survived the Pol Pot period; the Vietnamese-installed government trained or retrained about 40,000.

PUBLISHING AND BROADCAST MEDIA

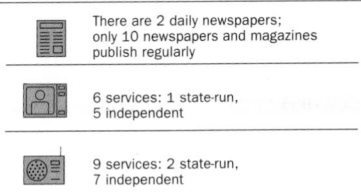

There are 2 daily newspapers; only 10 newspapers and magazines publish regularly

6 services: 1 state-run, 5 independent

9 services: 2 state-run, 7 independent

HEALTH

No welfare state health benefits

1 per 10,000 people

Circulatory and infectious diseases, cancers

The Cambodian health system was effectively destroyed in the Pol Pot period; only 50 doctors survived, and Cambodia's health indicators were among the worst in the world.

Conditions have since improved, but AIDS is widespread, affecting even children in rural areas. Infant mortality remains high, and malaria and cholera are endemic. In 2000, Unicef helped mount an immunization campaign against tetanus, a major cause of neonatal mortality.

SPENDING

GDP/cap. increase

CONSUMPTION AND SPENDING

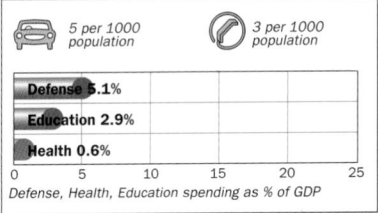

5 per 1000 population

3 per 1000 population

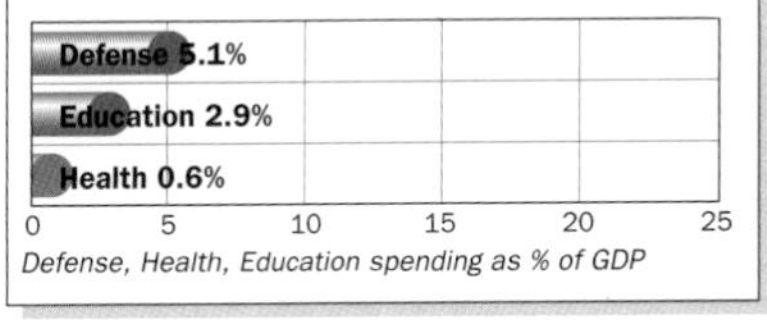
Defense 5.1%
Education 2.9%
Health 0.6%
0
5
10
15
20
25
Defense, Health, Education spending as % of GDP

New industries such as textiles, in which female garment workers may earn $40 a month in vast workshops, help to attract migrants to the towns, although they risk unemployment and homelessness. Cambodians in rural areas face more severe poverty, exacerbated by land shortage.

WORLD RANKING

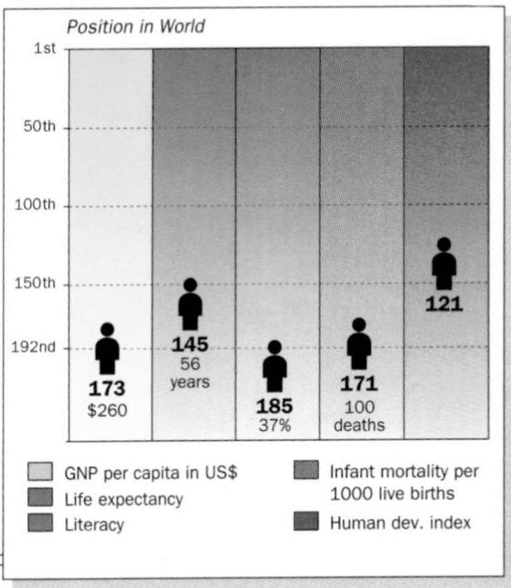
Position in World
1st
50th
100th
150th
192nd
173
$260
145
56 years
185
37%
171
100 deaths
121
GNP per capita in US$
Life expectancy
Literacy
Infant mortality per 1000 live births
Human dev. index

C

CAMEROON

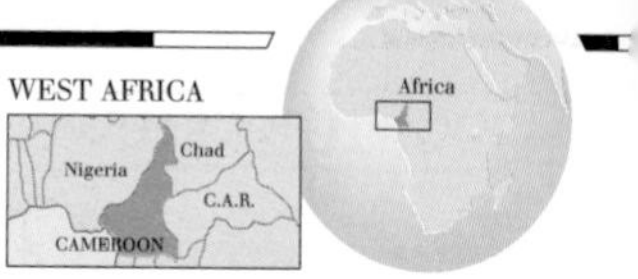

WEST AFRICA
Africa
Nigeria
Chad
C.A.R.
CAMEROON

OFFICIAL NAME: Republic of Cameroon **CAPITAL:** Yaoundé
POPULATION: 15.1 million **CURRENCY:** CFA franc **OFFICIAL LANGUAGES:** French and English

C

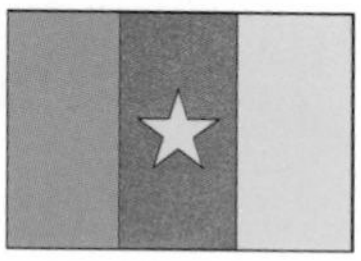

1960 | 1961 | May 20 | CAM | +1 | +237 | .cm

Savanna landscape below Mindif Pic in Cameroon's far north. From here, the land slopes down to the hot, arid Lake Chad basin.

LOCATED ON THE CENTRAL West African coast, over half of Cameroon is forested, with equatorial rainforest to the south, and evergreen forest and wooded savanna north of the Sanaga river. Most cities are located in the south, although there are densely populated areas around Mount Cameroon, a dormant volcano. For 30 years Cameroon was effectively a one-party state. Democratic elections in 1992 returned the former ruling party to power.

CLIMATE

Tropical equatorial

WEATHER CHART

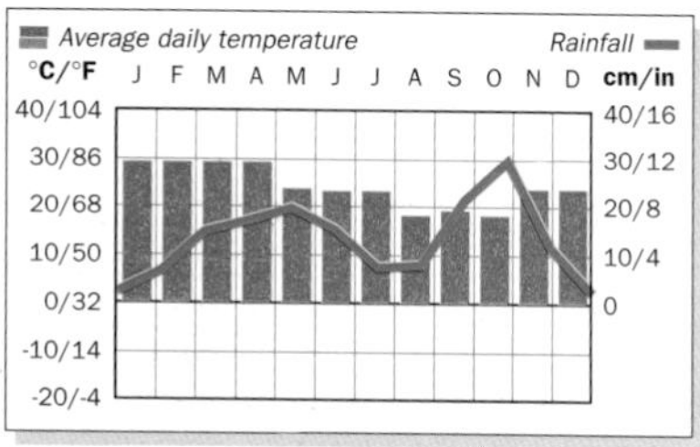

Average daily temperature
Rainfall
°C/°F
J F M A M J J A S O N D
cm/in
40/104
30/86
20/68
10/50
0/32
-10/14
-20/-4
40/16
30/12
20/8
10/4
0

Climate varies from the equatorial south, with 500 cm (200 in) of rain a year, to the drought-beset Sahelian north.

TRANSPORTATION

Drive on right

Douala International 434,744 passengers

58 ships 12,900 grt

THE TRANSPORTATION NETWORK

4288 km (2664 miles)

Trans-African Highway

1016 km (631 miles)

2090 km (1299 miles)

Major projects are the east–west Trans-African Highway and the realigning of the Douala–Nkongsamba railroad.

TOURISM

Visitors : Population 1:112

135,000 visitors

Up 32% in 1998

MAIN TOURIST ARRIVALS

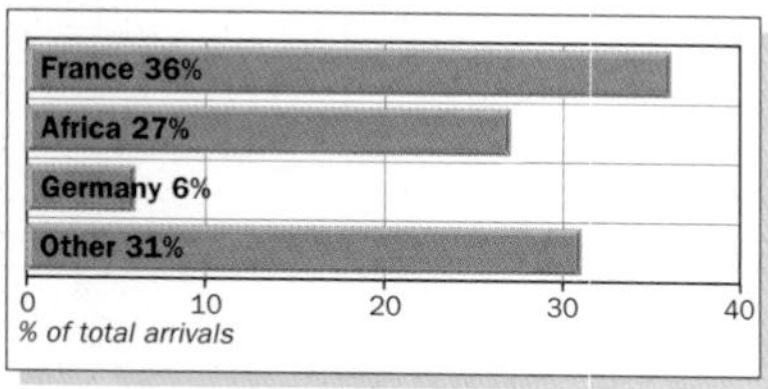

France 36%
Africa 27%
Germany 6%
Other 31%
0
10
20
30
40
% of total arrivals

In 1989, the first tourism minister was appointed to boost the still small industry. Some package tours visit the northern game parks. A new airport near Yaoundé will replace the present one. There are beach hotels near Kribi.

PEOPLE

Pop. density low

Bamileke, Fang, Fulani, French, English

32/km² (84/mi²)

THE URBAN/RURAL POPULATION SPLIT

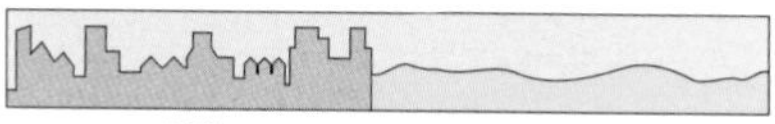

48%
52%

RELIGIOUS PERSUASION

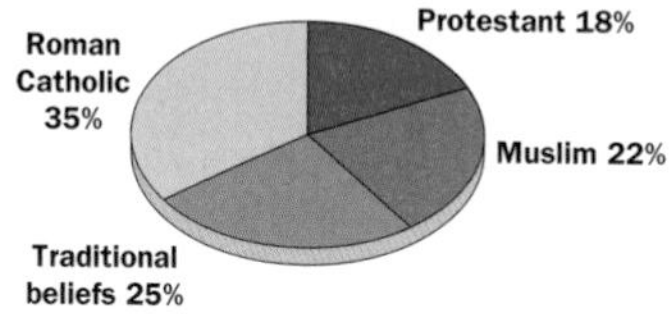

Roman Catholic 35%
Protestant 18%
Muslim 22%
Traditional beliefs 25%

Cameroon is ethnically diverse – there are 230 groups, no single group being dominant. The largest is the Bamileke of the central southwest region, but this group has never held political power. When President Ahidjo, a northern Fulani, retired, he was replaced by Paul Biya of the southeastern Bulu-Beti group. The north–south enmity which affects many other west African states is also present in Cameroon, albeit diminished by the great diversity of peoples. There are tensions between the French- and English-speaking communities, with sections of the latter demanding independence.

POLITICS

Multiparty elections

1997/2002

President Paul Biya

AT THE LAST ELECTION
National Assembly 180 seats

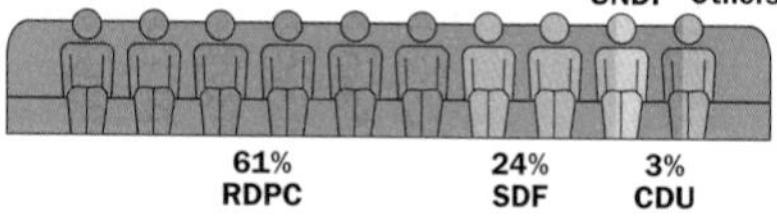

7% UNDP
5% Others
61% RDPC
24% SDF
3% CDU

RDPC = Cameroon People's Democratic Rally **SDF** = Social Democratic Front **UNDP** = National Union for Democracy and Progress **CDU** = Cameroon Democratic Union

A Senate is to be created under the 1995 constitution.

President Biya's RDPC narrowly won control of the new parliament in multiparty elections in 1992, which were boycotted by the main opposition SDF. The SDF candidate John Fru Ndi also disputed Biya's claim of victory in a presidential election that year. In legislative elections in May 1997 the RDPC's apparent landslide victory was condemned by the opposition as the product of fraud and intimidation, as was Biya's reelection as president that October.

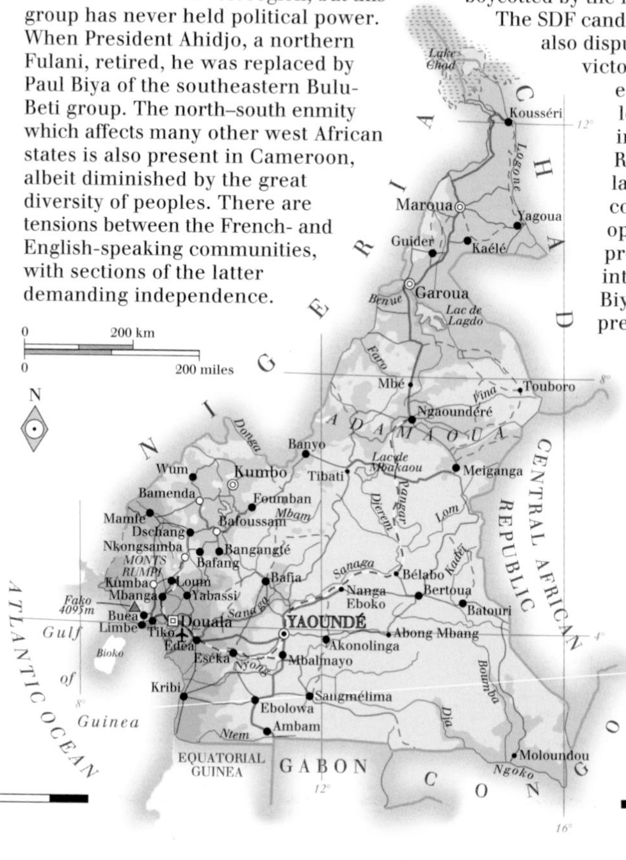

0
200 km
0
200 miles
N
Lake Chad
CHAD
NIGERIA
Kousséri
Logone
Maroua
Yagoua
Guider
Kaélé
Benue
Garoua
Lac de Lagdo
Faro
Mbé
Vina
Touboro
Ngaoundéré
ADAMAOUA
Donga
Banyo
Tibati
Lac de Mbakaou
Meiganga
Djerem
Wum
Kumbo
Bamenda
Foumban
Mbam
Mamfe
Dschang
Bafoussam
Nkongsamba
Bangangté
MONTS RUMPI
Bafang
Kumba
Loum
Mbanga
Yabassi
Bafia
Sanaga
Nanga Eboko
Bélabo
Bertoua
Batouri
Kadei
Lom
Fako 4095m
Buea
Limbe
Tiko
Douala
YAOUNDÉ
Akonolinga
Abong Mbang
Edéa
Eséka
Nyong
Mbalmayo
Gulf of Guinea
Bioko
ATLANTIC OCEAN
Kribi
Sangmélima
Ebolowa
Ambam
Ntem
Dja
Boumba
Ngoko
Moloundou
EQUATORIAL GUINEA
GABON
CONGO
CENTRAL AFRICAN REPUBLIC

CAMEROON

Total Land Area : 465 400 sq. km (179 691 sq. miles)

POPULATION

over 1 000 000
over 500 000
over 100 000
over 50 000
over 10 000
under 10 000

LAND HEIGHT

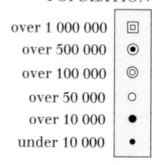

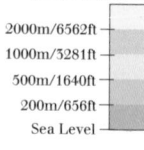

2000m/6562ft
1000m/3281ft
500m/1640ft
200m/656ft
Sea Level

WORLD AFFAIRS

Joined UN in 1960

BDEAC | Comm | OIC | LCBC | FZ

Cameroon's most important relationship continues to be with France, although the country has attempted to diversify its international links, joining the Commonwealth in 1995. A territorial dispute with Nigeria of long duration concerns sovereignty over the oil-rich Bakassi peninsula, where there were clashes in 1996 and 1998.

AID

Recipient

$434m (receipts) — Up 2% in 1999

France is by far the most important donor, even having twice paid up Cameroon's back debts to the IMF to prevent its being blacklisted. Lack of funding has forced many development projects to be abandoned. Despite poor economic performance, relations with the IMF are improving.

DEFENSE

No compulsory military service

$154m — Up 3% in 1999

The 11,500-strong army has been active in supporting the regime and maintaining order in the face of prodemocratic protests since before independence. Military equipment and training comes mainly from France. There is also a 9000-strong paramilitary gendarmerie.

ECONOMICS

Inflation 5.5% p.a. (1990–1999)

$8.8bn — 654.42–698.69 CFA francs

SCORE CARD

❑ WORLD GNP RANKING	89th
❑ GNP PER CAPITA	$600
❑ BALANCE OF PAYMENTS	$–396m
❑ INFLATION	0.1%
❑ UNEMPLOYMENT	30%

STRENGTHS

French and US companies exploit moderate oil reserves. Very diversified agriculture includes timber, cocoa, bananas, and coffee. Self-sufficiency in food. Strong informal sector. Private sector in relatively good state. Electricity is 95% HEP.

WEAKNESSES

Massive fuel smuggling from Nigeria affects refinery profits. Inflated civil service. Widespread corruption.

EXPORTS

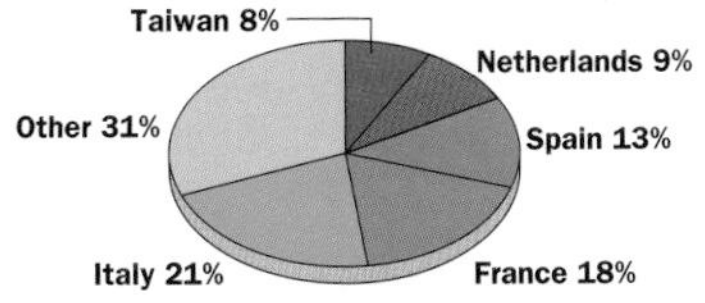
Taiwan 8%
Netherlands 9%
Spain 13%
France 18%
Italy 21%
Other 31%

IMPORTS

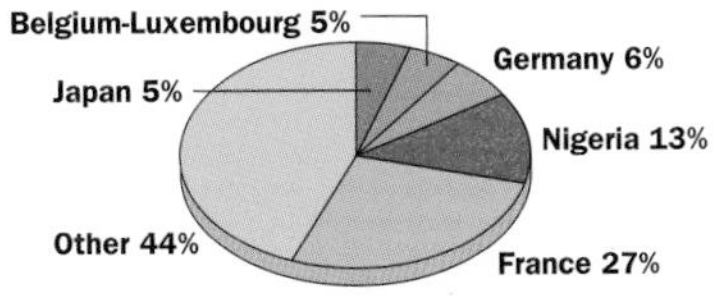
Belgium-Luxembourg 5%
Germany 6%
Japan 5%
Nigeria 13%
France 27%
Other 44%

RESOURCES

Electric power 627,000 kw

89,055 tonnes

90,000 b/d (reserves 400,000,000 bbl)

5.9m cattle, 3.9m sheep, 30m chickens

Oil, coal, tin, natural gas, bauxite, iron, uranium, gold

New oil discoveries may be able to bolster declining extraction rates. In spite of large bauxite deposits, much is imported for the Edea smelter, which takes 50% of national electricity output.

ENVIRONMENT

Sustainability rank: 76th

5% (2% partially protected)

0.2 tonnes per capita

The 1999 Yaoundé Declaration should help to protect part of Cameroon's 22 million hectares of forest, threatened by commercial logging.

MEDIA

TV ownership low

Daily newspaper circulation 7 per 1000 people

PUBLISHING AND BROADCAST MEDIA

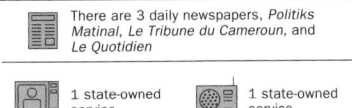

There are 3 daily newspapers, *Politiks Matinal, Le Tribune du Cameroun,* and *Le Quotidien*

1 state-owned service — 1 state-owned service

There are frequent allegations of censorship and violence against journalists. English-language media are generally more outspoken.

CRIME

Death penalty used

Cameroon does not publish prison figures — Up 238% 1996–1998

Armed robbery and burglary in Douala and Yaoundé are rising fast. The police are known to use torture.

EDUCATION

School leaving age: 12

76% — 33,177 students

The French-speaking majority has failed in its attempt to take over the bilingual system. Cameroon has a high literacy rate compared with much of the rest of Africa.

CHRONOLOGY

One of the great trading emporia of west Africa, Cameroon was divided between the French and British in 1919, after 30 years of German rule.

- ❑ **1955** Revolt; French kill 10,000.
- ❑ **1960** French sector independent.
- ❑ **1961** British south joins Cameroon (north joins Nigeria). Federal system established – abolished in 1972.
- ❑ **1982** Ahidjo dies; Paul Biya president.
- ❑ **1983–1984** Coup attempts. Heavy casualties; 50 plotters executed.
- ❑ **1990** Demonstrations and strikes; declaration of multiparty state.
- ❑ **1992** Multiparty elections.
- ❑ **1997** President and ruling RDPC returned in disputed elections.
- ❑ **2000** World Bank funding approved for oil and pipeline project, despite environmental fears.

C

HEALTH

No welfare state health benefits

1 per 10,000 people

Malaria, diarrheal and respiratory diseases

A sharp fall in government health provision means that more people are using the private health sector or traditional practitioners.

SPENDING

GDP/cap. increase

CONSUMPTION AND SPENDING

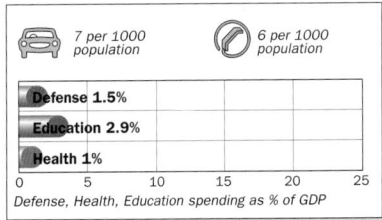

7 per 1000 population — *6 per 1000 population*

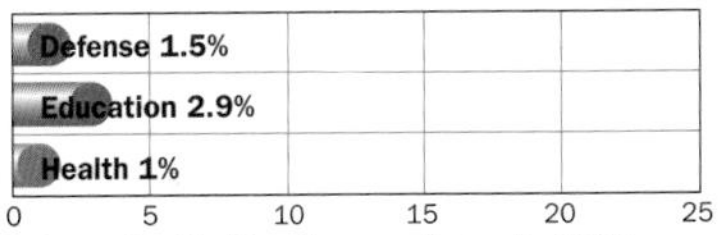
Defense 1.5%
Education 2.9%
Health 1%
0
5
10
15
20
25

Defense, Health, Education spending as % of GDP

Wealth is unevenly distributed and has been declining since the end of the oil boom. There is still a very wealthy, albeit small, sector of the population.

WORLD RANKING

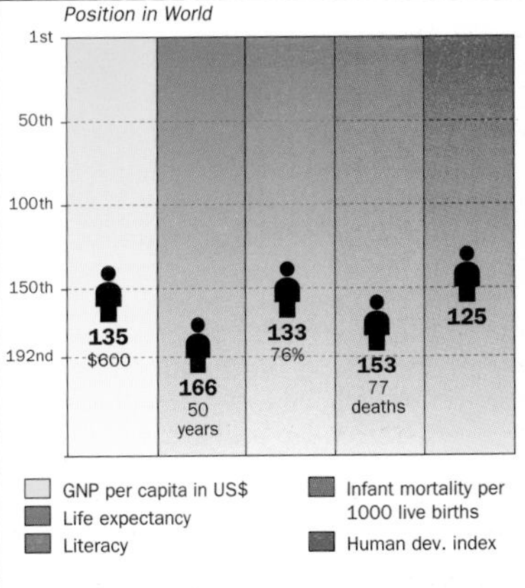
Position in World
1st
50th
100th
150th
192nd
135
$600
166
50
years
133
76%
153
77
deaths
125
GNP per capita in US$
Life expectancy
Literacy
Infant mortality per 1000 live births
Human dev. index

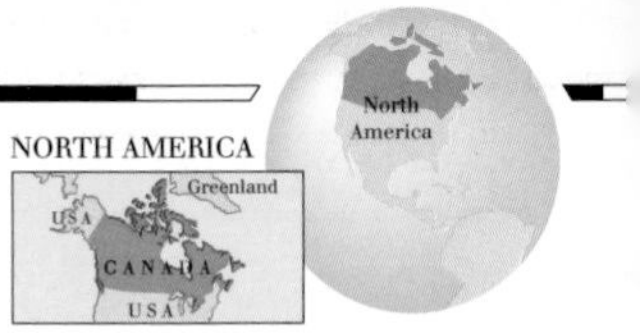
NORTH AMERICA
North America
Greenland
USA
CANADA
USA

CANADA

Official Name: Canada **Capital:** Ottawa **Population:** 31.1 million
Currency: Canadian dollar **Official languages:** English and French

C

1867
1949
July 1
CDN
-3.5 to -8
+1
.ca

CANADA IS THE WORLD'S third-largest country, stretching north to Cape Columbia on Ellesmere Island, south to Lake Erie, and across five time zones from Newfoundland to the Pacific seaboard. The interior lowlands around Hudson Bay make up 80% of Canada's land area and include the vast Canadian Shield, with the plains of Saskatchewan and Manitoba and the Rocky Mountains to the west. The St. Lawrence, Yukon, Mackenzie, and Fraser Rivers are among the world's 40 largest. The St. Lawrence river and Great Lakes lowlands are the most populous areas. An Inuit homeland, Nunavut, was created in 1999, covering nearly a quarter of Canada's land area, formerly the eastern part of Northwest Territories. French-speaking Québec's relationship with the rest of the country causes recurring constitutional arguments.

CLIMATE

Continental/subarctic/mountain

WEATHER CHART

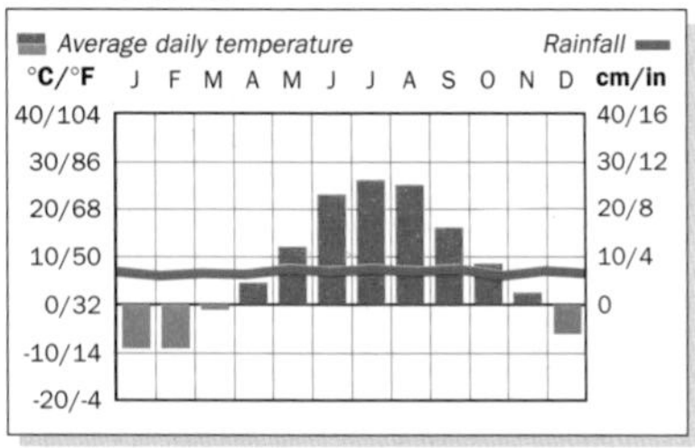
Average daily temperature
Rainfall
°C/°F
J F M A M J J A S O N D
cm/in
40/104
30/86
20/68
10/50
0/32
-10/14
-20/-4
40/16
30/12
20/8
10/4
0

Canada's climate ranges from polar and subpolar in the north, to cool in the south. Summers in the interior are hotter, and winters colder and longer than on the coast, with temperatures well below freezing and deep snow. The Pacific coast around Vancouver has the warmest winters, where temperatures rarely fall below zero.

TRANSPORTATION

Drive on right

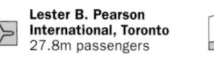

Lester B. Pearson International, Toronto
27.8m passengers

835 ships
2.5m grt

THE TRANSPORTATION NETWORK

318,371 km (197,826 miles)	16,571 km (10,297 miles)
14,000 km (8700 miles)	3769 km (2342 miles)

Canada's size means that the emergence of a national economy depended on the development of an efficient system of transportation. The Trans-Canada Highway and two transcontinental rail systems are the east–west backbones of the road and rail networks, which also reach into the far north. Air services are well developed and expanding. Easy access to the cheap transportation of the Great Lakes–St. Lawrence Seaway system helped Ontario and Québec dominate the economy for most of the 20th century.

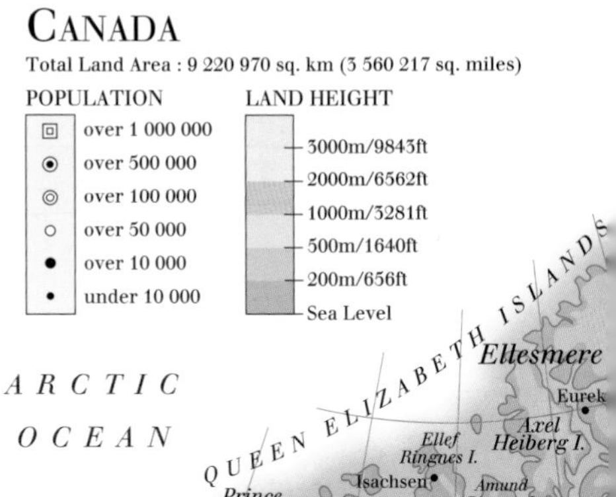
CANADA
Total Land Area : 9 220 970 sq. km (3 560 217 sq. miles)
POPULATION
over 1 000 000
over 500 000
over 100 000
over 50 000
over 10 000
under 10 000
LAND HEIGHT
3000m/9843ft
2000m/6562ft
1000m/3281ft
500m/1640ft
200m/656ft
Sea Level
ARCTIC OCEAN
QUEEN ELIZABETH ISLANDS
Ellesmere

Prince Patrick I.
Mould Bay
SVERDRUP ISLANDS
Isachsen
Ellef Ringnes I.
Amund Ringnes I.
Axel Heiberg I.
PARRY ISLANDS
Melville I.
Bathurst I.
Cornwallis I.
Resolute
Beaufort Sea
Banks I.
Viscount Meville Sound
Sachs Harbour
Somerset I.
Prince of Wales I.
Inuvik
Amundsen Gulf
Victoria I.
Wollaston Peninsula
M'Clintock Channel
Boothia Peninsula
USA (ALASKA)
Yukon
Dawson
Klondike
MACKENZIE MOUNTAINS
Cambridge Bay
Kugluktuk
King William I.
Spence Bay
Queen Maud Gulf
Gjoa Haven
Great Bear Lake
YUKON TERRITORY
Mount Logan 5959m
NORTHWEST TERRITORIES
NUNAVUT
Whitehorse
ROCKY MOUNTAINS
CASSIAR MOUNTAINS
Watson Lake
Mackenzie
Yellowknife
Rankin Inlet
PACIFIC OCEAN
Great Slave Lake
Hay River
Fort Smith
Dubawnt
COAST MOUNTAINS
Peace
BRITISH COLUMBIA
Lake Athabasca
Prince Rupert
Fort St. John
Athabasca
Churchill
Queen Charlotte Is
Fort McMurray
Grande Prairie
York Factory
Ocean Falls
Prince George
ALBERTA
SASKATCHEWAN
Thompson
Nelson
Queen Charlotte Sound
St. Albert
Fort Saskatchewan
Edmonton
Flin Flon
MANITOBA
Campbell River
Fraser
Leduc
Wetaskiwin
Camrose
Red Deer
Lloydminster
N. Saskatchewan
Prince Albert
Lake Winnipeg
Lake Winnipegosis
Kamloops
North Battleford
Saskatoon
Vancouver I.
Vernon
Kelowna
Airdrie
Nanaimo
Vancouver
Calgary
Victoria
Chilliwack
Penticton
S. Saskatchewan
Yorkton
Medicine Hat
Regina
Portage la Prairie
Cranbrook
Moose Jaw
Lethbridge
Swift Current
Brandon
Winnipeg
Weyburn
Estevan
Red R.
Lake of the Woods
140°
130°
120°
110°
100°
N
0 400 km
0 400 miles
UNITED STATES OF AMERI

TOURISM

Visitors : Population 1:1.5

20.4m visitors

Up 5% in 2000

MAIN TOURIST ARRIVALS

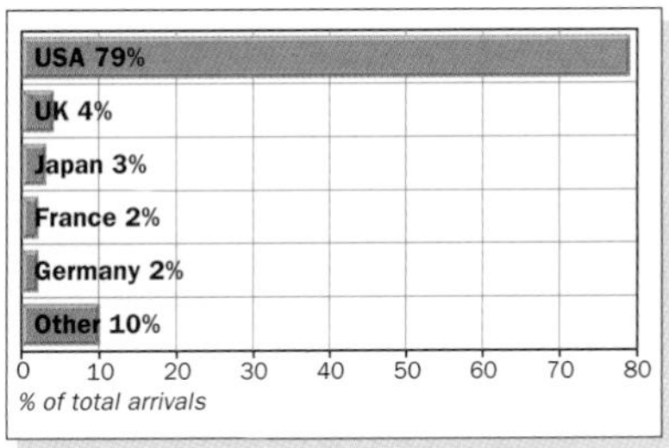
USA 79%
UK 4%
Japan 3%
France 2%
Germany 2%
Other 10%
0
10
20
30
40
50
60
70
80
% of total arrivals

Most tourist visitors come from the USA, often on short tours. Efforts to attract European visitors are based around campaigns emphasizing Canada's unpolluted natural beauty. Bizarrely, the fictional home of the eponymous hero of *Anne of Green Gables* on Prince Edward Island is a magnet for tourists from Japan, where the novels enjoy enormous popularity.

PEOPLE

Pop. density low

English, French, Chinese, Italian, German, Ukrainian, Portuguese, Inuktitut, Cree

3/km²
9/mi²

THE URBAN/RURAL POPULATION SPLIT

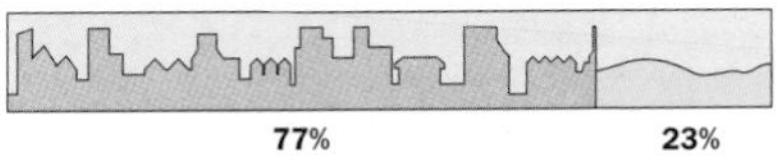
77%
23%

RELIGIOUS PERSUASION

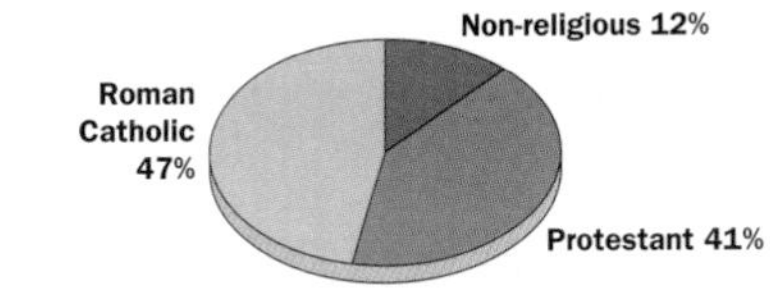
Non-religious 12%
Roman Catholic 47%
Protestant 41%

ETHNIC MAKEUP

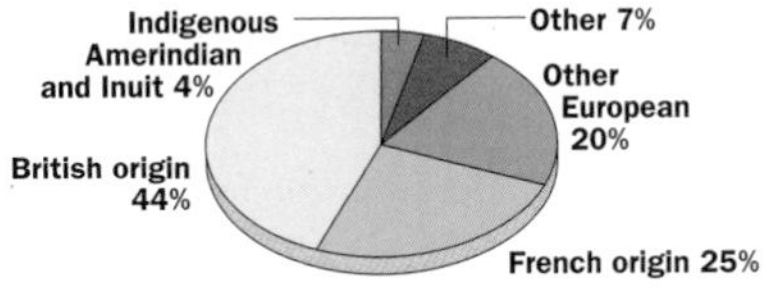
Indigenous Amerindian and Inuit 4%
Other 7%
Other European 20%
British origin 44%
French origin 25%

Relations between French-speaking Québécois and the English-speaking majority in Canada have been the dominant ethnic issue of the past 40 years. Support for separatist parties increased mainly because of the failure of Canada's other provinces to deal with Québec's demand to be recognized as a "distinct society," with powers to preserve its culture and language from further anglicization. Québec's still controversial 1977 language law made French the province's official language. Two-thirds of Canada's population live in the 5% of its land area taken up by the Great Lakes–St. Lawrence lowlands.

A dude ranch in British Columbia.
Many tourists are attracted by Canada's wide choice of outdoor pursuits.

POPULATION AGE BREAKDOWN

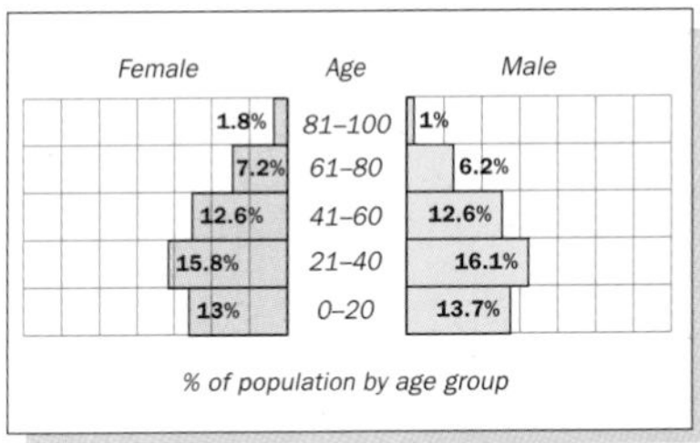
Female
Age
Male
1.8%
81–100
1%
7.2%
61–80
6.2%
12.6%
41–60
12.6%
15.8%
21–40
16.1%
13%
0–20
13.7%
% of population by age group

However, Canada's ethnic mix has changed significantly in the past 25 years, due to a move from a restrictive immigration policy to one which welcomes those with money or skills. Significant numbers of Asians have moved to Canada. The government promotes a policy which encourages each group to maintain its own culture. Canada is now officially a "mosaic" of communities.

The largest element of the indigenous population is the 800,000 people of native Amerindian descent, known in Canada as First Nations. There are also 213,000 Métis (French–Amerindians) and an Inuit population of some 50,000 in the north. In 1992 the Inuit successfully settled their long-standing land claim, and in 1999 the Nunavut area, with only 25,000 mainly Inuit inhabitants, gained the status of a territory, the first part of Canada to be governed by indigenous Canadians in modern history. A Supreme Court land rights ruling in 1997, establishing the principle of "aboriginal title," opened the way for the return of ancestral lands claimed by native Amerindian nations, and in 1998 the federal government formally apologized for their past mistreatment.

Canada has a long tradition of state welfare more akin to Scandinavia than the USA. Unemployment provision and health care, supported by high taxes, are still generous, despite recent cutbacks. The government has sought to end inequalities. Measures include the "pay-equity" laws, which aim to specify pay rates for jobs done mainly by women – such as receptionists – equivalent to similar skill jobs for men. Women are well represented at most levels of business and government.

Baffin Bay
Davis Strait
Baffin Island
Cumberland Peninsula
Hall Peninsula
Iqaluit
Meta Incognita Peninsula
Foxe Peninsula
Coral Harbour
Ivujivik
Péninsula D'ungava
Ungava Bay
LABRADOR SEA
NEWFOUNDLAND
Labrador
Schefferville
Smallwood Res.
Happy Valley-Goose Bay
QUEBEC
Belcher Is
Labrador City
St John's
Winisk
La Grande Rivière
LAURENTIAN MOUNTAINS
Corner Brook
Newfoundland
James Bay
Sept-Iles
Gulf of St. Lawrence
ST PIERRE & MIQUELON (to France)
Cabot Strait
Moosonee
PRINCE EDWARD ISLAND
Prince Edward I.
Sydney
Cape Breton I.
Chicoutimi
Jonquière
NEW BRUNSWICK
Charlottetown
Moncton
Québec
Fredericton
Dartmouth
Halifax
Timmins
Saint John
NOVA SCOTIA
Trois-Rivières
Sherbrooke
Yarmouth
Laval
Hull
Montréal
Verdun
Wawa
Sudbury
North Bay
OTTAWA
Sault Sainte Marie
L. Huron
Peterborough
Oshawa
Kingston
Toronto
L. Ontario
Kitchener
Niagara Falls
Hamilton
St. Catherines
Windsor
London
L. Erie
L. Michigan
ATLANTIC OCEAN

CHRONOLOGY

Peopled for centuries by indigenous Inuits and Amerindians, Canada began to experience extensive European settlement following the landing of the English expedition led by John Cabot in 1497 and the French landing of Jacques Cartier in 1534.

- **1754** British fight French and Indian War. France forced to relinquish St. Lawrence and Québec settlements to Britain.
- **1774** Act of Québec recognizes Roman Catholicism, French language, culture, and traditions.
- **1775–1783** American War of Independence. Canada becomes refuge for loyalists to British Crown.
- **1867** Federation of Canada created under British North America Act.
- **1885** Transcontinental railroad completed.
- **1897** Klondike gold rush begins.
- **1914–1918, 1939–1945** Canada supports Allies in both world wars.
- **1931** Autonomy within Commonwealth.
- **1949** Founder member of NATO. Newfoundland joins Federation.
- **1968** Liberal Party under Pierre Trudeau in power. Separatist Parti Québécois (PQ) formed to demand complete separation from federation.
- **1970s** Québec secessionist movement grows, accompanied by terrorist attacks.
- **1976** In Québec, PQ wins elections
- **1977** French made official language.
- **1980** Separation of Québec rejected at referendum. Trudeau prime minister again.
- **1982** UK transfers all powers relating to Canada in British law.
- **1984** Trudeau resigns. Elections won by PCP. Brian Mulroney prime minister until 1993.
- **1987** Meech Lake Accord.
- **1989** Canadian–USA Free Trade Agreement.
- **1992** Charlottetown Agreement on provincial–federal issues rejected at referendum. Canada, Mexico, and USA finalize terms for NAFTA.
- **1993** Crushing election defeat of PCP, rise of regional parties.
- **1994** PQ regains power in Québec. NAFTA takes effect.
- **1995** Narrow "no" vote in second Québec sovereignty referendum.
- **1995** Fishing dispute with EU.
- **1997** Regional considerations again dominate federal election; Liberals retain power; election victory based on support in Ontario.
- **1998** PQ only narrowly holds power in Québec.
- **2000** November, early elections. Liberals retain power.

POLITICS

Multiparty elections

2000/2005 — HM Queen Elizabeth II

AT THE LAST ELECTION

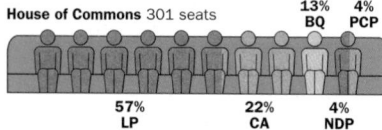

House of Commons 301 seats

13% BQ
4% PCP
57% LP
22% CA
4% NDP

LP = Liberal Party **CA** = Canadian Reform Conservative Alliance **BQ** = Bloc Québécois **NDP** = New Democratic Party **PCP** = Progressive Conservative Party **Ind** = Independents

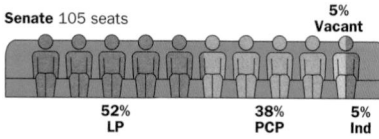

Senate 105 seats

5% Vacant
52% LP
38% PCP
5% Ind

Senators are appointed for life by the governor-general in Council, to a usual maximum of 105; the prime minister may appoint an extra 8 senators.

Canada is a federal multiparty democracy.

Main Political Issues

The unity of the state

Opposition to federal government is not confined to Québec – the 1997 and 2000 federal elections confirmed support for greater autonomy for Canada's western provinces – but Canada has agonized over separatist tendencies in francophone Québec almost since the foundation of the state. Québec did not take part in the 1997 Calgary conference, where a Canadian unity framework was agreed by the other provinces, together with recognition of Québec's "unique character." A series of earlier proposals, to recognize Québec as a distinct society and strengthen the powers of all the federal provinces, had failed to gain ratification or been rejected by the electorate. The Parti Québécois (PQ), back in power at provincial level since 1994, advocates another referendum on separatism, despite losing those held in 1980 and 1995. The Supreme Court has ruled, however, that secession would require federal approval and the agreement of at least seven of the ten provinces. The April 2000 Clarity Act set strict criteria for any pro-secession referendum result to be valid.

North American integration

The North American Free Trade Agreement (NAFTA), a hotly debated issue in Canada when it was being negotiated in the early 1990s, has produced a trade boom, especially for Ontario. However, Canadians have problems competing for foreign investment with Mexico, where labor costs, social welfare, and environmental standards are lower. Most Canadians oppose such ideas as a currency union and ever closer integration with the USA.

Niagara Falls *is situated between Lakes Erie and Ontario on the Canada–USA border. Horseshoe Falls, in Canada, are 49m (160 ft) high and 790 m (2591 ft) across.*

Profile

Until recently, Canadian politics was traditionally dominated by two main parties, the PCP and LP, which had few major ideological differences. The third party, the NDP (which has never held federal power), advocated greater government intervention than the other two.

The 1990s brought a major political shift – the eclipse of the PCP, three successive LP victories (1993, 1997, and November 2000), and an eventual realignment on the right, based on the emergence of the populist Reform Party (RP) in the western provinces. The trend away from mainstream politics, toward parties representing strong regional interests, left the LP with few seats outside its strongholds in the east. The Bloc Québécois (BQ), espousing the separatist cause at federal level, was the second-largest party in the federal parliament between 1994 and 1997. Since then the role of official opposition has been held by the RP and then by its successor party, the Canadian Alliance, which was formed in March 2000 and includes some leading former PCP figures.

Bernard Landry, *the outspoken separatist premier of Québec.*

Stockwell Day, *the leader of the CA opposition.*

Jean Chrétien, *prime minister since 1993.*

WORLD AFFAIRS

Joined UN in 1945

Comm | G7 | OECD | NAFTA | NATO

Canada's most important relationship is with the USA, its main trading partner. There are tensions, however. Specific disputes include those over dealings with Cuba and over environmental matters. Canada fears and resents pollution damage from oil transported between Alaska and the rest of the USA, and from industrial plants on the US border. Currently, disputes between Canada and the USA over the prohibitive tariff imposed on Canadian soft-wood lumber exports are the major cause of friction.

In the forefront on debt relief for the poorest countries, Canada also led the world in campaigning to outlaw anti-personnel landmines worldwide, hosting the December 1997 Ottawa conference which agreed an international treaty.

AID

Donor

US$1.70bn (donations)

Little change in 1999

Canada's aid budget, one of the first areas of government spending earmarked for cuts in the 1990s, was given extra funding again at the end of the decade. NGOs supported by the Canadian International Development Agency (CIDA) are prominent on global development issues, and most Canadians support aid.

Aid now aims to provide know-how skills, rather than funding for large-scale development projects. CIDA has pioneered a theme-based approach, stressing human rights, basic needs, gender issues, and good governance. The regional focus of aid has gradually shifted from Africa, to include programs in the 1990s to support recovery and reform in former communist countries, and toward the development needs of the Indian subcontinent.

DEFENSE

No compulsory military service

US$7.50bn

Down 2% in 1999

CANADIAN ARMED FORCES

114 main battle tanks (*Leopard* C–1/C–2)	20,900 personnel
12 frigates, 4 destroyers, and 14 patrol boats	9000 personnel
140 combat aircraft (122 CF–18)	13,500 personnel
None	

Canada cooperates closely with the USA on North American defense issues.

Defense spending was cut after the end of the Cold War, and many Canadians continue to advocate further reductions. Canada withdrew its forces stationed in Europe in 1992. The focus of defense planning is now the creation of rapid reaction forces. Canadian troops have served in many UN peacekeeping operations, most recently in Kosovo, East Timor, and Sierra Leone. Their involvement in Somalia, however, which ended in 1993, was tarnished by a scandal over racism, torture, and murder which shocked the whole country.

ECONOMICS

Inflation 1.4% p.a. (1990–1999)

US$614bn

1.451–1.502 Canadian dollars

SCORE CARD

- ❑ WORLD GNP RANKING..........................9th
- ❑ GNP PER CAPITA ....US$20,140
- ❑ BALANCE OF PAYMENTS ....US$–2.27bn
- ❑ INFLATION 1.7%
- ❑ UNEMPLOYMENT....................................6%

EXPORTS

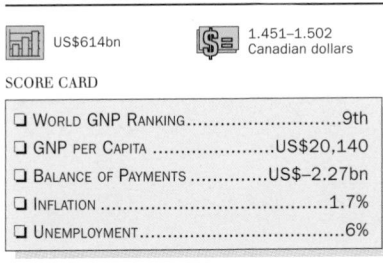

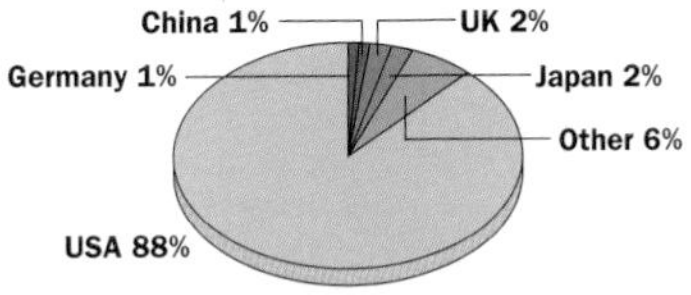
China 1%
UK 2%
Germany 1%
Japan 2%
Other 6%
USA 88%

IMPORTS

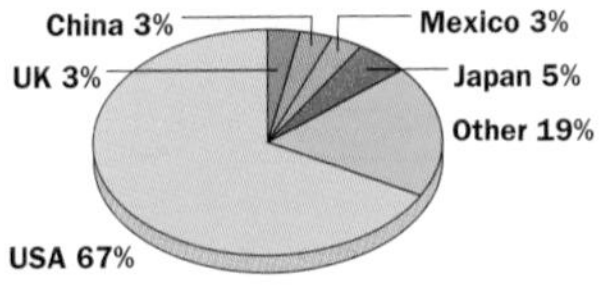
China 3%
Mexico 3%
UK 3%
Japan 5%
Other 19%
USA 67%

STRENGTHS

A broad and rich resource base. Provides exports, raw materials for manufacturing sector, and massive cheap energy, notably HEP; also large oil and gas reserves. Agriculture and forestry contribute 3% of GDP, mining 4%. Successful manufacturing sector, contributes 17% of GDP, especially forestry products, transportation equipment, and chemicals. Strong recovery and growth from mid-1990s. Free access to huge US and Mexican markets through NAFTA. Low inflation.

WEAKNESSES

Problems of competitiveness; higher taxes, more regulations, lower productivity relative to NAFTA; other threats from globalization. Vulnerable to price fluctuations for raw material exports. Federal and provincial budget deficits are still high.

ECONOMIC PERFORMANCE INDICATOR

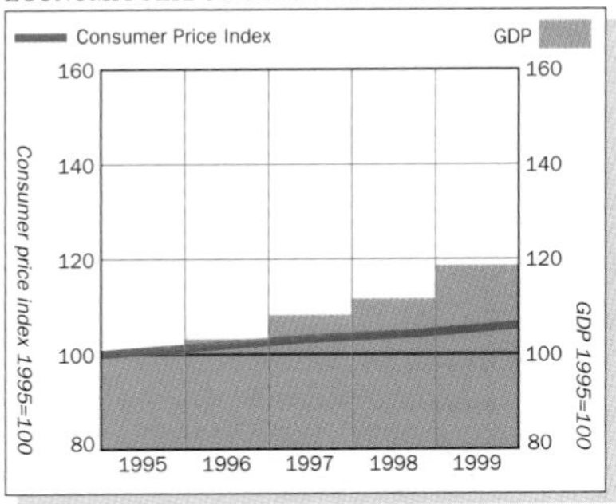
Consumer Price Index
GDP
160
140
120
100
80
Consumer price index 1995=100
GDP 1995=100
1995
1996
1997
1998
1999

PROFILE

Canada has an enormous resource base, and the UN rates it as having one of the highest standards of living in the world. Since the mid-1980s, however, its manufactured exports have faced increasing competition, while prices for its primary exports fluctuate. Real growth averaged 3.5% a year for most of the 1980s, but then stagnated for five years, while budget deficits rose, forcing restructuring at both federal and provincial levels. Many of Canada's welfare programs were cut back, while the defense budget was sharply reduced. Growth resumed after 1993 and strengthened through the end of the decade. As a consequence of Canada's membership of NAFTA, its firms have had to become more competitive to maintain exports. Most have been successful, with better productivity and a shift to high tech, and unemployment, at almost 10% in the mid-1990s, fell back to just over 6% by the end of 2000.

CANADA : MAJOR BUSINESSES

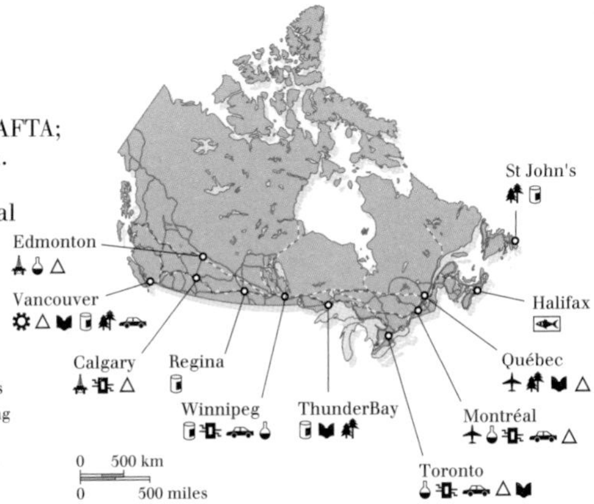
St John's
Edmonton
Vancouver
Halifax
Calgary
Regina
Québec
Winnipeg
ThunderBay
Montréal
Toronto
0 500 km
0 500 miles

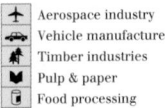

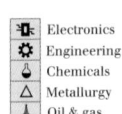

- Aerospace industry
- Vehicle manufacture
- Timber industries
- Pulp & paper
- Food processing
- Fish processing
- Electronics
- Engineering
- Chemicals
- Metallurgy
- Oil & gas

RESOURCES

Electric power 114m kw

1.03m tonnes

2.7m b/d (reserves 6,400,000,000 bbl)

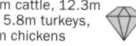

12.7m cattle, 12.3m pigs, 5.8m turkeys, 145m chickens

Coal, oil, gas, gold, zinc, uranium, nickel, potash, asbestos, gypsum

ELECTRICITY GENERATION

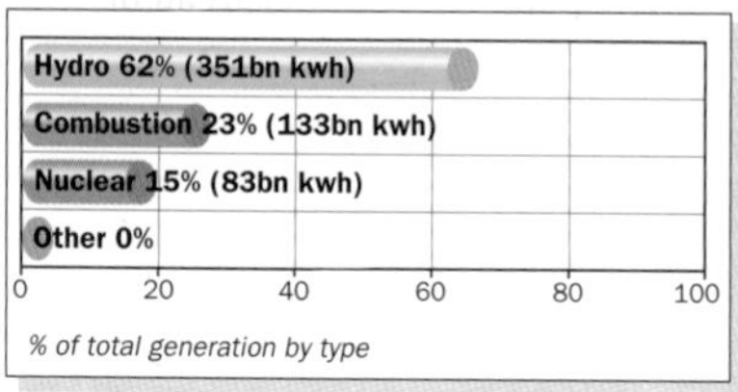

Hydro 62% (351bn kwh)
Combustion 23% (133bn kwh)
Nuclear 15% (83bn kwh)
Other 0%
0
20
40
60
80
100
% of total generation by type

Canada is a country of enormous natural resources. It is the world's largest exporter of forest products and a top exporter of fish, furs, and wheat. Minerals have played a key role in Canada's transformation into an urban–industrial economy. Alberta, British Columbia, Québec, and Saskatchewan are the principal mining regions. Ontario and the Northwest (NWT) and Yukon Territories are also significant producers. Canada is the world's largest producer of zinc and uranium, the second-largest of nickel, asbestos, potash, and gypsum. Oil and gas are exploited in Alberta, off the Atlantic coast, and in the northwest – huge additional reserves are thought to exist in the high Arctic. Most exports go to the USA. Canada is also one of the world's top hydroelectricity producers.

CANADA : LAND USE

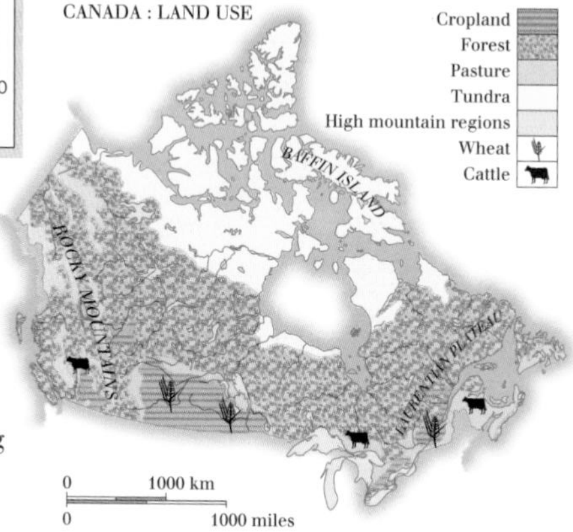

Cropland
Forest
Pasture
Tundra
High mountain regions
Wheat
Cattle
BAFFIN ISLAND
ROCKY MOUNTAINS
LAURENTIAN PLATEAU
0
1000 km
0
1000 miles

ENVIRONMENT

Sustainability rank: 3rd

10% (2% partially protected)

16.6 tonnes per capita

ENVIRONMENTAL TREATIES

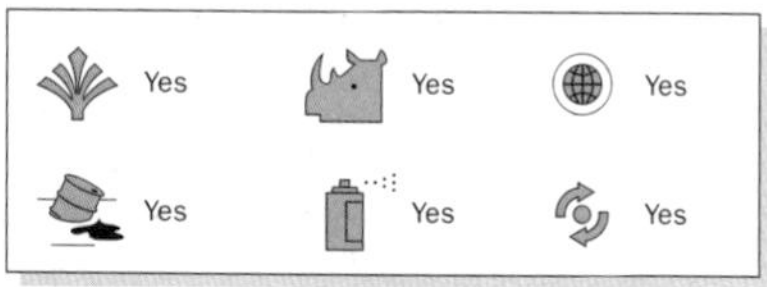

Yes
Yes
Yes
Yes
Yes
Yes

With a population of only some 31 million living in the world's third-largest country, Canada is justly renowned for vast tracts of wilderness untroubled by industrial pollution or pollution caused by intensive farming methods. A major conservation issue is the battle to stop the logging of virgin forest in northern Ontario and on the west coast. Notable successes were achieved in the late 1990s, pressuring timber companies to adopt more sustainable policies, and a landmark agreement in early 2001 promised protection for British Columbia's coastal Great Bear Rainforest.

Canadians have tighter pollution controls than the neighboring USA. Ontario, the most polluted province, has imposed stricter limits on oil refineries and (from 2001) on electricity-generating plants. Carbon dioxide emissions (mainly from cars) are the world's third-highest per person. Canada has accepted a target of a 6% cut by 2010. Production of hazardous waste is also higher than the European average.

MEDIA

TV ownership high

Daily newspaper circulation 158 per 1000 people

PUBLISHING AND BROADCAST MEDIA

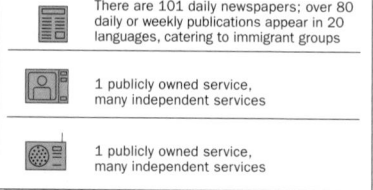

There are 101 daily newspapers; over 80 daily or weekly publications appear in 20 languages, catering to immigrant groups

1 publicly owned service, many independent services

1 publicly owned service, many independent services

The public Canadian Broadcasting Corporation (CBC) runs two national TV channels, in English and French; the Canadian Alliance wants it partially privatized. Local cable services often include multilingual or ethnic channels. Canadian TV is renowned for its news and sports coverage. *La Presse* is the leading French-language daily and the *Globe and Mail* the leading serious newspaper in English.

***Autumn in the tundra** in northern Canada. Trees such as the black spruce are subject to the effects of acid rain originating in the USA's northern industrial regions.*

CRIME

Death penalty not used

33,882 prisoners

Down 7% 1996–1998

CRIME RATES

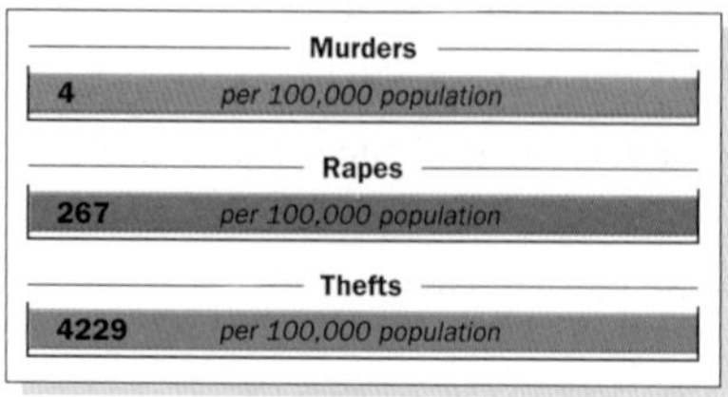

Murders
4
per 100,000 population
Rapes
267
per 100,000 population
Thefts
4229
per 100,000 population

Rates for serious crime are lower in Canada than in the USA. Canadians ascribe this to their far stricter gun control laws, which were further tightened in the 1990s. Newfoundland police began carrying guns routinely only in 1998, and as such were the last force in North America to do so. There have been careful efforts to maintain the inner cities as crime-free zones. The ghetto problems of US inner cities have largely been avoided. However, Canada does have a rising narcotics problem, and youth crime is also growing.

EDUCATION

School leaving age: 16

99%

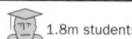

1.8m students

THE EDUCATION SYSTEM

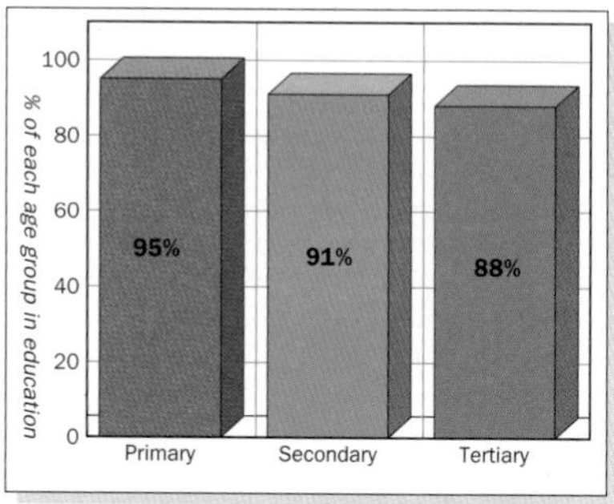

100
80
60
40
20
0
% of each age group in education
95%
91%
88%
Primary
Secondary
Tertiary

Education is a responsibility of the provinces and is accorded high priority. The period of free compulsory school attendance varies, but is a minimum of nine years. The prime medium of instruction is English in all provinces except francophone Québec. In several other provinces, French-speaking students are entitled to be taught in French. Multicultural education also helps maintain the cultural identity of immigrant groups.

Canada has 76 universities and some 200 other higher education institutions. Nearly all high school graduates go on to some form of higher education – the highest proportion in the industrialized world. The emphasis placed on education is also reflected in the fact that Canada's total education expenditure as a percentage of GDP is among the highest in the world.

QUÉBEC'S DISTINCT SOCIETY AND SEPARATISM

QUÉBEC IS CANADA'S largest province, with an area of 1,667,926 sq km (594,860 sq miles). Its population, 7.3 million at the 1994 census, includes more than five million of Canada's 6.1 million French Canadians, most of whom are Catholics. The province's capital is Québec City. Its leading commercial center, Montréal, has suffered a decline in prestige compared with Toronto, neighboring Ontario's main city, which is overwhelmingly English-speaking. Québec has massive hydroelectric power resources and vast areas of forest, and its principal industries include timber, pulp and paper, and mining, particularly for iron ore. Consequently, environmental protection legislation is relatively lax, and there is conflict with those seeking to protect First Nation lands from devastation by logging and massive dam schemes.

Conquered by the British in the 18th century, the Québecois retained the French civil code under the 1774 Québec Act, but French Canadians only gradually recovered minority language rights suppressed after an unsuccessful rebellion in the 1830s. A so-called "quiet revolution" began in the 1960s, based initially on militant trade unionism. This brought far-reaching changes in the social, economic, and political balance in Québec. The wage gap closed, and francophones now slightly out-earn anglophones, partly because many of the best-educated anglophones tend to leave the province. Francophone-owned businesses were built up through the "Québec Inc" project. The anglophone dominance in government and the civil service was reversed, and higher education opportunities for francophones expanded. Québec now has four French-language and three English-language universities.

E. PRINCE ARTHUR STREET
GROCER
BEER
ARRET
STOP

***Bilingual street signs** in Québec have now largely been replaced by French-only signs.*

RESTAURANT
CAFÉ DE PARIS

***French shop signs** above the streets of Québec City.*

Francophone militancy was also channeled into party politics, fueled by resentment at a harsh security clampdown against the guerrilla Québec Liberation Front in the early 1970s. The Parti Québécois (PQ), unexpectedly gained control of the provincial Assembly in 1976, and a French language charter, Bill 101, was enacted almost immediately. French became not only the official language but compulsory in government and on public signs. Non-francophones protested, and the Canadian Supreme Court ruled in 1988 that part of the language charter violated their human rights, but the provincial government managed to keep these rules in force on a "temporary" basis.

The PQ's other important initiative was sovereignty for Québec. After its defeat in a referendum in 1980, the idea was revived in the 1990s amid long-running disputes about the Canadian constitution and provincial–federal relationships. The PQ, promising a second referendum (and backed by its newly formed counterpart at federal level, the BQ), returned to power in Québec in 1994. The following year, 60% of Québec's francophone majority voted in favor of sovereignty in association with Canada, a high-water mark for separatism; the proposition was defeated by the narrowest of margins by the non-francophone vote. After the PQ's disappointing showings in the 1998 provincial and 2000 federal elections, even francophones, still fiercely protective of their language and culture, appeared increasingly disposed to settle for a federal compromise which acknowledged Québec's "unique character."

HEALTH

Welfare state health benefits

1 per 476 people

Heart and respiratory diseases, cancers, accidents

The comprehensive state health service is funded from national insurance.

Rising costs are the result of an aging population and the spread of more sophisticated and expensive treatments. Health care was the main issue of the 2000 election campaign. Popular backing for retaining the present publicly funded system has encouraged the LP government to restore spending to earlier levels, after a period of cuts made in an effort to reduce the budget deficit. About 25% of Canadians use private health facilities.

SPENDING

GDP/cap. increase

CONSUMPTION AND SPENDING

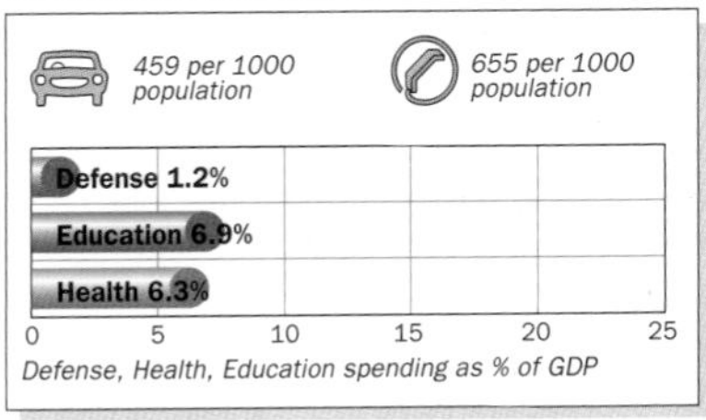
459 per 1000 population
655 per 1000 population
Defense 1.2%
Education 6.9%
Health 6.3%
0
5
10
15
20
25
Defense, Health, Education spending as % of GDP

Despite strains caused by recession during the early 1990s – including a rise in unemployment to over 10% – life for most Canadians remains very good.

The UN ranks Canada as one of the best countries in the world in which to live. In its overall assessment of human development indicators such as income, education, and life expectancy, Canada consistently comes out top, or near top, and ahead of the USA.

However, disadvantaged groups do exist, in particular among indigenous Canadians. Unemployment, poor housing, and mortality rates for Amerindians and Inuits are well above those for other Canadians; the Inuit suicide rate is three times higher. Those Amerindians who live on reserves are the poorest group.

WORLD RANKING

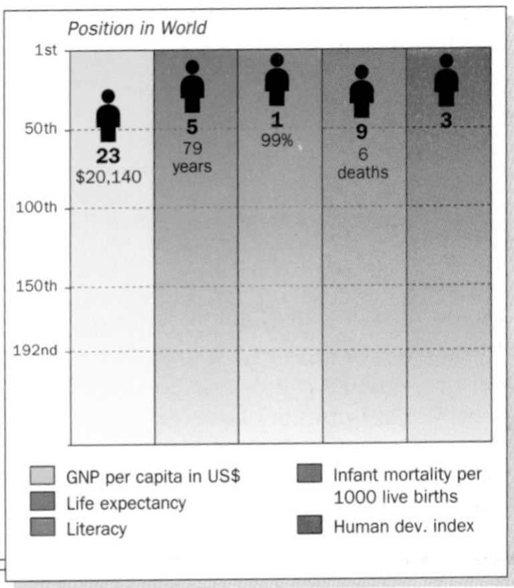
Position in World
1st
50th
100th
150th
192nd
23
$20,140
5
79 years
1
99%
9
6 deaths
3
GNP per capita in US$
Life expectancy
Literacy
Infant mortality per 1000 live births
Human dev. index

CAPE VERDE

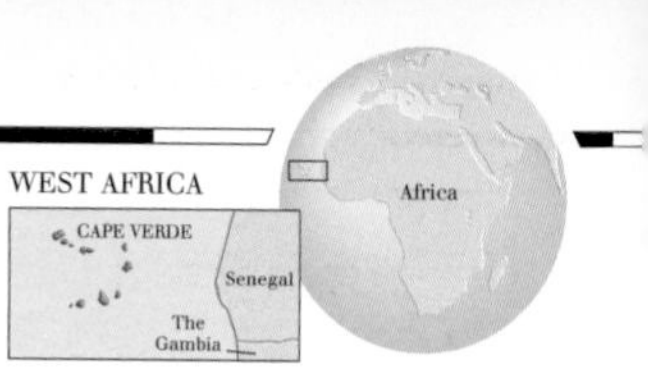
WEST AFRICA
CAPE VERDE
Senegal
The Gambia
Africa

OFFICIAL NAME: Republic of Cape Verde **CAPITAL:** Praia
POPULATION: 428,000 **CURRENCY:** Cape Verde escudo **OFFICIAL LANGUAGE:** Portuguese

C

1975 | 1975 | July 5 | CV | -1 | +238 | .cv

THE CAPE VERDE ARCHIPELAGO off the west coast of Africa became independent of Portugal in 1975. Most of the islands are mountainous and volcanic; the low-lying islands of Sal, Boa Vista, and Maio have agricultural potential, though they are prone to debilitating droughts. Around 50% of the population lives on São Tiago. A period of single-party socialist rule followed independence. Cape Verde held its first multiparty elections in 1991.

CLIMATE

Tropical oceanic

WEATHER CHART

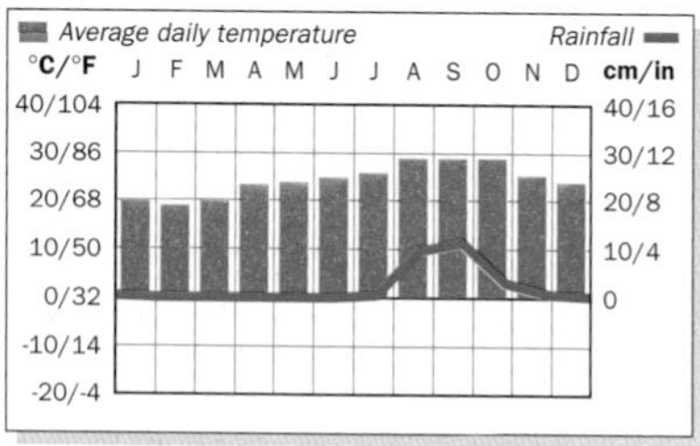
Average daily temperature
Rainfall
°C/°F
J F M A M J J A S O N D
cm/in
40/104
30/86
20/68
10/50
0/32
-10/14
-20/-4
40/16
30/12
20/8
10/4
0

Cape Verde has a very dry climate, subject to droughts that sometimes last for years at a time.

TRANSPORTATION

Drive on right

Amílcar Cabral, Sal Island 492,804 passengers

37 ships 19,900 grt

THE TRANSPORTATION NETWORK

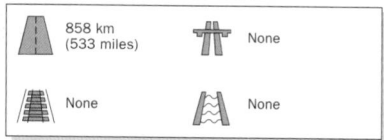

858 km (533 miles)

None

None

None

Cape Verde has a strategic position on international sea and air routes, which it is beginning to exploit.

TOURISM

Visitors : Population 1:5.8

74,000 visitors

Up 68% in 2000

MAIN TOURIST ARRIVALS

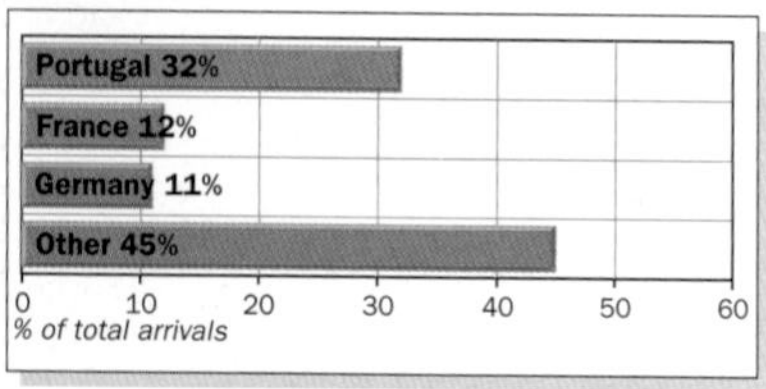
Portugal 32%
France 12%
Germany 11%
Other 45%
0 10 20 30 40 50 60
% of total arrivals

Tourism has not been a government priority and remains on a modest scale. The islands of São Tiago, Santo Antão, Fogo, and Brava have tourist potential, offering a combination of mountain scenery and extensive beaches.

PEOPLE

Pop. density medium

Portuguese Creole, Portuguese

106/m² (275/mi²)

THE URBAN/RURAL POPULATION SPLIT

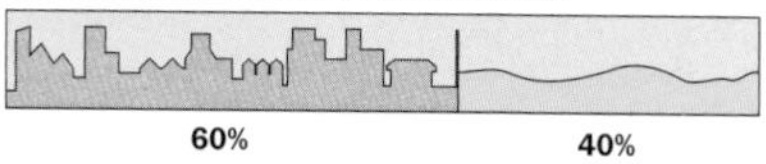
60%
40%

ETHNIC MAKEUP

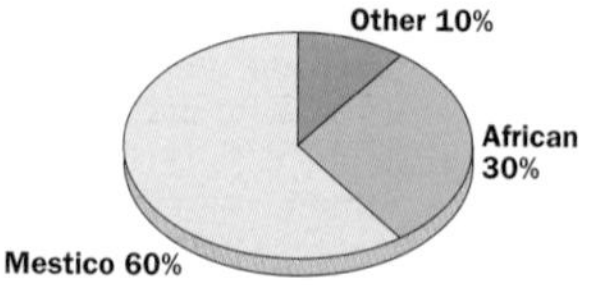
Other 10%
African 30%
Mestico 60%

The majority of the population is Portuguese–African *mestico*; the remainder is largely African, descended either from slaves or from more recent immigrants from the mainland. The Creolization of the culture has led to a relative lack of ethnic tension, though there is some bad feeling between islands. African traditions of the extended family as well as the Roman Catholic Church have helped to ensure the vitality of family life. However, women outnumber men in Cape Verde, with many single mothers acting as head of the household and main breadwinner.

POLITICS

Multiparty elections

2001/2006

President Pedro Pires

AT THE LAST ELECTION

National Assembly 72 seats

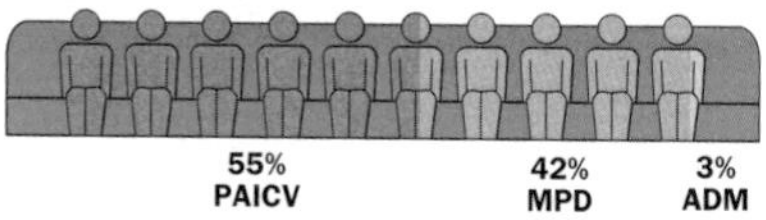
55% PAICV
42% MPD
3% ADM

PAICV = African Party for the Independence of Cape Verde
MPD = Movement for Democracy
ADM = Democratic Alliance for Change

Cape Verde experienced a peaceful transition to multipartyism in 1991, when elections brought the MPD to power. Although there had previously been a decade of single-party rule under the PAICV, it had in fact operated a liberal system in which opposition and dissent were tolerated. The large Cape Verdean diaspora had an important influence in effecting the transition to multiparty politics.

The MPD was defeated in legislative elections in January 2001, when the PAICV was returned to power with an absolute majority. Pedro Pires of the PAICV was elected president the following month, beating his MPD rival by just 17 votes. The main issue for the current government is that of economic survival, particularly during periods of drought.

WORLD AFFAIRS

Joined UN in 1975

CPLP | ECOWAS | OIF | NAM | OAU

Cape Verde wishes to diversify its international contacts in order to secure aid, while maintaining good relations with Portugal, the former colonial power, although the latter is not a major donor. Within the region, Cape Verde seeks to restore normal relations with Guinea-Bissau, having withdrawn from a proposed union in 1980, and to improve contacts with other mainland states, such as Senegal.

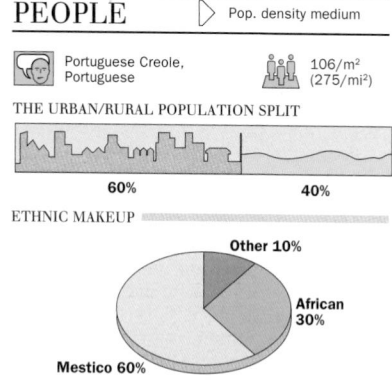

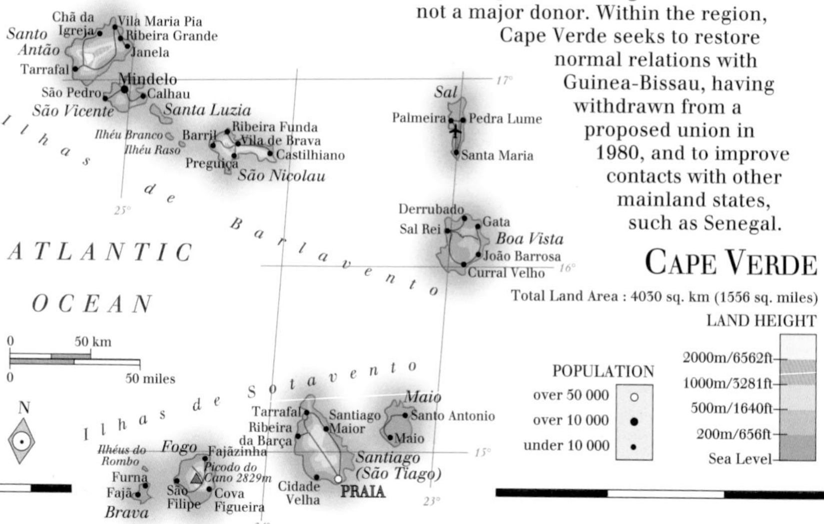
Santo Antão
Chã da Igreja
Vila Maria Pia
Ribeira Grande
Janela
Tarrafal
Mindelo
São Pedro
Calhau
São Vicente
Santa Luzia
Ilhéu Branco
Ilhéu Raso
Barril
Ribeira Funda
Vila de Brava
Castilhiano
Preguiça
São Nicolau
Ilhas de Barlavento
Sal
Palmeira
Pedra Lume
Santa Maria
Derrubado
Sal Rei
Gata
Boa Vista
João Barrosa
Curral Velho
ATLANTIC OCEAN
0 50 km
0 50 miles
N
Ilhas de Sotavento
Tarrafal
Ribeira da Barça
Santiago
Maior
Maio
Santo Antonio
Maio
Santiago (São Tiago)
PRAIA
Cidade Velha
Ilhéus do Rombo
Fogo
Fajãzinha
Pico do Cano 2829m
Furna
Fajã
Brava
São Filipe
Cova Figueira
CAPE VERDE
Total Land Area : 4030 sq. km (1556 sq. miles)
LAND HEIGHT
2000m/6562ft
1000m/3281ft
500m/1640ft
200m/656ft
Sea Level
POPULATION
over 50 000
over 10 000
under 10 000

AID

Recipient

$136m (receipts)

Up 5% in 1999

The most important donor is the EU, which has provided substantial food aid in the wake of recent droughts, as well as funding aid programs. The World Bank is also a major source, as are the Netherlands, Sweden, Germany, France, and Italy. Aid finances almost all development in Cape Verde, which is one of the least industrialized countries in the world.

DEFENSE

Compulsory military service

$7m

Up 75% in 1999

After independence, small armed forces were established, now consisting of a 1000-strong army, a small air force, and a naval coastguard. They have never been called upon to play a political role; their main duties are to protect territorial waters against illegal fishing and to curb smuggling.

ECONOMICS

Inflation 5.1% p.a. (1990–1999)

$569m

109.7–118.2 Cape Verde escudos

SCORE CARD

- World GNP Ranking 167th
- GNP per Capita $1330
- Balance of Payments .... $-58m
- Inflation 4.3%
- Unemployment 35%

Strengths

Strategic geographical position, off the westernmost tip of Africa, close to the mid-Atlantic where Africa is nearest to Latin America. This has military and economic advantages, including shipping maintenance and air travel. Low debt-servicing costs.

Weaknesses

Permanent threat of drought and water supply problems, despite desalination plants. Lack of agricultural land and dependency on food aid. Difficulties of communications between islands.

EXPORTS

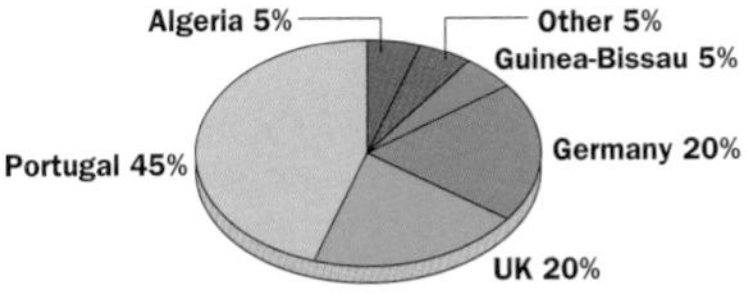
Algeria 5%
Other 5%
Guinea-Bissau 5%
Portugal 45%
Germany 20%
UK 20%

IMPORTS

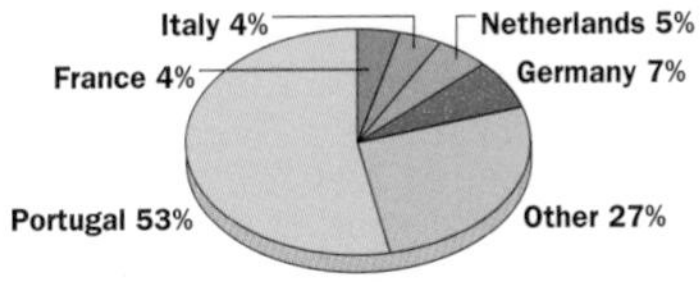
Italy 4%
Netherlands 5%
France 4%
Germany 7%
Portugal 53%
Other 27%

***Portuguese colonial-style architecture** on Fogo, one of the larger islands. The volcano in its center is the highest point in Cape Verde.*

RESOURCES

Electric power 7000 kw

10,039 tonnes

Not an oil producer

636,000 pigs, 112,000 goats, 417,000 chickens

Salt, pozzolana

Cape Verde has no known strategic resources. With no oil or gas and no possibility of hydroelectric power, it depends on imported petroleum for energy. However, experimental projects have been carried out to investigate the potential of wave power, windmills, and biogas.

ENVIRONMENT

Not available

None

0.3 tonnes per capita

Cape Verde has recently suffered several years of persistent drought, which has affected food production and reduced livestock herds. It is a very active member of CILSS, which struggles against drought in the Sahel region. Environmental initiatives include reforestation, soil conservation, and a water resources program.

MEDIA

TV ownership low

There are no daily newspapers

PUBLISHING AND BROADCAST MEDIA

There are no daily newspapers. Independent publications suffer from financial pressures

1 state-controlled service

1 state-controlled service

The government publishes three weeklies, but there are no daily newspapers. Press freedom is guaranteed by law. TV and radio broadcasting are in Portuguese and Creole, with the cooperation of the Portuguese service RTPI.

CRIME

Death penalty not used

Cape Verde does not publish prison figures

Little change from year to year

Crime is not a serious problem, even in urban centers, though smuggling is fairly widespread.

CHRONOLOGY

Cape Verde was a Portuguese colony from 1462 until 1975, and was ruled jointly with Guinea-Bissau.

- **1961** Joint struggle for independence of Cape Verde and Guinea-Bissau begins.
- **1974** Guinea-Bissau independent.
- **1975** Independence.
- **1981** Final split from Guinea-Bissau.
- **1991** MPD wins first multiparty poll.
- **2001** General election returns PAICV to power.

EDUCATION

School leaving age: 13

74%

Not available

At independence, education became a priority; 80% of children now attend elementary school, and more than 60% go on to secondary education.

HEALTH

No welfare state health benefits

1 per 3448 people

Heart disease, tuberculosis, typhoid, and accidents

Health care has improved since the colonial period, and polio has been virtually eradicated.

SPENDING

GDP/cap. increase

CONSUMPTION AND SPENDING

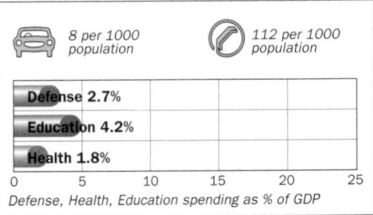

8 per 1000 population

112 per 1000 population

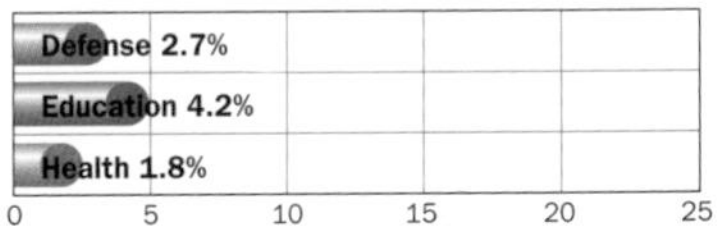
Defense 2.7%
Education 4.2%
Health 1.8%
0
5
10
15
20
25

Defense, Health, Education spending as % of GDP

In comparison with the 90% of the population engaged in primary production, the small business class in Praia is well-off.

WORLD RANKING

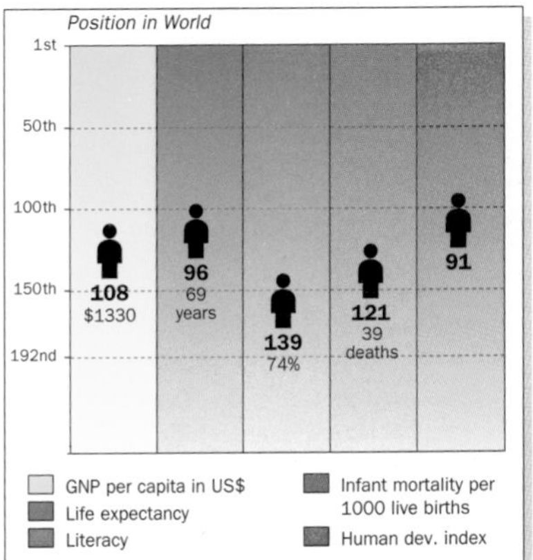
Position in World
1st
50th
100th
150th
192nd
108
$1330
96
69 years
139
74%
121
39 deaths
91
GNP per capita in US$
Life expectancy
Literacy
Infant mortality per 1000 live births
Human dev. index

CENTRAL AFRICAN REPUBLIC

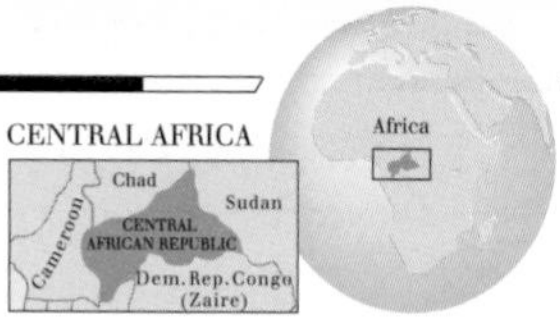
CENTRAL AFRICA
Chad
Sudan
CENTRAL AFRICAN REPUBLIC
Cameroon
Dem. Rep. Congo (Zaire)
Africa

OFFICIAL NAME: Central African Republic **CAPITAL:** Bangui
POPULATION: 3.6 million **CURRENCY:** CFA franc **OFFICIAL LANGUAGE:** French

C

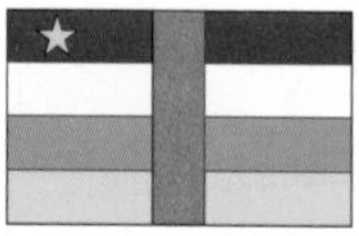

1960 | 1960 | Dec 1 | RCA | +1 | +236 | .cf

LANDLOCKED AT THE WESTERN end of the Sahel, the Central African Republic (CAR) is a low plateau stretching north from one of Africa's great rivers, the Ubangi, which forms its border with Dem. Rep. Congo (formerly Zaire). Almost all the population lives in the equatorial, rainforested south. "Emperor" Bokassa's eccentric rule from 1965 to 1979 was followed by military dictatorship. Democracy was restored in 1993.

CLIMATE

Tropical equatorial

WEATHER CHART

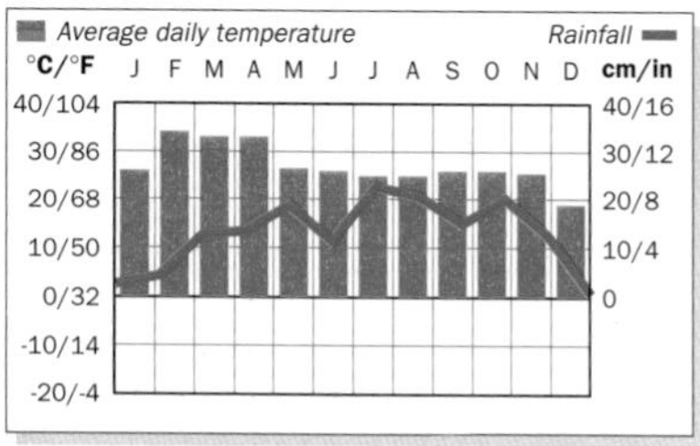
Average daily temperature
Rainfall
°C/°F
J F M A M J J A S O N D
cm/in
40/104
30/86
20/68
10/50
0/32
-10/14
-20/-4
40/16
30/12
20/8
10/4
0

The south is equatorial, the north has a savanna-type climate, and the far north lies within the Sahel.

TRANSPORTATION

Drive on right

Mpoko, Bangui 56,804 passengers

Has no fleet

THE TRANSPORTATION NETWORK

429 km (267 miles)

Trans-African Highway

None

800 km (497 miles)

The CAR has a limited transportation system, depending on the river link to Brazzaville, Congo, and rail from there to Pointe-Noire and the Congo river ports.

TOURISM

Visitors : Population 1:360

10,000 visitors

Up 43% in 1999

MAIN TOURIST ARRIVALS

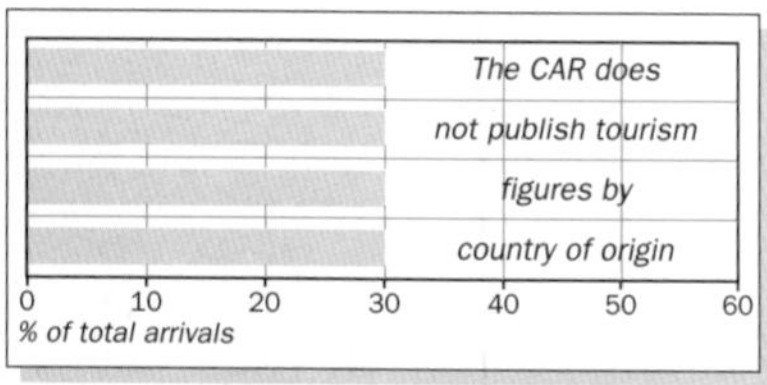
The CAR does not publish tourism figures by country of origin
0
10
20
30
40
50
60
% of total arrivals

Tourist promotion is small-scale, but since 1979 there has been a modest increase in national park safaris. A new runway in Bangui will permit air charters, chiefly from France.

PEOPLE

Pop. density low

Sango, Banda, Gbaya, French

6/km² (15/mi²)

THE URBAN/RURAL POPULATION SPLIT

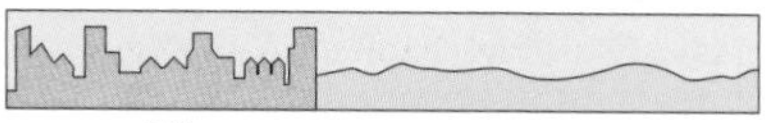
41%
59%

ETHNIC MAKEUP

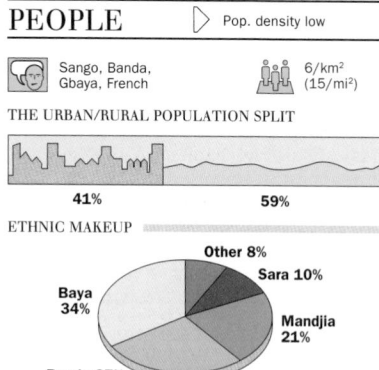

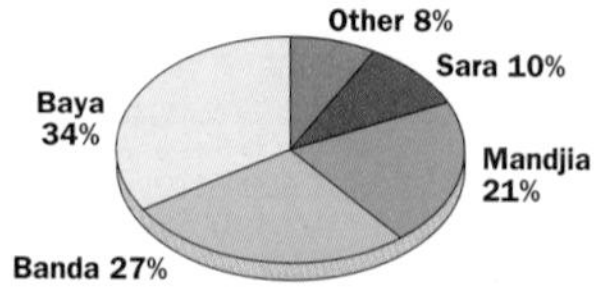
Other 8%
Sara 10%
Mandjia 21%
Banda 27%
Baya 34%

Although the Baya and the Banda are the largest ethnic groups, the lingua franca is Sango. This is spoken by the southern riverine minorities, who provided the political leaders from independence until 1993 (Presidents Dacko and Kolingba and "Emperor" Bokassa). President Patasse is from the interior. Resentment against the river peoples occasionally flares up, as happened after the coup attempt in 2001. Women, as in other non-Muslim African countries, have considerable power. Elizabeth Domitien was prime minister from 1975 to 1976 and Ruth Rolland ran for president in 1993.

POLITICS

Multiparty elections

1998/2003

President Ange-Félix Patasse

AT THE LAST ELECTION

National Assembly 109 seats

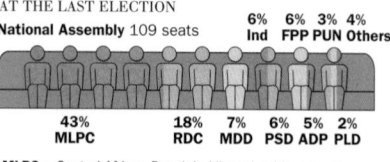

6% Ind
6% FPP
3% PUN
4% Others
43% MLPC
18% RDC
7% MDD
6% PSD
5% ADP
2% PLD

MLPC = Central African People's Liberation Movement **RDC** = Central African Democratic Rally **MDD** = Movement for Democracy and Development **Ind** = Independents **PSD** = Social Democratic Party **FPP** = Patriotic Front for Progress **ADP** = Alliance for Democracy and Progress **PUN** = National Unity Party **PLD** = Liberal Democratic Party

Democratic elections in 1993 ended four years of Gen. Kolingba's single-party rule, bringing in Ange-Félix Patasse as president. Patasse was Bokassa's prime minister during the 1970s, but he was jailed for dissent and subsequently went into exile in Paris. Army mutinies in 1996 prompted the formation of a government of national unity, but fighting continued, including an incident in Bangui when two French soldiers were killed. A French-led multinational force kept the peace from February 1997. It was replaced by a UN force (UNMICAR) in April 1998. Patasse's party, the MLPC, remains the most important in the new parliament after the 1998 elections but needs the support of opposition parties to maintain a workable coalition. A coup attempt in 2001, allegedly organized by Kolingba, provoked fierce fighting in Bangui.

WORLD AFFAIRS

Joined UN in 1960

BDEAC | CEMAC | FZ | LCBC | OAU

Apart from keeping up the momentum of its improving political image in international life, the CAR is anxious to continue good relations with France, whose financial help will be needed for some time, and with Cameroon and Congo, which provide its main outlets to the sea. Troops from Libya, Chad, and Dem. Rep. Congo (former Zaire) supported President Patasse against the coup in 2001.

AID

Recipient

$117m (receipts)

Down 3% in 1999

Almost all development projects are funded from external aid. France, the former colonial power, provides two-thirds of the total. EU countries (notably Belgium, Italy, and Germany), Japan, and (since 1989) the USA and Israel, are major donors. The CAR also receives assistance from the IMF and the World Bank.

DEFENSE

Compulsory military service

$45m

Down 10% in 1999

The 3000-strong army, which is well equipped, mostly with French hardware, is a heavy drain on the budget. Military service is selective. French officers fill senior army posts. In 1996, 1400 resident French troops intervened to quell the army rebellions; the garrison began to withdraw in 1997. UNMICAR forces were deployed from 1997 to 2000.

CENTRAL AFRICAN REPUBLIC

POPULATION

- over 500 000
- over 50 000
- over 10 000
- under 10 000

Total Land Area : 622 980 sq. km (240 530 sq. miles)

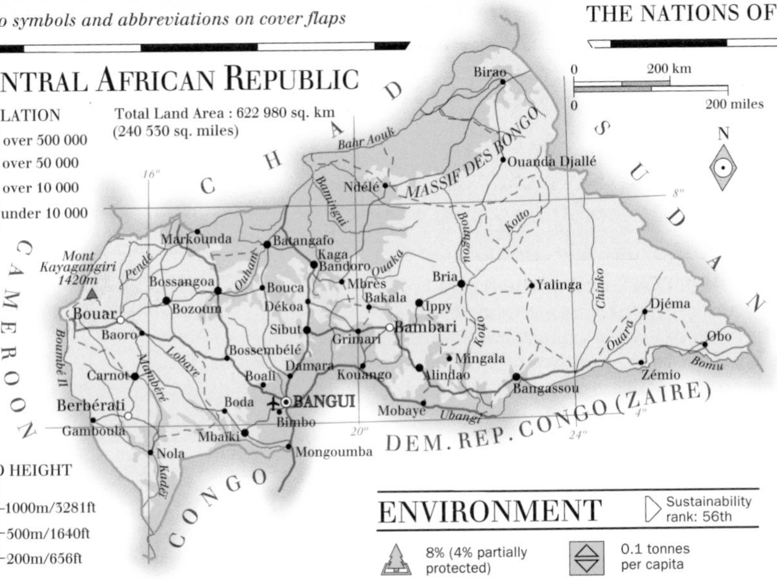

CHAD
SUDAN
CAMEROON
CONGO
DEM. REP. CONGO (ZAIRE)
200 km
200 miles
Birao
Ouanda Djallé
Ndélé
MASSIF DES BONGO
Markounda
Batangafo
Kaga Bandoro
Mont Kayagangiri 1420m
Bossangoa
Bouca
Mbrès
Bria
Yalinga
Bouar
Bozoum
Dékoa
Bakala
Ippy
Djéma
Baoro
Sibut
Grimari
Bambari
Obo
Bossembélé
Mingala
Zémio
Carnot
Boali
Damara
Kouango
Alindao
Bangassou
Berbérati
Boda
BANGUI
Mobaye
Gamboula
Bimbo
Mbaïki
Nola
Mongoumba
Ubangi
Bomu
Kotto
Chinko
LAND HEIGHT
1000m/3281ft
500m/1640ft
200m/656ft

CHRONOLOGY

The French established the colony of Ubangi-Chari in 1905 and gave it autonomy as the CAR in 1958.

- **1960** Independence under David Dacko; one-party state.
- **1965** Coup by Jean-Bédel Bokassa.
- **1977** Bokassa crowned "Emperor."
- **1979** French help reinstate Dacko.
- **1981** Gen. Kolingba ousts Dacko.
- **1996** Government of national unity formed following army rebellion.
- **2001** Coup attempt.

C

ECONOMICS

Inflation 4.9% p.a. (1990–1999)

$1bn

654.42–698.69 CFA francs

SCORE CARD

World GNP Ranking	153rd
GNP per Capita	$290
Balance of Payments	$-42m
Inflation	-1.9%
Unemployment	6%

STRENGTHS

Self-sufficiency in food. Some diversity of export earnings (diamonds, cotton, timber, iron, coffee). Status as transit zone in central Africa. Trans-African Highway and waterways.

WEAKNESSES

Landlocked. Poor infrastructure. Not enough trained people to run economy.

EXPORTS

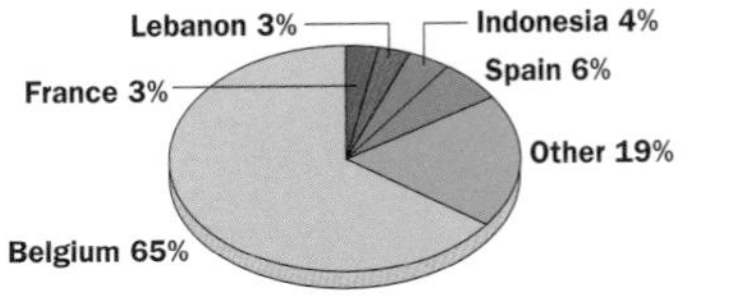

Lebanon 3%
Indonesia 4%
Spain 6%
France 3%
Other 19%
Belgium 65%

IMPORTS

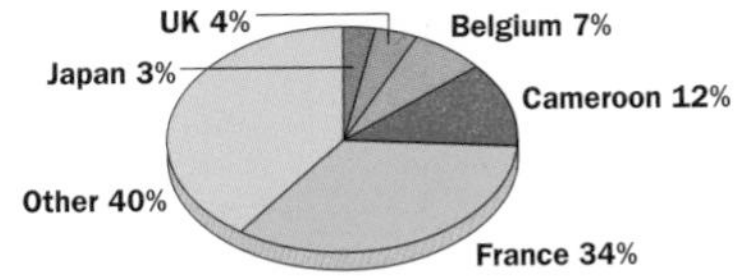

UK 4%
Belgium 7%
Japan 3%
Cameroon 12%
Other 40%
France 34%

RESOURCES

Electric power 43,000 kw

12,860 tonnes

Not an oil producer and has no refineries

2.95m cattle, 2.6m goats, 650,000 pigs, 4.1m chickens

Diamonds, gold, uranium, iron, copper, manganese

Cotton and diamonds are the CAR's major exports. Other minerals are potentially important.

ENVIRONMENT

Sustainability rank: 56th

8% (4% partially protected)

0.1 tonnes per capita

There has been an attempt to impose a conservationist forest policy. Hunting of elephants was banned in 1985 as numbers had fallen from 80,000 in the mid-1970s to just over 13,000.

MEDIA

TV ownership low

Daily newspaper circulation 2 per 1000 people

PUBLISHING AND BROADCAST MEDIA

There are 3 daily newspapers, *E Le Songo, Le Citoyen,* and *Le Novateur*

1 state-owned service

1 state-owned service

The three weeklies and three daily newspapers have only limited circulation. A small opposition press has developed with multipartyism, but is inhibited by lack of resources.

CRIME

Death penalty not used

CAR does not publish prison figures

Crime is rising

Human rights abuses have been reduced dramatically since the excesses of the Bokassa years. The level of criminality is usually low. The major criminal problem appears to be the increase in urban robbery resulting from continued political instability from 1996.

Baskets of cotton, *Meme village. Cotton is one of the Central African Republic's most significant export crops.*

EDUCATION

School leaving age: 14

47%

3684 students

Schooling, on the French model, is compulsory, but in practice is only received by 68% of 6–14 year olds.

HEALTH

No welfare state health benefits

1 per 10,000 people

Communicable and parasitic diseases, malnutrition

Colonial neglect and postcolonial maladministration have resulted in a poorly developed health system.

SPENDING

GDP/cap. increase

CONSUMPTION AND SPENDING

1 per 1000 population

3 per 1000 population

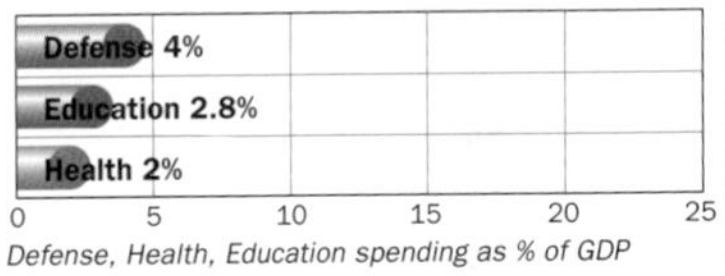

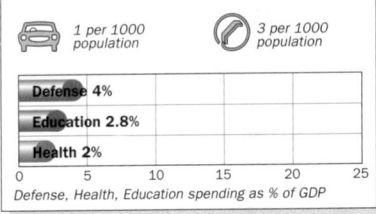

Defense 4%
Education 2.8%
Health 2%
0
5
10
15
20
25
Defense, Health, Education spending as % of GDP

There is a small political–military elite in the CAR, which came into being only in postcolonial days. For its members Paris is the chosen destination and style leader.

WORLD RANKING

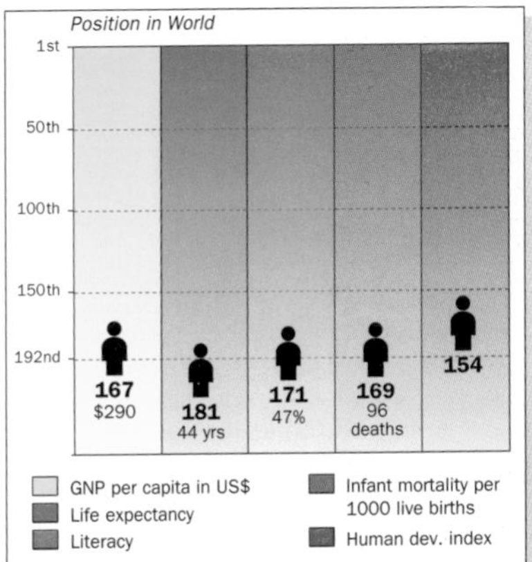

Position in World
1st
50th
100th
150th
192nd
167
$290
181
44 yrs
171
47%
169
96 deaths
154
GNP per capita in US$
Life expectancy
Literacy
Infant mortality per 1000 live births
Human dev. index

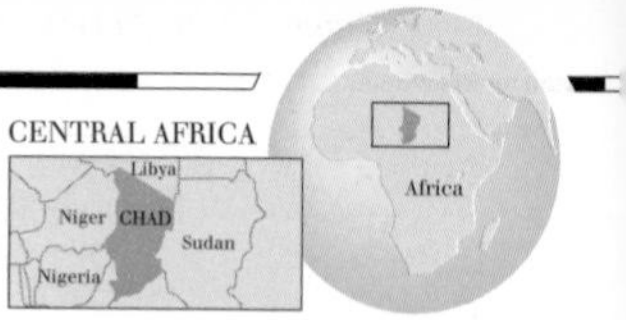
CENTRAL AFRICA
Libya
Niger
CHAD
Sudan
Nigeria
Africa

CHAD

OFFICIAL NAME: Republic of Chad **CAPITAL:** N'Djamena **POPULATION:** 7.7 million
CURRENCY: CFA franc **OFFICIAL LANGUAGES:** Arabic and French

C

1960 | 1960 | Aug 11 | TCH | +1 | +235 | .td

LANDLOCKED IN NORTH central Africa, Chad has had a turbulent history since independence from France in 1960. Intermittent periods of civil war, involving French and Libyan troops, followed a military coup in 1975. Following a coup in 1990, an interim government commenced the transition to multipartyism, now enshrined in a new constitution. The discovery of large oil reserves could eventually have a dramatic impact on the economy. The tropical, cotton-producing south is the most populous region.

CLIMATE

Hot desert/steppe

WEATHER CHART

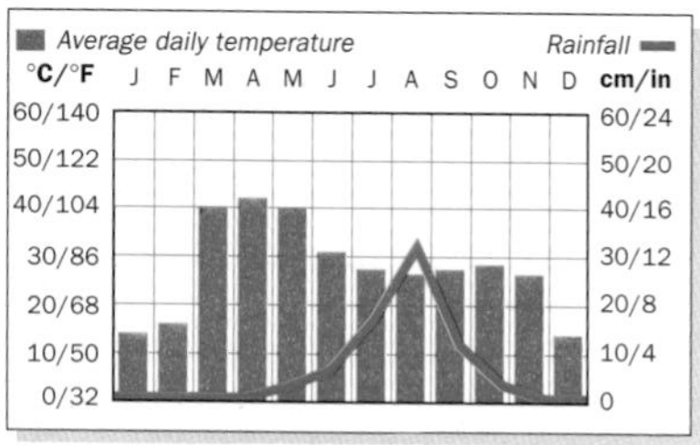
Average daily temperature
Rainfall
°C/°F
J F M A M J J A S O N D
cm/in
60/140
50/122
40/104
30/86
20/68
10/50
0/32
60/24
50/20
40/16
30/12
20/8
10/4
0

There are three distinct zones: the tropical south, the central semiarid Sahelian belt, and the desert north.

TRANSPORTATION

Drive on right

N'Djamena International 7760 passengers

Has no fleet

THE TRANSPORTATION NETWORK

267 km (166 miles)	None
None	2000 km (1243 miles)

Chad has a limited transportation infrastructure. The nearest rail links are in Nigeria and Cameroon.

TOURISM

Visitors : Population 1:193

40,000 visitors

Down 15% in 2000

MAIN TOURIST ARRIVALS

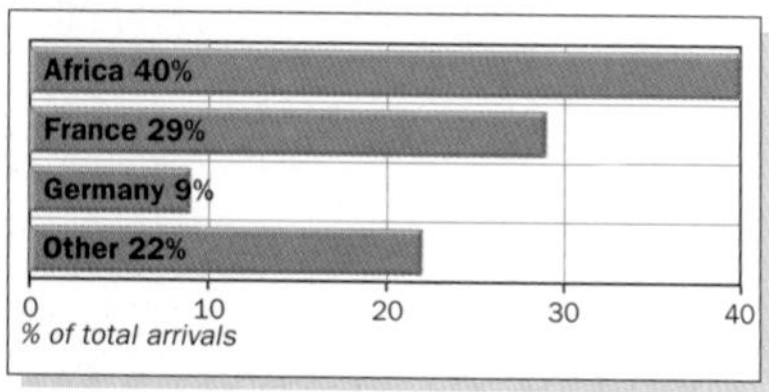
Africa 40%
France 29%
Germany 9%
Other 22%
0
10
20
30
40
% of total arrivals

Tourism is virtually nonexistent. The national parks and game reserves are the main potential attractions. The prehistoric rock painting of the Tibesti plateau and the Muslim cities of central Chad attract the adventurous.

***Watering hole at Oum Hadjer,** a village on the Batha watercourse in central Chad, 145 km (90 miles) east of Ati.*

PEOPLE

Pop. density low

French, Sara, Arabic, Maba

6/km² (16/mi²)

THE URBAN/RURAL POPULATION SPLIT

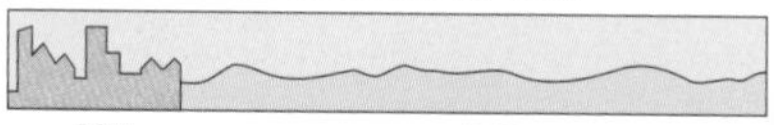
23%
77%

RELIGIOUS PERSUASION

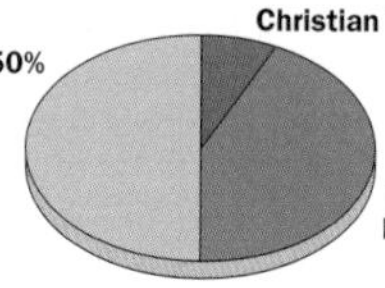
Christian 7%
Muslim 50%
Traditional beliefs 43%

About half the population, mainly the Sara-speaking and related peoples, is concentrated in the south in one-fifth of the national territory. Most of the rest are located in the central sultanates. The northern third of Chad has a population of only 100,000 people, mainly nomadic Muslim Toubou.

POLITICS

Multiparty elections

1997/2002

President Idriss Déby

AT THE LAST ELECTION

National Assembly 125 seats

3% UDR
2% Vacant
51% MPS
23% URD
12% UNDR
2% RDP
7% Others

MPS = Patriotic Salvation Movement **URD** = Union for Renewal and Democracy **UNDR** = National Union for Development and Renewal **UDR** = Union for Democracy and the Republic **RDP** = Rally for Democracy and Progress

Idriss Déby overthrew President Hissène Habré in 1990 after an armed invasion from Sudan. He promised multipartyism, and in 1992 legalized political parties for the first time since the early 1960s. After many delays, the transitional process led to a successful referendum in 1996 on a new constitution based on the French model. President Déby was confirmed in office in elections in 1996 and again in 2001. His ruling MPS won 63 seats in parliament in the 1997 elections, just achieving an overall majority. Despite the government's attempts to restore peace, a new rebellion broke out in the north in early 1999, among the nomadic Toubou people.

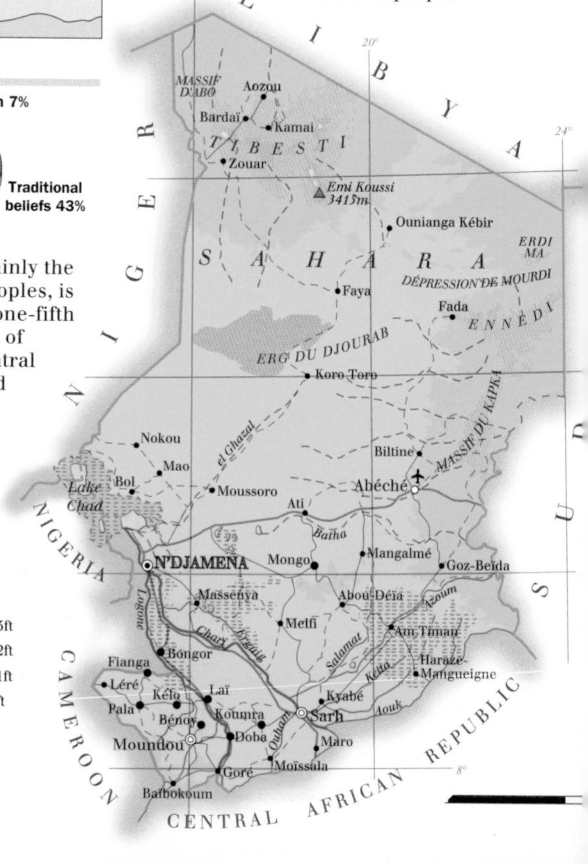
LIBYA
NIGER
NIGERIA
CAMEROON
CENTRAL AFRICAN REPUBLIC
SUDAN
MASSIF D'ABO
Aozou
Bardaï
Kamai
TIBESTI
Zouar
Emi Koussi 3415m
Ounianga Kébir
SAHARA
ERDI MA
DÉPRESSION DE MOURDI
Faya
Fada
ENNEDI
ERG DU DJOURAB
Koro Toro
Nokou
Mao
Bol
Lake Chad
Moussoro
Biltine
Abéché
Ati
Batha
N'DJAMENA
Mongo
Mangalmé
Goz-Beïda
Massenya
Abou-Déïa
Melfi
Am Timan
Haraze-Mangueigne
Bongor
Fianga
Léré
Kélo
Laï
Pala
Bénoy
Koumra
Sarh
Kyabé
Moundou
Doba
Maro
Goré
Moïssala
Baïbokoum
Logone
Chari
Salamat
MASSIF DU KAPKA

CHAD

Total Land Area : 1 259 200 sq. km (486 177 sq. miles)

POPULATION

- over 500 000
- over 100 000
- over 50 000
- over 10 000
- under 10 000

LAND HEIGHT

- 3000m/9843ft
- 2000m/6562ft
- 1000m/3281ft
- 500m/1640ft
- 200m/656ft
- 100m/328ft

N

0 200 km
0 200 miles

WORLD AFFAIRS

Joined UN in 1960

CILSS | FZ | LCBC | OAU | OIC

Chad's most important relationship is with France. Libya occupied the uranium-rich Aozou strip in 1973–1994.

AID

Recipient

$188m (receipts) — Up 13% in 1999

France is by far the major donor. Other sources include Libya, the EU, the USA, the IMF, and the Arab members of OPEC. Without assistance to cover civil servants' pay over recent years, the administration would have collapsed.

DEFENSE

Compulsory military service

$47m — Down 27% in 1999

On seizing power, Déby swelled the existing army with irregulars. The policy has now been reversed and the army reduced to 25,000, including former rebels. France provides military aid and personnel.

ECONOMICS

Inflation 7.6% p.a. (1990–1999)

$1.6bn — 654.42–698.69 CFA francs

SCORE CARD

- ❑ World GNP Ranking........145th
- ❑ GNP per Capita........$210
- ❑ Balance of Payments........$-161m
- ❑ Inflation........-6.8%
- ❑ Unemployment........Widespread underemployment

Strengths

Recent discovery of large oil deposits could transform Chad's poor financial situation. Cotton industry; potential for other agriculture in south. Strategic trading location in heart of Africa. Deposits of natron and uranium.

Weaknesses

Underdevelopment and poverty. Lack of transportation infrastructure. Political instability. Frequent droughts.

EXPORTS

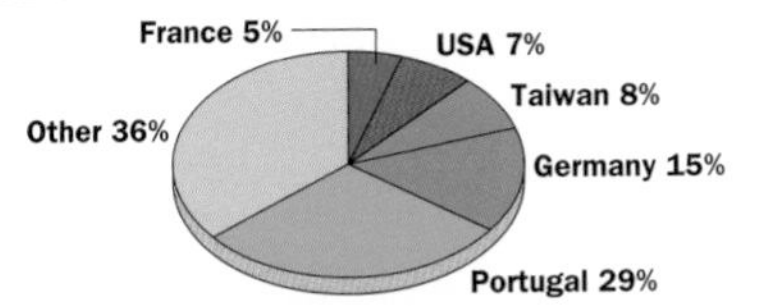
France 5%
USA 7%
Taiwan 8%
Other 36%
Germany 15%
Portugal 29%

IMPORTS

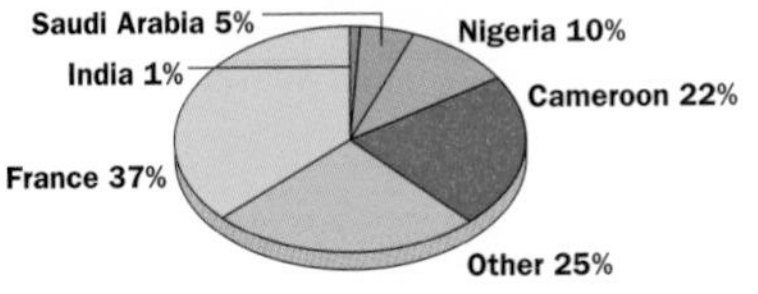
Saudi Arabia 5%
Nigeria 10%
India 1%
Cameroon 22%
France 37%
Other 25%

RESOURCES

Electric power 29,000 kw

85,000 tonnes — Reserves currently unexploited

5.58m cattle, 4.97m goats, 2.43m sheep, 4.8m chickens — Natron, uranium, oil, kaolin, soda, rock salt

A consortium of ESSO, Shell, and ELF has discovered large oil reserves in the south, mostly near Doba, which could make Chad a major African producer. Natron, found north of Lake Chad, is the only mineral currently exploited. There is uranium in the Aozou strip.

ENVIRONMENT

Not available

9% — 0.02 tonnes per capita

President Déby's government has made protection of the environment a priority, with anti-desertification measures such as tree-planting campaigns and aid-funded irrigation schemes. There is concern about potential environmental damage which may result from the planned Chad–Cameroon oil pipeline.

MEDIA

TV ownership low

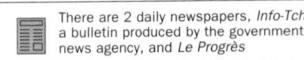

Daily newspaper circulation 0.2 per 1000 people

PUBLISHING AND BROADCAST MEDIA

There are 2 daily newspapers, *Info-Tchad*, a bulletin produced by the government news agency, and *Le Progrès*

1 state-controlled service — 1 state-controlled service

Broadcasting is controlled by the government, which sometimes allows the airing of opposition views. There are a few independent publications, of which the best known is the weekly *N'Djamena-Hebdo*.

CRIME

Death penalty used

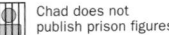

Chad does not publish prison figures — Crime is rising

The easy availability of weapons in the region in the past two decades has meant that local disputes, usually over water or grazing, often now lead to gun battles. Armed robbery, smuggling, and vandalism are widespread. In several areas, the activities of disaffected former rebels threaten security.

EDUCATION

School leaving age: 12

43% — 3446 students

Education is based on the French model, although there are Koranic schools in the north. Primary schooling is officially compulsory, but enrollment is only 46%. Recently, World Bank aid has been directed at elementary schooling.

CHRONOLOGY

France extended its domination of the area now known as Chad after ousting the last Arab ruler in 1900.

- ❑ **1960** Independence. One-party state.
- ❑ **1973** Libyans seize Aozou strip.
- ❑ **1975** Coup by Gen. Félix Malloum.
- ❑ **1979–1982** North–south civil war.
- ❑ **1980** Goukouni Oueddei in power.
- ❑ **1982** Hissène Habré (northerner) defeats Oueddei.
- ❑ **1990** Idriss Déby overthrows Habré, who flees to Senegal.
- ❑ **1994** Libya relinquishes Aozou strip.
- ❑ **1996** National cease-fire; new constitution.
- ❑ **1997** Déby's MPS largest party in new parliament.
- ❑ **1999** Rebellion in north.
- ❑ **2001** Heavy fighting continues. Déby reelected.

C

HEALTH

Welfare state health benefits

1 per 20,000 people — Diarrheal, parasitic, and communicable diseases

There are few city hospitals and under 300 smaller health centers; half are run by religious groups or charities.

SPENDING

GDP/cap. increase

CONSUMPTION AND SPENDING

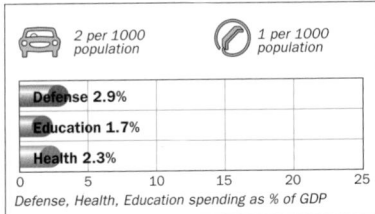

2 per 1000 population — 1 per 1000 population

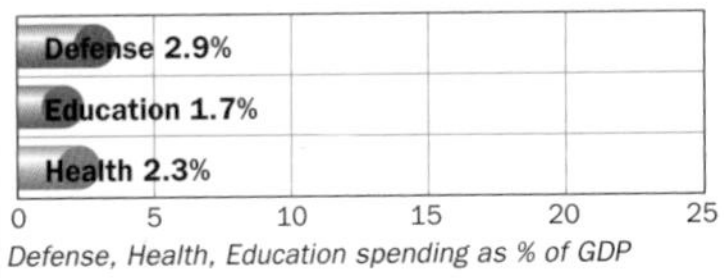
Defense 2.9%
Education 1.7%
Health 2.3%
0
5
10
15
20
25
Defense, Health, Education spending as % of GDP

Poverty is almost universal in Chad; the middle class is very small. There are few wealthy individuals. Habré looted the treasury when he was overthrown in 1990.

WORLD RANKING

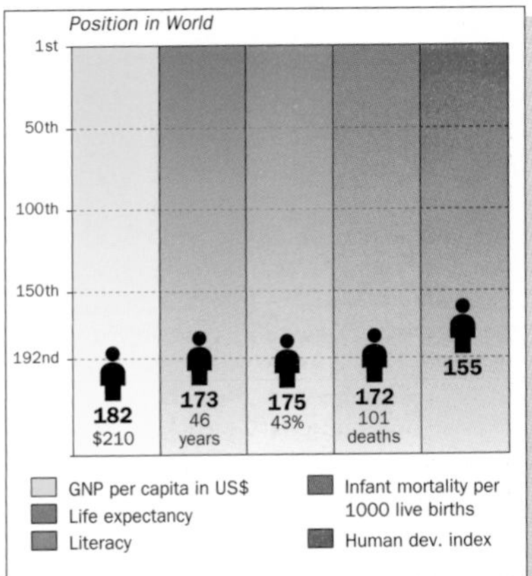
Position in World
1st
50th
100th
150th
192nd
182
$210
173
46 years
175
43%
172
101 deaths
155
GNP per capita in US$
Life expectancy
Literacy
Infant mortality per 1000 live births
Human dev. index

CHILE

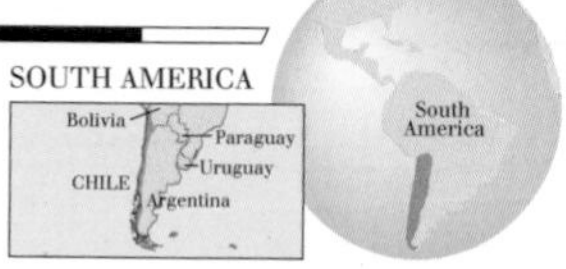
SOUTH AMERICA
Bolivia
Paraguay
Uruguay
CHILE
Argentina
South America

OFFICIAL NAME: Republic of Chile **CAPITAL:** Santiago
POPULATION: 15.2 million **CURRENCY:** Chilean peso **OFFICIAL LANGUAGE:** Spanish

C

1818 | 1883 | Sept 18 | RCH | -4 | +56 | .cl

CHILE EXTENDS IN A narrow ribbon 4350 km (2700 miles) down the Pacific coast of South America. The plains of the central pampa lie between a coastal range and the Andes; most of the population lives in the fertile heartland around Santiago. Glaciers are a prominent feature of the southern Andes, as are fjords, lakes, and deep sea channels. In 1989, Chile returned to elected civilian rule, following a popular rejection of the Pinochet dictatorship. A collapse in copper prices, coupled with weaker export markets, has interrupted the high growth seen in the 1990s.

General Pinochet, *a dictatorial president rejected by popular referendum in 1989.*

Ricardo Lagos *was narrowly elected president in 2000.*

CLIMATE

Desert/mountain/maritime

WEATHER CHART

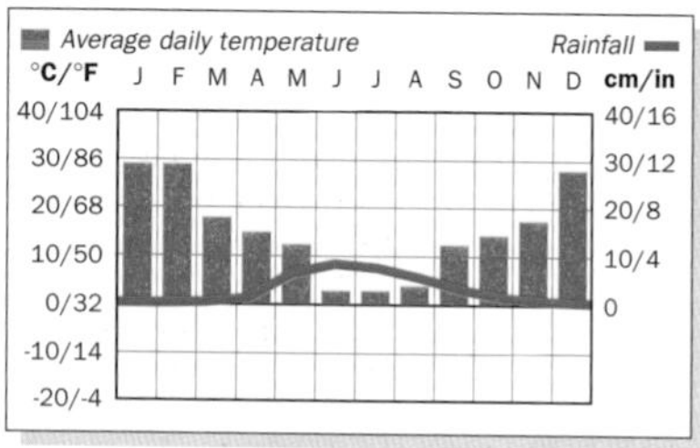
Average daily temperature
Rainfall
°C/°F
J F M A M J J A S O N D
cm/in
40/104
30/86
20/68
10/50
0/32
-10/14
-20/-4
40/16
30/12
20/8
10/4
0

Chile has an immensely varied climate. The north, which includes the world's driest desert, the Atacama, is frequently cloudy and cool for its latitude. The central regions have an almost Mediterranean climate, with changeable winters and hot, dry summers. The higher reaches of the Andes have a typically alpine climate, with glaciers and year-round snow. The south is the wettest region.

TRANSPORTATION

Drive on right

Comodoro Arturo Merino Benítez, Santiago
5.91m passengers

472 ships
753,000 grt

THE TRANSPORTATION NETWORK

11,012 km (6843 miles)

3455 km (2146 miles)

2084 km (1295 miles)

725 km (450 miles)

The state railroad is being upgraded with private capital assistance: suburban services into Santiago are being improved, and line repairs and better rolling stock will shorten journeys from Santiago to Temuco. Sections of the Pan-American Highway, the sole arterial road running from the Peruvian border to Puerto Montt, are being upgraded. The USA's open skies agreement with Chile reached in 1999, the first with a South American country, gives Chile strong regional and international links.

TOURISM

Visitors : Population 1:9.4

1.6m visitors

Down 8% in 1999

MAIN TOURIST ARRIVALS

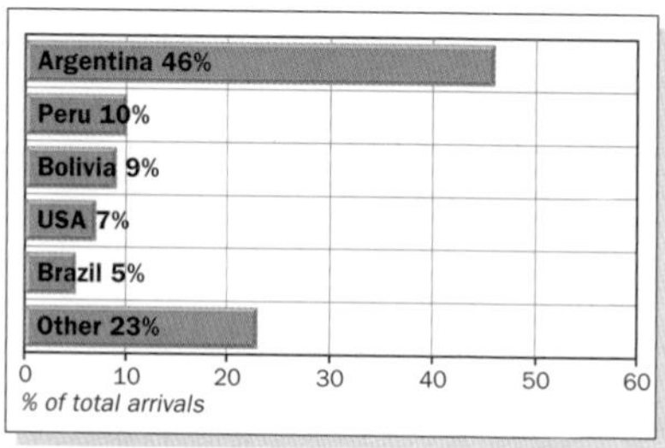
Argentina 46%
Peru 10%
Bolivia 9%
USA 7%
Brazil 5%
Other 23%
0 10 20 30 40 50 60
% of total arrivals

The Pinochet years saw a dramatic decline in tourists from the USA and Europe, although the numbers from neighboring countries held up. Since 1989, visitors have returned, but in 1999 some 60% of them still came from Argentina and Peru. Investment in the sector totaled $2.17 billion in the first half of 2000, up 3.8% on the same period in 1999. Accordingly, Chile is making more of its stunning Andean scenery, its immensely long coastline and a number of exceptional sites, including Chuquicamata, the world's largest copper mine, the Elqui Valley wine-growing region, and the spectacular glaciers and fjords of southern Chile. Easter Island in the Pacific is another major attraction.

Peaks in the Paine range, southern Chile. *Fjords, glaciers, and myriad islands typify Chile's very wet, wild, and stormy south.*

PEOPLE

Pop. density low

Spanish, Amerindian languages

20/km² (53/mi²)

THE URBAN/RURAL POPULATION SPLIT

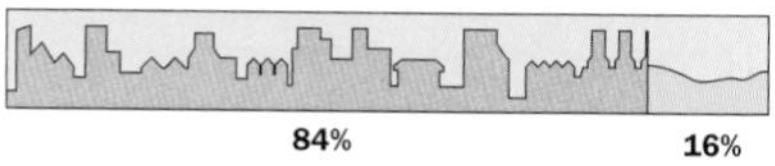
84%
16%

RELIGIOUS PERSUASION

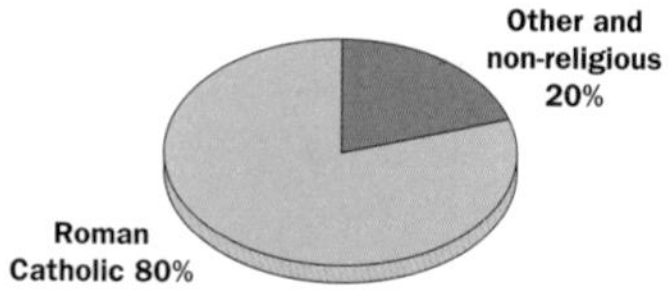
Other and non-religious 20%
Roman Catholic 80%

ETHNIC MAKEUP

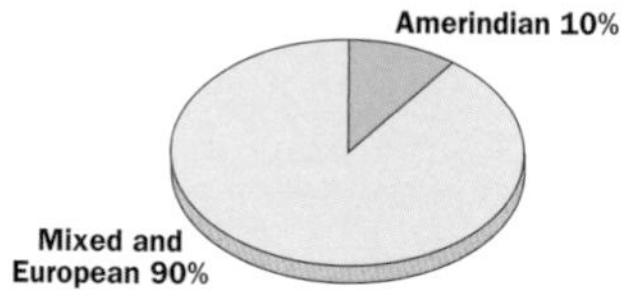
Amerindian 10%
Mixed and European 90%

One-third of Chile's population lives in Santiago, where rapid growth has created large slums. Chile has relatively few immigrants; most people are of mixed Spanish–Amerindian descent. A Commission for Historic Truth was set up in 2000 to address the problems of Amerindians. There are some 80,000 Mapuche Amerindians around Temuco in the south, 20,000 Aymara in the northern Chilean Andes, and 2000 Rapa Nui on Easter Island.

Over 25% of working women are employed in domestic service.

POPULATION AGE BREAKDOWN

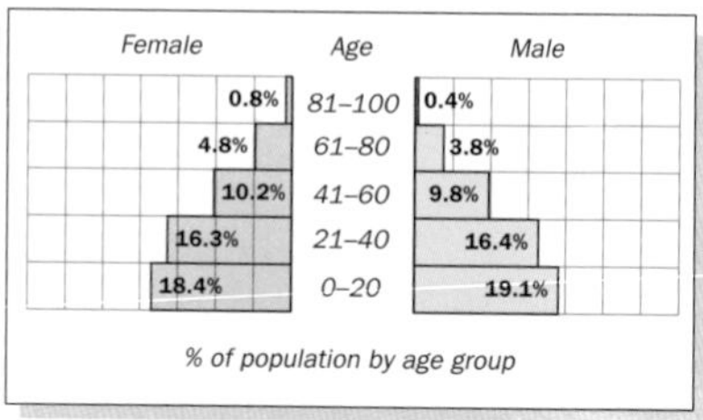
Female
Age
Male
0.8%
81–100
0.4%
4.8%
61–80
3.8%
10.2%
41–60
9.8%
16.3%
21–40
16.4%
18.4%
0–20
19.1%
% of population by age group

C

Juan Fernández Is
I. Alejandro Selkirk
San Juan Bautista
I. Robinson Crusoe
0 100 km
0 100 miles
Easter I.
Terevaka
Hanga Roa
0 10 km
0 10 miles
PERU
BOLIVIA
ARGENTINA
PACIFIC OCEAN
Arica
Iquique
Alacama Desert
Chuquicamata
Calama
Antofagasta
Chañaral
Nevado Ojos del Salado 6880m
Copiapó
Vallenar
La Serena
Coquimbo
Elqui
Ovalle
Illapel
Los Andes
Viña del Mar
Quilpué
Valparaíso
SANTIAGO
Llolleo
Puente Alto
San Bernardo
Rancagua
Curicó
Rengo
Talca
San Javier de Loncomilla
Linares
Parral
Talcahuano
San Carlos
Concepción
Chillán
Los Ángeles
Curanilahue
Mulchén
Bío Bío
Traiguén
Victoria
Temuco
Lautaro
Valdivia
La Unión
Puerto Varas
Puerto Montt
Isla de Chiloé
Castro
Puerto Aisén
Coihaique
Lago General Carrera
Chile Chico
Isla Wellington
Cerro Paine
Puerto Natales
Punta Arenas
Porvenir
Strait of Magellan
Beagle Channel
I. Picton
I. Nueva
I. Lennox
Cape Horn
Drake Passage
CHILE
Total Land Area : 748 800 sq. km (289 112 sq. miles)
POPULATION
over 1 000 000
over 100 000
over 50 000
over 10 000
under 10 000
LAND HEIGHT
4000m/13124ft
2000m/6562ft
1000m/3281ft
200m/656ft
Sea Level
N
0 300 km
0 300 miles

POLITICS

Multiparty elections

L. House 1997/2001
U. House 1997/2001

President Ricardo Lagos Escobar

AT THE LAST ELECTION

Chamber of Deputies 120 seats

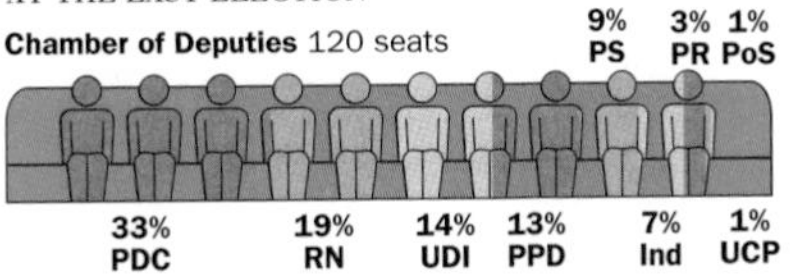
9% PS
3% PR
1% PoS
33% PDC
19% RN
14% UDI
13% PPD
7% Ind
1% UCP

PDC = Christian Democratic Party **RN** = National Renewal Party **UDI** = Independent Democratic Union **PPD** = Party for Democracy **PS** = Socialist Party of Chile **Ind** = Independents **PR** = Radical Party **UCP** = Progressive Center Union **PoS** = Party of South **App** = Appointed **SL** = Senator-for-Life

Senate 49 seats

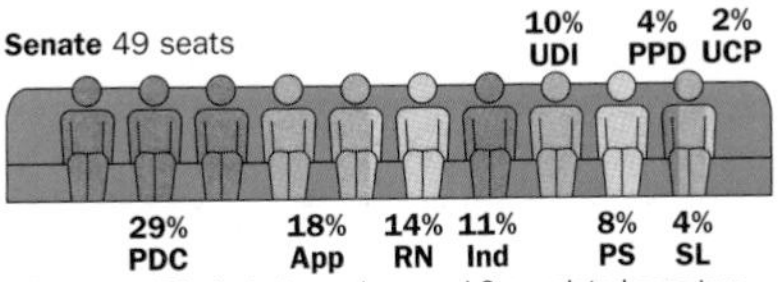
10% UDI
4% PPD
2% UCP
29% PDC
18% App
14% RN
11% Ind
8% PS
4% SL

There are 38 elected members and 9 appointed senators. Former presidents Pinochet and Frei are senators-for-life

After 16 years of military rule under Pinochet, Chile returned to multiparty democracy in 1989.

Main political issues

Pinochet factor and democracy

President Lagos has a mandate to curb the power of the military through radical constitutional reform. However, rapid progress was not expected until Pinochet was out of the way. He returned to Chile in March 2000 after the UK government ruled that he was too mentally incapacitated to be extradited to Spain to face human rights charges. His return was celebrated by right-wing supporters, but ultimately led to moves to bring him to justice. He subsequently lost his immunity from prosecution, but charges against him were suspended in 2001. Few Chileans believed that he would be prosecuted under the sluggish judicial system.

Human rights abuse trials

The right-wing-dominated Senate, and some judges, have frustrated efforts to accelerate justice for crimes committed under the military dictatorship. The ongoing campaign to press for the reopening of hundreds of pending cases is resisted by the army, although an amnesty was granted in 2000 to individual army officers volunteering information on the "disappeared."

Profile

Chilean politics is still strongly affected by the legacy of the military dictatorship of 1973–1989, which began when Pinochet's coup overthrew the elected Marxist government of Salvador Allende.

The CIA backed the Pinochet coup, anxious to halt Allende's program of nationalization of the largely US-owned copper mines. As a result thousands of Chileans were killed by the military or "disappeared," and a further 80,000 were taken as political prisoners.

Pinochet's nationalist politics drew on the example of Franco's Spain, while his economic policy was one of the first experiments in the free-market Chicago School of monetarism. Chile's business and middle classes prospered, while opposition, which was brutally suppressed by the DINA secret police, came most visibly from the Church and the urban poor.

In 1988 Pinochet, attempting to secure a popular mandate for continuing his regime, was surprised when the population emphatically voted for democracy. Pinochet stepped down, but remained head of the army. Patricio Aylwin won presidential elections held in 1989, heading Concertación, a center-left coalition dominated by the PDC and PS parties.

Under Aylwin, politics became more stable, partly as a result of a cross-party consensus on economic policy. Continued growth and some progressive social measures attracted the support of the trade unions. These policies were continued under Eduardo Frei of the PS party, who was elected president in 1993.

When Pinochet retired as army chief in 1998, heated disagreements over his entry to the Congress as a senator-for-life split Concertación on broadly left and right lines. Disagreements over Pinochet's subsequent arrest and detention in Europe on human rights charges further complicated the picture. Ricardo Lagos of the PS emerged as front runner for the 1999 presidential elections, in which both the PS and the PDC presented themselves as the guarantors of peace and democracy. Right-wing opposition parties, however, also began to downplay their past links with Pinochet to broaden their electoral appeal. Lagos narrowly won a run-off poll in January 2000, but Concertación for the first time faced a well-organized opposition.

CHRONOLOGY

The Spanish first attempted the conquest of Chile against the fierce indigenous Araucanian people in 1535. Santiago was founded in 1541. Chile was subject to Spanish rule until independence in 1818.

- **1817–1818** Bernardo O'Higgins leads republican Army of the Andes in victories against royalist forces.
- **1879–1883** War of the Pacific with Bolivia and Peru. Chile gains valuable nitrate regions.
- **1891–1924** Parliamentary republic ends with growing political chaos.

C

CHRONOLOGY *continued*

- 1936–1946 Communist, Radical, and Socialist parties form influential Popular Front coalition.
- 1943 Chile backs USA in World War II.
- 1946–1964 Right-wing Chilean presidents follow US McCarthy policy and marginalize the left.
- 1970 Salvador Allende elected. Reforms provoke strong reaction from the right.
- 1973 Allende dies in army coup. Brutal dictatorship of General Pinochet.
- 1988 Referendum votes "no" to Pinochet staying in power.
- 1989 Democracy peacefully restored; Pinochet steps down after Aylwin election victory.
- 1998 Pinochet detained in UK pending extradition to Spain on human rights charges.
- 2000 Ricardo Lagos (PS) sworn in as president. Pinochet, deemed unfit to face trial, returns to Chile. Charges there are suspended in 2001.

WORLD AFFAIRS

Joined UN in 1945

APEC | G15 | NAM | OAS | RG

Chile's most important relationship remains with its main trading partner, the USA, which supplies its critical copper industry. The relationship has not always been easy. Under Allende, the USA actively worked against the government, fearing that the spread of socialism would jeopardize its investments in Chile and the rest of Latin America. Pinochet's human rights record eventually became an embarrassment. Relations are now good.

In 1999, in response to Pinochet's detention in the UK and planned extradition to Spain to stand trial on human rights charges, Chile argued that this amounted to an infringement of its sovereignty and the jurisdiction of its courts. Relations with Spain and the UK improved in 2000 following Pinochet's return to Chile.

Chile, with Bolivia, is an associate member of the MERCOSUR trade bloc, but jealously guards its right to pursue its own bilateral economic agreements, most recently with the USA, the EU, and South Korea. Border disputes with Bolivia and Peru are ongoing.

AID

Recipient

$69m (receipts) | Down 34% in 1999

The majority of aid is in the form of debts rescheduled by the World Bank at the instigation of the USA.

DEFENSE

Compulsory military service

$2.7bn | Down 12% in 1999

CHILEAN ARMED FORCES

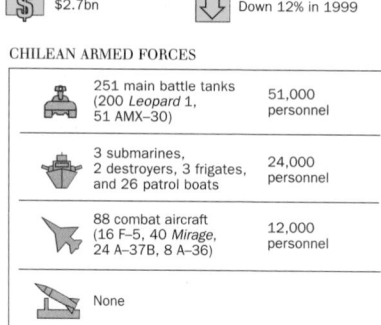

251 main battle tanks (200 *Leopard* 1, 51 AMX–30)	51,000 personnel
3 submarines, 2 destroyers, 3 frigates, and 26 patrol boats	24,000 personnel
88 combat aircraft (16 F-5, 40 *Mirage*, 24 A-37B, 8 A-36)	12,000 personnel
None	

The Defense Ministry has no effective control over the armed forces, who are mostly funded from copper exports of Codelco, the state copper giant. However, the military has recently seen its funds dwindle and equipment deteriorate, and there are signs that it wants to put the years of military rule (1973–1989) behind it, by adopting a dual stance on human rights. It has fought a rearguard action to prevent Pinochet from being tried, but some senior officers have indicated that those accused of offenses committed after the 1978 amnesty law, passed by the dictatorship, might face trial. Dozens of top military still face investigation. Military service, at 19 years of age, is for 12 months (army) or 22 months (navy and air force).

ECONOMICS

Inflation 8% p.a. (1990–1999)

$69.6bn | 529.80–573.75 Chilean pesos

SCORE CARD

WORLD GNP RANKING	44th
GNP PER CAPITA	$4630
BALANCE OF PAYMENTS	$-80m
INFLATION	3.3%
UNEMPLOYMENT	9%

EXPORTS

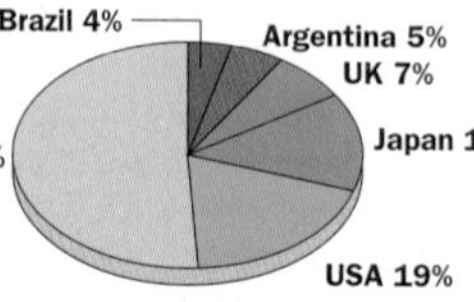

Brazil 4%
Argentina 5%
UK 7%
Japan 14%
USA 19%
Other 51%

IMPORTS

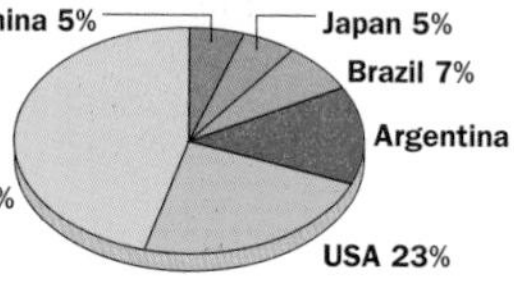

China 5%
Japan 5%
Brazil 7%
Argentina 14%
USA 23%
Other 46%

STRENGTHS

World's largest copper producer. Fresh fruit exports. Strong investment inflows allowing rapid economic growth. Highest credit rating due to fiscal and monetary stability and highly liquid financial system. Development of non-traditional industries such as wine and fresh and prepared fish.

WEAKNESSES

Dependence on USA as single largest trading partner. Prolonged weakness in Asian export markets. Vulnerability of copper revenues, representing 40% of exports, to low world market prices.

PROFILE

Competing ideologies have battled over Chile's economy. Allende's socialism brought huge corporations into the state sector. The Pinochet dictatorship introduced radical monetarist policies. Drastic cutting of the state sector and the selling-off of state enterprises at below market value led to large profits for investors and speculators. Tough economic measures, irrespective of the social consequences, brought Chile's inflation rate down from 400%.

The Aylwin and Frei governments continued with neo-liberal policies, including privatizing the pension system. However, some 30 companies, including the large Codelco copper company, remain in the state sector. The latest privatizations aim to improve the infrastructure. Recent poor copper prices have highlighted the need for more diversification.

ECONOMIC PERFORMANCE INDICATOR

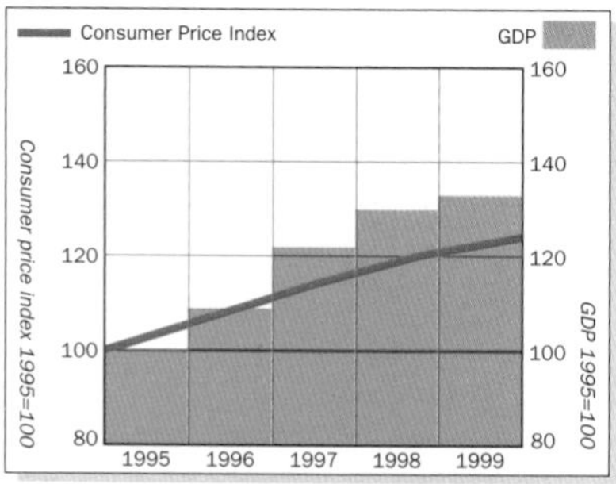

Consumer Price Index
GDP
160
140
120
100
80
Consumer price index 1995=100
GDP 1995=100
1995
1996
1997
1998
1999

CHILE : MAJOR BUSINESSES

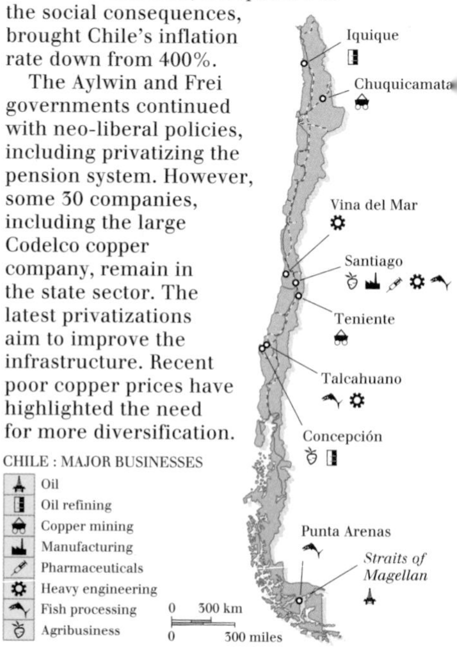

Iquique
Chuquicamata
Vina del Mar
Santiago
Teniente
Talcahuano
Concepción
Punta Arenas
Straits of Magellan
Oil
Oil refining
Copper mining
Manufacturing
Pharmaceuticals
Heavy engineering
Fish processing
Agribusiness
0 300 km
0 300 miles

RESOURCES

Electric power 7.5m kw

6.08m tonnes

5414 b/d (reserves 106,725,600 bbl)

4.14m sheep, 4.07m cattle, 2.47m pigs, 70m chickens

Coal, copper, gold, silver, iron, molybdenum, iodine

ELECTRICITY GENERATION

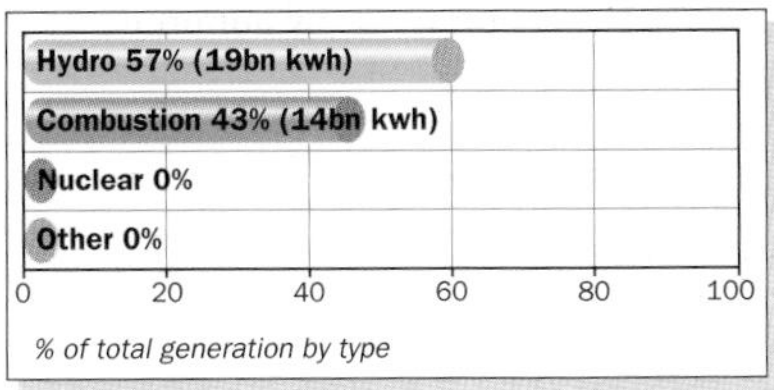
Hydro 57% (19bn kwh)
Combustion 43% (14bn kwh)
Nuclear 0%
Other 0%
0
20
40
60
80
100
% of total generation by type

Chile is the world's largest producer of copper, which accounts for a large proportion of its export revenues. There are important deposits of lithium, molybdenum, and especially of gold. Chile also has reserves of natural gas, oil, and coal, and plenty of hydroelectric potential. In addition, it leads the world in fishmeal production, and has a flourishing wine industry.

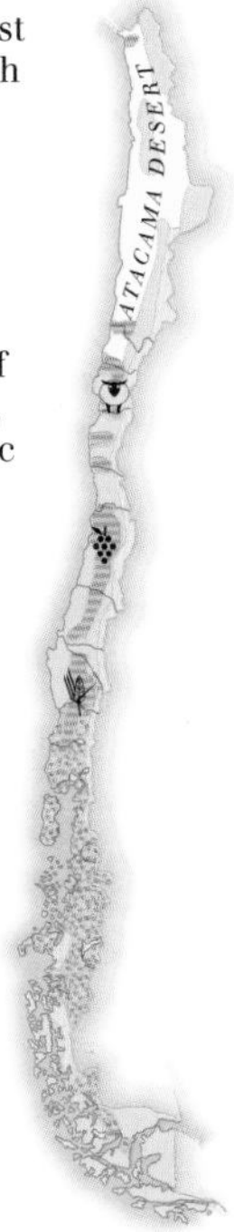
ATACAMA DESERT

CHILE : LAND USE

- Cropland
- Pasture
- Forest
- Desert
- High mountain regions
- Wheat
- Fruits - cash crop
- Sheep

0 300 km

0 300 miles

ENVIRONMENT

Sustainability rank: 31st

19% (7% partially protected)

4.1 tonnes per capita

ENVIRONMENTAL TREATIES

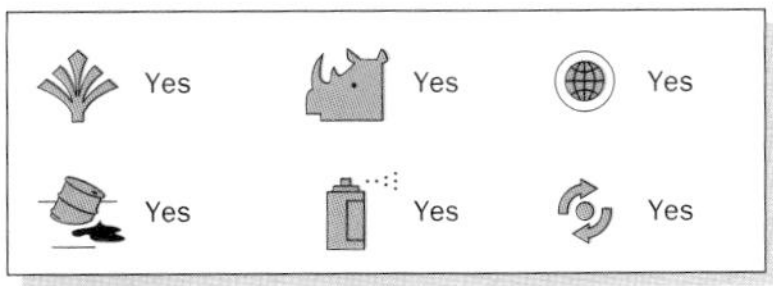
Yes
Yes
Yes
Yes
Yes
Yes

Environmental concerns do not rank highly on the political agenda. Severe smogs still cover Santiago, due in part to diesel fumes from the city's 14,500 buses. The chief concern is logging in the south by Japanese and other foreign companies. The huge growth of the salmon industry, which fences off sea lakes, is resulting in dolphins losing their natural habitats. Overfishing of swordfish has led to friction with the EU, particularly Spain.

MEDIA

TV ownership medium

Daily newspaper circulation 98 per 1000 people

PUBLISHING AND BROADCAST MEDIA

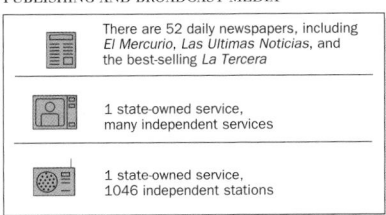

There are 52 daily newspapers, including *El Mercurio, Las Ultimas Noticias*, and the best-selling *La Tercera*

1 state-owned service, many independent services

1 state-owned service, 1046 independent stations

A long-delayed liberalized press law was finally introduced in 2001. Military courts will no longer be able to try journalists, and political authorities will be denied the special procedures used to sue reporters for slander.

CRIME

Death penalty not used

21,514 prisoners

Up 3% 1996–1998

CRIME RATES

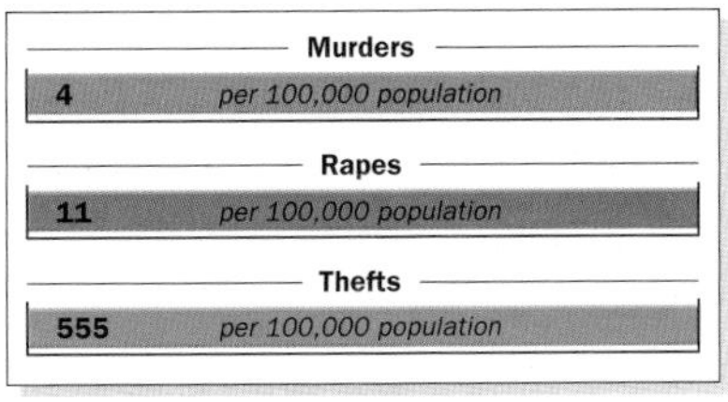
Murders
4 per 100,000 population
Rapes
11 per 100,000 population
Thefts
555 per 100,000 population

The judiciary has been slow to pursue human rights cases from the Pinochet regime, despite the discoveries during the 1990s of mass graves of victims of the DINA (secret police). Mapuche leaders were among the "disappeared." Levels of child abuse are exceptionally high, although now starting to fall.

EDUCATION

School leaving age: 13

96%

325,614 students

THE EDUCATION SYSTEM

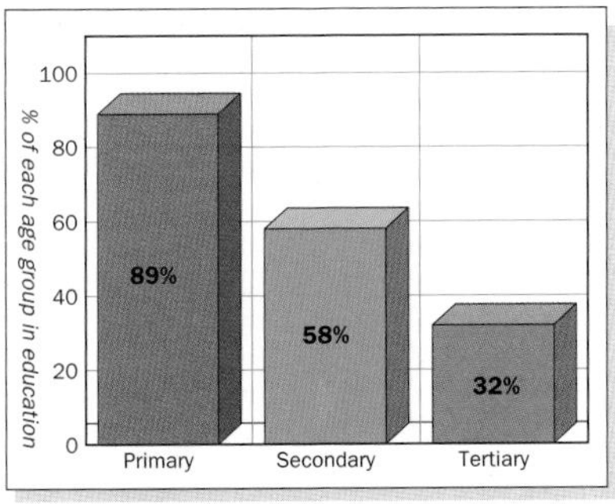
100
80
60
40
20
0
% of each age group in education
89%
58%
32%
Primary
Secondary
Tertiary

Economic growth has permitted public spending on education to increase substantially. Free primary education is officially compulsory for eight years. Human rights issues now appear in school curricula. Many new private universities offer vocational courses.

HEALTH

Welfare state health benefits

1 per 909 people

Heart diseases, cancers, crime

Sustained growth in recent years has seen increased public spending on health.

The public health service covers 80% of people, but is mostly found in urban areas. Rich people have private care. Infant mortality has fallen to one-third of the 1980 level.

SPENDING

GDP/cap. increase

CONSUMPTION AND SPENDING

88 per 1000 population

207 per 1000 population

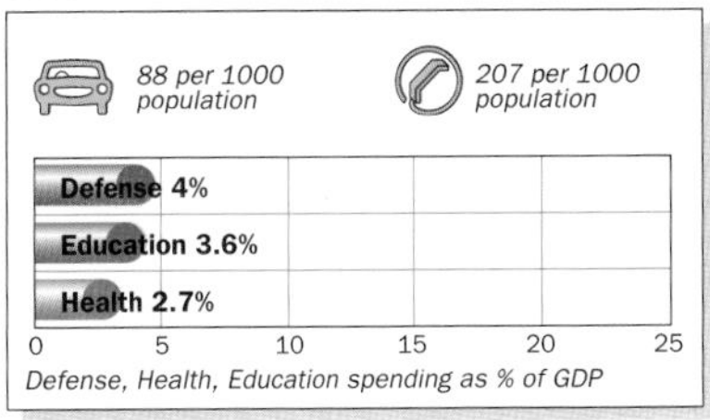
Defense 4%
Education 3.6%
Health 2.7%
0
5
10
15
20
25
Defense, Health, Education spending as % of GDP

Chile's traditionally large middle class did well under Pinochet and the economic policies of the Chicago School. The wealthiest sections benefited considerably from the sale of state assets at 40%–50% of their true market value. Five years into the regime, wealth had become highly concentrated, with just nine economic conglomerates controlling the assets of the top 250 businesses, 82% of banking, and 64% of all financial loans. The regime's artificially high domestic interest rates enabled those with access to international finance to earn an estimated $800 million between 1977 and 1980, simply by borrowing abroad and lending at home. These groups have retained their position.

The poor, by contrast, are over 15% worse off than in 1970, with an estimated four million people living just above the UN poverty line and one million below it.

WORLD RANKING

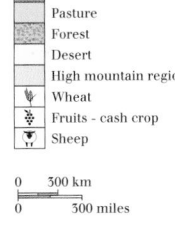

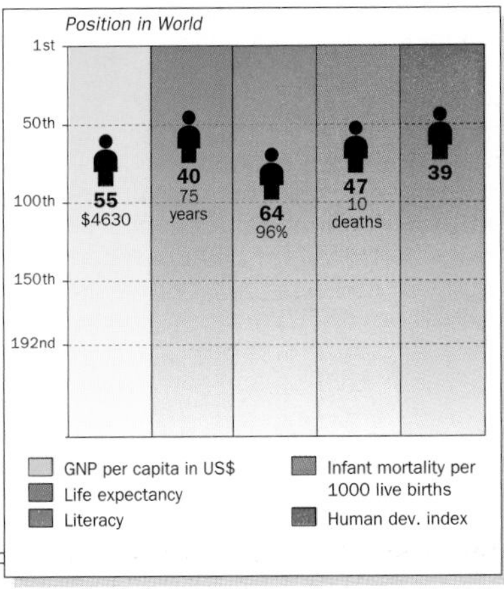
Position in World
1st
50th
100th
150th
192nd
55
$4630
40
75
years
64
96%
47
10
deaths
39
GNP per capita in US$
Life expectancy
Literacy
Infant mortality per 1000 live births
Human dev. index

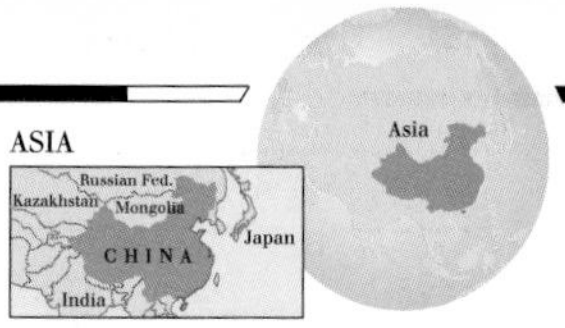
ASIA
Asia
Russian Fed.
Kazakhstan
Mongolia
CHINA
Japan
India

China

Official Name: People's Republic of China **Capital:** Beijing
Population: 1.3 billion **Currency:** Renminbi (known as yuan) **Official Language:** Mandarin

C

1949
1999
Oct 1
VRC
+8
+86
.cn

Li River (Xi Jiang), Guangxi, China's most beautiful region. Its spectacular scenery has encouraged large-scale tourist development.

COVERING A VAST AREA of eastern Asia, China is bordered by 14 countries; to the east it has a long Pacific coastline. Two-thirds of China is uplands. The southwestern mountains include the Tibetan Plateau; in the northwest, the Tien Shan Mountains separate the Tarim and Dzungarian basins. The low-lying east is home to two-thirds of the population. China was dominated by Mao Zedong from the founding of the Communist People's Republic in 1949 until his death in 1976. Despite the major disasters of the 1950s Great Leap Forward and the 1960s Cultural Revolution, it became an industrial and nuclear power. Today, China is rapidly developing a market-oriented economy, but political liberalization is not on the agenda. The current leadership remains set on enforcing single-party rule, as were veterans such as "elder statesman" Deng Xiaoping, who died in 1997.

CLIMATE

Mountain/tropical/continental/steppe

WEATHER CHART

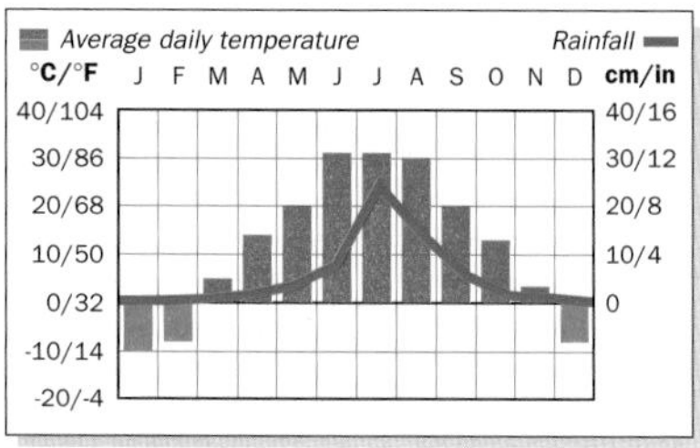
Average daily temperature
Rainfall
°C/°F
J F M A M J J A S O N D
cm/in
40/104
30/86
20/68
10/50
0/32
-10/14
-20/4
40/16
30/12
20/8
10/4
0

China is divided into two main climatic regions. The north and west are semiarid or arid, with extreme temperature variations. The south and southeast are warmer and more humid, with year-round rainfall.

Winter temperatures vary with latitude and are warmest on the subtropical southeast coast, where they average about 16°C (60°F). Summer temperatures are more uniform, rising above 21°C (70°F) throughout China; on the southeast coast, the July average is about 30°C (86°F). In the north and west, temperate summers contrast with harsh winters. In northern Manchuria, rivers freeze for five months and temperatures can fall to –25°C (–13°F). In the deserts of Xinjiang province, temperatures range from –11°C (12°F) in winter to 33°C (91°F) in summer.

Summer and autumn are China's wettest seasons. Winds from the Pacific during the summer monsoon bring rains to most of the country. The south and east also have wet winters, but elsewhere the winter monsoon brings cold, dry air from Siberia.

Floods are frequent and sometimes catastrophic, as in 1998. Droughts can be even more devastating; that of 1959–1962 contributed to a famine which killed millions.

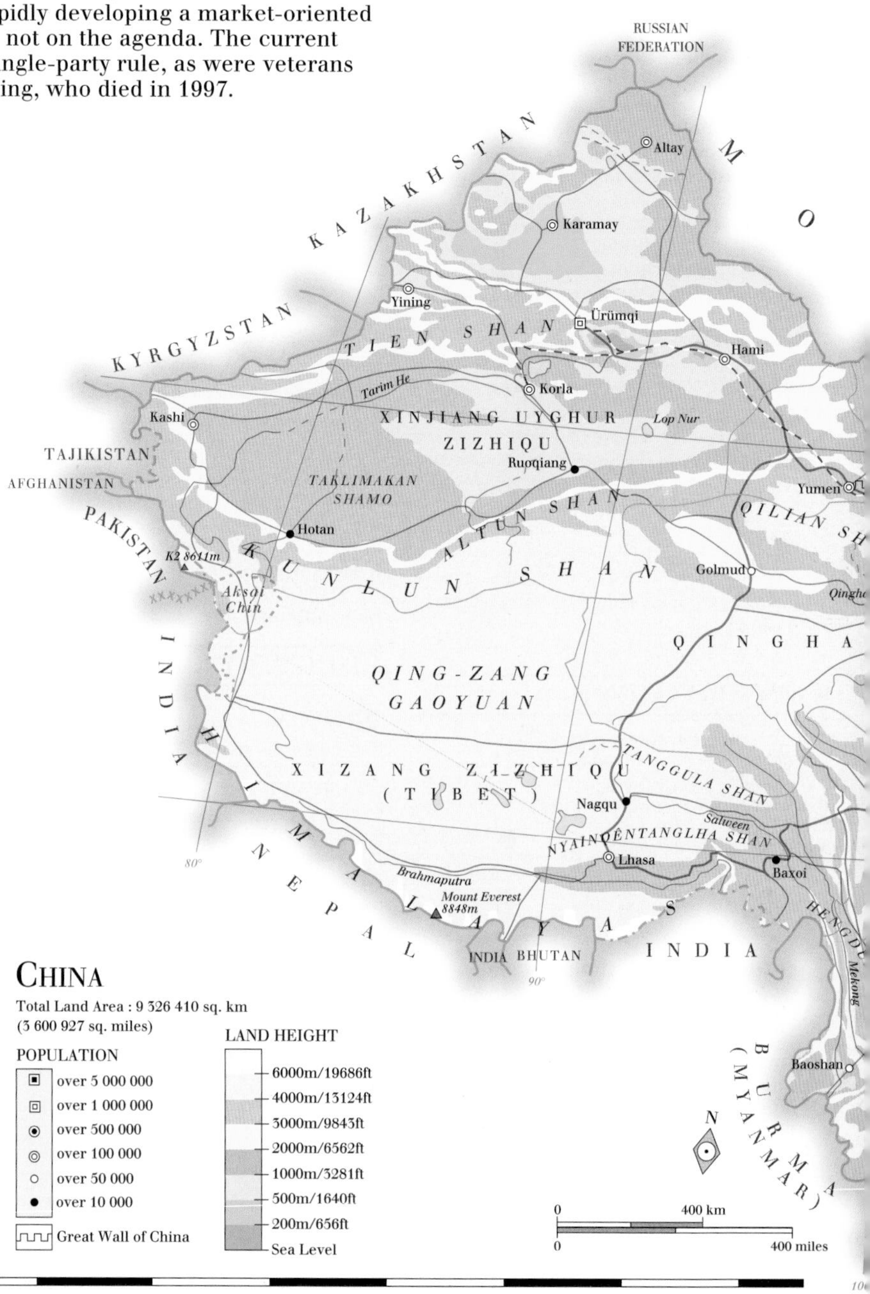
RUSSIAN FEDERATION
Altay
KAZAKHSTAN
Karamay
Yining
Ürümqi
KYRGYZSTAN
TIEN SHAN
Hami
Tarim He
Korla
Kashi
XINJIANG UYGHUR ZIZHIQU
Lop Nur
TAJIKISTAN
AFGHANISTAN
Ruoqiang
TAKLIMAKAN SHAMO
Yumen
PAKISTAN
Hotan
ALTUN SHAN
QILIAN SHAN
K2 8611m
KUNLUN SHAN
Golmud
Aksai Chin
QINGHAI
QING-ZANG GAOYUAN
INDIA
TANGGULA SHAN
XIZANG ZIZHIQU (TIBET)
Nagqu
Salween
NYAINQENTANGLHA SHAN
Lhasa
Baxoi
80°
Brahmaputra
Mount Everest 8848m
HIMALAYAS
NEPAL
INDIA
BHUTAN
90°
Mekong
HENGDUAN
BURMA (MYANMAR)
Baoshan
N
CHINA
Total Land Area : 9 326 410 sq. km (3 600 927 sq. miles)
POPULATION
over 5 000 000
over 1 000 000
over 500 000
over 100 000
over 50 000
over 10 000
Great Wall of China
LAND HEIGHT
6000m/19686ft
4000m/13124ft
3000m/9843ft
2000m/6562ft
1000m/3281ft
500m/1640ft
200m/656ft
Sea Level
0
400 km
0
400 miles

C

TOURISM

Visitors : Population 1:41

31.2m visitors

Up 16% in 2000

MAIN TOURIST ARRIVALS

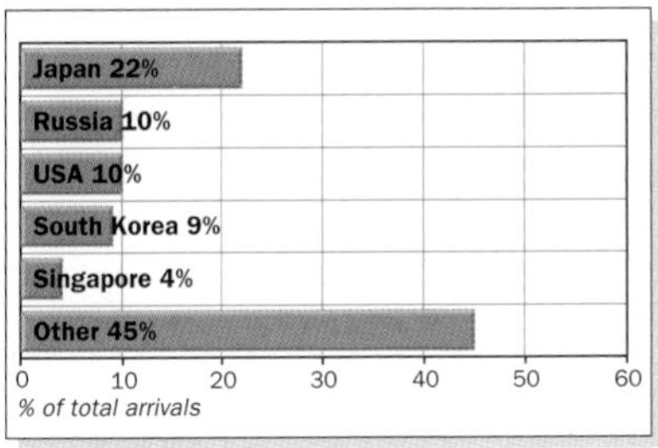
Japan 22%
Russia 10%
USA 10%
South Korea 9%
Singapore 4%
Other 45%
0 10 20 30 40 50 60
% of total arrivals

The easing of restrictions since the 1980s has led to the rapid growth of all kinds of tourism, from luxury tours to budget packages and backpacking. Hong Kong is a major entry point. Most of China is now open to visitors, and there have been some moves to allow tourists into Tibet, although access to Xinjiang in western China, and other areas, is sometimes impossible. The Great Wall, the Forbidden City in Beijing, and the terracotta warriors at Xi'an remain among the top attractions. In recent years more and more Chinese have been able to travel abroad.

RUSSIAN FEDERATION
XIAO HINGGAN LING
DA HINGGAN LING
Heihe
Manzhouli
Hulun Nur
Amur
Jiamusi
Qiqihar
HEILONGJIANG
MANCHURIA
Harbin
Jixi
L. Khanka
Baicheng
Mudanjiang
Xilinhot
Changchun
Jilin
JILIN
Siping
SEA OF JAPAN
Shenyang
Fushun
Tonghua
NORTH KOREA
Fuxin
LIAONING
Benxi
Anshan
Jinzhou
Dandong
Hohhot
Zhangjiakou
Baotou
Huang He
BEIJING (PEKING)
Tangshan
Korea Bay
Datong
Baoding
Tianjin
Bo Hai
Dalian
Liaodong Bandao
Shijiazhuang
HEBEI
Yantai
Shandong Bandao
Yinchuan
Taiyuan
Zibo
Weifang
NINGXIA
SHANXI
Jinan
Qingdao
YELLOW SEA
Xining
Lanzhou
Handan
SHANDONG
Luoyang
Kaifeng
Xuzhou
Lianyungang
GANSU
Baoji
Xi'an
Zhengzhou
HENAN
Hongze Hu
JIANGSU
SHAANXI
Nanyang
Bengbu
Huainan
Nanjing
Guangyuan
Xinyang
ANHUI
Wuxi
Suzhou
Shanghai
Hefei
Wuhu
Tai Hu
Chang Jiang (Yangtze Kiang)
Shashi
Wuhan
Hangzhou
Ningbo
Chengdu
HUBEI
Chongqing
Dongting Hu
Poyang Hu
ZHEJIANG
Zigong
Nanchang
Wenzhou
EAST CHINA SEA
Xiangtan
Changsha
JIANGXI
HUNAN
Guiyang
Hengyang
Fuzhou
Panzhihua
FUJIAN
Quanzhou
GUIZHOU
Taiwan Strait
Kunming
Shaoguan
TAIWAN
Liuzhou
Xi Jiang
Wuzhou
GUANGDONG
Shantou
GUANGXI
Guangzhou
Nanning
Hong Kong (Xianggang)
Macao (Aomen)
VIETNAM
Zhanjiang
Leizhou Bandao
Gulf of Tongking
SOUTH CHINA SEA
Haikou
HAINAN
Hainan Dao
GOBI
MONGOLIA
NEI MONGOL ZIZHIQU
SICHUAN

TRANSPORTATION

Drive on right

Chek Lap Kok, Hong Kong 18.2m passengers

3214 ships 16.5m grt

THE TRANSPORTATION NETWORK

271,300 km (168,578 miles)	24,474 km (15,207 miles)
67,394 km (41,879 miles)	110,263 km (68,514 miles)

Roads and railroads have been extended since 1949 to provide a basic national network. The transportation system is now being modernized and expanded to support the push for economic growth. The Ninth Five-Year Plan (1996–2000) provided for 8100 km (5000 miles) of new railroad. Beijing and Shanghai are to get a high-speed rail link. In 2001, plans were announced to connect the Tibetan capital, Lhasa, to the railroad system by extending the track from Golmud in Qinghai province. If and when it is completed, this will present one of the highest railroads in the world.

Container shipping is growing fast. Shanghai handled one-third of all Chinese container traffic before the reversion of Hong Kong (which is the world's biggest container port) to Chinese rule in 1997. The inland waterway system, which was hitherto in a state of disrepair, is being upgraded and now handles one-third of all internal freight. The Yangtze River (Chang Jiang) is navigable by ships of over 1000 tonnes for more than 1000 km (620 miles) from the coast. This capacity is planned to increase under the Three Gorges dam project.

Many small airlines have sprung up since the state monopoly ended in 1988. Hong Kong's new airport opened in July 1999. Air transportation is growing rapidly, like private car ownership, as wealth increases. Bicycles are still the main mode of personal transportation.

Li River (Xi Jiang) valley. *Irrigation helps Chinese farmers to feed 20% of the world's people, using only 7% of the world's farmland.*

PEOPLE

Pop. density medium

Mandarin, Wu, Cantonese, Hsiang, Min, Hakka, Kan

137/km² (355/mi²)

THE URBAN/RURAL POPULATION SPLIT

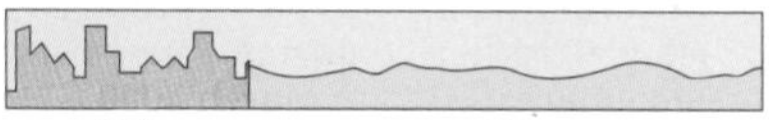
32%
68%

RELIGIOUS PERSUASION

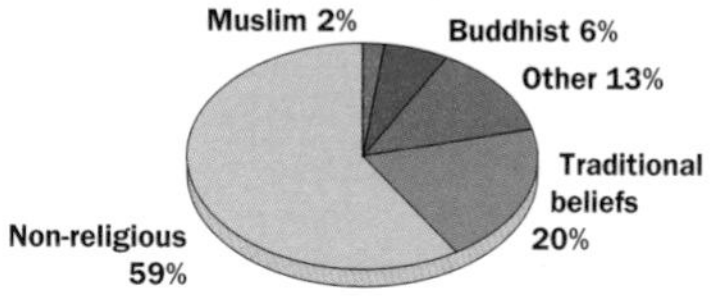
Muslim 2%
Buddhist 6%
Other 13%
Traditional beliefs 20%
Non-religious 59%

ETHNIC MAKEUP

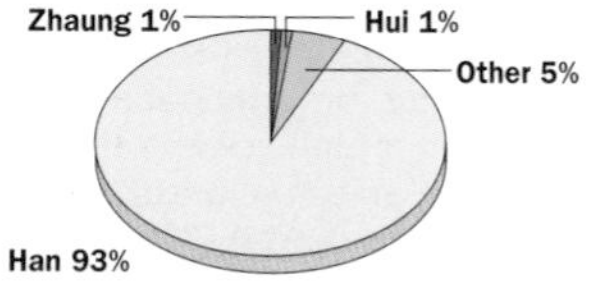
Zhaung 1%
Hui 1%
Other 5%
Han 93%

About 93% of China's population are Han Chinese. The rest belong to one of 55 minority nationalities, or recognized ethnic groups. The minorities have disproportionate political significance because many, like the Mongolians, Tibetans, or Muslim Uyghurs in Xinjiang, live in strategic border areas.

The deeply resented policy of resettling Han Chinese in remote regions has led to ruthlessly suppressed uprisings in Xinjiang and Tibet. Han Chinese are now a majority in Xinjiang and Nei Mongol Zizhiqu (Inner Mongolia). Tibetan calls for greater political and cultural autonomy get much more international attention.

A one-child policy was adopted in 1979. Most Han Chinese still face strict family planning controls, though these are widely flouted. Cases of female infanticide at birth have produced a demographic imbalance, and rules were relaxed for minorities after some small groups came near to extinction.

Chinese society is patriarchal in practice, and generations tend to live together. However, economic change is putting pressure on family life, breaking down the social controls of the Mao era. Divorce and unemployment are rising; materialism has replaced the puritanism of the past. The Falun Gong spiritual movement, perceived as a rival to CCP authority, was banned in 1999.

POPULATION AGE BREAKDOWN

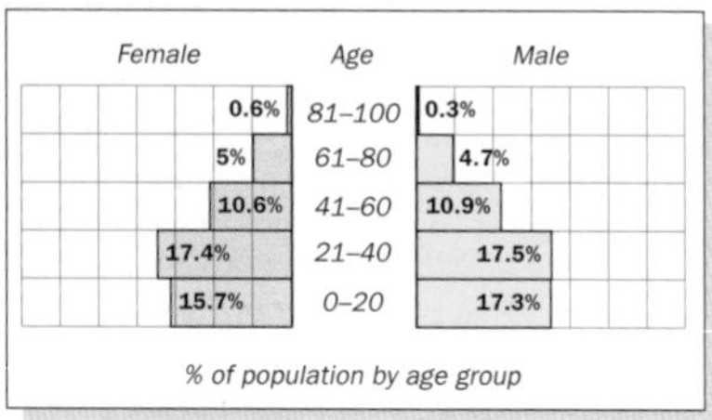
Female
Age
Male
0.6%
81–100
0.3%
5%
61–80
4.7%
10.6%
41–60
10.9%
17.4%
21–40
17.5%
15.7%
0–20
17.3%
% of population by age group

POLITICS

No multiparty elections

1998/2003

President Jiang Zemin

AT THE LAST ELECTION

National People's Congress 2979 seats

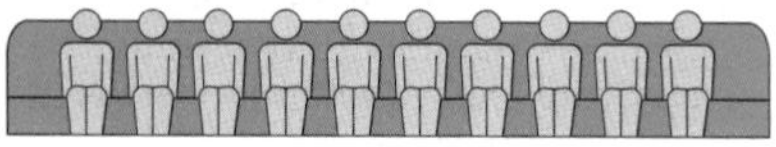

The Communist Party of China (CCP) is the only permitted party

China is a single-party state, dominated by the CCP, the world's largest political party. The National People's Congress, indirectly elected every five years, is theoretically the supreme organ of state power. It appoints the president and executive State Council, headed by the prime minister. The real focus of power, however, is the 22-member politburo of the CCP and, in particular, its standing committee of seven.

Main Political Issues

Economic change and CCP authority

After the death of Mao Zedong in 1976, China embarked on economic reform, while seeking to secure the dominance of the CCP and avoid political upheaval. The "great helmsman" of this process for two decades was Deng Xiaoping, China's paramount leader, even after he had relinquished all official posts, until his death in 1997. Advocating a fast-track move to a "socialist market economy," Deng and his followers looked to South Korea and Taiwan as achieving high growth without political reform. At the 1997 party congress the reformers, led by Jiang Zemin, by now both head of state and party leader, took their opportunity to realign formal party policy with their desire to privatize large areas of state-run industry. Economic reform still poses a real threat to the CCP's central authority. The 22 provinces, particularly those in the southeast, are acting increasingly independently of Beijing. At a popular level, there is growing rural discontent over widening wealth differentials.

Conservatives versus reformers

Conservatives within the CCP, while recognizing a need for economic change, wanted it to be slower and more tightly controlled by the center.

Nanjing Donglu (Nanking Road), *in central Shanghai, is one of China's most famous shopping streets. A magnet for foreign investment, Shanghai is China's largest city.*

The prodemocracy protests of 1989, culminating in the Tiananmen Square massacre, enabled the conservatives under the then premier Li Peng to gain the upper hand for a while. Deng moved to restore the balance and his longevity shifted the advantage toward his heir apparent, President Jiang Zemin. Jiang has gone on to strengthen his own power base and international stature, while premier Zhu Rongji spearheads the economic reform and anti-corruption campaigns, but Li Peng, since 1998 the president of the parliament, still commands support among conservatives within the state and party leadership.

Profile

The death in 1997 of Deng Xiaoping marked in effect the passing of the dominance of the "Immortals" – those who took part with Mao Zedong in the 1934–1935 Long March. Deng, the architect of China's economic reforms, had worked hard behind the scenes forming alliances to promote his reformist ideas and followers. The foremost of these, Jiang Zemin, has consolidated his position as president and CCP general secretary since Deng's death. The profound economic changes under way, transferring much of the huge state economic system into private ownership, are a challenge to the CCP's ability to monopolize power, but the party has allowed no political opposition to surface.

Deng Xiaoping *was China's paramount leader until his death in 1997.*

Jiang Zemin, *CCP leader and China's president since Deng resigned the post.*

Li Peng, *president of the National People's Congress.*

Zhu Rongji, *premier, reformer, and a protégé of Deng Xiaoping.*

C

WORLD AFFAIRS

Joined UN in 1945

APEC | IAEA | IBRD | ADB | SCO

The push for economic modernization, and concerns about regional stability, dominate Chinese foreign policy. Investment, technology, and trade considerations outweigh ideology.

Despite the human rights issue, relations with the West have recovered since the 1989 Tiananmen Square massacre. US President Clinton visited China in mid-1998. Two years later the US agreed to give China permanent Most Favored Nation (MFN) trading status.

China, like Russia, opposed NATO's use of force against Yugoslavia in 1999, and now has significant trade and military contacts with Russia. Relations with Vietnam have been normalized. While seeking to restrain North Korea, China has developed diplomatic and economic links with South Korea.

Taiwan remains a thorny issue. Beijing strongly opposes anything that would perpetuate the division of China or imply Taiwanese statehood. Periodic displays of bellicosity disrupt cross-strait cooperation. Threats of military action were renewed during Taiwan's presidential election in March 2000, but China later said that reunification might not take place for 20 years. Most of its southern neighbors – particularly Vietnam and the Philippines – are alarmed by China's territorial claims to the Spratly Islands, far out in the South China Sea.

AID

Recipient

$2.32bn (receipts) — Down 1% in 1999

In the 1970s aid was an important part of Chinese diplomacy, going mostly to Africa, but other communist and southeast Asian states were also recipients. Aid flows outward have almost ceased since the late 1970s, as the economic reform process has turned China itself into a major aid recipient. Japan is the biggest bilateral donor to China, but the potential of the Chinese market means that most developed states provide aid. A significant portion of funding is used to finance high-tech imports. The 1989 Tiananmen Square massacre led to a temporary suspension of aid disbursements by the West.

DEFENSE

Compulsory military service

$39.9bn — Up 4% in 1999

CHINESE ARMED FORCES

7060 main battle tanks (5500 T–59, T–69, T–79, T–88, T–98)	1.7m personnel
65 submarines, 20 destroyers, 40 frigates, and 368 patrol boats	220,000 personnel
Over 3000 combat aircraft (300 Q–5, 1500 J–6, 700 J–7, 250 J–8, 40 Su–30)	420,000 personnel
ICBM (20 DF–5), IRBM (20 DF–4, 38 DF–3A, 8 DF–21), SLBM (12 CSS–N–3), SRBM (20 DF–15, 40 DF–11), 1 SSBN	

The People's Liberation Army (PLA), closely linked with the ruling CCP, numbered as many as three million personnel in 1996, and appeared unassailable. A key instrument of ensuring the party's dominance, it was used in 1967 to restore order after the chaos of the Cultural Revolution, and in 1989 to suppress prodemocracy protests in Tiananmen Square, as well as to stamp out dissent in Tibet. However, the PLA is being cut back as part of a modernization process, reducing both its numbers and its involvement in the economy through army-run industries.

China has a large weapons industry, and has extended its nuclear weapons capability to include the neutron bomb. It is a significant arms exporter.

ECONOMICS

Inflation 8.2% p.a. (1990–1999)

$979.9bn — 8.2795–8.2774 yuan

SCORE CARD

❑ WORLD GNP RANKING	7th
❑ GNP PER CAPITA	$780
❑ BALANCE OF PAYMENTS	$15.7bn
❑ INFLATION	–1.4%
❑ UNEMPLOYMENT	3% (official)

STRENGTHS

Huge domestic market. Self-sufficiency in food. Mineral reserves. Diversified industrial sector. Low wage costs. Rapid sustained growth. Growing export sector. Hong Kong as financial center.

ECONOMIC PERFORMANCE INDICATOR

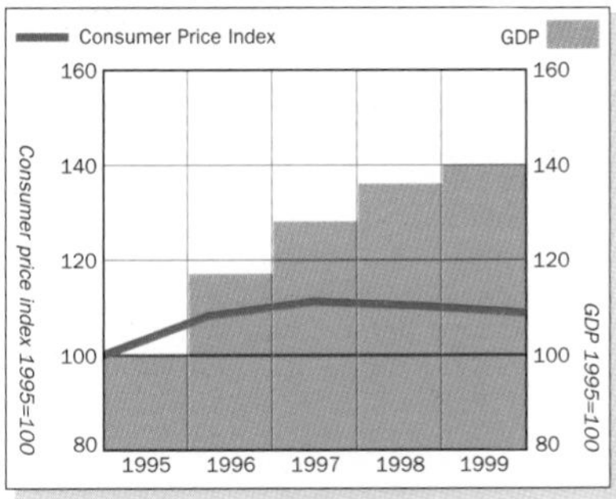
Consumer Price Index
GDP
160
140
120
100
80
1995
1996
1997
1998
1999
Consumer price index 1995=100
GDP 1995=100

EXPORTS

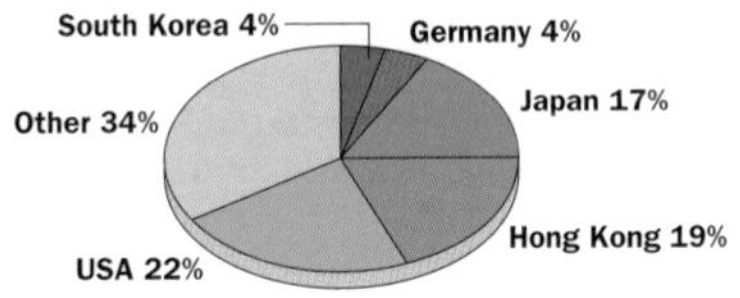
South Korea 4%
Germany 4%
Japan 17%
Other 34%
Hong Kong 19%
USA 22%

IMPORTS

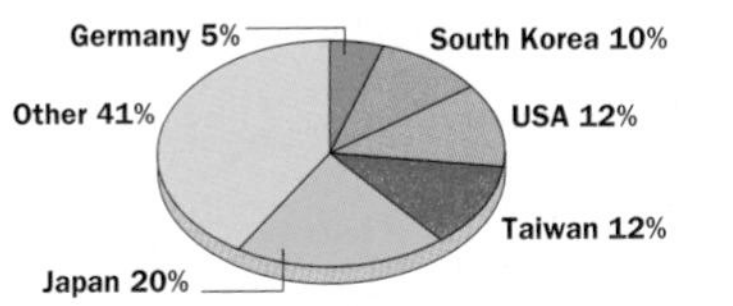
Germany 5%
South Korea 10%
Other 41%
USA 12%
Taiwan 12%
Japan 20%

WEAKNESSES

Massive underemployment, rising unemployment, and migration to cities. Unevenly distributed resources. Poor transportation. Debt-ridden state sector.

CHINA : MAJOR BUSINESSES

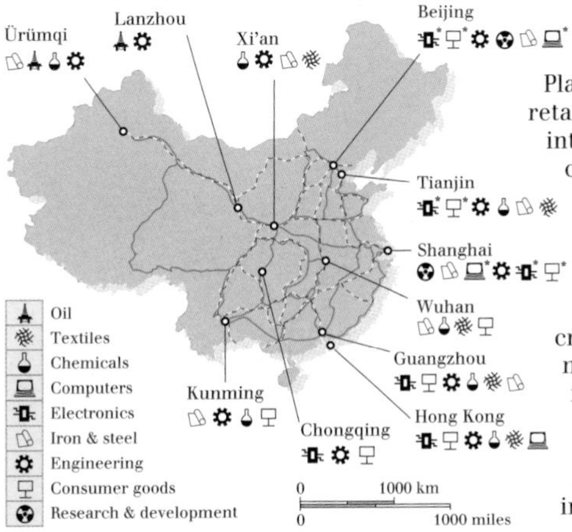
Ürümqi
Lanzhou
Xi'an
Beijing
Tianjin
Shanghai
Wuhan
Guangzhou
Hong Kong
Chongqing
Kunming
Oil
Textiles
Chemicals
Computers
Electronics
Iron & steel
Engineering
Consumer goods
Research & development
0 1000 km
0 1000 miles

* significant multinational ownership

PROFILE

China's shift from a centrally planned to a market-oriented economy has steamed ahead since the 1980s, notably in the south, where liberalization has gone furthest.

Growth had to be curbed on several occasions to control inflation. In the Ninth Five-Year Plan (1996–2000) the government retained strict controls, promoting intensive growth. The 1997 party congress boosted the process of privatizing the huge state-owned sector. Pledges not to devalue the renminbi helped to retain foreign investment flows during the 1997–1999 crisis of confidence in emerging markets. In 2000 a trade deal was forged with the EU, and the USA normalized trade relations, as China pressed to join the WTO. An unprecedented growth in imports was recorded for 2000.

C

MINORITIES IN THE AUTONOMOUS REGIONS

AUTONOMOUS REGIONS OF CHINA

XINJIANG UYGHUR ZIZHIQU
INNER MONGOLIA (NEI MONGOL ZIZHIQU)
NINGXIA
TIBET (XIZANG ZIZHIQU)
GUANGXI

CHINA'S CONSTITUTION states that "regional autonomy is practiced in areas where people of minority nationalities live in compact communities." The Manchu, Miao, Yi, and many others among the 55 recognized ethnic minorities are not regarded as meeting this criterion, but there are five areas which do officially have the status of autonomous region or *zizhiqu*. The two most westerly such regions, sparsely populated Tibet and the home of the Uyghur people in Xinjiang are both particularly sensitive border areas, and opposition to Chinese rule there has been suppressed.

TIBET

The vast mountainous region of Tibet has China's lowest population density, at only two inhabitants per sq km, spread across an area of 1,220,000 sq km, with Lhasa as its capital. Tibetans were officially recorded as making up 95% of its total population of 2.2 million at the 1990 census, and Han Chinese, whose immigration has aroused strong local resentment, as under 4%, though another census in 1995 gave a total population figure of nearly three million.

Tibet was part of the Manchu empire from the 18th century until 1911, but exercised full control over most of its affairs under the feudal rule of the Dalai Lama, spiritual head of Tibetan Buddhism. The forces of China invaded Tibet in 1950, and ruthlessly crushed the 1959 independence uprising. The Dalai Lama fled to India amid an exodus of refugees and established a government in exile, but has recently come close to accepting Chinese rule in an effort to win greater real self-government and cultural freedom for the Tibetan people. In 1965 Tibet was made a region of China, known as Xizang Zizhiqu. Opponents of Chinese rule were imprisoned or executed and many Buddhist monasteries were destroyed. Clashes between nationalists and Chinese troops in 1987 led to a renewed clampdown. In 1988, in an apparently more conciliatory spirit, the Chinese government accepted Tibetan as a "major official language."

In 1995, there was further tension when the Chinese authorities detained a young boy whom Tibetan Buddhists had recognized as the latest incarnation of their second-ranking spiritual leader, the Panchen Lama. The Chinese government named its own candidate to this office instead, which Tibetans regarded as an unwarranted interference in their religious life. The offense was compounded when China in June 1999 reportedly initiated a search for the next Dalai Lama.

XINJIANG UYGHUR

Consisting largely of desert, and bordering on Kyrgyzstan and Kazakhstan, the Xinjiang Uyghur Zizhiqu has a total area of 1,647,000 sq km, or nearly 18% of China's total land mass. Han Chinese are narrowly in the majority in its population of 15.4 million, the total number of (mainly Muslim) Uyghurs being only 7.2 million. Dissent has been firmly suppressed, and restrictions imposed on traveling to the area. The regional capital, Urumqi, is an industrial city noted for iron and steel, oil, and chemicals.

The Kumbum dagoba at the Palkhor Tschöde monastery, Gyangze (Chiang-tzu), Tibet. At the tip of this 15th-century structure is a Buddhist chapel.

INNER MONGOLIA

Inner Mongolia, or Nei Mongol Zizhiqu, occupies most of the area in northern China along the long land border with Mongolia (i.e. Outer Mongolia, as seen from the Chinese perspective). Han Chinese are the majority in a total population of 21.1 million, of whom 4.8 million, or less than a quarter, are ethnic Mongolian.

NINGXIA HUI

The smallest of all the autonomous regions, Ningxia Hui Zizhiqu occupies an area of only 170 sq km, just south of Nei Mongol Zizhiqu. Its capital is at Yinchuan. The population was 4.7 million at the 1990 census. Many of the Hui people, who number some 8.6 million in all, live outside the region.

GUANGXI ZHUANG

This autonomous region, unlike the others, lies close to China's booming economic heartland, in the south between Guangdong province and the border with Vietnam. Relatively small in terms of area (220 sq km), it is by far the largest autonomous region in terms of population, with a density of 192 per sq km and 42.5 million inhabitants at the 1990 census. The capital is Nanning. The Zhuang people, although China's largest ethnic minority, number only 15.5 million, and thus are substantially in the minority in the region.

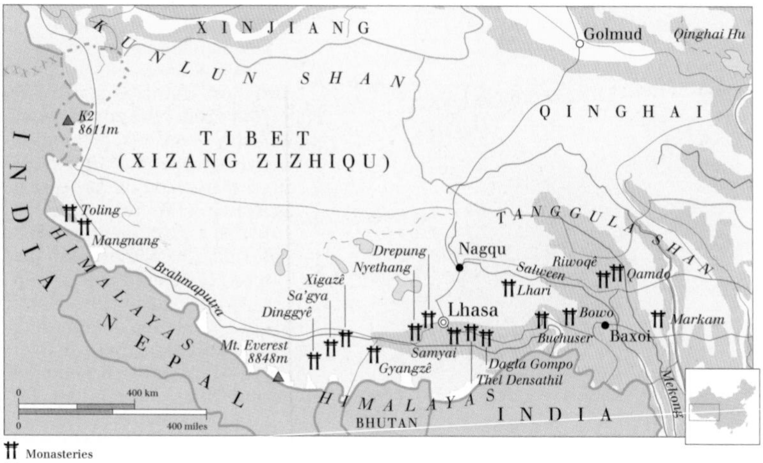
XINJIANG
Golmud
Qinghai Hu
KUNLUN SHAN
QINGHAI
K2 8611m
TIBET (XIZANG ZIZHIQU)
INDIA
Toling
Mangnang
HIMALAYAS
Brahmaputra
Drepung
Nyethang
Nagqu
Xigazê
Sa'gya
Dinggyê
Lhasa
Salween
Riwoqê
Qamdo
Lhari
Bowo
Baxoi
Markam
Buchuser
Samyai
Gyangzê
Dagla Gompo
Thel Densathil
Mt. Everest 8848m
NEPAL
TANGGULA SHAN
Mekong
HIMALAYAS
BHUTAN
INDIA
0 400 km
0 400 miles

Monasteries

SPECIAL ECONOMIC ZONES, OPEN CITIES, AND SPECIAL ADMINISTRATIVE REGIONS

Economic reforms first instituted by Deng Xiaoping in 1978 began opening China to foreign business. This has spread from a small number of zones operating under special tax regimes, to other cities all along the coastal belt and inland, and has fueled an extraordinary urban investment boom.

Nanchang
Changsha
HUNAN
JIANGXI
0 500 km
0 500 miles
Hengyang
Ganzhou
Fuzhou
FUJIAN
Quanzhou
Shaoguan
Xiamen
GUANGXI
GUANGDONG
TAIWAN
Wuzhou
Xi Jiang
Guangzhou
Shantou
Shenzen
Zhuhai
SOUTH CHINA SEA
Macao
Hong Kong
Zhanjiang
Haikou
HAINAN
Special Economic Zones (SEZs)
Special Administrative Regions (SARs)

Special economic zones

The creation of five special economic zones (SEZs) on the south coast was a major early milestone. Shenzhen, the trail-blazer for the concept, was established in 1980, adjoining Kowloon in Hong Kong. Also in Guangdong province are Zhuhai, adjoining Macao, and Shantou further east, while Xiamen SEZ is in Fujian province opposite Taiwan. These locations reflect the aim of attracting investment from the 30 million Chinese overseas, especially in Hong Kong and Taiwan, whose ancestral homes were in Guangdong and Fujian. The fifth and least dynamic of the SEZs comprises the southern island province of Hainan.

Foreign investment

Foreign direct investment reached over $45 billion in 1998, more than for any other country except the USA. The inflow then began falling, for the first time for a decade. Most investment goes into the Open Coastal Belt, based on 14 cities, from Dalian in the north to Zhanjiang and Beihai in the south, which were picked in the mid-1980s for the dual role of "windows," opening to the outside world, and "radiators," spreading the development of an export-oriented economy.

Among the most successful development areas is the great port of Shanghai, where the stock exchange reopened in 1990. Investors in the city's Pudong New Zone, on the east bank of the Huangpu River, enjoy more preferential conditions than in the SEZs, including the right to sell goods and financial services. Pudong has attracted major foreign companies keen to establish a foothold in the potentially massive Chinese market, including General Motors, NEC, Sharp Hitachi, Siemens, Unilever, BASF, and Pilkington. Pudong also forms the "dragon head" for a chain of open cities, extending up the Yangtze River valley, where foreign investment has been encouraged since 1990. Since 1992 China has also designated a new set of open cities, this time in areas around its land borders, adjoining Russia, Mongolia, Kazakhstan, Burma, and Vietnam, to develop infrastructure and promote trade and the growth of export-oriented industries.

Industrial growth in Guangdong

Guangdong province, with Guangzhou and Shenzhen at its heart, promises to become Asia's largest industrial region. One in ten of the world's top 500 multinational companies has invested in the Guangzhou Economic and Technical Development District (GET). Shenzhen, meanwhile, was the first Chinese city to start selling state-owned apartments freehold. It is being revamped as the science and technology city of the future, complete with parks, pedestrian precincts, civic amenities, and a sophisticated communications infrastructure, although its original incentive package of tax concessions for investors is being phased out.

Hong Kong and Macao SARs

The success of Shenzhen contrasts with Hong Kong, recession-hit after its reversion to Chinese sovereignty in mid-1997 (although high growth was recorded there in 2000). As a British colony, Hong Kong had flourished through its textile industry, subsequently expanding into electronics, but it was above all a trade and financial services center. This role is preserved under its status as a special administrative region (SAR). Hong Kong's population is estimated at 6.69 million, in an area of only 1095 sq km. Its Basic Law guarantees a high level of autonomy for 50 years under the "one country, two systems" formula, and GDP per capita in 1998 stood at some $22,200, even after that year's 5% negative economic growth. Its Chinese-appointed chief executive, Tung Chee-hwa, has been unpopular, however – increasingly at odds with members of his administration (several of whom resigned in 2000–2001), and with the region's Legislative Council. The number of directly elected seats on the Council was increased somewhat (to 24 out of 60) for the September 2000 elections, half of which were won by the opposition Democratic Party, but public apathy produced a low turnout. English and Chinese are both official languages, and the freely convertible Hong Kong dollar remains as the SAR's currency.

China's other SAR, Macao, ceased to be a Portuguese colony at midnight on 19–20 December 1999. Macao too has free port status, its own currency, the pataca, two official languages (Portuguese and Chinese), a partly elective Legislative Assembly, and a guarantee under its Basic Law that the "one country, two systems" formula will apply for 50 years. Macao's area of only 21.45 sq km was due to increase by 20% on completion of the Nam Van lakes project. The population of 414,128 at the 1996 census, including more than 100,000 people with Portuguese nationality, had a per capita GDP of $7330, but the economy, based on tourism and gambling, has recently been in decline.

***Hong Kong's** return to Chinese sovereignty after 157 years of British rule, took place at midnight on 30th June 1997.*

C

CHRONOLOGY

China has the world's oldest continuous civilization. Its recorded history begins 4000 years ago with the Shang dynasty, founded in the north in 1766 BCE. Succeeding dynasties expanded China's boundaries; it reached its greatest extent under the Manchu (Qing) dynasty in the 18th century. Chinese isolationism frustrated Europe's attempts to expand into the empire until the 19th century, when China had fallen behind the industrializing West. For the previous 3000 years, it had been one of the world's most advanced nations.

- **1839–1860** Opium Wars with Britain. China defeated; forced to open ports to foreigners.
- **1850–1873** Internal rebellions against Manchu empire.
- **1895** Defeat by Japan in war over Korean peninsula.
- **1900** Boxer Rebellion to expel all foreigners suppressed.
- **1911** Manchu empire overthrown by nationalists led by Sun Yat-sen. Republic of China declared.
- **1912** Sun Yat-sen forms National People's Party (Guomindang).
- **1916** Nationalists factionalize. Sun Yat-sen sets up government in Guangdong. Rest of China under control of rival warlords.
- **1921** CCP founded in Shanghai.
- **1923** CCP joins Soviet-backed Guomindang to fight warlords.
- **1925** Chiang Kai-shek becomes Guomindang leader on death of Sun Yat-sen.
- **1927** Chiang turns on CCP. CCP leaders escape to rural south.
- **1930–1934** Mao Zedong formulates strategy of peasant-led revolution.
- **1931** Japan invades Manchuria.
- **1934** Chiang forces CCP out of its southern bases. Start of 12,000-km (7450-mile) Long March.
- **1935** Long March ends in Yanan, Shaanxi province. Mao becomes CCP leader.
- **1937–1945** War against Japan: CCP Red Army in north, Guomindang in south. Japan defeated.
- **1945–1949** War between Red Army and Guomindang. US-backed Guomindang retreats to Taiwan.
- **1949** 1 October, Mao proclaims People's Republic of China.
- **1950** Invasion of Tibet. Mutual assistance treaty with USSR.
- **1950–1958** Land reform; culminates in setting up of communes. First Five-Year Plan (1953–1958) fails.
- **1958** "Great Leap Forward" to boost production fails; contributes to millions of deaths during 1959–1961 famine. Mao resigns ⇨

RESOURCES

Electric power 225m kw

36.3m tonnes

3.2m b/d (reserves 24,000,000,000 bbl)

612m ducks, 438m pigs, 203m geese, 3.63bn chickens

Coal, oil, natural gas, salt, iron, molybdenum, titanium, tungsten

ELECTRICITY GENERATION

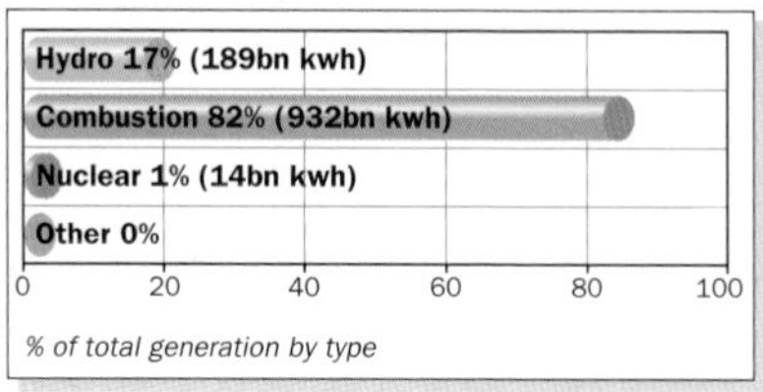
Hydro 17% (189bn kwh)
Combustion 82% (932bn kwh)
Nuclear 1% (14bn kwh)
Other 0%
0
20
40
60
80
100
% of total generation by type

China dominates the world market in molybdenum, titanium, and tungsten; it has the world's largest deposits of more than a dozen minerals, and commercial deposits of most others.

China is the world's largest coal producer, with reserves of about 800 billion tonnes, primarily in the Shaanxi and Sichuan basins. Annual output of over 1.3 billion tonnes, used mainly for power generation, considerably exceeds demand, and many mines face closure.

Power generation, previously well behind demand, expanded rapidly to create overcapacity by the late 1990s. Nuclear power capacity in 1998 was just over 2000 MW from three reactors, with major expansion to 50,000 MW planned by 2020. The world's largest hydropower plant, the "Three Gorges" scheme on the Yangtze River, is due for completion in 2009, but faces sustained controversy over its proposed benefits, costs, and environmental consequences.

Crude oil production has risen only slightly since reaching 160 million tonnes in 1997. Eastern oilfields are depleted, and hopes now center on enormous reserves in the Tarim basin in the far west. Gas production was 25.2 billion cubic m (900 billion cubic feet) in 1999.

CHINA : LAND USE

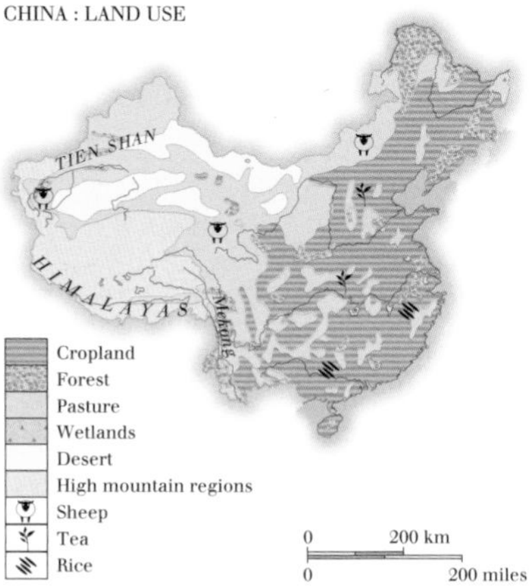
TIEN SHAN
HIMALAYAS
Mekong
Cropland
Forest
Pasture
Wetlands
Desert
High mountain regions
Sheep
Tea
Rice
0
200 km
0
200 miles

ENVIRONMENT

Sustainability rank: 108th

6%

2.9 tonnes per capita

ENVIRONMENTAL TREATIES

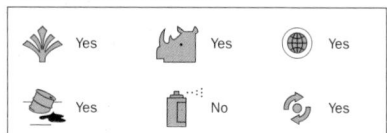

Yes	Yes	Yes
Yes	No	Yes

Climate and geology mean that natural disasters are quite frequent in China. However, their impact is often made worse by human actions. The economic policies of the 1950s turned drought into a devastating famine, while poor building standards helped push the death toll in the 1976 Tangshan earthquake to over 500,000.

Economic growth is the priority of China's leaders. Industrial pollution and environmental degradation, already widespread, are increasing. However, the environment is a growing concern among educated Chinese. The unsuccessful 1992 campaign to stop the Three Gorges hydroelectric scheme was revived with growing open criticism in the late 1990s. The government is becoming less suspicious of Western pressure for environmental controls, and is taking steps to respond to acute problems of urban air pollution and water quality in particular.

MEDIA

TV ownership high

Daily newspaper circulation 42 per 1000 people

PUBLISHING AND BROADCAST MEDIA

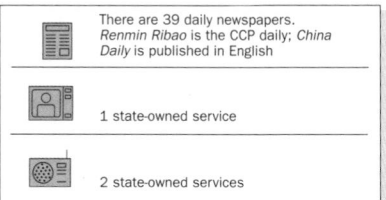

There are 39 daily newspapers. *Renmin Ribao* is the CCP daily; *China Daily* is published in English

1 state-owned service

2 state-owned services

China's more open, market-oriented economy has allowed people increasing access to nonofficial sources of information. TV ownership is rising and satellite-dish owners can choose what to view, while Internet access makes central control even more difficult. New rules in April 2000 require all Internet sites to obtain official approval and make them responsible if they carry information in breach of secrecy laws. The printed media remain on a tight rein. The ideological influence of the huge-circulation party newspaper *Renmin Ribao* (*People's Daily*) and the trade union *Workers' Daily* is much diminished, but papers considered to be undesirable have their licenses removed in periodic clean-ups. Beijing and the provinces have their own dailies.

CHRONOLOGY *continued*

as CCP chairman; succeeded by Liu Shaoqi.

- **1960** Sino-Soviet split.
- **1961–1965** More pragmatic economic approach led by Liu and Deng Xiaoping.
- **1966** Cultural Revolution initiated by Mao to restore his supreme power. Youthful Red Guards attack all authority. Mao rules, with Military Commission under Lin Biao and State Council under Zhou Enlai.
- **1967** Army intervenes to restore order amid countrywide chaos. Liu and Deng purged from party.
- **1969** Mao regains chair of CCP. Lin Biao designated his successor, but quickly attacked by Mao.
- **1971** Lin dies in plane crash.
- **1972** US President Nixon visits. More open foreign policy initiated by Zhou Enlai.
- **1973** Mao's wife Jiang Qing, Zhang Chunquio, and other "Gang of Four" members elected to CCP politburo. Deng Xiaoping rehabilitated.
- **1976** Death of Zhou Enlai. Mao strips Deng of posts. September, Mao dies. October, Gang of Four arrested.
- **1977** Deng regains party posts, begins to extend power base.
- **1978** Decade of economic modernization launched. Open door policy to foreign investment; farmers allowed to farm for profit.
- **1980** Deng emerges as China's paramount leader. Economic reform gathers pace, but hopes for political change suppressed.
- **1983–1984** Conservative elderly leaders attempt to slow reform.
- **1984** Industrial reforms announced.
- **1989** Prodemocracy demonstrations in Tiananmen Square. Crushed by army; 1000–5000 dead. Beijing under martial law.
- **1992–1995** Trials of prodemocracy activists continue. Plans for market economy accelerated.
- **1993** Jiang Zemin president.
- **1997** February, Deng Xiaoping dies at 92. July, UK hands back Hong Kong. September, five-yearly party congress confirms Jiang's leadership and reformist policies.
- **1999** China develops neutron bomb. Portugal hands back Macao. Friction over Taiwanese claim of statehood. Clampdown on Falun Gong sect.
- **2000** Taiwanese presidential election causes tension. USA normalizes trade relations.
- **2001** Major diplomatic incident with USA when Chinese pilot is killed and US spy-plane is forced down on Hainan Island. Beijing awarded 2008 Olympic Games.

CRIME

Death penalty used

1.24m prisoners

Down 33% from 1990–1996

CRIME RATES

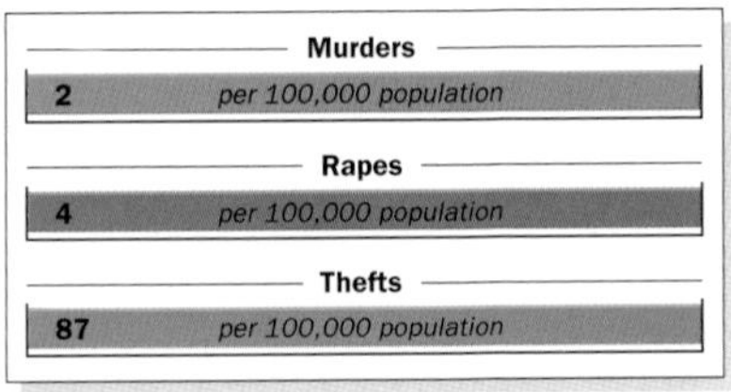
Murders
2
per 100,000 population
Rapes
4
per 100,000 population
Thefts
87
per 100,000 population

China's legal system is a mix of custom and statute. Economic reform and social changes have been paralleled by a rise in corruption and violent crime. The death penalty is used extensively – China carries out more executions than the rest of the world combined. Many party officials were condemned in the largest ever anti-corruption trial in 2000. There was a crackdown on human trafficking after the breaking of smuggling rings bringing Chinese into Europe. China's poor human rights record was brought to the fore by the 1989 Tiananmen Square massacre. Although many detainees have been released since that clampdown on dissent, many political prisoners remain.

EDUCATION

School leaving age: 15

84%

6.1m students

THE EDUCATION SYSTEM

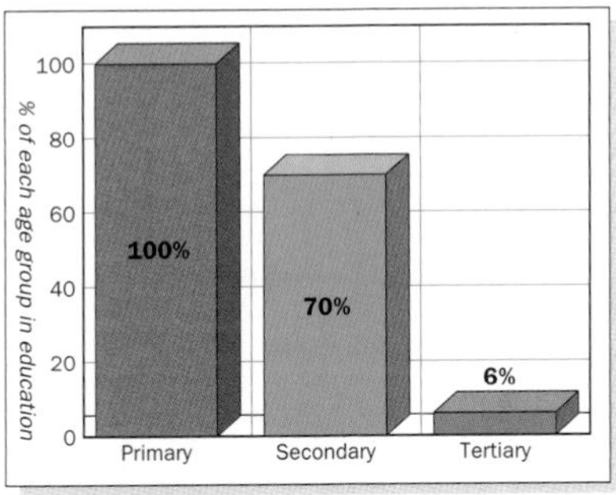
100
80
60
40
20
0
% of each age group in education
100%
70%
6%
Primary
Secondary
Tertiary

The government set a target of nine years of education for all – despite the expansion of education since 1949, illiteracy and semiliteracy are still widespread. School attendance fell when fees at all levels were introduced in the 1980s, but now most children of secondary school age are in school – including those catching up with primary education. Selection for higher education is now based on academic rather than political criteria. The government legalized private schools, permitted since the early 1980s, in May 2001, in an effort to regulate, and profit from, "illegal" institutions. The number of private schools is believed to have tripled since the early 1990s, and about seven million pupils are thought to attend them.

HEALTH

Welfare state health benefits

1 per 500 people

Cardiovascular and diarrheal diseases, cancers, tuberculosis

Economic changes threaten China's network of primary health care, which, combining traditional and Western medicine, used to extend to the remotest regions. The system of universal state employment was accompanied by a free health system, and the Chinese enjoyed a life expectancy on a par with many richer countries. The change to a market-oriented economy, however, has produced a two-tier system. A gaping divide exists between city and rural provision, fees for treatment are rising, and fewer people are covered by free health care as a benefit of state employment.

SPENDING

GDP/cap. increase

CONSUMPTION AND SPENDING

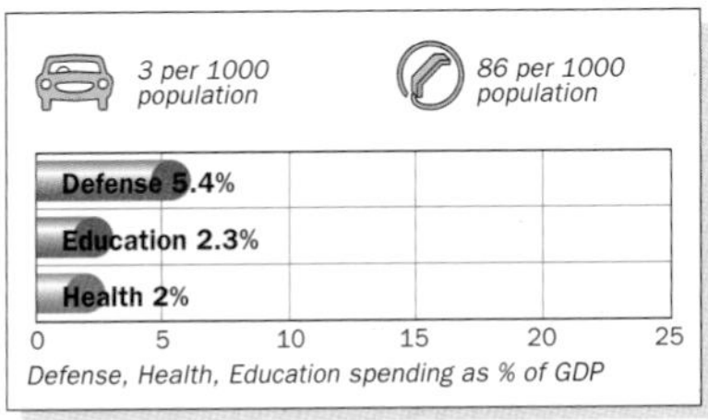
3 per 1000 population
86 per 1000 population
Defense 5.4%
Education 2.3%
Health 2%
0
5
10
15
20
25
Defense, Health, Education spending as % of GDP

The majority of Chinese are still farmers, whose living standards are threatened by rising production costs. Economic change has led to widening wealth disparities. The burgeoning small-business class and employees of companies with foreign investment have benefited most. They mainly live in the east, especially the southeast, where there are a number of millionaires. The main losers are the 150 million "surplus" agricultural workers, many of whom have migrated to the cities in search of jobs. By July 2001, there were more mobile phones in China than in the USA, 120.6 million in total, nearly one for every ten Chinese.

WORLD RANKING

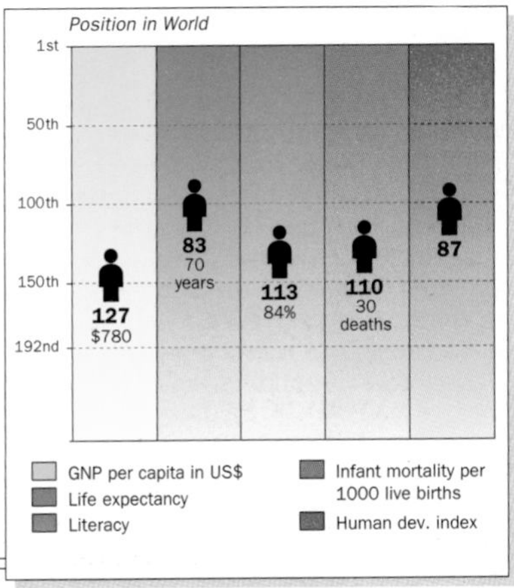
Position in World
1st
50th
100th
150th
192nd
127
$780
83
70
years
113
84%
110
30
deaths
87
GNP per capita in US$
Life expectancy
Literacy
Infant mortality per 1000 live births
Human dev. index

COLOMBIA

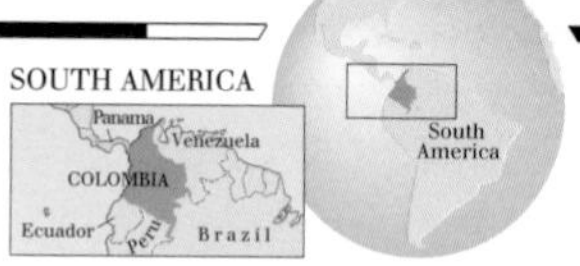
SOUTH AMERICA
Panama
Venezuela
COLOMBIA
Ecuador
Peru
Brazil
South America

OFFICIAL NAME: Republic of Colombia **CAPITAL:** Bogotá
POPULATION: 42.3 million **CURRENCY:** Colombian peso **OFFICIAL LANGUAGE:** Spanish

C

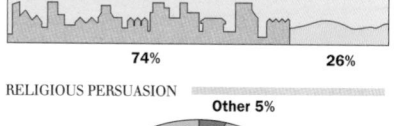

1819 | 1903 | July 20 | CO | -5 | +57 | .co

LYING IN NORTHWEST South America, Colombia has coastlines on both the Caribbean and the Pacific. The east of the country is densely forested and sparsely populated, and separated from the western coastal plains by the Andes mountains. The Andes divide into three ranges (*cordilleras*) in Colombia. The eastern range is divided from the two western ranges by the densely populated Magdalena river valley. The Colombian lowlands are very wet, hot, and fertile, supporting two harvests and allowing many crops to be planted at any time of year. A multiparty democracy since 1957, Colombia is noted for its coffee, emeralds, gold, and narcotics trafficking.

CLIMATE

Tropical/mountain

WEATHER CHART

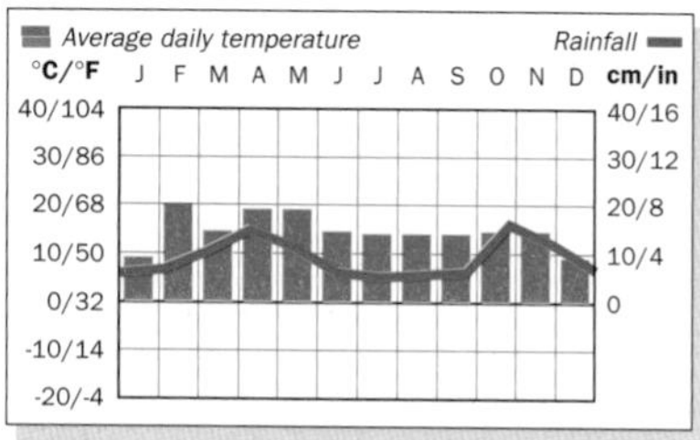
Average daily temperature
Rainfall
°C/°F
J F M A M J J A S O N D
cm/in
40/104
30/86
20/68
10/50
0/32
-10/14
-20/4
40/16
30/12
20/8
10/4
0

Most of Colombia is wet, and the hot Pacific coastal areas receive up to 500 cm (200 in) of rain a year. The Caribbean coast is a little drier. The Andes have three climatic regions: the *tierra caliente* (hot lowlands), *tierra templada* (temperate uplands), and *tierra fría* (cold highlands); the last has year-round springlike conditions such as those found in Bogotá. The equatorial east has two wet seasons.

TRANSPORTATION

Drive on right

El Dorado, Bogotá
4.66m passengers

112 ships
111,700 grt

THE TRANSPORTATION NETWORK

13,868 km (8617 miles)

Caribbean Trunk Highway

2113 km (1313 miles)

18,140 km (11,272 miles)

Roads in the north are in reasonable condition. Those in the south and east tend to be rutted and badly affected by the frequent rains. The civil war means that roads are frequently blocked by the guerrillas and the military. Most of the railroad is closed.

Rivers are an important means of transportation; the Magdalena, Orinoco, Atrato, and Amazon river systems are all extensively navigable. Plans exist to connect Colombia to the Pan-American Highway.

TOURISM

Visitors : Population 1:80

530,000 visitors

Down 3% in 2000

MAIN TOURIST ARRIVALS

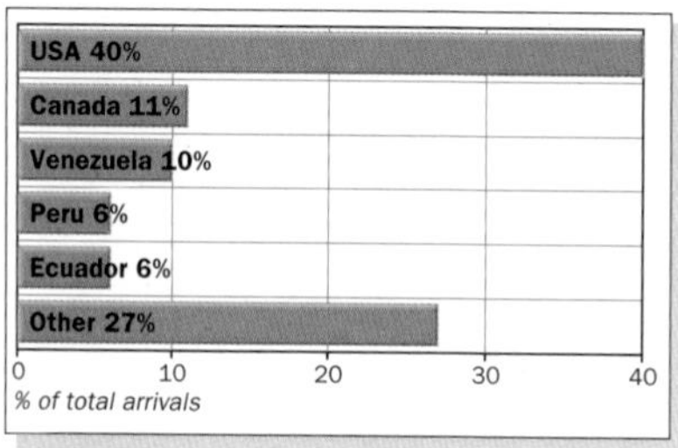
USA 40%
Canada 11%
Venezuela 10%
Peru 6%
Ecuador 6%
Other 27%
0
10
20
30
40
% of total arrivals

Tourism in Colombia is largely limited to the beaches of the Caribbean coast. Cartagena, Barranquilla, and Santa Marta are the main resorts. Cartagena has also been developed as a major Latin American conference center.

The expansion of tourism has been limited by Colombia's political instability and the prevalence of narcotics-related crime. The well-publicized activities of drugs cartels in Medellín and Cali, and instances of kidnappings in Bogotá are major deterrents for travelers.

Limited infrastructure makes many regions of the country, particularly Amazonia to the east of the Andes, almost inaccessible. The Caribbean coast is also barely exploited.

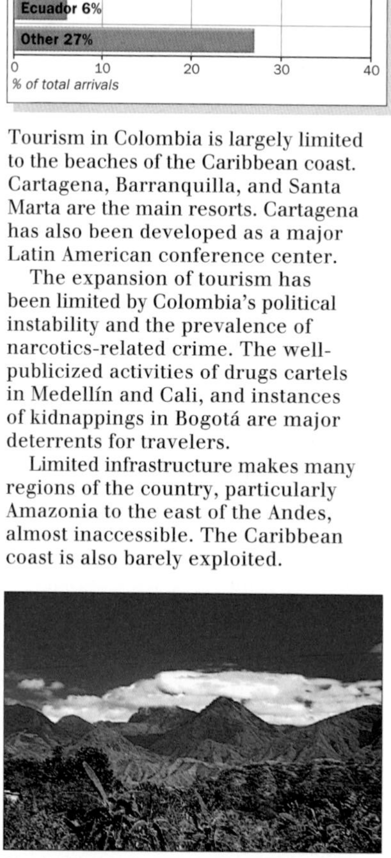

Simón Bolívar and Cristóbal Colón, twin peaks with a height of over 19,030 feet in the heart of the Colombian Andes.

PEOPLE

Pop. density low

Spanish, Amerindian languages, English Creole

41/km² (105/mi²)

THE URBAN/RURAL POPULATION SPLIT

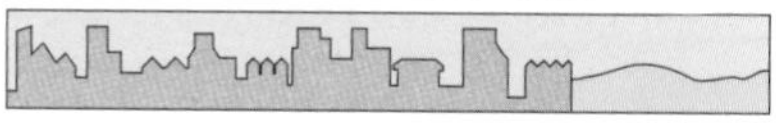
74%
26%

RELIGIOUS PERSUASION

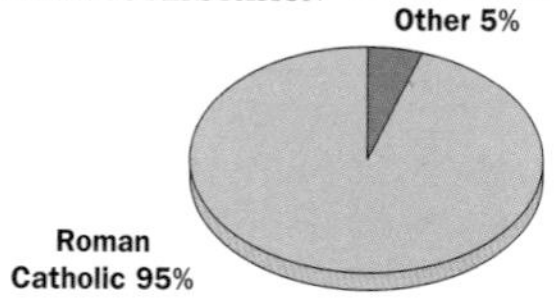
Other 5%
Roman Catholic 95%

ETHNIC MAKEUP

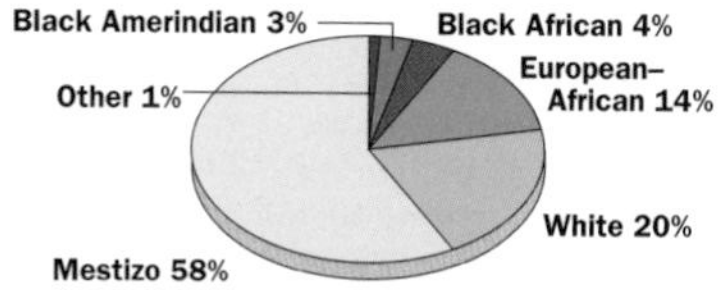
Black Amerindian 3%
Black African 4%
Other 1%
European–African 14%
White 20%
Mestizo 58%

The majority of Colombians are people of mixed blood. An estimated 450,000 indigenous Amerindians are largely concentrated in the southwest and Amazonia, although some communities are scattered throughout the country. A small black population lives along both coasts, particularly in Chocó, Colombia's poorest region. Blacks are the most unrepresented group.

Some progress has been made in giving Amerindians a greater political voice. In 1991, constitutional reforms reserved two seats in the Senate for indigenous representatives, and Amerindian pressure groups are increasingly active. Harassment by landowners and narcotics traffickers continues in Amazonia, and very few investigations into suspected human rights violations against Amerindians have led to prosecutions.

Women in Colombia have a higher profile than in much of the rest of Latin America. Many are prominent in the professions, though few reach the top in politics. The traditional extended Catholic family is still the norm. Regional identity is strong.

POPULATION AGE BREAKDOWN

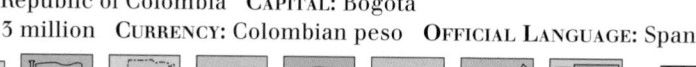

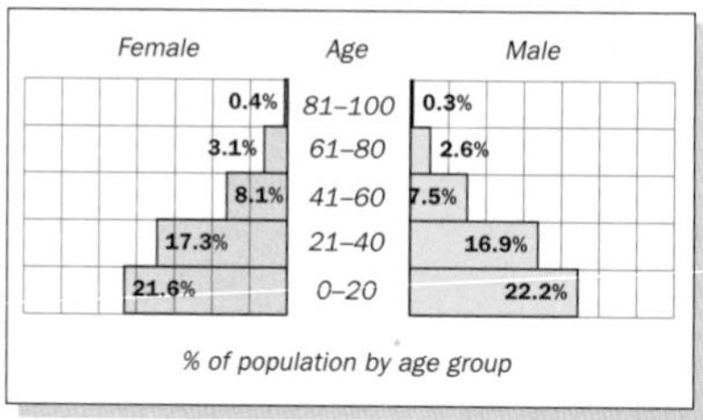
Female
Age
Male
0.4%
81–100
0.3%
3.1%
61–80
2.6%
8.1%
41–60
7.5%
17.3%
21–40
16.9%
21.6%
0–20
22.2%
% of population by age group

C

POLITICS

Multiparty elections

L. House 1998/2002
U. House 1998/2002

President Andres Pastrana Arango

Colombia is a presidential democracy, with a bicameral Congress. Presidents may not serve two consecutive terms.

MAIN POLITICAL ISSUES

Peace process

The largest guerrilla group – the Armed Revolutionary Force of Colombia (FARC) – and the National Liberation Army (ELN) are suspicious of the government's stated intention of negotiating an end to the guerrilla war, while continuing to fight against them. FARC in particular, however, has taken steps toward becoming part of the political process. Right-wing paramilitaries and the army favor a military solution. Meanwhile whole areas of the country remain effectively ungovernable.

Relations with the USA

Latest UN figures show that coca cultivation grew from 78,000 to 112,000 hectares in 1991–1999; the USA's $1.3 billion military aid package approved in 2000 supports the government's "Plan Colombia" anti-drug program to spray 60,000 hectares and intensify military operations against the narcotics industry.

AT THE LAST ELECTION

House of Representatives 161 seats

61%
PL
32%
PSC
7%
Others

PL = Liberal Party **PSC** = Social Conservative Party **Ind** = Independents **Reps** = Representatives of the Amerindian communities

Senate 102 seats

57%
PL
27%
PSC
13%
Ind
3%
Reps

Two special representatives of the Amerindian communities are appointed to the Senate, and one is elected.

PROFILE

The PSC and the PL, with few ideological differences, have shared power for the past 40-odd years. Pervasive official corruption and the violence associated with drugs cartels, guerrillas, paramilitaries, and the military, have seriously weakened public confidence in the state and the government, and have deterred foreign investors. President Pastrana's attempt in early 2000 to reform the Congress foundered on opposition from the house itself.

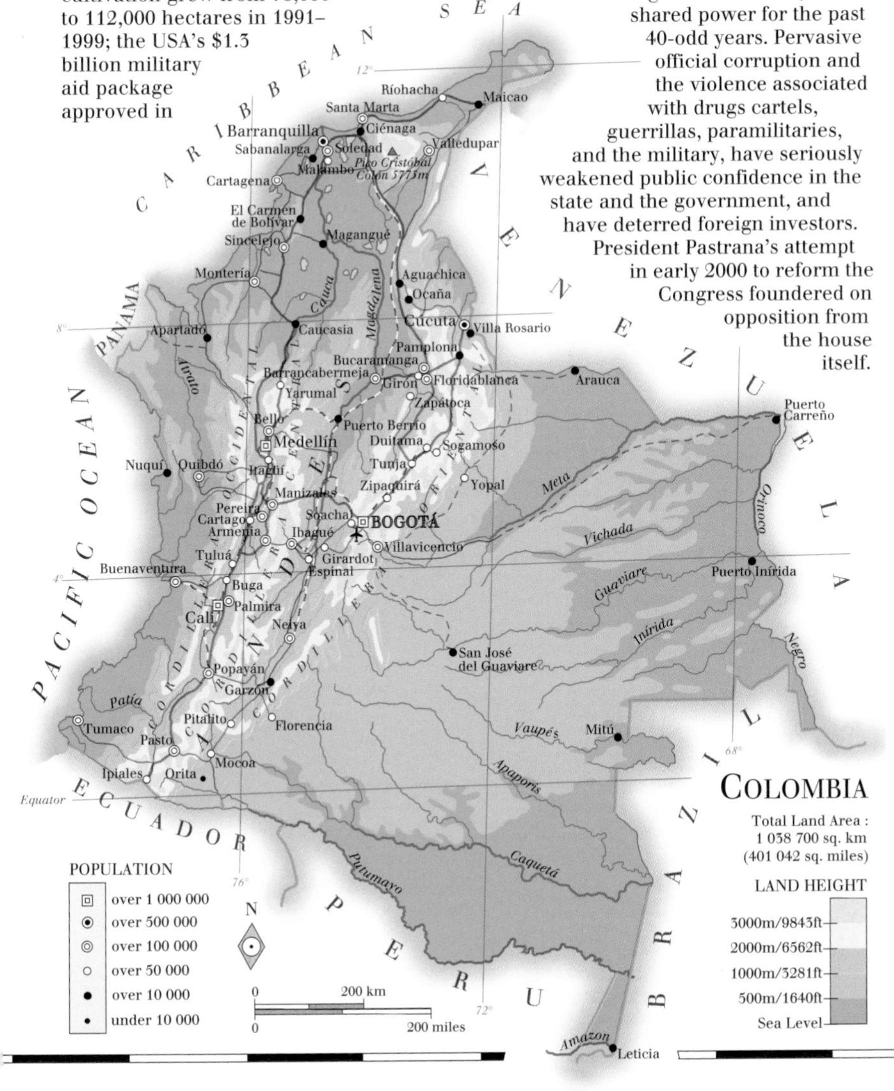
CARIBBEAN SEA
PACIFIC OCEAN
PANAMA
VENEZUELA
ECUADOR
PERU
BRAZIL
Ríohacha
Maicao
Santa Marta
Barranquilla
Ciénaga
Sabanalarga
Soledad
Malambo
Pico Cristóbal Colón 5775m
Valledupar
Cartagena
El Carmen de Bolívar
Magangué
Sincelejo
Montería
Aguachica
Ocaña
Apartadó
Caucasia
Cúcuta
Villa Rosario
Pamplona
Bucaramanga
Barrancabermeja
Girón
Floridablanca
Arauca
Yarumal
Zapatoca
Puerto Carreño
Bello
Puerto Berrío
Medellín
Duitama
Sogamoso
Nuquí
Quibdó
Itagüí
Tunja
Zipaquirá
Yopal
Manizales
Pereira
Soacha
Cartago
BOGOTÁ
Armenia
Ibagué
Villavicencio
Tuluá
Girardot
Espinal
Buenaventura
Puerto Inírida
Buga
Palmira
Cali
Neiva
San José del Guaviare
Popayán
Garzón
Tumaco
Pitalito
Florencia
Mitú
Pasto
Mocoa
Ipiales
Orita
Leticia
Equator
Cauca
Magdalena
Atrato
Meta
Vichada
Orinoco
Guaviare
Inírida
Negro
Vaupés
Apaporis
Patía
Caquetá
Putumayo
Amazon
COLOMBIA
Total Land Area : 1 038 700 sq. km (401 042 sq. miles)
LAND HEIGHT
3000m/9843ft
2000m/6562ft
1000m/3281ft
500m/1640ft
Sea Level
POPULATION
over 1 000 000
over 500 000
over 100 000
over 50 000
over 10 000
under 10 000
N
0
200 km
200 miles

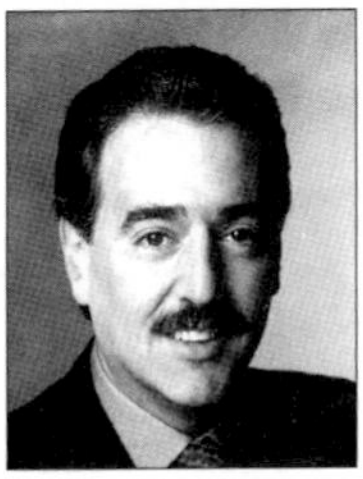

Andres Pastrana Arango, elected president in 1998.

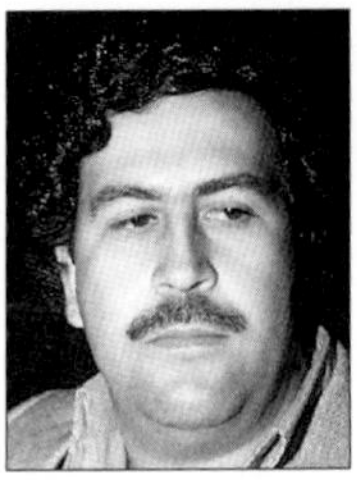

Pablo Escobar, ex-leader of Medellín drugs cartel, gunned down in 1993.

WORLD AFFAIRS

Joined UN in 1945

ACS | AP | AmCC | OAS | RG

Relations with the USA, Colombia's main export market and source of aid, have been strained in recent years. The USA has intervened directly to attack Colombia's narcotics business, making its elimination a condition of aid. Rapprochement with the Pastrana government led to the December 1998 military accord entailing further US training, equipment, and intelligence in the antinarcotics war. In October 1999 US and Colombian officials claimed a major success in smashing the largest drug-trafficking cartel. However, the boundary between this aim and the targeting of guerrilla groups is increasingly blurred.

Countries sharing borders with Colombia fear a "spillover" of violence and refugees due to "Plan Colombia."

AID

Recipient

$301m (receipts)

Up 80% in 1999

Critics say that US military aid for the narcotics war, which constitutes about 75% of total US aid, is also used against left-wing guerrillas. An IDB investment fund aids the peace process.

CHRONOLOGY

In 1525, Spain began the conquest of Colombia, which became its chief source of gold.

- **1819** Simón Bolívar defeats the Spanish at Boyacá. Republic of Gran Colombia formed with Venezuela, Ecuador, and Panama.
- **1830** Venezuela and Ecuador split away during revolts and civil wars.
- **1849** The Centralist Conservative and federalist Liberal parties are established.
- **1861–1886** Liberals hold monopoly on power.
- **1886–1930** Conservative rule.
- **1899–1903** Liberal "War of 1000 Days" revolt fails; 120,000 die.

C

CHRONOLOGY *continued*

- **1903** Panama secedes, but is not recognized by Colombia until 1921.
- **1930** Liberal President Olaya Herrera elected by coalition in first peaceful change of power.
- **1946** Conservatives take over.
- **1948** Shooting of Liberal mayor of Bogotá and riot known as *El Bogotazo* spark civil war, *La Violencia*, to 1957; 300,000 killed.
- **1953–1957** Military dictatorship of Rojas Pinilla.
- **1958** Conservatives and Liberals agree to alternate government in a National Front until 1974. Other parties banned.
- **1965** Left-wing guerrilla National Liberation Army and Maoist Popular Liberation Army founded.
- **1966** Pro-Soviet FARC guerrilla group formed.
- **1968** Constitutional reform allows new parties, but two-party parity continues. Guerrilla groups proliferate from now on.
- **1984** Minister of justice assassinated for attempting to enforce antidrugs campaign.
- **1985** M-19 guerrillas blast way into Ministry of Justice; 11 judges and 90 others killed. Patriotic Union (UP) party formed.
- **1986** Liberal Virgilio Barco Vargas wins presidential elections, ending power-sharing. UP wins ten seats in parliament. Right-wing paramilitary start murder campaign against UP politicians. Violence by both left-wing groups and death squads run by drugs cartels continues.
- **1989** M-19 reaches peace agreement with government, including the granting of a full pardon. Becomes legal party.
- **1990** UP and PL presidential candidates are murdered during the general election. Liberal César Gaviria is elected on an antidrugs platform.
- **1991** New constitution legalizes divorce, prohibits extradition of Colombian nationals. Indigenous peoples' democratic rights guaranteed, but territorial claims are not addressed.
- **1992–1993** Medellín drugs cartel leader, Pablo Escobar, captured, escapes and shot dead by police.
- **1995–1996** President Samper cleared of charges of receiving Cali cartel drug funds for elections.
- **1998** Andres Pastrana Arango elected to succeed Samper.
- **1999** Earthquake kills thousands.
- **2001** USA-backed spraying of illegal coca plantations begins in south; destruction of food crops by herbicides provokes resentment among peasant farmers.

DEFENSE

Compulsory military service

$2.16bn

Down 16% in 1999

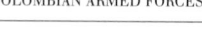

COLOMBIAN ARMED FORCES

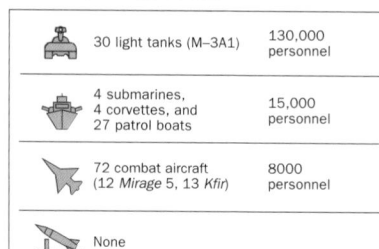

30 light tanks (M–3A1)	130,000 personnel
4 submarines, 4 corvettes, and 27 patrol boats	15,000 personnel
72 combat aircraft (12 *Mirage* 5, 13 *Kfir*)	8000 personnel
None	

The military is powerful, but rarely intervenes directly in politics. Human rights groups accuse the armed forces and their paramilitary allies of gross and systematic abuses, involving torture and murder, in their fight against guerrilla groups and the production of narcotics. The government reorganized the high command in 1998 in a bid to boost the peace process but the military remained suspicious, in particular opposing a FARC-controlled "demilitarized zone." It has successfully exploited increased tensions to expand substantially under President Pastrana, with numbers set to rise still more.

Colombia participates in the joint Latin American Defense Force. The USA supplies most arms and training, especially through "Plan Colombia."

ECONOMICS

Inflation 22.7% p.a. (1990–1999)

$90bn

1875–2236 Colombian pesos

SCORE CARD

- World GNP Ranking 37th
- GNP per Capita $2170
- Balance of Payments .... $-979m
- Inflation 11.2%
- Unemployment 20%

EXPORTS

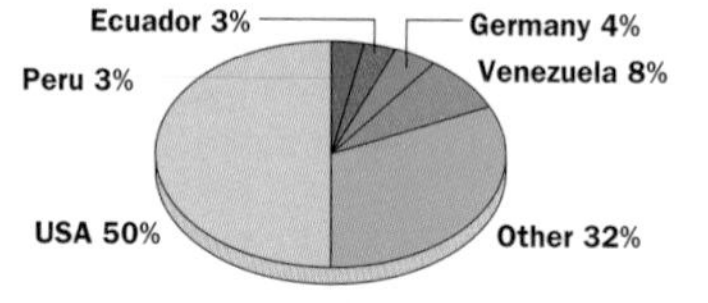
Ecuador 3%
Germany 4%
Peru 3%
Venezuela 8%
USA 50%
Other 32%

IMPORTS

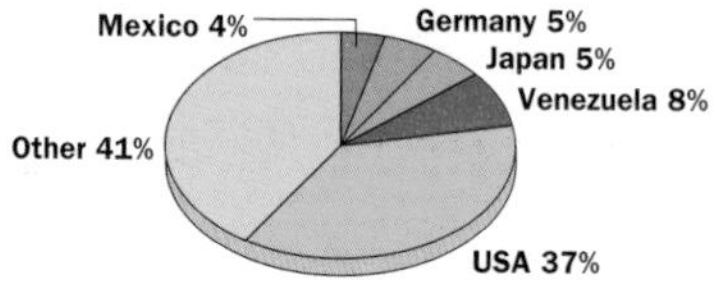
Mexico 4%
Germany 5%
Japan 5%
Venezuela 8%
Other 41%
USA 37%

ECONOMIC PERFORMANCE INDICATOR

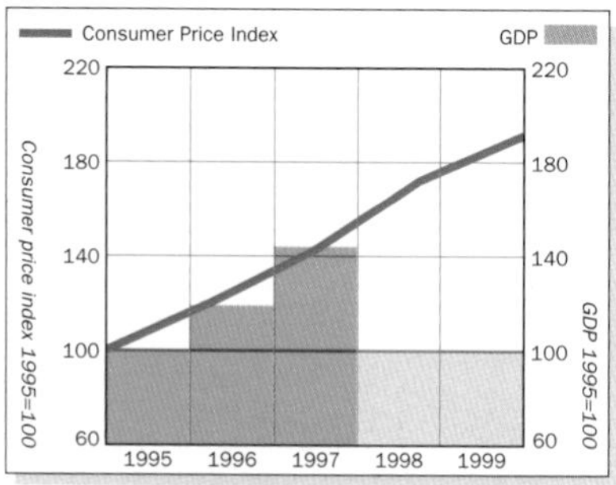
Consumer Price Index
GDP
220
180
140
100
60
Consumer price index 1995=100
GDP 1995=100
1995
1996
1997
1998
1999

Strengths

Substantial oil and coal deposits plus well-developed hydroelectric power makes Colombia almost self-sufficient in energy. Healthy and diversified export sector – especially coffee and coal. Light manufactures. Worldwide market for cocaine.

Weaknesses

Narcotics-related violence, corruption, and political instability discourage foreign investors. Domestic industry uncompetitive owing to protection. High unemployment. Coffee and oil subject to world price fluctuations.

Profile

Of all the Latin American economies, Colombia's is probably the closest to the US model. The state has traditionally played a relatively minor role and

Colombia has a successful private export sector. A thorough program of privatization has reduced the state's involvement further.

Regional disparities remain marked. Most wealth is found in the Bogotá, Medellín, and Cali regions. Rural areas are largely underdeveloped. The main obstacle to growth is the instability caused by the narcotics business and the protracted civil war. Given stability and investment, Colombia's potential for growth is considerable.

COLOMBIA : MAJOR BUSINESSES

Pulp and paper
Narcotics
Steel
Chemicals
Vehicle assembly
Food processing
Textiles
Oil
Barranquilla
Medellín
Bogotá
Cali
Ibagué
Orito
0 200 km
0 200 miles
* significant multinational ownership

C

RESOURCES

Electric power 11.7m kw

199,227 tonnes

710,000 b/d (reserves 2,600,000,000 bbl)

26m cattle, 2.8m pigs, 100m chickens

Oil, natural gas, coal, silver, emeralds, gold, platinum

ELECTRICITY GENERATION

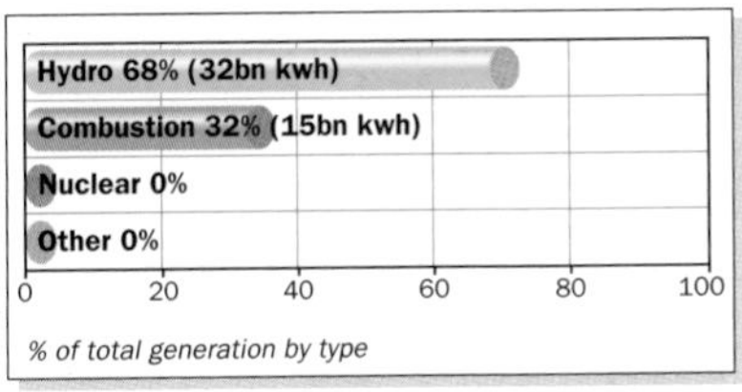
Hydro 68% (32bn kwh)
Combustion 32% (15bn kwh)
Nuclear 0%
Other 0%
0
20
40
60
80
100
% of total generation by type

Colombia has substantial oil reserves but needs increasing investment to maintain production. Coal and gas are important, and it is a major producer of gold, platinum, silver, and emeralds.

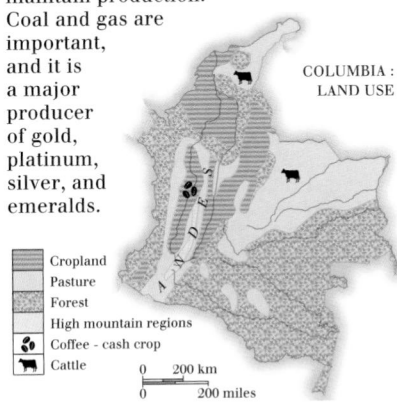

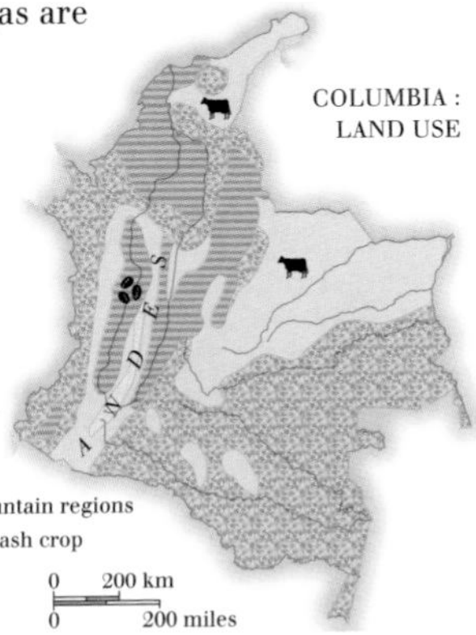
COLUMBIA : LAND USE
ANDES
Cropland
Pasture
Forest
High mountain regions
Coffee - cash crop
Cattle
0 200 km
0 200 miles

ENVIRONMENT

Sustainability rank: 36th

9%

1.8 tonnes per capita

ENVIRONMENTAL TREATIES

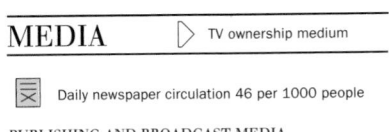

Yes	Yes	Yes
Yes	Yes	No

Cattle-ranching, logging, coca growing, and spraying cause soil degradation and loss of natural habitats.

MEDIA

TV ownership medium

Daily newspaper circulation 46 per 1000 people

PUBLISHING AND BROADCAST MEDIA

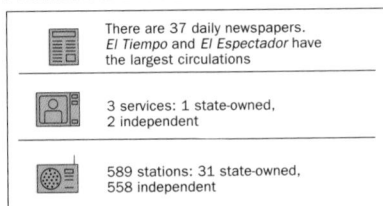

There are 37 daily newspapers. *El Tiempo* and *El Espectador* have the largest circulations

3 services: 1 state-owned, 2 independent

589 stations: 31 state-owned, 558 independent

The independent press is small. Journalists have been murdered by paramilitaries and held by guerrillas.

CRIME

Death penalty not used

28,968 prisoners

Up 35% 1996–1998

CRIME RATES

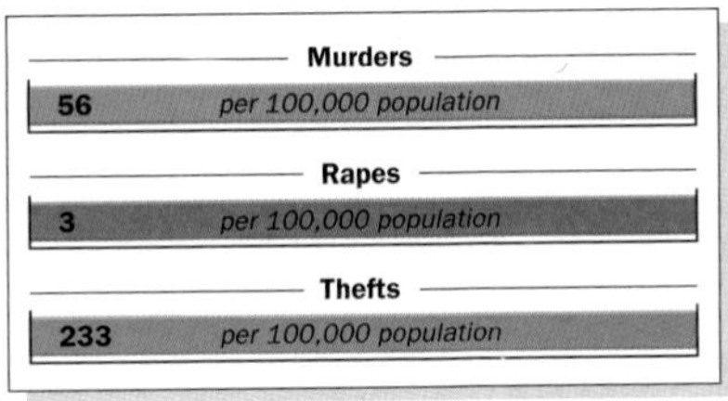
Murders
56 per 100,000 population
Rapes
3 per 100,000 population
Thefts
233 per 100,000 population

Colombia is one of the most violent countries in the world. Amnesty International identified right-wing paramilitaries as the authors of 61% of all gross human rights violations between September 1998 and March 2000; another 23% were linked to paramilitaries acting jointly with members of the security forces. Armed groups assassinated 20 mayoral candidates and 20 mayors, and kidnapped 200 other candidates, in regional and local elections in 2000. NGOs estimate that some 1.5 million people have been displaced over the last 12 years. Homicide is the main cause of death among young men in cities; overall, it rates after cancer in the mortality stakes. Most violence is narcotics-related, and Barracabermeja, Bogotá, Cali, and Medellín are dangerous places; the army, police, paramilitaries, and guerrillas are thought to be involved. Frequent armed robberies and kidnappings make wealthy residents extremely security conscious. A relatively new phenomenon is that of "social cleansing," the murder of street children and beggars by armed gangs, some in Bogotá funded by businesses.

EDUCATION

School leaving age: 12

92%

644,188 students

THE EDUCATION SYSTEM

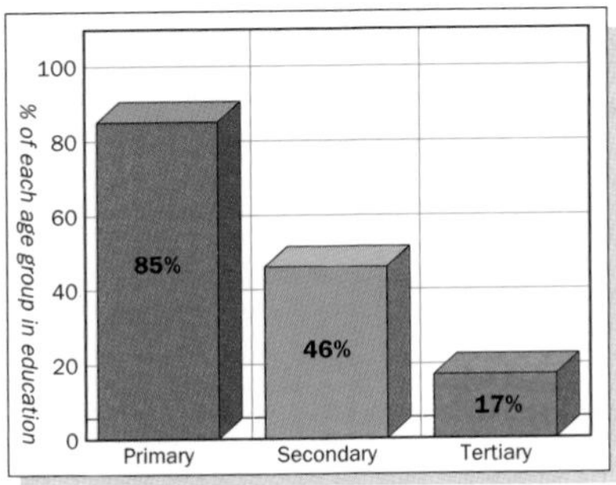
100
80
60
40
20
0
% of each age group in education
85%
46%
17%
Primary
Secondary
Tertiary

Education in Colombia is free and compulsory, and is a mix of French and US models, with a *baccalauréat* examination taken at the end of secondary school. Provision in rural areas is poor and absenteeism high. Where provided, public and university education is generally of a high standard, but the resources available to public education have decreased due to budget cuts. The rich send their children to private schools and universities in the USA.

HEALTH

Welfare state health benefits

1 per 909 people

Heart diseases, cancers, violence, accidents

Budget cuts have reduced health spending. Private care is growing. Only 16% of Colombians benefit from any social security system, rather fewer than in most Latin American states. Rural areas have little health provision, since most doctors work in the larger cities. A polio vaccination campaign has largely eradicated the virus from Colombia, except in coastal regions.

SPENDING

GDP/cap. increase

CONSUMPTION AND SPENDING

43 per 1000 population

160 per 1000 population

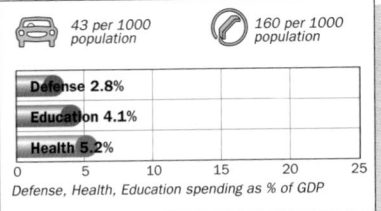

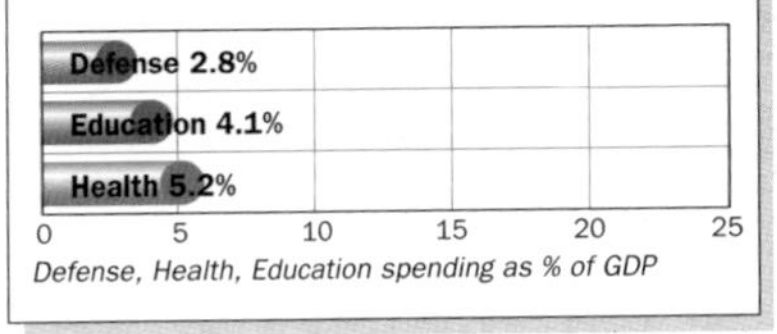
Defense 2.8%
Education 4.1%
Health 5.2%
0
5
10
15
20
25
Defense, Health, Education spending as % of GDP

There is little social mobility; the historically wealthy Spanish families are still dominant in political and business life, but the entry of drug-related money has created new layers of rich in cities and among landowners. Drug money also finances the import of consumer goods such as TV sets, computers, and perfume. The wealthy go to the USA for medical treatment and educate their children overseas. The rural poor are mostly landless. The inhabitants of shanty towns in Barranquilla, Buenaventura, Cali, and Cartagena form the poorest groups.

WORLD RANKING

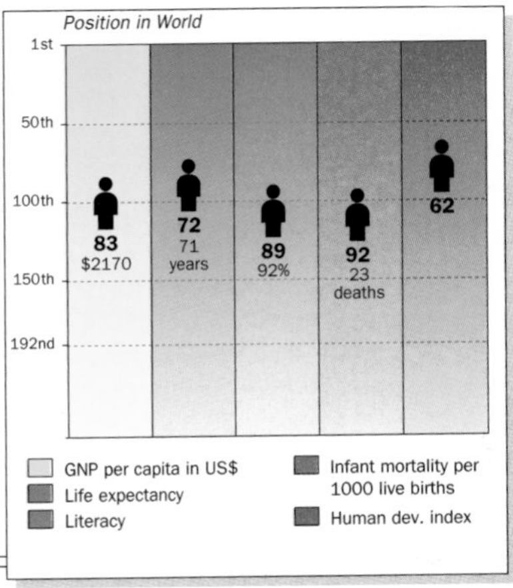
Position in World
1st
50th
100th
150th
192nd
83
$2170
72
71 years
89
92%
92
23 deaths
62
GNP per capita in US$
Life expectancy
Literacy
Infant mortality per 1000 live births
Human dev. index

COMOROS

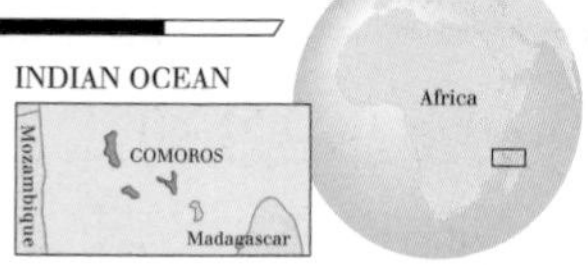
INDIAN OCEAN
Mozambique
COMOROS
Madagascar
Africa

OFFICIAL NAME: Federal Islamic Republic of the Comoros **CAPITAL:** Moroni
POPULATION: 694,000 **CURRENCY:** Comoros franc **OFFICIAL LANGUAGES:** Arabic and French

1975 | 1975 | July 6 | COM | +3 | +269 | .km

THE ARCHIPELAGO REPUBLIC of the Comoros lies off the east African coast, between Mozambique and Madagascar. It consists of three main islands and a number of islets. Most of the population are subsistence farmers. In 1975, the Comoros Islands, except for Mayotte, became independent of France. Since then instability has plagued this poor region, with several coups and counter-coups, and repeated attempts at secession by smaller islands.

Moroni, the capital, on Grande Comore. The Comoros Islands are fertile and heavily forested. Many are ringed by coral reefs.

CLIMATE

Tropical oceanic

WEATHER CHART

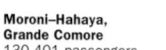

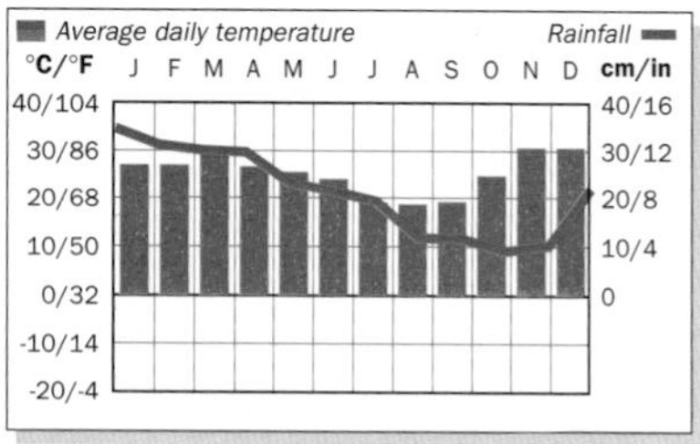
Average daily temperature
Rainfall
°C/°F
J F M A M J J A S O N D
cm/in
40/104
30/86
20/68
10/50
0/32
-10/14
-20/-4
40/16
30/12
20/8
10/4
0

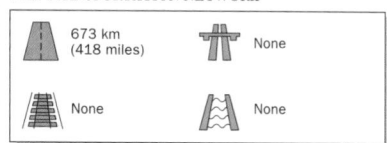

The islands are tropical; it is hot and humid on the coasts and cooler higher up, notably on Mount Kartala.

TRANSPORTATION

Drive on right

Moroni–Hahaya, Grande Comore 130,401 passengers

3 ships 2959 grt

THE TRANSPORTATION NETWORK

673 km (418 miles)

None

None

None

Recent projects have included the development of the port at Moroni and upgrading the international airport.

TOURISM

Visitors : Population 1:29

24,000 visitors

Down 11% in 1999

MAIN TOURIST ARRIVALS

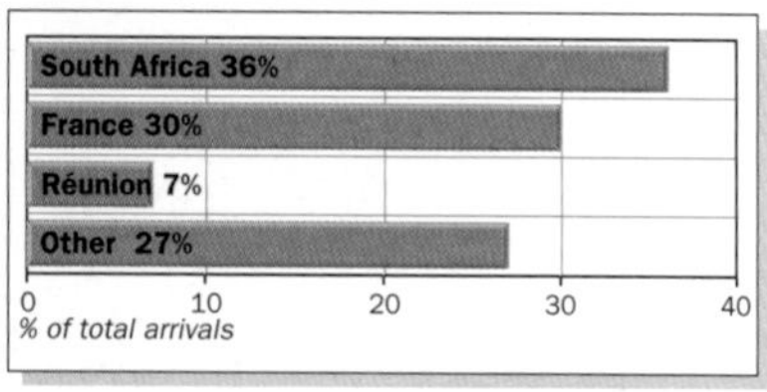
South Africa 36%
France 30%
Réunion 7%
Other 27%
0
10
20
30
40
% of total arrivals

In 1988, Sun International of South Africa joined a major project to build four hotels designed to attract 12,000 visitors a year. However, political instability has wrecked the islands' tourism prospects.

PEOPLE

Pop. density high

Arabic, Comoran, French

311/km² (806/mi²)

THE URBAN/RURAL POPULATION SPLIT

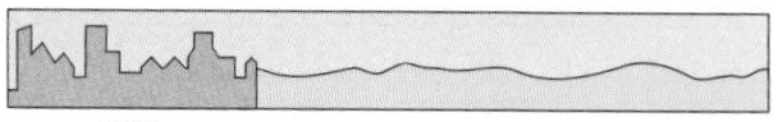
33%
67%

RELIGIOUS PERSUASION

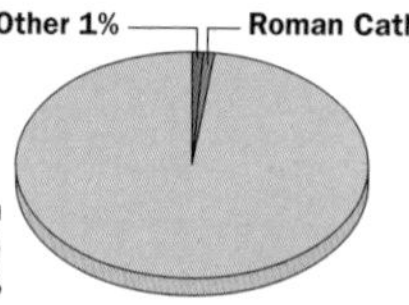
Other 1%
Roman Catholic 1%
Muslim (mainly Sunni) 98%

The Comoros has absorbed Polynesians, Africans, Indonesians, Persians, and Arabs over time, as well as immigrants from Portugal, Holland, France, and India. Some communities retain their individual character; for instance, Mwali (Mohéli) is still primarily African. Ethnic tension is rare, partly owing to the unifying force of Islam, the predominant religion. A more potent divisive factor, especially on Anjouan, is regionalism.

POLITICS

No multiparty elections

1996/2000 (postponed)

President Assoumani Azzali

AT THE LAST ELECTION

Federal Assembly 43 seats

2% Ind
91% RND
5% FNJ
2% VA

RND = Rassemblement national pour la developpement
FNJ = Front national pour la justice **Ind** = Independent
VA= Votes annulled

The Senate was abolished under the 1996 constitution.

The islands' attempts to introduce democracy have been consistently undermined by repeated coups. The island of Anjouan has been at the center of the country's troubles since it unilaterally declared independence in August 1997, with rival militias favoring either cohabitation with Grande Comore or reattachment to France. Renewed violence in April 1999 provided Colonel Assoumani Azzali with the pretext to install himself as president. A "new Comoran entity," with each separate island largely autonomous, was established in late 2000 by the Fomboni declaration. A timetable for a return to democracy was agreed in February 2001.

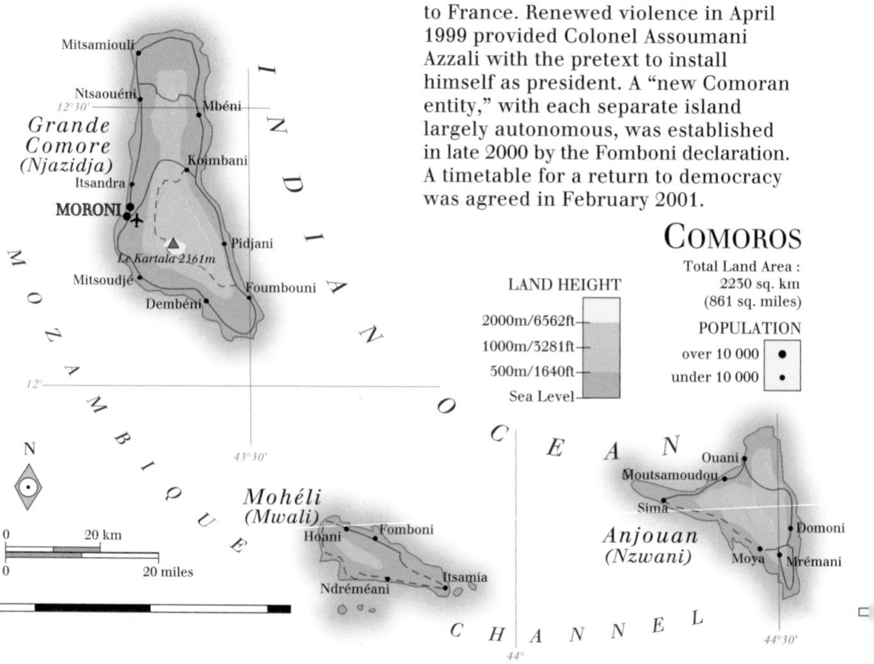
COMOROS
Total Land Area : 2230 sq. km (861 sq. miles)
LAND HEIGHT
2000m/6562ft
1000m/3281ft
500m/1640ft
Sea Level
POPULATION
over 10 000
under 10 000
Mitsamiouli
Ntsaouéni
Mbéni
Grande Comore (Njazidja)
Koimbani
Itsandra
MORONI
Pidjani
Le Kartala 2361m
Mitsoudjé
Foumbouni
Dembéni
INDIAN OCEAN
MOZAMBIQUE CHANNEL
12°30'
12°
43°30'
44°
44°30'
N
0
20 km
20 miles
Mohéli (Mwali)
Hoani
Fomboni
Itsamia
Ndrémeani
Ouani
Moutsamoudou
Sima
Anjouan (Nzwani)
Domoni
Moya
Mrémani

C

WORLD AFFAIRS

Joined UN in 1975

AL | OIC | OAU | COI | FZ

France remains the Comoros' main benefactor, although economic ties with South Africa have strengthened in recent years – a by-product of sanctions-busting during apartheid days. An OAU assessment team visited strife-torn Anjouan in February 1999, but had to be evacuated after fighting on the island intensified.

AID

Recipient

$21m (receipts)

Down 40% in 1999

Foreign aid, mainly from France, the EU, the World Bank, and the IMF, accounts for over 40% of GDP. Because of its Islamic links, the Comoros also gets aid from Arab states and OPEC. In 1998 major donors attacked the government for spending more than 70% on "political superstructure."

DEFENSE

No compulsory military service

$3m (estimated)

No significant change

France and South Africa finance the small presidential guard, the principal security force. Mauritian aid was also sought after clashes on Anjouan.

ECONOMICS

Inflation 3.8% p.a. (1990–1999)

$189m

485–528 Comoros francs

SCORE CARD

❑ WORLD GNP RANKING	183rd
❑ GNP PER CAPITA	$350
❑ BALANCE OF PAYMENTS	$–19m
❑ INFLATION	3%
❑ UNEMPLOYMENT	20%

STRENGTHS

Vanilla, ylang-ylang, and cloves are the main cash crops.

WEAKNESSES

Subsistence level farming. Over 50% of food requirements are imported. Lack of basic infrastructure, especially electricity and transportation. Open to allegations of financial mismanagement. The persistent political instability is hindering the growth of tourism.

EXPORTS

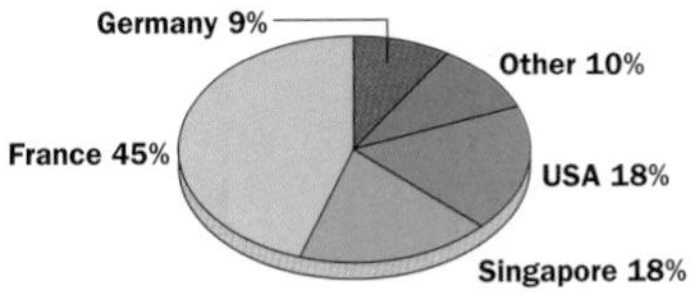
Germany 9%
Other 10%
France 45%
USA 18%
Singapore 18%

IMPORTS

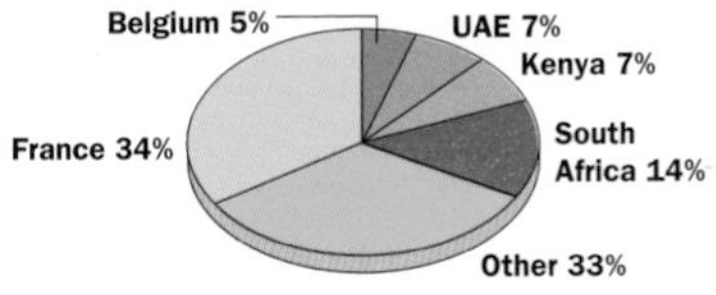
Belgium 5%
UAE 7%
Kenya 7%
France 34%
South Africa 14%
Other 33%

RESOURCES

Electric power 5000 kw

12,500 tonnes

Not an oil producer

140,000 goats, 52,000 cattle, 490,000 chickens

None

There are few strategic resources. An HEP plant is under construction on Anjouan, but most fuel for energy is still imported. Fishing remains a neglected source of future growth.

ENVIRONMENT

Not available

None

0.1 tonnes per capita

The environment is not a major priority in the Comoros; natural disasters, such as the volcanic eruption in 1977 which left 20,000 people homeless, are of more immediate concern. The government is promoting tourism and recognizes the long-term commercial value of imposing environmental controls on new developments.

MEDIA

TV ownership low

There are no daily newspapers

PUBLISHING AND BROADCAST MEDIA

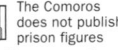

There are 2 weekly newspapers, the state-owned *Al Watwan* and the independent *La Gazette des Comores*

No TV service

1 state-controlled service, some independent services

France promises to fund the islands' first TV station. Radio is strictly controlled, and there is no single national newspaper.

CRIME

Death penalty used

The Comoros does not publish prison figures

Crime is rising

Civil unrest by youths in May 1998 led to police curfews and roadblocks in Moroni. Lawlessness between rival militias escalated throughout the year on the island of Anjouan.

EDUCATION

School leaving age: 16

60%

348 students

There is a very limited education system beyond secondary level. Schools are equipped to teach only basic literacy, hygiene, and agricultural techniques. Pupil–teacher ratios are high.

CHRONOLOGY

The Comoros was ruled by matrilineally inherited sultanates until shortly before becoming a French protectorate in 1886.

- ❑ **1961** Internal self-government.
- ❑ **1975** Independence.
- ❑ **1978** Mercenaries restore Ahmed Abdallah to power.
- ❑ **1989** Abdallah assassinated.
- ❑ **1992** Chaotic first multiparty polls.
- ❑ **1996** Mohammed Taki Abdoulkarim elected president.
- ❑ **1997** Anjouan separatists beat off government troops.
- ❑ **1999** Col. Azzali seizes power. Anjouan militias clash.
- ❑ **2000** Fomboni declaration signed with Anjouan.
- ❑ **2001** President Azzali promises return to civilian government by early 2002.

HEALTH

No welfare state health benefits

1 per 10,000 people

Malaria, infectious intestinal and bacterial diseases

Health care is rudimentary, other than two maternity clinics and 30 recently renovated health centers.

SPENDING

GDP/cap. decrease

CONSUMPTION AND SPENDING

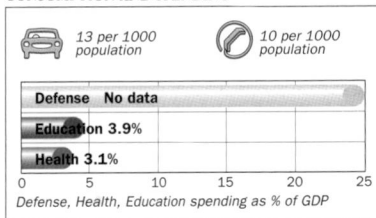

13 per 1000 population

10 per 1000 population

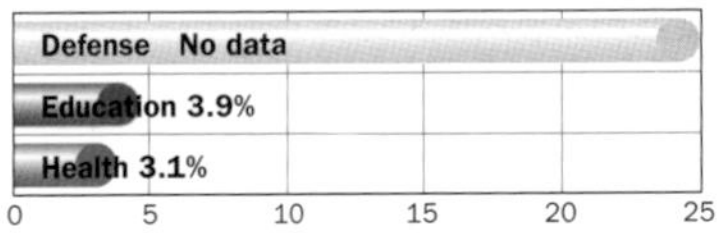
Defense No data
Education 3.9%
Health 3.1%
0
5
10
15
20
25

Defense, Health, Education spending as % of GDP

A political and business elite controls most of the wealth. Bridegrooms win social status according to the size of their weddings. Unpaid government workers went on strike in 1998.

WORLD RANKING

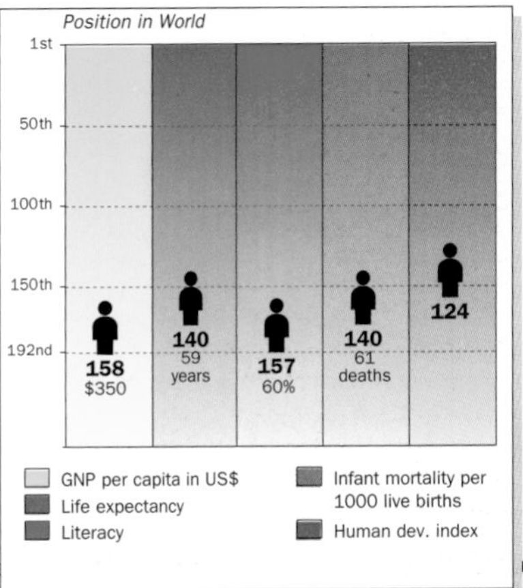
Position in World
1st
50th
100th
150th
192nd
158
$350
140
59 years
157
60%
140
61 deaths
124
GNP per capita in US$
Life expectancy
Literacy
Infant mortality per 1000 live births
Human dev. index

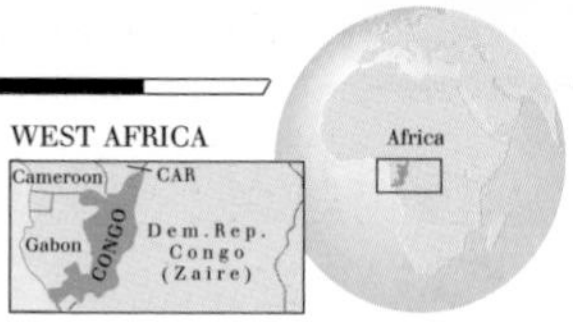

WEST AFRICA
Cameroon
CAR
Gabon
CONGO
Dem. Rep. Congo (Zaire)
Africa

CONGO

OFFICIAL NAME: The Republic of the Congo **CAPITAL:** Brazzaville
POPULATION: 2.9 million **CURRENCY:** CFA franc **OFFICIAL LANGUAGE:** French

C

1960 | 1960 | Aug 15 | RCB | +1 | +242 | .cg

STRADDLING THE EQUATOR in west central Africa, Congo achieved independence from France in 1960. However, it soon fell under a Marxist–Leninist regime with a one-party form of government which discouraged much foreign investment. Multiparty democracy was achieved in 1991, but has since been overtaken by years of feuding and violence.

CLIMATE

Tropical equatorial

WEATHER CHART

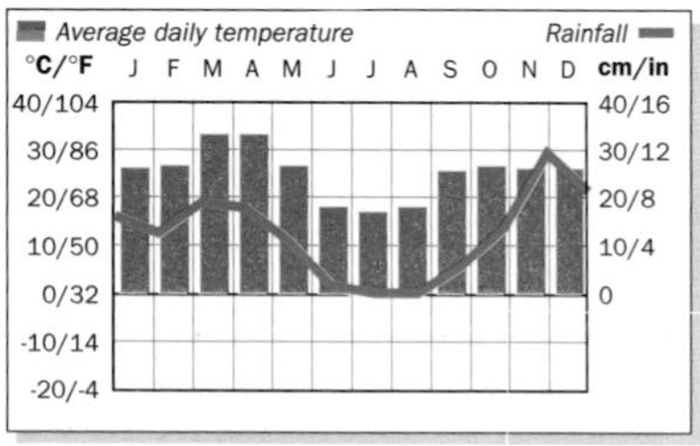

Average daily temperature
Rainfall
°C/°F
J F M A M J J A S O N D
cm/in
40/104
30/86
20/68
10/50
0/32
-10/14
-20/-4
40/16
30/12
20/8
10/4
0

In most years there are two wet seasons and two dry seasons in Congo. The rainfall is heaviest in the coastal regions south of the equator.

TRANSPORTATION

Drive on right

Brazzaville International 259,840 passengers

20 ships 3800 grt

THE TRANSPORTATION NETWORK

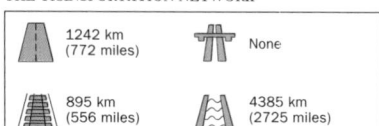

1242 km (772 miles)

None

895 km (556 miles)

4385 km (2725 miles)

Pointe-Noire is a major port, used by the Central African Republic, Chad, and Cameroon. The Congo Ocean Railroad (to Brazzaville) reopened in 2000. There are plans for a second, and larger, international airport near Ewo.

TOURISM

Visitors : Population 1:112

26,000 visitors

Up 420% in 2000

MAIN TOURIST ARRIVALS

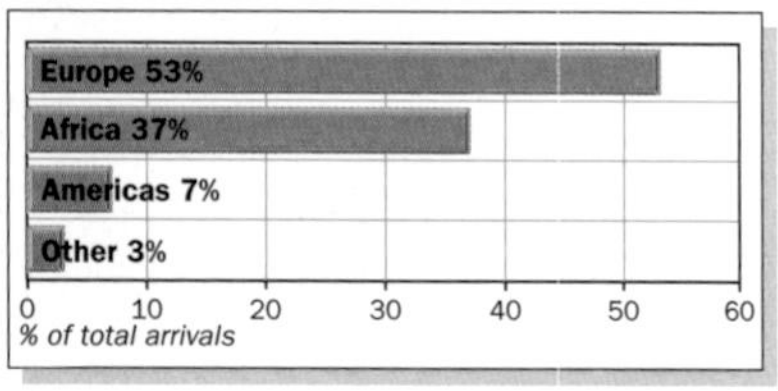

Europe 53%
Africa 37%
Americas 7%
Other 3%
0
10
20
30
40
50
60
% of total arrivals

The Marxist–Leninist regime did not seek to develop tourism, and visitors, mostly on safaris and business-related trips, are still rare, though increasing.

The Loufoulakari Falls, near Brazzaville. Swamps and mangroves border many of the rivers in the Congo's northern region.

PEOPLE

Pop. density low

Kongo, Teke, Lingala, French

8/km² (22/mi²)

THE URBAN/RURAL POPULATION SPLIT

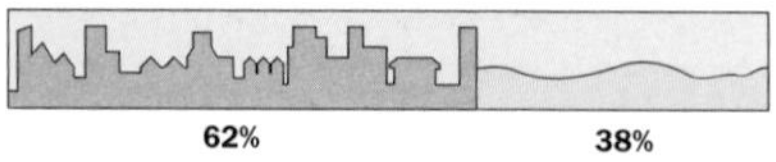

62%
38%

ETHNIC MAKEUP

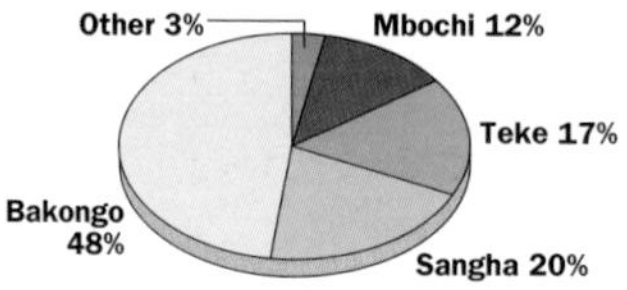

Other 3%
Mbochi 12%
Teke 17%
Bakongo 48%
Sangha 20%

Congo is one of the most tribally conscious countries in Africa. The main tensions are between the Bakongo, who live in the north, and the Mbochi, who are concentrated in the more prosperous south. Since the 1950s, women have achieved considerable freedom.

POLITICS

No multiparty elections

L. House 1993/2000
U. House 1995/2000
(both postponed)

President Denis Sassou-Nguesso

AT THE LAST ELECTION

National Assembly 125 seats (suspended in 1997)

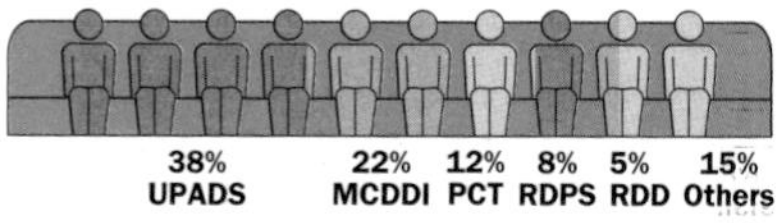

38% UPADS
22% MCDDI
12% PCT
8% RDPS
5% RDD
15% Others

UPADS = Pan-African Union for Social Democracy
MCDDI = Congolese Movement for Democracy and Integral Development **PCT** = Congolese Labour Party
RDPS = Rally for Democratic and Social Progress
RDD = Rally for Democracy and Development

Senate 60 seats (suspended in 1997)

Elections to the Senate are indirect, with one-third of members elected every two years. The Senate is dominated by UPADS

Multiparty elections in 1992–1993, won by Lissouba and his UPADS party, were strongly disputed by opposition parties. Thousands subsequently died in fighting in 1997, and former Marxist dictator Sassou-Nguesso seized power that October. A cease-fire, agreed in December 1999, restored relative calm.

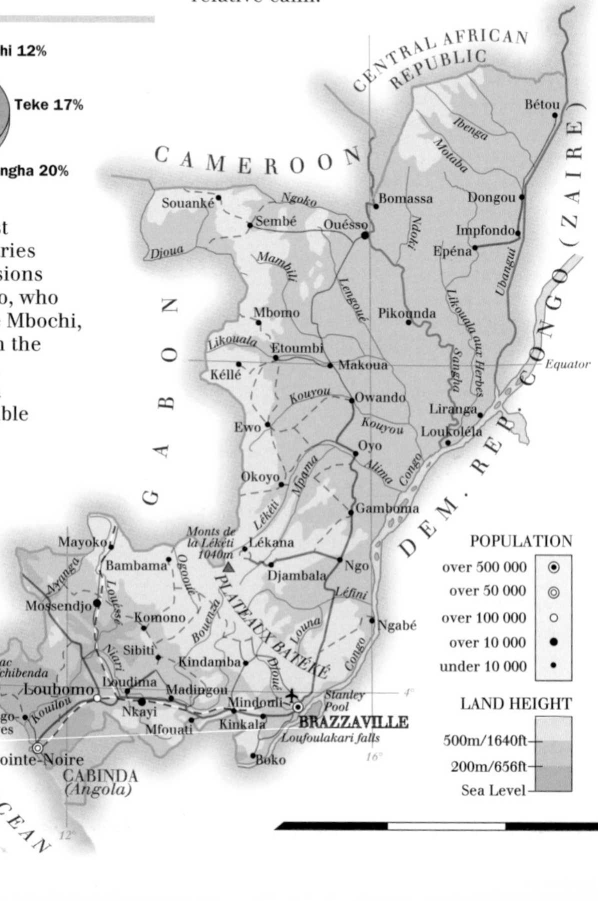

CENTRAL AFRICAN REPUBLIC
CAMEROON
GABON
DEM. REP. CONGO (ZAIRE)
ATLANTIC OCEAN
CABINDA (Angola)
Bétou
Bomassa
Dongou
Impfondo
Épéna
Souanké
Sembé
Ouésso
Mbomo
Pikounda
Etoumbi
Makoua
Kéllé
Owando
Ewo
Oyo
Okoyo
Gamboma
Lékana
Mayoko
Bambama
Djambala
Ngo
Mossendjo
Komono
Ngabé
Sibiti
Kindamba
Loubomo
Nzambi
Madingo-Kayes
Pointe-Noire
Nkayi
Madingou
Mfouati
Mindouli
Kinkala
BRAZZAVILLE
Loufoulakari falls
Boko
Stanley Pool
Monts de la Lékéti 1040m
PLATEAUX BATÉKÉ
Lac Tchibenda
Equator
Liranga
Loukoléla
POPULATION
over 500 000
over 50 000
over 100 000
over 10 000
under 10 000
LAND HEIGHT
500m/1640ft
200m/656ft
Sea Level

CONGO

Total Land Area : 341 500 sq. km (131 853 sq. miles)

N

0 100 km
0 100 miles

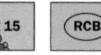

WORLD AFFAIRS

Joined UN in 1960

BDEAC | CEMAC | FZ | NAM | ACP

Carefully balancing relations with France and the USA is a priority, since both seek to extend their stakes in the oil industry; nevertheless relations with old Eastern bloc allies remain strong. Congo has been susceptible in recent years to political instability and wars in the neighboring Democratic Republic of Congo (former Zaire) and Angola.

AID

Recipient

$140m (receipts) | Up 115% in 1999

Before 1990, the USSR, Cuba, and China were the major donors. Most aid now comes from France. High levels of 1970s debt mean that, despite its oil, Congo remains dependent on aid.

DEFENSE

No compulsory military service

$73m | Down 12% in 1999

The militias of the various political forces were being integrated into the 8000-strong army, until fighting broke out again between them in mid-1997. The air force numbers 1200, and is equipped with 12 MiG-21s.

ECONOMICS

Inflation 8.6% p.a. (1990–1999)

$1.6bn | 654.42–698.69 CFA francs

SCORE CARD

❑ World GNP Ranking	144th
❑ GNP per Capita	$550
❑ Balance of Payments	$–252m
❑ Inflation	–16.9%
❑ Unemployment	Widespread underemployment

STRENGTHS

Increase in importance of oil, now providing 90% of export revenues. Significant timber supplies. Skilled and well-trained workforce helps sustain substantial industrial base in the capital and Pointe-Noire.

WEAKNESSES

$4 billion debt by late 1980s. Large refugee population. Top-heavy bureaucracy. Overdependence on oil. Political instability.

EXPORTS

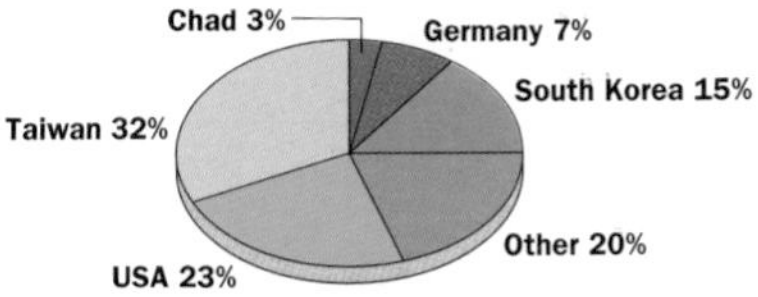
Chad 3%
Germany 7%
South Korea 15%
Taiwan 32%
Other 20%
USA 23%

IMPORTS

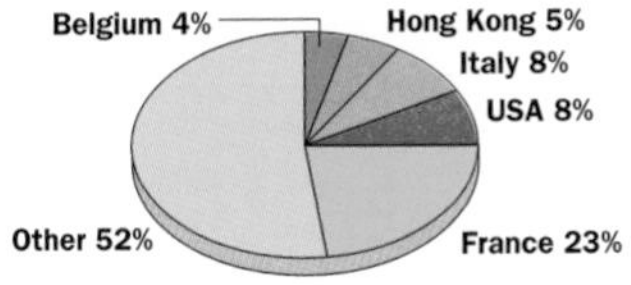
Belgium 4%
Hong Kong 5%
Italy 8%
USA 8%
Other 52%
France 23%

RESOURCES

Electric power 118,000 kw

38,181 tonnes | 275,000 b/d (reserves 1,500,000,000 bbl)

285,000 goats, 116,000 sheep, 1.9m chickens | Oil, natural gas, zinc, gold, copper, potash, diamonds

Oil is by far the Congo's most important resource. Natural gas reserves have yet to be exploited. There are some deposits of diamonds and potash. Bauxite and iron ore reserves are not large enough to be profitably mined and phosphate production was abandoned in 1977. Chinese aid has helped build two hydroelectric dams, on the Bouenza and Djoué rivers. A third is currently being built on the Léfini at Imboulou.

ENVIRONMENT

Not available

5% | 0.1 tonnes per capita

The Yaoundé Declaration should help control exploitation of tropical timber. Congo has been used in the past as a dumping ground for dangerous toxic waste from the West.

MEDIA

TV ownership low

Daily newspaper circulation 8 per 1000 people

PUBLISHING AND BROADCAST MEDIA

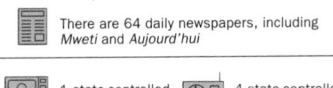

There are 64 daily newspapers, including *Mweti* and *Aujourd'hui*

1 state-controlled service | 4 state-controlled services

Two dailies, two weeklies, and national television and radio stations are all state-owned. During World War II, Radio Brazzaville was vital to Charles de Gaulle's forces.

CRIME

Death penalty not used

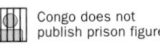

Congo does not publish prison figures | Crime is rising

Armed robbery and smuggling are widespread. Years of conflict and instability in neighboring countries mean that guns are easily available.

EDUCATION

School leaving age: 16

81% | 13,806 students

Originally pioneered by French Roman Catholic missions, schools are still subject to inspection from Paris.

CHRONOLOGY

The kingdoms of Teke and Loango were incorporated as the Middle Congo (part of French Equatorial Africa) between 1880 and 1883.

- ❑ **1960** Independence.
- ❑ **1964** Marxist–Leninist National Revolution Movement (MNR) becomes sole legal party.
- ❑ **1977** Yhompi-Opango head of state after President Ngoumbi's murder.
- ❑ **1979** Col. Denis Sassou-Nguesso president.
- ❑ **1992** Pascal Lissouba elected president.
- ❑ **1993** Elections: Lissouba's UPADS party gains majority.
- ❑ **1997** Lissouba ousted by Sassou-Nguesso.
- ❑ **1999** December, cease-fire signed.
- ❑ **2001** Draft constitution approved by parliament, subject to popular referendum.

C

HEALTH

Welfare state health benefits

1 per 3333 people | Diarrheal, parasitic and respiratory diseases, malaria

The health service, set up by French military doctors at the start of the 20th century, has been devastated by civil war.

SPENDING

GDP/cap. decrease

CONSUMPTION AND SPENDING

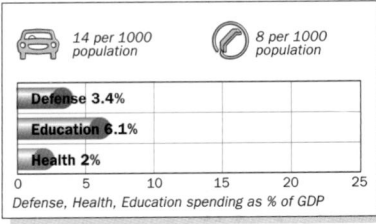

14 per 1000 population | *8 per 1000 population*

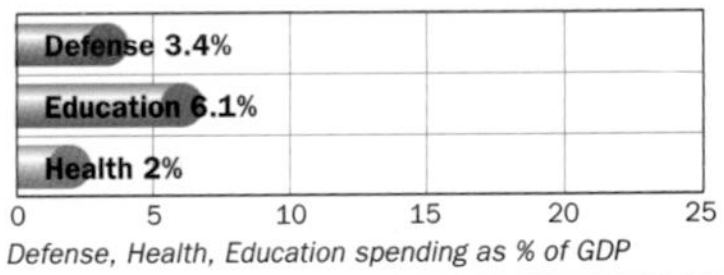
Defense 3.4%
Education 6.1%
Health 2%
0
5
10
15
20
25
Defense, Health, Education spending as % of GDP

Wealth generated from oil extraction has sustained an active and confident middle class. French-label products are considered to be status symbols.

WORLD RANKING

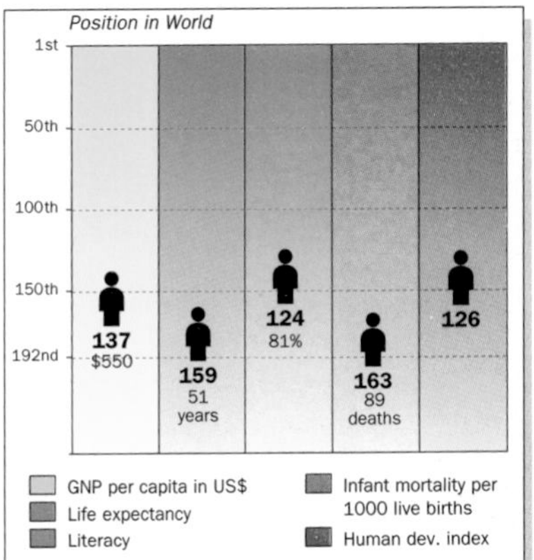
Position in World
1st
50th
100th
150th
192nd
137
$550
159
51
years
124
81%
163
89
deaths
126
GNP per capita in US$
Life expectancy
Literacy
Infant mortality per 1000 live births
Human dev. index

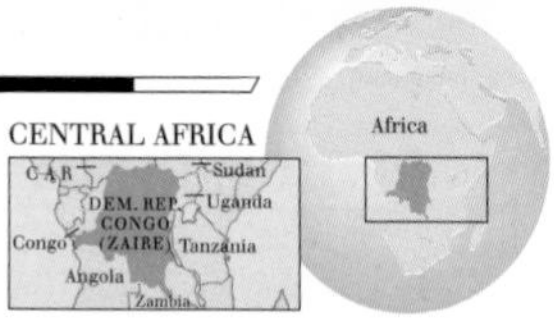
CENTRAL AFRICA
Africa
CAR
Sudan
DEM. REP. CONGO (ZAIRE)
Uganda
Congo
Tanzania
Angola
Zambia

CONGO (DEMOCRATIC REPUBLIC)

OFFICIAL NAME: Democratic Republic of the Congo **CAPITAL:** Kinshasa
POPULATION: 51.7 million **CURRENCY:** Congolese franc **OFFICIAL LANGUAGE:** French & English

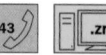

1960 | 1960 | June 6 | CGO | +1 | +243 | .zr

LYING IN EAST CENTRAL AFRICA, the Democratic Republic of Congo (DRC), known as Zaire from 1971 to 1997, is one of Africa's largest countries. The rainforested basin of the Congo River occupies 60% of the land area. On independence in 1960, civil war broke out. The notoriously corrupt Genertal Mobutu ruled from 1965 until his overthrow in 1997 by rebel forces under Laurent-Désiré Kabila. A rebellion launched in 1998 plunged the countryinto renewed chaos. Peace initiatives were revitalized by Joseph Kabila's succession in January 2001.

***The Congo River** is navigable for 1357 km (848 miles) and provides one of the most convenient ways of traveling in the country.*

CLIMATE

▷ Tropical equatorial/ wet & dry

WEATHER CHART

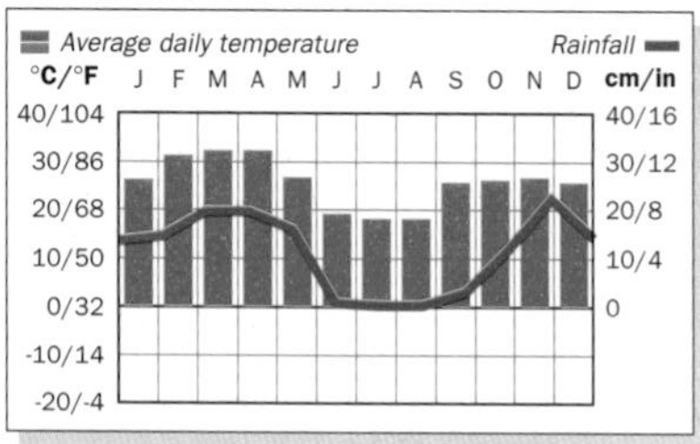
Average daily temperature
Rainfall
°C/°F
J F M A M J J A S O N D
cm/in
40/104
30/86
20/68
10/50
0/32
-10/14
-20/-4
40/16
30/12
20/8
10/4
0

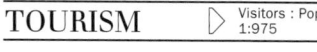

The climate is tropical and humid. Temperatures average 25°C (77°F) and vary little through the year. Annual rainfall is around 150–200 cm (59–79 in); mountainous areas are wetter. The equator passes through the north of the country, causing marked regional variations. To its south, well-differentiated wet and dry seasons are October–May and June–September respectively. North of the equator, a short dry season lasts from December to February; the rest of the year is wet.

TRANSPORTATION

▷ Drive on right

N'Djili, Kinshasa
525,000 passengers

20 ships
12,900 grt

THE TRANSPORTATION NETWORK

157,000 km (97,555 miles)

30 km (19 miles)

3641 km (2263 miles)

15,000 km (9321 miles)

The Congo River and its many tributaries provide the main means of communication. The size of the country and the fact that most of it is covered by dense rainforest have severely limited the development of road and rail networks. Many forest settlements are inaccessible except by air. Road maintenance, always poor, has virtually ceased outside the main towns since 1990, isolating even more settlements away from the main rivers.

TOURISM

▷ Visitors : Population 1:975

53,000 visitors

Up 86% 1995–1998

MAIN TOURIST ARRIVALS

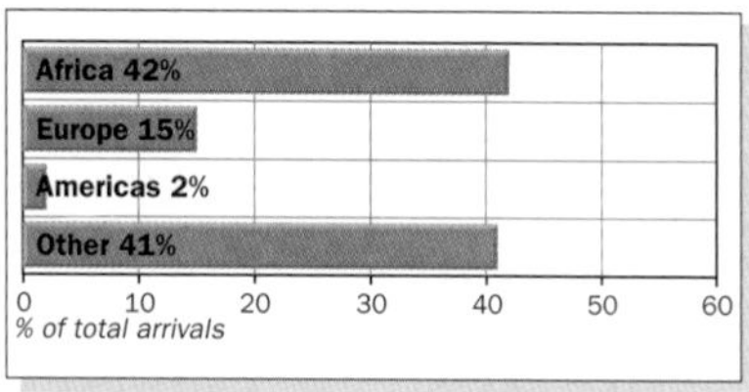
Africa 42%
Europe 15%
Americas 2%
Other 41%
0
10
20
30
40
50
60
% of total arrivals

Political turmoil and widespread anarchy since early 1997 ensure that the country remains off the itinerary for most travelers.

Potential tourist attractions consist mainly of scenery – mountains and lakes – and wildlife, but there are few facilities for tourists even in the capital. The Congo, 16 km (10 miles) wide in places, is Africa's longest river after the Nile. Visitors were formerly also attracted by the vibrant music of Kinshasa's many bands.

The once-large number of visitors on business has also collapsed as a consequence of the chronic instability of the 1990s.

PEOPLE

▷ Pop. density low

Kiswahili, Tshiluba, Kikongo, Lingala, French

23/km² (59/mi²)

THE URBAN/RURAL POPULATION SPLIT

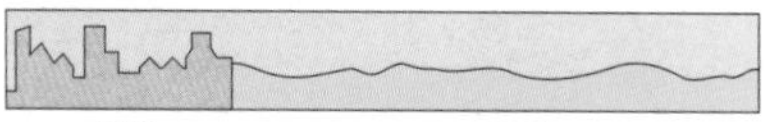
30%
70%

RELIGIOUS PERSUASION

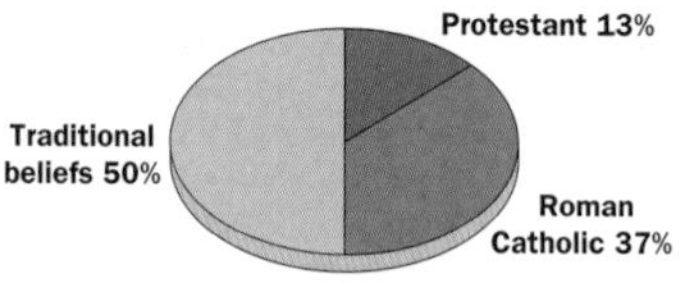
Protestant 13%
Traditional beliefs 50%
Roman Catholic 37%

ETHNIC MAKEUP

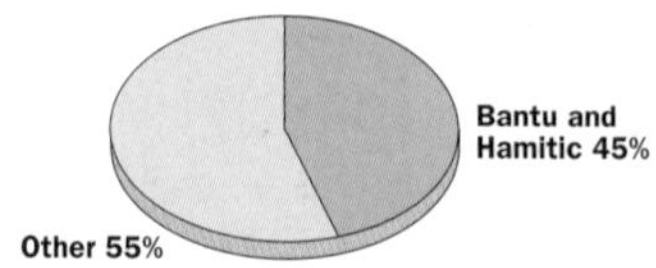
Bantu and Hamitic 45%
Other 55%

The Shaba mining area and major urban centers are densely populated, while the rainforests have a density of fewer than three people per square km, mostly subsisting on the margins of the cash economy. There is great ethnic diversity, with more than 12 main groups and around 190 smaller ones. The majority are of Bantu origin, but there are also large Hamitic and Nilotic populations, mainly in the north and northeast. The original inhabitants, the forest pygmies, today form a tiny and marginalized group.

Ethnic tensions inherited from the colonial period were contained under Mobutu until the 1990s. Ethnic violence in southeastern provinces in 1993 cost many thousands of lives, and a Hutu refugee influx from Rwanda the following year provoked serious tension among Tutsis in eastern areas; wide-scale revenge killings soon became commonplace. Regarded by Mobutu as foreigners, Tutsis provided the backbone of the 1996–1997 insurgency that overthrew him, and subsequently turned against Laurent Kabila also.

POPULATION AGE BREAKDOWN

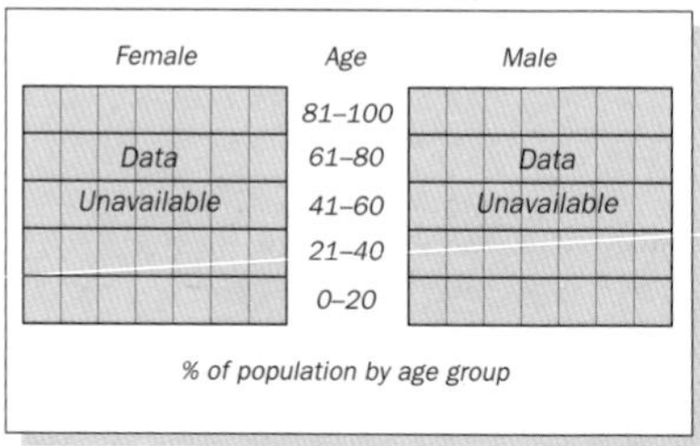
Female
Age
Male
81–100
61–80
41–60
21–40
0–20
Data Unavailable
Data Unavailable
% of population by age group

C

CONGO, DEMOCRATIC REPUBLIC (ZAIRE)

Total Land Area : 2 267 600 sq. km
(875 520 sq. miles)

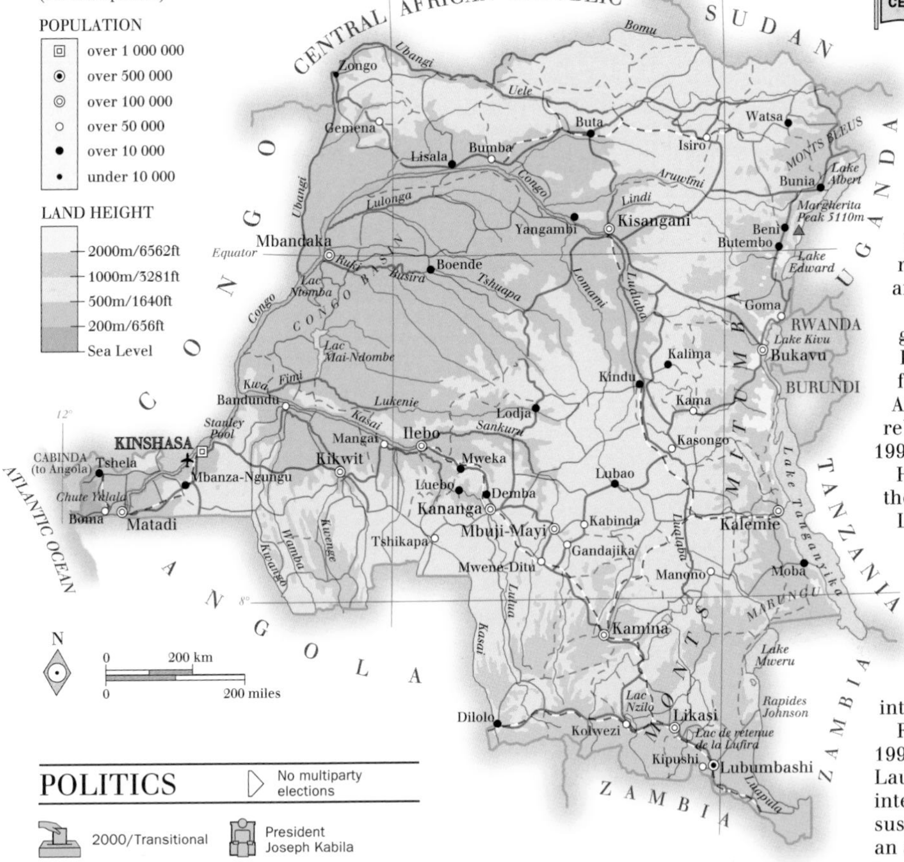
POPULATION
over 1 000 000
over 500 000
over 100 000
over 50 000
over 10 000
under 10 000
LAND HEIGHT
2000m/6562ft
1000m/3281ft
500m/1640ft
200m/656ft
Sea Level
N
200 km
200 miles
CENTRAL AFRICAN REPUBLIC
SUDAN
UGANDA
RWANDA
BURUNDI
TANZANIA
ZAMBIA
ANGOLA
CONGO
CABINDA (to Angola)
ATLANTIC OCEAN
KINSHASA
Zongo
Gemena
Lisala
Bumba
Buta
Isiro
Watsa
Bunia
Lake Albert
Margherita Peak 5110m
Beni
Butembo
Lake Edward
Goma
Lake Kivu
Bukavu
Kisangani
Yangambi
Mbandaka
Equator
Boende
Lac Ntomba
Lac Mai-Ndombe
Bandundu
Stanley Pool
Tshela
Mbanza-Ngungu
Boma
Matadi
Chute Yelala
Kikwit
Mangai
Ilebo
Lodja
Mweka
Luebo
Demba
Kananga
Tshikapa
Mbuji-Mayi
Kabinda
Gandajika
Mwene-Ditu
Lubao
Kasongo
Kama
Kindu
Kalima
Kalemie
Moba
Manono
Kamina
Dilolo
Kolwezi
Likasi
Lac Nzilo
Kipushi
Lubumbashi
Lac de retenue de la Lufira
Lake Mweru
Rapides Johnson
Lake Tanganyika
Ubangi
Uele
Bomu
Congo
Aruwimi
Lindi
Lulonga
Ruki
Busira
Tshuapa
Lomami
Lualaba
Kwa
Fimi
Kasai
Lukenie
Sankuru
Lulua
Kwango
Kwenge
Wamba
Luapula
MONTS BLEUS
MITUMBA
MONTS
MARUNGU
CONGO BASIN

POLITICS

No multiparty elections

2000/Transitional

President Joseph Kabila

AT THE LAST ELECTION

Constituent and Legislative Assembly 300 seats

The last legislative poll was in 1987 when members were chosen from Mobutu's Popular Revolutionary Movement (**MPR**). An interim legislature was appointed in July/August 2000 with 300 members chosen by Laurent Kabila.

The authoritarian regime of Laurent-Désiré Kabila continues under his son.

MAIN POLITICAL ISSUE
Securing peace and democracy

Promises of multiparty democracy from 1990 were largely subverted as Mobutu clung to power. Change engendered by his overthrow by Kabila in 1997 proved just as elusive. Elections scheduled for 1999 did not take place as fighting spiraled, with the government in true control of only half of the country. The death of Kabila in 2001 brought all factions together for peace talks.

PROFILE

Laurent Kabila's commitment to pluralist democracy came under question as he soon dissolved parliament and scrapped the constitution. A new Constituent and Legislative Assembly did not convene until August 2000. Meanwhile Kabila's ethnic Tutsi supporters rose in armed rebellion against him in August 1998. As neighboring countries joined the fighting, the war became a regional crisis. In 2000 the UN agreed to send a substantial peacekeeping mission, but its arrival was consistently delayed by Kabila.

Kabila's murder in January 2001 resulted in a vacuum that exposed the extent of his grip on power. His son Joseph, head of the armed forces, was rapidly appointed as his successor. Sworn in a few days later, Joseph Kabila promised to promote political pluralism and economic liberalization. He faces a daunting challenge.

***Joseph Kabila,** who succeeded his father as president in 2001.*

***Mobutu,** the ousted dictator, held power from 1965–1997.*

WORLD AFFAIRS

Joined UN in 1960

CEPGL | COMESA | OIF | G24 | OAU

For almost 25 years, the then Zaire was one of the leading African allies of the West, and of the USA and France in particular, while managing to maintain close ties with communist states. Relations with African countries were more problematic, complicated by Mobutu's support for the UNITA rebels in Angola, and for Morocco's annexation of Western Sahara.

From the late 1980s, Mobutu was a growing embarrassment to the West. Diplomatic efforts by France, which feared losing influence in central Africa, did not save the regime when rebel forces closed in on Kinshasa in 1997, forcing him into exile.

However, the former supporters in the east of successful rebel leader Laurent Kabila turned on him a year later. A savage rebellion backed by Rwanda and Uganda brought frantic intra-African efforts to arrange a peace settlement. Angola, Zimbabwe, Namibia, Chad, and Sudan were all nonetheless drawn into the conflict on Kabila's side.

Fighting continued despite the July 1999 cease-fire signed in Lusaka. Laurent Kabila attracted intense international criticism in 2000 for suspending the accords, taking an autocratic approach to a new transitional assembly, and obstructing the arrival of the UN peacekeeping mission, MONUC. His death and the succession of his son in 2001 sparked a fresh spate of peace initiatives. Ugandan, Rwandan, and Burundian troop withdrawals began in spring 2001.

AID

Recipient

$132m (receipts)

Up 5% in 1999

The regime's importance to the West during the Cold War brought in aid revenues on a large scale. Between 1970 and 1989, it received $8.3 billion in economic aid – including $1.1 billion from the USA and $6.9 billion from other OECD states – as well as large-scale military assistance. By 1990, changing political priorities led the USA to act on long-deferred problems of human rights abuses and misappropriation of aid. It suspended all but humanitarian aid; most other donors quickly followed suit, and the IMF declared the government "noncooperative" over its $10 billion foreign debt. Joseph Kabila's accession in early 2001 improved the country's international standing, and Belgium restarted aid donations.

C

CHRONOLOGY

The modern Congo was the site of the Kongo and other powerful African kingdoms and a focus of the slave trade. Belgium's King Leopold II claimed most of the Congo basin after 1876 as his personal possession.

- ❑ **1885** Brutal colonization of Congo Free State (CFS) as King Leopold's private fief.
- ❑ **1908** Belgium takes over CFS after international outcry.
- ❑ **1960** Independence of Republic of Congo. Katanga (Shaba) province secedes. UN intervenes.
- ❑ **1963** Katanga secession collapses.
- ❑ **1965** General Joseph-Désiré Mobutu seizes power.
- ❑ **1970** Mobutu elected president; his MPR becomes sole legal party.
- ❑ **1971** Country renamed Zaire.
- ❑ **1977–1978** Two invasions by former Katanga separatists repulsed with Western help.
- ❑ **1982** Opposition parties set up Union for Democracy and Social Progress (UDPS).
- ❑ **1986–1990** Civil unrest and foreign criticism of human rights abuses.
- ❑ **1990** Belgium suspends aid after security forces kill prodemocracy demonstrators. Mobutu announces transition to multiparty rule.
- ❑ **1991** Opposition leader Etienne Tshisekedi heads short-lived "crisis government" formed by Mobutu.
- ❑ **1992–1993** Rival governments claim legitimacy.
- ❑ **1994** Combined High Council of the Republic–Transitional Parliament established, elects Kengo wa Dondo as prime minister.
- ❑ **1995** Regime demands international assistance to support a million Rwandan Hutu refugees.
- ❑ **1996** Major insurgency launched in east by Alliance of Democratic forces for the Liberation of the Congo (AFDL) including Laurent Kabila's Popular Revolutionary Party (PRP), with disaffected ethnic Tutsi Banyamulunge.
- ❑ **1997** Forces led by Kabila sweep south and west. Mobutu flees. Kabila takes power. Country renamed DRC. Mobutu dies in exile.
- ❑ **1998** Banyamulunge join Kabila's opponents and launch rebellion in the east, backed by Rwanda and Uganda. Southern African states, give military backing to Kabila.
- ❑ **2000** UN approves peacekeeping mission; arrival stalled by Kabila.
- ❑ **2001** January, Laurent Kabila assassinated; succeeded by son Joseph. Peace talks start, with troop withdrawals from front line, but progress slow.

DEFENSE

No compulsory military service

$411m

Up 11% in 1999

Although the military strongly backed Mobutu's regime, it offered no real resistance when Laurent Kabila's insurgents swept the country in 1996–1997. Government troops, poorly paid and undisciplined, but supported by foreign allies, have been fighting in the civil war since 1998, led by Kabila's son and successor Joseph Kabila. The UN peacekeeping force, MONUC, had established a small presence by 2001.

CONGOLESE ARMED FORCES

60 main battle tanks (20 PRC Type–59, 40 PRC Type–62)	55,000 personnel
6 patrol boats	900 personnel
None	None
None	

ECONOMICS

Inflation 1423.1% p.a. (1990–1998)

$5.4bn

4.50–4.4999 Congolese francs

SCORE CARD

❑ World GNP Ranking	107th
❑ GNP per Capita	$110
❑ Balance of Payments	$-561m
❑ Inflation	15%
❑ Unemployment	Very high

EXPORTS

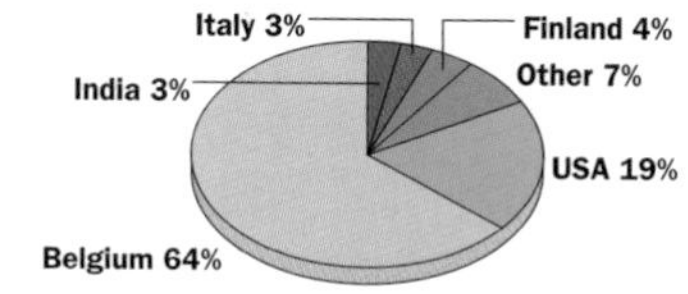

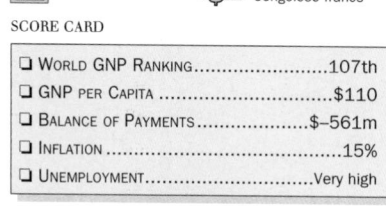

Italy 3%
Finland 4%
India 3%
Other 7%
USA 19%
Belgium 64%

IMPORTS

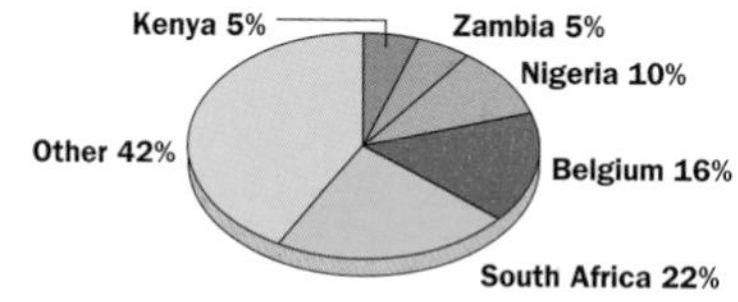

Kenya 5%
Zambia 5%
Nigeria 10%
Other 42%
Belgium 16%
South Africa 22%

ECONOMIC PERFORMANCE INDICATOR

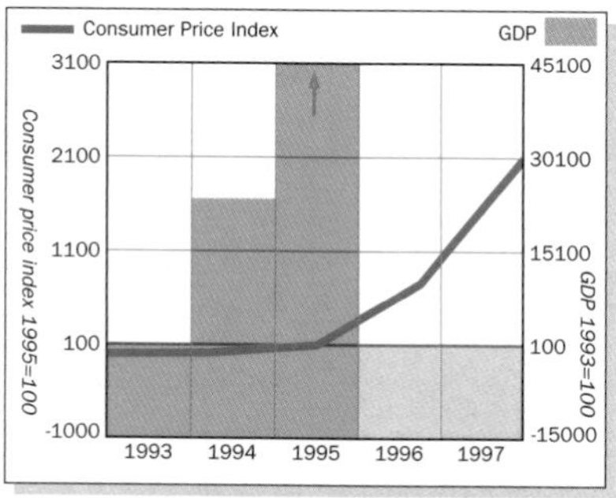

Consumer Price Index
GDP
3100
2100
1100
100
-1000
45100
30100
15100
100
-15000
Consumer price index 1995=100
GDP 1993=100
1993
1994
1995
1996
1997

Strengths

Rich resource base. Minerals – notably copper, cobalt, diamonds – provide 85% of export earnings. Energy: oil; possibly Africa's largest hydropower potential. Rich soil; much unutilized arable land. Trade surplus in peacetime.

Weaknesses

Legacy of decades of mismanagement and corruption: $10 billion foreign debt; inadequate, disintegrating social and transportation infrastructures; lack of food self-sufficiency. Political instability. Hyperinflation. Loss of export income. Withdrawal of foreign investment.

Profile

By the mid-1990s political instability, systematic corruption and long-term mismanagement had brought what is potentially a leading African economy to a state of collapse. Real GDP was falling by 10% or more each year. The government budget ran record deficits, and inflation ran virtually out of control from 1994 onwards. Lack of spares and power cuts have since closed many mines and halted most other industry. Strikes and riots over plummeting living standards hastened the flight of foreign capital. Subsistence farming and petty trade keep most people going. But even if the new regime can restore political stability, the immediate outlook is grim. Resumption of essential large-scale aid and debt relief will depend on difficult reforms and paying off arrears to the IMF and other creditors. The Kabila regime, despite its originally Marxist background, claims to want an effective free-market economy.

CONGO, DEM. REP. (ZAIRE) : MAJOR BUSINESSES

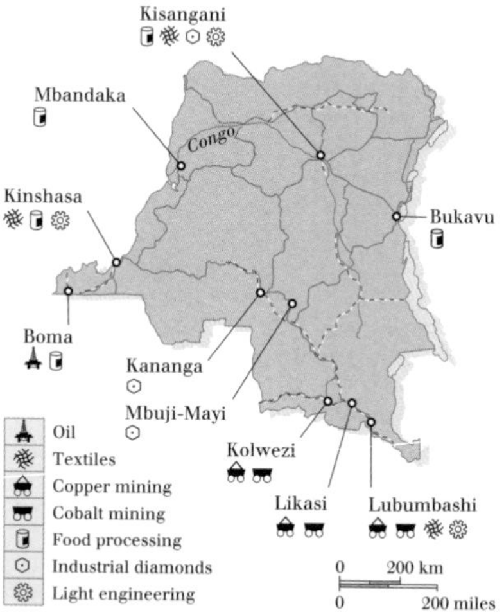

Kisangani
Mbandaka
Congo
Kinshasa
Bukavu
Boma
Kananga
Mbuji-Mayi
Kolwezi
Likasi
Lubumbashi
Oil
Textiles
Copper mining
Cobalt mining
Food processing
Industrial diamonds
Light engineering
0 200 km
0 200 miles

C

RESOURCES

Electric power 3.2m kw

162,961 tonnes

23,078 b/d (reserves 193,782,360 bbl)

4.3m goats, 1.05m pigs, 20m chickens

Copper, diamonds, oil, coltan, cobalt, zinc, uranium, manganese

ELECTRICITY GENERATION

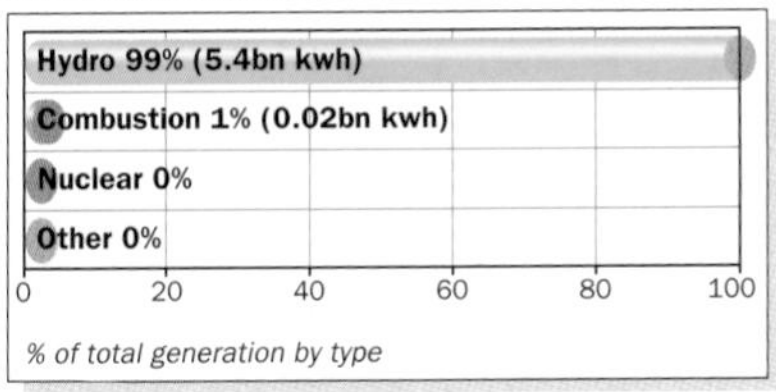
Hydro 99% (5.4bn kwh)
Combustion 1% (0.02bn kwh)
Nuclear 0%
Other 0%
0
20
40
60
80
100
% of total generation by type

What should be a prosperous country, with its rich resources, is instead one of the world's poorest states, exploited and mismanaged by its rulers for decades and damaged further by instability since 1990. In the 1980s, the country was the world's largest cobalt exporter and second-largest industrial diamond exporter. Since 1990, copper and cobalt output has collapsed and diamond smuggling is booming. There are oil reserves, and hydroelectric installations, with sufficient potential capacity to export power, should provide regular energy supplies, but instead lack of maintenance has shut down many turbines and most urban areas face power cuts. Despite rich soils and the fact that 60% of people are involved in farming, the country is not even self-sufficient in food.

CONGO, DEM. REP. (ZAIRE) : LAND USE

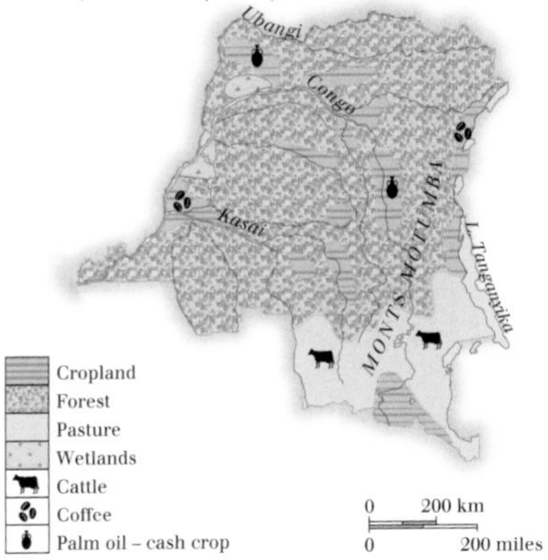
Ubangi
Congo
Kasai
MONTS MITUMBA
L. Tanganyika
Cropland
Forest
Pasture
Wetlands
Cattle
Coffee
Palm oil – cash crop
0
200 km
0
200 miles

ENVIRONMENT

Not available

5%

0.1 tonnes per capita

ENVIRONMENTAL TREATIES

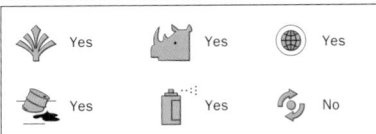

Yes	Yes	Yes
Yes	Yes	No

Rainforests cover over 60% of the country, representing almost 6% of the world's and 50% of Africa's remaining woodlands. They are home to several endangered species. The poor transportation network has so far prevented large-scale commercial exploitation of timber, but clearance for fuelwood is a problem. The collapse of many urban refuse and sewage disposal systems has led to major health and pollution problems. Environmental damage caused by the civil war is estimated at $320 million.

MEDIA

TV ownership low

Daily newspaper circulation 3 per 1000 people

PUBLISHING AND BROADCAST MEDIA

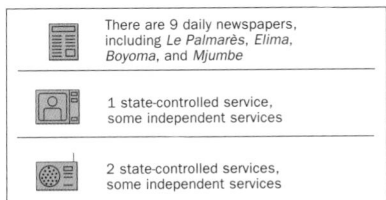

There are 9 daily newspapers, including *Le Palmarès*, *Elima*, *Boyoma*, and *Mjumbe*

1 state-controlled service, some independent services

2 state-controlled services, some independent services

Unlike the broadcast media, the press is privately owned. Opposition politics coverage widened after 1990, but press criticism of Mobutu or the security forces remained muted. One newspaper's offices were burnt down in 1993 after it published strongly anti-Mobutu material. The post-Mobutu regime has also been accused of such tendencies. Foreign broadcasts are banned.

CRIME

Death penalty used

Congo, Dem. Rep. does not publish prison figures

Violence and crime have risen rapidly since 1990

CRIME RATES

All types of crime are on the increase

Political crisis and economic collapse exacerbate long-standing problems of corruption and human rights abuses. Violence and crime of all kinds, including extortion, robbery, rape, and murder, are widespread and on the increase, and in war zones most law and order have broken down. Ethnic violence, suppressed after 1965, resurfaced in the 1990s, in the south and between the Hema and Lendu tribes in the northeast.

EDUCATION

Schooling is not compulsory

61%

93,266 students

THE EDUCATION SYSTEM

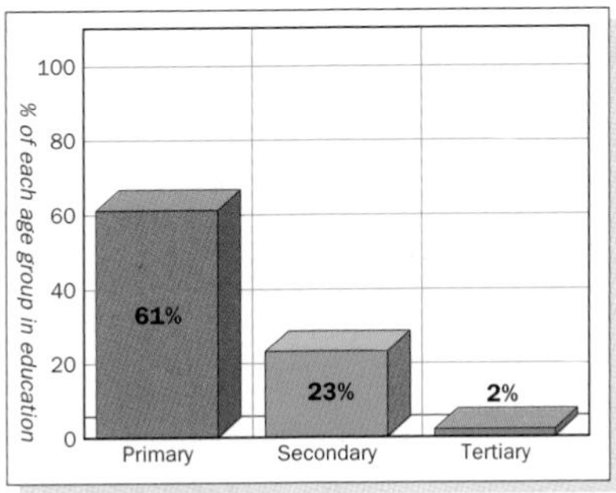
100
80
60
40
20
0
% of each age group in education
61%
23%
2%
Primary
Secondary
Tertiary

In 1997 just over 37% of secondary age children were attending classes, but this has dropped sharply during the civil war. Provision by the state, as with health care, is patchy and has faced sharp budget cuts since 1980. About 70% of schooling is now provided by the Roman Catholic Church.

HEALTH

No welfare state health benefits

1 per 10,000 people

Malaria, respiratory, and diarrheal diseases

State services have now virtually collapsed. Disease and death rates are rising, especially in rural areas. A new health insurance plan was announced in 2001, designed to enable greater access to health care. As of December 1999, just over one million people were estimated to be HIV/AIDS infected.

SPENDING

GDP/cap. decrease

CONSUMPTION AND SPENDING

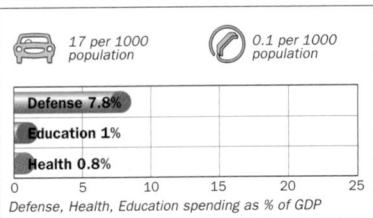

17 per 1000 population

0.1 per 1000 population

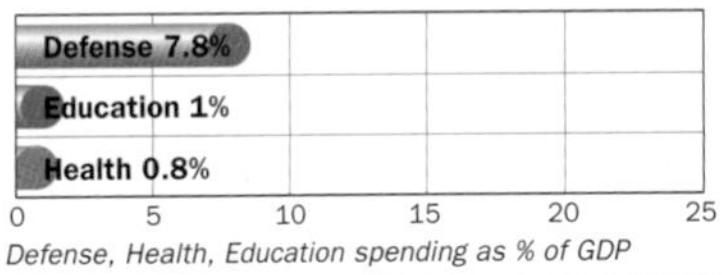
Defense 7.8%
Education 1%
Health 0.8%
0
5
10
15
20
25
Defense, Health, Education spending as % of GDP

Before his death in exile in 1997, ex-dictator Mobutu was one of the world's richest men, worth an estimated $4 billion. Most of his former subjects live in poverty, exacerbated by civil war.

WORLD RANKING

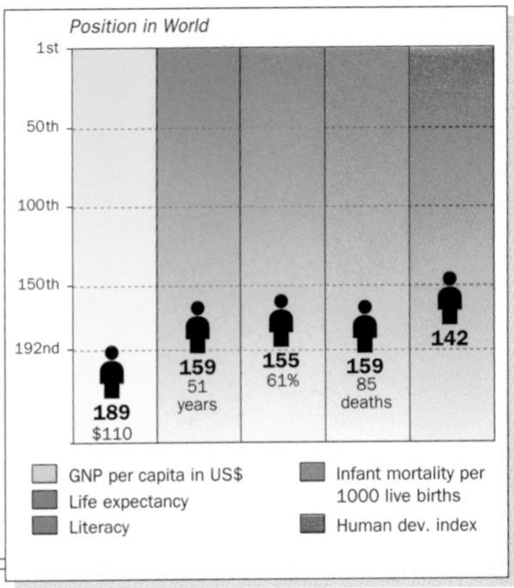
Position in World
1st
50th
100th
150th
192nd
189
$110
159
51
years
155
61%
159
85
deaths
142
GNP per capita in US$
Life expectancy
Literacy
Infant mortality per
1000 live births
Human dev. index

COSTA RICA

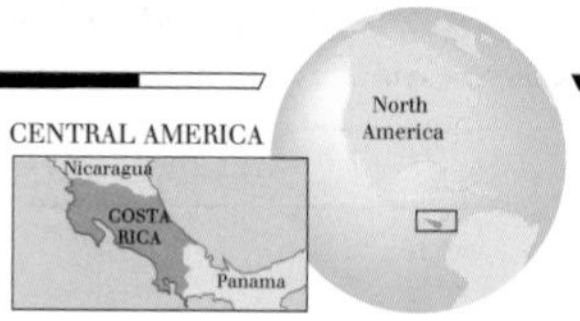
CENTRAL AMERICA
Nicaragua
COSTA RICA
Panama
North America

OFFICIAL NAME: The Republic of Costa Rica **CAPITAL:** San José
POPULATION: 4 million **CURRENCY:** Costa Rican colón **OFFICIAL LANGUAGE:** Spanish

C

1838 | 1838 | Sept 15 | CR | -6 | +506 | .cr

LOCATED IN CENTRAL AMERICA between Nicaragua and Panama, Costa Rica was under Spanish rule until 1821 and gained full independence in 1838. From 1948 until the end of the 1980s, it had the most developed welfare state in Central America. Costa Rica is nominally a multiparty democracy, but two parties dominate. Coffee and bananas are the major exports. Its army was abolished in 1948; the 1949 constitution then forbade national armies.

CLIMATE

Tropical wet & dry

WEATHER CHART

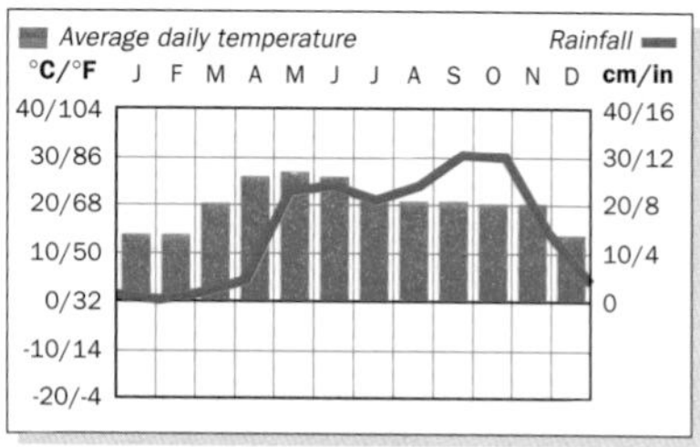
Average daily temperature
Rainfall
°C/°F J F M A M J J A S O N D cm/in
40/104
30/86
20/68
10/50
0/32
-10/14
-20/-4
40/16
30/12
20/8
10/4
0

The Caribbean coast has heavy rainfall, while the Pacific coast is much drier. The central uplands are temperate.

TRANSPORTATION

Drive on right

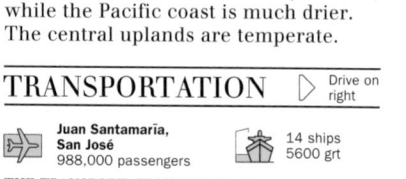

Juan Santamaría, San José
988,000 passengers

14 ships
5600 grt

THE TRANSPORTATION NETWORK

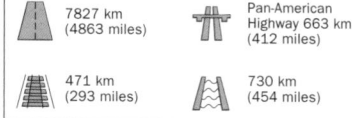

7827 km (4863 miles)

Pan-American Highway 663 km (412 miles)

471 km (293 miles)

730 km (454 miles)

A 42-km (25-mile) stretch of highway to the international airport, and the airport itself, are being modernized.

TOURISM

Visitors : Population 1:3.6

1.1m visitors

Up 7% in 2000

MAIN TOURIST ARRIVALS

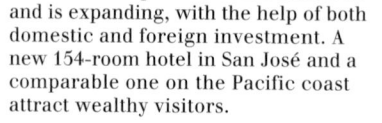

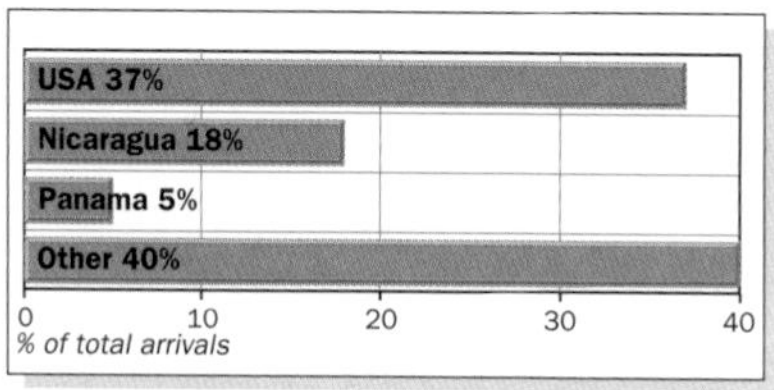
USA 37%
Nicaragua 18%
Panama 5%
Other 40%
0
10
20
30
40
% of total arrivals

Tourism brought in $1 billion in 1999 and is expanding, with the help of both domestic and foreign investment. A new 154-room hotel in San José and a comparable one on the Pacific coast attract wealthy visitors.

PEOPLE

Pop. density medium

Spanish, English Creole, Bribri, Cabecar

78/km² (203/mi²)

THE URBAN/RURAL POPULATION SPLIT

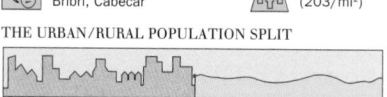

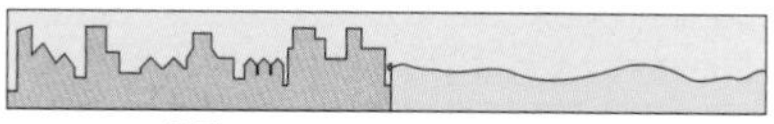
51%
49%

RELIGIOUS PERSUASION

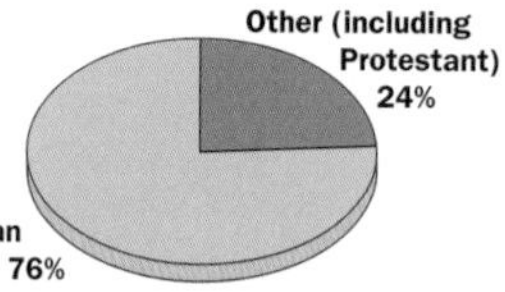
Other (including Protestant) 24%
Roman Catholic 76%

The majority of the population is *mestizo*, of partly Spanish origin. One-third of people in the Puerto Limón area are black and often English-speaking. There are only about 5000 indigenous Indians.

POLITICS

Multiparty elections

1998/2002

President Miguel Angel Rodriguez

AT THE LAST ELECTION

Legislative Assembly 57 seats

3% DFP
2% IN
51% PUSC
39% PLN
3% ML
2% PANLA

PUSC = Social Christian Unity Party **PLN** = National Liberation Party **ML** = Liberty Movement **DFP** = Democratic Force Party **PANLA** = National Action Workers' Party of Alajuela **IN** = National Integration

Politics has been long dominated by the PUSC and PLN, both of which have close ties to major banana- and coffee-growing families. Historically the USA has exercised a very powerful influence on politics. The PLN held power from 1982 until 1990, when President Rafael Calderón pursued austerity policies. In 1994, José María Figueres of the PLN won the presidency promising reforms, but soon came under pressure from international financial organizations to reduce the budget deficit. He reached a consensus with the PUSC on harsh structural adjustment measures which made him highly unpopular.

In the 1998 presidential and legislative elections the pendulum swung back to the PUSC. President Miguel Angel Rodriguez launched a three-year plan in 1999 to reduce inflation and poverty, create thousands of jobs, and stimulate foreign investment in state companies.

WORLD AFFAIRS

Joined UN in 1945

ACS | Geplac | RG | OAS | San José

Trade ties with the USA and protection of prices for coffee and bananas are priorities. Trade ties have been agreed with Chile and sought with Canada. Tensions with Nicaragua over their mutual border were resolved in 2000, but illegal immigrants remain an issue.

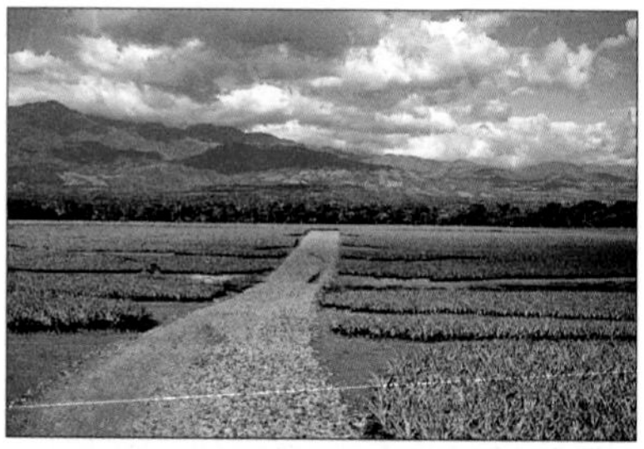

Pineapple plantation near Buenos Aires, crossed by the Pan-American Highway which runs for 663 km (414 miles) through Costa Rica.

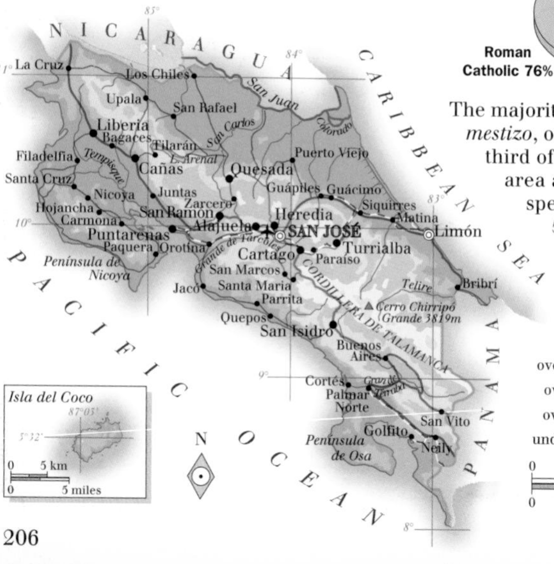
NICARAGUA
CARIBBEAN SEA
PACIFIC OCEAN
PANAMA
La Cruz
Los Chiles
Upala
San Rafael
Liberia
Bagaces
Filadelfia
Santa Cruz
Tilarán
Cañas
Quesada
Puerto Viejo
Nicoya
Juntas
Zarcero
Guápiles
Guácimo
Hojancha
Carmona
San Ramón
Alajuela
Heredia
SAN JOSÉ
Siquirres
Matina
Limón
Puntarenas
Paquera
Orotina
Cartago
Turrialba
Paraíso
Península de Nicoya
San Marcos
Santa María
Parrita
Jacó
Quepos
Telire
Bribrí
Cerro Chirripó Grande 3819m
San Isidro
Buenos Aires
Cortés
Palmar Norte
Golfito
San Vito
Neily
Península de Osa
Isla del Coco
N

COSTA RICA

Total Land Area : 51 060 sq. km (19 714 sq. miles)

POPULATION	LAND HEIGHT
over 100 000	3000m/9843ft
over 50 000	2000m/6562ft
over 10 000	1000m/3281ft
under 10 000	500m/1640ft
	200m/656ft
	Sea level

0 50 km
0 50 miles

AID

Recipient

$27m (receipts)

Loan repayments exceeded aid received in 1999

During the 1980s Costa Rica was a large recipient of US aid designed to inoculate it against left-wing insurgencies in El Salvador, Guatemala, and neighboring Nicaragua. Peace in the region has led to a sharp decline in such aid, especially given the country's relatively high per capita income. World Bank aid will help modernize Juan Santamaría international airport.

DEFENSE

No compulsory military service

$69m

Down 2% in 1999

Costa Rica emerged from the 1948 civil war as a neutral, demilitarized modern state. A 4400-strong Civil Guard is complemented by a largely military-trained police force. Spending on security has long been the lowest in the region. Lack of a common command structure hinders the influence of the security forces but also renders them less open to public control. Right-wing paramilitary groups are known to exist.

ECONOMICS

Inflation 16.7% p.a. (1990–1999)

$12.8bn

297.5–317.5 colones

SCORE CARD

❑ WORLD GNP RANKING	78th
❑ GNP PER CAPITA	$3570
❑ BALANCE OF PAYMENTS	$-460m
❑ INFLATION	10%
❑ UNEMPLOYMENT	6%

EXPORTS

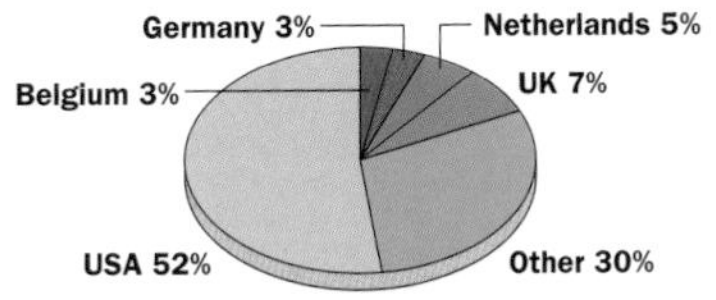
Germany 3%
Netherlands 5%
Belgium 3%
UK 7%
USA 52%
Other 30%

IMPORTS

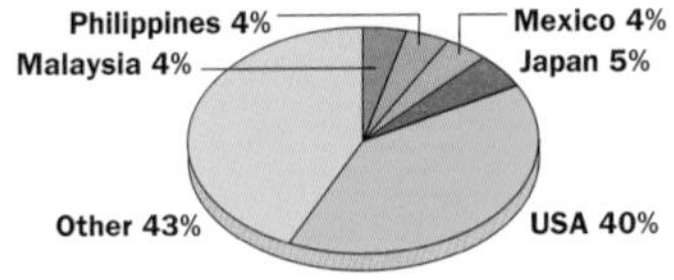
Philippines 4%
Mexico 4%
Malaysia 4%
Japan 5%
Other 43%
USA 40%

STRENGTHS

Major coffee, beef, and banana exports. Expanding tourism also fueling construction. Strong inward investment. Favorable WTO ruling on banana access to EU market.

WEAKNESSES

Coffee, beef, and bananas all vulnerable to falling prices. History of high inflation. Dependence on imported oil. Large domestic debt. Competitiveness hindered by insufficient investment in infrastructure. State monopolies have deterred investment in energy, telecommunications, and insurance sectors. Inefficient management.

RESOURCES

Electric power 1.4m kw

33,613 tonnes

Not an oil producer

1.69m cattle, 290,000 pigs, 17m chickens

Bauxite, gold, silver, manganese, mercury

Costa Rica has large bauxite deposits at Boruca – aluminum smelting is an important industry. Small quantities of gold, silver, manganese, and mercury are also mined. Self-sufficiency in energy is being pursued through the development of hydroelectric power. Forests cover 34% of the country.

ENVIRONMENT

Sustainability rank: 26th

14% (3% partially protected)

1.6 tonnes per capita

Despite good environmental regulation, reckless economic development has contributed to extensive deforestation. Pasture land now covers some 45% of the territory and pesticide abuse by agribusiness has poisoned rivers and threatened species. Urban sprawl has degraded the fertile central valley.

MEDIA

TV ownership medium

Daily newspaper circulation 88 per 1000 people

PUBLISHING AND BROADCAST MEDIA

There are 8 daily newspapers, including *La Nación*, *La República*, *La Prensa Libre*, and *Diario Extra*

8 stations: 1 state-owned, 7 independent

State-owned and independent stations

The media are free but dominated by conservative opinion. Entry into journalism is strictly licensed.

CRIME

Death penalty not used

3927 prisoners

Up 71% 1989–1994

Costa Rica is the least violent Central American country. Attacks on and kidnappings of tourists are rare but have dented its image as a safe haven. Drug cartels use the country to transfer cocaine to the USA and Europe. Police show hostility toward immigrants from neighboring countries.

CHRONOLOGY

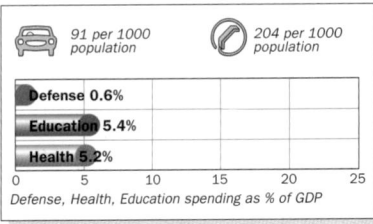

Costa Rica, ruled since the 16th century by Spain, became an independent state in 1838.

- ❑ **1948** Disputed elections lead to civil war; ended by Social Democratic Party (later the PLN) forming provisional government under José Ferrer. Army abolished.
- ❑ **1949** New constitution promulgated.
- ❑ **1987** Central American Peace Plan initiated by President Arias.
- ❑ **1998** PUSC returns to power.

C

EDUCATION

School leaving age: 18

96%

78,819 students

Costa Rica has the highest literacy rate in the isthmus, and is home to the University of Central America.

HEALTH

Welfare state health benefits

1 per 1111 people

Heart diseases, accidents, cancers, perinatal deaths

The public health system is one of the most developed in Latin America. Health was allocated 29.3% of total public spending in 1999.

SPENDING

GDP/cap. increase

CONSUMPTION AND SPENDING

91 per 1000 population

204 per 1000 population

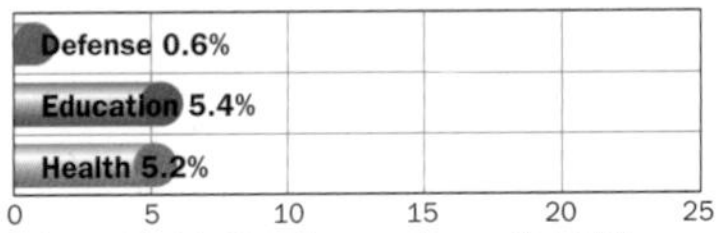
Defense 0.6%
Education 5.4%
Health 5.2%
0
5
10
15
20
25

Defense, Health, Education spending as % of GDP

The plantation-owning families are the wealthiest group; official figures claim that one-fifth of Costa Rica's population is living in poverty.

WORLD RANKING

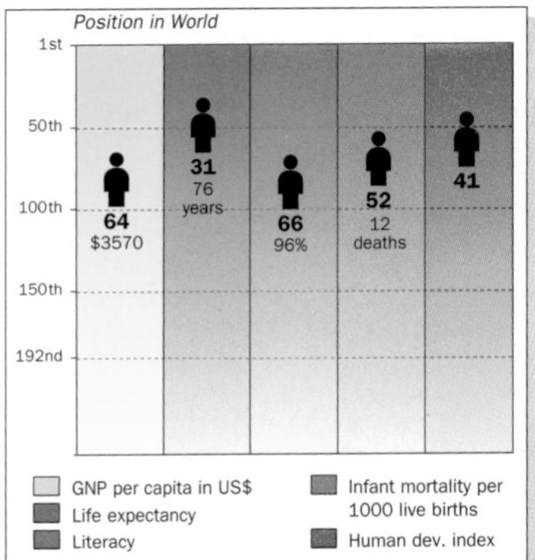
Position in World
1st
50th
100th
150th
192nd
64
$3570
31
76
years
66
96%
52
12
deaths
41
GNP per capita in US$
Life expectancy
Literacy
Infant mortality per 1000 live births
Human dev. index

CROATIA

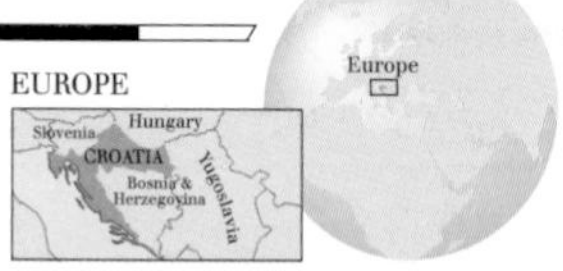
Europe
EUROPE
Slovenia
Hungary
CROATIA
Bosnia & Herzegovina
Yugoslavia

OFFICIAL NAME: Republic of Croatia **CAPITAL:** Zagreb
POPULATION: 4.5 million **CURRENCY:** Kuna **OFFICIAL LANGUAGE:** Croatian

1991
1991
May 30
HR
+1
+385
.hr

LOCATED TO THE SOUTH of Slovenia and west of Yugoslavia, Croatia includes the historic regions of Istria, Dalmatia, and Slavonia. Its Adriatic coastline is vital for tourism and shipping. During the breakup of the former Yugoslavia, Croatia fought to defend its own territory and was involved in the Bosnian war. Military offensives in 1995 ended Serb control over several enclaves, while Eastern Slavonia was administered by the UN until its return to Croatia in 1998.

Dubrovnik, Dalmatia. *This historic city on the Adriatic coast was shelled and besieged by the Yugoslav federal army in 1991.*

CLIMATE

Mediterranean/ continental

WEATHER CHART

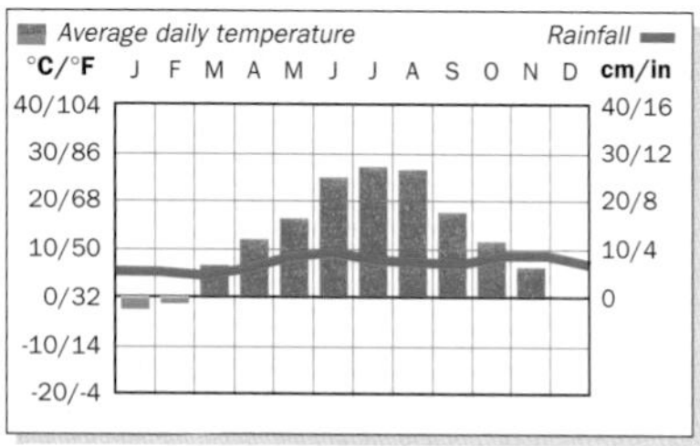
Average daily temperature
Rainfall
°C/°F
J F M A M J J A S O N D
cm/in
40/104
30/86
20/68
10/50
0/32
-10/14
-20/-4
40/16
30/12
20/8
10/4
0

Northern Croatia has a temperate continental climate. Its Adriatic coast has a Mediterranean climate.

TRANSPORTATION

Drive on right

Pleso International, Zagreb
1.08m passengers

260 ships
896,400 grt

THE TRANSPORTATION NETWORK

23,497 km (14,600 miles)

330 km (205 miles)

2726 km (1694 miles)

785 km (488 miles)

Zagreb's importance as a regional road and rail hub suffered during the 1990s from conflict and sanctions against Yugoslavia. A 1998 peace accord with Bosnia allows the latter to use the port of Ploce on the Adriatic.

TOURISM

Visitors : Population 1.3:1

5.8m visitors

Up 53% in 2000

MAIN TOURIST ARRIVALS

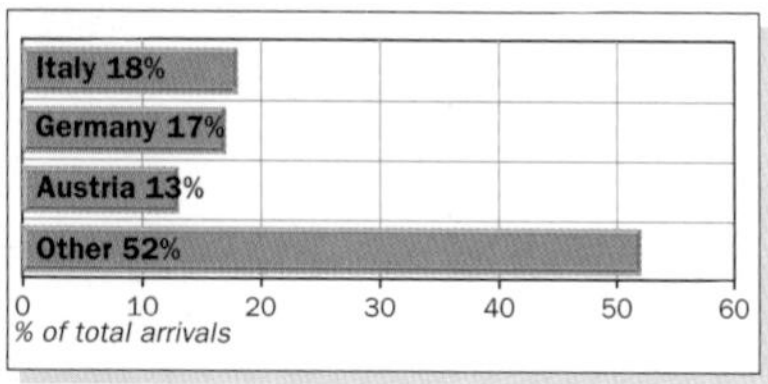
Italy 18%
Germany 17%
Austria 13%
Other 52%
0
10
20
30
40
50
60
% of total arrivals

Tourism continued its recovery in 2000, after a regional setback caused by the 1999 Kosovo conflict.

PEOPLE

Pop. density medium

Croatian

80/km² (206/mi²)

THE URBAN/RURAL POPULATION SPLIT

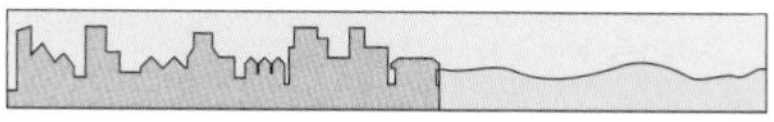
57%
43%

RELIGIOUS PERSUASION

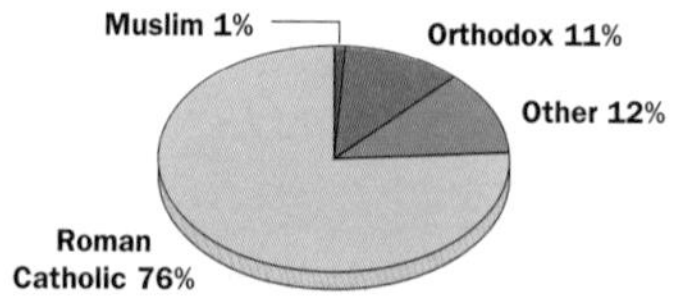
Muslim 1%
Orthodox 11%
Other 12%
Roman Catholic 76%

Before the breakup of Yugoslavia, Croats made up nearly 80% of the population, and Serbs 12%. In 1991, the Serbs, alienated by Croatian nationalism, proclaimed the Republic of Serbian Krajina in areas where they formed a majority. Croatian forces retook most Serb-held territory in offensives in 1995, precipitating a huge exodus of Serb refugees. One rebel Serb enclave, Eastern Slavonia, was placed under UN administration until its reintegration into Croatia in January 1998. Many of the 250,000 Bosnian refugees who fled to Croatia have now settled there.

WORLD AFFAIRS

Joined UN in 1992

CE | WTO | PfP | CEI | OSCE

Tudjman's nationalist stance after independence worked against closer relations with the West. Croatia's military successes in 1995, hastening the end of the Bosnian war, were reflected in the Bosnian peace accord. Tudjman's successors seek closer cooperation with the EU. In 2000 Croatia joined NATO's Partnership for Peace program.

AID

Recipient

$48m (receipts)

Up 23% in 1999

EU states have spent over $1 billion on reconstruction in Croatia since 1991.

DEFENSE

Compulsory military service

$776m

Down 29% in 1999

10,000 soldiers of the Croat Defense Association (HOS), not part of the Croatian armed forces proper, remained in Bosnia under the 1995 peace accord.

POLITICS

Multiparty elections

2000/2004

President Stipe Mesic

AT THE LAST ELECTION

House of Representatives 151 seats

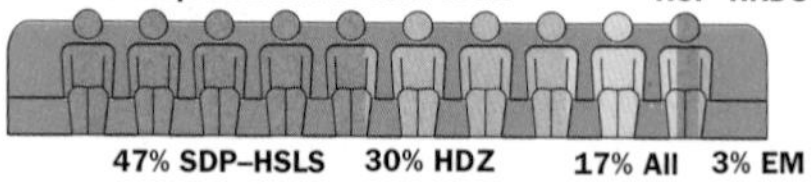
3% HSP–HKDU
47% SDP–HSLS
30% HDZ
17% All
3% EM

SDP–HSLS = *SDP*–Social Democratic Party, *HSLS*–Croatian Social Liberal Party **HDZ** = Croatian Democratic Union **All** = Alliance (*HSS*–Croatian Peasant Party, *IDS*–Istrian Democratic Assembly, *HNS*–Croatian People's Party, *LS*–Liberal Party, *ASH*–Croatian Social Democrats' Action) **HSP–HKDU** = *HSP*–Croatian Party of Rights, *HKDU*–Croatian Christian Democratic Union **EM** = Ethnic Minorities

Six seats are reserved for representatives of Croats living abroad (all are currently held by the HDZ). Five seats are reserved for ethnic minorities (one is currently held by the HSS).

Croatia left the former Yugoslavia in 1991 under the direction of the right-wing HDZ led by Franjo Tudjman. However, the country suffered growing international isolation because of its nationalist stance and ambiguous support for the 1995 Bosnian peace accord. The HDZ was left rudderless after Tudjman's death in December 1999 and, mired in corruption and spying scandals, was swept from power in elections in January 2000 by left-leaning parties. The eclipse of the HDZ was confirmed in presidential elections the following month, won by one-time Yugoslav federal president Stipe Mesic. The new government's priorities were to rehabilitate Croatia internationally and to reduce the authoritarian powers of the presidency.

C

ECONOMICS

Inflation 104.9% p.a. (1990–1999)

$20.2bn

7.663–8.087 kuna

SCORE CARD

- World GNP Ranking 63rd
- GNP per Capita $4530
- Balance of Payments $1.47bn
- Inflation 3.7%
- Unemployment 20%

Strengths

Moderate growth as economy made recovery from 1998–1999 recession. Program to reduce government spending backed by IMF.

Weaknesses

War damage estimated at $50 billion. Slow privatization until 2001. High and persistent unemployment.

EXPORTS

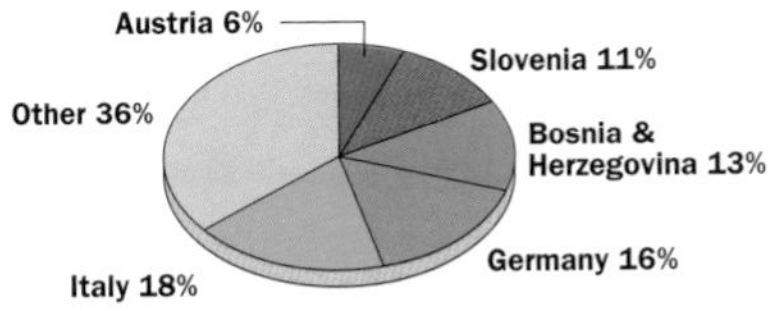

Austria 6%
Slovenia 11%
Other 36%
Bosnia & Herzegovina 13%
Germany 16%
Italy 18%

IMPORTS

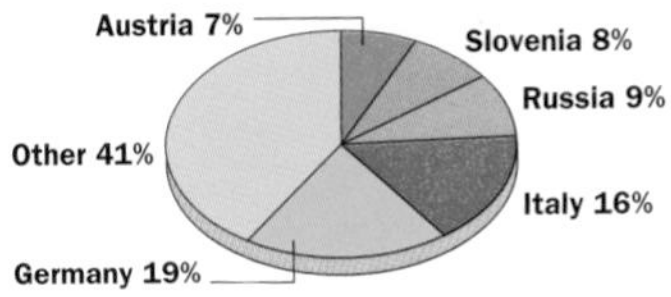

Austria 7%
Slovenia 8%
Russia 9%
Other 41%
Italy 16%
Germany 19%

RESOURCES

Electric power 3.6m kw

19,885 tonnes

29,995 b/d (reserves 43,802,880 bbl)

1.36m pigs, 630,000 turkeys, 10.9m chickens

Coal, bauxite, iron, oil, china clay, natural gas

Croatia generates 40% of its energy needs from combustion and 60% from hydroelectric sources. It has very few minerals, although it does have oil and gas fields. The rich fishing grounds of the Adriatic are a major resource.

ENVIRONMENT

Sustainability rank: 39th

7%

4.4 tonnes per capita

Croatia was the first Yugoslav republic to create reserves in order to protect endangered and unique wetlands.

MEDIA

TV ownership high

Daily newspaper circulation 115 per 1000 people

PUBLISHING AND BROADCAST MEDIA

There are 16 daily newspapers, published locally, including *Vecernji List* in Zagreb and *Slobodna Dalmacija* in Split

1 state-controlled service

4 services: 1 state-controlled, 3 independent

The three TV channels are state-owned. Media freedoms were eroded by the centralization of power under Tudjman.

CRIME

Death penalty not used

2572 prisoners

Down 4% 1996–1998

Under Tudjman, former Croat HOS militiamen escaped prosecution for "ethnic cleansing" in Bosnia, but the post-Tudjman government ordered a number of arrests.

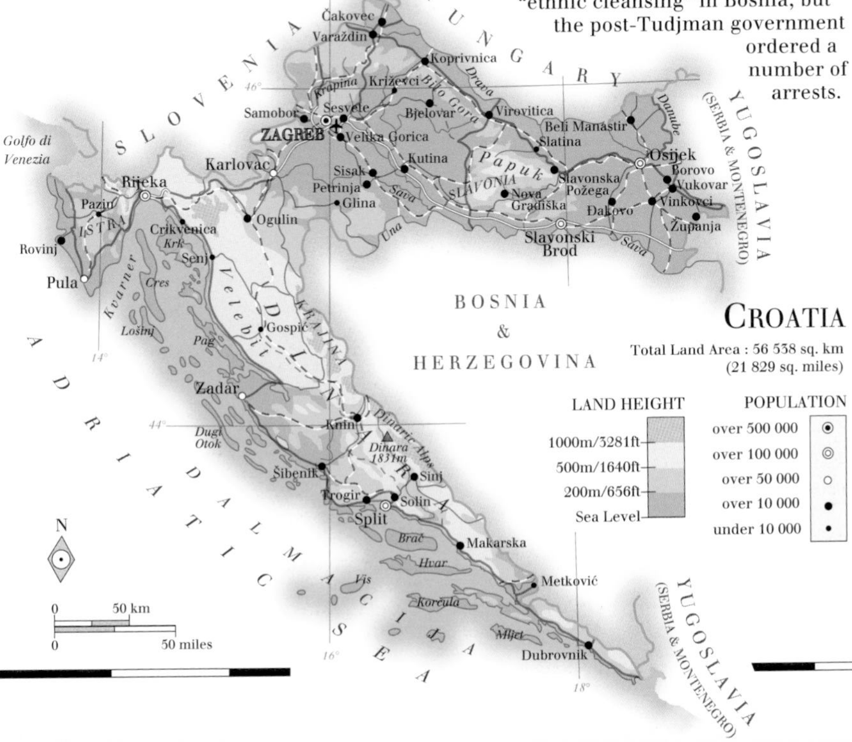

HUNGARY
SLOVENIA
YUGOSLAVIA (SERBIA & MONTENEGRO)
BOSNIA & HERZEGOVINA
ADRIATIC SEA
DALMACIA
Golfo di Venezia
Čakovec
Varaždin
Koprivnica
Križevci
Krapina
Bjelovar
Virovitica
Beli Manastir
Slatina
Osijek
Borovo
Vukovar
Vinkovci
Županja
Samobor
Sesvete
ZAGREB
Velika Gorica
Kutina
Sisak
Petrinja
Glina
Karlovac
Rijeka
Pazin
ISTRA
Rovinj
Pula
Crikvenica
Krk
Senj
Cres
Lošinj
Pag
Ogulin
Gospić
Zadar
Dugi Otok
Knin
Dinara 1831m
Šibenik
Trogir
Split
Solin
Sinj
Brač
Hvar
Makarska
Vis
Korčula
Mljet
Metković
Dubrovnik
Nova Gradiška
Slavonska Požega
Đakovo
Slavonski Brod
Sava
Una
Drava
Danube
Papuk
SLAVONIA
Velebit
Kvarner
KRAJINA
Dinaric Alps
N
0 50 km
0 50 miles
CROATIA
Total Land Area : 56 538 sq. km (21 829 sq. miles)
LAND HEIGHT
1000m/3281ft
500m/1640ft
200m/656ft
Sea Level
POPULATION
over 500 000
over 100 000
over 50 000
over 10 000
under 10 000

CHRONOLOGY

In 1945–1991 Croatia was a republic of the Yugoslav federation.

- **1991** Independence. Rebel Croatian Serb republic proclaimed.
- **1992** Tudjman president. Involvement in Bosnian civil war.
- **1995** Krajina and Western Slavonia recaptured.
- **1997** Tudjman reelected.
- **1998** Eastern Slavonia reintegrated.
- **1999** Death of Tudjman.
- **2000** Center-left wins elections.

EDUCATION

School leaving age: 15

98%

85,752 students

The education system is well-developed. There are four universities, at Zagreb, Rijeka, Osijek, and Split.

HEALTH

Welfare state health benefits

1 per 500 people

Cerebrovascular and heart diseases, cancers

Most Croats are covered by a health insurance scheme. However, an extra strain on already scarce funds is created by the demands of refugees and disabled war veterans.

SPENDING

GDP/cap. increase

CONSUMPTION AND SPENDING

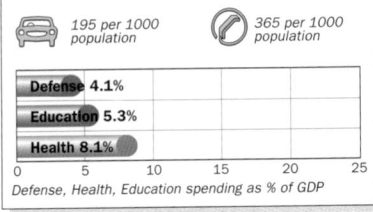

195 per 1000 population

365 per 1000 population

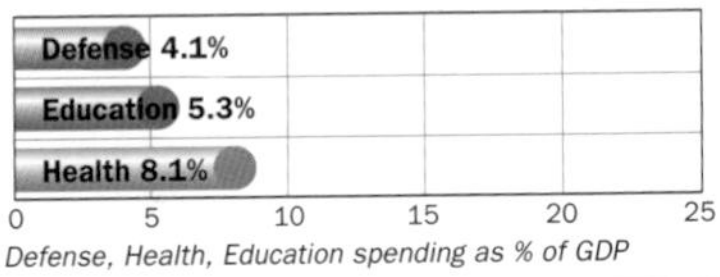

Defense 4.1%
Education 5.3%
Health 8.1%
0
5
10
15
20
25
Defense, Health, Education spending as % of GDP

Wage rises in the mid-1990s and again in 1999 led to spending booms. Consumers' high expectations were reined in by tighter wage policies.

WORLD RANKING

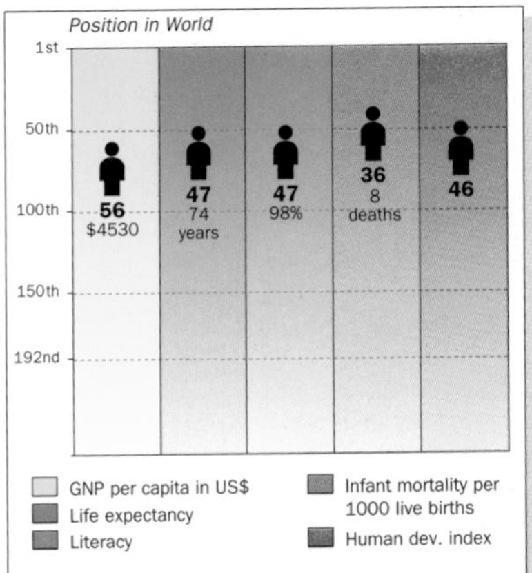

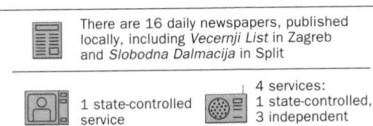

Position in World
1st
50th
100th
150th
192nd
56
$4530
47
74 years
47
98%
36
8 deaths
46
GNP per capita in US$
Life expectancy
Literacy
Infant mortality per 1000 live births
Human dev. index

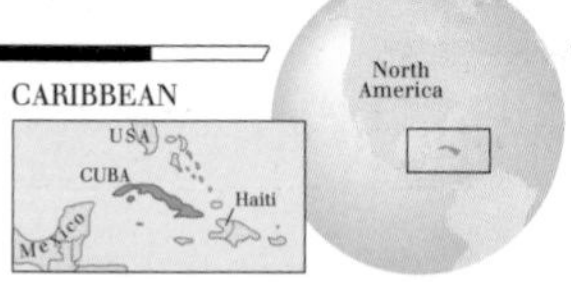
CARIBBEAN
USA
CUBA
Haiti
Mexico
North America

CUBA

OFFICIAL NAME: Republic of Cuba **CAPITAL:** Havana
POPULATION: 11.2 million **CURRENCY:** Cuban peso **OFFICIAL LANGUAGE:** Spanish

C

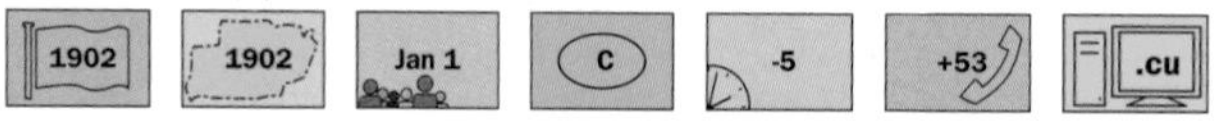
1902
1902
Jan 1
C
-5
+53
.cu

THE CARIBBEAN'S LARGEST island, Cuba has widely cultivated lowlands which fall between three mountainous areas. The fertile soil of the lowlands supports the sugar cane, rice, and coffee plantations. Sugar, the country's major export, suffers from underinvestment, low yields, and fluctuating world prices. A former Spanish colony, Cuba is the only communist state in the Caribbean. Since the collapse of communism in the Soviet Union, the USA sees Cuba as less of a threat, in marked contrast to 1962, when the deployment of Soviet nuclear missiles on the island brought the two superpowers close to war. Veteran president Fidel Castro is still very much in control.

Valle de Viñales, Pinar del Río province. *Cuba's undulating countryside is ideal for growing the main export crop, sugar.*

CLIMATE

Tropical oceanic

WEATHER CHART

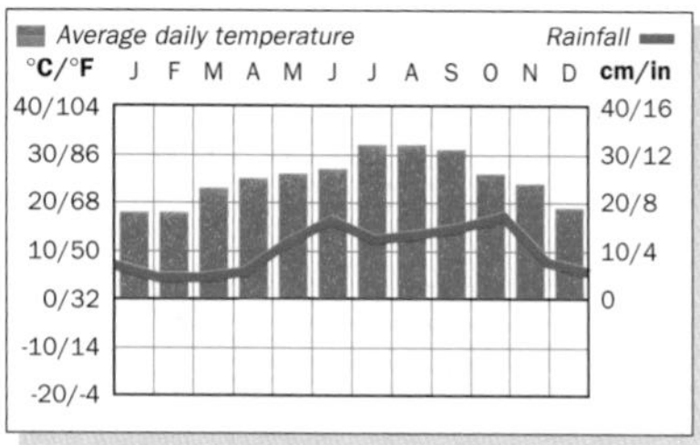
Average daily temperature
Rainfall
°C/°F
J F M A M J J A S O N D
cm/in
40/104
30/86
20/68
10/50
0/32
-10/14
-20/-4
40/16
30/12
20/8
10/4
0

Cuba's subtropical climate is hot all year round and very hot in the summer. Rainfall is heaviest in the mountains, which receive up to 250 cm (98 in) a year. Generally, the north is wetter than the south; the Guantánamo area receives only 20 cm (8 in) of rainfall annually. In winter, the west is affected sometimes by cold air from the USA, but only for a day or two at a time.

TRANSPORTATION

Drive on right

José Martí, Havana 2.43m passengers

105 ships 158,000 grt

THE TRANSPORTATION NETWORK

29,820 km (18,529 miles)

638 km (396 miles)

14,331 km (8905 miles)

240 km (149 miles)

Public transportation in Cuba has been extremely cheap, although fuel shortages have made it increasingly erratic and unreliable. Cubans rely mostly on traditional black bicycles, imported by the thousand from China. Havana owes much of its charm to the number of 45-year-old Chevrolets and Oldsmobiles still being driven around. This is another result of sanctions, but keeps the many inventive local spare-parts workshops in business.

TOURISM

Visitors : Population 1:6.6

1.7m visitors

Up 9% in 2000

MAIN TOURIST ARRIVALS

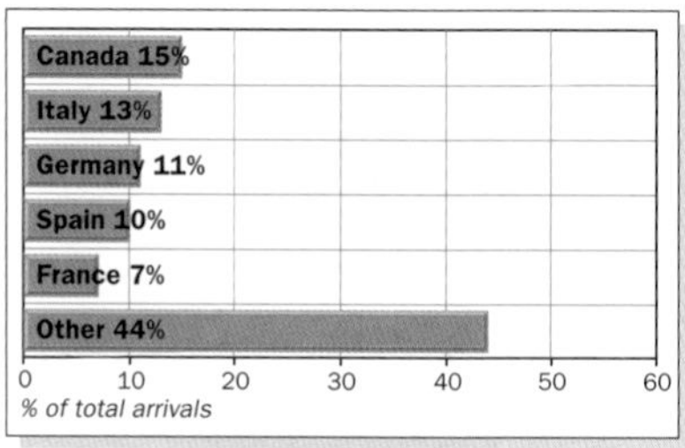
Canada 15%
Italy 13%
Germany 11%
Spain 10%
France 7%
Other 44%
0
10
20
30
40
50
60
% of total arrivals

Tourism began to develop after 1977 (when the USA relaxed some travel restrictions) and Cuba is now among the Caribbean's most popular holiday destinations. Tourism has supplanted sugar as the most important motor of the economy and largest generator of foreign exchange. Official estimates are that the number of arrivals will rise to more than five million by 2010. The government seeks to promote family tourism by cracking down on prostitutes who target Havana's main hotels.

GULF OF MEXICO
Straits of Florida
ATLANTIC OCEAN
CARIBBEAN SEA
HAVANA
(La Habana)
Guanabo
Marianao
Mariel
Guanabacoa
Matanzas
Varadero
Cárdenas
Archipiélago de Sabana
Archipiélago de los Colorados
Guanajay
Artemisa
San Cristóbal
Minas de Matahambre
Consolación del Sur
Pinar del Río
La Fé
C. San Antonio
Yucatan Channel
Golfo de Batabanó
Nueva Gerona
Isla de la Juventud
Santa Fé
Archipiélago de los Canarreos
Cayo Largo
Bay of Pigs
Jovellanos
Perico
Colón
Hanábana
Sagua la Grande
Cifuentes
Santo Domingo
Santa Clara
Caibarién
Placetas
Cienfuegos
Juraguá
Cabaiguán
Sancti Spíritus
Taguasco
Condado
Ciego de Ávila
Chambas
Morón
Archipiélago de Camagüey
Cayo Sabinal
Cayo Romano
Esmeralda
Céspedes
Florida
Nuevitas
Camagüey
Vertientes
Crucero Contramaestre
Guáimaro
Las Tunas
Puerto Padre
Jesús Menéndez
Santa Cruz del Sur
Archipiélago de los Jardines de la Reina
Golfo de Guacanayabo
Manzanillo
Bayamo
Niquero
Bartolomé Masó
Salado
Cauto
Palma Soriano
Sierra Maestra
Pico Turquino 1994 m
22°
84°
82°
80°
78°
20°

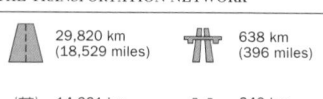

Guanabo, *25 km east of Havana, is a low-key holiday resort favored by Cubans. The most modern cars in Cuba are imported, along with computers, in exchange for sugar in a special trading deal with Japan.*

CUBA

Total Land Area : 110 860 sq. km (42 803 sq. miles)

POPULATION
- over 1 000 000
- over 500 000
- over 100 000
- over 50 000
- over 10 000
- under 10 000

LAND HEIGHT
- 1000m/3281ft
- 500m/1640ft
- 200m/656ft
- Sea Level

N

0 50 km

0 50 miles

PEOPLE

Pop. density medium

Spanish

101/km² (262/mi²)

THE URBAN/RURAL POPULATION SPLIT

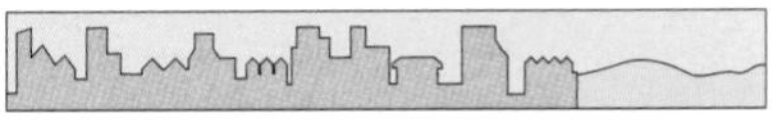
75%
25%

RELIGIOUS PERSUASION

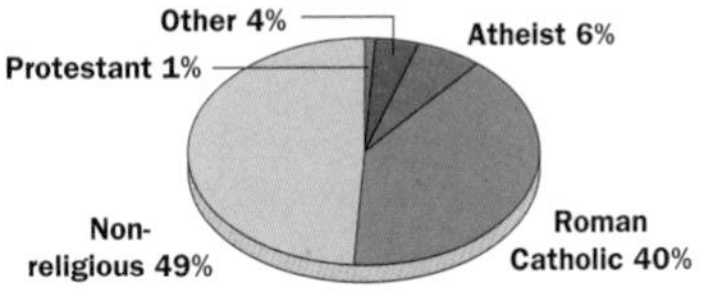
Other 4%
Atheist 6%
Protestant 1%
Non-religious 49%
Roman Catholic 40%

ETHNIC MAKEUP

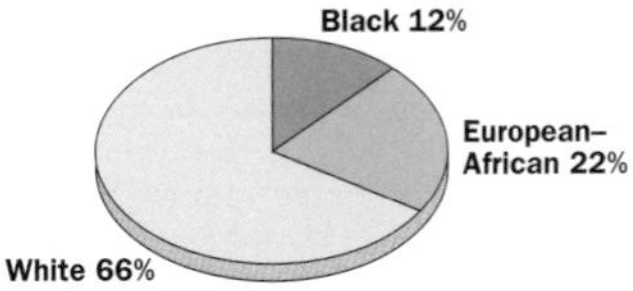
Black 12%
European–African 22%
White 66%

Ethnic tension in Cuba is minimal. About 70% of Cubans are of Spanish descent, mainly from the settlers, but also from the more recent influx of exiles from Franco's Spain. The black population is descended from the slaves and migrants from neighboring states, in particular Jamaica.

Living standards in Cuba fell dramatically in the early 1990s after the collapse of the east European communist bloc, previously its main trading partner, and rationing for most basic foodstuffs was introduced subsequently. The "dollarization" of the economy in recent years has led to great divisions between those who survive on pesos and the more than 50% of the population who have access to dollars. Since the early 1990s the number of those trying to leave, legally or otherwise, has risen markedly.

An increasing number of women are playing prominent roles in politics, the professions, and the armed forces. Child-care facilities are widespread.

POPULATION AGE BREAKDOWN

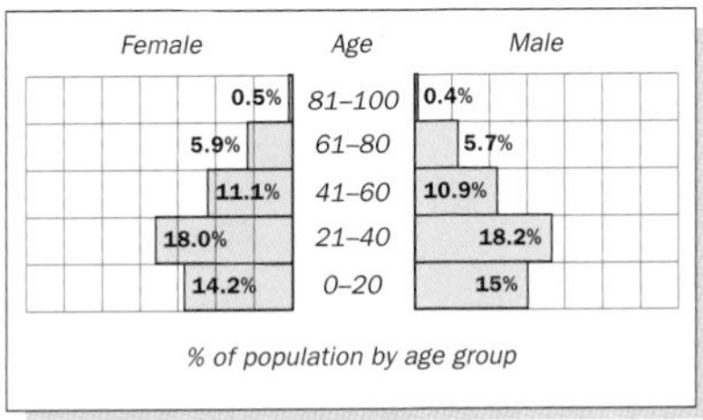
Female
Age
Male
0.5%
81–100
0.4%
5.9%
61–80
5.7%
11.1%
41–60
10.9%
18.0%
21–40
18.2%
14.2%
0–20
15%
% of population by age group

WORLD AFFAIRS

Joined UN in 1945

ACP | IAEA | SELA | NAM | ACS

Since the 1962 stand-off, when Cuba accepted Soviet missiles targeted at US cities, Cuba has been considered a danger by the USA. The end of aid from Moscow after 1991, following the collapse of the USSR, and the US trade blockade increased Cuba's economic isolation despite routine votes in the UN condemning sanctions. The embargo has been progressively loosened since 1999 and now allows for more flights, direct mail, essential medicines, and more food imports. The celebrated case of Elian Gonzalez, a shipwrecked Cuban boy forcibly returned to his Cuban father by the US authorities in June 2000, briefly saw a mutual policy agreement. However, relations remain tense, especially since the inauguration of right-wing US President George W. Bush in 2001.

Relations with Europe are also strained, due to the treatment of dissidents in Cuba, particularly in 1999, and to Castro's refusal to join a trade pact with the EU when Cuba joined the ACP in 2000.

C

POLITICS

No multiparty elections

1998/2003

President Fidel Castro Ruz

AT THE LAST ELECTION

National Assembly of the People's Power 601 seats

100%
PCC

PCC = Cuban Communist Party

Fidel Castro has led Cuba since 1959 and founded its one-party communist system set out in the 1976 constitution.

Main Political Issues

The succession

The aging Fidel Castro remains firmly in place but his successor is a major issue. Some observers predict that a younger, collective, and reform-minded leadership would normalize relations with the USA and steer Cuba towards Western-style democracy. Others warn that Castro's departure could lead to a power vacuum, vulnerable to social unrest and internal divisions between reformers and communist hardliners.

Moa
Baracoa
El Salvador
Guantánamo
GUANTANAMO BAY
(to US)
Windward Passage

Democracy

The trial in 1999 of four moderate dissidents was part of a tough clampdown on internal opposition. This has reduced hopes for the type of opening seen in the economic sphere and threatens diplomatic and economic ties. It offers the USA justification for its trade embargo.

Profile

The 1959 popular revolution, led by Castro, toppled the corrupt Batista dictatorship and launched a far-reaching program of social, economic, and political reforms.

In the 1990s the revolution seemed under siege in the wake of the collapse of the Soviet Union and tightened trade sanctions by the USA. Supporters continue to see Cuba as living proof of the triumph of socialist development over adversity, but critics view the Castro administration as an intolerant dictatorship.

***Raúl Castro,** brother of Fidel and the minister of defence.*

***Fidel Castro,** Cuba's leader since 1959. The USA is keen to oust his regime.*

AID

Recipient

$58m (receipts)

Down 28% in 1999

Spain, France, and UNICEF have provided aid. A 1998 agreement with Japan rescheduled debt over 20 years, and a 2001 agreement with China secured a loan of $400 million.

CHRONOLOGY

Originally inhabited by the Arawak people, Cuba was claimed for Spain by Columbus in 1492. Development of the sugar industry from the 18th century, using imported slave labor, made Cuba the world's third-largest producer by 1860.

- **1868** End of the slave trade.
- **1868–1878** Ten Years' War for independence from Spain.
- **1895** Second war of independence. Thousands die in Spanish concentration camps.
- **1898** In support of Cuban rebels USA declares war on Spain to protect strong American financial interests in Cuba.
- **1899** USA takes Cuba and installs military interim government.
- **1901** USA is granted intervention rights and military bases, including Guantánamo Bay naval base.

CHRONOLOGY *continued*

- **1902** Tomás Estrada Palma takes over as first Cuban president. USA leaves Cuba, but intervenes in 1906–1909 and 1919–1924.
- **1909** Liberal presidency of José Miguel Goméz. Economy prospers; US investment in tourism, gambling, and sugar.
- **1925–1933** Dictatorship of President Gerardo Machado.
- **1933** Years of guerrilla activity end in revolution. Sgt. Fulgencio Batista takes over; military dictatorship.
- **1955** Fidel Castro exiled after two years' imprisonment for subversion.
- **1956–1958** Castro returns to lead a guerrilla war in the Sierra Maestra.
- **1959** Batista flees. Castro takes over; brother, Raúl, is deputy; Che Guevara third in rank. Wholesale nationalizations; Cuba reorganized on Soviet model.
- **1961** USA breaks off relations. US-backed invasion of Bay of Pigs by anti-Castro Cubans fails. Cuba declares itself Marxist–Leninist.
- **1962** US economic and political blockade. Missile crisis: Soviet deployment of nuclear weapons in Cuba leads to extreme Soviet–US tension; war averted by Khrushchev ordering withdrawal of weapons.
- **1965** Che Guevara resigns to pursue foreign liberation wars. One-party state formalized.
- **1972** Cuba joins COMECON (communist economic bloc).
- **1976** New socialist constitution. Cuban troops in Angola until 1991.
- **1977** Sends troops to Ethiopia.
- **1980** 125,000 Cubans, including "undesirables" (criminals or people with learning disabilities), flee to the USA.
- **1982** USA tightens sanctions and bans flights and tourism to Cuba.
- **1983** US invasion of Grenada. Cuba involved in clashes with US forces.
- **1984** Agreement with USA on Cuban emigration and repatriation of "undesirables" is short-lived.
- **1986** Soviet-style *glasnost* rejected.
- **1988** UN's second veto of US attempt to accuse Cuba of human rights violations. Diplomatic relations established with EU.
- **1989** Senior military executed for arms and narcotics smuggling.
- **1991** Preferential trade agreement with USSR ends. Severe rationing.
- **1992–1993** USA tightens blockade. All former Soviet military leave.
- **1994–1995** Economic reforms to boost foreign trade and investment.
- **1996** US Helms-Burton Act tightens sanctions.
- **1998** Visit of Pope John Paul II.
- **1999** Leading moderate dissidents put on trial.

DEFENSE

Compulsory military service

$750m

Down 2% in 1999

CUBAN ARMED FORCES

900 main battle tanks (T–34, T–54/55, T–62)	45,000 personnel
5 patrol boats	3000 personnel
130 combat aircraft (MiG 21/23/29)	10,000 personnel
None	

From 1959 to the 1980s, Cuba's efficient military, well represented in the Council of Ministers and the Politburo, was one of the achievements of the revolution. Under Castro's brother Raúl, it succeeded in repelling the US-sponsored Bay of Pigs invasion in 1961, and saw effective action in Africa in the 1970s, preventing South Africa from taking control of Angola and Somalia from occupying the Ogaden region in Ethiopia.

Today, with communist regimes collapsed around the world, it has lost much of its prestige. Russia is still the main source of arms. A siege mentality associated with the US economic embargo keeps the military on the alert for perceived internal and external threats.

ECONOMICS

Not available

$18.3bn

21.00 Cuban pesos

SCORE CARD

- World GNP Ranking 71st
- GNP per Capita $1650
- Balance of Payments .... In deficit
- Inflation 0.3%
- Unemployment 6%

EXPORTS

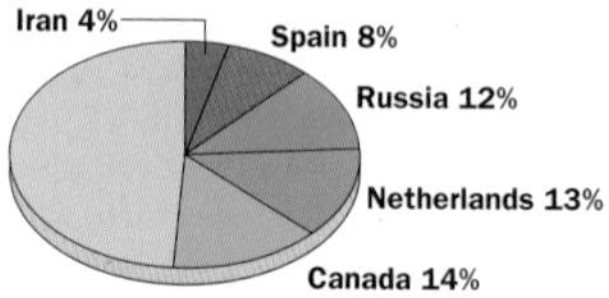
Iran 4%
Spain 8%
Russia 12%
Netherlands 13%
Canada 14%
Other 49%

IMPORTS

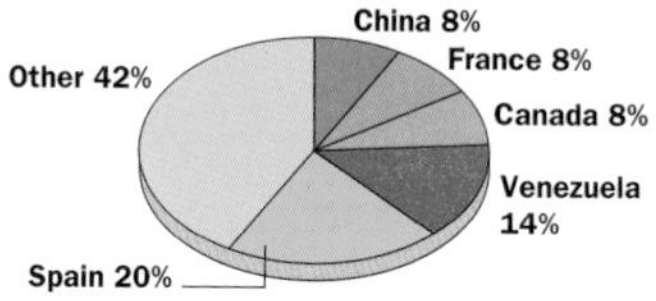
China 8%
France 8%
Canada 8%
Venezuela 14%
Spain 20%
Other 42%

Strengths

Buoyant tourism attracts strong foreign investment. Major exporter of sugar and nickel. Premium Cuban cigars. Strengthening banking sector.

Weaknesses

Cuba denied a major market and investment capital by US trade embargo. Acute shortage of hard currency. Vulnerability of sugar and nickel to world price fluctuations. Difficult terms of trade and weak legal framework deters investment. Infrastructure is deficient. Shortages of fuel, fertilizers, spare parts, and other essential inputs.

Profile

For a period after 1959, the state-controlled economy oscillated between concentration on sugar and stabs at industrialization. Total state control was reimposed in 1986 after a brief flirtation with market opening. The collapse of the USSR meant the loss of some $5 billion in annual aid and led to a deep recession in the early 1990s. A cautious adoption of some capitalist-style reforms in the mid-1990s, including the free use of the US dollar, stimulated the growth of a dollarized sector centered on tourism, which has attracted strong foreign investment. Tourism has replaced sugar as the motor of the economy, and benefits some 160,000 self-employed and small businesses. Foreign companies are also involved in joint ventures in banking and the oil and gas sectors. There is a very large informal sector.

ECONOMIC PERFORMANCE INDICATOR

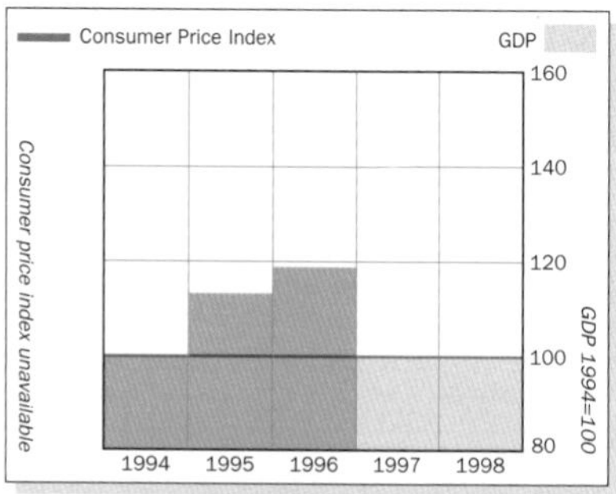
Consumer Price Index
GDP
Consumer price index unavailable
GDP 1994=100
160
140
120
100
80
1994
1995
1996
1997
1998

CUBA : MAJOR BUSINESSES

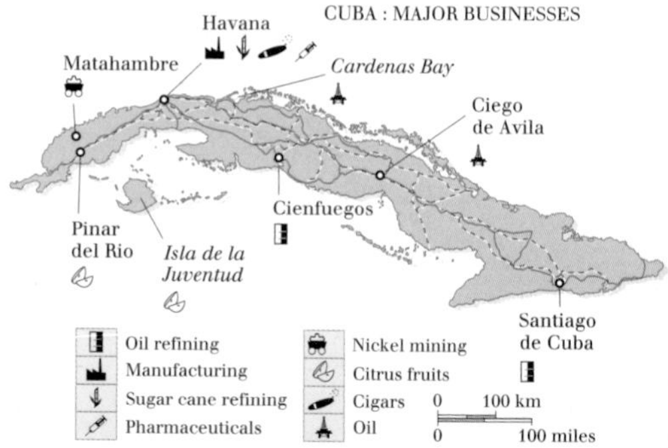
Havana
Matahambre
Cardenas Bay
Ciego de Avila
Cienfuegos
Pinar del Rio
Isla de la Juventud
Santiago de Cuba
Oil refining
Manufacturing
Sugar cane refining
Pharmaceuticals
Nickel mining
Citrus fruits
Cigars
Oil
0
100 km
100 miles

C

RESOURCES

Electric power 4m kw

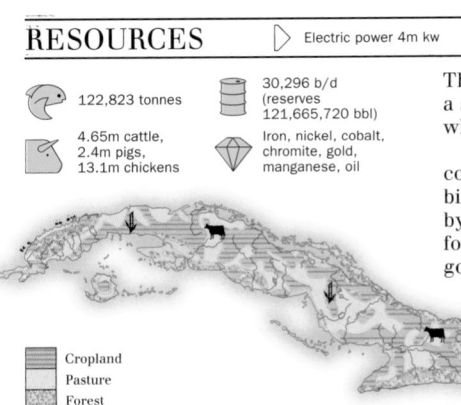

122,823 tonnes

30,296 b/d (reserves 121,665,720 bbl)

4.65m cattle, 2.4m pigs, 13.1m chickens

Iron, nickel, cobalt, chromite, gold, manganese, oil

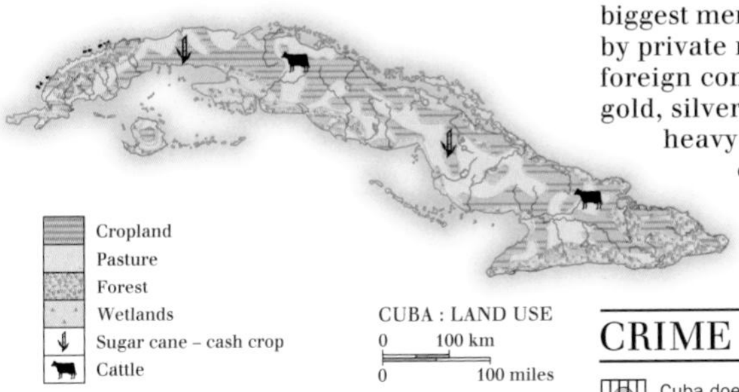
Cropland
Pasture
Forest
Wetlands
Sugar cane – cash crop
Cattle
CUBA : LAND USE
0 100 km
0 100 miles

ELECTRICITY GENERATION

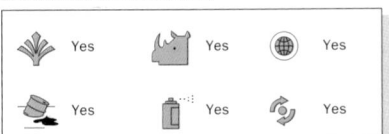

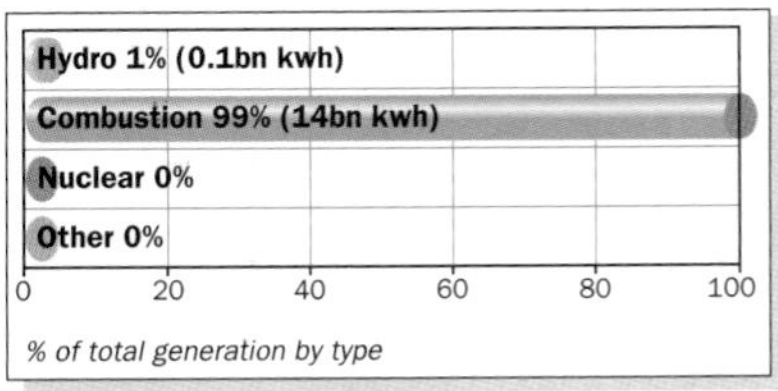
Hydro 1% (0.1bn kwh)
Combustion 99% (14bn kwh)
Nuclear 0%
Other 0%
0 20 40 60 80 100
% of total generation by type

The collapse of the USSR precipitated a steep decline in sugar production, which reached a 50-year low in 1998.

Cuba seeks to expand nickel and cobalt production, traditionally its biggest merchandise exports, assisted by private mining ventures. Several foreign companies are prospecting for gold, silver, and other metals, and for heavy crude oil and gas, through concessions. Work at Juraguá on a Russian-built nuclear reactor was abandoned in December 2000.

ENVIRONMENT

Sustainability rank: 35th

17% (2% partially protected)

2.3 tonnes per capita

ENVIRONMENTAL TREATIES

Yes	Yes	Yes
Yes	Yes	Yes

At the time of the revolution in 1959, only 14% of the country's forest cover remained, but a strong drive to replant has raised the tree cover level to over 20%. The intensive use of irrigation without adequate drainage has caused salinization and waterlogging. There is regional concern about the never-completed nuclear reactor at Juraguá.

MEDIA

TV ownership medium

Daily newspaper circulation 118 per 1000 people

PUBLISHING AND BROADCAST MEDIA

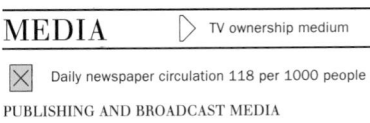

There are 17 regional daily newspapers. *Granma*, published by the government, has the biggest circulation

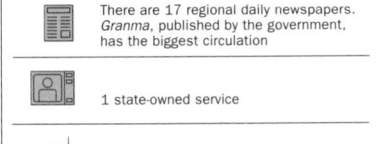

1 state-owned service

1 state-owned service

A catch-all anti-crime law restricts and penalizes investigative reporting by independent journalists which is judged to be assisting the US foreign policy against Cuba.

CRIME

Death penalty used

Cuba does not publish prison figures

Crime is rising

CRIME RATES

Cuba does not publish official statistics for murders, rapes, or thefts

Violent crime is officially viewed as a threat to national stability. In 1999 the penal code was amended to extend the death penalty to certain drug offences, robbery involving firearms, attacks on security officers, and sexual corruption of minors. A security crackdown is targeted at prostitutes and hustlers who thrive on tourism. Tensions associated with widening inequality have led to growing crime, especially theft from within state factories.

EDUCATION

School leaving age: 16

97%

111,587 students

THE EDUCATION SYSTEM

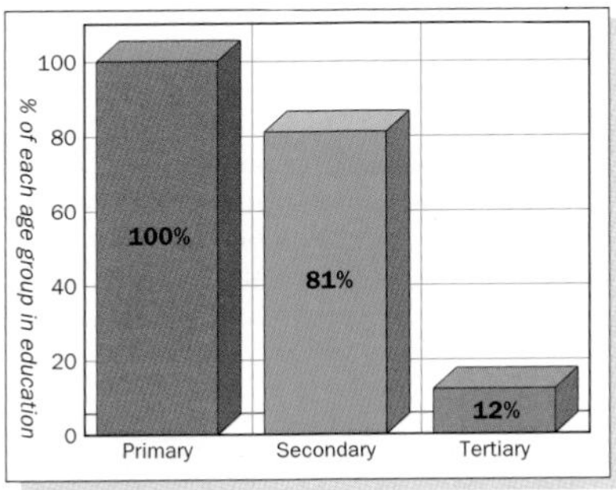
100
80
60
40
20
0
% of each age group in education
100%
81%
12%
Primary
Secondary
Tertiary

Education, which is universal and free at all levels, combines academic with manual work, in line with Marxist–Leninist principles. The high priority given to education under Castro, which is reflected in the high literacy rate, is now being promoted to attract foreign investment in high-tech industries, particularly biotechnology. Spending on education was increased in the late 1990s to around 11.5% of the budget.

HEALTH

Welfare state health benefits

1 per 189 people

Heart & cerebrovascular diseases, cancers, nutritional disorders

Spending on health accounted for around 10% of government expenditure in the late 1990s. Average life expectancy in Cuba is among the highest in Latin America, which is a reflection of its efficient, countrywide health service. The US trade embargo has led to shortages of hospital equipment and raw materials for drugs. The latter are normally supplied by Havana's sizable pharmaceuticals industry. Cuba's advanced surgery techniques attract patients from overseas.

SPENDING

GDP/cap. decrease

CONSUMPTION AND SPENDING

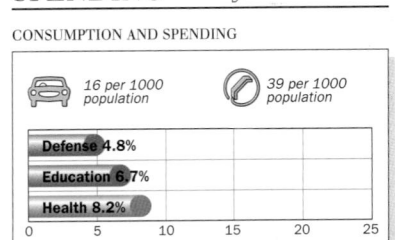

16 per 1000 population

39 per 1000 population

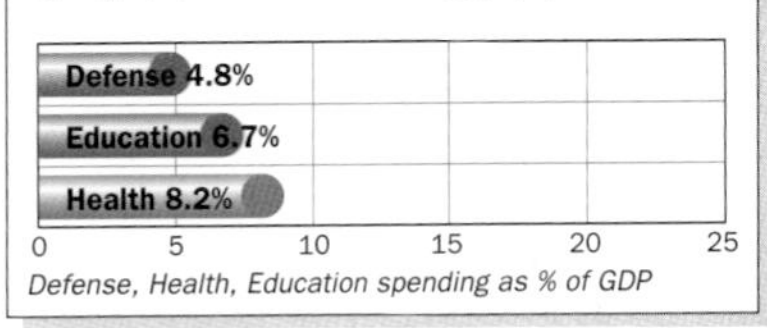
Defense 4.8%
Education 6.7%
Health 8.2%
0 5 10 15 20 25
Defense, Health, Education spending as % of GDP

Under Batista, there were huge wealth disparities, and Cuba was a playground for the rich. The 1959 revolution succeeded in reducing the disparities, partly by taking over all businesses, from oil companies to barbers' shops, and partly by prescribing not only minimum but also maximum wages. Economic regulations have varied since then; for a brief period in 1985, different wage rates were allowed in an attempt to provide incentives for hard workers, but this decision was reversed in 1986. Economic liberalization in the mid-1990s has created a large gulf between some 50% of the population with access to US dollars and those in the peso economy, who have to subsist on low salaries.

WORLD RANKING

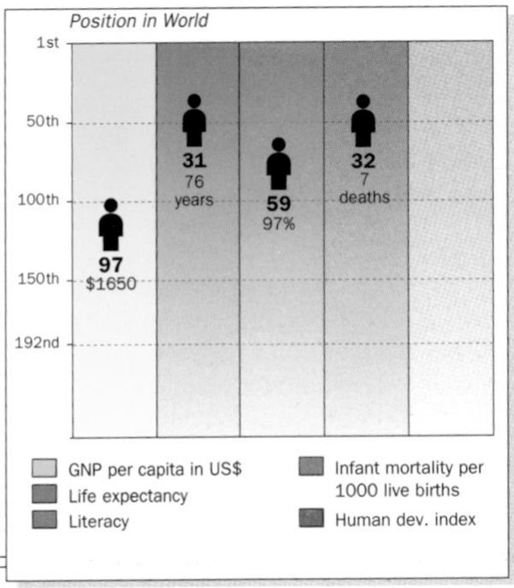
Position in World
1st
50th
100th
150th
192nd
97
$1650
31
76
years
59
97%
32
7
deaths
GNP per capita in US$
Life expectancy
Literacy
Infant mortality per 1000 live births
Human dev. index

CYPRUS

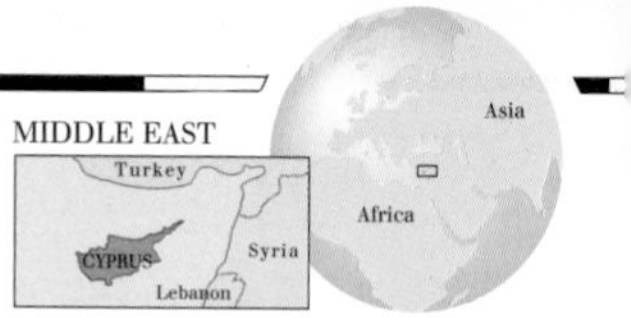
MIDDLE EAST
Turkey
CYPRUS
Syria
Lebanon
Asia
Africa

OFFICIAL NAME: Republic of Cyprus **CAPITAL:** Nicosia **POPULATION:** 786,000
CURRENCY: Cyprus pound (Turkish lira in TRNC) **OFFICIAL LANGUAGES:** Greek and Turkish

C

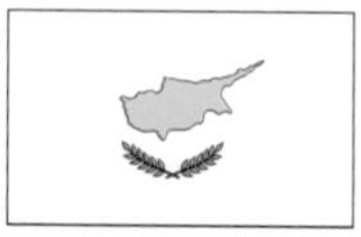

1960 | 1974 | Oct 1 | CY | +2 | +357 | .cy

THE ISLAND OF Cyprus, which rises from a central plateau to a high point at Mount Olympus, lies south of Turkey in the eastern Mediterranean. Cyprus was partitioned in 1974, following an invasion by Turkish troops. The south of the island is the Greek Cypriot Republic of Cyprus (Cyprus); the self-proclaimed Turkish Republic of Northern Cyprus (TRNC) is recognized only by Turkey.

CLIMATE

Mediterranean

WEATHER CHART

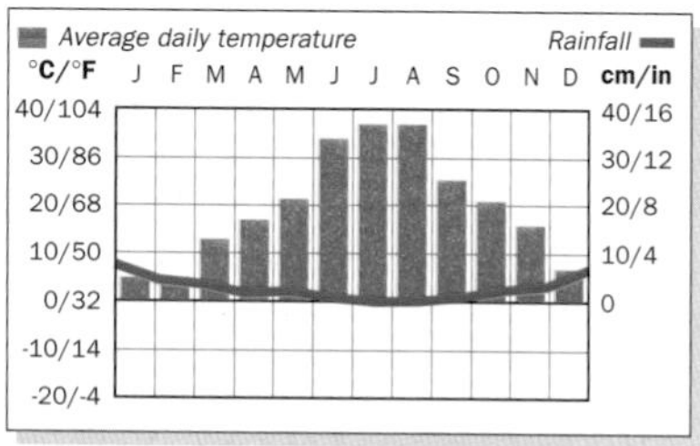
Average daily temperature
Rainfall
°C/°F J F M A M J J A S O N D cm/in
40/104 40/16
30/86 30/12
20/68 20/8
10/50 10/4
0/32 0
-10/14
-20/-4

The climate is typically Mediterranean: summers are hot and dry and winters mild, though there is mountain snow.

TRANSPORTATION

Drive on left

Larnaca 4.36m passengers | 1602 ships 23.3m grt

THE TRANSPORTATION NETWORK

6249 km (3883 miles)	178 km (111 miles)
None	None

Travel between the two zones is impeded. The south regards the airport at Ercan as an illegal point of entry.

TOURISM

Visitors : Population 3.4:1

2.7m visitors | Up 10% in 2000

MAIN TOURIST ARRIVALS

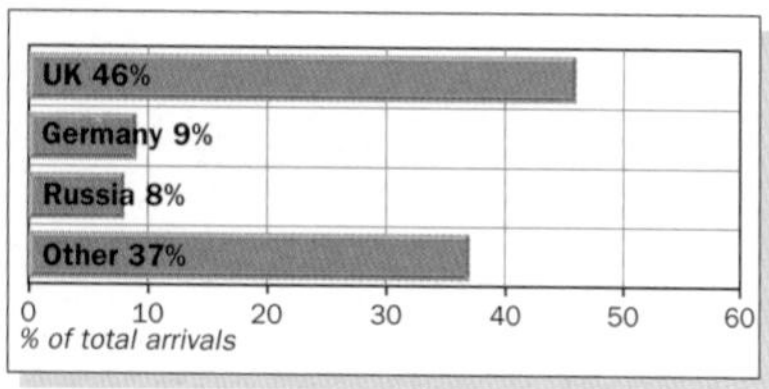
UK 46%
Germany 9%
Russia 8%
Other 37%
0 10 20 30 40 50 60
% of total arrivals

Tourism expanded rapidly in the 1980s in the south, and more recently in the north. A ten-year plan aims to double the number of visitors by 2010. Tourists come for beaches, archeology, or the abundant wildlife, notably on the Akamas peninsula and the Troodos mountains.

PEOPLE

Pop. density medium

Greek, Turkish | 85/km² (220/mi²)

THE URBAN/RURAL POPULATION SPLIT

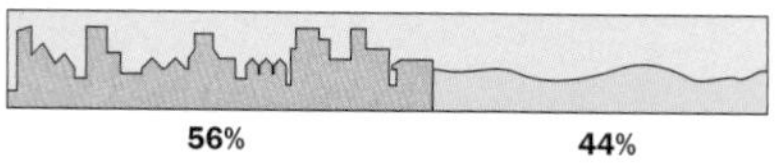
56%
44%

ETHNIC MAKEUP

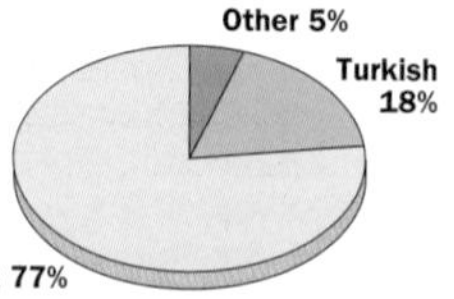
Other 5%
Turkish 18%
Greek 77%

Cyprus's Greek majority, who make up 77% of the population, are Christian. The 18% Turkish minority are Muslim. Some are the descendants of Turks who settled on the island from the 16th century, under the rule of the Ottoman Empire. Turkish Cypriots have been isolated following the 1974 partitioning, since when they have officially been recognized only by Turkey, which has resettled thousands of mainland Turks on the island. Both communities have suffered great upheavals: in 1974, 200,000 Greek Cypriots were forced to flee from the north to the south, while 65,000 Turkish Cypriots fled in the other direction.

Wage levels are on average three times higher in the south, where eastern European contract labor is brought in to staff the hotel industry. Unemployment levels in the north, meanwhile, are rising.

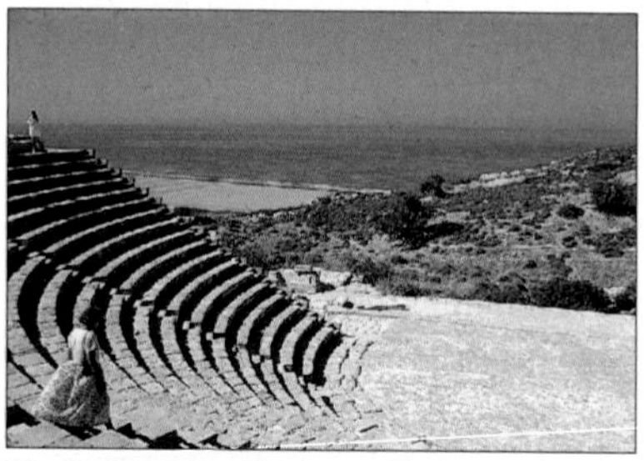

The 2nd-century theater at Curium, 14 km (19 miles) west of Limassol. Curium was the site of a flourishing Mycenaean colony before 1100 BCE.

POLITICS

Multiparty elections

2001/2006 Cyprus
1998/2003 TRNC

President Glafcos Clerides (Cyprus)
President Rauf Denktash (TRNC)

AT THE LAST ELECTION

House of Representatives 80 seats

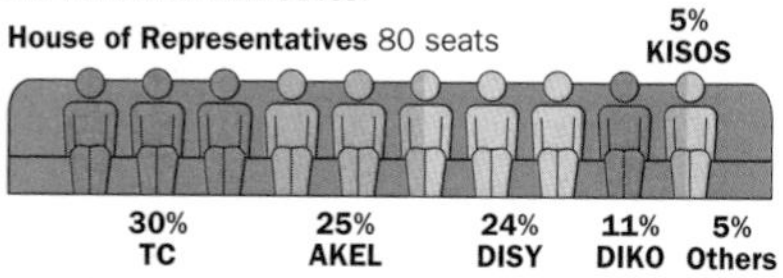
5% KISOS
30% TC
25% AKEL
24% DISY
11% DIKO
5% Others

TC = Reserved for Turkish Cypriots **AKEL** = Progressive Party of the Working People **DISY** = Democratic Rally **DIKO** = Democratic Party **KISOS** = Movement of Social Democrats

The 24 seats reserved for Turkish Cypriots have not been occupied since December 1963

Legislative Assembly (TRNC) 50 seats

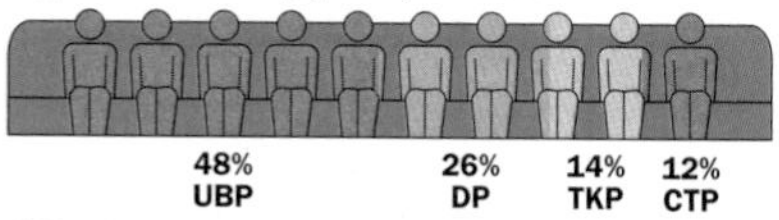
48% UBP
26% DP
14% TKP
12% CTP

UBP = National Unity Party **DP** = Democrat Party
TKP = Social Welfare Party **CTP** = Republican Turkish Party

The UN-backed proposal of a two-zone federation for Cyprus is supported by both the Greek and Turkish governments, eager to solve the dispute. Under this plan, each community would have its own territory but share a number of government functions and ministries. TRNC president Rauf Denktash, mindful of the Greek Cypriots' repression of the Turks prior to 1974, is unwilling to accept a plan that does not ensure full sovereignty and political equality for Turks. Greek Cypriots, in turn, fear the plan would give too much influence over their affairs to the small Turkish minority, who would be able to veto all government decisions.

WORLD AFFAIRS

Joined UN in 1960

CE | Comm | IBRD | NAM | OSCE

The presence of 1210 UN troops since 1974 staffing the "Green Line" (only the Middle East and Kashmir have longer-standing peacekeeping forces) costs $43 million a year. Only Turkey recognizes the TRNC. Cyprus applied to join the EU in 1990; formal negotiations opened in 1998.

AID

Recipient

$50m (receipts) (Cyprus) | Up 2% 1997–1999 (Cyprus)

Cyprus receives aid from international agencies, as well as from the EU and individual countries such as the UK. The TRNC is dependent on aid from Turkey of more than $60 million a year.

CYPRUS

Total Land Area : 9251 sq. km (3572 sq. miles)

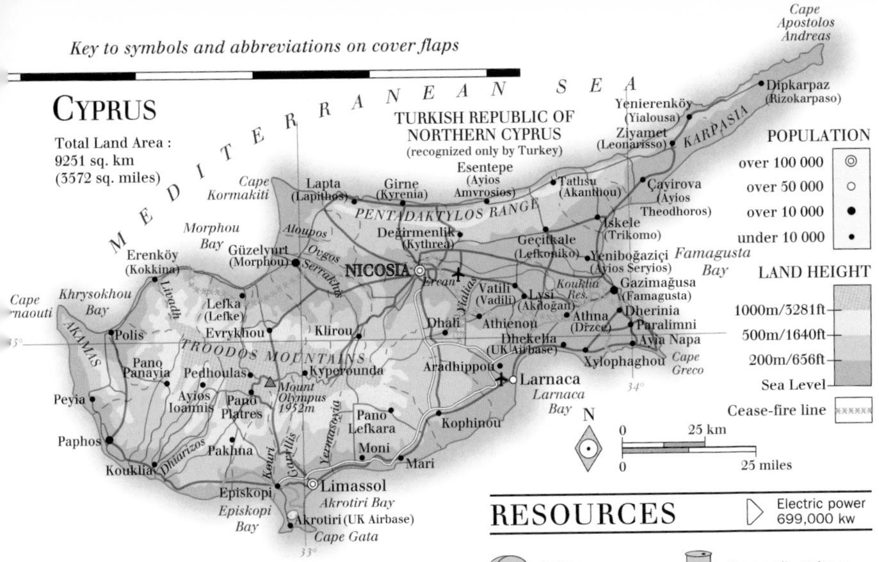
MEDITERRANEAN SEA
TURKISH REPUBLIC OF NORTHERN CYPRUS
(recognized only by Turkey)
Cape Apostolos Andreas
Dipkarpaz (Rizokarpaso)
Yenierenköy (Yialousa)
Ziyamet (Leonarisso)
KARPASIA
Esentepe (Ayios Amvrosios)
Tatlısu (Akanthou)
Çayirova (Ayios Theodhoros)
Cape Kormakiti
Lapta (Lapithos)
Girne (Kyrenia)
PENTADAKTYLOS RANGE
Değirmenlik (Kythrea)
Iskele (Trikomo)
Geçitkale (Lefkoniko)
Yeniboğaziçi (Ayios Seryios)
Famagusta Bay
Gazimağusa (Famagusta)
Morphou Bay
Güzelyurt (Morphou)
Erenköy (Kokkina)
NICOSIA
Ercan
Vatili (Vadili)
Lysi (Akdogan)
Kouklia Res.
Athna (Dizce)
Dherinia
Paralimni
Ayia Napa
Cape Greco
Xylophaghou
Cape Arnaouti
Khrysokhou Bay
Polis
Lefka (Lefke)
Evrykhou
Klirou
Dhali
Athienou
Dhekelia (UK Airbase)
AKAMAS
TROODOS MOUNTAINS
Pano Panayia
Pedhoulas
Kyperounda
Aradhippou
Larnaca
Larnaca Bay
Peyia
Ayios Ioannis
Pano Platres
Mount Olympus 1952m
Pano Lefkara
Kophinou
Paphos
Pakhna
Moni
Mari
Kouklia
Limassol
Episkopi
Episkopi Bay
Akrotiri Bay
Akrotiri (UK Airbase)
Cape Gata
POPULATION
over 100 000
over 50 000
over 10 000
under 10 000
LAND HEIGHT
1000m/3281ft
500m/1640ft
200m/656ft
Sea Level
Cease-fire line
N
0 25 km
0 25 miles

DEFENSE

Compulsory military service

$530m

Up 4% in 1999 (Cyprus)

In addition to UN forces and two British bases, there are 36,000 Turkish troops in northern Cyprus and 1250 Greek troops in the buffer zone. The 10,000-strong Greek Cypriot army and the 5000-strong Turkish Cypriot army both rely heavily on conscripts.

ECONOMICS

Inflation 3.5% p.a. (1990–1999)

$9.1bn

0.5752–0.6116 Cyprus pounds

SCORE CARD

- ❑ WORLD GNP RANKING..........88th
- ❑ GNP PER CAPITA..........$11,950
- ❑ BALANCE OF PAYMENTS..........$234m
- ❑ INFLATION..........1.6%
- ❑ UNEMPLOYMENT..........3%

STRENGTHS

Booming tourism industry, accounting for over 20% of GDP. Manufacturing sector and provision of services to Middle Eastern countries.

WEAKNESSES

Pressure for tighter supervision of offshore finance and crackdown on tax evasion. Limited liberalization. TRNC starved of foreign investment.

EXPORTS

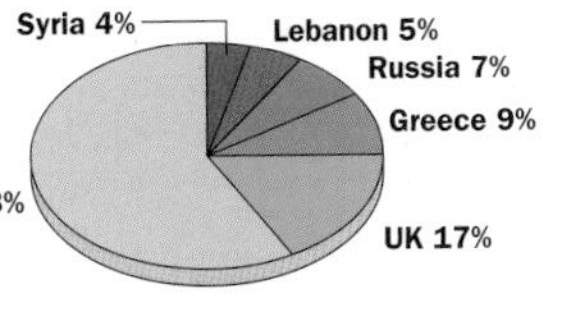
Syria 4%
Lebanon 5%
Russia 7%
Greece 9%
Other 58%
UK 17%

IMPORTS

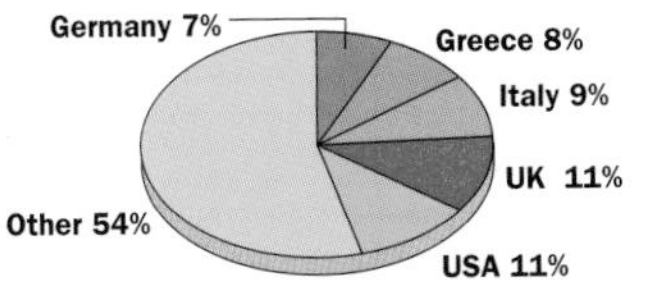
Germany 7%
Greece 8%
Italy 9%
UK 11%
Other 54%
USA 11%

RESOURCES

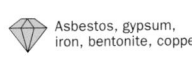

Electric power 699,000 kw

3358 tonnes

Not an oil producer

455,000 pigs, 322,000 goats, 3.8m chickens

Asbestos, gypsum, iron, bentonite, copper

Cyprus continues to supply electricity to TRNC, but has not been paid for this. The possibility of offshore oil and gas to the south has attracted interest. Water is precious but new desalinization plants have reduced shortages.

ENVIRONMENT

Not available

0.2% partially protected

8 tonnes per capita

Campaigners demand that the 155 sq km (60 sq miles) of the Akamas peninsula be fully protected from the threat of being sold for tourist development. Akamas is home to an unusual variety of plant and bird life, and contains breeding sites of the rare green turtle.

MEDIA

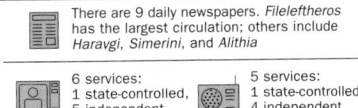

TV ownership high

Daily newspaper circulation 111 per 1000 people

PUBLISHING AND BROADCAST MEDIA

There are 9 daily newspapers. *Fileleftheros* has the largest circulation; others include *Haravgi*, *Simerini*, and *Alithia*

6 services: 1 state-controlled, 5 independent

5 services: 1 state-controlled, 4 independent

Cyprus's press is lively and tends to be highly politicized. The radio and TV services for British troops based in Cyprus are also popular.

CRIME

Death penalty not used

202 prisoners

Up 6% 1992–1996

Crime rates are low and violence is rare. The unruly and sometimes violent behavior of foreign forces has on occasions led Cypriots to object to their presence. The arrest of a Cypriot politician during protests at a UK military base in 2001 provoked riots.

CHRONOLOGY

Cyprus came, in turn, under the domination of Egypt, Greece, the Byzantines, the Ottomans, and the UK.

- ❑ **1960** Independence from UK.
- ❑ **1963** Turkish Cypriots abandon parliament.
- ❑ **1974** President Makarios deposed by Greek military junta. Turkey invades. Partition.
- ❑ **1983** Self-proclamation of TRNC.
- ❑ **1998** Talks on EU membership start, following 1990 application to join.

C

EDUCATION

School leaving age: 15

97%

9982 students

Education is free and compulsory up to the age of 15. Many Greek Cypriots go abroad to university.

HEALTH

Welfare state health benefits

1 per 392 people

Heart diseases, accidents, cancers

Health care is more advanced in the south; sophisticated surgery is carried out at Lefkosia General Hospital.

SPENDING

GDP/cap. increase

CONSUMPTION AND SPENDING

308 per 1000 population

545 per 1000 population

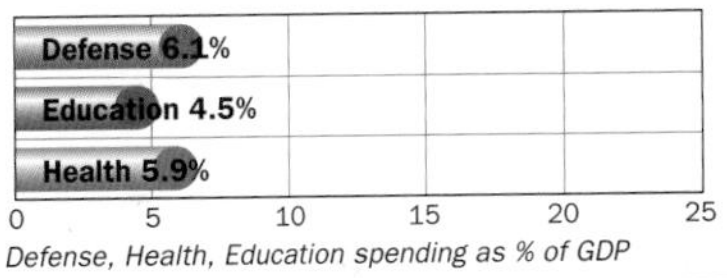
Defense 6.1%
Education 4.5%
Health 5.9%
0
5
10
15
20
25

Defense, Health, Education spending as % of GDP

The average income per capita in the southern part of Cyprus is higher than in Greece and Portugal, but slightly lower than that in Spain.

WORLD RANKING

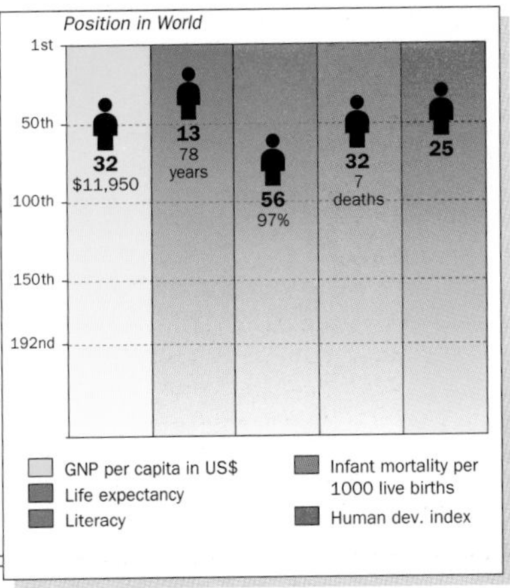
Position in World
1st
50th
100th
150th
192nd
32
$11,950
13
78
years
56
97%
32
7
deaths
25
GNP per capita in US$
Life expectancy
Literacy
Infant mortality per 1000 live births
Human dev. index

CZECH REPUBLIC

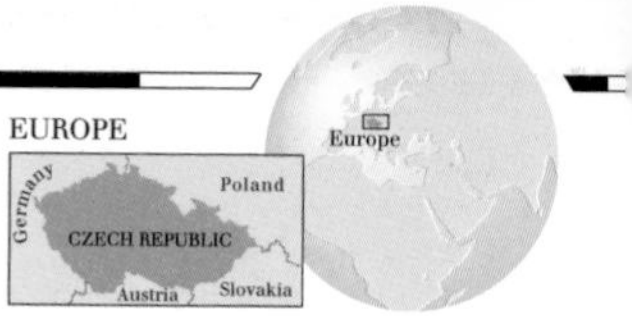
EUROPE
Europe
Germany
Poland
CZECH REPUBLIC
Austria
Slovakia

C

OFFICIAL NAME: Czech Republic **CAPITAL:** Prague
POPULATION: 10.2 million **CURRENCY:** Czech koruna **OFFICIAL LANGUAGE:** Czech

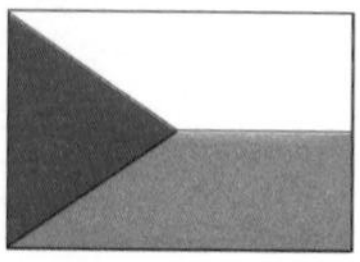

1993 | 1993 | Oct 28 | CZ | +1 | +420 | .cz

LANDLOCKED IN CENTRAL Europe, the Czech Republic comprises the territories of Bohemia and Moravia, and for most of the 20th century it was part of Czechoslovakia. In 1989, the "Velvet Revolution" ended four decades of communist rule, and free elections followed in 1990. In 1993 the Czech Republic and Slovakia peacefully dissolved their federal union to become two independent states.

CLIMATE

Continental

WEATHER CHART

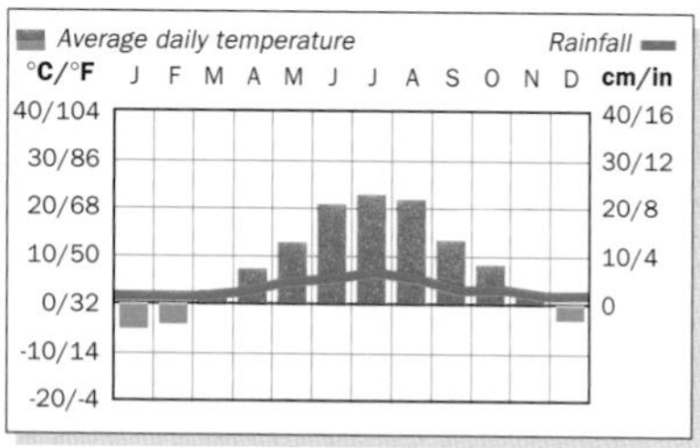
Average daily temperature
Rainfall
°C/°F
J F M A M J J A S O N D
cm/in
40/104
30/86
20/68
10/50
0/32
-10/14
-20/-4
40/16
30/12
20/8
10/4
0

The Czech climate is more moderate than that of Slovakia, though easterly winds bring low temperatures in winter.

TRANSPORTATION

Drive on right

Ruzyné, Prague 4.81m passengers

18 ships 228,000 grt

THE TRANSPORTATION NETWORK

127,693 km (79,345 miles)

498 km (309 miles)

9365 km (5819 miles)

677 km (421 miles)

There are new expressways and rail links to Germany. Prague is a busy regional center for passenger air traffic.

TOURISM

Visitors : Population 1:1.8

5.7m visitors

Up 2% in 2000

MAIN TOURIST ARRIVALS

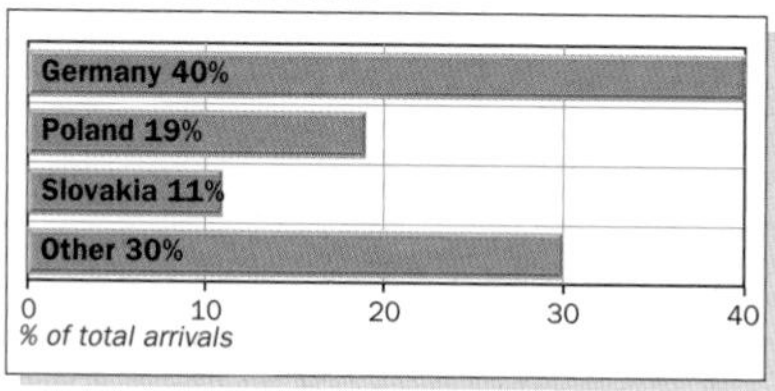
Germany 40%
Poland 19%
Slovakia 11%
Other 30%
0
10
20
30
40
% of total arrivals

Revenues from tourism amount to nearly $4 billion a year and are an invaluable source of foreign earnings for the Czech economy. Germans are the most numerous among the millions of visiting tourists, mainly from Europe. Prague, which rivals Paris as the most beautiful capital in Europe, is still the main destination for visitors, although a growing proportion now seek other attractions such as spa towns and skiing in the Carpathian Mountains.

PEOPLE

Pop. density medium

Czech, Slovak, Hungarian

129/km² (335/mi²)

THE URBAN/RURAL POPULATION SPLIT

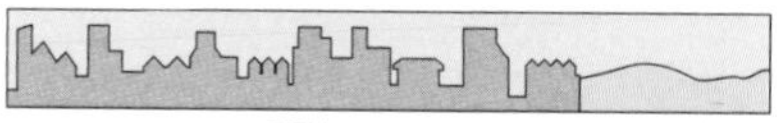
75%
25%

RELIGIOUS PERSUASION

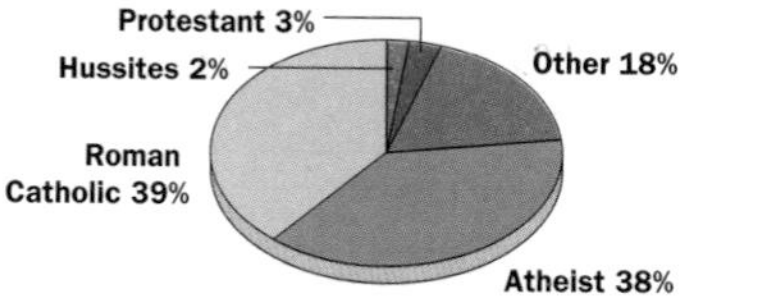
Protestant 3%
Hussites 2%
Other 18%
Roman Catholic 39%
Atheist 38%

Czechs make up over 80% of the population, while the next largest group is Moravians. Some 300,000 Slovaks were left in the country after partition, but dual citizenship is now permitted. Ethnic tensions are few, although the Roma community faces discrimination. A new commercial elite is emerging alongside ex-communist entrepreneurs. Divorce rates are high.

POLITICS

Multiparty elections

L. House 1998/2002
U. House 2000/2002

President Vaclav Havel

AT THE LAST ELECTION

Chamber of Deputies 200 seats

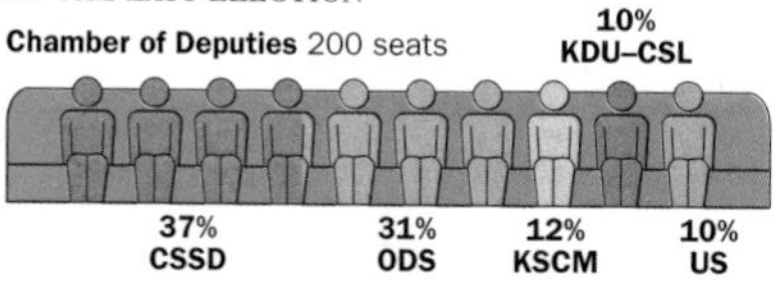
10%
KDU–CSL
37%
CSSD
31%
ODS
12%
KSCM
10%
US

CSSD = Czech Social Democratic Party **ODS** = Civic Democratic Party **KSCM** = Communist Party of Bohemia and Moravia **KDU–CSL** = Christian Democratic Union–Czech People's Party **US** = Freedom Union **QC** = Quad Coalition, comprising the KDU-CSL, the US, the Civic Democratic Alliance (ODA), and the Democratic Union (DEU)
Ind = Independents

Senate 81 seats

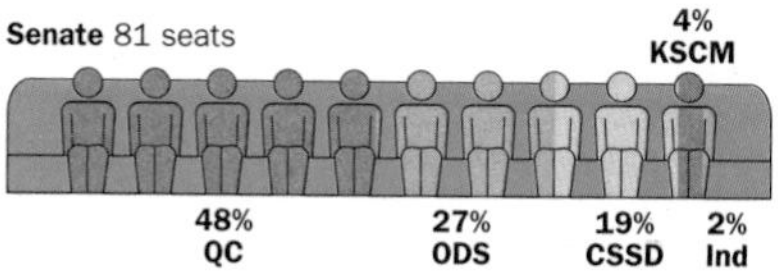
4%
KSCM
48%
QC
27%
ODS
19%
CSSD
2%
Ind

In 1990, Civic Forum won free elections and dissident playwright Vaclav Havel became president. By 1991, Civic Forum had split and Vaclav Klaus's ODS was the dominant party. It continued with economic reforms and privatization, and oversaw the split with the Slovak Republic in 1993, but lost its overall majority in the 1996 elections. Klaus resigned in 1997 amid a scandal over party funding and was then replaced by Josef Tosovsky. Milos Zeman formed a new social democrat-led government after elections in June 1998.

CZECH REPUBLIC

Total Land Area : 78 864 sq. km (30 449 sq. miles)

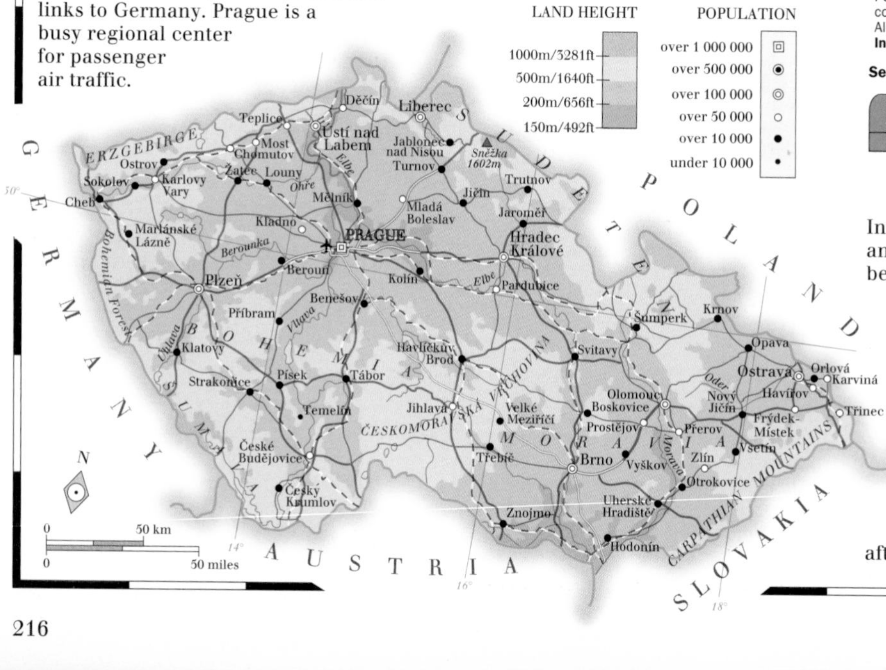
LAND HEIGHT
1000m/3281ft
500m/1640ft
200m/656ft
150m/492ft
POPULATION
over 1 000 000
over 500 000
over 100 000
over 50 000
over 10 000
under 10 000
GERMANY
POLAND
SLOVAKIA
AUSTRIA
ERZGEBIRGE
SUDETEN
BOHEMIA
ČESKOMORAVSKÁ VRCHOVINA
MORAVIA
CARPATHIAN MOUNTAINS
Bohemian Forest
ŠUMAVA
PRAGUE
Děčín
Liberec
Ústí nad Labem
Teplice
Most
Chomutov
Jablonec nad Nisou
Turnov
Sněžka 1602m
Ostrov
Sokolov
Karlovy Vary
Žatec
Louny
Cheb
Mělník
Trutnov
Jičín
Mladá Boleslav
Jaroměř
Kladno
Mariánské Lázně
Hradec Králové
Beroun
Plzeň
Kolín
Pardubice
Benešov
Příbram
Šumperk
Krnov
Opava
Klatovy
Havlíčkův Brod
Svitavy
Ostrava
Orlová
Karviná
Havířov
Strakonice
Písek
Tábor
Olomouc
Nový Jičín
Třinec
Temelín
Jihlava
Velké Meziříčí
Boskovice
Frýdek-Místek
Prostějov
Přerov
Vsetín
České Budějovice
Třebíč
Brno
Vyškov
Zlín
Otrokovice
Český Krumlov
Znojmo
Uherské Hradiště
Hodonín
Elbe
Ohře
Berounka
Vltava
Morava
Oder
N
0
50 km
50 miles

C

WORLD AFFAIRS

Joined UN in 1993

CE | CEFTA | NATO | OECD | OSCE

The Czech Republic began formal negotiations on EU membership in 1998. It joined NATO in 1999. Good relations with Germany are a priority. A 1997 joint declaration resolved the issue of property restitution for Germans expelled in 1945. Austria and Germany strongly opposed the opening of the Temelín nuclear plant in 2000.

AID

Recipient

$318m (receipts)

Up 197% 1997–1999

Aid for economic restructuring has been crucial for modernizing infrastructure such as telecommunications.

DEFENSE

Compulsory military service

$1.16bn

Down 1% in 1999

The split with Slovakia left an oversized, expensive military. In 1994, plans to cut the military by 20,000 were approved. Professional soldiers with a communist past were the first to go. The Czech armaments industry has a long tradition based on precision engineering, and the country is the world's 12th-largest arms exporter.

ECONOMICS

Inflation 12.4% p.a. (1990–1999)

$51.6bn

35.912–37.627 Czech koruny

SCORE CARD

❑ World GNP Ranking	48th
❑ GNP per Capita	$5020
❑ Balance of Payments	$1.07bn
❑ Inflation	2.1%
❑ Unemployment	9%

Strengths

Skilled industrial labor force. Good industrial base. Speed of privatization of state industries. Attractive to German investors. Draw of Prague for tourists.

Weaknesses

Lack of diversification in sectors usually attractive to overseas investors. Limited restructuring, banking sector problems. Pressure to cut government expenditure to reduce serious budget deficit.

EXPORTS

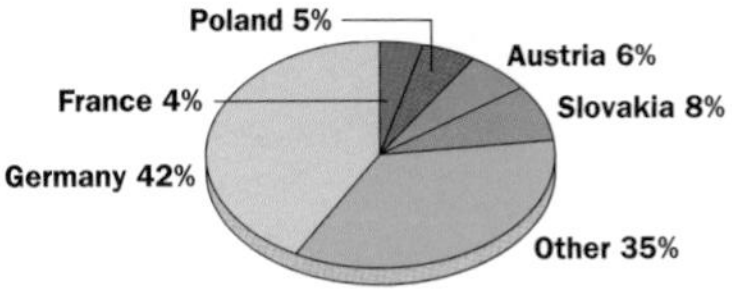
Poland 5%
Austria 6%
France 4%
Slovakia 8%
Germany 42%
Other 35%

IMPORTS

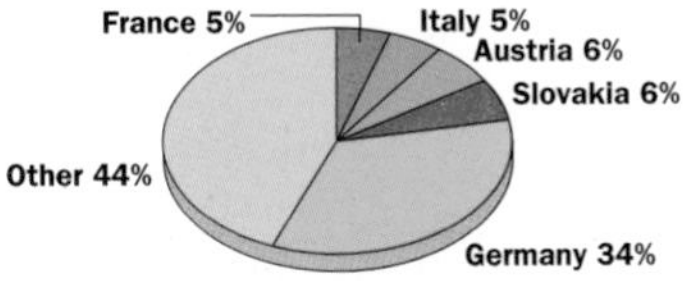
France 5%
Italy 5%
Austria 6%
Slovakia 6%
Other 44%
Germany 34%

RESOURCES

Electric power 13.9m kw

20,881 tonnes

3268 b/d (reserves 88,293,840 bbl)

3.69m pigs, 1.57m cattle, 29.5m chickens

Oil, natural gas, copper, lead, zinc, coal, uranium

Copper, lead, zinc, and coal are the Czech Republic's chief resources. The government is aiming to phase out the worst-polluting coal-fired power stations. Opposition to a planned 2000 MW Soviet-designed nuclear power station at Temelín delayed its completion until late 2000.

ENVIRONMENT

Sustainability rank: 29th

16%

12.2 tonnes per capita

Pollution from the power, chemical, and cement industries and the new Temelín nuclear plant are key concerns.

MEDIA

TV ownership high

Daily newspaper circulation 254 per 1000 people

PUBLISHING AND BROADCAST MEDIA

There are 21 daily newspapers. *Mladá Fronta Dnes* has the largest circulation

4 services: 1 state-owned, 3 independent

1 state-owned service, over 44 independent services

Government-influenced appointments of senior media officials provoked mass protests and a change in the law in 2001.

CRIME

Death penalty not used

19,508 prisoners

Up 8% 1996–1998

Prostitution is becoming a growing problem, especially in regions bordering Austria and Germany.

EDUCATION

School leaving age: 15

99%

207,221 students

Schooling has reverted to the pre-1945 system. Charles University in Prague was founded in the 13th century.

HEALTH

No welfare state health benefits

1 per 333 people

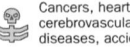

Cancers, heart and cerebrovascular diseases, accidents

Health care expenditure as a share of GDP has increased by 30% since 1990. Wealthy Czechs travel to Germany for complex surgery.

***The Vltava River** in Prague. Millions of tourists, mainly from Europe and the USA, visit Prague every year.*

CHRONOLOGY

Formerly part of the Austro-Hungarian empire, the Republic of Czechoslovakia was established in 1918. It was invaded by Hitler in 1939.

- ❑ **1968** "Prague Spring." Invasion by Warsaw Pact countries.
- ❑ **1989** "Velvet Revolution."
- ❑ **1990** Elections; Vaclav Havel president.
- ❑ **1993** Division into Czech Republic and Slovakia.
- ❑ **1998** Start of EU membership negotiations.
- ❑ **1999** Joins NATO.

SPENDING

GDP/cap. increase

CONSUMPTION AND SPENDING

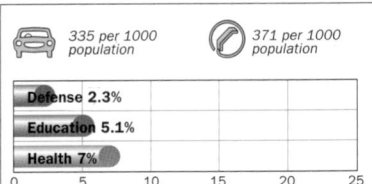

335 per 1000 population

371 per 1000 population

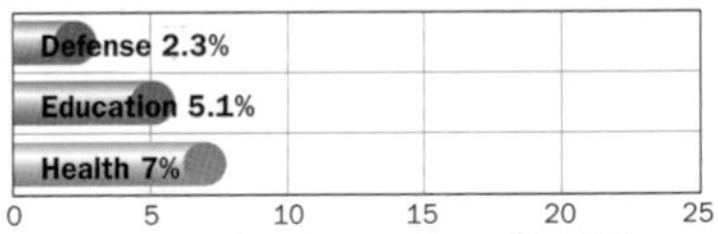
Defense 2.3%
Education 5.1%
Health 7%
0
5
10
15
20
25

Defense, Health, Education spending as % of GDP

A new entrepreneurial business class has emerged since the "Velvet Revolution" in 1989. Many Czechs have shares in privatized enterprises.

WORLD RANKING

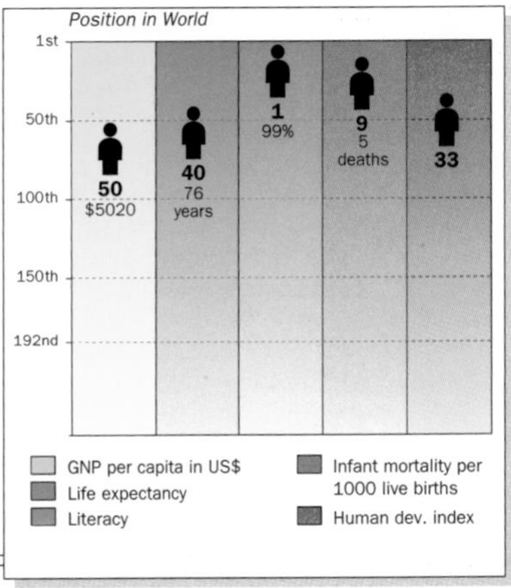
Position in World
1st
50th
100th
150th
192nd
50
$5020
40
76 years
1
99%
9
5 deaths
33
GNP per capita in US$
Life expectancy
Literacy
Infant mortality per 1000 live births
Human dev. index

DENMARK

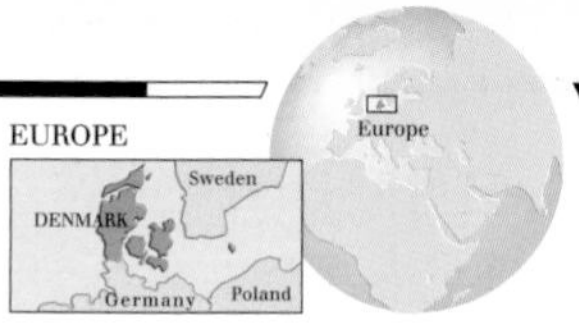
EUROPE
Europe
Sweden
DENMARK
Germany
Poland

OFFICIAL NAME: Kingdom of Denmark **CAPITAL:** Copenhagen (København)
POPULATION: 5.3 million **CURRENCY:** Danish krone **OFFICIAL LANGUAGE:** Danish

950
1944
April 16
DK
+1
+45
.dk

THE MOST SOUTHERLY COUNTRY in Scandinavia, Denmark occupies the Jutland (Jylland) peninsula, the islands of Sjælland, Fyn, Lolland, and Falster, and more than 400 smaller islands. Its terrain is among the flattest in the world. The Faeroe Islands and Greenland in the North Atlantic are self-governing associated territories. Politically, Denmark is stable, despite a preponderance of minority governments since 1945. It possesses a long liberal tradition and was one of the first countries to establish a welfare system, in the 1930s.

CLIMATE

Maritime

WEATHER CHART

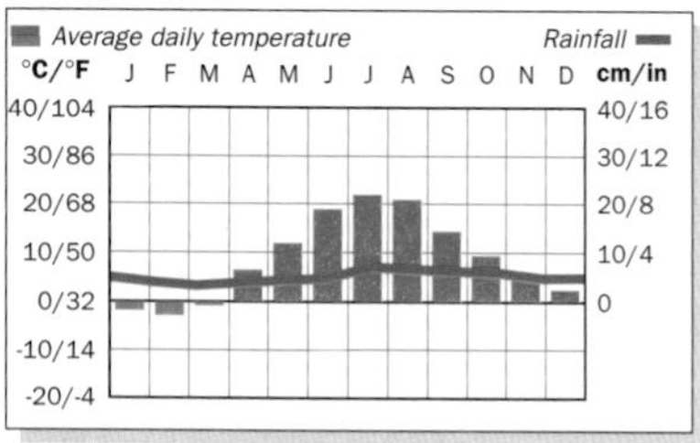
Average daily temperature
Rainfall
°C/°F
J F M A M J J A S O N D
cm/in
40/104
30/86
20/68
10/50
0/32
-10/14
-20/-4
40/16
30/12
20/8
10/4
0

Denmark's temperate, damp climate is one of the keys to its agricultural success. The Faeroes are windy, foggy, and cool. Greenland's climate ranges north–south from arctic to subarctic.

TRANSPORTATION

Drive on right

Kastrup, Copenhagen 17.4m passengers

1057 ships 5.9m grt

THE TRANSPORTATION NETWORK

71,437 km (44,389 miles)

843 km (524 miles)

2324 km (1444 miles)

417 km (259 miles)

There is an extensive, well-integrated transportation network of bus, rail, and ferry services. State-owned companies predominate, although privatization of some ferry and rail services have been mooted. Denmark wishes to reduce significant state transportation subsidies. A few private companies operate in the Faeroes and Greenland with state support.

Major new construction projects focus on bridge and tunnel links, such as the Storebælt project connecting the islands of Fyn and Sjælland. A 16-km (10-mile) Øresund road and rail link by bridge and tunnel, connecting Copenhagen with Malmö in Sweden, opened in July 2000. Copenhagen's new Metro light railway system is also nearly completed.

The island of Fyn, like the rest of Denmark, is flat and depends on coastal defenses to prevent flooding by the sea.

TOURISM

Visitors : Population 1:2.5

2.1m visitors

Up 3% in 2000

MAIN TOURIST ARRIVALS

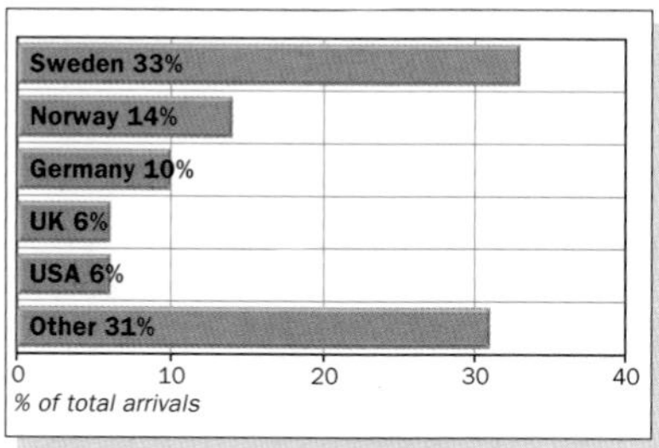
Sweden 33%
Norway 14%
Germany 10%
UK 6%
USA 6%
Other 31%
0
10
20
30
40
% of total arrivals

Denmark is a popular destination for Scandinavian and German tourists. Principal attractions are Copenhagen (with its Tivoli Gardens and fine 18th-century architecture), Legoland, the countryside, and seaside resorts. Greenland attracts wildlife tourists.

DENMARK
Total Land Area : 43 070 sq. km
(16 629 sq. miles)
POPULATION
over 1 000 000
over 100 000
over 10 000
under 10 000
LAND HEIGHT
175m/574ft
Sea Level
Ferry link
0
50 km
0
50 miles
N
Skagen
Skagerrak
Hirtshals
Hjørring
Frederikshavn
Løkken
Brønderslev
Jammerbugten
Læsø
Åbybro
Hanstholm
Fjerritslev
Ålborg
Thisted
Limfjorden
Kattegat
Mors
Ålborg Bugt
Nissum Bredning
Lemvig
Hobro
Skive
Randers
Struer
Viborg
Grenå
Holstebro
Gudenå
JYLLAND
Herning
Ikast
Silkeborg
Århus
Ebeltoft
Ringkøbing
Holmsland Klit
Ringkøbing Fjord
Skjern
Skjern Å
Brande
Yding Skovhøj 173m
Give
Samsø
Sejerø
Horsens
Grindsted
Vejle
Endelave
Varde
Fredericia
Middelfart
Kolding
Esbjerg
Brørup
Otterup
Odense
Storebælt
Ribe
Årup
Fyn
Ringe
Tøftlund
Haderslev
Kværndrup
Rømø
Lillebælt
Fåborg
Svendborg
Åbenrå
Vindeby
Tønder
Gråsten
Als
Sønderborg
Ærø
Langeland
GERMANY
Kiel Bay
to Fehmarn, Germany
NORTH SEA
Bornholm
Rønne
(continuation on same scale)
Helsingør
to Helsingborg
The Sound
Hundested
Hillerød
Nykøbing
Isefjord
Hørsholm
Holbæk
COPENHAGEN
Kalundborg
Roskilde
Tåstrup
Saltholm
Sjælland
Sorø
Køge
Slagelse
Ringsted
Korsør
Store Heddinge
Næstved
Præstø
Vordingborg
Møn
Nakskov
Falster
Maribo
Sakskøbing
Nykøbing-Falster
Lolland
Gedser
BALTIC SEA
SWEDEN

D

PEOPLE

Pop. density medium

Danish

125/km² (324/mi²)

THE URBAN/RURAL POPULATION SPLIT

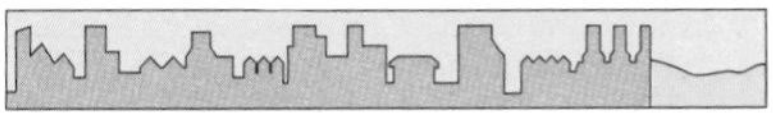
85%
15%

RELIGIOUS PERSUASION

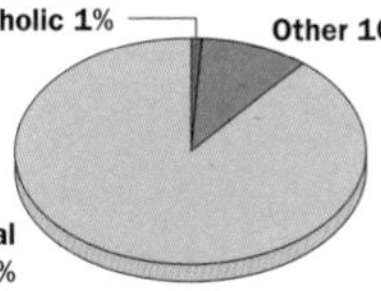
Roman Catholic 1%
Other 10%
Evangelical Lutheran 89%

ETHNIC MAKEUP

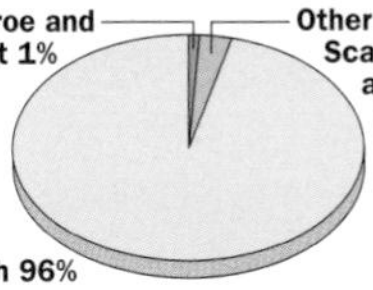
Faeroe and Inuit 1%
Other (including Scandinavian and Turkish) 3%
Danish 96%

Danish society is homogeneous. Out of a population of 5.3 million, just 250,000 are foreign citizens, mainly from other Scandinavian or EU states. The most visible minority groups are the Inuit, Greenland's indigenous inhabitants, and the Turkish community. Rising unemployment has engendered some ethnic tension, although racially motivated attacks are still rare.

Denmark has undergone profound social changes over the last 20 years, and the role of women has been transformed. Helped by Denmark's extensive social and educational provision, three-quarters of women now work in part-time or full-time jobs. Denmark provides the best state child support in Europe: almost half of children under two, and two-thirds of three- to six-year-olds, are in day nurseries.

Less than half the population lives in a nuclear family, in part reflecting the high divorce rate. Marriage is becoming less common; almost 40% of children are brought up by unmarried couples or single parents. Cohabiting couples now have the same legal rights as those who are married. In 1990, Denmark became the first country to allow registered partnerships between homosexual couples, effectively granting them the same legal status as heterosexual couples.

POPULATION AGE BREAKDOWN

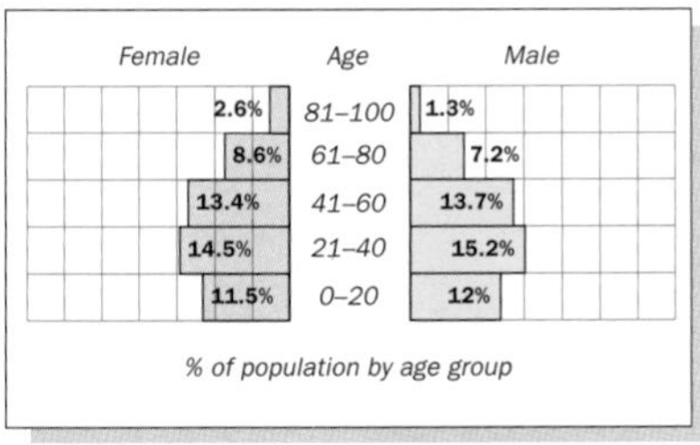
Female
Age
Male
2.6%
81–100
1.3%
8.6%
61–80
7.2%
13.4%
41–60
13.7%
14.5%
21–40
15.2%
11.5%
0–20
12%
% of population by age group

POLITICS

Multiparty elections

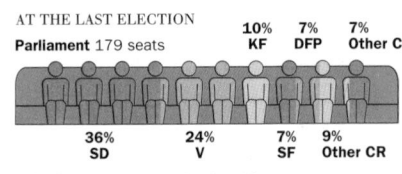

1998/2002

HM Queen Margrethe II

AT THE LAST ELECTION

Parliament 179 seats
10% KF
7% DFP
7% Other CL
36% SD
24% V
7% SF
9% Other CR

SD = Social Democrats V = Liberal Party KF = Conservative People's Party DFP = Danish People's Party SF = Socialist People's Party Other CR = Other Center Right Other CL = Other Center Left

Greenland and the Faeroe Islands send 4 members to the Parliament

Poul Nyrup Rasmussen, prime minister andSD leader.

Queen Margrethe, who succeeded to the throne in 1972.

Denmark is a constitutional monarchy and a multiparty democracy. The associated territories of Greenland and the Faeroe Islands have home rule.

MAIN POLITICAL ISSUES

Relations with the EU

In recent years, Denmark's left-of-center parties have been suspicious of further EU integration. In 1992 ratification of the Maastricht Treaty, approved by parliament, was rejected in a referendum, voters objecting to monetary union, a common defense force, and local election voting rights for European citizens living in Denmark. Later that year an EU summit allowed Denmark to opt out of monetary union, defense, and European citizenship. A referendum in 1993 finally approved the Treaty. Voters also approved the Amsterdam Treaty (successor to the Maastricht Treaty) in 1998, but in September 2000 a referendum on joining the euro (which Denmark had already decided not to introduce from its outset in 1999) produced a highly significant, and unexpected, "no" decision.

Immigration

In what many saw as a vindication of Danish liberal traditions, the then prime minister Poul Schlüter was forced to resign in 1993 over the "Tamilgate" affair. A judicial inquiry ruled that he had falsely denied in parliament that immigration officials were hindering the entry of the families of Tamil workers resident in Denmark. The position and integration into society of immigrants and refugees, who account for only 4% of the population, continues to be a controversial issue. The new far-right, anti-immigrant Danish People's Party won 13 seats in the 1998 election.

PROFILE

Denmark's intricate proportional electoral system ensures that parliament truly reflects voters' wishes, but also tends to lead to minority governments. SD governments were predominant until 1982. A decade of Conservative–Liberal rule followed. In 1993, the SD regained power, at the head of a center-left coalition. Although the coalition lost ground in the 1994 elections, it continued to lead a minority government coalition, with Prime Minister Poul Nyrup Rasmussen narrowly winning a fresh term of office at the 1998 general election. Policy differences between the two main political groups are few.

WORLD AFFAIRS

Joined UN in 1945

CE EU NATO OECD OSCE

Relations with the rest of Europe are the major foreign policy concern, notably the issue of a common defense policy and monetary union. Denmark decided against introducing the euro from January 1999, but the krone is pegged to the euro, and economic policies follow those of the participating states. Promoting economic ties with Norway, Sweden, and Finland is a priority, as are improving links with former Eastern bloc states, especially those on the Baltic – not least to assist pollution reduction, a serious concern. Denmark is also a strong supporter of Third World development, especially in Africa.

CHRONOLOGY

Founded in the 10th century, Denmark is Europe's oldest monarchy. It was the dominant Baltic power until the 17th century, when it was eclipsed by Sweden.

- ❑ **1815** Denmark forced to cede Norway to Swedish rule.
- ❑ **1849** Creation of first democratic constitution.
- ❑ **1864** Denmark forced to cede provinces of Schleswig and Holstein after losing war with Prussia.
- ❑ **1914–1918** Denmark neutral in World War I.
- ❑ **1915** Universal adult suffrage introduced. Rise of SD.
- ❑ **1920** Northern Schleswig votes to return to Danish rule.

D

CHRONOLOGY *continued*

- **1929** First full SD government takes power under prime minister Thorvald Stauning.
- **1930s** Implementation of advanced social welfare legislation and other liberal reforms under SD.
- **1939** Outbreak of World War II; Denmark reaffirms neutrality.
- **1940** Nazi occupation. National coalition government formed.
- **1943** Danish Resistance successes lead Nazis to take full control.
- **1944** Iceland declares independence from Denmark.
- **1945** Denmark recognizes Icelandic independence. After defeat of Nazi Germany, SD leads postwar coalition governments.
- **1948** Faeroes granted home rule.
- **1952** Founder member of the Nordic Council.
- **1953** Constitution reformed; single-chamber, proportionally elected parliament created.
- **1959** Denmark joins the European Free Trade Association (EFTA).
- **1973** Denmark joins European Communities.
- **1979** Greenland granted home rule.
- **1975–1982** SD's Anker Jorgensen heads series of coalitions; elections in 1977, 1979, and 1981. Final coalition collapses over economic policy differences.
- **1982** Poul Schlüter first Conservative prime minister since 1894.
- **1992** Referendum rejects Maastricht Treaty on European Union.
- **1993** Schlüter resigns over "Tamilgate" scandal. Center-left government led by Poul Nyrup Rasmussen. Danish voters ratify revised Maastricht Treaty.
- **1994** General election; Rasmussen heads SD-led minority coalition.
- **1998** General election narrowly returns coalition.
- **2000** Referendum rejects joining euro single currency.

AID

Donor

$1.7bn (donations) | Up 2% in 1999

In GNP terms, Denmark is the world's leading aid donor, contributing an average 1% of its national income since 1992. It supports both economic and social development projects and policy reforms. Aid is an important political issue; the current debate is over its use as a tool to promote democracy.

Denmark provides aid to Asia and Latin America, but its closest ties are with Africa. Tanzania is the largest single aid recipient. Denmark has also provided considerable support to the other southern African SADC states.

DEFENSE

Compulsory military service

$2.68bn | Down 8% in 1999

Denmark was neutral until 1945. Apart from NATO commitments, defense has a low priority; spending is less than 2% of GDP (well below the NATO average). Denmark provides troops for the NATO-led forces in former Yugoslavia and observers for other UN peacekeeping operations. One-quarter of its armed forces are conscripts, and its reserves include a Home Guard. Denmark has observer status at the WEU.

DANISH ARMED FORCES

248 main battle tanks (230 *Leopard* 1A5, 18 *Leopard* 2)	12,850 personnel
3 submarines, 3 corvettes, and 27 patrol boats	4060 personnel
69 combat aircraft (F-16A/B)	4900 personnel
None	

ECONOMICS

Inflation 2% p.a. (1990–1999)

$170.7bn | 7.4244–7.9499 Danish kroner

SCORE CARD

- World GNP Ranking 24th
- GNP per Capita $32,050
- Balance of Payments $2.17bn
- Inflation 2.5%
- Unemployment 6%

EXPORTS

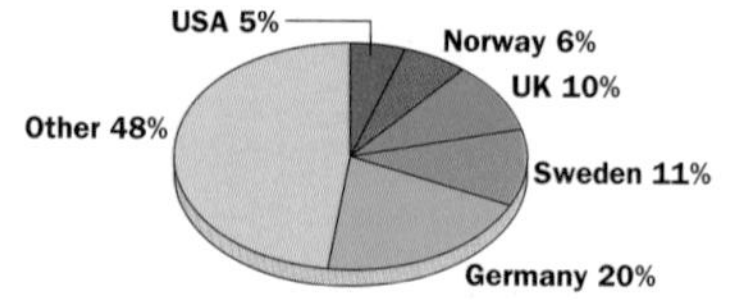
USA 5%
Norway 6%
UK 10%
Sweden 11%
Germany 20%
Other 48%

IMPORTS

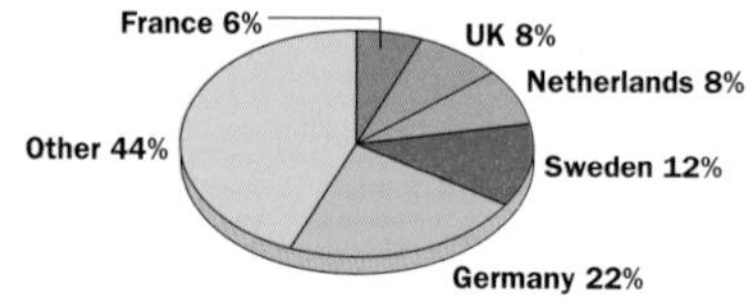
France 6%
UK 8%
Netherlands 8%
Sweden 12%
Germany 22%
Other 44%

Strengths
Low inflation. Unemployment halved from a high of 13% in 1994. Buoyant GDP growth in 1990s (average 3% per annum). Gas and oil reserves. Strong high-tech, high-profit manufacturing sector. Skilled workforce.

Weaknesses
Heavy tax burden. Weakening competitiveness and growing current-account deficit. Strong krone harms exports. Frequent minority governments.

Profile
Denmark's mix of a large state sector and a private sector has been successful. GDP per capita is one of the highest among the OECD countries.

A new minority center-right coalition in the 1980s introduced major changes. A stable exchange rate policy and tighter budget controls aimed to reduce inflation and reverse the balance-of-payments deficit. This policy mix proved successful, but recession in Europe in the early 1990s led to slower growth. An economic upturn since 1993, when a center-left coalition took office, was first led by private consumption and then buoyed by increased exports and business investment.

Voters have refused to accept EU monetary union, a "no" vote in the referendum on introducing the euro in September 2000 reinforcing this stance. However, Denmark does meet the EU's economic convergence criteria for monetary union, the krone being pegged to the euro, and economic policies follow those of the participating states.

ECONOMIC PERFORMANCE INDICATOR

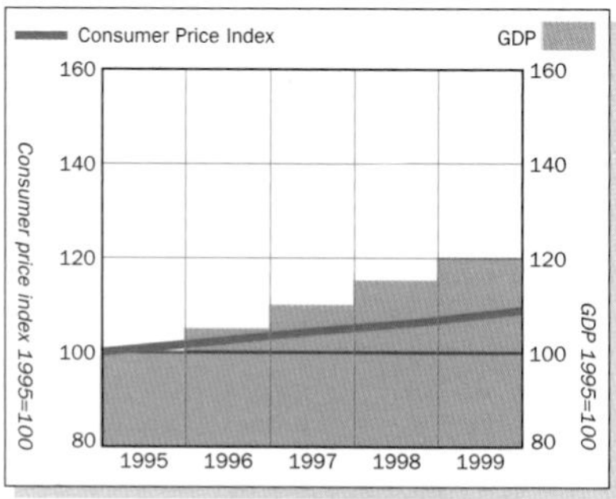
Consumer Price Index
GDP
160
140
120
100
80
1995
1996
1997
1998
1999
Consumer price index 1995=100
GDP 1995=100

DENMARK : MAJOR BUSINESSES

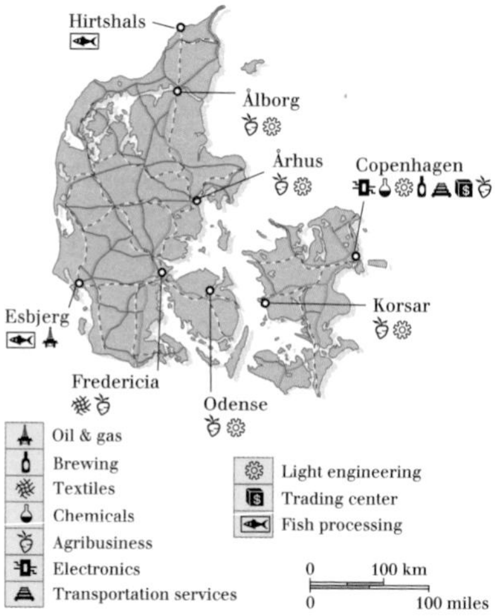
Hirtshals
Ålborg
Århus
Copenhagen
Esbjerg
Korsar
Fredericia
Odense
Oil & gas
Brewing
Textiles
Chemicals
Agribusiness
Electronics
Transportation services
Light engineering
Trading center
Fish processing
0
100 km
0
100 miles

RESOURCES

Electric power 11.8m kw

1.87m tonnes

370,000 b/d (reserves 1,100,000,000 bbl)

11.6m pigs, 1.85m cattle, 20m chickens

Natural gas, oil

ELECTRICITY GENERATION

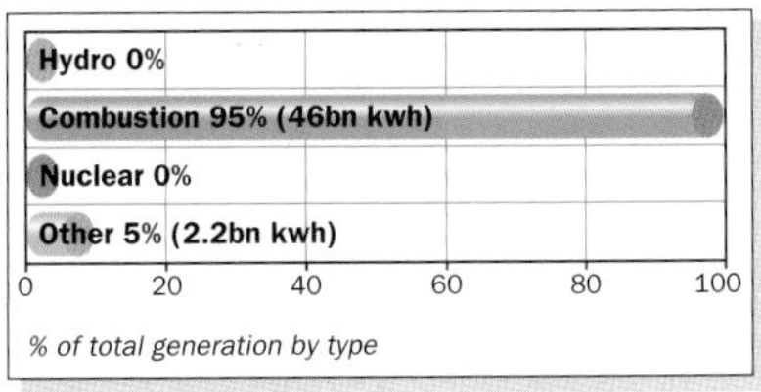
Hydro 0%
Combustion 95% (46bn kwh)
Nuclear 0%
Other 5% (2.2bn kwh)
0
20
40
60
80
100
% of total generation by type

Despite expansion of North Sea oil and gas output, Denmark is still an overall importer of energy. Agriculture is highly efficient, and Denmark is the world's biggest exporter of pork.

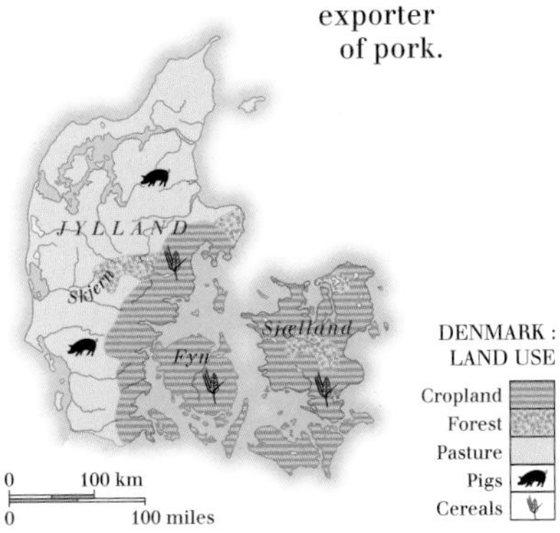
JYLLAND
Skjern
Fyn
Sjælland
DENMARK : LAND USE
Cropland
Forest
Pasture
Pigs
Cereals
0
100 km
0
100 miles

HEALTH

Welfare state health benefits

1 per 345 people

Heart diseases, cancers, accidents

Denmark was one of the first countries to introduce a state social welfare system. The national health service, which still provides free treatment for almost everything, is the main reason for Denmark's high taxes – in 2000 almost a quarter of government spending was allocated to social services. Any attempts to reduce expenditure will meet with strong opposition. Repeated surveys show that most Danes prefer their system to those based on private health insurance. In the early 1980s, Denmark had the highest incidence of AIDS in Europe, but after peaking in 1993, it has dropped markedly, due to the free availability of drug therapy.

D

ENVIRONMENT

Sustainability rank: 10th

32%

10.9 tonnes per capita

ENVIRONMENTAL TREATIES

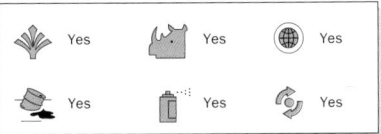

Yes Yes Yes

Yes Yes Yes

Popular and governmental concern for the environment has resulted in some of the strictest regulations in Europe, including those aimed at reducing ozone-destroying emissions and water pollution. Fears that they may be eroded have led to ambivalence toward the EU. In 1993, Denmark persuaded the EU to locate its new Environmental Agency in Copenhagen. It hopes to extend its own standards to the rest of Europe and met its 2000 target of recycling 54% of all waste a year early.

CRIME

Death penalty not used

3421 prisoners

Down 6% 1996–1998

CRIME RATES

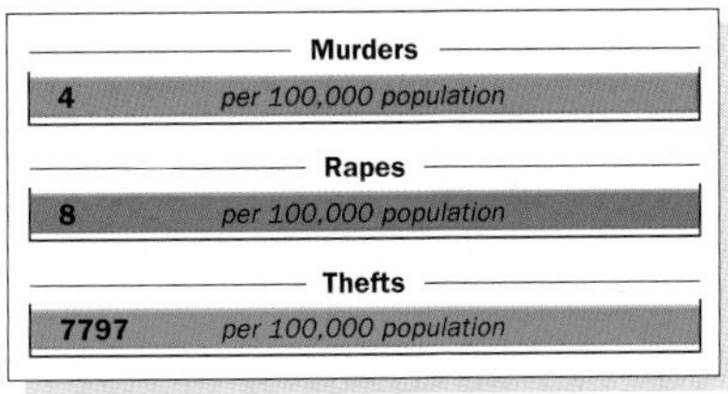
Murders
4 per 100,000 population
Rapes
8 per 100,000 population
Thefts
7797 per 100,000 population

The main concern is that Mafia-style organized crime could be imported from eastern Europe. Computer hacking, drug trafficking, and rival motor cycle gangs are problems.

SPENDING

GDP/cap. increase

CONSUMPTION AND SPENDING

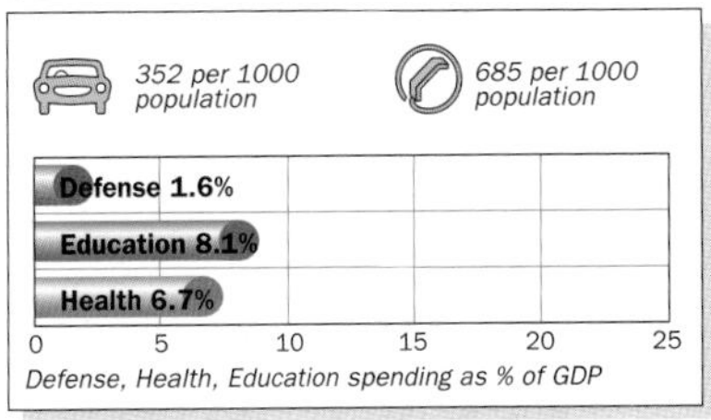
352 per 1000 population
685 per 1000 population
Defense 1.6%
Education 8.1%
Health 6.7%
0
5
10
15
20
25
Defense, Health, Education spending as % of GDP

Most Danes are comfortably off. Income distribution is more even than in many Western countries and social mobility is high. Free higher education means that access to the professions is more a question of ability than wealth or connections. Denmark is one of the world's most egalitarian societies. The generous social security system means that Danes suffer little from social deprivation. Rasmussen's government has created more kindergarten places and increased time off for those with young children. Refugees and recent immigrants tend to be the most disadvantaged members of Danish society.

MEDIA

TV ownership high

Daily newspaper circulation 311 per 1000 people

PUBLISHING AND BROADCAST MEDIA

There are 36 daily newspapers, including *BT, Politiken, Ekstra Bladet,* and *Berlingske Tidende*

52 services: 1 state-owned, 1 publicly financed, and 50 independent

1 state-owned service, 250 independent local services

The media has a long history of political independence, and objectivity is prized. Most of the press has a political viewpoint, but expression of this is largely limited to editorials. The tone of both TV and the press is serious; Denmark does not have a scandal-mongering tabloid press as found in the USA, the UK, and Germany. Invasion of privacy laws are strict.

EDUCATION

School leaving age: 16

99%

174,975 students

THE EDUCATION SYSTEM

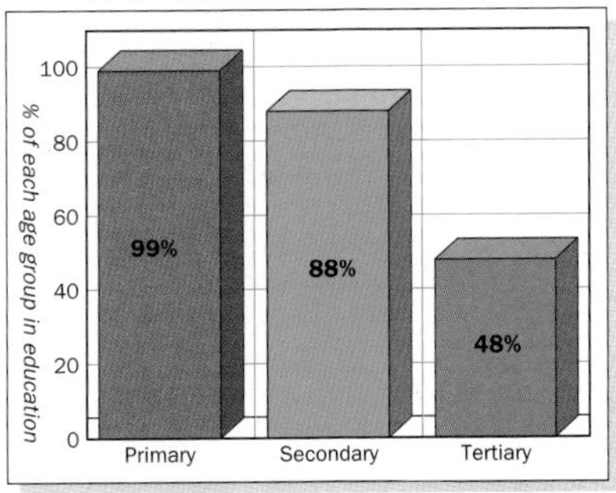
100
80
60
40
20
0
% of each age group in education
99%
88%
48%
Primary
Secondary
Tertiary

The educational level is generally high, in part reflecting the need for a skilled workforce. Formal schooling begins at age seven and is mandatory for nine years. However, most children receive preschool education, and over 90% of pupils go on at the age of 16 to further academic or vocational training. Traditional folk high schools offer a wide range of further education options, but no professional qualifications.

WORLD RANKING

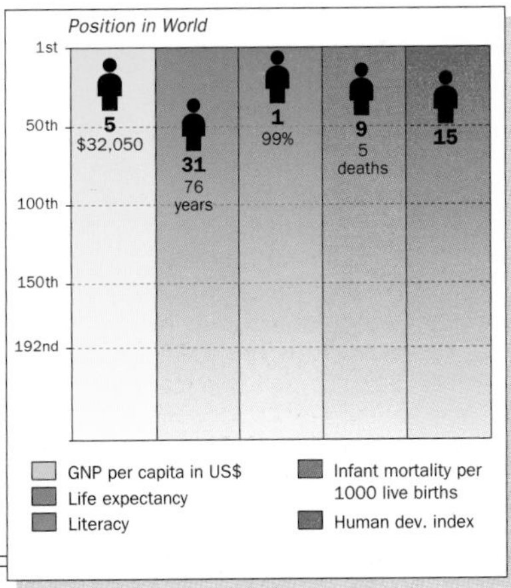
Position in World
1st
50th
100th
150th
192nd
5
$32,050
31
76 years
1
99%
9
5 deaths
15
GNP per capita in US$
Life expectancy
Literacy
Infant mortality per 1000 live births
Human dev. index

DJIBOUTI

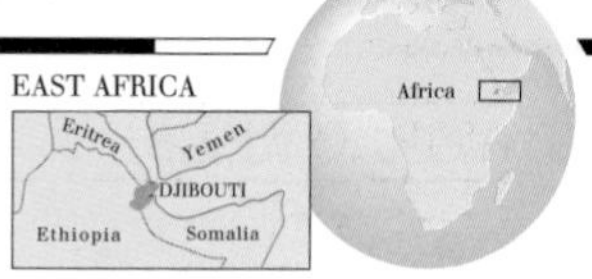
EAST AFRICA
Africa
Eritrea
Yemen
DJIBOUTI
Ethiopia
Somalia

OFFICIAL NAME: Republic of Djibouti **CAPITAL:** Djibouti
POPULATION: 638,000 **CURRENCY:** Djibouti franc **OFFICIAL LANGUAGES:** Arabic and French

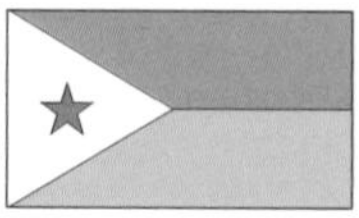

1977 | 1977 | June 27 | DJI | +3 | +253 | .dj

A CITY STATE WITH a desert hinterland, Djibouti lies in northeast Africa on the strait linking the Red Sea and the Indian Ocean. Known from 1967 as the French Territory of the Afars and Issas, Djibouti became independent in 1977. Its economy relies on the main port, the railroad to Addis Ababa, and French aid. A guerrilla war which erupted in 1991 as a result of tension between the Issas in the south and the Afars in the north has largely been resolved.

CLIMATE

Hot desert

WEATHER CHART

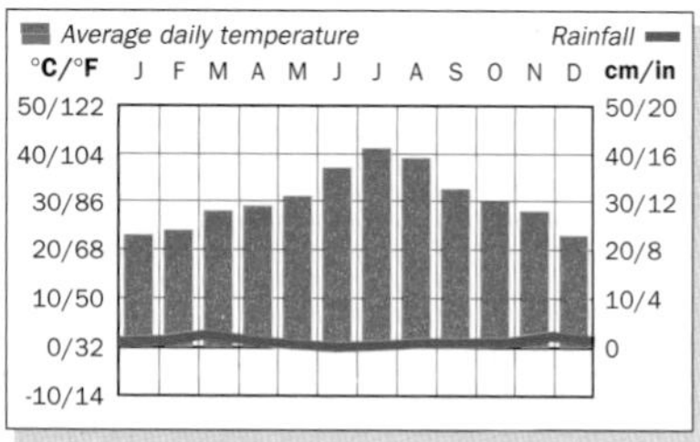
Average daily temperature
Rainfall
°C/°F J F M A M J J A S O N D cm/in
50/122 40/104 30/86 20/68 10/50 0/32 -10/14
50/20 40/16 30/12 20/8 10/4 0

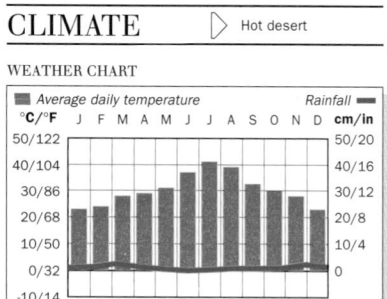

Despite extremely low rainfall, the monsoon season is characterized by very humid conditions. Even locals find the heat in June–August hard to bear.

TRANSPORTATION

Drive on right

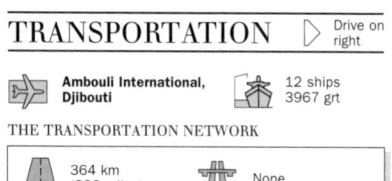

Ambouli International, Djibouti

12 ships 3967 grt

THE TRANSPORTATION NETWORK

364 km (226 miles)

None

121 km (75 miles)

None

Djibouti's port, created by the French in the 19th century and now a modern container facility, is its key asset. Landlocked Ethiopia's vital link to the sea is the Addis Ababa–Djibouti railroad.

TOURISM

Visitors : Population 1:30

21,000 visitors

Little change 1995–1998

MAIN TOURIST ARRIVALS

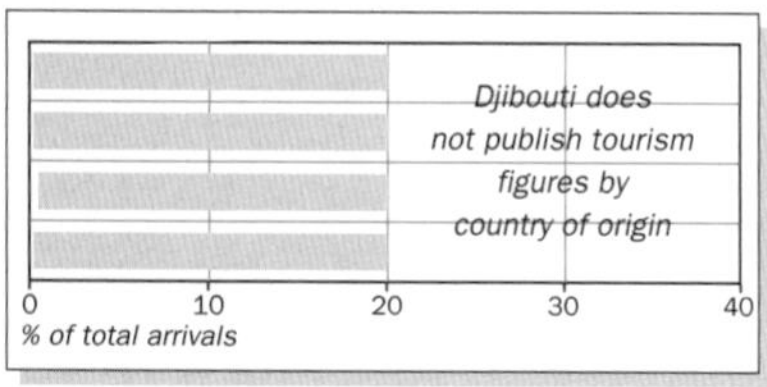
Djibouti does not publish tourism figures by country of origin
0 10 20 30 40
% of total arrivals

Most visitors are passing through on their way to Ethiopia, or coming to see relatives working in Djibouti port.

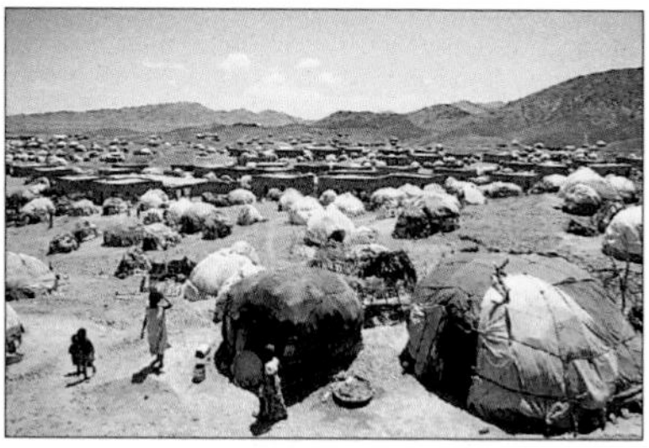

Nomadic Djiboutian village, close to Balho near the Ethiopian border.

PEOPLE

Pop. density low

Somali, Afar, French, Arabic

28/km² (71/mi²)

THE URBAN/RURAL POPULATION SPLIT

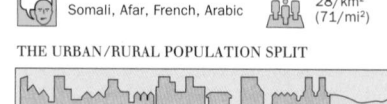

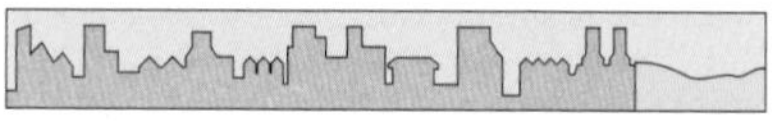
83%
17%

ETHNIC MAKEUP

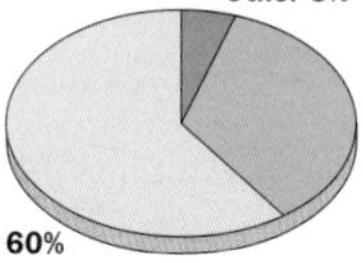
Other 5%
Afar 35%
Issa 60%

The main ethnic groups are the Afars and Issas; tension between these groups developed into a guerrilla war in 1991. The population was swelled in 1992 by 20,000 Somali refugees. The rural people are mostly nomadic.

POLITICS

Multiparty elections

1997/2002

President Ismael Omar Guelleh

AT THE LAST ELECTION

National Assembly 65 seats

100% RPP–FRUD

RPP–FRUD = Alliance of the Popular Rally for Progress (RPP) and the Front for the Restoration of Unity and Democracy (FRUD)

President Hassan Gouled Aptidon, an Issa, backed by France, dominated politics from independence in 1977 until his retirement in 1999. Afar fears of Issa domination erupted in 1991, when the Afar guerrilla group FRUD took control of much of the country. The French intervened militarily to keep Gouled in power, but forced him to hold elections in 1992, won by the RPP. The FRUD became a legal political party following a 1996 peace agreement. An alliance of the RPP and FRUD won the elections in 1997. Presidential elections in April 1999 were won by Ismael Omar Guelleh, a former close aide of Gouled, amid opposition claims of electoral fraud.

DJIBOUTI

Total Land Area : 23 180 sq. km (8950 sq. miles)

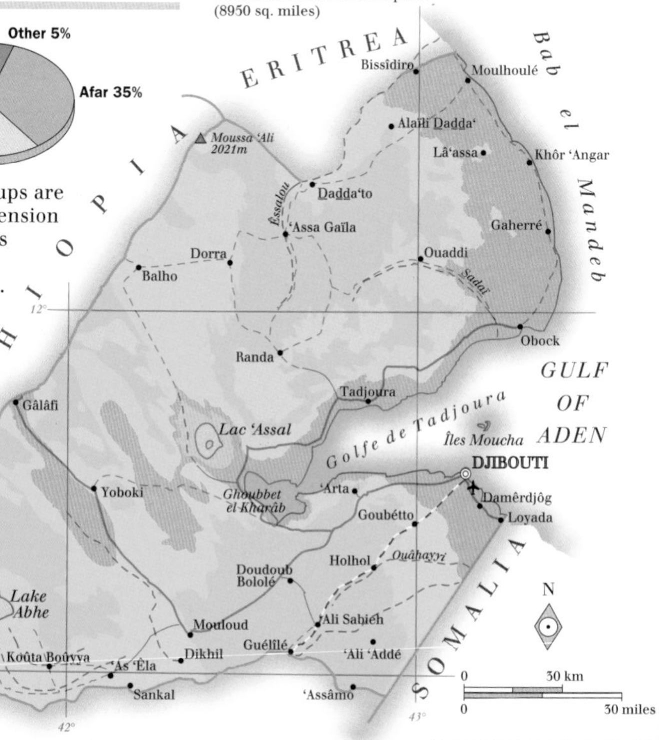
ERITREA
ETHIOPIA
SOMALIA
Bab el Mandeb
GULF OF ADEN
Golfe de Tadjoura
Bissîdiro
Moulhoulé
Alaïli Dadda'
Lâ'assa
Khôr 'Angar
Moussa 'Ali 2021m
Dadda'to
'Assa Gaïla
Gaherré
Ouaddi
Dorra
Balho
Obock
Randa
Tadjoura
Gâlâfi
Lac 'Assal
Îles Moucha
DJIBOUTI
Ghoubbet el Kharâb
'Arta
Yoboki
Damêrdjôg
Loyada
Goubétto
Holhol
Doudoub Bololé
Lake Abhe
Mouloud
'Ali Sabîeh
Dikhil
Guélilé
'Ali 'Addé
Koûta Boûyya
As 'Ela
Sankal
'Assâmo
N
0 30 km
0 30 miles

POPULATION
- over 100 000
- under 10 000

LAND HEIGHT
- 1000m/3281ft
- 500m/1640ft
- 200m/656ft
- Sea Level
- -200m/656ft

WORLD AFFAIRS

Joined UN in 1977

AL | OIF | IGAD | OAU | OIC

France, with a key military presence, is pressing for greater democratization. Djibouti, Ethiopia, and Eritrea all seek to contain Afar secessionism. In 2000 the southern town of Arta hosted the Somali reconciliation conference.

AID

Recipient

$75m (receipts) | Down 7% in 1999

France is the major donor, effectively financing one-third of government expenditure. Djibouti has also received aid from Saudi Arabia and Kuwait.

DEFENSE

No compulsory military service

$22m | No change in 1999

The size of the armed forces is a state secret, but is estimated at 9600 personnel; former FRUD guerrillas were integrated into the army. There is a 3200-strong French garrison.

ECONOMICS

Inflation 4.4% p.a. (1990–1998)

$511m | 172.25–174.80 Djibouti francs

SCORE CARD

- ❑ WORLD GNP RANKING........................170th
- ❑ GNP PER CAPITA $790
- ❑ BALANCE OF PAYMENTS......................$-23m
- ❑ INFLATION 3%
- ❑ UNEMPLOYMENT.................................50%

STRENGTHS

Free port in key Red Sea location; large profits from 1991 Gulf War and from 1992 US and UN intervention in Somalia. Continuing development of Djibouti and Tadjoura port facilities.

WEAKNESSES

Dependence on French aid and garrison. Civil war has delayed planned Saudi investment. Other ports on Red Sea now providing stiff competition.

EXPORTS

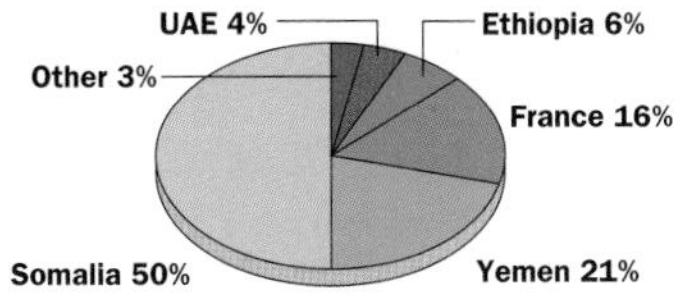
UAE 4%
Ethiopia 6%
Other 3%
France 16%
Somalia 50%
Yemen 21%

IMPORTS

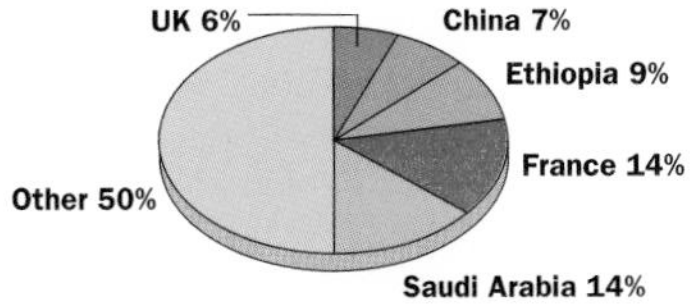
UK 6%
China 7%
Ethiopia 9%
France 14%
Other 50%
Saudi Arabia 14%

RESOURCES

Electric power 85,000 kw

340 tonnes | Not an oil producer

513,000 goats, 465,000 sheep, 269,000 cattle | Gypsum, mica, amethyst, sulfur, natural gas

The few mineral resources are scarcely exploited. Geothermal energy is being developed and natural gas has recently been found. The guerrilla war delayed attempts to develop underground water supplies for agriculture.

ENVIRONMENT

Not available

0.4% | 0.6 tonnes per capita

The concentration of business around Djibouti port means that inland desert areas are not threatened. Ecological issues are not a national concern.

MEDIA

TV ownership low

There are no daily newspapers

PUBLISHING AND BROADCAST MEDIA

There are no daily newspapers. The weekly *La Nation de Djibouti* is published by the government

1 state-controlled service | 1 state-controlled service

Djibouti is a member of the Arab Satellite Communications Organization. The media are largely state-controlled, but there is one opposition newspaper.

CRIME

Death penalty not used

Djibouti does not publish prison figures | Up 74% 1996–1998

The government has accused FRUD of atrocities, but the state's own human rights record has been criticized by Amnesty International. While drug smuggling and prostitution are rife, petty crime, rather than violence, is the norm.

EDUCATION

School leaving age: 12

65% | 161 students

Schooling is mostly in French, although there has been a growing emphasis on Islamic teaching, particularly as Saudi Arabia has declared an interest in providing aid for education. Djibouti has no university.

HEALTH

Welfare state health benefits

1 per 5000 people | Respiratory and heart diseases

AIDS is a growing problem in Djibouti port, with its large prostitute population. UN estimates for 1999 suggested that there were some 37,000 AIDS and HIV sufferers. Small French-financed hospitals cater for the urban elite.

CHRONOLOGY

The French set up a coaling station at Djibouti in the 1880s, to balance the British presence in Aden.

- ❑ **1917** Railroad from Addis Ababa reaches Djibouti port.
- ❑ **1977** Independence.
- ❑ **1981–1992** One-party state.
- ❑ **1989** Eruption of violence between Afars and Issas.
- ❑ **1991** FRUD launches armed insurrection.
- ❑ **1994** Peace agreement with FRUD.
- ❑ **1999** Ismael Omar Guelleh becomes president.
- ❑ **2000** Coup attempt by police officers fails.

SPENDING

GDP/cap. decrease

CONSUMPTION AND SPENDING

15 per 1000 population | *14 per 1000 population*

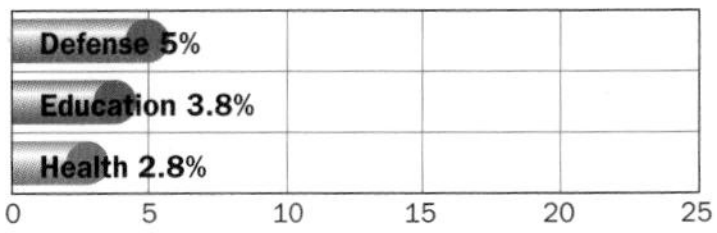
Defense 5%
Education 3.8%
Health 2.8%
0
5
10
15
20
25

Defense, Health, Education spending as % of GDP

As happens in many African states, the wealth in Djibouti tends to be concentrated among those closest to government. Djiboutians working in the ports also do well, although much port labor is expatriate. The guerrilla war has had little effect on port life, since it is almost completely isolated from the rest of the country. The nomads of the interior are the poorest group.

Trade in the mild narcotic *qat*, or "green gold," which is grown in Ethiopia and shipped through Djibouti, is highly lucrative, to the extent that the state is now taking its share of the profits. In Djibouti, *qat* chewing is an age-old social ritual.

WORLD RANKING

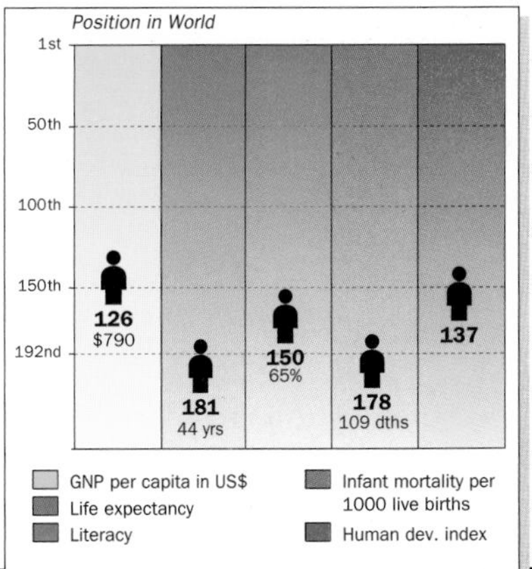
Position in World
1st
50th
100th
150th
192nd
126
$790
181
44 yrs
150
65%
178
109 dths
137
GNP per capita in US$
Life expectancy
Literacy
Infant mortality per 1000 live births
Human dev. index

D

DOMINICA

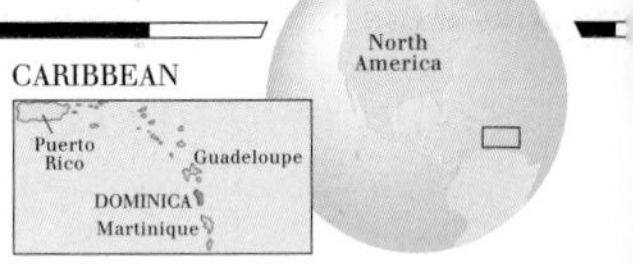
CARIBBEAN
North America
Puerto Rico
Guadeloupe
DOMINICA
Martinique

OFFICIAL NAME: Commonwealth of Dominica **CAPITAL:** Roseau
POPULATION: 73,000 **CURRENCY:** Eastern Caribbean dollar **OFFICIAL LANGUAGE:** English

1978 | 1978 | Nov 3 | WD | -4 | +1767 | .dm

D

DOMINICA IS RENOWNED as the Caribbean island that resisted European colonization until the 18th century, when it was controlled first by the French then, from 1759, by the British. Known as the "Nature Island" due to its spectacular, lush, and abundant flora and fauna, which are protected by extensive national parks, Dominica is the most mountainous of the Lesser Antilles. Located between Guadeloupe and Martinique in the West Indian Windward Islands group, its volcanic origin has given it very fertile soils and the second-largest boiling lake in the world.

CLIMATE

Tropical oceanic

WEATHER CHART

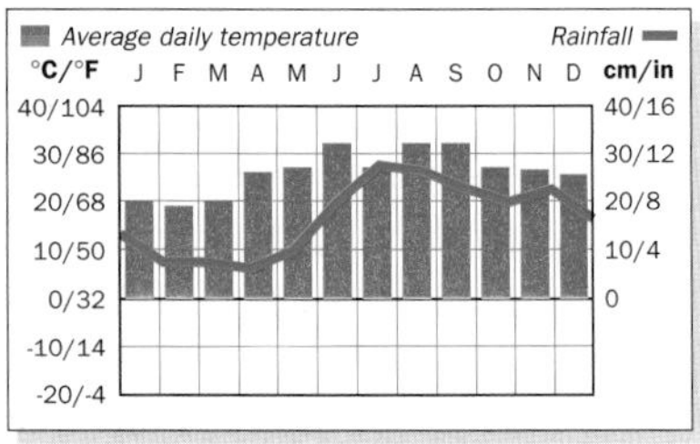
Average daily temperature
Rainfall
°C/°F
J F M A M J J A S O N D
cm/in
40/104
30/86
20/68
10/50
0/32
-10/14
-20/-4
40/16
30/12
20/8
10/4
0

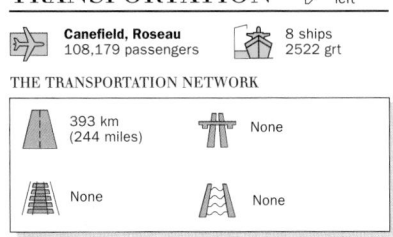

Like the other Windward Islands in the Eastern Caribbean, Dominica is subject to constant trade winds. The rainy season is in the summer, and tropical depressions and hurricanes are likely between June and November. Short, thundery showers in the late afternoon and evening are common throughout the year.

TRANSPORTATION

Drive on left

Canefield, Roseau 108,179 passengers

8 ships 2522 grt

THE TRANSPORTATION NETWORK

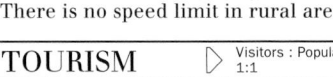

393 km (244 miles)

None

None

None

Both airports take only small propeller aircraft. Roads are well maintained. There is no speed limit in rural areas.

TOURISM

Visitors : Population 1:1

74,000 visitors

Up 12% in 1999

MAIN TOURIST ARRIVALS

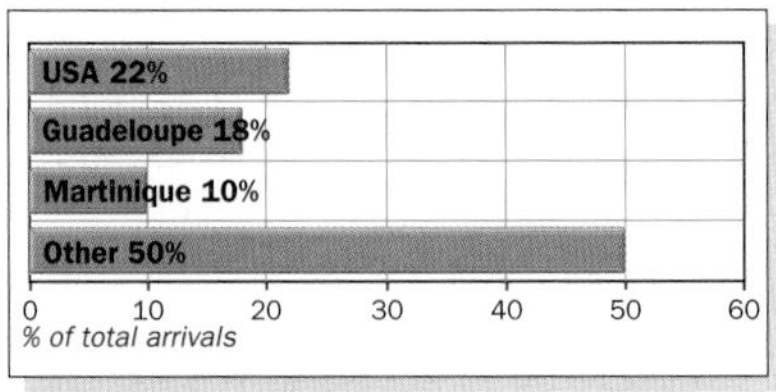
USA 22%
Guadeloupe 18%
Martinique 10%
Other 50%
0
10
20
30
40
50
60
% of total arrivals

The national parks, with their rare indigenous birds, hot springs, and sulfur pools, are a major attraction for tourists. However, the lack of an airport able to take commercial jetliners (visitors take connecting flights from Barbados or Antigua) has made Dominica less accessible to mass-market tourism than its Caribbean neighbors.

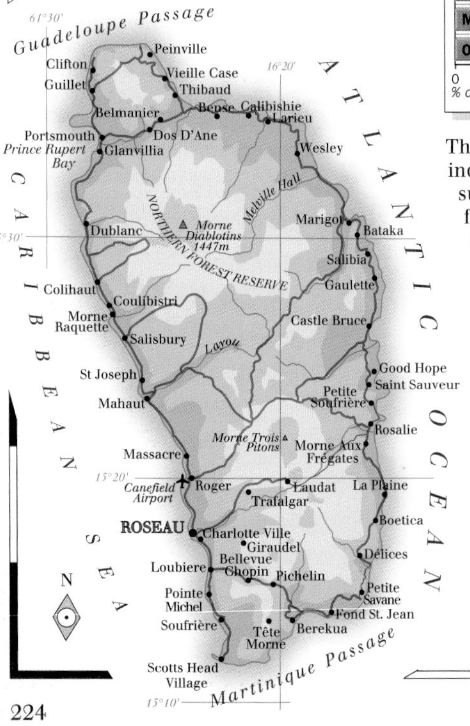
Guadeloupe Passage
Peinville
Clifton
Guillet
Vieille Case
Thibaud
Belmanier
Bense
Calibishie
Larieu
Portsmouth
Prince Rupert Bay
Dos D'Ane
Glanvillia
Wesley
Melville Hall
NORTHERN FOREST RESERVE
Morne Diablotins 1447m
Marigot
Bataka
Dublanc
Salibia
Gaulette
Colihaut
Coulibistri
Morne Raquette
Castle Bruce
Salisbury
Layou
Good Hope
Saint Sauveur
St Joseph
Mahaut
Petite Soufrière
Morne Trois Pitons
Morne Aux Frégates
Rosalie
Massacre
Canefield Airport
Roger
Laudat
La Plaine
Trafalgar
ROSEAU
Charlotte Ville
Giraudel
Boetica
Bellevue Chopin
Délices
Loubiere
Pichelin
Pointe Michel
Petite Savane
Fond St. Jean
Soufrière
Tête Morne
Berekua
Scotts Head Village
Martinique Passage
ATLANTIC OCEAN
CARIBBEAN SEA
N

DOMINICA

Total Land Area : 750 sq. km (290 sq. miles)

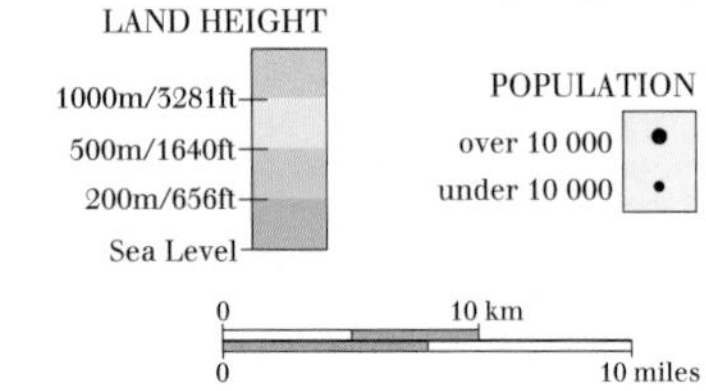
LAND HEIGHT
1000m/3281ft
500m/1640ft
200m/656ft
Sea Level
POPULATION
over 10 000
under 10 000
0
10 km
0
10 miles

PEOPLE

Pop. density medium

French Creole, English

97/km² (252/mi²)

THE URBAN/RURAL POPULATION SPLIT

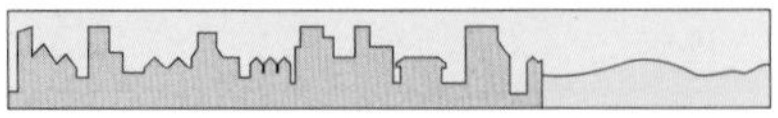
70%
30%

RELIGIOUS PERSUASION

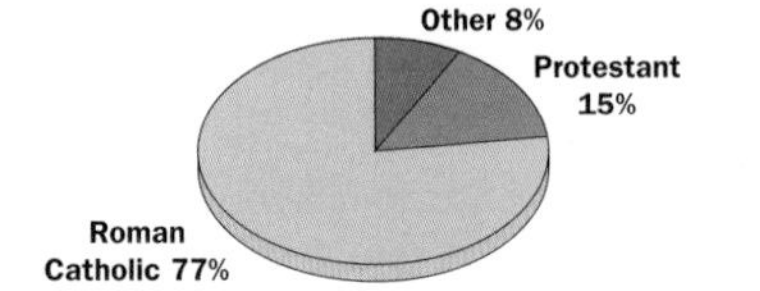
Other 8%
Protestant 15%
Roman Catholic 77%

The majority of Dominicans are descendants of Africans brought over to work the banana plantations. The Carib Territory on the northeast of the island forms the only surviving Carib population in the Caribbean.

POLITICS

Multiparty elections

2000/2005

President Vernon Shaw

AT THE LAST ELECTION

House of Assembly 30 seats

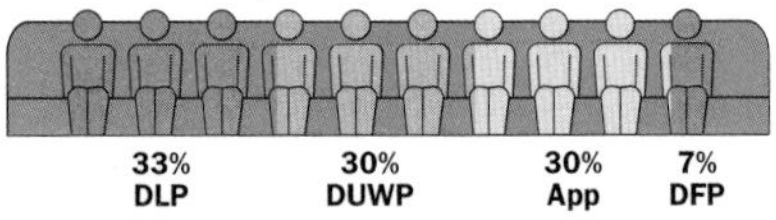
33% DLP
30% DUWP
30% App
7% DFP

DLP = Dominica Labour Party **DUWP** = Dominica United Workers' Party **App** = Appointed **DFP** = Dominica Freedom Party

9 senators are appointed to the House of Assembly by the head of state.

Politicians tend to come from the professional classes – usually young lawyers and doctors. Occasionally the larger farmers, who provide most party funding, stand for elections. The center-left DUWP narrowly won the 1995 elections, ending 15 consecutive years of rule by the right-wing DFP. A further swing to the left produced a DLP victory in January 2000 and its leader Rosie Douglas became prime minister. On his sudden death in October Pierre Charles replaced him. The main political issue is how to cope with the ending of preferential banana exports to the EU.

WORLD AFFAIRS

Joined UN in 1978

ACS | Comm | Caricom | OAS | OECS

Dominica has close links with France and the USA. Preferential access to the EU for Caribbean bananas, crucial for Dominica's economy, was contested by the USA, which obtained a WTO ruling in its favor in 1999.

Inshore fishing boats, which mostly supply the domestic market, on a typical Dominican beach.

AID

Recipient

US$10m (receipts) | Down 47% in 1999

The European Development Fund allocated money in 1998 for sustainable tourism projects; Japan and Taiwan gave aid for firefighting and education.

DEFENSE

No compulsory military service

Defense forces were officially disbanded in 1981 | Not applicable

Dominica has no armed forces, but it does participate in the US-sponsored Regional Security System.

ECONOMICS

Inflation 3.2% p.a. (1990–1999)

US$238m | 2.7 Eastern Caribbean dollars

SCORE CARD

❏ World GNP Ranking	178th
❏ GNP per Capita	US$3260
❏ Balance of Payments	US$–18m
❏ Inflation	1.2%
❏ Unemployment	20%

Strengths

Banana exports; though this sector has declined since the loss of EU preferential access. Offshore business center and "economic citizenship" scheme. Growing services sector.

Weaknesses

Dependence on US and EU markets for its banana crop, threatened by WTO ruling. Low productivity in public sector. Poor infrastructure.

EXPORTS

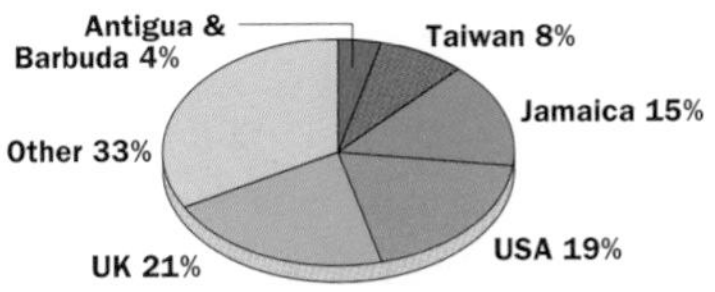
Antigua & Barbuda 4%
Taiwan 8%
Jamaica 15%
Other 33%
USA 19%
UK 21%

IMPORTS

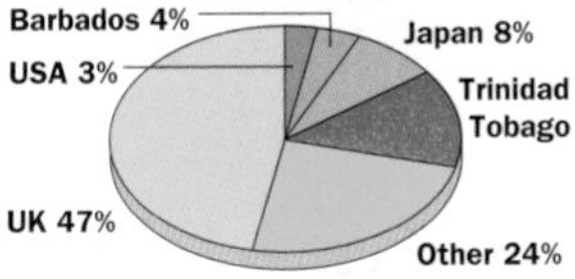
Barbados 4%
Japan 8%
USA 3%
Trinidad & Tobago 14%
UK 47%
Other 24%

RESOURCES

Electric power 8000 kw

855 tonnes | Not an oil producer

13,400 cattle, 9700 goats, 7600 sheep, 190,000 chickens | None

Dominica has no natural resources. A hydroelectric power plant in the Morne Trois Pitons national park provides most of the island's power.

ENVIRONMENT

Not available

9% | 1.1 tonnes per capita

Increased agriculture and timber harvesting is threatening Dominica's rainforest; already there is more land under cultivation than planned by the government. The current promotion of the rainforest as a tourist attraction poses a threat, as does a possible expansion in HEP generators. Two species of parrot – the imperial, or sisserou, and the red-necked – are threatened, despite conservation orders. Endangered hawksbill turtles, living on coral reefs off the island, are traditionally hunted.

MEDIA

TV ownership medium

There are no daily newspapers

PUBLISHING AND BROADCAST MEDIA

There are no daily newspapers. The dominant newspaper is the weekly *Chronicle*, which takes a center-left editorial stance

No TV service | 4 services: 1 state-owned, 3 independent

Local franchises, offering cable TV with selected US networks, serve one-third of the island. Broadcasts from other Caribbean states can also be received. There are four newspapers.

CRIME

Death penalty used

Dominica does not publish prison figures | Down 7% 1996–1998

Dominica has a lower crime rate than most of its Caribbean neighbors. Burglary and armed robbery are the major concerns; murders are rare. Justice is based on British common law and administered by the Eastern Caribbean Supreme Court, which is based on the island of St. Lucia.

EDUCATION

School leaving age: 16

94% | 484 students

Dominican education is based on the British model, and retains the selective 11-plus exam for entrance into high school. Students go on to the University of the West Indies or, increasingly, to colleges in the USA and the UK.

CHRONOLOGY

Colonized first by the French, Dominica came under British control in 1759.

- ❏ **1975** Morne Trois Pitons national park established.
- ❏ **1978** Independence from UK. Patrick John first prime minister.
- ❏ **1980** Eugenia Charles, the Caribbean's first woman prime minister, elected.
- ❏ **1981** Two coup attempts, backed by Patrick John, foiled.
- ❏ **1995** Opposition DUWP defeats DFP. Dame Eugenia Charles retires after 27 years in politics.
- ❏ **2000** DLP wins elections.

D

HEALTH

Welfare state health benefits

1 per 2174 people | Heart and respiratory diseases, cancers

There are numerous health centers. Difficult communications hamper emergency hospital access for people living in the interior.

SPENDING

GDP/cap. increase

CONSUMPTION AND SPENDING

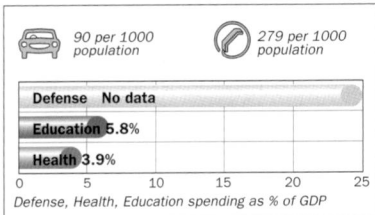

90 per 1000 population | *279 per 1000 population*

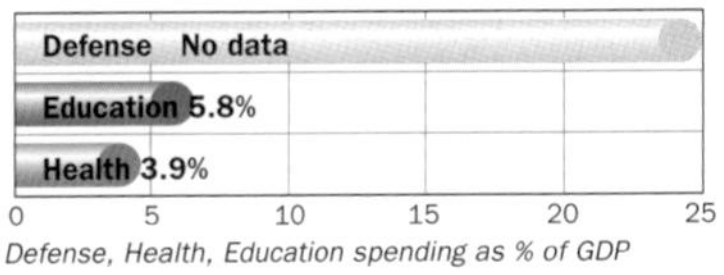
Defense No data
Education 5.8%
Health 3.9%
0 5 10 15 20 25
Defense, Health, Education spending as % of GDP

Wealth disparities are not as marked in Dominica as they are on the larger Caribbean islands, but the alleviation of poverty has become a major plank of government policy. Measures taken include increased benefits and help for the country's pensioners.

WORLD RANKING

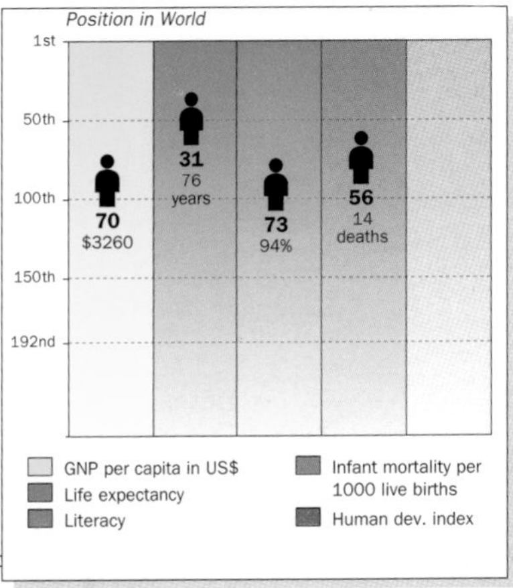
Position in World
1st
50th
100th
150th
192nd
70
$3260
31
76 years
73
94%
56
14 deaths
GNP per capita in US$
Life expectancy
Literacy
Infant mortality per 1000 live births
Human dev. index

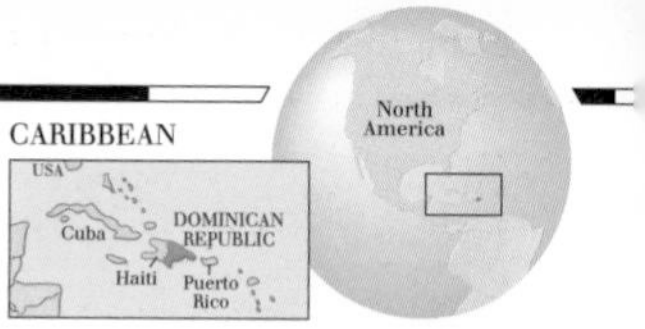
CARIBBEAN
USA
Cuba
DOMINICAN REPUBLIC
Haiti
Puerto Rico
North America

DOMINICAN REPUBLIC

OFFICIAL NAME: Dominican Republic **CAPITAL:** Santo Domingo
POPULATION: 8.5 million **CURRENCY:** Dominican Republic peso **OFFICIAL LANGUAGE:** Spanish

1865 | 1865 | Feb 27 | DOM | -4 | +1809 | .do

D

THE LARGEST TOURIST destination in the Caribbean, the Dominican Republic lies 970 km (600 miles) southeast of Florida. Once ruled by Spain, it occupies the eastern two-thirds of the island of Hispaniola and boasts both the highest point (Pico Duarte, 3175 m – 10,420 feet) and the lowest point (Lake Enriquillo, 44 m – 144 feet – below sea level) in the West Indies. Spanish-speaking, it seeks closer ties with the anglophone Caribbean.

View south from Pico Duarte along the fertile banks of the Río Yaque del Norte.

CLIMATE

Tropical equatorial/ oceanic

WEATHER CHART

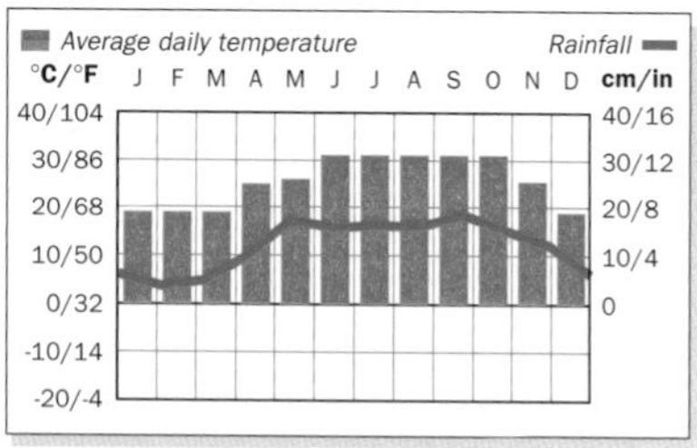
Average daily temperature
Rainfall
°C/°F
J F M A M J J A S O N D
cm/in
40/104
30/86
20/68
10/50
0/32
-10/14
-20/-4
40/16
30/12
20/8
10/4
0

The trade winds blow all year round, providing relief from the tropical heat and humidity. The hurricane season runs from June until November.

TRANSPORTATION

Drive on right

Aeropuerto International de las Américas, Santo Domingo 2.72m passengers

20 ships 9000 grt

THE TRANSPORTATION NETWORK

6224 km (3867 miles)

None

1600 km (994 miles)

None

Urban and rural transportation is poor; railroads are mainly for transporting sugar cane and ores. An international consortium in 1999 won a 30-year concession to operate four airports.

TOURISM

Visitors : Population 1:2.9

3m visitors

Up 12% in 2000

MAIN TOURIST ARRIVALS

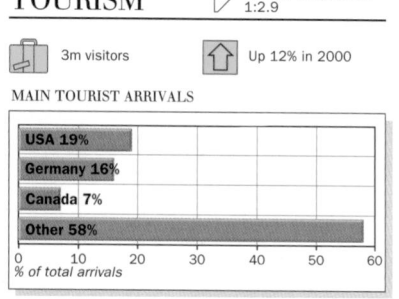

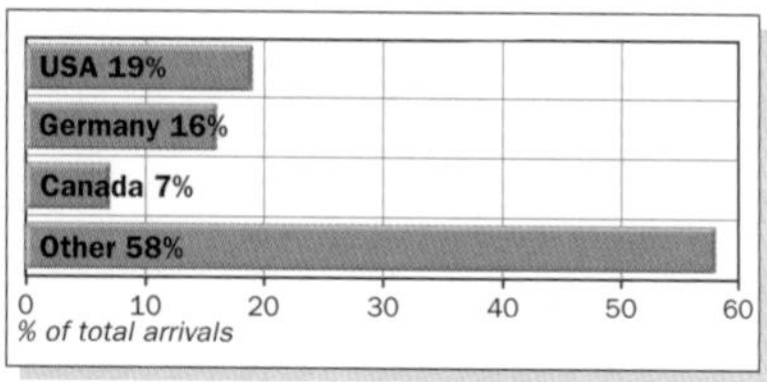
USA 19%
Germany 16%
Canada 7%
Other 58%
0
10
20
30
40
50
60
% of total arrivals

Ample accommodation and excellent beaches attract many tourists each year, mainly from Europe and North America.

PEOPLE

Pop. density medium

Spanish, French Creole

176/km² (455/mi²)

THE URBAN/RURAL POPULATION SPLIT

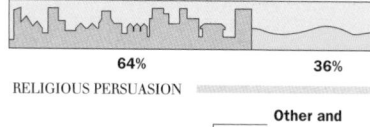

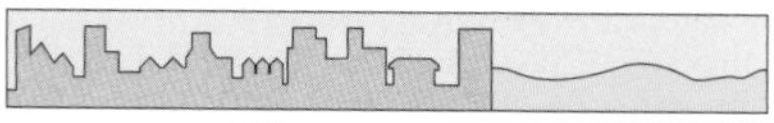
64%
36%

RELIGIOUS PERSUASION

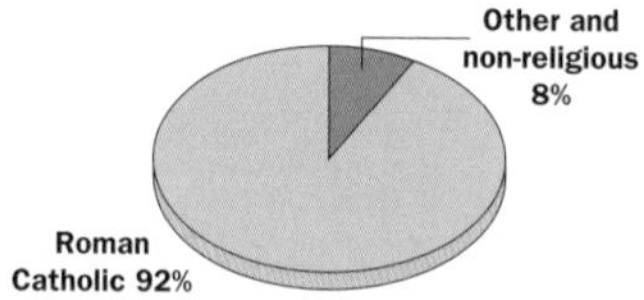
Other and non-religious 8%
Roman Catholic 92%

The white population, primarily the descendants of Spanish settlers, still owns most of the land. The mixed race majority – about 73% – controls much of the republic's commerce, and forms the bulk of the professional middle classes. Blacks, the descendants of Africans, are mainly small-scale farmers and often the victims of latent racism, especially in business. Women in the black community work the farms; in the white and mixed race communities women are starting to appear in the professions.

POLITICS

Multiparty elections

L. House 1998/2002
U. House 1998/2002

President Hipolito Mejia

AT THE LAST ELECTION

Chamber of Deputies 149 seats

56% PRD
34% PLD
10% PRSC

PRD = Dominican Revolutionary Party **PLD** = Dominican Liberation Party **PRSC** = Christian Social Reform Party

Senate 30 seats

80% PRD
13% PLD
7% PRSC

Joaquín Balaguer of the PRSC, a political patriarch since the 1960s and representative of the white elite and the military, achieved a bogus victory in a 1994 poll. He was forced to agree to fresh elections in 1996 which were narrowly won by Leonel Fernández of the more moderate PLD. The PRSC and PLD later joined forces against the opposition center-left PRD, which won control of the Congress in 1998. The PRD called for a fair presidential election in 2000; it was won by the PRD candidate, Hipolito Mejia.

DOMINICAN REPUBLIC

Total Land Area : 48 380 sq. km (18 679 sq. miles)

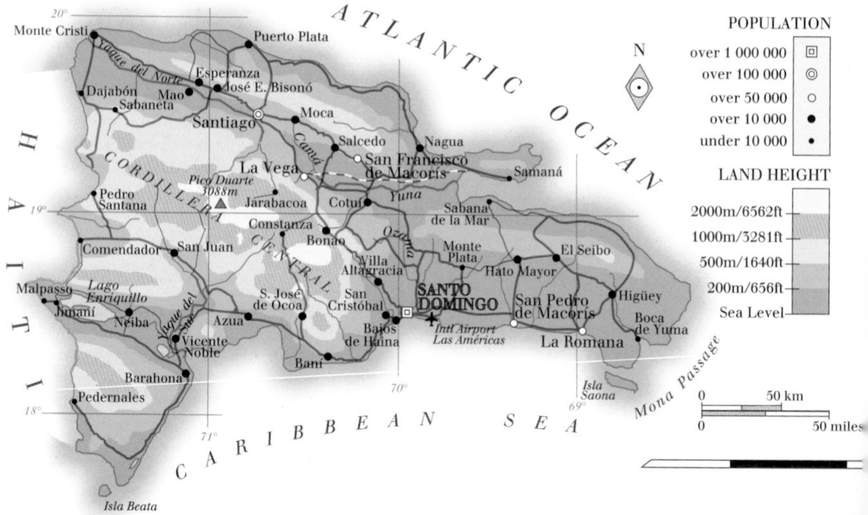
ATLANTIC OCEAN
CARIBBEAN SEA
HAITI
Monte Cristi
Puerto Plata
Esperanza
José E. Bisonó
Dajabón
Mao
Sabaneta
Santiago
Moca
Salcedo
Nagua
San Francisco de Macorís
Samaná
La Vega
Pico Duarte 3088m
Jarabacoa
Cotuí
Yuna
Sabana de la Mar
Pedro Santana
Constanza
Bonao
Comendador
San Juan
Monte Plata
Hato Mayor
El Seibo
Villa Altagracia
Malpasso
Lago Enriquillo
Jimaní
Neiba
S. José de Ocoa
San Cristóbal
SANTO DOMINGO
Intl Airport Las Américas
San Pedro de Macorís
Higüey
Boca de Yuma
La Romana
Azua
Vicente Noble
Bajos de Haina
Baní
Barahona
Pedernales
Isla Saona
Mona Passage
Isla Beata
Yaque del Norte
Yaque del Sur
CORDILLERA CENTRAL
Camú
Ozama
N
POPULATION
over 1 000 000
over 100 000
over 50 000
over 10 000
under 10 000
LAND HEIGHT
2000m/6562ft
1000m/3281ft
500m/1640ft
200m/656ft
Sea Level
0 50 km
0 50 miles

WORLD AFFAIRS

Joined UN in 1945

ACS | Geplac | IBRD | OAS | SELA

Relations with Haiti, with which it shares the island of Hispaniola, are important. The Dominican Republic favors a "strategic alliance" between the Caribbean and Central America.

AID

Recipient

$195m (receipts) | Up 63% in 1999

Multilateral and bilateral aid of some $235 million was granted in 1998 to repair severe hurricane damage.

DEFENSE

No compulsory military service

$114m | Down 1% in 1999

The military has economic and political interests, but no longer holds the defense portfolio. It focuses on illegal immigration from Haiti. The main arms supplier is the USA.

ECONOMICS

Inflation 9.9% p.a. (1990–1999)

$16.1bn | 15.75–16.12 Dominican Republic pesos

SCORE CARD

❑ WORLD GNP RANKING	74th
❑ GNP PER CAPITA	$1920
❑ BALANCE OF PAYMENTS	$-336m
❑ INFLATION	6.5%
❑ UNEMPLOYMENT	14%

STRENGTHS

Sustained tourism growth. Mining – mainly of nickel and gold – and sugar are major sectors. Hand-made cigars, which are the biggest sellers in USA. Large hidden economy based on transshipment of narcotics to USA.

WEAKNESSES

Major sectors severely affected by fluctuating world prices and cutbacks in US import quotas. Poor creditworthiness. Failure to diversify. Stalled privatizations.

EXPORTS

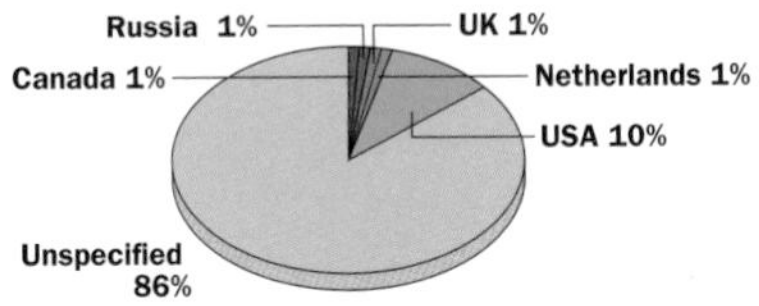
Russia 1%
UK 1%
Canada 1%
Netherlands 1%
USA 10%
Unspecified 86%

IMPORTS

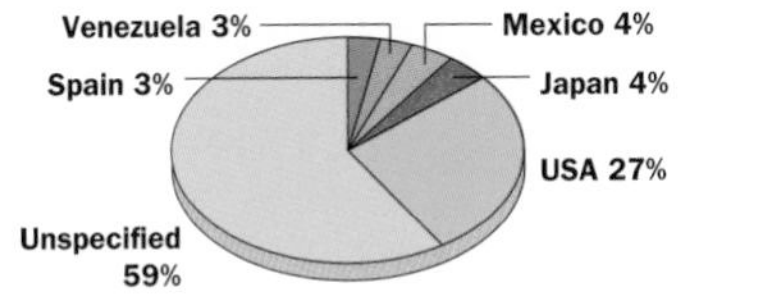
Venezuela 3%
Mexico 4%
Spain 3%
Japan 4%
USA 27%
Unspecified 59%

RESOURCES

Electric power 1.5m kw

15,276 tonnes | Not an oil producer

1.9m cattle, 900,000 pigs, 46m chickens | Ferro-nickel, bauxite, copper, gold, silver

Hydroelectric generators are the only domestic source of power, but power cuts are frequent. The Dominican Republic is a net energy importer. Attempts at oil prospecting have not been successful. Under the terms of the San José Agreement, oil is imported from Mexico and Venezuela on preferential terms. The Dominican Republic's quota from Venezuela was increased under the 2000 Caracas Accord.

ENVIRONMENT

Sustainability rank: 72nd

25% (10% partially protected) | 1.7 tonnes per capita

Forests are threatened by destructive agricultural practices and also by the use of wood as fuel by rural communities. Deforestation has accelerated soil erosion.

MEDIA

TV ownership medium

Daily newspaper circulation 52 per 1000 people

PUBLISHING AND BROADCAST MEDIA

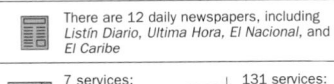

There are 12 daily newspapers, including *Listín Diario, Ultima Hora, El Nacional,* and *El Caribe*

7 services: 1 state-owned, 6 independent | 131 services: 1 state-owned, 130 independent

Television broadcasts from both Mexico and the USA can easily be received in the Dominican Republic.

CRIME

Death penalty not used

Dominican Republic does not publish prison figures | Thefts decreased 1996–1998

Drug cartels are increasingly using the Dominican Republic as a transshipment point to the USA. Narcotics trafficking and arms smuggling are linked to the high levels of violent crime.

EDUCATION

School leaving age: 14

84% | 176,995 students

State schools are badly underfunded. The state university of Santo Domingo suffered a financial crisis in 1999. The rich send their children to study in the USA and Spain.

HEALTH

Welfare state health benefits

1 per 455 people | Heart attacks, infectious and parasitic diseases

Wealthy Dominicans fly to Cuba and the USA for treatment. The poor rely on a basic public service, inadequately provided by 146 state hospitals.

CHRONOLOGY

The 1697 Franco-Spanish partition of Hispaniola left Spain with the eastern two-thirds of the island, now the Dominican Republic.

- ❑ **1865** Independence from Spain.
- ❑ **1930–1961** Gen. Molina dictator.
- ❑ **1965** Civil war. US intervention.
- ❑ **1966** Joaquín Balaguer's first of seven presidential terms over next 30 years.
- ❑ **1996** Center-left PRD candidate succeeds Balaguer.
- ❑ **1998** Major hurricane damage.
- ❑ **2000** Hipolito Mejia of PRD wins presidency.

D

SPENDING

GDP/cap. increase

CONSUMPTION AND SPENDING

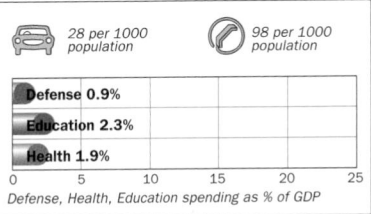

28 per 1000 population | 98 per 1000 population

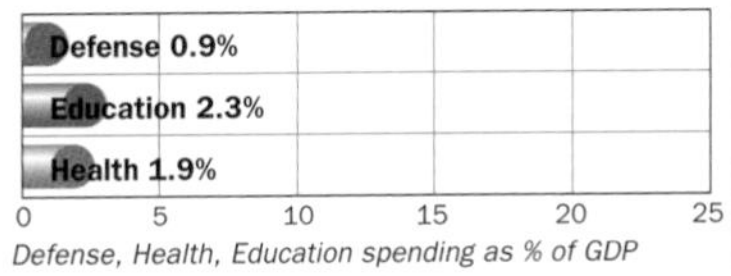
Defense 0.9%
Education 2.3%
Health 1.9%
0
5
10
15
20
25

Defense, Health, Education spending as % of GDP

Great disparities exist between rich and poor. The government in 1998 announced a seven-year plan to relieve poverty and reduce the level of malnutrition currently affecting well over two million people. Black Dominicans remain at the bottom of the economic and social ladder, accounting for the major proportion of small farmers and unemployed. Haitian immigrants are poorly paid, badly treated, and are liable to be deported at short notice. Mixed races have shown most upward mobility in recent years, but, nevertheless, the old Spanish families still form the wealthiest section of society and retain their grip on valuable estates.

WORLD RANKING

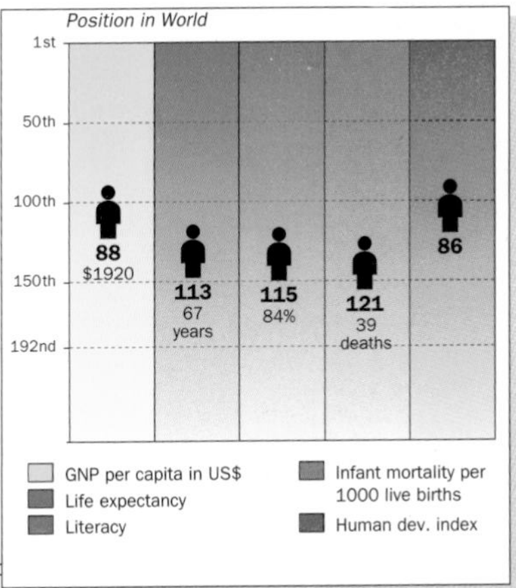
Position in World
1st
50th
100th
150th
192nd
88
$1920
113
67 years
115
84%
121
39 deaths
86
GNP per capita in US$
Life expectancy
Literacy
Infant mortality per 1000 live births
Human dev. index

ECUADOR

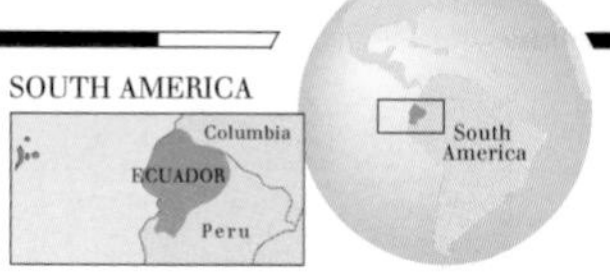
SOUTH AMERICA
Columbia
ECUADOR
Peru
South America

OFFICIAL NAME: Republic of Ecuador **CAPITAL:** Quito
POPULATION: 12.5 million **CURRENCY:** US dollar **OFFICIAL LANGUAGE:** Spanish

1830 | 1941 | Aug 10 | EC | -5 | +593 | .ec

ONCE PART OF THE INCA heartland, Ecuador lies on the western coast of South America. It was ruled by Spain from 1533, when the last Inca emperor was executed, until independence in 1830. Most Ecuadorians live either in the lowland coastal region or in the Andean Sierra. The Amazonian Amerindians are now pressing for their land rights to be recognized. Massive depreciation of the sucre forced the government to dollarize the currency in 2000.

CLIMATE

Tropical/mountain

WEATHER CHART

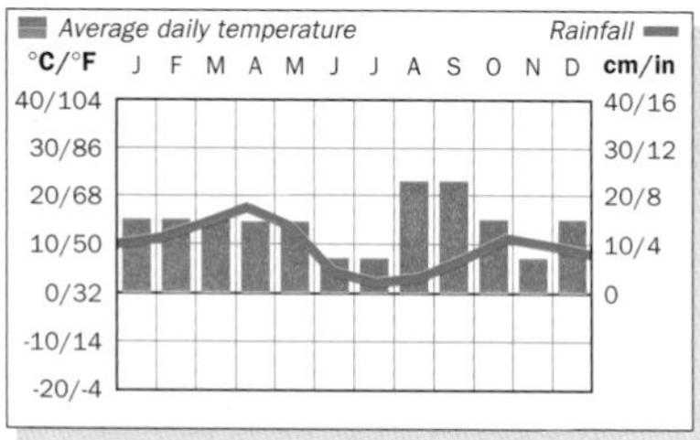
Average daily temperature
Rainfall
°C/°F J F M A M J J A S O N D cm/in
40/104 40/16
30/86 30/12
20/68 20/8
10/50 10/4
0/32 0
-10/14
-20/-4

Climate varies from hot equatorial in the Amazon forests, to dry heat in the south and "perpetual spring" in Quito.

TRANSPORTATION

Drive on right

Mariscal Sucre, Quito 1.71m passengers

167 ships 171,300 grt

THE TRANSPORTATION NETWORK

8165 km (5073 miles)

Pan-American Highway

956 km (594 miles)

1500 km (932 miles)

The road network and railroad are grossly underfunded. Serious political unrest in 2000–2001 blocked roads.

TOURISM

Visitors : Population 1:20

615,000 visitors

Up 21% in 2000

MAIN TOURIST ARRIVALS

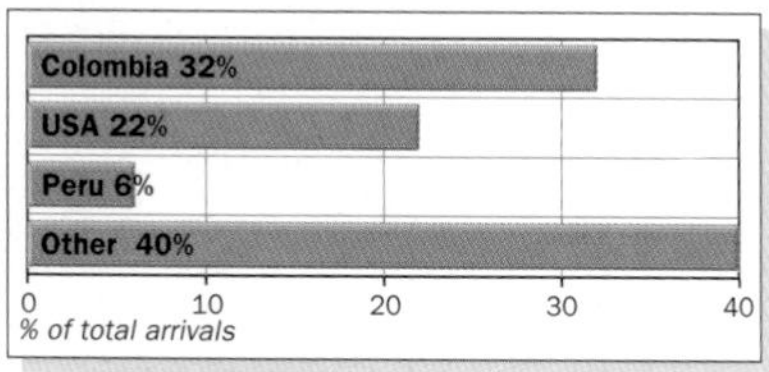
Colombia 32%
USA 22%
Peru 6%
Other 40%
0 10 20 30 40
% of total arrivals

Tourism is growing. Quito, once the capital of the Inca empire, has restored many of its Spanish imperial buildings, including 86 churches. Access to the Galapagos Islands is restricted to 40,000 visitors a year.

PEOPLE

Pop. density low

Spanish, Quechua, other Amerindian languages

46/km² (118/mi²)

THE URBAN/RURAL POPULATION SPLIT

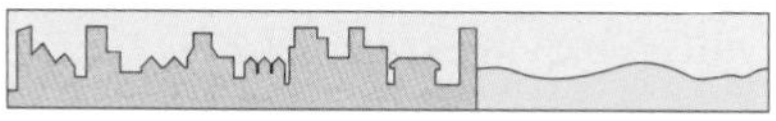
62%
38%

RELIGIOUS PERSUASION

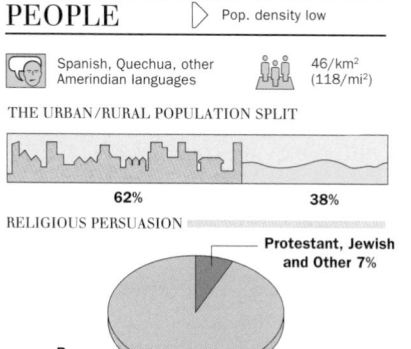

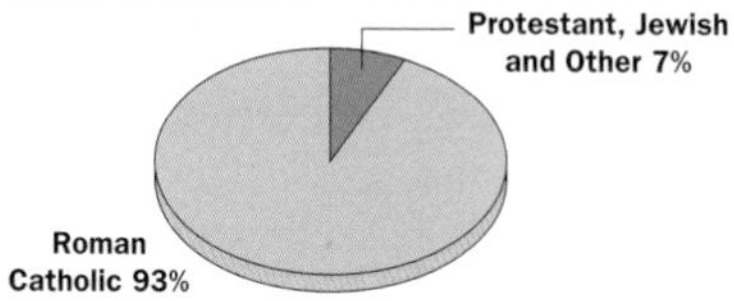
Protestant, Jewish and Other 7%
Roman Catholic 93%

Over half of the population is of Indian–Spanish extraction (*mestizo*). Black communities exist on the coast. The Amerindians, who make up about one-quarter of the population, are pressing for Ecuador to be described as a plurinational state, where different indigenous communities are recognized as distinct nationalities. The result is a strong and largely unified Amerindian movement which is at the forefront of social protests.

POLITICS

Multiparty elections

1998/2002

President Gustavo Noboa

AT THE LAST ELECTION

National Congress 121 seats

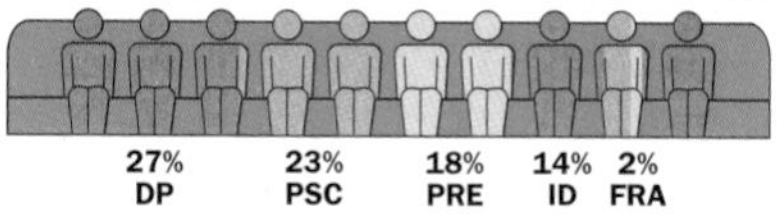
4% NMN–PP
12% Other
27% DP
23% PSC
18% PRE
14% ID
2% FRA

DP = Popular Democracy **PSC** = Social Christian Party
PRE = Ecuadorean Roldosist Party **ID** = Democratic Left
NMN–PP = New Country–Pachakutik Movement
FRA = Alfarist Radical Front

101 provincial members are elected for two-year terms, and 20 national members are directly elected for four-year terms.

After the instability and corruption of the late 1990s, a new broad-based alliance was formed in 1999. Severe austerity reforms provoked widespread protests; the army intervened and Vice President Gustavo Noboa took over the presidency in 2000. Repression, negotiation, and a state of emergency were Noboa's response in 2000–2001 to popular protests at the dollarization of the economy and IMF-backed austerity.

WORLD AFFAIRS

Joined UN in 1945

AP | AmCC | NAM | OAS | RG

Access to US and EU markets for bananas and oil prices are major concerns. There are serious security problems on the border with Colombia.

ECUADOR

Total Land Area : 276 840 sq. km (106 888 sq. miles)

POPULATION
- over 1 000 000
- over 500 000
- over 100 000
- over 50 000
- over 10 000
- under 10 000

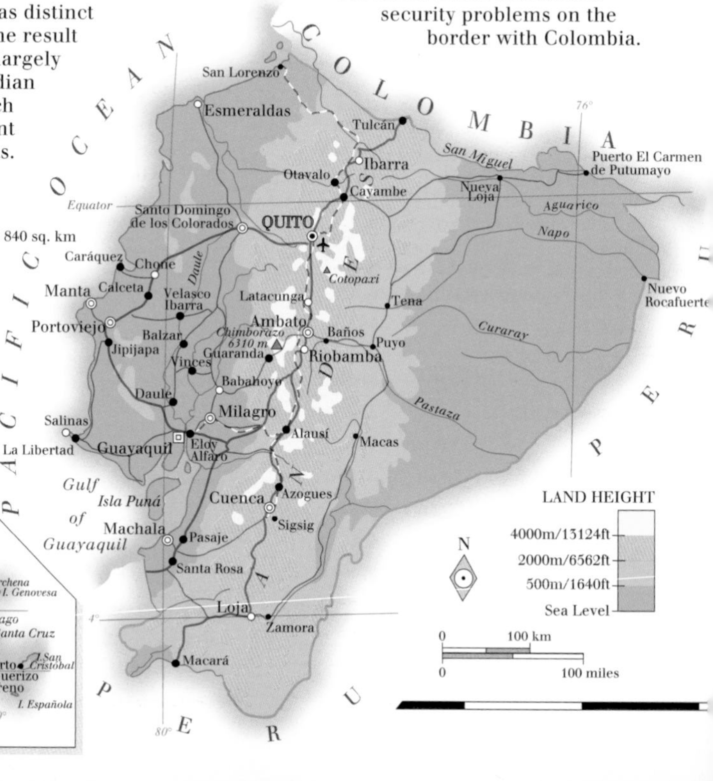
PACIFIC OCEAN
COLOMBIA
PERU
San Lorenzo
Esmeraldas
Tulcán
Ibarra
Otavalo
Cayambe
San Miguel
Nueva Loja
Puerto El Carmen de Putumayo
Aguarico
Napo
Equator
Santo Domingo de los Colorados
QUITO
Cotopaxi
Caráquez
Chone
Manta
Calceta
Velasco Ibarra
Latacunga
Tena
Nuevo Rocafuerte
Portoviejo
Jipijapa
Balzar
Ambato
Chimborazo 6310 m
Baños
Puyo
Curaray
Guaranda
Riobamba
Vinces
Babahoyo
Daule
Milagro
Pastaza
Salinas
La Libertad
Guayaquil
Eloy Alfaro
Alausí
Macas
Gulf of Guayaquil
Isla Puná
Cuenca
Azogues
Sigsig
Machala
Pasaje
Santa Rosa
Loja
Zamora
Macará
LAND HEIGHT
4000m/13124ft
2000m/6562ft
500m/1640ft
Sea Level
0 100 km
0 100 miles

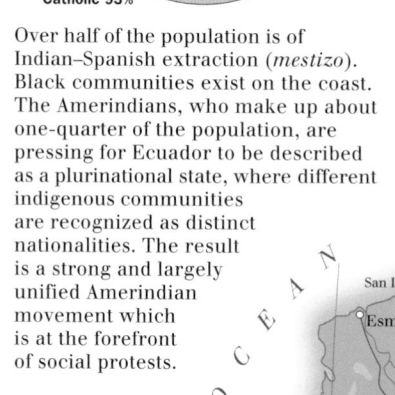

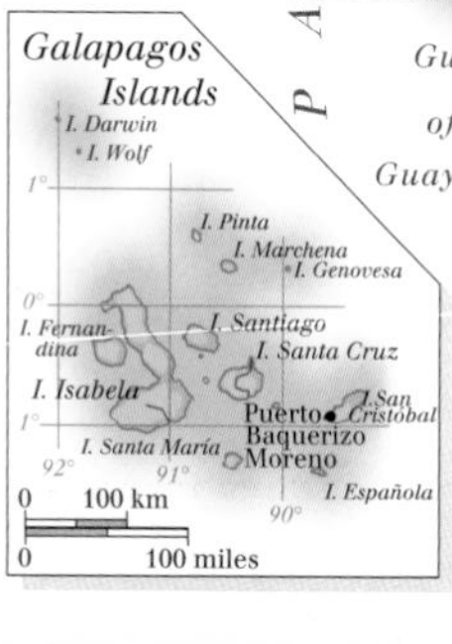
Galapagos Islands
I. Darwin
I. Wolf
I. Pinta
I. Marchena
I. Genovesa
I. Fernandina
I. Santiago
I. Santa Cruz
I. Isabela
I. San Cristóbal
Puerto Baquerizo Moreno
I. Santa María
I. Española
0 100 km
0 100 miles

***Quito is the highest** capital in the world after La Paz in Bolivia. It lies in an Andean valley, lined with 30 volcanoes.*

AID

Recipient

$146m (receipts)

Down 17% in 1999

Aid from the USA, the EU, and the World Bank alleviates the heavy foreign debt burden. The Galapagos Islands receive generous grants from UNESCO.

DEFENSE

Compulsory military service

$339m

Down 38% in 1999

From the mid-1970s the army kept out of politics until its intervention in 2000. Moves to reduce the military's 50% "royalty" share of oil revenues, its prime source of funding, have raised tensions.

ECONOMICS

Inflation 33.8% p.a. (1990–1999)

$16.8bn

Currency is US dollar

SCORE CARD

❑ WORLD GNP RANKING	73rd
❑ GNP PER CAPITA	$1360
❑ BALANCE OF PAYMENTS	$955m
❑ INFLATION	52.2%
❑ UNEMPLOYMENT	11%

STRENGTHS

Net oil exporter. World's biggest banana producer. Fishing industry.

WEAKNESSES

Poor infrastructure and land productivity. Energy crises. High inflation. Financial instability. Confusion over adoption of US dollar as official currency in 2000.

EXPORTS

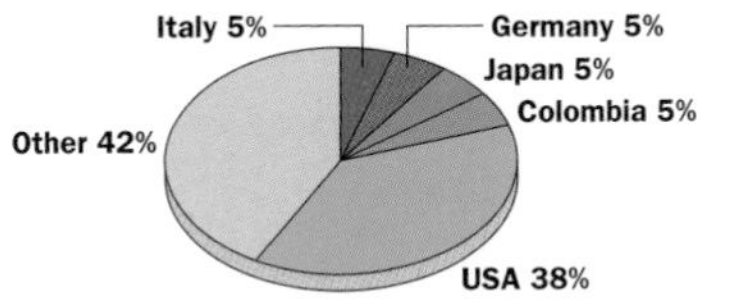
Italy 5%
Germany 5%
Japan 5%
Colombia 5%
Other 42%
USA 38%

IMPORTS

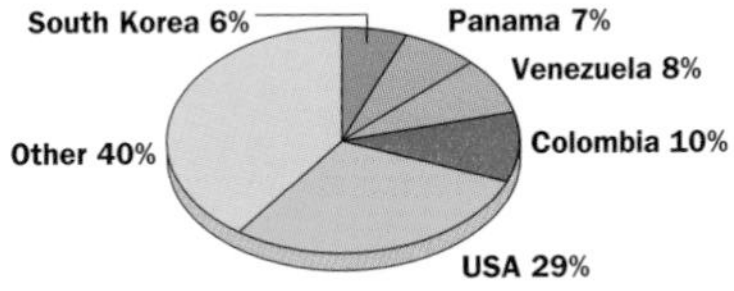
South Korea 6%
Panama 7%
Venezuela 8%
Colombia 10%
Other 40%
USA 29%

RESOURCES

Electric power 2.8m kw

688,297 tonnes

405,000 b/d (reserves 2,100,000,000 bbl)

5.11m cattle, 2.87m pigs, 2.13m sheep, 130m chickens

Oil, natural gas, gold, silver, copper, zinc

The government is encouraging faster oil exploration and higher output. Ecuador left OPEC in 1992. Overfishing is threatening mackerel and squid stocks.

ENVIRONMENT

Sustainability rank: 44th

43%

1.8 tonnes per capita

Oil drilling in new areas of Amazonia threatens indigenous tribes. Tourism, some of it illegal, has upset the delicate ecosystems of the Galapagos Islands; the land iguana has become sterile and black coral is stolen in quantity for souvenirs. The breaching of the *Jessica* oil tanker just offshore in 2001 raised concerns about shipping oil through ecologically sensitive areas.

MEDIA

TV ownership medium

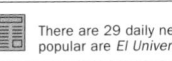

Daily newspaper circulation 70 per 1000 people

PUBLISHING AND BROADCAST MEDIA

There are 29 daily newspapers. The most popular are *El Universo* and *El Comercio*

67 independent services

1 state-owned, 320 independent stations

The press is largely independent. It is highly regionalized, based either in the Quito region or around Guayaquil on the coast. The latter is also a center for commercial radio stations. There are ten cultural and ten religious radio stations.

CRIME

Death penalty not used

Ecuador does not publish prison figures

Up 14% 1996–1998

Right-wing paramilitaries were blamed for the murders of a trade union leader in November 1998 and a left-wing congressman in February 1999. The paramilitaries are rumored to be supported by Colombians. Left-wing urban guerrillas are also reported. Unprecedented numbers of citizens are applying for arms permits and the illegal arms trade is thriving.

EDUCATION

School leaving age: 15

91%

206,541 students

Some 20% of Ecuadorians in the relevant age group receive higher education at 16 universities.

Programs have been launched to combat high levels of adult illiteracy in rural areas. Secondary schools are badly underfunded.

CHRONOLOGY

Alternating republican and military governments ruled Ecuador from independence in 1830 to 1978.

- ❑ **1941–1942** Loss of mineral-rich El Oro region to Peru.
- ❑ **1948–1960** Prosperity from bananas.
- ❑ **1972** Oil production starts.
- ❑ **1979** Return to democracy.
- ❑ **1992** Amerindians win land in Amazonia.
- ❑ **1996–1997** Abdalá Bucarám Ortíz removed from presidency on grounds of mental incapacity.
- ❑ **1998–1999** Jamil Mahuad of DP wins elections; forms new majority alliance. Economic crisis.
- ❑ **2000** Army sides with Amerindian protestors. Vice president Gustavo Noboa replaces Mahuad.

E

HEALTH

Welfare state health benefits

1 per 588 people

Malnutrition, intestinal infectious diseases, pneumonia, accidents

Health care is seriously underfunded. Some services exist in poor urban districts but are still unavailable in many rural areas. Severe budget cuts mean that any improvement will depend on more outside aid.

SPENDING

GDP/cap. increase

CONSUMPTION AND SPENDING

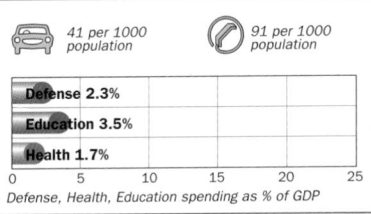

41 per 1000 population

91 per 1000 population

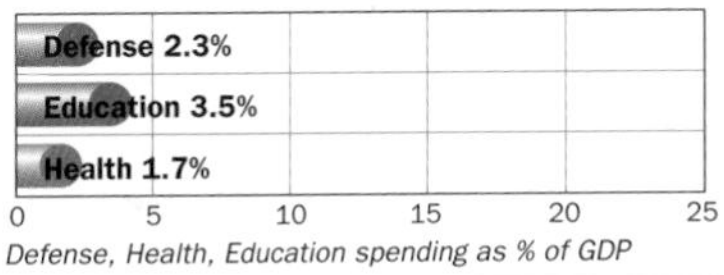
Defense 2.3%
Education 3.5%
Health 1.7%
0
5
10
15
20
25

Defense, Health, Education spending as % of GDP

An estimated 60% of the population live in poverty, but disparity between rich and poor is not as great as in other South American countries.

WORLD RANKING

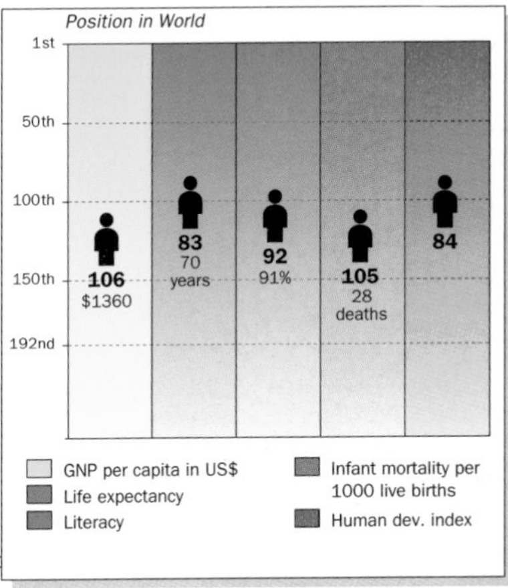
Position in World
1st
50th
100th
150th
192nd
106
$1360
83
70 years
92
91%
105
28 deaths
84
GNP per capita in US$
Life expectancy
Literacy
Infant mortality per 1000 live births
Human dev. index

EGYPT

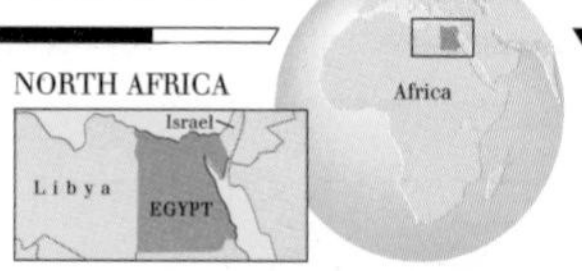
NORTH AFRICA
Israel
Libya
EGYPT
Africa

OFFICIAL NAME: Arab Republic of Egypt **CAPITAL:** Cairo
POPULATION: 68.5 million **CURRENCY:** Egyptian pound **OFFICIAL LANGUAGE:** Arabic

1936 | 1982 | July 23 | ET | +2 | +20 | .eg

OCCUPYING THE NORTHEAST corner of Africa, Egypt is bisected by the highly fertile Nile valley separating the arid western desert from the smaller semiarid eastern desert. Egypt's 1979 peace treaty with Israel brought security, the return of the Sinai, and large injections of US aid. Its essentially pro-Western military-backed regime is now being challenged by an increasingly influential Islamic fundamentalist movement.

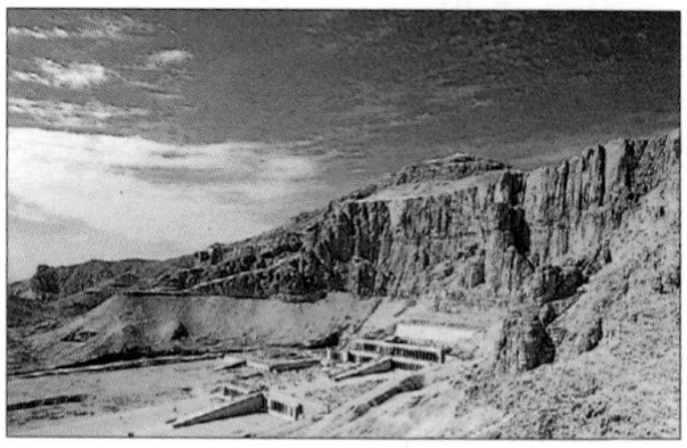

18th-Dynasty Temple of Queen Hatshepsut dating from the Middle Kingdom, c.1480 BCE. It is at Deir el-Bahri on the west bank of the Nile opposite Thebes, Egypt's capital at the time.

CLIMATE

Hot desert/ Mediterranean

WEATHER CHART

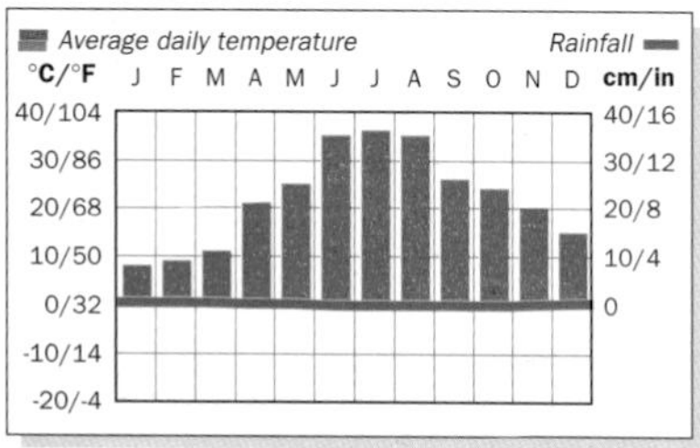
Average daily temperature
Rainfall
°C/°F
J F M A M J J A S O N D
cm/in
40/104
30/86
20/68
10/50
0/32
-10/14
-20/-4
40/16
30/12
20/8
10/4
0

Summers are very hot, especially in the south, but winters are cooler. The only significant rain falls in winter along the Mediterranean coast.

TRANSPORTATION

Drive on right

Cairo International 8.30m passengers

379 ships 1368 grt

THE TRANSPORTATION NETWORK

49,684 km (30,872 miles)	None
5024 km (3122 miles)	Suez Canal, 3500 km (2175 miles)

Egypt's cities are linked by adequate roads, but railroads are the main transportation arteries. The Suez Canal is a vital international shipping lane. Cairo's metro opened in 1987.

TOURISM

Visitors : Population 1:13

5.1m visitors

Up 14% in 2000

MAIN TOURIST ARRIVALS

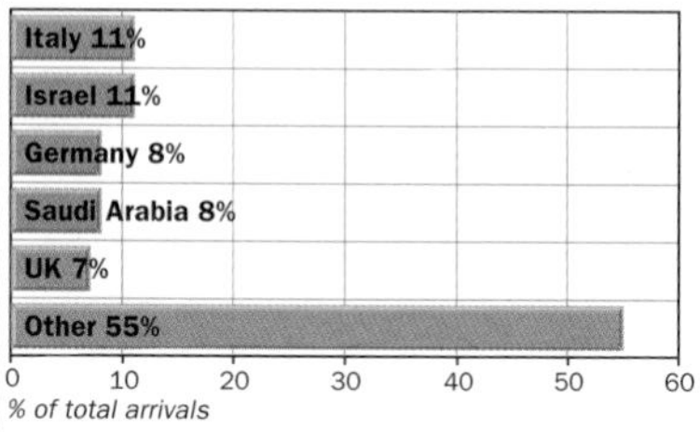
Italy 11%
Israel 11%
Germany 8%
Saudi Arabia 8%
UK 7%
Other 55%
0
10
20
30
40
50
60
% of total arrivals

Egypt's wealth of antiquities from its ancient civilizations have made it a key tourist destination since the 1880s. Today, it also offers Nile cruises and some of the world's best subaqua diving, notably at the coral reefs near Hurghada on the Red Sea.

In the mid-1990s, however, the industry went into sharp decline when militant Islamists, whose aim was to pressure the government into moving the state more toward Islam, began attacking Western tourists; in an attack in Luxor in November 1997 58 tourists were killed. The result was a sharp decline in the number of visitors and a major dent in foreign exchange earnings, the business convention trade being particularly affected.

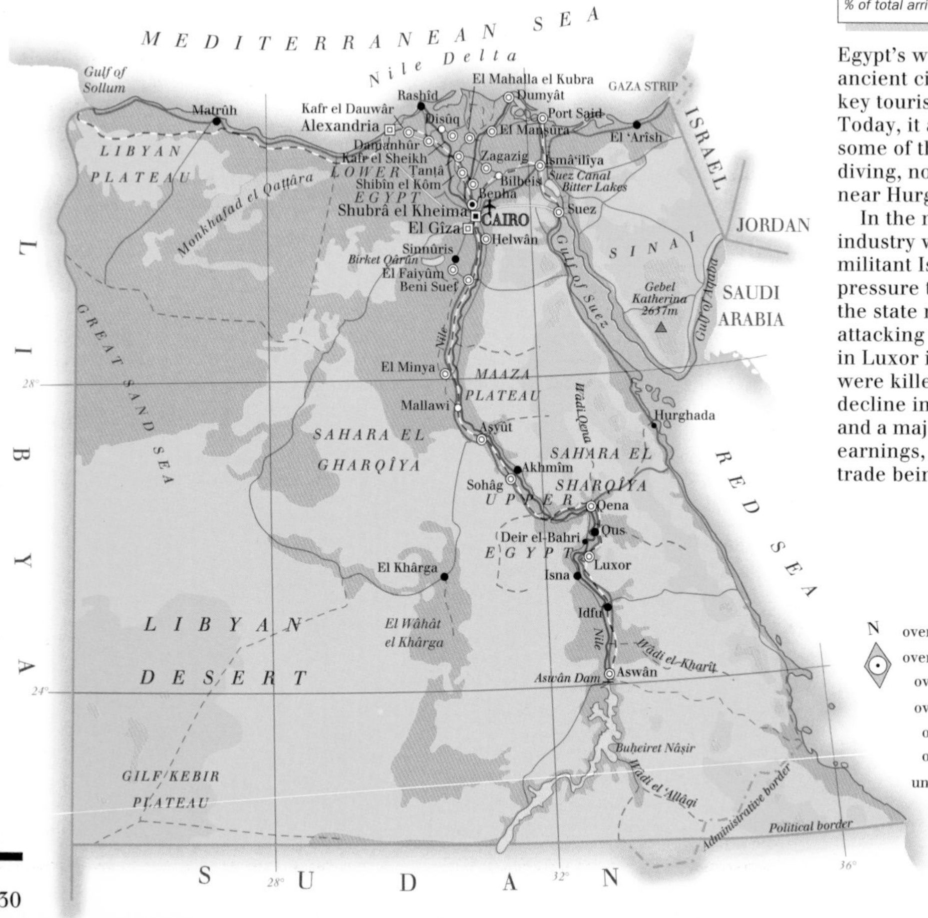
MEDITERRANEAN SEA
Nile Delta
Gulf of Sollum
Matrûh
Kafr el Dauwâr
Alexandria
Rashîd
El Mahalla el Kubra
Dumyât
GAZA STRIP
Port Said
Disûq
El Mansûra
El 'Arîsh
Damanhûr
Kafr el Sheikh
Zagazig
Ismâ'ilîya
Tanta
Bilbeis
Suez Canal
Bitter Lakes
Shibîn el Kôm
LOWER EGYPT
Benha
Shubrâ el Kheima
CAIRO
Suez
El Gîza
Helwân
LIBYAN PLATEAU
Monkhafad el Qattâra
ISRAEL
JORDAN
SINAI
Sinnûris
Birket Qârûn
El Faiyûm
Beni Suef
Gulf of Suez
Gulf of Aqaba
Gebel Katherina 2637m
SAUDI ARABIA
LIBYA
GREAT SAND SEA
Nile
El Minya
MAAZA PLATEAU
Mallawi
Wadi Qena
Hurghada
Asyût
SAHARA EL GHARQÎYA
Akhmîm
SAHARA EL SHARQÎYA
Sohâg
UPPER EGYPT
Qena
Qus
Deir el-Bahri
Luxor
Isna
El Khârga
RED SEA
Idfu
El Wâhât el Khârga
LIBYAN DESERT
Wadi el-Kharît
Aswân Dam
Aswân
Buheirat Nâsir
Wadi el 'Allâqi
GILF KEBIR PLATEAU
Administrative border
Political border
SUDAN
28°
32°
36°
24°

EGYPT

Total Land Area : 995 450 sq. km (384 343 sq. miles)

POPULATION

- over 5 000 000
- over 1 000 000
- over 500 000
- over 100 000
- over 50 000
- over 10 000
- under 10 000

LAND HEIGHT

- 2000m/6562ft
- 1000m/3281ft
- 500m/1640ft
- 200m/656ft
- Sea Level
- -200m/-656ft

0 200 km
0 200 miles

PEOPLE

Pop. density medium

Arabic, French, English, Berber

69/km² (178/mi²)

THE URBAN/RURAL POPULATION SPLIT

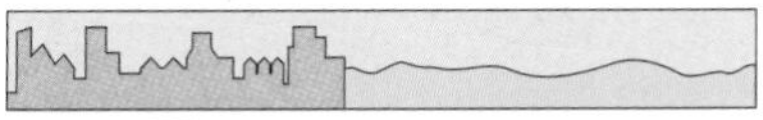
45%
55%

RELIGIOUS PERSUASION

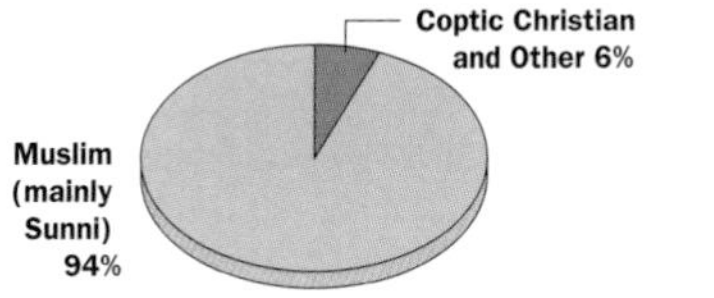
Coptic Christian and Other 6%
Muslim (mainly Sunni) 94%

ETHNIC MAKEUP

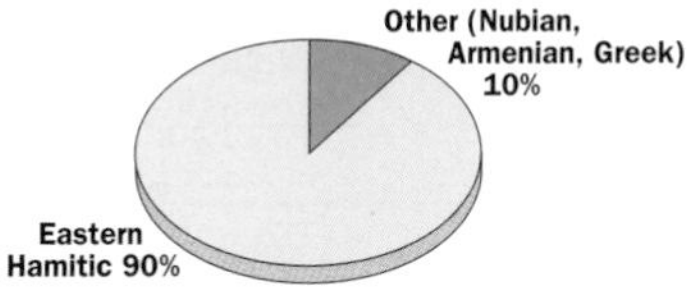
Other (Nubian, Armenian, Greek) 10%
Eastern Hamitic 90%

Egypt has a long tradition of ethnic and religious tolerance, though the rise in Islamic fundamentalism has sparked sectarian clashes between Muslims and Coptic Christians. Most Egyptians speak Arabic, though many also have French or English as a second language. There are Berber-speaking communities in the western oases. Small colonies of Greeks and Armenians live in the larger towns. Islam is the dominant religion, followed by Coptic Christianity. Although many Jews left Egypt for Israel after 1948, a small community remains in Cairo.

Cairo is the second-most populous city in Africa, and a key social question in Egypt is the high birthrate. In 1985 the government set up the National Population Council, which made birth control readily available. Since then, the birthrate has dropped from 39 to fewer than 25 per 1000 people, but population growth is still high. The population is predicted to reach almost 100 million by 2025. The growing influence of Islamic fundamentalists, who oppose contraception, could see the rate accelerate once more.

Egyptian women have been among the most liberated in the Arab world, and under a law passed in 2000 they now have the right to initiate divorce proceedings. The steady rise of Islamic fundamentalism, however, threatens their position, particularly in rural areas.

POPULATION AGE BREAKDOWN

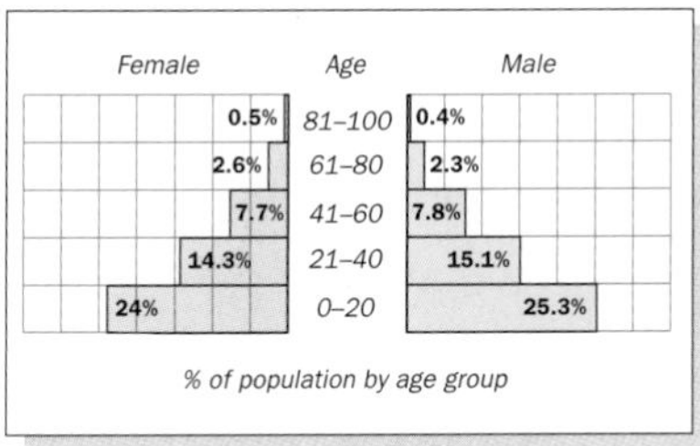
Female
Age
Male
0.5%
81–100
0.4%
2.6%
61–80
2.3%
7.7%
41–60
7.8%
14.3%
21–40
15.1%
24%
0–20
25.3%
% of population by age group

POLITICS

Multiparty elections

2000/2005

President Mohammed Hosni Mubarak

AT THE LAST ELECTION

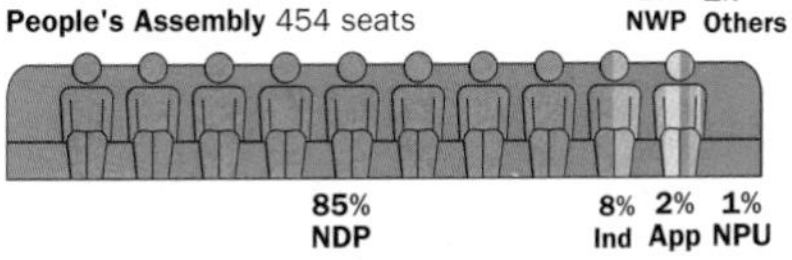
People's Assembly 454 seats
2% NWP
1% Others
85% NDP
8% Ind
2% App
1% NPU

NDP = National Democratic Party **Ind** = Independents **App** = Appointed **NWP** = New Wafd Party **NPU** = National Progressive Unionist Party

444 members of the Assembly are elected and 10 appointed by the head of state

Egypt is a multiparty system in theory. In practice, the ruling NDP, backed by the military, runs a one-party state.

MAIN POLITICAL ISSUES

Islamic fundamentalism

The NDP government is engaged in a struggle against Islamist terrorist groups seeking to turn Egypt into a Muslim theocracy along Iranian lines. Extremists have been responsible for numerous attacks on police and tourists. The fundamentalist message, with promises of improved conditions, has proved attractive to both urban and rural poor. Mosques are often the main providers of education and health services that parallel the state's. Although the government uses draconian measures to counter the terrorist threat, and banned the only legal Islamic party, the Labor Party, in May 2000, it continues to allow religious organizations to pursue their social programs.

The state of emergency

The ruling NDP in 1994 extended the national state of emergency in force since the assassination of President Sadat by Islamic terrorists in 1981. Emergency laws have been invoked to justify the ban on religious parties, especially the Muslim Brotherhood. Opposition parties accused the NDP of using existing laws to ensure its electoral success in general elections held in 1995. Human rights groups claim that emergency powers are routinely applied to silence the NDP's political opponents.

***Hosni Mubarak,** president since the assassination of Anwar Sadat in 1981.*

***Gemal Abd al-Nasser,** pan-Arab nationalist, president from 1954 to 1970.*

PROFILE

Egypt has been politically stable since World War II, with just three leaders since 1954 when Nasser came to power. Anwar Sadat was assassinated in 1981, but was immediately replaced by Hosni Mubarak, a man in the same mold. The NDP retains its grip on the political process by means of the state of emergency, and has close links with the military. Elections in 2000 were more transparent, and the Islamic opposition fared slightly better than before, but many candidates elected as independents then joined the NDP.

While Nasser promoted Arab socialism, influenced by the Soviet model, Sadat and Mubarak encouraged private enterprise and a liberalized economy. However, there has been no parallel liberalization in politics – one reason for the growing success of Islamist militants.

WORLD AFFAIRS

Joined UN in 1945

AL | Damasc | OAPEC | OAU | OIC

Following the 1979 peace treaty with Israel, Egypt developed closer relations with the USA. Its political and military support for the US-led response to Iraq's invasion of Kuwait in 1990 was critical to the success of Operation Desert Storm in 1991. Egypt received a massive economic reward from Saudi Arabia for its participation.

Relations with Iran are tense. Iran actively supports the Islamist groups operating against the NDP government, and characterizes Egypt as a corrupt state under US influence. Egypt is concerned that the international boycott and air exclusion zones imposed on Iraq are simply allowing Iran to extend its influence in the Middle East. President Mubarak now advocates a diplomatic solution, and has opposed recent US-led air strikes against Iraq and against supposed terrorist targets elsewhere.

Egypt's diplomatic service is the Arab world's largest, and many Egyptians, such as former UN Secretary-General Boutros Boutros Ghali, have served on international bodies. The headquarters of the Arab League are in Cairo.

AID

Recipient

$1.58bn (receipts)

Down 19% in 1999

Egypt has received massive levels of US military aid since the late 1970s, and currently heads the list of US aid recipients, having overtaken Israel. Egypt was also equal top for all aid from OECD countries until the late 1990s.

E

CHRONOLOGY

Egypt's centuries-old Ottoman occupation ended in 1914, when the country came under British rule. It became fully independent in 1936. Army officers led by Lieutenant Colonel Nasser seized power in 1952.

- **1953** Political parties dissolved, monarchy abolished. Republic proclaimed with General Mohammed Neguib as president.
- **1954** Nasser deposes Neguib to become president.
- **1956** Suez Crisis over nationalization of Suez Canal. Israeli, British, and French forces invade, but withdraw after pressure from UN and USA.
- **1957** Suez Canal reopens after UN salvage fleet clears blockade.
- **1958** Egypt merges with Syria as United Arab Republic.
- **1960–1970** Building of Aswan Dam.
- **1961** Syria breaks away from union with Egypt.
- **1967** Six-Day War with Israel; loss of Sinai.
- **1970** Nasser dies of heart attack. Succeeded by Anwar Sadat.
- **1971** Readopts the name Egypt. Islam becomes state religion.
- **1972** Soviet military advisers dismissed from Egypt.
- **1974–1975** USA brokers partial Israeli withdrawal from Sinai.
- **1977** Sadat visits Jerusalem for first-ever meeting with Israeli prime minister.
- **1978** Camp David accords, brokered by US, signed by Egypt and Israel.
- **1979** Egypt and Israel sign peace treaty, alienating most Arab states.
- **1981** Sadat assassinated by Islamist extremists. Succeeded by Hosni Mubarak.
- **1982** Last Israeli troops leave Sinai.
- **1986** President Mubarak meets Israeli Prime Minister Shimon Peres to discuss Middle East peace.
- **1988** Novelist Naguib Mahfuz wins Nobel Prize for Literature.
- **1989** After 12-year rift, Egypt and Syria resume diplomatic relations.
- **1990–1991** Egypt participates in UN operation to liberate Kuwait.
- **1991** Damascus Declaration provides for a defense pact among Egypt, Syria, and GCC countries against Iraq.
- **1994–1998** Islamist extremists begin campaign of terrorism, killing civilians and tourists. Government steps up counter-measures.
- **1999** Banned Gamaat Islamiya ends campaign to overthrow government.
- **2000** Egypt recalls ambassador to Israel because of escalating Israeli aggression against Palestinians.

E

DEFENSE

Compulsory military service

$2.99bn

Up 3% in 1999

EGYPTIAN ARMED FORCES

3960 main battle tanks (T–54/55, M1A1 *Abrams*, *Ramses* II, T–62, M–60)	320,000 personnel
4 submarines, 1 destroyer, 40 patrol boats, and 10 frigates	18,500 personnel
580 combat aircraft (*Alpha Jet*, PRC J-6, F-4E, *Mirage* 5E2)	30,000 personnel
None	

Egypt's armed forces, the largest in the Arab world, are battle-hardened from successive wars with Israel and from participation in Operation Desert Storm to liberate Kuwait in 1991. More than 500,000 reservists augment the regular troops.

After the 1978 Camp David framework agreements were reached with Israel, Egypt stopped buying Soviet weapons and aircraft, and turned instead to Western suppliers. Cooperation with the USA has reaped dividends in the form of access to more sophisticated defense equipment and improved training. Egypt has a small arms industry and sells light weapons, notably its version of the Soviet-developed AK-47 assault rifle, to other developing countries.

ECONOMICS

Inflation 8.8% p.a. (1990–1999)

$86.5bn

3.421–3.890 Egyptian pounds

SCORE CARD

World GNP Ranking	39th
GNP per Capita	$1380
Balance of Payments	$–1.63bn
Inflation	3.1%
Unemployment	12%

EXPORTS

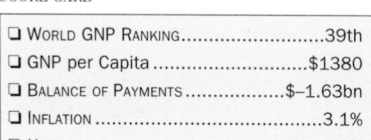

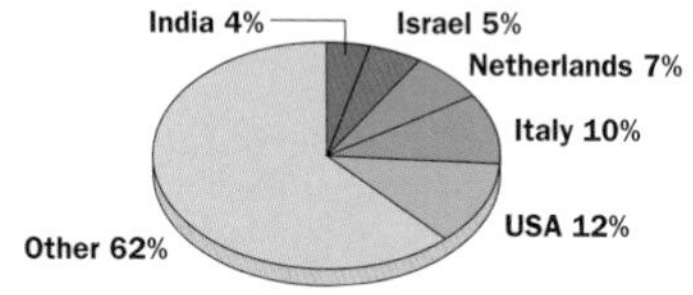
India 4%
Israel 5%
Netherlands 7%
Italy 10%
USA 12%
Other 62%

IMPORTS

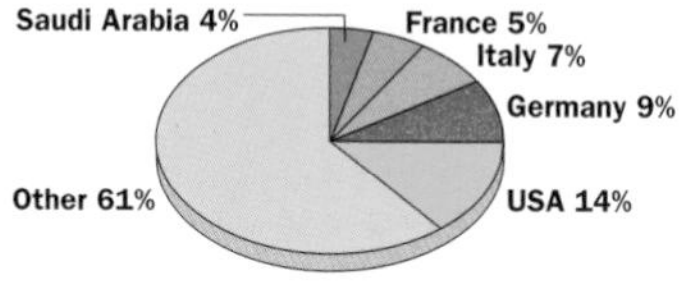
Saudi Arabia 4%
France 5%
Italy 7%
Germany 9%
USA 14%
Other 61%

ECONOMIC PERFORMANCE INDICATOR

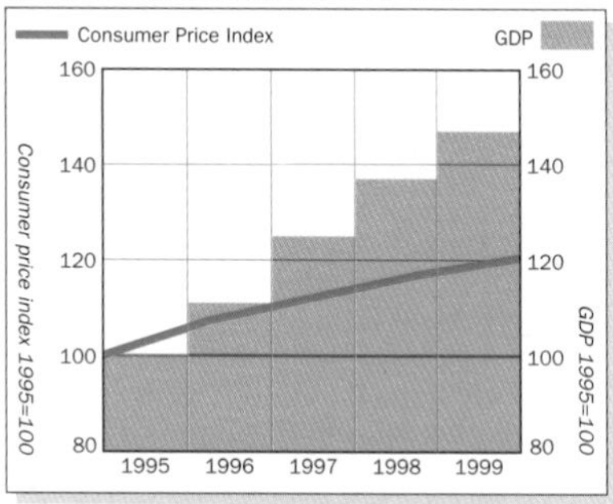
Consumer Price Index
GDP
160
140
120
100
80
Consumer price index 1995=100
GDP 1995=100
1995
1996
1997
1998
1999

Strengths

Oil and gas revenues. Tourist industry. Remittances from Egyptians working overseas. Suez Canal tolls. Agricultural produce, especially cotton. Light industry and manufacturing.

Weaknesses

Remittances from Egyptians working overseas vulnerable to regional recession. Dependence on imported technology. High birthrate.

Profile

Under President Nasser, Egypt followed an economic policy inspired by the Soviet model. Rigid and highly centralized, it gave Egypt one of the largest public sectors of all developing countries. Economic restrictions were first relaxed in 1974. President Sadat's open-door policy allowed joint ventures with foreign partners for the first time, although the business classes were the only ones to profit. Most Egyptians suffered from new austerity measures.

Under President Mubarak, economic reform has quickened and there is more awareness of poverty and the high levels of unemployment. Priorities now are to encourage manufacturing, sustain economic growth, and reduce the gap between rich and poor.

EGYPT : MAJOR BUSINESSES

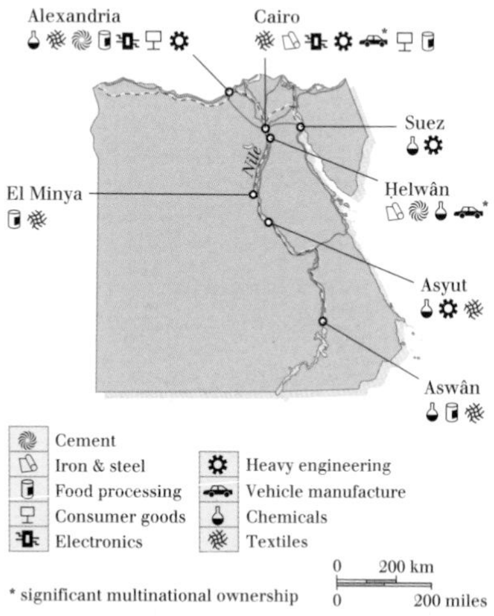
Alexandria
Cairo
Suez
Helwân
El Minya
Asyut
Aswân
Nile
Cement
Iron & steel
Food processing
Consumer goods
Electronics
Heavy engineering
Vehicle manufacture
Chemicals
Textiles
* significant multinational ownership
0 200 km
0 200 miles

RESOURCES

Electric power 16.8m kw

418,694 tonnes

795,000 b/d (reserves 2,900,000,000 bbl)

9.2m ducks, 9.1m geese, 88m chickens

Natural gas, oil, phosphates, manganese, uranium

ELECTRICITY GENERATION

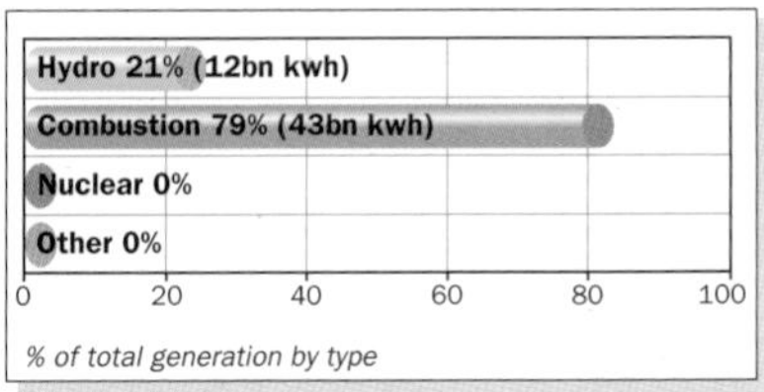
Hydro 21% (12bn kwh)
Combustion 79% (43bn kwh)
Nuclear 0%
Other 0%
0
20
40
60
80
100
% of total generation by type

Oil and gas are Egypt's most valuable resources. Oil multinationals are involved in new explorations, but more competitive oil-rich countries, such as Algeria and Yemen, are more profitable; 55% of Egypt's oil production is consumed locally.

Most electricity is derived from coal and hydroelectric power. The Aswan Dam, built between 1960 and 1970 and with a maximum output of 10 billion kwh, provides the bulk of hydroelectricity. Within four years, revenue from it had covered its construction costs. The USA gave aid in 2000 to upgrade the power plant, with work going ahead in 2001.

EGYPT : LAND USE

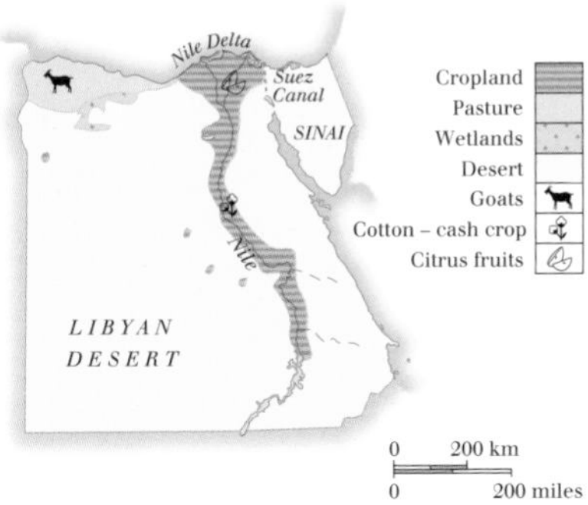
Nile Delta
Suez Canal
SINAI
Nile
LIBYAN DESERT
Cropland
Pasture
Wetlands
Desert
Goats
Cotton – cash crop
Citrus fruits
0 200 km
0 200 miles

ENVIRONMENT

Sustainability rank: 67th

1% (0.7% partially protected)

2 tonnes per capita

ENVIRONMENTAL TREATIES

Yes Yes Yes

Yes Yes Yes

Egypt suffers from a chronic lack of water. The Nile, the only perennial source, is increasingly saline because of its much-reduced flow, due to irrigation use and the Aswan Dam. The main cities suffer heavy industrial pollution, and environmental controls are few. In Cairo a sewerage system has improved sanitary conditions.

MEDIA

TV ownership medium

Daily newspaper circulation 38 per 1000 people

Pressure from Islamists has resulted in more airtime for Islamic sermons. Severe restrictions were imposed in 1998, after criticism of the government's security clampdown. Egypt was the first Arab state to have its own satellite, Nilesat 101, and is now the center of a flourishing satellite TV industry.

PUBLISHING AND BROADCAST MEDIA

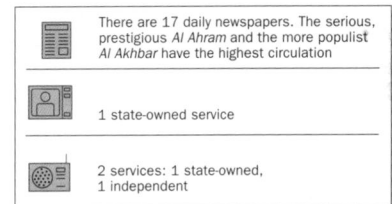

There are 17 daily newspapers. The serious, prestigious *Al Ahram* and the more populist *Al Akhbar* have the highest circulation

1 state-owned service

2 services: 1 state-owned, 1 independent

CRIME

Death penalty used

Egypt does not publish prison figures

Crime is rising

CRIME RATES

Murders
2 *per 100,000 population*

Rapes
0.03 *per 100,000 population*

Thefts
60 *per 100,000 population*

Terrorist attacks have tarnished Egypt's reputation as a law-abiding country; street crime and muggings were previously rare.

Intercommunity violence – in particular between Muslims and Christians – has become more common, as have attacks on Western tourists by Islamic extremists. Human rights groups have criticized the police for their abuse of current emergency laws, which results in the routine torture and death in police custody of scores of political prisoners.

EDUCATION

School leaving age: 14

55%

850,051 students

THE EDUCATION SYSTEM

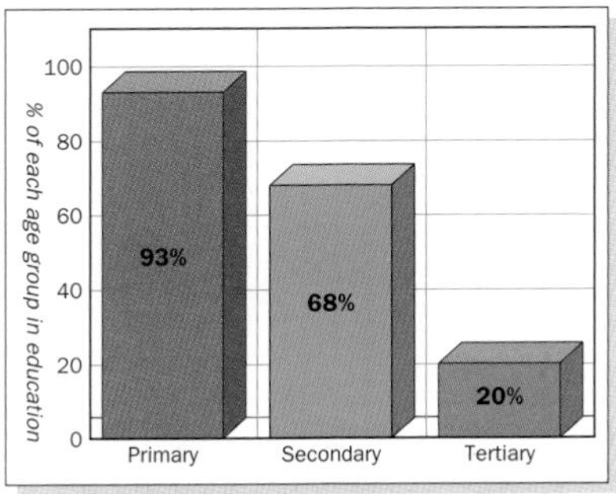
% of each age group in education
100
80
60
40
20
0
93%
68%
20%
Primary
Secondary
Tertiary

Most Egyptians attend elementary school until the age of 11, but not many complete secondary education. A small majority of men, but a minority of women, are literate. A government initiative to improve girls' primary education was launched in 2000. The quality of the education given by Egyptian universities is widely respected in the Arab world.

HEALTH

Welfare state health benefits

1 per 625 people

Digestive, respiratory, and heart diseases, perinatal deaths

Health care, although improved, remains basic – there is only one hospital bed for every 500 people. Patient–doctor ratios are among the lowest in the Arab world. Islamic medical centers based on the mosque organization are spreading, and are replacing the state system. Female circumcision was banned in public hospitals in 1996, although this move was challenged in the courts.

SPENDING

GDP/cap. increase

CONSUMPTION AND SPENDING

23 per 1000 population

75 per 1000 population

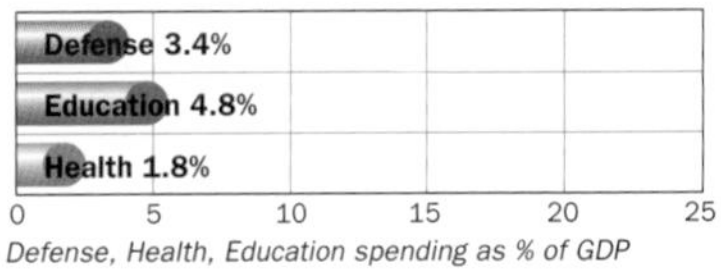
Defense 3.4%
Education 4.8%
Health 1.8%
0
5
10
15
20
25
Defense, Health, Education spending as % of GDP

Wealth disparities are highly marked in Egypt. The largely urban Coptic Christian community is the group with the country's highest standard of living. Most Egyptians remain subsistence farmers wih low incomes. The return of many unemployed workers from the Gulf states to their mainly rural homes has further depressed conditions in the countryside.

WORLD RANKING

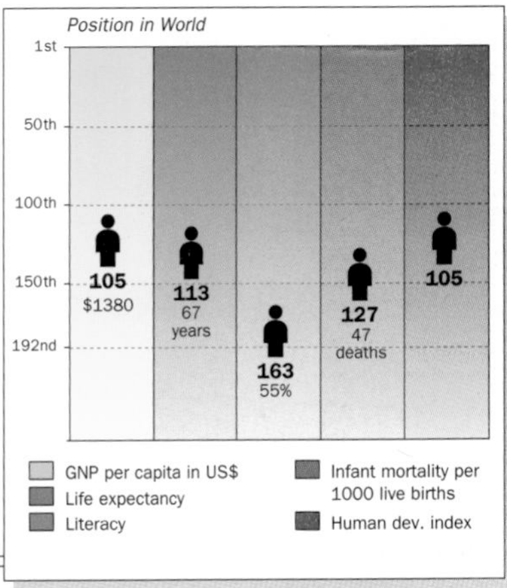
Position in World
1st
50th
100th
150th
192nd
105
$1380
113
67
years
163
55%
127
47
deaths
105
GNP per capita in US$
Life expectancy
Literacy
Infant mortality per 1000 live births
Human dev. index

El Salvador

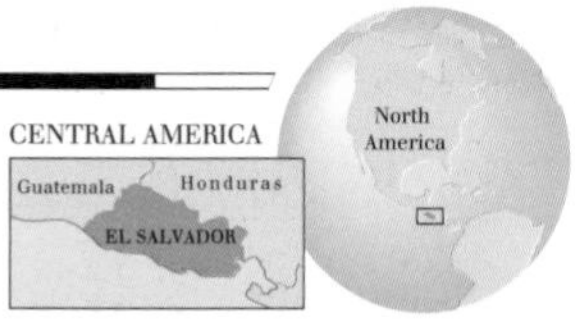
CENTRAL AMERICA
Guatemala
Honduras
EL SALVADOR
North America

Official Name: Republic of El Salvador **Capital:** San Salvador
Population: 6.3 million **Currency:** Salvadorean colón & US dollar **Official Language:** Spanish

1841 | 1841 | Sept 15 | ES | -6 | +503 | .sv

THE SMALLEST AND MOST DENSELY populated Central American republic, El Salvador won full independence in 1841. Located on the Pacific coast, it lies within a zone of seismic activity. Between 1979 and 1991, El Salvador was ravaged by a civil war between US-backed right-wing government forces and left-wing FMLN guerrillas. Since the UN-brokered peace agreement, the country has been concentrating on rebuilding its shattered economy.

View over the capital, San Salvador. It lies in a depression in the southern and higher of El Salvador's two mountain ranges, which is punctuated by more than 20 volcanoes.

CLIMATE

Tropical wet & dry

WEATHER CHART

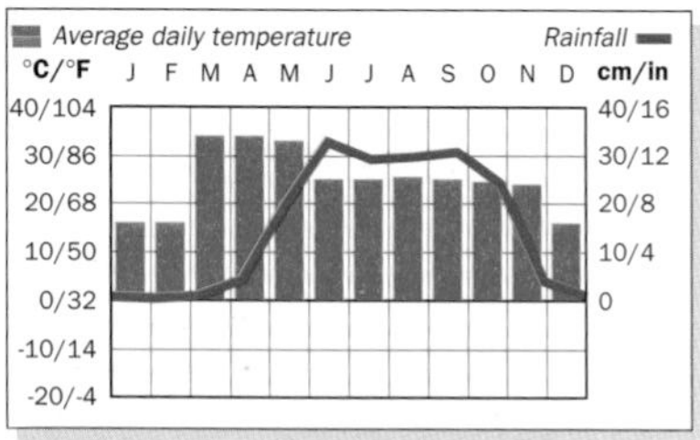
Average daily temperature
Rainfall
°C/°F
J F M A M J J A S O N D
cm/in
40/104
30/86
20/68
10/50
0/32
-10/14
-20/-4
40/16
30/12
20/8
10/4
0

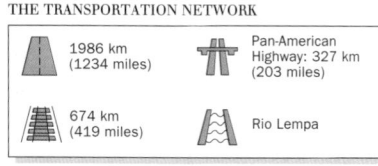

The tropical coastal *tierra caliente* is very hot, with seasonal rains. The low hills are cooler at night; the higher *tierra templada* is drier and also cooler.

TRANSPORTATION

Drive on right

Cuscatlan, San Salvador 1.37m passengers

12 ships 1500 grt

THE TRANSPORTATION NETWORK

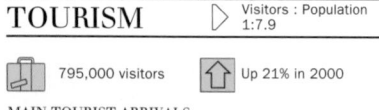

1986 km (1234 miles)

Pan-American Highway: 327 km (203 miles)

674 km (419 miles)

Rio Lempa

A succession of earthquakes in 2001 further deteriorated the road and rail networks, already poor in rural areas. Reconstruction will take many years.

TOURISM

Visitors : Population 1:7.9

795,000 visitors

Up 21% in 2000

MAIN TOURIST ARRIVALS

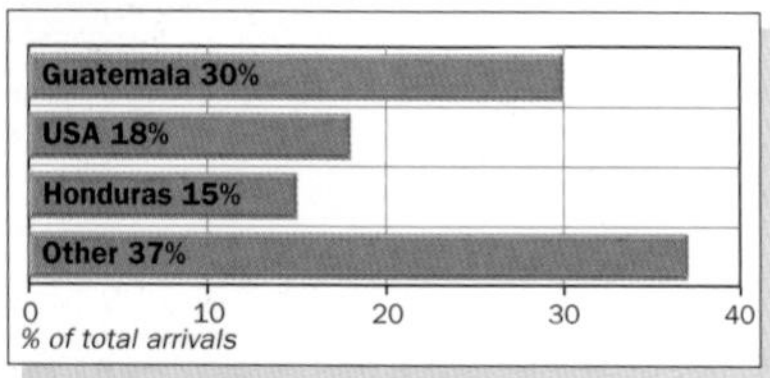
Guatemala 30%
USA 18%
Honduras 15%
Other 37%
0
10
20
30
40
% of total arrivals

Peace has brought visitors back to the unspoiled beach resorts. However, high prices for rooms and air travel, along with crime, hinder tourist expansion.

PEOPLE

Pop. density high

Spanish

304/km² (788/mi²)

THE URBAN/RURAL POPULATION SPLIT

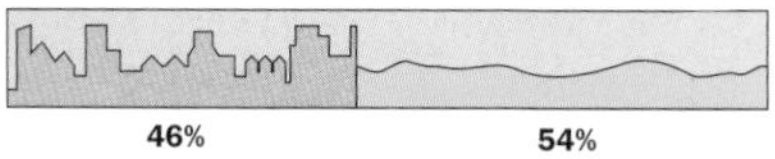
46%
54%

RELIGIOUS PERSUASION

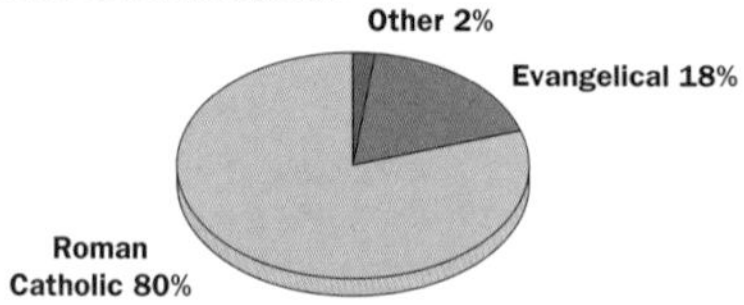
Other 2%
Evangelical 18%
Roman Catholic 80%

Salvadorans are largely a *mestizo* people; there are few ethnic tensions. The civil war was fought over gross economic disparities, which still exist.

POLITICS

Multiparty elections

2000/2003

President Francisco Flores

AT THE LAST ELECTION

Legislative Assembly 84 seats

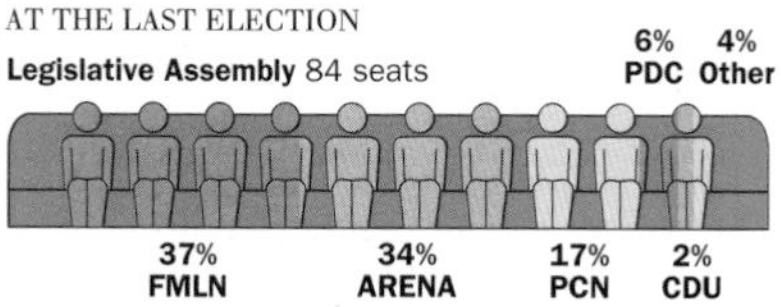
6% PDC
4% Other
37% FMLN
34% ARENA
17% PCN
2% CDU

FMLN = Farabundo Martí National Liberation Front **ARENA** = Nationalist Republican Alliance **PCN** = National Conciliation Party **PDC** = Christian Democratic Party **CDU** = United Democratic Center

El Salvador had traditionally been dominated by the centrist PDC and right-wing ARENA. The latter, however, now faces greater opposition from the FMLN, leftist former guerrillas, who in 1997 won the mayorship of San Salvador and half the state capitals.

In the 1999 presidential election the FMLN, split between center-left pragmatists and hardliners, came a poor second to ARENA's Francisco Flores, who promised reduced poverty and income redistribution. By March 2000, however, with the economy in difficulties, election voters punished ARENA by returning the FMLN as the largest party in parliament.

WORLD AFFAIRS

Joined UN in 1945

ACS | Geplac | IBRD | OAS | San José

El Salvador was an international pariah in the 1980s, because of the human rights abuses committed by its military death squads. Today it cooperates with its neighbors in pressing the USA on key issues such as trade and immigration, and, in 2001, for aid in coping with three earthquakes. In 2000 it co-signed a free trade treaty with Guatemala, Honduras, and Mexico. The final issue arising from a territorial dispute with Honduras was settled in 1998, when those affected were permitted to choose between Honduran and Salvadoran citizenship.

AID

Recipient

$183m (receipts)

Up 2% in 1999

Post-civil war aid focused on efforts to secure peace and achieve national reconciliation by funding rebuilding and refugee resettlement programs. The current emphasis is on a shift toward supporting growth.

The UN received a slow international response in 2001 to its appeal for $34.8 million in emergency housing, medicine, and disaster prevention programs after El Salvador's devastating earthquakes.

DEFENSE

Compulsory military service

$171m

Up 5% in 1999

Between 1979 and 1991, the role of the US-backed military was to fight an unrestricted war against the FMLN. Human rights were in effect suspended and governments that opposed the military were overthrown. Under the peace accords the military agreed to withdraw from politics and internal security matters, but it remains a potent force capable of intervention.

E

ECONOMICS

Inflation 8.1% p.a. (1990–1999)

$11.8bn

8.745–8.740 colones

SCORE CARD

❑ World GNP Ranking	79th
❑ GNP per Capita	$1920
❑ Balance of Payments	$-84m
❑ Inflation	0.5%
❑ Unemployment	8%

Strengths

Coffee exports. Offshore assembly *maquila* industry. Sizable family remittances from USA.

Weaknesses

Exports uncompetitive. High tax evasion and unemployment. Low savings. Vast reconstruction needed after earthquakes in 2001.

EXPORTS

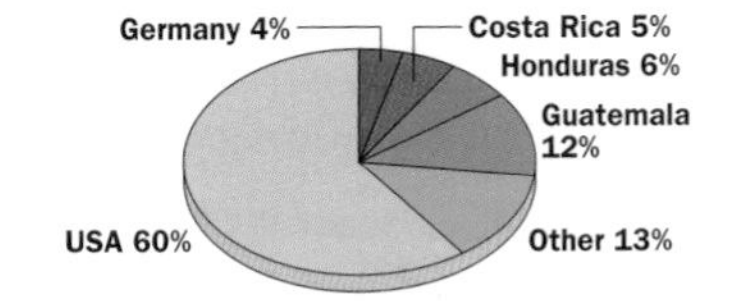
Germany 4%
Costa Rica 5%
Honduras 6%
Guatemala 12%
USA 60%
Other 13%

IMPORTS

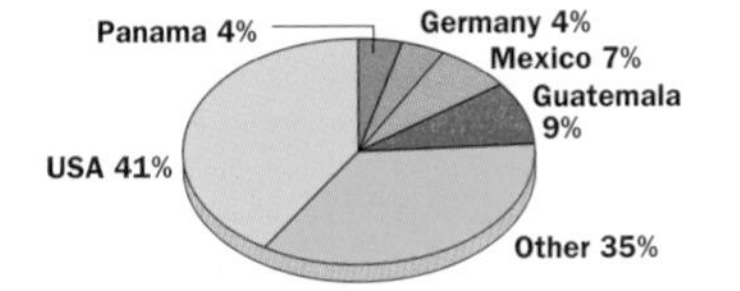
Panama 4%
Germany 4%
Mexico 7%
Guatemala 9%
USA 41%
Other 35%

RESOURCES

Electric power 980,000 kw

10,987 tonnes

Not an oil producer

1.21m cattle, 368,200 pigs, 8.1m chickens

Salt, limestone, gypsum

No significant resources. Several volcanoes facilitate abundant and relatively cheap geothermal energy.

ENVIRONMENT

Sustainability rank: 84th

1% (0.2% partially protected)

1 tonne per capita

Deforestation has led to erosion and desertification – worsening landslides during the earthquakes of 2001. Overuse of pesticides is a major problem.

MEDIA

TV ownership medium

Daily newspaper circulation 48 per 1000 people

PUBLISHING AND BROADCAST MEDIA

There are 8 daily newspapers. *El Diario de Hoy* has the highest circulation

11 channels: 2 state-owned, 9 independent

66 stations: 1 state-owned, 65 independent

The media is owned by powerful groups, such as the Dutriz family. Intimidation and self-censorship exist.

CRIME

Death penalty not used

5995 prisoners

Falling, but still high by regional standards

A corrupt judiciary and police force have failed to stem a postwar crime wave fueled by readily available arms; armed robberies, kidnappings, and murders deter investment and tourism. Uncompleted elements of the peace accords, particularly land transfers, often lead to violence.

EDUCATION

School leaving age: 15

79%

112,004 students

Education is based on the US system and is limited in rural areas. During the civil war, state universities were closed by the military and replaced by private universities which continue to thrive despite their low standards. A 1995 reform bill tried to address the negative impact of deregulation.

CHRONOLOGY

El Salvador was Spanish until 1821. Part of the United Provinces of Central America in 1823–1839, it became fully independent in 1841.

- ❑ **1932** Army crushes popular insurrection led by Farabundo Martí.
- ❑ **1944–1979** Army rules through PCN.
- ❑ **1979** Reformist officers overthrow PCN government.
- ❑ **1981** Left-wing Farabundo Martí National Liberation Movement (FMLN) launches civil war.
- ❑ **1991** UN-brokered peace. FMLN recognized as a political party.
- ❑ **1997** Leftist wins San Salvador mayoralty.
- ❑ **2001** Devastating earthquakes kill hundreds; dollarization of economy.

HEALTH

Welfare state health benefits

1 per 1000 people

Accidents, violence, circulatory diseases, infections

Health spending, almost halved during the civil war, has been slow to recover. The wealthy go to the USA for surgery.

SPENDING

GDP/cap. increase

CONSUMPTION AND SPENDING

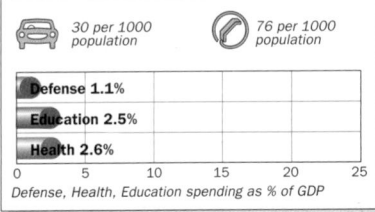

30 per 1000 population

76 per 1000 population

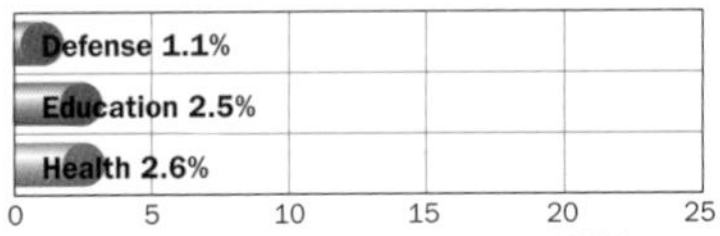
Defense 1.1%
Education 2.5%
Health 2.6%
0
5
10
15
20
25

Defense, Health, Education spending as % of GDP

Gross wealth disparities see 20% of the population owning 70% of national wealth. Land distribution remains highly skewed, and some three million – nearly half the population – live in poverty.

WORLD RANKING

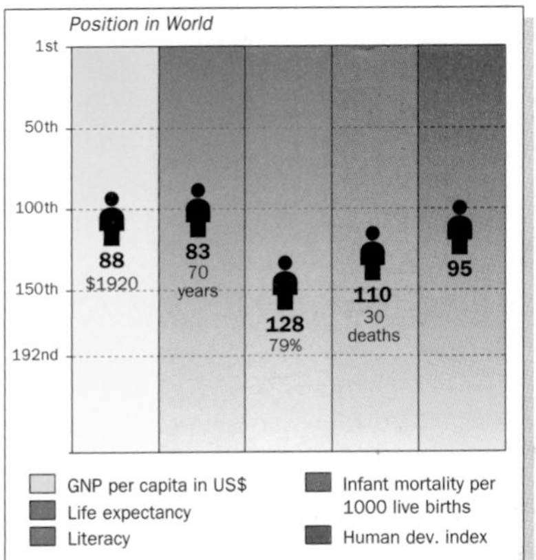
Position in World
1st
50th
100th
150th
192nd
88
$1920
83
70 years
128
79%
110
30 deaths
95
GNP per capita in US$
Life expectancy
Literacy
Infant mortality per 1000 live births
Human dev. index

EL SALVADOR

Total Land Area : 20 720 sq. km (8000 sq. miles)

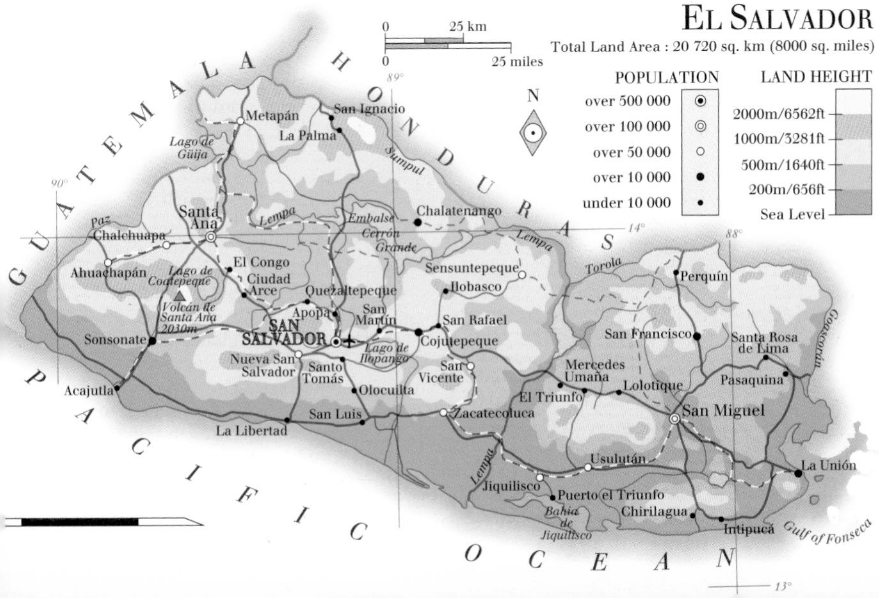
0
25 km
25 miles
POPULATION
over 500 000
over 100 000
over 50 000
over 10 000
under 10 000
LAND HEIGHT
2000m/6562ft
1000m/3281ft
500m/1640ft
200m/656ft
Sea Level
N
GUATEMALA
HONDURAS
PACIFIC OCEAN
Metapán
San Ignacio
La Palma
Lago de Güija
Santa Ana
Chalatenango
Chalchuapa
Ahuachapán
El Congo
Ciudad Arce
Quezaltepeque
Apopa
SAN SALVADOR
Nueva San Salvador
Santo Tomás
Sonsonate
Acajutla
La Libertad
San Luis
Olocuilta
Cojutepeque
Sensuntepeque
Ilobasco
San Rafael
San Vicente
Zacatecoluca
Mercedes Umaña
El Triunfo
Lolotique
San Francisco
Perquín
Santa Rosa de Lima
Pasaquina
San Miguel
Usulután
Jiquilisco
Puerto el Triunfo
Chirilagua
Intipucá
La Unión
Gulf of Fonseca
Lempa
Torola
Goascorán
Cerrón Grande
Lago de Ilopango
Volcán de Santa Ana 2030m

EQUATORIAL GUINEA

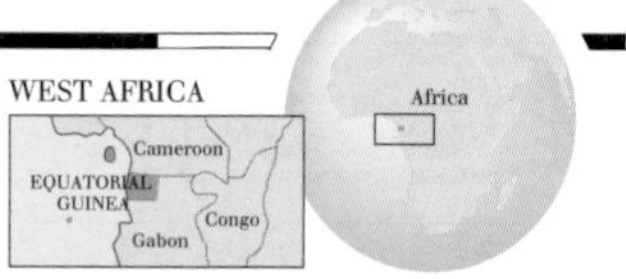
WEST AFRICA
Africa
Cameroon
EQUATORIAL GUINEA
Gabon
Congo

OFFICIAL NAME: Republic of Equatorial Guinea **CAPITAL:** Malabo
POPULATION: 453,000 **CURRENCY:** CFA franc **OFFICIAL LANGUAGE:** Spanish

1968
1968
Oct 12
GQ
+1
+240
.gq

COMPRISING FIVE ISLANDS and the territory of Río Muni on the west coast of Africa, Equatorial Guinea lies just north of the equator. Mangrove swamps border the mainland coast. The republic gained its independence in 1968 after 190 years of Spanish rule. Multipartyism was accepted in 1991, but the fairness of subsequent general elections has been questioned.

Bioko, formerly Fernando Po. Although the volcanic land is very fertile, cocoa production fell by 90% during the Macías years.

CLIMATE

Tropical equatorial

WEATHER CHART

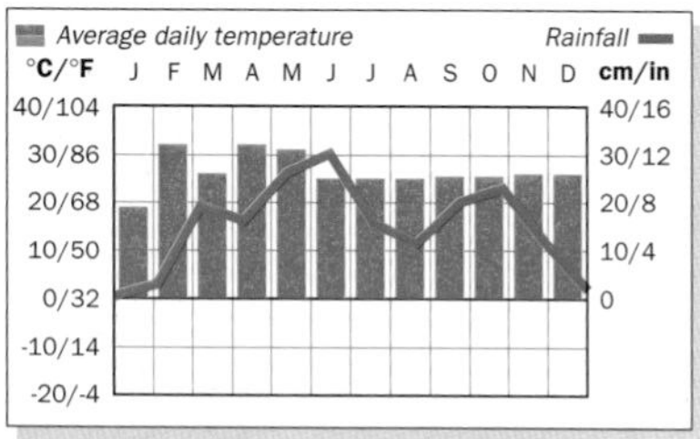
Average daily temperature
Rainfall
°C/°F
J F M A M J J A S O N D
cm/in
40/104
30/86
20/68
10/50
0/32
-10/14
-20/-4
40/16
30/12
20/8
10/4
0

The island of Bioko is extremely wet and humid, with an annual rainfall of 200 cm (79 in), while the mainland is only marginally drier and cooler.

TRANSPORTATION

Drive on right

Malabo

87 ships 58,506 grt

THE TRANSPORTATION NETWORK

508 km (316 miles)

None

None

None

Apart from once- or twice-weekly IBERIA flights to Madrid, all air links are through neighboring countries. The Chinese financed the Ncue–Mongomo Highway project in the 1980s.

TOURISM

Not available

Tourism receipts totalled $2 million in 1998

Numbers are increasing slowly

MAIN TOURIST ARRIVALS

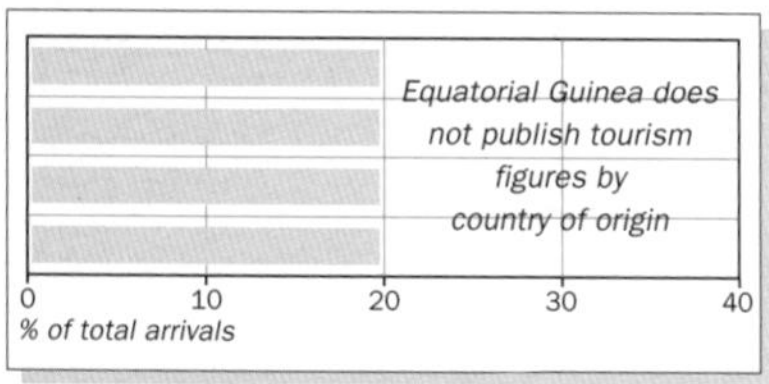
Equatorial Guinea does not publish tourism figures by country of origin
0
10
20
30
40
% of total arrivals

Equatorial Guinea is only of interest to the adventurous, independent tourist, despite the potential attraction of its beaches and the island of Bioko's spectacular mountain scenery.

PEOPLE

Pop. density low

Spanish, Fang, Bubi

16/km² (42/mi²)

THE URBAN/RURAL POPULATION SPLIT

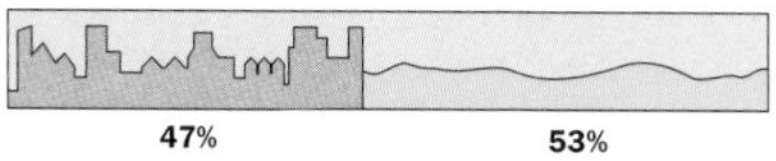
47%
53%

RELIGIOUS PERSUASION

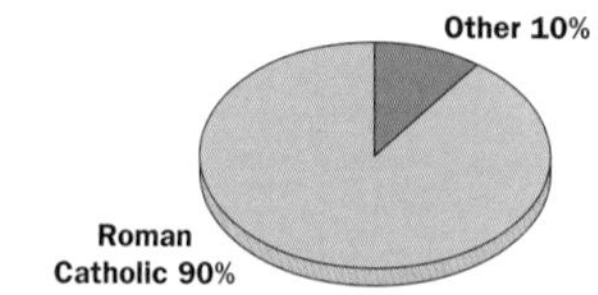
Other 10%
Roman Catholic 90%

The mainland has a majority of Fang, a people who also inhabit Cameroon and north Gabon. Bioko is populated by a majority of Bubi and a minority of Creoles, known as *Fernandinos*. The Macías dictatorship consolidated the power of the Fang, especially the Mongomo clan, from which both Macías and his successor Obiang come. The extended family has maintained its solidarity, despite disruptive social pressure during the Macías dictatorship.

POLITICS

Multiparty elections

1999/2004

President Teodoro Obiang Nguema Mbasogo

AT THE LAST ELECTION

House of Representatives of the People 80 seats

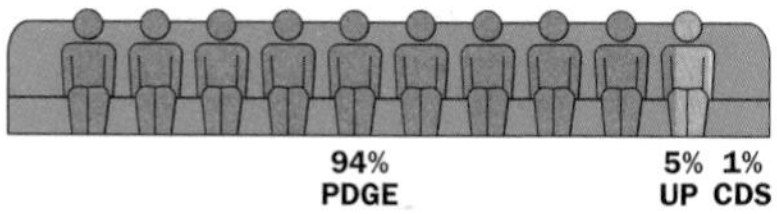
94% PDGE
5% UP
1% CDS

PDGE = Equatorial Guinea Democratic Party **UP** = Popular Union **CDS** = Convergence for Social Democracy

Despite officially being a multiparty state since 1991, some of the several exiled political parties have not yet found it safe to return – opposition leaders who publicize themselves tend to be arrested. The ruling PDGE was set up in 1987 by Teodoro Obiang Nguema Mbasogo, nephew of the dictator Francisco Macías Nguema, whom he overthrew in 1979. It replaced Macías' National Workers' Party (PUNT). The PDGE benefits from heavy government patronage, receiving 3% of all salaries.

The movement toward multipartyism – which was initiated in 1988 following the first elections for 20 years – has been marked by instability. The 1993 parliamentary elections were boycotted by the main opposition parties, while the presidential poll in 1996, in which Obiang was the only candidate, was declared farcical by foreign observers. The 1999 legislative elections were won easily by the PDGE, but denounced by the opposition.

EQUATORIAL GUINEA

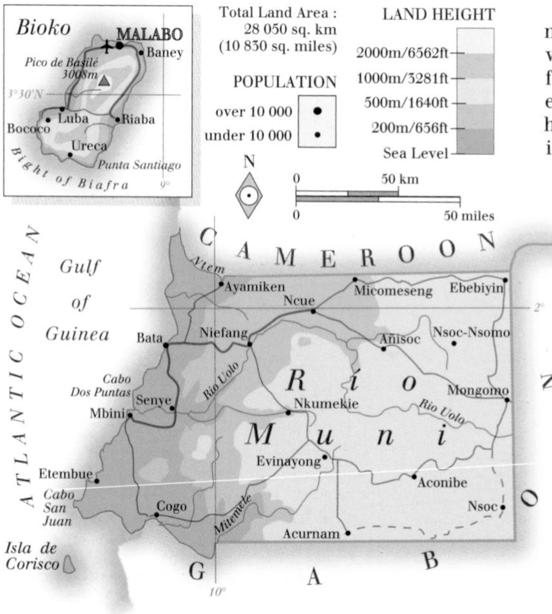
Bioko
MALABO
Baney
Pico de Basilé 3008m
Luba
Riaba
Bococo
Ureca
Punta Santiago
Bight of Biafra
Total Land Area : 28 050 sq. km (10 830 sq. miles)
POPULATION
over 10 000
under 10 000
LAND HEIGHT
2000m/6562ft
1000m/3281ft
500m/1640ft
200m/656ft
Sea Level
N
0
50 km
50 miles
CAMEROON
ATLANTIC OCEAN
Gulf of Guinea
Ntem
Ayamiken
Micomeseng
Ebebiyin
Ncue
Niefang
Bata
Añisoc
Nsoc-Nsomo
Río Uolo
Río Muni
Cabo Dos Puntas
Senye
Mbini
Nkumekie
Mongomo
Evinayong
Etembue
Cabo San Juan
Cogo
Mitemele
Aconibe
Nsoc
Acurnam
Isla de Corisco
GABON

E

WORLD AFFAIRS

Joined UN in 1968

BDEAC | ACP | FZ | NAM | OAU

After a period of extreme isolation at the time of the Macías dictatorship, Equatorial Guinea sought to rebuild links, especially its relationship with Spain, the former colonial power and traditionally a haven for political dissenters. However, the international community remains wary of the Obiang regime. Joining the Franc Zone in 1988 did not bring the expected benefits. Spain has become suspicious of French commercial ambitions in the country.

AID

Recipient

$20m (receipts) — Down 20% in 1999

Equatorial Guinea is poorly developed and therefore heavily dependent on aid. Inefficiency, corruption, and a shortage of skilled people hinder the planning and implementation of projects, and the government's political record threatens funding. France, Italy, Spain, the World Bank, and Arab funds are all important sources of aid. An IMF program was suspended in 1997 after the government failed to implement reforms.

DEFENSE

No compulsory military service

$10m — Up 43% in 1999

The main concern for the military and paramilitary force is internal security. Cuba and North Korea provided Macías with a presidential guard, while Obiang has been protected by Moroccan troops. Nigeria, Cameroon, and Gabon have interests in maintaining the autonomy of the Malabo and Río Muni regions.

RESOURCES

Electric power 5000 kw

6090 tonnes

115,000 b/d (reserves 3,600,000 bbl)

36,000 sheep, 30,000 ducks, 245,000 chickens

Oil, natural gas, gold

There are estimated to be ten years of oil and gas reserves at current production levels. President Obiang has pledged to use income from oil to promote development. Bata is served by a 3.2 MW hydropower station.

ENVIRONMENT

Not available

None — 1.5 tonnes per capita

The government has failed to take any serious measures to stop timber companies depleting the rainforest.

MEDIA

TV ownership low

Daily newspaper circulation 5 per 1000 people

PUBLISHING AND BROADCAST MEDIA

There is no regular daily press. The formerly daily newspaper *Poto Poto* now appears irregularly

1 state-owned service

3 services: 1 state-owned, 2 independent

The press remains tightly controlled, with little liberalization, despite the state's adoption of multipartyism. The press association was closed down by the police in February 2001.

CRIME

Death penalty used

Equatorial Guinea does not publish prison figures

Little change from year to year

The level of recorded crime is relatively low, although many offences do not get reported. Many human rights abuses still occur.

ECONOMICS

Inflation 13.1% p.a. (1990–1999)

$516m

654.42–698.69 CFA francs

SCORE CARD

❑ WORLD GNP RANKING	169th
❑ GNP PER CAPITA	$1170
❑ BALANCE OF PAYMENTS	$-344m
❑ INFLATION	–23.6%
❑ UNEMPLOYMENT	30%

EXPORTS

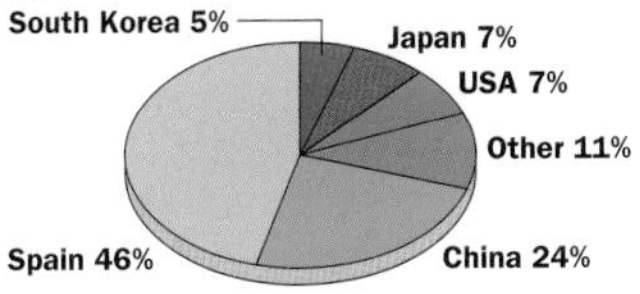
South Korea 5%
Japan 7%
USA 7%
Other 11%
Spain 46%
China 24%

IMPORTS

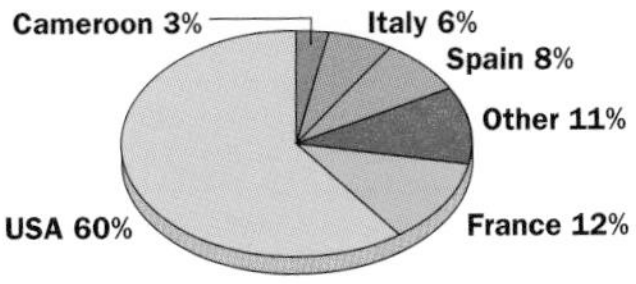
Cameroon 3%
Italy 6%
Spain 8%
Other 11%
USA 60%
France 12%

STRENGTHS

Fertile soils. Timber. Cocoa and coffee. Extensive territorial waters, with potential for fisheries. The economy is strengthening as oil and gas reserves are exploited.

WEAKNESSES

Lasting effects of economic regression under Macías dictatorship. Maladministration and ideological attacks on the educated have restricted growth; under Macías, cocoa production slumped by 90%. Deterioration of rural economy under successive brutal regimes. Undeveloped natural resources.

CHRONOLOGY

Equatorial Guinea remained a backwater of Spanish colonialism until development began after 1939.

- ❑ **1968** Independence. President Macías begins reign of terror.
- ❑ **1979** Coup puts nephew in power.
- ❑ **1991** Multiparty constitution.
- ❑ **1999** Ruling party wins majority in election condemned as fraudulent.
- ❑ **2001** Government resigns en masse following allegations of mismanagement and corruption.

EDUCATION

School leaving age: 11

83% — 578 students

Education declined in the Macías years, when attendance rates fell from 90% to 55%. Although education is declared the state's first priority, funding is poor.

HEALTH

No welfare state health benefits

1 per 4000 people

Diarrheal and respiratory diseases, malaria

Life expectancy has risen from 37 years in 1960 to 51 years in 1999. There are 25 doctors to every 100,000 people.

SPENDING

GDP/cap. increase

CONSUMPTION AND SPENDING

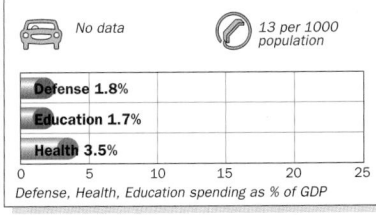

No data — *13 per 1000 population*

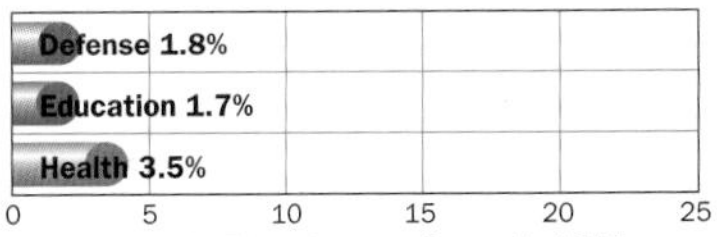
Defense 1.8%
Education 1.7%
Health 3.5%
0
5
10
15
20
25

Defense, Health, Education spending as % of GDP

What wealth there is in Equatorial Guinea tends to be concentrated in the ruling clan. There is also a remnant of the former Spanish plutocracy.

WORLD RANKING

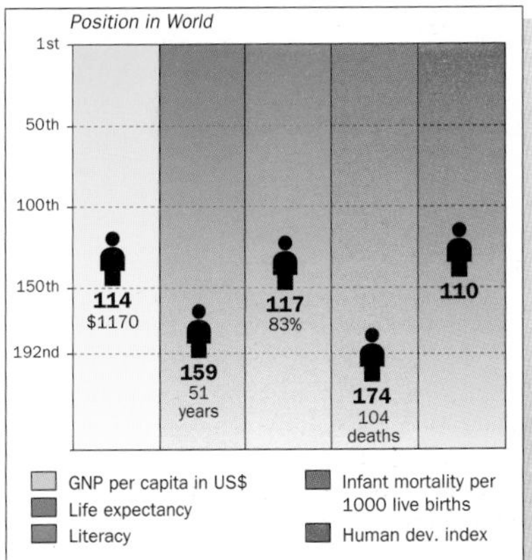
Position in World
1st
50th
100th
150th
192nd
114
$1170
159
51 years
117
83%
174
104 deaths
110
GNP per capita in US$
Life expectancy
Literacy
Infant mortality per 1000 live births
Human dev. index

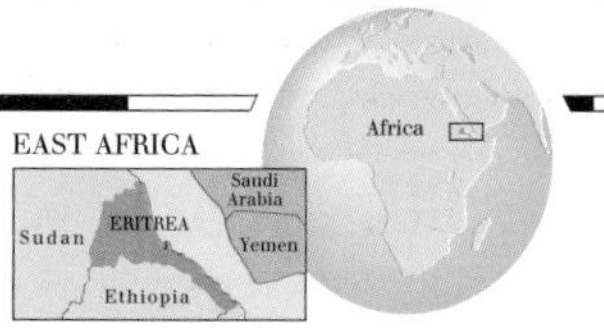
EAST AFRICA
Africa
Saudi Arabia
Sudan
ERITREA
Yemen
Ethiopia

ERITREA

OFFICIAL NAME: State of Eritrea **CAPITAL:** Asmara
POPULATION: 3.9 million **CURRENCY:** Nakfa **OFFICIAL LANGUAGE:** Tigrinya

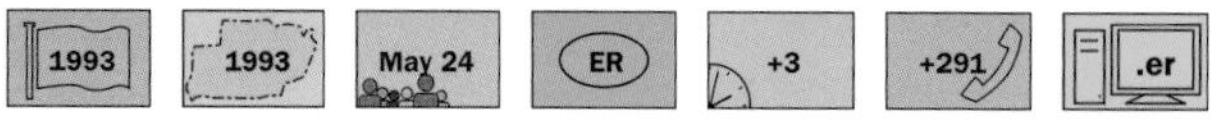
1993
1993
May 24
ER
+3
+291
.er

LYING ON THE SHORES of the Red Sea, Eritrea's landscape is one of rugged mountains, bush, and desert. A former Italian colony later annexed by Ethiopia, Eritrea fought a long war to win independence in 1993. Like its southern neighbor, Eritrea is prone to recurring droughts and the threat of famine. War with Ethiopia in 1998–2000 brought heavy losses on both sides, until the signing of a comprehensive peace agreement in December 2000.

CLIMATE

Hot desert/mountain

WEATHER CHART

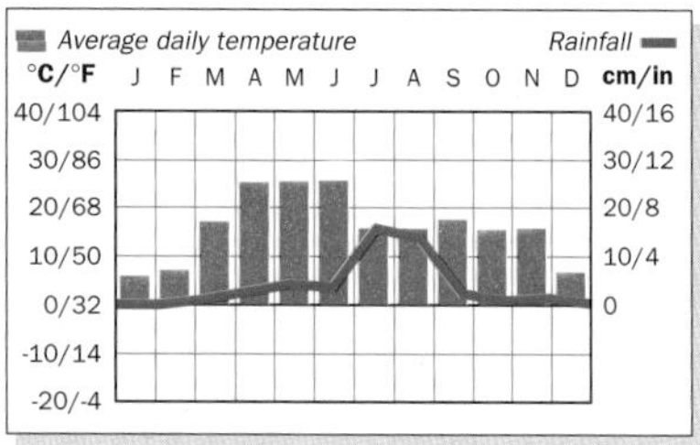
Average daily temperature
Rainfall
°C/°F J F M A M J J A S O N D cm/in
40/104
30/86
20/68
10/50
0/32
-10/14
-20/-4
40/16
30/12
20/8
10/4
0

Eritrea's harvest is dependent on mid-year rainfall in the highlands. Lowland temperatures may exceed 50°C (122°F).

TRANSPORTATION

Drive on right

Yohannes IV, Asmara
93,007 passengers

7 ships
7335 grt

THE TRANSPORTATION NETWORK

874 km (543 miles)

None

117 km (73 miles)

None

All transportation infrastructure requires massive investment. Ports have potential as transit points for Ethiopia.

TOURISM

Visitors : Population 1:56

70,000 visitors

Up 23% in 2000

MAIN TOURIST ARRIVALS

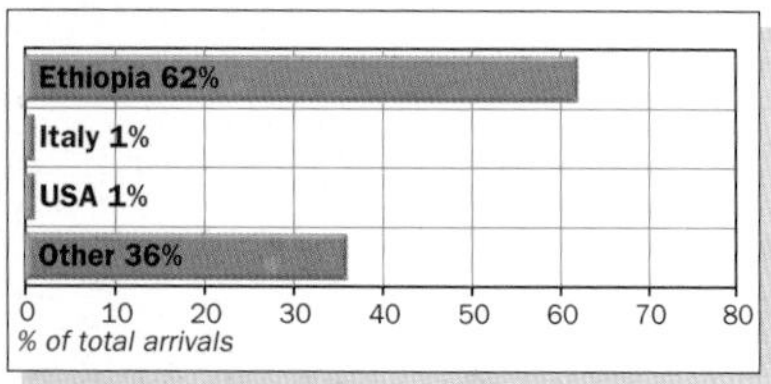
Ethiopia 62%
Italy 1%
USA 1%
Other 36%
0 10 20 30 40 50 60 70 80
% of total arrivals

There is currently very little tourism, but Eritrea has considerable long-term potential, especially along the Red Sea coast, with its underwater attractions, and in the spectacular Danakil depression. Guides are essential.

PEOPLE

Pop. density low

Tigrinya, English, Tigre, Afar, Arabic, Bilen, Kunama, Nara, Saho, Hadareb

33/km² (86/mi²)

THE URBAN/RURAL POPULATION SPLIT

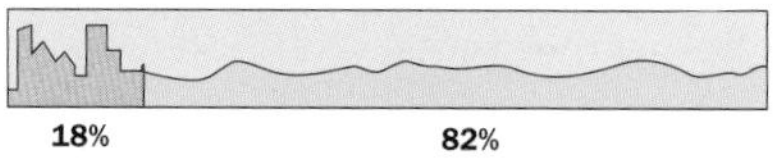
18%
82%

RELIGIOUS PERSUASION

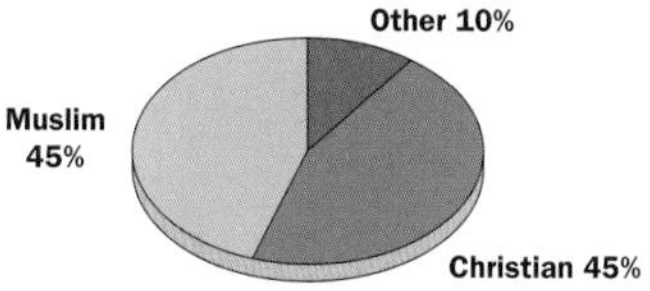
Other 10%
Muslim 45%
Christian 45%

Tigrinya-speakers, mainly Orthodox Christians, form the largest of Eritrea's nine main ethnic groups. A strong sense of nationhood has been forged by the 30-year struggle for independence. Women played an important role in the war; from 1973, 30,000 fought alongside men, some in positions of command. The nomadic peoples of the Danakil desert remain fiercely independent. Subsistence farmers account for 80% of the population.

ERITREA

Total Land Area : 117 680 sq. km (45 405 sq. miles)

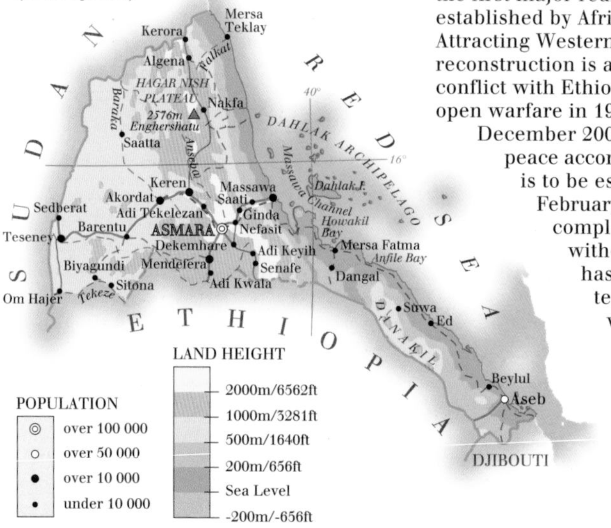
Mersa Teklay
Kerora
Algena
SUDAN
RED SEA
HAGAR NISH PLATEAU
Baraka
Nakfa
2576m
Enghershatu
DAHLAK ARCHIPELAGO
Saatta
Massawa Channel
Keren
Dahlak K.
Massawa
Saati
Akordat
Sedberat
Adi Tekelezan
Ginda
Howakil Bay
Barentu
Tesenev
ASMARA
Nefasit
Dekemhare
Adi Keyih
Mersa Fatma
Anfile Bay
Biyagundi
Mendefera
Senafe
Sitona
Adi Kwala
Dangal
Om Hajer
Tekeze
Suwa
Ed
ETHIOPIA
DANAKIL
Beylul
Aseb
DJIBOUTI
LAND HEIGHT
2000m/6562ft
1000m/3281ft
500m/1640ft
200m/656ft
Sea Level
-200m/-656ft
POPULATION
over 100 000
over 50 000
over 10 000
under 10 000
N
0 100 km
0 100 miles

POLITICS

No multiparty elections

Elections not yet held

President Issaias Afewerki

AT THE LAST ELECTION

National Assembly 150 seats

The National Assembly comprises 75 PFDJ central committee members and 75 directly elected members, including 11 seats reserved for women. Elections expected in 1997 under the new constitution have not yet taken place

A former Italian colony, Eritrea came under a temporary British mandate in 1941, until the UN passed the mandate to Ethiopia in a federation set up in 1952. Ethiopia annexed the country in 1961 prompting a long secessionist struggle. In 1991, the Eritrean People's Liberation Front (EPLF) and its Tigrean allies finally defeated the Ethiopian regime. A referendum held in 1993 overwhelmingly endorsed independence.

Pending multiparty elections, the country is run by a core leadership from the EPLF (now the People's Front for Democracy and Justice – PFDJ), who conducted the military campaign. A new constitution adopted in May 1997 forbids parties based on religious or ethnic affiliations. Issaias Afewerki, a Christian, has been careful to include Muslims in his transitional cabinet. His government came under unprecedented criticism from within the PFDJ in 2001.

WORLD AFFAIRS

Joined UN in 1993

COMESA | IBRD | IGAD | NAM | OAU

Eritrea's secession represented the first major redrawing of borders established by Africa's colonizers. Attracting Western and Arab aid for reconstruction is a priority. A border conflict with Ethiopia erupted into open warfare in 1998. Under the December 2000 UN-sponsored peace accord, a new border is to be established. In February 2001 Ethiopia completed its troop withdrawal. Eritrea has resolved other territorial disputes with Yemen and Sudan.

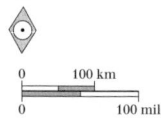

AID

Recipient

$148m (receipts)

Down 11% in 1999

The economy is highly aid-dependent, and 75% of the population survive on food aid. This is an obvious and pressing need, given the country's vulnerability to famine, but Western donors have been less generous with aid for the $2 billion reconstruction costs. Emergency UN aid was requested in mid-2000 to assist over a million people displaced by the Ethiopian incursion. WHO supplied emergency medical aid.

DEFENSE

Compulsory military service

$309m

Up 4% in 1999

Defense expenditure is massive. The 54,000-strong permanent army (of whom about a third are women) is swelled by vast numbers of conscripts. Troops were being reintegrated into the economy on "food for work" schemes until the latest war with Ethiopia, which inflicted heavy losses. An international arms embargo was imposed over this conflict.

ECONOMICS

Inflation 9.4% p.a. (1993–1998)

$779m

9.5–10.2 nakfa

SCORE CARD

- ❑ WORLD GNP RANKING........................160th
- ❑ GNP PER CAPITA..............................$200
- ❑ BALANCE OF PAYMENTS....................$-282m
- ❑ INFLATION.......................................0.9%
- ❑ UNEMPLOYMENT.........Widespread underemployment

STRENGTHS

Resourceful, hard-working population. Strategic position on Red Sea – tourism and transportation. Potential for mining and oil industry. Government committed to cutting dependence on food aid.

WEAKNESSES

Legacy of war – infrastructure and equipment destroyed. Port of Massawa heavily bombed. Dependent on aid. Most of population living at subsistence level. Susceptibility to drought and famine. 750,000 refugees have now returned.

EXPORTS

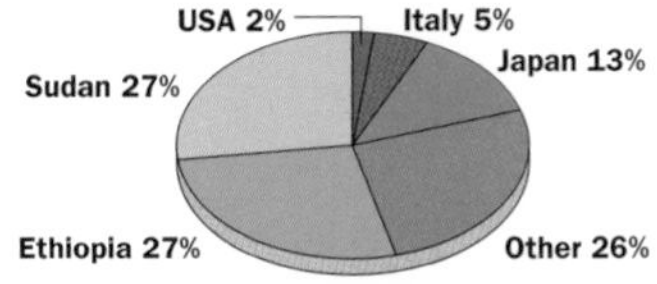
USA 2%
Italy 5%
Japan 13%
Sudan 27%
Ethiopia 27%
Other 26%

IMPORTS

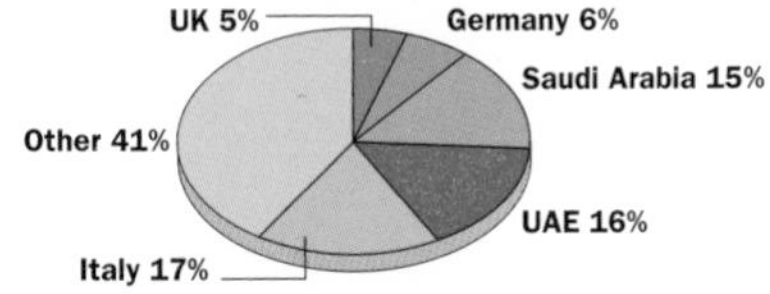
UK 5%
Germany 6%
Saudi Arabia 15%
Other 41%
UAE 16%
Italy 17%

RESOURCES

Electric power: Included within Ethiopian figures

978 tonnes

Not an oil producer; oil refinery at Assab

1.6m goats, 1.54m sheep, 1.4m cattle, 4.5m chickens

Copper, potash, gold, iron, silver, zinc, oil, silica, granite, marble

Eritrea has substantial copper reserves, and lesser ones of silver, zinc, and gold. High-quality silica, granite, and marble deposits could be exploited. Onshore and offshore oil deposits are believed to exist, but exploration work is at an early stage. There is potential for power generation from geothermal sources.

ENVIRONMENT

Not available

5%

0.03 tonnes per capita

Deforestation and soil erosion are major problems. The Ethiopian army uprooted trees to destroy the cover they provided for Eritrean soldiers. Since 1991, 22 million seedlings have been grown in a replanting scheme. The Red Sea coast is a conservation priority.

MEDIA

TV ownership low

There are no daily newspapers

PUBLISHING AND BROADCAST MEDIA

New Eritrea, owned by the PFDJ, is published every 3 days in English, Tigrinya, and Arabic

1 state-controlled service

1 state-controlled service

The media is largely controlled by the PFDJ, which runs both the radio and TV services. Independent newspapers are not encouraged.

CRIME

Death penalty used

Eritrea does not publish prison figures

Crime levels remain low

Crime has not been a major problem since independence. The judiciary and police answer to the PFDJ. There are a number of political prisoners.

EDUCATION

School leaving age: 13

56%

3096 students

Very few schools functioned during the war. There is one university. In an attempt to reduce potential ethnic tension, all children above the age of 11 are being taught in English.

HEALTH

No welfare state health benefits

1 per 20,000 people

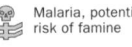

Malaria, potential risk of famine

The risk of famine overrides normal health concerns. Eritreans built their own hospitals during the independence struggle. Health provision is basic.

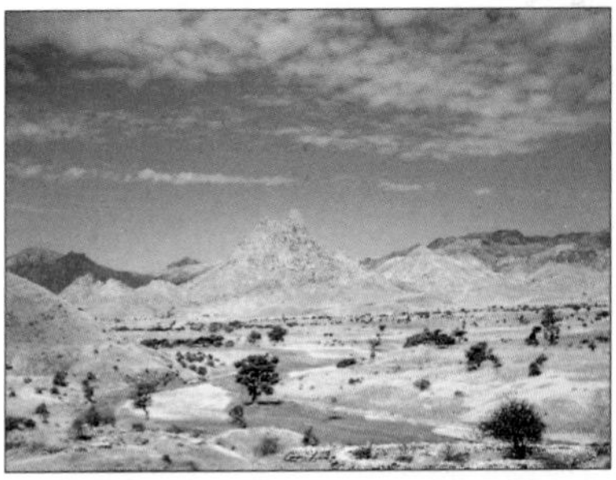

Seasonal river beds *carry rain from the Ethiopian highlands into Eritrea, providing essential irrigation for agriculture.*

E

CHRONOLOGY

British military rule replaced Italian colonial authority in 1941.

- ❑ **1952** Eritrea absorbed by Ethiopia.
- ❑ **1961** Beginning of armed struggle.
- ❑ **1987** EPLF refuses offer of autonomy; fighting intensifies.
- ❑ **1991** EPLF takes Asmara.
- ❑ **1993** Formal independence.
- ❑ **1998** Border war with Ethiopia.
- ❑ **2000** OAU peace treaty signed.
- ❑ **2001** Ethiopia completes troop withdrawal from Eritrea.

SPENDING

GDP/cap. increase

CONSUMPTION AND SPENDING

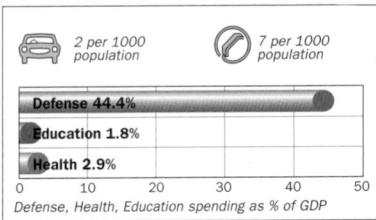

2 per 1000 population

7 per 1000 population

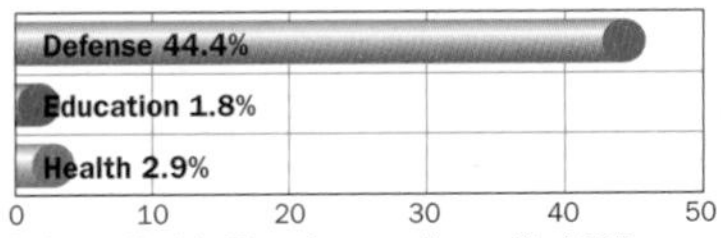
Defense 44.4%
Education 1.8%
Health 2.9%
0
10
20
30
40
50

Defense, Health, Education spending as % of GDP

Over 80% of Eritrea's population are subsistence farmers. A few of the 150,000 refugees who fled to Arab and Western countries have built up some personal savings.

WORLD RANKING

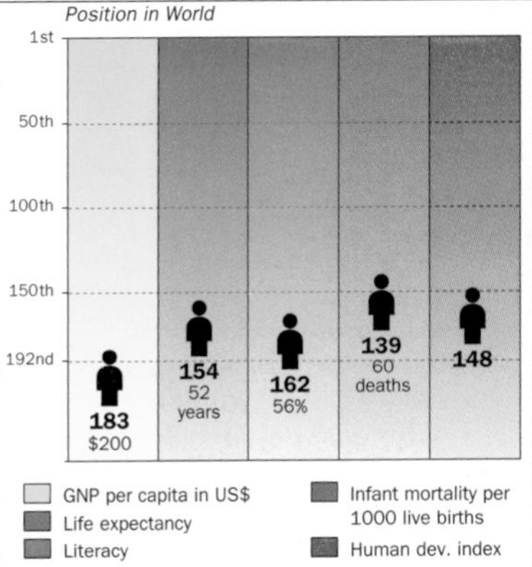
Position in World
1st
50th
100th
150th
192nd
183
$200
154
52 years
162
56%
139
60 deaths
148
GNP per capita in US$
Life expectancy
Literacy
Infant mortality per 1000 live births
Human dev. index

ESTONIA

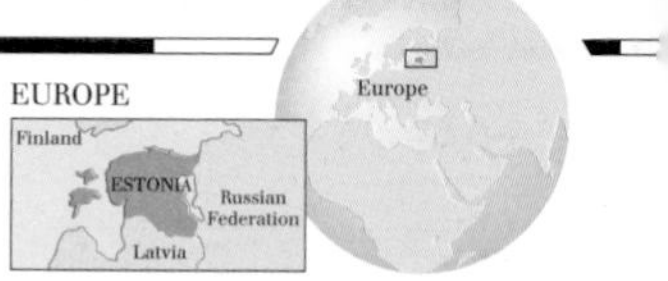
EUROPE
Europe
Finland
ESTONIA
Russian Federation
Latvia

OFFICIAL NAME: Republic of Estonia **CAPITAL:** Tallinn
POPULATION: 1.4 million **CURRENCY:** Kroon **OFFICIAL LANGUAGE:** Estonian

1991 | 1991 | Feb 24 | EST | +2 | +372 | .ee

TRADITIONALLY THE MOST Western-oriented of the Baltic states, Estonia is bordered by Latvia and the Russian Federation. Its terrain is flat, boggy, and partly wooded, and includes more than 1500 islands. Estonia formally regained its independence as a multiparty democracy in 1991. In contrast to the peoples of Latvia and Lithuania, Estonians are Finno-Ugric and their language is related to Finnish.

CLIMATE
Continental

WEATHER CHART

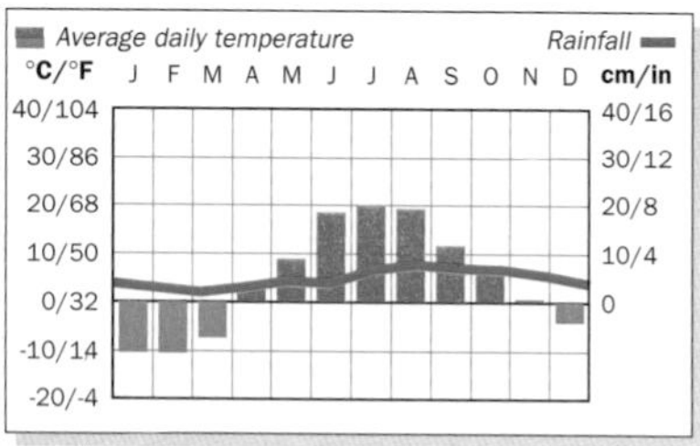
Average daily temperature
Rainfall
°C/°F
J F M A M J J A S O N D
cm/in
40/104
30/86
20/68
10/50
0/32
-10/14
-20/-4
40/16
30/12
20/8
10/4
0

Estonia's coastal location gives it cool summers, and cold winters when the Baltic Sea freezes.

TRANSPORTATION
Drive on right

Tallinn Ulemiste 551,989 passengers

239 ships 522,000 grt

THE TRANSPORTATION NETWORK

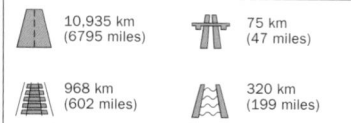

10,935 km (6795 miles)

75 km (47 miles)

968 km (602 miles)

320 km (199 miles)

Railroads have improved and buses are reliable. Baltic ferries link Tallinn with Finland, Sweden, and Germany.

TOURISM
Visitors : Population 1:1.3

1.1m visitors

Up 16% in 2000

MAIN TOURIST ARRIVALS

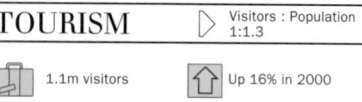

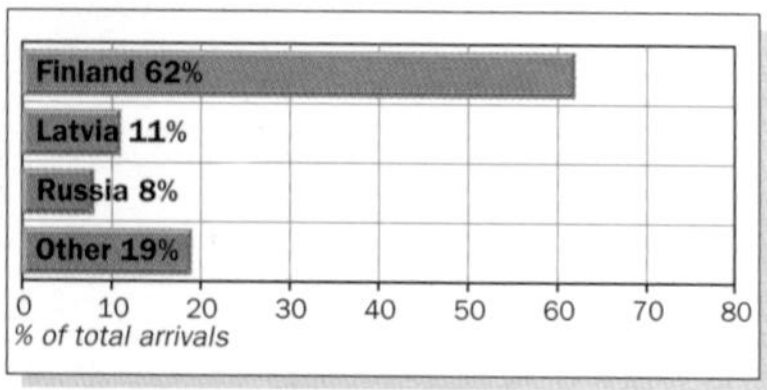
Finland 62%
Latvia 11%
Russia 8%
Other 19%
0 10 20 30 40 50 60 70 80
% of total arrivals

Estonia is particularly popular with Finns. Water sports, winter sports, folk and architectural heritage, and nature tours, are the main attractions. Tallinn's medieval center is a major draw for tourists on short visits.

PEOPLE
Pop. density low

Estonian, Russian

31/km² (80/mi²)

THE URBAN/RURAL POPULATION SPLIT

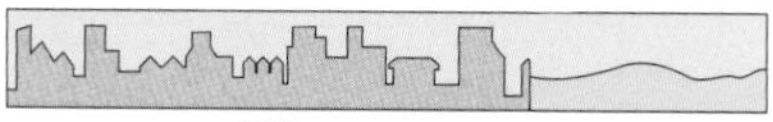
69%
31%

ETHNIC MAKEUP

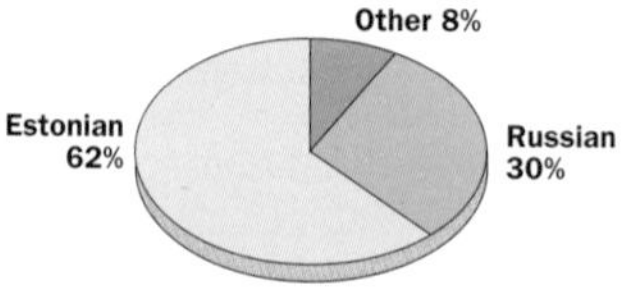
Other 8%
Estonian 62%
Russian 30%

Following decades of Soviet rule, there existed an uneasy relationship between Estonians and the Russian minority. Rules on citizenship, introduced in 1992 and 1995, excluded many ethnic Russians who could not meet the Estonian language and minimum residency requirements. Over 100,000 took Russian rather than Estonian citizenship. A 2000 language law met international demands for an end to discrimination against the Russian-speaking minority. Estonians are predominantly Protestant. Families are small; divorce rates are high.

POLITICS
Multiparty elections

1999/2003

President Lennart Meri

AT THE LAST ELECTION

Parliament 101 seats

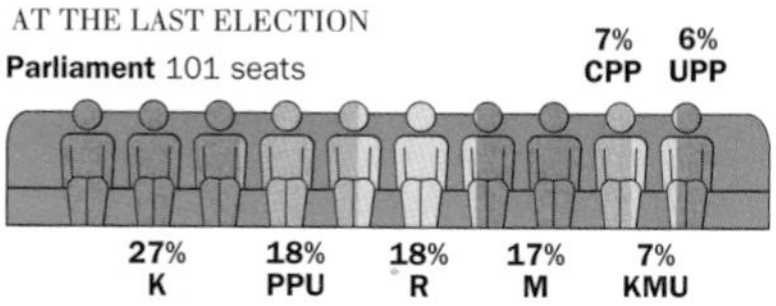
7% CPP
6% UPP
27% K
18% PPU
18% R
17% M
7% KMU

K = Centre Party **PPU** = Pro Patria Union **R** = Reform Party **M** = Moderates **CPP** = Rural People's Party **KMU** = Coalition Party **UPP** = United People's Party

Coalition government has been the norm since the end of communist rule. In elections in 1999 the Centre Party won the most seats, on a platform of graduated income tax to help overcome wealth disparities. However, Mart Laar, who had led the government in power from 1992 to 1995, became prime minister, leading a center-right coalition of the PPU, the Reform, and the Moderate parties. There was no place for the outgoing prime minister, Mart Siiman, despite his economic successes over the previous two years. Laar's government committed itself to pursuing free-market reforms. The battle to get measures through parliament, with only a slim majority, eased as the economy grew strongly from the beginning of 2000.

ESTONIA

Total Land Area : 45 125 sq. km (17 423 sq. miles)

LAND HEIGHT
- 200m/565ft
- Sea Level

POPULATION
- over 500 000
- over 100 000
- over 50 000
- over 10 000
- under 10 000

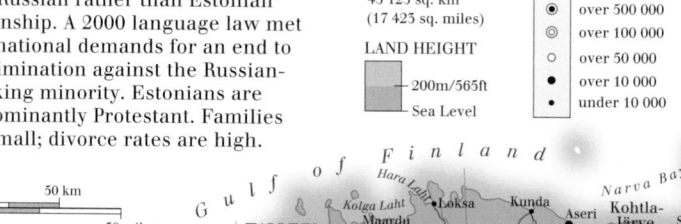

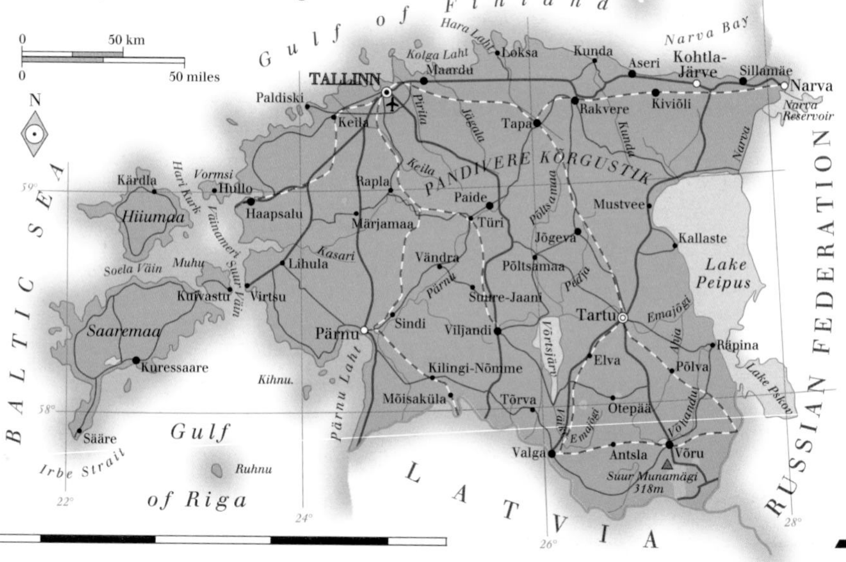
Gulf of Finland
Narva Bay
TALLINN
Paldiski
Maardu
Loksa
Kunda
Aseri
Kohtla-Järve
Sillamäe
Narva
Narva Reservoir
Keila
Tapa
Rakvere
Kiviõli
PANDIVERE KÕRGUSTIK
Kärdla
Hiiumaa
Vormsi
Haapsalu
Rapla
Paide
Türi
Märjamaa
Mustvee
Jõgeva
Kallaste
Lake Peipus
Lihula
Vändra
Põltsamaa
Kuivastu
Virtsu
Pärnu
Sindi
Viljandi
Suure-Jaani
Tartu
Emajõgi
Räpina
Põlva
Elva
Saaremaa
Kuressaare
Kihnu
Kilingi-Nõmme
Mõisaküla
Tõrva
Otepää
Võhandu
Lake Pskov
Valga
Antsla
Võru
Suur Munamägi 318m
Sääre
Irbe Strait
Gulf of Riga
Ruhnu
BALTIC SEA
LATVIA
RUSSIAN FEDERATION
0 50 km
0 50 miles
N

WORLD AFFAIRS

Joined UN in 1991

CBSS | CE | EAPC | OSCE | PfP

Estonia's trade with the West has been growing, and "fast track" negotiations on full EU membership began in 1998. Ties with other Baltic countries and with Scandinavia have been particularly emphasized. Integration with the EU and NATO is the top priority.

Estonia has now accepted the de facto border with Russia, having effectively ceded a portion of its territory during the Soviet period.

AID

Recipient

$83m (receipts) | Up 28% 1997–1999

Although an aid recipient, since 1997 Estonia has also been an aid donor, mainly through technical assistance.

DEFENSE

Compulsory military service

$71m | Up 16% in 1999

The government agreed in July 2000 to shorten compulsory military service from 12 to eight months. Initial US opposition to full membership of NATO has now been changed to support for the Baltic states' entry into the organization.

ECONOMICS

Inflation 62.7% p.a. (1990–1999)

$4.9bn | 15.609–16.675 krooni

SCORE CARD

❑ WORLD GNP RANKING	111th
❑ GNP PER CAPITA	$3400
❑ BALANCE OF PAYMENTS	$295m
❑ INFLATION	3.3%
❑ UNEMPLOYMENT	13%

STRENGTHS

Improved productivity and stable currency are pegged to the euro. Simplicity of tax regime. More advantage is being taken of natural resources, including timber and oil shale. Transportation infrastructure has been upgraded. Exports growing.

WEAKNESSES

Poor raw materials base. Dependence on imported energy supplies.

EXPORTS

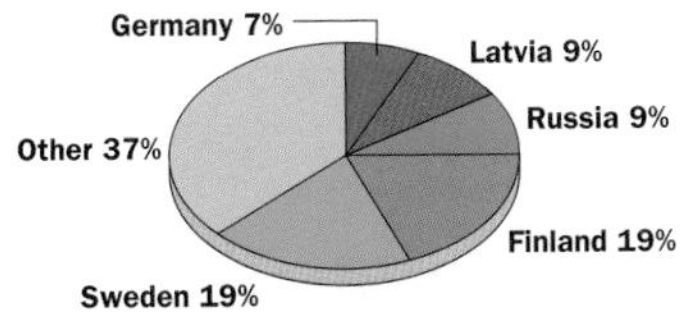
Germany 7%
Latvia 9%
Russia 9%
Other 37%
Finland 19%
Sweden 19%

IMPORTS

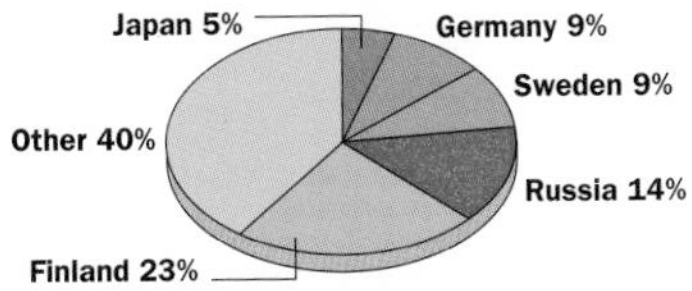
Japan 5%
Germany 9%
Sweden 9%
Other 40%
Russia 14%
Finland 23%

RESOURCES

Electric power 2.7m kw

123,873 tonnes | Oil figures not published

285,600 cattle, 281,200 pigs, 2.46m chickens | Oil shale, coal, peat, phosphorite

The chief energy resource is oil shale. Phosphorite mining has been stopped. Timber is processed to make paper.

ENVIRONMENT

Sustainability rank: 27th

12% | 13.1 tonnes per capita

Industrial pollution comes especially from power stations burning oil shale. Danger of radioactive leaks from former Soviet bases remains. Water supply and sewage treatment have improved.

MEDIA

TV ownership high

Daily newspaper circulation 174 per 1000 people

PUBLISHING AND BROADCAST MEDIA

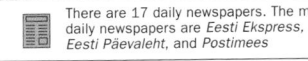

There are 17 daily newspapers. The main daily newspapers are *Eesti Ekspress, Eesti Päevaleht,* and *Postimees*

5 services: 1 state-owned, 4 independent | 8 services: 1 state-owned, 7 independent

The media are mostly pro-government. The number of Russian-language programs is declining. Estonians have been able to receive Finnish satellite TV for some years.

CRIME

Death penalty not used

4034 prisoners | Up 31% 1996–1998

Robbery and narcotics are the main crime problems. Generally, however, crime levels are still relatively low.

EDUCATION

School leaving age: 16

99% | 43,468 students

Education is becoming increasingly Westernized. There are 34 higher-education establishments in Estonia.

HEALTH

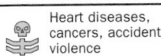

Welfare state health benefits

1 per 323 people | Heart diseases, cancers, accidents, violence

The health system, improved since the collapse of communism, is better than that of most former Soviet republics.

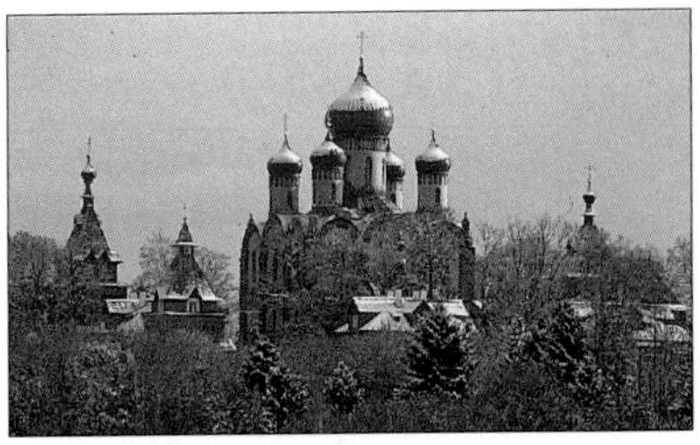

***The Russian Orthodox convent** of Pühtitsa at Kuremäe in Estonia's marshy north. Most of the population is Evangelical Lutheran.*

CHRONOLOGY

After Swedish and then Russian rule, Estonia briefly enjoyed independence from 1921 until its incorporation into the Soviet Union in 1940.

- ❑ **1990** Unilateral declaration of independence; achieved in 1991.
- ❑ **1992** First multiparty elections: election of center-right government.
- ❑ **1996** President Lennart Meri wins second term of office.
- ❑ **1997** December, EU agrees to open membership negotiations.
- ❑ **1999** Elections result in new center-right government.

E

SPENDING

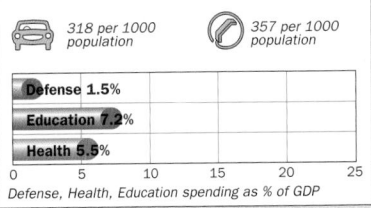

GDP/cap. decrease

CONSUMPTION AND SPENDING

318 per 1000 population | *357 per 1000 population*

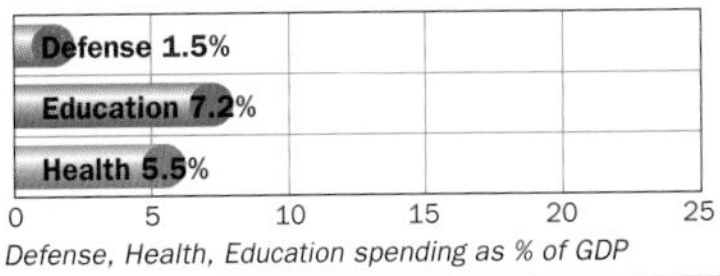
Defense 1.5%
Education 7.2%
Health 5.5%
0
5
10
15
20
25
Defense, Health, Education spending as % of GDP

Market reforms have led to increased prosperity. A few have become very rich. Average wages are higher than in other Baltic states.

WORLD RANKING

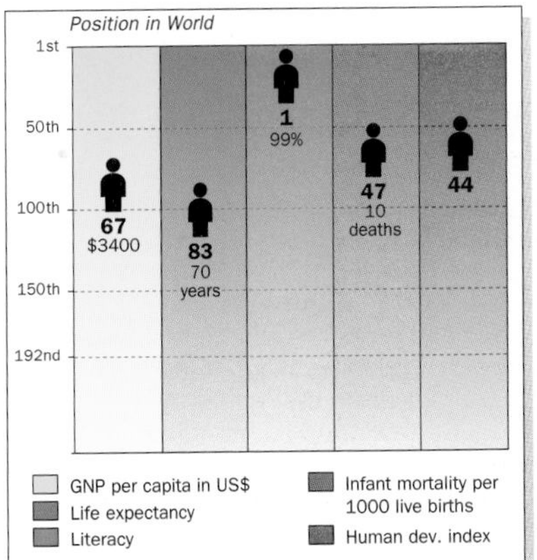
Position in World
1st
50th
100th
150th
192nd
67
$3400
83
70
years
1
99%
47
10
deaths
44
GNP per capita in US$
Life expectancy
Literacy
Infant mortality per 1000 live births
Human dev. index

ETHIOPIA

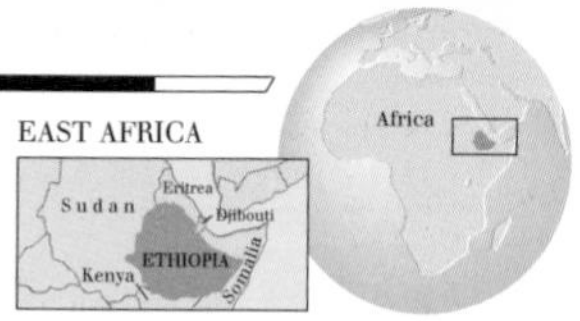
EAST AFRICA
Africa
Sudan
Eritrea
Djibouti
ETHIOPIA
Kenya
Somalia

OFFICIAL NAME: Federal Democratic Republic of Ethiopia **CAPITAL:** Addis Ababa
POPULATION: 62.6 million **CURRENCY:** Ethiopian birr **OFFICIAL LANGUAGE:** Amharic

1896
1993
May 28
ETH
+3
+251
.et

LOCATED IN NORTHEAST Africa, the former empire of Ethiopia is the cradle of an ancient civilization, which adopted Orthodox Christianity in the 4th century. It has been landlocked since 1993, when Eritrea, on the Red Sea, seceded. Ethiopia is mountainous except for desert lowlands in the northeast and southeast, and is prone to devastating drought and famine. A long civil war ended in 1991 with the defeat of the Stalinist military dictatorship that had ruled since 1974. A free-market, multiparty democratic system now provides substantial regional autonomy. War with Eritrea in 1998–2000 brought heavy losses on both sides, before a peace agreement was signed in December 2000 and arbitrators were brought in to redefine the border.

CLIMATE

Mountain/steppe

WEATHER CHART

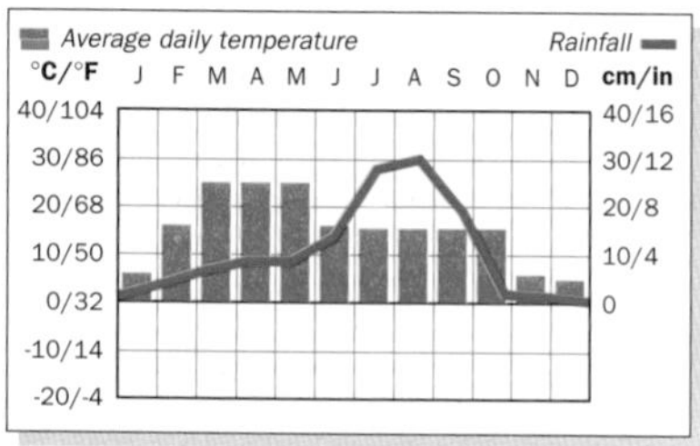
Average daily temperature
Rainfall
°C/°F J F M A M J J A S O N D cm/in
40/104
30/86
20/68
10/50
0/32
-10/14
-20/-4
40/16
30/12
20/8
10/4
0

In general, the climate is moderate, except in the lowlands of the Danakil and the Ogaden deserts, which are hot all year round and can suffer severe drought. The highlands are temperate, with night frost in the mountains. The single rainy season in the west brings twice as much rain as do the two wet seasons in the east. During these cloudy periods, thunderstorms occur almost daily.

TRANSPORTATION

Drive on right

Bole International, Addis Ababa
940,400 passengers

12 ships
82,503 grt

THE TRANSPORTATION NETWORK

4275 km (2656 miles)

Trans-East Africa Highway

681 km (423 miles)

None

The single railroad linking Addis Ababa with Djibouti has grown in strategic importance due to the conflict with Eritrea. Ethiopia's main access to the sea by road has been through the Red Sea ports of Assab and Massawa, now part of an independent Eritrea. Inland, pack mules and donkeys are widely used. Ethiopian Airlines has good services to much of Africa, and to European and US cities.

TOURISM

Visitors : Population 1:501

125,000 visitors

Up 36% in 2000

MAIN TOURIST ARRIVALS

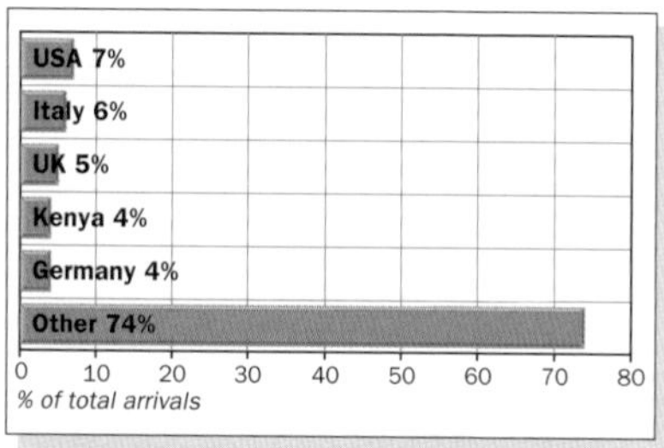
USA 7%
Italy 6%
UK 5%
Kenya 4%
Germany 4%
Other 74%
0 10 20 30 40 50 60 70 80
% of total arrivals

Despite Ethiopia's unique attractions, tourism is on a small scale, although since 1991 there has been a sizable increase in the number of visitors, mostly on organized tours. Several new hotels are being built. The Rift Valley lakes, Lake Tana, the Gonder castles, and the Blue Nile gorge, with its spectacular scenery, are popular tourism destinations, but guides are essential. Ancient churches and cities such as Aksum, the royal capital of the first Ethiopian kingdom, are now accessible. Visitors are also attracted to the five national parks.

Lalibela lies 120 km (75 miles) northwest of Desē in Ethiopia's plateau region, and is famous for the rock-hewn churches created by King Lalibela of the Zagwe dynasty.

PEOPLE

Pop. density medium

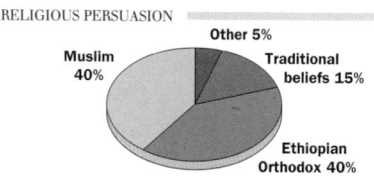

Amharic, Tigrinya, Galla, Sidamo, Somali, English, Arabic

56/km² (146/mi²)

THE URBAN/RURAL POPULATION SPLIT

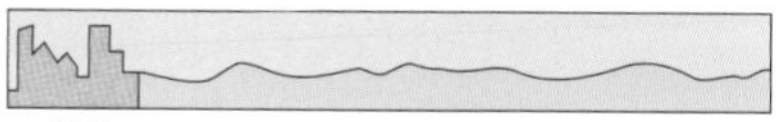
17%
83%

RELIGIOUS PERSUASION

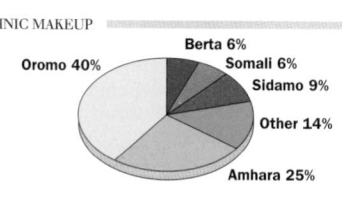

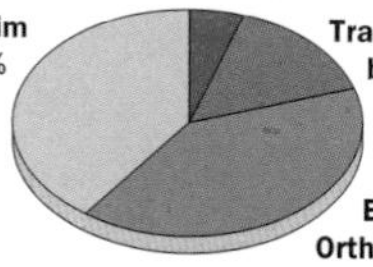
Other 5%
Traditional beliefs 15%
Muslim 40%
Ethiopian Orthodox 40%

ETHNIC MAKEUP

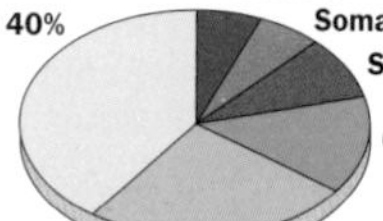
Berta 6%
Oromo 40%
Somali 6%
Sidamo 9%
Other 14%
Amhara 25%

There are 76 ethnic nations in Ethiopia, speaking 286 languages. Oromos (or Gallas) form the largest group. whereas less than 5% of the population are Tigreans.

Civil war was sparked by fighting between different ethnic groups, but they later united in opposition to the Mengistu regime. Ethnic tensions are still near the surface, in spite of the new federal structure, and there have been reports of boundary disputes in several regions. The Oromos withdrew from the Tigrean-dominated government in 1992. Hostility to the government has also been voiced by disaffected Amharas, who had been dominant for several centuries, and by the Orthodox Church. The aspirations of ethnic Somalis in the southeast are another source of tension.

Most of the small Jewish community, which has lived in Ethiopia for 2000 years, was evacuated to Israel in 1991, but more than 20,000 remain, waiting for Israel to offer them citizenship.

The participation of women in rural organizations is increasing, reflecting the key role women played in the war.

POPULATION AGE BREAKDOWN

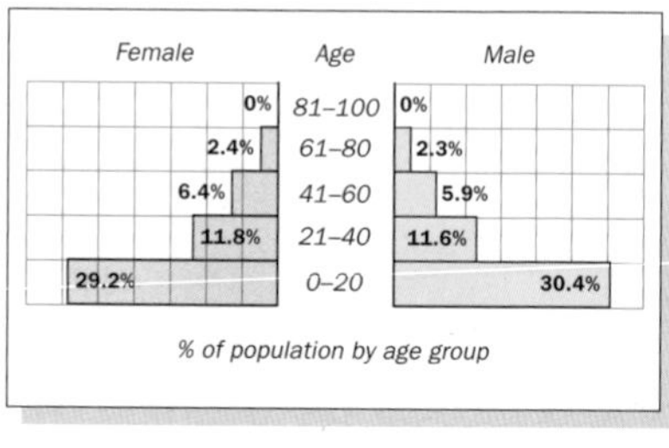
Female
Age
Male
0%
81–100
0%
2.4%
61–80
2.3%
6.4%
41–60
5.9%
11.8%
21–40
11.6%
29.2%
0–20
30.4%
% of population by age group

Key to symbols and abbreviations on cover flaps

ETHIOPIA

Total Land Area : 1 110 000 sq. km (428 571 sq. miles)

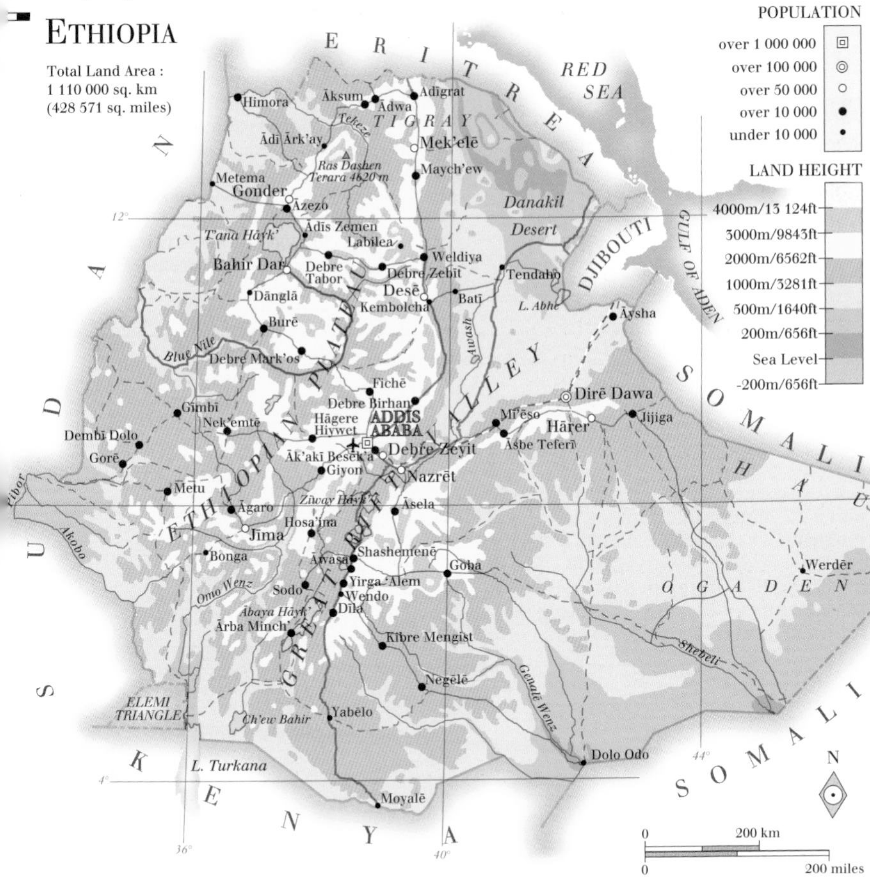
POPULATION
over 1 000 000
over 100 000
over 50 000
over 10 000
under 10 000
LAND HEIGHT
4000m/13 124ft
3000m/9843ft
2000m/6562ft
1000m/3281ft
500m/1640ft
200m/656ft
Sea Level
-200m/656ft
ERITREA
RED SEA
TIGRAY
Himora
Āksum
Ādwa
Ādigrat
Mek'elē
Ādī Ārk'ay
Ras Dashen Terara 4620m
Maych'ew
Metema
Gonder
Āzezo
Danakil Desert
DJIBOUTI
GULF OF ADEN
T'ana Hāyk'
Ādīs Zemen
Labilea
Weldiya
Bahir Dar
Debre Tabor
Debre Zebīt
Tendaho
Desē
Kembolcha
Batī
L. Abhe
Dānglā
Āysha
Burē
Blue Nile
Debre Mark'os
Awash
Fichē
Debre Birhan
Dirē Dawa
Gīmbī
Nek'emtē
Hāgere Hiywet
ADDIS ABABA
Mī'ēso
Hārer
Jijiga
Dembī Dolo
Āsbe Teferī
Gorē
Āk'akī Besek'a
Debre Zeyit
Giyon
Nazrēt
Metu
ETHIOPIAN PLATEAU
GREAT RIFT VALLEY
Āgaro
Ziway Hāyk'
Āsela
Jīma
Hosa'ina
Akobo
Bonga
Āwasa
Shashemenē
Goba
HAUD
OGADEN
Werdēr
Omo Wenz
Sodo
Yirga 'Alem
Wendo
Ābaya Hāyk'
Dīla
Ārba Minch'
Kibre Mengist
Shebelē
Negēlē
Genalē Wenz
ELEMI TRIANGLE
Ch'ew Bahir
Yabēlo
SUDAN
SOMALIA
Dolo Odo
L. Turkana
KENYA
Moyalē
N
0
200 km
200 miles

WORLD AFFAIRS

Joined UN in 1945

COMESA | G24 | IGAD | NAM | OAU

Landlocked since the secession of Eritrea, Ethiopia needs continued access to the Red Sea ports of Massawa and Assab, and maintained cordial relations with Eritrea until a border dispute escalated into armed conflict in 1998. A peace accord reached two years later allowed for the demarcation of a new border.

Addis Ababa is the headquarters of the OAU and of the UN Economic Commission for Africa. Ethiopia is active in regional diplomacy, including numerous attempts at brokering peace in Somalia, although tension with Somali factions during 1998 and 1999 escalated into armed intervention by Ethiopia.

The government's official policy is one of non-interference in the affairs of neighboring countries, although Sudan and Somalia have accused Ethiopia of supporting southern rebels. Links with other African states have been strengthened, as have those with the USA, the EU, and Israel.

E

POLITICS

Multiparty elections

L. House 2000/2005
U. House 2000/2005

President Negaso Gidada

AT THE LAST ELECTION

House of People's Representatives 550 seats

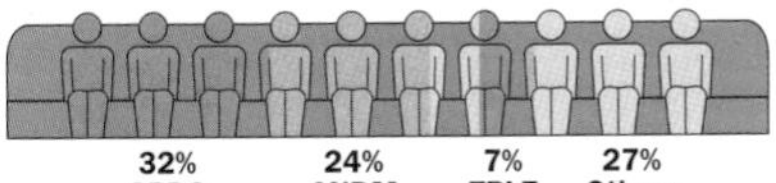
8% Vacant
2% Ind
32% OPDO
24% ANDM
7% TPLF
27% Others

OPDO = Oromo People's Democratic Organization
ANDM = Amhara National Democratic Movement
TPLF = Tigray People's Liberation Front **Ind** = Independents

The Ethiopian People's Revolutionary Democratic Front (EPRDF) includes all the main parties and controls over 90% of the lower house.

Federal Council 108 seats

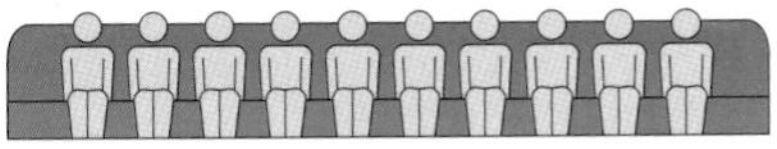

The Federal Council is elected indirectly on a nonparty basis.

The transitional period which followed the collapse of the Mengistu military dictatorship in 1991 ended in 1995 with multiparty elections.

MAIN POLITICAL ISSUE
Ethnic representation

The 1994 constitution establishing a nine-state federation grants the states considerable autonomy, including the right to secede, as Eritrea did in 1993. The EPRDF government believes this to be the best way to prevent secessionist conflict and maintain national unity. The ruling broad-based coalition government is ideologically led by Tigrean politicians.

PROFILE

The current government, reelected in 2000, succeeded that set up in 1991 by the EPRDF, the strongest of the groups that fought Mengistu's Marxist regime and chiefly responsible for winning the civil war. Prime Minister Meles Zenawi is the leader of the Tigrean People's Liberation Front, the largest group within the EPRDF. There is growing opposition from the Oromos and Amharas to the dominance of Tigreans. The nine states are largely governed by elected governments dominated by local liberation movements.

***Prime Minister Meles Zenawi,** leader of the EPRDF, which ousted the Mengistu regime.*

***Mengistu Haile Mariam,** who ran Ethiopia on Soviet lines from 1977–1991.*

CHRONOLOGY

After repelling a devastating Muslim invasion in 1523, Ethiopia developed as an isolated empire until Egyptian and Sudanese incursions in the 1850s led to its renewed political power under Emperor Teodros. His successor, Menelik II, doubled the empire southward and eastward.

- **1896** Italian invasion of Tigre defeated. Europeans recognize Ethiopia's independence.
- **1913** Menelik II dies.
- **1916** His son, Lij Iyasu, is deposed for his conversion to Islam and a proposed alliance with Turkey. Menelik's daughter, Zauditu, becomes empress with Ras Tafari as regent.
- **1923** Joins League of Nations.
- **1930** Zauditu dies. Ras Tafari crowned Emperor Haile Selassie.
- **1936** Italians occupy Ethiopia. League of Nations fails to react.
- **1941** British oust Italians and restore Haile Selassie, who sets up a constitution, parliament, and cabinet, but retains personal power and the feudal system.
- **1952** Eritrea, ruled by Italy until 1941, then under British mandate, federated with Ethiopia.

E

CHRONOLOGY *continued*

- **1962** Unitary state created; Eritrea loses its autonomy within the Ethiopian state despite the demands of secessionists.
- **1972–1974** Famine kills 200,000.
- **1974** Strikes and army mutinies at Haile Selassie's autocratic rule and country's economic decline. Dergue (Military Committee) stages coup.
- **1975** Becomes socialist state: nationalizations, worker cooperatives, and health reforms.
- **1977** Colonel Mengistu Haile Mariam takes over. Somali invasion of Ogaden defeated with Soviet and Cuban help.
- **1978–1979** Thousands of political opponents killed or imprisoned.
- **1984** Workers' Party of Ethiopia (WPE) set up on Soviet model. One million die in famine after drought and years of war. Live Aid concert raises funds for relief.
- **1986** Eritrean rebels now control the whole northeastern coast.
- **1987** Serious drought again threatens famine.
- **1988** Eritrean and Tigrean People's Liberation Fronts (EPLF and TPLF) begin new offensives. Mengistu's budget is for "Everything to the War Front." Diplomatic relations with Somalia restored.
- **1989** Military coup attempt fails. TPLF in control of most of Tigre. TPLF and Ethiopian People's Revolutionary Movement form alliance – EPRDF.
- **1990** Military gains by opponents of Mengistu regime. Moves toward market economy and restructuring of ruling party to include non-Marxists. Distribution of food aid for victims of new famine is hampered by government and rebel forces.
- **1991** Mengistu accepts military defeat and flees country. EPRDF enters Addis Ababa, sets up provisional government, promising representation for all ethnic groups. Outbreaks of fighting continue, between mainly Tigrean EPRDF and opposing groups.
- **1993** Eritrean independence recognized following referendum.
- **1995** Transitional rule ends. EPRDF wins landslide in multiparty elections, sets up first democratic government. New nine-state federation is formed.
- **1998–2000** Tensions with Eritrea escalate into a border war.
- **2000** OAU peace treaty signed. Haile Selassie's remains buried in Trinity Cathedral, Addis Ababa.
- **2001** Ethiopia completes troop withdrawal from Eritrea.

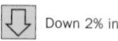

AID

Recipient

$633m (receipts)

Down 2% in 1999

The World Food Program and the EU are the largest sources of assistance, while the USA has taken over from Italy and the former Soviet Union as the major bilateral donor. Aid per capita is low by regional standards. However, long-term development assistance and balance of payments support look set to continue their recent growth. Aid is now playing an increasingly important part in the economy. The emphasis – at least until the 2000 drought disaster – was shifting from food aid toward credit for infrastructure development.

DEFENSE

No compulsory military service

$444m

Up 15% in 1999

Ethiopia is one of the most heavily militarized states in Africa. Its sizable standing army is boosted by conscription at times of crisis. Heavy losses have been sustained in fighting with Eritrea and a 12-month international arms embargo was imposed following the Ethiopian advance in May 2000. The government is trying to gain control of the many ethnic and clan-based militias throughout the country.

ETHIOPIAN ARMED FORCES

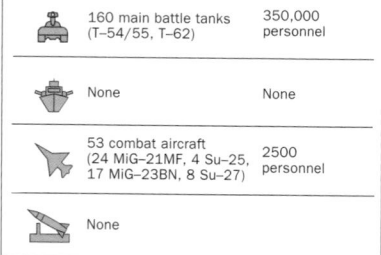

160 main battle tanks (T–54/55, T–62)	350,000 personnel
None	None
53 combat aircraft (24 MiG–21MF, 4 Su–25, 17 MiG–23BN, 8 Su–27)	2500 personnel
None	

ECONOMICS

Inflation 7.6% p.a. (1990–1999)

$6.5bn

7.999–8.225 Ethiopian birr

SCORE CARD

World GNP Ranking	100th
GNP per Capita	$100
Balance of Payments	$134m
Inflation	8.2%
Unemployment	63%

EXPORTS

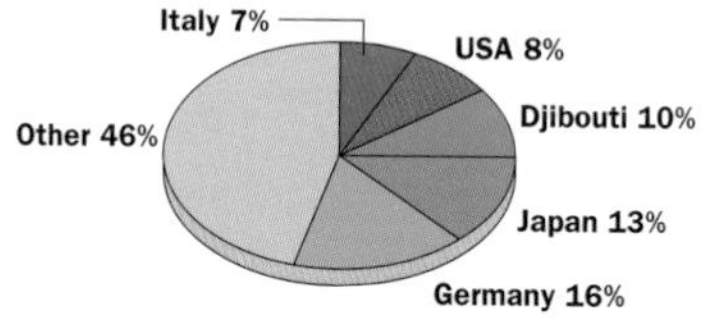

Italy 7%
USA 8%
Djibouti 10%
Other 46%
Japan 13%
Germany 16%

IMPORTS

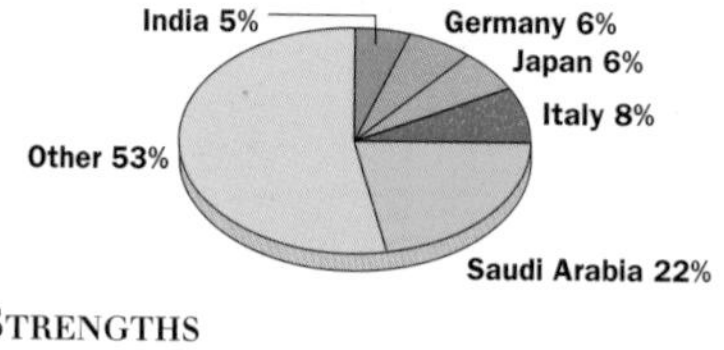

India 5%
Germany 6%
Japan 6%
Italy 8%
Other 53%
Saudi Arabia 22%

Strengths

Increased economic aid in 1990s. End of total state control. Coffee production.

Weaknesses

Overwhelming dependence on agriculture. Periodic serious droughts. War-damaged infrastructure. Massive displacement of population by war and drought. Small industrial base. Lack of skilled workers. Legacy of Mengistu regime's centrally planned economy.

Profile

After the end of the civil war in 1991, Ethiopia began moving toward a

ECONOMIC PERFORMANCE INDICATOR

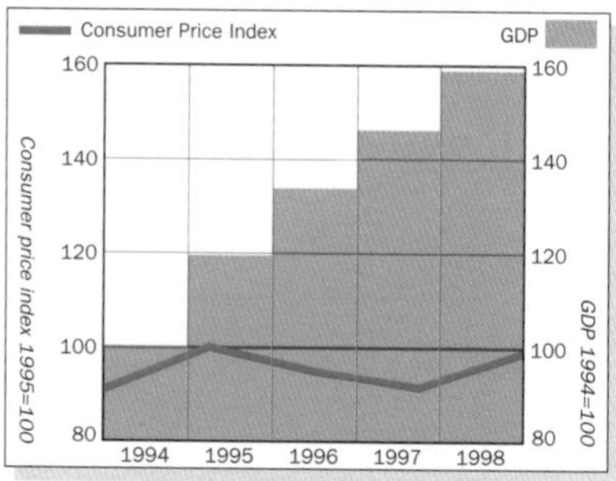

Consumer Price Index
GDP
160
140
120
100
80
1994
1995
1996
1997
1998
Consumer price index 1995=100
GDP 1994=100

market economy by encouraging foreign investment and reforming land tenure. Economic decline was reversed in 1993 as agricultural and industrial output grew, with foreign aid used to fund the purchase of parts and raw materials for manufacturing. These gains were undermined by war with Eritrea in 1998–2000 and the renewed danger of severe drought-related famine in 2000.

ETHIOPIA : MAJOR BUSINESSES

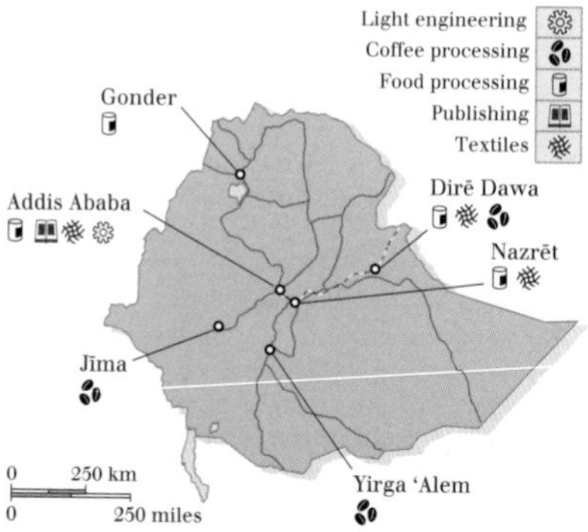

Light engineering
Coffee processing
Food processing
Publishing
Textiles
Gonder
Addis Ababa
Dirē Dawa
Nazrēt
Jīma
Yirga 'Alem
0 250 km
0 250 miles

RESOURCES

Electric power 456,000 kw

10,414 tonnes

Oil reserves currently unexploited

35.1m cattle, 22.1m sheep, 17m goats, 55.6m chickens

Oil, gold, platinum, copper, potash, iron, natural gas

ELECTRICITY GENERATION

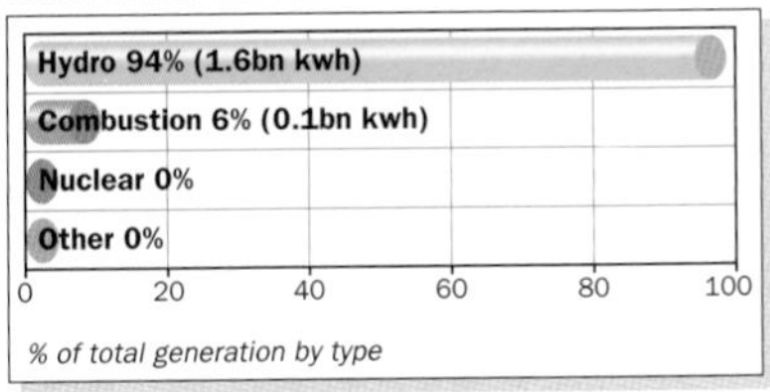
Hydro 94% (1.6bn kwh)
Combustion 6% (0.1bn kwh)
Nuclear 0%
Other 0%
0
20
40
60
80
100
% of total generation by type

Manpower and financial constraints have prevented a systematic survey of mineral resources. At present, mining contributes less than 1% of GDP. Ethiopia has great potential for hydroelectric power which, in the long run, could offset a domestic reliance on fuelwood and slow massive deforestation and soil erosion. Current exploration for oil and gas has revealed reserves in the Ogaden, but exploitation has not begun. When Eritrea seceded in 1993, Ethiopia lost other substantial oil reserves and many oil concessions.

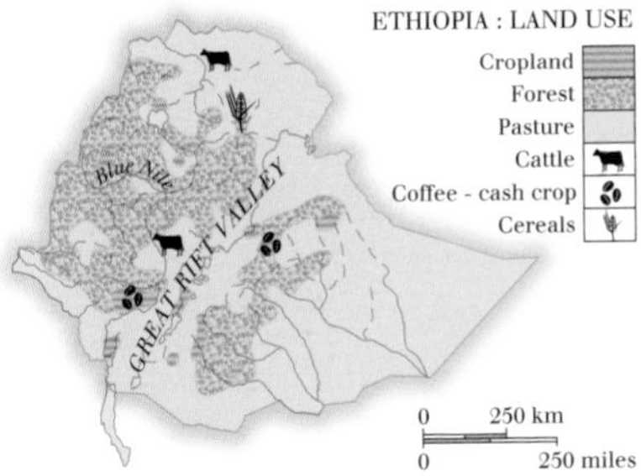
ETHIOPIA : LAND USE
Cropland
Forest
Pasture
Cattle
Coffee - cash crop
Cereals
Blue Nile
GREAT RIFT VALLEY
0 250 km
0 250 miles

ENVIRONMENT

Sustainability rank: 119th

6%

0.1 tonnes per capita

ENVIRONMENTAL TREATIES

No | Yes | Yes

Yes | No | No

Deforestation for fuelwood and the resultant rapid soil erosion, particularly in the highlands, are serious problems. Forest cover has fallen from 40% in 1900 to only 2% today. Dung is being used for fuel, instead of as a fertilizer. The amount used – with a fertilizing value of $123 million a year – would increase annual grain harvests by up to 1.5 million tonnes. Local projects include terracing hillsides to prevent soil and water run-off – 36,000 km (22,370 miles) of terraces were built in Tigray in 1992.

MEDIA

TV ownership low

Daily newspaper circulation 2 per 1000 people

The government remains uneasy about the post-Mengistu independent press, which has become prolific and critical, although circulation is small. Legal action has been taken to silence several publications. All main newspapers and the TV broadcasting station are government-owned and operated.

PUBLISHING AND BROADCAST MEDIA

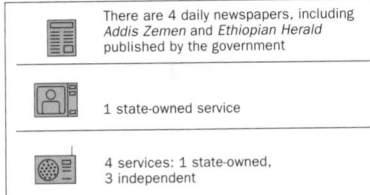

There are 4 daily newspapers, including *Addis Zemen* and *Ethiopian Herald* published by the government

1 state-owned service

4 services: 1 state-owned, 3 independent

CRIME

Death penalty used

13,585 prisoners

Up 9% 1996–1998

CRIME RATES

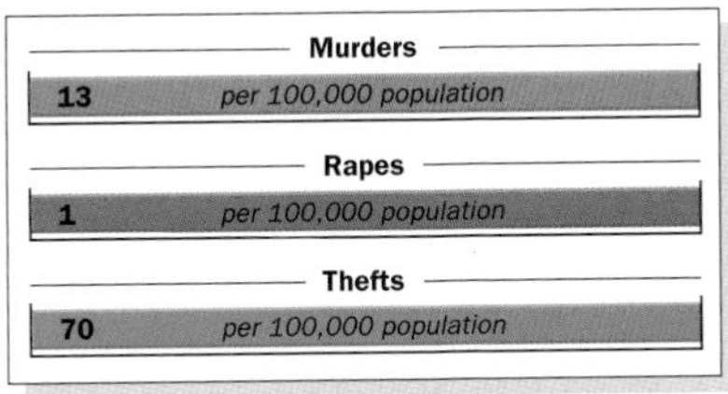
Murders
13 per 100,000 population
Rapes
1 per 100,000 population
Thefts
70 per 100,000 population

A number of human rights abuses by the transitional government have been documented by the independent Ethiopian Human Rights Council. These include detention without trial, "disappearances," and extrajudicial killings. There is some concern over indiscipline among EPRDF forces, who provide a de facto police force in many regions. In many rural areas, the state system has yet to replace traditional forms of justice.

EDUCATION

School leaving age: 13

38%

42,226 students

THE EDUCATION SYSTEM

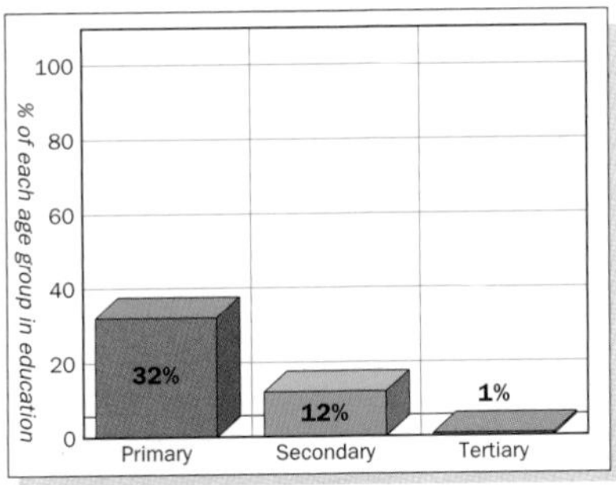
100
80
60
40
20
0
% of each age group in education
32%
12%
1%
Primary
Secondary
Tertiary

Secondary education is in English and Amharic. Schools are basic and classes crowded; education was severely disrupted during the civil war. Addis Ababa University, a center of political activity (usually anti-EPRDF), suffers periodic closures and the dismissal of leading academics.

HEALTH

No welfare state health benefits

1 per 20,000 people

Diarrheal and respiratory diseases, tuberculosis, malaria

Only about half of the population lives within 12 km (8 miles) of a health unit. Hospital building, distribution of resources to rural areas, outpatient visits, and referrals are all very slow. Skin and eye diseases are common, and incidence of HIV/AIDS is rising. Mission hospitals are of a reasonably high standard. The use of traditional remedies is widespread.

SPENDING

GDP/cap. increase

CONSUMPTION AND SPENDING

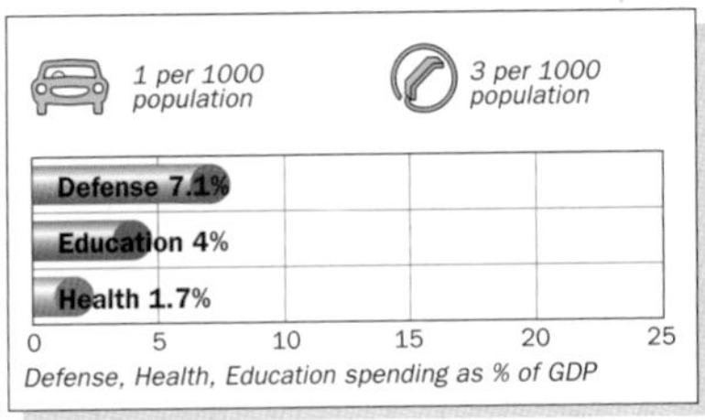
1 per 1000 population
3 per 1000 population
Defense 7.1%
Education 4%
Health 1.7%
0
5
10
15
20
25
Defense, Health, Education spending as % of GDP

Most Ethiopians are extremely poor; many of the country's wealthier families having fled into exile in recent years. Ethiopian Christian culture places more value on maintaining traditional social structures than on realising individual ambition. Living at subsistence level and a reliance on traditional agriculture remain the general expectation.

WORLD RANKING

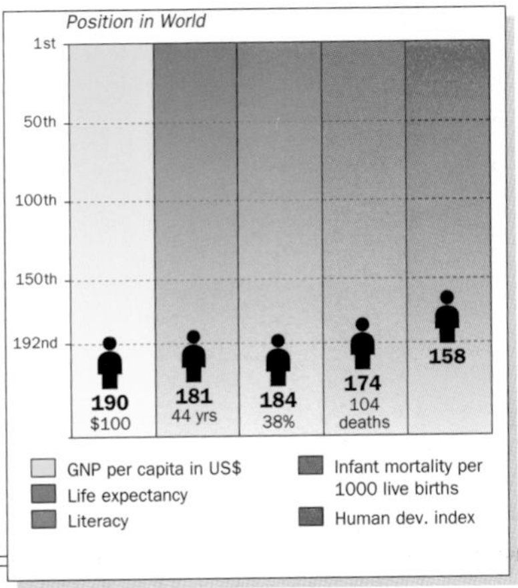
Position in World
1st
50th
100th
150th
192nd
190
$100
181
44 yrs
184
38%
174
104
deaths
158
GNP per capita in US$
Life expectancy
Literacy
Infant mortality per 1000 live births
Human dev. index

E

FIJI

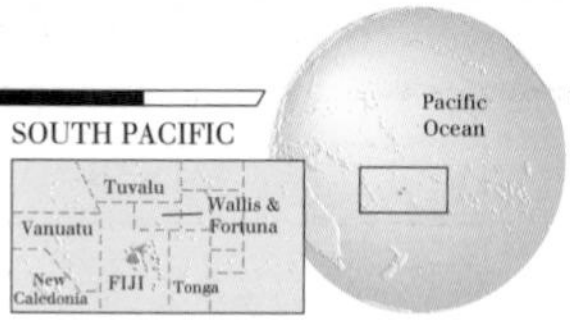
SOUTH PACIFIC
Pacific Ocean
Tuvalu
Wallis & Fortuna
Vanuatu
New Caledonia
FIJI
Tonga

OFFICIAL NAME: Republic of Fiji **CAPITAL:** Suva
POPULATION: 817,000 **CURRENCY:** Fiji dollar **OFFICIAL LANGUAGE:** English

1970 | 1970 | Oct 10 | FJI | +12 | +679 | .fj

FIJI IS A VOLCANIC ARCHIPELAGO in the southern Pacific Ocean, comprising two main islands and nearly 900 smaller islands and islets. The introduction of ethnic Indian workers by the British in 1879–1916 was to have dramatic consequences. Between 1946 and 1997 Indo-Fijians outnumbered Melanesian Fijians. A series of coups led by Fijian supremacists between 1987 and 2000 led to a mass exodus of ethnic Indians, the most recent seriously damaging the economy.

CLIMATE

Tropical oceanic

WEATHER CHART

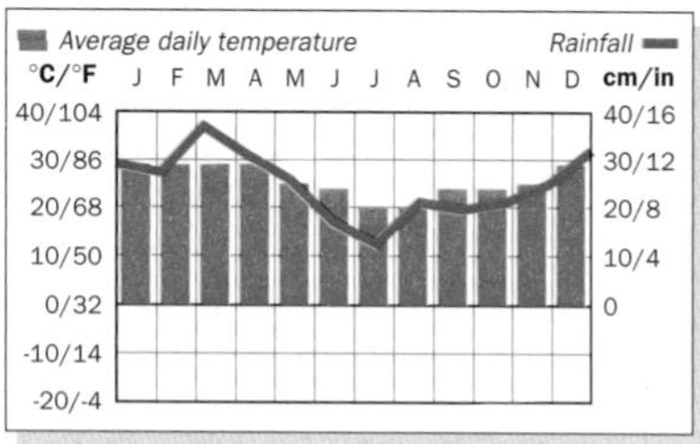
Average daily temperature
Rainfall
°C/°F
J F M A M J J A S O N D
cm/in
40/104
30/86
20/68
10/50
0/32
-10/14
-20/-4
40/16
30/12
20/8
10/4
0

The eastern sides of the main islands are wettest, having more than twice the annual rainfall of the western flanks. Fiji lies in a cyclone path.

TRANSPORTATION

Drive on left

Nadi International 1.18m passengers

53 ships 29,300 grt

THE TRANSPORTATION NETWORK

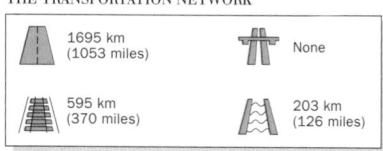

1695 km (1053 miles)

None

595 km (370 miles)

203 km (126 miles)

On the axis of Australian–US west coast air routes, Fiji is well served by international flights. An international airport is proposed for Vanua Levu.

TOURISM

Visitors : Population 1:2.8

294,000 visitors

Down 28% in 2000

MAIN TOURIST ARRIVALS

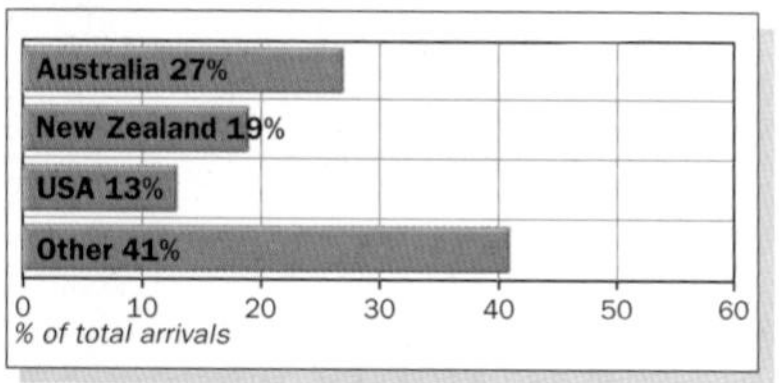
Australia 27%
New Zealand 19%
USA 13%
Other 41%
0
10
20
30
40
50
60
% of total arrivals

Tourism – once Fiji's greatest earner – has been adversely affected by political instability. 7500 jobs in the tourism sector were lost in 2000.

PEOPLE

Pop. density low

Fijian, English, Hindi, Urdu, Tamil, Telugu

45/km² (116/mi²)

THE URBAN/RURAL POPULATION SPLIT

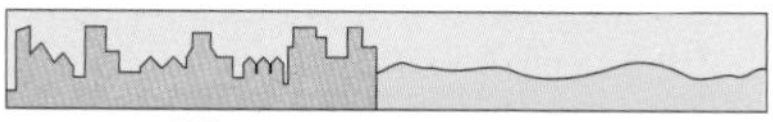
49%
51%

RELIGIOUS PERSUASION

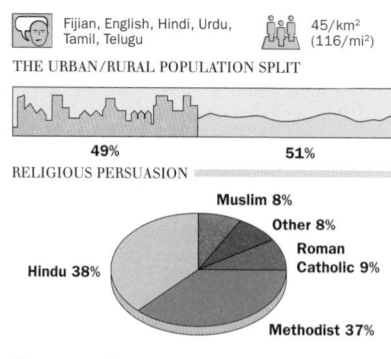

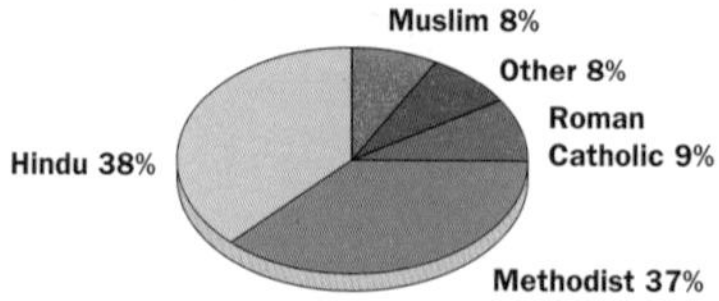
Muslim 8%
Other 8%
Roman Catholic 9%
Hindu 38%
Methodist 37%

The once delicate balance between ethnic and Indo-Fijians has been shattered by the exodus of the latter group in 1987–1989 and 2000–2001. The lawlessness in 2000 exaggerated ethnic tensions and brought racist rhetoric back to the political mainstream. A substantial population of Polynesians live on Rotuma and have traditionally pressed for autonomy. Women are lobbying for more rights.

POLITICS

Multiparty elections

L. House 2001/2006
U. House 2001/2003

President Ratu Josefa Iloilo

AT THE LAST ELECTION

House of Representatives 71 seats

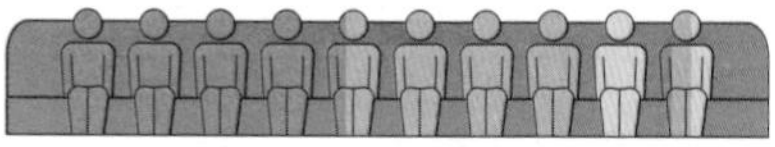
3% NLUP
4% Other
44% SDL
38% FLP
8% MV
3% Ind

SDL = Fijian People's Party **FLP** = Fiji Labor Party
MV = Conservative Alliance (Matanitu Vanua)
NLUP = New Labor Unity Party **Ind** = Independents

Senate 32 seats

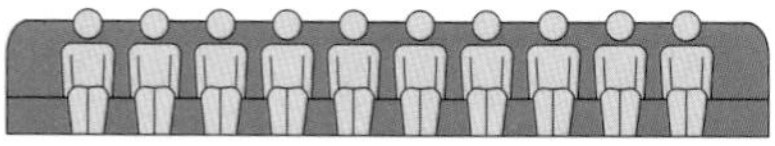

The Senate is appointed by the president

The issue of political representation for Fiji's large Indian minority has dominated politics since the 1980s, and the 1987 coup was justified as defending ethnic Fijian land rights. The traditional Great Council of Chiefs emerged as the power-broker after the May 2000 coup; despite lacking constitutional powers it was consulted at every turn. It ensured that the Indian-dominated FLP government, elected in 1999, was barred from returning to power and that the multi-ethnic 1997 constitution remained buried.

FIJI

Total Land Area : 18 270 sq. km (7054 sq. miles)

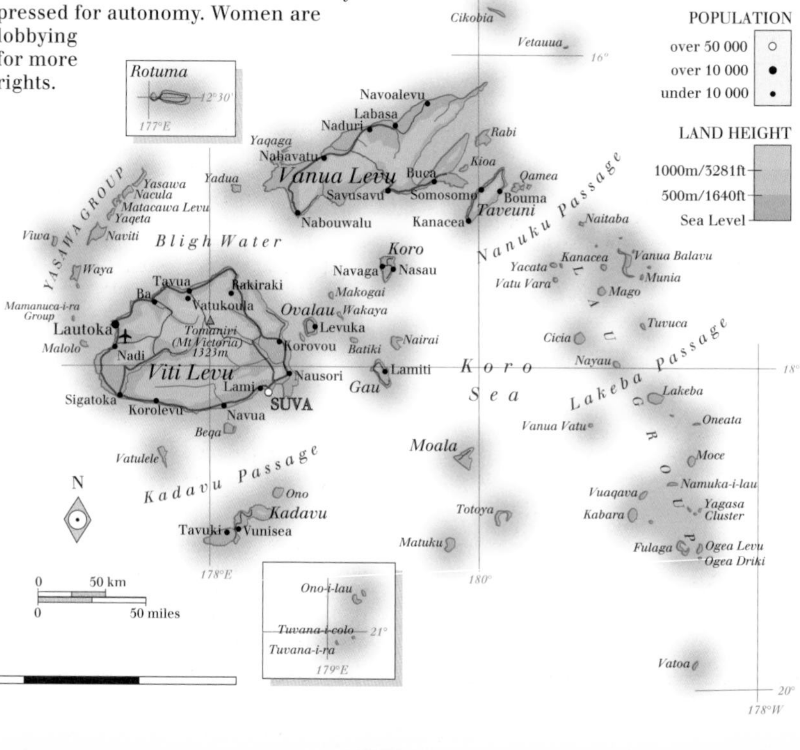
POPULATION
over 50 000
over 10 000
under 10 000
LAND HEIGHT
1000m/3281ft
500m/1640ft
Sea Level
Rotuma
12°30'
177°E
Cikobia
Vetauua
16°
Navoalevu
Labasa
Naduri
Rabi
Yaqaga
Nabavatu
Kioa
Vanua Levu
Buca
Qamea
Savusavu
Somosomo
Bouma
Taveuni
Nabouwalu
Kanacea
Yadua
Yasawa
Nacula
Matacawa Levu
Yaqeta
Naviti
YASAWA GROUP
Viwa
Waya
Bligh Water
Koro
Navaga
Nasau
Nanuku Passage
Naitaba
Kanacea
Vanua Balavu
Yacata
Munia
Vatu Vara
Mago
Makogai
Tavua
Rakiraki
Ba
Vatukoula
Ovalau
Wakaya
Mamanuca-i-ra Group
Lautoka
Levuka
Tomaniivi (Mt Victoria) 1323m
Nairai
Tuvuca
Cicia
Malolo
Nadi
Korovou
Batiki
Nayau
Viti Levu
Nausori
Lamiti
Koro Sea
Lakeba Passage
18°
Lami
Gau
SUVA
Lakeba
Sigatoka
Korolevu
Navua
Vanua Vatu
Oneata
Beqa
Moala
LAU GROUP
Moce
Vatulele
Kadavu Passage
Namuka-i-lau
N
Ono
Vuaqava
Yagasa Cluster
Kadavu
Totoya
Kabara
Tavuki
Vunisea
Matuku
Fulaga
Ogea Levu
Ogea Driki
178°E
180°
0
50 km
50 miles
Ono-i-lau
Tuvana-i-colo
21°
Tuvana-i-ra
179°E
Vatoa
20°
178°W

WORLD AFFAIRS

Joined UN in 1970

ACP | CP | IBRD | PC | PIF

Fiji's international reputation has been severely damaged by its discrimination against Indo-Fijians and the recent coups. Fiji was again suspended from the Commonwealth in 2000.

AID

Recipient

US$34m (receipts) — Down 6% in 1999

Fiji traditionally received a lot of overseas aid, but international disquiet at the 2000 coup has led to drastic cuts.

DEFENSE

No compulsory military service

US$35m — Up 3% in 1999

Of the almost entirely ethnic Fijian military, significant numbers – around 20% – are assigned to UN duties and have served in Lebanon and Egypt.

ECONOMICS

Inflation 3.5% p.a. (1990–1999)

US$1.8bn — 1.9899–2.1764 Fiji dollars

SCORE CARD

World GNP Ranking	142nd
GNP per Capita	US$2310
Balance of Payments	US$–55m
Inflation	2%
Unemployment	6%

Strengths

Relatively well-diversified economy, with strong tourist infrastructure. Location on Pacific air routes. Many regional and international organizations located in Suva.

Weaknesses

2000 coup caused dramatic contraction in economy – 12.5%. Migration of many Indo-Fijian professionals. Sugar crops vulnerable to drought. Major exports – sugar, copra, and gold – subject to large fluctuations in world prices.

EXPORTS

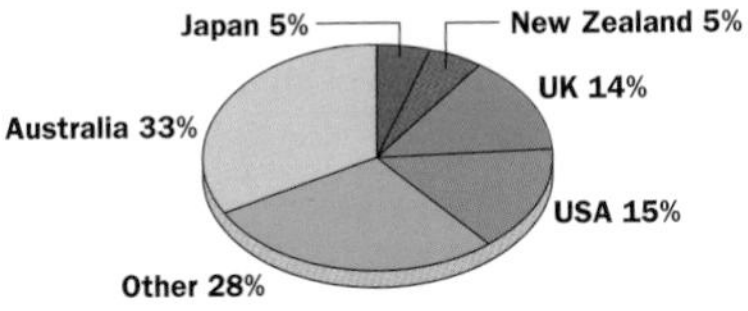
Japan 5%
New Zealand 5%
UK 14%
Australia 33%
USA 15%
Other 28%

IMPORTS

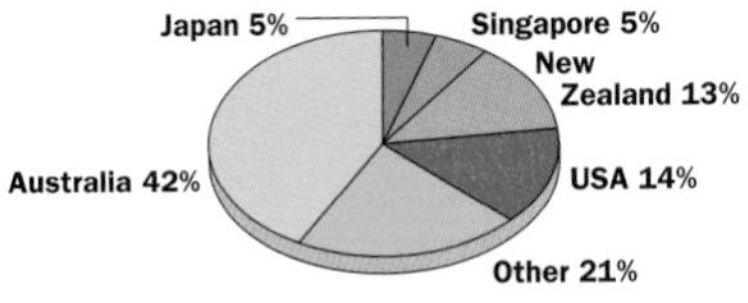
Japan 5%
Singapore 5%
New Zealand 13%
Australia 42%
USA 14%
Other 21%

***Cane field** on the west side of Viti Levu, between Nadi and Lautoka. Sugar accounts for about one-third of Fiji's exports.*

RESOURCES

Electric power 200,000 kw

36,374 tonnes — Not an oil producer

344,636 cattle, 235,000 goats, 3.9m chickens — Gold, silver

The varied terrain allows diversified agriculture. Gold and minerals are mined. A hydroelectric station at Monasavu provides 95% of electricity.

ENVIRONMENT

Sustainability rank: 55th

0.3% — 1 tonne per capita

Governments are environmentally aware. Tourism is damaging coral reefs. Fiji was downwind of French Pacific nuclear tests. Fertilizers are overused.

MEDIA

TV ownership low

Daily newspaper circulation 51 per 1000 people

PUBLISHING AND BROADCAST MEDIA

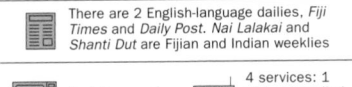

There are 2 English-language dailies, *Fiji Times* and *Daily Post. Nai Lalakai* and *Shanti Dut* are Fijian and Indian weeklies

1 state-owned service — 4 services: 1 state-controlled, 3 independent

Press freedoms are championed by the government, and cases of corruption are often reported in the media. However, the police have blocked politically sensitive broadcasts.

CRIME

Death penalty not used

961 prisoners — Up 17% 1992–1998

Usually theft and drink-related violence top the crime list. The 2000 coup spurred Fijians to settle old scores by force.

EDUCATION

Schooling is not compusory

93% — 7908 students

Education, originally modeled on the British system, is now mostly run by local committees and is increasingly racially segregated. Attendance, although high, is not compulsory.

CHRONOLOGY

The British decision to import Indian sugar workers in 1879–1916 dramatically changed Fijian society.

- **1970** Independence from Britain.
- **1987** Election win for Indo-Fijian coalition. Sitiveni Rabuka's coups secure minority ethnic Fijian rule. Ejected from Commonwealth.
- **1989** Mass Indo-Fijian emigration.
- **1990** Constitution discriminating against Indo-Fijians introduced.
- **1992** Rabuka wins legislative polls.
- **1997** Census shows ethnic Fijians outnumber Indo-Fijians. Fiji rejoins Commonwealth. New constitution.
- **1999** General election won by FLP. First Indo-Fijian prime minister.
- **2000** Civilian-led coup; new ethnic Fijian government.
- **2001** Nationalists win elections.

F

HEALTH

Welfare state health benefits

1 per 1905 people — Cerebrovascular and heart diseases, cancers, accidents

Medical treatment is provided for all at a nominal charge. Fiji is free of almost all tropical diseases, but AIDS affects 0.07% of the adult population.

SPENDING

GDP/cap. increase

CONSUMPTION AND SPENDING

58 per 1000 population — *101 per 1000 population*

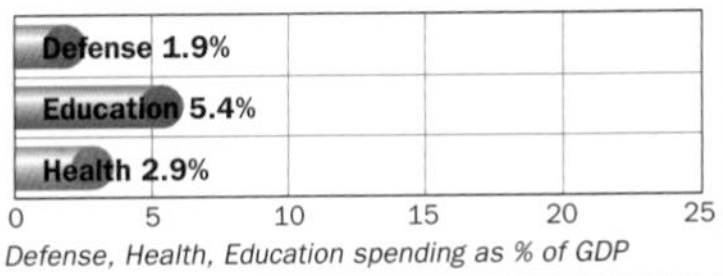
Defense 1.9%
Education 5.4%
Health 2.9%
0
5
10
15
20
25
Defense, Health, Education spending as % of GDP

Ostentatious displays of wealth are rare in Fiji; prestige derives from family and landholdings. The professional middle class, traditionally dominated by Indo-Fijians, is becoming more mixed.

WORLD RANKING

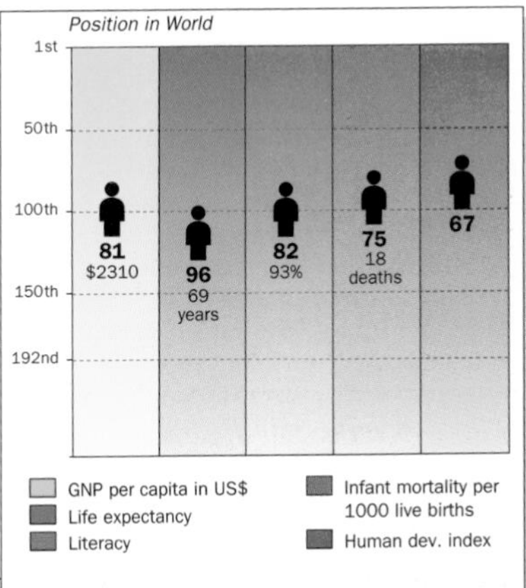
Position in World
1st
50th
100th
150th
192nd
81
$2310
96
69 years
82
93%
75
18 deaths
67
GNP per capita in US$
Life expectancy
Literacy
Infant mortality per 1000 live births
Human dev. index

FINLAND

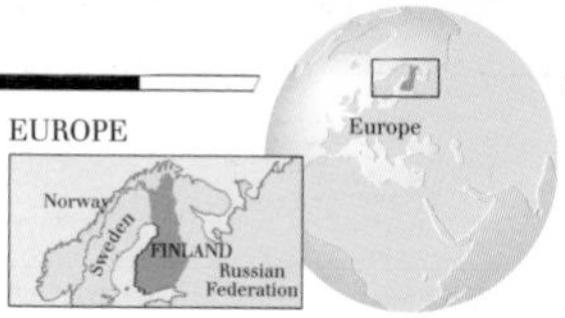
EUROPE
Europe
Norway
Sweden
FINLAND
Russian Federation

OFFICIAL NAME: Republic of Finland **CAPITAL:** Helsinki **POPULATION:** 5.2 million
CURRENCY: Euro (markka until 2002) **OFFICIAL LANGUAGES:** Finnish and Swedish

1917 | 1947 | Dec 6 | FIN | +2 | +358 | .fi

BORDERED TO THE north and west by Norway and Sweden, and to the east by Russia, Finland is a low-lying country of forests and 187,888 lakes. Politics are based on consensus, and the country has been stable despite successive short-lived coalitions. Russia annexed Finland in 1809, ruling it until 1917, and subsequently Finland accepted a close relationship with the USSR as the price of maintaining its independence. It joined the European Union in 1995 and, despite popular suspicion of Brussels bureaucracy, Finland was among the 11 EU states to introduce the euro from 1999.

CLIMATE

Subarctic/continental

WEATHER CHART

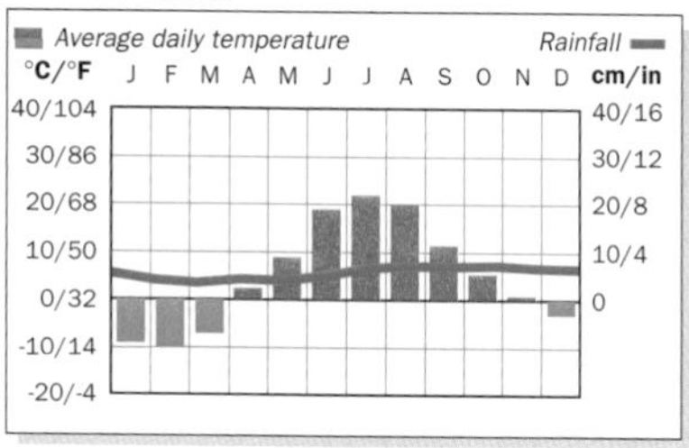
Average daily temperature
Rainfall
°C/°F
J F M A M J J A S O N D
cm/in
40/104
30/86
20/68
10/50
0/32
-10/14
-20/-4
40/16
30/12
20/8
10/4
0

North of the Arctic Circle the climate is extreme. Temperatures fall to –30°C (–22°F) in the six-month winter and rise to 27°C (81°F) during the 73 days of summer midnight sun. In the south, summers are mild and short, winters are cold.

TRANSPORTATION

Drive on right

Helsinki-Vantaa, 8.6m passengers

284 ships 1.6m grt

THE TRANSPORTATION NETWORK

49,853 km (30,977 miles)	473 km (294 miles)
5836 km (3626 miles)	6715 km (4172 miles)

The transportation system is well integrated. The railroad connects with the Swedish and Russian networks. There are frequent air services to most neighboring states, and links with Baltic states are being expanded. With one of the densest domestic networks in Europe, internal air travel is important, particularly north of the Arctic Circle.

With 187,888 lakes and a major river network, Finland has Europe's largest inland waterway system. It still carries freight, but is now used mainly for recreation. Finland's international ports handle around 70 million tonnes a year. Kotka is the chief export port. Helsinki, with five specialized harbors, handles most imports.

TOURISM

Visitors : Population 1:1.9

2.7m visitors

Up 10% in 2000

MAIN TOURIST ARRIVALS

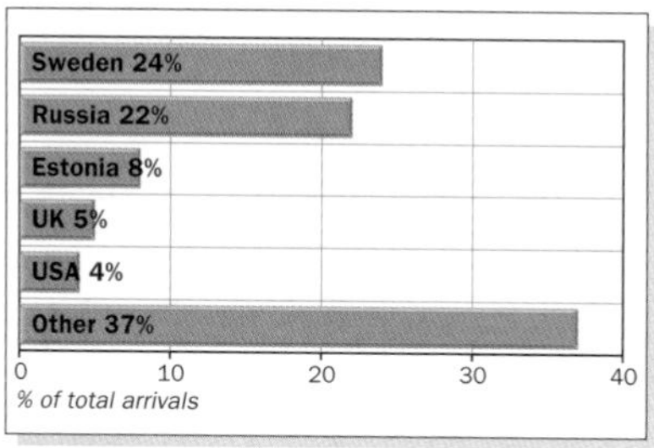
Sweden 24%
Russia 22%
Estonia 8%
UK 5%
USA 4%
Other 37%
0
10
20
30
40
% of total arrivals

The scenery of the southern lakes and the vast forests of its Arctic north are Finland's main attractions. Helsinki is an important cultural center and hosts an annual arts festival. There are many first-class restaurants and its opera house has an international reputation. Most tourists try a sauna, a Finnish invention, and the local vodka, which is reputedly among the world's finest.

Visitors come largely from neighboring Sweden. Since 1990, the number of visitors from the Baltic states and Russia has risen and Finland is attracting more British tourists.

A summer's night at Kilpisjärvi, "The Way of the Four Winds," which lies at the point where Finland, Sweden, and Norway meet.

PEOPLE

Pop. density low

Finnish, Swedish, Sami

17/km² (44/mi²)

THE URBAN/RURAL POPULATION SPLIT

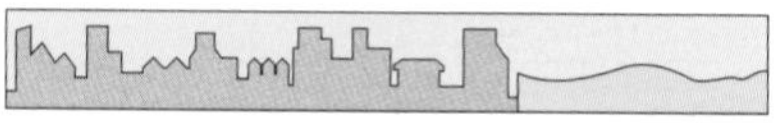
67%
33%

RELIGIOUS PERSUASION

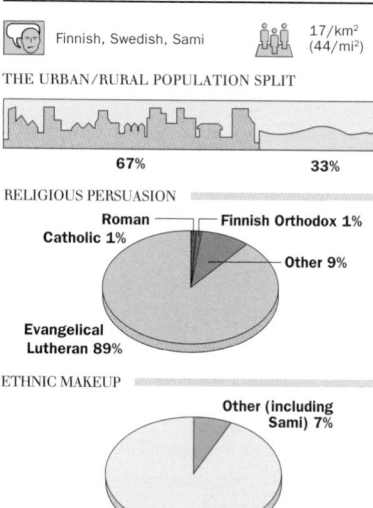

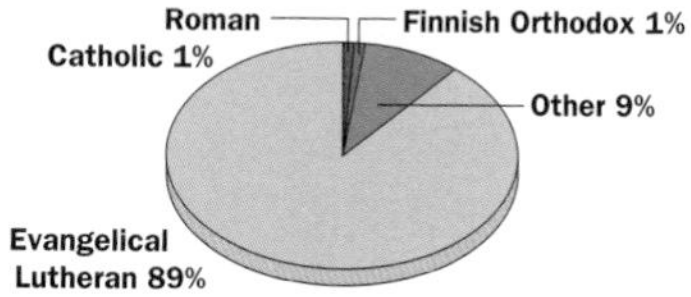
Roman Catholic 1%
Finnish Orthodox 1%
Other 9%
Evangelical Lutheran 89%

ETHNIC MAKEUP

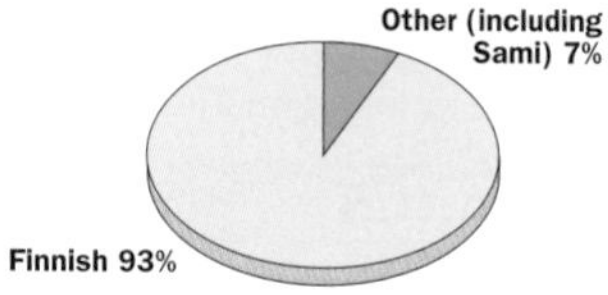
Other (including Sami) 7%
Finnish 93%

Most Finns are of Scandinavian–Baltic extraction. Finnish belongs to the small Finno-Ugric linguistic group and is a legacy of the country's early Asian invaders. These tribes integrated with local and surrounding European peoples, but preserved their distinct language. Sami, also a Finno-Ugric language, is spoken by the small Sami population, who live above the Arctic Circle. Around 6% of the population speak Swedish, most of whom live in the southwestern coastal regions and on the Åland Islands.

More than 50% of Finns live in the five southernmost districts around Helsinki. Families tend to be close-knit, although divorce rates are high. The sauna is an integral part of everyday life; there are 1.5 million saunas among 5.2 million Finns.

Finnish women have a long tradition of political and economic participation. They were the first in Europe to get the vote, in 1906, and the first in the world able to stand for parliament. Almost 50% of women now work outside the home, and the president and one-third of the cabinet are female.

POPULATION AGE BREAKDOWN

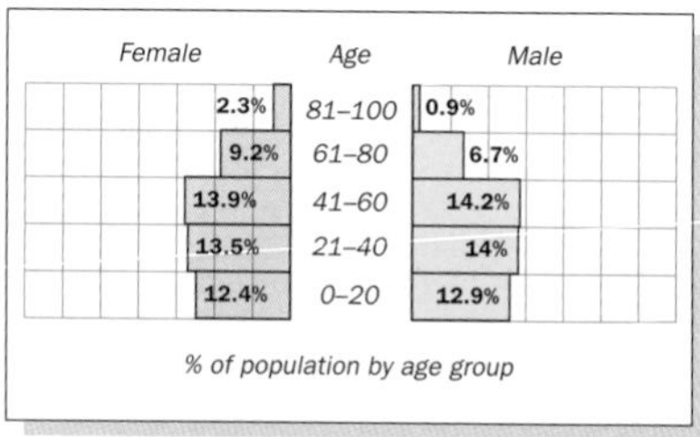
Female
Age
Male
2.3%
81–100
0.9%
9.2%
61–80
6.7%
13.9%
41–60
14.2%
13.5%
21–40
14%
12.4%
0–20
12.9%
% of population by age group

POLITICS

Multiparty elections

1999/2003 | President Tarja Halonen

Finland's constitution combines parliamentary government with a strong presidency. The external territory of the Åland Islands, inhabited by Swedish-speakers, has internal self-government.

AT THE LAST ELECTION

Parliament 200 seats

5% G
7% Others
26% SDP
24% KESK
23% KOK
10% VL
5% SFP

SDP = Social Democratic Party **KESK** = Center Party
KOK = National Coalition Party **VL** = Left-wing Alliance
SFP = Swedish People's Party **G** = Greens

Tarja Halonen, who became Finland's first female president in 2000.

Prime Minister Paavo Lipponen, *heads the SDP-led coalition.*

MAIN POLITICAL ISSUES

EU membership

Finland joined the EU in 1995, many Finns supporting entry as a way of identifying with western Europe. The small but influential farming community was hostile to membership. Others feared that welfare cuts would be more far-reaching if the economy was liberalized in line with EU expectations. In the event, after a dose of austerity, EU membership became associated with greater prosperity from the late 1990s. Finland's decision to join the euro in January 1999 contrasted with the nonmembership of its closest EU neighbor, Sweden.

Unemployment

The victory of SDP candidate Martti Ahtisaari in the 1994 presidential election was a sign of discontent with the conservative coalition then in power, whose handling of the recession resulted in record unemployment levels and welfare cuts. The 1995 general election led to the return of an SDP-led coalition which continued many of the previous government's austerity policies. Unemployment has since been substantially reduced.

PROFILE

Proportional representation has led to government by coalition, usually dominated by the SDP or KESK. The emphasis on consensus has favored stability but resulted in slow decision-making. The current "rainbow" coalition comprises five parties from across the political spectrum.

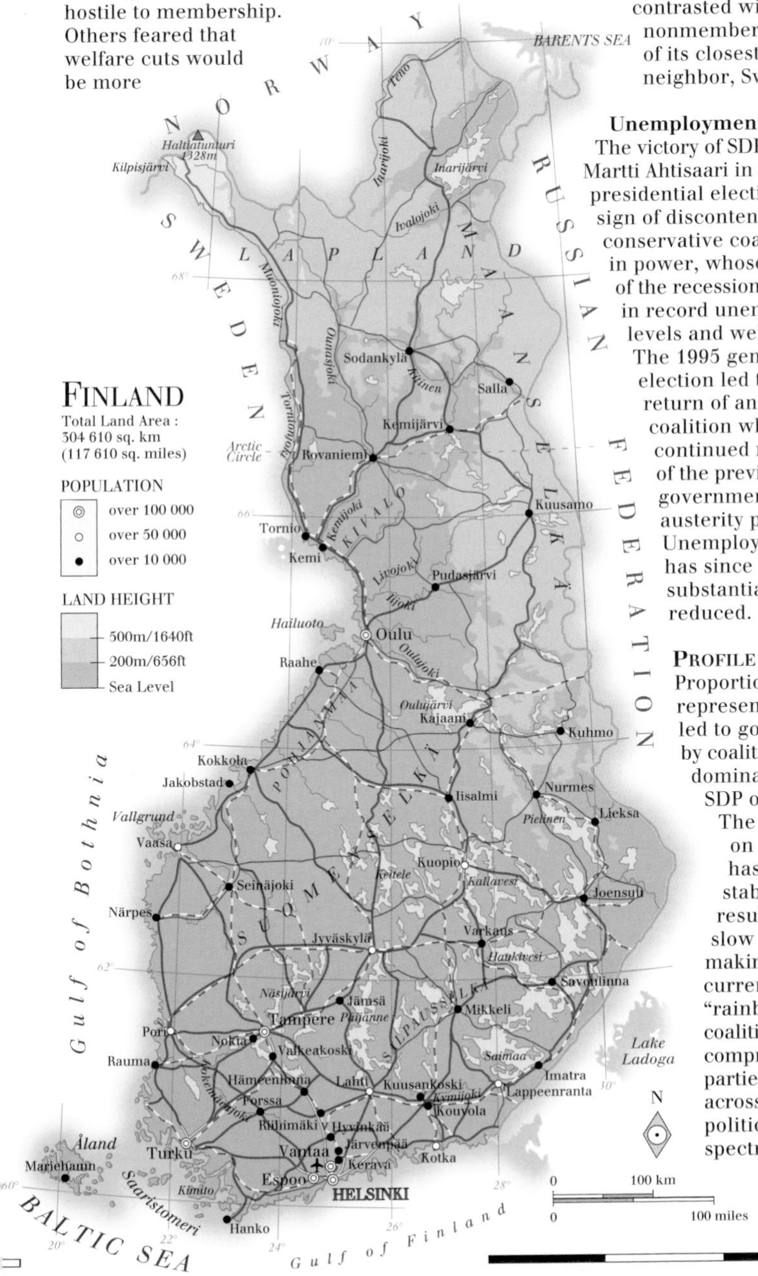
FINLAND
Total Land Area : 304 610 sq. km (117 610 sq. miles)
POPULATION
over 100 000
over 50 000
over 10 000
LAND HEIGHT
500m/1640ft
200m/656ft
Sea Level
NORWAY
BARENTS SEA
SWEDEN
RUSSIAN FEDERATION
LAPLAND
MAANSELKÄ
KIVALO
POHJANMAA
SUOMENSELKÄ
SALPAUSSELKÄ
Haltiatunturi 1328m
Kilpisjärvi
Inarijärvi
Sodankylä
Salla
Kemijärvi
Rovaniemi
Arctic Circle
Kuusamo
Tornio
Kemi
Pudasjärvi
Hailuoto
Oulu
Raahe
Kajaani
Kuhmo
Kokkola
Jakobstad
Vallgrund
Vaasa
Iisalmi
Nurmes
Lieksa
Kuopio
Joensuu
Seinäjoki
Närpes
Jyväskylä
Varkaus
Savonlinna
Jämsä
Tampere
Mikkeli
Pori
Nokia
Valkeakoski
Rauma
Hämeenlinna
Lahti
Kuusankoski
Imatra
Lappeenranta
Kouvola
Forssa
Riihimäki
Hyvinkää
Järvenpää
Turku
Vantaa
Kerava
Kotka
Åland
Mariehamn
Espoo
HELSINKI
Hanko
Lake Ladoga
Gulf of Bothnia
BALTIC SEA
Gulf of Finland
Saaristomeri
0 100 km
0 100 miles

WORLD AFFAIRS

Joined UN in 1955

CE | EU | OECD | OSCE | PfP

After carefully balancing its relations with the USSR and the West during the Cold War, Finland has now decided that its national interest lies within western Europe. In addition to joining the EU, it has observer status at the WEU. However, acknowledging historical and geographical realities, the government is also keen to maintain a special relationship with Russia.

AID

Donor

$416m (donations) | Up 5% in 1999

Finland allocated an average of 0.33% of GNP to aid in 1995–1998 (well below the UN target of 0.7%). The main recipients are China, Bosnia and Herzegovina, and southern Africa.

CHRONOLOGY

Finland's history has been closely linked with the competing interests of Sweden and Russia.

- **1323** Treaty of Pähkinäsaari. Finland part of Swedish Kingdom.
- **1809** Treaty of Fredrikshamn, Sweden cedes Finland to Russia. Finland becomes a Grand Duchy enjoying considerable autonomy.
- **1812** Helsinki becomes capital.
- **1863** Finnish becomes an official language alongside Swedish.
- **1865** Grand Duchy acquires its own monetary system.
- **1879** Conscription law lays the foundation for a Finnish army.
- **1899** Czar Nicholas II begins process of Russification. Labor Party founded.
- **1900** Gradual imposition of Russian as the official language begins.
- **1901** Finnish army disbanded, Finns ordered into Russian units. Disobedience campaign prevents men being drafted into the army.

F

F

CHRONOLOGY *continued*

- **1903** Labor Party becomes SDP.
- **1905** National strike forces restoration of 1899 status quo.
- **1906** Parliamentary reform. Universal suffrage introduced.
- **1910** Responsibility for important legislation passed to Russian Duma.
- **1917** Russian revolution allows Finland to declare independence.
- **1918** Civil war between Bolsheviks and right-wing government. General Gustav Mannerheim leads government to victory at Battle of Tampere.
- **1919** Finland becomes republic. Kaarlo Ståhlberg elected president with wide political powers.
- **1920** Treaty of Tartu: USSR recognizes Finland's borders.
- **1921** London Convention. Åland Islands become part of Finland.
- **1939** August, Hitler–Stalin nonaggression pact gives USSR a free hand in Finland. November, Soviet invasion; strong Finnish resistance in ensuing Winter War.
- **1940** Treaty of Moscow. Finland cedes a tenth of national territory.
- **1941** Finnish troops join Germany in its invasion of USSR.
- **1944** June, Red Army invades. August, President Risto Ryti resigns. September, Finland, led by Marshal Mannerheim, signs armistice.
- **1946** President Mannerheim resigns, Juho Paasikivi president.
- **1948** Signs friendship treaty with USSR. Agrees to resist any attack on USSR made through Finland by Germany or its allies.
- **1952** Payment of $570 million in war reparations completed.
- **1956** Uhro Kekkonen, leader of the Agrarian Party, becomes president.
- **1956–1991** A series of coalition governments involving SDP and Agrarians, renamed KESK in 1965, hold power.
- **1981** President Kekkonen resigns.
- **1982** Mauno Koivisto president.
- **1989** USSR recognizes Finnish neutrality for first time.
- **1991** Non-SDP government elected. Austerity measures.
- **1992** January, signs ten-year agreement with Russia which, for first time since World War II, involves no military agreement.
- **1994** SDP candidate Martti Ahtisaari elected president.
- **1995** Finland joins EU. General election returns SDP-led coalition under Paavo Lipponen.
- **1999** Finland among first 11 countries to introduce euro. General election returns Lipponen's coalition to power.
- **2000** Tarja Halonen elected as first woman president.

DEFENSE

Compulsory military service

$1.7bn

Down 12% in 1999

Finland is a neutral country. Its armed forces, the majority of whom are conscripts, are backed up by 500,000 active reservists and 3400 border guards. Russia's instability has reinforced concern about border security, the main defense issue. Finland participates in NATO's Partnerships for Peace program and has WEU observer status. Military service lasts for up to 12 months.

FINNISH ARMED FORCES

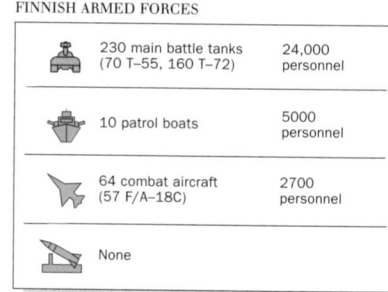

230 main battle tanks (70 T–55, 160 T–72)	24,000 personnel
10 patrol boats	5000 personnel
64 combat aircraft (57 F/A–18C)	2700 personnel
None	

ECONOMICS

Inflation 2% p.a. (1990–1999)

$127.8bn

5.932–6.333 markkaa

SCORE CARD

❑ World GNP Ranking	29th
❑ GNP per Capita	$24,730
❑ Balance of Payments	$6.94bn
❑ Inflation	1.2%
❑ Unemployment	10%

EXPORTS

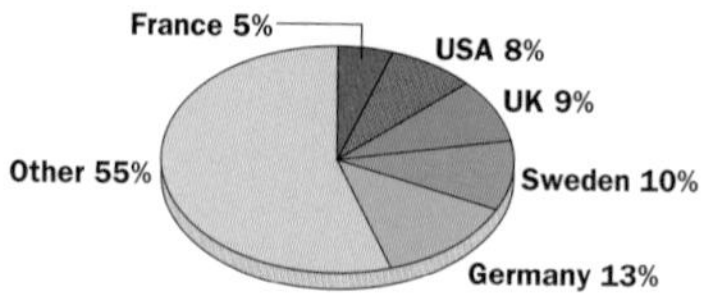
France 5%
USA 8%
UK 9%
Sweden 10%
Germany 13%
Other 55%

IMPORTS

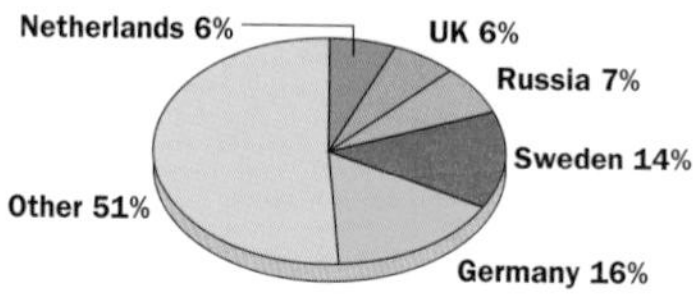
Netherlands 6%
UK 6%
Russia 7%
Sweden 14%
Germany 16%
Other 51%

Strengths

Industry export- and quality-oriented. Large high-tech sector, especially Nokia mobile phones and Internet services. World leader in pulp and paper. Exports quick to recover from recession. Low inflation, now less than 2% a year. Improved foreign investment incentives. Gateway to Russian and Baltic economies. Membership of eurozone. Strong recent economic growth.

Weaknesses

Severe recession in 1991–1993 when real GDP declined 15%. Danger of economy overheating following more recent period of rapid growth. High level of public and foreign debt. High unemployment. Small domestic market. Peripheral position in Europe.

Profile

Finland is a wealthy market economy, but has a powerful recent experience of the worst recession in 60 years in the early 1990s. The collapse of the former Soviet Union was largely responsible for that downturn. Whereas it had once taken more than a quarter of Finland's exports, Russia took only 4% of Finland's exports in 1999.

A rapid rise in unemployment and business failures after 1990 pushed up government spending, but the floating of the markka in 1992, and austerity measures including welfare benefit cuts, higher taxes, and wage restraints, improved competitiveness.

Unemployment has fallen, but is still high, and there is now a risk of the economy overheating. Finland was one of the 11 EU countries to introduce the euro in January 1999.

ECONOMIC PERFORMANCE INDICATOR

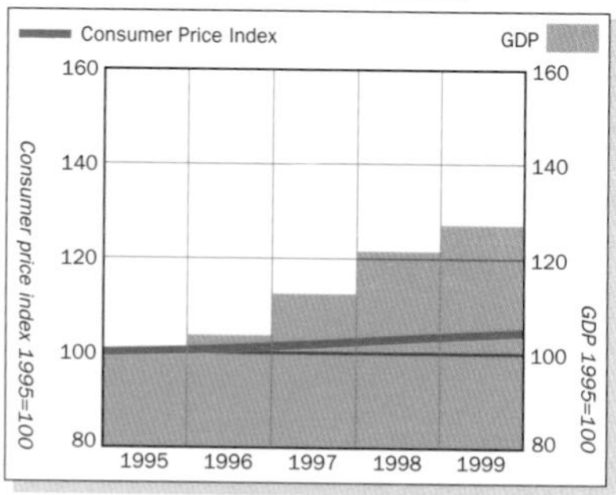
Consumer Price Index
GDP
Consumer price index 1995=100
GDP 1995=100
160
140
120
100
80
1995
1996
1997
1998
1999

FINLAND : MAJOR BUSINESSES

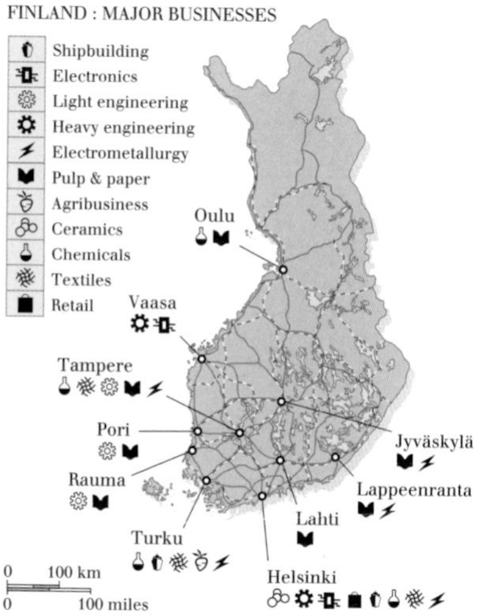
Shipbuilding
Electronics
Light engineering
Heavy engineering
Electrometallurgy
Pulp & paper
Agribusiness
Ceramics
Chemicals
Textiles
Retail
Oulu
Vaasa
Tampere
Pori
Rauma
Turku
Jyväskylä
Lappeenranta
Lahti
Helsinki
0 100 km
0 100 miles

RESOURCES

Electric power 14.2m kw

196,513 tonnes

Not an oil producer; refines 200,000 b/d

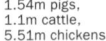

1.54m pigs, 1.1m cattle, 5.51m chickens

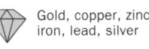

Gold, copper, zinc, iron, lead, silver

ELECTRICITY GENERATION

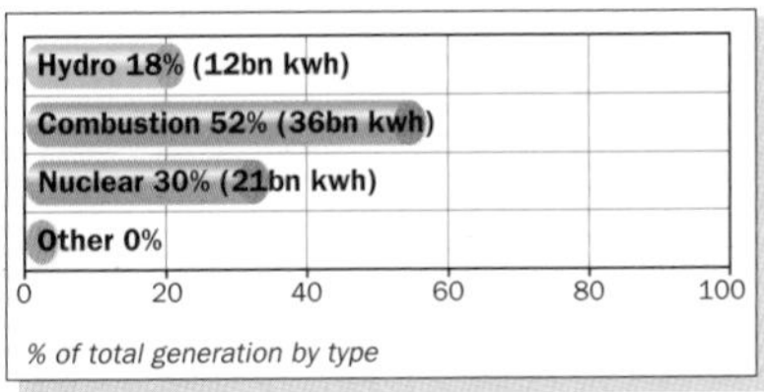
Hydro 18% (12bn kwh)
Combustion 52% (36bn kwh)
Nuclear 30% (21bn kwh)
Other 0%
0
20
40
60
80
100
% of total generation by type

Finland's trees are its prime natural resource. Commercial forests cover 65% of the land, and wood products account for 30% of exports. Finland has no oil, but has significant hydroelectric resources. Industry's high energy demands are met chiefly by thermal and nuclear power. A fifth nuclear power station is planned. Oil import costs have risen since 1990, when the collapse of the USSR ended a 42-year agreement on the exchange of Finnish manufactures for Soviet oil.

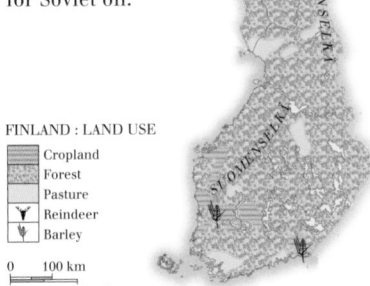

FINLAND : LAND USE

LAPLAND
MAANSELKÄ
SUOMENSELKÄ
Cropland
Forest
Pasture
Reindeer
Barley
0 100 km
0 100 miles

ENVIRONMENT

Sustainability rank: 1st

6%

11 tonnes per capita

ENVIRONMENTAL TREATIES

Yes Yes Yes

Yes Yes Yes

Finland has strict laws on industrial emissions. Energy efficiency is a priority; nearly half of all homes are connected to district heating systems. Growing public concern about nuclear safety has led to opposition to the planned fifth nuclear plant and to proposals for the greater use of waste materials in energy generation. The government is funding nuclear safety programs in Russia. Rising levels of pollution in the Baltic are of concern.

MEDIA

TV ownership high

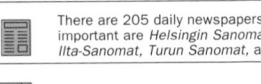

Daily newspaper circulation 455 per 1000 people

PUBLISHING AND BROADCAST MEDIA

There are 205 daily newspapers. The most important are *Helsingin Sanomat, Aamulehti, Ilta-Sanomat, Turun Sanomat,* and *Kaleva*

2 services: 1 state-owned, 1 independent

5 services: 1 state-owned, 4 independent

Nine out of ten adult Finns read a daily paper, the world's third-highest per capita ratio. Regional papers dominate; the only national is the independent *Helsingin Sanomat*. There is no censorship, but the press shows restraint in criticizing the government.

CRIME

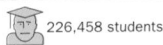

Death penalty not used

3018 prisoners

Down 1% 1996–1998

CRIME RATES

Murders

0.4 *per 100,000 population*

Rapes

9 *per 100,000 population*

Thefts

2919 *per 100,000 population*

The jump in unemployment in the early 1990s was seen as one of the causes of rising crime. There is concern about links with organized crime in Russia.

EDUCATION

School leaving age: 16

99%

226,458 students

THE EDUCATION SYSTEM

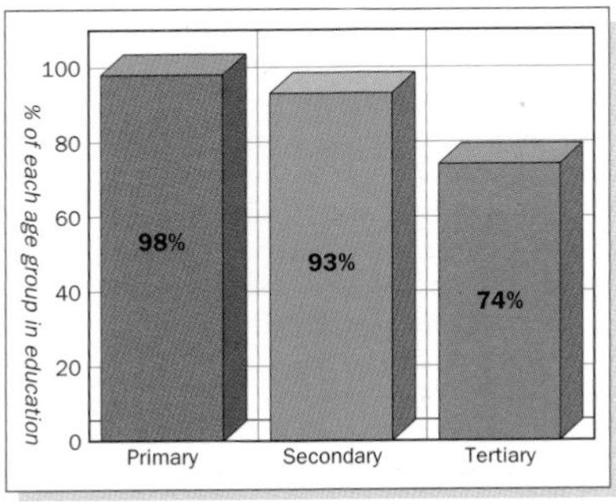
100
80
60
40
20
0
% of each age group in education
98%
93%
74%
Primary
Secondary
Tertiary

Compulsory education, introduced in 1921, lasts from seven to 16 years of age. By 1977/1978 the whole country had transferred to a new comprehensive system. Almost all children receive preschool education and also go on to three years of upper secondary education. Tough examinations mean that only 35% of entrants qualify to attend one of the 20 universities.

HEALTH

Welfare state health benefits

1 per 333 people

Cerebrovascular and heart diseases, cancers, suicides

14% of total government expenditure is spent on Finland's well-developed health system. Every Finn is legally guaranteed access to a local health center which is staffed by up to four doctors, as well as nurses and a midwife. Most non-hospital medical costs are covered by national health insurance; hospital fees are moderate. Diabetes and osteoporosis are increasing, and obesity is a growing health problem.

SPENDING

GDP/cap. increase

CONSUMPTION AND SPENDING

403 per 1000 population

557 per 1000 population

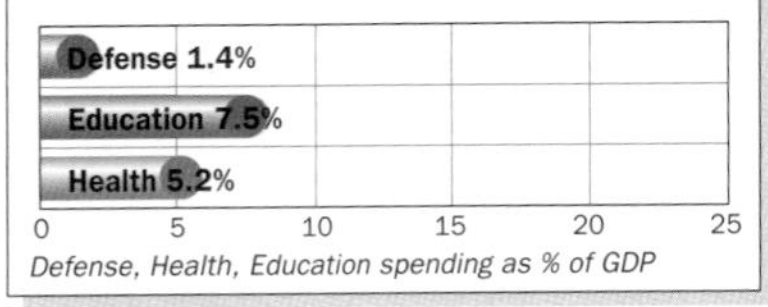
Defense 1.4%
Education 7.5%
Health 5.2%
0
5
10
15
20
25
Defense, Health, Education spending as % of GDP

Income disparities are more marked in Finland than in other Scandinavian countries. However, the economic boom and labor shortages of the 1980s led to a sharp rise in all living standards. Personal consumption reached Swedish levels, and many families were able to take two vacations a year. Social security benefits were extended.

During the deep recession which began in 1990, this improvement was reversed. Wealth disparities widened and expenditure cuts led to lower social security benefits for the jobless. Those in work had to accept lower pay rises and higher taxes. Average real disposable incomes dropped sharply. The situation has started to improve again now that the economy is posting strong growth.

Estonian immigrants form the poorest group in Finnish society.

WORLD RANKING

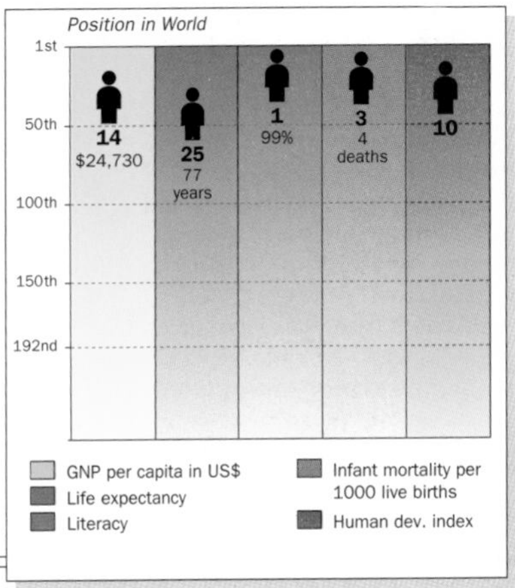
Position in World
1st
50th
100th
150th
192nd
14
$24,730
25
77
years
1
99%
3
4
deaths
10
GNP per capita in US$
Life expectancy
Literacy
Infant mortality per 1000 live births
Human dev. index

F

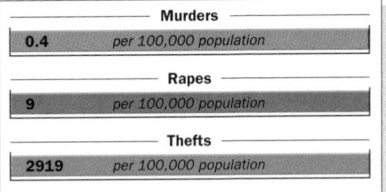

FRANCE

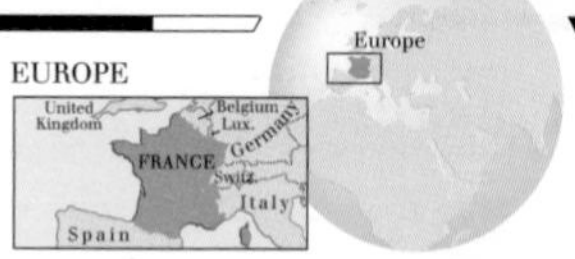
Europe
EUROPE
United Kingdom
Belgium
Lux.
Germany
FRANCE
Switz.
Italy
Spain

OFFICIAL NAME: French Republic **CAPITAL:** Paris **POPULATION:** 59.1 million
CURRENCY: Euro (French franc until 2002) **OFFICIAL LANGUAGE:** French

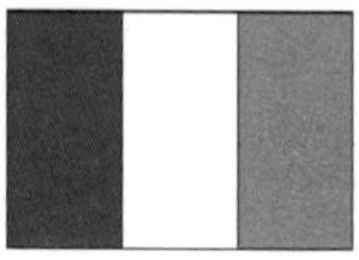

486 | 1919 | July 14 | F | +1 | +33 | .fr

STRADDLING WESTERN EUROPE from the English Channel to the Mediterranean, France was Europe's first modern republic, and possessed a colonial empire second only to that of the UK. Today, it is one of the world's major industrial powers and its fourth-largest exporter. Industry is the leading economic sector, but the agricultural lobby remains powerful – French farmers will mount the barricades in defense of their interests. France's focus is very much on Europe. Together with Germany it was a founder member of the European Economic Community (EEC), and has supported successive steps to build a more closely integrated European Union. Paris, the French capital, is generally considered one of the world's most beautiful cities. It has been home to some of the most influential artists, writers, and film-makers of the modern era.

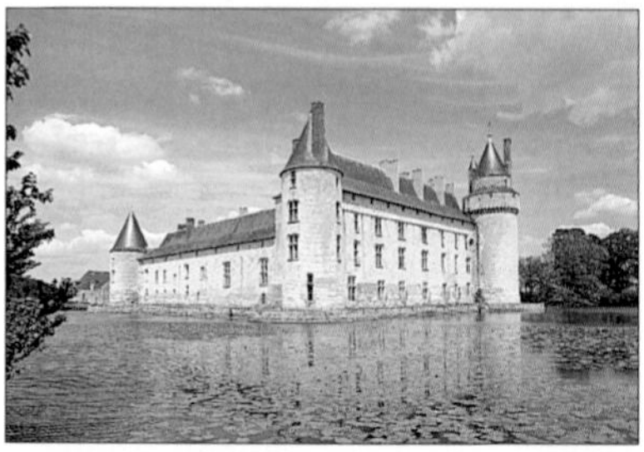

***Le Plessis-Bourré, Loire Valley.** The region is famous for its many chateaux, which attract thousands of visitors every year.*

F

CLIMATE

Maritime/Mediterranean/ mountain/continental

WEATHER CHART

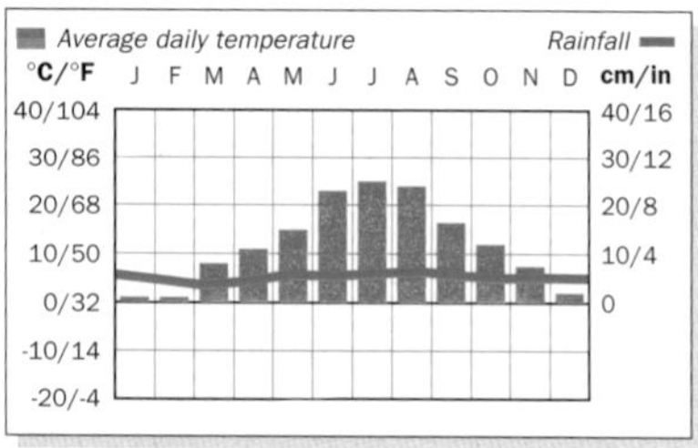
Average daily temperature
Rainfall
°C/°F
J F M A M J J A S O N D
cm/in
40/104
30/86
20/68
10/50
0/32
-10/14
-20/-4
40/16
30/12
20/8
10/4
0

France's climate differs significantly from region to region. The northwest, in particular Brittany, is mild but damp. The east has hot summers and stormy winters, whereas summers in the south are dry and hot, and forest fires are frequent.

TRANSPORTATION

Drive on right

Charles de Gaulle, Paris 43.6m passengers

4.1m grt

THE TRANSPORTATION NETWORK

893,300 km (555,070 miles)	10,300 km (6400 miles)
31,589 km (19,629 miles)	14,932 km (9278 miles)

France led the world in high-speed train technology in 1983 with the TGV (*train à grande vitesse*) from Paris to Lyon. TGV lines have since been extended further south, and link up with Belgium, Italy, Spain, the Mediterranean, and the Channel Tunnel; a Paris–Strasbourg line is planned for 2005. On the expanding network of *autoroutes* motorists pay tolls for the convenience of rapid journeys. France is also a major center for commercial airline traffic, thanks partly to the importance of tourism.

TOURISM

Visitors : Population 1.3:1

75.5m visitors

Up 3% in 2000

MAIN TOURIST ARRIVALS

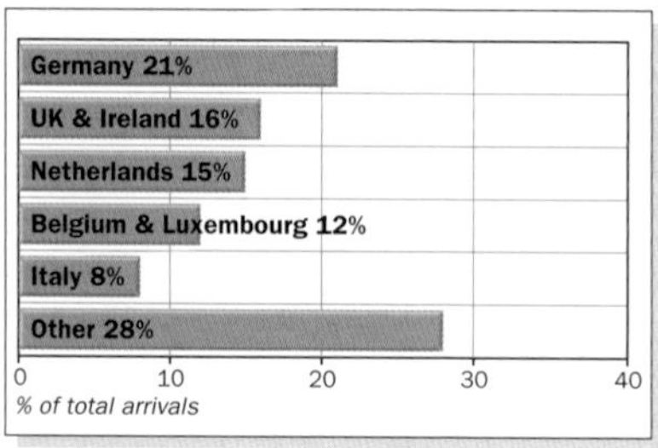
Germany 21%
UK & Ireland 16%
Netherlands 15%
Belgium & Luxembourg 12%
Italy 8%
Other 28%
0
10
20
30
40
% of total arrivals

France is the world's leading tourist destination, with over 75 million visitors a year. It tops the list for tourists from many of its neighboring countries, including Germans, British, Italians, and Dutch. Most French people also prefer to take vacations in their own country, although many do visit Spain and Italy.

Paris is the most visited city in Europe. Its attractions include the Eiffel Tower, Nôtre Dame cathedral, Eurodisney, the Centre Pompidou, and the Louvre, the world's most popular art museum.

Other destinations throughout the country attract tourists for a wide variety of reasons such as wine production, historic and archaeological sites, and good beaches. There are also developed resorts for skiing and hiking in the Alps and Pyrenees, and sailing off the varied coastline is also popular. Modern tourism was all but invented on the Côte d'Azur, when royalty and other notables flocked to fashionable resorts such as Nice at the end of the 19th century. Cannes hosts the world's leading film festival, and has a growing business convention trade.

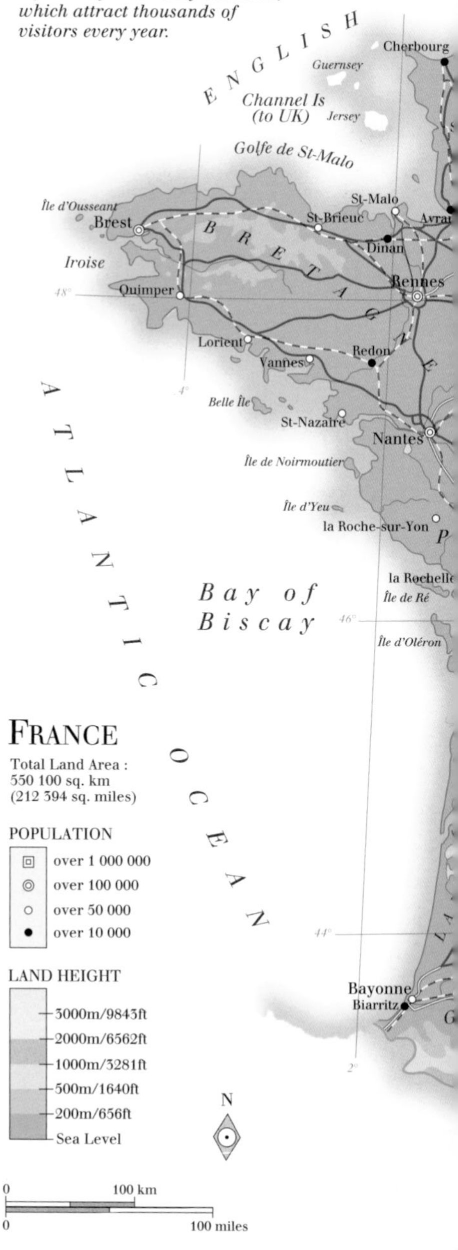
ENGLISH
Cherbourg
Guernsey
Channel Is (to UK)
Jersey
Golfe de St-Malo
St-Malo
Île d'Ousseant
Brest
St-Brieuc
Dinan
BRETAGNE
Iroise
Quimper
Rennes
Lorient
Vannes
Redon
Belle Île
St-Nazaire
Nantes
Île de Noirmoutier
Île d'Yeu
la Roche-sur-Yon
la Rochelle
Île de Ré
Bay of Biscay
Île d'Oléron
ATLANTIC OCEAN
Bayonne
Biarritz
FRANCE
Total Land Area : 550 100 sq. km (212 394 sq. miles)
POPULATION
over 1 000 000
over 100 000
over 50 000
over 10 000
LAND HEIGHT
3000m/9843ft
2000m/6562ft
1000m/3281ft
500m/1640ft
200m/656ft
Sea Level
N
0
100 km
0
100 miles

F

PEOPLE

Pop. density medium

French, Provençal, German, Breton, Catalan, Basque

107/km² (278/mi²)

There is a strong national identity, and compulsory use of French has traditionally been promoted as a unifying force. The cultural traditions of Bretons, Flemings, Alsatians, Basques, Occitans, Catalans, and Corsicans are now respected, but the Constitutional Court has struck down legislation on the use of regional language in government. There are some five million immigrants, 25% of whom are now naturalized citizens.

Despite France's traditional freedom of thought, high unemployment led to a rise in intolerance, exploited politically in the 1980s. Large antiracist rallies countered racist National Front (FN) propaganda, however, and youth solidarity among "black, blanc, beur" ("black, white, Arab") was boosted by the 1998 World Cup success of the multiracial national soccer team.

The Roman Catholic Church is still dominant, but there are sizable Protestant, Jewish, and Muslim minorities. Abortion and birth control were both legalized in the 1970s, despite strong Catholic opposition, and couples now commonly live together before marriage. Some two million unmarried couples of two or more years' standing, including gay couples, gained legal status with social and tax rights under 1998 legislation recognizing the civil solidarity pact.

Women did not get the vote until 1944, but now have the same legal rights as men. They are still under-represented in parliament, although there was a woman prime minister, Edith Cresson, in 1991–1992, and women took five senior cabinet posts in the incoming Socialist-led government in 1997. A new "parity" law in 2000 requires an equal number of male and female candidates on party electoral lists. Women are also gaining more advancement in the professions.

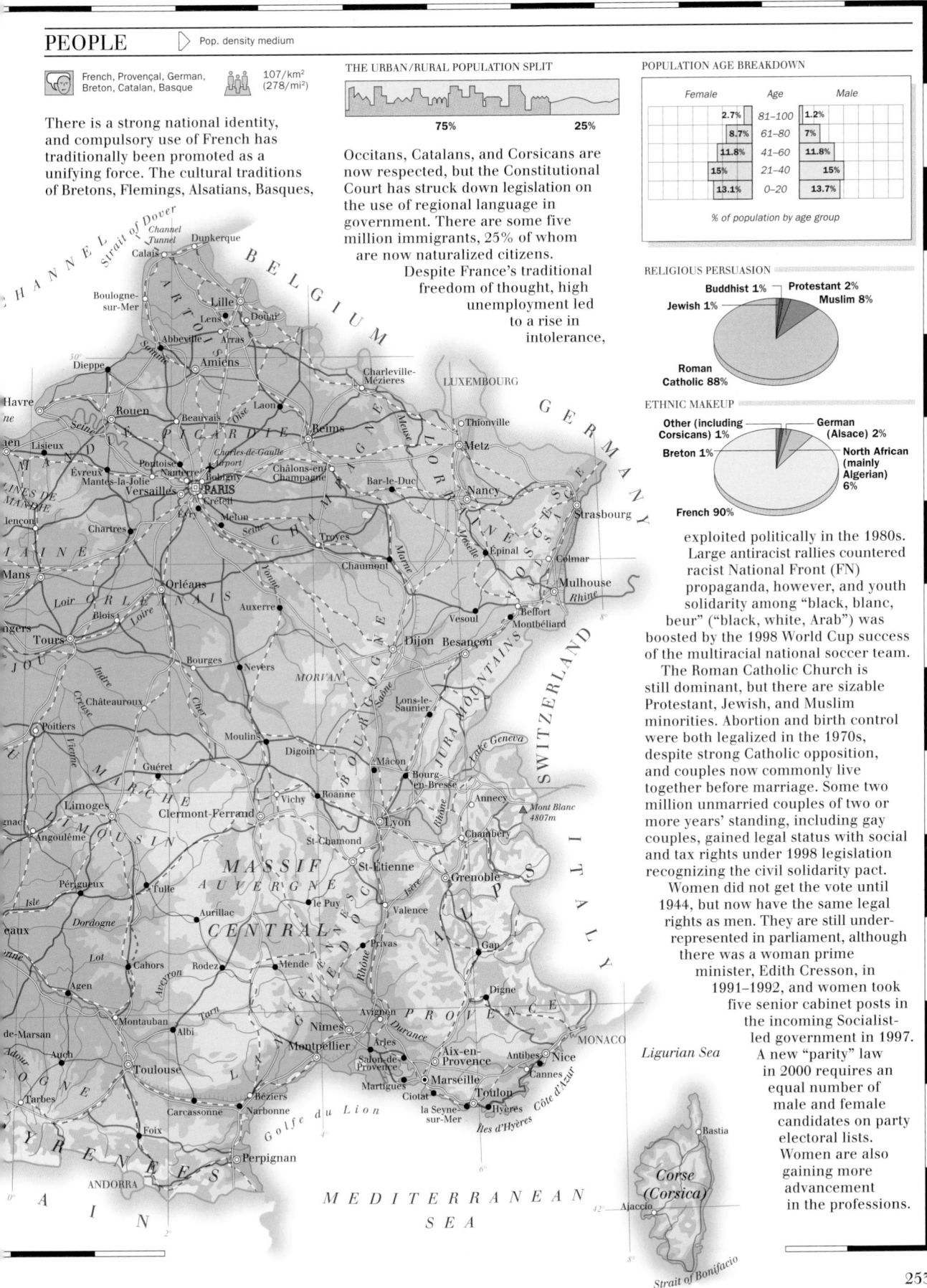

THE URBAN/RURAL POPULATION SPLIT

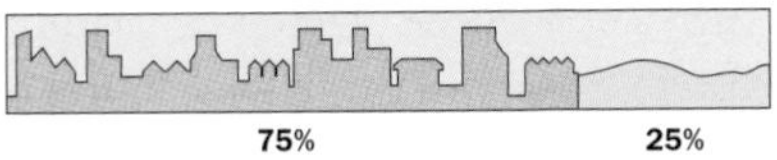
75%
25%

POPULATION AGE BREAKDOWN

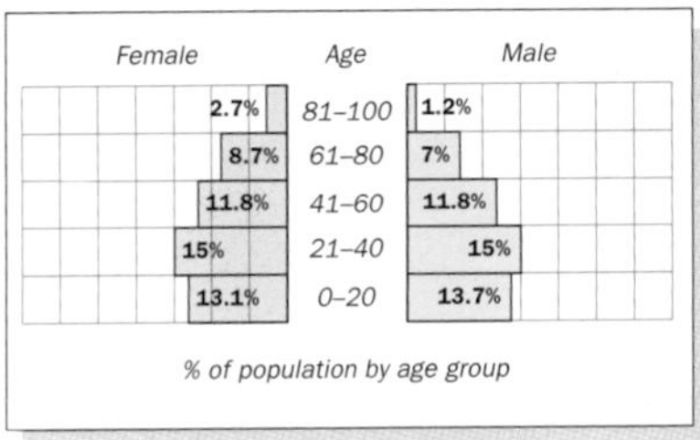
Female
Age
Male
2.7%
81–100
1.2%
8.7%
61–80
7%
11.8%
41–60
11.8%
15%
21–40
15%
13.1%
0–20
13.7%
% of population by age group

RELIGIOUS PERSUASION

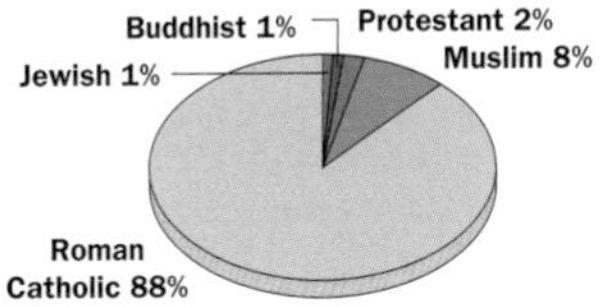
Buddhist 1%
Protestant 2%
Muslim 8%
Jewish 1%
Roman Catholic 88%

ETHNIC MAKEUP

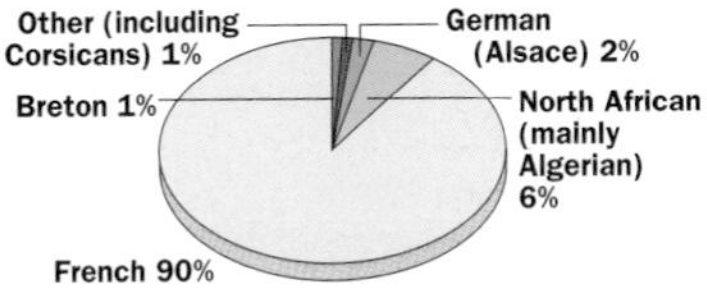
Other (including Corsicans) 1%
German (Alsace) 2%
Breton 1%
North African (mainly Algerian) 6%
French 90%

CHANNEL
Strait of Dover
Channel Tunnel
Calais
Dunkerque
BELGIUM
Boulogne-sur-Mer
ARTOIS
Lille
Lens
Douai
Arras
Abbeville
Somme
Amiens
Dieppe
Charleville-Mézieres
LUXEMBOURG
GERMANY
Rouen
Seine
Beauvais
Oise
Laon
PICARDIE
Reims
Meuse
Thionville
Metz
LORRAINE
Lisieux
Pontoise
Nanterre
Charles-de-Gaulle Airport
Bobigny
Évreux
Mantes-la-Jolie
Versailles
PARIS
Créteil
Évry
Melun
Châlons-en-Champagne
Bar-le-Duc
Nancy
Strasbourg
Chartres
Seine
CHAMPAGNE
Troyes
Marne
Moselle
Épinal
VOSGES
ALSACE
Colmar
Mulhouse
Rhine
Chaumont
Orléans
ORLÉANAIS
Loir
Blois
Loire
Auxerre
Yonne
Vesoul
Belfort
Montbéliard
Tours
Dijon
Besançon
Bourges
Nevers
MORVAN
BOURGOGNE
JURA MOUNTAINS
SWITZERLAND
Indre
Châteauroux
Creuse
Cher
Lons-le-Saunier
Poitiers
Vienne
Moulins
Digoin
Saône
Lake Geneva
Mâcon
Bourg-en-Bresse
Guéret
MARCHE
Vichy
Roanne
Annecy
Mont Blanc 4807m
Limoges
Clermont-Ferrand
Lyon
Rhône
Chambéry
LIMOUSIN
Angoulême
St-Chamond
St-Étienne
MASSIF CENTRAL
AUVERGNE
Grenoble
Isère
ALPES
ITALY
Périgueux
Tulle
Le Puy
Valence
Aurillac
Dordogne
Privas
Gap
Lot
Cahors
Rodez
Mende
Aveyron
CÉVENNES
Rhône
Agen
Digne
Tarn
Montauban
Albi
Avignon
PROVENCE
Nîmes
Durance
Arles
Montpellier
MONACO
Auch
Toulouse
Salon-de-Provence
Aix-en-Provence
Antibes
Nice
Cannes
Martigues
Marseille
Côte d'Azur
Tarbes
Béziers
Ciotat
Toulon
Carcassonne
Narbonne
Golfe du Lion
la Seyne-sur-Mer
Hyères
Îles d'Hyères
Foix
Ligurian Sea
Bastia
PYRENEES
Perpignan
ANDORRA
Corse (Corsica)
SPAIN
MEDITERRANEAN SEA
Ajaccio
Strait of Bonifacio

F

CHRONOLOGY

The French Revolution of 1789–1794 overthrew a monarchy that had lasted for more than 1300 years. It ushered in a period of alternating republicanism, Napoleonic imperialism, and monarchism. In 1870 the founding of the Third Republic established France firmly in the republican tradition.

- **1914–1918** 1.4 million Frenchmen killed in World War I.
- **1918–1939** Economic recession and political instability; 20 prime ministers and 44 governments.
- **1940** Capitulation to Germany. Puppet Vichy regime. General de Gaulle leads “Free French” abroad.
- **1944** Liberation of France.
- **1946–1958** Fourth Republic. Political instability: 26 governments. Nationalizations. France takes leading role in EEC formation.
- **1958** Fifth Republic. De Gaulle becomes president with strong executive powers.
- **1960** Most French colonies gain independence.
- **1962** Algerian independence after bitter war with France.
- **1966** France withdraws from NATO military command.
- **1968** General strike and riots over education policy and low wages. National Assembly dissolved; Gaullist victory in June elections.
- **1969** De Gaulle resigns after defeat in referendum on regional reform; replaced by Georges Pompidou.
- **1974** Valéry Giscard d’Estaing president. Center-right coalition.
- **1981** Left wins elections; François Mitterrand president.
- **1983–1986** Government U-turn on economic policy.
- **1986** *Cohabitation* between socialist president and new right-wing government led by Jacques Chirac. Privatization program introduced.
- **1988** Mitterrand wins second term. PS-led coalition returns.
- **1991** Edith Cresson becomes first woman prime minister.
- **1993** Center-right wins elections. Second period of *cohabitation.*
- **1995** Jacques Chirac president.
- **1995–1996** Controversial series of Pacific nuclear tests.
- **1996** Unpopular austerity measures to prepare economy for European monetary union.
- **1997** Center-right loses elections. PS-led government takes office in reversed *cohabitation.* Lionel Jospin prime minister.
- **1998–1999** Extensive privatization program.
- **1999** France introduces euro.
- **2000** 35-hour week becomes law.

POLITICS

Multiparty elections

L. House 1997/2002
U. House 1998/2001

President Jacques Chirac

AT THE LAST ELECTION

National Assembly 577 seats

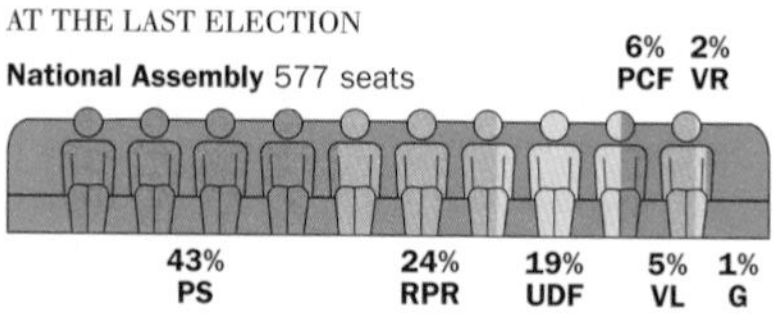
6% PCF
2% VR
43% PS
24% RPR
19% UDF
5% VL
1% G

PS = Socialist Party **RPR** = Rally for the Republic **UDF** = Union for French Democracy **PCF** = Communist Party of France **VL** = Various Left **VR** = Various Right **G** = Greens **UC** = Centrist Union **Rep** = Republicans and Independents **RDSE** = European Democratic and Social Rally **RCC** = Republicans, Communists, and Citizens **Ind** = Independents

Senate 321 seats

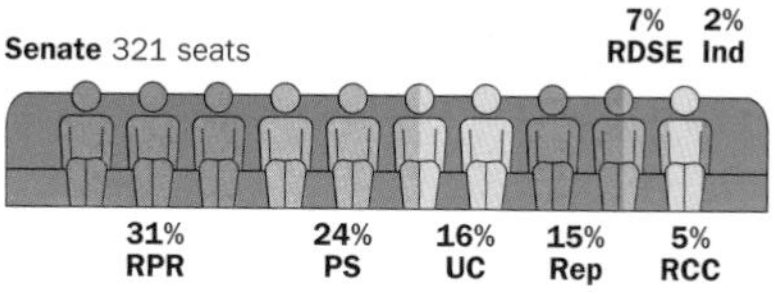
7% RDSE
2% Ind
31% RPR
24% PS
16% UC
15% Rep
5% RCC

France is a multiparty democracy. The president has strong executive powers, but rules in tandem with a government and prime minister chosen by the *Assemblée Nationale*. Until changes agreed in 2000, the president and parliament were elected according to separate timetables, with the president serving a seven-year term. Traditionally presidents attend to foreign policy and defense issues, while the government focuses on domestic and economic policy, but in early 2000 Prime Minister Lionel Jospin defended his active involvement in foreign affairs.

MAIN POLITICAL ISSUES

The presidential system

The executive presidency has had to come to terms with *cohabitation*, first between a Socialist president and right-wing governments in 1986–1988 and 1993–1995, and, since June 1997, between the Gaullist President Chirac and a socialist government. Both Jospin and Chirac backed new rules to make the presidential and *Assemblée* terms run concurrently, for five years each, starting from the 2002 elections.

Racism and “exclusion”

When unemployment rates are high, the racist right has been able to profit by blaming immigrants. Legislation on immigration has been tightened. There is concern too about inner city deprivation and violence. “Exclusion” of the unemployed and homeless is widely recognized as divisive. Resenting economic austerity policies, the electorate in 1997 chose a government which promised greater social concern. Unemployment fell below 10% in 2000 for the first time in a decade. Realignment of the defeated right-wing parties did open the possibility of more mainstream acceptance of the racist National Front (FN), although complex party splits largely ruled this out.

European integration and globalization

Opposition to European integration grew in the early 1990s, fueled by fears of losing French sovereignty and identity, while opponents of “globalization” tap into similar concerns that French jobs and culture are under threat. Now part of the euro single currency, the French look for benefits in terms of stability and economic growth. The most strident opponent of EU integration is the FN.

PROFILE

Two decades of right-of-center government, under the presidencies of de Gaulle, Pompidou, and Giscard d’Estaing, ended in 1981 with the united left victory. François Mitterrand became president and a PS-led government nationalized many of France’s most famous businesses, while local government was decentralized. However, the failure of its reflationary economic policy forced the PS to change course, adopting monetarist policies instead. Badly tainted by scandal and loss of direction, the PS suffered a crushing electoral defeat in 1993 and lost the presidency in 1995 to the right-of-center Chirac. The PS returned to government two years later when its leader Lionel Jospin reached pre-election agreements with the Communists, Greens, and other left-wing groups. By 2001, Chirac and Jospin were openly behaving as rivals with a view to their expected presidential election contest in 2002.

The far left has declined since 1945, when the PCF had 25% of the vote, but the racist FN has built up its following to around 15%. This gave it only one seat at the 1997 elections, but had a disproportionate political impact.

Jacques Chirac, *elected president of France in 1995.*

Dominique Voynet *former environment minister who leads the Green Party.*

Lionel Jospin, *who became prime minister in 1997.*

WORLD AFFAIRS

Joined UN in 1945

EU | G7 | NATO | OECD | OSCE

French foreign policy has followed two, apparently contradictory, strands since World War II – maintenance of a strongly independent line and furtherance of French interests within a united Europe. France's leading role within the EU was a way of combining the two strands, but after 1989 the weight of a reunited Germany within Europe created something of a backlash against European integration on the French nationalist right. This swelled the minority "no" vote in the 1992 Maastricht referendum almost to the point of rejecting the Treaty on European Union. However, the Franco-German thrust toward greater European integration remains the keystone of French foreign policy. France also supported broadening of the EU to include Scandinavia as well as further enlargement to the east.

France seeks to offset US dominance in both foreign affairs and culture. It left NATO's military command in 1966, maintained an independent nuclear deterrent (which it insisted on testing in the Pacific in 1995–1996 despite a wave of international criticism), and sought a role in the post-Cold War world as a counterweight to US influence in the Middle East and Africa.

AID

Donor

$5.64bn (donations)

Down 2% in 1999

France is one of the world's major aid donors. Its motives are not simply commercial; it also wishes to maintain the influence of the French language, particularly in west Africa, which has been the main aid recipient. Médecins sans Frontières reflects a long French tradition of NGO aid agencies.

ECONOMICS

Inflation 1.6% p.a. (1990–1999)

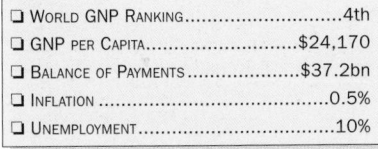

$1453bn

6.5442–6.9869 francs

SCORE CARD

❑ WORLD GNP RANKING	4th
❑ GNP PER CAPITA	$24,170
❑ BALANCE OF PAYMENTS	$37.2bn
❑ INFLATION	0.5%
❑ UNEMPLOYMENT	10%

EXPORTS

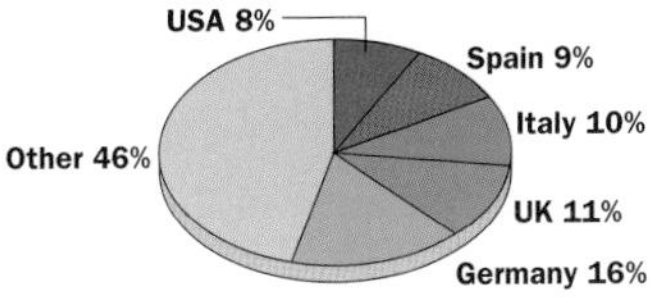
USA 8%
Spain 9%
Italy 10%
UK 11%
Germany 16%
Other 46%

IMPORTS

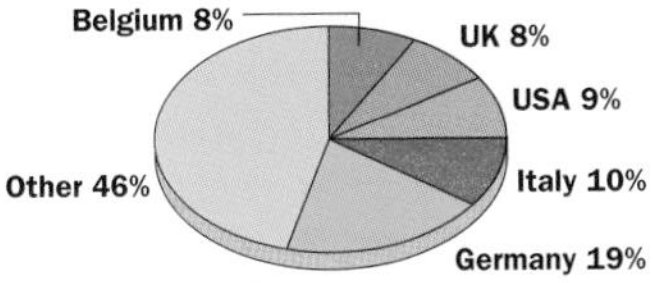
Belgium 8%
UK 8%
USA 9%
Italy 10%
Germany 19%
Other 46%

STRENGTHS

Engineering, reflected in the TGV and nuclear industries. Specializations such as cars (Citroën, Peugeot, and Renault) and telecommunications (Alcatel). Defense sector a major exporter, as are pharmaceutical and chemical industries. Success in attracting inward investment. Strong technocratic traditions: unlike in USA or UK, top graduates are attracted into engineering. Luxury goods, cosmetics, perfumes, and quality wines. Most agriculture well modernized; France is Europe's leading agricultural producer.

WEAKNESSES

High taxes, social charges, and labor costs. France is losing its positions in traditional industries such as iron and steel, metallurgy, and textiles. Some major high-tech industries, such as telecommunications, run partly to further national pride, rather than on a strictly commercial basis.

ECONOMIC PERFORMANCE INDICATOR

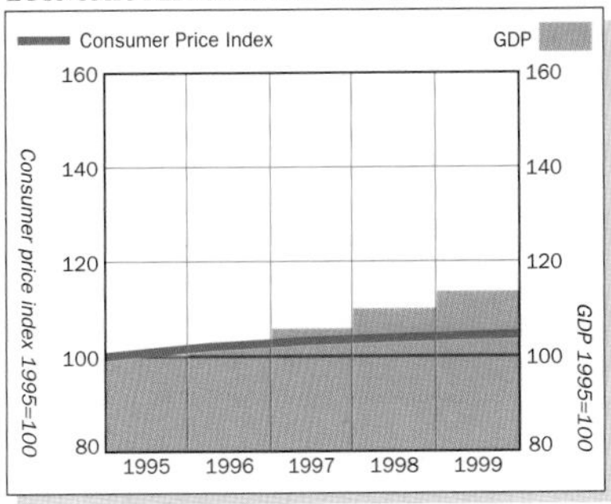
Consumer Price Index
GDP
160
140
120
100
80
Consumer price index 1995=100
GDP 1995=100
1995
1996
1997
1998
1999

PROFILE

At first slow to industrialize, protectionist France started competing in world markets and modernizing its industry in the 1950s and 1960s. Integration in western Europe, starting with the coal and steel industry in the 1950s, placed France at the heart of the EU. It was one of the 11 EU countries to introduce the euro in 1999. One of the world's top exporters, its foreign trade balance runs a healthy surplus. France has a long tradition of state involvement in running the economy. Nationalization of key industries began in the late 1930s, with a fresh burst in 1981–1983, but since then both right-of-center and socialist governments have pursued privatization with vigor, reaching into the defense industry, aviation, banking, telecommunications, and insurance. Regional hubs are of growing economic significance. France is the EU's largest agricultural producer, and its farmers are a powerful political lobby. Active trade unions succeeded in getting a maximum 35-hour week introduced in 2000.

FRANCE : MAJOR BUSINESSES

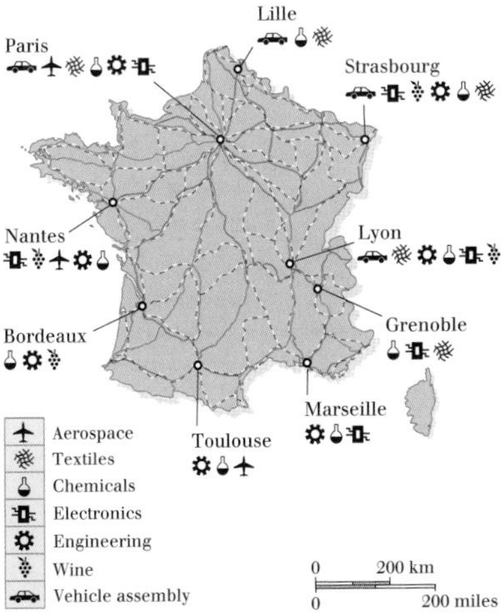
Lille
Paris
Strasbourg
Nantes
Lyon
Bordeaux
Grenoble
Marseille
Toulouse
Aerospace
Textiles
Chemicals
Electronics
Engineering
Wine
Vehicle assembly
0 200 km
0 200 miles

DEFENSE

No compulsory military service

$37.9bn

Down 7% in 1999

FRENCH ARMED FORCES

834 main battle tanks (635 AMX-30B2, 199 *Leclerc*)	169,300 personnel
1 carrier, 11 submarines, 1 cruiser, 4 destroyers, 29 frigates, & 40 patrol boats	49,490 personnel
517 combat aircraft (352 *Mirage* F-1B/1C/1CR, 66 *Jaguar*, 99 *Alpha Jet*)	60,500 personnel
64 SLBM in 4 SSBN	

France was a founder member of NATO, but left its miltary command in 1966 in opposition to US domination. It maintained an independent nuclear deterrent through the Cold War, but had a rapprochement with NATO in the 1990s. Joint participation with Germany in European army units is partly symbolic of reconciliation, as well as an expression of the need for an EU defense structure.

The influence of the army, once very strong, is now much diminished. The government began the phasing out of compulsory military service in 1996.

France has one of the world's largest and most export-oriented defense industries, producing its own tanks, jet fighter aircraft, and missiles.

F

RESOURCES

Electric power 112.3m kw

829,914 tonnes

35,689 b/d (reserves 104,236,800 bbl)

42m turkeys, 23.8m ducks, 20.2m cattle, 233m chickens

Coal, oil, natural gas, iron, zinc

ELECTRICITY GENERATION

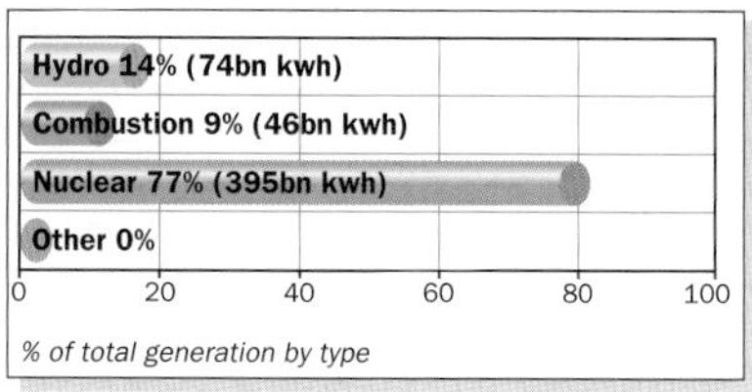
Hydro 14% (74bn kwh)
Combustion 9% (46bn kwh)
Nuclear 77% (395bn kwh)
Other 0%
0
20
40
60
80
100
% of total generation by type

France is the world's most committed user of nuclear energy, which provides over three-quarters of its electricity requirements. The policy reflects a desire for national energy self-sufficiency. Coal, once plentiful in the north and Lorraine, is now mostly exhausted, as are the gas fields off the southwest coast.

FRANCE : LAND USE

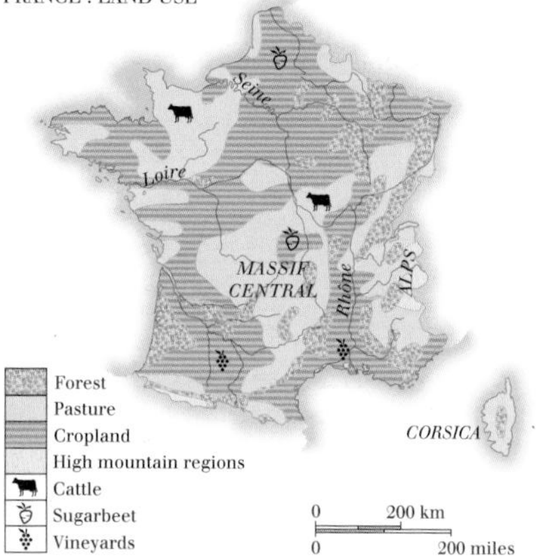
Seine
Loire
MASSIF CENTRAL
Rhône
ALPS
CORSICA
Forest
Pasture
Cropland
High mountain regions
Cattle
Sugarbeet
Vineyards
0 200 km
0 200 miles

ENVIRONMENT

Sustainability rank: 13th

11% (9% partially protected)

6 tonnes per capita

ENVIRONMENTAL TREATIES

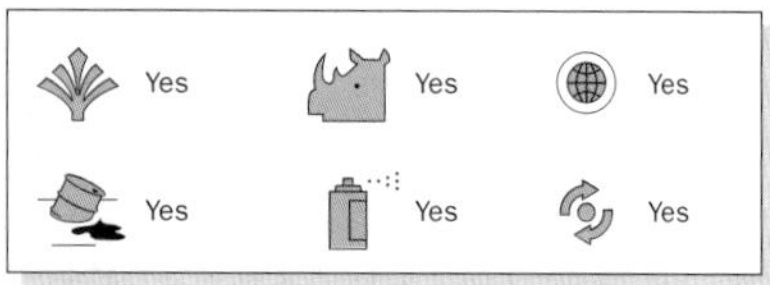
Yes
Yes
Yes
Yes
Yes
Yes

Awareness of "green" issues has risen with a series of campaigns against major infrastructure projects. Nuclear power's importance, however, puts the environmentalist lobby in perspective. Transportation of oil by sea poses the threat of pollution of the Atlantic coast. Brittany's beaches and fisheries were severely affected by the wreck of the *Erika* in December 1999. Severe storms devastated woodlands in 2000, focusing attention on the dangers of global warming.

THE IMPACT OF MODERN TRANSPORTATION

While the French regions retain distinctive characteristics, the country's modern transportation and telecommunications network, with Paris at its hub, has brought the main provincial cities within easy reach of the capital. It also helps France to play a central role in European business.

The autoroute network

The toll-charging autoroutes, or freeways, with a speed limit of 130 km/h (81 mph), now reach almost every corner of the map except the Cherbourg peninsula and Brittany in the north-west. They have relieved the previous generation of town-to-town highways of much of their former traffic congestion, but have also encouraged the upsurge in trans-European heavy freight vehicle movement, carrying through traffic to and from Spain, Italy, Switzerland, Germany, the Benelux countries, and the Channel ports. There has been much controversy about the environmental impact of several as yet uncompleted cross-country links, notably the E11 route south from Clermont-Ferrand to join the Mediterranean network.

French leadership in high-speed trains

French pride in leading-edge engineering, and a capacity for ambitious centralized planning and state-backed investment, have been apparent in its high speed train system, the *train à grande vitesse* (TGV). Rivaled only by the Japanese "bullet train" as the fastest in passenger service, the TGV can run at sustained speeds of over 300 km/h (186 mph). It has hit domestic airline traffic hard on some of the prime routes, by offering a combination of comfort and shorter door-to-door journey times in many instances. During the 1990s, some double-decker trains were introduced, to help meet high demand for seats, and a new generation of TGV trains was unveiled by the engineers Alstom in 1998–1999.

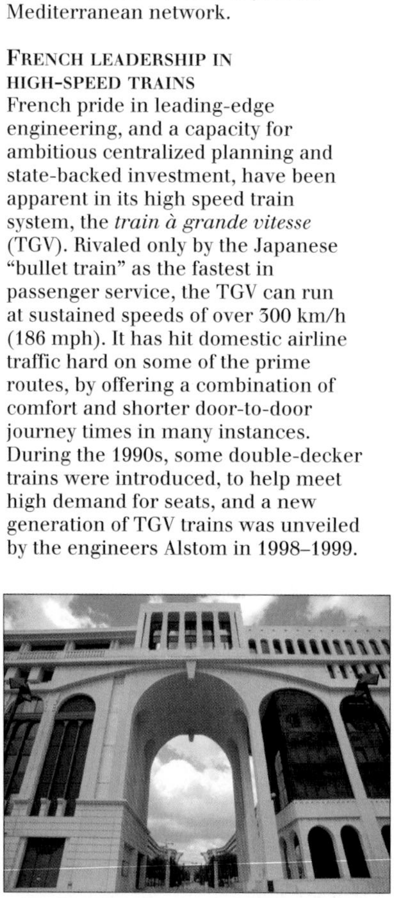

The first element was the TGV south-east. Construction began in 1975 and the Paris–Lyon section came into service in 1983, with subsequent extensions southward, culminating in the high-profile opening in 2001 of the direct service from Paris to Marseille. By the end of the 1980s a western route from Paris, initially to Le Mans,

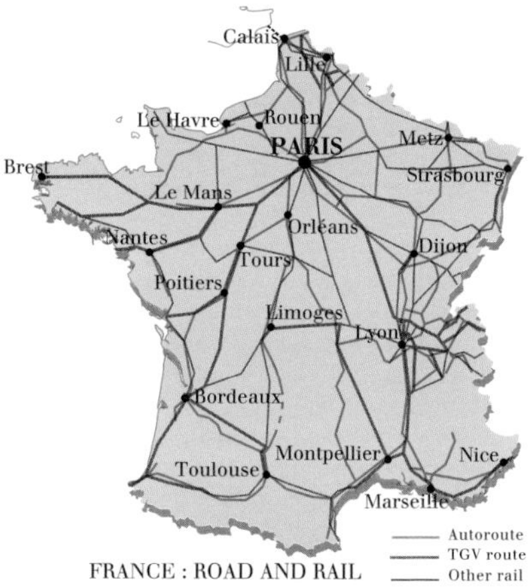
Calais
Lille
Le Havre
Rouen
PARIS
Metz
Brest
Strasbourg
Le Mans
Orléans
Nantes
Dijon
Tours
Poitiers
Limoges
Lyon
Bordeaux
Montpellier
Nice
Toulouse
Marseille
Autoroute
TGV route
Other rail

FRANCE : ROAD AND RAIL

was also in service. The northern Paris–Lille route opened in 1993 with extensions to Brussels, Calais, and the Channel Tunnel.

Extending the train network

The existing TGV lines, which use mainly modernized but also some purpose-built track, are a highly profitable part of the French rail network. Seeing the likely economic benefits, many towns have lobbied hard to be included. The next planned line, however, from Paris east to Strasbourg, has faced more opposition as well as escalating cost estimates. Construction began in early 1999, aiming for completion in six to seven years. To make money, this line will need to provoke a big shift in existing traveling habits. The French government's commitment is also in part a strategic political decision, designed to reinforce Strasbourg's role "at the heart of European integration."

A link via Tours to Bordeaux is intended to be part of the next stage, along with further international links – from Lyon to Turin, from Marseille and Montpellier to Barcelona, and via Strasbourg to Stuttgart and Frankfurt and thus into the German high-speed ICE train network.

Modern office blocks *in Montpellier, a city whose new dynamic image owes much to its transportation links and investment in communications technology.*

MEDIA

TV ownership high

Daily newspaper circulation 218 per 1000 people

PUBLISHING AND BROADCAST MEDIA

There are 117 daily newspapers, including *Le Monde*, *Libération*, and *Le Figaro*. *Ouest-France* has the highest circulation

8 services: 3 state-controlled, 5 independent

7 services: 3 state-controlled, 4 independent

TV and radio were freed from direct state influence in the 1980s. Two of the main TV channels are still state-owned, but TF1 was privatized in 1987. Canal Plus mixes pay-per-view and advertising-backed services. A Breton-language station started up in 2000. Commercial channels have multiplied with the growth of satellite and cable.

The once innovative Minitel electronic communications system is now overshadowed by the Internet. Circulation of prestigious national newspapers has dwindled and regional papers too have suffered from a gradual shift to electronic media.

CRIME

Death penalty not used

53,697 prisoners

Down 1% 1996–1998

CRIME RATES

Crime	Rate	
Murders	4	per 100,000 population
Rapes	13	per 100,000 population
Thefts	3917	per 100,000 population

The Code Napoléon, enacted by Bonaparte in 1804, still forms the basis of French law. Criminal justice is based on inquisitorial rather than adversarial principles. The *juge d'instruction* has considerable powers to examine witnesses and assess evidence. The press are not restricted by *sub judice* rules in reporting trials and can speak freely of suspects. Political corruption cases, reaching the higher echelons of government, attract much attention.

Public concern about rising petty crime and violence has encouraged successive governments to promote tough policing.

HEALTH

Welfare state health benefits

1 per 333 people

Heart and cerebrovascular diseases, cancers, accidents

The French consume more medicines per capita than any other nation, and a significant number take medically approved, and prescribed, cures at health spas. French health care was rated most efficient in the world by WHO in 2000. Under the national health system patients pay for treatment, and then get the majority of the cost reimbursed by an insurance company paid by the social services. Although health awareness has risen in recent years, a 1992 law banning smoking in public places is widely ignored and alcoholism remains a problem, with cirrhosis of the liver not uncommon as a cause of death.

SPENDING

GDP/cap. increase

CONSUMPTION AND SPENDING

469 per 1000 population

582 per 1000 population

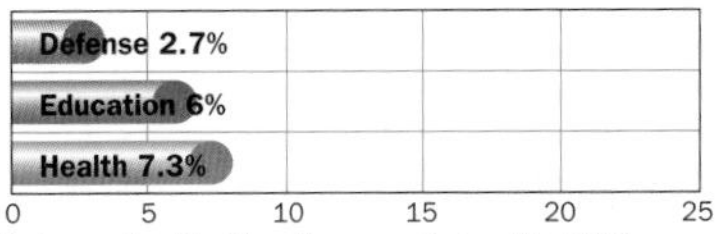
Defense 2.7%
Education 6%
Health 7.3%
0
5
10
15
20
25
Defense, Health, Education spending as % of GDP

EDUCATION

School leaving age : 16

99%

2.1m students

THE EDUCATION SYSTEM

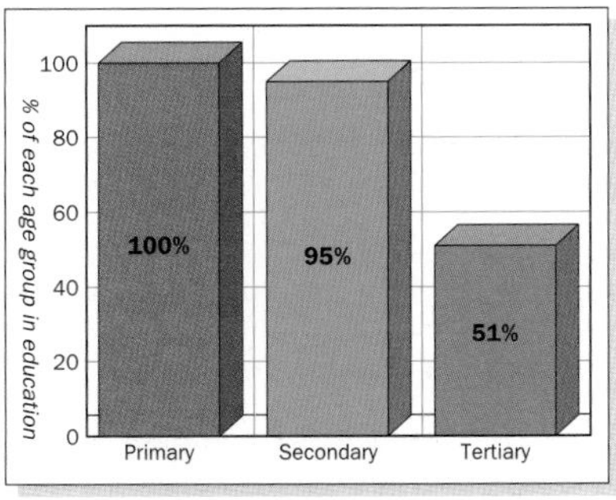
100
80
60
40
20
0
% of each age group in education
100%
95%
51%
Primary
Secondary
Tertiary

Education is highly centralized, a situation which is slowly generating a desire for greater flexibility. The education ministry organizes the curriculum, sets examinations, including the *baccalauréat*, and decides staffing issues. Roman Catholic schools, which take most of the 17% of privately educated children (but are not fee paying and receive large state subsidies), are the exception. However, they are still obliged to follow the national curriculum.

The focus in the classroom remains the acquisition of a broad range of knowledge. Pupils' academic records are impressive, despite frequent staff strikes.

France has more than 70 universities – 13 in Paris – and higher education bodies with 1.2 million students. Entry is not competitive, but based on passing the secondary-level exam, the *baccalauréat*. Most students attend the university nearest to home. The universities have not been given the funds or staff to cope with the huge increase in student numbers in recent years. The 150 *Grandes Écoles*, the most influential tertiary institutions, are outside the university system, and each takes just a few hundred carefully selected students. They groom the future governing elite, opening the way for their successful graduates to gain the top civil service and professional jobs.

Massif Central, Auvergne. *The Massif's lonely granite plateaus and extinct volcanoes are France's oldest rock formations.*

Wealth and income disparities in France are higher than in most OECD states. The Socialists narrowed the gap a little in the 1980s with the introduction of the legal minimum wage (*le* SMIC). Most tax is indirect – a result of a long French tradition of income-tax evasion. Major tax cuts announced in 2000 aimed to redress the imbalance of income tax on the rich and poor. The wealthy take exotic vacations to the Himalayas, the Andes, and Polynesia. The French lag behind their European neighbors in using the Internet; fewer than one-fifth of the population had done so by 2001.

WORLD RANKING

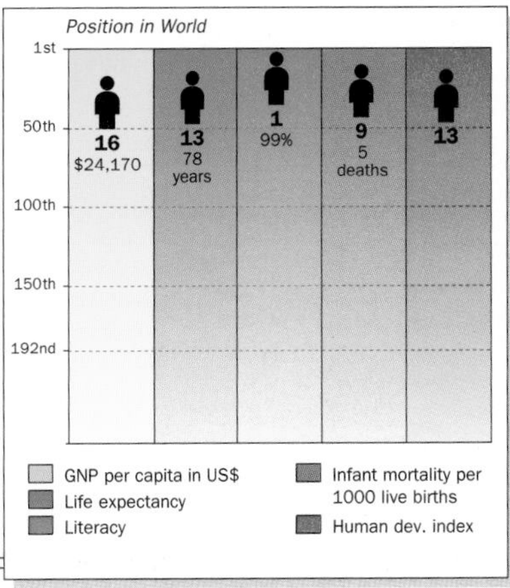
Position in World
1st
50th
100th
150th
192nd
16
$24,170
13
78 years
1
99%
9
5 deaths
13
GNP per capita in US$
Life expectancy
Literacy
Infant mortality per 1000 live births
Human dev. index

F

GABON

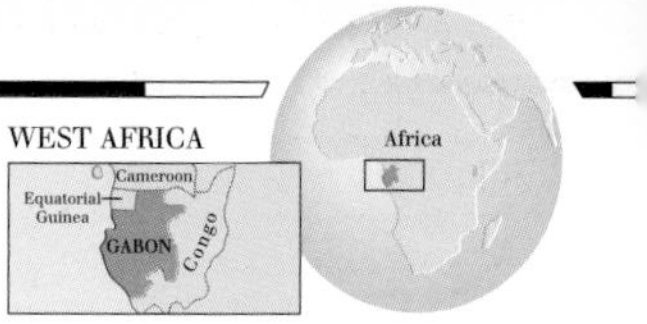
WEST AFRICA
Cameroon
Equatorial Guinea
GABON
Congo
Africa

OFFICIAL NAME: The Gabonese Republic **CAPITAL:** Libreville
POPULATION: 1.2 million **CURRENCY:** CFA franc **OFFICIAL LANGUAGE:** French

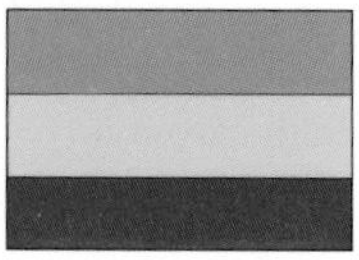

1960 | 1960 | Aug 17 | G | +1 | +241 | .ga

AN EQUATORIAL COUNTRY on the west coast of Africa, Gabon's major economic activity is the production of oil. Only a small area of Gabon is cultivated, and more than two-thirds of it constitute one of the world's finest virgin rainforests. Gabon became independent of France in 1960. A single-party state from 1968, it returned to multiparty democracy in 1990. Gabon's population is small, and the government is encouraging its increase.

CLIMATE

Tropical equatorial

WEATHER CHART

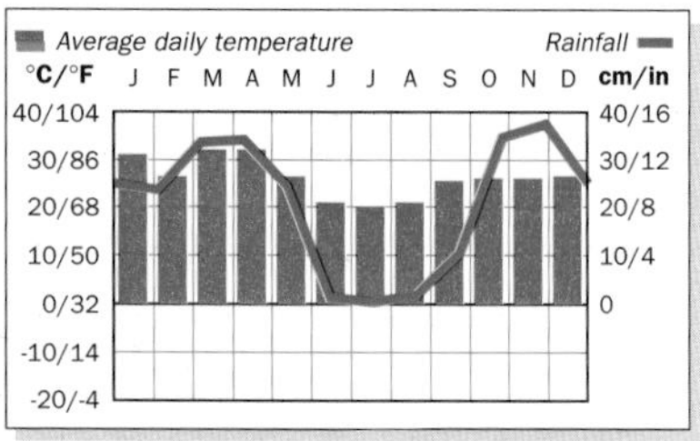
Average daily temperature
Rainfall
°C/°F
J F M A M J J A S O N D
cm/in
40/104
30/86
20/68
10/50
0/32
-10/14
-20/-4
40/16
30/12
20/8
10/4
0

The climate is heavily equatorial – hot all year round with a long rainy season from October to May. The cold Benguela current lowers coastal temperatures.

TRANSPORTATION

Drive on right

Léon M'Ba, Libreville 807,159 passengers

5 ships 26,532 grt

THE TRANSPORTATION NETWORK

629 km (391 miles)

30 km (19 miles)

814 km (506 miles)

1600 km (994 miles)

The Trans-Gabon Railroad from Owendo port near Libreville to Massoukou is the key transportation link.

Air transportation is well developed, and most big companies have airstrips.

TOURISM

Visitors : Population 1:6.9

175,000 visitors

Down 10% in 1999

MAIN TOURIST ARRIVALS

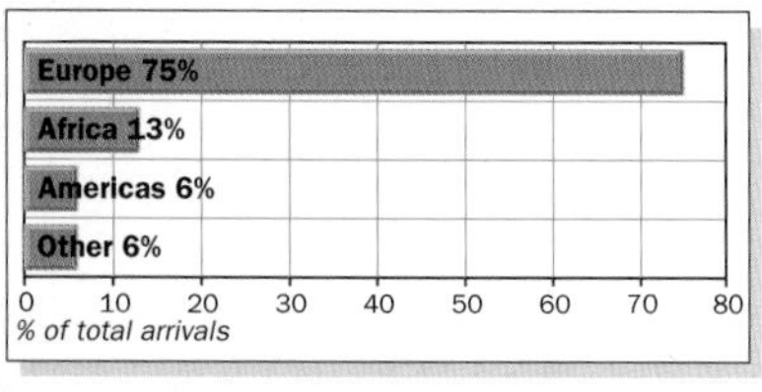
Europe 75%
Africa 13%
Americas 6%
Other 6%
0 10 20 30 40 50 60 70 80
% of total arrivals

Despite Libreville's many hotels, Gabon has little tourism, in part a reflection of its lack of good beaches.

PEOPLE

Pop. density low

Fang, French, Punu, Sira, Nzebi, Mpongwe

5/km² (12/mi²)

THE URBAN/RURAL POPULATION SPLIT

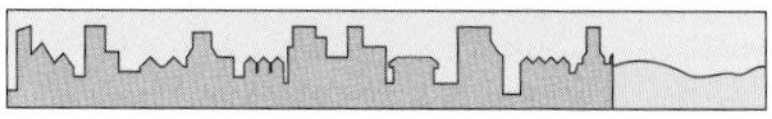
80%
20%

ETHNIC MAKEUP

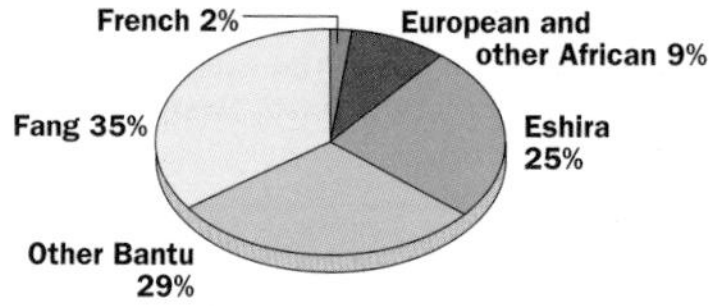
French 2%
European and other African 9%
Fang 35%
Eshira 25%
Other Bantu 29%

The largest ethnic group in Gabon is the Fang, who live mainly in the north, but they have yet to gain control of government. President Omar Bongo, from a subgroup of the minority Bateke in the southeast, has artfully united the common interests of other ethnic groups to keep the Fang from power. The Myene group around Port-Gentil consider themselves as the aristocrats of Gabonese society owing to their long-standing ex-colonial contacts. Oil wealth has led to the growth of a distinct bourgeoisie.

POLITICS

Multiparty elections

L. House 1996/2001
U. House 1997/2003

President Omar Bongo

AT THE LAST ELECTION

National Assembly 120 seats

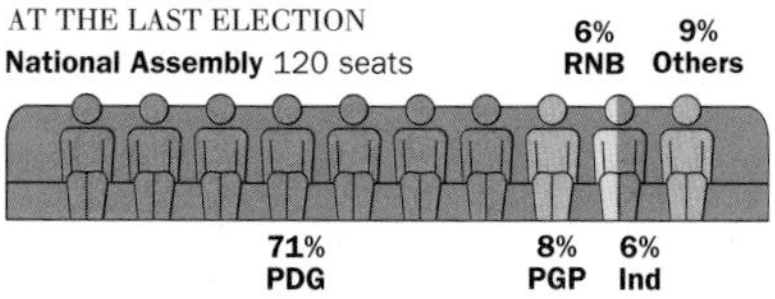
6% RNB
9% Others
71% PDG
8% PGP
6% Ind

PDG = Gabonese Democratic Party
PGP = Gabonese Progress Party
Ind = Independents
RNB = National Rally of Woodcutters

Senate 91 seats

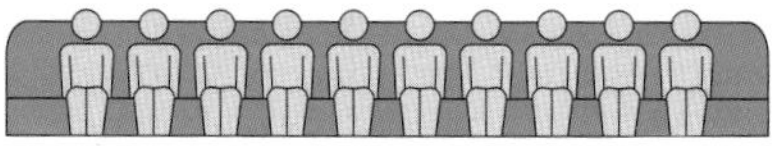

The Senate is indirectly elected by regional councils.

Gabon has had a multiparty constitution since 1990, when elections confirmed in power the former sole ruling party – Omar Bongo's PDG. Bongo, in power since 1967, won the first multiparty presidential poll in 1993, but its fairness was widely disputed. In parliamentary elections in 1996 the PDG again won a majority. Bongo was reelected president in 1998, this time for a seven-year term. Jean-François Ntoutoume-Emane was appointed prime minister, replacing Paulin Obame-Nguema in January 1999.

WORLD AFFAIRS

Joined UN in 1960

FZ | G24 | OAU | OIC | ACP

Gabon still maintains close links with France, although US companies are also making inroads into Gabon's oil-rich economy. In regional terms, Gabon remains influential in francophone Africa, although relations further afield, particularly with OPEC (Gabon was chair in 1993), are also important.

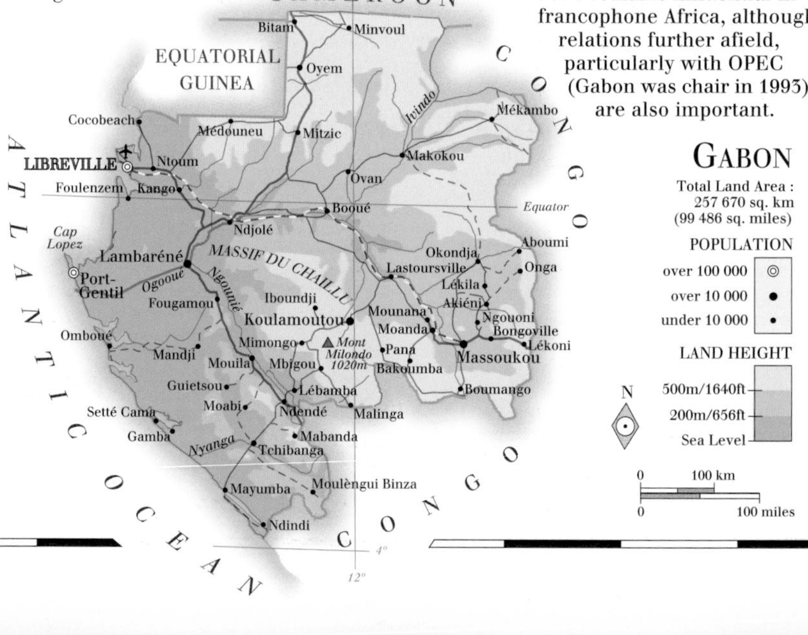
CAMEROON
EQUATORIAL GUINEA
CONGO
ATLANTIC OCEAN
Bitam
Minvoul
Oyem
Cocobeach
Médouneu
Mitzic
Mékambo
Ivindo
LIBREVILLE
Ntoum
Makokou
Foulenzem
Kango
Ovan
Booué
Equator
Ndjolé
Cap Lopez
Lambaréné
MASSIF DU CHAILLU
Okondja
Aboumi
Port-Gentil
Ogooué
Lastoursville
Onga
Lékila
Akiéni
Fougamou
Iboundji
Koulamoutou
Mounana
Ngouoni
Bongoville
Moanda
Omboué
Mimongo
Mont Milondo 1020m
Pana
Lékoni
Mandji
Mouila
Mbigou
Bakoumba
Massoukou
Guietsou
Lébamba
Boumango
Moabi
Ndendé
Malinga
Setté Cama
Gamba
Nyanga
Mabanda
Tchibanga
Mayumba
Moulèngui Binza
Ndindi
4°
12°
GABON
Total Land Area : 257 670 sq. km (99 486 sq. miles)
POPULATION
over 100 000
over 10 000
under 10 000
LAND HEIGHT
500m/1640ft
200m/656ft
Sea Level
N
0 100 km
0 100 miles

AID

Recipient

$48m (receipts) | Up 7% in 1999

France is by far the major aid donor, providing two-thirds of total receipts. For a middle-income country with one of the highest GNPs per capita in the developing world, Gabon has benefited from considerable aid.

Its indebtedness is the result of excessive borrowing encouraged by Western banks in the 1970s. Much aid goes to servicing this debt.

DEFENSE

No compulsory military service

$135m | No change in 1999

President Bongo's background in the military is reflected in Gabon's large defense budget and prestige weaponry, which includes French *Mirage* jets. France guarantees Gabon's security and keeps a 680-strong garrison in Libreville. A recruitment drive was launched in April 2001 to recruit 1500 18- to 25-year-olds by 2006.

ECONOMICS

Inflation 5.8% p.a. (1990–1999)

$4bn | 654.42–698.69 CFA francs

SCORE CARD

❑ World GNP Ranking	117th
❑ GNP per Capita	$3300
❑ Balance of Payments	$100m
❑ Inflation	–8.6%
❑ Unemployment	21%

Strengths

Oil and a relatively small population give Gabon a high per capita GNP. The country's other abundant resources – including some of the world's best tropical hardwoods – are just beginning to be tapped.

Weaknesses

Large debt burden incurred in the 1970s. Continuing dependence on French technical assistance.

EXPORTS

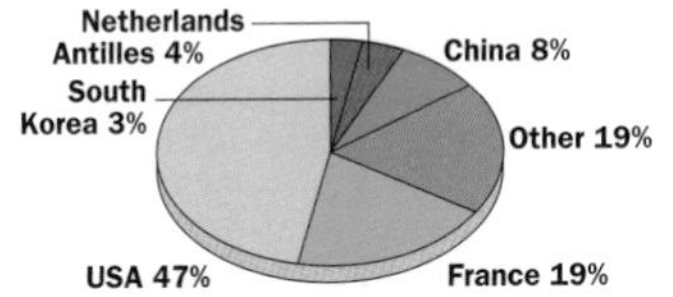
Netherlands Antilles 4%
China 8%
South Korea 3%
Other 19%
USA 47%
France 19%

IMPORTS

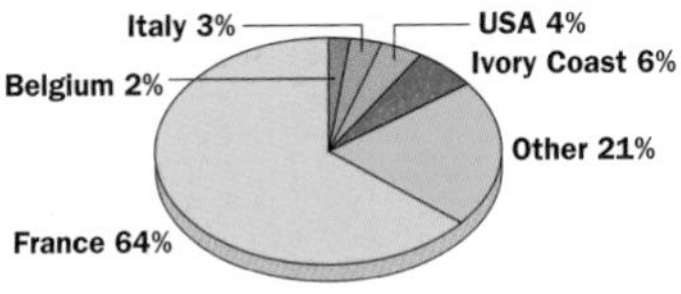
Italy 3%
USA 4%
Ivory Coast 6%
Belgium 2%
Other 21%
France 64%

RESOURCES

Electric power 378,000 kw

44,772 tonnes | 325,000 b/d (reserves 2,500,000,000 bbl)

213,000 pigs, 198,000 sheep, 3.2m chickens | Oil, manganese, uranium, gold, iron, natural gas

Oil is the major export earner. Gabon also has large deposits of uranium and over 100 years' reserves of manganese. The unexploited iron ore deposits at Bélinga are the world's largest.

ENVIRONMENT

Sustainability rank: 49th

3% | 3 tonnes per capita

The Trans-Gabon Railroad has sliced through one of the world's finest virgin rainforests and has opened the interior to indiscriminate exploitation of rare woods such as oleoirme. Gabon abandoned plans for nuclear power following the 1986 Chernobyl disaster.

MEDIA

TV ownership high

Daily newspaper circulation 30 per 1000 people

PUBLISHING AND BROADCAST MEDIA

There are 2 daily newspapers, *L'Union* and *Gabon-Matin*

3 services: 1 state-owned, 2 independent | 7 services: 2 state-controlled, 5 independent

The media are mostly government-controlled. There was a crackdown in 1998 on independent media, which in the 1990s had become quite diverse. The move raised concerns about freedom of expression.

CRIME

Death penalty used

Gabon does not publish prison figures | Recorded crime rose sharply from 1992–1996

Urban crime rates (Gabon is one of Africa's most urbanized nations) have been growing. Gabon's human rights record has improved in recent years.

***Albert Schweitzer Hospital,** Lambaréné, on the lower Ogooué River. Schweitzer won a Nobel Prize for his pioneering work in Africa.*

CHRONOLOGY

Gabon became a French colony in 1886, administered as part of French Equatorial Africa.

- ❑ **1960** Independence. Léon M'ba president.
- ❑ **1964** Military coup. French intervene to reinstate M'ba.
- ❑ **1967** Albert-Bernard (later Omar) Bongo president.
- ❑ **1968** Single-party state instituted.
- ❑ **1990** Multiparty democracy.
- ❑ **1998** Bongo reelected president.

G

EDUCATION

School leaving age: 16

71% | 4655 students

Education follows the French system. Université Omar Bongo in Libreville, founded in the 1970s, now has more than 4000 students.

HEALTH

No welfare state health benefits

1 per 5000 people | Heart and diarrheal diseases, pneumonia, accidents

Oil revenues have allowed substantial investment in the health service, which is now among the best in Africa.

SPENDING

GDP/cap. increase

CONSUMPTION AND SPENDING

22 per 1000 population | *32 per 1000 population*

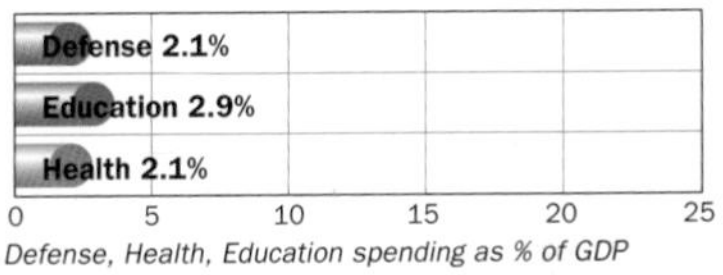
Defense 2.1%
Education 2.9%
Health 2.1%
0
5
10
15
20
25
Defense, Health, Education spending as % of GDP

Oil wealth has led to the growth of an affluent bourgeoisie class. Menial and low-income jobs are done by immigrant workers.

WORLD RANKING

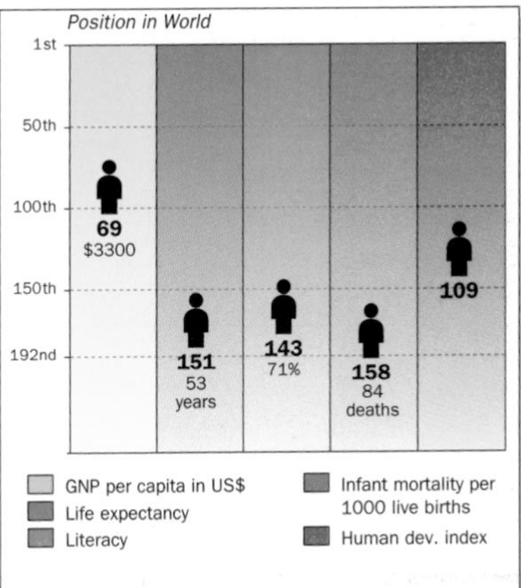
Position in World
1st
50th
100th
150th
192nd
69
$3300
151
53 years
143
71%
158
84 deaths
109
GNP per capita in US$
Life expectancy
Literacy
Infant mortality per 1000 live births
Human dev. index

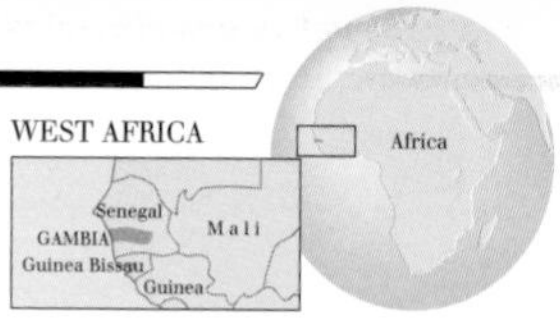
WEST AFRICA
Africa
Senegal
Mali
GAMBIA
Guinea Bissau
Guinea

GAMBIA

OFFICIAL NAME: Republic of the Gambia **CAPITAL:** Banjul
POPULATION: 1.3 million **CURRENCY:** Dalasi **OFFICIAL LANGUAGE:** English

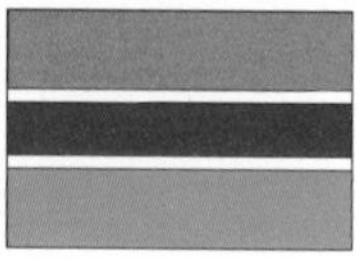

1965 | 1965 | Feb 18 | WAG | 0 | +220 | .gm

A NARROW COUNTRY on the western coast of Africa, the Gambia was renowned as a stable democracy until an army coup in 1994. Agriculture accounts for 65% of GDP, yet many Gambians are leaving rural areas for the towns, where average incomes are four times higher. Its position as a semi-enclave within Senegal seems likely to endure, following the failure of an experiment in federation in the 1980s.

CLIMATE
Tropical wet & dry

WEATHER CHART

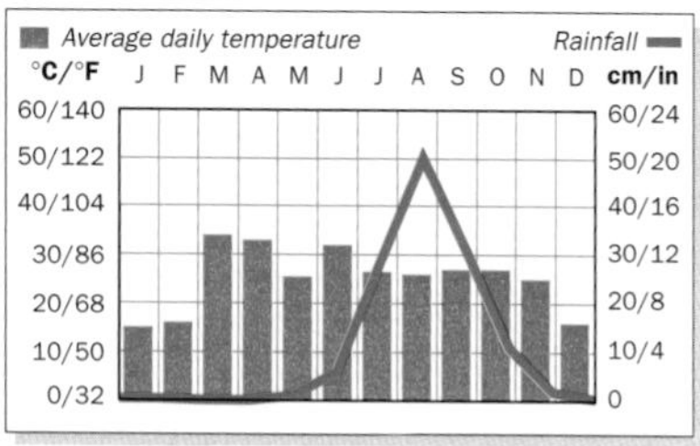
Average daily temperature
Rainfall
°C/°F J F M A M J J A S O N D cm/in
60/140 50/122 40/104 30/86 20/68 10/50 0/32
60/24 50/20 40/16 30/12 20/8 10/4 0

The subtropical and sunny dry season is punctuated by intermittent hot *harmattan* winds.

TRANSPORTATION
Drive on right

Yundum International, Banjul 317,885 passengers

8 ships 1884 grt

THE TRANSPORTATION NETWORK

956 km (594 miles)

None

None

400 km (249 miles)

The river Gambia carries more traffic than the roads – ships of up to 3000 tonnes can reach Georgetown. Yundum airport was upgraded by NASA in 1989 for US space shuttle emergency landings.

TOURISM
Visitors : Population 1:14

91,000 visitors

Up 14% in 1998

MAIN TOURIST ARRIVALS

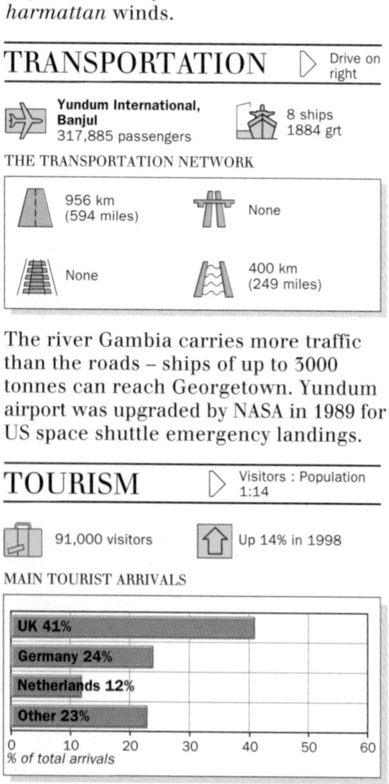
UK 41%
Germany 24%
Netherlands 12%
Other 23%
0 10 20 30 40 50 60
% of total arrivals

A successful tourist industry offers sunshine, beaches, and resort hotel life. Most visitors are Europeans escaping winter, including many single women.

PEOPLE
Pop. density medium

Mandinka, Fulani, Wolof, Diola, Soninke, English

131/km² (338/mi²)

THE URBAN/RURAL POPULATION SPLIT

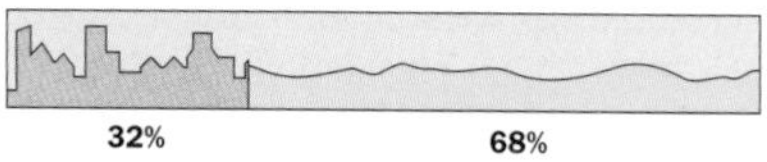
32%
68%

ETHNIC MAKEUP

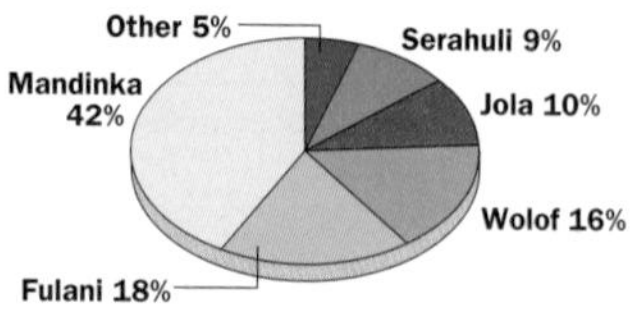
Other 5%
Serahuli 9%
Mandinka 42%
Jola 10%
Wolof 16%
Fulani 18%

Until the 1994 coup, led by Lieutenant Colonel Yahya Jammeh, the 1962–1994 government of President Sir Dawda Jawara had tried to offset minority resentment of the Mandinka's domination of politics, distributing political offices fairly according to ethnic origins. Jammeh, a fervent Muslim, is from the minority Jola (or Diola) community, numerous across the border in Senegal, where they are active in a local rebellion. About 85% of Gambians follow Islam, although there is no official state religion. There is a yearly influx of migrants, who come from Senegal, Guinea, and Mali to trade in groundnuts. The Gambia is still a very poor country, with 80% of the labor force engaged in agriculture. Women are active as traders in an otherwise male-dominated society.

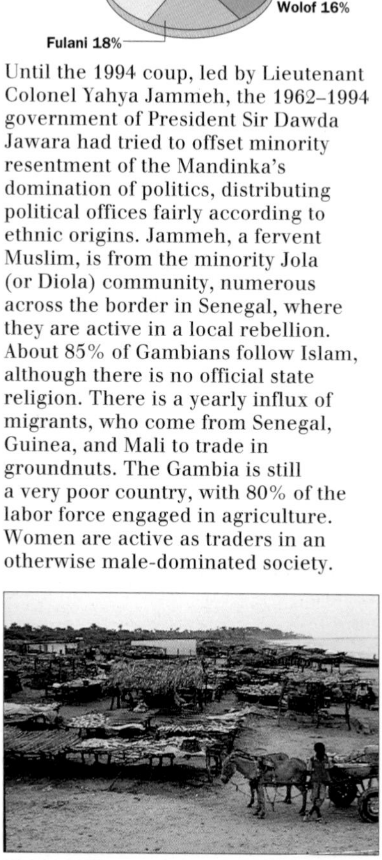

Fishing village. *Overfishing in the waters off the Gambia and Senegal, mainly by distant nations, is a growing problem.*

POLITICS
Multiparty elections

1997/2001

President Yahya Jammeh

AT THE LAST ELECTION

National Assembly 49 seats

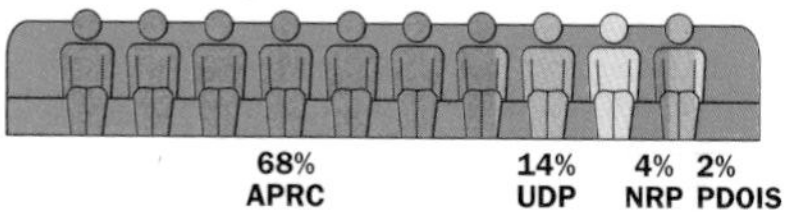
8% Nom
4% Ind
68% APRC
14% UDP
4% NRP
2% PDOIS

APRC = Alliance for Patriotic Reorientation and Construction
UDP = United Democratic Party **Nom** = Nominated
NRP = National Reconciliation Party **Ind** = Independents
PDOIS = People's Democratic Organization for Independence and Socialism

The People's Progressive Party (PPP) was in government from 1962 until 1994, for most of which time the Gambia was one of Africa's few democracies. A ban, imposed after the 1994 coup on the PPP and the three main parties which had been in opposition, was lifted in 2001 in time for elections.

During the army's coup, Sir Dawda Jawara took refuge aboard a visiting US warship, and he then went into exile in Britain. The coup's leaders claimed that it had been initiated in a bid to end corruption and pledged to preserve democracy. In the new government several portfolios went to civil servants who had served in the Jawara administration. Military leader Yahya Jammeh was elected president in controversial elections in September 1996, and the following January his APRC won the majority of seats in a parliamentary election. In January 2000 the government claimed to have foiled a military coup.

WORLD AFFAIRS
Joined UN in 1965

CILSS | Comm | ECOWAS | OAU | OIC

President Jammeh has vigorously cultivated new partnerships following strong Commonwealth and Western criticism of his coup in 1994. Also, close ties have been forged with Nigeria as a counterweight to Senegal, with which relations have sometimes been strained since the collapse of the 1982–1989 confederation.

AID
Recipient

$33m (receipts)

Down 13% in 1999

Western aid flows, suspended after the 1994 coup, have largely resumed. The World Bank, the IMF, the AfDB, the UK, the USA, Japan, Libya, Egypt, the Gulf states, Cuba, and Taiwan are all significant donors.

GAMBIA

Total Land Area : 10 000 sq. km (3861 sq. miles)

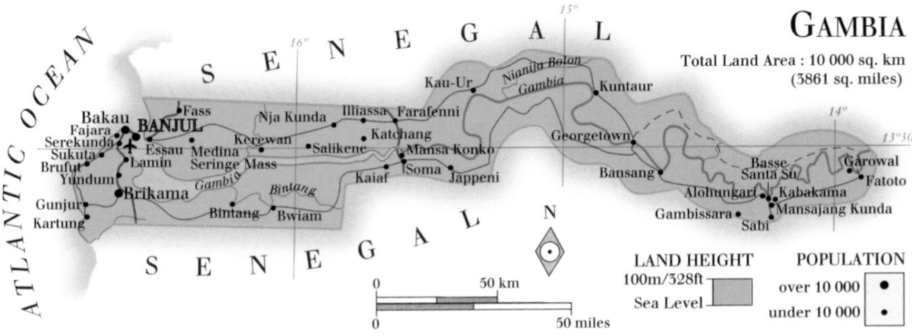
ATLANTIC OCEAN
SENEGAL
SENEGAL
Bakau
BANJUL
Fajara
Serekunda
Sukuta
Brufut
Yundum
Brikama
Gunjur
Kartung
Fass
Essau
Lamin
Medina
Seringe Mass
Kerewan
Nja Kunda
Illiassa
Farafenni
Salikene
Katchang
Mansa Konko
Soma
Kaiaf
Jappeni
Bintang
Bwiam
Kau-Ur
Kuntaur
Georgetown
Bansang
Basse Santa Su
Garowal
Fatoto
Alohungari
Kabakama
Mansajang Kunda
Gambissara
Sabi
Gambia
Bintang
Nianija Bolon
N
0 50 km
0 50 miles
LAND HEIGHT
100m/328ft
Sea Level
POPULATION
over 10 000
under 10 000

DEFENSE

No compulsory military service

$16m

Up 7% in 1999

The Gambia National Army, with two infantry battalions, takes about half of the defense budget; the rest finances the 600-strong gendarmerie. Most arms are bought from the UK, although supplies are now increasingly coming from Nigeria too. A defense pact with Senegal collapsed along with the federation in 1989.

ECONOMICS

Inflation 3.7% p.a. (1990–1999)

$415m

11.575–15.275 dalasis

SCORE CARD

- ❑ WORLD GNP RANKING 171st
- ❑ GNP PER CAPITA $330
- ❑ BALANCE OF PAYMENTS ....$–46m
- ❑ INFLATION 3.8%
- ❑ UNEMPLOYMENT ....Widespread underemployment

STRENGTHS

Low tariffs make the Gambia a focus of regional trade. Natural deep-water harbor at Banjul, one of the finest on the west African coast. Well-managed economy, favorably viewed by donors.

WEAKNESSES

Small size of market can inhibit investment. Smuggling: deprives government of significant revenues. Lack of resources, little agricultural diversification; consequent over-reliance on groundnuts, the main crop.

EXPORTS

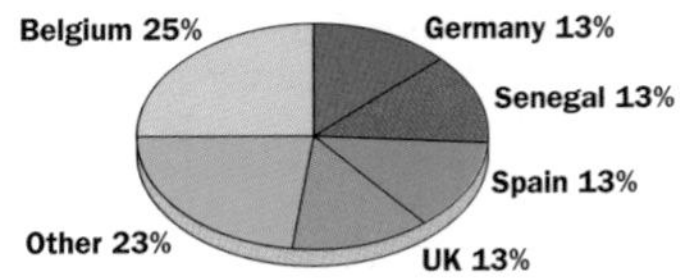
Belgium 25%
Germany 13%
Senegal 13%
Spain 13%
UK 13%
Other 23%

IMPORTS

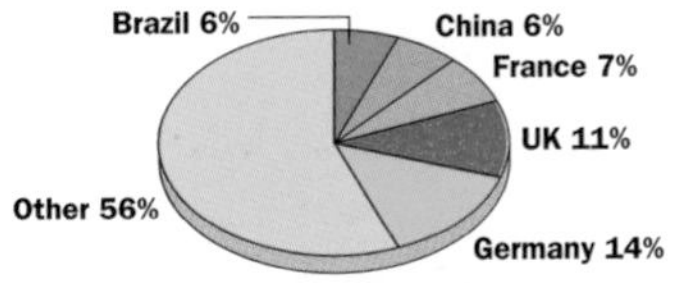
Brazil 6%
China 6%
France 7%
UK 11%
Germany 14%
Other 56%

RESOURCES

Electric power 29,000 kw

32,258 tonnes

Not an oil producer

360,000 cattle, 265,000 goats, 680,000 chickens

Ilmenite, zirconium, rutile, kaolin, tin, oil

The Gambia river is one of Africa's few good waterways, but it is underused owing to its separation from its natural hinterland by the Gambia–Senegal border. Irrigation is at present provided by a single dam; plans for further dams for power generation have met with opposition. Oil deposits are believed to exist offshore.

ENVIRONMENT

Not available

2%

0.2 tonnes per capita

The impact of tourism and of overfishing in Gambian waters are major concerns, as are desertification and deforestation.

MEDIA

TV ownership low

Daily newspaper circulation 2 per 1000 people

PUBLISHING AND BROADCAST MEDIA

There are 2 daily newspapers, the independent *Daily Observer* and the government-owned *Gambia Daily*

1 state-owned service

9 services: 1 state-owned, 8 independent

Journalists and newspaper proprietors have suffered low-level harassment since the 1994 coup, and a popular private radio station has been closed down.

CRIME

Death penalty not used

The Gambia does not publish prison figures

General crime levels are low but rising

Crime levels are relatively low in what is a peaceful society compared with many other states in the region.

EDUCATION

Schooling is not compulsory

37%

1591 students

The aims are to increase enrollment to 75% in primary and 20% in secondary schools, and to improve teacher quality. A university was established in 1998.

CHRONOLOGY

Mandinka traders brought Islam in the 13th century and were the main influence until the 18th century. The 1700s and 1800s saw colonial rivalry between Britain and France.

- ❑ **1888** British possession.
- ❑ **1959** Dawda Jawara founds PPP.
- ❑ **1965** Independence from Britain.
- ❑ **1970** Republic; Jawara president.
- ❑ **1981** Senegalese troops help crush army coup attempt.
- ❑ **1982–1989** Federation with Senegal.
- ❑ **1994** Jawara ousted in army coup.
- ❑ **1996** Yahya Jammeh wins presidential election.
- ❑ **2000** Military coup foiled.
- ❑ **2001** $2 million anti-poverty program launched by government.

HEALTH

No welfare state health benefits

1 per 20,000 people

Malaria, tuberculosis, parasitic diseases

Most people have access to basic medicines, but these are no longer free. Advanced medical care in the public sector is limited. An influx of Cuban doctors has helped extend services.

SPENDING

GDP/cap. increase

CONSUMPTION AND SPENDING

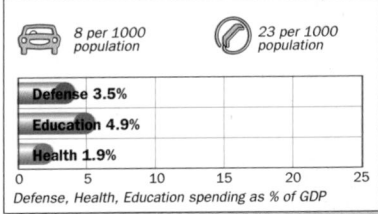

8 per 1000 population

23 per 1000 population

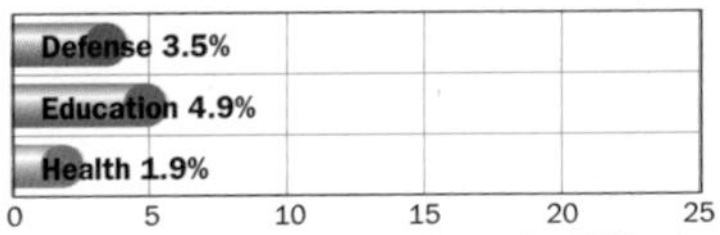
Defense 3.5%
Education 4.9%
Health 1.9%
0
5
10
15
20
25

Defense, Health, Education spending as % of GDP

Public service and the professions have created wealth and some people are comfortably off, but great wealth is not a feature of Gambian life. Unemployed young men in Banjul are regarded as the underclass.

WORLD RANKING

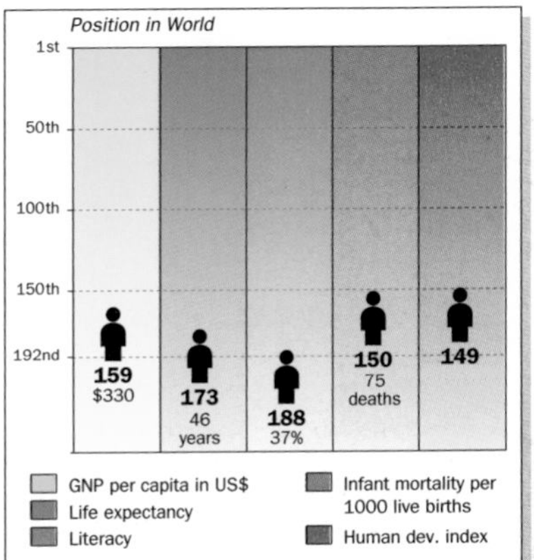
Position in World
1st
50th
100th
150th
192nd
159
$330
173
46 years
188
37%
150
75 deaths
149
GNP per capita in US$
Life expectancy
Literacy
Infant mortality per 1000 live births
Human dev. index

GEORGIA

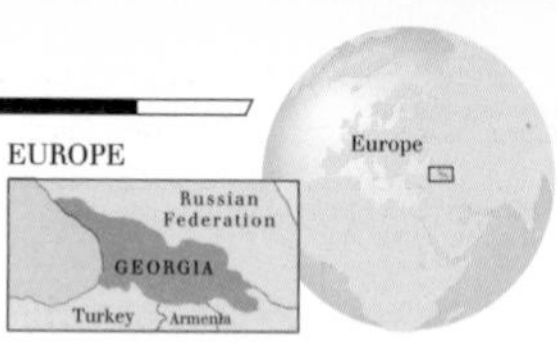
EUROPE
Russian Federation
GEORGIA
Turkey
Armenia
Europe

OFFICIAL NAME: Republic of Georgia **CAPITAL:** Tbilisi
POPULATION: 5 million **CURRENCY:** Lari **OFFICIAL LANGUAGE:** Georgian

1991 | 1991 | May 26 | GE | +4 | +995 | .ge

SITUATED ON THE EASTERN coast of the Black Sea, Georgia is largely mountainous. Its coastline stretches from Abkhazia in the north to Ajaria in the south. Georgia was one of the first republics to demand independence from Moscow, but has been plagued over recent years by civil war and ethnic disputes in Abkhazia and South Ossetia. The birthplace of Stalin, Georgia is primarily agricultural and is famous for its wine.

CLIMATE

Mountain/subtropical

WEATHER CHART

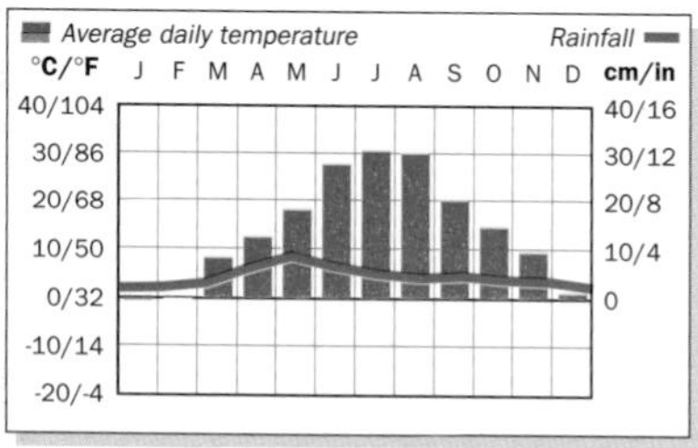
Average daily temperature
Rainfall
°C/°F
J F M A M J J A S O N D
cm/in
40/104
30/86
20/68
10/50
0/32
-10/14
-20/-4
40/16
30/12
20/8
10/4
0

Georgia's climate is continental inland and subtropical along the coast, where grapes, citrus fruit, and tea are grown.

Tbilisi, Georgia's capital since the 5th century. Its buildings rise in steep terraces from both banks of the River Kura.

TRANSPORTATION

Drive on right

Novo Alexeyevka, Tbilisi 316,226 passengers

95 ships 117,800 grt

THE TRANSPORTATION NETWORK

19,354 km (12,026 miles)

None

1545 km (960 miles)

None

Civil war has seriously disrupted transportation. A new rail route and oil pipeline from Baku to the Black Sea ports of Poti and Supsa was opened in 1999.

TOURISM

Visitors : Population 1:13

384,000 visitors

Up 21% in 1999

MAIN TOURIST ARRIVALS

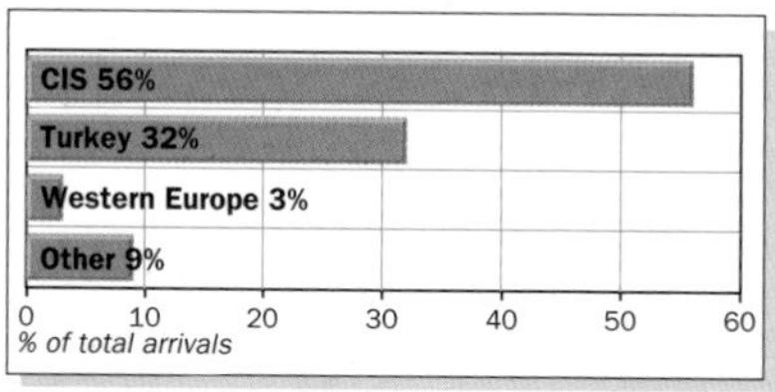
CIS 56%
Turkey 32%
Western Europe 3%
Other 9%
0
10
20
30
40
50
60
% of total arrivals

The volatile political situation has discouraged tourism, but numbers are rising again. Most tourists still come from former Soviet states.

PEOPLE

Pop. density medium

Georgian, Russian

72/km² (186/mi²)

THE URBAN/RURAL POPULATION SPLIT

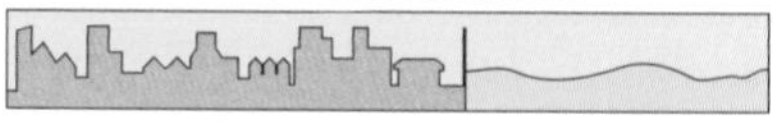
60%
40%

ETHNIC MAKEUP

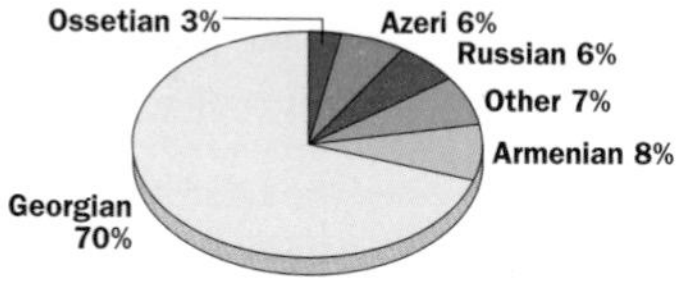
Ossetian 3%
Azeri 6%
Russian 6%
Other 7%
Armenian 8%
Georgian 70%

Georgia is a paternalistic society, with strong family and cultural traditions. Approximately 70% of the population is Georgian, with Armenian, Russian, Azeri, Ossetian, Greek, and Abkhaz minorities. More than 300,000 people were displaced by the violent internal conflicts of the 1990s.

POLITICS

Multiparty elections

1999/2003

President Eduard Shevardnadze

AT THE LAST ELECTION
Parliament 235 seats

56% CUG
24% AGUR
7% ISG
5% AD
8% Others

CUG = Citizens' Union of Georgia **AGUR** = All Georgian Union of Revival **ISG** = Industry Will Save Georgia **AD** = Abkhazian Deputies

10 Abkhazian seats were not contested in 1999.

The political situation remains volatile. Eduard Shevardnadze, reelected as president in 2000, has been the target of several assassination attempts. He came to power in 1992 amid civil war with the "Zviadists," supporters of the ex-president Zviad Gamsakhurdia, who committed suicide while under fire in late 1993.

Fighting raged simultaneously in Abkhazia, where ethnic Abkhazians attempted to secede; ethnic Georgians were expelled. Fighting still flares up sporadically. A UN-brokered peace process begun in mid-2000 soon stalled over the basic issue of the future status of Abkhazia.

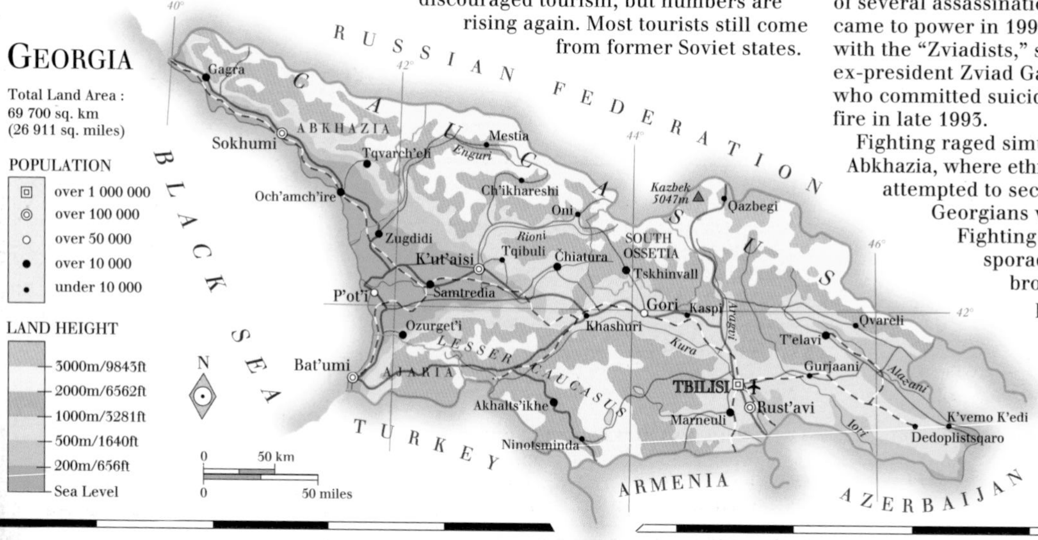
GEORGIA
Total Land Area : 69 700 sq. km (26 911 sq. miles)
POPULATION
over 1 000 000
over 100 000
over 50 000
over 10 000
under 10 000
LAND HEIGHT
3000m/9843ft
2000m/6562ft
1000m/3281ft
500m/1640ft
200m/656ft
Sea Level
0 50 km
0 50 miles
RUSSIAN FEDERATION
BLACK SEA
TURKEY
ARMENIA
AZERBAIJAN
CAUCASUS
LESSER CAUCASUS
ABKHAZIA
AJARIA
SOUTH OSSETIA
Gagra
Sokhumi
Och'amch'ire
Tqvarch'eli
Mestia
Enguri
Zugdidi
Ch'ikhareshi
Oni
Kazbek 5047m
Qazbegi
Rioni
K'ut'aisi
Tqibuli
Chiatura
Tskhinvali
P'ot'i
Samtredia
Gori
Kaspi
Aragvi
Ozurget'i
Khashuri
Kura
Qvareli
T'elavi
Gurjaani
Alazani
Bat'umi
TBILISI
Rust'avi
Marneuli
Iori
K'vemo K'edi
Dedoplistsqaro
Akhalts'ikhe
Ninotsminda

WORLD AFFAIRS

Joined UN in 1992

BSEC | CIS | CE | OSCE | PfP

Relations with Russia are strained over Abkhazia, instability in the Caucasus region, and oil pipeline issues.

AID

Recipient

$239m (receipts)

Up 44% in 1999

As well as aid for infrastructure projects, Georgia receives Western support for institutional and financial sector reform.

DEFENSE

Compulsory military service

$111m

Down 1% in 1999

The government's security police are CIA-trained. Russia, whose intervention helped end the Zviadist conflict in 1993, retained four military bases in Georgia, including one in Abkhazia. Russian troops, numbering over 9000, began a reluctant withdrawal in 2000. Abkhazia remains the army's main concern.

ECONOMICS

Not available

$3.4bn

1.96 lari

SCORE CARD

❑ WORLD GNP RANKING	125th
❑ GNP PER CAPITA	$620
❑ BALANCE OF PAYMENT	$–220m
❑ INFLATION	19.1%
❑ UNEMPLOYMENT	15%

STRENGTHS

Gateway to West for Azeri oil through pipelines across Georgia to Black Sea and Mediterranean ports. Hyperinflation brought under control in mid-1990s.

WEAKNESSES

War damage and severance of links with other ex-Soviet republics. Large black economy and influential Mafia. Drought and currency crisis in 1998. Serious budget deficit problems. Negative trade balance.

EXPORTS

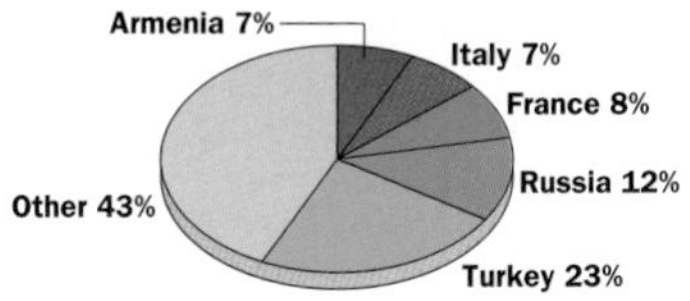
Armenia 7%
Italy 7%
France 8%
Russia 12%
Turkey 23%
Other 43%

IMPORTS

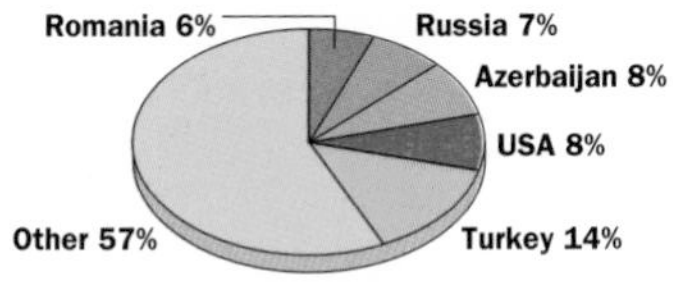
Romania 6%
Russia 7%
Azerbaijan 8%
USA 8%
Turkey 14%
Other 57%

RESOURCES

Electric power 4.6m kw

6933 tonnes

2687 b/d (reserves 36,292,560 bbl)

1.12m cattle, 553,300 sheep, 8.47m chickens

Manganese, coal, oil, natural gas, zinc, cobalt, vanadium

Known oil reserves are as yet barely developed. Georgia is dependent on Russia for much of its energy supply, although a new US–Georgian oil refinery was opened in eastern Georgia in 1998. Georgia is a predominantly agricultural country, and food processing and wine production continue to be the major industries. Manganese and small quantities of zinc, cobalt, and vanadium are mined.

ENVIRONMENT

Not available

3%

0.8 tonnes per capita

Radiation from materials left by departing Russian soldiers is a growing problem, as is Black Sea pollution and the protection of upland pastures.

MEDIA

TV ownership high

Daily newspaper circulation figures not available

PUBLISHING AND BROADCAST MEDIA

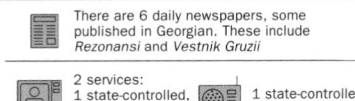

There are 6 daily newspapers, some published in Georgian. These include *Rezonansi* and *Vestnik Gruzii*

2 services: 1 state-controlled, 1 independent

1 state-controlled service

Government newspapers receive subsidies. The main independent TV channel, Rustavi–2, overcame licensing restrictions to reopen in 1998.

CRIME

Death penalty not used

7750 prisoners

Up 7% 1996–1998

Organized crime under the control of Mafia-style groups has flourished since independence in 1991. The judicial system currently favors Shevardnadze and his supporters.

EDUCATION

School leaving age: 14

99%

163,345 students

Since independence, education has stressed Georgian language and history. All levels of education are seriously underfunded. Tbilisi University was formerly of a high standard.

HEALTH

Welfare state health benefits

1 per 263 people

Circulatory and respiratory diseases, cancers, accidents

The health system was limited under the control of the Soviet Union. Internal strife and a lack of resources have prevented any recent investment.

CHRONOLOGY

A Russian protectorate from 1763, Georgia was absorbed into the Russian empire in 1801. It was established as an independent state under a Menshevik socialist government in 1918.

- ❑ **1920** Recognized by Soviet Russia as an independent state.
- ❑ **1921** Soviet Red Army invades. Effectively part of USSR.
- ❑ **1922–1936** Incorporated into Transcaucasian Soviet Federative Socialist Republic (TSFSR).
- ❑ **1989** Pro-independence riots in Tbilisi put down by Soviet troops.
- ❑ **1990** Declares sovereignty.
- ❑ **1991** Independence. Zviad Gamsakhurdia elected president.
- ❑ **1992** Gamsakhurdia flees Tbilisi. Shevardnadze elected chair of Supreme Soviet and State Council.
- ❑ **1992–1993** Abkhazia conflict.
- ❑ **1995** Shevardnadze narrowly survives assassination attempt, subsequently elected president.
- ❑ **1999** Opening of pipeline from Caspian to Black Sea.
- ❑ **2000** Shevardnadze reelected. Russian troop withdrawal begins.

SPENDING

GDP/cap. decrease

CONSUMPTION AND SPENDING

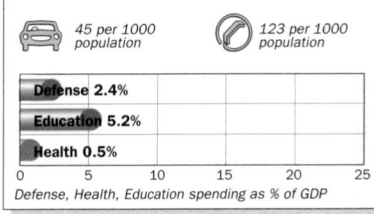

45 per 1000 population

123 per 1000 population

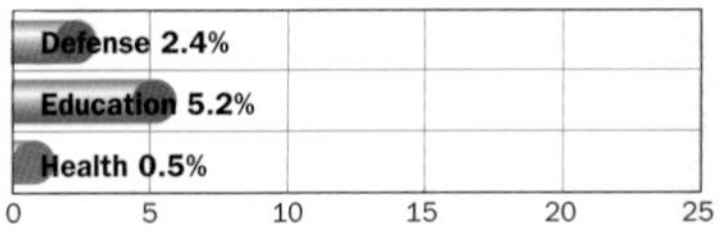
Defense 2.4%
Education 5.2%
Health 0.5%
0
5
10
15
20
25

Defense, Health, Education spending as % of GDP

A small elite of the population are wealthy and extravagant, but most Georgians live in poverty. Wages and welfare are often in arrears.

WORLD RANKING

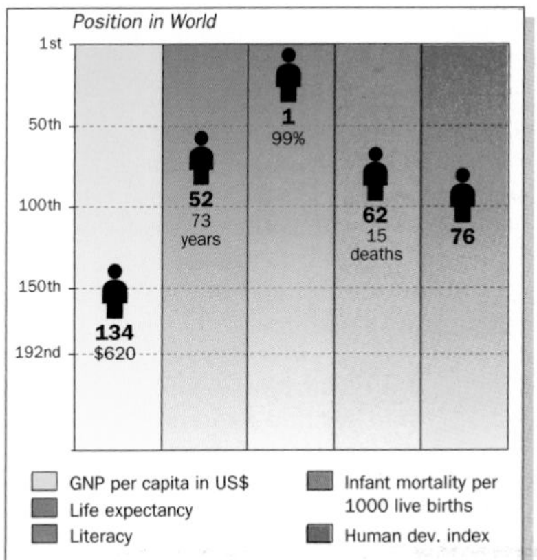
Position in World
1st
50th
100th
150th
192nd
134
$620
52
73
years
1
99%
62
15
deaths
76
GNP per capita in US$
Life expectancy
Literacy
Infant mortality per 1000 live births
Human dev. index

G

EUROPE
Europe
Netherlands
Denmark
Belgium
GERMANY
Poland
Czech Rep.
Luxembourg
France
Switz.
Austria

GERMANY

OFFICIAL NAME: Federal Republic of Germany **CAPITAL:** Berlin **POPULATION:** 82.2 million
CURRENCY: Euro (Deutsche mark until 2002) **OFFICIAL LANGUAGE:** German

1871 | 1990 | Oct 3 | D | +1 | +49 | .de

WITH COASTLINES on both the Baltic and North Seas, Germany is bordered by nine countries. Plains and rolling hills in the north give way to more mountainous terrain in the south. Europe's foremost industrial power, and its most populous country apart from Russia, Germany is the world's second-biggest exporter. Unified in the 1870s, it was divided after the defeat of the Nazi regime in 1945. The communist-ruled east was part of the Soviet bloc until the collapse of the East German regime in 1989, which paved the way for reunification in 1990. Tensions created by wealth differences between east and west were then exacerbated by record levels of unemployment. The government committed itself to European union and adopted the single currency, the euro, even though the stable Deutsche mark had been a symbol of German pride.

CLIMATE

Continental/maritime

WEATHER CHART

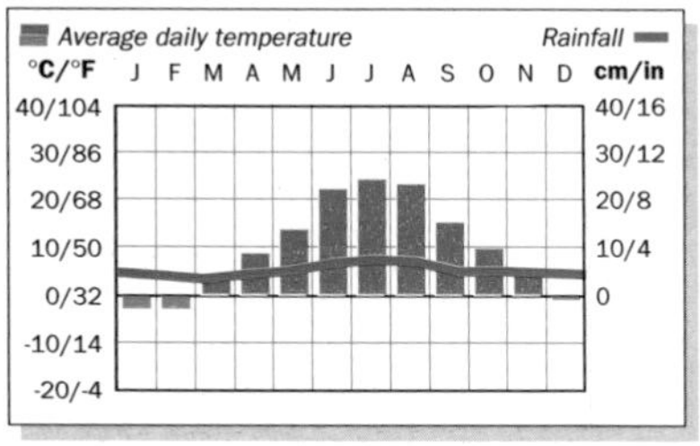
Average daily temperature
Rainfall
°C/°F
J F M A M J J A S O N D
cm/in
40/104
30/86
20/68
10/50
0/32
-10/14
-20/-4
40/16
30/12
20/8
10/4
0

Germany has a broad climatic range. The upper Rhine valley is very mild and suitable for wine-making. The Bavarian Alps, the Harz Mountains, and the Black Forest are by contrast cold, with heavy falls of snow in winter.

TRANSPORTATION

Drive on right

Frankfurt/Main International 45.8m passengers

1158 ships 8.1m grt

THE TRANSPORTATION NETWORK

650,891 km (404,444 miles)

11,400 km (7084 miles)

37,559 km (23,339 miles)

7467 km (4640 miles)

Germany virtually invented the modern highway with the first *Autobahnen* in the 1930s. These have since become Europe's most elaborate highway network. Despite protests from environmentalists there are generally no tolls and few speed limits. The efficient railroad system has been restructured as a first step toward privatization. Germany's high-speed ICE railroad opened its main north–south routes in 1991 and has expanded greatly since then. Urban transportation systems are highly efficient.

TOURISM

Visitors : Population 1:4.3

19m visitors

Up 11% in 2000

MAIN TOURIST ARRIVALS

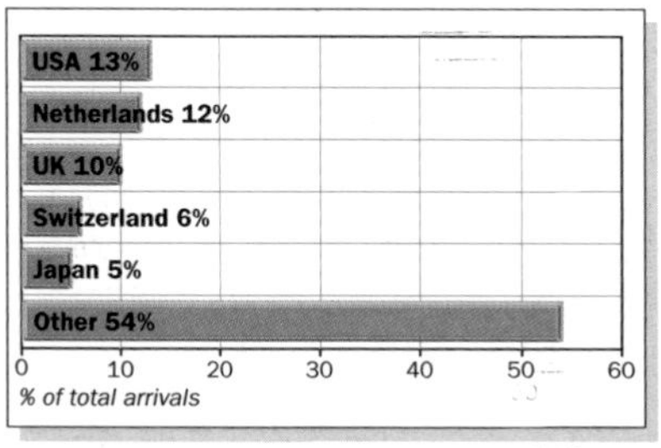
USA 13%
Netherlands 12%
UK 10%
Switzerland 6%
Japan 5%
Other 54%
0
10
20
30
40
50
60
% of total arrivals

Northerly beaches and a colder climate make Germany less of a tourist destination than France or Italy. Skiing in the Bavarian Alps, the historic castles of the Rhine valley, the Black Forest, and Germany's excellent beer are all major attractions. Berlin, even before 1989, drew tourists with its rich cultural life and its Wall separating capitalist West and communist East. Now capital of the reunified Germany, and with a dynamic and vibrant atmosphere, it has undergone massive reconstruction.

***The Stillach Valley, Allgäu Alps,** Bavaria (Bayern). Alarm at acid rain damage to Germany's forests sparked off the rise of the Greens, who joined the government in 1998.*

GERMANY

Total Land Area : 349 520 sq. km (134 910 sq. miles)

POPULATION
- over 1 000 000
- over 500 000
- over 100 000
- over 10 000

LAND HEIGHT
- 2000m/6562ft
- 1000m/3281ft
- 500m/1640ft
- 200m/656ft
- Sea Level

0 100 km
0 100 miles

N
NORTH SEA
Nordfriesische Inseln
Helgoland
German Bight
Helgoländer Bucht
Ostfriesische Inseln
Cuxhaven
Aurich
Emden
Wilhelmshaven
Bremerhav
Oldenburg
Breme
NETHERLANDS
NORDDEU
NIEDERSACH
Ems
Weser
Ibbenbüren
Osnabrück
Rheine
Melle
Münster
Bielefeld
NORDRHEIN-WESTFALEN
Recklinghausen
Hamm
Paderbo
Gelsenkirchen
Herne
Bochum
Lippstadt
Moers
Oberhausen
Dortmund
Duisburg
Essen
Witten
RUHR
Hagen
Mülheim
Wuppertal
Mönchengladbach
Remscheid
Düsseldorf
Solingen
VALLEY
Bergisch Gladbach
Leverkusen
Köln
Siegen
Aachen
Bonn
Marburg an der Lahn
RHEINISCHES SCHIEFERGEBIRGE
Wetzlar
HESSE
EIFEL
Koblenz
BELGIUM
LUXEMBOURG
Frankfurt am Main
Offenbach
Wiesbaden
Mainz
Darmstadt
Mosel
RHEINLAND-PFALZ
Trier
Bensheim
Kaiserslautern
Mannheim
SAARLAND
Ludwigshafen
Heidelberg
Saarbrücken
Heilbronn
Karlsruhe
Pforzheim
Rastatt
BADEN-WÜRTTEMB
FRANCE
Offenburg
Reut
BLACK FOREST
SCHWARZWALD
Freiburg im Breisgau
Friedrichshafe
Lake Const
SWITZERLAND

PEOPLE

Pop. density high

German

235/km² (609/mi²)

THE URBAN/RURAL POPULATION SPLIT

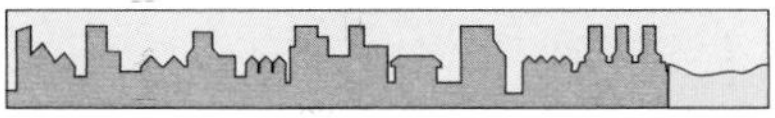
87%
13%

RELIGIOUS PERSUASION

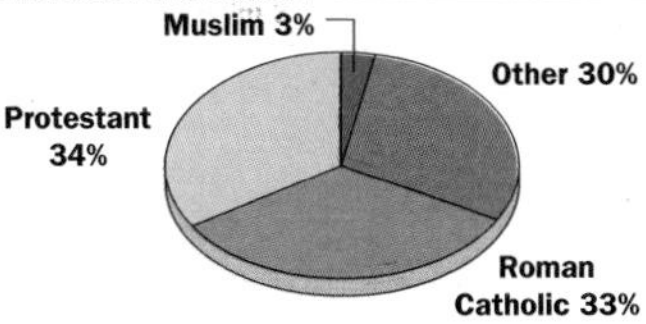
Muslim 3%
Other 30%
Protestant 34%
Roman Catholic 33%

ETHNIC MAKEUP

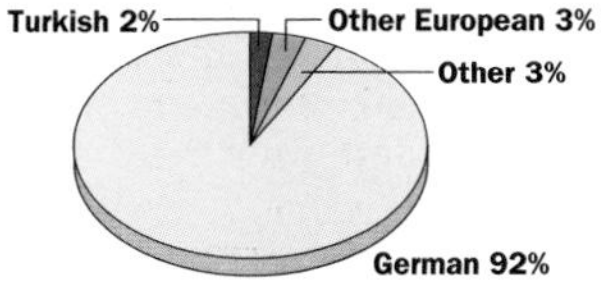
Turkish 2%
Other European 3%
Other 3%
German 92%

BALTIC SEA
Fehmarnbelt
Fehmarn
Mecklenburger Bucht
Sassnitz
Stralsund
Pomeranian Bay
Greifswald
Rostock
Lübeck
Wismar
MECKLENBURG-VORPOMMERN
Oderhaff
Schwerin
Schweriner See
Neubrandenburg
Plauer See
Müritz
TIEFLAND
Elbe
BRANDENBURG
Oder
POLAND
Stendal
BERLIN
Fürstenwalde
Wolfsburg
Brandenburg
Potsdam
Köpenick
Frankfurt an der Oder
Braunschweig
FLÄMING
Magdeburg
Salzgitter
SACHSEN-ANHALT
Bernburg
Dessau
Cottbus
Saale
Spree
Nordhausen
Halle
Leipzig
Meissen
Bautzen
Görlitz
THÜRINGEN
Dresden
Pirna
Erfurt
SACHSEN
Jena
Gera
Chemnitz
Zwickau
ERZGEBIRGE
CZECH REPUBLIC
Bamberg
Weiden
Erlangen
Nürnberg
BOHEMIAN FOREST
BAYERN
Regensburg
Ingolstadt
Danube
Landshut
Passau
Ulm
Augsburg
Inn
Dachau
München
Germering
Chiemsee
Rosenheim
Kaufbeuren
Kempten
BAYRISCHE ALPEN
AUSTRIA
Zugspitze 2962m

The majority of German-speakers live in Germany itself, although Austria and the greater part of Switzerland are German-speaking, as are parts of eastern France. Germans share a common language, but they speak it in a variety of dialects, reflecting a strong sense of regionalism. The north is still largely Protestant, while the south and southwest, particularly Bavaria (Bayern), have strong Catholic traditions.

The large immigrant population now totals some 7.4 million, the 2.1 million Turks forming the largest single group. *Gastarbeiter* (guest workers) recruited from the mid-1950s to mid-1970s provided much of the labor on which the former West Germany's economic recovery was built. Legislation in 1999 improved the rights of their children to obtain German nationality.

Germany's once liberal asylum laws were tightened in 1993 in response to domestic tension over a new influx, this time of ethnic Germans and others fleeing Russia and eastern Europe after the collapse of communism. Germany took in more refugees from the war in the former Yugoslavia than all other Western countries put together. Extreme right-wing parties sought to whip up and exploit anti-immigrant feeling among disaffected groups including the young unemployed.

Family ties in Germany are little different from those in the USA or the UK. Millions of couples live together in common-law arrangements, although this is frowned on by the Catholic Church. In rural districts, notably in Bavaria (Bayern), more traditional habits are still observed. The birthrate is one of Europe's lowest, and the population would have fallen were it not for the influx of immigrants since the 1950s.

Germany has a tradition of strong feminism. Women have full rights under the law and play a bigger role in politics than in most other European countries. In the *Bundestag* (Federal Assembly) elected in 1998, 30% of the members were women. There are six women ministers in the government. From 2001, women were permitted to take on combat roles in the armed forces. However, they are less well represented in top jobs in business and industry. Abortion remains a charged issue. Women in former East Germany once had the right to abortion on demand, but the Constitutional Court, after strong Roman Catholic lobbying, overruled a relatively liberal 1992 compromise law for the whole country. The current regulations, dating from mid-1995, allow abortions (but only after counseling) within three months of conception.

POPULATION AGE BREAKDOWN

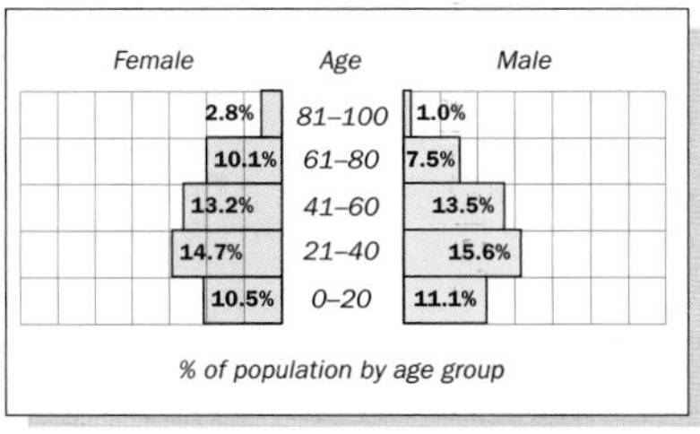
Female
Age
Male
2.8%
81–100
1.0%
10.1%
61–80
7.5%
13.2%
41–60
13.5%
14.7%
21–40
15.6%
10.5%
0–20
11.1%
% of population by age group

G

CHRONOLOGY

German unification in the 19th century brought together a mosaic of states with a common linguistic, but varied political, heritage.

- **1815** German Confederation under nominal Austrian leadership.
- **1834** Zollverein Customs Union of 18 states, including Prussia.
- **1862** Otto von Bismarck appointed Prussian chancellor.
- **1864–1870** Prussia defeats Austrians, Danes, and French; north German states under Prussian control.
- **1871** Southern states join Prussian-led unified German Empire under Wilhelm I.
- **1870s** Rapid industrialization.
- **1890** Kaiser Wilhelm II accedes, with aspirations for German world role. Bismarck sacked.
- **1914–1918** World War I.
- **1918** Germany signs armistice; Weimar Republic created.
- **1919** Treaty of Versailles: colonies lost and reparations paid. Rhineland demilitarized.

CHRONOLOGY *continued*

- ❑ **1923** France occupies Ruhr; financial collapse and hyperinflation.
- ❑ **1929** World recession brings mass unemployment.
- ❑ **1933** Hitler chancellor after Nazis become largest party in elections. One-party rule; rearmament.
- ❑ **1935** Nuremberg Laws; official persecution of Jews begins.
- ❑ **1936** German entry into Rhineland. Axis alliance with Italy.
- ❑ **1938** Annexation of Austria and Sudetenland.
- ❑ **1939** Invasion of Poland starts World War II.
- ❑ **1940** France, Belgium, the Netherlands, and Norway invaded.
- ❑ **1941** USSR invaded.
- ❑ **1942–1943** Germans defeated by Red Army at Stalingrad.
- ❑ **1945** German surrender; Allies control four occupation zones.
- ❑ **1949** Germany divided: communist East led by Walter Ulbricht 1951–1971, Erich Honecker 1971–1989; liberal democratic West led by CDU's Konrad Adenauer, first Chancellor, 1949–1963.
- ❑ **1955** West Germany joins NATO.
- ❑ **1961** Berlin Wall built.
- ❑ **1966–1969** West German grand coalition of CDU and SPD.
- ❑ **1969–1982** SPD-led West German governments under Willy Brandt (1969–1974), Helmut Schmidt (1974–1982).
- ❑ **1973** Both Germanies join UN.
- ❑ **1982** Helmut Kohl West German chancellor, CDU–FDP coalition.
- ❑ **1989** Fall of Berlin Wall.
- ❑ **1990** Reunification of Germany. First all-German elections since 1933; Kohl heads government.
- ❑ **1996** Rising concern over jobs.
- ❑ **1998** Gerhard Schröder heads coalition of SPD and Greens.
- ❑ **1999** Euro introduced.
- ❑ **2000** Disgrace of Kohl in party funding scandal.

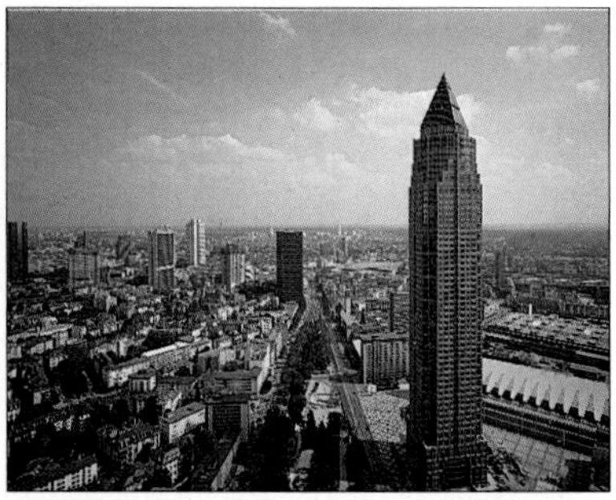

***The Messeturm**, Frankfurt, the tallest office building in Europe. Frankfurt is Germany's financial services center and home to many of its leading companies.*

POLITICS

Multiparty elections

1998/2002

President Johannes Rau

AT THE LAST ELECTION

Federal Assembly 669 seats

6% FDP
45% SPD
37% CDU/CSU
7% A/G
5% PDS

SPD = Social Democratic Party of Germany **CDU/CSU** = Christian Democratic Union/Christian Social Union **A/G** = Alliance 90/Greens **FDP** = Free Democratic Party **PDS** = Party of Democratic Socialism

Federal Council 69 seats

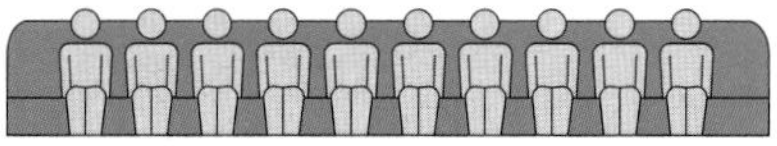

Each of the 16 states (*Länder*) is represented by between 3 and 6 members in the Federal Council (*Bundesrat*), who are appointed after the elections in each Land.

Germany is a federal democratic republic of 16 *Länder* (states). The government is led by the federal chancellor, elected by the *Bundestag* (Federal Assembly). The president's role is largely ceremonial. The "Basic Law" of West Germany, drawn up in 1948, became the 1990 federal constitution of reunified Germany.

Main Political Issues

East and west

Most Germans supported reunification after the fall of the Berlin Wall in 1989, but feelings soured as the true costs became clear. Over DM1000 billion have been spent on reconstruction in the east, financed partly by a "solidarity surcharge" on income tax, but the tenth anniversary of reunification in November 2000 was less a celebration than a reflection on past mistakes. The east remains poorer, and people moving west, still seen as "ossis," may find it hard to fit in. Support for the former communist PDS is confined almost entirely to the east.

The economy

Germans, used to constant growth since the 1950s, were shocked by recession in the 1990s. Public spending was reined in in mid-decade to meet targets for European monetary union, despite unrest as unemployment peaked at over four million. A return to growth enabled the SPD, in power from 1998, to tackle pension reform in less of a crisis atmosphere.

Far-right violence

Unemployment and resentment of "foreigners" led to a rise in support for far-right parties. Foreign workers, particularly Turks, and asylum seekers have been subject to shocking attacks. The problem of racism, even if no worse than in many other European states, is particularly sensitive, given Germany's history.

Profile

Germany's politics are now strongly democratic, with a long tradition of federative association. Before unification in 1871, Germany was a mass of separate principalities, kingdoms, and city states, a tradition in many ways maintained by Bismarck in his unification constitution. The 1933–1945 Nazi period, during which the federal system was abolished, was very much a hiatus. The Allies reestablished the federal system in West Germany in 1949; in the east, the *Länder* were restored after reunification in 1990. In many ways, the *Länder* are at the heart of German political life. Each *Land* has its own elected parliament and largely controls its own finances. In addition German cities have larger budgets than their European counterparts and city mayors wield considerable power. By general consensus the system delivers efficient and commercially astute government. There have been few major differences on domestic policy between the postwar ruling coalitions. All parties support the social market economy on which German prosperity was built.

Nationally, Germany has enjoyed stable governments, with coalitions of the center-left and center-right each holding sway for long periods since the "grand coalition" of 1966–1969. In September 1998 the electorate chose moderate SPD leader Gerhard Schröder in a vote for change, instead of approving yet another term for long-serving CDU Chancellor Helmut Kohl. Although the SPD-led government soon lost popularity, its CDU opponents were overwhelmed by a party-funding scandal in 2000. Kohl was disgraced. His successor as CDU leader, Angela Merkel, is the first person from the former East Germany to lead the party.

***Helmut Kohl**, long-serving chancellor until 1998.*

***Gerhard Schröder**, elected chancellor in place of Kohl in 1998.*

***Joschka Fischer**, popular foreign minister.*

WORLD AFFAIRS

Joined UN in 1973

EU | G7 | NATO | OECD | OSCE

Before reunification, Germany played only a modest part in international politics. The focus of West Germany was integration in Western Europe and, gradually, a more flexible *Ostpolitik* – to improve relations with the Soviet bloc, which had 400,000 troops stationed in East Germany.

Since 1990, the emphasis has changed and Germany has begun to voice a foreign policy which reflects its position as the most powerful country in Europe. The united Germany has inevitably shifted more of its attention eastward. German influence in central and eastern Europe is based primarily on trade and, above all, investment in the region's post-communist economies. Germany also remains a leading proponent of deepening as well as widening European union.

AID

Donor

$5.52bn (donations)

Down 1% in 1999

Unlike the USA, the UK, and France, Germany's aid programs are not directly motivated by its desire for political influence in the world's poorer regions. Most are multilateral, although there is also a strong tradition of direct aid. Much comes from church organizations such as the Protestant Brot für die Welt. Many German volunteers and missionaries work overseas on aid programs.

DEFENSE

Compulsory military service

$31.1bn

Down 8% in 1999

US and UK troops are being withdrawn. The large German army, designed for national defense, is being slimmed down to focus more on mobility and providing support to allied states. The Constitutional Court ruled in 1994 that army units could take part in collective defense activities abroad. German participation in the 1999 NATO bombing of Serbia was its first military action abroad since 1945.

GERMAN ARMED FORCES

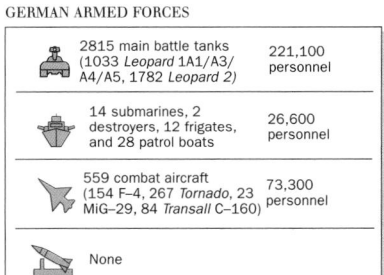

2815 main battle tanks (1033 *Leopard* 1A1/A3/ A4/A5, 1782 *Leopard 2)*	221,100 personnel
14 submarines, 2 destroyers, 12 frigates, and 28 patrol boats	26,600 personnel
559 combat aircraft (154 F–4, 267 *Tornado*, 23 MiG–29, 84 *Transall* C–160)	73,300 personnel
None	

ECONOMICS

Inflation 1.9% p.a. (1991–1999)

$2104bn

1.9513–2.0833 Deutsche marks

SCORE CARD

❑ World GNP Ranking	3rd
❑ GNP per Capita	$25,620
❑ Balance of Payments	$20.9bn
❑ Inflation	0.6%
❑ Unemployment	12%

EXPORTS

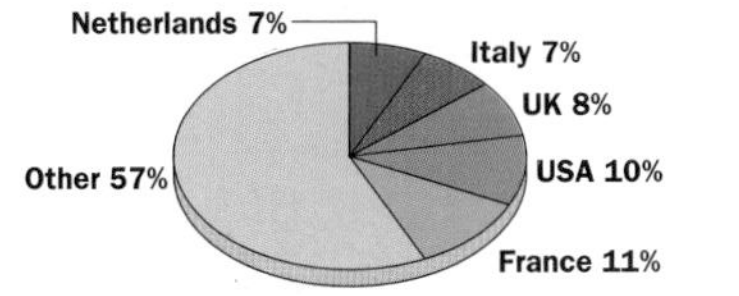
Netherlands 7%
Italy 7%
UK 8%
USA 10%
France 11%
Other 57%

IMPORTS

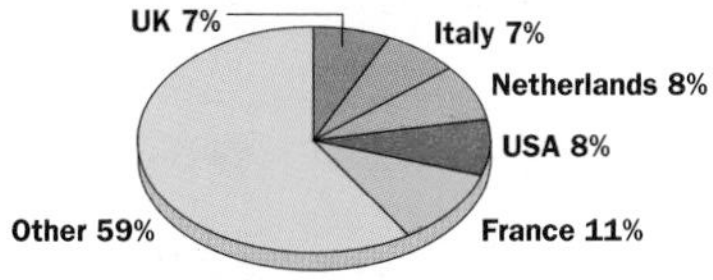
UK 7%
Italy 7%
Netherlands 8%
USA 8%
France 11%
Other 59%

Strengths

Europe's major industrial power and, until 1990s, most successful economy. Efficient industry benefits from low inflation environment. Return to growth by 2000. Workers and managers live up to reputation for thoroughness and hard work. Strong sectors are cars, heavy engineering, electronics, and chemicals.

Weaknesses

Underestimation of the costs of updating inefficient eastern German economy. High welfare costs; pension obligations (despite reforms in 2001) with an aging population. Competition from efficient

ECONOMIC PERFORMANCE INDICATOR

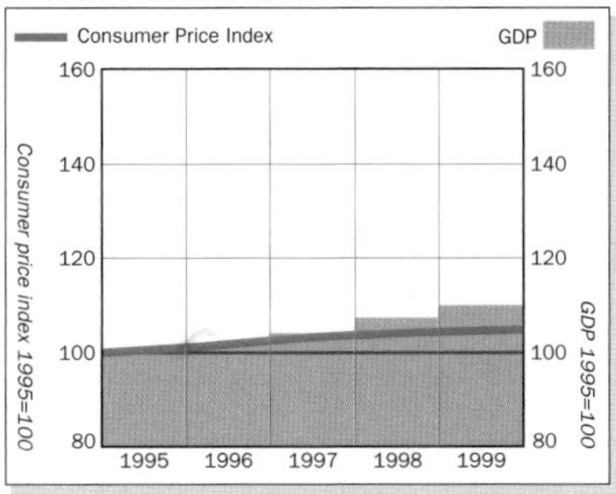
Consumer Price Index
GDP
160
140
120
100
80
1995
1996
1997
1998
1999
Consumer price index 1995=100
GDP 1995=100

Asian economies. Relatively few small firms, a short working week, poorly developed service sector.

Profile

West Germany's remarkable postwar recovery, to become the world's third-strongest economy, was based on the concept of a social market economy, under which the state provided welfare and ensured workers' rights, while the economy was largely in private hands. Major banks and businesses are privately owned, except for Volkswagen, partly state-owned. After reunification in 1990, massive investment went into the former East Germany, where state concerns were sold off. Rebuilding the east remains a great challenge.

The government of Helmut Kohl also successfully put the case for completing European monetary union, and the euro was introduced from 1999. The SPD-led government elected in 1998 undertook to tackle unemployment, which has fallen from its peak of 12.7% in 1997, and to maintain growth, which reached a ten-year high of 3.1% in 2000. The sale of "third generation" mobile phone operators' licenses raised over $46 billion, helping to reduce the budget deficit. Major tax reforms aimed to balance the budget by 2006.

GERMANY : MAJOR BUSINESSES

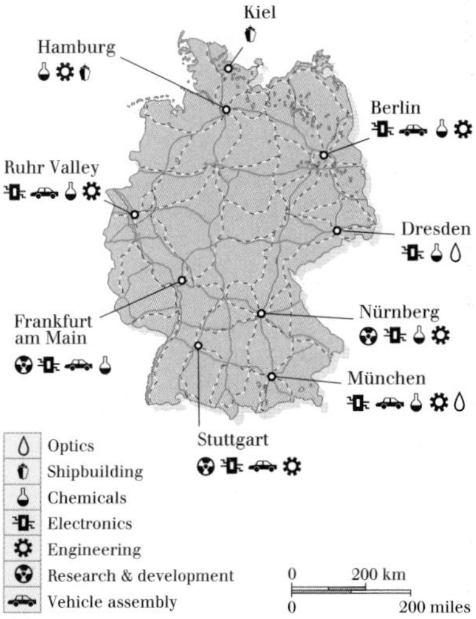
Kiel
Hamburg
Berlin
Ruhr Valley
Dresden
Nürnberg
Frankfurt am Main
München
Stuttgart
Optics
Shipbuilding
Chemicals
Electronics
Engineering
Research & development
Vehicle assembly
0 200 km
0 200 miles

Potsdamer Platz, Berlin, was rapidly reconstructed as the commercial center of the capital after reunification.

RESOURCES

Electric power 115.4m kw

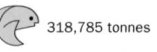

318,785 tonnes

56,220 b/d (reserves 205,252,800 bbl)

27m pigs, 14.6m cattle, 7.3m turkeys, 103m chickens

Coal, oil, natural gas, copper, salt, potash, tin, nickel

ELECTRICITY GENERATION

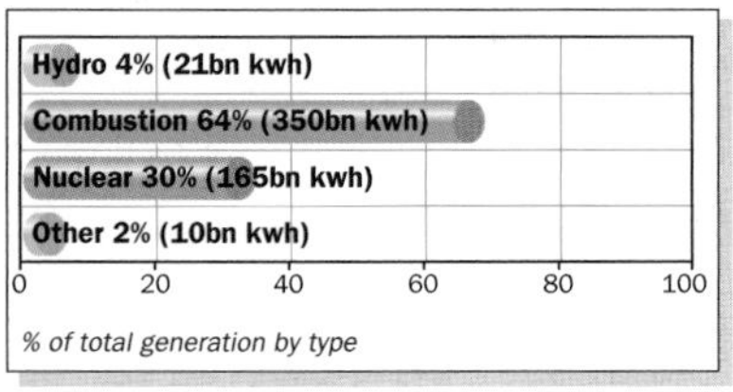

Hydro 4% (21bn kwh)
Combustion 64% (350bn kwh)
Nuclear 30% (165bn kwh)
Other 2% (10bn kwh)
0
20
40
60
80
100
% of total generation by type

With relatively few natural resources, Germany imports over 50% of its energy needs, mainly oil and gas. Coal, the basis of industrialization, now accounts for under a quarter of energy consumption. West Germany invested less heavily than France in nuclear power, and Soviet-built stations in the east have been shut down. The "red–green" coalition government decided in mid-2000 to phase out nuclear power (which provides over 30% of electricity). Renewable resources account for 2% of primary energy consumption, but 6% of electricity production (with a target of 50% by 2050); Germany is a world leader in wind power.

GERMANY : LAND USE

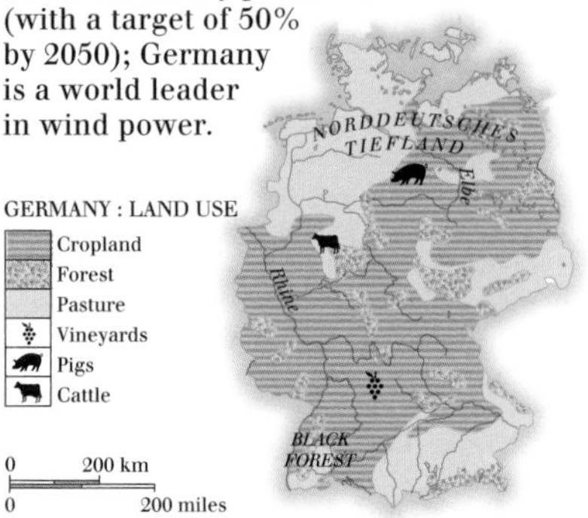

NORDDEUTSCHES TIEFLAND
Elbe
Rhine
BLACK FOREST
Cropland
Forest
Pasture
Vineyards
Pigs
Cattle
0 200 km
0 200 miles

ENVIRONMENT

Sustainability rank: 15th

27%

10.4 tonnes per capita

ENVIRONMENTAL TREATIES

Yes · Yes · Yes

Yes · Yes · Yes

Germans are among the world's most environmentally conscious people. Environmental campaigns led by the Green Party, which emerged as a powerful political force in the 1980s, have influenced the policies of all major parties. At national level, the Greens are a significant force in the *Bundestag*; they joined the SPD-led federal government coalition in 1998, and are strongly represented in *Land* parliaments and local councils.

Germany has some of the strictest pollution controls in the world, with ambitious targets for reducing carbon dioxide emissions, compelling businesses to become more energy-efficient. Germans recycle half of their waste paper, and three-quarters of their used tires and glass.

The nuclear debate has been vigorously fought and won by the Greens; a gradual program of closing existing nuclear power stations was approved in 2001, although waste disposal is still an issue. Fears in the 1980s that up to 50% of trees were sick or dying because of car fumes and industrial pollution led to Germany becoming the first European country to insist that new cars be fitted with catalytic converters. The east had the highest per capita rate of sulfur emissions in the world, but these have been reduced by the closure of industrial plants and the elimination of the noxious Trabant cars.

MEDIA

TV ownership high

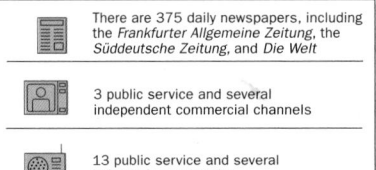

Daily newspaper circulation 311 per 1000 people

PUBLISHING AND BROADCAST MEDIA

There are 375 daily newspapers, including the *Frankfurter Allgemeine Zeitung*, the *Süddeutsche Zeitung*, and *Die Welt*

3 public service and several independent commercial channels

13 public service and several independent networks

TV is supervised by the political parties to ensure a balance of views. Satellite and cable TV have taken much of the audience once shared between the main public service channels, ARD and ZDF. Media conglomerates such as Kirch and Bertelsmann have expanded abroad. Newspapers are mostly regional and serious. An exception is *Bild Zeitung*, a right-wing, sensationalist tabloid, which sells 4.5 million copies daily.

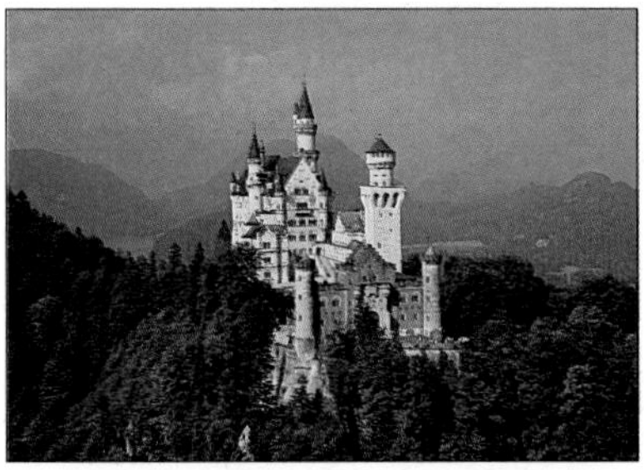

Neuschwanstein Castle, Bayern (Bavaria), *one of Germany's major tourist attractions. It was built for the eccentric King Ludwig II.*

EDUCATION

School leaving age : 18

99%

2.1m students

THE EDUCATION SYSTEM

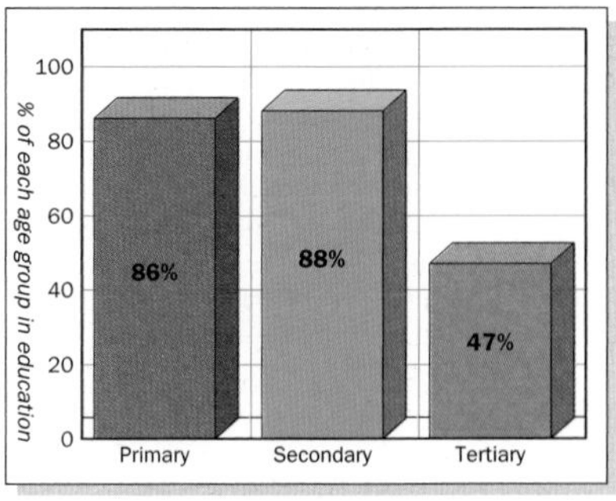

100
80
60
40
20
0
% of each age group in education
86%
88%
47%
Primary
Secondary
Tertiary

Nearly one-tenth of total government expenditure goes on education, which is run by the *Länder*. They coordinate teaching policies, but have autonomy within their borders. The German approach to education stresses academic and vocational achievement. Sporting or cultural activities tend to be organized informally. Nearly all schools have Internet access.

Those who wish to go to university attend the upper-secondary *Gymnasien* to prepare for the *Abitur* exam. Since this was made easier, resources have been strained as thousands more have decided to go to university. They were taking an average of seven years to complete their diploma, until new legislation added shorter bachelor's and master's degrees as in other countries. Research is done as much by major companies as by the universities.

CRIME

Death penalty not used

68,396 prisoners

Down 3% 1996–1998

CRIME RATES

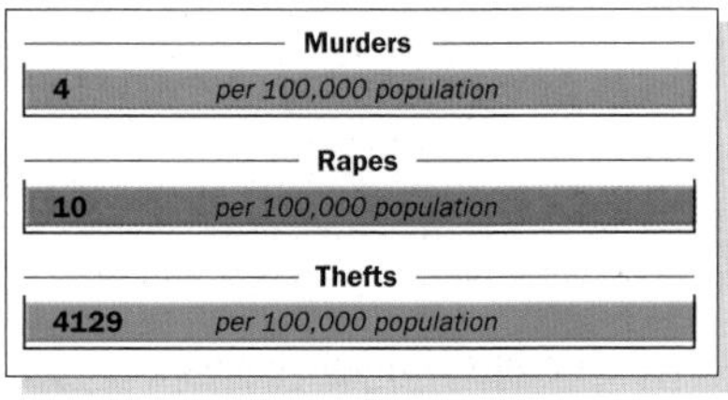

Murders
4 per 100,000 population
Rapes
10 per 100,000 population
Thefts
4129 per 100,000 population

Crime rates in Germany are lower than in most other European countries. This is largely the result of a genuine respect for the law, coupled with a strong police force. Recently, however, higher unemployment has led to an increase in petty theft and a wave of violence, notably against immigrants.

German politicians, once with an enviably clean reputation, have suffered several corruption scandals. Civil service corruption remains rare. People convicted under environmental laws can face ten-year jail sentences.

BERLIN, REUNIFICATION, AND CENTRAL EUROPE

THE SO-CALLED "BONN REPUBLIC," created in West Germany in the postwar period, ended symbolically in September 1999. Bonn could justifiably claim to have been home for some 50 years to Germany's only enduringly successful parliamentary democracy. The decision to move the capital to Berlin, however, symbolizing German unity, was enshrined in the 1990 unification treaty only months after the fall of the Berlin Wall in November 1989. It took time to confirm that both government and parliament would be transferred – the lower house of parliament, the *Bundestag*, only voted to move in 1994 – but five years after that vote, in the same month that Federal Chancellor Schröder moved into his office in Berlin, the *Bundestag* held its first full session there.

***The dramatic glass dome** of the new Reichstag building in Berlin.*

PROSPECTS FOR BERLIN

The parliament's new home is the former *Reichstag* building, impressively redesigned by English architect Norman Foster. Topped with a transparent dome and lit up at night from within, it epitomizes the emphasis on architectural and engineering achievements in modern Berlin. New government, commercial, and tourist facilities have brought a lengthy construction boom in Berlin, which with a population of some 3.5 million is Germany's largest city. The proliferation of cultural and artistic activity has also contributed to a strong sense of excitement, boosting the city's image with the international media and the public. Berlin nevertheless faces many problems, including an unemployment rate well above the national average and the need to revitalize its declining industrial base. The outward movement of business and population, from central urban areas to surrounding regions, has been an established trend for decades in major western German cities, but is now happening much more rapidly in Berlin, whose western half was for years an enclave within East Germany. The city also has a long way to go in attracting major companies to make their headquarters there; only 12 of the largest German companies are located in Berlin, compared with over 40 each in Hamburg, Munich, and Frankfurt.

COSTLY REUNIFICATION

The costs of reconstruction of the former East Germany far outweighed initial expectations. Achievements stand out in telecommunications and rail transportation, but most infrastructure in the east is still well below the standard of the west, despite subsidies amounting to the transfer to the east of some 7% of GDP of western *Länder* per year for a decade. Unemployment is higher, labor productivity lower, and living conditions less attractive to the majority of Germans.

GERMANY'S NEW CENTER OF GRAVITY

The transfer of the capital reinforces the shift in Germany's center of gravity brought about by reunification. Coinciding with the collapse of communism across the whole former Soviet bloc came a revival of interest in Germany's role in central Europe or *Mitteleuropa*. In the former communist countries German economic influence is now particularly strong. West Germany was firmly anchored in Western Europe, in economic terms by the European Economic Community (now the European Union), and in a political–military sense by its membership of the NATO alliance. The imminent eastward expansion of the EU, however, suggests the emergence of France–Germany–Poland as a new and powerful axis in the Europe of the 21st century.

Arbeit!

***Unemployed** Germans demonstrate for the right to work.*

HEALTH

Welfare state health benefits

1 per 286 people

Heart and cerebro-vascular diseases, cancers, accidents

The German social security system, first pioneered by Bismarck, is one of the most comprehensive in the world. Health insurance is compulsory, and employer and employee contributions are high. Although most hospitals are run by the *Länder*, some are still owned by Germany's wealthy churches. Almost one-third of health spending is now private.

Germans are increasingly health-conscious, paying great attention to diet. Nearly a million people go on cures every year to the country's 200-plus spas. In the east there is a higher incidence of lung diseases, the legacy of industrial pollution.

SPENDING

GDP/cap. increase

CONSUMPTION AND SPENDING

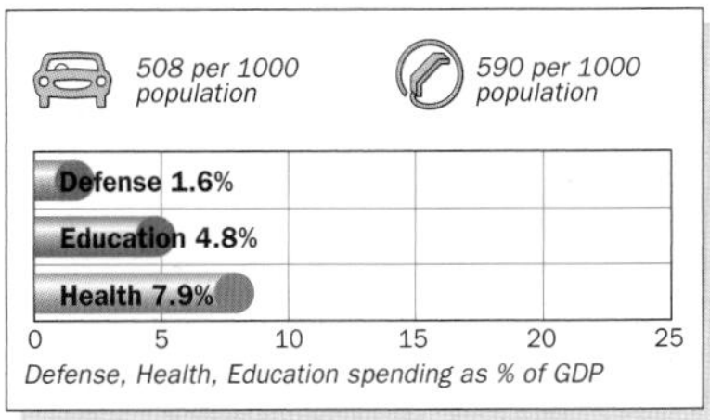
508 per 1000 population
590 per 1000 population
Defense 1.6%
Education 4.8%
Health 7.9%
0
5
10
15
20
25
Defense, Health, Education spending as % of GDP

The effects of the Nazi period, which discredited many of the ruling class, and the destruction of the property of millions of families in the war, explain the relatively classless nature of society. Status is now more closely linked to wealth than to birth. In the west, there are fewer disparities than in most of Europe; workers are generally well paid and social security is generous. Wages in the east, however, are 10% below western rates, and a disproportionate number of unemployed live on welfare benefit. Most Germans own a mobile phone, and almost a third of them had accessed the Internet by 2001.

WORLD RANKING

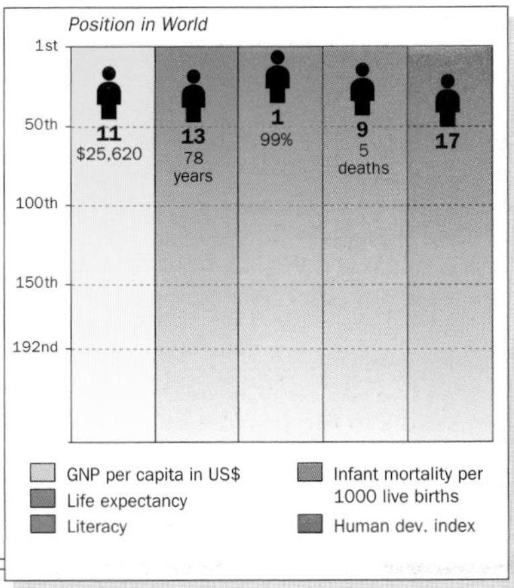
Position in World
1st
50th
100th
150th
192nd
11
$25,620
13
78
years
1
99%
9
5
deaths
17
GNP per capita in US$
Life expectancy
Literacy
Infant mortality per 1000 live births
Human dev. index

GHANA

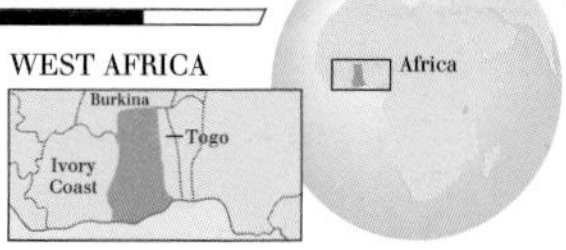
WEST AFRICA
Africa
Burkina
Togo
Ivory Coast

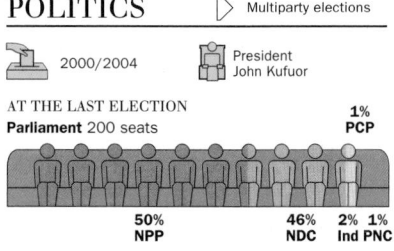

OFFICIAL NAME: Republic of Ghana **CAPITAL:** Accra
POPULATION: 20.2 million **CURRENCY:** Cedi **OFFICIAL LANGUAGE:** English

1957 | 1957 | March 6 | GH | 0 | +233 | .gh

THE HEARTLAND OF THE ancient Ashanti kingdom, modern Ghana is a union of the former British colony of the Gold Coast and the British-administered part of the UN Trust Territory of Togoland. Ghana gained independence in 1957, the first British colony to do so. Multiparty democracy was embraced in 1992, and the handover of power to the main opposition party in 2000 confirmed the shift away from Ghana's recent history of intermittent military rule.

CLIMATE

Tropical wet & dry/ equatorial

WEATHER CHART

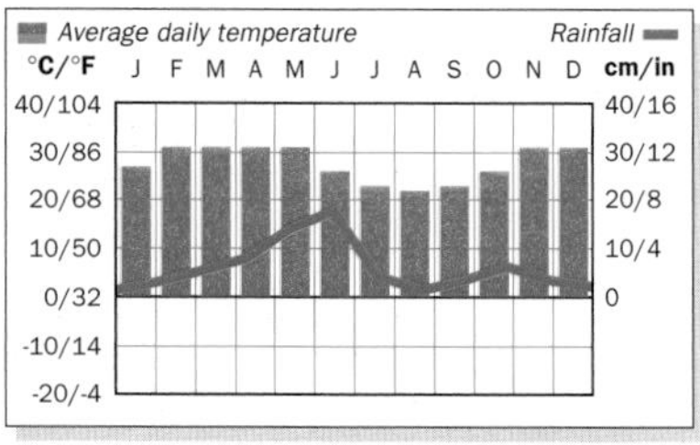
Average daily temperature
Rainfall
°C/°F
J F M A M J J A S O N D
cm/in
40/104
30/86
20/68
10/50
0/32
-10/14
-20/-4
40/16
30/12
20/8
10/4
0

Southern Ghana has two rainy seasons: from April to July and September to November. The drier north has just one, from April to September.

TRANSPORTATION

Drive on right

Kotoka International, Accra
673,661 passengers

205 ships
115,500 grt

THE TRANSPORTATION NETWORK

11,653 km (7241 miles)

30 km (19 miles)

1300 km (808 miles)

168 km (104 miles)

In 1983, work began to restore Ghana's roads, which had fallen into disrepair in the 1960s and 1970s; the network is now improving.

TOURISM

Visitors : Population 1:54

373,000 visitors

Up 7% in 1999

MAIN TOURIST ARRIVALS

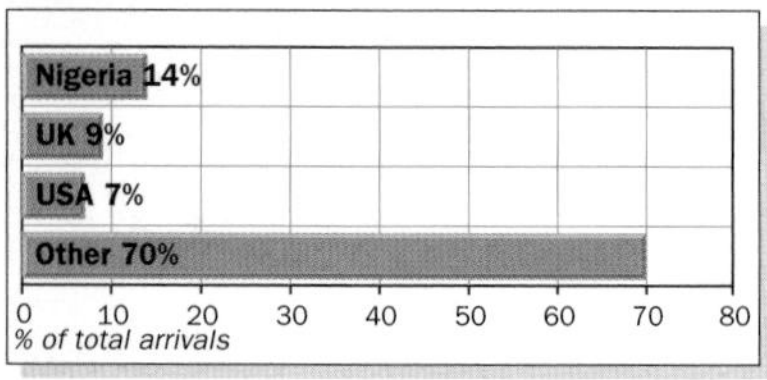
Nigeria 14%
UK 9%
USA 7%
Other 70%
0 10 20 30 40 50 60 70 80
% of total arrivals

Tourism is still small-scale; most visitors come from the rest of Africa, the UK, and the USA. Good beaches and old coastal forts are major attractions.

PEOPLE

Pop. density medium

Twi, Fanti, Ewe, Ga, Adangbe, Gurma, Dagomba (Dagbani)

88/km² (227/mi²)

THE URBAN/RURAL POPULATION SPLIT

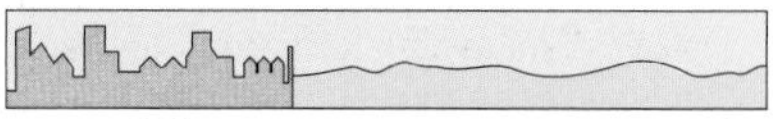
38%
62%

RELIGIOUS PERSUASION

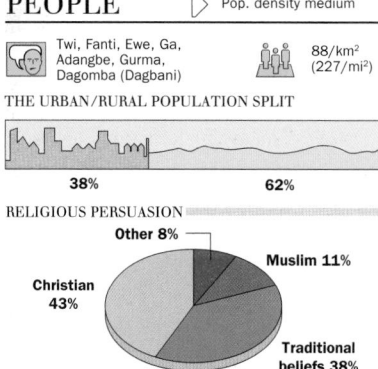

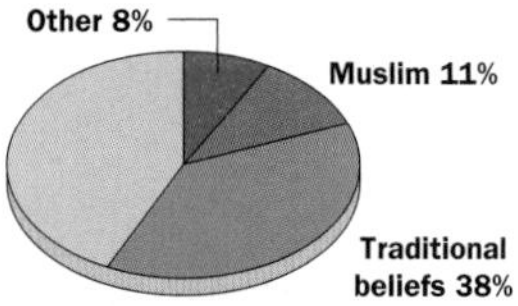
Other 8%
Muslim 11%
Christian 43%
Traditional beliefs 38%

Ghana contains various cultural-linguistic groups. The largest is the Akan, who include the Ashanti and Fanti peoples. Other important groups are the Mole-Dagbani in the north, Ga-Adangbe around Accra, and Ewe in the southeast. There are few tribal tensions. Family ties are strong.

POLITICS

Multiparty elections

2000/2004

President John Kufuor

AT THE LAST ELECTION

Parliament 200 seats

1% PCP
50% NPP
46% NDC
2% Ind
1% PNC

NPP = New Patriotic Party **NDC** = National Democratic Congress **Ind** = Independents **PNC** = People's National Convention **PCP** = People's Convention Party

Ghana's return to multiparty rule in 1992 marked the legitimization of the military government of Jerry Rawlings. An air force flight-lieutenant of Ewe-Scottish descent and one of the great survivors of African politics, Rawlings staged coups in 1979 and 1981, and led the 1981–1992 Provisional National Defense Council (PNDC) military government. As the NDC candidate, Rawlings won 58% of the vote in the 1992 presidential election. Opposition parties boycotted the following parliamentary elections, which the NDC won easily. Elections in 1996 gave Rawlings a further and final term of office. In December 2000 the opposition NPP gained a historic victory when it stripped the NDC of its parliamentary majority and NPP candidate John Kufuor won the presidency.

WORLD AFFAIRS

Joined UN in 1957

Comm | ECOWAS | G24 | IAEA | OAU

Good relations with the West, which provides the bulk of Ghana's military and development aid, are a priority. Ghana has played a significant part in UN peacekeeping operations. It was also the main contributor, after Nigeria, to the ECOWAS forces (ECOMOG) in war-torn Liberia from 1990 to 1997. Ghana maintains good relations with its French-speaking neighbors, despite periods of strain with Togo.

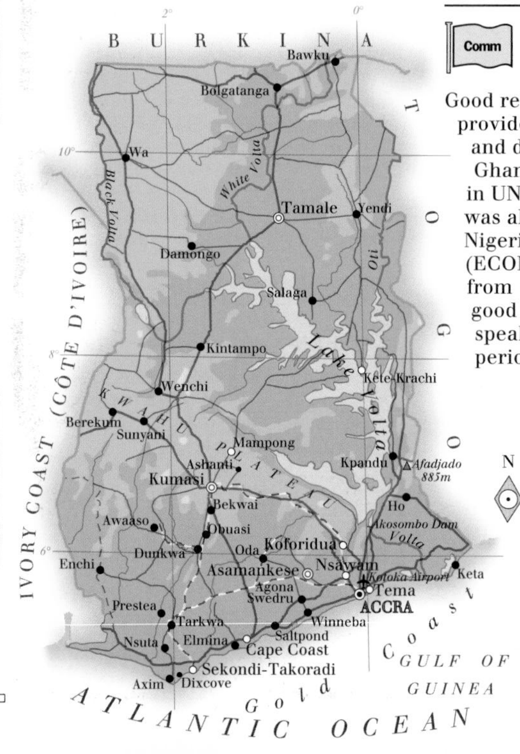
BURKINA
TOGO
IVORY COAST (CÔTE D'IVOIRE)
Bawku
Bolgatanga
Wa
White Volta
Black Volta
Tamale
Yendi
Damongo
Oti
Salaga
Kintampo
Lake Volta
Kete-Krachi
Wenchi
KWAHU PLATEAU
Berekum
Sunyani
Mampong
Ashanti
Kumasi
Kpandu
Afadjado 885m
Bekwai
Ho
Awaso
Obuasi
Akosombo Dam
Volta
Dunkwa
Oda
Koforidua
Enchi
Asamankese
Nsawam
Kotoka Airport
Keta
Agona Swedru
Tema
ACCRA
Prestea
Tarkwa
Winneba
Saltpond
Nsuta
Elmina
Cape Coast
Sekondi-Takoradi
Axim
Dixcove
Gold Coast
GULF OF GUINEA
ATLANTIC OCEAN
N

GHANA

Total Land Area : 230 020 sq. km (88 810 sq. miles)

LAND HEIGHT: 500m/1640ft; 200m/656ft; Sea Level

POPULATION: over 500 000; over 100 000; over 50 000; over 10 000; under 10 000

0 100 km
0 100 miles

AID
Recipient

$607m (receipts) | Down 13% in 1999

A largely successful economic recovery program backed by World Bank and IMF aid began in 1983. Between 1984 and 1989, Ghana received $3.5 billion, the third-largest recipient of World Bank aid after India and China, and inflows continue to rise.

DEFENSE
No compulsory military service

$121m | Down 12% in 1999

In 1966, 1972, 1979, and 1981, the military mounted successful coups, and there have also been several unsuccessful coups. Outside Ghana, the 5000-strong army has been deployed mainly in UN and ECOWAS operations. Ghana's navy is small, with four patrol boats. The air force has 19 combat aircraft.

ECONOMICS
Inflation 27.4% p.a. (1990–1999)

$7.45bn | 3500–7275 cedis

SCORE CARD

❑ World GNP Ranking	97th
❑ GNP per Capita	$400
❑ Balance of Payments	$–766m
❑ Inflation	12.4%
❑ Unemployment	20%

Strengths
GNP rose by 5% a year throughout the 1990s, following economic recovery policies begun in 1983. Second-largest gold producer in Africa. Since 1996, Ashanti Goldfields Co Ltd has expanded into a multinational active in 12 African countries. Cocoa production accounts for 15% of world total.

Weaknesses
High budget deficits and debt repayments; the cedi was devalued in 1983 and has since tended to float downward. Foreign investors generally invest solely in gold mining. High inflation levels.

EXPORTS

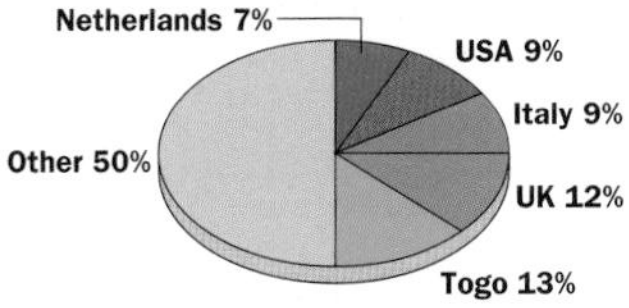
Netherlands 7%
USA 9%
Italy 9%
UK 12%
Togo 13%
Other 50%

IMPORTS

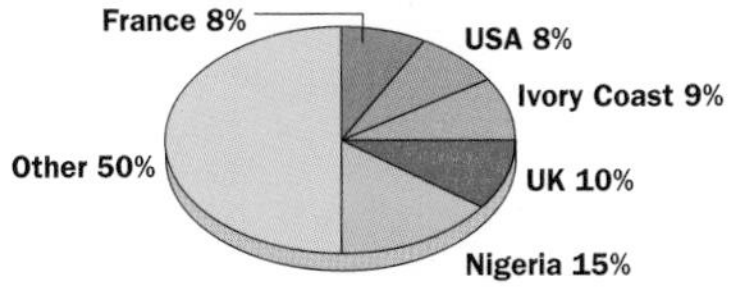
France 8%
USA 8%
Ivory Coast 9%
UK 10%
Nigeria 15%
Other 50%

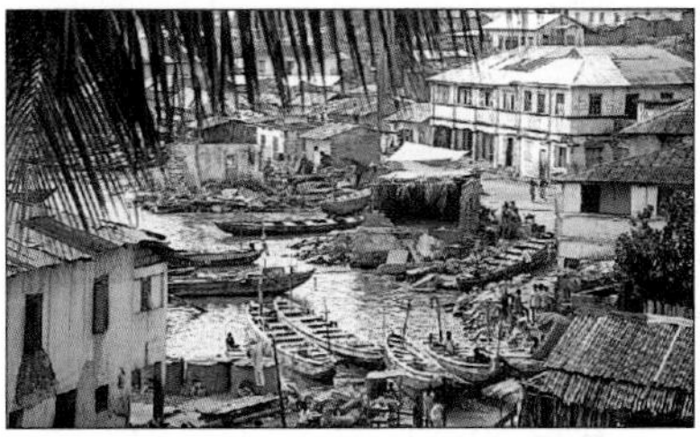

***Dixcove harbor,** close to Ghana's most southerly cape. The majority of Ghanaians lead a traditional subsistence existence.*

RESOURCES
Electric power 1.2m kw

446,883 tonnes | Reserves of 500,000 bbl

2.8m goats, 2.57m sheep, 1.29m cattle, 18m chickens | Gold, diamonds, bauxite, manganese

Gold production has expanded strongly since the mid-1980s; by 1993, gold had overtaken cocoa as the major export. Diamonds, bauxite, and manganese are also exported. Hydropower from the Volta Dam is exported to Togo and Benin, but is hit by periodic droughts.

ENVIRONMENT
Sustainability rank: 63rd

5% | 0.3 tonnes per capita

Cutting of wood for fuel, timber, and farming has destroyed 70% of forests. Devastation caused by mining is now being tackled under a World Bank project.

MEDIA
TV ownership medium

Daily newspaper circulation 14 per 1000 people

PUBLISHING AND BROADCAST MEDIA

There are 2 daily newspapers, the *Ghanaian Times* and the *Daily Graphic*

1 state-controlled service | 1 state-controlled service

New independent weeklies reflect the increase in private press ownership. Radio and TV tend to follow government reporting guidelines.

CRIME
Death penalty used

Ghana does not publish prison figures | Up 8% 1990–1996

The judiciary has little independence and the government often resorts to ad hoc "people's tribunals." Corruption is now less of a problem.

EDUCATION
School leaving age: 14

72% | 9609 students

All sectors of the education system are oversubscribed. There are a few high-quality boarding schools and four universities.

CHRONOLOGY
In 1874 Kumasi, capital of the Ashanti kingdom, was sacked by a British force to create the Gold Coast colony.

- ❑ **1957** Independence under Kwame Nkrumah.
- ❑ **1964** Single-party state.
- ❑ **1966** Army coup.
- ❑ **1972–1979** "Kleptocracy" of General Acheampong. Executed 1979.
- ❑ **1979** Flight Lieutenant Jerry Rawlings' coup. Civilian Hilla Limann wins elections.
- ❑ **1981** Rawlings takes power again.
- ❑ **1992, 1996** Rawlings and NDC win multiparty elections.
- ❑ **2000** Opposition NPP wins elections; John Kufuor wins presidency.

G

HEALTH
No welfare state health benefits

1 per 16,700 people | Malaria, diarrheal diseases, tuberculosis

The health of most of the population has benefited more from improvements in public hygiene than in medical care. Private health care is available.

SPENDING
GDP/cap. increase

CONSUMPTION AND SPENDING

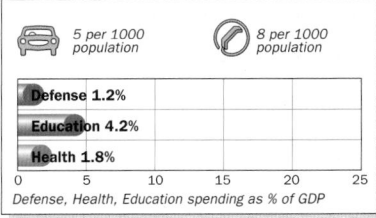

5 per 1000 population | *8 per 1000 population*

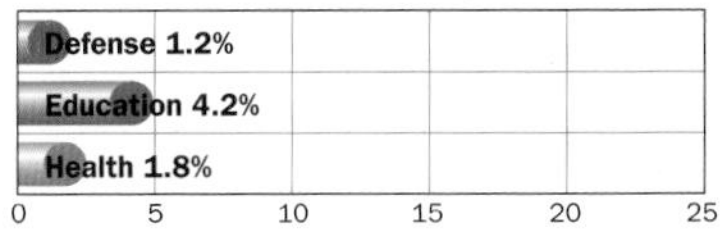
Defense 1.2%
Education 4.2%
Health 1.8%
0
5
10
15
20
25

Defense, Health, Education spending as % of GDP

Political uncertainty brought few opportunities for advancement, and many Ghanaians emigrated, but the situation is now improving. The main economic disparity is still between the poorer rural north and the richer, more urban, south.

WORLD RANKING

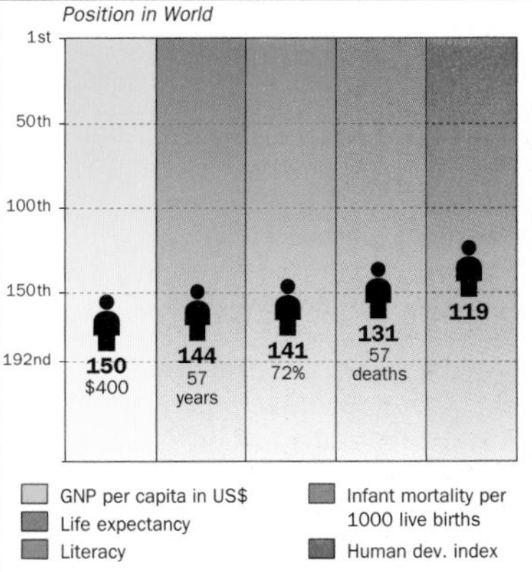
Position in World
1st
50th
100th
150th
192nd
150
$400
144
57 years
141
72%
131
57 deaths
119
GNP per capita in US$
Life expectancy
Literacy
Infant mortality per 1000 live births
Human dev. index

GREECE

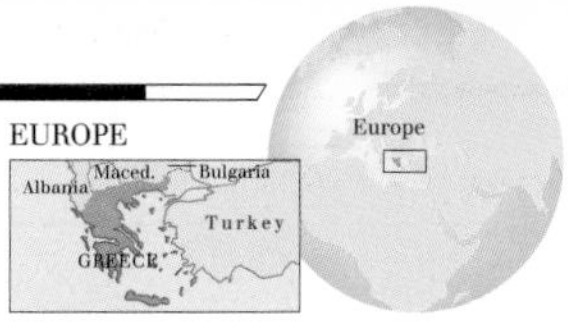
EUROPE
Albania
Maced.
Bulgaria
Turkey
GREECE
Europe

OFFICIAL NAME: Hellenic Republic **CAPITAL:** Athens **POPULATION:** 10.6 million
CURRENCY: Euro (drachma until 2002) **OFFICIAL LANGUAGE:** Greek

1829 | 1947 | March 25 | GR | +2 | +30 | .gr

THE SOUTHERNMOST country of the Balkans, Greece is surrounded by the Aegean, Ionian, and Cretan seas. Its mainly mountainous territory includes more than 2000 islands. Only one-third of the land is cultivated. There is a strong seafaring tradition, and some of the world's biggest ship-owners are Greek. Greece is rich in minerals – including chromium, whose occurrence is rare. Relations with Turkey, marked by conflict and territorial disputes, have improved in recent years. To the north, however, upheavals in Albania and the conflicts in former Yugoslavia have made for greater instability.

CLIMATE

Mediterranean

WEATHER CHART

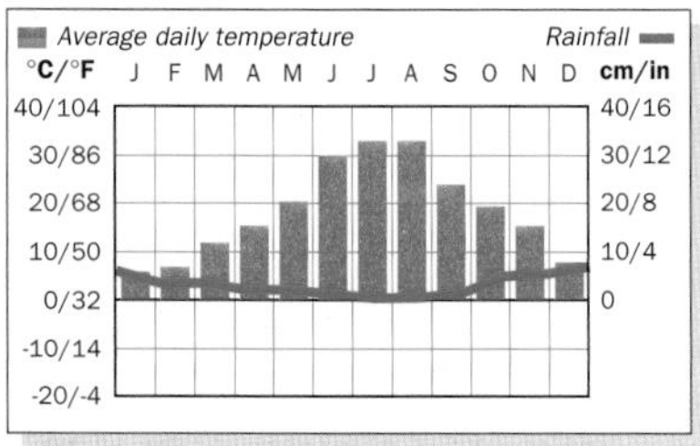
Average daily temperature
Rainfall
°C/°F
J F M A M J J A S O N D
cm/in
40/104
30/86
20/68
10/50
0/32
-10/14
-20/-4
40/16
30/12
20/8
10/4
0

The climate varies from region to region. The northwest is alpine, while parts of Crete border on the subtropical. The large central plain experiences high summer temperatures. Water is a problem, since many rivers have been diverted underground by earthquakes.

TRANSPORTATION

Drive on right

Athinai, Athens
6.3m passengers

1545 ships
25.2m grt

THE TRANSPORTATION NETWORK

107,406 km (66,739 miles)

470 km (292 miles)

2299 km (1429 miles)

80 km (50 miles)

The easiest and cheapest method of transportation between the islands and the mainland is by boat or hovercraft. A major ferry disaster in 2000 prompted government moves to improve standards. Greece has 444 ports, of which 123 are large enough to handle passenger or freight traffic. Piraeus is the main port. A new airport at Spata, 30 km east of Athens, opened in 2001. Greece has a good, if increasingly congested, road network. Two expressway routes are nearing completion, with the help of EU funds, as is the upgrading of the Athens metro. An interurban bus system and a fleet of air-conditioned tourist Pullmans offer an extensive service.

TOURISM

Visitors : Population 1.2:1

12.5m visitors

Up 3% in 2000

MAIN TOURIST ARRIVALS

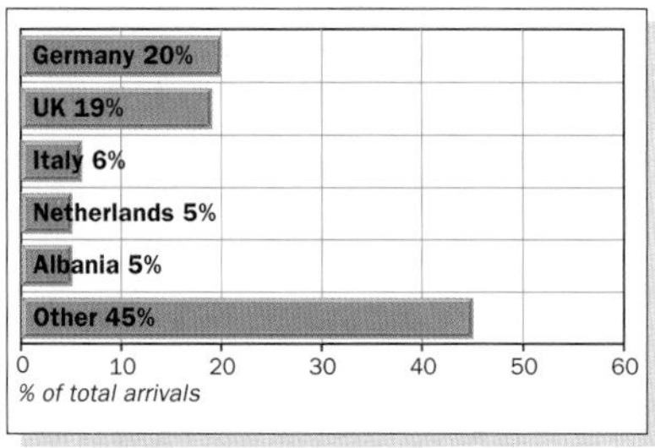
Germany 20%
UK 19%
Italy 6%
Netherlands 5%
Albania 5%
Other 45%
0
10
20
30
40
50
60
% of total arrivals

Tourism is a mainstay of the Greek economy, with an annual turnover of some $10 billion, and is a major source of foreign exchange. Until recently, the state gave grants for hotel development and many third-grade hotels were built, especially on Crete and Rhodes. Smaller islands also tried to encourage tourism, but few have sufficient water supplies or sandy beaches. Visitor numbers fell in the mid-1990s as people chose cheaper vacations elsewhere. The tourist industry is now being encouraged to raise standards and move upmarket, and is also promoting year-round activity holidays and conference tourism. The 2004 Olympics, to be held in Athens, are a stimulus to upgrade the city's facilities.

The theater at Dodona. *Classical sites such as this amphitheater in northwestern Greece, have helped to make tourism one of Greece's most important industries.*

PEOPLE

Pop. density medium

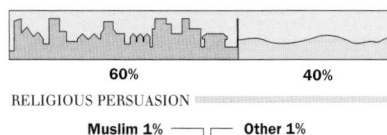

Greek, Turkish, Macedonian, Albanian

81/km² (210/mi²)

THE URBAN/RURAL POPULATION SPLIT

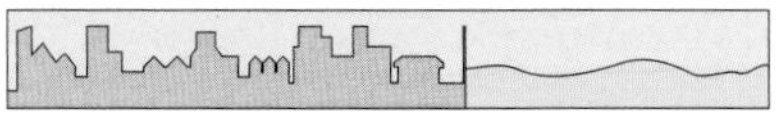
60%
40%

RELIGIOUS PERSUASION

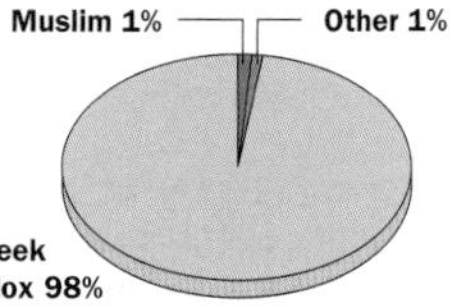
Muslim 1%
Other 1%
Greek Orthodox 98%

ETHNIC MAKEUP

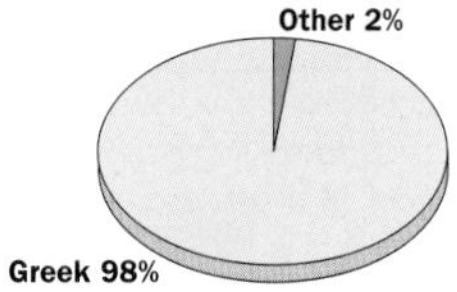
Other 2%
Greek 98%

The Greeks were for many centuries a largely agrarian and seafaring nation. The German occupation during World War II, and the civil war that followed, destroyed much of the fabric of rural life and there was rapid urbanization after the 1950s. There was also extensive emigration in the 1950s and 1960s to northern Europe, Australia, the USA, Canada, and southern Africa. However, many people returned to Greece in the 1980s, putting pressure on the labor market. The socialist PASOK governments of 1981–1989 spent large sums, mostly from EU sources, on developing the infrastructure and business life of the rural regions with a view to halting emigration to the cities. The policy was mostly successful, but a majority still lives in or near the capital, Athens, and Thessaloníki in the north.

Some 98% of the population belong to the Greek Orthodox Church. Civil marriage and divorce only became legal in 1982. There are minorities of Muslims, Roman Catholics, and Jews, and a recent influx of illegal immigrants, mainly from Albania.

POPULATION AGE BREAKDOWN

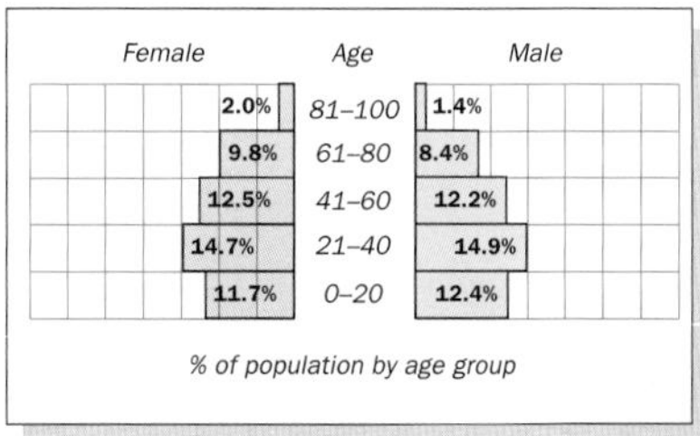
Female
Age
Male
2.0%
81–100
1.4%
9.8%
61–80
8.4%
12.5%
41–60
12.2%
14.7%
21–40
14.9%
11.7%
0–20
12.4%
% of population by age group

POLITICS

Multiparty elections

2000/2004

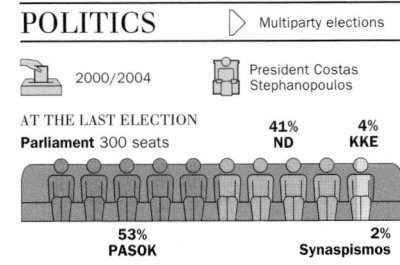

President Costas Stephanopoulos

AT THE LAST ELECTION

Parliament 300 seats

41% **ND**

4% **KKE**

53% **PASOK**

2% **Synaspismos**

PASOK = Pan-Hellenic Socialist Movement
ND = New Democracy **KKE** = Communist Party of Greece
Synaspismos = Left Coalition

Greece is a multiparty democracy. A military government was in power between 1967 and 1974.

MAIN POLITICAL ISSUES

Closer European union

The socialist government's chief priority in the late 1990s was to qualify for euro membership. This was achieved in time for the introduction of the common currency in 2001, although not without widespread protests and industrial unrest over the austerity policies which it entailed. Currently the poorest EU country, Greece could lose funding to new members, especially if Turkey joins.

Relations with Macedonia

In 1995, Greece finally recognized the sovereignty of the Former Yugoslav Republic of Macedonia. The crisis in Macedonia in 2001 over ethnic Albanian separatism increased Greek regional security concerns.

Albanian refugees

Thousands of Albanians of Greek descent entered Greece illegally after 1990. Willing to work for very low wages, they swelled Greece's thriving black economy. Eventually a 1998 legalization program resulted in the registration of 375,000 Albanians.

PROFILE

Although PASOK has held power continuously since 1993, its economic policies differ little from the previous conservative government. Kostas Simitis has led the party since the resignation and death in 1996 of its founder Andreas Papandreou. PASOK only narrowly won the election held in April 2000.

Kostas Simitis, *prime minister since January 1996.*

Andreas Papandreou, *founded PASOK, prime minister 1981–1989, 1993–1996.*

G

WORLD AFFAIRS

Joined UN in 1945

EU NATO OECD OSCE CE

Although closely allied to the West, Greece has sympathies with Russians and Serbs, who share its Orthodox heritage. Greece withdrew from NATO's military command in 1974, in protest at its failure to prevent the Turkish invasion of Cyprus, but has since rejoined. Cyprus remains a sore point in Greece's otherwise improving relations with Turkey. The current priority is Greece's role within an expanding EU. In 2000 Greek claims for compensation for victims of Nazi war crimes led to a diplomatic dispute with Germany.

AID

Donor

$194m (donations) Up 8% in 1999

Greece's contribution to overseas development assistance is the lowest in Western Europe. However, Greek companies have been active as investors elsewhere in the southern Balkans. Greece receives regional development assistance from the EU, especially from the EU's structural and cohesion funds, its share of which was estimated to amount to around $3.5 billion over the period 1994–1999. Some of the money has been used to reverse the decline of northeast Greece – the EU's least developed region. Greece supplied some emergency humanitarian aid to Turkey following the severe earthquake devastation of 1999.

GREECE

Total Land Area : 130 850 sq. km (50 521 sq. miles)

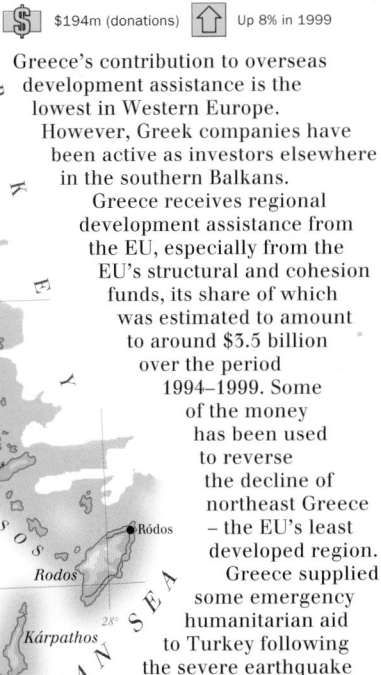

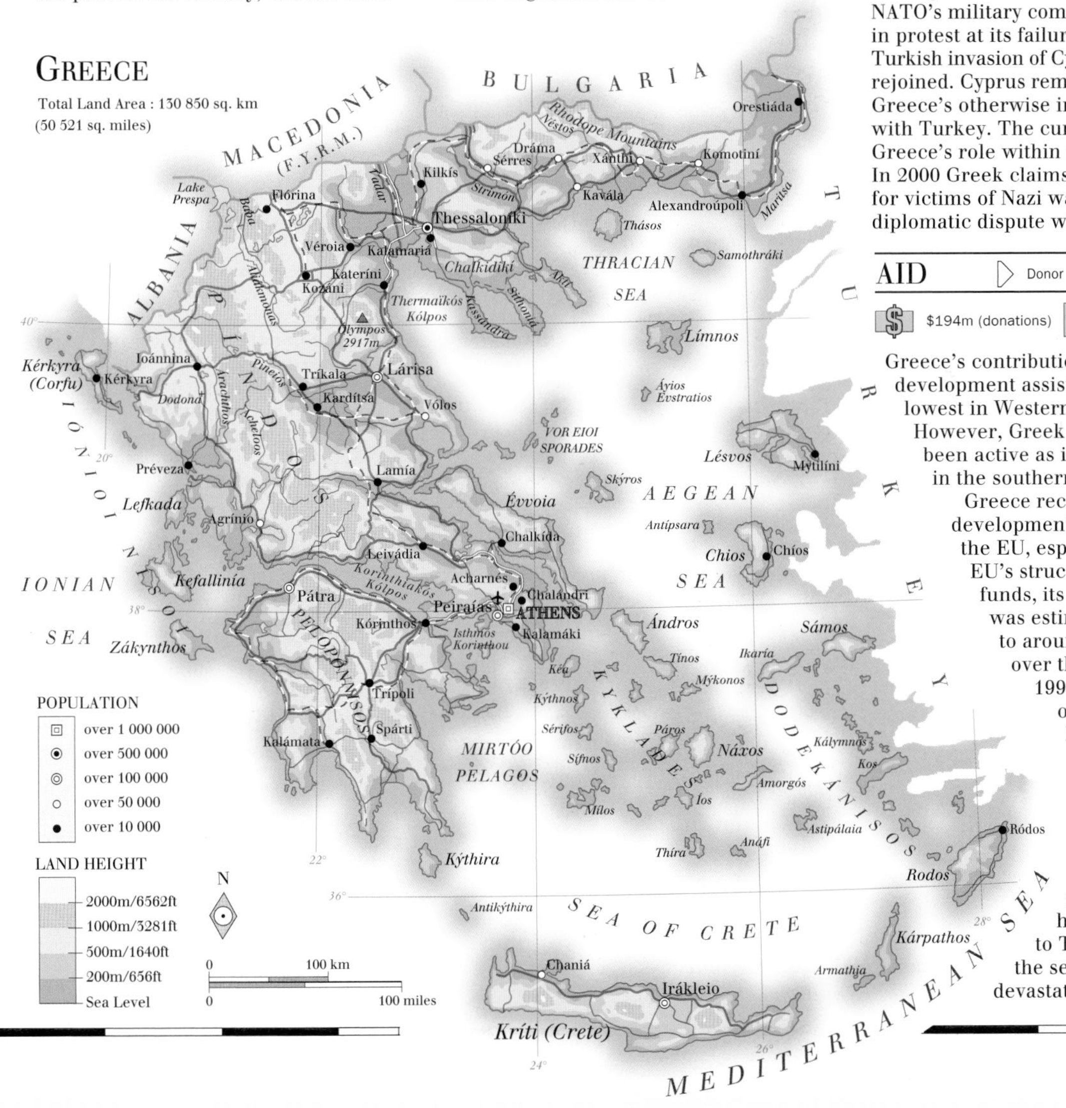
BULGARIA
MACEDONIA (F.Y.R.M.)
ALBANIA
TURKEY
Orestiáda
Rhodope Mountains
Néstos
Dráma
Sérres
Xánthi
Komotiní
Kilkís
Strimón
Kavála
Alexandroúpoli
Maritsa
Lake Prespa
Flórina
Thessaloníki
Thásos
Vérioia
Kalamaria
Chalkidikí
THRACIAN SEA
Samothráki
Kateríni
Kozáni
Thermaïkós Kólpos
Olympos 2917m
Límnos
PÍNDOS
Ioánnina
Kérkyra (Corfu)
Kérkyra
Tríkala
Lárisa
Kardítsa
Vólos
Dodoní
Áyios Evstratios
VOREIOI SPORADES
Lésvos
Mytilíni
Préveza
Lamía
Skýros
AEGEAN SEA
Lefkada
Agrínio
Évvoia
Antipsara
Chalkída
Chíos
IONIAN SEA
IÓNIOI NÍSOI
Kefallinía
Leivádia
Korinthiakós Kólpos
Acharnés
Pátra
Chalándri
Peiraías
ATHENS
Kórinthos
Isthmos Korinthou
Kalamáki
Zákynthos
PELOPÓNNISOS
Ándros
Sámos
Tínos
Ikaría
Mýkonos
Kéa
Kýthnos
Trípoli
KYKLADES
DODEKANISOS
Sérifos
Páros
Spárti
Kalámata
Náxos
Kálymnos
Kos
MIRTÓO PELAGOS
Sífnos
Amorgós
Mílos
Íos
Astipálaia
Rodos
Ródos
Kýthira
Thíra
Anáfi
Antikýthira
SEA OF CRETE
Kárpathos
Chaniá
Irákleio
Armathia
Kríti (Crete)
MEDITERRANEAN SEA
POPULATION
over 1 000 000
over 500 000
over 100 000
over 50 000
over 10 000
LAND HEIGHT
2000m/6562ft
1000m/3281ft
500m/1640ft
200m/656ft
Sea Level
N
0 100 km
0 100 miles

CHRONOLOGY

Greece was occupied by Nazi Germany between 1941 and 1944. After liberation by the Allies, communists and royalists fought a five-year civil war. This ended with communist defeat, and King Paul became the constitutional monarch.

- ❑ **1964** King Constantine succeeds his father, King Paul.
- ❑ **1967** Military coup. King in exile. Colonel Giorgios Papadopoulos becomes premier.
- ❑ **1973** Greece declared a republic, with Papadopoulos as president. Papadopoulos overthrown in military coup. Lieutenant General Ghizikis becomes president. Adamantios Androutsopoulos prime minister.
- ❑ **1974** Greece leaves NATO in protest at Turkish occupation of northern Cyprus. "Colonels' regime" falls. Constantinos Karamanlis becomes premier and his ND party wins subsequent elections.
- ❑ **1975** Konstantinos Tsatsou becomes president.
- ❑ **1977** Elections: ND reelected.
- ❑ **1980** Karamanlis president. Georgios Rallis prime minister. Greece rejoins NATO.
- ❑ **1981** PASOK wins elections. Andreas Papandreou first-ever socialist premier. Greece joins European Communities.
- ❑ **1985** Proposals to limit power of president. Karamanlis resigns. Christos Sartzetakis president. Greece and Albania reopen borders, closed since 1940.
- ❑ **1985–1989** Civil unrest caused by economic austerity program.
- ❑ **1988** Cabinet implicated in financial scandal. Leading members resign.
- ❑ **1989** Defense agreement with USA. Two inconclusive elections lead to formation of all-party coalition.
- ❑ **1990** Coalition government collapses. ND wins elections. Konstantinos Mitsotakis prime minister; Karamanlis president.
- ❑ **1990–1992** Strikes against economic reform.
- ❑ **1992** EU persuaded to withhold recognition of Former Yugoslav Republic of Macedonia (FYRM).
- ❑ **1993** PASOK wins election, Andreas Papandreou premier.
- ❑ **1995** Kostas Stephanopoulos elected president; recognition of sovereignty of FYRM.
- ❑ **1996** Andreas Papandreou resigns as prime minister; succeeded by Kostas Simitis.
- ❑ **1997–1998** Protest at austerity measures.
- ❑ **2000** April, PASOK led by Simitis wins general election.
- ❑ **2001** January, introduction of euro.

G

DEFENSE

▷ Compulsory military service

$5.21bn

Down 13% in 1999

Greece spends a higher percentage of GDP on defense than any other NATO country, its main concern being the perceived threat from Turkey. Despite flare-ups over islands in the Dodecanese, and the stationing on Cyprus of Greek S-300 anti-aircraft missiles (later moved to Crete), tensions with Turkey are now less acute. In 1998 a law was passed on the conscription of women (for four days a year) for the defense of border regions.

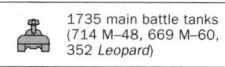

GREEK ARMED FORCES

1735 main battle tanks (714 M-48, 669 M-60, 352 *Leopard*)	110,000 personnel
8 submarines, 4 destroyers, 12 frigates, and 42 patrol boats	19,000 personnel
458 combat aircraft (A-7, F-5, F-4E, F-16, *Mirage* F-1, *Mirage* 2000)	30,170 personnel
None	

ECONOMICS

▷ Inflation 9.5% p.a. (1990–1999)

$127.6bn

329.51–362.94 drachmas

SCORE CARD

❑ World GNP Ranking	30th
❑ GNP per Capita	$12,110
❑ Balance of Payments	$–4.86bn
❑ Inflation	2.6%
❑ Unemployment	10%

EXPORTS

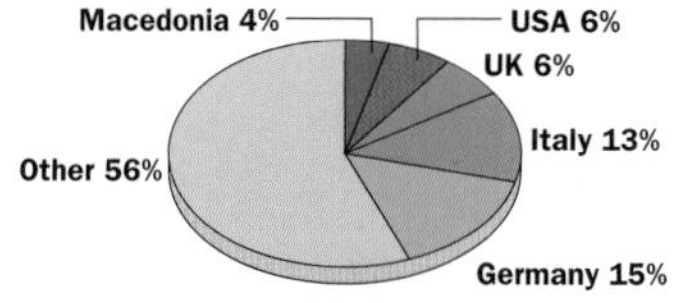
Macedonia 4%
USA 6%
UK 6%
Italy 13%
Other 56%
Germany 15%

IMPORTS

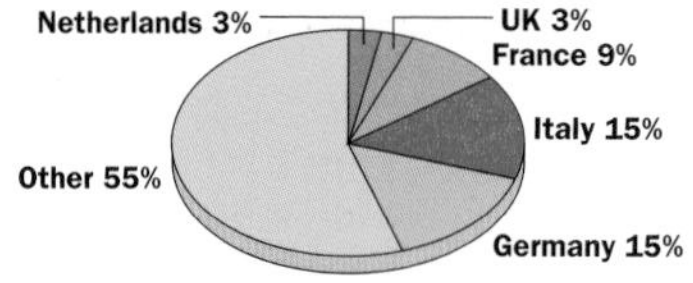
Netherlands 3%
UK 3%
France 9%
Italy 15%
Other 55%
Germany 15%

Strengths

One of the major tourist destinations in Europe. Efficient agricultural exporter. Shipping: the world's largest beneficially owned fleet.

Weaknesses

High levels of public debt. Until recently, interest rates and bureaucratic banking system discouraged private initiative. State-owned sector, often poorly managed, remains large, as does the black economy.

Profile

Greece took longer than most other European countries to recover from World War II. It was not until the 1960s that any substantial investment occurred. The Colonels' dictatorship curbed inflationary pressures by the introduction of a wage freeze. When civilian government was restored in 1974, a spate of high wage settlements and the oil price shocks of 1973 and 1979 drove inflation to above 20%. Greece's largest companies made substantial losses, until the socialists' controversial austerity program of 1986–1987 reined in labor costs.

Greece was the only one of the 12 EU countries seeking to introduce the euro in 1999 which failed to meet the economic convergence criteria. It then tackled the problems with determination, balancing the budget and bringing inflation under control, although public-sector debt remains high. In January 2001 Greece became the 12th member of the eurozone. Unemployment is still high.

ECONOMIC PERFORMANCE INDICATOR

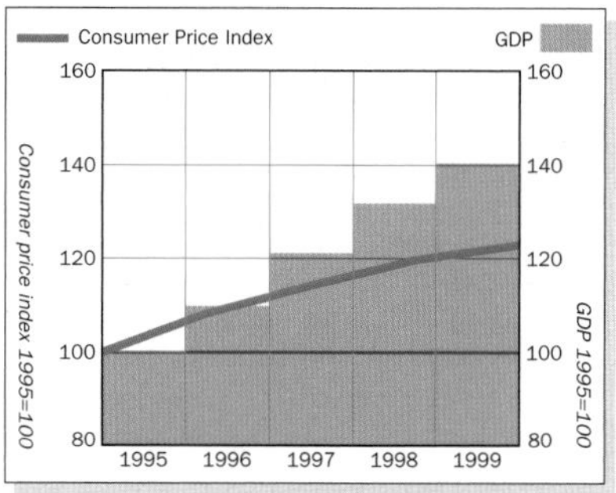
Consumer Price Index
GDP
160
140
120
100
80
Consumer price index 1995=100
GDP 1995=100
1995
1996
1997
1998
1999

GREECE : MAJOR BUSINESSES

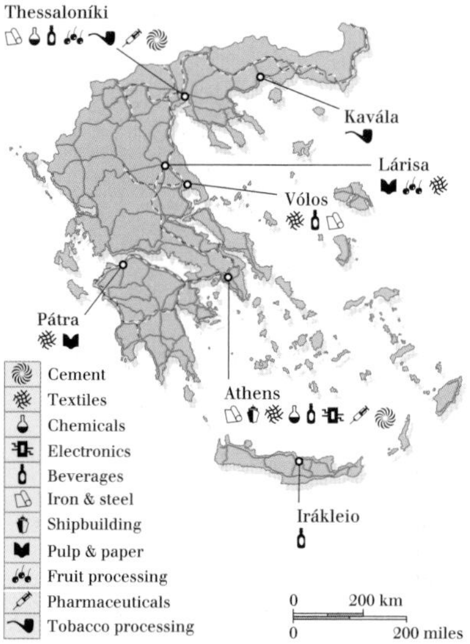
Thessaloníki
Kavála
Lárisa
Vólos
Pátra
Athens
Irákleio
Cement
Textiles
Chemicals
Electronics
Beverages
Iron & steel
Shipbuilding
Pulp & paper
Fruit processing
Pharmaceuticals
Tobacco processing
0
200 km
0
200 miles

RESOURCES

Electric power 9.6m kw

214,228 tonnes

8742 b/d (reserves 12,766,080 bbl)

9m sheep, 5.3m goats, 28m chickens

Oil, gas, coal, iron, bauxite, marble, nickel, magnesite, chromium

ELECTRICITY GENERATION

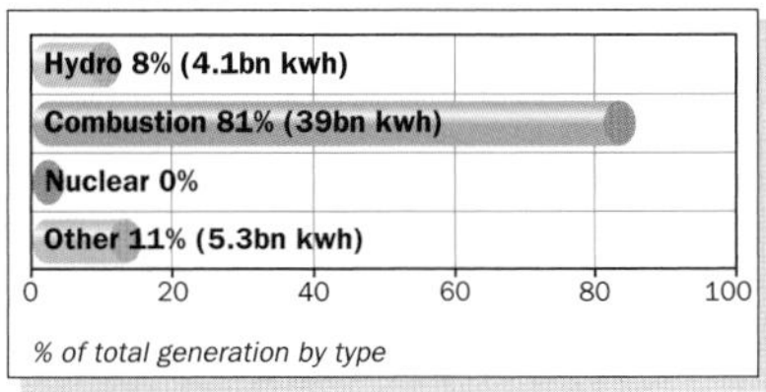

Hydro 8% (4.1bn kwh)
Combustion 81% (39bn kwh)
Nuclear 0%
Other 11% (5.3bn kwh)
0
20
40
60
80
100
% of total generation by type

Greece has an oil and gas field off the coast of Thasos island. There may also be exploitable reserves in eastern waters, ownership of which is contested by Turkey. Coal, iron, and other mining contributes less than 2% to GDP. Greece is a leading producer of marble.

ENVIRONMENT

Sustainability rank: 41st

2% (0.2% partially protected)

8.3 tonnes per capita

ENVIRONMENTAL TREATIES

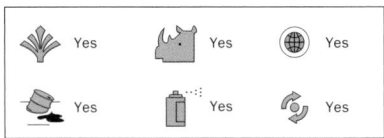

Yes Yes Yes

Yes Yes Yes

Local fishing interests have formed a successful anti-pollution organization, HELMEPA. Smog in Athens is irritating to the eyes and throat and highly damaging to ancient monuments: the Parthenon in Athens has suffered more erosion in the last two decades than in the previous 2000 years. Forest fires regularly cause havoc, damaging flora and fauna.

MEDIA

TV ownership high

Daily newspaper circulation 153 per 1000 people

PUBLISHING AND BROADCAST MEDIA

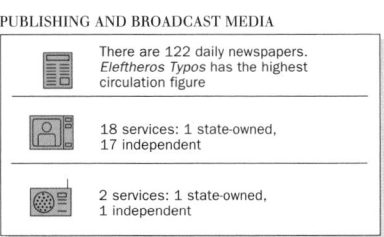

There are 122 daily newspapers. *Eleftheros Typos* has the highest circulation figure

18 services: 1 state-owned, 17 independent

2 services: 1 state-owned, 1 independent

The state had a monopoly on radio and TV until 1990. Since then the number of private TV networks has grown rapidly. Commercial broadcasting has made politicians far more answerable to the electorate than ever before. It has also had a cultural impact, with the import of more foreign, particularly US, programs.

GREECE : LAND USE

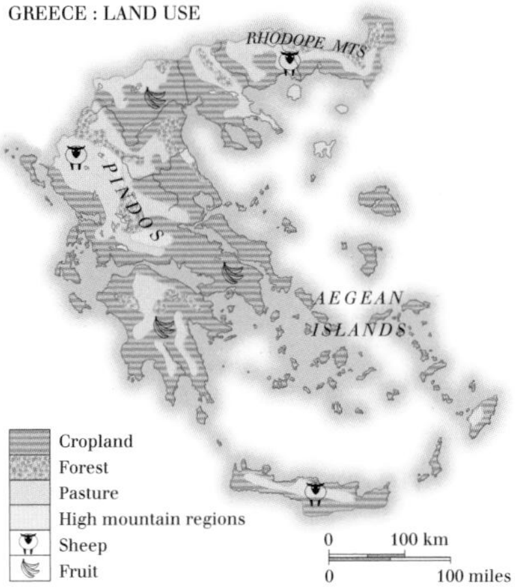

RHODOPE MTS
PINDOS
AEGEAN ISLANDS
Cropland
Forest
Pasture
High mountain regions
Sheep
Fruit
0
100 km
0
100 miles

CRIME

Death penalty not used

5897 prisoners

Up 10% 1996–1998

CRIME RATES

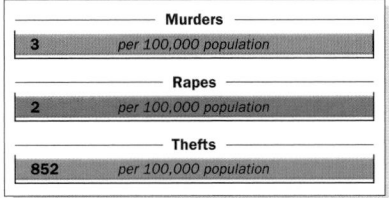

Murders	3	per 100,000 population
Rapes	2	per 100,000 population
Thefts	852	per 100,000 population

An influx of migrants is blamed for an increase in violent crime. The terrorist group November 17 has assassinated more than 20 people. There is corruption in the police force.

EDUCATION

School leaving age: 15

97%

363,150 students

THE EDUCATION SYSTEM

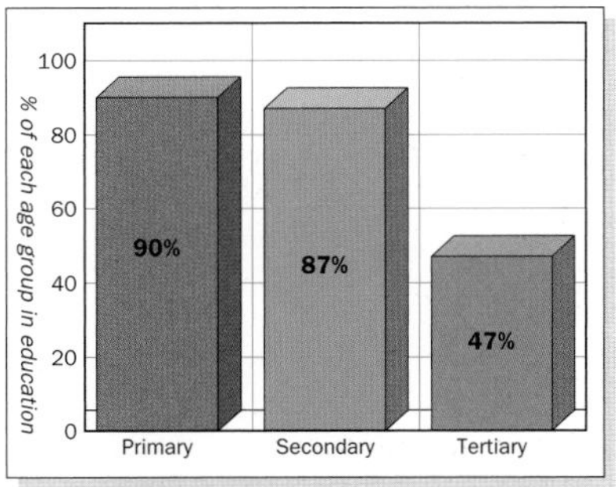

100
80
60
40
20
0
% of each age group in education
90%
87%
47%
Primary
Secondary
Tertiary

Some 9% of total government spending is on education, which is free and officially compulsory for nine years. Teachers are poorly paid and qualifications are low. University places are limited and many students go abroad for tertiary education. Technical courses, funded by the EU, have increased since the 1990s.

HEALTH

Welfare state health benefits

1 per 250 people

Heart and cerebrovascular diseases, cancers, accidents

The socialists (PASOK) introduced a National Health Service and a national pharmaceuticals industry. Some 12% of government expenditure goes on health, and every Greek is entitled to sickness benefit. Greece now has the third-highest number of doctors per head of population in the EU; however, primary care is poor, as is that in state hospitals. In the early 1990s the ND attempted to upgrade private medicine and to incorporate its activities with those in state hospitals. Many Greeks needing major surgery go abroad for treatment.

SPENDING

GDP/cap. increase

CONSUMPTION AND SPENDING

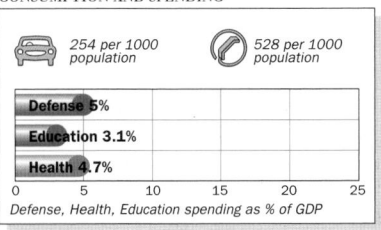

254 per 1000 population

528 per 1000 population

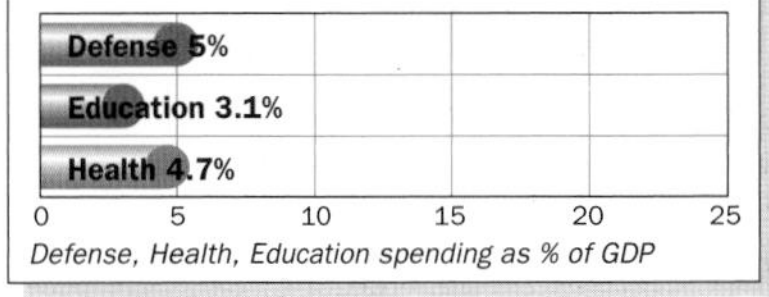

Defense 5%
Education 3.1%
Health 4.7%
0
5
10
15
20
25
Defense, Health, Education spending as % of GDP

Greek society changed dramatically in the postwar period. Formerly a largely agricultural society living in isolated communities, it was rapidly urbanized in the 1950s. Former agricultural workers made fortunes, many by grabbing opportunities presented by the shipping industry. Among these were the now prominent Niarchos and Onassis families.

The advent of the republic in 1975 reflected the social changes which had occurred since the war. New wealth and success became more admired than aristocratic birth or prestige. Greece is now a socially mobile society. Living standards have improved universally since the 1950s.

WORLD RANKING

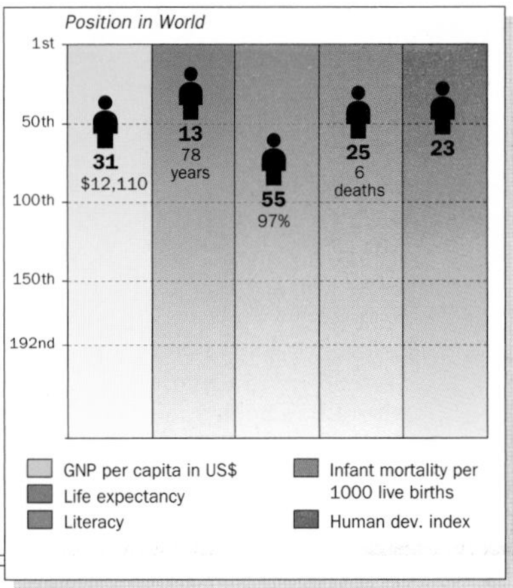

Position in World
1st
50th
100th
150th
192nd
31
$12,110
13
78 years
55
97%
25
6 deaths
23
GNP per capita in US$
Life expectancy
Literacy
Infant mortality per 1000 live births
Human dev. index

G

GRENADA

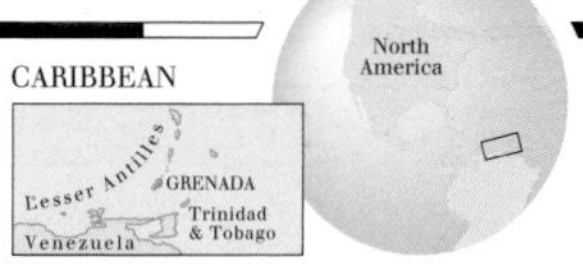
CARIBBEAN
North America
Lesser Antilles
GRENADA
Trinidad & Tobago
Venezuela

OFFICIAL NAME: Grenada **CAPITAL:** St. George's
POPULATION: 99,500 **CURRENCY:** Eastern Caribbean dollar **OFFICIAL LANGUAGE:** English

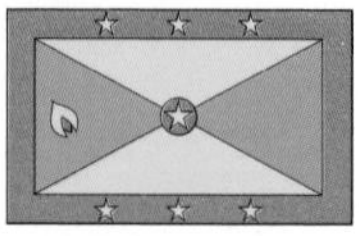

1974 | 1974 | Feb 7 | WG | -4 | +1473 | .gd

THE MOST SOUTHERLY of the Windward Islands, Grenada also includes the islands of Carriacou and Petite Martinique. It is the world's second-largest nutmeg producer. Grenada became a focus of international attention in 1983 when the USA, with token backing from several Caribbean states, mounted an invasion to sever its growing links with Castro's Cuba. Grenada is one of the seven members of the OECS.

G

CLIMATE

Tropical oceanic

WEATHER CHART

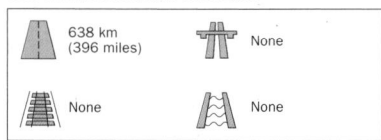

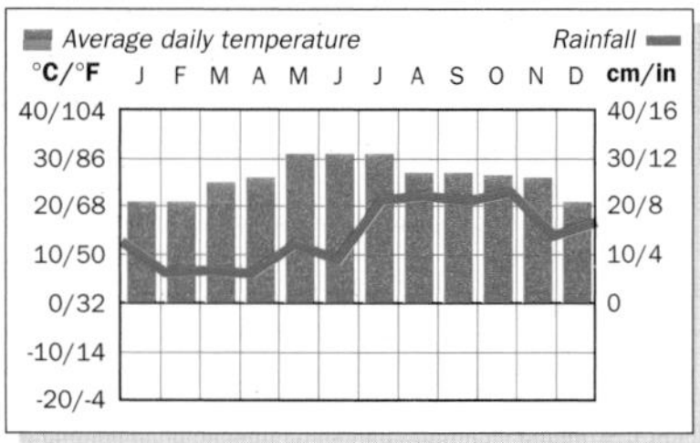
Average daily temperature
Rainfall
°C/°F J F M A M J J A S O N D cm/in
40/104
30/86
20/68
10/50
0/32
-10/14
-20/-4
40/16
30/12
20/8
10/4
0

Rainfall totals 150 cm (59 in) on the coast, and twice that in the mountains. Hurricanes occur in the rainy season.

TRANSPORTATION

Drive on left

Point Salines, St. George's 434,966 passengers

5 ships 887 grt

THE TRANSPORTATION NETWORK

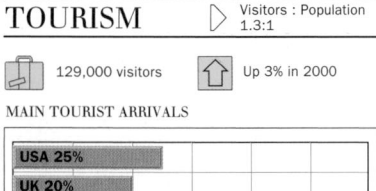

638 km (396 miles)

None

None

None

Roads in the interior are poor. The airport is being expanded and a new cruise ship port is planned.

TOURISM

Visitors : Population 1.3:1

129,000 visitors

Up 3% in 2000

MAIN TOURIST ARRIVALS

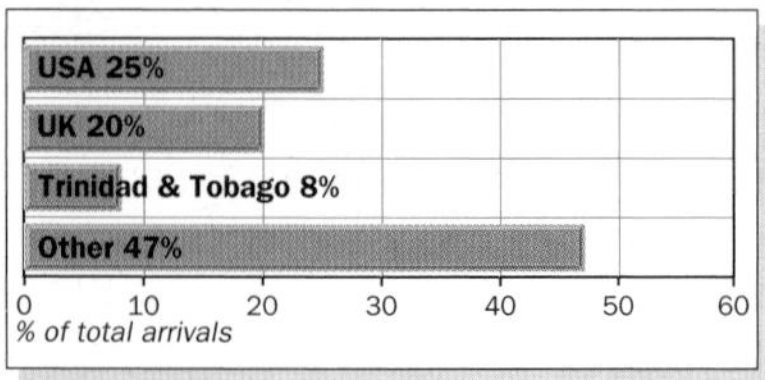
USA 25%
UK 20%
Trinidad & Tobago 8%
Other 47%
0 10 20 30 40 50 60
% of total arrivals

Tourism has developed since the 1984 completion of the international airport, though there has been a concurrent decline in the arrival of cruise ships; the Crown Dynasty company folded in 1999, with a major impact on tourist numbers.

PEOPLE

Pop. density high

English, English Creole

293/km² (758/mi²)

THE URBAN/RURAL POPULATION SPLIT

37%
63%

RELIGIOUS PERSUASION

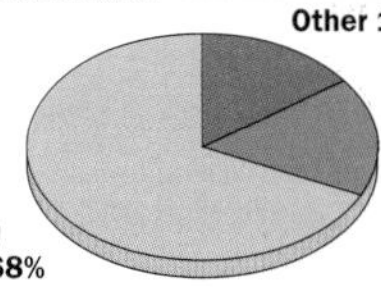
Other 15%
Anglican 17%
Roman Catholic 68%

Most Grenadians are descendants of Africans brought over to work sugar plantations in the 16th to 19th centuries. Intermarriage between this group and the small numbers of Europeans and indigenous Amerindians has meant that there is little racial tension. As in other Caribbean states, extended families with absentee fathers are not uncommon.

GRENADA

Total Land Area : 340 sq. km (131 sq. miles)

POPULATION
- over 10 000
- under 10 000

LAND HEIGHT
- 500m/1640ft
- 200m/656ft
- Sea Level

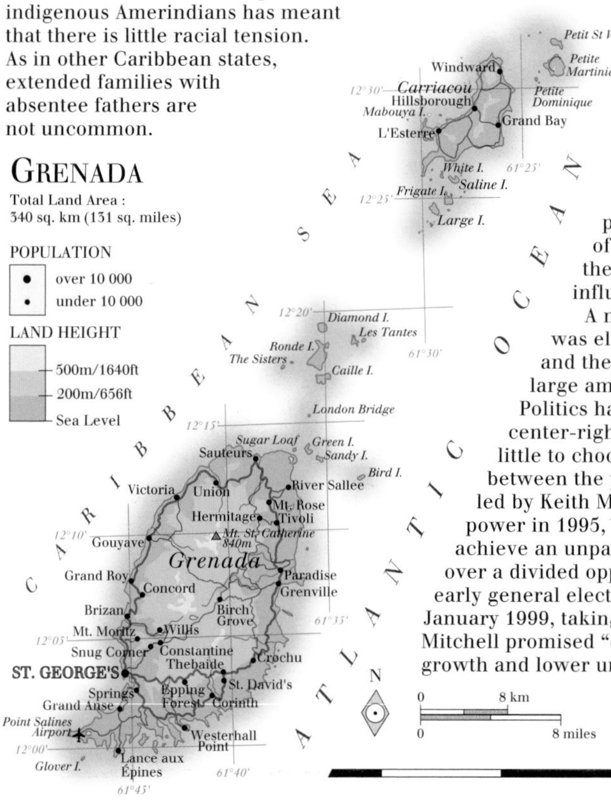
CARIBBEAN SEA
ATLANTIC OCEAN
Petit St Vincent I.
Petite Martinique
Windward
Carriacou
Hillsborough
Mabouya I.
L'Esterre
Petite Dominique
Grand Bay
White I.
Frigate I.
Saline I.
Large I.
Diamond I.
Les Tantes
Ronde I.
The Sisters
Caille I.
London Bridge
Sugar Loaf
Green I.
Sandy I.
Bird I.
Sauteurs
Victoria
Union
River Sallee
Mt. Rose
Hermitage
Tivoli
Mt. St. Catherine 840m
Gouyave
Grenada
Grand Roy
Paradise
Concord
Grenville
Birch Grove
Brizan
Mt. Moritz
Willis
Snug Corner
Constantine
Thebaide
Crochu
ST. GEORGE'S
Springs
Epping Forest
St. David's
Grand Anse
Corinth
Point Salines Airport
Westerhall Point
Glover I.
Lance aux Épines
0 8 km
0 8 miles

POLITICS

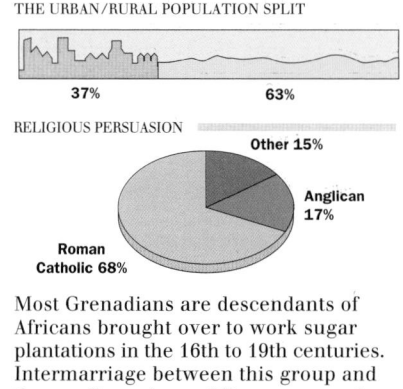

Multiparty elections

1999/2004

HM Queen Elizabeth II

AT THE LAST ELECTION

House of Representatives 15 seats

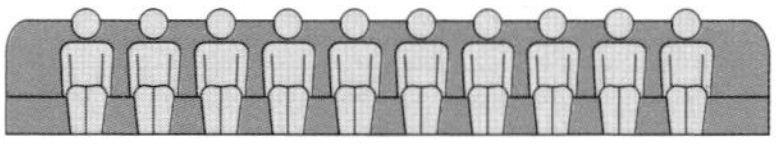

100% NNP

NNP = New National Party

Senate 13 seats

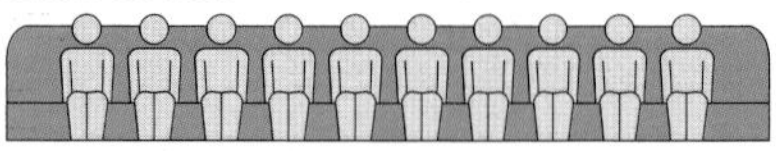

The members of the Senate are appointed by the prime minister and the leader of the opposition

The past 25 years have seen Grenada move from a position of political isolation toward integration with the rest of the region. The late Sir Eric Gairy, when prime minister, was as well known for his eccentric requests to the UN Security Council – he once asked it to investigate UFOs on the island – as for his intimidation of political opponents by means of organized gangs. Gairy was overthrown in 1979 by armed militants of the New Jewel Movement led by Maurice Bishop, a charismatic socialist who in turn was deposed and executed by former allies in 1983. This coup was the pretext for the US invasion, the primary motive of which was to end the perceived Cuban influence in Grenada. A new government was elected in 1984, and the USA provided large amounts of aid. Politics has since been center-right, and there is little to choose ideologically between the parties. The NNP, led by Keith Mitchell, gained power in 1995, and went on to achieve an unparalleled victory over a divided opposition in the early general election held in January 1999, taking all 15 seats. Mitchell promised "explosive" growth and lower unemployment.

WORLD AFFAIRS

Joined UN in 1974

ACS | Caricom | Comm | OAS | OECS

Priorities are the relations with the rest of the Windward Islands group, access to the EU for bananas, and strategies with Indonesia aimed at steadying world nutmeg prices. Since 1983, it has supported US policy in the Caribbean.

AID

Recipient

US$10m (receipts)

Up 67% in 1999

The main aid sources are the UK, the EU, the USA, Japan, and Taiwan. Cuba, before the 1983 invasion, helped build the airport at Point Salines.

DEFENSE

No compulsory military service

Minimal expenditure

Defense spending is falling

The People's Revolutionary Army, created by Maurice Bishop in the wake of his 1979 coup, was replaced in 1983 by a paramilitary defense unit trained by the USA and the UK.

ECONOMICS

Inflation 2.6% p.a. (1990–1999)

US$334m

2.70 Eastern Caribbean dollars

SCORE CARD

❑ World GNP Ranking	173rd
❑ GNP per Capita	US$3440
❑ Balance of Payments	US$–58m
❑ Inflation	0.2%
❑ Unemployment	15%

Strengths

Second-largest producer of nutmeg after Indonesia. Important sectors are tourism, bananas, construction, and financial services.

Weaknesses

Weak tax base, lack of diversification. Poor infrastructure. Low productivity. Large avoidance of customs duties. Smuggling.

EXPORTS

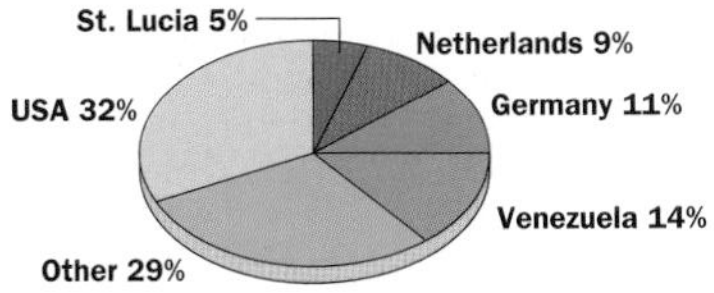
St. Lucia 5%
Netherlands 9%
Germany 11%
Venezuela 14%
Other 29%
USA 32%

IMPORTS

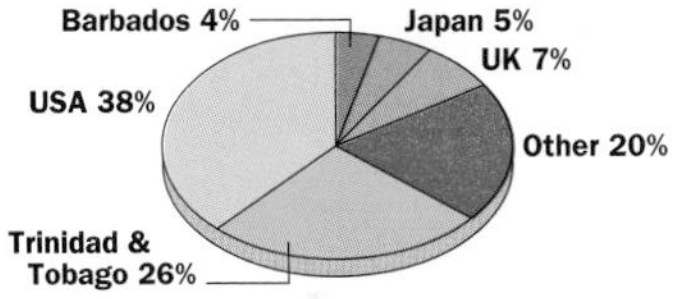
Barbados 4%
Japan 5%
UK 7%
Other 20%
Trinidad & Tobago 26%
USA 38%

RESOURCES

Electric power 15,000 kw

1408 tonnes

Not an oil producer

13,000 sheep, 7000 goats, 220,000 chickens

None

Grenada has no strategic resources and has to import most of its energy. Its major asset is the nutmeg industry, which accounts for almost one-quarter of total world production.

ENVIRONMENT

Not available

None

1.9 tonnes per capita

Tourism threatens some key environmental sites, including a remnant of rainforest. Resort projects have caused serious beach erosion, in turn requiring costly coastal defenses. An environmental levy on visitors is opposed by cruise companies.

MEDIA

TV ownership high

There are no daily newspapers

PUBLISHING AND BROADCAST MEDIA

There are no daily newspapers. The *Grenadian Voice* and the *Grenada Guardian* are published weekly

1 partly state-owned service

3 services: 1 partly state-owned, 2 independent

The government sold a 60% share in the then Grenada Broadcasting Corporation (GBC) in 1999. There is an independent private press.

CRIME

Death penalty not used

Grenada does not publish prison figures

Up 345% 1989–1996

The doubling of poverty during the 1990s and high unemployment have contributed to a rising crime rate. Narcotics trafficking is also a growing problem. However, while there is street crime, the level of violence is low.

EDUCATION

School leaving age: 16

96%

535 students

Education follows the former British selective 11-plus system. Many students go on to the University of the West Indies, or to college in the USA.

HEALTH

Welfare state health benefits

1 per 2000 people

Heart diseases, cancers, nutritional disorders

After 1979, Cuban physicians provided a basic health care system. There are free weekly clinics in each district, and treatment in subsidized state hospitals now matches the Caribbean average. In 1999 Cuba began its promised expansion of the general hospital.

St George's harbor. *The newest hotel developments are on the beaches to the south of the capital.*

CHRONOLOGY

A French colony from 1650, Grenada was captured by the British in 1762.

- ❑ **1951** Universal suffrage introduced.
- ❑ **1967–1974** Internal self-government. Full independence from the UK.
- ❑ **1979** Coup. Maurice Bishop prime minister. Growing links with Cuba.
- ❑ **1983** US invasion establishes pro-US administration.
- ❑ **1999** NNP reelected, taking all 15 seats in House of Representatives.

SPENDING

GDP/cap. increase

CONSUMPTION AND SPENDING

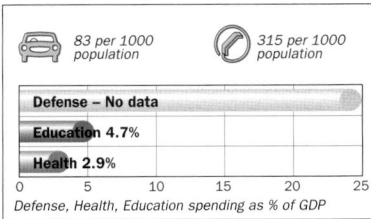

83 per 1000 population

315 per 1000 population

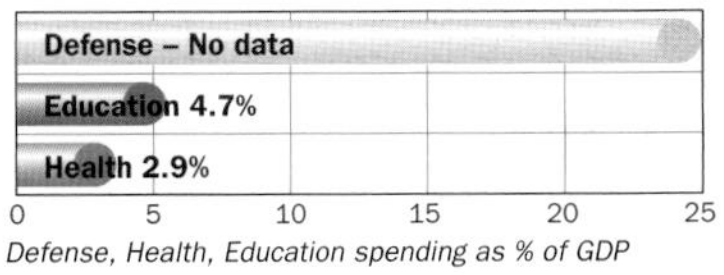
Defense – No data
Education 4.7%
Health 2.9%
0
5
10
15
20
25
Defense, Health, Education spending as % of GDP

Wealth disparities in Grenada are less marked than in most Caribbean states, but poverty is growing. The wealthiest groups are those in control of the nutmeg trade.

WORLD RANKING

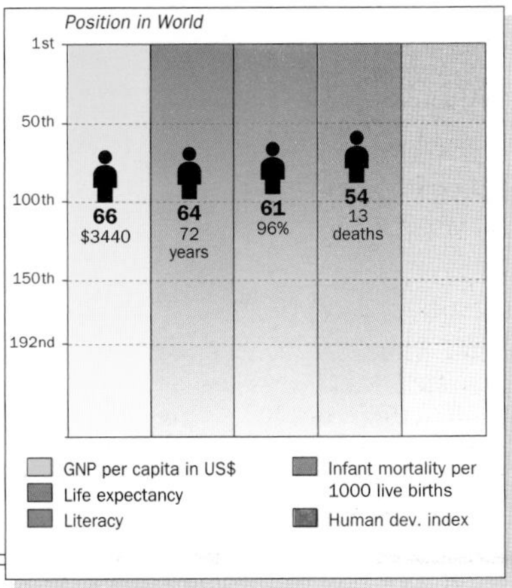
Position in World
1st
50th
100th
150th
192nd
66
$3440
64
72
years
61
96%
54
13
deaths
GNP per capita in US$
Life expectancy
Literacy
Infant mortality per 1000 live births
Human dev. index

G

GUATEMALA

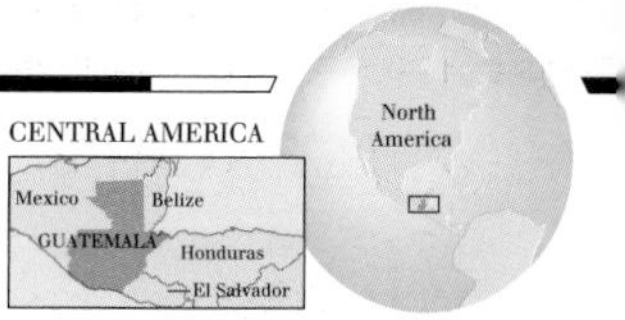
CENTRAL AMERICA
North America
Mexico
Belize
GUATEMALA
Honduras
El Salvador

OFFICIAL NAME: Republic of Guatemala **CAPITAL:** Guatemala City
POPULATION: 11.4 million **CURRENCY:** Quetzal **OFFICIAL LANGUAGE:** Spanish

1838 | 1838 | Sept 15 | GCA | -6 | +502 | .gt

THE LARGEST AND MOST POPULOUS of the states of the Central American isthmus, Guatemala was home to the ancient Maya civilization. Its fertile Pacific and Caribbean coastal lowlands give way to the highlands which dominate the country. Independent since 1838, Guatemala's history since 1954 has been one of military rule. Civilian rule was restored in 1986, but 90% of the population live below the poverty line.

G

CLIMATE

Tropical equatorial/ wet & dry

WEATHER CHART

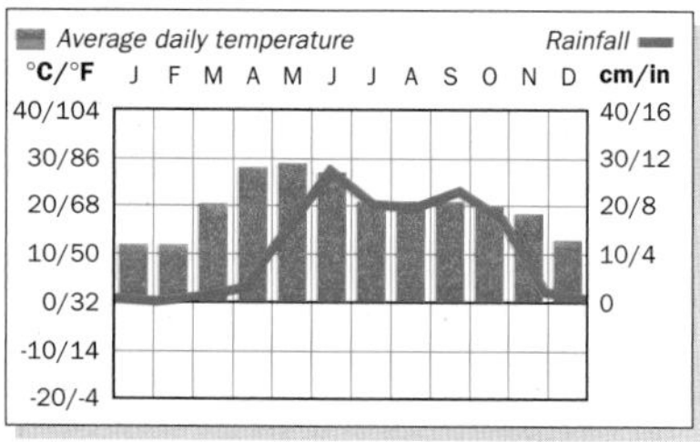
Average daily temperature
Rainfall
°C/°F
J F M A M J J A S O N D
cm/in
40/104
30/86
20/68
10/50
0/32
-10/14
-20/-4
40/16
30/12
20/8
10/4
0

The climate varies with altitude: daytime temperatures average 28°C (82°F) in tropical coast areas and 20°C (68°F) in the more temperate central highlands.

TRANSPORTATION

Drive on right

La Aurora, Guatemala City 939,000 passengers

5 ships 800 grt

THE TRANSPORTATION NETWORK

3616 km (2247 miles)	140 km (87 miles)
1994 km (1239 miles)	260 km (162 miles)

Good roads link the major towns. The railroad and two international airports are attracting foreign investment.

TOURISM

Visitors : Population 1:14

826,000 visitors

No change in 2000

MAIN TOURIST ARRIVALS

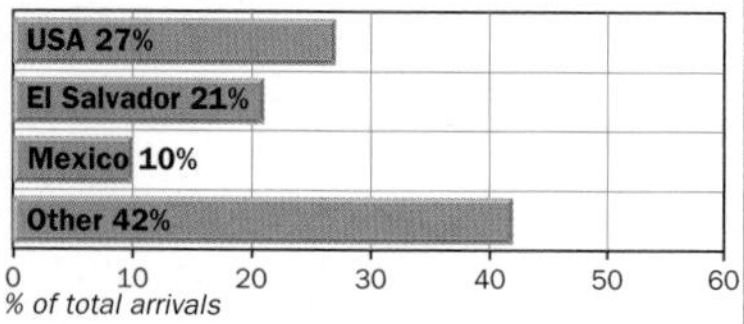
USA 27%
El Salvador 21%
Mexico 10%
Other 42%
0
10
20
30
40
50
60
% of total arrivals

Tourism rapidly revived after the military excesses in the 1980s, but postwar crime, including an increase in mob violence, deters visitors. Mayan ruins are the top attractions.

PEOPLE

Pop. density medium

Quiché, Mam, Cakchiquel, Kekchí, Spanish

105/km² (272/mi²)

THE URBAN/RURAL POPULATION SPLIT

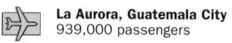

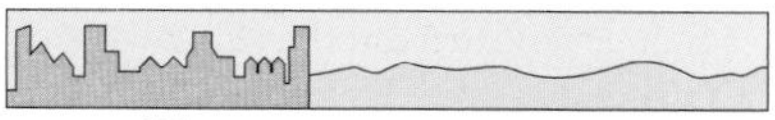
40%
60%

ETHNIC MAKEUP

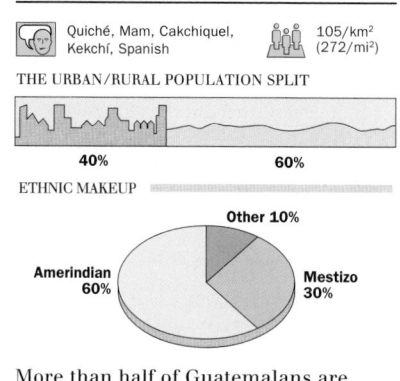

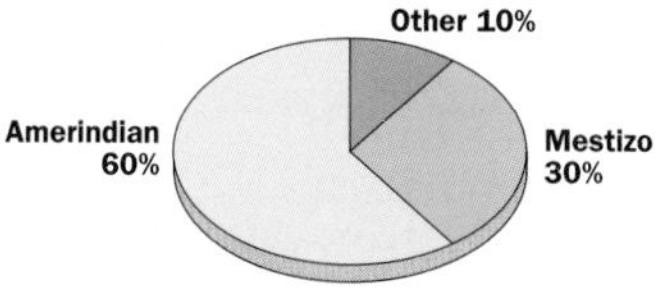
Other 10%
Amerindian 60%
Mestizo 30%

More than half of Guatemalans are Amerindians, descendants of the original Mayas. Culture and language distinguish them from *ladino* groups. *Ladinos* include a white elite, a large mixed race group, and also Amerindians rejecting traditional dress and language to avoid discrimination. Political power and 65% of land are held by a few *ladino* families. Amerindians mainly live in the highlands, by subsistence farming. In a 1999 plebiscite, *ladinos* rejected proposed reforms recognizing 23 Amerindian languages and the right of Amerindians to have judicial hearings in their own languages.

POLITICS

Multiparty elections

1999/2003

President Alfonso Portillo

AT THE LAST ELECTION

Congress of the Republic 113 seats

56% FRG
32% PAN
9% NNA
3% Others

FRG = Guatemalan Republican Front **PAN** = National Advancement Party **NNA** = New Nation Alliance

A military government which came to power in 1954 with US backing brutally suppressed opposition and persecuted the highland Amerindians until the return of democracy in 1986. Civil war effectively continued until President Arzú of the PAN concluded a peace agreement with the Guatemalan National Revolutionary Unity (URNG) guerrillas in 1996. The 36-year war had claimed 200,000 lives, mostly innocent civilians. In presidential elections in 1999 Alfonso Portillo of the right-wing FRG, running on a strong law and order platform, defeated the PAN candidate.

Efraín Ríos Montt, military ruler in 1982–1986, remains a force in politics and in 2001 was elected president of the Congress, despite being investigated by a Spanish court on charges of genocide. Constant tension exists between the legislative and executive branches of government.

GUATEMALA

Total Land Area : 108 430 sq. km (41 865 sq. miles)

POPULATION

- over 1 000 000
- over 100 000
- over 50 000
- over 10 000

LAND HEIGHT

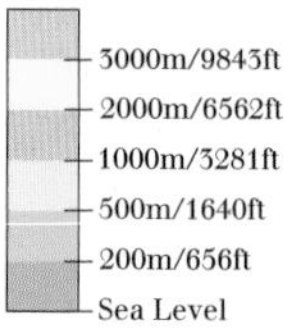
3000m/9843ft
2000m/6562ft
1000m/3281ft
500m/1640ft
200m/656ft
Sea Level

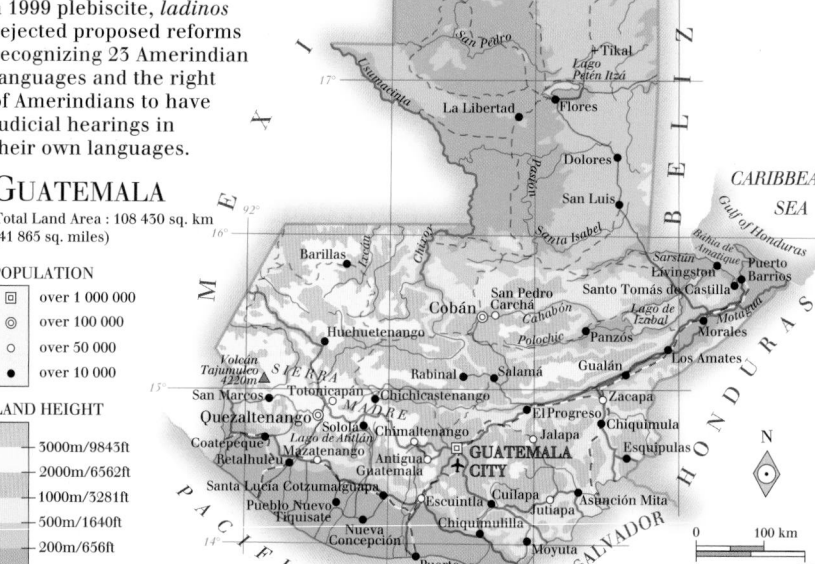

MEXICO
BELIZE
CARIBBEAN SEA
Gulf of Honduras
HONDURAS
EL SALVADOR
PACIFIC OCEAN
San Pedro
Tikal
Lago Petén Itzá
Usumacinta
La Libertad
Flores
Pasión
Dolores
San Luis
Santa Isabel
Bahía de Amatique
Sarstún
Livingston
Puerto Barrios
Santo Tomás de Castilla
Barillas
Chixoy
Cobán
San Pedro Carchá
Cahabón
Lago de Izabal
Motagua
Morales
Huehuetenango
Polochic
Panzós
Los Amates
Rabinal
Salamá
Gualán
SIERRA MADRE
Totonicapán
Chichicastenango
Zacapa
Quezaltenango
Sololá
Chimaltenango
El Progreso
Chiquimula
Jalapa
Lago de Atitlán
Mazatenango
Antigua Guatemala
GUATEMALA CITY
Esquipulas
Santa Lucía Cotzumalguapa
Escuintla
Cuilapa
Jutiapa
Asunción Mita
Pueblo Nuevo Tiquisate
Chiquimulilla
Nueva Concepción
Moyuta
Puerto San José
100 km
100 miles
N

WORLD AFFAIRS

Joined UN in 1945

ACS | Geplac | NAM | OAS | San José

Economic relations with the USA and neighboring states are priorities. A UN mission deployed to oversee the 1996 peace accord is still in place. A claim to half of Belize was revived in early 2000.

AID

Recipient

$293m (receipts)

Up 26% in 1999

In 1998 the government agreed the disbursement of the remaining $926 million of the $1.9 billion pledged by the international donors for postwar reconstruction. 8.4 million quetzales were loaned in hurricane relief.

DEFENSE

Compulsory military service

$149m

Down 6% in 1999

A damning "truth commission" report in 1999 found the armed forces and their allies guilty of 93% of human rights violations during the civil war. The army remains largely unreformed and a potent sociopolitical force.

ECONOMICS

Inflation 10.9% p.a. (1990–1999)

$18.6bn

7.6616–7.7815 quetzales

SCORE CARD

❑ World GNP Ranking	69th
❑ GNP per Capita	$1680
❑ Balance of Payments	$-1.03bn
❑ Inflation	4.9%
❑ Unemployment	8%

STRENGTHS

Main exports are coffee, sugar, beef, bananas, and cardamom. Privatizations boost foreign investor confidence.

WEAKNESSES

Traditional exports vulnerable to world price changes. Shaky financial system. Inequalities in land and wealth limit domestic market. Tax evasion.

EXPORTS

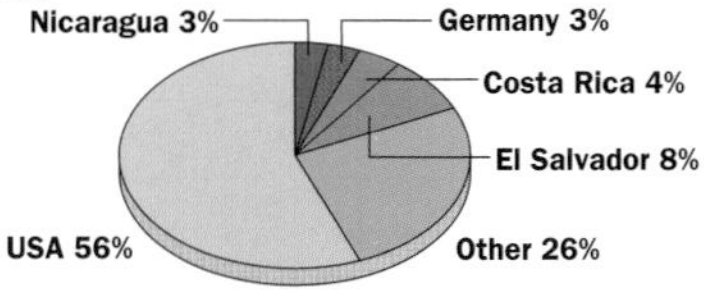
Nicaragua 3%
Germany 3%
Costa Rica 4%
El Salvador 8%
USA 56%
Other 26%

IMPORTS

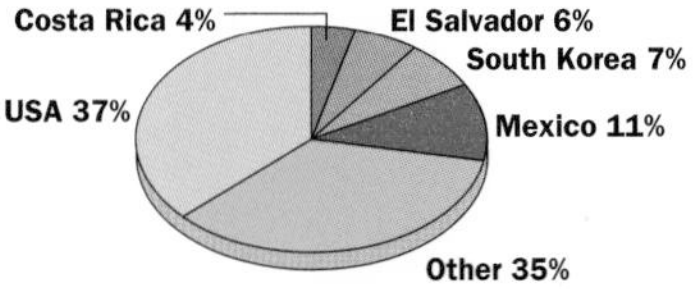
Costa Rica 4%
El Salvador 6%
South Korea 7%
USA 37%
Mexico 11%
Other 35%

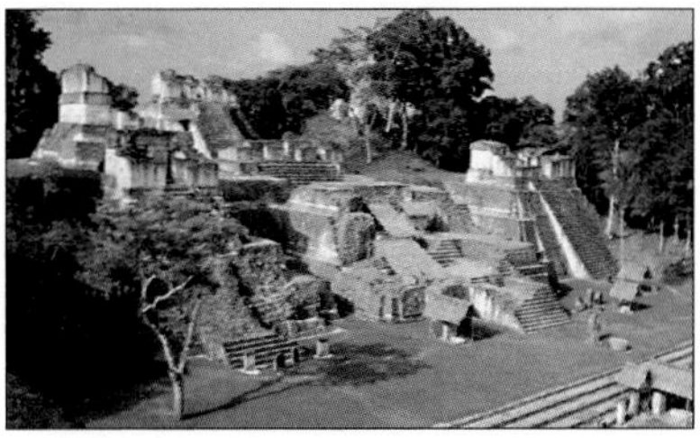

North Acropolis, Tikal, Petén. One of the largest lowland Maya cities, Tikal was virtually abandoned by about 900CE.

RESOURCES

Electric power 938,000 kw

11,303 tonnes

19,549 b/d (reserves 199,836,000 bbl)

2.3m cattle, 825,000 pigs, 24m chickens

Oil, antimony, lead, tungsten, nickel, copper

Agriculture provides 25% of GDP and about 70% of export earnings. Guatemala is the world's largest producer of cardamom. The civil war hindered the exploitation of oil reserves and hydroelectric potential.

ENVIRONMENT

Sustainability rank: 61st

17% (0.5% partially protected)

0.8 tonnes per capita

Forest cover has been halved to 35% since 1954 due to intensive agriculture. The excessive use of pesticides, many banned in the USA, threaten health. Pollution and waste are serious problems, especially in the capital, Guatemala City.

MEDIA

TV ownership medium

Daily newspaper circulation 33 per 1000 people

PUBLISHING AND BROADCAST MEDIA

There are 7 daily newspapers, including *Prensa Libre, Siglo Veintiuno, El Gráfico,* and the state *Diario de Centroamérica*

5 services: 1 state-owned, 4 independent

85 stations: 5 state-owned, 80 independent

Powerful groups own the media, but newspapers can be hard-hitting. There is less military, government, or private-sector control over radio stations.

CRIME

Death penalty used

Guatemala does not publish prison figures

Crime is rising

Violence is high. In 2000 the Interior Ministry purged the police, which had been corrupted by drug-trafficking.

EDUCATION

School leaving age: 14

69%

80,228 students

Education is only for the privileged. A literacy rate of 69% makes Guatemala one of the worst educated countries in Latin America.

CHRONOLOGY

The site of the Maya civilization, Guatemala declared independence from Spain in 1821. It became a fully independent nation in 1838.

- ❑ **1954** US-backed coup topples reformist government.
- ❑ **1966–1984** Counterinsurgency war; highlands "pacification."
- ❑ **1986–1993** Return of civilian rule; President Serrano elected. Flees country after abortive "self-coup."
- ❑ **1996** President Arzú elected; peace deal with URNG guerrillas, ending 36 years of civil war.
- ❑ **1998** Bishop Juan Gerardi, human rights campaigner, murdered.
- ❑ **1999** "Truth Commission" blames army for most human rights abuses. Portillo and FRG win elections.

G

HEALTH

Welfare state health benefits

1 per 1111 people

Gastrointestinal infections, tuberculosis, heart disease, violence

Health spending is a budget priority as a result of pressure from the UN and multilateral lenders. Gastrointestinal and other infections directly linked to poverty remain the main causes of death.

SPENDING

GDP/cap. increase

CONSUMPTION AND SPENDING

52 per 1000 population

55 per 1000 population

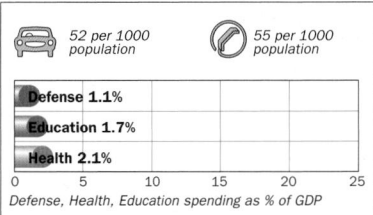

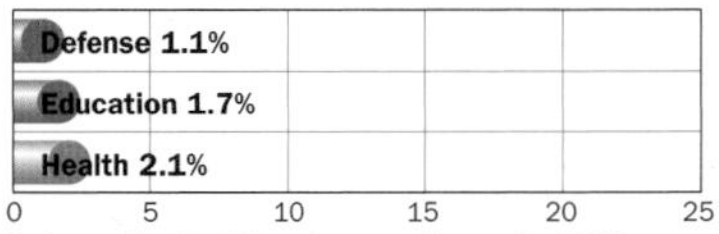
Defense 1.1%
Education 1.7%
Health 2.1%
0
5
10
15
20
25

Defense, Health, Education spending as % of GDP

Poverty has risen since 1980: 90% of the population now live below the poverty line. The richest 10% control an estimated 46% of the country's national wealth.

WORLD RANKING

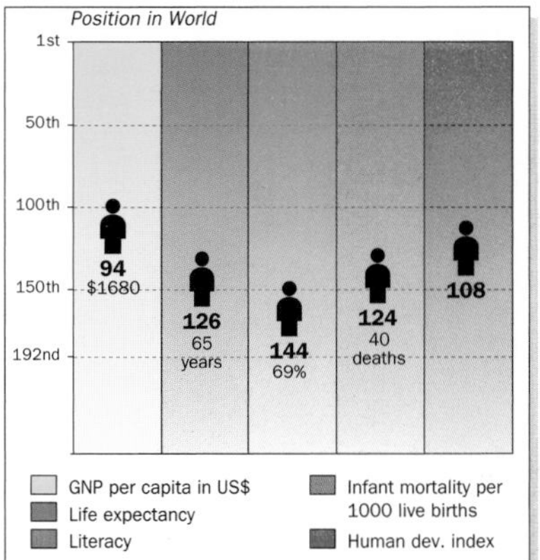
Position in World
1st
50th
100th
150th
192nd
94
$1680
126
65 years
144
69%
124
40 deaths
108
GNP per capita in US$
Life expectancy
Literacy
Infant mortality per 1000 live births
Human dev. index

Guinea

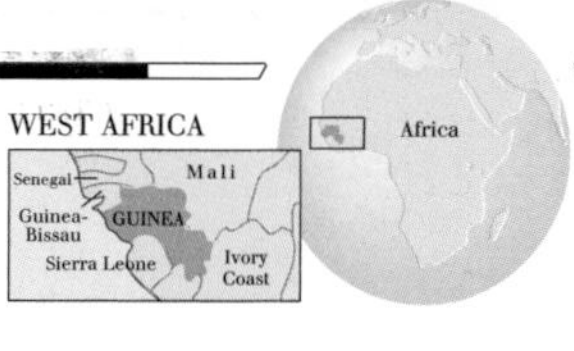
WEST AFRICA
Senegal
Mali
Guinea-Bissau
GUINEA
Sierra Leone
Ivory Coast
Africa

Official Name: Republic of Guinea **Capital:** Conakry
Population: 7.4 million **Currency:** Guinea franc **Official Language:** French

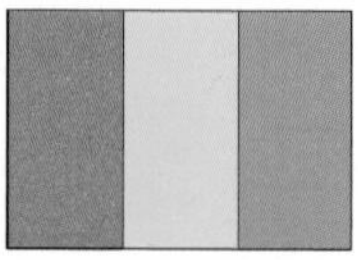

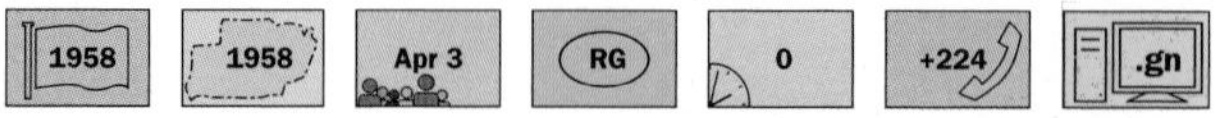
1958
1958
Apr 3
RG
0
+224
.gn

Guinea lies on the western coast of Africa. The central densely forested or savanna highlands slope down to coastal plains and swamps in the west and to the semidesert of the north. Military rule, established in 1984, ended with legislative elections in 1995; however, the results were disputed.

CLIMATE

Tropical monsoon

WEATHER CHART

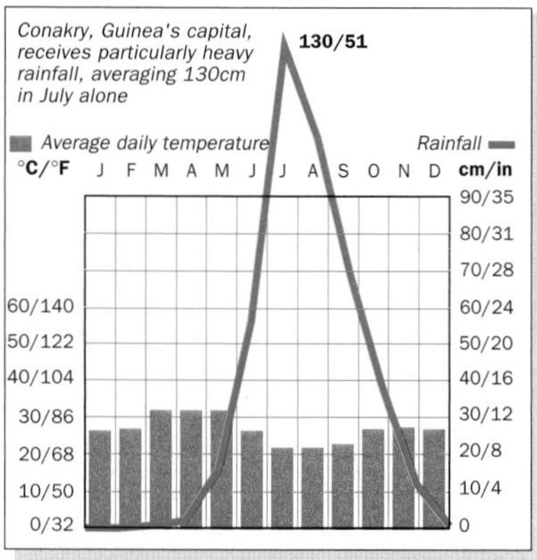
Conakry, Guinea's capital, receives particularly heavy rainfall, averaging 130cm in July alone
130/51
Average daily temperature
Rainfall
°C/°F
J F M A M J J A S O N D
cm/in
90/35
80/31
70/28
60/140
60/24
50/122
50/20
40/104
40/16
30/86
30/12
20/68
20/8
10/50
10/4
0/32
0

Guinea's climate is similar to Sierra Leone's. Conakry's six-month rainy season peaks dramatically in July.

TRANSPORTATION

Drive on right

Conakry–Gbessia 316,866 passengers

30 ships 11,200 grt

THE TRANSPORTATION NETWORK

5033 km (3127 miles)

None

1045 km (649 miles)

1295 km (805 miles)

Major roads and rail lines are being rebuilt with World Bank and French aid. Much of the rail network is exclusively for the use of the bauxite industry.

A small mosque in Conakry. *Muslims make up 85% of the population; 8% are Christian. The remainder follow traditional beliefs.*

TOURISM

Visitors : Population 1:224

33,000 visitors

Up 22% in 2000

MAIN TOURIST ARRIVALS

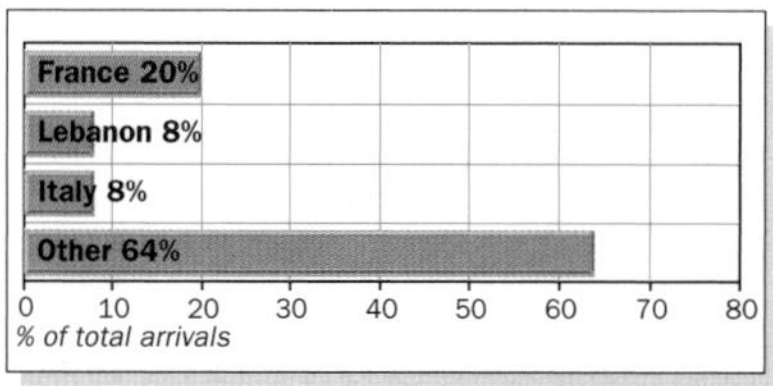
France 20%
Lebanon 8%
Italy 8%
Other 64%
0
10
20
30
40
50
60
70
80
% of total arrivals

Limited infrastructure means that Guinea cannot exploit the tourist potential of its beaches, scenery, and rich culture.

PEOPLE

Pop. density low

Fulani, Malinke, Soussou, French

30/km² (78/mi²)

THE URBAN/RURAL POPULATION SPLIT

32%
68%

ETHNIC MAKEUP

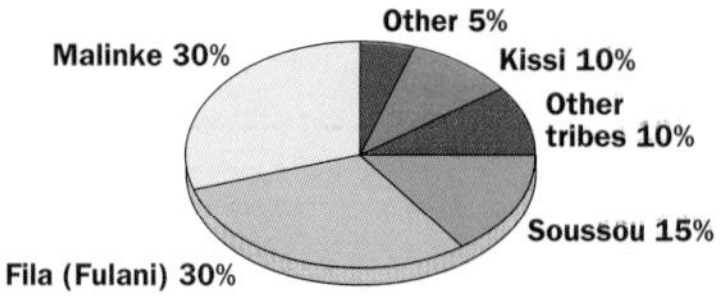
Other 5%
Malinke 30%
Kissi 10%
Other tribes 10%
Soussou 15%
Fila (Fulani) 30%

Since the death of Marxist dictator Sekou Touré in 1984, traditional rivalries have reemerged between ethnic groups. The two largest groups are the Fulani, based in the highland region of Fouta Djallon, and the Malinke, who lost the power they had held under Touré, and have suffered reprisals. Today, the coastal peoples, including the Soussou, are dominant, benefiting from renewed rivalry between the Malinke and Fulani.

The extended family system survived the climate of suspicion generated by paid informers under Sekou Touré. Women acquired influence within his Marxist party, but a Muslim revival since 1984 has reversed this trend.

Hundreds of thousands of refugees, fleeing from conflicts in neighboring countries, are now caught up in fighting in the southern border region.

POLITICS

Multiparty elections

1995/2000 (postponed indefinitely)

President Lansana Conté

AT THE LAST ELECTION

National Assembly 114 seats

8% UNR
2% UPG
62% PUP
17% RPG
8% PRP
3% Others

PUP = Party of Unity and Progress **RPG** = Rally of the Guinean People **PRP** = Party of Renewal and Progress **UNR** = Union for the New Republic **UPG** = Union for the Prosperity of Guinea

The death in 1984 of Sekou Touré, who headed the Marxist single-party regime of the Guinea Democratic Party (PDG) from 1958, opened the way for the military to intervene, with promises of multiparty elections. In 1990, a referendum overwhelmingly approved democratic changes, but the military appointed a Transitional Committee to run the country, delaying elections until the end of 1993, when incumbent leader, General Lansana Conté, won with 52% of the votes. His closest rival, the Malinke leader Alpha Condé, who had been in exile until 1992, received 20% of the votes. Opposition parties alleged that the elections had been rigged, and serious violence broke out. A disputed victory for Conté's PUP in the 1995 legislative elections was followed by a further win for Conté in the December 1998 presidential election.

Fighting escalated into civil war in 2000, with cross-border incursions in the south from rebels based in Sierra Leone and Liberia.

WORLD AFFAIRS

Joined UN in 1958

ECOWAS | OIF | OAU | OIC | OMVG

A growing concern is balancing the interests of its two major aid donors, France and the USA. Relations with neighboring Liberia deteriorated in 2000 following accusations of playing host to Liberian rebels.

AID

Recipient

$238m (receipts)

Down 34% in 1999

In 1969, the World Bank funded the Boké bauxite project, then one of its most ambitious projects. Since 1986, Western aid has grown to finance over 85% of all development projects. The 1997–2000 World Bank/IMF structural reform program foresees an annual growth rate of 5%.

G

GUINEA

Total Land Area : 245 860 sq. km (94 926 sq. miles)

POPULATION

- ◉ over 500 000
- ○ over 50 000
- ● over 10 000
- • under 10 000

LAND HEIGHT

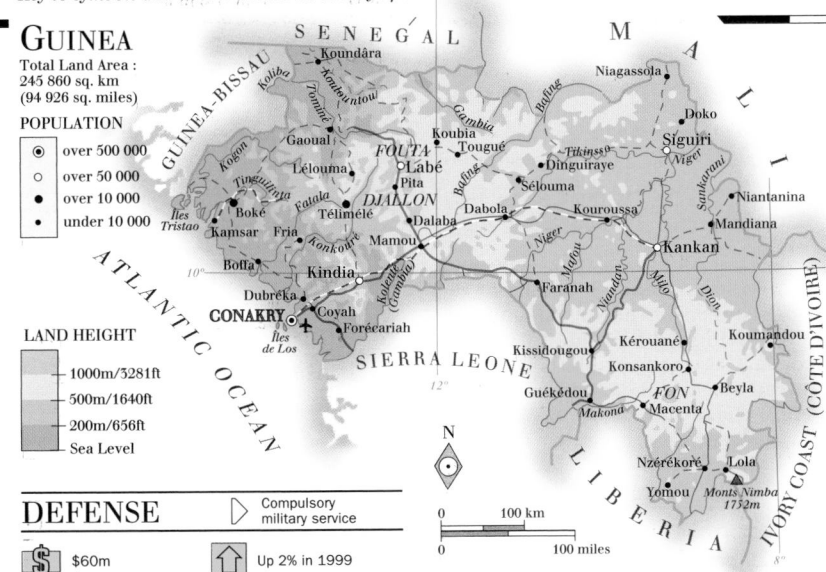

- 1000m/3281ft
- 500m/1640ft
- 200m/656ft
- Sea Level

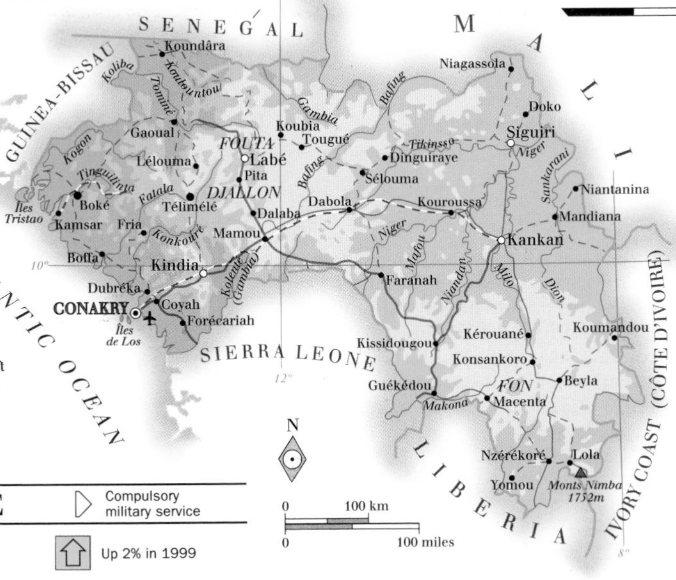

SENEGAL
MALI
GUINEA-BISSAU
ATLANTIC OCEAN
SIERRA LEONE
LIBERIA
IVORY COAST (CÔTE D'IVOIRE)
Koundâra
Niagassola
Doko
Siguiri
Koubia
Tougué
Gaoual
Labé
Pita
Lélouma
Dinguiraye
Sélouma
FOUTA DJALLON
Niantanina
Mandiana
Boké
Télimélé
Dalaba
Dabola
Kouroussa
Kamsar
Fria
Mamou
Kankan
Boffa
Kindia
Faranah
Dubréka
CONAKRY
Coyah
Forécariah
Îles de Los
Îles Tristao
Kissidougou
Kérouané
Koumandou
Konsankoro
Guékédou
FON
Macenta
Beyla
Nzérékoré
Lola
Yomou
Monts Nimba 1752m
Niger
Gambia
Milo
N
0 100 km
0 100 miles

DEFENSE

Compulsory military service

$60m

Up 2% in 1999

Defense forces consist of an army and a militia, partly merged since the 1984 coup, a gendarmerie, and a tiny navy and airforce. China, North Korea, and the Eastern bloc used to be the main arms procurement markets. Weaponry is now supplied by France and the USA.

ECONOMICS

Inflation 5.6% p.a. (1990–1999)

$3.6bn

1367–1880 Guinea francs

SCORE CARD

- ❑ WORLD GNP RANKING........................123rd
- ❑ GNP PER CAPITA $490
- ❑ BALANCE OF PAYMENTS....................$–152m
- ❑ INFLATION 4.3%
- ❑ UNEMPLOYMENT..........Widespread underemployment

STRENGTHS

Natural resources including bauxite, gold, and diamonds. Major iron ore deposits at Mount Nimba. Good soil and climate give high cash-crop yields. Relatively low inflation.

WEAKNESSES

Legacy of maladministration from Touré years. Poor infrastructure. 1990–1997 Liberian civil war set back major joint projects. Current refugee situation a drain on resources.

EXPORTS

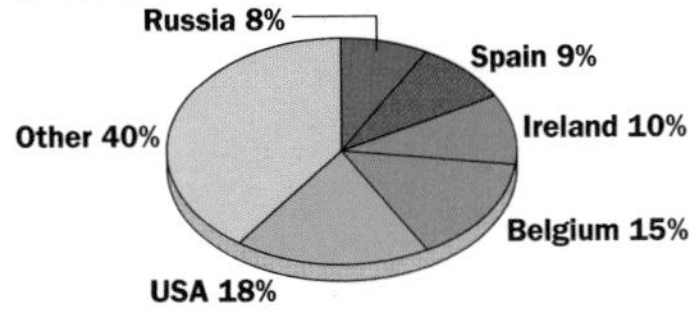

Russia 8%
Spain 9%
Ireland 10%
Belgium 15%
USA 18%
Other 40%

IMPORTS

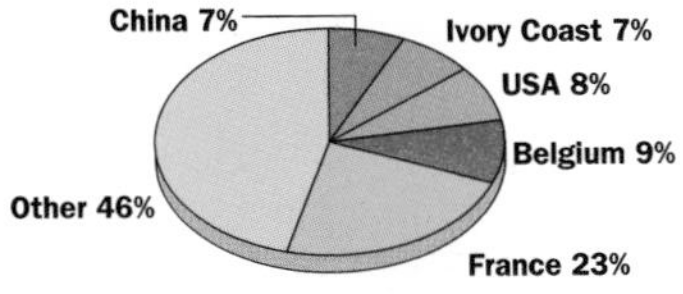

China 7%
Ivory Coast 7%
USA 8%
Belgium 9%
France 23%
Other 46%

RESOURCES

Electric power 186,000 kw

102,589 tonnes

Not an oil producer

2.37m cattle, 864,000 goats, 8.9m chickens

Bauxite, diamonds, gold, iron

Bauxite accounts for over 90% of export earnings. Guinea, with 30% of known world reserves, is the world's largest producer after Australia. Demand for electricity for bauxite processing is high. Gold production has grown steadily since 1995.

ENVIRONMENT

Not available

1%

0.2 tonnes per capita

Uncontrolled deforestation, particularly of large areas of rainforest, is the major long-term problem.

MEDIA

TV ownership low

Daily newspaper circulation 2 per 1000 people

PUBLISHING AND BROADCAST MEDIA

There is 1 daily newspaper, *Fonike*

1 state-owned service

1 state-owned service

Guinea's limited broadcast media are state-owned. The main newspaper, *Horoya*, is a weekly. There has been a slight relaxation in censorship.

CRIME

Death penalty used

Guinea does not publish prison figures

Up 20% in 1992

The death penalty was reintroduced in 2001 in an attempt to crack down on spiraling crime. Cross-border diamond smuggling is at the root of anarchy in the south.

CHRONOLOGY

France colonized Guinea in 1890, strongly opposed by the Fulani Muslim empire of Fouta Djallon.

- ❑ **1958** Full independence under Sekou Touré.
- ❑ **1984** Sekou Touré dies. Army coup.
- ❑ **1993–1995** Disputed elections.
- ❑ **1998** Conté reelected president.
- ❑ **2000** Cross-border attacks from Sierra Leone and Liberia place Guinea in a state of civil war.

EDUCATION

School leaving age: 13

41%

8151 students

French was readopted as the main teaching language in 1984, after Sekou Touré's Marxist-inspired experiments.

HEALTH

No welfare state health benefits

1 per 5000 people

Malaria, diarrheal and respiratory diseases, tuberculosis

Health provision is very poor, reflected in Guinea's high infant mortality rate and low average life expectancy. Private health care was legalized in 1984.

SPENDING

GDP/cap. increase

CONSUMPTION AND SPENDING

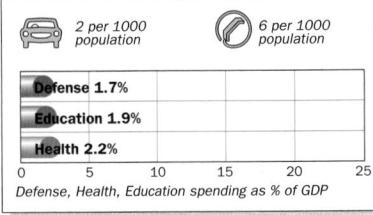

2 per 1000 population

6 per 1000 population

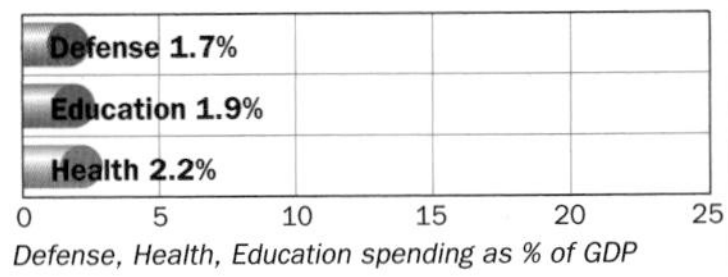

Defense 1.7%
Education 1.9%
Health 2.2%
0
5
10
15
20
25
Defense, Health, Education spending as % of GDP

Private enterprise has brought with it a new business class and Guinea now has some wealthy exiles, but much of the country remains poor and underdeveloped; GNP is below $500 per capita.

WORLD RANKING

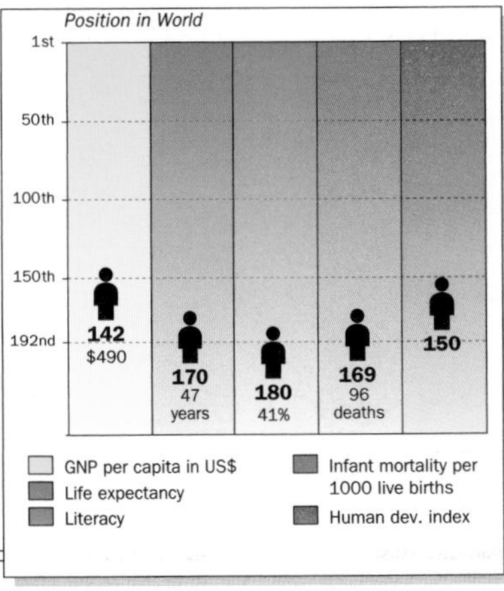

Position in World
1st
50th
100th
150th
192nd
142
$490
170
47 years
180
41%
169
96 deaths
150
GNP per capita in US$
Life expectancy
Literacy
Infant mortality per 1000 live births
Human dev. index

G

GUINEA-BISSAU

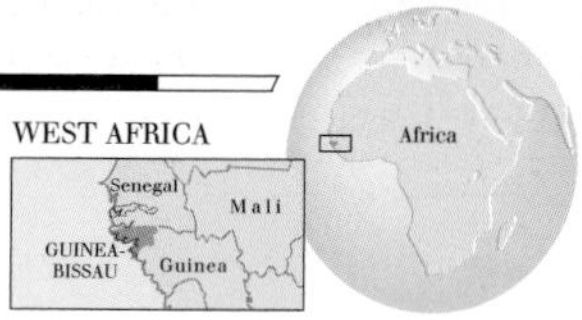
WEST AFRICA
Africa
Senegal
Mali
GUINEA-BISSAU
Guinea

OFFICIAL NAME: Republic of Guinea-Bissau **CAPITAL:** Bissau
POPULATION: 1.2 million **CURRENCY:** Guinea peso **OFFICIAL LANGUAGE:** Portuguese

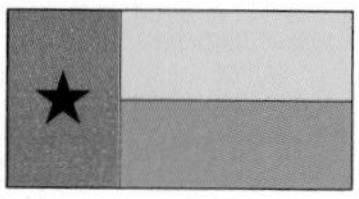

1974 | 1974 | Sept 24 | GNB | 0 | +245 | .gw

LYING ON AFRICA'S west coast, impoverished Guinea-Bissau, a former Portuguese territory, is bordered by Senegal to the north and Guinea to the south and east. Apart from savanna highlands in the northeast, the country is low-lying. The PAIGC initiated a process of change to multiparty democracy in 1990, and elections were held in 1994. A military coup in 1999 followed army rebellion the previous year, but legislative and presidential elections have since been held.

CLIMATE

Tropical monsoon

WEATHER CHART

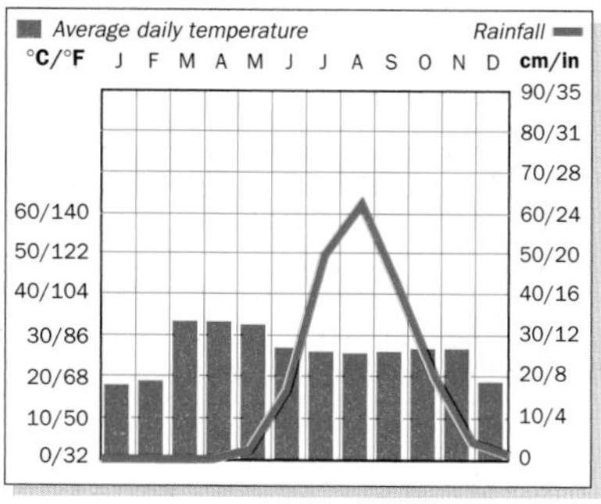
Average daily temperature
Rainfall
°C/°F
J F M A M J J A S O N D
cm/in
90/35
80/31
70/28
60/140
60/24
50/122
50/20
40/104
40/16
30/86
30/12
20/68
20/8
10/50
10/4
0/32
0

The climate is tropical. The north is affected by the Sahel, the wetter south by the Atlantic. Droughts can occur.

TRANSPORTATION

Drive on right

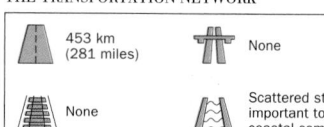

Bissalanca International, Bissau

23 ships 6079 grt

THE TRANSPORTATION NETWORK

453 km (281 miles)

None

None

Scattered stretches important to coastal commerce

The many waterways and islands make water transportation as vital as the roads. Both are being improved.

TOURISM

Not available

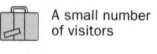

A small number of visitors

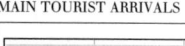

No significant change from year to year

MAIN TOURIST ARRIVALS

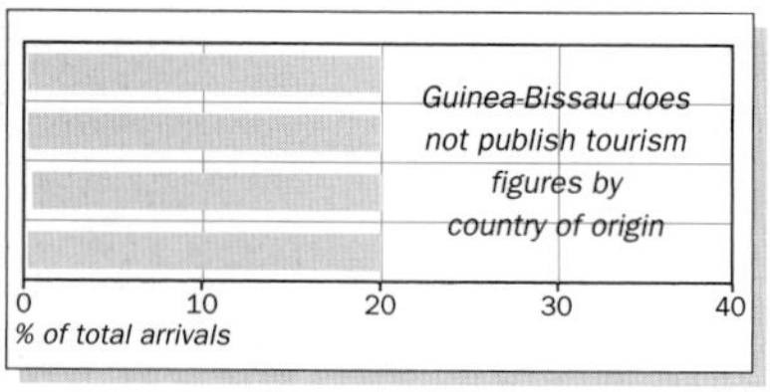
Guinea-Bissau does not publish tourism figures by country of origin
0
10
20
30
40
% of total arrivals

Lack of tourist facilities means that the country remains a destination for only the most independent of travelers.

PEOPLE

Pop. density low

Portuguese Creole, Balante, Fulani, Malinke, Portuguese

43/km² (111/mi²)

THE URBAN/RURAL POPULATION SPLIT

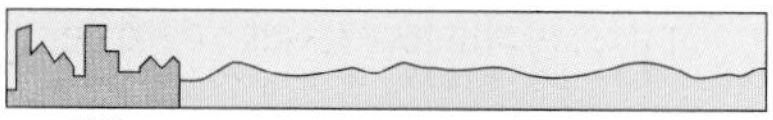
23%
77%

RELIGIOUS PERSUASION

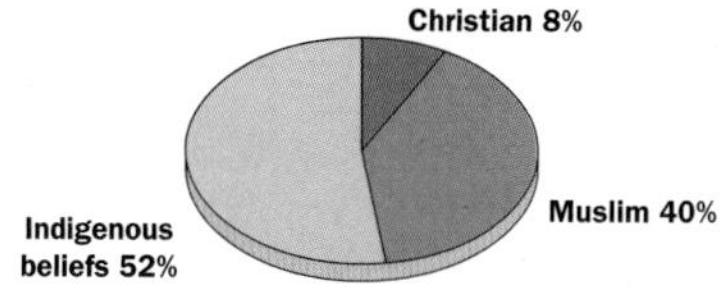
Christian 8%
Muslim 40%
Indigenous beliefs 52%

About 98% of Guinea-Bissau's people come from indigenous ethnic groups. The largest is the southern Balante, who form almost one-third of the population. Mixed-race *mestiço* and European minorities make up just 2% of the population. Although small in number, the *mestiços* – many of whom derive from Cape Verde, Portugal's other former west African colony – still dominate the bureaucracy. Resentment at this, especially among the Balante, who provided most of the PAIGC troops in the independence war, was one cause of the 1980 coup. The majority of the population live and work on small family farms, grouped in self-contained villages. The bulk of the urban population live in the capital, Bissau.

POLITICS

Multiparty elections

1999/2003

President Kumba Yalla

AT THE LAST ELECTION

National People's Assembly 102 seats

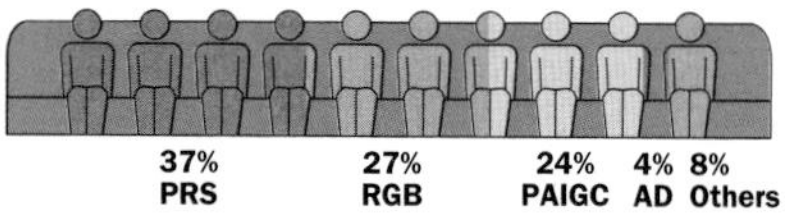
37% PRS
27% RGB
24% PAIGC
4% AD
8% Others

PRS = Party for Social Renewal **RGB** = Guinea-Bissau Resistance **PAIGC** = African Party for the Independence of Guinea and Cape Verde **AD** = Alliance for Democracy

Twenty years of one-party rule ended in 1994, when opposition groups disputed the ruling PAIGC's win in multiparty elections. A period of instability led to an army rebellion in 1998 and eight months of fighting between loyalists of President João Bernardo Vieira and the army chief, General Ansumane Mane, during which about half the population was displaced. Peace was restored by ECOWAS troops and a national unity government was formed, only to be overthrown by the army in May 1999. Mane, the coup leader, convened elections in November which saw victory for the PRS. The party's candidate Kumba Yalla was elected president in January 2000. The following November, Mane was killed in another, failed, coup attempt.

WORLD AFFAIRS

Joined UN in 1974

ECOWAS | CPLP | OIF | OAU | OIC

Relations with Sierra Leone and Liberia are extremely tense due to the activities of various rebel militias along the southern borders. Senegalese and Guinean troops intervened in mid-1998 to suppress an anti-government army rebellion.

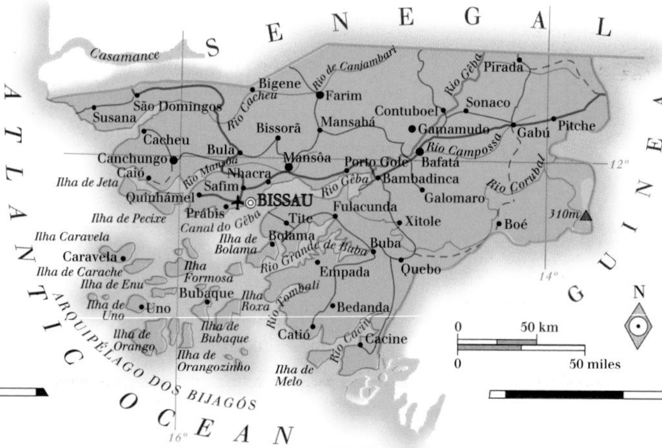
SENEGAL
GUINEA
ATLANTIC OCEAN
ARQUIPÉLAGO DOS BIJAGÓS
Casamance
São Domingos
Susana
Bigene
Rio Cacheu
Farim
Rio de Canjambari
Pirada
Rio Gêba
Sonaco
Contuboel
Gamamudo
Gabú
Pitche
Rio Campossa
Bafatá
Bissorã
Mansabá
Cacheu
Bula
Canchungo
Caió
Mansôa
Porto Gole
Nhacra
Safim
Ilha de Jeta
Quinhámel
BISSAU
Rio Gêba
Bambadinca
Galomaro
Rio Corubal
Ilha de Pecixe
Prábis
Canal do Gêba
Tite
Fulacunda
Xitole
Boé
310m
Ilha Caravela
Caravela
Ilha de Bolama
Bolama
Buba
Rio Grande de Buba
Ilha de Carache
Ilha Formosa
Empada
Quebo
Ilha de Enu
Bubaque
Ilha Roxa
Rio Tombali
Ilha de Uno
Uno
Bedanda
Ilha de Orango
Ilha de Bubaque
Catió
Cacine
Rio Cacine
Ilha de Orangozinho
Ilha de Melo
12°
14°
16°
N
0 50 km
0 50 miles

GUINEA-BISSAU

Total Land Area : 28 120 sq. km (10 857 sq. miles)

POPULATION

over 100 000

over 10 000

under 10 000

LAND HEIGHT

200m/656ft

Sea Level

AID

Recipient

$52m (receipts) — Down 46% in 1999

Portugal is Guinea-Bissau's largest aid donor. Balance of payments support is critical to the economy. Export earnings rarely top $20 million, and import and debt service costs amount to over $100 million. Donor support was frozen in 1991 beause of the country's World Bank arrears, but the governent pushed ahead with economic reforms begun in the mid-1980s, and the World Bank and the IMF agreed a $790 million debt relief package in 2001. Education, the infrastructure, and health care are the main targets of project aid.

DEFENSE

Compulsory military service

$6m — Up 20% in 1999

There are around 9000 troops. The army led coups in 1980 and 1999, and suffered internal rebellions in 1998 and 2000, continuing a history of military interference in politics. ECOWAS soldiers have intervened to restore order on a number of occasions.

ECONOMICS

Inflation 37.6% p.a. (1990–1999)

$194m — 654.42–698.69 Guinea pesos

SCORE CARD

- WORLD GNP RANKING........................181st
- GNP PER CAPITA..............................$160
- BALANCE OF PAYMENTS......................$-30m
- INFLATION......................................–0.7%
- UNEMPLOYMENT.......Widespread underemployment

STRENGTHS

Minimal at present, but good potential in fisheries and timber. Offshore oil potential.

WEAKNESSES

Lack of sufficiency in rice staple. Few exports, mainly cashew nuts, groundnuts. Minimal industry. Lack of entrepreneurial business class. High illiteracy. Poor state economic management.

EXPORTS

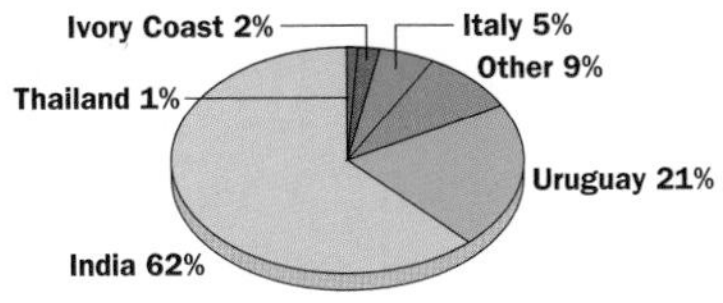
Ivory Coast 2%
Italy 5%
Other 9%
Thailand 1%
Uruguay 21%
India 62%

IMPORTS

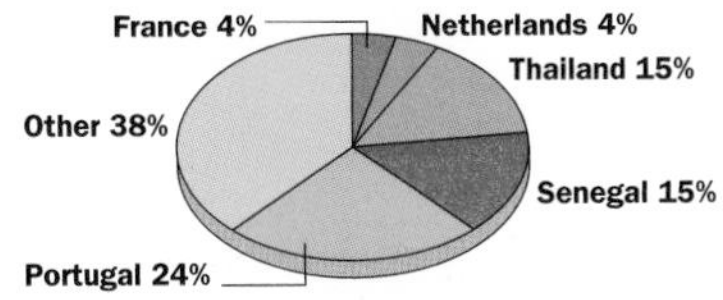
France 4%
Netherlands 4%
Thailand 15%
Other 38%
Senegal 15%
Portugal 24%

***Bafatá, the chief town** in central Guinea-Bissau. It lies on the Gêba River and is also an important inland port.*

RESOURCES

Electric power 11,000 kw

7250 tonnes — Not an oil producer

520,000 cattle, 340,000 pigs, 850,000 chickens — Bauxite, phosphates

Fish and timber are the main natural resources, but local exploitation is only 10% of the sustainable levels of 250,000 tonnes and 100,000 tonnes a year. Considerable hydropower potential is also underexploited.

ENVIRONMENT

Not available

None — 0.2 tonnes per capita

Drought and locust plagues are serious natural hazards. A small population and minimal industry mean that there are few serious environmental problems.

MEDIA

TV ownership low

Daily newspaper circulation 5 per 1000 people

PUBLISHING AND BROADCAST MEDIA

There is 1 daily newspaper, *Nô Printcha*, published by the government

1 state-owned service — 3 services: 1 state-owned, 2 independent

Only one newspaper, *Baguerra*, and one magazine, *Expresso-Bissau*, are independently owned. Portugal helps to fund the TV service, started in 1989.

CRIME

Death penalty not used

Guinea-Bissau does not publish prison figures — Up 66% in 1992

The death penalty was abolished in 1993. Reform of the legal system is in progress to make it more independent of the PAIGC. The government has been criticized for human rights abuses.

EDUCATION

School leaving age: 13

39% — 404 students

Around 65% of children receive rudimentary education. Guinea-Bissau has no university.

CHRONOLOGY

Explored by the Portuguese in the 15th century, Portuguese Guinea was established in 1879. A war for independence began in the 1960s.

- **1974** Independence. PAIGC takes power.
- **1980** Military coup.
- **1990** Multiparty politics accepted.
- **1994** Multiparty elections.
- **1998** Army rebellion led by General Mane. ECOWAS intervention.
- **1999** Transitional government. May, army seizes power. November, PRS defeats PAIGC in elections.
- **2000** Kumba Yalla president. Mane killed in failed coup attempt.

G

HEALTH

No welfare state health benefits

1 per 5000 people — Parasitic, diarrheal, and communicable diseases, malaria

Guinea-Bissau's health statistics are among the world's worst, due partly to the minimal medical facilities. Average life expectancy is just 45 years; infant mortality is 127 per 1000 live births; the maternal death rate is high. In mid-2000 the AfDB provided $500,000 in funding for an emergency health program.

SPENDING

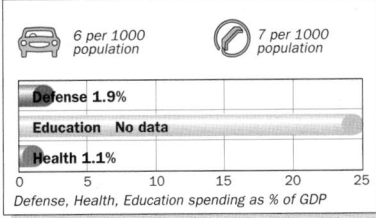

GDP/cap. increase

CONSUMPTION AND SPENDING

6 per 1000 population — *7 per 1000 population*

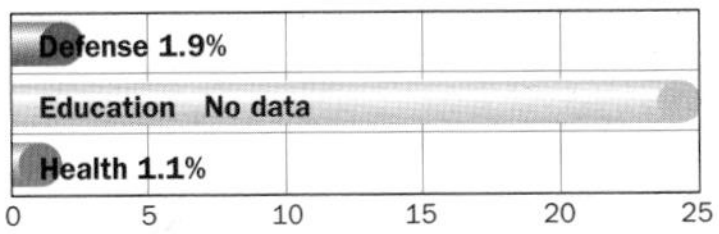
Defense 1.9%
Education No data
Health 1.1%
0
5
10
15
20
25

Defense, Health, Education spending as % of GDP

Living conditions for the majority of Guinea-Bissau's people are extremely poor; over 70% of the population are unable to meet their basic needs. The tiny elite is mainly *mestiço*.

WORLD RANKING

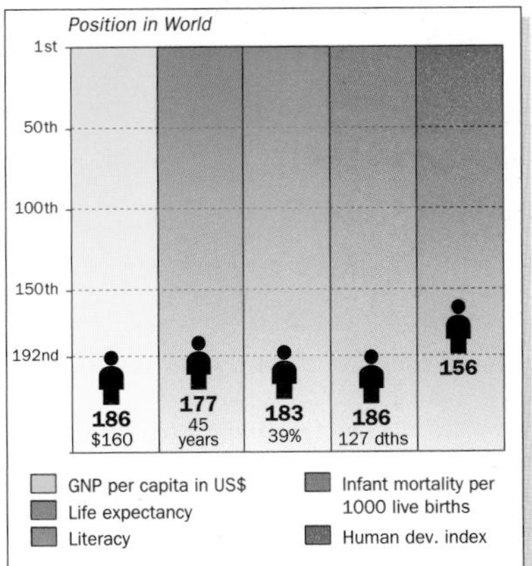
Position in World
1st
50th
100th
150th
192nd
186
$160
177
45 years
183
39%
186
127 dths
156
GNP per capita in US$
Life expectancy
Literacy
Infant mortality per 1000 live births
Human dev. index

GUYANA

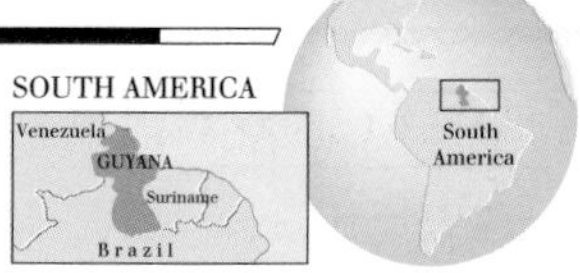
SOUTH AMERICA
Venezuela
GUYANA
Suriname
Brazil
South America

OFFICIAL NAME: Cooperative Republic of Guyana **CAPITAL:** Georgetown
POPULATION: 861,000 **CURRENCY:** Guyana dollar **OFFICIAL LANGUAGE:** English

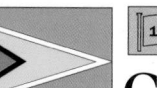

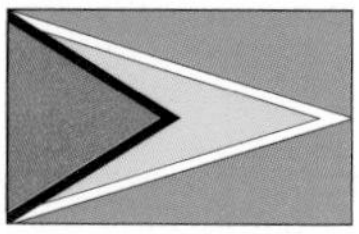

1966 | 1966 | Feb 23 | GUY | -4 | +592 | .gy

GUYANA LIES ON the northeast coast of South America, bordered by Venezuela, Brazil, and Suriname. Dense interior rainforest covers some three-quarters of its territory, but this is diminishing at a worrying rate as a result of logging. Independence from the UK came in 1966. Exports of sugar, bauxite, rice, gold, and timber sustain the economy. The vast majority of Guyana's population lives on the narrow coastal plain partially reclaimed from the sea.

CLIMATE

Tropical equatorial

WEATHER CHART

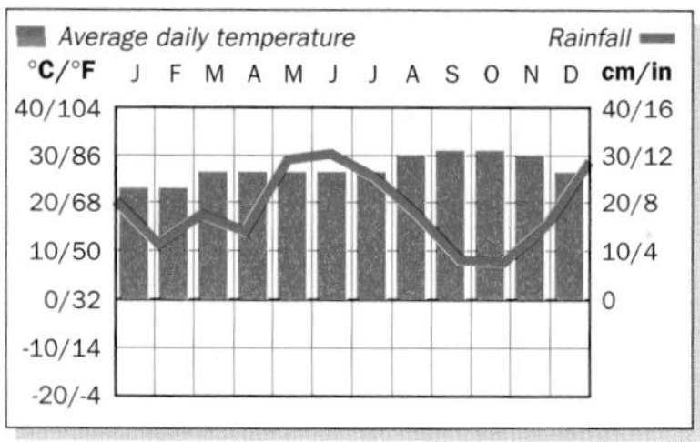
Average daily temperature
Rainfall
°C/°F
J F M A M J J A S O N D
cm/in
40/104
30/86
20/68
10/50
0/32
-10/14
-20/-4
40/16
30/12
20/8
10/4
0

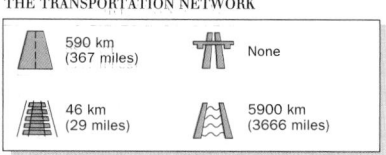

The lowlands are very humid with a constant temperature. The highlands are a little cooler, especially at night.

TRANSPORTATION

Drive on left

Timehri International, Georgetown 270,500 passengers

62 ships 16,260 grt

THE TRANSPORTATION NETWORK

590 km (367 miles)

None

46 km (29 miles)

5900 km (3666 miles)

Reliable travel to the interior is by air or river; most paved roads are coastal. The only international airport is Timehri.

TOURISM

Visitors : Population 1:11

75,000 visitors

Up 10% in 1999

MAIN TOURIST ARRIVALS

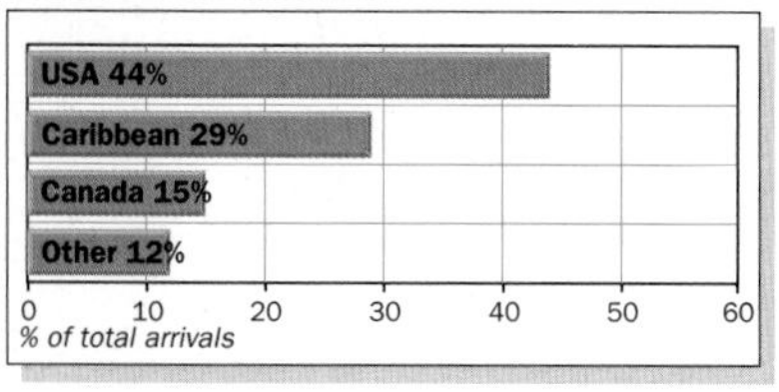
USA 44%
Caribbean 29%
Canada 15%
Other 12%
0 10 20 30 40 50 60
% of total arrivals

The government promotes tourism, but the number of tourists is modest. Guyana means Land of Many Waters; the Kaieteur Falls are among the world's most impressive. Old Dutch wooden architecture characterizes Georgetown.

Modest homes, Georgetown. Most buildings are made of wood. The cathedral is one of the world's tallest freestanding wooden buildings.

PEOPLE

Pop. density low

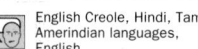

English Creole, Hindi, Tamil, Amerindian languages, English

4/km² (11/mi²)

THE URBAN/RURAL POPULATION SPLIT

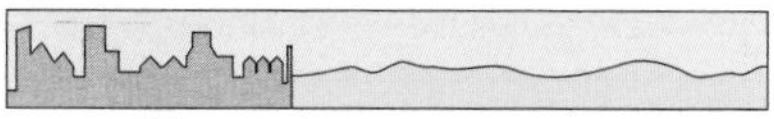
38%
62%

ETHNIC MAKEUP

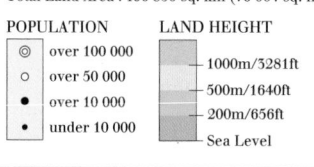

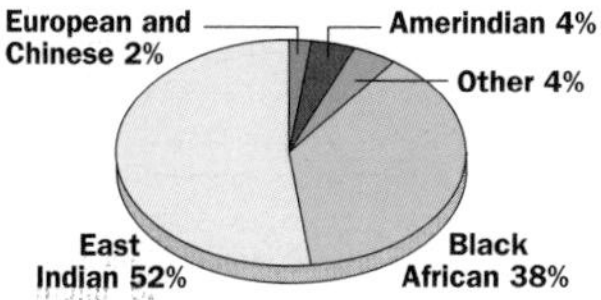
European and Chinese 2%
Amerindian 4%
Other 4%
East Indian 52%
Black African 38%

Tension exists between the Afro-Guyanese, descended from Africans brought over in the 17th to 19th centuries, and the Indo-Guyanese, descendants of south Asian laborers brought from India in the 19th century. This is currently displayed in the hostility existing between the opposition PNC, representing Afro-Guyanese, and the ruling PPP, traditionally representing the Indo-Guyanese.

POLITICS

Multiparty elections

2001/2006

President Bharrat Jagdeo

AT THE LAST ELECTION

National Assembly 65 seats

3% GAP–WPA
2% TUF
52% PPP–CIVIC
41% PNC
2% ROAR

PPP–CIVIC = People's Progressive Party–CIVIC
PNC = People's National Congress
GAP–WPA = Guyana Action Party–Working People's Alliance
ROAR = Rise Organize and Rebuild **TUF** = The United Force

The success of the PPP in the 1992 elections, widely seen as the first fair poll since independence, ended the dominance of the pro-Afro-Guyanese PNC. Veteran PPP leader Cheddi Jagan, a Marxist before adopting free-market policies, died in office in 1997. The PNC violently contested the succession of his wife Janet. A Caricom-brokered peace restored calm, though tension flared in early 2001 when the High Court condemned the 1997 poll. Violence erupted once again when elections confirmed Janet Jagan's successor, Bharrat Jagdeo, as president.

GUYANA

Total Land Area : 196 850 sq. km (76 004 sq. miles)

POPULATION	LAND HEIGHT
over 100 000	1000m/3281ft
over 50 000	500m/1640ft
over 10 000	200m/656ft
under 10 000	Sea Level

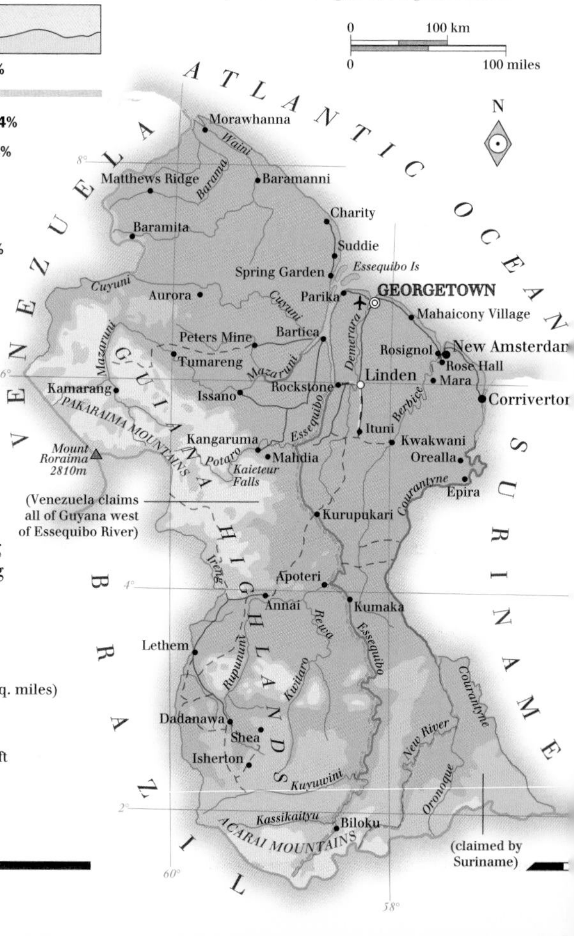
0 100 km
0 100 miles
N
ATLANTIC OCEAN
VENEZUELA
SURINAME
BRAZIL
GUIANA HIGHLANDS
PAKARAIMA MOUNTAINS
ACARAI MOUNTAINS
Morawhanna
Matthews Ridge
Baramanni
Charity
Baramita
Suddie
Essequibo Is
Spring Garden
Parika
GEORGETOWN
Mahaicony Village
Aurora
Peters Mine
Bartica
Tumareng
Rosignol
New Amsterdam
Rose Hall
Mara
Linden
Kamarang
Issano
Rockstone
Corriverton
Ituni
Kangaruma
Kwakwani
Mount Roraima 2810m
Mahdia
Kaieteur Falls
Orealla
Epira
(Venezuela claims all of Guyana west of Essequibo River)
Kurupukari
Apoteri
Annai
Kumaka
Lethem
Dadanawa
Shea
Isherton
Biloku
(claimed by Suriname)
Waini
Barama
Cuyuni
Mazaruni
Essequibo
Demerara
Berbice
Potaro
Courantyne
Ireng
Rupununi
Rewa
Kuyuwini
Kassikaityu
New River
Oronoque

WORLD AFFAIRS

Joined UN in 1966

ACS | OIC | Caricom | Comm | OAS

Rescheduling debt with Western creditor states is paramount. Also important are the long-standing border dispute with Venezuela and closer integration with the Caribbean.

AID

Recipient

US$27m (receipts)

Down 71% in 1999

Most aid comes from the USA, the EU, and the UK. Recent grants covered public health projects, business development, and protection of the rainforest.

DEFENSE

No compulsory military service

US$7m

Down 13% in 1999

The security forces, which include a small land army, benefit from financial support and training provided by the US and UK governments.

ECONOMICS

Inflation 14.3% p.a. (1990–1999)

US$651m

179.6–180.5 Guyana dollars

SCORE CARD

❑ WORLD GNP RANKING	164th
❑ GNP PER CAPITA	US$760
❑ BALANCE OF PAYMENTS	US$–135m
❑ INFLATION	7.5%
❑ UNEMPLOYMENT	12%

STRENGTHS

Gold, rice, sugar, diamonds, bauxite, and timber production. Good tourism potential. Debt reduction plan agreed with multilateral agencies.

WEAKNESSES

High per capita foreign debt. Political instability dents investor confidence. Currency vulnerable to exchange rate pressure. Main exports vulnerable to fluctuations in international commodity prices. Weak manufacturing base.

EXPORTS

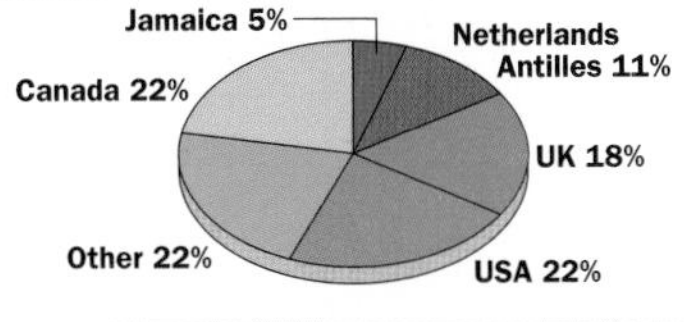
Jamaica 5%
Netherlands Antilles 11%
Canada 22%
UK 18%
Other 22%
USA 22%

IMPORTS

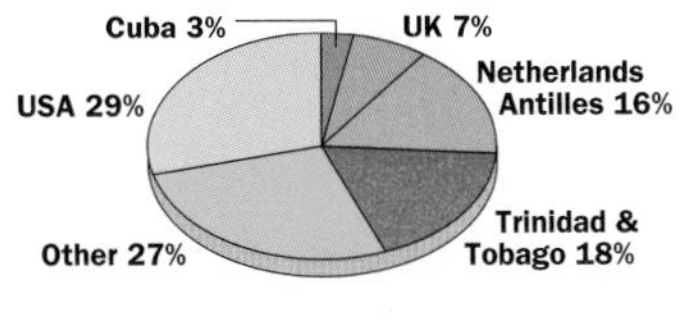
Cuba 3%
UK 7%
Netherlands Antilles 16%
USA 29%
Trinidad & Tobago 18%
Other 27%

RESOURCES

Electric power 114,000 kw

57,409 tonnes

Not an oil producer

220,000 cattle, 130,000 sheep, 11.6m chickens

Bauxite, gold, diamonds, gemstones, oil, manganese, uranium

Gold, bauxite, diamonds, and timber are major resources. Offshore and onshore prospecting for oil has not reduced the need for petroleum imports for electricity generation. More hydroelectric power plants are being constructed.

ENVIRONMENT

Not available

0.05%

1.2 tonnes per capita

The state of disrepair of the 18th-century sea defense system threatens the urbanized coastline that lies below sea level. Commercial logging threatens to deplete the rainforest. The pollution of rivers due to gold and diamond mining is now a serious problem.

MEDIA

TV ownership medium

Daily newspaper circulation 50 per 1000 people

PUBLISHING AND BROADCAST MEDIA

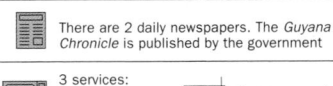

There are 2 daily newspapers. The *Guyana Chronicle* is published by the government

3 services: 1 state-owned, 2 independent

1 state-owned service

The PPP and the PNC both publish periodicals. The government owns one TV service and the sole radio service as well as publishing a daily newspaper.

CRIME

Death penalty used

1396 prisoners

Down 12% 1996–1998

The police are strongly criticized for corruption and ineffectiveness in the face of rising urban crime. Serious violence between PNC and PPP–CIVIC supporters erupted in 1998, 1999, and 2001.

EDUCATION

School leaving age: 14

98%

8965 students

Education is based on the British system. Entry to high schools is by 11-plus examination. There is a state-financed university, though many students go to the USA or the UK.

HEALTH

Welfare state health benefits

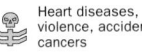

1 per 303 people

Heart diseases, violence, accidents, cancers

Nearly all of Guyana's population have access to the country's mainly state-run health service. The referral system is relatively good.

CHRONOLOGY

During the 17th and 18th centuries, the Dutch founded three colonies, Essequibo, Demerara, and Berbice, in the region. In 1814, these came under British control, and were later combined to form British Guiana.

- ❑ **1953** First universal elections won by PPP under Cheddi Jagan; parliament later suspended by UK.
- ❑ **1964** PNC dominates ruling coalition parties.
- ❑ **1966** Independence from UK.
- ❑ **1973** PPP boycotts parliament, accusing PNC of electoral fraud.
- ❑ **1992** Fair elections won by PPP. Jagan president.
- ❑ **1997–1998** Jagan dies in office; PNC rejects his widow Janet's election victory. Political crisis.
- ❑ **1999** Caricom-brokered peace deal. Janet Jagan resigns due to illness.
- ❑ **2001** Political violence flares again.

G

SPENDING

GDP/cap. increase

CONSUMPTION AND SPENDING

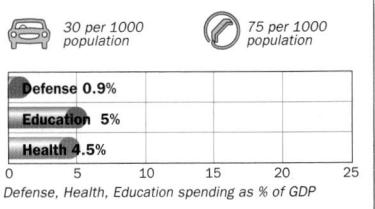

30 per 1000 population

75 per 1000 population

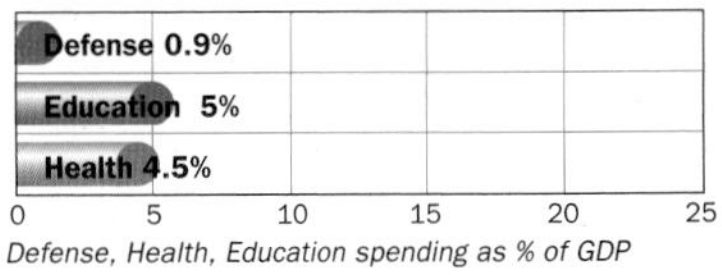
Defense 0.9%
Education 5%
Health 4.5%
0
5
10
15
20
25
Defense, Health, Education spending as % of GDP

Significant urban and rural poverty in Guyana has forced the government to make provision in the budget for poverty alleviation. Redundancies in the public sector exacerbate the problem. The poorest group in society are Amerindian subsistence farmers. There are a few very affluent urban families who derive their wealth not only from business but also from rural farming interests.

WORLD RANKING

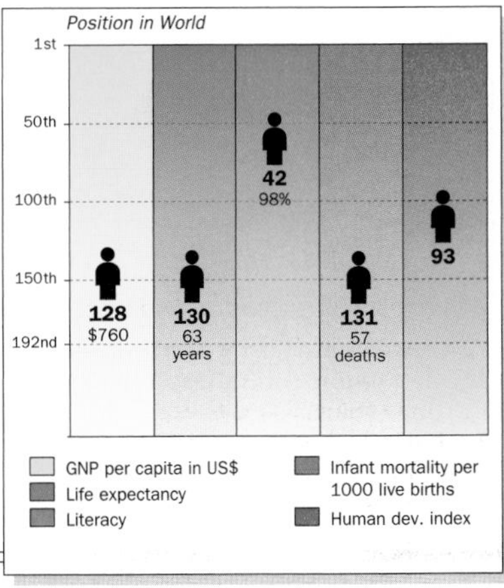
Position in World
1st
50th
100th
150th
192nd
128
$760
130
63
years
42
98%
131
57
deaths
93
GNP per capita in US$
Life expectancy
Literacy
Infant mortality per 1000 live births
Human dev. index

HAITI

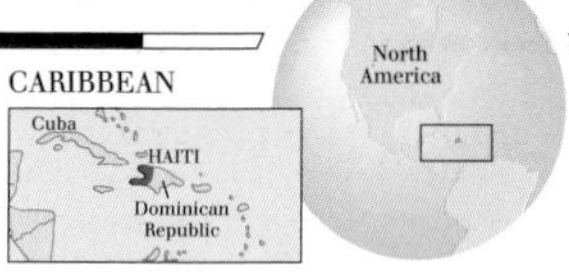
CARIBBEAN
North America
Cuba
HAITI
Dominican Republic

OFFICIAL NAME: Republic of Haiti **CAPITAL:** Port-au-Prince **POPULATION:** 8.2 million
CURRENCY: Gourde **OFFICIAL LANGUAGES:** French and French Creole

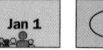

1804 | 1844 | Jan 1 | RH | -5 | +509 | .ht

HAITI OCCUPIES the western third of the Caribbean island of Hispaniola. A former Spanish colony, in 1804 it was the first Caribbean state to become independent, and has been in a state of political chaos virtually ever since. Democracy did not materialize with the exile of the dictator Jean-Claude Duvalier in 1986. Elections were held in 1990, but by 1991 the military were back in power and were ousted in 1994 only through US intervention.

CLIMATE

Tropical equatorial/ oceanic

WEATHER CHART

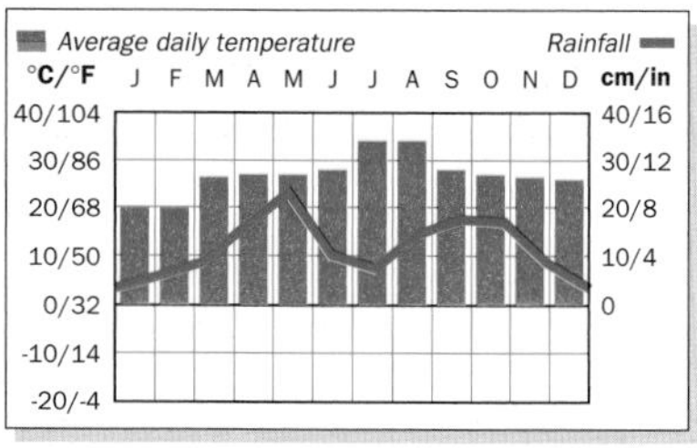
Average daily temperature
Rainfall
°C/°F
J F M A M J J A S O N D
cm/in
40/104
30/86
20/68
10/50
0/32
-10/14
-20/-4
40/16
30/12
20/8
10/4
0

Haiti lies mostly in the rain shadow of the central mountains, so humidity is lower than the Caribbean average.

TRANSPORTATION

Drive on right

Port-au-Prince 545,000 passengers

5 ships 1300 grt

THE TRANSPORTATION NETWORK

1011 km (628 miles)	None
None	100 km (62 miles)

Roads are poor, especially in the interior. Ferries provide the main transportation to the southern peninsula.

TOURISM

Visitors : Population 1:57

143,000 visitors

Down 3% in 1999

MAIN TOURIST ARRIVALS

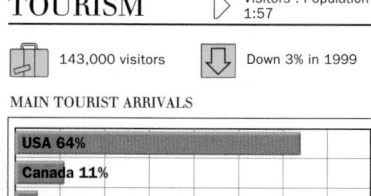

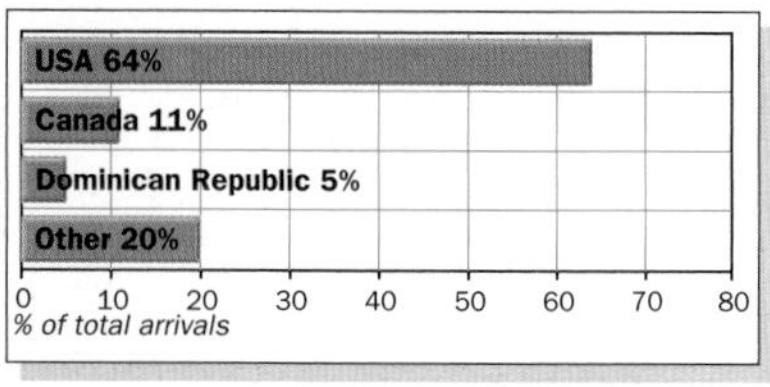
USA 64%
Canada 11%
Dominican Republic 5%
Other 20%
0 10 20 30 40 50 60 70 80
% of total arrivals

Haiti's location, history, and culture provided much of its attraction for tourists in the 1960s and 1970s. Political instability and violence in the 1980s, however, led to the industry's near collapse and it has yet to recover.

PEOPLE

Pop. density high

French Creole, French

298/km² (761/mi²)

THE URBAN/RURAL POPULATION SPLIT

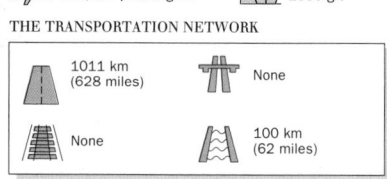

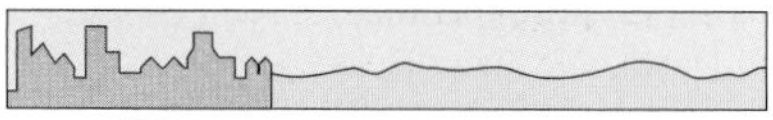
35%
65%

RELIGIOUS PERSUASION

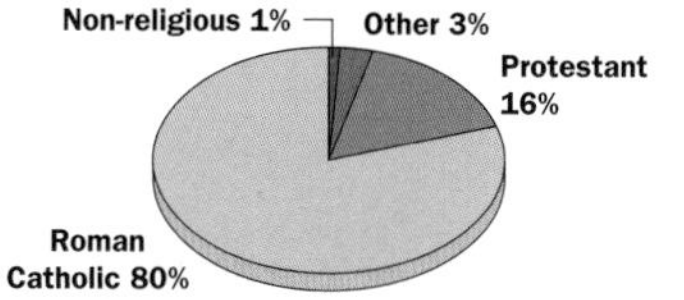
Non-religious 1%
Other 3%
Protestant 16%
Roman Catholic 80%

Most Haitians are the descendants of Africans; a few have European roots, primarily French. The majority of the population lives in extreme poverty: Haiti is the poorest country in the Americas, and Port-au-Prince has the worst slums in the Caribbean. Social tensions run high, and focus on class rather than race. In recent years, the combination of political repression and a collapsing economy led many to emigrate illegally to the USA, or across the border to neighboring Dominican Republic.

POLITICS

Multiparty elections

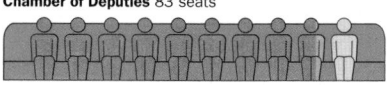

L. House 2000/2002
U. House 2000/2002

President Jean-Bertrand Aristide

AT THE LAST ELECTION

Chamber of Deputies 83 seats

87% Lavalas coalition | 2% Vacant | 11% Others

Senate 27 seats

96% Lavalas coalition | 4% Others

A wealthy elite, backed by the military, supported the dictatorships of the Duvaliers and regularly financed coups after "Baby Doc" Duvalier's overthrow in 1986. UN sanctions followed the 1991 coup and US forces restored the elected president, Jean-Bertrand Aristide, in 1994. His left-wing Lavalas party won legislative elections in 1995 and René Préval was installed as the new president, with the party's backing, in 1996. A backlash against austerity policies instigated at the insistence of the USA forced the prime minister to step down in 1997 and soured relations between the presidency and the legislature. New elections, finally held in May 2000, resulted in a strongly disputed but decisive victory for the Lavalas coalition. A similarly controversial presidential poll in November was won by Aristide; his victory was rejected by the opposition.

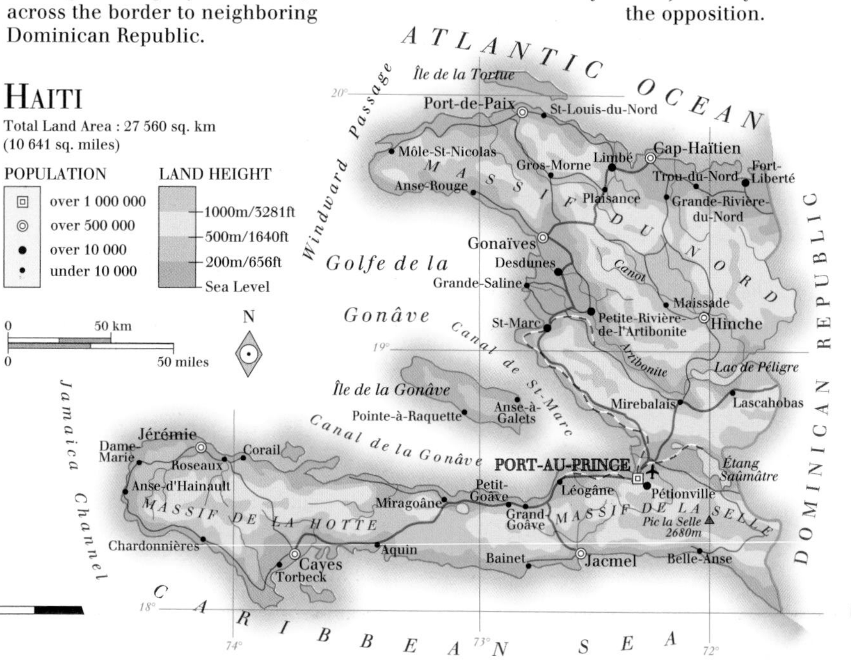
HAITI
Total Land Area : 27 560 sq. km (10 641 sq. miles)
POPULATION
over 1 000 000
over 500 000
over 10 000
under 10 000
LAND HEIGHT
1000m/3281ft
500m/1640ft
200m/656ft
Sea Level
0 50 km
0 50 miles
N
ATLANTIC OCEAN
Île de la Tortue
Windward Passage
Port-de-Paix
St-Louis-du-Nord
Môle-St-Nicolas
MASSIF DU NORD
Anse-Rouge
Gros-Morne
Limbé
Cap-Haïtien
Fort-Liberté
Trou-du-Nord
Plaisance
Grande-Rivière-du-Nord
Gonaïves
Desdunes
Golfe de la Gonâve
Grande-Saline
Canot
Maïssade
St-Marc
Petite-Rivière-de-l'Artibonite
Hinche
Canal de St-Marc
Artibonite
Lac de Péligre
Île de la Gonâve
Anse-à-Galets
Pointe-à-Raquette
Mirebalais
Lascahobas
Canal de la Gonâve
Jamaica Channel
Jérémie
Dame-Marie
Corail
Roseaux
Anse-d'Hainault
PORT-AU-PRINCE
Étang Saumâtre
Petit-Goâve
Léogâne
Pétionville
MASSIF DE LA HOTTE
Miragoâne
Grand-Goâve
MASSIF DE LA SELLE
Pic la Selle 2680m
Chardonnières
Aquin
Cayes
Torbeck
Bainet
Jacmel
Belle-Anse
DOMINICAN REPUBLIC
CARIBBEAN SEA
20°
19°
18°
74°
73°
72°

WORLD AFFAIRS

Joined UN in 1945

ACS | ACP | Geplac | OAS | WTO

After years of sanctions, economic links with the outside world have been largely restored. Illegal immigration to the USA and relations with the Dominican Republic are major issues.

AID

Recipient

$263m (receipts) | Down 35% in 1999

The IMF granted $21 million in emergency aid in 1998 for hurricane damage. The IDB approved loans for water and health problems, and Taiwan granted $60.4 million in aid.

DEFENSE

No compulsory military service

$50m | Up 2% in 1999

In 1994, the military were ousted and democracy was restored. The armed forces and police were disbanded and an interim public security force was created. A 5300-strong new national police force has now been formed, funded and trained by the USA.

ECONOMICS

Inflation 22.2% p.a. (1990–1999)

$3.6bn | 17.46–21.00 gourdes

SCORE CARD

❑ World GNP Ranking	122nd
❑ GNP per Capita	$460
❑ Balance of Payments	$-38m
❑ Inflation	8.7%
❑ Unemployment	70%

Strengths

Coffee exports. Remittances by Haitians living abroad. US demand for goods assembled in Haiti. Large profits from the transshipment of narcotics to USA.

Weaknesses

Huge tax avoidance. Foreign investment and promised aid deterred by political instability.

EXPORTS

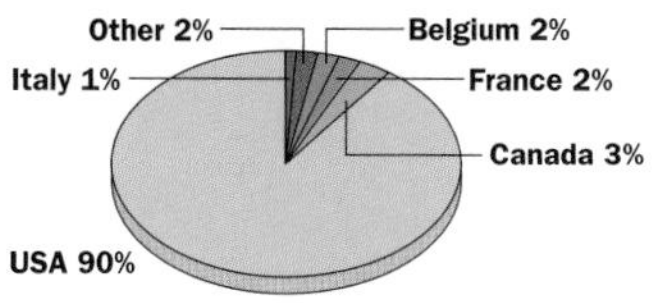
Other 2%
Belgium 2%
Italy 1%
France 2%
Canada 3%
USA 90%

IMPORTS

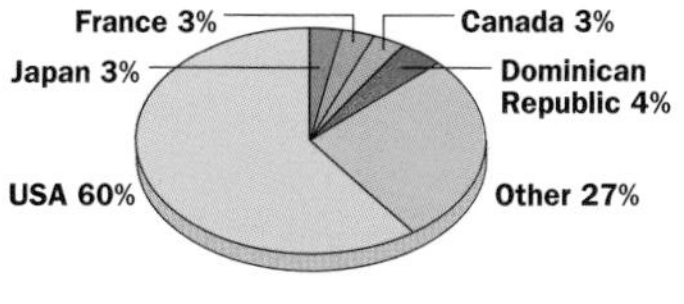
France 3%
Canada 3%
Japan 3%
Dominican Republic 4%
USA 60%
Other 27%

Haiti: the poorest country in the Americas. In remote villages, most houses are made of earth and do not have glass in their windows.

RESOURCES

Electric power 153,000 kw

5630 tonnes | Not an oil producer

1.62m goats, 1.3m cattle, 800,000 pigs, 5m chickens | Marble, limestone, clay, silver, gold, natural asphalt

Haiti has no strategic resources. Under prolonged economic sanctions, it had to find unofficial sources of oil; much was imported from Europe.

ENVIRONMENT

Sustainability rank: 122nd

1% | 0.2 tonnes per capita

One-third of soil is seriously eroded and forest cover is now only 1.5% of total land area. The removal of 4000 tonnes of toxic waste, illegally dumped in 1988 near Gonaïves, finally began in 1998.

MEDIA

TV ownership low

Daily newspaper circulation 3 per 1000 people

PUBLISHING AND BROADCAST MEDIA

There are 2 daily newspapers, *Le Nouvelliste* and *Le Matin*

4 services: 1 state-owned, 3 independent | 18 services: 1 state-owned, 17 independent

Under military rule, the media were largely controlled through intimidation. The transition to multiparty democracy has produced a more open press.

CRIME

Death penalty not used

Haiti does not publish prison figures | Crime is rising

Extrajudicial killings, torture, and brutality continue, despite the ending of military dictatorship. Narcotics trafficking is highly organized. Police are inexperienced and the judicial system is slow and open to corruption.

EDUCATION

School leaving age: 12

50% | 6288 students

The run-down state education system is based on the French; the *baccalauréat* pass rate in 1998 was under 10%. The wealthy educate their children abroad.

CHRONOLOGY

In 1697, Spain ceded the west of Hispaniola to France. Ex-slave Toussaint l'Ouverture's rebellion in 1791 led to independence in 1804.

- ❑ **1915–1934** US occupation.
- ❑ **1957–1971** François "Papa Doc" Duvalier's brutal dictatorship.
- ❑ **1971–1986** His son Jean-Claude, "Baby Doc," rules; eventually flees.
- ❑ **1986–1988** Military rule.
- ❑ **1990** Jean-Bertrand Aristide elected; exiled in 1991 coup.
- ❑ **1994–1995** US forces oust military. Aristide reinstated; elections.
- ❑ **1997–1999** Political deadlock.

2000 Lavalas coalition and Aristide reelected.

H

HEALTH

No welfare state health benefits

1 per 5000 people | Malaria, other parasitic diseases, tuberculosis

Most Haitians cannot afford health care. In rural areas, help is often sought from voodoo priests.

SPENDING

GDP/cap. decrease

CONSUMPTION AND SPENDING

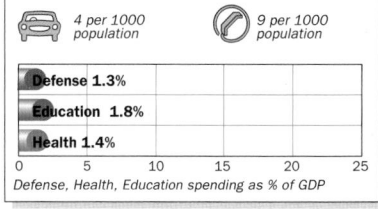

4 per 1000 population | *9 per 1000 population*

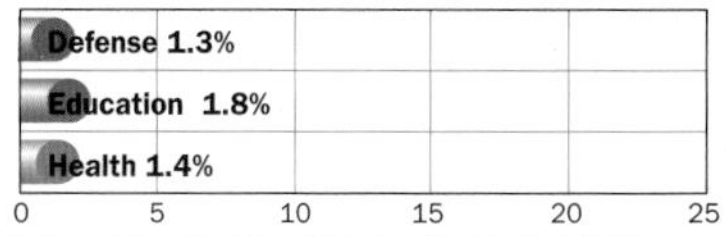
Defense 1.3%
Education 1.8%
Health 1.4%
0
5
10
15
20
25

Defense, Health, Education spending as % of GDP

Haiti's rigid class structure maintains extreme disparities of wealth between a few affluent families and the mass of the population, who live in slums without running water or proper sanitation. According to the UN, around 80% of Haitians cannot meet their basic daily needs.

WORLD RANKING

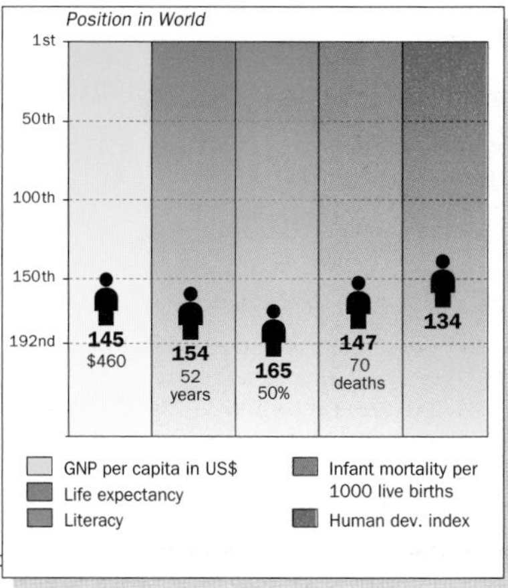
Position in World
1st
50th
100th
150th
192nd
145
$460
154
52 years
165
50%
147
70 deaths
134
GNP per capita in US$
Life expectancy
Literacy
Infant mortality per 1000 live births
Human dev. index

HONDURAS

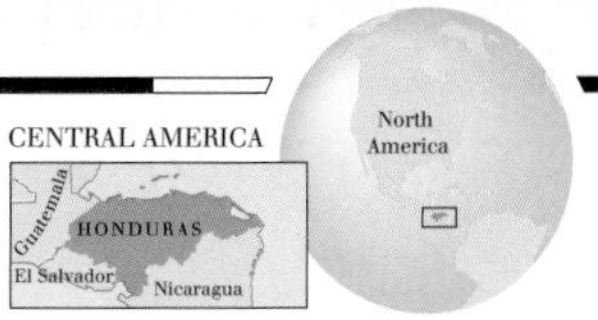
CENTRAL AMERICA
North America
Guatemala
HONDURAS
El Salvador
Nicaragua

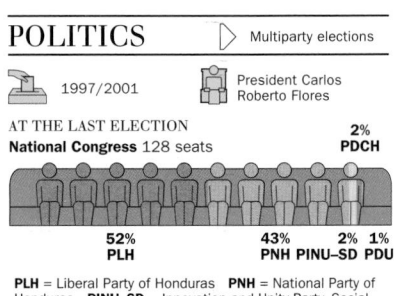

OFFICIAL NAME: Republic of Honduras **CAPITAL:** Tegucigalpa
POPULATION: 6.35 million **CURRENCY:** Lempira **OFFICIAL LANGUAGE:** Spanish

1838 | 1838 | Sept 15 | HN | -6 | +504 | .hn

STRADDLING THE Central American isthmus, Honduras has only a short Pacific coast. Its long Caribbean shoreline includes the virtually uninhabited Mosquito Coast, while most of the rest of the country is mountainous. After a succession of military governments it returned to full civilian rule in 1984. In 1998 Honduras was devastated by Hurricane Mitch, which resulted in the death of at least 5600 people and damage estimated at some $3 billion.

CLIMATE

Tropical equatorial

WEATHER CHART

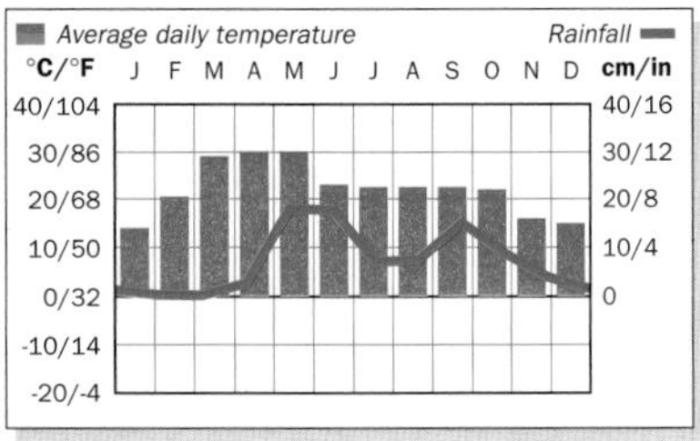
Average daily temperature
Rainfall
°C/°F
J F M A M J J A S O N D
cm/in
40/104
30/86
20/68
10/50
0/32
-10/14
-20/-4
40/16
30/12
20/8
10/4
0

Honduras' Caribbean coastline is generally extremely hot. The central highlands are much cooler.

TRANSPORTATION

Drive on right

Toncontín, Tegucigalpa 404,000 passengers

1465 ships 1.1m grt

THE TRANSPORTATION NETWORK

3126 km (1942 miles)	None
996 km (619 miles)	465 km (289 miles)

In 1998 Hurricane Mitch destroyed roads and bridges across the country; reconstruction will take many years.

TOURISM

Visitors : Population 1:16

408,000 visitors

Up 10% in 2000

MAIN TOURIST ARRIVALS

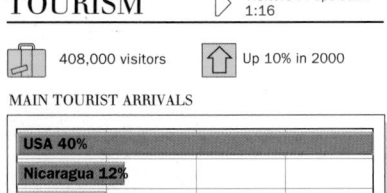

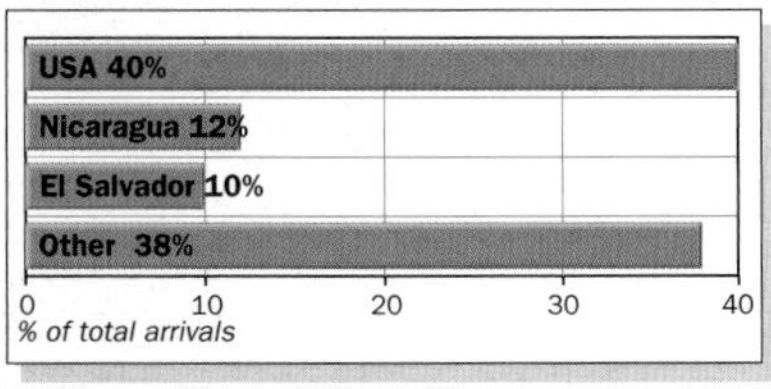
USA 40%
Nicaragua 12%
El Salvador 10%
Other 38%
0
10
20
30
40
% of total arrivals

Caribbean coast resorts and the Bay Islands are popular, while exploring the remote region inland from the Mosquito Coast and jungle rafting appeal to the adventurous. The ruined Maya temples of Copán are a major draw.

PEOPLE

Pop. density medium

Spanish, Black Carib, English Creole

58/km² (150/mi²)

THE URBAN/RURAL POPULATION SPLIT

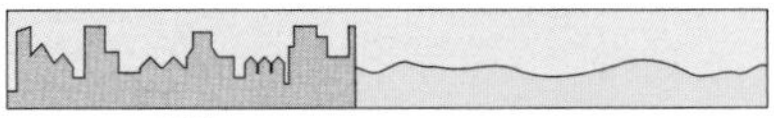
46%
54%

ETHNIC MAKEUP

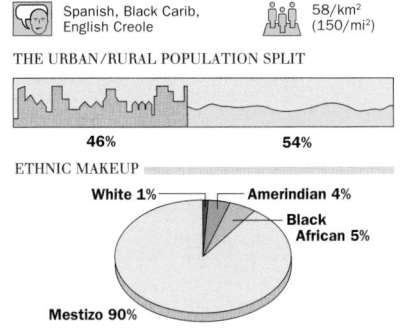

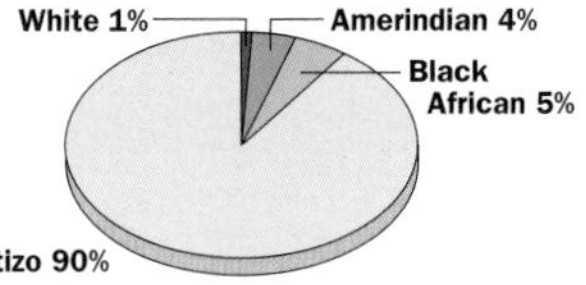
White 1%
Amerindian 4%
Black African 5%
Mestizo 90%

As in most of Central America, very few pure indigenous groups remain. The estimated 45,000 Miskito Amerindians, and an English-speaking *garífuna* (black) population on the Caribbean coast united in 1999 to oppose a constitutional amendment allowing foreigners to buy land in coastal areas, traditionally their communal lands. Poverty is at the root of social tension; whites still have the best opportunities.

Rural poverty and strong Roman Catholicism (97% are Roman Catholic) mean that the family is a powerful unifying force. The status of women is low; many work in domestic service.

POLITICS

Multiparty elections

1997/2001

President Carlos Roberto Flores

AT THE LAST ELECTION

National Congress 128 seats

2% PDCH
52% PLH
43% PNH
2% PINU–SD
1% PDU

PLH = Liberal Party of Honduras **PNH** = National Party of Honduras **PINU–SD** = Innovation and Unity Party–Social Democracy **PDCH** = Honduran Christian Democratic Party **PDU** = Party of Democratic Unification

The traditional power brokers have been the military, the US embassy, and the United Fruit Company, the biggest banana producer in Honduras.

The military held power intermittently from the mid-1950s, until pressure from the US government forced it to allow a return to civilian rule in 1984. However, during the 1980s, US President Reagan effectively converted the country into a US "aircraft carrier" to counter a perceived communist threat from El Salvador and Nicaragua. Peace in the region then saw a cut in US aid.

The PNH and PLH, with few real ideological differences, have tended to alternate in power. Presidents, able to serve only one four-year term, have tended to be weak. The PLH government of President Carlos Reina introduced unpopular austerity measures in 1994, but also began reducing the autonomy of the military by abolishing conscription. His PLH successor Carlos Flores, elected in 1997, continued this "demilitarization" process by naming a civilian defense minister in 1999. Reconstruction after the devastation of Hurricane Mitch in 1998 will be a long-term undertaking.

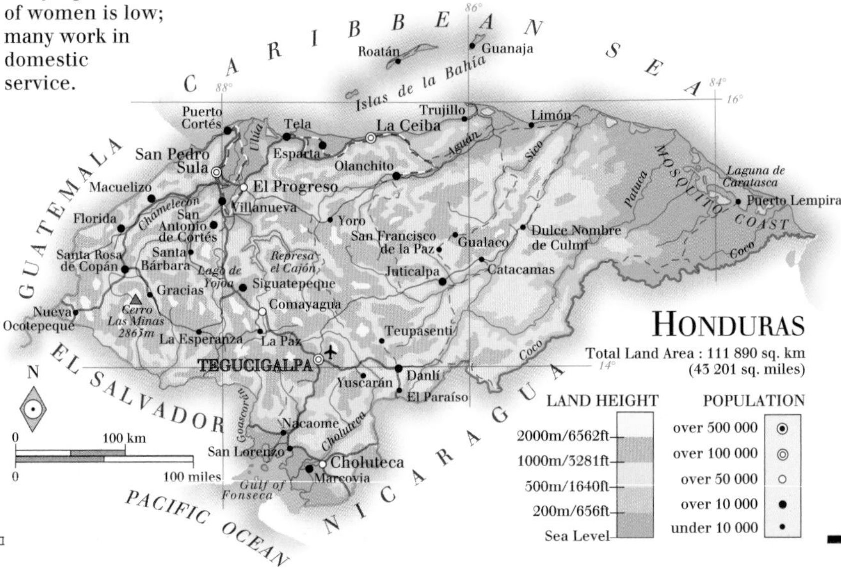
CARIBBEAN SEA
Roatán
Guanaja
Islas de la Bahía
Puerto Cortés
Tela
Trujillo
La Ceiba
Limón
San Pedro Sula
Esparta
Olanchito
Laguna de Caratasca
Macuelizo
El Progreso
Villanueva
Puerto Lempira
MOSQUITO COAST
Florida
San Antonio de Cortés
Yoro
San Francisco de la Paz
Gualaco
Dulce Nombre de Culmí
Santa Rosa de Copán
Santa Bárbara
Lago de Yojoa
Represa el Cajón
Siguatepeque
Juticalpa
Catacamas
Gracias
Comayagua
Nueva Ocotepeque
Cerro Las Minas 2863m
La Esperanza
La Paz
Teupasenti
TEGUCIGALPA
Danlí
Yuscarán
El Paraíso
Nacaome
San Lorenzo
Choluteca
Marcovia
Gulf of Fonseca
PACIFIC OCEAN
GUATEMALA
EL SALVADOR
NICARAGUA
Ulúa
Aguán
Sico
Patuca
Coco
Chamelecón
Goascorán
Choluteca
N
0 100 km
0 100 miles
HONDURAS
Total Land Area : 111 890 sq. km (43 201 sq. miles)
LAND HEIGHT
2000m/6562ft
1000m/3281ft
500m/1640ft
200m/656ft
Sea Level
POPULATION
over 500 000
over 100 000
over 50 000
over 10 000
under 10 000

WORLD AFFAIRS

Joined UN in 1945

ACS | Geplac | NAM | OAS | San José

Hurricane aid, and trade with and immigration to the USA are key issues. In 2001 free trade was agreed with El Salvador, Guatemala, and Mexico.

AID

Recipient

$817m (receipts) — Up 155% in 1999

Aid from the IMF and the World Bank on favorable terms followed the 1998 earthquake. Western countries agreed debt relief of $1.2 billion.

DEFENSE

No compulsory military service

$95m — Down 4% in 1999

Until 1994 the military operated with virtual impunity. The first civilian defense minister was appointed in 1999, completing the "demilitarization" process begun with the return to civilian rule in 1984.

ECONOMICS

Inflation 19.7% p.a. (1990–1999)

$4.8bn — 14.62–15.10 lempiras

SCORE CARD

- World GNP Ranking........113th
- GNP per Capita........$760
- Balance of Payments........$–333m
- Inflation........11.7%
- Unemployment........12%

STRENGTHS

Coffee, flowers, fruit. Economic boost due to hurricane reconstruction. Barely exploited mineral deposits. Hardwoods.

WEAKNESSES

Servicing of foreign debt. Vulnerability of coffee exports. Banana industry yet to recover from hurricane damage. Slow rate of privatizations. Corruption. Lack of land reform. High unemployment and underemployment. Weak industrial base. Overdependence on hydroelectric power.

EXPORTS

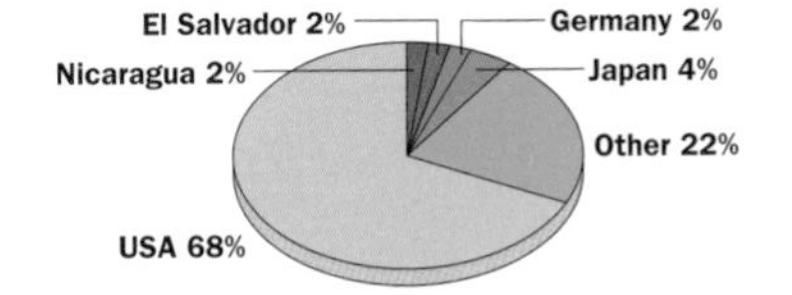
El Salvador 2%
Germany 2%
Nicaragua 2%
Japan 4%
Other 22%
USA 68%

IMPORTS

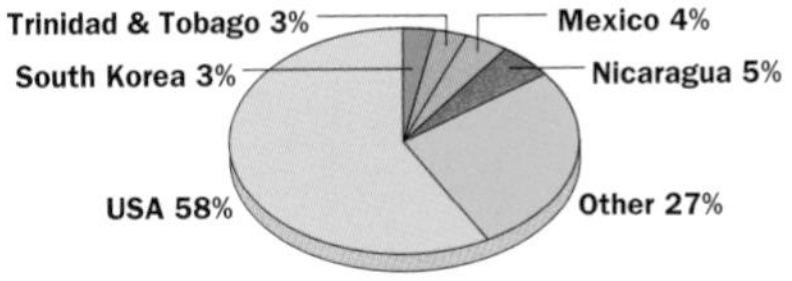
Trinidad & Tobago 3%
Mexico 4%
South Korea 3%
Nicaragua 5%
USA 58%
Other 27%

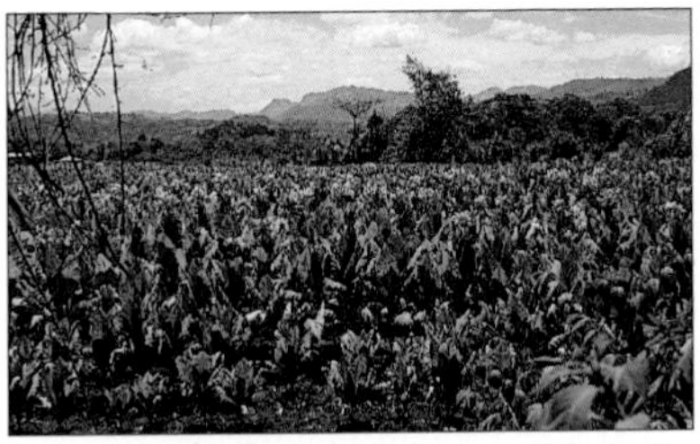

***Tobacco field.** As an export earner tobacco is overshadowed by coffee, shrimps, and melons.*

RESOURCES

Electric power 615,000 kw

23,585 tonnes — Not an oil producer

1.95m cattle, 800,000 pigs, 18m chickens — Lead, zinc, silver, gold, copper, iron, tin, coal

The banana industry was devastated by Hurricane Mitch in 1998. Oil and mineral deposits are being explored. Hydroelectric supply is erratic.

ENVIRONMENT

Sustainability rank: 64th

10% — 0.8 tonnes per capita

The unregulated timber, cotton, and cattle industries, land colonization, and pesticides have led to ecological crisis.

MEDIA

TV ownership medium

Daily newspaper circulation 55 per 1000 people

PUBLISHING AND BROADCAST MEDIA

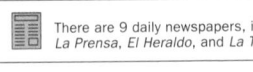

There are 9 daily newspapers, including *La Prensa*, *El Heraldo*, and *La Tribuna*

6 independent services — 5 services: 1 state-owned, 4 independent

Self-censorship, dependence on US sources, corruption, and intimidation guarantee a largely compliant media.

CRIME

Death penalty not used

Honduras does not publish prison figures — Violent crime is rising

Drug crime is a major problem. Some 100 youth gangs in Tegucigalpa are blamed for rising violence.

EDUCATION

School leaving age: 12

75% — 54,106 students

State-run education follows the US system, although the drop-out rate from secondary schools is high.

HEALTH

No welfare state health benefits

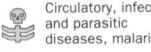

1 per 1250 people — Circulatory, infectious, and parasitic diseases, malaria

Only 66% of people have easy access to health services. Plans were announced in 2000 to privatize the health service.

CHRONOLOGY

Honduras was a Spanish possession until 1821. In 1823, it formed the United Provinces of Central America with four neighboring nations.

- **1838** Declares full independence.
- **1890s** US banana plantations set up.
- **1932–1949** Dictatorship of General Tiburcio Carías Andino of PNH.
- **1954–1957** Elected PLH president Villeda Morales deposed, reelected.
- **1963** Military coup.
- **1969** 13-day Football War with El Salvador sparked by World Cup.
- **1980–1983** PLH wins elections but General Gustavo Alvarez holds real power. Military maneuvers with USA. Trades unionists arrested; death squads operate.
- **1984** Return to democracy.
- **1988** 12,000 Contra rebels forced out of Nicaragua into Honduras.
- **1995** Military defies human rights charges.
- **1998** Hurricane Mitch wreaks havoc.
- **1999** Appointment of first civilian defense minister.

H

SPENDING

GDP/cap. increase

CONSUMPTION AND SPENDING

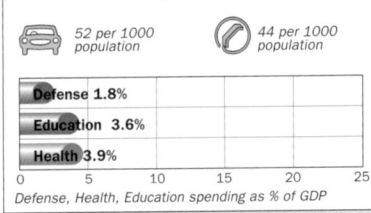

52 per 1000 population — *44 per 1000 population*

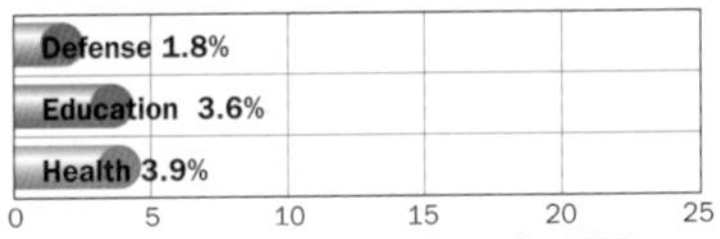
Defense 1.8%
Education 3.6%
Health 3.9%
0
5
10
15
20
25

Defense, Health, Education spending as % of GDP

The social structure of Honduras is characterized by great inequalities: 4% of people own 60% of the land. Relief agencies estimate that 85% of people now live below the poverty line, compared with 80% before the devastation of Hurricane Mitch.

WORLD RANKING

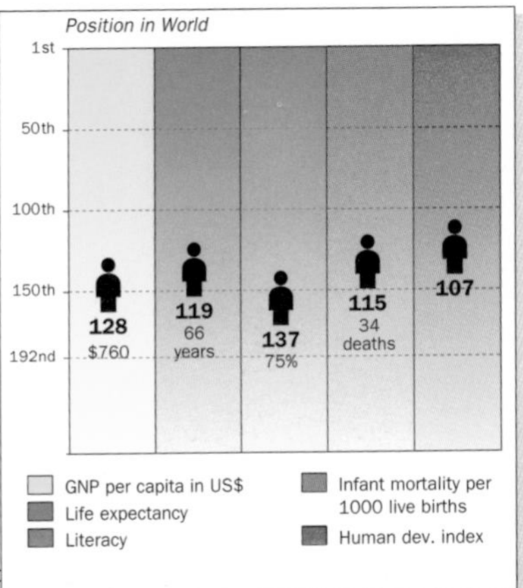
Position in World
1st
50th
100th
150th
192nd
128
$760
119
66 years
137
75%
115
34 deaths
107
GNP per capita in US$
Life expectancy
Literacy
Infant mortality per 1000 live births
Human dev. index

HUNGARY

Europe
EUROPE
Slovakia
Ukraine
Austria
HUNGARY
Romania
Slovenia
Croatia
Yugo.

OFFICIAL NAME: Republic of Hungary **CAPITAL:** Budapest
POPULATION: 10 million **CURRENCY:** Forint **OFFICIAL LANGUAGE:** Hungarian

1918 | 1947 | Aug 20 | H | +1 | +36 | .hu

LYING AT THE HEART of central Europe, Hungary is landlocked and has borders with seven states. Historically, Hungary has been a cosmopolitan cultural center, and during its years of market socialism was more prosperous than the other Eastern Bloc countries. Economic and political reforms have brought it closer to the EU, which it expects to join in the first "wave" of eastward enlargement; Hungary has also become a member of the NATO alliance. In foreign policy it is particularly sensitive about the treatment of Hungarian minorities in neighboring states.

CLIMATE

Continental

WEATHER CHART

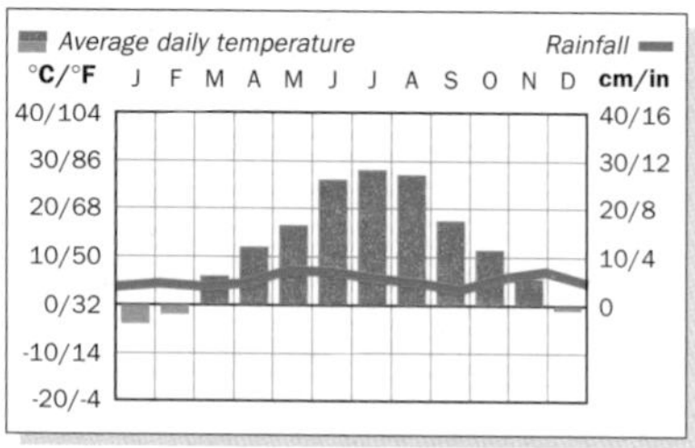
Average daily temperature
Rainfall
°C/°F J F M A M J J A S O N D cm/in
40/104
30/86
20/68
10/50
0/32
-10/14
-20/-4
40/16
30/12
20/8
10/4
0

Hungary has a continental climate, with wet springs, late summers, and cold, cloudy winters. There are no great differences of weather and climate within the country. Conditions in summer and winter may, however, differ from one year to the next. The transition between seasons tends to be sudden.

TRANSPORTATION

Drive on right

Budapest Ferihegy 4.32m passengers

2 ships 15,300 grt

THE TRANSPORTATION NETWORK

80,680 km (50,132 miles)

438 km (272 miles)

7988 km (4964 miles)

1373 km (853 miles)

Freight travels mainly via the rail link from Budapest to the Austrian border. Most foreign investment is located along this corridor. A direct link to Slovenia opened in mid-2001. The Budapest–Vienna expressway was the first of four big EU-backed road projects to be completed.

TOURISM

Visitors : Population 1.6:1

15.6m visitors

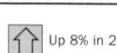

Up 8% in 2000

MAIN TOURIST ARRIVALS

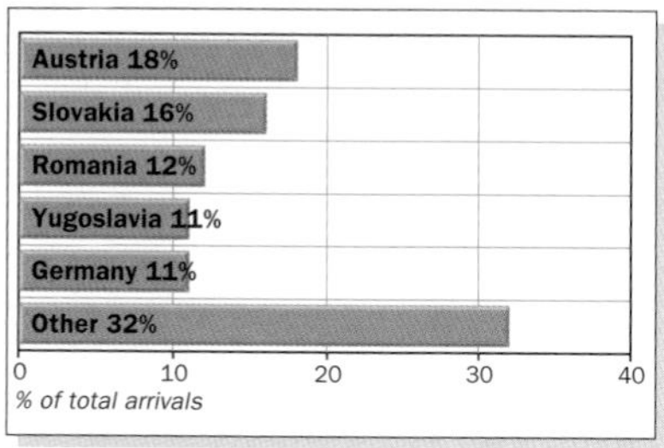
Austria 18%
Slovakia 16%
Romania 12%
Yugoslavia 11%
Germany 11%
Other 32%
0
10
20
30
40
% of total arrivals

Lake Balaton, the traditional summer holiday destination, was a magnet for East European visitors during the communist period. Since then, Hungary has invested heavily in its tourist facilities, and the number of travel agents and hotels has risen dramatically. Germans and Austrians are most numerous among the new clientele the country now attracts. Budapest's baths, some of which date from the Ottoman period, are a distinctive feature, and the capital also promotes itself as an international business convention center.

SLOVAKIA
UKRAINE
ROMANIA
YUGOSLAVIA (SERBIA AND MONTENEGRO)
CROATIA
SLOVENIA
AUSTRIA
Ózd
Kazincbarcika
Miskolc
Salgótarján
Balassagyarmat
Bükk
Kékes 1014m
Eger
Mátra
Gyöngyös
Nyíregyháza
Hajdúböszörmény
Debrecen
Mosonmagyaróvár
Neusiedler See
Győr
Sopron
Esztergom
Vác
Danube
Little Alföld
Tatabánya
Gödöllő
BUDAPEST
Jászberény
Kiskörei-víztároló
Pápa
Szombathely
Székesfehérvár
Szolnok
Cegléd
Ajka
Veszprém
Dunaújváros
Nagykőrös
Kecskemét
Bakony
Balaton
Zalaegerszeg
Kiskunfélegyháza
Békéscsaba
Szentes
Gyula
Orosháza
Nagykanizsa
Kaposvár
Szekszárd
Kiskunhalas
Hódmezővásárhely
Szeged
Makó
Komló
Mecsek
Pécs
Baja
Drava
Tisza
Great Alföld
0 50 km
0 50 miles
N
HUNGARY
Total Land Area : 92 340 sq. km (35 652 sq. miles)
POPULATION
over 1 000 000
over 500 000
over 100 000
over 50 000
over 10 000
LAND HEIGHT
500m/1640ft
200m/656ft
80m/262ft

PEOPLE

Pop. density medium

Hungarian

108/km² (280/mi²)

THE URBAN/RURAL POPULATION SPLIT

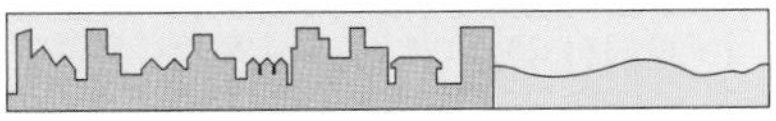
64%
36%

RELIGIOUS PERSUASION

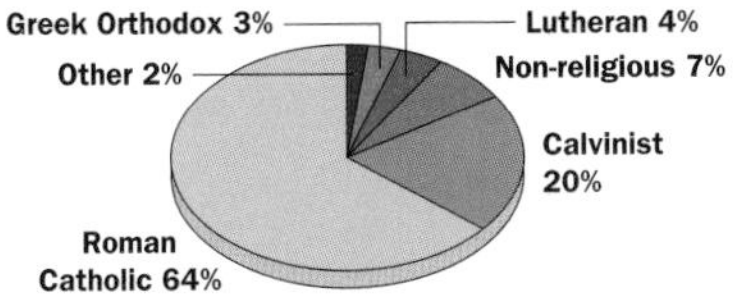
Greek Orthodox 3%
Lutheran 4%
Other 2%
Non-religious 7%
Calvinist 20%
Roman Catholic 64%

ETHNIC MAKEUP

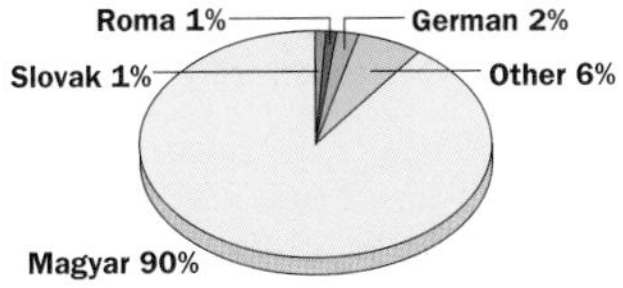
Roma 1%
German 2%
Slovak 1%
Other 6%
Magyar 90%

Hungary is ethnically homogeneous, although there are small minorities of Germans, Slovaks, Roma, Serbs, Croats, Romanians, and Hungarian Jews. There is little ethnic tension at home, although there is considerable concern about the treatment of Hungarian minorities in Romanian Transylvania, Serbian Vojvodina, and Slovakia. New legislation in June 2001 gave them special status in Hungary, including the right to work there for three months per year. The 100,000-strong Jewish community in Hungary is the largest in the region, although a mere fraction of the pre-Holocaust numbers, and is the target of occasional anti-Semitic outbursts. Prejudice against Roma is widespread and several major discrimination rows flared up in 2000. The new bourgeoisie has benefited from the market economy, but for the unskilled and unemployed life is tougher than under communism. Hungary has the highest suicide rate in the world.

POPULATION AGE BREAKDOWN

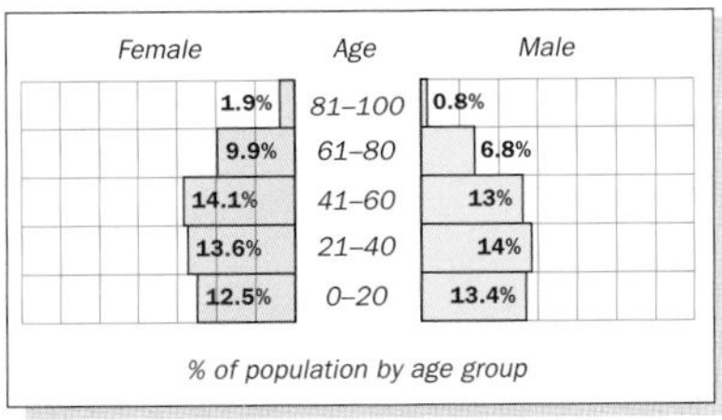
Female
Age
Male
1.9%
81–100
0.8%
9.9%
61–80
6.8%
14.1%
41–60
13%
13.6%
21–40
14%
12.5%
0–20
13.4%
% of population by age group

POLITICS

Multiparty elections

1998/2002

President Ferenc Mádl

AT THE LAST ELECTION

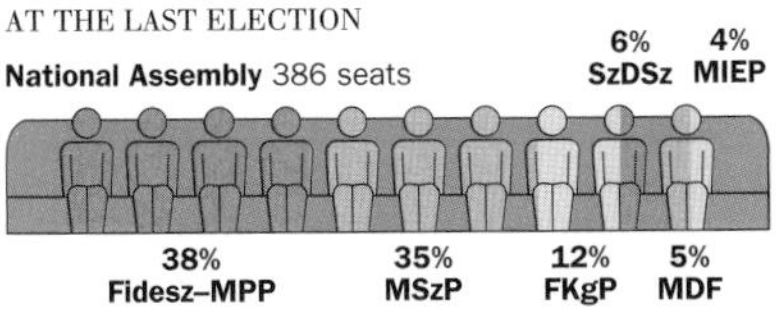
National Assembly 386 seats
6% SzDSz
4% MIEP
38% Fidesz–MPP
35% MSzP
12% FKgP
5% MDF

Fidesz–MPP = Young Democrats–Hungarian Civic Party **MSzP** = Hungarian Socialist Party **FKgP** = Independent Smallholders' Party **SzDSz** = Alliance of Free Democrats **MDF** = Hungarian Democrat Forum **MIEP** = Hungarian Justice and Life Party

Hungary has been a multiparty democracy since 1990.

MAIN POLITICAL ISSUE

Social welfare versus free-market economics

Reforms to assist transition to a market economy have led to strong economic recovery in the Budapest area and the western part of the country. Widening income differentials between young, skilled workers and those in education, health, and other state sectors have provoked protests and strikes, as the new prosperity eludes others.

PROFILE

Hungary's governments since the fall of communism have been relatively stable coalitions. The electoral pendulum has swung at four-yearly intervals, first to the Christian democratic nationalists of the MDF, then back to the former communists, and in 1998 to a liberal-led center-right.

MDF leader József Antall, prime minister from 1990, was the dominant figure in Hungarian democratic politics until his death in 1993. However, party disintegrations and disappointing economic results led to an increase in apathy and disillusionment among voters. After the 1994 general election, when Hungarians voted the former communists back into power, the victorious MSzP under Gyula Horn nevertheless preferred to work in coalition in order to ease the passage of economic and social reforms through parliament. The right-of-center coalition led by Viktor Orban, which has held office since Horn's narrow defeat in the 1998 election, has driven the country toward completing its transition to a market economy ready for EU membership.

***Ferenc Mádl,** known as "Mr. Professor," was elected president in 2000.*

***Viktor Orbán,** who became the country's youngest-ever premier in 1998.*

***The Hungarian parliament buildings** in Budapest, viewed across the Danube from the castle area of the city.*

WORLD AFFAIRS

Joined UN in 1955

CE | CEFTA | NATO | OECD | OSCE

Hungary joined NATO's Partnership for Peace program and gained WEU associate status in 1994. In a 1997 referendum 85% of voters endorsed joining NATO, and in March 1999 Hungary became a full NATO member, with Poland and the Czech Republic. Joining the EU is a slower process. With an association agreement since early 1994, in 1998 Hungary was one of six applicant countries to open formal membership negotiations.

Hungary has a cooperation and friendship treaty with Russia, but relations have been strained by Hungary's open courting of the West. Difficult relations with Slovakia and Romania have been eased by friendship treaties concluded in the mid-1990s.

CHRONOLOGY

The region today occupied by Hungary was first settled by the Finno-Ugrian Magyar peoples from the 8th century. In the 16th and 17th centuries, it came under Austrian domination, lasting until 1867, when Austria-Hungary was formed.

- **1918** Hungarian Republic created as successor state to Austria-Hungary.
- **1919** Béla Kún leads a short-lived communist government. Romania intervenes militarily and hands power to Admiral Horthy.
- **1938–1941** Hungary gains territory from Czechoslovakia, Yugoslavia, and Romania in return for supporting Nazi Germany.
- **1941** Hungary drawn into World War II on Axis side when Hitler attacks Soviet Union.
- **1944** Nazi Germany preempts Soviet advance on Hungary by invading. Deportation of Hungarian Jews and Roma to extermination camps begins. Soviet Red Army enters in October. Horthy forced to resign.
- **1945** Liberated by Red Army. Soviet-formed provisional government

H

CHRONOLOGY *continued*

installed. Imre Nagy introduces land reform.

- ❑ **1947** Communists emerge as largest party in second postwar election.
- ❑ **1948** Forcible merger of Social Democrats with communists to establish Hungarian Socialist Workers' Party (HSWP) in 1956.
- ❑ **1949** New constitution; formally becomes People's Republic.
- ❑ **1950–1951** First Secretary Mátyás Rákosi uses authoritarian powers to collectivize agriculture and industrialize the economy.
- ❑ **1953** Imre Nagy, Rákosi's rival, becomes premier and reduces political terror.
- ❑ **1955** Nagy deposed by Rákosi.
- ❑ **1956** Rákosi out. Student demonstrations, demanding withdrawal of Soviet troops and Nagy's return, become popular uprising. Nagy appointed premier and János Kádár First Secretary. Nagy announces Hungary will leave Warsaw Pact. Three days later, Soviet forces suppress protests. About 25,000 killed. Kádár becomes premier.
- ❑ **1958** Nagy executed.
- ❑ **1968** Kádár introduces New Economic Mechanism to bring market elements to socialism.
- ❑ **1986** Police suppress commemoration of 1956 uprising. Democratic opposition demands Kádár resign.
- ❑ **1987** Party reformers establish MDF as a political movement.
- ❑ **1988** Kádár ousted. Protests force suspension of plans for Nagymaros Dam on the Danube.
- ❑ **1989** End of one-party state as parliament votes to allow independent parties. Posthumous rehabilitation of Nagy, who is given state funeral. Round table talks between HSWP and opposition.
- ❑ **1990** József Antall's MDF wins multiparty elections decisively. Speed of economic reform hotly debated. Árpád Göncz president.
- ❑ **1991** Warsaw Pact dissolved. Last Soviet troops leave.
- ❑ **1994** Hungary joins NATO's Partnership for Peace program. Former communist MSzP wins general election. Austerity program prompts protests.
- ❑ **1998** EU entry negotiations open. Elections; Viktor Orbán (Fidesz-MPP) forms right-of-center coalition.
- ❑ **1999** Joins NATO. Airspace used in NATO bombing of Yugoslavia.
- ❑ **2000** Tisza river polluted by Romanian industries upstream. June, Ferenc Mádl succeeds Göncz as president.

H

AID

Recipient

$248m (receipts)

Up 63% 1997–1999

Hungary received substantial Western aid in 1990–1996, but by the end of the decade was considered able to attract investment mainly on commercial terms. EU and World Bank assistance moved to focus on targeting disadvantaged social groups, raising environmental standards, and strengthening market institutions.

DEFENSE

Compulsory military service

$745m

Up 11% in 1999

Troop numbers were more than halved, and conventional arms and the military hierarchy were updated in advance of NATO membership in 1999. The emphasis has switched toward more flexibility and rapid response. Almost immediately on joining NATO, Hungary permitted it to use its airspace to bomb Yugoslavia. Military service has been shortened to six months with effect from 2002.

HUNGARIAN ARMED FORCES

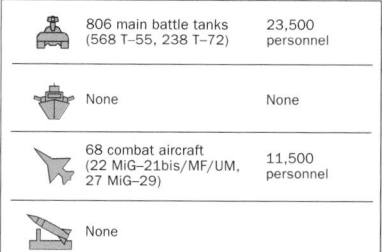

806 main battle tanks (568 T-55, 238 T-72)	23,500 personnel
None	None
68 combat aircraft (22 MiG-21bis/MF/UM, 27 MiG-29)	11,500 personnel
None	

ECONOMICS

Inflation 20.6% p.a. (1990–1999)

$46.8bn

254.02–282.34 forint

SCORE CARD

- ❑ World GNP Ranking......51st
- ❑ GNP per Capita......$4640
- ❑ Balance of Payments......$2.1bn
- ❑ Inflation......10.3%
- ❑ Unemployment......10%

EXPORTS

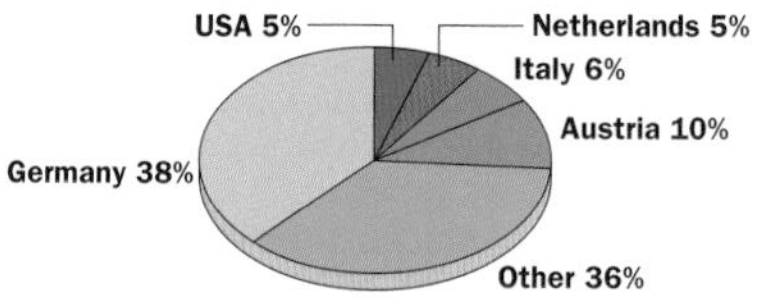
USA 5%
Netherlands 5%
Italy 6%
Austria 10%
Germany 38%
Other 36%

IMPORTS

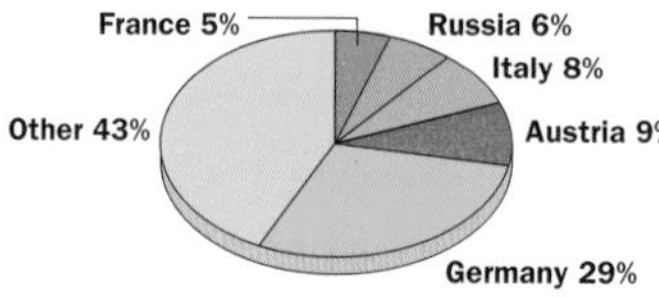
France 5%
Russia 6%
Italy 8%
Austria 9%
Other 43%
Germany 29%

Strengths

Openness to foreign direct investment, especially since 1998. Favorable tax regime, streamlined bureaucracy. Strong export-led growth in late 1990s continued into 2000. High industrial production, especially at new, state-of-the-art factories. Currency fully convertible from mid-2001. Inflation dropping.

Weaknesses

Low energy efficiency. East–west split as development bypasses rural eastern areas. Widening income differentials. Money laundering is a challenge to finance industry regulators; Hungary is on OECD blacklist.

ECONOMIC PERFORMANCE INDICATOR

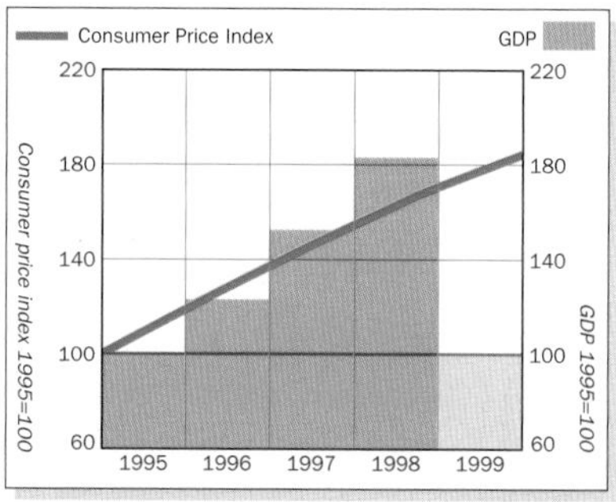
Consumer Price Index
GDP
220
180
140
100
60
Consumer price index 1995=100
GDP 1995=100
1995
1996
1997
1998
1999

Profile

The collapse of COMECON (communist economic bloc) caused a reorientation of trade toward western Europe. Exports increased rapidly and competitiveness has improved. However, the economy did not recover to its pre-1989 level until 1999. Privatization has reduced the state-owned share of the economy, from 85% to 15%, and has helped cut external debt.

HUNGARY : MAJOR BUSINESSES

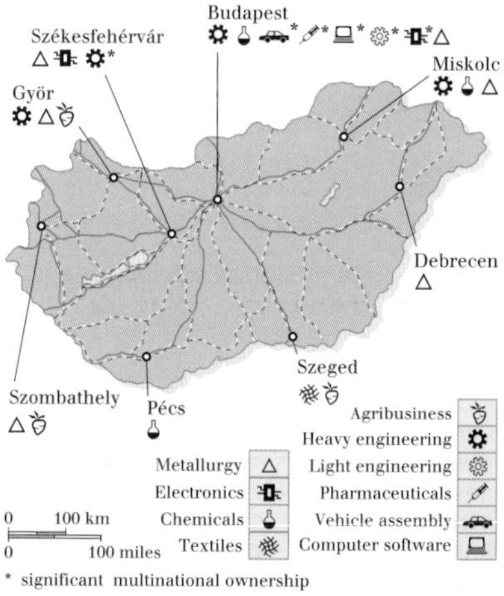
Budapest
Székesfehérvár
Miskolc
Györ
Debrecen
Szeged
Szombathely
Pécs
Agribusiness
Heavy engineering
Metallurgy
Light engineering
Electronics
Pharmaceuticals
Chemicals
Vehicle assembly
Textiles
Computer software
0 100 km
0 100 miles
* significant multinational ownership

RESOURCES

Electric power 7m kw

21,916 tonnes

27,268 b/d (reserves 29,865,600 bbl)

5.3m pigs, 2.3m ducks, 26m chickens

Bauxite, coal, oil, natural gas, lignite

ELECTRICITY GENERATION

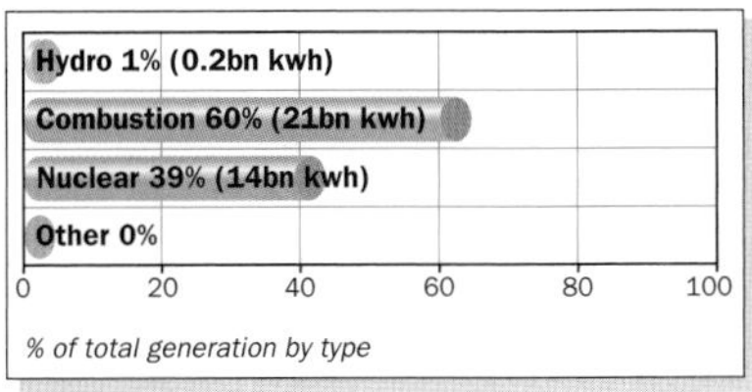
Hydro 1% (0.2bn kwh)
Combustion 60% (21bn kwh)
Nuclear 39% (14bn kwh)
Other 0%
0
20
40
60
80
100
% of total generation by type

HUNGARY : LAND USE

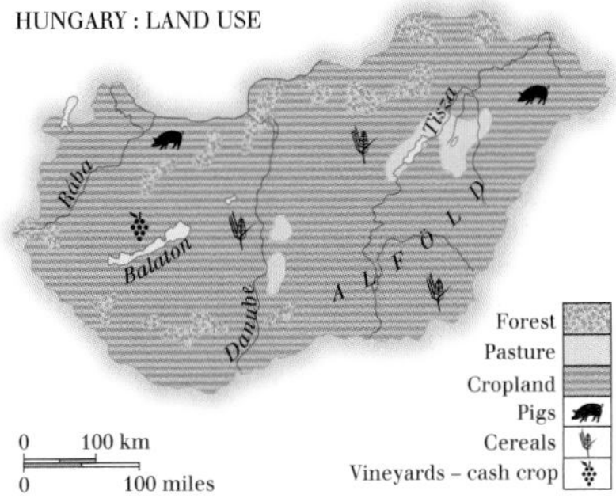
Rába
Balaton
Danube
Tisza
A L F Ö L D
Forest
Pasture
Cropland
Pigs
Cereals
Vineyards – cash crop
0 100 km
0 100 miles

Hungary has bauxite, brown coal, lignite, and natural gas reserves. It depends for about 40% of its electricity on nuclear energy from the Paks complex, north of Baja. Fertile farmlands provide grains, sugar beet, and potatoes. Wine production is also important.

ENVIRONMENT

Sustainability rank: 21st

7% (5% partially protected)

5.9 tonnes per capita

ENVIRONMENTAL TREATIES

Yes	Yes	Yes
Yes	Yes	No

A high sulfur content in Hungary's fossil fuels exacerbates the serious air pollution in industrial zones. The energy industry must meet new standards by 2005. A "green card" system has been introduced to favor the use of cars with catalytic convertors and reduce serious pollution from older vehicles.

Industrial pollution of the Sajo, Tisza, and Danube river systems, sometimes originating in neighboring countries, is a major problem.

MEDIA

TV ownership high

Daily newspaper circulation 186 per 1000 people

PUBLISHING AND BROADCAST MEDIA

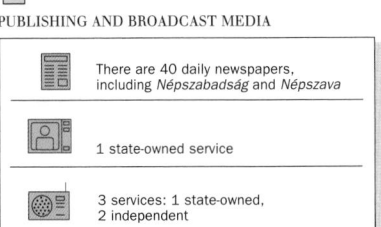

There are 40 daily newspapers, including *Népszabadság* and *Népszava*

1 state-owned service

3 services: 1 state-owned, 2 independent

Newspapers and magazines are fiercely independent and critical of government policy. In 1994 the Constitutional Court declared that state interference in the media was unlawful. Allegations of interference persist. The boards controlling state TV and radio must have equal representation from government and opposition under a 1996 media law, but the government has been accused of bending or ignoring the rules.

CRIME

Death penalty not used

12,455 prisoners

Up 30% 1996–1998

CRIME RATES

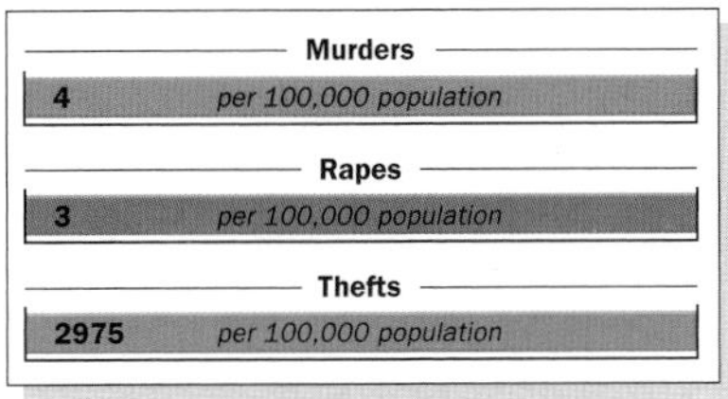
Murders
4 per 100,000 population
Rapes
3 per 100,000 population
Thefts
2975 per 100,000 population

An alarming trend in the late 1990s was the increase in murders of elderly people for financial gain. Organized crime, money laundering, and smuggling of illegal immigrants are rising.

EDUCATION

School leaving age: 16

99%

194,607 students

THE EDUCATION SYSTEM

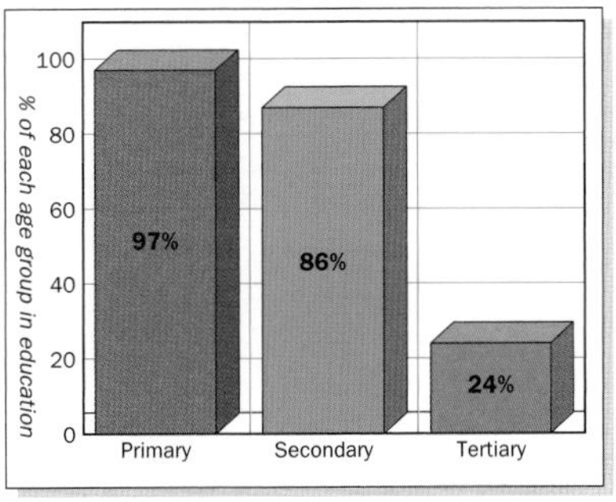
100
80
60
40
20
0
% of each age group in education
97%
86%
24%
Primary
Secondary
Tertiary

Education is free and compulsory from the ages of six to 16. Bilingual schools have been established in southern Hungary to promote the languages of the national minorities. In 1999–2000 a major transformation of the education system took place, as a result of which, with effect from 2000, there are 30 universities and colleges run by the state, 26 run by the church, and six colleges run by various foundations.

HEALTH

Welfare state health benefits

1 per 286 people

Heart and cerebrovascular diseases, cancers, accidents

Medical treatment has traditionally been free to all, although there is a charge toward prescription costs. State sickness benefits remain relatively generous. Spending on the health service has fallen in recent years in real terms; at $600 per capita, it is only one-third the OECD average, and there is concern that Hungary's health care sector is among the least developed of OECD countries. The ratio of doctors to patients is high, but there is a shortage of nurses. Family physician services are being privatized rapidly under a law passed in 2000.

H

SPENDING

GDP/cap. increase

CONSUMPTION AND SPENDING

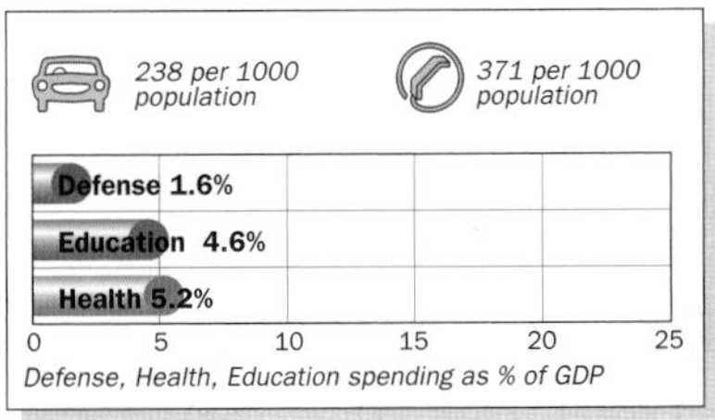
238 per 1000 population
371 per 1000 population
Defense 1.6%
Education 4.6%
Health 5.2%
0
5
10
15
20
25
Defense, Health, Education spending as % of GDP

Hungary enjoys a higher standard of living than other former communist countries except Slovenia, and demand for luxury goods is rising. Access to mobile phones and the Internet is relatively high. Real wages, which fell by 15% in the mid-1990s, had regained most of this ground by 2000. Hungarians still have to work longer hours to pay for basic consumer goods than workers in western Europe. Salaries in the public services have not kept pace with the rising cost of living, and as a result there is a growing disparity between those working in the state and private sectors. The Roma minority suffers particularly over access to housing, which is in short supply.

WORLD RANKING

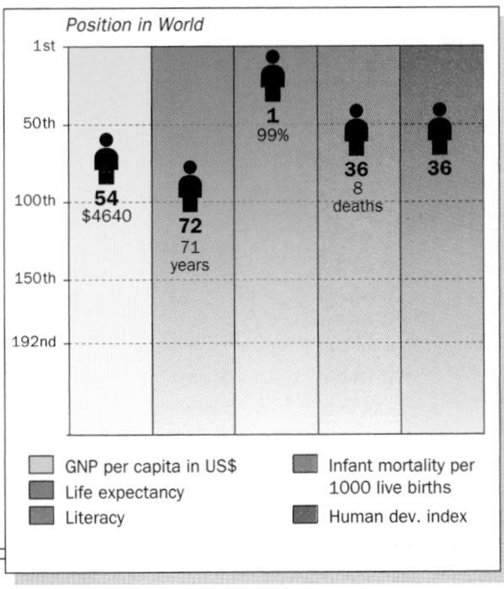
Position in World
1st
50th
100th
150th
192nd
54
$4640
72
71 years
1
99%
36
8 deaths
36
GNP per capita in US$
Life expectancy
Literacy
Infant mortality per 1000 live births
Human dev. index

ICELAND

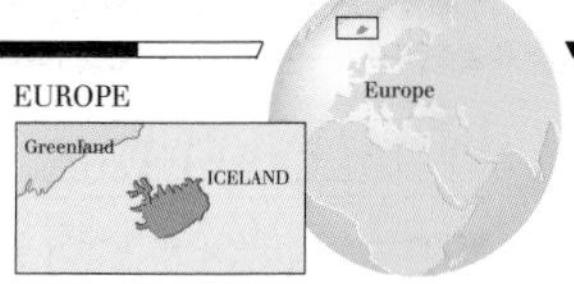
EUROPE
Europe
Greenland
ICELAND

OFFICIAL NAME: Republic of Iceland **CAPITAL:** Reykjavík
POPULATION: 281,000 **CURRENCY:** Icelandic króna **OFFICIAL LANGUAGE:** Icelandic

1944
1944
June 17
IS
0
+354
.is

EUROPE'S WESTERNMOST country, Iceland has a strategic location in the North Atlantic, just south of the Arctic Circle. Its position, on the rift where the North American and European continental plates are pulling apart, accounts for its 200 volcanoes and its numerous geysers and solfataras. Previously a Danish possession, Iceland became fully independent in 1944. Most settlements are along the coast, where ports remain ice-free in winter.

CLIMATE

Subarctic

WEATHER CHART

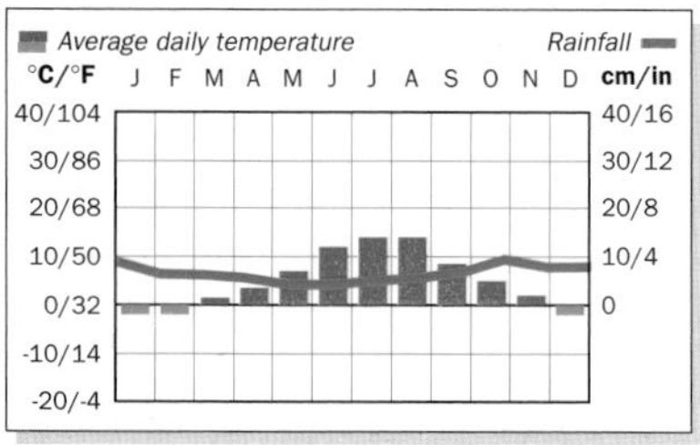
Average daily temperature
Rainfall
°C/°F
J F M A M J J A S O N D
cm/in
40/104
30/86
20/68
10/50
0/32
-10/14
-20/-4
40/16
30/12
20/8
10/4
0

Iceland sits in the Gulf Stream. Winters are consequently mild. Summers are cool, with fine, long sunny days.

TRANSPORTATION

Drive on right

Keflavík International, Reykjavík
1.32m passengers

979 ships
216,391 grt

THE TRANSPORTATION NETWORK

3439 km (2137 miles)	None
None	None

Icelanders rely entirely on cars and internal airplane and helicopter flights. Most freight moves by sea. The only main road is the island ring road.

TOURISM

Visitors : Population 1.1:1

303,000 visitors

Up 15% in 2000

MAIN TOURIST ARRIVALS

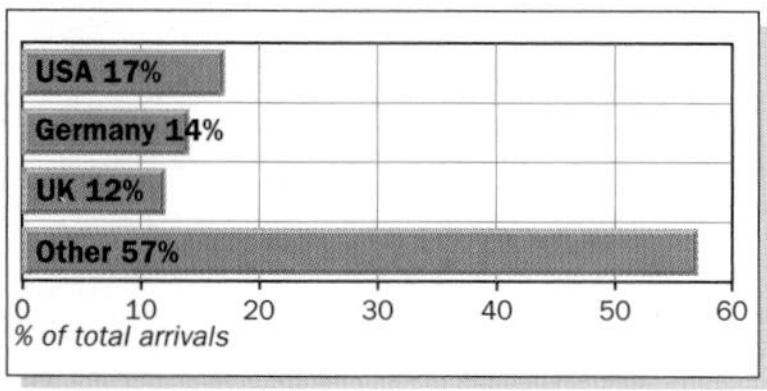
USA 17%
Germany 14%
UK 12%
Other 57%
0
10
20
30
40
50
60
% of total arrivals

Iceland is promoting itself, especially in Japan, as an upmarket destination for tourists who are attracted by its spectacular scenery, glaciers, green valleys, fjords, and hot springs.

PEOPLE

Pop. density low

Icelandic

3/km² (7/mi²)

THE URBAN/RURAL POPULATION SPLIT

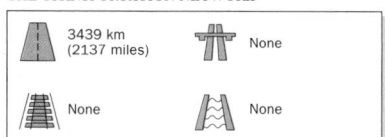

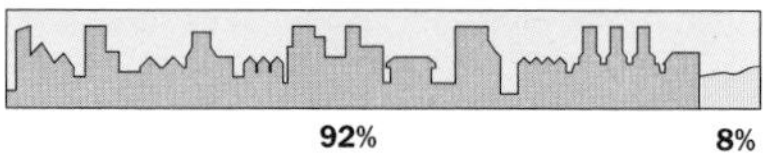
92%
8%

RELIGIOUS PERSUASION

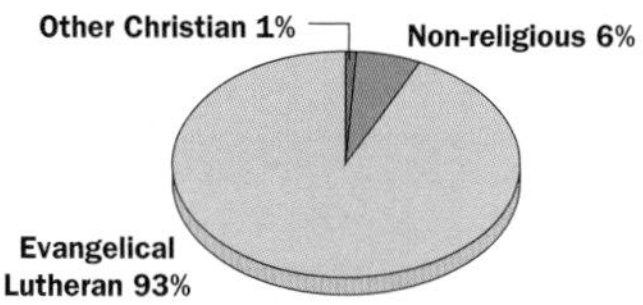
Other Christian 1%
Non-religious 6%
Evangelical Lutheran 93%

Descended from Norwegians and Celts, Icelanders form an ethnically homogeneous society. Almost all follow the Evangelical Lutheran Church. More than half the population live in or near Reykjavík. Living standards are high, and there are few social tensions.

POLITICS

Multiparty elections

1999/2003

President Olafur Ragnar Grimsson

AT THE LAST ELECTION

Parliament 63 seats

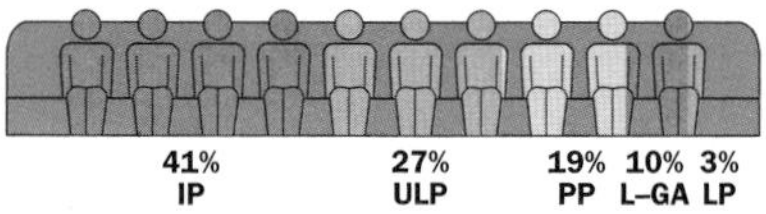
41% IP
27% ULP
19% PP
10% L–GA
3% LP

IP = Independence Party **ULP** = United Left Party
PP = Progressive Party **L–GA** = Left–Green Alliance
LP = Liberal Party

From independence Iceland has been ruled by coalitions, but in the 1980s the traditional four-party system began to splinter. After the 1991 election, a new IP/Social Democratic coalition promoted market-led reforms. Arguments over whether or not to join the EU were defused in 1992 with the successful negotiation of the EEA, giving Iceland access to the key EU market.

The coalition collapsed after the 1995 general election, when both parties had lost support, and was replaced by a center-right government led by the IP, with David Oddsson as prime minister. He has successfully built on a recovery under way since 1994 and strengthened his position in the 1999 general election.

ICELAND

Total Land Area : 100 250 sq. km (38 707 sq. miles)

POPULATION
- over 50 000
- over 10 000
- under 10 000

LAND HEIGHT
- 1000m/3281ft
- 500m/1640ft
- 200m/656ft
- Sea Level
- Ice Cap

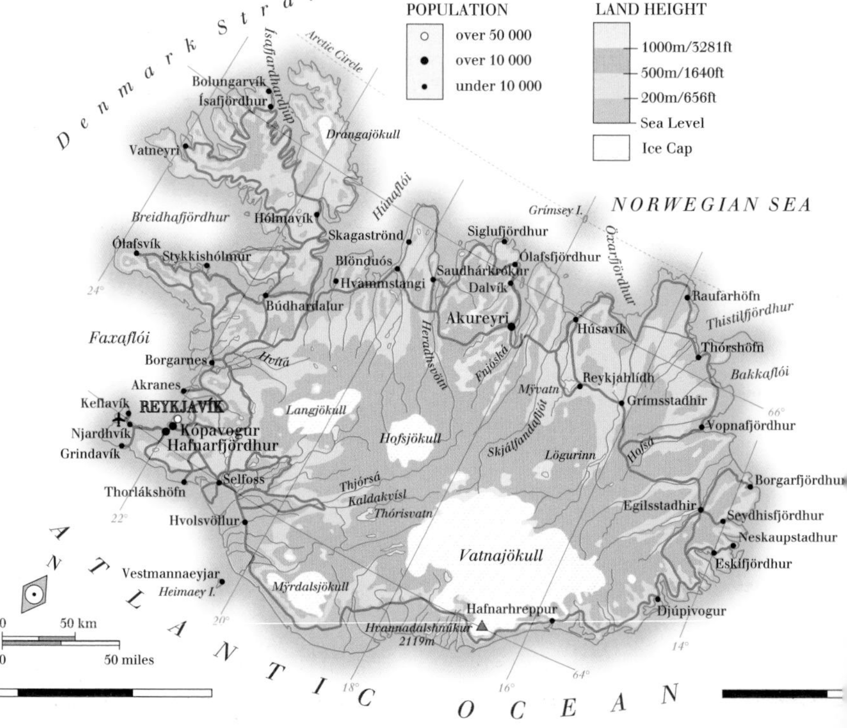
Denmark Strait
Arctic Circle
Ísafjardhardjúp
Bolungarvík
Ísafjördhur
Drangajökull
Vatneyri
Breidhafjördhur
Hólmavík
Húnaflói
Grímsey I.
NORWEGIAN SEA
Öxarfjördhur
Skagaströnd
Siglufjördhur
Ólafsvík
Stykkishólmur
Blönduós
Ólafsfjördhur
Hvammstangi
Saudhárkrókur
Dalvík
Raufarhöfn
Thistilfjördhur
Búdhardalur
Heradhsvötn
Akureyri
Fnjóská
Húsavík
Faxaflói
Borgarnes
Hvítá
Thórshöfn
Bakkaflói
Akranes
Mývatn
Reykjahlídh
Grímsstadhir
Keflavík
REYKJAVÍK
Langjökull
Njardhvík
Kópavogur
Hafnarfjördhur
Skjálfandafljót
Vopnafjördhur
Grindavík
Hofsjökull
Lögurinn
Jökulsá
Selfoss
Borgarfjördhur
Thorlákshöfn
Thjórsá
Kaldakvísl
Thórisvatn
Egilsstadhir
Hvolsvöllur
Seydhisfjördhur
Neskaupstadhur
Vatnajökull
Eskifjördhur
Vestmannaeyjar
Heimaey I.
Mýrdalsjökull
Hafnarhreppur
Djúpivogur
Hvannadalshnúkur 2119m
ATLANTIC OCEAN
0 50 km
0 50 miles

WORLD AFFAIRS

Joined UN in 1946

CE | NATO | OECD | OSCE | EEA

Although a member of NATO and EFTA, Iceland has traditionally maintained arm's length relations with the EU and the USA. Major disputes have concerned fishing rights. It left the International Whaling Commission in 1992 when a commercial whaling ban was continued, but rejoined in 2001. Links with other Nordic states are strong.

AID

Donor

$6m (donations)

Down 14% in 1994

Aid donations are modest, and form a smaller proportion of the budget than in other Scandinavian states.

DEFENSE

No compulsory military service

Coastguard is only military force

Not applicable

A NATO member and an associate WEU member, Iceland has no armed forces. US troops are based at Keflavík.

ECONOMICS

Inflation 3.3% p.a. (1990–1999)

$8.2bn

72.61–84.74 Icelandic krónur

SCORE CARD

❑ WORLD GNP RANKING	94th
❑ GNP PER CAPITA	$29,540
❑ BALANCE OF PAYMENTS	$–591m
❑ INFLATION	3.2%
❑ UNEMPLOYMENT	3%

STRENGTHS

High-tech fishing industry with exclusive access to prime fishing grounds. Strong economic recovery in late 1990s; low inflation and unemployment. Very cheap geothermal power.

WEAKNESSES

Over 70% of export earnings derived from fish. Large state-owned banking sector restricts market flexibility.

EXPORTS

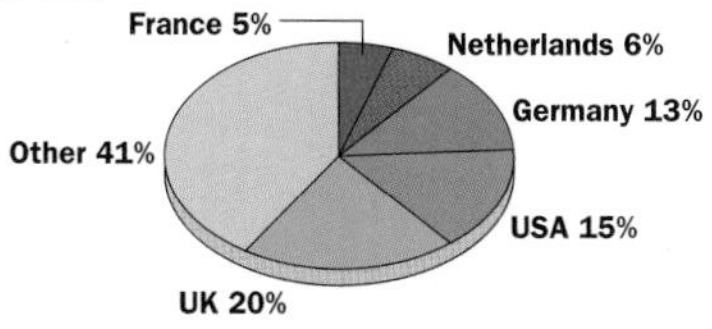
France 5%
Netherlands 6%
Germany 13%
USA 15%
UK 20%
Other 41%

IMPORTS

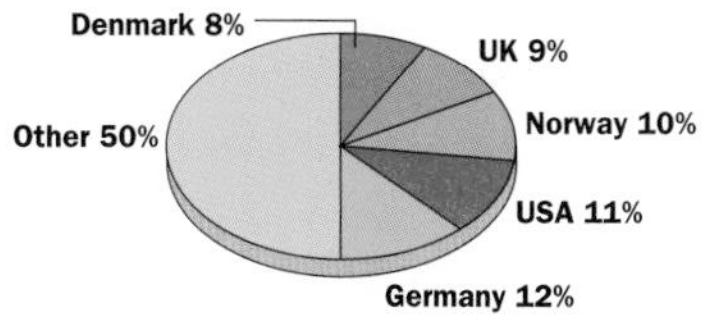
Denmark 8%
UK 9%
Norway 10%
USA 11%
Germany 12%
Other 50%

***Lava towers,** near Lake Mývatn in northern Iceland – an area of grassy lowlands. Iceland's center consists of lava desert and glaciers.*

RESOURCES

Electric power 1.2m kw

2.21m tonnes

Not an oil producer

490,538 sheep, 77,330 horses, 191,000 chickens

Diatomite

Iceland has virtually no minerals. All energy needs are met by geothermal and hydroelectric sources. It has implemented measures to try to restore once abundant fish stocks.

ENVIRONMENT

Sustainability rank: 9th

9% (7% partially protected)

7.9 tonnes per capita

Iceland has no nuclear or coal-fired power stations. Pollution levels are low. Believing that minke whales eat valuable cod stocks, Iceland resumed whale hunting in 1992. The 1996 eruption of the Loki volcano under Vatna glacier caused extensive flooding and damage.

MEDIA

TV ownership high

Daily newspaper circulation 535 per 1000 people

PUBLISHING AND BROADCAST MEDIA

There are 4 daily newspapers, including *Dagbladid-Visir* and *Morgunbladid*, which has the largest circulation

12 services: 1 state-owned, 11 independent

17 services: 1 state-owned, 16 independent

Iceland is renowned for having one of the highest per capita newspaper circulations in the world.

CRIME

Death penalty not used

113 prisoners

Crime rates are fairly stable

Crime rates are comparatively low. The rate of alcohol-related murders is higher than the European average.

EDUCATION

School leaving age: 16

99%

7908 students

Icelanders buy more books per capita than any other nation. Education is state-run; some 40% of school students go on to university at Reykjavík or Akureyri, or to colleges in the USA.

CHRONOLOGY

Settled in the 9th century by Norwegians, Iceland was ruled by Denmark from 1380 to 1944, becoming fully self-governing in 1918.

- ❑ **1940–1945** Occupied by UK and USA.
- ❑ **1944** Independence as republic.
- ❑ **1949** Founder member of NATO.
- ❑ **1951** US air base built at Keflavík despite strong local opposition.
- ❑ **1972–1976** Extends fishing limits to 50 miles; two "cod wars" with UK.
- ❑ **1975** Sets 200-mile fishing limit.
- ❑ **1980** Vigdís Finnbogadóttir world's first elected woman head of state.
- ❑ **1985** Declares nuclear-free status.
- ❑ **1995–1999** Formation of center-right coalition under David Oddsson after general election; reelected in 1999.

I

HEALTH

Welfare state health benefits

1 per 307 people

Heart disease, cancers, accidents

The state health system is free to all Icelanders. Iceland, like most of Western Europe, has one of the lowest infant mortality rates and one of the highest longevity rates in the world.

SPENDING

GDP/cap. increase

CONSUMPTION AND SPENDING

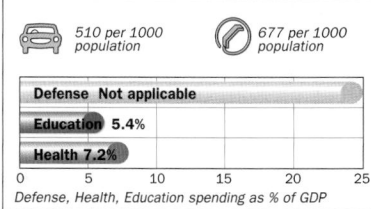

510 per 1000 population

677 per 1000 population

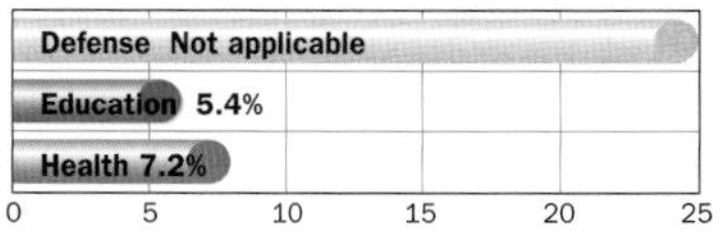
Defense Not applicable
Education 5.4%
Health 7.2%
0
5
10
15
20
25

Defense, Health, Education spending as % of GDP

Wealth distribution in Iceland is comparatively even and social mobility is high. Domestic heating, extracted from geothermal sources, is provided at almost no cost.

WORLD RANKING

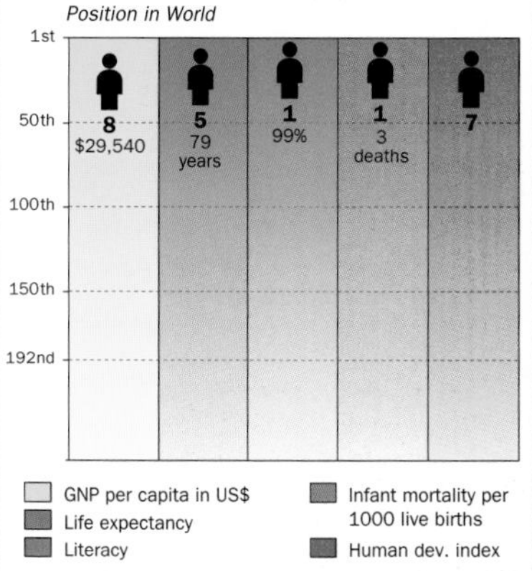
Position in World
1st
50th
100th
150th
192nd
8
$29,540
5
79 years
1
99%
1
3 deaths
7
GNP per capita in US$
Life expectancy
Literacy
Infant mortality per 1000 live births
Human dev. index

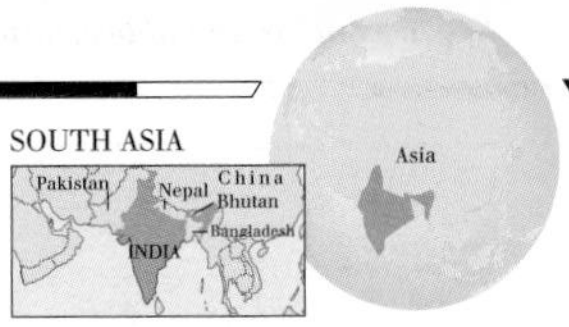
SOUTH ASIA
Pakistan
Nepal
China
Bhutan
Bangladesh
INDIA
Asia

INDIA

OFFICIAL NAME: Republic of India **CAPITAL:** New Delhi
POPULATION: 1 billion **CURRENCY:** Indian rupee **OFFICIAL LANGUAGES:** Hindi and English

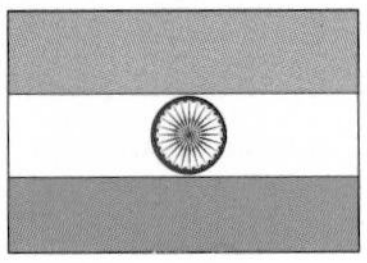

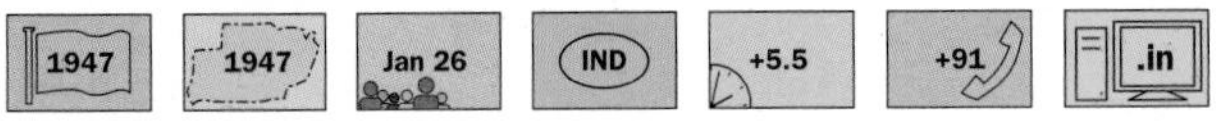
1947
1947
Jan 26
IND
+5.5
+91
.in

SEPARATED FROM the rest of Asia by the Himalaya mountain range, India forms a subcontinent. As well as the Himalayas, there are two other main geographical regions, the Indo-Gangetic plain, which lies between the foothills of the Himalayas and the Vindhya Mountains, and the central–southern plateau. India is the world's largest democracy and second most populous country after China. The birthrate has recently been falling, but even at its current level India's population will probably overtake China's by 2030. After years of protectionism, India is opening up its economy to the outside world. The hope is that the free market will go some way to alleviating one of the country's major problems, poverty.

CLIMATE

Tropical/subtropical/desert/mountain/monsoon

WEATHER CHART

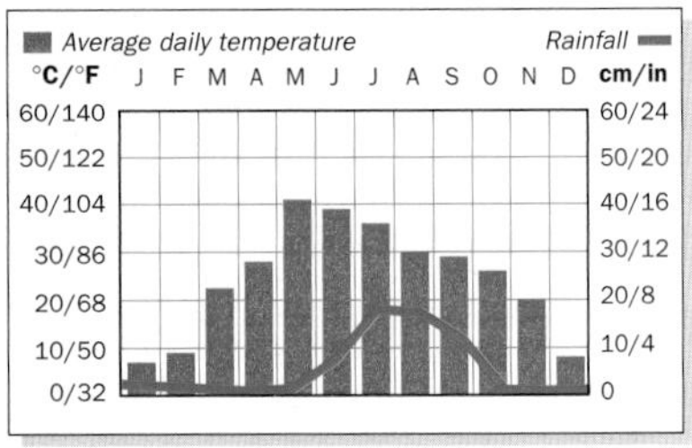
Average daily temperature
Rainfall
°C/°F
J F M A M J J A S O N D
cm/in
60/140
50/122
40/104
30/86
20/68
10/50
0/32
60/24
50/20
40/16
30/12
20/8
10/4
0

During the hot season, temperatures in the north can reach 40°C (104°F). The monsoon breaks in June and peters out in September or October. In the cool season, average temperatures are 5°C–15°C (41°F–59°F) in the north and the weather is mainly dry. The south has a less variable climate. Chennai (Madras) is always hot. Average temperatures range from 24°C (75°F) in January to 32°C (90°F) in May and June.

TRANSPORTATION

Drive on left

Mumbai International
11.3m passengers

947 ships
6.8m grt

THE TRANSPORTATION NETWORK

1.52m km (942,666 miles)	33,500 km (20,816 miles)
62,810 km (39,030 miles)	16,180 km (10,054 miles)

India's state-owned railroad system, the largest in Asia, spans all the major cities. Rail carries 40% of passenger traffic and 65% of freight. Strict controls on diesel emissions from cars and buses to check pollution were enforced in 2001. Cycle and scooter rickshaws are common in urban centers. Kolkata (Calcutta) still has rickshaws pulled by hand.

INDIA
Total Land Area : 2 973 190 sq. km
(1 147 949 sq. miles)
POPULATION
over 5 000 000
over 1 000 000
over 500 000
over 100 000
over 10 000
LAND HEIGHT
5000m/16 405ft
4000m/13 124ft
3000m/9843ft
2000m/6562ft
1000m/3281ft
500m/1640ft
200m/656ft
Sea Level
0 200 km
0 200 miles
N
Aksai Chin
Line of control
KARAKORAM RANGE
Indus
Srinagar
JAMMU & KASHMIR
Jammu
CHINA (TIBET)
Amritsar
Jalandhar
Ludhiana
HIMACHAL PRADESH
Chandigarh
PUNJAB
Nanda Devi 7816m
HARYANA
Meerut
PAKISTAN
THAR DESERT
NEPAL
Delhi
NEW DELHI
Faridabad
Bareilly
Bikaner
Agra
UTTAR PRADESH
Gorakhpur
Jaipur
Lucknow
RAJASTHAN
Jodhpur
Gwalior
Yamuna
Kanpur
Patna
Allahabad
Ganges
Varanasi
BIHAR
Dhanbad
Kota
Rann of Kachch
GUJARAT
Gulf of Kachch
Jamnagar
Rajkot
Ahmadabad
Vindhya Range
Bhopal
Indore
Jabalpur
MADHYA PRADESH
Chota Nagpur Plateau
Ranchi
Jamshedpur
Vadodara
Narmada
Bilaspur
Mahanadi
Surat
Tapi
Satpura Range
Raipur
Diu
Gulf of Khambhat
Pimpri
Amravati
Nagpur
ORISSA
Nashik
MAHARASHTRA
Godavari
Nanded
ARABIAN SEA
Thane
Kalyan
Mumbai (Bombay)
Pune
DECCAN
Nizamabad
Warangal
Visakhapatnam
Solapur
ANDHRA PRADESH
Hyderabad
Rajahmundry
KARNATAKA
Kolhapur
Vijayawada
Krishna
Kurnool
Guntur
Tungabhadra
Panji
GOA
Hubli
Bellary
Anantapur
Cuddapah
Western Ghats
Eastern Ghats
Chennai (Madras)
Mangalore
Bangalore
Vellore
Mysore
Calicut
Salem
Pondicherry
Amindivi Is
KERALA
Coimbatore
TAMIL NADU
Tiruchchirappalli
LAKSHADWEEP (Laccadive Is)
Kavaratti I.
Kalpeni I.
Trichur
Dindigal
Madurai
Cochin
Palk Strait
Trivandrum
Tuticorin
Gulf of Mannar
SRI LANKA
Minicoy I.
Nagercoil
INDIAN OCEAN
North Andaman
ANDAMAN ISLANDS
Middle Andaman
South Andaman
Port Blair
Little Andaman
NICOBAR ISLANDS
Great Nicobar
(continuation on same scale)

A religious festival. *Such festivals are a frequent occurrence and form an important part of Hindu culture.*

ARUNACHAL PRADESH
BHUTAN
Kangchenjunga
8598m
Darjiling
Shiliguri
Brahmaputra
Guwahati
ASSAM
Imphal
BANGLADESH
Ganges
Calcutta
(Kolkata)
Mouths of the Ganges
BURMA
(MYANMAR)
BAY OF
BENGAL

TOURISM

Visitors : Population 1:384

2.6m visitors

Up 6% in 2000

MAIN TOURIST ARRIVALS

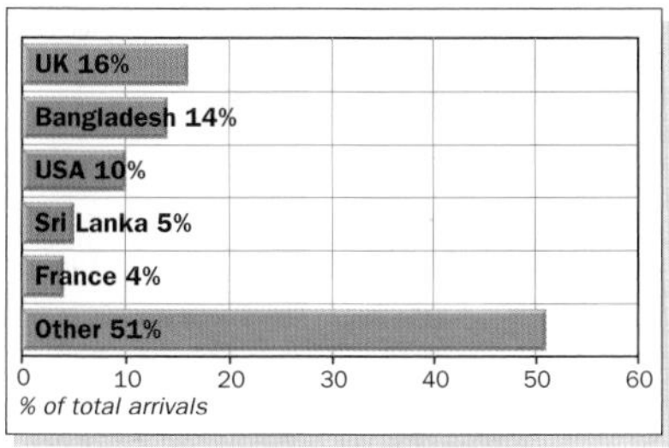
UK 16%
Bangladesh 14%
USA 10%
Sri Lanka 5%
France 4%
Other 51%
0
10
20
30
40
50
60
% of total arrivals

Tourism is India's sixth-largest foreign exchange earner. More luxury hotels are being built, and wildlife and adventure tourism are being promoted. However, India still has only a small share of the world tourism market. The inauguration in early 1999 of the first bus service between India and Pakistan is expected to raise tourist revenues.

PEOPLE

Pop. density high

Hindi, English, Urdu, Bengali, Marathi, Telugu, Tamil, Bihari, Gujarati, Kanarese

341/km² (883/mi²)

THE URBAN/RURAL POPULATION SPLIT

28%
72%

RELIGIOUS PERSUASION

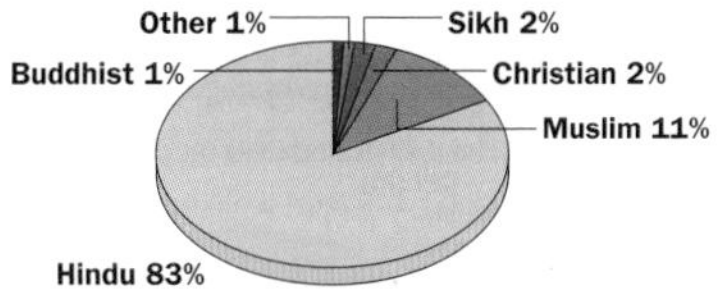
Other 1%
Sikh 2%
Buddhist 1%
Christian 2%
Muslim 11%
Hindu 83%

ETHNIC MAKEUP

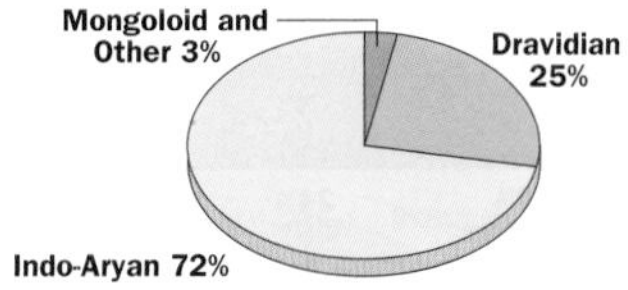
Mongoloid and Other 3%
Dravidian 25%
Indo-Aryan 72%

India is the world's second most populous country after China, officially passing the one billion mark in 2000. Despite a major birth control program, the decrease in population growth has been marginal. Nationwide awareness campaigns aim to promote the idea of smaller families. India's planners consider the rise in the population the most significant brake on development. Cultural and religious pressures encourage large families, however, and the extended family is seen as an essential security for old age.

The fertile rice-growing areas of the Gangetic plain and delta are very densely populated. The northern state of Uttar Pradesh has the largest population, followed by neighboring Bihar and the western state of Maharashtra. Maharashtra is also the most urbanized state, with more than half of its people living in towns or cities. Elsewhere, most Indians live in rural areas, although poverty continues to drive many to the swelling cities.

The overwhelming majority of the population are Hindus. Each Hindu belongs to one of thousands of castes and subcastes. Hindus are born into their caste, and caste largely determines whom they marry and their future status and occupation. Various attempts to reform the system have met with violent opposition.

POPULATION AGE BREAKDOWN

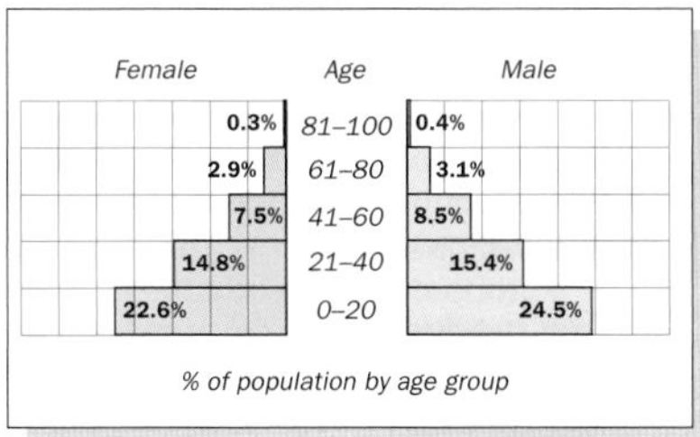
Female
Age
Male
0.3%
81–100
0.4%
2.9%
61–80
3.1%
7.5%
41–60
8.5%
14.8%
21–40
15.4%
22.6%
0–20
24.5%
% of population by age group

CHRONOLOGY

The origins of an Indus valley civilization may be traced back to the third millennium BCE. By the 3rd century BCE, the Mauryan kingdom under Ashoka encompassed most of modern India. Following the Battle of Plassey in 1757, British rule – through the East India Company – was consolidated.

- ❑ **1885** Formation of Indian National Congress.
- ❑ **1919** Act of parliament introduces "responsible government."
- ❑ **1920–1922** Mahatma Gandhi's first civil disobedience campaign.
- ❑ **1935** Government of India Act grants autonomy to provinces.
- ❑ **1936** First elections under new constitution.
- ❑ **1942–1943** "Quit India" movement.
- ❑ **1947** August, independence and partition into India and Pakistan. Jawarhalal Nehru becomes first prime minister.
- ❑ **1948** Assassination of Mahatma Gandhi. War with Pakistan over Kashmir. India becomes a republic.
- ❑ **1951–1952** First general election won by Congress party.
- ❑ **1957** Congress party reelected. First elected communist state government installed in Kerala.
- ❑ **1960** Bombay divided into states of Gujarat and Maharashtra.
- ❑ **1962** Congress party reelected. Border war with China.
- ❑ **1964** Death of Nehru. Lal Bahadur Shastri becomes prime minister.
- ❑ **1965** Second war with Pakistan over Kashmir.
- ❑ **1966** Shastri dies; Indira Gandhi (daughter of Jawarhalal Nehru) becomes prime minister.
- ❑ **1969** Congress party splits into two factions; larger faction led by Indira Gandhi.
- ❑ **1971** Indira Gandhi's Congress party wins elections. Third war with Pakistan, over creation of Bangladesh.
- ❑ **1972** Simla (peace) Agreement signed with Pakistan.
- ❑ **1974** Explosion of first nuclear device in underground test.
- ❑ **1975–1977** Imposition of state of emergency.
- ❑ **1977** Congress loses general election. People's Party (JD) takes power at the center.
- ❑ **1978** New political group, Congress (Indira) – Congress (I) – formally established.
- ❑ **1980** Indira Gandhi's C(I) wins general election.
- ❑ **1984** Indian troops storm Sikh Golden Temple in Amritsar. Assassination of Indira Gandhi ➪

I

I I

ECONOMICS

Inflation 14.7% p.a (1990–1999)

$125bn

7050–9675 rupiahs

SCORE CARD

- World GNP Ranking 31st
- GNP per Capita $600
- Balance of Payments $5.79bn
- Inflation 20.5%
- Unemployment 6%

ECONOMIC PERFORMANCE INDICATOR

Consumer Price Index
GDP
400
300
200
100
0
Consumer price index 1995=100
GDP 1995=100
1995
1996
1997
1998
1999

EXPORTS

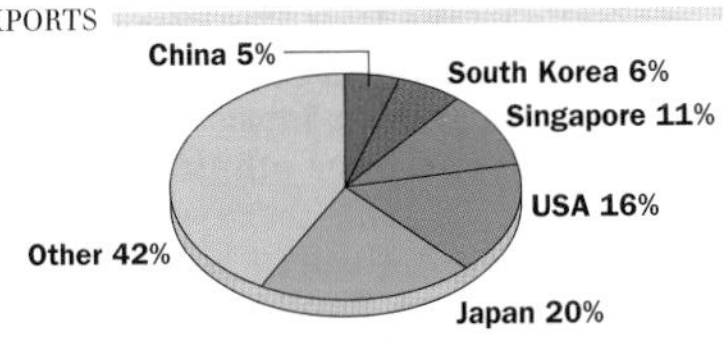

China 5%
South Korea 6%
Singapore 11%
USA 16%
Japan 20%
Other 42%

IMPORTS

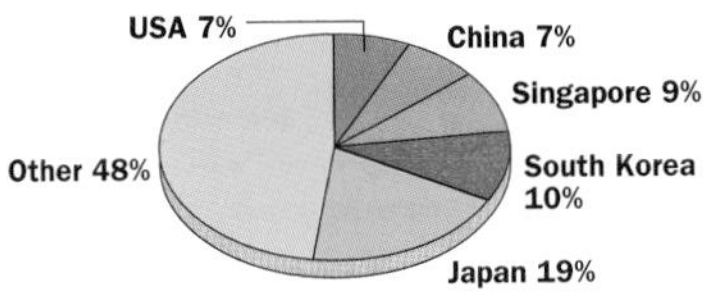

USA 7%
China 7%
Singapore 9%
South Korea 10%
Japan 19%
Other 48%

Strengths

Varied resources, especially oil. Signs of return to high growth.

Weaknesses

Red tape; corruption. Major debt burden. Collapse of investor confidence.

Profile

Under Suharto the economy grew rapidly, fueled largely by oil, until its collapse in 1997–1998. State-owned corporations played a significant role, protected from foreign competition. Non-oil exports, especially manufactures, were diversified, but the debt burden used up a third of export earnings. Promised reform was delayed by conflict between advocates of deregulation and "technologists" who favored industrialization over profit for state concerns. Further reforms have been stymied by the PKB's poor parliamentary representation. Corruption remains rife, embroiling Wahid himself in 2001.

INDONESIA : MAJOR BUSINESSES

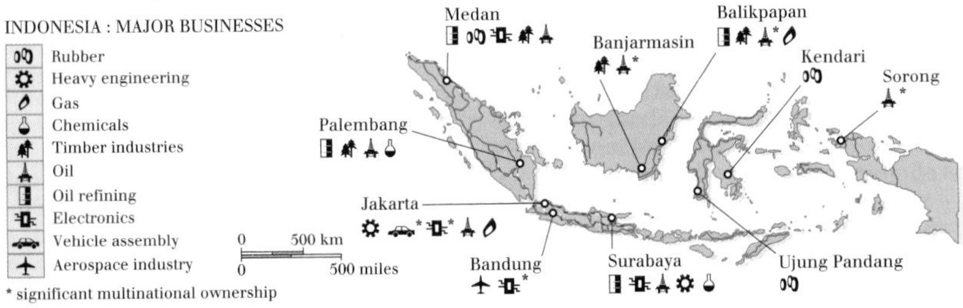

Rubber
Heavy engineering
Gas
Chemicals
Timber industries
Oil
Oil refining
Electronics
Vehicle assembly
Aerospace industry
Medan
Banjarmasin
Balikpapan
Kendari
Sorong
Palembang
Jakarta
Bandung
Surabaya
Ujung Pandang
0 500 km
0 500 miles

* significant multinational ownership

RESOURCES

Electric power 21.3m kw

4.4m tonnes

1.4m b/d (reserves 5,000,000,000 bbl)

28.2m ducks, 15.2m goats, 1bn chickens

Oil, natural gas, tin, bauxite, nickel, copper, gold, coal

ELECTRICITY GENERATION

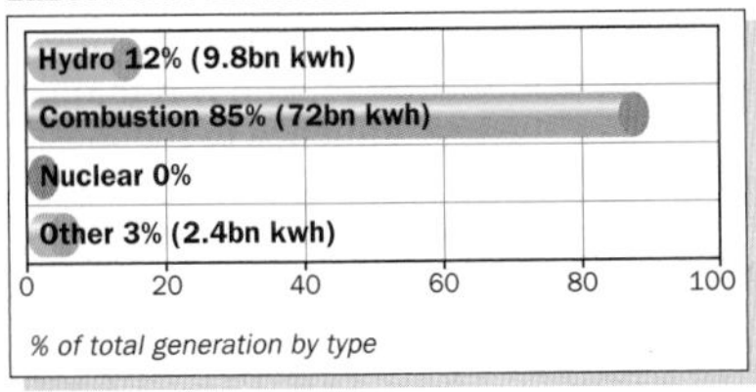

Hydro 12% (9.8bn kwh)
Combustion 85% (72bn kwh)
Nuclear 0%
Other 3% (2.4bn kwh)
0
20
40
60
80
100
% of total generation by type

Indonesia is rich in energy sources. The main export earners are oil and liquefied natural gas – the country is the world's largest LNG exporter. However, oil output has been falling. Combined with rapid growth in domestic energy demand, this could turn the country into an oil importer in the next decade. The government is therefore encouraging extending exploration into remote regions. It is also considering developing geothermal and nuclear energy sources. Indonesia's other main resources are coal, bauxite, and nickel, and agricultural products such as rubber and palm oil. With 75% of the land classified as forest, timber production is also significant.

INDONESIA : LAND USE

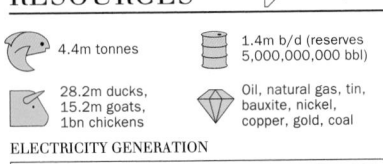

Cropland
Forest
Pasture
Wetlands
Rice
Nutmeg - cash crop
Cattle
Sumatra
Kalimantan
Sulawesi
Maluku
Irian Jaya
Laut Jawa
Laut Banda
Java
Timor
PACIFIC OCEAN
0 500 km
0 500 miles

CHRONOLOGY

Hindu, Buddhist, and Islamic interest preceded European rivalries over valuable spices. The Dutch won control by the 17th century. By 1910, the Dutch East Indies encompassed present-day Indonesia.

- **1930s** Dutch repress nationalists.
- **1942–1945** Japanese occupation. Sukarno works with Japanese while promoting independence.
- **1945** Declaration of independence.
- **1945–1949** Nationalist guerrilla war.
- **1949** Dutch grant independence under President Sukarno.
- **1957–1959** Sukarno introduces authoritarian Guided Democracy.
- **1962** Dutch relinquish Irian Jaya.
- **1965** Communist PKI alliance with military ends. Army led by General Suharto crushes abortive coup and acts to eliminate PKI; up to one million killed.
- **1966** Sukarno hands over power to General Suharto.
- **1968** Suharto becomes president.
- **1975** Invasion of East Timor; becomes 27th province in 1976.
- **1984** Muslim protests in Jakarta trigger Islamic movement.
- **1989** Unrest in Java and Sumbawa.
- **1991** Indonesian troops massacre pro-independence demonstrators in East Timor.
- **1996** Anti-government demonstrations in Jakarta.
- **1997** Economic recession. Smog across region from forest fires.
- **1998** Suharto resigns amid unrest.
- **1999** Election victory for opposition led by Megawati Sukarnoputri. East Timor referendum backing independence triggers violent backlash. UN appoints transitional authority. Abdurrahman Wahid elected president, Megawati named vice president.
- **2001** July, Wahid removed, replaced by Megawati.

ENVIRONMENT

Sustainability rank: 86th

11% (3% partially protected)

1.3 tonnes per capita

ENVIRONMENTAL TREATIES

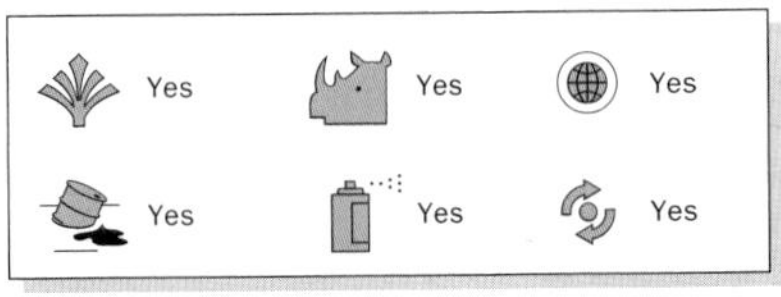

Yes
Yes
Yes
Yes
Yes
Yes

Environmental legislation is poorly enforced. The worst problem relates to the rich tropical forests, threatened by excessive logging, and the disappearance of rare flora and fauna. Smog from forest fires created a regional health alert in 1997. Frequent oil spillages in the Malacca Strait are a hazard.

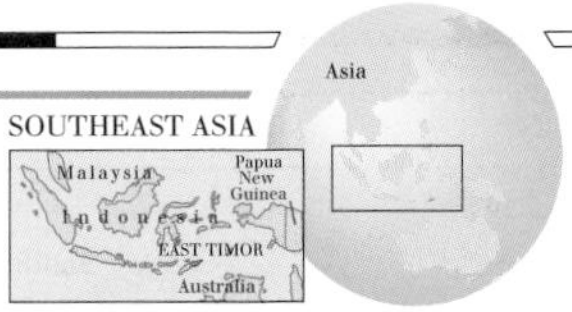
Asia
SOUTHEAST ASIA
Malaysia
Papua New Guinea
Indonesia
EAST TIMOR
Australia

EAST TIMOR

OFFICIAL NAME: East Timor **CAPITAL:** Dili **POPULATION:** 750,000

2001 | 50/km² (129/mi²) | Tetum (Portuguese/Austronesian), Bahasa Malay, Portuguese | US dollar | 2001

The island of Timor has a narrow coastal plain giving way to forested highlands. Timor's mountain backbone rises to 2963 m (9715 feet). The eastern half of the island was colonized from 1520 by the Portuguese, then occupied from 1975 by Indonesia, which proclaimed East Timor its 27th province and hunted down all resistance. A referendum in 1999 launched a turbulent transition to independence.

The economy suffered extensive damage in 1999 to towns and communications. Coffee is the main cash crop, corn the staple food. Oil under the Timor Sea could transform East Timor's prospects.

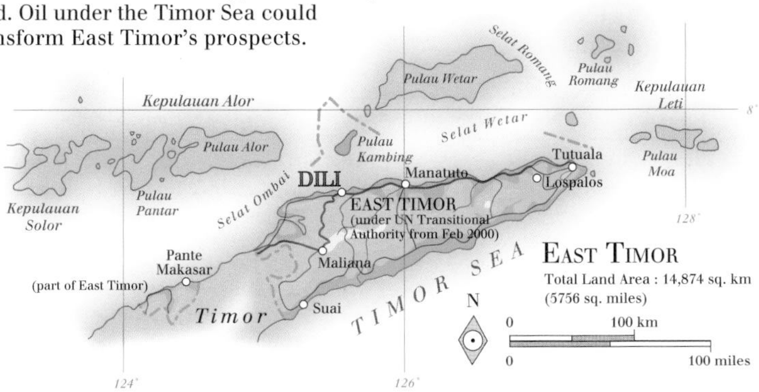
Selat Romang
Pulau Wetar
Pulau Romang
Kepulauan Leti
Kepulauan Alor
Pulau Alor
Pulau Kambing
Selat Wetar
Tutuala
Pulau Moa
Lospalos
Manatuto
DILI
Selat Ombai
Kepulauan Solor
Pulau Pantar
EAST TIMOR
(under UN Transitional Authority from Feb 2000)
Pante Makasar
(part of East Timor)
Maliana
Suai
Timor
TIMOR SEA
EAST TIMOR
Total Land Area : 14,874 sq. km
(5756 sq. miles)
N
0
100 km
0
100 miles
124°
126°
128°
8°

CLIMATE

The climate is tropical, with heavy rain from December to March, then dry and increasingly hot weather for the rest of the year, especially in the north.

PEOPLE

RELIGIONS: Christian (over 90% Roman Catholic); some Muslims, others.
ETHNIC MIX: Various Papuan groups; 2% Chinese. In the 1990s Indonesian settlers became numerous, accounting for 20% of the population by 1999.

POLITICS

Massacres and destruction by pro-Indonesian militias followed the 1999 vote for independence by almost 80% of a 98% turnout. A UN administration (UNTAET) was set up to oversee the transitional period leading to elections in August 2001, dominated by Fretilin (the guerrilla movement against Indonesian rule), and independence by the end of the year. The death penalty was abolished. Xanana Gusmão, veteran leader of Fretilin, is the leading candidate for president.

I

MEDIA

TV ownership medium

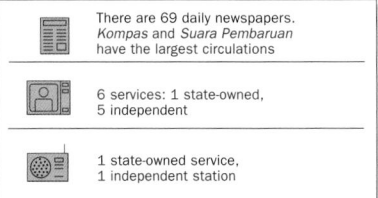

Daily newspaper circulation 23 per 1000 people

PUBLISHING AND BROADCAST MEDIA

There are 69 daily newspapers. *Kompas* and *Suara Pembaruan* have the largest circulations

6 services: 1 state-owned, 5 independent

1 state-owned service, 1 independent station

The 1999 press law prohibits censorship, but journalists can still be fined for violating "religious and moral norms." Independent press and broadcasting have flourished since 1998.

CRIME

Death penalty used

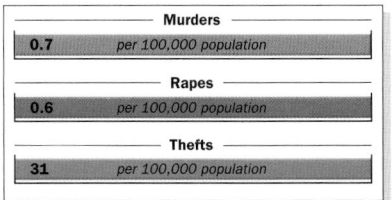

43,980 prisoners

Down 31% 1992–1996

CRIME RATES

Murders
0.7 *per 100,000 population*

Rapes
0.6 *per 100,000 population*

Thefts
31 *per 100,000 population*

Suppression of secessionists is harsh. Militias ransacked Timor in 1999 and remain active.

EDUCATION

School leaving age: 15

87%

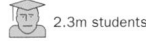

2.3m students

THE EDUCATION SYSTEM

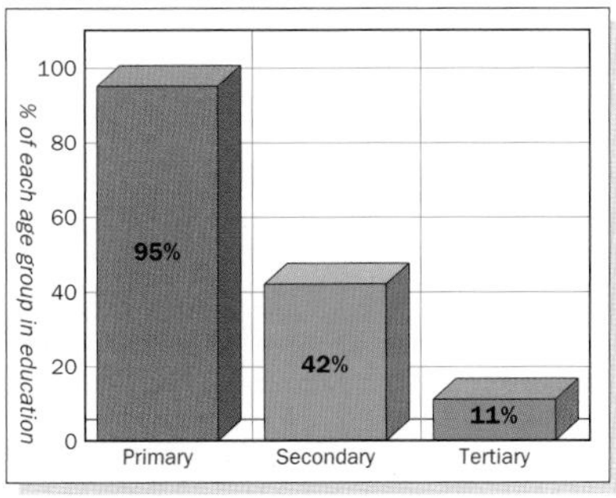
100
80
60
40
20
0
% of each age group in education
95%
42%
11%
Primary
Secondary
Tertiary

Primary education is compulsory, and is often provided by Islamic schools, but children in many rural areas are still deprived of secondary education.

HEALTH

Welfare state health benefits

1 per 5000 people

Lower respiratory and diarrheal diseases

An extensive network of clinics, down to village level, means that access to health care is reasonable. As a result, health indicators have improved significantly. The death rate declined from 2% in 1965 to 0.9% in 1990, while infant mortality more than halved. East Timorese driven from their homes in the violence of 1999 face problems of disease and hunger.

SPENDING

GDP/cap. increase

CONSUMPTION AND SPENDING

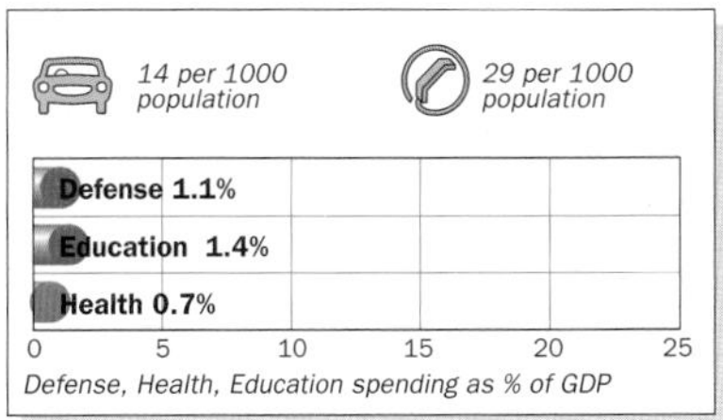
14 per 1000 population
29 per 1000 population
Defense 1.1%
Education 1.4%
Health 0.7%
0
5
10
15
20
25
Defense, Health, Education spending as % of GDP

Since 1998 attempts have been made in the courts to tackle the issues of corruption and concentration of wealth in the hands of close associates and relatives of former President Suharto.

WORLD RANKING

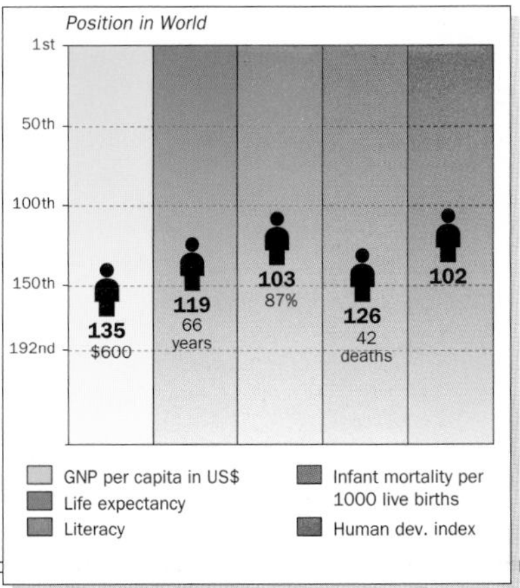
Position in World
1st
50th
100th
150th
192nd
135
$600
119
66 years
103
87%
126
42 deaths
102
GNP per capita in US$
Life expectancy
Literacy
Infant mortality per 1000 live births
Human dev. index

IRAN

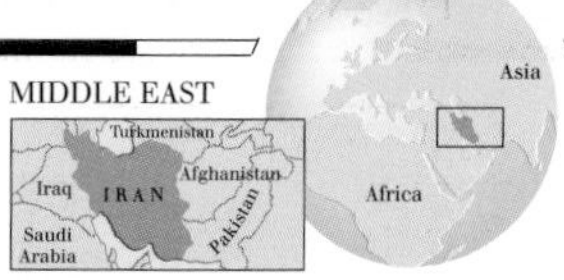
MIDDLE EAST
Turkmenistan
Iraq
IRAN
Afghanistan
Pakistan
Saudi Arabia
Asia
Africa

OFFICIAL NAME: Islamic Republic of Iran **CAPITAL:** Tehran
POPULATION: 67.7 million **CURRENCY:** Iranian rial **OFFICIAL LANGUAGE:** Farsi (Persian)

1502 | 1990 | Feb 11 | IR | +3.5 | +98 | .ir

IRAN IS SURROUNDED by turbulent neighbors, with republics of the former Soviet Union to the north, Afghanistan and Pakistan to the east, and Iraq and Turkey to the west. The south faces the Persian Gulf and the Gulf of Oman. Since 1979, when a revolution led by Ayatollah Khomeini deposed the shah, Iran has become the world's largest theocracy and the leading center for militant Shi'a Islam. Iran's active support for Islamic fundamentalist movements has led to strained relations with central Asian, Middle Eastern, and north African states, as well as the USA and western Europe.

***The Reshteh-ye Kuhhā-ye Alborz** (Elburz Mountains). Their Caspian Sea slopes are rainy and forested; the southern slopes are dry.*

CLIMATE

Mountain/cold desert

WEATHER CHART

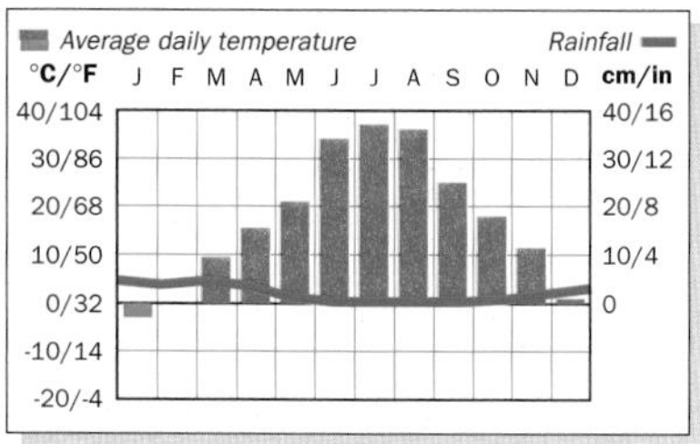
Average daily temperature
Rainfall
°C/°F
J F M A M J J A S O N D
cm/in
40/104
30/86
20/68
10/50
0/32
-10/14
-20/-4
40/16
30/12
20/8
10/4
0

The area bordering the Caspian Sea is Iran's most temperate region. Most of the country has a desert climate.

TRANSPORTATION

Drive on right

Mehrabad International, Tehran
1.16m passengers

382 ships
3.3m grt

THE TRANSPORTATION NETWORK

49,440 km (30,721 miles)	470 km (292 miles)
6398 km (3976 miles)	904 km (562 miles)

Adequate roads link main towns, but rural areas are less well served. Most freight travels by rail. A ferry runs from Bandar-e Abbas to the UAE.

PEOPLE

Pop. density low

Farsi (Persian), Azerbaijani, Gilaki, Mazanderani, Kurdish, Baluchi, Arabic, Turkmen

41/km² (107/mi²)

THE URBAN/RURAL POPULATION SPLIT

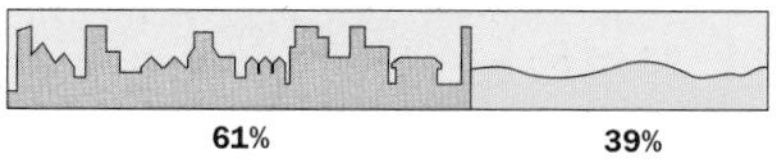
61%
39%

RELIGIOUS PERSUASION

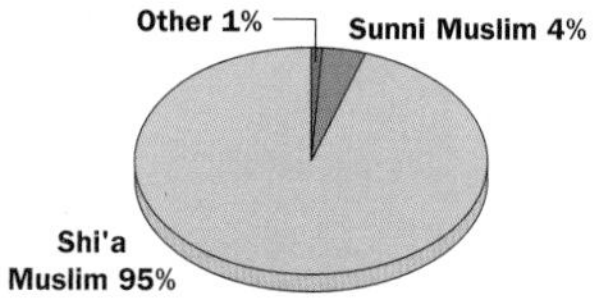
Other 1%
Sunni Muslim 4%
Shi'a Muslim 95%

ETHNIC MAKEUP

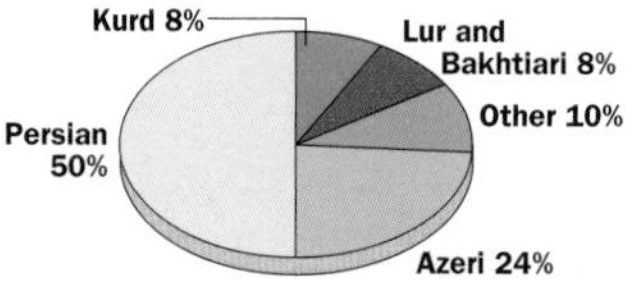
Kurd 8%
Lur and Bakhtiari 8%
Other 10%
Persian 50%
Azeri 24%

The population comprises several ethnic groups. The people of the north and center – about half of all Iranians – speak Farsi (Persian), while about a quarter speak related languages, including Kurdish in the west and Baluchi in the southeast. Another quarter of the population speaks Turkic languages, primarily the Azeris and the Turkmen in the northwest. Smaller groups, such as the Circassians and Georgians, are found in the northern provinces.

Until the 16th century, much of Iran followed the Sunni interpretation of Islam, but since then the Shi'a sect has been dominant. Religious minorities, accounting for just 1% of the population, include followers of the Bahai faith, who suffer discrimination, Zoroastrians, Christians, and Jews. The regime has a remarkably liberal attitude to refugees of the Muslim faith. Nearly three million Afghan refugees were received during the height of the Afghan civil war, although many have since been repatriated. In Khorosan province in the east, refugees account for nearly a quarter of the population; near the Turkish border they constitute half the total population. Many are young, resulting in intense competition with Iranians for jobs and consequent ethnic tensions.

One of the main consequences of the 1979 Islamic revolution was to reverse the policy of female emancipation. The revolution restricted the public role of women and enforced a strict dress code, obliging women to wear the ankle-length *hijab* and keep their heads covered with a scarf. More liberal attitudes have gradually emerged, and reform of the divorce laws has been proposed, under which it would become possible for proceedings to be initiated by the wife.

POPULATION AGE BREAKDOWN

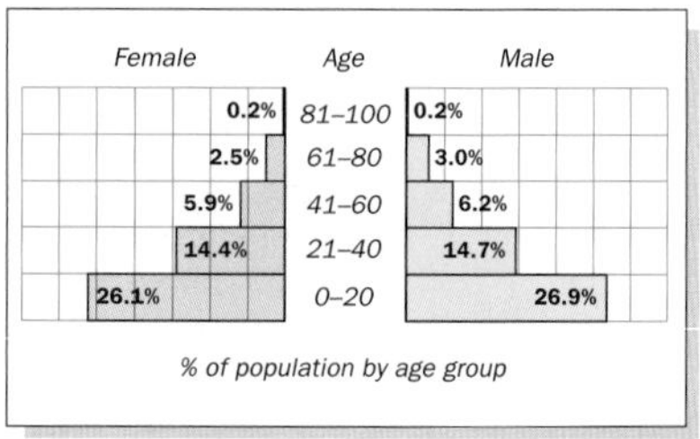
Female
Age
Male
0.2% 81–100 0.2%
2.5% 61–80 3.0%
5.9% 41–60 6.2%
14.4% 21–40 14.7%
26.1% 0–20 26.9%
% of population by age group

TOURISM

Visitors : Population 1:40

1.7m visitors

Up 29% in 2000

MAIN TOURIST ARRIVALS

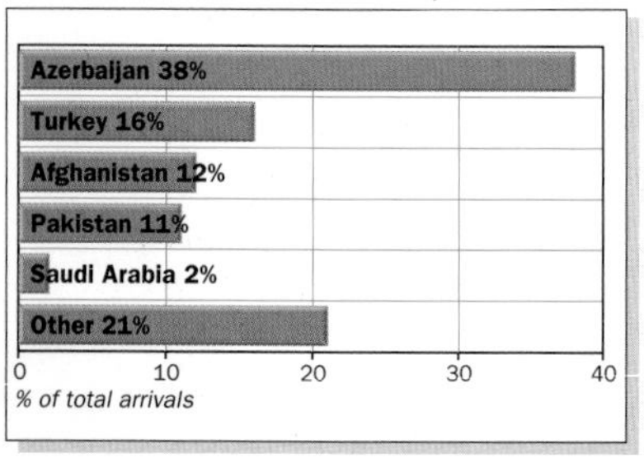
Azerbaijan 38%
Turkey 16%
Afghanistan 12%
Pakistan 11%
Saudi Arabia 2%
Other 21%
0
10
20
30
40
% of total arrivals

Iran's historical heritage, mosques, and bazaars formerly attracted sizable numbers of tourists. This flow was cut off by the 1979 revolution, which deterred visitors, especially from the West. In the 1990s, however, there was a rise in the number of business people visiting Iran. Procedures at Tehran's Mehrabad airport have been simplified and the capital's hotels refurbished. In late 1998 President Khatami's more liberal regime welcomed a delegation of US tourists, despite conservative groups.

POLITICS

Multiparty elections

2000/2004

President Mohammad Khatami

AT THE LAST ELECTION

Consultative Council (Majlis) 290 seats

2%
Rel
65%
IIPF
17%
C
11%
Ind
5%
Vacant

IIPF = Islamic Iran Participation Front (reformists)
C = Coalition of Followers of the Line of Imam (conservatives)
Ind = Independents **Rel** = Religious Minorities

Iran is a theocracy. Tension exists between the conservative mullahs and the reformist government.

Main Political Issue

Mosque versus secular state

A power struggle between the clergy and the secular state has arisen from the ill-defined division of power between the two. The conservative faction in parliament lost its overall majority in 1996 and has been steadily displaced by reformists, who in 2000 made sweeping gains in parliamentary elections. In

Ayatollah Khamenei, *who became spiritual leader after the death of Ayatollah Khomeini.*

Mohammad Khatami, *reformist president, in office since 1997.*

2001 reformist president Mohammad Khatami was reelected, this time with an overwhelming 77% of the vote.

Khatami is committed to modernizing the economy, but is strongly opposed by the mullahs, for whom adherence to religious values is more important than material welfare. Student proreform protests were heavily suppressed by hardliners, who remain a force, despite the 2000 elections, through the powerful Council of Guardians.

Profile

Iran's religious revolution of 1979 was fueled by popular outrage at the corruption, repression, and inequalities of the shah's regime. Since the time of Ayatollah Khomeini, successive Iranian governments have maintained that the clergy have a religious duty to establish a just social system. Accordingly, the legislature, the executive, and the judiciary may, in theory, be overruled by the religious leadership; former president Hashemi Rafsanjani's moderate policies were questioned by radical clergymen advocating "permanent revolution." However, the mullahs' failure to address Iran's economic problems has eroded their political standing. Reformists were encouraged by the election of President Khatami in 1997, but the clergy remains powerful. Huge student demonstrations in 1999 and 2000 in favor of reform were offset by crackdowns on reformist politicians and newspapers. The mullahs, so far unbowed by reformist election victories, have continued to confront the modernizers.

WORLD AFFAIRS

Joined UN in 1945

ECO | G24 | NAM | OIC | OPEC

Following the 1979 revolution, Iran assumed international significance as the voice of militant Shi'a Islam. Iran is accused of backing terrorist activity by Muslim extremists and fostering unrest throughout the Middle East and central Asia. In 1995 the USA took action by imposing sanctions against Iran.

Under President Khatami, Iran has tried to convey a less confrontational image. Improved relations with Saudi Arabia, troubled since Iran's seizure of the islands of Abu Musa and the Tumbs in 1970, resulted in the signing of a pact in 2001. Relations with the West have also improved. In 1999 Khatami visited Italy, the first Iranian leader since the fall of the shah to be officially welcomed by a Western government.

Iran's most pressing security preoccupation is with Iraq, which allows *mujahideen* guerrillas to mount attacks on Iran from its territory.

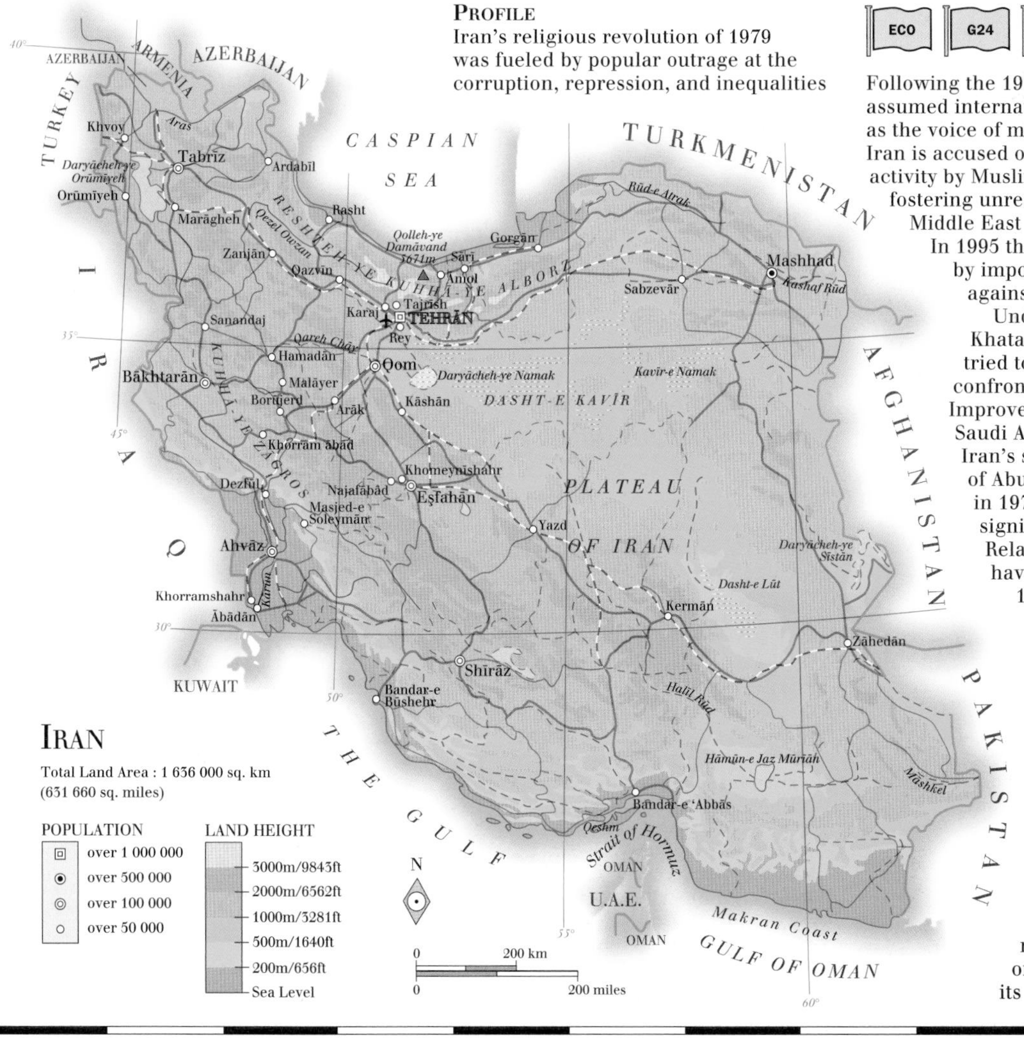
AZERBAIJAN
ARMENIA
AZERBAIJAN
TURKEY
CASPIAN SEA
TURKMENISTAN
IRAQ
AFGHANISTAN
PAKISTAN
KUWAIT
THE GULF
GULF OF OMAN
U.A.E.
OMAN
Khvoy
Tabrīz
Ardabīl
Orūmīyeh
Marāgheh
Rasht
Zanjān
Qazvīn
Gorgān
Sārī
Āmol
Karaj
Tajrīsh
TEHRAN
Rey
Mashhad
Sabzevār
Sanandaj
Hamadān
Qom
Bākhtarān
Malāyer
Borūjerd
Arāk
Kāshān
Khorram ābād
Khomeynīshahr
Najafābād
Eşfahān
Masjed-e Soleymān
Dezfūl
Ahvāz
Khorramshahr
Ābādān
Yazd
Kermān
Zāhedān
Shīrāz
Bandar-e Būshehr
Bandar-e 'Abbās
Qeshm
Strait of Hormuz
Makran Coast
Qolleh-ye Damāvand 5671m
RESHTEH-YE KŪHHĀ-YE ALBORZ
KŪHHĀ-YE ZAGROS
DASHT-E KAVĪR
PLATEAU OF IRAN
Daryācheh-ye Namak
Kavīr-e Namak
Dasht-e Lūt
Daryācheh-ye Sīstān
Hāmūn-e Jaz Mūrīān
Daryācheh-ye Orūmīyeh
Aras
Qezel Owzan
Qareh Chāy
Kārūn
Rūd-e Atrak
Kashaf Rūd
Halīl Rūd
Māshkel
N
0
200 km
0
200 miles
IRAN
Total Land Area : 1 636 000 sq. km (631 660 sq. miles)
POPULATION
over 1 000 000
over 500 000
over 100 000
over 50 000
LAND HEIGHT
3000m/9843ft
2000m/6562ft
1000m/3281ft
500m/1640ft
200m/656ft
Sea Level

CHRONOLOGY

Persia was ruled by the shahs as an absolute monarchy until 1906, when the first constitution was approved. The Pahlavis took power in 1925 and changed the country's name to Iran in 1935.

- **1957** SAVAK, shah's secret police, established to control opposition.
- **1964** Ayatollah Khomeini is exiled to Iraq for criticizing secular state.
- **1971** Shah celebrates 2500th anniversary of Persian monarchy.
- **1975** Agreement with Iraq over Shatt al 'Arab waterway.
- **1977** Khomeini's son dies. Anti-shah demonstrations during mourning.
- **1978** Riots and strikes. Khomeini settles in Paris.
- **1979** Shah goes into exile. Ayatollah Khomeini returns from exile in France and declares an Islamic republic. Students seize 63 hostages at US embassy in Tehran.
- **1980** Shah dies in exile. Start of eight-year Iran–Iraq war.
- **1981** US hostages released. Hojatoleslam Ali Khamenei elected president.
- **1985** Khamenei reelected.
- **1987** Around 275 Iranian pilgrims killed in riots in Mecca.
- **1988** USS *Vincennes* shoots down Iranian airliner; 290 killed. End of Iran–Iraq war.
- **1989** Khomeini issues *fatwa* condemning Salman Rushdie to death for blasphemy. Khomeini dies. President Ali Khamenei appointed Supreme Religious Leader. Hashemi Rafsanjani elected president.
- **1990** Earthquake in northern Iran kills 45,000 people.
- **1992** *Majlis* elections.
- **1993** Rafsanjani reelected president.
- **1995** Imposition of US sanctions.
- **1996** *Majlis* elections. Society for Combatant Clergy loses ground to more liberal Servants of Iran's Construction.
- **1997** Earthquake south of Mashhad kills 1500 people. Mohammad Khatami elected president.
- **1998** Khatami government dissociates itself from *fatwa* against Salman Rushdie.
- **1999** First nationwide local elections since 1979. President Khatami visits Italy and becomes the first Iranian leader to be welcomed by a Western government since 1979.
- **2000** Sweeping election victory for reformists. Crackdown on reformist newspapers.
- **2001** Khatami reelected, winning 77% of vote.

I

AID

Recipient

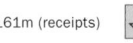

$161m (receipts) | Down 2% in 1999

As an oil exporter, Iran does not qualify for much aid and hardliners are opposed to money from the West. However, Iran receives some UN aid for its millions of refugees from Afghanistan and Iraq.

Concern that Iran supports Muslim terrorism has recently affected aid programs. In 1994, the World Bank suspended loans. US sanctions imposed in 1995 ended bilateral assistance, although European oil companies have more recently announced new deals.

DEFENSE

Compulsory military service

$5.71bn | Down 3% in 1999

Iran has more than 500,000 men under arms, including the 125,000-strong Revolutionary Guard Corps (*Pasdaran Inquilab*), and is regarded by neighboring states as a serious military threat. The testing of medium-range cruise and ballistic missiles in 1998 heightened concern over Iran's possible military objectives.

Before the 1979 revolution Iran was part of a pro-Western alliance structure. The long war with Iraq in the 1980s diminished the military power of the revolutionary regime.

IRANIAN ARMED FORCES

1135 main battle tanks (M-47/48/60A1, *Chieftain* Mk3/5, T-54/55/62/72)	325,000 personnel
5 submarines, 3 frigates, 63 patrol boats	18,000 personnel
291 combat aircraft (F-4D/E, F-5E/F, Su-24, F-14, F-7, MiG-29)	45,000 personnel
None	

A new defense agreement with Russia allowing for the sale of arms to Iran was reached in 2000.

ECONOMICS

Inflation 27% p.a. (1990–1999)

$113.7bn | 1752.5–1747.5 Iranian rials

SCORE CARD

- World GNP Ranking 33rd
- GNP per Capita $1810
- Balance of Payments .... $-1.9bn
- Inflation 21%
- Unemployment 25%

EXPORTS

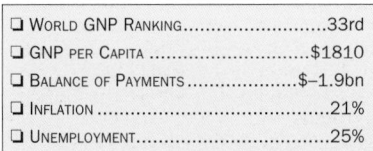

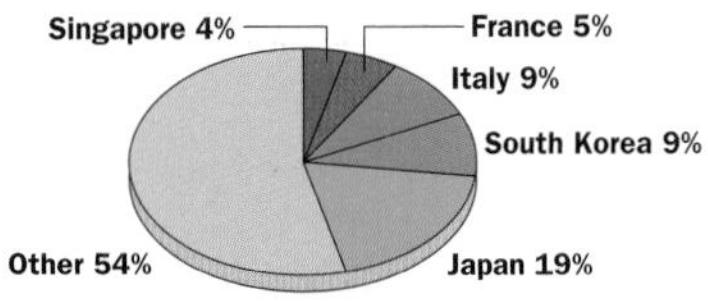
Singapore 4%
France 5%
Italy 9%
South Korea 9%
Japan 19%
Other 54%

IMPORTS

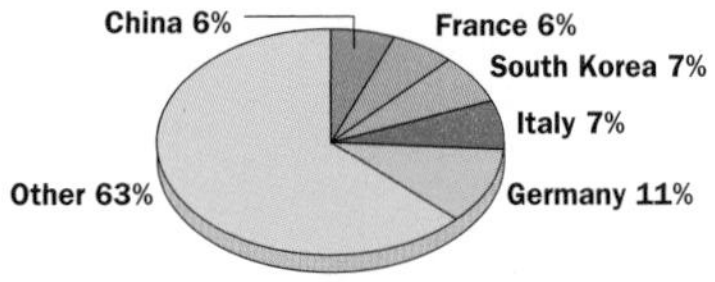
China 6%
France 6%
South Korea 7%
Italy 7%
Germany 11%
Other 63%

STRENGTHS

OPEC's second-biggest oil producer; soaring world oil prices in 2000. Potential for related industries and increased production of traditional exports: carpets, pistachio nuts, and caviar.

WEAKNESSES

Theocratic authorities restrict contact with West and access to technology. High unemployment and inflation. Excessive foreign debts.

ECONOMIC PERFORMANCE INDICATOR

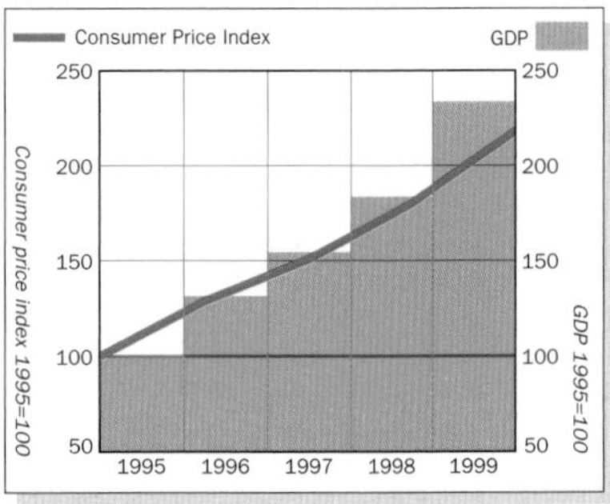
Consumer Price Index
GDP
Consumer price index 1995=100
GDP 1995=100
250
200
150
100
50
1995
1996
1997
1998
1999

PROFILE

With few industries other than oil, US sanctions and fluctuations in oil prices made foreign earnings volatile; higher prices in 2000 held out the prospect of being able to invest in diversification.

IRAN : MAJOR BUSINESSES

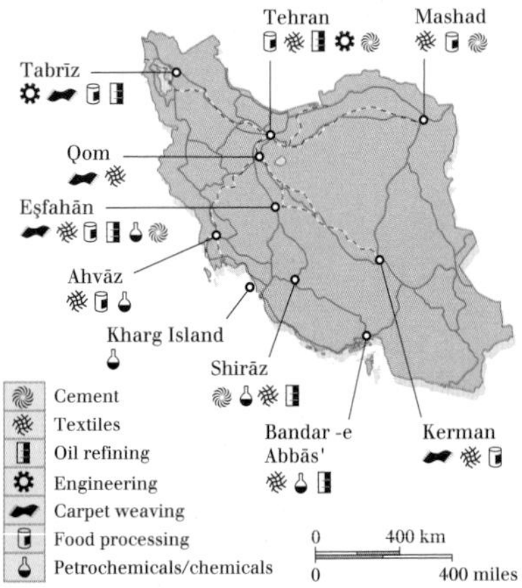
Tehran
Mashad
Tabrīz
Qom
Eşfahān
Ahvāz
Kharg Island
Shirāz
Bandar -e Abbās'
Kerman
Cement
Textiles
Oil refining
Engineering
Carpet weaving
Food processing
Petrochemicals/chemicals
0
400 km
0
400 miles

RESOURCES

Electric power 29.4m kw

380,200 tonnes

3.8m b/d (reserves 89,700,000,000 bbl)

55m sheep, 26m goats, 8.1m cattle, 230m chickens

Iron, copper, lead, oil, zinc, chromite, coal, manganese, gypsum

ELECTRICITY GENERATION

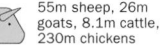

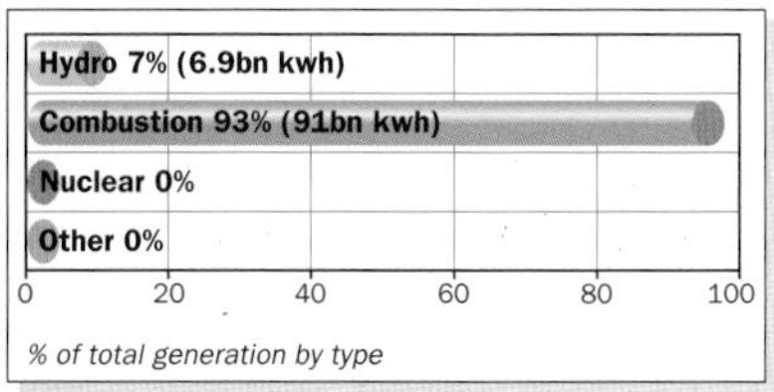
Hydro 7% (6.9bn kwh)
Combustion 93% (91bn kwh)
Nuclear 0%
Other 0%
0
20
40
60
80
100
% of total generation by type

Iran has substantial oil reserves. It also has metal, coal, and salt deposits, but these are relatively undeveloped. The agricultural sector is an important part of Iran's economy. Principal crops are wheat, barley, rice, sugar beet, tobacco, and pistachio nuts.

Iran was once an opium exporter, but its cultivation and use have since been banned. The vodka industry has also been closed down. Enough wool is produced to supply the carpet weaving industry. Iran has insufficient livestock to supply the domestic meat market and has to import large quantities. The Caspian Sea fisheries are controlled by the state, which sells caviar for export.

IRAN : LAND USE

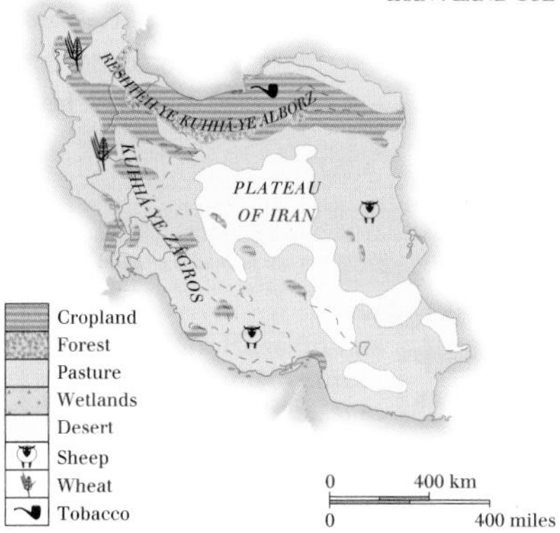
RESHTEH-YE KUHHA-YE ALBORZ
KUHHA-YE ZAGROS
PLATEAU OF IRAN
Cropland
Forest
Pasture
Wetlands
Desert
Sheep
Wheat
Tobacco
0
400 km
0
400 miles

ENVIRONMENT

Sustainability rank: 105th

5% (3% partially protected)

4.9 tonnes per capita

ENVIRONMENTAL TREATIES

Yes	Yes	Yes
Yes	Yes	No

War damage to southern Iran, especially at Bandar Khomeini, the tanker terminal at Kharg Island, and the refinery at Abadan, has caused significant environmental damage. Environmental issues are not of concern to the religious leadership.

MEDIA

TV ownership medium

Daily newspaper circulation 26 per 1000 people

PUBLISHING AND BROADCAST MEDIA

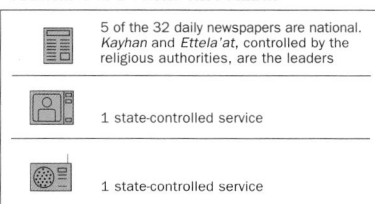

5 of the 32 daily newspapers are national. *Kayhan* and *Ettela'at*, controlled by the religious authorities, are the leaders

1 state-controlled service

1 state-controlled service

Radio and TV are state-controlled. Satellite dishes are banned. Closures of reformist newspapers by the conservative Council of Guardians, and prosecutions of their editors, peaked in 2000.

CRIME

Death penalty used

Iran does not publish prison figures

Little change from year to year

CRIME RATES

Iran does not publish crime statistics. However, general crime rates are relatively low.

Revolutionary guards enforce law and order. More than 100 offenses carry the death sentence. Executions, of both men and women, are common for political "crimes." Iran is accused by Western governments of supporting international terrorism by Muslim extremists abroad. In 2000 the government finally admitted that narcotics addiction, prostitution, and the violent abuse of women were rife.

EDUCATION

School leaving age: 11

77%

579,070 students

THE EDUCATION SYSTEM

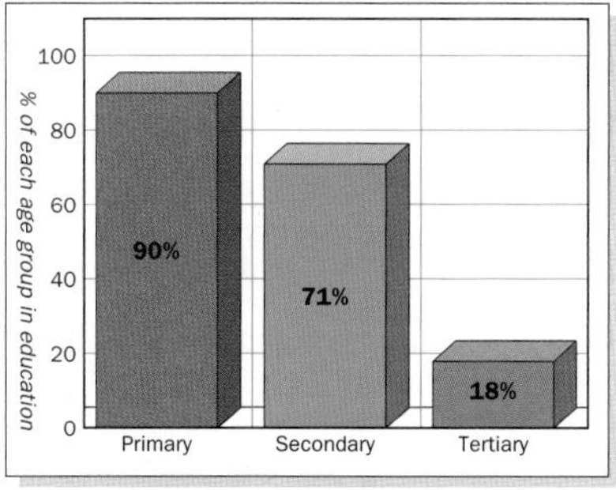
100
80
60
40
20
0
% of each age group in education
90%
71%
18%
Primary
Secondary
Tertiary

Most of the population is literate. Primary education, which lasts for five years from the age of six, is free, as are universities, but a small fee is charged for secondary education. Most schools are single-sex. There are 36 universities. Students are strong supporters of liberalization and the reformist agenda of President Khatami.

HEALTH

Welfare state health benefits

1 per 1250 people

Heart and respiratory diseases, injuries, neonatal deaths

Although an adequate system of primary health care exists in the cities, conditions in rural areas are basic. The major problem facing the nation's health is the fast-growing population. Under Khomeini, having children became a political and religious duty, but the high birthrate has now forced the introduction of birth control programs, and sterilization and contraception are now officially promoted. Growing drug addiction has resulted in rehabilitation programs and anti-drug propaganda.

SPENDING

GDP/cap. increase

CONSUMPTION AND SPENDING

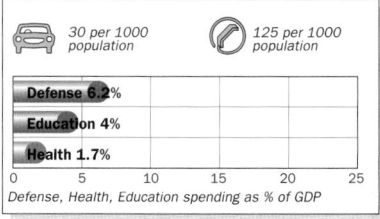

30 per 1000 population

125 per 1000 population

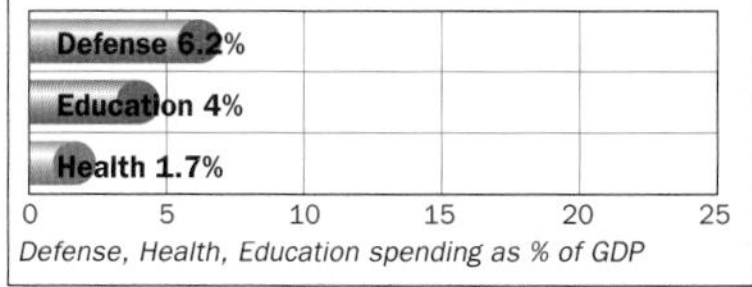
Defense 6.2%
Education 4%
Health 1.7%
0
5
10
15
20
25
Defense, Health, Education spending as % of GDP

After the 1979 revolution, living standards in Iran declined markedly. A shortage of foreign exchange has stifled imports of consumer goods. Rationing, brought in during the war with Iraq, is still partly in force, and smuggling from the Arab Gulf states is rife. Unemployment is high, and few Iranians are able to gain access to modern technology such as telephones. Official figures for income per capita do not relate to conditions on the ground. In reality, oil wealth fails to reach the economically deprived. Private businesses have gradually emerged in Iran since the launch in 1994 of the country's first private savings and loans associations.

WORLD RANKING

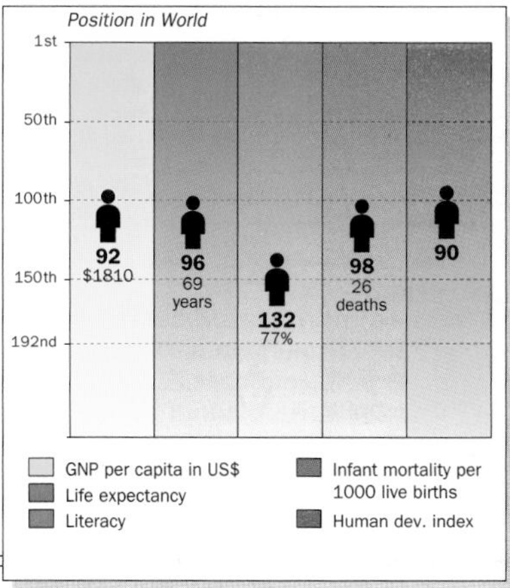
Position in World
1st
50th
100th
150th
192nd
92
$1810
96
69
years
132
77%
98
26
deaths
90
GNP per capita in US$
Life expectancy
Literacy
Infant mortality per 1000 live births
Human dev. index

I

I

CHRONOLOGY

Iraq became independent in 1932. In 1958, the Hashemite dynasty was overthrown when King Faisal died in a coup led by the military under Brigadier Kassem. He was initially supported by the Iraqi Ba'ath Party.

- ❑ **1961** Start of Kurdish rebellion. Iraq claims sovereignty over Kuwait on the eve of Kuwait's independence.
- ❑ **1963** Kassem overthrown. Colonel Abd as-Salem Muhammad Aref takes power. Kuwait's sovereignty recognized.
- ❑ **1964** Ayatollah Khomeini, future leader of Iran, takes refuge at Najaf in Iraq.
- ❑ **1966** Aref is succeeded by his brother, Abd ar-Rahman.
- ❑ **1968** Ba'athists under Ahmad Hassan al-Bakr take power.
- ❑ **1970** Revolutionary Command Council agrees manifesto on Kurdish autonomy.
- ❑ **1972** Nationalization of Western-controlled Iraq Petroleum Company.
- ❑ **1978** Iraq and Syria form economic and political union.
- ❑ **1979** Saddam Hussein replaces al-Bakr as president.
- ❑ **1980** Outbreak of Iraq–Iran war.
- ❑ **1982** Shi'a leader Mohammed Baqir al-Hakim, exiled in Tehran, forms Supreme Council of the Islamic Revolution in Iraq.
- ❑ **1988** Iraq and Iran agree cease-fire. Iraqi chemical weapons attack on Kurdish village of Halabja.
- ❑ **1990** British journalist Farzad Bazoft hanged for spying. Iraq and Iran restore diplomatic relations. Iraq invades Kuwait. UN imposes trade sanctions.
- ❑ **1991** Gulf War. US-led military coalition defeats Iraq and liberates Kuwait. Iraqi regime suppresses Shi'a rebellion.
- ❑ **1992** Western powers proclaim air exclusion zone over southern Iraq.
- ❑ **1993** Iraqi attempts to recover military equipment from Kuwait provoke Western air attacks.
- ❑ **1994** Outbreak of Kurdish civil war. Iraq recognizes Kuwaiti sovereignty.
- ❑ **1995** Government minister Gen. Hussein Kamil defects to Jordan, and is murdered on his return to Iraq in January 1996.
- ❑ **1996** First legislative elections since 1989 are won by ruling Ba'ath Party. UN supervises limited sales of Iraq oil to purchase humanitarian supplies.
- ❑ **1998–1999** UN weapons inspection teams refused reentry into Iraq; USA and UK mount punitive air strikes.

DEFENSE

▷ Compulsory military service

$1.5bn

Up 5% in 1999

IRAQI ARMED FORCES

2200 main battle tanks (T–55/62, PRC Type–59, 700 T–72)	375,000 personnel
6 patrol boats	2000 personnel
310 combat aircraft (est) (*Mirage* F1EQ5, Su–7/20/25, MiG–21/23/25/29)	35,000 personnel
None	

Iraq's military defeat by the US-led coalition in 1991 led to the destruction of much of its arsenal. Since then UN Security Council resolutions have required the elimination of the bulk of Iraq's weapons of mass destruction, and inspection teams have sought with some effect to enforce this. There is a shortage in Iraq of high-tech weaponry that could match the kind acquired by Kuwait and Saudi Arabia from US and other Western suppliers since the Gulf War. The army is large, but poorly trained and equipped; military service, lasting between 18 months and two years, is compulsory for all men at the age of 18. The military relies on tanks and aircraft from the former Soviet Union and China. The air force has some French *Mirage* fighters and US helicopters.

ECONOMICS

▷ Not available

$20bn

0.3109–0.3124 Iraqi dinars

SCORE CARD

❑ World GNP Ranking	64th
❑ GNP per Capita	$950
❑ Balance of Payments	Not available
❑ Inflation	135%
❑ Unemployment	Not available

EXPORTS

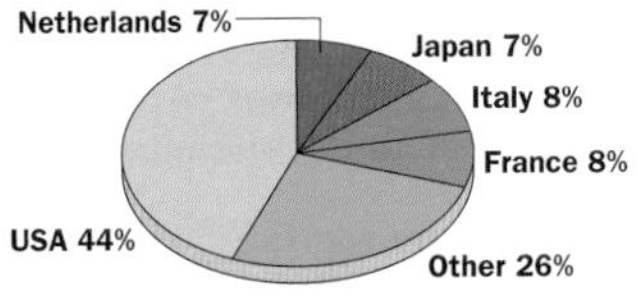
Netherlands 7%
Japan 7%
Italy 8%
France 8%
USA 44%
Other 26%

IMPORTS

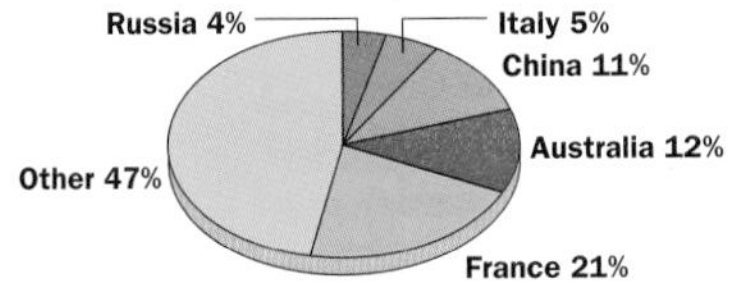
Russia 4%
Italy 5%
China 11%
Australia 12%
Other 47%
France 21%

Strengths
Second-largest crude oil and natural gas reserves in OPEC. Large labor force.

Weaknesses
Inability to sell oil on the international market; Iraq's gross national product halved by UN sanctions. Once-thriving agricultural sector devastated by war.

Profile
Before 1990, Iraq was the world's third-largest oil supplier. Under sanctions, oil was produced only for domestic consumption. Limited oil exports under strict UN supervision were resumed for the first time in December 1996, and in 2000 the UN Security Council approved a resolution permitting Iraq to buy parts and equipment for the oil industry.

The denial of Western assistance following the 1991 Gulf War has stifled Iraq's economy, although the recent resumption of informal economic links with France and Russia may lead to some improvement. The once thriving agricultural sector was badly affected by the war. The manufacturing industry is at a standstill. The introduction of draconian penalties, including the death sentence, have failed to curb the black market or halt the sharp depreciation in the value of the dinar.

ECONOMIC PERFORMANCE INDICATOR

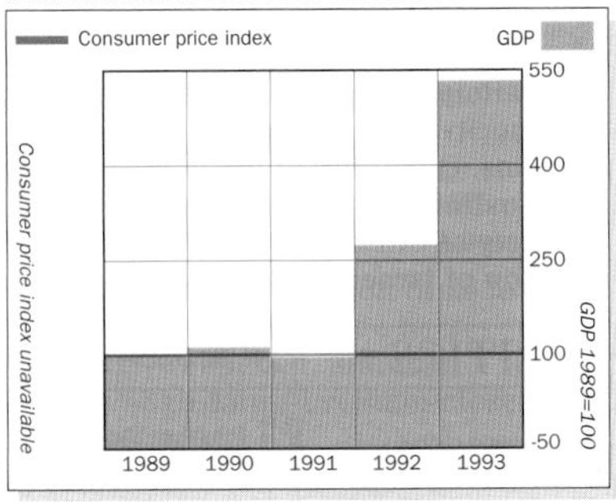
Consumer price index
GDP
550
400
250
100
-50
Consumer price index unavailable
GDP 1989=100
1989
1990
1991
1992
1993

IRAQ : MAJOR BUSINESSES

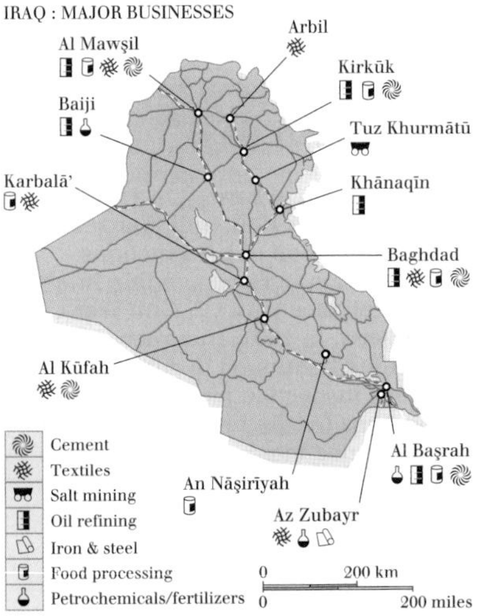
Al Mawşil
Arbil
Kirkūk
Baiji
Tuz Khurmātū
Karbalā'
Khānaqīn
Baghdad
Al Kūfah
Al Başrah
An Nāşirīyah
Az Zubayr
Cement
Textiles
Salt mining
Oil refining
Iron & steel
Food processing
Petrochemicals/fertilizers
0
200 km
0
200 miles

RESOURCES

Electric power 9.5m kw

34,702 tonnes

2.6m b/d (reserves 112,500,000,000 bbl)

6.1m sheep, 1.35m goats, 1.15m cattle, 19m chickens

Oil, natural gas, sulfur

ELECTRICITY GENERATION

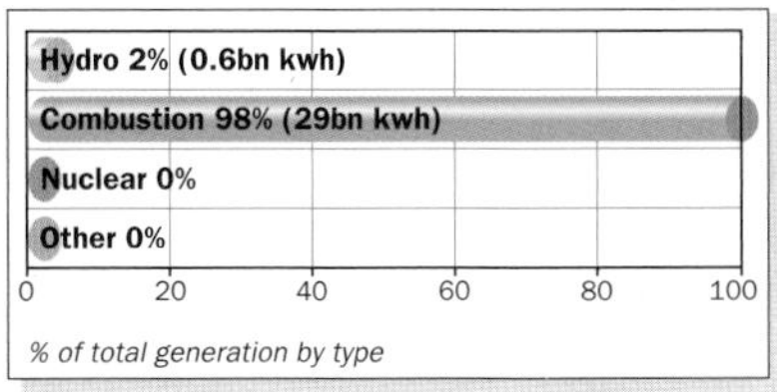
Hydro 2% (0.6bn kwh)
Combustion 98% (29bn kwh)
Nuclear 0%
Other 0%
0
20
40
60
80
100
% of total generation by type

Iraq has huge reserves of oil and gas. The oil industry is controlled by the Iraqi National Oil Company. Total gas reserves, many of which are associated with oil, are proven to be 3.11 trillion cubic meters (110 trillion cubic feet), with estimates of a further 4.25 trillion cubic meters (150 trillion cubic feet). Most electricity is generated from oil, although hydroelectric power also makes a small contribution. Reserves of phosphates, sulfur, gypsum, and salt are also exploited.

Before the invasion of Kuwait and subsequent war, Iraq was supplying 80% of the world's trade in dates. Production is now sharply down. Food is now produced simply for domestic consumption. Iraq has, however, achieved a degree of self-sufficiency in such crops as wheat, rice, and sugar.

IRAQ : LAND USE

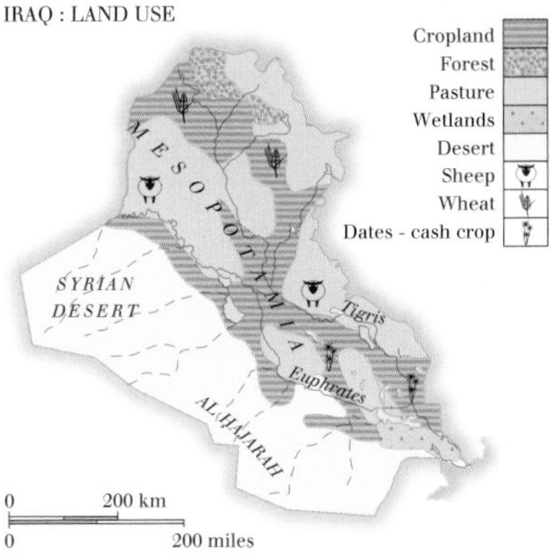
Cropland
Forest
Pasture
Wetlands
Desert
Sheep
Wheat
Dates - cash crop
MESOPOTAMIA
SYRIAN DESERT
Tigris
Euphrates
AL HIJARAH
0
200 km
0
200 miles

ENVIRONMENT

Not available

None

4.2 tonnes per capita

ENVIRONMENTAL TREATIES

No No No

No No No

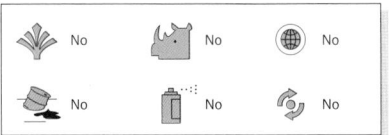

Wars with Iran and with the US-led alliance over the Kuwait occupation led to massive environmental damage. Hundreds of thousands of land mines remain in the Kuwait border regions, posing lethal hazards to farmers, livestock, and wild animals. The north has been affected by chemical weapons, used by the regime against the Kurds. In the south, an entire wetland ecosystem is being destroyed by a program to drain the marshes for largely political reasons.

MEDIA

TV ownership medium

Daily newspaper circulation 20 per 1000 people

PUBLISHING AND BROADCAST MEDIA

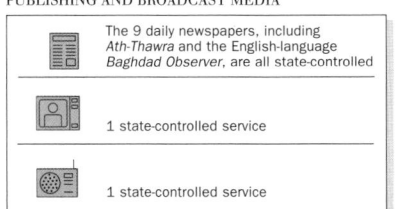

The 9 daily newspapers, including *Ath-Thawra* and the English-language *Baghdad Observer*, are all state-controlled

1 state-controlled service

1 state-controlled service

The media are strictly controlled, although rebel groups circulate clandestine newspapers. Saddam Hussein's son Uday controls two newspapers, one of which is the influential *Babil*, which opposes UN Gulf War resolutions. All foreign journalists are vetted. Opposition groups began satellite broadcasts with US assistance in 2001.

CRIME

Death penalty used

Iraq does not publish prison figures

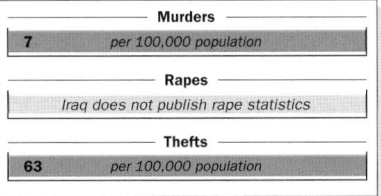

Up 28% in 1992

CRIME RATES

Murders

7 per 100,000 population

Rapes

Iraq does not publish rape statistics

Thefts

63 per 100,000 population

Iraq was formerly a law-abiding society, but economic collapse has sent crime rates soaring, especially in cities. Theft has been made a capital offense, encouraging thieves to murder in order to escape detection.

EDUCATION

School leaving age: 12

56%

209,818 students

THE EDUCATION SYSTEM

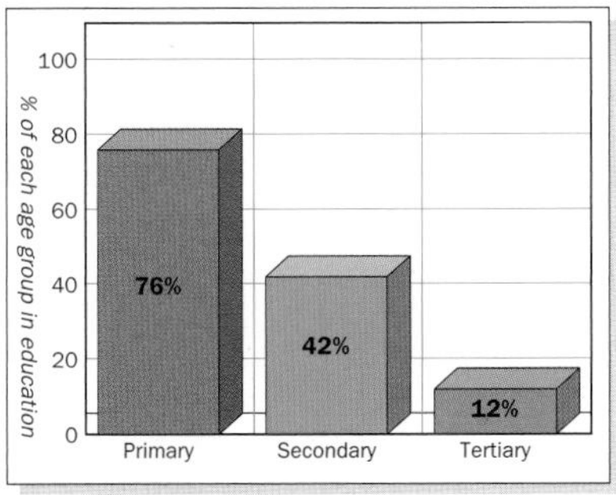
100
80
60
40
20
0
% of each age group in education
76%
42%
12%
Primary
Secondary
Tertiary

Education is free and universal, except in remote rural areas. Primary education has been made compulsory in an effort to reduce illiteracy. There are six universities. Academics authorized the organized plunder of antiquities and university equipment from Kuwait during the 1990 occupation. University scientists work closely with the regime on weapons research programs.

HEALTH

Welfare state health benefits

1 per 1667 people

Pneumonia, influenza, cancers, heart diseases

An effect of UN sanctions has been to aggravate the shortage of medical supplies and equipment, and deaths among children and the elderly have spiraled sharply. The increase in the number of children born with birth defects since 1991 is attributed to the use of depleted uranium shells during the Gulf War.

SPENDING

GDP/cap. decrease

CONSUMPTION AND SPENDING

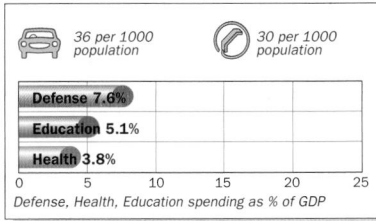

36 per 1000 population

30 per 1000 population

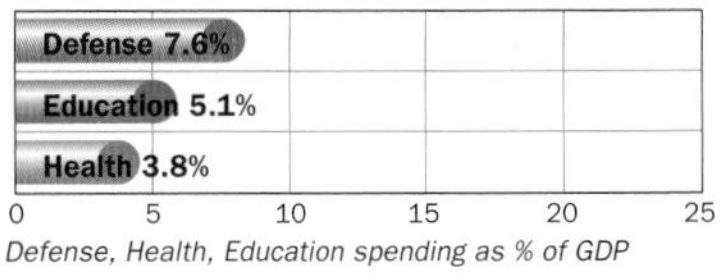
Defense 7.6%
Education 5.1%
Health 3.8%
0
5
10
15
20
25
Defense, Health, Education spending as % of GDP

Vulnerable sections of society have been particularly affected by UN sanctions. Middle-class citizens and traders are able to benefit from Iraq's open border with Jordan.

WORLD RANKING

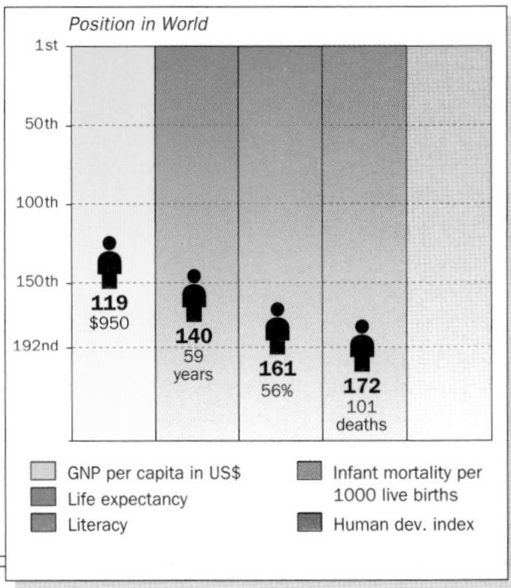
Position in World
1st
50th
100th
150th
192nd
119
$950
140
59
years
161
56%
172
101
deaths
GNP per capita in US$
Life expectancy
Literacy
Infant mortality per 1000 live births
Human dev. index

I

IRELAND

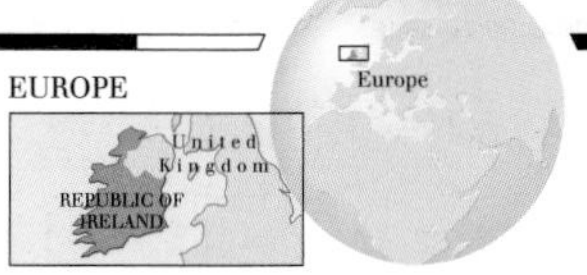
EUROPE
Europe
United Kingdom
REPUBLIC OF IRELAND

OFFICIAL NAME: Republic of Ireland **CAPITAL:** Dublin
POPULATION: 3.7 million **CURRENCY:** Euro (Punt until 2002) **OFFICIAL LANGUAGES:** Irish

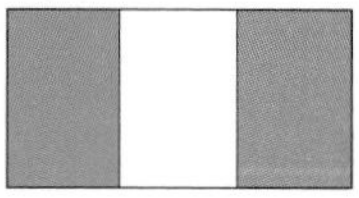

1922 | 1922 | March 17 | IRL | 0 | +353 | .ie

LYING IN THE Atlantic Ocean, off the west coast of Britain, the Irish Republic occupies about 85% of the island of Ireland. Low coastal mountain ranges surround a central basin with lakes, hills, and peat bogs. Centuries of struggle against English colonialism led to the formation of the Irish Free State in 1922 and full sovereignty in 1937. Hopes for the resolution of the Northern Ireland conflict center on the 1998 Good Friday accord, to which Ireland is a party.

CLIMATE

Maritime

WEATHER CHART

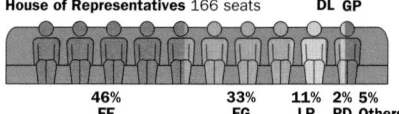

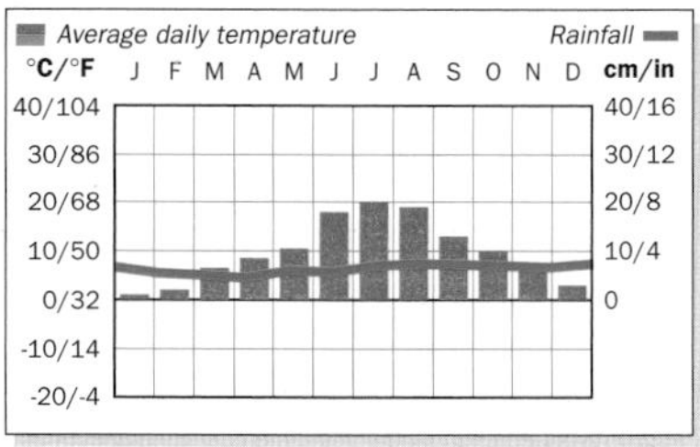
Average daily temperature
Rainfall
°C/°F J F M A M J J A S O N D cm/in
40/104
30/86
20/68
10/50
0/32
-10/14
-20/-4
40/16
30/12
20/8
10/4
0

Moderated by the Gulf Stream, the Irish climate is mild, equable, and wet. The mean annual temperature is 12°C (54°F).

TRANSPORTATION

Drive on left

Dublin International 12.8m passengers

150 ships 183,809 grt

THE TRANSPORTATION NETWORK

87,043 km (54,086 miles)

115 km (71 miles)

1919 km (1192 miles)

710 km (441 miles)

EU funds have improved road networks, especially around Dublin, which still, however, suffers from congestion.

TOURISM

Visitors : Population 1.8:1

6.7m visitors

Up 5% in 2000

MAIN TOURIST ARRIVALS

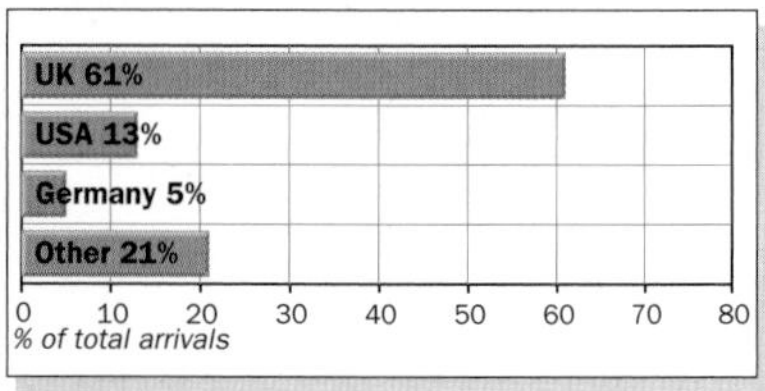
UK 61%
USA 13%
Germany 5%
Other 21%
0 10 20 30 40 50 60 70 80
% of total arrivals

Tourist numbers have increased steadily in recent years and exceed six million a year. Vibrant Dublin attracts many on "city breaks." Other draws are scenery, Ireland's "clean" environmental image, and the relaxed lifestyle.

PEOPLE

Pop. density medium

English, Irish Gaelic

54/km² (139/mi²)

THE URBAN/RURAL POPULATION SPLIT

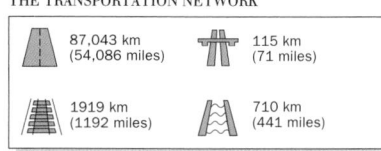

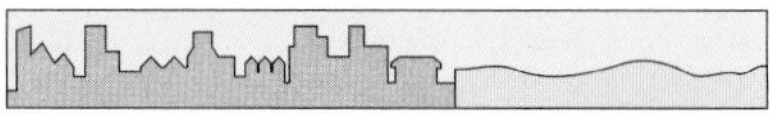
59%
41%

RELIGIOUS PERSUASION

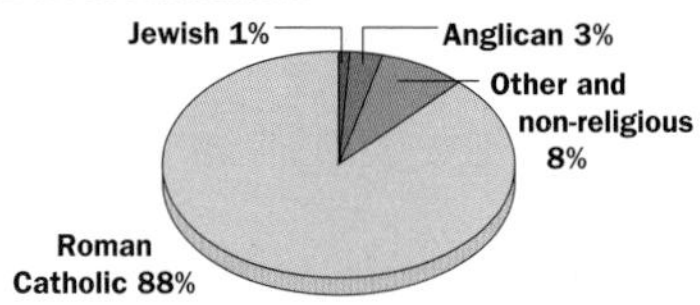
Jewish 1%
Anglican 3%
Other and non-religious 8%
Roman Catholic 88%

The population is 95% ethnic Irish. The influence of the Roman Catholic Church is declining. Ireland is now a country of net immigration, against the trend of the past 150 years.

POLITICS

Multiparty elections

L. House 1997/2002
U. House 1997/2002

President Mary McAleese

AT THE LAST ELECTION

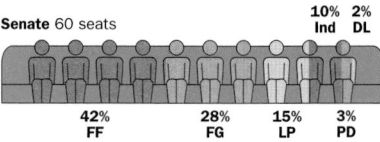

House of Representatives 166 seats

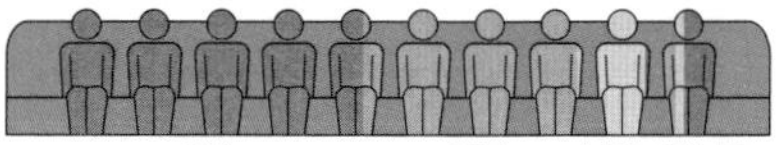
46% FF
33% FG
11% LP
2% PD
5% Others
2% DL
1% GP

FF = Fianna Fail FG = Fine Gael LP = Labour Party
DL = Democratic Left PD = Progressive Democrats
GP = Green Party Ind = Independents

Senate 60 seats

42% FF
28% FG
15% LP
3% PD
10% Ind
2% DL

In 1973, an FG/LP coalition took power, marking the end of FF as the traditional party of government – a role it had held since 1932. FF and FG/LP governments since then have tended to be short-lived. Since 1989, FF has needed PD support to govern. In 1994, the FF/LP government fell once more and was replaced by an FG/LP/DL coalition, led by FG leader John Bruton. However, an early general election in 1997 returned FF to office, under Bertie Ahern as *taoiseach* (prime minister).

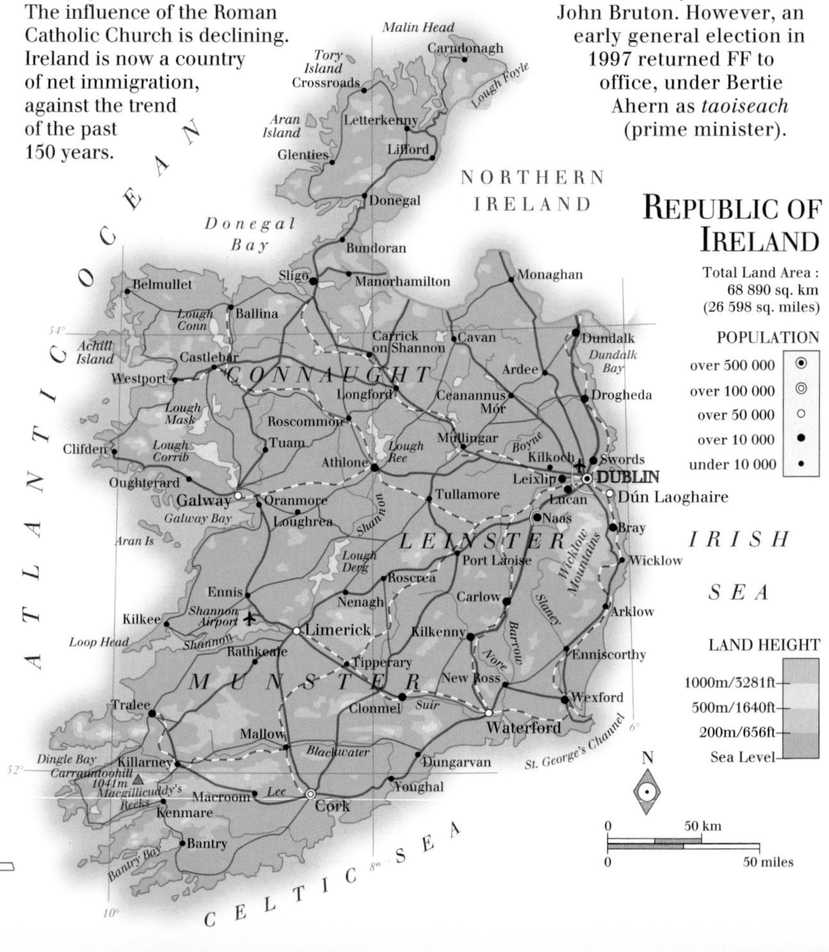
ATLANTIC OCEAN
CELTIC SEA
IRISH SEA
NORTHERN IRELAND
CONNAUGHT
LEINSTER
MUNSTER
Malin Head
Carndonagh
Lough Foyle
Tory Island
Crossroads
Aran Island
Letterkenny
Lifford
Glenties
Donegal
Donegal Bay
Bundoran
Sligo
Manorhamilton
Monaghan
Belmullet
Lough Conn
Ballina
Achill Island
Castlebar
Westport
Carrick on Shannon
Cavan
Dundalk
Dundalk Bay
Ardee
Drogheda
Longford
Ceanannus Mór
Lough Mask
Roscommon
Tuam
Lough Corrib
Clifden
Mullingar
Lough Ree
Athlone
Boyne
Kilkock
Swords
Leixlip
DUBLIN
Lucan
Dún Laoghaire
Oughterard
Galway
Oranmore
Galway Bay
Loughrea
Tullamore
Naas
Bray
Aran Is
Shannon
Lough Derg
Roscrea
Port Laoise
Wicklow Mountains
Wicklow
Ennis
Nenagh
Carlow
Kilkee
Shannon Airport
Limerick
Kilkenny
Slaney
Barrow
Arklow
Loop Head
Rathkeale
Nore
Enniscorthy
Tipperary
New Ross
Wexford
Tralee
Clonmel
Suir
Waterford
Mallow
Blackwater
St. George's Channel
Dingle Bay
Killarney
Carrauntoohill 1041m
Macgillicuddy's Reeks
Dungarvan
Macroom
Lee
Youghal
Cork
Kenmare
Bantry
Bantry Bay
REPUBLIC OF IRELAND
Total Land Area : 68 890 sq. km (26 598 sq. miles)
POPULATION
over 500 000
over 100 000
over 50 000
over 10 000
under 10 000
LAND HEIGHT
1000m/3281ft
500m/1640ft
200m/656ft
Sea Level
N
0 50 km
0 50 miles

WORLD AFFAIRS

Joined UN in 1955

CE | ESA | EU | OECD | OSCE

Ireland, the UK, and the USA are involved in the Northern Ireland peace process. A 2001 referendum rejected the EU's Nice treaty, embarrassing the government.

AID

Donor

$245m (donations) — Up 23% in 1999

Africa is the main recipient of Irish aid. Ireland is a big recipient of EU aid.

DEFENSE

No compulsory military service

$745m — Up 1% in 1999

Ireland is determined to maintain its neutrality, despite EU moves to establish a common European defense policy. It has observer status at the WEU.

ECONOMICS

Inflation 3.4% p.a. (1990–1999)

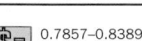

$80.6bn — 0.7857–0.8389 punts

SCORE CARD

- ❑ WORLD GNP RANKING..........40th
- ❑ GNP PER CAPITA..........$21,470
- ❑ BALANCE OF PAYMENTS..........$305m
- ❑ INFLATION..........1.6%
- ❑ UNEMPLOYMENT..........6%

STRENGTHS

The "Celtic tiger" – one of Europe's fastest-growing economies: real GDP growth of 9% a year in the latter half of the 1990s. Trade surplus. Low inflation. Efficient agriculture and food processing. Expanding high-tech sector; electronics account for 25% of exports. Large recipient of EU infrastructure aid. Highly educated workforce.

WEAKNESSES

Many key sectors owned by overseas multinationals. Danger of economy overheating. Housing shortage. Rapid growth is now straining the nation's infrastructure.

EXPORTS

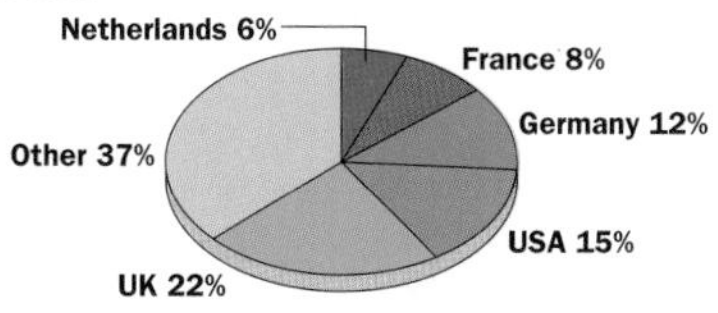
Netherlands 6%
France 8%
Germany 12%
Other 37%
USA 15%
UK 22%

IMPORTS

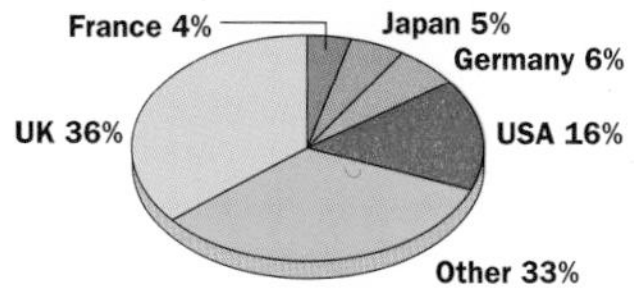
France 4%
Japan 5%
Germany 6%
UK 36%
USA 16%
Other 33%

RESOURCES

Electric power 4.4m kw

329,496 tonnes

Not an oil producer; refines 56,000 b/d

6.71m cattle, 5.39m sheep, 1.76m pigs, 11.5m chickens

Lead, zinc, natural gas, silver, coal

Oil has been found off the south coast. Studies suggest that this may be in commercially exploitable quantities.

ENVIRONMENT

Sustainability rank: 17th

1% — 10.2 tonnes per capita

The main environmental concerns are overexploitation of the country's peat bogs for fuel and the recent expansion of conifer plantations. While Ireland's levels of forest cover will increase in the next few years, most new planting is of conifers. In 1994 stringent new laws increased pollution controls. A small windpower industry is expanding.

MEDIA

TV ownership high

Daily newspaper circulation 149 per 1000 people

PUBLISHING AND BROADCAST MEDIA

There are 6 daily newspapers. These include the *Irish Times* and the *Irish Independent*

2 services: 1 state-owned, 1 independent

3 services: 1 state-owned, 2 independent

Censorship of media coverage of Sinn Féin was finally lifted in 1994. There is wide access to British newspapers, TV, and radio.

CRIME

Death penalty not used

2032 prisoners — Down 20% 1996-1998

Rural Ireland has the EU's lowest crime rate. Growing urban crime and narcotics are a problem in Dublin and Cork.

EDUCATION

School leaving age: 15

99% — 134,566 students

The Roman Catholic Church runs many schools. Increased education spending has resulted in a skilled workforce.

***Clew Bay in County Mayo,** on the western coast of Ireland, viewed from the slopes of neighboring Croagh Patrick.*

CHRONOLOGY

English colonization, begun in 1167, was reinforced after 1558 by anti-Catholic legislation and settlement of Scottish Protestants in the north.

- ❑ **1845–1855** Famine. One million die, 1.5 million emigrate.
- ❑ **1919–1921** Anglo-Irish war after republican Sinn Féin proclaims Irish independence.
- ❑ **1922** Irish Free State established.
- ❑ **1973** FG/LP alliance wins elections ending FF's ascendancy since 1932.
- ❑ **1990** Mary Robinson elected first woman president.
- ❑ **1995** Referendum favors divorce.
- ❑ **1998** Good Friday accord on Northern Ireland.
- ❑ **2001** Voters reject EU "Nice" treaty on expansion.

I

HEALTH

Welfare state health benefits

1 per 455 people — Heart diseases, cancers, accidents

Free care is means tested; about one-third of people qualify. Others pay to visit their doctor and for prescriptions, and there is a modest charge for hospital care.

SPENDING

GDP/cap. increase

CONSUMPTION AND SPENDING

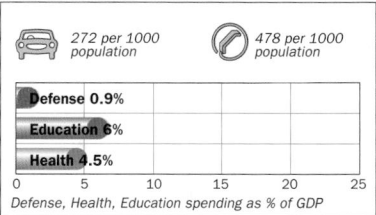

272 per 1000 population — *478 per 1000 population*

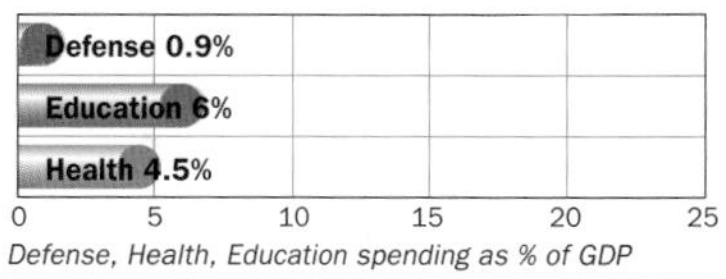
Defense 0.9%
Education 6%
Health 4.5%
0
5
10
15
20
25
Defense, Health, Education spending as % of GDP

Living standards for those with jobs are rising steadily. Welfare for those not in work is low by OECD standards.

WORLD RANKING

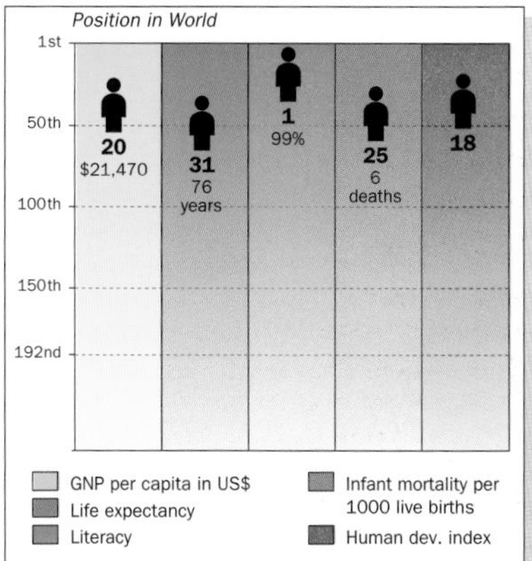
Position in World
1st
50th
100th
150th
192nd
20
$21,470
31
76
years
1
99%
25
6
deaths
18
GNP per capita in US$
Life expectancy
Literacy
Infant mortality per 1000 live births
Human dev. index

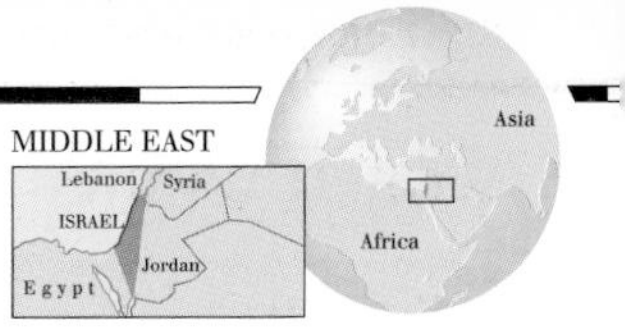
MIDDLE EAST
Lebanon
Syria
ISRAEL
Jordan
Egypt
Asia
Africa

ISRAEL

OFFICIAL NAME: State of Israel **CAPITAL:** Jerusalem (not internationally recognized)
POPULATION: 6.2 million **CURRENCY:** Shekel **OFFICIAL LANGUAGES:** Hebrew and Arabic

1948 | 1994 | May 12 | IL | +2 | +972 | .il

CREATED AS A NEW STATE in 1948 with the backing of the USA and other Allied powers, Israel is bordered by Egypt, Jordan, Syria, and Lebanon. The Dead Sea on the Israel–Jordan border is the lowest point on the Earth's land surface. After wars with its Arab neighbors, Israel has unilaterally extended its boundaries. Resolving the Israeli–Palestinian conflict hinges on the future of the West Bank and East Jerusalem, under a "land for peace" deal.

CLIMATE

Hot desert/ Mediterranean

WEATHER CHART

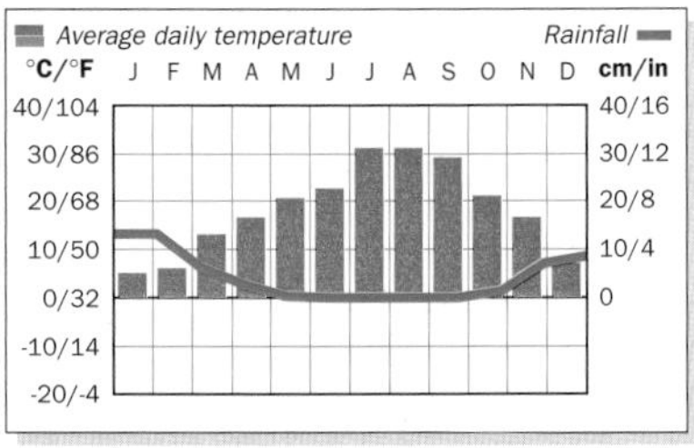
Average daily temperature
Rainfall
°C/°F
J F M A M J J A S O N D
cm/in
40/104
30/86
20/68
10/50
0/32
-10/14
-20/4
40/16
30/12
20/8
10/4
0

Summers are hot and dry. The wet season is between November and March, when the weather is mild.

TRANSPORTATION

Drive on right

Ben-Gurion International, Tel Aviv–Yafo 8.9m passengers

53 ships 751,600 grt

THE TRANSPORTATION NETWORK

15,965 km (9920 miles)

56 km (35 miles)

663 km (412 miles)

None

Railroads are being extended. There are three commercial ports. Ben Gurion international airport is being expanded.

TOURISM

Visitors : Population 1:2.6

2.4m visitors

Up 4% in 2000

MAIN TOURIST ARRIVALS

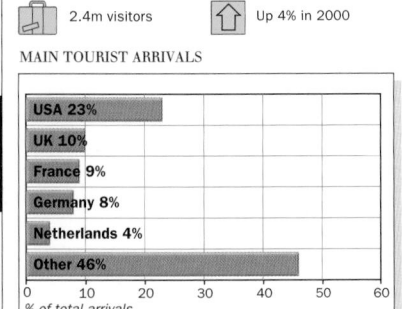

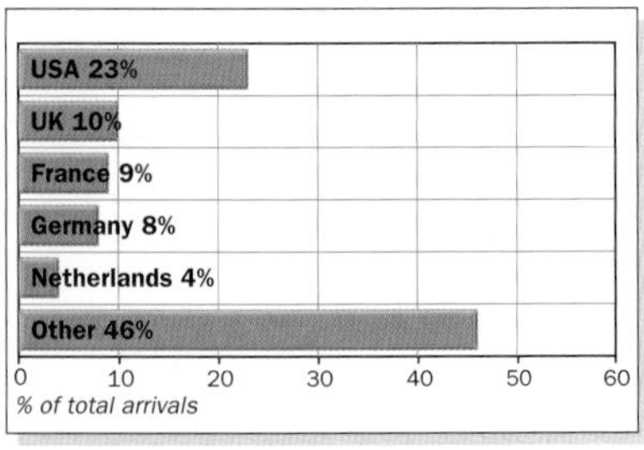
USA 23%
UK 10%
France 9%
Germany 8%
Netherlands 4%
Other 46%
0
10
20
30
40
50
60
% of total arrivals

Tourism has been damaged by the sustained violence of the Israeli–Palestinian conflict.

PEOPLE

Pop. density high

Hebrew, Arabic, Yiddish, German, Russian, Polish, Romanian, Persian

305/km² (790/mi²)

THE URBAN/RURAL POPULATION SPLIT

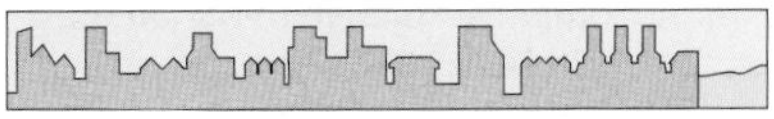
91%
9%

RELIGIOUS PERSUASION

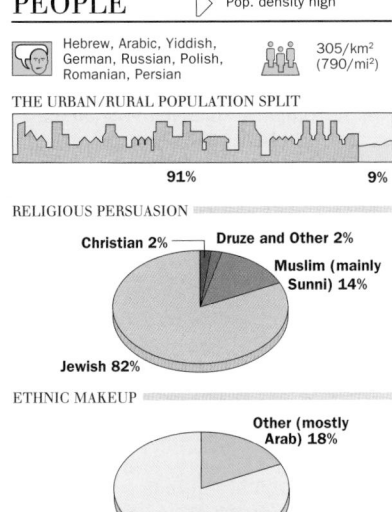

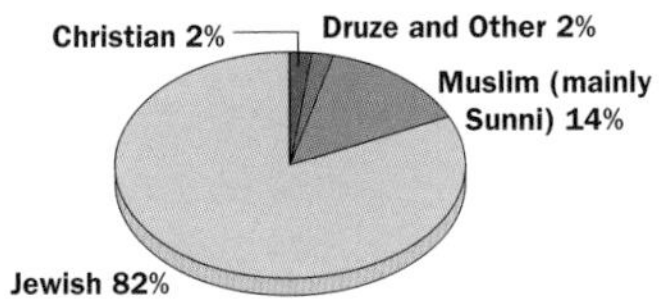
Christian 2%
Druze and Other 2%
Muslim (mainly Sunni) 14%
Jewish 82%

ETHNIC MAKEUP

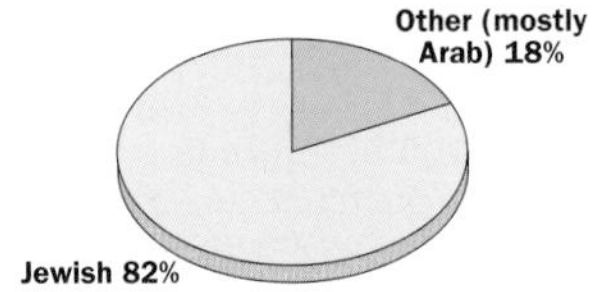
Other (mostly Arab) 18%
Jewish 82%

Large numbers of Jewish immigrants settled in Palestine before Israel was founded. After World War II, immigration increased massively. Sephardic Jews from the Middle East and Mediterranean are now probably in the majority, but Ashkenazi Jews, most of central European origin, still dominate society. Hundreds of thousands of Russian Jews have arrived since 1989. Israel's non-Jewish population totals more than one million. Many take part in the democratic process, but remain sidelined in Israeli life. There are tensions between secular and Orthodox Jews over religious observance and the pursuit of a viable peace agreement with the Palestinians.

POPULATION AGE BREAKDOWN

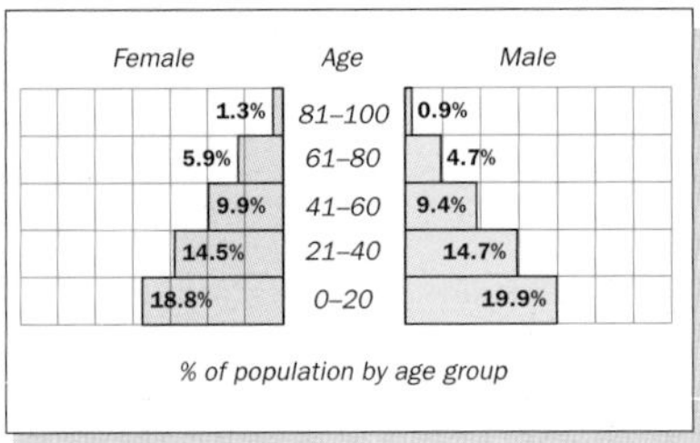
Female
Age
Male
1.3%
81–100
0.9%
5.9%
61–80
4.7%
9.9%
41–60
9.4%
14.5%
21–40
14.7%
18.8%
0–20
19.9%
% of population by age group

POLITICS

Multiparty elections

1999/2003

President Moshe Katzav

AT THE LAST ELECTION
Parliament 120 seats

8% M
4% NRP
22% One Isr
16% Li
14% Sh
5% YB
31% Others

One Isr = One Israel **Li** = Likud **Sh** = Shas
M = Meretz–Democratic Israel **YB** = Yisrael Ba'aliya
NRP = National Religious Party
The One Israel alliance comprises Labor, Gesher, and Meymad

Israel is a multiparty democracy.

MAIN POLITICAL ISSUES

Peace with the Palestinians

Whether Israel's security should be based on military and police strength, or on "land for peace" deals with Palestinians and neighboring countries, is a central issue. Most Jewish settlers in the West Bank and Gaza adamantly oppose returning territory. Religious parties led calls to bring down the government in early 2000 over the transfer of sensitive areas. The renewed Israeli–Palestinian conflict later that year swung popular opinion toward a less compromising approach.

Peace with Syria

The 1999–2001 Labor government favored negotiating with Syria over the conquered Golan Heights, and withdrew all its forces from the "security zone" in neighboring southern Lebanon in 2000. The victory of Ariel Sharon in prime ministerial elections in 2001 took dealings with Syria off the agenda.

PROFILE

In 1996, 1999, and 2001 the prime minister was elected by direct popular vote. In 2001 Labor leader Ehud Barak was defeated by hard-liner Ariel Sharon, who then formed a national unity government comprising his right-wing Likud party, the centrist Labor party, and a number of smaller parties.

Ariel Sharon, *the hard-line prime minister since 2001.*

Yasser Arafat, *the militant-turned-moderate leader of the PLO.*

I

WORLD AFFAIRS

Joined UN in 1949

EBRD | IAEA | IBRD | WTO

Israel is technically at war with all Arab states except Egypt and Jordan; it withdrew from southern Lebanon in 2000. It maintains a close relationship with the USA. Its harsh reprisals against Palestinian unrest are widely condemned.

AID

Recipient

$906m (receipts) — Down 24% 1997–1999

Israel receives massive military and economic aid from the USA. Large ad hoc donations are also received from Jewish NGOs.

ISRAEL

Total Land Area : 20 330 sq. km (7849 sq. miles)

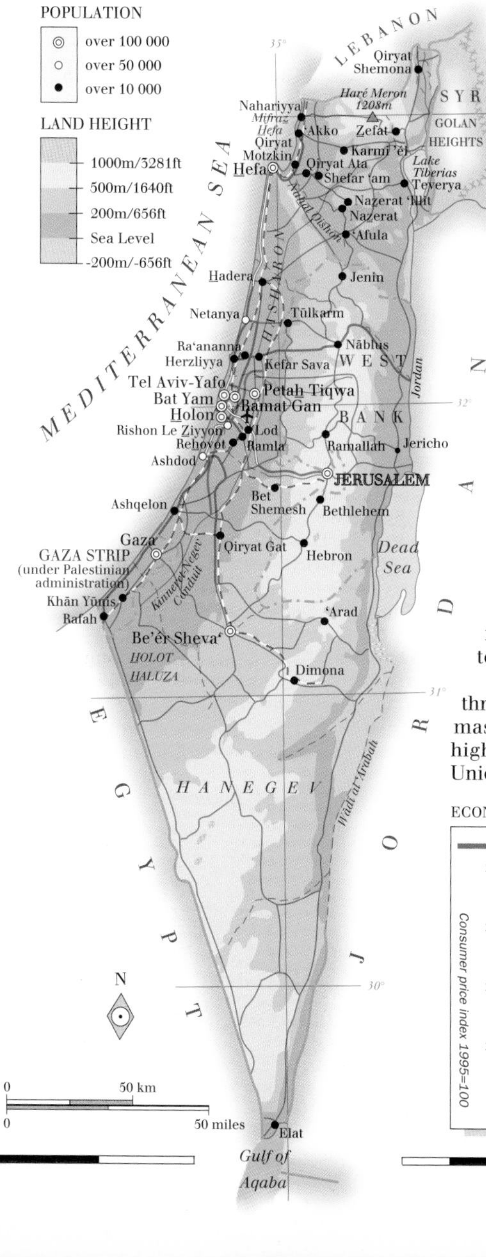
POPULATION
over 100 000
over 50 000
over 10 000
LAND HEIGHT
1000m/3281ft
500m/1640ft
200m/656ft
Sea Level
-200m/-656ft
LEBANON
SYRIA
GOLAN HEIGHTS
MEDITERRANEAN SEA
Qiryat Shemona
Haré Meron 1208m
Nahariyya
Mifraz Hefa
'Akko
Zefat
Qiryat Motzkin
Karmi'él
Hefa
Qiryat Ata
Shefar'am
Lake Tiberias
Teverya
Nazerat 'Illit
Nazerat
'Afula
Hadera
Jenin
Netanya
Tūlkarm
Nāblus
Ra'anana
Herzliyya
Kefar Sava
WEST BANK
Tel Aviv-Yafo
Petah Tiqwa
Bat Yam
Ramat Gan
Holon
Rishon Le Ziyyon
Lod
Rehovot
Ramla
Ramallah
Jericho
Ashdod
JERUSALEM
Bet Shemesh
Bethlehem
Ashqelon
Gaza
GAZA STRIP (under Palestinian administration)
Qiryat Gat
Hebron
Dead Sea
Khān Yūnis
Rafah
'Arad
Be'ér Sheva'
HOLOT HALUZA
Dimona
HANEGEV
EGYPT
JORDAN
Jordan
Wādī al 'Arabah
Elat
Gulf of Aqaba
N
0 50 km
0 50 miles

DEFENSE

Compulsory military service

$8.85bn — Down 5% in 1999

Israel is the only known nuclear-armed power in the Middle East. It has a small regular defense force, which can be boosted by nearly 600,000 reservists. Equipped with some of the latest US technology, it is vastly superior in firepower to the armies of its Arab neighbors. However, countering the Palestinian *intifada* necessitates new tactics – counter-insurgency and riot control, rather than conventional tactics.

ISRAELI ARMED FORCES

3900 main battle tanks (*Centurion*, *Merkava* I/II/III, M-48A5/60A3, *Magach* 7)	130,000 personnel
2 submarines, 47 patrol boats	6500 personnel
696 combat aircraft (50 F-4E-2000, 73 F-15, 237 F-16)	36,000 personnel
Widely believed that Israel has a nuclear capacity with up to 100 warheads. Delivery via *Jericho* 1 and *Jericho* 2 missiles	

ECONOMICS

Inflation 10.7% p.a. (1990–1999)

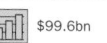

$99.6bn — 4.1598–4.0435 sheqalim

SCORE CARD

- ❑ WORLD GNP RANKING........................35th
- ❑ GNP PER CAPITA..........................$16,310
- ❑ BALANCE OF PAYMENTS....................$–2.6bn
- ❑ INFLATION.................................5.2%
- ❑ UNEMPLOYMENT...............................9%

STRENGTHS

Strong government commitment to economic reform. Huge potential of agriculture, manufacturing, and high-tech industry. Important banking sector. Sizable aid from USA and international Jewish organizations.

WEAKNESSES

Rising unemployment. Large defense budget. History of regional and internal instability inhibits foreign investment. Little trade with Arab neighbors. Incidents of corruption.

PROFILE

The government is seeking ways to reduce massive state spending. The state owns most of the land and controls over 20% of all industries and services. Public companies are being privatized and there are plans to end restrictive labor practices. Agriculture is highly specialized and profitable, but has been eclipsed by high-tech industries. The state is now aiming to boost the service sector.

Israel's economy expanded through the 1990s, benefiting from mass immigration of Jews, many highly educated, from the former Soviet Union. Although unemployment levels rose as a result of immigration, new skills and contacts also helped the Israeli economy toward sustained export-led growth. Pockets of poverty remained in "development towns."

The Palestinian uprising from 2000 seriously damaged the economy, hitting trade, tourism, and investment.

ECONOMIC PERFORMANCE INDICATOR

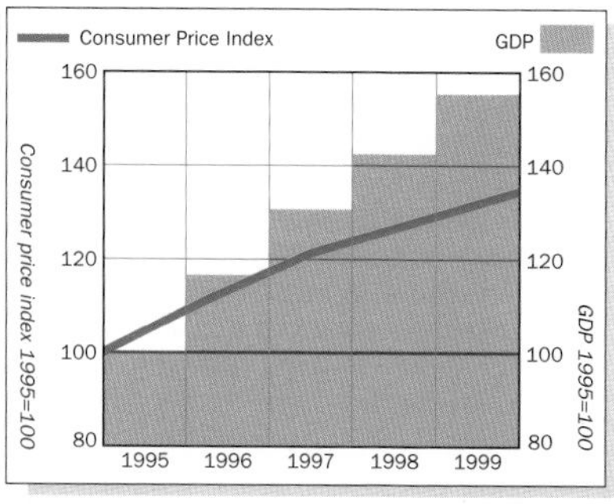
Consumer Price Index
GDP
160
140
120
100
80
Consumer price index 1995=100
GDP 1995=100
1995
1996
1997
1998
1999

EXPORTS

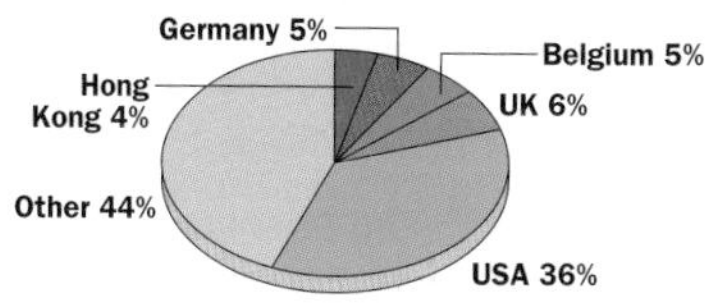
Germany 5%
Belgium 5%
Hong Kong 4%
UK 6%
Other 44%
USA 36%

IMPORTS

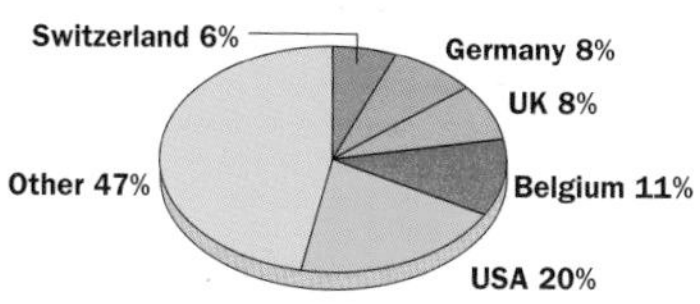
Switzerland 6%
Germany 8%
UK 8%
Other 47%
Belgium 11%
USA 20%

ISRAEL : MAJOR BUSINESSES

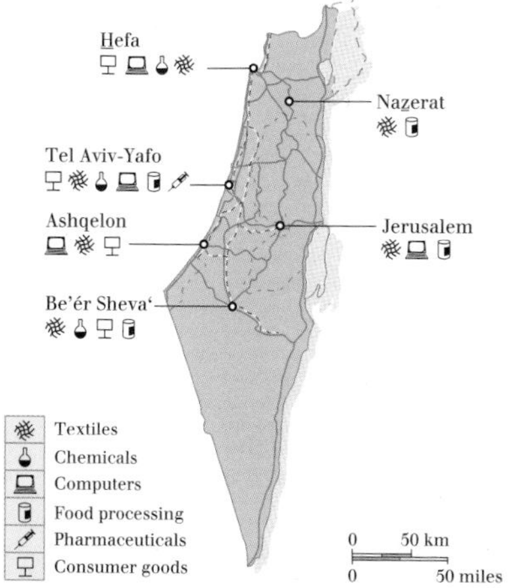
Hefa
Nazerat
Tel Aviv-Yafo
Ashqelon
Jerusalem
Be'ér Sheva'
Textiles
Chemicals
Computers
Food processing
Pharmaceuticals
Consumer goods
0 50 km
0 50 miles

I

ISRAEL AND THE PALESTINIANS

THE CONFLICT BETWEEN ISRAEL and the Palestinians – the Arab population of the pre-1948 British mandated territory of Palestine – is crucial in Middle East politics. In 1948 nearly a million Palestinians became refugees, and 300,000 more left territories occupied by Israel in 1967. The Palestine Liberation Organization (PLO) led by Yasser Arafat claimed to be the Palestinians' "sole legitimate representative." Not until the 1993 accords did they begin getting self-rule in the West Bank and Gaza – inhabited by over two million Palestinians and 300,000 Jewish settlers. A timetable agreed in 1999 promised to complete this in a year and resolve "permanent status" issues. Palestinians expected this to entail full statehood. A descent into conflict in the latter part of 2000 left these hopes for peace in ruins.

BACKGROUND

In 1947 the UN approved a plan to partition Palestine, to create separate Jewish and Arab states. This was accepted by the Jewish side but not the Arabs. When the British Mandate ended in May, Arab states invaded Palestine but were pushed back well beyond the UN partition lines by Israeli forces. The 1949 armistices left only East Jerusalem, the West Bank (5900 sq km), and the Egyptian-administered coastal Gaza Strip (1000 sq km) not in Israeli hands. Jordan declared East Jerusalem and the West Bank to be part of its territory, only renouncing this claim formally in 1988.

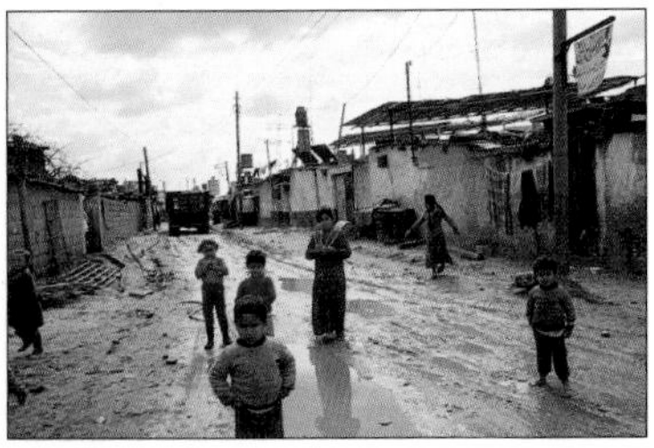

***Poor slum housing** in Gaza.*

GAZA STRIP

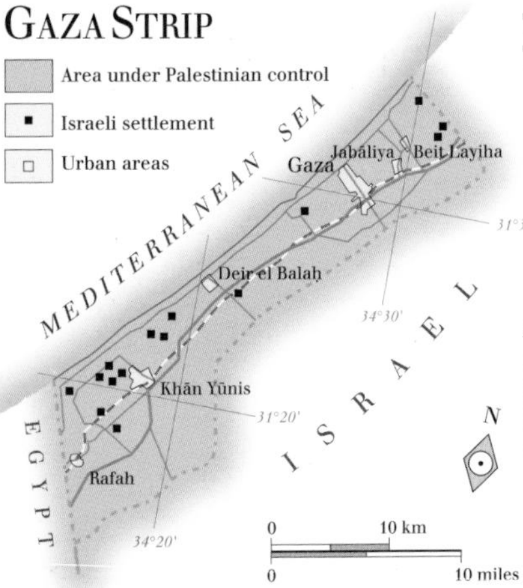
Area under Palestinian control
Israeli settlement
Urban areas
MEDITERRANEAN SEA
Gaza
Jabāliya
Beit Lāyiha
31°30'
Deir el Balah
34°30'
ISRAEL
Khān Yūnis
31°20'
EGYPT
Rafah
34°20'
N
0
10 km
10 miles

In the 1967 Six-Day War Israel took East Jerusalem, the West Bank, and Gaza. Jewish settlers began moving in, regarding these occupied territories as part of the biblical-era Land of Israel. Plans for Palestinian autonomy were part of the 1978 Camp David agreement, but failed to materialize. Diplomatically, there was deadlock. The PLO didn't recognize Israel's right to exist until 1988, while Israel refused to "negotiate with terrorists."

PALESTINIAN AUTONOMY

Turning away from armed struggle, the PLO in 1993 concluded a historic "land for peace" deal with Israel, the "Oslo Accords." The two sides formally recognized one another, and Arafat and Israeli Prime Minister Rabin signed a Declaration of Principles in Washington D.C. A five-year timetable for "permanent status" negotiations would tackle the future of Jewish settlements and the Palestinian demand for East Jerusalem as their capital. Palestinians were to get interim self-rule, initially in Gaza and Jericho (achieved in 1994), and gradually in the whole West Bank. This meant Palestinian police taking over responsibility for security from the Israeli military, who had been struggling since 1987 to end an insurrection led by the radical Islamic organization Hamas. The Palestinian National Authority (PNA) was established on Palestinian territory, based in Gaza. Arafat – its chairman – made a triumphal return in July 1994 and won a mandate in January 1996 as president of the 88-member Palestinian Legislative Council elected at the same time.

THE DERAILING OF THE PEACE PROCESS

The "Oslo B" accord extended PNA rule from Gaza and Jericho to six more West Bank towns in 1995. After repeated delays Israel also relinquished control of Hebron (but not of rural areas). Mutual mistrust and violence, however, threatened to derail the peace process before it reached the stage of "final status" talks. Arafat risked losing credibility among radical Palestinians. Attacks by rogue Hamas guerrillas, including suicide bombings in Israel, overshadowed elections there in mid-1996. A new right-wing government adopted a tougher stance and did little to restrain the Jewish settlers, who fiercely opposed the whole "land for peace" deal.

WEST BANK

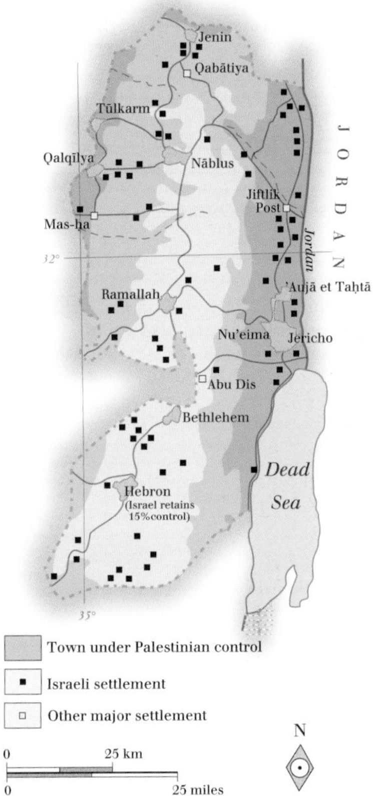
Jenin
Qabātiya
Tūlkarm
Qalqīlya
Nāblus
Jiftlik Post
Mas-ha
JORDAN
Jordan
32°
'Aujā et Taḥtā
Ramallah
Nu'eima
Jericho
Abu Dis
Bethlehem
Dead Sea
Hebron (Israel retains 15% control)
35°
Town under Palestinian control
Israeli settlement
Other major settlement
0
25 km
25 miles
N

After Israel's 1999 elections, a Labor-led government in 2000 under new prime minister Ehud Barak established with the PNA an ambitious timetable for a permanent agreement. Intensive US diplomacy helped keep this plan alive until the eleventh hour, but heavy-handed Israeli retaliation to violent incidents in September–October 2000 provoked Palestinian rage and a return to the tactics of *intifada* (uprising). In a bitter climate of atrocity, retaliation, and counter-strike, Israeli policy hardened under a new government headed by Ariel Sharon, who was elected prime minister in 2001.

***Bethlehem,** situated in the troubled West Bank, is just one of the many holy places that remain a principal attraction for visitors.*

I

RESOURCES

Electric power 7.8m kw

23,274 tonnes

100 b/d (reserves 7,320,000 bbl)

4.9m turkeys, 1.4m geese, 28m chickens

Natural gas, oil, salt, potash, copper, gold, magnesium, bromine

ELECTRICITY GENERATION

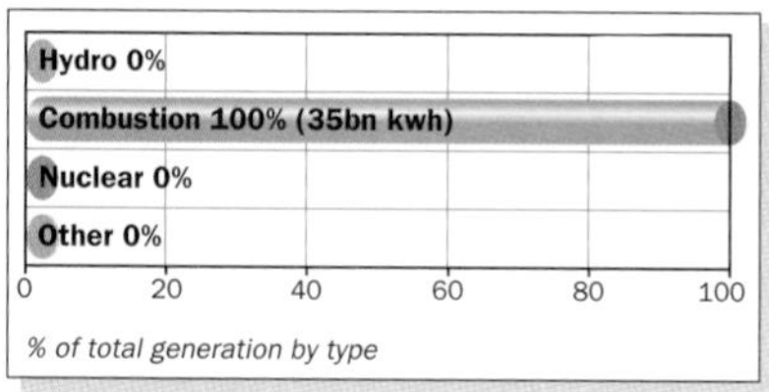

Hydro 0%
Combustion 100% (35bn kwh)
Nuclear 0%
Other 0%
0
20
40
60
80
100
% of total generation by type

The country's most valuable deposits of minerals are potash, bromine (of which Israel is the world's largest exporter), and other salts mined near the Dead Sea. Reserves of copper ore and gold were discovered in 1988. In the coastal plain, mixed farming, vineyards, and citrus groves are plentiful. Former desert areas now have extensive irrigation systems supporting specialized agriculture.

Israel's most critical resource is water. Shortages have forced Israel to purchase water, transported in plastic bags, from Turkey.

Jordan
Dead Sea
HANAGEV
0
50 km
0
50 miles

ISRAEL : LAND USE

- Cropland
- Forest
- Pasture
- Desert
- Sheep
- Citrus fruit – cash crop

ENVIRONMENT

Sustainability rank: 53rd

15%

10.4 tonnes per capita

Since 1993–1994, designated Environment Year, the government has aimed to promote recycling schemes, the cleanup of rivers, and a healthier urban environment.

ENVIRONMENTAL TREATIES

Yes	Yes	Yes
Yes	Yes	Yes

MEDIA

TV ownership high

Daily newspaper circulation 288 per 1000 people

PUBLISHING AND BROADCAST MEDIA

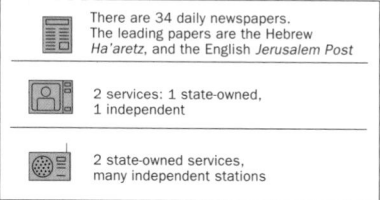

There are 34 daily newspapers. The leading papers are the Hebrew *Ha'aretz*, and the English *Jerusalem Post*

2 services: 1 state-owned, 1 independent

2 state-owned services, many independent stations

The left-wing press favors the peace process. The number of private radio stations, many right-wing, is rising.

CRIME

Death penalty not used

10,179 prisoners

Down 13% 1996–1998

CRIME RATES

Murders
2 per 100,000 population

Rapes
14 per 100,000 population

Thefts
3994 per 100,000 population

The vast majority of violent attacks are due to the Israeli–Palestinian conflict rather than individual criminal acts.

EDUCATION

School leaving age: 15

96%

198,766 students

THE EDUCATION SYSTEM

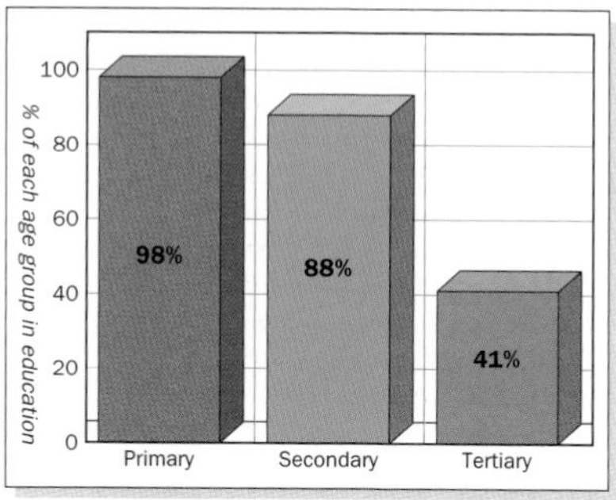

100
80
60
40
20
0
% of each age group in education
98%
88%
41%
Primary
Secondary
Tertiary

A highly educated population has been the engine of Israel's economic growth. State schools have religious (Jewish), secular, and Arab streams. Ultra-orthodox and Sephardic Jews increasingly run their own private ventures.

HEALTH

Welfare state health benefits

1 per 217 people

Heart and cerebrovascular diseases, cancers

The ratio of doctors to the total population in Israel is one of the highest in the world. Primary health care reaches all communities. Israel's hospitals have pioneered many innovative treatments.

CHRONOLOGY

The creation of Israel in Palestine in 1948 realized the Zionist dream of a Jewish homeland.

- ❑ **1967** Six-Day War; Israel takes West Bank, Gaza, Sinai, Golan Heights.
- ❑ **1973** Egypt and Syria attack Israel.
- ❑ **1978** Camp David accords with Egypt.
- ❑ **1978** Formal peace treaty, Sinai returned to Egypt.
- ❑ **1982** Israel invades Lebanon.
- ❑ **1987** Palestinians launch *intifada.*
- ❑ **1993** Oslo Accords.
- ❑ **1994** Palestinian autonomy begins in Gaza and Jericho.
- ❑ **1995** Prime minister Yitzhak Rabin assassinated: replaced by Peres.
- ❑ **1996** Palestinian elections. Benjamin Netanyahu (Likud) first directly elected Israeli prime minister.
- ❑ **1998** Israel stalls on US-backed plan to revive peace process.
- ❑ **1999** Ehud Barak (Labor) elected prime minister. Renewed peace process with Palestinians and Syria.
- ❑ **2000** Israeli forces withdraw from southern Lebanon. Large-scale violent Israeli–Palestinian clashes.
- ❑ **2001** Ariel Sharon (Likud) elected prime minister; forms unity government. Conflict worsens.

I

SPENDING

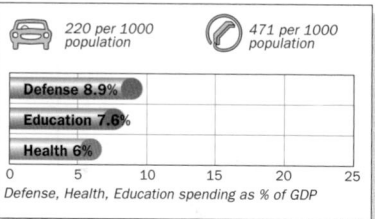

GDP/cap. increase

CONSUMPTION AND SPENDING

220 per 1000 population

471 per 1000 population

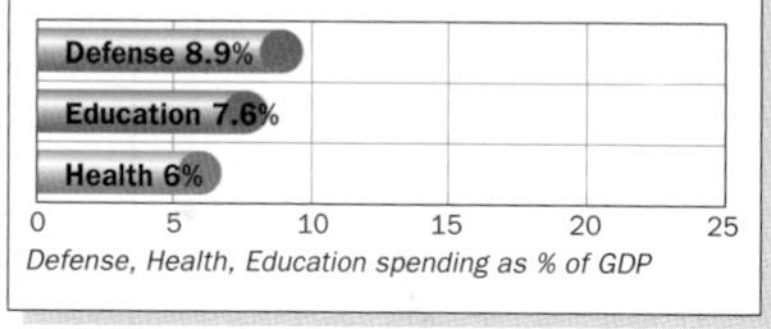

Defense 8.9%
Education 7.6%
Health 6%
0
5
10
15
20
25
Defense, Health, Education spending as % of GDP

Income per head is high, but taxation is heavy. In theory, those living in communes (*kibbutzim*) eschew personal material wealth.

WORLD RANKING

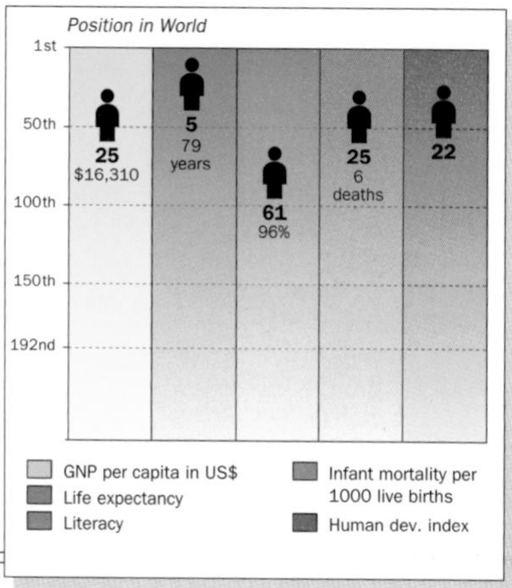

Position in World
1st
50th
100th
150th
192nd
25
$16,310
5
79
years
61
96%
25
6
deaths
22
GNP per capita in US$
Life expectancy
Literacy
Infant mortality per 1000 live births
Human dev. index

ITALY

OFFICIAL NAME: Italian Republic **CAPITAL:** Rome **POPULATION:** 57.3 million
CURRENCY: Euro (Italian lira until 2002) **OFFICIAL LANGUAGE:** Italian

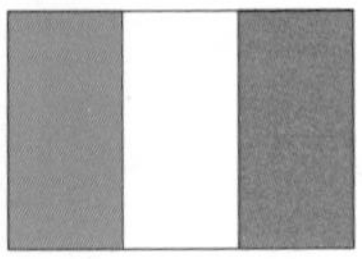

1870 | 1947 | June 2 | I | +1 | +39 | .it

THE BOOT-SHAPED Italian peninsula stretches 800 km (496 miles) southwards into the Mediterranean, while the Alps form a natural boundary to the north. Italy also includes Sicily, Sardinia, and several smaller islands. The south is an area of seismic activity, with two famous volcanoes, Vesuvius and Etna. Rival city states flourished in Renaissance Italy, a unified country only in Roman times and since 1870. Fascist rule under Mussolini from 1922 ended with Italy's defeat in World War II. The Christian Democrats (CD) then dominated Italy's notoriously short-lived governments for decades, until in the 1990s the established parties and patronage systems were shaken up by corruption investigations. New groupings emerged, power alternating between a right-wing coalition and a broad center-left "Olive Tree" alliance.

CLIMATE

Mediterranean/mountain

WEATHER CHART

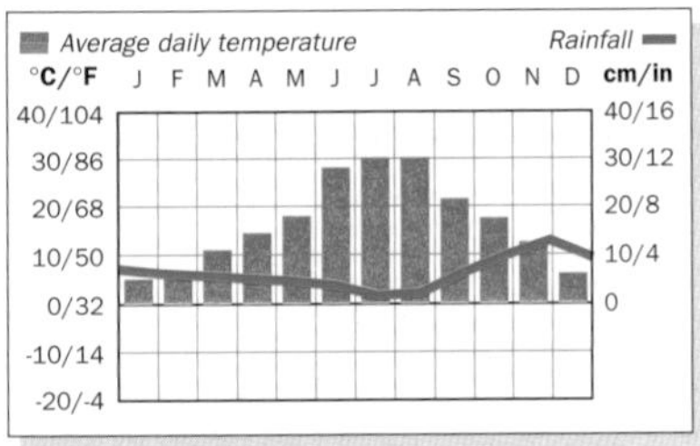

Average daily temperature
Rainfall
°C/°F
J F M A M J J A S O N D
cm/in
40/104
30/86
20/68
10/50
0/32
-10/14
-20/-4
40/16
30/12
20/8
10/4
0

A Mediterranean climate in the south contrasts with more temperate conditions in the north. Summers are hot and dry, especially in the south; Sardinia and Sicily have highs of more than 30°C (86°F). The Adriatic coast suffers from cold winds such as the *bora*. Southern winters are mild; northern ones are cooler and wetter, with heavy snow in the mountains.

TRANSPORTATION

Drive on right

Leonardo da Vinci (Fiumicino), Rome 24m passengers

1329 ships 6.8m grt

THE TRANSPORTATION NETWORK

654,676 km (406,796 miles)

6957 km (4323 miles)

16,108 km (10,010 miles)

2400 km (1491 miles)

Italy's roads, which carry the bulk of its trade via Switzerland and Austria, are badly congested. The *autostrada* (expressway) network lacks key links, and serious bottlenecks affect the main north–south artery. Construction of the high-speed TAV train from Naples to Turin is behind schedule and over budget, with the first (Naples–Rome) section still not open in 2001.

TOURISM

Visitors : Population 1:1.4

41.2m visitors

Up 13% in 2000

MAIN TOURIST ARRIVALS

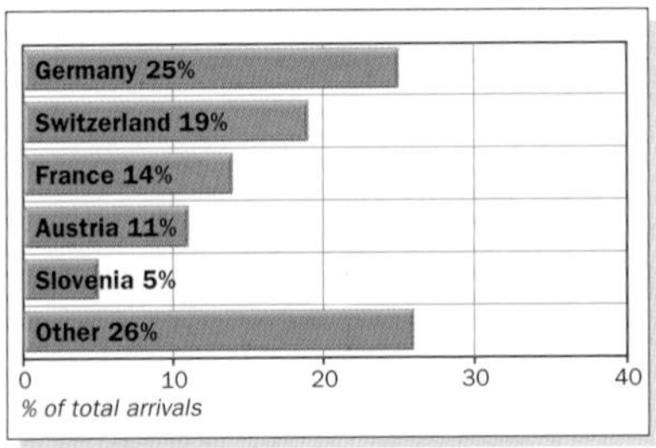

Germany 25%
Switzerland 19%
France 14%
Austria 11%
Slovenia 5%
Other 26%
0
10
20
30
40
% of total arrivals

Italy has been a tourist destination since the 16th century. Roman popes consciously aimed to make their city the most beautiful in the world to attract travelers. In the 18th century, Italy was the focus of any Grand Tour. Today, its many unspoiled centers of Renaissance and ancient culture continue to make Italy one of the world's major tourism destinations. The industry accounts for 3% of Italy's GDP, and employs a million people – 5% of the workforce.

Most visitors travel to the northern half of Italy, to cities such as Venice and Florence, and to Rome. Tourists are also drawn to the northern lakes, while beach resorts such as Rimini attract a large, youthful crowd in summer. Italy is also growing in popularity as a skiing destination. In the south the breathtaking ruins of Roman Pompeii are a particular magnet for visitors.

Fears have been expressed about the detrimental impact of tourism on Italy's environment. The pressure of visitors to Venice is such that in summer one-way systems for pedestrians have to be introduced and day-trippers are often turned away.

Europe
EUROPE
SWITZERLAND
FRANCE
Mont Blanc 4807m
Gran Paradiso 4061m
Aosta
Biella
Varese
Lake Maggiore
Lago di Como
Como
Lecco
Bergamo
Lago di Garda
Brescia
Monza
Milano
Vercelli
Novara
Torino
Asti
Alessandria
Piacenza
Mantova
Parma
Reggio nell' Emilia
Modena
Cueno
Appennino Ligure
Genova
Rapallo
Savona
Golfo di Genova
La Spezia
Carrara
Massa
MONACO
Imperia
San Remo
Viareggio
Pistoia
Pisa
Livorno
LIGURIAN SEA
Isola d'Elba
Arcipelago Toscano
Corsica (FRANCE)
Porto Torres
Olbia
Sassari
Alghero
Macomer
Nuoro
Sardegna (Sardinia)
Monti del Gennargentu
Oristano
Arbatax
Iglesias
Carbonia
Cagliari
Sant Antioco

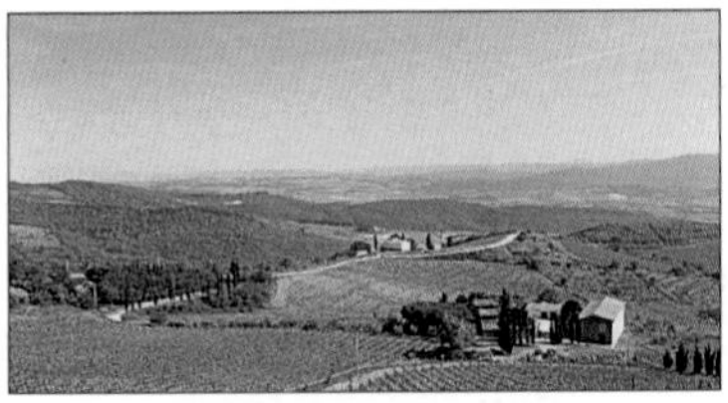

Tuscan landscape. *Chianti wine is produced in this region, where many northern Europeans own holiday homes.*

ITALY

Total Land Area : 294 060 sq. km (113 536 sq. miles)

POPULATION

over 1 000 000
over 500 000
over 100 000
over 50 000
over 10 000

LAND HEIGHT

3000m/9843ft
2000m/6562ft
1000m/3281ft
500m/1640ft
200m/656ft
Sea Level

SLOVENIA
Udine
Trieste
Monfalcone
Venezia
Golfo di Venezia
Ravenna
Rimini
Cesena
SAN MARINO
Pesaro
Fano
Sengallia
Ancona
ADRIATIC SEA
Fabriano
Perugia
Assisi
Lago Trasimeno
Ascoli Piceno
Teramo
Terni
Pescara
L'Aquila
ROME
Tivoli
Avezzano
di Ostia
Vasto
Rodi Garganico
San Severo
Manfredonia
Campobasso
Foggia
Latina
Barletta
Teracina
Benevento
Andria
Bari
Golfo di Gaeta
Monopoli
Napoli
Avellino
Isloe Ponziane
Torre del Greco
I. d'Ischia
Castellamare di Stabia
Isola di Capri
Salerno
Potenza
La Murge
Brindisi
Taranto
Lecce
Strait of Otranto
Golfo di Salerno
Penisola Salentina
Golfo di Taranto
Castrovillari
TYRRHENIAN SEA
Rossano
Cosenza
Paola
La Sila
Crotone
Nicastro
Catanzaro
I. de Ustica
Isole Eolie
Stretto di Messina
I. Lupari
Vulcano
IONIAN SEA
Messina
Locri
Reggio di Calabria
Palermo
Trapani
Barcellona
Alcamo
Sicilia (Sicily)
Mt Etna 3323m
Taormina
Egadi
Marsala
Corleone
Acireale
Castelvetrano
Sciacca
Enna
Caltanissetta
Catania
Augusta
Agrigento
Caltagirone
Siracusa
Licata
Gela
Ragusa
Vittoria
Pantelleria
MEDITERRANEAN SEA
N
0
100 km
100 miles

PEOPLE

Pop. density medium

Italian, German, French, Rhaeto-Romanic, Sardinian

195/km² (505/mi²)

THE URBAN/RURAL POPULATION SPLIT

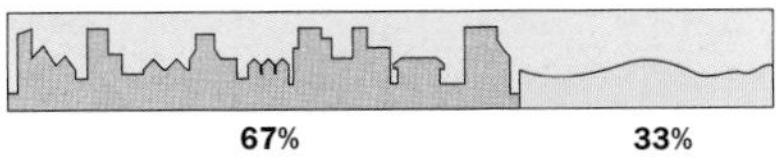
67%
33%

RELIGIOUS PERSUASION

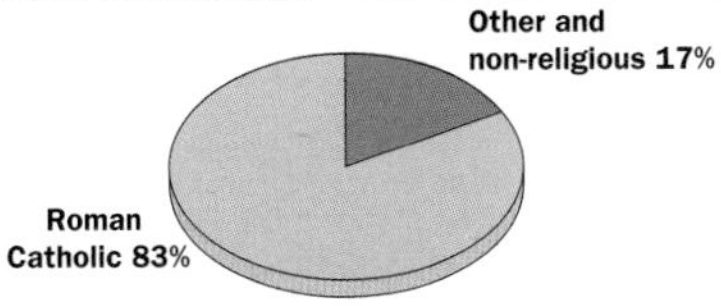
Other and non-religious 17%
Roman Catholic 83%

ETHNIC MAKEUP

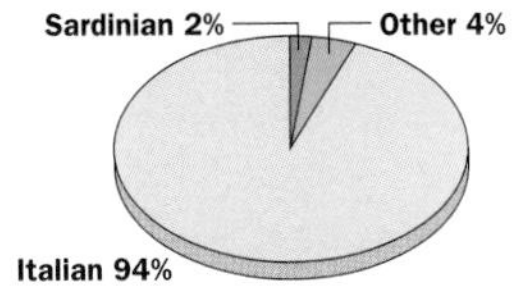
Sardinian 2%
Other 4%
Italian 94%

Italy is a remarkably homogeneous society. Most Italians are Roman Catholics and Italy has far fewer ethnic minorities than its EU neighbors; most are fairly recent immigrants from Ethiopia, the Philippines, and Egypt. A sharp rise in illegal immigration in the 1980s and 1990s, from north and west Africa, Turkey, and Albania, generated a right-wing backlash and tighter controls. It became a major election issue and a factor in the rise of the federalist Northern League. Stringent measures against illegal immigrants were introduced in 1995.

Difficult economic conditions caused many Italians to emigrate in the 1950s and 1960s. There are now five million Italians living abroad. About half live in other EU countries, the rest mainly in the USA, South America, and Australia. Most migrants then, as now, are from the poorer south – the Mezzogiorno. Within Italy, prejudice still exists in the north against southern Italians.

Sport – especially soccer – has an unusual ability to bring out a strong sense of national identity among Italians. In other spheres, with state institutions viewed as inefficient and corrupt, most people feel a stronger allegiance to the region, or the community, and above all to the family. The extended family remains Italy's key social and economic support system. Most Italians live at home before marriage. Marriage rates are among the highest in Europe and divorce rates the lowest. Catholicism, however, has not stopped Italy having the lowest birthrate and one of the highest abortion rates in the EU.

Italians tend to dress well. Their preoccupation with style reflects the traditional importance of *bella figura* – image, cutting a dash – in Italian life as much as the high living standards which most now enjoy.

POPULATION AGE BREAKDOWN

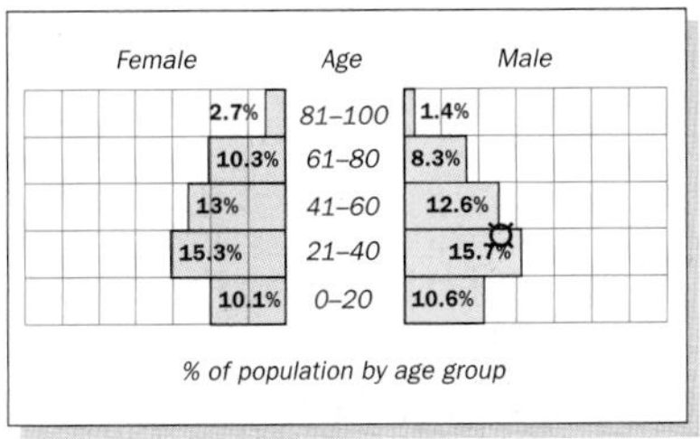
Female
Age
Male
2.7%
81–100
1.4%
10.3%
61–80
8.3%
13%
41–60
12.6%
15.3%
21–40
15.7%
10.1%
0–20
10.6%
% of population by age group

CHRONOLOGY

Previously a collection of independent city states, dukedoms, and monarchies, Italy became a unified state in 1870.

- **1922** Mussolini asked to form government by king.
- **1928** One-party rule by Fascists.
- **1929** Lateran Treaties with Vatican recognize sovereignty of Holy See.
- **1936–1937** Axis formed with Nazi Germany. Abyssinia (Ethiopia) conquered.
- **1939** Albania annexed.
- **1940** Italy enters World War II on German side.
- **1943** Invaded by Allies. Mussolini imprisoned by Victor Emmanuel III. Armistice with Allies. Italy declares war on Germany.

I

CHRONOLOGY *continued*

- **1945** Mussolini released; establishes puppet regime in north; executed by Italian partisans.
- **1946** Referendum votes in favor of Italy becoming a republic.
- **1947** Italy signs peace treaty, ceding border areas to France and Yugoslavia, Dodecanese to Greece, and giving up colonies.
- **1948** Elections: DC under De Gaspieri heads coalition.
- **1949** Founder member of NATO.
- **1950** Agreement with USA on US bases in Italy.
- **1951** Joins European Coal and Steel Community.
- **1957** Founder member of European Economic Community. Aided by funds from that organization and by Marshall Aid, industrial growth accelerates.
- **1964** DC government under Aldo Moro forms coalition with Socialist Party (PSI).
- **1969** Red Brigades, extreme left terrorist group, formed.
- **1972** Support for extreme right reaches postwar peak (9%). Rise in urban terrorism by both extreme left and right.
- **1976** Communist Party (PCI) support reaches a peak of 34% under Enrico Berlinguer's Eurocommunist philosophy.
- **1978** Aldo Moro abducted and murdered by Red Brigades.
- **1980** Extreme right bombing of Bologna station kills 84, wounds 200.
- **1983–1987** Center-left coalition formed under Bettino Craxi.
- **1990** NL attacks immigration policies and subsidies for the south.
- **1992** Corruption scandal, involving bribes for public contracts, uncovered in Milan. Government members accused.
- **1994** General election: DC support collapses; coalition government formed between Silvio Berlusconi's Forza Italia, NL, and neo-fascists.
- **1995–1996** Technocrat government tackles budget, pensions, media, and regional issues.
- **1996** Center-left Olive Tree alliance wins general election; Romano Prodi prime minister.
- **1998** May, Italy qualifies to join euro currency from January 1999. October, Prodi government falls, Massimo D'Alema prime minister.
- **1999** Carlo Ciampi president.
- **2000** April, D'Alema replaced by Giuliano Amato.
- **2001** May, Berlusconi victory in general election. June, right-wing government includes "post-fascist" National Alliance.

I

POLITICS

Multiparty elections

L. House 2001/2006
U. House 2001/2006

President Carlo Azeglio Ciampi

AT THE LAST ELECTION

Chamber of Deputies 630 seats

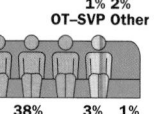

1%
OT–SVP
58%
FA
38%
OTA
2%
RC
1%
Other

FA = Freedom Alliance (includes Forza Italia, National Alliance – **NA**, and Northern League –**NL**)
OTA = Olive Tree Alliance (includes Democrats of the Left – **DS** (formerly Communist Party (**PCI**) then changed to **PDS**) and Party of Italian Communists – **PDCI**)
RC = Communist Refoundation **OT–SVP** = Olive Tree–South Tyrolese People's Party **Nom** = Nominated

Senate 324 seats

1%
OT–SVP
2%
Other
55%
FA
38%
OTA
3%
Nom
1%
RC

The Senate comprises 315 elected members and several life senators

Italy is a multiparty democracy.

Main Political Issues

Corruption

The 1990s *mani pulite* (clean hands) investigations, initially concerned with financial scandals in Milan, went on to reveal a nationwide network of corruption permeating political and business life. The issue destroyed the old political order, and many public figures were disgraced. Silvio Berlusconi, who emerged as a leading figure in the country's new political makeup, was himself dogged by bribery-related charges. Although he was acquitted on several counts during 2000, his return to power the following year left the corruption issue still simmering.

Institutional Reform

Substantial electoral reforms, moving away from proportional representation, were approved before the 1994 elections. However, the center-left alliance elected in 1996 failed to win cross-party support for further constitutional reforms. A 1999 referendum proposed to strengthen the first-past-the-post system further and abolish the 25% of seats still elected by proportional representation. Although few voters opposed it, the proposal fell due to low turnout, as did a similar referendum in May 2000.

Romano Prodi, *ex-premier (1996–1999) who heads European Commission.*

Umberto Bossi, *leader of the regionalist Northern League.*

Silvio Berlusconi, *conservative prime minister, elected for a second time in 2001.*

The church of Santa Maria della Salute *marks the entrance to Venice. The city state managed to retain its independence until Napoleon Bonaparte's invasion of Italy.*

Profile

A coalition of Berlusconi's Forza Italia, the neo-fascist NA, and the secessionist NL won elections in 1994, but collapsed by the end of that year. A technocratic government, led by Lamberto Dini, took over until 1996, when fresh elections resulted in an historic victory for the center-left Olive Tree alliance headed by Romano Prodi.

Success in qualifying for membership of the single European currency crowned the Prodi government's achievements in the economic sphere after two years in office.

The separatist NL leader Umberto Bossi failed to rouse mass support for his declaration in September 1996 of an independent northern state of "Padania."

Prodi, who survived one crisis in late 1997, eventually fell in October 1998, after the communists challenged his government's budget. Massimo D'Alema of the Left Democrats (DS – formerly the reformed communist PDS) then took over until April 2000 and Giuliano Amato for the final year until the May 2001 elections, retaining a broadly similar coalition formula. Aware of the strength of the challenge from Berlusconi and the right, Amato then agreed to stand aside so that the popular mayor of Rome, Francesco Rutelli, could lead the center-left campaign. The eventual right-wing victory was essentially Berlusconi's personal triumph, although his government, formed in June 2001, included Umberto Bossi's xenophobic Northern League and Gianfranco Fini's "post-fascist" National Alliance.

WORLD AFFAIRS

Joined UN in 1955

EU | G7 | NATO | OECD | OSCE

Italy was one of the founders of the EU and remains one of its most committed members. Its strategic position in the Mediterranean also made it a central member of NATO, whose South European Command is based in Naples. Despite a pro-Western orientation, Italy often plays a mediatory role both within eastern Europe and the Middle East. Italy's dependence on Libya for energy supplies made it especially keen to see UN sanctions lifted.

Italy's major concern in the 1990s was upheaval in Albania and conflict in the former Yugoslavia. The use of Italian bases for air strikes against Yugoslavia over the Kosovo conflict in 1999 demonstrated Italy's commitment to NATO.

AID

Donor

$1.81bn (donations)

Down 21% in 1999

Aid to former Yugoslavia and Albania in particular aims to stave off a feared flood of "economic" migrants. Italian military personnel have run relief operations through successive upheavals. The massive Kosovo refugee crisis of 1998–1999 gave a fresh focus to this issue.

DEFENSE

Compulsory military service

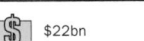

$22bn

Down 8% in 1999

ITALIAN ARMED FORCES

699 main battle tanks (*Leopard* 1A1, *Leopard* 1A5, *Centauro* B-1, *Ariete*)	153,000 personnel
7 submarines, 1 carrier, 1 cruiser, 4 destroyers, 24 frigates, and 9 patrol boats	38,000 personnel
336 combat aircraft (116 *Tornado*, 91 F-104, 104 AMX)	59,600 personnel
None	

Since the ending of the Cold War, conflicts in former Yugoslavia have helped refocus defense priorities. A "New Model Defense" was announced in 1992, and a 1999 draft law, phasing out conscription by 2005 and also introducing women soldiers, was approved by the legislature in 2000. The law would also replace the current defense force with a professional army. This is to play a rapid-intervention role on NATO's southern flank, while the navy fulfills Mediterranean coastal functions rather than retaining ocean-going capabilities. Defense spending remains low, despite pressures to modernize weapons systems.

ECONOMICS

Inflation 4% p.a. (1990–1999)

$1163bn

1931.4–2062.4 lire

SCORE CARD

- ❑ WORLD GNP RANKING.........................6th
- ❑ GNP PER CAPITA.........................$20,170
- ❑ BALANCE OF PAYMENTS....................$8.2bn
- ❑ INFLATION......................................1.7%
- ❑ UNEMPLOYMENT.................................12%

EXPORTS

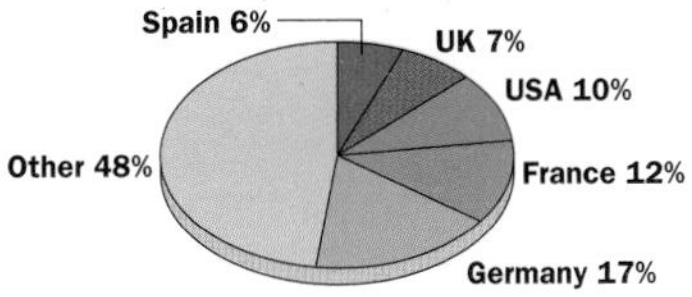
Spain 6%
UK 7%
USA 10%
France 12%
Germany 17%
Other 48%

IMPORTS

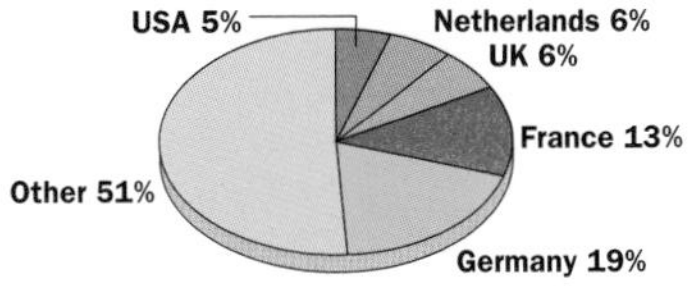
USA 5%
Netherlands 6%
UK 6%
France 13%
Germany 19%
Other 51%

STRENGTHS

Highly competitive, innovative small- to medium-size business sector. World leader in industrial and product design, textiles, and household appliances. Several highly innovative firms include Fiat (cars), Montedison (plastics), Olivetti (communications), and Benetton (clothes). Strong agriculture and tourism sectors, prestigious fashion houses.

WEAKNESSES

Public deficit and government debt remain high. Slow growth. Inefficient public sector undergoing major privatizations. Uneven wealth distribution: northern Italy far richer than the south, which suffers three times more unemployment. Poor record on tax collection, although much improved in 1999–2001. Relatively small companies facing foreign competition. Heavy dependence on imported energy.

PROFILE

Since World War II, Italy has developed from a mainly agricultural society into a world industrial power. The economy is characterized by a large state sector, a mass of family-owned businesses, relatively high levels of protectionism, and strong regional differences. Italy also has relatively few multinationals compared with other G7 economies.

The fascist-era Institute for Industrial Reconstruction (IRI), a state-owned holding company, progressively privatized its electronics, steel, telecommunications, engineering, shipbuilding, transportation, and aerospace companies, until closing down itself in 2000. The National Hydrocarbons Group (ENI), one of the world's top players in the energy and chemicals sectors, has been privatized, as has Telecom Italia, and the electricity corporation Enel. City and regional authorities own utilities, banks, and other businesses.

ECONOMIC PERFORMANCE INDICATOR

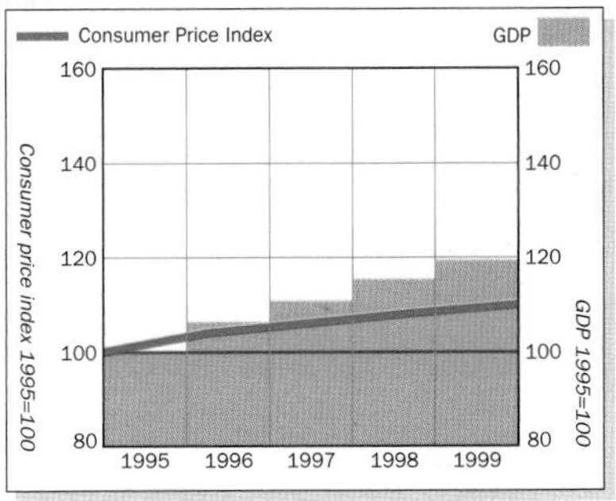
Consumer Price Index
GDP
160
140
120
100
80
Consumer price index 1995=100
GDP 1995=100
1995
1996
1997
1998
1999

Family-owned businesses, which are the backbone of the private sector, include Fiat, whose interests include aero engines, telecommunications, and bioengineering, as well as cars. Similar businesses tend to congregate, encouraging local competition which has translated into national success.

The Mezzogiorno remains an exception. State attempts to attract new investment have met with success in areas immediately south of Rome, but elsewhere organized crime has deterred investors and siphoned off state funds. Anger at the misuse of state funds in the south has been a powerful factor in the growth of the NL with its demands for autonomy. One-third of Italian tax revenue is generated in Italy's industrial heartland of Milan.

ITALY : MAJOR BUSINESSES

Milano
Torino
Venezia
Bologna
Genova
Firenze
Rome
Napoli
Palermo
Textiles
Chemicals
Garments
Electronics
Pharmaceuticals
Light engineering
Defence industries
Vehicle manufacture
Aerospace industries
0
200 km
0
200 miles

I

***Remains of the Greek theater** at Taormina, eastern Sicily. It was rebuilt by the Romans in the 2nd century CE. Today, the theater is the venue for an annual arts festival.*

RESOURCES

Electric power 68.2m kw

562,196 tonnes

90,000 b/d (reserves 600,000,000 bbl)

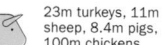

23m turkeys, 11m sheep, 8.4m pigs, 100m chickens

Coal, oil, lignite, pyrites, fluorite, barytes, bauxite

ELECTRICITY GENERATION

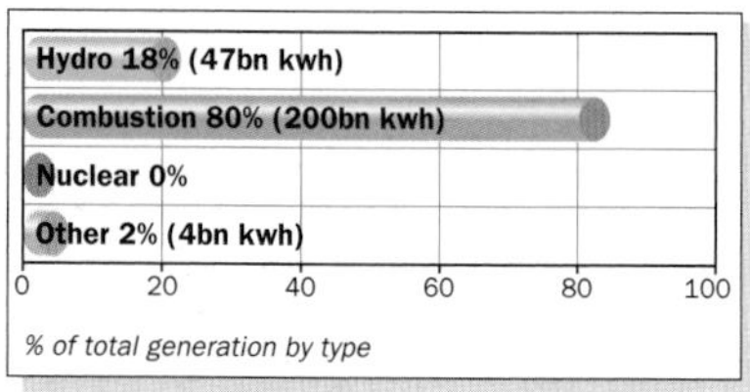
Hydro 18% (47bn kwh)
Combustion 80% (200bn kwh)
Nuclear 0%
Other 2% (4bn kwh)
0
20
40
60
80
100
% of total generation by type

Italy has very few natural resources. It produces just 1% of its oil needs and is highly vulnerable to both fluctuations in world prices and political instability in its north African suppliers. It has reduced its exposure since 1973, when oil accounted for 71% of its needs. Even so, oil still accounts for 56% of energy consumption. Some power is generated from hydro and geothermal sources. Nuclear power was rejected in a 1987 referendum, and development has effectively been abandoned. Italy's mineral assets are small and the sector contributes little to national wealth.

ITALY : LAND USE

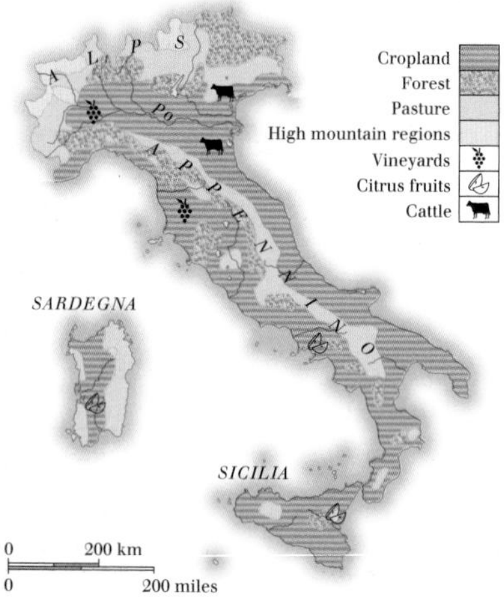
A L P S
Po
A P P E N N I N O
SARDEGNA
SICILIA
Cropland
Forest
Pasture
High mountain regions
Vineyards
Citrus fruits
Cattle
0
200 km
0
200 miles

ENVIRONMENT

Sustainability rank: 37th

7%

7.4 tonnes per capita

ENVIRONMENTAL TREATIES

Yes Yes Yes

Yes Yes Yes

Italy has extensive environmental legislation, but has faced problems in enforcing directives. Wildlife successes include the return of the endangered lynx and brown bear, and growing numbers of wolves in the Appenines. The hunting of migrant birds, a popular sport in Italy, attracts international criticism. The use of drift nets, prone to catching dolphins and turtles as well as fish, has been made illegal under EU law. The right-wing government of the mid-1990s, returned to office in 2001, is suspicious of energy taxes and laws on waste recycling, not wanting to restrict business competitiveness. Green Party members in government in the Olive Tree alliance from 1996 to 2001 had insisted on a more active environmental stance.

Pollution in cities such as Naples and Rome is a major concern. Bans on traffic for up to seven hours during windless days are not uncommon. Acid rain has also damaged forests; 10% of trees are affected.

MEDIA

TV ownership high

Daily newspaper circulation 104 per 1000 people

PUBLISHING AND BROADCAST MEDIA

There are 78 daily newspapers. The leading nationals are *Corriere della Serra* and *La Repubblica*

1 publicly owned service, 16 independent national networks, over 900 independent stations

1 publicly owned service, over 2100 independent stations

Italy's media are dominated by a few conglomerates, notably the Fininvest Group owned by Prime Minister Silvio Berlusconi and Carlo de Benedetti's Ferruzzi group. It has traditionally been highly politicized. Until the exposures of the corruption investigations brought reform in the 1990s, this was particularly true of the state TV RAI channels. Like the rest of the state sector, they were apportioned between the main parties: RAI 1 to the Christian Democrats, RAI 2 to the Socialists, and RAI 3 to the former Communist Party. All the media reflect the Italian love of sport, especially soccer. *La Gazzetta dello Sport* has one of the largest circulations of the national dailies.

CRIME

Death penalty not used

47,323 prisoners

Down 1% 1996–1998

CRIME RATES

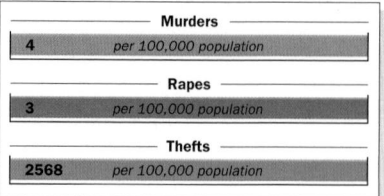

Murders
4 per 100,000 population

Rapes
3 per 100,000 population

Thefts
2568 per 100,000 population

Over 25% of prisoners are foreigners, many held for drugs offenses. There is a huge backlog of cases. Organized crime has been weakened by the anti-corruption drive and a cleaned-up bureaucracy. The Sicilian Mafia, the *Cosa Nostra*, in particular, was hit hard by arrests and trials in which former members provided key evidence. However, the *Cosa Nostra* and its counterparts in Naples and Calabria – *Camorra* and *'ndrangheta* – still control wholesale agricultural markets and much of the narcotics trade, bleed businesses of protection money, and manipulate public works contracts.

EDUCATION

School leaving age: 16

98%

1.9m students

THE EDUCATION SYSTEM

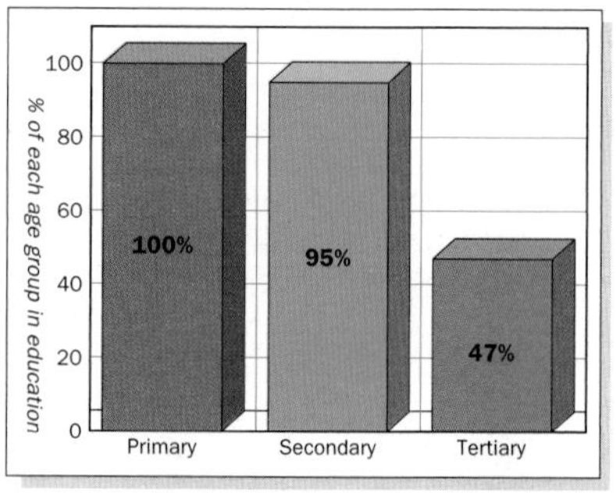
100
80
60
40
20
0
% of each age group in education
100%
95%
47%
Primary
Secondary
Tertiary

Schooling is state-run, apart from a few religious and elite private institutions. The pupil–teacher ratio in Italian schools is one of the best in Europe. In 1993, the minimum school leaving age was raised from 14 to 16 years, bringing Italy into line with the rest of Europe. However, the dropout rate in schools – as high as 50% in Sicily – remains a problem. An educational credit system aims to tackle shortcomings in information technology training.

Universities in Italy are oversubscribed. Rome has 180,000 students, only 30% of whom gain a degree. Many Italian educationalists wish to restrict entry. Another concern is the fact that Italy devotes only 1.4% of its GNP to research, compared with a European average of 2.5%.

REGIONALISM AND NORTHERN SEPARATISM

THE ECONOMIC DIVISION of Italy into the more dynamic and prosperous north and the impoverished south or Mezzogiorno is a source of continuing tension. It helps to explain why, in a country as homogeneous as Italy in terms of ethnicity, language, and religion, there is a strong demand for more devolution of power to regional level. In the mid-1990s, a political party calling for the breakup of the country was able to gain a significant following. The Northern League (NL), created in 1991 and built around the earlier Lombard League, won over 10% of the vote in the 1996 election. Although it had lost momentum by 2001, many northern Italians still feel real resentment that their taxes fund substantial subsidies to the south.

***Run-down housing** in the poor, rural area of Calabria in southern Italy.*

REGIONS WITH MORE DYNAMIC ECONOMIES

GDP per capita is almost three times higher in the richest northern areas, such as Bologna in Emilia-Romagna and Milan in Lombardy, than in southern areas such as Reggio di Calabria. After the 1996 recession, the north achieved more rapid growth, creating more new jobs faster. Lombardy and Piedmont attract the lion's share of inward investment. Turin, the capital of Piedmont and home of Fiat, is boosting its industrial image by completing high speed rail links and staging the Winter Olympics in 2006. Some southern areas try to attract investment by emphasizing that labor is cheaper there, and getting unions to accept lower wages locally in so-called "territorial pacts," but poor infrastructure remains a major obstacle. A road–rail bridge to Sicily remains a distant dream.

PADANIA

The NL invented in the 1990s the idea of creating a "Republic of Padania" to secede from the rest of Italy (Rome, its surrounding Lazio region, and the south). The NL leader Umberto Bossi declared Padania's "independence" in a ceremony in September 1996 after a pilgrimage the length of the river Po, the symbolic artery of "Padania," from Piedmont in northwest Italy to the Adriatic south of Venice. Bossi declared that independence was to take effect a year later, supposedly to allow time to negotiate with the Italian government on an agreed separation. Meanwhile the NL set up a self-styled government and parliament, a national guard, and a flag. Mantua was described as the capital, but it remained unclear precisely how far its intended territory extended. Usually understood to refer to the nine most northerly regions, as far south as Florence and the rest of Tuscany, it was sometimes defined by the NL as also including the Umbria and Marche regions.

Aosta
Trento
Milano
Venezia
Trieste
Torino
Genova
Bologna
PADANIA
Firenze
Ancona
Perugia

The Italian government refused to take the Padania idea seriously, dismissing it as a publicity stunt. NL leaders were subsequently persuaded, by a series of bad local election results including losing the mayorships of Mantua and Milan, that the time was not right to press forward with their project. Some of its impetus – the desire of northern businesses to be at the center of European Union integration, not held back by the south – also disappeared when Italy qualified to join the European single currency, the euro, in 1999.

***Shopping center** in Milan, Italy's center of fashion and commerce.*

HEALTH

Welfare state health benefits

1 per 169 people

Heart and cerebro-vascular diseases, cancers, accidents

Italy's health care system was rated by WHO in 2000 as the second most efficient in the world.

Standards of health care vary across the country, as the services are run by the regions. The state-run health system introduced in the 1970s initially provided services free at the point of use, but charges have been levied since 1988 for some dental and prescription costs; patients also have to pay a daily hospital charge and a yearly health fee. AIDS patients are exempt.

SPENDING

GDP/cap. increase

CONSUMPTION AND SPENDING

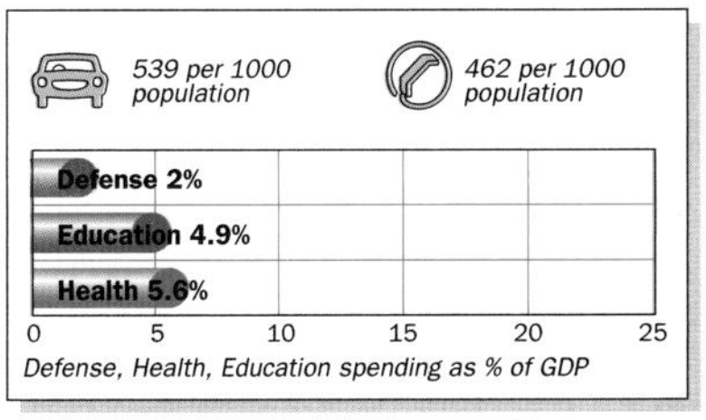
539 per 1000 population
462 per 1000 population
Defense 2%
Education 4.9%
Health 5.6%
0
5
10
15
20
25
Defense, Health, Education spending as % of GDP

Italians, particularly in the north, are today among the world's wealthiest people in terms of disposable income. This is a result not only of economic growth, but also of the structure of Italian society.

Many Italians have more than one job. The extended families in which most people still live often have access to more than one income. Few people have mortgages, and savings and tax avoidance levels are high.

The main exceptions are in parts of the south. Although inward investment has been attracted to the Bari area, many people still live in poverty in other places, such as Naples and the Calabria region, where investment has been lowest, unemployment is highest, and even tourism is underdeveloped.

WORLD RANKING

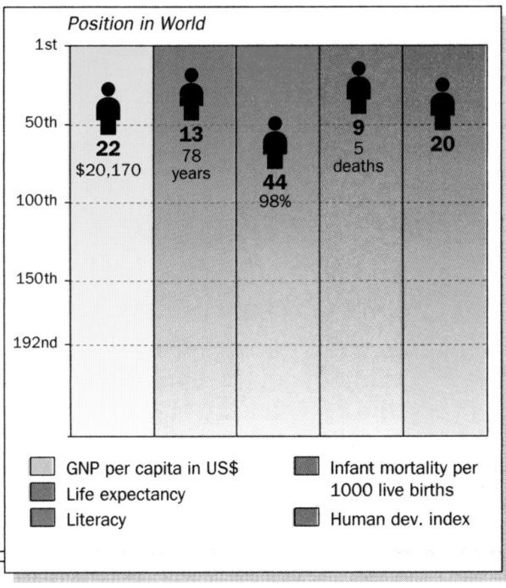
Position in World
1st
50th
100th
150th
192nd
22
$20,170
13
78
years
44
98%
9
5
deaths
20
GNP per capita in US$
Life expectancy
Literacy
Infant mortality per 1000 live births
Human dev. index

JAMAICA

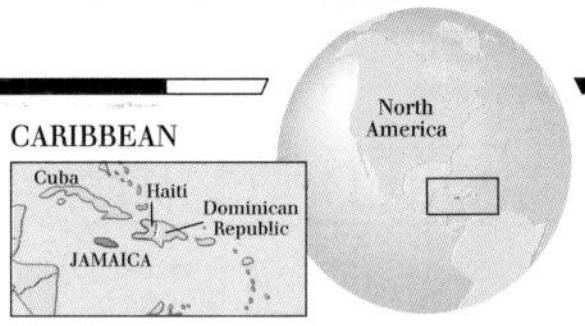
CARIBBEAN
North America
Cuba
Haiti
Dominican Republic
JAMAICA

OFFICIAL NAME: Jamaica **CAPITAL:** Kingston
POPULATION: 2.6 million **CURRENCY:** Jamaican dollar **OFFICIAL LANGUAGE:** English

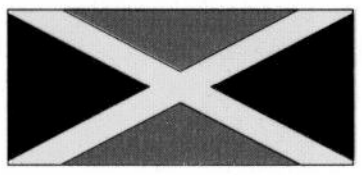

1962 | 1962 | Aug 5 | JA | -5 | +1876 | .jm

FIRST COLONIZED BY the Spanish and then, from 1655, by the English, Jamaica is located in the Caribbean, 145 km (90 miles) south of Cuba. It was the first of the Caribbean island countries to become independent in the postwar years, and remains an active force in Caribbean politics. Jamaica is also influential on the world music scene; *reggae* and *ragga* (or dancehall) developed in the tough conditions of Kingston's poor districts.

CLIMATE

Tropical oceanic

WEATHER CHART

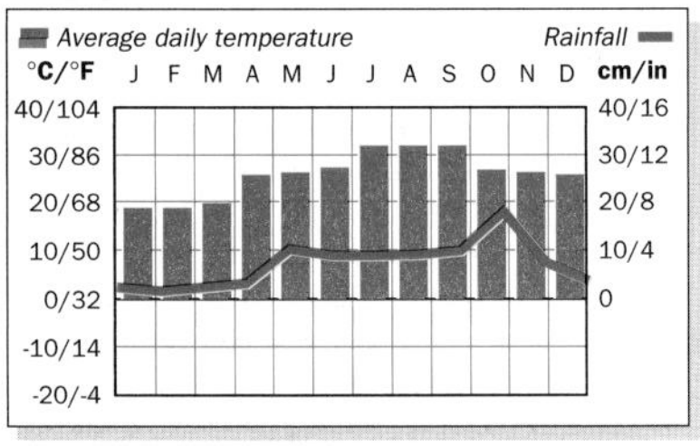
Average daily temperature
Rainfall
°C/°F J F M A M J J A S O N D cm/in
40/104
30/86
20/68
10/50
0/32
-10/14
-20/-4
40/16
30/12
20/8
10/4
0

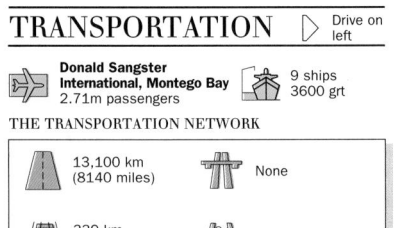

Tropical and humid conditions at sea level give way to temperate weather in mountain areas. Rainfall is seasonal, with marked regional variations.

TRANSPORTATION

Drive on left

Donald Sangster International, Montego Bay 2.71m passengers

9 ships 3600 grt

THE TRANSPORTATION NETWORK

13,100 km (8140 miles)

None

339 km (211 miles)

None

Kingston's harbor has been expanded and its airport improved. Main roads encircle the island. Private buses provide public transportation.

TOURISM

Visitors : Population 1:2

1.3m visitors

Up 6% in 2000

MAIN TOURIST ARRIVALS

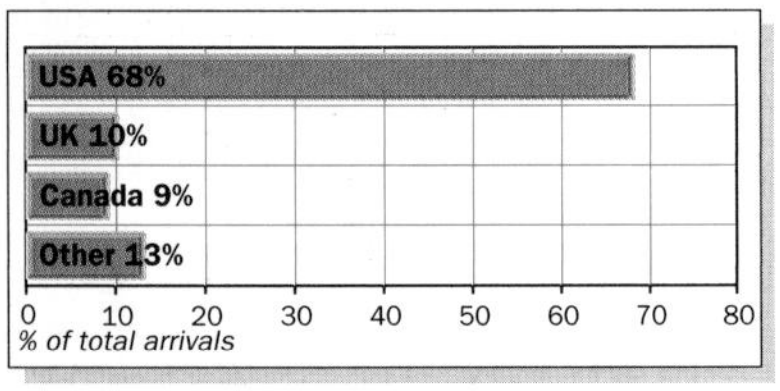
USA 68%
UK 10%
Canada 9%
Other 13%
0 10 20 30 40 50 60 70 80
% of total arrivals

Tourism is the major earner of foreign exchange. Most tourists stay in large, enclosed beach resorts. Recent bouts of social unrest have damaged the sector.

PEOPLE

Pop. density high

English Creole, English

240/km² (622/mi²)

THE URBAN/RURAL POPULATION SPLIT

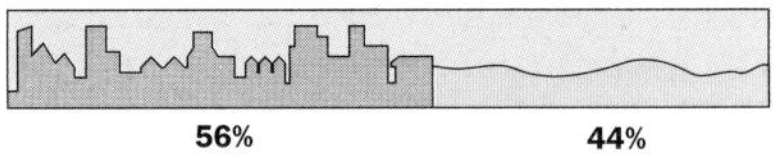
56%
44%

RELIGIOUS PERSUASION

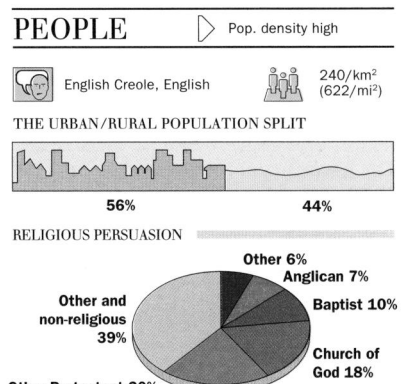

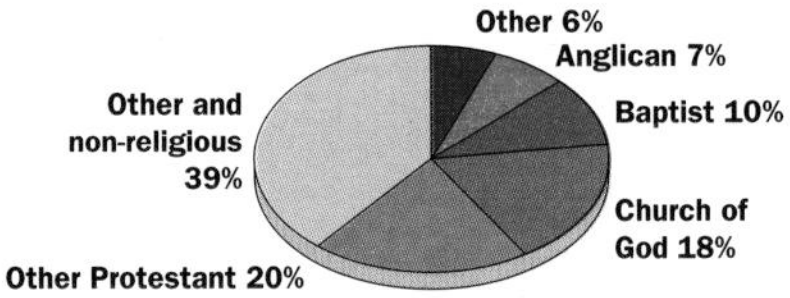
Other 6%
Anglican 7%
Baptist 10%
Church of God 18%
Other Protestant 20%
Other and non-religious 39%

Jamaicans are a broad ethnic mix. Most are the descendants of Africans brought to the island between the 16th and 19th centuries, but there are minorities of Europeans, Indians, Chinese, and Arabs. Jamaica is also home to the Rastafarians, worshippers of the former Emperor of Ethiopia.

Most social tension is the result of the marked disparities in wealth. The Caribbean women's rights movement originated in Jamaica, and today many women hold senior positions in economic and political life.

Although life revolves around the family, absentee fathers are common. Many career women are single parents by choice. Life in the ghettos of Kingston is often violent and based largely on gun law. Kingston slums have their own patois.

***Bauxite mine and terminal,** Runaway Bay. Bauxite – from which aluminum is extracted – is the main source of foreign income.*

POLITICS

Multiparty elections

L. House 1997/2002
U. House 1998/2003

HM Queen Elizabeth II

AT THE LAST ELECTION

House of Representatives 60 seats

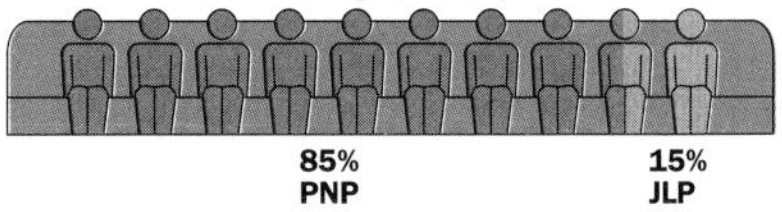
85% PNP
15% JLP

PNP = People's National Party **JLP** = Jamaica Labour Party

Senate 21 seats

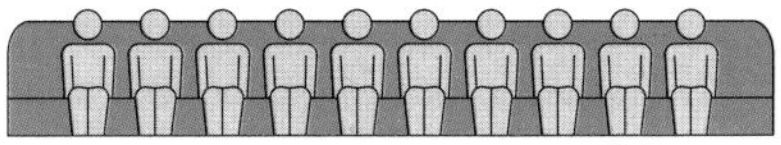

The members of the Senate are appointed. Thirteen members are chosen by the prime minister and 8 by the leader of the opposition

The country's political complexion changed markedly in the late 1980s, as the ideologies of the once socialist PNP and the conservative JLP converged toward a moderate free-market economic approach. A general election in December 1997 gave the PNP government a third consecutive term in office. The party subsequently swept the local elections in 1998.

Violent disturbances in 1998 and 1999 were in response to the government's attempts to deal with economic recession and a large fiscal deficit. The unrest, which led to several deaths, gave new life to the internally troubled JLP, as it then identified itself with opposition to fuel tax increases.

WORLD AFFAIRS

Joined UN in 1962

ACS | Caricom | Geplac | Comm | OAS

Anti-drugs cooperation with the USA and future relations within Caricom and the Commonwealth predominate.

AID

Recipient

US$18m (receipts)

Down 74% in 1998

Most aid comes from the USA, the EU, and the UK. It includes both project loans and balance of payments support.

DEFENSE

No compulsory military service

US$51m

Up 13% in 1999

Jamaica's defense force buys its arms from the USA, but is trained by the UK. Today, the defense force is used against narcotics smugglers and to assist the police to break up unrest, as in 1999.

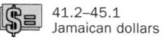

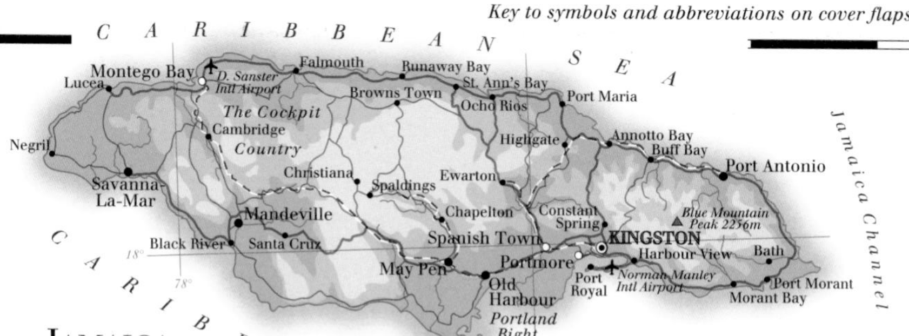
CARIBBEAN SEA
Montego Bay
Lucea
D. Sangster Intl Airport
Falmouth
Runaway Bay
St. Ann's Bay
Browns Town
Ocho Rios
Port Maria
The Cockpit Country
Cambridge
Negril
Highgate
Annotto Bay
Buff Bay
Port Antonio
Christiana
Ewarton
Spaldings
Savanna-La-Mar
Mandeville
Chapelton
Constant Spring
Blue Mountain Peak 2256m
Black River
Santa Cruz
Spanish Town
KINGSTON
Harbour View
Bath
May Pen
Portmore
Port Royal
Norman Manley Intl Airport
Port Morant
Old Harbour
Morant Bay
Portland Bight
Jamaica Channel
POPULATION
over 500 000
over 50 000
over 10 000
under 10 000
LAND HEIGHT
2000m/6562ft
1000m/3281ft
500m/1640ft
200m/656ft
Sea Level
0
40 km
40 miles
N

JAMAICA

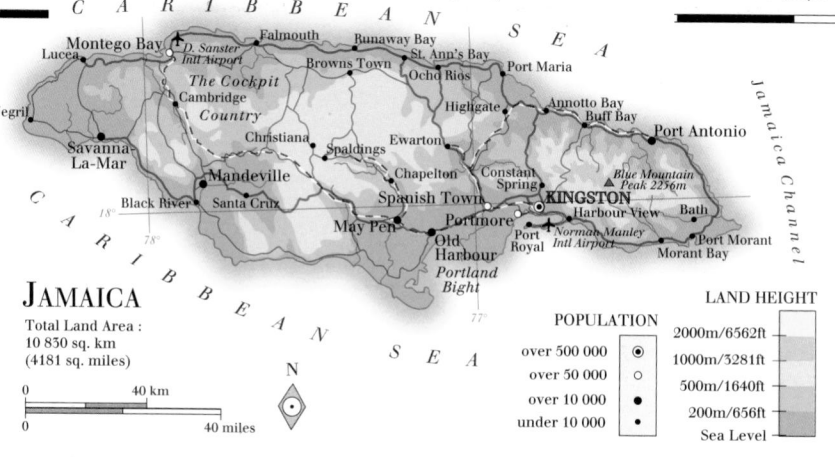

Total Land Area :
10 830 sq. km
(4181 sq. miles)

CHRONOLOGY

Spain occupied the island in 1510, wiping out the indigenous Arawak population. Britain seized it in 1655.

- ❑ **1958–1961** West Indies Federation.
- ❑ **1962** Independence under JLP.
- ❑ **1972** PNP elected. Reforms fail; street violence begins.
- ❑ **1980** Unpopular IMF austerity measures lead to JLP election win.
- ❑ **1991–1995** PNP returned and austerity continues.
- ❑ **1999** Violent protests over fuel tax increases.

ECONOMICS

Inflation 27.6% p.a. (1990–1999)

US$6.3bn

41.2–45.1 Jamaican dollars

SCORE CARD

❑ World GNP Ranking	101st
❑ GNP per Capita	US$2430
❑ Balance of Payments	US$–255m
❑ Inflation	6%
❑ Unemployment	16%

Strengths

Relatively diversified economy. Mining and refining of bauxite for aluminum. Tourism. Agriculture, including sugar, bananas, rum, and coffee. Light manufacturing and data processing for US companies are growing sectors.

Weaknesses

Banking and insurance sectors. Financing of sugar production. Stagnant growth. High debt burden.

EXPORTS

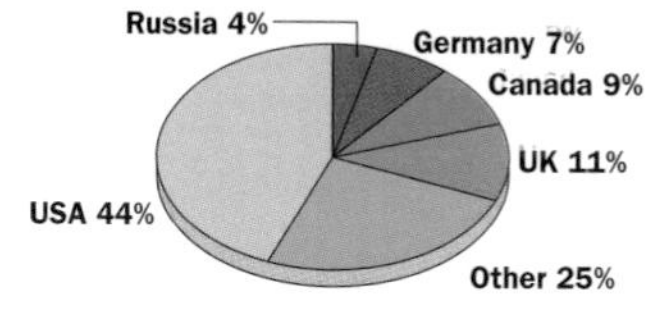
Russia 4%
Germany 7%
Canada 9%
UK 11%
USA 44%
Other 25%

IMPORTS

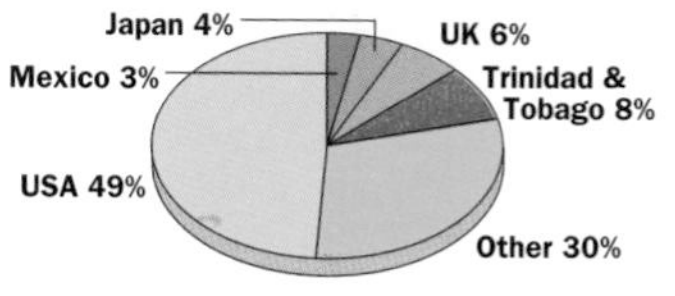
Japan 4%
UK 6%
Mexico 3%
Trinidad & Tobago 8%
USA 49%
Other 30%

RESOURCES

Electric power 1.2m kw

11,458 tonnes

Not an oil producer; refines 32,000 b/d

440,000 goats, 400,000 cattle, 10m chickens

Bauxite, marble, gypsum, silica, clay

Jamaica is the world's third-largest producer of bauxite. Sugar and bananas are major exports.

ENVIRONMENT

Sustainability rank: 88th

None

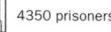

4.3 tonnes per capita

Acidic dust from bauxite processing is a major problem, as is urban pollution in Kingston and its bay. Broad-leaved tropical forests have largely disappeared.

MEDIA

TV ownership medium

Daily newspaper circulation 63 per 1000 people

PUBLISHING AND BROADCAST MEDIA

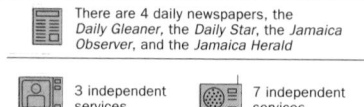

There are 4 daily newspapers, the *Daily Gleaner*, the *Daily Star*, the *Jamaica Observer*, and the *Jamaica Herald*

3 independent services

7 independent services

The government has loosened its hold on broadcasting. The Jamaican press is one of the most influential in the Caribbean.

CRIME

Death penalty used

4350 prisoners

Down 18% 1996–1998

Armed crime is a major problem. Many murders are the result of armed robberies linked to narcotics gangs competing for territory. Much of the world crack trade is still controlled from Jamaica. Large areas of Kingston are ruled by violent gang leaders. The armed police are also frequently accused of the arbitrary shooting of suspects.

An agreement to create a new Caribbean Court of Justice raised the likelihood of executions being carried out. The last hangings were in 1988.

EDUCATION

School leaving age: 12

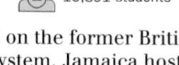

87%

15,891 students

Education is based on the former British 11-plus selection system. Jamaica hosts the largest of the three campuses of the University of the West Indies.

HEALTH

No welfare state health benefits

1 per 769 people

Cerebrovascular and heart diseases, cancers, diabetes

The once-efficient state health service is now seriously underfunded. There are fewer doctors and nurses than in the 1980s. Hospitals generally have a shortage of drugs and there is only rudimentary medical equipment.

SPENDING

GDP/cap. increase

CONSUMPTION AND SPENDING

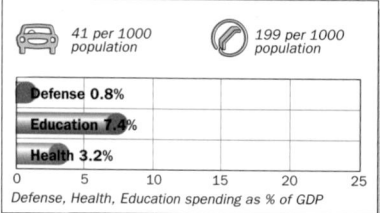

41 per 1000 population

199 per 1000 population

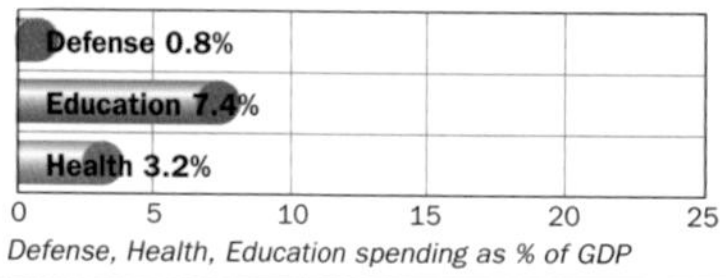
Defense 0.8%
Education 7.4%
Health 3.2%
0
5
10
15
20
25
Defense, Health, Education spending as % of GDP

Wealth disparities are highly marked in Jamaica, although better education has seen an increase in the number of Afro-Jamaicans taking more lucrative, white-collar jobs. The poorest in Jamaica, mostly migrants from rural areas, live in the slums of Kingston.

WORLD RANKING

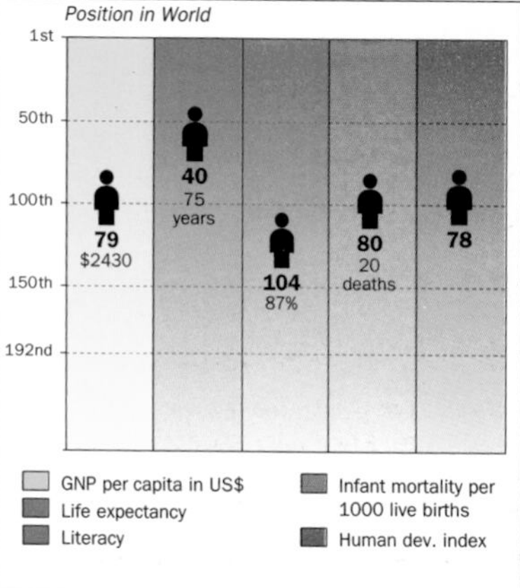
Position in World
1st
50th
100th
150th
192nd
79
$2430
40
75 years
104
87%
80
20 deaths
78
GNP per capita in US$
Life expectancy
Literacy
Infant mortality per 1000 live births
Human dev. index

J

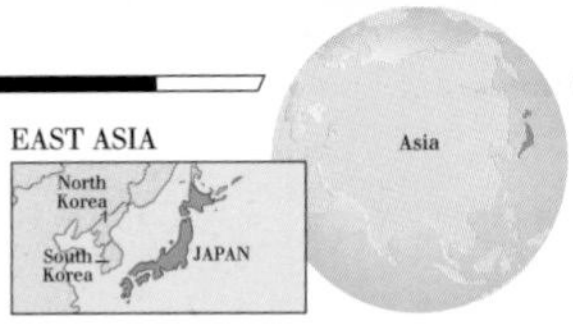
EAST ASIA
Asia
North Korea
South Korea
JAPAN

JAPAN

OFFICIAL NAME: Japan **CAPITAL:** Tokyo
POPULATION: 126.7 million **CURRENCY:** Yen **OFFICIAL LANGUAGE:** Japanese

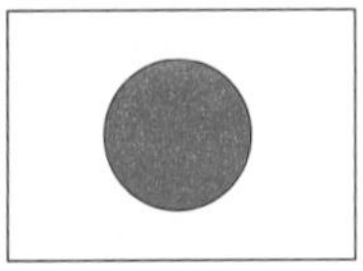

1590 | 1972 | Dec 23 | J | +9 | +81 | .jp

A CONSTITUTIONAL MONARCHY, with an emperor as ceremonial head of state, Japan is located off the east Asian coast in the north Pacific. It comprises four principal islands and more than 3000 smaller islands. Sovereignty over the most southerly islands in the Kurile chain is disputed with the Russian Federation. The terrain is mostly mountainous, with fertile coastal plains; over two-thirds is woodland. The Pacific coast is vulnerable to tsunamis – tidal waves triggered by submarine earthquakes. Most cities are located by the sea; Tokyo, Kawasaki, and Yokohama together constitute the most populous and heavily industrialized area. Hokkaido is the most rural of the main islands. Japan's power in the global economy, with annual trade surpluses exceeding $100 billion and massive overseas investments, has been shaken since the early 1990s by a series of bad debt crises, bankruptcies in the financial sector, and prolonged recession since 1997.

***Traditional paddy field** in Hokkaido. Rice farming is among the most protected sectors of the Japanese economy.*

CLIMATE

Continental/subtropical

WEATHER CHART

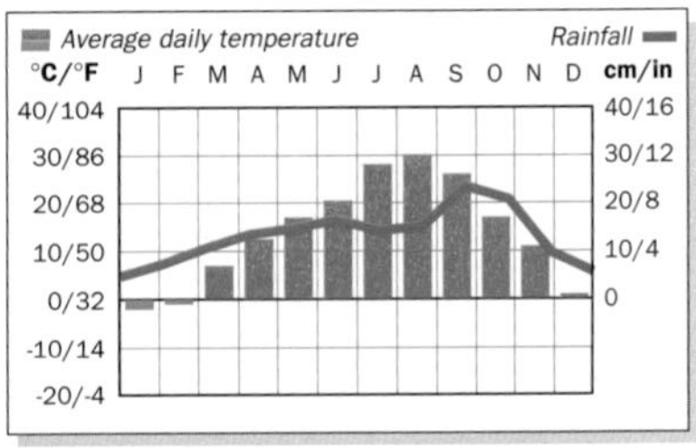
Average daily temperature
Rainfall
°C/°F
J F M A M J J A S O N D
cm/in
40/104
30/86
20/68
10/50
0/32
-10/14
-20/-4
40/16
30/12
20/8
10/4
0

The Sea of Japan has a moderating influence on Japan's climate. Winters are less cold than on the Asian mainland. and rainfall is much higher. Spring is perhaps the most pleasant season, with warm, sunny days without the sultry, oppressive heat and rainfall of the summer. Recent freak storms and heavy floods have raised concern over the implications of global climate change.

TRANSPORTATION

Drive on left

Haneda, Tokyo 54.34m passengers

8922 ships 17.8m grt

THE TRANSPORTATION NETWORK

863,003 km (536,244 miles)	6114 km (3799 miles)
20,165 km (12,531 miles)	1770 km (1100 miles)

Railroads are the most important means of transportation in Japan. The *Shinkansen*, known in the West as the bullet train, is the second-fastest in the world. It is renowned as much for its reliability – timed to the second – as for its speed. The Tokyo–Chitose air route is the busiest in the world.

JAPAN

Total Land Area : 376 520 sq. km (145 374 sq. miles)

POPULATION

- over 5 000 000
- over 1 000 000
- over 500 000
- over 100 000
- over 50 000
- over 10 000

LAND HEIGHT

- 1500m/4921ft
- 1000m/3281ft
- 500m/1640ft
- Sea Level

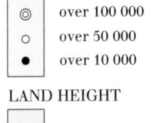

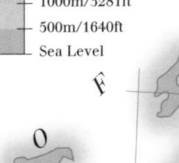

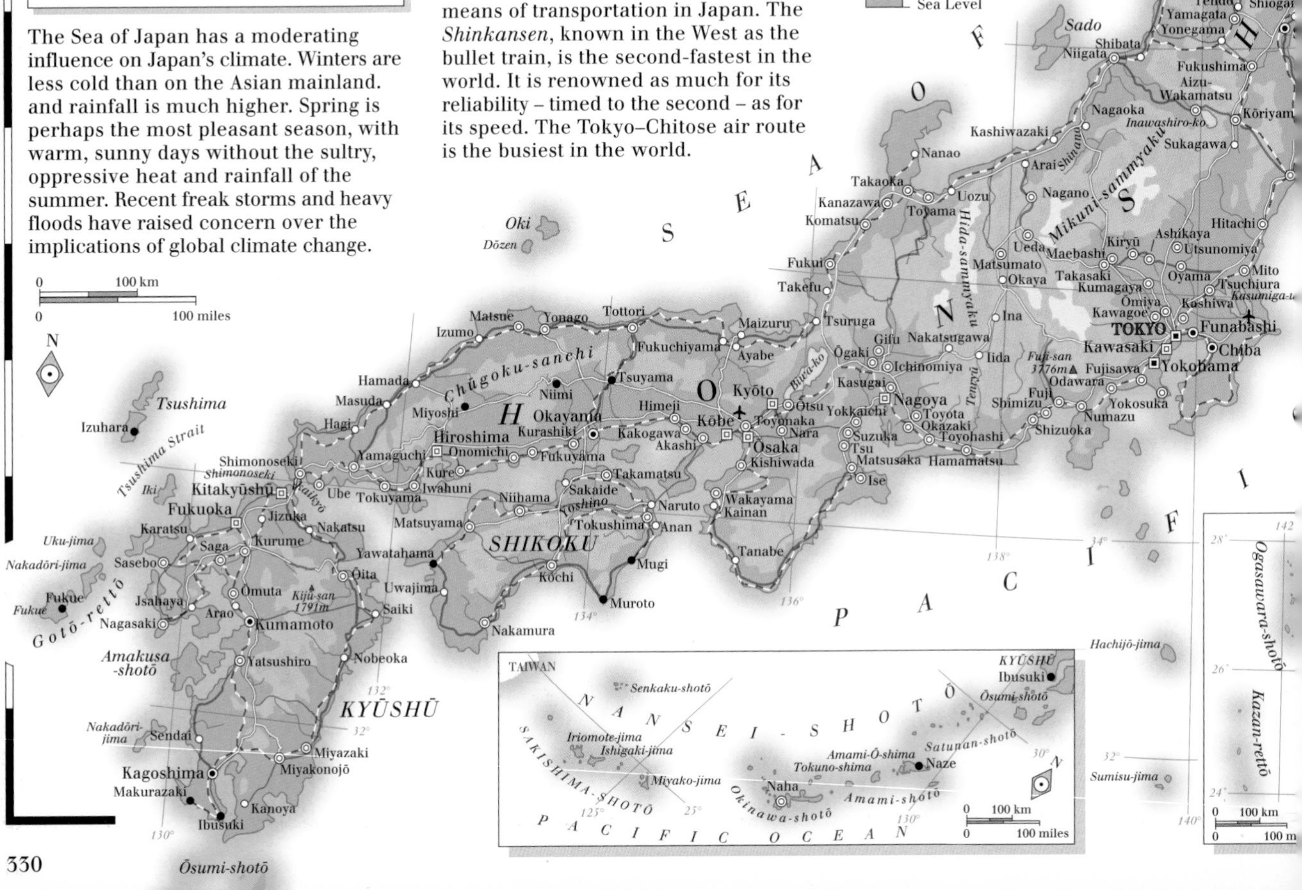
0 100 km
0 100 miles
N
SEA OF JAPAN
PACIFIC OCEAN
Sapporo
Hakodate
Okushiri-tō
Muroran
Goshogawara
Hirosaki
Noshiro
Ogata
Akita
Sakata
Tsuruoka
Sado
Niigata
Shibata
Fukushima
Aizu-Wakamatsu
Kōriyama
Nagaoka
Kashiwazaki
Nanao
Takaoka
Kanazawa
Komatsu
Toyama
Uozu
Nagano
Matsumoto
Okaya
Ueda
Maebashi
Takasaki
Kumagaya
Utsunomiya
Hitachi
Mito
Tsuchiura
TOKYO
Kawasaki
Yokohama
Chiba
Funabashi
Odawara
Yokosuka
Shizuoka
Numazu
Hamamatsu
Toyohashi
Okazaki
Toyota
Nagoya
Gifu
Ōgaki
Ichinomiya
Yokkaichi
Suzuka
Tsu
Matsusaka
Ise
Kyōto
Ōtsu
Nara
Ōsaka
Kōbe
Himeji
Akashi
Kakogawa
Kishiwada
Wakayama
Tanabe
Fukui
Takefu
Tsuruga
Maizuru
Ayabe
Fukuchiyama
Tottori
Yonago
Matsue
Izumo
Hamada
Masuda
Hagi
Miyoshi
Niimi
Tsuyama
Okayama
Kurashiki
Fukuyama
Onomichi
Hiroshima
Kure
Iwakuni
Tokuyama
Ube
Yamaguchi
Shimonoseki
Kitakyūshū
Fukuoka
Tsushima
Izuhara
Tsushima Strait
Iki
Karatsu
Saga
Kurume
Nakatsu
Sasebo
Nagasaki
Ōmuta
Kumamoto
Ōita
Yatsushiro
Nobeoka
Miyazaki
Miyakonojō
Sendai
Kagoshima
Makurazaki
Ibusuki
Kanoya
KYŪSHŪ
SHIKOKU
Matsuyama
Niihama
Takamatsu
Sakaide
Tokushima
Anan
Kōchi
Mugi
Muroto
Nakamura
Uwajima
Yawatahama
Oki
Dōzen
Chūgoku-sanchi
Mikuni-sammyaku
Hida-sammyaku
Fuji-san 3776m
Amakusa-shotō
Gotō-rettō
Ōsumi-shotō
Hachijō-jima
TAIWAN
NANSEI-SHOTŌ
SAKISHIMA-SHOTŌ
Senkaku-shotō
Iriomote-jima
Ishigaki-jima
Miyako-jima
Okinawa-shotō
Naha
Amami-shotō
Amami-Ō-shima
Naze
Tokuno-shima
Satunan-shotō
Ibusuki
Ogasawara-shotō
Kazan-rettō
Sumisu-jima

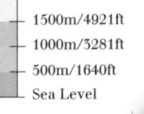

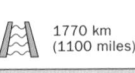

Iturup
Kuril'sk
PACIFIC OCEAN
0 50 km
0 50 miles
Kunashir
KURILE IS
Kitami
Asahikawa
Takikawa
Kussharo-ko
Asahi-dake 2290m
HABOMAI IS
Kushiro
Obihiro
Horoshiri-dake 2051m
The Kurile islands are administered by the Russian Federation, but claimed by Japan
PACIFIC OCEAN

TOURISM

Visitors : Population 1:27

4.8m visitors

Up 7% in 2000

MAIN TOURIST ARRIVALS

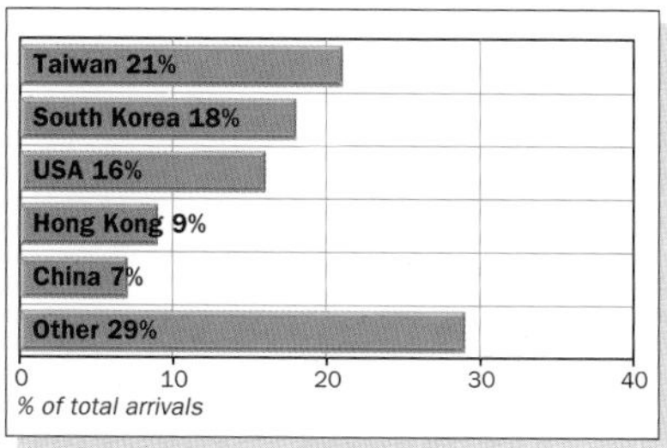
Taiwan 21%
South Korea 18%
USA 16%
Hong Kong 9%
China 7%
Other 29%
0
10
20
30
40
% of total arrivals

Japan is expensive for foreign tourists, despite reductions in the yen exchange rate. Most come from Taiwan, South Korea, the USA, and, increasingly, China. The ancient imperial capital, Kyoto, and the temples and gardens of Nara are popular tourist destinations. Other attractions include the extraordinary variety of energetic high-tech urban living in Tokyo and Osaka. Traditional agricultural life can be found in rural areas such as Tohoku in northern Honshu. Wilderness areas of Hokkaido attract mainly Japanese climbers and hikers.

High Street, Ginza District, Tokyo. *Japan's well-policed cities are among the safest in the world.*

PEOPLE

Pop. density high

Japanese, Korean, Chinese

337/km² (872/mi²)

THE URBAN/RURAL POPULATION SPLIT

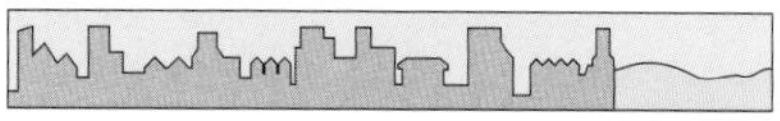
79%
21%

RELIGIOUS PERSUASION

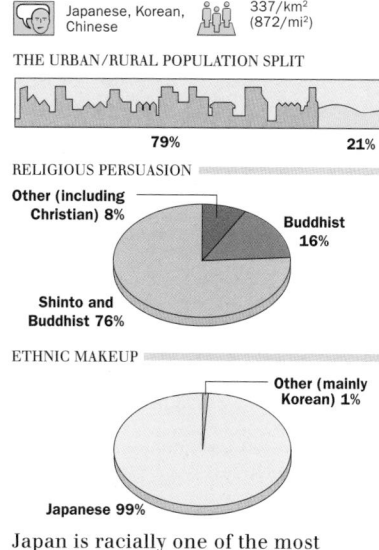

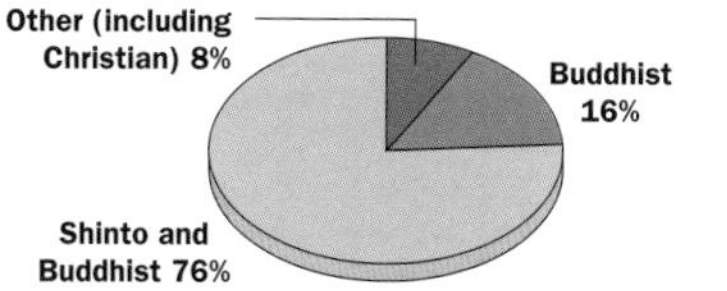
Other (including Christian) 8%
Buddhist 16%
Shinto and Buddhist 76%

ETHNIC MAKEUP

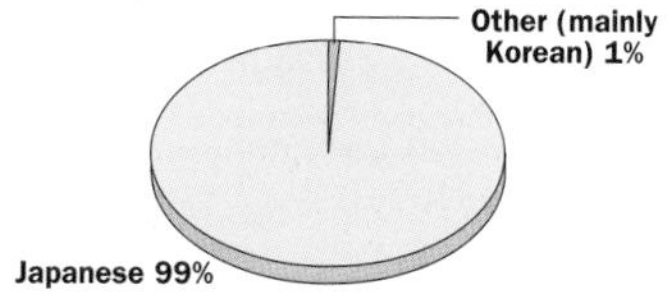
Other (mainly Korean) 1%
Japanese 99%

Japan is racially one of the most homogeneous societies in the world. Its sense of order is reflected in the tradition of the lifetime employer. Many Japanese men define themselves by the company they work for rather than their job. An employer's influence stretches into employees' social time, and even to encouraging and approving marriages.

Traditionally women run the home and supervise the all-important education of their children. Many pursue careers until marriage, then continue to work part-time. However, trends are changing and some women are beginning to take on long-term careers, particularly in the medical and legal professions. Takako Doi became the country's first female political party leader in 1991.

Social form remains extremely important in Japanese society. Respect for elders and for social and business superiors is strongly ingrained. There is little tradition of generation rebellion, but the youth market is powerful and current fashions are geared toward teenagers. Many may still follow their parents' lifestyles, but established attitudes are under challenge. Working for the same company for life, and giving up evenings and weekends to entertain company clients, became harder to justify in the economically turbulent 1990s.

POPULATION AGE BREAKDOWN

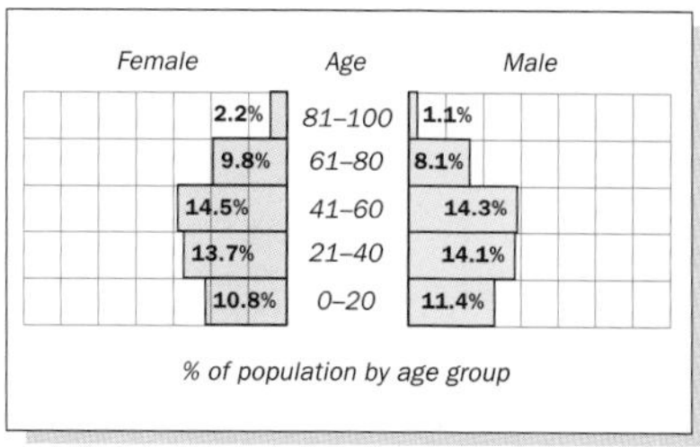
Female
Age
Male
2.2%
81–100
1.1%
9.8%
61–80
8.1%
14.5%
41–60
14.3%
13.7%
21–40
14.1%
10.8%
0–20
11.4%
% of population by age group

CHRONOLOGY

Japan's tendency to limit its contacts with the outside world ended in 1853, when a US naval squadron coerced trading concessions from the last of the Tokugawa shoguns.

- **1868** Meiji Restoration; overthrow of Tokugawa regime and restoration of imperial power.
- **1872** Modernization along Western lines. Japan's strong military tradition becomes state-directed.
- **1889** Constitution modeled on Bismarck's Germany adopted.
- **1894–1895** War with China; ends in Japanese victory.
- **1904–1905** War with Russia; ends in Japanese victory. Formosa (Taiwan) and Korea annexed.
- **1914** Joins World War I on Allied side. Sees limited naval action.
- **1919** Versailles peace conference gives Japan limited territorial gains in the Pacific.
- **1923** Yokohama earthquake kills 140,000.
- **1927** Japan enters period of radical nationalism, and introduces the notion of a "coprosperity sphere" in southeast Asia under Japanese control. Interpreted in the USA as a threat to its Pacific interests.
- **1931** Chinese Manchuria invaded and renamed Manchukuo.
- **1937** Japan launches full-scale invasion of China proper.
- **1938** All political parties placed under one common banner; Japan effectively ruled by militarists.
- **1939** Undeclared border war with Soviet Union; Japan defeated.
- **1940** Fall of France in Europe; Japan occupies French Indo-China.
- **1941** USA imposes total trade embargo, including oil, on Japan thereby threatening to stifle its military machine. Japan responds in December by launching attack on US fleet at Pearl Harbor and invading US, British, and Dutch possessions in the Pacific.
- **1942** Japan loses decisive naval battle of Midway.
- **1945** Huge US bombing campaign culminates in atomic bombing of Hiroshima and Nagasaki. Soviet Union declares war on Japan. Emperor Hirohito surrenders, gives up divine status. Japan placed under US military government with General MacArthur installed as supreme commander of Allied Powers in Japan.
- **1947** New Japanese constitution: modeled on USA's, but retains emperor in ceremonial role.
- **1950** Korean War. US army contracts lead to quick expansion of Japanese economy. ➩

CHRONOLOGY *continued*

- **1952** Treaty of San Francisco. Japan regains independence. Industrial production recovers to 15% above 1936 levels.
- **1955** Merger of conservative parties to form LDP which governs for next 38 years.
- **1964** Tokyo Olympics. Bullet train (*Shinkansen*) inaugurated. Japan admitted to OECD.
- **1973** Oil crisis. Economic growth cut. Government-led economic reassessment decides to concentrate on high-tech industries.
- **1976** LDP shaken by Lockheed bribery scandal; in subsequent election it remains in power but loses outright majority for first time.
- **1979** Second oil crisis. Growth continues at 6% per year.
- **1980** Elections: restoration of LDP overall majority.
- **1982** Honda establishes first car factory in USA.
- **1988** Japan becomes world's largest aid donor and overseas investor.
- **1989** Death of Emperor Hirohito. Recruit–Cosmos bribery scandal leads to resignation of Prime Minister Noburo Takeshita; replaced by Sosuke Uno, who is in turn forced to resign over sexual scandal. Tokyo stock market crash.
- **1991–1992** LDP torn by factional disputes, further financial scandals, and the issue of electoral reform.
- **1993** Reformists split from LDP and create new parties. Elections; LDP loses power. Morihiro Hosokawa becomes prime minister at head of seven-party coalition.
- **1994** Hosokawa resigns. Withdrawal of SDPJ causes collapse of coalition. New three-party coalition includes LDP and SDPJ. Opposition parties unified by creation of Shinshinto. Implementation of far-reaching political and electoral reforms designed to eradicate "money politics."
- **1995** Kobe earthquake kills more than 5000 people.
- **1996** Elections: LDP minority government. Copper trader Yasuo Yamanaka sentenced to eight years in prison for incurring losses of $2.6 billion while acting for the Sumitomo Corporation.
- **1997** Severe economic recession.
- **1998** Crisis over reform of banking and financial system.
- **2000** April, Prime Minister Keizo Obuchi falls into coma, replaced by Yoshiro Mori. June, LDP loses overall majority in general election.
- **2001** April, LDP turns to populist right-winger Junichiro Koizumi as prime minister; five women appointed to cabinet.

J

POLITICS

Multiparty elections

L. House 2000/2004
U. House 2001/2004

Emperor Tsegu no Miya Akihito

AT THE LAST ELECTION

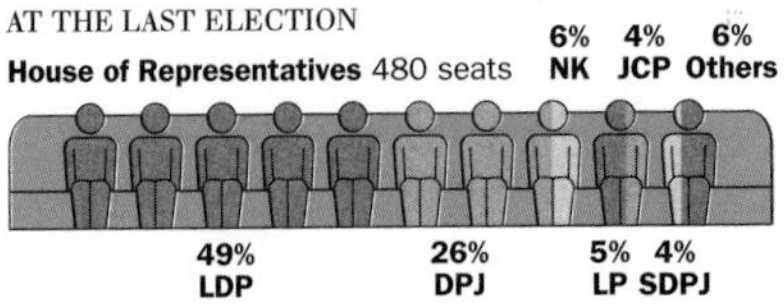
House of Representatives 480 seats
6% NK
4% JCP
6% Others
49% LDP
26% DPJ
5% LP
4% SDPJ

LDP = Liberal Democratic Party **DPJ** = Democratic Party of Japan **NK** = New Komeito **LP** = Liberal Party **JCP** = Japan Communist Party **SDPJ** = Social Democratic Party of Japan

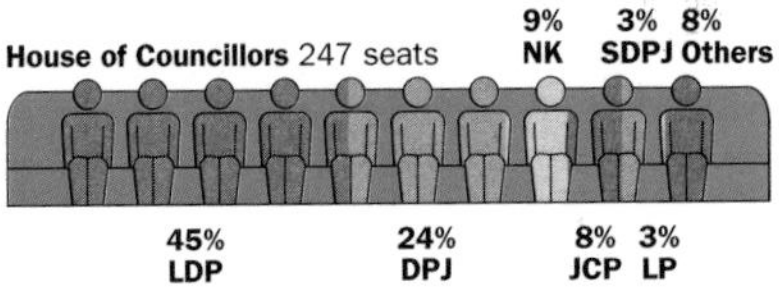
House of Councillors 247 seats
9% NK
3% SDPJ
8% Others
45% LDP
24% DPJ
8% JCP
3% LP

Japan is a multiparty democracy. The Emperor has a purely ceremonial role.

Main Political Issues

LDP strength and opposition weakness

Japanese postwar politics was dominated by a system of patronage, linking big business, the bureaucracy, and the ruling LDP, until the 1993 elections. Numerous scandals and public disaffection with the LDP then saw the party briefly ousted from government. Far-reaching electoral reforms adopted in 1994 abolished multimember constituencies. This weakened the system of LDP factions (although these later returned), striking at the "money politics" by which they were financed. A shortlived unification of opposition groups, creating a Shinshinto alliance, then promised a realignment toward a two-party system. Adroit maneuvering, however, restored the LDP's position, which was bolstered by its hold on the centralized bureaucracy.

Junichiro Koizumi, populist premier who is spearheading economic reform.

Yoshiro Mori, prime minister (2000–2001), but not liked by the voters.

Foreign Minister Makiko Tanaka, one of a record five women in Koizumi's cabinet.

Emperor Akihito. He acceded in 1989 on the death of his father, Hirohito.

The military issue

The Japanese constitution enshrines pacifism. This prohibition of the use of force is a matter of hot debate within Japan; critics such as Shintaro Ishihara, elected as Tokyo governor in 1999, argue that its economic power should be better reflected in foreign policy and the defense arena.

Profile

Morihiro Hosokawa, becoming the first non-LDP prime minister in 1993, was helped by the fact that he was not associated with the tainted world of Tokyo politics. Four LDP prime ministers had resigned because they were implicated in scandals, or had failed to stamp out corruption. Hosokawa too, however, was accused of financial irregularities, and resigned in 1994. His government, a fragile coalition, nevertheless laid the basis for electoral reform, apologized for Japan's war crimes, and began the process of institutional deregulation.

In 1996, the LDP returned to power in a coalition including the SDPJ, with Ryutaro Hashimoto as prime minister. Elections later that year were principally a contest for the center-right vote. The LDP emerged as the largest party ahead of Shinshinto, formed two years earlier by Ichiro Ozawa as a merger of opposition groups. Hashimoto formed a minority LDP government, but was replaced as LDP leader in mid-1998 by Keizo Obuchi. His coalition was shattered in April 2000 when Ozawa withdrew his repeatedly sidelined Liberal Party, and Obuchi himself fell into a coma and died. His successor as prime minister and LDP leader, Yoshiro Mori, led a lack-luster campaign in a general election in June 2000, from which the LDP emerged with a reduced representation but still as the largest party and the main force in government. Mori's unpopularity finally led to his replacement as LDP leader (and prime minister) in April 2001 by charismatic newcomer Junichiro Koizumi.

WORLD AFFAIRS

Joined UN in 1956

APEC | G7 | IAEA | WTO | OECD

After years of limiting its role on the world stage, Japan began to make its influence felt in the 1990s. Its eventual aim is a seat on the UN's Security Council, which would be commensurate with its economic influence. Tentative moves were made in 1993, with Japanese forces joining UN peacekeepers in Cambodia. However, the lobby that fears a resurgence of militarism in Japan is still strong. Relations with the West are seriously strained over Japan's continuing to carry out "scientific" whale hunts in the Pacific. In Asia, Japan remains burdened by the legacy of its wartime aggression, exacerbated by revision of school history texts downplaying its crimes.

AID

Donor

$15.32bn (donations)

Up 44% in 1999

Japan's aid donations are the largest of any single country in the world. Most aid goes to Asia and the Pacific, particularly China. Polynesian islands are heavily dependent on Japanese aid in support of their main livelihood, fishing. In 2001, Japan admitted to "buying" support for whaling.

DEFENSE

No compulsory military service

$40.38bn

Up 5% in 1999

JAPANESE ARMED FORCES

1070 main battle tanks (20 Type-61, 860 Type-74, 190 Type-90)	148,500 personnel
16 submarines, 13 frigates, 42 destroyers, 3 patrol boats	42,600 personnel
331 combat aircraft (F-1, F-4EJ, F-15J/DJ)	44,200 personnel
None	

Article 9 of the Japanese constitution renounces war as a means of settling international disputes. The defense establishment in Japan has not recovered from the effects of World War II, and in the postwar period any military activity in Japan has aroused fierce debate. Involvement even in UN peacekeeping duties, which Japan first undertook in Cambodia in 1993, is hotly contested by pacifists. Japan's Self-Defense Forces, however, have grown quite large. Shots fired in March 1999, to deter an intrusion by two North Korean vessels, fueled fresh debate about the use of force.

ECONOMICS

Inflation 0.1% p.a. (1990–1999)

$4055bn

102.36–114.20 yen

ECONOMIC PERFORMANCE INDICATOR

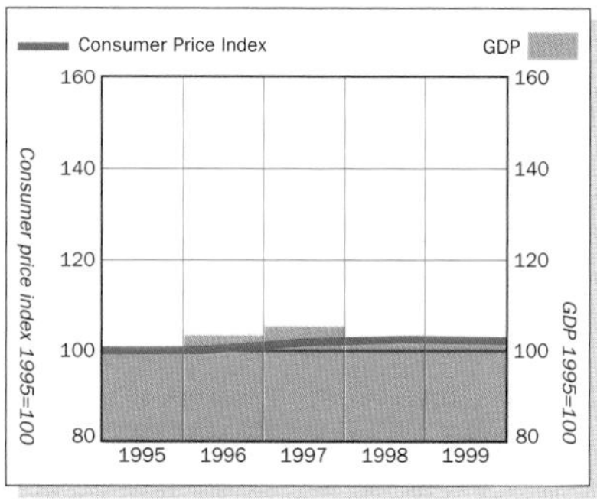
Consumer Price Index
GDP
160
140
120
100
80
1995 1996 1997 1998 1999
Consumer price index 1995=100
GDP 1995=100

STRENGTHS

Major producer of high-tech electronic products and cars. Commitment to long-term research and development. Talent for developing ideas from EU and USA. Global spread of business, including plants in key markets of EU and USA. Once-revolutionary management and production techniques. *Keiretsu* – vertically integrated families of companies who agree to cooperate in business – keep non-Japanese companies out of Japanese markets.

WEAKNESSES

Heavy dependence on imported oil. Trade surplus a source of international tension. Financial system in need of reform, burdened by high level of bad debts and lack of transparency.

PROFILE

Since the early 1990s Japan's economic strengths have been overshadowed by its difficulties. Recession has brought a serious crisis since 1997.

The Tokyo stock market crash in 1990, ended a period of remarkable economic growth. The contraction in demand stemmed the flow of imports, industrial production fell, and corporate profits were sharply down. However, the overall economy continued to grow, companies did not shed great amounts of labor, and research and development spending went up. The government stepped in with a five-year economic plan of infrastructure spending.

Japan's trade surplus climbed to $100 billion a year by 1993. Pushed to do more to encourage imports, for the sake of relations with the USA and the EU, Japan shifted from concentrating almost totally on export-led growth to stimulating the domestic economy.

Problems in the financial sector remained acute. The collapse of securities firm Yamaichi in November 1997 was followed by more bankruptcies, and even corporations such as Hitachi reported record losses. Unemployment continued to rise, despite government efforts to increase spending to try to boost the economy. Industry leaders began to argue that Japan needed a fundamental change in thinking. The new Koizumi government agreed, and pressed ahead with stringent economic reforms, acknowledging the inevitable adverse side-effects. Unable to compete with other Asian countries in terms of low production costs for basic manufacturing, it would depend on catching up with modern service industries and creating a more knowledge-based economy.

SCORE CARD

❑ WORLD GNP RANKING	2nd
❑ GNP PER CAPITA	$32,030
❑ BALANCE OF PAYMENTS	$107bn
❑ INFLATION	–0.3%
❑ UNEMPLOYMENT	5%

EXPORTS

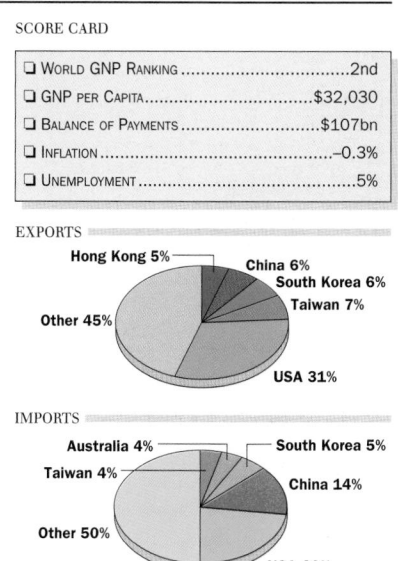

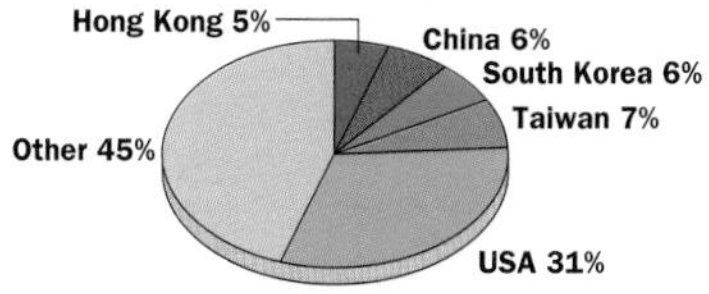
Hong Kong 5%
China 6%
South Korea 6%
Taiwan 7%
Other 45%
USA 31%

IMPORTS

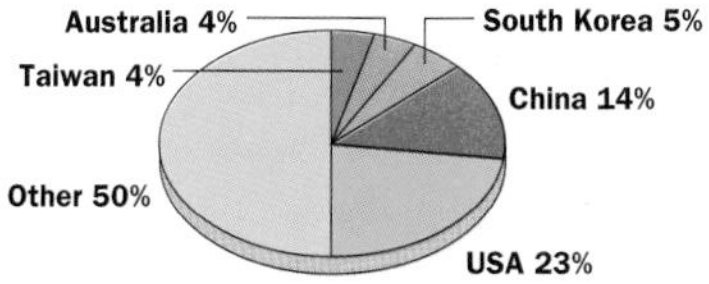
Australia 4%
South Korea 5%
Taiwan 4%
China 14%
Other 50%
USA 23%

JAPAN : MAJOR BUSINESSES

- Research & development
- Vehicle manufacture
- Heavy engineering
- Consumer goods
- Shipbuilding
- Iron & steel
- Electronics
- Chemicals
- Brewing
- Textiles
- Computers
- Banking & Finance

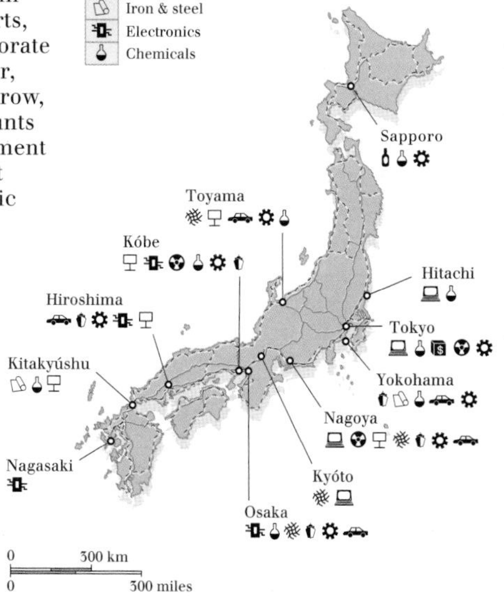
Sapporo
Toyama
Kóbe
Hitachi
Hiroshima
Tokyo
Kitakyúshu
Yokohama
Nagoya
Nagasaki
Kyóto
Osaka
0 300 km
0 300 miles

J

RESOURCES

Electric power 235m kw

6.7m tonnes

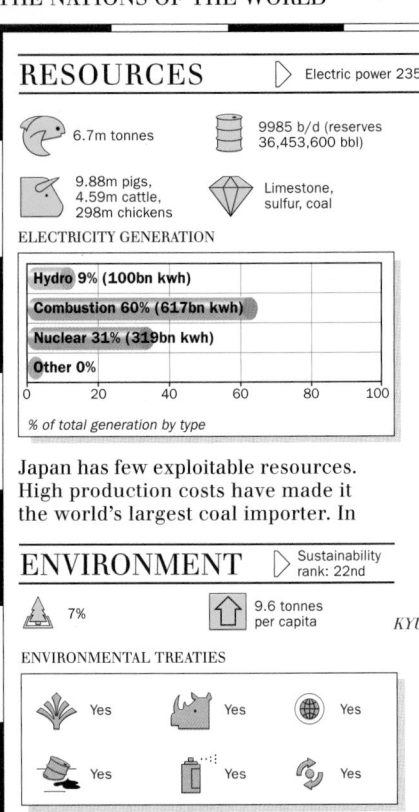

9985 b/d (reserves 36,453,600 bbl)

9.88m pigs, 4.59m cattle, 298m chickens

Limestone, sulfur, coal

ELECTRICITY GENERATION

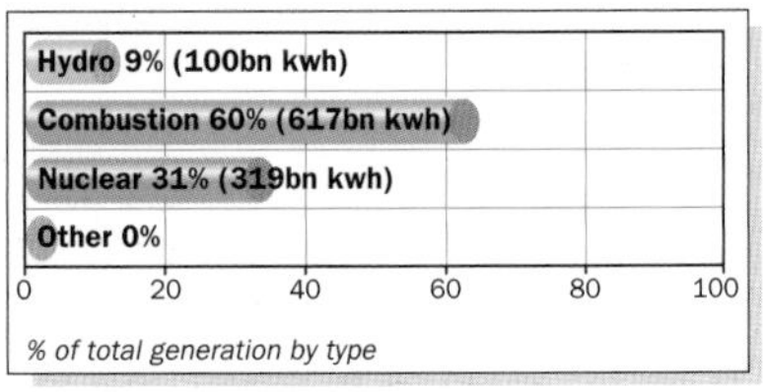
Hydro 9% (100bn kwh)
Combustion 60% (617bn kwh)
Nuclear 31% (319bn kwh)
Other 0%
0
20
40
60
80
100
% of total generation by type

Japan has few exploitable resources. High production costs have made it the world's largest coal importer. In an attempt to reduce dependence on imported fuels, Japan has developed alternative energy sources. It is now the world's fourth-biggest generator of nuclear power. However, environmentalists strongly oppose any expansion of this sector. Nuclear safety became a priority issue after a serious accident at the Tokaimura plant in 1999.

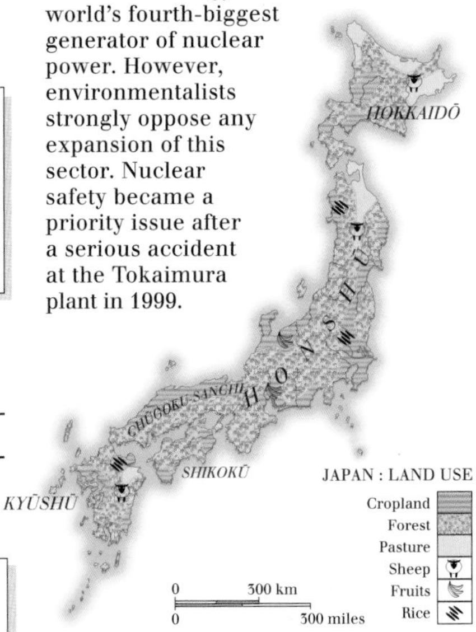
HOKKAIDŌ
HONSHU
CHŪGOKU-SANCHI
SHIKOKU
KYŪSHŪ
JAPAN : LAND USE
Cropland
Forest
Pasture
Sheep
Fruits
Rice
0
300 km
0
300 miles

ENVIRONMENT

Sustainability rank: 22nd

7%

9.6 tonnes per capita

ENVIRONMENTAL TREATIES

Yes	Yes	Yes
Yes	Yes	Yes

Japan supports moves to establish a global foundation to aid sustainable development in the Third World. In 1997 it played host to the Kyoto climate conference, although it only agreed to a modest cut in its "greenhouse gas" emissions. It faces strong criticism for its consumption of tropical timber, overfishing, and continuing to catch whale species under the umbrella of "scientific research."

Traditional Japanese respect for nature has spawned a vigorous grassroots ecological movement which prevented a second runway at Tokyo's Narita airport, and opposes nuclear power expansion and waste processing. The most serious environmental disasters have been a nuclear accident at Tokaimura in 1999 and the breakup in early 1997 of a Russian oil tanker along Japan's western shoreline.

***Datsetsusan National Park**, Hokkaido. Japan's northerly island is the least populous of the main group.*

MEDIA

TV ownership high

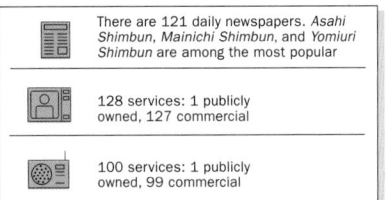

Daily newspaper circulation 578 per 1000 people

PUBLISHING AND BROADCAST MEDIA

There are 121 daily newspapers. *Asahi Shimbun*, *Mainichi Shimbun*, and *Yomiuri Shimbun* are among the most popular

128 services: 1 publicly owned, 127 commercial

100 services: 1 publicly owned, 99 commercial

The Japanese are among the world's most avid newspaper readers; daily sales exceed 70 million, and average circulation was the highest in the world in 1999. Major newspapers are issued in simultaneous editions in the main urban centers. Most dailies are owned by large media groups who also have TV and cable interests. Weekly newspapers carry more tabloid journalism. Over 36 billion copies of magazines and 1.5 billion books are sold in Japan every year. *Non Non*, a women's magazine, is the best-selling title, and lifestyle magazines are a growing sector of the market.

Japan has redefined much of the world's media. It invented the personal stereo and created the huge computer games market. From the early 1990s this market showed exponential growth. Nintendo, a leading games company, became one of the most profitable in Japan. Ironically, the Internet has been slow to take off in Japan. The government injected $100 billion into the IT sector in 2000.

EDUCATION

School leaving age: 15

99%

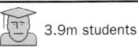

3.9m students

THE EDUCATION SYSTEM

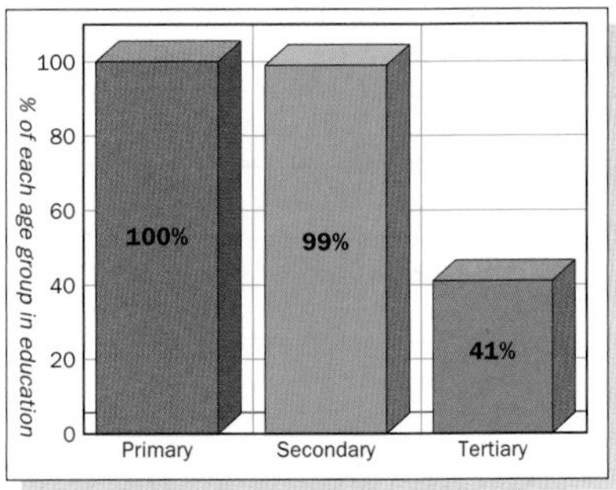
100
80
60
40
20
0
% of each age group in education
100%
99%
41%
Primary
Secondary
Tertiary

The Japanese education system is highly pressurized and competitive. One of the key dividing lines is between university graduates, who get the most coveted white-collar jobs, and nongraduates, who have difficulty reaching management level.

Competition for university places is intense, and starts with the choice of kindergarten, which the Japanese attend from the age of four. Academic pressure diminishes once at university. Graduates from Tokyo, Kyoto, Waseda, and Keio, which are the most prestigious universities, have access to top civil service and business jobs. The system succeeds in producing a uniformly well-educated workforce. However, it has also been criticized for not fostering individual responsibility, flexibility, or entrepreneurship.

CRIME

Death penalty used

46,622 prisoners

Up 11% 1996–1998

CRIME RATE

Murders

1 per 100,000 population

Rapes

1 per 100,000 population

Thefts

1417 per 100,000 population

Japan has one of the lowest crime rates in the Western world. Cities are safe, with police kiosks at frequent intervals on street corners. However, young people are becoming more involved in crime, and drug abuse is increasing.

The major crime problem is fraud and the activities of the *kumi*, organized Mafia-style syndicates whose members are known as *yakuza*. The authorities have been reluctant to challenge these groups, seeking to contain rather than eradicate their activities. *Kumi* are suspected of having connections with the political extreme right.

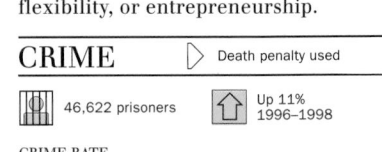

URBAN STRESS AND GARDENS OF HARMONY

A QUARTER OF JAPAN'S entire population lives in the Tokyo Metropolitan Area, which sprawls south to merge with Kawasaki and Yokohama. The average commuter faces a journey of well over an hour each way, some 30% longer than the typical London commute, between the business center and high-density housing in outlying areas. Although the city's public transportation system rightly enjoys a reputation for efficiency and punctuality, passengers in Tokyo have to put up with serious overcrowding during peak hours. Rail staff may even be employed to help shove them into the carriages, although longer-term measures have been taken recently to lengthen both trains and platforms.

HIGH DENSITY URBAN DEVELOPMENT

People migrated steadily to Tokyo between the 1950s and 1970s. In the 1980s the demand for Tokyo office space was so great that new buildings were crammed into every available piece of land. The property boom then ended abruptly at the close of that decade, migration to Tokyo slowed, and the trend was actually reversed in the 1990s. However, one legacy of the previous buildup is a city where housing is twice as expensive as in the USA as a proportion of average earnings. Apartments tend to be small, and several other features of overcrowded urban living strike the visitor, including the so-called "capsule hotels" providing the bare minimum space for sleeping. Tokyo has few open spaces and parks – just 2.6 sq m per person, one tenth of that in London and even less in comparison with Washington D.C.'s 46 sq m.

Aware of both the advantages and the disadvantages of city life, most Japanese acknowledge that Tokyo is an extremely crowded physical environment which leaves much to be desired. On the other hand it is relatively safe, offers the convenience of services available around the clock, and has a rich cultural life.

***The peaceful surroundings** of the Toji-in temple gardens, in Kyoto.*

CALM IN THE TRADITIONAL GARDEN

One respite from urban stress, firmly established in Japanese culture, is to visit a traditional garden. The guiding principle of garden design is the creation of a controlled and harmonious environment, intended to nourish the spirit and allow anxiety to subside, making room for quiet reflection. Among the inspirations behind the Japanese garden is the reverence paid in Shinto animist beliefs to special "spirit places" in the landscape, such as gnarled trees, waterfalls, and islands. Sacred places, created to communicate with the gods, feature sacred stones for the gods from above, and sacred ponds for those from beyond the sea. Complex principles were also brought in by Buddhist monks for creating outdoor spaces along Zen principles, and mirroring a spiritual passage from the noisy city to the inner sanctuary, using the concepts of entry, threshold, and enclosure.

The five main styles, with different combinations of water, garden plants, stones, waterfalls, trees, and bridges, are represented by the gardens of the Heian aristocrats, Zen Buddhist gardens arranged with sand and stones such as the famous Ryoanji garden in Kyoto, tea gardens providing the setting for the rituals of the tea ceremony, enclosed Tsubo gardens, and Edo strolling gardens such as the Meiji in Tokyo.

***High density housing** in the Shinjuku district of Tokyo.*

HEALTH

Welfare state health benefits

1 per 526 people

Heart and circulatory diseases, cancers, accidents

Japan's health care system, which is ranked by the WHO as the best in the world, delivers some of the highest longevity and lowest infant mortality rates. The poorest in society receive free treatment; expensive high-tech hospital facilities can also offer the latest techniques. Contributory national health insurance is based on earnings-related premiums. and the cost of medical care for the elderly and the self-employed is subsidized, though the rapidly aging population presents a major future funding challenge.

SPENDING

GDP/cap. increase

CONSUMPTION AND SPENDING

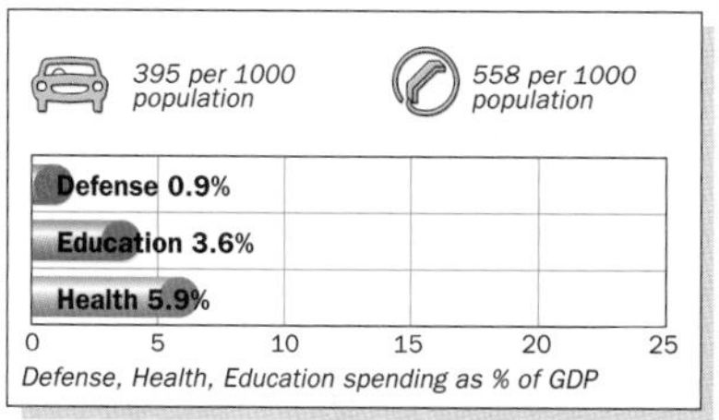
395 per 1000 population
558 per 1000 population
Defense 0.9%
Education 3.6%
Health 5.9%
0
5
10
15
20
25
Defense, Health, Education spending as % of GDP

Measured in consumer goods, the Japanese are wealthy; car ownership is only low because city parking is so restricted. Most households have substantial savings, enabling them to withstand economic recession.

The country's wealthiest men, however, remain extremely wealthy; the fortunes of the top ten averaged $7 billion in 2000. The richest, software king Masayoshi Son, tripled his fortune in one year, to $19.4 billion. Tokyo living costs are high and most who work there live outside the city center, facing a long, cramped commuter journey. Girls and young women still living in their parents' homes are one group with high disposable income.

WORLD RANKING

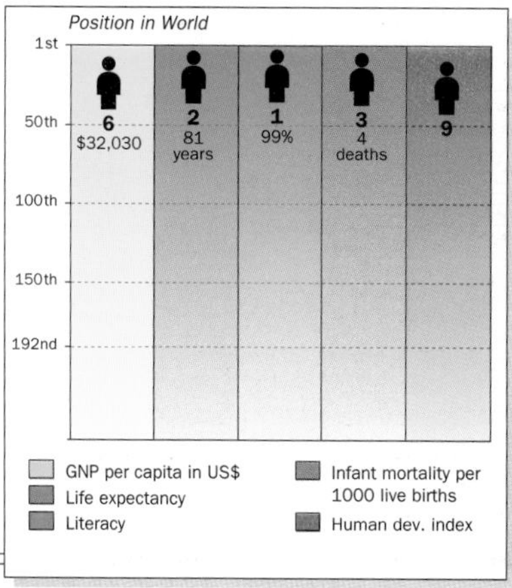
Position in World
1st
50th
100th
150th
192nd
6
$32,030
2
81 years
1
99%
3
4 deaths
9
GNP per capita in US$
Life expectancy
Literacy
Infant mortality per 1000 live births
Human dev. index

J

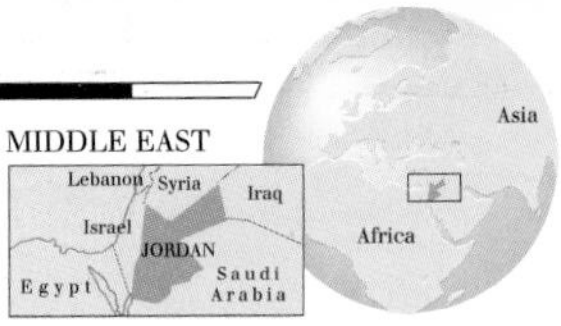
MIDDLE EAST
Lebanon
Syria
Iraq
Israel
JORDAN
Egypt
Saudi Arabia
Asia
Africa

JORDAN

OFFICIAL NAME: Hashemite Kingdom of Jordan **CAPITAL:** Amman
POPULATION: 6.7 million **CURRENCY:** Jordanian dinar **OFFICIAL LANGUAGE:** Arabic

1946 | 1967 | May 25 | HKJ | +2 | +962 | .jo

SHARING BORDERS WITH Iraq, Syria, Israel, and Saudi Arabia, Jordan has just 26 km (16 miles) of coastline on the Gulf of Aqaba. Jordan formally includes the West Bank of the Jordan river and East Jerusalem in its territory, but Israel has occupied these areas since 1967. Jordan ceded its claim to the West Bank to the PLO in 1988. Phosphates, and tourism associated with important historical sites such as Petra, are the mainstays of the economy.

CLIMATE

Hot desert/steppe/ Mediterranean

WEATHER CHART

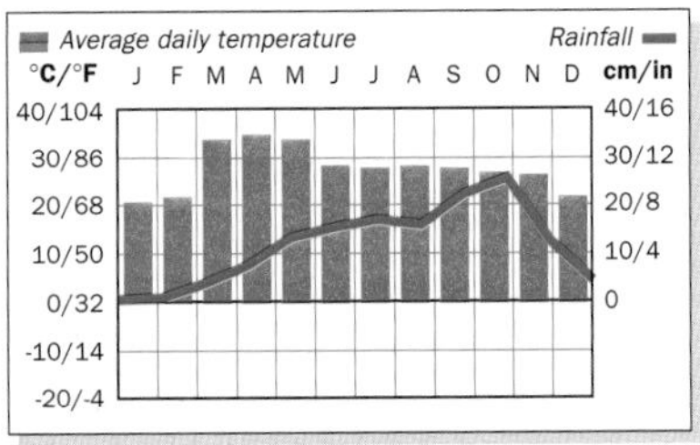
Average daily temperature
Rainfall
°C/°F
J F M A M J J A S O N D
cm/in
40/104
30/86
20/68
10/50
0/32
-10/14
-20/-4
40/16
30/12
20/8
10/4
0

Summers are hot and dry, winters cool and wet. Areas below sea level are very hot in summer and warm in winter.

TRANSPORTATION

Drive on right

Queen Alia International, Amman
2.23m passengers

10 ships
42,100 grt

THE TRANSPORTATION NETWORK

8000 km (4971 miles)

None

293 km (182 miles)

None

Adequate roads link main cities. A railroad links the port of Aqaba with the Syrian capital, Damascus.

TOURISM

Visitors : Population 1:4.7

1.4m visitors

Up 5% in 2000

MAIN TOURIST ARRIVALS

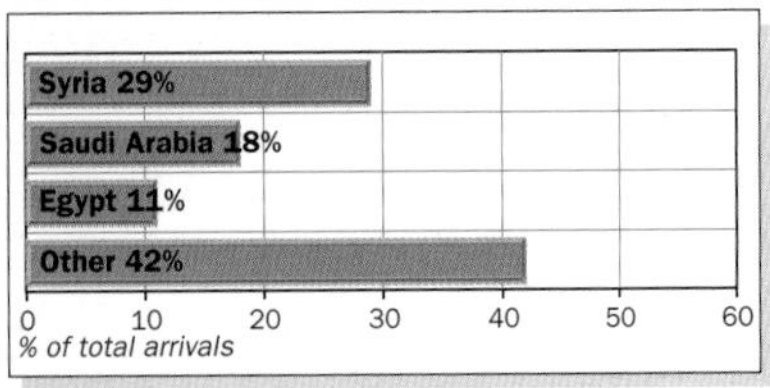
Syria 29%
Saudi Arabia 18%
Egypt 11%
Other 42%
0
10
20
30
40
50
60
% of total arrivals

Aqaba offers fine beaches, water sports, and subaqua diving, while the ancient city of Petra attracts those visitors interested in Nabatean remains. Amman is developing as a center for Arabic culture and the arts.

PEOPLE

Pop. density medium

Arabic

75/km² (195/mi²)

THE URBAN/RURAL POPULATION SPLIT

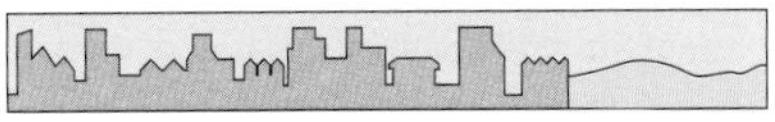
74%
26%

ETHNIC MAKEUP

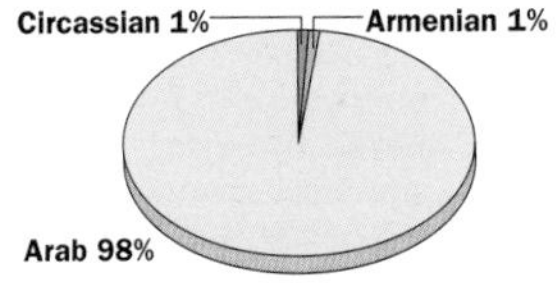
Circassian 1%
Armenian 1%
Arab 98%

Jordan is a predominantly Muslim country drawn from Bedouin roots, with a Christian minority. About half the population are Palestinian in origin. The monarchy's power base lies among the rural tribes, which also provide the backbone of the military. National identity is strong.

POLITICS

Multiparty elections

L. House 1997/2001
U. House 1997/2001

HM King Abdullah II

AT THE LAST ELECTION

House of Deputies 80 seats

62%
Ind
20%
IAF
3%
AAP
15%
Others

Ind = Independents **IAF** = Islamic Action Front
AAP = Al-Ahd Party

Senate 40 seats

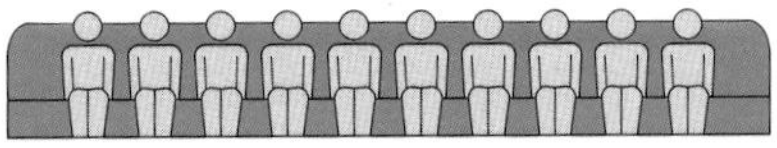

The members of the Senate (Majlis Al-Aayan) are appointed by the king

King Abdullah II acceded to the throne in February 1999 upon the death of his father, King Hussein. Although lacking in political experience, he is respected by the army and enjoys the support of Jordan's tribal leaders. Multiparty elections, initiated in 1993, have benefited pro-government parties, despite a strong Islamist opposition lobby. The appointment in 2000 of Prime Minister Ali Abu al-Ragheb marked a shift toward a modernizing and pro-business government.

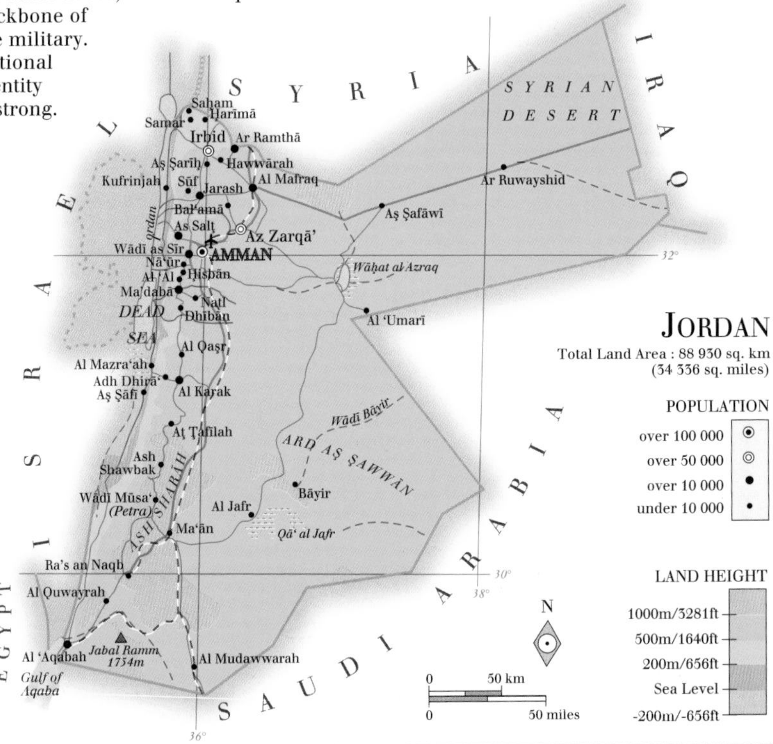
SYRIA
SYRIAN DESERT
IRAQ
ISRAEL
SAUDI ARABIA
EGYPT
Saham
Harimā
Samar
Irbid
Ar Ramthā
Aş Şarīh
Hawwārah
Kufrinjah
Sūf
Al Mafraq
Jarash
Ar Ruwayshid
Aş Şafāwī
Bal'amā
As Salt
Az Zarqā'
Wādī as Sīr
AMMAN
Nā'ūr
Al 'Āl
Hisbān
Wāhat al Azraq
Ma'dabā
Natl
DEAD SEA
Dhībān
Al 'Umarī
Al Qaşr
Al Mazra'ah
Adh Dhirā'
Aş Şāfī
Al Karak
Wādī Bāyir
Aţ Ţafīlah
ARḌ AŞ ŞAWWĀN
Ash Shawbak
Bāyir
Wādī Mūsā (Petra)
Al Jafr
Ma'ān
Qā' al Jafr
Ra's an Naqb
Al Quwayrah
Al 'Aqabah
Jabal Ramm 1754m
Al Mudawwarah
Gulf of Aqaba
32°
30°
36°
38°
N
0 50 km
0 50 miles
JORDAN
Total Land Area : 88 930 sq. km (34 336 sq. miles)
POPULATION
over 100 000
over 50 000
over 10 000
under 10 000
LAND HEIGHT
1000m/3281ft
500m/1640ft
200m/656ft
Sea Level
-200m/-656ft

WORLD AFFAIRS

Joined UN in 1955

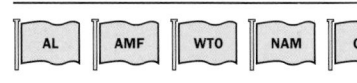

AL | AMF | WTO | NAM | OIC

Jordan's position as a key player in Middle East politics is under question since the death of King Hussein. Policy toward the emerging Palestinian state is uncertain since its relations with Israel remain much less aggressive than those of other Arab countries. The USA signed a ten-year free trade agreement with Jordan in 2000.

Jordan has been at the forefront of the rehabilitation of Iraq. It refused to join the anti-Iraq coalition formed by the Gulf states in 1991.

AID

Recipient

$430m (receipts)

Up 5% in 1999

The Gulf states undertook to restore aid to Jordan after King Hussein moved to distance himself from Iraq in 1995.

DEFENSE

No compulsory military service

$588m

Up 5% in 1999

The armed forces are loyal to the monarchy. They have a reputation for thorough training and professionalism. The forces are dependent on Western support for credit in purchasing advanced arms and equipment, but Jordanian forces played no part in the 1991 Gulf War.

ECONOMICS

Inflation 3.5% p.a. (1990–1999)

$7.7bn

0.71 Jordanian dinars

SCORE CARD

❑ WORLD GNP RANKING	96th
❑ GNP PER CAPITA	$1630
❑ BALANCE OF PAYMENTS	$14m
❑ INFLATION	0.6%
❑ UNEMPLOYMENT	15%

STRENGTHS

Major exporter of phosphates. Skilled workforce. Recovery of tourist industry after 1991 Gulf War. The port of Aqaba is a special economic zone.

WEAKNESSES

Reliant on imports of energy. Poor export to import ratio. Unemployment, exacerbated by influx of refugees from Kuwait after Gulf crisis. Little arable land.

EXPORTS

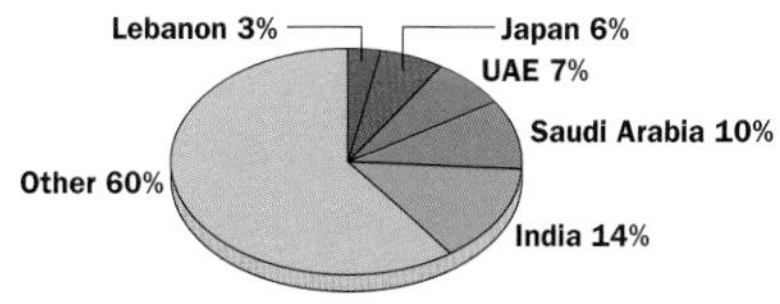
Lebanon 3%
Japan 6%
UAE 7%
Saudi Arabia 10%
India 14%
Other 60%

IMPORTS

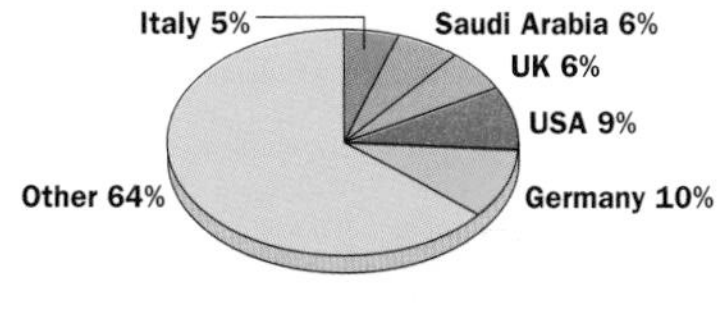
Italy 5%
Saudi Arabia 6%
UK 6%
USA 9%
Germany 10%
Other 64%

RESOURCES

Electric power 1.3m kw

552 tonnes

Low levels of oil production (reserves 4,000,000 bbl)

1.6m sheep, 630,000 goats, 25m chickens

Oil, phosphates, potash

Oil deposits have been discovered. Phosphates, livestock, and crops such as tomatoes, wheat, olives, and vegetables are the main resources.

ENVIRONMENT

Sustainability rank: 96th

3%

3.5 tonnes per capita

Conservation is a government priority. Rare animals are protected and species that became extinct in the wild in the 1950s are being reintroduced into controlled environments.

MEDIA

TV ownership medium

Daily newspaper circulation 42 per 1000 people

PUBLISHING AND BROADCAST MEDIA

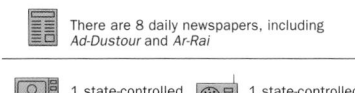

There are 8 daily newspapers, including *Ad-Dustour* and *Ar-Rai*

1 state-controlled service

1 state-controlled service

A restrictive press and publications law was enacted in 1998. Radio and TV are controlled by the state.

CRIME

Death penalty used

Jordan does not publish prison figures

Up 344% 1996–1998

Jordan is largely peaceful. Crime levels are generally low, although theft in urban areas is rising.

EDUCATION

School leaving age: 15

90%

112,959 students

Men and women receive the same education. Jordanian teachers work all over the Middle East.

HEALTH

Welfare state health benefits

1 per 588 people

Heart, digestive, and respiratory diseases, accidents, cancers

Health care is subsidized by the government. Hospitals are well distributed throughout the country.

CHRONOLOGY

Jordan, previously the British mandated territory of Transjordan, became independent in 1946.

- ❑ **1953** Hussein appointed king.
- ❑ **1967** Israel seizes West Bank territories.
- ❑ **1970** Massive crackdown on PLO in Jordan.
- ❑ **1988** Jordan cedes claims to West Bank to PLO.
- ❑ **1994** Peace treaty with Israel.
- ❑ **1999** Death of King Hussein; succession of King Abdullah II.

The King's Highway, *seen from the castle at Al Karak. This strategic fortress was built by Crusader knights in the 12th century.*

J

SPENDING

GDP/cap. increase

CONSUMPTION AND SPENDING

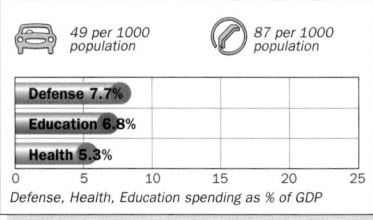

49 per 1000 population

87 per 1000 population

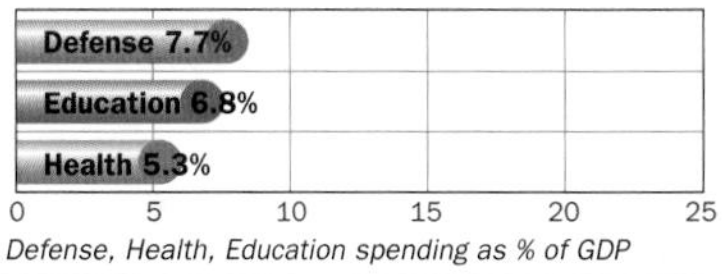
Defense 7.7%
Education 6.8%
Health 5.3%
0
5
10
15
20
25
Defense, Health, Education spending as % of GDP

Poverty is relatively rare, though refugee camps still exist and 25% unemployment damaged many family incomes in the late 1990s.

WORLD RANKING

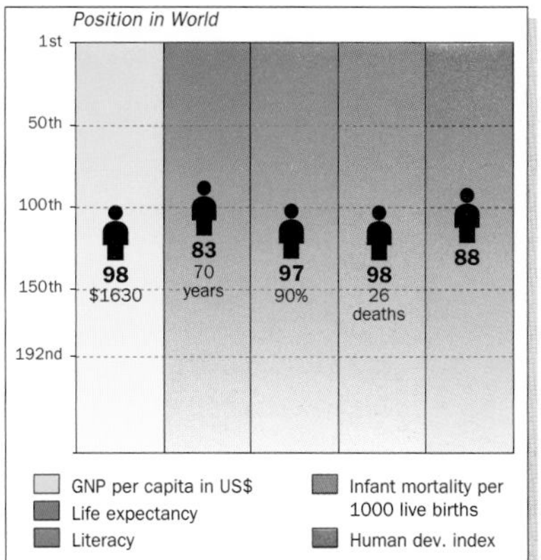
Position in World
1st
50th
100th
150th
192nd
98
$1630
83
70 years
97
90%
98
26 deaths
88
GNP per capita in US$
Life expectancy
Literacy
Infant mortality per 1000 live births
Human dev. index

KAZAKHSTAN

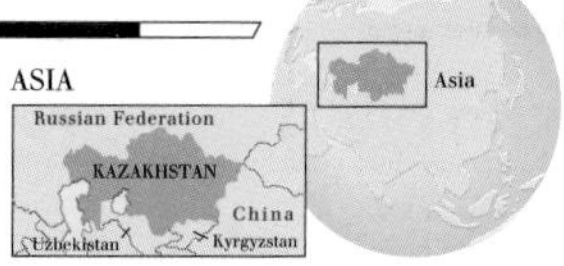
ASIA
Asia
Russian Federation
KAZAKHSTAN
China
Uzbekistan
Kyrgyzstan

OFFICIAL NAME: Republic of Kazakhstan **CAPITAL:** Astana
POPULATION: 16.2 million **CURRENCY:** Tenge **OFFICIAL LANGUAGE:** Kazakh

1991 | 1991 | Oct 25 | KZ | +5 to +6 | +7 | .kz

THE SECOND-LARGEST of the former Soviet republics, Kazakhstan extends almost 2000 km (1240 miles) from the Caspian Sea in the west to the Altai Mountains in the east and 1300 km (806 miles) north to south. It borders Russia to the north and China to the east. Kazakhstan was the last Soviet republic to declare its independence, in 1991. In 1999, elections confirmed the former communist Nursultan Nazarbayev and his supporters in power. Kazakhstan has considerable economic potential, and many Western companies seek to exploit its mineral resources.

***The Altai Mountains**, eastern Kazakhstan. Subject to harsh continental winters, the Altai range is a cold, inhospitable place. Rivers carry meltwater down onto the vast steppe.*

CLIMATE

Cold desert/steppe

WEATHER CHART

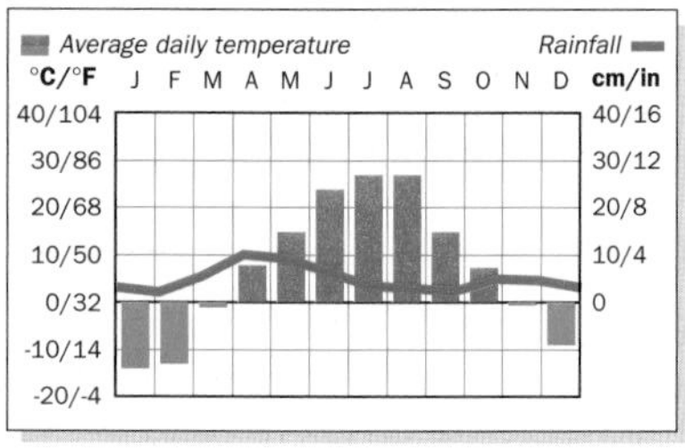
Average daily temperature
Rainfall
°C/°F
J F M A M J J A S O N D
cm/in
40/104
30/86
20/68
10/50
0/32
-10/14
-20/-4
40/16
30/12
20/8
10/4
0

Kazakhstan has a continental climate with large temperature variations: average January temperatures range from –18°C (0°F) on the northern Kazakh steppe to –3°C (27°F) in the deserts 1300 km (800 miles) to the south; July temperatures average 19°C (66°F) and 30°C (86°F) respectively. As the Caspian Sea never freezes, winters are mildest on Kazakhstan's southwestern coast.

TRANSPORTATION

Drive on right

Astana

18 ships 9253 grt

THE TRANSPORTATION NETWORK

103,272 km (64,170 miles)	None
13,601 km (8452 miles)	3900 km (2423 miles)

Transportation networks focus on the north and east, the key economic areas. Most of the roads in Kazakhstan are in urgent need of repair. The railroads link into the Russian system and most international flights go via Moscow, although there are direct flights to Germany. In 1998 measures to restructure and privatize the railroad were announced.

TOURISM

Not available

Visitors are mainly on business

Gradually increasing

MAIN TOURIST ARRIVALS

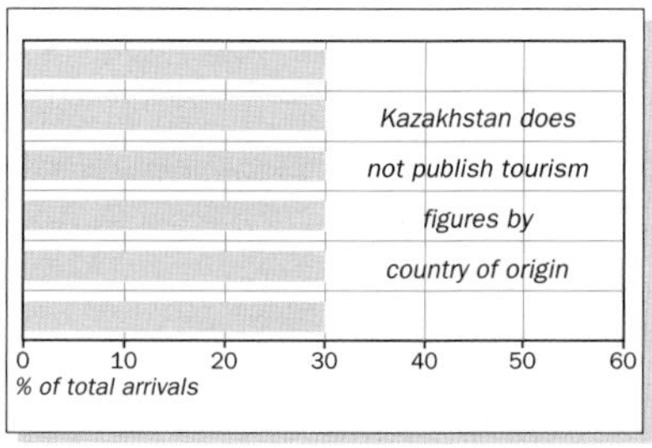
Kazakhstan does not publish tourism figures by country of origin
0
10
20
30
40
50
60
% of total arrivals

The number of visitors to Kazakhstan is increasing, but very few come solely as tourists. The majority are business travelers, and a dense web of contacts with foreign companies has evolved. Of the central Asian states, Kazakhstan has cultivated the closest links with the West. Most foreign businesses are concentrated in Almaty.

KAZAKHSTAN

Total Land Area : 2 717 300 sq. km (1 049 150 sq. miles)

RUSSIAN FEDERATION
Petropavlovsk
Kostanay
Rudnyy
Kokshetau
Shchuchinsk
Pavlodar
Yermak
Ekibastuz
Irtysh
Kushmurun
Dzhetygara
Ishim
Atbasar
ASTANA
Semipalatinsk
Leninogorsk
Zyryanovsk
Ust'-Kamenogorsk
Shar
Gora Belukha 4506m
Ural'sk
Aksay
Aktyubinsk
KIRGHIZ STEPPE
Alga
Uli
Temir
Emba
Ural
Ozero Tengiz
Temirtau
Karaganda
Saran'
Shakhtinsk
Arkalyk
Karkaralinsk
Ozero Zaysan
Torghay
Atyrau
Chelkar
KAZAKHSKIY MELKOSOPOCHNIK
Ayaguz
Nikol'skiy
Zhezkazgan
Balkhash
Ozero Balkhash
Ozero Alakol'
Aral'sk
Caspian Sea
Beyneu
Fort-Shevchenko
Novokazalinsk
Dzhusaly
Syr Darya
Aral Sea
PESKI MUYUNKUM
Taldykorgan
Tekeli
Ili
Aktau
USTYURT PLATEAU
Zhanaozen
Kzylorda
Panfilov
Shu
Almaty
UZBEKISTAN
Turkestan
Kentau
Karatau
Taraz
Ayrs'
Shymkent
KYRGYZSTAN
CHINA
TURKMENISTAN
POPULATION
over 500 000
over 100 000
over 50 000
over 10 000
under 10 000
LAND HEIGHT
3000m/9843ft
2000m/6562ft
1000m/3281ft
500m/1640ft
200m/656ft
Sea Level
-200m/-656ft
0 200 km
0 200 miles

PEOPLE

Pop. density low

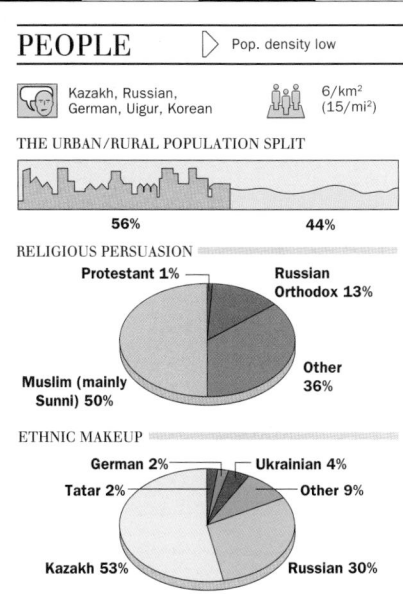

Kazakh, Russian, German, Uigur, Korean

6/km² (15/mi²)

THE URBAN/RURAL POPULATION SPLIT

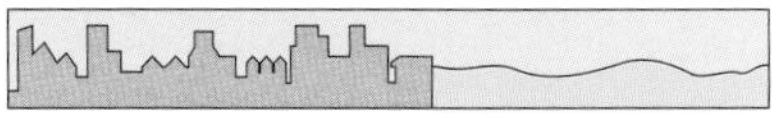
56%
44%

RELIGIOUS PERSUASION

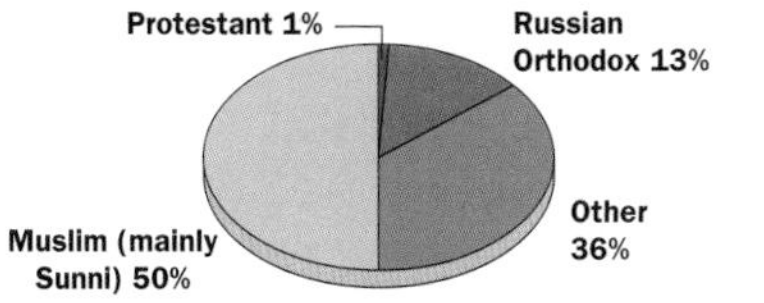
Protestant 1%
Russian Orthodox 13%
Other 36%
Muslim (mainly Sunni) 50%

ETHNIC MAKEUP

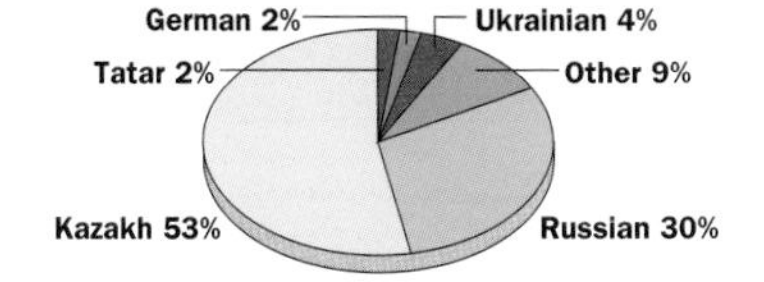
German 2%
Ukrainian 4%
Tatar 2%
Other 9%
Kazakh 53%
Russian 30%

Kazakhstan's ethnic diversity arose from the forced settlement during the Soviet era of Germans, Tatars, and Russians. By 1959, Kazakhs were outnumbered by ethnic Russians. This balance has been redressed by the immigration of ethnic Kazakhs from neighboring states and the departure in the 1990s of some 1.5 million ethnic Russians. In addition, a majority of ethnic Germans have opted to live in Germany, although in 2000 the government announced a campaign to try to lure some of them back.

POPULATION AGE BREAKDOWN

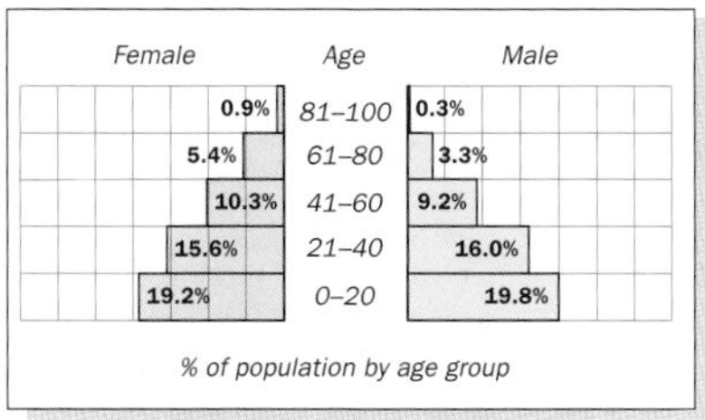
Female
Age
Male
0.9%
81–100
0.3%
5.4%
61–80
3.3%
10.3%
41–60
9.2%
15.6%
21–40
16.0%
19.2%
0–20
19.8%
% of population by age group

In 1995, ethnic Russians criticized the country's new constitution for preventing dual citizenship with Russia and refusing to recognize Russian as an official language. Central control over ethnic Russians has been reinforced by shifting the capital to Astana (formerly Akmola) in the north, where the majority of ethnic Russians reside.

Few Kazakhs retain their traditional nomadic life. Commitment to Islam and loyalty to the clan remain strong.

POLITICS

Multiparty elections

L. House 1999/2004
U. House 1999/2002

President Nursultan Nazarbayev

AT THE LAST ELECTION

Majlis 77 seats

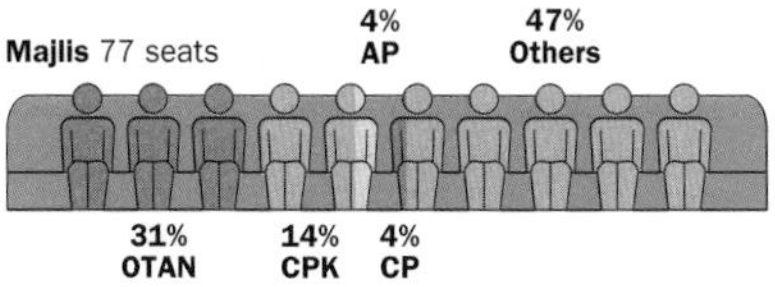
4% AP
47% Others
31% OTAN
14% CPK
4% CP

OTAN = Fatherland Republican Party of Kazakhstan
CPK = Civil Party of Kazakhstan **AP** = Agrarian Party
CP = Communist Party of Kazakhstan

Senate 39 seats

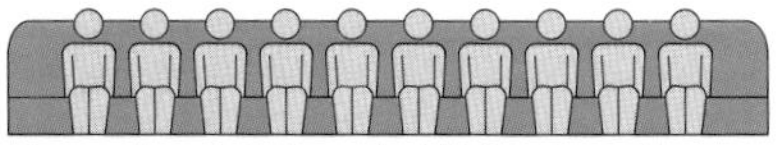

Two members elected by each of 16 districts, and 7 nominated by the president

Legislative authority is vested in the bicameral Parliament. The president, who must be fluent in Kazakh, has supreme executive power.

Main Political Issue
Presidential powers

The increased powers of President Nazarbayev are the focus of political controversy, prompting his critics to accuse him of developing a personality cult. The 1995 constitution strengthened presidential powers, conferring a veto over the decisions of the Constitutional Council. Also in 1995 Nazarbayev, who was due to face reelection in 1996, won a referendum which extended his term of office until 2000. However, in 1998 the legislature approved constitutional amendments forcing him to hold a presidential election in 1999. Although reelected, Nazarbayev was tarnished by allegations of voting irregularities.

Profile

Despite a democratic government, the president enjoys political dominance, and the patronage of the Kazakh clans is still important. Since coming to power in 1989, Nazarbayev has concentrated on market reforms. His political credibility was badly shaken in 1994, when allegations of widespread fraud led to the annulment of legislative elections. New elections were held in 1995, but Nazarbayev faces mounting domestic and international criticism of his attempts to expand the scope of presidential powers. In June 2000 the Assembly granted him special powers to advise future presidents after his term expires in 2006.

***President Nursultan Nazarbayev**, who steered Kazakhstan to independence.*

***Kasymzhomart Tokayev**, prime minister since 1999.*

WORLD AFFAIRS

Joined UN in 1992

CIS | SCO | EAPC | OIC | OSCE

Maintaining close ties with other former Soviet republics is a priority. Relations with Russia, although strained at times by Moscow's concern over Kazakhstan's ethnic Russians, have been cemented by a 25-year cooperation treaty.

The largest of the former Soviet central Asian republics, Kazakhstan has recently assumed a broader role in the region, offering military assistance to both Kyrgyzstan and Uzbekistan in 2000 as a "guarantor of peace." President Nazarbayev was the first chairman of the Eurasian Economic Community, set up in October 2000.

Kazakhstan's rich mineral resources have attracted investors from Europe, the USA, and Asia, particularly South Korea. Relations with China have improved, with agreements in 1998 and 1999 on border issues.

AID

Recipient

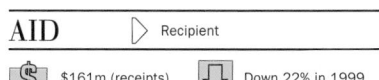

$161m (receipts)

Down 22% in 1999

Kazakhstan joined the IMF and the World Bank in 1992, and is also a member of the EBRD. Most multilateral and bilateral aid is aimed at supporting economic reform and improving health care, transportation and communications.

CHRONOLOGY

Once part of the Mongol empire, Kazakhstan was absorbed by the Russian empire in the 19th century. Ethnic Russians began to settle on land used by nomadic Kazakhs. Russian settlement intensified after the 1917 Revolution and Kazakhstan was subjected to intensive industrial and agricultural development.

- **1916** Rebellion against Russian rule brutally suppressed.
- **1917** Russian Revolution inspires civil war in Kazakhstan between Bolsheviks, anti-Bolsheviks, and Kazakh nationalists.
- **1918** Kazakh nationalists set up autonomous republic.
- **1920** Bolsheviks take control. Kirghiz Autonomous Soviet Socialist Republic (ASSR) set up within Russian Soviet Federative Socialist Republic.
- **1925** Kirghiz ASSR renamed Kazakh ASSR.
- **1936** Kazakhstan becomes full union republic of the USSR as Kazakh SSR.

K

CHRONOLOGY *continued*

- **1930s** Stalin's collectivization program leads to increase in Russian settlement and the deaths of an estimated one million Kazakhs.
- **1941–1945** Large-scale deportations of Germans, Jews, Crimean Tatars, and others to Kazakhstan.
- **1950s** Nuclear test site set up at Semipalatinsk; 500 nuclear explosions follow before testing ends in 1991.
- **1954–1960** Khrushchev's policy to plow "Virgin Lands" for grain most vigorously followed in Kazakhstan. Russian settlement reaches a peak.
- **1986** Riots in Almaty after an ethnic Russian, Gennadi Kolbin, appointed head of Kazakhstan Communist Party (CPK) to replace Kazakh, Dinmukhamed Kunyev.
- **1989** Kolbin replaced by Nursultan Nazarbayev, an ethnic Kazakh and chair of Council of Ministers. Reform of political and administrative system.
- **1990** CPK wins elections to Supreme Soviet by overwhelming majority. Nazarbayev appointed first president of Kazakhstan. Kazakhstan declares sovereignty.
- **1991** Kazakhstan votes to preserve USSR as union of sovereign states. USSR authorities hand control of enterprises in Kazakhstan to Kazakh government. CPK ordered to cease activities in official bodies following abortive August coup in Moscow. CPK restructures itself as Socialist Party of Kazakhstan (SPK). Independence of Republic of Kazakhstan declared; joins CIS.
- **1992** Opposition demonstrations against dominance of reformed communists in Supreme Soviet, now Supreme *Kenges*. Nationalist groups form Republican Party, Azat.
- **1993** Adoption of new constitution. Introduction of new currency, the tenge.
- **1994** Legislative elections annulled after proof of widespread voting irregularities.
- **1995** Adoption of new constitution broadening presidential powers; referendum extends Nazarbayev's term until 2000; legislative elections.
- **1998** Legislature approves constitutional amendments, including the holding of early presidential election.
- **1999** Nazarbayev reelected president for a further seven-year term.

K

DEFENSE

Compulsory military service

$504m — Down 1% in 1999

KAZAKH ARMED FORCES

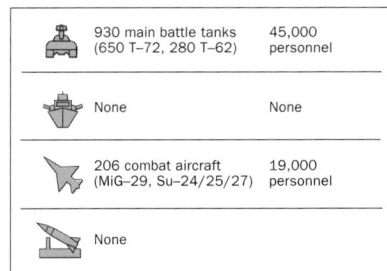

930 main battle tanks (650 T–72, 280 T–62)	45,000 personnel
None	None
206 combat aircraft (MiG–29, Su–24/25/27)	19,000 personnel
None	

As a former nuclear power and the largest of the five former Soviet central Asian republics, Kazakhstan is a potential guarantor of regional peace and stability. Kazakhstan ratified the START-I nuclear reduction treaty in 1992 and the NPT in 1993, but the process of disarmament has been delayed, due mainly to financial problems. In 1993, the USA agreed to grant Kazakhstan $84 million to dismantle its nuclear weapons. In 1995, Kazakhstan announced that all its nuclear weapons had been transferred to Russia or destroyed. Later that year military relations with Russia were sealed with a landmark agreement under which Kazakh and Russian armed forces were to be unified.

ECONOMICS

Inflation 255.9% p.a. (1990–1999)

$18.7bn — 138.55–145.56 tenge

SCORE CARD

World GNP Ranking	68th
GNP per Capita	$1250
Balance of Payments	$–171m
Inflation	8.2%
Unemployment	4%

ECONOMIC PERFORMANCE INDICATOR

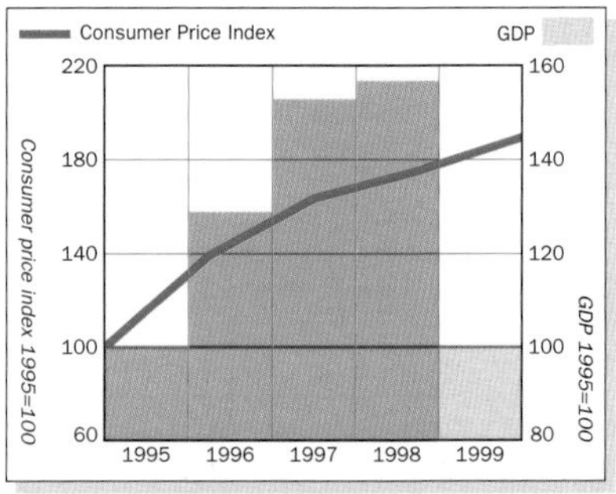
Consumer Price Index
GDP
220
180
140
100
60
160
140
120
100
80
1995
1996
1997
1998
1999
Consumer price index 1995=100
GDP 1995=100

EXPORTS

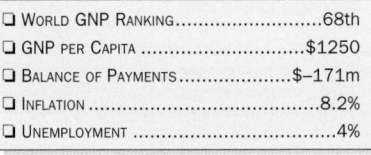

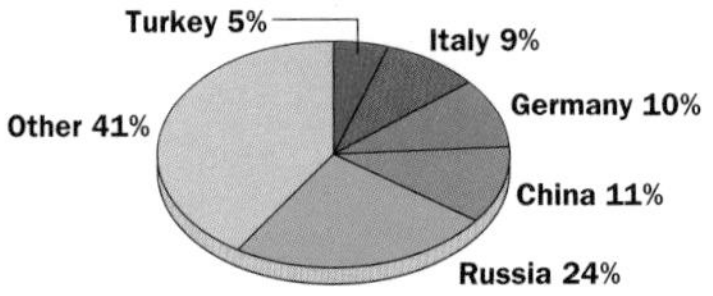
Turkey 5%
Italy 9%
Germany 10%
China 11%
Russia 24%
Other 41%

IMPORTS

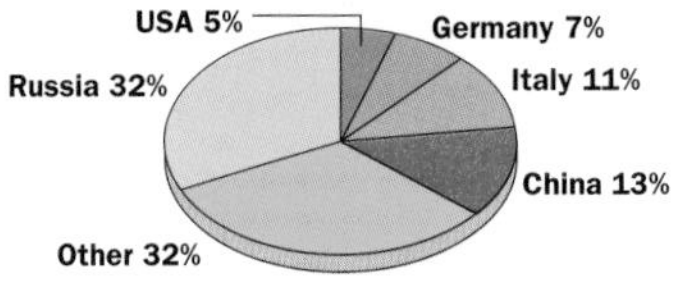
USA 5%
Germany 7%
Italy 11%
China 13%
Other 32%
Russia 32%

Strengths

Mineral resources, notably oil and gas, and bismuth and cadmium, used in electronics industry. Joint oil and gas ventures with Western companies. Mass privatization program launched in 1994.

Weaknesses

Collapse of former Soviet economic and trading system. Reliance on imported consumer goods. Rapid introduction of the tenge in 1993 increased instability and fueled sharp price rises. Inefficient industrial plants.

Profile

Kazakhstan has moved faster than other former Soviet republics to establish a market economy. Prices have been freed, foreign trade deregulated, and the tax system reformed. Growth has still been elusive. Unemployment and inflation have risen sharply, due in large part to the collapse of the wider Soviet economy.

Foreign direct investment is mainly in the energy sector. Outdated equipment and inadequate distribution networks mean that energy has to be imported, although Kazakhstan exports fossil fuel.

An oil price boom set the tone for the country's first "five-year plan" in 2000, part of Nazarbayev's "Kazakhstan 2030" program. It promised long-term land leases, although not full private ownership, from 2001.

KAZAKHSTAN : MAJOR BUSINESSES

Petropavlovsk
Karaganda
Aktyubinsk
Semipalatinsk
Atyrau
Almaty
Shymkent
Oil
Steel
Textiles
Chemicals
Oil refining
Coal mining
Food processing
Light engineering
Pharmaceuticals
0 500 km
0 500 miles
* significant multinational ownership

RESOURCES

Electric power 19m kw

41,367 tonnes

745,000 b/d (reserves 8,000,000,000 bbl)

9.78m sheep, 4m cattle, 1.03m pigs, 17.9m chickens

Oil, gas, manganese, gold, silver, coal, iron, tungsten, chromite, bismuth, cadmium

ELECTRICITY GENERATION

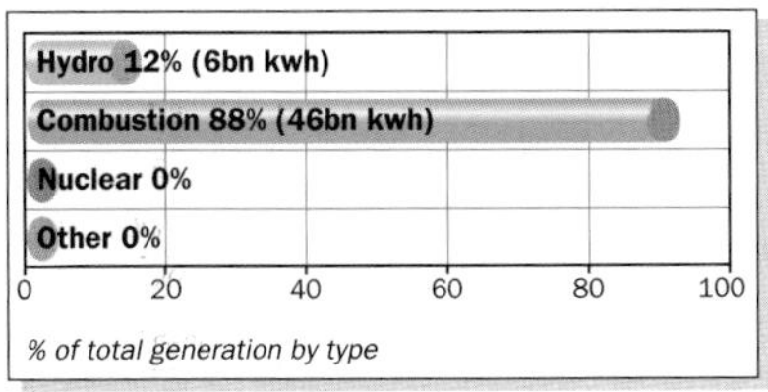

Hydro 12% (6bn kwh)
Combustion 88% (46bn kwh)
Nuclear 0%
Other 0%
0
20
40
60
80
100
% of total generation by type

Mining is the single most important industry in Kazakhstan. The US company Chevron has been developing the huge Tengiz oilfield since 1993. Joint ventures to exploit substantial oil and gas reserves in the Caspian Sea were agreed with Russia in 1995, and the USA and Japan in 1998. Kazakhstan also possesses vast iron ore and gold reserves.

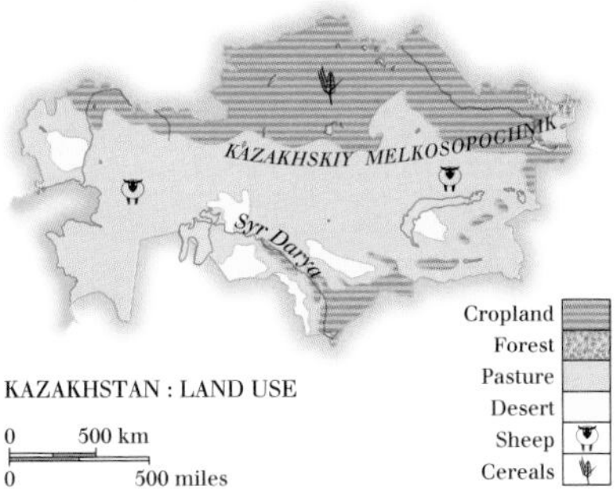

KAZAKHSKIY MELKOSOPOCHNIK
Syr Darya
Cropland
Forest
Pasture
Desert
Sheep
Cereals
0
500 km
0
500 miles

KAZAKHSTAN : LAND USE

ENVIRONMENT

Sustainability rank: 91st

3%

8 tonnes per capita

ENVIRONMENTAL TREATIES

No Yes Yes

No No Yes

Environmental damage caused by intensive industrial and agricultural development is a major concern. The eastern cities are heavily polluted and farmlands are being eroded. The Aral Sea, polluted by overuse of fertilizers, has shrunk by 50% owing to the diversion of rivers for irrigation.

In 1991, environmental pressure groups succeeded in ending more than 40 years of nuclear testing at Semipalatinsk. The green lobby is now pressing for tighter pollution controls.

MEDIA

TV ownership medium

Daily newspaper circulation 30 per 1000 people

PUBLISHING AND BROADCAST MEDIA

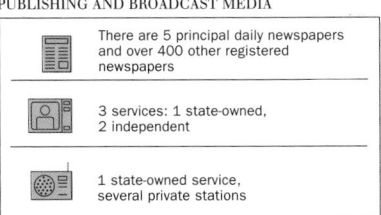

There are 5 principal daily newspapers and over 400 other registered newspapers

3 services: 1 state-owned, 2 independent

1 state-owned service, several private stations

The state-owned media compete with independent publications and privately owned radio and television stations, many of which are controlled by members of President Nazarbayev's family. All reports pertaining to ethnic minorities are censored. There are more than 400 registered newspapers, though Kazakh-language publications account for less than half of the market.

CRIME

Death penalty used

Kazakhstan does not publish prison figures

Crime levels are rising

CRIME RATES

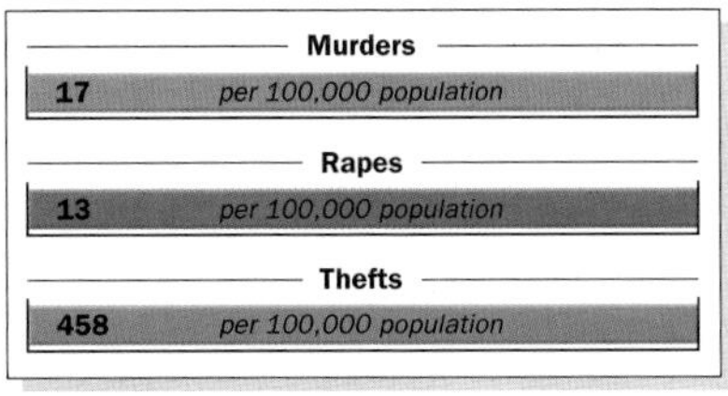

Murders
17 per 100,000 population
Rapes
13 per 100,000 population
Thefts
458 per 100,000 population

Narcotics smuggling is increasing. Corruption is rife. A moratorium on the death penalty was imposed from 1998.

EDUCATION

School leaving age: 17

99%

419,460 students

THE EDUCATION SYSTEM

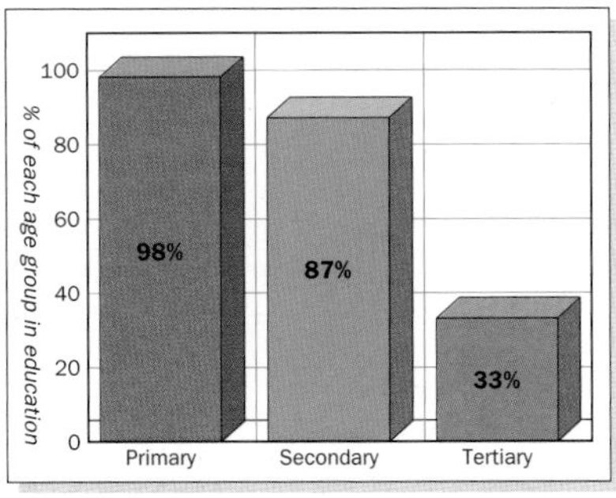

100
80
60
40
20
0
% of each age group in education
98%
87%
33%
Primary
Secondary
Tertiary

Education remains based on the Soviet model. Since the adoption of Kazakh as the state language in 1995, Russian is gradually being replaced by Kazakh as the main medium of instruction in schools, but there is a shortage of Kazakh textbooks and Kazakh-speaking teachers to replace the Russian speakers. There are a large number of higher-education institutions and medical schools.

HEALTH

No welfare state health benefits

1 per 286 people

Heart attacks, cancers, accidents, violence, tuberculosis

Kazakhstan's ill-equipped and poorly funded health system has produced one of the highest infant mortality rates in central Asia.

The health system is limited in terms of both facilities and coverage. Rural people have minimal access to clinics. The country's size means that extending coverage and improving the quality of care will be costly. Attempts are therefore being made to attract foreign investment into the health sector. Many doctors have emigrated to Russia.

SPENDING

GDP/cap. decrease

CONSUMPTION AND SPENDING

66 per 1000 population

108 per 1000 population

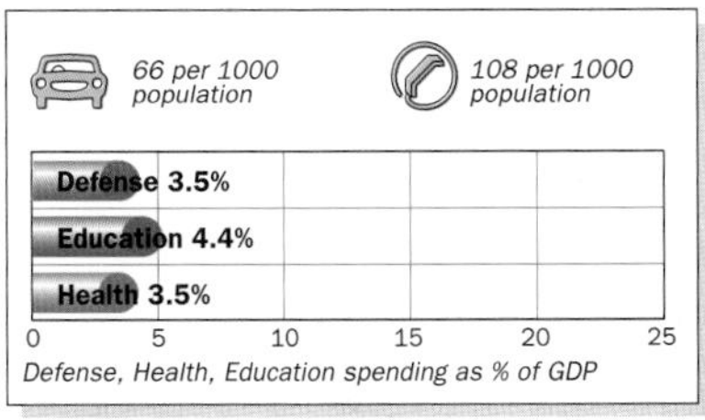

Defense 3.5%
Education 4.4%
Health 3.5%
0
5
10
15
20
25
Defense, Health, Education spending as % of GDP

Life for the majority of Kazakhs has always been hard, and has grown even more difficult since 1989. Living standards have deteriorated and unemployment has risen as a result of market-oriented reforms within Kazakhstan. The liberalization of the economy also fueled sharp price rises for essential commodities.

The rural population, the poorest group in Kazakhstan, has been badly affected. The small wealthy elite is made up mainly of former communist officials, many of whom have benefited from privatization, or belong to President Nazarbayev's clan. In 1995, the government banned Kazakhs from carrying out any foreign currency transactions.

WORLD RANKING

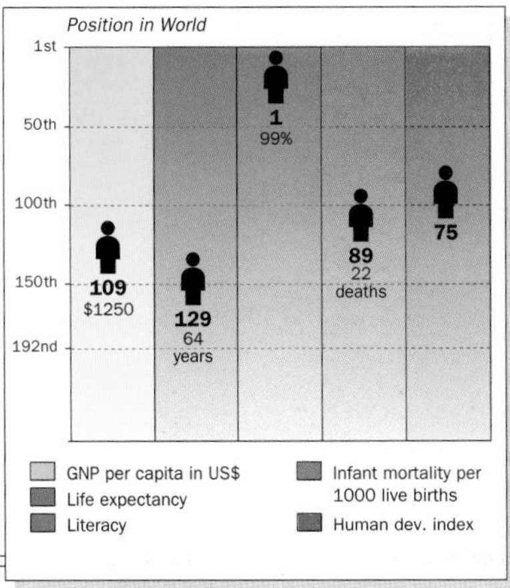

Position in World
1st
50th
100th
150th
192nd
109
$1250
129
64
years
1
99%
89
22
deaths
75
GNP per capita in US$
Life expectancy
Literacy
Infant mortality per 1000 live births
Human dev. index

K

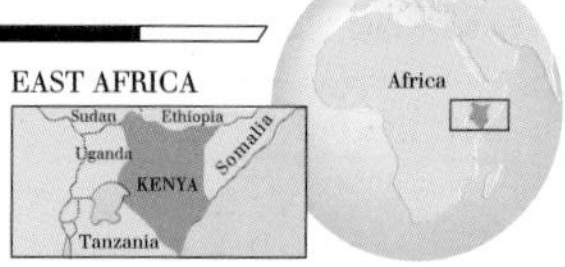
EAST AFRICA
Sudan
Ethiopia
Uganda
KENYA
Somalia
Tanzania
Africa

KENYA

OFFICIAL NAME: Republic of Kenya **CAPITAL:** Nairobi
POPULATION: 30.1 million **CURRENCY:** Kenya shilling **OFFICIAL LANGUAGES:** Swahili and English

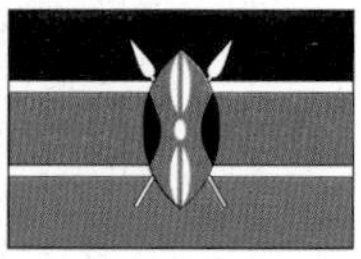

1963 | 1963 | Dec 12 | EAK | +3 | +254 | .ke

KENYA STRADDLES the equator on Africa's east coast. Its central plateau is bisected by the Great Rift Valley. The land to the north is desert, while to the east lies a fertile coastal belt. After independence from the UK in 1963, politics was dominated by Jomo Kenyatta, who was succeeded in 1978 by President Daniel arap Moi, whose divide-and-rule policies have drawn accusations of favoritism and of fomenting ethnic hatreds. His KANU won elections easily in 1992 and 1997, amid accusations of electoral fraud. Economic mainstays are tourism and agriculture, but high population growth is a major problem.

***Kenyatta Conference Center,** Nairobi. The modern skyline of the business center contrasts sharply with the slums on the city's outskirts.*

CLIMATE

Steppe/mountain/ tropical

WEATHER CHART

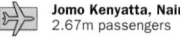

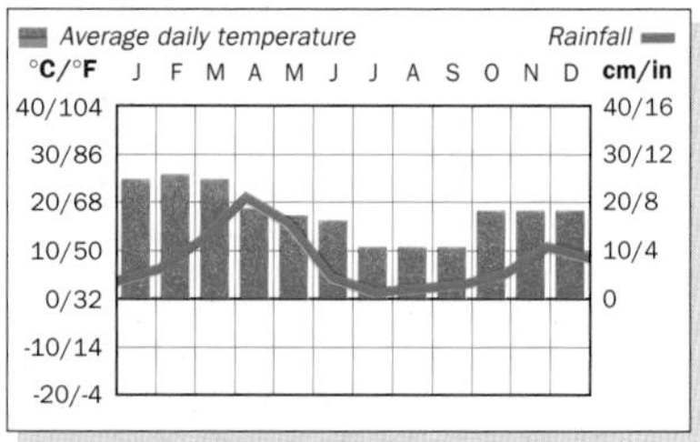
Average daily temperature
Rainfall
°C/°F
J F M A M J J A S O N D
cm/in
40/104
30/86
20/68
10/50
0/32
-10/14
-20/-4
40/16
30/12
20/8
10/4
0

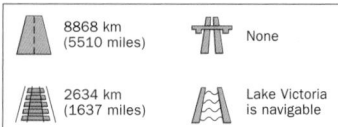

The coast and Great Rift Valley are hot and humid, the plateau interior is temperate, and the northeastern desert hot and dry. Rain generally falls from April to May and October to November.

TRANSPORTATION

Drive on left

Jomo Kenyatta, Nairobi
2.67m passengers

39 ships
20,900 grt

THE TRANSPORTATION NETWORK

8868 km (5510 miles)

None

2634 km (1637 miles)

Lake Victoria is navigable

Kenya's railroads, ports, and main airport are currently being upgraded, while in addition a five-year road improvement program was begun in 2000.

***Great Rift Valley,** Kenya. This huge crack in the Earth's crust runs from the River Jordan right through Africa to the Zambezi River.*

TOURISM

Visitors : Population 1:32

943,000 visitors

Up 10% in 1999

Tourism is vital to the economy and a key foreign exchange earner. However, after enjoying a boom in package safaris and beach holidays during the 1980s, Kenya saw visitor numbers decline during most of the 1990s. The main factors were world recession, reports of instability, the much-publicized murder of several tourists, and the 1998 US embassy bombing.

MAIN TOURIST ARRIVALS

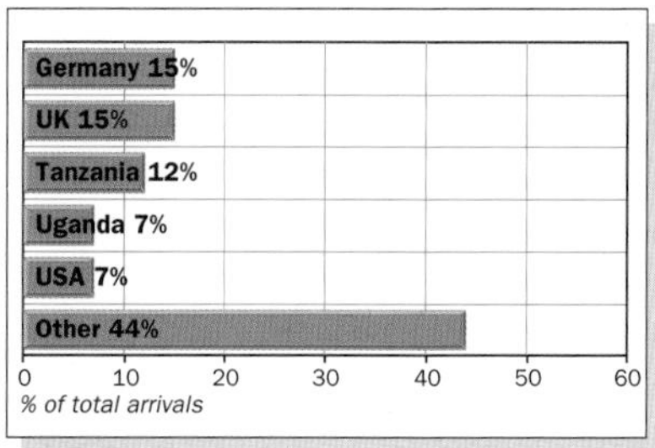
Germany 15%
UK 15%
Tanzania 12%
Uganda 7%
USA 7%
Other 44%
0
10
20
30
40
50
60
% of total arrivals

KENYA

Total Land Area : 566 970 sq. km (218 907 sq. miles)

POPULATION

- over 1 000 000
- over 500 000
- over 100 000
- over 50 000
- over 10 000
- under 10 000

LAND HEIGHT

- 3000m/9843ft
- 2000m/6562ft
- 1000m/3281ft
- 500m/1640ft
- 200m/656ft
- Sea Level

SUDAN
ETHIOPIA
SOMALIA
UGANDA
TANZANIA
ELEMI TRIANGLE
Lokitaung
Lake Turkana (Lake Rudolf)
Moyale
Daua
Mandera
AWARA PLAIN
Lodwar
CHALBI DESERT
Marsabit
BOKHOL PLAIN
Wajir
Maralal
Kapenguria
Kitale
Tambach
Lake Baringo
Isiolo
Bungoma
Eldoret
Kabarnet
Meru
Kakamega
Busia
Nyahururu
Nanyuki
Kirinyaga 5199m
Kisumu
Kapsabet
Londiani
Nakuru
Nyeri
Garissa
Winam Gulf
Kericho
Njoro
Embu
Rusinga I.
Mfanganu I.
Homa Bay
Elburgon
Murang'a
Kisii
Naivasha
Lake Naivasha
Thika
Lake Victoria
Karungu Bay
Narok
NAIROBI
Kitui
Machakos
LOITA HILLS
Lake Magadi
Magadi
Lamu
Pate Island
Manda Island
Garsen
Namanga
Oloitokitok
Ungama Bay
Malindi
Voi
Taveta
Kilifi
Mombasa
Kwale
INDIAN OCEAN
GREAT RIFT VALLEY
NYIKA
YATTA PLATEAU
NYIRI DESERT
Tana
Galana
Lugards Falls
Chandlers Falls
Lorian Swamp
Equator
N
0
100 km
100 miles

PEOPLE

Pop. density medium

Swahili, English, Kikuyu, Luo, Kamba

53/km² (138/mi²)

THE URBAN/RURAL POPULATION SPLIT

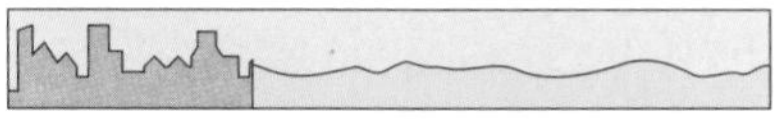
32%
68%

RELIGIOUS PERSUASION

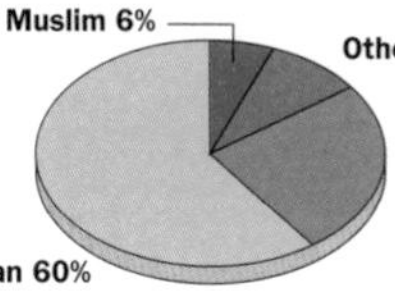
Muslim 6%
Other 9%
Traditional beliefs 25%
Christian 60%

ETHNIC MAKEUP

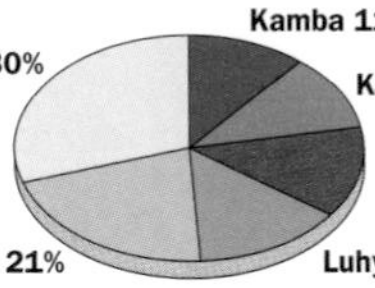
Kamba 11%
Other 30%
Kalenjin 11%
Luo 13%
Kikuyu 21%
Luhya 14%

Kenya's ethnic diversity, with about 70 different groups, reflects its past as a focus of population movements. Asians, Europeans, and Arabs form 1% of the population. The rural majority retains strong clan and extended family links, although these are being weakened by urban migration. Poverty, severe drought, and a high population growth rate are the root causes of the land hunger which has recently been fueling a surge in ethnic violence. Much violence is concentrated in western Kenya, where Kikuyu, the formerly dominant tribe, are the main targets of attacks by Kalenjin, Masai, and Pokor groups. Several hundred thousand Kikuyu are believed to have been displaced from their villages.

POPULATION AGE BREAKDOWN

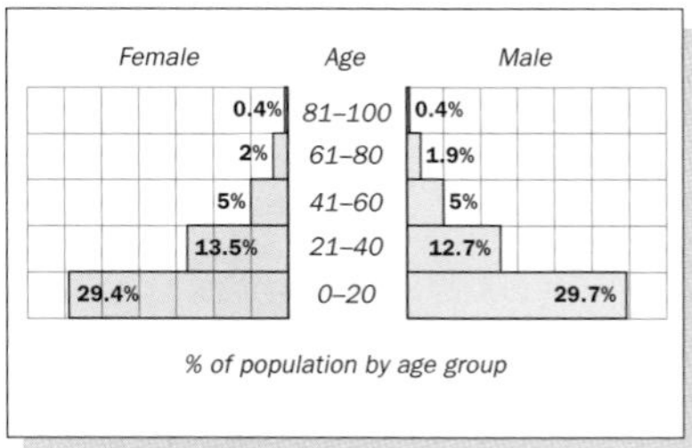
Female
Age
Male
0.4%
81–100
0.4%
2%
61–80
1.9%
5%
41–60
5%
13.5%
21–40
12.7%
29.4%
0–20
29.7%
% of population by age group

POLITICS

Multiparty elections

1997/2002

President Daniel arap Moi

AT THE LAST ELECTION

National Assembly 224 seats

8% FORD–K
2% Saf
51% KANU
18% DP
10% NDP
7% SDP
4% Others

KANU = Kenya African National Union
DP = Democratic Party **NDP** = National Development Party
FORD–K = Forum for the Restoration of Democracy–Kenya
SDP = Social Democratic Party **Saf** = Safina
Others include FORD–People, Kenya Social Congress, Shirikisho, FORD–Asili, and two ex-officio members.

The National Assembly comprises 210 elected members, 12 nominated by the president, and two ex-officio.

Kenya has been led by President Daniel arap Moi since 1978, and became a multiparty democracy in 1992.

MAIN POLITICAL ISSUE
Ethnic violence

The ethnic polarization of political parties in Kenya and rising poverty are fueling ethnic violence. Determined to ensure KANU dominance, President Moi, a Kalenjin, is turning the party into an alliance of smaller ethnic groups opposed to the once dominant Kikuyu. The latter are the largest ethnic group, the main victims of violence, and the main supporters of the opposition.

PROFILE

After 1982, President Moi's efforts to entrench KANU in power provoked demands at home for the introduction of multiparty politics, and condemnation abroad for the human rights abuses committed. Forced in 1992 to concede free elections, Moi helped ensure KANU's victory by curtailing the campaign period. His reelection in December 1997 was marred by widespread allegations of intimidation and electoral fraud.

Moi has attempted to break down barriers with some opponents. In 1999, he appointed paleontologist Richard Leakey, a former political opponent, to head a drive against official corruption. Leakey stepped down in March 2001, saying that he had completed his task. Also in 2001, the NDP joined the government.

***President Daniel arap Moi**, Kenya's leader since 1978.*

***Mwai Kibaki**, opposition leader.*

AID

Recipient

$308m (receipts)

Down 35% in 1999

Kenya has been a major recipient of aid from donors including the UK, Japan, the EU, the World Bank, and the IMF. Little, however, has trickled down to the majority of the population. This is partly because of the high proportion of aid tied to construction projects and donor-country firms, and partly because of mismanagement and official corruption. In 1996 Western creditor governments decided to link aid disbursements to improvements in human rights, and in 2001 the IMF and the World Bank withheld all aid pending anti-corruption reforms.

CHRONOLOGY

From the 10th century, Arab coastal settlers mixed with indigenous peoples in the region. Britain's need for a route to landlocked Uganda led to the formation in 1895 of the British East African Protectorate in the coastal region.

- **1900–1918** White settlement.
- **1920** Interior becomes British colony.
- **1930** Jomo Kenyatta goes to UK; stays 14 years.
- **1944** Kenyan African Union (KAU) formed; Kenyatta returns to lead it.
- **1952–1956** *Mau Mau*, Kikuyu-led violent campaign to restore African lands. State of emergency; 13,000 people killed.
- **1953** KAU banned. Kenyatta jailed.
- **1960** State of emergency ends. Tom Mboya and Oginga Odinga form KANU.
- **1961** Kenyatta freed; takes up presidency of KANU.
- **1963** KANU wins elections. Kenyatta prime minister. Full independence declared.
- **1964** Republic of Kenya formed with Kenyatta as president and Odinga as vice president.
- **1966** Odinga defects to form Kenya People's Union (KPU).

WORLD AFFAIRS

Joined UN in 1963

Comm | COMESA | EAC | IGAD | OAU

Relations with neighboring states and with key Western donors are Kenya's priorities. The US embassy closed temporarily in 1998 after a terrorist bombing caused carnage there. In 1991, human rights concerns were partly responsible for a two-year suspension of aid. Talks were held in spring 2001 in an effort to end Kenya's border dispute with Sudan. Relations with Rwanda improved in 2000, when it was agreed to reopen the Kenyan embassy in Kigali and to establish a joint commission for bilateral relations. Kenya is greatly concerned by the situation in Burundi and Congo (former Zaire), as well as by tensions in Sudan, Somalia, and Ethiopia.

K

CHRONOLOGY *continued*

- **1969** KANU sole party to contest elections (also 1974). Tom Mboya of KANU assassinated. Unrest. KPU banned and Odinga arrested.
- **1978** Kenyatta dies. Vice President Daniel arap Moi succeeds him.
- **1982** Kenya declared a one-party state. Opposition to Moi. Abortive air force coup. Odinga rearrested.
- **1986** Open "queue-voting" replaces secret ballot in first stage of general elections. Other measures to extend Moi's powers incite opposition.
- **1988** Moi wins third term and extends his control over judiciary.
- **1990** Government implicated in deaths of foreign minister Robert Ouko and Anglican archbishop. Riots. Odinga and others form FORD, outlawed by government.
- **1991** Arrest of FORD leaders and attempts to stop prodemocracy demonstrations. Donors suspend aid. Moi agrees to introduce multiparty system. Ethnic violence on increase.
- **1992** FORD splits into factions led by ex-minister Kenneth Matiba and Odinga. Opposition weakness helps Moi win December elections.
- **1994** Odinga dies.
- **1997** December, Moi wins further term in widely criticized elections.
- **1998** Bomb explodes at US embassy in Nairobi, killing 230 and wounding thousands.
- **1999** Moi appoints paleontologist Richard Leakey to lead government drive against corruption.
- **2000** Worst drought since 1947.
- **2001** Leakey resigns. Drought threatens starvation for millions.

DEFENSE

No compulsory military service

$327m — Up 2% in 1999

KENYAN ARMED FORCES

76 main battle tanks (Vickers Mk 3)	18,200 personnel
4 patrol boats	1000 personnel
30 combat aircraft (10 F-5)	3000 personnel
None	

Destabilization of the northeastern border by the Somali civil war is the main defense issue. The army has recently been deployed to suppress tribal fighting in the Rift Valley. Military assistance is given by the UK and the USA.

ECONOMICS

Inflation 14.9% p.a. (1990–1999)

$10.7bn

72.80–78.05 Kenya shillings

SCORE CARD

World GNP Ranking	82nd
GNP per Capita	$360
Balance of Payments	$-363m
Inflation	2.6%
Unemployment	50%

EXPORTS

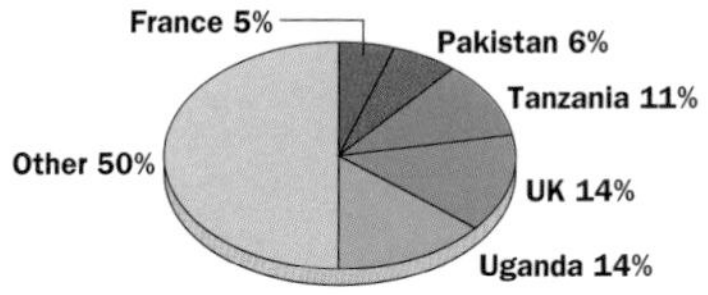
France 5%
Pakistan 6%
Tanzania 11%
Other 50%
UK 14%
Uganda 14%

IMPORTS

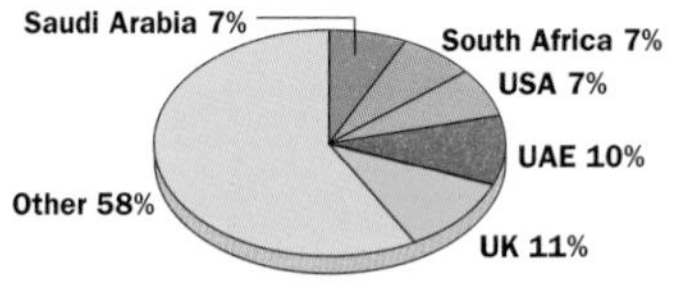
Saudi Arabia 7%
South Africa 7%
USA 7%
UAE 10%
Other 58%
UK 11%

ECONOMIC PERFORMANCE INDICATOR

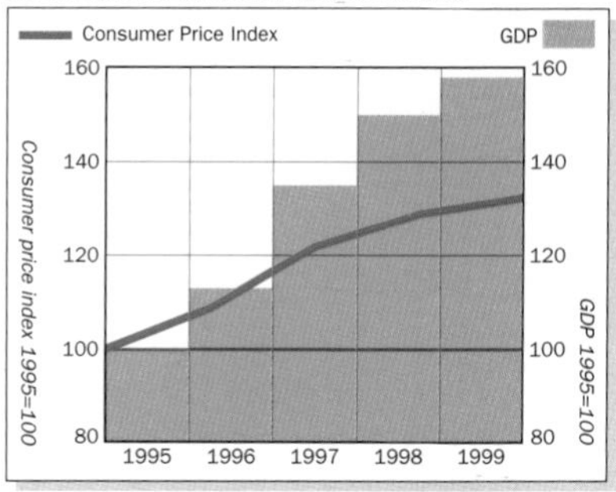
Consumer Price Index
GDP
160
140
120
100
80
Consumer price index 1995=100
GDP 1995=100
1995
1996
1997
1998
1999

Strengths

Tourism – largest foreign exchange earner. Broad agricultural base, especially cash crops such as coffee and tea. East Africa's largest, most diversified manufacturing sector.

Weaknesses

Fluctuating world prices for coffee and tea. Corruption. Poor recent GDP growth. High population growth. Land shortage means uneconomic small units. Country's image problem affects tourism.

Profile

Kenya has been hailed as an example to the rest of Africa of the benefits of a mainly free-market economy. Government involvement has been relatively limited, and recently further reduced by privatization. Foreign investment has been encouraged, with some success. Tourism has become the leading foreign exchange earner over the past 20 years, despite suffering serious setbacks in the 1990s. Manufacturing now accounts for 21% of GDP, and is the most diversified sector in east Africa, but needs to expand rapidly so as to create more jobs.

Economic growth was good by African standards during the 1980s, averaging over 4% a year. However, it was barely sufficient to compensate for one of the world's highest population growth rates, approximately 3.5%, although the UN estimates that this rate will fall to 2.2% in the early 2000s. For the majority of Kenyans, farming ever-smaller landholdings or earning a living in the informal sector, life has become harsher. The situation was exacerbated in 2001 by a ban on all trade with Somalia, which affects exports of the mild narcotic, qat, widely grown in Kenya. Severe drought since 2000 has crippled the agricultural sector and put 20 million people at risk of starvation.

Other problems, including inflation, a heavy debt burden ($7.4 billion in 1997), and growing dependence on balance of payments support had come to a head in the early 1990s, when economic growth gave way to recession. Real GDP growth fell to 0.4% in 1992 and has remained low, typically at 1.2% in 1997. The rise in poverty-linked violence and political unrest hit tourism; earnings fell by 15% in the early 1990s, and the industry has yet to recover fully.

Partly as a response to pressure from donors, including the 1991–1993 freeze on balance of payments support, the government has implemented some economic liberalization measures. These include floating the Kenya shilling, raising interest rates, and giving exporters direct access to their hard currency earnings. However, sustained growth is likely to remain elusive until Kenya overcomes the official corruption which drains vital resources, and the poor image affecting its tourist industry.

KENYA : MAJOR BUSINESSES

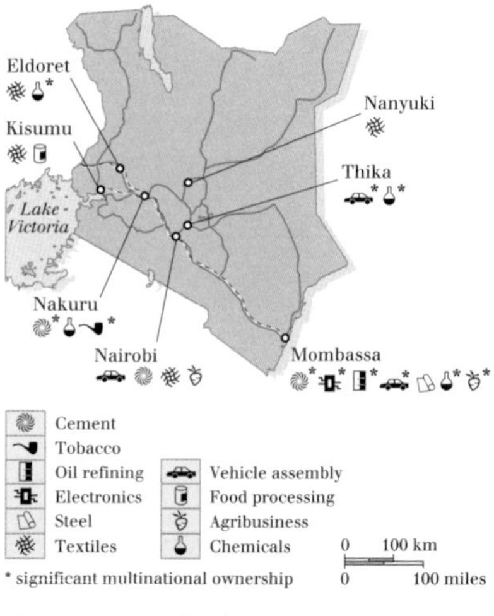
Eldoret
Kisumu
Lake Victoria
Nakuru
Nairobi
Nanyuki
Thika
Mombassa
Cement
Tobacco
Oil refining
Electronics
Steel
Textiles
Vehicle assembly
Food processing
Agribusiness
Chemicals
0 100 km
0 100 miles

* significant multinational ownership

RESOURCES

Electric power 809,000 kw

161,183 tonnes

Not an oil producer; refines 90,000 b/d

13.8m cattle, 7.7m goats, 5.9m sheep, 31m chickens

Soda ash, fluorite, limestone, rubies, gold, vermiculite

ELECTRICITY GENERATION

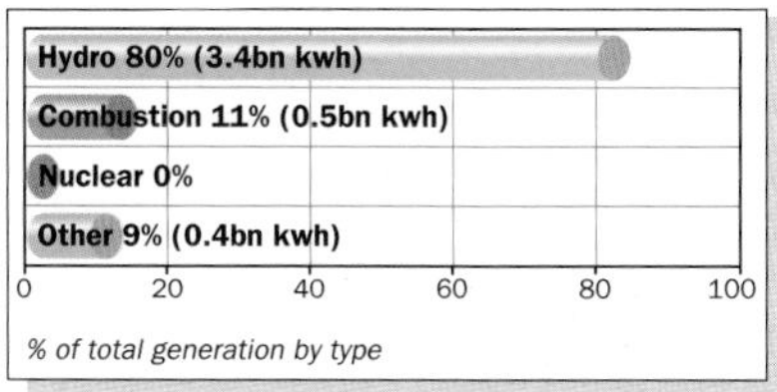
Hydro 80% (3.4bn kwh)
Combustion 11% (0.5bn kwh)
Nuclear 0%
Other 9% (0.4bn kwh)
0
20
40
60
80
100
% of total generation by type

Agriculture is still the largest sector of the economy. Kenya's varied topography means that tropical, subtropical, and temperate crops may be grown. Coffee and tea, the main export crops, have been affected by falling world prices. Efforts to reduce dependence on these have led to the growth of a successful export-oriented horticultural industry.

Kenya has few mineral resources, though oil exploration has revealed deposits in Turkana District. Hydroelectric and geothermal sources are being developed to reduce energy imports – currently 70% of total requirements. However, droughts caused power shortages in 2000 and 2001, leading to the imposition of daily power cuts.

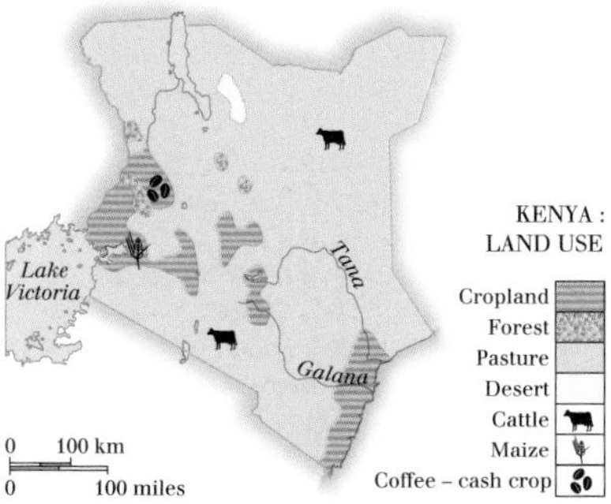
KENYA : LAND USE
Lake Victoria
Tana
Galana
Cropland
Forest
Pasture
Desert
Cattle
Maize
Coffee – cash crop
0 100 km
0 100 miles

ENVIRONMENT

Sustainability rank: 82nd

6%

0.3 tonnes per capita

ENVIRONMENTAL TREATIES

	Yes		Yes		Yes
	Yes		Yes		No

The importance to tourism of wildlife conservation is recognized, and recent elephant protection schemes have been a success, but proposed national reserves compete with agriculture for land. Opposition to government plans to reallocate some national park land to squatters is growing.

MEDIA

TV ownership low

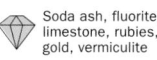

Daily newspaper circulation 9 per 1000 people

PUBLISHING AND BROADCAST MEDIA

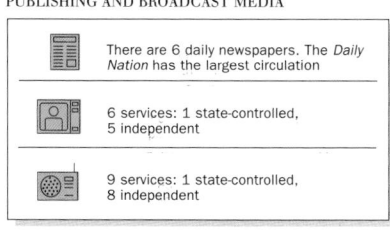

There are 6 daily newspapers. The *Daily Nation* has the largest circulation

6 services: 1 state-controlled, 5 independent

9 services: 1 state-controlled, 8 independent

Government intolerance of criticism is long-standing and includes plays and novels as well as the media. Ngugi wa Thiongo, Kenya's most famous novelist, was exiled for his criticism of KANU.

CRIME

Death penalty used

Kenya does not publish prison figures

Up 15% in 1992

CRIME RATES

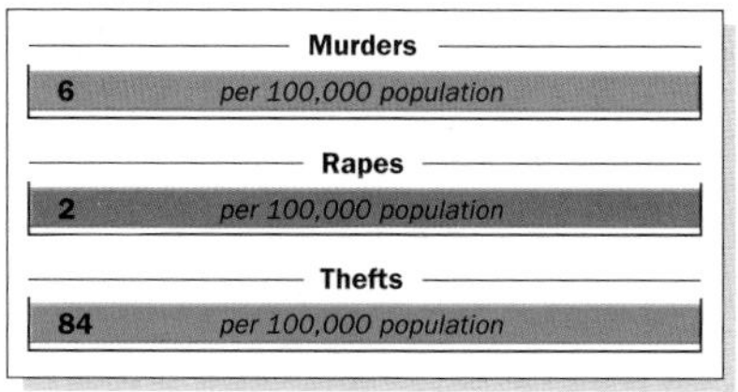
Murders
6 per 100,000 population
Rapes
2 per 100,000 population
Thefts
84 per 100,000 population

Nairobi's high crime levels are spreading countrywide, as a result of worsening poverty, ethnic violence, and rising banditry in the northeast. An increase in the use of guns underlies the rapid increase in violent crime.

EDUCATION

School leaving age: 14

82%

35,421 students

THE EDUCATION SYSTEM

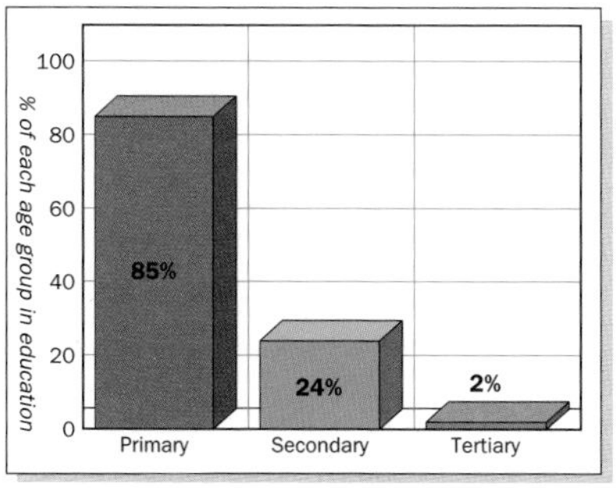
100
80
60
40
20
0
% of each age group in education
85%
24%
2%
Primary
Secondary
Tertiary

The education system is loosely based on the British model. Primary education, from six to 14 years of age, is free and compulsory; some 85% of children attend. The drop-out rate at secondary level is high, with only about 24% attendance. In higher education, the emphasis is on vocational training. There are five state universities.

HEALTH

No welfare state health benefits

1 per 10,000 people

Respiratory and diarrheal diseases, malaria

The health system comprises a mixture of state and private facilities, the latter mainly run by charities and missions. The state system has been badly hit by recession, worsening the already limited access of the rural majority. Poverty-related illnesses, particularly among women and children, are increasing. HIV and AIDS reached epidemic proportions in some areas in the 1990s, and according to a UN estimate, 13.95% of the adult population was infected with HIV at the end of 1999. Kenya has ten doctors and 23 qualified nurses for every 100,000 people.

SPENDING

GDP/cap. increase

CONSUMPTION AND SPENDING

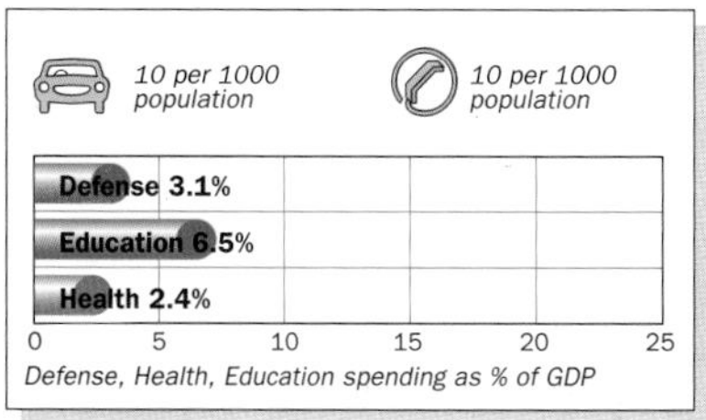
10 per 1000 population
10 per 1000 population
Defense 3.1%
Education 6.5%
Health 2.4%
0
5
10
15
20
25
Defense, Health, Education spending as % of GDP

Wealth disparities in Kenya are large and growing, exacerbated by land hunger and migration to the cities, where jobs are few and existence depends on the informal economy. More than half of all town-dwellers live in slums, and the slum dwellers of Nairobi's Amarthi Valley are among Africa's poorest, worst-nourished people. Their lives contrast sharply with those of the country's elite – top government officials with access to patronage; white Kenyans, who derive their wealth largely from agricultural estates; and the largely Asian business community. Wealthy Kenyans often send their children abroad for higher education.

WORLD RANKING

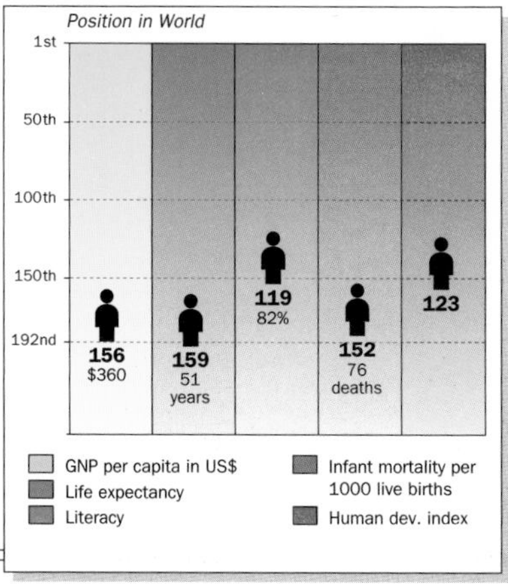
Position in World
1st
50th
100th
150th
192nd
156
$360
159
51
years
119
82%
152
76
deaths
123
GNP per capita in US$
Life expectancy
Literacy
Infant mortality per 1000 live births
Human dev. index

K

KIRIBATI

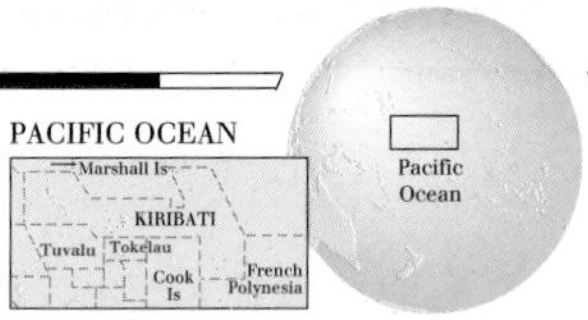
PACIFIC OCEAN
Marshall Is
KIRIBATI
Tuvalu
Tokelau
Cook Is
French Polynesia
Pacific Ocean

OFFICIAL NAME: Republic of Kiribati **CAPITAL:** Bairiki (Tarawa Atoll)
POPULATION: 92,000 **CURRENCY:** Australian dollar **OFFICIAL LANGUAGE:** English

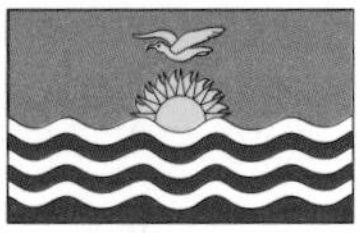

1979 | 1979 | July 12 | KIR | +12 | +686 | .ki

FORMERLY PART OF THE colony of the Gilbert and Ellice Islands, the Gilberts became independent from Britain in 1979 and took the name Kiribati (pronounced "Kir-ee-bahs"). British interest in the Gilbert Islands rested solely on the exploitation of the phosphate deposits on Banaba; these ran out in 1980. In 1981, Kiribati won damages (but not the costs of litigation) from the British for decades of phosphate exploitation.

Banreaba Island, Tarawa atoll. *None of the atolls is more than 8 m (26 ft) high except Banaba, once the source of phosphates.*

CLIMATE

Tropical oceanic

WEATHER CHART

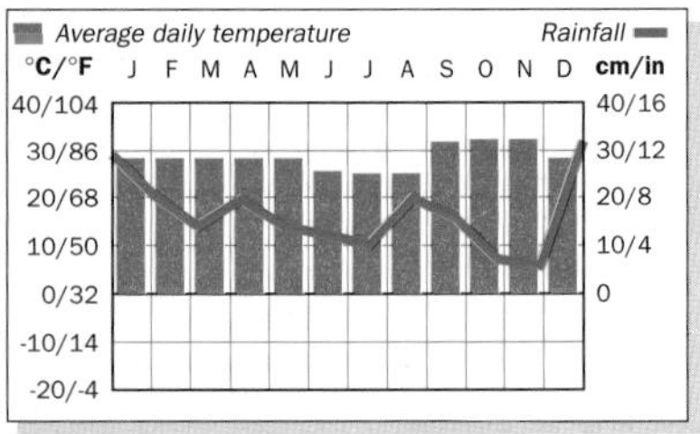
Average daily temperature
Rainfall
°C/°F
J F M A M J J A S O N D
cm/in
40/104
30/86
20/68
10/50
0/32
-10/14
-20/4
40/16
30/12
20/8
10/4
0

Kiribati's small land area in the vast Pacific means that some atolls can often go for months without rain. In March 1999, a nationwide drought emergency was declared.

TRANSPORTATION

Drive on right

Bonriki International, Tarawa
51,000 passengers

4200 grt

THE TRANSPORTATION NETWORK

483 km (300 miles)

None

None

5 km (3 miles)

Kiribati has a limited air link with Fiji. Transportation around and between the atolls is provided mostly by small canoes.

TOURISM

Visitors : Population 1:92

1000 visitors

No change in 2000

MAIN TOURIST ARRIVALS

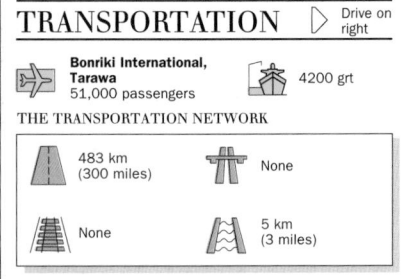

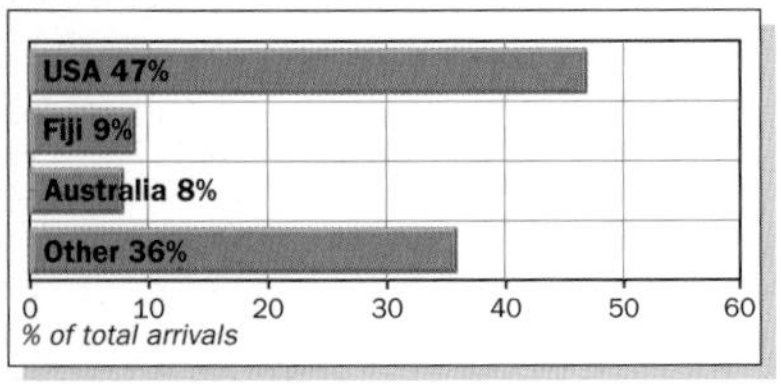
USA 47%
Fiji 9%
Australia 8%
Other 36%
0
10
20
30
40
50
60
% of total arrivals

Kiritimati, which has a weekly air service to Honolulu, attracts a small but steady stream of visitors.

PEOPLE

Pop. density medium

English, Micronesian dialect

130/km² (336/mi²)

THE URBAN/RURAL POPULATION SPLIT

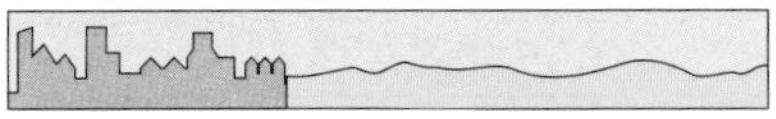
37%
63%

RELIGIOUS PERSUASION

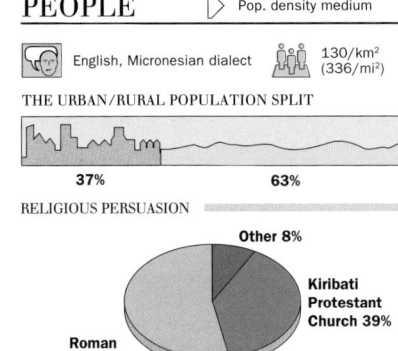

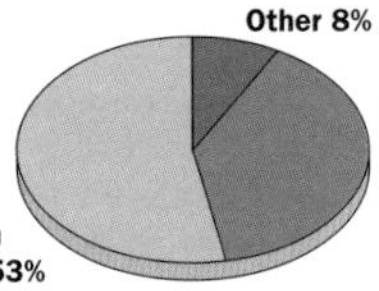
Other 8%
Kiribati Protestant Church 39%
Roman Catholic 53%

Locals still refer to themselves as Gilbertese. Almost all Gilbertese are Micronesian, although the inhabitants of Banaba employed anthropologists to establish their racial distinctness. Tension with the Banabans is intense, mostly fueled by the historic value of Banaba's phosphate deposits. Most Gilbertese are poor. Many go to Nauru as guest workers, living in barrack-room conditions, or work as merchant shipping crew. Those who stay at home go through a circular migration from the outlying islands to Tarawa, returning to see relatives. Women play a prominent role, especially on outlying islands, where they run most of the farms.

POLITICS

Multiparty elections

1998/2002

President Teburoro Tito

AT THE LAST ELECTION

House of Assembly 42 seats

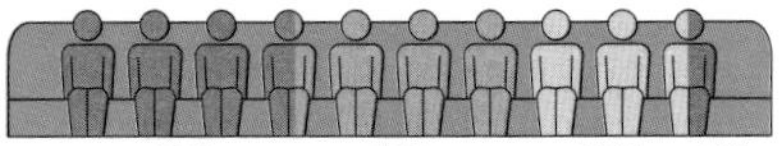
36% Ind
33% MTM
26% NPP
5% App

Ind = Independents **MTM** = Maneaban Te Mauri
NPP = National Progressive Party **App** = Appointed

The House of Assembly has one appointed member and one ex-officio member

The traditional chiefs still effectively rule Kiribati, through a party system on the British model. Victory for the MTM in the 1994 elections ended 15 years of rule by the NPP. The main concern is the economy, which is extremely vulnerable to any fluctuations in world demand for coconuts. The overpopulation of Tarawa is the other major issue. Possible restrictions on travel to the island have been discussed. In part, the problem of migration is caused by the poverty and lack of opportunity on the outer islands. A resettlement program, aiming to move people out of Tarawa, began in 1998.

KIRIBATI

Total Land Area : 710 sq. km (274 sq. miles)

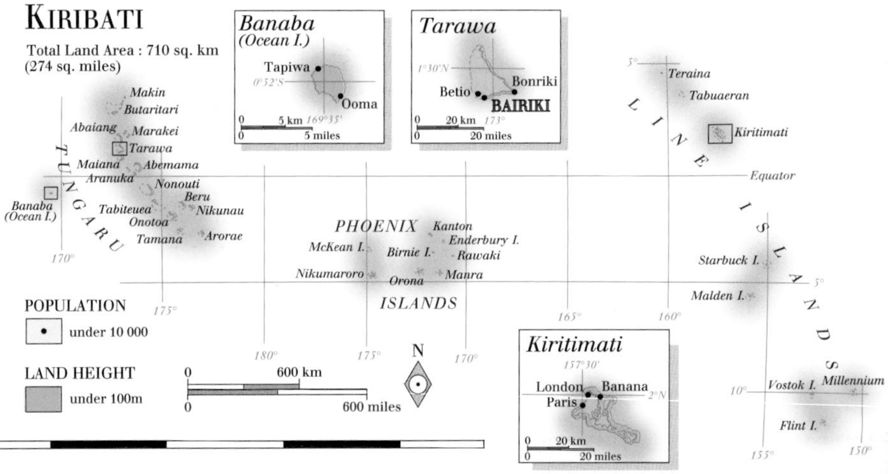
Banaba (Ocean I.)
Tapiwa
Ooma
5 km
5 miles
Tarawa
Betio
Bonriki
BAIRIKI
20 km
20 miles
Makin
Butaritari
Abaiang
Marakei
Tarawa
Maiana
Abemama
Aranuka
Nonouti
Beru
Nikunau
Tabiteuea
Onotoa
Tamana
Arorae
TUNGARU
Banaba (Ocean I.)
PHOENIX ISLANDS
Kanton
Enderbury I.
Rawaki
McKean I.
Birnie I.
Nikumaroro
Orona
Manra
Teraina
Tabuaeran
Kiritimati
LINE ISLANDS
Equator
Starbuck I.
Malden I.
Vostok I.
Millennium
Flint I.
Kiritimati
London
Banana
Paris
20 km
20 miles
N
POPULATION
under 10 000
LAND HEIGHT
under 100m
600 km
600 miles

WORLD AFFAIRS

Joined UN in 1999

ACP | Comm | PC | PIF | ADB

Kiribati has little international significance because of its tiny size and remote location, but is able to make its voice heard regionally through the Pacific Islands Forum. In 1986, Kiribati was a signatory to a deal between the USA and a number of Pacific Island states that resulted in the USA paying $60 million in return for access to Pacific fishing grounds. In the Cold War era Kiribati played the USSR off against the USA, extracting a high price for fishing leases, which allowed boats to spy on US nuclear testing on the neighboring Kwajalein atoll in the Marshall Islands.

AID

Recipient

US$21m (receipts)

Up 24% in 1999

Aid is mostly offered for small projects to improve infrastructure. New Zealand is the most generous donor, granting US$1.7 million in 2000.

DEFENSE

No compulsory military service

Kiribati has no defense budget

Not applicable

Australia and New Zealand provide *de facto* protection, with regular antisubmarine patrols.

ECONOMICS

Inflation 3.9% p.a. (1990–1999)

US$81m

1.5282–1.7997 Australian dollars

SCORE CARD

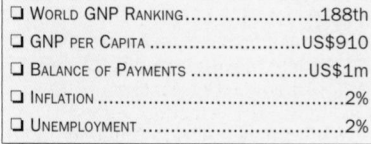

❑ WORLD GNP RANKING	188th
❑ GNP PER CAPITA	US$910
❑ BALANCE OF PAYMENTS	US$1m
❑ INFLATION	2%
❑ UNEMPLOYMENT	2%

STRENGTHS

Subsistence economy; little need to import food. Coconuts provide some export income: the EU is the biggest market. Fisheries have limited potential. Upgraded port facilities at Betio.

WEAKNESSES

Lack of resources since Banaba's phosphate deposits ran out. Isolation, and large distances between islands. Heavy dependence on international aid. Almost no economic potential.

EXPORTS

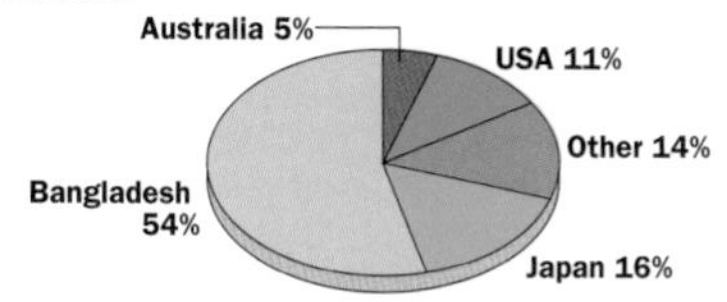
Australia 5%
USA 11%
Other 14%
Bangladesh 54%
Japan 16%

IMPORTS

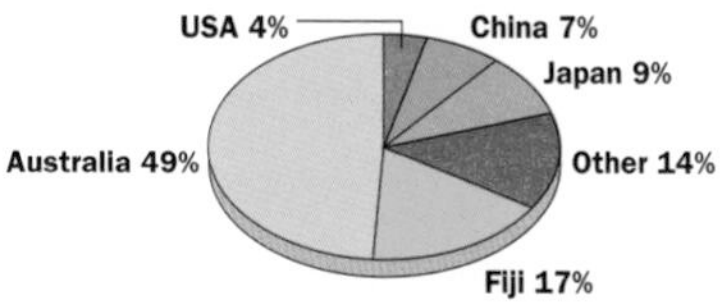
USA 4%
China 7%
Japan 9%
Australia 49%
Other 14%
Fiji 17%

RESOURCES

Electric power 2000 kw

23,052 tonnes

Not an oil producer

12,000 pigs, 365,000 chickens

None

Phosphate deposits on Banaba ran out in 1980. All energy supplies have to be imported. An underwater agriculture scheme is under development.

ENVIRONMENT

Not available

39% (including marine and semi-protected areas)

0.3 tonnes per capita

Rising sea levels cause coastal erosion and ultimately threaten Kiribati's existence. The coral reef, which protects Tarawa from the sea and which holds important inshore fish stocks in the lagoon, is threatened by untreated effluent. Approaches have been made by international – mainly US – companies seeking to dump industrial waste into the lagoons.

MEDIA

TV ownership low

There are no daily newspapers

PUBLISHING AND BROADCAST MEDIA

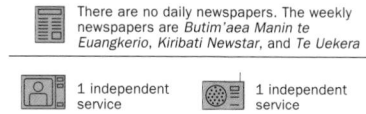

There are no daily newspapers. The weekly newspapers are *Butim'aea Manin te Euangkerio, Kiribati Newstar,* and *Te Uekera*

1 independent service

1 independent service

The independent *Newstar* competes with the state-owned *Te Uekera* and the Protestant Church's paper. Churches also produce monthly newsletters.

CRIME

Death penalty not used

91 prisoners

Crime is minimal

Crime, apart from brawls resulting from drunkenness, is minimal. The islands' judicial system is based on the British model.

EDUCATION

School leaving age: 15

98%

Not available

Education is British-inspired and compulsory from six to 15. The best students go on to university in Fiji.

CHRONOLOGY

The British established the phosphate-producing colony of the Gilbert and Ellice Islands in 1892.

- ❑ **1957** First British nuclear tests take place near Kiritimati.
- ❑ **1979** Independence as two states, Kiribati and Tuvalu.
- ❑ **1981** Kiribati wins damages for phosphate mining from UK.
- ❑ **1986** Kiribati–US fishing deal.
- ❑ **1994** NPP loses election.
- ❑ **1998** Elections confirm Teburoro Tito in power.
- ❑ **1999** National drought emergency.

HEALTH

Welfare state health benefits

1 per 7600 people

Heart diseases, diabetes

Most Gilbertese are healthy, thanks to a home-grown diet and free medical care. Those on Tarawa import tinned food because of a lack of agricultural land, and nutrition is becoming a problem.

SPENDING

GDP/cap. increase

CONSUMPTION AND SPENDING

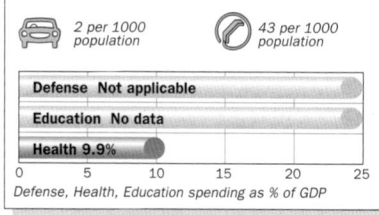

2 per 1000 population

43 per 1000 population

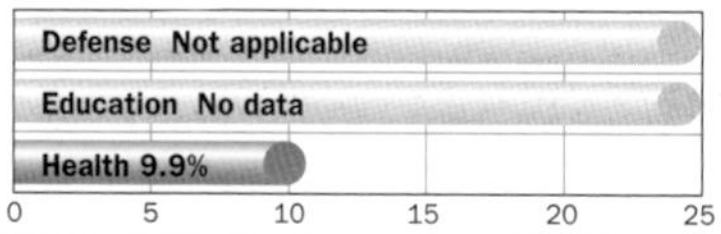
Defense Not applicable
Education No data
Health 9.9%
0
5
10
15
20
25

Defense, Health, Education spending as % of GDP

Life in Kiribati is modest. Most Gilbertese live by subsistence farming and fishing. Civil servants in Bairiki form the wealthiest group. The cost of living in Tarawa is higher than in the outlying islands due to the need to import food, although fish is abundant and cheap everywhere.

WORLD RANKING

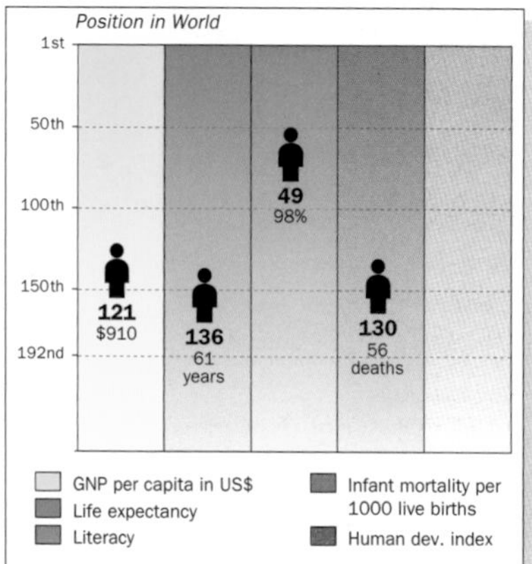
Position in World
1st
50th
100th
150th
192nd
121
$910
136
61 years
49
98%
130
56 deaths
GNP per capita in US$
Life expectancy
Literacy
Infant mortality per 1000 live births
Human dev. index

K

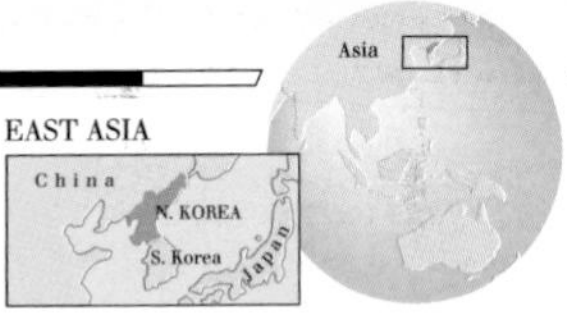
Asia
EAST ASIA
China
N. KOREA
S. Korea
Japan

NORTH KOREA

OFFICIAL NAME: Democratic People's Republic of Korea **CAPITAL:** Pyongyang
POPULATION: 24 million **CURRENCY:** North Korean won **OFFICIAL LANGUAGE:** Korean

1948 | 1953 | Sept 9 | DRK | +9 | +850 | .kp

Comprising the northern half of the Korean peninsula, North Korea is separated from the US-dominated South by an armistice line straddling the 38th parallel. Much of the country is mountainous; the Chaeryong and Pyongyang plains in the southwest are the most fertile regions. An independent communist republic from 1948, it remains largely isolated. With its economy starved of capital, it now faces a food crisis requiring large-scale international assistance.

CLIMATE

Continental

WEATHER CHART

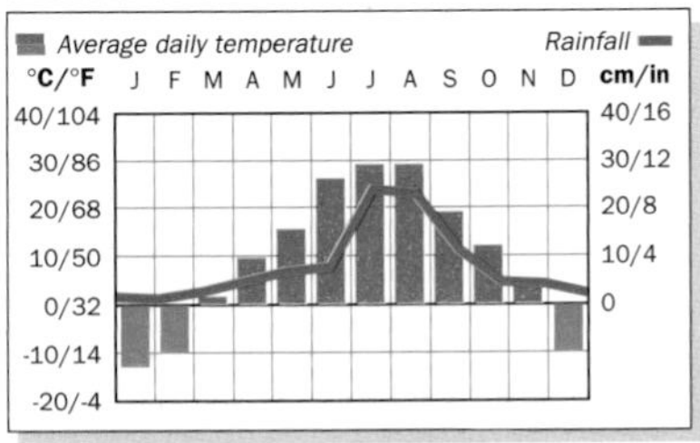
Average daily temperature
Rainfall
°C/°F
J F M A M J J A S O N D
cm/in
40/104
30/86
20/68
10/50
0/32
-10/14
-20/-4
40/16
30/12
20/8
10/4
0

North Korea has a typically continental climate. Winters in the north can be extreme.

TRANSPORTATION

Drive on right

Sunan, Pyongyang

182 ships 631,000 grt

THE TRANSPORTATION NETWORK

1997 km (1241 miles)

524 km (326 miles)

5214 km (3240 miles)

2253 km (1400 miles)

The railroad network built by the occupying Japanese is heavily relied on. Highways are open only to very limited, officially approved traffic. Improving relations with South Korea in 2000 led to plans to construct cross-border links.

TOURISM

Visitors : Population 1:185

130,000 visitors

Up 2% 1995–1998

MAIN TOURIST ARRIVALS

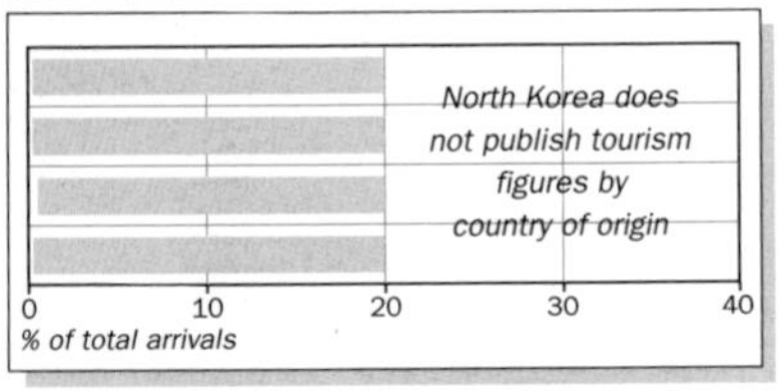
North Korea does not publish tourism figures by country of origin
0
10
20
30
40
% of total arrivals

Economic need has forced limited tourism. South Korean firms have developed resorts such as Mt. Kumgang.

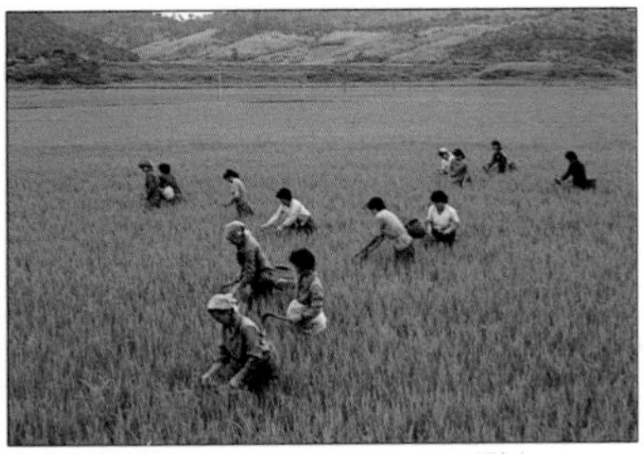

Rice paddy-field. The hot, wet summers are ideal for rice growing. Most farms are run as cooperatives.

PEOPLE

Pop. density medium

Korean, Chinese

199/km² (516/mi²)

THE URBAN/RURAL POPULATION SPLIT

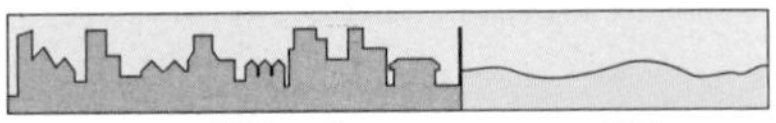
60%
40%

ETHNIC MAKEUP

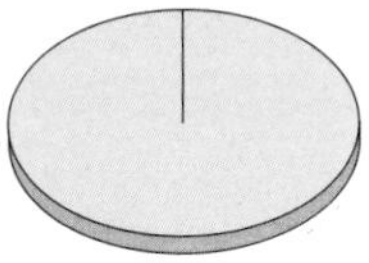
Korean 100%

The Korean peninsula is unusual in having been inhabited by a single ethnic group for the last 2000 years. There is a tiny Chinese minority in North Korea.

The religions practiced under strict state control are Buddhism, Christianity, and Chondogyo, a combination of Confucianism, Buddhism, and Christianity which is peculiar to Korea.

North Koreans live highly regulated lives. Divorce is nonexistent and extramarital sex highly frowned upon. Women form more than 50% of the workforce, but are also expected to run the home; it is not uncommon for them to rise at 4 a.m., and end their working day at 7 p.m. From an early age, children are looked after by an extensive system of state-run crèches. The privileged lifestyle of the political elite – some 200,000 in number – is rumored to be a source of popular resentment.

POLITICS

No multiparty elections

1998/2003

Eternal President Kim Il Sung

AT THE LAST ELECTION

Supreme People's Assembly 687 seats

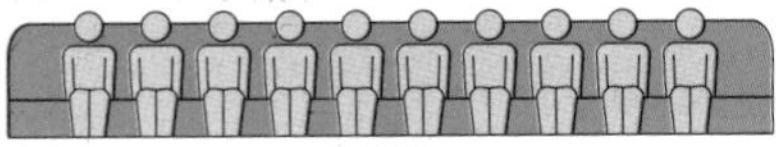
100%
DFRF

DFRF = Democratic Front for the Reunification of the Fatherland
The Democratic Front for the Reunification of the Fatherland (led by the Korean Workers' Party – **KWP**) was the sole party permitted to take part in the 1998 elections.

The three million-strong KWP is the only legal party; membership is essential for individual advancement. Kim Il Sung, the subject of a lavish personality cult, died in 1994 after almost 50 years as leader. Since then the key question has been how his son and chosen successor, Kim Jong Il, will handle the leadership. He lacks his father's authority, and has yet to seal the succession; in 1998 Kim Il Sung, by now four years dead, was declared "Eternal President."

WORLD AFFAIRS

Joined UN in 1991

NAM

The collapse of Soviet communism in 1991 destroyed North Korea's framework of foreign relations, leaving China as its closest ally. A nuclear missile program hampered moves to thaw relations with the West, and is still a source of concern. A breakthrough in North–South relations came in 2000, with their leaders' first direct encounter since the 1953 armistice. Several countries have since established diplomatic links, and many US trade sanctions have been lifted. In 2001 Kim Jong Il paid a landmark visit to Russia.

AID

Recipient

$201m (receipts)

Up 84% in 1999

Rice harvests were badly damaged by alternate drought and flood in the mid-1990s, precipitating a famine. A massive international aid effort has been required to stave off starvation.

DEFENSE

Compulsory military service

$2.1bn

Up 1% in 1999

North Korea is thought to have manufactured nuclear weapons prior to the 1994 freeze on its nuclear program. It developed, and exports, missiles.

K

NORTH KOREA

Total Land Area : 120 410 sq. km (46 490 sq. miles)

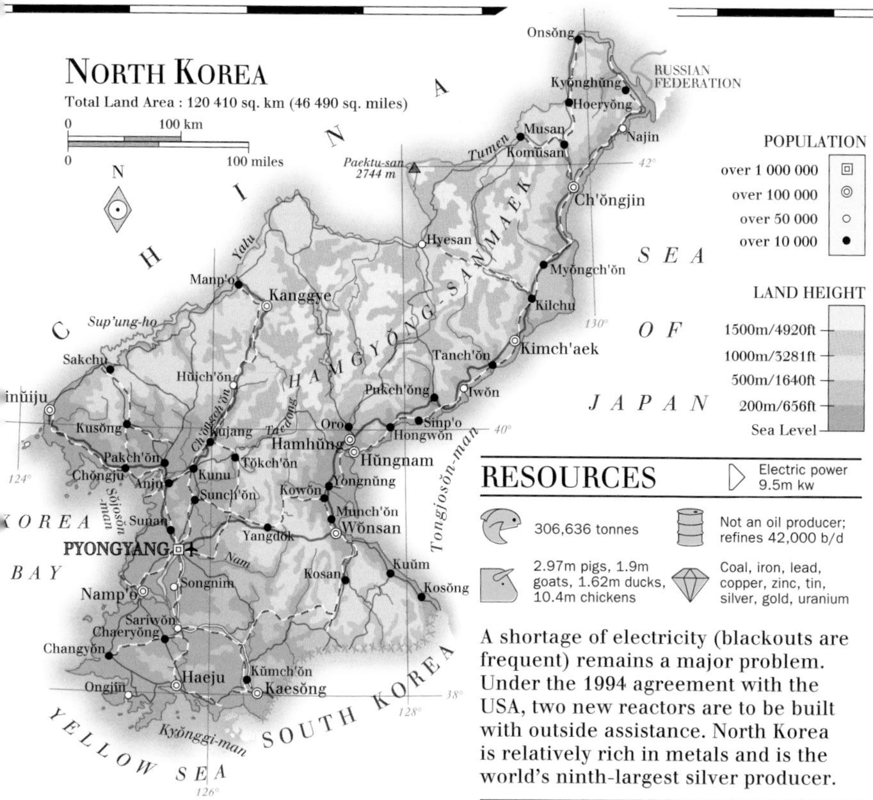
0
100 km
0
100 miles
N
C H I N A
RUSSIAN FEDERATION
Onsŏng
Kyŏnghŭng
Hoeryŏng
Musan
Komusan
Tumen
Najin
Paektu-san 2744 m
Ch'ŏngjin
Hyesan
Yalu
Manp'o
Kanggye
Myŏngch'ŏn
Kilchu
Kimch'aek
Tanch'ŏn
Sup'ung-ho
Sakchu
Hŭich'ŏn
HAMGYŎNG-SANMAEK
Pukch'ŏng
Iwŏn
Sinŭiju
Kusŏng
Kujang
Oro
Hamhŭng
Sinp'o
Hongwŏn
Hŭngnam
Pakch'ŏn
Chŏngju
Anju
Kunu
Tŏkch'ŏn
Sunch'ŏn
Kowŏn
Yŏngnŭng
Munch'ŏn
Wŏnsan
KOREA BAY
Sunan
PYONGYANG
Yangdŏk
Tongjosŏn-man
Namp'o
Songnim
Kosan
Kŭum
Kosŏng
Sariwŏn
Chaeryŏng
Changyŏn
Haeju
Kŭmch'ŏn
Kaesŏng
Ongjin
Kyŏnggi-man
SOUTH KOREA
YELLOW SEA
SEA OF JAPAN
POPULATION
over 1 000 000
over 100 000
over 50 000
over 10 000
LAND HEIGHT
1500m/4920ft
1000m/3281ft
500m/1640ft
200m/656ft
Sea Level

CHRONOLOGY

Annexed by Japan in 1910, the peninsula was divided in 1945 at the 38th parallel; North Korea was made an independent state in 1948.

- ❑ **1950–1953** Korean War.
- ❑ **1994** Withdrawal from IAEA. Kim Il Sung dies; declared "Eternal President" four years later.
- ❑ **1997** Threat of famine worsens. Kim Jong Il becomes party leader.
- ❑ **2000** Historic North–South summit.

RESOURCES

Electric power 9.5m kw

306,636 tonnes

Not an oil producer; refines 42,000 b/d

2.97m pigs, 1.9m goats, 1.62m ducks, 10.4m chickens

Coal, iron, lead, copper, zinc, tin, silver, gold, uranium

A shortage of electricity (blackouts are frequent) remains a major problem. Under the 1994 agreement with the USA, two new reactors are to be built with outside assistance. North Korea is relatively rich in metals and is the world's ninth-largest silver producer.

EDUCATION

School leaving age: 15

95%

390,000 students

English is compulsory as a second language at the age of 14. Kim Il Sung, Pyongyang, is the only university.

HEALTH

Welfare state health benefits

1 per 370 people

Heart disease, cancers, digestive diseases

Health care is free. Reasonable life expectancy is now threatened by malnutrition and outright starvation.

K

ECONOMICS

Not available

$20bn

2.2 won

SCORE CARD

- ❑ WORLD GNP RANKING..........................64th
- ❑ GNP PER CAPITA $1390
- ❑ BALANCE OF PAYMENTS ....*Closed economy;*
- ❑ INFLATION ....*does not publish*
- ❑ UNEMPLOYMENT ....*any figures*

STRENGTHS

Other than minerals, strengths are now few.

WEAKNESSES

GNP has declined steadily since 1990. The acute shortage of foreign capital and technology has been catastrophic.

EXPORTS

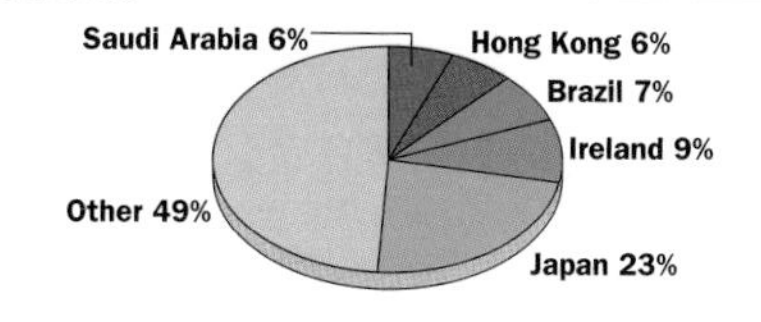
Saudi Arabia 6%
Hong Kong 6%
Brazil 7%
Ireland 9%
Other 49%
Japan 23%

IMPORTS

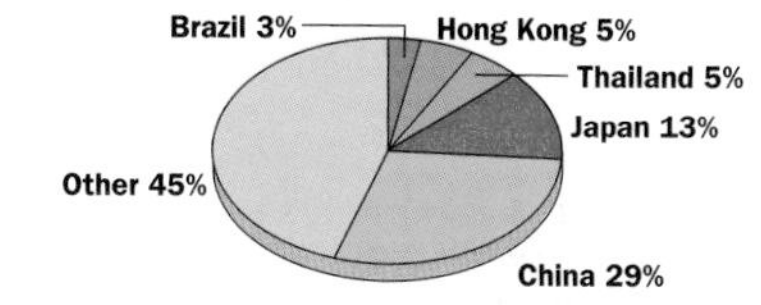
Brazil 3%
Hong Kong 5%
Thailand 5%
Japan 13%
Other 45%
China 29%

ENVIRONMENT

Not available

3% (0.1% partially protected)

11.4 tonnes per capita

Excessive use of fertilizers and unchecked pollution from heavy industry are the major problems.

MEDIA

TV ownership medium

Daily newspaper circulation 199 per 1000 people

PUBLISHING AND BROADCAST MEDIA

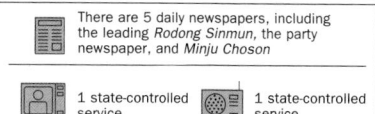

There are 5 daily newspapers, including the leading *Rodong Sinmun*, the party newspaper, and *Minju Choson*

1 state-controlled service

1 state-controlled service

TV consists mostly of musical shows praising Kim Il Sung and Kim Jong Il, and anti-American tirades directed against the Korean War.

CRIME

Death penalty used

North Korea does not publish prison figures

Low level of violent street crime

At an individual level, crime is officially said to hardly exist. The criminal code is weighted to protect the state against "subversion," rather than the rights of the individual. North Korea has a very poor human rights record and there is a *gulag* of more than 100,000 "subversives," where whole families are sent along with those accused, and where torture is routine.

SPENDING

GDP/cap. decrease

CONSUMPTION AND SPENDING

No data

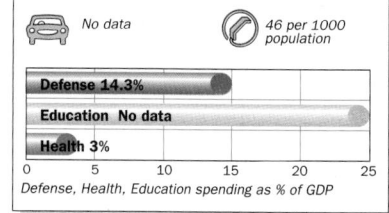

46 per 1000 population

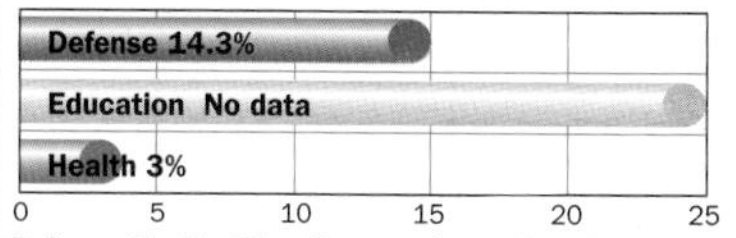
Defense 14.3%
Education No data
Health 3%
0
5
10
15
20
25

Defense, Health, Education spending as % of GDP

An elite within the KWP lives well, with access to specialist shops and consumer goods such as VCRs. Ownership of telephones, private cars, and, in many areas, bicycles, is forbidden.

WORLD RANKING

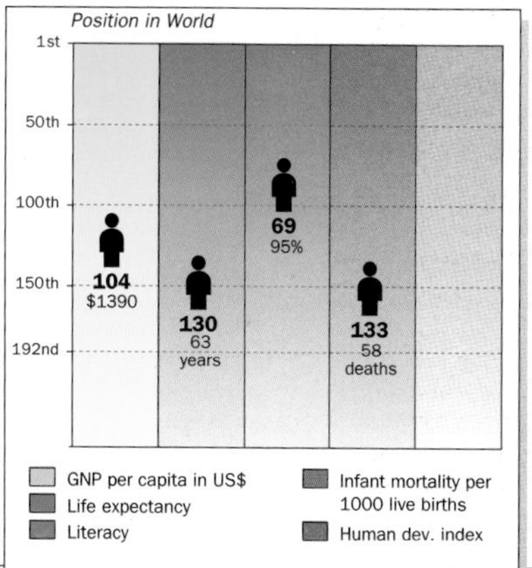
Position in World
1st
50th
100th
150th
192nd
104
$1390
130
63
years
69
95%
133
58
deaths
GNP per capita in US$
Life expectancy
Literacy
Infant mortality per 1000 live births
Human dev. index

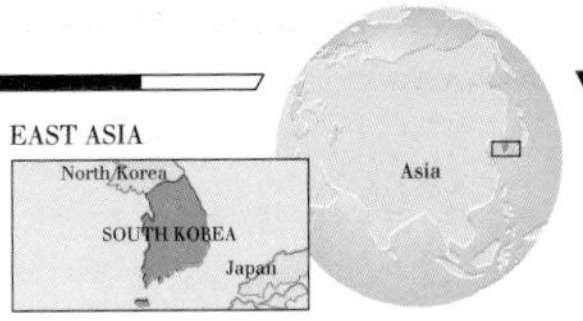
EAST ASIA
North Korea
SOUTH KOREA
Japan
Asia

SOUTH KOREA

OFFICIAL NAME: Republic of Korea **CAPITAL:** Seoul
POPULATION: 46.8 million **CURRENCY:** South Korean won **OFFICIAL LANGUAGE:** Korean

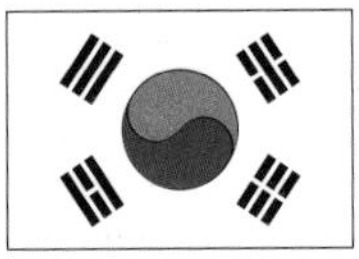

1948
1953
Aug 15
ROK
+9
+82
.kr

SOUTH KOREA OCCUPIES the southern half of the Korean peninsula in East Asia. Over 80% of its terrain is mountainous and two-thirds is forested. Rice is the major agricultural product, grown by over 85% of South Korea's three million farmers. The whole peninsula was annexed by Japan from 1910 to 1945. The split between South Korea and the communist North originated with the arrival of rival US and Soviet armies in 1945. Although the two states have discussed reunification, the legacy of hostility arising from the 1950–1953 Korean War remains a major obstacle.

CLIMATE

Continental

WEATHER CHART

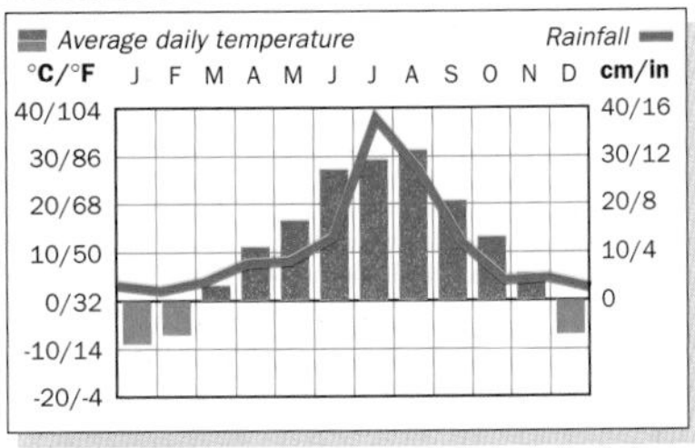
Average daily temperature
Rainfall
°C/°F
J F M A M J J A S O N D
cm/in
40/104
30/86
20/68
10/50
0/32
-10/14
-20/-4
40/16
30/12
20/8
10/4
0

South Korea has four distinct seasons. Winters are dry and can be bitterly cold. Summers are hot and humid, especially during July and August.

TRANSPORTATION

Drive on right

Kimpo International, Seoul 33.37m passengers

2381 ships 5.7m grt

THE TRANSPORTATION NETWORK

64,808 km (40,270 miles)

1996 km (1240 miles)

3098 km (1925 miles)

1609 km (1000 miles)

South Korea has an efficient and highly integrated public transportation system. A toll-based nationwide motor expressway network joins most major urban centers. Air travel has expanded rapidly as a convenient way to traverse the mountainous interior. Korean Air competes with Asiana. Buses, trains, boats, and planes are integrated in one timetable, and have a reputation for punctuality. A high-speed rail link will connect Seoul and Pusan. The collapse of a major road bridge in Seoul in 1994 raised questions about the quality of some of the constructions.

Improving relations with North Korea in 2000 produced proposals for the construction of cross-border rail and road links and for what would be the first connecting flights since 1953, but these have been slow to materialize.

TOURISM

Visitors : Population 1:8.8

5.3m visitors

Up 14% in 2000

MAIN TOURIST ARRIVALS

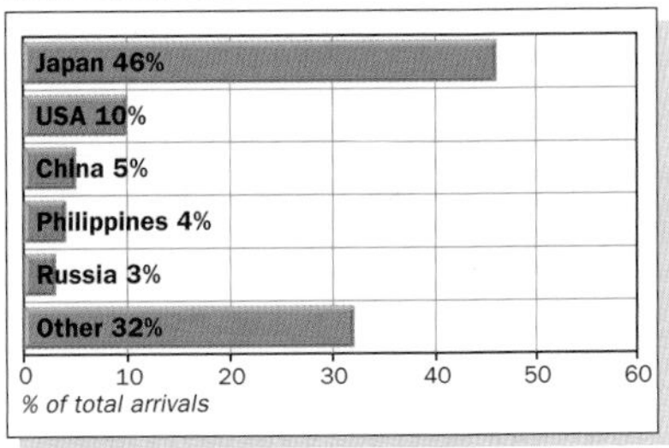
Japan 46%
USA 10%
China 5%
Philippines 4%
Russia 3%
Other 32%
0 10 20 30 40 50 60
% of total arrivals

Overseas tourism to South Korea has increased ten-fold since 1969. Most visitors are Japanese, who come for the golf and Seoul's nightlife; Cheju-do is a favored honeymoon destination. Whereas visiting relations of US army personnel once made up 13% of all tourists, today Los Angeles-based Korean–Americans make up the greatest proportion of US visitors. However, despite the publicity generated by the 1988 Olympics, and the decision to make 1994 "Visit Korea Year," South Korea is still not seen in the West as a prime tourist destination.

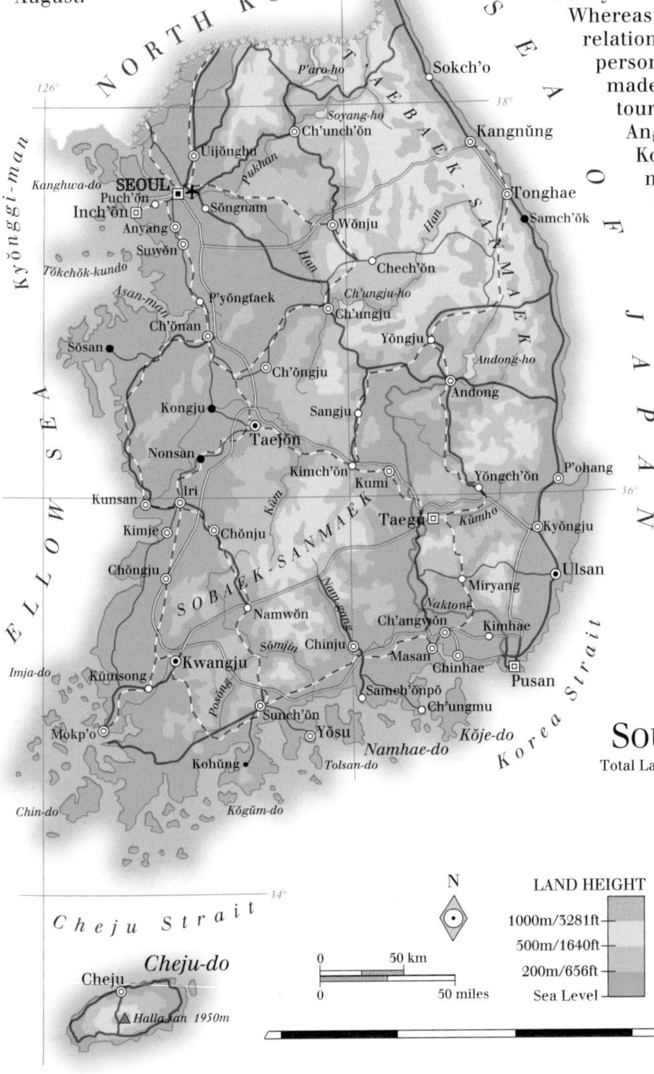
NORTH KOREA
SEA OF JAPAN
YELLOW SEA
Kyŏnggi-man
Cheju Strait
Korea Strait
TAEBAEK-SANMAEK
SOBAEK-SANMAEK
SEOUL
Inch'ŏn
Puch'ŏn
Anyang
Suwŏn
Ŭijŏngbu
Sŏngnam
Ch'unch'ŏn
Sokch'o
Kangnŭng
Tonghae
Samch'ŏk
Wŏnju
Chech'ŏn
Ch'ungju
P'yŏngtaek
Ch'ŏnan
Sŏsan
Ch'ŏngju
Yŏngju
Andong
Kongju
Taejŏn
Sangju
Nonsan
Kimch'ŏn
Kumi
Kunsan
Iri
Kimje
Chŏnju
Taegu
Yŏngch'ŏn
P'ohang
Kyŏngju
Ulsan
Chŏngju
Miryang
Namwŏn
Ch'angwŏn
Kimhae
Chinju
Masan
Chinhae
Pusan
Kwangju
Kŭmsong
Mokp'o
Sunch'ŏn
Samch'ŏnpŏ
Ch'ungmu
Yŏsu
Kohŭng
Kŏje-do
Namhae-do
Tolsan-do
Kŏgŭm-do
Chin-do
Hŭksan-kundo
Imja-do
Kanghwa-do
Tŏkchŏk-kundo
Asan-man
Cheju
Cheju-do
Halla-san 1950m
P'aro-ho
Soyang-ho
Ch'ungju-ho
Andong-ho
Han
Pukhan
Kŭm
Naktong
Kŭmho
Nam-gang
Sŏmjin
Posŏng
126°
128°
38°
36°
34°
N
0 50 km
0 50 miles

SOUTH KOREA

Total Land Area : 98 730 sq. km (38 120 sq. miles)

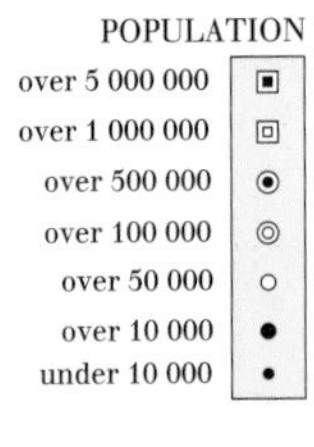
POPULATION
over 5 000 000
over 1 000 000
over 500 000
over 100 000
over 50 000
over 10 000
under 10 000
LAND HEIGHT
1000m/3281ft
500m/1640ft
200m/656ft
Sea Level

PEOPLE

Population density high

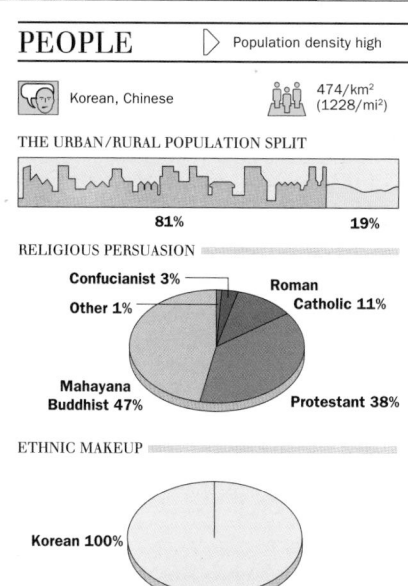

Korean, Chinese

474/km² (1228/mi²)

THE URBAN/RURAL POPULATION SPLIT

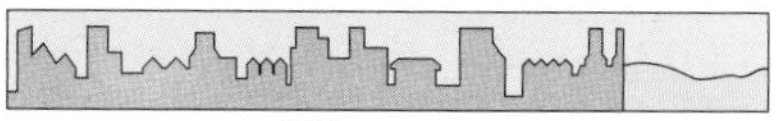
81%
19%

RELIGIOUS PERSUASION

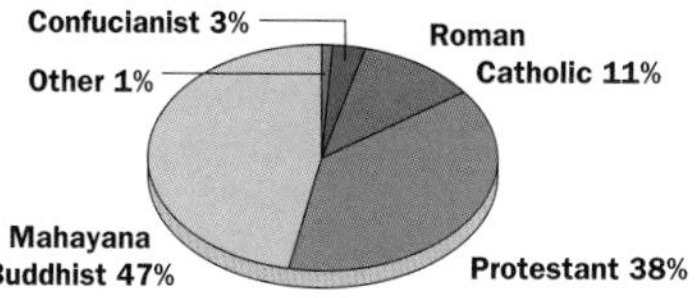
Confucianist 3%
Other 1%
Roman Catholic 11%
Mahayana Buddhist 47%
Protestant 38%

ETHNIC MAKEUP

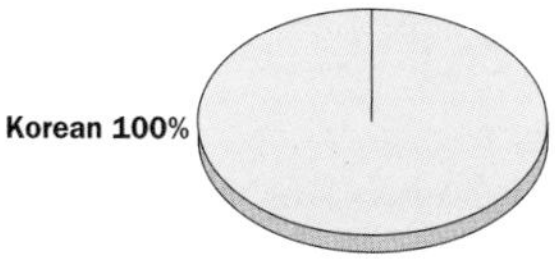
Korean 100%

The Korean peninsula is unusual in having been inhabited by one ethnic group for the last 2000 years. Family life is a central and clearly defined part of Korean society. Most Koreans can trace their ancestry back thousands of years. This is significant, as those of the same surname group (rather than the same surname – 60% of Koreans are called Lee, Kim or Pak) may not marry. A tiny minority practice Chundo Kyo, a religion peculiar to Korea combining elements of Shamanism, Buddhism, and Christianity. Pressure on housing has led to an increase in nuclear families and fewer traditional households. Women play a traditional role in society: it is still not respectable for those who are married to have a job.

One result of economic growth has been an increase in illegal immigrants from the poorer Asian countries, who take menial jobs that Koreans now refuse to do.

POPULATION AGE BREAKDOWN

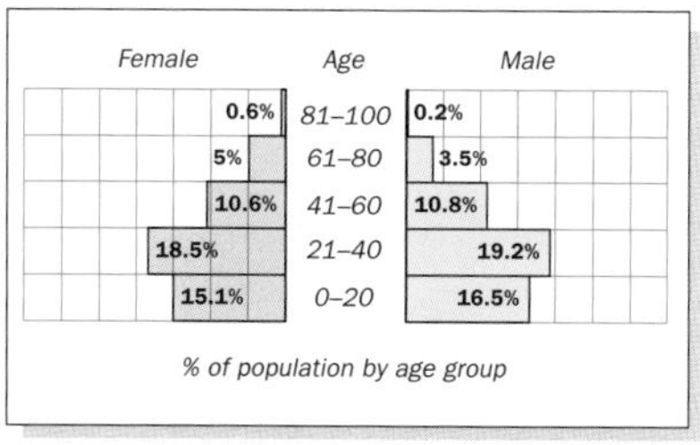
Female
Age
Male
0.6%
81–100
0.2%
5%
61–80
3.5%
10.6%
41–60
10.8%
18.5%
21–40
19.2%
15.1%
0–20
16.5%
% of population by age group

POLITICS

Multiparty elections

2000/2004

President Kim Dae Jung

AT THE LAST ELECTION

National Assembly 273 seats

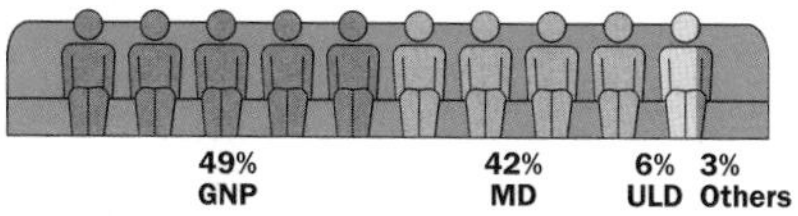
49% GNP
42% MD
6% ULD
3% Others

GNP = Grand National Party **MD** = Millennium Democratic Party **ULD** = United Liberal Democrats

Officially a democracy since its inception, in practice South Korea was ruled by military dictators until 1987.

Main Political Issues

The economy

South Korea's economy, once one of the most impressive in the world, was severely shaken by the regional crisis of late 1997. Severe financial austerity and retrenchment failed to prevent large-scale bankruptcies in 2000.

Relations with North Korea

The sudden flowering of North–South relations in 2000 soon lost popularity. Expensive cross-border projects, and promises of aid for the impoverished North, raised fears of the mounting cost for the embattled southern economy.

Profile

South Korea's politics changed radically in 1987 with the introduction of direct presidential elections, a parliament with enhanced powers, and a free press.

In 1993, the first nonmilitary leader in 30 years, Kim Young Sam, became president. He launched a popular anti-corruption campaign, targeting former presidents Chun Doo Hwan and Roh Tae Woo. Kim's ruling New Korea Party (NKP) (formerly the Democratic Liberal Party – DLP) was returned to power with a reduced majority in 1996, but the economic crisis of 1997 saw the resignation of the cabinet amid a steel scandal. Veteran opposition leader Kim Dae Jung was elected president later that year in the first peaceful transfer of power to an opposition politician in South Korea's history. Supporters of the new president gained ground in legislative elections in 2000, but political instability continued, with three successive prime ministers serving in that year alone.

President Kim Dae Jung. *A veteran activist, he has won the Nobel Peace Prize.*

Lee Han Dong, *the "lion" of the conservatives and premier since 2000.*

WORLD AFFAIRS

Joined UN in 1991

APEC | CP | IAEA | OECD | WTO

Since the birth of South Korea, relations with North Korea have been the major concern of foreign policy. A historic summit meeting in 2000 in Pyongyang, North Korea, opened a new phase in relations, and cross-border diplomatic and economic cooperation momentarily flourished. However, although the ultimate goal of both Koreas remains reunification, doubts have been raised about the social and economic costs of union. On top of this, military tensions persist, and a large detachment of US troops remains on the border. Relations with China, the closest ally of North Korea, have improved. Japan is also a major trading partner, although South Koreans harbor resentment over the 1910–1945 Japanese annexation.

AID

Donor

$50m (donations)

Down 69% in 1998

Once a massive recipient of US aid, and then of Japanese war reparations, South Korea emerged in the 1970s and 1980s as a major aid donor. However, the economic crisis which hit South Korea in 1997–1998 forced it to seek international financial assistance to salvage key sectors of its threatened economy.

CHRONOLOGY

The Yi dynasty, founded in Seoul in 1392, ruled the kingdom of Korea until 1910. However, Korea became a vassal state of China in 1644.

- **1860** Korea reacts to French and British occupation of Peking by preventing Western influence; becomes the "Hermit Kingdom."
- **1904–1905** Russo-Japanese War. Japan conquers Korea.
- **1910** Japan annexes Korea.
- **1919** Independence protests violently suppressed.
- **1945** US and Soviet armies arrive. Korea split at 38°N. South comes under de facto US rule.
- **1948** Republic of South Korea created; Syngman Rhee becomes president at head of an increasingly authoritarian regime.
- **1950** Hostilities between North and South, each aspiring to rule a united Korea. North invades, sparking Korean War. USA, with UN backing, enters on South's side; China unofficially assists North. In 1951 fighting stabilizes near 38th parallel.
- **1953** Armistice; *de facto* border at cease-fire line, close to the 38th parallel.

➪

K

CHRONOLOGY *continued*

- **1960** Syngman Rhee resigns in face of popular revolt.
- **1961** Military coup leads to authoritarian junta led by Park Chung Hee.
- **1963** Pressure for civilian government. Park reelected as president (also in 1967 and 1971). Strong manufacturing base and exports drive massive economic development program.
- **1965** Links restored with Japan.
- **1966** 45,000 troops engaged in South Vietnam.
- **1972** Martial law stifles political opposition. New constitution with greater presidential powers.
- **1979** Park assassinated. General Chun Doo Hwan, intelligence chief, leads coup. Kim Young Sam, opposition leader, expelled from parliament.
- **1980** Chun chosen as president. Kim Dae Jung and other opposition leaders arrested.
- **1986** Car exports start.
- **1987** Emergence of prodemocracy movement. Roh Tae Woo, Chun's chosen successor, elected president.
- **1988** Inauguration of Sixth Republic which includes genuine multiparty democracy. Restrictions on foreign travel lifted.
- **1990** Government party and two opposition parties, including Kim Young Sam's, merge to form DLP.
- **1991** South Korea joins UN.
- **1992** Diplomatic links with China established. December, Kim Young Sam elected president.
- **1996** Chun sentenced to death on charges of organizing 1979–1980 overthrow of the civilian government; Roh given a 22½-year prison term. Both sentences were rescinded.
- **1997** Violent protests against new labor laws. Steel scandal brings down government. Economic crisis.
- **1998** Kim Dae Jung president.
- **2000** Historic North–South summit in Pyongyang. Lee Han Dong appointed premier.

Seoul lit up at night. The city is home to more than ten million people – one-quarter of South Korea's population. Seoul means "capital."

DEFENSE

Compulsory military service

$12.09bn

Up 16% in 1999

SOUTH KOREAN ARMED FORCES

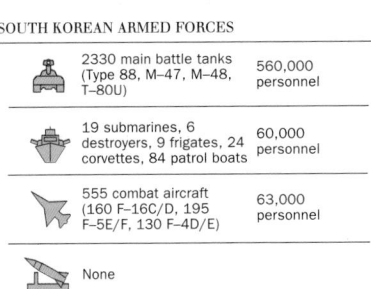

2330 main battle tanks (Type 88, M-47, M-48, T-80U)	560,000 personnel
19 submarines, 6 destroyers, 9 frigates, 24 corvettes, 84 patrol boats	60,000 personnel
555 combat aircraft (160 F-16C/D, 195 F-5E/F, 130 F-4D/E)	63,000 personnel
None	

The main defense concern is the North Korean regime. South Korea has fewer troops, tanks, artillery, and aircraft than the North, but it claims parity through the permanent presence of 35,000 US troops on its territory and its superior technology. The manufacture of missiles capable of striking any target in North Korea was legalized in 2001. However, US computer simulations question South Korea's ability to resist an invasion by the North, since Seoul is only 55km (35 miles) from the demilitarized zone.

In the mid-1990s, the army's standing and role in national politics was sharply downgraded, due to a vigorous government campaign to investigate corruption in the armed forces, especially pertaining to arms procurement, and past military involvement in politics.

ECONOMICS

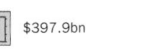

Inflation 5.8% p.a. (1990–1999)

$397.9bn

1132.8–1265.0 South Korean won

SCORE CARD

- World GNP Ranking..........13th
- GNP per Capita..........$8490
- Balance of Payments..........$40.6bn
- Inflation..........0.8%
- Unemployment..........6%

EXPORTS

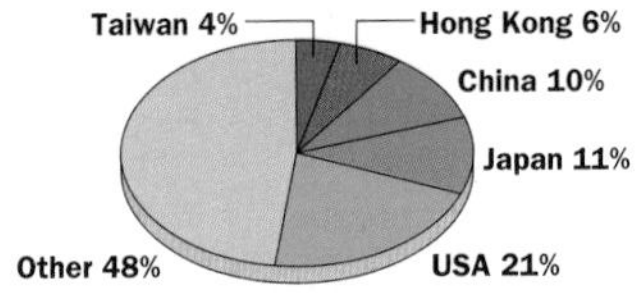
Taiwan 4%
Hong Kong 6%
China 10%
Japan 11%
USA 21%
Other 48%

IMPORTS

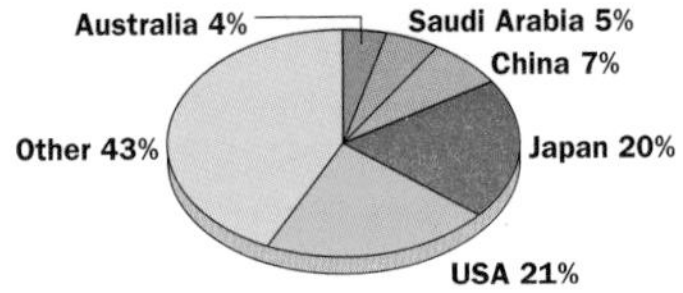
Australia 4%
Saudi Arabia 5%
China 7%
Japan 20%
USA 21%
Other 43%

Strengths

World's most successful shipbuilder, with 45% of the market. Continuing benefits of highly valued yen, making Korean exports more competitive than Japan's. Strong demand from China for Korean goods, particularly cars.

Weaknesses

Financial sector lacking in openness. High level of indebtedness and vulnerability to international capital movements. Increasingly militant workforce since 1997. State sector a burden on the economy. Strong competition from Japan.

Profile

South Korea's economic miracle began with centralized planning. Conglomerates known as *chaebol*, such as Samsung, achieved impressive growth rates in strategic industries such as car manufacturing, shipbuilding, and semiconductors. A well-educated workforce and cheap state credit gave Korea a competitive edge. The government then encouraged foreign investment and an emphasis on smaller industries to maintain growth. In 1996 South Korea joined the OECD. The following year, however, a major financial crisis and the threat of a debt implosion forced the government to turn to the IMF for a huge credit agreement.

ECONOMIC PERFORMANCE INDICATOR

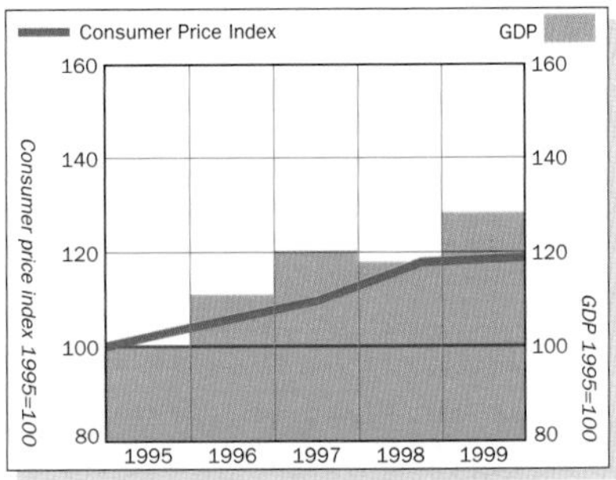
Consumer Price Index
GDP
160
140
120
100
80
Consumer price index 1995=100
GDP 1995=100
1995
1996
1997
1998
1999

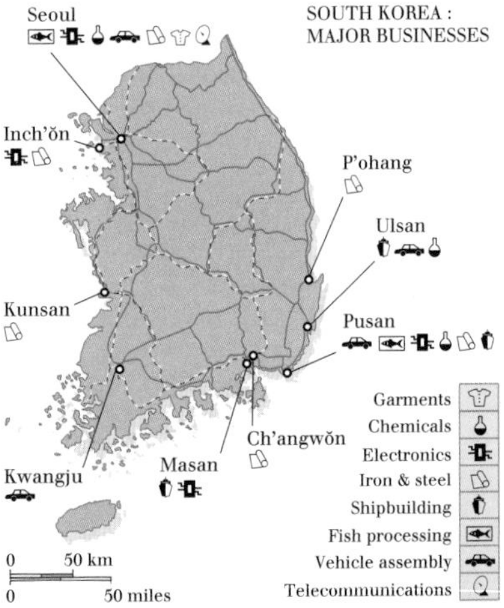
SOUTH KOREA : MAJOR BUSINESSES
Seoul
Inch'ŏn
P'ohang
Ulsan
Kunsan
Pusan
Ch'angwŏn
Masan
Kwangju
Garments
Chemicals
Electronics
Iron & steel
Shipbuilding
Fish processing
Vehicle assembly
Telecommunications
0 50 km
0 50 miles

RESOURCES

Electric power 45.3m kw

2.6m tonnes

Not an oil producer; refines 1.15m b/d

7.86m pigs, 4.26m ducks, 97m chickens

Coal, iron, lead, zinc, tungsten, gold, graphite, fluorite

ELECTRICITY GENERATION

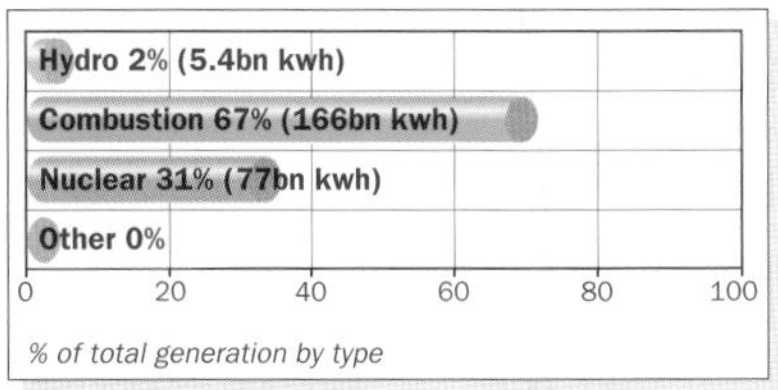
Hydro 2% (5.4bn kwh)
Combustion 67% (166bn kwh)
Nuclear 31% (77bn kwh)
Other 0%
0
20
40
60
80
100
% of total generation by type

South Korea has few natural resources. It has to import all of its oil and has built a series of nuclear reactors for generating electricity. Under the terms of the 1994 agreement between North Korea and the USA, two South Korean reactors are also to be built in North Korea which, in the event of reunification, will be connected to the national grid.

Agriculture remains a highly protected sector. Plans announced in 1994 to open up the rice market led to massive demonstrations in Seoul.

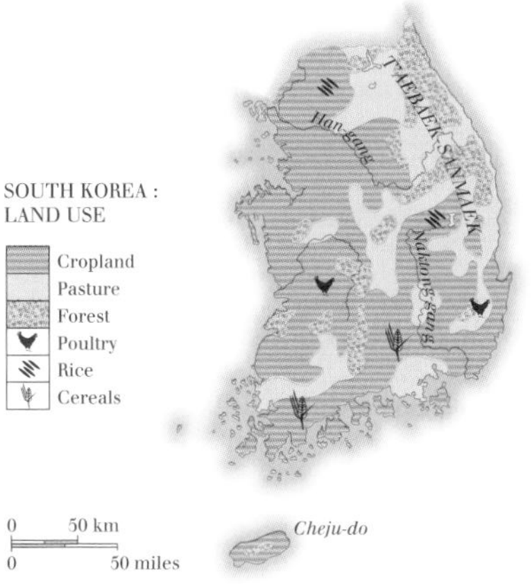
SOUTH KOREA : LAND USE
Cropland
Pasture
Forest
Poultry
Rice
Cereals
Han-gang
TAEBAEK-SANMAEK
Naktong-gang
Cheju-do
0 50 km
0 50 miles

ENVIRONMENT

Sustainability rank: 95th

7%

9.9 tonnes per capita

ENVIRONMENTAL TREATIES

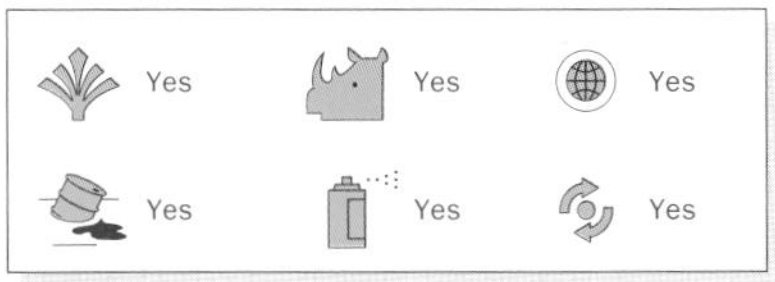
Yes
Yes
Yes
Yes
Yes
Yes

Environmental groups in southeast Asia have expressed concern at South Korea's fast-track nuclear power program. Rapid industrialization has resulted in environmental problems. In September 1998 the government agreed to sign the Kyoto Protocol, which aims to reduce carbon dioxide emissions, indicating its recognition of the problem of air pollution in urban areas, particularly in Seoul. Rivers in rural areas have been polluted by fertilizers and chemicals.

CRIME

Death penalty used

61,019 prisoners

Up 12% 1996–1998

CRIME RATES

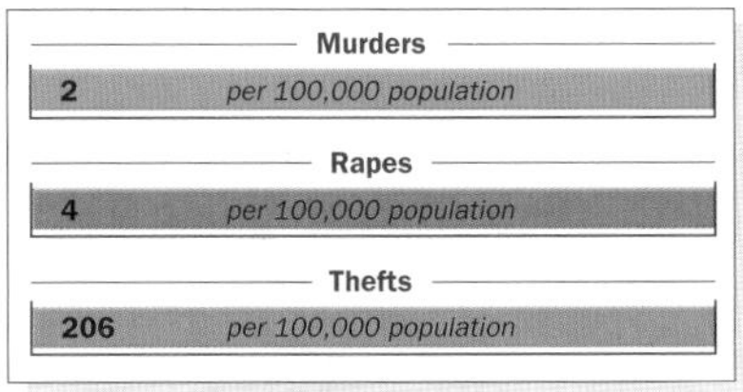
Murders
2 per 100,000 population
Rapes
4 per 100,000 population
Thefts
206 per 100,000 population

The government has begun to treat corruption as a crime. Otherwise, crime rates are relatively low and cases of violent crime uncommon. Since 1987, the internal security forces' operations have been restricted, although left-wing activists are still harassed. Striking workers and student demonstrators are subjected to tear gas and other methods of crowd control.

HEALTH

Welfare state health benefits

1 per 769 people

Cancers, accidents, heart and cerebro-vascular diseases, TB

The health service has improved in line with economic growth. Most hospitals are equipped with modern facilities, and many offer advanced treatments comparable with those in the USA and western Europe. Health indicators such as infant mortality and longevity have improved accordingly.

SPENDING

GDP/cap. increase

CONSUMPTION AND SPENDING

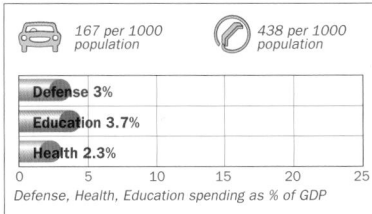

167 per 1000 population

438 per 1000 population

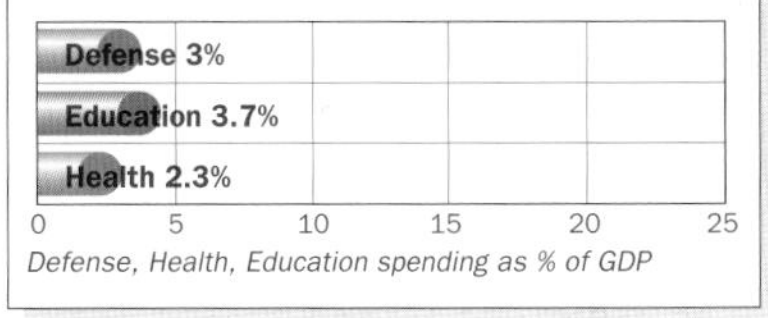
Defense 3%
Education 3.7%
Health 2.3%
0
5
10
15
20
25
Defense, Health, Education spending as % of GDP

Most South Koreans have benefited from economic growth, but since the 1997 recession have been worse off. The Cholla region in the southwest remains the poorest.

MEDIA

TV ownership high

Daily newspaper circulation 394 per 1000 people

PUBLISHING AND BROADCAST MEDIA

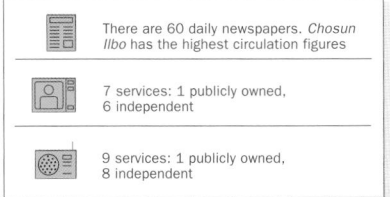

There are 60 daily newspapers. *Chosun Ilbo* has the highest circulation figures

7 services: 1 publicly owned, 6 independent

9 services: 1 publicly owned, 8 independent

South Korea's media have been freed of most restrictions since the advent of full multiparty democracy. However, criticisms of the armed forces are still frowned upon, and journalists tend to avoid altogether the subject of the role of the military in society. Caution also has to be exercised in reporting facts about North Korea. In the past, South Korean journalists who have made favorable mention of the North Korean communist regime have suffered harassment and intimidation.

EDUCATION

School leaving age: 15

98%

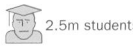

2.5m students

THE EDUCATION SYSTEM

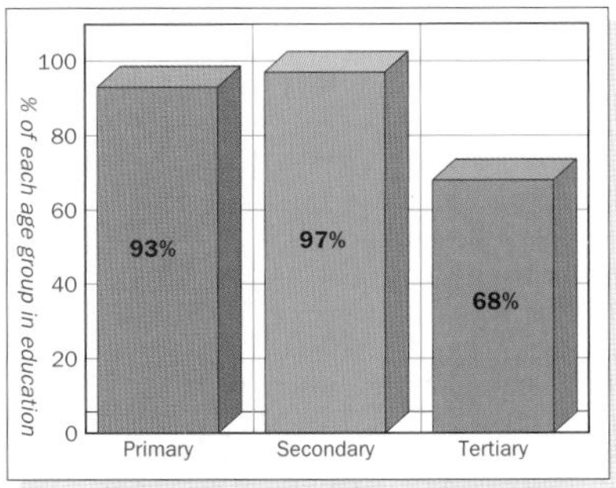
100
80
60
40
20
0
% of each age group in education
93%
97%
68%
Primary
Secondary
Tertiary

South Korea began a concentrated education program in the 1950s, and a well-educated workforce has been the foundation of South Korea's impressive economic growth. Secondary education, which begins at 12 years of age, comprises two three-year cycles, of which one is compulsory. Tertiary enrollment is nearly 70% – one of the highest rates in the world.

WORLD RANKING

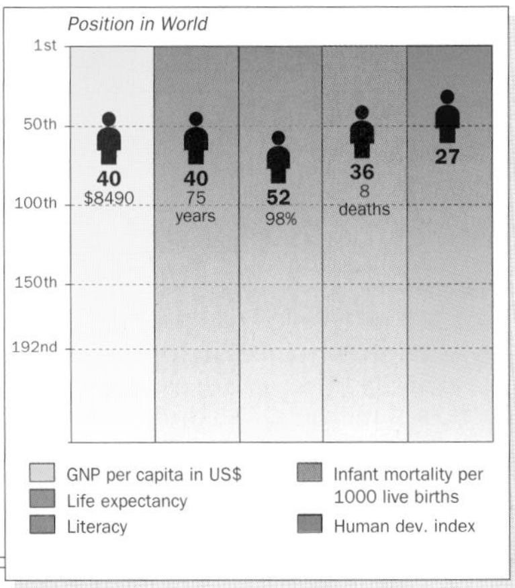
Position in World
1st
50th
100th
150th
192nd
40
$8490
40
75 years
52
98%
36
8 deaths
27
GNP per capita in US$
Life expectancy
Literacy
Infant mortality per 1000 live births
Human dev. index

K

KUWAIT

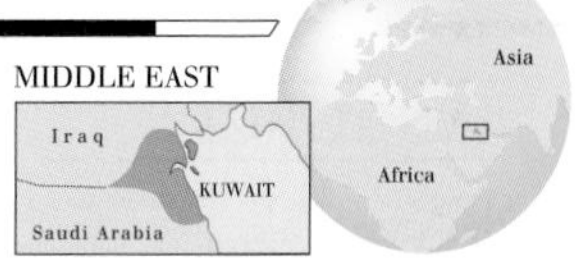
MIDDLE EAST
Iraq
KUWAIT
Saudi Arabia
Asia
Africa

OFFICIAL NAME: State of Kuwait **CAPITAL:** Kuwait City
POPULATION: 2 million **CURRENCY:** Kuwaiti dinar **OFFICIAL LANGUAGE:** Arabic

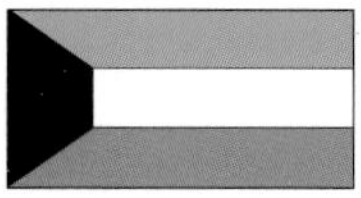

1961 | 1961 | Feb 25 | KWT | +3 | +965 | .kw

Saffar Towers in the business center of Kuwait City. The postwar cost of rebuilding Kuwait's economy is put at $25 billion.

AT THE NORTHWEST EXTREME of the Gulf, Kuwait is dwarfed by its neighbors Iraq, Iran, and Saudi Arabia. The flat, almost featureless landscape conceals huge oil and gas reserves, which put Kuwait among the world's first oil-rich states. In 1990 Iraq invaded, claiming Kuwait as its 19th province. A US-led alliance, under the aegis of the UN, expelled Iraqi forces following a short war in 1991. Since its liberation, Kuwait has built a wall separating its territory from Iraq.

CLIMATE

Hot desert

WEATHER CHART

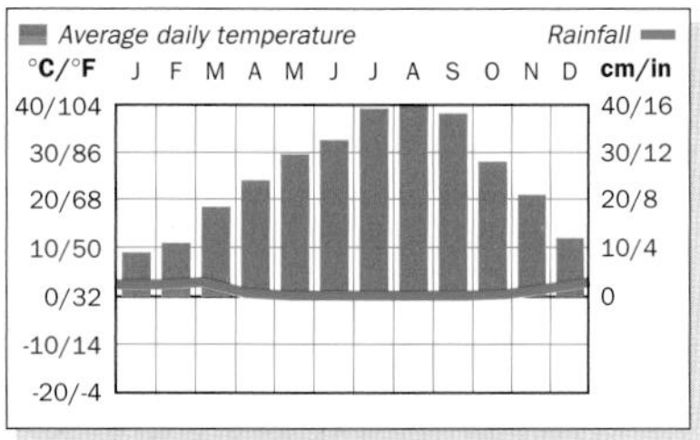
Average daily temperature
Rainfall
°C/°F
J F M A M J J A S O N D
cm/in
40/104
30/86
20/68
10/50
0/32
-10/14
-20/-4
40/16
30/12
20/8
10/4
0

Summer temperatures can soar to over 40°C (104°F), but winters can be cold, with frost at night.

TRANSPORTATION

Drive on right

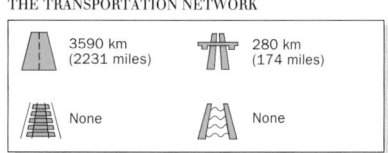

Kuwait International, Kuwait City 3.8m passengers

202 ships 2.5m grt

THE TRANSPORTATION NETWORK

3590 km (2231 miles)

280 km (174 miles)

None

None

Kuwait has a system of radial expressways around the capital and good connecting roads to Saudi Arabia.

TOURISM

Visitors : Population 1:26

77,000 visitors

Up 12% 1995–1998

MAIN TOURIST ARRIVALS

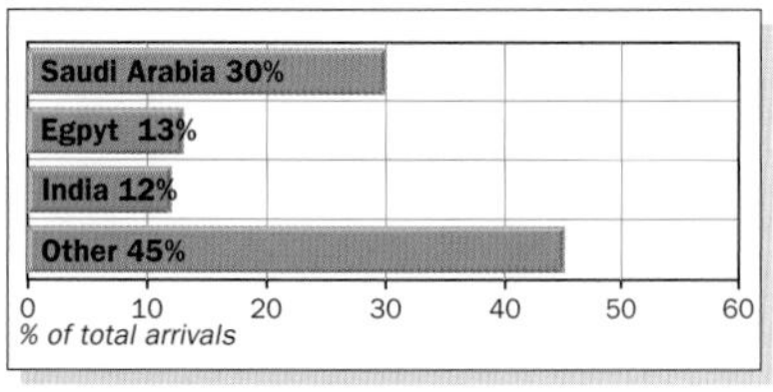
Saudi Arabia 30%
Egypt 13%
India 12%
Other 45%
0
10
20
30
40
50
60
% of total arrivals

Most Western visitors to Kuwait go specifically to see relatives working in the oil industry. The limited tourism from neighboring Arab states, notably Saudi Arabia, has not recovered since the 1990–1991 Gulf War.

PEOPLE

Pop. density medium

Arabic, English

112/km² (291/mi²)

THE URBAN/RURAL POPULATION SPLIT

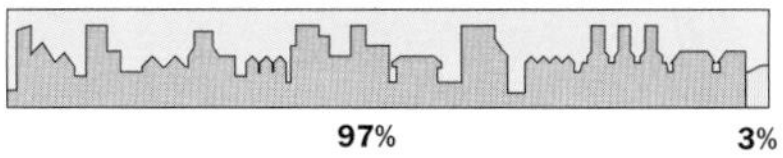
97%
3%

ETHNIC MAKEUP

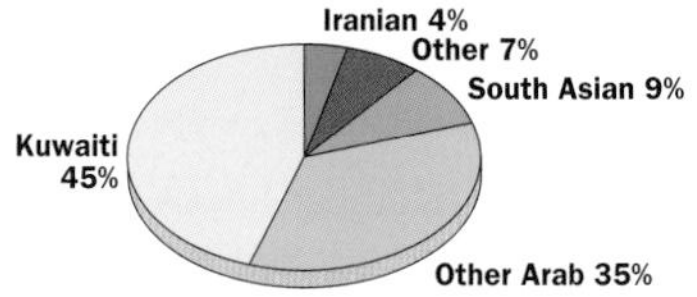
Iranian 4%
Other 7%
South Asian 9%
Kuwaiti 45%
Other Arab 35%

Kuwait is a conservative Sunni Muslim society (27% of the population are Shi'ite). Women have considerable freedom, although the amir's decree providing for female enfranchisement has been repeatedly rejected by the National Assembly.

Kuwait's oil wealth has drawn in thousands of workers from south Asia and other Arab countries. The PLO's support for the Iraqi invasion led to most Palestinians, hitherto more numerous in Kuwait than elsewhere in the Arabian peninsula, being driven out. Now native Kuwaitis are outnumbered by resident foreign nationals.

POLITICS

No multiparty elections

1999/2003

Amir Shaikh Jabir al-Ahmad al-Jabir al-Sabah

AT THE LAST ELECTION

National Assembly 50 seats

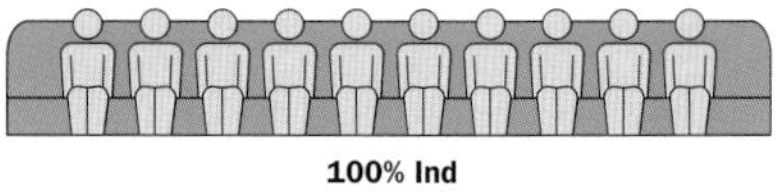
100% Ind

The electorate comprises civilian men over 21 years of age whose families have been resident in Kuwait since before 1921. Elections on July 3, 1999, were contested by independents. The 50 seats were split evenly between Islamists, liberals, and government supporters.

In 1992 Amir Shaikh Jabir restored the National Assembly. There was then a government of "national unity" until 1999, when elections strengthened the amir's Islamist and liberal opponents. The Council of Ministers resigned in 2001 in the face of Assembly criticism. In the new cabinet the ruling al-Sabah family still holds the top posts.

KUWAIT

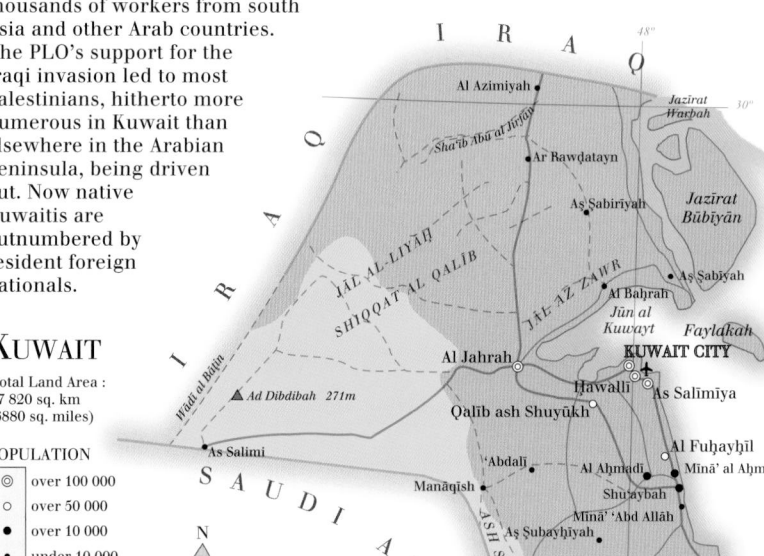

Total Land Area : 17 820 sq. km (6880 sq. miles)

POPULATION

- ◎ over 100 000
- ○ over 50 000
- ● over 10 000
- • under 10 000

LAND HEIGHT

- 200m/656ft
- Sea Level

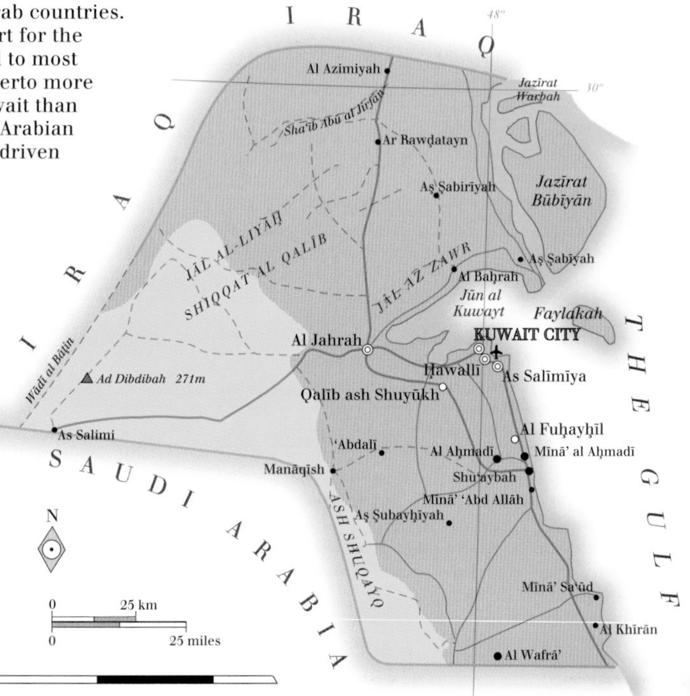
IRAQ
IRAQ
Al Azimiyah
Jazirat Warbah
Sha'ib Abu al Jirfan
Ar Rawdatayn
As Sabiriyah
Jazirat Būbiyān
JĀL AL-LIYĀH
SHIQQAT AL QALĪB
JĀL AZ ZAWR
As Sabiyah
Al Bahrah
Jūn al Kuwayt
Faylakah
Al Jahrah
KUWAIT CITY
Hawallī
As Salimiya
Wādī al Bāṭin
Ad Dibdibah 271m
Qalīb ash Shuyūkh
Al Fuḥayḥīl
Mīnā' al Aḥmadī
'Abdalī
Al Aḥmadī
Manāqīsh
Shu'aybah
Mīnā' 'Abd Allāh
As Salimi
Aṣ Ṣubayḥiyah
ASH SHUQAYQ
SAUDI ARABIA
THE GULF
Mīnā' Sa'ūd
Al Khīrān
Al Wafrā'
N
0
25 km
25 miles
48°
30°

WORLD AFFAIRS

Joined UN in 1963

AL | Damasc | GCC | OIC | OPEC

Kuwait's strategic importance is as a major exporter of crude oil and natural gas. As such, it has always maintained very close links with the West, which have deepened since the war with Iraq, and on which it depends for its future security. Kuwait still awaits the return of POWs and Kuwaiti nationals detained by Iraq.

AID

Donor

$147m (donations) | Down 47% in 1999

The Kuwait Fund for Arab Economic Development continued to give aid even during the invasion crisis.

DEFENSE

Compulsory military service

$3.28bn | Down 11% in 1999

In August 1990 Kuwait's 11,000-strong, partly volunteer army was easily overrun by vastly superior Iraqi forces. Since its liberation, defense pacts have been signed with the USA, the UK, France, and Russia. Kuwait is rearming fast, with weapons purchased from major Western suppliers.

ECONOMICS

Inflation 2% p.a. (1990–1999)

$35.2bn | 0.3043–0.3055 Kuwaiti dinars

SCORE CARD

❑ WORLD GNP RANKING	54th
❑ GNP PER CAPITA	$22,110
❑ BALANCE OF PAYMENTS	$5.06bn
❑ INFLATION	2%
❑ UNEMPLOYMENT	2%

STRENGTHS
Recovery of oil and gas production. Benefits from return of high oil prices after the collapse of 1986. Large overseas investments. Stable banking system.

WEAKNESSES
Adverse consequences of Iraqi invasion. Strategic vulnerability deters investment. Reliance on imported skilled labor, food, and raw materials. Delays in enacting privatization package.

EXPORTS

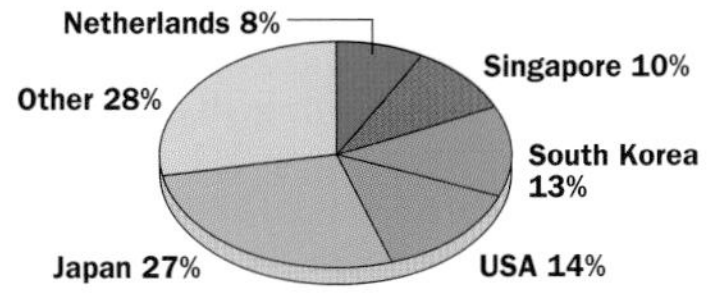
Netherlands 8%
Singapore 10%
Other 28%
South Korea 13%
Japan 27%
USA 14%

IMPORTS

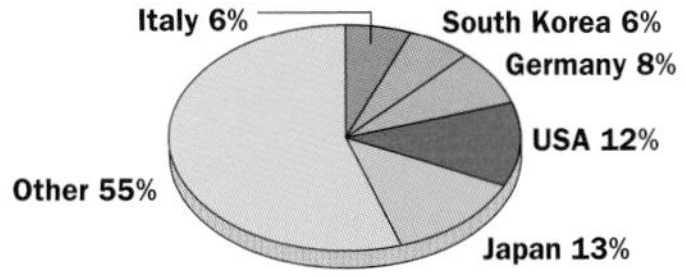
Italy 6%
South Korea 6%
Germany 8%
USA 12%
Other 55%
Japan 13%

RESOURCES

Electric power 7m kw

7980 tonnes | 2.2m b/d (reserves 96,500,000,000 bbl)

450,000 sheep, 155,000 goats, 33m chickens | Oil, natural gas, salt

The oil industry is Kuwait's most profitable sector, accounting for over 80% of export earnings. Although badly hit by the Gulf War, when a number of wells were deliberately fired, it was quickly rehabilitated. Kuwait also possesses valuable reserves of natural gas. Other resources are dates, fish, ammonia, and chemicals.

ENVIRONMENT

Sustainability rank: 116th

2% | 28.2 tonnes per capita

The Iraqi invasion and the subsequent war caused an ecological disaster. Although the effects of this did not prove as grave as some observers first feared, marine life has been damaged and many thousands of hectares of cultivated land have been obliterated. Millions of land mines still litter border areas. Water is scarce.

MEDIA

TV ownership high

Daily newspaper circulation 377 per 1000 people

PUBLISHING AND BROADCAST MEDIA

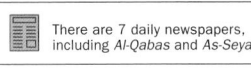

There are 7 daily newspapers, including *Al-Qabas* and *As-Seyassah*

1 state-controlled service | 1 state-controlled service

Radio and TV are state-controlled, but satellite TV is freely available. Press freedom exists in theory.

CRIME

Death penalty used

36 prisoners | Up 8% 1996–1998

Isolated acts of terrorism related to the war still occur. There have been reports of human rights abuses.

EDUCATION

School leaving age: 14

83% | 29,509 students

Kuwaiti citizens receive free education from nursery to university. Since the liberation, more emphasis has been placed on technology in the curriculum.

CHRONOLOGY

Kuwait traces its independence to 1710, but was under British rule from the late 18th century until 1961. The government denies any historical link with Iraq.

- ❑ **1961** Independence from UK. Iraq claims Kuwait.
- ❑ **1976** Amir suspends National Assembly.
- ❑ **1990** Iraqi invasion.
- ❑ **1991** Liberation following Gulf War.
- ❑ **1992** National Assembly elections.
- ❑ **1999** Elections; Islamists and liberals win most seats.

HEALTH

Welfare state health benefits

1 per 526 people | Heart diseases, accidents, cancers, perinatal deaths

Despite theft of equipment during the Iraqi invasion, Kuwait has restored its Western-standard health care service. Nationals receive free treatment.

SPENDING

GDP/cap. increase

CONSUMPTION AND SPENDING

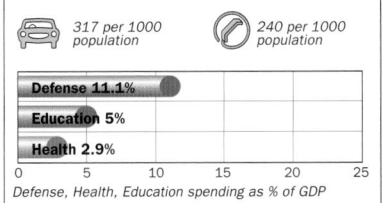

317 per 1000 population | *240 per 1000 population*

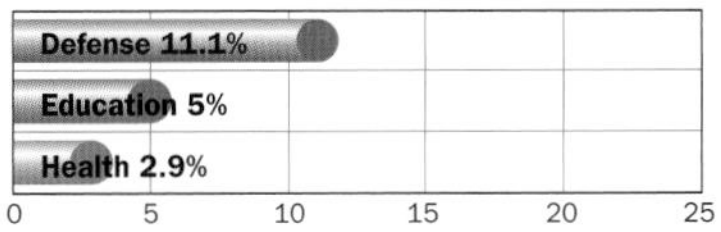
Defense 11.1%
Education 5%
Health 2.9%
0
5
10
15
20
25

Defense, Health, Education spending as % of GDP

As well as the oil-rich elite, most Kuwaitis enjoy high incomes, and the government has repeatedly rescued citizens who have suffered stock market or other financial losses. School and university leavers are guaranteed jobs. Capital is easily transferred abroad and there are effectively no exchange controls.

WORLD RANKING

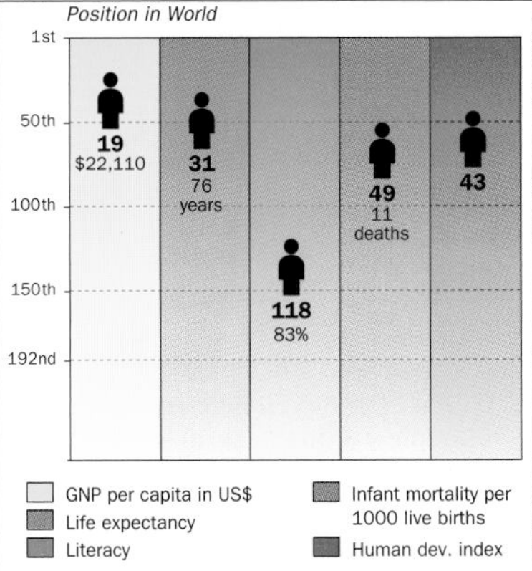
Position in World
1st
50th
100th
150th
192nd
19
$22,110
31
76
years
118
83%
49
11
deaths
43
GNP per capita in US$
Life expectancy
Literacy
Infant mortality per 1000 live births
Human dev. index

K

KYRGYZSTAN

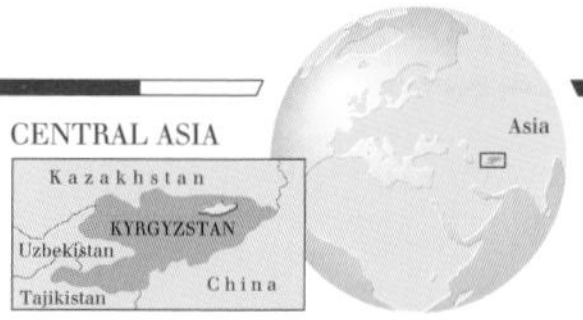
CENTRAL ASIA
Asia
Kazakhstan
KYRGYZSTAN
Uzbekistan
China
Tajikistan

OFFICIAL NAME: Kyrgyz Republic **CAPITAL:** Bishkek
POPULATION: 4.7 million **CURRENCY:** Som **OFFICIAL LANGUAGES:** Kyrgyz and Russian

1991 | 1991 | Aug 31 | KS | +6 | +996 | .kg

KYRGYZSTAN IS A SMALL and very mountainous state in central Asia. It is the least urbanized of the former Soviet republics (the rural population is growing faster than the towns) and was among the last to develop its own cultural nationalism. Its moderate government is treading uncertainly between Kyrgyz nationalist pressures and ensuring that the minority Russians are not alienated, since they tend to possess the skills necessary to run a market-based economy.

CLIMATE

Mountain

WEATHER CHART

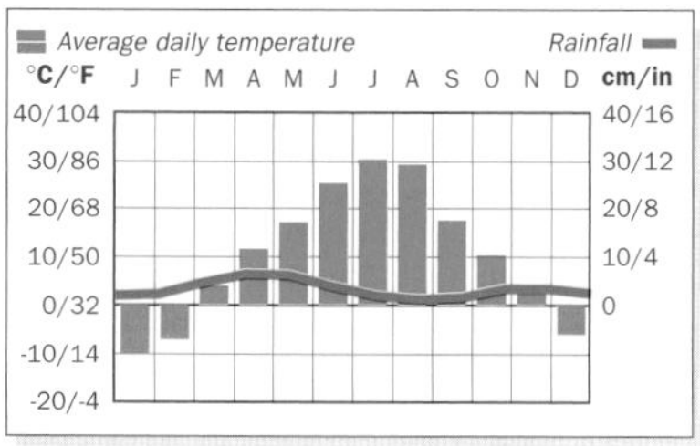
Average daily temperature
Rainfall
°C/°F J F M A M J J A S O N D cm/in
40/104 40/16
30/86 30/12
20/68 20/8
10/50 10/4
0/32 0
-10/14
-20/-4

Conditions vary from permanent snow and cold deserts at altitude to hot deserts in low regions. Intermediate slopes and valleys receive some rain.

TRANSPORTATION

Drive on right

Bishkek International — Has no fleet

THE TRANSPORTATION NETWORK

16,854 km (10,473 miles) — 140 km (87 miles)

417 km (259 miles) — 600 km (373 miles)

Kyrgyzstan does not have the financial budget to improve on its poor mountain road network.

TOURISM

Visitors : Population 1:68

69,000 visitors — Up 17% in 1999

MAIN TOURIST ARRIVALS

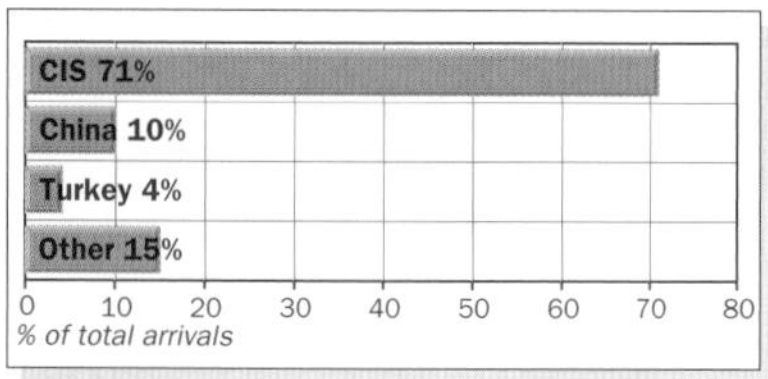
CIS 71%
China 10%
Turkey 4%
Other 15%
0 10 20 30 40 50 60 70 80
% of total arrivals

Tourism is undeveloped; most visitors are people on business, or working on multilateral aid projects. Tourism promotion centers on the country's position on the Silk Road trade route.

PEOPLE

Pop. density low

Kyrgyz, Russian — 24/km² (61/mi²)

THE URBAN/RURAL POPULATION SPLIT

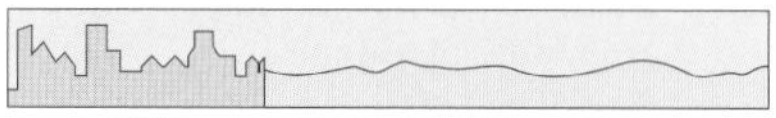
34%
66%

ETHNIC MAKEUP

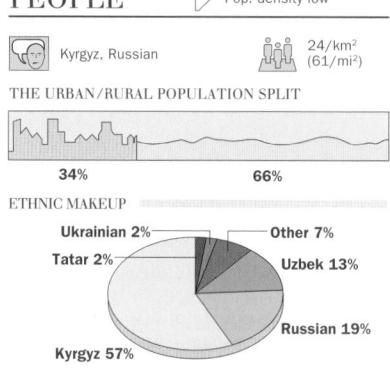

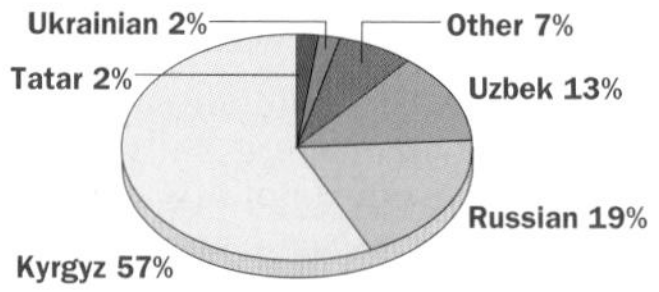
Ukrainian 2%
Other 7%
Tatar 2%
Uzbek 13%
Russian 19%
Kyrgyz 57%

Like other former Soviet republics, Kyrgyzstan has witnessed the rise of militant nationalism. Relations are most strained with the large Uzbek minority. The preference given to Kyrgyz in the political system and in particular in the land laws, which exclude all others from full title, has aggravated ethnic tensions. The trend in politics is toward greater Islamization, which is linking religion and race issues more closely and adding pressure on "foreigners," particularly ethnic Russians, to leave.

Since 1989 a high birthrate has enabled the Kyrgyz to resume their position as the main ethnic group, replacing the Russian community which until recently controlled the economy. However, the government moved to stem the tide of Russian emigration by declaring Russian an official language with full equal status with effect from 2000.

Loess landscape, Naryn valley. *Kyrgyzstan is dominated by the ice-capped Tien Shan Mountains, but valleys are green and fertile.*

POLITICS

Multiparty elections

L. House 2000/2005
U. House 2000/2005
President Askar Akayev

AT THE LAST ELECTION

Legislative Assembly 60 seats

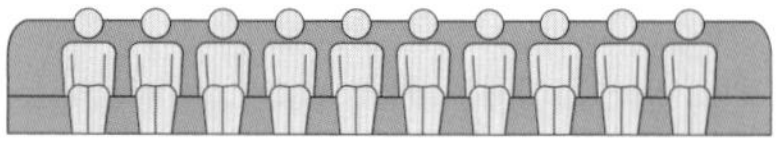

Election results by party were announced only for the 15 national list seats. The other 45 seats are elected on a constituency basis. The Party of Communists of Kyrgyzstan is the largest party and the Union of Democratic Forces the second-largest.

Assembly of People's Representatives 45 seats

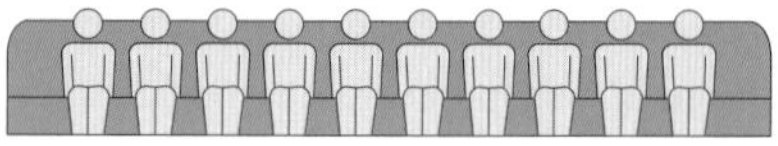

The members represent Kyrgyzstan's different regional and ethnic communities.

In 1991 Kyrgyzstan was the first former Soviet republic to ban the Communist Party. It was revived in 1992 as the Party of Communists of Kyrgyzstan. Relations with the large Uzbek minority have remained calm since serious clashes in 1990.

President Akayev has been accused of fostering a personality cult. Already in power under the Soviet regime before independence he was reelected in 1995 and in 2000, after objections to a third term were overruled by the Constitutional Court.

Accusations of fraud during the 2000 parliamentary and presidential elections destroyed the regime's already tarnished democratic credentials. The main opposition leader Felix Kulov was imprisoned just weeks before the presidential poll. Akayev's free-market economic policies have shown few tangible results.

WORLD AFFAIRS

Joined UN in 1992

CIS | SCO | OIC | OSCE | EAPC

Kyrgyzstan is working to reduce its dependence on Russia. Turkey is developing close links aimed at restraining Iranian fundamentalist influence in the region. Relations with Uzbekistan, which allegedly supports some of the antigovernment forces in Kyrgyzstan, are tense, although in 2000 both countries joined with Tajikistan to combat Islamist militants in the region.

AID

Recipient

$267m (receipts) — Up 24% in 1999

The USA and Japan are the main aid donors. The World Bank is also an important source of financial assistance.

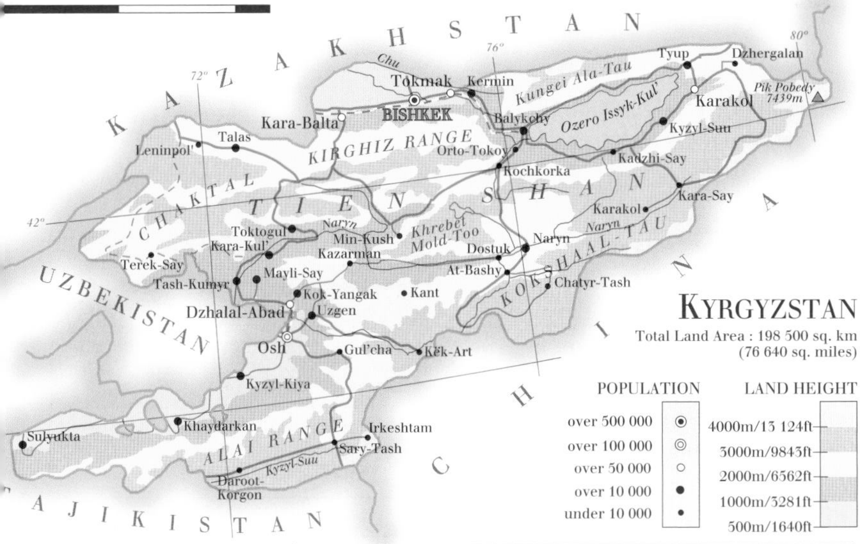
KAZAKHSTAN
Chu
Tokmak
Kermin
Tyup
Dzhergalan
Kungei Ala-Tau
Ozero Issyk-Kul'
Karakol
Pik Pobedy 7439m
BISHKEK
Kara-Balta
Balykchy
Kyzyl-Suu
Talas
Leninpol'
KIRGHIZ RANGE
Orto-Tokoy
Kadzhi-Say
Kochkorka
TIEN SHAN
CHATKAL
Kara-Say
Karakol
Toktogul
Kara-Kul'
Naryn
Min-Kush
Kazarman
Khrebet Mold-Too
Dostuk
Naryn
KOKSHAAL-TAU
Terek-Say
Tash-Kumyr
Mayli-Say
At-Bashy
Chatyr-Tash
UZBEKISTAN
Kok-Yangak
Kant
Dzhalal-Abad
Uzgen
Osh
Gul'cha
Kek-Art
CHINA
Kyzyl-Kiya
Khaydarkan
Irkeshtam
Sulyukta
ALAI RANGE
Sary-Tash
Kyzyl-Suu
Daroot-Korgon
TAJIKISTAN
KYRGYZSTAN
Total Land Area : 198 500 sq. km (76 640 sq. miles)
POPULATION
over 500 000
over 100 000
over 50 000
over 10 000
under 10 000
LAND HEIGHT
4000m/13 124ft
3000m/9843ft
2000m/6562ft
1000m/3281ft
500m/1640ft

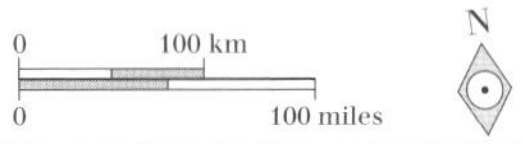
0
100 km
0
100 miles
N

DEFENSE

Compulsory military service

$51m

Down 23% in 1999

In 1992, a national army was set up and a defense treaty was signed with five other CIS states. The army is weak and not influential in politics.

ECONOMICS

Inflation 129.7% p.a. (1990–1999)

$1.5bn

45.429–48.237 soms

SCORE CARD

- ❑ WORLD GNP RANKING........................148th
- ❑ GNP PER CAPITA $300
- ❑ BALANCE OF PAYMENTS....................$-371m
- ❑ INFLATION 35.9%
- ❑ UNEMPLOYMENT 6%

STRENGTHS

Agricultural self-sufficiency. Private land ownership since 2000. Gold and mercury exports. Hydropower potential.

WEAKNESSES

Dominant state and collective farming mentality. Sharp decline since breakup of USSR, on which it depended for trade and supplies. Chronic inflation.

EXPORTS

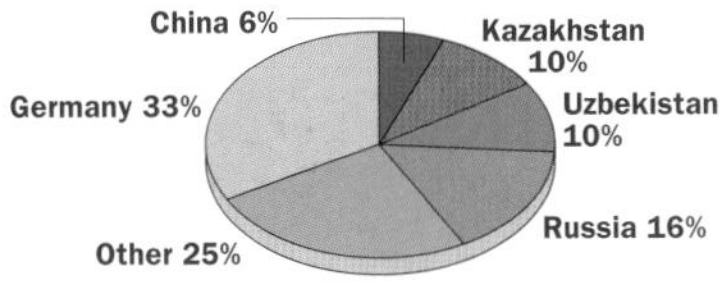
China 6%
Kazakhstan 10%
Germany 33%
Uzbekistan 10%
Russia 16%
Other 25%

IMPORTS

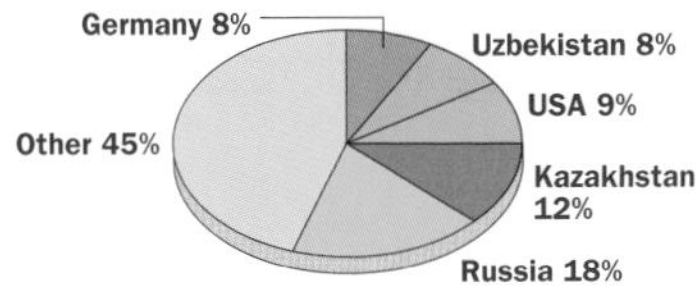
Germany 8%
Uzbekistan 8%
USA 9%
Other 45%
Kazakhstan 12%
Russia 18%

RESOURCES

Electric power 3.7m kw

300 tonnes

1704 b/d (reserves 36,709,800 bbl)

4.44m sheep, 955,000 cattle, 2.3m chickens

Coal, antimony, gas, oil, tin, mercury, iron, uranium, zinc, gold

Kyrgyzstan has small quantities of commercially exploitable coal, oil, and gas, and great hydroelectric power potential. Energy policy, which relies on Western aid and technology, is primarily aimed at developing these further in order to reduce dependence on supplies from Russia, and eventually to achieve self-sufficiency in energy.

ENVIRONMENT

Sustainability rank: 98th

4%

1.4 tonnes per capita

The major problem is the salination of the soil caused by excessive irrigation of cotton crops. Kyrgyzstan has a poor record in limiting industrial pollution.

MEDIA

TV ownership low

Daily newspaper circulation 15 per 1000 people

PUBLISHING AND BROADCAST MEDIA

There are 4 daily newspapers, including *Kyrgyz Tuusu, Slovo Kyrgyzstana*, and *Vechernii Bishkek*

1 state-owned service

4 services: 1 state-owned, 3 independent

Television programming is mainly from Russia. The Kyrgyz press is the most liberal in central Asia.

CRIME

Death penalty not used

13,786 prisoners

The crime rate is rising

Ethnic tension fuels violence. The narcotics trade flourishes. A 1998 moratorium on the death penalty was extended in 2000 for a further year.

CHRONOLOGY

The Kyrgyz first developed a recognizable ethnic consciousness in the late 18th century.

- ❑ **1860s** Expansion of Russian Empire into Kyrgyz lands.
- ❑ **1924** Incorporated in USSR.
- ❑ **1991** Independence from USSR.
- ❑ **1995** New constitution adopted.
- ❑ **2000** Legislative and presidential elections; Akayev reelected.

EDUCATION

School leaving age: 16

97%

49,744 students

Replacing Russian as the main teaching language is proving an enormous task. Russian is likely to survive at tertiary level, as the Kyrgyz language lacks key technical and scientific terms.

HEALTH

Welfare state health benefits

1 per 323 people

Heart diseases, cancers, accidents, violence, tuberculosis

Kyrgyzstan has one of the least developed public health systems in central Asia. Infant mortality is high.

SPENDING

GDP/cap. decrease

CONSUMPTION AND SPENDING

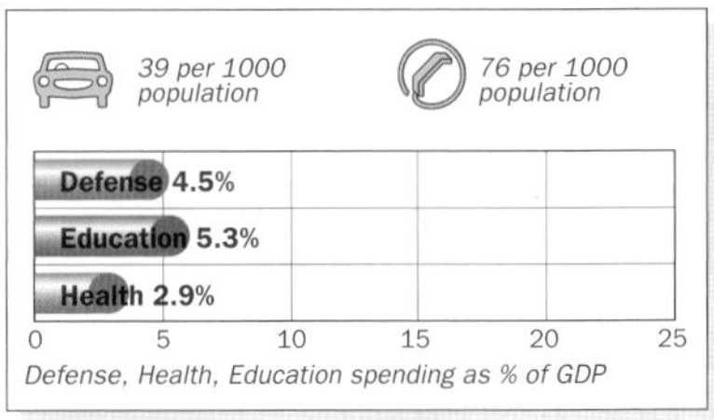
39 per 1000 population
76 per 1000 population
Defense 4.5%
Education 5.3%
Health 2.9%
0
5
10
15
20
25
Defense, Health, Education spending as % of GDP

In 2000, almost 90% of the population were estimated as living in poverty. The old Communist Party *nomenklatura* are the main beneficiaries of privatization.

WORLD RANKING

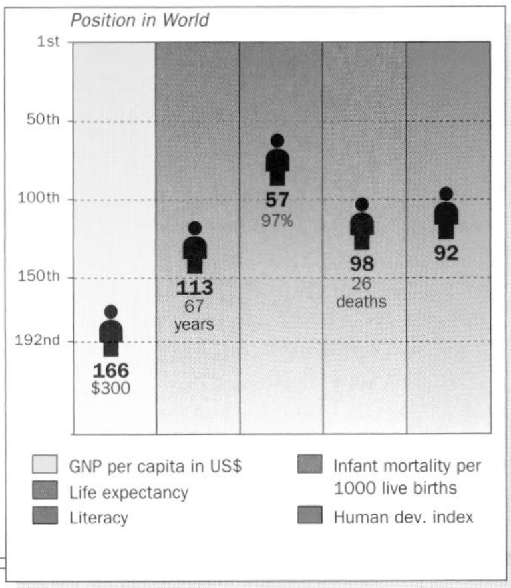
Position in World
1st
50th
100th
150th
192nd
166
$300
113
67
years
57
97%
98
26
deaths
92
GNP per capita in US$
Life expectancy
Literacy
Infant mortality per 1000 live births
Human dev. index

K

LAOS

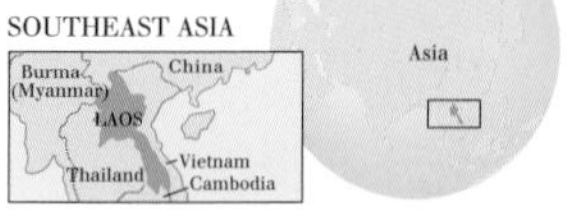
SOUTHEAST ASIA
Burma (Myanmar)
China
LAOS
Thailand
Vietnam
Cambodia
Asia

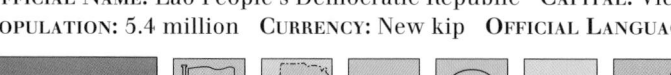

OFFICIAL NAME: Lao People's Democratic Republic **CAPITAL:** Vientiane
POPULATION: 5.4 million **CURRENCY:** New kip **OFFICIAL LANGUAGE:** Lao

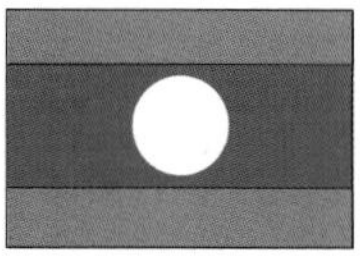

1953 | 1953 | Dec 2 | LAO | +7 | +856 | .la

LAOS IS A LANDLOCKED country bordered by Vietnam, Cambodia, Thailand, Burma, and China. The Mekong river forms its main thoroughfare and feeds the fertile lowlands of the Mekong valley. Independence from France in 1953 was followed by two decades of civil war, and heavy bombing by US forces during the Vietnam War. The communist Lao People's Revolutionary Party (LPRP) has held power since 1975. The government began to introduce market-oriented reforms in 1986. A transfer of power to a younger generation within the LPRP took place during the 1990s.

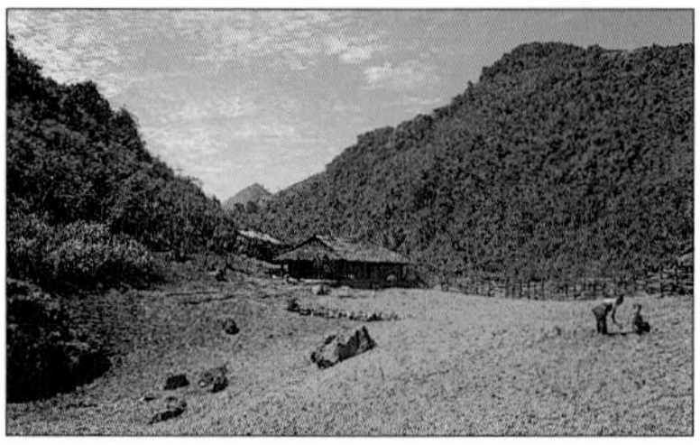

Farm in northeastern Laos. *The only lowlands are along the Mekong river. Three-quarters of Laotians are subsistence farmers.*

CLIMATE

Tropical monsoon

WEATHER CHART

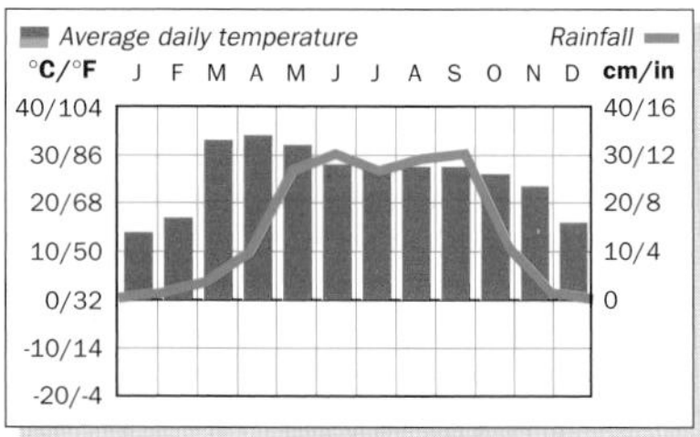
Average daily temperature
Rainfall
°C/°F
J F M A M J J A S O N D
cm/in
40/104
30/86
20/68
10/50
0/32
-10/14
-20/-4
40/16
30/12
20/8
10/4
0

The tropical southerly monsoon brings heavy rains from May to September. For the rest of the year Laos has dry northerly winds and sunny skies.

TRANSPORTATION

Drive on right

Wattay, Vientiane 165,000 passengers

1 ship 2400 grt

THE TRANSPORTATION NETWORK

9674 km (6011 miles)

None

None

4600 km (2858 miles)

Access to Laos is by air or the only main road, via Thailand, across the Mekong bridge at Vientiane, which opened in 1994. A bridge at Paksé opened in 2000. Freight goes mainly by river; there is no railroad and roads are poor and few.

PEOPLE

Pop. density low

Lao, Mon-Khmer, Yao, Vietnamese, Chinese, French

23/km² (61/mi²)

THE URBAN/RURAL POPULATION SPLIT

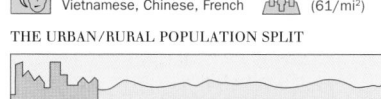

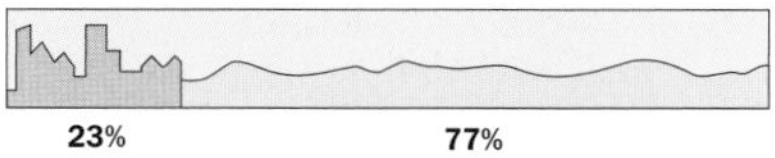
23%
77%

RELIGIOUS PERSUASION

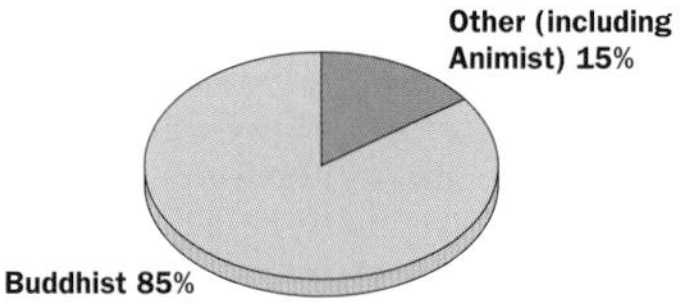
Other (including Animist) 15%
Buddhist 85%

ETHNIC MAKEUP

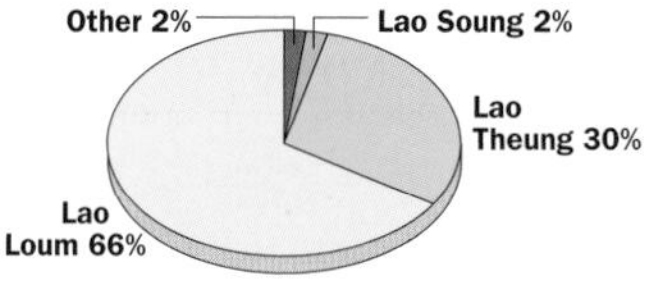
Other 2%
Lao Soung 2%
Lao Theung 30%
Lao Loum 66%

POPULATION AGE BREAKDOWN

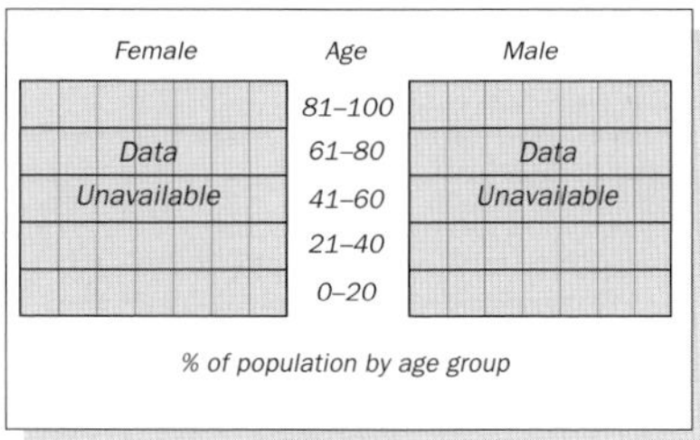
Female
Age
Male
81–100
61–80
41–60
21–40
0–20
Data Unavailable
Data Unavailable
% of population by age group

There are more than 60 ethnic groups in Laos and this considerable diversity has hindered national integration. Society is broadly divided by altitude rather than by region.

The lowland Laotians (*Lao Loum*), who make up the majority of the population and are mostly ethnic Lao, reside in the river valleys along the Mekong river and practice wet rice agriculture. The upland Laotians (*Lao Theung*) live in the hills above the valleys and practice slash and burn agriculture. Efforts by the government in Vientiane to alter this traditional form of farming, which can destroy forests and watersheds, have been resisted by the people.

Similarly, the mountain-top Laotians (*Lao Soung*), who include the Hmong, Yao, and Man groups, have resisted government efforts to introduce substitutes for traditional cash crops such as opium. The Hmong, in particular, have never been reconciled to rule from Vientiane. Tens of thousands fled to Thailand, and the USA, when the LPRP took power in 1975. Today, the government continues to face small pockets of Hmong resistance.

Two-thirds of the population speak Lao, and a large number of tribal dialects are also spoken. Buddhism is the main religion, but there are some Christians and animists.

TOURISM

Visitors : Population 1:18

300,000 visitors

Up 16% in 2000

Tourists were first allowed into Laos in 1989; numbers have risen rapidly since then. Mass tourism is discouraged and preference given to small package tours. In early 1999 tourists from neighboring countries were allowed to enter Laos using border passes at international checkpoints under the guidance of Lao tour companies. Hotels are few, and travel outside Vientiane is difficult.

MAIN TOURIST ARRIVALS

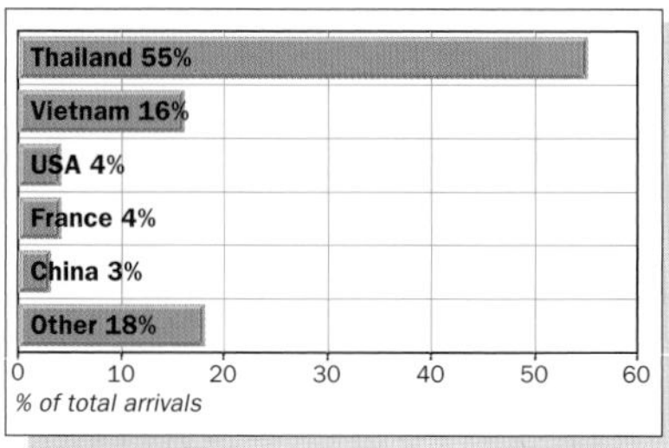
Thailand 55%
Vietnam 16%
USA 4%
France 4%
China 3%
Other 18%
0
10
20
30
40
50
60
% of total arrivals

Bounnyang Vorachit, *prime minister since 2001.*

Gen. Khamtay Siphandone, *president and head of the LPRP.*

POLITICS

No multiparty elections

1997/2002

President Khamtay Siphandone

AT THE LAST ELECTION

National Assembly 99 seats

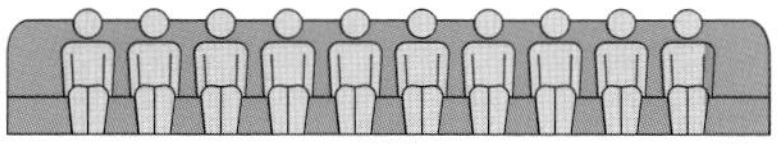

99% **LPRP** — **1%** **Ind**

LPRP = Lao People's Revolutionary Party (the sole legal political party) **Ind** = Independent
Many candidates ran as independents, but were effectively approved by the LPRP

Laos is a one-party state under the direct control and administration of the communist LPRP.

MAIN POLITICAL ISSUES

Political reform

Reforms are currently being introduced to modernize key state functions. The country's first written constitution was adopted in 1991, and a modern legal infrastructure has been introduced.

The LPRP has begun to relax its total hold on power. The executive branch of government, which relies on the LPRP for broad guidelines, is heavily dominated by the military, although civilian membership of the Council of Ministers rose in 2001. The National Assembly, once simply a rubber stamp for LPRP edicts, now takes more initiative.

Central control

Tensions continue to be felt between the communist government in Vientiane and the rural areas, where the rank and file of the LPRP and the military have their roots. There is particular resistance to central attempts to alter traditional farming methods.

PROFILE

Laos has been ruled by the same circle of communist revolutionaries, one of the world's most durable and closely knit hierarchies, since 1975.

The vacuum left by the death in 1992 of long-time LPRP leader Kaysone Phomvihane was quickly filled by his protégés. The military, the LPRP, and the executive branch remain closely intertwined, with party chairman General Khamtay Siphandone becoming the country's president in February 1998. Economic setbacks in the late 1990s forced some leaders to resign.

Despite limited moves toward political reform, the LPRP, which is modeled on the Communist Party of Vietnam, continues to dominate political life at every level.

The long-standing problem of corruption, sometimes at high levels, has become a matter of concern as Laos has opened to foreign investors. Economic reform has not been accompanied by political liberalization.

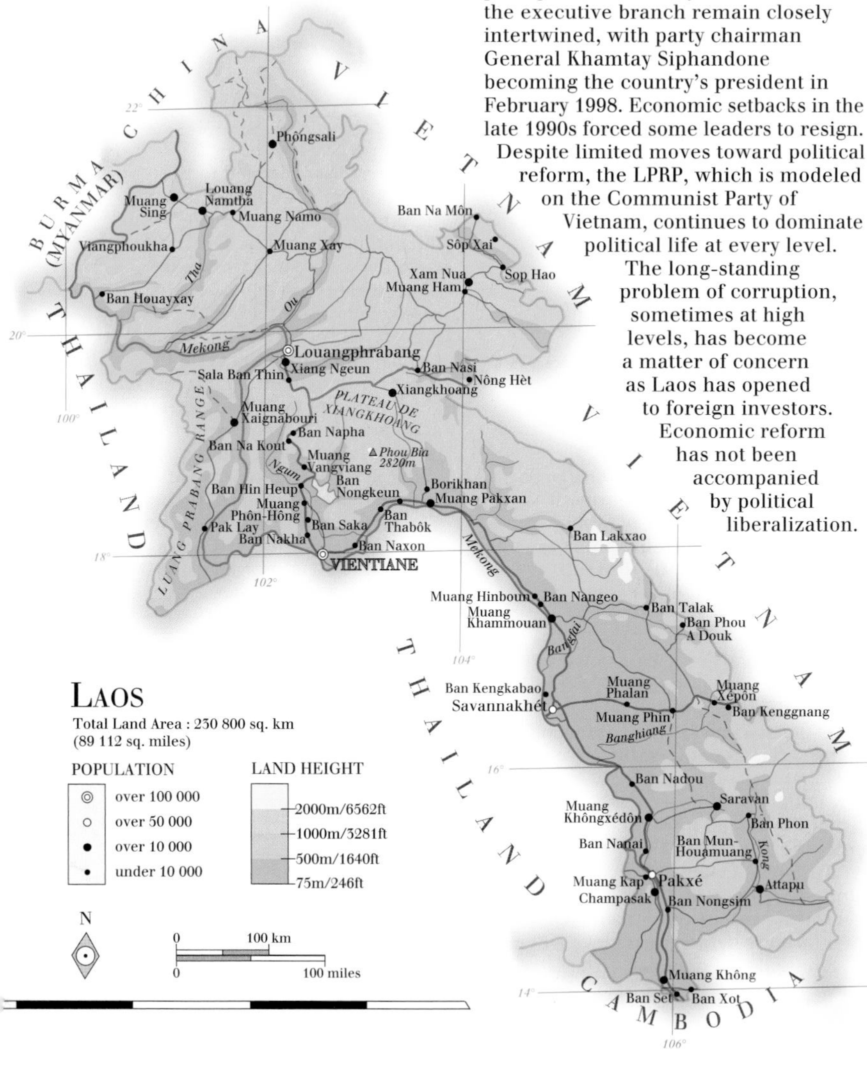
LAOS
Total Land Area : 230 800 sq. km
(89 112 sq. miles)
POPULATION
over 100 000
over 50 000
over 10 000
under 10 000
LAND HEIGHT
2000m/6562ft
1000m/3281ft
500m/1640ft
75m/246ft
N
0 100 km
0 100 miles
CHINA
VIETNAM
BURMA (MYANMAR)
THAILAND
CAMBODIA
Phôngsali
Louang Namtha
Muang Sing
Muang Namo
Viangphoukha
Muang Xay
Ban Houayxay
Ban Na Môn
Sôp Xai
Xam Nua
Muang Ham
Sop Hao
Mekong
Louangphrabang
Xiang Ngeun
Sala Ban Thin
Ban Nasi
Nông Hèt
Xiangkhoang
PLATEAU DE XIANGKHOANG
Muang Xaignabouri
Ban Napha
Ban Na Kont
Muang Vangviang
Phou Bia 2820m
Ban Nongkeun
Borikhan
Muang Pakxan
Ban Hin Heup
Muang Phôn-Hông
Pak Lay
Ban Saka
Ban Thabôk
Ban Nakha
Ban Naxon
VIENTIANE
LUANG PRABANG RANGE
Ban Lakxao
Muang Hinboun
Ban Nangeo
Muang Khammouan
Ban Talak
Ban Phou A Douk
Ban Kengkabao
Savannakhét
Muang Phalan
Muang Phin
Muang Xépôn
Ban Kenggnang
Banghiang
Ban Nadou
Saravan
Muang Khôngxédôn
Ban Phon
Ban Nanai
Ban Mun-Houamuang
Kong
Muang Kap
Champasak
Pakxé
Attapu
Ban Nongsim
Muang Không
Ban Set
Ban Xot

WORLD AFFAIRS

Joined UN in 1955

ASEAN | CP | OIF | Mekong River | NAM

From the time of the communist takeover in 1975, Vietnam was Laos's most important ally. In the late 1980s, however, the party leadership began to seek improved relations with the West in particular, building up close ties with Japan and achieving a rapprochement both with Thailand and with two former enemies, the USA and France. The motivation was mainly the need for foreign aid.

Following the collapse of communism in eastern Europe in the 1990s, Laos turned to its northern neighbor, China, for ideological support and in order to counterbalance the growing influence of Thailand. At the same time, the government was careful not to jeopardize links with Vietnam.

In 1992, Laos acceded to the Treaty of Amity and Concord of ASEAN, marking the beginning of a new relationship with former adversaries. Laos was admitted to full membership of ASEAN in 1997.

L

CHRONOLOGY

In the late 19th century, France established control over the three small kingdoms of Champasak, Louangphrabang, and Vientiane.

- **1893** Franco-Siamese treaty establishes French control over all territory east of the Mekong.
- **1899** Creation of a unified Laos under the French.
- **1941** Japanese seize power from Vichy French in Indo-China.
- **1946** French rule resumed.
- **1950** Lao Patriotic Front (LPF) set up to oppose French rule. Gains support of newly formed communist Lao People's Party (LPP).
- **1953** Independence as a constitutional monarchy backed by France and the USA.
- **1963** LPF begins armed struggle against royal government through its armed wing, the Pathet Lao.
- **1964** US bombing of North Vietnamese sanctuaries in Laos.
- **1973** LPRP (formerly the LPF) and royal government form a coalition after withdrawal of US forces from Indo-China.
- **1975** LPRP seizes power, abolishes monarchy, and proclaims Lao People's Democratic Republic. Premier Kaysone Phomvihane adopts policies for "socialist transformation" of economy.
- **1977** The Treaty of Friendship and Cooperation, providing for mutual ➪

CHRONOLOGY *continued*

security, signed with Vietnam. Relations cool with China.

- **1978** Popular unrest and resistance to collectivization. Former king and crown prince are arrested and die in captivity. Almost 50,000 Laotians flee to Thailand.
- **1979** Softer economic line adopted and the speed of "socialist transformation" slows.
- **1986** Fourth Party Congress introduces market-oriented economic reforms.
- **1988** Brief border war with Thailand. Restoration of diplomatic relations with China.
- **1989** National elections held. All candidates approved by LPRP. Rapprochement with Thailand.
- **1990** Counteroffensives against right-wing, largely Hmong, guerrilla bases located in the outer provinces. Most agricultural collectives and state farms disbanded. Arrest of three former officials for promoting multiparty democracy.
- **1991** A constitution providing for a National Assembly, confirming the leading role of the LPRP, and enshrining the right of private ownership, is promulgated. Kaysone steps down as prime minister and takes up post of president. Khamtay Siphandone becomes prime minister.
- **1992** Death of President Kaysone; Khamtay becomes LPRP leader.
- **1994** Thailand–Laos bridge opens over Mekong – first direct road link between the two countries.
- **1995** Death of former president Souphanouvong – the Red Prince.
- **1997** Laos becomes a member of ASEAN.
- **1998** Former prime minister Khamtay becomes president.
- **1999** October, student-led demonstration in Vientiane demanding greater political freedom.
- **2001** Prime Minister Sisavat Keobounphan resigns over economic mismanagement.

AID

Recipient

$294m (receipts) | Up 5% in 1999

Laos has one of the highest per capita aid inflows in the developing world. However, severe problems have been encountered in the implementation of aid programs. In the 1980s, Laos was heavily dependent on the USSR and Vietnam for aid. Today, donors include the IMF, the World Bank, the ADB, France, Sweden, Australia, and Japan.

DEFENSE

Compulsory military service

$22m | Down 35% in 1999

The armed forces are estimated by the West to number around 30,000 personnel. This total is further swelled by a paramilitary militia. Eighteen months' military service is compulsory for all Laotian men.

The military and the ruling LPRP have close links. Defense forces are deployed to ensure border security and control the narcotics trade along the Thai border. However, recent allegations of narcotics smuggling across the Laotian–Thai border have implicated sections of the army. In 1977, Laos signed a treaty with Vietnam, providing for mutual assistance in the event of a threat to national security.

LAOTIAN ARMED FORCES

30 main battle tanks (T–54/55, T–34/85)	25,000 personnel
16 patrol boats	600 personnel
14 combat aircraft (12 MiG–21 bis)	3500 personnel
None	

ECONOMICS

Inflation 22.9% p.a. (1990–1999)

$1.5bn | 6550–7600 new kips

SCORE CARD

World GNP Ranking	147th
GNP per Capita	$290
Balance of Payments	$–150m
Inflation	128.4%
Unemployment	6%

EXPORTS

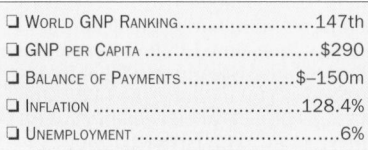

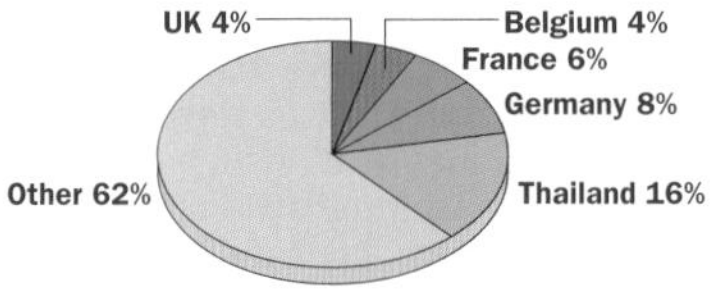
UK 4%
Belgium 4%
France 6%
Germany 8%
Other 62%
Thailand 16%

IMPORTS

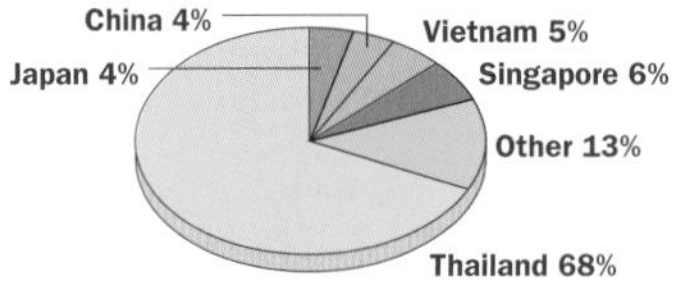
China 4%
Vietnam 5%
Japan 4%
Singapore 6%
Other 13%
Thailand 68%

ECONOMIC PERFORMANCE INDICATOR

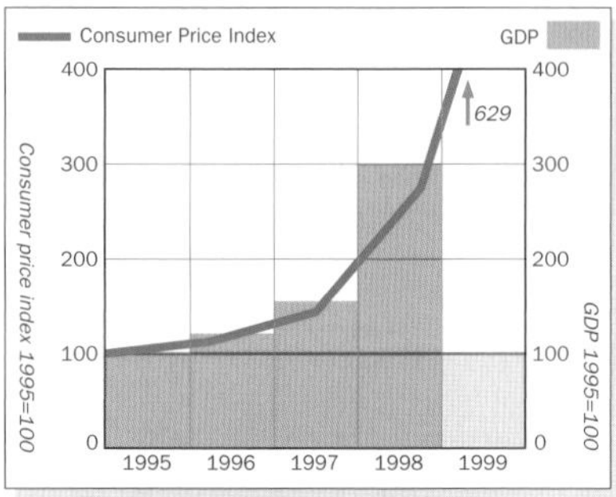
Consumer Price Index
GDP
400
300
200
100
0
629
Consumer price index 1995=100
GDP 1995=100
1995
1996
1997
1998
1999

Strengths

Rising levels of overseas (mostly Thai) investment. Potential of garment manufacturing, timber plantations, mining, wood processing, tourism, banking, and aviation. Minerals and possible oil and gas deposits.

Weaknesses

One of the world's least developed countries. Lack of technical expertise. Imbalance in sources of foreign investment – most is Thai. Problems in targeting aid efficiently.

Profile

The LPRP began introducing market-oriented reforms in 1986. The collapse of the Soviet Union speeded up this process in the early 1990s. Price controls on rice and other crops were removed, and farmers helped to achieve a degree of food self-sufficiency.

The reforms also led to the privatization of a number of state-owned companies, including the national brewery. The national currency – the kip – was floated, interest rates eased, and trade restrictions lifted. Foreign investment was encouraged, Laos being the first country in Indo-China to do this. However, most foreign interest has been confined to the service sector and natural resource exploitation, such as logging and mining.

In 1998 the economy was hit by the financial crisis in southeast Asia. The value of the kip fell by over 80%, forcing up inflation, which was running at about 100% a year. Recovery since then has been uneven.

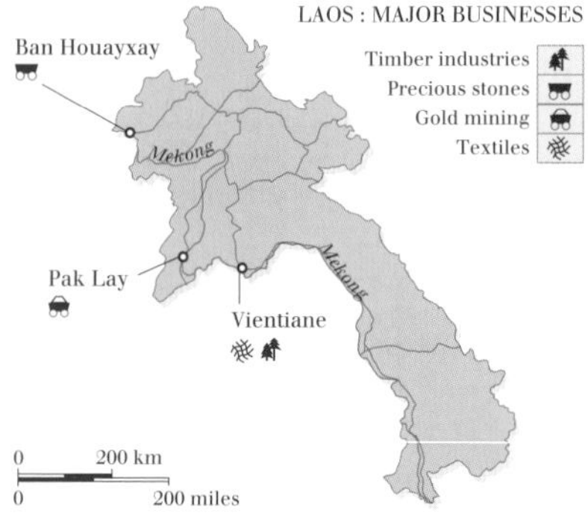
LAOS : MAJOR BUSINESSES
Timber industries
Precious stones
Gold mining
Textiles
Ban Houayxay
Mekong
Pak Lay
Vientiane
Mekong
0
200 km
0
200 miles

RESOURCES

Electric power 256,000 kw

40,000 tonnes

Not an oil producer

1.63m ducks, 1.1m pigs, 1m buffaloes, 12m chickens

Tin, gypsum, iron, coal, copper, potash, lead, limestone, antimony

Laos's most important agricultural resources are timber and coffee. The country is rich in minerals, and important deposits include tin and gypsum (which are exported), iron ore, copper, potash, limestone, antimony, manganese, lead, and salt. An increasing number of foreign companies have been awarded concessions to mine for gold and precious stones.

ELECTRICITY GENERATION

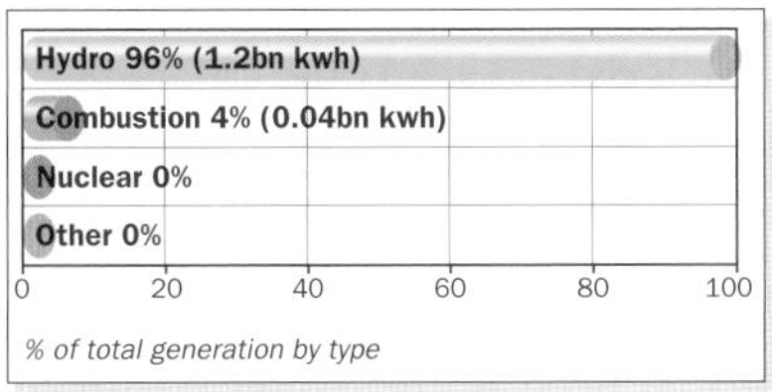
Hydro 96% (1.2bn kwh)
Combustion 4% (0.04bn kwh)
Nuclear 0%
Other 0%
0
20
40
60
80
100
% of total generation by type

The country's first oil and gas exploration agreements with oil multinationals were negotiated in the early 1990s. Laos's principal source of electricity is hydroelectric power. Surpluses are exported to Thailand.

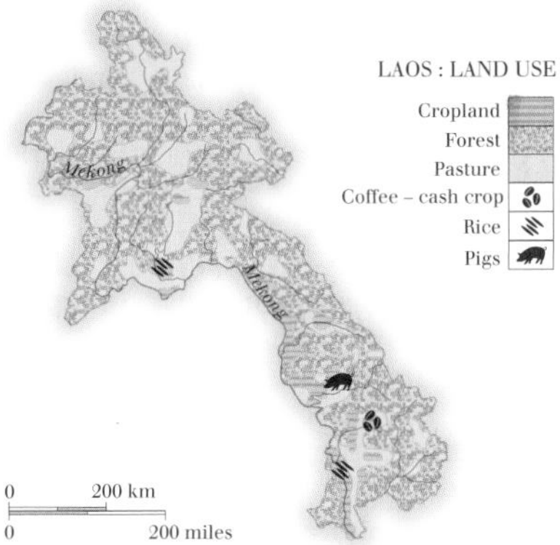
LAOS : LAND USE
Cropland
Forest
Pasture
Coffee – cash crop
Rice
Pigs
Mekong
Mekong
0
200 km
0
200 miles

ENVIRONMENT

Not available

None

0.1 tonnes per capita

Bombing and the use of defoliants in the Vietnam War did serious ecological damage. Slash and burn farming and illegal logging are destroying forests.

ENVIRONMENTAL TREATIES

No	No	Yes
No	No	No

MEDIA

TV ownership low

Daily newspaper circulation 4 per 1000 people

PUBLISHING AND BROADCAST MEDIA

There are 3 daily newspapers, including the government-published *Vientiane Mai*

2 services: 1 fully state-owned, 1 partly state-owned

2 services: 1 state-owned, 1 independent

Newspapers in Laos are owned and controlled by the LPRP; one is published by the Lao People's Army. Revelations of corruption by state officials are not uncommon, but criticism of the party and its leaders remains taboo. TV services began in 1983, and there are now three channels, one of them mainly Thai-owned.

CRIME

Death penalty used

Laos does not publish prison figures

Rising overall, particularly corruption

CRIME RATES

Most crime is rising. However the trend in mountain regions is hard to establish.

Laos is the world's third-largest opium producer. Since 1990, attempts have been made to combat the production and trafficking of illegal drugs. The USA has provided funds to replace poppies with alternative cash crops in the mountainous northeastern provinces.

EDUCATION

School leaving age: 15

49%

12,732 students

THE EDUCATION SYSTEM

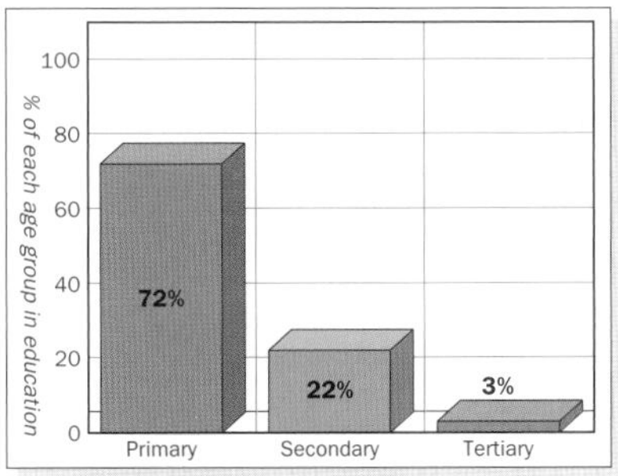
100
80
60
40
20
0
% of each age group in education
72%
22%
3%
Primary
Secondary
Tertiary

Education was badly disrupted by the years of civil war. To combat low literacy rates, which are 32% for women and 63% for men, adult education is currently being expanded and new schools are being built. Since 1990, private schools have been allowed to help meet demand.

HEALTH

Welfare state health benefits

1 per 5000 people

Diarrheal, respiratory, and parasitic diseases, malaria, influenza

Since 1975, public health care has developed steadily. However, more health education is needed in rural areas to improve standards of nutrition and sanitation, whose poor levels are reflected in the standard indicators of health and longevity for Laos. Infant mortality is about 10% and life expectancy is just over 50 years. Malaria and hemorrhagic fever are on the increase.

SPENDING

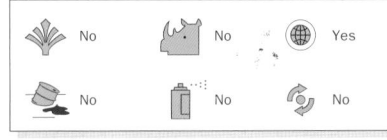

GDP/cap. increase

CONSUMPTION AND SPENDING

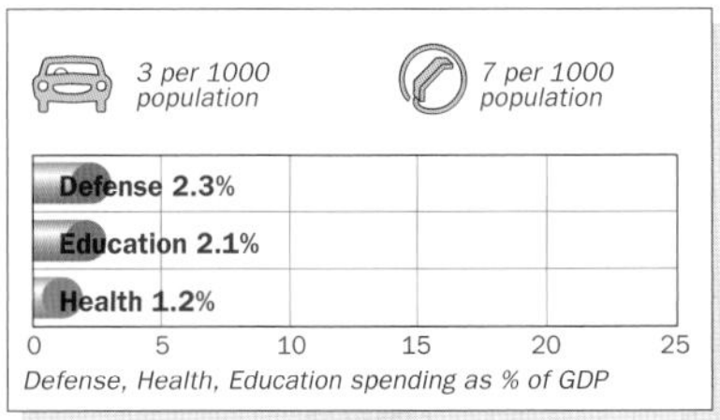
3 per 1000 population
7 per 1000 population
Defense 2.3%
Education 2.1%
Health 1.2%
0
5
10
15
20
25
Defense, Health, Education spending as % of GDP

There are large inequalities of wealth throughout Laos. A rapidly expanding group of Laotian entrepreneurs is profiting from the gradual liberalization of the country's economy. The elite tend to live in French-style villas. Mercedes are not uncommon in the capital, and the number of motorcycles has increased significantly in recent years.

Development is unevenly spread around the country. Many in the highlands and mountainous regions lead a subsistence existence, while farmers in the fertile Mekong valley are relatively well-off. Most homes along the Mekong have TV sets which can receive broadcasts from Thai stations. Bribes are a key part of most bureaucrats' incomes.

WORLD RANKING

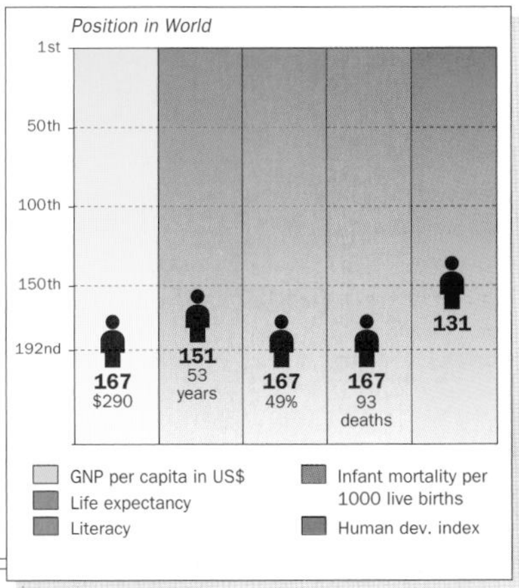
Position in World
1st
50th
100th
150th
192nd
167
$290
151
53
years
167
49%
167
93
deaths
131
GNP per capita in US$
Life expectancy
Literacy
Infant mortality per 1000 live births
Human dev. index

L

LATVIA

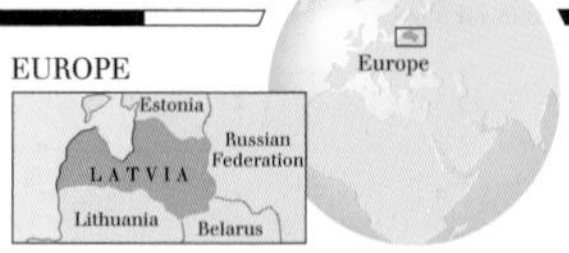

EUROPE
Europe
Estonia
Russian Federation
LATVIA
Lithuania
Belarus

OFFICIAL NAME: Republic of Latvia **CAPITAL:** Riga
POPULATION: 2.4 million **CURRENCY:** Lat **OFFICIAL LANGUAGE:** Latvian

1991 | 1991 | Nov 18 | LV | +2 | +371 | .lv

LYING BETWEEN Estonia and Lithuania, Latvia is situated on the eastern coast of the Baltic Sea. To the east it borders the Russian Federation and Belarus. The whole country is a low-lying plain, which nowhere rises above 300 meters (975 ft). Latvia's independence was recognized by Moscow in 1991. Defense-related industries and agriculture play an important role in the economy. Only just over half of the population are ethnic Latvians.

CLIMATE

Continental

WEATHER CHART

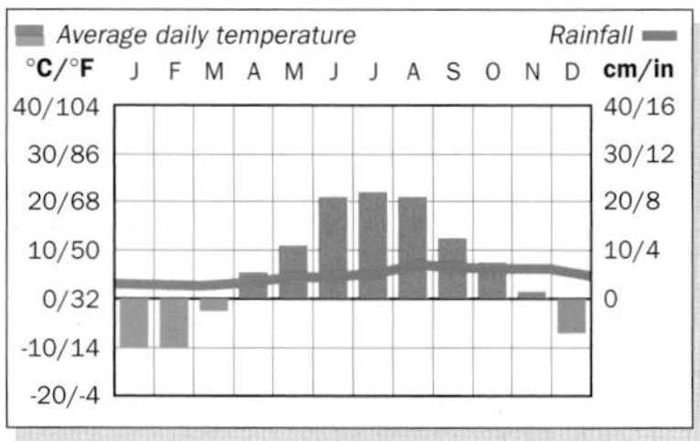

Average daily temperature
Rainfall
°C/°F
J F M A M J J A S O N D
cm/in
40/104
30/86
20/68
10/50
0/32
-10/14
-20/-4
40/16
30/12
20/8
10/4
0

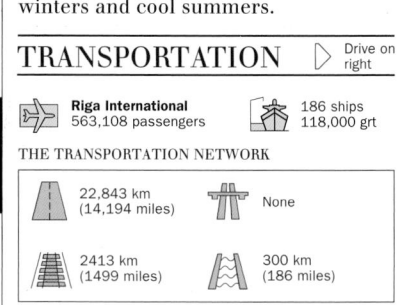

Latvia's coastal position means that the climate is temperate, with cold winters and cool summers.

TRANSPORTATION

Drive on right

Riga International 563,108 passengers

186 ships 118,000 grt

THE TRANSPORTATION NETWORK

22,843 km (14,194 miles)

None

2413 km (1499 miles)

300 km (186 miles)

Riga has the busiest container port in the Baltic. The EU-backed Via Baltica highway, linking Poland and Finland, runs north–south through Latvia. An east–west link of similar standard is a priority.

***The Russian Orthodox Cathedral** in Riga. Used as a planetarium during the Soviet era, its interior has now been restored.*

TOURISM

Visitors : Population 1:4.9

490,000 visitors

Down 14% in 1999

MAIN TOURIST ARRIVALS

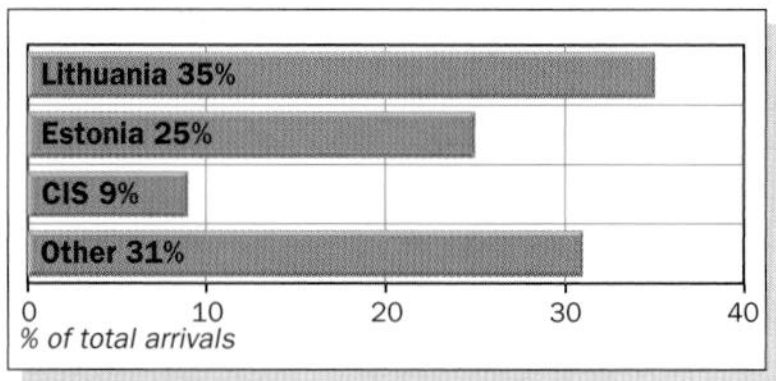

Lithuania 35%
Estonia 25%
CIS 9%
Other 31%
0
10
20
30
40
% of total arrivals

Riga is the main tourist destination, with many hotels and restaurants. Its medieval center is being restored.

PEOPLE

Pop. density low

Latvian, Russian

37/km² (96/mi²)

THE URBAN/RURAL POPULATION SPLIT

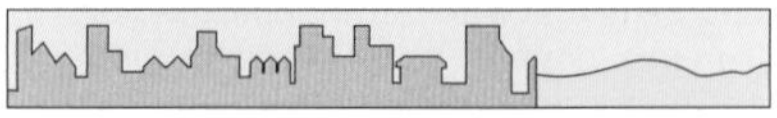

69%
31%

ETHNIC MAKEUP

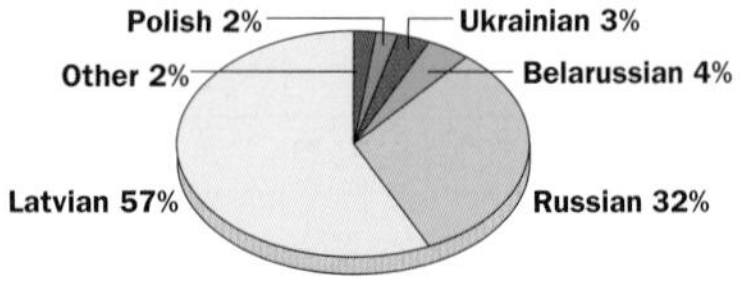

Polish 2%
Ukrainian 3%
Other 2%
Belarussian 4%
Latvian 57%
Russian 32%

Latvians make up just over half the population, but are a minority in Riga. Naturalization procedures were simplified in 1998, easing tension with the country's large minority population of ethnic Russians, but a restrictive language law reopened the controversy. In mid-2000 Latvian was proclaimed the only official language for the public and private sectors. The divorce rate is high.

POLITICS

Multiparty elections

1998/2002

President Vaira Vike-Freiberga

AT THE LAST ELECTION

Parliament 100 seats

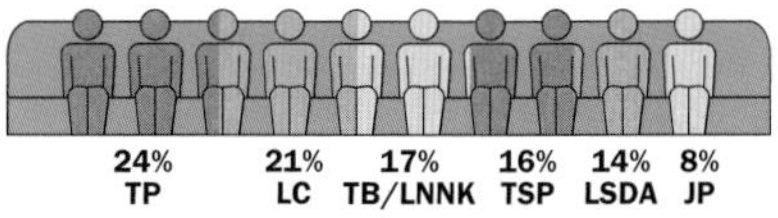

24% TP
21% LC
17% TB/LNNK
16% TSP
14% LSDA
8% JP

TP = People's Party **LC** = Latvia's Way **TB/LNNK** = Fatherland and Freedom **TSP** = National Harmony Party **LSDA** = Social Democratic Party **JP** = New Party

The 1998 general election boosted center-right parties, all in favor of EU membership and continuing market reforms. The largest single party was the recently formed TP, led by former premier Andris Skele, whose 1995–1997 government prepared the way for economic recovery. The TP was excluded from the new government, but this coalition was short-lived, the populist Skele taking over again in 1999. In May 2000, however, Riga's high-profile mayor, Andris Berzins, was appointed as prime minister, as Skele's coalition disintegrated.

LATVIA

Total Land Area : 64 589 sq. km (24 938 sq. miles)

POPULATION
- over 500 000
- over 100 000
- over 50 000
- over 10 000
- under 10 000

LAND HEIGHT
- 200m/656ft
- Sea Level

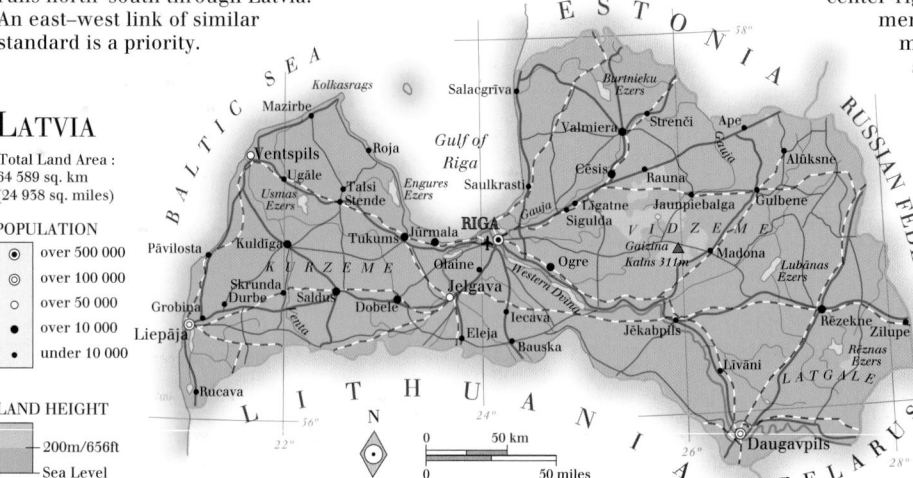

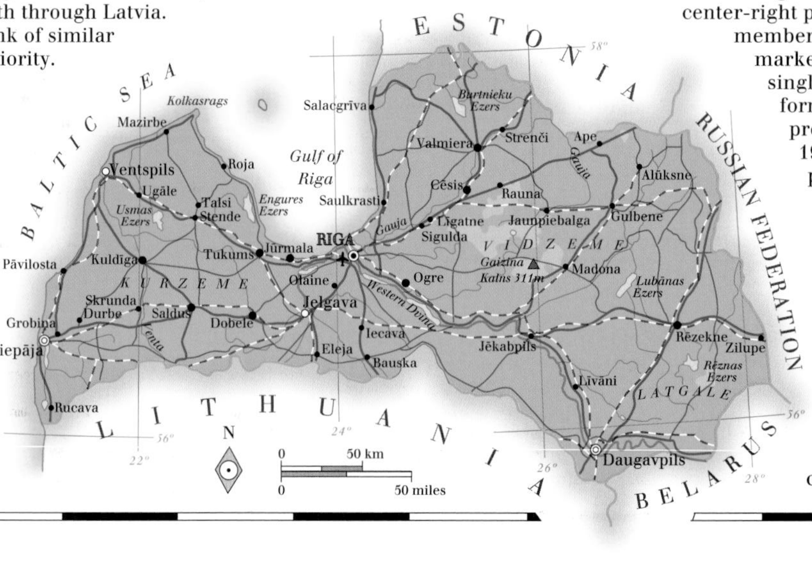

ESTONIA
RUSSIAN FEDERATION
BELARUS
LITHUANIA
BALTIC SEA
Gulf of Riga
Kolkasrags
Mazirbe
Ventspils
Ugāle
Usmas Ezers
Roja
Talsi
Stende
Engures Ezers
Saulkrasti
Salacgrīva
Burtnieku Ezers
Valmiera
Strenči
Ape
Gauja
Alūksne
Cēsis
Rauna
Līgatne
Sigulda
Jaunpiebalga
Gulbene
RIGA
Jūrmala
Tukums
Pāvilosta
Kuldīga
KURZEME
VIDZEME
Gaizina Kalns 311m
Madona
Lubānas Ezers
Olaine
Ogre
Western Dvina
Jelgava
Skrunda
Durbe
Saldus
Dobele
Grobiņa
Liepāja
Venta
Iecava
Eleja
Bauska
Jēkabpils
Rēzekne
Zilupe
Rēznas Ezers
Līvāni
LATGALE
Rucava
Daugavpils
N
0 50 km
0 50 miles

WORLD AFFAIRS

Joined UN in 1991

CE | CBSS | OSCE | EAPC | PfP

Latvia is one of six "second wave" candidates for admission to the EU which began membership negotiations in 2000. It also has US backing for entry to NATO. Relations with Russia have been strained. Laws passed in 2000 making Latvian the only official language angered the sizable Russian minority.

AID

Recipient

$96m (receipts) — Up 19% 1997–1999

Aid to Latvia comes mainly from the World Bank, the IMF, and the EU. Most goes toward improving the country's infrastructure.

DEFENSE

Compulsory military service

$58m — Up 45% in 1999

Building up the military is a priority, and there is now US backing for entry into NATO. Latvia has been participating in NATO's Partnership for Peace program. In February 2000, Russian forces finished dismantling their last military installation in Latvia, the Skrunda radar station.

ECONOMICS

Inflation 57.9% p.a. (1990–1999)

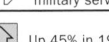

$5.9bn — 0.5863–0.6178 lati

SCORE CARD

- World GNP Ranking 105th
- GNP per Capita $2430
- Balance of Payments .... $–641m
- Inflation 2.4%
- Unemployment 10%

Strengths

Industrial production improving after slump. Service sector now providing more than half of GDP. Inflation under control. Foreign investment rising.

Weaknesses

Dependence on imported oil and natural gas for energy. Lack of raw materials. Farming is technically backward after the dismantling of the collective farms.

EXPORTS

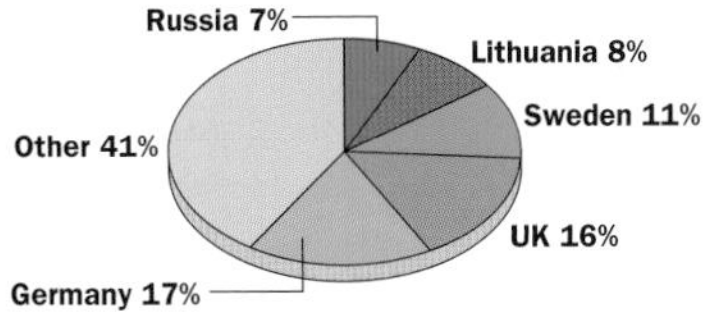
Russia 7%
Lithuania 8%
Sweden 11%
UK 16%
Germany 17%
Other 41%

IMPORTS

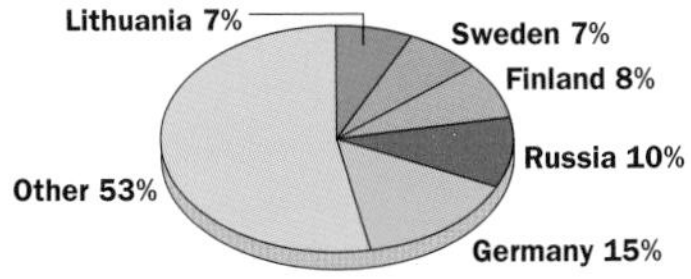
Lithuania 7%
Sweden 7%
Finland 8%
Russia 10%
Germany 15%
Other 53%

RESOURCES

Electric power 2.1m kw

106,027 tonnes — Not an oil producer

437,000 turkeys, 404,900 pigs, 2.8m chickens — Amber, dolomite, gravel, gypsum, limestone, peat, sand

Latvia has very limited natural resources, and is dependent on imports (mainly from Russia) to meet its energy needs. Peat is still burned for energy. Electricity comes chiefly from hydroelectric power and imports from Lithuania and Estonia. Offshore oil exploration is planned. Ventspils deep-water port is being promoted as an oil terminal.

ENVIRONMENT

Sustainability rank: 32nd

13% — 3.3 tonnes per capita

Peat extraction has damaged valuable bog habitat. Pollution of the Baltic Sea and air and water quality in industrial centers are also of concern.

Environmental issues featured in pre-independence protests and have retained a high profile.

MEDIA

TV ownership high

Daily newspaper circulation 247 per 1000 people

PUBLISHING AND BROADCAST MEDIA

There are 23 daily newspapers, including *Diena* and *Neatkariga Rita Avize*

2 services: 1 state-owned, 1 independent — 16 services: 1 state-owned, 15 independent

The press is now relatively free from state interference. Previously, the media were predominantly in Russian. Since 1991 the state, aiming to broaden the use of the official language, has actively promoted Latvian publications.

CRIME

Death penalty not used

9608 prisoners — Down 2% 1996–1998

Organized crime is a growing problem, but general crime levels are lower than in other former Soviet states.

EDUCATION

School leaving age: 15

99% — 56,187 students

Schools have opened for many minority ethnic groups. There are more than 50,000 students in higher education.

CHRONOLOGY

Latvia was dominated by Germany and, briefly, Sweden before Russia completed its conquest in 1795.

- **1917** Opposes Russian Bolshevik revolution. Declares independence.
- **1918–1920** Invaded by Bolsheviks and Germany.
- **1920** Gains independence.
- **1944** Incorporated into USSR.
- **1989** Popular Front (PLF) wins elections; declares independence.
- **1991** Independence recognized.
- **1995** TP-led coalition formed.
- **1998** Elections; LC-led coalition. Naturalization procedure eased.
- **1999** First woman president. Andris Skele of TP returns as premier.
- **2000** Skele resigns; replaced by Andris Berzins.

HEALTH

Welfare state health benefits

1 per 294 people — Heart diseases, cancers, accidents, respiratory diseases

The state-run system suffers shortages of medicines and equipment. Some improvements have been made, but it is still seriously underfunded.

SPENDING

GDP/cap. decrease

CONSUMPTION AND SPENDING

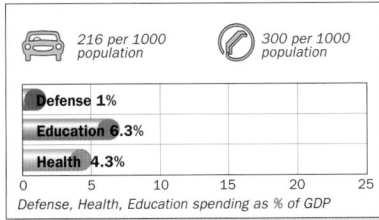

216 per 1000 population — *300 per 1000 population*

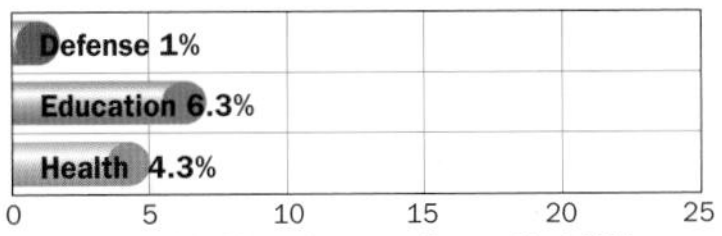
Defense 1%
Education 6.3%
Health 4.3%
0
5
10
15
20
25

Defense, Health, Education spending as % of GDP

The old bureaucracy has retained its privileged status and contacts, and remains the wealthiest group. Farmers are among the poorest.

WORLD RANKING

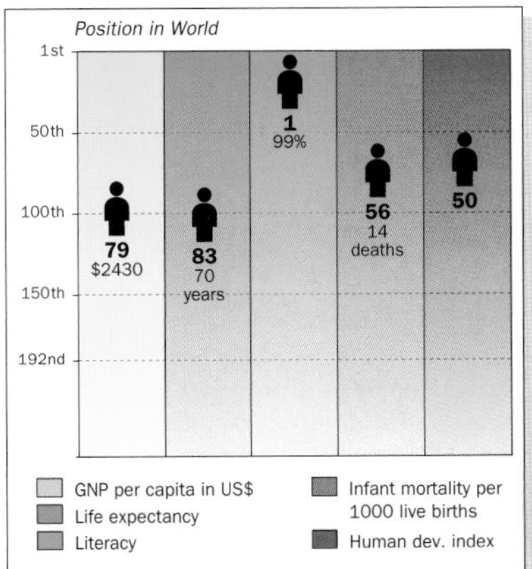
Position in World
1st
50th
100th
150th
192nd
79
$2430
83
70
years
1
99%
56
14
deaths
50
GNP per capita in US$
Life expectancy
Literacy
Infant mortality per 1000 live births
Human dev. index

L

LEBANON

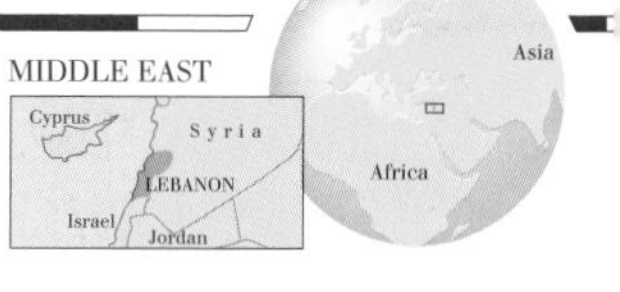
MIDDLE EAST
Cyprus
Syria
LEBANON
Israel
Jordan
Asia
Africa

OFFICIAL NAME: Republic of Lebanon **CAPITAL:** Beirut
POPULATION: 3.3 million **CURRENCY:** Lebanese pound **OFFICIAL LANGUAGE:** Arabic

1941 | 1941 | Nov 22 | RL | +2 | +961 | .lb

LEBANON IS DWARFED BY its two powerful neighbors, Syria and Israel. The country's coastal strip is fertile and the hinterland mountainous. Although in the minority, Maronite Christians have traditionally ruled Lebanon. A civil war between Muslim and Christian factional groups which began in 1975 threatened to lead to the breakup of the state. However, Saudi Arabia brokered a peace agreement in 1989; politics became more stable and reconstruction began.

CLIMATE

Mediterranean/mountain

WEATHER CHART

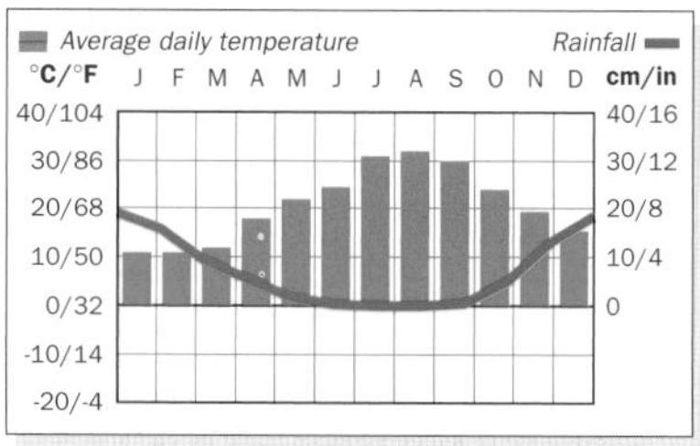
Average daily temperature
Rainfall
°C/°F
J F M A M J J A S O N D
cm/in
40/104
30/86
20/68
10/50
0/32
-10/14
-20/-4
40/16
30/12
20/8
10/4
0

Winters are mild and summers hot, with high humidity on the coast. Snow falls on high ground in the winter.

TRANSPORTATION

Drive on right

Beirut International, Khaldeh
2.22m passengers

106 ships
263,500 grt

THE TRANSPORTATION NETWORK

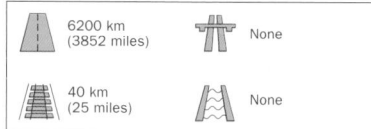

6200 km (3852 miles)

None

40 km (25 miles)

None

The redevelopment of Beirut could see it regain its position as one of the Middle East's major entrepôts.

TOURISM

Visitors : Population 1:4.4

742,000 visitors

Up 10% in 2000

MAIN TOURIST ARRIVALS

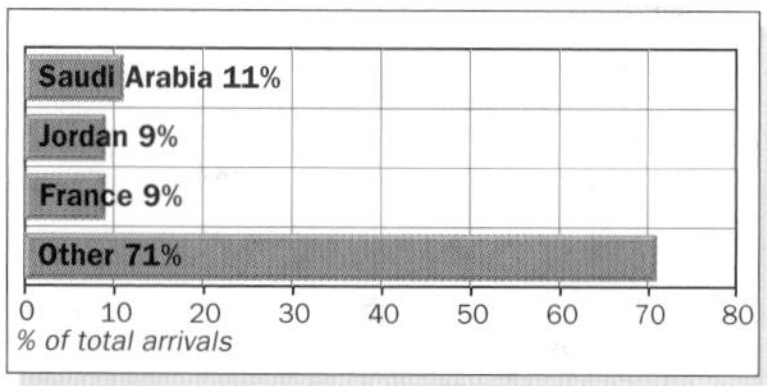
Saudi Arabia 11%
Jordan 9%
France 9%
Other 71%
0 10 20 30 40 50 60 70 80
% of total arrivals

Tourists have gradually returned since the devastation of the civil war. Beirut remains the main destination, its battle scars even adding to its attraction. In 1998 the USA lifted its restrictions on travel by US citizens to Lebanon.

PEOPLE

Pop. density high

Arabic, French, Armenian, Assyrian

323/km² (835/mi²)

THE URBAN/RURAL POPULATION SPLIT

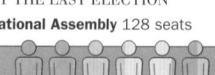

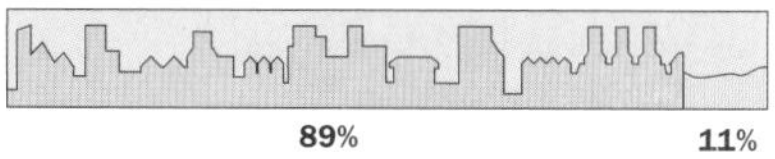
89%
11%

RELIGIOUS PERSUASION

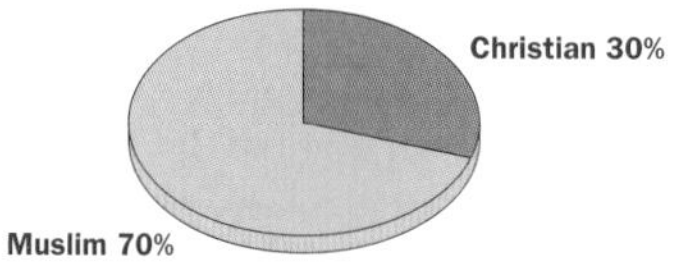
Christian 30%
Muslim 70%

The Lebanese population is fragmented in religious terms into subsects of Christians and Muslims, but retains a strong sense of national identity. There has been a large Palestinian refugee population in the country since 1948. Islamic fundamentalism is influential among poorer Shi'a Muslims, who constitute the largest single group.

POLITICS

Multiparty elections

2000/2004

President Émile Lahoud

AT THE LAST ELECTION

National Assembly 128 seats

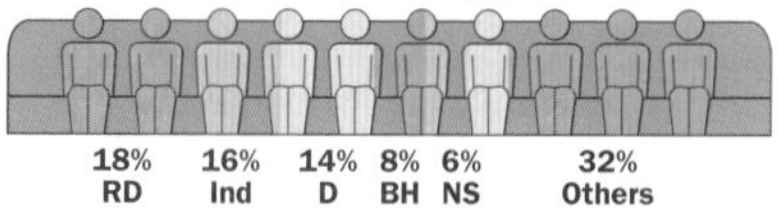
6%
MLU
18%
RD
16%
Ind
14%
D
8%
BH
6%
NS
32%
Others

RD = Resistance and Development List **Ind** = Independents **D** = Dignity **BH** = Baalbek–Hermel List **NS** = National Struggle List **MLU** = Mount Lebanon Unity

The Arab-brokered 1989 Taif peace agreement ending the civil war redressed the constitutional balance between Christians and Muslims and guaranteed power-sharing. Relative stability has been maintained under Rafiq al-Hariri, who won the first postwar legislative elections in 1992. Gen. Émile Lahoud was elected president in 1998. After a brief term as premier by Salim al-Hoss, Hariri was elected to a third term in 2000. Syria remains the main power-broker in Lebanon, especially following the withdrawal of Israeli troops in 2000.

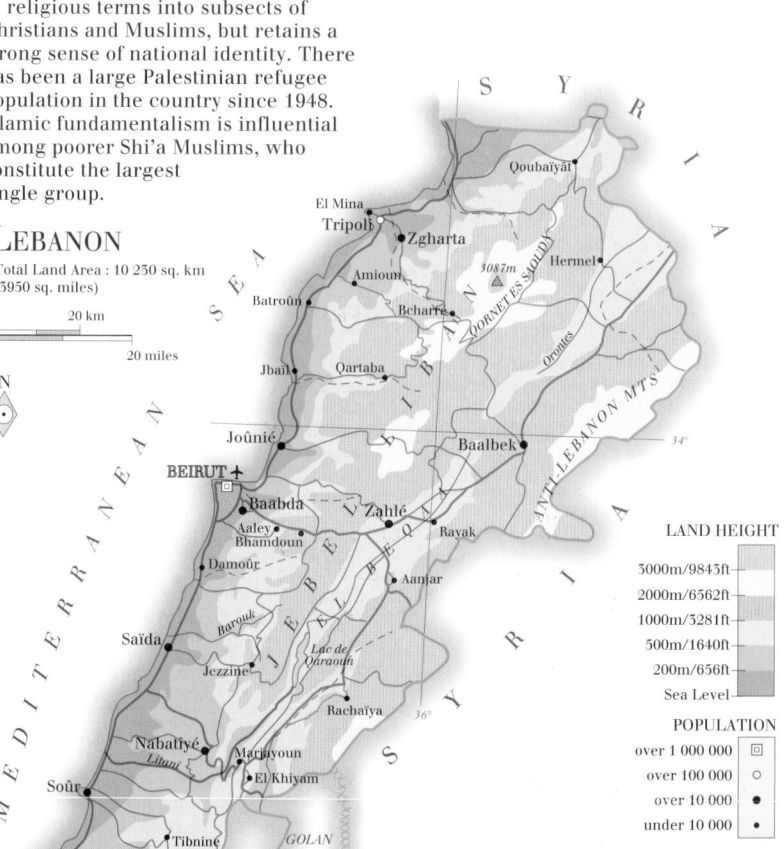

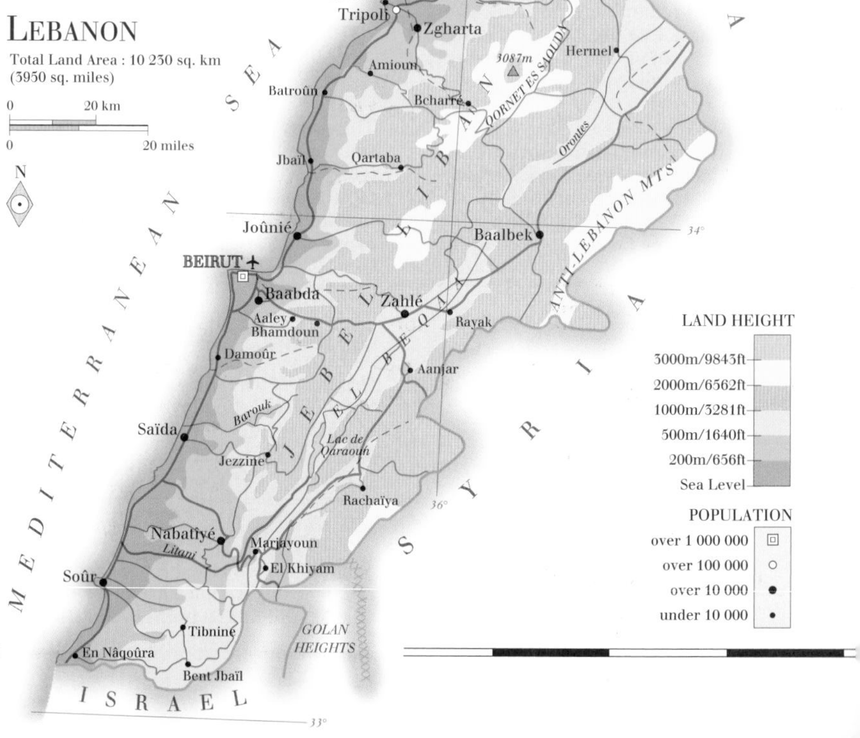
LEBANON
Total Land Area : 10 230 sq. km (3950 sq. miles)
0 20 km
0 20 miles
N
SYRIA
MEDITERRANEAN SEA
ISRAEL
GOLAN HEIGHTS
El Mina
Tripoli
Zgharta
Qoubaïyât
Hermel
Amioun
3087m
Batroûn
Becharré
QORNET ES SAOUDA
Orontes
Jbail
Qartaba
LIBAN
ANTI-LEBANON MTS
Jounié
Baalbek
BEIRUT
Baabda
Zahlé
Aaley
Bhamdoun
Rayak
Damoûr
Aanjar
BEQAA
JEBEL
Barouk
Saïda
Lac de Qaraoun
Jezzine
Rachaïya
Nabatîyé
Litani
Marjayoun
El Khiyam
Soûr
Tibnine
En Nâqoûra
Bent Jbaïl
34°
36°
33°
LAND HEIGHT
3000m/9843ft
2000m/6562ft
1000m/3281ft
500m/1640ft
200m/656ft
Sea Level
POPULATION
over 1 000 000
over 100 000
over 10 000
under 10 000

L

WORLD AFFAIRS
Joined UN in 1945

AL | G24 | OIF | NAM | OIC

The 1989 Taif Agreement ending the civil war has left Syria with enormous influence in domestic politics. Continuing tension in Israel still threatens peace.

Until mid-2000, when Israeli troops withdrew, clashes in the south between Israeli occupying forces (and their proxy militias) and the *Hezbollah* militia were frequent and bloody. A UN force now patrols the border; anti-Israeli rhetoric remains the political lingua franca.

AID
Recipient

$194m (receipts) — Down 18% in 1999

The government has sought billions of dollars for reconstruction. The World Bank prefers working through NGOs.

DEFENSE
Compulsory military service

$563m — Down 4% in 1999

The army has over 60,000 troops. *Hezbollah* guerrillas rapidly regained control of southern Lebanon after the Israeli withdrawal in 2000. There is a UN peacekeeping force on the Israeli border. Syrian forces, whose dominant security role had been formalized in 1991, withdrew from Beirut in 2001.

ECONOMICS
Inflation 24% p.a. (1990–1998)

$15.8bn — 1507.5–1507.0 Lebanese pounds

SCORE CARD

- ❑ World GNP Ranking..........75th
- ❑ GNP per Capita..........$3700
- ❑ Balance of Payments..........$-4809m
- ❑ Inflation..........8%
- ❑ Unemployment..........18%

Strengths
Peace will allow Lebanon to regain its position as an Arab center for banking and services. Potentially a major producer of wine and fruit. Tight fiscal policy has kept inflation down.

Weaknesses
Dependent on imported oil and gas. Agriculture still at 40% of prewar levels. High public debt. Alleged Syrian "dumping" of cheap produce.

EXPORTS

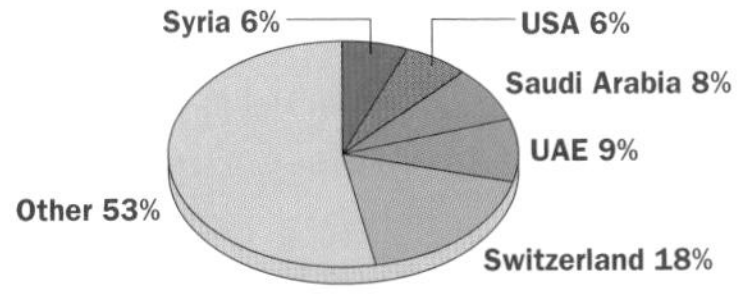
Syria 6%
USA 6%
Saudi Arabia 8%
UAE 9%
Other 53%
Switzerland 18%

IMPORTS

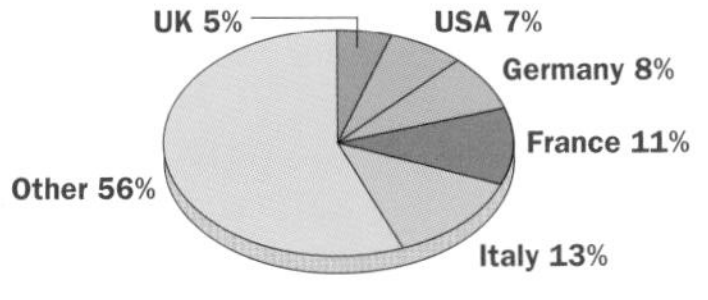
UK 5%
USA 7%
Germany 8%
France 11%
Other 56%
Italy 13%

RESOURCES
Electric power 1.3m kw

3955 tonnes — Not an oil producer; refines 37,500 b/d

445,000 goats, 380,000 sheep, 32m chickens — Lignite, iron ore

Wine, cotton, fruit, and vegetables are the main crops. Thermal power stations are fueled by imported petroleum.

ENVIRONMENT
Sustainability rank: 109th

None — 4.3 tonnes per capita

Rebuilding Beirut's basic infrastructure and ridding the country of mines are the government's priorities.

MEDIA
TV ownership high

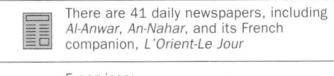

Daily newspaper circulation 141 per 1000 people

PUBLISHING AND BROADCAST MEDIA

There are 41 daily newspapers, including *Al-Anwar*, *An-Nahar*, and its French companion, *L'Orient-Le Jour*

5 services: 1 state-controlled, 4 independent — 1 state-owned service

In the late 1990s the government banned news and political programs on private satellite television channels.

CRIME
Death penalty used

Lebanon does not publish prison figures — Up 202% 1996–1998

The kidnapping of hostages and the breakdown of law during the civil war made Beirut a dangerous city for visitors.

Politically motivated violence has recently declined, though the risk of urban terrorism remains. Rural areas untouched by the conflict have low levels of crime.

***The Corniche, Beirut,** was rebuilt after the civil war by US consultant engineers and architects in a privately financed scheme.*

CHRONOLOGY
Under French mandate from 1920, Lebanon declared independence in 1941, achieving full autonomy in 1946.

- ❑ **1975** Civil war erupts.
- ❑ **1982** Israeli invasion.
- ❑ **1989** Taif Agreement ends civil war.
- ❑ **1992** First election in 20 years. Rafiq al-Hariri prime minister.
- ❑ **1996** Israeli attack kills over 100 civilians at UN base in Qana.
- ❑ **1998** Émile Lahoud president.
- ❑ **2000** Israeli forces withdraw. Hariri reelected by a landslide.

EDUCATION
School leaving age: 15

86% — 81,588 students

Lebanon has one of the highest literacy rates in the Arab world. Education was severely disrupted by the war.

HEALTH
Welfare state health benefits

1 per 435 people — Heart disease, infectious and parasitic diseases

An adequate system of primary health care exists. Hospital staffing is returning to prewar levels.

SPENDING
GDP/cap. increase

CONSUMPTION AND SPENDING

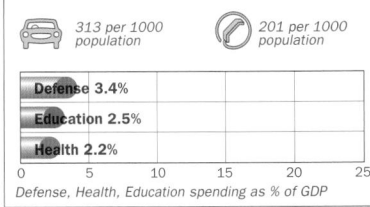

313 per 1000 population — *201 per 1000 population*

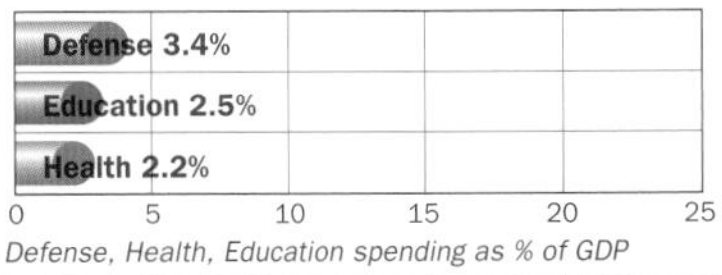
Defense 3.4%
Education 2.5%
Health 2.2%
0
5
10
15
20
25
Defense, Health, Education spending as % of GDP

Average income per capita statistics conceal the fact that a huge gulf exists between the poor and a small, massively rich elite.

WORLD RANKING

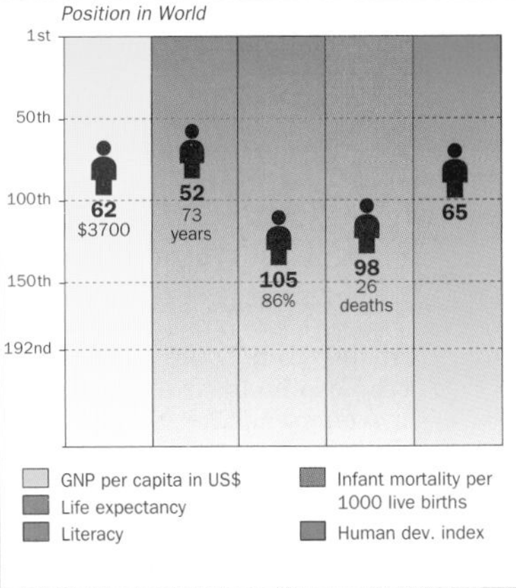
Position in World
1st
50th
100th
150th
192nd
62
$3700
52
73
years
105
86%
98
26
deaths
65
GNP per capita in US$
Life expectancy
Literacy
Infant mortality per 1000 live births
Human dev. index

L

LESOTHO

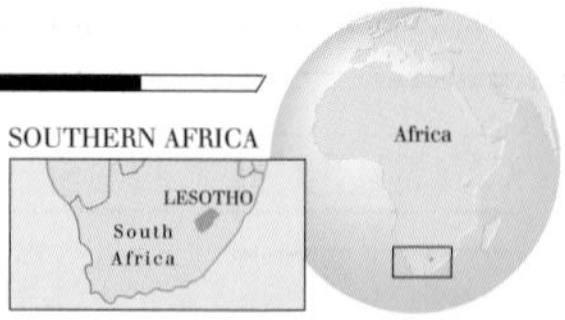
SOUTHERN AFRICA
LESOTHO
South Africa
Africa

OFFICIAL NAME: Kingdom of Lesotho **CAPITAL:** Maseru
POPULATION: 2.2 million **CURRENCY:** Loti **OFFICIAL LANGUAGES:** English and Sesotho

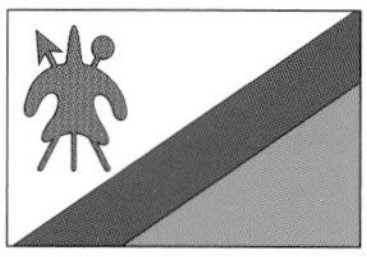

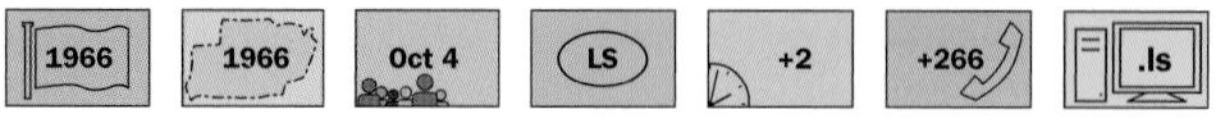
1966
1966
Oct 4
LS
+2
+266
.ls

A MOUNTAINOUS AND landlocked country entirely surrounded by South Africa, Lesotho is economically dependent on its larger neighbor. However, Lesotho is beginning to benefit from the export of energy from the recently completed Highlands Water Scheme. Elections in 1993 ended a period of military rule, but South Africa had to send in its troops when serious political unrest erupted in 1998.

CLIMATE

Mountain

WEATHER CHART

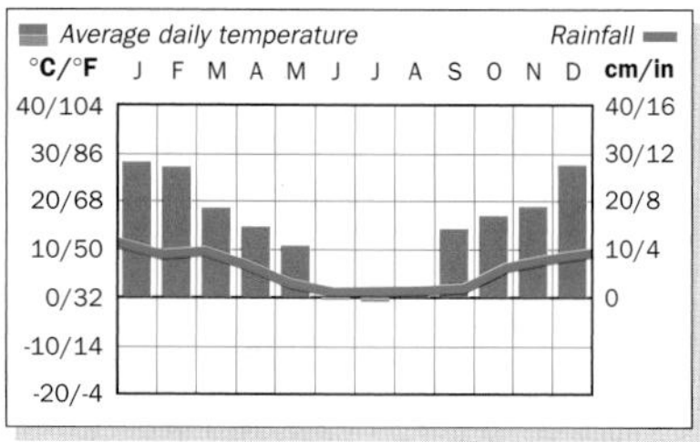
Average daily temperature
Rainfall
°C/°F
J F M A M J J A S O N D
cm/in
40/104
30/86
20/68
10/50
0/32
-10/14
-20/-4
40/16
30/12
20/8
10/4
0

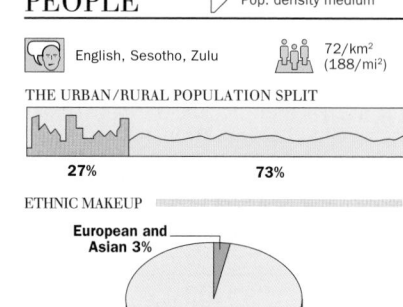

Drought is often followed by torrential rain storms. Snow is frequent in winter in the mountains.

TRANSPORTATION

Drive on left

Moshoeshoe International, Maseru 43,000 passengers

Has no fleet

THE TRANSPORTATION NETWORK

887 km (551 miles)	None
3 km (2 miles)	None

Lesotho has to rely on South African road and rail outlets. New roads have been constructed to service the Highlands Water Scheme.

TOURISM

Visitors : Population 1:12

186,000 visitors

Up 24% in 1999

MAIN TOURIST ARRIVALS

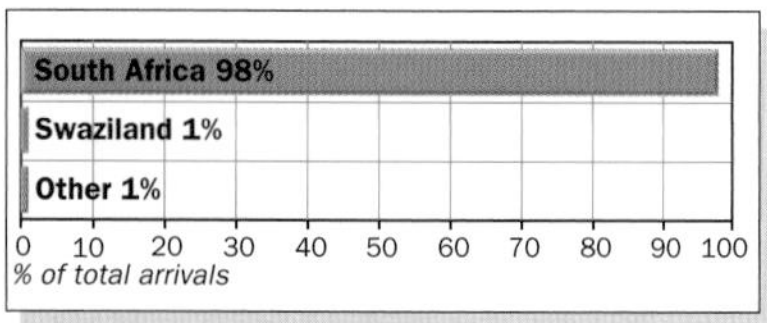
South Africa 98%
Swaziland 1%
Other 1%
0 10 20 30 40 50 60 70 80 90 100
% of total arrivals

Tourists, mainly from South Africa are attracted to Lesotho by its dramatic mountain scenery and for watersports on artificially created lakes. However, political violence in 1998 deterred many visitors.

PEOPLE

Pop. density medium

English, Sesotho, Zulu

72/km² (188/mi²)

THE URBAN/RURAL POPULATION SPLIT

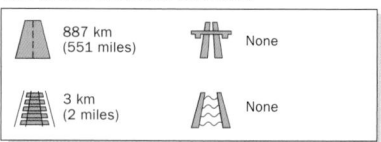

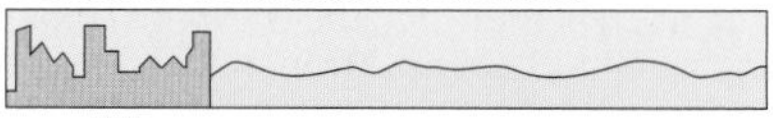
27%
73%

ETHNIC MAKEUP

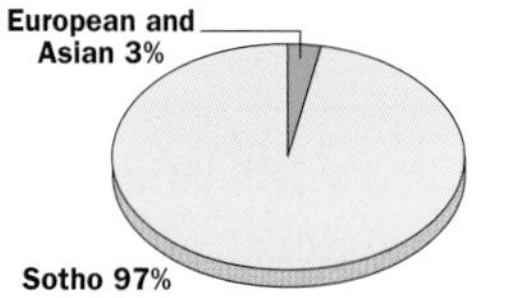
European and Asian 3%
Sotho 97%

The overwhelming majority of the population are Sotho, though there are also small minority communities of European, south Asian, and Chinese origin. Ethnic homogeneity and a strong sense of national identity have tended to minimize ethnic tension. However, in 1991 rioters attacked south Asian and Chinese storekeepers, whose control of business they resented. The export of male contract labor to South African mines means that women head 72% of households; they also run farming, regarded by Lesotho men as "women's work."

POLITICS

Multiparty elections

L. House 1998/2002
U. House 1998/2003

HM King Letsie III

AT THE LAST ELECTION

National Assembly 80 seats

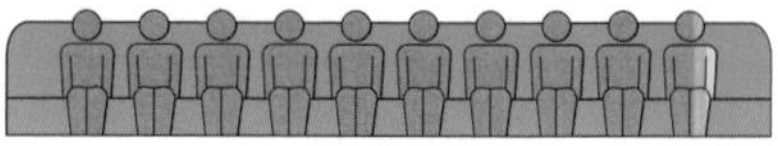
1%
BNP
98%
LCD
1%
Vacant

LCD = Lesotho Congress for Democracy Party
BNP = Basotho National Party

Senate 33 seats

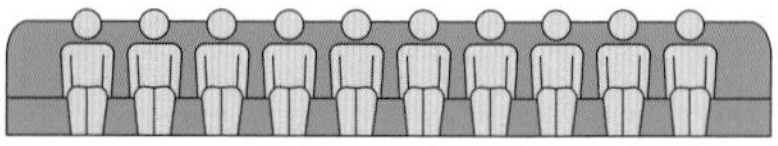

The Senate comprises 22 principal chiefs and 11 other members named by the king

The armed forces have been key political players in Lesotho since a bloodless coup in 1986. Although direct military rule ended in 1993, and a free and peaceful general election resulted in a sweeping victory for the Basotho Congress Party (BCP), the army maintained its powers over national security. Tensions between the army and the civilian administration escalated in 1994, when mutinous troops killed the deputy prime minister. King Moshoeshoe II was restored to the throne, and was succeeded by his son Letsie III in 1996.

Accusations of vote rigging and mass protests greeted a general election win in 1998 by the LCD. After an attempted coup in September, the South African military intervened to restore democracy, brokering an agreement between the king and Lesotho's 12 parties. However, elections scheduled for 2000 were postponed until 2002.

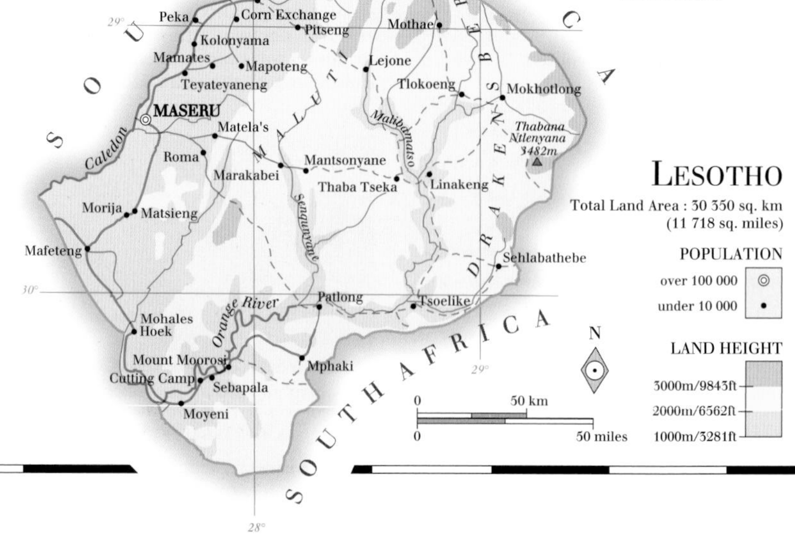
SOUTH AFRICA
Joel's Drift
Ohobela
Oxbow
Butha Buthe
Hlotse
Peka
Corn Exchange
Pitseng
Kolonyama
Mothae
Mamates
Mapoteng
Lejone
Teyateyaneng
Tlokoeng
Mokhotlong
MASERU
MALUTI
Matela's
Malibamatso
Thabana Ntlenyana 3482m
Caledon
Roma
Mantsonyane
Marakabei
Thaba Tseka
Linakeng
DRAKENSBERG
Morija
Matsieng
Senqunyane
Mafeteng
Sehlabathebe
Orange River
Patlong
Tsoelike
Mohales Hoek
Mount Moorosi
Cutting Camp
Mphaki
Sebapala
Moyeni
SOUTH AFRICA
29°
30°
28°
N
0 50 km
0 50 miles
LESOTHO
Total Land Area : 30 350 sq. km (11 718 sq. miles)
POPULATION
over 100 000
under 10 000
LAND HEIGHT
3000m/9843ft
2000m/6562ft
1000m/3281ft

WORLD AFFAIRS

Joined UN in 1966

Comm | ACP | NAM | OAU | SADC

Foreign policy is dominated by the nature of Lesotho's relationship with South Africa. Lesotho currently has duty-free access to the EU for most manufactured goods, and also has preferential access to US and Scandinavian markets.

AID

Recipient

$31m (receipts) — Down 53% in 1999

Aid, mostly devoted to agricultural development, accounts for 26% of Lesotho's GNP; about half comes from the Southern Africa Customs Union (SACU). Other donors include the World Bank, the EU, and the UK.

DEFENSE

No compulsory military service

$34m — Down 19% in 1999

Lesotho's 2000-strong army relied on South African assistance to quell political violence in 1998.

ECONOMICS

Inflation 9.6% p.a. (1990–1999)

$1.2bn — 6.158–7.570 maloti

SCORE CARD

❑ World GNP Ranking	152nd
❑ GNP per Capita	$550
❑ Balance of Payments	$–280m
❑ Inflation	7.3%
❑ Unemployment	50%

Strengths

Potential of educated workforce. Boom in textiles and other manufacturing. Membership of SACU. Future revenues from water sales.

Weaknesses

Dependent on South Africa. Weak agricultural sector. Loss of workers to mining in South Africa. Retail sector suffered badly during 1998 disturbances.

EXPORTS

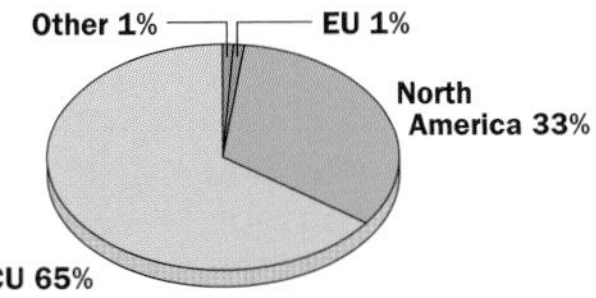
Other 1%
EU 1%
North America 33%
SACU 65%

IMPORTS

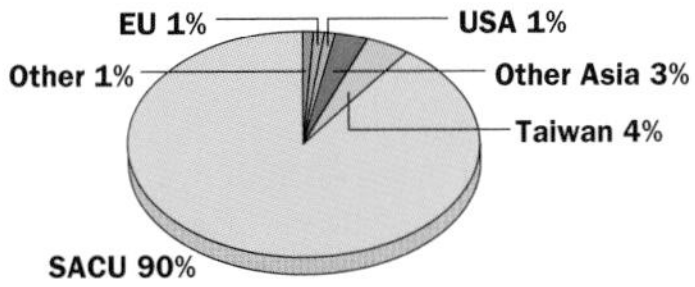
EU 1%
USA 1%
Other 1%
Other Asia 3%
Taiwan 4%
SACU 90%

Landscape near Mohales Hoek *in Lesotho's lowest lands – over 1300 m (4260 ft) above sea level. This spiral aloe grows only in Lesotho.*

RESOURCES

Not available

44 tonnes — Not an oil producer

750,000 sheep, 580,000 goats, 1.8m chickens — Diamonds

The Highlands Water hydroelectric scheme has the capacity to supply all of Lesotho's energy requirements, as well as 63.3 cubic m (2200 cubic feet) of water per second for South African use. Diamonds are mined in the northeast.

ENVIRONMENT

Not available

1% — Not available

Climate and overgrazing have seriously eroded the land. The Highlands Water Scheme has flooded acres of peasant farmland. Supporters of this massive dam project stress encouragement for wildlife in reservoirs and on bird-friendly pylons.

MEDIA

TV ownership low

Daily newspaper circulation 8 per 1000 people

PUBLISHING AND BROADCAST MEDIA

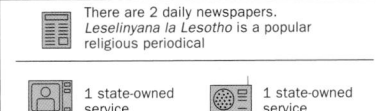

There are 2 daily newspapers. *Leselinyana la Lesotho* is a popular religious periodical

1 state-owned service — 1 state-owned service

State control of the media was used for political ends in 1998. The *Mirror* is the only independent paper.

CRIME

Death penalty used

Lesotho does not publish prison figures — Large rise in 1998

The 1998 political crisis increased crime levels, which previously were much lower than in South Africa.

EDUCATION

School leaving age: 13

83% — 4614 students

Lesotho has very high school enrollment levels and one of the highest literacy rates in Africa.

CHRONOLOGY

As Basutoland, Lesotho became a British Crown colony in 1884.

- ❑ **1966** Independent kingdom.
- ❑ **1986** Military coup.
- ❑ **1990** King Moshoeshoe II exiled. Son installed as Letsie III.
- ❑ **1993** Free elections.
- ❑ **1994** Return of Moshoeshoe II.
- ❑ **1996** Letsie III succeeds to throne.
- ❑ **1998** New LCD wins polls. South Africa intervenes after coup attempt, and reconciles king and parties.
- ❑ **2000** Elections postponed.
- ❑ **2001** Election registration starts for promised 2002 elections.

HEALTH

Welfare state health benefits

1 per 10,000 people — Tuberculosis, parasitic diseases, nutritional disorders

Private health organizations and NGOs account for half of all health services. A government-operated flying doctor service covers the highlands. The main endemic disease is tuberculosis. Political conflict in late 1998 ruined whole communities, and led to 35,000 children needing emergency food aid.

L

SPENDING

GDP/cap. increase

CONSUMPTION AND SPENDING

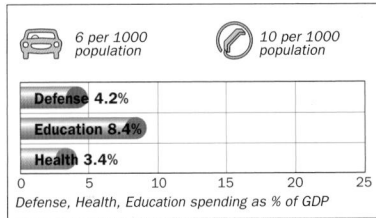

6 per 1000 population — *10 per 1000 population*

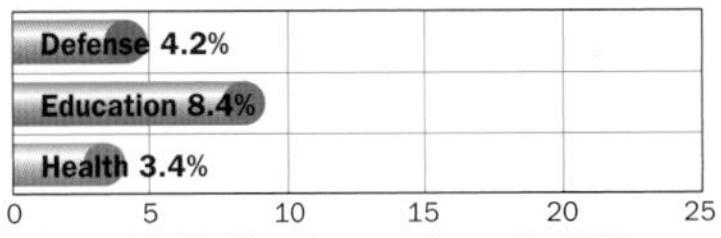
Defense 4.2%
Education 8.4%
Health 3.4%
0
5
10
15
20
25

Defense, Health, Education spending as % of GDP

Social mobility is limited in Lesotho; the ruling elite keeps a tight control on power and wealth. Over 90% of the population live below the poverty line and many are migrant laborers.

WORLD RANKING

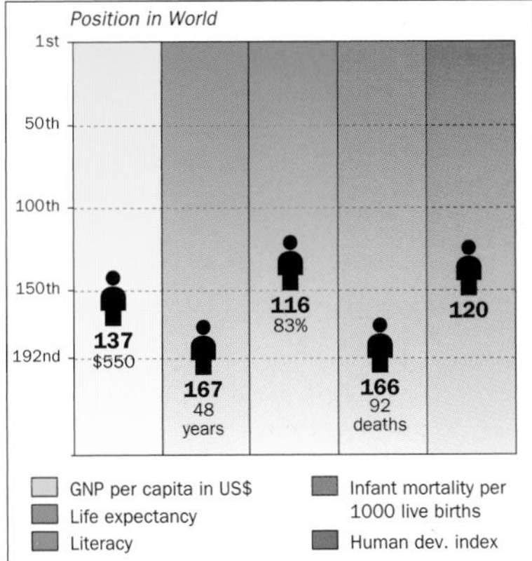
Position in World
1st
50th
100th
150th
192nd
137
$550
167
48
years
116
83%
166
92
deaths
120
GNP per capita in US$
Life expectancy
Literacy
Infant mortality per 1000 live births
Human dev. index

LIBERIA

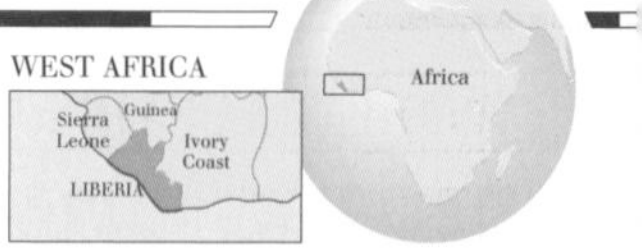
WEST AFRICA
Sierra Leone
Guinea
Ivory Coast
LIBERIA
Africa

OFFICIAL NAME: Republic of Liberia **CAPITAL:** Monrovia
POPULATION: 3.2 million **CURRENCY:** Liberian dollar **OFFICIAL LANGUAGE:** English

1847 | 1847 | July 26 | LB | 0 | +231 | .lr

FOUNDED IN 1847 by freed slaves from the USA, Liberia today is struggling to recover from a civil war which reduced it to anarchy between 1990 and 1996. Facing the Atlantic in equatorial west Africa, most of its coastline is characterized by lagoons and mangrove swamps. Inland, a grassland plateau supports the limited agriculture (just 1% of land is arable). Liberia has the world's largest flag of convenience merchant fleet.

CLIMATE

Tropical equatorial

WEATHER CHART

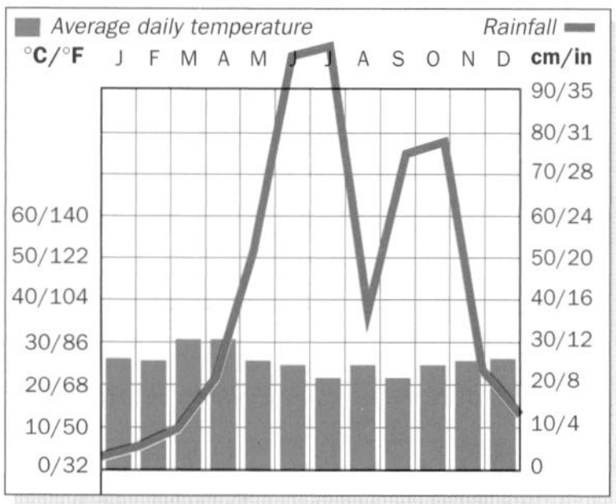
Average daily temperature
Rainfall
°C/°F
J F M A M J J A S O N D
cm/in
90/35
80/31
70/28
60/24
50/20
40/16
30/12
20/8
10/4
0
60/140
50/122
40/104
30/86
20/68
10/50
0/32

There is one long rainy season from May to October, except in the southeast which has two separate rainy seasons. Temperatures are consistently high. During the dry season, when the dust-laden *harmattan* wind blows, they rise even higher inland.

TRANSPORTATION

Drive on right

Roberts Field International, Monrovia

1717 ships 60.5m grt

THE TRANSPORTATION NETWORK

657 km (408 miles)	None
480 km (298 miles)	None

Most roads in Liberia are unpaved. The 480-km (298-mile) railroad was built to transport iron ore and carries little other traffic. Roberts Field airport was built by the USA during World War II.

TOURISM

Not available

Tourists deterred by civil war

Little change from year to year

MAIN TOURIST ARRIVALS

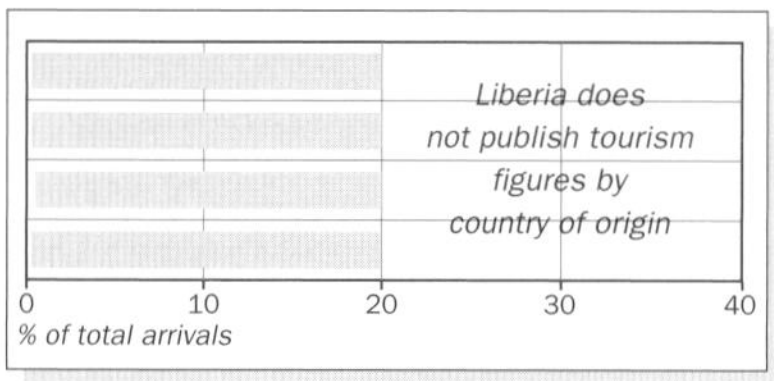
Liberia does not publish tourism figures by country of origin
0
10
20
30
40
% of total arrivals

As a result of the civil war and continuing insecurity, tourism, never a significant activity in Liberia, is now non-existent.

PEOPLE

Pop. density low

Kpelle, Vai, Bassa, Kru, Grebo, Kissi, Gola, Loma, English

33/km² (86/mi²)

THE URBAN/RURAL POPULATION SPLIT

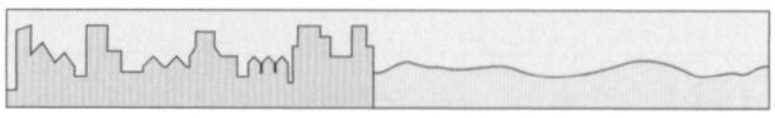
48%
52%

ETHNIC MAKEUP

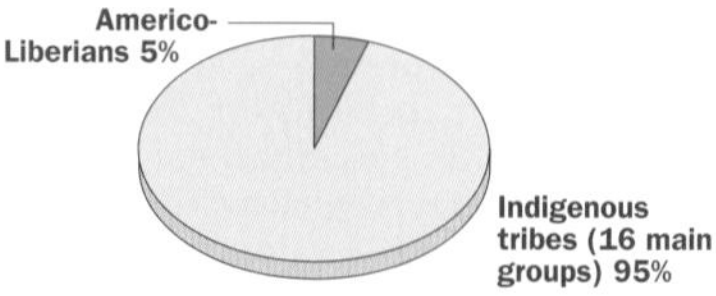
Americo-Liberians 5%
Indigenous tribes (16 main groups) 95%

A key distinction in Liberia has been between Americo-Liberians, the descendants of those freed from slavery (known as "civilized persons"), and the majority indigenous "tribals." The latter were long held in contempt by the Americos, but intermarriage and political assimilation since 1944 have softened attitudes. Intertribal tension in Liberia is now a much more serious problem, and was the main cause of the civil war which erupted in 1990.

POLITICS

Multiparty elections

L. House 1997/2003
U. House 1997/2006

President Charles Taylor

AT THE LAST ELECTION

House of Representatives 64 seats

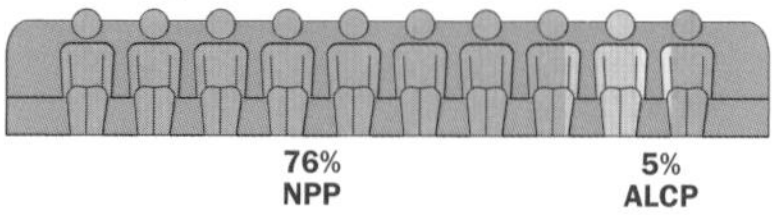
11% UP
8% Others
76% NPP
5% ALCP

NPP = National Patriotic Party **UP** = Unity Party
ALCP = All Liberia Coalition Party

Senate 26 seats

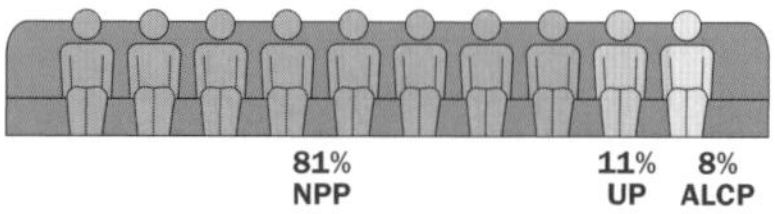
81% NPP
11% UP
8% ALCP

Liberian politics collapsed after 1990 into a chaotic, bloody, and many-sided conflict. A peace agreement finally signed in 1996 provided for presidential and legislative elections in 1997, won by Charles Taylor and his NPP, formerly the National Patriotic Front of Liberia (NPFL), the predominant armed faction. Some 700,000 refugees began returning, but instability continued, and intense fighting broke out in the north in mid-2000 following the formation of a new rebel faction, Liberians United for Reconciliation and Democracy. Thousands of civilians fled the area in early 2001 as fighting escalated.

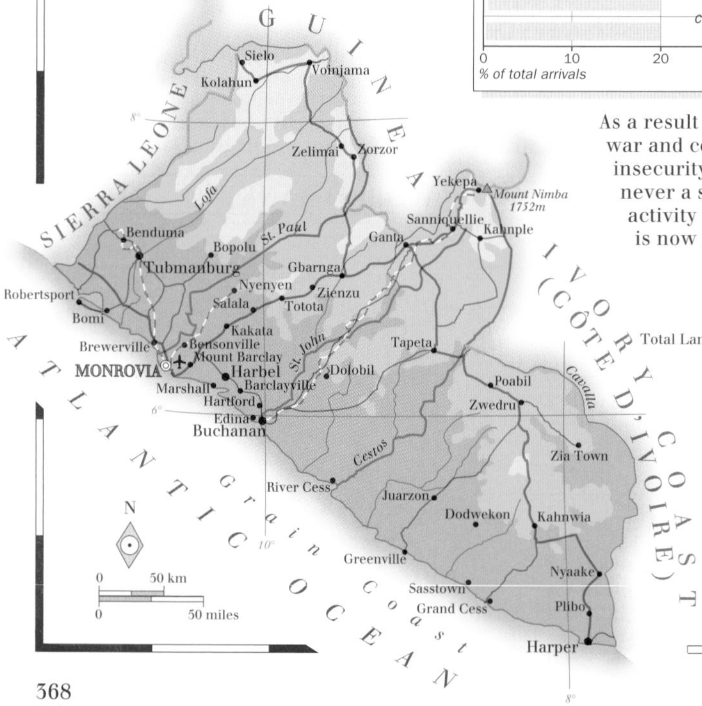
GUINEA
SIERRA LEONE
IVORY COAST (CÔTE D'IVOIRE)
ATLANTIC OCEAN
Grain Coast
Sielo
Voinjama
Kolahun
Zelimai
Zorzor
Lofa
Yekepa
Mount Nimba 1752m
Sanniquellie
Kahnple
Ganta
Bendums
Bopolu
St. Paul
Tubmanburg
Gbarnga
Nyenyen
Zienzu
Salala
Totota
Robertsport
Bomi
Kakata
Bensonville
Brewerville
Mount Barclay
St. John
Tapeta
MONROVIA
Harbel
Dolobil
Marshall
Barclayville
Hartford
Poabil
Cavalla
Edina
Buchanan
Zwedru
Cestos
Zia Town
River Cess
Juarzon
Dodwekon
Kahnwia
Greenville
Nyaake
Sasstown
Grand Cess
Plibo
Harper
N
0
50 km
50 miles

LIBERIA

Total Land Area : 96 320 sq. km
37 189 sq. miles

POPULATION
over 100 000
over 10 000
under 10 000

LAND HEIGHT
1000m/3281ft
500m/1640ft
200m/656ft
Sea Level

WORLD AFFAIRS

Joined UN in 1945

ACP | ECOWAS | IAEA | NAM | OAU

The ECOWAS peacekeeping force ECOMOG, backed chiefly by Nigeria and Ghana, arrived in 1990. It was pressure from ECOWAS that kept the UN-led peace process on track in the mid-1990s. The UN imposed sanctions in 2001, accusing Liberia of fomenting war in west Africa. Diplomatic relations with neighboring Guinea and Sierra Leone were broken off abruptly in 2001.

AID

Recipient

US$94m (receipts) — Up 29% in 1999

Liberia remains heavily dependent on foreign aid. In mid-2000 the EU cut an aid package, accusing the regime of selling arms to rebels in Sierra Leone.

DEFENSE

No compulsory military service

US$25m — Down 46% in 1999

Peace agreements in 1995 and 1996 provided for the demobilization of the various warring factions and the formation of a single national army.

ECONOMICS

Not available

US$1bn — 1 Liberian dollar

SCORE CARD

- WORLD GNP RANKING....................154th
- GNP PER CAPITA....................US$330
- BALANCE OF PAYMENTS....................US$–145m
- INFLATION....................9.1%
- UNEMPLOYMENT....................70%

STRENGTHS

Potential for reviving the Firestone rubber plantation and huge LAMCO iron ore mine. Tropical timber, but reserves are declining.

WEAKNESSES

Little commercial activity, and low confidence. Political instability. UN sanctions on diamond trade from 2001.

EXPORTS

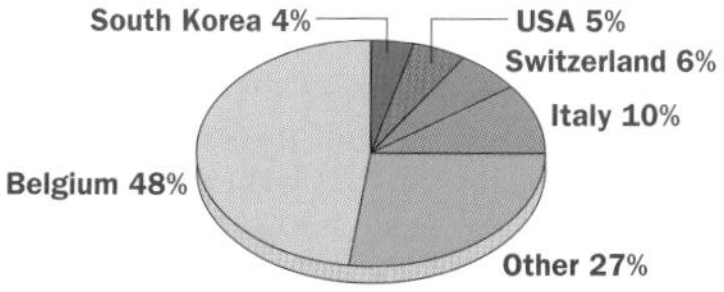
South Korea 4%
USA 5%
Switzerland 6%
Italy 10%
Belgium 48%
Other 27%

IMPORTS

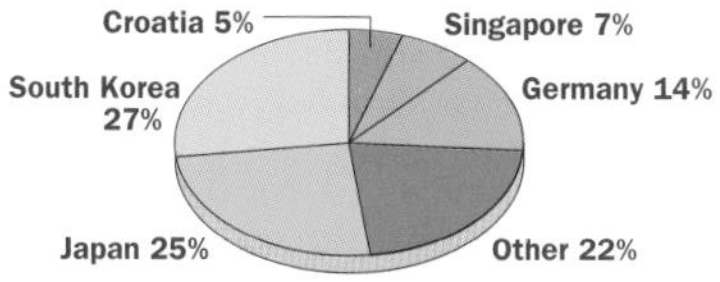
Croatia 5%
Singapore 7%
South Korea 27%
Germany 14%
Japan 25%
Other 22%

Village near Gbarnga. *The Kpelle, the largest of Liberia's 16 indigenous ethnic groups, are concentrated in this part of Liberia.*

RESOURCES

Electric power 332,000 kw

- 8580 tonnes
- Not an oil producer
- 220,000 goats, 210,000 sheep, 3.5m chickens
- Iron ore, diamonds, gold, barytes, kyanite, columbite, manganese

Liberia has an estimated billion tonnes of iron ore reserves at Mount Nimba, but even when peaceful conditions return, the current state of world demand would barely justify exploitation.

ENVIRONMENT

Not available

1% — 0.1 tonnes per capita

The NPFL and other armed groups cut down tropical forests to help finance their armies.

MEDIA

TV ownership low

Daily newspaper circulation 16 per 1000 people

PUBLISHING AND BROADCAST MEDIA

There are 6 daily newspapers, including the independent *Daily Observer*

1 partly state-owned service — 10 services: 4 state-owned, 6 independent

The Monrovia press has been freer since the fall of Doe in 1990, but distribution problems in a state of war lessened the impact of newspapers.

CRIME

Death penalty used

Liberia does not publish prison figures — Crime is rampant. There are no enforcing agencies

Human rights have figured little in Liberian life, and after 1990 they disappeared altogether. The warring factions regularly massacred civilians, press-ganged armies, and displaced thousands into seeking refuge in neighboring states.

EDUCATION

School leaving age: 16

54% — 5095 students

Originally based on the US model, the education system effectively collapsed during the civil war.

CHRONOLOGY

Between 1816 and 1892, 22,000 liberated slaves, most from the USA, settled in Liberia, established as a republic in 1847.

- **1980** Coup. President assassinated by Samuel Doe.
- **1990** Outbreak of civil war.
- **1991** Doe assassinated.
- **1996** Second peace agreement.
- **1997** Charles Taylor president.
- **1999** Withdrawal of ECOMOG.
- **2001** Borders with Guinea and Sierra Leone closed. Conflict with rebels escalates.

HEALTH

No welfare state health benefits

1 per 9350 people — Communicable, diarrheal, parasitic, and heart diseases

Very few people have access to basic health care. Liberia's infant mortality rate remains among the highest in the world.

SPENDING

GDP/cap. decrease

CONSUMPTION AND SPENDING

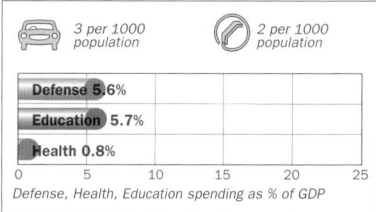

3 per 1000 population — *2 per 1000 population*

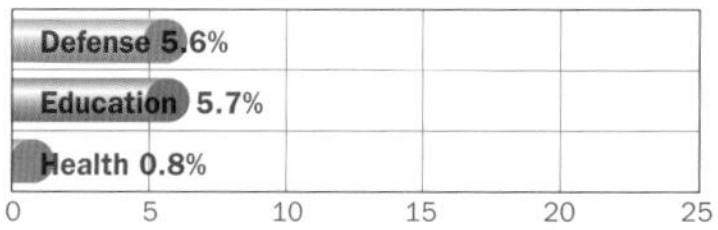
Defense 5.6%
Education 5.7%
Health 0.8%
0
5
10
15
20
25

Defense, Health, Education spending as % of GDP

Power and wealth have a very direct connection in Liberia. Both the Americo-Liberian regimes and the Doe regime which replaced them, saw the state as a source of plunder in the form of well-paid jobs and kick-backs from contracts. The factions in the 1990–1996 civil war sought similar power. Most ordinary Liberians live in rural poverty.

WORLD RANKING

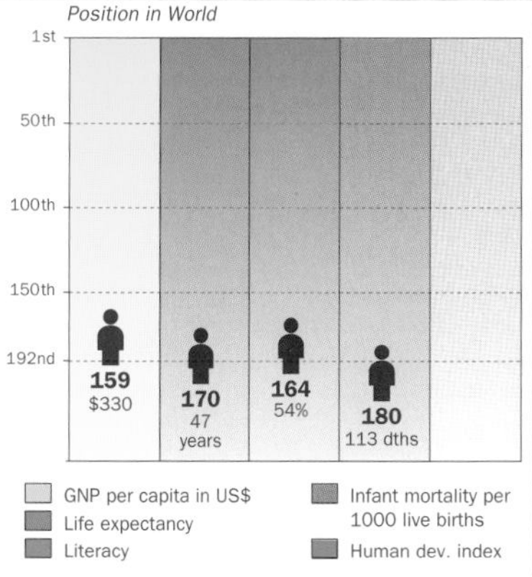
Position in World
1st
50th
100th
150th
192nd
159
$330
170
47 years
164
54%
180
113 dths
GNP per capita in US$
Life expectancy
Literacy
Infant mortality per 1000 live births
Human dev. index

L

LIBYA

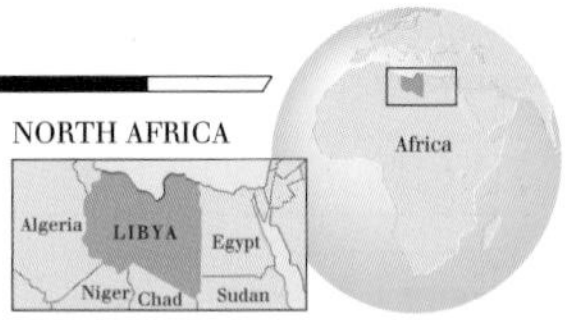
NORTH AFRICA
Africa
Algeria
LIBYA
Egypt
Niger
Chad
Sudan

OFFICIAL NAME: Great Socialist People's Libyan Arab Jamahiriyah
CAPITAL: Tripoli **POPULATION:** 5.6 million **CURRENCY:** Libyan dinar **OFFICIAL LANGUAGE:** Arabic

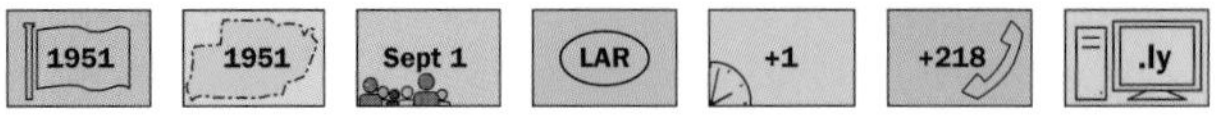
1951
1951
Sept 1
LAR
+1
+218
.ly

LIBYA IS SITUATED between Egypt and Algeria on the Mediterranean coast of north Africa, with Chad and Niger on its southern borders. Apart from the coastal strip and the mountains in the south, it is desert or semidesert. Libya's strategic position in north Africa and its abundant oil and gas resources made it an important trading partner for European states. It has for many years been politically marginalized by the West for its links with terrorist groups, but UN sanctions were suspended in 1999, when it handed over the two men suspected of the 1988 Lockerbie bombing.

Roman amphitheater, Sabratah. *Libya's impressive classical heritage testifies to its importance in ancient times.*

CLIMATE

Hot desert

WEATHER CHART

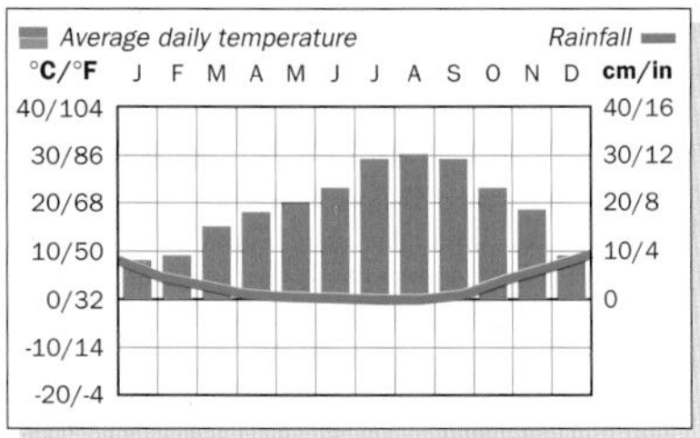
Average daily temperature
Rainfall
°C/°F
J F M A M J J A S O N D
cm/in
40/104
30/86
20/68
10/50
0/32
-10/14
-20/-4
40/16
30/12
20/8
10/4
0

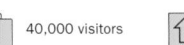

The coastal region has a warm, temperate climate, with mild, wet winters and hot, dry summers.

TRANSPORTATION

Drive on right

Tripoli International

144 ships 567,000 grt

THE TRANSPORTATION NETWORK

47,590 km (29,571 miles)

None

None

None

The National Coast Road runs 1825 km (1135 miles) between the Tunisian and Egyptian borders, linking the principal urban centers. There are no railroads, but some are planned. Since sanctions were lifted in 1999, international airlines have resumed flights to Libya.

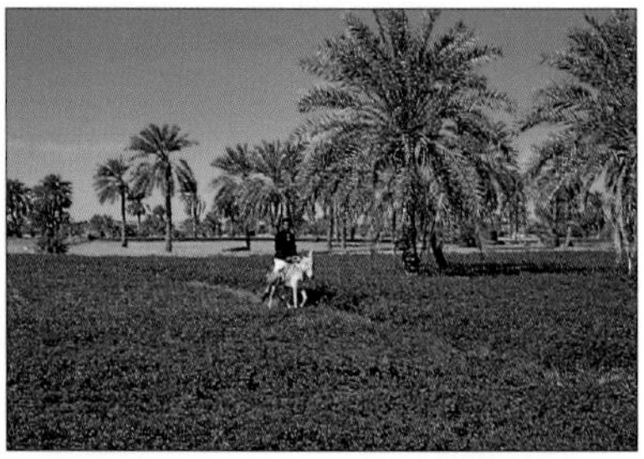

Al Kufrah Oasis. *As 90% of Libya is arid rock and sand, oases provide essential agricultural land, besides being tourist attractions.*

TOURISM

Visitors : Population 1:140

40,000 visitors

Up 25% in 1999

Libya possesses a rich Roman and Greek heritage, centered on the ancient Roman coastal towns of Labdah (Leptis Magna) and Sabratah near Tripoli, and Shahhat (Cyrene) further east. There are fine beaches at Tripoli. A $2–3 billion investment program launched in 2000 aims to attract thousands of visitors. Western tourists have begun to return since sanctions were lifted in 1999.

MAIN TOURIST ARRIVALS

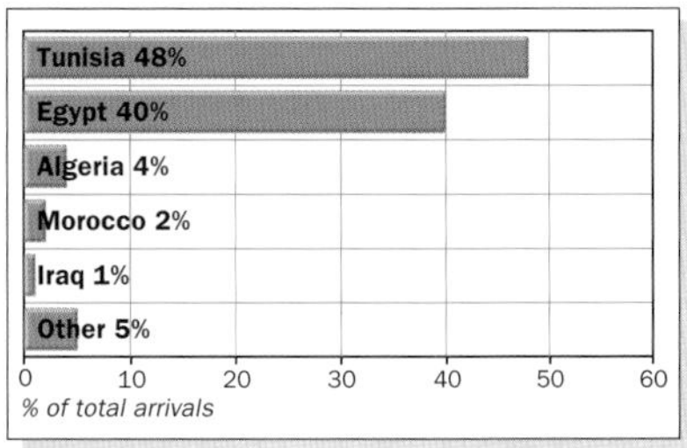
Tunisia 48%
Egypt 40%
Algeria 4%
Morocco 2%
Iraq 1%
Other 5%
0
10
20
30
40
50
60
% of total arrivals

PEOPLE

Pop. density low

Arabic, Tuareg

3/km² (8/mi²)

THE URBAN/RURAL POPULATION SPLIT

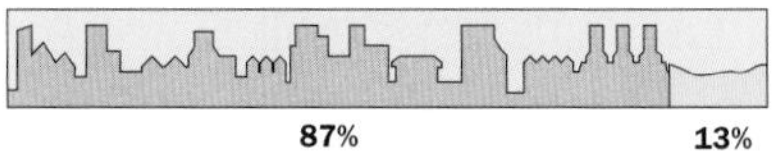
87%
13%

RELIGIOUS PERSUASION

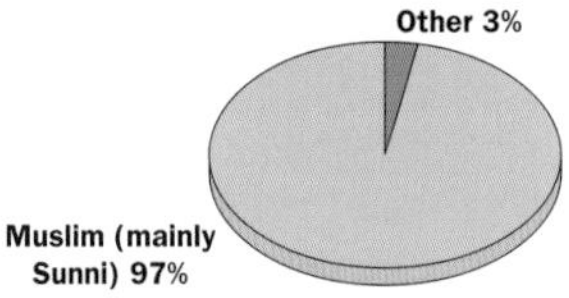
Other 3%
Muslim (mainly Sunni) 97%

ETHNIC MAKEUP

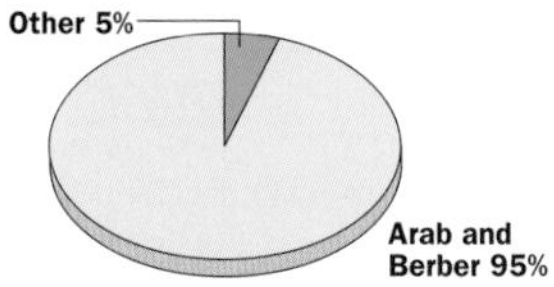
Other 5%
Arab and Berber 95%

POPULATION AGE BREAKDOWN

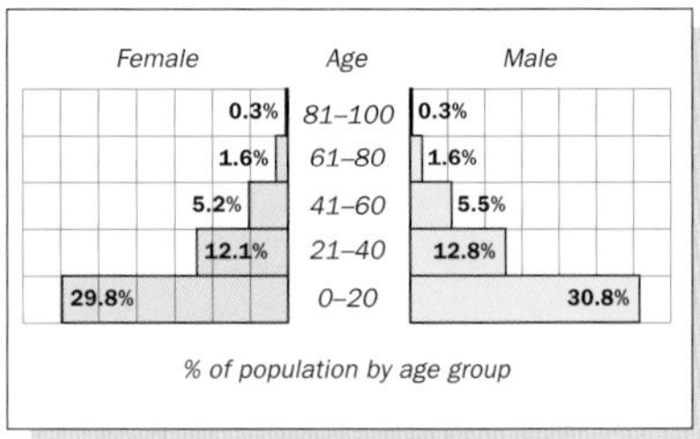
Female
Age
Male
0.3%
81–100
0.3%
1.6%
61–80
1.6%
5.2%
41–60
5.5%
12.1%
21–40
12.8%
29.8%
0–20
30.8%
% of population by age group

Arabs and Berbers, split into many tribal groupings, form 95% of the population. They were artificially brought together when Libya was created in 1951 by the unification of three historic Ottoman provinces. The pro-Western monarchy then set up perpetuated the dominance of Cyrenaican tribes and the Sanusi religious order.

The 1969 revolution brought to the fore Arab nationalist Colonel Gaddafi, who embodied the character and aspirations of the rural Sirtica tribes from Fazzan: fierce independence, deep Islamic convictions, belief in a communal lifestyle, and hatred for the urban rich. His revolution wiped out private enterprise and the middle class, banished European settlers and Jews, undermined the religious Muslim establishment, and imposed a form of popular democracy through the *jamahiriyah* (state of the masses). However, resentment of the regime grew as it became clear that power now lay mainly with the Sirtica tribes, especially Gaddafi's own clan, the Qadhadhfa.

Since the revolution, Libya has become a society where most are city-dwellers. Jews have been invited to return as investors, and immigrants from sub-Saharan Africa have been drawn in to provide low-cost labor. However, clashes in 2000, in which 100 died, highlighted unresolved social issues.

L

POLITICS

No multiparty elections

Not applicable

Leader of the Revolution Col. Muammar al-Gaddafi

LEGISLATIVE OR ADVISORY BODIES

General People's Congress 750 seats

The constitution makes no provision for direct elections. Last renewal May 2000

Executive power is exercised by the General People's Committee. The General People's Congress elects the head of state, the Leader of the Revolution.

MAIN POLITICAL ISSUES

Repression

Political dissidents, including Islamist militants, have been violently suppressed. Libyan dissidents have been murdered abroad, allegedly by government agents. Political parties were banned in 1971, but opposition groups are active in Egypt and Sudan.

The regime's public image

In the past few years, the regime has made an effort to improve its image. Measures have included the freeing of some political prisoners, allowing exiles to visit the country, and permitting foreign travel.

PROFILE

In 1977, a new form of direct democracy was promulgated, through which some 2000 People's Congresses sought to involve every adult in policy-making. In theory, their wishes are carried out by popular committees. In practice, ultimate control rests with Colonel Gaddafi and his collaborators, many of whom date from the 1969 revolution. In recent years some are thought to have been alienated from Gaddafi, including his deputy, Major Abdessalem Jalloud, who in 1994 was reportedly marginalized after expressing differences with him. In 1995, another of Gaddafi's close associates, Khoueldi Hamidi, a defense commander, was also said to have become disillusioned with Gaddafi. In 2000, Gaddafi embraced African unity – an unpopular concept among most Libyans, increasing Gaddafi's alienation from his fomer associates. He is now believed to rely on members of his own clan, particularly his five sons.

Colonel Gaddafi, *Libya's leader since 1969, shies from official titles.*

Ex-King Idris *deposed by Colonel Gaddafi in 1969.*

WORLD AFFAIRS

Joined UN in 1955

AL | AMU | NAM | OIC | OPEC

Gaddafi's regime was by 2001 indicating a less confrontational stance than that which had left it isolated for decades, in particular its support for various terrorist groups, and its strong opposition to the ongoing Middle East peace process. UN sanctions imposed in 1992 were eased in 1999, after Libya finally handed over two men accused of involvement in the 1988 bombing of a US airliner over Lockerbie, Scotland. The conviction of one of them in January 2001, by a Scottish court sitting at The Hague, prompted calls for the complete removal of sanctions. The UK resumed relations in 1999, when Libya admitted responsibility for the London shooting of a policewoman in 1984. Relations also improved with other EU countries and even the USA.

L

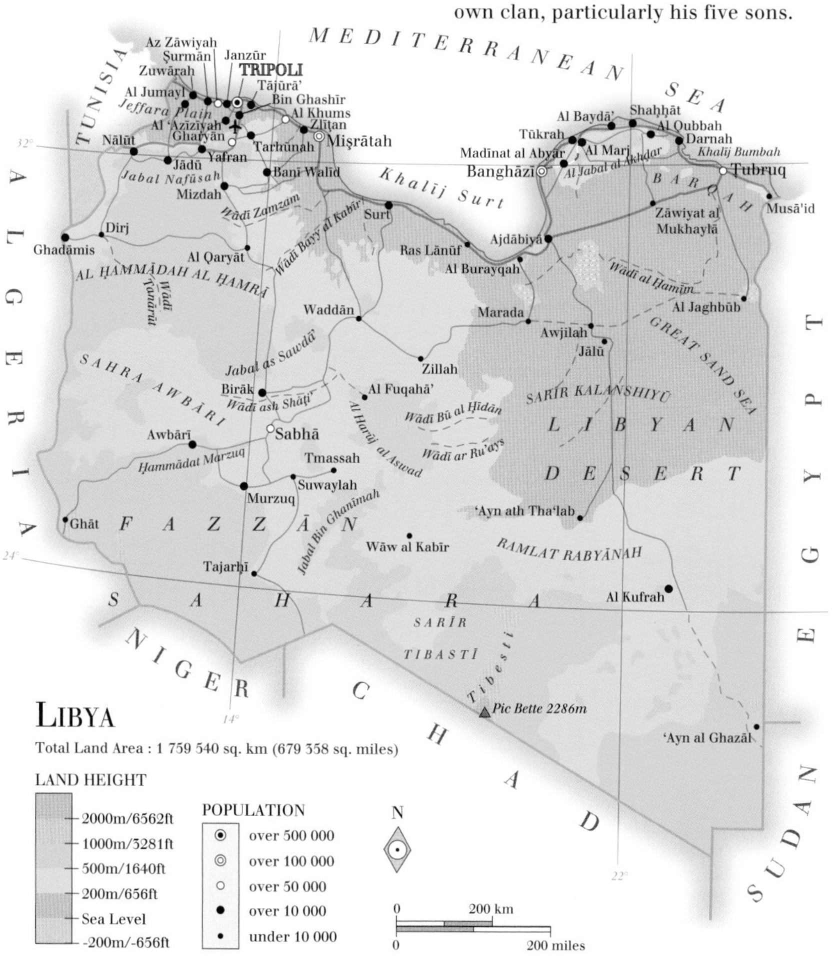
MEDITERRANEAN SEA
TRIPOLI
Az Zāwiyah
Şurmān
Janzūr
Zuwārah
Tājūrā'
Al Jumayl
Bin Ghashīr
Jeffara Plain
Al Khums
Al 'Azīzīyah
Zlītan
Gharyān
Mişrātah
Nālūt
Tarhūnah
Yafran
Jādū
Banī Walīd
Jabal Nafūsah
Mizdah
Wādī Zamzam
Khalīj Surt
Surt
Dirj
Ghadāmis
Al Qaryāt
Wādī Bayy al Kabīr
AL ḨAMMĀDAH AL ḨAMRĀ
Wādī Tanārūt
Ras Lānūf
Al Burayqah
Ajdābiyā
Waddān
Marada
Awjilah
Jālū
Zillah
Jabal as Sawdā'
SAHRĀ AWBĀRĪ
Birāk
Wādī ash Shāţi'
Al Fuqahā'
Sabhā
Awbārī
Ḩammādat Marzuq
Tmassah
Suwaylah
Murzuq
Ghāt
FAZZĀN
Jabal Bin Ghanīmah
Al Harūj al Aswad
Wādī Bū al Ḩidān
Wādī ar Ru'ays
Wāw al Kabīr
Tajarhī
SARĪR KALANSHIYŪ
LIBYAN DESERT
'Ayn ath Tha'lab
RAMLAT RABYĀNAH
Al Kufrah
SARĪR TIBASTĪ
Tibesti
Pic Bette 2286m
'Ayn al Ghazāl
SAHARA
Al Bayḑā'
Shaḩḩāt
Al Qubbah
Darnah
Tūkrah
Al Marj
Madīnat al Abyār
Banghāzī
Al Jabal al Akhḑar
Khalīj Bumbah
Tubruq
BAR QAH
Mūsā'id
Zāwiyat al Mukhaylā
Wādī al Ḩamīm
Al Jaghbūb
GREAT SAND SEA
TUNISIA
ALGERIA
NIGER
CHAD
SUDAN
EGYPT
LIBYA
Total Land Area : 1 759 540 sq. km (679 358 sq. miles)
LAND HEIGHT
2000m/6562ft
1000m/3281ft
500m/1640ft
200m/656ft
Sea Level
-200m/-656ft
POPULATION
over 500 000
over 100 000
over 50 000
over 10 000
under 10 000
N
0
200 km
200 miles

CHRONOLOGY

Italy occupied Libya and expelled the Turks in 1911. Britain and France agreed to a UN plan for an independent monarchy in 1951.

- **1969** King Idris deposed in coup by Revolutionary Command Council led by Colonel Gaddafi. Tripoli Charter sets up revolutionary alliance with Egypt and Sudan.
- **1970** UK and US military ordered out. Property belonging to Italians and Jews confiscated. Western oil company assets nationalized, a process completed in 1973.
- **1973** Libya forms abortive union with Egypt. Gaddafi launches Cultural Revolution. Libya occupies Aozou Strip in Chad.
- **1974** Libya forms union of Libya and Tunisia.
- **1977** Official name changed to the Great Socialist People's Libyan Arab Jamahiriyah.
- **1979** Members of Revolution Command Council replaced by elected officials. Gaddafi remains Leader of the Revolution.

CHRONOLOGY *continued*

- **1981** USA shoots down two Libyan aircraft over Gulf of Sirte.
- **1984** Gunman at Libyan embassy in London kills British policewoman; UK severs diplomatic relations with Libya (until 1999). Libya signs Oudja Accord with Morocco for an Arab Africa Federation.
- **1985** Libya expels 30,000 foreign workers. Tunisia cuts diplomatic links.
- **1986** US aircraft bomb Libya, killing 101 people and destroying Gaddafi's residence.
- **1988** Army and police abolished. Pan-Am airliner explodes over Lockerbie, Scotland; allegations of Libyan complicity.
- **1989** Arab Maghreb Union established with Algeria, Morocco, Mauritania, and Tunisia. Libya and Chad cease-fire in Aozou Strip.
- **1990** Libya expels Palestinian splinter group led by Abu Abbas.
- **1991** Opening of first branch of Great Man-Made River project.
- **1992–1993** UN sanctions imposed as Libya fails to hand over Lockerbie suspects; sanctions made stricter.
- **1994** Religious leaders obtain right to issue religious decrees (*fatwas*) for first time since 1969. Return of Aozou strip to Chad.
- **1996** US legislation imposes penalties on foreign companies investing in Libya's energy sector.
- **1999** Lockerbie suspects handed over for trial in the Netherlands under Scottish law; UN sanctions eased.
- **2000** Gaddafi announces plans to form United States of Africa.
- **2001** Lockerbie trial verdict:` one suspect convicted. Sanctions eased further.

AID

Recipient

$7m (receipts) | No change in 1999

As an oil-exporting state, Libya fails to qualify for international aid, despite being a developing country. During the 1970s, Colonel Gaddafi aided several African liberation movements, such as the ANC in South Africa. He backed Hissène Habré's forces in Chad, and helped dissidents by training them in his Pan-African legion. He has also financed or supplied arms to the PLO in the Middle East, Irish republicans in Northern Ireland, the Moros in the southern Philippines, and the Basques, Corsicans, and other separatist causes in Europe. In 1993, Libya granted aid totaling $27 million, despite UN sanctions and a lack of surplus resources.

DEFENSE

Compulsory military service

$1.31bn | Down 12% in 1999

LIBYAN ARMED FORCES

2210 main battle tanks (1600 T-54/55, 350 T-62, 260 T-72)	45,000 personnel
2 submarines, 2 frigates, and 16 patrol boats	8000 personnel
426 combat aircraft (40 MiG-23BN, 15 MiG-23U, 58 *Mirage*, 45 Su-20/22)	23,000 personnel
None	

The armed forces suffered a blow in 1987 with the loss of thousands of men and equipment worth $1.4 billion in the Chad civil war. The costly border war with Chad ended in 1994 with the return of the Aozou Strip to Chad. In 1989 the armed forces were replaced by "the Armed People." Conscription is selective, and can last up to two years. In addition, there is a People's Militia numbering 40,000. Attempts to depoliticize the army received a setback following confirmation of an abortive military coup in 1993. UN sanctions resulted in the concentration of military hardware that is outdated. Despite the suspension of the sanctions in 1999, fresh arms contracts would still be too controversial for most potential suppliers.

ECONOMICS

Not available

$29.2bn | 0.4595–0.5423 Libyan dinars

SCORE CARD

- World GNP Ranking..........58th
- GNP per Capita..........$5220
- Balance of Payments..........$1.48bn
- Inflation..........18%
- Unemployment..........30%

EXPORTS

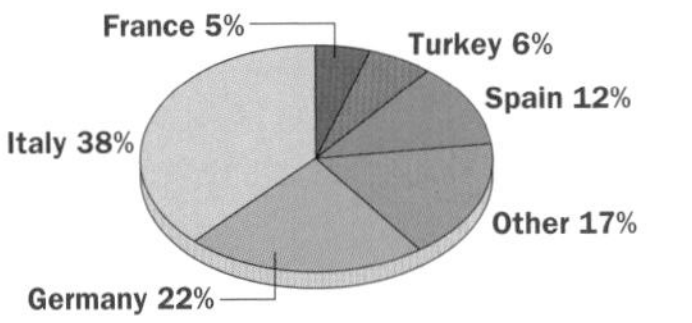
France 5%
Turkey 6%
Spain 12%
Italy 38%
Other 17%
Germany 22%

IMPORTS

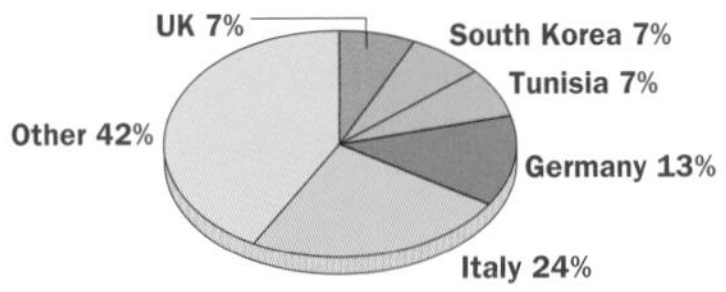
UK 7%
South Korea 7%
Tunisia 7%
Other 42%
Germany 13%
Italy 24%

ECONOMIC PERFORMANCE INDICATOR

Consumer Price Index
GDP
160
140
120
100
80
Consumer price index unavailable
GDP 1993=100
1993
1994
1995
1996
1997

Strengths
Oil and gas production. High investment in downstream industries – petrochemicals, refineries, fertilizers, and aluminum smelting.

Weaknesses
Single-resource economy subject to oil-market fluctuations. Most food is imported. Reliance on foreign labor. Lack of water for agriculture. History of international unreliability.

Profile
Western oil companies had close business ties with Libya until the imposition in 1992 of UN sanctions over the Lockerbie affair. In 1993, Gaddafi called for the program of privatization, authorized by the General People's Congress in late 1992, to be revived, but there have been few tangible results. An ambitious program of industrialization was launched in the 1970s. Gaddafi's most controversial economic project has been the Great Man-Made River. Started in 1984 and engineered by European and Korean companies, this scheme was designed to bring underground water from the Sahara to the coast, but the pipes are already corroding, with water leaking into the sand.

LIBYA : MAJOR BUSINESSES

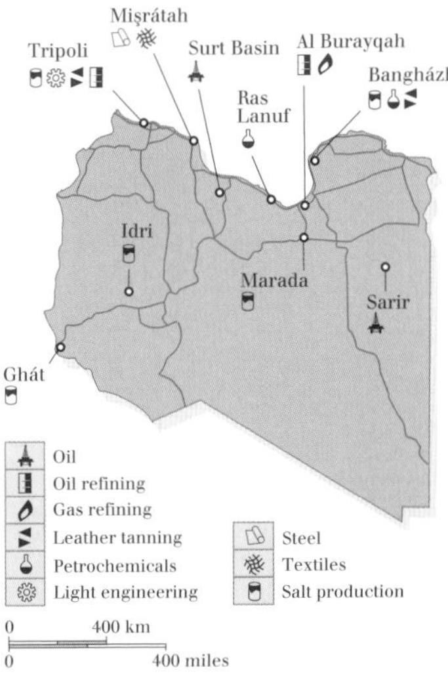
Mişrátah
Tripoli
Surt Basin
Al Burayqah
Bangházh
Ras Lanuf
Idri
Marada
Sarir
Ghát
Oil
Oil refining
Gas refining
Leather tanning
Petrochemicals
Light engineering
Steel
Textiles
Salt production
0
400 km
0
400 miles

RESOURCES

Electric power 4.6m kw

32,849 tonnes

1.5m b/d (reserves 29,500,000,000 bbl)

6.45m sheep, 2.25m goats, 24.8m chickens

Oil, natural gas, iron, potassium, gypsum, magnesium, sulfur

ELECTRICITY GENERATION

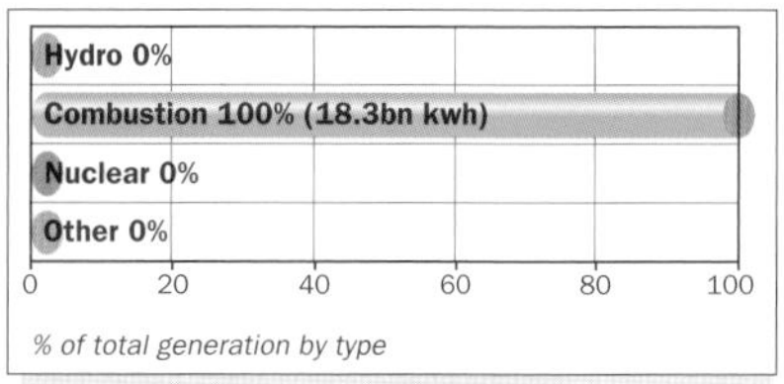

Hydro 0%
Combustion 100% (18.3bn kwh)
Nuclear 0%
Other 0%
0
20
40
60
80
100
% of total generation by type

Libya's economy depends almost entirely on petroleum and natural gas resources. It has considerable crude oil reserves and is likely to remain an oil-exporting country well into the 21st century. Natural gas potential is more limited but, provided links are developed with other north African states, the future is assured. Libya also has reserves of iron ore, potassium, sulfur, magnesium, and gypsum. The Great Man-Made River project means that the area of irrigated land has grown, but 90% of Libya is desert. Animal husbandry is the basis of farming, but some cereal crops are grown, as well as dates, olives, and citrus fruits. Cement production is sufficient to meet national demand; raw materials are local, but most other manufacturing inputs are imported.

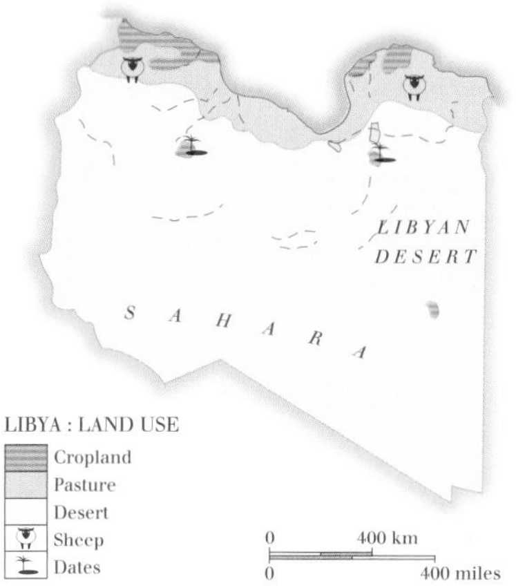

LIBYAN DESERT
S A H A R A
LIBYA : LAND USE
Cropland
Pasture
Desert
Sheep
Dates
0
400 km
0
400 miles

ENVIRONMENT

Sustainability rank: 118th

1% (0.1% partially protected)

8.4 tonnes per capita

ENVIRONMENTAL TREATIES

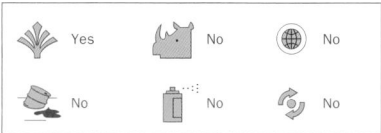

Yes No No

No No No

The UN Development Program has described Libya as more than 90% "wasteland." Both nature and man have conspired against the environment. Apart from two coastal strips – the Jafara Plain and the Al Jabal al-Akhdar in Cyrenaica – together with the Fazzan Oasis, most of Libya is desert. Much of the irrigated area is saline because of unwise use of naturally occurring water from artesian wells. Near Tripoli, seawater has penetrated the water table as far as 20 km (12 miles) inland.

MEDIA

TV ownership medium

Daily newspaper circulation 14 per 1000 people

PUBLISHING AND BROADCAST MEDIA

There are 4 daily newspapers, including *Al-Fajr al-Jadid*, published by the Jamahiriyah News Agency (JANA)

1 state-controlled service

2 services: 1 state-controlled, 1 independent

Libya's press and TV are a mouthpiece for the leadership. Satellite TV and the Internet are widely available, but heavily censored. The main daily newspaper is published in Arabic and has a circulation of 40,000 readers. The TV station broadcasts mostly in Arabic. Radio broadcasts in Swahili, Hausa, Fulani, and Amharic were due to begin in 1999, but were postponed.

CRIME

Death penalty used

Libya does not publish prison figures

Down 3% 1996–1998

CRIME RATES

Murders
2 per 100,000 population

Rapes
5 per 100,000 population

Thefts
315 per 100,000 population

Policing is often in the hands of gangs appointed by Gaddafi's lieutenants to root out student protestors and other dissidents. Hit squads allegedly operate abroad against Libyan exiles.

EDUCATION

School leaving age: 15

80%

72,899 students

THE EDUCATION SYSTEM

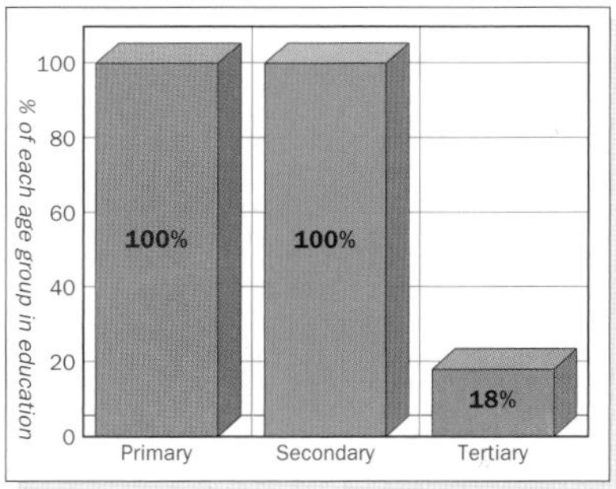

100
80
60
40
20
0
% of each age group in education
100%
100%
18%
Primary
Secondary
Tertiary

Some one million Libyans are in formal education. It is compulsory between the ages of six and 15, and rates of attendance are very high, but it varies in quality and can be rudimentary in rural areas. Secondary education, from the age of 15, lasts for three years. There are 13 universities, and institutes for vocational training. The literacy rate has more than doubled from a level of 39% in 1970.

HEALTH

Welfare state health benefits

1 per 769 people

Pneumonia, diarrheal diseases, accidents, cancers

An adequate system of free primary health care exists except in remote areas, and there are two big hospitals, in Benghazi and Tripoli. However, hospitals lack equipment, and there is a shortage of medical supplies.

SPENDING

GDP/cap. decrease

CONSUMPTION AND SPENDING

159 per 1000 population

101 per 1000 population

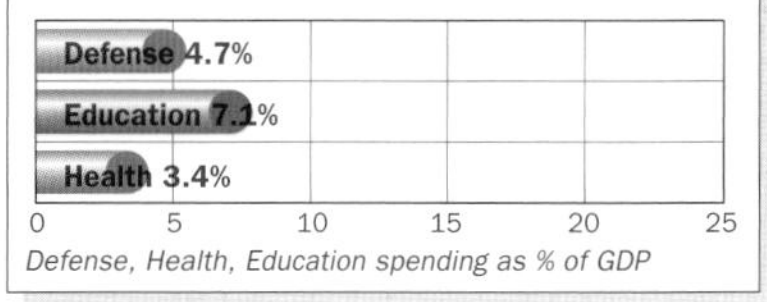

Defense 4.7%
Education 7.1%
Health 3.4%
0
5
10
15
20
25
Defense, Health, Education spending as % of GDP

There is widespread poverty after years of import constraints; UN sanctions worsened the situation. Gaddafi refuses to use oil revenues for basic expenses, such as salaries – teachers earn about $1200 a year.

WORLD RANKING

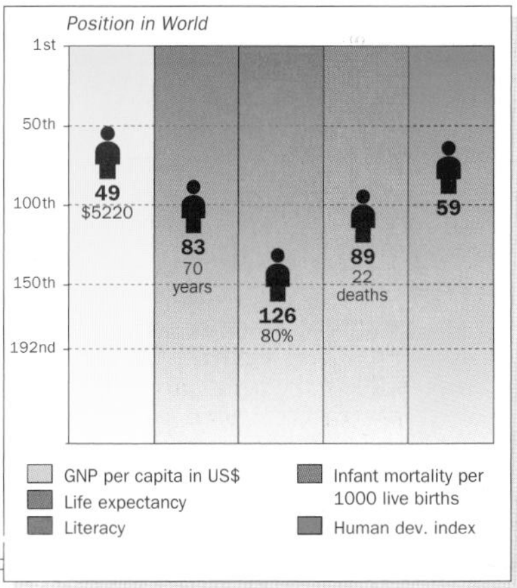

Position in World
1st
50th
100th
150th
192nd
49
$5220
83
70
years
126
80%
89
22
deaths
59
GNP per capita in US$
Life expectancy
Literacy
Infant mortality per 1000 live births
Human dev. index

L

LIECHTENSTEIN

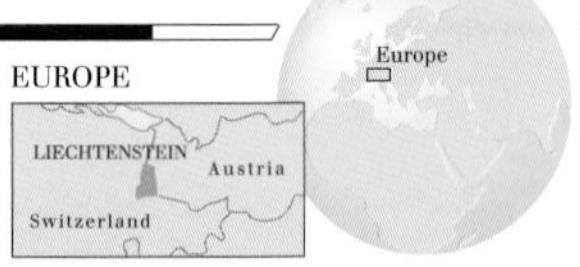
EUROPE
Europe
LIECHTENSTEIN
Austria
Switzerland

OFFICIAL NAME: Principality of Liechtenstein **CAPITAL:** Vaduz
POPULATION: 32,200 **CURRENCY:** Swiss franc **OFFICIAL LANGUAGE:** German

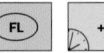

1719 | 1719 | Aug 15 | FL | +1 | +423 | .li

PERCHED IN THE ALPS between Switzerland and Austria, Liechtenstein is rare among small states in having both a thriving banking sector and a well-diversified manufacturing economy. It is closely allied to Switzerland, which handles its foreign relations and defense. Life in Liechtenstein is stable and conservative. Its banking secrecy laws and low taxes make it home to many overseas trusts, banks, and investment companies.

CLIMATE

Mountain

WEATHER CHART

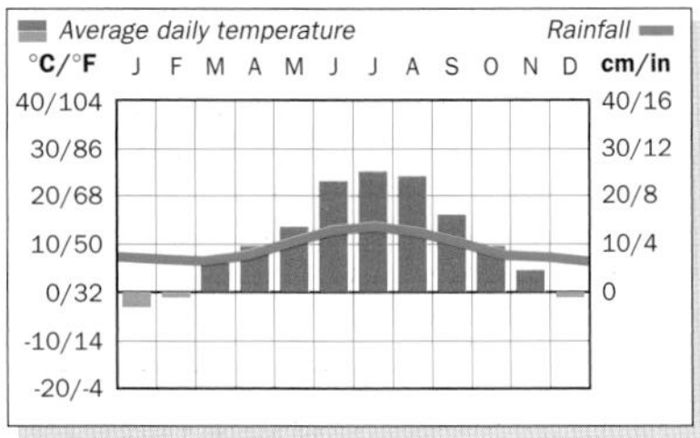
Average daily temperature
Rainfall
°C/°F
J F M A M J J A S O N D
cm/in
40/104
30/86
20/68
10/50
0/32
-10/14
-20/-4
40/16
30/12
20/8
10/4
0

Climate varies with altitude. Excellent skiing conditions are the result of heavy settling snow from December to March. Summers are warm and wet.

TRANSPORTATION

Drive on right

None | Has no fleet

THE TRANSPORTATION NETWORK

250 km (155 miles)	None
19 km (12 miles)	26 km (16 miles)

Public transportation in Liechtenstein is mostly by the postal bus network. The single-track railroad has few stops. Zürich, a two-hour drive away, is the nearest airport.

TOURISM

Visitors : Population 1.9:1

61,000 visitors | Up 2% in 2000

MAIN TOURIST ARRIVALS

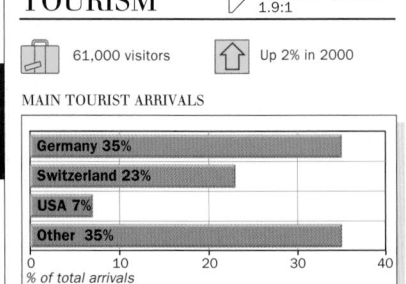

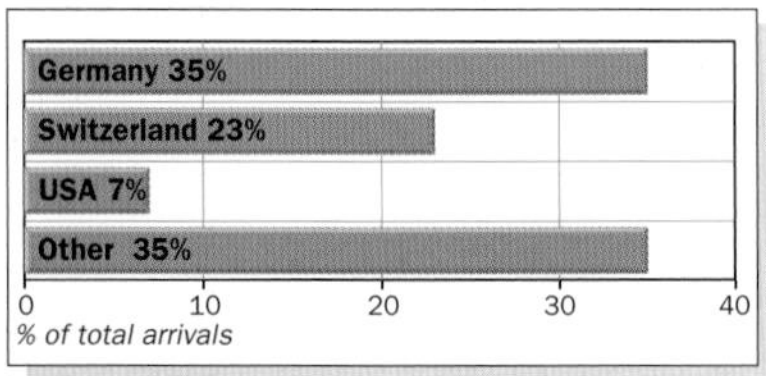
Germany 35%
Switzerland 23%
USA 7%
Other 35%
0
10
20
30
40
% of total arrivals

Liechtenstein's alpine scenery attracts skiers in the winter, and climbers and hikers in the summer.

PEOPLE

Pop. density high

German, Alemannish dialect, Italian | $201/km^2$ ($521/mi^2$)

THE URBAN/RURAL POPULATION SPLIT

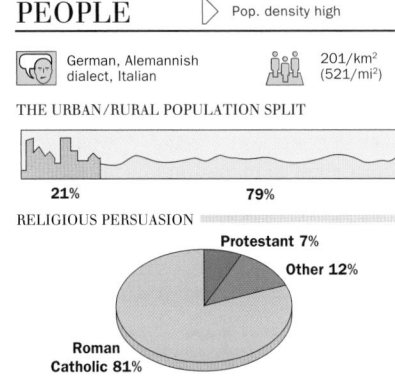

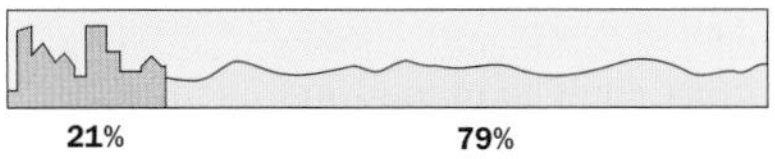
21%
79%

RELIGIOUS PERSUASION

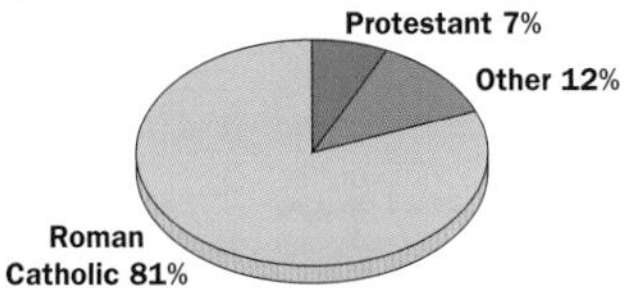
Protestant 7%
Other 12%
Roman Catholic 81%

Liechtenstein's role as a financial center accounts for the many foreign residents (over 35% of the population), of whom half are Swiss and the rest mostly German. The high standard of living results in few ethnic or social tensions. Family life is highly traditional; women received the vote only in 1984, after much controversy. A proposal the following year that equal rights for women be enshrined in the constitution was rejected in a referendum by a large majority.

POLITICS

Multiparty elections

2001/2005 | Prince Hans-Adam II von und zu Liechtenstein

AT THE LAST ELECTION

Parliament 25 seats

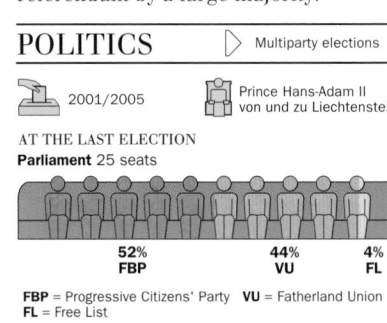

52% FBP
44% VU
4% FL

FBP = Progressive Citizens' Party **VU** = Fatherland Union
FL = Free List

Between 1938 and 1997 the VU and the FBP alternated as coalition leaders, except briefly in 1993. This partnership ended in 1997 when Mario Frick, at the age of 28 Europe's youngest premier, formed a VU-only government. In elections in 2001 the FBP under Otmar Hasler overtook the VU. Referenda have increasingly been used to decide policy issues.

WORLD AFFAIRS

Joined UN in 1990

CE | EEA | IAEA | OSCE | WTO

Liechtenstein effectively gave up control of its external relations when in 1924 it signed a Customs Union Treaty with Switzerland. The terms of this agreement requires Swiss approval for any treaty arrangements between Liechtenstein and a third state. The country became a member of the UN only in 1990. It joined EFTA and the EBRD in 1991, and has been a participant in the EEA since 1995. However, Swiss rejection of EU membership in 1992 effectively ended any prospect of Liechtenstein joining the EU in the foreseeable future.

AID

Donor

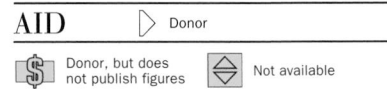

Donor, but does not publish figures | Not available

Although overseas aid donations are small and aid issues have little political importance, Liechtenstein has helped to fund shelter and reconstruction projects in former Yugoslavia and local development projects in Bulgaria.

LIECHTENSTEIN

Total Land Area : 160 sq. km (62 sq. miles)

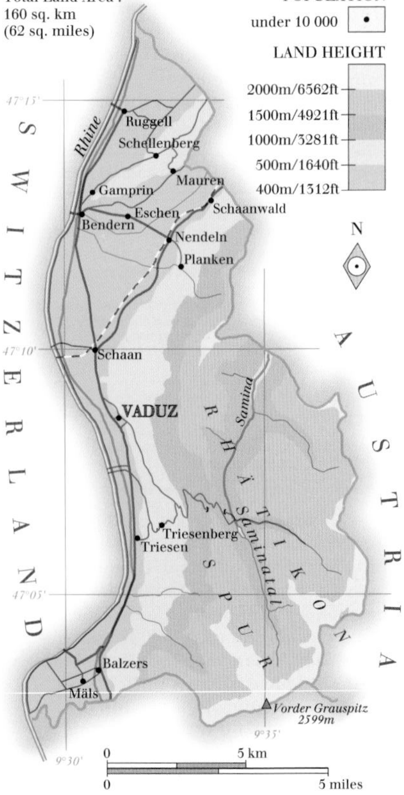
POPULATION
under 10 000
LAND HEIGHT
2000m/6562ft
1500m/4921ft
1000m/3281ft
500m/1640ft
400m/1312ft
SWITZERLAND
AUSTRIA
Rhine
Ruggell
Schellenberg
Mauren
Gamprin
Eschen
Schaanwald
Bendern
Nendeln
Planken
Schaan
VADUZ
RHÄTIKON
Samina
Saminatal
Triesenberg
Triesen
Balzers
Mäls
Vorder Grauspitz 2599m
0 5 km
0 5 miles

Alpine scenery near Vaduz. *The state budget includes 2% allocated to restoring mountain vegetation and coordinating land use.*

DEFENSE

No compulsory military service

No defense force | Not applicable

There has been no standing army since 1868, and there is only a small police force. *De facto* protection is provided by Switzerland. In theory, any male under 60 is liable for military service during a national emergency, although this law has never been invoked.

ECONOMICS

Inflation 2.9% p.a. (1985–1996)

$1.2bn | 1.6007–1.6205 Swiss francs

SCORE CARD

❑ World GNP Ranking	151st
❑ GNP per Capita	$40,000
❑ Balance of Payments	Included in Swiss total
❑ Inflation	0.5%
❑ Unemployment	2%

Strengths

Stability and customs union with Switzerland make Liechtenstein a favored tax haven; its lack of EU membership makes the banking sector less vulnerable to future changes in EU banking laws. The economy is well diversified; chemicals, furniture, coatings for the electro-optical industry, construction services, and precision instruments are all thriving sectors.

Weaknesses

Very few. Need to balance integration with other countries with safeguarding economic independence.

EXPORTS

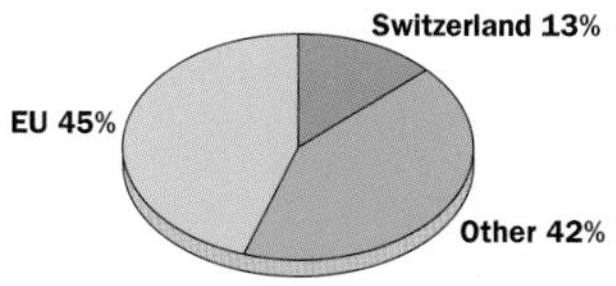
Switzerland 13%
EU 45%
Other 42%

IMPORTS

With a limited domestic market, Liechtenstein's industry is export-oriented. Liechtenstein has a customs union with Switzerland and does not publish separate import figures.

RESOURCES

Electric Power: Included in Swiss total

None | Not an oil producer

6000 cattle, 3000 pigs, 2900 sheep, 280 goats | None

Liechtenstein has to import most of its energy. Almost all of its electricity comes from German power stations.

ENVIRONMENT

Not available

38% partially protected | Not available

Protection of Liechtenstein's alpine scenery is high enough on the political agenda for one of the five councillors, or ministers, to have responsibility for the environment. As in Switzerland, the greatest worry is the effect of high rates of car use and of through traffic. However, a 1988 trial in providing free public bus transportation proved a failure, as Liechtensteiners remained firmly wedded to their automobiles.

MEDIA

TV ownership high

Daily newspaper circulation 602 per 1000 people

PUBLISHING AND BROADCAST MEDIA

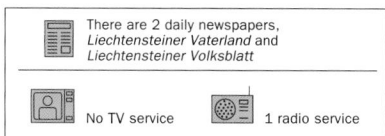

There are 2 daily newspapers, *Liechtensteiner Vaterland* and *Liechtensteiner Volksblatt*

No TV service | 1 radio service

The two newspapers, although free of formal state control, are both run by political parties: the *Vaterland* by the VU; the *Volksblatt* by the FBP. Both have circulations of around 10,000.

CRIME

Death penalty not used

Liechtenstein does not publish prison figures | Crime does not pose any great problems

Crime is a minor problem, a result of the relatively even distribution of wealth and high average living standard. Liechtenstein has also taken great care to protect its tax-haven status by careful regulation of its financial sector. It has avoided major scandals, and took steps in 2000 to tighten precautions against the growing problem of money laundering.

EDUCATION

School leaving age: 16

99% | Not available

Education, modeled on the German system, includes two types of school at secondary level – the more academic *Gymnasium* and the *Realschule*. Liechtenstein has no university; students go on to colleges in Austria, Switzerland, or Germany, or to business schools in the USA.

CHRONOLOGY

In 1719 Liechtenstein became an independent principality of the Holy Roman Empire.

- ❑ **1924** Customs union with Switzerland.
- ❑ **1990** Joins UN.
- ❑ **1995** Joins EEA.
- ❑ **1997** End of VU-FBP coalition dominant since 1938. Mario Frick now heads VU government.
- ❑ **2001** FBP wins majority in elections; Otmar Hasler premier.

HEALTH

Welfare state health benefits

1 per 948 people | Heart and respiratory diseases, cancers

Although clinics and hospitals are few, the health system provides advanced care. Many Liechtensteiners have private health insurance arrangements, so that they have access to Swiss medical expertise and facilities as well as their own.

SPENDING

GDP/cap. increase

CONSUMPTION AND SPENDING

657 per 1000 population | *609 per 1000 population*

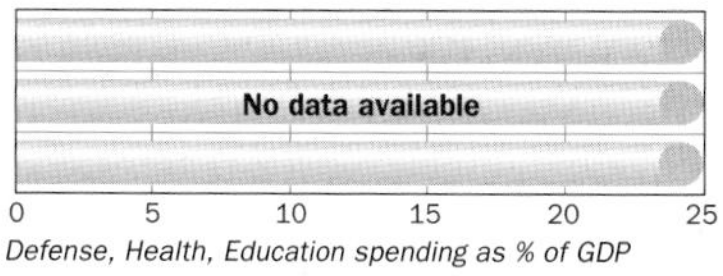
No data available
0
5
10
15
20
25
Defense, Health, Education spending as % of GDP

Unlike other tax havens, Liechtenstein displays a more conservative prosperity. Private deposit accounts are not a key part of its banking business, but an increase in money-laundering activities and the country's appearance on a blacklist of financial centers led to a ban on anonymous accounts in mid-2000.

WORLD RANKING

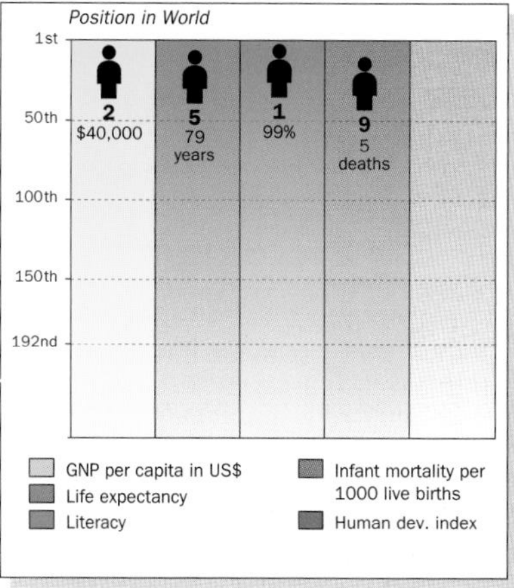
Position in World
1st
50th
100th
150th
192nd
2
$40,000
5
79 years
1
99%
9
5 deaths
GNP per capita in US$
Life expectancy
Literacy
Infant mortality per 1000 live births
Human dev. index

L

LITHUANIA

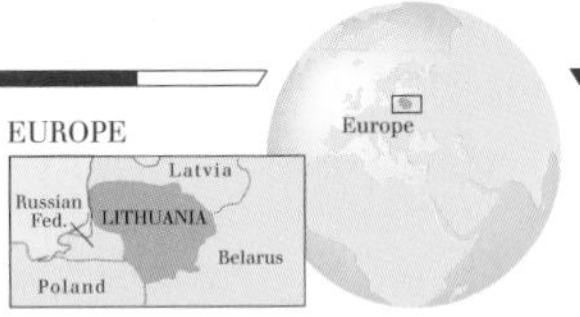
EUROPE
Europe
Latvia
Russian Fed.
LITHUANIA
Belarus
Poland

OFFICIAL NAME: Republic of Lithuania **CAPITAL:** Vilnius
POPULATION: 3.7 million **CURRENCY:** Litas **OFFICIAL LANGUAGE:** Lithuanian

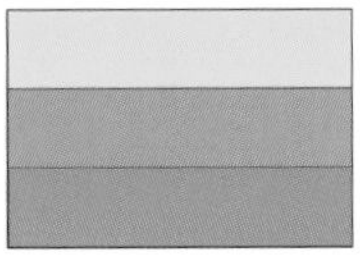

1991 | 1991 | Feb 16 | LT | +2 | +370 | .lt

LYING ON THE EASTERN COAST of the Baltic Sea, Lithuania is bordered by Latvia, Belarus, Poland, and the Kaliningrad area of the Russian Federation. Its terrain is mostly flat with many lakes, moors, and bogs. Now a multiparty democracy, Lithuania achieved independence from the former USSR in 1991. Industrial production and agriculture are the mainstays of the economy. Russia finally withdrew all its troops from Lithuania in 1993.

CLIMATE

Continental

WEATHER CHART

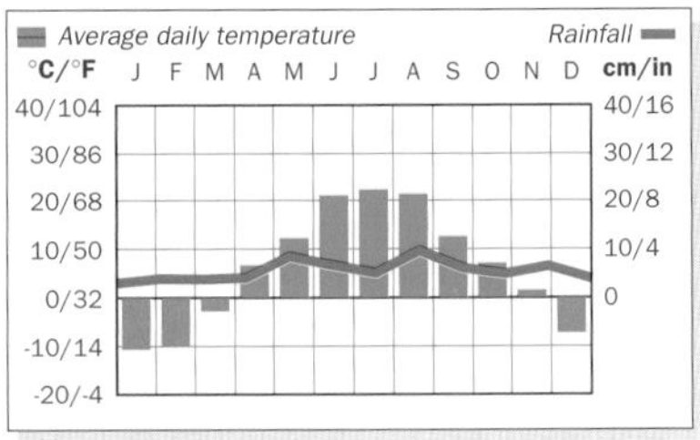
Average daily temperature
Rainfall
°C/°F
J F M A M J J A S O N D
cm/in
40/104
30/86
20/68
10/50
0/32
-10/14
-20/-4
40/16
30/12
20/8
10/4
0

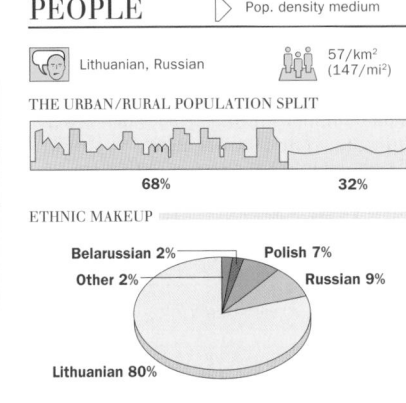

Lithuania's coastal position moderates an otherwise continental-type climate. Summers are cool.

TRANSPORTATION

Drive on right

Vilnius International 480,708 passengers

206 ships 481,100 grt

THE TRANSPORTATION NETWORK

64,951 km (40,359 miles)	417 km (259 miles)
1905 km (1184 miles)	600 km (373 miles)

Rail track and signaling are being improved and roads upgraded. Flights to the West are increasing.

TOURISM

Visitors : Population 1:3

1.2m visitors

Down 14% in 2000

MAIN TOURIST ARRIVALS

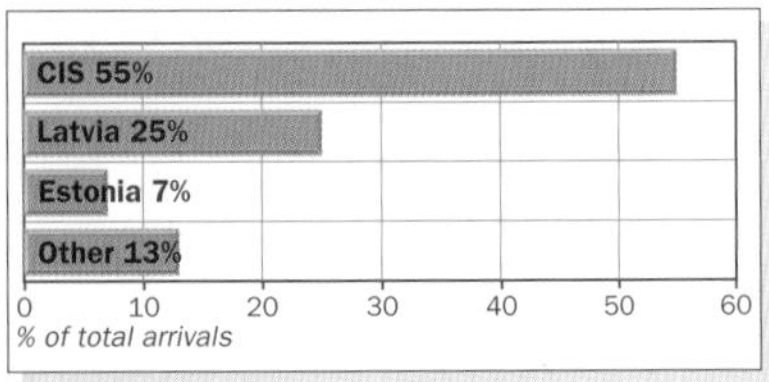
CIS 55%
Latvia 25%
Estonia 7%
Other 13%
0
10
20
30
40
50
60
% of total arrivals

Tourism has expanded in recent years. Vilnius is well preserved; its historic center survived German and Russian occupation. Trakai, the capital of the Grand Duchy in the 16th century, is also popular with visitors.

PEOPLE

Pop. density medium

Lithuanian, Russian

57/km² (147/mi²)

THE URBAN/RURAL POPULATION SPLIT

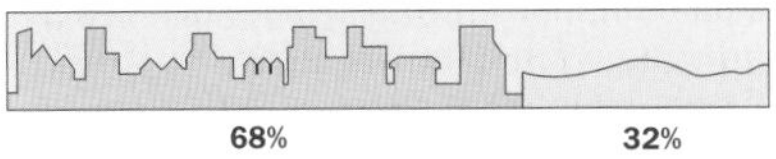
68%
32%

ETHNIC MAKEUP

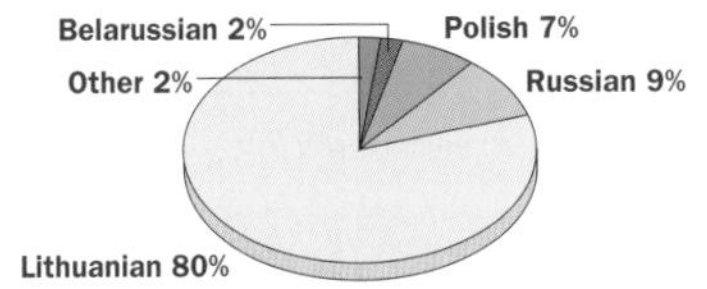
Belarussian 2%
Polish 7%
Other 2%
Russian 9%
Lithuanian 80%

Relations with ethnic Russians are best of all the Baltic states, but there are fewer of them. The mainly Catholic population has strong historical links with Poland, although there has been tension between Lithuanians and Poles in recent years. Relations with the Jewish minority remain strained. More than 90% of non-ethnic Lithuanians have been granted citizenship.

POLITICS

Multiparty elections

2000/2004

President Valdas Adamkus

AT THE LAST ELECTION

Parliament 141 seats

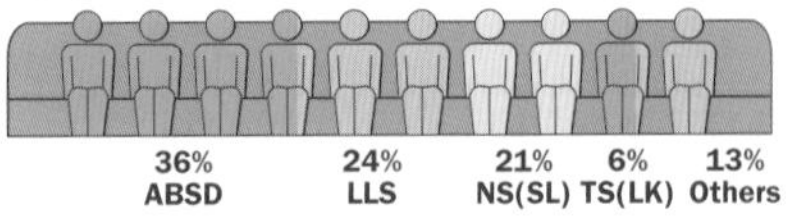
36% ABSD
24% LLS
21% NS(SL)
6% TS(LK)
13% Others

ABSD = A. Brazauskas Social Democratic Coalition
LLS = Lithuanian Liberal Union
NS(SL) = New Union (Social Liberals)
TS(LK) = Homeland Union (Lithuanian Conservatives)

Lithuania was the most politically stable of the three Baltic republics in the 1990s. Strongly nationalist when it reestablished independence from the disintegrating Soviet Union in 1991, it unexpectedly voted the former communists back into office in 1992 and 1993. Former communist leader Algirdas Brazauskas held the presidency for five years until returning emigré businessman Valdas Adamkus was elected in 1998. Meanwhile the conservative TS(LK) had won the 1996 legislative elections in the wake of a banking scandal, but their popularity dwindled as successive prime ministers were forced to resign. The TS(LK) suffered a massive defeat in the 2000 legislative elections. Adamkus controversially bypassed the Social Democrats, the largest bloc in the new Parliament, in favor of a pro-market coalition. This collapsed in mid-2001 and Brazauskas became prime minister in a government dominated by his Social Democrats.

LITHUANIA

Total Land Area : 65 200 sq. km (25 174 sq. miles)

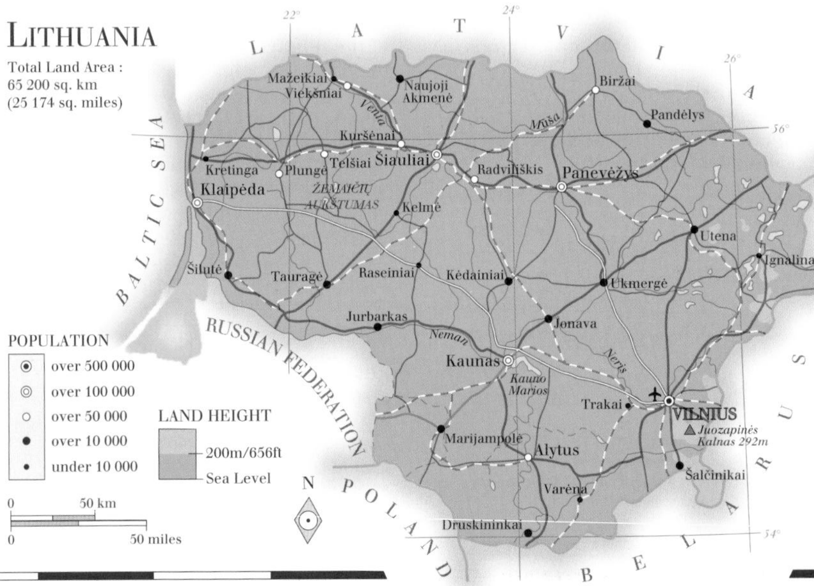
LATVIA
BALTIC SEA
RUSSIAN FEDERATION
POLAND
BELARUS
Mažeikiai
Viekšniai
Naujoji Akmenė
Biržai
Pandėlys
Venta
Mūša
Kuršėnai
Kretinga
Plungė
Telšiai
Šiauliai
Radviliškis
Panevėžys
Klaipėda
ŽEMAIČIŲ AUKŠTUMAS
Kelmė
Utena
Ignalina
Šilutė
Tauragė
Raseiniai
Kėdainiai
Ukmergė
Jurbarkas
Jonava
Neman
Neris
Kaunas
Kauno Marios
Trakai
VILNIUS
Juozapinės Kalnas 292m
Marijampolė
Alytus
Šalčininkai
Varėna
Druskininkai
22°
24°
26°
56°
54°
POPULATION
over 500 000
over 100 000
over 50 000
over 10 000
under 10 000
LAND HEIGHT
200m/656ft
Sea Level
N
0
50 km
0
50 miles

WORLD AFFAIRS

Joined UN in 1991

CE | CBSS | WTO | OSCE | PfP

As a "second wave" applicant, Lithuania began EU membership negotiations in 2000. It currently has the best relations with Russia of all the Baltic states, but is keen for all three to join NATO.

AID

Recipient

$129m (receipts) — Up 26% 1997–1999

Aid, mostly from the IMF and the EU, is used for infrastructure projects and to promote private enterprise.

DEFENSE

Compulsory military service

$106m — Down 24% in 1999

Lithuania's security is in the hands of its army, the small navy and air force, and a large National Guard formed to patrol its frontiers. Twelve months' military service is compulsory. The USA is now supporting Lithuania's entry into NATO.

ECONOMICS

Inflation 90.7% p.a. (1990–1999)

$9.8bn — 4.0011–3.9990 litai

SCORE CARD

❑ World GNP Ranking	84th
❑ GNP per Capita	$2640
❑ Balance of Payments	$-1.19bn
❑ Inflation	0.8%
❑ Unemployment	10%

STRENGTHS

Privatization has stimulated the economy to some extent. Inflation under control.

WEAKNESSES

Agriculture is in the doldrums following de-collectivization. Exports badly hit by Russian economic crisis. Poor raw materials base. Need to import oil and natural gas from Russia. Difficulty in attracting significant foreign investment.

EXPORTS

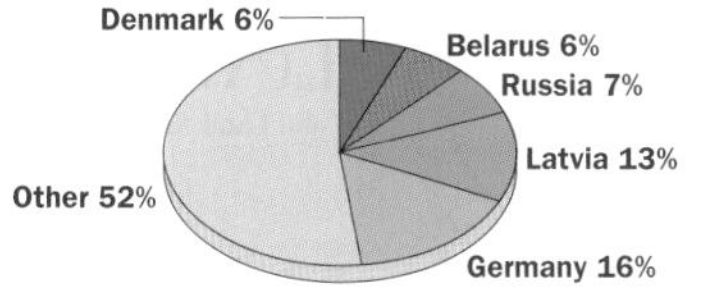
Denmark 6%
Belarus 6%
Russia 7%
Latvia 13%
Other 52%
Germany 16%

IMPORTS

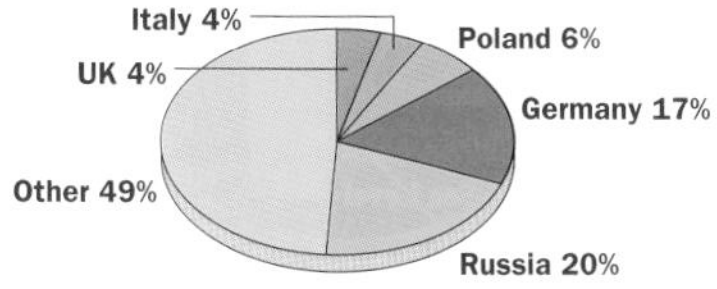
Italy 4%
UK 4%
Poland 6%
Germany 17%
Other 49%
Russia 20%

One of Lithuania's 3000 lakes. The entire country is low-lying. Its coast, fringed by sand dunes and pine forests, is famous for amber.

RESOURCES

Electric power 5.8m kw

19,837 tonnes

4251 b/d (reserves 13,966,560 bbl)

936,100 pigs, 897,800 cattle, 6m chickens

Sand, gravel, clay, limestone, gypsum

Lithuania has significant reserves of peat and materials used in construction industry. The Ignalina nuclear plant provides more than 80% of the country's electricity. Oil is mostly imported from Russia.

ENVIRONMENT

Sustainability rank: 23rd

10% — 4.1 tonnes per capita

Radioactive leaks and the risk of accident at the giant Chernobyl-type nuclear plant at Ignalina cause much concern. Only one of the two reactors is due to close, in 2004. The EU is pressing (and paying) for decommissioning as soon as possible.

MEDIA

TV ownership high

Daily newspaper circulation 93 per 1000 people

PUBLISHING AND BROADCAST MEDIA

There are 19 daily newspapers, including *Lietuvos Rytas* and *Respublika*

10 services: 1 state-owned, 9 independent

24 services: 1 state-owned, 23 independent

The mainstream media, Russian under communism, now publish and broadcast mainly in Lithuanian.

CRIME

Death penalty not used

13,228 prisoners — Up 15% 1996–1998

Levels of crime are low compared with other parts of the former USSR. Robbery is a growing problem.

EDUCATION

School leaving age: 15

99% — 83,645 students

Teaching at all levels is in Lithuanian, making access to higher education harder for minorities; 8% of the population are graduates.

CHRONOLOGY

Russia annexed Lithuania in 1795. The suppression of rebellions in 1831 and 1863 failed to undermine its nationalist movement.

- ❑ **1915** Occupied by German troops.
- ❑ **1918** Independence declared.
- ❑ **1926** Military coup; one-party rule.
- ❑ **1940** Annexed by Soviet Union.
- ❑ **1941–1944** Nazi occupation.
- ❑ **1945** Incorporated into USSR.
- ❑ **1991** Achieves full independence.
- ❑ **1992** First multiparty elections.
- ❑ **1993** Russian troops withdraw.
- ❑ **1996** Prime minister forced from office by banking scandal. General election; conservative TS(LK) wins.
- ❑ **1998** Valdas Adamkus president.
- ❑ **2000** Brief center-left coalition.
- ❑ **2001** Ex-president Brazauskas becomes prime minister.

HEALTH

Welfare state health benefits

1 per 256 people

Heart disease, cancers, accidents, tuberculosis

The 1997 reorganization of the health service involves replacing state funding with finance from insurance funds.

SPENDING

GDP/cap. decrease

CONSUMPTION AND SPENDING

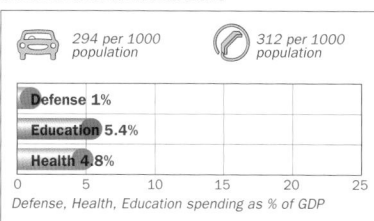

294 per 1000 population — *312 per 1000 population*

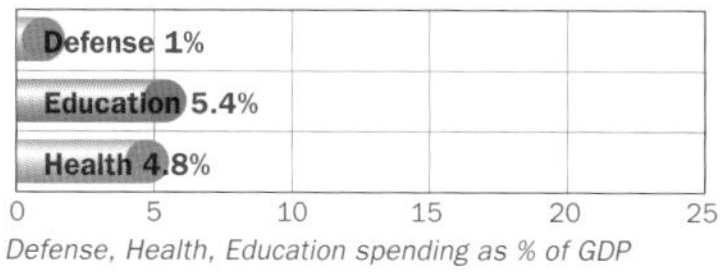
Defense 1%
Education 5.4%
Health 4.8%
0
5
10
15
20
25

Defense, Health, Education spending as % of GDP

Lithuanians are on average poorer than their neighbors in the other Baltic states. Since 1991 a large gap has opened between the incomes of rich and poor.

WORLD RANKING

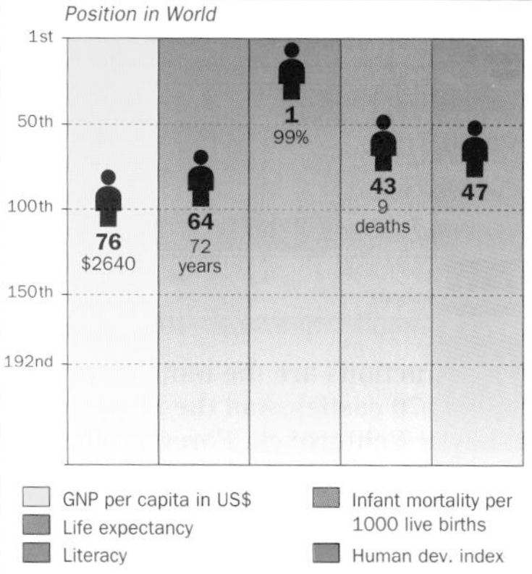
Position in World
1st
50th
100th
150th
192nd
76
$2640
64
72
years
1
99%
43
9
deaths
47
GNP per capita in US$
Life expectancy
Literacy
Infant mortality per 1000 live births
Human dev. index

L

MACEDONIA

EUROPE
Europe
Yugoslavia
Bulgaria
Albania
MACEDONIA
Greece

OFFICIAL NAME: Former Yugoslav Republic of Macedonia **CAPITAL:** Skopje
POPULATION: 2 million **CURRENCY:** Macedonian denar **OFFICIAL LANGUAGE:** Macedonian

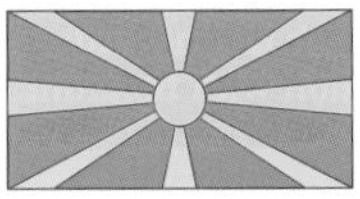

1991 | 1991 | Aug 2 | MK | +1 | +389 | .mk

THE FORMER YUGOSLAV REPUBLIC of Macedonia (FYRM) is landlocked in southeastern Europe. Despite the signing of an accord in 1995, Greece remains suspicious that it harbors ambitions about absorbing northern Greece – also called Macedonia – in a "Greater Macedonia." A militant movement among ethnic Albanians erupted into violent conflict in 2001, threatening the survival of the multi-ethnic governing coalition.

A fisherman's hut on Lake Dojran. The lake lies on the border with Greece in southeastern Macedonia and is shared by the two countries.

CLIMATE

Continental

WEATHER CHART

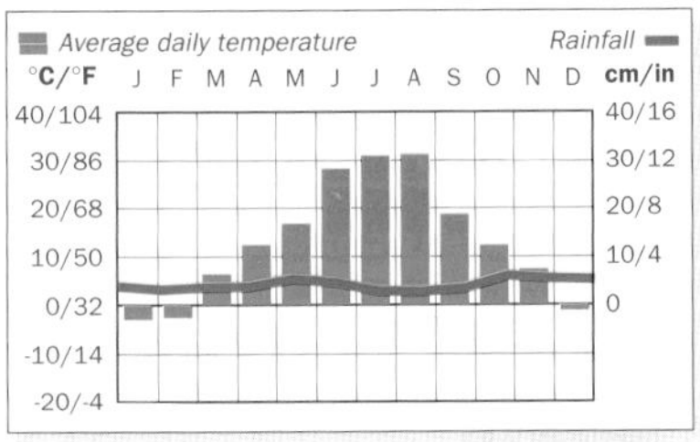
Average daily temperature
Rainfall
°C/°F
J F M A M J J A S O N D
cm/in
40/104
30/86
20/68
10/50
0/32
-10/14
-20/-4
40/16
30/12
20/8
10/4
0

The FYRM has a continental climate. Winter snow supports skiing.

TRANSPORTATION

Drive on right

Skopje International 840,985 passengers

Has no fleet

THE TRANSPORTATION NETWORK

5540 km (3442 miles)

133 km (83 miles)

699 km (434 miles)

None

An east–west road and rail route from Tirana in Albania through Macedonia to Sofia in Bulgaria will reduce reliance on Yugoslavian routes.

TOURISM

Visitors : Population 1:8.9

224,000 visitors

Up 24% in 2000

MAIN TOURIST ARRIVALS

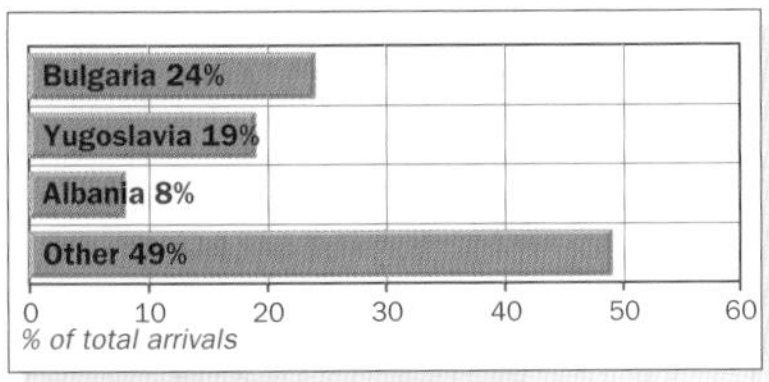
Bulgaria 24%
Yugoslavia 19%
Albania 8%
Other 49%
0
10
20
30
40
50
60
% of total arrivals

The major attraction is the ecclesiastical center of Ohrid, situated on Europe's deepest lake, with Roman and Byzantine ruins. Other lake resorts and skiing in the Sara mountains in the northwest, have potential once stability is restored.

PEOPLE

Pop. density medium

Macedonian, Albanian, Serbo-Croat

78/km² (201/mi²)

THE URBAN/RURAL POPULATION SPLIT

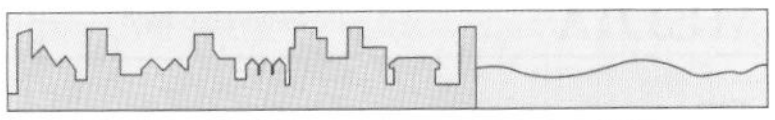
62%
38%

ETHNIC MAKEUP

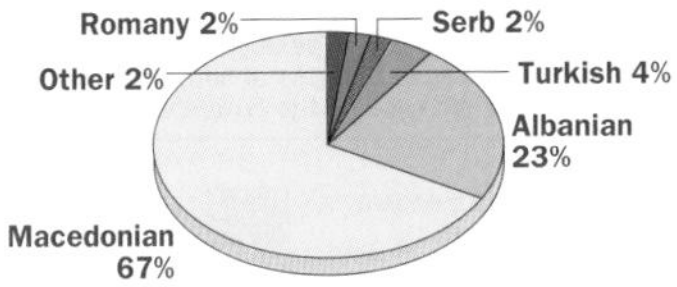
Romany 2%
Serb 2%
Other 2%
Turkish 4%
Albanian 23%
Macedonian 67%

Slav Macedonians, speaking a language akin to Bulgarian, are in the majority. The large Albanian minority claims to amount to over one-third of the population, but it was recorded as forming only 23% at the time of the 1994 census. Tensions rose in 1999, when an influx of ethnic Albanians fleeing from Kosovo threatened to change the ethnic balance.

Macedonians are mostly Eastern Orthodox, but there are a substantial number of Slavic Muslims, whose ancestors converted during the Ottoman occupation. Ethnic Albanians are mostly Muslim.

POLITICS

Multiparty elections

1998/2002

President Boris Trajkovski

AT THE LAST ELECTION

Assembly of the Republic 120 seats

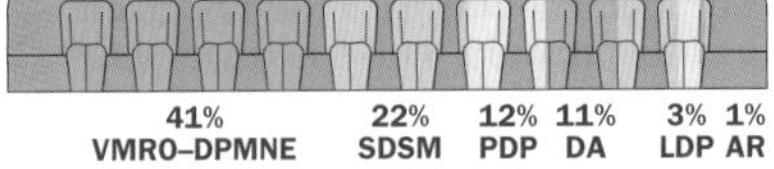
9% DPA
1% SPM
41% VMRO–DPMNE
22% SDSM
12% PDP
11% DA
3% LDP
1% AR

VMRO–DPMNE = Democratic Party for Macedonian National Unity **SDSM** = Social Democratic Alliance of Macedonia **PDP** = Party of Democratic Prosperity **DA** = Democratic Alternative **DPA** = Democratic Party of Albanians **LDP** = Liberal Democratic Party **AR** = Romany Alliance **SPM** = Socialist Party of Macedonia

The early 1990s were overshadowed by the dispute with Greece over the state's name, but this was resolved and an accord signed in 1995 which also confirmed the existing common frontier as an inviolable international border. Former communists held power until the late 1990s. Other political parties are fragmented along nationalist lines. The ethnic Albanian DPA, pursuing recognition as a constituent nation within the FYRM, opposes the resort to guerrilla struggle by the militant National Liberation Army, which emerged only in 2001.

President Boris Trajkovski, elected in December 1999 as the candidate of the nationalist VMRO–DPMNE, put together a broad multi-ethnic coalition. Its survival was threatened as open conflict with Albanian militants escalated in mid-2001.

WORLD AFFAIRS

Joined UN in 1993

CE | IAEA | EAPC | PfP | OSCE

Macedonia's hosting of NATO troops in the Kosovo war in 1999 placed it firmly in the Western fold. Nationalists resented EU and NATO pressure to compromise over inter-ethnic conflict in 2001.

AID

Recipient

$273m (receipts)

Up 197% in 1999

The World Bank and EU are the main channels for economic development assistance, apart from crisis aid and military support. A major boost in EU aid was agreed in March 2001. Regional security fears limit foreign investment.

DEFENSE

Compulsory military service

$67m

Down 7% in 1999

Rebuilding the army since independence has depended heavily on officer training in NATO countries. Conflict with ethnic Albanian militants in 2001 severely tested army discipline.

M

ECONOMICS

Inflation 94.2% p.a. (1990–1999)

$3.3bn

59.85–66.26 Macedonian denars

SCORE CARD

- ❑ WORLD GNP RANKING........................126th
- ❑ GNP PER CAPITA.............................$1660
- ❑ BALANCE OF PAYMENTS.....................$–109m
- ❑ INFLATION.....................................–1.3%
- ❑ UNEMPLOYMENT...............................35%

EXPORTS

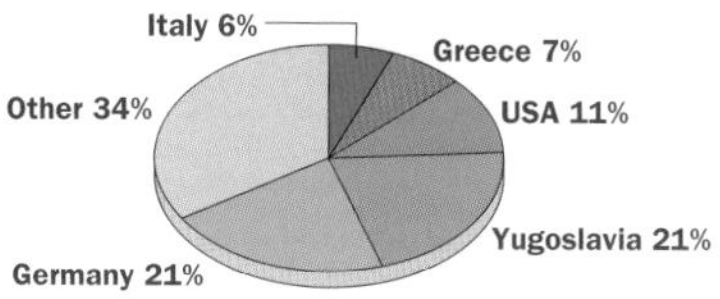
Italy 6%
Greece 7%
Other 34%
USA 11%
Yugoslavia 21%
Germany 21%

IMPORTS

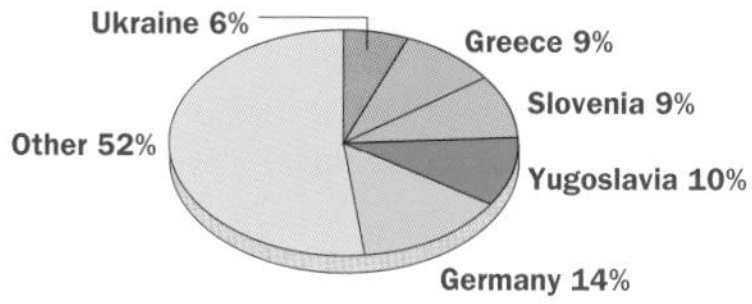
Ukraine 6%
Greece 9%
Slovenia 9%
Other 52%
Yugoslavia 10%
Germany 14%

STRENGTHS
Growth in private sector and foreign investment. Mineral resources.

WEAKNESSES
Poorest of former Yugoslav republics. Loss of trade in mid-1990s due to Greek embargo and sanctions on Yugoslavia. Dependence on oil, gas, and machinery imports. Disruption caused by Kosovo conflict and 2001 violence.

FORMER YUGOSLAV REPUBLIC OF MACEDONIA

Total Land Area : 25 715 sq. km (9929 sq. miles)

LAND HEIGHT
- 2000m/6562ft
- 1000m/3281ft
- 500m/1640ft
- 50m/164ft

POPULATION
- over 500 000
- over 100 000
- over 50 000
- over 10 000
- under 10 000

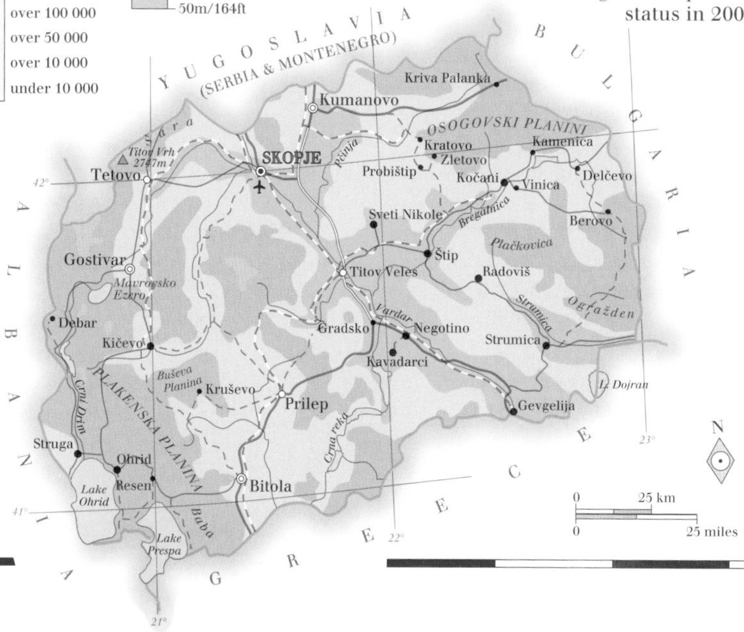
YUGOSLAVIA
(SERBIA & MONTENEGRO)
BULGARIA
ALBANIA
GREECE
Kriva Palanka
Kumanovo
OSOGOVSKI PLANINI
Kratovo
Zletovo
Kamenica
SKOPJE
Pčinja
Probištip
Kočani
Delčevo
Vinica
Šar
Titov Vrh 2747m
Tetovo
Sveti Nikole
Bregalnica
Berovo
Štip
Plačkovica
Gostivar
Titov Veles
Radoviš
Mavrovsko Ezero
Strumica
Ogražden
Debar
Vardar
Gradsko
Negotino
Strumica
Kičevo
Kavadarci
Buševa Planina
Kruševo
PLAKENSKA PLANINA
L. Dojran
Prilep
Crni Drim
Gevgelija
Crna reka
Struga
Ohrid
Lake Ohrid
Resen
Bitola
Lake Prespa
Baba
42°
41°
21°
22°
23°
N
0 25 km
0 25 miles

RESOURCES

Electric power 1.5m kw

1137 tonnes

Not an oil producer

1.55m sheep, 290,000 cattle, 3.34m chickens

Coal, copper, bauxite, iron, antimony, chromium, lead, zinc

Minerals remain underexploited. South-facing fertile plains produce early fruit and vegetables for EU markets.

ENVIRONMENT

Sustainability rank: 100th

7%

5.5 tonnes per capita

Industrial pollution affects water quality. The Titov Veles lead and zinc smelter is the worst culprit for toxic waste.

MEDIA

TV ownership medium

Daily newspaper circulation 21 per 1000 people

PUBLISHING AND BROADCAST MEDIA

There are 4 daily newspapers, including the government-funded Albanian *Flaka e Vellazerimit*

3 services: 1 state-owned, 2 independent

1 state-owned, also independent services

Newspaper sales have expanded rapidly. In 2001, two independent newspapers "voluntarily" ceased publication.

CRIME

Death penalty not used

Macedonia does not publish prison figures

Down 11% 1996–1998

Cigarette smuggling is dominated by Albanian gangs also involved in the illegal arms trade and heroin trafficking.

EDUCATION

School leaving age: 15

94%

30,754 students

An Albanian-language university first established at Tetovo in 1994 was finally granted special status in 2000.

CHRONOLOGY

After partition of the former Ottoman province between Serbia, Bulgaria, and Greece in 1912–1913, what is now Macedonia was part of Yugoslavia until 1991.

- ❑ **1944** Tito establishes republic, stressing Macedonian identity.
- ❑ **1945** Adoption of standardized Macedonian language.
- ❑ **1989–1990** Multiparty elections.
- ❑ **1991** Independence declared. EU recognition delayed by Greeks.
- ❑ **1995** Accord with Greece.
- ❑ **1998–1999** Right-wing VMRO–DPMNE coalition wins elections.
- ❑ **1999** Upheaval over Kosovo conflict.
- ❑ **2001** Conflict with ethnic Albanian militants.

HEALTH

Welfare state health benefits

1 per 435 people

Heart and cerebrovascular diseases, cancers

In theory, the state guarantees universal health care, but effective and speedy treatment is increasingly only available in the private sector.

SPENDING

GDP/cap. decrease

CONSUMPTION AND SPENDING

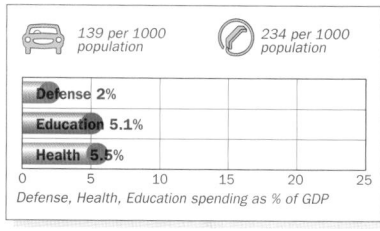

139 per 1000 population

234 per 1000 population

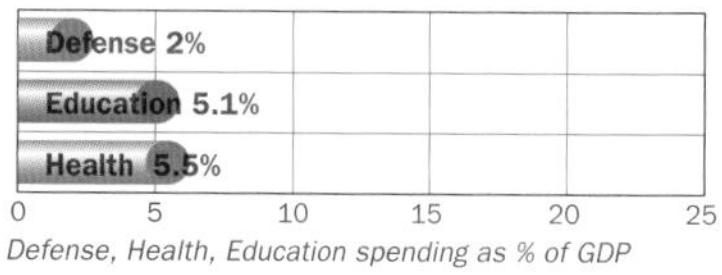
Defense 2%
Education 5.1%
Health 5.5%
0
5
10
15
20
25

Defense, Health, Education spending as % of GDP

Incomes have fallen by more than two-thirds since 1990, although smuggling and organized crime have made a few people conspicuously wealthy.

WORLD RANKING

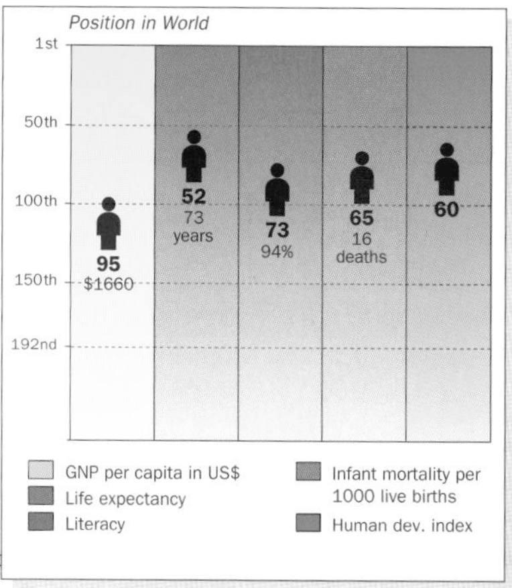
Position in World
1st
50th
100th
150th
192nd
95
$1660
52
73 years
73
94%
65
16 deaths
60
GNP per capita in US$
Life expectancy
Literacy
Infant mortality per 1000 live births
Human dev. index

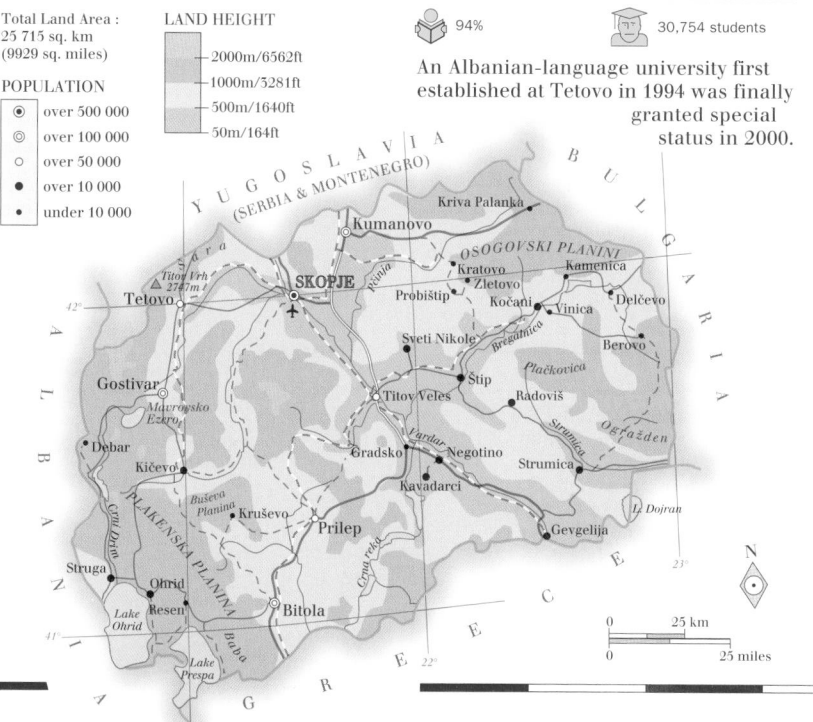

M

MADAGASCAR

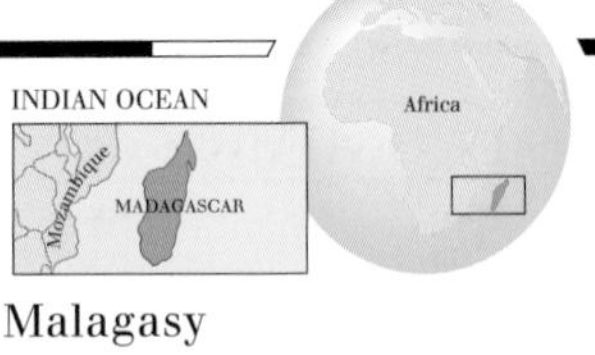
INDIAN OCEAN
Africa
Mozambique
MADAGASCAR

OFFICIAL NAME: Republic of Madagascar **CAPITAL:** Antananarivo
POPULATION: 15.9 million **CURRENCY:** Malagasy franc **OFFICIAL LANGUAGES:** French and Malagasy

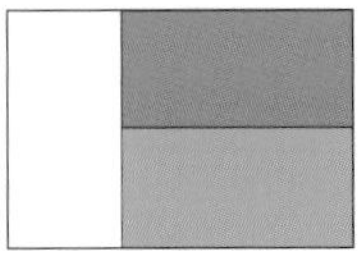

1960 | 1960 | June 26 | RM | +3 | +261 | .mg

LYING IN THE INDIAN Ocean, Madagascar is the world's fourth-largest island. Its isolation means that there is a host of unique wildlife and plants. To the east, the large central plateau drops precipitously through forested cliffs to the coast; in the west, gentler gradients give way to fertile plains. It became independent from France in 1960, and after 18 years of radical socialism under Didier Ratsiraka, became a multiparty democracy. It is heavily dependent on the IMF as it tries to rebuild its agriculture-based economy.

CLIMATE

Tropical

WEATHER CHART

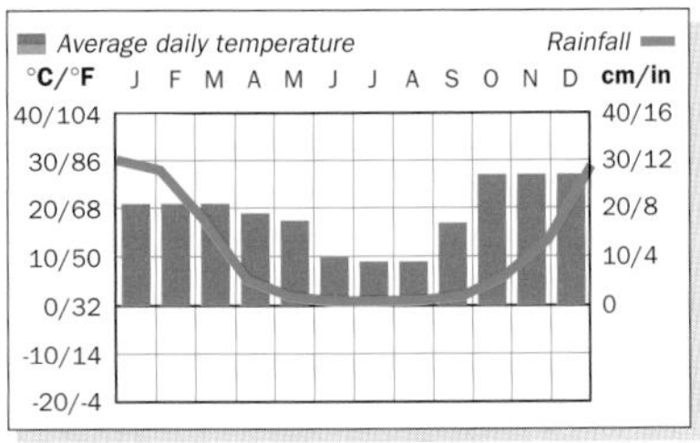
Average daily temperature
Rainfall
°C/°F J F M A M J J A S O N D cm/in
40/104
30/86
20/68
10/50
0/32
-10/14
-20/-4
40/16
30/12
20/8
10/4
0

Tropical Madagascar often has cyclones. The coastal lowlands are humid; rainfall averages 200 cm (79 in) in the east, but under 80 cm (31 in) in the southwest. The central plateau is cooler, with 100–150 cm (39–59 in) of rain a year.

TRANSPORTATION

Drive on right

Ivato, Antananarivo 678,366 passengers

101 ships 41,700 grt

THE TRANSPORTATION NETWORK

5781 km (3592 miles)

None

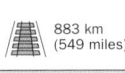

883 km (549 miles)

600 km (373 miles)

An extensive domestic air network – due for privatization – compensates for the facts that many roads are impassable during the rains and the rail network is very limited. Toamasina port handles about 70% of total traffic.

PEOPLE

Pop. density low

Malagasy, French

27/km² (71/mi²)

THE URBAN/RURAL POPULATION SPLIT

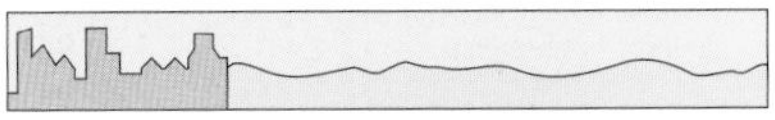
29%
71%

RELIGIOUS PERSUASION

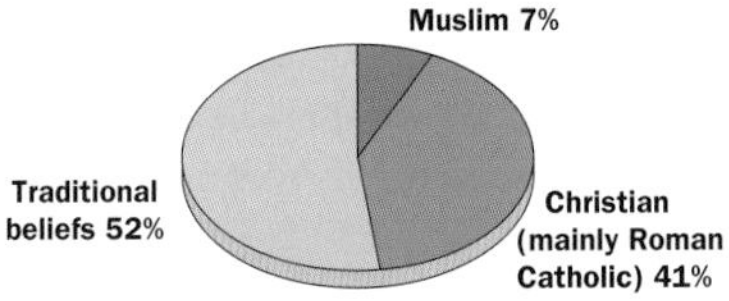
Muslim 7%
Traditional beliefs 52%
Christian (mainly Roman Catholic) 41%

The people of Madagascar, like their language, Malagasy, are essentially Malay–Indonesian in origin. Their ancestors migrated across the Indian Ocean in successive waves from the 1st century. Later migrants from the African mainland intermixed and provided the many African words in Malagasy. Arab traders provided another ingredient to the mix. The main ethnic division is between the central plateau and *côtier* peoples. Of more pronounced Malay extraction, the plateau Merina were Madagascar's historic rulers. They remain the social elite – to the resentment of the poorer *côtiers*. President Didier Ratsiraka owes much of his political longevity to the fact that he is a *côtier*. The extended family remains the focus of social life for the rural majority.

POLITICS

Multiparty elections

L. House 1998/2003
U. House 2001/2007

President Didier Ratsiraka

AT THE LAST ELECTION

National Assembly 150 seats

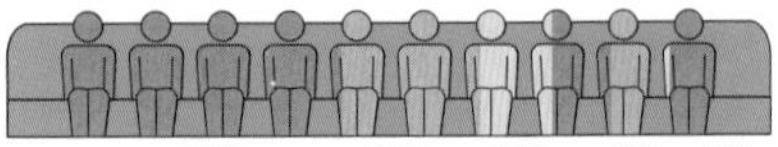
9% AVI
2% MFM
42% Arema
22% Ind
11% LF
7% RPSD
7% Others

Arema = Association pour la renaissance de Madagascar **Ind** = Independents **LF** = Leader–Torch (Fanilo) **AVI** = "People are judged by the work they do" **RPSD** = Rally for Socialism and Democracy **MFM** = Militant Party for the Development of Madagascar

Senate 90 seats

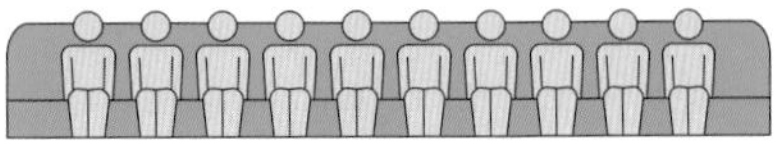

Two-thirds of Senate members are elected by regional governments; the remainder are nominated by the president.

Former dictator Didier Ratsiraka was returned to power in elections in 1997, and extended the presidential powers in a new constitution in 1998.

TOURISM

Visitors : Population 1:99

160,000 visitors

Up 16% in 2000

MAIN TOURIST ARRIVALS

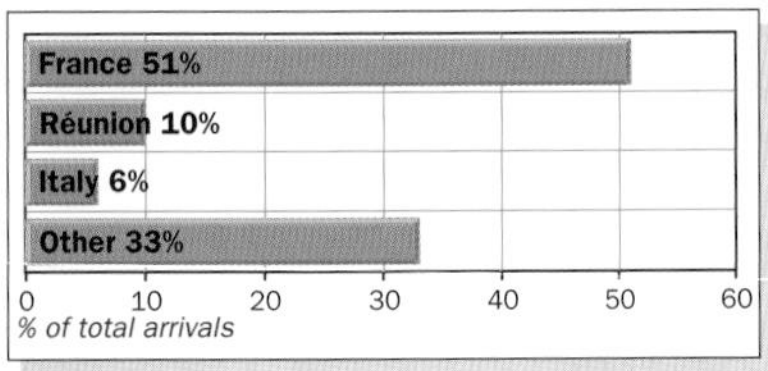
France 51%
Réunion 10%
Italy 6%
Other 33%
0 10 20 30 40 50 60
% of total arrivals

With 5000 km (3100 miles) of tropical beaches and unique flora and fauna, Madagascar has great tourism potential. An important foreign exchange earner, tourism nonetheless remains underdeveloped. Tourist arrivals increased after the marked decline of 1991, thanks partly to restored political stability.

MADAGASCAR

Total Land Area : 581 540 sq. km (224 533 sq. miles)

POPULATION

- over 500 000
- over 100 000
- over 50 000
- over 10 000
- under 10 000

LAND HEIGHT

- 2000m/6562ft
- 1000m/3281ft
- 500m/1640ft
- 200m/656ft
- Sea Level

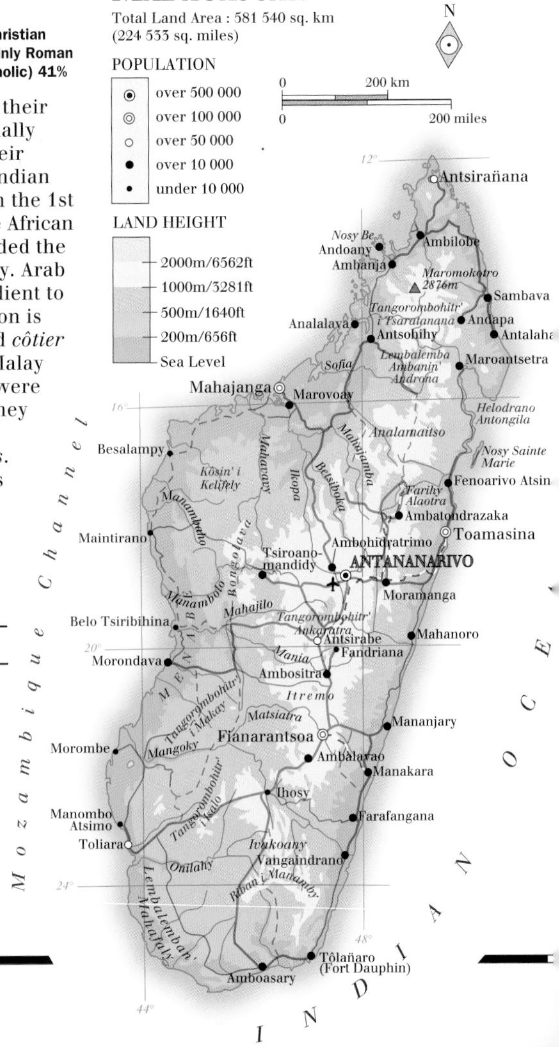
N
0 200 km
0 200 miles
Antsirañana
Nosy Be
Andoany
Ambanja
Ambilobe
Maromokotro 2876m
Sambava
Tangoromohitr' i Tsaratanana
Andapa
Antalaha
Analalava
Antsohihy
Sofia
Lembalemba Ambanin' Androna
Maroantsetra
Mahajanga
Marovoay
Helodrano Antongila
Analamaitso
Besalampy
Kôsin' i Kelifely
Mahavavy
Ikopa
Betsiboka
Mahajamba
Nosy Sainte Marie
Fenoarivo Atsinanana
Manambaho
Fariny Alaotra
Ambatondrazaka
Toamasina
Maintirano
Bongolava
Tsiroanomandidy
Ambohidratrimo
ANTANANARIVO
Moramanga
Manambolo
Mahajilo
Belo Tsiribihina
Tangoromohitr' Ankaratra
Antsirabe
Mahanoro
Fandriana
Morondava
Mania
Ambositra
Itremo
Tangoromohitr' i Makay
Matsiatra
Mananjary
Morombe
Mangoky
Fianarantsoa
Ambalavao
Manakara
Ihosy
Manombo Atsimo
Farafangana
Toliara
Onilahy
Ivakoany
Vangaindrano
Mananara
Lembalemban' Mahafaly
Tôlañaro (Fort Dauphin)
Amboasary
Mozambique Channel
INDIAN OCEAN
12°
16°
20°
24°
44°
48°

WORLD AFFAIRS

Joined UN in 1960

COMESA | OIF | IAEA | COI | OAU

Once-close ties with Moscow and North Korea waned as Madagascar cemented relations with its main Western trading partners, especially France and the USA. Since Zafy left office, cooperation with the IMF has improved too. Regionally, Madagascar has reestablished ties with South Africa and in 1994 joined COMESA.

AID

Recipient

$358m (receipts)

Down 28% in 1999

In 1999 the IMF pledged assistance for fiscal and economic reforms. Emergency aid became a high priority after cyclone damage and heavy floods in early 2000.

DEFENSE

Compulsory military service

$43m

Down 4% in 1999

The army, a key political force, aims to maintain a stable, unitary state. In 1992, it acted against federalist *côtiers*.

ECONOMICS

Inflation 20.6% p.a. (1990–1999)

$3.7bn

6435–6220 Malagasy francs

SCORE CARD

- ❑ WORLD GNP RANKING........................120th
- ❑ GNP PER CAPITA.................................$250
- ❑ BALANCE OF PAYMENTS....................$-301m
- ❑ INFLATION..9.9%
- ❑ UNEMPLOYMENT.......Widespread underemployment

STRENGTHS

Varied agricultural base; vanilla, coffee, and clove exports. Offshore oil and gas. Prawns. Tourism. Literate workforce.

WEAKNESSES

Losing out to cheaper vanilla exporters. Vulnerability to drought and cyclone damage, severe in early 2000. Economic reforms yet to bear fruit. Not self-sufficient in rice, the food staple.

EXPORTS

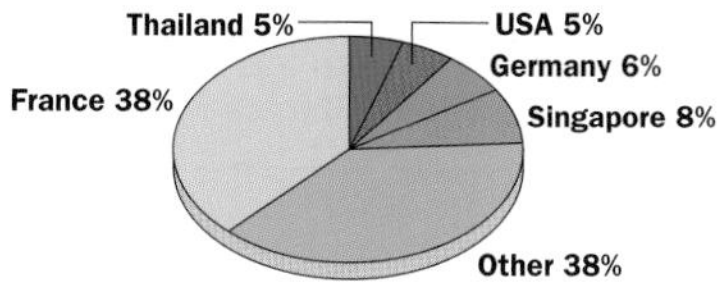

Thailand 5%
USA 5%
Germany 6%
France 38%
Singapore 8%
Other 38%

IMPORTS

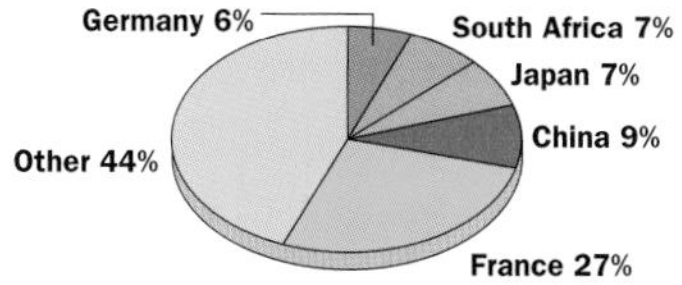

Germany 6%
South Africa 7%
Japan 7%
Other 44%
China 9%
France 27%

***Tôlañaro** (also known as Fort Dauphin), a port on the southeast coast. This was the area first settled by the French in the 16th century.*

RESOURCES

Electric power 220,000 kw

124,973 tonnes

Not an oil producer

10.4m cattle, 3.9m ducks, 3.1m geese, 20m chickens

Chromite, graphite, oil, mica, iron, bitumen, gemstones, marble, gas

Electricity is hydrogenerated. There are underexploited mineral reserves and offshore oil and gas. There were large finds of high quality sapphires in 1998.

ENVIRONMENT

Sustainability rank: 113th

3% (1% partially protected)

0.1 tonnes per capita

Madagascar's environment is a unique resource; 80% of its plant and many animal species, such as the lemur, are found nowhere else. Aid donations help to combat deforestation and soil erosion.

MEDIA

TV ownership low

Daily newspaper circulation 5 per 1000 people

PUBLISHING AND BROADCAST MEDIA

There are 5 daily newspapers, including the *Madagascar Tribune* and *Midi-Madagasikara*

1 state-owned service

1 state-owned service, many independent stations

Even before the return of multiparty democracy in 1993, there was a flourishing opposition press. There are 127 local radio stations.

CRIME

Death penalty not used

20,136 prisoners

Down 68% 1992–1994

Urban crime levels are rising, with theft a particular concern. The army faces accusations of abusing human rights and of shooting federalists in 1993.

EDUCATION

School leaving age: 13

67%

26,715 students

Madagascar boasts one of Africa's highest literacy rates. Universal primary education will soon be based on French, not Malagasy. About 40% of children attend secondary school.

CHRONOLOGY

Increasing European contacts after the 16th century culminated in the 1895 French invasion. Madagascar became a French colony and the Merina monarchy was abolished.

- ❑ **1947–1948** French troops kill thousands in nationalist uprisings.
- ❑ **1960** Independence.
- ❑ **1975** Radical socialist Didier Ratsiraka takes power.
- ❑ **1990** Multiparty political reforms.
- ❑ **1991** Opposition *Forces Vives* (CFV) coalition set up; led by Albert Zafy. Mass strikes against regime.
- ❑ **1992** Civilian rule restored.
- ❑ **1993** Zafy's CFV defeats Ratsiraka's coalition, the MFM, in free elections.
- ❑ **1996** Zafy impeached.
- ❑ **1997** Ratsiraka elected president.
- ❑ **1998** New constitution adopted.

HEALTH

Welfare state health benefits

1 per 3333 people

Malaria, enteric, and respiratory diseases

Private health care was legalized in 1993. State care is free but inadequate. Malaria is at epidemic levels. There are outbreaks of bubonic plague.

SPENDING

GDP/cap. increase

CONSUMPTION AND SPENDING

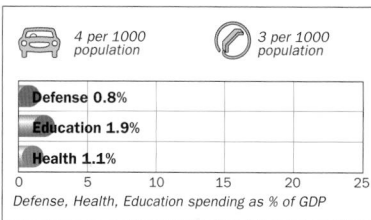

4 per 1000 population

3 per 1000 population

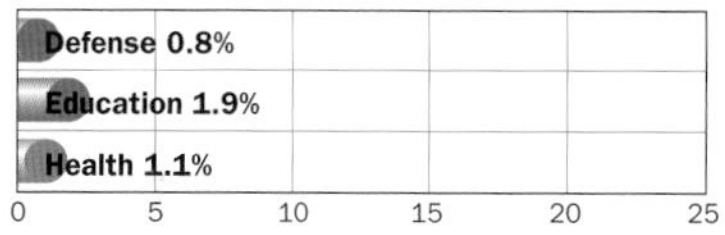

Defense 0.8%
Education 1.9%
Health 1.1%
0
5
10
15
20
25

Defense, Health, Education spending as % of GDP

Most of Madagascar's people are terribly poor, although central plateau dwellers are richer than the *côtier* farmers and fishermen.

WORLD RANKING

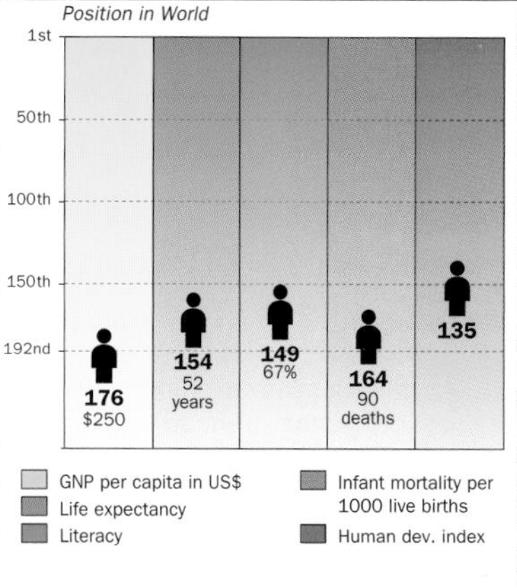

Position in World
1st
50th
100th
150th
192nd
176
$250
154
52 years
149
67%
164
90 deaths
135
GNP per capita in US$
Life expectancy
Literacy
Infant mortality per 1000 live births
Human dev. index

M

MALAWI

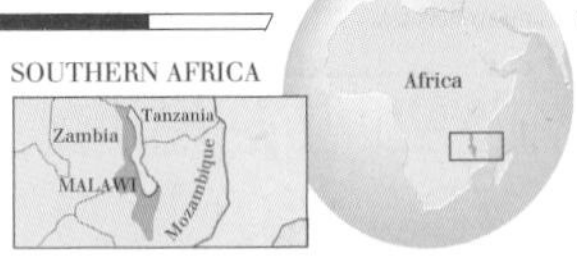
SOUTHERN AFRICA
Africa
Tanzania
Zambia
MALAWI
Mozambique

OFFICIAL NAME: Republic of Malawi **CAPITAL:** Lilongwe
POPULATION: 10.9 million **CURRENCY:** Malawi kwacha **OFFICIAL LANGUAGE:** English

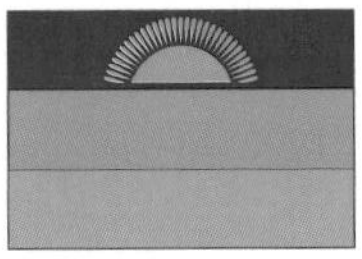

1964 | 1964 | July 6 | MW | +2 | +265 | .mw

LANDLOCKED IN SOUTHEAST Africa, Malawi borders the Great Rift Valley. One-fifth of the country is submerged under Africa's third-largest expanse of water, Lake Nyasa. In the 1980s Malawi hosted large numbers of Mozambican refugees, at some cost to its fragile economy. A former British colony, Malawi established democracy in 1994 after three decades of one-party rule under Hastings Banda. Bakili Muluzi was reelected president in June 1999.

CLIMATE

Tropical wet & dry

WEATHER CHART

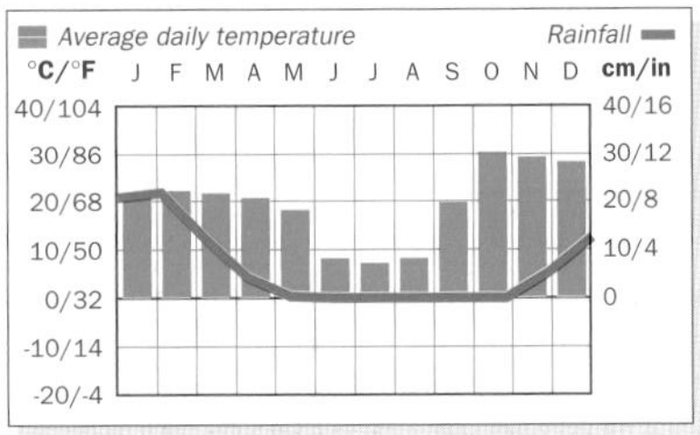
Average daily temperature
Rainfall
°C/°F
J F M A M J J A S O N D
cm/in
40/104
30/86
20/68
10/50
0/32
-10/14
-20/-4
40/16
30/12
20/8
10/4
0

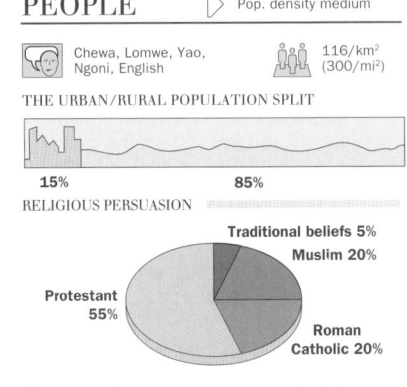

The south is hot and humid. The rest of Malawi is warm and very sunny in the dry season, but cooler in the highlands.

TRANSPORTATION

Drive on left

Kamuzu International, Lilongwe
198,924 passengers

Has no fleet

THE TRANSPORTATION NETWORK

5254 km (3265 miles)

None

797 km (495 miles)

144 km (89 miles)

The Kamuzu Highway has been upgraded, and the Nacala Rail Corridor, a vital link to the sea, has attracted private investment.

TOURISM

Visitors : Population 1:48

228,000 visitors

Down 10% in 2000

MAIN TOURIST ARRIVALS

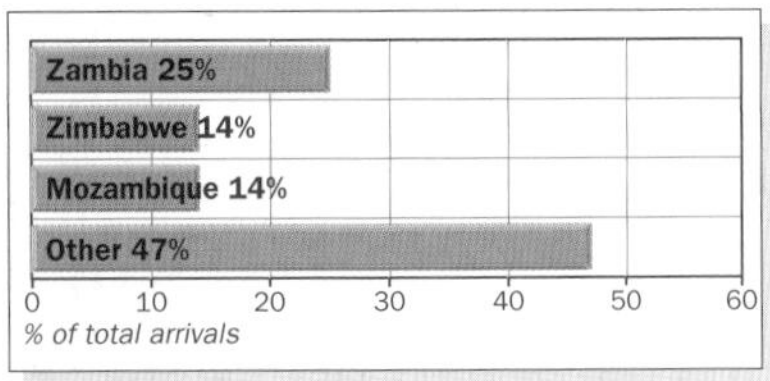
Zambia 25%
Zimbabwe 14%
Mozambique 14%
Other 47%
0
10
20
30
40
50
60
% of total arrivals

The national parks and Lake Nyasa's fishing and water sports are the main tourist attractions. The opening of international airports at Blantyre and Lilongwe has increased accessibility.

PEOPLE

Pop. density medium

Chewa, Lomwe, Yao, Ngoni, English

116/km² (300/mi²)

THE URBAN/RURAL POPULATION SPLIT

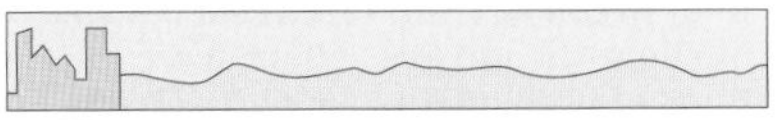
15%
85%

RELIGIOUS PERSUASION

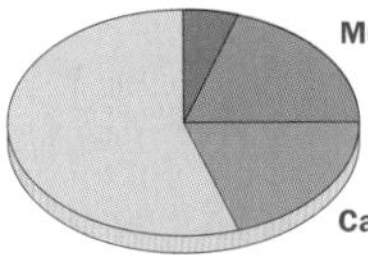
Traditional beliefs 5%
Muslim 20%
Protestant 55%
Roman Catholic 20%

Ethnicity has not been exploited for political ends as has been the case in neighboring states. Most Malawians share a common Bantu origin. Of the various groups, the Chewa are dominant in the central region, Nyanja in the south, Tumbuka in the north, the mostly Muslim Yao in the southeast, and the Ngoni, a Zulu offshoot, in the lowlands. Other groups include the Chieoka and Tonga. Northerners felt ignored by Banda and his MCP, but the UDF government has largely succeeded in reducing the resulting tensions.

The election of President Muluzi, a member of Malawi's 20% Muslim minority, arguably signals the failure of Banda's plan to enforce Protestant domination in Malawi. Many of Malawi's Muslim Asians work in the retailing sector.

***Fruit and vegetable sellers** offering their wares on the Mozambican border. The south of the country is intensively cultivated.*

POLITICS

Multiparty elections

1999/2004

President Bakili Muluzi

AT THE LAST ELECTION

National Assembly 193 seats

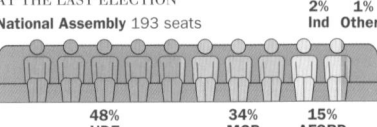

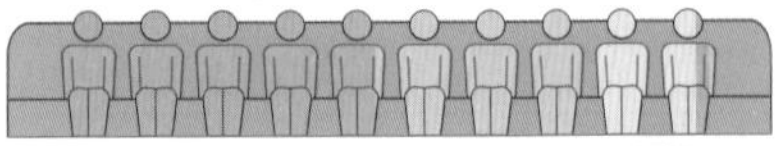
2% Ind
1% Others
48% UDF
34% MCP
15% AFORD

UDF = United Democratic Front **MCP** = Malawi Congress Party **AFORD** = Alliance for Democracy **Ind** = Independents

From independence in 1964 Malawi was ruled by the autocratic Hastings Banda. His single-party regime outlawed dissent; torture and imprisonment without trial were common. In 1992 international aid was suspended because of the regime's human rights record. A referendum in 1993 forced Banda to introduce multiparty politics. In 1994 elections saw the mainly southern-based UDF under Bakili Muluzi score a dramatic victory. In simultaneous presidential polls Muluzi, a wealthy businessman, resoundingly beat Banda, thus ending one of the world's longest-lasting dictatorships. Muluzi shrewdly recruited several prominent MCP politicians to his team. He vowed to restore personal and religious freedom, liberalize and revive the shattered economy, and improve Malawi's regional standing. Muluzi was narrowly reelected in June 1999, but opposition leader Gwanda Chakuamba contested the results, and violence against Muslims and UDF supporters erupted in the north.

WORLD AFFAIRS

Joined UN in 1964

Comm | COMESA | NAM | OAU | SADC

Malawi aims to protect its restored status as a recipient of Western aid. In 1998 the UK pledged to support President Muluzi's fiscal policies and anti-poverty drive. Malawi also wants to preserve ties with South Africa, unbroken since 1967, a unique record in black Africa. One in ten Mozambicans fled to Malawi as refugees in the 1980s.

AID

Recipient

$446m (receipts)

Up 3% in 1999

Non-humanitarian aid resumed with the advent of democracy, and international donors have pledged $1.2 billion. The World Food Program launched an emergency aid program in April 2001 to help flood victims.

M

DEFENSE

No compulsory military service

$27m | Up 4% in 1999

The government is confident of the loyalty of the 5000-strong military. In the last days of Banda rule, the military lost confidence in the ruling party, forcing the pace of democratization. In 1993, it disarmed the Young Pioneers, a militarized section of the MCP.

ECONOMICS

Inflation 34.3% p.a. (1990–1999)

$2bn | 46.43–80.40 kwacha

SCORE CARD

- WORLD GNP RANKING........................140th
- GNP PER CAPITA $180
- BALANCE OF PAYMENTS...................$–450m
- INFLATION 44.9%
- UNEMPLOYMENT ....Widespread underemployment

STRENGTHS

Tobacco, earning 76% of foreign exchange. Tea and sugar production. Unexploited bauxite, asbestos, and coal reserves. Much tourism potential.

WEAKNESSES

Agriculture vulnerable to drought and price fluctuations. Only 14% of GDP derived from industry. Small domestic market, few skilled workers. Strain of housing Mozambican refugees.

EXPORTS

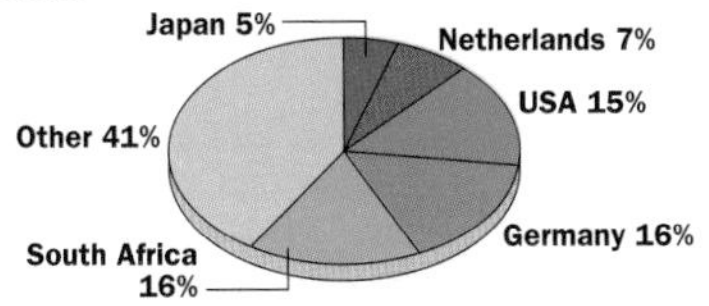
Japan 5%
Netherlands 7%
USA 15%
Other 41%
Germany 16%
South Africa 16%

IMPORTS

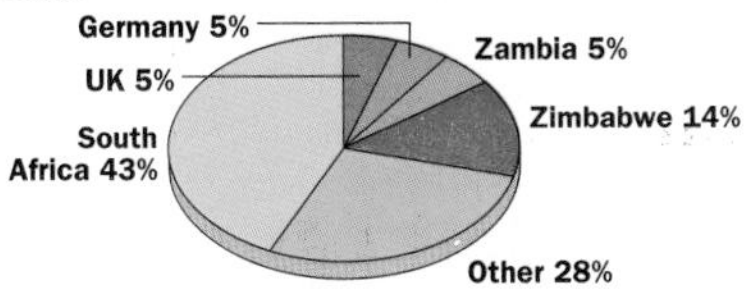
Germany 5%
Zambia 5%
UK 5%
Zimbabwe 14%
South Africa 43%
Other 28%

RESOURCES

Electric power 185,000 kw

56,564 tonnes | Not an oil producer

1.27m goats, 760,000 cattle, 15m chickens | Coal, limestone, gemstones, bauxite, graphite, uranium

One 215 MW hydropower plant on Shire River accounts for nearly 85% of generating capacity, but only 3% of total energy use. Most rely on fuelwood for their energy needs. Malawi now encourages privatization, crop diversification, improved irrigation, and regional economic integration via the SADC to exploit its naturally limited resources. A deep-seam coal mine currently operates at Rumphi.

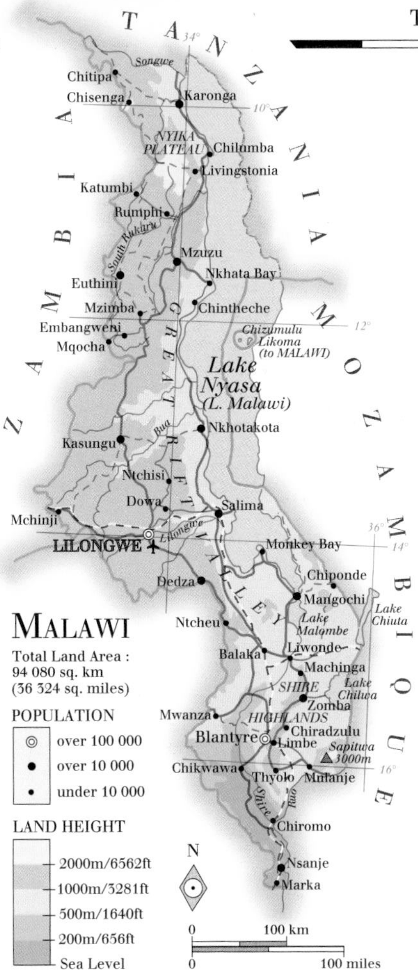
TANZANIA
ZAMBIA
MOZAMBIQUE
Songwe
Chitipa
Chisenga
Karonga
NYIKA PLATEAU
Chilumba
Livingstonia
Katumbi
Rumphi
South Rukuru
Mzuzu
Nkhata Bay
Euthini
Mzimba
Chintheche
Embangweni
Mqocha
Chizumulu
Likoma (to MALAWI)
Lake Nyasa (L. Malawi)
Nkhotakota
Kasungu
Ntchisi
Dowa
Salima
Mchinji
LILONGWE
Monkey Bay
Dedza
Chiponde
Mangochi
Lake Chiuta
GREAT RIFT VALLEY
Ntcheu
Lake Malombe
Liwonde
Balaka
Machinga
Lake Chilwa
SHIRE HIGHLANDS
Zomba
Mwanza
Blantyre
Chiradzulu
Limbe
Sapitwa 3000m
Chikwawa
Thyolo
Mulanje
Shire
Ruo
Chiromo
Nsanje
Marka
N
0 100 km
0 100 miles

MALAWI

Total Land Area : 94 080 sq. km (36 324 sq. miles)

POPULATION

- over 100 000
- over 10 000
- under 10 000

LAND HEIGHT

- 2000m/6562ft
- 1000m/3281ft
- 500m/1640ft
- 200m/656ft
- Sea Level

ENVIRONMENT

Sustainability rank: 92nd

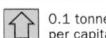

11% | 0.1 tonnes per capita

Drought, devastating agriculture in 1992, eclipses all other problems. Ecological husbandry now attracts tourism.

MEDIA

TV ownership low

Daily newspaper circulation 3 per 1000 people

PUBLISHING AND BROADCAST MEDIA

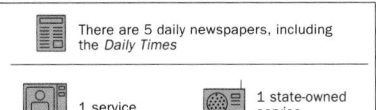

There are 5 daily newspapers, including the *Daily Times*

1 service | 1 state-owned service

The first TV company was launched in 1999. In 1998 President Muluzi accused newspapers of "spreading despondency."

CRIME

Death penalty used

Malawi does not publish prison figures | Up 10% in 1990

Urban crime is on the increase. The proliferation of weapons, particularly guns, is contributing to a rise in cases of armed robbery.

CHRONOLOGY

After strong Scottish missionary activity, Malawi came under British rule as Nyasaland in 1891.

- **1964** Independence under Hastings Banda.
- **1966** One-party state.
- **1992** Antigovernment riots. Illegal prodemocracy groups unite.
- **1993** Referendum for multipartyism.
- **1994** Muluzi's UDF wins elections.
- **1999** Muluzi reelected president.
- **2001** Floods leave many homeless.

EDUCATION

School leaving age: 14

60% | 5561 students

Primary-level education is widespread, with 73% of boys and 60% of girls attending school regularly.

HEALTH

Welfare state health benefits

1 per 20,000 people | Infectious, parasitic, and respiratory diseases

Access to health services is difficult and HIV/AIDS is a growing problem.

SPENDING

GDP/cap. increase

CONSUMPTION AND SPENDING

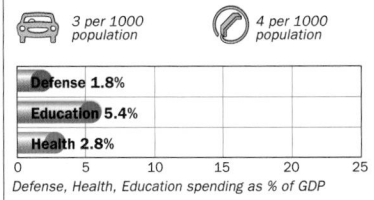

3 per 1000 population | 4 per 1000 population

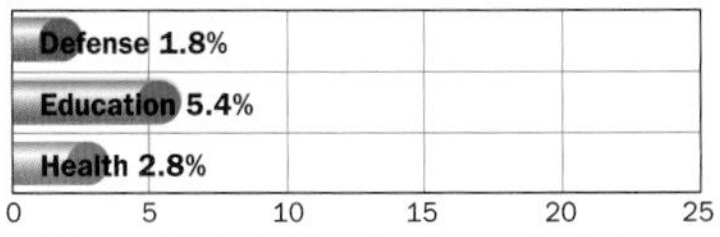
Defense 1.8%
Education 5.4%
Health 2.8%
0
5
10
15
20
25

Defense, Health, Education spending as % of GDP

The ousted MCP elite grew wealthy, allegedly through embezzlement. However, 80% of Malawians remain mired in poverty, and are forced to survive on less than $1 a day.

WORLD RANKING

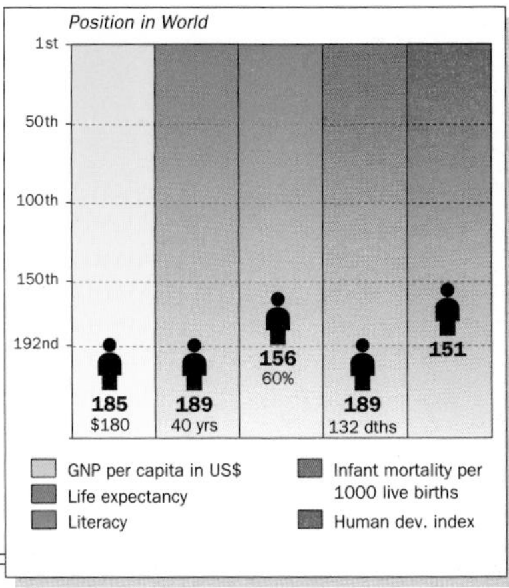
Position in World
1st
50th
100th
150th
192nd
185
$180
189
40 yrs
156
60%
189
132 dths
151
GNP per capita in US$
Life expectancy
Literacy
Infant mortality per 1000 live births
Human dev. index

M

MALAYSIA

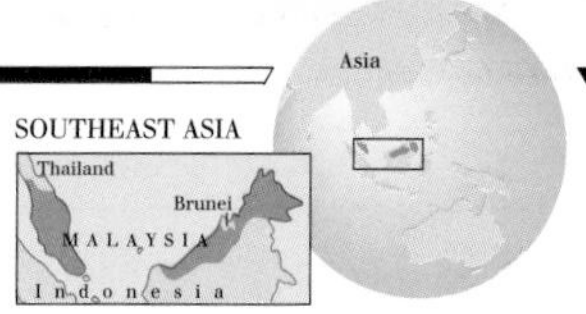
Asia
SOUTHEAST ASIA
Thailand
Brunei
MALAYSIA
Indonesia

OFFICIAL NAME: Federation of Malaysia **CAPITAL:** Kuala Lumpur
POPULATION: 22.2 million **CURRENCY:** Ringgit **OFFICIAL LANGUAGE:** Bahasa Malaysia

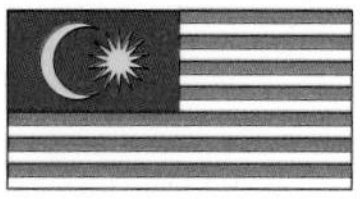

1963 | 1965 | Aug 31 | MAL | +8 | +60 | .my

COMPRISING THE THREE territories of Peninsular Malaysia, Sarawak, and Sabah, Malaysia stretches over 2000 km (1240 miles) from the Malay Peninsula to the northeastern end of the island of Borneo. It shares borders with Thailand, Indonesia, and the enclave states of Singapore and Brunei. A central mountain chain divides Peninsular Malaysia, separating fertile western plains from an eastern coastal belt. Sarawak and Sabah have swampy coastal plains rising to mountains on the border with Indonesia. Putrajaya, just south of Kuala Lumpur, is a high-tech new development intended as the future capital.

CLIMATE

Tropical equatorial

WEATHER CHART

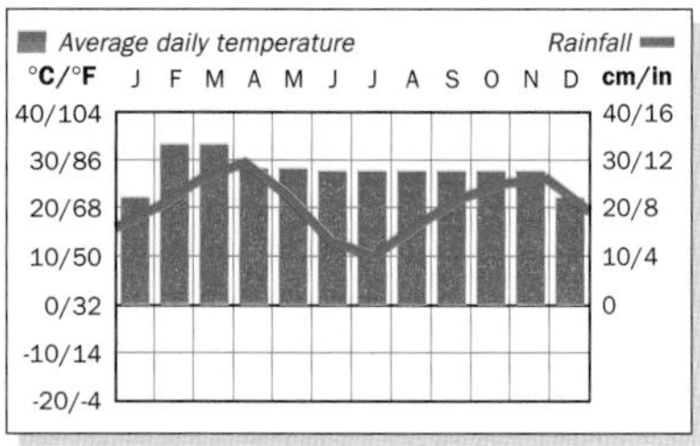
Average daily temperature
Rainfall
°C/°F J F M A M J J A S O N D cm/in
40/104
30/86
20/68
10/50
0/32
-10/14
-20/-4
40/16
30/12
20/8
10/4
0

The whole of Malaysia has an equatorial climate. The country has rainfall throughout the year; it falls on between 150 and 200 days almost everywhere. However, there are two distinct rainy seasons, when the heaviest rain falls - from March to May and from September to November. Coastal areas are also subject to the alternating southwest and northeast monsoon winds.

***Tea plantations** and colonial-style houses and gardens make Cameron Highlands, in Peninsular Malaysia, one of Asia's most popular mountain resorts.*

TRANSPORTATION

Drive on left

Subang International, Kuala Lumpur 15.17m passengers

828 ships 5.2m grt

THE TRANSPORTATION NETWORK

70,970 km (44,099 miles)	580 km (360 miles)
1622 km (1008 miles)	7296 km (4534 miles)

A major north-south highway has been built and in Kuala Lumpur a new mass transit system is being constructed to extend to its outer suburbs. Malaysia's "national car," the Proton, has been a success; since 1985, national car ownership has tripled. Several ports are being updated: 90% of the country's trade is seaborne.

TOURISM

Visitors : Population 1:2.2

10.2m visitors

Up 29% in 2000

MAIN TOURIST ARRIVALS

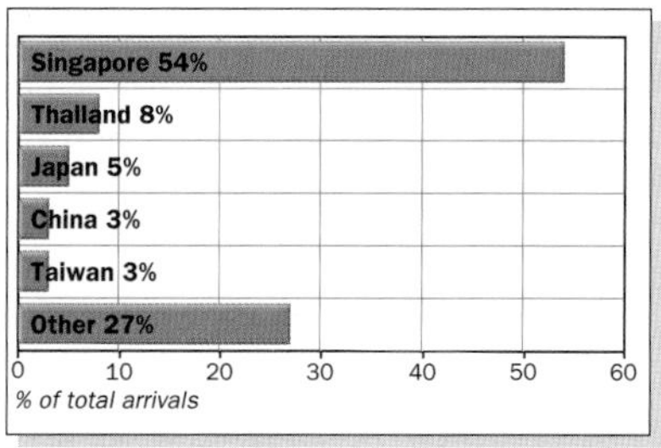
Singapore 54%
Thailand 8%
Japan 5%
China 3%
Taiwan 3%
Other 27%
0 10 20 30 40 50 60
% of total arrivals

Malaysia is southeast Asia's major tourist destination. Most tourists come for the excellent tropical beaches on the east coast, to hike in the Cameron Highlands, or to trek in the world's oldest rainforests in Borneo. There has recently been an increase in the international business convention trade, and hotel capacity has been growing at 10% a year.

By 1990, when the government ran the Visit Malaysia Year campaign, tourism had become Malaysia's third-biggest foreign exchange earner. Two other such campaigns were launched in 1994 and 1998. However, the resurgence since 1999 of pro-Islamic parties, which favor stricter dress codes for women and a ban on alcohol, has deterred some Western tourists. In 2000 Malaysia backed an integrated tourism package with Thailand, Indonesia, and Singapore to enable tourists to visit the four countries under a common program.

MALAYSIA

Total Land Area : 328 550 sq. km (126 853 sq. miles)

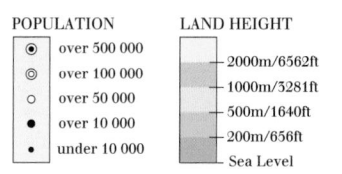

POPULATION	LAND HEIGHT
over 500 000	2000m/6562ft
over 100 000	1000m/3281ft
over 50 000	500m/1640ft
over 10 000	200m/656ft
under 10 000	Sea Level

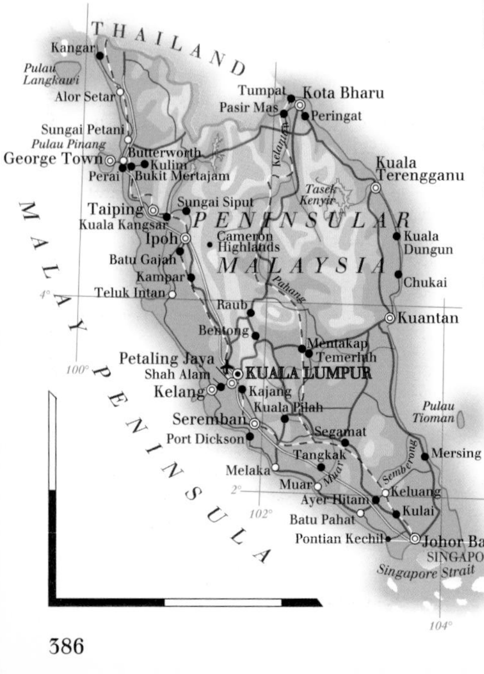
THAILAND
Kangar
Pulau Langkawi
Alor Setar
Tumpat
Kota Bharu
Pasir Mas
Peringat
Sungai Petani
Pulau Pinang
George Town
Butterworth
Kulim
Perai
Bukit Mertajam
Kuala Terengganu
Taiping
Sungai Siput
Kuala Kangsar
Tasek Kenyir
PENINSULAR MALAYSIA
Ipoh
Cameron Highlands
Kuala Dungun
Batu Gajah
Kampar
Chukai
Teluk Intan
MALAY PENINSULA
Raub
Kuantan
Bentong
Mentakap
Temerloh
Petaling Jaya
Shah Alam
KUALA LUMPUR
Kelang
Kajang
Kuala Pilah
Seremban
Port Dickson
Segamat
Pulau Tioman
Tangkak
Mersing
Melaka
Muar
Keluang
Ayer Hitam
Kulai
Batu Pahat
Pontian Kechil
Johor Baharu
SINGAPORE
Singapore Strait

Kepulauan Anambas (INDONESIA)
Kepulauan Natuna (INDONESIA)
SOUTH CHINA SEA
Selat Serasan
Teluk Datu
Pulau Beruit
SARAWAK
Bintulu
Sibu
Kuching
Bandar Sri Aman
Rajang
Penunungan Boyeh Kapuas
Kepulauan Tambelan (INDONESIA)
INDON

PEOPLE

Pop. density medium

Bahasa Malaysia, Malay, Chinese, Tamil, English

68/km² (175/mi²)

THE URBAN/RURAL POPULATION SPLIT

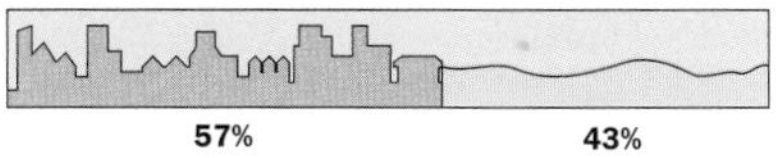
57%
43%

RELIGIOUS PERSUASION

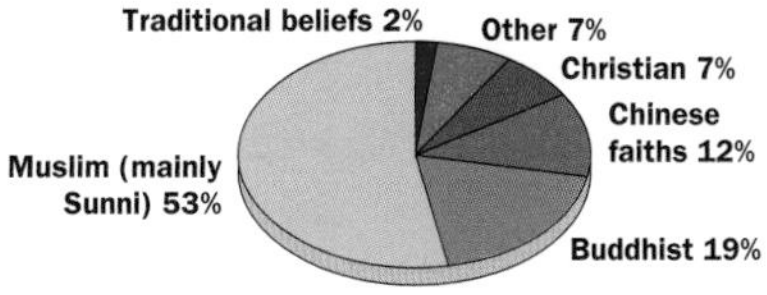
Traditional beliefs 2%
Other 7%
Christian 7%
Chinese faiths 12%
Muslim (mainly Sunni) 53%
Buddhist 19%

ETHNIC MAKEUP

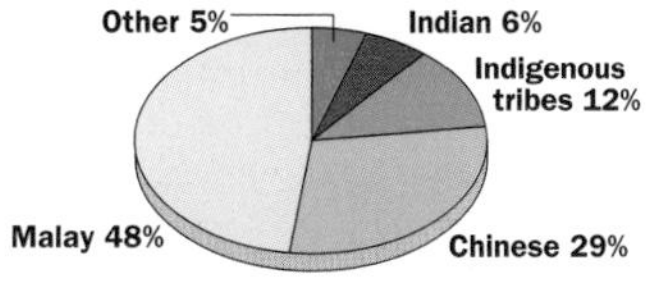
Other 5%
Indian 6%
Indigenous tribes 12%
Malay 48%
Chinese 29%

POPULATION AGE BREAKDOWN

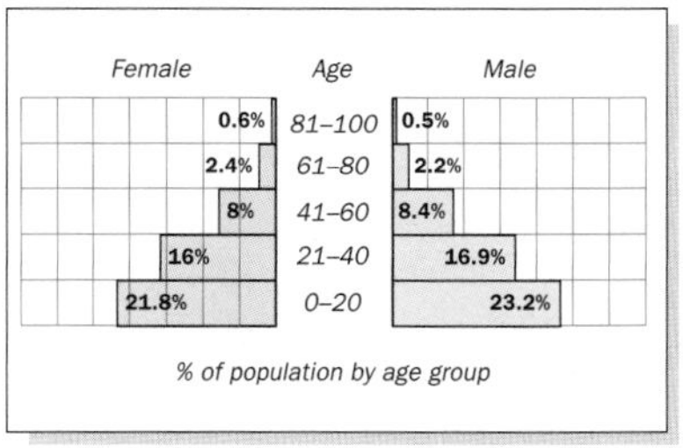
Female
Age
Male
0.6% 81–100 0.5%
2.4% 61–80 2.2%
8% 41–60 8.4%
16% 21–40 16.9%
21.8% 0–20 23.2%
% of population by age group

The key distinction in Malaysian society is between the indigenous Malays, termed the "Bumiputras" (literally, sons of the soil), and the Chinese. The Malays form the largest group, accounting for just under half of the population. However, the Chinese have traditionally controlled most business activity. The New Economic Policy (NEP), introduced in the 1970s, was designed to address this imbalance by offering positive opportunities to the Malays through the education system and by making jobs available to them in both the state and private sectors. There are estimated to be more than one million Indonesian and Filipino immigrants in Malaysia, attracted by its labor shortages and a dearth of employment in their own countries. In addition, nearly 255,000 Vietnamese refugees were offered temporary refuge in Malaysia between 1975 and 1997; most have now been resettled in third countries, but around 6000 remain. Gender discrimination was only outlawed in 2001. Muslim women are encouraged to take the veil.

POLITICS

Multiparty elections

L. House 1999/2004
U. House Varying

Sultan Salehuddin Abdul Aziz

AT THE LAST ELECTION

House of Representatives 193 seats

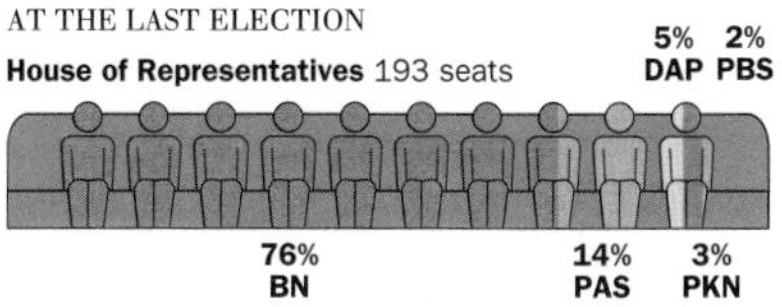
5% DAP
2% PBS
76% BN
14% PAS
3% PKN

BN = National Front (dominated by the United Malays National Organization – **UMNO**) **PAS** = Pan-Malaysian Islamic Party **DAP** = Democratic Action Party **PKN** = National Justice Party (Keadilan) **PBS** = United Sabah Party

The DAP, the PAS and the PKN form the Alternative Front.

Senate 69 seats

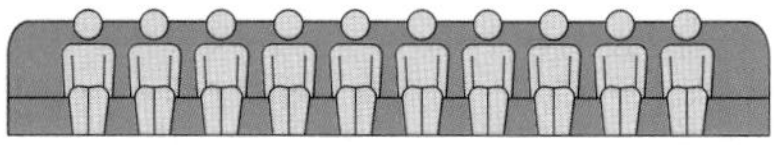

The Senate comprises 26 members indirectly elected by the State Legislative Assemblies, and 43 appointed by the head of state

Balabac Strait
Pulau Banggi
Kudat
SULU SEA
Gunung Kinabalu 4094m
Telukan Labuk
Kota Kinabalu
Labuk
Sandakan
Sibutu Passage
Pulau Labuan
Victoria
Kinabatangan
Brunei Bay
SABAH
Banjaran Brassey
Telukan Lahad Datu
Tawau
CELEBES SEA
Borneo
N
0
100 km
200 miles
116°
118°
4°
2°

Supreme power rests in theory with the monarch, who acts on the advice of parliament. Opposition parties, while legal, are under tight control.

Main Political Issue

Malay dominance of government

The current administration of Mahathir Mohamed has declared that it no longer wishes to discriminate positively in favor of Malays, but the Chinese community accuses the government of corruption and uncompetitive practices, declaring that Malays are still favored for the placing of government contracts. It is further alienated by the more restrictive Islamic society.

Profile

Malaysia has long been dominated by the United Malays National Organization (UMNO), part of the ruling BN coalition, since Malay independence in 1957. It controls a huge network of patronage.

However, the economic crisis of 1997–1998 and recent dissent within the ruling coalition have shaken Mahathir's authority. In 1998 Anwar Ibrahim, deputy prime minister and once Mahathir's chosen successor, was dismissed after challenging the government's economic policy and calling for political reform. He was found guilty of corruption in April 1999, and sentenced to six years' imprisonment (lengthened to 15 years in 2000 after his conviction for sodomy). The initial verdict sparked riots and gained support for the new opposition PKN headed by Anwar's wife, Wan Azizah. PKN activists have been hounded by the government. In elections in 1999, the BN coalition retained its large majority but Mahathir's own UMNO lost ground. In an attempt to regain popularity among the Islamic community, the government, although officially secular, appointed officials to oversee the country's 5000 mosques.

Anwar Ibrahim, in 1998 controversially dismissed by Mahathir.

Mahathir Mohamed, prime minister since 1981.

WORLD AFFAIRS

Joined UN in 1957

APEC | ASEAN | Comm | G15 | OIC

Mahathir sees himself as one of the developing world's leading voices. He maintains a strongly anti-US line in his public speeches and has chastised the West for failing to control currency traders, whom he blames for the Asian economic crisis. Mahathir's pro-Malay policies have caused tensions with Singapore, exacerbated by the latter's dependence on Malaysia for water.

AID

Recipient

$143m (receipts)

Down 29% in 1999

Most Western aid to Malaysia was used until recently to finance large infrastructure projects. The economic crisis which affected southeast Asia in 1997–1998 has forced Malaysia to seek foreign assistance to support an economic recovery program.

M

CHRONOLOGY

The former British protectorate of Malaya, made up of 11 states, gained independence in 1957. The federation of Malaysia, incorporating Singapore, Sarawak, and Sabah, was founded in 1963.

- ❑ **1965** Singapore leaves federation, reducing Malaysian states to 13.
- ❑ **1970** Malay–Chinese ethnic tension forces resignation of Prime Minister Tunku Abdul Rahman. New prime minister, Tun Abdul Razak, creates the BN coalition.
- ❑ **1976-1978** Guerrilla attacks by banned Communist Party of Malaya (CPM), based in southern Thailand.
- ❑ **1976** Tun Abdul Razak dies. Succeeded by his deputy.
- ❑ **1977** Unrest in Kelantan following expulsion of its chief minister from Pan-Malaysian Islamic Party (PAS). National emergency declared. PAS expelled from BN.
- ❑ **1978** Elections consolidate BN power. PAS marginalized. Government rejects plans for Chinese university.
- ❑ **1978-1989** Unrestricted asylum given to Vietnamese refugees.
- ❑ **1981** Mahathir Mohamed becomes prime minister.
- ❑ **1982** General election returns BN with increased majority.
- ❑ **1985** BN defeated by PBS in Sabah state elections.
- ❑ **1986** PBS joins BN coalition. Dispute between Mahathir and his deputy, Dakuk Musa, triggers general election, won by BN.
- ❑ **1987** Detention without trial of 106 politicians from all parties suspected of Chinese sympathies. Media censored.
- ❑ **1989** Disaffected UMNO members join PAS. Screening of Vietnamese refugees introduced. CPM signs peace agreement with Malaysian and Thai governments.
- ❑ **1990** General election. BN returned to power with reduced majority.
- ❑ **1993** Sultans lose powers, including legal immunity.
- ❑ **1995** BN wins landslide victory in the country's ninth general election.
- ❑ **1997** A major financial crisis ends a decade of spectacular economic growth.
- ❑ **1998–1999** Deputy Prime Minister Anwar Ibrahim dismissed from office. Launches *Reformasi* (reform) movement. Found guilty of corruption, later convicted of sodomy and six-year sentence extended to 15 years; his wife, Wan Azizah, forms National Justice Party to continue democracy campaign. UMNO loses ground in November 1999 general election.

DEFENSE

No compulsory military service

$3.16bn

Up 67% in 1999

MALAYSIAN ARMED FORCES

26 light tanks (*Scorpion*)	80,000 personnel
4 frigates and 41 patrol boats	8000 personnel
84 combat aircraft (25 *Hawk*, 17 MiG–29, 9 MB–339, 8 F/A–18D)	8000 personnel
None	

The main defense concerns are Singapore, with its large and highly mechanized army, and more recently, though to a lesser extent, Indonesia. Also important to Malaysia is the growing Chinese influence in the South China Sea.

The military is entirely composed of Malays. Budget plans for 1999 allocated almost 10% of projected expenditure to defense. Malaysia is an important market for Western arms suppliers. However, in 1994 Malaysia signed an agreement to buy Russian MiG-29 fighter aircraft and became the first noncommunist state in southeast Asia to operate Russian military equipment. Patrolling east and west Malaysia is a key function of the navy, which is large by regional standards.

ECONOMICS

Inflation 3.9% p.a. (1990–1999)

$76.9bn

3.8 ringgits

SCORE CARD

❑ World GNP Ranking	42nd
❑ GNP per Capita	$3390
❑ Balance of Payments	$12.6bn
❑ Inflation	2.7%
❑ Unemployment	3%

EXPORTS

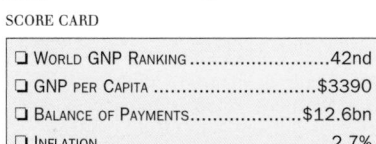

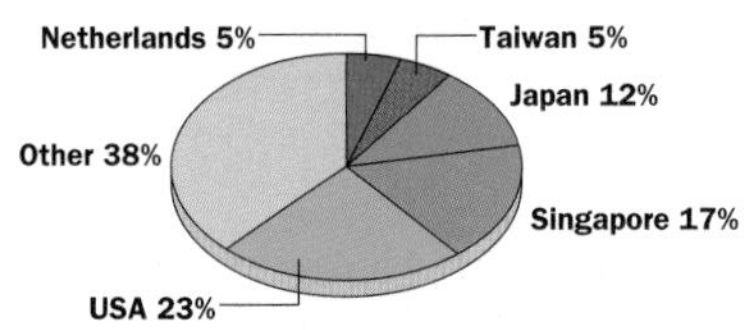
Netherlands 5%
Taiwan 5%
Japan 12%
Other 38%
Singapore 17%
USA 23%

IMPORTS

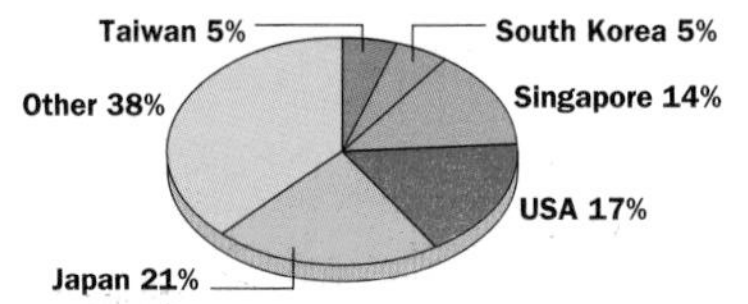
Taiwan 5%
South Korea 5%
Other 38%
Singapore 14%
USA 17%
Japan 21%

Strengths

Electronics: major disk-drive producer. Heavy industries such as steel. Palm oil. Latex and rubber; electrical machinery and appliances; chemical products.

ECONOMIC PERFORMANCE INDICATOR

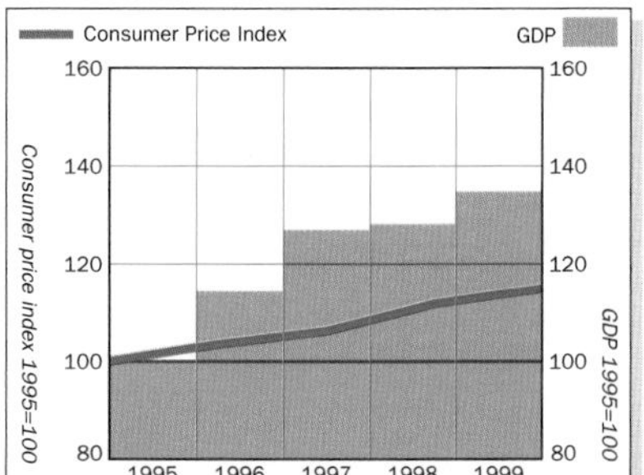
Consumer Price Index
GDP
160
140
120
100
80
Consumer price index 1995=100
GDP 1995=100
1995
1996
1997
1998
1999

Weaknesses

High level of debt. Shortage of skilled labor. High interest rates deter private investors. High government budget spending. Competition from NICs.

Profile

From 1987, for almost a decade, Malaysia expanded faster than any other southeast Asian nation, at an average yearly rate of 8%, with much of the growth state-directed. However, plans for full industrialization, named "Vision 2020," were revised after the 1997 financial crisis. Nevertheless, growth in the next few years was expected to exceed 7.5%. A project for a Multimedia Super Corridor (MSC), located south of Kuala Lumpur and aimed at attracting world-class companies, is expected to be completed by 2003.

MALAYSIA : MAJOR BUSINESSES

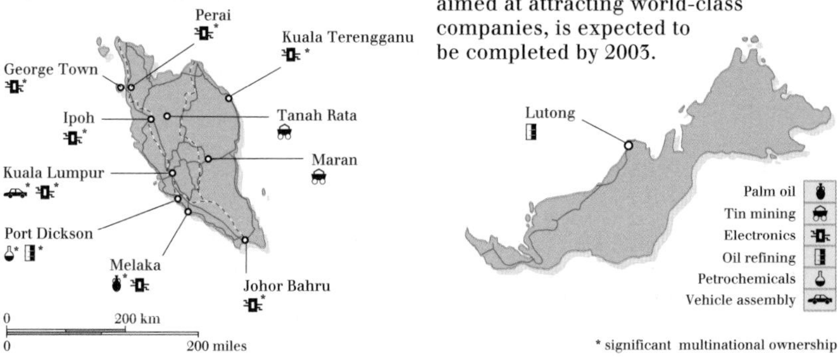
Perai
Kuala Terengganu
George Town
Ipoh
Tanah Rata
Maran
Kuala Lumpur
Port Dickson
Melaka
Johor Bahru
Lutong
0
200 km
200 miles
Palm oil
Tin mining
Electronics
Oil refining
Petrochemicals
Vehicle assembly

* significant multinational ownership

RESOURCES

Electric power 12.8m kw

1.28m tonnes

805,000 b/d (reserves 3,900,000,000 bbl)

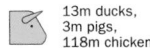

13m ducks, 3m pigs, 118m chickens

Natural gas, oil, tin, bauxite, copper, iron, coal

ELECTRICITY GENERATION

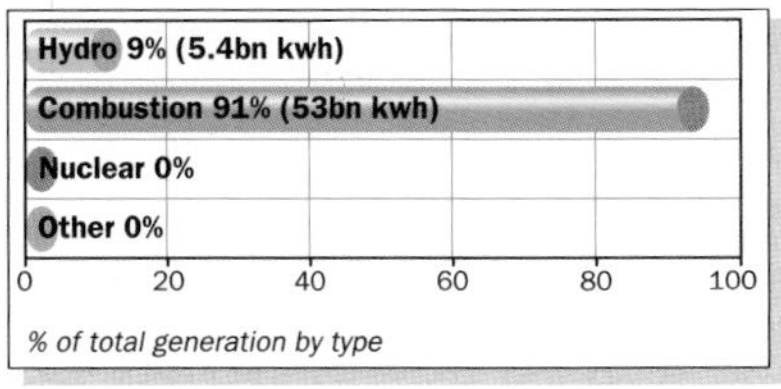
Hydro 9% (5.4bn kwh)
Combustion 91% (53bn kwh)
Nuclear 0%
Other 0%
0
20
40
60
80
100
% of total generation by type

Thailand has overtaken Malaysia as the world's major rubber producer. Palm oil, of which Malaysia is the world's largest producer, is now a more important export product. Malaysia is a significant exporter of oil and natural gas. Oil reserves are offshore from Sabah and Sarawak. The good quality of the oil means that most is exported, while crude imports are refined. Malaysia accounts for nearly half of world timber exports, most of which come from Sarawak.

PENINSULAR MALAYSIA

MALAYSIA : LAND USE

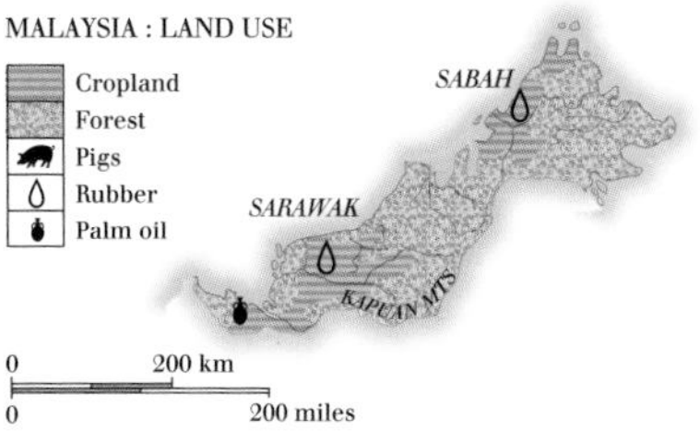
Cropland
Forest
Pigs
Rubber
Palm oil
SABAH
SARAWAK
KAPUAN MTS
0
200 km
0
200 miles

ENVIRONMENT

Sustainability rank: 52nd

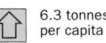

5%

6.3 tonnes per capita

ENVIRONMENTAL TREATIES

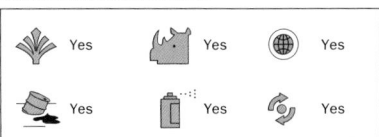

Yes	Yes	Yes
Yes	Yes	Yes

Logging is the overwhelming concern. World Bank estimates suggest that trees are being cut down at four times the sustainable rate. Indigenous forest communities are being destroyed, and some species of wood are near extinction. In 1992, Sarawak began to take action to diversify its economy, but logging profits are hard to resist.

In September 1997, smog caused by burning forests and scrub in Indonesia created a pollution and health alert across the whole region.

Traditional lifestyles are threatened by grandiose modernization schemes, and the Bakun dam project, shelved in 1997 due to a lack of investment confidence, was restarted in 2000.

MEDIA

TV ownership medium

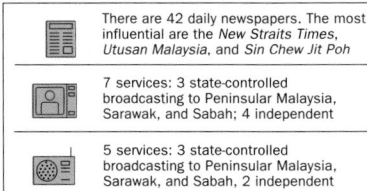

Daily newspaper circulation 163 per 1000 people

PUBLISHING AND BROADCAST MEDIA

There are 42 daily newspapers. The most influential are the *New Straits Times*, *Utusan Malaysia*, and *Sin Chew Jit Poh*

7 services: 3 state-controlled broadcasting to Peninsular Malaysia, Sarawak, and Sabah; 4 independent

5 services: 3 state-controlled broadcasting to Peninsular Malaysia, Sarawak, and Sabah, 2 independent

Almost all the newspapers are controlled by UMNO, the dominant political party. The party owns the Straits group, which includes the most influential press. Radio and TV are also strictly controlled, under the 1987 Broadcasting Act, and Western commercials are banned. Singaporean TV can be received in the south.

CRIME

Death penalty used

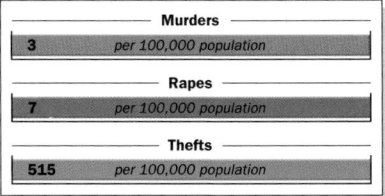

20,324 prisoners

Up 80% 1996–1998

CRIME RATES

Murders	
3	*per 100,000 population*
Rapes	
7	*per 100,000 population*
Thefts	
515	*per 100,000 population*

The judiciary and UMNO maintain close links. The death sentence for possession of narcotics is mandatory. Kelantan state has attempted to implement the Islamic penal code, including stoning for adulterers and amputation for thieves.

EDUCATION

School leaving age: 14

88%

230,000 students

THE EDUCATION SYSTEM

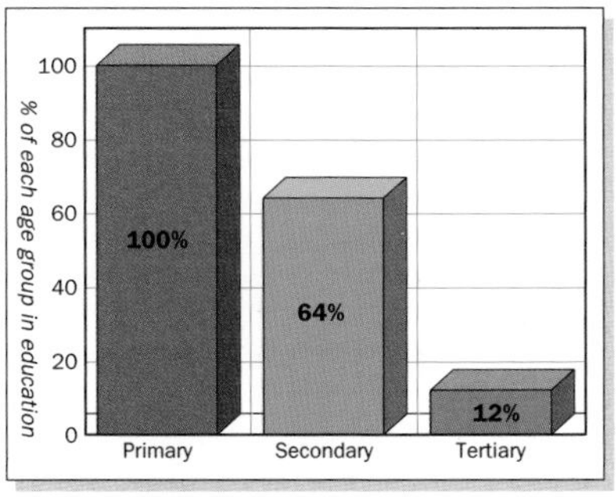
100
80
60
40
20
0
% of each age group in education
100%
64%
12%
Primary
Secondary
Tertiary

There is free schooling at government-assisted schools for children between the ages of six and 18.

Malays are favored above other communities, especially at tertiary level, where a quota system gives them preference for places. The Chinese community has its own schools, but plans for a private Chinese university were vetoed by the government. Many students, particularly the Chinese, complete their studies in the UK or the USA.

HEALTH

Welfare state health benefits

1 per 2000 people

Heart diseases, cancers

There is growing disparity between the modern facilities available in cities and the traditional medicine practiced in rural and outlying areas. Traditional practices such as acupuncture and herbal medicine continue to be used by the Chinese community.

SPENDING

GDP/cap. increase

CONSUMPTION AND SPENDING

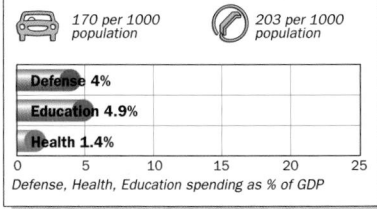

170 per 1000 population

203 per 1000 population

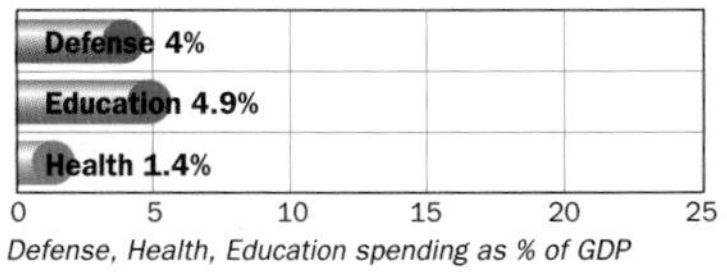
Defense 4%
Education 4.9%
Health 1.4%
0
5
10
15
20
25
Defense, Health, Education spending as % of GDP

The Chinese remain the wealthiest community in Malaysia. However, following riots in 1970, the UMNO government embarked on a deliberate program of achieving 30% Malay ownership of the corporate sector. Many Malays earned quick profits from preferential privatization share allocations in the early 1990s.

WORLD RANKING

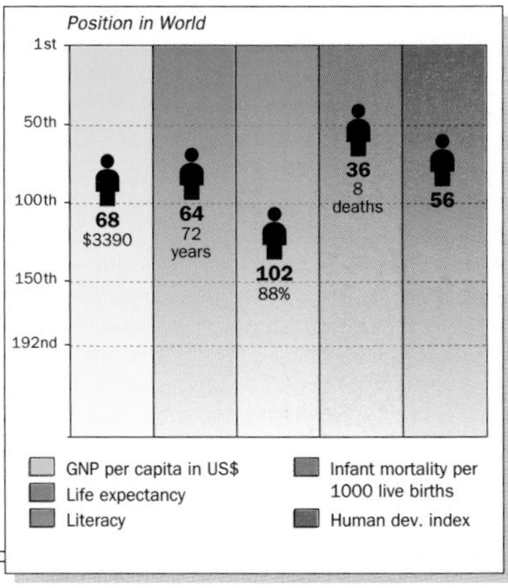
Position in World
1st
50th
100th
150th
192nd
68
$3390
64
72 years
102
88%
36
8 deaths
56
GNP per capita in US$
Life expectancy
Literacy
Infant mortality per 1000 live births
Human dev. index

M

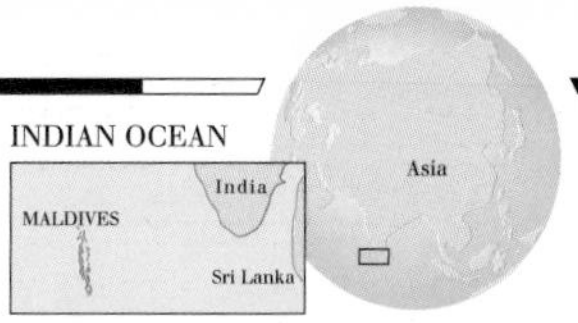
INDIAN OCEAN
India
MALDIVES
Sri Lanka
Asia

MALDIVES

OFFICIAL NAME: Republic of Maldives **CAPITAL:** Male'
POPULATION: 286,000 **CURRENCY:** Rufiyaa **OFFICIAL LANGUAGE:** Dhivehi

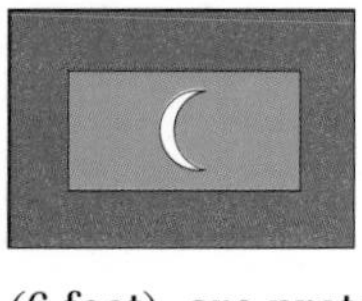

1965 | 1965 | July 26 | MV | +5 | +960 | .mv

THE MALDIVES IS AN archipelago of 1190 small coral islands set in the Indian Ocean southwest of India. The islands, none of which rise above 1.8 m (6 feet), are protected by encircling reefs or *faros*. Only 200 are inhabited. Tourism has grown in recent years, though vacation islands are separate from settled islands. In 1998, President Maumoon Abdul Gayoom, who has survived three coup attempts, was elected for a fifth term in office.

Traditional Maldivian trading yacht. The 1190 coral islands are grouped in natural atolls, derived from the Maldivian word 'atolu'.

CLIMATE

Tropical oceanic

WEATHER CHART

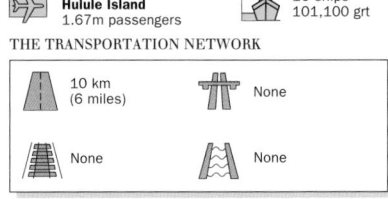

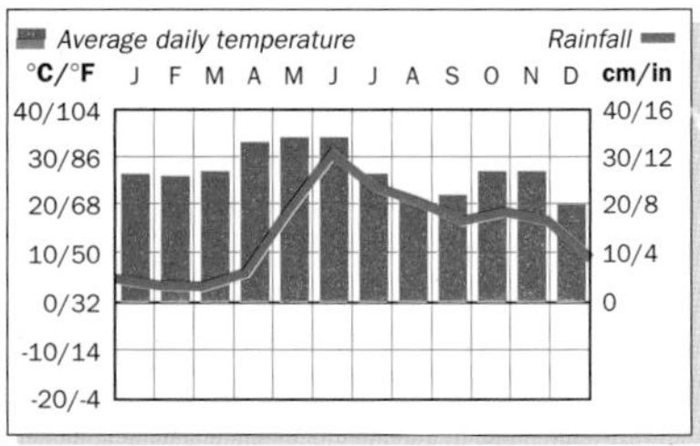
Average daily temperature
Rainfall
°C/°F
J F M A M J J A S O N D
cm/in
40/104
30/86
20/68
10/50
0/32
-10/14
-20/-4
40/16
30/12
20/8
10/4
0

The Maldives has a tropical climate with abundant rainfall and high temperatures throughout the year. The northern islands are occasionally affected by violent storms caused by tropical cyclones. Most rain falls in the southern islands.

TRANSPORTATION

Drive on left

Male' International, Hulule Island 1.67m passengers

10 ships 101,100 grt

THE TRANSPORTATION NETWORK

10 km (6 miles)

None

None

None

It is possible to walk across Male' island in 20 minutes. Inter-island travel is mostly by ferry and traditional *dhoni*.

TOURISM

Visitors : Population 1.6:1

467,000 visitors

Up 9% in 2000

MAIN TOURIST ARRIVALS

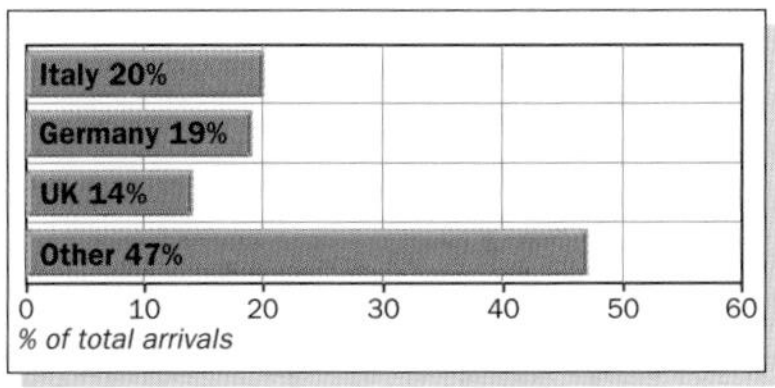
Italy 20%
Germany 19%
UK 14%
Other 47%
0 10 20 30 40 50 60
% of total arrivals

Tourism is the largest source of foreign exchange, accounting for almost 20% of GDP. The first resort was opened in 1972, and hotels financed by local and foreign capital have since been built on the uninhabited islands. There are now nearly half a million visitors a year.

POLITICS

No multiparty elections

1999/2004

President Maumoon Abdul Gayoom

AT THE LAST ELECTION

Citizens' Assembly 50 seats

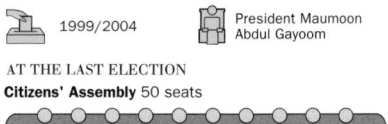

There are no political parties. 42 members of the Majlis (Assembly) are elected, and 8 appointed by the president

Politics in the Maldives is restricted to a small group of influential families. Most were already dominant under the sultanate. Formal parties with ideological objectives are virtually non-existent, politics being organized around family and clan loyalties.

Former president Ibrahim Nasir abolished the premiership in 1975 and substantially strengthened the presidency. The main figure now is Maumoon Abdul Gayoom, a wealthy businessman who has been president since 1978. His brother-in-law, Ilyas Ibrahim, is regarded as his main rival.

A young Westernized elite has increased the pressure for political reform. Under a constitution effective since 1998, rival candidates may seek to be parliament's presidential nominee; only one name then goes forward for popular endorsement in a referendum.

PEOPLE

Pop. density high

Dhivehi (Maldivian)

953/km² (2469/mi²)

THE URBAN/RURAL POPULATION SPLIT

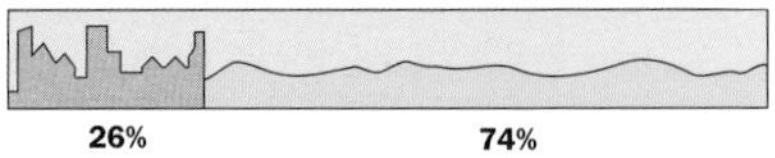
26%
74%

RELIGIOUS PERSUASION

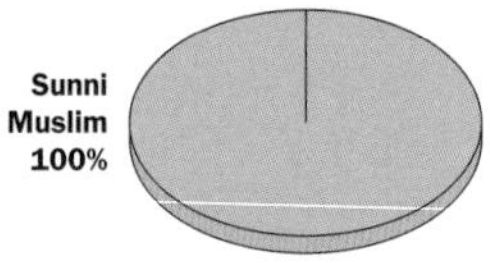
Sunni Muslim 100%

It is believed that the islands were inhabited as early as 1500 BCE. Aryan immigrants arrived around 500 BCE. The islands were then discovered by Arab traders. The people, who are all Sunni Muslims, live on only 200 of the 1190 islands. About 25% of the total population live on the island capital of Male'. It is estimated that 12,000 guest workers from neighboring Sri Lanka and India work in the Maldives. The country's new-found prosperity has seen the emergence of a commercial elite.

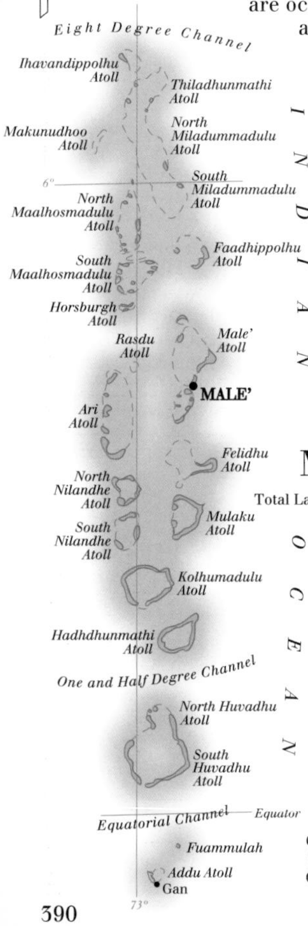
Eight Degree Channel
Ihavandippolhu Atoll
Thiladhunmathi Atoll
Makunudhoo Atoll
North Miladummadulu Atoll
South Miladummadulu Atoll
North Maalhosmadulu Atoll
Faadhippolhu Atoll
South Maalhosmadulu Atoll
Horsburgh Atoll
Rasdu Atoll
Male' Atoll
MALE'
Ari Atoll
Felidhu Atoll
North Nilandhe Atoll
Mulaku Atoll
South Nilandhe Atoll
Kolhumadulu Atoll
Hadhdhunmathi Atoll
One and Half Degree Channel
North Huvadhu Atoll
South Huvadhu Atoll
Equatorial Channel
Equator
Fuammulah
Addu Atoll
Gan
INDIAN OCEAN

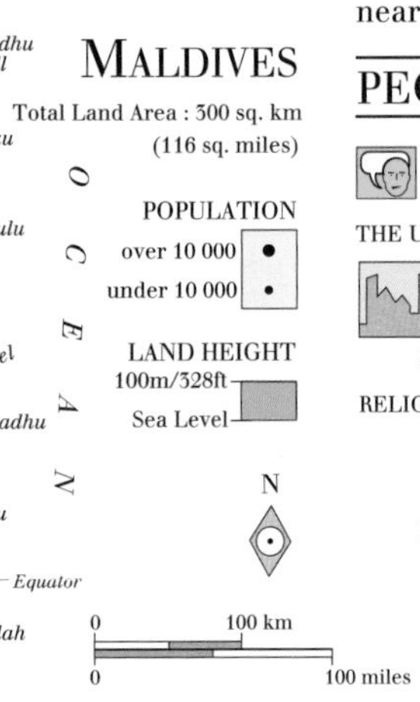
MALDIVES
Total Land Area : 300 sq. km (116 sq. miles)
POPULATION
over 10 000
under 10 000
LAND HEIGHT
100m/328ft
Sea Level
N
0 100 km
0 100 miles

WORLD AFFAIRS

Joined UN in 1965

Comm | NAM | OIC | SAARC | WTO

The Maldives is a long-standing member of the NAM. The government continues to support it and rejects the view that the organization does not have a role to play in the post-Cold War world. The Maldives' international standing was enhanced in 1990, when it hosted the fifth SAARC summit meeting, held in Male'.

AID

Recipient

$31m (receipts) — Up 24% in 1999

Aid has helped to finance the development of port and airport facilities. Japan is the most important bilateral aid donor. In 1991, India, Pakistan, and the USA supplied relief aid to help victims of violent storms which caused damage estimated at $30 million.

DEFENSE

No compulsory military service

$41m — Up 5% in 1999

The British military presence ended in 1975, when troops were withdrawn from the staging post on Gan, in the Addu atoll. The Maldives follows a policy of nonalignment, but in 1988 called on India for military assistance to help suppress a coup attempt.

ECONOMICS

Inflation 8% p.a. (1990–1999)

$322m — 11.06–11.77 rufiyaa

SCORE CARD

- ❑ WORLD GNP RANKING........................174th
- ❑ GNP PER CAPITA..............................$1200
- ❑ BALANCE OF PAYMENTS.......................$-60m
- ❑ INFLATION...3%
- ❑ UNEMPLOYMENT...................................1%

STRENGTHS

Boom in tourism. Thriving fishing industry, especially tuna. Shipping. Clothing. Coconut production. Economic reforms since 1989 have eased import restrictions and encouraged foreign investment.

WEAKNESSES

Too dependent on fluctuating tourist industry. Growing trade deficit. Skilled labor shortage. Small manufacturing base. Cottage industries employ 25% of workforce; little scope for expansion.

EXPORTS

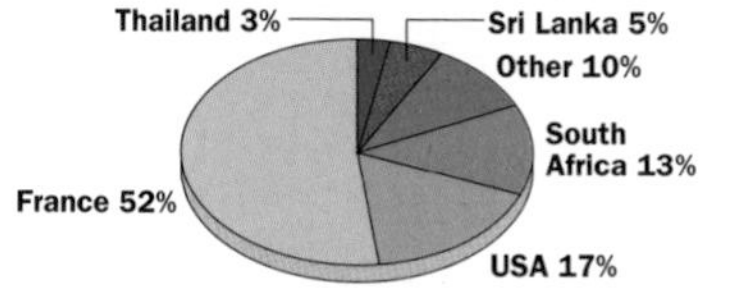
Thailand 3%
Sri Lanka 5%
Other 10%
South Africa 13%
France 52%
USA 17%

IMPORTS

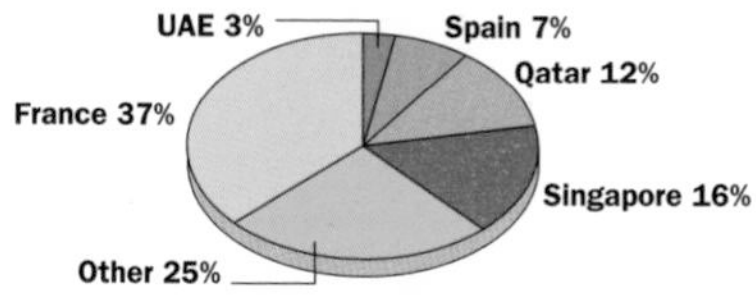
UAE 3%
Spain 7%
Qatar 12%
France 37%
Singapore 16%
Other 25%

RESOURCES

Electric power 25,000 kw

107,676 tonnes — Not an oil producer

31,000 cattle, 20,000 goats, 11,000 sheep — None

Natural resources include abundant stocks of fish, particularly tuna. Fishing, still carried out by the traditional pole and line method to help conserve stocks, employs over 20% of the working population. Coconut production is also important. All oil products and virtually all staple foods are imported.

ENVIRONMENT

Not available

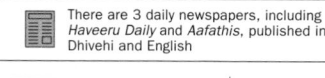

None — 1.2 tonnes per capita

Rising sea levels due to global warming and climate change threaten the islands, which have an average height of just 1.5 m (5 feet). A sea wall has been built around the capital island.

Other environmental concerns are sewerage, waste disposal, and the mining of coral for building.

MEDIA

TV ownership low

Daily newspaper circulation 19 per 1000 people

PUBLISHING AND BROADCAST MEDIA

There are 3 daily newspapers, including *Haveeru Daily* and *Aafathis*, published in Dhivehi and English

1 state-owned service — 2 services

There is a marked degree of press censorship. In the past, journalists and satirists have been imprisoned. There are three daily newspapers.

CRIME

Death penalty not used

The Maldives does not publish prison figures — Up 90% 1992–1996

The Maldives is a strict Islamic society. Narcotics crimes are heavily punished. Political prisoners are banished to outer islands. The judiciary and executive are closely linked.

CHRONOLOGY

The Maldives was a British protectorate from 1887 and gained its independence in 1965.

- ❑ **1932** First written constitution.
- ❑ **1968** Sultanate abolished. Declared a republic. Ibrahim Nasir elected as first president.
- ❑ **1978** Gayoom becomes president.
- ❑ **1994** Nonparty legislative elections.
- ❑ **1998** New constitution; Gayoom reelected for fifth five-year term.

EDUCATION

Schooling is not compulsory

96% — Not available

Primary education has been improved. Secondary education is less developed in the outer islands; the first school outside Male' was opened in 1992.

HEALTH

Welfare state health benefits

1 per 1358 people — Infectious and parasitic diseases, tuberculosis, perinatal deaths

There is a lack of general equipment and facilities. Health care is less developed on the outlying islands.

SPENDING

GDP/cap. increase

CONSUMPTION AND SPENDING

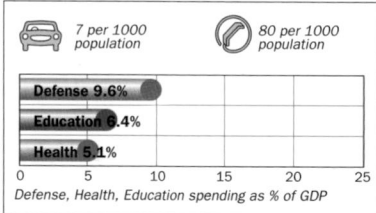

7 per 1000 population — *80 per 1000 population*

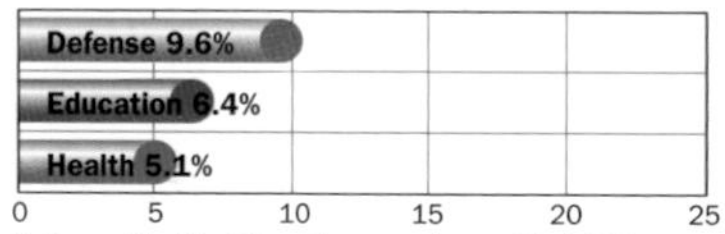
Defense 9.6%
Education 6.4%
Health 5.1%
0
5
10
15
20
25

Defense, Health, Education spending as % of GDP

Great disparities of wealth exist between the people who live in the capital, Male', and those who live on the more distant outer islands.

WORLD RANKING

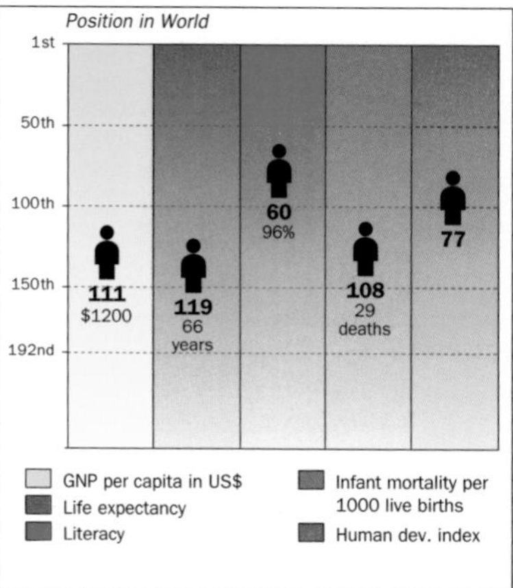
Position in World
1st
50th
100th
150th
192nd
111
$1200
119
66
years
60
96%
108
29
deaths
77
GNP per capita in US$
Life expectancy
Literacy
Infant mortality per 1000 live births
Human dev. index

M

MALI

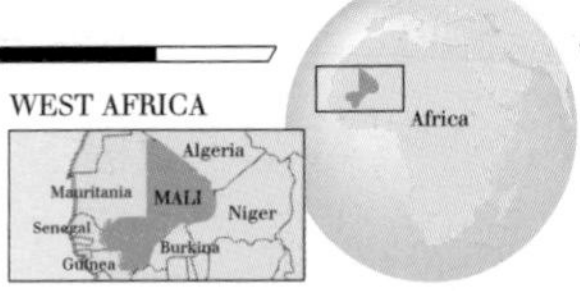
WEST AFRICA
Africa
Algeria
Mauritania
MALI
Niger
Senegal
Burkina
Guinea

OFFICIAL NAME: Republic of Mali **CAPITAL:** Bamako
POPULATION: 11.2 million **CURRENCY:** CFA franc **OFFICIAL LANGUAGE:** French

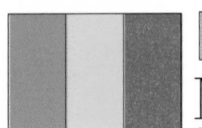

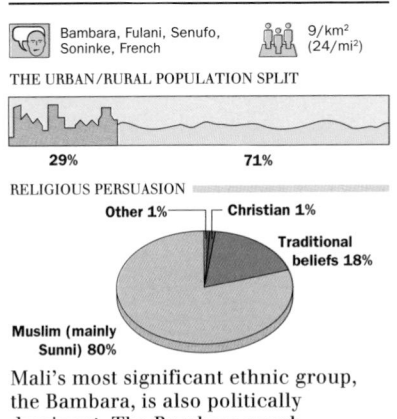

1960 | 1960 | Sept 22 | RMM | 0 | +223 | .ml

MALI IS LANDLOCKED in the heart of west Africa. Its mostly flat terrain comprises virtually uninhabited Saharan plains in the north and more fertile savanna land in the south, where most of the population live. The Niger river irrigates the central and southwestern regions. Mali achieved independence from France in 1960. Multiparty democratic elections under a new constitution, in 1992 and then in 1997, provoked accusations of severe irregularities.

CLIMATE

Hot desert/steppe

WEATHER CHART

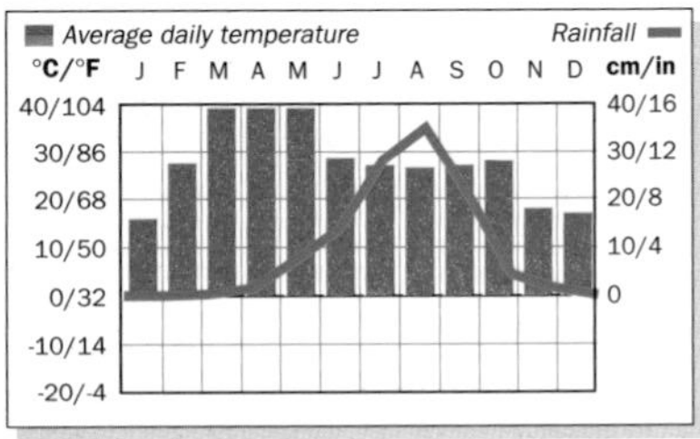
Average daily temperature
Rainfall
°C/°F
J F M A M J J A S O N D
cm/in
40/104
30/86
20/68
10/50
0/32
-10/14
-20/-4
40/16
30/12
20/8
10/4
0

In the south, intensely hot, dry weather precedes the westerly rains. Mali's northern half is almost rainless.

TRANSPORTATION

Drive on right

Bamako–Senou 381,034 passengers

Has no fleet

THE TRANSPORTATION NETWORK

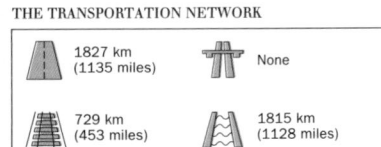

1827 km (1135 miles)

None

729 km (453 miles)

1815 km (1128 miles)

Mali is linked by rail with the port of Dakar in Senegal, and by good roads to the port of Abidjan in Ivory Coast.

TOURISM

Visitors : Population 1:123

91,000 visitors

Up 5% in 2000

MAIN TOURIST ARRIVALS

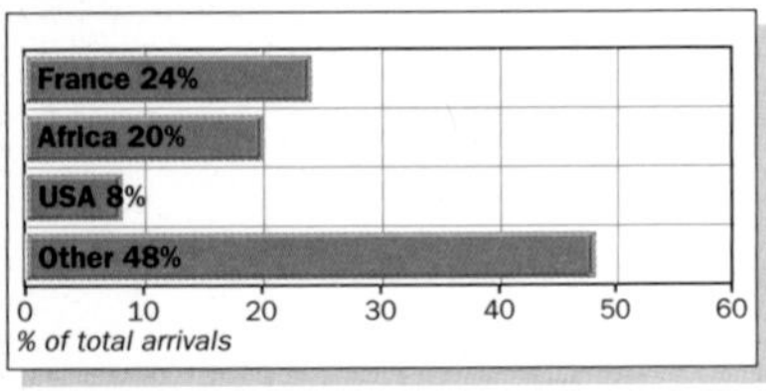
France 24%
Africa 20%
USA 8%
Other 48%
0
10
20
30
40
50
60
% of total arrivals

Tourism is largely safari-oriented, though the historic cities of Djénné, Gao, and Mopti, lying on the banks of the Niger river, also attract visitors. A national domestic airline began operating in 1990.

PEOPLE

Pop. density low

Bambara, Fulani, Senufo, Soninke, French

9/km² (24/mi²)

THE URBAN/RURAL POPULATION SPLIT

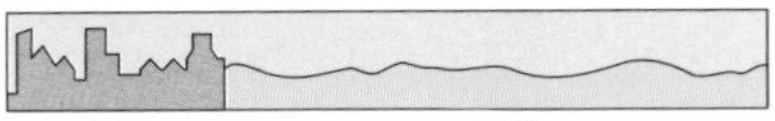
29%
71%

RELIGIOUS PERSUASION

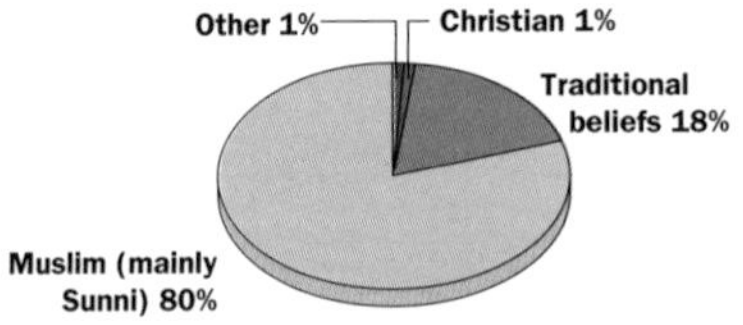
Other 1%
Christian 1%
Traditional beliefs 18%
Muslim (mainly Sunni) 80%

Mali's most significant ethnic group, the Bambara, is also politically dominant. The Bambara speak the *lingua franca* of the Niger river, which is shared with other groups including the Malinke. The relationship between the Bambara–Malinke majority and the Tuareg nomads of the Saharan north is tense and sometimes violent. The extended family is a vital social security system and link between the urban and rural poor. There are a few powerful women in Mali but, in general, women have little status.

POLITICS

Multiparty elections

1997/2002

President Alpha Oumar Konaré

AT THE LAST ELECTION

National Assembly 147 seats

87%
ADEMA
5%
PARENA
8%
Others

ADEMA = Alliance for Democracy in Mali
PARENA = Party for National Renewal
Others = Democratic and Social Convention, Party for Democracy and Progress, Union for Democracy and Development, Convention for Progress and the People, Democracy and Justice Party, National Democratic Rally

The successful transition to multiparty politics in 1992 followed the overthrow in the previous year of Moussa Traoré, Mali's dictator for 23 years. The army's role was crucial in leading the coup, while Colonel Touré, who acted as interim president, was responsible for the swift return to civilian rule in less than a year. The change marked Mali's first experience of multipartyism. Maintaining good relations with the Tuaregs, after a peace agreement in 1991, is a key issue. However, the main challenge facing President Alpha Oumar Konaré's government is to alleviate poverty while placating the opposition, which accuses his government of fraud in the 1997 general election. Konaré's economic austerity measures have met with opposition.

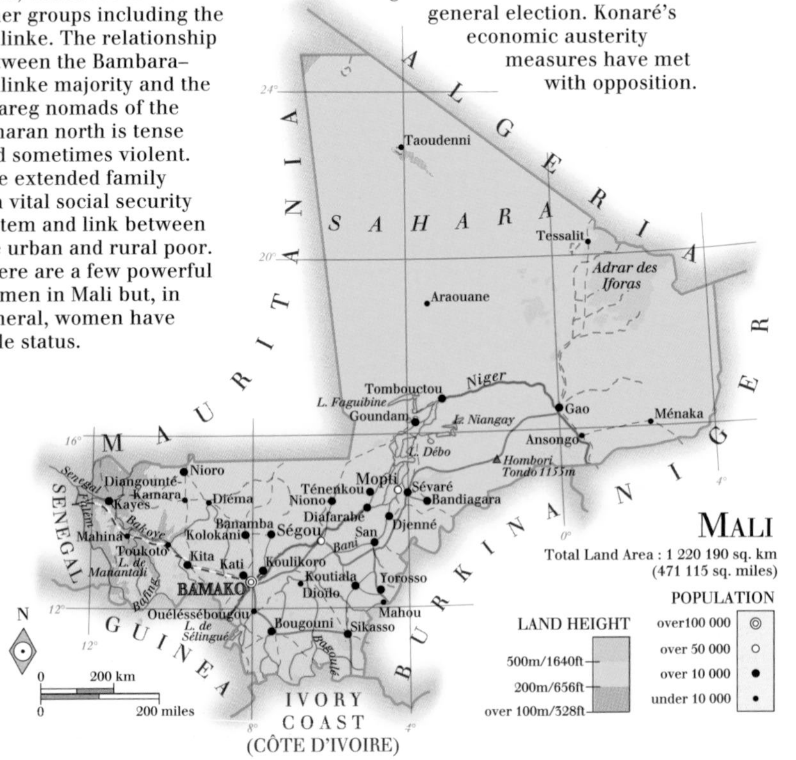
ALGERIA
MAURITANIA
SAHARA
NIGER
BURKINA
GUINEA
SENEGAL
IVORY COAST (CÔTE D'IVOIRE)
Taoudenni
Tessalit
Adrar des Iforas
Araouane
Tombouctou
Niger
L. Faguibine
Goundam
L. Niangay
Gao
Ménaka
Ansongo
L. Débo
Hombori Tondo 1155m
Nioro
Diangounté-Kamara
Kayes
Diéma
Ténenkou
Mopti
Sévaré
Niono
Bandiagara
Diafarabé
Djenné
Banamba
Kolokani
Ségou
San
Bani
Mahina
Toukoto
L. de Manantali
Bakoye
Kita
Kati
Koulikoro
Koutiala
Yorosso
BAMAKO
Dioïla
Ouéléssébougou
L. de Sélingué
Bougouni
Sikasso
Mahou
Bagoé
Bafing
N
0 200 km
0 200 miles
MALI
Total Land Area : 1 220 190 sq. km (471 115 sq. miles)
LAND HEIGHT
500m/1640ft
200m/656ft
over 100m/328ft
POPULATION
over100 000
over 50 000
over 10 000
under 10 000

M

WORLD AFFAIRS

Joined UN in 1960

ECOWAS | FZ | OAU | OIC | OIF

Mali concentrates on maintaining good relations with the ECOWAS countries to its south and northern neighbors such as Algeria. Relations with Libya, which is suspected of fomenting Tuareg revolt, are tense. There are good relations with the USA, and other Western aid providers.

AID

Recipient

$354m (receipts) — Up 1% in 1999

Mali is highly dependent on foreign aid, which comes from France, the EU, China, a few Arab states, the USA and international lending institutions.

DEFENSE

Compulsory military service

$34m — Down 6% in 1999

Mali's 7800-strong armed forces have stayed out of politics since the overthrow of President Traoré in 1991.

ECONOMICS

Inflation 8.1% p.a. (1990–1999)

$2.6bn — 654.42–698.69 CFA francs

SCORE CARD

❑ WORLD GNP RANKING	134th
❑ GNP PER CAPITA	$240
❑ BALANCE OF PAYMENTS	$–178m
❑ INFLATION	–1.2%
❑ UNEMPLOYMENT	Widespread underemployment

STRENGTHS

Producer of high-quality cotton. Irrigation potential from the Niger and Senegal rivers. Rapid expansion of gold production now under way.

WEAKNESSES

Serious poverty and underdevelopment. Landlocked status and vast size of country present considerable communications problems. Drought-prone climate.

EXPORTS

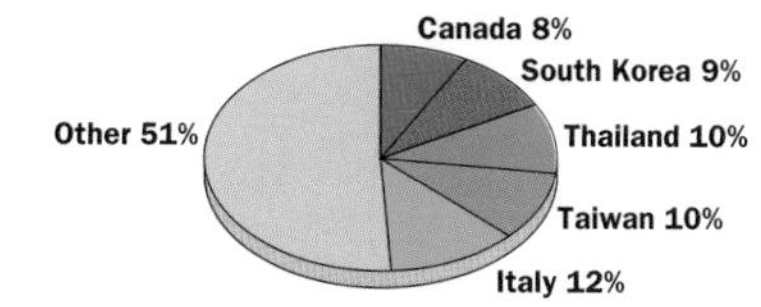
Canada 8%
South Korea 9%
Thailand 10%
Taiwan 10%
Italy 12%
Other 51%

IMPORTS

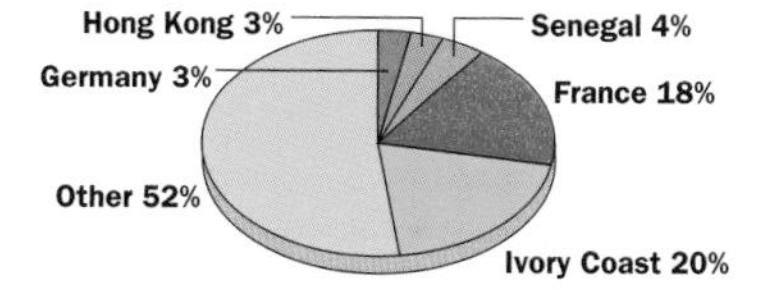
Hong Kong 3%
Senegal 4%
Germany 3%
France 18%
Other 52%
Ivory Coast 20%

Village near Bandiagara. *These low, broken hills typical of the east and southeast of Mali are the homeland of the Dogon people.*

RESOURCES

Electric power 114,000 kw

99,610 tonnes — Not an oil producer

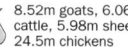

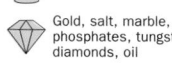

8.52m goats, 6.06m cattle, 5.98m sheep, 24.5m chickens — Gold, salt, marble, phosphates, tungsten, diamonds, oil

Gold deposits are now being mined, and prospecting is under way for tungsten, diamonds, and oil. The exploitation of other natural resources is hampered by Mali's poor infrastructure and landlocked situation. Almost all electric power comes from the Selingue dam on the Niger. When the Manantali dam, on the Senegal, comes into operation in April 2002, there should be a surplus.

ENVIRONMENT

Sustainability rank: 71st

4% — 0.05 tonnes per capita

Severe drought in 1983 destroyed herds and accelerated desertification and deforestation. The Selingue dam seriously affects the levels of the Niger, even in years of good rainfall.

MEDIA

TV ownership low

Daily newspaper circulation 1 per 1000 people

PUBLISHING AND BROADCAST MEDIA

There are 5 daily newspapers, including the pro-government *L'Essor – La Voix du Peuple*

3 services: 1 state-owned, 2 independent — 15 services: 1 state-owned, 14 independent

Even before the 1991 coup, previously rigid controls were being relaxed. The 1992 Constitution guarantees the freedom of the press, and Mali's broadcast and print media are now among the freest in Africa.

CRIME

Death penalty not used

Mali does not publish prison figures — Crime is rising slowly

Crime is not particularly prevalent compared with some other countries in the region, owing at least in part to the relative lack of urbanization. In towns, robbery, juvenile delinquency, and smuggling are problems.

CHRONOLOGY

Mali was a major trans-Saharan trading empire. The French colonized the area between 1881 and 1895.

- ❑ **1960** Independence.
- ❑ **1968** Coup by Gen. Moussa Traoré.
- ❑ **1990** Prodemocracy demonstrations.
- ❑ **1991** Traoré arrested.
- ❑ **1992** Free multiparty elections.
- ❑ **1997** President Konaré and ADEMA party reelected in disputed polls.
- ❑ **1999** Traoré's death sentence commuted to life imprisonment.

EDUCATION

School leaving age: 16

41% — 13,847 students

Only 25% of children go to primary school and just 7% to secondary school. A ten-year program to raise education levels for girls was launched in 2001.

HEALTH

No welfare state health benefits

1 per 10,000 people — Malaria, pneumonia, parasitic and diarrheal diseases

A four-year program began in 1998, with the aim of higher immunization rates for children and more health care access.

SPENDING

GDP/cap. increase

CONSUMPTION AND SPENDING

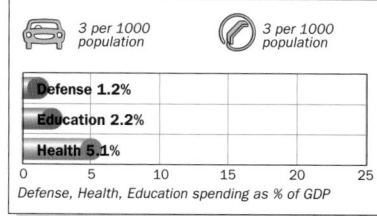

3 per 1000 population — *3 per 1000 population*

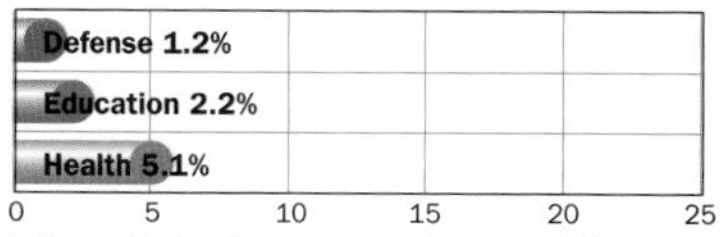
Defense 1.2%
Education 2.2%
Health 5.1%
0
5
10
15
20
25

Defense, Health, Education spending as % of GDP

Poverty is widespread, and wealth is limited to a very small group; Malians disapprove of flaunted wealth and public ostentation is rare.

WORLD RANKING

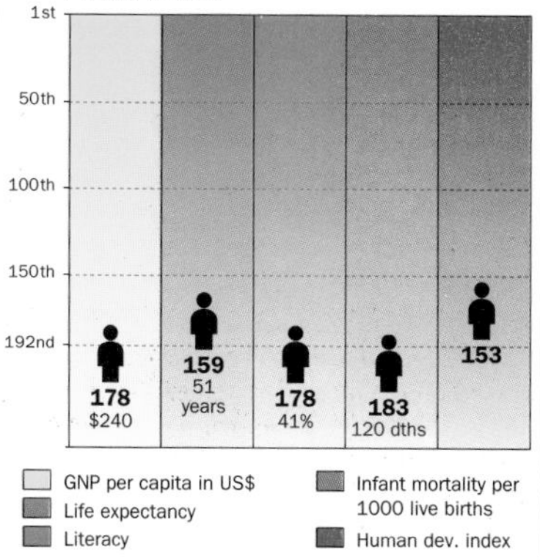
Position in World
1st
50th
100th
150th
192nd
178
$240
159
51 years
178
41%
183
120 dths
153
GNP per capita in US$
Life expectancy
Literacy
Infant mortality per 1000 live births
Human dev. index

M

MALTA

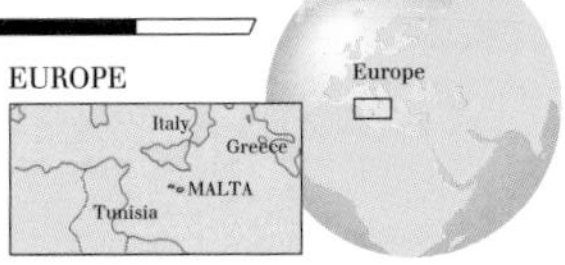
EUROPE
Europe
Italy
Greece
MALTA
Tunisia

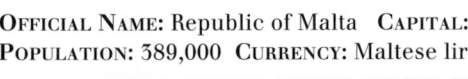

OFFICIAL NAME: Republic of Malta **CAPITAL:** Valletta
POPULATION: 389,000 **CURRENCY:** Maltese lira **OFFICIAL LANGUAGES:** English and Maltese

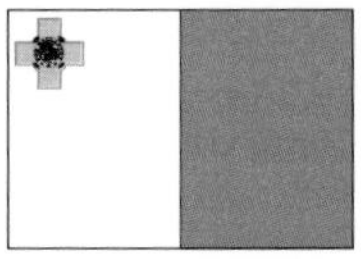

1964 | 1964 | Sept 21 | M | +1 | +356 | .mt

THE MALTESE ARCHIPELAGO is strategically located, lying between Europe and north Africa. Controlled throughout its history by successive colonial powers, Malta finally gained independence from the UK in 1964. The islands are mainly low-lying, with rocky coastlines; only Malta, Gozo (Ghawdex), and Kemmuna are inhabited. Tourism is Malta's chief source of income, with an influx of tourists each year of over three times the islands' population.

CLIMATE

Mediterranean

WEATHER CHART

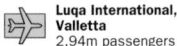

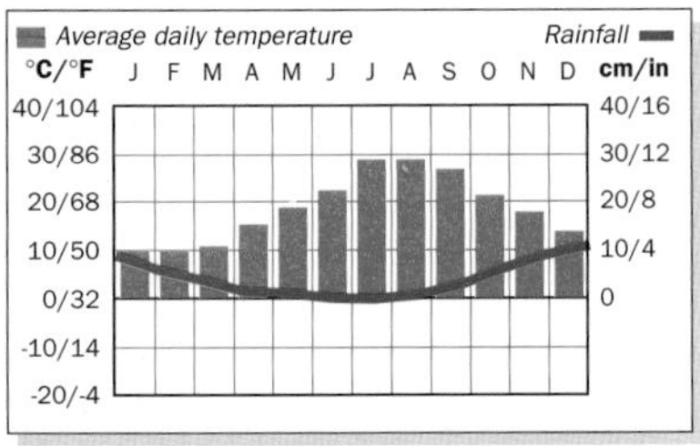
Average daily temperature
Rainfall
°C/°F
J F M A M J J A S O N D
cm/in
40/104
30/86
20/68
10/50
0/32
-10/14
-20/-4
40/16
30/12
20/8
10/4
0

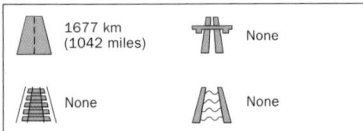

The climate is typical of the southern Mediterranean – with at least six hours of sunshine a day, even in winter.

TRANSPORTATION

Drive on left

Luqa International, Valletta
2.94m passengers

3189 ships
28.6m grt

THE TRANSPORTATION NETWORK

1677 km (1042 miles)

None

None

None

Malta Freeport at Marsaxlokk exploits Malta's strategic shipping location in the Mediterranean. In summer, a five-minute helicopter flight from the international airport links the islands of Malta and Gozo. There is a well-developed public transportation system, with ferry and hovercraft services and buses on both islands.

Traditionally painted **luzzus** *at St. Julian's harbor. The fish caught are now only for domestic and tourist consumption.*

TOURISM

Visitors : Population 3.1:1

1.2m visitors

No change in 2000

MAIN TOURIST ARRIVALS

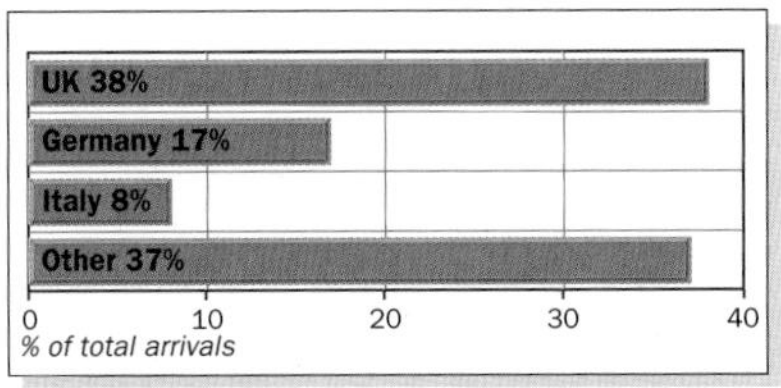
UK 38%
Germany 17%
Italy 8%
Other 37%
0
10
20
30
40
% of total arrivals

Tourism is vital to the economy and accounts for more than 30% of GDP, even though most visitors are budget holidaymakers. In addition to beaches and scenery, there are the historical attractions of Mdina and Valletta. Development on the quieter island of Gozo is limited to luxury-grade hotels.

PEOPLE

Pop. density high

Maltese, English

1216/km² (3148/mi²)

THE URBAN/RURAL POPULATION SPLIT

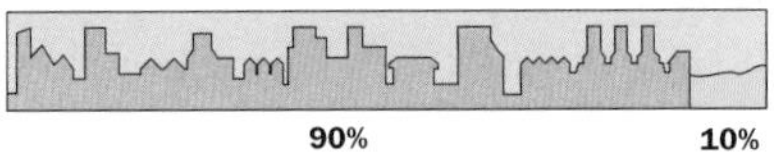
90%
10%

RELIGIOUS PERSUASION

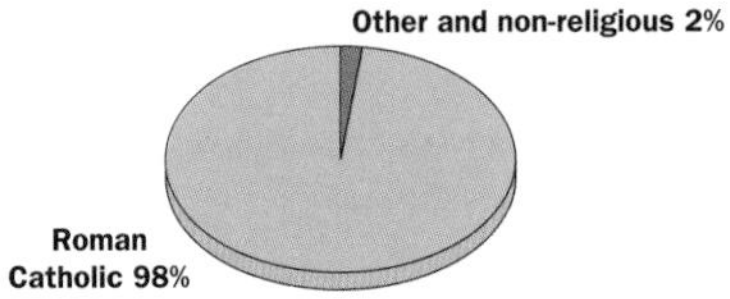
Other and non-religious 2%
Roman Catholic 98%

Malta's population has been subject over the centuries to diverse Arabic, Sicilian, Norman, Spanish, English, and Italian influences. Today, much of the younger Maltese population goes abroad to find work, especially to the USA or Australia; opportunities for them on the islands are few.

The Maltese are staunch Roman Catholics, on a percentage basis more so than virtually any other nation. The remainder are mainly Anglicans, who are included within the diocese of Gibraltar. Divorce is illegal.

POLITICS

Multiparty elections

1998/2003

President Guido de Marco

AT THE LAST ELECTION

House of Representatives 65 seats

54%
NP
46%
MLP

NP = Nationalist Party **MLP** = Malta Labour Party

Maltese politics is strongly adversarial and evenly split between the right-wing NP and the left-wing MLP. The latter dominated the government in the 1970s and 1980s, ensuring state control of industry and pursuing a nonaligned foreign policy.

The 1990s, however, saw a switch in favor of the NP, with Prime Minister Edward Fenech Adami at the helm in 1987–1996 and since 1998. Under Fenech Adami, Malta moved toward ever closer ties with Europe, and favors a free-market approach to its economy. The NP secured reelection in 1992, largely due to a rise in living standards. A modernized MLP ended the NP's nine-year reign in 1996. Under Alfred Sant, a leading writer and Harvard MBA, it diluted traditional links with the unions and "froze" Malta's EU application. However, the MLP's small parliamentary majority undermined the government, and the NP won early elections in 1998. Fenech Adami has now reset Malta on its course for membership of the EU.

WORLD AFFAIRS

Joined UN in 1964

CE | Comm | IBRD | NAM | OSCE

Malta has made the most of its location on the fringe of Europe, with a staunchly nonaligned foreign policy. Ties are traditionally strong with the Arab world and north Africa, and relations with Libya remain good. There are also close commercial links with Russia and China.

However, it is the island's relationship with Europe that has dominated recent policy. Malta's bid for EU membership, launched in 1990, was derailed by the anti-EU MLP government in 1996. With the application frozen, Malta was denied a place in the "first wave" of potential EU members. However, the return to power of the pro-EU NP in 1998 restarted the bid and Malta joined talks in March 2000 as part of the "second wave."

M

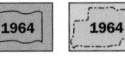

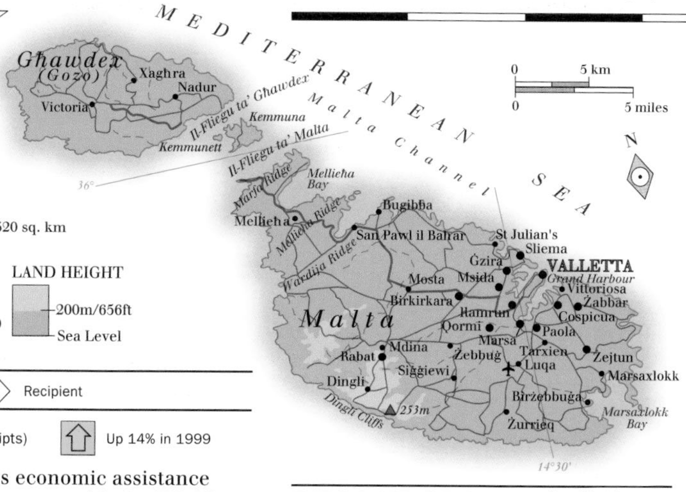
MEDITERRANEAN SEA
Ghawdex (Gozo)
Xaghra
Nadur
Victoria
Il-Fliegu ta' Ghawdex
Kemmuna
Kemmunett
Il-Fliegu ta' Malta
Malta Channel
Mellieħa Bay
Marfa Ridge
Mellieħa Ridge
Mellieħa
Buġibba
San Pawl il Baħar
Wardija Ridge
St Julian's
Sliema
Gżira
Msida
VALLETTA
Grand Harbour
Vittoriosa
Żabbar
Mosta
Birkirkara
Ħamrun
Qormi
Cospicua
Paola
Malta
Mdina
Rabat
Marsa
Tarxien
Żebbuġ
Siġġiewi
Luqa
Żejtun
Marsaxlokk
Dingli
Dingli Cliffs
253m
Birżebbuġa
Żurrieq
Marsaxlokk Bay
0 5 km
0 5 miles
N
36°
14°30'

MALTA

Total Land Area : 320 sq. km (124 sq. miles)

POPULATION: ● over 10 000 • under 10 000

LAND HEIGHT: 200m/656ft; Sea Level

AID

Recipient

$25m (receipts) | Up 14% in 1999

Malta receives economic assistance under an agreement with the EU. The UK is the main bilateral source of aid.

DEFENSE

No compulsory military service

$27m | Down 10% in 1999

The Maltese army, advised by the Libyans in the 1980s, now receives training and equipment from Italy, Germany, and the UK.

ECONOMICS

Inflation 3.1% p.a. (1990–1999)

$3.5bn | 0.4133–0.4357 Maltese liri

SCORE CARD

- ❑ WORLD GNP RANKING........124th
- ❑ GNP PER CAPITA........$9210
- ❑ BALANCE OF PAYMENTS........$–128m
- ❑ INFLATION........2.1%
- ❑ UNEMPLOYMENT........6%

STRENGTHS

Tourism and naval dockyards. Schemes to attract foreign high-tech industry. Malta Freeport container distribution center. Offshore banking. Strategic position between Europe and Africa, on main Mediterranean shipping lines.

WEAKNESSES

Cut-rate competition from Africa and Asia in traditional textile industry. Need to import almost all requirements.

EXPORTS

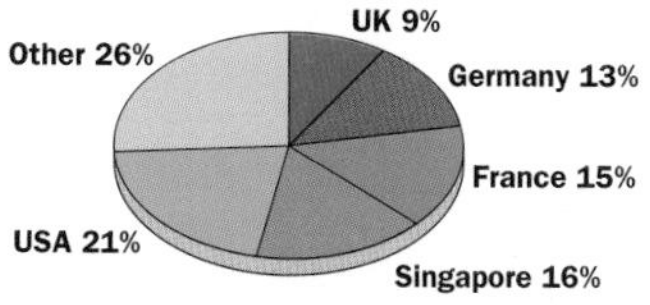
UK 9%
Germany 13%
France 15%
Singapore 16%
USA 21%
Other 26%

IMPORTS

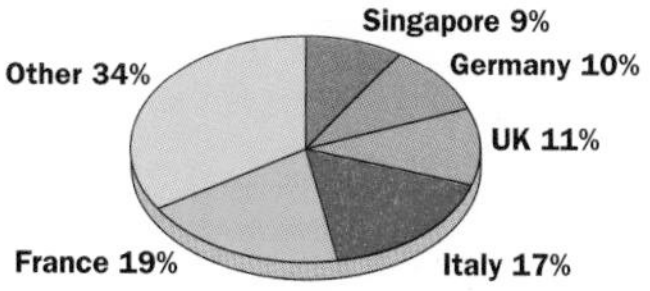
Singapore 9%
Germany 10%
UK 11%
Italy 17%
France 19%
Other 34%

RESOURCES

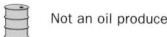

Electric power 250,000 kw

2667 tonnes | Not an oil producer

69,000 pigs, 19,000 cattle, 820,000 chickens | Stone, sand

Malta is dependent on desalination plants for most of its water supply. All oil has to be imported, mostly from Libya. However, there are petroleum reserves currently under exploration in Maltese waters.

ENVIRONMENT

Not available

None | 4.7 tonnes per capita

The main environmental concern is linked to the tourist industry. A lack of planning controls in the 1970s was responsible for unsightly beach developments. These are now tightly controlled, particularly on Gozo.

MEDIA

TV ownership high

Daily newspaper circulation 127 per 1000 people

PUBLISHING AND BROADCAST MEDIA

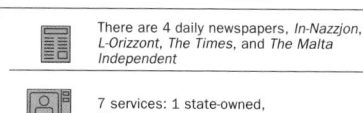

There are 4 daily newspapers, *In-Nazzjon*, *L-Orizzont*, *The Times*, and *The Malta Independent*

7 services: 1 state-owned, 6 independent

12 services: 1 state-owned, 11 independent

The Maltese press is largely party politically oriented. Two of the three main press groups are affiliated to the NP or MLP; one is independent.

CRIME

Death penalty not used

196 prisoners | Down 19% 1992–1996

Crime rates are low compared with those on the European mainland. There has been an increase in narcotics transshipment and associated crimes.

CHRONOLOGY

Ancient Malta was dominated by Phoenicians, Carthaginians, Greeks, and Romans, and was later ruled by the Arabs, Norman Sicily, Spain, France, and, finally, the UK.

- ❑ **1947** Internal self-government.
- ❑ **1964** Full independence from UK.
- ❑ **1971** Dom Mintoff's MLP in power.
- ❑ **1987–1996** Edward Fenech Adami (NP) is premier.
- ❑ **1998** Early elections bring pro-EU Fenech Adami back to power after brief MLP interlude.

EDUCATION

School leaving age: 16

92% | 8260 students

One-third of pupils attend non-state schools, including heavily subsidized church-run institutions. There is a state university in Valletta.

HEALTH

Welfare state health benefits

1 per 383 people | Cerebrovascular and heart diseases, cancers, diabetes

Malta has five state-run and a couple of private hospitals. Diabetes is prevalent, as on other Mediterranean islands.

SPENDING

GDP/cap. increase

CONSUMPTION AND SPENDING

495 per 1000 population | *512 per 1000 population*

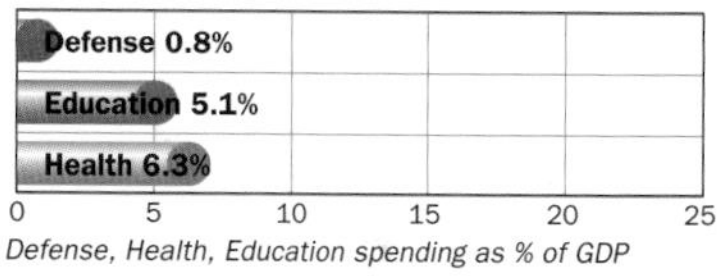
Defense 0.8%
Education 5.1%
Health 6.3%
0
5
10
15
20
25
Defense, Health, Education spending as % of GDP

Remittances from Maltese working abroad are an important source of income for many island families.

WORLD RANKING

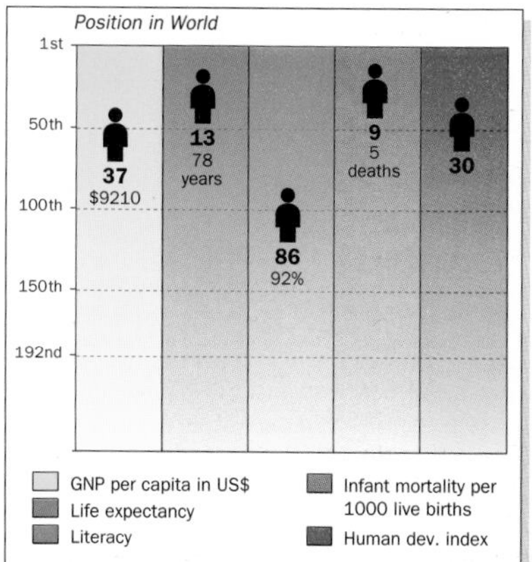
Position in World
1st
50th
100th
150th
192nd
37
$9210
13
78 years
86
92%
9
5 deaths
30
GNP per capita in US$
Life expectancy
Literacy
Infant mortality per 1000 live births
Human dev. index

M

Marshall Islands

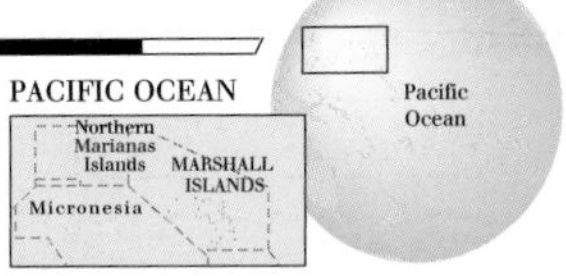
PACIFIC OCEAN
Pacific Ocean
Northern Marianas Islands
MARSHALL ISLANDS
Micronesia

Official Name: Republic of the Marshall Islands **Capital:** Majuro
Population: 68,100 **Currency:** US dollar **Official Languages:** English and Marshallese

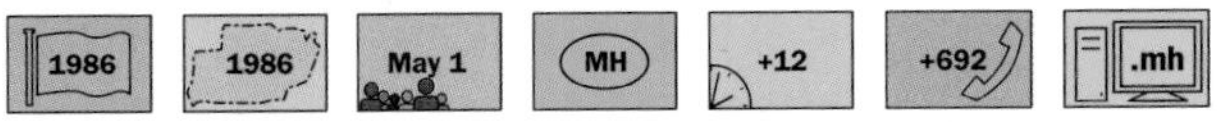
1986
1986
May 1
MH
+12
+692
.mh

THE MARSHALL ISLANDS comprise a group of 34 widely scattered atolls in the central Pacific Ocean, formerly under US rule as part of the UN Trust Territory of the Pacific Islands. An agreement which granted internal sovereignty in free association with the USA became operational in 1986, and the Trust was formally dissolved in 1990. The economy is almost entirely dependent on US aid and rent for the US missile base on Kwajalein atoll.

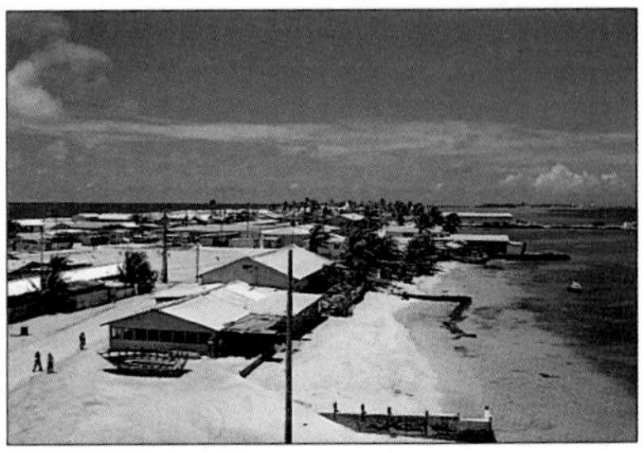

Ebeye District on Kwajalein atoll.
Population pressures on the island have led to the disappearance of most tree and grass cover.

CLIMATE

Tropical oceanic

WEATHER CHART

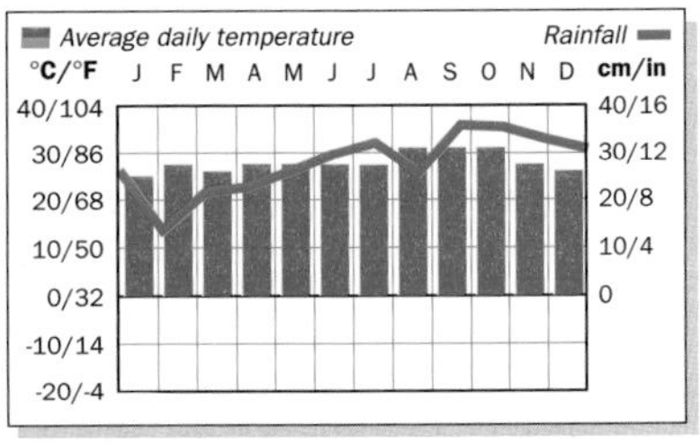
Average daily temperature
Rainfall
°C/°F
J F M A M J J A S O N D
cm/in
40/104
30/86
20/68
10/50
0/32
-10/14
-20/-4
40/16
30/12
20/8
10/4
0

The climate is tropical oceanic with little seasonal variation; temperatures average around 30°C (86°F).

TRANSPORTATION

Drive on right

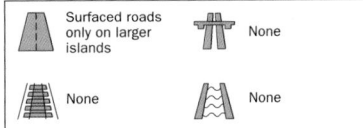

Majuro International

207 ships 6.4m grt

THE TRANSPORTATION NETWORK

Surfaced roads only on larger islands	None
None	None

The transportation system is limited, although there is some inter-island shipping. State carrier Air Marshalls has experienced economic difficulties.

TOURISM

Visitors : Population 1:14

5000 visitors

No change in 2000

MAIN TOURIST ARRIVALS

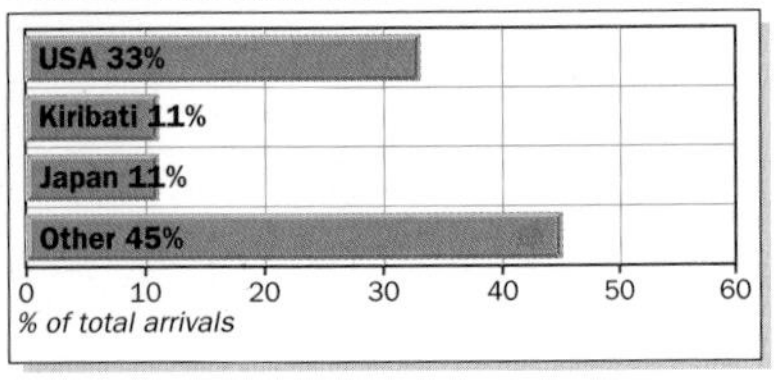
USA 33%
Kiribati 11%
Japan 11%
Other 45%
0 10 20 30 40 50 60
% of total arrivals

In the late 1990s major resort complexes were established on Majuro and on Mili Atoll. Attractions include diving, game-fishing, and exploring the sites and relics of World War II battles.

PEOPLE

Pop. density high

Marshallese, English, Japanese, German

376/km² (975/mi²)

THE URBAN/RURAL POPULATION SPLIT

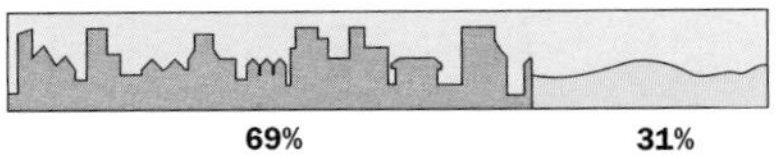
69%
31%

ETHNIC MAKEUP

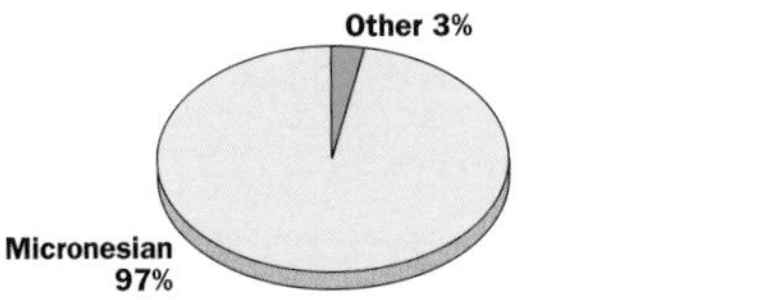
Other 3%
Micronesian 97%

Of the 34 atolls making up the Marshall Islands, 24 are inhabited. Majuro, the capital and commercial center, is home to almost half of the population, many of whom live in its overcrowded slums. The other main center of population is Ebeye Island in the Kwajalein atoll, where tensions are high due to poor living conditions. Most of Kwajalein atoll's inhabitants were forcibly relocated onto Ebeye in 1947 to make way for a US missile tracking, testing, and interception base; many still travel daily to work at the base. Life on the outlying islands is still centered around subsistence agriculture and fishing. Society is traditionally matrilineal.

POLITICS

Multiparty elections

1999/2003

President Kessai Note

AT THE LAST ELECTION

Parliament 33 seats

55% UDP
45% K

UDP = United Democratic Party **K** = Pro-Kabua Grouping
The 33 members are elected from 25 districts

Council of Chiefs 12 seats

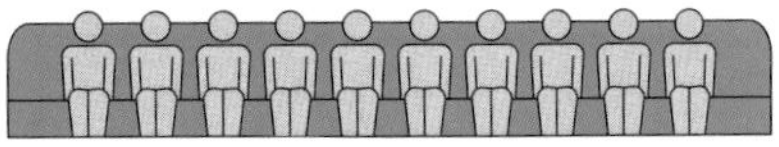

All 12 members are high chiefs

Politics is traditionally dominated by chiefs. Amata Kabua, the islands' high chief and first president until his death in December 1996, was succeeded in early 1997 by his cousin Imata Kabua. However, the 1999 elections were won by the United Democratic Party, whose presidential candidate, commoner and former parliamentary speaker Kessai Note, was elected to office in early January 2000. Just over a year later Imata Kabua returned to lead an unsuccessful vote of no confidence in Note's administration – only the second in the islands' history. The vote was motivated by criticism of the government approach to the crucial renegotiation of the Compact of Free Association with the USA. The original treaty, which provided most of the islands' revenue and defense, was to expire at the end of 2001.

Marshall Islands

Total Land Area : 181 sq. km (70 sq. miles)

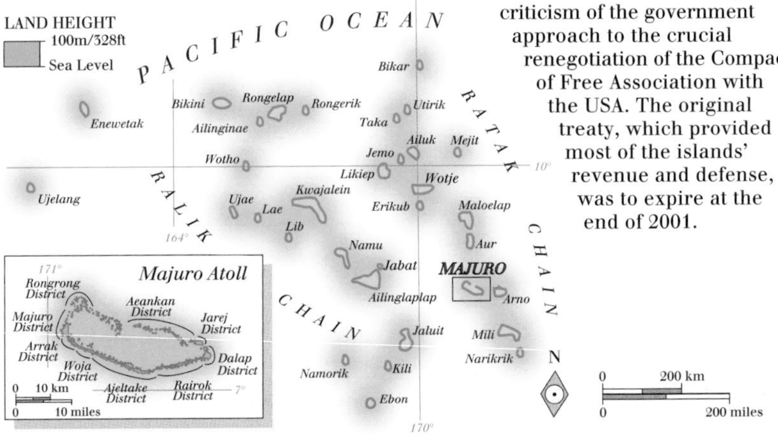
LAND HEIGHT
100m/328ft
Sea Level
PACIFIC OCEAN
Bokak
Bikar
Enewetak
Bikini
Rongelap
Rongerik
Utirik
Ailinginae
Taka
Ailuk
Mejit
Wotho
Jemo
Likiep
Wotje
Ujelang
Ujae
Lae
Kwajalein
Erikub
Maloelap
Lib
Namu
Aur
Jabat
MAJURO
Ailinglaplap
Arno
Jaluit
Mili
Namorik
Kili
Narikrik
Ebon
RATAK CHAIN
RALIK CHAIN
164°
170°
10°
Majuro Atoll
171°
Rongrong District
Aeankan District
Majuro District
Jarej District
Arrak District
Woja District
Dalap District
Ajeltake District
Rairok District
7°
0 10 km
0 10 miles
N
0 200 km
0 200 miles

WORLD AFFAIRS

Joined UN in 1991

IAEA | PIF | ACP | PC | ADB

The 15-year Compact of Free Association has made ties to the USA of central importance. From 1986 to 2001 the USA was to provide $1 billion in return for the use of Kwajalein atoll as a missile firing range; it has also determined the islands' foreign and defense policies. Taiwan has become a source of funding for development, provoking controversy on the issue of diplomatic recognition.

AID

Recipient

$63m (receipts) | Up 26% in 1999

US aid accounts for around two-thirds of the islands' revenue. Australia and Taiwan also provide some assistance.

DEFENSE

No compulsory military service

USA is responsible for defense | Not applicable

There is no defense force. All defense is provided by the USA under the Compact of Free Association. The USA does not have offensive weapons sited in the Marshalls, but its navy patrols regularly.

ECONOMICS

Inflation 6.3% p.a. (1990–1999)

$99m | Currency is US dollar

SCORE CARD

- ❑ WORLD GNP RANKING........186th
- ❑ GNP PER CAPITA........$1950
- ❑ BALANCE OF PAYMENTS........$-6m
- ❑ INFLATION........4.8%
- ❑ UNEMPLOYMENT........31%

STRENGTHS

US guarantee against economic collapse to preserve strategic influence. Aid from the USA, on which islands almost totally depend. Copra. Huge tourism potential.

WEAKNESSES

High unemployment. Dependence on imports, which are 11 times greater than exports. All fuel has to be imported. Vulnerability to storm damage. Large state sector employs 75% of workers.

EXPORTS

The Marshall Islands' main export partners are the USA, Australia, and Japan.

IMPORTS

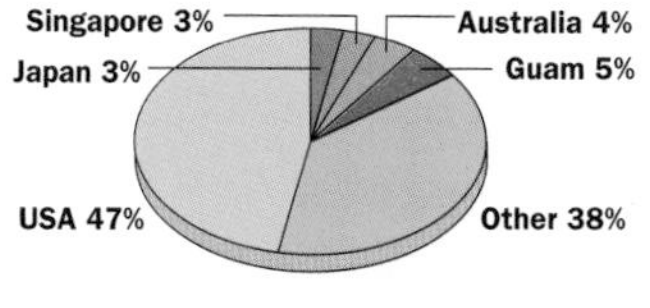
Singapore 3%
Australia 4%
Japan 3%
Guam 5%
USA 47%
Other 38%

RESOURCES

Not available

405 tonnes | Not an oil producer

Not available | Phosphates

There are few known strategic resources. Exploratory tests have revealed some high-grade phosphate deposits, but not in economically viable quantities. Small diesel generators are used for electricity production.

ENVIRONMENT

Not available

None | Not available

Between 1946 and 1958, Bikini, Enewetak, and neighboring atolls were rendered uninhabitable by a series of US nuclear military tests. Enewetak residents were allowed to return in 1980, and Rongelap was declared habitable in 2001. A 1999 tribunal adopted stringent standards for further decontamination. The USA has now paid out over $101 million to victims of nuclear testing. Nuclear waste imports were banned in 1999. The effects of rising sea levels are a major concern. Erosion affects beaches and soil is being lost and also contaminated by brackish water.

MEDIA

TV ownership low

There are no daily newspapers

PUBLISHING AND BROADCAST MEDIA

There are no daily newspapers. The one weekly newspaper, the *Marshall Islands Journal*, is privately owned

2 independent services | 2 services: 1 state-owned, 1 independent

Radio is the major source of information in the Marshalls. The main TV service is subscription-only. The US personnel stationed on Kwajalein have their own TV and radio stations.

CRIME

Death penalty not used

The Marshalls do not publish prison figures | Little change from year to year

Crime levels are generally low; however, the rate is up in Ebeye. Outlying islands are crime-free.

EDUCATION

School leaving age: 14

91% | Not available

Education, compulsory between the ages of six and 14 years, is based on the US model. The number of secondary school graduates exceeds the availability of suitable employment in the Marshall Islands. Many go on to university in the USA.

CHRONOLOGY

After a period under Spanish rule, the Marshall Islands became a German protectorate in 1885; Japan took possession at the start of World War I. The islands were transferred to US control in 1945.

- ❑ **1946** US nuclear testing begins.
- ❑ **1947** UN Trust Territory of the Pacific established.
- ❑ **1961** Kwajalein becomes US army missile range.
- ❑ **1979** Constitution approved in referendum. Government set up.
- ❑ **1986** Compact of Free Association with US operational.
- ❑ **1990** Trust terminated by UN.
- ❑ **1997** Imata Kabua elected president after death in office of Amata Kabua, his cousin.
- ❑ **2000** Kessai Note president after opposition election victory.

HEALTH

No welfare state health benefits

1 per 3294 people | Respiratory, heart, and diarrheal diseases

Medical facilities are rudimentary. Complex operations are performed in Hawaii. Levels of malnutrition and Vitamin A deficiency are high.

SPENDING

Not available

CONSUMPTION AND SPENDING

No data | *62 per 1000 population*

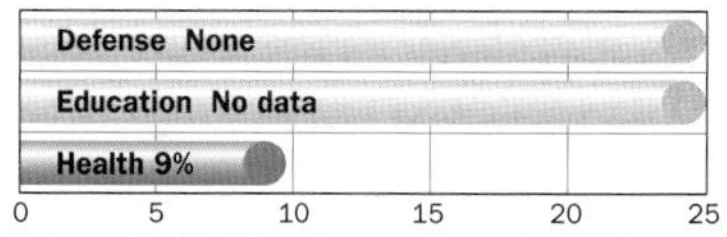
Defense None
Education No data
Health 9%
0
5
10
15
20
25

Defense, Health, Education spending as % of GDP

Wealth disparities are small. Very few citizens can afford luxuries such as air conditioning and cars.

WORLD RANKING

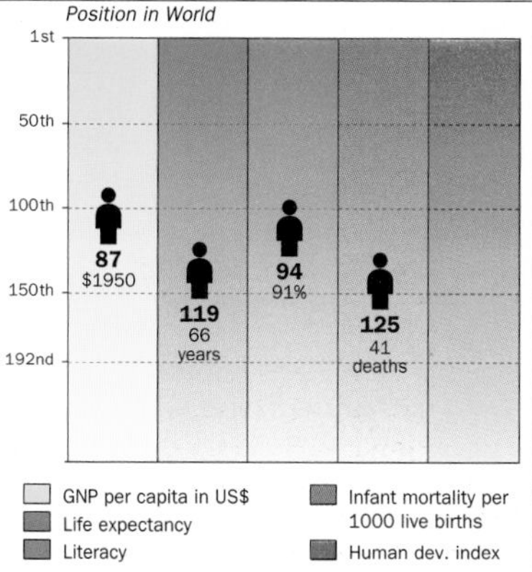
Position in World
1st
50th
100th
150th
192nd
87
$1950
119
66
years
94
91%
125
41
deaths
GNP per capita in US$
Life expectancy
Literacy
Infant mortality per 1000 live births
Human dev. index

M

Mauritania

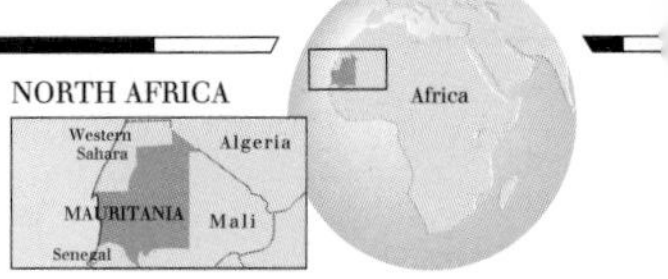
NORTH AFRICA
Western Sahara
Algeria
MAURITANIA
Mali
Senegal
Africa

Official Name: Islamic Republic of Mauritania **Capital:** Nouakchott
Population: 2.7 million **Currency:** Ouguiya **Official Languages:** Arabic and French

1960 | 1960 | Nov 28 | RIM | 0 | +222 | .mr

LOCATED IN NORTHWEST AFRICA, Mauritania is a member of both the OAU and the Arab League. Formerly a French colony, the country has taken a strongly Arab direction since 1964; today, it is the Maures who control political life and dominate the minority black population. The Sahara extends across two-thirds of Mauritania's territory; the only productive land is that drained by the Senegal river in the south and southwest.

CLIMATE
Hot desert

WEATHER CHART

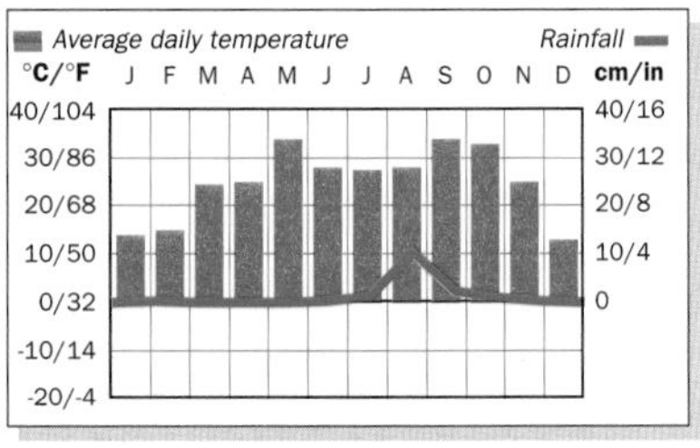
Average daily temperature
Rainfall
°C/°F
J F M A M J J A S O N D
cm/in
40/104
30/86
20/68
10/50
0/32
-10/14
-20/-4
40/16
30/12
20/8
10/4
0

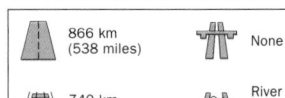

The dusty Saharan *harmattan* wind often aggravates the very hot, dry conditions. Some rain falls in the south.

TRANSPORTATION
Drive on right

Nouakchott

140 ships
47,959 grt

THE TRANSPORTATION NETWORK

866 km (538 miles)

None

740 km (460 miles)

River Senegal is navigable by small craft

The transportation system is limited and unevenly developed. There are two major roads, but shifting sands mean that they require constant maintenance.

TOURISM
Visitors : Population 1:113

24,000 visitors

Little change from year to year

MAIN TOURIST ARRIVALS

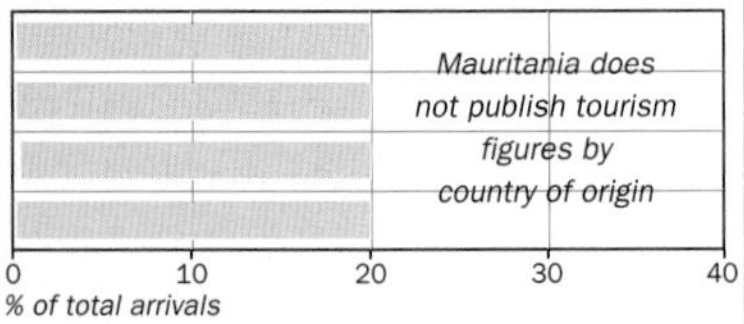
Mauritania does not publish tourism figures by country of origin
0
10
20
30
40
% of total arrivals

There are few tourists apart from desert safari enthusiasts. The more mountainous areas are especially dramatic, but access is difficult. Nouakchott has some hotels.

PEOPLE
Pop. density low

Hassaniyah Arabic, Wolof, French

3/km² (7/mi²)

THE URBAN/RURAL POPULATION SPLIT

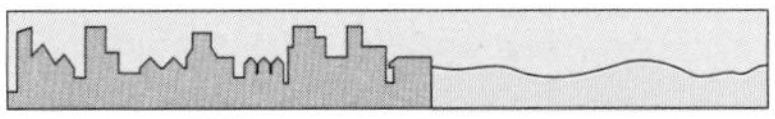
56%
44%

RELIGIOUS PERSUASION

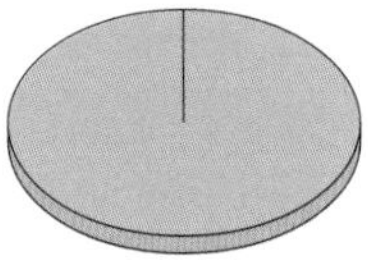
Muslim (Sunni) 100%

The politically dominant Maures make up the majority of the population. The black population is composed of the Havalin, the Senegalese, and the Peulh, Tukolor, and Wolof groups. Ethnic tension centers on the oppression of blacks by Maures. The old black bourgeoisie has now been superseded by a Maurish class; tens of thousands of blacks are estimated to be in slavery. The arrival of 200,000 Maures from Senegal in 1989 caused ethnic tension to come to a head. There were attacks on Senegalese in Mauritania and many fled or were deported to refugee camps along the Senegal River.

Family solidarity among nomads is particularly strong.

POLITICS
Multiparty elections

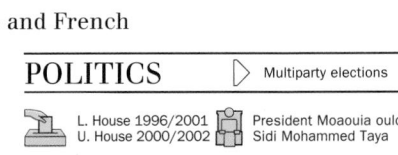

L. House 1996/2001
U. House 2000/2002

President Moaouia ould Sidi Mohammed Taya

AT THE LAST ELECTION

National Assembly 79 seats

89% PRDS
10% Ind
1% AC

PRDS = Democratic and Social Republican Party
Ind = Independents **AC** = Action for Change

Senate 56 seats

96% PRDS
2% Ind
2% AC

The Senate is indirectly elected.

Mauritania officially adopted multiparty democracy in 1991. However, the 1992 and 1997 presidential elections simply returned to power the incumbent military ruler, President Moaouia ould Sidi Mohammed Taya, with around 90% of the vote. Legislative elections have been boycotted by the opposition parties, which accuse the government of electoral fraud. There have been frequent government changes in recent years. The opposition parties are mainly Maure-led. The blacks of the south support exiled parties, such as the Dakar-based African Liberation Forces of Mauritania (FLAM).

Mauritania

Total Land Area : 1 025 520 sq. km (395 953 sq. miles)

POPULATION
- over 500 000
- over 10 000
- under 10 000

LAND HEIGHT
- 500m/1640ft
- 200m/656ft
- Sea Level

N

0 200 km
0 200 miles

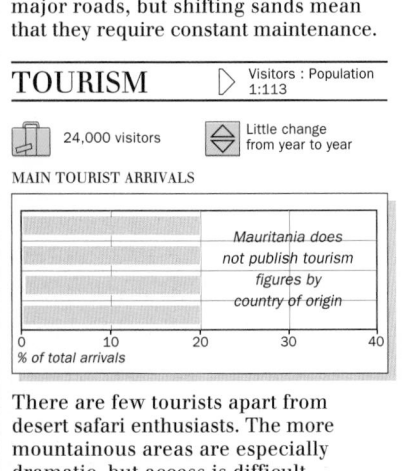

WESTERN SAHARA
ALGERIA
ATLANTIC OCEAN
SAHARA
MALI
SENEGAL
Bîr Mogreïn
'Aïn Ben Tili
Sebkhet Iguetti
Sebkhet Oumm ed Drous Telli
Fdérik
Zouérat
Kediet ej Jill 915m
Nouâdhibou
Atâr
Chinguetti
Ouadane
Et Tidra
Akjoujt
Sebkhet Te-n-Dghâmcha
NOUAKCHOTT
Ouâd Nâga
Moudjéria
Magta' Lahjar
Tidjikja
Tîchît
Boutilimit
Boûmdeïd
Tâmchekket
Oualâta
Keur Massène
Lac Rkiz
Aleg
Guérou
Kiffa
'Ayoûn el 'Atroûs
Néma
Rosso
Bogué
Bababé
Mbagne
Kaédi
Mbout
Kankossa
Tintâne
Tîmbédra
Amourj
Kobenni
Djiguéni
Bassikounou
Ould Yenjé
Sélibabi
Senegal
24°
20°
16°
4°
8°
12°
16°

WORLD AFFAIRS

Joined UN in 1961

AL | CILSS | OAU | OIF | OIC

Mauritania seeks to maintain a balance between sub-Saharan Africa and the Arab world, but has had tensions with all its neighbors. It has now effectively withdrawn from the Western Sahara dispute. Relations with Senegal have improved since the conflicts of 1989.

AID

Recipient

$219m (receipts) — Up 27% in 1999

France, Germany, the IMF, OPEC, and Iraq are all donors. Most aid is used for development projects, such as the EU-funded Trans-Mauritanian Highway.

DEFENSE

Compulsory military service

$24m — Down 8% in 1999

The 15,000-strong army is a strain on Mauritania's budget. Troops are used increasingly in public works projects. France is the main arms supplier.

ECONOMICS

Inflation 6% p.a. (1990–1999)

$1bn — 223.33–250.97 ouguiyas

SCORE CARD

❑ World GNP Ranking	156th
❑ GNP per Capita	$390
❑ Balance of Payments	$77m
❑ Inflation	4.1%
❑ Unemployment	23%

Strengths
Iron from the Cominor mine at Zouérat. Largest gypsum deposits in the world. Copper, yet to be properly exploited. Offshore fishing among the best in West Africa.

Weaknesses
"Debt-distressed," with a debt of nearly $2 billion. Poor land. Drought, locust attacks, fluctuating commodity prices. Very hot, dry desert climate.

EXPORTS

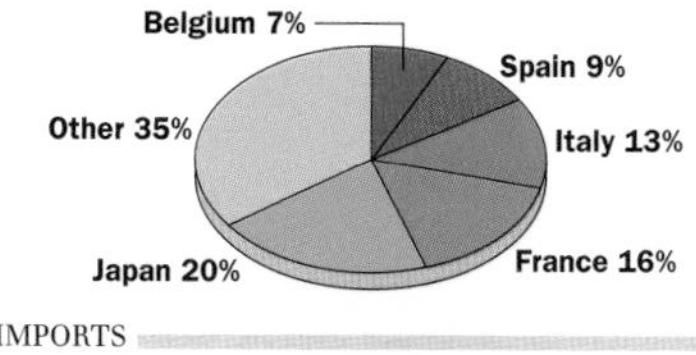
Belgium 7%
Spain 9%
Other 35%
Italy 13%
Japan 20%
France 16%

IMPORTS

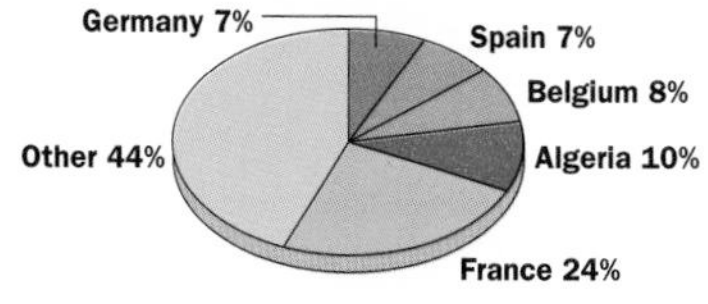
Germany 7%
Spain 7%
Belgium 8%
Other 44%
Algeria 10%
France 24%

***Mauritania's extreme aridity** means that only 1% of the land is arable. Two-thirds of the country is part of the Sahara desert; sparse vegetation over the rest supports some livestock.*

RESOURCES

Electric power 105,000 kw

82,000 tonnes — Not an oil producer

6.2m sheep, 4.13m goats, 1.44m cattle, 4.1m chickens — Iron, gypsum, copper, gold, phosphates, yttrium, diamonds

Iron continues to be exploited, despite low world prices. There are some gold and diamond deposits. Mining and fisheries represent 99.7% of exports. Electricity generation expanded by 40% between 1989 and 1996, and further expansion is expected to come from the Manantali dam. Phosphates have been found near the Senegal river. Offshore oil exploration started in April 2001.

ENVIRONMENT

Not available

2% (0.2% partially protected) — 1.2 tonnes per capita

The chief environmental problem in Mauritania is that of the encroaching Sahara desert, a situation worsened by the droughts of 1973 and 1983, which caused widespread loss of grazing land. The consequent exodus of people away from the land has led to Nouakchott's population increasing from 20,000 in 1960 to almost a million today.

MEDIA

TV ownership medium

Daily newspaper circulation 0.5 per 1000 people

PUBLISHING AND BROADCAST MEDIA

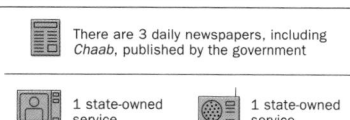

There are 3 daily newspapers, including *Chaab*, published by the government

1 state-owned service — 1 state-owned service

The press is heavily censored, and the broadcast media are state-owned. *Chaab*, the government newspaper, is also published in French (*Horizons*).

CRIME

Death penalty used

Mauritania does not publish prison figures — Down 23% 1992–1996

The main problems are smuggling and robbery. Levels of violence are lower than the west African average.

CHRONOLOGY

Once part of the Islamic Almoravid state, Mauritania became a French colony in 1814.

- ❑ **1960** Independence; one-party state.
- ❑ **1972** Peace with Polisario in war waged over Western Sahara.
- ❑ **1984** Colonel Moaouia Taya takes power in bloodless coup.
- ❑ **1992** First multiparty elections.
- ❑ **1997** Taya reelected as president.

EDUCATION

School leaving age: 12

42% — 8496 students

Despite improvements in education, over half the population continues to be illiterate. Arabic has been compulsory in all schools since 1988.

HEALTH

No welfare state health benefits

1 per 10,000 people — Diarrheal and respiratory diseases, influenza, tuberculosis

Historic regional inequalities persist and the best facilities are in the capital. The overall level of care is on a par with neighboring states.

SPENDING

GDP/cap. increase

CONSUMPTION AND SPENDING

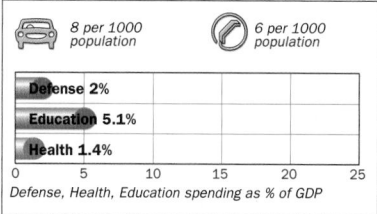

8 per 1000 population — *6 per 1000 population*

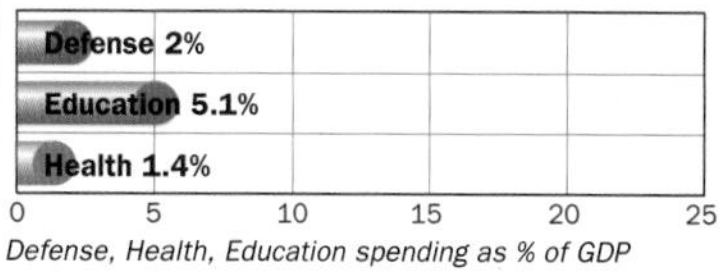
Defense 2%
Education 5.1%
Health 1.4%
0
5
10
15
20
25
Defense, Health, Education spending as % of GDP

The small ruling Maures elite form the richest sector. Wealthy Maures travel to Mecca, Saudi Arabia, to perform the *haj* (Muslim pilgrimage).

WORLD RANKING

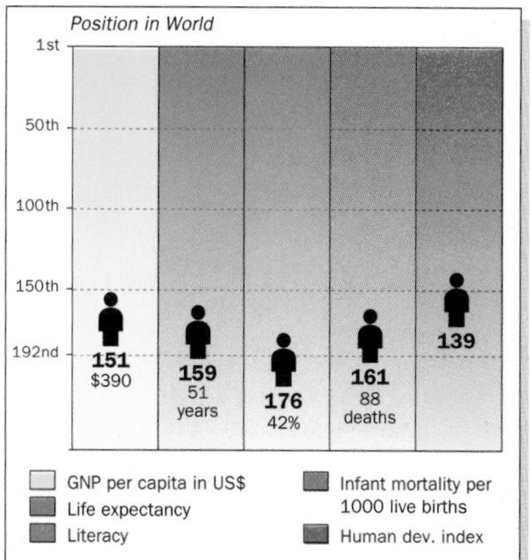
Position in World
1st
50th
100th
150th
192nd
151
$390
159
51 years
176
42%
161
88 deaths
139
GNP per capita in US$
Life expectancy
Literacy
Infant mortality per 1000 live births
Human dev. index

M

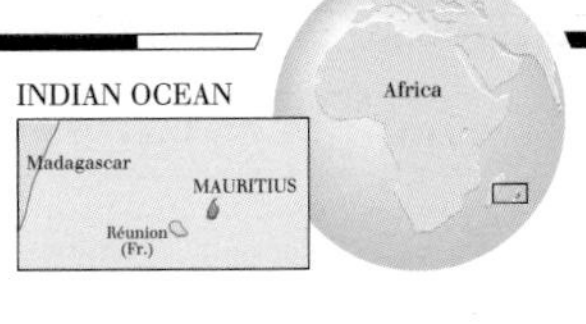
INDIAN OCEAN
Africa
Madagascar
MAURITIUS
Réunion (Fr.)

MAURITIUS

OFFICIAL NAME: Mauritius **CAPITAL:** Port Louis
POPULATION: 1.2 million **CURRENCY:** Mauritian rupee **OFFICIAL LANGUAGE:** English

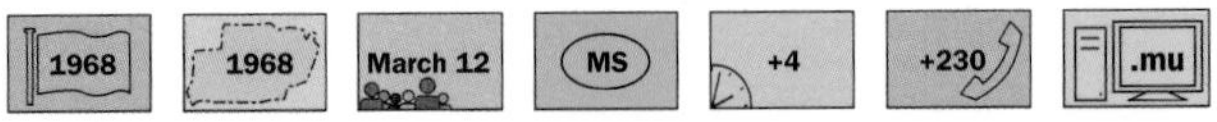
1968
1968
March 12
MS
+4
+230
.mu

THE ISLANDS THAT MAKE UP Mauritius lie in the Indian Ocean east of Madagascar. The main island, from which the country takes its name, is of volcanic origin and surrounded by coral reefs. Along with Rodrigues to the east, the country includes the Agalega Islands and the Cargados Carajos Shoals (500 km – 300 miles – to the north). Mauritius has enjoyed considerable economic success following recent industrial diversification and the expansion of tourism.

CLIMATE

Tropical oceanic

WEATHER CHART

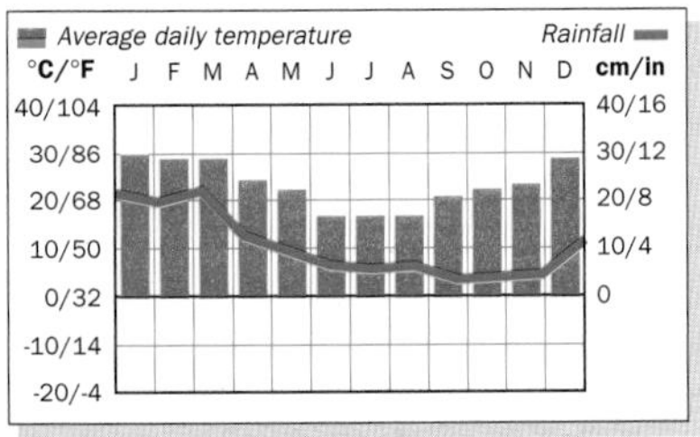
Average daily temperature
Rainfall
°C/°F J F M A M J J A S O N D cm/in
40/104
30/86
20/68
10/50
0/32
-10/14
-20/-4
40/16
30/12
20/8
10/4
0

The climate is subtropical and humid. December to March are the hottest and wettest months. Tropical cyclones are an occasional threat at this time.

TRANSPORTATION

Drive on left

Sir Seewoosagur Ramgoolam International 870,000 passengers

51 ships 206,000 grt

THE TRANSPORTATION NETWORK

1834 km (1140 miles)

36 km (22 miles)

None

None

Roads are extensive, but often congested. Plans exist for a monorail link between Port Louis and Curepipe.

TOURISM

Visitors : Population 1:1.8

656,000 visitors

Up 14% in 2000

MAIN TOURIST ARRIVALS

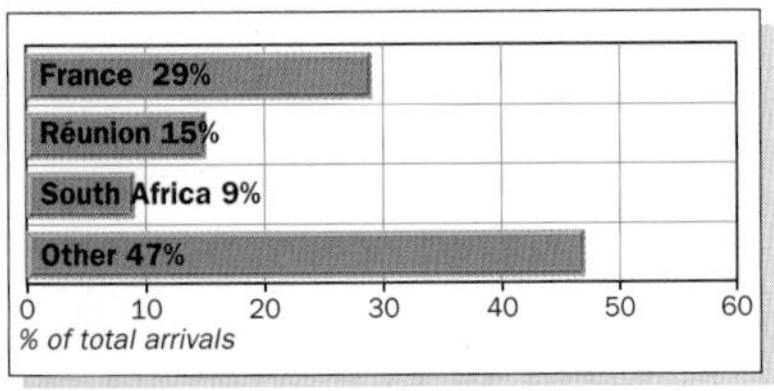
France 29%
Réunion 15%
South Africa 9%
Other 47%
0 10 20 30 40 50 60
% of total arrivals

Tourism expanded rapidly in the 1990s. Spectacular beaches, water sports, and big game fishing are major attractions. Almost 30% of visitors each year come from France.

PEOPLE

Pop. density high

French Creole, Hindi, Urdu, Tamil, Chinese, English, French

645/km² (1671/mi²)

THE URBAN/RURAL POPULATION SPLIT

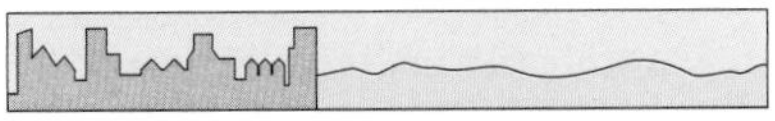
41%
59%

RELIGIOUS PERSUASION

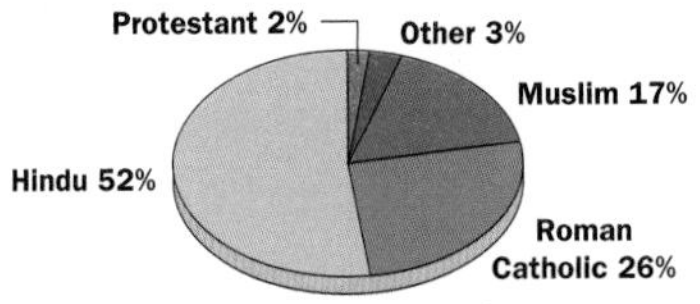
Protestant 2%
Other 3%
Muslim 17%
Hindu 52%
Roman Catholic 26%

Mauritius is one of the world's most densely populated countries. The majority of the population descend from indentured Indian laborers brought over in the 19th century. Creoles make up 27% of the population, while 3% are of Chinese origin. Clashes between Hindus, Muslims, and Creoles no longer occur, although Creoles complain of discrimination.

POLITICS

Multiparty elections

2000/2005

President Cassam Uteem

AT THE LAST ELECTION

National Assembly 70 seats

11% PTr/PMXD
3% MR
83% MSM/MMM
3% OPR

MSM/MMM = Mauritian Socialist Movement/Mauritian Militant Movement **PTr/PMXD** = Labour Party/Mauritian Social Democratic Party of Xavier Duval **OPR** = Organization of the People of Rodrigues **MR** = Mouvement Rodriguais

62 members of the National Assembly are directly elected, and up to eight are appointed from the highest losers

Mauritius became a republic in 1992. Navin Ramgoolam of the PTr became prime minister in 1995, promoting regional integration and economic liberalization to attract investment. However, corruption scandals led to early elections in 2000. The PTr was defeated and Sir Anerood Jugnauth, Ramgoolam's predecessor, now heads a new coalition between his MSM and the former opposition MMM.

WORLD AFFAIRS

Joined UN in 1968

Comm | COMESA | COI | OAU | SADC

Mauritius hosted a francophone nations summit in 1995, and the first OAU human rights conference in 1999. Links with South Africa and India are important. Disputes persist over UK-administered Diego Garcia and the French-ruled island of Tromelin.

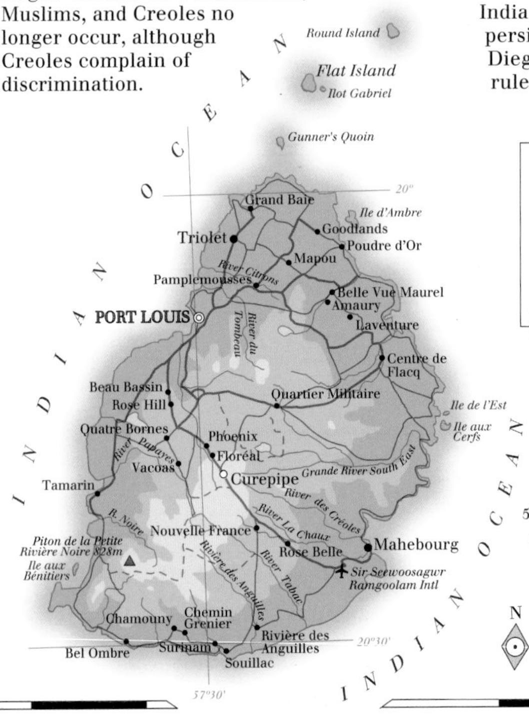
INDIAN OCEAN
Round Island
Flat Island
Ilot Gabriel
Gunner's Quoin
Grand Baie
Ile d'Ambre
Goodlands
Triolet
Poudre d'Or
Mapou
Pamplemousses
River Citrons
Belle Vue Maurel
Amaury
Laventure
PORT LOUIS
River du Tombeau
Centre de Flacq
Beau Bassin
Rose Hill
Quartier Militaire
Ile de l'Est
Ile aux Cerfs
Quatre Bornes
Phoenix
Floréal
Vacoas
Curepipe
Grande River South East
Tamarin
River des Créoles
River La Chaux
Nouvelle France
Mahebourg
Piton de la Petite Rivière Noire 828m
Ile aux Bénitiers
Rose Belle
Sir Seewoosagur Ramgoolam Intl
Chamouny
Chemin Grenier
Rivière des Anguilles
Bel Ombre
Surinam
Souillac
20°
20°30'
57°30'
N

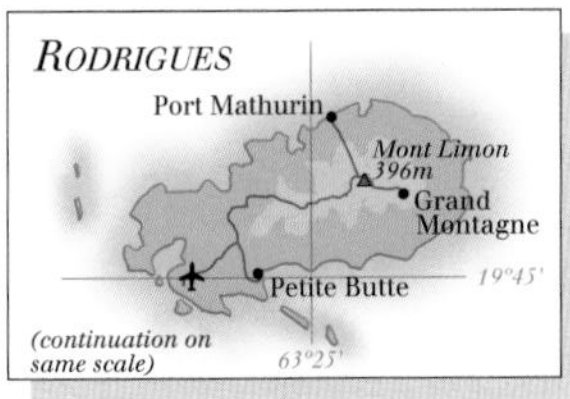
RODRIGUES
Port Mathurin
Mont Limon 396m
Grand Montagne
Petite Butte
19°45'
63°25'
(continuation on same scale)

MAURITIUS

Total Land Area : 1860 sq. km (718 sq. miles)

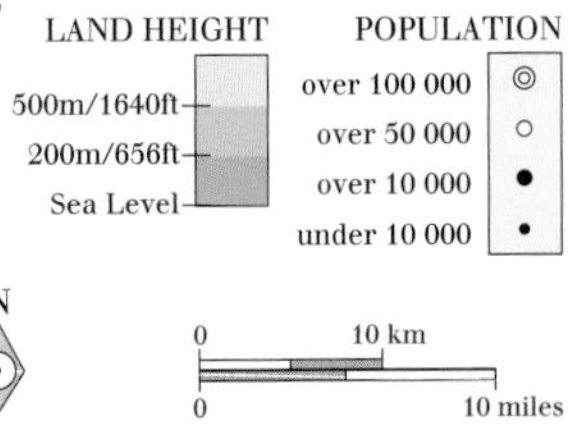
LAND HEIGHT
500m/1640ft
200m/656ft
Sea Level
POPULATION
over 100 000
over 50 000
over 10 000
under 10 000
0 10 km
0 10 miles

AID

Recipient

$42m (receipts) — Up 5% in 1999

Aid is predominantly bilateral, with France and the UK as the main donors. Mauritius also receives aid from Norway, from the EU under the Lomé Convention, and from other international organizations. The World Bank assisted a five-year conservation program, starting in 1990, and promised $53 million toward transforming Port Louis into a free port.

DEFENSE

No compulsory military service

$91m — Up 2% in 1999

Mauritius has no standing defense forces. There is, however, a 1000-strong special police mobile unit to ensure internal security. There is also a coastguard numbering 500.

ECONOMICS

Inflation 6.3% p.a. (1990–1999)

$4.2bn — 25.415–27.820 Mauritian rupees

SCORE CARD

❑ WORLD GNP RANKING	116th
❑ GNP PER CAPITA	$3540
❑ BALANCE OF PAYMENTS	$–52m
❑ INFLATION	6.9%
❑ UNEMPLOYMENT	10%

STRENGTHS

Strong economic growth. The sugar industry accounts for 30% of export earnings. Export Processing Zone (EPZ), especially for clothing manufacture. Tourism. Highly educated work force. Ranked as the most competitive economy in Africa by the World Economic Forum in 1999. Development as offshore financial center.

WEAKNESSES

Vulnerability to fluctuating world sugar price and droughts. 75% of food requirements are imported. Few crops other than sugar can be grown. Lack of strategic resources. Remoteness.

EXPORTS

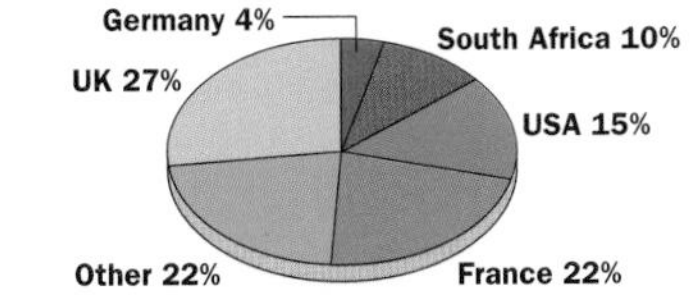
Germany 4%
South Africa 10%
UK 27%
USA 15%
Other 22%
France 22%

IMPORTS

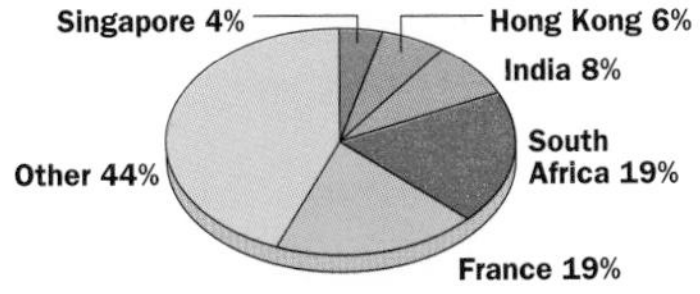
Singapore 4%
Hong Kong 6%
India 8%
South Africa 19%
Other 44%
France 19%

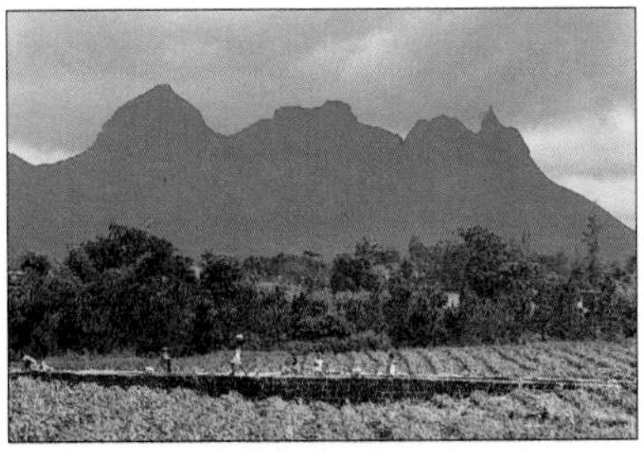

Villagers at a water source *in the center of Mauritius island. Mauritius' main rivers are used for hydropower generation.*

RESOURCES

Electric power 364,000 kw

13,852 tonnes — Not an oil producer

94,000 goats, 29,400 cattle, 4.4m chickens — None

Mauritius has to import oil, so the government has invested heavily in alternative indigenous energy schemes, including HEP generation, and power stations fueled by bagasse (a by-product of the sugar industry). Industrialization and agricultural diversification make up for limited natural resources.

ENVIRONMENT

Sustainability rank: 46th

5% (0.1% partially protected) — 1.5 tonnes per capita

Rapid industrialization as well as unchecked hotel building have caused environmental problems. Coral reefs are under threat from both coral sand mining and the discharging of untreated sewage into the sea.

MEDIA

TV ownership medium

Daily newspaper circulation 76 per 1000 people

PUBLISHING AND BROADCAST MEDIA

There are 10 daily newspapers. *Le Quotidien, L'Express,* and *Le Mauricien* have the largest circulations

1 independent service — 1 independent service

Mauritius has an active press, subject to few regulations and with a wide readership. Newspapers are published in English, French, Creole, Hindi, Chinese, and Tamil. Opposition parties complain that TV and radio broadcasts are consistently biased toward the government.

CRIME

Death penalty not used

1056 prisoners — Up 4% 1996–1998

Crime rates on the main island are fairly low. There has been a small increase in thefts and drug smuggling. Outlying islands are virtually crime-free.

CHRONOLOGY

Mauritius was colonized and ruled by the Dutch in the 17th century, the French (1710–1810), and the British.

- ❑ **1959** First full elections.
- ❑ **1968** Independence. Riots between Creoles and Muslims.
- ❑ **1982–1995** Sir Anerood Jugnauth prime minister; forms MSM.
- ❑ **1992** Becomes a republic.
- ❑ **1995** Elections won by PTr–MMM.
- ❑ **2000** Return of Jugnauth.

EDUCATION

School leaving age: 12

85% — 6419 students

Educational provision is good, and 91% of Mauritians under 30 are literate. The University of Mauritius has about 2000 students.

HEALTH

Welfare state health benefits

1 per 1111 people — Circulatory and heart diseases, cancers, accidents, malnutrition

Free health care is universally available. There are 14 state hospitals and six private clinics.

SPENDING

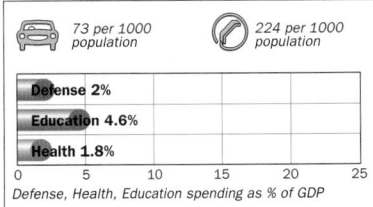

GDP/cap. increase

CONSUMPTION AND SPENDING

73 per 1000 population — *224 per 1000 population*

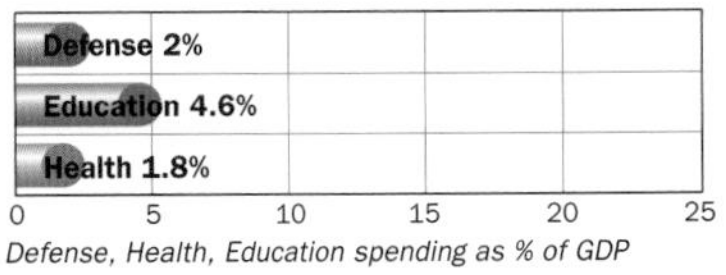
Defense 2%
Education 4.6%
Health 1.8%
0
5
10
15
20
25
Defense, Health, Education spending as % of GDP

French-descended hotel and plantation owners form the country's wealthiest social group. Government employees are well paid.

WORLD RANKING

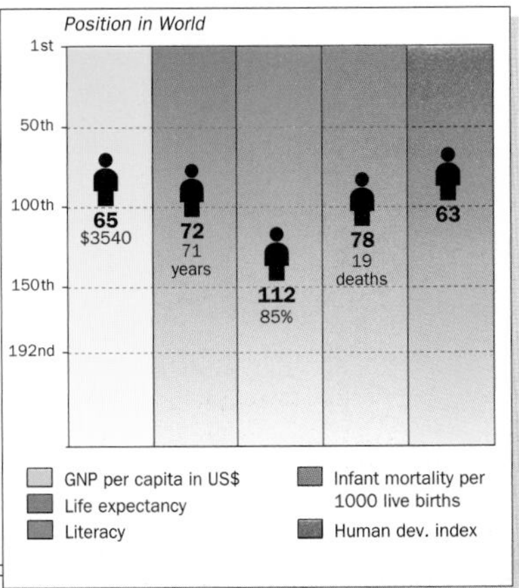
Position in World
1st
50th
100th
150th
192nd
65
$3540
72
71
years
112
85%
78
19
deaths
63
GNP per capita in US$
Life expectancy
Literacy
Infant mortality per 1000 live births
Human dev. index

M

MEXICO

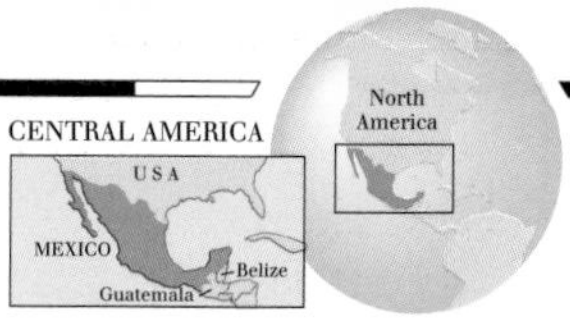
CENTRAL AMERICA
USA
MEXICO
Belize
Guatemala
North America

OFFICIAL NAME: United States of Mexico **CAPITAL:** Mexico City
POPULATION: 98.9 million **CURRENCY:** Mexican peso **OFFICIAL LANGUAGE:** Spanish

1836
1848
Sept 16
MEX
-6
+52
.mx

INCREASINGLY CONSIDERED a part of North rather than Central America, Mexico straddles the southern end of the continent. Coastal plains along its Pacific and Caribbean seaboards rise into an arid central plateau, which includes one of the world's biggest conurbations, Mexico City, built on the site of the Aztec capital, Tenochtitlán. Colonized by the Spanish for its silver mines, Mexico achieved independence in 1836. In the "Epic Revolution" of 1910–1920, in which 250,000 died, much of modern Mexico's structure was established. In 1994, Mexico signed the North American Free Trade Agreement (NAFTA).

***The cathedral of Santa Prisca** at Taxco near Cuernavaca. It was built in Spanish Churriguera style between 1748 and 1758.*

CLIMATE

Tropical/mountain/desert

WEATHER CHART

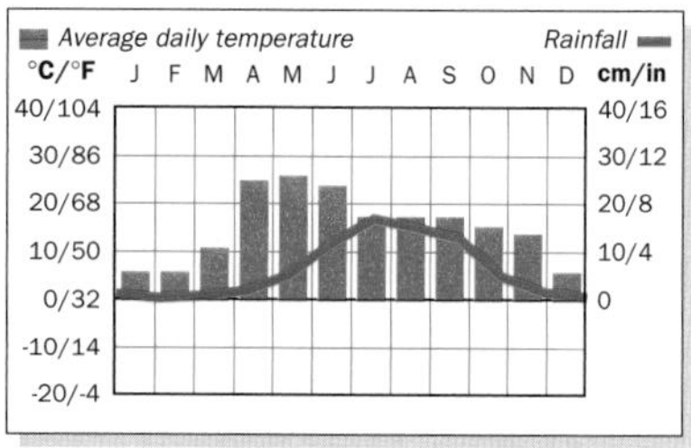
Average daily temperature
Rainfall
°C/°F
J F M A M J J A S O N D
cm/in
40/104
30/86
20/68
10/50
0/32
-10/14
-20/-4
40/16
30/12
20/8
10/4
0

The plateau and high mountains are warm for much of the year. The Pacific coast has a tropical climate.

TRANSPORTATION

Drive on right

Benito Juárez International, Mexico City
20.45m passengers

626 ships
1.1m grt

THE TRANSPORTATION NETWORK

96,221 km (59,789 miles)

6335 km (3936 miles)

26,595 km (16,526 miles)

2900 km (1802 miles)

A privately financed $14 billion road network, some 6000 km (3730 miles) of toll roads, is seriously underused and a commercial failure. Regional travel is mainly by bus; the unreliable railroad is largely for freight. In 2000 the Federal Competition Commission ordered a holding company owning Aeroméxico and Mexicana de Aviación, which control 80% of domestic flights, to be broken up, to reduce high ticket prices and foster tourism.

TOURISM

Visitors : Population 1:4.8

20.6m visitors

Up 8% in 2000

MAIN TOURIST ARRIVALS

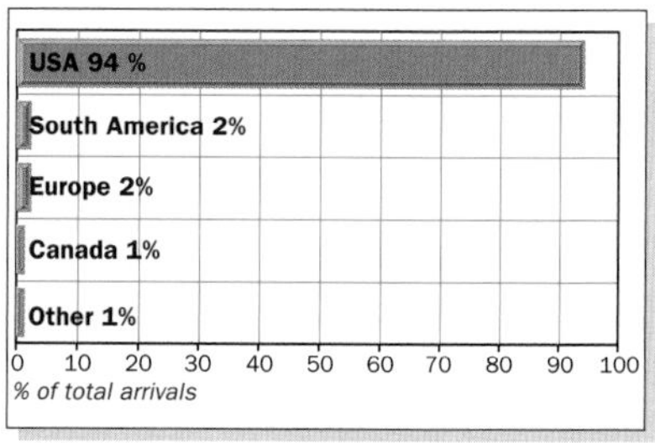
USA 94 %
South America 2%
Europe 2%
Canada 1%
Other 1%
0 10 20 30 40 50 60 70 80 90 100
% of total arrivals

Tourism is one of the largest employment sectors in Mexico, and a major source of foreign exchange. Attractions include excellent beach resorts such as Acapulco on the Pacific coast, and the new resorts of the Peninsula de Yucatán on the Caribbean coast. Impressive coastal scenery, volcanoes, the Sierra Madre mountains, and archaeological remains of Aztec and Mayan civilizations, designated as World Heritage sites, are major draws, as are the many Spanish colonial cities, such as Morelia and Guadalajara, which have remained virtually intact since conquest.

UNITED STATES OF AMERICA
Tijuana
Mexicali
Ensenada
Ciudad Juárez
Isla Ángel de la Guarda
Isla del Tiburón
Hermosillo
Isla Cedros
Bahía Sebastián Vizcaíno
BAJA CALIFORNIA
Golfo de California
Chihuahua
BOLSÓN DE MAPIMÍ
ALTIPLANICIE MEXICANA
SIERRA MADRE OCCIDENTAL
SIERRA MADRE ORIENTAL
Ciudad Obregón
Nuevo Laredo
Monclova
Reynosa
Matamoros
Monterrey
Saltillo
Gómez Palacio
Torreón
Guasave
Los Mochis
Culiacán
Durango
Ciudad Victoria
Mazatlán
Zacatecas
Tampico
San Luis Potosí
Aguascalientes
Tepic
Islas Marías
León
Guanajuato
Irapuato
Querétaro
Guadalajara
Puerto Vallarta
Salamanca
Celaya
Lago de Chapala
Pachuca
Poza Rica
MEXICO CITY
Jalapa
Veracruz
Morelia
Uruapan
Toluca
Cuernavaca
Puebla
Volcán Pico de Orizaba 5700m
Balsas
Coatzacoalcos
Minatitlán
Villahermosa
Oaxaca
ISTMO DE TEHUANTEPEC
Tuxtla Gutiérrez
Acapulco
SIERRA MADRE DEL SUR
Golfo de Tehuantepec
Tapachula
GULF OF MEXICO
Bahía de Campeche
Mérida
Campeche
PENINSULA DE YUCATÁN
Yucatan Channel
Isla de Cozumel
CARIBBEAN SEA
BELIZE
GUATEMALA
Usumacinta
Hondo
Grijalva
Río Grande
Yaqui
Conchos
Pánuco
Grande de Santiago
PACIFIC OCEAN
MEXICO
Total Land Area : 1 908 690 sq. km (736 945 sq. miles)
LAND HEIGHT
3000m/9843ft
2000m/6562ft
1000m/3281ft
500m/1640ft
200m/656ft
Sea Level
POPULATION
over 5 000 000
over 1 000 000
over 500 000
over 100 000
over 50 000
N
0 200 km
0 200 miles

PEOPLE

Pop. density medium

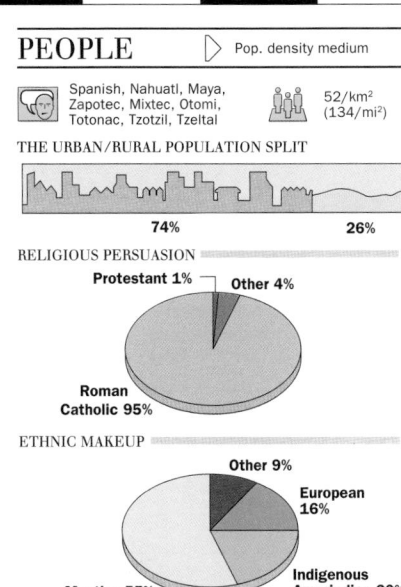

Spanish, Nahuatl, Maya, Zapotec, Mixtec, Otomi, Totonac, Tzotzil, Tzeltal

52/km² (134/mi²)

THE URBAN/RURAL POPULATION SPLIT

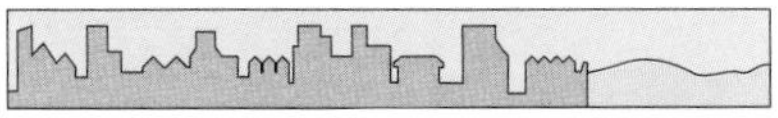
74%
26%

RELIGIOUS PERSUASION

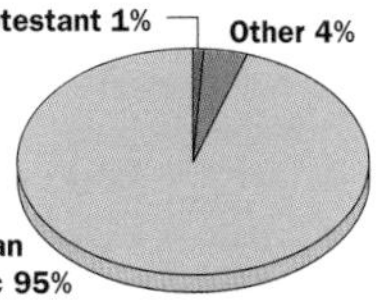
Protestant 1%
Other 4%
Roman Catholic 95%

ETHNIC MAKEUP

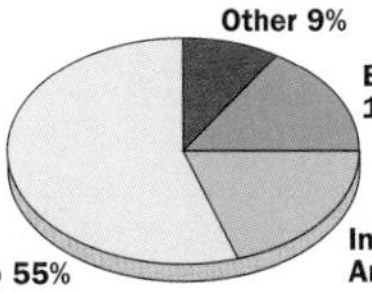
Other 9%
European 16%
Indigenous Amerindian 20%
Mestizo 55%

While most Mexicans are *mestizo*, it is Mexico's Amerindian culture which is promoted by the state. This obscures the fact that rural Amerindians are largely segregated from Hispanic society, a situation that dates back to the Spanish colonial period and which has only

POPULATION AGE BREAKDOWN

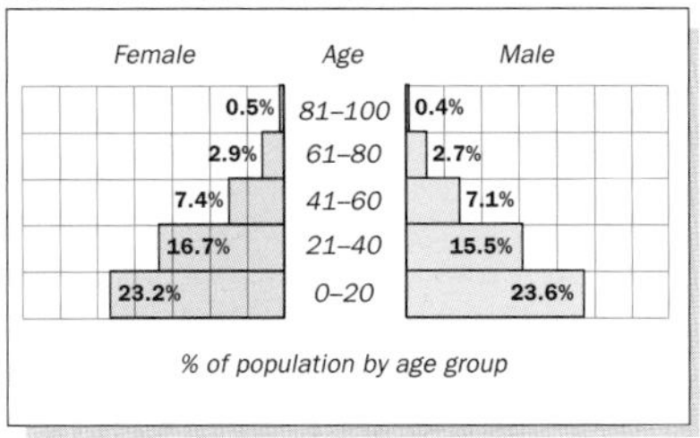
Female
Age
Male
0.5%
81–100
0.4%
2.9%
61–80
2.7%
7.4%
41–60
7.1%
16.7%
21–40
15.5%
23.2%
0–20
23.6%
% of population by age group

recently been seriously challenged. The 1994 Chiapas *Zapatista* EZLN guerrilla uprising was on behalf of Amerindian rights, and in protest against the poverty of landless Amerindians. In an unofficial EZLN plebiscite in 1999, up to three million Mexicans said that Amerindians should play an active part in the country's development and that their rights should be recognized in the constitution.

The small black community, which is concentrated along the eastern coast, is well integrated.

As in much of Latin America, men retain their dominance in business and relatively few women take part in the political process.

WORLD AFFAIRS

Joined UN in 1945

G15 | NAFTA | OECD | OAS | RG

NAFTA has effectively bound together the economies of Mexico and the USA, and has created complications in bilateral relations. Sectors of US business and trade unions are hostile to the agreement, since competitive Mexican imports have undercut some US farmers and manufacturers. Job losses have also occurred in the USA as multinationals have relocated south to benefit from lower Mexican labor rates. Large-scale illegal immigration from Mexico to the USA has led to tougher policing on the border. Another point of friction is the limited success of bilateral law enforcement, which has aided powerful Mexican narcotics cartels supplying the US market.

Mexico also seeks stronger trade links with MERCOSUR, the South American common market linking Argentina, Brazil, Paraguay, and Uruguay, and has signed free trade agreements with the EU and EFTA.

AID

Recipient

$34m (receipts)

Up 127% in 1999

Mexico receives modest aid. Some European and US NGOs provide assistance, particularly for literacy campaigns in poorer areas.

POLITICS

Multiparty elections

L. House 2000/2003
U. House 2000/2006

President Vicente Fox

AT THE LAST ELECTION

Chamber of Deputies 500 seats

45% PAN–PVEM
42% PRI
13% PRD–PT

PAN–PVEM = Alliance for Change (National Action Party and Green Party) **PRI** = Institutional Revolutionary Party **PRD–PT** = Alliance for Mexico (Party of the Democratic Revolution and Labor Party)

Senate 128 seats

45% PRI
42% PAN–PVEM
13% PRD–PT

Mexico was a multiparty democracy in name only until 1997, when reforms culminated in a PAN presidency in 2000.

Main Political Issues

President Fox's ability to govern

The opposition PRI still holds important congressional commissions. It will use these to frustrate the government's legislative program. President Vicente Fox is also at odds with his own PAN.

Chiapas peace

Fox quickly began to honor conditions set down by the *Zapatista* National Liberation Army (EZLN) for new peace talks, releasing some prisoners and withdrawing some troops from Chiapas. Opposition by the local PRI, the army, and paramilitaries in the state, and fiscal restraint will hinder needed economic and social reform.

Future of PRI

Since its defeat in the 2000 presidential elections, the PRI has been faction-ridden and rudderless. Its fragmentation is possible, despite its strength in the bicameral Congress and at state level.

Profile

The PRI dominated Mexico from 1929. Regional elections in the 1990s showed the strength of opposition parties, and after grudging electoral reform, the PRI lost its monopoly on power in 1997. President Fox's PAN became the largest party in the Chamber of Deputies in the 2000 elections, but it lacks an overall majority. Fox promised a broadly conceived "government of transition."

Vicente Fox, elected president in 2000, ending 70 years of PRI dominance.

***Sub-commander Marcos,** leader of the* Zapatista *National Liberation Army.*

CHRONOLOGY

The Aztec kingdom of Montezuma II was defeated in war by the Spaniard, Hernán Cortés, in 1521. By 1546, the Spaniards had discovered large silver mines at Zacatecas. Mexico, then known as New Spain, became a key part of the Spanish colonial empire.

- **1810** Fr. Miguel Hidalgo leads abortive rising against Spanish.
- **1821** Spanish viceroy forced to leave by Agustín de Iturbide.
- **1822** Federal Republic established.
- **1823** Texas opened to US immigration.
- **1829** Spanish military expedition fails to regain control.
- **1836** USA is first country to recognize Mexico's independence. Spain follows suit. Texas declares its independence from Mexico.
- **1846** War breaks out with USA.
- **1848** Loses modern-day New Mexico, Arizona, Nevada, Utah, California, and part of Colorado.
- **1858–1861** War of Reform won by anticlerical Liberals.
- **1862** France, Britain, and Spain launch military expedition.

M

CHRONOLOGY *continued*

- **1863** French troops capture Mexico City. Maximilian of Austria established as Mexican emperor.
- **1867** Mexico recaptured by Benito Juárez. Maximilian shot.
- **1876** Porfirio Díaz president. Economic growth; rail system built.
- **1901** First year of oil production.
- **1910–1920** Epic Revolution provoked by excessive exploitation by foreign companies and desire for land reform. 250,000 killed.
- **1911** Díaz overthrown by Francisco Madero. Guerrilla war breaks out in north. Emilio Zapata leads peasant revolt in the south.
- **1913** Madero murdered.
- **1917** New constitution limits power of Church. Minerals and subsoil rights reserved for the nation.
- **1926–1929** *Cristero* rebellion led by militant Catholic priests.
- **1929** National Revolutionary Party (later PRI) formed.
- **1934** General Cárdenas president. Land reform accelerated, cooperative farms established, railroads nationalized, and US and UK oil companies expelled.
- **1940s** US war effort helps Mexican economy to grow.
- **1970** Accelerating population growth reaches 3% a year.
- **1982** Mexico declares it cannot repay its foreign debt of over $800 billion. IMF insists on economic reforms to reschedule the debt.
- **1984** Government contravenes constitution by relaxing laws on foreign investment.
- **1985** Earthquake in Mexico City. Official death toll 7000. Economic cost estimated at $425 million.
- **1988** Carlos Salinas de Gortari, minister of planning during the earthquake, elected president.
- **1990** Privatization program begun.
- **1994–1995** Guerrilla rebellion in southern Chiapas state brutally suppressed by army. 100 dead. Mexico joins NAFTA. PRI presidential candidate Luis Colosio murdered. Ernesto Zedillo replaces him and is elected. Economic crisis.
- **1997** Watershed elections; end of PRI's monopoly on power in Congress.
- **1999** Austerity budget and controversial bail-out of the banking system approved with PAN support.
- **2000** July, PAN wins presidency and elections, ending 70 years of PRI rule. December, President Vicente Fox takes office.
- **2001** EZLN guerrillas and supporters make 16-day motorcade from Chiapas to Mexico City to push for an indigenous rights law.

DEFENSE

Compulsory military service

$4.29bn — Up 10% in 1999

Mexico has no ambitions beyond its borders, and the army acts to defend internal security. The military has, on the whole, avoided direct interference in politics. Most arms procurement is from the USA and France. In 1994, the role of controlling the border with the USA was passed to the police.

The *Zapatista* rebellion in Chiapas in 1994 elicited a brutal response from the army, acting on PRI orders. The increasing militarization of the state over the next six years hindered the peace process and led to a proliferation of paramilitaries, with the tacit blessing of the local PRI, who are blamed by human rights groups for the massacre of Amerindians. The PAN government has withdrawn some forces from key areas of the state.

MEXICAN ARMED FORCES

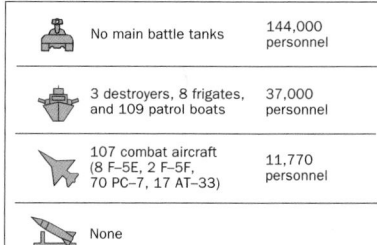

No main battle tanks	144,000 personnel
3 destroyers, 8 frigates, and 109 patrol boats	37,000 personnel
107 combat aircraft (8 F-5E, 2 F-5F, 70 PC-7, 17 AT-33)	11,770 personnel
None	

ECONOMICS

Inflation 19.5% p.a. (1990–1999)

$428.9bn — 9.480–9.609 Mexican pesos

SCORE CARD

World GNP Ranking	12th
GNP per Capita	$4440
Balance of Payments	$-14.02bn
Inflation	16.6%
Unemployment	2%

EXPORTS

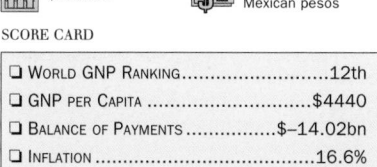

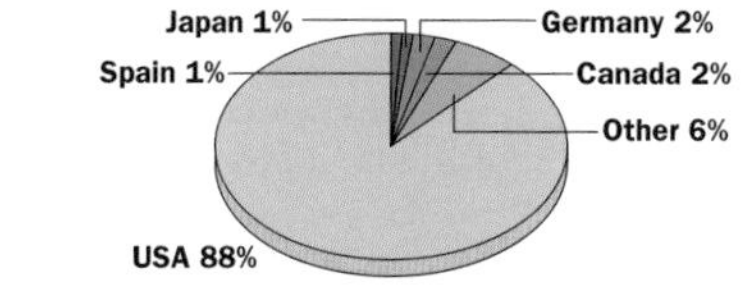
Japan 1%
Germany 2%
Spain 1%
Canada 2%
Other 6%
USA 88%

IMPORTS

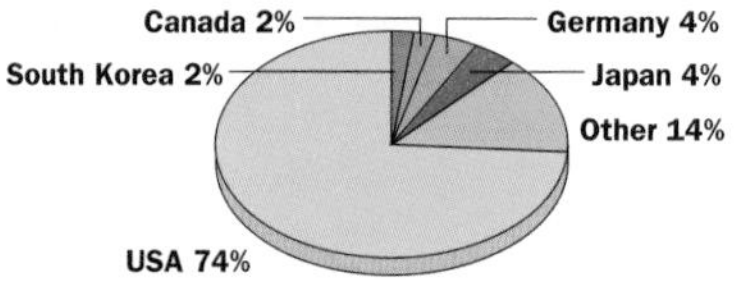
Canada 2%
Germany 4%
South Korea 2%
Japan 4%
Other 14%
USA 74%

Strengths
Global oil producer, with substantial reserves. Extensive mineral resources. Strong foreign direct investment. Diversification of exports. NAFTA membership. Low overheads.

Weaknesses
Debt burden. Vulnerable currency. Corruption. Affected by oil price changes and US slowdown. Weak tax system.

Profile
While in power, the PRI effectively ran the economy. The debt crisis of the 1980s, however, forced privatizations. The 1994 peso crisis needed a US-led $20 billion international bail-out and resulted in a severe slump. The Zedillo government launched tough reforms, but a global loss of confidence in "emerging markets" impacted growth.

ECONOMIC PERFORMANCE INDICATOR

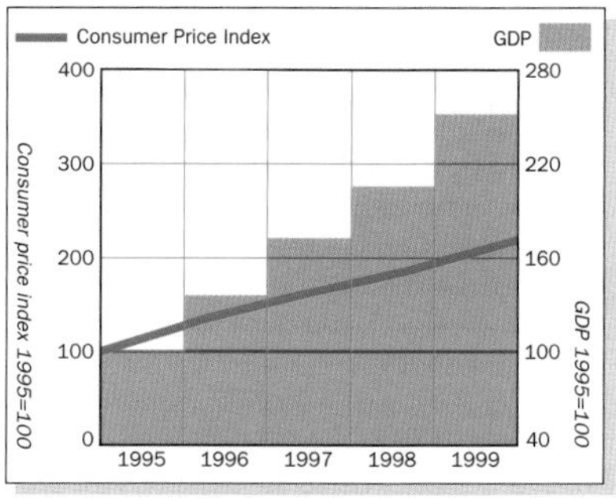
Consumer Price Index
GDP
Consumer price index 1995=100
GDP 1995=100
0
100
200
300
400
40
100
160
220
280
1995
1996
1997
1998
1999

Tighter fiscal management was rewarded by 2000, when investor confidence improved. The government and central bank have pledged to retain the tight fiscal and monetary stance, and tackle rampant tax evasion, but President Fox's election pledges to reduce poverty and tackle other social problems will place pressure on him to increase spending. Worries also remain about oil, which accounts for one-third of government revenues, the peso, and exports in the event of a US recession.

MEXICO : MAJOR BUSINESSES

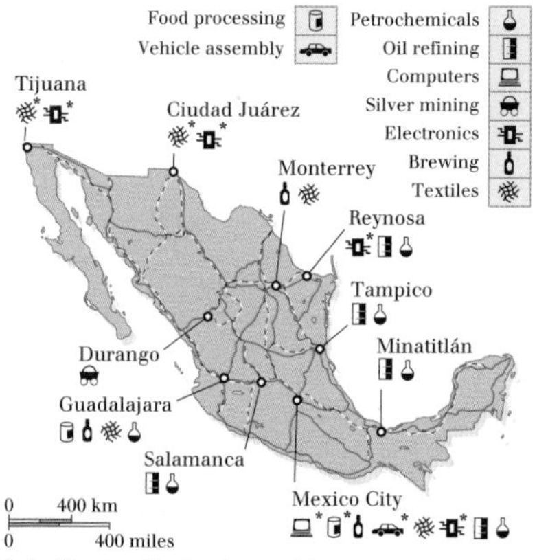
Food processing
Vehicle assembly
Petrochemicals
Oil refining
Computers
Silver mining
Electronics
Brewing
Textiles
Tijuana
Ciudad Juárez
Monterrey
Reynosa
Tampico
Durango
Minatitlán
Guadalajara
Salamanca
Mexico City
0 400 km
0 400 miles
* significant multinational ownership

RESOURCES

Electric power 46.3m kw

1.53m tonnes

3.5m b/d (reserves 28,300,000,000 bbl)

30.3m cattle, 13.7m pigs, 9.6m goats, 476m chickens

Oil, gas, gold, silver, copper, coal, fluorite, mercury, antimony

ELECTRICITY GENERATION

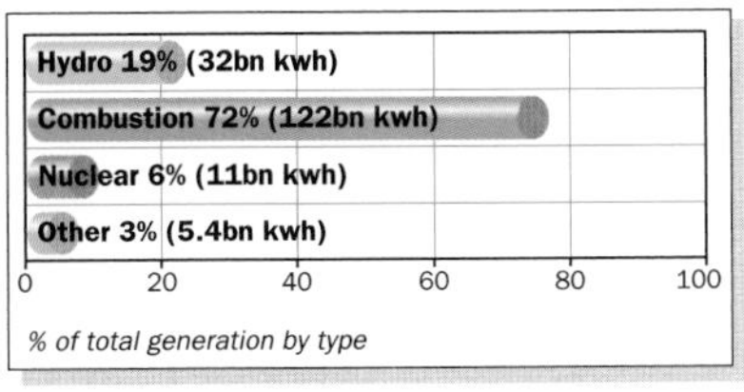
Hydro 19% (32bn kwh)
Combustion 72% (122bn kwh)
Nuclear 6% (11bn kwh)
Other 3% (5.4bn kwh)
0
20
40
60
80
100
% of total generation by type

MEXICO : LAND USE

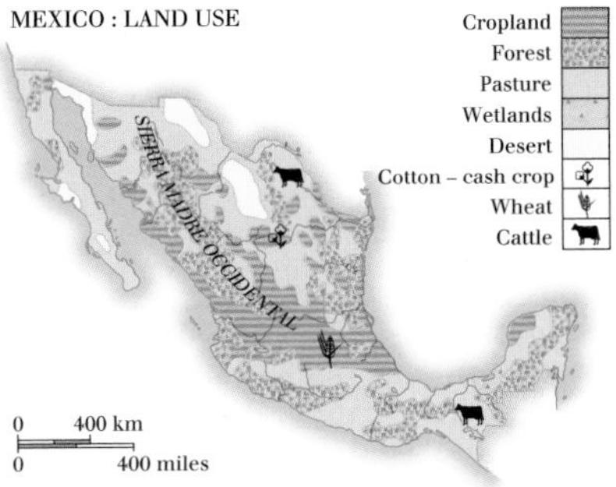
Cropland
Forest
Pasture
Wetlands
Desert
Cotton – cash crop
Wheat
Cattle
SIERRA MADRE OCCIDENTAL
0 400 km
0 400 miles

Mexico is one of the largest oil exporters outside the OPEC cartel. Most oil production comes from offshore drilling platforms in the Gulf of Mexico. The industry was state-owned and state-run by PEMEX, the world's fifth-largest oil company, employing 120,000 people. The decision to privatize petrochemical plants has provoked serious social unrest, and further sell-offs and deregulation remain politically highly sensitive. Despite its oil reserves, Mexico has embarked on a nuclear power program and projects to modernize the national electricity grid and boost natural gas production to overcome an energy crisis.

ENVIRONMENT

Sustainability rank: 73rd

4% (4% partially protected)

4 tonnes per capita

ENVIRONMENTAL TREATIES

Yes Yes Yes

Yes Yes Yes

The largely unplanned conurbation of Mexico City struggles to accommodate around 20 million inhabitants as the absence of environmental controls contributes to perhaps the world's worst air quality and waste problems. PEMEX (the state petroleum company) stands accused of massive pollution.

Maquiladoras – assembly plants on the Mexico–US border – have no effective environmental controls and are usually surrounded by insanitary slums. Environmentalists oppose the intense development of tourism along the coast.

MEDIA

TV ownership high

Daily newspaper circulation 97 per 1000 people

PUBLISHING AND BROADCAST MEDIA

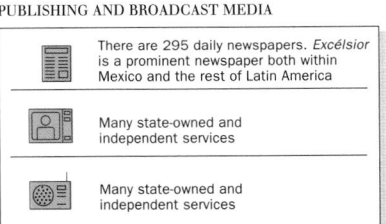

There are 295 daily newspapers. *Excélsior* is a prominent newspaper both within Mexico and the rest of Latin America

Many state-owned and independent services

Many state-owned and independent services

The PRI has historically manipulated the media, being accused in the 2000 elections of denying opponents airtime.

CRIME

Death penalty not used

83,520 prisoners

Little change from year to year

CRIME RATES

Mexico does not publish murder, theft, or rape statistics

Northern Mexico is a major center for narcotics shipments to the USA. Anti-drugs police are accused by the USA of corruption. Guns are rife and minor incidents may end in shootings. The high crime rate in Mexico City is a major political issue. Reforms of the corrupt judiciary and the whole police force are considered top priorities.

EDUCATION

School leaving age: 14

91%

1.6m students

THE EDUCATION SYSTEM

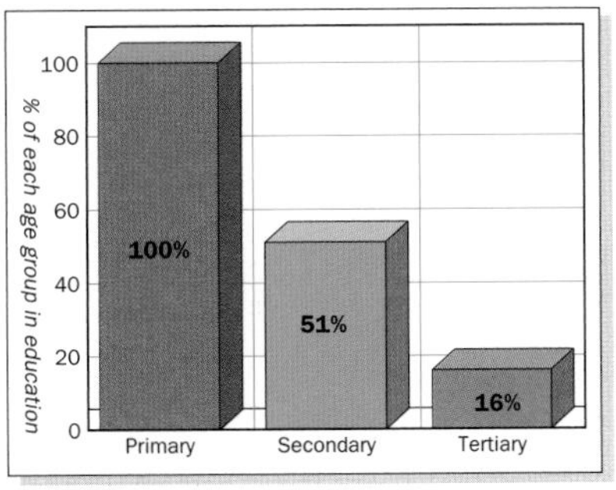
100
80
60
40
20
0
% of each age group in education
100%
51%
16%
Primary
Secondary
Tertiary

Public education, officially compulsory for the first six years, is underfunded and rural provision is poor. The system is a mixture of the French and US models. There is a well-developed public university system.

HEALTH

Welfare state health benefits

1 per 625 people

Heart disease, accidents, cancers, violence

The national health care system is basic and badly underfunded, although an ambitious scheme was launched in 1996 to improve access to health services in marginalized areas. Mexico has a good reputation for surgery and dentistry, but this is mostly in the private sector. The rich also go to the USA for treatment.

SPENDING

GDP/cap. increase

CONSUMPTION AND SPENDING

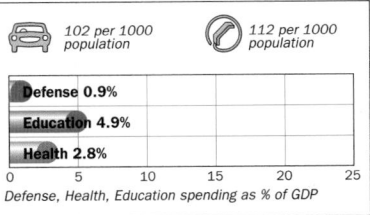

102 per 1000 population

112 per 1000 population

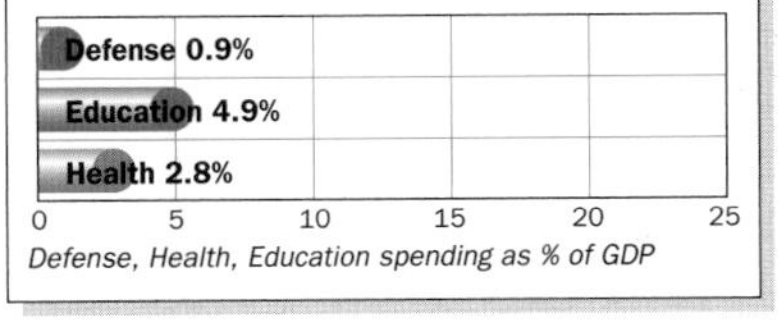
Defense 0.9%
Education 4.9%
Health 2.8%
0
5
10
15
20
25
Defense, Health, Education spending as % of GDP

Mexico has enormous wealth disparities, from the few dollar-billionaires to the 13% living in extreme poverty. There is little social mobility; the old Spanish families retain their hold on institutions. In the past, the wealthy did not generally pay taxes and often benefited from the large state machine. Tax evasion remains a serious problem.

Rural Amerindians are probably the most disadvantaged group. In the last decade, poverty has forced them into city slums to work in factories or *maquiladoras*, where conditions and pay are poor. Generally, real wages have fallen by 71% in the last ten years. The 1994 Chiapas rebellion was fed by demands for more land and more assistance in farming it. The flow of poor rural migrants to the USA stems largely from the need to subsidize families back home.

WORLD RANKING

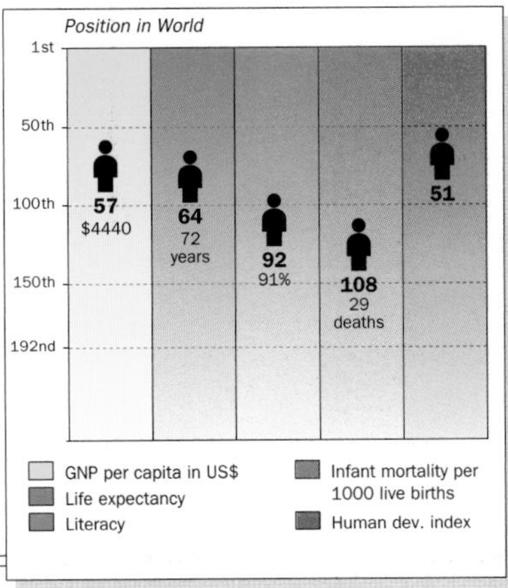
Position in World
1st
50th
100th
150th
192nd
57
$4440
64
72
years
92
91%
108
29
deaths
51
GNP per capita in US$
Life expectancy
Literacy
Infant mortality per 1000 live births
Human dev. index

M

MICRONESIA

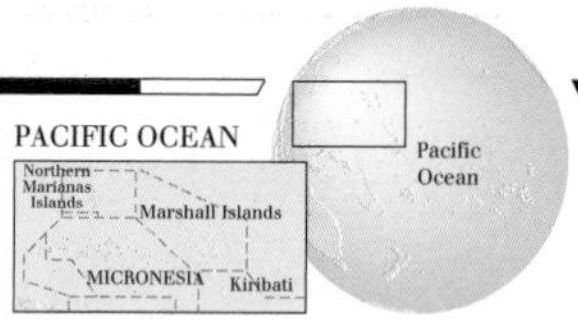
PACIFIC OCEAN
Pacific Ocean
Northern Marianas Islands
Marshall Islands
MICRONESIA
Kiribati

OFFICIAL NAME: Federated States of Micronesia **CAPITAL:** Palikir (Pohnpei Island)
POPULATION: 133,000 **CURRENCY:** US dollar **OFFICIAL LANGUAGE:** English

1986 | 1986 | May 10 | FSM | +10 to +11 | +691 | .fm

THE FEDERATED STATES of Micronesia (FSM), situated in the Pacific Ocean, encompasses all the Caroline Islands except Palau. It is composed of four island cluster states: Pohnpei, Kosrae, Chuuk, and Yap. The FSM was formerly under US rule as part of the UN Trust Territory of the Pacific Islands. An agreement which granted internal sovereignty in free association with the USA became operational in 1986, and the Trust was formally dissolved in 1990. The islands continue to receive considerable aid from the USA.

CLIMATE

Tropical oceanic

WEATHER CHART

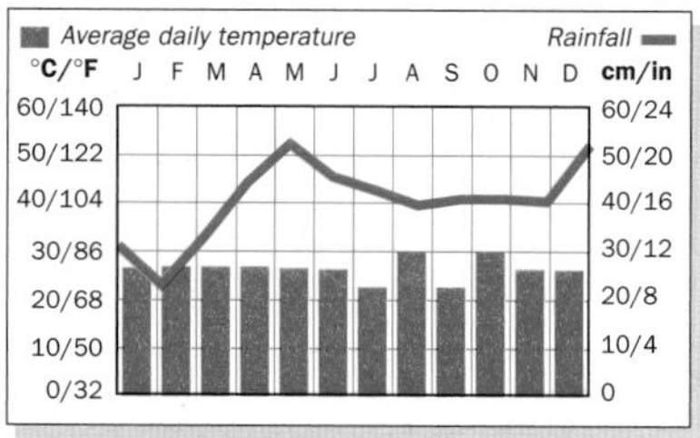
Average daily temperature
Rainfall
°C/°F
J F M A M J J A S O N D
cm/in
60/140
50/122
40/104
30/86
20/68
10/50
0/32
60/24
50/20
40/16
30/12
20/8
10/4
0

The islands are humid and fairly hot all year round, and the daily temperature range is small. Rainfall is abundant.

TRANSPORTATION

Drive on right

Pohnpei 44,834 passengers

19 ships 10,400 grt

THE TRANSPORTATION NETWORK

42 km (26 miles)

None

None

None

The inauguration in 2000 of flights by a Boeing 737 opened the way for greater air traffic between the islands. Shipping is mainly used for bulk cargoes and copra. Some island roads are surfaced with coral.

Micronesia, aerial view of rock islands. *Like many Pacific states, Micronesia fears rising sea levels as a result of global warming.*

TOURISM

Visitors : Population 1:6.7

20,000 visitors

Up 82% in 1994–1996

MAIN TOURIST ARRIVALS

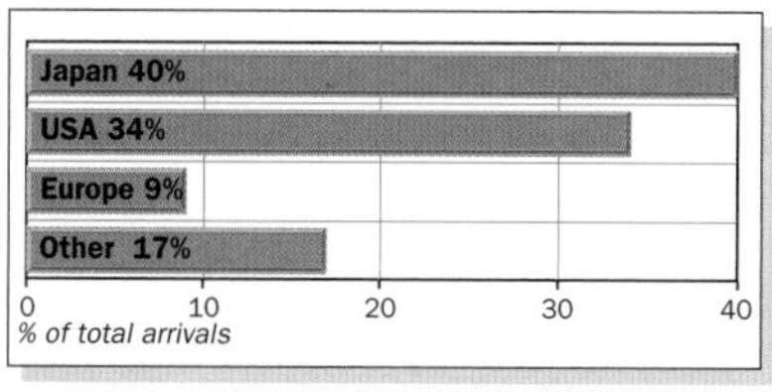
Japan 40%
USA 34%
Europe 9%
Other 17%
0
10
20
30
40
% of total arrivals

Outlying islands remain untouched and unspoiled. Chuuk's underwater war wreckage and Kosrae's beaches attract visitors. Lack of infrastructure tends to hinder the growth of tourism.

PEOPLE

Pop. density medium

Trukese, Pohnpeian, Mortlockese, Losrean, English

190/km² (491/mi²)

THE URBAN/RURAL POPULATION SPLIT

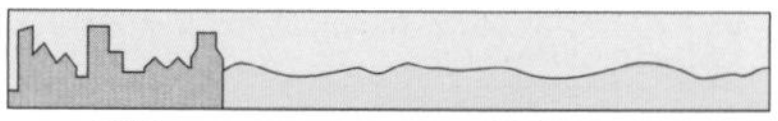
28%
72%

RELIGIOUS PERSUASION

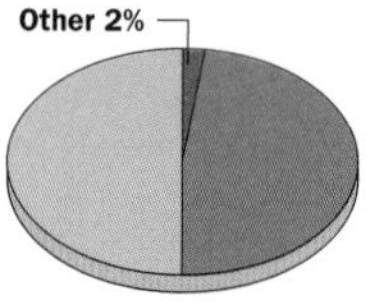
Other 2%
Roman Catholic 50%
Protestant 48%

The Micronesians are physically, linguistically, and culturally diverse. Melanesians live on Yap, and Polynesians occupy southwestern atolls in Pohnpei state. Most islanders live without electricity or running water, and many are effectively recipients of US welfare. Society is traditionally matrilineal.

POLITICS

Multiparty elections

2001/2003

President Leo Falcam

AT THE LAST ELECTION

Congress 14 seats

There are no political parties. Congress has 14 members, 10 senators directly elected for a two-year term and four "at-large" senators (one from each state) who are elected for a four-year term

Under the federal structure, the president and vice president are elected from among the four "at-large" senators (one from each state) by the federal legislature. However, the power of the traditional chiefs in politics remains very strong. Increasing Micronesia's economic independence is the key political issue and it dominated negotiations throughout 2000 and 2001 on the outline of the next Compact of Free Association with the USA.

MICRONESIA

Total Land Area : 702 sq. km (271 sq. miles)

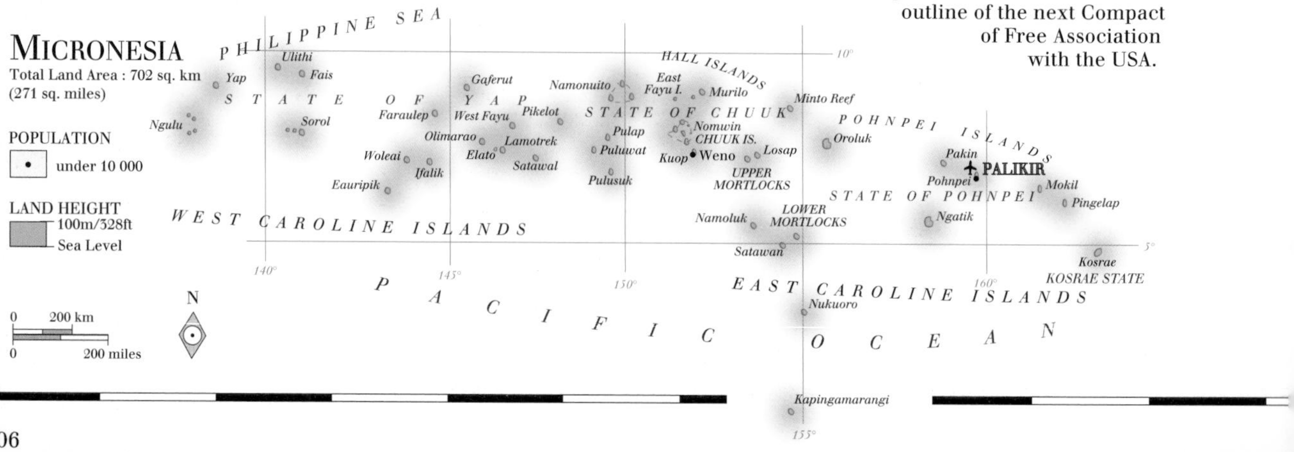
POPULATION
under 10 000
LAND HEIGHT
100m/328ft
Sea Level
0 200 km
0 200 miles
N
PHILIPPINE SEA
Ulithi
Fais
Yap
STATE OF YAP
Ngulu
Sorol
Gaferut
Faraulep
West Fayu
Pikelot
Olimarao
Lamotrek
Elato
Satawal
Woleai
Ifalik
Eauripik
Namonuito
East Fayu I.
Murilo
HALL ISLANDS
STATE OF CHUUK
Pulap
Puluwat
Pulusuk
Nomwin
CHUUK IS.
Kuop
Weno
Losap
UPPER MORTLOCKS
LOWER MORTLOCKS
Namoluk
Satawan
Minto Reef
POHNPEI ISLANDS
Oroluk
Pakin
PALIKIR
Pohnpei
Mokil
Pingelap
STATE OF POHNPEI
Ngatik
Kosrae
KOSRAE STATE
WEST CAROLINE ISLANDS
EAST CAROLINE ISLANDS
Nukuoro
Kapingamarangi
PACIFIC OCEAN
10°
5°
140°
145°
150°
155°
160°

WORLD AFFAIRS

Joined UN in 1991

ADB | PIF | ACP | PC | IBRD

Micronesia's most important relationship is with the USA, which administered the islands from 1947 as part of the UN Trust Territory of the Pacific Islands. Under the Compact of Free Association, the USA has exclusive control over the FSM's foreign and defense policies. Alternative funds were sought to compensate for the reduction in annual aid under the Compact with the USA after 2001. Japan is also important, with the Tokyo government providing aid, and the FSM has recently cultivated strong links with China.

AID

Recipient

$108m (receipts)

Up 35% in 1999

The USA is the principal donor of aid, which funds hospitals, schools, food stamps, and construction projects.

DEFENSE

No compulsory military service

USA is responsible for defense

Not applicable

Defense is entirely in the hands of the USA. Airstrips in the FSM were used by the USA in the Vietnam War.

ECONOMICS

Inflation 3.5% p.a. (1990–1999)

$212m

Currency is US dollar

SCORE CARD

- ❑ WORLD GNP RANKING........................180th
- ❑ GNP PER CAPITA............................$1830
- ❑ BALANCE OF PAYMENTS.......................$15m
- ❑ INFLATION...................................3%
- ❑ UNEMPLOYMENT................................8%

STRENGTHS

Access to US economy, especially for garment manufacture through preferential trading rights. Construction industry is the largest private-sector activity. Tourism, fishing, and copra production. US strategic interest in Micronesia, and US budget subsidies.

WEAKNESSES

Dependence on USA for imports, especially for fuel. Heavy indebtedness. Acute shortage of water limits development potential. High levels of underemployment.

EXPORTS

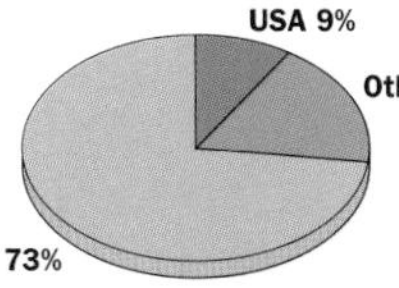
USA 9%
Other 18%
Japan 73%

IMPORTS

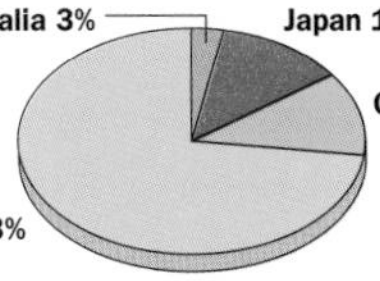
Australia 3%
Japan 12%
Other 12%
USA 73%

RESOURCES

Not available

9428 tonnes

Not an oil producer

32,000 pigs, 13,900 cattle, 4000 goats, 185,000 chickens

None

The FSM is entirely dependent on external sources for its energy supply. Almost all electricity is produced by small diesel generators. The main resources are copra and valuable fish stocks, especially tuna.

ENVIRONMENT

Not available

None

Not available

The FSM does not face pollution on the scale of that in the neighboring Marshall Islands. However, Chuuk suffers serious droughts; occasionally water rationing has had to be introduced for short periods. The growth of marine-based tourism is monitored by the South Pacific Environment Program, which aims to promote sustainable development.

MEDIA

TV ownership medium

There are no daily newspapers

PUBLISHING AND BROADCAST MEDIA

There are no daily newspapers. *The National Union* is a popular fortnightly

4 services: 1 state-owned, 3 independent

1 state-owned service

Press freedoms have not been infringed since the strongly criticized expulsion of a Canadian journalist in 1997.

CRIME

Death penalty not used

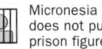

Micronesia does not publish prison figures

Little change from year to year

Crime is rare and the outlying islands are crime-free. Some alcohol-related assault occurs on Chuuk.

EDUCATION

School leaving age: 14

89%

1461 students

Education is compulsory between the ages of six and 14 years. Most university students are supported by US grants and a large number attend US colleges.

CHRONOLOGY

The Caroline Islands were first colonized by the Spanish. Sold to Germany in 1899, the islands were occupied by Japan from 1914 and served as an important base in World War II. US control of the islands began in 1945.

- ❑ **1947** UN Trust Territory of the Pacific Islands established.
- ❑ **1979** Becomes independent.
- ❑ **1986** Compact of Free Association with USA operational.
- ❑ **1990** Official termination of trusteeship agreement.
- ❑ **1991** Joins UN.
- ❑ **1995** President Bailey Olter reelected.
- ❑ **1997** Jacob Nena formally succeeds Olter as president after the latter is incapacitated by a stroke.

HEALTH

Welfare state health benefits

1 per 2311 people

Heart, cerebrovascular, and intestinal diseases

Basic health care is accessible to all. Diabetes and drug abuse are growing problems. An increase in imported food has led to dietary problems.

SPENDING

Not available

CONSUMPTION AND SPENDING

No data

80 per 1000 population

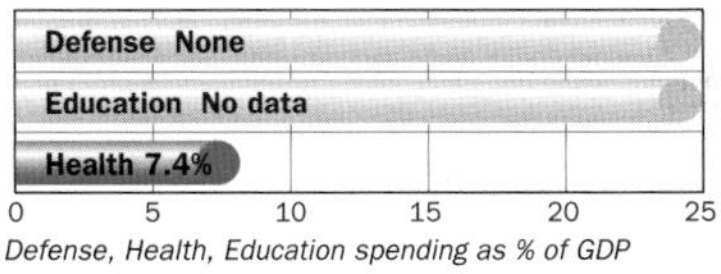
Defense None
Education No data
Health 7.4%
0
5
10
15
20
25
Defense, Health, Education spending as % of GDP

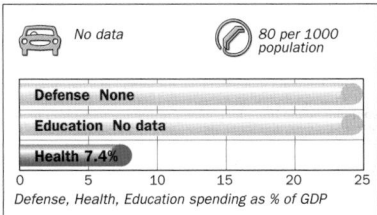

The gap between rich and poor is increasing as Micronesia's businessmen and local officials exploit US aid donations.

WORLD RANKING

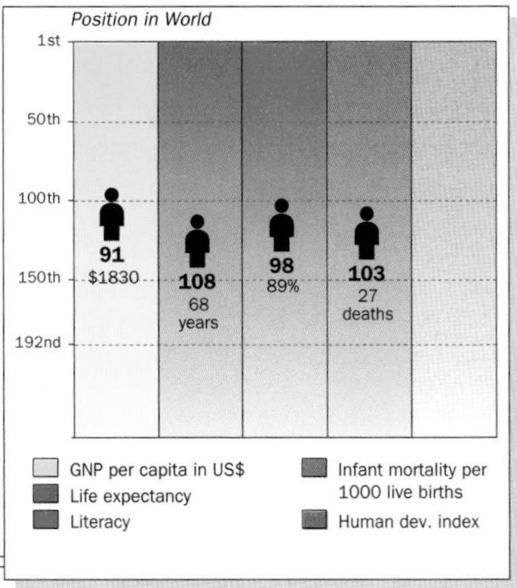
Position in World
1st
50th
100th
150th
192nd
91
$1830
108
68 years
98
89%
103
27 deaths
GNP per capita in US$
Life expectancy
Literacy
Infant mortality per 1000 live births
Human dev. index

M

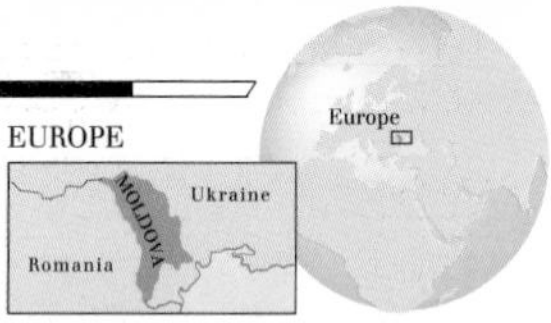
EUROPE
Europe
MOLDOVA
Ukraine
Romania

MOLDOVA

OFFICIAL NAME: Republic of Moldova **CAPITAL:** Chişinău
POPULATION: 4.4 million **CURRENCY:** Leu **OFFICIAL LANGUAGE:** Romanian

1991 | 1991 | Aug 27 | MD | +2 | +373 | .md

MOSTLY UNDULATING steppe country, Moldova is the smallest and most densely populated of the former Soviet republics. Once a part of Romania, it was incorporated into the Soviet Union in 1940. Independence in 1991 brought with it the expectation that Moldova would be reunited with Romania. In a 1994 plebiscite, however, Moldovans voted against the proposal. Most of its population is engaged in intensive agriculture.

Agricultural landscape. *Warm summers and even rainfall are ideal for cereal and fruit farming. Moldova is famous for its wine.*

CLIMATE

Continental

WEATHER CHART

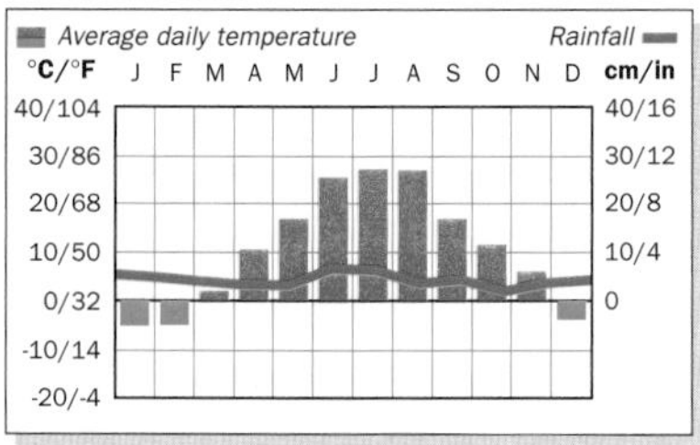
Average daily temperature
Rainfall
°C/°F
J F M A M J J A S O N D
cm/in
40/104
30/86
20/68
10/50
0/32
-10/14
-20/-4
40/16
30/12
20/8
10/4
0

Warm summers, mild winters, and moderate rainfall give Moldova an ideal climate for cultivation.

TRANSPORTATION

Drive on right

Chişinău International 233,269 passengers

Small Black Sea fleet

THE TRANSPORTATION NETWORK

10,738 km (6672 miles)

None

1140 km (708 miles)

424 km (263 miles)

"Transport Corridor Europe–Caucasus–Asia" (TRAGECA) is planned. Railroads and roads have deteriorated.

TOURISM

Visitors : Population 1:259

17,000 visitors

Up 21% in 2000

MAIN TOURIST ARRIVALS

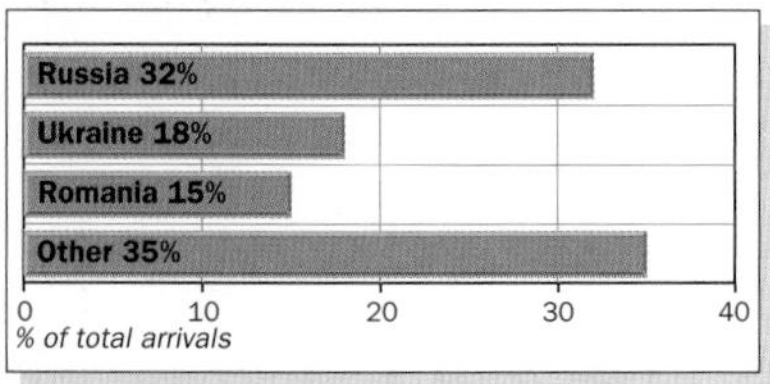
Russia 32%
Ukraine 18%
Romania 15%
Other 35%
0
10
20
30
40
% of total arrivals

Few tourists go to Moldova, although some visitors to Romania do combine the two. Hopes for expansion of tourism focus on vineyards and underground wine vault "streets" as the main attractions.

PEOPLE

Pop. density medium

Moldovan, Romanian, Russian

131/km² (338/mi²)

THE URBAN/RURAL POPULATION SPLIT

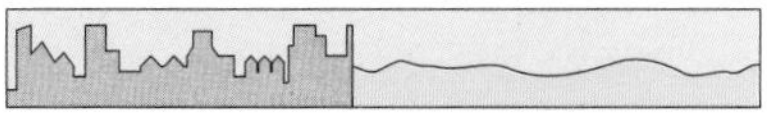
46%
54%

ETHNIC MAKEUP

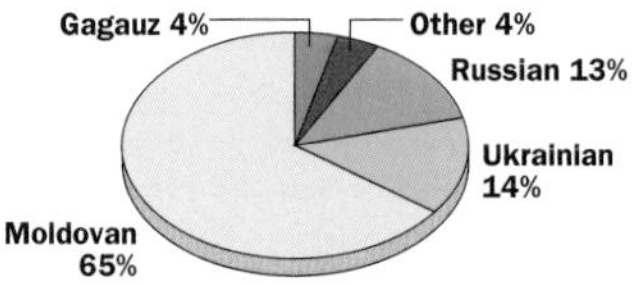
Gagauz 4%
Other 4%
Russian 13%
Ukrainian 14%
Moldovan 65%

Moldovans are ethnically identical to Romanians. There are 153,000 Gagauz (Orthodox Christian Turks) in the south, and a population of mixed Russian–Moldovan–Ukrainian parentage on the eastern bank of the Dniester.

POLITICS

Multiparty elections

2001/2005

President Vladimir Voronin

AT THE LAST ELECTION

Parliament 101 seats

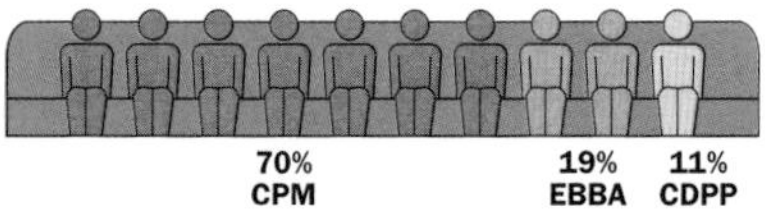
70% CPM
19% EBBA
11% CDPP

CPM = Communist Party of Moldova
EBBA = Electoral Bloc Braghis Alliance
CDPP = Christian-Democratic People's Party

Moldova declared its independence from the Soviet Union in 1991.

Petru Lucinschi, a centrist favoring a free-market economy, won presidential elections in late 1996. His government was hampered by the strength of the left in Parliament, especially after 1998 when the revived CPM won most seats. In 2000 Parliament voted to end direct presidential elections, but then became deadlocked over the election of a successor to Lucinschi. This forced fresh legislative elections in 2001, which gave the CPM an overwhelming majority, and two months later the Parliament chose CPM leader Vladimir Voronin as the new president.

Transdniestria (on the eastern bank of the river Dniester) and Gagauzia (in the south) declared themselves as republics in 1990. While Gagauzia accepted autonomous status as provided for in the 1994 constitution, Transdniestria still seeks independence.

UKRAINE
ROMANIA
Edineț
Soroca
Rîşcani
Drochia
Florești
Dniester
Rezina
Ribnița
Bălți
Sîngerei
Prut
Răutel
Fălești
Dubăsari Reservoir
Orhei
Călărași
Dubăsari
Ungheny
429m
Strășeni
Nisporeni
CHIȘINĂU
Bîc
Tiraspol
Hîncești
Tighina
Slobozia
Cogîlnic
Leova
Cimișlia
Căușeni
Basarabeasca
Comrat
Ialpug
Ciadîr-Lunga
Taraclia
Cahul
Vulcănești
48°
46°
28°
N
0 50 km
0 50 miles

MOLDOVA

Total Land Area : 33 700 sq. km (13 000 sq. miles)

POPULATION

- over 500 000
- over 100 000
- over 50 000
- over 10 000
- under 10 000

LAND HEIGHT

200m/656ft
80m/262ft

M

WORLD AFFAIRS

Joined UN in 1992

BSEC | CE | CIS | EAPC | OSCE

Moldova has not sought NATO membership, and in 2001 showed interest in joining a Union State with Russia and Belarus. Ties with countries in the Black Sea Economic Zone, including Romania and Ukraine, are being developed. The creation of a free economic zone near the mouth of the Danube is under discussion.

AID

Recipient

$102m (receipts) — Up 200% in 1999

IMF and World Bank support resumed in early 1999. The EU, Romania, Turkey, and Bulgaria are also important sources of aid.

DEFENSE

Compulsory miltary service

$6m — Down 89% in 1999

Under a 1999 accord Russian forces in Transdniestria are to be withdrawn by end-2005. In 1999 plans were announced to cut army personnel by 30%. Military service was cut from 18 to 12 months.

ECONOMICS

Inflation 142.1% p.a. (1990–1999)

$1.5bn — 11.666–12.395 lei

SCORE CARD

❑ World GNP Ranking	146th
❑ GNP per Capita	$410
❑ Balance of Payments	$-33m
❑ Inflation	38%
❑ Unemployment	2%

Strengths

Agriculture – notably wine, tobacco, and cotton – and food processing. Light manufacturing.

Weaknesses

Dependent on Russia as source of raw materials and fuel, and main market for exports. Dramatic shrinking of economy since independence. Isolated location; weak transportation network. Slow pace of reform. Cumbersome bureaucracy. Strong black economy. Foreign debt – over 50% of GDP – costs 20% of export earnings to service.

EXPORTS

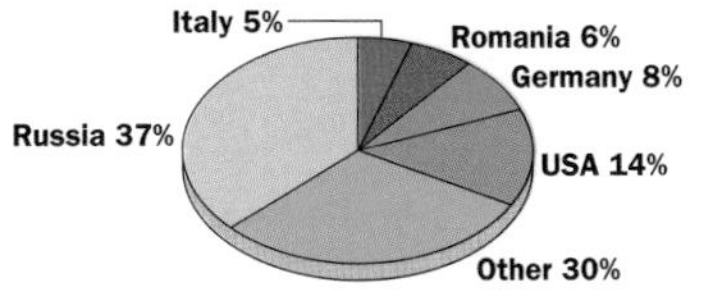
Italy 5%
Romania 6%
Germany 8%
Russia 37%
USA 14%
Other 30%

IMPORTS

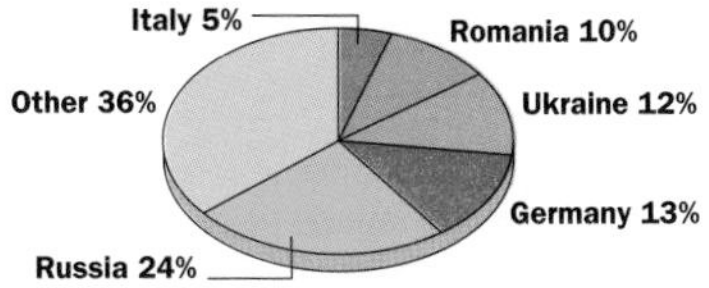
Italy 5%
Romania 10%
Other 36%
Ukraine 12%
Germany 13%
Russia 24%

RESOURCES

Electric power 1m kw

1272 tonnes

Oil and gas reserves not exploited

974,000 sheep, 705,000 pigs, 13.5m chickens

Lignite, phosphates, gypsum, oil, natural gas

Moldova has few mineral resources. It has to import all its fuel and most of its electricity.

ENVIRONMENT

Sustainability rank: 59th

1% — 2.4 tonnes per capita

Overuse of agricultural chemicals and pesticides on tobacco farms is a problem, as is soil erosion. There is little spending on environmental improvement.

MEDIA

TV ownership high

Daily newspaper circulation 60 per 1000 people

PUBLISHING AND BROADCAST MEDIA

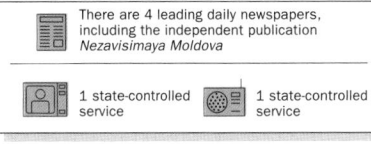

There are 4 leading daily newspapers, including the independent publication *Nezavisimaya Moldova*

1 state-controlled service — 1 state-controlled service

The many new publications represent widely differing interest groups. Russian-language broadcasting is restricted.

CRIME

Death penalty not used

10,363 prisoners — Up 5% 1996–1998

Crime rates have risen as the economic situation has deteriorated. The unstable situation in Transdniestria has meant that crime, including smuggling of Russian arms, has been able to spread to neighboring regions.

EDUCATION

School leaving age: 17

99% — 93,759 students

Since 1990 moves have been made to switch from a Soviet to a Romanian (French-inspired) system. Engineering is the largest university faculty.

HEALTH

Welfare state health benefits

1 per 278 people — Circulatory diseases, cancers, accidents

The centralized health service is poor by regional standards. There are serious shortages of medical supplies.

CHRONOLOGY

Modern Moldova corresponds roughly to the eastern part of the Romanian principality of Moldavia, which existed for 500 years from 1359. Most of it was annexed by Russia in 1812 as Bessarabia.

- ❑ **1918** Bessarabia joins Romania.
- ❑ **1924** Moldovan Autonomous Soviet Republic formed within USSR.
- ❑ **1940** Romania cedes Bessarabia to Ukrainian and Moldovan SSRs.
- ❑ **1941–1945** Bessarabia again under Romanian control.
- ❑ **1945** Returns to Soviet control.
- ❑ **1990** Declares sovereignty.
- ❑ **1991** Independence.
- ❑ **1993–1994** Pro-unification parties' election defeat; referendum rejects Romanian unification. Rejoins CIS.
- ❑ **1996** Lucinschi elected president.
- ❑ **1998** Communist revival at general election.
- ❑ **2001** CPM wins big majority. Voronin becomes president.

SPENDING

GDP/cap. decrease

CONSUMPTION AND SPENDING

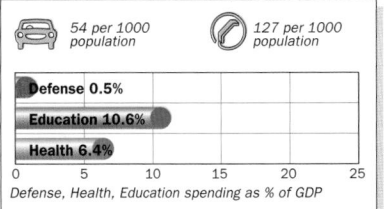

54 per 1000 population — *127 per 1000 population*

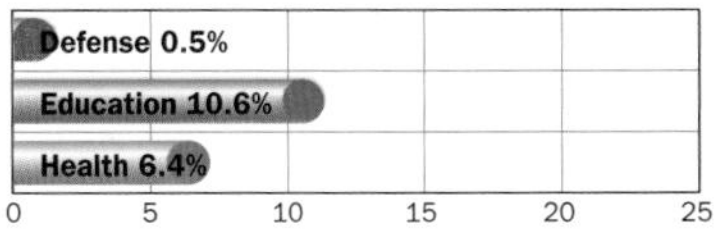
Defense 0.5%
Education 10.6%
Health 6.4%
0
5
10
15
20
25

Defense, Health, Education spending as % of GDP

Former communist officials have been well placed to benefit from the sale of state-owned businesses. Car ownership is low but rising. However, pensions and wages are often months in arrears. In 1998 the benefits for low-income families and veterans were scrapped. Ethnic Gagauz (Orthodox Christian Turks) are the poorest group.

WORLD RANKING

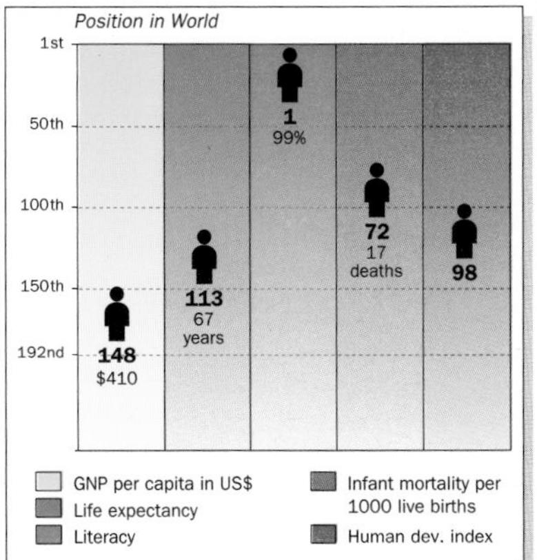
Position in World
1st
50th
100th
150th
192nd
148
$410
113
67
years
1
99%
72
17
deaths
98
GNP per capita in US$
Life expectancy
Literacy
Infant mortality per 1000 live births
Human dev. index

M

MONACO

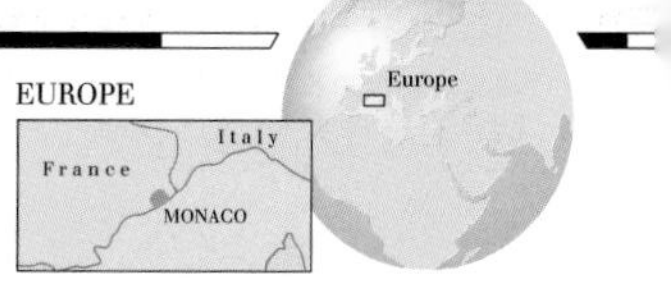
EUROPE
Europe
Italy
France
MONACO

OFFICIAL NAME: Principality of Monaco **CAPITAL:** Monaco **POPULATION:** 32,000
CURRENCY: Euro (French franc until 2002) **OFFICIAL LANGUAGE:** French

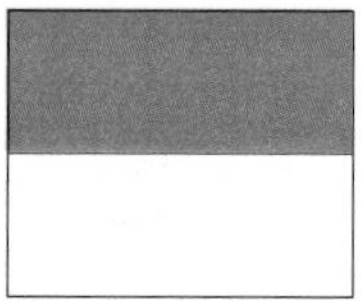

1861 | 1861 | Nov 19 | MC | +1 | +377 | .mc

MONACO IS A TINY ENCLAVE on the Côte d'Azur in southeastern France. Its destiny changed radically in 1863, when Prince Charles III, after whom Monte Carlo is named, opened the casino. Today, Monaco is a lucrative banking and services center, as well as a tourist destination. Prince Rainier's marriage to film star Grace Kelly, and some astute management of the economy, successfully transformed Monaco into a center for the international jet set. In 1962, the prince's absolute authority was abolished by a new, democratic constitution.

CLIMATE

Mediterranean

WEATHER CHART

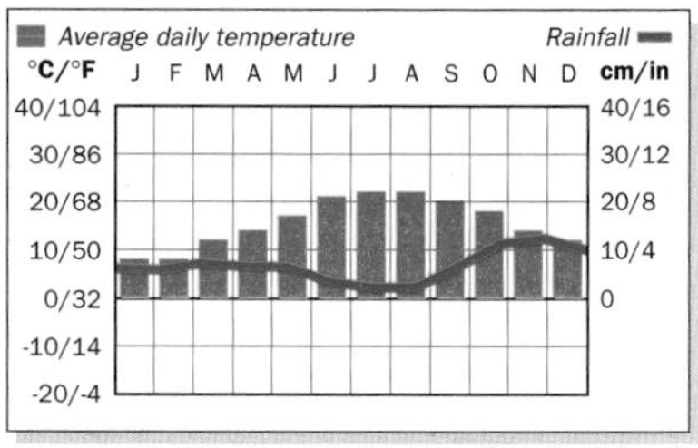
Average daily temperature
Rainfall
°C/°F J F M A M J J A S O N D cm/in
40/104
30/86
20/68
10/50
0/32
-10/14
-20/-4
40/16
30/12
20/8
10/4
0

Summers are hot and dry; days with 12 hours of sunshine are not uncommon. Winters are mild and sunny.

TRANSPORTATION

Drive on right

Héliport de Monaco, Fontvieille 141,932 passengers

8 ships

THE TRANSPORTATION NETWORK

50 km (31 miles)

None

2 km (1 mile)

None

A new underground railroad system connecting to Cap d'Ail in France was opened in 1999 and increased the principality's area by 2%. Work has begun on a FFr 1.8 billion floating jetty extension on the west side of Condamine port.

TOURISM

Visitors : Population 9.5:1

300,000 visitors

Up 8% in 2000

MAIN TOURIST ARRIVALS

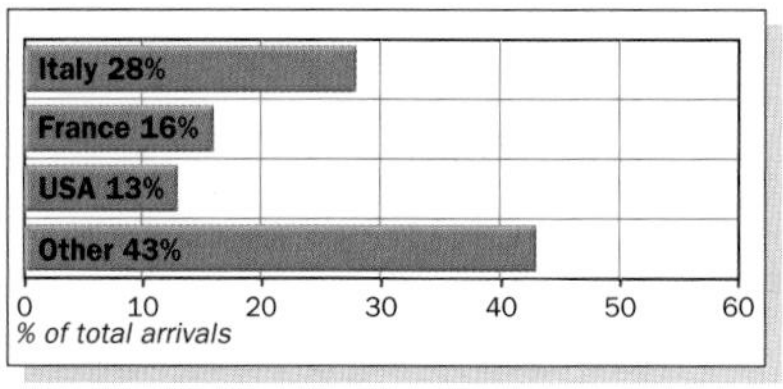
Italy 28%
France 16%
USA 13%
Other 43%
0 10 20 30 40 50 60
% of total arrivals

Huge numbers of tourists, greatly outnumbering the inhabitants, are attracted to Monaco, most coming from France and Italy. Almost all are day-trippers drawn by the casinos and Monaco's conspicuous high society. Around 75% of hotel rooms are classed as "four-star deluxe," and the principality is a particular favorite of wealthy Italians. The Grimaldi Forum conference center, which opened in 2000, hopes to attract more business travelers.

A number of social and sporting events draw particularly large crowds each spring, including the Rose Ball (March), the Tennis Open (April), and the Grand Prix (May).

PEOPLE

Pop. density high

French, Italian, Monégasque, English

16,253/km² (42,095/mi²)

THE URBAN/RURAL POPULATION SPLIT

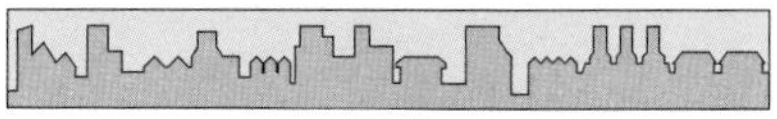
100%

RELIGIOUS PERSUASION

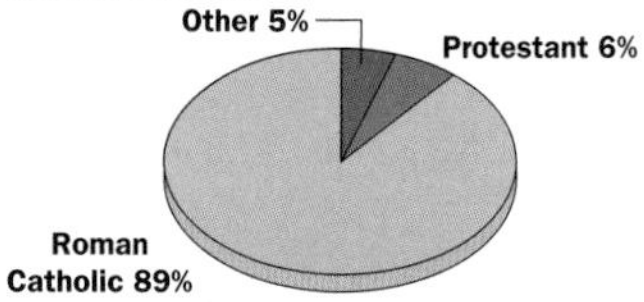
Other 5%
Protestant 6%
Roman Catholic 89%

Less than a fifth of Monaco's residents are Monégasque. Around half are French, the rest Italian, American, British, and Belgian. Monégasques enjoy considerable privileges, including housing subsidies to protect them from Monaco's high property prices, and the right of first refusal before a job can be offered to a foreigner. Women have equal status, but only acquired the vote in the constitutional changes of 1962.

POLITICS

Multiparty elections

1998/2003

HSH Prince Rainier III

AT THE LAST ELECTION

National Council 18 seats

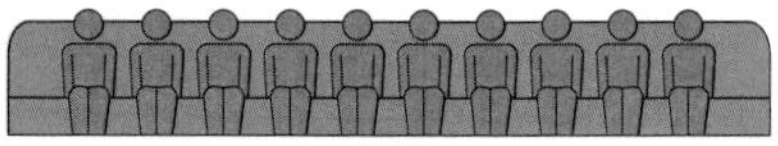
100%
NDU

NDU = National and Democratic Union
There are no formal political parties

The Grimaldi princes have been hereditary rulers of Monaco for more than 700 years. Prince Rainier III renounced absolute rule in 1962 but retains considerable power. The executive minister of state is appointed by the Prince from a list of French diplomats. National Council elections – based on personalities rather than parties – were last held in 1998.

WORLD AFFAIRS

Joined UN in 1993

FZ | IAEA | OSCE | OIF

A key concern is to protect both banking secrecy and the liberal tax regime from EU regulation, though the principality did introduce the euro in 1999. France is particularly critical, and French citizens have been banned from banking in Monaco since 1962.

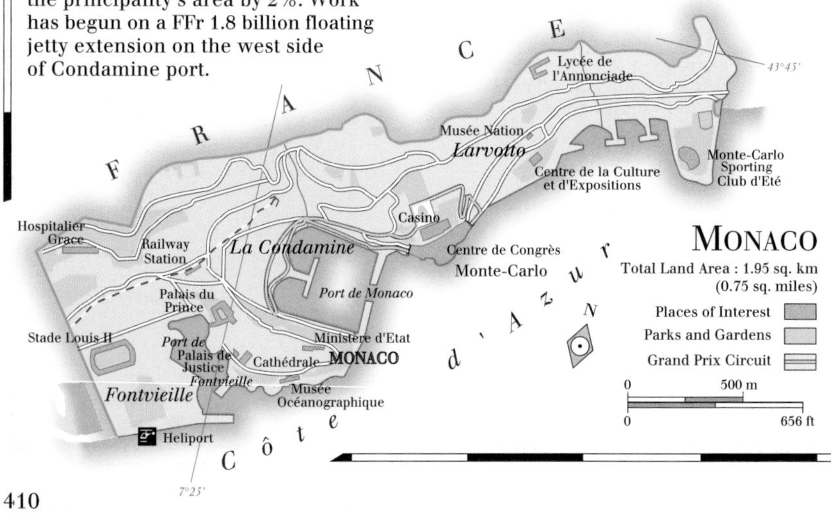
F R A N C E
Lycée de l'Annonciade
43°45'
Musée National
Larvotto
Monte-Carlo Sporting Club d'Eté
Centre de la Culture et d'Expositions
Casino
Hospitalier Grace
Railway Station
La Condamine
Centre de Congrès Monte-Carlo
Port de Monaco
Palais du Prince
Stade Louis II
Port de Fontvieille
Palais de Justice
Ministère d'Etat
Cathédrale
MONACO
Musée Océanographique
Fontvieille
Heliport
Côte d'Azur
N
7°25'
MONACO
Total Land Area : 1.95 sq. km (0.75 sq. miles)
Places of Interest
Parks and Gardens
Grand Prix Circuit
0 500 m
0 656 ft

M

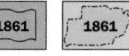

Monte Carlo with its luxury hotels and yacht harbor. The only space for new development is on land reclaimed from the sea.

AID

Not applicable

Monaco has no aid receipts or donations

Not applicable

Monaco neither receives nor gives aid, and the issue is not of concern to Monégasques.

DEFENSE

No compulsory military service

France responsible for defense

Not applicable

Monaco has no armed forces and no defense budget. France, as the protecting power, bears responsibility for the defense of the principality.

ECONOMICS

Inflation 2.6% p.a. (1985–1996)

$4.9bn

6.544–6.987 French francs

SCORE CARD

❑ WORLD GNP RANKING	112th
❑ GNP PER CAPITA	$11,000
❑ BALANCE OF PAYMENTS	Included in French total
❑ INFLATION	Included in French total
❑ UNEMPLOYMENT	3%

STRENGTHS

Strict banking confidentiality and low taxes attract billions of dollars of overseas deposits. Strong tourism sector. Assets managed by Monaco banks increased by 18% a year in the late 1990s. No formal debt and reserves of over FFr 15 billion. Very low unemployment.

WEAKNESSES

Continuing vulnerability to money-laundering despite revised banking secrecy laws under the 1994 accord with France obliging banks to furnish details of suspicious accounts. Subject to fluctuations of French and Italian economies. Dependence on VAT for 55% of revenues. Pressure from EU states to end privileged banking and tax laws. Total dependence on imports because of lack of natural resources.

EXPORTS/IMPORTS

Monaco has a full customs union with France.

RESOURCES

Electric power: Included in French total

4 tonnes

Not an oil producer

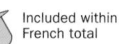

Included within French total

None

Monaco has no strategic resources and imports all its energy from France. It has no agricultural land.

ENVIRONMENT

Not available

None

4.4 tonnes per capita

Monaco has built the most extensive underground car parking facilities in the world to tackle congestion. The quality of the built environment around the harbor occasionally arouses local passions. Important populations of red coral are under threat from land reclamation and pollution.

MEDIA

TV ownership high

Daily newspaper circulation 251 per 1000 people

PUBLISHING AND BROADCAST MEDIA

There is 1 daily newspaper. *Nice-Matin*, a regional French newspaper, publishes a Monaco edition

2 services

4 services: 1 part-owned by French state, 3 independent

In addition to its domestic radio and TV, Monaco receives all the mainstream French and Italian channels.

CRIME

Death penalty not used

Monaco does not publish prison figures

Down 11% 1996–1998

Low crime rates make it safe for the rich to sport their furs and jewelry in public. In late 1998 the appeals court upheld Monaco's first conviction of an individual for money laundering.

EDUCATION

School leaving age: 16

99%

Not available

The education system is essentially the same as that of France, with students studying for the *baccalauréat* exam. Most go on to university in France, but then return to claim good jobs in Monaco. The Catholic Church exerts considerable influence and is still responsible for primary schooling.

HEALTH

Welfare state health benefits

1 per 333 people

Heart and cerebrovascular diseases, cancers

Most medical care is provided by private health insurance. Doctors train in France. The Princess Grace Hospital can serve 60,000 people, also catering for patients from outside Monaco.

CHRONOLOGY

In 1297, the Grimaldis established themselves as the principality's hereditary rulers.

- ❑ **1861** Independent under French protection.
- ❑ **1911** Constitution promulgated.
- ❑ **1949** Rainier III accedes to throne.
- ❑ **1962** Constitution rewritten: end of absolute authority of the prince.
- ❑ **1963** Democratic legislative elections held for first time.
- ❑ **1982** Princess Grace dies following a car accident.

SPENDING

GDP/cap. increase

CONSUMPTION AND SPENDING

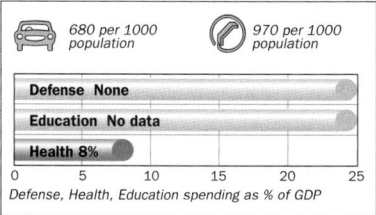

680 per 1000 population

970 per 1000 population

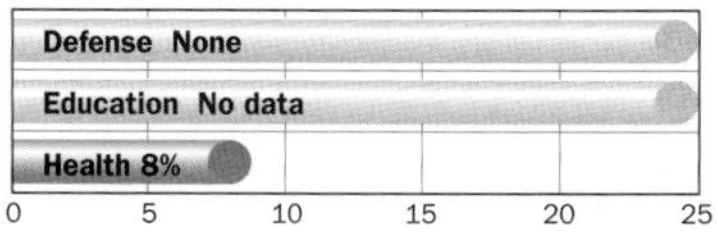
Defense None
Education No data
Health 8%
0
5
10
15
20
25

Defense, Health, Education spending as % of GDP

Monaco's image abroad has changed dramatically since Prince Rainier acceded in 1949. From being considered a simple gambling spot, it is now ranked as one of the world's most glamorous international jetset destinations. In part, this was the result of Rainier's wedding to Grace Kelly, then a leading Hollywood star, which brought Monaco to the attention of US high society. More important was Rainier's work in turning Monaco into a major tax haven and an up-market resort, by making the most of its Mediterranean coastal location. Many tax exiles have taken up residence, among them Luciano Pavarotti and Wall Street investment guru Bob Beckman.

WORLD RANKING

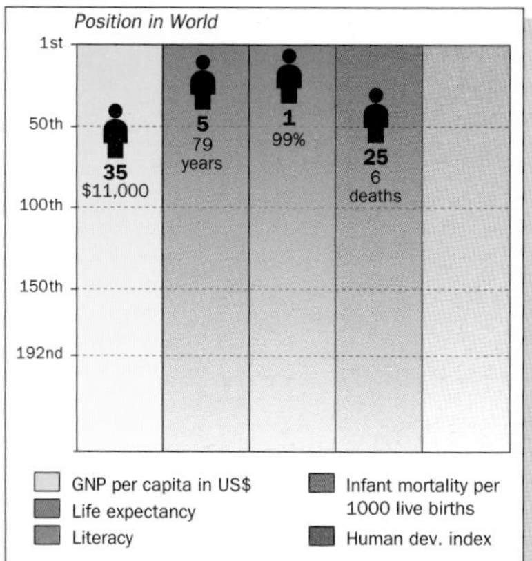
Position in World
1st
50th
100th
150th
192nd
35
$11,000
5
79
years
1
99%
25
6
deaths
GNP per capita in US$
Life expectancy
Literacy
Infant mortality per 1000 live births
Human dev. index

M

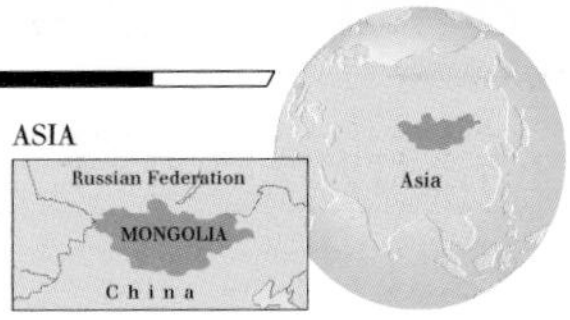
ASIA
Russian Federation
MONGOLIA
China
Asia

MONGOLIA

OFFICIAL NAME: Mongolia **CAPITAL:** Ulan Bator **POPULATION:** 2.7 million
CURRENCY: Tugrik (tögrög) **OFFICIAL LANGUAGE:** Khalkha Mongol

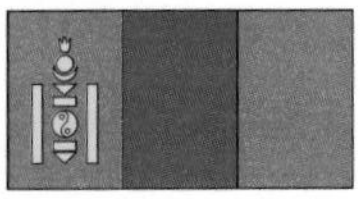

1924 | 1924 | July 11 | MGL | +8 | +976 | .mn

LANDLOCKED BETWEEN Russia and China, Mongolia rises from the semiarid Gobi Desert to mountainous steppe. The traditionally nomadic Mongols were first unified by Genghis Khan in 1206. Mongolia achieved independence from China as a communist state in 1924 and was officially aligned with the USSR from 1936. In 1990, it abandoned communist rule and widespread poverty ensued. Particularly harsh winters in 1999–2001 devastated the rural economy.

CLIMATE

Mountain/cold desert/steppe

WEATHER CHART

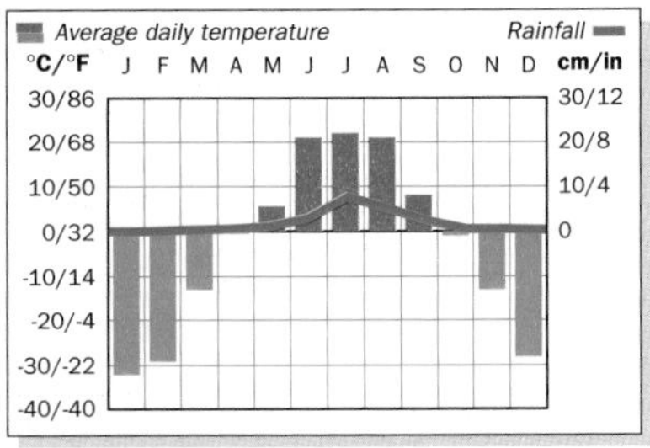
Average daily temperature
Rainfall
°C/°F
J F M A M J J A S O N D
cm/in
30/86
20/68
10/50
0/32
-10/14
-20/-4
-30/-22
-40/-40
30/12
20/8
10/4
0

Temperature variations are extreme. Dry summers combine with severe winters, known as *zud*, to devastate livestock, as happened in 1999 and 2000.

TRANSPORTATION

Drive on right

Buyant-Ukhaa, Ulan Bator

Has no fleet

THE TRANSPORTATION NETWORK

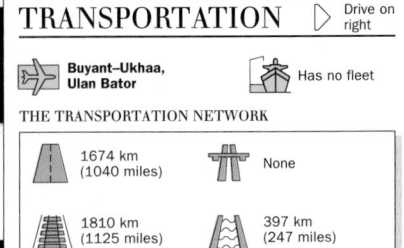

1674 km (1040 miles)

None

1810 km (1125 miles)

397 km (247 miles)

Lack of investment has left Mongolia's infrastructure to decay, increasing transportation and distribution costs. Links to China and the Pacific are priorities. Gasoline shortages have meant a large increase in the use of animal labor.

Traditional* gers *in the Gobi Desert.
Many Mongolians still choose to pursue a nomadic lifestyle, living in felt tents called gers.

TOURISM

Visitors : Population 1:17

158,000 visitors

Down 1% in 2000

MAIN TOURIST ARRIVALS

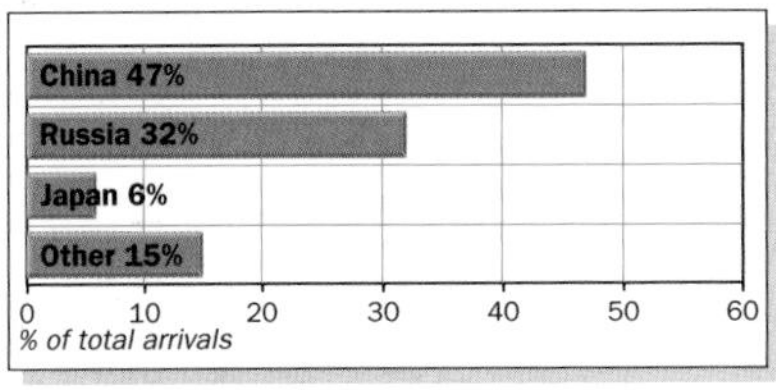
China 47%
Russia 32%
Japan 6%
Other 15%
0
10
20
30
40
50
60
% of total arrivals

Tourism has expanded since the easing of visa restrictions in 1991. Under communism, all travel was arranged through the state agency, Zhuuichin, but private companies are now entering the market.

PEOPLE

Pop. density low

Khalkha Mongolian, Turkic, Chinese, Russian

2/km² (4/mi²)

THE URBAN/RURAL POPULATION SPLIT

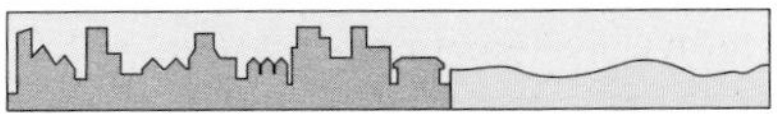
58%
42%

ETHNIC MAKEUP

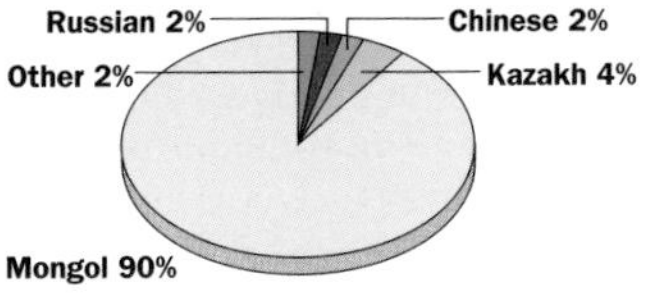
Russian 2%
Chinese 2%
Other 2%
Kazakh 4%
Mongol 90%

Khalkh Mongols, who adhere to Tibetan Buddhism, are the main ethnic group. Although economic pressures keep many people near urban centers, most remain nomadic. One-third live in Ulan Bator. Turkic Kazakhs in the west form the largest minority, but emigration to Kazakhstan since 1990 has reduced their numbers. Tensions exist with the Chinese and Russian minorities.

POLITICS

Multiparty elections

2000/2004

President Natsagyn Bagabandi

AT THE LAST ELECTION

State Great Hural 76 seats

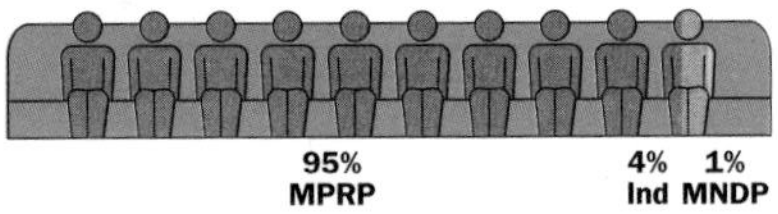
95%
MPRP
4%
Ind
1%
MNDP

MPRP = Mongolian People's Revolutionary Party
Ind = Independents
MNDP = Mongolian National Democratic Party

The end of communism and the advent of democracy in 1990 revolutionized Mongolian politics. The shock of economic reform led many Mongolians to look back to the certainties of the communist era. In 1992 the democrats lost power to the renamed communists (MPRP), but their failure to revive the economy swung the pendulum back in favor of a democratic coalition in 1996. An uneasy cohabitation between President Natsagyn Bagabandi of the MPRP, who took office in 1997, and an MNDP-led government existed from 1998 until the sweeping MPRP election victory in 2000.

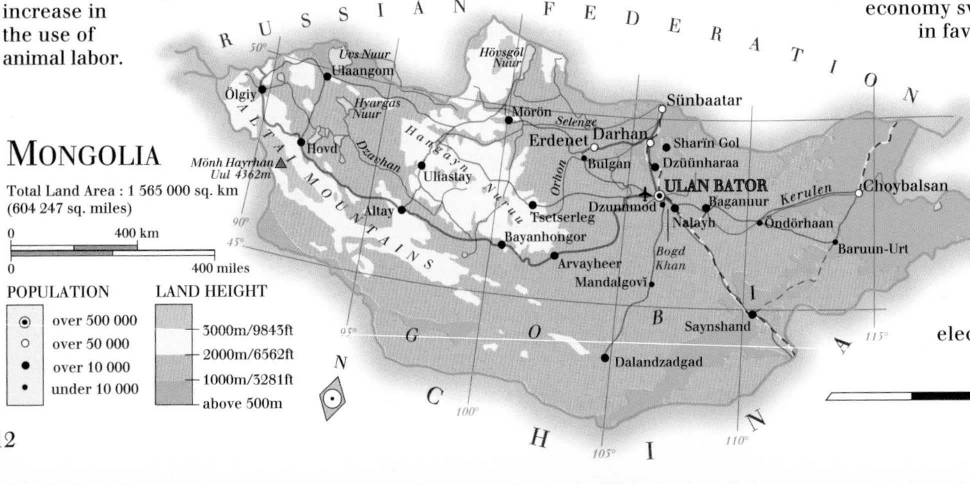
RUSSIAN FEDERATION
MONGOLIA
Total Land Area : 1 565 000 sq. km (604 247 sq. miles)
0
400 km
0
400 miles
POPULATION
over 500 000
over 50 000
over 10 000
under 10 000
LAND HEIGHT
3000m/9843ft
2000m/6562ft
1000m/3281ft
above 500m
Uvs Nuur
Ulaangom
Ölgiy
Hövsgöl Nuur
Hyargas Nuur
Mörön
Selenge
Sünbaatar
Darhan
Erdenet
Sharïn Gol
Bulgan
Dzüünharaa
Hovd
Mönh Hayrhan Uul 4362m
ALTAI MOUNTAINS
Dzavhan
Hangayn Nuruu
Uliastay
Orhon
ULAN BATOR
Kerulen
Choybalsan
Altay
Tsetserleg
Dzuunmod
Baganuur
Nalayh
Öndörhaan
Bayanhongor
Arvayheer
Bogd Khan
Baruun-Urt
Mandalgovi
Saynshand
Dalandzadgad
GOBI
CHINA
N

WORLD AFFAIRS
Joined UN in 1961

IAEA | IBRD | NAM | ADB | WTO

Closer relations with Japan and other east Asian states have failed to dilute Mongolia's traditional ties with Russia and China. There are residual tensions with China, as a majority of Mongols reside in the adjoining Chinese province of Inner Mongolia, but there is no longer a fear of Chinese designs on Mongolian sovereignty.

AID
Recipient

$219m (receipts)

Up 8% in 1999

A large balance of payments deficit and severe weather make aid vital. The main donors are the USA and Japan.

DEFENSE
Compulsory military service

$19m

Down 10% in 1999

The last Soviet forces left in 1992. However, ties are still strong, and under agreements reached in 2000 and 2001 Russia is helping to reform the greatly reduced and poorly equipped Mongolian forces.

ECONOMICS
Inflation 66.6% p.a. (1990–1999)

$927m

1072.4–1097.0 tugriks

SCORE CARD

- World GNP Ranking 157th
- GNP per Capita $390
- Balance of Payments .... $–112m
- Inflation 7.6%
- Unemployment 5%

Strengths
Copper and cashmere. Largely untapped coal and oil reserves. Traditional and efficient rural economy.

Weaknesses
Harsh winters ravaged livestock between 1999 and 2001. Decaying infrastructure. Rising poverty.

EXPORTS

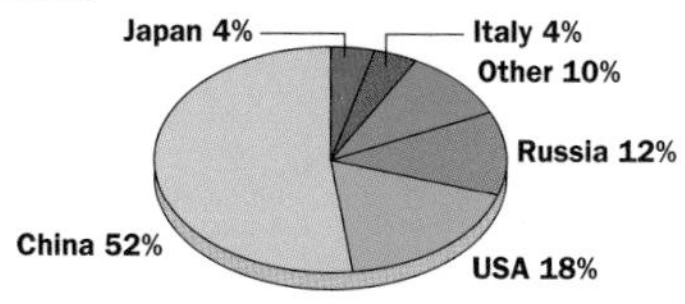
Japan 4%
Italy 4%
Other 10%
Russia 12%
China 52%
USA 18%

IMPORTS

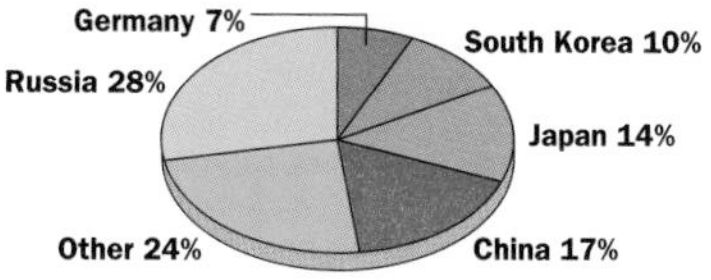
Germany 7%
South Korea 10%
Russia 28%
Japan 14%
Other 24%
China 17%

RESOURCES
Electric power 901,000 kw

181 tonnes

Contracts have recently been signed with oil prospectors

14m sheep, 10m goats, 3.5m cattle, 3.1m horses

Oil, coal, copper, lead, fluorite, tungsten, tin, gold, uranium

Under communism, Mongolia's vast mineral resources were barely exploited, and prospecting has only recently begun. A uranium-mining joint venture with Russia has been established. Mongolia is rich in oil, with sufficient reserves to meet future domestic needs. In 1999 an oil extraction agreement was signed with China.

ENVIRONMENT
Sustainability rank: 50th

10%

3.3 tonnes per capita

Industrial pollution around Ulan Bator is a health hazard. Lake Hövsgöl is seriously polluted. Renewed efforts were launched in 2001 to preserve the Bogd Khan, the world's oldest protected area, dating from 1788, from illegal logging, hunting, and air pollution.

MEDIA
TV ownership medium

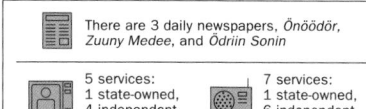

Daily newspaper circulation 27 per 1000 people

PUBLISHING AND BROADCAST MEDIA

There are 3 daily newspapers, *Önöödör, Zuuny Medee*, and *Ödriin Sonin*

5 services: 1 state-owned, 4 independent

7 services: 1 state-owned, 6 independent

Since 1990, Mongolia's press has enjoyed unlimited freedom; there are no slander or libel laws. Legislation enacted in January 1999 eased remaining curbs on the media. However, the shortage of paper and fuel supplies has restricted the number of publications and their distribution.

CRIME
Death penalty used

Mongolia does not publish prison figures

Down 1% 1996–1998

Crime rose rapidly in the early 1990s, particularly organized crime and muggings by knife gangs. Ulan Bator is the most dangerous area, especially for foreigners; Russians, Chinese, and dollar-carrying US tourists are the main targets.

EDUCATION
School leaving age: 16

99%

50,961 students

Education is modeled on the former Soviet system. The majority of teachers are women on low salaries. Private-sector schools emphasizing Mongol culture are beginning to open.

CHRONOLOGY

In the 17th century, the Manchus took control of Mongolia. It stayed in Chinese hands until 1911.

- **1919** China reoccupies Mongolia.
- **1924** Independent communist state.
- **1989–1990** Prodemocracy protests; communist election defeat.
- **1992** Former communists, renamed MPRP, returned to power.
- **1996** Democratic Union coalition wins general election.
- **1997** MPRP wins presidency.
- **1999–2001** Severe winters.
- **2000** Landslide electoral victory for MPRP.

HEALTH
Welfare state health benefits

1 per 385 people

Heart, parasitic, and respiratory diseases

Shortages of drugs and equipment have renewed interest in traditional Mongolian herbal medicine. As well as the state-run system, some Buddhist monasteries provide health care.

SPENDING
GDP/cap. increase

CONSUMPTION AND SPENDING

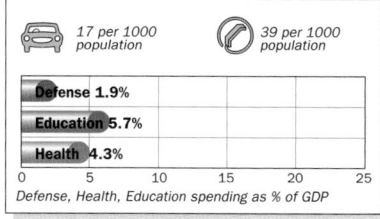

17 per 1000 population

39 per 1000 population

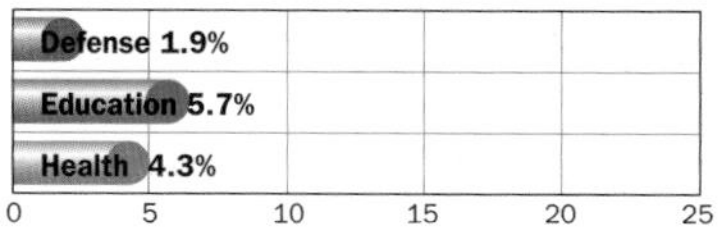
Defense 1.9%
Education 5.7%
Health 4.3%
0
5
10
15
20
25

Defense, Health, Education spending as % of GDP

Economic liberalization has fueled great disparities in wealth. An estimated one-third of the population still live below the poverty line; the poorest cannot even afford to buy bread. Starvation threatened after the severe winters of 1999–2001.

WORLD RANKING

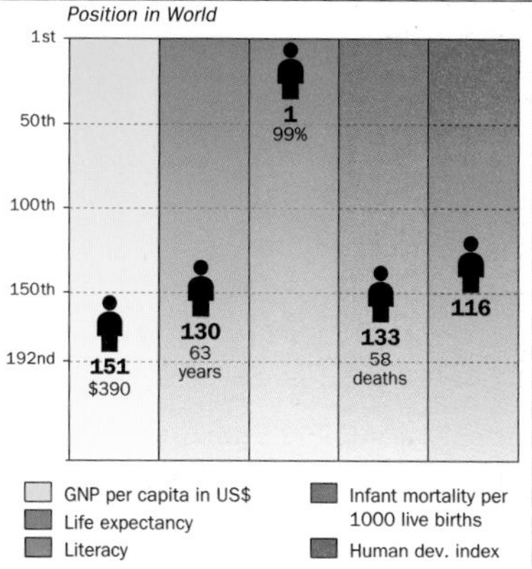
Position in World
1st
50th
100th
150th
192nd
151
$390
130
63
years
1
99%
133
58
deaths
116
GNP per capita in US$
Life expectancy
Literacy
Infant mortality per 1000 live births
Human dev. index

M

MOROCCO

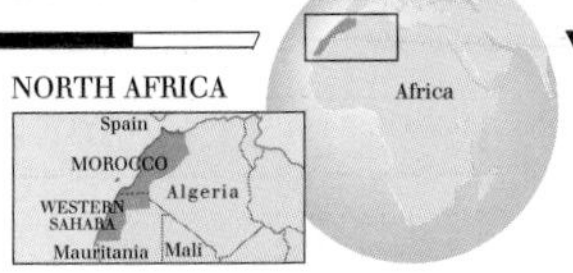

NORTH AFRICA
Spain
MOROCCO
Algeria
WESTERN SAHARA
Mauritania
Mali
Africa

OFFICIAL NAME: Kingdom of Morocco **CAPITAL:** Rabat
POPULATION: 28.4 million **CURRENCY:** Moroccan dirham **OFFICIAL LANGUAGE:** Arabic

1956 | 1956 | July 30 | MA | 0 | +212 | .ma

MOROCCO IS SITUATED IN northern Africa, but at its northernmost point lies only 12 km (8 miles) from mainland Europe, across the Strait of Gibraltar. Morocco's northern regions have a Mediterranean climate, while the south comprises semiarid desert. The late King Hassan's international prestige gave Morocco status out of proportion to its wealth. The main issues the country faces are the internal threat of Islamic militancy and the unresolved fate of Western Sahara, the former Spanish colony occupied by Morocco since 1975. The key economic strengths are tourism, phosphate production, and agriculture.

CLIMATE

Hot desert/mountain/ Mediterranean

WEATHER CHART

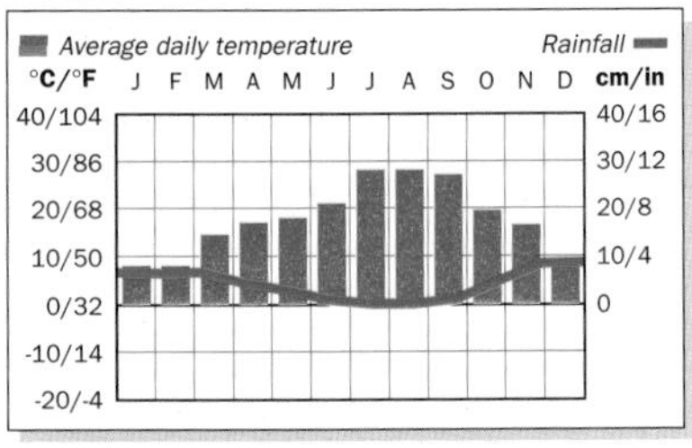

Average daily temperature
Rainfall
°C/°F
J F M A M J J A S O N D
cm/in
40/104
30/86
20/68
10/50
0/32
-10/14
-20/-4
40/16
30/12
20/8
10/4
0

The climate ranges from warm and temperate in the north to semiarid in the south, but temperatures are cooler in the mountains, especially in the high Atlas. During the summer, the effects of the *sirocco* and *chergui*, hot winds from the Sahara, are felt.

TRANSPORTATION

Drive on right

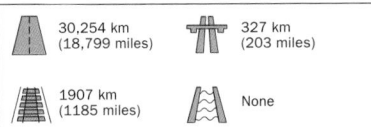

Mohammed V, Casablanca 3.42m passengers

496 ships 444,000 grt

THE TRANSPORTATION NETWORK

30,254 km (18,799 miles)

327 km (203 miles)

1907 km (1185 miles)

None

Morocco has six international airports. A highway links Rabat and Casablanca, and plans for a new trans-Sahara highway from Tangiers to Lagos, Nigeria, were announced in mid-2000. In rural areas, however, roads tend to peter out.

TOURISM

Visitors : Population 1:6.9

4.1m visitors

Up 7% in 2000

MAIN TOURIST ARRIVALS

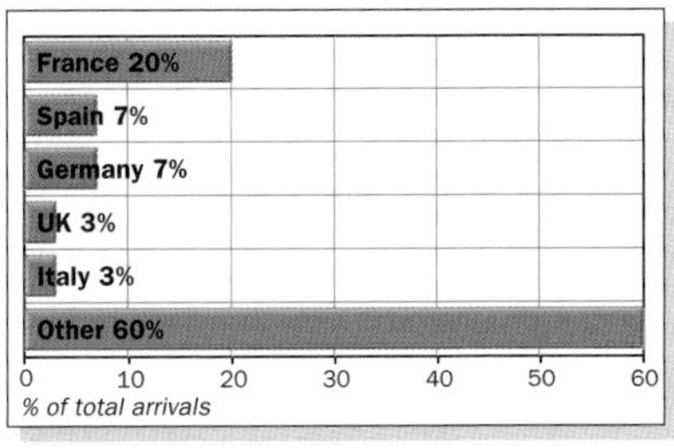

France 20%
Spain 7%
Germany 7%
UK 3%
Italy 3%
Other 60%
0 10 20 30 40 50 60
% of total arrivals

Tourism is vital to the Moroccan economy. Good beaches abound; Agadir has 300 days of sunshine a year. Fès and Marrakech offer cultural interest, while the Atlas mountains attract walkers and skiers. Desert safaris are offered in the Sahara. Most Western tourists come from France, Germany, and Spain.

M

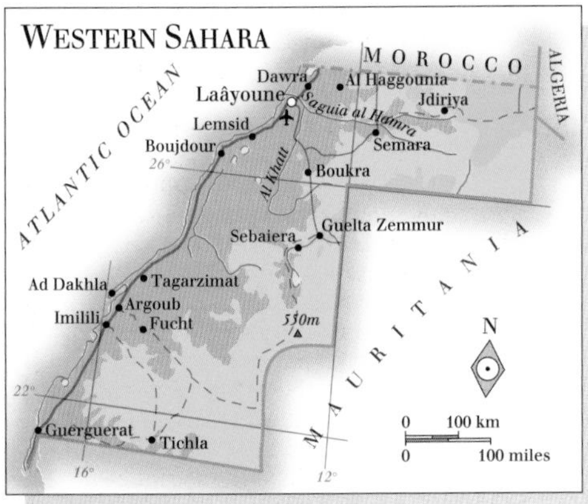

WESTERN SAHARA
MOROCCO
ALGERIA
ATLANTIC OCEAN
MAURITANIA
Dawra
Al Haggounia
Laâyoune
Jdiriya
Lemsid
Saguia al Hamra
Boujdour
Semara
Boukra
Al Khatt
Sebaiera
Guelta Zemmur
Ad Dakhla
Tagarzimat
Argoub
Imilili
Fucht
530m
Guerguerat
Tichla
26°
22°
16°
12°
N
0 100 km
0 100 miles

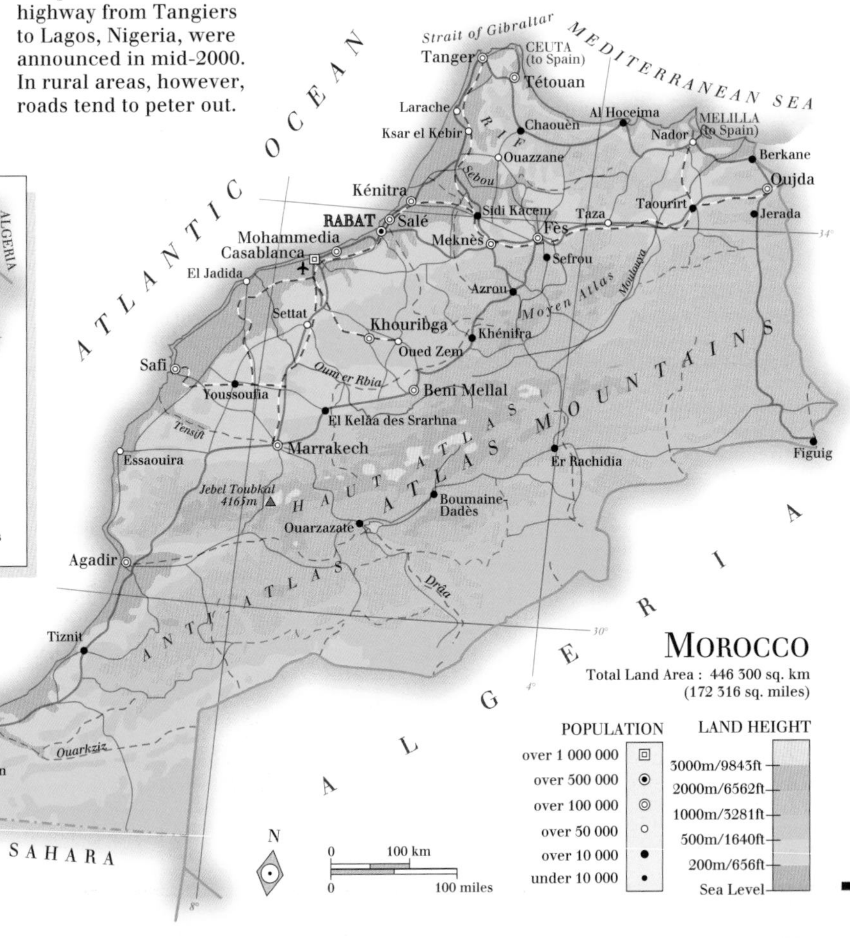

Strait of Gibraltar
MEDITERRANEAN SEA
ATLANTIC OCEAN
Tanger
CEUTA (to Spain)
Tétouan
Larache
Ksar el Kebir
Chaouèn
Al Hoceima
Nador
MELILLA (to Spain)
Berkane
Oujda
Ouazzane
RIF
Sebou
Kénitra
RABAT
Salé
Sidi Kacem
Taza
Taourirt
Jerada
Mohammedia
Casablanca
Meknès
Fès
Sefrou
El Jadida
Azrou
Moyen Atlas
Moulouya
Settat
Khouribga
Khénifra
Oued Zem
Safi
Oum er Rbia
Beni Mellal
Youssoufia
El Kelâa des Srarhna
Tensift
Marrakech
Essaouira
Er Rachidia
Figuig
ATLAS MOUNTAINS
HAUT ATLAS
Jebel Toubkal 4165m
Boumaine-Dadès
Ouarzazate
Agadir
ANTI ATLAS
Drâa
Tiznit
ALGERIA
Tan-Tan
Ouarkziz
WESTERN SAHARA
N
0 100 km
0 100 miles
MOROCCO
Total Land Area : 446 300 sq. km (172 316 sq. miles)
POPULATION
over 1 000 000
over 500 000
over 100 000
over 50 000
over 10 000
under 10 000
LAND HEIGHT
3000m/9843ft
2000m/6562ft
1000m/3281ft
500m/1640ft
200m/656ft
Sea Level

PEOPLE

Pop. density medium

Arabic, Berber (Shluh, Tamazight, Riffian), French, Spanish

64/km² (165/mi²)

THE URBAN/RURAL POPULATION SPLIT

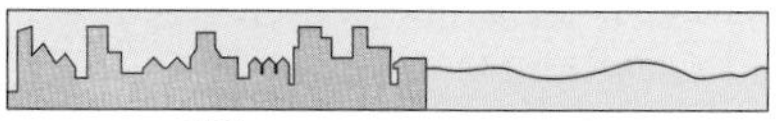
55%
45%

RELIGIOUS PERSUASION

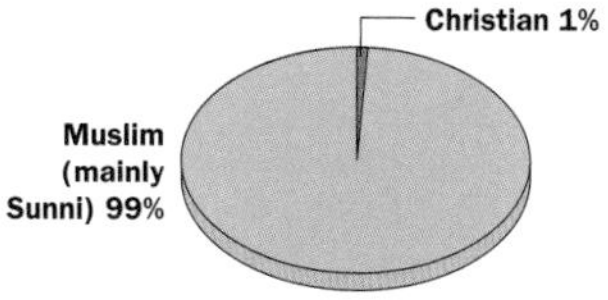
Christian 1%
Muslim (mainly Sunni) 99%

ETHNIC MAKEUP

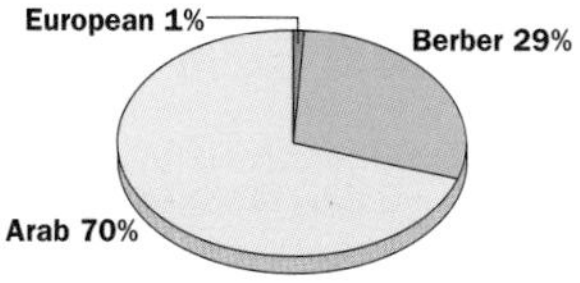
European 1%
Berber 29%
Arab 70%

Morocco, the westernmost of the Maghreb states, is the main refuge for descendants of the original Berber inhabitants of northwest Africa. About 35% of Moroccans are Berber-speaking. They live mainly in mountain villages, while the Arab majority inhabit the lowlands. Before independence from France, 450,000 Europeans lived in Morocco; numbers have since greatly diminished. Some 45,000 Jews enjoy religious freedom and full civil rights – a position in society unique among Arab countries. Most people speak Arabic, and French is also spoken in urban areas. Sunni Islam is the religion of most of the population. The king is the spiritual leader through his position as Commander of the Faithful. Female emancipation has been slow to take root in Morocco, but women are starting to take a more prominent role in society.

POPULATION AGE BREAKDOWN

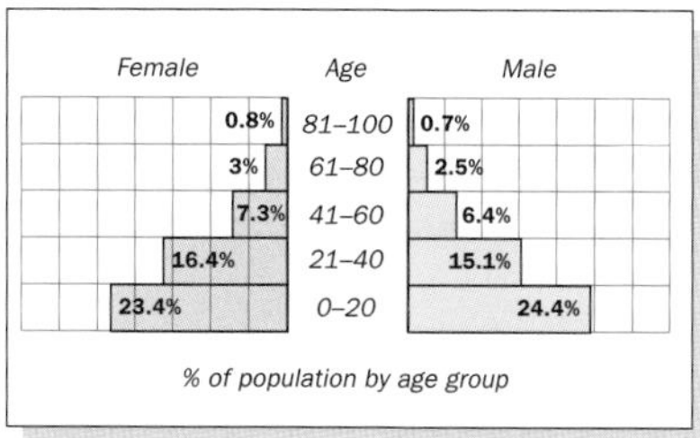
Female
Age
Male
0.8%
81–100
0.7%
3%
61–80
2.5%
7.3%
41–60
6.4%
16.4%
21–40
15.1%
23.4%
0–20
24.4%
% of population by age group

POLITICS

Multiparty elections

L. House 1997/2002
U. House 2000/2003

HM King Mohammed VI

AT THE LAST ELECTION

House of Representatives 325 seats

3% MPCD
1% PSD
31% K
31% W
30% C
3% FFD
1% Others

K = Koutla bloc (includes Socialist Union of Popular Forces and Istiqlal) **W** = Wifaq bloc (includes Constitutional Union & Popular Movement) **C** = Center bloc (includes National Rally of Independents and Democratic Popular Movement) **MPCD** = Constitutional & Democratic Popular Movement **FFD** = Democratic Forces Front **PSD** = Democratic Socialist Party

House of Councillors 270 seats

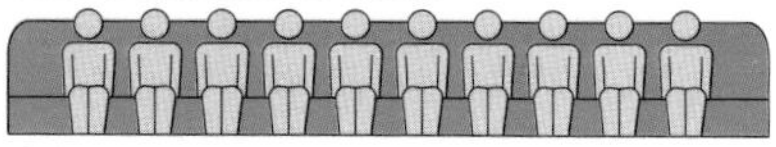

An indirectly elected House of Councillors was formed in December 1997

Morocco is a constitutional monarchy with a bicameral legislature.

Main Political Issues

The post-Hassan monarchy

The new king, Mohammed VI, is seen as a less dominating figure than his late father King Hassan II. His accession has encouraged expectations of change.

Islamic militancy

Under Hassan the government dealt ruthlessly with Islamic militants, but it had begun to take a less repressive stance, and Mohammed VI and the government in office since 1998 have ushered in further liberalizing moves. In May 2000 Abdessalam Yassine, spiritual leader of the banned Islamic movement Justice and Good Deeds, was released after ten years' imprisonment without trial. Popular support for Islamic fundamentalism is fueled by the fear that Morocco is losing its Islamic identity. Pro-Islamist rallies in March 2000 far outnumbered those by supporters of greater rights for women.

Profile

Although the majority party in parliament now chooses the government, the king reserved the right to appoint or dismiss the prime minister. Legislative elections in November 1997 left parliament split three ways, with only nine seats going to Islamists. The eventual formation of a socialist-led government was seen as the clearest expression to date of the increasing role of the party system.

Abderrahmane el Youssoufi*, prime minister since 1998.*

King Mohammed VI*, who succeeded his father, Hassan II.*

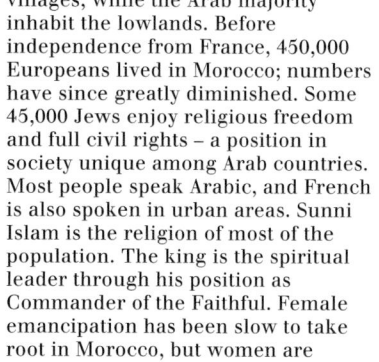

The town of Boumaine-Dadès *lies in the southern foothills of the Atlas Mountains. The region's outstanding scenery makes it one of Morocco's major tourist attractions.*

WORLD AFFAIRS

Joined UN in 1956

AL | AMU | IBRD | NAM | OIC

Morocco's important role in the quest for lasting peace in the Middle East was underlined by Israeli prime minister Yitzhak Rabin's visit to Rabat following the signing in Washington of the 1993 peace accord with the Palestine Liberation Organization. King Hassan's foreign policy was ambiguous, for while he negotiated with Israel he also headed the Jerusalem Committee of the Islamic Conference Organization (OIC). Generally more pro-Western than other Arab states, Morocco has also earned respect by protecting its Jewish minority.

International disapproval has focused on Morocco's occupation since 1975 of the former Spanish colony of Western Sahara. Resistance by Polisario Front guerrillas who are fighting for an independent Western Sahara, commenced in 1983 and has continued, despite a UN-brokered peace plan in 1991. In 1994, the UN approved plans for a voter identification process, to lead to a referendum on self-determination. The whole process was so frequently obstructed that UN representative James Baker proposed in 2001 that Western Sahara should become part of Morocco as an autonomous area for a 10-year trial period.

Relations with the EU have been strengthened with the signing of an association agreement in late 1995, envisaging free trade in industrial goods within 12 years. However, a fisheries dispute with the EU involving Spanish and Portuguese fishing rights off the Moroccan coast remains to be resolved.

AID

Recipient

$678m (receipts)

Up 28% in 1999

Saudi Arabia wrote off $2.7 billion of Moroccan debt after the Gulf War. The World Bank has given help to Morocco, but the country receives little aid.

M

CHRONOLOGY

Independence from France in 1956 was only the first step in ending colonial rule for the oldest kingdom in the Arab world, even though the present Alaoui dynasty has been in power for three centuries.

- ❑ **1956** France recognizes Moroccan independence under Sultan Mohammed Ibn Yousif. Morocco joins UN. Spain renounces control over most of its territories.
- ❑ **1957** Sultan Mohammed king.
- ❑ **1961** Hassan succeeds his father.
- ❑ **1967** Morocco backs Arab cause in Six-Day War with Israel.
- ❑ **1969** Spain returns Ifni to Morocco.
- ❑ **1972** King Hassan survives assassination attempt.
- ❑ **1975** International Court of Justice grants right of self-determination to Western Saharan people. King Hassan orders Moroccan forces to seize Saharan capital.
- ❑ **1976** Morocco and Mauritania partition Western Sahara.
- ❑ **1979** Mauritania renounces claim to part of Western Sahara, which is added to Morocco's territory.
- ❑ **1984** King Hassan signs Oujda Treaty with Col. Gaddafi of Libya as first step toward a Maghreb union. Morocco leaves OAU after criticism of its role in Western Sahara.
- ❑ **1986** Morocco abrogates Oujda Treaty.
- ❑ **1987** Defensive wall around Western Sahara.
- ❑ **1989** Arab Maghreb Union (AMU) creates no-tariff zone between Morocco, Algeria, Tunisia, Libya, and Mauritania.
- ❑ **1990** Morocco condemns Iraq's invasion of Kuwait.
- ❑ **1991** Morocco accepts UN plan for referendum in Western Sahara.
- ❑ **1992** New constitution grants majority party in parliament right to choose the government.
- ❑ **1993** First general election for nine years. After major parties refuse his invitation, king appoints nonparty government.
- ❑ **1994** King Hassan replaces veteran prime minister Karim Lamrani with Abdellatif Filali.
- ❑ **1995** Islamist opposition leader Mohamed Basri returns to Morocco after 28 years of exile.
- ❑ **1998** Socialists enter government with Abderrahmane el Youssoufi as prime minister.
- ❑ **1999** Death of King Hassan. Mohammed VI enthroned. Liberalization program announced.
- ❑ **2000–2001** UN plan for Western Sahara founders; UN special representative proposes a ten-year trial period as part of Morocco.

M

DEFENSE

Compulsory military service

$1.76bn

Up 4% in 1999

MOROCCAN ARMED FORCES

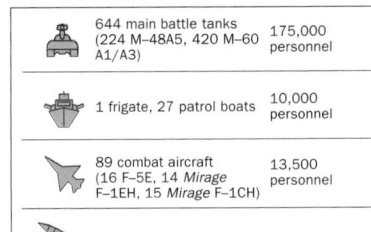

644 main battle tanks (224 M-48A5, 420 M-60 A1/A3)	175,000 personnel
1 frigate, 27 patrol boats	10,000 personnel
89 combat aircraft (16 F-5E, 14 *Mirage* F-1EH, 15 *Mirage* F-1CH)	13,500 personnel
None	

Morocco's long struggle in Western Sahara against Polisario Front guerrillas has given the kingdom's forces a formidable reputation. Moroccans have also fought as mercenaries in the Gulf. In the 1980s, Moroccan sappers constructed a 2500-km (1550-mile) defensive wall to cordon off Western Sahara in an attempt to prevent incursions from Polisario guerrillas based in Algeria. The Polisario forces themselves number some 3000–6000.

Morocco's pro-Western stance has allowed its forces access to sophisticated weapons and training from the West, particularly the USA – unlike neighboring north African states, which are dependent on the former Soviet bloc.

The air force was formed in 1956 and flies US and European aircraft, notably Mirage interceptors. The navy uses Western-supplied ships, but is insignificant in regional terms. In addition, there are 42,000 paramilitaries.

Over 4% of national income is spent on defense – a relatively high figure for a developing country. Military service, lasting 18 months, is compulsory.

ECONOMICS

Inflation 3.2% p.a. (1990–1999)

$33.7bn

10.076–10.563 Moroccan dirhams

SCORE CARD

❑ World GNP Ranking	55th
❑ GNP per Capita	$1190
❑ Balance of Payments	$-236m
❑ Inflation	0.7%
❑ Unemployment	19%

EXPORTS

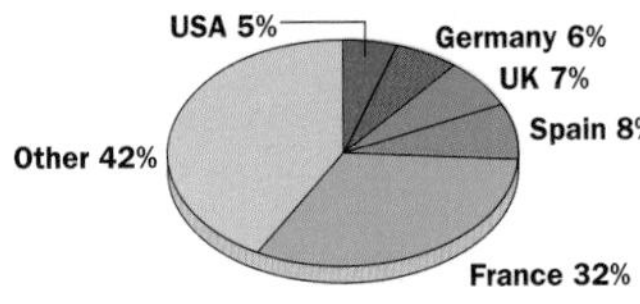
USA 5%
Germany 6%
UK 7%
Spain 8%
Other 42%
France 32%

IMPORTS

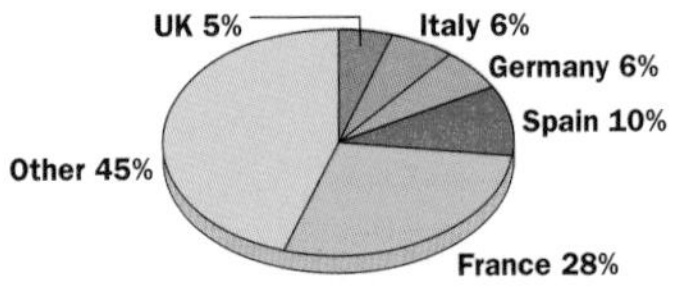
UK 5%
Italy 6%
Germany 6%
Spain 10%
Other 45%
France 28%

ECONOMIC PERFORMANCE INDICATOR

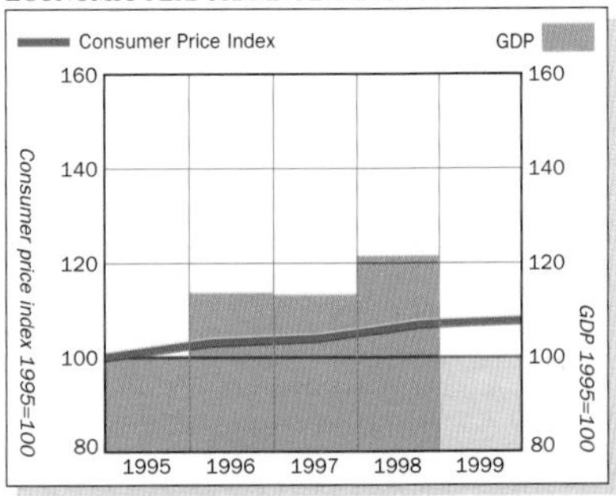
Consumer Price Index
GDP
160
140
120
100
80
Consumer price index 1995=100
GDP 1995=100
1995
1996
1997
1998
1999

Strengths

Probusiness policies and abundant labor attract foreign investment. Low inflation. Tourist industry (already important), phosphates, and agriculture all have great potential.

Weaknesses

High unemployment and population growth. Droughts have hit agriculture. Cannabis production (providing Europe's main source of resin) complicates closer EU links.

Profile

The government's large-scale privatization program, which began in 1992, was designed to attract investment, particularly from Europe. Severe drought in 1995 made austerity measures necessary. The new socialist-led government has given social policy a higher priority. Expected revenue from oil reserves will be channeled into the development of rural areas.

MOROCCO : MAJOR BUSINESSES

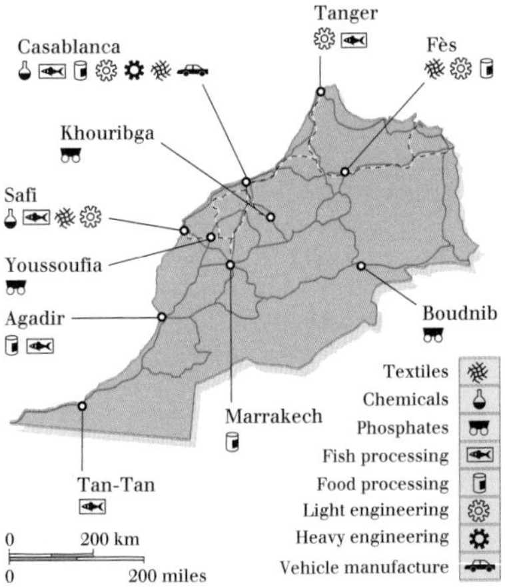
Tanger
Fès
Casablanca
Khouribga
Safi
Youssoufia
Agadir
Boudnib
Marrakech
Tan-Tan
Textiles
Chemicals
Phosphates
Fish processing
Food processing
Light engineering
Heavy engineering
Vehicle manufacture
0
200 km
0
200 miles

RESOURCES

Electric power 4m kw

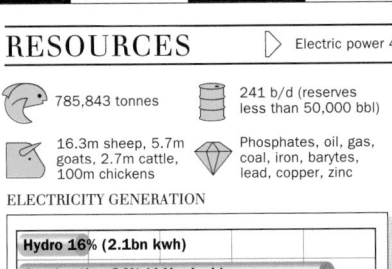

785,843 tonnes

241 b/d (reserves less than 50,000 bbl)

16.3m sheep, 5.7m goats, 2.7m cattle, 100m chickens

Phosphates, oil, gas, coal, iron, barytes, lead, copper, zinc

ELECTRICITY GENERATION

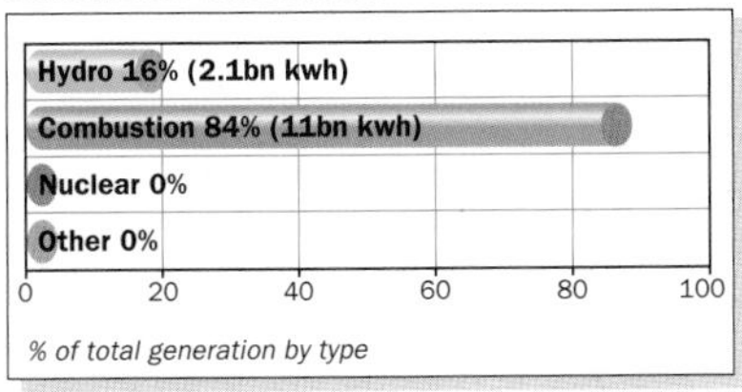
Hydro 16% (2.1bn kwh)
Combustion 84% (11bn kwh)
Nuclear 0%
Other 0%
0
20
40
60
80
100
% of total generation by type

Morocco possesses 75% of the world's phosphate reserves. The discovery of large oil and gas deposits in the northeastern desert in mid-2000 could yield an annual revenue of $400 million.

MOROCCO : LAND USE

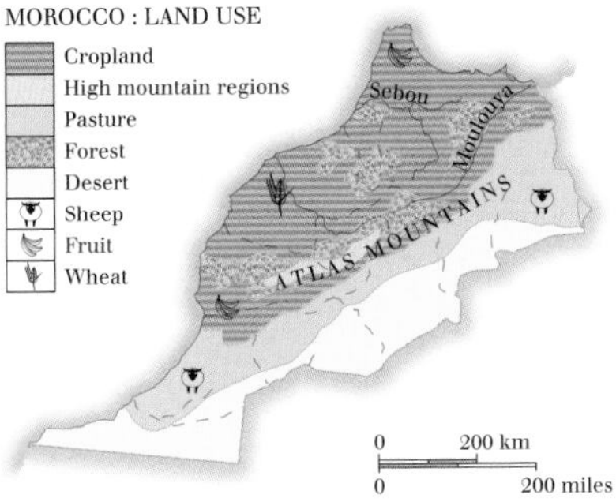
Cropland
High mountain regions
Pasture
Forest
Desert
Sheep
Fruit
Wheat
Sebou
Moulouya
ATLAS MOUNTAINS
0
200 km
0
200 miles

ENVIRONMENT

Sustainability rank: 89th

1% (0.7% partially protected)

1.3 tonnes per capita

ENVIRONMENTAL TREATIES

Yes	Yes	Yes
Yes	Yes	No

Morocco's wealth of plant and animal life has suffered severely from long periods of drought, most recently in the early 1980s and early 1990s. The unplanned development of tourist resorts is posing a threat to fragile coastal ecosystems.

MEDIA

TV ownership medium

Daily newspaper circulation 27 per 1000 people

PUBLISHING AND BROADCAST MEDIA

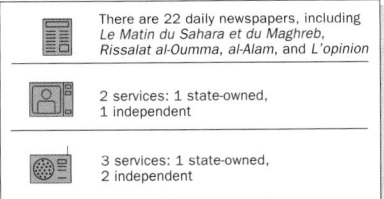

There are 22 daily newspapers, including *Le Matin du Sahara et du Maghreb*, *Rissalat al-Oumma*, *al-Alam*, and *L'opinion*

2 services: 1 state-owned, 1 independent

3 services: 1 state-owned, 2 independent

The succession of Mohammed VI fueled hopes of a more liberal climate, but the media remain strictly controlled. In 2000, the outspoken French-language weekly *Demain* was banned. The sports pages, especially the soccer reports, are the most dynamic sections of the press. State-owned TV began transmissions in Arabic and French in 1962. Radio broadcasts are in Arabic, Berber, French, Spanish, and English from Rabat and Tangier. Morocco can receive broadcasts from Spanish radio stations, and the main Spanish television stations can also be received in the north.

CRIME

Death penalty used

21,332 prisoners

Crime rose sharply 1991–1994

CRIME RATES

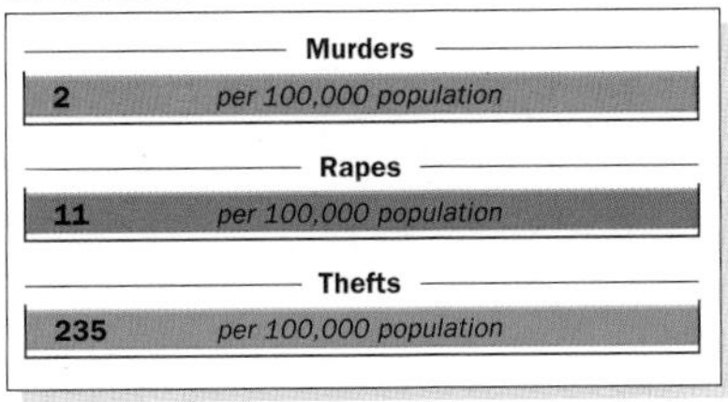
Murders
2 per 100,000 population
Rapes
11 per 100,000 population
Thefts
235 per 100,000 population

Urban crime is increasing, but muggings are rare. Apart from a 1990 strike that led to 40 deaths in Fès, there has been little civil unrest. Prisons are overcrowded, and conditions are poor.

EDUCATION

School leaving age: 16

49%

311,743 students

THE EDUCATION SYSTEM

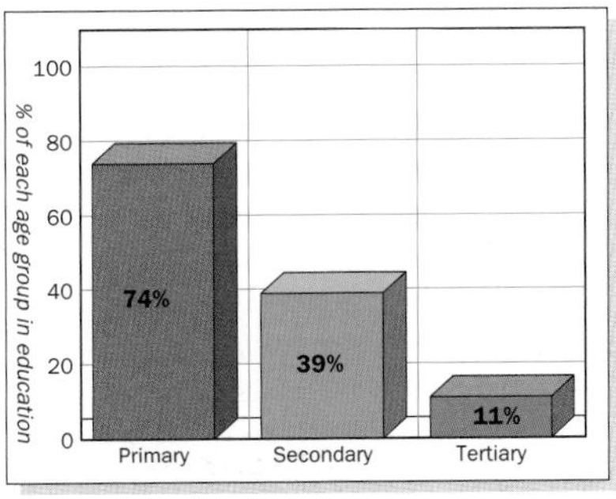
100
80
60
40
20
0
% of each age group in education
74%
39%
11%
Primary
Secondary
Tertiary

Literacy is much lower among the rural population (only 14%) than in the cities. The literacy level and elementary school enrollment rates are well below average for countries with similar living standards; child labor is widely used. There are both state-controlled and private schools. In 1988 the secondary school graduation examination, the *baccalauréat*, was replaced by a system of continuous assessment.

HEALTH

Welfare state health benefits

1 per 2500 people

Neonatal causes, cerebrovascular and heart diseases

Despite recent progress, child mortality and nutritional standards for the poorest Moroccans remain well below average. There is one doctor for every 2500 Moroccans and one hospital bed for every 1000 people. Outside the cities, primary health care is virtually nonexistent, with the result that people depend on traditional remedies for illnesses. All employees are required to contribute to a social welfare fund, which operates a system of benefits in the event of illness, occupational accidents, and old age.

SPENDING

GDP/cap. increase

CONSUMPTION AND SPENDING

41 per 1000 population

53 per 1000 population

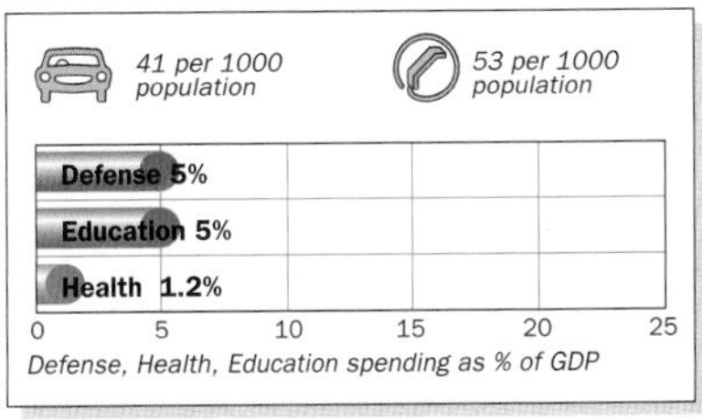
Defense 5%
Education 5%
Health 1.2%
0
5
10
15
20
25
Defense, Health, Education spending as % of GDP

Income per head is considerably lower than in the neighboring countries of Algeria and Tunisia. Almost one in five Moroccans live below the poverty line, and the rural–urban gap in wealth is considerable; just over half of the population live in rural areas. A period of drought in the 1990s accelerated urban drift.

Unrest has largely been avoided owing to the fact that Morocco has a thriving informal sector. This provides jobs in clothes manufacturing, food processing, goods transportation, and the hotel and building trades. In addition, there is work to be found in the illegal hashish trade and the smuggling of alcohol and Western goods.

WORLD RANKING

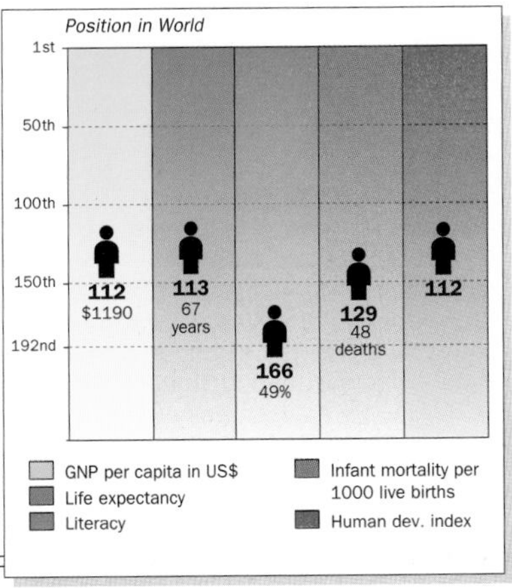
Position in World
1st
50th
100th
150th
192nd
112
$1190
113
67
years
166
49%
129
48
deaths
112
GNP per capita in US$
Life expectancy
Literacy
Infant mortality per 1000 live births
Human dev. index

M

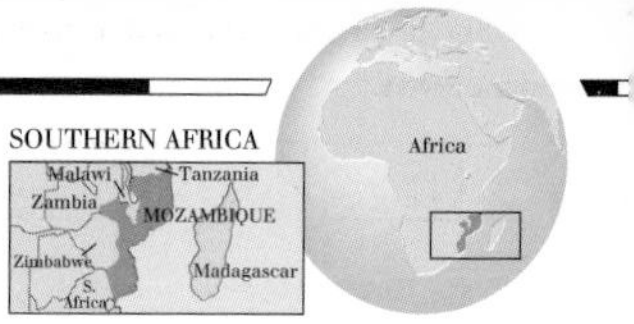
SOUTHERN AFRICA
Malawi
Tanzania
Zambia
MOZAMBIQUE
Zimbabwe
Madagascar
S. Africa
Africa

MOZAMBIQUE

OFFICIAL NAME: Republic of Mozambique **CAPITAL:** Maputo
POPULATION: 19.7 million **CURRENCY:** Metical **OFFICIAL LANGUAGE:** Portuguese

1975 | 1975 | June 25 | MOC | +2 | +258 | .mz

SITUATED ON THE SOUTHEAST African coast, Mozambique is bisected by the Zambezi River. South of the Zambezi lies a semiarid savanna lowland. The more fertile north-central delta provinces around Tete are home to most of Mozambique's ethnically diverse population. Following independence from Portugal in 1975, Mozambique was torn apart by civil war between the (then Marxist) FRELIMO government and the South African-backed Mozambique National Resistance (RENAMO). The conflict finally ended in 1992 after UN arbitration. Multiparty elections in 1994 returned FRELIMO to power. Devastating floods in 2000 and 2001 have created a desperate situation for this impoverished country.

CLIMATE

Tropical wet & dry

WEATHER CHART

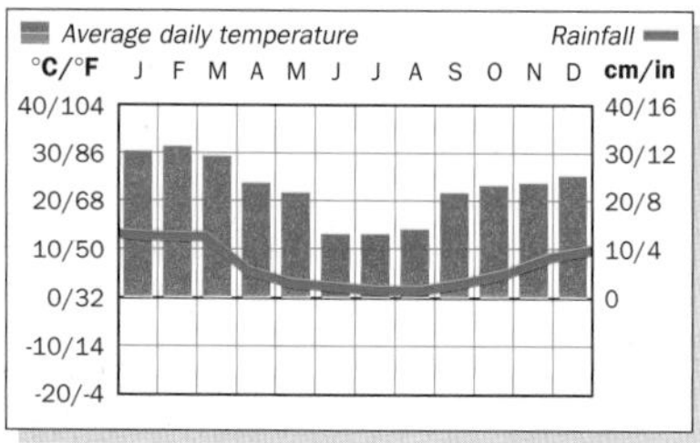
Average daily temperature
Rainfall
°C/°F
J F M A M J J A S O N D
cm/in
40/104
30/86
20/68
10/50
0/32
-10/14
-20/-4
40/16
30/12
20/8
10/4
0

In theory, Mozambique has a rainy and a dry season. However, in the 1980s, frequent failure of the rains contributed to two disastrous famines. The coast south of Beira and the highlands adjoining Malawi and Zimbabwe are the wettest areas. The northern coast is dry, the moist trade winds being blocked by Madagascar. The Zambezi valley is the driest region. Devastating floods occurred in 2000 and 2001.

TRANSPORTATION

Drive on left

Mavalane International, Maputo 390,882 passengers

124 ships 35,300 grt

THE TRANSPORTATION NETWORK

5685 km (3532 miles)

None

3114 km (1935 miles)

3750 km (2330 miles)

The billion-dollar Maputo Corridor, launched in 1995, reconnects South African industrial centers with the Mozambican coast, and should also facilitate port modernization. CFM, the state-owned railroad company, is cooperating with other neighboring states. The national airline is returning profits. Even so, millions of land mines still hamper access, damaged bridges have yet to be rebuilt, and remote communities remain isolated.

***Tea picking.** Other important cash crops are cashew nuts, cotton, sugar, copra, and citrus fruits. Agriculture employs 85% of workers.*

TOURISM

Not available

Tourism has still not recovered after war

Little change from year to year

MAIN TOURIST ARRIVALS

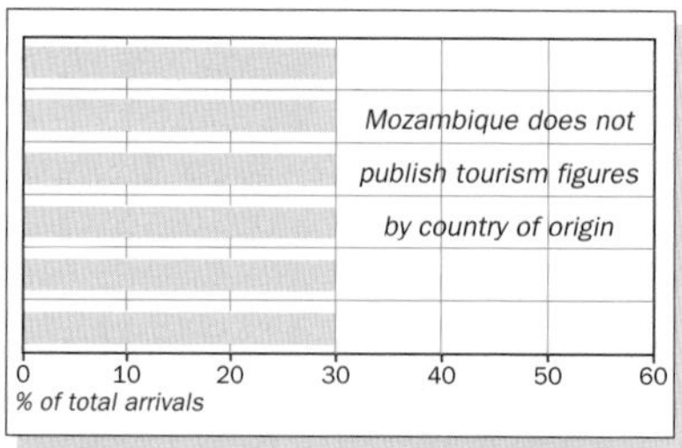
Mozambique does not publish tourism figures by country of origin
0
10
20
30
40
50
60
% of total arrivals

Mozambique used to attract around 300,000 South Africans and Rhodesians a year in the 1970s, but the tourist industry was destroyed by the civil war and is only slowly being rebuilt. Land mines still render travel outside the capital hazardous, while food shortages, poor infrastructure, and costly international flights are added obstacles. Further setbacks followed the floods in 2000.

Given political stability, though, Mozambique could yet exploit its excellent beaches and game reserves, which include the Gorongosa Game Park. Some hotel groups are once more targeting Maputo as a luxury tourist and conference venue.

PEOPLE

Pop. density low

Makua, Tsonga, Sena, Lomwe, Portuguese

25/km² (65/mi²)

THE URBAN/RURAL POPULATION SPLIT

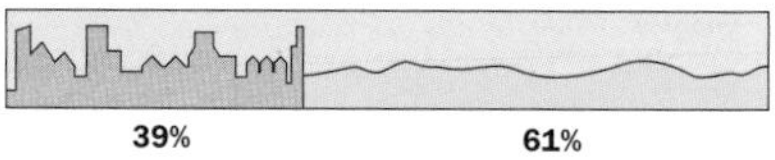
39%
61%

RELIGIOUS PERSUASION

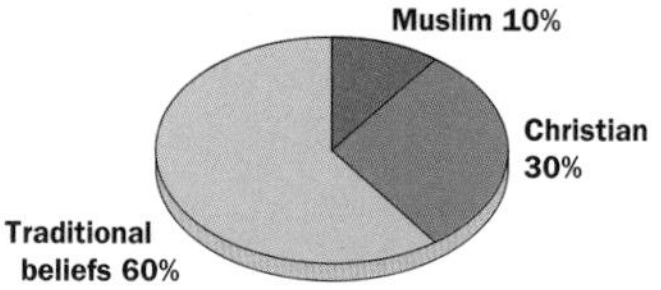
Muslim 10%
Christian 30%
Traditional beliefs 60%

ETHNIC MAKEUP

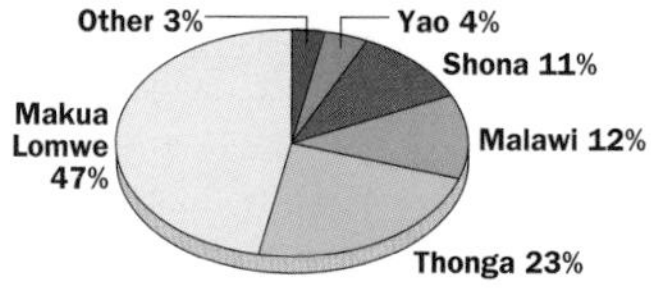
Other 3%
Yao 4%
Shona 11%
Malawi 12%
Makua Lomwe 47%
Thonga 23%

Mozambique is ethnically diverse, with the overwhelming black African majority divided into numerous groups, and tiny minorities of whites, mixed-race groups, and Asians. However, the predominant social tensions are regional: RENAMO, strong in the north and central regions, accuses the FRELIMO government of consistently favoring the south. Antiwhite feelings are growing too, as "Africanists" claim that whites enjoy excessive political influence – incendiary charges in a country where life expectancy is below 50 years and poverty is endemic.

Mozambican society centers on the extended family. In some provinces, notably Zambezia, Cabo Delgado, and Tete, this is matriarchal. Polygamy is fairly widespread among men who can support second wives. FRELIMO pays special attention to women's rights. Many women served in FRELIMO armies, and are now protected by divorce, child-custody, and husband-desertion laws. The Mozambican Women's Organization encourages participation in political life.

POPULATION AGE BREAKDOWN

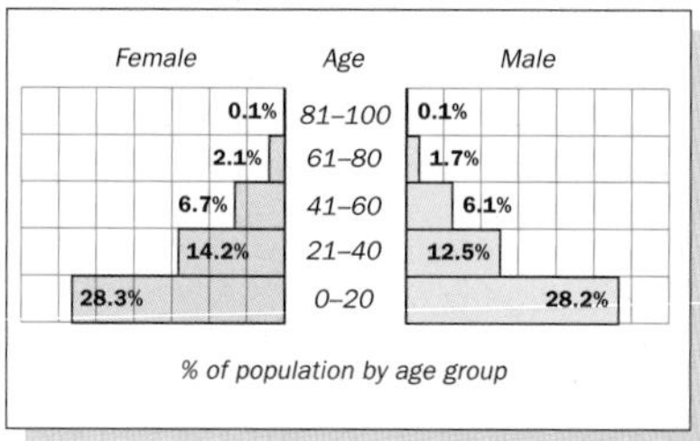
Female
Age
Male
0.1%
81–100
0.1%
2.1%
61–80
1.7%
6.7%
41–60
6.1%
14.2%
21–40
12.5%
28.3%
0–20
28.2%
% of population by age group

M

POLITICS

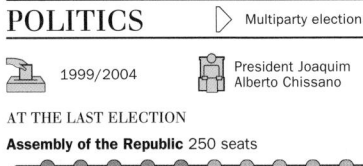

Multiparty elections

1999/2004

President Joaquim Alberto Chissano

AT THE LAST ELECTION

Assembly of the Republic 250 seats

53% FRELIMO **47% RENAMO**

FRELIMO = Front for the Liberation of Mozambique
RENAMO = Mozambique National Resistance

MAIN POLITICAL ISSUES

The move to democracy

In 1993, the UN secured, with difficulty, the $260 million and the 7500-strong multinational forces required to demobilize Mozambique's warring factions and to stage the first democratic elections.

Despite last-minute hitches, elections were held in 1994 which returned FRELIMO to power. However, support for RENAMO was stronger than had been anticipated. Their leader Afonso Dhlakama polled strongly in the presidential elections in both 1994 and 1999, contesting President Chissano's claim of victory.

Reconstruction

The government faces an enormous task in rebuilding a country where devastating floods came on top of the ravages of civil war. The fighting had left 900,000 dead, one million refugees, and an estimated 90% of the remaining population living below the poverty line.

Joaquim Chissano, *president since 1986, has pushed towards political pluralism.*

Afonso Dhlakama, *RENAMO leader, has turned from militarism to politics.*

PROFILE

Between 1977 and 1990, Mozambique was a one-party state ruled by the Soviet-backed FRELIMO. It had campaigned for independence from Portugal since the 1960s. White South Africa and Southern Rhodesia (now Zimbabwe) both backed anti-Marxist RENAMO rebels, who fought against FRELIMO. Changing international realities persuaded FRELIMO to adopt a democratic constitution in 1990. Meanwhile, RENAMO lost its external sponsors. Today little distinguishes the two ideologically. Although FRELIMO is the biggest party in parliament, RENAMO is clearly popular, and demands recognition for its 15 years of struggle. New groups, such as the antiwhite PALMO, COINMO, and UNAMO, have recently emerged; FRELIMO is pushing ahead with plans to decentralize power. Continuing disputes between RENAMO and the FRELIMO government about provincial representation since the 1999 elections have rekindled fears for the future of multiparty democracy.

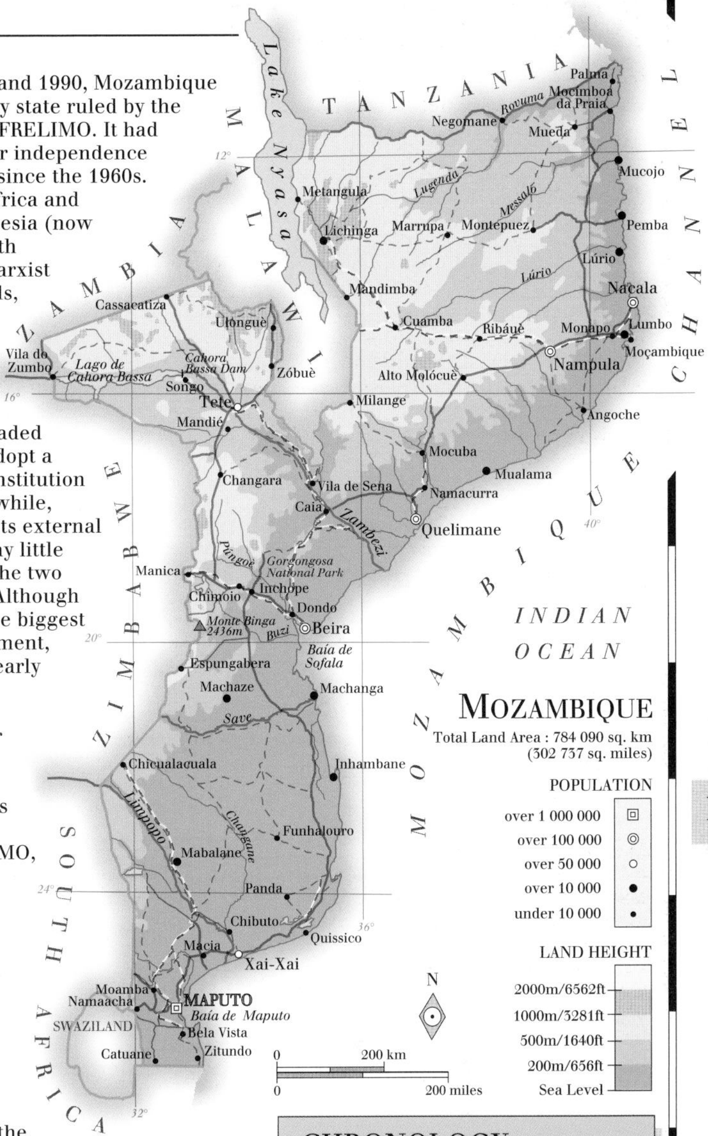
TANZANIA
MALAWI
ZAMBIA
ZIMBABWE
SOUTH AFRICA
SWAZILAND
MOZAMBIQUE CHANNEL
INDIAN OCEAN
Lake Nyasa
Lago de Cahora Bassa
Rovuma
Lugenda
Messalo
Lúrio
Zambezi
Pungoè
Búzi
Save
Limpopo
Changane
Palma
Mocimboa da Praia
Negomane
Mueda
Mucojo
Pemba
Metangula
Lichinga
Marrupa
Montepuez
Lúrio
Nacala
Mandimba
Cuamba
Ribáuè
Monapo
Lumbo
Moçambique
Nampula
Alto Molócuè
Cassacatiza
Ulóngué
Vila do Zumbo
Cahora Bassa Dam
Songo
Zóbuè
Tete
Milange
Mandié
Angoche
Mocuba
Mualama
Changara
Vila de Sena
Namacurra
Caia
Quelimane
Manica
Gorongosa National Park
Chimoio
Inchope
Dondo
Monte Binga 2436m
Beira
Baía de Sofala
Espungabera
Machaze
Machanga
Chicualacuala
Inhambane
Funhalouro
Mabalane
Panda
Chibuto
Quissico
Macia
Xai-Xai
Moamba
Namaacha
MAPUTO
Baía de Maputo
Bela Vista
Catuane
Zitundo
MOZAMBIQUE
Total Land Area : 784 090 sq. km (302 737 sq. miles)
POPULATION
over 1 000 000
over 100 000
over 50 000
over 10 000
under 10 000
LAND HEIGHT
2000m/6562ft
1000m/3281ft
500m/1640ft
200m/656ft
Sea Level
N
0 200 km
0 200 miles

WORLD AFFAIRS

Joined UN in 1975

Comm | CPLP | OAU | OIC | SADC

Mozambique was a key Cold War battleground between Soviet-backed Marxism, and capitalism sponsored by the USA and South Africa. The resulting civil war devastated the country between 1977 and 1992.

In the early 1980s, however, the FRELIMO government's position began to shift as Soviet aid became erratic. Responding to President Samora Machel's overtures, the USA lifted its ban on economic assistance in 1984. Britain agreed to train FRELIMO's forces in 1987. South Africa continued to support RENAMO until at least 1990, despite its 1984 pledge. Zimbabwean troops helped Mozambique guard the strategically important Beira and Limpopo corridors, but left in 1993.

In 1995, the UN withdrew its 6000 peacekeepers and a democratic Mozambique joined the Commonwealth, despite having no formal links with the old British Empire. President Chissano became deputy head of the SADC, but regional tensions persisted, with Mozambique accusing South Africans of gun-running, and Swaziland claiming Maputo Province as its own.

CHRONOLOGY

The Portuguese tapped the local trade in slaves, gold, and ivory in the 16th century and made Mozambique a colony in 1752. Large areas were run by private companies until 1929.

- **1964** FRELIMO starts war of liberation.
- **1975** Independence. FRELIMO leader Samora Machel is president.
- **1976** Resistance movement RENAMO set up inside Mozambique by Rhodesians.
- **1976–1980** Mozambique closes Rhodesian border and supports Zimbabwean freedom fighters. Reprisals by RENAMO.
- **1977** FRELIMO constitutes itself as Marxist–Leninist party.
- **1980** South Africa takes over backing of RENAMO.

M

CHRONOLOGY *continued*

- **1982** Zimbabwean troops arrive to guard Mutare–Beira corridor.
- **1984** Nkomati Accord: South Africa agrees to stop support for RENAMO, and Mozambique for ANC, but fighting continues.
- **1986** RENAMO declares war on Zimbabwe. Tanzanian troops reinforce FRELIMO. Machel dies in mysterious air crash in South Africa. Joaquim Chissano replaces him.
- **1988** Nkomati Accord reactivated. Mozambicans allowed back to work in South African mines.
- **1989** War and malnutrition said to claim one million lives. FRELIMO drops Marxism–Leninism.
- **1990** Multipartyism and free-market economy in new constitution. RENAMO breaches cease-fire.
- **1992** Chissano signs peace agreement with RENAMO.
- **1994** Democratic elections return FRELIMO to power.
- **1995** Joins Commonwealth. Economic reforms begun.
- **1999** G7 chooses Mozambique as flagship for international debt relief initiative. RENAMO disputes results of December elections.
- **2000–2001** Thousands displaced by devastating floods.

AID

Recipient

$118m (receipts) — Down 89% in 1999

Mozambique is the world's second most aid-dependent country. Aid accounts for fully 60% of national earnings, and pays for the food needs of some seven million citizens. In 1999, Mozambique became one of only four countries to receive the G7 debt relief scheme for HIPCs, which is worth nearly $3 billion. The main donor states are Italy, the UK, the USA, Sweden, Denmark, the Netherlands, Norway, and, recently, South Africa. Debts from earlier Soviet aid have been written off.

DEFENSE

Compulsory military service

$94m — Up 15% in 1999

About 2.5 million men were deemed "fit for military service" in 1998, but since the civil war ended in 1992, the military's once dominant role in society has greatly diminished. Military figures, once prominent in the FRELIMO government, have been largely stripped of political influence.

Mozambique's new post-peace, British-trained permanent army was formally inaugurated in August 1994. Truly national in character, and only 3–5000 strong, it consists of both former government and RENAMO troops.

However, one byproduct of reorganization was the demobilization of some 75,000 battle-hardened soldiers. Their severance pay ended in mid-1996, and it has not been easy to retrain them, or reintegrate them into civilian life. Some have turned to banditry.

The war's end also saw the departure of external forces, such as the Zimbabwean troops who once guarded strategic railroads against RENAMO attack, and about 6000 UN peacekeepers.

MOZAMBICAN ARMED FORCES

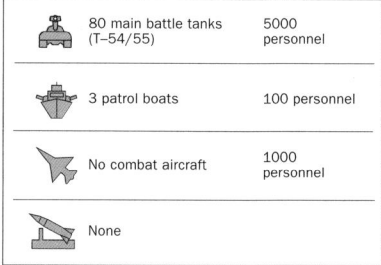

80 main battle tanks (T–54/55)	5000 personnel
3 patrol boats	100 personnel
No combat aircraft	1000 personnel
None	

M

ECONOMICS

Inflation 36.4% p.a. (1990–1999)

$3.8bn — 13,208–17,175 meticais

SCORE CARD

World GNP Ranking	119th
GNP per Capita	$220
Balance of Payments	$-429m
Inflation	2%
Unemployment	50%

EXPORTS

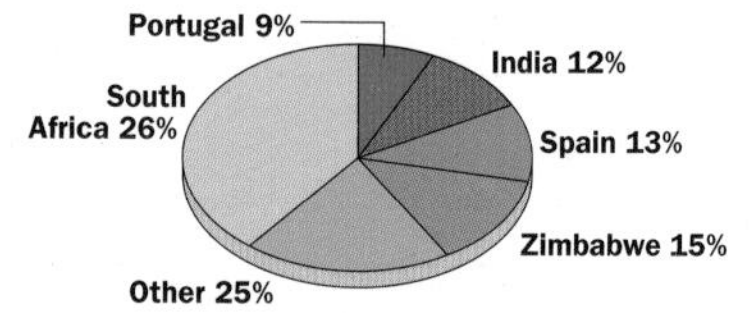

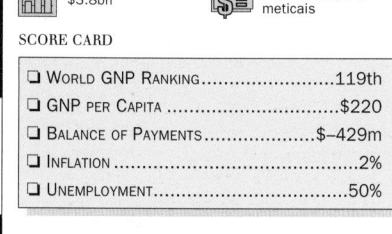

Portugal 9%
India 12%
South Africa 26%
Spain 13%
Zimbabwe 15%
Other 25%

IMPORTS

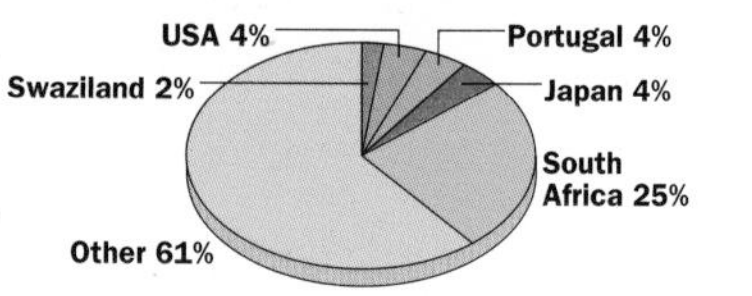

USA 4%
Portugal 4%
Swaziland 2%
Japan 4%
South Africa 25%
Other 61%

Strengths

Following IMF advice, the government has adopted privatization, exchange rate reforms, and trade liberalization. This has enabled Mozambique to attract aid and increase exports.

ECONOMIC PERFORMANCE INDICATOR

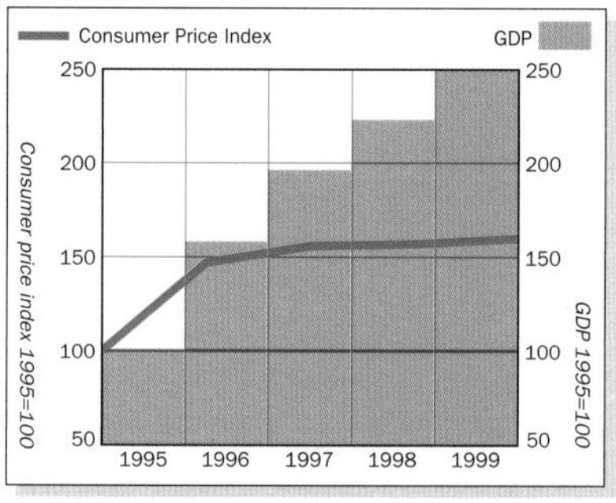

Consumer Price Index
GDP
250
200
150
100
50
1995
1996
1997
1998
1999
Consumer price index 1995=100
GDP 1995=100

Massive rural development programs target agriculture, which employs 85% of the workforce. The fisheries industry has great potential. Improved transportation links with Maputo, Africa's second-largest harbor, will help it to service southern Africa's landlocked regions.

Weaknesses

Overseas aid is essential to prevent at least half the population starving. Over-dependence on foreign donors and companies is another long-term concern. The country is susceptible to drought, floods, and cyclones. Destroyed transportation links hinder the exploitation of minerals. Skilled workers often choose to work in other countries; their absence has delayed the return to normal economic activity.

Profile

Although Mozambique has enormous problems, the government in 1995 produced an optimistic plan, based on World Bank recommendations, to eradicate poverty and raise annual GDP growth to 8–9% by 2000. Devastation resulting from the floods of 2000 and 2001 has effectively destroyed such hopes, and GDP growth for 2000 is put at less than 4%.

MOZAMBIQUE : MAJOR BUSINESSES

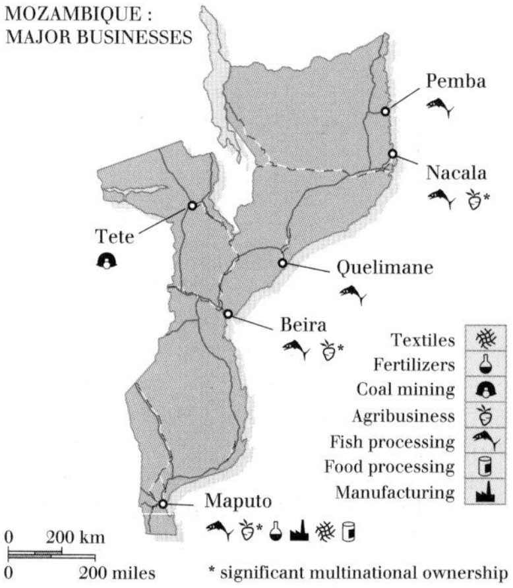

Pemba
Nacala
Tete
Quelimane
Beira
Maputo
Textiles
Fertilizers
Coal mining
Agribusiness
Fish processing
Food processing
Manufacturing
0 200 km
0 200 miles

* significant multinational ownership

RESOURCES

Electric power 2.4m kw

39,579 tonnes

Not an oil producer

1.32m cattle, 670,000 ducks, 28m chickens

Coal, iron, tantalite, uranium, gold, bauxite titanium, copper, gas

ELECTRICITY GENERATION

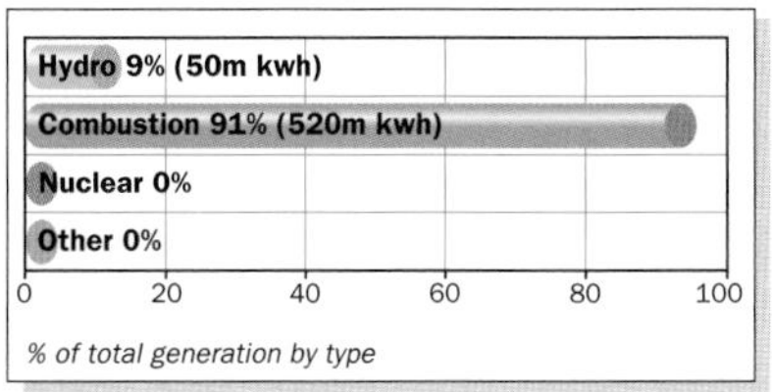
Hydro 9% (50m kwh)
Combustion 91% (520m kwh)
Nuclear 0%
Other 0%
0
20
40
60
80
100
% of total generation by type

Mineral reserves of coal, iron, bauxite, uranium, and gas are under-exploited, due to poor transportation. Cotton could overtake cashew nuts as the chief crop. Fishing is a vital sector; shrimps are a lucrative export. Electricity supplies are being restored, and the Mozal aluminum smelter opened in 2000.

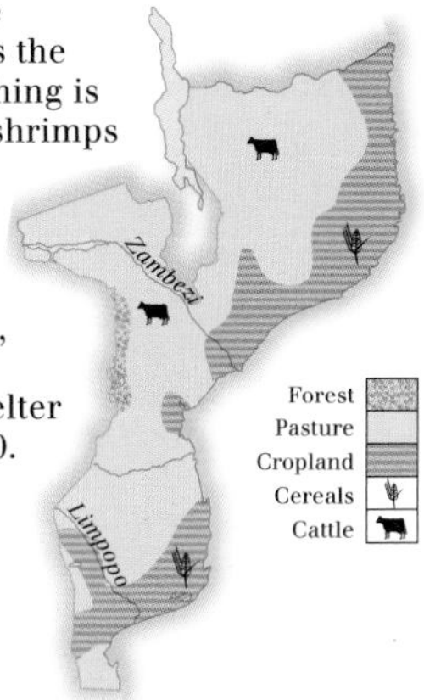
Zambezi
Limpopo
Forest
Pasture
Cropland
Cereals
Cattle
0 200 km
0 200 miles

MOZAMBIQUE : LAND USE

ENVIRONMENT

Sustainability rank: 77th

6%

0.1 tonnes per capita

ENVIRONMENTAL TREATIES

No	Yes	Yes
Yes	Yes	No

Floods followed by droughts are often devastating. The floods of early 2000, resulting from a combination of cyclones and torrential rain, affected an estimated one million people. More than 200,000 were displaced by the floods of 2001. The worst drought in living memory was in 1982–1984; it killed 100,000 and left four million people close to starvation. Civil war pushed rural populations toward the cities and coasts, resulting in overcrowding, disease, pollution, and desertification on abandoned farms. However, ecological concerns are still low on the agenda.

MEDIA

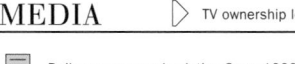

TV ownership low

Daily newspaper circulation 3 per 1000 people

PUBLISHING AND BROADCAST MEDIA

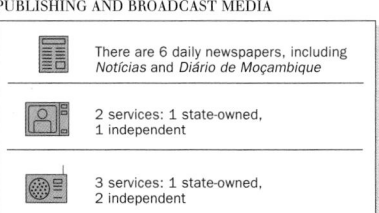

There are 6 daily newspapers, including *Notícias* and *Diário de Moçambique*

2 services: 1 state-owned, 1 independent

3 services: 1 state-owned, 2 independent

The press, hitherto a FRELIMO publicity machine, has enjoyed greater freedom in the 1990s. The killing in 2000 of a popular and outspoken editor, Carlos Cardoso, shocked the country. TV sets are still a rarity. The state-owned radio station broadcasts in Portuguese, English, and vernacular languages.

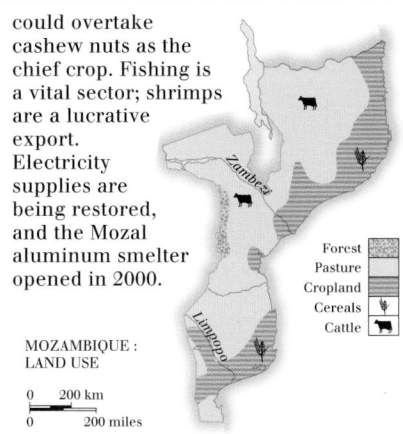

CRIME

Death penalty not used

9608 prisoners

Crime is rising

CRIME RATES

Murders

4 *per 100,000 population*

Rapes

Mozambique does not publish rape statistics

Thefts

36 *per 100,000 population*

Mozambique is awash with weapons. There are many bandits, often former soldiers, in rural areas; road travel is unsafe. Senior officials stand accused of misappropriating food aid money.

EDUCATION

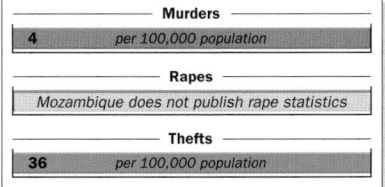

School leaving age: 14

44%

7143 students

THE EDUCATION SYSTEM

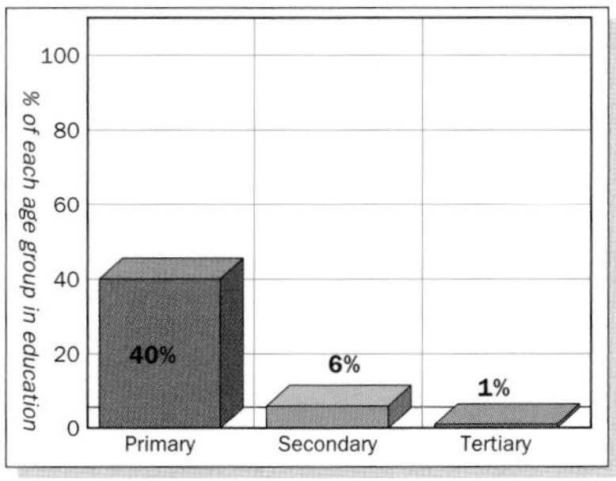
100
80
60
40
20
0
% of each age group in education
40%
6%
1%
Primary
Secondary
Tertiary

At independence, between 85% and 95% of the adult population were illiterate, and school closures during the civil war created a lost generation of uneducated people. A target of educating at least 86% of children was set for 2000, concentrating on rural areas. The government used World Bank/IMF debt relief to strengthen the education budget in 2001.

HEALTH

Welfare state health benefits

1 per 50,000 people

Tuberculosis, gastroenteric infections, pneumonia

Thousands of people lost limbs from land mines, or suffered other appalling injuries and psychological trauma, during Mozambique's savage civil war. Happily, health services have improved since the war's end. Preventive medicines and antenatal care are provided free. Doctors serve a mandatory two years in rural areas. Many private clinics have been established since 1987. However, in 1999 cholera, a lingering byproduct of war, was reported in Beira, and in Niassa, Cabo Delgado, and Nampula provinces. An estimated one million Mozambicans have AIDS.

SPENDING

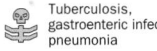

GDP/cap. increase

CONSUMPTION AND SPENDING

1 per 1000 population

4 per 1000 population

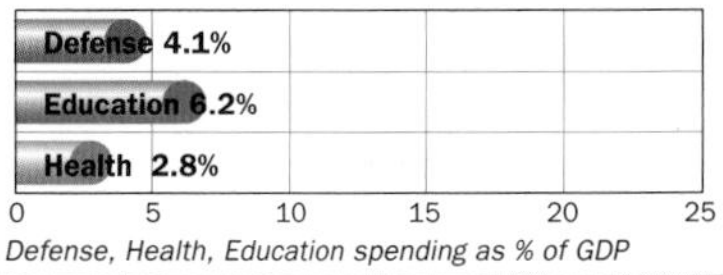
Defense 4.1%
Education 6.2%
Health 2.8%
0
5
10
15
20
25
Defense, Health, Education spending as % of GDP

Mozambique is one of the world's poorest countries, with over 90% of the people living below the breadline even before the floods of 2000 and 2001, which left thousands homeless. Measures adopted in the 1990s to attract Western aid made conditions tougher, raising the price of rice by 600%. The recent export boom has generally bypassed the traditional subsistence farmer. Only the higher echelons of FRELIMO, RENAMO, and other political parties have cars, air-conditioning, and brick-built apartments. Free-market reforms, however, are gradually increasing access to consumer goods.

WORLD RANKING

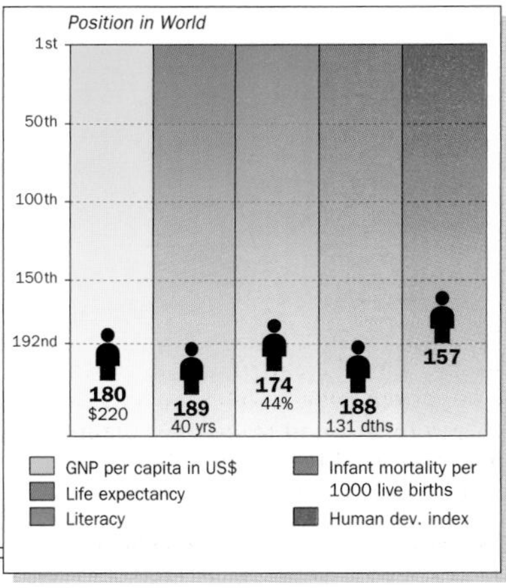
Position in World
1st
50th
100th
150th
192nd
180
$220
189
40 yrs
174
44%
188
131 dths
157
GNP per capita in US$
Life expectancy
Literacy
Infant mortality per 1000 live births
Human dev. index

M

NAMIBIA

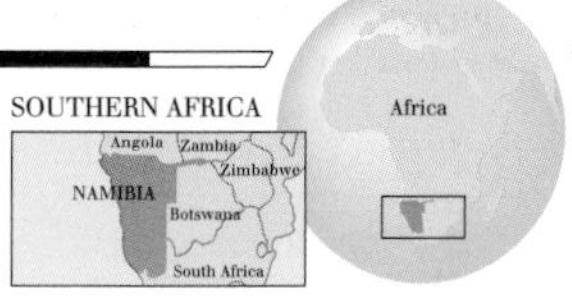
SOUTHERN AFRICA
Africa
Angola
Zambia
Zimbabwe
NAMIBIA
Botswana
South Africa

OFFICIAL NAME: Republic of Namibia **CAPITAL:** Windhoek
POPULATION: 1.7 million **CURRENCY:** Namibian dollar **OFFICIAL LANGUAGE:** English

1990 | 1994 | March 21 | NAM | +2 | +264 | .na

LOCATED IN SOUTHWESTERN Africa, Namibia has an arid coastal strip formed by the Namib Desert. After many years of guerrilla warfare, Namibia won independence from South Africa in 1990. Despite the move away from apartheid, Namibia's economy remains reliant on the expertise of the small white population, a legacy of the previously poor education for blacks. Namibia is Africa's fourth-largest minerals producer.

CLIMATE

Hot desert/steppe

WEATHER CHART

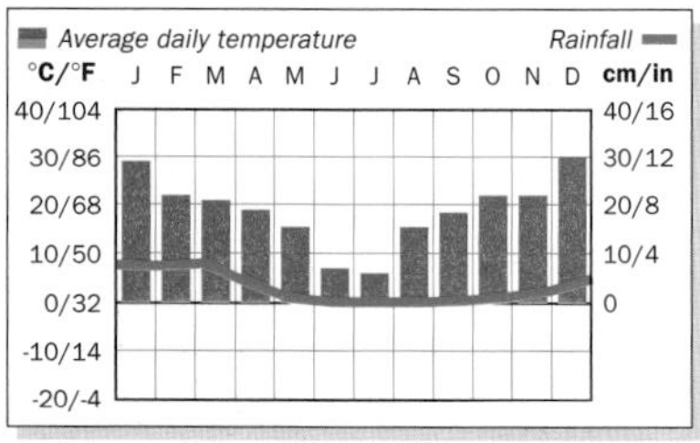
Average daily temperature
Rainfall
°C/°F
J F M A M J J A S O N D
cm/in
40/104
30/86
20/68
10/50
0/32
-10/14
-20/-4
40/16
30/12
20/8
10/4
0

Namibia is almost rainless. The coast is usually shrouded in thick, cold fog unless the hot, very dry *berg* blows.

TRANSPORTATION

Drive on left

Windhoek International 492,957 passengers

105 ships 54,794 grt

THE TRANSPORTATION NETWORK

5250 km (3262 miles)

None

2382 km (1480 miles)

None

Large-scale industry is well served by road and rail. Plans exist to build a new harbor at Walvis Bay.

TOURISM

Visitors : Population 1:2.8

614,000 visitors

Up 54% 1995–1998

MAIN TOURIST ARRIVALS

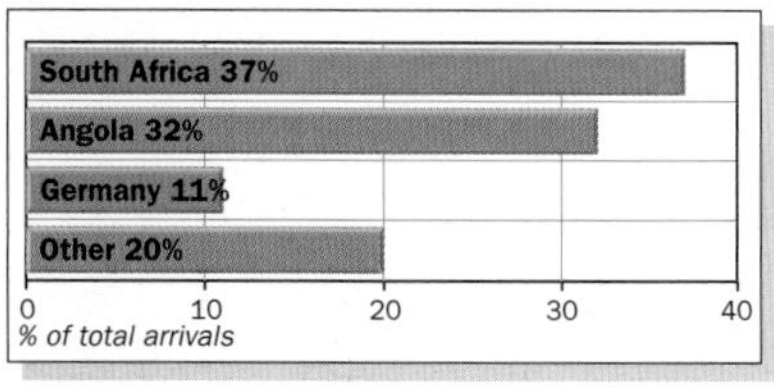
South Africa 37%
Angola 32%
Germany 11%
Other 20%
0
10
20
30
40
% of total arrivals

Tourists, largely from South Africa, make a very limited contribution to GDP. German tourists come to see Windhoek's German sector. There are plans to limit tourists to 300,000 a year to preserve Namibia's fragile desert ecology.

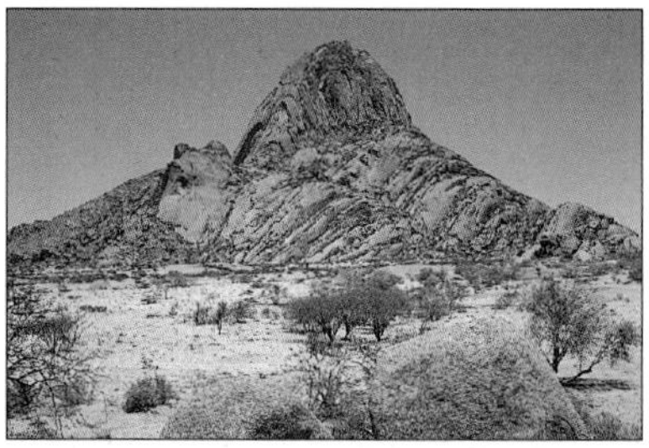

Spitzkoppe, west of Karibib. *Unique scenery such as this is attracting increasing numbers of tourists to Namibia.*

PEOPLE

Pop. density low

Ovambo, Kavango, English, Bergdama, German

2/km² (5/mi²)

THE URBAN/RURAL POPULATION SPLIT

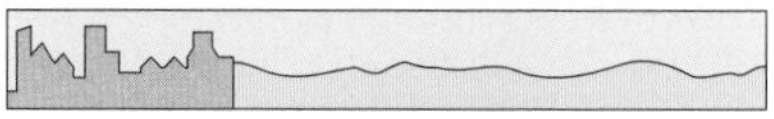
30%
70%

ETHNIC MAKEUP

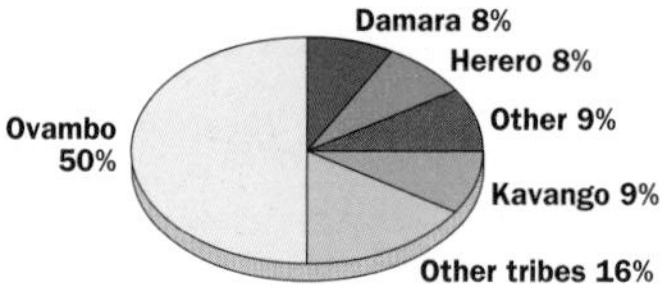
Damara 8%
Herero 8%
Other 9%
Kavango 9%
Other tribes 16%
Ovambo 50%

The largest ethnic group, the Ovambo, tend to live in the sparsely populated north of the country. Whites – 60% of whom speak Afrikaans – are concentrated in Windhoek. The capital is also home to a wealthy century-old German community. Namibia's original inhabitants, the San and Khoi (once called Bushmen) now constitute a tiny, marginalized minority.

The ethnic strife predicted in 1990 has not materialized. For the most part, black Namibians, predominantly subsistence farmers, have accepted the greater wealth of the white community. Families are large in Namibia; many black women have six or more children. The constitution supports gender equality and discriminates in favor of women; few, however, have official jobs or own property. Homosexuality is not tolerated.

POLITICS

Multiparty elections

L. House 1999/2004
U. House 1998/2004

President Sam Nujoma

AT THE LAST ELECTION

National Assembly 72 seats

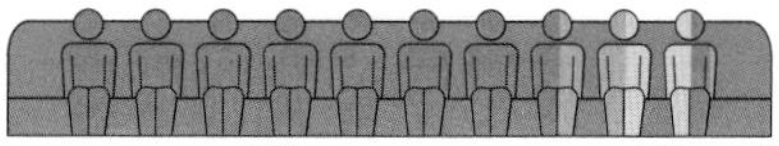
10% CoD
3% UDF
76% SWAPO
10% DTA
1% MAG

SWAPO = South West Africa People's Organization **CoD** = Congress of Democrats **DTA** = Democratic Turnhalle Alliance **UDF** = United Democratic Front **MAG** = Monitor Action Group

Six additional nonvoting members may be appointed to the National Assembly by the president

National Council 26 seats

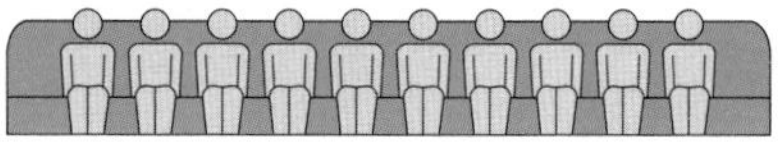

Two members are elected by each of the 13 Regional Councils to the National Council

SWAPO guerrillas fought for and won independence from South Africa in 1990. Namibia switched from a system of apartheid to a state-wide, multiparty democracy. The center-left SWAPO has dominated politically ever since. In 1998 a constitutional amendment allowed President Nujoma to run for a third term, which he duly won in late 1999. SWAPO's main opposition comes from the center-right DTA, a coalition of 11 parties favoring free-market practices.

WORLD AFFAIRS

Joined UN in 1990

Comm | COMESA | NAM | OAU | SADC

In 1992, South Africa settled its border dispute with Namibia, and in 1994 relinquished control of the enclave of Walvis Bay – Namibia's only deep-water port. South Africa has also written off Namibia's earlier debts. Withdrawal of Namibian troops from the war-torn Congo (former Zaire) began in 2001.

AID

Recipient

US$178m (receipts)

Down 1% in 1999

The UN provides most aid; Germany is the main unilateral donor. Around one-third of aid is spent on education.

DEFENSE

No compulsory military service

US$120m

Up 28% in 1999

Fishing grounds are patrolled to prevent raids by foreign trawlers. Soldiers performed a peacekeeping role in Congo (former Zaire).

N

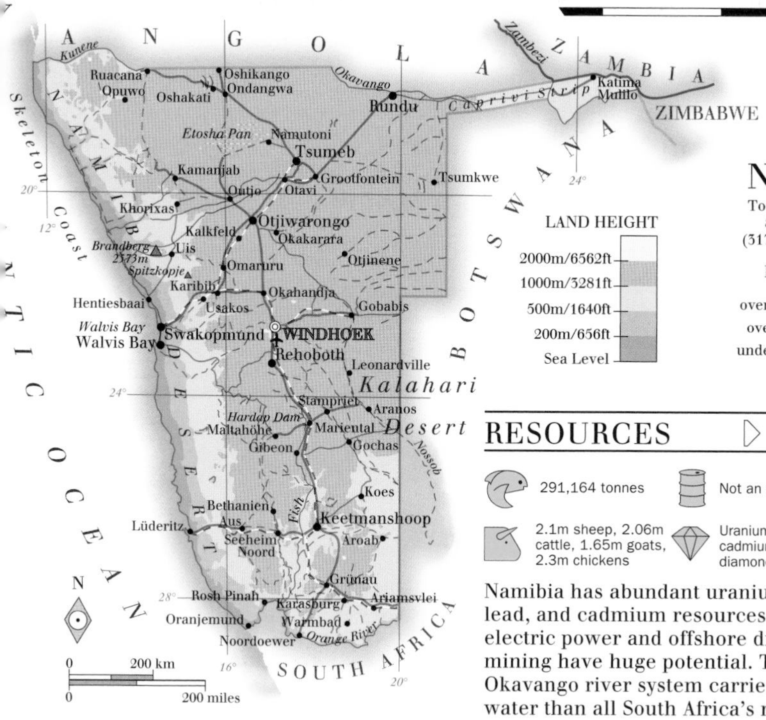
ANGOLA
Kunene
Ruacana
Opuwo
Oshakati
Oshikango
Ondangwa
Okavango
Rundu
Caprivi Strip
Zambezi
ZAMBIA
Katima Mulilo
ZIMBABWE
BOTSWANA
Etosha Pan
Namutoni
Tsumeb
Tsumkwe
Kamanjab
Grootfontein
Outjo
Otavi
Skeleton Coast
Khorixas
Kalkfeld
Otjiwarongo
Okakarara
Brandberg 2573m
Uis
Spitzkopje
Omaruru
Otjinene
Karibib
Okahandja
Hentiesbaai
Usakos
Gobabis
Walvis Bay
Swakopmund
WINDHOEK
Rehoboth
Leonardville
Kalahari Desert
NAMIB DESERT
ATLANTIC OCEAN
Stampriet
Aranos
Hardap Dam
Maltahöhe
Mariental
Gibeon
Gochas
Nossob
Koes
Fish
Bethanien
Lüderitz
Aus
Keetmanshoop
Seeheim Noord
Aroab
Grünau
Rosh Pinah
Karasburg
Ariamsvlei
Oranjemund
Warmbad
Orange River
Noordoewer
SOUTH AFRICA
N
200 km
200 miles
LAND HEIGHT
2000m/6562ft
1000m/3281ft
500m/1640ft
200m/656ft
Sea Level

NAMIBIA

Total Land Area : 823 290 sq. km (317 872 sq. miles)

POPULATION

over 100 000
over 10 000
under 10 000

CHRONOLOGY

In 1915, South Africa took over the former German colony as a League of Nations' mandate known as South West Africa.

- **1966** Apartheid laws imposed. SWAPO begins armed struggle.
- **1968** Renamed Namibia.
- **1973** UN recognizes SWAPO.
- **1990** Independence.
- **1994** South Africa relinquishes Walvis Bay.
- **1999** President Sam Nujoma wins third term.

ECONOMICS

Inflation 9.8% p.a. (1990–1999)

US$3.2bn

6.158–7.570 Namibian dollars

SCORE CARD

- World GNP Ranking 129th
- GNP per Capita ....US$1890
- Balance of Payments ....US$162m
- Inflation 8.6%
- Unemployment..................................40%

STRENGTHS
Varied mineral resources. Market conditions attractive to private investors. Rich fishing grounds. Potential of Walvis Bay as conduit for landlocked neighbors. Low external debt.

WEAKNESSES
Most goods imported. Fluctuations in mineral prices. Recessionary ripple effect of currency pegged to South African rand. Lack of skilled labor; high unemployment. Severe drought in 1996.

EXPORTS

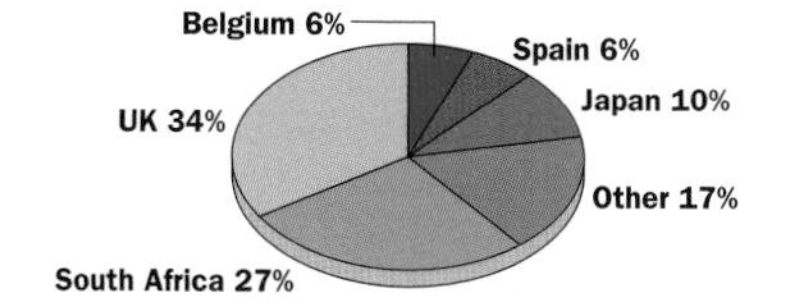
Belgium 6%
Spain 6%
Japan 10%
UK 34%
Other 17%
South Africa 27%

IMPORTS

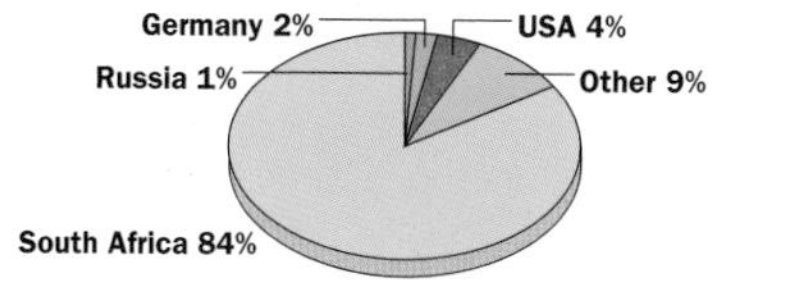
Germany 2%
USA 4%
Russia 1%
Other 9%
South Africa 84%

RESOURCES

Not available

291,164 tonnes

Not an oil producer

2.1m sheep, 2.06m cattle, 1.65m goats, 2.3m chickens

Uranium, lead, gold, cadmium, oil, copper, diamonds, zinc, silver,

Namibia has abundant uranium, lead, and cadmium resources. Hydro-electric power and offshore diamond mining have huge potential. The Okavango river system carries more water than all South Africa's rivers combined. Large oil deposits were discovered in 2000.

ENVIRONMENT

Not available

13%

Not available

Illegal poaching and anthrax deposits are threatening the unique Namibian desert-adapted elephant (fewer than 50 remain) and the black rhino. Vast expanses of the fragile, unspoiled Namib and Kalahari Desert ecosystems are protected. The government is generally sensitive to environmental issues (the annual seal-cull to protect fish stocks is an exception) and wishes to attract ecotourists rather than invest in mass-market developments.

MEDIA

TV ownership low

Daily newspaper circulation 19 per 1000 people

PUBLISHING AND BROADCAST MEDIA

There are 4 daily newspapers, including *The Namibian* and *Die Republikein*

2 independent services

5 independent services

State radio transmits in 11 languages, including German and English. An active press targets corrupt politicians.

CRIME

Death penalty not used

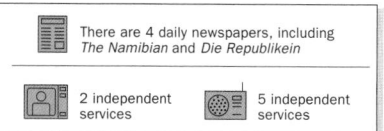

Namibia does not publish prison figures

Down 1% 1996–1998

Burglary and theft are rising, particularly in urban areas. Ostrich smuggling to the USA is common.

EDUCATION

School leaving age: 16

82%

11,344 students

Nearly 90% of children attend primary school, but illiteracy among black adults remains a legacy of apartheid.

HEALTH

Welfare state health benefits

1 per 5000 people

AIDS, respiratory, heart, and intestinal diseases

Preventive care and rural health care have top priority. Most areas lack safe water. AIDS is the leading cause of death.

SPENDING

GDP/cap. increase

CONSUMPTION AND SPENDING

47 per 1000 population

64 per 1000 population

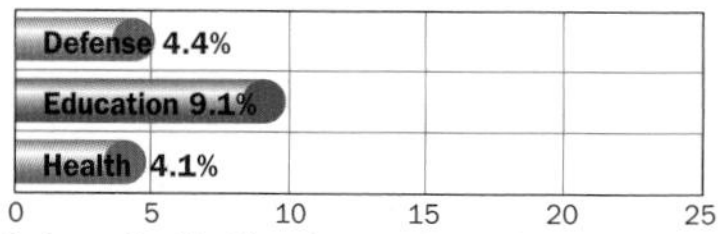
Defense 4.4%
Education 9.1%
Health 4.1%
0
5
10
15
20
25

Defense, Health, Education spending as % of GDP

Gross disparities in wealth persist throughout Namibia: the top 1% of households consumes as much as the poorest 50%.

WORLD RANKING

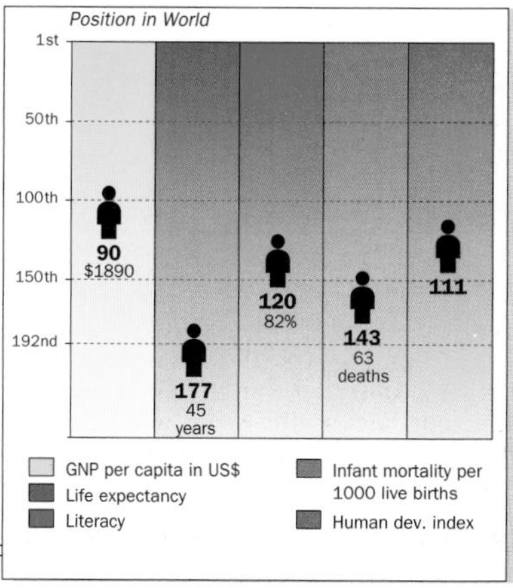
Position in World
1st
50th
100th
150th
192nd
90
$1890
177
45 years
120
82%
143
63 deaths
111
GNP per capita in US$
Life expectancy
Literacy
Infant mortality per 1000 live births
Human dev. index

N

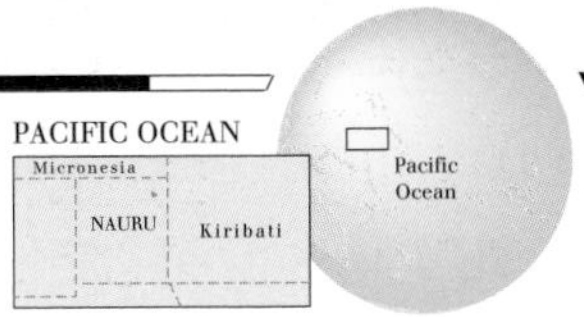
PACIFIC OCEAN
Micronesia
NAURU
Kiribati
Pacific Ocean

NAURU

OFFICIAL NAME: Republic of Nauru **CAPITAL:** *No official capital*
POPULATION: 11,800 **CURRENCY:** Australian dollar **OFFICIAL LANGUAGE:** Nauruan

1968 | 1968 | Jan 31 | NAU | +12 | +674 | .nr

NAURU, THE WORLD'S smallest republic, lies in the Pacific Ocean, 4000 km (2480 miles) northeast of Australia. A former British colony, Nauru was exploited for its phosphates by the UK, Australia, and New Zealand. After independence in 1968, the phosphates industry made Nauruans among the wealthiest people in the world. Economic mismanagement and the approaching end of phosphate reserves have left Nauru facing financial ruin, prompting economic reform.

CLIMATE

Tropical oceanic

WEATHER CHART

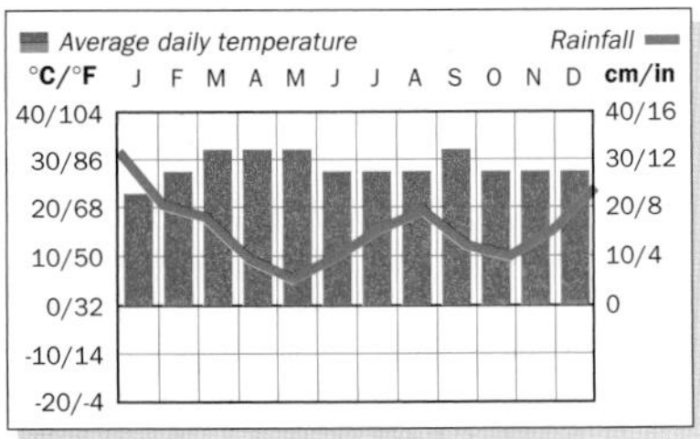
Average daily temperature
Rainfall
°C/°F
J F M A M J J A S O N D
cm/in
40/104
30/86
20/68
10/50
0/32
-10/14
-20/-4
40/16
30/12
20/8
10/4
0

Nauru's tiny size means that rain clouds often miss the island; years can pass without rain.

TRANSPORTATION

Drive on left

Nauru Island International

3 ships 1000 grt

THE TRANSPORTATION NETWORK

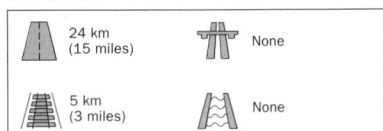

24 km (15 miles)	None
5 km (3 miles)	None

Nauru operates its own airline with a Boeing 737 flown by Australian pilots. The Nauru Pacific Line provides infrequent commercial services to Australia. However, all external travel is very expensive. Nauru has no harbor: to load cargoes of phosphates, ships have to dock, engines still running, with huge concrete caissons floating out at sea. The circular ring road is often littered with abandoned cars, as it has been much cheaper for Nauruans to import new vehicles than to attempt to repair existing ones. The number of car accident fatalities is one of the highest in the South Pacific.

TOURISM

Not available

Minimal tourist arrivals

Little variation from year to year

MAIN TOURIST ARRIVALS

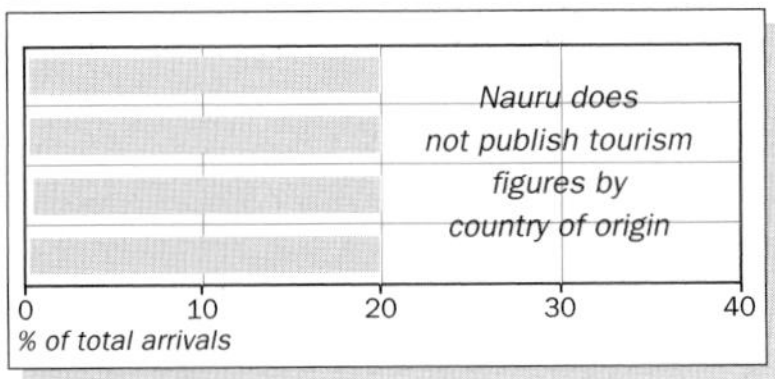
Nauru does not publish tourism figures by country of origin
0
10
20
30
40
% of total arrivals

Even if Nauru had any conventional tourist attractions, the enormous cost of getting there would dissuade most tourists from making the journey. The main feature of interest on the island is the bizarre lunar landscape created by over 80 years of phosphate extraction. There are no beaches and only a few basic hotels.

NAURU

Total Land Area : 21.2 sq. km (8.2 sq. miles)

LAND HEIGHT
200m/565ft
Sea Level

Urban area
Phosphate mineworks

0 1 km
0 1 mile

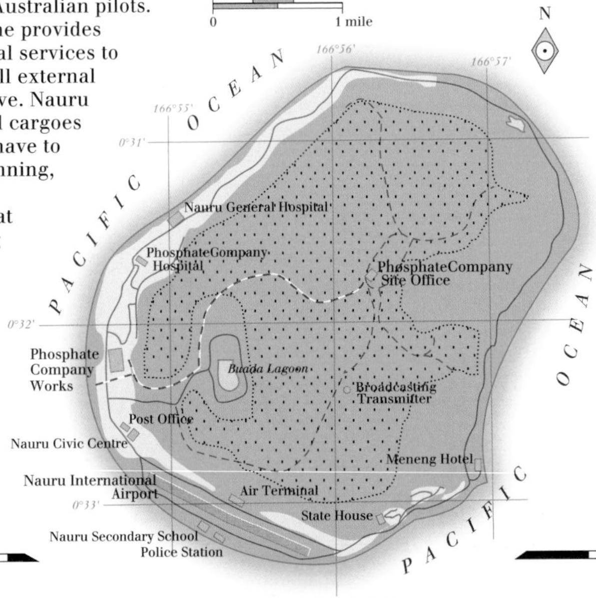
N
PACIFIC OCEAN
PACIFIC OCEAN
166°55'
166°56'
166°57'
0°31'
0°32'
0°33'
Nauru General Hospital
Phosphate Company Hospital
Phosphate Company Site Office
Phosphate Company Works
Buada Lagoon
Broadcasting Transmitter
Post Office
Nauru Civic Centre
Meneng Hotel
Nauru International Airport
Air Terminal
State House
Nauru Secondary School
Police Station

PEOPLE

Pop. density high

Nauruan, Kiribati, Chinese, Tuvaluan, English

564/km² (1461/mi²)

THE URBAN/RURAL POPULATION SPLIT

Nauru is 100% semi-urban

ETHNIC MAKEUP

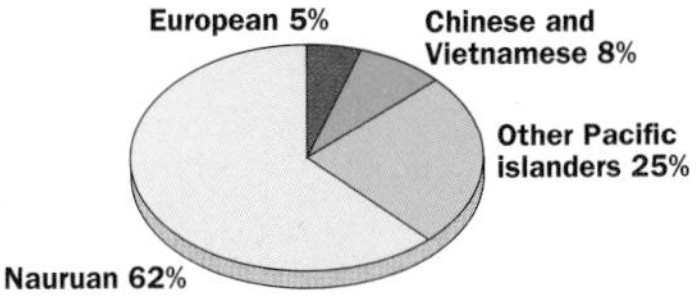
European 5%
Chinese and Vietnamese 8%
Other Pacific islanders 25%
Nauruan 62%

Indigenous Nauruans are a homogenous blend of Mela-, Micro-, and Polynesian strands. They have traditionally been employed in government service, while a large imported workforce – mainly from Kiribati – mines the phosphates.

A society of just over 10,000 people, Nauru is mostly self-regulating. There is some tension between younger Nauruans, who go to Australia to study but have little incentive to do well, and their parents, who fought hard for independence. As the phosphates run out, an increasing feeling of futility is gripping the young. Many see their future in Australia or New Zealand, but fear a drop in living standards and the loss of the luxury of sovereignty. It was the latter which led Nauruans to reject the offer of resettlement on an island off the Queensland coast of Australia.

POLITICS

Multiparty elections

2000/2003

President Rene Harris

AT THE LAST ELECTION

Parliament 18 seats

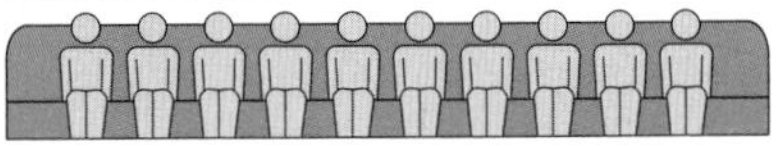

All members are elected as independents

Parliament is based on the British Westminster model, but traditional leaders are the dominant figures. Members of the legislature often switch between temporary groupings based more on personalities than ideologies. Hammer DeRoburt became the island's first president in 1968, dominating the political landscape until a 1989 vote of no confidence.

Since DeRoburt's downfall the presidency (elected by parliament) has changed hands frequently in a more volatile political atmosphere.

N

WORLD AFFAIRS

Joined UN in 1999

Comm | PC | PIF | ADB | ACP

The case for compensation for phosphate exploitation brought by Nauru against the UK government was rejected in 1992 after the longest suit in British legal history. However, an Australian settlement that year brought payments eventually totaling A$107 million. Nauru's main concern is participation in the Pacific Islands Forum and the management of trust funds to support Nauruans when phosphate deposits run out. Nauru joined the UN in 1999. It seeks a voice on environmental issues.

AID

Recipient

US$7m (receipts)

Up 250% in 1999

Nauru receives or donates little aid, except as a member of the Pacific Islands Forum.

DEFENSE

No compulsory military service

Australia responsible for defense

Not applicable

Nauru has no defense force. Australia, under a *de facto* arrangement, is responsible for the island's security.

ECONOMICS

Not available

US$80m

1.5282–1.7997 Australian dollars

SCORE CARD

- ❑ WORLD GNP RANKING........................189th
- ❑ GNP PER CAPITA ....US$7270
- ❑ BALANCE OF PAYMENTS ....Not available
- ❑ INFLATION ....–4%
- ❑ UNEMPLOYMENT ....Minimal unemployment

STRENGTHS

Considerable investments overseas. Tax haven. Offshore banking potential. Trust funds for post-phosphate era. Strong Australian dollar.

WEAKNESSES

Phosphate revenues due to end in 2003. High cost of rehabilitating the 80% of the island where mining occurred. Virtually no other resources. Bad investment decisions in 1990s.

EXPORTS

Nauru's only export commodity is phosphates, in which it trades with Australia and New Zealand.

IMPORTS

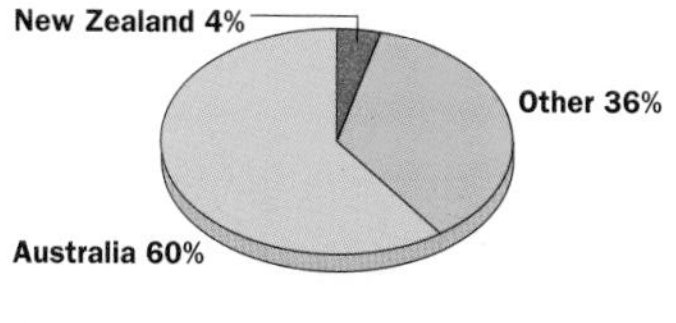
New Zealand 4%
Other 36%
Australia 60%

RESOURCES

Electric power 10,000 kw

400 tonnes

Not an oil producer

2.1m sheep, 2800 pigs, 5000 chickens

Guano (phosphates)

Since 1888 Nauru has been exploited by the Germans, British, Australians, New Zealanders, and recently by Nauruans themselves, for its valuable phosphate reserves. Extraction has destroyed 80% of the island, and the deposits have been virtually exhausted. Nauru has no other resources. The island is entirely dependent on outside energy supplies and the cost of oil is 50% higher than the Pacific average, since Nauru does not lie on any shipping routes. Most electricity is produced by small diesel generators.

ENVIRONMENT

Not available

None

Not available

Nauru is an environmental disaster area. Mining has destroyed 80% of its ecosystem and, like other Pacific islands, it faces the increasing threat of rising sea levels. Also of concern is contamination from the nearby former French nuclear test sites in the Pacific.

MEDIA

TV ownership low

There are no daily newspapers

PUBLISHING AND BROADCAST MEDIA

There are no daily newspapers. The *Nasero Bulletin* is published fortnightly

1 state-owned service

1 state-owned service

Nauru has one national TV broadcasting service and one radio station. Both are state-run.

CRIME

Death penalty not used

Nauru does not publish prison figures

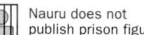

Crime levels are rising slightly

Theft is almost nonexistent. Assaults and dangerous driving as a result of drunkenness are the major problems.

***Nauru is almost circular** with a 16-km (10-mile) ring road. The overcrowded coastal strip is the sole habitable land.*

CHRONOLOGY

Colonized by Germany in 1888, from 1919 the island was administered jointly by the UK, Australia, and New Zealand.

- ❑ **1968** Independence.
- ❑ **1970** Gains phosphate control.
- ❑ **1992** Australia agrees compensation for phosphate extraction.

EDUCATION

School leaving age: 16

99%

Not available

Many Nauruans attend boarding school in Australia from a young age. Few go on to university.

HEALTH

Welfare state health benefits

1 per 700 people

Tuberculosis, vitamin deficiencies, diabetes

A diet of processed imported foods and widespread obesity are the major problems. Over one-third of the population suffers from non-insulin-dependent diabetes. Industrial accidents are treated in Australia.

SPENDING

GDP/cap. increase

CONSUMPTION AND SPENDING

No data

157 per 1000 population

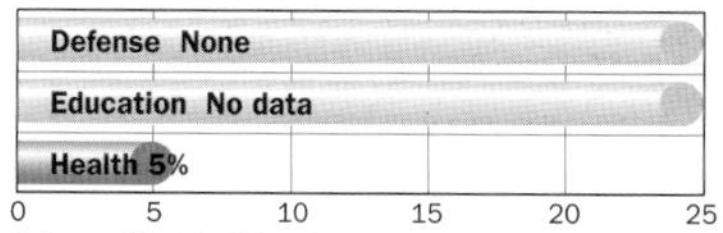
Defense None
Education No data
Health 5%
0
5
10
15
20
25

Defense, Health, Education spending as % of GDP

Nauru is carrying out a major economic adjustment program, to be funded by the ADB. The program is intended to allow it to adjust to the loss of income when its phosphate reserves are exhausted.

WORLD RANKING

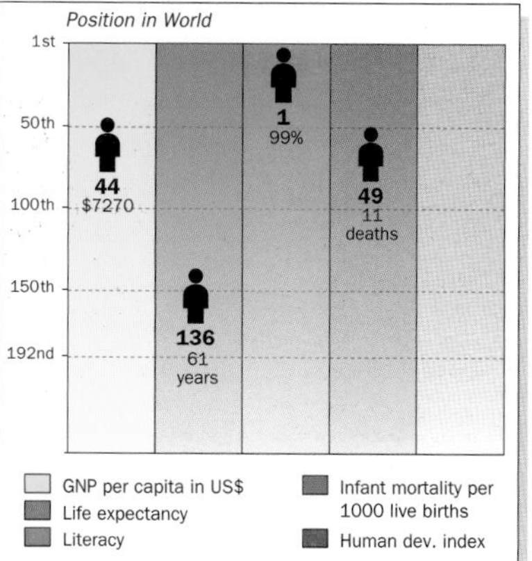
Position in World
1st
50th
100th
150th
192nd
44
$7270
136
61
years
1
99%
49
11
deaths
GNP per capita in US$
Life expectancy
Literacy
Infant mortality per 1000 live births
Human dev. index

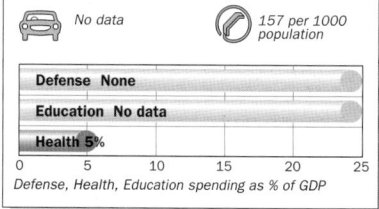

N

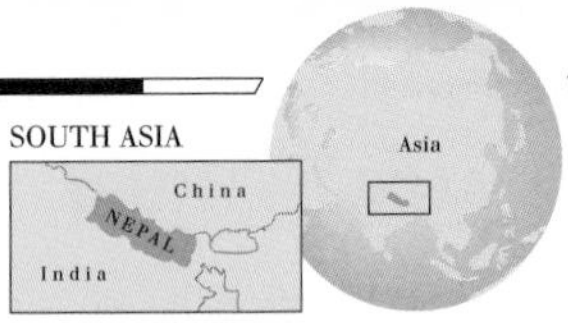
SOUTH ASIA
China
NEPAL
India
Asia

NEPAL

OFFICIAL NAME: Kingdom of Nepal **CAPITAL:** Kathmandu
POPULATION: 23.9 million **CURRENCY:** Nepalese rupee **OFFICIAL LANGUAGE:** Nepali

1769 · 1769 · Dec 28 · NEP · +5.75 · +977 · .np

ON THE SHOULDER of the southern Himalayas, Nepal is surrounded by India and China. It was ruled by an absolute monarchy until 1990; since then its politics have become increasingly turbulent. The mainly agricultural economy is heavily dependent on the prompt arrival of the monsoon. Hopes for development have been invested in hydroelectric power, despite the adverse impact of large dams. Backpackers, a major source of tourist income, also cause environmental problems.

CLIMATE

Mountain/subtropical

WEATHER CHART

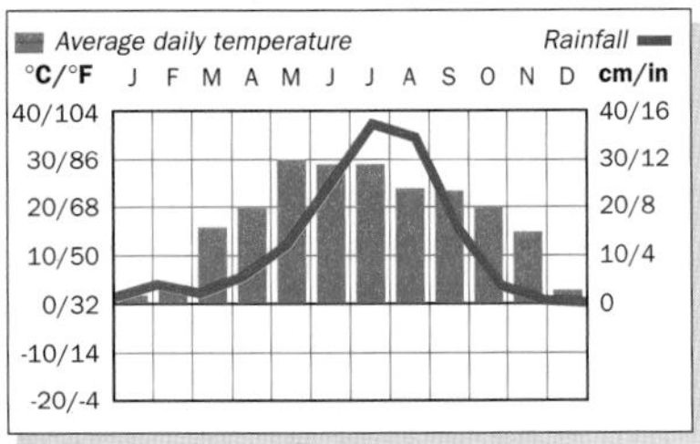
Average daily temperature
Rainfall
°C/°F J F M A M J J A S O N D cm/in
40/104
30/86
20/68
10/50
0/32
-10/14
-20/-4
40/16
30/12
20/8
10/4
0

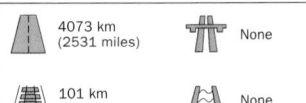

The warm July to October monsoon affects the whole country, causing flooding in the hot Terai plain, but generally decreases northward and westward. The rest of the year is dry, sunny and mild, except in the Himalayas, where valley temperatures in winter may average –10°C (14°F).

TRANSPORTATION

Drive on left

Tribhuvan International, Kathmandu 800,000 passengers

Has no fleet

THE TRANSPORTATION NETWORK

4073 km (2531 miles)

None

101 km (63 miles)

None

Domestic flights link the main towns. There are paved roads in the south and in the Kathmandu valley; only one runs north to China. Two short stretches of railroad cross into India.

Himalayan harvest. *Steep mountainsides and easily eroded soils mean that most fields are terraced. A majority of Nepalese are farmers.*

TOURISM

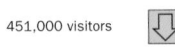

Visitors : Population 1:53

451,000 visitors

Down 8% in 2000

MAIN TOURIST ARRIVALS

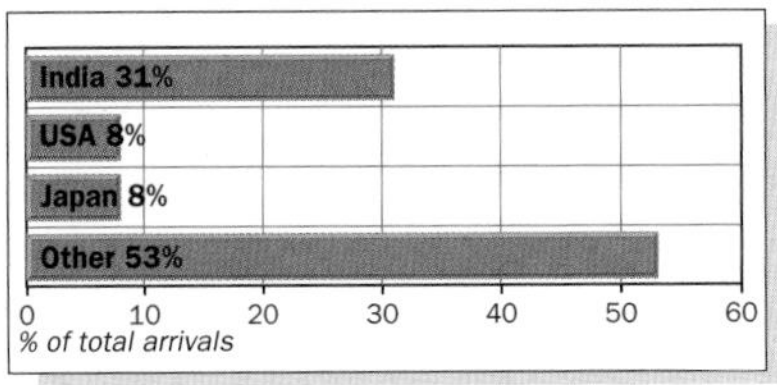
India 31%
USA 8%
Japan 8%
Other 53%
0 10 20 30 40 50 60
% of total arrivals

A serious conflict exists in Nepal between the wish to preserve the environment and the desire for tourist revenue. Recent terrorist activity such as the 1999 hijacking of an Air India aircraft bound for Nepal, and the Maoist insurgency, which resurfaced with a much higher public profile in 2001, threatens to deter visitors. A law was passed in 2000 banning child labor in the tourism industry.

PEOPLE

Pop. density medium

Nepali, Maithilli, Bhojpuri

175/km² (452/mi²)

THE URBAN/RURAL POPULATION SPLIT

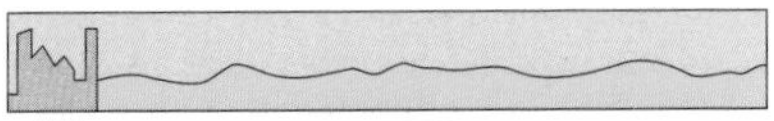
12%
88%

RELIGIOUS PERSUASION

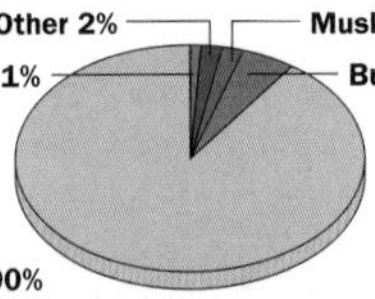
Other 2%
Muslim 3%
Christian 1%
Buddhist 4%
Hindu 90%

There are few tensions among diverse ethnic groups such as the Sherpas in the north, "Hill Hindu" Brahmins and Chhettris, Newars, and others in the Kathmandu valley, and Terai in the south. The Sherpa and other Buddhist women are less restricted than Hindus. Polygamy is practiced in the hills. Since 1990 many ethnic Nepalese refugees from Bhutan have settled in Nepal.

POLITICS

Multiparty elections

L. House 1999/2004
U. House 2001/2003

HM King Gyanendra Bir Bikram Shah Dev

AT THE LAST ELECTION

House of Representatives 205 seats

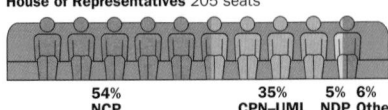

54% NCP
35% CPN–UML
5% NDP
6% Other

NCP = Nepali Congress Party **CPN–UML** = Communist Party of Nepal–United Marxist-Leninist **NDP** = National Democratic Party **App** = Appointed by the king

National Council 60 seats

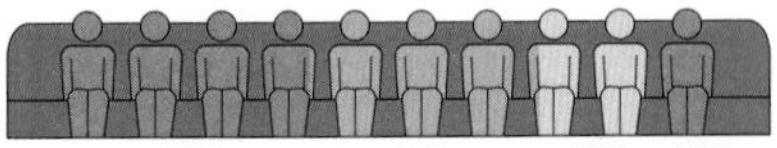
38% CPN-UML
35% NCP
17% App
10% Other

A multiparty system introduced in 1990 produced a short-lived communist government in 1994, then a series of unstable coalitions until the NCP won elections in 1999. Nepal was shocked in June 2001 by the killing of King Birendra and members of his family in a palace massacre. Gyanendra, his brother, became king amid growing unrest. Maoist rebels, already a threat to government authority in some rural areas, pressed for Girija Prasad Koirala to resign as prime minister, and Sher Bahadur Deuba replaced him in July.

WORLD AFFAIRS

Joined UN in 1955

CP · IBRD · NAM · SAARC · ADB

Nepal's security relations with India are questioned by the UML which is more pro-Chinese. The NCP government has revived links with India, on which Nepal depends for its external trade. Relations with Bhutan are strained over ethnic Nepali Bhutanese refugees in Nepal.

AID

Recipient

$344m (receipts)

Down 15% in 1999

Nepal's strategic position has made it a focus for powerful donors, including the USA, China, India, Japan, and member states of the CIS.

DEFENSE

No compulsory military service

$42m

Up 8% in 1999

The army, at 46,000 men, is small and has no tanks or combat aircraft. Weapons come from India and the UK, in whose own army the Nepalese Gurkhas serve.

N

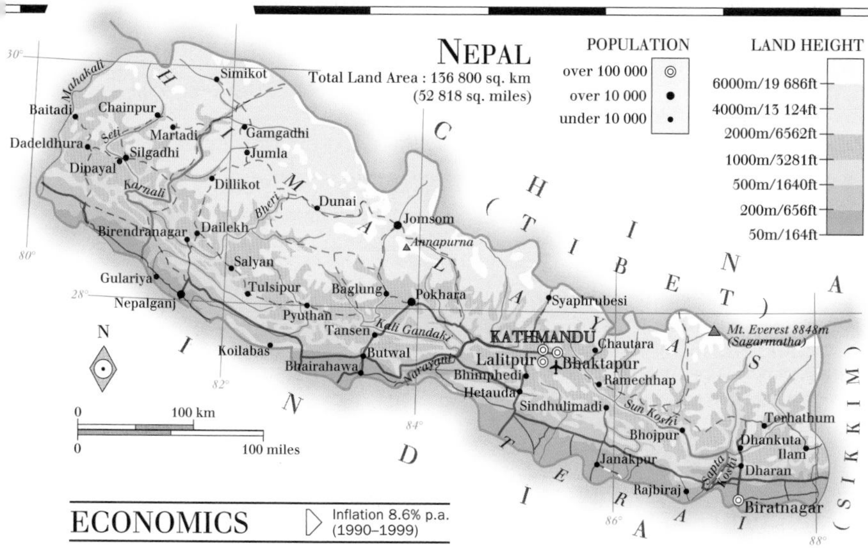
NEPAL
Total Land Area : 136 800 sq. km (52 818 sq. miles)
POPULATION
over 100 000
over 10 000
under 10 000
LAND HEIGHT
6000m/19 686ft
4000m/13 124ft
2000m/6562ft
1000m/3281ft
500m/1640ft
200m/656ft
50m/164ft
CHINA (TIBET)
INDIA
SIKKIM
KATHMANDU
Simikot
Baitadi
Chainpur
Dadeldhura
Martadi
Gamgadhi
Silgadhi
Jumla
Dipayal
Dillikot
Dunai
Jomsom
Annapurna
Birendranagar
Dailekh
Salyan
Gulariya
Nepalganj
Tulsipur
Baglung
Pokhara
Pyuthan
Tansen
Syaphrubesi
Mt. Everest 8848m (Sagarmatha)
Chautara
Koilabas
Butwal
Bhairahawa
Lalitpur
Bhaktapur
Bhimphedi
Hetauda
Ramechhap
Sindhulimadi
Terhathum
Bhojpur
Dhankuta
Ilam
Janakpur
Dharan
Rajbiraj
Biratnagar
0 100 km
0 100 miles

ECONOMICS

Inflation 8.6% p.a. (1990–1999)

$5.2bn

68.72–74.58 Nepalese rupees

SCORE CARD

- World GNP Ranking........108th
- GNP per Capita........$220
- Balance of Payments........$-57m
- Inflation........8%
- Unemployment........5%

Strengths
Self-sufficiency in grain most years. Economic liberalization under NCP government. Potential for hydroelectric power generation. Low debt level.

Weaknesses
Agricultural dependency: only 10% of GDP from manufacturing. Landlocked status. Low savings rate. Absence of active entrepreneurial class.

EXPORTS

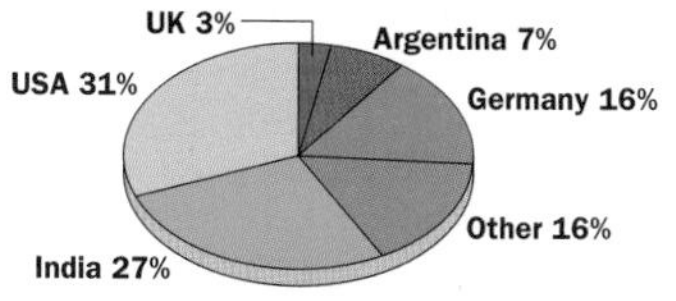
UK 3%
Argentina 7%
USA 31%
Germany 16%
Other 16%
India 27%

IMPORTS

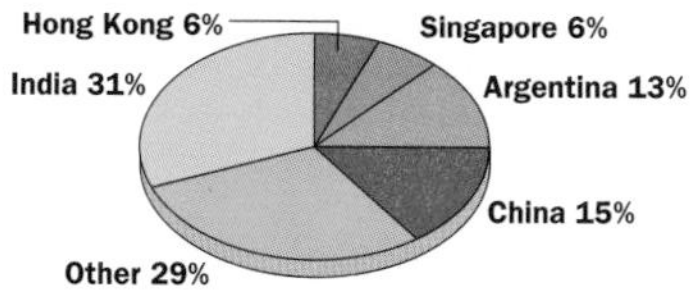
Hong Kong 6%
Singapore 6%
India 31%
Argentina 13%
China 15%
Other 29%

RESOURCES

Electric power 317,000 kw

23,206 tonnes

Not an oil producer

7.0m cattle, 6.2m goats, 3.5m buffaloes, 17.8m chickens

Mica, lignite, copper, cobalt, iron

The first privately owned power plant, situated near Ramechhap, opened in mid-2000.

ENVIRONMENT

Sustainability rank: 66th

8% (1% partially protected)

0.1 tonnes per capita

Kathmandu has chronic traffic and pollution problems. Deforestation and soil erosion are serious. The native tiger is fast disappearing. Approval of the controversial Arun III hydroelectric project was granted in mid-2000.

MEDIA

TV ownership low

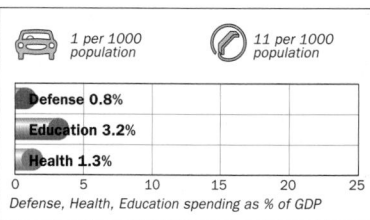

Daily newspaper circulation 11 per 1000 people

PUBLISHING AND BROADCAST MEDIA

There are 29 daily newspapers, including the leading *Gorkhapatra, Nepali Hindi Daily*, and *Rising Nepal*

1 limited state-owned service

1 state-owned and 1 independent service

The Nepal TV service began broadcasting in 1986; under 25% of the population receives it. The press is mainly Kathmandu-based with low circulations. The *Sunday Dispatch* is the paper most critical of government.

CRIME

Death penalty not used

Nepal does not publish prison figures

Down 80% 1996–1998

Petty theft and smuggling are the main problems. The legal provision for detention without trial is used, and police suppression of demonstrations is often brutal.

EDUCATION

School leaving age: 11

42%

99,300 students

Over 80% of boys attend school in Nepal, but still only a minority of girls. Nepal's literacy rate is among the lowest in the world.

CHRONOLOGY

The foundations of the Nepalese state were laid in 1769, when King Prithvi Narayan Shah conquered the region.

- **1816–1923** Establishment of quasi-British protectorate.
- **1959** First multiparty constitution.
- **1960** Constitution suspended.
- **1962–1990** *Panchayat* non-party system.
- **1972** Birendra succeeds to throne.
- **1991** NCP victory in elections.
- **1994** First communist government.
- **1995–1998** Succession of weak coalition governments.
- **1999** NCP election victory. Maoist insurgency in rural areas.
- **2001** June, Birendra and family killed in palace shootings. Gyanendra crowned amid unrest.

HEALTH

Welfare state health benefits

1 per 20,000 people

Respiratory and diarrheal diseases, maternal deaths

There are about 100 *dharmi-jhankri* (faith healers) for every health worker. Maternal mortality is high, the result of harmful traditional birth practices; a re-education program for midwives has been established.

SPENDING

GDP/cap. increase

CONSUMPTION AND SPENDING

1 per 1000 population

11 per 1000 population

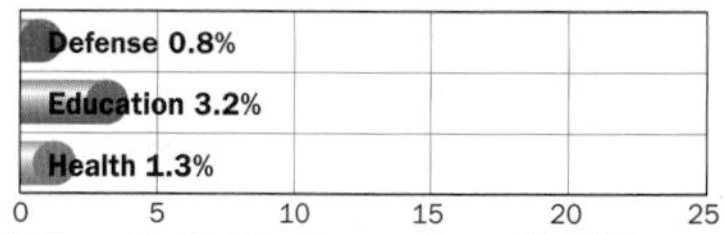
Defense 0.8%
Education 3.2%
Health 1.3%
0
5
10
15
20
25

Defense, Health, Education spending as % of GDP

Nepal is one of the poorest countries in the world. Bonded labor was abolished in mid-2000, releasing 36,000 people.

WORLD RANKING

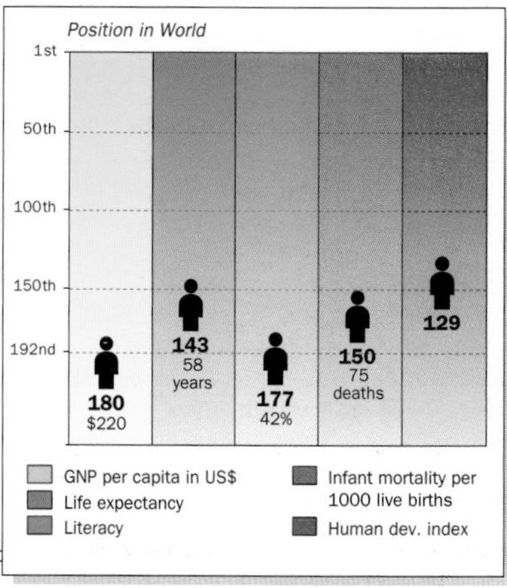
Position in World
1st
50th
100th
150th
192nd
180
$220
143
58 years
177
42%
150
75 deaths
129
GNP per capita in US$
Life expectancy
Literacy
Infant mortality per 1000 live births
Human dev. index

N

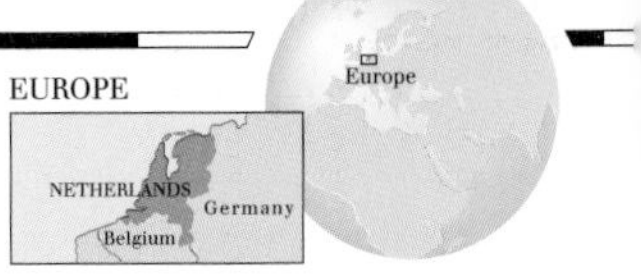
EUROPE
Europe
NETHERLANDS
Germany
Belgium

NETHERLANDS

OFFICIAL NAME: Kingdom of the Netherlands **CAPITALS:** Amsterdam, The Hague
POPULATION: 15.8 million **CURRENCY:** Euro (Netherlands guilder until 2002) **OFFICIAL LANGUAGE:** Dutch

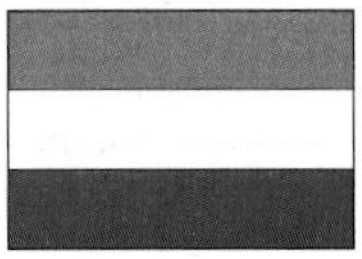

1815
1839
April 30
NL
+1
+31
.nl

THE NETHERLANDS IS LOCATED at the delta of four major rivers in northwest Europe. The few hills in the eastern and southern part of the country fall into a flat coastal area, bordered by the North Sea to the north and west. This is protected by a giant infrastructure of dunes, dikes, and canals, as 27% of the coast is below sea level. The Netherlands became one of the world's first confederative republics after Spain recognized its independence in 1648. Its highly successful economy has a long trading tradition, and Rotterdam is the world's largest port.

CLIMATE

Maritime

WEATHER CHART

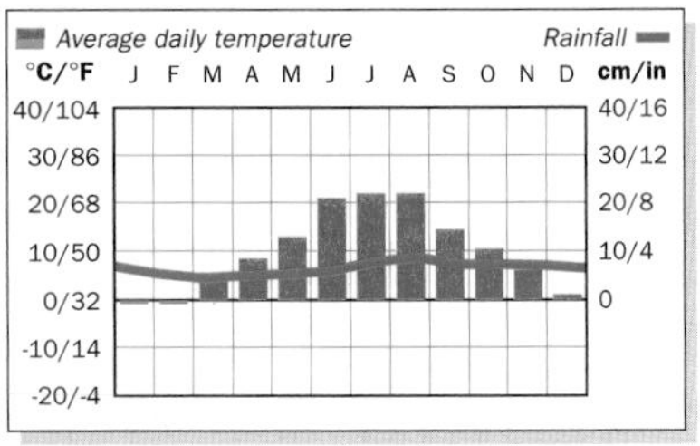
Average daily temperature
Rainfall
°C/°F
J F M A M J J A S O N D
cm/in
40/104
30/86
20/68
10/50
0/32
-10/14
-20/-4
40/16
30/12
20/8
10/4
0

The Netherlands has a temperate climate, with mild winters which rarely fall much below freezing, and cool summers with a mean temperature of 20°C (68°F). The country's coastal areas have the mildest climate, though northerly gales are fairly frequent, particularly in autumn and winter.

TRANSPORTATION

Drive on right

Schiphol, Amsterdam 36.77m passengers

1214 ships 4.3m grt

THE TRANSPORTATION NETWORK

113,018 km (70,226 miles)

2235 km (1389 miles)

2808 km (1745 miles)

5043 km (3134 miles)

Rotterdam, the key transshipment port for northern Europe, is also the world's largest. Schiphol airport is one of the air transportation hubs of Europe. A high-speed passenger rail line is under construction that will link Amsterdam and Rotterdam with Brussels and Paris, and a high-speed freight line is under construction from Rotterdam to Germany.

TOURISM

Visitors : Population 1:1.5

10.2m visitors

Up 3% in 2000

MAIN TOURIST ARRIVALS

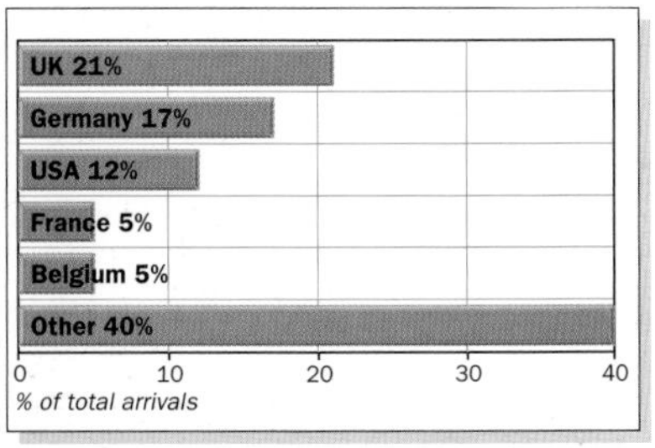
UK 21%
Germany 17%
USA 12%
France 5%
Belgium 5%
Other 40%
0
10
20
30
40
% of total arrivals

Tourism is a major business in the Netherlands. Visitors go mainly to Amsterdam, although cities such as Groningen and Maastricht are growing in popularity. Amsterdam caters for a diverse tourism market. Its world-famous museums include the Rijksmuseum, with its collection of Vermeers and Rembrandts, while its network of canals is popular. Amsterdam is also renowned for its liberal attitude to sex; its red-light district draws millions every year. In the past decade, the city has become a center for the European gay community, with celebrations on 30 April (Queen's Day – the monarch's official birthday) and in August (Amsterdam Pride). A thriving club scene and liberal drug laws draw enthusiasts from neighboring countries. In spring and summer, the tulip fields and North Sea beaches attract large numbers of visitors.

Windmill at Baambrugge, *near Amsterdam. A century ago there were 10,000 in the country compared with today's 1000. A protective ring of 900 mills kept Amsterdam from flooding.*

PEOPLE

Pop. density high

Dutch, Frisian

466/km² (1206/mi²)

THE URBAN/RURAL POPULATION SPLIT

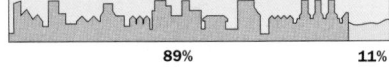

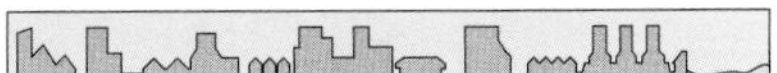
89%
11%

RELIGIOUS PERSUASION

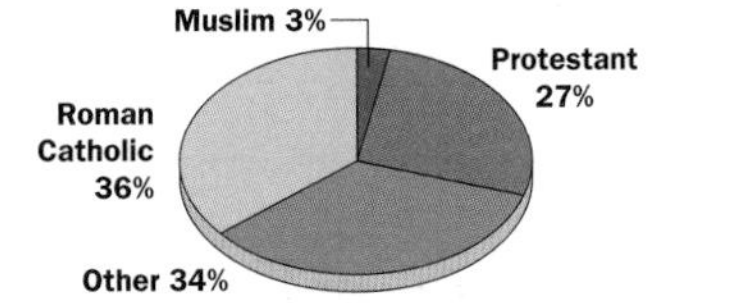
Muslim 3%
Protestant 27%
Roman Catholic 36%
Other 34%

ETHNIC MAKEUP

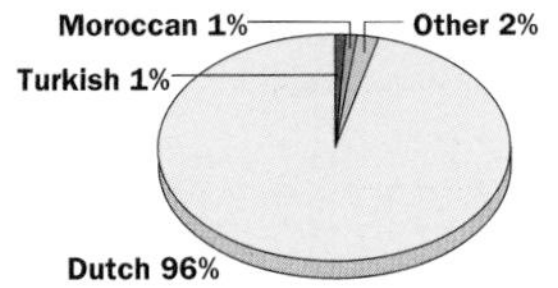
Moroccan 1%
Other 2%
Turkish 1%
Dutch 96%

The Dutch see their country as the most tolerant in Europe and it has a long history of welcoming refugees seeking religious and political asylum. In the 20th century, immigrants from former colonies settled in the Netherlands and became fully accepted as citizens. They came first from Indonesia and then from Suriname and the Netherlands Antilles. The small Turkish community, however, does not enjoy full citizenship.

The tradition of tolerance is reflected in liberal attitudes to sexuality. In 2001 same-sex marriages were legalized, giving gay couples full equality, including the right of adoption (after three years of marriage).

The state does not try to impose a particular morality on its citizens. Drug taking is seen as a matter of personal choice, and in 2001 the Netherlands became the first country in the world to legalize euthanasia, albeit under strict conditions.

Women enjoy equal rights and hold 37% of seats in the Second Chamber of the States-General, but are not well represented in the boardroom.

POPULATION AGE BREAKDOWN

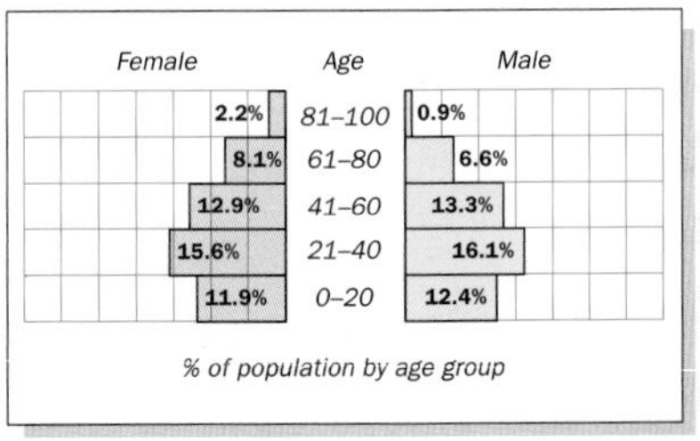
Female
Age
Male
2.2%
81–100
0.9%
8.1%
61–80
6.6%
12.9%
41–60
13.3%
15.6%
21–40
16.1%
11.9%
0–20
12.4%
% of population by age group

POLITICS

Multiparty elections

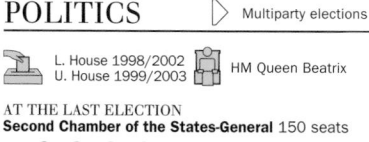

L. House 1998/2002
U. House 1999/2003

HM Queen Beatrix

AT THE LAST ELECTION
Second Chamber of the States-General 150 seats

30%	26%	19%	9%	7%	9%
PvdA	**VVD**	**CDA**	**D66**	**GL**	**Others**

PvdA = Labour Party **VVD** = People's Party for Freedom and Democracy **CDA** = Christian Democratic Appeal **D66** = Democrats 66 **GL** = Green Left

First Chamber of the States-General 75 seats

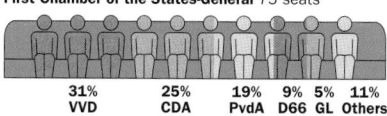

31%	25%	19%	9%	5%	11%
VVD	**CDA**	**PvdA**	**D66**	**GL**	**Others**

The First Chamber of the States-General is indirectly elected

The Netherlands is a constitutional monarchy. Legislative power is vested in parliament, and the monarch has only nominal power.

MAIN POLITICAL ISSUES

The future of social welfare

Despite cutbacks in the 1980s, the Dutch still had one of Europe's most generous welfare systems. Most political parties accepted that levels of welfare could not be maintained indefinitely. The debate thus focuses on how much and in which areas cuts should be made.

Queen Beatrix, who acceded in 1980 and rebuilt support for the Dutch monarchy.

Wim Kok, won the 1994 elections and is the first labour prime minister since 1977.

Political refugees

In recent years, a rising number of people have sought political asylum in the Netherlands. Increasingly this has led to concerns over the costs involved, and worries that this trend might lead to a rise in support for extreme right-wing nationalist parties. Since 1994 asylum laws have been tightened in the Netherlands, as in neighboring countries.

PROFILE

Dutch politics are characterized by coalitions and a high degree of consensus. Most Dutch agree on the social function of government and readily accept relatively high taxes and a generous social security system. Political debate is more a question of the emphasis and focus of policy than of ideology.

The CDA has traditionally led two-party coalition governments, either with the left-of-center PvdA or with the right-wing VVD. However, after the 1994 election the CDA found itself out in the cold as the PvdA, the VVD, and the left-liberal D66 formed a left–right government – dubbed the "purple coalition" (i.e. a mix of red and blue) – under PvdA leader Wim Kok. This administration was reelected in 1998, and survived a mid-1999 crisis, when D66 was persuaded to remain in the coalition, despite the Senate's rejection of its cherished project for wider use of referendums.

Wim Kok's coalition has continued a general policy which has become known as the "polder model." Formulated in the early 1980s, this concentrates on job creation, pay moderation, economic deregulation, and generous social protection.

NORTH SEA
WADDENEILANDEN
Waddenzee
Schiermonnikoog
Ameland
Terschelling
Vlieland
Texel
IJSSELMEER
Ems
Delfzijl
Groningen
Leeuwarden
Harlingen
Hoogezand
Sappemeer
Stadskanaal
Assen
Den Helder
Heerenveen
Emmen
Meppel
Hoogeveen
Enkhuizen
Alkmaar
Hoorn
Purmerend
Lelystad
Zwolle
Beverwijk
Velsen
Zaanstad
Almere
Haarlem
AMSTERDAM
Almelo
Amstelveen
Aalsmeer
Huizen
Hilversum
Apeldoorn
Deventer
Hengelo
Enschede
Katwijk aan Zee
Leiden
Nieuwkoop
Maarssen
Amersfoort
'S-GRAVENHAGE (THE HAGUE)
Alphen aan de Rijn
Utrecht
Zeist
Barneveld
Ede
Rheden
Zoetermeer
Delft
Gouda
Nieuwegein
Doetinchem
Arnhem
Neder-Rijn
Lek
Schiedam
Vlaardingen
Rotterdam
Spijkenisse
Zwijndrecht
Tiel
Goeree
Ridderkerk
Waal
Oss
Nijmegen
Overflakkee
Dordrecht
Schouwen
Maas
Oosterhout
's-Hertogenbosch
Oosterschelde
Noord-Beveland
Tholen
Breda
Walcheren
Middelburg
Vlissingen
Goes
Zuid-Beveland
Roosendaal
Tilburg
Helmond
Westerschelde
Bergen op Zoom
Eindhoven
Venlo
Terneuzen
Roermond
BELGIUM
GERMANY
Sittard
Geleen
Heerlen
Kerkrade
Maastricht
NETHERLANDS
Total Land Area :
33 920 sq. km
(13 097 sq. miles)
N
0
40 km
40 miles
POPULATION
over 1 000 000
over 500 000
over 100 000
over 50 000
over 10 000
LAND HEIGHT
100m/328ft
Sea Level
-100m/-328ft

WORLD AFFAIRS

Joined UN in 1945

Benelux | EU | NATO | OECD | OSCE

Political and monetary integration within the EU have strong popular support. In 1995, internal border controls were lifted under the Schengen Convention. In 1999 the Netherlands was one of the 11 EU states to introduce the euro. Former finance minister Wim Duisenberg was appointed the first president of the European Central Bank. The International Court of Justice and the International Criminal Tribunal for the former Yugoslavia sit in The Hague, as will the International Criminal Court.

AID

Donor

$3.13bn (donations)

Up 3% in 1999

The Netherlands is one of the few countries to exceed the UN target of devoting 0.7% of GNP to development aid: in 1998, 0.8% of GNP was so allocated. The government actively pursues a policy of linking foreign aid and human rights. It also gives priority to projects which link longer-term development goals with efforts to manage and reduce inter-group conflict.

CHRONOLOGY

Suppression of Protestantism by the ruling Spanish Habsburgs led to the revolt of the Netherlands and the declaration of independence of the northern provinces as a republic in 1581, recognized by Spain in 1648.

- **1813** Dutch oust French after 18 years of French rule and choose to become a constitutional monarchy.
- **1815** United Kingdom of Netherlands formed to include Belgium and Luxembourg.
- **1839** Recognition of 1830 secession of Catholic southern provinces as Belgium.
- **1848** New constitution – ministers to be accountable to parliament.
- **1897–1901** Wide-ranging social legislation enacted. Development of strong trade unions.
- **1898** Wilhelmina succeeds to throne, ending Luxembourg union, where male hereditary Salic Law is in force.
- **1914–1918** Dutch neutrality respected in World War I.
- **1922** Women fully enfranchised.
- **1940** Dutch assert neutrality in World War II, but Germany invades. Fierce resistance.
- **1942** Japan invades Dutch East Indies.
- **1944–1945** "Winter of starvation" in German-occupied western provinces.
- **1945** Liberation. International Court of Justice set up in The Hague.
- **1946–1958** PvdA leads center-left coalitions. Marshall Aid from USA speeds reconstruction.
- **1948** Juliana becomes queen.
- **1949** Joins NATO. Most of East Indies colonies gain independence as Indonesia.
- **1957** Founder member of EEC.
- **1960** Economic union with Belgium and Luxembourg comes into effect.
- **1973** PvdA wins power after 15 years spent mainly in opposition. Center-left coalition.
- **1977–1981** CDA/VVD coalition.
- **1980** CDA alliance of the "confessional" parties forms a single party. Beatrix becomes queen.
- **1982** PvdA rejects deployment of US cruise missiles in Netherlands. CDA/VVD center-right coalition under Ruud Lubbers.
- **1989** VVD refuses to support finance for 20-year National Environment Policy (NEP). Elections. Lubbers forms CDA/PvdA center-left coalition.
- **1990** NEP introduced.
- **1992** Licensed brothels legalized.
- **1994** Elections. Wim Kok of PvdA heads coalition with VVD and D66.
- **1999** Netherlands among 11 EU countries to introduce euro.
- **2001** Euthanasia and gay marriage legalized.

DEFENSE

No compulsory military service

$6.95bn — Down 3% in 1999

DUTCH ARMED FORCES

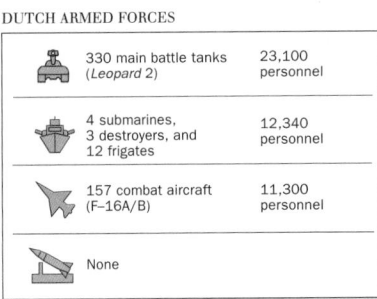

330 main battle tanks (*Leopard* 2)	23,100 personnel
4 submarines, 3 destroyers, and 12 frigates	12,340 personnel
157 combat aircraft (F–16A/B)	11,300 personnel
None	

The Dutch military has undergone major restructuring since the end of the Cold War with the aim of making it a rapidly deployable, more flexible military force as befits a NATO member state. Compulsory military service was abolished in 1996 and personnel cut by 44%, with the number of army divisions reduced from three to two. In 1995, a joint Dutch–German army corps numbering 28,000 was inaugurated. The armed forces' new role was evidenced when it sent troops to take part in the international peace implementation force and then the stabilization force in Bosnia. The Netherlands also has a large defense industry, which specializes in submarines, weapons systems, and aircraft.

ECONOMICS

Inflation 1.9% p.a. (1990–1999)

$397.4bn — 2.1986–2.3473 guilders

SCORE CARD

- World GNP Ranking 14th
- GNP per Capita $25,140
- Balance of Payments $22.6bn
- Inflation 2.2%
- Unemployment 3%

EXPORTS

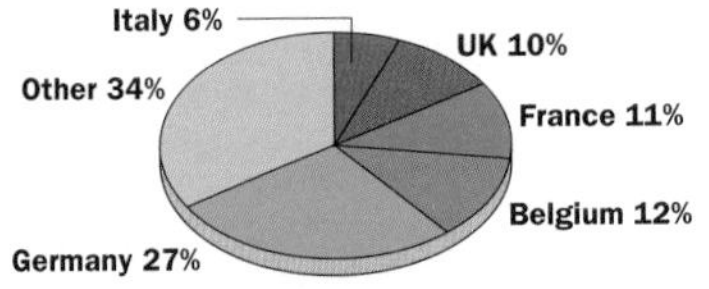

Italy 6%
UK 10%
Other 34%
France 11%
Belgium 12%
Germany 27%

IMPORTS

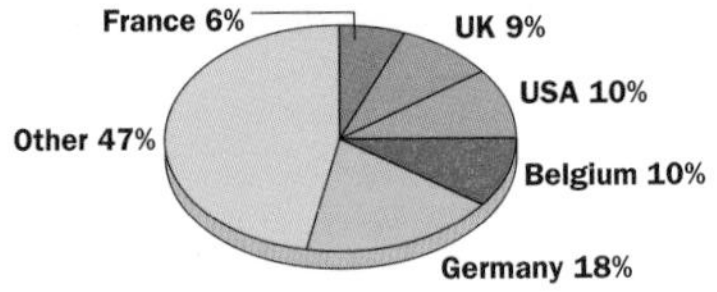

France 6%
UK 9%
USA 10%
Other 47%
Belgium 10%
Germany 18%

Strengths

Highly skilled, educated, multilingual workforce. Sophisticated infrastructure. Many blue-chip multinationals, including Philips and Shell. Strong consensus between employers and employees. Low inflation. Tradition of high-tech innovation, including development of music cassette and CD.

Weaknesses

Costly welfare system, resulting in high taxes and social insurance premiums; one-third of national income spent on social security. High labor costs.

Profile

Trade has been central to the success of the economy since the 16th century. Most goods travel through Rotterdam, the world's biggest port. As well as high-tech industries such as electronics, telecommunications and chemicals, there is a successful agricultural sector. Productivity rates are high and agricultural produce such as cheese, vegetables, meat, and flowers are significant export earners. Job creation schemes have reduced unemployment to half the EU average, though many people receive sick or disability pay.

ECONOMIC PERFORMANCE INDICATOR

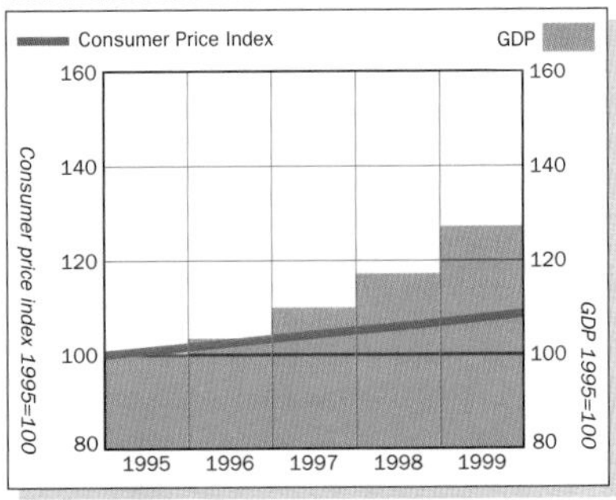

Consumer Price Index
GDP
160
140
120
100
80
Consumer price index 1995=100
GDP 1995=100
1995
1996
1997
1998
1999

NETHERLANDS : MAJOR BUSINESSES

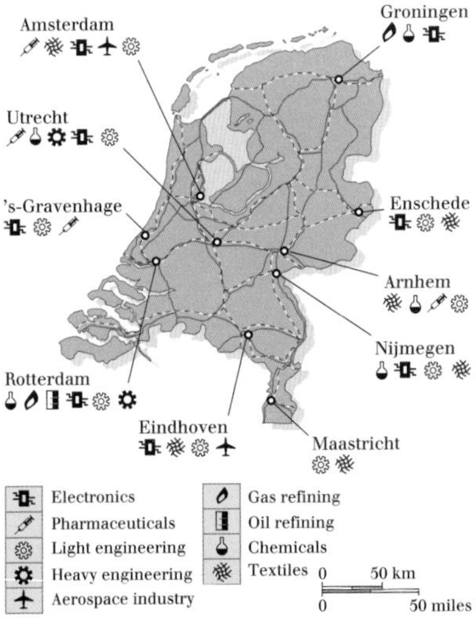

Amsterdam
Groningen
Utrecht
's-Gravenhage
Enschede
Arnhem
Nijmegen
Rotterdam
Eindhoven
Maastricht
Electronics
Pharmaceuticals
Light engineering
Heavy engineering
Aerospace industry
Gas refining
Oil refining
Chemicals
Textiles
0 50 km
0 50 miles

N

RESOURCES

▷ Electric power 20.1m kw

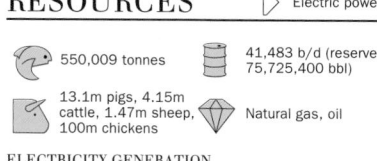

550,009 tonnes

41,483 b/d (reserves 75,725,400 bbl)

13.1m pigs, 4.15m cattle, 1.47m sheep, 100m chickens

Natural gas, oil

ELECTRICITY GENERATION

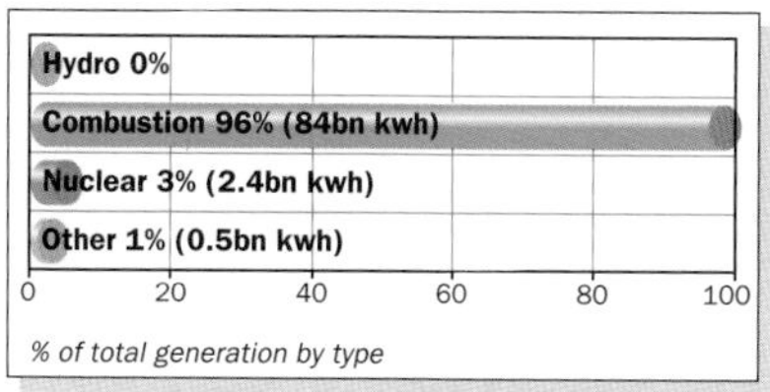
Hydro 0%
Combustion 96% (84bn kwh)
Nuclear 3% (2.4bn kwh)
Other 1% (0.5bn kwh)
0
20
40
60
80
100
% of total generation by type

There are large natural gas reserves in the north. There is some oil production from offshore drilling in the North Sea.

NETHERLANDS : LAND USE

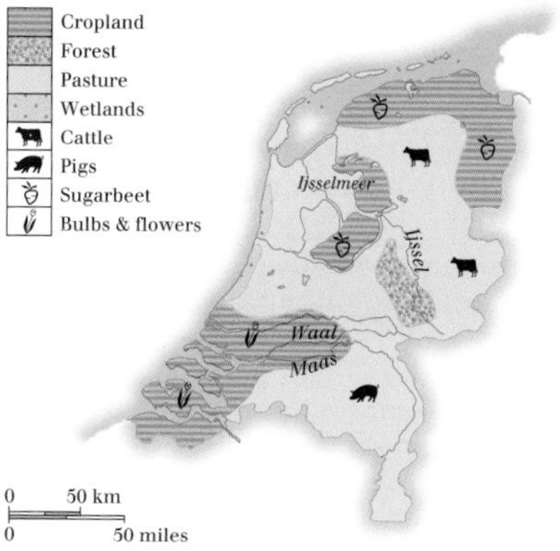
Cropland
Forest
Pasture
Wetlands
Cattle
Pigs
Sugarbeet
Bulbs & flowers
IJsselmeer
IJssel
Waal
Maas
0
50 km
0
50 miles

ENVIRONMENT

▷ Sustainability rank: 12th

7%

10.5 tonnes per capita

ENVIRONMENTAL TREATIES

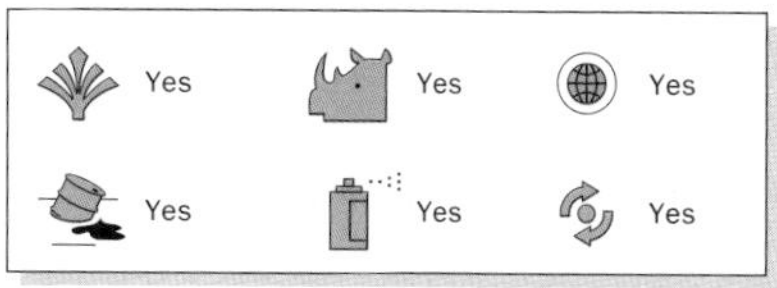
Yes
Yes
Yes
Yes
Yes
Yes

There is a strong environmental tradition, a legacy in part of living in one of the most densely populated states in the world. NGOs such as Greenpeace are well supported and the Green Left party is well represented in parliament.

The Dutch recycle domestic trash, have a good record on energy efficiency, and have developed innovative projects in housing and local transportation. An eco-tax on energy users was introduced in 1996 – the first of its kind in the West – though big businesses are exempt.

Serious flooding of the rivers Maas and Waal (an arm of the Rhine) in 1993 and 1995 raised concern about the state of the country's flood defenses and the use of flood plains for development.

MEDIA

▷ TV ownership high

Daily newspaper circulation 305 per 1000 people

PUBLISHING AND BROADCAST MEDIA

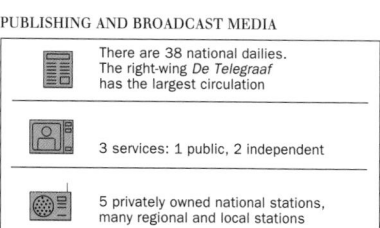

There are 38 national dailies. The right-wing *De Telegraaf* has the largest circulation

3 services: 1 public, 2 independent

5 privately owned national stations, many regional and local stations

Newspaper circulation is high. While editorially independent, broadcasting is strongly regulated. Dutch law does not recognize a right of reply or a right to protect information sources.

CRIME

▷ Death penalty not used

10,143 prisoners

Down 16% 1996–1998

CRIME RATES

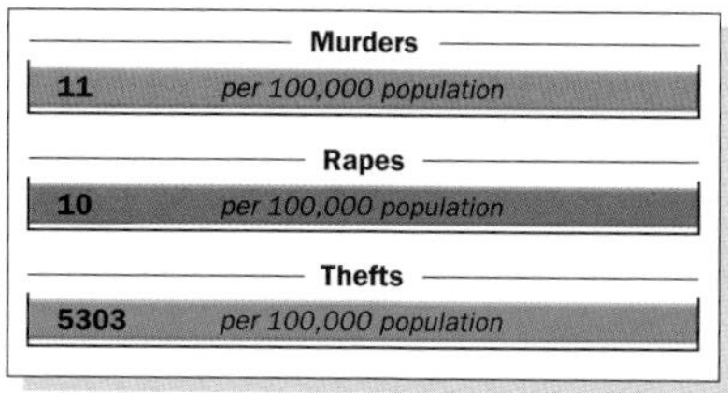
Murders
11 per 100,000 population
Rapes
10 per 100,000 population
Thefts
5303 per 100,000 population

The Netherlands treats the use of hard drugs more as a medical and social than a criminal issue. Other member states of Europe's Schengen Convention, particularly France, fear that this makes Dutch ports a soft point of entry for narcotics. Possessing cannabis for personal use has been decriminalized – stopping short of actual legalization.

EDUCATION

▷ School leaving age: 18

99%

468,970 students

THE EDUCATION SYSTEM

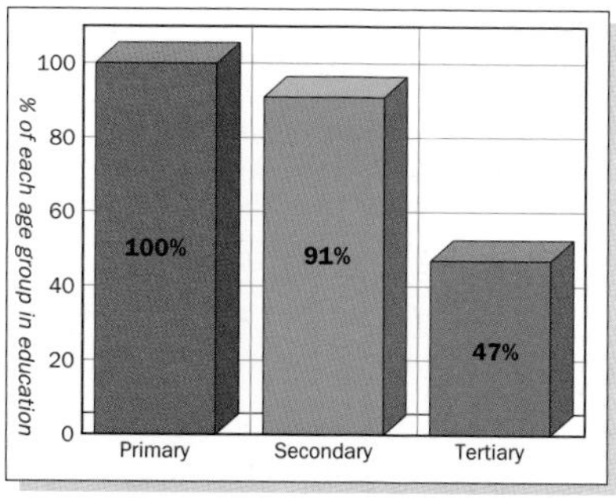
100
80
60
40
20
0
% of each age group in education
100%
91%
47%
Primary
Secondary
Tertiary

Corporate funding plays an important part in university research.

Public, municipally run schools attract 35% of pupils, and private (mostly denominational) schools are attended by 65%. Both types are fully funded by the state.

HEALTH

▷ Welfare state health benefits

1 per 385 people

Heart and respiratory diseases, cancers

Health care in the Netherlands is largely funded by the state, though around 25% of funding comes from private sources. High spending ensures that the care that is offered is among the best in the world. However, there are fears that the Dutch may have to accept lower standards in future, particularly since the population is aging. Major health problems are similar to those in the rest of western Europe. Incidence of AIDS is higher than in Sweden or the UK but lower than in Switzerland, France, or Spain.

SPENDING

▷ GDP/cap. increase

CONSUMPTION AND SPENDING

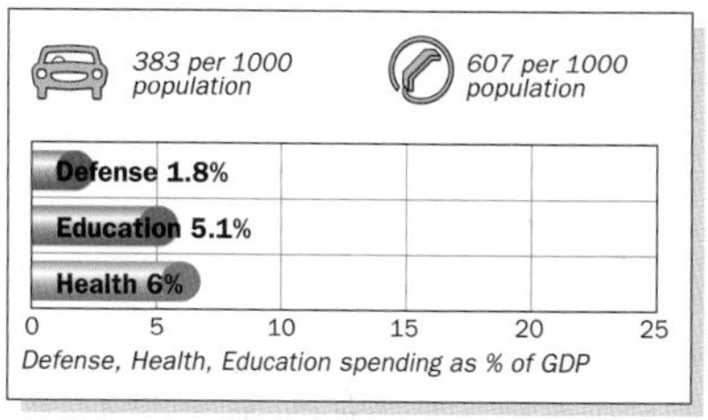
383 per 1000 population
607 per 1000 population
Defense 1.8%
Education 5.1%
Health 6%
0
5
10
15
20
25
Defense, Health, Education spending as % of GDP

The Netherlands is, per capita, one of the richest countries in the world. Oil executives, stock market traders, and businessmen are among the wealthiest sector of the population. A progressive taxation system and extensive social welfare mean that wealth is quite evenly distributed. A small elite have considerable inherited wealth, but extravagant displays of affluence are rare.

Class does not play a big part in Dutch society. Most citizens would consider themselves middle class. Immigrant communities are the exception; they often live on the edges of towns in deprived areas. The poorest group of all are the illegal immigrants.

WORLD RANKING

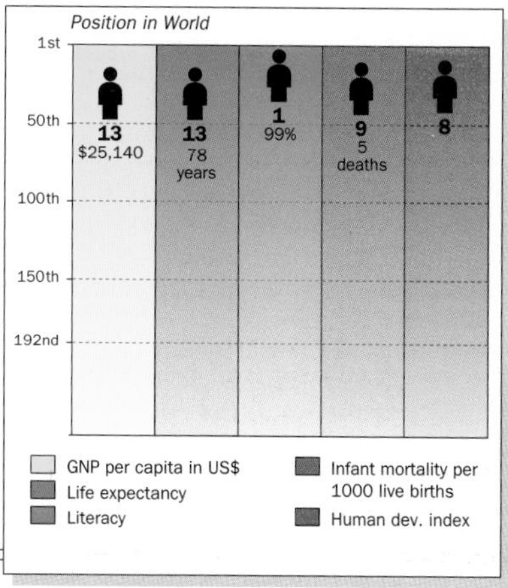
Position in World
1st
50th
100th
150th
192nd
13
$25,140
13
78
years
1
99%
9
5
deaths
8
GNP per capita in US$
Life expectancy
Literacy
Infant mortality per 1000 live births
Human dev. index

N

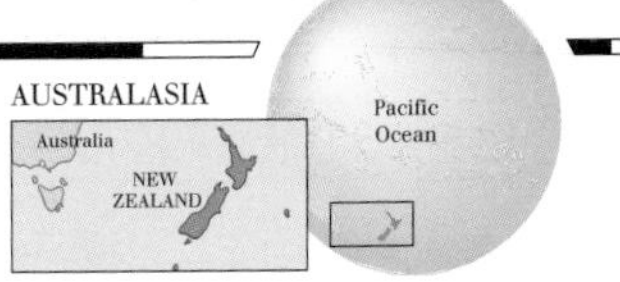
AUSTRALASIA
Pacific Ocean
Australia
NEW ZEALAND

NEW ZEALAND

OFFICIAL NAME: Dominion of New Zealand **CAPITAL:** Wellington
POPULATION: 3.9 million **CURRENCY:** New Zealand dollar **OFFICIAL LANGUAGES:** English and Maori

1947
1947
Feb 6
NZ
+12
+64
.nz

LYING IN THE SOUTH PACIFIC, 1600 km (992 miles) southeast of Australia, New Zealand comprises the main North and South Islands, separated by the Cook Strait, and a number of smaller islands. South Island is the more mountainous; North Island contains hot springs and geysers, and the bulk of the population. The political tradition is liberal and egalitarian, and has been dominated by the National and Labour Parties. Radical, and often unpopular, reforms since 1984 have restored economic growth, speeded up economic diversification, and strengthened New Zealand's position within the Pacific Rim countries.

CLIMATE

Maritime/subtropical

WEATHER CHART

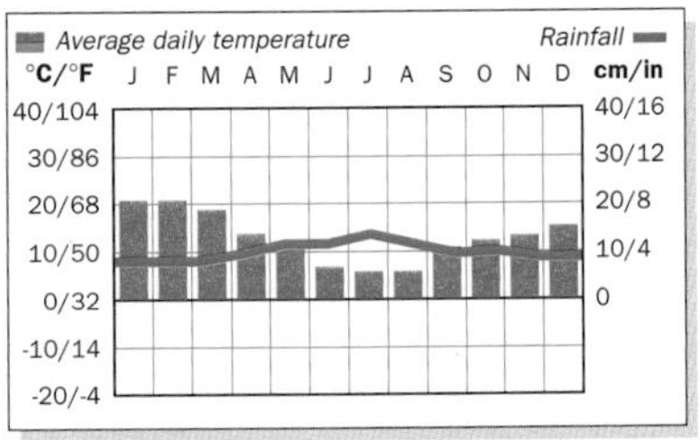
Average daily temperature
Rainfall
°C/°F
J F M A M J J A S O N D
cm/in
40/104
30/86
20/68
10/50
0/32
-10/14
-20/-4
40/16
30/12
20/8
10/4
0

New Zealand's climate is generally temperate and damp, with an average temperature of 12°C (54°F). There are differences between the islands, which extend north–south nearly 2000 km (1240 miles). The extreme north is almost subtropical; southern winters are cold. It is windy: Wellington is particularly known for bouts of blustery weather that can last for days.

TRANSPORTATION

Drive on left

Auckland International 7.50m passengers

173 ships 336,278 grt

THE TRANSPORTATION NETWORK

53,568 km (33,286 miles)

144 km (89 miles)

3900 km (2423 miles)

1609 km (1000 miles)

Although both the main islands are well served by transportation services, the more populous North Island's road and rail network is more extensive than the South's. Air and ferry services complement the land networks and provide links between the North and South Islands, as well as with the numerous smaller islands. Cargo ferry services are particularly important for Antarctic bases in the Ross Dependency. Links with New Zealand's other associated territories – the Cook Islands, Niue, and the Tokelau atolls – are underdeveloped.

TOURISM

Visitors : Population 1:2.2

1.8m visitors

Up 11% in 2000

MAIN TOURIST ARRIVALS

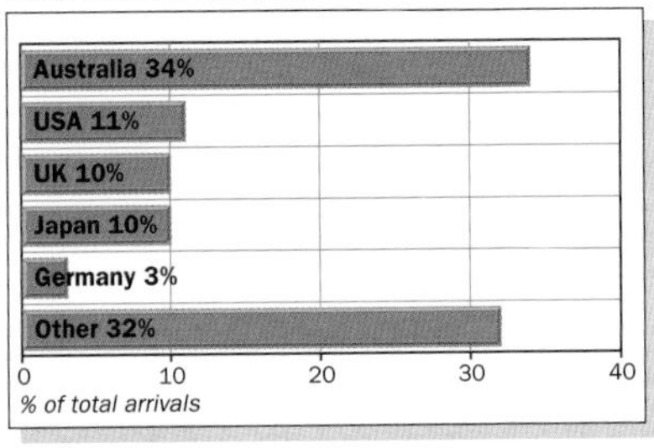
Australia 34%
USA 11%
UK 10%
Japan 10%
Germany 3%
Other 32%
0
10
20
30
40
% of total arrivals

New Zealand's prime attraction is its scenery. Unspoiled and, relative to the country's size, the most varied in the world, it offers mountains, fjords and lakes, glaciers, rainforests, beaches, boiling mud pools, and geysers. Other attractions are the Maori culture and outdoor activities such as river rafting, fishing, skiing, whale watching, and bungee jumping – a local invention.

Tourists come mainly from Australia, the USA, Japan, and the UK. The tourism industry is the largest single foreign-exchange earner, generating NZ$4 billion and attracting nearly two million visitors each year. Tourism continues to grow, although the industry was hit by the 1997–1998 Asian economic crisis which saw the number of Asian tourists drop by 10%.

Mount Egmont, an extinct volcano, is one of the numerous popular natural attractions of New Zealand's North Island.

PEOPLE

Pop. density low

English, Maori

15/km² (38/mi²)

THE URBAN/RURAL POPULATION SPLIT

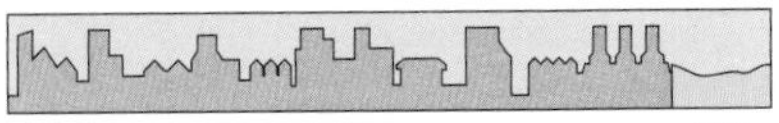
87%
13%

RELIGIOUS PERSUASION

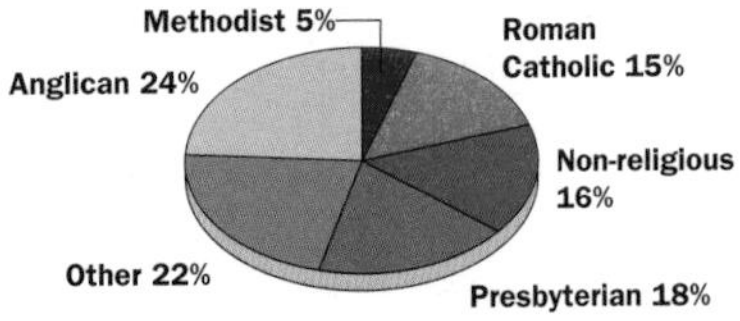
Methodist 5%
Roman Catholic 15%
Anglican 24%
Non-religious 16%
Other 22%
Presbyterian 18%

ETHNIC MAKEUP

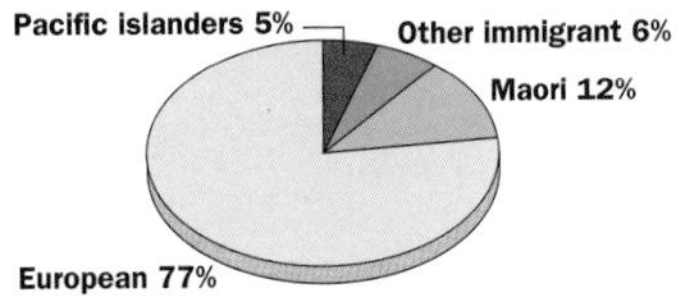
Pacific islanders 5%
Other immigrant 6%
Maori 12%
European 77%

New Zealand is a country of migrants. The first settlers, the Maoris, migrated from Polynesia about 1200 years ago. Today's majority European population is mainly descended from British migrants who settled after 1840. Newer migrants include Asians from Hong Kong and Malaysia, and Polynesians. The government is keen to attract skilled South Americans, Russians, Chinese, and Africans to revitalize the economy.

The living standards and unemployment rates of the Maoris compare adversely with those of the European-descended majority, and relations can be tense. The crown signed the Waikato Raupatu Claims Settlement Act and officially apologized to the Maoris in 1995. In 1998 the Waitangi Tribunal ordered the return of confiscated land.

New Zealand became the first country in the world to give women the vote – in 1893. In 2001, the prime minister, the leader of the opposition, and the governor-general were all positions filled by women.

POPULATION AGE BREAKDOWN

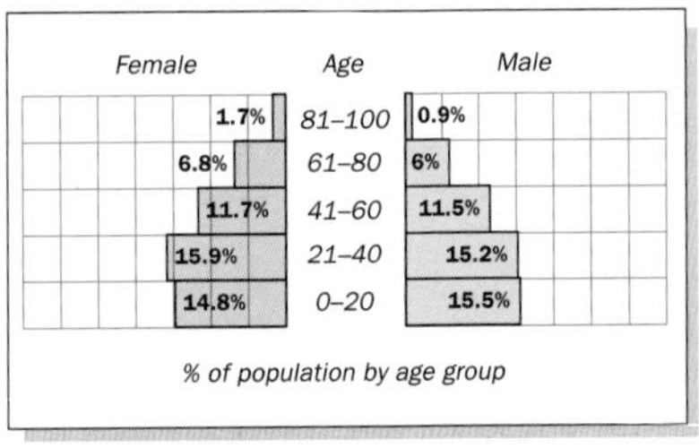
Female
Age
Male
1.7%
81–100
0.9%
6.8%
61–80
6%
11.7%
41–60
11.5%
15.9%
21–40
15.2%
14.8%
0–20
15.5%
% of population by age group

N

POLITICS

Multiparty elections

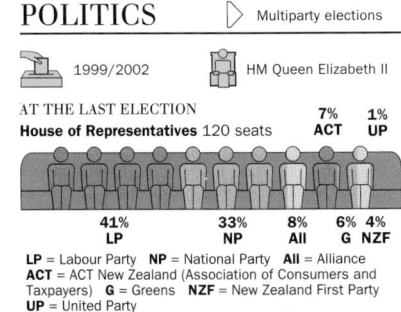

1999/2002 — HM Queen Elizabeth II

AT THE LAST ELECTION

House of Representatives 120 seats

41% LP
33% NP
8% All
7% ACT
6% G
4% NZF
1% UP

LP = Labour Party **NP** = National Party **All** = Alliance **ACT** = ACT New Zealand (Association of Consumers and Taxpayers) **G** = Greens **NZF** = New Zealand First Party **UP** = United Party

Helen Clark, *LP leader and prime minister since 1999.*

Jenny Shipley, *NP leader, and first woman prime minister (1997–1999).*

New Zealand is a single-chamber parliamentary democracy. The Cook Islands and Niue are self-governing territories.

MAIN POLITICAL ISSUE

Electoral reform

New Zealand shifted to a system of proportional representation (PR) for the 1996 general election. Endorsement of this reform in a referendum in 1993 reflected widespread disillusionment with the NP and LP. The new German-style system strengthened the role of smaller parties. As predicted, the first election to use the system in 1996 produced a coalition government led by the NP. Forced into a minority position in 1998, the NP has, unsuccessfully, called for a review of the PR system.

PROFILE

The NP and the LP dominated the old first-past-the-post system. Since 1984 the economy has undergone massive reforms; cuts to the welfare system and privatization of public assets have been unpopular. Jenny Shipley became the country's first woman prime minister in 1997 as leader of the NP. She headed a coalition with the small NZF, but headed a minority administration from 1998 when the coalition broke down. A new minority coalition of the LP and the Alliance assumed power under LP leader Helen Clark in November 1999.

WORLD AFFAIRS

Joined UN in 1945

Comm | APEC | OECD | PIF | PC

Many New Zealanders are strongly committed to the British crown and the Commonwealth, but the UK's EU involvement has forced New Zealand to reorient its trade and foreign policy toward its Pacific Rim neighbors, especially Australia, now New Zealand's largest trading partner. Their 1983 Closer Economic Relationship (CER) treaty was strengthened in 1996 by the signing of a mutual recognition agreement. Relations with Asia are growing in importance. The 1997–1998 Asian economic crisis significantly affected trade, particularly tourism. Relations with the USA are improving after a low point when New Zealand's antinuclear stance led to its exclusion from the ANZUS pact. Official ties with France, cut in 1985 after French agents bombed Greenpeace's *Rainbow Warrior* in Auckland harbor, were restored in 1997.

AID

Donor

US$134m (donations)

Up 3% in 1999

Over half of New Zealand's overseas aid is bilateral. Particular areas of focus are the Pacific states and Pacific-wide organizations. New Zealand is a major supporter of the Pacific Islands Forum, the University of the South Pacific, and the Pacific Environment Program. It also offers scholarships to overseas students for study or training in New Zealand.

NORTH ISLAND
SOUTH ISLAND
TASMAN SEA
SOUTH PACIFIC OCEAN
Great Exhibition Bay
Kaitaia
Whangarei
Dargaville
Little Barrier I.
Great Barrier I.
Kaipara Harbour
Colville Channel
Hauraki Gulf
Great Mercury I.
Waiheke I.
Coromandel Peninsula
Takapuna
Auckland
Manurewa
Papatoetoe
Manukau Harbour
Papakura
Pukekohe
Bay of Plenty
Mount Maunganui
White I.
Tauranga
Hamilton
Cambridge
Whakatane
Ruatoria
L. Rotorua
Rotorua
Tokoroa
Murupara
Gisborne
Taupo
L. Taupo
L. Waikaremoana
North Taranaki Bight
Taumarunui
New Plymouth
Mt Taranaki (Mt Egmont) 2518m
Mt Ruapehu 2797m
Cape Egmont
Wairoa
Hawke Bay
Mahia Peninsula
Hawera
Napier
Hastings
South Taranaki Bight
Wanganui
Fielding
Palmerston North
Levin
Golden Bay
D'Urville Island
Kapiti I.
Paraparaumu
Masterton
Tasman Bay
Porirua
Upper Hutt
L. Wairarapa
Lower Hutt
WELLINGTON
Nelson
Blenheim
Cook Strait
Karamea Bight
Westport
Buller
Wairau
Reefton
Clarence
Greymouth
Kaikoura
Hokitika
Hurunui
Waimakariri
Rakaia
Rangiora
Pegasus Bay
Mount Cook 3744m
Christchurch
SOUTHERN ALPS
CANTERBURY PLAINS
Banks Peninsula
L. Tekapo
Ashburton
Rangitata
L. Pukaki
L. Ohau
Twizel
Timaru
L. Hawea
Canterbury Bight
L. Wanaka
Wanaka
Waitaki
L. Wakatipu
Queenstown
Oamaru
L. Te Anau
Alexandra
Te Anau
Clutha
Taieri
Resolution I.
Waiau
Oreti
Mataura
Mosgiel
Otago Peninsula
Dunedin
Gore
Balclutha
Invercargill
Foveaux Strait
Stewart Island
Halfmoon Bay
36°
40°
44°
168°
172°
176°
Chatham Is
Petre Bay
Waitangi
Chatham I.
Pitt Strait
Pitt I.
(continuation on same scale)
NEW ZEALAND
Total Land Area : 268 670 sq. km (103 733 sq. miles)
LAND HEIGHT
2000m/6562ft
1000m/3281ft
500m/1640ft
200m/656ft
Sea Level
POPULATION
over 500 000
over 100 000
over 50 000
over 10 000
under 10 000
N
0
100 km
100 miles

CHRONOLOGY

A former British colony, New Zealand became a dominion in 1907, self-governing from 1926, and fully independent in 1947.

- **1962** Western Samoa (now Samoa) gains independence.
- **1965** Cook Islands become self-governing.
- **1975** Conservative NP wins elections. Economic austerity program introduced.
- **1976** Immigration cut by over 80%.
- **1984** LP elected; David Lange prime minister. Auckland harbor headland restored to Maoris.
- **1985** New Zealand prohibits nuclear vessels from ports and waters. French agents sink Greenpeace ship *Rainbow Warrior* in Auckland harbor.
- **1986** USA suspends military obligations under ANZUS Treaty.
- **1987** LP wins elections. Introduction of controversial privatization plan. Nuclear ban enshrined in legislation.
- **1989** Cabinet split. Lange resigns. Succeeded by Geoffrey Palmer.
- **1990** Palmer resigns. LP defeated by NP in elections. James Bolger prime minister.
- **1991** Widespread protests at spending cuts.
- **1992** Maoris win South Island fishing rights. Majority vote for electoral reform in referendum.
- **1993** Docking of first French naval ship for eight years. NP returned with single-seat majority in election. Proportional representation introduced by referendum.
- **1994** Senior-level US contacts restored; agrees not to send nuclear-armed ships to New Zealand ports. Maoris reject government ten-year land claims settlement of NZ$1 billion.
- **1995** Waitangi Day celebrations abandoned after Maori protests. Crown apologizes to Maoris and signs Waikato Raupatu Claims Act. UK warship visits resume.
- **1996** NP forms coalition to preserve overall legislative majority. First general election under new proportional representation system.
- **1997** NP forms coalition with New Zealand First (NZF) party. Bolger resigns. Jenny Shipley becomes first woman prime minister.
- **1998** Shipley sacks NZF leader Winston Peters as deputy prime minister, and forms minority government when coalition splits. Waitangi Tribunal orders government to return to Maoris NZ$6.1 million of confiscated land.
- **1999** November, LP led by Helen Clark wins general election.

DEFENSE

No compulsory military service

US$824m

Down 8% in 1999

Military cuts announced in May 2001 emphasized the aim to refocus defense policy on small-scale peacekeeping. The move put renewed stress on the 1951 security pact with Australia and the USA (ANZUS). The 1984 decision to refuse access to nuclear warships from 1985 damaged defense cooperation with the USA and other Western powers for ten years, forcing New Zealand to seek closer links with Australia. Senior level contacts were resumed in 1994, the USA announcing that it would not send nuclear-armed warships to New Zealand ports. Since then, the UK has also resumed naval visits.

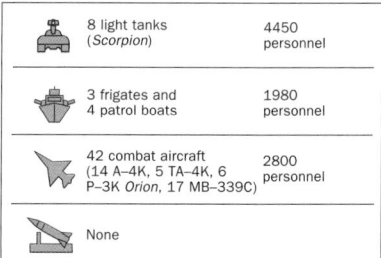

NEW ZEALAND ARMED FORCES

8 light tanks (*Scorpion*)	4450 personnel
3 frigates and 4 patrol boats	1980 personnel
42 combat aircraft (14 A-4K, 5 TA-4K, 6 P-3K *Orion*, 17 MB-339C)	2800 personnel
None	

New Zealand's defense strategy centers on protection against low-level economic threats, terrorism, regional security, and peacekeeping.

ECONOMICS

Inflation 1.4% p.a. (1990–1999)

US$53.3bn

1.92–2.26 New Zealand dollars

SCORE CARD

❑ World GNP Ranking	47th
❑ GNP per Capita	US$13,990
❑ Balance of Payments	US$-4.33bn
❑ Inflation	-0.1%
❑ Unemployment	7%

EXPORTS

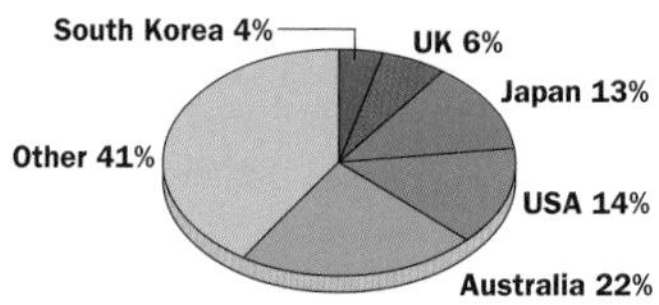
South Korea 4%
UK 6%
Japan 13%
Other 41%
USA 14%
Australia 22%

IMPORTS

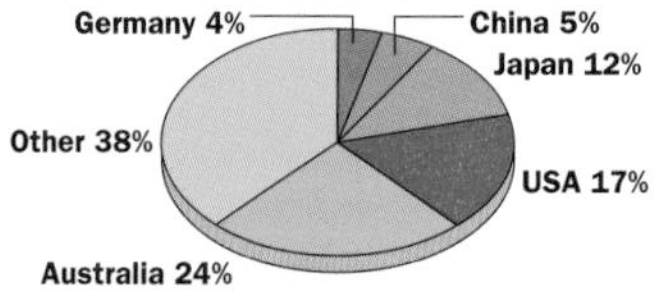
Germany 4%
China 5%
Japan 12%
Other 38%
USA 17%
Australia 24%

Strengths

Modern agricultural sector; world's biggest exporter of butter and (per capita) of wool. Rapidly expanding tourist sector. Manufacturing, with emphasis on high tech. One of world's most open economies. Strong trade links within Pacific Rim.

Weaknesses

One of the highest levels of public debt outside developing world. Continuing reliance on imported manufactured goods and foreign investment.

Profile

Since 1984, New Zealand has changed from being one of the most regulated to one of the most open economies in the world. Radical reforms and drastic cuts in social security and related government spending helped to restore growth and cut inflation to minimal. Diversification into new markets and products recovered after the 1997–1998 Asian economic crisis. Prime Minister Clark dropped objections in 2001 to the idea of a unified Australia–New Zealand dollar. High public debt and poor levels of private investment remain a problem.

ECONOMIC PERFORMANCE INDICATOR

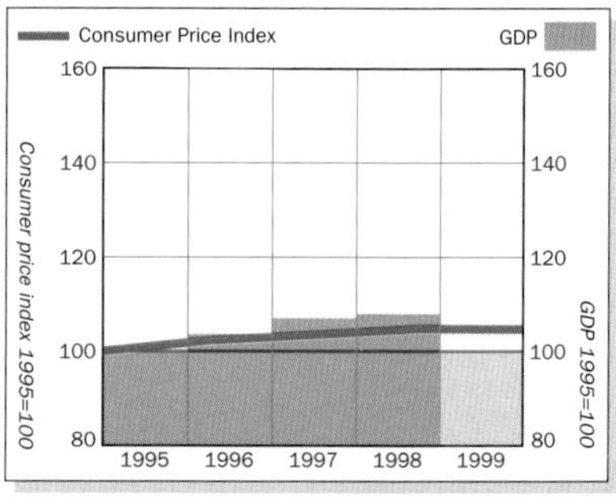
Consumer Price Index
GDP
160
140
120
100
80
Consumer price index 1995=100
GDP 1995=100
1995
1996
1997
1998
1999

NEW ZEALAND : MAJOR BUSINESSES

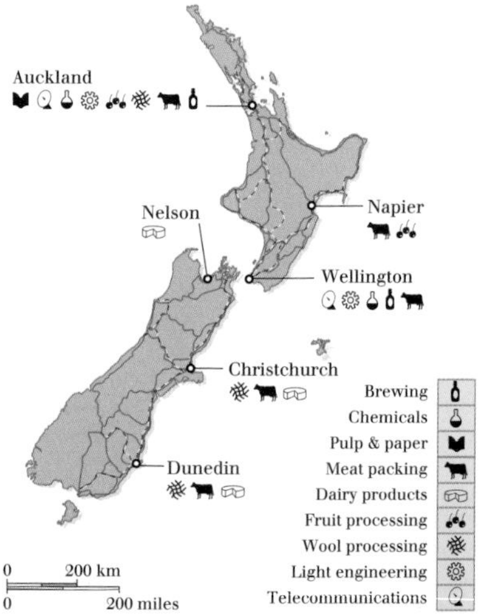
Auckland
Nelson
Napier
Wellington
Christchurch
Dunedin
Brewing
Chemicals
Pulp & paper
Meat packing
Dairy products
Fruit processing
Wool processing
Light engineering
Telecommunications
0
200 km
0
200 miles

RESOURCES

Electric power 7.5m kw

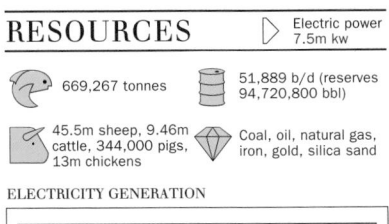

669,267 tonnes

51,889 b/d (reserves 94,720,800 bbl)

45.5m sheep, 9.46m cattle, 344,000 pigs, 13m chickens

Coal, oil, natural gas, iron, gold, silica sand

ELECTRICITY GENERATION

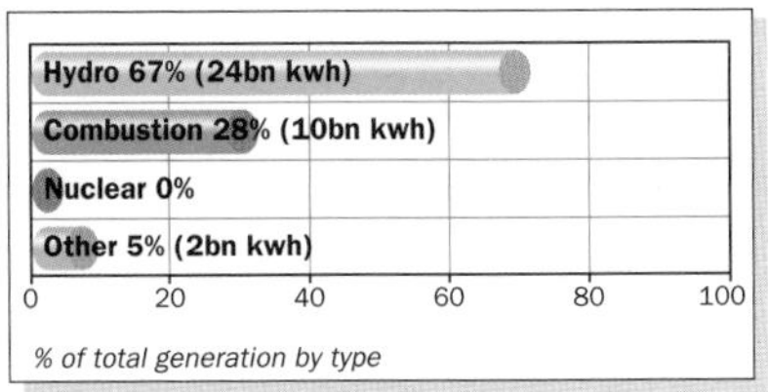
Hydro 67% (24bn kwh)
Combustion 28% (10bn kwh)
Nuclear 0%
Other 5% (2bn kwh)
0
20
40
60
80
100
% of total generation by type

New Zealand's rich pastures, a result of even rainfall throughout the year, have traditionally been its key resource. The sheep, wool, and dairy products on which the country's wealth was built are still important. Newer export industries include products such as fruit, vegetables, fish, cork, wood, and textile fibers.

New Zealand is well endowed with energy resources. It has coal, oil, and natural gas reserves, but most energy is generated by hydroelectric plants.

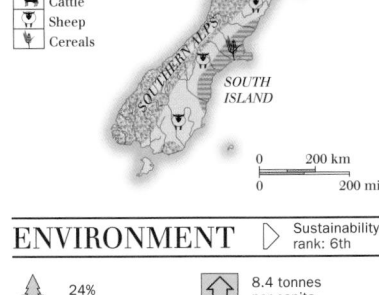

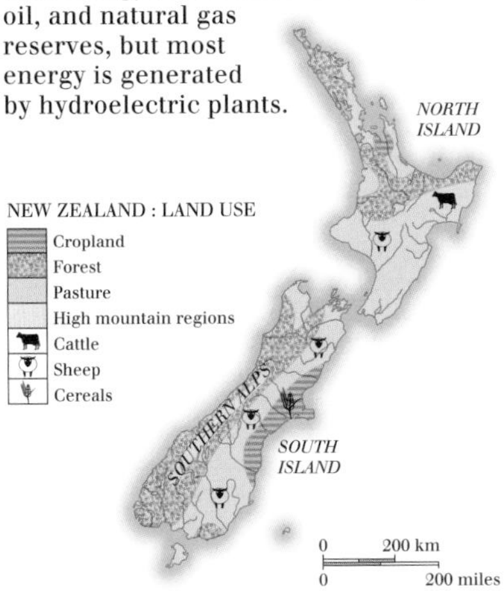
NEW ZEALAND : LAND USE
Cropland
Forest
Pasture
High mountain regions
Cattle
Sheep
Cereals
NORTH ISLAND
SOUTH ISLAND
SOUTHERN ALPS
0
200 km
0
200 miles

ENVIRONMENT

Sustainability rank: 6th

24%

8.4 tonnes per capita

ENVIRONMENTAL TREATIES

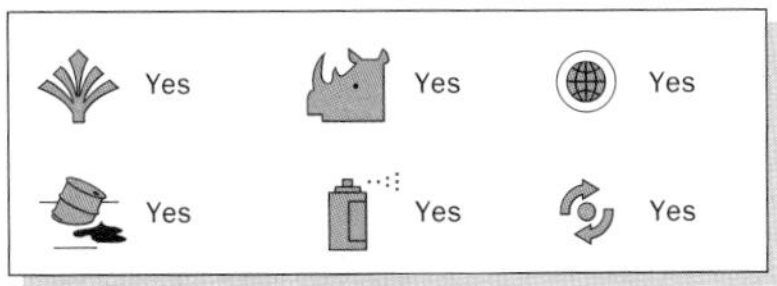
Yes
Yes
Yes
Yes
Yes
Yes

New Zealand's isolation, small population, and limited industry have helped to keep it one of the world's most pollution-free countries. It was a leading opponent of French nuclear testing in the Pacific and has banned nuclear vessels from its ports. Ozone depletion over Antarctica, deforestation, and protection of native flora and fauna are major issues.

MEDIA

TV ownership high

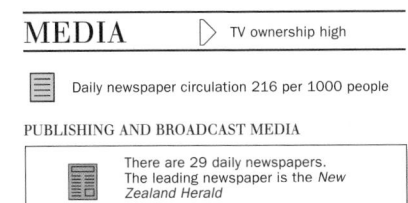

Daily newspaper circulation 216 per 1000 people

PUBLISHING AND BROADCAST MEDIA

There are 29 daily newspapers. The leading newspaper is the *New Zealand Herald*

7 services: 1 state-owned, 6 independent

3 services: 1 state-owned, 2 independent

Deregulated in 1988, New Zealand television is one of the most liberal media in the world. Ruia Mai, the first Maori-language radio station, began broadcasting in 1996.

CRIME

Death penalty not used

4553 prisoners

Down 3% 1992–1996

CRIME RATES

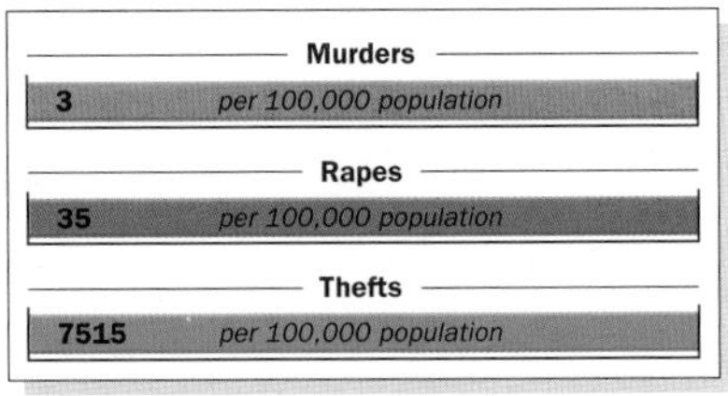
Murders
3
per 100,000 population
Rapes
35
per 100,000 population
Thefts
7515
per 100,000 population

Crime rates in New Zealand's urban areas have increased in recent years. However, overall, the country remains one of the world's safest and most peaceful places in which to live.

EDUCATION

School leaving age:16

99%

169,656 students

THE EDUCATION SYSTEM

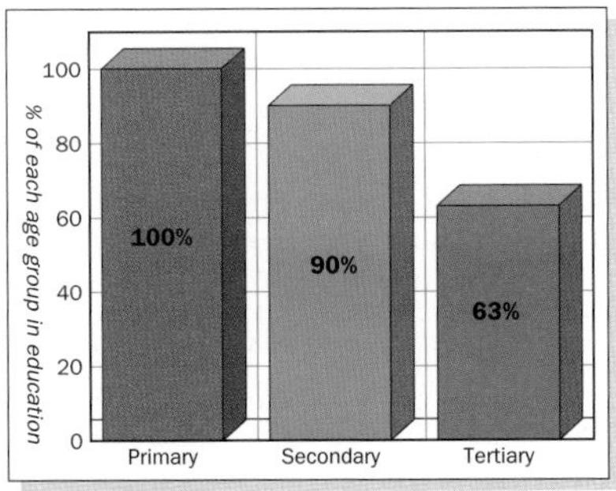
100
80
60
40
20
0
% of each age group in education
100%
90%
63%
Primary
Secondary
Tertiary

Education is free, and compulsory between six and 16. A number of schools are composite, providing both primary and secondary education. New Zealand has one of the highest proportions of the population with tertiary qualifications in the OECD. However, it has one of the worst rates of adult literacy in the developed world. A government initiative, More than Words, was launched in 2000.

HEALTH

Welfare state health benefits

1 per 435 people

Heart disease, cancers, accidents

In 1936 New Zealand was the first country to introduce a full welfare state. Government efforts since 1991 to impose UK-style market systems on the health service have been very unpopular. While life expectancy continues to improve, the nation's OECD health ranking is falling. In comparison with other OECD countries New Zealand has high mortality rates for heart disease, respiratory disease, breast and bowel cancer, motor vehicle accidents, and suicide.

SPENDING

GDP/cap. increase

CONSUMPTION AND SPENDING

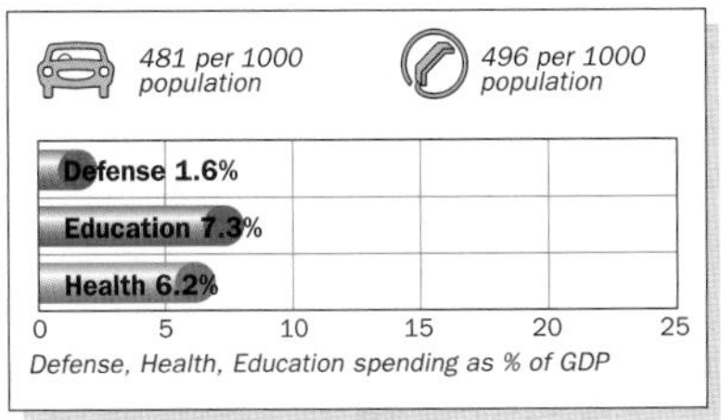
481 per 1000 population
496 per 1000 population
Defense 1.6%
Education 7.3%
Health 6.2%
0
5
10
15
20
25
Defense, Health, Education spending as % of GDP

The years since 1984 have been very difficult for New Zealanders, who are used to affluence within a generous welfare state. A rash of economic and social reforms has held back wages, raised unemployment, and cut welfare benefits. Even so, average living standards are still high, and a strong egalitarian tradition means that wealth remains quite evenly distributed.

The quality of life in New Zealand is among the world's highest, in terms of access to basic necessities, and a pure, healthy, urban and rural environment. Social mobility is fairly high. Wealthier people tend to spend their money on houses close to the water. Yachts are a major status symbol.

WORLD RANKING

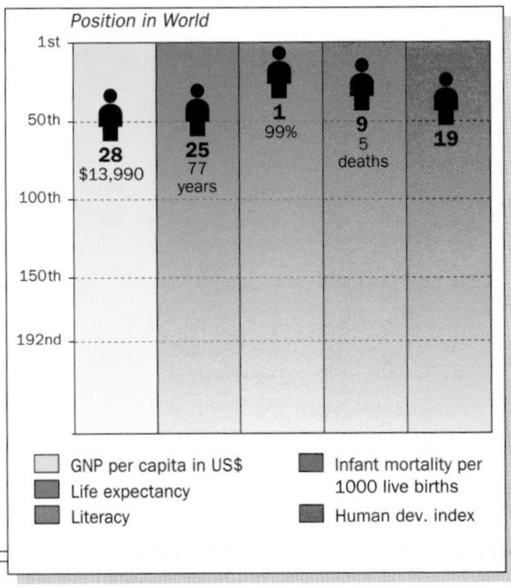
Position in World
1st
50th
100th
150th
192nd
28
$13,990
25
77
years
1
99%
9
5
deaths
19
GNP per capita in US$
Life expectancy
Literacy
Infant mortality per 1000 live births
Human dev. index

N

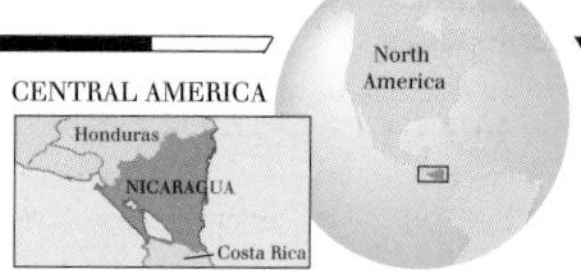
CENTRAL AMERICA
North America
Honduras
NICARAGUA
Costa Rica

NICARAGUA

OFFICIAL NAME: Republic of Nicaragua **CAPITAL:** Managua
POPULATION: 5.1 million **CURRENCY:** Córdoba oro **OFFICIAL LANGUAGE:** Spanish

1838 | 1838 | Sept 15 | NIC | -6 | +505 | .ni

BOUNDED BY THE Pacific Ocean to the west and the Caribbean Sea to the east, Nicaragua lies at the heart of Central America. After more than 40 years of dictatorship, the Sandinista revolution in 1978 led to 11 years of civil war, which almost destroyed the economy. The Sandinistas lost elections unexpectedly in 1990, and right-wing parties have held power since then. The Sandinistas remain the main opposition on the left, despite a party split.

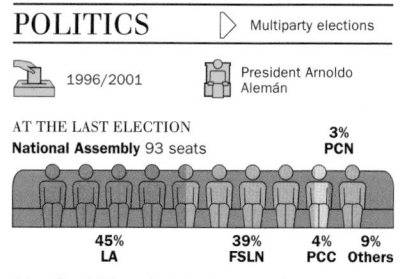

Oil refinery at Bluefields, on the Caribbean coast. Under the Sandinistas, most crude oil came from the Soviet Union, via Cuba.

CLIMATE

Tropical equatorial/ wet & dry

WEATHER CHART

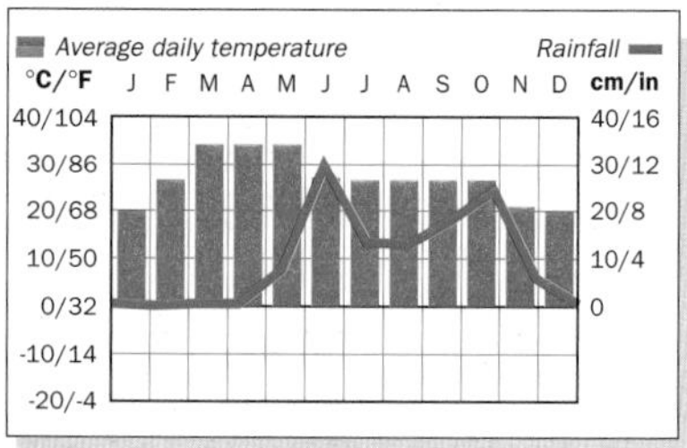
Average daily temperature
Rainfall
°C/°F
J F M A M J J A S O N D
cm/in
40/104
30/86
20/68
10/50
0/32
-10/14
-20/-4
40/16
30/12
20/8
10/4
0

The climate is tropical and often violent, as evidenced by Hurricane Mitch in 1998. Earthquakes also occur.

TRANSPORTATION

Drive on right

Augusto C. Sandino International, Managua 729,001 passengers

28 ships 4300 grt

THE TRANSPORTATION NETWORK

1818 km (1130 miles)

Pan-American Highway: 384 km (239 miles)

None

2220 km (1379 miles)

Nicaragua lacks a Caribbean deep-water port. Hurricane Mitch damaged major roads and destroyed 35 key bridges.

TOURISM

Visitors : Population 1:10

486,000 visitors

Up 4% in 2000

MAIN TOURIST ARRIVALS

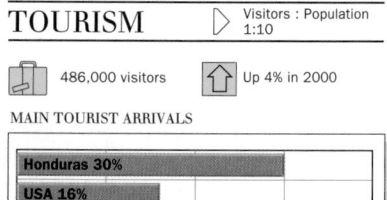

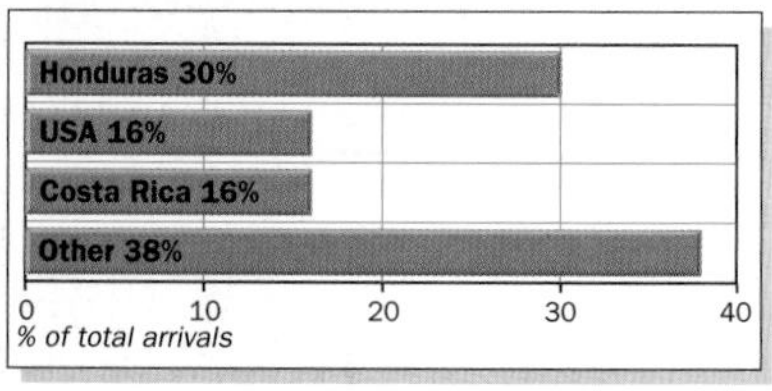
Honduras 30%
USA 16%
Costa Rica 16%
Other 38%
0
10
20
30
40
% of total arrivals

The civil war caused the near-collapse of tourism, and slow recovery has been interrupted by the devastation caused by Hurricane Mitch. Foreign direct investment in the sector grew in 1997–1998.

PEOPLE

Pop. density low

Spanish, English Creole, Miskito

43/km² (111/mi²)

THE URBAN/RURAL POPULATION SPLIT

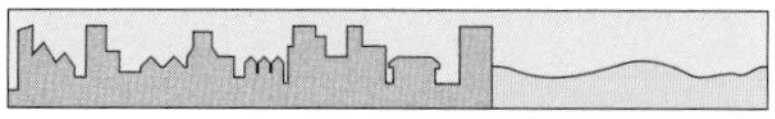
64%
36%

ETHNIC MAKEUP

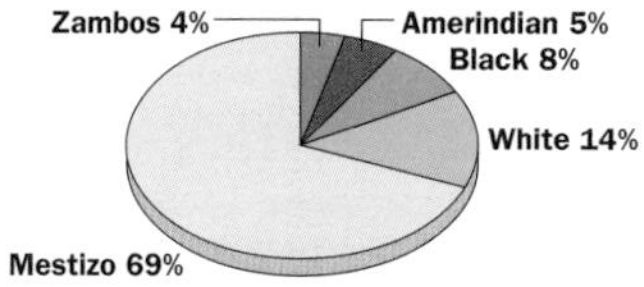
Zambos 4%
Amerindian 5%
Black 8%
White 14%
Mestizo 69%

The Caribbean regions, which in 1987 achieved limited autonomy, are isolated from the more populous Pacific regions. The indigenous Miskito tribes and the descendants of Africans, brought over by Spanish colonists in the 18th century to work the plantations, are concentrated along the Caribbean coast, where English Creole is widely spoken. The Sandinista revolution improved the status of women through changes in the legal system and the incorporation of women into economic and political life. However, poverty and lack of permanent employment have since forced many women into prostitution.

POLITICS

Multiparty elections

1996/2001

President Arnoldo Alemán

AT THE LAST ELECTION

National Assembly 93 seats

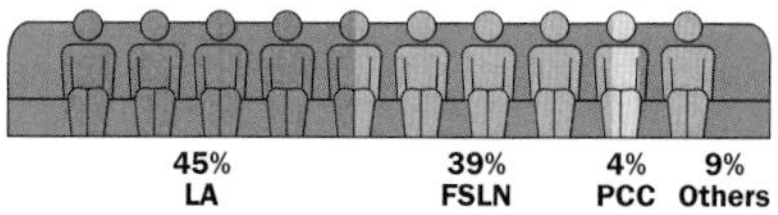
3% PCN
45% LA
39% FSLN
4% PCC
9% Others

LA = Liberal Alliance (includes the Liberal Constitutionalist Party – **PLC**) **FSLN** = Sandinista National Liberation Front **PCC** = Christian Road Party **PCN** = Conservative Party of Nicaragua

Defeated in the 1990 and 1996 polls by right-wing parties, the FSLN underwent an internal crisis. The Liberal Alliance government of President Arnoldo Alemán, which took office in 1997, promised to unite the country but quickly became unpopular due to austerity measures and allegations of corruption. Two-party domination, strengthened by a controversial pact between the ruling PLC and FSLN in 2000, has weakened democracy.

NICARAGUA

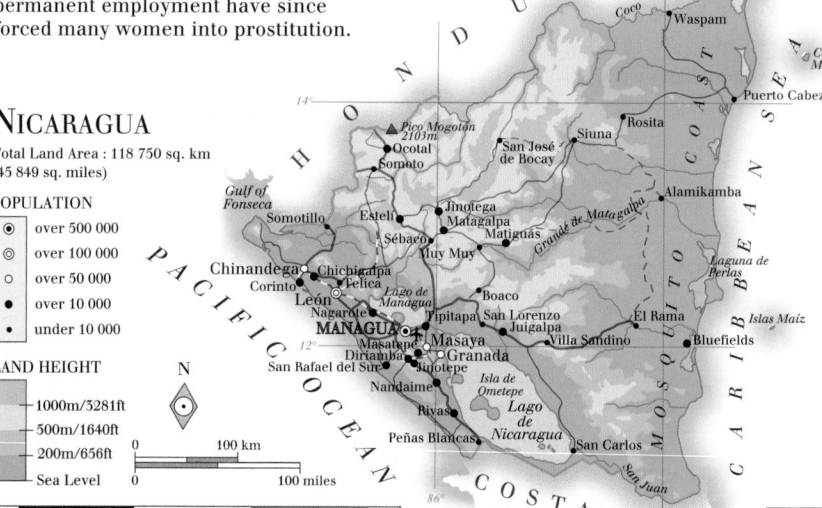

Total Land Area : 118 750 sq. km (45 849 sq. miles)

POPULATION
- over 500 000
- over 100 000
- over 50 000
- over 10 000
- under 10 000

LAND HEIGHT
- 1000m/3281ft
- 500m/1640ft
- 200m/656ft
- Sea Level

0 100 km
0 100 miles

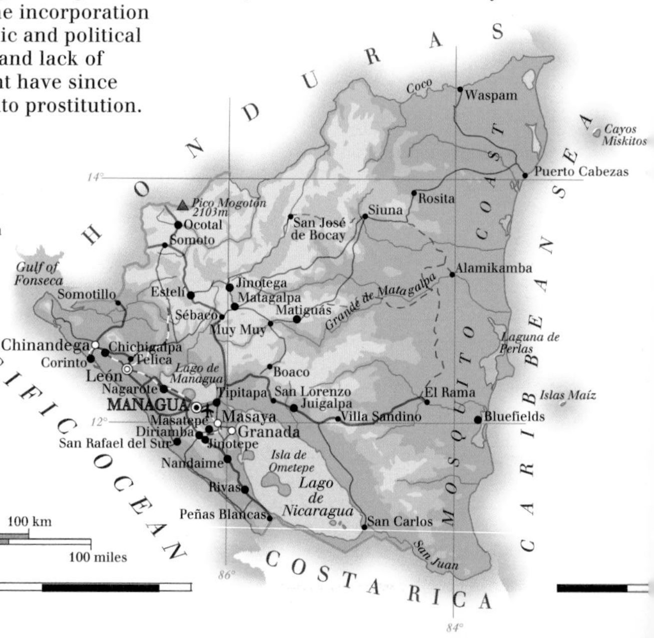
HONDURAS
PACIFIC OCEAN
COSTA RICA
CARIBBEAN SEA
MOSQUITO COAST
Waspam
Coco
Cayos Miskitos
Puerto Cabezas
Rosita
Siuna
Pico Mogotón 2103m
Ocotal
Somoto
San José de Bocay
Alamikamba
Gulf of Fonseca
Somotillo
Estelí
Jinotega
Matagalpa
Matiguás
Grande de Matagalpa
Sébaco
Muy Muy
Chinandega
Chichigalpa
Telica
Corinto
León
Lago de Managua
Boaco
Nagarote
Tipitapa
San Lorenzo
Juigalpa
El Rama
Islas Maíz
Laguna de Perlas
MANAGUA
Masatepe
Masaya
Villa Sandino
Bluefields
Diriamba
Granada
San Rafael del Sur
Jinotepe
Nandaime
Isla de Ometepe
Rivas
Lago de Nicaragua
Peñas Blancas
San Carlos
San Juan
14°
12°
86°
84°

WORLD AFFAIRS

Joined UN in 1945

ACS | Geplac | NAM | OAS | San José

Main issues are debt relief in the wake of Hurricane Mitch, cooperation with neighboring countries for increased US trade access, and the treatment of over 300,000 Nicaraguan immigrants in Costa Rica. A free-trade agreement with Mexico is important. A dispute over the common border with Costa Rica was resolved in 2000. Ongoing border and navigation rights disputes exist with Honduras and Colombia.

AID

Recipient

$675m (receipts) | Up 18% in 1999

Hurricane Mitch damage produced new World Bank and IDB loans. Cuba, France, Finland, and Spain pardoned all or part of Nicaragua's debt. The USA and the Paris Club of international creditors canceled outstanding obligations when it was included in the IMF-run Highly Indebted Poor Countries initiative.

DEFENSE

Compulsory military service

$25m | Down 17% in 1999

FSLN forces that overthrew the Somoza regime formed the basis of the army, which expanded to some 134,000 troops during the civil war, but was cut to 10,000 by 1995. Senior Sandinistas were among officers retired in 1998. The army is to be involved in more community-based roles focused on the defense of natural resources and mine clearance.

ECONOMICS

Inflation 38.6% p.a. (1990–1999)

$2bn | 12.301–12.900 córdobas oro

SCORE CARD

❑ WORLD GNP RANKING	138th
❑ GNP PER CAPITA	$410
❑ BALANCE OF PAYMENTS	$–652m
❑ INFLATION	11.2%
❑ UNEMPLOYMENT	11%

STRENGTHS

Coffee, sugar, and grain exports. Foreign aid and public and private reconstruction work after Hurricane Mitch will benefit tourism, energy, services, and construction.

WEAKNESSES

Heavy debt burden. Main exports subject to commodity price fluctuations. High unemployment. Poor energy supply and infrastructure. Lack of investment and diversification. Weak banks. Delays in privatization. Skewed land ownership and protracted disputes over property. Corruption.

EXPORTS

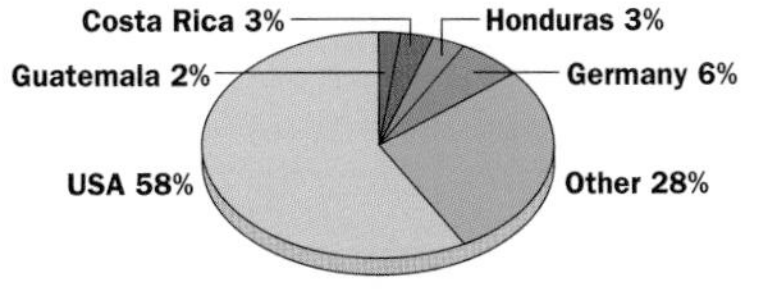
Costa Rica 3%
Honduras 3%
Guatemala 2%
Germany 6%
USA 58%
Other 28%

IMPORTS

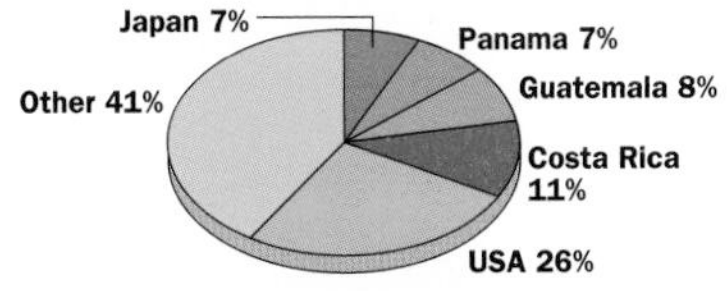
Japan 7%
Panama 7%
Guatemala 8%
Other 41%
Costa Rica 11%
USA 26%

RESOURCES

Electric power 457,000 kw

16,130 tonnes | Not an oil producer

1.66m cattle, 400,000 pigs, 10m chickens | Gold, silver, lead, zinc, copper, tungsten, salt

Nicaragua has small quantities of gold and silver. New thermal generation projects are planned to overcome energy deficits. There is possible offshore oil.

ENVIRONMENT

Sustainability rank: 43rd

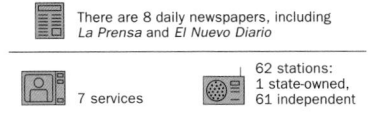

7% | 0.7 tonnes per capita

Deforestation over large areas and the widespread use of pesticides are major problems.

MEDIA

TV ownership medium

Daily newspaper circulation 30 per 1000 people

PUBLISHING AND BROADCAST MEDIA

There are 8 daily newspapers, including *La Prensa* and *El Nuevo Diario*

7 services | 62 stations: 1 state-owned, 61 independent

Since the civil war, radio, TV, and newspapers have tended to ally themselves with the government or the opposition; there is little room for political neutrality.

CRIME

Death penalty not used

3046 prisoners | Crime is rising

Former combatants have menaced parts of central and northern regions. Violent crime is rising, as is drug-trafficking.

CHRONOLOGY

Nicaragua became independent in 1838. Guerrilla forces, led by General Sandino, opposed the US marine presence in the early 1930s.

- ❑ **1978–1990** FSLN ends 44-year Somoza dictatorship; civil war between FSLN and Contras.
- ❑ **1998** Hurricane Mitch devastates country.

EDUCATION

School leaving age: 12

69% | 56,558 students

The Sandinista "Literacy Crusade" achieved dramatic results in the 1980s, but has long since died away. Student protests in recent years have been for increases in the education budget.

HEALTH

Welfare state health benefits

1 per 1250 people | Heart and intestinal infectious diseases, accidents, tuberculosis

The standard of health care improved substantially in the 1980s under the Sandanista government. However, real spending on health fell by 71% between 1988 and 1993 and still has to recover.

SPENDING

GDP/cap. increase

CONSUMPTION AND SPENDING

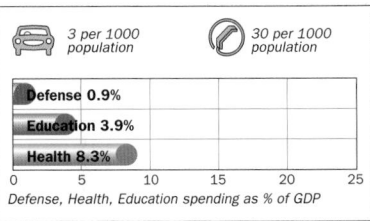

3 per 1000 population | *30 per 1000 population*

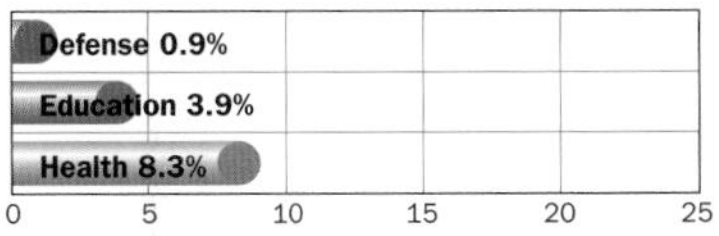
Defense 0.9%
Education 3.9%
Health 8.3%
0
5
10
15
20
25

Defense, Health, Education spending as % of GDP

A UNDP study in 1998 revealed that 44% of Nicaragua's population have to survive on the equivalent of less than US$1 a day.

WORLD RANKING

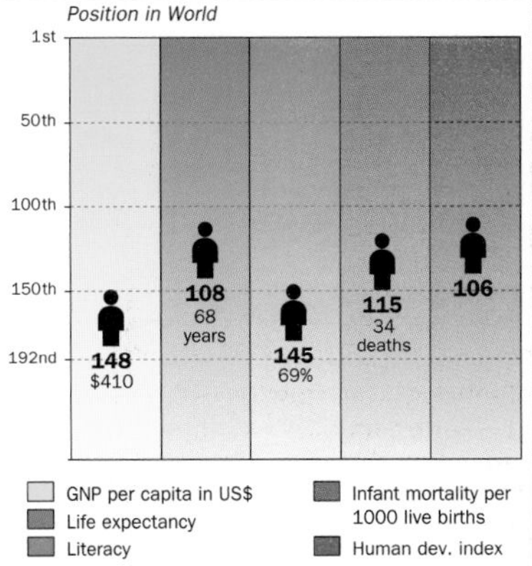
Position in World
1st
50th
100th
150th
192nd
148
$410
108
68
years
145
69%
115
34
deaths
106
GNP per capita in US$
Life expectancy
Literacy
Infant mortality per 1000 live births
Human dev. index

N

NIGER

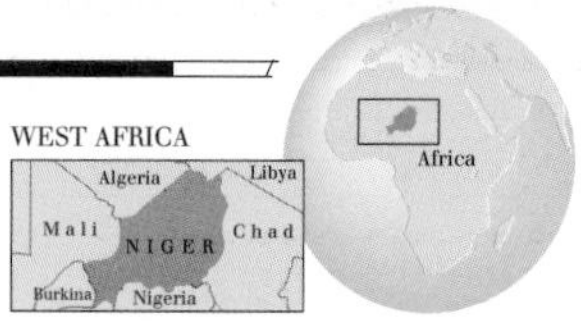
WEST AFRICA
Algeria
Libya
Mali
NIGER
Chad
Burkina
Nigeria
Africa

OFFICIAL NAME: Republic of Niger **CAPITAL:** Niamey
POPULATION: 10.7 million **CURRENCY:** CFA franc **OFFICIAL LANGUAGE:** French

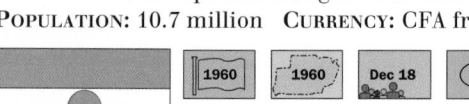

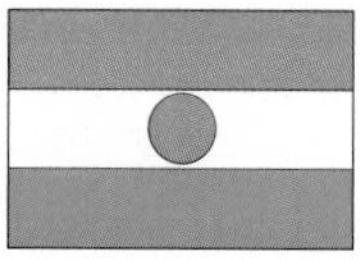

1960 | 1960 | Dec 18 | RN | +1 | +227 | .ne

LANDLOCKED IN THE WEST of Africa, Niger is linked to the sea by the Niger river. Saharan conditions prevail in the northern regions, in the area around the Aïr mountains, and, particularly, in the vast uninhabited northeast. Niger was ruled by one-party or military regimes until 1992 when a multiparty constitution was introduced, but a much-troubled democratic process was disrupted by military coups in 1996 and 1999.

CLIMATE

Hot desert/steppe

WEATHER CHART

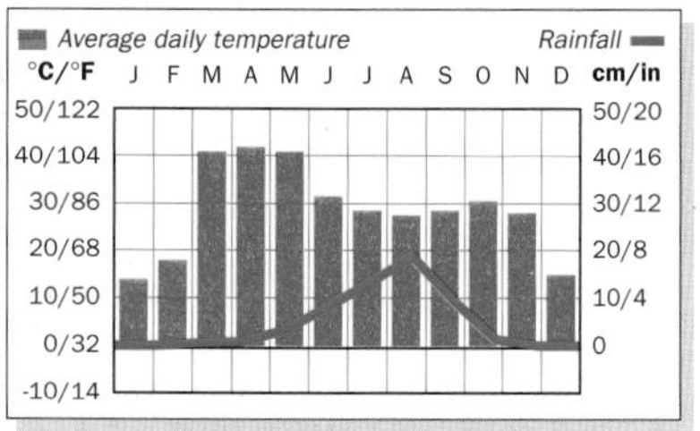
Average daily temperature
Rainfall
°C/°F
J F M A M J J A S O N D
cm/in
50/122
40/104
30/86
20/68
10/50
0/32
-10/14
50/20
40/16
30/12
20/8
10/4
0

The Saharan north is virtually rainless. The south, in the Sahel belt, has an unreliable rainy season, preceded by a period of extreme daytime heat.

TRANSPORTATION

Drive on right

Niamey International 96,928 passengers

Has no fleet

THE TRANSPORTATION NETWORK

798 km (496 miles)

Trans-Sahara Highway: 428 km (266 miles)

None, but shares administration of Benin's railroad

300 km (186 miles)

A very small proportion of Niger's road network is paved. There are international airports at Niamey and Agadez. There is no railroad.

TOURISM

Visitors : Population 1:214

50,000 visitors

Up 16% in 2000

MAIN TOURIST ARRIVALS

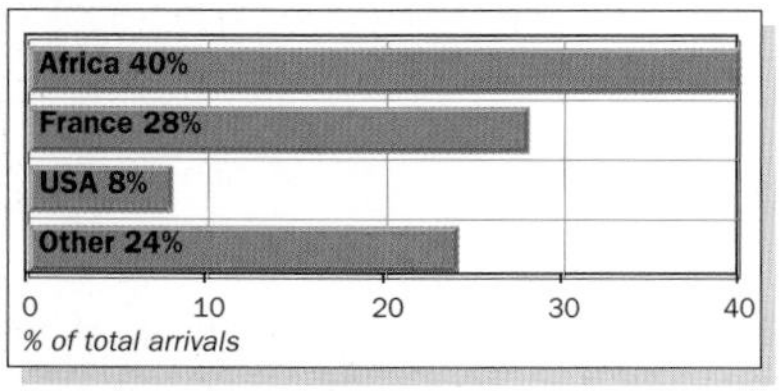
Africa 40%
France 28%
USA 8%
Other 24%
0
10
20
30
40
% of total arrivals

The Aïr mountains, southern Hausa cities, and Saharan Tuareg culture attract some tourists in spite of Niger's limited infrastructure and its instability.

PEOPLE

Pop. density low

Hausa, Djerma, Fulani, Tuareg, Teda, French

8/km² (22/mi²)

THE URBAN/RURAL POPULATION SPLIT

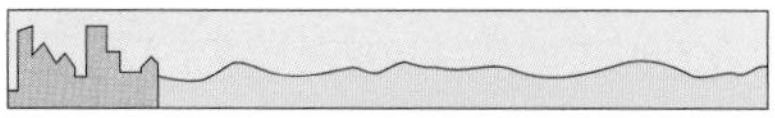
20%
80%

ETHNIC MAKEUP

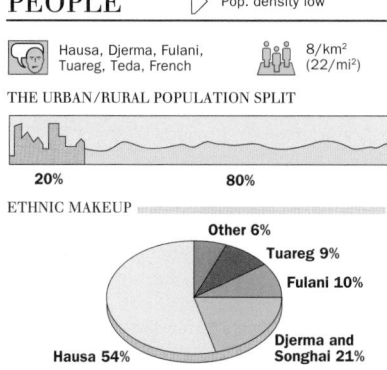

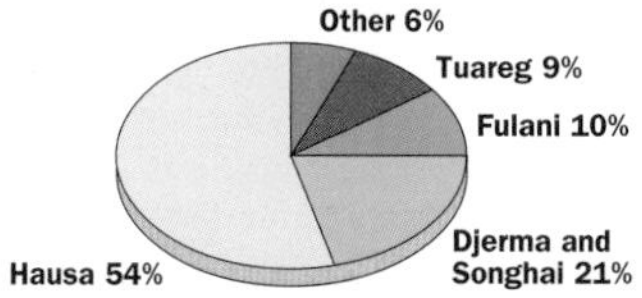
Other 6%
Tuareg 9%
Fulani 10%
Djerma and Songhai 21%
Hausa 54%

Considerable tensions exist in Niger between the Tuaregs in the north and the southern groups. The Tuaregs' sense of alienation from mainstream Nigerien politics has increased since the 1973 and 1984 droughts, which disrupted the Tuaregs's nomadic way of life. A five-year rebellion by northern Tuaregs ended in 1995 with a peace agreement. In eastern Niger, Toubou and Arab groups have also been in revolt.

A more subtle antagonism exists between the Djerma and Hausa groups. The Djerma elite from the southwest dominated politics for many years, until 1993 when control passed to the Hausa majority.

Niger is an overwhelmingly Islamic society. Women have, on the whole, only limited rights and restricted access to education.

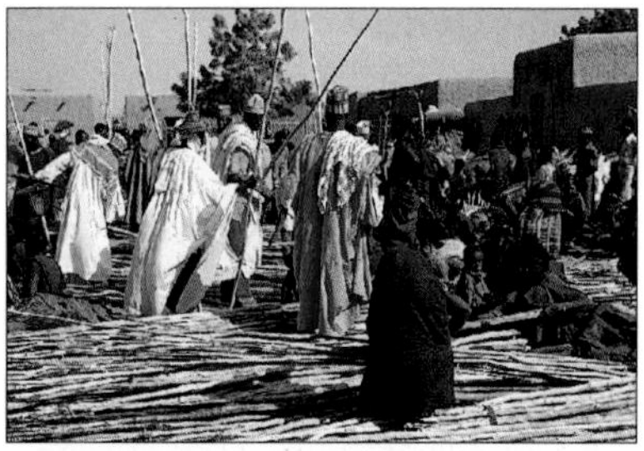

***Testing boating poles in the market** at Ayorou on the River Niger, the country's only major permanent watercourse.*

POLITICS

Multiparty elections

1999/2004

President Mamadou Tandja

AT THE LAST ELECTION

National Assembly 83 seats

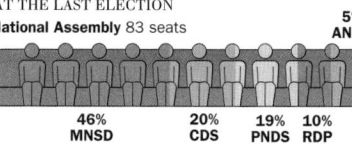

5%
ANDP
46%
MNSD
20%
CDS
19%
PNDS
10%
RDP

MNSD = National Movement for the Development of Society **CDS** = Democratic and Social Convention **PNDS** = Niger Party for Democracy and Socialism **RDP** = Rally for Democracy and Progress **ANDP** = Niger Alliance for Democracy and Progress

The death in 1987 of the military dictator, President Seyni Kountché, paved the way for prodemocracy demonstrations and eventually led to multiparty elections in 1993. An ensuing power struggle between President Mahamane Ousmane and his political opponents provoked a military coup in 1996. Gen. Ibrahim Barre Mainassara promulgated a new constitution and won a presidential election condemned as fraudulent by the opposition. Mainassara was assassinated by his presidential guard in early 1999. The new military leadership drew up yet another constitution. MNSD leader Mamadou Tandja won the presidential poll later that year. His party, allied with the CDS of former president Ousmane, dominates the new legislature.

WORLD AFFAIRS

Joined UN in 1960

CILSS | ECOWAS | FZ | OAU | OIC

Relations with Libya and Algeria have improved since the end of the Tuareg rebellion in 1995. ECOWAS members and the OAU condemned the 1999 coup, as did all key donors, led by France.

AID

Recipient

$187m (receipts)

Down 36% in 1999

France is the principal donor, followed by the IMF and Arab funds. Most aid was frozen immediately following the 1999 coup, but in late 2000 the IMF approved a three-year loan under its Poverty Reduction and Growth Facility.

DEFENSE

Compulsory military service

$28m

Up 8% in 1999

Niger's armed forces and paramilitary elements total 10,700. Politics has been dominated by the military since 1974.

N

Key to symbols and abbreviations on cover flaps

NIGER

Total Land Area : 1 266 700 sq. km (489 073 sq. miles)

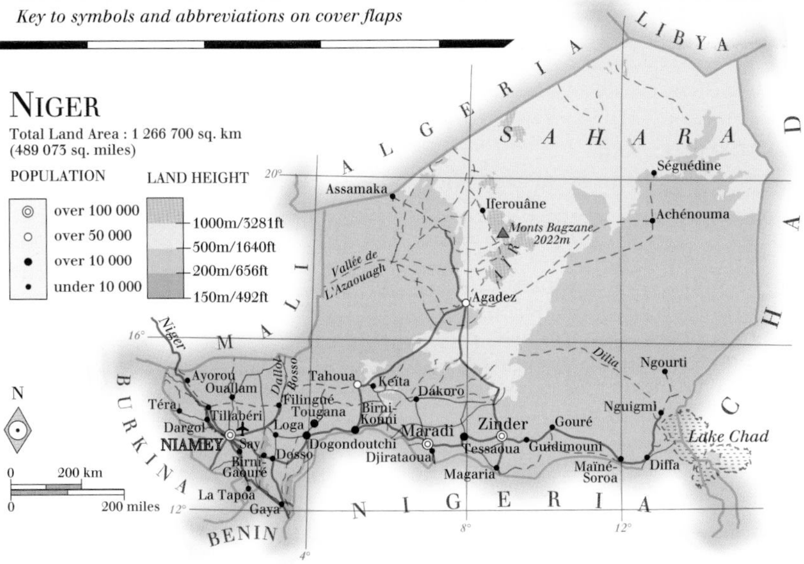
POPULATION
over 100 000
over 50 000
over 10 000
under 10 000
LAND HEIGHT
1000m/3281ft
500m/1640ft
200m/656ft
150m/492ft
N
0
200 km
0
200 miles
LIBYA
ALGERIA
SAHARA
CHAD
MALI
BURKINA
BENIN
NIGERIA
Assamaka
Iferouâne
Séguédine
Achénouma
Monts Bagzane 2022m
Vallée de L'Azaouagh
Agadez
AÏR
Niger
Ayorou
Ouallam
Téra
Tillabéri
Dargol
NIAMEY
Say
Birni-Gaouré
Dosso
La Tapoa
Gaya
Filingué
Tougana
Loga
Tahoua
Keïta
Dakoro
Birni-Konni
Maradi
Dogondoutchi
Djirataoua
Zinder
Tessaoua
Magaria
Gouré
Guidimouni
Maïné-Soroa
Diffa
Nguigmi
Ngourti
Dilia
Lake Chad
Dallol Bosso

CHRONOLOGY

The powerful Islamic Sokoto Empire dissolved as the French took Niger over between 1883 and 1901.

- **1960** Independence.
- **1968** French open uranium mines.
- **1973** Drought; 60% of livestock die.
- **1974** Military coup. General Kountché bans political parties.
- **1984** New drought; Niger river dries up. Uranium boom ends.
- **1987** Kountché dies. General Ali Saibou eases transition to democracy.
- **1990–1995** Tuareg rebellion.
- **1992** Multiparty constitution.
- **1993** Democratic elections.
- **1996** Military coup. Staged elections.
- **1999** New constitution. General Mainassara assassinated. Multiparty elections won by Mamadou Tandja.
- **2001** Hunting banned in effort to save wildlife.

ECONOMICS

Inflation 6.4% p.a. (1990–1999)

$1.97bn

654.42–698.69 CFA francs

SCORE CARD

- World GNP Ranking 139th
- GNP per Capita $190
- Balance of Payments .... $–174m
- Inflation .... –2.3%
- Unemployment .... Not available

STRENGTHS

Vast uranium deposits; gold and oil discoveries in late 1990s revived hopes for economic viability.

WEAKNESSES

Aid-dependent. Collapse of uranium prices in 1980s created large debt burden. Only 3% of land cultivable. Weak infrastructure. Frequent droughts. Political instability.

EXPORTS

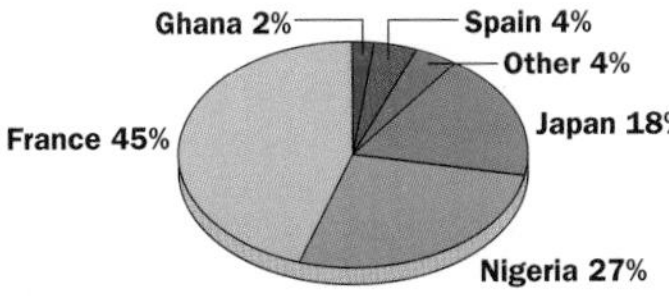
Ghana 2%
Spain 4%
Other 4%
Japan 18%
France 45%
Nigeria 27%

IMPORTS

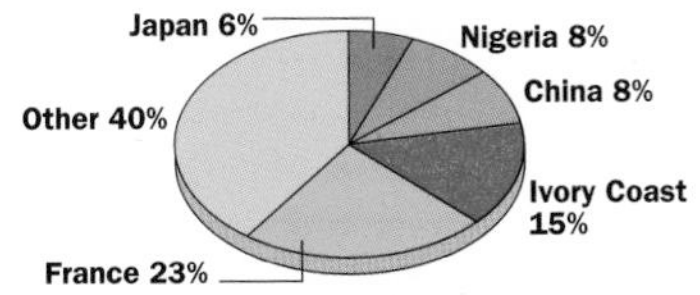
Japan 6%
Nigeria 8%
China 8%
Other 40%
Ivory Coast 15%
France 23%

ENVIRONMENT

Sustainability rank: 111th

8%

0.1 tonnes per capita

Serious droughts intensify desertification. Hunting was banned in 2001, in an effort to preserve the wildlife population.

MEDIA

TV ownership low

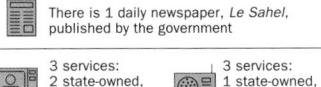

Daily newspaper circulation 0.2 per 1000 people

PUBLISHING AND BROADCAST MEDIA

There is 1 daily newspaper, *Le Sahel*, published by the government

3 services: 2 state-owned, 1 independent

3 services: 1 state-owned, 2 independent

The government controls most broadcasting. The BBC World Service's Hausa programming is influential.

CRIME

Death penalty not used

Niger does not publish prison figures

Down 36% 1996–1998

Rural banditry is common, often involving access to grazing and water. Urban crime levels are low, but in border areas smuggling is a way of life.

EDUCATION

School leaving age: 15

16%

4513 students

Local languages are emphasized more strongly than in most francophone states. School attendance is only 30%.

RESOURCES

Electric power 63,000 kw

6341 tonnes

Not an oil producer

6.6m goats, 4.3m sheep, 2.2m cattle, 20m chickens

Uranium, tin, gypsum, coal, salt, tungsten, oil, iron, phosphates, gold

During the 1970s, Niger's uranium mines boomed, but output collapsed in the 1980s when world prices slumped. Other mining is small-scale and oil reserves, discovered in the Lake Chad area, are not yet commercially viable. Salt is a traditionally exploited resource, as are such plant resources as the doum and palmyra palms.

HEALTH

No welfare state health benefits

1 per 20,000 people

Malaria, tuberculosis, meningitis, measles, malnutrition

In spite of progress in rural health care, immunization, malaria control, and child nutrition are still limited.

SPENDING

GDP/cap. increase

CONSUMPTION AND SPENDING

4 per 1000 population

2 per 1000 population

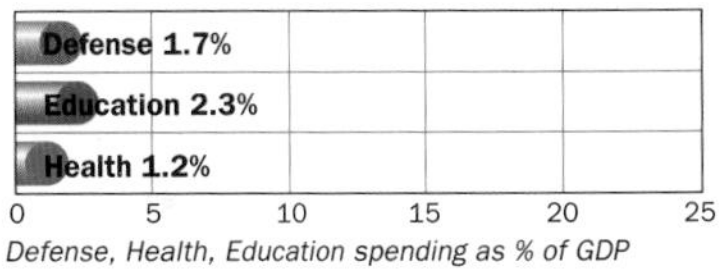
Defense 1.7%
Education 2.3%
Health 1.2%
0
5
10
15
20
25
Defense, Health, Education spending as % of GDP

A small circle of secretive trading families controls much of Niger's wealth. They are successful in evading taxation.

WORLD RANKING

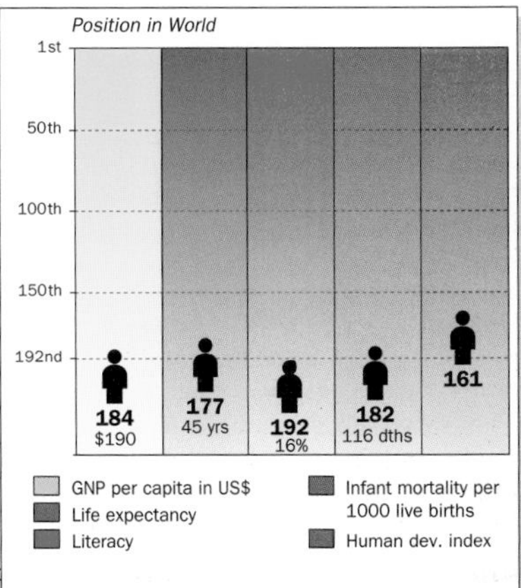
Position in World
1st
50th
100th
150th
192nd
184
$190
177
45 yrs
192
16%
182
116 dths
161
GNP per capita in US$
Life expectancy
Literacy
Infant mortality per 1000 live births
Human dev. index

N

NIGERIA

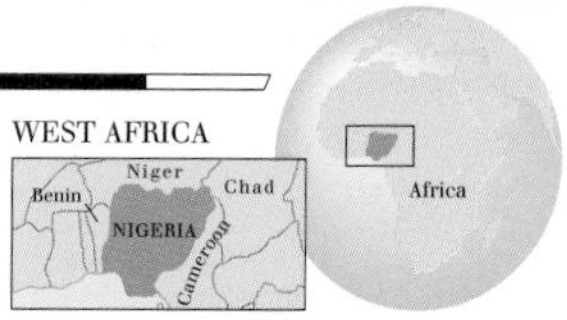

WEST AFRICA
Niger
Benin
Chad
NIGERIA
Cameroon
Africa

OFFICIAL NAME: Federal Republic of Nigeria **CAPITAL:** Abuja
POPULATION: 112 million **CURRENCY:** Naira **OFFICIAL LANGUAGE:** English

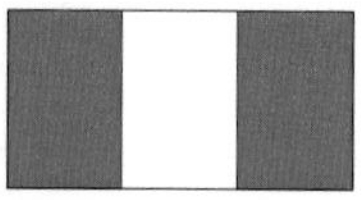

1960 | 1961 | Oct 1 | NGR | +1 | +234 | .ng

Village beneath Tengele Peak in Bauchi State. A large proportion of Nigerians live from subsistence agriculture.

AFRICA'S MOST POPULOUS state, Nigeria gained its independence from Britain in 1960. Bordered by Benin, Niger, Chad, and Cameroon, its terrain varies from tropical rainforest and swamps in the south to savanna in the north. Nigeria has been dominated by military governments since 1966. After many delays, a promised return to civilian rule came about in 1999, with the election as president of Olusegun Obasanjo, a former general who had been head of state from 1976 to 1979. Nigeria is OPEC's fourth-largest oil producer, but it has experienced a fall in living standards since the 1970s oil boom.

CLIMATE

Tropical/steppe

WEATHER CHART

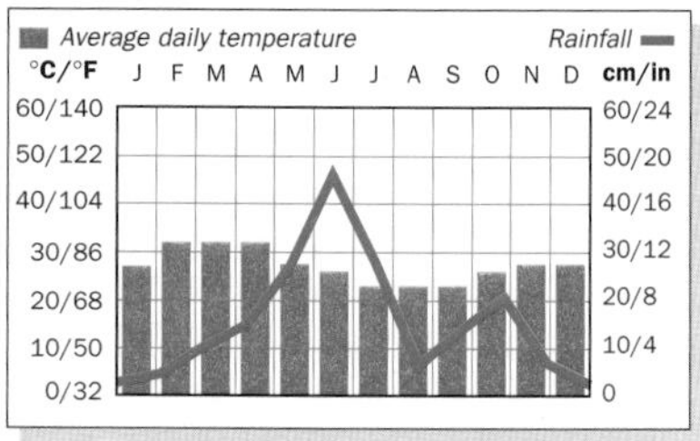

Average daily temperature
Rainfall
°C/°F
J F M A M J J A S O N D
cm/in
60/140
50/122
40/104
30/86
20/68
10/50
0/32
60/24
50/20
40/16
30/12
20/8
10/4
0

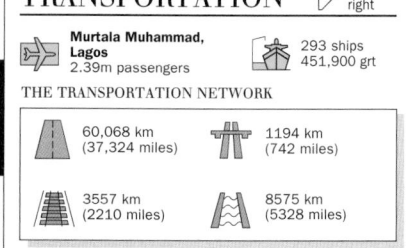

The south is hot, rainy, and humid for most of the year. The arid north experiences only one, uncomfortably humid, rainy season from May to September. Its very hot dry season is marked by the *harmattan* wind. The Jos Plateau and the eastern highlands are cooler than the rest of Nigeria. Forcados, in the Niger delta, gets most rain, with 380 cm (150 in) a year.

TRANSPORTATION

Drive on right

Murtala Muhammad, Lagos
2.39m passengers

293 ships
451,900 grt

THE TRANSPORTATION NETWORK

60,068 km (37,324 miles)

1194 km (742 miles)

3557 km (2210 miles)

8575 km (5328 miles)

Nigeria relies almost entirely on road transportation. During the oil-boom years of the 1970s, new long-distance roads and stretches of freeway were built. The road network is now badly maintained and in urgent need of repair. The road accident rate is among the world's highest and there is severe and chronic traffic congestion in Lagos. In mid-2000 plans for a new trans-Sahara highway from Lagos to Tangiers, Morocco, were announced. Work started in 2001 on a $40 million ports project that will link the five southeastern states.

TOURISM

Visitors : Population 1:151

739,000 visitors

Up 21% in 1998

Nigeria has attempted to build a tourist industry, but numbers remain low. Year-round tropical temperatures and poor infrastructure have limited its growth. The major deterrent to visitors, however, is crime. Travel can be hazardous, and Lagos has one of the world's highest crime rates.

MAIN TOURIST ARRIVALS

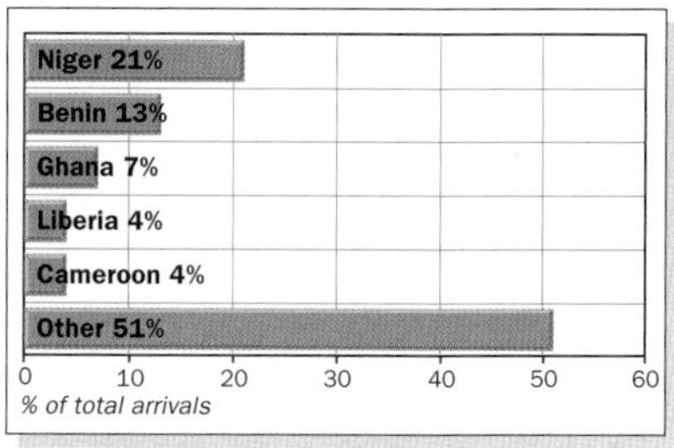

Niger 21%
Benin 13%
Ghana 7%
Liberia 4%
Cameroon 4%
Other 51%
0
10
20
30
40
50
60
% of total arrivals

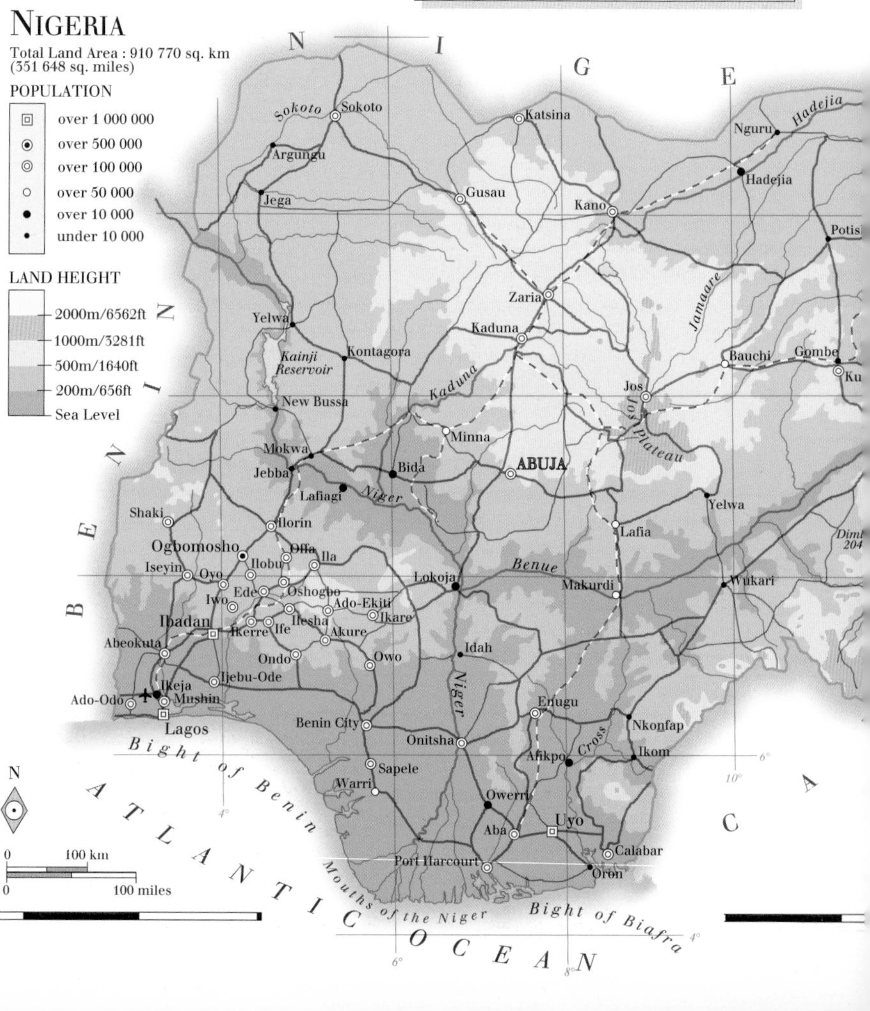

NIGERIA
Total Land Area : 910 770 sq. km (351 648 sq. miles)
POPULATION
over 1 000 000
over 500 000
over 100 000
over 50 000
over 10 000
under 10 000
LAND HEIGHT
2000m/6562ft
1000m/3281ft
500m/1640ft
200m/656ft
Sea Level
N
0
100 km
0
100 miles
N I G E R
B E N I N
C H A D
C A
Bight of Benin
Bight of Biafra
Mouths of the Niger
A T L A N T I C O C E A N
Sokoto
Sokoto
Argungu
Jega
Gusau
Katsina
Nguru
Hadejia
Hadejia
Kano
Potis
Zaria
Jamaare
Yelwa
Kainji Reservoir
Kontagora
Kaduna
Kaduna
Bauchi
Gombe
Ku
Jos
Jos Plateau
New Bussa
Minna
Mokwa
Jebba
Bida
ABUJA
Lafiagi
Niger
Yelwa
Shaki
Ilorin
Ogbomosho
Offa
Lafia
Ilobu
Ila
Iseyin
Oyo
Ede
Oshogbo
Lokoja
Benue
Makurdi
Wukari
Iwo
Ado-Ekiti
Ibadan
Ikerre
Ife
Ilesha
Ikare
Akure
Abeokuta
Ondo
Owo
Idah
Ijebu-Ode
Ikeja
Ado-Odo
Mushin
Lagos
Niger
Enugu
Nkonfap
Benin City
Onitsha
Cross
Ikom
Afikpo
Sapele
Warri
Owerri
Uyo
Aba
Calabar
Port Harcourt
Oron

PEOPLE

Pop. density medium

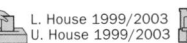

Hausa, English, Yoruba, Ibo

122/km² (317/mi²)

THE URBAN/RURAL POPULATION SPLIT

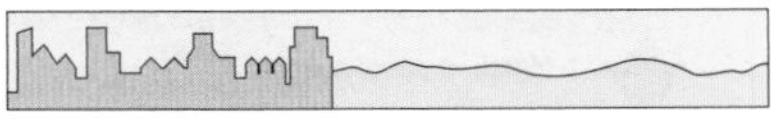
43%
57%

RELIGIOUS PERSUASION

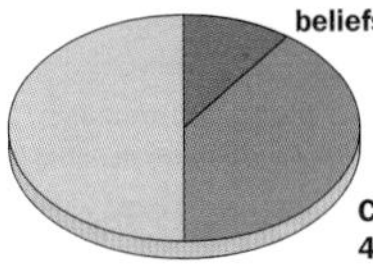
Traditional beliefs 10%
Muslim 50%
Christian 40%

ETHNIC MAKEUP

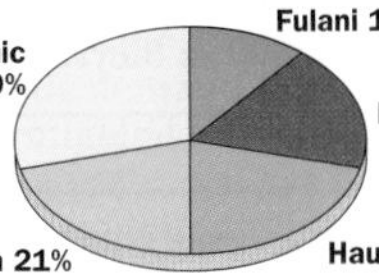
Fulani 11%
Other ethnic groups 29%
Ibo 18%
Yoruba 21%
Hausa 21%

Until fighting erupted between Hausas and Yorubas in the southwest in mid-1999, Nigeria had enjoyed some success in containing tensions caused by ethnic, religious, and linguistic diversity. There is intense rivalry among the Hausa, Yoruba, and Ibo, the three main ethnic groups, as well as among the 245 smaller ones. Religion is a particular source of tension. Outbreaks of violence, in the north particularly, are frequently attributable to clashes between Islamist militants and Christian proselytizers. When the northern state of Zamfara introduced *sharia* – Islamic law – in 1999, President Obasanjo, a Christian, refused to attend the ceremony. Proposals to introduce *sharia* in other northern states sparked violence in 2000 and over 400 deaths in Kaduna. Traditionally, except in the Islamic north, women have possessed independent economic status. In recent years they have, however, been subjected to some prejudice in professional circles.

POPULATION AGE BREAKDOWN

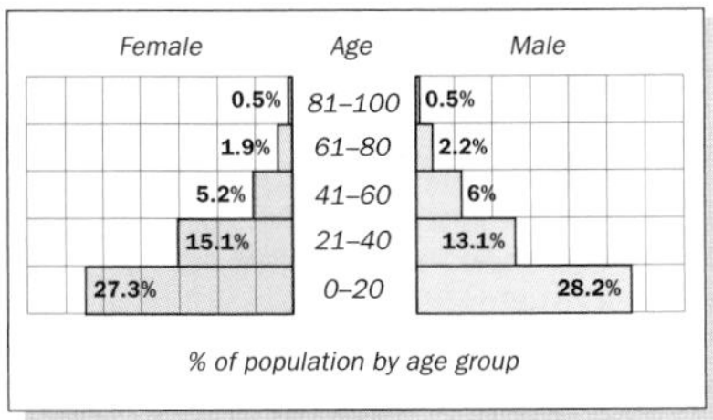
Female
Age
Male
0.5% 81–100 0.5%
1.9% 61–80 2.2%
5.2% 41–60 6%
15.1% 21–40 13.1%
27.3% 0–20 28.2%
% of population by age group

POLITICS

Multiparty elections

L. House 1999/2003
U. House 1999/2003

President Olusegun Obasanjo

AT THE LAST ELECTION

House of Representatives 360 seats

60% PDP
19% APP
18% AD
3% Vacant

PDP = People's Democratic Party **APP** = All People's Party **AD** = Alliance for Democracy

Senate 109 seats

61% PDP
21% APP
17% AD
1% Vacant

Since May 1999 Nigeria has had a civilian constitution, after 16 years of military dictatorships. President Olusegun Obasanjo and his PDP promise national reconciliation.

MAIN POLITICAL ISSUES

Corruption

Corruption has been identified as a major cause of Nigeria's debt levels. Bureaucrats demand lucrative kickbacks when granting contracts. Accusations at all levels of government peaked with the impeachment in mid-2000 of the Senate president. President Obasanjo has promised to stamp out corruption.

Ethnic tensions

The Obasanjo regime faces difficulties in reversing the rivalries among the Hausa, Yoruba, and Ibo. The situation deteriorated in early 2000 with ethnic violence involving Yoruba separatists, and rioting between Christians and the majority Muslims in the north so severe that state governments backed off from proposals on implementing *sharia* law. However, by 2001 ten northern states had introduced the Islamic code.

PROFILE

The sudden death of military ruler Sani Abacha in 1998, followed by that of the imprisoned Chief Moshood Abiola, the presumed winner of the annulled 1993 presidential elections, left General Abdulsalam Aboubakar to usher in civilian rule. Olusegun Obasanjo, a popular general who was head of state in 1976–1979, won elections held in 1999.

Olusegun Obasanjo, *elected president in 1999.*

General Abacha. *Head of state from 1993 until 1998.*

CHRONOLOGY

Before formal colonization by the British, begun only in 1861, Nigeria was a collection of African states owing their considerable wealth to trans-Saharan and transatlantic trade. During the 18th century the principal commodity was slaves: over 15,000 people a year were exported from the Bight of Benin and another 15,000 from the Bight of Biafra.

- ❑ **1885** Royal Niger Company given official responsibility for British sphere of influence along Niger and Benue rivers. British armed forces coerce local rulers into accepting British rule.
- ❑ **1897** West Africa Frontier Force (WAFF) established; subjugation of the north begins.
- ❑ **1898** The Royal Niger Company's charter revoked.
- ❑ **1900** British Protectorate of Northern Nigeria established.
- ❑ **1906** Lagos incorporated into the Protectorate of Southern Nigeria.
- ❑ **1914** Protectorates of Northern and Southern Nigeria joined to form colony of Nigeria.
- ❑ **1960** Independence. Nigeria established as a federation.
- ❑ **1961** Northern part of UK-administered UN Trust Territory of the Cameroons incorporated as part of Nigeria's Northern Region.
- ❑ **1966** January, first military coup, led by Major General Ironsi. July, counter-coup mounted by group of northern army officers. Ironsi murdered. Thousands of Ibo in Northern Region massacred. General Gowon in control of north and west.
- ❑ **1967–1970** Civil war. Lieutenant Colonel Ojukwu calls for secession of oil-rich east under the new name Biafra. Over one million Nigerians die before secessionists defeated by federal forces.
- ❑ **1970** General Gowon in power.
- ❑ **1975** Gowon toppled in bloodless coup. Brig. Mohammed takes power.
- ❑ **1976** Murtala Mohammed murdered in abortive coup. Succeeded by General Olusegun Obasanjo.
- ❑ **1978** Political parties legalized, on condition they represent national, not tribal, interests.
- ❑ **1979** Elections won by Alhaji Shehu Shagari and the National Party of Nigeria (NPN), marking return to civilian government.
- ❑ **1983** Military coup. Major General Mohammed Buhari heads Supreme Military Council.
- ❑ **1985** Major General Ibrahim Babangida heads bloodless coup, promising a return to democracy.
- ❑ **1993** August, elections annulled; Babangida resigns; military sets ⇨

N

CHRONOLOGY *continued*

- **1972** EC membership rejected in popular referendum by 3% majority. Bratteli resigns. Center coalition government takes power. Lars Korvald prime minister.
- **1973** Elections. Bratteli returns to power as prime minister.
- **1976** Bratteli succeeded by Odvar Nordli.
- **1981** Nordli resigns owing to ill health. Gro Harlem Brundtland becomes first woman prime minister. Elections bring to power Norway's first Conservative Party (H) government for 53 years. Kare Willoch prime minister.
- **1983** Conservatives form coalition with SP and KrF.
- **1985** Election. Willoch's H–SP–KrF coalition returned. Norway agrees to suspend commercial whaling.
- **1986** 100,000 demonstrate for better working conditions. Brundtland forms minority DNA government. Currency devalued by 12%.
- **1989** Brundtland resigns. H–KrF coalition in power. Soviet Union agrees exchange of information after fires on Soviet nuclear submarines off Norwegian coast.
- **1990** H–KrF coalition breaks up over closer ties with EU (formerly EC). Brundtland and DNA in power.
- **1991** Olaf V dies; succeeded by son, King Harald V.
- **1994** EEA comes into effect. Referendum rejects EU membership.
- **1996** Brundtland resigns; replaced by Thorbjørn Jagland (also DNA).
- **1997** DNA loses ground in general election; Kjell Magne Bondevik forms center-right coalition.
- **2000** Jens Stoltenberg (DNA) prime minister at head of three-party coalition.

AID

Donor

$1.37bn (donations)

Up 4% in 1999

Norway has been granting more than the UN development target of 0.7% of GNP in aid every year since 1975. Although Norway's ratio of aid to GNP has declined somewhat, to 0.92% in 1999, it remains one of the highest in the world. The vast majority of Norway's bilateral aid goes to the least developed countries of southeast Africa, south Asia, and Central America, though Palestine and Bosnia are also important recipients. The Norwegian government allocates funds to various multilateral assistance programs, as well. The 1999 budget included a debt relief program to help reduce developing country indebtedness.

DEFENSE

Compulsory military service

$3.15bn

Down 7% in 1999

Plans have been announced to almost halve the size of Norway's conscript army, which traditionally has absorbed most of the defense budget. It joined NATO in 1949. The overriding defense issue is the stability of Russia and the security of their common border. Five Russian diplomats were expelled in 1998 after a double agent revealed that Russia had extensive information on Norwegian defenses and oil industry.

NORWEGIAN ARMED FORCES

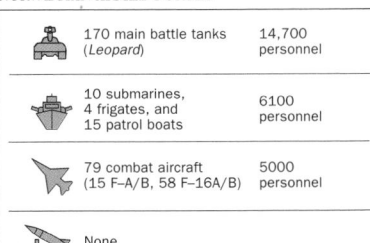

170 main battle tanks (*Leopard*)	14,700 personnel
10 submarines, 4 frigates, and 15 patrol boats	6100 personnel
79 combat aircraft (15 F-A/B, 58 F-16A/B)	5000 personnel
None	

ECONOMICS

Inflation 2.1% p.a. (1990–1999)

$149bn

8.0372–8.8185 Norwegian kroner

SCORE CARD

World GNP Ranking	26th
GNP per Capita	$33,470
Balance of Payments	$-2.16bn
Inflation	2.3%
Unemployment	3%

EXPORTS

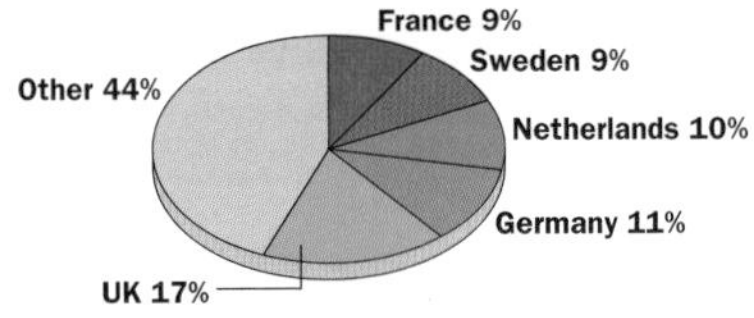
France 9%
Sweden 9%
Netherlands 10%
Germany 11%
UK 17%
Other 44%

IMPORTS

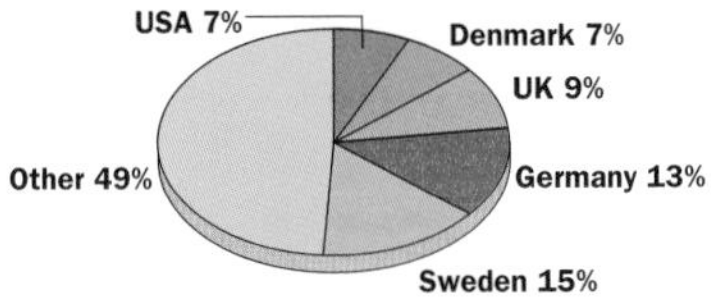
USA 7%
Denmark 7%
UK 9%
Germany 13%
Sweden 15%
Other 49%

ECONOMIC PERFORMANCE INDICATOR

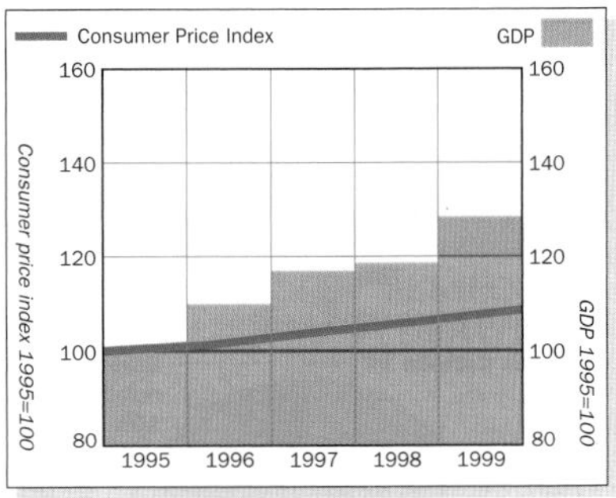
Consumer Price Index
GDP
160
140
120
100
80
Consumer price index 1995=100
GDP 1995=100
1995
1996
1997
1998
1999

Strengths

Western Europe's biggest producer and exporter of oil and natural gas. Mineral reserves. Hydroelectric power satisfies much of country's energy demands, allowing most oil to be exported. Soaring world oil prices in 2000. Petroleum fund for current profits to provide for future generations. Large merchant shipping fleet. Low inflation and unemployment compared with rest of Europe.

Weaknesses

Overdependence on oil revenue. Small home market and relatively remote location. Shortage of skilled labor. Harsh climate limits agriculture.

Profile

The state is interventionist by nature. In 1991, it stepped in to rescue most of the main commercial banks, which had been hit by bad loans. It began returning them to the private sector in 1994. The state also manages the distribution of offshore oil and gas licenses, and maintains control of over 50% of these through its own company, Statoil, although plans to privatize Statoil were announced in 2000.

Norway's immediate future prosperity is guaranteed by its offshore sector. There is a shortage of skilled labor, partly eased by the arrival of workers from other Scandinavian countries, but creating upward pressure on wages. Continuing the strong regional policy of redirecting resources from the more prosperous south to the isolated north is likely to remain a priority, both for social and strategic reasons.

NORWAY : MAJOR BUSINESSES

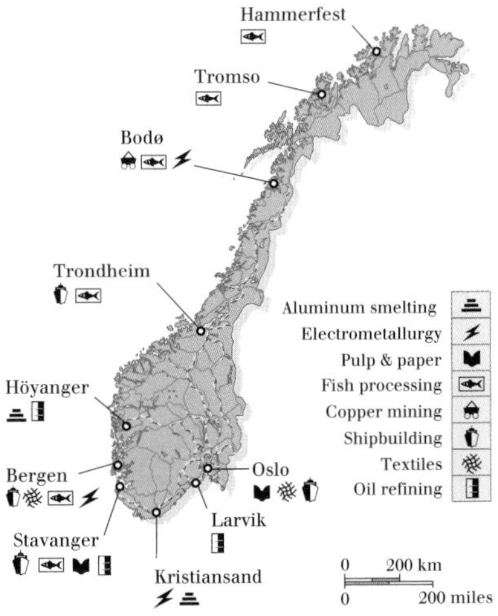
Hammerfest
Tromso
Bodø
Trondheim
Höyanger
Bergen
Stavanger
Kristiansand
Larvik
Oslo
Aluminum smelting
Electrometallurgy
Pulp & paper
Fish processing
Copper mining
Shipbuilding
Textiles
Oil refining
0 200 km
0 200 miles

RESOURCES

Electric power 27.8m kw

3.22m tonnes

3.4m b/d (reserves 9,400,000,000 bbl)

2.4m sheep, 1.04m cattle, 23.3m chickens

Oil, natural gas, iron, coal, copper, lead, zinc

ELECTRICITY GENERATION

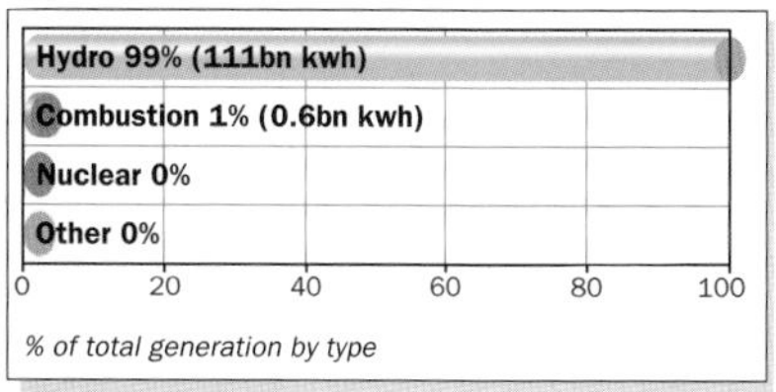
Hydro 99% (111bn kwh)
Combustion 1% (0.6bn kwh)
Nuclear 0%
Other 0%
0
20
40
60
80
100
% of total generation by type

Norway is Europe's largest oil producer; it also has sizable gas reserves. Most of Norway's electricity is produced by hydropower. In summer, the HEP surplus is exported. Fish and forestry are traditionally significant sectors; salmon farming, managed with particular efficiency, has grown rapidly. With agriculture, they account for only 2.5% of GDP and 5% of the workforce, but to many Norwegians they are sufficiently important to merit the rejection of membership of the EU.

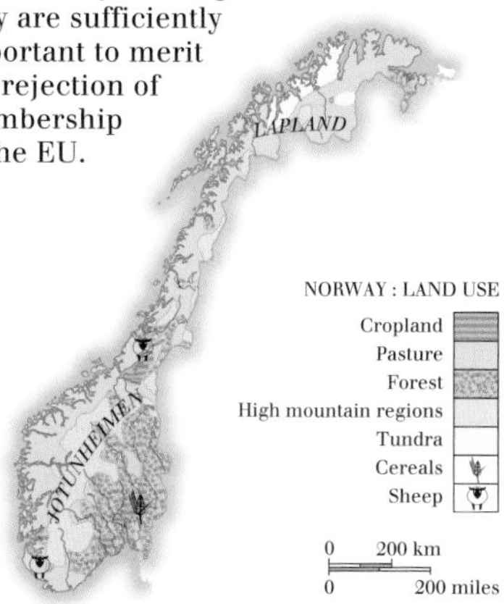
LAPLAND
JOTUNHEIMEN
NORWAY : LAND USE
Cropland
Pasture
Forest
High mountain regions
Tundra
Cereals
Sheep
0 200 km
0 200 miles

ENVIRONMENT

Sustainability rank: 2nd

31%

15.6 tonnes per capita

ENVIRONMENTAL TREATIES

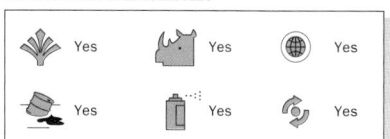

Yes	Yes	Yes
Yes	Yes	Yes

In 1986 northern Norway suffered radioactive contamination after the Chernobyl nuclear disaster. Norway has introduced a tax on carbon dioxide emissions and was instrumental in securing agreement on the 1997 Kyoto Protocol which aims to reduce greenhouse gas emissions. In 1993, it lifted a ban on fishing minke whales, arguing that the species was not threatened. It drew further criticism when it allowed the export of whale products from 2001.

MEDIA

TV ownership high

Daily newspaper circulation 590 per 1000 people

PUBLISHING AND BROADCAST MEDIA

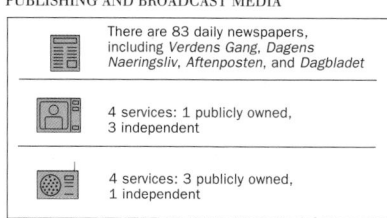

There are 83 daily newspapers, including *Verdens Gang, Dagens Naeringsliv, Aftenposten,* and *Dagbladet*

4 services: 1 publicly owned, 3 independent

4 services: 3 publicly owned, 1 independent

Over 80 daily newspapers have a total circulation of over two million, the second-highest per head in the world. *Verdens Gang*, the leading daily, has a circulation of 370,000.

CRIME

Death penalty not used

2398 prisoners

Up 7% 1996–1998

CRIME RATES

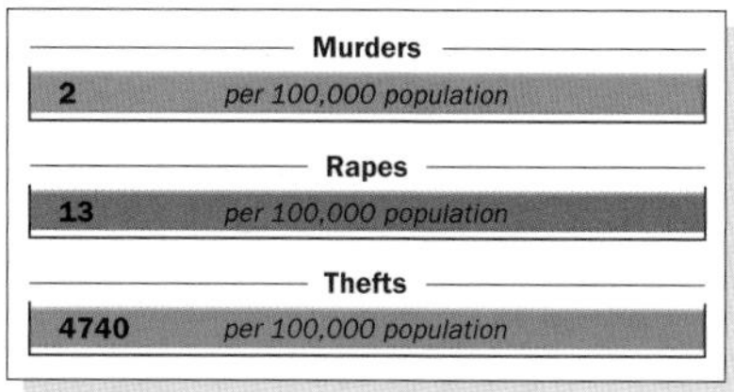
Murders
2 per 100,000 population
Rapes
13 per 100,000 population
Thefts
4740 per 100,000 population

Norway has low levels of crime, even by Scandinavian standards. Violent crime barely exists – the murder rate is one-fifth of that of Sweden, and there are considerably fewer assaults and robberies.

EDUCATION

School leaving age: 15

99%

185,320 students

THE EDUCATION SYSTEM

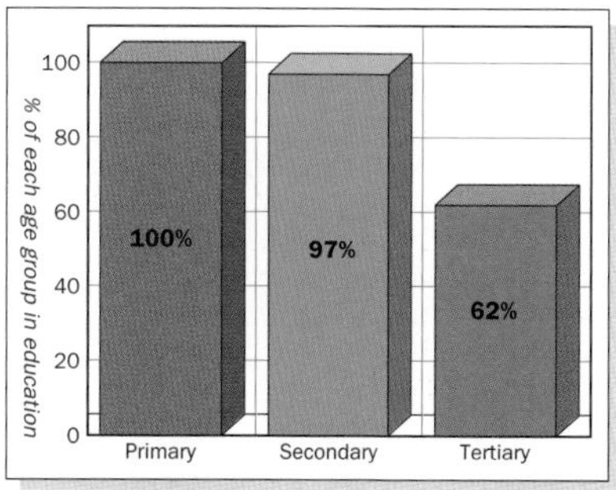
100
80
60
40
20
0
% of each age group in education
100%
97%
62%
Primary
Secondary
Tertiary

The period of compulsory schooling was increased from nine to ten years, with effect from the school year 1997/1998. Most schools are run by municipalities. There are four universities; specialized colleges include the Nordic College of Fisheries. Promotion of continuing education kept youth unemployment down during the early 1990s recession.

HEALTH

Welfare state health benefits

1 per 400 people

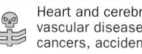

Heart and cerebro-vascular diseases, cancers, accidents

The WHO ranks Norway as providing the world's third-best health care. The country's infant mortality rate is among the world's lowest, and life expectancy at birth is one of the highest. Spending, however, is no higher than the OECD average.

Telemedicine (online remote audio and image diagnosis) allows remote northern hospitals to obtain specialist consultations without having to send patients to the regional hospital.

Reports in 1998 indicated that hospitals had carried out sterilization experiments on insane and mentally retarded patients in 1974–1994.

SPENDING

GDP/cap. increase

CONSUMPTION AND SPENDING

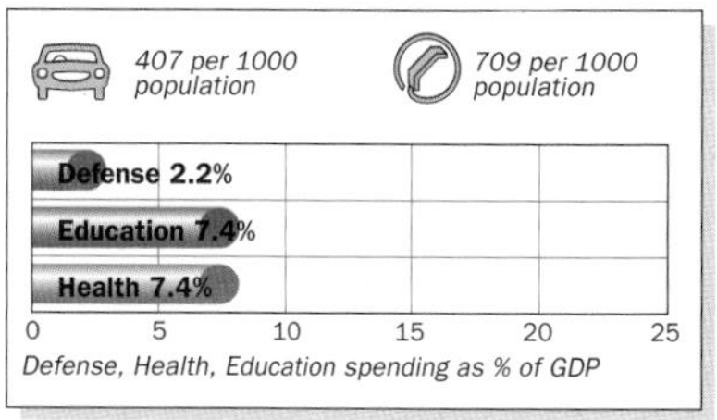
407 per 1000 population
709 per 1000 population
Defense 2.2%
Education 7.4%
Health 7.4%
0
5
10
15
20
25
Defense, Health, Education spending as % of GDP

In terms of income distribution, the Scandinavian countries are the most egalitarian in the world, and the richest 10% of Norway's population owns much less of the country's wealth than is the case in other developed countries. Homelessness and social deprivation are very rare. Recent refugees from the Bosnian conflict are the most disadvantaged group.

The discrepancy between men's and women's pay is greater than in either Sweden or Finland, although still well below the European average. Social provision has been maintained even through economic recession. Benefits are generous.

WORLD RANKING

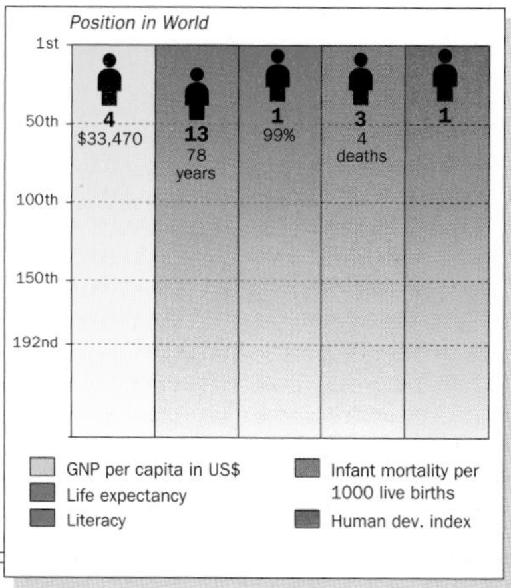
Position in World
1st
50th
100th
150th
192nd
4
$33,470
13
78 years
1
99%
3
4 deaths
1
GNP per capita in US$
Life expectancy
Literacy
Infant mortality per 1000 live births
Human dev. index

N

See also OVERSEAS TERRITORIES p.640

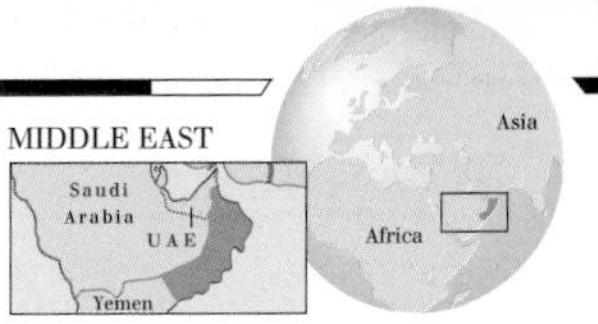
MIDDLE EAST
Asia
Saudi Arabia
UAE
Africa
Yemen

OMAN

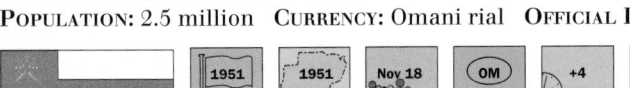

OFFICIAL NAME: Sultanate of Oman **CAPITAL:** Muscat
POPULATION: 2.5 million **CURRENCY:** Omani rial **OFFICIAL LANGUAGE:** Arabic

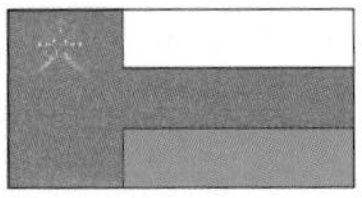

1951 | 1951 | Nov 18 | OM | +4 | +968 | .om

SHARING BORDERS with Yemen, the United Arab Emirates and Saudi Arabia, Oman occupies a strategic position at the entrance to the Gulf. It is the least developed of the Gulf states. The most densely populated areas are the northern coast and the southern Salalah plain. Oil exports have given Oman modest prosperity under a paternalistic sultan, who defeated a Marxist-led insurgency in the 1970s.

CLIMATE

Hot desert

WEATHER CHART

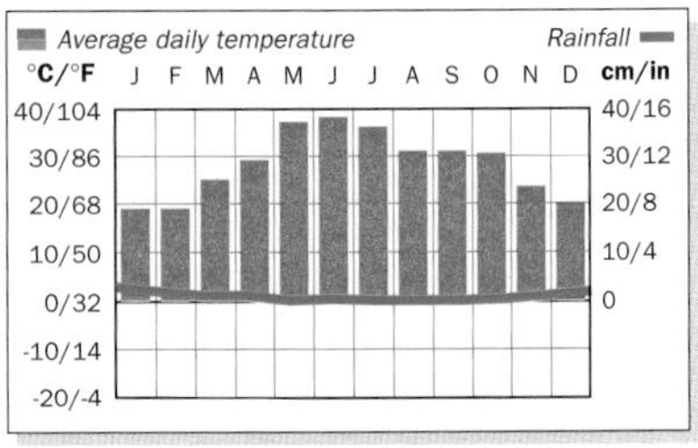
Average daily temperature
Rainfall
°C/°F
J F M A M J J A S O N D
cm/in
40/104
30/86
20/68
10/50
0/32
-10/14
-20/-4
40/16
30/12
20/8
10/4
0

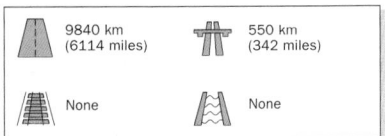

In the north temperatures often climb above 45°C (113°F) in summer. The south has a monsoon climate.

TRANSPORTATION

Drive on right

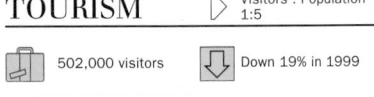

Seeb International, Muscat 2.8m passengers

20 ships 15,000 grt

THE TRANSPORTATION NETWORK

9840 km (6114 miles)

550 km (342 miles)

None

None

A major dual carriageway linking the Rusayl and Nizwa industrial complexes is nearing completion.

TOURISM

Visitors : Population 1:5

502,000 visitors

Down 19% in 1999

MAIN TOURIST ARRIVALS

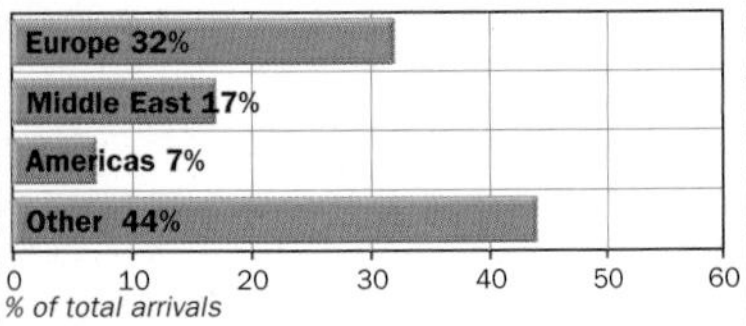
Europe 32%
Middle East 17%
Americas 7%
Other 44%
0
10
20
30
40
50
60
% of total arrivals

Until the late 1980s, Oman was closed to all but business or official visitors. The sultanate's rich cultural heritage, fine beaches, and luxury hotels are now enjoyed by thousands of Western visitors each year.

PEOPLE

Pop. density low

Arabic, Baluchi

12/km² (30/mi²)

THE URBAN/RURAL POPULATION SPLIT

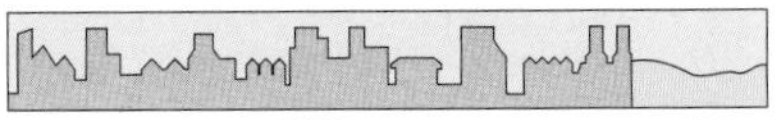
82%
18%

RELIGIOUS PERSUASION

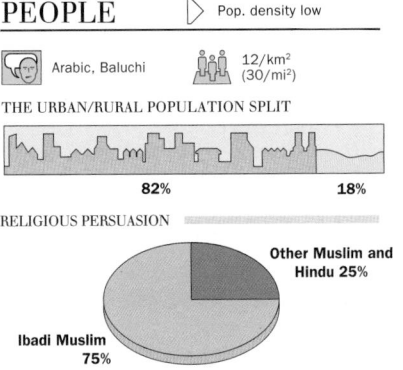

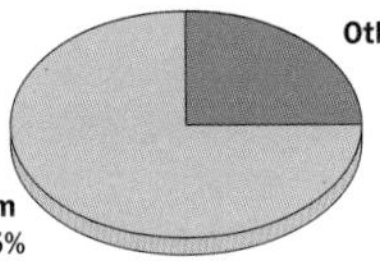
Other Muslim and Hindu 25%
Ibadi Muslim 75%

Native Omanis, who include Arab refugees who fled Zanzibar in the 1960s, make up three-quarters of the population. Baluchis are the largest foreign grouping. Expatriates pose no threat to the regime and Westerners enjoy considerable freedom. Urban drift has taken place, and most Omanis now live in cities. Oman has a number of distinct minorities; the most numerous are the Jebalis in Dhofar – nomadic herdsmen who speak a language resembling Ethiopian. Many Dhofaris supported the Marxist-led insurgents in the 1970s, but they are now considered loyal. Most Omanis are Ibadi Muslims who follow an appointed leader, the Imam. Ibadism does not oppose freedom for women, and a few enjoy positions of authority; two were elected to the 82-seat Consultative Council in September 2000.

POLITICS

No multiparty elections

2000/2003

Sultan Qaboos bin Said

LEGISLATIVE OR ADVISORY BODIES

Consultative Council 82 seats

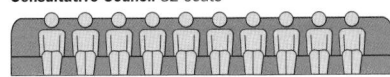

There are no political parties. The members of the Consultative Council (Majlis ash-shoura) were directly elected for the first time in 2000 by electoral committees in each province, and included two women.

Sultan Qaboos is an authoritarian but paternalistic monarch, whose dynasty traces its roots to the 18th century. As well as being head of state, the sultan is prime minister and minister for foreign affairs, defense, and finance. Family members hold other key positions. The regime faces no serious challenge, although Qaboos keeps a careful eye on the religious right wing. In 1991, he created the Consultative Council (*Majlis ash-shoura*), which gives a semblance of democracy. From 2000 its members were directly elected by provincial committees, rather than being appointed. Major political issues include the planned privatization of medium-sized government projects, and improving Oman's self-defense capability.

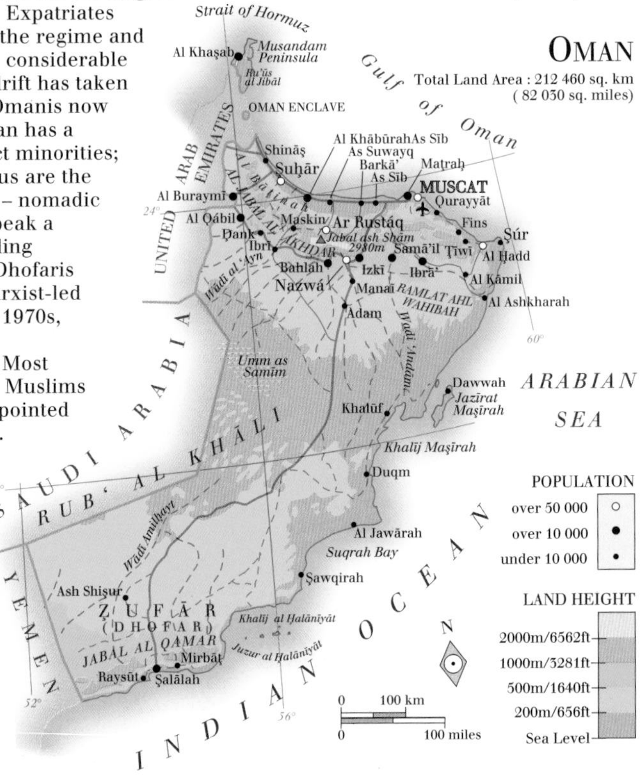
OMAN
Total Land Area : 212 460 sq. km (82 030 sq. miles)
Strait of Hormuz
Al Khaşab
Musandam Peninsula
Ru'ūs al Jibāl
OMAN ENCLAVE
Gulf of Oman
UNITED ARAB EMIRATES
Shināş
Şuhār
Al Khābūrah
As Sīb
As Suwayq
Barkā'
Maţraḩ
MUSCAT
Qurayyāt
Al Buraymī
Al Qābil
Ḑank
'Ibrī
Maskin
Ar Rustāq
Jabal ash Shām 2980m
Samā'il
Ţīwī
Şūr
Fins
Al Ḩadd
Bahlāʼ
Nazwá
Izkī
Ibrā'
Manaḩ
Al Kāmil
Al Ashkharah
RAMLAT AHL WAHIBAH
Adam
Wādī 'Andam
Wādī al 'Ayn
AL JABAL AL AKHḐAR
Umm as Samīm
SAUDI ARABIA
RUB' AL KHĀLĪ
Dawwah
Jazīrat Maşīrah
ARABIAN SEA
Khalūf
Khalīj Maşīrah
Duqm
Al Jawārah
Suqrah Bay
Şawqirah
Wādī Ámilhayt
Ash Shişur
ZUFĀR (DHOFAR)
JABAL AL QAMAR
Khalīj al Ḩalānīyāt
Juzur al Ḩalānīyāt
Mirbāţ
Raysūt
Şalālah
YEMEN
INDIAN OCEAN
N
0 100 km
0 100 miles
POPULATION
over 50 000
over 10 000
under 10 000
LAND HEIGHT
2000m/6562ft
1000m/3281ft
500m/1640ft
200m/656ft
Sea Level

WORLD AFFAIRS

Joined UN in 1971

AL | AMF | Damasc | GCC | OIC

Relations with Israel are maintained. Oman is firmly pro-Western, but has ties with Iran and calls for an easing of sanctions against Iraq. A founding member of the GCC, Oman clarified the demarcation of its border with Saudi Arabia in 1992, and Yemen in 1997.

A watchtower above an oasis. *Most of Oman is gravelly desert. The only large area of cultivation is the 20-km-wide Al Batinah plain.*

AID

Recipient

$40m (receipts)

Down 2% in 1999

Oman is a recipient of World Bank, US, and UK overseas assistance. Agencies face difficulty in allocating aid to Oman as it has yet to hold a census. Oman itself donated aid to anticommunist causes in the 1970s.

DEFENSE

No compulsory military service

$1.63bn

Down 9% in 1999

The UK is the main supplier of equipment. In the 1991 Gulf War, Oman provided communications and services to US and UK forces. Oman's Defense Council, established in 1996, has replenished tanks, ships, and aircraft in recent years. Baluchi mercenaries supplement army strength.

ECONOMICS

Inflation 0.2% p.a. (1990–1999)

$11bn

0.3851 Omani rials

SCORE CARD

- ❑ World GNP Ranking........................81st
- ❑ GNP per Capita $4876
- ❑ Balance of Payments.................$–2.97bn
- ❑ Inflation 0.4%
- ❑ Unemployment ....Not available

Strengths

Oil industry, led by Royal Dutch/Shell. Has benefited from staying out of OPEC and selling oil at spot prices without quotas. Soaring world oil prices in 2000 signified recovery from 1986 collapse. Rich Indian Ocean coastal waters have potential for sizable fishing industry.

Weaknesses

Overdependence on oil (90% of GNP), with less than 20 years' known reserves. Services sector less well-developed than in United Arab Emirates. Foreign workers needed in all economic sectors.

EXPORTS

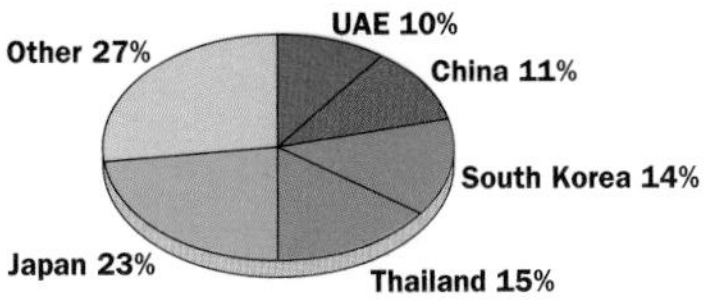
Other 27%
UAE 10%
China 11%
South Korea 14%
Japan 23%
Thailand 15%

IMPORTS

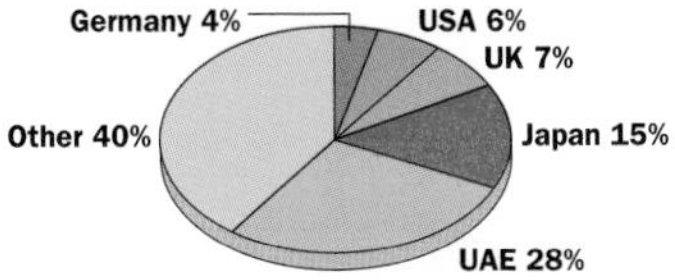
Germany 4%
USA 6%
UK 7%
Other 40%
Japan 15%
UAE 28%

RESOURCES

Electric power 2.1m kw

117,049 tonnes

960,000 b/d (reserves 5,500,000,000 bbl)

729,000 goats, 180,000 sheep, 3.4m chickens

Oil, natural gas, copper, chromite, marble, gypsum

Oman's policy of limiting oil production to conserve resources was abandoned in 1993 following a number of exploration successes.

ENVIRONMENT

Not available

16%

8.2 tonnes per capita

Overpumping of groundwater causes sea water to seep into traditional irrigation areas. Nature reserves and anti-hunting laws protect rich wildlife.

MEDIA

TV ownership high

Daily newspaper circulation 28 per 1000 people

PUBLISHING AND BROADCAST MEDIA

There are 5 daily newspapers, including *Al-Watan, Oman Daily Newspaper*, and the English-language *Oman Daily Observer*

1 state-controlled service

2 state-controlled services

Nothing critical of the government may be published in Oman, despite a 1984 law allowing for "freedom of opinion."

CRIME

Death penalty used

Oman does not publish prison figures

Up 334% 1996–1998

Reckless driving by young Omani males is a problem. A "flying court" serves remote communities.

CHRONOLOGY

The present Albusaidi dynasty has ruled in Oman since 1749.

- ❑ **1932** Sultan bin Taimur in power.
- ❑ **1970** Sultan Qaboos bin Said seizes power from his father.
- ❑ **1975** Suppression of Dhofar revolt.
- ❑ **1991** Consultative Council set up.
- ❑ **1993** Limits on oil production lifted.
- ❑ **2000** Consultative Council members elected for first time.

EDUCATION

Schooling is not compulsory

72%

16,032 students

Education has improved since 1970, but rural illiteracy is still high. Over 100 new schools have been built since 1996.

HEALTH

Welfare state health benefits

1 per 769 people

Heart and cerebrovascular diseases, accidents

There is a policy of replacing expatriate medical staff with Omani nationals. Rural areas are served by clinics.

SPENDING

GDP/cap. increase

CONSUMPTION AND SPENDING

97 per 1000 population

90 per 1000 population

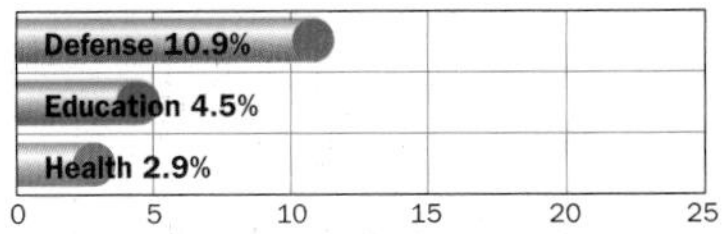
Defense 10.9%
Education 4.5%
Health 2.9%
0
5
10
15
20
25

Defense, Health, Education spending as % of GDP

Omanis in urban areas enjoy the same high living standards that are to be found in other Gulf states. Hunting trips to Pakistan are popular among the rich Omani elite, and a *khanjar*, a curved dagger, is seen as a status symbol.

WORLD RANKING

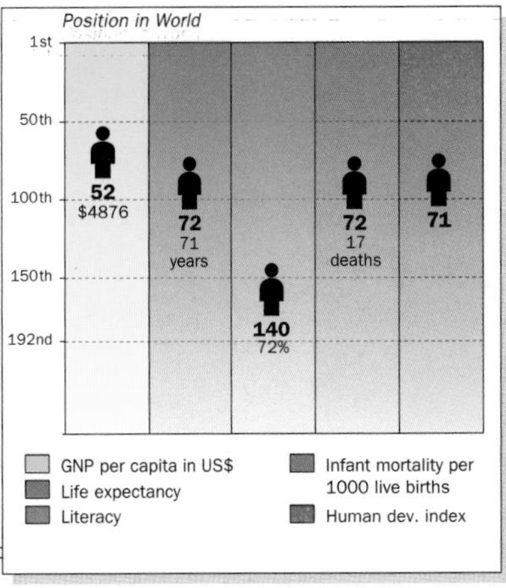
Position in World
1st
50th
100th
150th
192nd
52
$4876
72
71
years
140
72%
72
17
deaths
71
GNP per capita in US$
Life expectancy
Literacy
Infant mortality per 1000 live births
Human dev. index

O

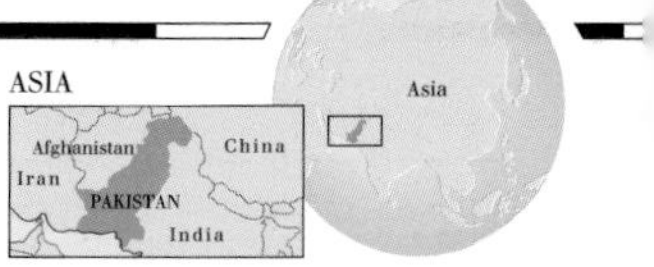
ASIA
Asia
Afghanistan
China
Iran
PAKISTAN
India

PAKISTAN

OFFICIAL NAME: Islamic Republic of Pakistan **CAPITAL:** Islamabad
POPULATION: 156.5 million **CURRENCY:** Pakistani rupee **OFFICIAL LANGUAGE:** Urdu

1947 | 1971 | March 23 | PK | +5 | +92 | .pk

ONCE A PART OF BRITISH INDIA, Pakistan was created in 1947 in response to the demand for an independent and predominantly Muslim Indian state. Initially the new nation included East Pakistan, present-day Bangladesh, which seceded from Pakistan in 1971. Eastern and southern Pakistan, the flood plain of the Indus river, is highly fertile and produces cotton, the basis of the large textile industry.

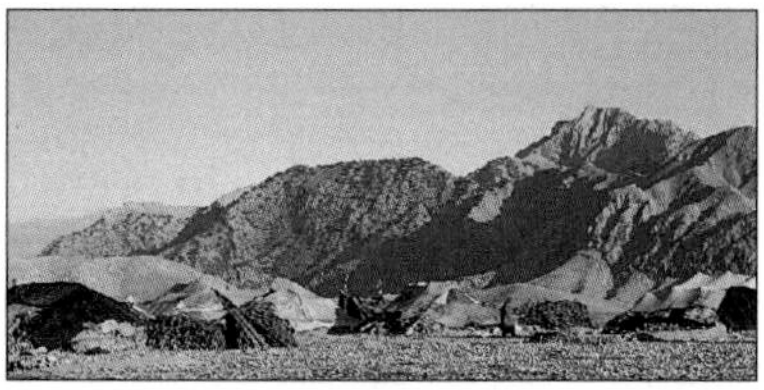

Barren landscape in Kachhi, Baluchistan. *This area of Pakistan has some of the highest May-to-September temperatures in the world.*

CLIMATE

Mountain/steppe/ hot desert

WEATHER CHART

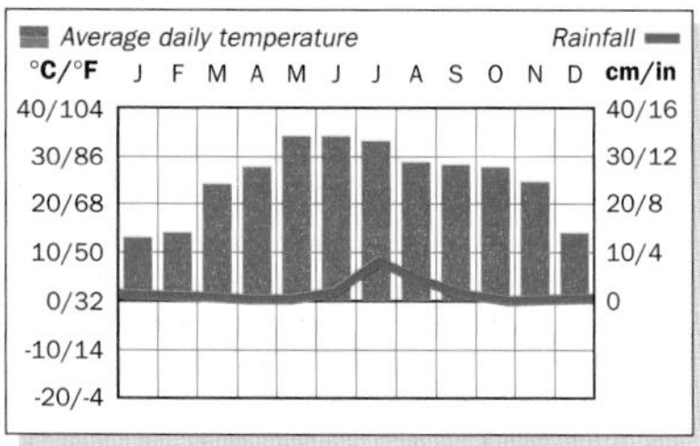
Average daily temperature
Rainfall
°C/°F
J F M A M J J A S O N D
cm/in
40/104
30/86
20/68
10/50
0/32
-10/14
-20/-4
40/16
30/12
20/8
10/4
0

Temperatures can soar to 50°C (122°F) in Sindh and Baluchistan and fall to –20°C (–4°F) in the northern mountains.

TRANSPORTATION

Drive on left

Karāchi International 4.94m passengers

57 ships 401,200 grt

THE TRANSPORTATION NETWORK

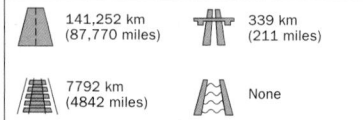

141,252 km (87,770 miles)

339 km (211 miles)

7792 km (4842 miles)

None

Most roads are poorly maintained. A modern highway linking Islamabad and Lahore was inaugurated in 1997.

TOURISM

Visitors : Population 1:288

543,000 visitors

Up 26% in 2000

MAIN TOURIST ARRIVALS

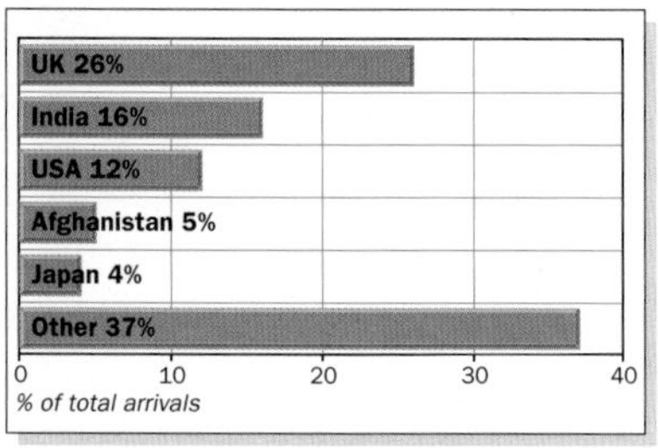
UK 26%
India 16%
USA 12%
Afghanistan 5%
Japan 4%
Other 37%
0
10
20
30
40
% of total arrivals

Relatively few tourists visit Pakistan, despite its rich cultural heritage and unspoiled natural beauty.

PEOPLE

Pop. density high

Punjabi, Sindhi, Pashtu, Urdu, Baluchi, Brahui

203/km² (526/mi²)

THE URBAN/RURAL POPULATION SPLIT

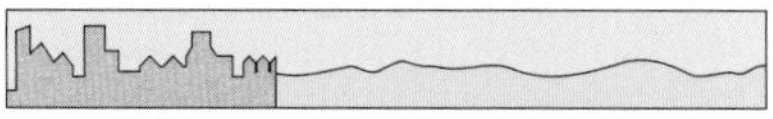
36%
64%

RELIGIOUS PERSUASION

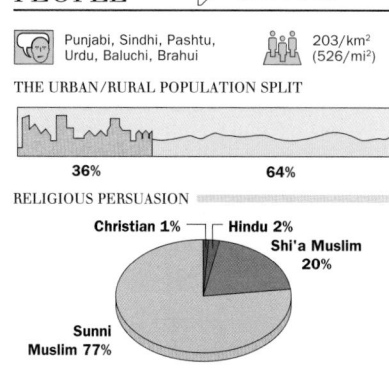

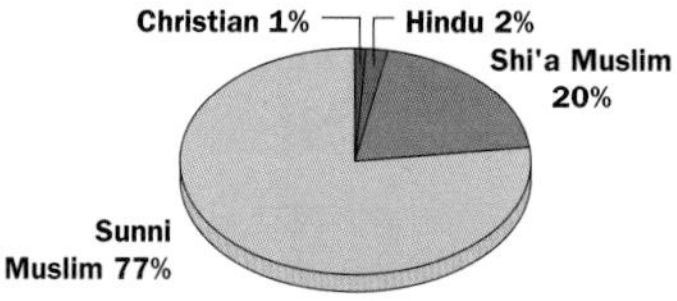
Christian 1%
Hindu 2%
Shi'a Muslim 20%
Sunni Muslim 77%

ETHNIC MAKEUP

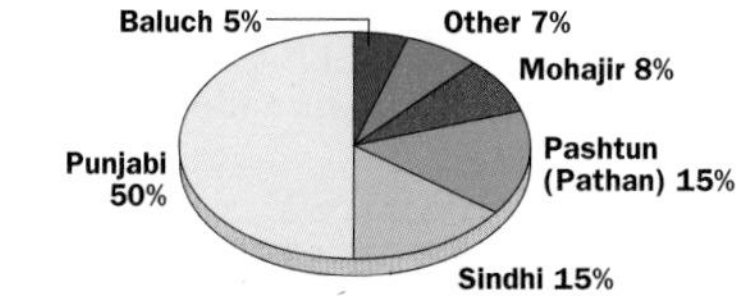
Baluch 5%
Other 7%
Mohajir 8%
Pashtun (Pathan) 15%
Sindhi 15%
Punjabi 50%

POPULATION AGE BREAKDOWN

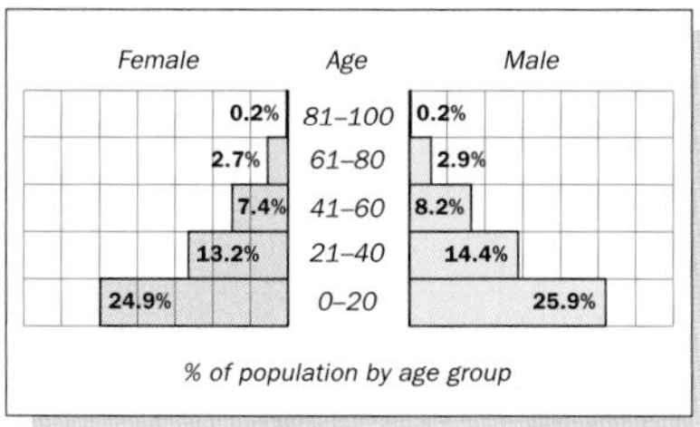
Female
Age
Male
0.2%
81–100
0.2%
2.7%
61–80
2.9%
7.4%
41–60
8.2%
13.2%
21–40
14.4%
24.9%
0–20
25.9%
% of population by age group

Punjabis account for 50% of the population, while Sindhis, Pathans, and Baluch are also prominent. *Mohajirs* – Urdu-speaking immigrants from pre-partition India – predominate in Karachi and Hyderabad. Punjabi political and military dominance of the centralized state has spawned many separatist and autonomy movements. Pathans have frequently threatened to establish a homeland with ethnic kin in Afghanistan. Tensions between the Baluch and Pathan refugees from Afghanistan sporadically erupt into violence, as do those between native Sindhis and immigrant *mohajirs*.

The gap between rich and poor, as exemplified by the feudal land-owning class, which dominates the ruling elite and their serfs, is considerable. There is an expanding middle class of small-scale traders and manufacturers.

Recent years have witnessed a marked increase in Islamist militancy, accompanied by growing discrimination against religious minorities. After the 1999 coup, the Musharraf regime trod a fine line in trying to avoid conflict with Islamic militants, both over issues such as the strict application of Islamic *sharia* law, and over foreign policy.

The extended family is an enduring institution, and ties between its members are strong, reflected in the dynastic and nepotistic nature of the political system. Although some women hold prominent positions, and Benazir Bhutto has twice been prime minister, relatively few are allowed to work by their religiously conservative menfolk. Pakistan has one of the world's lowest ratios of females to males, implying widespread neglect and some female infanticide. Amnesty International criticized Pakistan in 2000 for its failure to give women's rights sufficient protection. Women's rights groups are mainly based in cities, and have made little overall impact.

64°
A F
Hāmūn
CHĀGAI HILLS
Hāmūn-i Māshkel
SANDY DES
BALUCH
IRAN
SIĀHĀN R
Rakh.
CENTRAL MA
Turbat
Dasht Kaur
Gwādar
ARABIA

POLITICS

No multiparty elections

L. and U. Houses 1997/not known

President Pervez Musharraf

AT THE LAST ELECTION

National Assembly (dissolved) 237 seats

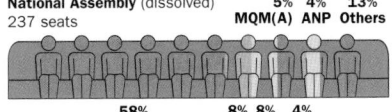

5% MQM(A)
4% ANP
13% Others
58% PML
8% W
8% PPP
4% N-M

PML = Pakistan Muslim League **W** = Women **PPP** = Pakistan People's Party **MQM(A)** = Mohajir Qaumi Movement (A) Haq Parast Group **ANP** = Awami National Party **N-M** = Non-Muslim minorities **Others** include Baluchistan National Party, Jamiat-Ulema-e-Pakistan, Pakistan People's Party Jamhoori Watan Party (Republican Nation Party), National People's Party, and independents

Senate (dissolved) 87 seats

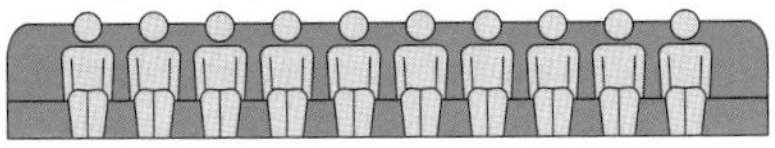

The Senate is indirectly elected

The military suspended multiparty democracy in 1999. The National Assembly was dissolved in June 2001.

MAIN POLITICAL ISSUES

The army
The popularity of the October 1999 coup indicated the loss of respect for the country's much-abused democratic institutions. The national security council (NSC) acts as a cabinet under General Pervez Musharraf.

Corruption
Charges of corruption have entrapped former prime minister Benazir Bhutto and members of the ousted government of Nawaz Sharif, who was himself found guilty of treason in 2000.

Ethnic violence
Violence in Sindh between Sindhis and Urdu-speaking *Mohajirs* killed thousands of people in the 1990s. Islamic groups are active, and sectarian violence between Sunnis and minority Shi'as has risen sharply since 1994.

PROFILE

Throughout the 1990s fragile coalitions were forced to rule in cooperation with the president and the army, and are hampered by a large bureaucracy. The military regime which removed Nawaz Sharif in 1999 remains committed to restoring democracy by 2002, but faces growing calls for accelerating the transition from all opposition parties. In June 2001 Musharraf appointed himself president.

Benazir Bhutto, PPP leader and former prime minister.

Pervez Musharraf, military ruler and self-styled president.

WORLD AFFAIRS

Joined UN in 1947

IAEA | ECO | NAM | OIC | SAARC

Although anxious to avoid war with India, Pakistan supports the separatist movement spearheaded by the largely Muslim Kashmiris. Border fighting flared up in mid-1999, briefly threatening full-scale war, and incidents on the border continue. Musharraf traveled to India in July 2001 to meet Indian Prime Minister A. B. Vajpayee, but their talks foundered on the Kashmir issue.

In 1998 Pakistan carried out a series of nuclear tests in response to similar tests by India, provoking international condemnation and the imposition of US sanctions. Pakistan's membership of the Commonwealth was suspended after the 1999 coup.

One of only three countries to recognize the Afghan *taliban* regime, Pakistan in September 2001 urged the *taliban* to hand over terrorism suspect Osama bin Laden, and came under great pressure to back US-led action against the regime.

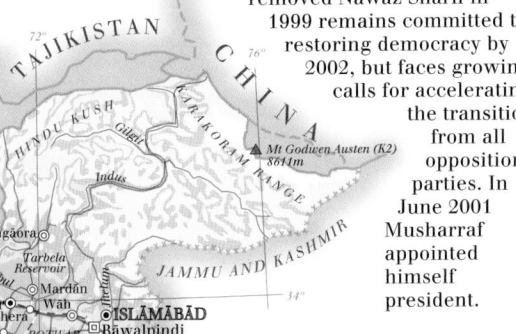

PAKISTAN
Total Land Area : 770 880 sq. km (297 637 sq. miles)
LAND HEIGHT
6000m/19 686ft
4000m/13 124ft
3000m/9843ft
2000m/6562ft
1000m/3281ft
500m/1640ft
200m/656ft
Sea Level
POPULATION
over 5 000 000
over 1 000 000
over 500 000
over 100 000
over 50 000
over 10 000
0 200 km
0 200 miles
TAJIKISTAN
CHINA
HINDU KUSH
KARAKORAM RANGE
Mt Godwin Austen (K2) 8611m
JAMMU AND KASHMIR
Gilgit
Indus
Mingāora
Tarbela Reservoir
Khyber Pass
Kabul
Mardān
Peshāwar
Wah
ISLĀMĀBĀD
Nowshera
Kohāt
Rāwalpindi
POTWAR PLATEAU
New Mīrpur
Jhelum
Chakwāl
Khāriān
Miānwāli
Lāla Mūsa
Gujrāt
Siālkot
Wazīrābād
Daska
Khushāb
Gujrānwāla
Sargodha
Shekhūpura
Dera Ismāīl Khān
Chiniot
Lahore
Faisalābād
Jhang
Kasūr
Leiah
PUNJAB
Shorkot
Sāhīwāl
Okāra
Kamālia
Pākpattan
Khānewāl
Chīchāwatni
Multān
Mandi Būrewāla
Dera Ghāzi Khān
Muzaffargarh
Chishtiān Mandi
Bahāwalpur
Ahmadpur East
Khānpur
Rahīmyār Khān
Sādiqābād
Chaman
TOBA KĀKAR RANGE
Zhob
Quetta
Sibi
KACHHI
CENTRAL BRAHUI RANGE
SULAIMAN RANGE
Jacobābād
Shāhdādkot
Shikārpur
Lārkāna
Kambar
Sukkur
Khairpur
KIRTHAR RANGE
Nawābshāh
SINDH
Tando Ādam
Hyderābād
Karāchi
THAR DESERT
INDIA
RANN OF KUTCH
Mouths of the Indus
ARABIAN SEA
AFGHANISTAN

Rice paddy fields, *with monsoon rains threatening from the Himalayas. Rice is Pakistan's second most valuable agricultural export after cotton.*

CHRONOLOGY

From the 8th to the 16th centuries, Islamic rule extended to northwest and northeast India. Punjab and Sindh, annexed by the British East India Company in the 1850s, were ceded to the British Raj in 1857.

- **1906** Muslim League founded as organ of Indian Muslim separatism.
- **1947** Partition of India. Muhammad Ali Jinnah first governor-general of Pakistan, divided by 1600 km (994 miles) of Indian territory into East and West Pakistan. Millions displaced by large-scale migration.
- **1948** First Indo-Pakistan war over Kashmir.
- **1949** New Awami League (AL) demands East Pakistan's autonomy.
- **1956** Constitution establishes Pakistan as an Islamic republic.
- **1958** Martial law. General Muhammad Ayub Khan takes over; elected president two years later.

P

CHRONOLOGY *continued*

- **1965** Second Indo-Pakistan war over Kashmir.
- **1970** Ayub Khan resigns. General Agha Yahya Khan takes over. First direct elections won by AL; West Pakistani parties reject results. Military crackdown in East Pakistan. War with India over East Pakistan.
- **1971** East Pakistan secedes as Bangladesh. PPP leader Zulfikar Ali Bhutto becomes Pakistan's president.
- **1972** Simla (peace) agreement with India.
- **1973** Bhutto, now prime minister, initiates Islamic socialism.
- **1977** General election. Riots over allegations of vote rigging. General Zia ul-Haq stages military coup.
- **1979** Bhutto executed.
- **1986** Bhutto's daughter Benazir returns from exile to lead PPP.
- **1988** Zia killed in air crash. Bhutto wins general election.
- **1990** Ethnic violence in Sindh. President dismisses Bhutto. Nawaz Sharif becomes premier.
- **1991** Muslim *sharia* law incorporated in legal code.
- **1992** Violence between Sindhis and *Mohajirs* escalates in Sindh.
- **1993** President Khan and prime minister Sharif resign. Elections; Bhutto returns to power.
- **1996** President dismisses Bhutto.
- **1997** PML wins landslide election victory; Sharif elected prime minister. President's power to dismiss prime minister removed.
- **1998** Nuclear tests.
- **1999–2000** Military coup. Sharif found guilty of treason and exiled to Saudi Arabia.
- **2001** June, National Assembly suspended, Gen. Musharraf appoints himself president. July, talks between Musharraf and Indian Prime Minister Vajpayee.

AID

Recipient

$732m (receipts) — Down 30% in 1999

Pakistan is heavily dependent on aid, although the government has a long history of misdirecting aid payments. Aid intended for major projects has regularly been used to fund the current-account deficit. In mid-1998 the IMF agreed to help Pakistan meet its international debt obligations after the USA and other Western aid donors cut off aid in protest against Pakistan's nuclear tests. The USA subsequently agreed to resume some aid, but the economy was badly damaged. Japan and Germany are among other main bilateral donors. Aid is also provided by the World Bank and the ADB.

DEFENSE

No compulsory military service

$3.52bn — Down 14% in 1999

Pakistan has emerged as a significant regional arms trader. It established itself as a nuclear power after conducting a number of successful nuclear tests in May 1998. Defense spending has a high priority, accounting for about a quarter of all government expenditure. The USA was the most important arms supplier until sanctions were imposed in 1990 and 1998. Pakistan's other main defense procurements are from France, the UK, and China. The army has been highly significant in politics throughout the period since independence, even when not actually in power in a military regime. Two years prior to the 1999 coup, it had already assumed a formal role in civilian decision-making by its inclusion in a National Security Council.

PAKISTANI ARMED FORCES

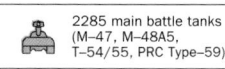

2285 main battle tanks (M–47, M–48A5, T–54/55, PRC Type–59)	550,000 personnel
10 submarines, 8 frigates, and 9 patrol boats	22,000 personnel
353 combat aircraft (52 *Mirage* 5, 42 Q–5)	40,000 personnel
Capability undisclosed; weapons tested in May 1998	

ECONOMICS

Inflation 10.6% p.a. (1990–1999)

$62.9bn — 51.88–57.60 Pakistani rupees

SCORE CARD

World GNP Ranking	45th
GNP per Capita	$470
Balance of Payments	$–2.2bn
Inflation	4.1%
Unemployment	7%

EXPORTS

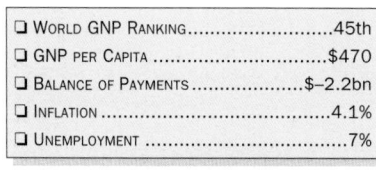

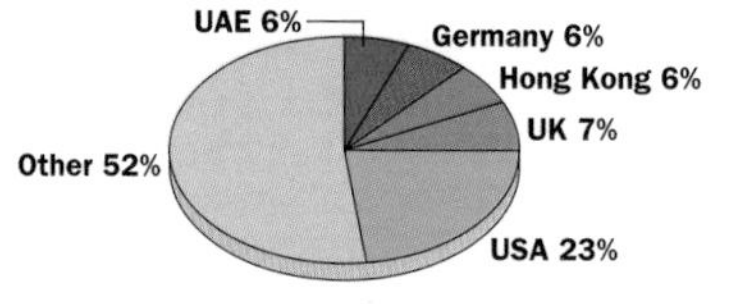
UAE 6%
Germany 6%
Hong Kong 6%
UK 7%
Other 52%
USA 23%

IMPORTS

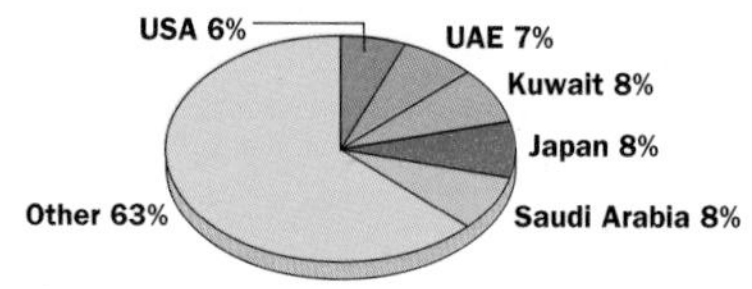
USA 6%
UAE 7%
Kuwait 8%
Japan 8%
Other 63%
Saudi Arabia 8%

ECONOMIC PERFORMANCE INDICATOR

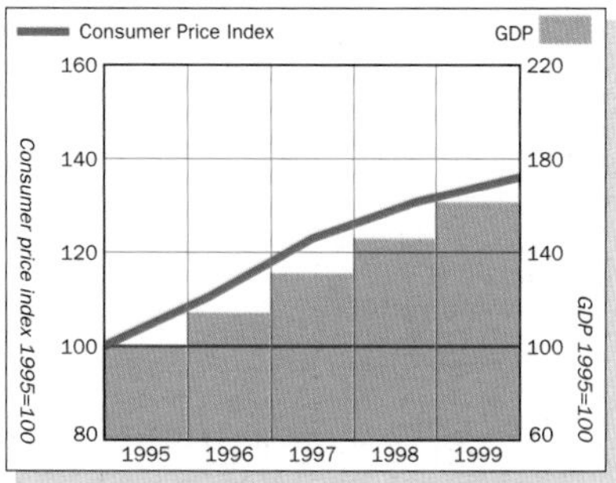
Consumer Price Index
GDP
Consumer price index 1995=100
GDP 1995=100
160
140
120
100
80
220
180
140
100
60
1995
1996
1997
1998
1999

Strengths
Gas, water, coal, oil. Substantial untapped natural resources. Low labor costs. Potentially huge market. One of the world's leading producers of cotton and a major exporter of rice.

Weaknesses
Production and sales of cotton and rice vulnerable to weather conditions. History of inefficient and haphazard government economic policies. Weak and overstretched infrastructure.

Profile
Pakistan has yet to show progress in tackling its considerable economic problems. Although successive governments have reversed the nationalization policies instituted in the 1970s, private enterprise has been stifled by the rules of a massive bureaucracy. There is some foreign investment in previously state-only sectors such as banking, and water and other utilities. However, corruption at all levels of government undermined economic confidence throughout the 1990s, and it was particularly acute under the administration of Benazir Bhutto. Efforts by the military government to tackle corruption and poverty were praised by the World Bank in 2001. Defense spending remains high.

PAKISTAN : MAJOR BUSINESSES

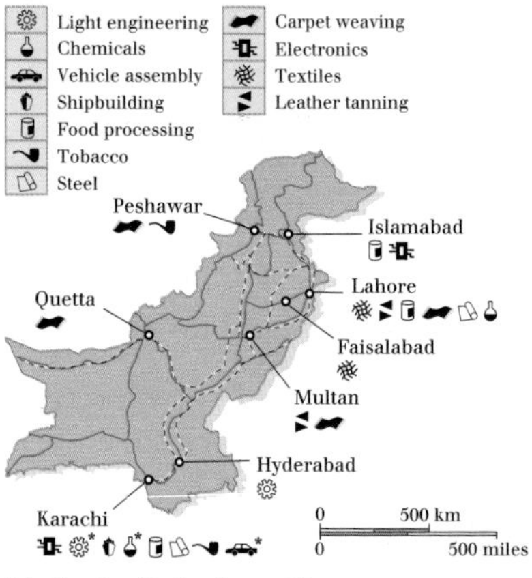
Light engineering
Chemicals
Vehicle assembly
Shipbuilding
Food processing
Tobacco
Steel
Carpet weaving
Electronics
Textiles
Leather tanning
Peshawar
Islamabad
Lahore
Quetta
Faisalabad
Multan
Hyderabad
Karachi
0
500 km
0
500 miles

* significant multinational ownership

RESOURCES

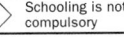

Electric power 14.7m kw

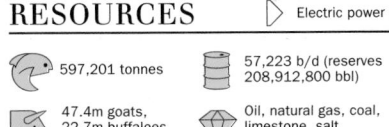

597,201 tonnes

57,223 b/d (reserves 208,912,800 bbl)

47.4m goats, 22.7m buffaloes, 148m chickens

Oil, natural gas, coal, limestone, salt, gypsum, silica sand

ELECTRICITY GENERATION

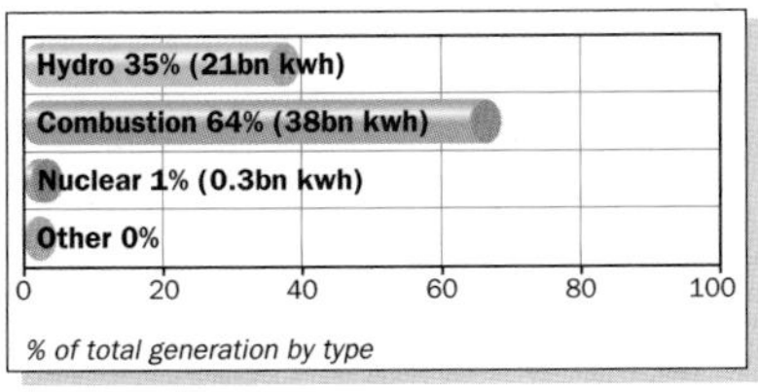
Hydro 35% (21bn kwh)
Combustion 64% (38bn kwh)
Nuclear 1% (0.3bn kwh)
Other 0%
0
20
40
60
80
100
% of total generation by type

Apart from cotton and rice, Pakistan's major resources are oil, coal, gas, and water. The state hopes that the privatization of the utilities industries will reduce energy imports and shortages – peak electricity demand, for example, exceeds supply by 20%. Steps are being taken to attract more foreign investment in oil and gas exploration, extraction, and distribution. Pakistan's current refining capacity falls well below the present 280,000 b/d demand, let alone the projected future demand.

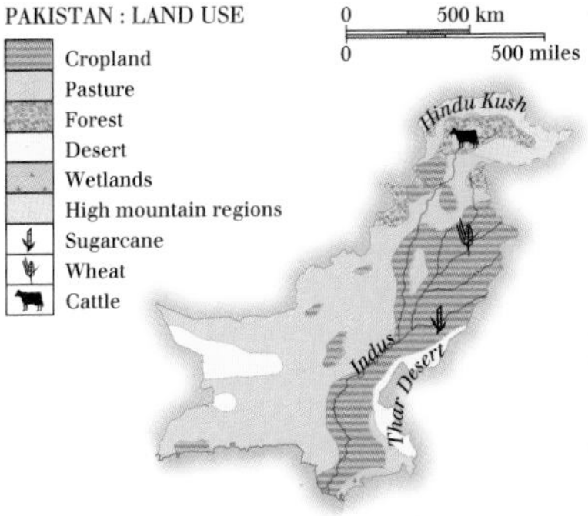
PAKISTAN : LAND USE
0
500 km
0
500 miles
Cropland
Pasture
Forest
Desert
Wetlands
High mountain regions
Sugarcane
Wheat
Cattle
Hindu Kush
Indus
Thar Desert

ENVIRONMENT

Sustainability rank: 85th

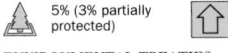

5% (3% partially protected)

0.8 tonnes per capita

ENVIRONMENTAL TREATIES

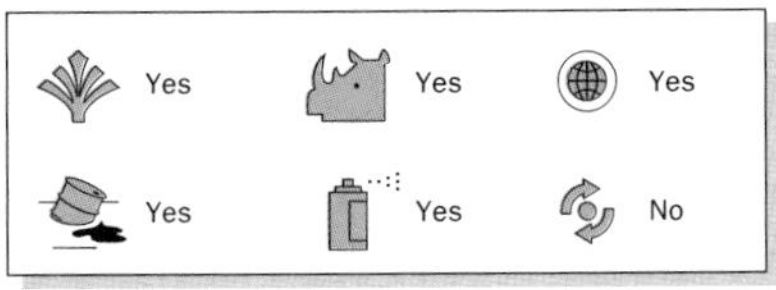
Yes
Yes
Yes
Yes
Yes
No

Tough measures are in force to curb illegal logging. Urban pollution affects many cities. Local groups increasingly voice environmental concerns.

MEDIA

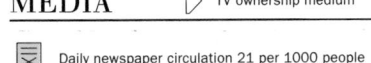

TV ownership medium

Daily newspaper circulation 21 per 1000 people

PUBLISHING AND BROADCAST MEDIA

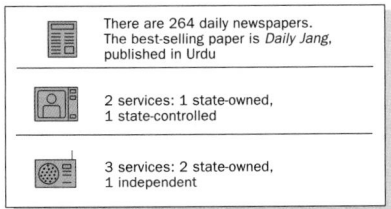

There are 264 daily newspapers. The best-selling paper is *Daily Jang*, published in Urdu

2 services: 1 state-owned, 1 state-controlled

3 services: 2 state-owned, 1 independent

State-run services dominate the mass media. Journalists who challenge official views are systematically harassed.

EDUCATION

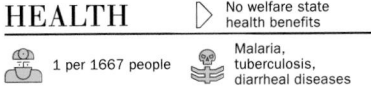

Schooling is not compulsory

46%

1.05m students

THE EDUCATION SYSTEM

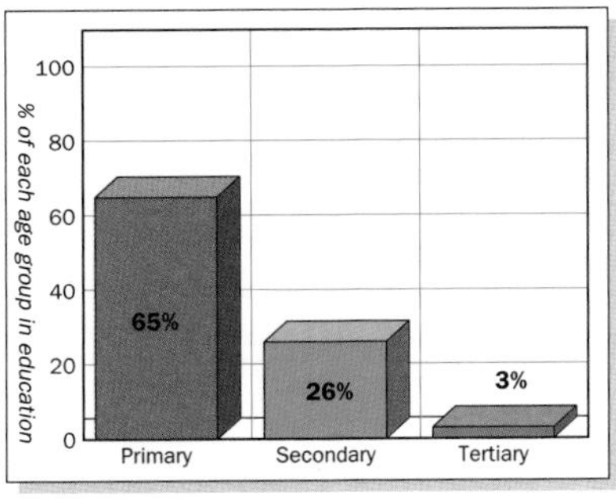
100
80
60
40
20
0
% of each age group in education
65%
26%
3%
Primary
Secondary
Tertiary

Although universal free primary education is a constitutional right, education is not compulsory. Literacy rates in Pakistan are among the lowest in the world. The education system is heavily Islamized, and weighted toward educating males; a large majority of children enrolled in primary schools are boys. The 23 universities, 99 professional colleges, and 675 arts and sciences colleges all have a heavy preponderance of arts students. Wealthy parents frequently choose to send their children abroad for higher education, mainly to colleges in the UK or the USA.

HEALTH

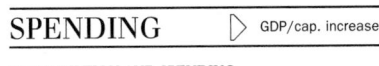

No welfare state health benefits

1 per 1667 people

Malaria, tuberculosis, diarrheal diseases

Availability of doctors and hospital beds is among the lowest in the world, and there is a shortage of equipment and medicines. Uncontrolled counterfeit drugs are common. A specialized cancer hospital in Lahore, opened in 1995, offers modern facilities and advanced treatment. Pakistan has a high incidence of heroin addicts due largely to its proximity to Afghanistan.

SPENDING

GDP/cap. increase

CONSUMPTION AND SPENDING

5 per 1000 population

22 per 1000 population

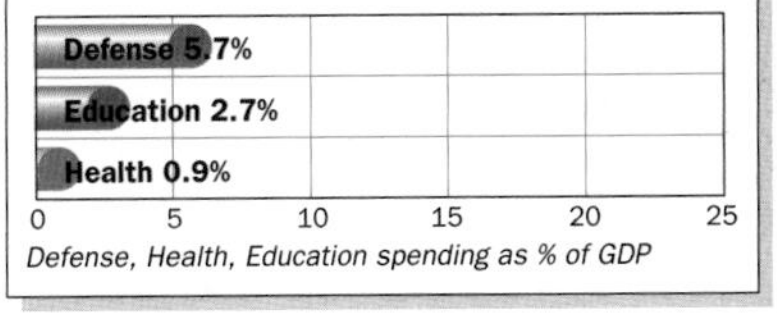
Defense 5.7%
Education 2.7%
Health 0.9%
0
5
10
15
20
25
Defense, Health, Education spending as % of GDP

Members of the bureaucratic and political elite tend to be extremely rich, as are some of the top military. Despite Pakistan's considerable economic potential, much of its population lives below the poverty line.

CRIME

Death penalty used

44,640 prisoners

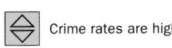

Crime rates are high

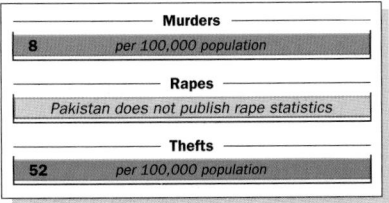

CRIME RATES

Murders

8 *per 100,000 population*

Rapes

Pakistan does not publish rape statistics

Thefts

52 *per 100,000 population*

Compared with similar Islamic states, there is a high incidence of murder, kidnapping, narcotics trafficking, rape, and robbery. Corruption, and the abuse of women are major causes for concern; rising numbers of women are being reported killed or threatened with death for refusing to accept arranged marriages. Torture of prisoners and deaths in custody are frequent, as is the rape of women prisoners. The most dangerous area is Sindh, where severe factional violence continues to terrorize Karachi. Militant sectarian groups are also blamed for a recent rise in crime in Punjab. Heavily armed *dacoits* (bandits) still hold sway in the interior. Pressure from Islamic parties has forced the government of North West Frontier Province to replace British-based civil law by the rulings of *sharia* courts.

WORLD RANKING

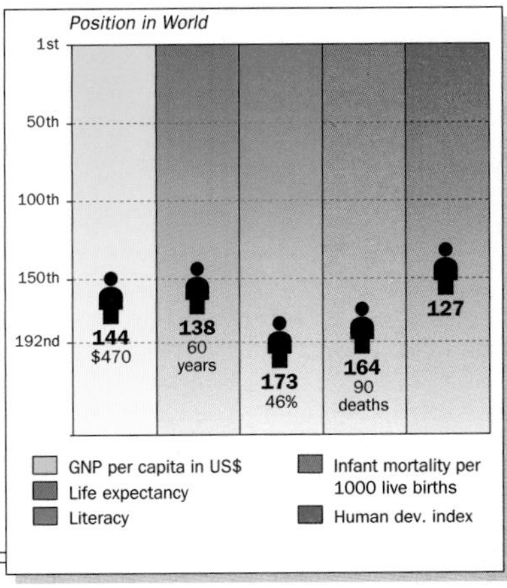
Position in World
1st
50th
100th
150th
192nd
144
$470
138
60
years
173
46%
164
90
deaths
127
GNP per capita in US$
Life expectancy
Literacy
Infant mortality per 1000 live births
Human dev. index

P

PALAU

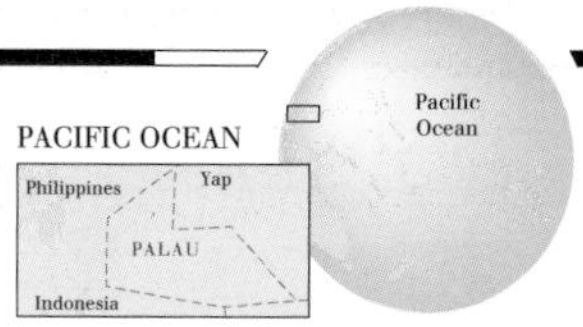
PACIFIC OCEAN
Philippines
Yap
PALAU
Indonesia
Pacific Ocean

OFFICIAL NAME: Republic of Palau **CAPITAL:** Koror
POPULATION: 18,800 **CURRENCY:** US dollar **OFFICIAL LANGUAGES:** Palauan and English

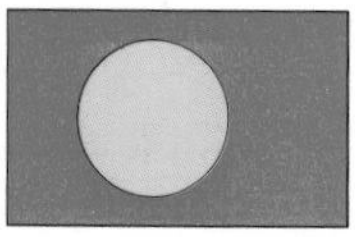

1994 | 1994 | Oct 1 | PAL | +9 | +680 | .pw

THE REPUBLIC OF PALAU (locally known as Belau) is situated in the western Pacific and comprises more than 300 islands in the Caroline Islands archipelago, only nine of which are inhabited. Formerly a part of the US-administered Trust Territory of the Pacific Islands, Palau became independent in association with the USA in 1994, but continues to be heavily dependent on US aid.

CLIMATE

Tropical oceanic

WEATHER CHART

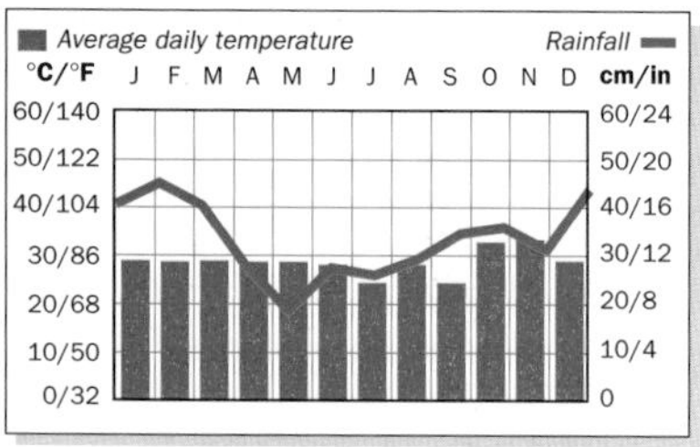
Average daily temperature
Rainfall
°C/°F
J F M A M J J A S O N D
cm/in
60/140
50/122
40/104
30/86
20/68
10/50
0/32
60/24
50/20
40/16
30/12
20/8
10/4
0

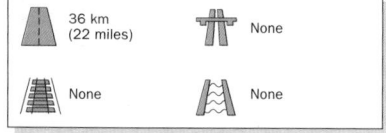

The islands are humid, with fairly constant temperatures and heavy rainfall all year round. The mean temperature is 27°C (81°F).

TRANSPORTATION

Drive on right

Palau International, Koror — Has no fleet

THE TRANSPORTATION NETWORK

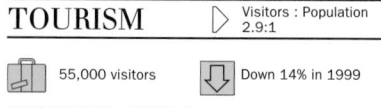

36 km (22 miles) — None — None — None

Limited air links and local shipping connect the islands. Better road access across Babelthuap island is planned.

TOURISM

Visitors : Population 2.9:1

55,000 visitors — Down 14% in 1999

MAIN TOURIST ARRIVALS

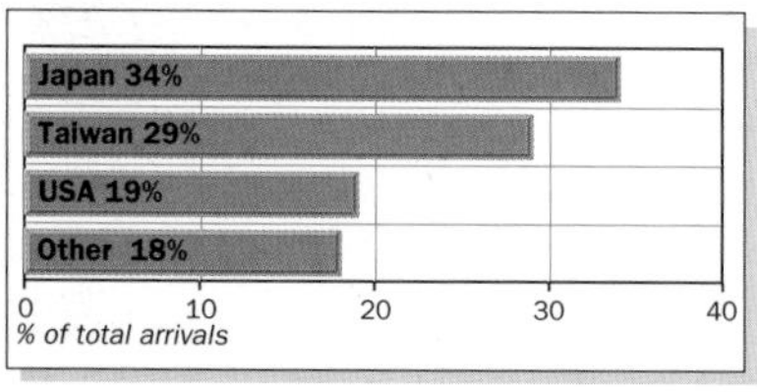
Japan 34%
Taiwan 29%
USA 19%
Other 18%
0
10
20
30
40
% of total arrivals

Tourism is becoming more important. Improved transportation access is planned, amid concerns about impact on traditional culture. Several islands have battle sites from the Pacific War. The outlying islands remain unspoiled.

PEOPLE

Pop. density low

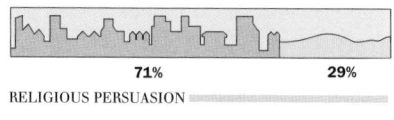

Palauan, English, Japanese, Angaur, Tobi, Sonsorolese — 37/km² (96/mi²)

THE URBAN/RURAL POPULATION SPLIT

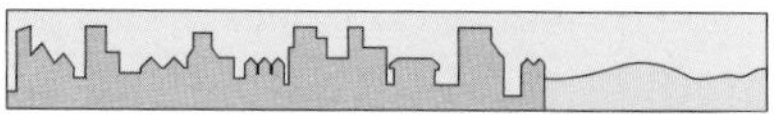
71%
29%

RELIGIOUS PERSUASION

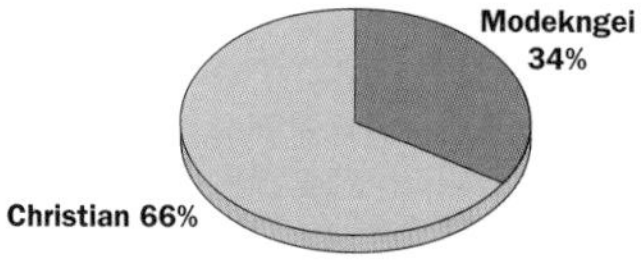
Modekngei 34%
Christian 66%

Palauans can claim a diverse genetic heritage. Palau was first colonized by southeast Asian peoples some 3000 years ago. There has also been mixing with other Melanesian and Polynesian peoples. More recently, low-skilled Filipinos have added to the population. Immigration from south Asia was banned in 2001 due to rising tensions.

Some 70% of Palauans live on the island city of Koror (a new capital is being constructed on neighboring Babelthuap island). The thinly scattered remaining population are linguistically diverse, with distinct separate languages in the most southern islands. Cultural influence from the USA and Japan has been strong, though in the more remote islands a more traditional way of life has been maintained. Society remains largely matrilineal. One-third of Palauans practice the indigenous Modekngei religion.

***Palau's islands** have many idyllic beaches, but tourism remains underdeveloped due to a lack of resources and the country's remoteness.*

POLITICS

Multiparty elections

L. House 2000/2004
U. House 2000/2004
President Tommy Remengesau

AT THE LAST ELECTION

House of Delegates 16 seats

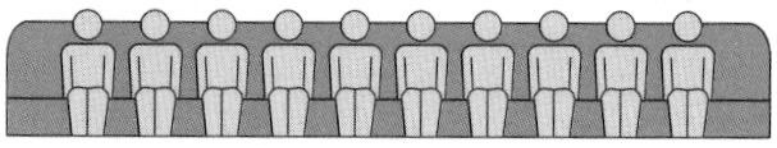

One member is elected to the House of Delegates to represent each of the 16 states

Senate 14 seats

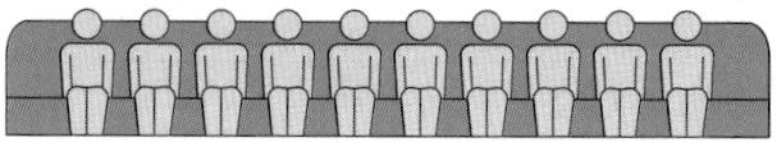

The 14 senators represent geographical districts, according to population

The Compact of Free Association with the USA formed the basis of Palau's independence. One clause, requiring the transit and storage of nuclear materials, was the subject of several referenda until a simple majority in 1993 brought sovereignty the following year. Vice President Tommy Remengesau was elected president in November 2000.

WORLD AFFAIRS

Joined UN in 1994

PC | PIF | IBRD | ACP

The USA has exclusive control over Palau's foreign affairs and defense policies under the 1994 conditions of the Compact of Free Association. Cordial relations with the Pacific Islands Forum were restored in 1999 after tensions caused by Palau's bid to give Japan the right to veto the establishment of a whale sanctuary in the South Pacific.

AID

Recipient

$29m (receipts) — Down 67% in 1999

Palau's economy is heavily dependent upon the USA. Receipt of aid was a crucial factor in Palau's decision to enter into the 1994 Compact of Free Association with the USA after the end of the UN trusteeship. Palau will receive up to US$700 million over 15 years from the USA in return for furnishing military facilities.

DEFENSE

No compulsory military service

There are no armed forces — Not applicable

Under the 1994 Compact of Free Association, the USA is responsible for Palau's defense.

P

ECONOMICS

▷ Inflation 6.4% p.a. (1994–1998)

$82m

Currency is US dollar

SCORE CARD

- ❑ WORLD GNP RANKING........................187th
- ❑ GNP PER CAPITA $5000
- ❑ BALANCE OF PAYMENTS.....................$–25m
- ❑ INFLATION.................................Not available
- ❑ UNEMPLOYMENT 7%

STRENGTHS

Preferential trading rights give access to US economy. Tourism, fishing, and copra production. Some minerals (especially gold). Increasing trade with Philippines. High per capita income.

WEAKNESSES

Heavy dependence on US aid. High levels of underemployment. Remote location. Limited resources for education. Aid dependent culture. Limited but expanding transportation infrastructure.

EXPORTS

Palau does not publish export figures by country

IMPORTS

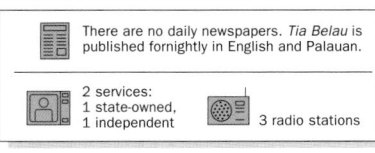

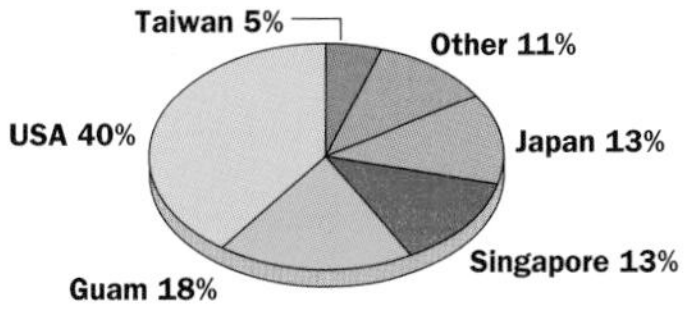
Taiwan 5%
Other 11%
USA 40%
Japan 13%
Singapore 13%
Guam 18%

RESOURCES

▷ Electric power 62,000 kw

1500 tonnes

Not an oil producer

Not available

Gold

On some islands the soil is highly fertile, although the terrain of the larger islands makes farming difficult. Some islands are densely forested. Palau has copra and some gold deposits. There is also the possibility of exploitation of reserves of minerals on the seabed. Palau has a small fishing industry with the potential for development.

PALAU

Total Land Area : 508 sq. km (196 sq. miles)

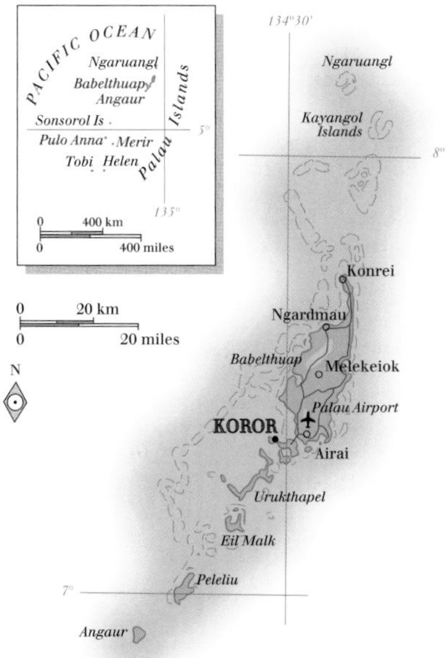
PACIFIC OCEAN
Ngaruangl
Babelthuap
Angaur
Sonsorol Is.
Pulo Anna
Merir
Tobi
Helen
Palau Islands
400 km
400 miles
134°30'
Ngaruangl
Kayangol Islands
Konrei
Ngardmau
Babelthuap
Melekeiok
Palau Airport
KOROR
Airai
Urukthapel
Eil Malk
Peleliu
Angaur
20 km
20 miles
N

ENVIRONMENT

▷ Not available

None

13.9 tonnes per capita

Palau suffers from inadequate facilities for the disposal of solid waste. Sand and coral dredging and illegal fishing practices pose a significant threat to the marine ecosystem. Palau and its surrounding waters are Micronesia's richest habitat; however, there is concern about the commercial export of fruit bats to neighboring islands as a delicacy. Typhoons sometimes cause severe damage to infrastructure.

MEDIA

▷ TV ownership high

There are no daily newspapers

PUBLISHING AND BROADCAST MEDIA

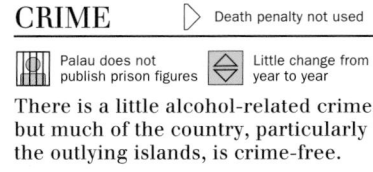

There are no daily newspapers. *Tia Belau* is published fornightly in English and Palauan.

2 services:
1 state-owned,
1 independent

3 radio stations

The country's TV and radio stations tend to deal in material which is largely derived from the USA.

CRIME

▷ Death penalty not used

Palau does not publish prison figures

Little change from year to year

There is a little alcohol-related crime, but much of the country, particularly the outlying islands, is crime-free.

EDUCATION

▷ School leaving age: 14

92%

305 students

Elementary education is compulsory between the ages of six and 14. The Micronesian Occupational college, based in Palau, provides two-year training programs.

CHRONOLOGY

The Caroline Islands were colonized in turn by Spain, Germany, and Japan before being transferred to US control in 1945.

- ❑ **1947** UN Trust Territory of the Pacific Islands established.
- ❑ **1982** Palau signs Compact of Free Association with USA.
- ❑ **1993** Compact approved.
- ❑ **1994** Palau becomes independent in free association with the USA on October 1.

HEALTH

▷ No welfare state health benefits

1 per 83 people

Heart, cerebro-vascular, and intestinal diseases

Basic health care is available. Many outlying islands do not have easy access to qualified doctors and therefore often rely on nurses or traditional health remedies. An epidemic of mosquito-borne dengue fever hit Palau in 2000.

SPENDING

▷ Not available

CONSUMPTION AND SPENDING

No data

19 per 1000 population

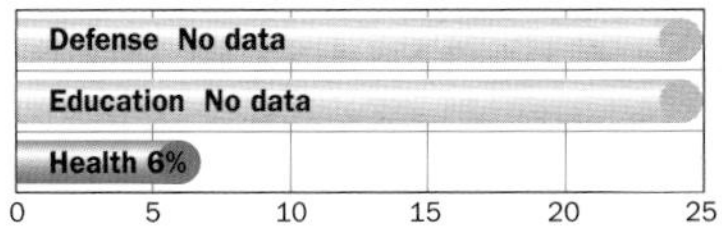
Defense No data
Education No data
Health 6%
0
5
10
15
20
25

Defense, Health, Education spending as % of GDP

The gap between rich and poor is steadily growing, as entrepreneurs and government officials exploit US aid and develop the tourist industry. In 2001, a program providing cheap rental housing for low-income families received a US grant of $200,000.

WORLD RANKING

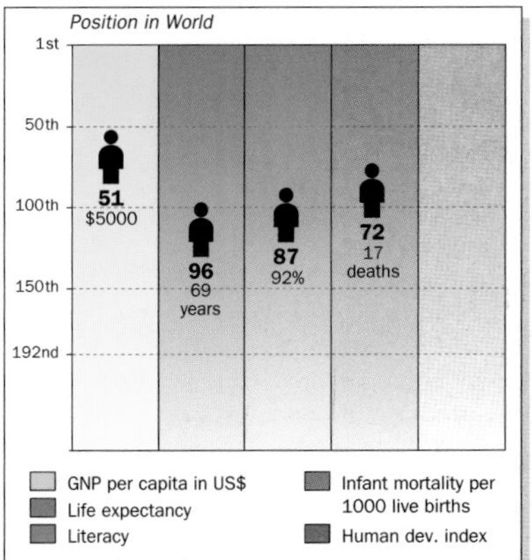
Position in World
1st
50th
100th
150th
192nd
51
$5000
96
69
years
87
92%
72
17
deaths
GNP per capita in US$
Life expectancy
Literacy
Infant mortality per 1000 live births
Human dev. index

P

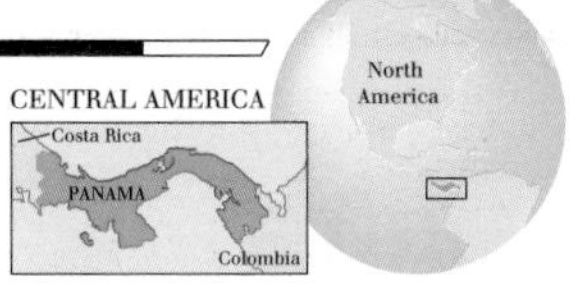

CENTRAL AMERICA
North America
Costa Rica
PANAMA
Colombia

Panama

Official Name: Republic of Panama **Capital:** Panama City
Population: 2.9 million **Currency:** Balboa **Official Language:** Spanish

1903 | 1903 | Nov 3 | PA | -5 | +507 | .pa

PANAMA IS THE SOUTHERNMOST of the seven countries occupying the isthmus that joins North and South America. The rainforests of the southeastern Darien Peninsula are some of the wildest areas left in the Americas. Elected governments have held power since the US invasion of 1989. Panama's traditional economic strength is its banking sector. The USA returned control of the Panama Canal Zone to Panama on 31 December 1999.

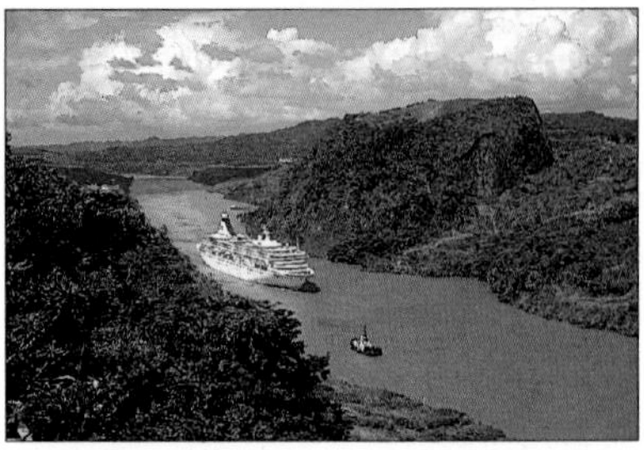

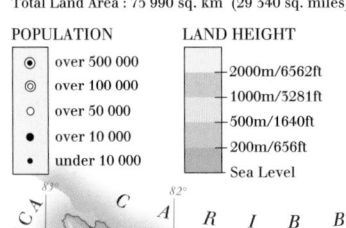

Cruise liner on the Panama Canal. The canal shortens the sea route from the east coast of the USA to Japan by 4800 km (3000 miles).

Climate

Tropical wet & dry

WEATHER CHART

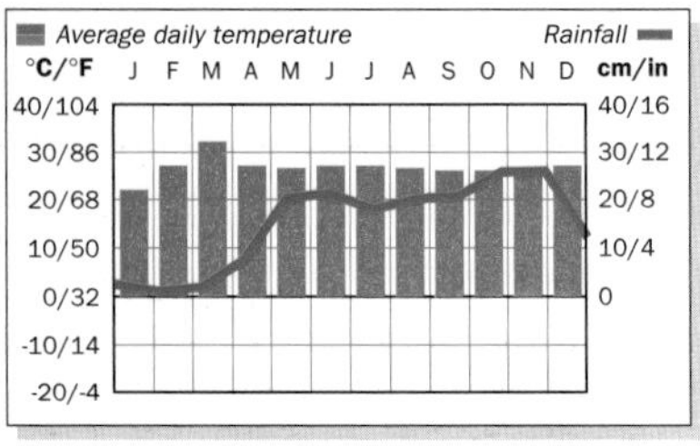

Average daily temperature
Rainfall
°C/°F
J F M A M J J A S O N D
cm/in
40/104
30/86
20/68
10/50
0/32
-10/14
-20/-4
40/16
30/12
20/8
10/4
0

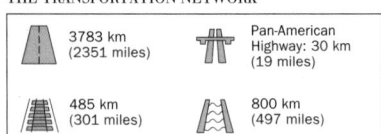

Panama has a humid tropical climate; rainfall is twice as heavy on the Caribbean coast as on the Pacific coast.

Transportation

Drive on right

Tocumen International, Panama City
898,000 passengers

6143 ships
98.2m grt

THE TRANSPORTATION NETWORK

3783 km (2351 miles)

Pan-American Highway: 30 km (19 miles)

485 km (301 miles)

800 km (497 miles)

The 80-km (50-mile) Panama Canal carries some 5% of all ocean-going trade. Many roads are in a poor state of repair. A new container port is planned for Colón, as is the modernization of the canal railroad.

Tourism

Visitors : Population 1:6.1

479,000 visitors

Up 5% in 2000

MAIN TOURIST ARRIVALS

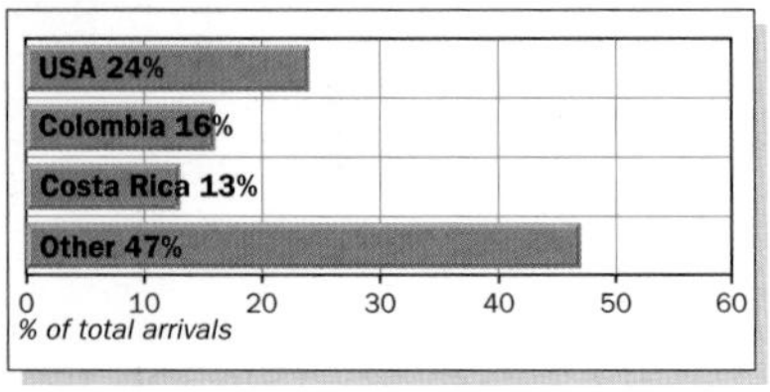

USA 24%
Colombia 16%
Costa Rica 13%
Other 47%
0
10
20
30
40
50
60
% of total arrivals

Portobelo and Panama City have old Spanish colonial buildings. In 2000, new cruise ship facilities opened in Colón.

People

Pop. density low

Spanish, English Creole, Amerindian languages, Chibchan

38/km² (99/mi²)

THE URBAN/RURAL POPULATION SPLIT

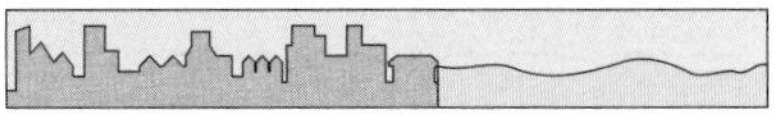

57%
43%

ETHNIC MAKEUP

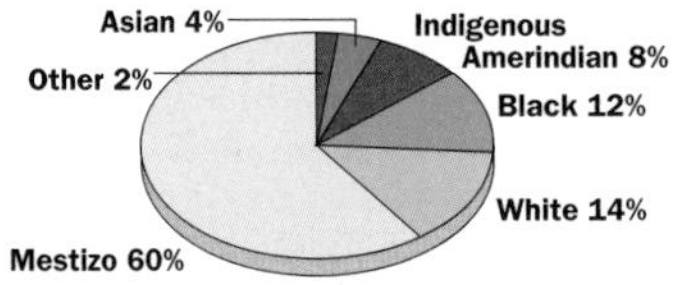

Asian 4%
Indigenous Amerindian 8%
Other 2%
Black 12%
White 14%
Mestizo 60%

The northwest coast has a large black community, mostly descended from African immigrants who worked the plantations. The majority speak English Creole rather than Spanish. About 8% of the population are Amerindians mainly from the Guaymies, Chocoes, Kunas, and Ngobe-Buglé tribes. Roman Catholicism and the extended family remain strong, although the canal and the former US military bases have given society a cosmopolitan outlook.

Politics

Multiparty elections

1999/2004

President Mireya Moscoso

AT THE LAST ELECTION

Legislative Assembly 71 seats

58% NN
34% UP
8% AO

NN = New Nation (comprises the Democratic Revolutionary Party (**PRD**), the Solidarity Party, the National Liberal Party, and the Papa Egoro Movement)
UP = Union for Panama (comprises the Arnulfisto Party (**PA**), MOLIRENA, the Party for Democratic Change, and MORENA)
AO = Action for the Opposition (comprises the Christian Democratic Party, the Liberal Party, the Popular Nationalist Party, and the Civil Renovation Party)

In 1989, the USA invaded Panama and arrested its ruler, General Manuel Noriega, for narcotics smuggling. US forces installed the compliant Endara government, criticized for corruption. The 1994 presidential and legislative elections were won by Ernesto Pérez Balladares and the PRD, Noriega's old party, but the new government was largely pro-US and attracted widespread discontent due to its economic reforms. A 1998 referendum denied Balladares a second consecutive term by 64% to 34%. In May 1999 opposition leader Mireya Moscoso of the PA was elected as Panama's first woman president. She promised social justice for the poor, but has followed an IMF-backed program and seen her popularity decline.

Panama

Total Land Area : 75 990 sq. km (29 340 sq. miles)

POPULATION	LAND HEIGHT
over 500 000	2000m/6562ft
over 100 000	1000m/3281ft
over 50 000	500m/1640ft
over 10 000	200m/656ft
under 10 000	Sea Level

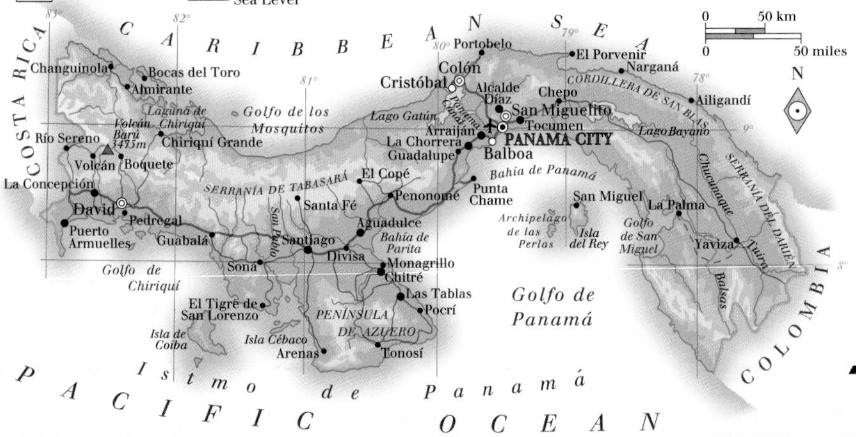

CARIBBEAN SEA
PACIFIC OCEAN
COSTA RICA
COLOMBIA
Changuinola
Bocas del Toro
Almirante
Laguna de Chiriquí
Volcán Barú 3475m
Chiriquí Grande
Golfo de los Mosquitos
Río Sereno
Volcán
Boquete
La Concepción
David
Pedregal
Puerto Armuelles
Guabalá
Golfo de Chiriquí
SERRANÍA DE TABASARÁ
Santa Fé
Santiago
Soná
El Tigre de San Lorenzo
Isla de Coiba
Isla Cébaco
Arenas
PENÍNSULA DE AZUERO
Tonosí
Las Tablas
Pocrí
Chitré
Monagrillo
Divisa
Aguadulce
Bahía de Parita
Penonomé
El Copé
Portobelo
Colón
Cristóbal
Lago Gatún
Alcalde Díaz
Chepo
San Miguelito
Tocumen
Arraiján
La Chorrera
Guadalupe
PANAMA CITY
Balboa
Bahía de Panamá
Punta Chame
Archipiélago de las Perlas
Isla del Rey
San Miguel
Golfo de San Miguel
La Palma
Yaviza
Golfo de Panamá
El Porvenir
Narganá
Ailigandí
CORDILLERA DE SAN BLAS
Lago Bayano
SERRANÍA DEL DARIÉN
Istmo de Panamá
0 50 km
0 50 miles
N

WORLD AFFAIRS

Joined UN in 1945

RG | Geplac | NAM | OAS | San José

The Canal Zone reverted to Panama on 31 December 1999. The USA, which had maintained 14 military bases there, has re-based its anti-narcotics activities in Florida after failing to reach agreement to allow some troops to stay on in Panama. Discussions continue.

Panama has had observer status with the Andean Community since 1995.

AID

Recipient

$14m (receipts)

Down 36% in 1999

The IDB pledged $3.3 million in 2000 to convert a former US base; Japan has loaned $1 million for the project.

DEFENSE

No compulsory military service

$128m

Up 5% in 1999

The National Guard and defense forces were disbanded in 1990 following the 1989 US invasion. They were replaced by the Public Force, numbering some 11,800 in 1999 and comprising the National Police, the National Air Service, and the National Maritime Service.

ECONOMICS

Inflation 2.1% p.a. (1990–1999)

$8.7bn

1 balboa

SCORE CARD

❑ World GNP Ranking	90th
❑ GNP per Capita	$3080
❑ Balance of Payments	$–1.33bn
❑ Inflation	1.3%
❑ Unemployment	14%

Strengths

Colón Free Trade Zone second-largest in world. Strong banking, financial, insurance, and other allied services. Banana, shrimp exports. Merchant shipping payments for sailing under the Panamanian flag.

Weaknesses

History of political instability and corruption. Large foreign debt. High unemployment, underemployment. Poor infrastructure.

EXPORTS

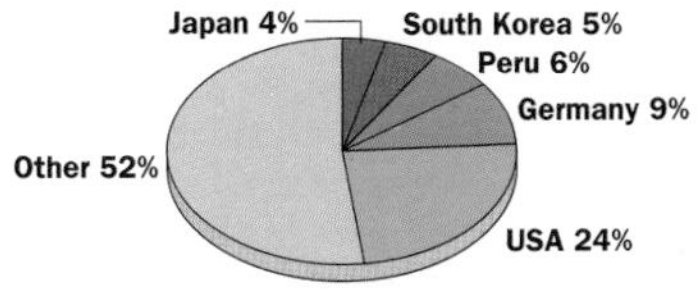
Japan 4%
South Korea 5%
Peru 6%
Germany 9%
Other 52%
USA 24%

IMPORTS

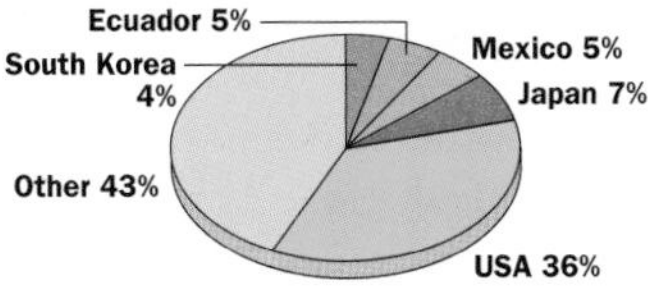
Ecuador 5%
South Korea 4%
Mexico 5%
Japan 7%
Other 43%
USA 36%

RESOURCES

Electric power 960,000 kw

169,718 tonnes

Not an oil producer; refines 100,000 b/d

1.36m cattle, 278,300 pigs, 11.8m chickens

Copper, coal, gold, silver, manganese, salt, clay

The Petaquilla area, west of the canal, has great copper and gold potential. To reduce the country's dependence on oil imports, the government has stepped up hydroelectric production; four state energy plants were privatized in 1999. Tropical hardwoods are being cut down at an alarming rate.

ENVIRONMENT

Sustainability rank: 34th

19%

2.9 tonnes per capita

The destruction of rainforests is proceeding at an increasingly rapid rate, resulting in widespread soil erosion. Large numbers of rare bird and animal species are threatened. Sewage from Panama City and Colón is discharged directly into coastal waters, canals, and ditches. Stretches of mangrove swamps are cut down for urban development, shrimp farms, and resorts.

MEDIA

TV ownership medium

Daily newspaper circulation 62 per 1000 people

PUBLISHING AND BROADCAST MEDIA

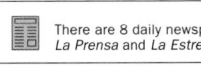

There are 8 daily newspapers, including *La Prensa* and *La Estrella de Panamá*

5 independent services

1 state-owned service, over 200 independent stations

A more independent press has flourished since Noriega's overthrow. Radio reaches the greatest number.

CRIME

Death penalty not used

5595 prisoners

Down 44% 1996–1998

Panama City and Colón have high crime levels. Money laundering, narcotics trafficking, and corruption are rife.

EDUCATION

School leaving age: 15

92%

80,980 students

Schooling is based on the US model. Provision for the urban poor, blacks, and indigenous people is limited.

CHRONOLOGY

On independence from Spain in 1821, Panama was incorporated into Gran Colombia. Panama gained independence from Colombia with US support in 1903.

- ❑ **1903** USA buys concession for Panama Canal.
- ❑ **1914–1939** Canal opens to traffic. US protectorate status ended.
- ❑ **1968–1981** Rule of Colonel Torrijos Herrera.
- ❑ **1989** Indicted drug trafficker General Noriega annuls elections to retain power. US invasion.
- ❑ **1994** PRD wins presidency and is largest party in parliament.
- ❑ **1999** PA's Mireya Moscoso elected first woman president. December, control of Canal Zone reverts from USA to Panama.

HEALTH

Welfare state health benefits

1 per 588 people

Heart disease, cancers, violence, accidents, tuberculosis

Primary health care is accessible to some two-thirds of the rural population. The isolation of many villages hinders efforts to improve the system.

SPENDING

GDP/cap. increase

CONSUMPTION AND SPENDING

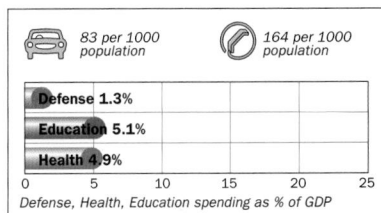

83 per 1000 population

164 per 1000 population

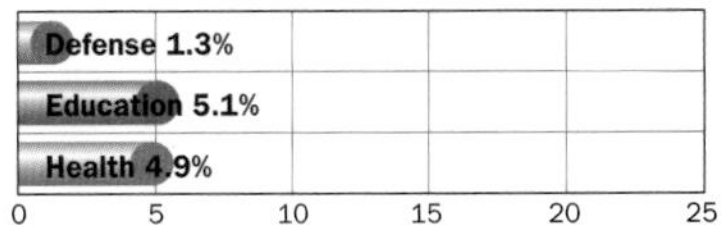
Defense 1.3%
Education 5.1%
Health 4.9%
0
5
10
15
20
25

Defense, Health, Education spending as % of GDP

Wealth disparities are large. More than 40% of the population are estimated to live below the poverty line – clustered in the cities rather than in rural areas.

WORLD RANKING

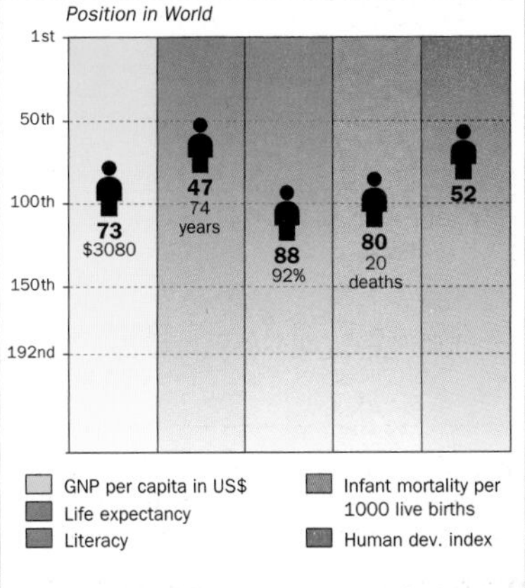
Position in World
1st
50th
100th
150th
192nd
73
$3080
47
74
years
88
92%
80
20
deaths
52
GNP per capita in US$
Life expectancy
Literacy
Infant mortality per 1000 live births
Human dev. index

Papua New Guinea

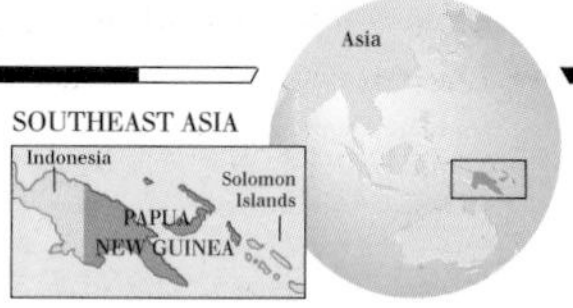
Asia
SOUTHEAST ASIA
Indonesia
Solomon Islands
PAPUA NEW GUINEA

Official name: Independent State of Papua New Guinea **Capital:** Port Moresby
Population: 4.8 million **Currency:** Kina **Official language:** English

1975 | 1975 | Sept 16 | PNG | +10 | +675 | .pg

THE MOST LINGUISTICALLY diverse country in the world, with approximately 750 languages, Papua New Guinea (PNG) achieved independence from Australia in 1975. The country occupies the eastern end of New Guinea, the world's third-largest island, and several other groups of islands. Much of the country is still isolated and much of the rural population experiences basic living conditions.

CLIMATE

Tropical equatorial/monsoon

WEATHER CHART

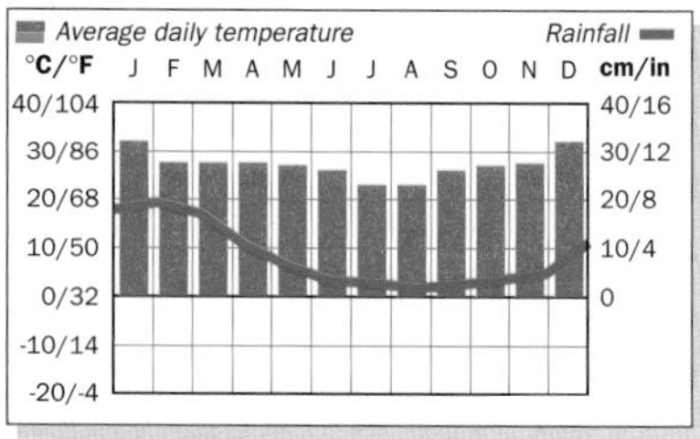
Average daily temperature
Rainfall
°C/°F
J F M A M J J A S O N D
cm/in
40/104
30/86
20/68
10/50
0/32
-10/14
-20/-4
40/16
30/12
20/8
10/4
0

Unvaryingly hot lowlands contrast with snow on Mount Victoria. Severe weather followed El Niño of 1997–1998.

TRANSPORTATION

Drive on left

Jacksons, Port Moresby 745,000 passengers

102 ships 61,000 grt

THE TRANSPORTATION NETWORK

686 km (426 miles)

None

None

10,940 km (6798 miles)

Infrastructure is improving with the construction and upgrading of major link roads, airports, and port facilities.

Papua New Guinea's 600 or so outer islands are mainly high and volcanic, with lush vegetation and fringing coral reefs.

TOURISM

Visitors : Population 1:83

58,000 visitors

Down 13% in 2000

MAIN TOURIST ARRIVALS

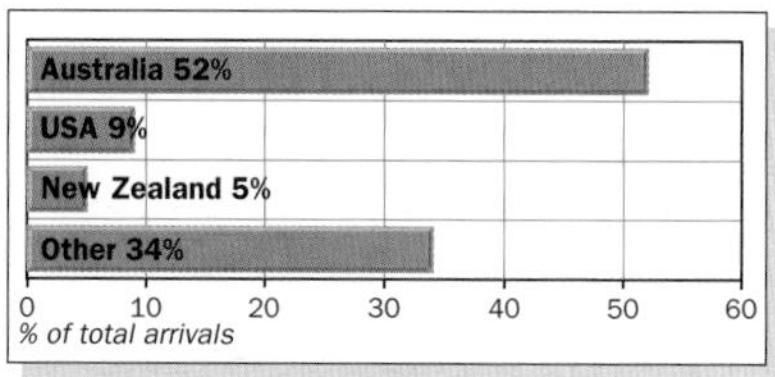
Australia 52%
USA 9%
New Zealand 5%
Other 34%
0
10
20
30
40
50
60
% of total arrivals

Tourism has great potential. However, it is hampered by the high rates of poverty-related violent crime, particularly in urban centers.

PEOPLE

Pop. density low

Pidgin English, Papuan, English, Motu, 750 (est) native languages

11/km² (27/mi²)

THE URBAN/RURAL POPULATION SPLIT

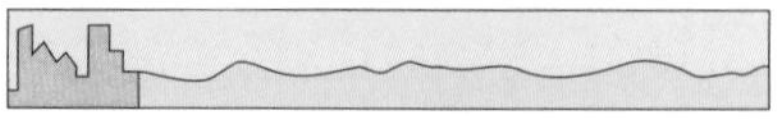
17%
83%

RELIGIOUS PERSUASION

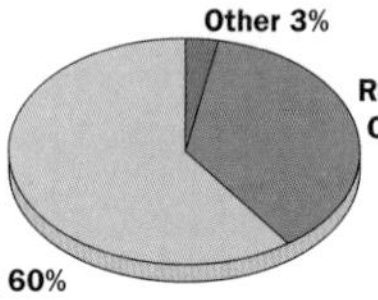
Other 3%
Roman Catholic 37%
Protestant 60%

PNG has an extraordinary diversity of peoples, with around 750 different language groups and even more tribes. The key distinction is between the lowlanders, with frequent contacts with the outside world, and the very isolated highlanders. Highland tribes see all strangers as potentially hostile. Vendettas can last for generations and tribal battles are not infrequent. A majority of people are nominally Christian, but indigenous beliefs and practices are widespread.

POLITICS

Multiparty elections

1997/2002

HM Queen Elizabeth II

AT THE LAST ELECTION

National Parliament 109 seats

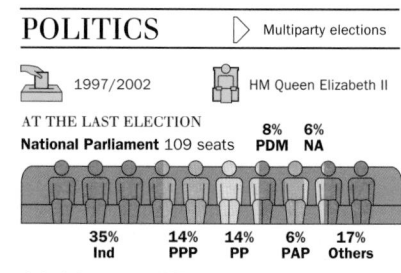

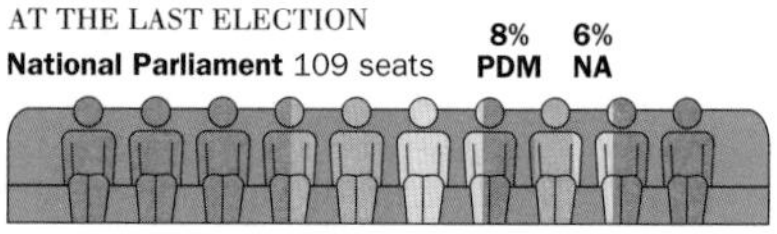
8% PDM
6% NA
35% Ind
14% PPP
14% PP
6% PAP
17% Others

Ind = Independents **PPP** = People's Progress Party
PP = Pangu Pati **PDM** = People's Democratic Movement
NA = National Alliance **PAP** = People's Action Party

PNG's many political parties lack clear ideological foundations, creating long-term political instability. The patronage required to maintain coalition groupings tended to encourage corruption. Prime Minister Sir Mekere Morauta has worked to overhaul the precarious system, and in May 2001 following many political realignments within parliament, his PDM claimed the first ever simple majority. A ten-year insurgency by separatists on Bougainville ended with the 1998 cease-fire, and Morauta has promised autonomy for the island and a future referendum on independence. Elsewhere, strong local traditions and communications problems have made centralization difficult.

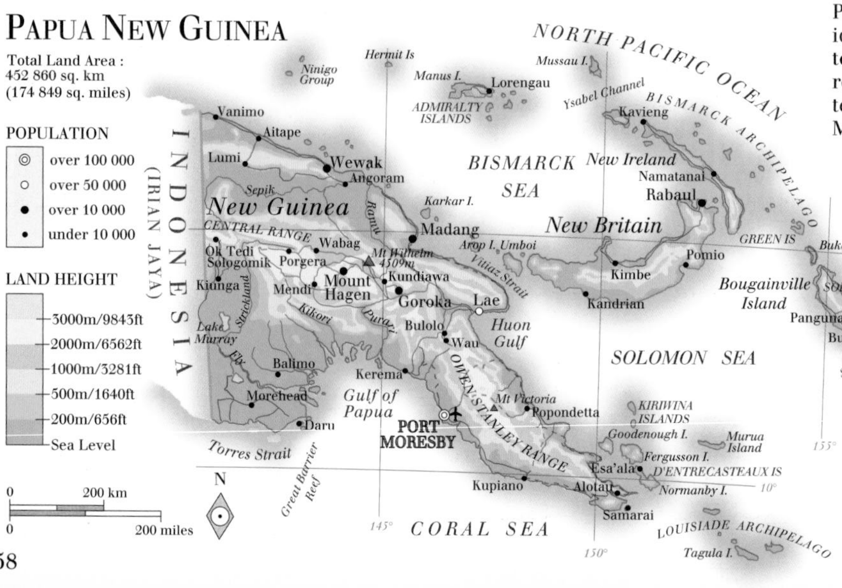
Papua New Guinea
Total Land Area : 452 860 sq. km (174 849 sq. miles)
POPULATION
over 100 000
over 50 000
over 10 000
under 10 000
LAND HEIGHT
3000m/9843ft
2000m/6562ft
1000m/3281ft
500m/1640ft
200m/656ft
Sea Level
0 200 km
0 200 miles
NORTH PACIFIC OCEAN
BISMARCK ARCHIPELAGO
BISMARCK SEA
SOLOMON SEA
CORAL SEA
LOUISIADE ARCHIPELAGO
INDONESIA (IRIAN JAYA)
New Guinea
New Britain
New Ireland
Bougainville Island
PORT MORESBY
Vanimo
Aitape
Lumi
Wewak
Angoram
Madang
Karkar I.
Mount Hagen
Goroka
Lae
Kundiawa
Wabag
Porgera
Mendi
Kiunga
Ok Tedi
Sologomik
Balimo
Kerema
Morehead
Daru
Bulolo
Wau
Kavieng
Namatanai
Rabaul
Kimbe
Kandrian
Pomio
Lorengau
Manus I.
ADMIRALTY ISLANDS
Mussau I.
Hermit Is
Ninigo Group
Buka I.
Arawa
Kieta
Panguna
Buin
SOLOMON IS
GREEN IS
Popondetta
Kupiano
Alotau
Samarai
Esa'ala
Goodenough I.
Fergusson I.
Normanby I.
D'ENTRECASTEAUX IS
KIRIWINA ISLANDS
Murua Island
Tagula I.
Gulf of Papua
Huon Gulf
Torres Strait
Great Barrier Reef
Mt Wilhelm 4509m
Mt Victoria
OWEN STANLEY RANGE
CENTRAL RANGE
Sepik
Fly
Strickland
Purari
Ramu
Kikori
Lake Murray
Vitiaz Strait
Ysabel Channel
Arop I.
Umboi
145°
150°
155°
5°
10°

WORLD AFFAIRS

Joined UN in 1975

APEC | Comm | NAM | PC | PIF

Accusations of PNG support for separatists in West Papua (Irian Jaya), the neighboring Indonesian province, have strained relations. A pro-Taiwan policy, in return for aid funding, provoked Chinese anger in 1999.

AID

Recipient

$216m (receipts) | Down 40% in 1999

Australia is the major aid donor. The World Bank in 2000 endorsed Morauta's reforms with a $90 million loan.

DEFENSE

No compulsory military service

$59m | Up 4% in 1999

Fears of exploitation at the hands of international aid donors led to an abortive army mutiny in March 2001.

ECONOMICS

Inflation 7.1% p.a. (1990–1999)

$3.8bn | 2.679–3.035 kina

SCORE CARD

❑ WORLD GNP RANKING	118th
❑ GNP PER CAPITA	$810
BALANCE OF PAYMENTS	$95m
❑ INFLATION	14.9%
❑ UNEMPLOYMENT	5%

STRENGTHS
Significant mineral reserves of copper, gold, nickel, cobalt, oil, and natural gas. A proposed gas pipeline between the highlands and Australia is expected to net $219 million a year. Agriculture sustains the population.

WEAKNESSES
Agricultural production and mining were significantly disrupted by severe droughts caused by El Niño of 1997–1998. Poor transportation and banking infrastructures. Political instability. Foreign exploitation of resources.

EXPORTS

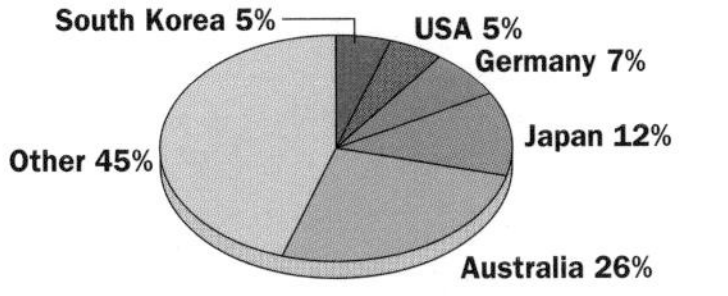
South Korea 5%
USA 5%
Germany 7%
Japan 12%
Other 45%
Australia 26%

IMPORTS

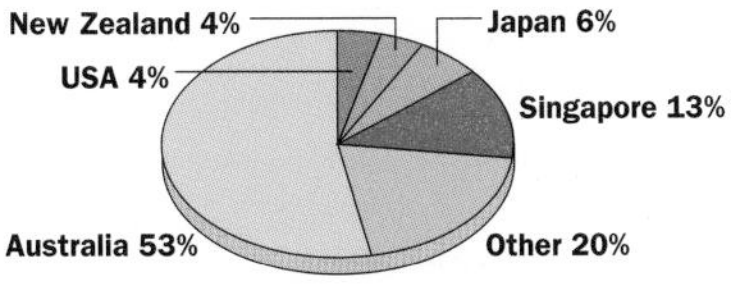
New Zealand 4%
Japan 6%
USA 4%
Singapore 13%
Australia 53%
Other 20%

RESOURCES

Electric power 490,000 kw

45,025 tonnes | 70,000 b/d (reserves 300,000,000 bbl)

1.55m pigs, 86,000 cattle, 9000 ducks, 3.6m chickens | Copper, gold, silver, gas, oil, nickel, chromite, cobalt

Papua New Guinea is rich in minerals. The Ok Tedi mine in the Star Mountains is the most productive in the country. The Porgera gold mine is one of the world's largest. In 1998 production at both mines was significantly affected by drought. Prospecting has revealed extensive oil and natural gas reserves.

ENVIRONMENT

Sustainability rank: 62nd

None | 0.5 tonnes per capita

Deforestation and heavy-metal pollution are major issues. Cyanide poisoning from an Australian-owned mine in 2000 caused serious water pollution. Subduction of continental plates has forced the relocation of thousands of people from the low-lying islands.

MEDIA

TV ownership low

Daily newspaper circulation 15 per 1000 people

PUBLISHING AND BROADCAST MEDIA

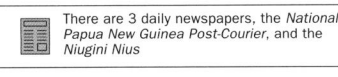

There are 3 daily newspapers, the *National*, *Papua New Guinea Post-Courier*, and the *Niugini Nius*

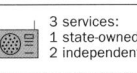

2 independent services | 3 services: 1 state-owned, 2 independent

The dismissal of the head of the National Broadcasting Commission in 2001 raised concerns over the freedom of the media.

CRIME

Death penalty not used

PNG does not publish prison figures | Up 22% in 1992

Violent crime by gangs of "Rascals" is very common. A cultural tradition of vendettas persists in rural communities.

EDUCATION

School leaving age: 16

64% | 13,663 students

Education is not compulsory. Equipment charges and fees have been introduced. Universities are suffering funding cuts.

HEALTH

Welfare state health benefits

1 per 10,000 people | Malaria, pneumonia, diarrheal diseases

The health system has suffered from recent cuts. HIV and tuberculosis co-infections are at crisis level. Life expectancy rates are among the lowest in the Pacific. Access to clean water and sanitation are major issues.

CHRONOLOGY

The British annexed the southeast and the Germans the northeast of the island of New Guinea in 1884.

- ❑ **1904** Australia takes over British sector; renamed Papua in 1906.
- ❑ **1914** German sector occupied by Australia.
- ❑ **1942–1945** Japanese occupation.
- ❑ **1964** National Parliament created.
- ❑ **1971** Renamed Papua New Guinea.
- ❑ **1975** Independence under Michael Somare, leader since 1972.
- ❑ **1988** Bougainville Revolutionary Army begins guerrilla campaign.
- ❑ **1997** El Niño effect causes severe drought and tsunamis. Sir Julius Chan resigns as prime minister over the use of Western-led mercenaries in Bougainville.
- ❑ **2000** Loloata Understanding promises autonomy for Bougainville.
- ❑ **2001** PDM claims parliamentary majority. Final peace agreement with Bougainville ratified after three-year cease-fire.

SPENDING

GDP/cap. increase

CONSUMPTION AND SPENDING

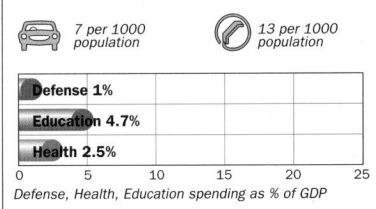

7 per 1000 population | *13 per 1000 population*

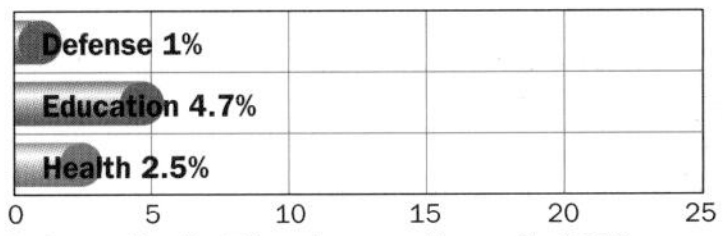
Defense 1%
Education 4.7%
Health 2.5%
0
5
10
15
20
25

Defense, Health, Education spending as % of GDP

There is a growing gap between the country's rich and poor, particularly in urban areas. The government has cut expenditure on public services in order to raise capital for investing in basic infrastructure, education, and public health.

WORLD RANKING

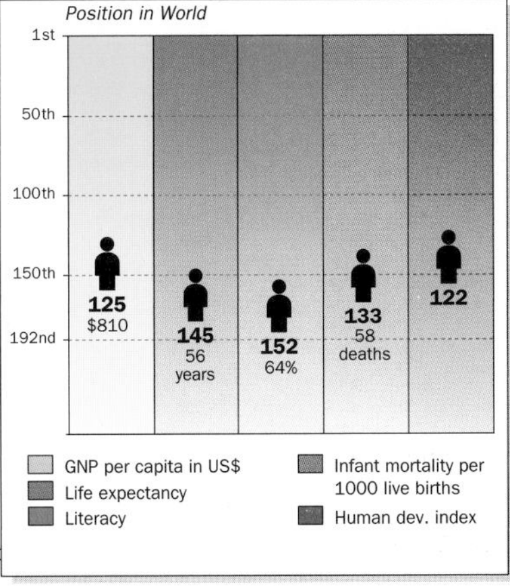
Position in World
1st
50th
100th
150th
192nd
125
$810
145
56
years
152
64%
133
58
deaths
122
GNP per capita in US$
Life expectancy
Literacy
Infant mortality per 1000 live births
Human dev. index

P

Paraguay

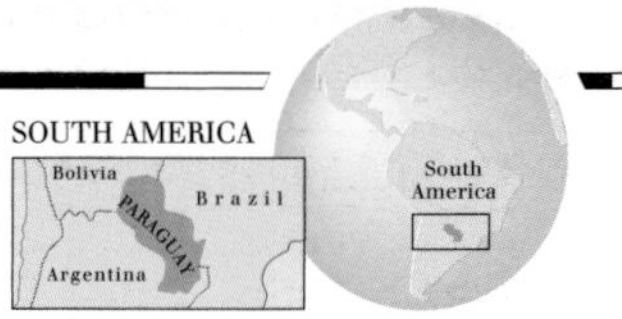
SOUTH AMERICA
Bolivia
Brazil
PARAGUAY
Argentina
South America

Official Name: Republic of Paraguay **Capital:** Asunción
Population: 5.5 million **Currency:** Guaraní **Official Language:** Spanish

1811 | 1938 | May 14 | PY | -4 | +595 | .py

LANDLOCKED IN SOUTH America and a Spanish possession until 1811, Paraguay gained large tracts of land from Bolivia in 1938. From then until the overthrow in 1989 of General Alfredo Stroessner, South America's longest-surviving dictator, it experienced periods of anarchy and military rule. The Paraguay river divides the eastern hills and fertile plains, where 90% of people live, from the almost uninhabited Chaco in the west. Paraguay's economy is largely agricultural.

CLIMATE

Tropical/subtropical

WEATHER CHART

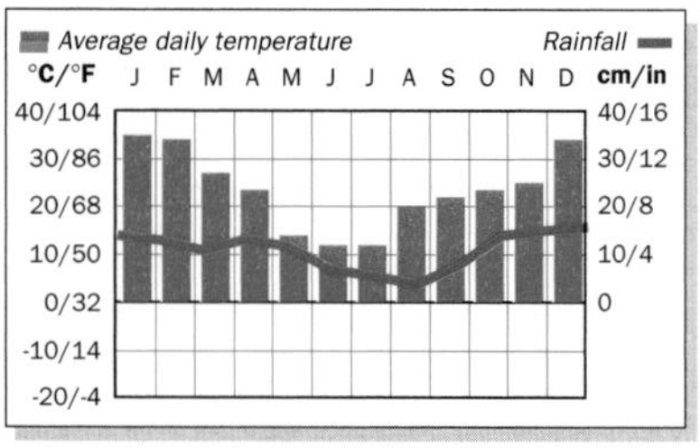
Average daily temperature
Rainfall
°C/°F
J F M A M J J A S O N D
cm/in
40/104
30/86
20/68
10/50
0/32
-10/14
-20/-4
40/16
30/12
20/8
10/4
0

Paraguay is subtropical, with all parts experiencing floods and droughts, but the Chaco is generally drier and hotter.

TRANSPORTATION

Drive on right

Silvio Pettirossi International, Asunción 320,000 passengers

47 ships 44,900 grt

THE TRANSPORTATION NETWORK

15,000 km (9321 miles)

Pan-American Highway: 700 km (435 miles)

370 km (230 miles)

3100 km (1926 miles)

Roads badly need upgrading. The government wants to part-privatize the near-paralyzed FCCAL (railroad).

TOURISM

Visitors : Population 1:25

221,000 visitors

Down 18% in 2000

MAIN TOURIST ARRIVALS

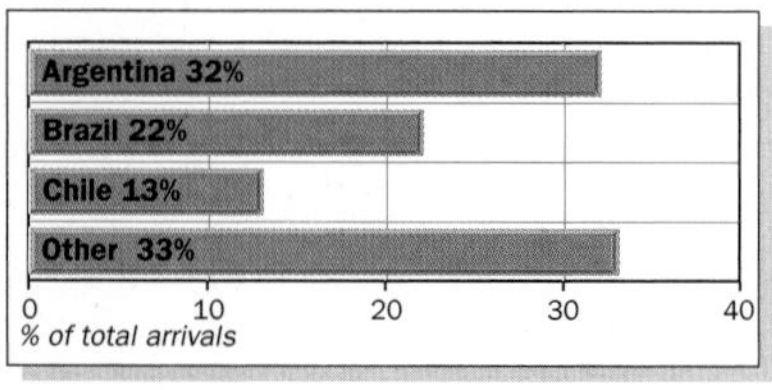
Argentina 32%
Brazil 22%
Chile 13%
Other 33%
0
10
20
30
40
% of total arrivals

Tourist numbers are small. Most visitors are cross-border day-trippers from Brazil and Argentina, who flock to Ciudad del Este to buy cheap, mainly Far Eastern, electrical goods. The Chaco attracts tourists for safaris.

PEOPLE

Pop. density low

Guaraní, Spanish

14/km² (36/mi²)

THE URBAN/RURAL POPULATION SPLIT

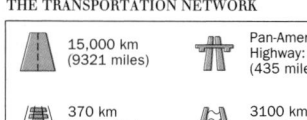

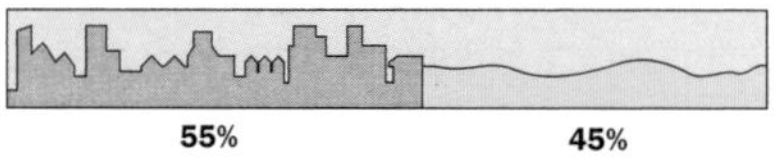
55%
45%

ETHNIC MAKEUP

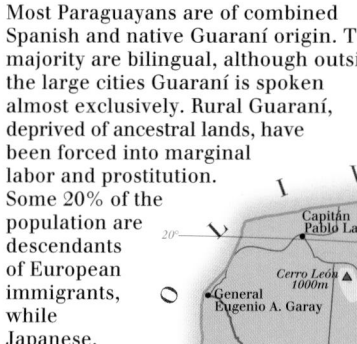

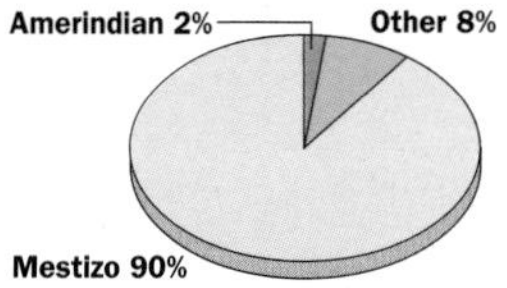
Amerindian 2%
Other 8%
Mestizo 90%

Most Paraguayans are of combined Spanish and native Guaraní origin. The majority are bilingual, although outside the large cities Guaraní is spoken almost exclusively. Rural Guaraní, deprived of ancestral lands, have been forced into marginal labor and prostitution. Some 20% of the population are descendants of European immigrants, while Japanese, Koreans, and South Africans are more recent arrivals.

POLITICS

Multiparty elections

L. House 1998/2003
U. House 1998/2003

President Luis Gonzalez Macchi

AT THE LAST ELECTION

Chamber of Deputies 80 seats

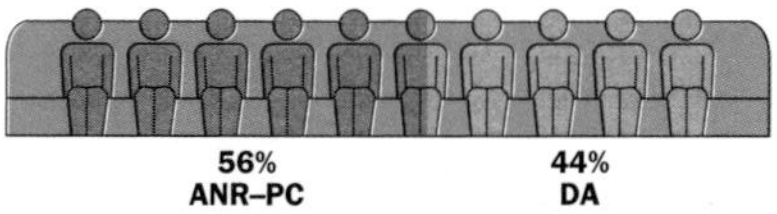
56%
ANR–PC
44%
DA

ANR–PC = National Republican Association–Colorado Party
DA = Democratic Alliance
The Democratic Alliance is a coalition led by the Authentic Radical Liberal Party (**PLRA**)

Senate 45 seats

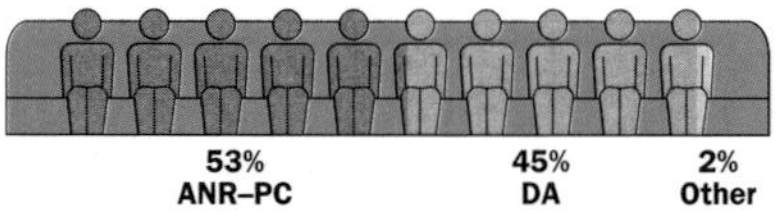
53%
ANR–PC
45%
DA
2%
Other

A 1989 coup ended General Stroessner's 34-year dictatorship. In 1993, his PC won the first free elections in 60 years, but with continued reliance on the military. The PC again won in 1998, despite the last-minute annulment of former army chief General Lino Oviedo's presidential candidacy. Unrest in 1999 after the assassination of Vice President Luis Argaña, Oviedo's main opponent in the PC, forced the resignation of President Raúl Cubas, a supporter of Oviedo. A fragile coalition government survived a coup in May 2000 led by Oviedo – his third such attempt since 1993. Vice-presidential elections in August 2000 led to an unprecedented cohabitation between a PC president and his PLRA deputy.

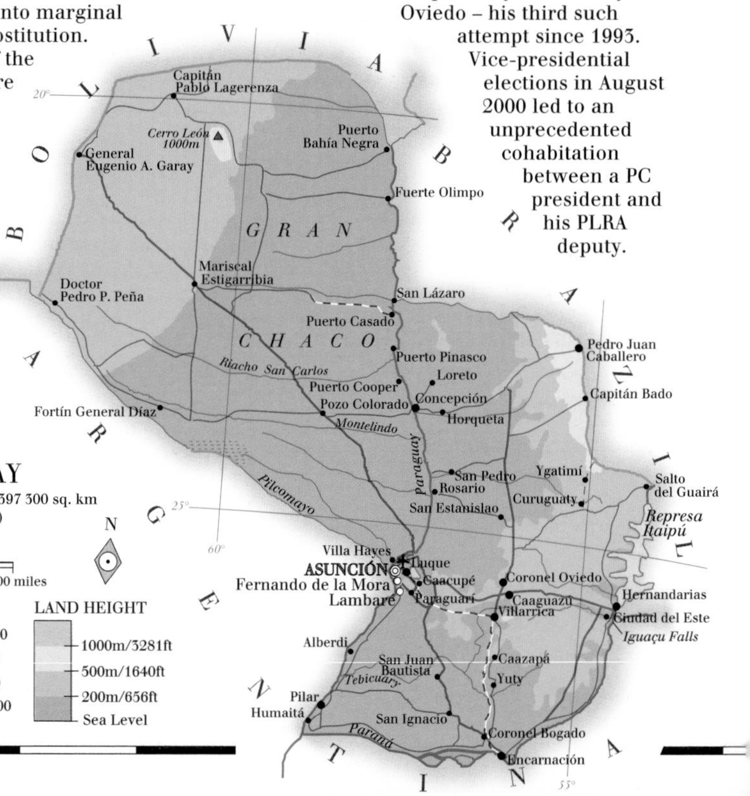
BOLIVIA
BRAZIL
ARGENTINA
Capitán Pablo Lagerenza
Cerro León 1000m
Puerto Bahía Negra
General Eugenio A. Garay
Fuerte Olimpo
GRAN
Mariscal Estigarribia
Doctor Pedro P. Peña
San Lázaro
Puerto Casado
CHACO
Pedro Juan Caballero
Puerto Pinasco
Riacho San Carlos
Loreto
Puerto Cooper
Pozo Colorado
Concepción
Capitán Bado
Fortín General Díaz
Horqueta
Montelindo
Paraguay
San Pedro
Ygatimí
Salto del Guairá
Rosario
Pilcomayo
Curuguaty
San Estanislao
Represa Itaipú
Villa Hayes
Luque
ASUNCIÓN
Caacupé
Coronel Oviedo
Fernando de la Mora
Lambaré
Paraguarí
Caaguazú
Villarrica
Hernandarias
Ciudad del Este
Iguaçu Falls
Alberdi
San Juan Bautista
Caazapá
Tebicuary
Yuty
Pilar
Humaitá
San Ignacio
Paraná
Coronel Bogado
Encarnación
20°
25°
60°
55°

PARAGUAY

Total Land Area : 397 300 sq. km (153 398 sq. miles)

0 100 km
0 100 miles

N

POPULATION
- over 100 000
- over 50 000
- over 10 000
- under 10 000

LAND HEIGHT
- 1000m/3281ft
- 500m/1640ft
- 200m/656ft
- Sea Level

WORLD AFFAIRS

Joined UN in 1945

IBRD | IAEA | Geplac | Mercosr | RG

The main aims are fairer integration in the MERCOSUR common market and good relations with the USA.

AID

Recipient

$78m (receipts) — Up 3% in 1999

The World Bank offers development aid, the IMF conditional loans. NGO charities run small programs in rural areas.

DEFENSE

Compulsory military service

$128m — Down 5% in 1999

Under Stroessner, the military controlled political and economic life. In 1994–1995, Congress tried to limit its powers, but President Juan Carlos Wasmosy endorsed its political and institutional role. The pact between the military and the PC, in power since 1947, has been weakened by factionalism.

ECONOMICS

Inflation 13.4% p.a. (1990–1999)

$8.4bn — 3318–3545 guaraníes

SCORE CARD

❑ WORLD GNP RANKING	93rd
❑ GNP PER CAPITA	$1560
❑ BALANCE OF PAYMENTS	$-106m
❑ INFLATION	6.8%
❑ UNEMPLOYMENT	12%

STRENGTHS

Electricity exporter – earnings obtain foreign exchange. Self-sufficiency in wheat and other staple foodstuffs. Cotton, oilseeds, notably soybeans.

WEAKNESSES

Reliance on agriculture and Brazilian and Argentine markets. No hydrocarbons produced. Weak banking and financial sectors. High unemployment. Political instability deters foreign investment.

EXPORTS

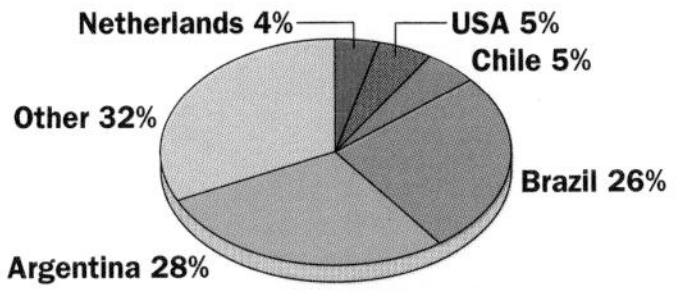
Netherlands 4%
USA 5%
Chile 5%
Other 32%
Brazil 26%
Argentina 28%

IMPORTS

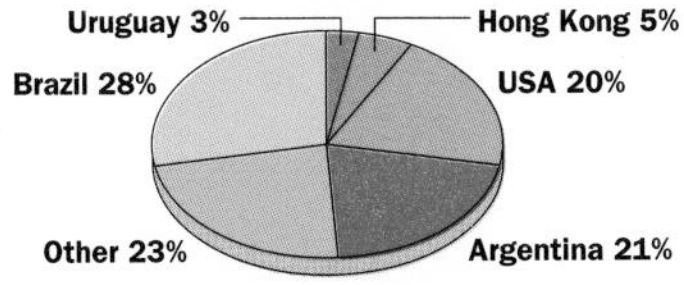
Uruguay 3%
Hong Kong 5%
Brazil 28%
USA 20%
Other 23%
Argentina 21%

The Iguaçu Falls, on the border with Brazil and Argentina, are composed of over 20 cataracts, separated by rocks and tree-covered islands.

RESOURCES

Electric power 6.5m kw

28,000 tonnes — Not an oil producer

9.91m cattle, 2.7m pigs, 710,000 ducks, 25m chickens — Gypsum, marble, clay, kaolin, iron, manganese, uranium

The joint Paraguay–Brazil Itaipú hydroelectric dam is the world's largest. The massive Yacyretá dam is operated with Argentina.

ENVIRONMENT

Sustainability rank: 54th

4% — 0.8 tonnes per capita

Apart from the destruction of forests for farming and for dams, a major ecological worry is the smuggling abroad of endangered species.

MEDIA

TV ownership medium

Daily newspaper circulation 43 per 1000 people

PUBLISHING AND BROADCAST MEDIA

There are 7 daily newspapers, including *ABC Color, Noticias, Popular,* and *Ultima Hora*

4 independent services — 21 independent services

The media, historically sponsored by political parties, flourished after the fall of Stroessner, publishing details of corruption and abuses of human rights. The constitution nominally protects the rights of columnists to air their views.

CRIME

Death penalty not used

Paraguay does not publish prison figures — Down 3% 1996–1998

Paraguay is the contraband capital of Latin America, with trade in everything from cars to cocaine. Jungle airstrips near Brazil provide a route for narcotics.

EDUCATION

School leaving age: 12

93% — 42,302 students

Education is compulsory to the age of 12; only about 28% go on to secondary school. Provisions for education are limited in remote rural areas.

CHRONOLOGY

Paraguay was controlled by Spain from 1536 until 1811.

- ❑ **1864–1870** Loses War of the Triple Alliance against Argentina, Brazil, and Uruguay.
- ❑ **1928–1935** Two Chaco Wars against Bolivia over disputed territory.
- ❑ **1938** Boundary with Bolivia fixed; Paraguay awarded large tracts.
- ❑ **1954–1989** Rule of Gen. Stroessner; repressive military regime.
- ❑ **1993** First democratic elections.
- ❑ **1996** Coup attempt by General Lino Oviedo.
- ❑ **1998–1999** Raúl Cubas elected president; resigns after assassination of vice president; Cubas and Oviedo leave country.
- ❑ **2000** Further failed coup attempt by Oviedo.

HEALTH

Welfare state health benefits

1 per 909 people — Heart disease, cancers, obstetric causes, tuberculosis

Hepatitis, typhoid, dysentery, and tuberculosis are endemic and leprosy is common. Medical care is expensive.

SPENDING

GDP/cap. increase

CONSUMPTION AND SPENDING

14 per 1000 population — *55 per 1000 population*

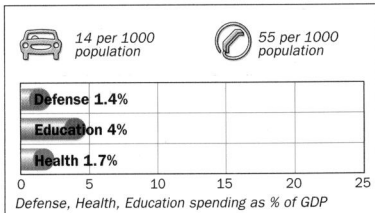

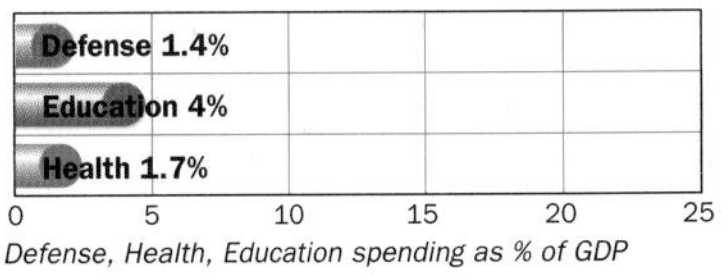
Defense 1.4%
Education 4%
Health 1.7%
0
5
10
15
20
25

Defense, Health, Education spending as % of GDP

Income inequality is great and rural poverty serious. Top military ranks and business and landed elites control wealth.

WORLD RANKING

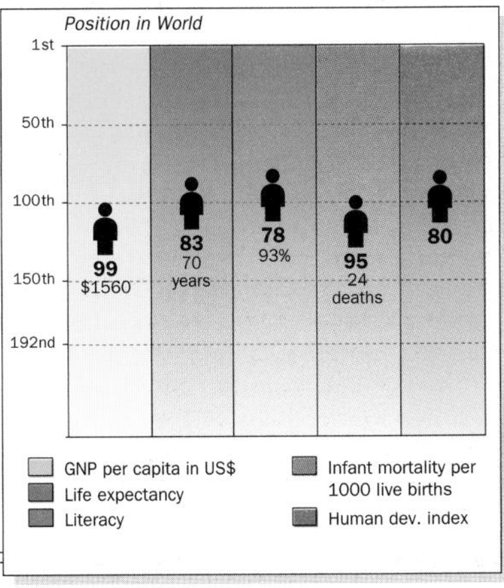
Position in World
1st
50th
100th
150th
192nd
99
$1560
83
70 years
78
93%
95
24 deaths
80
GNP per capita in US$
Life expectancy
Literacy
Infant mortality per 1000 live births
Human dev. index

P

PERU

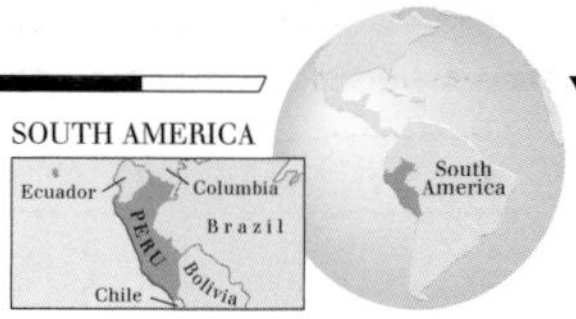
SOUTH AMERICA
Ecuador
Columbia
Brazil
PERU
Chile
Bolivia
South America

OFFICIAL NAME: Republic of Peru **CAPITAL:** Lima **POPULATION:** 25.7 million
CURRENCY: Nuevo sol (new sol) **OFFICIAL LANGUAGES:** Spanish and Quechua

1824
1941
July 28
PE
-5
+51
.pe

LYING JUST SOUTH of the equator, on the Pacific coast of South America, Peru became independent of Spain in 1824. It rises from an arid coastal strip to the Andes, dominated in the south by volcanoes; about half of Peru's population live in mountain regions. Peru's border with Bolivia to the south runs through Lake Titicaca, the highest navigable lake in the world. In 1995, Peru was involved in a brief border war with Ecuador, its northern neighbor, and the issue was finally settled in 1998.

CLIMATE

Tropical/mountain/desert

WEATHER CHART

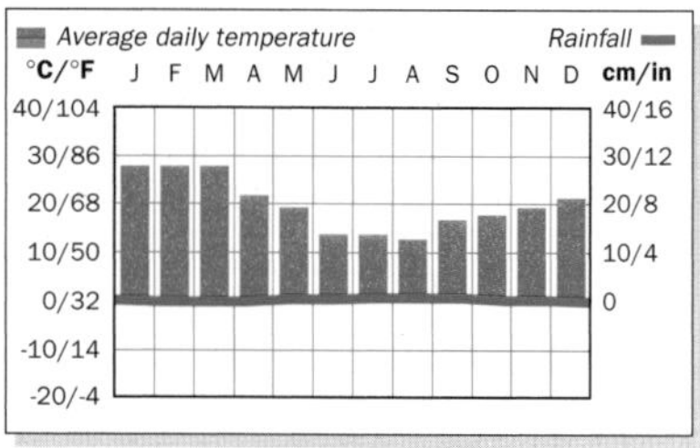
Average daily temperature
Rainfall
°C/°F
J F M A M J J A S O N D
cm/in
40/104
30/86
20/68
10/50
0/32
-10/14
-20/-4
40/16
30/12
20/8
10/4
0

Peru has several distinct climatic regions. The arid or desert coastal region experiences the *garúa*, persistent low cloud and fog, giving Lima cool "winters" even though it is close to the equator. The temperate slopes of the Andes have large daily temperature ranges and one rainy season, while the tropical Amazon Basin receives year-round rains.

TRANSPORTATION

Drive on right

Jorge Chávez International, Lima
2.57m passengers

719 ships
269,700 grt

THE TRANSPORTATION NETWORK

8700 km (5406 miles)

Pan-American Highway: 2495 km (1550 miles)

1639 km (1018 miles)

8600 km (5344 miles)

The World Bank in 2001 estimated that Peru had a public infrastructure deficit of $7 billion. Most roads remain unpaved. Work on a transcontinental highway from Ilo, a free port on the Pacific, via Puerto Suárez in Bolivia, to the port of Portos in Brazil is ongoing. The two rail networks, the Central and Southern, are as yet unconnected. The La Oroya–Huancayo line is the world's highest stretch of standard-gauge railroad. River transportation provides major access to Iquitos in Amazonia. As well as four important international airports, there are more than 130 airstrips scattered throughout the country.

Spanish colonial church near Urubamba. *The River Urubamba with its deep gorges was known as the Sacred Valley to the Incas.*

TOURISM

Visitors : Population 1:25

1m visitors

Up 9% in 2000

MAIN TOURIST ARRIVALS

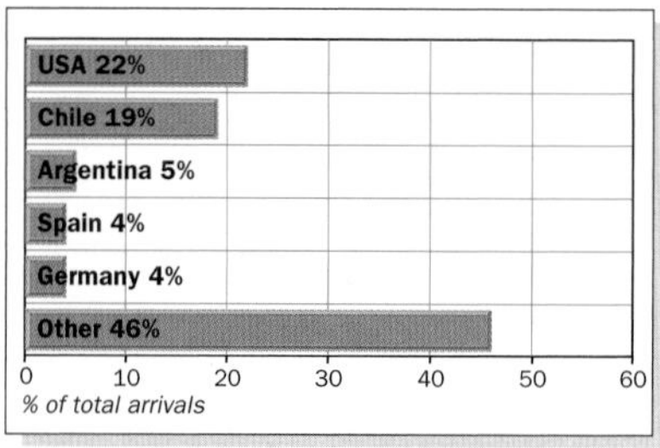
USA 22%
Chile 19%
Argentina 5%
Spain 4%
Germany 4%
Other 46%
0
10
20
30
40
50
60
% of total arrivals

Tourism is gradually recovering, after being plunged into crisis in the early 1990s by guerrilla activity, crime, and cholera fears. The heavily indebted industry has been unable to take full advantage of new investment opportunities, but privatization programs have seen the sale of state hotels. Visitors face poor infrastructure and accommodation to see incomparable sites such as the Inca ruins at Machu Picchu in the Andes. Tourism to the Amazon is also growing, but environmentalists are concerned about the impact on indigenous people. The patterns in the desert made by the Nazca people (known as the Nazca lines), dating from the 2nd century BCE, are also a major attraction. Lake Titicaca and the Spanish colonial architecture of Lima are other draws.

PEOPLE

Pop. density low

Spanish, Quechua, Aymará

20/km² (52/mi²)

THE URBAN/RURAL POPULATION SPLIT

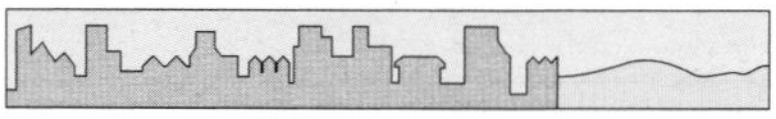
72%
28%

RELIGIOUS PERSUASION

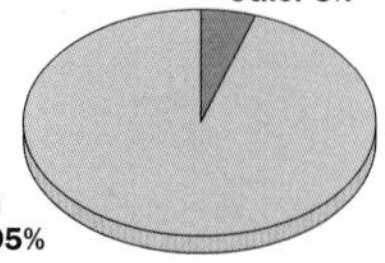
Other 5%
Roman Catholic 95%

ETHNIC MAKEUP

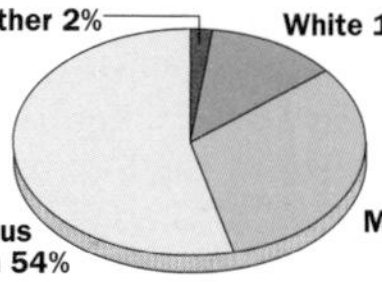
Other 2%
White 12%
Indigenous Amerindian 54%
Mestizo 32%

Most Peruvians are Amerindian or *mestizo*. The small elite of Spanish descendants retain a strong hold on the economy, power, and social standing. A few Chinese and Japanese live in the northern cities.

Previously remote Andean Amerindians are increasingly informed of events in Lima and the coastal strip by radio and by relatives in cities. This has compensated for problems associated with the marginalization of their native Quechua and Aymará languages in a Spanish-speaking culture. A further 250,000 Amazonian Amerindians live in the eastern lowlands. Together with the small community of Africans (descendants of plantation workers), they tend to suffer the worst discrimination in towns.

The extended family remains strong. A part of traditional native Amerindian traditions, its role as a social bond was strengthened by Roman Catholicism. In recent years, economic difficulties have raised its profile as the key social support system for most Peruvians.

POPULATION AGE BREAKDOWN

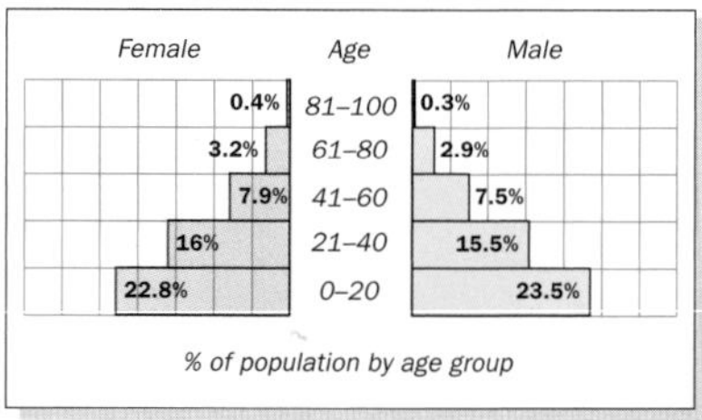
Female
Age
Male
0.4%
81–100
0.3%
3.2%
61–80
2.9%
7.9%
41–60
7.5%
16%
21–40
15.5%
22.8%
0–20
23.5%
% of population by age group

P

POLITICS

Multiparty elections

2001/2006

President Alejandro Toledo

Alberto Fujimori, *president 1990–2000, ran an increasingly autocratic regime.*

President Alejandro Toledo, *Peru's first Amerindian head of state, elected in 2001.*

AT THE LAST ELECTION

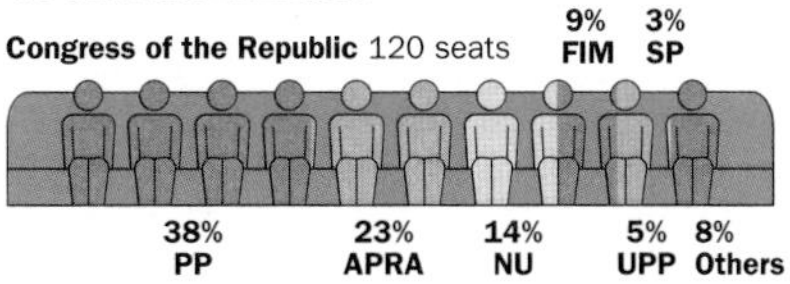
Congress of the Republic 120 seats
9% FIM
3% SP
38% PP
23% APRA
14% NU
5% UPP
8% Others

PP = Peru Posible **APRA** = American Popular Revolutionary Alliance **NU** = National Unity **FIM** = Independent Moralizing Front **UPP** = Union for Peru **SP** = Somos Peru

Peru is a multiparty democracy in which the president holds executive power.

MAIN POLITICAL ISSUES

Democracy

Former President Alberto Fujimori appeared in 2000 to have secured an unconstitutional third term. His reelection, boycotted in the second round by popular opposition candidate Alejandro Toledo, provoked domestic protests but muted criticism worldwide. Soon after, however, a bribery scandal involving his powerful secret service chief led to his unexpected resignation and self-exile in Japan. An interim government of national unity under an appointed president took office until the holding of fresh elections. None of the candidates, however, had distinctive policies, making it all the more probable that in the future, government will depend on fragile alliances and political horsetrading.

Corruption

The bribery scandal that brought down Fujimori was the tip of the iceberg. Corruption oils the wheels of power and is endemic in politics, the judiciary, and business, and in the military and police.

Reform of military

Senior officers loyal to Fujimori and his security chief, Vladimiro Montesinos, have been sacked, but the military, and the militarized police, need reforming to make them professional forces. The likelihood of this happening soon is slim.

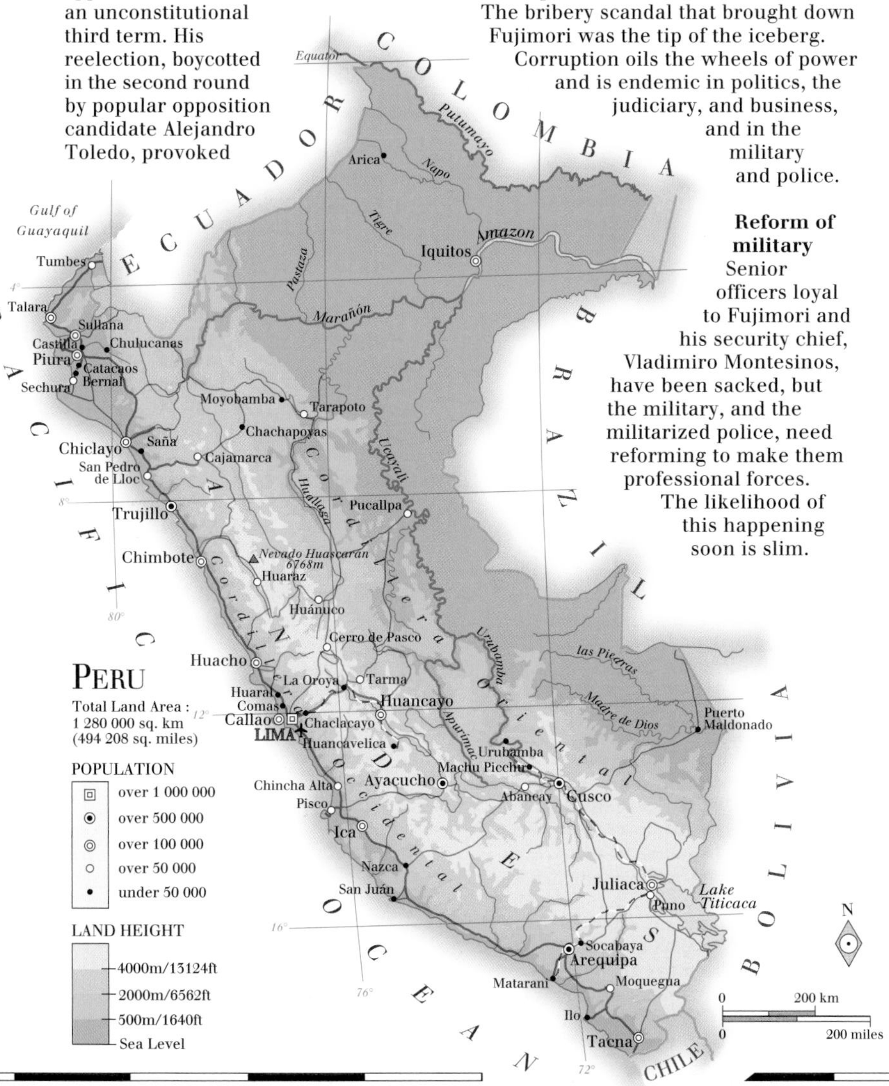
PERU
Total Land Area : 1 280 000 sq. km (494 208 sq. miles)
POPULATION
over 1 000 000
over 500 000
over 100 000
over 50 000
under 50 000
LAND HEIGHT
4000m/13124ft
2000m/6562ft
500m/1640ft
Sea Level
COLOMBIA
ECUADOR
BRAZIL
BOLIVIA
CHILE
PACIFIC OCEAN
Gulf of Guayaquil
Equator
Putumayo
Napo
Tigre
Pastaza
Amazon
Marañón
Ucayali
Huallaga
Urubamba
Apurímac
las Piedras
Madre de Dios
Lake Titicaca
Arica
Iquitos
Tumbes
Talara
Sullana
Castilla
Chulucanas
Piura
Catacaos
Bernal
Sechura
Moyobamba
Tarapoto
Chachapoyas
Chiclayo
Saña
Cajamarca
San Pedro de Lloc
Trujillo
Pucallpa
Chimbote
Nevado Huascarán 6768m
Huaraz
Huánuco
Cerro de Pasco
Huacho
La Oroya
Tarma
Huaral
Comas
Callao
Chaclacayo
Huancayo
LIMA
Huancavelica
Puerto Maldonado
Urubamba
Machu Picchu
Chincha Alta
Ayacucho
Pisco
Abancay
Cusco
Ica
Nazca
San Juán
Juliaca
Puno
Socabaya
Arequipa
Matarani
Moquegua
Ilo
Tacna
N
0 200 km
0 200 miles

PROFILE

The long tradition of large parties dominating politics ended with Fujimori's election in 1990. His "self-coup" created a compliant legislature and judiciary, and the approval of a new constitution permitted his reelection in 1995. His popularity was greatly boosted by successes against hyperinflation and the *Sendero Luminoso* (Shining Path) guerrillas. It faded in the late 1990s as he tightened his personal control of the government, and appeared increasingly reliant on the army. Few checks on the executive remained, and Fujimori was able to obtain his third term in 2000. However, blatant electoral fraud and the corrupt use of power were exposed when his security service chief Montesinos was videoed bribing opposition legislators. Fujimori's position was irrevocably damaged, and he resigned in November, having fled to Japan. Fresh presidential and legislative elections in April 2001 were won by populist Alejandro Toledo and his Peru Posible party.

CHRONOLOGY

Francisco Pizarro's arrival in 1532 during a war of succession between two Inca rulers marked the start of the Spanish colonization of Peru, and the end of the Inca empire.

- **1821** Independence proclaimed in Lima after its capture by Argentine liberator, José de San Martín, who had just freed Chile.
- **1824** Spain suffers final defeats at battles of Junín and Ayacucho by Simón Bolívar and General Sucre, liberators of Venezuela and Colombia.
- **1836–1839** Peru and Bolivia joined in short-lived confederation.
- **1866** Peruvian–Spanish War.
- **1879–1884** War of the Pacific. Chile defeats Peru and Bolivia. Peru loses territory in south.
- **1908** Augusto Leguía y Salcedo's dictatorial rule begins.
- **1924** Dr. Víctor Raúl Haya de la Torre founds nationalist APRA in exile in Mexico.
- **1930** Leguía ousted. APRA moves to Peru as first political party.
- **1931–1945** APRA banned.
- **1939–1945** Moderate, pro-US civilian government.
- **1948** Gen. Manuel Odría takes power. APRA banned again.
- **1956** Civilian government restored.
- **1962–1963** Two military coups.
- **1963** Election of Fernando Belaúnde Terry. Land reform, but military used to suppress communist-inspired insurgency.

P

CHRONOLOGY *continued*

- **1968** Military junta takes over. Attempts to alleviate poverty. Large-scale nationalizations.
- **1975–1978** New right-wing junta.
- **1980** Belaúnde reelected. Maoist *Sendero Luminoso* (Shining Path) begins armed struggle.
- **1981–1998** Border war with Ecuador over Cordillera del Cóndor, given to Peru by a 1942 protocol. Ecuador wants access to Amazon.
- **1982** Deaths and "disappearances" start to escalate as army cracks down on guerrillas and narcotics.
- **1985** Electoral win for left-wing APRA under Alán García Pérez.
- **1987** Peru bankrupt. Plans to nationalize banks blocked by new *Libertad* movement led by writer Mario Vargas Llosa.
- **1990** Over 3000 political murders. Alberto Fujimori, an independent, elected president on anticorruption platform. Severe austerity program.
- **1992–95** Fujimori "self-coup." New constitution. Fujimori reelected.
- **1996–1997** Left-wing Tupac Amarú guerrillas seize hundreds of hostages at Japanese ambassador's residence in four-month siege.
- **2000** November, Fujimori resigns amid corruption scandal despite having won controversial third term in May; seeks refuge in Japan.
- **2001** Fresh presidential elections, won by Alejandro Toledo in run-off against García.

WORLD AFFAIRS

Joined UN in 1945

AP | AmCC | NAM | OAS | RG

Cooperation with the USA, the main source of aid, extends to the war on cocaine, although Peru remains one of the world's largest coca producers. Reported incursions by guerrillas, paramilitaries, and drug-traffickers make the security of the border with Colombia a problem. Membership of the Andean Pact trade bloc offers the prospect of closer links with MERCOSUR.

AID

Recipient

$452m (receipts) | Down 10% in 1999

The USA mostly aids anti-narcotics work. $1.3 billion in recent loans from the IDB, the World Bank, and Japan were conditional on specific health and educational targets being met and progress on privatizations. State management of aid has been criticized.

DEFENSE

Compulsory military service

$888m | Down 12% in 1999

In no other country in Latin America did a president have so much control over the armed forces. The military, in power from 1968 to 1980, supported President Fujimori's 1992 presidential coup. A quarter of national territory remained under states of emergency until early 2000, despite the defeat of the *Sendero Luminoso* guerrillas. Fujimori's control over promotions and the National Intelligence Service (SIN) guaranteed a loyal armed forces leadership. After his resignation and the dissolution of the SIN in late 2000, the interim government moved to cut back military influence and removed key officers. The 1998 peace accord with Ecuador rankled with sections of the military command. The US military advises on anti-drug programs.

PERUVIAN ARMED FORCES

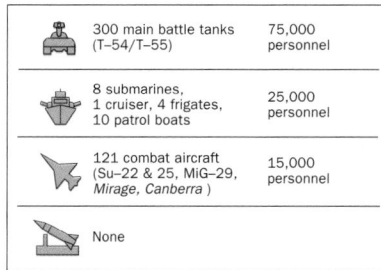

Army	300 main battle tanks (T-54/T-55)	75,000 personnel
Navy	8 submarines, 1 cruiser, 4 frigates, 10 patrol boats	25,000 personnel
Air force	121 combat aircraft (Su-22 & 25, MiG-29, *Mirage, Canberra*)	15,000 personnel
Missiles	None	

ECONOMICS

Inflation 31% p.a. (1990–1999)

$53.7bn | 3.5120–3.5268 new soles

SCORE CARD

World GNP Ranking	46th
GNP per Capita	$2130
Balance of Payments	$-3.8bn
Inflation	3.5%
Unemployment	8%

EXPORTS

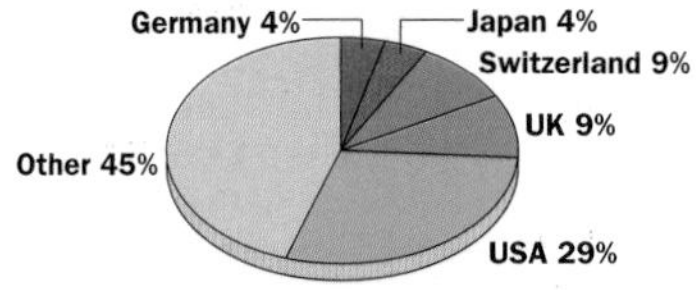
Germany 4%
Japan 4%
Switzerland 9%
UK 9%
Other 45%
USA 29%

IMPORTS

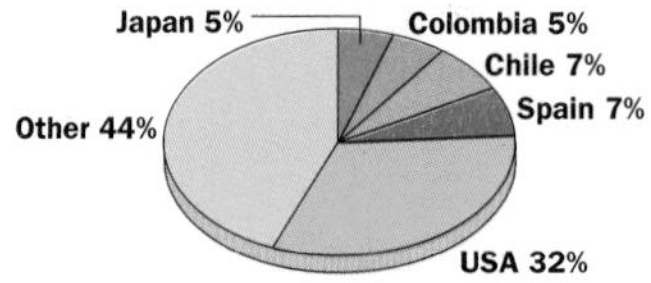
Japan 5%
Colombia 5%
Chile 7%
Spain 7%
Other 44%
USA 32%

ECONOMIC PERFORMANCE INDICATOR

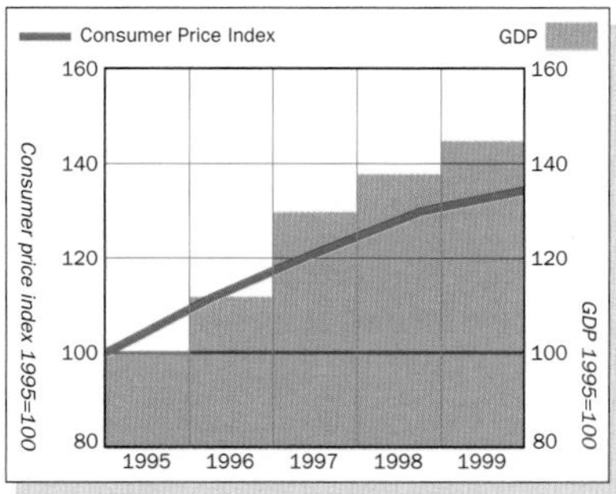
Consumer Price Index
GDP
160
140
120
100
80
Consumer price index 1995=100
GDP 1995=100
1995
1996
1997
1998
1999

Strengths

Abundant mineral resources, including oil. Rich fish stocks in the Pacific. Wide climatic variation, allowing diverse and productive agriculture; cotton and coffee are important. Well-developed textile industry.

Weaknesses

Over-dependence on metals and commodities whose fluctuating prices undermine trade and investment. Stalled privatization. Corruption and poor infrastructure deterring investment. Weak banks.

Profile

Wealth and economic activity in Peru are largely confined to the cities of the coastal plain. The inhabitants of the Andean uplands are subsistence farmers or coca producers.

Peru's strict fiscal and monetary policy continued under Fujimori. In 1998, three external shocks – the disruption of fishing by El Niño-generated storms, the Asian economic crises, and Russian-provoked turmoil in emerging markets – hit growth hard, as did depressed world commodity prices. In 1999 another three-year loan package was arranged with the IMF.

New president Alejandro Toledo has declared that he wants an "all-out war on poverty."

PERU : MAJOR BUSINESSES

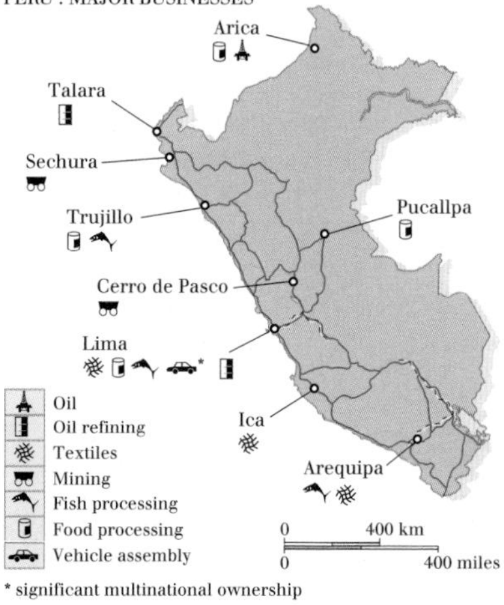
Arica
Talara
Sechura
Trujillo
Pucallpa
Cerro de Pasco
Lima
Ica
Arequipa
Oil
Oil refining
Textiles
Mining
Fish processing
Food processing
Vehicle assembly
0 400 km
0 400 miles

* significant multinational ownership

RESOURCES

Electric power 5.2m kw

7.88m tonnes

105,000 b/d (reserves 300,000,000 bbl)

14.4m sheep, 4.9m cattle, 2.8m pigs, 81.3m chickens

Oil, coal, lead, zinc, silver, iron, gold, copper

ELECTRICITY GENERATION

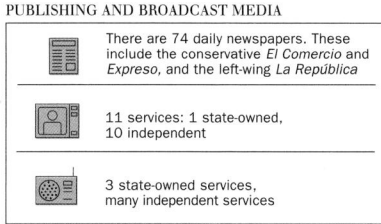

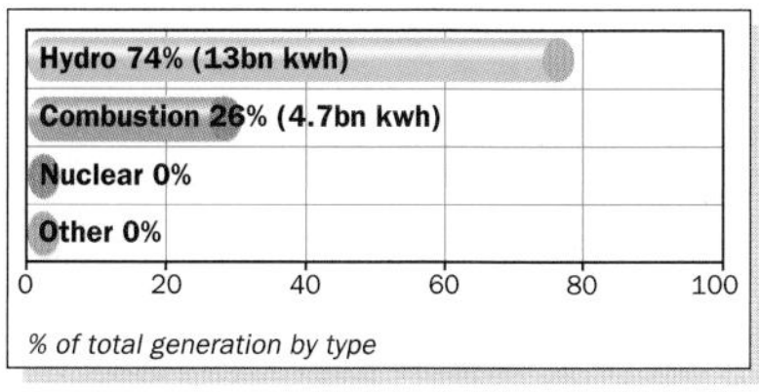
Hydro 74% (13bn kwh)
Combustion 26% (4.7bn kwh)
Nuclear 0%
Other 0%
0
20
40
60
80
100
% of total generation by type

Peru is an important exporter of copper and lead. Development of the huge Antamina copper and zinc deposit is under way. Development of the $3 billion Camisea hydrocarbon project is ongoing. The full extent of the large oil reserves still needs to be explored. A priority is the further development of hydroelectric power.

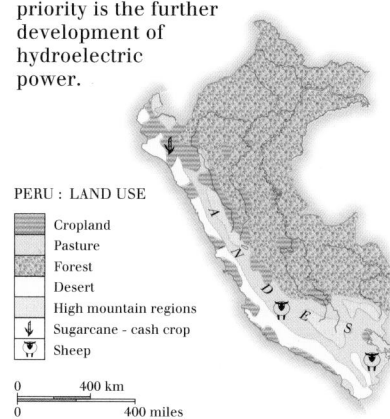

A N D E S

PERU : LAND USE

- Cropland
- Pasture
- Forest
- Desert
- High mountain regions
- Sugarcane - cash crop
- Sheep

0 400 km

0 400 miles

ENVIRONMENT

Sustainability rank: 38th

3%

1.2 tonnes per capita

ENVIRONMENTAL TREATIES

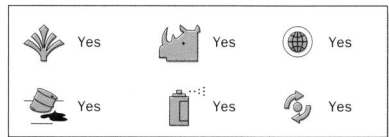

Yes	Yes	Yes
Yes	Yes	Yes

Environmentalists have long been concerned about coastal industrial pollution and the activities of the fishing industry. Over-fishing of anchovies almost resulted in their extinction in the 1970s. Today, attention has switched to the rising number of dolphins being caught in drift nets. Unchecked urban and industrial pollution, especially in Lima, is a major problem.

Environmentalists fear that Peru's and the USA's policy of using powerful air-sprayed herbicides to destroy coca crops is adding to river pollution in the Andes, where mining also causes severe environmental problems.

MEDIA

TV ownership medium

Daily newspaper circulation 84 per 1000 people

PUBLISHING AND BROADCAST MEDIA

There are 74 daily newspapers. These include the conservative *El Comercio* and *Expreso*, and the left-wing *La República*

11 services: 1 state-owned, 10 independent

3 state-owned services, many independent services

The chairman of TV Channel 10 and the editor of *Expreso* were videoed accepting bribes from Montesinos.

CRIME

Death penalty not used

19,236 prisoners

Down 81% 1992–1998

CRIME RATES

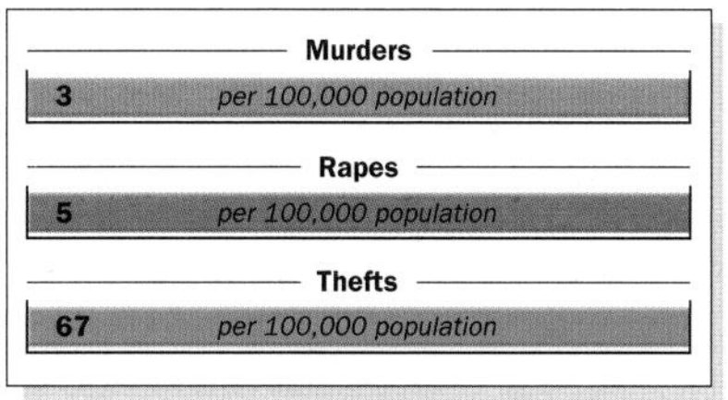
Murders
3
per 100,000 population
Rapes
5
per 100,000 population
Thefts
67
per 100,000 population

Kidnappings, murders, armed robberies, and drug-related crime remain serious problems, especially in Lima. Corruption is deep-seated in the police and security forces. Despite the near-destruction of the left-wing *Sendero Luminoso* guerrillas, main cities frequently have curfews and those who can afford it protect themselves with high-security homes and armed guards.

EDUCATION

School leaving age: 12

90%

657,586 students

THE EDUCATION SYSTEM

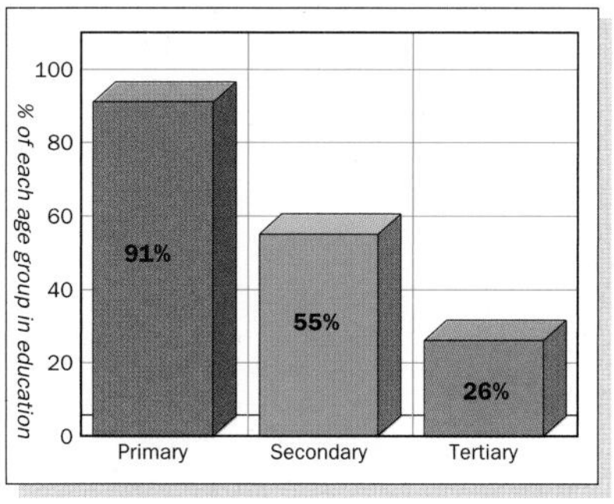
100
80
60
40
20
0
% of each age group in education
91%
55%
26%
Primary
Secondary
Tertiary

Education is based on the US system; spending has been declining. The provision of state education, especially for the poor, remains a major challenge. State and private universities are accessible to a small minority.

HEALTH

Welfare state health benefits

1 per 1111 people

Respiratory, heart, infectious, and parasitic diseases

The poor public health system almost collapsed in the 1980s. In many areas primary care is non-existent. Advanced treatment is available only to private patients in city clinics. Goiter, a thyroid abnormality, is widespread, especially in mountain areas. Infant mortality is rising due to social deprivation, diarrheal diseases, and tuberculosis. Malaria is again widespread, and cholera reached epidemic proportions in 1994. Thousands of poor women were forcibly sterilized in the late 1990s as part of a government program to lower the birthrate. Social welfare is compulsory, and benefits cover sickness, disability, and old age.

SPENDING

GDP/cap. increase

CONSUMPTION AND SPENDING

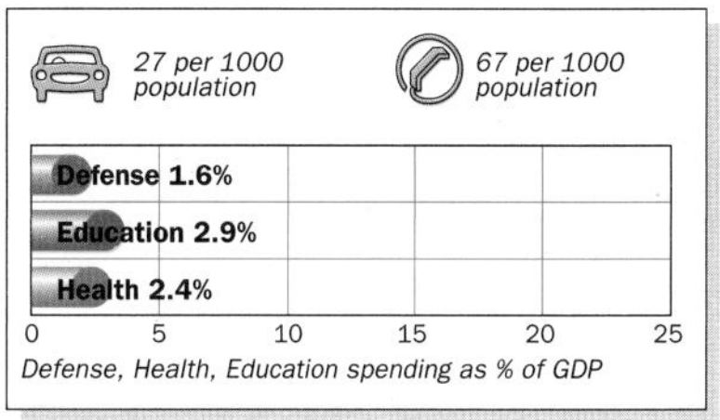
27 per 1000 population
67 per 1000 population
Defense 1.6%
Education 2.9%
Health 2.4%
0
5
10
15
20
25
Defense, Health, Education spending as % of GDP

Most wealth and power in Peru is still retained by old Spanish families. Indigenous peoples remain excluded from both. The rich live in a state of siege; a key status symbol is the number of armed guards and security cameras protecting family property. Overpopulation and rural migration accentuate poverty in Lima, where some 2.7 million people live in shanty towns, many of them lacking such basic utilities as running water and electricity. The UN estimates that over 30% of Peruvians live below the poverty line.

WORLD RANKING

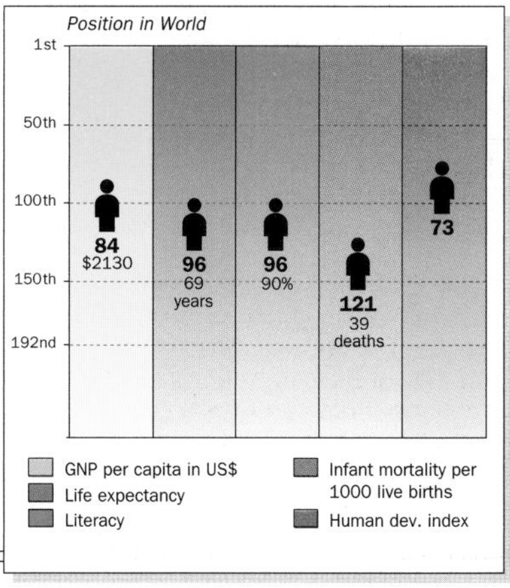
Position in World
1st
50th
100th
150th
192nd
84
$2130
96
69
years
96
90%
121
39
deaths
73
GNP per capita in US$
Life expectancy
Literacy
Infant mortality per 1000 live births
Human dev. index

P

PHILIPPINES

SOUTHEAST ASIA
China
Taiwan
PHILIPPINES
Malaysia
Asia

OFFICIAL NAME: Republic of the Philippines **CAPITAL:** Manila
POPULATION: 76 million **CURRENCY:** Philippine peso **OFFICIAL LANGUAGES:** English and Filipino

1946
1946
June 12
RP
+8
+63
.ph

LYING IN THE WESTERN Pacific Ocean, the Philippines is the world's second-largest archipelago after Indonesia. It comprises 7107 islands, of which 4600 are named and 1000 inhabited. There are three main island groupings: Luzon, Visayan, and the Mindanao and Sulu islands. Located on the Pacific "ring of fire," the country is subject to frequent earthquakes and volcanic activity. Economic growth outstripped population increase in the 1990s, until the 1997–1998 "Asian crisis," but efforts to build a stable democracy have been compromised by high-level corruption, leading to the ouster of President Estrada in 2001.

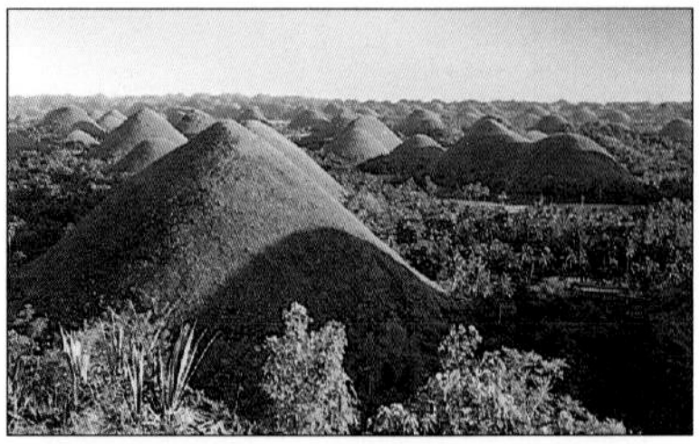

***Bohol Island** has over 1000 of these famous mounds, also known as "the chocolate hills."*

CLIMATE

Tropical monsoon/equatorial

WEATHER CHART

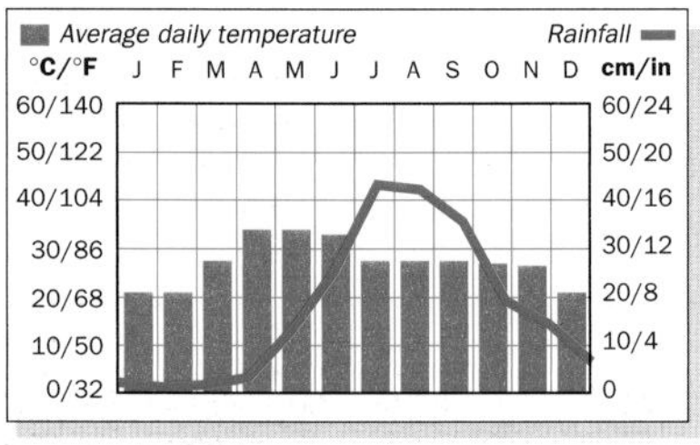
Average daily temperature
Rainfall
°C/°F
J F M A M J J A S O N D
cm/in
60/140
50/122
40/104
30/86
20/68
10/50
0/32
60/24
50/20
40/16
30/12
20/8
10/4
0

The Philippines is warm and humid all year. The rainy season lasts from June to October. Humidity falls from 85% in September to 71% in March.

TRANSPORTATION

Drive on right

Ninoy Aquino International, Manila
12.6m passengers

1726 ships
8.5m grt

THE TRANSPORTATION NETWORK

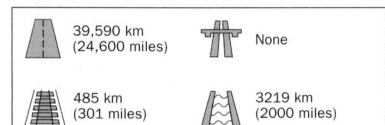

39,590 km (24,600 miles)	None
485 km (301 miles)	3219 km (2000 miles)

Basic infrastructure lacks investment and many main roads are in desperate need of repair. Chronic traffic congestion in Manila holds back economic growth.

Air travel is the only means of getting around the islands quickly. Philippines Airlines, privatized in 1992, has invested heavily in new aircraft and expanding its regional route network. Work began in 2000 on a spectacular new terminal at Manila's international airport, nearly trebling its capacity.

Subic Bay, a massive US naval base until 1992, is now being exploited as a commercial asset, thanks to its prime location. Opening on to the South China Sea, its deep natural harbor is being developed as a free port and enterprise zone. The Taiwanese are the biggest investors in this project.

TOURISM

Visitors : Population 1:35

2.2m visitors

Up 1% in 1999

MAIN TOURIST ARRIVALS

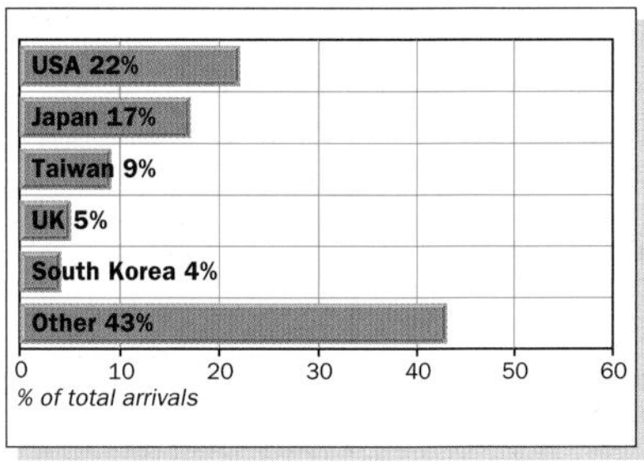
USA 22%
Japan 17%
Taiwan 9%
UK 5%
South Korea 4%
Other 43%
0
10
20
30
40
50
60
% of total arrivals

Tourism remains a smaller business in the Philippines than in the regional NICs. Dubious images conveyed by sex-tourism have become a liability as international pressure to end it intensifies, while Muslim secessionists have seized tourists on neighboring Malaysian islands as hostages. The tiny central island of Boracay is a popular resort, and Palawan retains most of its tropical rainforest and coral lagoons, although coral reefs elsewhere are badly damaged. The rice terraces of northern Luzon are another attraction.

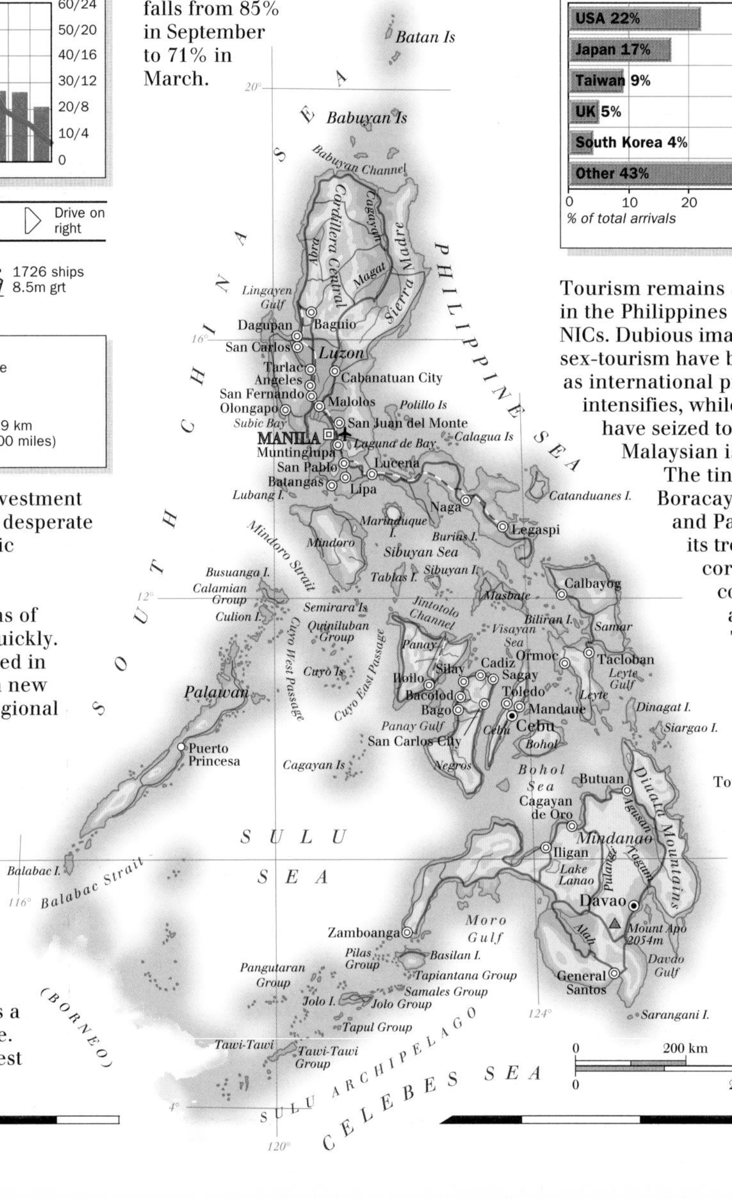
Batan Is
Babuyan Is
Babuyan Channel
SOUTH CHINA SEA
PHILIPPINE SEA
Cordillera Central
Cagayan
Sierra Madre
Abra
Magat
Lingayen Gulf
Dagupan
Baguio
San Carlos
Luzon
Tarlac
Angeles
Cabanatuan City
San Fernando
Olongapo
Malolos
Polillo Is
Subic Bay
San Juan del Monte
MANILA
Calagua Is
Muntinglupa
Laguna de Bay
San Pablo
Lucena
Batangas
Lipa
Lubang I.
Catanduanes I.
Naga
Marinduque I.
Burias I.
Legaspi
Mindoro Strait
Mindoro
Sibuyan Sea
Busuanga I.
Tablas I.
Sibuyan I.
Calamian Group
Culion I.
Masbate
Calbayog
Semirara Is
Jintotolo Channel
Quiniluban Group
Biliran I.
Samar
Cuyo West Passage
Visayan Sea
Panay
Ormoc
Tacloban
Cuyo Is
Silay
Cadiz
Leyte Gulf
Iloilo
Sagay
Bacolod
Toledo
Leyte
Palawan
Cuyo East Passage
Bago
Mandaue
Dinagat I.
Cebu
Siargao I.
Panay Gulf
San Carlos City
Puerto Princesa
Negros
Bohol
Cagayan Is
Bohol Sea
Butuan
Cagayan de Oro
Diuata Mountains
Agusan
Mindanao
SULU SEA
Iligan
Balabac I.
Balabac Strait
Lake Lanao
Davao
Zamboanga
Moro Gulf
Mount Apo 2954m
Pilas Group
Basilan I.
Davao Gulf
Pangutaran Group
Tapiantana Group
General Santos
Samales Group
Jolo I.
Jolo Group
Tapul Group
Sarangani I.
Tawi-Tawi
Tawi-Tawi Group
SULU ARCHIPELAGO
(BORNEO)
CELEBES SEA
20°
16°
12°
8°
4°
116°
120°
124°
N
0 200 km
0 200 miles

PHILIPPINES

Total Land Area : 298 170 sq. km (115 123 sq. miles)

POPULATION
over 1 000 000
over 500 000
over 100 000

LAND HEIGHT
2000m/6562ft
1000m/3281ft
500m/1640ft
200m/656ft
Sea Level

P

PEOPLE

Pop. density high

Filipino/Tagalog, Cebuano, Hiligaynon, Samaran, Ilocano, Bikol, English

255/km² (660/mi²)

THE URBAN/RURAL POPULATION SPLIT

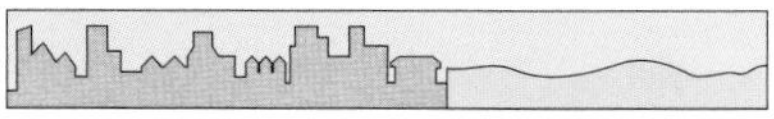
58%
42%

RELIGIOUS PERSUASION

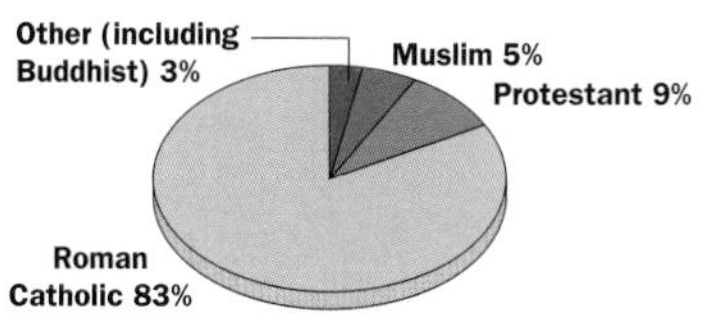
Other (including Buddhist) 3%
Muslim 5%
Protestant 9%
Roman Catholic 83%

ETHNIC MAKEUP

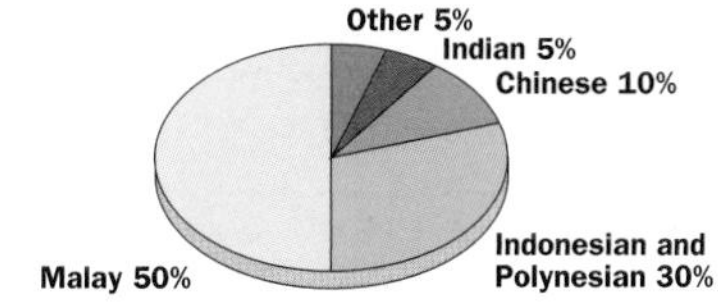
Other 5%
Indian 5%
Chinese 10%
Indonesian and Polynesian 30%
Malay 50%

POPULATION AGE BREAKDOWN

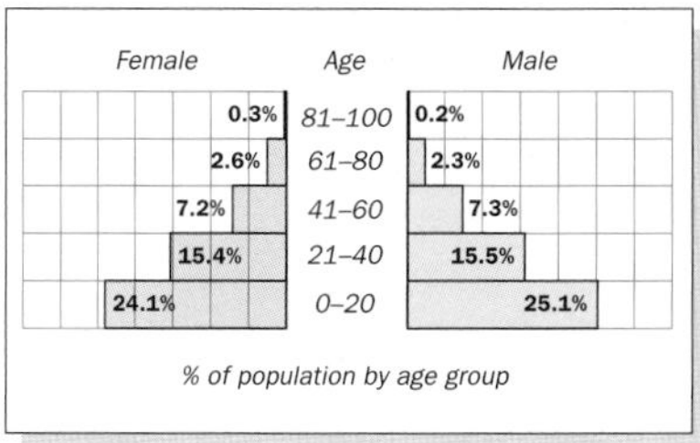
Female
Age
Male
0.3%
81–100
0.2%
2.6%
61–80
2.3%
7.2%
41–60
7.3%
15.4%
21–40
15.5%
24.1%
0–20
25.1%
% of population by age group

The Philippines encompasses more than 100 distinct ethnic groups. The national language, Filipino, is based on Tagalog, spoken by the largest of the various groups of Malay origin. Other Malay groups include Cebuano, Ilocan, Longgo, Bicolano, Waray, Pampangan, and Pangasinan. They are concentrated on the main island, Luzon, and are also a majority on Mindanao. Most Muslims live on Mindanao, but many are also found in the Sulu archipelago. The Chinese minority, which was well established by 1603, has remained significant in business and trade. More than 120 Chinese schools have ensured that it has retained a distinct identity.

There are also a number of cultural minorities who practice animist religions. They include the Ifugaos, Bontocks, Kalingas, and Ibalois on Luzon, the Manobo and Bukidnon on Mindanao, and the Mangyans on Palawan. Many of these groups speak Malayo-Polynesian dialects. Limited intermarriage with other peoples has meant that groups in the more remote regions have managed to retain their traditional ways of life.

The Philippines is the only Christian state in Asia; over 80% of Filipinos are Roman Catholics and the Church is the dominant cultural force in the country. It opposes state-sponsored family planning programs, which are designed to curb accelerating population growth.

Women have traditionally played a prominent part in Philippine public and professional life. Inheritance laws give them equal rights to men. Many go into politics, banking, and business, and in several professional sectors they form a majority.

POLITICS

Multiparty elections

L. House 2001/2004
U. House 2001/2004

President Gloria Macapagal Arroyo

AT THE LAST ELECTION

House of Representatives 222 seats

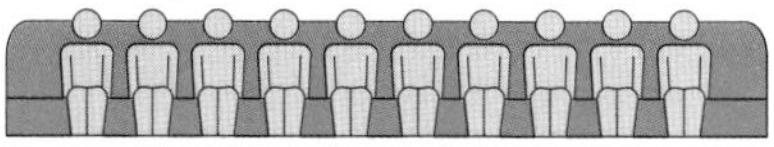

Results of the 2001 elections for the House of Representatives were unavailable, but the NUCD was thought to have won the largest number of seats

PP = People's Power Coalition, dominated by Lakas – National Union of Christian Democrats (**NUCD**)
PnM = Strength of the Masses coalition, dominated by Laban ng Masang Pilipino (**LAMP**) **Ind** = Independents

Senate 24 seats

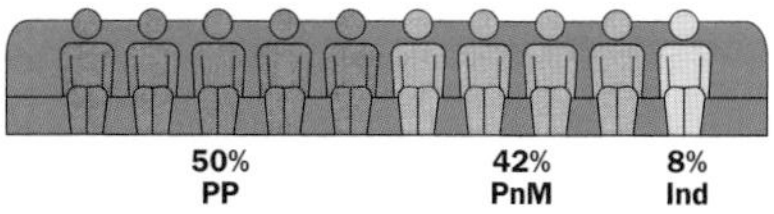
50% PP
42% PnM
8% Ind

The Philippines is a multiparty democracy.

MAIN POLITICAL ISSUES

Political stability

The downfall of the Marcos regime in 1986 through popular demonstration ensured a return to democracy. The subsequent two presidents passed on power smoothly to an elected successor, but flamboyant former film star Joseph Estrada was quickly mired in corruption scandals. Moves for his impeachment were overtaken by mass rallies in Manila. Forced from office in January 2001, he retained widespread support among the rural poor, questioning the legitimacy of Vice President Macapagal Arroyo's constitutional assumption of the presidency.

Communist and Muslim separatists

Communist and Muslim separatists have been fighting Manila-based governments for over 30 years, with more than 10,000 armed confrontations with rebels recorded by the army. Much of the support for secession has been fueled by the failure of successive governments to curb poverty.

Since 1992, the government has been seeking peace with all armed groups. The communist New People's Army (NPA), once regarded as a heroic army of the oppressed and as an alternative to traditional politics, has declined in significance, but launched new offensives in 2000. The Moro National Liberation Front (MNLF), representing secessionist Muslim rebels on Mindanao, signed a peace agreement in 1996. A militant breakaway Muslim Islamic Liberation Front (MILF) continued fighting, its clashes with troops forcing the government to abandon a massive irrigation project. Fighting reached a peak in 2000, but in mid-2001 the MILF joined the peace process.

PROFILE

The 21-year dictatorship of Ferdinand Marcos was shown by 1986 to have no popular legitimacy as "people power" massed in support of his opponent Corazon Aquino, who was declared the true winner of the presidential elections. Losing the backing of the USA, Marcos was forced into exile. Aquino succeeded in handing over power to Fidel Ramos through fair elections in 1992. His dependence on loose coalition arrangements in Congress created difficulties for the government's economic liberalization program. His successor in 1998, the populist Joseph Estrada of LAMP, was accused of links to a gambling syndicate, and impeachment proceedings began in late 2000. A repeat of the mass "people power" demonstrations of 1986 toppled him in 2001. Vice President Gloria Macapagal Arroyo of the NUCD led the united political opposition to Estrada, and was appointed to the presidency on his downfall.

***Joseph Estrada,** film-star-turned-president, ousted in 2001.*

***Gloria Arroyo,** succeeded Estrada in a popular uprising.*

P

WORLD AFFAIRS

Joined UN in 1945

APEC ASEAN G24 NAM WTO

Regional relationships are paramount, despite sporadic frictions with Malaysia. Manila's claim to the Spratly Islands conflicts notably with Beijing's. The recent Visiting Forces Agreement with the USA, and resumption of US naval visits since 1999, have improved security cooperation.

CHRONOLOGY

Ceded to the USA by Spain in 1898, the Philippines became self-governing in 1935. After Japanese occupation in World War II, in 1946 it became an independent republic.

- ❑ **1965** Ferdinand Marcos president.
- ❑ **1969–1972** Marcos reelected amid malpractice allegations.
- ❑ **1972** Marcos declares martial law. Opposition leaders arrested, National Assembly suspended, press censored.
- ❑ **1977** Ex-Liberal Party leader Benigno Aquino sentenced to death. Criticism forces Marcos to delay execution.
- ❑ **1978** Elections won by Marcos's New Society (KBL). He is named president and prime minister.
- ❑ **1980** Aquino allowed to travel to USA for medical treatment.
- ❑ **1981** Martial law ends. Marcos reelected president by referendum.
- ❑ **1983** Aquino shot dead on return from USA. Inquiry blames military conspiracy.
- ❑ **1986** USA compels presidential election. Result disputed. Army rebels led by General Fidel Ramos, and public demonstrations, bring Aquino's widow, Corazon, to power. Marcos exiled to USA.
- ❑ **1987** New constitution. Aquino-led coalition wins Congress elections.
- ❑ **1988** Marcos and wife Imelda indicted for massive racketeering.
- ❑ **1989** Marcos dies in USA.
- ❑ **1990** Imelda Marcos acquitted of fraud charges in USA. Earthquake in Baguio City leaves 1600 dead.
- ❑ **1991** Mt. Pinatubo erupts. USA leaves Clark Air Base.
- ❑ **1992** General Fidel Ramos wins presidential election. USA withdraws from Subic Bay base.
- ❑ **1996** Peace agreement with Muslim MNLF secessionists.
- ❑ **1998** Joseph Estrada president.
- ❑ **1999** First execution in 22 years.
- ❑ **2000** Death penalty suspended.
- ❑ **2001** Estrada overthrown by popular protest. Gloria Macapagal Arroyo assumes presidency. August, Muslim MILF joins peace process.

AID

Recipient

$690m (receipts) | Up 14% in 1999

The Philippines' main bilateral aid donors are the USA and Japan. Many NGOs operate in the outlying islands. Large remittances are also received from Filipinos working overseas. In 1975, there were 40,000 of these overseas contract workers. By 2001 they numbered over five million.

DEFENSE

No compulsory military service

$1.63bn | Up 7% in 1999

The military retains political influence. In early 1999 Estrada's government announced its intention to modernize the armed forces.

Until the early 1990s, a strong US military presence helped maintain defense spending below regional levels. Clark base was vacated in 1991 following the eruption of Mt. Pinatubo. Subic Bay, the naval facility, was relinquished by the USA in 1992.

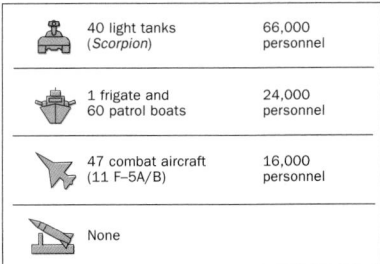

PHILIPPINE ARMED FORCES

40 light tanks (*Scorpion*)	66,000 personnel
1 frigate and 60 patrol boats	24,000 personnel
47 combat aircraft (11 F-5A/B)	16,000 personnel
None	

ECONOMICS

Inflation 8.6% p.a. (1990–1999)

$78bn | 40.3–50.0 Philippine pesos

SCORE CARD

- ❑ World GNP Ranking 41st
- ❑ GNP per Capita $1050
- ❑ Balance of Payments $7.91bn
- ❑ Inflation 6.7%
- ❑ Unemployment 10%

EXPORTS

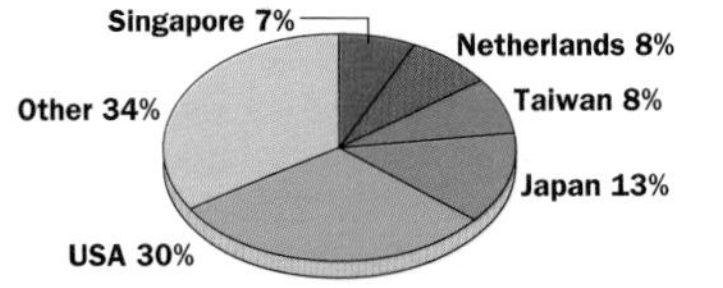
Singapore 7%
Netherlands 8%
Taiwan 8%
Japan 13%
USA 30%
Other 34%

IMPORTS

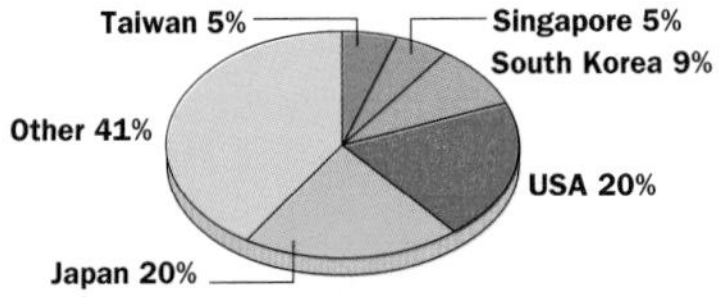
Taiwan 5%
Singapore 5%
South Korea 9%
USA 20%
Japan 20%
Other 41%

ECONOMIC PERFORMANCE INDICATOR

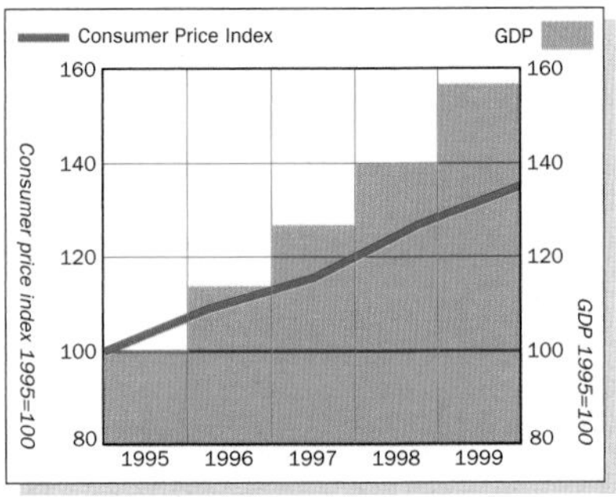
Consumer Price Index
GDP
Consumer price index 1995=100
GDP 1995=100
160
140
120
100
80
1995
1996
1997
1998
1999

Strengths

Now fully open to outside investment. Agricultural productivity rising. Strong pineapple and banana export industries. Substantial remittances from Filipinos working overseas.

Weaknesses

Power failures limit scope for expansion. Rudimentary infrastructure. Low domestic savings rates mean reliance on foreign finance. Low productivity in subsistence agriculture.

Profile

Once one of Asia's strongest economies, the Philippines has now fallen behind once much poorer countries such as Thailand, Malaysia, and South Korea. Around 50% of the rural population live on the poverty line, fueling many of the secessionist movements undermining the stability of successive governments.

The Ramos administration (1992–1998), backed by the IMF, deregulated the economy to encourage foreign investment, and tried to trim the power of the privately run monopolies whch form a major part of the economy. Raising per capita income to $1000 was achieved by 1995. Those living below the poverty line have fallen – officially – to under 30%. The objective of sustained economic growth receded dramatically when the whole region was hit by economic crisis in 1997. Ramos's successor, Estrada, made big populist promises but ran up a crippling budget deficit. Investor confidence plummeted amidst scandals and political crisis, and in 2001 the new government put many projects on hold.

PHILIPPINES : MAJOR BUSINESSES

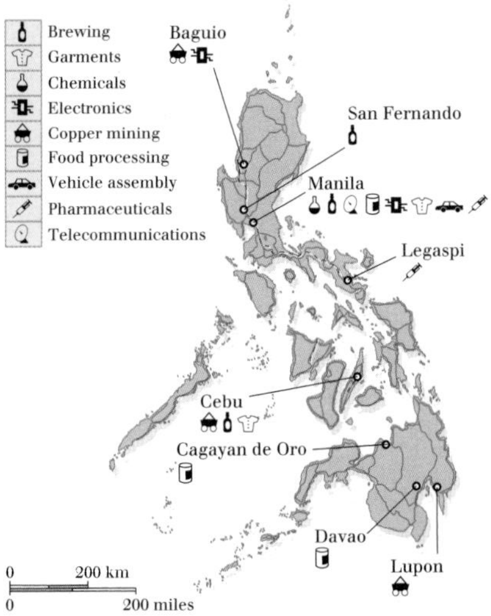
Brewing
Garments
Chemicals
Electronics
Copper mining
Food processing
Vehicle assembly
Pharmaceuticals
Telecommunications
Baguio
San Fernando
Manila
Legaspi
Cebu
Cagayan de Oro
Davao
Lupon
0 200 km
0 200 miles

RESOURCES

Electric power 11.1m kw

2.14m tonnes

862 b/d (reserves 204,908,760 bbl)

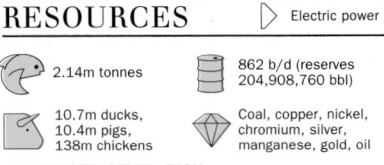

10.7m ducks, 10.4m pigs, 138m chickens

Coal, copper, nickel, chromium, silver, manganese, gold, oil

ELECTRICITY GENERATION

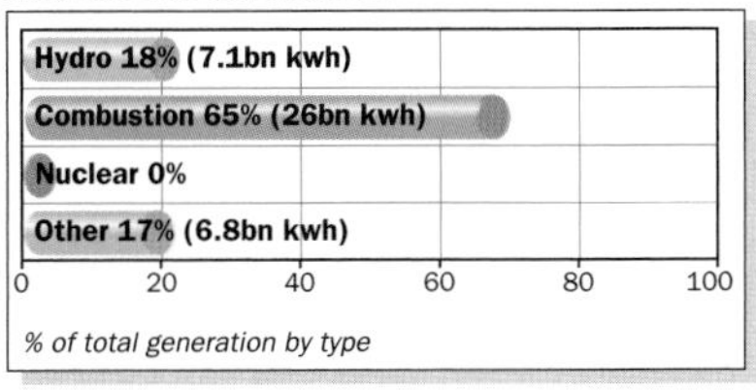

Hydro 18% (7.1bn kwh)
Combustion 65% (26bn kwh)
Nuclear 0%
Other 17% (6.8bn kwh)
0 20 40 60 80 100
% of total generation by type

The Philippines is the world's biggest supplier of refractory chrome. Copper is also a significant export. Substantial gold reserves have been mined since 1996. However, more than 90% of mineral potential remains undeveloped. Oil production off Palawan began in 1979. The Philippines is the world's second-biggest user of geothermal power after the USA. Almost 25% of electricity on Luzon is provided by this method. In 1989, timber exports were halted, although illegal logging continues to cause deforestation.

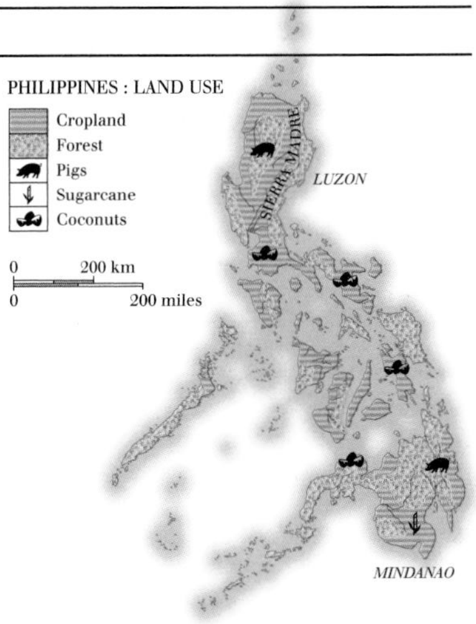

PHILIPPINES : LAND USE
Cropland
Forest
Pigs
Sugarcane
Coconuts
0 200 km
0 200 miles
SIERRA MADRE
LUZON
MINDANAO

ENVIRONMENT

Sustainability rank: 112th

5% (1% partially protected)

1.1 tonnes per capita

ENVIRONMENTAL TREATIES

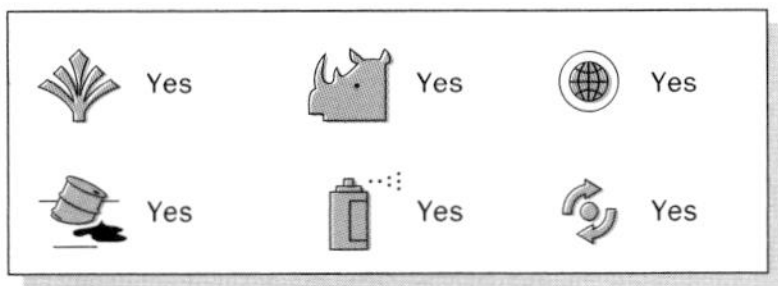

Yes
Yes
Yes
Yes
Yes
Yes

The environment has become a major issue in the Philippines. Most of the tropical rainforest has been destroyed, except for pockets such as the island of Palawan. Fishermen have dynamited unique coral habitats, and continue to use cyanide and muro-ami techniques to increase the size of their catches.

The government recognizes the costs of environmental damage, as soil run-off silts rivers and reduces the power generated by hydroelectric dams, and fast-depleting coral habitats reduce the attraction of the Philippines for tourists.

Logging has been banned, but enforcement is difficult; many loggers have their own private armies. In addition, continued use of slash and burn farming has aided deforestation.

MEDIA

TV ownership medium

Daily newspaper circulation 82 per 1000 people

PUBLISHING AND BROADCAST MEDIA

There are 47 daily newspapers. The most influential are the *Philippine Star* and the *Philippine Daily Globe*

7 services: 1 state-owned, 6 independent

17 services

The lifting of censorship following Corazon Aquino's election in 1986 led to a burgeoning of the media. As well as the national press, there are more than 250 regional newspapers in local dialects. State TV and radio broadcast in English and Filipino. Four independent television stations serve Metro Manila.

CRIME

Death penalty used

17,843 prisoners

Down 39% 1990–1994

CRIME RATES

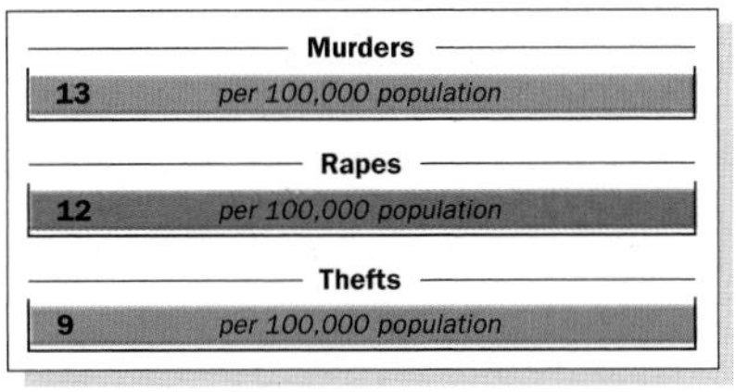

Murders
13 per 100,000 population
Rapes
12 per 100,000 population
Thefts
9 per 100,000 population

The death penalty, reinstated in 1993, was suspended again in 2000. Abductions of tourists from neighboring Malaysian islands made world news in April 2000.

EDUCATION

School leaving age: 12

95%

2.02m students

THE EDUCATION SYSTEM

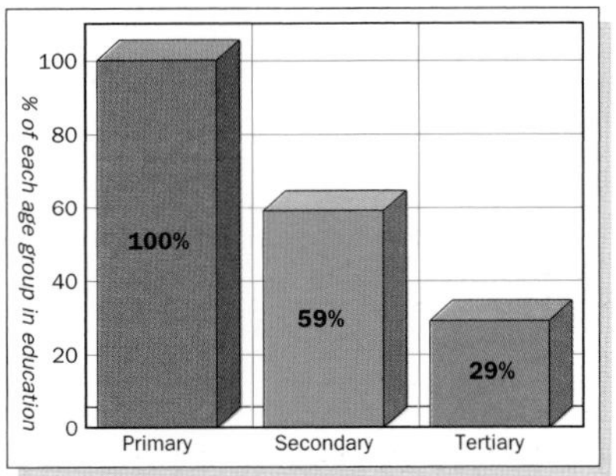

100
80
60
40
20
0
% of each age group in education
100%
59%
29%
Primary
Secondary
Tertiary

The Philippines has one of the highest literacy rates among developing countries. The education system is based on the US model, but with a higher proportion of private schools. The main teaching languages are English and Filipino/Tagalog.

Although there is a national curriculum up to age 15, sectarianism is common; the Chinese community has its own schools. Most colleges and universities are also run privately. The universities of San Carlos in Cebu city and Santo Tomas in Manila are Spanish colonial foundations, dating from 1595 and 1611 respectively.

HEALTH

No welfare state health benefits

1 per 10,000 people

Pneumonia, tuberculosis, violence, accidents, malaria, typhoid

Most general hospitals are privately run. Malaria, which was once a major problem, has been eradicated in all but remote areas. Poor sanitation and disease are common in the sprawling slums around Manila.

SPENDING

GDP/cap. increase

CONSUMPTION AND SPENDING

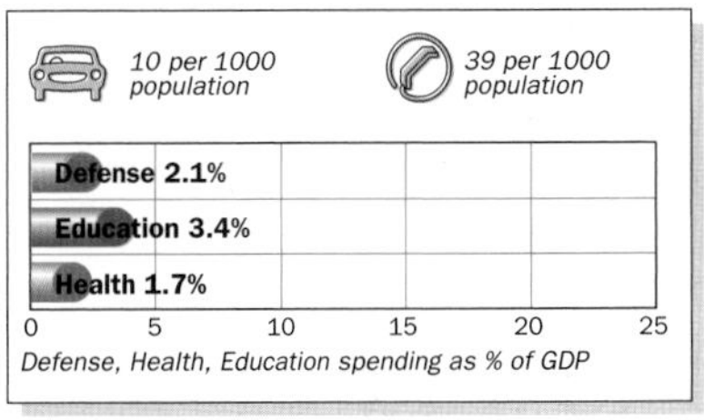

10 per 1000 population
39 per 1000 population
Defense 2.1%
Education 3.4%
Health 1.7%
0 5 10 15 20 25
Defense, Health, Education spending as % of GDP

The contrast between extremes of wealth and poverty is particularly marked. Wealth remains highly concentrated in a few select business families which are based in Manila.

WORLD RANKING

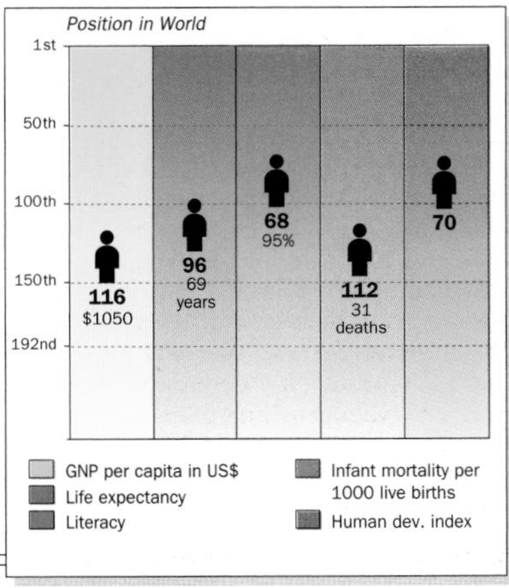

Position in World
1st
50th
100th
150th
192nd
116
$1050
96
69
years
68
95%
112
31
deaths
70
GNP per capita in US$
Life expectancy
Literacy
Infant mortality per 1000 live births
Human dev. index

P

POLAND

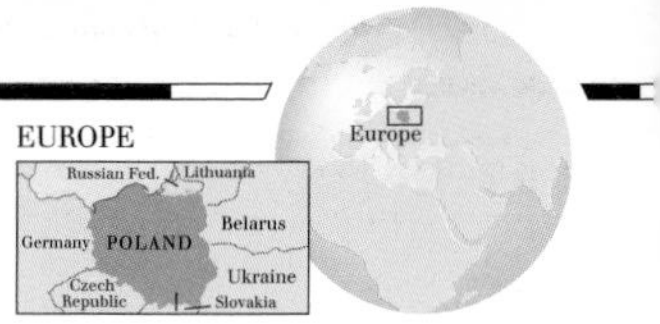
EUROPE
Europe
Russian Fed.
Lithuania
Belarus
Germany
POLAND
Czech Republic
Ukraine
Slovakia

OFFICIAL NAME: Republic of Poland **CAPITAL:** Warsaw
POPULATION: 38.8 million **CURRENCY:** Zloty **OFFICIAL LANGUAGE:** Polish

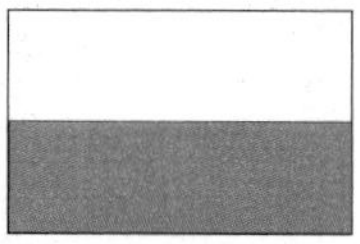

1918
1945
May 3
PL
+1
+48
.pl

LOCATED IN THE HEART OF EUROPE, Poland's low-lying plains extend from the Baltic shore in the north to the Tatra Mountains on its southern border with the Czech Republic and Slovakia. Since the collapse of communism, Poland has undergone massive social, economic, and political change. Opting for a radical form of economic "shock therapy" in the early 1990s to kick-start the switch to a market economy, it has experienced rapid growth, is one of the front runners in negotiations to join the EU, and has already been accepted as a member of NATO.

CLIMATE

Continental

WEATHER CHART

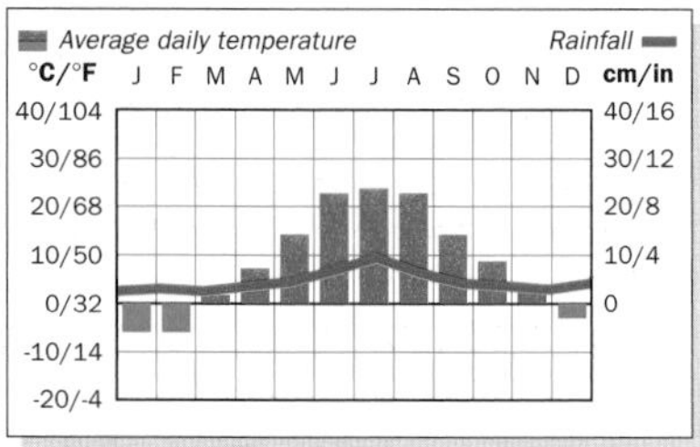
Average daily temperature
Rainfall
°C/°F
J F M A M J J A S O N D
cm/in
40/104
30/86
20/68
10/50
0/32
-10/14
-20/-4
40/16
30/12
20/8
10/4
0

Most of the country experiences a similar climate. Summers are hot, with heavy rainfall often accompanied by thunder. Winters are severe, with snow covering the ground on the southern mountains, for as much as 60–70 days in the east.

TRANSPORTATION

Drive on right

Okecie International, Warsaw
4m passengers

447 ships
1.4m grt

THE TRANSPORTATION NETWORK

249,966 km (155,321 miles)

268 km (167 miles)

22,891 km (14,224 miles)

3812 km (2369 miles)

The national airline LOT has increased its charter business as more middle-class Poles holiday abroad. Russian aircraft have all been replaced with Western models. A 15-year roads expansion program was begun in 1997. "Fast tram" systems for cities, and long-distance high-speed rail links, need major investment.

Telecommunications have been affected by the advent of mobile phones, and the privatization of Telekomunikacja Polska and the end of its monopoly on long-distance calls. The government plans to slim down the rail workforce and to commercialize and part-privatize Polish State Railways (PKP) by 2003.

The medieval administrative center of Lublin lies in Poland's southeastern agricultural heartland.

TOURISM

Visitors : Population 1:2.2

17.4m visitors

Down 3% in 2000

MAIN TOURIST ARRIVALS

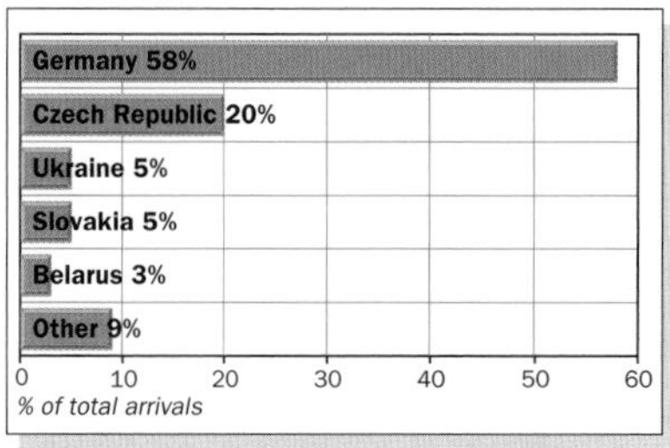
Germany 58%
Czech Republic 20%
Ukraine 5%
Slovakia 5%
Belarus 3%
Other 9%
0 10 20 30 40 50 60
% of total arrivals

Despite environmental problems, Poland is renowned for its skiing and hiking, especially in the Tatra Mountains. Kraków's medieval core has been preserved, while Toruń has restored its historic German Hanseatic buildings.

Warsaw's historic center has been reconstructed following the destruction of 80% of it by the German army in 1944. More hotels and restaurants are being opened.

Poznań has exploited its location between Warsaw and Berlin to create an international exhibition and business convention industry.

Airlines have increased their flights from the West to take advantage of the country's tourist potential.

PEOPLE

Pop. density medium

Polish

127/km² (330/mi²)

THE URBAN/RURAL POPULATION SPLIT

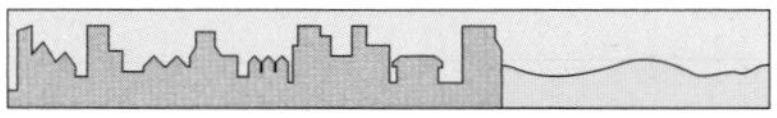
65%
35%

RELIGIOUS PERSUASION

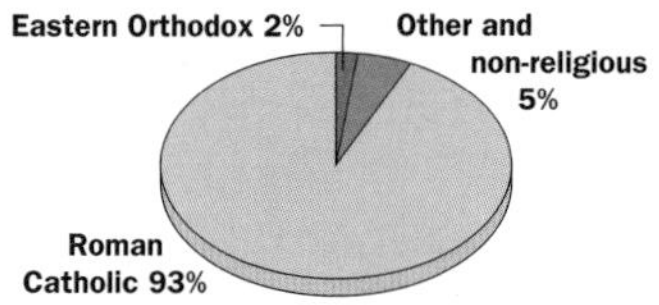
Eastern Orthodox 2%
Other and non-religious 5%
Roman Catholic 93%

ETHNIC MAKEUP

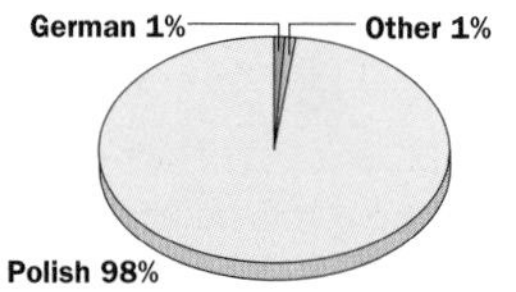
German 1%
Other 1%
Polish 98%

Poland has a strongly Roman Catholic population, and there is little ethnic diversity. The Church believes that stronger links with the West, especially through joining the EU, will weaken its influence. Abortion is still a major issue, and attempts to liberalize the law in 1996 were overturned by the Constitutional Tribunal.

Some small ethnic groups have opened schools and cultural and religious centers. Others, particularly the Germans in Silesia, are becoming more assertive. Jews are still resentful of past discrimination, and there is some evidence of residual anti-Semitism at a high level. The site of the Auschwitz concentration camp, near Kraków, has caused conflict between Jews and Catholics.

Wealth disparities are small, although the growing wealth of the entrepreneurial class is causing tension. The major political parties on left and right agree on continuing economic reform.

Women are prominent policy makers. Hanna Suchocka was prime minister in 1992–1993.

POPULATION AGE BREAKDOWN

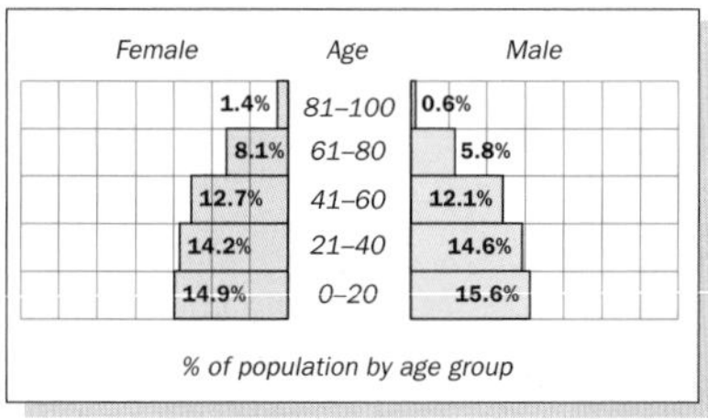
Female
Age
Male
1.4%
81–100
0.6%
8.1%
61–80
5.8%
12.7%
41–60
12.1%
14.2%
21–40
14.6%
14.9%
0–20
15.6%
% of population by age group

P

POLITICS

Multiparty elections

L. House 1997/2001
U. House 1997/2001

President Aleksander Kwasniewski

AT THE LAST ELECTION

Diet 460 seats

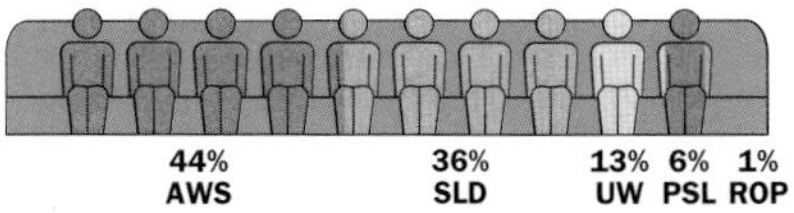
44%
AWS
36%
SLD
13%
UW
6%
PSL
1%
ROP

AWS = Solidarity Electoral Action **SLD** = Democratic Left Alliance **UW** = Freedom Union **PSL** = Polish Peasant Party **ROP** = Movement for Reconstruction of Poland **GM** = German Minority of Lower Silesia

Senate 100 seats

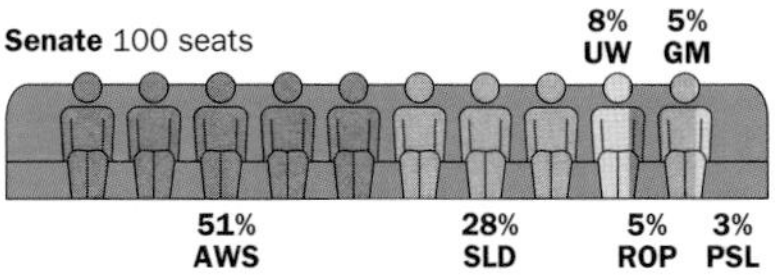
8%
UW
5%
GM
51%
AWS
28%
SLD
5%
ROP
3%
PSL

Since 1989, Poland has been a multiparty parliamentary democracy.

MAIN POLITICAL ISSUES

Coalition rule

Poland's emerging party system has been hindered by a superfluity of political factions, and sustaining coalitions has proved difficult. Parties are required to have at least 5% of the vote in order to gain a seat and 8% to be eligible to join a coalition government.

Church–state relations

The Catholic Church has been outspoken in its views on social and political policy. Debates over abortion, worship in schools, and values in the media have fueled a heated dialogue over the proper role of the Church. Abortion laws were eased in 1996 until the Constitutional Tribunal ruled that this move was unconstitutional.

PROFILE

From 1993 until 1997, successive governments were formed by the reformed communists of the SLD and the PSL, which pursued a policy of market reforms. Aleksander Kwasniewski, leader of the SLD, was elected president in 1995. More right-wing groups held sway for the 1997–2001 parliamentary term, with Jerzy Buzek, a member of Solidarity since its formation in 1980, as prime minister. His AWS alliance, a right-wing grouping with vocal Catholic and nationalist elements, formed a coalition with the liberal UW. A threatened split in early 1999 over controversial health service reforms was averted by the resignation of the health minister, but further contentious issues led to the resignation in May 2000 of the UW ministers. The AWS remained in office thereafter as a minority government. Buzek, who resisted pressure for early elections, came under attack from within the AWS itself. In May 2001 the Solidarity trade union wing voted to withdraw from politics.

Local government reform was introduced in July 1998. In subsequent local elections, the AWS won the most seats, but the SLD gained control of more of the provinces.

***Former president Lech Wałęsa.** He was awarded the Nobel Peace Prize in 1983.*

***President Aleksander Kwasniewski,** leader of the SLD, who was elected in 1995.*

WORLD AFFAIRS

Joined UN in 1945

CE | CEFTA | OECD | NATO | OSCE

Poland has good relations with the Baltic states and other countries of central Europe. It was admitted to NATO in 1999, and is among the region's "first wave" of applicants to join the EU, hoping for accession in 2004. A border treaty has been signed with Germany, recognizing the postwar border. The EU wants tighter controls along the eastern border with Belarus and Ukraine.

CHRONOLOGY

Poland has Europe's second-oldest written constitution. In 1795, it was partitioned between Austria-Hungary, Prussia, and Russia.

- ❑ **1918** Polish state recreated.
- ❑ **1921** Democratic constitution.
- ❑ **1926–1935** Pilsudski heads military coup. Nine years of authoritarian rule.
- ❑ **1939** Germany invades and divides Poland with Russia.
- ❑ **1941** First concentration camps built on Polish soil.
- ❑ **1944** Warsaw Uprising.
- ❑ **1945** Potsdam and Yalta Conferences set present borders and determine political allegiance to Soviet Union.
- ❑ **1947** Communists manipulate elections to gain power.

POLAND

Total Land Area : 304 460 sq. km (117 552 sq. miles)

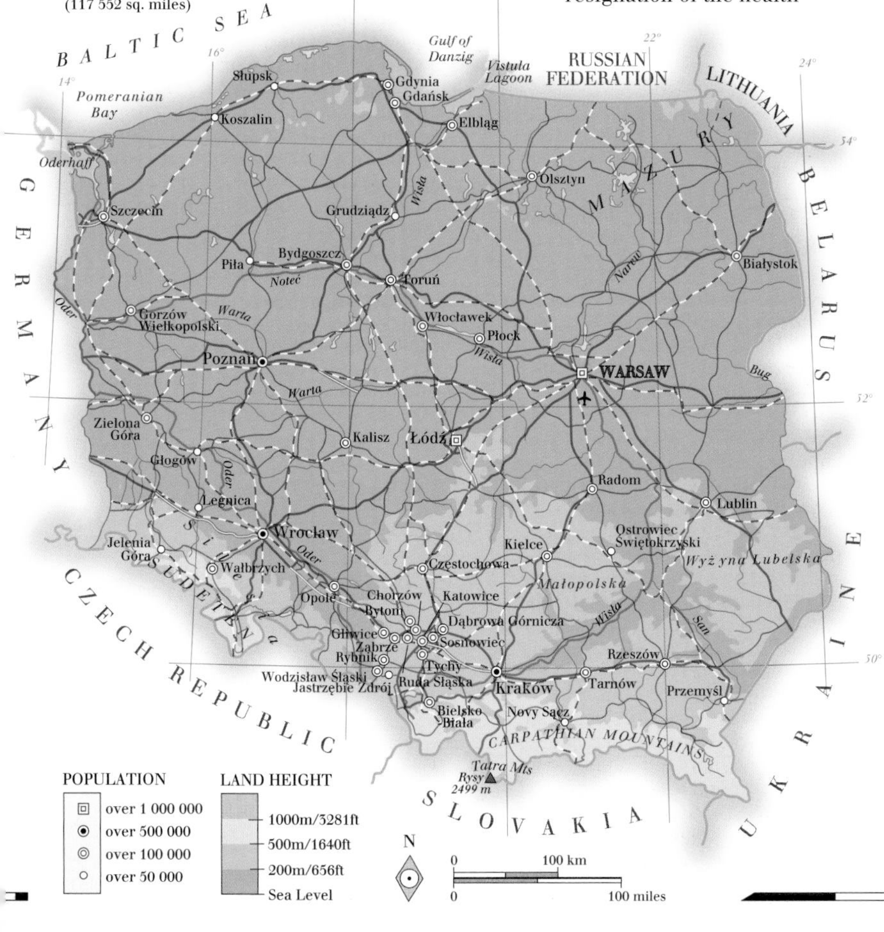
BALTIC SEA
Pomeranian Bay
Gulf of Danzig
Vistula Lagoon
RUSSIAN FEDERATION
LITHUANIA
BELARUS
UKRAINE
SLOVAKIA
CZECH REPUBLIC
GERMANY
Oderhaff
Słupsk
Gdynia
Gdańsk
Koszalin
Elbląg
Olsztyn
MAZURY
Szczecin
Grudziądz
Wisła
Bydgoszcz
Piła
Noteć
Toruń
Białystok
Narew
Gorzów Wielkopolski
Warta
Oder
Włocławek
Płock
Poznań
WARSAW
Bug
Zielona Góra
Kalisz
Łódź
Głogów
Radom
Legnica
Lublin
Wrocław
Jelenia Góra
Wałbrzych
SUDETEN
Kielce
Ostrowiec Świętokrzyski
Wyżyna Lubelska
Częstochowa
Małopolska
Opole
Chorzów
Bytom
Katowice
Gliwice
Zabrze
Rybnik
Dąbrowa Górnicza
Sosnowiec
San
Tychy
Rzeszów
Wodzisław Śląski
Jastrzębie Zdrój
Ruda Śląska
Kraków
Tarnów
Przemyśl
Bielsko Biała
Nowy Sącz
CARPATHIAN MOUNTAINS
Tatra Mts
Rysy 2499 m
POPULATION
over 1 000 000
over 500 000
over 100 000
over 50 000
LAND HEIGHT
1000m/3281ft
500m/1640ft
200m/656ft
Sea Level
N
0
100 km
100 miles

CHRONOLOGY *continued*

- **1956** More than 50 killed in rioting in Poznań.
- **1970** Food price increases lead to strikes and riots in the Baltic port cities. Hundreds are killed.
- **1979** Cardinal Karol Wojtyla of Kraków is elected pope and takes the name of John Paul II.
- **1980** Strikes force the government to negotiate with the Solidarity union. Resulting Gdańsk Accords grant the right to strike and to form free trade unions.
- **1981** Gen. Wojciech Jaruzelski becomes prime minister.
- **1981–1983** Martial law. Solidarity forced into underground existence. Many of its leaders, including Lech Waleşa, are interned.
- **1983** Waleşa awarded Nobel Peace Prize.
- **1986** Amnesty for political prisoners.
- **1987** Referendum rejects government austerity program.
- **1988** Renewed industrial unrest.
- **1989** Ruling party holds talks with Solidarity, which is relegalized. Partially free elections are held. First postwar noncommunist government formed.
- **1990** Launch of market reforms. Waleşa elected president.
- **1991** Free elections lead to fragmented parliament.
- **1992** Last Russian troops leave.
- **1993** Elections. Reformed communists head coalition government.
- **1994** Launch of mass privatization.
- **1995** Leader of reformed communists Aleksander Kwasniewski is elected president.
- **1996** Historic Gdańsk shipyard declared bankrupt and closed down.
- **1997** April, Parliament finally adopts new postcommunist constitution. September, legislative elections end former communist majority with big swing to AWS coalition. December, EU agrees to open membership negotiations.
- **1999** Joins NATO.
- **2000** AWS in minority government.
- **2001** Elections called for September.

AID

Recipient

$984m (receipts) | Up 54% 1997–1999

Large-scale aid for economic transformation was a phenomenon of the early 1990s. The IMF, the EBRD, and the EU all supported Poland's stabilization and reform program. EU aid now focuses on helping Poland to prepare to meet the environmental and other standards required of its members.

DEFENSE

Compulsory military service

$3.24bn | Down 7% in 1999

Poland joined NATO in March 1999. Its standing army is the largest in Europe after Russia's, and there are also large paramilitary units, including border guards. A 15-year program to modernize the armed forces was introduced by the government in 1997. A civilian alternative to military service was first offered in 1998, and military service was reduced from 18 months to a year from 1999.

POLISH ARMED FORCES

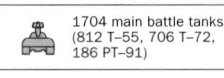

1704 main battle tanks (812 T–55, 706 T–72, 186 PT–91)	132,750 personnel
3 submarines, 2 frigates, 1 destroyer, and 25 patrol boats	16,860 personnel
267 combat aircraft (114 MiG–21, 25 MiG–23, 22 MiG–29, 99 Su–22)	46,200 personnel
None	

ECONOMICS

Inflation 25% p.a. (1990–1999)

$157bn | 4.1400–4.1325 zlotys

SCORE CARD

World GNP Ranking	25th
GNP per Capita	$4070
Balance of Payments	$–6.9bn
Inflation	7.3%
Unemployment	11%

EXPORTS

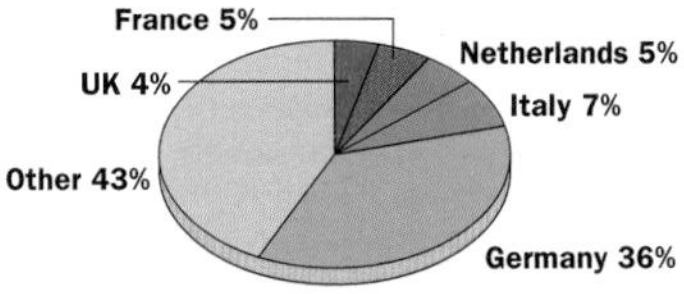
France 5%
Netherlands 5%
UK 4%
Italy 7%
Other 43%
Germany 36%

IMPORTS

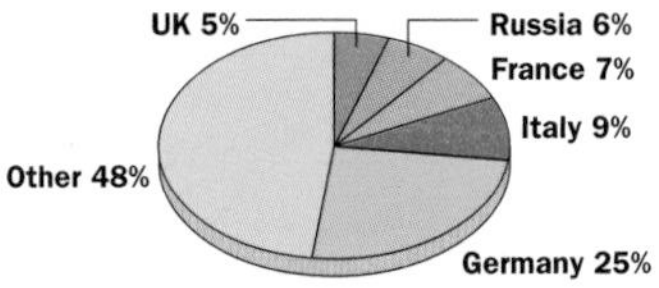
UK 5%
Russia 6%
France 7%
Italy 9%
Other 48%
Germany 25%

ECONOMIC PERFORMANCE INDICATOR

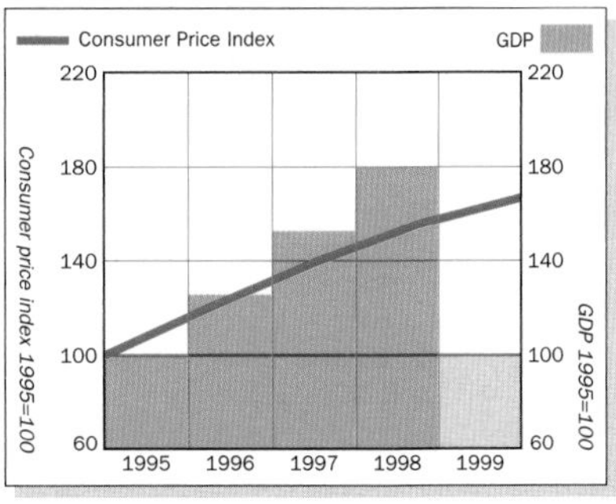
Consumer Price Index
GDP
220
180
140
100
60
Consumer price index 1995=100
GDP 1995=100
1995
1996
1997
1998
1999

Strengths
Restructuring of loss-making coal industry began in 1998. Successful privatizations accelerated again in late 1990s. High rates of foreign investment. Modernization of electricity supply and oil refining. Dynamic car industry.

Weaknesses
Agriculture suffers from lack of investment, tiny farms, and overmanning. Compensation for communist-era property expropriations unresolved. Steel, mining, shipbuilding, energy, and chemicals industries not competitive.

Profile
After a decade of economic crisis, the postcommunist government in 1990 drove through the most determined plan in the whole region to make the transition to a market economy. Most prices were freed, trade was opened and the zloty was made convertible. Economic growth and foreign investment soared, especially after

Western creditors agreed to cancel half of the country's foreign debt in 1994. Poland now attracts more foreign capital than any other country in central and eastern Europe.

There are still large-scale heavy industrial plants left over from the communist era, but some have been converted or reorganized successfully. Many state farms have been liquidated, but agricultural efficiency is improving only slowly. 26% of the workforce is employed in farming.

Economic growth slowed at the end of the 1990s, but was back to 4% in 2000. Inflation and unemployment remained relatively high.

POLAND : MAJOR BUSINESSES

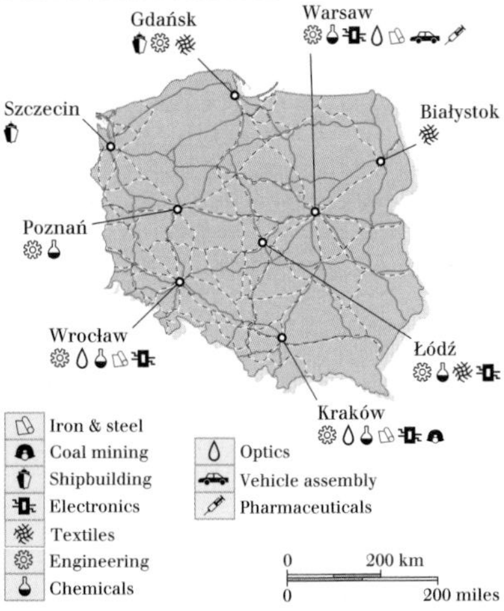
Gdańsk
Warsaw
Szczecin
Białystok
Poznań
Wrocław
Łódź
Kraków
Iron & steel
Coal mining
Shipbuilding
Electronics
Textiles
Engineering
Chemicals
Optics
Vehicle assembly
Pharmaceuticals
0
200 km
0
200 miles

P

RESOURCES

Electric power 29.5m kw

390,586 tonnes

5794 b/d (reserves 35,963,160 bbl)

6.2m cattle, 3.55m ducks, 49.5m chickens

Coal, copper, silver, sulfur, natural gas, lead, salt, iron

ELECTRICITY GENERATION

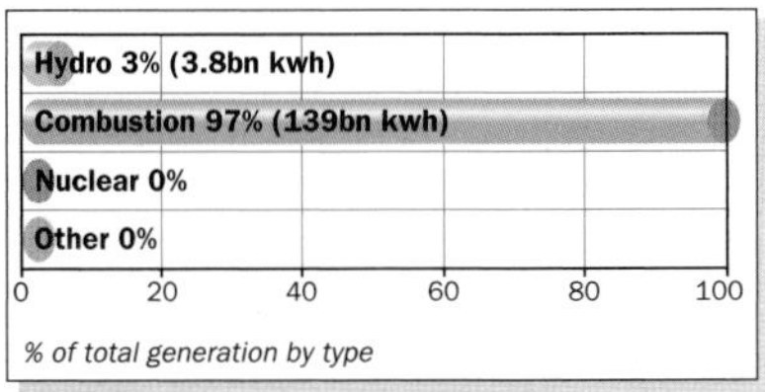
Hydro 3% (3.8bn kwh)
Combustion 97% (139bn kwh)
Nuclear 0%
Other 0%
0
20
40
60
80
100
% of total generation by type

Poland has significant quantities of coal, sulfur, copper, natural gas, silver, lead, and salt. It aims to achieve self-sufficiency and eventually to export fuels; plans are in place to privatize the fuel and energy industries. Coal supplies two-thirds of electricity generation. The amounts of copper ores mined is too small to affect world markets.

POLAND : LAND USE

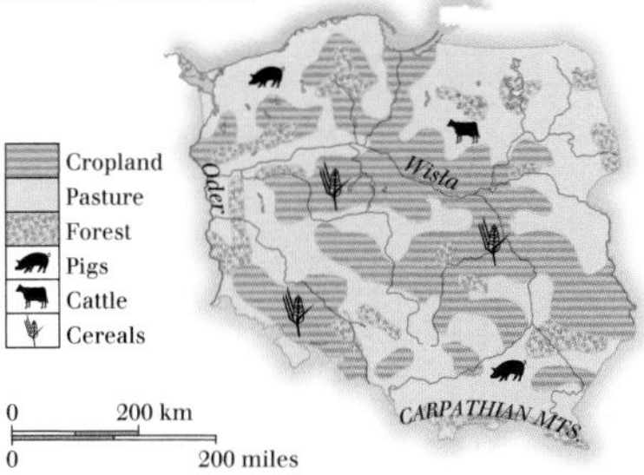
Cropland
Pasture
Forest
Pigs
Cattle
Cereals
Wisła
Oder
CARPATHIAN MTS
0
200 km
0
200 miles

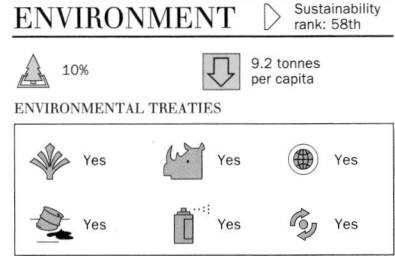

ENVIRONMENT

Sustainability rank: 58th

10%

9.2 tonnes per capita

ENVIRONMENTAL TREATIES

Yes Yes Yes

Yes Yes Yes

Pollution problems are serious, but improving. Upper Silesia and the Kraków area are still badly affected, but industry there only emits a third of the pollutants it emitted in 1990. Now that much heavy industry has been cleaned up or closed down, there is more concern about small factories, domestic coal fires, and the increased use of private cars.

Water pollution is a major problem, mainly from untreated sewage and industrial discharges. Rivers flowing into the Baltic are badly affected by nitrates and phosphates used in farming. Polish standards, themselves widely disregarded, need to be raised to meet EU minimum requirements.

MEDIA

TV ownership high

Daily newspaper circulation 113 per 1000 people

The constitution guarantees media freedom. *Gazeta Wyborcza*, set up by Solidarity in 1989, is still the leading daily, and its owners are expanding into other media. The head of election coverage at Polish Public Television (TVP) resigned in 2000, accused of favoring President Kwasniewski.

PUBLISHING AND BROADCAST MEDIA

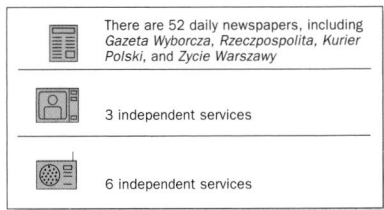

There are 52 daily newspapers, including *Gazeta Wyborcza, Rzeczpospolita, Kurier Polski*, and *Zycie Warszawy*

3 independent services

6 independent services

CRIME

Death penalty not used

65,819 prisoners

Up 19% 1996–1998

CRIME RATES

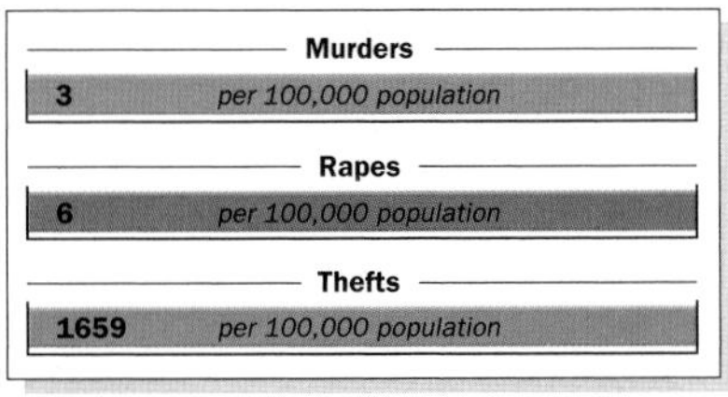
Murders
3 per 100,000 population
Rapes
6 per 100,000 population
Thefts
1659 per 100,000 population

Smuggling is the most significant problem, and Warsaw is a main center for this. Expensive cars are transferred eastward to Russia and drugs westward to Berlin. A National Remembrance Institute was set up in mid-2000 to investigate and prosecute the communist- and Nazi-era crimes of 1939–1989.

EDUCATION

School leaving age: 15

99%

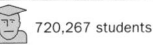

720,267 students

THE EDUCATION SYSTEM

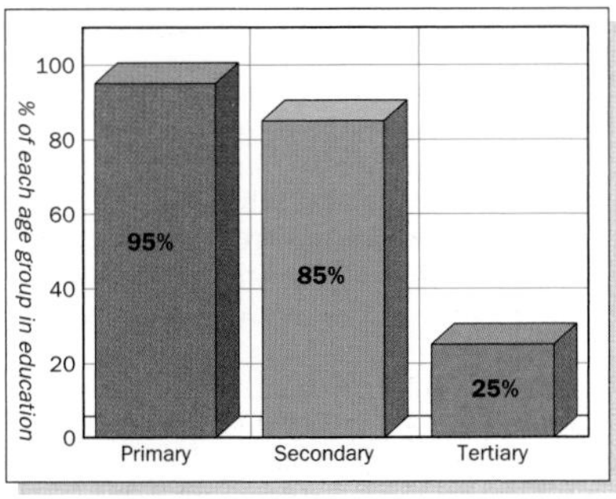
100
80
60
40
20
0
% of each age group in education
95%
85%
25%
Primary
Secondary
Tertiary

Education is free and compulsory for eight years from the age of seven. A standard curriculum is followed in all schools. Despite the high official literacy figures, a relatively large proportion of school-leavers still lack basic skills. At upper secondary level, exam-based selection separates the academic, technical, and vocational schools. Public spending on education fell in real terms in the 1990s. Since 1989 the Roman Catholic Church has been allowed to operate schools. Most of the almost 140 higher education institutions offer business-related courses.

HEALTH

Welfare state health benefits

1 per 435 people

Arteriosclerosis, heart disease, cancers, accidents

Fundamental reforms introduced in 1999 created a "market" health system, giving patients the right to choose where to go for treatment. Intended to be decentralized and less bureaucratic, the new system was confusing for some patients, with hospitals and doctors competing for business. Medical care is free for most people, but there are now a number of private health clinics.

SPENDING

GDP/cap. increase

CONSUMPTION AND SPENDING

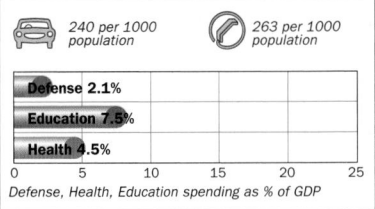

240 per 1000 population

263 per 1000 population

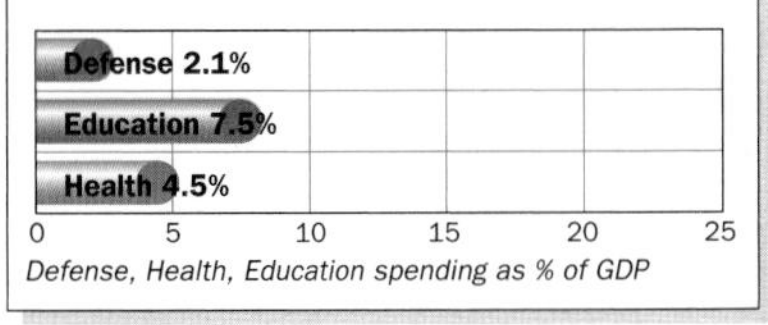
Defense 2.1%
Education 7.5%
Health 4.5%
0
5
10
15
20
25
Defense, Health, Education spending as % of GDP

Market reforms have led to some structural unemployment, and the inevitable hardship that this represents. More restructuring of heavy industry is planned. Pensioners have enjoyed benefits amounting to a higher percentage of GDP than in most countries, but state cutbacks are making private pensions more necessary.

P

WORLD RANKING

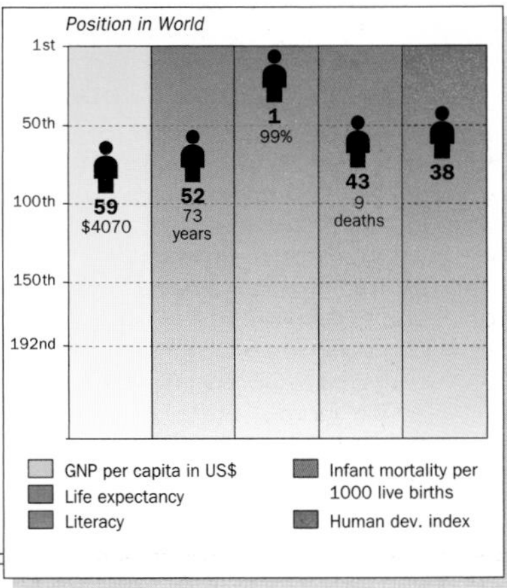
Position in World
1st
50th
100th
150th
192nd
59
$4070
52
73
years
1
99%
43
9
deaths
38
GNP per capita in US$
Life expectancy
Literacy
Infant mortality per 1000 live births
Human dev. index

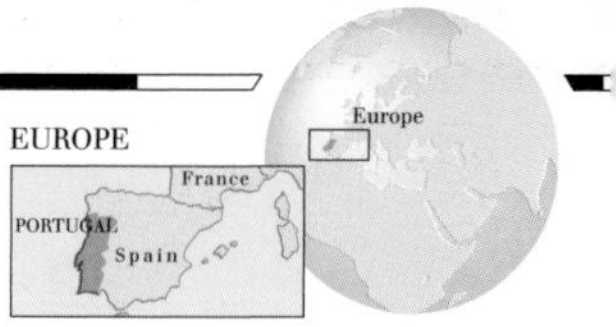
EUROPE
Europe
France
PORTUGAL
Spain

PORTUGAL

OFFICIAL NAME: Republic of Portugal **CAPITAL:** Lisbon **POPULATION:** 9.9 million
CURRENCY: Euro (escudo until 2002) **OFFICIAL LANGUAGE:** Portuguese

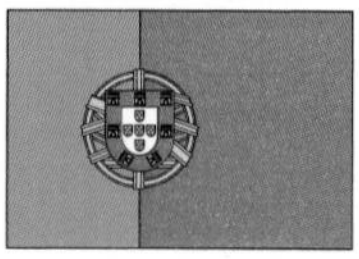

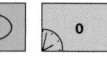

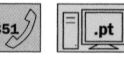

1640 | 1640 | June 10 | P | 0 | +351 | .pt

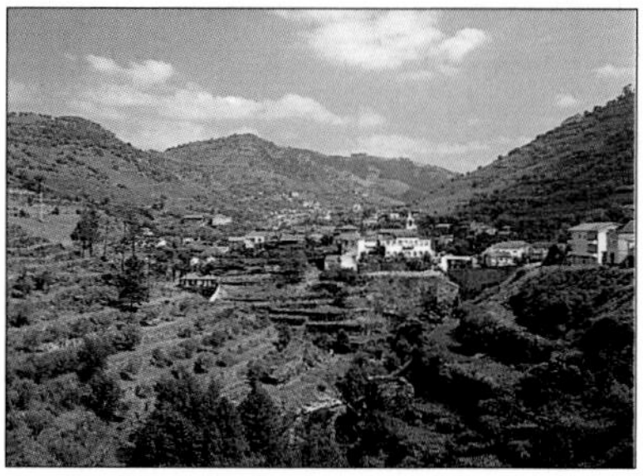

Santa Marta de Penanguiao, a small village in the heart of Portugal's wine-producing region, which is centered on the Douro valley.

PORTUGAL, WITH ITS long Atlantic coast, lies on the western side of the Iberian peninsula. The river Tagus divides the more mountainous north from the lower, undulating terrain to the south. In 1974, a bloodless military coup overthrew a long-standing conservative dictatorship. A constituent assembly was elected in 1975 and the armed forces withdrew from politics thereafter. Portugal then began a substantial program of economic modernization and accompanying social change. Membership of the EU has helped underpin this process.

CLIMATE

Mediterranean/ maritime

WEATHER CHART

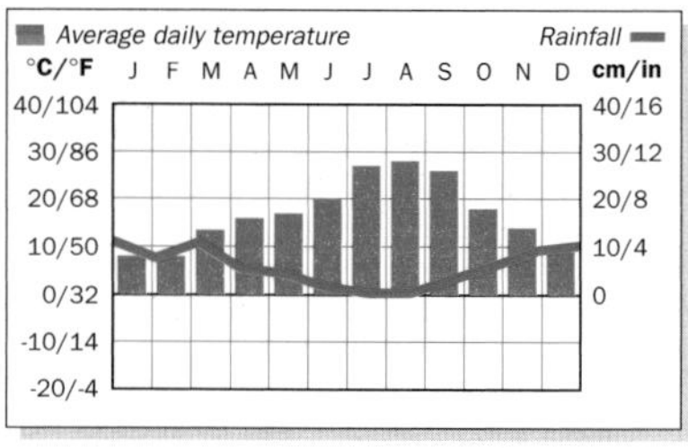
Average daily temperature
Rainfall
°C/°F J F M A M J J A S O N D cm/in
40/104
30/86
20/68
10/50
0/32
-10/14
-20/4
40/16
30/12
20/8
10/4
0

Portugal has a mild, Mediterranean climate, which is moderated by the influence of the Atlantic. Summers can be hot and sultry, while winters are relatively mild. Inland areas have more variable weather than coastal regions. Rainfall is generally higher in the mountainous north, while the central areas are more temperate. The southern Algarve region is predominantly dry and sunny.

TRANSPORTATION

Drive on right

Portela de Sacavem, Lisbon
8.67m passengers

442 ships
1.1m grt

THE TRANSPORTATION NETWORK

59,110 km (36,729 miles)

797 km (495 miles)

2813 km (1748 miles)

820 km (510 miles)

The road system has been extensively improved with grants from the EU. Road links with Spain remain limited, despite modernization schemes and the new southern Guadiana bridge. A third bridge over the Tagus estuary is planned; the 18-km Vasco da Gama bridge in Lisbon opened in 1998. Heavy traffic, poor road construction, and dangerous driving mean that Portugal has Europe's highest rate of road deaths. Lisbon's small, efficient metro complements its trams, but Porto's metro remains uncompleted.

TOURISM

Visitors : Population 1.2:1

12m visitors

Up 4% in 2000

MAIN TOURIST ARRIVALS

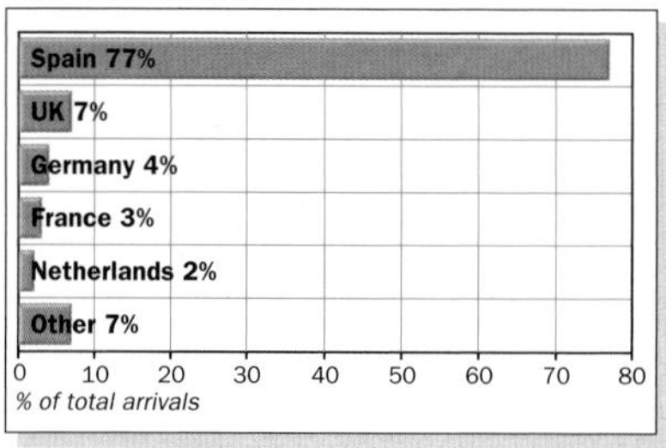
Spain 77%
UK 7%
Germany 4%
France 3%
Netherlands 2%
Other 7%
0 10 20 30 40 50 60 70 80
% of total arrivals

From the 1960s, Portugal's popularity as a tourist destination has been linked in part to qualities which reflected its relatively poor economic development, such as low prices and little crime. Thus some of the consequences of its substantial economic growth may have eroded some of the country's appeal, but since Portugal now has more than 12 million visitors a year, tourism remains a major income-earner. The most popular destination is the Algarve, the southernmost province, followed by the western resorts of Figueira da Foz and the Tróia Peninsula. Visitors are also attracted by Portugal's architecture, notably that dating from the Manueline period (1490–1520), and by its handicrafts, such as ceramics, lace, and tapestries. In addition, Portugal is noted for being the location of some of Europe's finest golf courses.

PORTUGAL

Total Land Area : 91 950 sq. km (35 502 sq. miles)

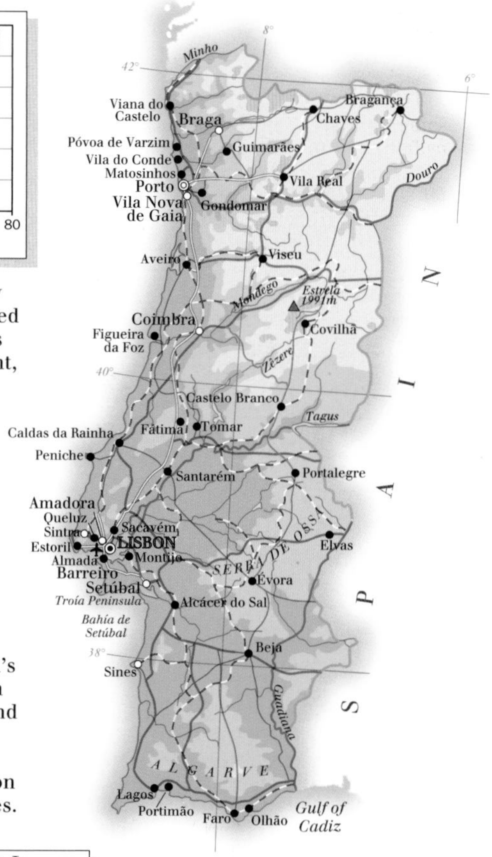
Minho
Viana do Castelo
Braga
Bragança
Chaves
Póvoa de Varzim
Vila do Conde
Guimarães
Matosinhos
Porto
Vila Real
Douro
Vila Nova de Gaia
Gondomar
Aveiro
Viseu
Mondego
Estrela 1991m
Coimbra
Figueira da Foz
Covilhã
Zêzere
Castelo Branco
Caldas da Rainha
Fátima
Tomar
Tagus
Peniche
Santarém
Portalegre
Amadora
Queluz
Sintra
Sacavém
Estoril
LISBON
Almada
Montijo
Elvas
Barreiro
Setúbal
SERRA DE OSSA
Évora
Tróia Peninsula
Alcácer do Sal
Bahía de Setúbal
Beja
Sines
Guadiana
ALGARVE
Lagos
Portimão
Faro
Olhão
Gulf of Cadiz
SPAIN

Azores
Corvo
Flores
São Jorge
Graciosa
Terceira
Faial
Pico
São Miguel
Ponta Delgada
Santa Maria
0 200 km
0 200 miles

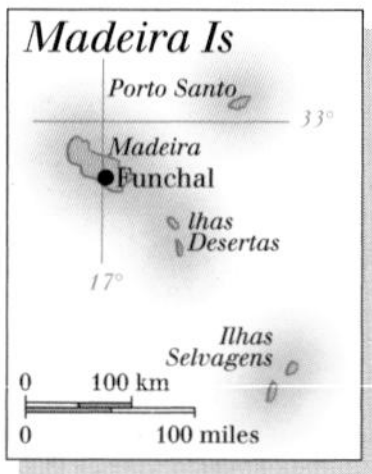
Madeira Is
Porto Santo
Madeira
Funchal
Ilhas Desertas
Ilhas Selvagens
0 100 km
0 100 miles

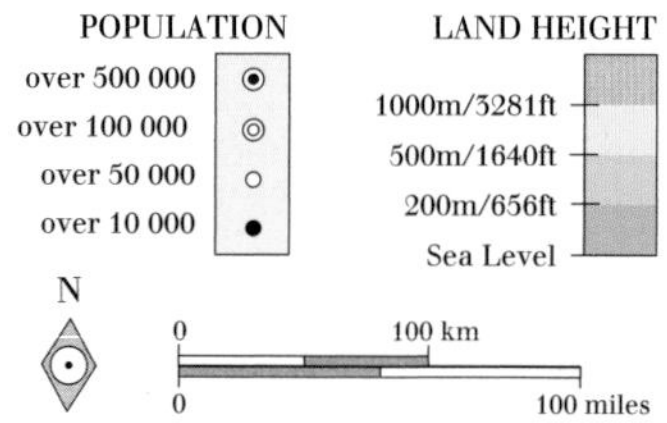
POPULATION
over 500 000
over 100 000
over 50 000
over 10 000
LAND HEIGHT
1000m/3281ft
500m/1640ft
200m/656ft
Sea Level
N
0 100 km
0 100 miles

P

PEOPLE

Population density medium

Portuguese

108/km² (279/mi²)

THE URBAN/RURAL POPULATION SPLIT

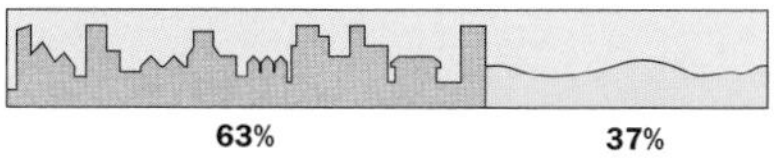
63%
37%

RELIGIOUS PERSUASION

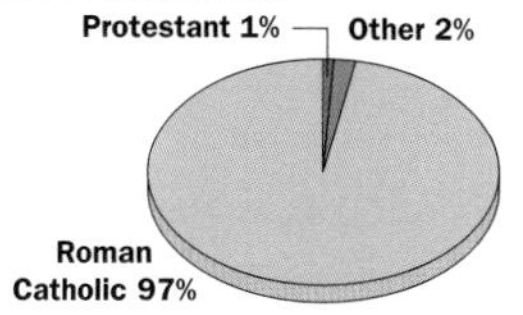
Protestant 1%
Other 2%
Roman Catholic 97%

ETHNIC MAKEUP

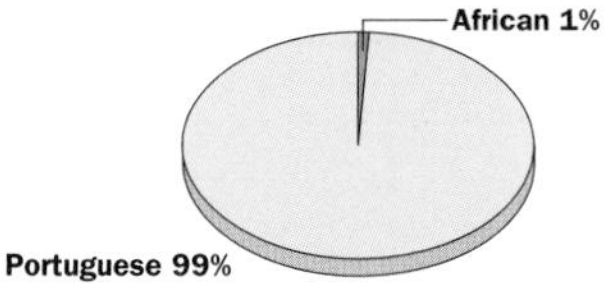
African 1%
Portuguese 99%

Portuguese society, once regarded as rather inward-looking, has become increasingly integrated into the rest of western Europe.

The Roman Catholic Church has lost some of its social influence, as shown by falling birthrates and more liberal attitudes to abortion, divorce, and unmarried mothers (almost one in five children are born outside marriage). Apart from large urban areas, the north is still devoutly Catholic.

Ethnic and religious tensions are limited. African immigrants, who come mainly from the former colonies, such as Angola, Mozambique, and Guinea, have been assimilated with relative ease.

Family ties remain all-important. Women got the vote only in 1976; now 60% of university students are women, and 63% of women of working age have jobs. Overall, democracy and rapid socioeconomic change have tended to produce a more egalitarian society.

POPULATION AGE BREAKDOWN

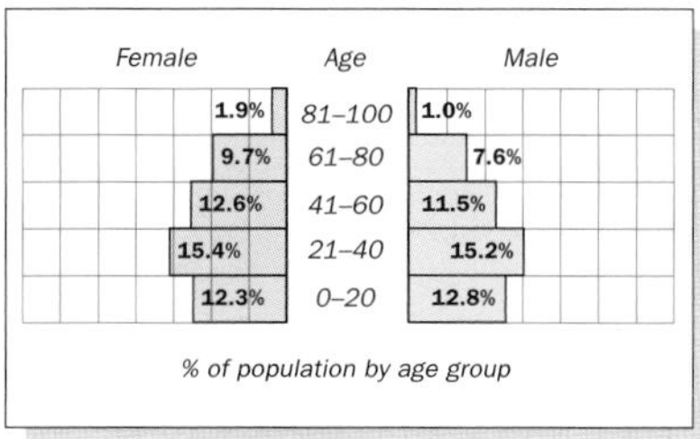
Female
Age
Male
1.9%
81–100
1.0%
9.7%
61–80
7.6%
12.6%
41–60
11.5%
15.4%
21–40
15.2%
12.3%
0–20
12.8%
% of population by age group

WORLD AFFAIRS

Joined UN in 1955

EU CE NATO OECD OSCE

Since 1986, Portugal's foreign policy has dealt mainly with the consequences of EU membership. It is a committed NATO member, though its relative strategic importance declined after Spain joined. Relations with its former African colonies, occasionally turbulent, are a high priority, as are those with Brazil. Portugal backed East Timor's struggle to reverse its annexation by Indonesia. Relations with China were cordial enough to ensure the smooth return of Macao to the latter at the end of 1999.

AID

Donor

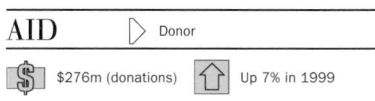

$276m (donations) Up 7% in 1999

Portugal is a major beneficiary of EU aid from the so-called structural funds. It currently earmarks 0.25% of its GDP for aid to developing countries. More than 60% goes to former colonies in Africa, especially Mozambique, where Portuguese funding helped rebuild the massive war-damaged Cahora Bassa dam and power station.

POLITICS

Multiparty elections

1999/2003

President Jorge Sampaio

AT THE LAST ELECTION

Assembly of the Republic 230 seats

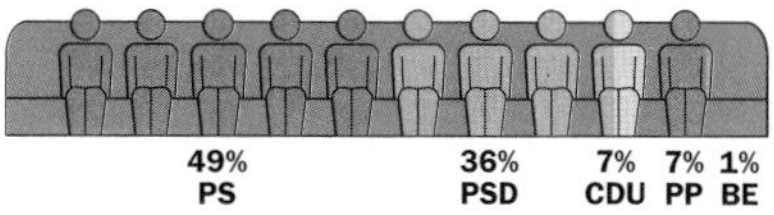
49% PS
36% PSD
7% CDU
7% PP
1% BE

PS = Socialist Party **PSD** = Social Democratic Party
CDU = United Democratic Coalition **PP** = People's Party
BE = Left Bloc

Portugal is a multiparty democracy.

Main Political Issues

Transformation

Portugal has been transformed in recent decades. The consolidation of democracy since the 1974 "carnation revolution" and EU membership since 1986 have brought Portugal into the European mainstream. There are high expectations about completing the "catching-up" process. Expo '98 in Lisbon showed off the new confidence. In 1999 Portugal was among the first 11 EU countries to introduce the euro.

Presidency and parliament

For ten years up to 1995, the presidency and the government were controlled by opposing parties, a situation which encouraged conflict and obstruction. The relationship has functioned more smoothly since then, with Socialist presidents and PS minority governments. Former PS leader Jorge Sampaio, who succeeded Mário Soares as president in 1996, was reelected comfortably in early 2001.

Profile

A decade of center-right government was brought to an end by the legislative elections of 1995 when the PSD was ousted from power by the PS. PS leader António Guterres was appointed prime minister at the head of a minority government. Having fought the election on a platform of social reform, the PS gave priority to reducing the budget deficit by cutting public spending. The success of these measures put the economy on a strong footing and secured enough popular support for the PS government to be returned to office with an increase in seats (but still just short of an overall majority) in 1999. A low turnout, however, reinforced growing concern about voter apathy.

President Jorge Sampãio, socialist president since 1996.

António Guterres, prime minister since 1995.

CHRONOLOGY

Portugal has existed as a nation state since the 11th century, although it was frequently challenged by Spain. It reached its zenith in the 16th century.

- **1755** Earthquake destroys Lisbon.
- **1793** Joins coalition against revolutionary France.
- **1807** France invades; royal family flees to Brazil.
- **1808** British troops arrive under Wellington. Start of Peninsular War.
- **1810** French leave Portugal.
- **1820** Liberal revolution.
- **1822** King John VI returns and accepts first Portuguese constitution. His son Dom Pedro declares independence of Brazil.
- **1834** Dom Pedro returns to Portugal to end civil war and installs his daughter as Queen Mary II.
- **1875–1876** Republican and Socialist parties founded.
- **1890** Land connection between Angola and Mozambique ended.
- **1891** Republican uprising in Porto.
- **1908** Assassination of King Carlos I and heir to the throne.
- **1910** Abdication of Manuel II and proclamation of the Republic. Church and state separated.
- **1916** Portugal joins allied side in World War I.
- **1917–1918** New Republic led by Sidónio Pais.

P

CHRONOLOGY *continued*

- 1926 Army overturns republic.
- 1928 António Salazar joins government as finance minister. Economy improves significantly.
- 1932 Salazar prime minister.
- 1933 Promulgation of the constitution of the "New State," instituting right-wing dictatorship.
- 1936–1939 Salazar assists Franco in Spanish Civil War.
- 1939–1945 Portugal neutral during World War II, but lets UK use air bases in Azores.
- 1949 Founder member of NATO.
- 1955 Joins UN.
- 1958 Américo Thómas appointed president, following the fraudulent defeat of General Humberto Delgado.
- 1961 India annexes Goa. Guerrilla warfare breaks out in Angola, Mozambique, and Guinea.
- 1970 Death of Salazar, incapacitated since 1968. Succeeded by Marcelo Caetano.
- 1971 Caetano attempts liberalization.
- 1974 Carnation Revolution – left-wing Armed Forces Movement overthrows Caetano.
- 1974–1975 Portuguese possessions in Africa attain independence. Some 750,000 Portuguese expatriates return to Portugal.
- 1975 Communist takeover foiled by moderates and Mário Soares' PS.
- 1975–1976 Indonesia seizes former Portuguese East Timor unopposed.
- 1976 General António Eanes elected president. Adoption of new constitution. Soares appointed prime minister.
- 1978 Period of non-party technocratic government instituted.
- 1980 Center-right wins elections. General Eanes reelected.
- 1982 Full civilian government formally restored.
- 1983 Soares becomes caretaker prime minister; PS is majority party.
- 1985 Anibal Cavaco Silva becomes prime minister. Minority PSD government.
- 1986 Soares elected president. Portugal joins EU, which funds major infrastructure and construction projects.
- 1987 Cavaco Silva wins absolute majority in parliament.
- 1991 Soares reelected president.
- 1995 PS wins elections; António Guterres becomes prime minister.
- 1996 Former PS leader Jorge Sampãio elected president.
- 1999 January, Portugal among first 11 EU countries to introduce euro. October, general election: ruling PS strengthens its position. December, Macao returned to China.
- 2001 Sampãio reelected.

DEFENSE

Compulsory military service

$2.28bn

Down 4% in 1999

Portugal has been a member of NATO since 1949. It has a small but relatively modern navy. The army and air force are less efficient. The government announced in 1999 that it planned to abolish compulsory miltary service (currently of four months, with a seven-month civilian alternative) during its current four-year term in office. The USA, which is the major arms supplier, has a strategic air base in the Azores.

PORTUGUESE ARMED FORCES

187 main battle tanks (86 M–48A5, 101 M–60)	25,650 personnel
3 submarines, 6 frigates, and 30 patrol boats	11,600 personnel
66 combat aircraft (40 *Alpha Jet*, 20 F–16A/B)	7400 personnel
None	

ECONOMICS

Inflation 5.6% p.a. (1990–1999)

$110.2bn

200.01–213.54 escudos

SCORE CARD

World GNP Ranking	34th
GNP per Capita	$11,030
Balance of Payments	$–9bn
Inflation	2.3%
Unemployment	5%

EXPORTS

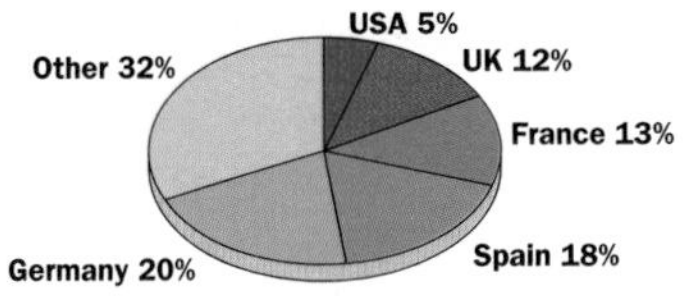
USA 5%
UK 12%
France 13%
Spain 18%
Germany 20%
Other 32%

IMPORTS

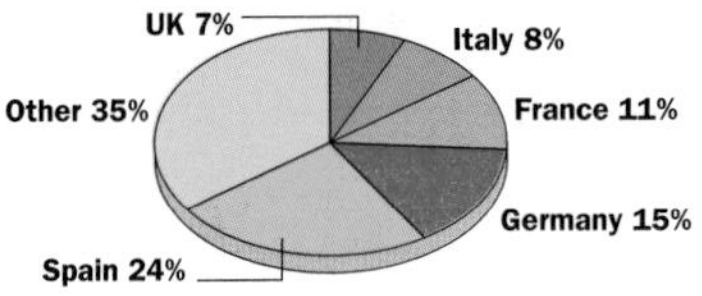
UK 7%
Italy 8%
France 11%
Germany 15%
Spain 24%
Other 35%

Strengths

Relatively low, if rapidly rising, labor costs. Flexible labor market. High domestic and direct foreign investment. Strong banking sector. Potential for growth of tourism, now earning 6% of GDP – highest ratio in EU. Clothing and shoe manufacturing now joined by cars (notably Volkswagens) and machinery as major exports. Fast-track improvement of transportation infrastructure. Good deep-water port at Lisbon. Wine, especially port. Tomatoes, citrus fruit, cork, sardines.

Weaknesses

High dependence on imported oil. Reliance on public works to drive economic growth. Large agricultural sector (5% of GDP, 10% of workforce) is most inefficient in EU. Outdated farming methods, small landholdings, low crop yields; product prices undercut by Spain.

Profile

EU membership in 1986 brought a sharp increase in foreign investment

ECONOMIC PERFORMANCE INDICATOR

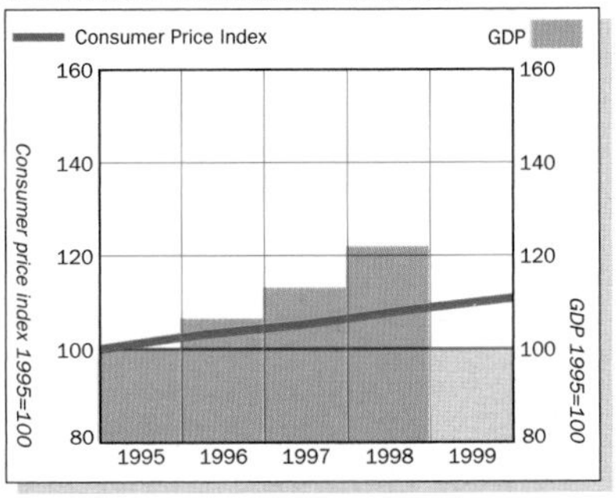
Consumer Price Index
GDP
160
140
120
100
80
1995
1996
1997
1998
1999
Consumer price index 1995=100
GDP 1995=100

to largely rural Portugal. Exports rose dramatically. The economy recorded growth of over 3% a year in the second half of the 1990s. Maintaining growth thereafter required a big emphasis on raising labor productivity.

At one time participation in EU monetary union seemed a distant prospect. In the event the socialist government of António Guterres which came to power in 1995 was able to meet the required economic criteria with relative ease, and in January 1999 Portugal was among the 11 EU countries which introduced the euro. While Portuguese wages are about 70% of the EU average, the unemployment rate is among the lowest in the EU.

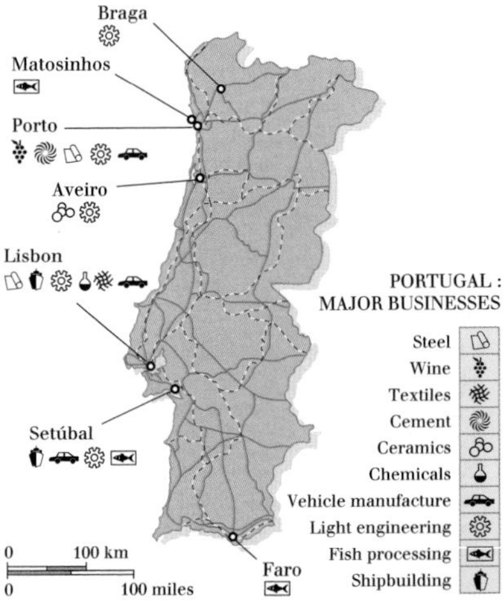
Braga
Matosinhos
Porto
Aveiro
Lisbon
Setúbal
Faro
0 100 km
0 100 miles
PORTUGAL : MAJOR BUSINESSES
Steel
Wine
Textiles
Cement
Ceramics
Chemicals
Vehicle manufacture
Light engineering
Fish processing
Shipbuilding

P

RESOURCES

Electric power 9.4m kw

229,108 tonnes

Not an oil producer; refines 294,000 b/d

7m turkeys, 5.85m sheep, 2.33m pigs, 28m chickens

Coal, limestone, granite, marble, tin, copper, tungsten

ELECTRICITY GENERATION

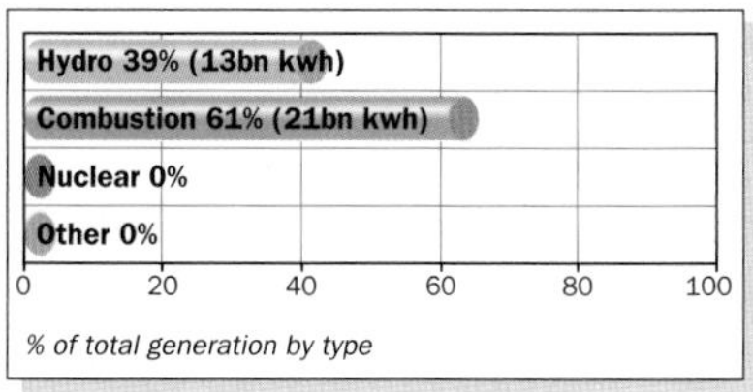
Hydro 39% (13bn kwh)
Combustion 61% (21bn kwh)
Nuclear 0%
Other 0%
0
20
40
60
80
100
% of total generation by type

Portugal is disadvantaged by a lack of natural resources, including water. Mining has historically been important, notably for tungsten, copper and tin. The last coal mine closed in the mid-1990s. The fish catch, once central to the economy, has been decling in recent years.

PORTUGAL : LAND USE

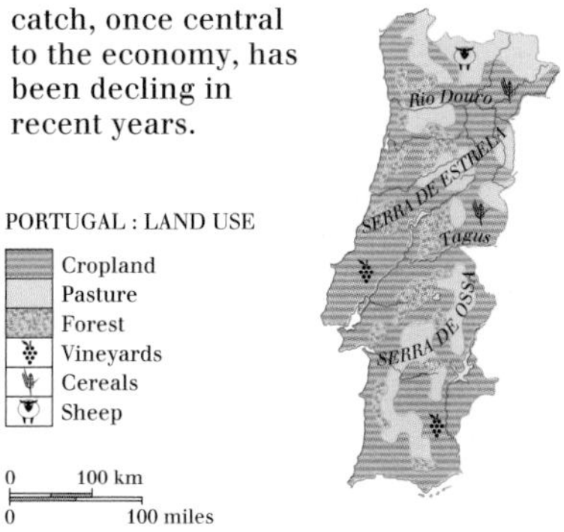
Cropland
Pasture
Forest
Vineyards
Cereals
Sheep
0
100 km
0
100 miles
Rio Douro
SERRA DE ESTRELA
Tagus
SERRA DE OSSA

ENVIRONMENT

Sustainability rank: 20th

6%

5.4 tonnes per capita

ENVIRONMENTAL TREATIES

Yes	Yes	Yes
Yes	Yes	Yes

The unrestricted development of tourist resorts in the Algarve and the huge investment in new harbor, road, and bridge developments are having detrimental effects on natural habitats. EU agricultural grants for projects such as draining meadows, and monoculture afforestation, notably of *Eucalyptus* and *Pinus*, are degrading biodiversity. Much toxic waste is dumped on any available land, as few official controls or infill sites exist. New waste management regulations are being introduced.

MEDIA

TV ownership high

Daily newspaper circulation 75 per 1000 people

PUBLISHING AND BROADCAST MEDIA

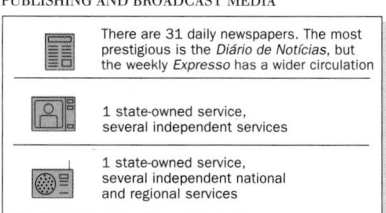

There are 31 daily newspapers. The most prestigious is the *Diário de Notícias*, but the weekly *Expresso* has a wider circulation

1 state-owned service, several independent services

1 state-owned service, several independent national and regional services

Newspaper circulations are low; most have only regional distribution. TV is the dominant medium. In 1992–1993 two independent TV stations began broadcasting alongside state-owned RTP. One, SIC, emphasized game shows and soaps. The other, the Catholic TVI, was sold in 1998 to Media Capital, one of four groups that control most of the press and broadcasting.

CRIME

Death penalty not used

12,150 prisoners

Down 21% 1996–1998

CRIME RATES

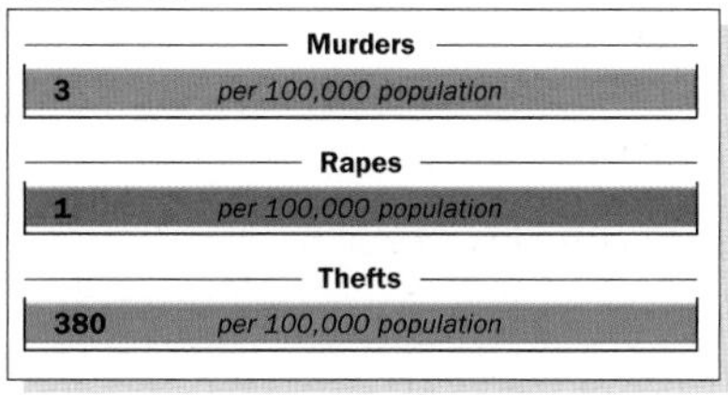
Murders
3
per 100,000 population
Rapes
1
per 100,000 population
Thefts
380
per 100,000 population

Portugal enjoys a low crime rate. Consumption and possession of small quantities of narcotics were decriminalized in mid-2000 and legalized a year later.

EDUCATION

School leaving age: 15

92%

319,525 students

THE EDUCATION SYSTEM

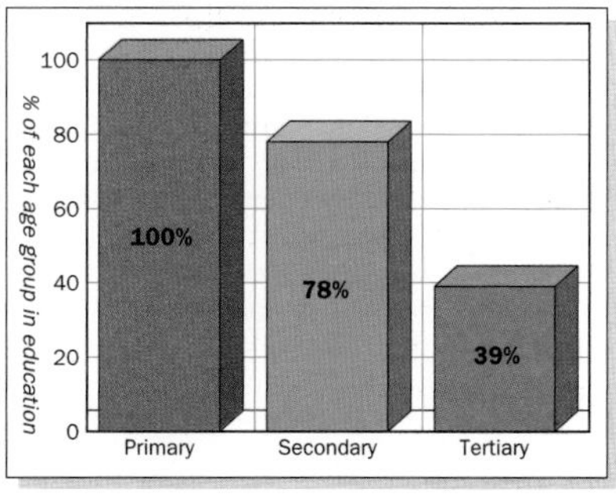
100
80
60
40
20
0
% of each age group in education
100%
78%
39%
Primary
Secondary
Tertiary

Portuguese is the seventh most widely spoken language in the world.

Free state education is available to all pupils between the ages of three and 15. Nursery provision has been greatly expanded, although the preschool stage is not compulsory. Middle-class parents rely heavily on the private sector. State universities have been expanded to ease the pressure on places. There are several prestigious private universities.

HEALTH

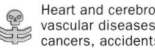

Welfare state health benefits

1 per 323 people

Heart and cerebro-vascular diseases, cancers, accidents

Of total government expenditure nearly 10% is spent on health.

Portugal has had a publicly funded, free national health service since 1979; Spending on health has increased markedly in recent years, but care remains below the EU average. There are strong regional differences in facilities. Larger urban hospitals are modern and well equipped. Private health care schemes, which are allowed to coexist, are both affordable and good value for money; over 40% of the population use the private system.

SPENDING

GDP/cap. increase

CONSUMPTION AND SPENDING

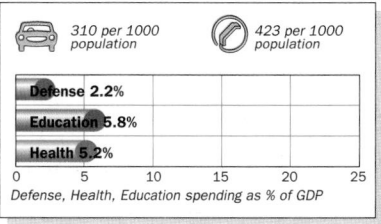

310 per 1000 population

423 per 1000 population

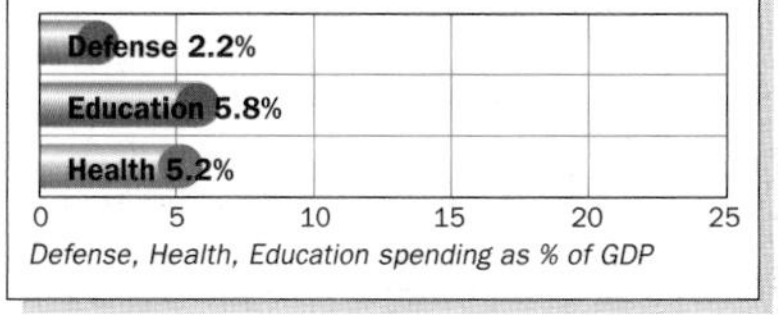
Defense 2.2%
Education 5.8%
Health 5.2%
0
5
10
15
20
25
Defense, Health, Education spending as % of GDP

Wealth differentials in Portugal are smaller than in most EU countries. The 1976 constitution committed Portugal to making the transition to socialism, and since then governments have introduced limited wealth redistribution measures.

Families owning land with tourist development potential, such as golf courses, have made large profits from rapid economic change. In the late 1990s growing prosperity and low interest rates led to a surge in property purchases. Average incomes, which were just over half the EU average in 1986, now stand at 74%. Over half the population now have mobile phones, mainly on prepayment systems, which were pioneered in Portugal.

WORLD RANKING

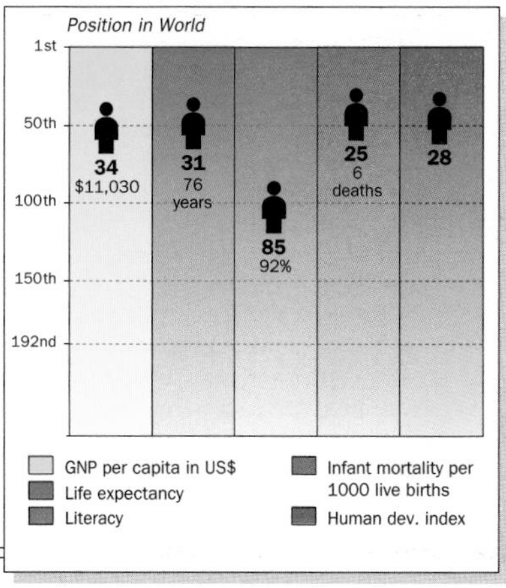
Position in World
1st
50th
100th
150th
192nd
34
$11,030
31
76
years
85
92%
25
6
deaths
28
GNP per capita in US$
Life expectancy
Literacy
Infant mortality per 1000 live births
Human dev. index

P

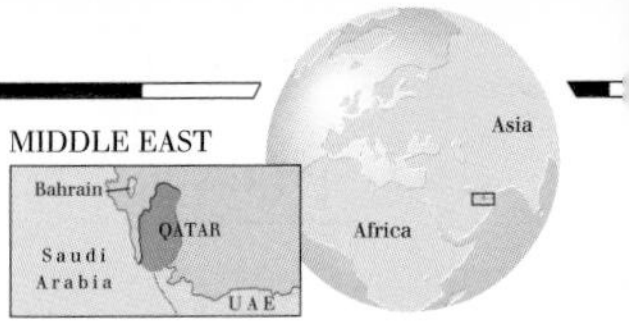
MIDDLE EAST
Bahrain
QATAR
Saudi Arabia
UAE
Asia
Africa

QATAR

OFFICIAL NAME: State of Qatar **CAPITAL:** Doha
POPULATION: 699,000 **CURRENCY:** Qatar riyal **OFFICIAL LANGUAGE:** Arabic

1971 | 1971 | Sept 3 | Q | +3 | +974 | .qa

PROJECTING NORTH FROM the Arabian peninsula into the Gulf, Qatar has land borders with Saudi Arabia and the United Arab Emirates, and a sea border with Bahrain. Most of the country is flat, semi-arid desert. Qatar is a founder member of OPEC, and its plentiful oil and natural gas reserves make it one of the wealthiest states in the region. The country enjoys political stability under the rule of the al-Thani clan.

CLIMATE

Hot desert

WEATHER CHART

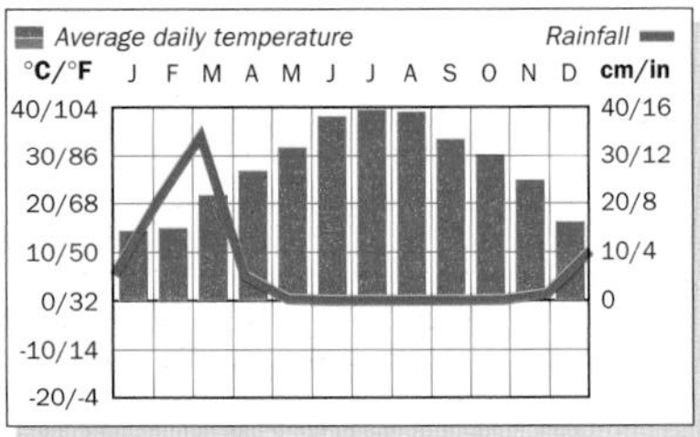
Average daily temperature
Rainfall
°C/°F
J F M A M J J A S O N D
cm/in
40/104
30/86
20/68
10/50
0/32
-10/14
-20/-4
40/16
30/12
20/8
10/4
0

The climate is hot and sultry, with midsummer temperatures reaching 44°C (111°F). Rainfall is rare.

TRANSPORTATION

Drive on right

Doha International
1.1m passengers

64 ships
744,131 grt

THE TRANSPORTATION NETWORK

1107 km (688 miles)

None

None

None

A good road network links Qatar to its neighbors. A new international airport was opened in Doha in 1997.

TOURISM

Visitors : Population 1:1.5

451,000 visitors

Up 6% in 1998

MAIN TOURIST ARRIVALS

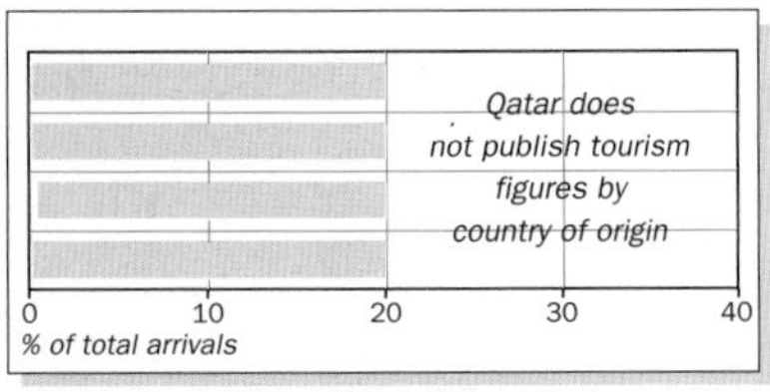
Qatar does not publish tourism figures by country of origin
0
10
20
30
40
% of total arrivals

Qatar attracts several thousand European visitors a year, who enjoy unspoiled beaches, duty-free shopping, modern hotels, and the desert hinterland. Alcohol is permitted in five-star hotels for non-Muslims.

PEOPLE

Pop. density medium

Arabic

64/km² (165/mi²)

THE URBAN/RURAL POPULATION SPLIT

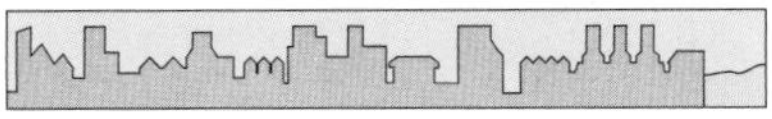
92%
8%

ETHNIC MAKEUP

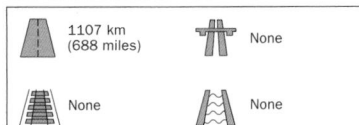

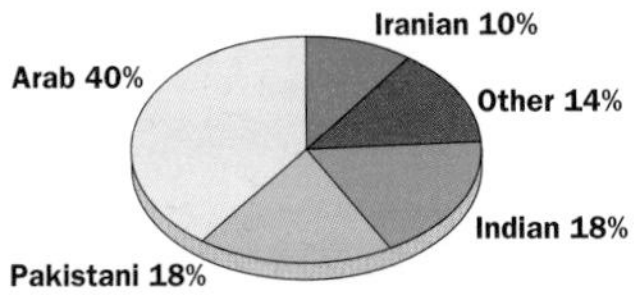
Iranian 10%
Arab 40%
Other 14%
Indian 18%
Pakistani 18%

Only one in five inhabitants is native-born. Most are guest workers from the Indian subcontinent, Iran, and the northern African countries. Western expatriates enjoy a high standard of living and take no part in politics.

Most Qataris are followers of the Wahhabi interpretation of Sunni Islam and espouse conservative religious views. However, women are not obliged to take the veil and can hold a driving license. Expatriate Christians are allowed freedom to worship but not to promote Christianity.

Since the advent of oil wealth, the Qataris, who were formerly nomadic Bedouins, have become a nation of city-dwellers. Almost 90% of the population now inhabit the capital Doha and its suburbs. As a result, northern Qatar is dotted with depopulated and abandoned villages.

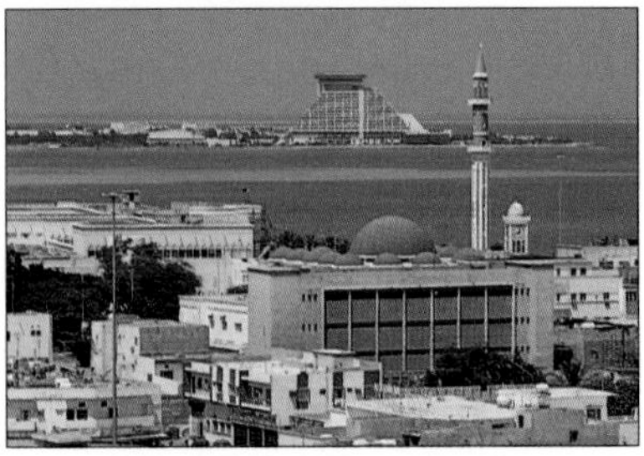

***Doha, the capital.** Although desert covers the whole country, Qatar now grows most of its own vegetables by tapping groundwater.*

POLITICS

No multiparty elections

Not applicable

Amir Shaikh Hamad bin Khalifa al-Thani

LEGISLATIVE OR ADVISORY BODIES

Advisory Council 35 seats

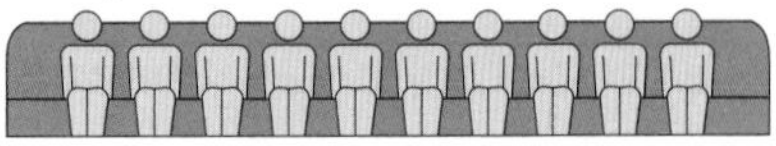

Qatar is an absolute monarchy and has no legislature. The amir rules with the assistance of the Council of Ministers and the Advisory Council.

Qatar is a traditional emirate. The government and religious establishment is dominated by the amir, Shaikh Hamad, who took power from his father, Shaikh Khalifa, in 1995. A failed coup against Hamad in early 1996 was linked with efforts to regain power by Khalifa, now based in the United Arab Emirates. The prodemocracy movement has called for reform of the 35-member Advisory Council. Shaikh Hamad responded by authorizing Qatar's first elections, to a new municipal council, in 1999, in which all adults, including women, were able to vote and stand as candidates. In early 2001 he promised the establishment of a directly elected parliament within the next 18 months.

WORLD AFFAIRS

Joined UN in 1971

AL | OIC | GCC | OAPEC | OPEC

Qatar is a founder member of the GCC. Since taking power in mid-1995, Shaikh Hamad has on occasion adopted an independent and at times belligerent, stance toward it, boycotting part of the GCC's annual summit in 1995 in protest at the appointment of a Saudi official. In the late 1990s Qatar agreed to supply liquefied natural gas (LNG) to Israel. Although keen to retain strong links with the West, the amir criticized the USA and the UK in early 1999 for their daily bombing of Iraq to force compliance with UN Gulf War resolutions. Within the quotas set by OPEC, Qatar has supported a moderate oil price. In 2001 Qatar reached an agreement on the border with Saudi Arabia, but lost its claim to the Hawar islands when the International Court of Justice ruled in Bahrain's favor.

AID

Recipient

$5m (receipts)

Up 400% 1997–1999

Qatar was a generous aid donor to developing countries during the 1970s and early 1980s, but this use of oil wealth subsequently dropped away.

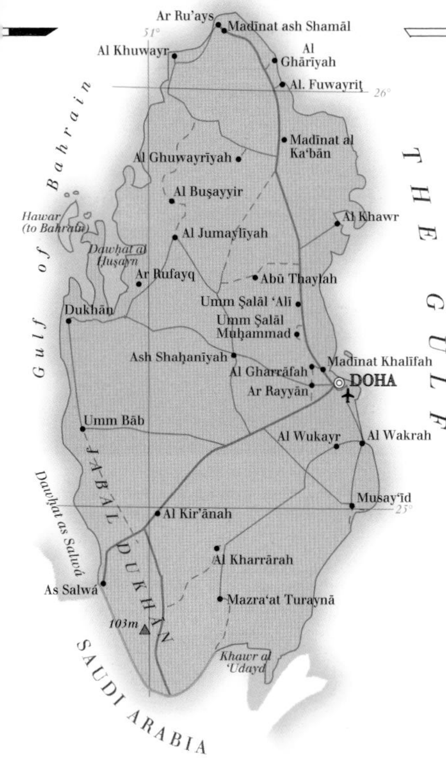
Ar Ru'ays
Madīnat ash Shamāl
Al Khuwayr
Al Ghārīyah
Al. Fuwayrit
Madīnat al Ka'bān
Al Ghuwayrīyah
Al Buşayyir
Al Khawr
Hawar (to Bahrain)
Al Jumaylīyah
Dawḩat al Ḩuşayn
Ar Rufayq
Abū Thaylah
Umm Şalāl 'Alī
Umm Şalāl Muḩammad
Dukhān
Ash Shaḩanīyah
Madīnat Khalīfah
Al Gharrāfah
DOHA
Ar Rayyān
Umm Bāb
Al Wukayr
Al Wakrah
Musay'īd
Al Kir'ānah
Al Kharrārah
As Salwá
Mazra'at Turaynā
103m
Khawr al 'Udayd
Gulf of Bahrain
THE GULF
JABAL DUKHAN
Dawḩat as Salwá
SAUDI ARABIA
51°
26°
25°

QATAR

Total Land Area : 11 000 sq. km (4247 sq. miles)

POPULATION
over 100 000
under 10 000

LAND HEIGHT
200m/1640ft
Sea Level

0 30 km
0 30 miles

N

DEFENSE

No compulsory military service

$1.47bn

Up 7% in 1999

The estimated 12,000-strong armed forces are too small to play a significant role in Qatari affairs, even in the event of political turmoil. A ten-year defense agreement with the USA provides for joint exercises, the stockpiling of US equipment, and US access to bases.

RESOURCES

Electric power 1.5m kw

5034 tonnes

795,000 b/d (reserves 13,200,000,000 bbl)

207,000 sheep, 179,000 goats, 50,000 camels

Oil, natural gas

Qatar has the smallest reserves of crude oil within OPEC but abundant reserves of gas (the third-largest in the world), including the world's largest field of gas unassociated with oil.

ENVIRONMENT

Not available

None

72.9 tonnes per capita

The desert hinterland supports little plant or animal life. Most native species are extinct in the wild. Oil pollution has damaged marine life. There are salt flats in the south.

MEDIA

TV ownership high

Daily newspaper circulation 161 per 1000 people

PUBLISHING AND BROADCAST MEDIA

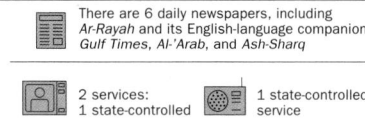

There are 6 daily newspapers, including *Ar-Rayah* and its English-language companion *Gulf Times*, *Al-'Arab*, and *Ash-Sharq*

2 services: 1 state-controlled

1 state-controlled service

Shaikh Hamad has relaxed press censorship. Qatari TV is the most independent in the region. Al Jazeera is a major news channel for the whole area.

CRIME

Death penalty used

6285 prisoners

Up 128% 1996–1998

Traditional Islamic punishments have deterred crime. However, narcotics trafficking is on the increase. The incidence of street crime is low.

CHRONOLOGY

The ruling al-Thanis, related to the Khalifa family of Bahrain, date back to the 18th century.

- ❑ **1971** Independence from the UK.
- ❑ **1972** Accession of Amir Khalifa.
- ❑ **1995** Shaikh Hamad overthrows Shaikh Khalifa.
- ❑ **1999** First ever polls, to elect new municipal council.

EDUCATION

Schooling is free but not compulsory

81%

8475 students

Education is free from primary to university level. The government finances students to study overseas.

HEALTH

Welfare state health benefits

1 per 699 people

Heart, circulatory, and infectious diseases, cancers

Primary health care is free to Qataris. Hospitals operate to Western standards of care and the government also funds treatment abroad.

SPENDING

GDP/cap. increase

CONSUMPTION AND SPENDING

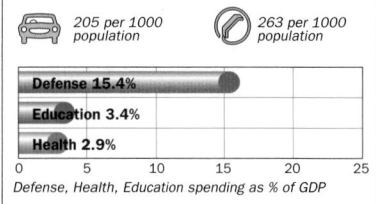

205 per 1000 population

263 per 1000 population

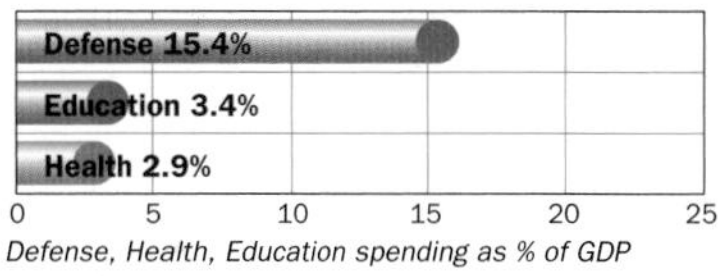
Defense 15.4%
Education 3.4%
Health 2.9%
0
5
10
15
20
25
Defense, Health, Education spending as % of GDP

Qataris have a high income per capita. There is no income tax, public services are free, and the government guarantees jobs for school-leavers. There are no exchange controls.

ECONOMICS

Inflation 2.8% p.a. (1990–1999)

$7.4bn

3.6408–3.6393 Qatar riyals

SCORE CARD

- ❑ WORLD GNP RANKING..........98th
- ❑ GNP PER CAPITA..........$11,570
- ❑ BALANCE OF PAYMENTS..........$-1.66bn
- ❑ INFLATION..........2.8%
- ❑ UNEMPLOYMENT..........Not available

EXPORTS

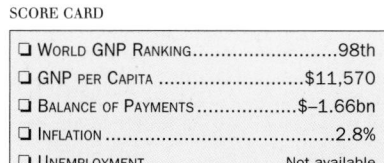

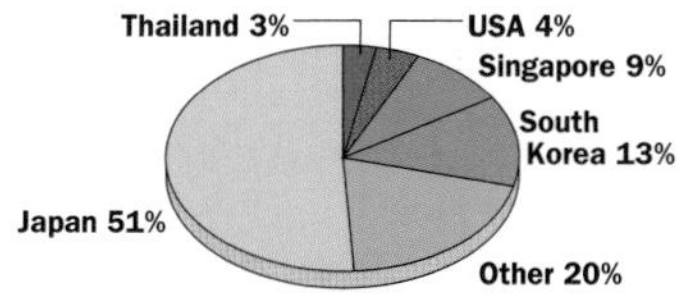
Thailand 3%
USA 4%
Singapore 9%
South Korea 13%
Japan 51%
Other 20%

IMPORTS

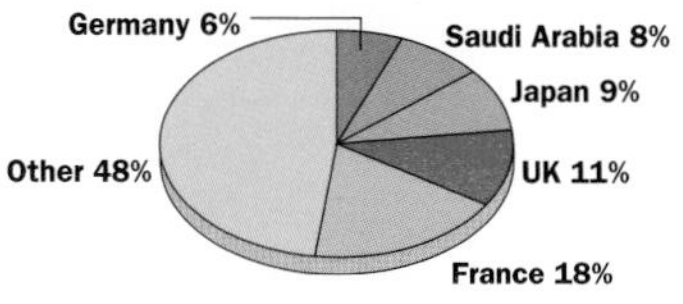
Germany 6%
Saudi Arabia 8%
Japan 9%
Other 48%
UK 11%
France 18%

STRENGTHS

A steady supply of crude oil and huge gas reserves, plus related industries. Soaring world oil prices in 2000. Modern infrastructure. Budget surplus.

WEAKNESSES

Dependence on foreign workforce. All raw materials imported. Virtually all water has to be desalinated. Large foreign reserves, but new industries depend on cementing agreements with foreign partners. Potential threat to security from Iraq and Iran makes some multinationals wary of investment.

WORLD RANKING

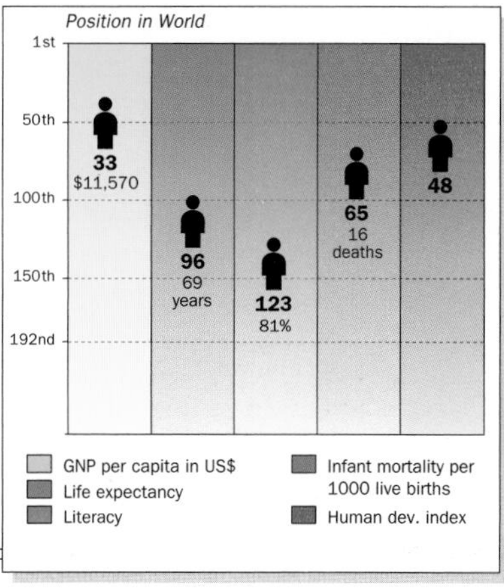
Position in World
1st
50th
100th
150th
192nd
33
$11,570
96
69 years
123
81%
65
16 deaths
48
GNP per capita in US$
Life expectancy
Literacy
Infant mortality per 1000 live births
Human dev. index

Q

ROMANIA

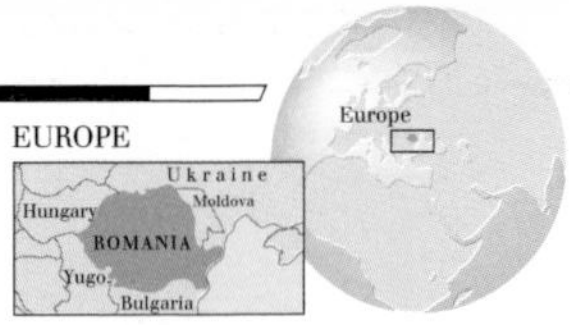
EUROPE
Europe
Ukraine
Moldova
Hungary
ROMANIA
Yugo.
Bulgaria

OFFICIAL NAME: Romania **CAPITAL:** Bucharest
POPULATION: 22.3 million **CURRENCY:** Leu **OFFICIAL LANGUAGE:** Romanian

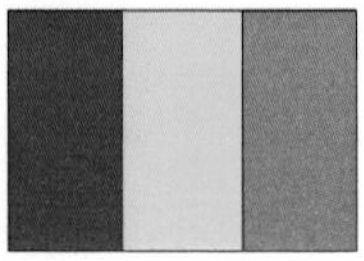

1878 | 1947 | Dec 1 | RO | +2 | +40 | .ro

ROMANIA LIES ON THE Black Sea coast, with the Danube as its southern border. The Carpathian Mountains form an arc across the country, curving around the upland basin of Transylvania. Long dominated by the Ottoman, Russian, and Habsburg empires, Romania became an independent monarchy in 1878. After World War II, this was supplanted by a communist People's Republic, headed from 1965 by Nicolae Ceauşescu. A coup in 1989 resulted in his execution and a limited democracy under Ion Iliescu. Although defeated in elections in 1996, Iliescu was returned to office in 2000.

***Village in northeastern Romania,** in the foothills of the Carpathian Mountains, close to the border with Ukraine. Corn and wheat are Romania's main crops.*

CLIMATE

Continental

WEATHER CHART

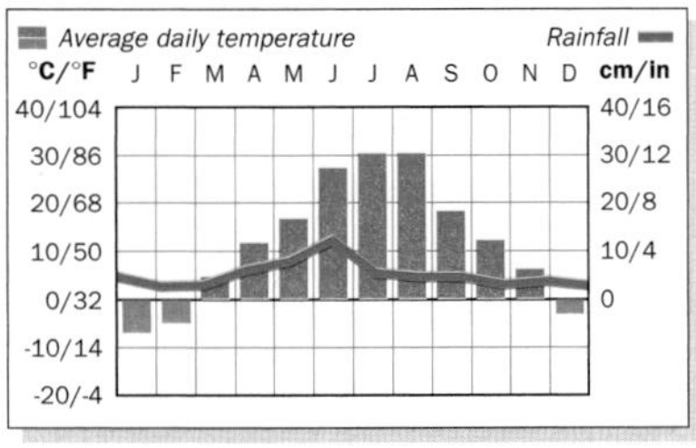
Average daily temperature
Rainfall
°C/°F
J F M A M J J A S O N D
cm/in
40/104
30/86
20/68
10/50
0/32
-10/14
-20/-4
40/16
30/12
20/8
10/4
0

Romania has a continental climate with two growing seasons. Rainfall is generally moderate, with most rain falling in spring and early summer. Very heavy spring rains occasionally destroy new crops. Snow is frequent in winter, which can be bitterly cold.

TRANSPORTATION

Drive on right

Bucharest–Otopeni International 1.68m passengers

389 ships 2.1m grt

THE TRANSPORTATION NETWORK

103,671 km (64,418 miles)

133 km (83 miles)

11,364 km (7062 miles)

1724 km (1071 miles)

The road network is inadequate, and traffic levels are rising. EBRD, EU, World Bank, and Japanese funding has focused on the expressway from Bucharest to Hungary, and on improving major roads. Modernization of the port of Constanţa to include a container port and new grain silo is also under way.

TOURISM

Visitors : Population 1:6.8

3.3m visitors

Up 2% in 2000

MAIN TOURIST ARRIVALS

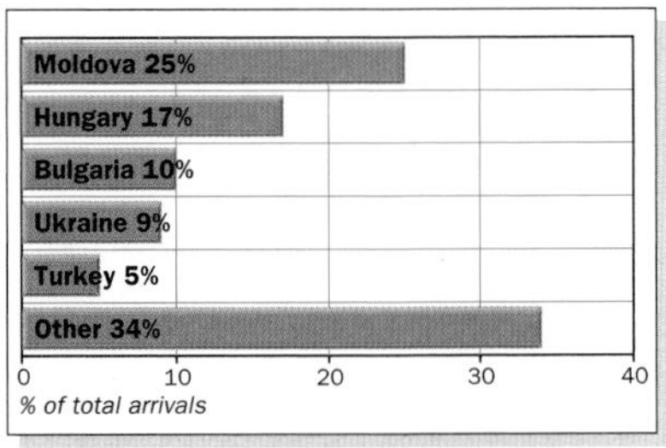
Moldova 25%
Hungary 17%
Bulgaria 10%
Ukraine 9%
Turkey 5%
Other 34%
0
10
20
30
40
% of total arrivals

The Black Sea, Danube delta, and Carpathian Mountains are the primary natural attractions, while Transylvania has a rich historical heritage. A theme park has been proposed which will exploit the Dracula legend. However, tourist facilities are generally poor. Under Ceauşescu, the need for foreign currency meant that tourist facilities came before Romanians' own housing needs. Today, privatization of property and an acute housing shortage have reduced the accommodation available to visitors.

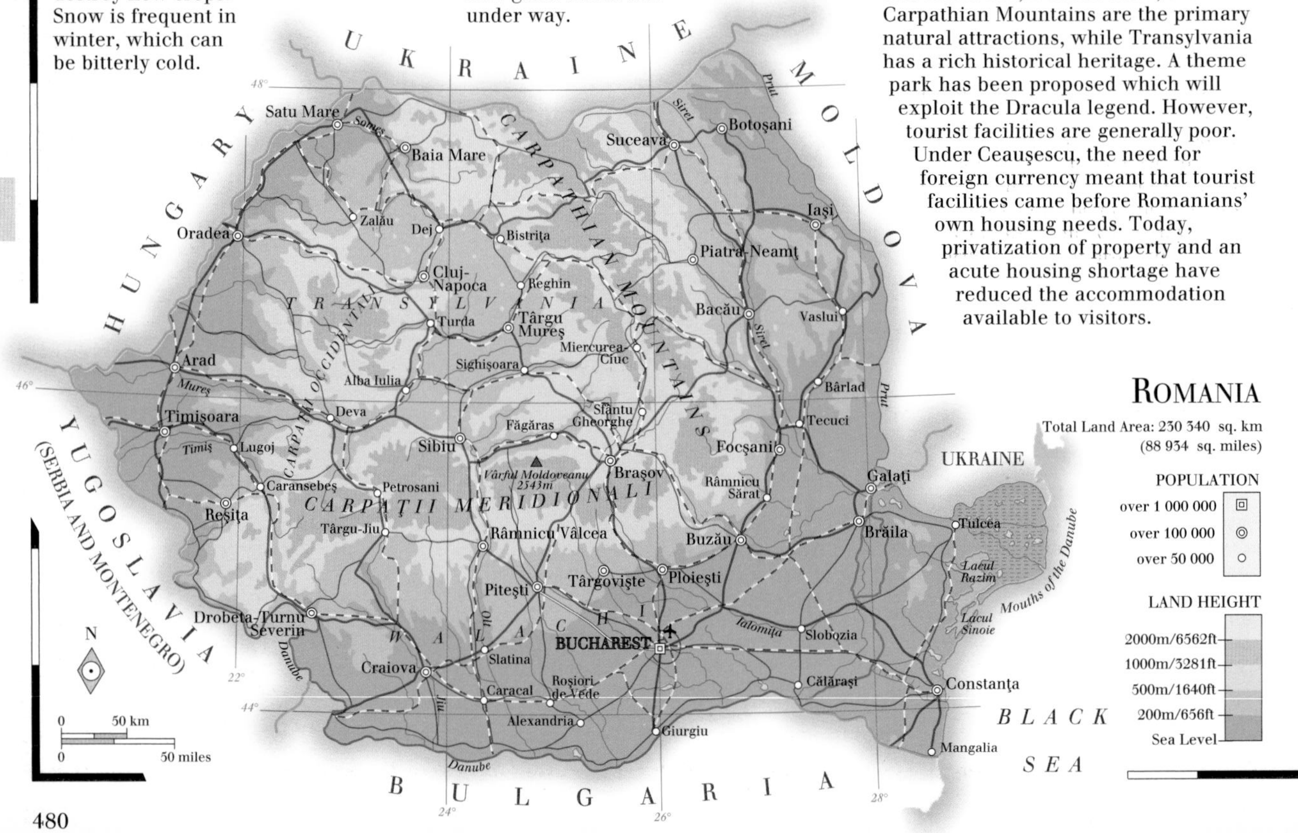
UKRAINE
MOLDOVA
HUNGARY
YUGOSLAVIA (SERBIA AND MONTENEGRO)
BULGARIA
BLACK SEA
CARPATHIAN MOUNTAINS
TRANSYLVANIA
CARPAŢII OCCIDENTALI
CARPAŢII MERIDIONALI
WALACHIA
Satu Mare
Baia Mare
Suceava
Botoşani
Zalău
Dej
Bistriţa
Iaşi
Oradea
Piatra-Neamţ
Cluj-Napoca
Reghin
Turda
Târgu Mureş
Bacău
Vaslui
Miercurea-Ciuc
Arad
Sighişoara
Alba Iulia
Bârlad
Deva
Sfântu Gheorghe
Tecuci
Timişoara
Făgăras
Lugoj
Sibiu
Focşani
Braşov
Vârful Moldoveanu 2543m
Caransebeş
Petrosani
Reşiţa
Râmnicu Sărat
Galaţi
Târgu-Jiu
Râmnicu Vâlcea
Brăila
Tulcea
Buzău
Târgovişte
Ploieşti
Piteşti
Lacul Razim
Mouths of the Danube
Drobeta-Turnu Severin
Slobozia
Lacul Sinoie
BUCHAREST
Slatina
Craiova
Călăraşi
Constanţa
Caracal
Roşiori de Vede
Alexandria
Giurgiu
Mangalia
Danube
Mureş
Timiş
Someş
Siret
Prut
Ialomiţa
Olt
Jiu
48°
46°
44°
22°
24°
26°
28°
N
0 50 km
0 50 miles
ROMANIA
Total Land Area: 230 340 sq. km (88 934 sq. miles)
POPULATION
over 1 000 000
over 100 000
over 50 000
LAND HEIGHT
2000m/6562ft
1000m/3281ft
500m/1640ft
200m/656ft
Sea Level

R

PEOPLE

Pop. density medium

Romanian, Hungarian, German

97/km² (251/mi²)

THE URBAN/RURAL POPULATION SPLIT

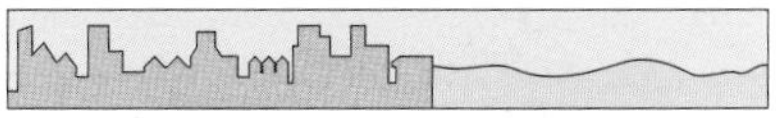
56%
44%

RELIGIOUS PERSUASION

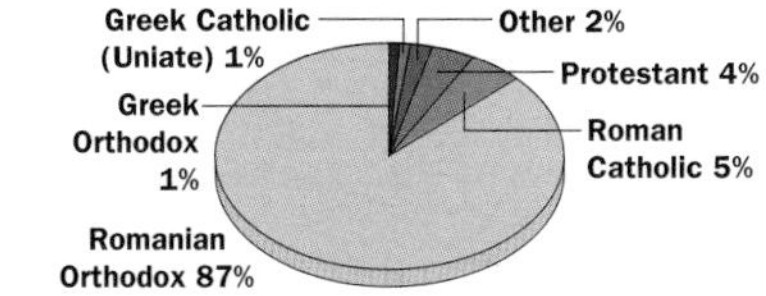
Greek Catholic (Uniate) 1%
Other 2%
Protestant 4%
Greek Orthodox 1%
Roman Catholic 5%
Romanian Orthodox 87%

ETHNIC MAKEUP

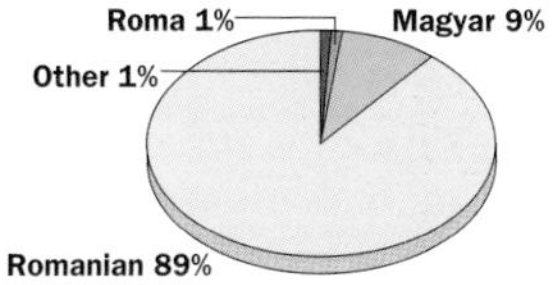
Roma 1%
Magyar 9%
Other 1%
Romanian 89%

Since 1989, Romanian nationalism has increased, aggravated by economic austerity measures. The incidence of ethnic violence has also risen, toward Roma and Hungarians in particular. Ethnic Hungarians, who form the largest minority group, are partly protected by the influence of the Hungarian state, whereas the Roma do not have any similar support and tend to suffer greater discrimination.

The population is currently decreasing, due to rising emigration since 1989, mainly for economic reasons, and to a falling birthrate since the early 1990s. The latter trend is in sharp contrast to the 1980s, when the Ceauşescu regime enforced a "pronatalist" policy, banning abortion and contraception; the birthrate rose, but the population as a whole did not grow significantly due to an increase in the mortality rate. Abortion was legalized in 1989; maternal death rates have recently declined. Adoptions by foreigners, spurred partly by shocking conditions in orphanages, were banned for a year in mid-2001, amid concerns about a "trade in children." Romania, the last country in Europe to lift its ban on homosexuality, did so in 1996, although public acts by homosexuals still receive harsher sentences.

POPULATION AGE BREAKDOWN

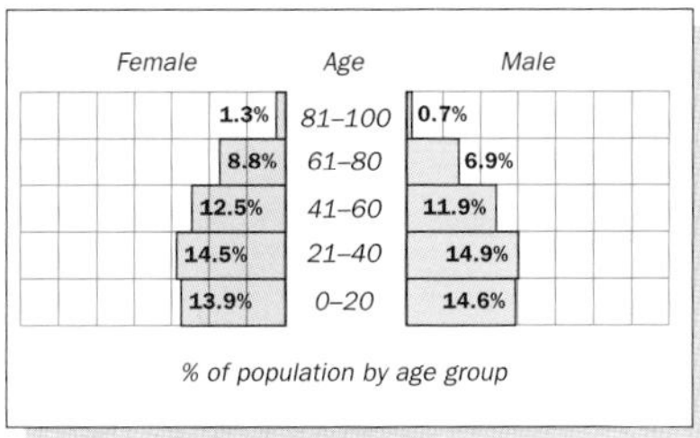
Female
Age
Male
1.3%
81–100
0.7%
8.8%
61–80
6.9%
12.5%
41–60
11.9%
14.5%
21–40
14.9%
13.9%
0–20
14.6%
% of population by age group

WORLD AFFAIRS

Joined UN in 1955

BSEC CE EBRD OSCE CEFTA

Romania's priority is building closer links with western Europe. In 1993, it signed an association agreement with the EU, and in 1995 formally applied for membership. Although not one of the front-runners with which the EU opened negotiations in 1998, it was among six "second wave" candidates which began membership negotiations in 2000.

In 1996 Romania signed a treaty of reconciliation and friendship with Hungary, with which relations had long been tense; Romania has resisted the demands of the Hungarian minority in Transylvania for greater autonomy. In 1997 Romania also signed a treaty with Ukraine recognizing the latter's sovereignty over parts of Bessarabia and Northern Bukovina.

AID

Recipient

$373m (receipts)

Up 89% 1997–1999

Western aid declined somewhat after the mid-1990s, reflecting uncertainty about the implementation of reform. A World Bank strategy in mid-2001 envisaged a significant increase in annual aid if its suggested reforms were given high priority.

POLITICS

Multiparty elections

L. House 2000/2004
U. House 2000/2004

President Ion Iliescu

AT THE LAST ELECTION

House of Deputies 345 seats

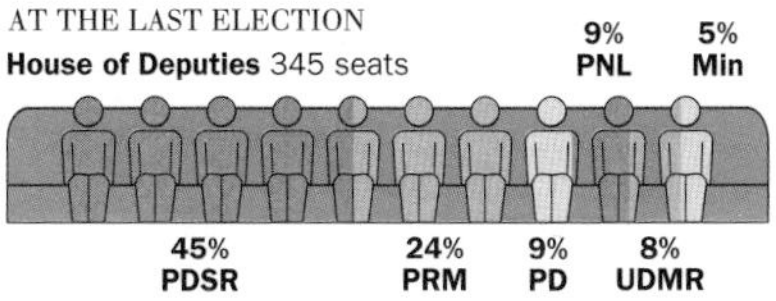
9% PNL
5% Min
45% PDSR
24% PRM
9% PD
8% UDMR

PDSR = Social Democracy Party of Romania
PRM = Greater Romania Party **PD** = Democratic Party
PNL = National Liberal Party
UDMR = Hungarian Democratic Union of Romania
Min = Minority representatives: 18 seats in the House of Deputies are reserved for national minorities

Senate 140 seats

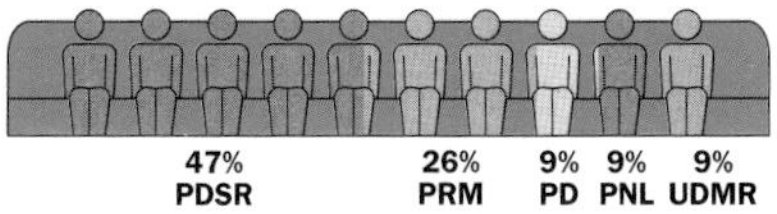
47% PDSR
26% PRM
9% PD
9% PNL
9% UDMR

Romania is a multiparty democracy led by a directly elected president.

MAIN POLITICAL ISSUES

Economic performance

Romanians have endured growing poverty, while the half-hearted attempts at economic reform failed to achieve structural change. Strikes are frequent and protests by miners have been especially forceful, notably against the center-right coalition in power in 1996–2000.

Ethnic tensions

Economic difficulties have led to increased ethnic tensions. The far right has made political gains and nationalism is increasingly accepted. Extreme right elements have even advocated labor camps for ethnic minorities. Roma have been victims of violent, racially motivated attacks.

PROFILE

The 1989 "revolution" left an old communist elite in power, with no group ready to introduce real democracy and start creating a market economy. Only the victory of the center-right in 1996 elections brought more far-reaching reform.

Many of the state assets privatized under the first Ion Iliescu regime remained closely linked to the ruling clique. Now nominally a social democrat, Iliescu retains the support of such conservative groups as miners and rural workers. The coalition parties in power after 1996 came a poor third in the 2000 elections behind Iliescu's PDSR and the extreme nationalist PRM; Iliescu won the presidential vote. In mid-2001 a party merger created a new ruling Social Democrat Party (PSD) based on the PDSR and the Social Democracy Party of Romania (PSDR).

Ion Iliescu, Romania's first post-communist president, reelected in 2001.

Adrian Nastase, prime minister since 2000.

CHRONOLOGY

Many foreign policy tensions stem from Romania's continually redrawn borders. It retains a Hungarian minority in Transylvania. Post-Soviet Moldova opted not to rejoin Romania.

- **1859** Unification of Moldavia and Wallachia forms basis of future Romania.
- **1878** Independence, but at cost of losing Bessarabia to Russia.
- **1916–1918** Enters World War I on Allied side. At end of war, gains substantial territory, including Transylvania from Hungary.

CHRONOLOGY *continued*

- **1924** Communists banned in unstable political arena. Rise of fascist "Iron Guard."
- **1938** King Carol establishes royal autocracy.
- **1940** Territory forcibly ceded to Soviet Union, Bulgaria, and Hungary. Coup by Iron Guard. King Carol abdicates in favor of son, Michael. Tripartite Pact with Germany.
- **1941** Enters war on Axis side, hoping to recover Bessarabia.
- **1944** Romania switches sides as Soviet troops reach border.
- **1945** Soviet-backed regime installed. Romanian Communist Party plays an increasing role.
- **1946** Romania regains Transylvania. Bessarabia goes to Soviet Union, which also demands huge reparations. Communist-led National Democratic Front wins majority in disputed elections.
- **1947** Michael forced to abdicate.
- **1948–1953** Centrally planned economy put in place.
- **1953** Leaders of Jewish community prosecuted for Zionism.
- **1958** Soviet troops withdraw.
- **1964** Prime Minister Gheorghiu-Dej declares national sovereignty. Proposes joint planning by all communist countries to lessen Soviet economic control.
- **1965** Ceauşescu party secretary after death of Gheorghiu-Dej.
- **1968–1980** Condemns Soviet invasion of Czechoslovakia; courts USA and European Communities.
- **1982** Ceauşescu vows to pay off foreign debt.
- **1989** Demonstrations; many killed by military. Armed forces join with opposition in National Salvation Front (NSF) to form government. Ion Iliescu declared president. Ceauşescu summarily tried and shot.
- **1990** NSF election victory. Political prisoners freed but many later reinterned.
- **1991** New constitution, providing for market reform, approved.
- **1992** Second free elections. NSF splits into factions. Nicolae Vacaroiu forms minority government.
- **1994** General strike demands faster economic reform.
- **1996** Reconciliation treaty with Hungary. Center right wins elections, breaking with communist past; Emil Constantinescu president.
- **1997** Treaty recognizes Ukraine's sovereignty over territory ruled by Romania in 1919–1940.
- **1998** Coalition differences, prime minister Victor Ciorbea resigns.
- **2000** December, Ion Iliescu and PDSR win elections.

DEFENSE

Compulsory military service

$607m

Down 33% in 1999

The military received limited funding under the Ceauşescu regime, and troops were routinely deployed as cheap labor. Romania was the first country to join NATO's Partnerships for Peace program in 1994. Since 1996 the government has actively sought membership of NATO itself, but Romania was not among the first three former Warsaw Pact countries to join the alliance in 1999.

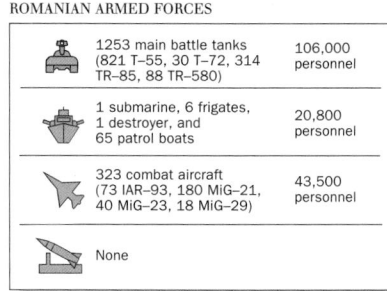

ROMANIAN ARMED FORCES

Army	1253 main battle tanks (821 T–55, 30 T–72, 314 TR–85, 88 TR–580)	106,000 personnel
Navy	1 submarine, 6 frigates, 1 destroyer, and 65 patrol boats	20,800 personnel
Air force	323 combat aircraft (73 IAR–93, 180 MiG–21, 40 MiG–23, 18 MiG–29)	43,500 personnel
Missiles	None	

ECONOMICS

Inflation 105.6% p.a. (1990–1999)

$33bn

18,250–25,925 lei

SCORE CARD

World GNP Ranking	56th
GNP per Capita	$1470
Balance of Payments	$–1.3bn
Inflation	45.8%
Unemployment	11%

EXPORTS

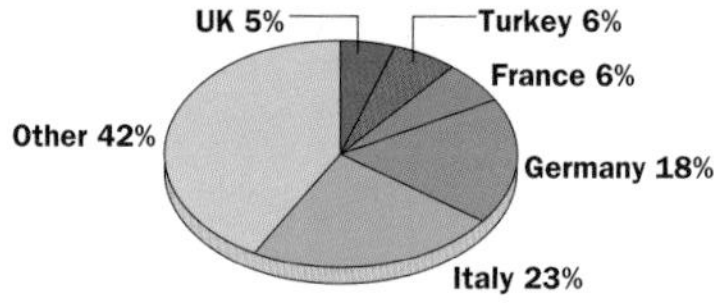
UK 5%
Turkey 6%
France 6%
Other 42%
Germany 18%
Italy 23%

IMPORTS

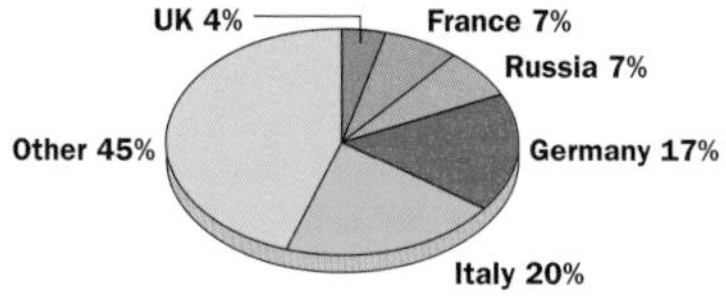
UK 4%
France 7%
Russia 7%
Other 45%
Germany 17%
Italy 20%

Strengths

Many foreign joint ventures. Oil reserves. Tourism potential. Fall in inflation.

Weaknesses

Slow transition from centrally planned to market economy. Delays in economic reform. Low foreign investment levels. Large bureaucracy.

Profile

Romania was relatively slow to launch economic reforms, and suffered severe recession for most of the 1990s. The chemical, petrochemical, metal, transportation, and food industries are the priority areas for liberalization and structural overhaul. The reform-oriented government elected in 1996 took tough measures to curb inflation and the budget deficit. Output fell sharply, a situation made worse by disruption to trade during the 1999 Kosovo conflict, and not until 2000 did an export-led recovery appear likely.

In the last decade, land reform has restored most farmland to private hands, and a program was launched in mid-2000 to complete the sell-off of all state farms by the end of 2001. Agriculture, severely undermechanized, still employs over 35% of the workforce.

Romania was the first east European country to open its economy to foreign investment, allowing 100% foreign ownership from 1990. Joint ventures, while now numerous, are small in scale; larger investors are put off by bureaucracy and doubts about stability. The privatization of state-owned enterprises, a priority for the center-right government elected in 1996, was delayed by problems in the sale of larger companies, but by 2000 the private sector accounted for over 60% of GDP.

ECONOMIC PERFORMANCE INDICATOR

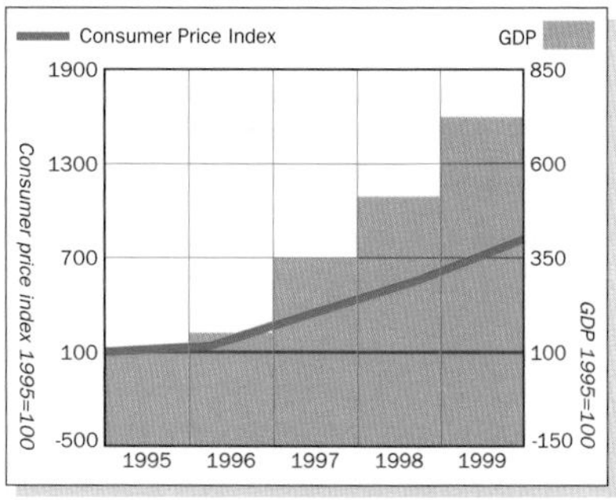
Consumer Price Index
GDP
1900
1300
700
100
-500
850
600
350
100
-150
Consumer price index 1995=100
GDP 1995=100
1995
1996
1997
1998
1999

ROMANIA : MAJOR BUSINESSES

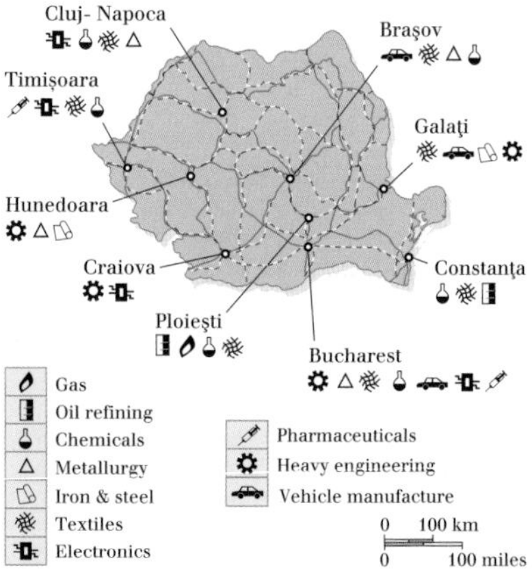
Cluj- Napoca
Braşov
Timişoara
Galaţi
Hunedoara
Craiova
Constanţa
Ploieşti
Bucharest
Gas
Oil refining
Chemicals
Metallurgy
Iron & steel
Textiles
Electronics
Pharmaceuticals
Heavy engineering
Vehicle manufacture
0 100 km
0 100 miles

R

RESOURCES

Electric power 22.8m kw

19,322 tonnes

130,000 b/d (reserves 1,400,000,000 bbl)

8m sheep, 6m pigs, 4m ducks, 72m chickens

Oil, coal, salt, iron, gas, methane, bauxite, copper, lead, zinc

ELECTRICITY GENERATION

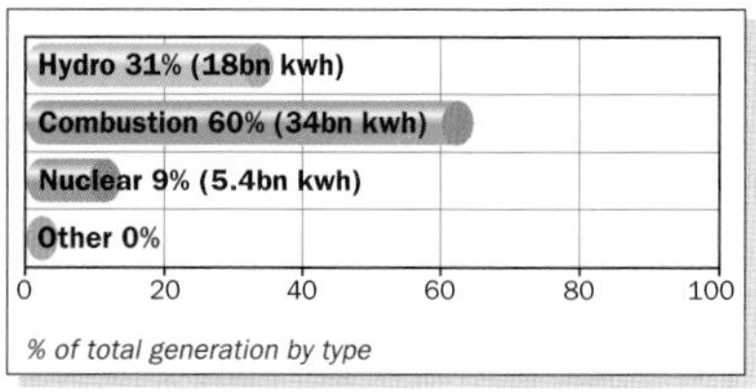
Hydro 31% (18bn kwh)
Combustion 60% (34bn kwh)
Nuclear 9% (5.4bn kwh)
Other 0%
0
20
40
60
80
100
% of total generation by type

Romania has large reserves of oil, but there is little left of proven gas reserves. Oil and gas production from onshore fields has fallen for 25 years and meets barely 40% of domestic demand. Since the mid-1990s efforts have been concentrated on developing offshore reserves in the Black Sea, opening up exploration and processing to foreign investors. Deposits of other minerals are small and contribute little to export earnings. Many coal mines have been shut down.

The electricity industry is outdated but does produce a surplus for export. An agreement in 2000 connected the national grid with that of Bulgaria. The removal of price ceilings since 1997, with a consequent doubling of prices, provides strong incentives to users to improve poor efficiency.

ROMANIA : LAND USE

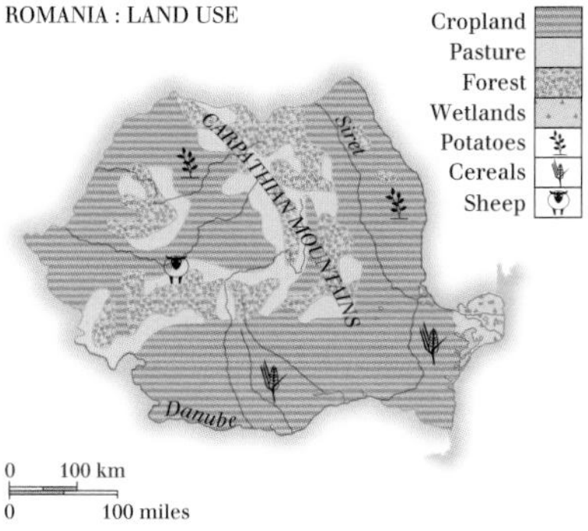
Cropland
Pasture
Forest
Wetlands
Potatoes
Cereals
Sheep
CARPATHIAN MOUNTAINS
Siret
Danube
0 100 km
0 100 miles

ENVIRONMENT

Sustainability rank: 80th

5% (4% partially protected)

4.9 tonnes per capita

ENVIRONMENTAL TREATIES

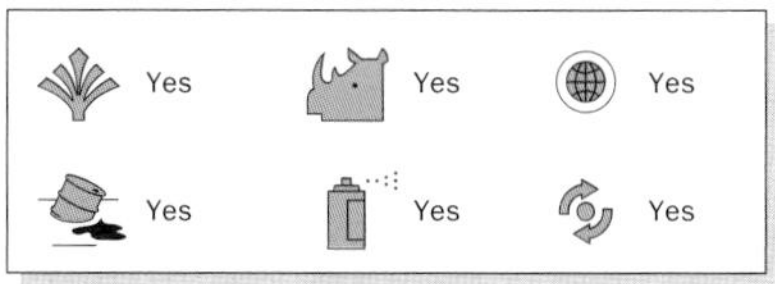
Yes
Yes
Yes
Yes
Yes
Yes

Saddled with the disastrous legacy of its communist-era industry, Romania needs help with a major cleanup. Air pollution, mainly from cement plant and power-station emissions but also from exhaust fumes and low-quality coal, is most serious in the south. Cyanide and heavy metal leaked from a gold mine in Baia Mare in 2000 created a transboundary pollution catastrophe in the Tisza river in Hungary. The Danube delta, despite serious pollution, is identified as a potential biosphere reserve.

CRIME

Death penalty not used

45,309 prisoners

Up 21% 1996–1998

CRIME RATES

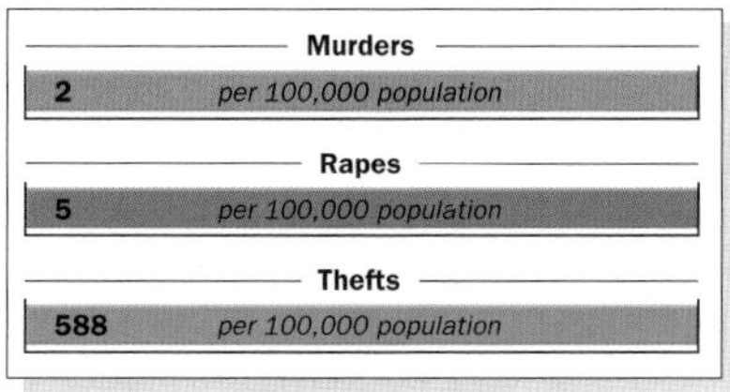
Murders
2 per 100,000 population
Rapes
5 per 100,000 population
Thefts
588 per 100,000 population

The black economy is the primary source of income for a third of the population. Levels of tax evasion are estimated to be among the highest in the world.

HEALTH

Welfare state health benefits

1 per 556 people

Heart & cerebrovascular diseases, cancers, accidents, tuberculosis

Average life expectancy is among the lowest in Europe; in the worst polluted parts of Transylvania it is as low as 61 years. The incidence of tuberculosis is the highest in Europe. After years of chronic state underfunding, there was a shift in 1999–2001 toward an insurance-based system.

SPENDING

GDP/cap. decrease

CONSUMPTION AND SPENDING

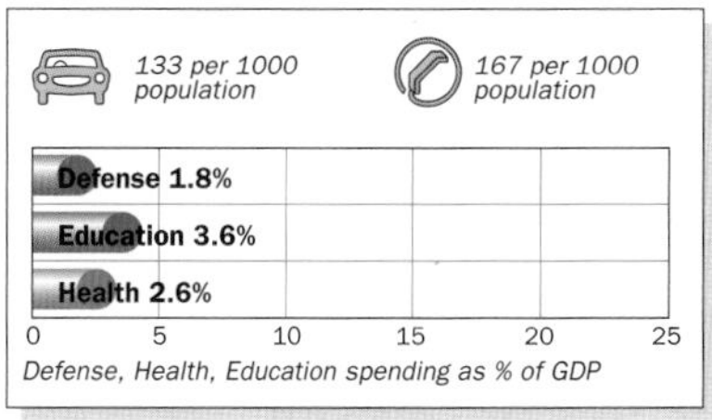
133 per 1000 population
167 per 1000 population
Defense 1.8%
Education 3.6%
Health 2.6%
0
5
10
15
20
25
Defense, Health, Education spending as % of GDP

Real incomes have been hit hard by a decade of economic decline; 40% live below the national poverty line. Most families own their own homes (often overcrowded) and many have small plots of land. Few rural homes have running water or sewerage.

MEDIA

TV ownership high

Daily newspaper circulation 298 per 1000 people

PUBLISHING AND BROADCAST MEDIA

There are 106 daily newspapers, including *Evenimentul Zilei, Adevărul, România Liberă, Curierul National*, and *Cotidianul*

5 services: 2 state-owned, 3 independent

4 services: 3 state-owned, 1 independent

Many of the newspapers which proliferated after 1989 are now closing, since rising prices mean that fewer can afford them. Political censorship was reimposed in 1994, and in practice the government controls the national independent TV service. The first satellite TV channel was launched in 1994, and the first exclusively Hungarian radio station in 1999.

EDUCATION

School leaving age: 14

98%

411,687 students

THE EDUCATION SYSTEM

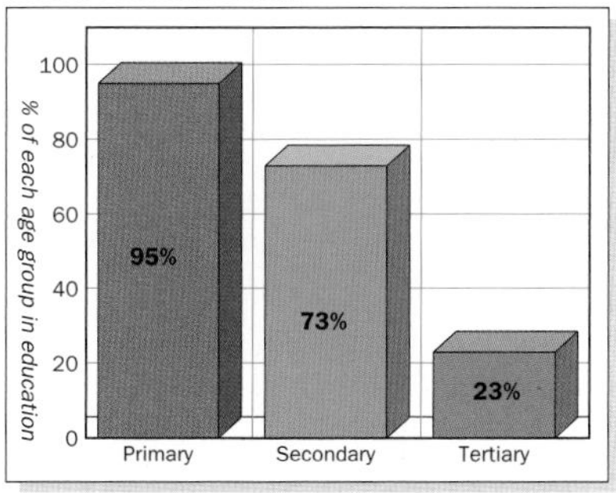
% of each age group in education
100
80
60
40
20
0
95%
73%
23%
Primary
Secondary
Tertiary

Attendance at primary and secondary schools is far below the European average. As university enrollment is no longer restricted, the number of tertiary students has risen rapidly. The government pledged in early 2000 to devote at least 4% of GDP to education. Improvements to teachers' pay helped end their general strike, called to protest against the chronic underfunding of the school system.

WORLD RANKING

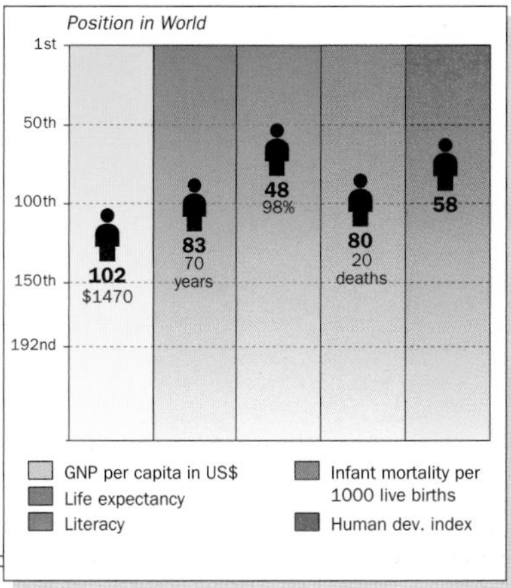
Position in World
1st
50th
100th
150th
192nd
102
$1470
83
70
years
48
98%
80
20
deaths
58
GNP per capita in US$
Life expectancy
Literacy
Infant mortality per 1000 live births
Human dev. index

R

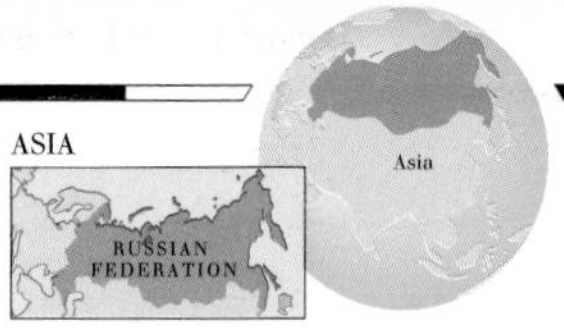
ASIA
Asia
RUSSIAN FEDERATION

Russian Federation

Official Name: Russian Federation **Capital:** Moscow
Population: 146.9 million **Currency:** Rouble **Official Language:** Russian

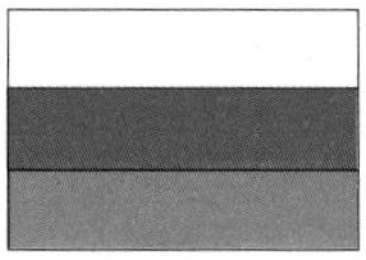

1991
1991
June 12
RUS
+1 to +11
+7
.ru

Russia's territory extends over 17 million sq km (6.6 million sq miles). This makes it by far the world's largest state, almost twice as big as either the USA or China. Bounded by the Arctic and Pacific Oceans on its northern and eastern coasts, it also has land boundaries with 13 countries. With the formal dissolution of the USSR in 1991, Russia became an independent sovereign state. Within the CIS, it maintains a traditionally dominant role in central Asia and Eurasia. Ethnic Russians make up 82% of the population, but there are around 150 smaller ethnic groups, many with their own national territories within Russia's borders. Regionalism and separatism are major political issues. The situation is complicated by the fact that many of these territories are rich in key resources such as oil, gas, gold, and diamonds.

The Kremlin, Moscow. *Rebuilt in 1475 by Ivan the Great, who commissioned architects from Pskov and Italy, it is enclosed by walls 4 km (1.5 miles) long and lies on the Moscow River.*

CLIMATE

Subarctic/continental/mountain/steppe

WEATHER CHART

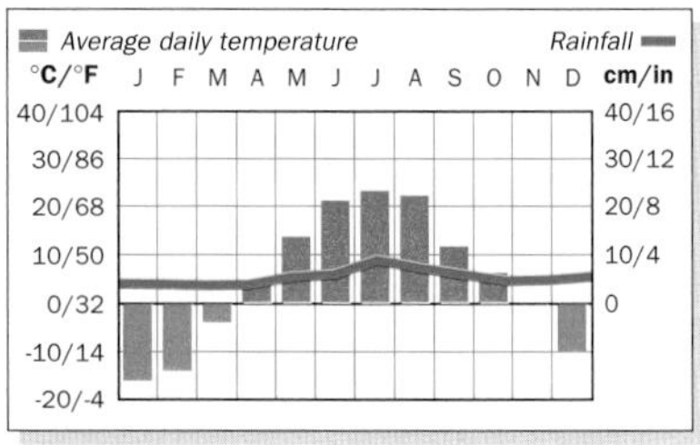
Average daily temperature
Rainfall
°C/°F
J F M A M J J A S O N D
cm/in
40/104
30/86
20/68
10/50
0/32
-10/14
-20/-4
40/16
30/12
20/8
10/4
0

Russia has a cold continental climate, characterized by two widely divergent main seasons. Spring and autumn are very brief periods of transition between warm summers and freezing winters. The country is open to the influences of the Arctic and Atlantic to the north and west. However, mountains to the south and east prevent any warming effects from the Indian and Pacific Oceans filtering across. Severe winters affect most regions. Winter temperatures vary surprisingly little from north to south, but fall sharply in eastern regions. The January temperature of –70°C (–94°F) recorded at Verkhoyansk in Siberia is the world record low outside Antarctica.

R

Housing in Moscow. *Living conditions in major cities are cramped, with two families often sharing one small flat.*

NORWAY
FINLAND
BARENTS SEA
Novaya Zemlya
Murmansk
Apatity
KOL'SKIY POLUOSTROV
KARELIYA
Gulf of Finland
Kaliningrad
POLAND
LITHUANIA
LATVIA
ESTONIA
St Petersburg
Ladozhskoye Ozero
Petrozavodsk
Onezhskoye Ozero
BELOYE MORE
Severodvinsk
Arkhangel'sk
Arctic Circle
Ostrov Kolguyev
Ostrov Vaygach
Nar'yan-Mar
Pskov
Novgorod
BELARUS
Smolensk
Cherepovets
Rybinskoye Vdkhr.
Tver'
Vologda
MOSCOW
Yaroslavl'
Kostroma
Ivanovo
Vladimir
Severnaya Dvina
Kotlas
K O M I
Pechora
Vorkuta
Salekhard
Nadym
Syktyvkar
Bryansk
Tula
Orel
Kursk
Ryazan'
Nizhniy Novgorod
Kirov
UKRAINE
Belgorod
Lipetsk
Voronezh
Tambov
MARIY EL
CHAVASH
Kazan'
MORDOVIYA
Bereznik
UDMURTSKAYA
Izhevsk
Perm'
Serov
SIBIRSKA
Khanty-Mansiysk
Penza
Ul'yanovsk
Kuybyshevskoye Vdkhr.
TATARSTAN
Naberezhnyye Chelny
SEA OF AZOV
Rostov-na-Donu
Mikhaylovka
Saratov
Don
Tol'yatti
Samara
Balakovo
BASHKORTOSTAN
Yekaterinburg
Nizhnevartovsk
ZAPADNO
RAVNINA
Tyumen'
Tobol'sk
BLACK SEA
Krasnodar
Volgograd
Volga
Maykop
ADYGEYA
Sochi
Stavropol'
Elista
Sterlitamak
Ufa
URAL MOUNTAINS
Orenburg
Ural
Chelyabinsk
Kurgan
Irtysh
KARACHAYEVO-CHERKESSKAYA
KABARDINO-BALKARSKAYA
KALMYKIYA
INGUSHSKAYA
Astrakhan'
Magnitogorsk
SEVERNAYA OSETIYA-ALANIYA
Nal'chik
Vladikavkaz
GEORGIA
Groznyy
CHECHENSKAYA
Orsk
Omsk
KAZAKHSTAN
CASPIAN SEA
DAGESTAN
Makhachkala
AZERBAIJAN
Rubtsovsk
Zemlya Georga
30°
40°
50°
60°
70°
80°
N
RUSSIAN FEDERATION
Total Land Area :
16 995 800 sq. km
(6 562 100 sq. miles)
POPULATION
over 5 000 000
over 1 000 000
over 500 000
over 100 000
over 50 000
over 10 000
LAND HEIGHT
3000m/9843ft
2000m/6562ft
1000m/3281ft
500m/1640ft
200m/656ft
Sea Level
-200m/-656ft
0
500 km
0
500 miles

TRANSPORTATION

Drive on right

Sheremetyevo, Moscow
9.56m passengers

4723 ships
11.1m grt

THE TRANSPORTATION NETWORK

336,000 km (208,780 miles)	None
86,031 km (53,460 miles)	101,000 km (62,758 miles)

Russia has a comprehensive transportation network. However, since 1991, all systems have seen some decline due to lack of funding. Cities are still served by good trolley and bus systems and Moscow has one of the most impressive subway systems in the world. In rural areas, car ownership is low and the population relies on an extensive bus service. About 20% of the railroad track should be renewed annually owing to frost and other damage. Shortage of funds means this is no longer done. The railroads are heavily used but seriously overburdened and liable to accidents and delays. New track has been laid for the Sokol (Falcon) high speed rail link between Moscow and St. Petersburg; the first trains using it, in December 2000, cut over an hour off the minimum journey time and further dramatic reductions are expected. Roads in major cities are deteriorating, as are interurban highways. Crime is a problem on railroads – notably the Trans-Siberian – and roads.

The former Aeroflot monopoly of air transportation has been broken up. Aeroflot now competes as Aeroflot Russian International Airlines, but hundreds of regional "babyflot" airlines run mainly domestic routes, some with alarming accident records.

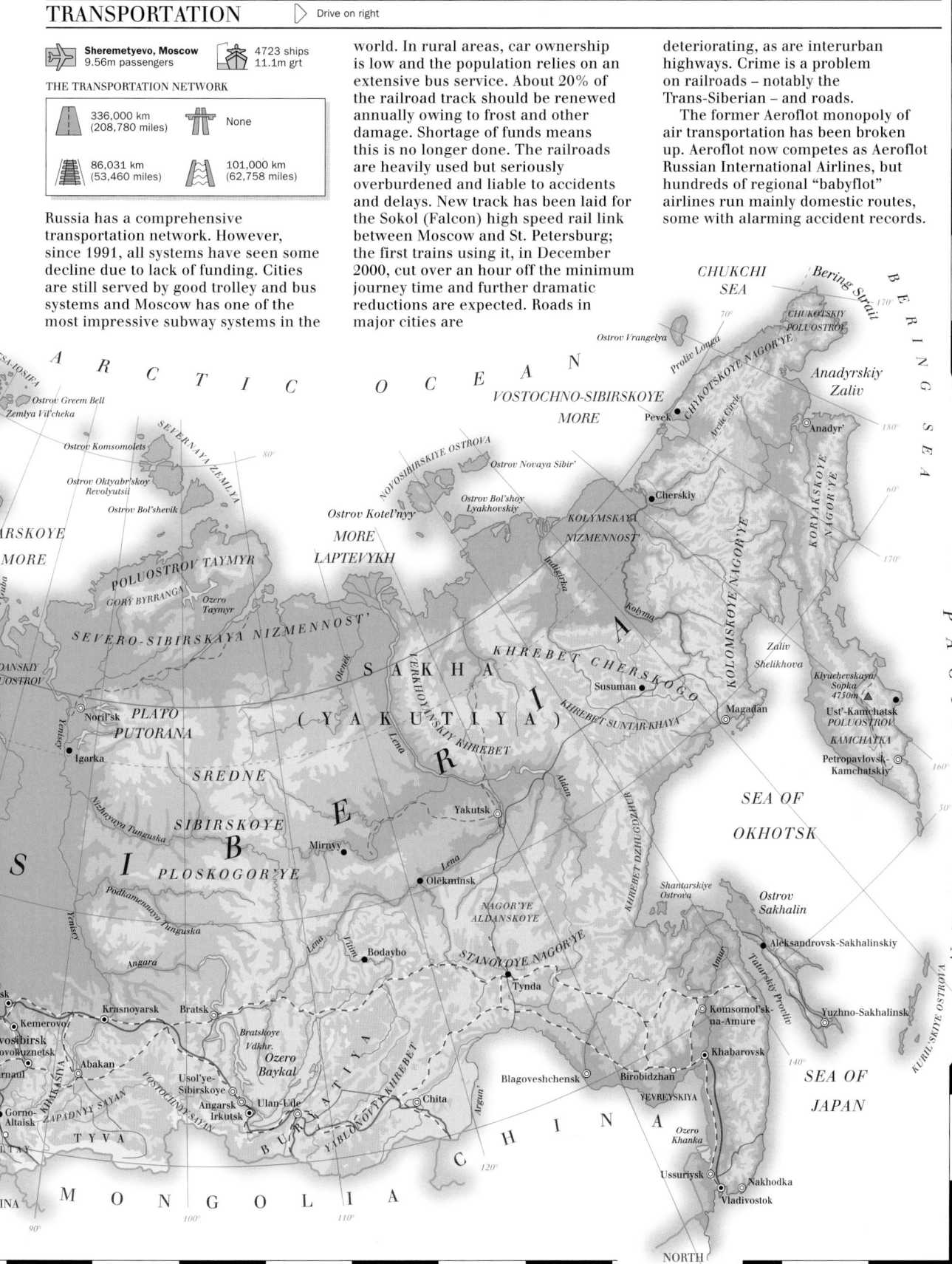

CHUKCHI SEA

Bering Strait

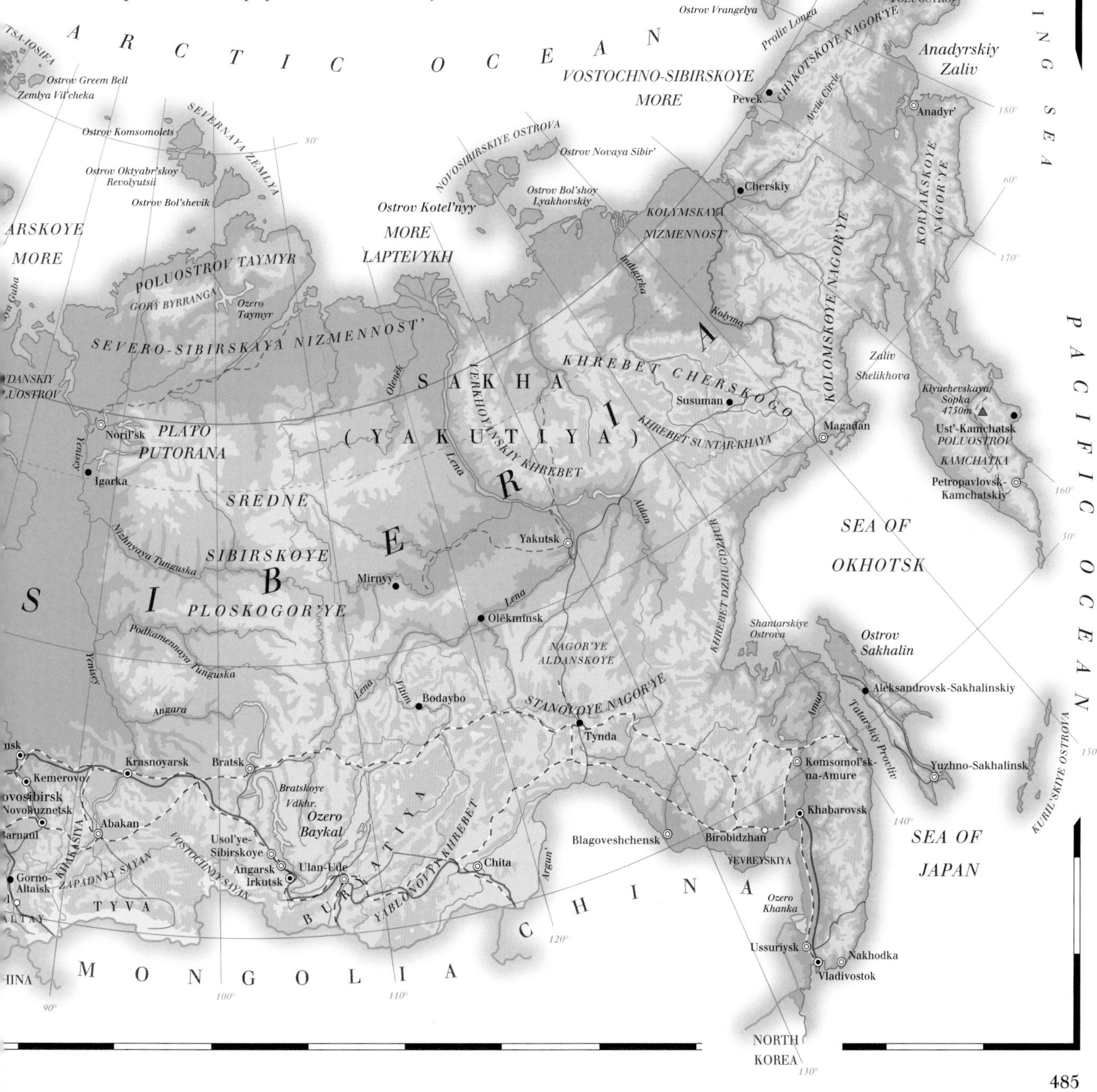
ARCTIC OCEAN
BERING SEA
PACIFIC OCEAN
VOSTOCHNO-SIBIRSKOYE MORE
MORE LAPTEVYKH
SEA OF OKHOTSK
SEA OF JAPAN
Ostrov Vrangelya
Proliv Longa
CHUKOTSKIY POLUOSTROV
CHYKOTSKOYE NAGOR'YE
Anadyrskiy Zaliv
Pevek
Anadyr'
Arctic Circle
Ostrov Greem Bell
Zemlya Vil'cheka
Ostrov Komsomolets
SEVERNAYA ZEMLYA
Ostrov Oktyabr'skoy Revolyutsii
Ostrov Bol'shevik
NOVOSIBIRSKIYE OSTROVA
Ostrov Novaya Sibir'
Ostrov Bol'shoy Lyakhovskiy
Ostrov Kotel'nyy
Cherskiy
KOLYMSKAYA NIZMENNOST'
KORYAKSKOYE NAGOR'YE
KOLOMSKOYE NAGOR'YE
POLUOSTROV TAYMYR
GORY BYRRANGA
Ozero Taymyr
SEVERO-SIBIRSKAYA NIZMENNOST'
Indigirka
Kolyma
KHREBET CHERSKOGO
Zaliv Shelikhova
Klyuchevskaya Sopka 4750m
Ust'-Kamchatsk
POLUOSTROV KAMCHATKA
Petropavlovsk-Kamchatskiy
SAKHA (YAKUTIYA)
SIBERIA
VERKHOYANSKIY KHREBET
KHREBET SUNTAR-KHAYA
Susuman
Magadan
Olenëk
Lena
Noril'sk
PLATO PUTORANA
Yenisey
Igarka
SREDNE SIBIRSKOYE PLOSKOGOR'YE
Nizhnyaya Tunguska
Yakutsk
Aldan
KHREBET DZHUGDZHUR
Mirnyy
Olëkminsk
Podkamennaya Tunguska
NAGOR'YE ALDANSKOYE
Shantarskiye Ostrova
Ostrov Sakhalin
Aleksandrovsk-Sakhalinskiy
Vitim
Bodaybo
STANOVOYE NAGOR'YE
Tynda
Angara
Amur
Tatarskiy Proliv
Komsomol'sk-na-Amure
Yuzhno-Sakhalinsk
KURIL'SKIYE OSTROVA
Krasnoyarsk
Bratsk
Kemerovo
Novosibirsk
Novokuznetsk
Barnaul
Abakan
KHAKASIYA
Bratskoye Vdkhr.
Ozero Baykal
BURYATIYA
YABLONOVYY KHREBET
Khabarovsk
Blagoveshchensk
Birobidzhan
YEVREYSKIYA
Usol'ye-Sibirskoye
Angarsk
Irkutsk
Ulan-Ude
Chita
Argun'
VOSTOCHNYY SAYAN
ZAPADNYY SAYAN
Gorno-Altaisk
TYVA
Ozero Khanka
Ussuriysk
Nakhodka
Vladivostok
CHINA
MONGOLIA
NORTH KOREA

TOURISM

Visitors : Population 1:6.9

21.2m visitors

Up 15% in 2000

MAIN TOURIST ARRIVALS

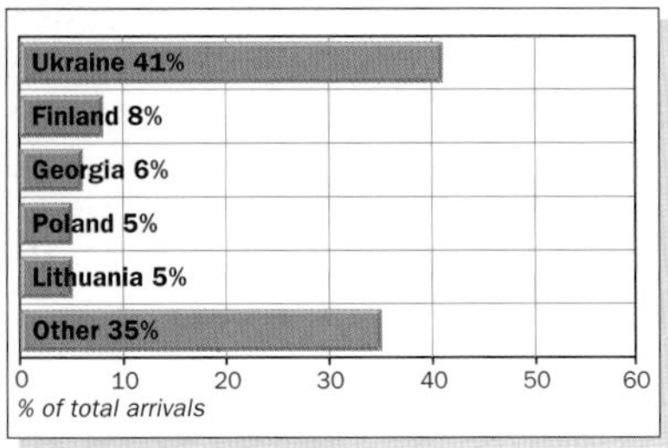
Ukraine 41%
Finland 8%
Georgia 6%
Poland 5%
Lithuania 5%
Other 35%
0 10 20 30 40 50 60
% of total arrivals

The privatization and breakup of the previous monopoly tourist agency, Intourist, has led to a vast expansion of tourism opportunities in Russia; each region is keen to earn hard currency and to attract rich visitors. By 2000 the total number of tourists a year had reached over 21 million.

At the luxury end of the market, trips from St. Petersburg to Tashkent on former president Brezhnev's official train are now available. River trips down the Volga and visits to medieval monasteries are increasingly popular. Tourists can also explore forests, or fish for salmon in the Kola peninsula. The defense sector has opened up to tourism and now offers flights in MiG jets, or drives in T–84 Russian tanks.

Moscow and St. Petersburg remain favorite destinations. Hotels in both cities tend either to cater for the well-off or to be of a basic standard. Near St. Petersburg, Novgorod has many fine churches and the Pskov area is celebrated as the setting for many of Pushkin's works, including *Eugene Onegin* and *Boris Godunov*.

Many parts of Russia remain inaccessible to most tourists. The communist ban on foreigners visiting the Urals has been lifted, but the area still has very few facilities. Resorts such as the subtropical Sochi on the Black Sea, where powerful Russians have *dachas* (country houses), have experienced a building boom.

PEOPLE

Pop. density low

Russian

9/km² (22/mi²)

THE URBAN/RURAL POPULATION SPLIT

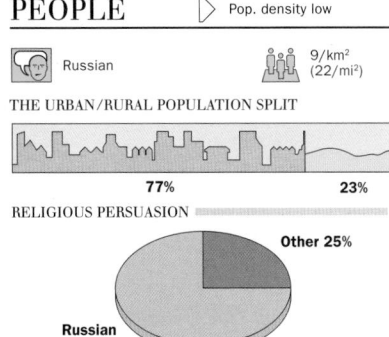

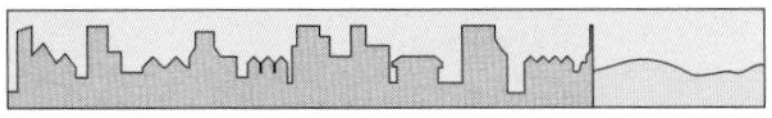
77%
23%

RELIGIOUS PERSUASION

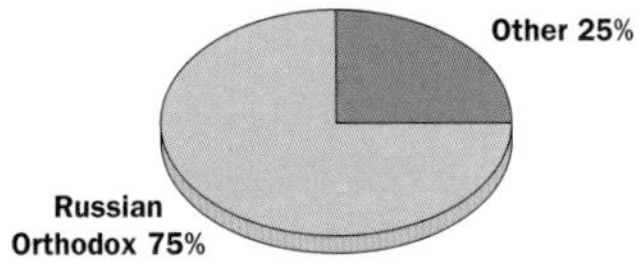
Other 25%
Russian Orthodox 75%

ETHNIC MAKEUP

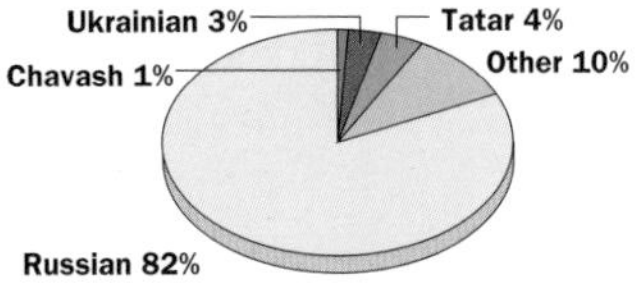
Ukrainian 3%
Tatar 4%
Chavash 1%
Other 10%
Russian 82%

In the former Soviet Union, Russians were just over 50% of the population, but in Russia they are an overwhelming majority. Although significant numbers of Russians still live in some of the neighboring former Soviet republics, notably Ukraine and Latvia, a rise in nationalism has persuaded many to return to Russia.

Within Russia there has also been an increase in ethnic tension, especially in the Caucasus. Hostility toward the Muslim Chechens is particularly acute. There are 57 nationalities with their own territories within the federation and 95 nationalities (but only 6% of the population) without a territory.

Social life in Russia has not changed significantly since the demise of communism. With the lifting of censorship, there has been a greater expression of sexuality and of political and religious views. The expensive rebuilding of Moscow's Church of Christ the Savior symbolized this change. The strong revival of the Russian Orthodox Church is boosted by legal recognition of its "special role" in Russia's history. All religious organizations were required to re-register by 1 January 2000, under conditions which many small minority faiths could not meet, and whereby a church deemed to "violate social order" would be banned.

One marked change of which Russians speak is the growing importance given to money. Mutual support systems of extended friendships are now in decline.

The position of women has changed little since the fall of communism. Many have suffered from the rise in unemployment, but this reflects the demise of part-time or badly paid jobs, rather than gender-motivated social change. Most Russians have very modest living standards and were further impoverished by the collapse of the economy in the late 1990s.

POPULATION AGE BREAKDOWN

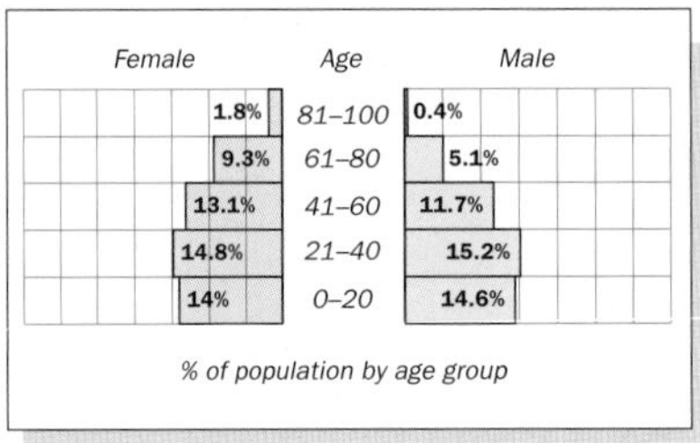
Female
Age
Male
1.8% 81–100 0.4%
9.3% 61–80 5.1%
13.1% 41–60 11.7%
14.8% 21–40 15.2%
14% 0–20 14.6%
% of population by age group

POLITICS

Multiparty elections

L. House 1999/2003
U. House Varying

President
Vladimir Putin

AT THE LAST ELECTION

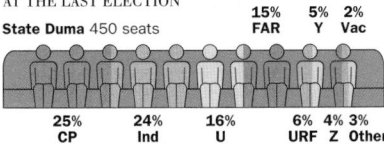

State Duma 450 seats

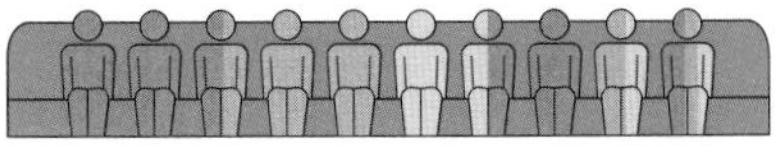
15% FAR
5% Y
2% Vac
25% CP
24% Ind
16% U
6% URF
4% Z
3% Others

CP = Communist Party **Ind** = Independents **U** = Unity
FAR = Fatherland–All Russia **URF** = Union of Right Forces
Y = Yabloko **Z** = Zhirinovsky's Bloc **Vac** = Vacant

Council of the Federation 178 seats

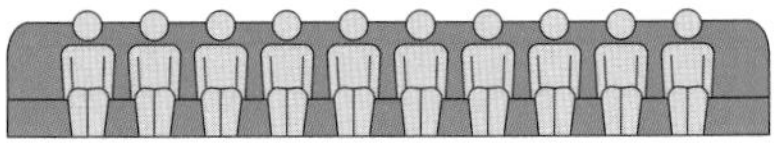

Each of 89 regions is represented in the Council of the Federation (Soviet Federatsii) by two members chosen by the regional legislature

The government is responsible to the elected parliament (*Duma*), but executive power lies firmly with the president.

Main Political Issues

Living standards

Russians are disillusioned at the failure of politicians to improve their living standards. The fall of communism swept away the securities which used to underpin life – long-term employment, guaranteed housing, and a basic diet – hitting the old particularly hard. Uneven and crisis-prone efforts at introducing a market economy under former president Yeltsin created much insecurity.

Crime and corruption

Crime levels rose alarmingly under the post-Soviet regime, and visitors began to be warned against walking the streets of St. Petersburg or Moscow after dark. Widespread bureaucratic corruption was countered by the power acquired by business tycoons, the so-called "oligarchs," who snapped up privatized industries at bargain prices. President Putin has launched a crusade against these oligarchs, but has shied away from a full-scale review of the privatization process.

Regionalism and separatism

Nation-based separatism is brutally suppressed. Nowhere has this been

Former president Boris Yeltsin, *renowned for his erratic behavior, stepped down in 1999.*

Mikhail Gorbachev, *whose restructuring ultimately led to the breakup of the Soviet Union.*

R

POLITICS *continued*

made clearer than by the ferocious military campaign in Chechnya.

Influence accumulated under the Yeltsin regime by Russia's 89 regional governors has been reversed by Putin's efforts to concentrate power in the presidency. Control of police and taxation has been centralized in seven huge federal districts, responsible only to Putin, and the governors have been stripped of their seats in the upper house, the Federation Council.

Russia's loss of Great Power status
The collapse of the economy and Russia's withdrawal from a global role after communism has badly dented Russian pride. It experienced particularly sharp rebuffs when its views were disregarded over NATO military action against Yugoslavia in 1999, and over US missile defense plans in 2001.

PROFILE
Since coming to power as acting president from the end of 1999, Vladimir Putin has greatly consolidated his position. Having stormed to victory in the first round of the March 2000 presidential elections, he has tackled the power of the business oligarchs, and of Russia's 89 regional governors, with his program of centralization. His support within the *Duma* has been consolidated by the transformation of the Unity bloc (which he formed for the December 1999 legislative elections) into an official party. A merger with the Fatherland bloc in April 2001 made Unity the largest single party in parliament. Although Putin's personal standing was shaken over criticism of his handling of the *Kursk* submarine disaster, in which 118 sailors died in August 2000, the marked improvement in the economy during his first year in office stood greatly to his credit in popular opinion. It also contributed to the standing of Prime Minister Mikhail Kasyanov, appointed in May 2000 with revitalizing the economy as his central task. The Communist Party, which until April 2001 was the single largest party in the *Duma*, remains powerful because of its effective organization and its ability to appeal to those who have suffered from the upheavals of the post-Soviet period. However, even with parliamentary allies, it has been unable to take power. Its leader Gennady Zyuganov has three times been beaten to the presidency.

Vladimir Putin *was handed power by Yeltsin in 1999, and was elected president in 2000.*

Mikhail Kasyanov, *economic reformist appointed prime minister in 2000.*

The conflict in Chechnya, which has damaged Putin's image internationally, has by contrast been a key element in his domestic appeal as a strong leader. He prosecuted the renewed war fiercely when first appointed prime minister in 1999, as a little-known former head of the Federal Security Service (FSB). The then president, Boris Yeltsin, had seen his own second term (1996–1999) overshadowed by his health problems, economic crisis, and corruption.

Dramatic changes of government personnel were a characteristic of this period, as Yeltsin confronted the *Duma* in both 1998 and 1999 and imposed his own choice of prime minister.

WORLD AFFAIRS

Joined UN in 1945

CE | CIS | IAEA | G8 | OSCE

In the first years after the breakup of the Soviet Union, Russia displayed little independent initiative in foreign affairs and allied itself closely to the USA. Its weak economy put it in no position to antagonize the Western powers.

From 1993 onwards, a more independent foreign policy emerged with a renewed skepticism about Western intentions, especially NATO's eastward expansion. In early 2000 President Putin gave some signs of wanting to reestablish Russia as a global alternative to the USA, but a new foreign policy doctrine announced that June accepted the pragmatic need to be nonconfrontational. Russia's limited resources should be concentrated, it said, in areas which could assist in solving internal problems. Russia remains anxious about the possible expansion of NATO up to its borders and – in common with China – feels particularly threatened by US plans for a new missile defense system. It resents Western criticism of Putin's military onslaught against Chechnya, which it regarded as a purely internal matter.

The 1999 NATO bombardment of Yugoslavia pushed relations with the West to a low ebb. Russia saw Yugoslavia as a natural ally, both being predominantly Orthodox Christian and Slavic, and struggling to emerge from communism.

The successor states of the USSR are regarded as "near abroad." Several CIS regimes are run by ex-communists with close links with Moscow, and the Belarus regime in particular is keen on reunion with Russia.

St. Basil's Cathedral, Moscow. *It was commissioned by Tsar Ivan the Terrible and built in 1555–1561. The exterior domes were decorated in the 1670s.*

AID

Recipient

$1.8bn (receipts) | Up 153% 1997–1999

Russia has received billions of dollars in aid from Western countries on several occasions to stave off government debt and to promote economic restructuring. Large-scale IMF credits were obtained during the economic crises of the mid-and late 1990s.

DEFENSE

Compulsory military service

$56.8bn | Down 1% in 1999

RUSSIAN ARMED FORCES

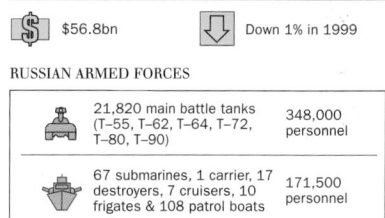

21,820 main battle tanks (T–55, T–62, T–64, T–72, T–80, T–90)	348,000 personnel
67 submarines, 1 carrier, 17 destroyers, 7 cruisers, 10 frigates & 108 patrol boats	171,500 personnel
1590 combat aircraft (MiG–23/25/29/31, Su–24/25/27)	184,600 personnel
776 ICBM, 19 SSBN, 100 ABM	

The loss of the 118-man *Kursk* submarine in August 2000 symbolized the long-term decline of Russia's military might.

Maintaining and using the enormous former communist war machine has proved too expensive, despite a rapid decline in numbers. Plans have been drafted to axe hundreds of thousands of troops by 2003, and conscription is set to be abolished in 2005. Public anger at conditions within the services has led to pay increases.

Spending on nuclear forces is limited to physical protection of warheads. The *Duma* ratified the Start II Nuclear Disarmament Treaty and the Comprehensive Test Ban Treaty in early 2000, but Russia sees new US missile defense proposals as destabilizing fundamentally the existing nuclear agreements.

Russia's northern and Pacific navy fleets are inactive and deteriorating fast.

R

ECONOMIC UPHEAVAL, REGIONALISM, AND CENTRALISM

THE RUSSIAN ECONOMY surprised many by its apparent recent recovery, recording growth of 7.7% in 2000. Massive problems remain, however, many of them relating to the sprawling and decaying industrial infrastructure, particularly in some remoter regions.

The Yeltsin regime in the 1990s failed to manage an effective reform and restructuring process. When matters came to a head in 1998, collapse was only narrowly averted, in a crisis which spotlighted the chronic weakness of central government finances. Since then, however, successive governments have overseen a real improvement in their own financial position. The combination of devaluation, an international rescue package, and default on domestic debt was further helped by increased tax revenue and the introduction of a uniform rate of income tax in 2001. When imports became much more expensive after the

***Residents of St. Petersburg** queue in the streets for basic foodstuffs.*

1998 devaluation, Russian-made goods started appearing in Moscow and St. Petersburg again, beginning with big increases in supplies of such things as electric kettles, bicycles, refrigerators, and washing machines. Middle-class Russians in the cities, who had found ways to survive the crisis, were eager buyers. Meanwhile, export earnings in the mining and oil and gas sectors were boosted by the low rouble and by the improvement in world prices. Gazprom, the giant company which monopolizes the gas industry, benefited most, while industries such as aluminum in Sakha (Yakutia) have become even more powerful in the local economy. The petroleum industry still suffers from high costs, because of both its own inefficiencies and the distance which pipelines have to cover to bring the output of distant fields to market.

For the majority of Russians, wages and pensions were paid with greater regularity after the 1998 crisis, but they were still a long way from catching up with the consequences of years of inflation. Teachers, for example, had had no pay increase for five years by 1999, when the state statistical committee itself calculated that almost 38% of Russians were trying to get by on incomes lower than the official subsistence level. Impoverished pensioners could commonly be seen attempting to sell their remaining possessions from makeshift stalls on street corners, at least in cities where enough people had money to buy them.

VICTIMS OF CHANGE

For many people in the provinces, the dismantling of the old command economy meant the disappearance of what was often the sole source of employment. Far-flung towns had been built exclusively around a particular heavy industry, such as steel, coal, shipbuilding, machine tools, or arms production. Many of these concerns, no longer with a market, were impossible to privatize. Their workers, put on short time or laid off, have been reduced to living on promises, state handouts, and barter arrangements. In cities in the Arctic north, people leave if they can; Murmansk, the largest, has lost a fifth of its population in a decade. In the far east, the collapse of heating and power systems around Vladivostok left residents freezing though the 2000–2001 winter, the bitterest for 70 years. The disappearance of proper welfare state provision in areas such as health care makes the situation even more catastrophic. Rates of alcoholism, drug abuse, and suicide have all risen. Most hard pressed are people with access to neither work nor land, living with children in small urban settlements. Wherever possible, however, people grow food to be as self-sufficient as possible, and use what they can for

***Heavy industries** have declined dramatically, and many factories now lie idle.*

***Poor maintenance** has resulted in cracks and leaks along Russia's network of oil pipelines.*

barter. Great reliance is also placed on family support networks. The relevance of the formal economy is thereby much reduced, while rents, transportation, and utility bills are still heavily subsidized. Even when cash changes hands, a large proportion of all purchases involves the black market in one way or another.

The running down of heavy industries has left some areas with massive environmental damage, among the most notorious instances being the pollution of rivers by toxic waste from the metallurgy industry in the Kola peninsula in the north. Problems of disposal of radioactive wastes affect northern coastal areas in particular, although the worst such legacy of the former Soviet Union – the effects of the nuclear accident at Chernobyl – has been left to Belarus and Ukraine.

REPUBLICS AND CENTRAL CONTROL

Some of the 21 republics which exist within the Russian Federation pressed hard in the 1990s to assert greater control over their mineral resources, believing that they could be managed more profitably at the region level, and resenting the outflow of their earnings. Regionalism based on dissatisfaction with central economic management began emerging as a key political issue.

Tatarstan is a case in point. Lying on the Volga some 1000 km east of Moscow, the republic (alone except for Chechnya) in 1992 refused to sign the treaty between the Russian Federation and its constituent parts. Instead, Tatar president Mintimer Shaimiev negotiated better autonomy terms in a 1994 agreement, whose detailed revenue-sharing provisions were extended for a further five years from 1999. Tatarstan also avoided rushing into privatization, conducted elsewhere in such a manner as to allow former managers effectively to appropriate huge assets. Its continuing control of the Tatneft oil company provides both a source of revenue and a route for foreign borrowing on relatively favorable terms.

President Putin, however, has acted swiftly and with determination to reverse the fragmentation of the Russian Federation. Before becoming president he was already closely identified with "firmness" in relaunching a brutal war in 1999 (ostensibly as an anti-terrorist operation) against Chechnya, the only republic to seek to secede. After his election in 2000 Putin's first major policy action was to group the federation's 89 regional administrative entities under seven federal districts headed by newly appointed presidential envoys. He has also asserted powers to disband regional legislators and dismiss regional governors, and removed the governors from the upper house of parliament, the Federation Council, although they do now sit on a new advisory State Council and have been given the right to stand for more than just two terms of office.

Recognizing the need to compromise with Putin's reassertion of central powers, Shaimiev (reelected for a third term in 2001) has reduced the recent emphasis on "Tatarization." Federal control over tax collection and spending is more evident again, as is the presence of federal agencies in the Tatar capital, Kazan. A push to reintroduce the Latin alphabet in place of Cyrillic in Tatar schools, launched in 2000, was deferred the following year. The population has at least as many ethnic Russians as Tatars, who – like the Chechens – are mainly Muslims and fiercely proud of their distinctive language and culture.

New gas pipelines being laid across the frozen expanses of Siberia.

ECONOMICS

Inflation 190.4% p.a. (1990–1999)

$329bn

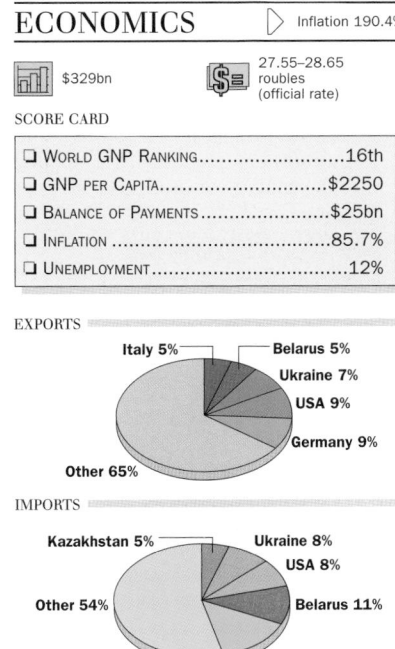

27.55–28.65 roubles (official rate)

SCORE CARD

❑ WORLD GNP RANKING	16th
❑ GNP PER CAPITA	$2250
❑ BALANCE OF PAYMENTS	$25bn
❑ INFLATION	85.7%
❑ UNEMPLOYMENT	12%

EXPORTS

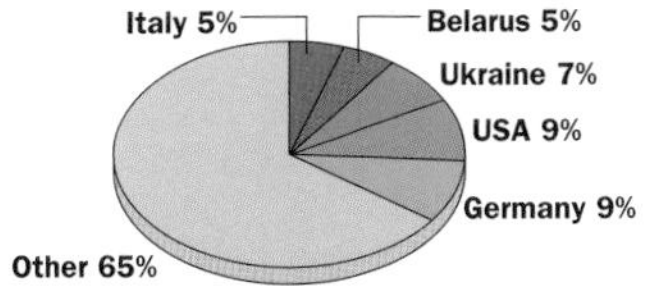
Italy 5%
Belarus 5%
Ukraine 7%
USA 9%
Germany 9%
Other 65%

IMPORTS

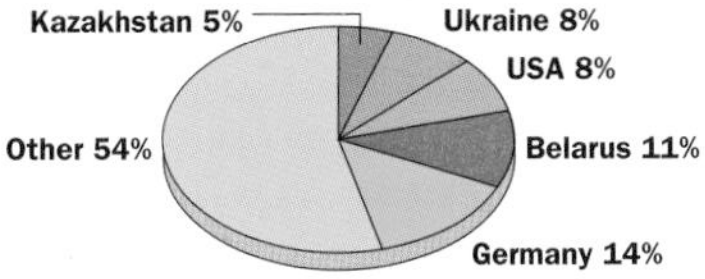
Kazakhstan 5%
Ukraine 8%
USA 8%
Belarus 11%
Germany 14%
Other 54%

STRENGTHS

Huge natural resources; in particular hydrocarbons, precious metals, fuel, timber. Enormous engineering and scientific base. Some dynamic small enterprises. Good potential for oil and natural gas.

WEAKNESSES

Privatization was exploited by former managers, who asset-stripped their companies. Organized crime syndicates control huge areas of the economy. Many of the skills developed under communism became irrelevant in the new economy, increasing popular disillusion. Lack of adequate legal infrastructure made transactions difficult. Russian companies keep billions of US dollars in Western bank accounts, an outflow of capital which damages the domestic economy.

ECONOMIC PERFORMANCE INDICATOR

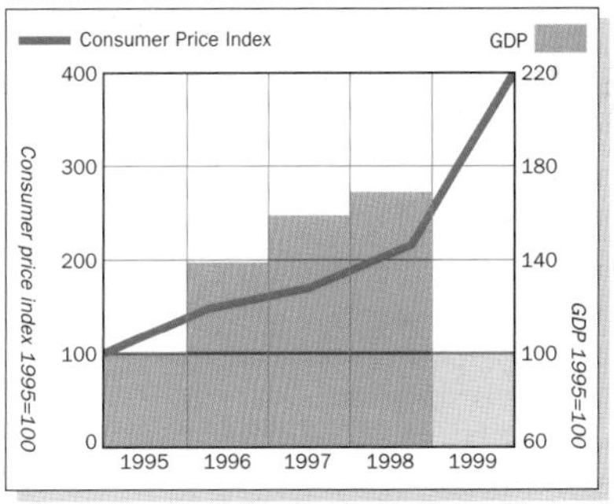
Consumer Price Index
GDP
Consumer price index 1995=100
GDP 1995=100
400
300
200
100
0
220
180
140
100
60
1995
1996
1997
1998
1999

Inflation in the 1990s undermined domestic savings and purchasing power. Tax evasion is widespread. The 1998 crisis hit investor confidence and made it more difficult to attract new foreign loans.

PROFILE

The collapse of industrial production, begun in the late 1980s, appeared to be bottoming out in the mid-1990s. However, the painfully won achievements of an IMF-backed stabilization program (defending the rouble, cutting inflation, and reducing the budget deficit) were swept away again in the 1998 crisis. Further IMF lending was then placed in jeopardy by reports that loans were being diverted into the hands of organized crime syndicates. Yeltsin oscillated between reform and appeasement of the hostile public and the communists in parliament. In 2000, Putin moved swiftly to start dismantling the power of the new economic elites. An upward turn in the economy saw higher industrial production and growth of 7.7% in GDP in 2000. A new 13% flat rate of income tax introduced in 2001 promised to help reduce widespread tax evasion. Putin has urged sweeping deregulation of the economy but the lack of industrial investment means that modernization faces enormous obstacles.

RUSSIAN FEDERATION : MAJOR BUSINESSES

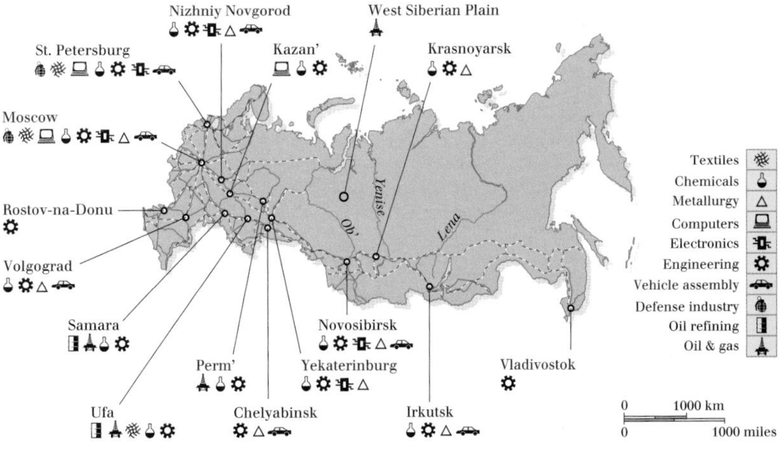
Nizhniy Novgorod
West Siberian Plain
St. Petersburg
Kazan'
Krasnoyarsk
Moscow
Rostov-na-Donu
Volgograd
Samara
Novosibirsk
Perm'
Yekaterinburg
Vladivostok
Ufa
Chelyabinsk
Irkutsk
Ob'
Yenisey
Lena
Textiles
Chemicals
Metallurgy
Computers
Electronics
Engineering
Vehicle assembly
Defense industry
Oil refining
Oil & gas
0
1000 km
0
1000 miles

R

CHRONOLOGY

The first Russian state (Rus) was in present-day Ukraine. Occupation by the Tatars (1240–1480) left a mark on the Russian language and character. From the 17th century, the Romanovs ruled.

- **1904–1905** Russian war against Japan; ends in defeat for Russia.
- **1905** Revolution.
- **1909–1914** Rapid economic expansion.
- **1914** Enters World War I against Germany.
- **1917** February Revolution; abdication of Nicholas II. October Revolution; Bolsheviks take over with Lenin as leader.
- **1918** July, Nicholas II and family shot.
- **1918–1920** Civil war.
- **1921** New Economic Policy; retreat from socialism.
- **1922** USSR established.
- **1924** Lenin dies. Leadership struggle eventually won by Stalin.
- **1928** First Five-Year Plan: forced industrialization and collectivization.
- **1929** Trotsky deported.
- **1936–1938** Show trials and campaigns against actual and suspected members of opposition. Millions sent to gulags in Siberia and elsewhere. Purges widespread.
- **1939** Hitler–Stalin pact gives USSR Baltic states, eastern Poland, and Bessarabia.
- **1941** Germany attacks USSR. Stalin unprepared. December, Battle of Moscow is first German defeat.
- **1943** February, great Soviet victory at Stalingrad.
- **1944–1945** Soviet offensive penetrates Balkans.
- **1945** Germany defeated. Under Yalta and Potsdam agreements eastern and southeastern Europe are Soviet zone of influence.
- **1947** Cold War begins; Stalin on defensive and fears penetration of Western capitalist values.
- **1953** Stalin dies.
- **1956** Hungarian uprising crushed. Krushchev's "secret speech" attacking Stalin at Party congress.
- **1957** Krushchev consolidates power. *Sputnik* launched.
- **1961** Yuri Gagarin first man in space.
- **1962** Cuban missile crisis.
- **1964** Krushchev ousted in coup, replaced by Leonid Brezhnev.
- **1975** Helsinki Final Act; confirms European frontiers as at end of World War II. Soviets agree human rights are concern of international community.
- **1979** Invades Afghanistan. Beginning of new intensification of Cold War.

RESOURCES

Electric power 211m kw

4.72m tonnes

6.5m b/d (reserves 48,600,000,000 bbl)

27.5m cattle, 18.3m pigs, 14m sheep, 340m chickens

Coal, oil, gas, gold, diamonds, iron, aluminum, manganese

ELECTRICITY GENERATION

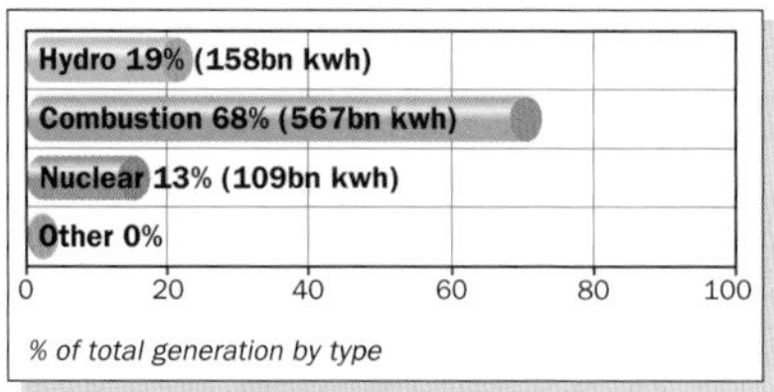

Hydro 19% (158bn kwh)
Combustion 68% (567bn kwh)
Nuclear 13% (109bn kwh)
Other 0%
0
20
40
60
80
100
% of total generation by type

Russia is a leading world producer of oil, natural gas, and electricity, among other resources. Confirmed reserves make Russia the world's leading country in terms of hydrocarbons, gold, other precious metals, diamonds, and timber.

Unlike some of the other republics of the ex-USSR, Russia has been reluctant to open its resources up to foreign concerns, fearing the loss of control to Western multinationals. The lack of investment and technology is a reason for underexploitation of many of the country's major resources. Geographical remoteness is another. Also, some of the richest energy and mineral deposits are located in national territories such as Tatarstan and Sakha Yakutia in Siberia. The regions' desire for greater autonomy has turned the ownership of these resources into a delicate political issue.

RUSSIAN FEDERATION : LAND USE

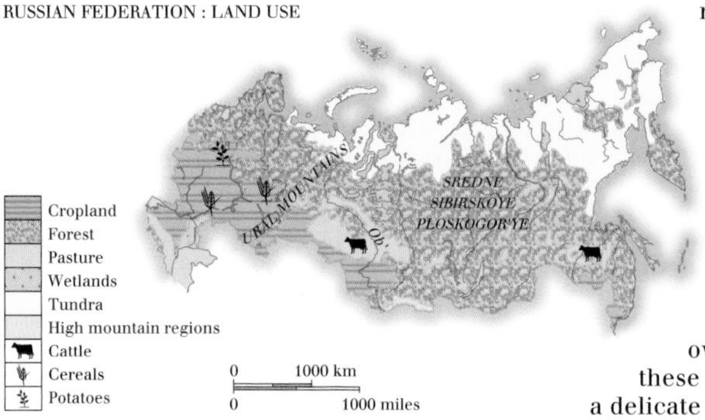

Cropland
Forest
Pasture
Wetlands
Tundra
High mountain regions
Cattle
Cereals
Potatoes
URAL MOUNTAINS
Ob
SREDNE SIBIRSKOYE PLOSKOGOR'YE
0 1000 km
0 1000 miles

ENVIRONMENT

Sustainability rank: 33rd

3%

9.8 tonnes per capita

ENVIRONMENTAL TREATIES

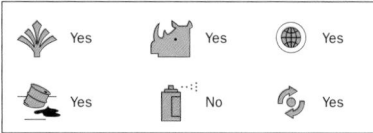

Yes	Yes	Yes
Yes	No	Yes

Although awareness of Russia's environmental problems has risen sharply, the resources, political will, and know-how to tackle them are still lacking. While Russia now has an active green movement, it has not as yet won significant support in general elections.

Each region has its own particular problems. The north risks contamination from the neglected Soviet-era nuclear submarine fleet and from nuclear waste containers dumped in the Barents Sea. Thousands of tonnes of chemical weapons have been dumped in the Baltic, although their exact location has not been revealed. Many fish species are now extinct in the River Volga in central Russia. In the Urals and the cities of European Russia, many chemical and heavy industrial plants do not treat their effluents at all. In June 2001 parliament approved a bill to allow the atomic energy ministry Minatom to earn $2 billion a year from storing and reprocessing foreign nuclear waste.

MEDIA

TV ownership high

Daily newspaper circulation 105 per 1000 people

PUBLISHING AND BROADCAST MEDIA

There are 285 daily newspapers, including *Izvestiya, Rossiiskaya Gazeta, Komsomolskaya Pravda*, and *Trud*

2 main national and regional services, partly state-owned, several independent channels

1 main state-run service, broadcasting 2 channels, 1 foreign broadcast service, several independents

Argumenty i Fakty, founded in 1987, is the best-selling weekly paper, with a circulation of nearly three million. The tabloid *Komsomolskaya Pravda* is the top-selling daily, whereas the once dominant Communist Party daily *Pravda* now sells barely 70,000 copies. The former Soviet state organ *Izvestiya* survives as an independent paper.

Public Russian Television (ORT), established in 1995 under part private ownership, runs two main TV channels. Bias in TV reporting, rife under Yeltsin, continues under Putin. Reporting events in Chechnya is subject to particular pressure. The NTV network, flagship of Media-Most, the media empire of exiled magnate Vladimir Gusinsky, was in 2001 taken over by the state-owned Gazprom's media division, while critical editorial staff were dismissed from the daily *Sevodnya* and weekly *Itogi*. Many Russians have satellite dishes and tune in to CNN and other Western channels.

R

CHRONOLOGY *continued*

- **1982** Brezhnev dies.
- **1985** Gorbachev in power. Start of *perestroika*, "restructuring." First of three USA–USSR summits resulting in arms reduction treaties. Nationality conflicts surface.
- **1988** Law of State Enterprises gives more power to enterprises; inflation and dislocation of economy.
- **1990** Gorbachev becomes Soviet president. First partly freely elected parliament (Supreme Soviet) meets.
- **1991** Boris Yeltsin elected president of Russia. Yeltsin and Muscovites resist hard-line communist coup. Gorbachev sidelined. CIS established; demise of USSR.
- **1992** Economic shock therapy.
- **1993** Yeltsin decrees dissolution of Supreme Soviet and uses force to disband parliament. Elections return conservative state *Duma*.
- **1994** Russian military offensive against Chechnya.
- **1995** Communists win elections.
- **1996** Yeltsin reelected despite strong Communist challenge; undergoes extensive heart surgery. Peace accord in Chechnya.
- **1998** Economic turmoil forces devaluation of rouble. Severe recession, rampant inflation.
- **1998–1999** Yeltsin repeatedly changes prime minister in successive political crises.
- **1999** December, parliamentary elections; Yeltsin resigns; Prime Minister Putin is acting president.
- **1999–2000** Terrorist violence blamed on Islamic separatists in Dagestan and Chechnya. Military offensive against Chechnya; fall of Chechen capital Grozny to Russian forces.
- **2000** Putin wins presidential election, consolidates power. Attack on "oligarchs" in big business. Improvement in economy. *Kursk* nuclear submarine disaster.
- **2001** April, party mergers make Putin's Unity party the largest grouping in parliament. July, Russian–Chinese friendship treaty.

Tundra in Russia's far east. *Russia has some of the largest uninhabited tracts of land in the world.*

CRIME

Death penalty used

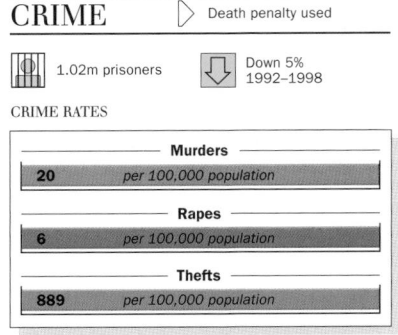

1.02m prisoners

Down 5% 1992–1998

CRIME RATES

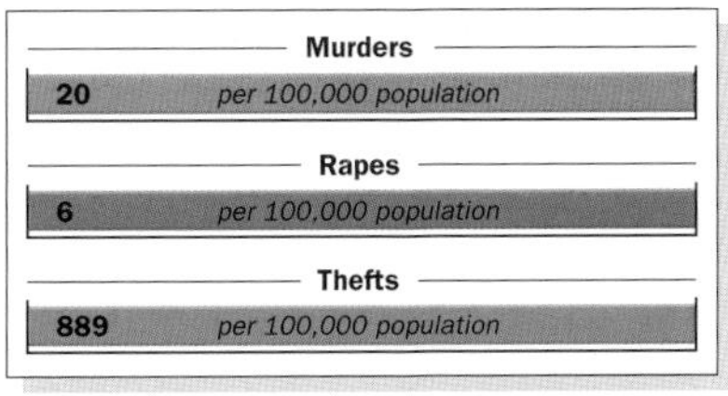
Murders
20
per 100,000 population
Rapes
6
per 100,000 population
Thefts
889
per 100,000 population

Despite official figures showing a drop in crime, in reality policing cannot keep pace with formidable problems.

Intergang violence accounts for a sharp rise in murders. Street crime has also increased in the larger cities. Corruption is rife, particularly in the regions. The Russian mafia profits from protection rackets, prostitution, smuggling operations, and narcotics, and is also active in western Europe. Public fear resulting from the rise in crime contributed to a temporary popularity in authoritarian political platforms.

With more than one million prisoners, overcrowding and poor conditions are major problems in Russian prisons.

EDUCATION

School leaving age: 15

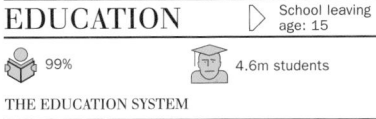

99%

4.6m students

THE EDUCATION SYSTEM

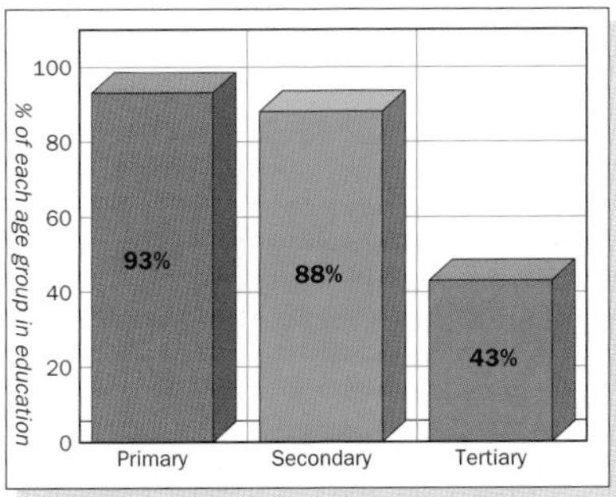
100
80
60
40
20
0
% of each age group in education
93%
88%
43%
Primary
Secondary
Tertiary

Schooling is free, and is compulsory for nine years up to age 15.

Attempts to change the Soviet-based curriculum, still widely in use, are hampered by lack of funds. Hundreds of private lycées, such as those run by the Orthodox Church, offer courses in west European languages. German in particular has made a comeback as a key language for international commerce. The state-subsidized higher education system is seriously underfunded, and some institutions have begun charging students. Prestigious institutions such as the Academy of Sciences have been forced to cut staff and research. Most academics have to rely on extramural earnings.

HEALTH

Welfare state health benefits

1 per 217 people

Heart disease, cancers, accidents, violence, tuberculosis

The health care system is in crisis and medicines are often in short supply.

Until 1991, state enterprises provided considerable health care for employees. Employers should now make payments through the Medical Insurance Fund, but many privatized concerns seek to cut costs. Local authorities lack the resources to take over these responsibilities. Bribing medical staff to obtain treatment is commonplace, and there is a lack of pharmaceutical products and drugs. Hospital patients are normally fed by their relatives.

SPENDING

GDP/cap. decrease

CONSUMPTION AND SPENDING

120 per 1000 population
210 per 1000 population

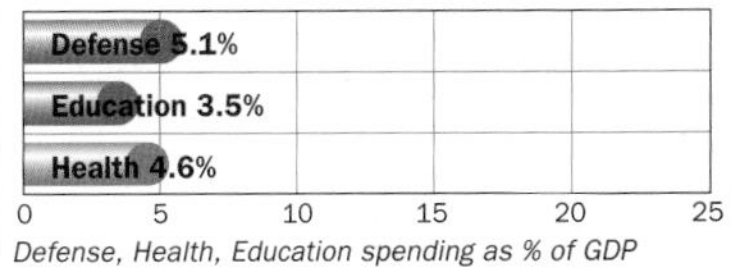
Defense 5.1%
Education 3.5%
Health 4.6%
0
5
10
15
20
25
Defense, Health, Education spending as % of GDP

Wealth disparities in Russia have increased sharply. A small minority of the population made huge profits from the dismantling of the old Soviet command economy. About 10% are thought to have benefited in some way.

A growing number of dollar millionaires flaunt their wealth, especially in Moscow. The bosses of organized crime are Russian society's wealthiest group. Russia is now the biggest buyer of Rolls Royces, while BMWs, Mercedes, and Volvos are relatively common in Moscow and St. Petersburg. A considerable amount of wealth is deposited abroad. There are now thousands of Russian offshore bank accounts; Northern Cyprus is a favorite location.

WORLD RANKING

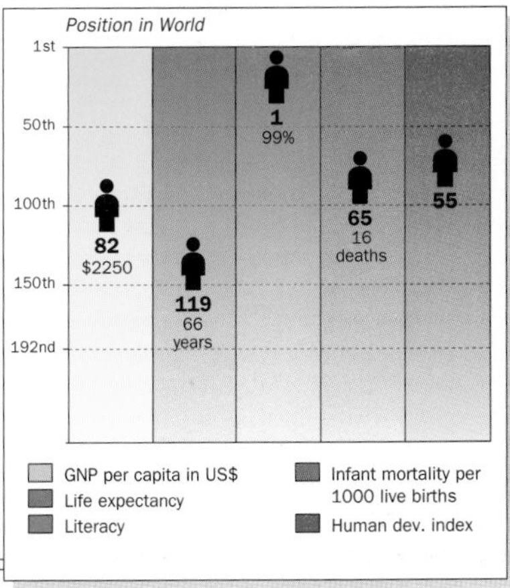
Position in World
1st
50th
100th
150th
192nd
82
$2250
119
66
years
1
99%
65
16
deaths
55
GNP per capita in US$
Life expectancy
Literacy
Infant mortality per 1000 live births
Human dev. index

R

RWANDA

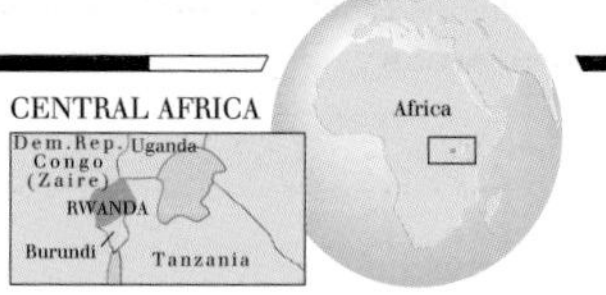
CENTRAL AFRICA
Africa
Dem. Rep. Congo (Zaire)
Uganda
RWANDA
Burundi
Tanzania

OFFICIAL NAME: Republic of Rwanda **CAPITAL:** Kigali
POPULATION: 7.7 million **CURRENCY:** Rwanda franc **OFFICIAL LANGUAGES:** French and Rwandan

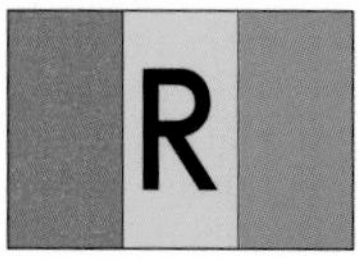
R

1962 | 1962 | July 1 | RWA | +2 | +250 | .rw

LANDLOCKED RWANDA lies just south of the equator in east central Africa. Since independence in 1962, ethnic tensions have dominated politics. In 1994, the violent death of the president led to appalling political and ethnic violence. Over half of the surviving population were displaced. The perpetrators of the genocide held sway in desperately overcrowded refugee camps in adjacent countries, greatly complicating the process of eventual repatriation and reintegration.

CLIMATE

Tropical wet & dry

WEATHER CHART

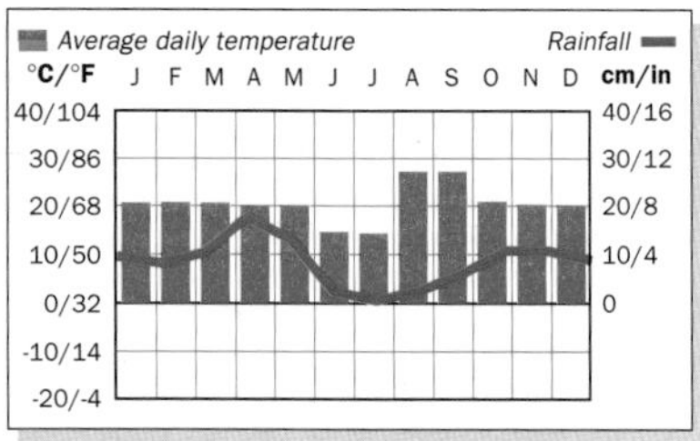
Average daily temperature
Rainfall
°C/°F J F M A M J J A S O N D cm/in
40/104 40/16
30/86 30/12
20/68 20/8
10/50 10/4
0/32 0
-10/14
-20/-4

Rwanda's climate is tropical, tempered by altitude. Two wet seasons allow for two harvests each year.

TRANSPORTATION

Drive on right

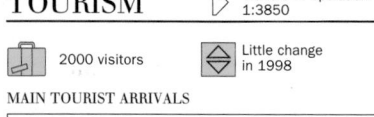

Kanombe International, Kigali 119,751 passengers

Has no fleet

THE TRANSPORTATION NETWORK

1000 km (621 miles)	None
None	Lake Kivu

The road network is well developed. The international airport near Kigali was completed in 1986.

TOURISM

Visitors : Population 1:3850

2000 visitors

Little change in 1998

MAIN TOURIST ARRIVALS

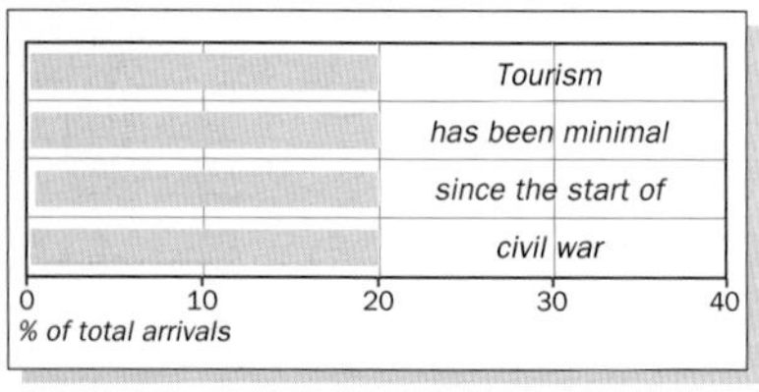
Tourism
has been minimal
since the start of
civil war
0 10 20 30 40
% of total arrivals

Tourism has effectively ceased as a result of the civil war. When peace is secured, Rwanda may be able to regain its status as a destination for wealthy wildlife enthusiasts. Top attractions are the mountain gorillas and Lake Kivu.

PEOPLE

Pop. density high

Kinyarwanda, French, Kiswahili, English

309/km² (799/mi²)

THE URBAN/RURAL POPULATION SPLIT

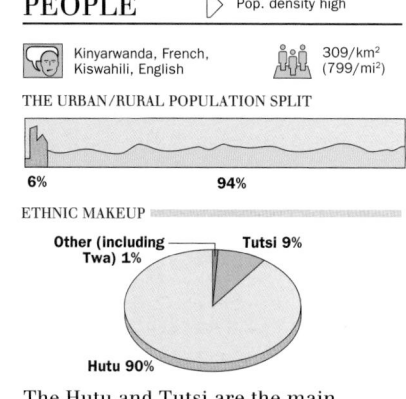

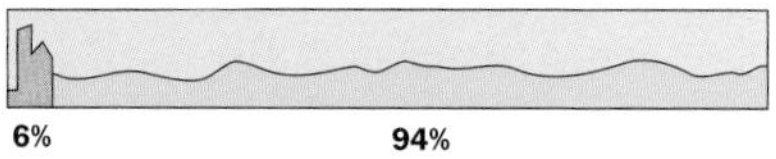
6%
94%

ETHNIC MAKEUP

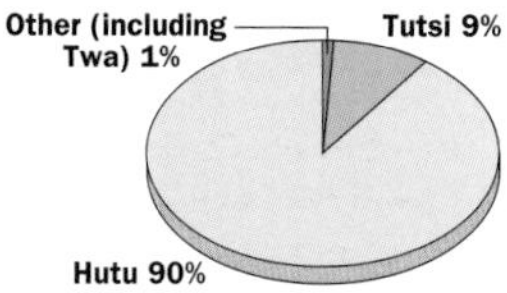
Other (including Twa) 1%
Tutsi 9%
Hutu 90%

The Hutu and Tutsi are the main groups; few of the Twa pygmies, the original inhabitants, remain. For over 500 years, the cattle-owning Tutsi were politically dominant, oppressing the land-owning Hutu majority. In 1959, violent revolt led to a reversal of the roles. The two groups have since been waging a spasmodic war. It is estimated that 800,000 people were killed in the violence of the mid-1990s, the majority of them Tutsi victims massacred by Hutus.

POLITICS

No multiparty elections

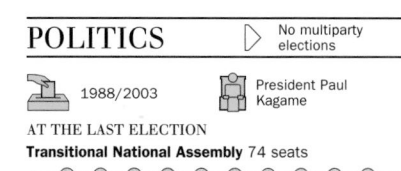

1988/2003

President Paul Kagame

AT THE LAST ELECTION

Transitional National Assembly 74 seats

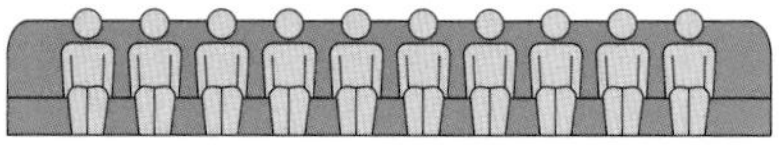

The last legislative election, to the National Development Council, took place in December 1988 when candidates were chosen from members of the National Republican Movement for Development and Democracy (MRND) list.
A Transitional National Assembly was set up in 1994. Polls due in 1999 were postponed until 2003.

In 1993 a peace accord to end the rebellion launched in 1990 by the Tutsi-dominated Rwandan Patriotic Front (FPR) was signed. However, the fragile peace process was halted in 1994 by the death of the president in a plane crash. Genocidal violence was unleashed between the mainly Hutu supporters of the old regime and its mainly, but not exclusively, Tutsi opponents. An estimated 800,000 died and millions fled the conflict, in which the FPR eventually gained control. Hutu were allocated key government posts, including the presidency, but when, in March 2000, the balance was shifted to increased Tutsi representation, President Pasteur Bizimungu resigned. Vice President Paul Kagame, the regime's dominant figure and the FPR leader, was formally elected president in April. Presidential and parliamentary elections are planned for end-2003, following the approval of a constitution.

RWANDA

Total Land Area : 24 950 sq. km (9633 sq. miles)

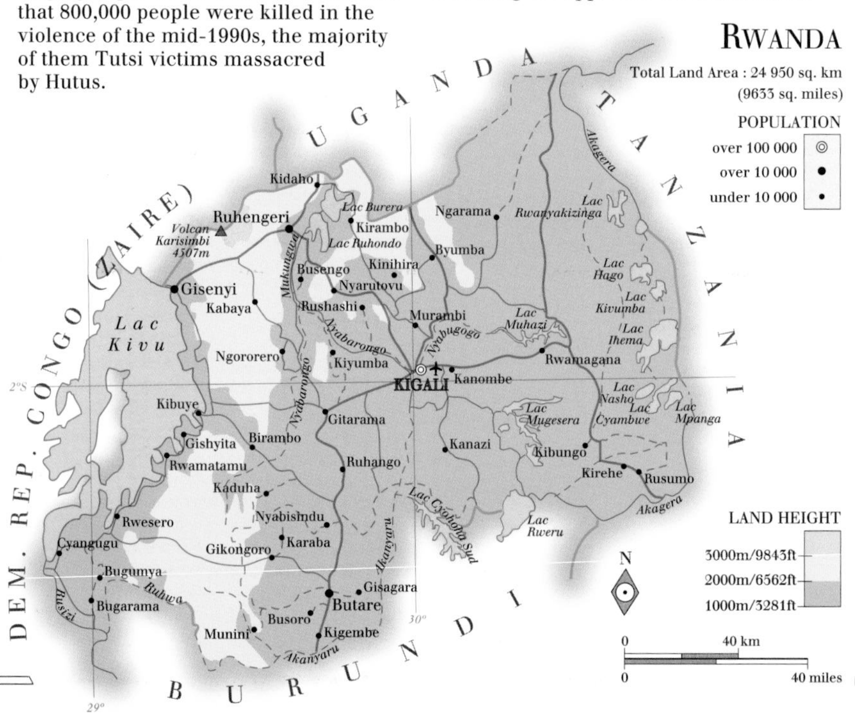
UGANDA
TANZANIA
DEM. REP. CONGO (ZAIRE)
BURUNDI
POPULATION
over 100 000
over 10 000
under 10 000
Kidaho
Ruhengeri
Volcan Karisimbi 4507m
Lac Burera
Kirambo
Lac Ruhondo
Ngarama
Rwanyakizinga
Byumba
Gisenyi
Kabaya
Busengo
Kinihira
Nyarutovu
Rushashi
Lac Kivu
Ngororero
Kiyumba
Murambi
Lac Muhazi
Lac Hago
Lac Kivumba
Lac Ihema
Rwamagana
KIGALI
Kanombe
Kibuye
Gitarama
Lac Mugesera
Lac Nasho
Lac Cyambwe
Lac Mpanga
Gishyita
Birambo
Kanazi
Kibungo
Rwamatamu
Ruhango
Kirehe
Rusumo
Kaduha
Akagera
Rwesero
Nyabisindu
Lac Rweru
Cyangugu
Karaba
Gikongoro
Bugumya
Gisagara
Butare
Bugarama
Busoro
Munini
Kigembe
Akanyaru
Nyabarongo
Mukungwa
Rusizi
Ruhwa
2°S
29°
30°
N
LAND HEIGHT
3000m/9843ft
2000m/6562ft
1000m/3281ft
0 40 km
0 40 miles

R

WORLD AFFAIRS

Joined UN in 1962

COMESA | CEPGL | OIF | NAM | OAU

Accused of abandoning Rwanda during 1994, the UN in 1995 set up a war crimes tribunal on the genocide; there have been several convictions. The continued presence, in 2001, of Rwandan troops in Congo (former Zaire) stalled peace talks.

AID

Recipient

$373m (receipts) — Up 7% in 1999

Large amounts of aid are required, particularly for the agricultural sector, which was severely disrupted by the war. Aid donors in November 2000 urged Rwanda to withdraw its troops from Congo (former Zaire).

DEFENSE

No compulsory military service

$135m — Down 6% in 1999

The Rwandan army is sufficiently powerful to make it a strong influence in the war-torn region. A national police force was established in 1999.

ECONOMICS

Inflation 16.3% p.a. (1990–1999)

$2.04bn — 336.06–359.03 Rwanda francs

SCORE CARD

- ❑ WORLD GNP RANKING........................137th
- ❑ GNP PER CAPITA $250
- ❑ BALANCE OF PAYMENTS....................$–143m
- ❑ INFLATION ....–2.4%
- ❑ UNEMPLOYMENT ....Few have formal employment

STRENGTHS

Currently none. Assuming stability, Rwanda could produce coffee and tea. Possible oil and gas reserves. Tourism potential.

WEAKNESSES

Economic activity completely disrupted by 1994 violence. Lengthy journey to Kenyan and Tanzanian ports means high transportation costs. Few resources.

EXPORTS

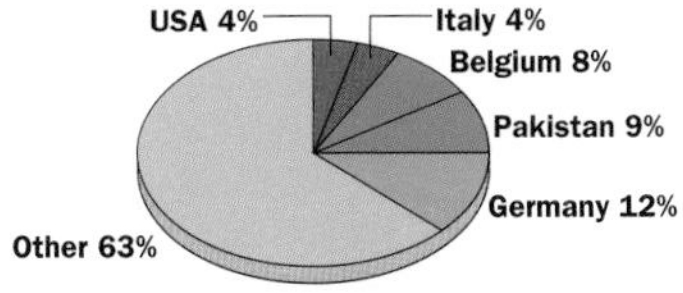
USA 4%
Italy 4%
Belgium 8%
Pakistan 9%
Germany 12%
Other 63%

IMPORTS

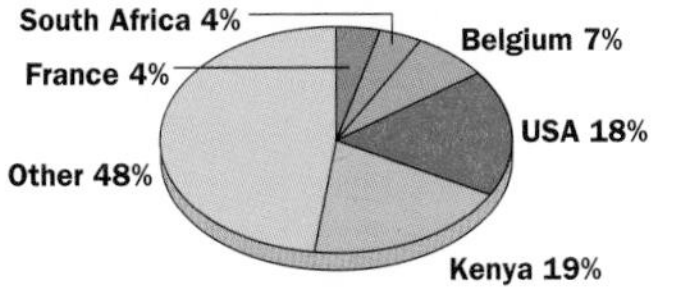
South Africa 4%
Belgium 7%
France 4%
USA 18%
Other 48%
Kenya 19%

Terraced hillside. *Before the war, Rwanda was the most densely populated country in Africa and its land was intensively cultivated.*

RESOURCES

Electric power 34,000 kw

3143 tonnes — Not an oil producer

725,000 cattle, 700,000 goats, 1.4m chickens — Tin, tungsten, gold, columbo-tantalite, methane gas

Gas deposits in Lake Kivu are likely to be explored with Congo (former Zaire). Only 20% of urban homes are on the national power grid.

ENVIRONMENT

Sustainability rank: 115th

15% — 0.1 tonnes per capita

Apart from the effects of war, soil erosion and forest loss are the major environmental problems. The tourist industry underpinned the preservation of the mountain gorilla.

MEDIA

TV ownership low

Daily newspaper circulation 0.1 per 1000 people

PUBLISHING AND BROADCAST MEDIA

There is 1 daily newspaper. The monthly *Inkingi* and *La Relève* are published in Kinyarwanda and French respectively

1 state-controlled service — 2 services: 1 state-controlled

The media have been used as an important propaganda tool by both sides in the political conflict.

CRIME

Death penalty used

Rwanda does not publish prison figures — Crime is rising

In 2001, 125,000 people were awaiting trial on genocide-related charges. A traditional system of participatory justice to alleviate the backlog of cases was introduced in 2000.

EDUCATION

School leaving age: 13

67% — 3389 students

Schools are run by the state and by Christian missions. Primary education is officially compulsory, but only 78% of children attended in 1997; just 8% go on to secondary schooling.

CHRONOLOGY

The Hutu majority began to arrive in the 14th century, the warrior Tutsi in the 15th. From 1890, German and then Belgian colonizers acted to reinforce Tutsi dominance.

- ❑ **1962** Independence. Hutu-led government.
- ❑ **1960s** Tutsi revolt; massacres by Hutu; thousands of Tutsi in exile.
- ❑ **1973** Coup by General Habyarimana.
- ❑ **1994** Habyarimana dies in plane crash. Genocidal violence unleashed by Hutu extremist regime, ousted by Tutsi-led FPR. Hutu refugee exodus.
- ❑ **1995** Start of war crimes tribunal.
- ❑ **1997** Refugees forcibly repatriated.
- ❑ **2000** Prominent Hutus leave office.
- ❑ **2001** Limited troop withdrawal from Congo (former Zaire) begins.

HEALTH

Welfare state health benefits

1 per 20,000 people — Malaria, measles, diarrheal diseases, violence

Rwanda has a network of 34 hospitals and 188 health centers. 11% of the population are estimated to be HIV-positive.

SPENDING

GDP/cap. decrease

CONSUMPTION AND SPENDING

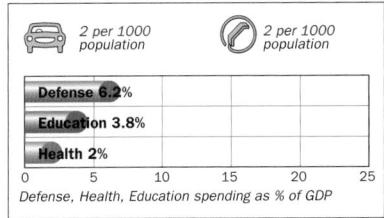

2 per 1000 population — *2 per 1000 population*

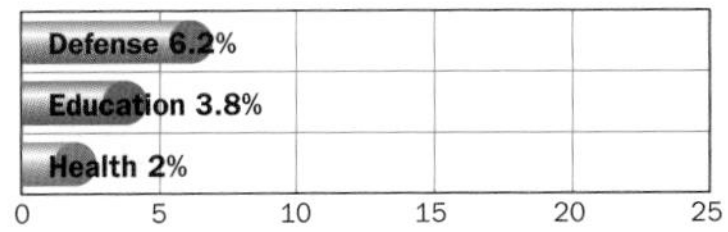
Defense 6.2%
Education 3.8%
Health 2%
0
5
10
15
20
25

Defense, Health, Education spending as % of GDP

Wealth is limited to the country's political elite. Most Rwandans are poor farmers; Twa pygmies and refugees are poorer still.

WORLD RANKING

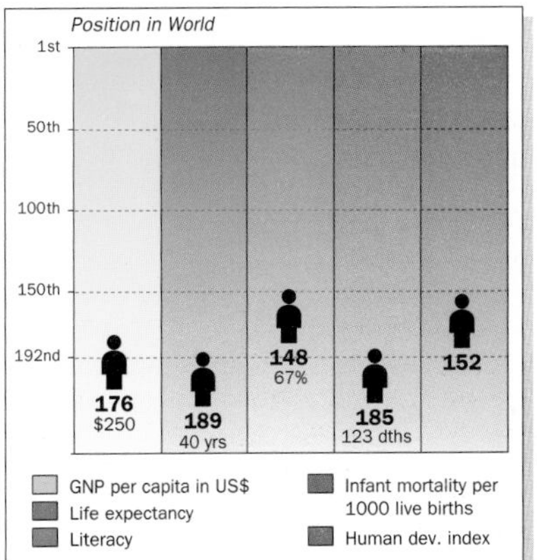
Position in World
1st
50th
100th
150th
192nd
176
$250
189
40 yrs
148
67%
185
123 dths
152
GNP per capita in US$
Life expectancy
Literacy
Infant mortality per 1000 live births
Human dev. index

R

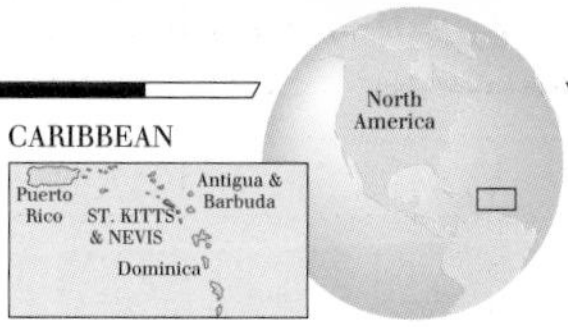
North America
CARIBBEAN
Puerto Rico
Antigua & Barbuda
ST. KITTS & NEVIS
Dominica

ST. KITTS & NEVIS

OFFICIAL NAME: Federation of Saint Christopher and Nevis **CAPITAL:** Basseterre
POPULATION: 41,000 **CURRENCY:** Eastern Caribbean dollar **OFFICIAL LANGUAGE:** English

1983 | 1983 | Sept 19 | KN | -4 | +1869 | .kn

ONE OF THE CARIBBEAN'S most popular tourist destinations, St. Kitts and Nevis, a former British colony, lies at the northern end of the Leeward Islands chain. St. Kitts is of volcanic origin; Mount Liamuiga, a dormant volcano with a crater 227 m (745 feet) deep, is the highest point on the island. Nevis, separated from St. Kitts by a channel 3 km (2 miles) wide, is the lusher but less developed of the two islands. In the 18th century, its famed hot and cold springs gained Nevis the title "the Spa of the Caribbean."

CLIMATE

Tropical oceanic

WEATHER CHART

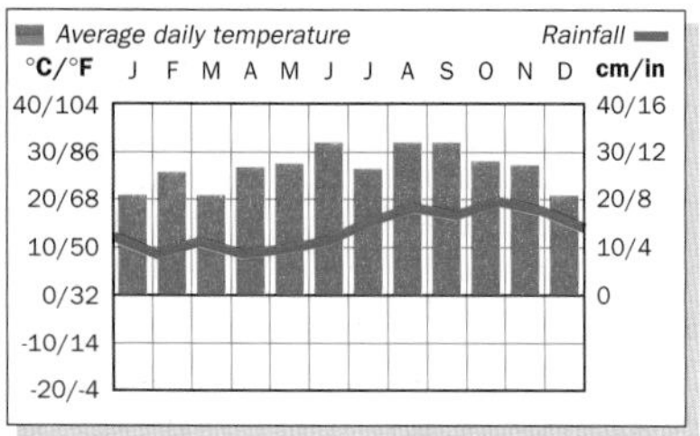
Average daily temperature
Rainfall
°C/°F
J F M A M J J A S O N D
cm/in
40/104
30/86
20/68
10/50
0/32
-10/14
-20/-4
40/16
30/12
20/8
10/4
0

A combination of high temperatures, trade breezes, and moderate rainfall in summer constitute St. Kitts' typically Caribbean climate.

TRANSPORTATION

Drive on left

Golden Rock International, Basseterre

1 ship 600 dwt

THE TRANSPORTATION NETWORK

136 km (85 miles) | None

58 km (36 miles) | None

Most roads on the islands follow the coast; just a few cross the interior. Access to the remote southeast peninsula of St. Kitts has been improved. The airport on St. Kitts takes large jets; Nevis airport accepts only light aircraft. Regular ferries connect both islands.

The southeastern peninsula of St. Kitts, looking across to Nevis in the background, on a typical December evening.

TOURISM

Visitors : Population 2:1

84,000 visitors

Down 10% in 1999

MAIN TOURIST ARRIVALS

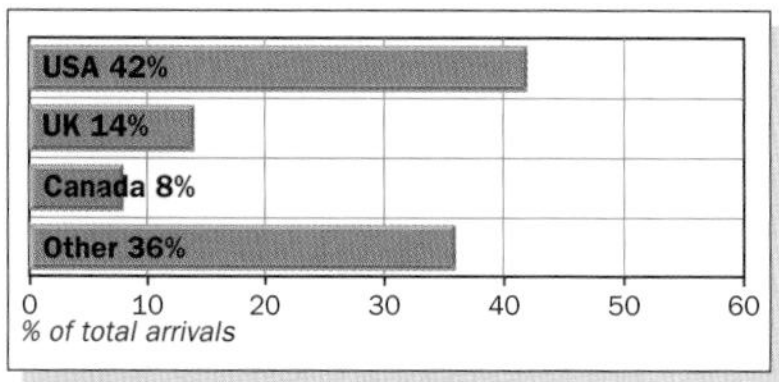
USA 42%
UK 14%
Canada 8%
Other 36%
0
10
20
30
40
50
60
% of total arrivals

St. Kitts has long targeted the mass US tourist market. Improvements to boost tourism include the opening up of the St. Kitts southern peninsula to large-scale tourist developments, and the expansion of the main port to accommodate two cruise ships simultaneously. Most visitors come for sand, sun, and the Caribbean mood, although in recent years safaris inland to see local wildlife and mineral springs have become more popular. On St. Kitts, the old Brimstone Hill fortress has been converted into a museum, as has the Nevis birthplace of Alexander Hamilton, one of the architects of the US constitution.

PEOPLE

Pop. density medium

English, English Creole

114/km² (295/mi²)

THE URBAN/RURAL POPULATION SPLIT

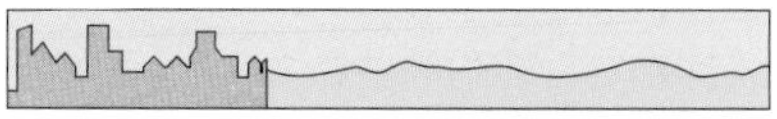
34%
66%

RELIGIOUS PERSUASION

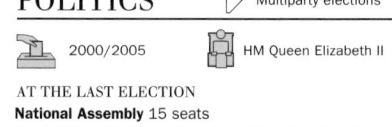

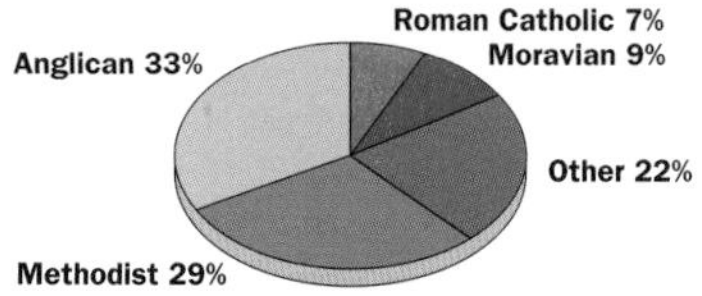
Roman Catholic 7%
Moravian 9%
Anglican 33%
Other 22%
Methodist 29%

Most of the population is descended from Africans brought over in the 17th century; intermarriage has blurred other racial lines. There are small numbers of Europeans and South Asians. High levels of emigration ensure a stable population size and provide a source of foreign currency.

POLITICS

Multiparty elections

2000/2005

HM Queen Elizabeth II

AT THE LAST ELECTION

National Assembly 15 seats

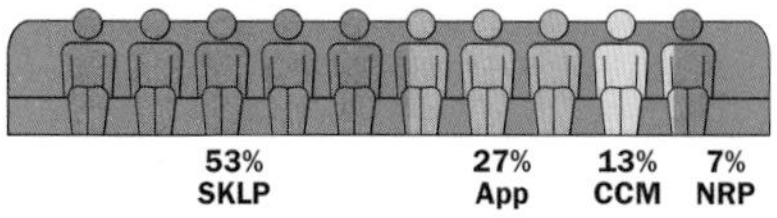
53% SKLP
27% App
13% CCM
7% NRP

SKLP = St. Kitts Labour Party **CCM** = Concerned Citizens' Movement **NRP** = Nevis Reformation Party **App** = Appointed

Nevis has its own legislature and executive, the Nevis Island Assembly, which exercises local power

The center-left SKLP ended 15 years of rule by the right-wing People's Action Movement (PAM) by winning the 1995 general election, and won a second term in 2000. A plan for secession by the Nevis government was narrowly defeated in a referendum in August 1998.

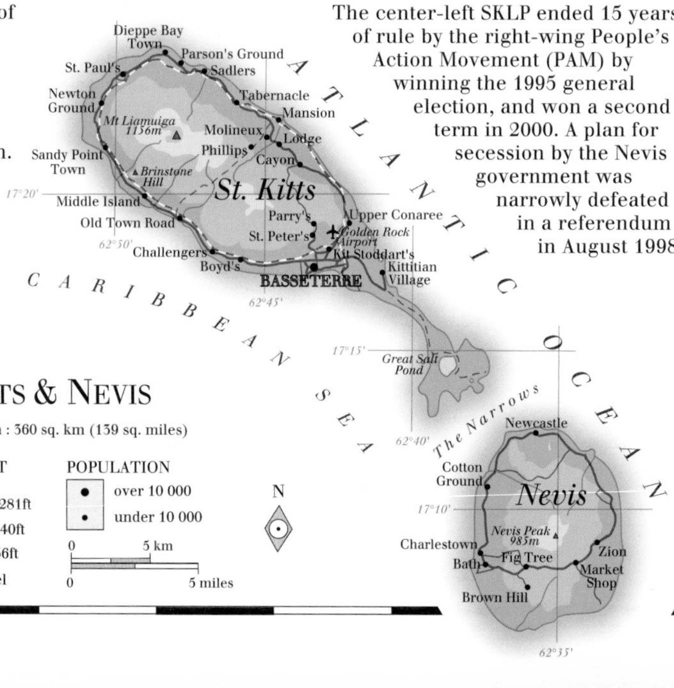
Dieppe Bay Town
Parson's Ground
Sadlers
St. Paul's
Tabernacle
Mansion
Newton Ground
Mt Liamuiga 1156m
Molineux
Lodge
Phillips
Cayon
Sandy Point Town
Brimstone Hill
St. Kitts
Middle Island
Old Town Road
Parry's
Upper Conaree
St. Peter's
Golden Rock Airport
Kit Stoddart's
Kittitian Village
Challengers
Boyd's
BASSETERRE
ATLANTIC OCEAN
CARIBBEAN SEA
Great Salt Pond
The Narrows
Newcastle
Cotton Ground
Nevis
Nevis Peak 985m
Charlestown
Zion
Fig Tree
Bath
Market Shop
Brown Hill
17°20'
17°15'
17°10'
62°50'
62°45'
62°40'
62°35'

ST. KITTS & NEVIS

Total Land Area : 360 sq. km (139 sq. miles)

LAND HEIGHT
- 1000m/3281ft
- 500m/1640ft
- 200m/656ft
- Sea Level

POPULATION
- over 10 000
- under 10 000

0 5 km
0 5 miles

N

WORLD AFFAIRS

Joined UN in 1983

ACS | Comm | Caricom | OAS | OECS

Resumption of hanging in 1998 after a 13-year moratorium drew strong international criticism. Suspected money laundering earned St. Kitts condemnation from G7 in 2000.

AID

Recipient

US$5m (receipts) — Down 29% in 1999

International aid in 1999 supported an economic recovery and relief program, following Hurricanes Georges and Lenny, which significantly damaged buildings and infrastructure. Most aid is from the USA, the EU, and the UK.

DEFENSE

No compulsory military service

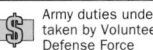

Army duties undertaken by Volunteer Defense Force — Not applicable

An army existed for six years before it was disbanded to cut government expenditure in 1981. A small paramilitary unit remains within the police; it made a token appearance with US forces during the 1983 invasion of Grenada.

ECONOMICS

Inflation 3.1% p.a. (1990–1999)

US$259m — 2.70 Eastern Caribbean dollars

SCORE CARD

- ❑ WORLD GNP RANKING........................177th
- ❑ GNP PER CAPITA ....US$6330
- ❑ BALANCE OF PAYMENTS..................US$–26m
- ❑ INFLATION 3.9%
- ❑ UNEMPLOYMENT 5%

STRENGTHS

Growing tourism industry – now 10% of GDP and set to expand further. Diversifying agricultural sector.

WEAKNESSES

Tourism and related industries prone to hurricane damage, most recently in 1998–1999. Agricultural exports sensitive to fluctuating world market.

EXPORTS

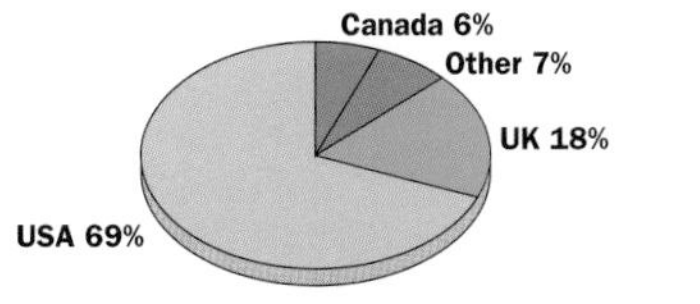
Canada 6%
Other 7%
UK 18%
USA 69%

IMPORTS

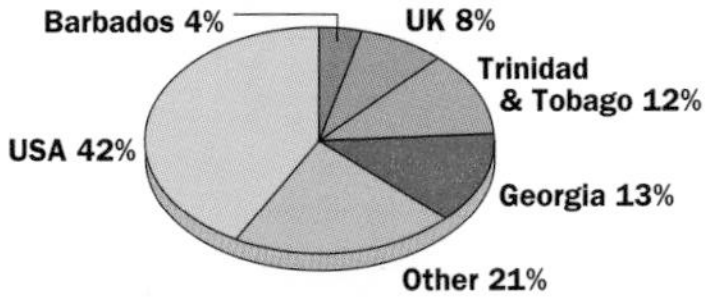
Barbados 4%
UK 8%
Trinidad & Tobago 12%
USA 42%
Georgia 13%
Other 21%

RESOURCES

Electric power 16,000 kw

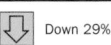

165 tonnes — Not an oil producer

14,500 goats, 8000 sheep, 3600 cattle, 60,000 chickens — None

St. Kitts has no strategic resources. Almost all energy has to be imported, mainly oil from Venezuela and Mexico. Sugar output declined rapidly in the 1990s. New crops, such as Sea Island cotton on Nevis, have been introduced. Offshore fishing has potential.

ENVIRONMENT

Not available

10% — 2.5 tonnes per capita

Hurricanes are the greatest environmental threat. Hurricane Georges alone caused damage in 1998 estimated at US$400 million. It was followed in 1999 by Hurricane Lenny. As in the rest of the Caribbean, benefits from encouraging tourism must be set against potential ecological damage. The government has shown sensitivity, with strict preservation orders on the remaining rainforest and on indigenous monkeys.

MEDIA

TV ownership high

There are no daily newspapers

PUBLISHING AND BROADCAST MEDIA

There are no daily newspapers. The two main newspapers are the weekly *The Democrat* and the twice-weekly *Labour Spokesman*

1 state-owned service — 4 services: 1 state-owned, 3 independent

The government proposes to privatize the state-owned TV and radio company. Two of the main newspapers, *The Democrat* and *The Labour Spokesman*, are funded by political parties.

CRIME

Death penalty used

St. Kitts does not publish prison figures — Up 5% 1996–1998

The judicial system is based on British common law. The police are UK-trained. Hanging was resumed in 1998, and plans agreed in 2001 to replace the role of the UK Privy Council with a Caribbean Court of Justice raised fears of more executions. Narcotics-related crimes are rising.

EDUCATION

School leaving age: 17

90% — 394 students

Education is based on the former British 11-plus selective system and is mostly state-run. Students attend the regional University of the West Indies, or go on to colleges in the USA and the UK.

CHRONOLOGY

A British colony since 1783 and part of the Leeward Islands Federation until 1956, St. Kitts and Nevis achieved independence in 1983.

- ❑ **1932** Pro-independence St. Kitts–Nevis–Anguilla Labour Party set up.
- ❑ **1967** Internal self-government.
- ❑ **1980** Anguilla formally separates from St. Kitts and Nevis.
- ❑ **1983** Independence from UK.
- ❑ **1995** Opposition SKLP wins election.
- ❑ **1998** Nevis referendum narrowly rejects secession.

HEALTH

Welfare state health benefits

1 per 1124 people — Heart and respiratory diseases, cancers

The government-run health service now provides rudimentary care on both St. Kitts and Nevis. The EU and France provided EC$8 million in 1998 for repairs to the main hospital at Basseterre, which was badly damaged by Hurricane Georges.

SPENDING

GDP/cap. increase

CONSUMPTION AND SPENDING

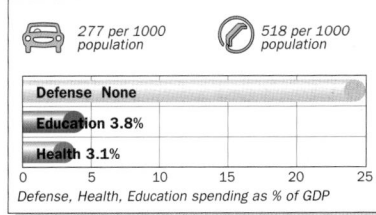

277 per 1000 population — *518 per 1000 population*

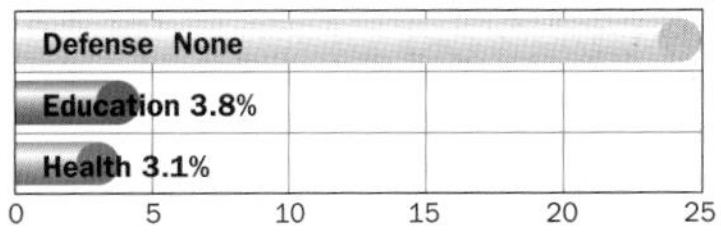
Defense None
Education 3.8%
Health 3.1%
0
5
10
15
20
25

Defense, Health, Education spending as % of GDP

Native professionals and civil servants have replaced expatriates over the past 20 years. They are now the best-paid group, but there are no great extremes of income. Status symbols include Japanese cars and TV satellite dishes.

WORLD RANKING

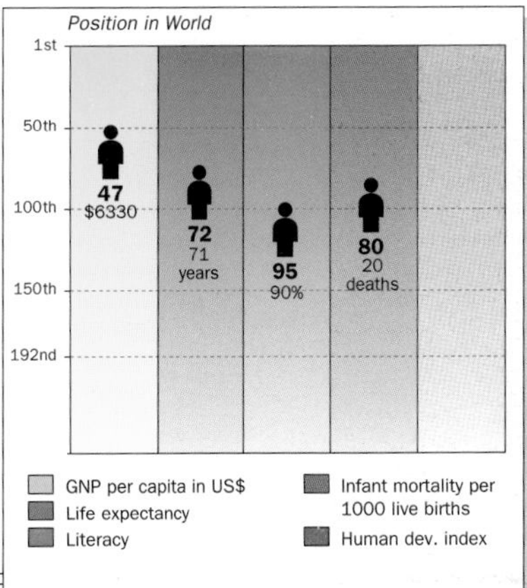
Position in World
1st
50th
100th
150th
192nd
47
$6330
72
71 years
95
90%
80
20 deaths
GNP per capita in US$
Life expectancy
Literacy
Infant mortality per 1000 live births
Human dev. index

S

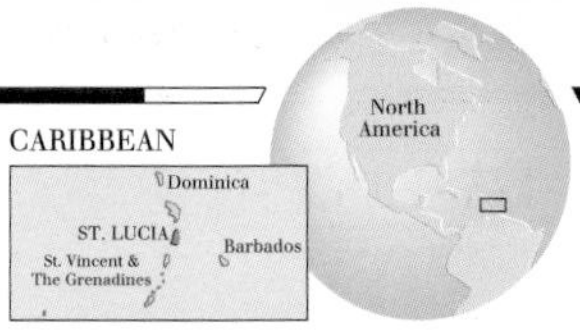

CARIBBEAN
Dominica
ST. LUCIA
Barbados
St. Vincent & The Grenadines
North America

ST. LUCIA

OFFICIAL NAME: Saint Lucia **CAPITAL:** Castries **POPULATION:** 156,300
CURRENCY: Eastern Caribbean dollar **OFFICIAL LANGUAGE:** English

1979 | 1979 | Feb 22 | WL | -4 | +1758 | .lc

ST. LUCIA IS ONE OF THE MOST beautiful islands of the Windward group of the Antilles. The twin Pitons, south of Soufrière, are one of the most striking natural features in the Caribbean. Ruled by the French and the British at different times in its past, St. Lucia retains the character of both. A multiparty democracy, it lives by banana-growing and tourism, with enticing beaches and a rich variety of wildlife in the rainforest.

CLIMATE

Tropical oceanic

WEATHER CHART

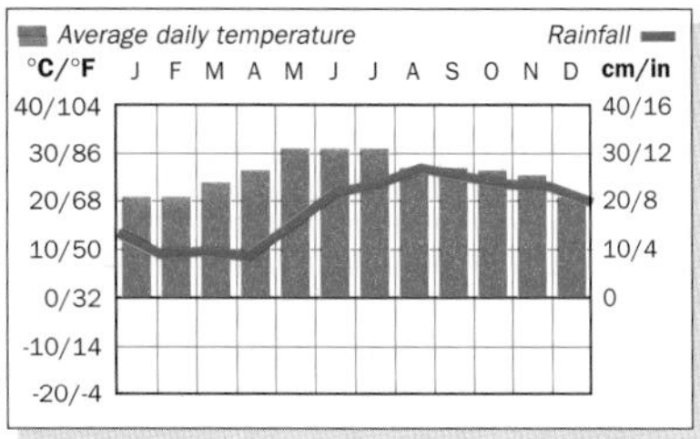

Average daily temperature
Rainfall
°C/°F
J F M A M J J A S O N D
cm/in
40/104
30/86
20/68
10/50
0/32
-10/14
-20/-4
40/16
30/12
20/8
10/4
0

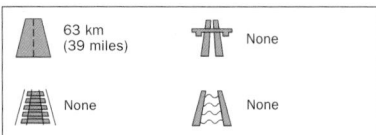

The dry season, from January to April, brings intense heat to sheltered parts of St. Lucia. During the rainy season, short warm showers can be expected daily. Rainfall is highest in the mountains.

TRANSPORTATION

Drive on left

Hewanorra International, Vieux Fort 447,269 passengers

3 ships 911 grt

THE TRANSPORTATION NETWORK

63 km (39 miles)

None

None

None

Roads are confined to the west and southeast coasts; only half are paved. Flights arrive from major European and North American cities, and other Caribbean locations. Direct passage to South America is largely by sea.

One of the twin Pitons south of Soufriére, marking the entrance to the Jalousie Plantation harbor.

TOURISM

Visitors : Population 1.7:1

259,000 visitors

Down 1% in 2000

MAIN TOURIST ARRIVALS

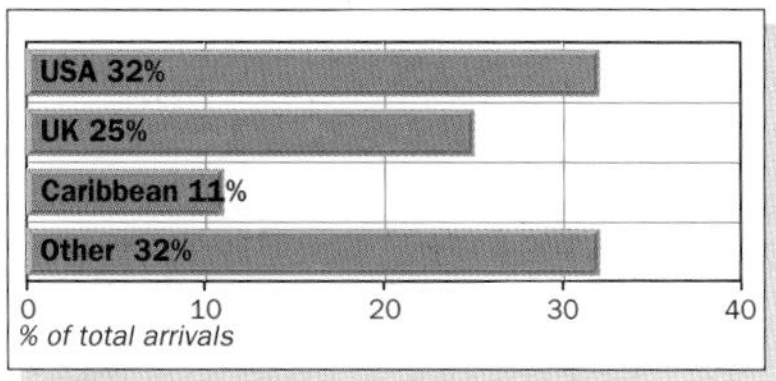

USA 32%
UK 25%
Caribbean 11%
Other 32%
0
10
20
30
40
% of total arrivals

Tropical beaches and typical Caribbean towns make St. Lucia a favorite destination for cruise ships and stay-over tourists. The number of hotel rooms continues to rise. The pristine rainforest has become the focus of nature tourism, with tours often organized by the National Trust.

PEOPLE

Pop. density high

English, French Creole

256/km² (663/mi²)

THE URBAN/RURAL POPULATION SPLIT

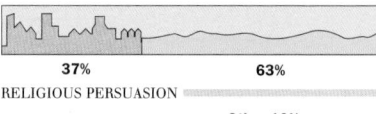

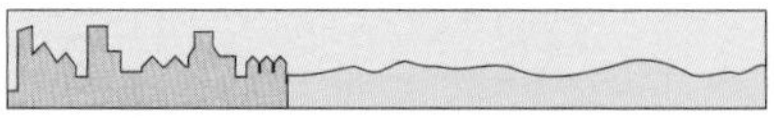

37%
63%

RELIGIOUS PERSUASION

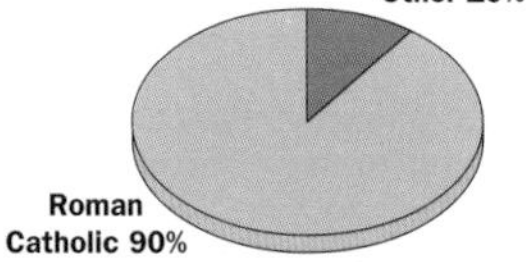

Other 10%
Roman Catholic 90%

St. Lucia has a rich, tension-free racial mix of descendants of Africans, Caribs, and European settlers. Despite relaxed attitudes, family life is central to most St. Lucians, many of whom are practicing Roman Catholics. Small families are the norm, but in rural districts, where women run many of the farms, absentee fathers are fairly common. In recent years, women have had greater access to higher education and have moved into professions. A bill to permit the occasional use of Creole in parliament was passed in 1998.

POLITICS

Multiparty elections

L. House 1997/2002
U. House 1997/2002

HM Queen Elizabeth II

AT THE LAST ELECTION

House of Assembly 18 seats

88% SLP
6% UWP
6% App

SLP = St. Lucia Labour Party **UWP** = United Workers' Party **App** = Appointed

Senate 11 seats

6 Senate members are nominated by the government, 3 by the opposition, and 2 by the governor-general on a non-party basis

Politics revolved for a long time around John Compton of the UWP and Julian Hunte of the SLP. A less personalized climate prevailed from 1996 with the emergence of new political figures. After losing heavily to the SLP in the 1997 general election, the UWP changed its leader three times in as many years.

WORLD AFFAIRS

Joined UN in 1979

ACS | Comm | Caricom | OECS | OAS

Relations with the USA were strained by the long-running, and ultimately successful, US campaign to end preferential access for Caribbean bananas to the EU. It is feared that from 2006 St. Lucia will be unable to compete with cheaper fruit from Central and South America. St. Lucia supports Japan, an aid donor, in its bid for a permanent seat on the UN Security Council. With the agreement in 2001 to form a Caribbean Court of Justice, one of the last constitutional ties to the UK was set to be cut.

AID

Recipient

US$26m (receipts)

Up 333% in 1999

The USA, the EU, and the UK are the main donors. China and Japan gave aid and grant loans in 1998.

DEFENSE

No compulsory military service

US$5m

Little change

The police force is supported by a small paramilitary unit. Training is provided by the USA and the UK.

S

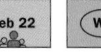

ST. LUCIA

Total Land Area : 620 sq. km (239 sq. miles)

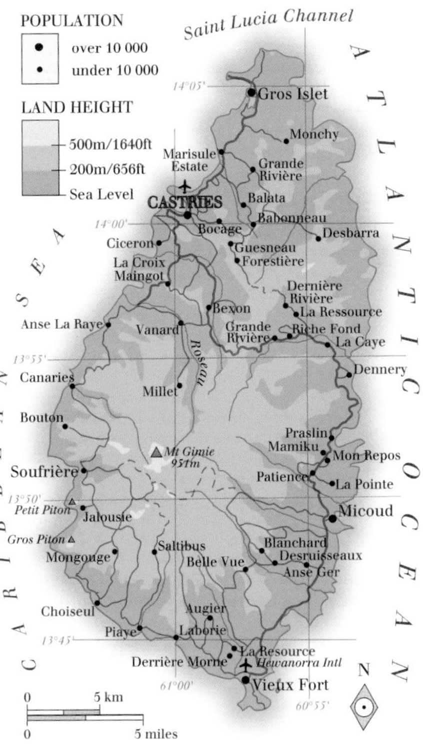
POPULATION
over 10 000
under 10 000
LAND HEIGHT
500m/1640ft
200m/656ft
Sea Level
Saint Lucia Channel
ATLANTIC OCEAN
CARIBBEAN SEA
Gros Islet
Monchy
Marisule Estate
Grande Rivière
CASTRIES
Balata
Babonneau
Bocage
Desbarra
Ciceron
Guesneau Forestière
La Croix Maingot
Dernière Rivière
Bexon
La Ressource
Anse La Raye
Vanard
Grande Rivière
Riche Fond
La Caye
Dennery
Canaries
Millet
Roseau
Bouton
Praslin
Mamiku
Mt Gimie 951m
Mon Repos
Soufrière
Patience
La Pointe
Petit Piton
Jalousie
Micoud
Gros Piton
Blanchard
Mongouge
Saltibus
Belle Vue
Desruisseaux
Anse Ger
Choiseul
Augier
Piaye
Laborie
La Resource
Derrière Morne
Hewanorra Intl
Vieux Fort
14°05'
14°00'
13°55'
13°50'
13°45'
61°00'
60°55'
N
0 5 km
0 5 miles

ECONOMICS

Inflation 2.7% p.a. (1990–1999)

US$590m

2.70 Eastern Caribbean dollars

SCORE CARD

- ❏ WORLD GNP RANKING........................166th
- ❏ GNP PER CAPITA ....US$3820
- ❏ BALANCE OF PAYMENTS.................US$–80m
- ❏ INFLATION 5.4%
- ❏ UNEMPLOYMENT.................................15%

STRENGTHS

Recently privatized banana industry. Tourism, fisheries potential.

WEAKNESSES

Most resorts foreign-owned. Preferential banana trade to be phased out by 2006.

EXPORTS

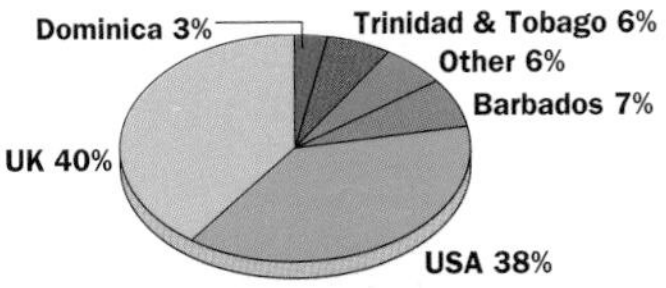
Dominica 3%
Trinidad & Tobago 6%
Other 6%
Barbados 7%
UK 40%
USA 38%

IMPORTS

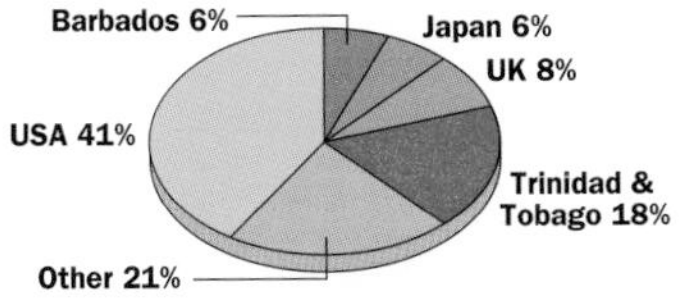
Barbados 6%
Japan 6%
UK 8%
USA 41%
Trinidad & Tobago 18%
Other 21%

RESOURCES

Electric power 22,000 kw

1313 tonnes

Not an oil producer

14,750 pigs, 12,500 sheep, 260,000 chickens

None

St. Lucia has no mineral resources and imports most of its energy. Plans exist to develop geothermal energy from the hot springs in the volcanic interior.

ENVIRONMENT

Not available

2% partially protected

1.3 tonnes per capita

St. Lucians are proud of their island, and environmental questions arouse fierce debate. In recent years, the greatest controversy surrounded the decision to allow a luxury hotel development on the ecologically important Jalousie Plantation, which encompasses the extraordinary twin Pitons and includes an important Amerindian archeological site. The issue illustrates a key problem in St. Lucia, where business pressures to develop tourism can outweigh vital environmental concerns. One notable conservation success has been the St. Lucian parrot. In 1978, there were 150 birds; strict laws against the trade in parrots ensured that by 1994 numbers had risen to over 400.

MEDIA

TV ownership medium

There are no daily newspapers

PUBLISHING AND BROADCAST MEDIA

There are no daily newspapers. *The Star* and *The Mirror* are published weekly

4 independent services

4 services: 1 state-owned, 3 independent

The privately owned press is free from government intervention. It is possible to receive TV programs from US, Mexican, and some Caribbean stations.

CRIME

Death penalty used

1016 prisoners

Crime is rising

Murder is rare, but narcotics-related deaths are increasing, as is violence in schools. The government in 1998 strengthened the police force to combat rising urban crime.

EDUCATION

School leaving age: 15

82%

2760 students

Education is based on the British system. St. Lucia has the most Nobel laureates per capita in the world, namely Sir Arthur Lewis (economics) and Derek Walcott (literature).

CHRONOLOGY

An excellent naval raiding base in the Caribbean in the 17th and 18th centuries, St. Lucia was fought over by France and Britain. Ownership alternated before it was finally ceded to Britain in 1814. French influence survives in St. Lucian patois and the local cuisine.

- ❏ **1958** Joins West Indies Federation.
- ❏ **1964** Sugar-growing ceases.
- ❏ **1979** Gains independence and joins Commonwealth.
- ❏ **1990** Establishes body with Dominica, Grenada, and St. Vincent to discuss forming a Windward Islands Federation.
- ❏ **1997** Hitherto ruling UWP reduced to one seat in general election.
- ❏ **2000** Blacklisted by OECD as international tax haven.

HEALTH

Welfare state health benefits

1 per 2857 people

Heart and respiratory diseases, cancers

Health care has improved since the 1960s. State hospitals are supplemented by private clinics.

SPENDING

GDP/cap. increase

CONSUMPTION AND SPENDING

95 per 1000 population

266 per 1000 population

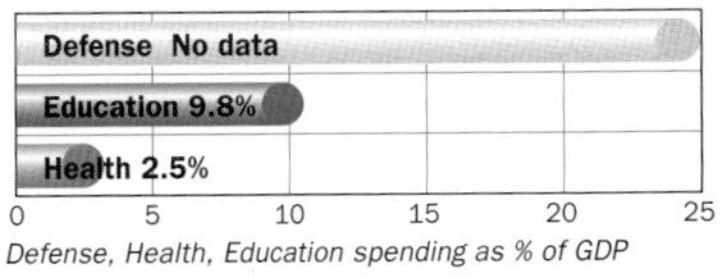
Defense No data
Education 9.8%
Health 2.5%
0
5
10
15
20
25

Defense, Health, Education spending as % of GDP

The island's large-scale banana growers and hotel owners form the richest section of society. Nearly one-fifth of households are considered to be poor.

WORLD RANKING

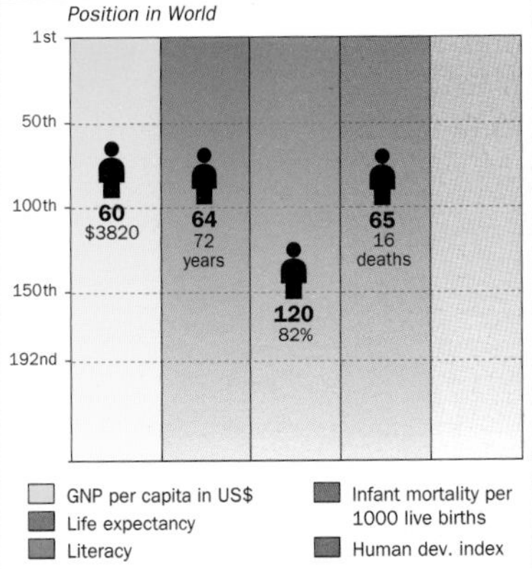
Position in World
1st
50th
100th
150th
192nd
60
$3820
64
72 years
120
82%
65
16 deaths
GNP per capita in US$
Life expectancy
Literacy
Infant mortality per 1000 live births
Human dev. index

S

St. Vincent & the Grenadines

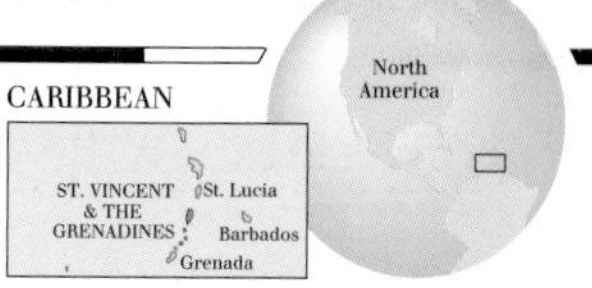
North America
CARIBBEAN
ST. VINCENT & THE GRENADINES
St. Lucia
Barbados
Grenada

Official Name: Saint Vincent and the Grenadines **Capital:** Kingstown
Population: 115,500 **Currency:** Eastern Caribbean dollar **Official Language:** English

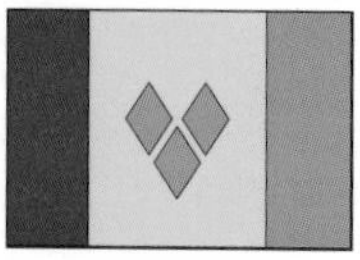

1979 | 1979 | Oct 27 | WV | -4 | +1784 | .vc

AMONG THE MOST ATTRACTIVE of the Windward Islands group, St. Vincent and the Grenadines is renowned as the Caribbean playground of the international jet set. Tourism and bananas are the economic mainstays, and St. Vincent is also the world's largest arrowroot producer. St. Vincent is mostly volcanic; the one remaining active volcano, La Soufrière, last erupted in 1979. The Grenadines are flat, mainly bare, coral reefs.

CLIMATE

Tropical oceanic

WEATHER CHART

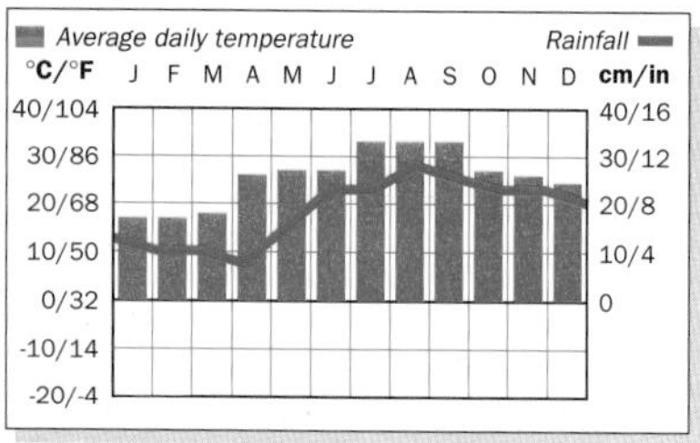
Average daily temperature
Rainfall
°C/°F J F M A M J J A S O N D cm/in
40/104
30/86
20/68
10/50
0/32
-10/14
-20/-4
40/16
30/12
20/8
10/4
0

Constant trade winds moderate St. Vincent's tropical climate. Rainfall is heaviest during the summer months. Tropical depressions and hurricanes are likely between June and November.

TRANSPORTATION

Drive on left

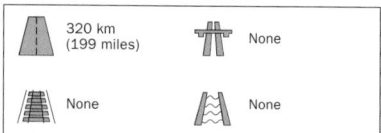

Arnos Vale, Kingstown | 1317 ships 7.9m grt

THE TRANSPORTATION NETWORK

320 km (199 miles)	None
None	None

Access by air is via neighboring islands. Paved roads encompass most of St. Vincent's coast. Port improvements have been completed in recent years. In 1992, an airport capable of taking executive jets was completed on Bequia.

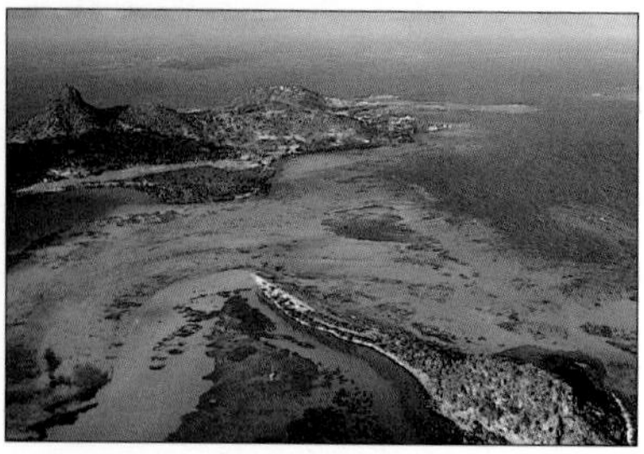

Aerial view of Union Island in the Grenadines chain. The government is developing the island as a major yachting center.

TOURISM

Visitors : Population 1:1.6

73,000 visitors | Up 7% in 2000

MAIN TOURIST ARRIVALS

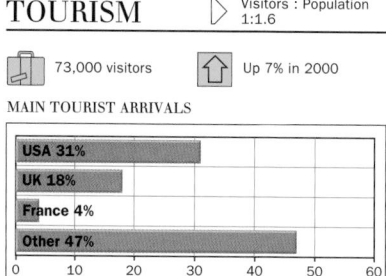

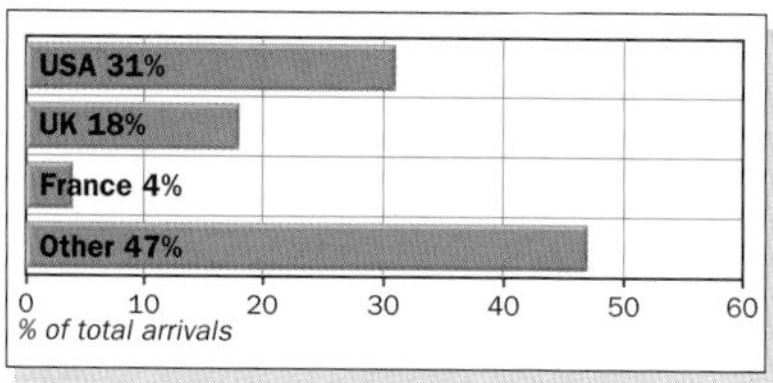
USA 31%
UK 18%
France 4%
Other 47%
0
10
20
30
40
50
60
% of total arrivals

Tourism is targeted at the jet set and cruise ship rather than the mass market, and is concentrated on the Grenadines. Mustique has attracted Mick Jagger and Princess Margaret among others. Union Island is a playground for the yachting rich, and luxury villas, apartments, a golf course, and a casino have been built on Canouan. Layou, on St. Vincent, is the site of pre-Columbian Amerindian petroglyphs.

PEOPLE

Pop. density high

English, English Creole | 340/km² (880/mi²)

THE URBAN/RURAL POPULATION SPLIT

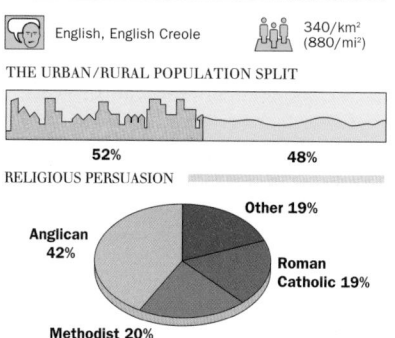

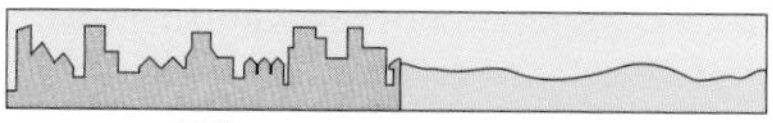
52%
48%

RELIGIOUS PERSUASION

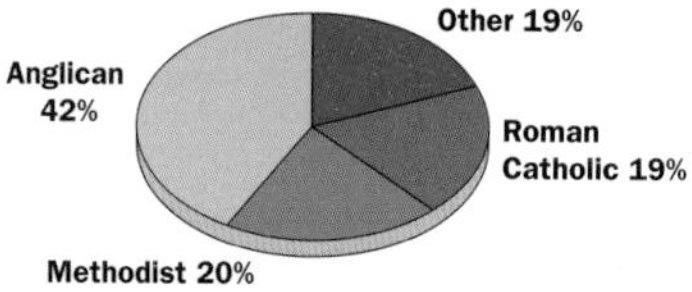
Other 19%
Anglican 42%
Roman Catholic 19%
Methodist 20%

Family life on St. Vincent is heavily influenced by the Anglican Church. Racial tensions are few, and intermarriage has meant that the original communities of descendants of African slaves, Europeans, and the few indigenous Caribs can no longer be distinguished. Many locals fear that traditional island life is being threatened by the expanding tourist industry.

POLITICS

Multiparty elections

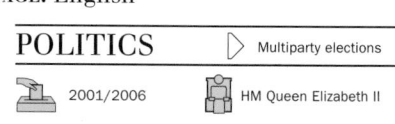

2001/2006 | HM Queen Elizabeth II

AT THE LAST ELECTION

House of Assembly 21 seats

57% ULP
29% App
14% NDP

ULP = Unity Labour Party **App** = Appointed **NDP** = New Democratic Party

Six senators are appointed to the House of Assembly by the governor-general

In March 2001, 17 years of rule by the NDP were overturned by a crushing electoral defeat. The leader of the long-term opposition ULP, Ralph Gonsalves, was appointed prime minister. A new Caribbean Court of Justice was agreed in 2001, but constitutional ties to the British monarchy remain, despite a strong republican movement.

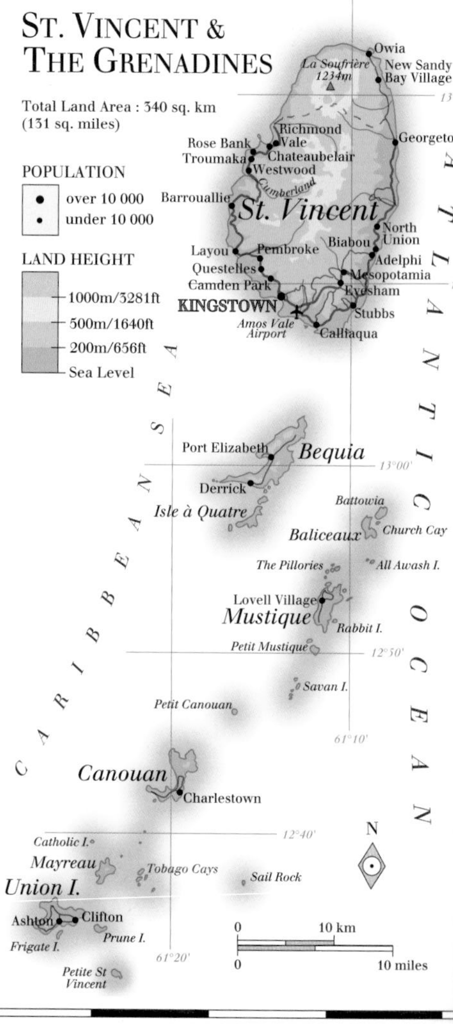
St. Vincent & The Grenadines
Total Land Area : 340 sq. km (131 sq. miles)
POPULATION
over 10 000
under 10 000
LAND HEIGHT
1000m/3281ft
500m/1640ft
200m/656ft
Sea Level
La Soufrière 1234m
Owia
New Sandy Bay Village
Richmond
Rose Bank
Vale
Troumaka
Chateaubelair
Westwood
Georgetown
Barrouallie
St. Vincent
North Union
Biabou
Layou
Pembroke
Questelles
Adelphi
Mesopotamia
Camden Park
Evesham
KINGSTOWN
Stubbs
Amos Vale Airport
Calliaqua
Port Elizabeth
Bequia
Derrick
Isle à Quatre
Battowia
Baliceaux
Church Cay
The Pillories
All Awash I.
Lovell Village
Mustique
Rabbit I.
Petit Mustique
Savan I.
Petit Canouan
Canouan
Charlestown
Catholic I.
Mayreau
Tobago Cays
Sail Rock
Union I.
Ashton
Clifton
Prune I.
Frigate I.
Petite St Vincent
CARIBBEAN SEA
ATLANTIC OCEAN
0 10 km
0 10 miles

WORLD AFFAIRS

Joined UN in 1980

ACS | Comm | Caricom | OAS | OECS

Relations with the USA are strained due to the successful US bid to end the EU's preferential treatment of Caribbean banana imports. St. Vincent supports a united move by Caricom to promote a presidential system of government in place of the British monarchy.

AID

Recipient

US$16m (receipts) — Down 20% in 1999

In 1998 the EU agreed grant aid of EC$15.5 million and the Caribbean Development Bank US$5.1 million in development and housing loans.

DEFENSE

No compulsory military service

US$3m — No significant change from year to year

St. Vincent has no army. Its small police force, trained by the USA and the UK, is part of the Windward and Leeward Islands' Regional Security System.

ECONOMICS

Inflation 2.3% p.a. (1990–1999)

US$301m — 2.70 Eastern Caribbean dollars

SCORE CARD

❑ WORLD GNP RANKING	176th
❑ GNP PER CAPITA	US$2640
❑ BALANCE OF PAYMENTS	US$-35m
❑ INFLATION	1%
❑ UNEMPLOYMENT	22%

STRENGTHS

Bananas, but preferential access to EU markets will end in 2006. Great tourist potential. Currency stability. Leading producer of arrowroot starch. Improving infrastructure.

WEAKNESSES

Little diversification. Strong potential competition from Central and South American banana producers.

EXPORTS

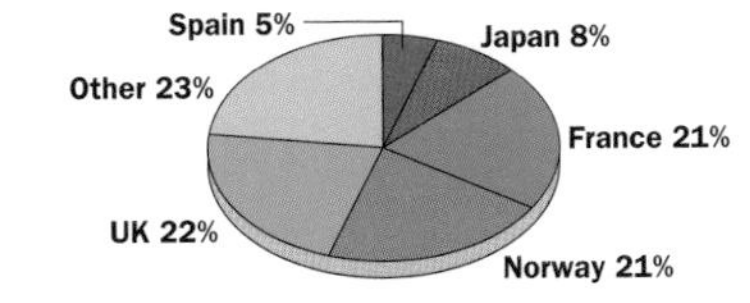
Spain 5%
Japan 8%
Other 23%
France 21%
UK 22%
Norway 21%

IMPORTS

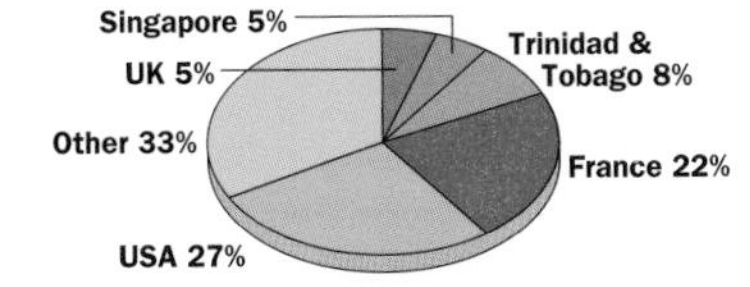
Singapore 5%
UK 5%
Trinidad & Tobago 8%
Other 33%
France 22%
USA 27%

RESOURCES

Electric power 16,000 kw

1410 tonnes — Not an oil producer

13,000 sheep, 9500 pigs, 200,000 chickens — None

There is a hydroelectric plant on the Cumberland river. Virtually all other energy requirements have to be imported. Some of the Grenadines have no fresh water sources.

ENVIRONMENT

Not available

21% (including marine and semi-protected areas) — 1.2 tonnes per capita

Hurricanes are the main environmental threat; Hurricane Emily destroyed 70% of the banana crop in 1987. The former inaccessibility of St. Vincent and the Grenadines meant that tourism was a minor environmental threat, and the untouched, idyllic landscape of islands such as Mustique was their attraction. Mustique is reasonably well protected – buildings have been restricted and further development is limited, since fresh water has to be shipped in. On Bequia, the new airport and consequent increase in visitors are seen as a mixed blessing. Schemes to develop Canouan have similarly been opposed by locals.

MEDIA

TV ownership medium

Daily newspaper circulation 9 per 1000 people

PUBLISHING AND BROADCAST MEDIA

There is 1 daily newspaper, *The Herald*. The main weekly newspaper is the independent *The Vincentian*

1 state-owned service — 1 state-owned service

Two of the six weekly papers are published by the political parties; the rest are independent. Freedom of the press is written into the constitution.

CRIME

Death penalty used

281 prisoners — Up 81% 1990–1994

Rape and robbery are the main local concerns, although on the outlying islands both are very rare. St. Vincent is used for narcotics transshipment to the USA.

EDUCATION

School leaving age: 15

82% — 677 students

State schools follow the former British 11-plus selective system. There are a few private schools. University students go on to the regional University of the West Indies in Jamaica, although increasing numbers are also studying in the USA and the UK.

CHRONOLOGY

In 1795, the local Carib population staged a revolt against the British, who deported them, leaving a largely black African population.

- ❑ **1951** Universal suffrage.
- ❑ **1969** Internal self-government.
- ❑ **1972** James Mitchell premier; holds balance of power between People's Political Party (PPP) and St. Vincent Labour Party (SVLP).
- ❑ **1974** PPP–SVLP coalition.
- ❑ **1979** Full independence under Milton Cato of SVLP. La Soufrière volcano erupts.
- ❑ **1984** NDP, founded by Mitchell in 1975, wins first of four terms.
- ❑ **2000** Mitchell resigns premiership.
- ❑ **2001** ULP wins landslide victory. Ralph Gonsalves prime minister.

HEALTH

Welfare state health beneifts

1 per 2174 people — Heart and respiratory diseases, cancers

Doctors train at the University of the West Indies. The system is a mixture of state and private hospitals and clinics; facilities are scarcer on the Grenadines.

SPENDING

GDP/cap. increase

CONSUMPTION AND SPENDING

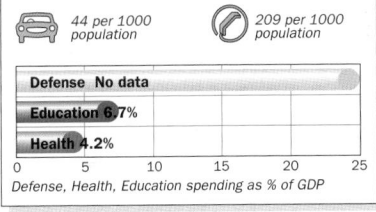

44 per 1000 population — *209 per 1000 population*

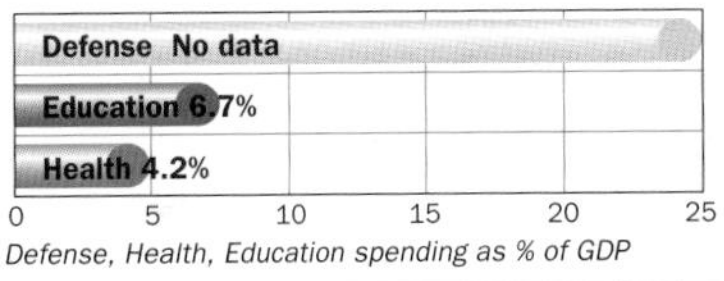
Defense No data
Education 6.7%
Health 4.2%
0 5 10 15 20 25
Defense, Health, Education spending as % of GDP

Jet-set wealth in the islands coexists with the low wages paid to most local workers. Union Island and Mustique in particular attract the wealthy, who favor jeeps and motor yachts.

WORLD RANKING

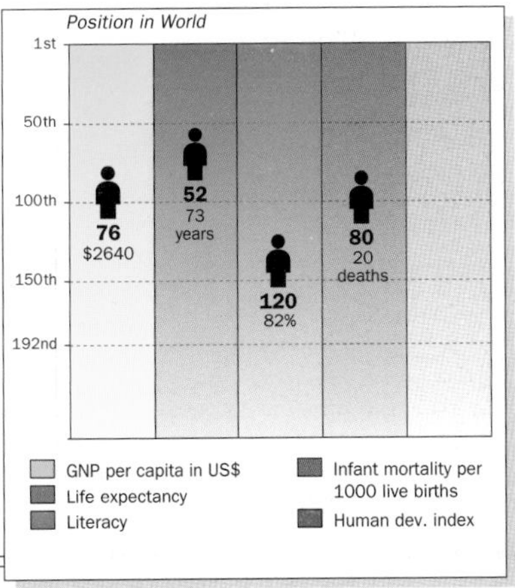
Position in World
1st
50th
100th
150th
192nd
76
$2640
52
73 years
120
82%
80
20 deaths
GNP per capita in US$
Life expectancy
Literacy
Infant mortality per 1000 live births
Human dev. index

S

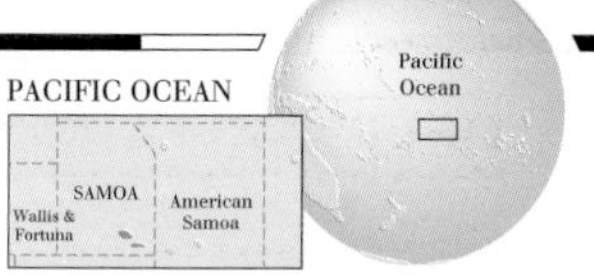
PACIFIC OCEAN
Pacific Ocean
SAMOA
Wallis & Fortuna
American Samoa

SAMOA

OFFICIAL NAME: Independent State of Samoa **CAPITAL:** Apia
POPULATION: 180,000 **CURRENCY:** Tala **OFFICIAL LANGUAGES:** Samoan and English

1962 | 1962 | June 1 | WS | -11 | +684 | .ws

SAMOA LIES IN THE HEART of the South Pacific, 2400 km (1490 miles) north of New Zealand. Four of its nine volcanic islands are inhabited – Apolima, Manono, Sava'ai (the largest), and Upolu (home to 72% of the population). Rainforests cloak the mountains; vegetable gardens and coconut plantations thrive around the coasts. High unemployment and low wages have made Samoa one of the world's least developed countries.

CLIMATE

Tropical oceanic

WEATHER CHART

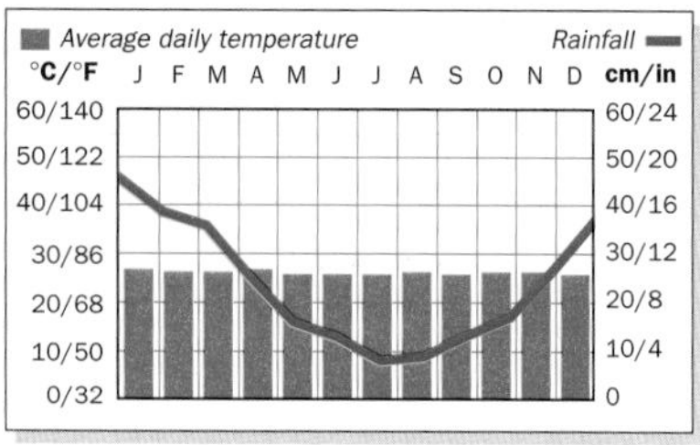
Average daily temperature
Rainfall
°C/°F
J F M A M J J A S O N D
cm/in
60/140
50/122
40/104
30/86
20/68
10/50
0/32
60/24
50/20
40/16
30/12
20/8
10/4
0

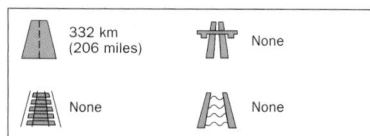

The climate is humid and temperatures rarely drop below 25°C (77°F). December to March is the hurricane season.

TRANSPORTATION

Drive on right

Faleolo Apia
271,240 passengers

7 ships
3300 grt

THE TRANSPORTATION NETWORK

332 km (206 miles)	None
None	None

Apia port has been improved with Japanese aid. International links are mainly by air. Ferries provide inter-island connections.

TOURISM

Visitors : Population 1:2

88,000 visitors

Up 4% in 2000

MAIN TOURIST ARRIVALS

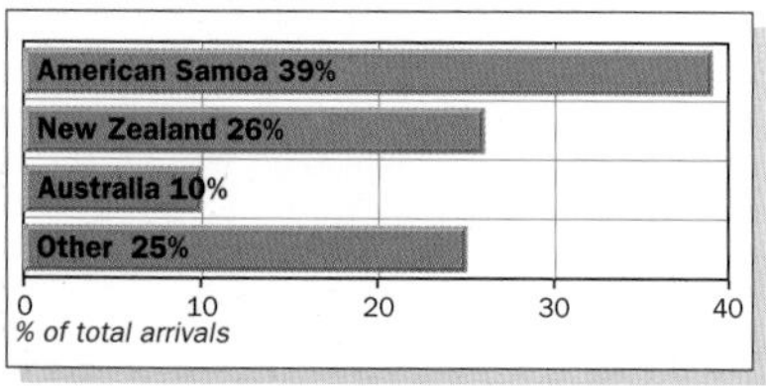
American Samoa 39%
New Zealand 26%
Australia 10%
Other 25%
0
10
20
30
40
% of total arrivals

Tourism is a rapidly growing industry. Small-scale village-based tourism is encouraged. Tourists are attracted by the climate and the easygoing *fa'a Samoa* (Samoan way of life).

PEOPLE

Pop. density medium

Samoan, English

64/km² (165/mi²)

THE URBAN/RURAL POPULATION SPLIT

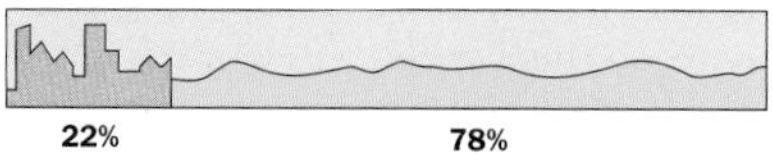
22%
78%

ETHNIC MAKEUP

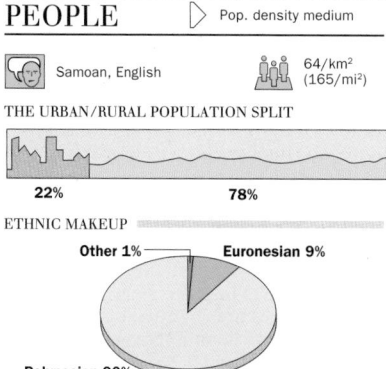

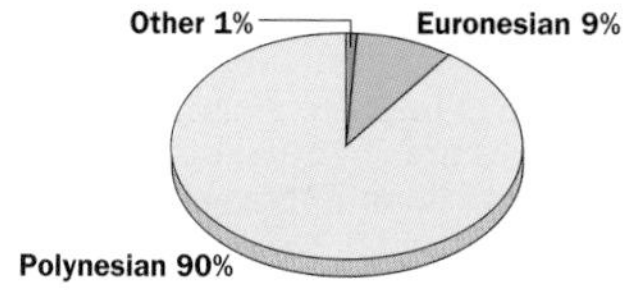
Other 1%
Euronesian 9%
Polynesian 90%

Ethnic Samoans – around 90% of the population – are the world's second-largest Polynesian group, after the Maoris. The *fa'a Samoa* – Samoan way of life – is communal and conservative. Extended family groups, in which most people live, own 80% of the land, and are not permitted to sell it. Each family is headed by a *matai*, or elected chief, who looks after its political and social interests. Large-scale migration to New Zealand and the USA reflects a lack of jobs and the attractions of Western life. Conflict between the *fa'a Samoa* and modern life is strongest among the young, who have a high suicide rate.

SAMOA

Total Land Area : 2830 sq. km (1093 sq. miles)

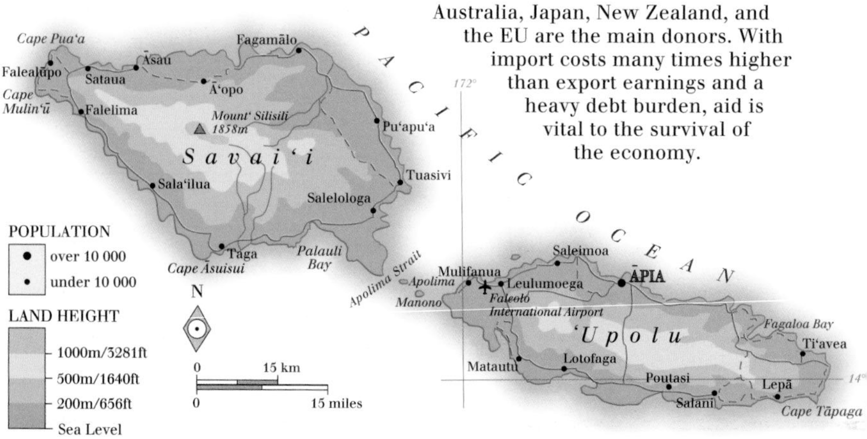
Cape Pua'a
Falealupo
Asau
Fagamālo
Sataua
A'opo
Cape Mulin'ū
Falelima
Mount Silisili 1858m
Pu'apu'a
S a v a i ' i
Sala'ilua
Tuasivi
Salelologa
Taga
Cape Asuisui
Palauli Bay
Apolima Strait
PACIFIC OCEAN
Saleimoa
Mulifanua
Apolima
Manono
Leulumoega
APIA
Faleolo International Airport
Fagaloa Bay
Ti'avea
'U p o l u
Mataut
Lotofaga
Poutasi
Lepā
Salani
Cape Tāpaga
172°
14°
POPULATION
over 10 000
under 10 000
LAND HEIGHT
1000m/3281ft
500m/1640ft
200m/656ft
Sea Level
N
0
15 km
15 miles

POLITICS

Multiparty elections

2001/2006

HH Susuga Malietoa Tanumafili II

AT THE LAST ELECTION

Legislative Assembly 49 seats

46% HRPP
27% SNDP
27% Ind

HRPP = Human Rights Protection Party **SNDP** = Samoan National Development Party **Ind** = Independents

The conservatism of the *fa'a Samoa* and the Church underpins Samoa's political stability. Allegiance to the two main parties is quite fluid. Until 1990, only the 1800 elected chiefs, or *matai*, could vote for the 47 ethnic Samoan seats in the Assembly; the other two seats are elected by non-Samoans. Universal suffrage was introduced at the 1991 elections. Tofilau Eti Alesana of the HRPP, prime minister twice since 1988, resigned in 1998 amid widespread protest against the government's autocratic style. His successor, Tuilaepa Sailele Malielegaoi, also of the HRPP, was reelected in 2001.

WORLD AFFAIRS

Joined UN in 1976

ACP | Comm | IBRD | PC | PIF

Australia is Samoa's main trading partner. New Zealand, the USA, Japan, Fiji, American Samoa, and the EU are also important. Relations with China have recently been established. Samoa has trade links with the Cook Islands, and supports a Polynesian free trade agreement.

AID

Recipient

$23m (receipts)

Down 36% in 1999

Australia, Japan, New Zealand, and the EU are the main donors. With import costs many times higher than export earnings and a heavy debt burden, aid is vital to the survival of the economy.

S

DEFENSE

No compulsory military service

Samoa has no army and few police

Not applicable

New Zealand looks after defense under a 1962 treaty. Internal order is mostly maintained by the *matai* (chiefs).

ECONOMICS

Inflation 4.5% p.a. (1990–1999)

$181m

3.0893–3.3389 tala

SCORE CARD

- ❑ WORLD GNP RANKING........................184th
- ❑ GNP PER CAPITA $1070
- ❑ BALANCE OF PAYMENTS $20m
- ❑ INFLATION 2.2%
- ❑ UNEMPLOYMENT.......Widespread underemployment

STRENGTHS

Light manufacturing expanding, attracting foreign, especially Japanese, firms. Tourism growing rapidly with improved infrastructures. Services expanding rapidly since 1989 launch of offshore banking. Tropical agriculture: taro, coconut cream, cocoa, copra are main exports.

WEAKNESSES

Development adversely affected by cyclones. Fluctuating international markets for copra and cocoa. Poor transportation facilities. Dependence on aid and expatriate remittances.

EXPORTS

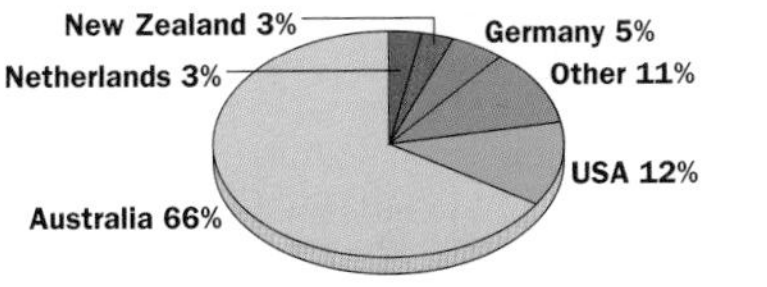
New Zealand 3%
Germany 5%
Netherlands 3%
Other 11%
USA 12%
Australia 66%

IMPORTS

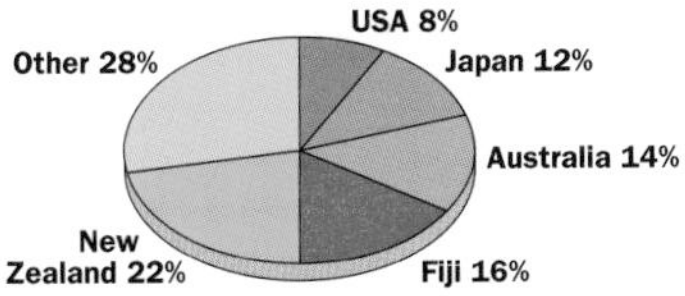
USA 8%
Other 28%
Japan 12%
Australia 14%
New Zealand 22%
Fiji 16%

RESOURCES

Electric power 19,000 kw

4590 tonnes

Not an oil producer

178,800 pigs, 26,000 cattle, 350,000 chickens

None

With no minerals, Samoa's main resources are its forests and tropical agriculture. The rainforests in lower-lying areas are increasingly exploited for timber. Mahogany and teak plantations are being developed. The volcanic soils, particularly on Upolu, support a wide range of staple and export crops. Two-thirds of the population work in agriculture.

Apia, the capital, on Upolu, Samoa's second-largest island. It has a central volcanic range of mountains and many rivers.

ENVIRONMENT

Not available

None

0.8 tonnes per capita

Strict logging regulations have been introduced to halt irreparable damage to the environment; over 80% of forests have been replaced by plantations. Overhunting and loss of habitat have endangered rare species of fruit bat and pigeon. Samoa is concerned about its marine resources and has taken a firm stance against driftnet fishing.

MEDIA

TV ownership medium

There are no daily newspapers

PUBLISHING AND BROADCAST MEDIA

There are no daily newspapers. The *Samoa Times* and the *Samoa Observer* are published five times a week

1 state-owned service

3 services: 1 state-owned, 2 independent

The independent media, notably the *Samoa Observer*, can face strong governmental opposition.

CRIME

Death penalty not used

238 prisoners

Down 79% 1992–1994

Alcohol-related violence is a problem at weekends; otherwise, violent crime is almost unknown. Theft is increasing in urban areas.

EDUCATION

School leaving age: 14

80%

562 students

Education is based on the New Zealand system. School attendance is universal and literacy levels high. A university was established in 1988. The use of corporal punishment is widespread.

HEALTH

No welfare state health benefits

1 per 2632 people

Heart and cerebrovascular diseases, pneumonia, suicide

The Samoan preference for being big went well with traditional diets. Diabetes and heart disease are rising as people change to Western-style foods.

CHRONOLOGY

Polynesians settled Samoa in about 1000 BCE. Western rivalry after 1830 led to the 1899 division of the islands into German Western and American Eastern Samoa.

- ❑ **1914** New Zealand occupies Western Samoa.
- ❑ **1962** Becomes first independent Polynesian nation.
- ❑ **1990** Cyclone Ofa leaves 10,000 people homeless.
- ❑ **1991** HRPP retains power in first election under universal adult suffrage.
- ❑ **1996 and 2001** HRPP returned to power in elections.
- ❑ **1997** The country's name is changed from Western Samoa to Samoa.

SPENDING

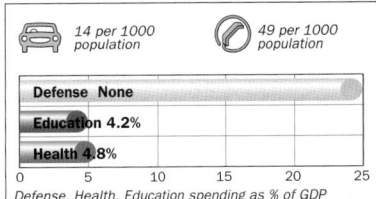

GDP/cap. increase

CONSUMPTION AND SPENDING

14 per 1000 population

49 per 1000 population

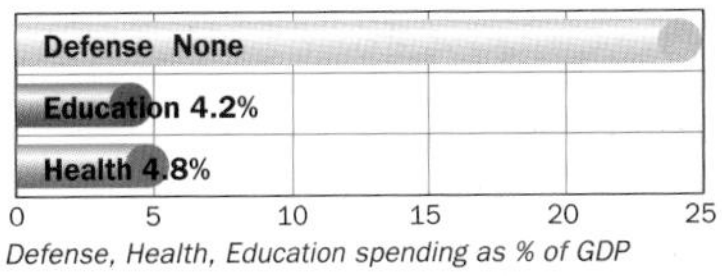
Defense None
Education 4.2%
Health 4.8%
0
5
10
15
20
25

Defense, Health, Education spending as % of GDP

One of the world's least developed nations according to the UN, Samoa has the lowest wages and the highest unemployment rates in Oceania. As a result, emigration is high. Some 60,000 Samoans live in New Zealand, 50,000 in the USA, and 10,000 in neighboring American Samoa, where generous US support makes life much easier. Most people depend on subsistence farming and the remittances of relatives for their livelihood. Two-thirds of those with a job work for the government.

WORLD RANKING

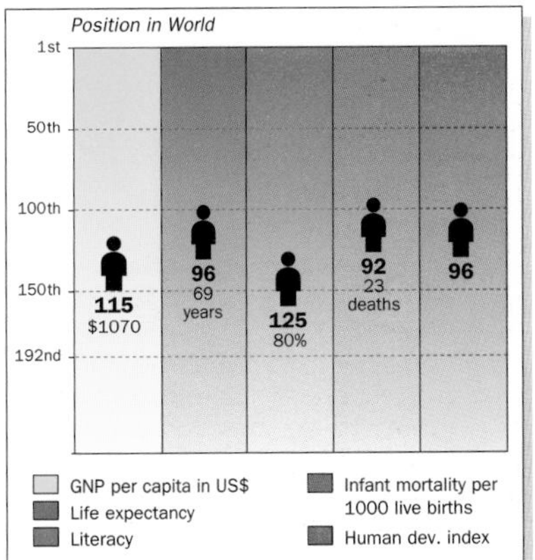
Position in World
1st
50th
100th
150th
192nd
115
$1070
96
69 years
125
80%
92
23 deaths
96
GNP per capita in US$
Life expectancy
Literacy
Infant mortality per 1000 live births
Human dev. index

S

SAN MARINO

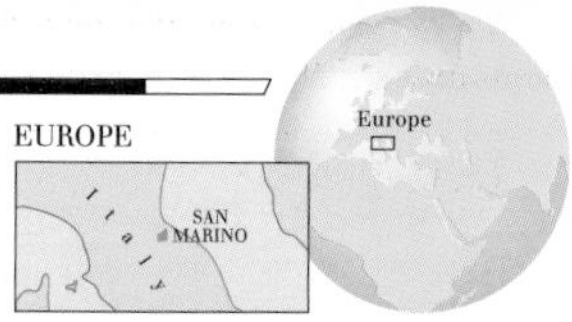
EUROPE
Italy
SAN MARINO
Europe

OFFICIAL NAME: Republic of San Marino **CAPITAL:** San Marino **POPULATION:** 26,900
CURRENCY: Euro (lira until 2002) **OFFICIAL LANGUAGE:** Italian

301 | 301 | Sept 3 | RSM | +1 | +378 | .sm

PERCHED ON THE SLOPES of Mount Titano in the Italian Appennines, tiny San Marino is the world's oldest republic; it has maintained its independence since the 4th century. The territory is divided into nine castles, or districts. One-third of Sammarinesi live in the northern town of Serravalle. Today San Marino makes its living through agriculture, tourism, and limited industry. Italy effectively controls most of its affairs.

***San Marino's** second fortress, la Cesta, built in the 13th century, dominates the republic from its highest pinnacle, 755 m above sea level.*

CLIMATE

Mediterranean

WEATHER CHART

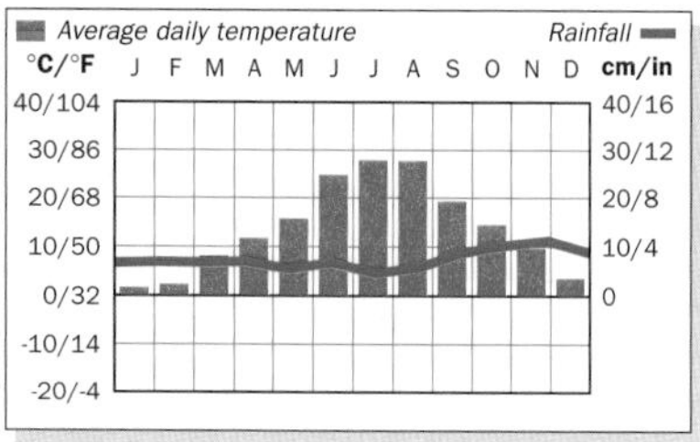
Average daily temperature
Rainfall
°C/°F
J F M A M J J A S O N D
cm/in
40/104
30/86
20/68
10/50
0/32
-10/14
-20/-4
40/16
30/12
20/8
10/4
0

San Marino's Mediterranean climate is moderated by cool sea breezes and its height above sea level. In summer, temperatures can reach 27°C (81°F), while in winter they fall to 7°C (45°F). There is rarely ever any snow.

TRANSPORTATION

Drive on right

None

Has no fleet

THE TRANSPORTATION NETWORK

237 km (147 miles)	Not available
2 km (1 mile)	None

The 24-km (15-mile) highway to Rimini, which has the nearest airport, is San Marino's most important link. Congestion is a major problem, especially during the annual Mille Miglia car rally. A funicular railroad climbs the east side of Mount Titano. The railroad to Rimini, closed since 1945, is being rebuilt.

PEOPLE

Pop. density high

Italian

442/km² (1144/mi²)

THE URBAN/RURAL POPULATION SPLIT

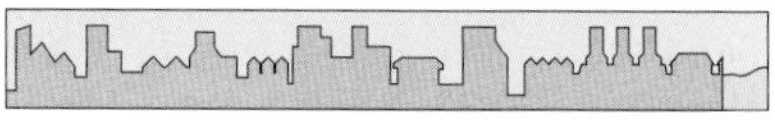
94%
6%

RELIGIOUS PERSUASION

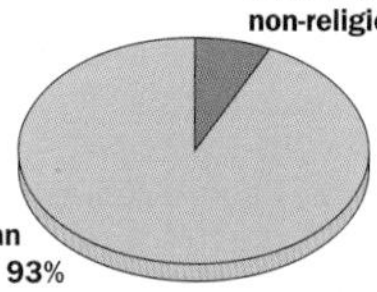
Other and non-religious 7%
Roman Catholic 93%

Citizenship requires 30 years' residence; it is no longer transmissible by marriage. Women gained the vote in 1960, but could not stand for public office until 1973. Around 20,000 live abroad, mainly in Italy. Some Sammarinesi speak a distinct regional dialect.

TOURISM

Visitors : Population 20:1

532,000 visitors

Little change in 1999

MAIN TOURIST ARRIVALS

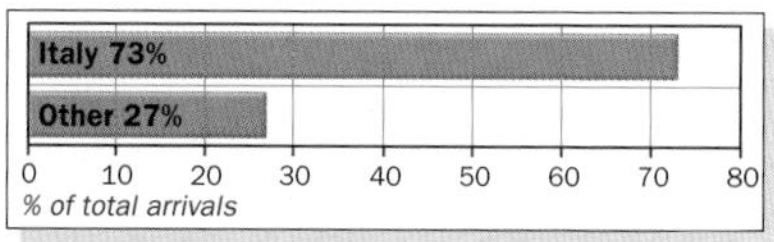
Italy 73%
Other 27%
0
10
20
30
40
50
60
70
80
% of total arrivals

Tourism is the mainstay of San Marino's economy, contributing more than half of government revenue and employment for 20% of the workforce. Earnings from tourism are the largest share of GDP. Every year half a million overnight visitors, and a further 2.5 million day visitors, are drawn by its mild climate and contrasting scenery, and come to sample its folklore and museums. The fortresses of Mount Titano – la Rocca, la Cesta, and Montale – built during the Middle Ages, command superb views and are the main attractions, along with the medieval city of San Marino itself. Many visitors to San Marino are day-trippers from Italy, although tourism is also boosted by the close proximity of the international airport at Rimini.

The San Marino tourist bureau is also attracting thousands of sports enthusiasts to the republic by hosting a series of top international sporting events. In March, both the Rimini–San Marino marathon and the Mille Miglia veteran car meeting are held. May heralds the San Marino Grand Prix, when thousands of Formula One fans descend on the country. June, meanwhile, attracts more motor-racing fans for the World Motocross Championships. A renowned crossbow competition is held to mark San Marino's national day, 3 September.

Efforts have been made to attract business meetings and conferences by means of extensive publicity in the Italian media.

***Religious procession.** The official state religion of San Marino is Roman Catholicism, in contrast to Italy, which has no state religion.*

SAN MARINO

Total Land Area : 61 sq. km (24 sq. miles)

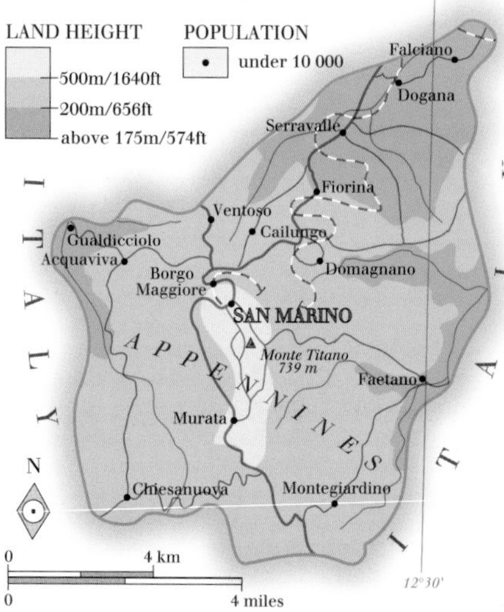
LAND HEIGHT
500m/1640ft
200m/656ft
above 175m/574ft
POPULATION
under 10 000
44°
Falciano
Dogana
Serravalle
Fiorina
Ventoso
Cailungo
Gualdicciolo
Acquaviva
Domagnano
Borgo Maggiore
SAN MARINO
APPENNINES
Monte Titano 739 m
Faetano
Murata
Chiesanuova
Montegiardino
ITALY
ITALY
N
0
4 km
0
4 miles
12°30'

POLITICS

Multiparty elections

2001/2006

Captains-Regent Luigi Lonfernini and Fabio Berardi

San Marino is a parliamentary democracy, headed by two captains-regent elected every six months. The party system is parallel to Italy's, with regular coalition governments. The PDCS holds the greatest share of seats in the Great and General Council and dominates the ruling coalition.

AT THE LAST ELECTION

Great and General Council 60 seats

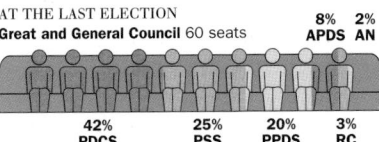

8% APDS
2% AN
42% PDCS
25% PSS
20% PPDS
3% RC

PDCS = San Marino Christian Democratic Party **PSS** = Socialist Party of San Marino **PPDS** = Progressive Democratic Party **APDS** = Popular Democratic Alliance **RC** = Communist Refoundation **AN** = National Alliance

WORLD AFFAIRS

Joined UN in 1992

CE | OSCE | IBRD | IMF

Foreign affairs are effectively decided by Italy, on which San Marino is entirely dependent. In 1992, San Marino acquired a seat at the UN.

AID

Neither

Neither an aid donor nor receiver

Not applicable

San Marino does not receive aid. However, annual subsidies from Italy and free access to the Italian market are essential to the economy.

DEFENSE

No compulsory military service

$1m

Little change in 1998

San Marino has a small territorial army and fortification guards. There is no compulsory military service, but males aged 16–55 may be called up in a national emergency.

ECONOMICS

Inflation 5.9% p.a. (1985–1996)

$190m

1932–2062 lire

SCORE CARD

❑ World GNP Ranking	182nd
❑ GNP per Capita	$7830
❑ Balance of Payments	$11m
❑ Inflation	2%
❑ Unemployment	4%

Strengths

Tourism, providing 60% of government revenue. Light industry, notably mechanical engineering and clothing, with emphasis on sportswear and high-quality prestige lines. Philately.

Weaknesses

Need to import all raw materials.

EXPORTS/IMPORTS

San Marino does not publish independent trade statistics; trade movements are included in the Italian totals.

RESOURCES

Electric Power: included in Italian total

Not available

Not an oil producer

Small numbers of cattle, pigs, sheep, and horses

None

San Marino has to import all its energy from Italy. It has no exploitable mineral resources now that the stone quarry on Mount Titano has been exhausted.

ENVIRONMENT

Not available

None

Not available

Mount Titano is a unique limestone outcrop in the surrounding Italian plain and so has a very localized ecosystem.

MEDIA

TV ownership high

Daily newspaper circulation 71 per 1000 people

PUBLISHING AND BROADCAST MEDIA

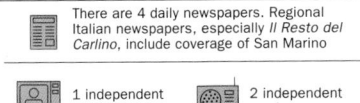

There are 4 daily newspapers. Regional Italian newspapers, especially *Il Resto del Carlino*, include coverage of San Marino

1 independent service

2 independent services

In 1993, a local TV station, San Marino RTV, began broadcasting. Sammarinesi can also receive Italian TV.

CRIME

Death penalty not used

San Marino does not publish prison figures

Little change from year to year

San Marino has a low crime rate. Justice is mainly administered in Italy. Until mid-1997 homosexuality was illegal.

EDUCATION

School leaving age: 14

99%

Not available

The government spends 13% of the budget on education. Secondary school pupils can go on to Italian universities.

HEALTH

Welfare state health benefits

1 per 375 people

Heart diseases, cancers, accidents

Health care is free and available to all. There is a hospital, but those requiring difficult operations normally go to Rimini for treatment.

CHRONOLOGY

Founded in the 4th century, the Republic of San Marino became one of many medieval Italian city states. It refused to join the unified Italian state created between 1860 and 1871.

- ❑ **1862** San Marino signs friendship treaty with Italy.
- ❑ **1914–1918** San Marino fights for Italy in World War I.
- ❑ **1940** Supports Axis powers and declares war on the Allies.
- ❑ **1943** Declares neutrality shortly before Italy surrenders.
- ❑ **1960** Women obtain vote.
- ❑ **1978** Coalition of San Marino Communist Party (PCS) and PSS – sole communist-led government in Western Europe.
- ❑ **1986** Financial scandals lead to a new PDCS/PCS government.
- ❑ **1988** Joins Council of Europe.
- ❑ **1990** PCS renames itself the PPDS.
- ❑ **1992** Joins UN. Collapse of communism in Europe sees PDCS/PPDS alliance replaced by a PDCS/PSS coalition government.
- ❑ **1999** Introduction of euro.

SPENDING

GDP/cap. increase

CONSUMPTION AND SPENDING

No data

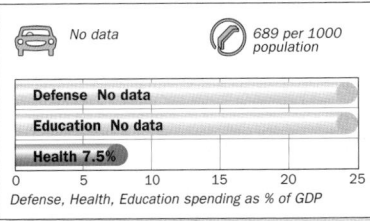

689 per 1000 population

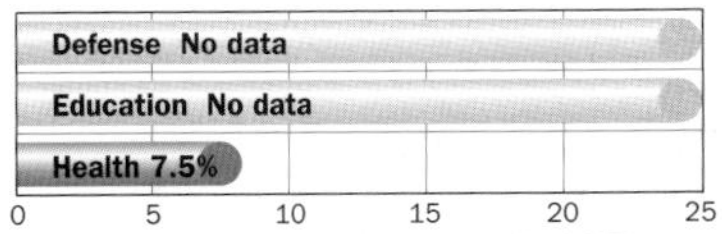
Defense No data
Education No data
Health 7.5%
0
5
10
15
20
25

Defense, Health, Education spending as % of GDP

Living standards are similar to those of northern Italy, while the unemployment rate is well below the Italian average.

WORLD RANKING

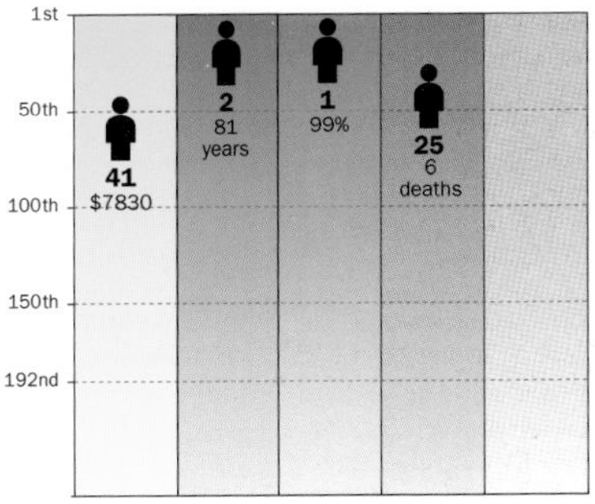
Position in World
1st
50th
100th
150th
192nd
41 $7830
2 81 years
1 99%
25 6 deaths
GNP per capita in US$
Life expectancy
Literacy
Infant mortality per 1000 live births
Human dev. index

S

São Tomé & Príncipe

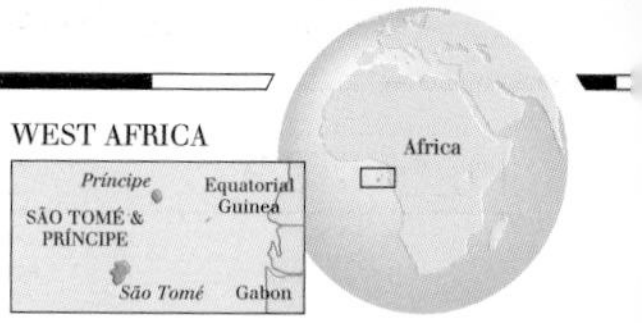
WEST AFRICA
Príncipe
SÃO TOMÉ & PRÍNCIPE
São Tomé
Equatorial Guinea
Gabon
Africa

Official Name: Democratic Republic of São Tomé and Príncipe **Capital:** São Tomé
Population: 159,900 **Currency:** Dobra **Official Language:** Portuguese

1975 | 1975 | July 12 | STP | 0 | +239 | .st

Composed of the main islands of São Tomé and Príncipe and surrounding islets, the republic is situated off the western coast of Africa. In 1975, a classic Marxist single-party regime was established following independence from Portugal, but a referendum in 1990 resulted in a 72% vote in favor of democracy. São Tomé's main concerns are to rebuild relations with Portugal and to seek closer ties with the EU and the USA.

CLIMATE

Tropical equatorial

WEATHER CHART

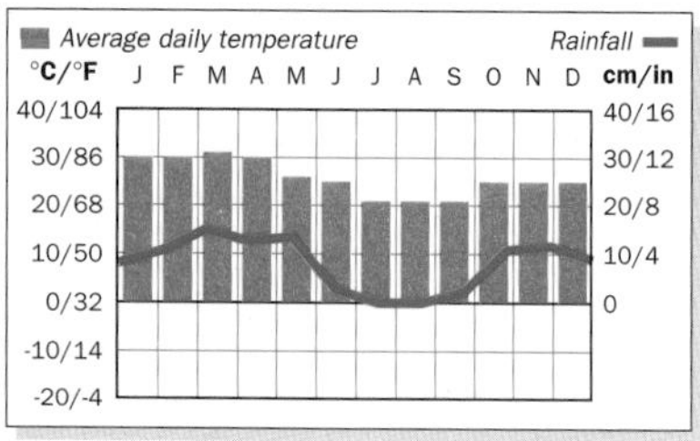
Average daily temperature
Rainfall
°C/°F J F M A M J J A S O N D cm/in
40/104
30/86
20/68
10/50
0/32
-10/14
-20/-4
40/16
30/12
20/8
10/4
0

The humid islands straddle the equator. Rainfall is 100 cm (39 in) on Príncipe and 500 cm (197 in) on São Tomé.

TRANSPORTATION

Drive on right

São Tomé International 23,000 passengers

10 ships 10,242 grt

THE TRANSPORTATION NETWORK

218 km (135 miles)

None

None

None

In 2000, plans were proceeding to construct a deep-water port at Agulhas Bay on Príncipe.

TOURISM

Visitors : Population 1:32

5000 visitors

Down 17% 1995–1998

MAIN TOURIST ARRIVALS

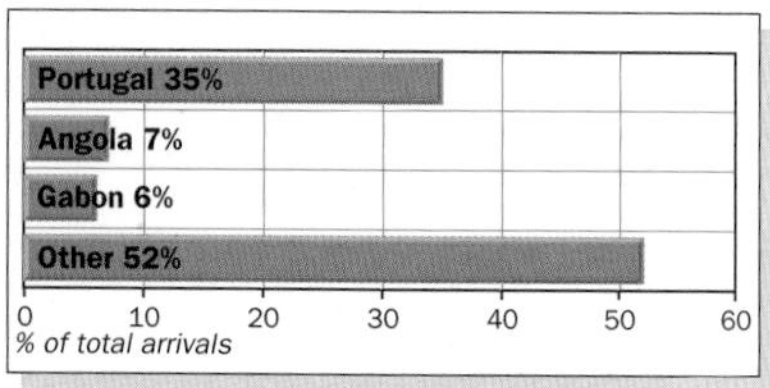
Portugal 35%
Angola 7%
Gabon 6%
Other 52%
0 10 20 30 40 50 60
% of total arrivals

Tourism is still small-scale, attracting wealthy Africans and Europeans. Despite recent foreign investment, the islands attract relatively few tourists annually. The first modern hotel opened in 1986.

PEOPLE

Pop. density medium

Portuguese Creole, Portuguese

167/km² (431/mi²)

THE URBAN/RURAL POPULATION SPLIT

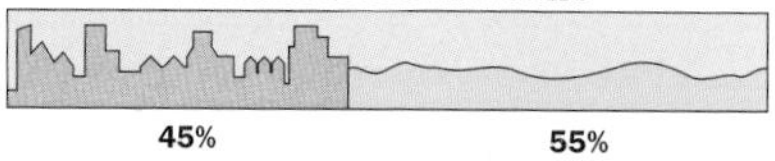
45%
55%

ETHNIC MAKEUP

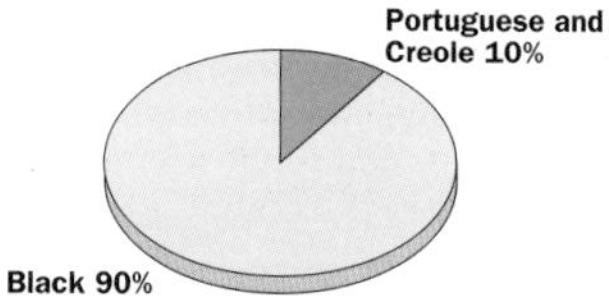
Portuguese and Creole 10%
Black 90%

The population is entirely descended from immigrants, since the islands were uninhabited when the Portuguese arrived in 1470. As the Portuguese settled, they imported Africans as slaves to work the sugar and cocoa plantations. The abolition of slavery in the 19th century, and the departure of 4000 Portuguese at independence, has resulted in a population which is 10% Portuguese and Creole and 90% black African, although Portuguese culture predominates. Blacks run the political parties. Society is well integrated and free of racial tensions. The main conflicts relate to class or differing ideologies. The extended family still offers the best, if not the only, form of social security. Women have a higher status than in most other African states; many have succeeded in attaining prominent positions in the professions.

***Lush vegetation on São Tomé.** The tropical climate is slightly moderated by the cool Benguela current.*

POLITICS

Multiparty elections

1998/2002

President Fradique de Menezes

AT THE LAST ELECTION

National Assembly 55 seats

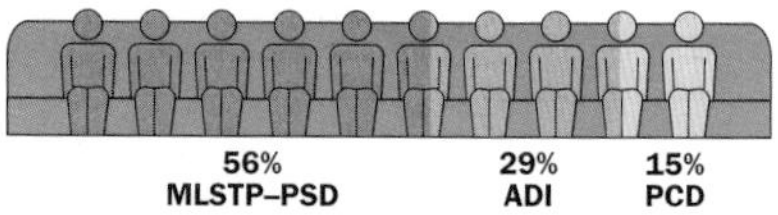
56% MLSTP–PSD
29% ADI
15% PCD

MLSTP–PSD = São Tomé and Príncipe Liberation Movement – Social Democratic Party **ADI** = Independent Democratic Action **PCD** = Democratic Convergence Party

In 1990, a new multiparty constitution swept away the Marxist single-party state that had existed since independence in 1975. The former leader Pinto da Costa, of the MLSTP, steered the way to multipartyism. The opposition PCD was swept to victory in 1991, and later that year Miguel Trovoada returned from 11 years' exile to be elected as an independent to the presidency. Early elections in 1994 saw the return to power of the MLSTP as the renamed MLSTP–PSD, which won again in 1998. The main political concerns are upholding the multiparty system and the development of the economy in the light of the undersea oil reserves, ownership of which was guaranteed when São Tomé and Nigeria reached agreement in 2000 over their common maritime border. In the July 2001 presidential elections, businessman Fradique de Menezes defeated former Marxist Pinto da Costa.

WORLD AFFAIRS

Joined UN in 1975

CPLP | ACP | OIF | NAM | OAU

São Tomé has achieved rapprochement with Portugal and seeks to maintain links with other former Portuguese colonies, notably Angola. It has always had close ties with Gabon and, while not dropping its ex-communist links, seeks closer relations with other central African states, France, and the USA.

AID

Recipient

$28m (receipts)

No change in 1999

São Tomé has one of the highest aid-to-population ratios in Africa. Joining the Lomé convention in the 1970s has meant that São Tomé has found new sources of aid fairly easily since the demise of communism worldwide. The World Bank and the IMF are the main donors.

S

DEFENSE

No compulsory military service

$1m

Little change

Since independence, the armed forces have figured prominently in national life. They have put down several attempted coups, notably in 1978, after which 2000 Angolan troops plus Soviet and Cuban advisers were invited in, and in 1988. In 1995, a group of army officers seized temporary control of the country. The national armed forces are believed to number 2000. With the collapse of the Eastern bloc, São Tomé now receives military assistance from the West.

ECONOMICS

Inflation 54.1% p.a. (1990–1999)

$40m

2318.6–2390.0 dobras

SCORE CARD

- ❑ WORLD GNP RANKING........................190th
- ❑ GNP PER CAPITA $270
- ❑ BALANCE OF PAYMENTS......................$–14m
- ❑ INFLATION 37.1%
- ❑ UNEMPLOYMENT.................................50%

EXPORTS

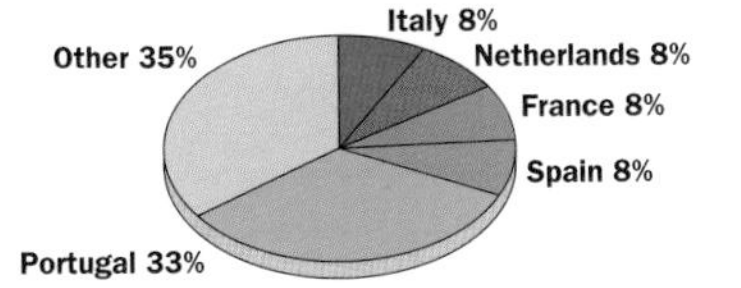
Italy 8%
Other 35%
Netherlands 8%
France 8%
Spain 8%
Portugal 33%

RESOURCES

Electric power 6000 kw

3338 tonnes

Not an oil producer

30,000 ducks, 4800 goats, 300,000 chickens

None

An offshore oil exploration agreement with Nigeria was signed in 2001. There are no mineral resources on the islands. São Tomé is very fertile; cocoa estates are finally back to pre-1975 productivity, and diversification of crops is now a priority. Príncipe has better ports, but its wild scenery makes it more suitable for tourism than farming.

IMPORTS

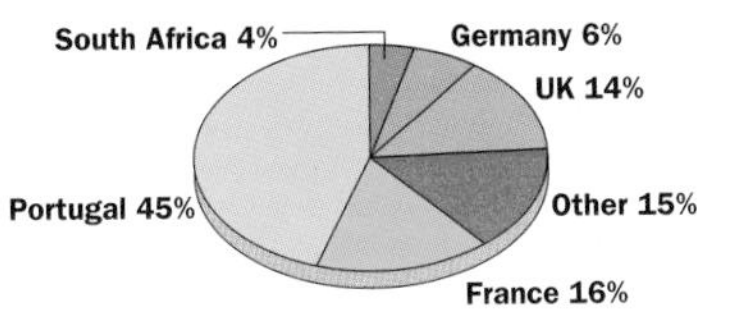
South Africa 4%
Germany 6%
UK 14%
Portugal 45%
Other 15%
France 16%

STRENGTHS

Legacy of Portuguese-built infrastructure. Potential for fisheries, agricultural, and oil development. Ability to attract substantial aid.

WEAKNESSES

Cocoa accounts for 90% of export earnings. Skillful diplomacy has attracted high levels of aid, but mismanagement of these funds has resulted in severe debt. Weak currency.

CHRONOLOGY

The entire preindependence history of the islands was as a Portuguese colony exploited by plantation owners.

- ❑ **1972–1973** Strikes by plantation workers.
- ❑ **1975** Independence as Marxist state. Plantations nationalized.
- ❑ **1978** Abortive coup.
- ❑ **1990** New democratic constitution.
- ❑ **1991–2000** Miguel Trovoada president for two terms.
- ❑ **1995** Príncipe granted autonomy.
- ❑ **2001** De Menezes wins presidency.

EDUCATION

School leaving age: 14

75%

Not available

Education is compulsory for 7–14-year-olds. All staff at the one technical and three secondary schools are foreigners.

HEALTH

No welfare state health benefits

1 per 3125 people

Malaria, other parasitic diseases, respiratory and diarrheal diseases

Although health care is not free, São Tomé has a better system of basic care than other African countries.

SPENDING

GDP/cap. increase

CONSUMPTION AND SPENDING

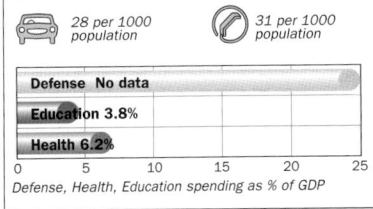

28 per 1000 population

31 per 1000 population

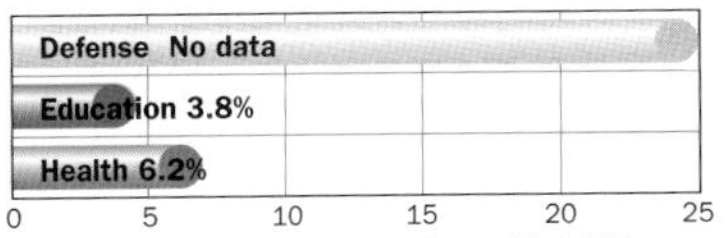
Defense No data
Education 3.8%
Health 6.2%
0
5
10
15
20
25

Defense, Health, Education spending as % of GDP

Wealth disparities are not conspicuous. There is a growing business class. Cocoa workers form the country's poorest group.

SÃO TOMÉ & PRÍNCIPE

Total Land Area : 960 sq. km (371 sq. miles)

POPULATION
- over 10 000
- under 10 000

LAND HEIGHT
- 1000m/3281ft
- 500m/1640ft
- 200m/656ft
- Sea Level

0 10 km
0 10 miles

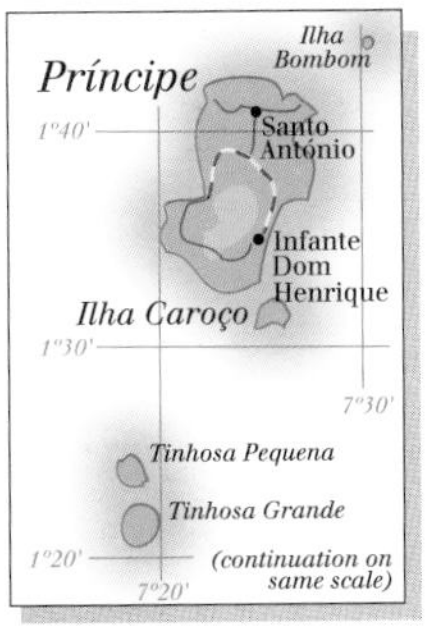
Príncipe
Ilha Bombom
Santo António
Infante Dom Henrique
Ilha Caroço
1°40'
1°30'
7°30'
Tinhosa Pequena
Tinhosa Grande
1°20'
7°20'
(continuation on same scale)

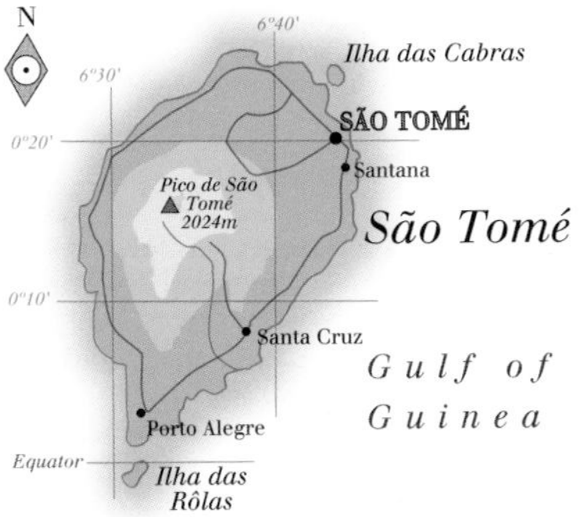
N
6°40'
6°30'
Ilha das Cabras
SÃO TOMÉ
0°20'
Santana
Pico de São Tomé 2024m
São Tomé
0°10'
Santa Cruz
Gulf of Guinea
Porto Alegre
Equator
Ilha das Rôlas

ENVIRONMENT

Not available

None

0.6 tonnes per capita

Fish conservation, deforestation for fuelwood, and potential tourism expansion are the major issues.

MEDIA

TV ownership medium

There are no daily newspapers

PUBLISHING AND BROADCAST MEDIA

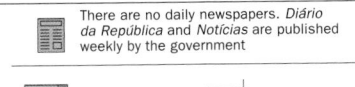

There are no daily newspapers. *Diário da República* and *Notícias* are published weekly by the government

1 state-controlled service

1 state-controlled service

Freedom of expression is respected. The state controls radio and TV stations. Radio ownership is high for Africa.

CRIME

Death penalty not used

99 prisoners

Crime is decreasing

Crime levels are fairly low owing to the tightly knit nature of the community. Urban robberies are a problem.

WORLD RANKING

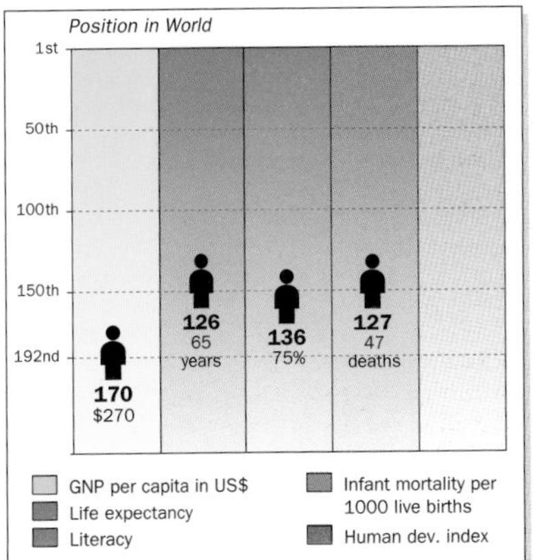
Position in World
1st
50th
100th
150th
192nd
170
$270
126
65 years
136
75%
127
47 deaths
GNP per capita in US$
Life expectancy
Literacy
Infant mortality per 1000 live births
Human dev. index

S

SAUDI ARABIA

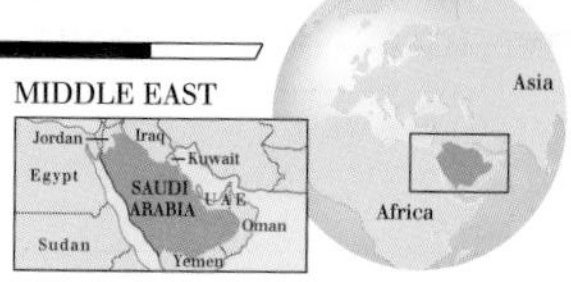
MIDDLE EAST
Jordan
Iraq
Kuwait
Egypt
SAUDI ARABIA
UAE
Oman
Sudan
Yemen
Asia
Africa

OFFICIAL NAME: Kingdom of Saudi Arabia **CAPITAL:** Riyadh
POPULATION: 21.6 million **CURRENCY:** Saudi riyal **OFFICIAL LANGUAGE:** Arabic

1932 | 1932 | Sept 23 | SA | +3 | +966 | .sa

OCCUPYING MOST OF THE Arabian peninsula, Saudi Arabia covers an area as large as western Europe. Over 95% of its land is desert, with the most arid part, known as the "Empty Quarter" or Rub al Khali, being in the southeast. Saudi Arabia has the world's largest oil and gas reserves and major refining and petrochemicals industries. It includes Islam's holiest cities, Medina and Mecca, visited each year by two million Muslims performing the pilgrimage known as the *haj*. The al-Sa'ud family have been Saudi Arabia's absolutist rulers since 1932.

CLIMATE

Hot desert

WEATHER CHART

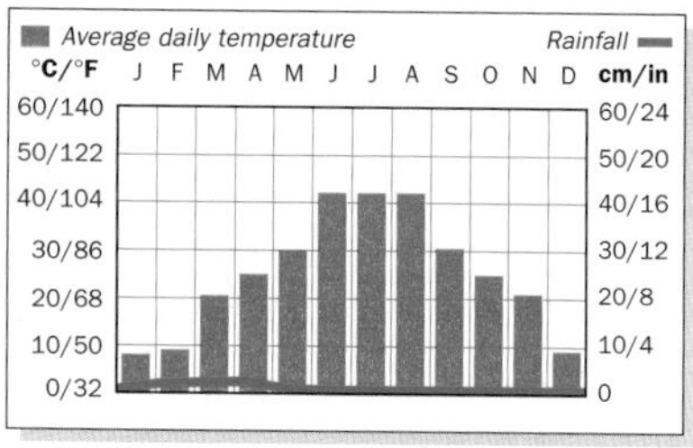
Average daily temperature
Rainfall
°C/°F
J F M A M J J A S O N D
cm/in
60/140
50/122
40/104
30/86
20/68
10/50
0/32
60/24
50/20
40/16
30/12
20/8
10/4
0

The kingdom's only reliable rainfall is in the southern Asir province, making agriculture viable there. The central plateau requires deep artesian wells to water crops. Inland, summer temperatures often soar above 48°C (118°F), but in winter, especially in the northwest, they may fall to freezing point.

TRANSPORTATION

Drive on right

King Abd al-Aziz International, Jiddah
10.3m passengers

279 ships
1.3m grt

THE TRANSPORTATION NETWORK

44,104 km (27,405 miles)

Trans-Arabian Highway

1392 km (865 miles)

None

Since the advent of oil wealth in the 1970s, a modern transportation infrastructure has been created, linking the main population centers to the Gulf states, Jordan, and Egypt.

TOURISM

Visitors : Population 1:5.8

3.7m visitors

Up 3% in 1998

MAIN TOURIST ARRIVALS

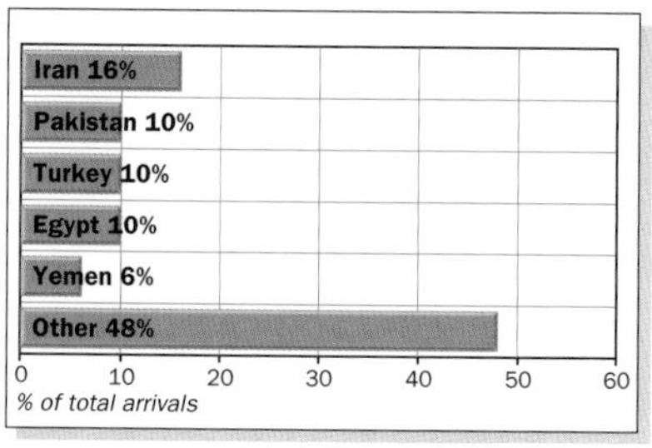
Iran 16%
Pakistan 10%
Turkey 10%
Egypt 10%
Yemen 6%
Other 48%
0
10
20
30
40
50
60
% of total arrivals

Saudi Arabia discourages foreign tourism. Until a limited relaxation in 2000, only Muslim pilgrims, business people, and foreign workers were permitted entry. Non-Muslims are banned from the holy cities of Mecca and Medina. Although strict quotas have been imposed to avoid overcrowding, stampedes of *haj* pilgrims in 1990, 1997, and 2001 killed and injured thousands. Many choose the port of Jiddah as a base from which to begin the pilgrimage. The *umra*, or little pilgrimage, is also popular, since it can be made at any time of year. An estimated $2.5 billion has been spent in recent years on improving *haj* facilities. Jizan on the Red Sea offers excellent scuba diving. The Hejaz railroad and the Nabatean ruins at Medain Salih are of archeological interest. To escape the summer heat, the government moves to mountainous Taif, used as a resort by the Saudis.

SAUDI ARABIA

Total Land Area : 2 114 690 sq. km (816 480 sq. miles)

POPULATION	LAND HEIGHT
over 1 000 000	3000m/9843ft
over 500 000	2000m/6562ft
over 100 000	1000m/3281ft
over 50 000	500m/1640ft
over 10 000	Sea Level
under 10 000	

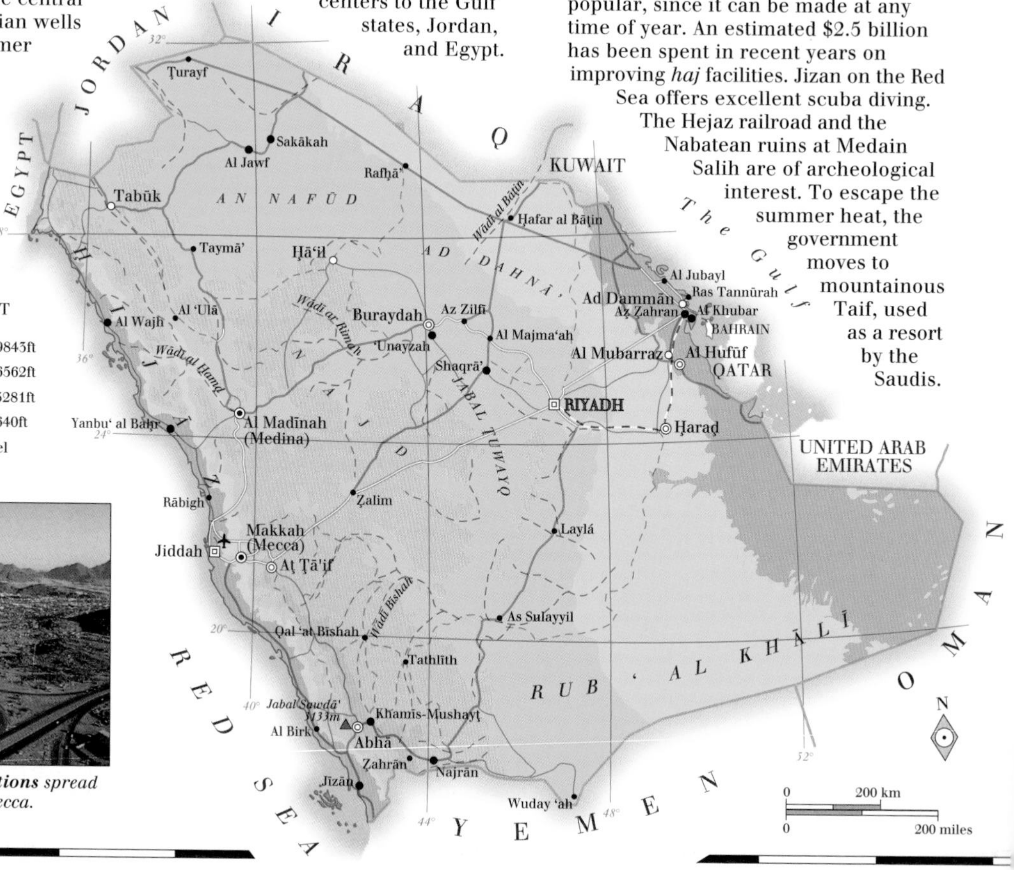
JORDAN
IRAQ
KUWAIT
EGYPT
The Gulf
BAHRAIN
QATAR
UNITED ARAB EMIRATES
OMAN
YEMEN
RED SEA
Turayf
Sakākah
Al Jawf
Rafḩā'
AN NAFŪD
Tabūk
Hafar al Bāṭin
Wādī al Bāṭin
Taymā'
Ḥā'il
AD DAHNĀ'
Al Jubayl
Ras Tannūrah
Ad Dammān
Az Zahrān
Al Khubar
Al 'Ulā
Al Wajh
Buraydah
Az Zilfī
Al Majma'ah
'Unayzah
Wādī ar Rimah
Wādī al Ḥamḍ
Al Mubarraz
Al Hufūf
Shaqrā'
JABAL TUWAYQ
RIYADH
Ḥaraḍ
Yanbu' al Baḥr
Al Madīnah (Medina)
NAJD
HIJAZ
Rābigh
Ẓalim
Laylá
Jiddah
Makkah (Mecca)
Aṭ Ṭā'if
As Sulayyil
Qal 'at Bīshah
Wādī Bīshah
Tathlīth
RUB' AL KHĀLĪ
Jabal Sawdā' 3133m
Khamis-Mushayṭ
Al Birk
Abhā
Ẓahrān
Najrān
Jīzān
Wuday 'ah
32°
28°
24°
20°
36°
40°
44°
48°
52°
N
0 200 km
0 200 miles

Network of modern road junctions spread out across the landscape near Mecca.

S

PEOPLE

Pop. density low

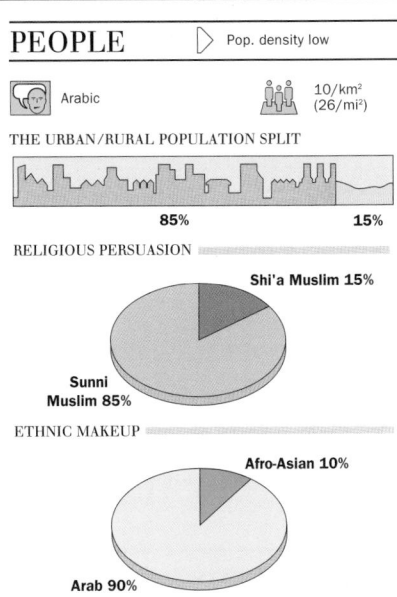

Arabic

10/km² (26/mi²)

THE URBAN/RURAL POPULATION SPLIT

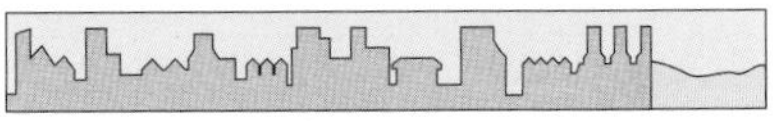

85% 15%

RELIGIOUS PERSUASION

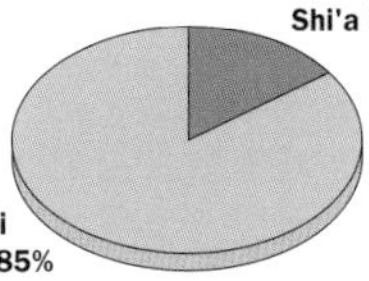
Shi'a Muslim 15%
Sunni Muslim 85%

ETHNIC MAKEUP

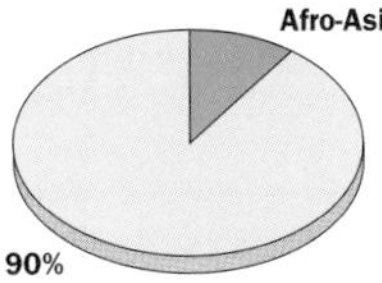
Afro-Asian 10%
Arab 90%

The Saudis, who take their name from the ruling al-Sa'ud family, were united by conquest between 1902 and 1932 by King Abd al-Aziz al-Sa'ud, who expelled the Turks. The vast majority of Saudis are Sunni Muslims who follow the *wahhabi* (puritan) interpretation of Islam and embrace *sharia* (Islamic law). The politically dominant Nejadi tribes from the central plateau around Riyadh are Bedouin in origin. The Hejazi tribes, from the south and west, have a more cosmopolitan, mercantile background, but are largely displaced from politics. In the eastern province there is a Shi'a minority of some 300,000, many of whom are employed in the oilfields. Women have to wear the veil, cannot hold a driving license, and have no role in public life. They are effectively barred from the workplace except as teachers and nurses. However, in 2000 Saudi Arabia decided to sign the UN convention on women's rights – provided it did not contradict *sharia*.

POPULATION AGE BREAKDOWN

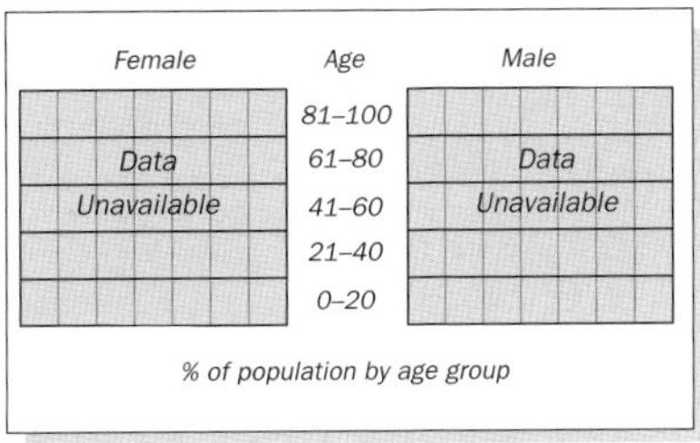
Female
Age
Male
81–100
61–80
41–60
21–40
0–20
Data Unavailable
Data Unavailable
% of population by age group

POLITICS

No multiparty elections

Not applicable

HM King Fahd ibn Abd al-Aziz

LEGISLATIVE OR ADVISORY BODIES

Consultative Council 120 seats

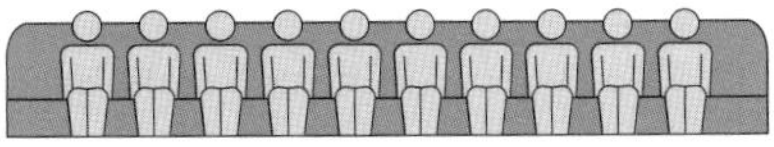

Saudi Arabia is an absolute monarchy. The king rules with the assistance of an appointed Council of Ministers and the Consultative Council

Saudi Arabia is an absolute monarchy. Since 1993 a Consultative Council (*Majlis ash-Shoura*) has been appointed by the king.

MAIN POLITICAL ISSUES

Questioning the ruling family

Following the 1991 Gulf War, a civil rights campaign emerged to challenge the authority of the ruling family, demanding closer adherence to Islamic values. The movement objected to the presence of US troops on Saudi territory and the consequent exposure to "corrupt" Western culture. The al-Sa'uds moved swiftly to quash the protest but exiled opponents have continued their activities using fax machines and e-mail. Osama bin Laden, formerly part of the inner circle, is now reportedly dedicated to overthrowing the ruling family from his base in Afghanistan.

The succession issue

The question of succession and the possibility of a future power struggle, rooted in rivalries endemic to the House of Sa'ud, emerged as major issues in early 1996, when King Fahd – suffering the effects of a stroke – formally ceded the management of day-to-day affairs to his half-brother, Crown Prince Abdullah. A few weeks later, Fahd resumed control.

PROFILE

The royal family rules by carefully manipulating appointments in all sectors of government. Frequent changes of personnel within the armed forces ensure that officers do not build personal followings. All influential cabinet portfolios, apart from those of oil and religious affairs, are held by members of the royal family.

Absolutist rule means that domestic politics are virtually nonexistent. The regime retains feudal elements: weekly *majlis*, or councils, are held where citizens can present petitions or grievances to leading members of the royal family. Large cash sums are often dispensed at these meetings.

The legitimacy of the regime is built on its adherence to Islamic values, and the backing of the *ulema* (scholars). It is the stress on Islam that colors Saudi life most. The 5000-strong *mutawa* (religious police) enforce the five-times-a-day call to prayer, when businesses must close. During Ramadan the *mutawa* are especially active.

WORLD AFFAIRS

Joined UN in 1945

AL | Damasc | GCC | OIC | OPEC

Saudi Arabia's strategic importance is derived largely from its oil reserves and worldwide investments. Relations with the USA are particularly close, and the Saudis remain important institutional investors in the West. After Iraq's invasion of Kuwait in 1990, it took a leading role in consolidating the Arab coalition against Iraq and sheltered the Kuwaiti royal family. It also provided military bases to the Western allies and supplied more troops than any other Arab country. However, the continued presence of foreign forces has provoked some hostility; in mid-1996 a bomb attack at a US military complex near Az Zahran killed 19 US personnel. Increasing rapprochement with Iran has also led to tensions with the USA.

Saudi Arabia has been an influential power broker in the civil war in Afghanistan, where its support ensured the success of the *taliban*. A pact signed with Yemen in June 2000 ended a simmering border dispute. As the guardian of Mecca, Saudi Arabia has immense importance as the spiritual center for more than a billion Muslims all over the world.

AID

Donor

$185m (donations)

Down 36% in 1999

Through the Saudi Fund for Development, generous loans and grants are made to other Arab and developing countries, mainly for infrastructure projects. Saudi Arabia promotes Islam through charitable foundations, especially in Africa, Asia, and the former Soviet Union. The royal purse also supports scientific and medical research. Since the liberation of Kuwait in 1991, Saudi Arabia has given large sums to countries that supported the US-led alliance, notably Egypt, Syria, Morocco, and Turkey. In addition, the Saudi government substantially reimbursed the USA and the UK for the cost of their expeditionary forces, as well as favoring companies from the allied countries for reconstruction contracts.

***King Fahd ibn Abd al-Aziz** acceded to the Saudi throne in 1982.*

***Crown Prince Abdullah,** commander of the National Guard.*

S

CHRONOLOGY

The unification of Saudi Arabia under King Abd al-Aziz (ibn-Sa'ud) was achieved in 1932. The kingdom remains the only country in the world which is named after its royal family.

- ❑ **1937** Oil reserves discovered near Riyadh.
- ❑ **1939** Ceremonial start of oil production at Az Zahran.
- ❑ **1953** King Sa'ud succeeds on the death of his father Abd al-Aziz.
- ❑ **1964** King Sa'ud abdicates in favor of his brother Faisal.
- ❑ **1967** Saudi Arabia joins Jordan and Iraq against Israel in Six-Day War.
- ❑ **1973** Saudi Arabia imposes oil embargo on Western supporters of Israel.
- ❑ **1975** King Faisal assassinated by a deranged nephew; succeeded by his brother Khalid.
- ❑ **1979** Muslim fundamentalists led by Juhaiman ibn Seif al-Otaibi seize Grand Mosque in Mecca, proclaim a *mahdi* (messiah) on first day of Islamic year 1400.
- ❑ **1981** Formation of Gulf Cooperation Council, with its secretariat in Riyadh.
- ❑ **1982** King Fahd succeeds on the death of his brother King Khalid. Promises to create consultative assembly.
- ❑ **1986** Opening of King Fahd Causeway to Bahrain. Sheikh Yamani sacked as oil minister.
- ❑ **1987** Diplomatic relations with Iran deteriorate after 402 people die in riots involving Islamic fundamentalists at Mecca during the *haj* (pilgrimage).
- ❑ **1989** Saudi Arabia signs nonaggression pact with Iraq. Saudi Arabia brokers political settlement to Lebanese civil war.
- ❑ **1990** Kuwaiti royal family seeks sanctuary in Taif after Iraqi invasion.
- ❑ **1990–1991** US, UK, French, Egyptian, and Syrian forces assemble in Saudi Arabia for Operation Desert Storm. Public executions are halted.
- ❑ **1991** Iraqis seize border town of Al Khafji, but are repulsed by Saudi, US, and Qatari forces.
- ❑ **1993** King Fahd appoints 60-man Consultative Council (*Majlis ash-Shoura*).
- ❑ **1996** King Fahd briefly relinquishes control to Crown Prince Abdullah. Bomb attack at US military complex in Az Zahran kills 19 US citizens.
- ❑ **1997, 2001** Consultative Council expanded, first to 90 then to 120 members.

DEFENSE

No compulsory military service

$21.9bn

Up 3% in 1999

Saudi Arabia's substantial military contribution to the 1991 Gulf War, at a cost of $55 billion, enhanced its image as a major regional power. Military equipment is purchased mostly from the USA, the UK, and France. Weapons systems are advanced and include Patriot missiles and AWACS early warning radar. However, skilled foreign personnel operate many of these: 1000 US Air Force troops are employed to keep AWACS flying. The air force is the elite branch of the military. It had one brief period of politicization in 1969 when officers attempted a coup. The paramilitary National Guard is drawn from tribal supporters of the al-Sa'ud regime. Its commander-in-chief is the crown prince rather than the defense minister.

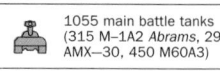

SAUDI ARABIAN ARMED FORCES

1055 main battle tanks (315 M-1A2 *Abrams*, 290 AMX–30, 450 M60A3)	75,000 personnel
4 frigates, 4 corvettes, and 26 patrol boats	15,500 personnel
417 combat aircraft (77 F-5, 166 F-15, 76 *Tornado* IDS, 24 *Tornado* ADV)	20,000 personnel
None	

ECONOMICS

Inflation 1.2% p.a. (1990–1999)

$139bn

3.7503–3.7505 Saudi riyals

SCORE CARD

❑ World GNP Ranking	27th
❑ GNP per Capita	$6900
❑ Balance of Payments	$-1.7bn
❑ Inflation	–1.4%
❑ Unemployment	6%

EXPORTS

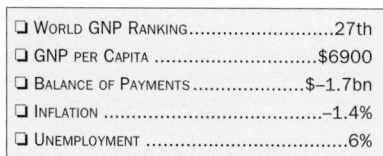

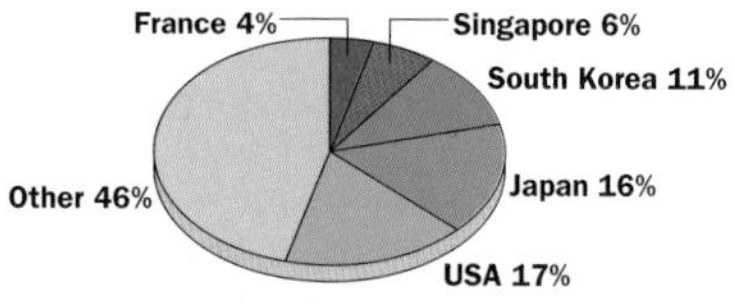
France 4%
Singapore 6%
South Korea 11%
Japan 16%
USA 17%
Other 46%

IMPORTS

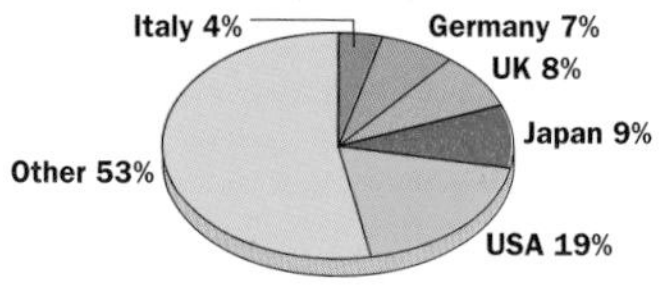
Italy 4%
Germany 7%
UK 8%
Japan 9%
USA 19%
Other 53%

Strengths

Vast oil and gas reserves. Soaring world oil prices in 2000 signified recovery from 1986 collapse. World-class associated industries. Accumulated surpluses and steady current income. Large income from two million pilgrims to Mecca annually.

Weaknesses

Lack of indigenous skilled workers. Food production requires heavy subsidy. Most consumer items and industrial raw materials imported. Up to 20% youth unemployment.

Profile

Since the 1970s, great efforts have been made to reduce dependence on oil exports and to provide employment for young Saudis. By the latter part of 2000, Saudi influence within OPEC was directed toward controlling a surge in oil prices to avoid recession in the industrialized countries or spurring a drive to develop alternative energy. Since 2000, foreigners have been allowed complete ownership of Saudi businesses and rights to property. Large sums have been spent on achieving a US-standard infrastructure, to provide the basis for a manufacturing economy. The economy, however, remains dependent on foreign workers.

ECONOMIC PERFORMANCE INDICATOR

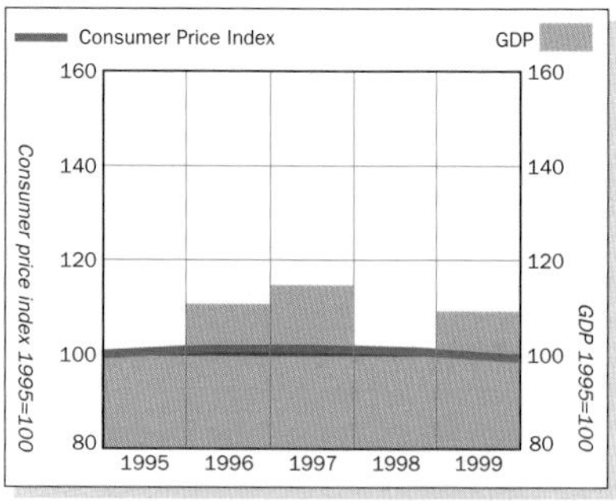
Consumer Price Index
GDP
Consumer price index 1995=100
GDP 1995=100
160
140
120
100
80
1995
1996
1997
1998
1999

SAUDI ARABIA : MAJOR BUSINESSES

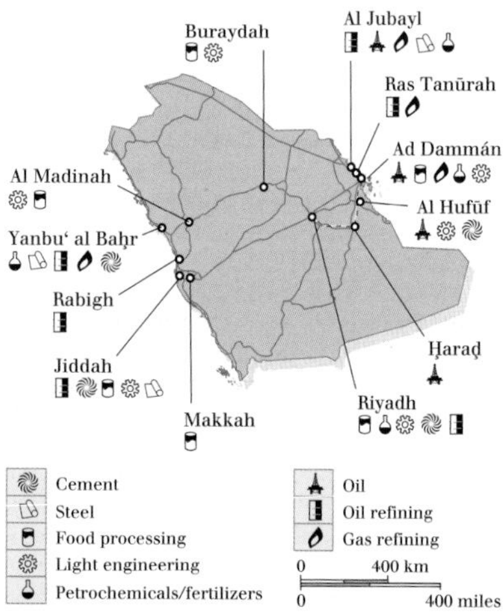
Buraydah
Al Jubayl
Ras Tanūrah
Ad Dammán
Al Madinah
Al Hufūf
Yanbu' al Baḥr
Rabigh
Jiddah
Ḥaraḍ
Riyadh
Makkah
Cement
Steel
Food processing
Light engineering
Petrochemicals/fertilizers
Oil
Oil refining
Gas refining
0
400 km
0
400 miles

RESOURCES

Electric power 21.7m kw

54,085 tonnes

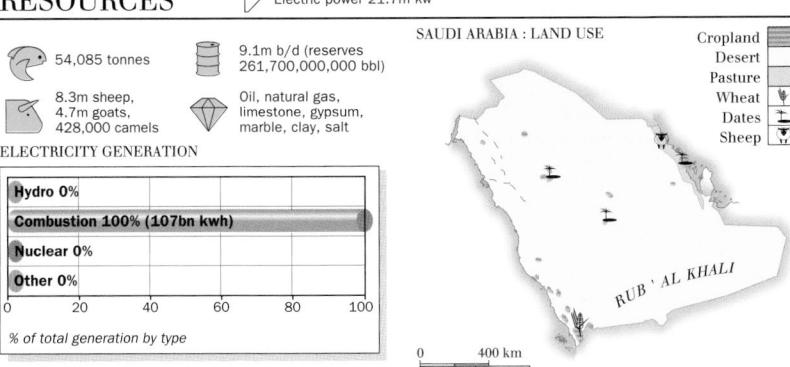

9.1m b/d (reserves 261,700,000,000 bbl)

8.3m sheep, 4.7m goats, 428,000 camels

Oil, natural gas, limestone, gypsum, marble, clay, salt

ELECTRICITY GENERATION

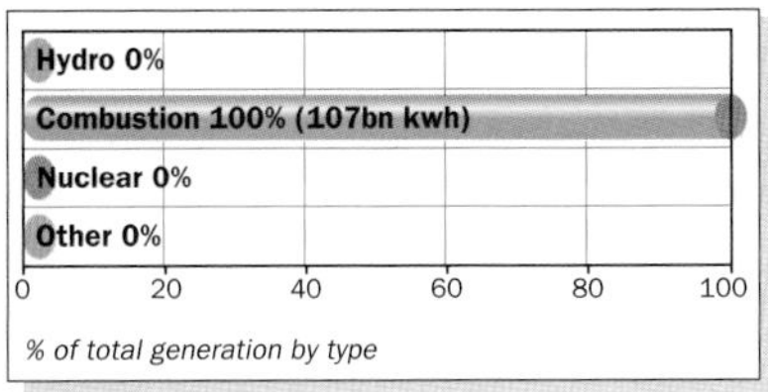
Hydro 0%
Combustion 100% (107bn kwh)
Nuclear 0%
Other 0%
0
20
40
60
80
100
% of total generation by type

SAUDI ARABIA : LAND USE

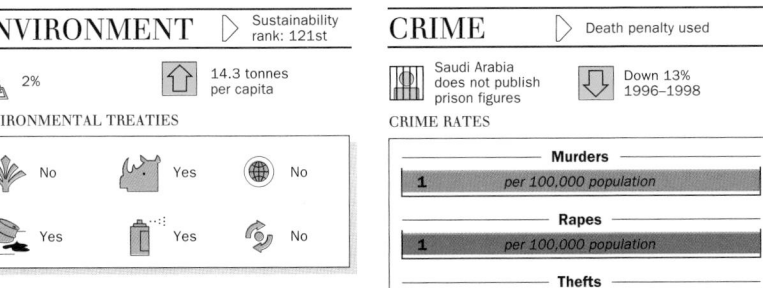

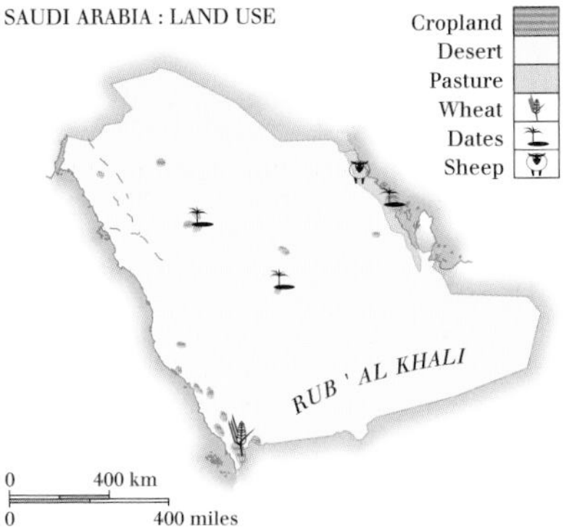
Cropland
Desert
Pasture
Wheat
Dates
Sheep
RUB ' AL KHALI
0
400 km
0
400 miles

With the world's biggest oil and gas reserves, Saudi Arabia plays a key role in the global economy and is among the top ten traders of all the world's major industrialized nations.

ENVIRONMENT

Sustainability rank: 121st

2%

14.3 tonnes per capita

ENVIRONMENTAL TREATIES

No | Yes | No

Yes | Yes | No

Pollution in the Gulf and Red Sea has threatened some wildlife and their habitats, as have hunters using high-velocity rifles and off-road vehicles. The government has taken steps to confine manufacturing to industrial estates. Environmental legislation is, nevertheless, poorly developed, although planning controls apply in the major cities.

MEDIA

TV ownership high

Daily newspaper circulation 59 per 1000 people

PUBLISHING AND BROADCAST MEDIA

There are 13 daily newspapers, in Arabic and English. The leading papers are *Ar-Riyadh*, *Sharq Al Awsat*, *Al-Jazirah*, and *Riyadh Daily*

2 state-owned services

2 services: 1 state-owned, 1 owned by a private oil company

The government imposes total press censorship and insists on strict morality. In 1994, private citizens were banned from owning satellite dishes. No allowance is made for Arab satellite broadcasts, which have recently been criticized for covering anti-Islamic issues. The international *Sharq Al Awsat* is a leading Arabic daily. Saudi investors own the influential press agency United Press International. In 2001 the government announced strict rules regarding state and religion on the Internet.

CRIME

Death penalty used

Saudi Arabia does not publish prison figures

Down 13% 1996–1998

CRIME RATES

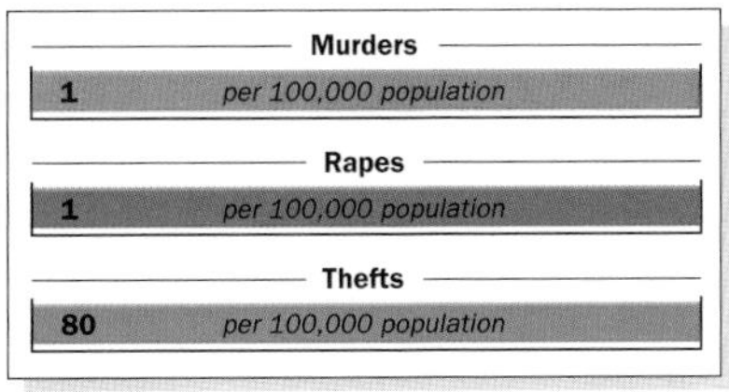
Murders
1
per 100,000 population
Rapes
1
per 100,000 population
Thefts
80
per 100,000 population

Strict Islamic punishments – stoning, amputation, and beheading – are enforced. Criticism for human rights abuses has increased, with an Amnesty International campaign in 2000.

EDUCATION

Schooling is free but not compulsory

77%

273,992 students

THE EDUCATION SYSTEM

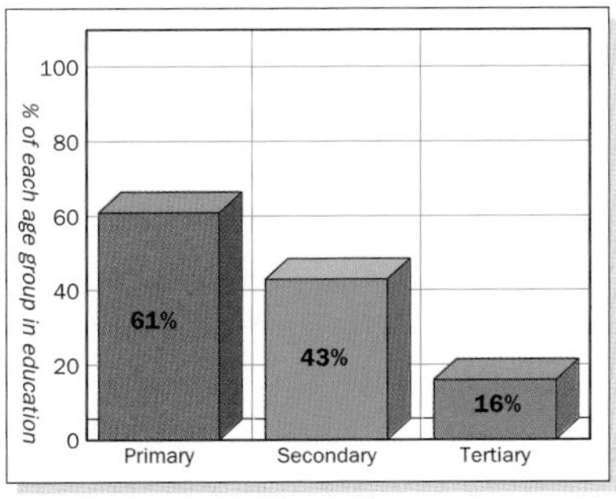
100
80
60
40
20
0
% of each age group in education
61%
43%
16%
Primary
Secondary
Tertiary

Growing numbers of Western-educated Saudis have intensified pressure for social and political change. In the 1950s, the then Crown Prince Faisal persuaded the religious establishment to give women equal opportunities in education. Much government money has gone into higher education and Islamic universities, though many Saudis still travel abroad to complete their studies.

HEALTH

Welfare state health benefits

1 per 588 people

Diarrheal, respiratory, heart, metabolic, and parasitic diseases

Infant mortality has dropped and endemic disease has been nearly eradicted. Health care outside major centers such as Riyadh and Jiddah still remains relatively undeveloped, given Saudi Arabia's huge economic resources. However, large sums have been spent on employing Western expertise. Many Saudis are still sent overseas by the government for treatment, especially for transplant operations, which pose some ethical problems for religious leaders. The private sector has also been encouraged.

SPENDING

GDP/cap. increase

CONSUMPTION AND SPENDING

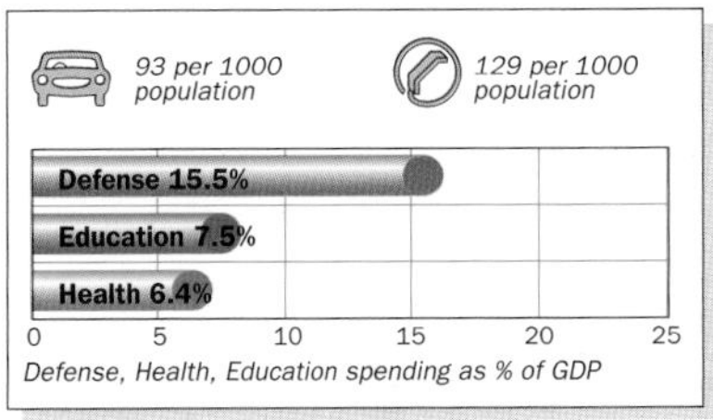
93 per 1000 population
129 per 1000 population
Defense 15.5%
Education 7.5%
Health 6.4%
0
5
10
15
20
25
Defense, Health, Education spending as % of GDP

Saudi citizens are among the most prosperous in the world. The al-Sa'uds have used their wealth to create a cradle-to-grave welfare system. Ownership of TVs, telephones, and VCRs is among the region's highest. The distribution of wealth is carefully controlled by the royal family through the *majlis* system. Petitioners attend weekly assemblies held by prominent royals and beg favors, which are usually granted. There is no stock market, although shares in public companies are traded privately. Many Saudis refuse for religious reasons to accept interest on deposits with banks, but Islamic banks offer profit-sharing investment schemes as an alternative.

WORLD RANKING

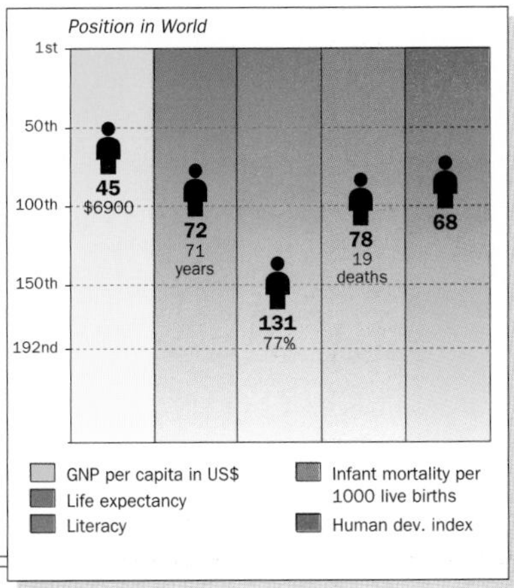
Position in World
1st
50th
100th
150th
192nd
45
$6900
72
71
years
131
77%
78
19
deaths
68
GNP per capita in US$
Life expectancy
Literacy
Infant mortality per 1000 live births
Human dev. index

S

SENEGAL

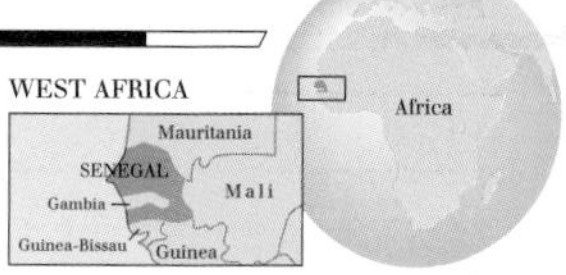
WEST AFRICA
Africa
Mauritania
SENEGAL
Mali
Gambia
Guinea-Bissau
Guinea

OFFICIAL NAME: Republic of Senegal **CAPITAL:** Dakar
POPULATION: 9.5 million **CURRENCY:** CFA franc **OFFICIAL LANGUAGE:** French

1960 | 1960 | April 4 | SN | 0 | +221 | .sn

SENEGAL'S CAPITAL, Dakar, lies on the westernmost cape of Africa. The country is mostly low, with open savanna and semidesert in the north and thicker savanna in the south. After independence from France in 1960, Senegal was ruled until 1981 by President Léopold Senghor. He was succeeded by his prime minister, Abdou Diouf, who held power for almost 20 years until his election defeat in March 2000.

CLIMATE

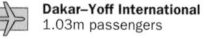

Steppe/tropical

WEATHER CHART

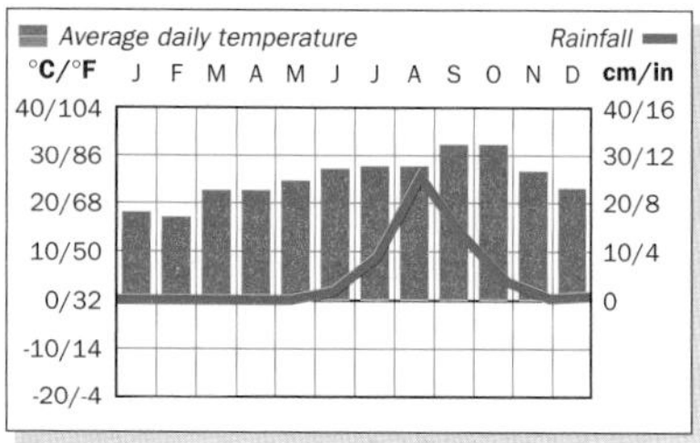
Average daily temperature
Rainfall
°C/°F
J F M A M J J A S O N D
cm/in
40/104
30/86
20/68
10/50
0/32
-10/14
-20/-4
40/16
30/12
20/8
10/4
0

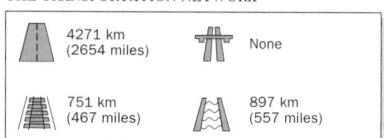

The coastal regions, which project into the path of the northern trade winds, are remarkably cool given their latitude.

TRANSPORTATION

Drive on right

Dakar–Yoff International 1.03m passengers

198 ships 51,000 grt

THE TRANSPORTATION NETWORK

4271 km (2654 miles)

None

751 km (467 miles)

897 km (557 miles)

Dakar is an important west African port, serving Senegal itself, Guinea, the hinterland of Mali, and southern Mauritania. The key rail link to Bamako, Mali's capital, was built in the 1920s.

TOURISM

Visitors : Population 1:26

369,000 visitors

Up 5% in 1999

MAIN TOURIST ARRIVALS

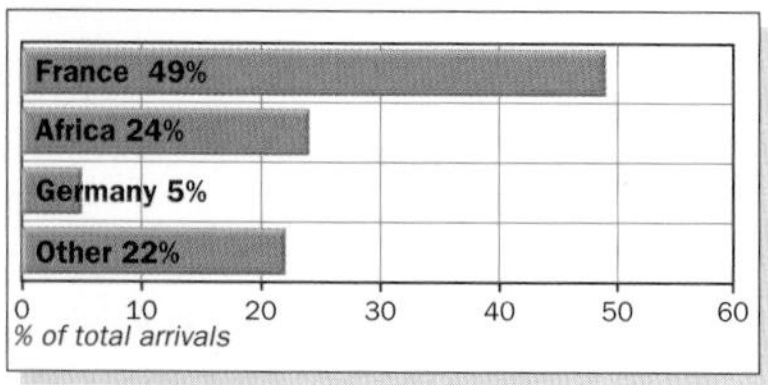
France 49%
Africa 24%
Germany 5%
Other 22%
0
10
20
30
40
50
60
% of total arrivals

In addition to French package tours to coastal resorts, tours for African–Americans to Gorée, an old slave island, are increasingly popular.

PEOPLE

Pop. density low

Wolof, Fulani, Serer, Diola, Malinke, Soninke, Arabic, French

49/km² (128/mi²)

THE URBAN/RURAL POPULATION SPLIT

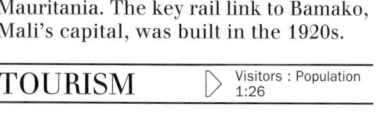

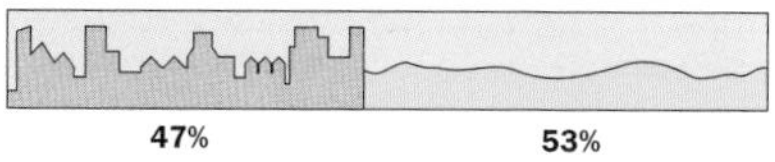
47%
53%

RELIGIOUS PERSUASION

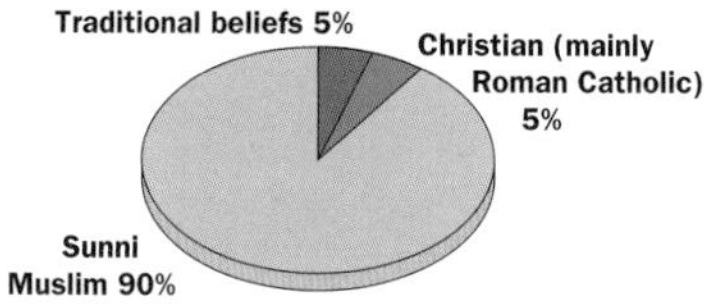
Traditional beliefs 5%
Christian (mainly Roman Catholic) 5%
Sunni Muslim 90%

Senegal has a fairly well-developed sense of nationhood, and intermarriage between groups has reduced ethnic tensions. Groups can still be identified regionally, however. Dakar is a Wolof area, the Senegal river is dominated by the Toucouleur, the Malinke mostly live in the east, and the Diola in Casamance. The Diola have felt excluded from politics, and this has led to a long-running rebellion in Casamance. A French-influenced class system is still prevalent. The 2001 constitution gave women property rights for the first time.

POLITICS

Multiparty elections

2001/2006

President Abdoulaye Wade

AT THE LAST ELECTION

National Assembly 120 seats

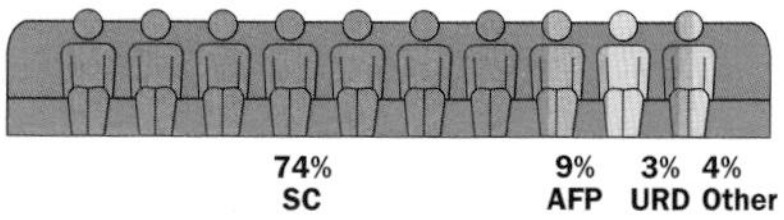
8% PS
2% AJ–PADS
74% SC
9% AFP
3% URD
4% Other

SC = Sopi Coalition (led by the Senegalese Democratic Party – **PDS**) **AFP** = Alliance of Progressive Forces **PS** = Senegalese Socialist Party **URD** = Union for Democratic Renewal **AJ–PADS** = And Jëf – African Party for Democracy and Socialism

Senegal has been a multiparty democracy since 1981 when, under the then new president Abdou Diouf, the constitution was amended to allow more than four political parties. However, the PS held power from the 1950s until 2000, and its influence has been pervasive. Presidential elections in 2000 marked a political watershed. Diouf was defeated by Abdoulaye Wade of the liberal democratic PDS, the dominant party in the "Sopi" (Change) coalition which went on to win a landslide victory in the 2001 legislative elections.

A new constitution, approved in 2001 by referendum, abolished the Senate and restricts the president to two terms.

WORLD AFFAIRS

Joined UN in 1960

CILSS | ECOWAS | FZ | OIC | OMVG

Maintaining good relations with France, Senegal's main ally and aid donor, is the major foreign affairs concern. Relations with neighboring Gambia, Mauritania, and Guinea-Bissau continue to be a constant preoccupation.

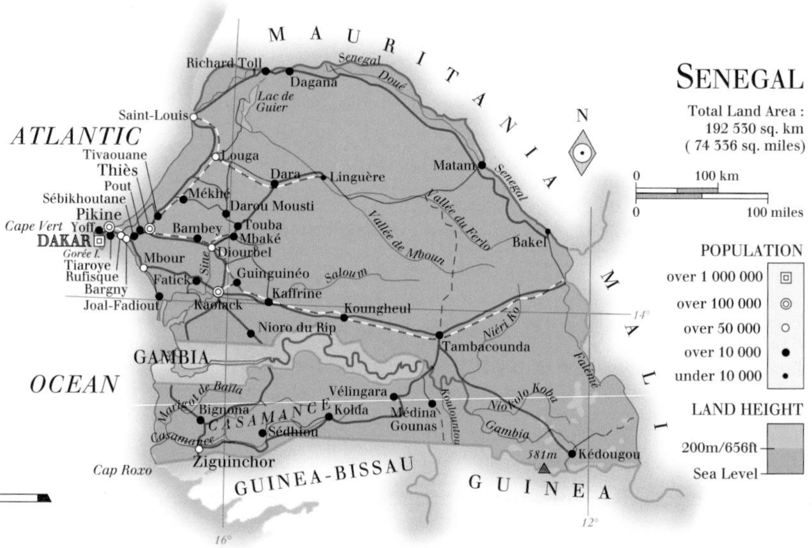
MAURITANIA
ATLANTIC
OCEAN
GAMBIA
GUINEA-BISSAU
GUINEA
MALI
Richard Toll
Dagana
Senegal
Doué
Lac de Guier
Saint-Louis
Louga
Tivaouane
Thiès
Pout
Sébikhoutane
Pikine
Cape Vert
Yoff
DAKAR
Gorée I.
Tiaroye
Rufisque
Bargny
Joal-Fadiout
Mékhé
Dara
Linguère
Darou Mousti
Bambey
Touba
Mbaké
Diourbel
Mbour
Fatick
Sine
Guinguinéo
Saloum
Kaffrine
Kaolack
Koungheul
Nioro du Rip
Matam
Vallée du Ferlo
Vallée de Mboun
Bakel
Tambacounda
Niéri Ko
Falémé
Vélingara
Kolda
Médina Gounas
Koulountou
Niokolo Koba
Gambia
Marigot de Baila
Bignona
CASAMANCE
Sédhiou
Casamance
Ziguinchor
Cap Roxo
581m
Kédougou
16°
14°
12°
N
SENEGAL
Total Land Area : 192 530 sq. km (74 336 sq. miles)
0
100 km
100 miles
POPULATION
over 1 000 000
over 100 000
over 50 000
over 10 000
under 10 000
LAND HEIGHT
200m/656ft
Sea Level

S

AID

Recipient

$534m (receipts) — Up 7% in 1999

Senegal is one of the highest recipients of aid per capita in Africa, mostly from France, the EU, and the World Bank. Aid is used to import 400,000 tonnes of rice annually, but also helps to finance a sizable civil service, now being cut back. An important structural adjustment program, backed by the IMF, was renewed for a further year in April 2001.

The mosque in Touba, *religious capital of the Muslim Mouride sect, which was founded in 1887 in Senegal's groundnut-growing district.*

CHRONOLOGY

France colonized Senegal, a major entrepôt from the 15th century, in 1890. Dakar was the capital of French West Africa.

- **1885** Gambia split off from Senegal.
- **1960** Independence under Senghor.
- **1966–1976** One-party state.
- **1981** Full multipartyism restored.
- **2000** Presidency won by Abdoulaye Wade in first ever defeat for PS.
- **2001** Referendum approves new constitution.

DEFENSE

Compulsory military service

$81m — Down 2% in 1999

France maintains an important naval base at Dakar. The armed forces total 9400, plus a paramilitary force of 4000, but the military has never intervened in politics. Senegalese troops took part in Operation Desert Storm in 1991, and intervened in conflicts in Liberia, Rwanda, and the Central African Republic. They also helped to quell revolts in Gambia and Guinea-Bissau.

ECONOMICS

Inflation 5% p.a. (1990–1999)

$4.7bn — 654.42–698.69 CFA francs

SCORE CARD

World GNP Ranking	115th
GNP per Capita	$500
Balance of Payments	$-304m
Inflation	0.8%
Unemployment	Widespread underemployment

EXPORTS

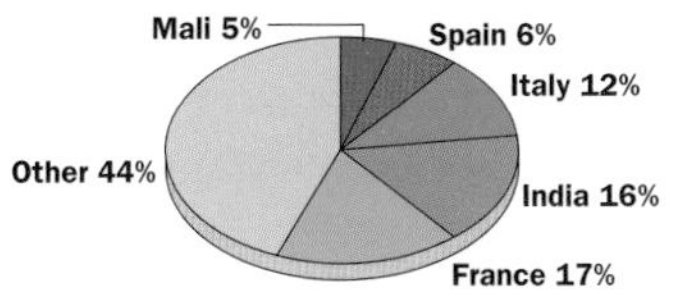
Mali 5%
Spain 6%
Italy 12%
Other 44%
India 16%
France 17%

IMPORTS

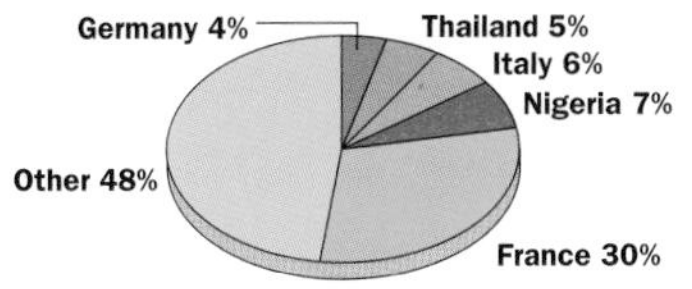
Germany 4%
Thailand 5%
Italy 6%
Nigeria 7%
Other 48%
France 30%

Strengths

Good infrastructure. Relatively strong industrial sector. First west African country with international credit rating.

Weaknesses

Few natural resources exploited, other than groundnuts, phosphates, and fish. Access to oil potential of Casamance region hampered by rebellion and poor transportation links. Inadequate diversification.

EDUCATION

School leaving age: 13

37% — 24,081 students

Illiteracy is Senegal's major educational challenge. There are universities at Dakar and St.-Louis.

HEALTH

No welfare state health benefits

1 per 10,000 people — Malaria, diarrheal diseases

The state health system is rudimentary. A successful education campaign helps to contain the incidence of HIV/AIDS.

SPENDING

GDP/cap. increase

CONSUMPTION AND SPENDING

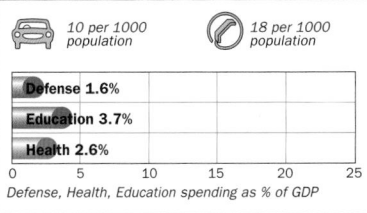

10 per 1000 population — *18 per 1000 population*

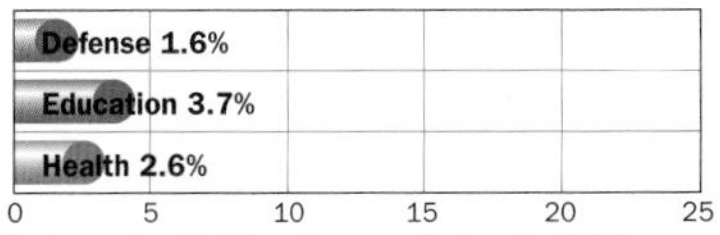
Defense 1.6%
Education 3.7%
Health 2.6%
0
5
10
15
20
25

Defense, Health, Education spending as % of GDP

Wealth disparities are considerable, and poverty is widespread. Those close to the government are the wealthiest group.

RESOURCES

Electric power 235,000 kw

507,040 tonnes — Not an oil producer

4.3m sheep, 3.6m goats, 3m cattle, 45m chickens — Phosphates, bauxite, salt, natural gas, marble, iron, copper

Senegal's electricity capacity is largely dependent on imported fuel; cheaper supplies are expected to become available soon from the Manantali dam in Mali. Initial explorations suggest that oil reserves may exist off Casamance.

MEDIA

TV ownership low

Daily newspaper circulation 5 per 1000 people

PUBLISHING AND BROADCAST MEDIA

There are 8 daily newspapers, including *Le Soleil, Wal Fadjiri,* and *Sud Quotidien*

2 services: 1 state-owned, 1 private — 5 services: 1 state-owned, 4 independent

The independent media flourished with multipartyism. Senegal had the first satirical journal in Africa with the founding of *Le Politicien* in 1978.

ENVIRONMENT

Sustainability rank: 87th

11% (6% partially protected) — 0.4 tonnes per capita

The damming of the Senegal river has caused concern that traditional farming practices, which rely on seasonal floods, may be disrupted. Two major droughts in 1973 and 1983 led to the advance of the Sahara desert in the west of the country.

CRIME

Death penalty not used

Senegal does not publish prison figures — Down 62% 1992–1998

Senegal has comparatively low crime rates, though levels are now rising in Dakar and the surrounding shanty towns, where gangs are based.

WORLD RANKING

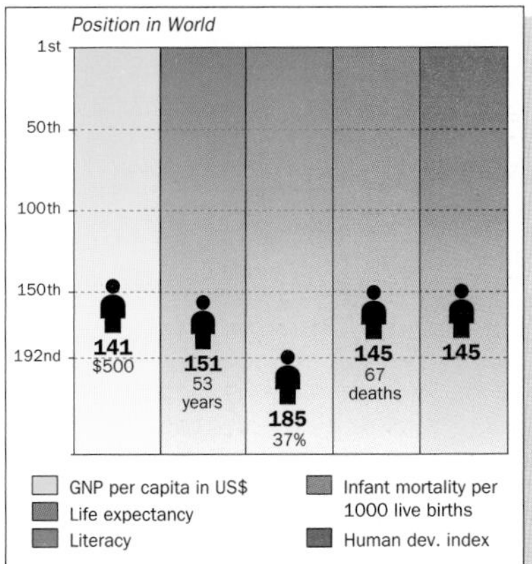
Position in World
1st
50th
100th
150th
192nd
141
$500
151
53 years
185
37%
145
67 deaths
145
GNP per capita in US$
Life expectancy
Literacy
Infant mortality per 1000 live births
Human dev. index

S

SEYCHELLES

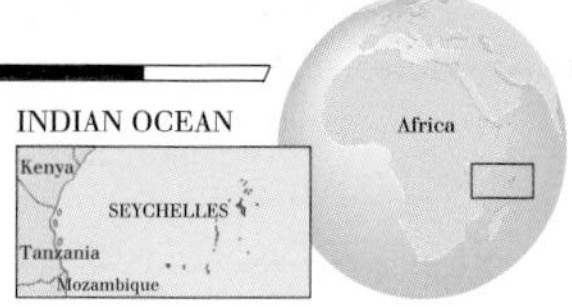
INDIAN OCEAN
Africa
Kenya
SEYCHELLES
Tanzania
Mozambique

OFFICIAL NAME: Republic of the Seychelles **CAPITAL:** Victoria
POPULATION: 79,300 **CURRENCY:** Seychelles rupee **OFFICIAL LANGUAGE:** Seselwa (French Creole)

1976
1976
June 18
SY
+4
+248
.sc

THE 115 ISLANDS of the Seychelles, lying in the Indian Ocean, support unique flora and fauna, including the giant tortoise and the world's largest seed, the *coco-de-mer*. Formerly a UK colony and then under one-party rule for 16 years, the Seychelles became a multiparty democracy in 1993. The economy relies on tourism.

CLIMATE

Tropical oceanic

WEATHER CHART

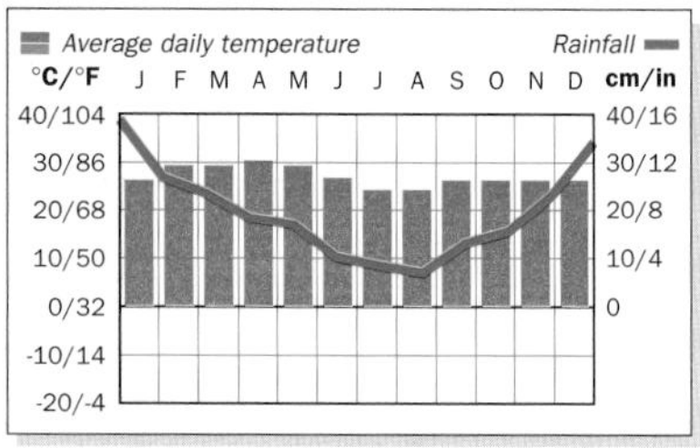
Average daily temperature
Rainfall
°C/°F
J F M A M J J A S O N D
cm/in
40/104
30/86
20/68
10/50
0/32
-10/14
-20/-4
40/16
30/12
20/8
10/4
0

The islands have a tropical oceanic climate, with only small temperature variations throughout the year.

TRANSPORTATION

Drive on left

Pointe Larue International, Mahé 155,000 passengers

16 ships 17,699 grt

THE TRANSPORTATION NETWORK

176 km (109 miles)	None
None	None

Nine islands have airstrips. The public transportation fleet and roads are being renewed. Victoria's deep-sea harbor is one of the best run in the region.

TOURISM

Visitors : Population 1.6:1

130,000 visitors

Up 4% in 2000

MAIN TOURIST ARRIVALS

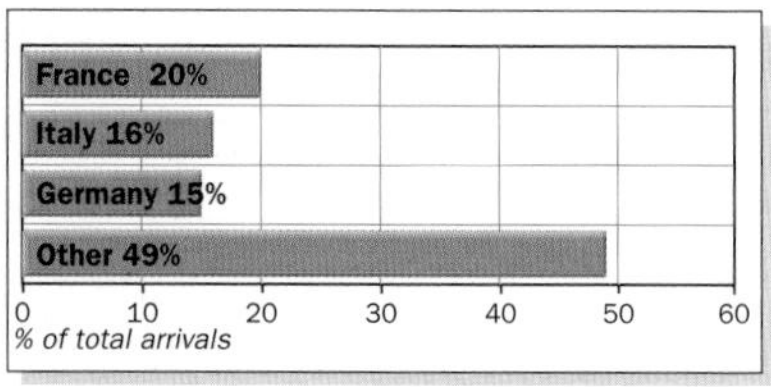
France 20%
Italy 16%
Germany 15%
Other 49%
0
10
20
30
40
50
60
% of total arrivals

Since Mahé international airport was opened in 1971, tourism has become the mainstay of the economy, and employs 30% of the workforce. New hotels must comply with laws to protect the islands' beauty and unique wildlife. There is substantial foreign investment.

PEOPLE

Pop. density high

French Creole, English, French

294/km² (761/mi²)

THE URBAN/RURAL POPULATION SPLIT

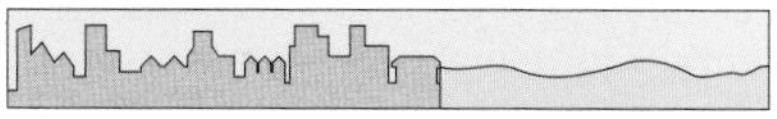
57%
43%

RELIGIOUS PERSUASION

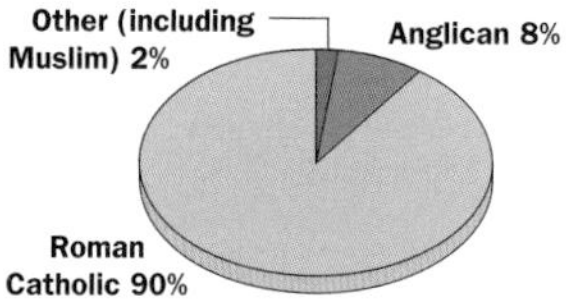
Other (including Muslim) 2%
Anglican 8%
Roman Catholic 90%

The Seychelles islands were uninhabited before French settlers arrived in the 1770s. Today, the population is markedly homogeneous as a result of intermarriage between different ethnic groups. The Creoles are the descendants of the French settlers and of the Africans who were settled on the islands by British administrators. There are small Chinese and Indian minorities.

Almost 90% of Seychellois live on Mahé. Population growth has been very low, as about 1000 people a year have been emigrating. The transition to democracy may reverse this trend.

POLITICS

Multiparty elections

1998/2003

President France-Albert René

AT THE LAST ELECTION

National Assembly 34 seats

88% SPPF
9% UO
3% DP

SPPF = Seychelles People's Progressive Front **UO** = United Opposition **DP** = Democratic Party

In 1993, the Seychelles returned to democracy after 16 years of one-party socialist rule under President René, who had seized power soon after independence. Opposition divisions in the 1993 elections allowed René to retain the presidency. His SPPF retained its majority in the 1998 elections – having dramatically abandoned its leftist ideology, and adopted wide-ranging reforms, encouraging privatization and legalizing trade unions. The highlight is a scheme to develop Seychelles as an International Trading Zone, with free-port facilities and new industry.

WORLD AFFAIRS

Joined UN in 1976

OIF Comm COI NAM OAU

The Seychelles is non-aligned, but its strategic location encourages competing world powers to seek its friendship. It claims the Chagos Archipelago from Britain. Trade accords exist with other Indian Ocean states.

SEYCHELLES

Total Land Area : 270 sq. km (104 sq. miles)

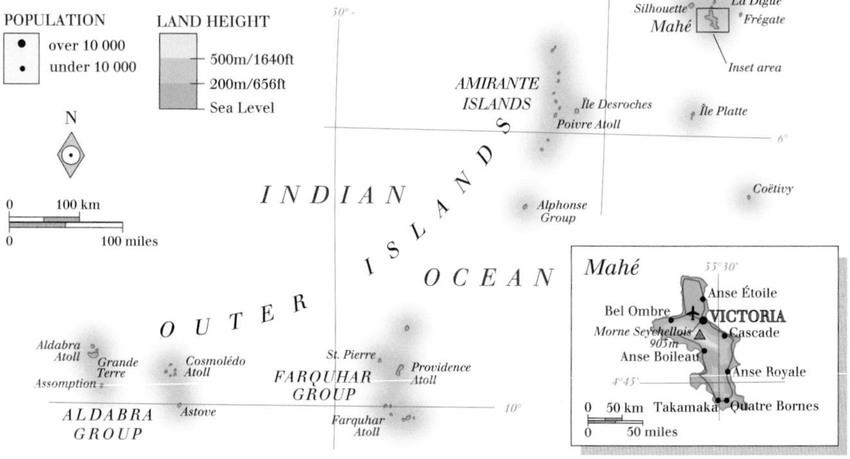
POPULATION
over 10 000
under 10 000
LAND HEIGHT
500m/1640ft
200m/656ft
Sea Level
N
0 100 km
0 100 miles
INNER ISLANDS
Île aux Vaches
Île Denis
Île Aride
Grand'Anse
Praslin
La Digue
Silhouette
Mahé
Frégate
Inset area
AMIRANTE ISLANDS
Île Desroches
Poivre Atoll
Île Platte
INDIAN OCEAN
OUTER ISLANDS
Alphonse Group
Coëtivy
Aldabra Atoll
Grande Terre
Assomption
Cosmolédo Atoll
Astove
ALDABRA GROUP
St. Pierre
Providence Atoll
FARQUHAR GROUP
Farquhar Atoll
Mahé
Anse Étoile
Bel Ombre
VICTORIA
Morne Seychellois 905m
Cascade
Anse Boileau
Anse Royale
Takamaka
Quatre Bornes
0 50 km
0 50 miles

AID

Recipient

$13m (receipts) — Down 46% in 1999

Multilateral agencies, notably the EU and the Arab Development Fund, support a range of development projects. In 1996, $13 million was spent on improving transportation links, protecting the environment, and rehabilitating Victoria Market. Bilateral aid comes from France, the USA, the UK, Australia, and Japan.

DEFENSE

No compulsory military service

$11m — No change in 1999

The Seychelles has a 200-strong army, and a paramilitary guard. The latter includes the coast guard made up of air and sea forces. The army, set up in 1977, was initially trained by Tanzania, and Tanzanian troops were brought in for three years after a coup attempt in 1981. North Korea provided advisers until 1989.

ECONOMICS

Inflation 1.5% p.a. (1990–1999)

$520m — 5.365–6.261 Seychelles rupees

SCORE CARD

- ❑ World GNP Ranking 168th
- ❑ GNP per Capita $6500
- ❑ Balance of Payments ....$-63m
- ❑ Inflation 2.6%
- ❑ Unemployment 9%

Strengths

Tourism. Fish exports, especially shrimps and tuna. Profitable re-export trade. International Trading Zone attracting foreign industrial interest. Copra, cinnamon, tea.

Weaknesses

Growing deficits in early 1990s, caused by drop in tourism following 1991 Gulf War, spending on hosting 1993 Indian Ocean Games, and cost of four elections. High debt servicing costs. Reliance on food imports, especially for tourist industry. Copra production declining. Reliance on expatriate labor.

EXPORTS

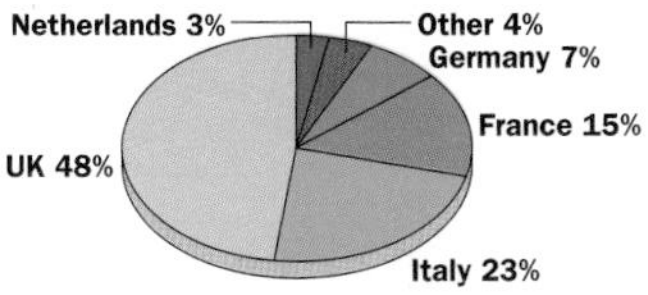
Netherlands 3%
Other 4%
Germany 7%
France 15%
UK 48%
Italy 23%

IMPORTS

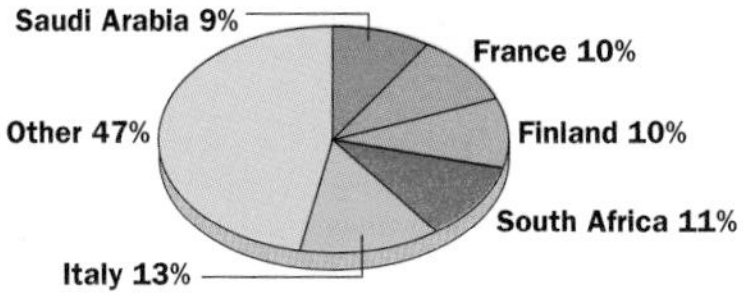
Saudi Arabia 9%
France 10%
Other 47%
Finland 10%
South Africa 11%
Italy 13%

One of the Inner Islands, which are home to most of the population. Unlike any other mid-ocean islands all but two are granitic.

RESOURCES

Electric power 28,000 kw

5928 tonnes — Not an oil producer

18,300 pigs, 5200 goats, 550,000 chickens — Phosphates (guano), salt, granite, natural gas

There are virtually no mineral resources. All fuel is imported; only three islands have electricity. Offshore discoveries of natural gas have spurred a search for oil. Natural habitat and free trade environment are tremendous assets.

ENVIRONMENT

Not available

95% — 2.6 tonnes per capita

The Seychelles has been praised for its commitment to conservation. It has two natural World Heritage sites, and helped promote the idea of whale sanctuaries.

MEDIA

TV ownership medium

Daily newspaper circulation 46 per 1000 people

PUBLISHING AND BROADCAST MEDIA

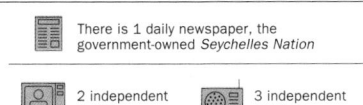

There is 1 daily newspaper, the government-owned *Seychelles Nation*

2 independent services — 3 independent services

The state broadcasting company has been reorganized and is now ostensibly free of government control. Privately owned periodicals are now permitted.

CRIME

Death penalty not used

1060 prisoners — Down 41% 1992–1996

Violent crime is rare in the Seychelles. The main concern is the increasing rate of petty theft.

EDUCATION

School leaving age: 16

84% — 1682 students

The 1995–2008 Educational and Training Plan places special emphasis on increasing levels of female enrollment. National Youth Service is mandatory for entry to higher education.

CHRONOLOGY

The French claimed the islands in 1756. Franco-British rivalry for control ended when France ceded them to Britain in 1815.

- ❑ **1952** Political parties formed, led by F. A. René (pro-independence) and James Mancham (pro-UK rule).
- ❑ **1965** UK returns Desroches, Aldabra, and Farquhar islands, which are leased to USA to 1976.
- ❑ **1976** Independence. Coalition with Mancham president, René premier.
- ❑ **1977** René takes over in coup.
- ❑ **1979** One-party socialist state.
- ❑ **1979–1987** Several coup attempts.
- ❑ **1992** Politicians in exile return.
- ❑ **1993** Democratic elections.
- ❑ **2001** René reelected in early presidential elections.

HEALTH

Welfare state health benefits

1 per 962 people — Heart and cerebrovascular diseases, cancers

State health care is free. Private medicine is allowed under new social legislation. Life expectancy is over 70 years.

SPENDING

GDP/cap. increase

CONSUMPTION AND SPENDING

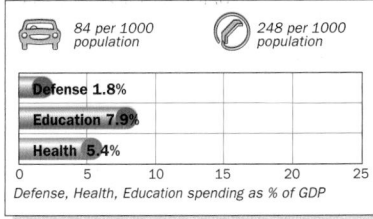

84 per 1000 population — *248 per 1000 population*

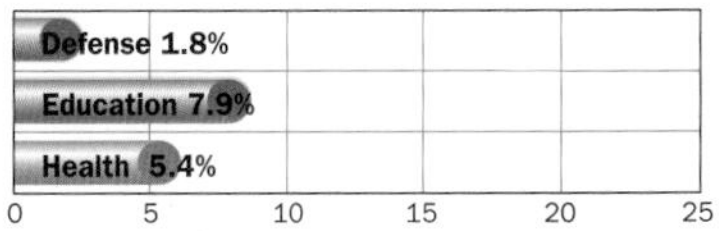
Defense 1.8%
Education 7.9%
Health 5.4%
0
5
10
15
20
25

Defense, Health, Education spending as % of GDP

Living standards are the highest among OAU states. There are no slums in the Seychelles, and the state welfare system caters for all.

WORLD RANKING

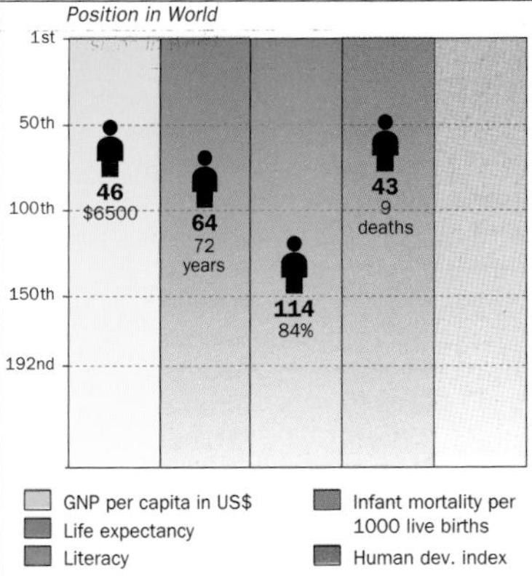
Position in World
1st
50th
100th
150th
192nd
46
$6500
64
72 years
114
84%
43
9 deaths
GNP per capita in US$
Life expectancy
Literacy
Infant mortality per 1000 live births
Human dev. index

S

SIERRA LEONE

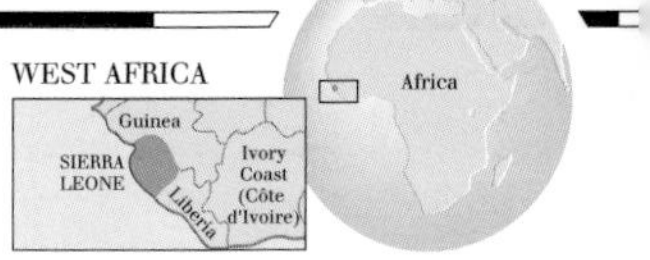
WEST AFRICA
Guinea
SIERRA LEONE
Liberia
Ivory Coast (Côte d'Ivoire)
Africa

OFFICIAL NAME: Republic of Sierra Leone **CAPITAL:** Freetown
POPULATION: 4.9 million **CURRENCY:** Leone **OFFICIAL LANGUAGE:** English

1961 | 1961 | April 27 | WAL | 0 | +232 | .sl

THE WEST AFRICAN state of Sierra Leone was founded by the British in 1787 for Africans freed from slavery. The terrain rises from coastal lowlands to mountains in the northeast. A democratic government took office in 1996 against a background of bloody rebellion. Sierra Leone soon plunged into a savage civil war. Although a 1999 peace agreement was short-lived, an ECOWAS-brokered accord signed in late 2000 seemed to be holding.

CLIMATE

Tropical equatorial/ monsoon

WEATHER CHART

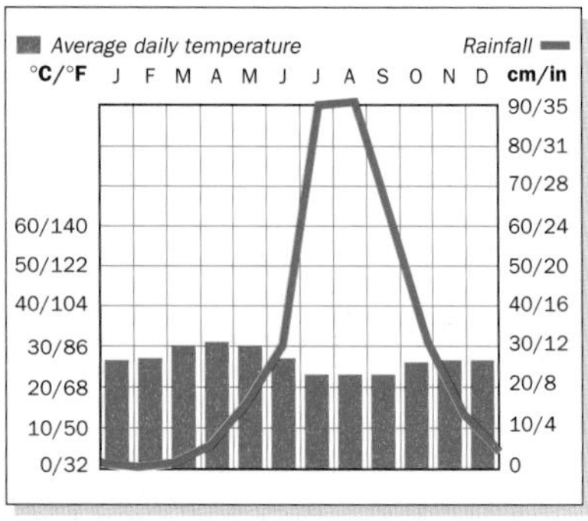
Average daily temperature
Rainfall
°C/°F
J F M A M J J A S O N D
cm/in
90/35
80/31
70/28
60/24
50/20
40/16
30/12
20/8
10/4
0
60/140
50/122
40/104
30/86
20/68
10/50
0/32

Coastal rainfall can be as high as 500 cm (197 in) a year, making Sierra Leone one of the wettest places in coastal west Africa. Humidity is consistently high – about 80% – during the rainy season. The dusty, northeasterly *harmattan* wind often blows during the hotter dry season from November to April. The northeastern savannas are drier, with 190–250 cm (75–98 in) of rain, and are one of the hottest areas.

TRANSPORTATION

Drive on right

Lungi International, Freetown 84,547 passengers

52 ships 18,792 grt

THE TRANSPORTATION NETWORK

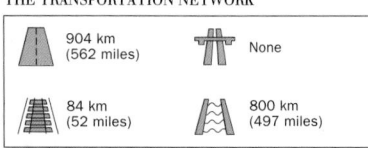

904 km (562 miles)	None
84 km (52 miles)	800 km (497 miles)

Little progress has been made in improving Sierra Leone's roads. The 300-km (190-mile) narrow-gauge railroad was abandoned in 1971 as uneconomic, although 84 km (52 miles) of track still runs to the closed iron ore mines at Marampa. Having failed in 1987, Sierra Leone's national airline resumed flights – to Paris only – in 1991. A limited ferry service across the estuary is the only link between Freetown and the airport.

TOURISM

Visitors : Population 1:490

10,000 visitors

Up 67% in 2000

MAIN TOURIST ARRIVALS

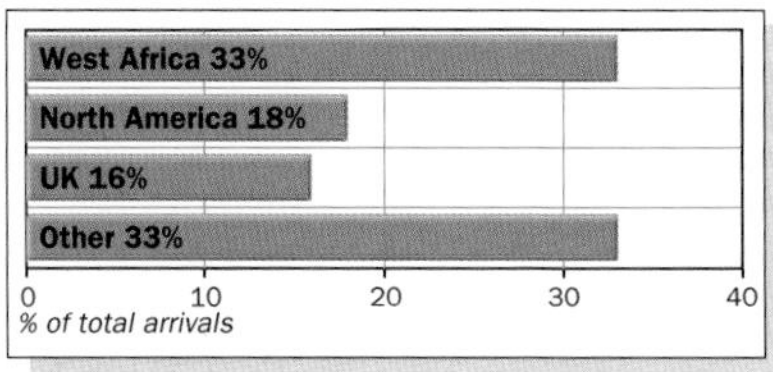
West Africa 33%
North America 18%
UK 16%
Other 33%
0
10
20
30
40
% of total arrivals

Sierra Leone has never attracted many tourists, apart from occasional cruise ship calls. Years of civil war have prevented the development of tourism. Among the chief potential attractions are the beaches along the Freetown peninsula, at present virtually undeveloped.

SIERRA LEONE

Total Land Area : 71 620 sq. km (27 652 sq. miles)

LAND HEIGHT

- 1000m/3281ft
- 500m/1640ft
- 200m/656ft
- Sea Level

POPULATION

- over 100 000
- over 10 000
- under 10 000

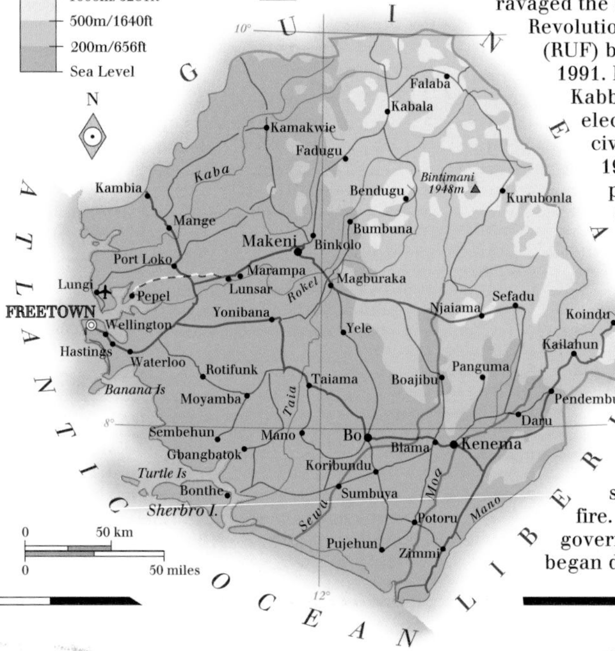
GUINEA
ATLANTIC OCEAN
LIBERIA
N
Falaba
Kabala
Kamakwie
Fadugu
Kaba
Kambia
Bendugu
Bintimani 1948m
Kurubonla
Mange
Bumbuna
Makeni
Binkolo
Port Loko
Marampa
Lungi
Pepel
Lunsar
Rokel
Magburaka
Sefadu
FREETOWN
Wellington
Yonibana
Njaiama
Koindu
Yele
Hastings
Kailahun
Waterloo
Rotifunk
Taiama
Boajibu
Panguma
Banana Is
Moyamba
Taia
Pendembu
Daru
Sembehun
Mano
Bo
Blama
Kenema
Gbangbatok
Koribundu
Turtle Is
Bonthe
Sumbuya
Sherbro I.
Moa
Mano
Sewa
Potoru
Pujehun
Zimmi
0
50 km
0
50 miles
10°
8°
12°

PEOPLE

Pop. density medium

Mende, Temne, Krio, English

68/km² (177/mi²)

THE URBAN/RURAL POPULATION SPLIT

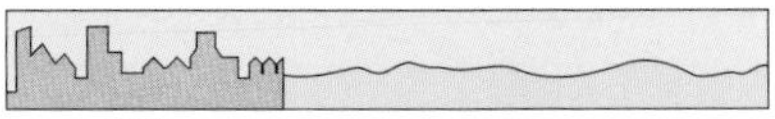
36%
64%

ETHNIC MAKEUP

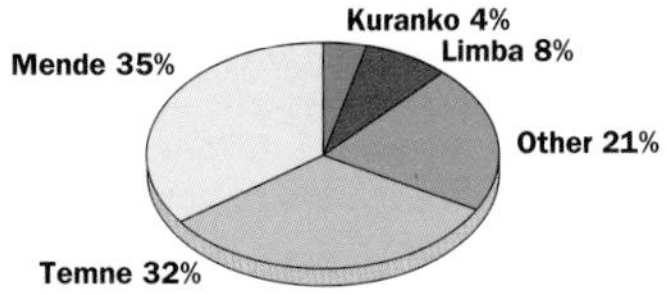
Kuranko 4%
Limba 8%
Mende 35%
Other 21%
Temne 32%

Freetown was founded as a settlement for people freed from slavery. Its citizens' British and North American origins account for Sierra Leone's strongly anglicized Creole culture. An estimated two million people were displaced by the civil war.

POLITICS

Multiparty elections

1996/2001

President Ahmad Tejan Kabbah

AT THE LAST ELECTION

National Assembly 80 seats

6% APC
4% DCP
34% SLPP
21% UNPP
15% PDP
15% App
5% NUP

SLPP = Sierra Leone People's Party **UNPP** = United People's Party **PDP** = People's Democratic Party **APC** = All People's Congress **NUP** = National Unity Party **DCP** = Democratic Centre Party **App** = Appointed: 12 paramount chiefs are indirectly elected to represent each province

A particularly savage civil war has ravaged the country since the Revolutionary United Front (RUF) began its rebellion in 1991. President Ahmad Kabbah was popularly elected at the head of a civilian government in 1996. A peace and power-sharing agreement was reached in July 1999, but collapsed in May 2000 when the RUF restarted its insurrection. Government forces, aided by a large UN and British force, in November 2000 secured a new cease-fire. The RUF and pro-government militia began disarming in 2001.

S

WORLD AFFAIRS

Joined UN in 1961

Comm | ECOWAS | MRU | OAU | OIC

UN peacekeepers and British forces assisted government forces during renewed fighting in 2000.

AID

Recipient

$74m (receipts) — Down 30% in 1999

Sierra Leone has not been able to fulfill the terms of an aid package agreed with the IMF in 1989. Funds have been diverted to cope with the humanitarian needs of refugees from Liberia, internal migrants fleeing the civil war, and the near-collapse of public services.

DEFENSE

No compulsory military service

$11m — Down 58% in 1999

The army is an ineffectual fighting force, prompting assistance from the UK with training in 2000. Both sides in the civil war have exploited child fighters.

ECONOMICS

Inflation 31.1% p.a. (1990–1999)

$653m — 1911–1899 leones

SCORE CARD

World GNP Ranking	163rd
GNP per Capita	$130
Balance of Payments	$–127m
Inflation	34.1%
Unemployment	Widespread

Strengths
Diamonds, although much of the output is smuggled; official exports resumed in late 2000 under a UN certification scheme. Some bauxite and rutile production.

Weaknesses
Years of instability affected the most productive areas, including diamond fields, with severe disruption of agricultural and mining sectors.

EXPORTS

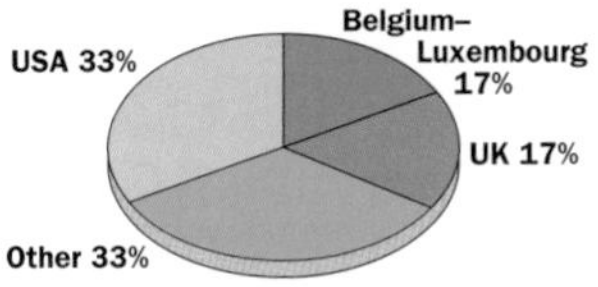
USA 33%
Belgium–Luxembourg 17%
UK 17%
Other 33%

IMPORTS

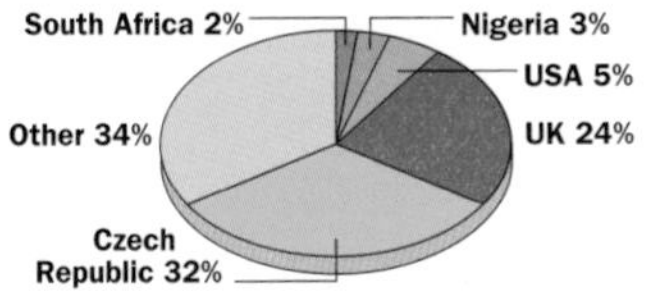
South Africa 2%
Nigeria 3%
USA 5%
UK 24%
Other 34%
Czech Republic 32%

RESOURCES

Electric power 126,000 kw

68,739 tonnes — Not an oil producer

400,000 cattle, 350,000 sheep, 6m chickens — Diamonds, rutile, bauxite, gold, titanium

The large diamond deposits need fresh investment as areas currently being mined become depleted. The southeast is the most fertile region.

ENVIRONMENT

Not available

1% — 0.1 tonnes per capita

Population pressures and the neglect resulting from years of civil war have depleted the land's productivity.

MEDIA

TV ownership low

Daily newspaper circulation 5 per 1000 people

PUBLISHING AND BROADCAST MEDIA

There is 1 daily newspaper, the *Daily Mail*, published by the government

1 state-controlled service — 1 state-controlled service

A broad range of periodicals is available. The government has promised press freedom, but the Internet is heavily censored.

CRIME

Death penalty used

Sierra Leone does not publish prison figures — Crime is rising

The civil war has resulted in savage atrocities and mass looting of resources. Illegal diamond mining and smuggling are lucrative crimes. After an international campaign the De Beers company introduced tighter rules against trade in diamonds from rebel-held areas, a potentially serious blow to RUF revenues.

EDUCATION

Schooling is not compulsory

36% — 4742 students

Freetown has a long tradition of education, and its university, Fourahbay College, became affiliated with Durham University in the UK in 1876. In recent times, its students have often been active in political dissent. Educational provision has inevitably deteriorated over the past decade.

HEALTH

No welfare state health benefits

1 per 14,300 people — Communicable diseases, malaria, malnutrition

Only traditional care is available outside the capital. WHO have ranked Sierra Leone's health care bottom in the world in terms of attainment and efficiency.

The main street, Kabala. *Sierra Leone is consistently at the bottom of the UN's Human Development Index.*

CHRONOLOGY

Freetown was founded in 1787 and became a British colony in 1808; the interior was annexed in 1896.

- **1961** Independence.
- **1978** Single-party republic.
- **1991** RUF rebellion starts.
- **1996** Civilian rule restored after 1992 army coup; Kabbah president.
- **1998** Kabbah restored following coup in 1997; fighting continues.
- **1999** Power-sharing agreement.
- **2000** November, new cease-fire after renewed fighting.
- **2001** RUF ends insurgency.

SPENDING

GDP/cap. decrease

CONSUMPTION AND SPENDING

4 per 1000 population — 4 per 1000 population

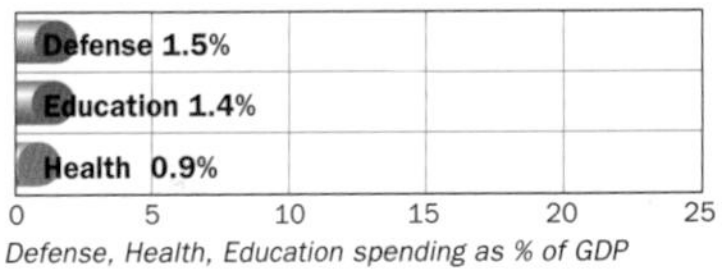
Defense 1.5%
Education 1.4%
Health 0.9%
0
5
10
15
20
25
Defense, Health, Education spending as % of GDP

In terms of quality of life, the UN has repeatedly ranked Sierra Leoneans as the world's poorest people. Any wealth is associated with political power.

WORLD RANKING

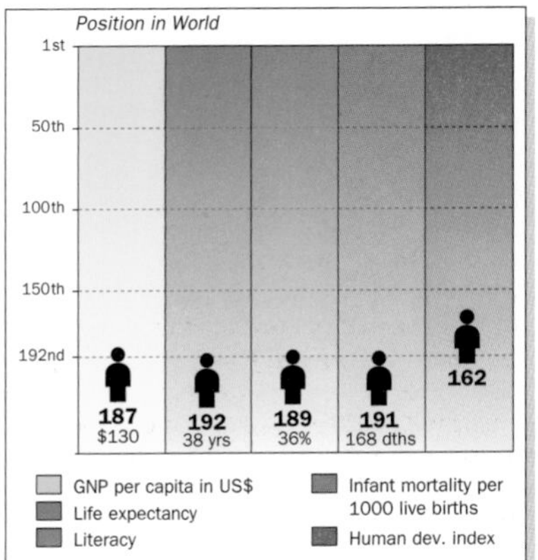
Position in World
1st
50th
100th
150th
192nd
187
$130
192
38 yrs
189
36%
191
168 dths
162
GNP per capita in US$
Life expectancy
Literacy
Infant mortality per 1000 live births
Human dev. index

S

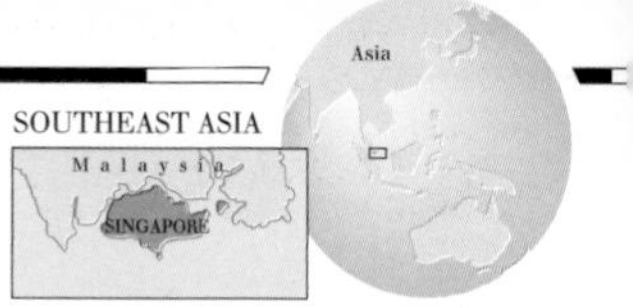

Asia
SOUTHEAST ASIA
Malaysia
SINGAPORE

SINGAPORE

OFFICIAL NAME: Republic of Singapore **CAPITAL:** Singapore **POPULATION:** 3.6 million
CURRENCY: Singapore dollar **OFFICIAL LANGUAGES:** Malay, English, Mandarin Chinese, and Tamil

1965 | 1965 | Aug 9 | SGP | +8 | +65 | .sg

AN ISLAND STATE linked to the southernmost tip of the Malay Peninsula by a causeway, Singapore was largely uninhabited between the 14th and 18th centuries. In 1819, an official of the British East India Company, Stamford Raffles, recognized the island's strategic position on key trade routes, and established Singapore as a trading settlement. Today, Singapore remains one of the most important entrepôts in Asia.

CLIMATE

Tropical equatorial

WEATHER CHART

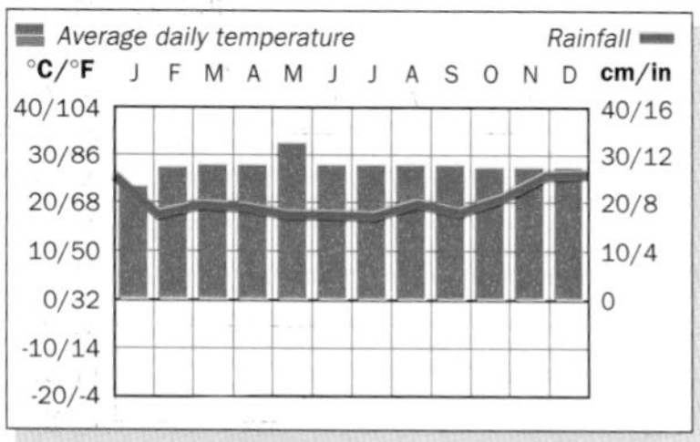

Average daily temperature
Rainfall
°C/°F
J F M A M J J A S O N D
cm/in
40/104
30/86
20/68
10/50
0/32
-10/14
-20/-4
40/16
30/12
20/8
10/4
0

The only variations in the hot, wet, and humid climate are the airless months of September and March, when the trade winds change direction.

TRANSPORTATION

Drive on left

Changi International 26m passengers | 1677 ships 20.4m grt

THE TRANSPORTATION NETWORK

3038 km (1888 miles) | 150 km (93 miles)
26 km (16 miles) | None

The Mass Rapid Transit System (subway), completed in 1991, is among the world's most efficient. Space for new roads has run out and monthly auctions are held to sell certificates entitling people to buy from a quota of new cars. The massive port at Pasir Panjang is being expanded on reclaimed land.

The financial center. More than a quarter of Singapore's GDP is generated by financial and business services.

TOURISM

Visitors : Population 1.7:1

6.3m visitors | Up 11% in 1999

MAIN TOURIST ARRIVALS

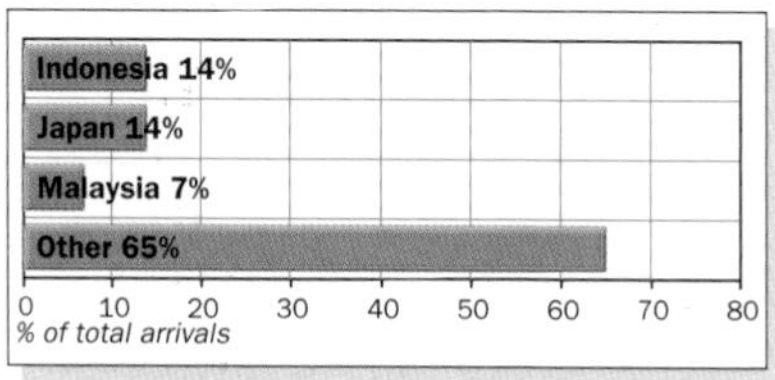

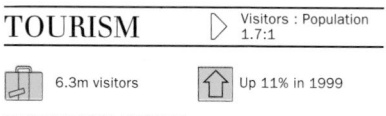

Indonesia 14%
Japan 14%
Malaysia 7%
Other 65%
0 10 20 30 40 50 60 70 80
% of total arrivals

The buildings of Chinatown, recognized as a picturesque tourist asset, are being restored. A Singaporean consortium is involved in developing a resort on Indonesia's Bintan island, some 45 km (28 miles) across the Strait of Singapore.

PEOPLE

Pop. density high

Mandarin Chinese, Malay, Tamil, English | 5902/km² (15,285/mi²)

THE URBAN/RURAL POPULATION SPLIT

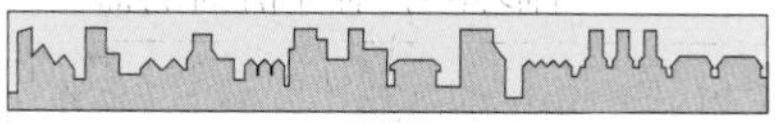

100%

ETHNIC MAKEUP

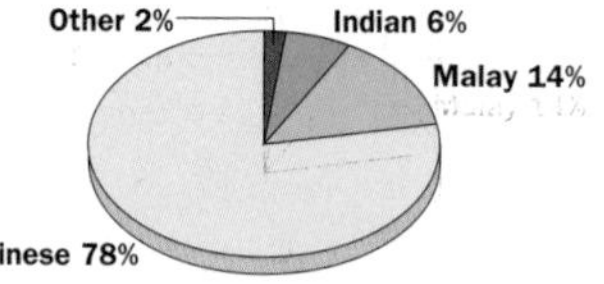

Other 2%
Indian 6%
Malay 14%
Chinese 78%

Singapore is dominated by the Chinese – the old-established English-speaking Straits Chinese and newer Mandarin speakers – who make up almost 80% of the community. Indigenous Malays are generally the poorest group, but today there is little overt ethnic tension. There is also a significant foreign workforce in Singapore.

Long-term plans to stabilize the population structure included the announcement in mid-2000 of cash bonuses for families with more than one child. Society is highly regulated and government campaigns to improve public behavior are frequent.

POLITICS

Multiparty elections

1997/2002 | President S. R. Nathan

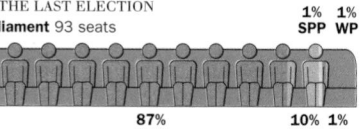

AT THE LAST ELECTION

Parliament 93 seats

1% SPP
1% WP
87% PAP
10% Nom
1% NC

PAP = People's Action Party **Nom** = Nominated
SPP = Singapore People's Party **WP** = Workers' Party
NC = Non-constituency member

In addition to the 83 elected members, up to six 'non-constituency' members may be nominated from the losers with the most votes and nine members may be nominated to ensure a wider representation in Parliament

Singapore is a multiparty democracy, although the ruling PAP effectively controls all parts of the political process and much of the economy. There are plans to create a national ideology ("shared values") based on Confucian traditions. In 1993, Ong Teng Cheong became the first president to be directly elected. The veteran politician, Lee Kuan Yew, prime minister for more than 30 years until his resignation in 1990, still exercises influence.

The PAP maintains its grip on power, having given Singaporeans one of the highest living standards in the world, based on a free-market economy. Its share of the vote has fallen since a massive peak in 1968, but it still regularly wins the overwhelming majority of seats in parliament. The first anti-government rally was permitted in 2001.

WORLD AFFAIRS

Joined UN in 1965

APEC | ASEAN | Comm | NAM | WTO

Singapore has established diplomatic relations with China while continuing to maintain close economic ties with Taiwan. In 1995, after 15 years of talks, Singapore and Malaysia finally agreed their territorial water boundary.

AID

Recipient

US$1m (receipts) | Down 93% 1996–1997

Aid is not an important issue in Singapore. The state does not provide aid to any states in southeast Asia.

DEFENSE

Compulsory military service

US$4.7bn | Down 5% in 1999

Despite Singapore's small size, its armed forces have a total strength of over 60,000.

S

ECONOMICS

Inflation 1.6% p.a. (1990–1999)

US$95.4bn

1.666–1.734 Singapore dollars

SCORE CARD

- ❑ WORLD GNP RANKING........................36th
- ❑ GNP PER CAPITA ....US$24,150
- ❑ BALANCE OF PAYMENTS ....US$21.3bn
- ❑ INFLATION ....–0.3%
- ❑ UNEMPLOYMENT 3%

EXPORTS

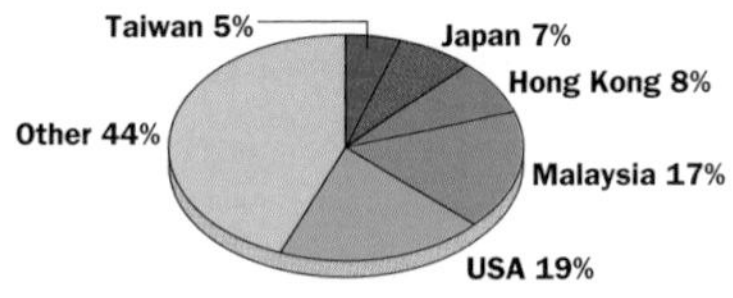
Taiwan 5%
Japan 7%
Hong Kong 8%
Other 44%
Malaysia 17%
USA 19%

IMPORTS

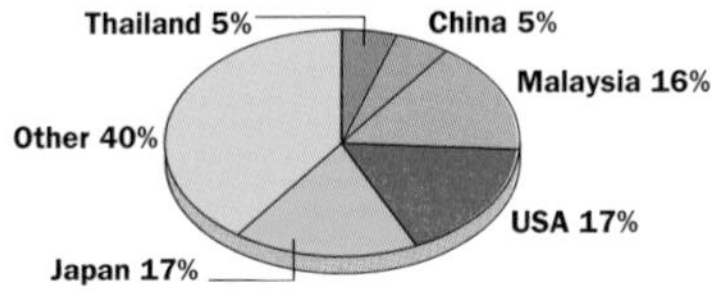
Thailand 5%
China 5%
Malaysia 16%
Other 40%
USA 17%
Japan 17%

STRENGTHS

Massive accumulated wealth is derived from success as an entrepôt and as a center of high-tech industries. Singapore is a major producer of computer disk drives. Huge state enterprises, such as TAMESEK, with over 450 companies, have proved highly flexible in responding to market conditions. World leader in new biotechnologies.

WEAKNESSES

Dependence on Malaysia for water. Almost all food and energy imported. Skills shortages, notably in engineering. Fluctuations in world electronics market caused recession in 2001. Lack of land.

RESOURCES

Electric power 5.6m kw

13,338 tonnes

Not an oil producer; refines 1.03m b/d

600,000 ducks, 190,000 pigs, 2m chickens

None

Singapore has no strategic resources and has to import almost all the energy and food it needs. Its main resources, on which its wealth as a center of commerce has been built, are its strategic position and its people.

ENVIRONMENT

Sustainability rank: 65th

None

21.9 tonnes per capita

There is a small green belt around the causeway. Singapore sees itself as a world leader in providing the perfect urban environment. There is no litter, thanks to instant heavy fines; chewing gum is banned by law.

MEDIA

TV ownership high

Daily newspaper circulation 324 per 1000 people

PUBLISHING AND BROADCAST MEDIA

There are 8 daily newspapers, including the *Straits Times* and *Lianhe Zaobao* in English and Chinese respectively

5 services: 4 independent, 1 US-controlled

6 privately owned services

The government is very sensitive to any criticism. However, it has declared its intention to partially liberalize the local media, as a part of "constructive competition." Foreigners may not own newspapers or broadcasting stations.

CRIME

Death penalty used

8500 prisoners

Down 23% 1996–1998

Crime is limited and punishment can be severe. The Triads are no longer a problem; the main issue is intellectual piracy.

CHRONOLOGY

In 1819, Sir Stamford Raffles set up a trading post in the village of Singapore; by 1826 it was Britain's colonial center in southeast Asia.

- ❑ **1959** PAP becomes ruling party.
- ❑ **1965** Independence.
- ❑ **1990** Lee Kuan Yew resigns as prime minister.
- ❑ **1993** Ong Teng Cheong first directly elected president.

EDUCATION

School leaving age: 15

92%

97,392 students

Schooling is not compulsory, but attendance is high. Education is seen as the key to a good salary, especially among the Chinese community.

HEALTH

Welfare state health benefits

1 per 714 people

Heart and cerebrovascular diseases, cancers

Singapore has an efficient modern health system. Incentives exist aimed at preserving the extended family, so that the elderly are cared for at home.

SPENDING

GDP/cap. increase

CONSUMPTION AND SPENDING

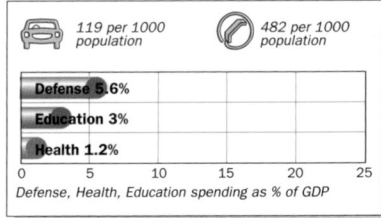

119 per 1000 population

482 per 1000 population

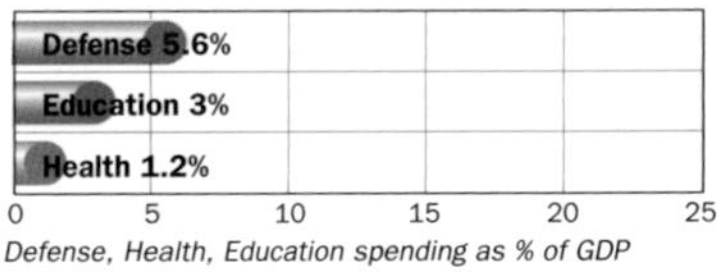
Defense 5.6%
Education 3%
Health 1.2%
0
5
10
15
20
25

Defense, Health, Education spending as % of GDP

Apartments are generally modest, despite the high standard of living. The 2001 "Singapore Share" scheme promised to give Singaporeans a share in the country's economy.

WORLD RANKING

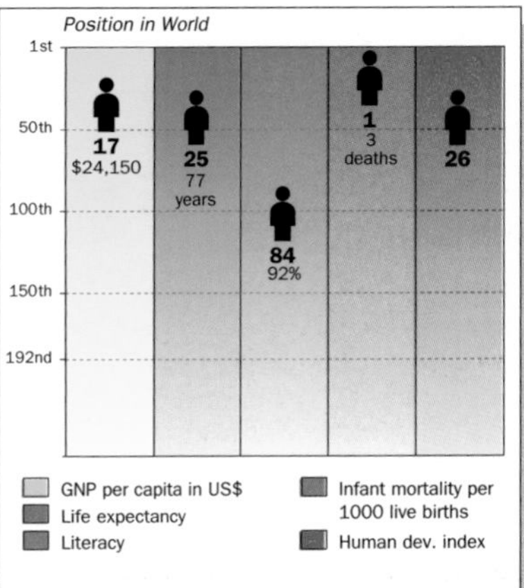
Position in World
1st
50th
100th
150th
192nd
17
$24,150
25
77 years
84
92%
1
3 deaths
26
GNP per capita in US$
Life expectancy
Literacy
Infant mortality per 1000 live births
Human dev. index

SINGAPORE

Total Land Area : 610 sq. km (236 sq. miles)

MALAYSIA
0 5 km
0 5 miles
N
Johore Strait
Causeway
Sembawang
Sarimbun Res.
Murai Res.
Lim Chu Kang
Kranji Res.
Seletar Res.
Sungai Seletar Res.
Pulau Ubin
Pulau Tekong Kechil
Pulau Tekong Res.
Punggol
Serangoon Harbour
Bukit Panjang
Serangoon
Changi
Pulau Tekong
Poyan Res.
Choa Chu Kang
Upper Peirce Res.
Kallang
Changi International Airport
Bukit Timah 176m
MacRitchie Res.
Jurong
Bedok Res.
Tengeh Res.
Jurong Lake
Bukit Timah
Jurong Town
1°20'
Jurong Industrial Estate
Pandan Res.
Queenstown
City
Geylang
Katong
104°
Strait of Singapore
SOUTH CHINA SEA
Pulau Pesek
Pulau Merlimau
Pasir Panjang
Pulau Pesek Kechil
Pulau Seraya
Pulau Retan Laut
Telok Blangah
Pulau Ayer Chawan
Keppel Harbour
Pulau Ayer Merbau
Pulau Sakra
Pulau Brani
Selat Pandan
Pulau Bukum
Sentosa
Urban Areas
Open Areas
Nature Reserve
Pulau Busing
Pulau Hantu
Pulau Tembakul
Pulau Sakijang Pelepah
Pulau Sakijang Bendera
Pulau Sudong
103°40'
Pulau Pawai
Pulau Semakau
Pulau Sebarok
103°50'
Pulau Senang

S

SLOVAKIA

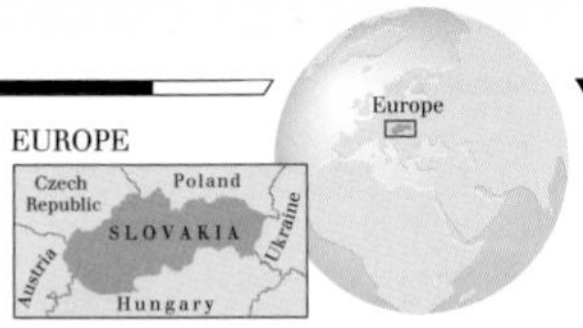
EUROPE
Europe
Czech Republic
Poland
SLOVAKIA
Ukraine
Austria
Hungary

OFFICAL NAME: Slovak Republic **CAPITAL:** Bratislava
POPULATION: 5.4 million **CURRENCY:** Koruna **OFFICAL LANGUAGE:** Slovak

1993 | 1993 | Oct 1 | SK | +1 | +421 | .sk

SLOVAKIA IS BORDERED by the Czech Republic, Austria, Poland, Hungary, and Ukraine. Southern lowlands contrast with the Carpathian mountain range, which extends along the Polish border. An independent democracy since 1993, Slovakia is the less developed half of the former Czechoslovakia. It is facing difficulties in making its heavy industry-based economy efficient.

Levoča, in northeastern Slovakia, dates from the 13th century and still retains its medieval street plan and town walls.

CLIMATE

Continental

WEATHER CHART

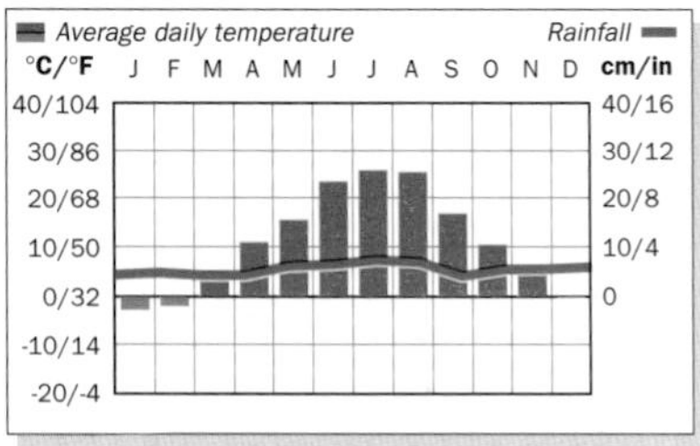
Average daily temperature
Rainfall
°C/°F
J F M A M J J A S O N D
cm/in
40/104
30/86
20/68
10/50
0/32
-10/14
-20/-4
40/16
30/12
20/8
10/4
0

Slovakia has a continental climate. Snowfalls are heavy in winter, while summers are moderately warm.

TRANSPORTATION

Drive on right

Milan Rastislav Stefanik, Bratislava 286,450 passengers

Has no fleet

THE TRANSPORTATION NETWORK

17,533 km (10,894 miles)

288 km (179 miles)

3662 km (2276 miles)

172 km (107 miles)

The Danube river is a vital artery. Trains are cheap and efficient, while buses and trams are the mainstay of urban transport.

TOURISM

Visitors : Population 1:5.1

1.1m visitors

Up 8% in 2000

MAIN TOURIST ARRIVALS

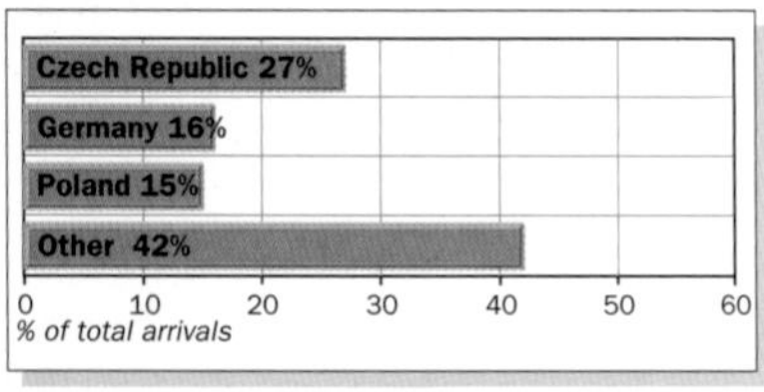
Czech Republic 27%
Germany 16%
Poland 15%
Other 42%
0
10
20
30
40
50
60
% of total arrivals

The Tatra Mountains are popular with skiers, hikers, and cavers. Tourists are also attracted to Bratislava, with its castle and old city, and to the many thermal-spring health spas. Most of the tourist industry has now been privatized.

PEOPLE

Pop. density medium

Slovak, Hungarian, Czech

110/km² (285/mi²)

THE URBAN/RURAL POPULATION SPLIT

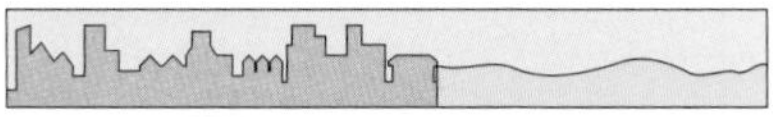
57%
43%

RELIGIOUS PERSUASION

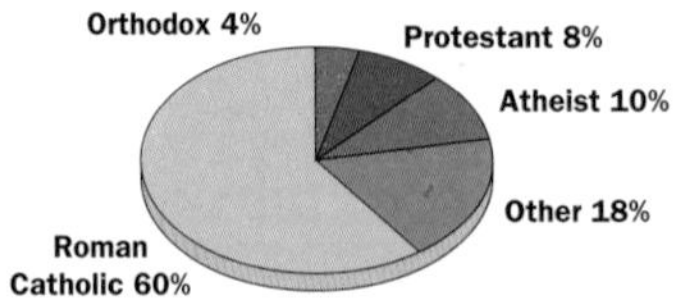
Orthodox 4%
Protestant 8%
Atheist 10%
Other 18%
Roman Catholic 60%

Slovaks dominate society, but 9% of the population is Hungarian, and there is a large Roma minority which faces discrimination. Tensions between Slovaks and Hungarians have lessened under the nine-party government which took office in 1998, including the Hungarian Coalition Party. There were 300,000 Slovaks living in the Czech lands in 1993. Dual citizenship is now permitted. Roman Catholicism remains a powerful social force.

POLITICS

Multiparty elections

1998/2002

President Rudolf Schuster

AT THE LAST ELECTION

National Council 150 seats

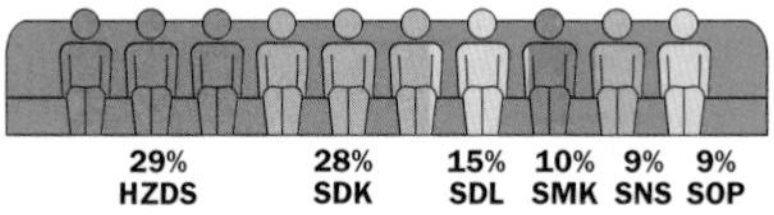
29% HZDS
28% SDK
15% SDL
10% SMK
9% SNS
9% SOP

HZDS = Movement for a Democratic Slovakia **SDK** = Slovak Democratic Coalition **SDL** = Party of the Democratic Left **SMK** = Hungarian Coalition Party **SNS** = Slovak National Party **SOP** = Party of Civic Understanding

The move which led to the separation of the two halves of the former Czechoslovakia in 1993 gathered momentum when Slovak leader Vladimir Meciar was tempted by independence as a way of enhancing his power base. The populist Meciar dominated Slovak politics until 1998, but clashed repeatedly with President Michal Kovac, both of them members of the HZDS.

A broad coalition led by center-right politician Mikulas Dzurinda won power in elections in September 1998. Slovakia's first direct presidential election in May 1999 was won by the pro-Western Rudolf Schuster, frustrating Meciar's bid for this office. The Hungarian minority has its own parties, one of which joined Dzurinda's ruling coalition, whereas the Roma have no official representation.

WORLD AFFAIRS

Joined UN in 1993

CE | CEFTA | OECD | EAPC | OSCE

The 1998 change of government reversed the pro-Russian Meciar years. Slovakia was among six "second wave" candidates which began EU membership talks in March 2000. It also became a member of the OECD in 2000.

AID

Recipient

$318m (receipts)

Up 375% 1997–1999

Foreign aid fell after the mid-1990s, but EU programs are now in place in preparation for EU membership.

DEFENSE

Compulsory military service

$329m

Down 22% in 1999

The Slovak armed forces include some 13,600 conscripts at any one time. Prime Minister Dzurinda, who took office in late 1998, has reversed Meciar's pro-Russian defense policies.

RESOURCES

Electric power 7.9m kw

2640 tonnes

1283 b/d (reserves 7,495,680 bbl)

1.59m pigs, 665,100 cattle, 13.1m chickens

Coal, lignite, gas, oil, antimony, copper, iron, mercury, zinc

44% of electricity was nuclear-generated, even before the Mochovce nuclear station began operations in 1998.

S

SLOVAKIA

Total Land Area : 49 036 sq. km (18 933 sq. miles)

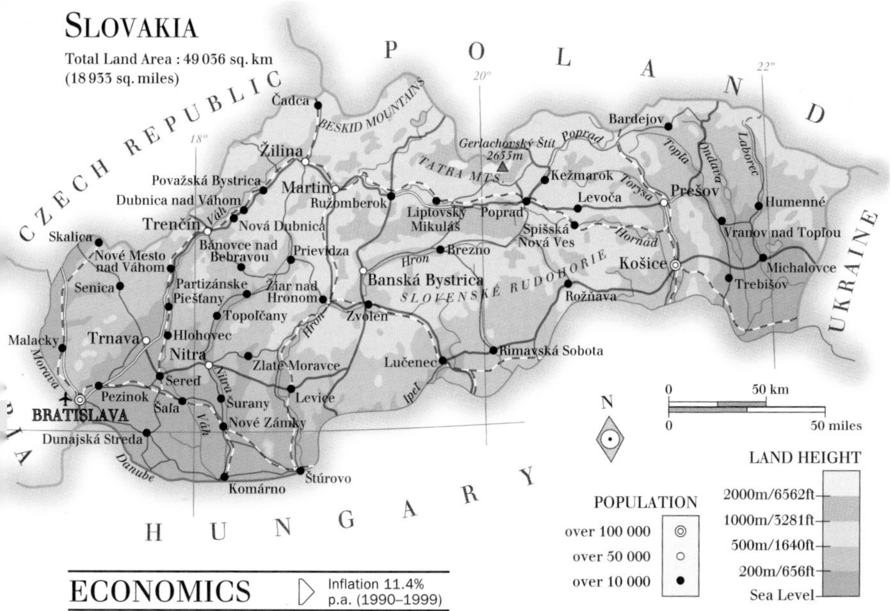

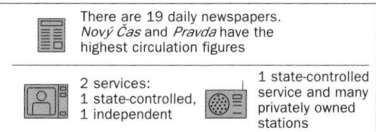

POLAND
CZECH REPUBLIC
UKRAINE
HUNGARY
AUSTRIA
BESKID MOUNTAINS
TATRA MTS.
Gerlachovský Štít 2655m
SLOVENSKÉ RUDOHORIE
Čadca
Žilina
Považská Bystrica
Dubnica nad Váhom
Martin
Ružomberok
Liptovský Mikuláš
Poprad
Kežmarok
Levoča
Bardejov
Prešov
Humenné
Vranov nad Topľou
Michalovce
Trebišov
Košice
Rožňava
Spišská Nová Ves
Brezno
Banská Bystrica
Zvolen
Trenčín
Nová Dubnica
Skalica
Nové Mesto nad Váhom
Bánovce nad Bebravou
Prievidza
Senica
Partizánske
Žiar nad Hronom
Piešťany
Topoľčany
Malacky
Trnava
Hlohovec
Nitra
Zlaté Moravce
Lučenec
Rimavská Sobota
Sereď
Pezinok
Šaľa
Šurany
Levice
BRATISLAVA
Nové Zámky
Dunajská Streda
Komárno
Štúrovo
Morava
Váh
Nitra
Hron
Ipeľ
Danube
Poprad
Topľa
Ondava
Laborec
Torysa
Hornád
N
0 50 km
0 50 miles
LAND HEIGHT
2000m/6562ft
1000m/3281ft
500m/1640ft
200m/656ft
Sea Level
POPULATION
over 100 000
over 50 000
over 10 000

CHRONOLOGY

Once part of the Austro-Hungarian empire, Slovakia and the Czech Lands formed the Republic of Czechoslovakia in 1918.

- ❑ **1939–1945** Separate Slovak state under pro-Nazi Jozef Tiso.
- ❑ **1945** Czechoslovak state restored.
- ❑ **1947** Communists seize power.
- ❑ **1968** "Prague Spring" ended by Warsaw pact invasion.
- ❑ **1989** "Velvet Revolution."
- ❑ **1990** Free multiparty elections.
- ❑ **1993** Jan 1, separate Slovak and Czech states established.
- ❑ **1994** HZDS election victory.
- ❑ **1998** Broad-based coalition wins general election.
- ❑ **1999** Rudolf Schuster defeats Meciar in direct presidential poll.
- ❑ **2000** EU negotiations begin.

ECONOMICS

Inflation 11.4% p.a. (1990–1999)

$20.3bn

42.33–46.88 Slovak koruny

SCORE CARD

❑ WORLD GNP RANKING	62nd
❑ GNP PER CAPITA	$3770
❑ BALANCE OF PAYMENTS	$–1.16bn
❑ INFLATION	10.6%
❑ UNEMPLOYMENT	20%

STRENGTHS

Increase in manufacturing, especially in Bratislava and surrounding area. Recent progress in cutting budget deficits and restructuring public and private sector. Growth in exports to EU. Potential for tourism, particularly skiing in the Tatra Mountains.

WEAKNESSES

High foreign indebtedness. Dependence on foreign trade makes the economy vulnerable to global recession. Heavy industry has found some new markets in the West, but struggles with poor productivity. Slow to attract foreign investment until 2000. Much poorer eastern region. Growing unemployment.

EXPORTS

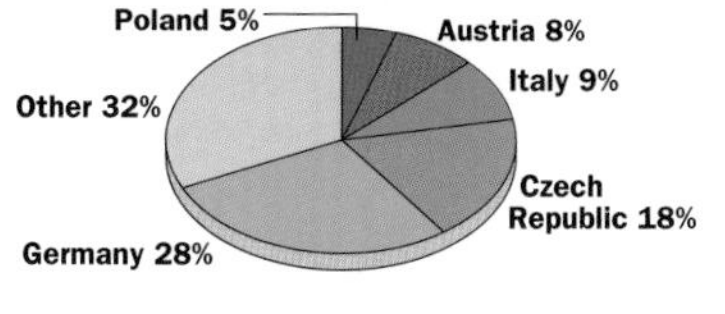

Poland 5%
Austria 8%
Italy 9%
Other 32%
Czech Republic 18%
Germany 28%

IMPORTS

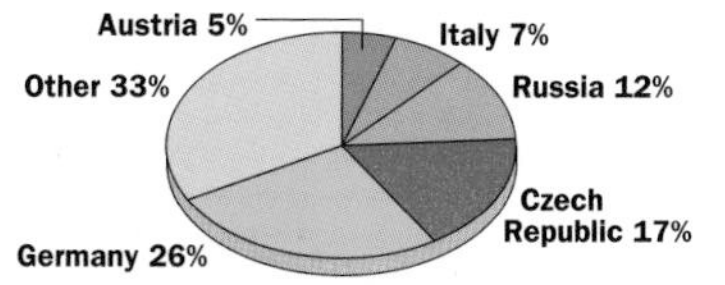

Austria 5%
Italy 7%
Other 33%
Russia 12%
Czech Republic 17%
Germany 26%

ENVIRONMENT

Sustainability rank: 18th

22%

7.1 tonnes per capita

The Gabcikovo dam and the Bohunice nuclear reactors, now scheduled for partial closure, have provoked criticism.

MEDIA

TV ownership high

Daily newspaper circulation 184 per 1000 people

PUBLISHING AND BROADCAST MEDIA

There are 19 daily newspapers. *Nový Čas* and *Pravda* have the highest circulation figures

2 services: 1 state-controlled, 1 independent

1 state-controlled service and many privately owned stations

The state news agency TASR, accused of lacking objectivity and depending on government funding, resisted the emergence of independent rival SITA.

CRIME

Death penalty not used

7979 prisoners

Down 6% 1996-1998

Organized crime has increased rapidly in recent years, as has "white collar crime" such as business fraud. A new law to control money laundering took effect in 2001. A former economics minister accused of embezzlement was murdered in 1999.

EDUCATION

School leaving age: 15

99%

101,764 students

Schooling now draws on pre-1939 Slovak traditions but it is not adequately resourced, especially in rural areas. There is a modern university in Bratislava.

HEALTH

Welfare state health benefits

1 per 333 people

Cancers, heart and cerebrovascular diseases, accidents

Rising demand and costs are straining the health service severely. Restoring viability is now a government priority.

SPENDING

GDP/cap. increase

CONSUMPTION AND SPENDING

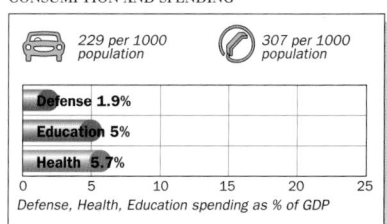

229 per 1000 population

307 per 1000 population

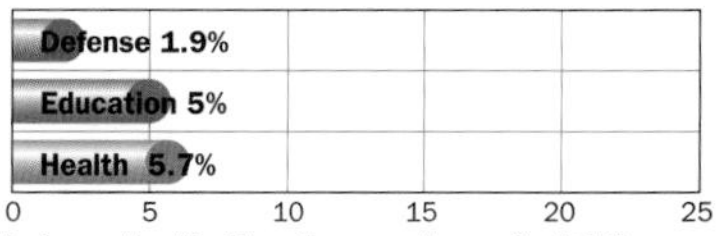

Defense 1.9%
Education 5%
Health 5.7%
0
5
10
15
20
25

Defense, Health, Education spending as % of GDP

A new elite is increasing demand for Western goods. Rural workers, Roma, and those living in the east are the poorest.

WORLD RANKING

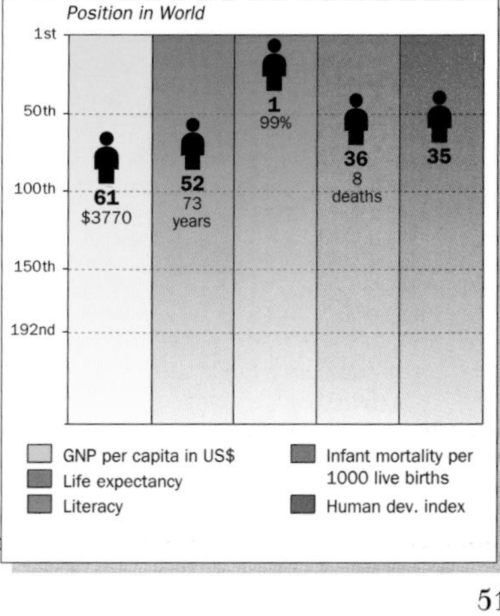

Position in World
1st
50th
100th
150th
192nd
61
$3770
52
73
years
1
99%
36
8
deaths
35
GNP per capita in US$
Life expectancy
Literacy
Infant mortality per 1000 live births
Human dev. index

S

SLOVENIA

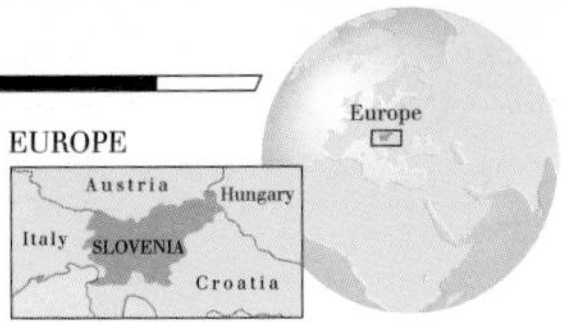
EUROPE
Europe
Austria
Hungary
Italy
SLOVENIA
Croatia

OFFICIAL NAME: Republic of Slovenia **CAPITAL:** Ljubljana
POPULATION: 2 million **CURRENCY:** Tolar **OFFICIAL LANGUAGE:** Slovene

1991 | 1991 | June 25 | SLO | +1 | +386 | .si

OF ALL THE FORMER Yugoslav republics, Slovenia has the closest links with western Europe. Located at the northeastern end of the Adriatic Sea, this small, Alpine country controls some of Europe's major transit routes. Slovenia's transition to independence in 1991 avoided the violence of the breakup of Yugoslavia. The most prosperous of the former communist European states, it is the only former Yugoslav republic on the "fast track" to EU membership.

CLIMATE

Continental/ Mediterranean

WEATHER CHART

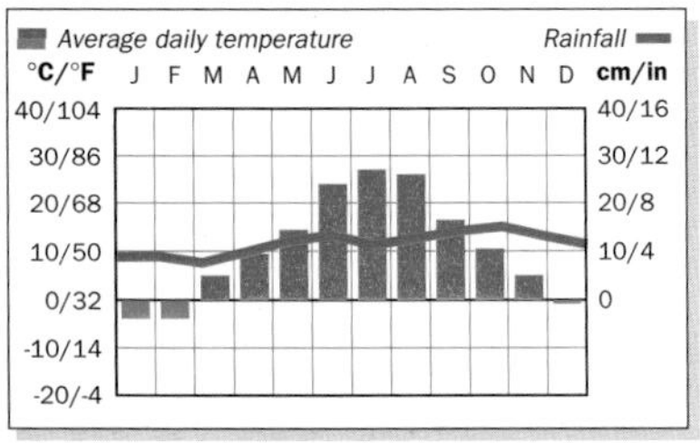
Average daily temperature
Rainfall
°C/°F
J F M A M J J A S O N D
cm/in
40/104
30/86
20/68
10/50
0/32
-10/14
-20/-4
40/16
30/12
20/8
10/4
0

Slovenia's interior has a continental climate. Its small coastal region has a mild Mediterranean climate.

TRANSPORTATION

Drive on right

Brnik International, Ljubljana 895,540 passengers

10 ships 1767 grt

THE TRANSPORTATION NETWORK

17,745 km (11,026 miles)	249 km (155 miles)
1202 km (747 miles)	None

Slovenia is strategically situated at some of Europe's major crossroads. In addition, its Adriatic ports provide Austria with its main maritime outlet.

TOURISM

Visitors : Population 1:1.8

1.1m visitors

Up 23% in 2000

MAIN TOURIST ARRIVALS

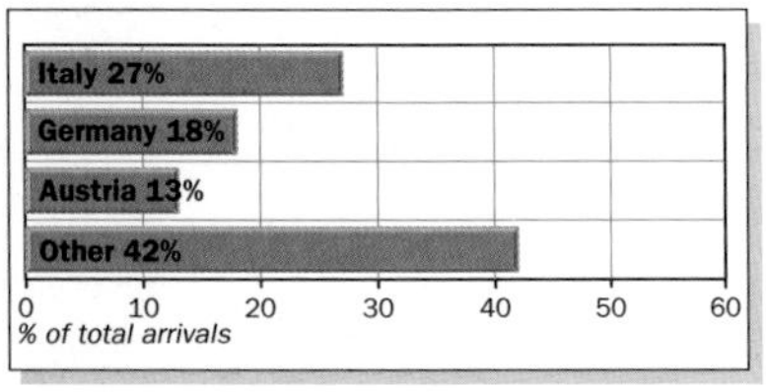
Italy 27%
Germany 18%
Austria 13%
Other 42%
0
10
20
30
40
50
60
% of total arrivals

Tourism contributes 9% of GDP and is rising. Attractions include the scenery and the sea, spas, and casinos. Disputes over ownership after denationalization have held up investment in hotels.

PEOPLE

Pop. density medium

Slovene, Serbo-Croat

99/km² (256/mi²)

THE URBAN/RURAL POPULATION SPLIT

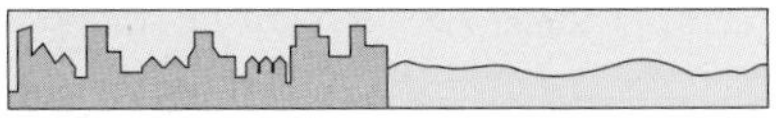
50%
50%

ETHNIC MAKEUP

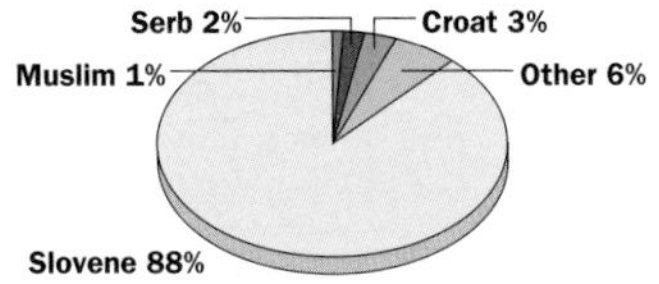
Serb 2%
Croat 3%
Muslim 1%
Other 6%
Slovene 88%

Slovenia is ethnically homogeneous; around 90% are Slovene. There are also small communities of Hungarians and Italians. The Slovene language is sufficiently different from Serbo-Croat to foster a separate identity from its Yugoslav neighbors. Slovenia has traditionally identified more with countries to the west than with its Balkan neighbors. Access to Italy and Austria during the 1970s and 1980s encouraged a separatist movement. These factors aided Slovenia's relatively peaceful secession from the former Yugoslavia in 1991.

POLITICS

Multiparty elections

L. House 2000/2004
U. House 1997/2002

President Milan Kučan

AT THE LAST ELECTION

National Assembly 90 seats

12% ZLSD
9% NSi
13% Others
38% LDS
16% SDS
10% SLS/SKD
2% MR

LDS = Liberal Democracy of Slovenia **SDS** = Social Democratic Party of Slovenia **ZLSD** = United List of Social Democrats **SLS/SKD** = Slovene People's Party/Christian Democrats of Slovenia **NSi** = New Slovenia – Christian People's Party **MR** = Minority representatives
Two seats are reserved for Italian and Hungarian minority representatives

National Council 40 seats

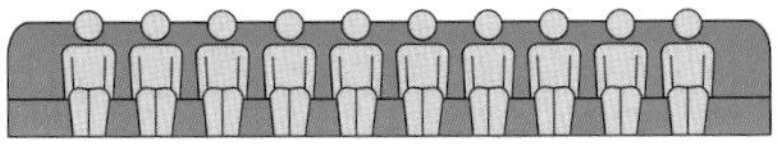

22 members of the National Council, which has an advisory role, are indirectly elected, and 18 are chosen by an electoral college to represent various interests

Slovenia has been strikingly stable since independence, with Milan Kučan as president. Fragmented party politics makes coalition governments essential. Janez Drnovsek, leader of the center-left LDS, has been prime minister almost continuously since 1992, apart from a six-month period in 2000 when the more right-wing SLS pulled out of the coalition. Andrej Bajuk, as SLS leader, then became prime minister, leaving his party after a failed attempt at electoral reform. Drnovsek returned to office following elections in 2000.

Many former communist officials still occupy top posts. Ownership of denationalized property remains an issue and there is still bitterness over the killing of opponents of Tito's partisans in the 1940s.

SLOVENIA

Total Land Area : 20 250 sq. km (7820 sq. miles)

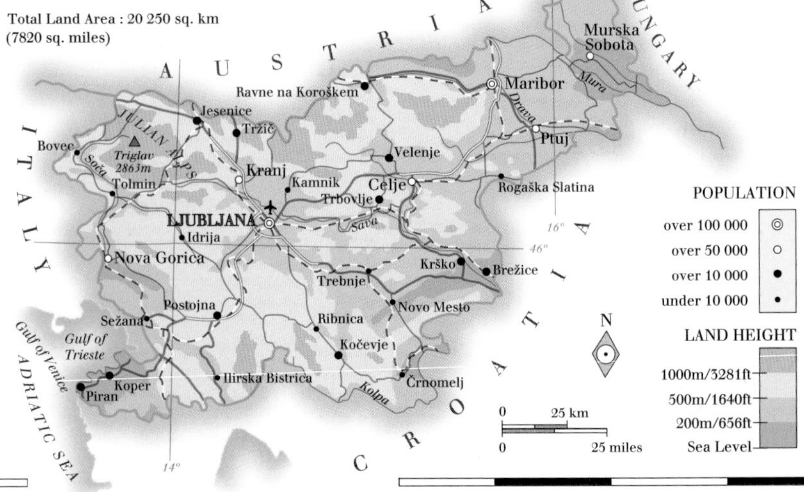
AUSTRIA
HUNGARY
ITALY
CROATIA
Murska Sobota
Maribor
Mura
Drava
Ptuj
Ravne na Koroškem
Jesenice
Tržič
Bovec
Triglav 2863m
JULIAN ALPS
Soča
Tolmin
Kranj
Kamnik
Velenje
Celje
Trbovlje
Rogaška Slatina
LJUBLJANA
Idrija
Sava
Nova Gorica
Krško
Brežice
Trebnje
Novo Mesto
Postojna
Sežana
Ribnica
Kočevje
Gulf of Trieste
Gulf of Venice
ADRIATIC SEA
Koper
Piran
Ilirska Bistrica
Kolpa
Črnomelj
0 25 km
0 25 miles
N
POPULATION
over 100 000
over 50 000
over 10 000
under 10 000
LAND HEIGHT
1000m/3281ft
500m/1640ft
200m/656ft
Sea Level

S

WORLD AFFAIRS

Joined UN in 1992

CE | EAPC | OSCE | PfP | WTO

Slovenia is on the "fast track" to EU membership, probably in 2004. It also aims to be part of the next round of NATO enlargement.

AID

Recipient

$31m (receipts)

Down 23% in 1999

EU and World Bank aid focuses on infrastructure, the environment, and agricultural reform, in preparation for EU membership.

DEFENSE

Compulsory military service

$337m

Up 4% in 1999

Troops staved off Yugoslav forces after secession in 1991. Defense spending will have to rise to reach NATO's required minimum of 2% of GDP.

ECONOMICS

Inflation 23.3% p.a. (1993–1999)

$19.9bn

198.5–227.5 tolars

SCORE CARD

❑ WORLD GNP RANKING	66th
❑ GNP PER CAPITA	$10,000
❑ BALANCE OF PAYMENTS	$–581m
❑ INFLATION	6.6%
❑ UNEMPLOYMENT	8%

EXPORTS

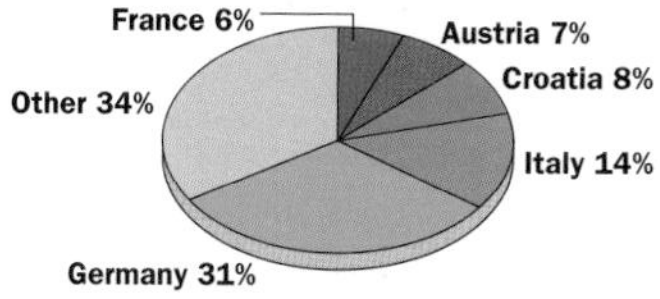

France 6%
Austria 7%
Croatia 8%
Other 34%
Italy 14%
Germany 31%

IMPORTS

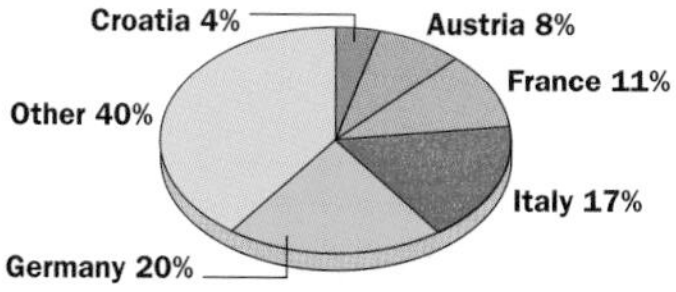

Croatia 4%
Austria 8%
France 11%
Other 40%
Italy 17%
Germany 20%

STRENGTHS

Stability. Competitive manufacturing industry. Exports to EU and to former Yugoslav markets. Revoz car plant very productive, making Renault Clios. Competitive port at Koper. Least indebted of central and eastern European states.

WEAKNESSES

Economy only partly liberalized. Capital market controls discourage foreign investment. Slower growth rates than other emerging markets. Disputes over denationalized property.

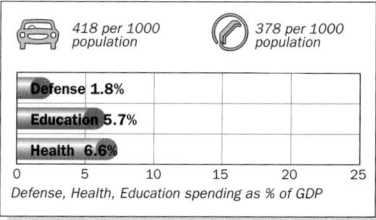

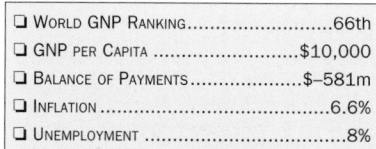

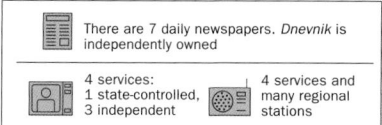

Lake Bled in the Julian Alps, *which lie astride the Slovenian–Italian border. The lake is a popular tourist destination.*

RESOURCES

Electric power 2.5m kw

3262 tonnes

20 b/d

552,155 pigs, 471,425 cattle, 8.55m chickens

Coal, lignite, lead, zinc, uranium, silver, mercury

Slovenia has come under pressure from Austria to close the nuclear plant at Krško, which provides one-third of Slovenia's power. It has deposits of brown coal and lignite, but they are difficult to extract and of poor quality.

ENVIRONMENT

Sustainability rank: 24th

6%

7.8 tonnes per capita

Protecting the country's alpine ecology is a priority. Pollution comes mainly from smelting, the chemicals industry, and burning brown coal and lignite.

MEDIA

TV ownership high

Daily newspaper circulation 199 per 1000 people

PUBLISHING AND BROADCAST MEDIA

There are 7 daily newspapers. *Dnevnik* is independently owned

4 services: 1 state-controlled, 3 independent

4 services and many regional stations

A free and critical press has developed. State broadcasters have a new ethical code, protecting journalists' sources. POP TV is a commercial success.

CRIME

Death penalty not used

630 prisoners

Up 52% 1996–1998

Slovenia has proportionately the lowest prison population in Europe. People-smuggling into western Europe is overtaking narcotics-smuggling as the focus of organized crime.

EDUCATION

School leaving age: 15

99%

51,009 students

School is compulsory from seven to 15 years of age, and standards are high. The university at Ljubljana was founded in 1595.

CHRONOLOGY

Slovenia was part of the Austro-Hungarian empire until 1918, when it joined the Kingdom of the Slavs, Croats, and Slovenes (Yugoslavia).

- ❑ **1949** Tito's break with Moscow.
- ❑ **1989** Parliament confirms right to secede. Calls multiparty elections.
- ❑ **1990** Control over army asserted, referendum approves secession.
- ❑ **1991** Independence declared; first republic to secede. Yugoslav federal army repelled.
- ❑ **1992** First multiparty elections. Milan Kučan president, Janez Drnovsek prime minister.
- ❑ **1993** Joins IMF and IBRD.
- ❑ **1998** EU membership talks begin.
- ❑ **2000** Drnovsek ousted; returns to office after elections.

HEALTH

Welfare state health benefits

1 per 476 people

Cerebrovascular and heart diseases, cancers, accidents,

National health care in Slovenia uses health centers and outpatient clinics to increase accessibility for patients.

SPENDING

GDP/cap. increase

CONSUMPTION AND SPENDING

418 per 1000 population

378 per 1000 population

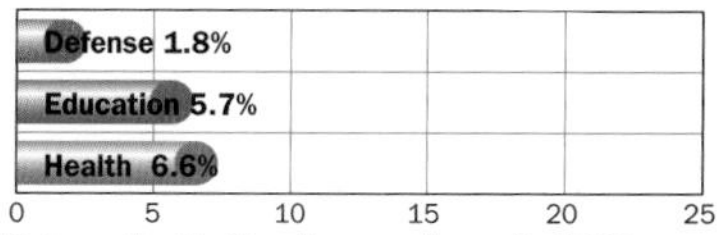

Defense 1.8%
Education 5.7%
Health 6.6%
0
5
10
15
20
25

Defense, Health, Education spending as % of GDP

Slovenia has the highest standard of living of the central and eastern European states, with earnings at 60% of the EU average.

WORLD RANKING

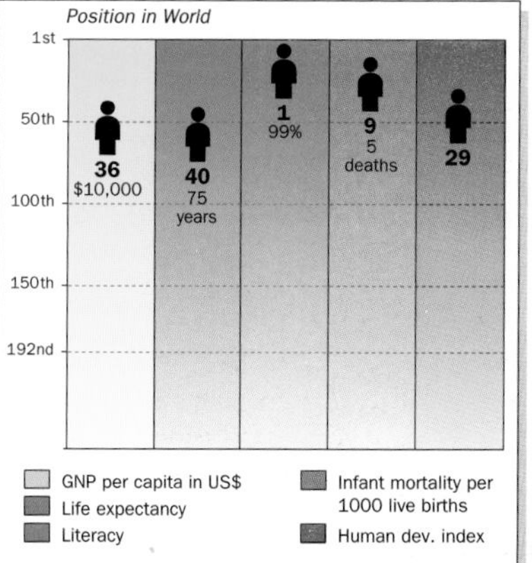

Position in World
1st
50th
100th
150th
192nd
36
$10,000
40
75
years
1
99%
9
5
deaths
29
GNP per capita in US$
Life expectancy
Literacy
Infant mortality per 1000 live births
Human dev. index

S

SOLOMON ISLANDS

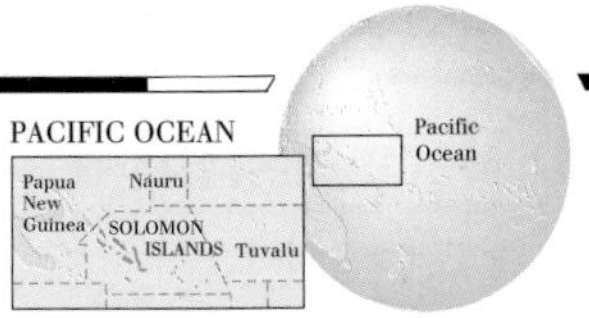
PACIFIC OCEAN
Papua New Guinea
Nauru
SOLOMON ISLANDS
Tuvalu
Pacific Ocean

OFFICIAL NAME: Solomon Islands **CAPITAL:** Honiara
POPULATION: 444,000 **CURRENCY:** Solomon Islands dollar **OFFICIAL LANGUAGE:** English

1978 | 1978 | July 7 | SLB | +11 | +677 | .sb

SCATTERED OVER 645,000 sq km (250,000 sq miles), the Solomons archipelago has several hundred islands, but most people live on the six largest – Guadalcanal, Malaita, New Georgia, Makira, Santa Isabel, and Choiseul. The Solomons have been settled since at least 1000 BCE; the Spanish arrived in 1568. Ethnic conflict between rival islanders ravaged the country from 1998 to 2000. Most of the Solomons are coral reefs. Just 1% of the land area is cultivable.

CLIMATE

Tropical equatorial

WEATHER CHART

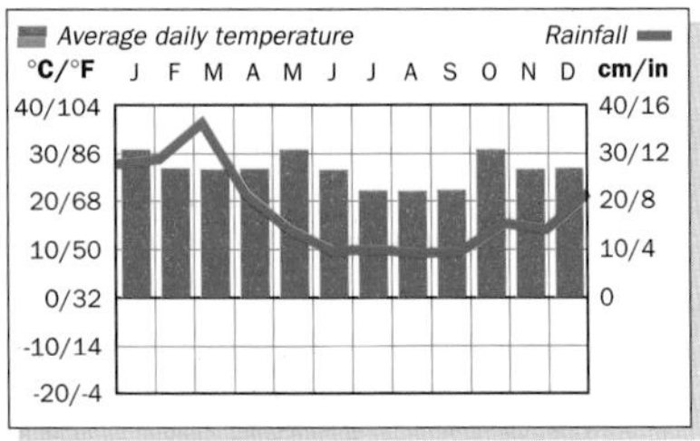
Average daily temperature
Rainfall
°C/°F
J F M A M J J A S O N D
cm/in
40/104
30/86
20/68
10/50
0/32
-10/14
-20/-4
40/16
30/12
20/8
10/4
0

There is little variation in the humid, subtropical climate, but ferocious cyclones can occur in the rainy season.

TRANSPORTATION

Drive on left

Henderson, Honiara 22,000 passengers

31 ships 1400 grt

THE TRANSPORTATION NETWORK

34 km (21 miles) | None | None | None

International flights from the principal airport, 13 km (8 miles) outside Honiara, were resumed in late 2000 after the ending of open hostilities.

Unloading seed coconuts near Munda on New Georgia in the Solomons' northern chain of islands. Coconuts are by far the largest and most commercially important crop.

TOURISM

Visitors : Population 1:21

21,000 visitors

Up 62% in 1999

MAIN TOURIST ARRIVALS

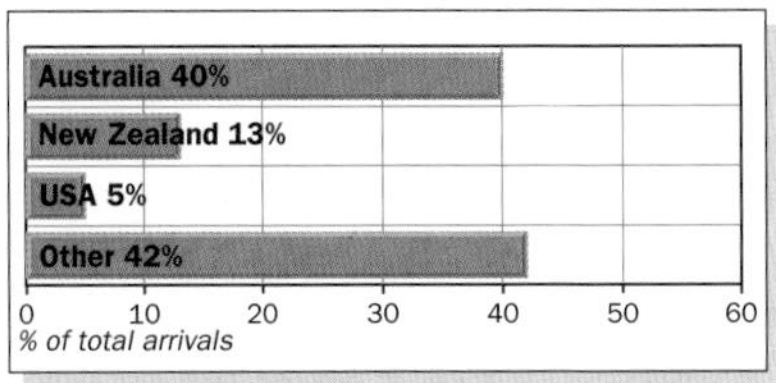
Australia 40%
New Zealand 13%
USA 5%
Other 42%
0
10
20
30
40
50
60
% of total arrivals

The importance of Guadalcanal during World War II and the tranquility of the outer islands used to attract tourists. However, ethnic conflict and the consequent warnings against visiting all but destroyed tourism in 1998. Lack of funding hampers recovery.

PEOPLE

Pop. density low

English, Pidgin English, Melanesian Pidgin

16/km² (41/mi²)

THE URBAN/RURAL POPULATION SPLIT

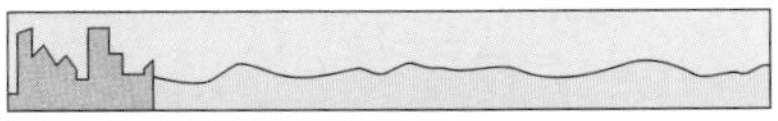
19%
81%

RELIGIOUS PERSUASION

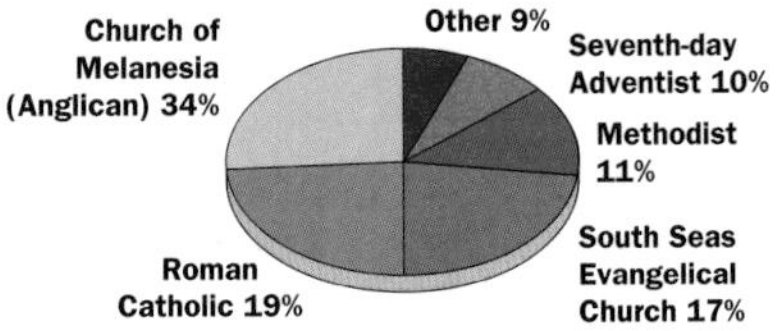
Church of Melanesia (Anglican) 34%
Other 9%
Seventh-day Adventist 10%
Methodist 11%
South Seas Evangelical Church 17%
Roman Catholic 19%

Almost all Solomon Islanders are Melanesian; relations between islands are tense. During the 1998–2000 conflict, 20,000 Malaitans were forced from their homes on Guadalcanal by native (Isatabu) militias. Authorities in outlying islands have pressed for greater autonomy. There are small communities of Micronesians who are descended from I-Kiribati temporarily relocated in 1957. Although the Islanders are nominally Christian, animist beliefs are widespread. More than 50 dialects are spoken.

POLITICS

Multiparty elections

1997/2001

HM Queen Elizabeth II

AT THE LAST ELECTION

National Parliament 50 seats

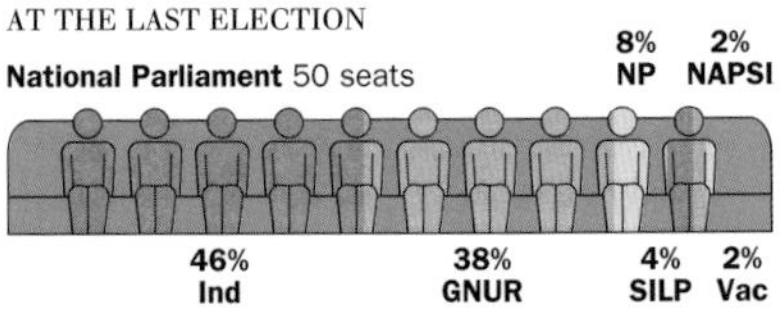
8% NP
2% NAPSI
46% Ind
38% GNUR
4% SILP
2% Vac

Ind = Independents **GNUR** = Group for National Unity and Reconciliation **NP** = National Party **SILP** = Solomon Islands Labour Party **NAPSI** = National Action Party of the Solomons **Vac** = Vacant

Parliament is based on the Westminster model, but with no dominant political class, prominent local figures – known as "big men" – stand as candidates and turnover of members is high, leading to fluid and unstable coalitions. The civil conflict on Guadalcanal led to the downfall of the government in June 2000; it was finally resolved with a tenuous peace treaty in October. New Prime Minister Manasseh Sogavare has striven to restore a semblance of stability with a new devolved "state system," which gives greater autonomy to the regions.

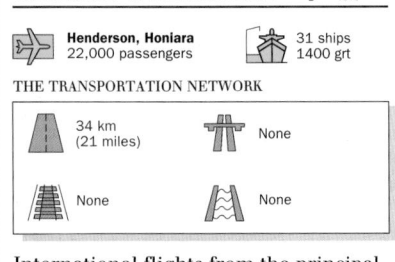

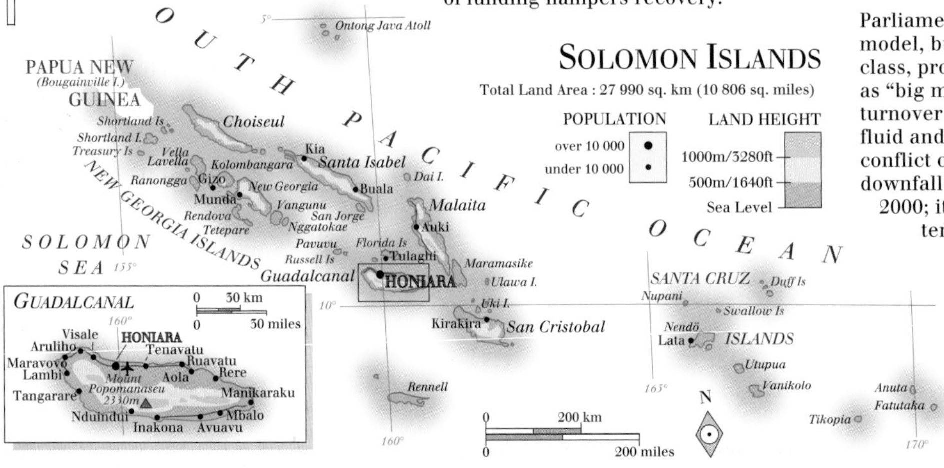
SOLOMON ISLANDS
Total Land Area : 27 990 sq. km (10 806 sq. miles)
POPULATION
over 10 000
under 10 000
LAND HEIGHT
1000m/3280ft
500m/1640ft
Sea Level
SOUTH PACIFIC OCEAN
PAPUA NEW GUINEA
(Bougainville I.)
Ontong Java Atoll
Shortland Is
Shortland I.
Treasury Is
Choiseul
Vella Lavella
Kolombangara
Ranongga
Gizo
Kia
Santa Isabel
Dai I.
Munda
New Georgia
Buala
Malaita
Vangunu
Rendova
San Jorge
Tetepare
Nggatokae
Auki
NEW GEORGIA ISLANDS
Pavuvu
Florida Is
Russell Is
Tulaghi
SOLOMON SEA
Guadalcanal
HONIARA
Maramasike
Ulawa I.
Uki I.
Kirakira
San Cristobal
Rennell
SANTA CRUZ ISLANDS
Duff Is
Nupani
Swallow Is
Nendö
Lata
Utupua
Vanikolo
Anuta
Fatutaka
Tikopia
200 km
200 miles
N
GUADALCANAL
30 km
30 miles
Visale
HONIARA
Aruliho
Tenavatu
Maravovo
Ruavatu
Lambi
Aola
Rere
Mount Popomanaseu 2330m
Tangarare
Manikaraku
Nduindui
Mbalo
Inakona
Avuavu
5°
10°
155°
160°
165°
170°

WORLD AFFAIRS

Joined UN in 1978

ACP | Comm | IBRD | PC | PIF

The intensification of violence on the islands in 2000 caused great concern around the Pacific, and heightened international mediation efforts, in which Australia was particularly involved. An Australian warship was the scene of Prime Minister Sogavare's election and of the ratification of the Townsville peace accord.

AID

Recipient

US$40m (receipts)

Down 7% in 1999

Aid has focused very specifically on restoring stability and rebuilding infrastructure after two years of brutal conflict. Regional powers Australia, New Zealand, and Taiwan are key in aiding recovery. Improved relations with Papua New Guinea brought aid of US$23 million between 1998 and 2001.

DEFENSE

No compulsory military service

Australia responsible for defense

Not applicable

Prime Minister Sogavare's Peace Plan 2000 includes the creation of a pan-ethnic security force. Under the Townsville accord security was overseen by unarmed peacekeepers from neighboring Pacific states. The rival militias are effectively in control on Guadalcanal and Malaita.

ECONOMICS

Inflation 8.5% p.a. (1990–1999)

US$320m

5.0564–5.1626 Solomon Islands dollars

SCORE CARD

- ❑ WORLD GNP RANKING........................175th
- ❑ GNP PER CAPITA ....US$750
- ❑ BALANCE OF PAYMENTS ....US$8m
- ❑ INFLATION 8.3%
- ❑ UNEMPLOYMENT...........Some underemployment

EXPORTS

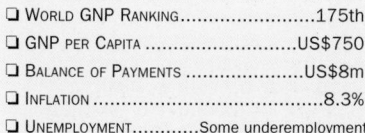

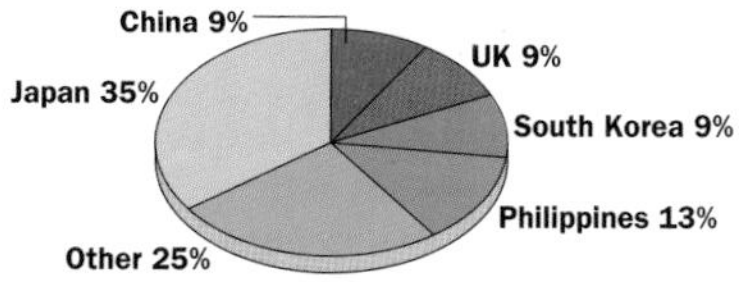
China 9%
UK 9%
Japan 35%
South Korea 9%
Philippines 13%
Other 25%

IMPORTS

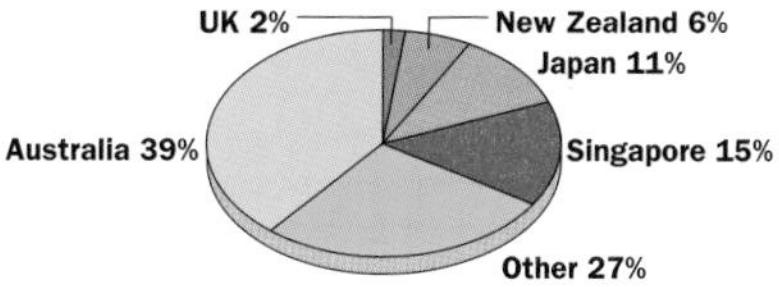
UK 2%
New Zealand 6%
Japan 11%
Australia 39%
Singapore 15%
Other 27%

STRENGTHS

Good mineral and agricultural resources. Influx of international aid.

WEAKNESSES

Economy near collapse after ethnic conflict. Destruction of infrastructure. Key gold mine shut by militias. Revenue from copra, gold, fish, and palm oil dried up. Social insecurity deters investment. Residual effects of 1997–1998 Asian crash.

RESOURCES

Electric power 12,000 kw

53,442 tonnes

Not an oil producer

58,000 pigs, 10,000 cattle, 185,000 chickens

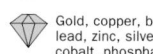

Gold, copper, bauxite, lead, zinc, silver, cobalt, phosphates

Bauxite deposits have been discovered on Rennell Island. In addition, there are traces of gold and copper on Guadalcanal. There is increasing concern over the exploitation of forest and marine resources.

ENVIRONMENT

Not available

None

0.4 tonnes per capita

The environmental movement is strong. Depletion of forest and marine resources are a major concern. In 1998 a sustainable forest harvesting policy was introduced, but the need to restore the economy puts pressure on environmentally sensitive areas.

MEDIA

TV ownership low

Daily newspaper circulation 16 per 1000 people

PUBLISHING AND BROADCAST MEDIA

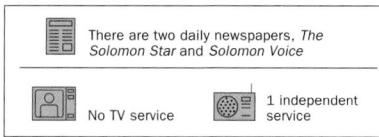

There are two daily newspapers, *The Solomon Star* and *Solomon Voice*

No TV service

1 independent service

The one radio station broadcasts in English and Pidgin. Islanders oppose TV as diluting their culture.

CRIME

Death penalty not used

150 prisoners

Crime is rising

Under the armed militias, extortion and gang-related violence have flourished, notably on Guadalcanal and Malaita.

CHRONOLOGY

Settled since before 1000 BCE by Melanesian peoples, the Solomons became a British colony in 1893.

- ❑ **1900** Britain acquires northern Solomons from Germany.
- ❑ **1942–1943** Japanese occupation.
- ❑ **1978** Independence from UK.
- ❑ **1983** Diplomatic relations with Taiwan established.
- ❑ **1998–2000** Civil conflict between Guadalcanal and Malaita islanders.

EDUCATION

School leaving age: 14

62%

Not available

Education is modeled on the British system. Tertiary students go to the University of the South Pacific in Fiji.

HEALTH

Welfare state health benefits

1 per 8719 people

Not available

The main hospital has seriously reduced services; local patients are now expected to provide their own food. Gang violence has spread on to wards.

SPENDING

GDP/cap. increase

CONSUMPTION AND SPENDING

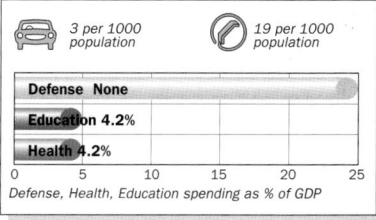

3 per 1000 population

19 per 1000 population

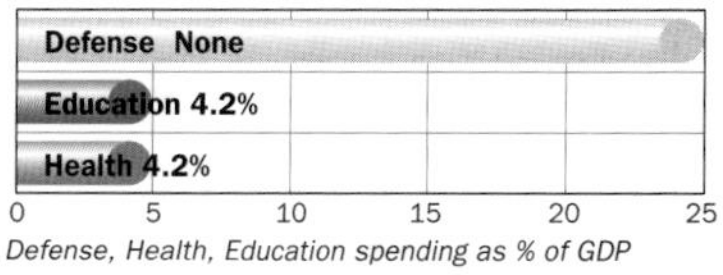
Defense None
Education 4.2%
Health 4.2%
0
5
10
15
20
25

Defense, Health, Education spending as % of GDP

Solomon Islanders in government jobs are the wealthiest group. Outlying islands are extremely poor.

WORLD RANKING

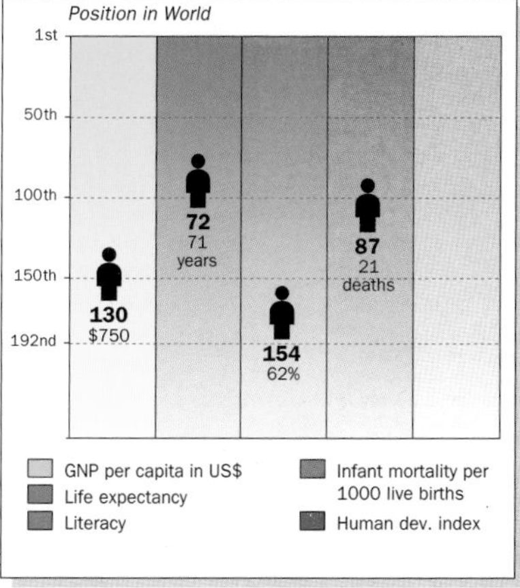
Position in World
1st
50th
100th
150th
192nd
130
$750
72
71
years
154
62%
87
21
deaths
GNP per capita in US$
Life expectancy
Literacy
Infant mortality per 1000 live births
Human dev. index

S

SOMALIA

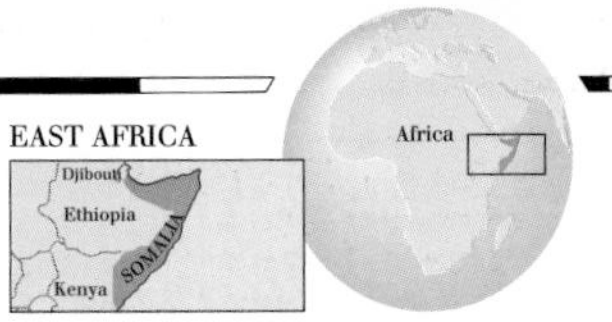
EAST AFRICA
Djibouti
Ethiopia
Kenya
SOMALIA
Africa

OFFICIAL NAME: Somali Democratic Republic **CAPITAL:** Mogadishu
POPULATION: 10.1 million **CURRENCY:** Somali shilling **OFFICIAL LANGUAGES:** Somali and Arabic

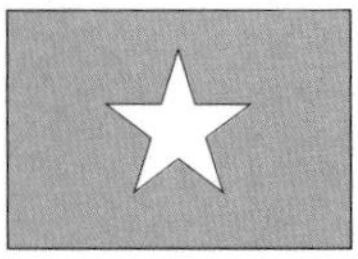

1960 | 1960 | Oct 21 | SO | +3 | +252 | .so

OCCUPYING THE HORN of Africa, Italian Somaliland and British Somaliland were united in 1960 to form an independent Somalia. Except in the more fertile south, the land is semiarid. Years of clan-based civil war have resulted in the collapse of central government, the frustration of US and UN intervention initiatives aimed at easing a huge refugee crisis, and mass starvation.

CLIMATE

Hot desert/steppe

WEATHER CHART

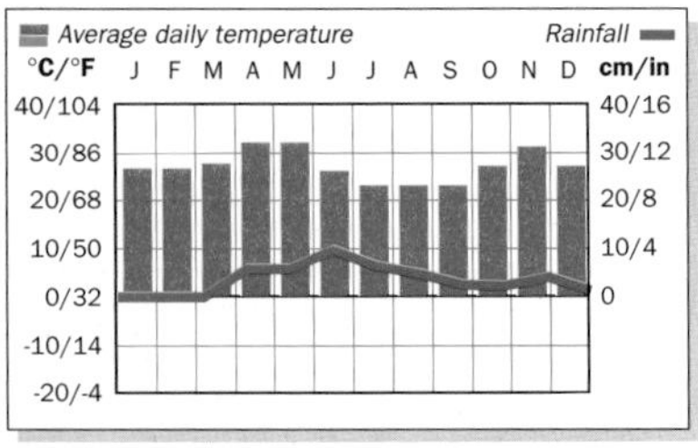
Average daily temperature
Rainfall
°C/°F
J F M A M J J A S O N D
cm/in
40/104
30/86
20/68
10/50
0/32
-10/14
-20/-4
40/16
30/12
20/8
10/4
0

Somalia is very dry. The northern coast is very hot and humid, the eastern less so. The interior has some of the world's highest mean yearly temperatures.

TRANSPORTATION

Drive on left

Mogadishu International

22 ships
11,400 grt

THE TRANSPORTATION NETWORK

2608 km (1621 miles) | None

None | None

About 50% of Somalis are nomads for whom the camel is the principal means of transportation. In 1990, the IDA agreed to repair the road network, but by 2001 no work had started on the seven-year project.

TOURISM

Visitors : Population 1:1010

10,000 visitors

No change in 1998

MAIN TOURIST ARRIVALS

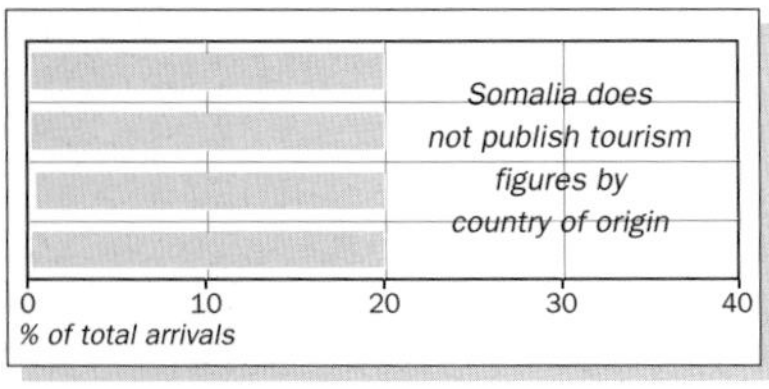
Somalia does not publish tourism figures by country of origin
0
10
20
30
40
% of total arrivals

Aid workers and foreign journalists are the only visitors. Land mines are a major hazard.

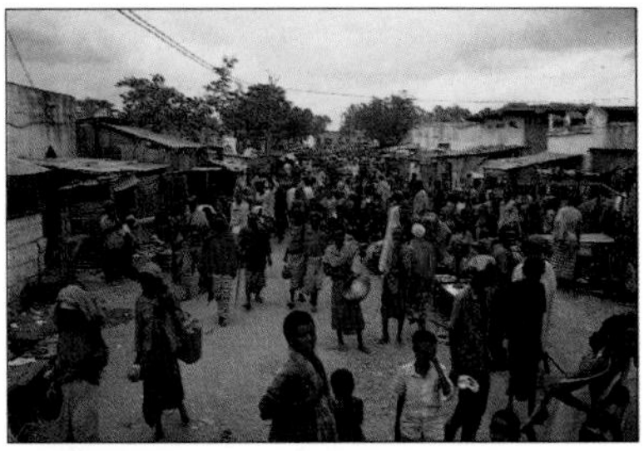

Baydhabo market. *Subsistence farming supports most people, despite chaos created by the fighting.*

PEOPLE

Pop. density low

Somali, Arabic, English, Italian

16/km² (42/mi²)

THE URBAN/RURAL POPULATION SPLIT

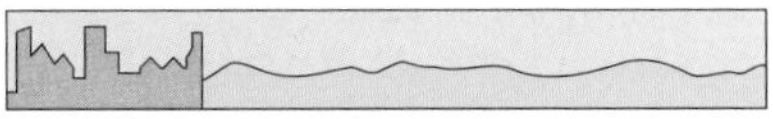
26%
74%

RELIGIOUS PERSUASION

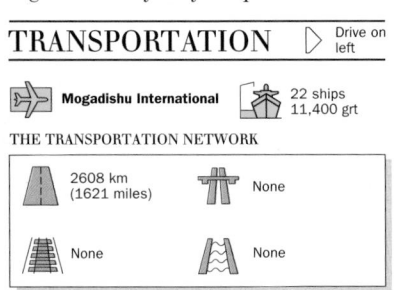

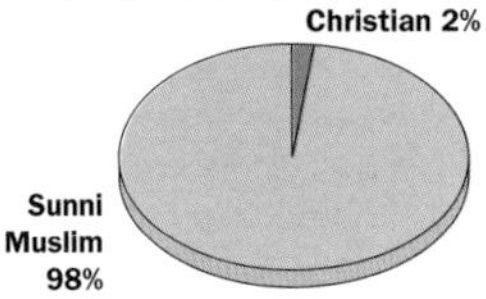
Christian 2%
Sunni Muslim 98%

The clan system is fundamental to Somalia. Shifting allegiances characterize its structure – a tendency stifled by Siad Barre's dictatorship but revived after his fall in 1991. His undermining of the traditional brokers of justice, the elders, contributed to the power vacuum that resulted in civil war, and his persecution of the Issaqs led to Somaliland's declaration of secession in 1991. However, the entire population is ethnic Somali, and national identity remains strong, shown by widespread opposition to the UN peacekeeping force.

POLITICS

No multiparty elections

1984/Uncertain

No internationally recognized head of state

AT THE LAST ELECTION

National Assembly (suspended)

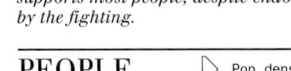

There has been no prospect of organizing new elections since the overthrow of Siad Barre. A transitional assembly was formed in 2000 on a non-party basis.

Somalia has remained in anarchy since the former dictator President Siad Barre fled in 1991. The unified state dissolved amid conflict in the south and separatism in the north.

The USA led a UN peacekeeping force to the south in 1992, but failed to loosen the grip of the warring factions. Throughout the 1990s rival warlords, including the powerful General Aideed, contended for supreme power. A National Salvation Council sank without trace in 1997.

A conference of businessmen and influential figures, held in neighboring Djibouti in 2000, established a transitional assembly and appointed former Barre minister Abdulkassim Salat Hassan as president. The new government, although warmly received in Mogadishu, was immediately rejected by most of the warlords and by the northern separatist authorities in "Somaliland" and "Puntland."

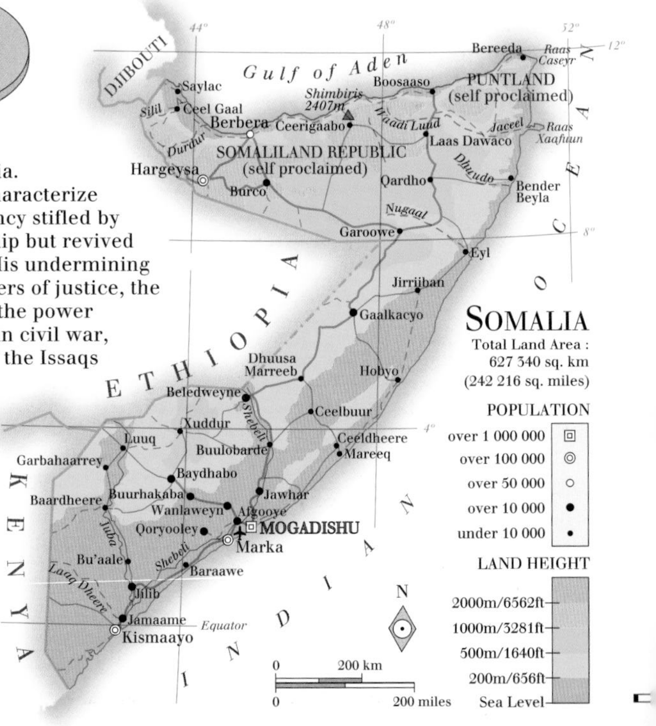
Gulf of Aden
DJIBOUTI
Saylac
Ceel Gaal
Berbera
Ceerigaabo
Shimbiris 2407m
Boosaaso
Bereeda
Raas Caseyr
PUNTLAND (self proclaimed)
Laas Dawaco
Raas Xaafuun
SOMALILAND REPUBLIC (self proclaimed)
Hargeysa
Burco
Qardho
Bender Beyla
Garoowe
Eyl
Jirriiban
Gaalkacyo
ETHIOPIA
Dhuusa Marreeb
Hobyo
Beledweyne
Ceelbuur
Xuddur
Luuq
Buulobarde
Ceeldheere
Mareeg
Garbahaarrey
Baydhabo
Jawhar
Baardheere
Buurhakaba
Wanlaweyn
Afgooye
Qoryooley
MOGADISHU
Marka
Bu'aale
Baraawe
Jilib
Jamaame
Kismaayo
Equator
KENYA
INDIAN OCEAN
SOMALIA
Total Land Area : 627 340 sq. km (242 216 sq. miles)
POPULATION
over 1 000 000
over 100 000
over 50 000
over 10 000
under 10 000
LAND HEIGHT
2000m/6562ft
1000m/3281ft
500m/1640ft
200m/656ft
Sea Level
0
200 km
200 miles
N

S

WORLD AFFAIRS

Joined UN in 1960

AL | IGAD | NAM | OAU | OIC

After the withdrawal in 1995 of the UN force, the international community appeared to abandon Somalia, although the formation of a transitional parliament in mid-2000 did receive international support. Ethiopia offered in mid-2001 to act as intermediary between the transitional government and warlords. The self-declared Somaliland Republic is pressing for international recognition.

AID

Recipient

$115m (receipts)

Up 44% in 1999

Mass starvation among the Somali population in 1991 finally prompted the UN to launch a large-scale humanitarian aid effort. In this the UN was largely effective, averting widescale starvation and restoring food security.

DEFENSE

No compulsory military service

$40m

Down 2% in 1999

Former soldiers have been urged to reenlist. Efforts to demobilize the estimated 75,000 militia began in 2000.

ECONOMICS

Not available

$835m

2555–2620 Somali shillings

SCORE CARD

- ❑ WORLD GNP RANKING........................158th
- ❑ GNP PER CAPITA $100
- ❑ BALANCE OF PAYMENTS....................$–157m
- ❑ INFLATION 81.9%
- ❑ UNEMPLOYMENT..........Widespread underemployment

STRENGTHS

Very few. Export of livestock to Arabian peninsula resumed in the north. Inflow of money from Somalis abroad. Growing market in stolen food aid.

WEAKNESSES

Every commodity, except arms, in extremely short supply. Little economic potential in the south. Destruction by drought of livestock. Mogadishu port closed by civil unrest until October 2000.

EXPORTS

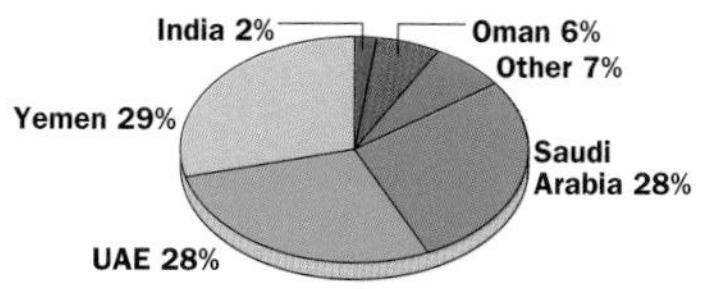
India 2%
Oman 6%
Other 7%
Yemen 29%
Saudi Arabia 28%
UAE 28%

IMPORTS

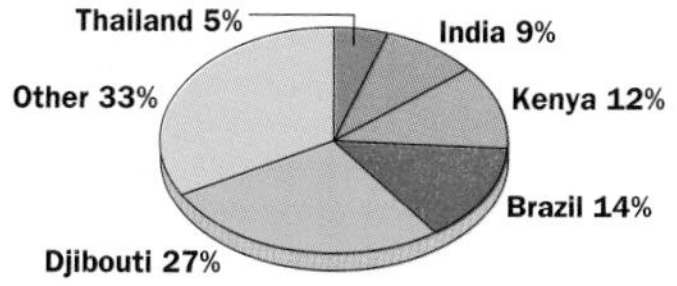
Thailand 5%
India 9%
Other 33%
Kenya 12%
Brazil 14%
Djibouti 27%

RESOURCES

Electric power 70,000 kw

15,700 tonnes

Not an oil producer

12m sheep, 11m goats, 5.8m camels, 4.5m cattle

Salt, tin, zinc, copper, gypsum, manganese, uranium, iron

Commercially exploitable minerals remain untapped. An oil exploration agreement was signed with a French oil group in February 2001.

ENVIRONMENT

Not available

0.3% partially protected

0.003 tonnes per capita

Human deprivation and starvation caused by the effects of drought and war on land and livestock outweigh all other ecological considerations.

MEDIA

TV ownership low

Daily newspaper circulation 1 per 1000 people

PUBLISHING AND BROADCAST MEDIA

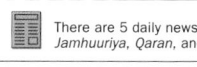

There are 5 daily newspapers, including *Jamhuuriya, Qaran,* and *Xiddigta Oktobar*

2 services: limited to the Mogadishu area

11 services: mostly political or religious

In Mogadishu there are three faction-run radio stations. Somali Television Network, an independent multichannel, multilingual service, began broadcasting in 1999. There are few newspapers, paper being in very short supply.

CRIME

Death penalty used

Somalia does not publish prison figures

Widespread breakdown in law and order since 1991

Armed clan factions (some, in remoter regions, engaged in family feuds rather than the war) and bandits rule large areas. The transitional government established a "national" police force in Mogadishu in 2001. *Sharia* (Islamic law), now the *de facto* system, is run in a makeshift fashion by elders.

EDUCATION

School leaving age: 14

24%

15,672 students

The system collapsed during the civil war. There were reports of improvised open-air schools starting up again in urban areas in 1993. Somali has been a written language only since 1972.

CHRONOLOGY

The lands of the Somalis became UK and Italian colonies in the 1880s.

- ❑ **1960** Unification at independence.
- ❑ **1964–1987** Conflict with Ethiopia over Ogaden region.
- ❑ **1969** Gen. Siad Barre takes power.
- ❑ **1991** Siad Barre ousted. Civil war and clan chaos. Mass starvation. Somaliland declares secession.
- ❑ **1992** Abortive US intervention.
- ❑ **1995** UN force withdrawn.
- ❑ **1997** Accord signed by 26 clan factions.
- ❑ **2000** National reconciliation conference appoints government; warlords dispute its authority.
- ❑ **2001** Somali Reconciliation and Restoration Council set up, with support from southern clan leaders.

HEALTH

No welfare state health benefits

1 per 25,000 people

Diarrheal, communicable, and parasitic diseases

The state-run system has collapsed entirely. A few very rudimentary facilities are run by foreign workers.

SPENDING

GDP/cap. decrease

CONSUMPTION AND SPENDING

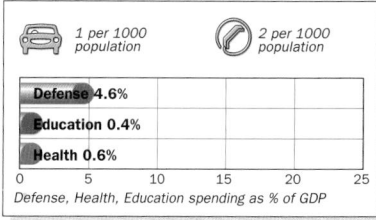

1 per 1000 population

2 per 1000 population

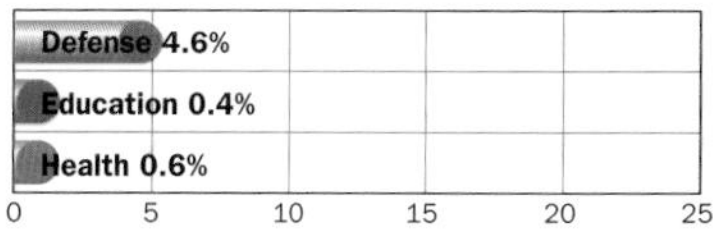
Defense 4.6%
Education 0.4%
Health 0.6%
0
5
10
15
20
25

Defense, Health, Education spending as % of GDP

Bandits and warlords gained rich pickings. Money sent by relatives living overseas is the main income for some people.

S

WORLD RANKING

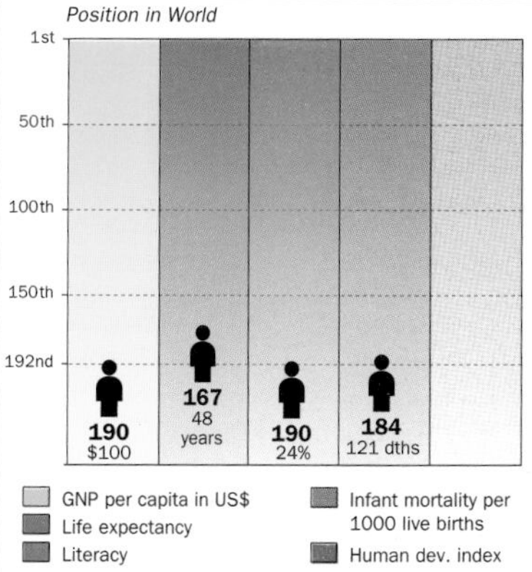
Position in World
1st
50th
100th
150th
192nd
190
$100
167
48 years
190
24%
184
121 dths
GNP per capita in US$
Life expectancy
Literacy
Infant mortality per 1000 live births
Human dev. index

SOUTH AFRICA

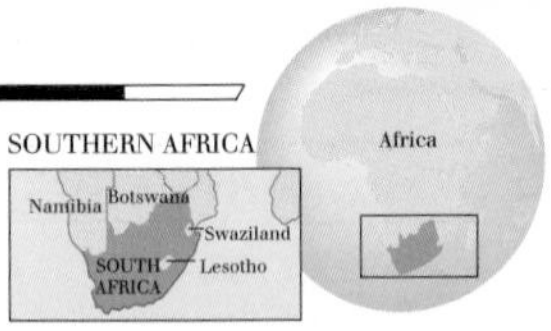
SOUTHERN AFRICA
Africa
Namibia
Botswana
Swaziland
SOUTH AFRICA
Lesotho

OFFICIAL NAME: Republic of South Africa **CAPITAL:** Pretoria
POPULATION: 40.4 million **CURRENCY:** Rand **OFFICIAL LANGUAGES:** Afrikaans and English

1934 | 1994 | April 27 | ZA | +2 | +27 | .za

RICH IN NATURAL RESOURCES, South Africa comprises a central plateau, or *veld*, bordered to the south and east by the Drakensberg Mountains. After eight decades of white minority rule, with racial segregation under the apartheid policy since 1948, South Africa held its first multiracial elections in 1994. The revolution in South Africa's politics began in 1990, when black freedom groups were legalized and the dismantling of apartheid began. The African National Congress (ANC), under Nelson Mandela and his successor Thabo Mbeki, is now the leading political movement.

***Nelson Mandela,** who became president of South Africa in April 1994.*

***Thabo Mbeki,** elected president in 1999 to succeed Mandela.*

CLIMATE

Desert/subtropical/ Mediterranean

WEATHER CHART

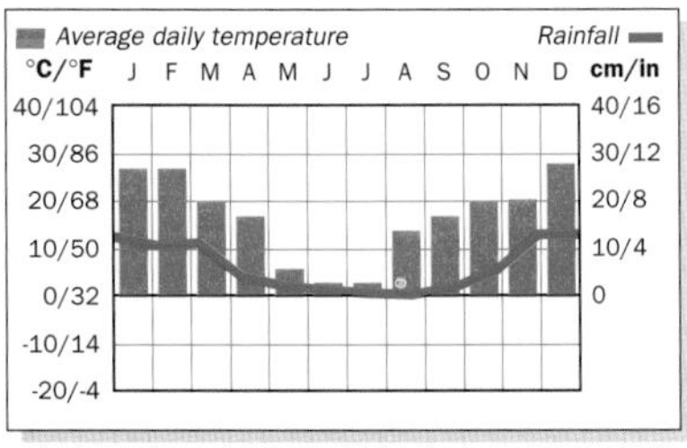
Average daily temperature
Rainfall
°C/°F
J F M A M J J A S O N D
cm/in
40/104
30/86
20/68
10/50
0/32
-10/14
-20/-4
40/16
30/12
20/8
10/4
0

Despite the moderating effects of oceans on three sides, the warm temperate climate is dry; 65% of the country has less than 50 cm (20 in) of rain a year. Drought is a periodic hazard.

TRANSPORTATION

Drive on left

Jan Smuts International, Johannesburg
11.3m passengers

192 ships
383,700 grt

THE TRANSPORTATION NETWORK

63,027 km (39,163 miles)	2032 km (1263 miles)
22,686 km (14,097 miles)	None

Priorities include expanding port capacity and cross-border rail networks such as the Maputo Corridor. In 1999 Swissair bought a 20% stake in South African Airways.

Cape Town, backed by the dramatic mountains of Cape Province.

TOURISM

Visitors : Population 1:6.7

6m visitors

No change in 2000

MAIN TOURIST ARRIVALS

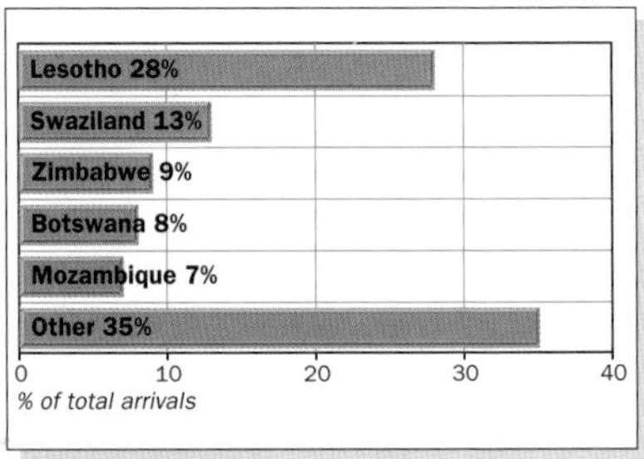
Lesotho 28%
Swaziland 13%
Zimbabwe 9%
Botswana 8%
Mozambique 7%
Other 35%
0
10
20
30
40
% of total arrivals

South Africa has huge tourist potential, with attractions ranging from beaches to mountains, from prize-winning vineyards to world renowned wildlife reserves. The enormous Kruger National Park boasts 137 species of mammal and 450 species of bird. Annual visitor numbers increased throughout the 1990s, but tourism is still recovering from its isolation during the apartheid era. Today, the key constraint on growth is rising crime. Studies suggest that by 2005 tourism could create an additional 450,000 jobs and contribute 10% toward GDP (compared with 4% in 1995).

PEOPLE

Pop. density low

English, Afrikaans, Zulu, Xhosa, Ndebele, Setswana, Siswati, North Sotho, South Sotho, Tsonga, Venda

33/km² (86/mi²)

THE URBAN/RURAL POPULATION SPLIT

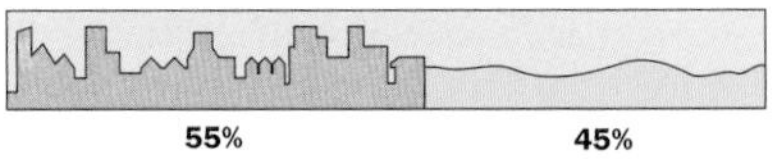
55%
45%

RELIGIOUS PERSUASION

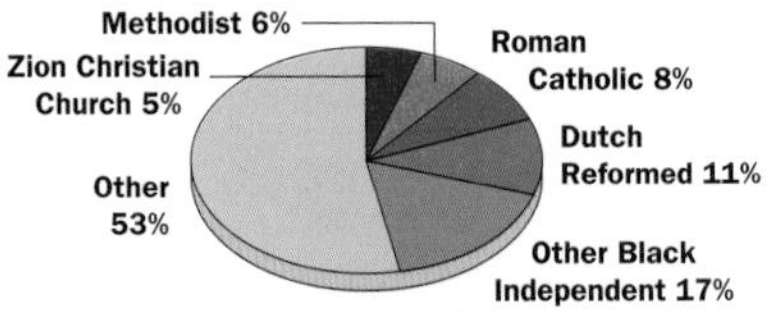
Methodist 6%
Zion Christian Church 5%
Roman Catholic 8%
Dutch Reformed 11%
Other 53%
Other Black Independent 17%

ETHNIC MAKEUP

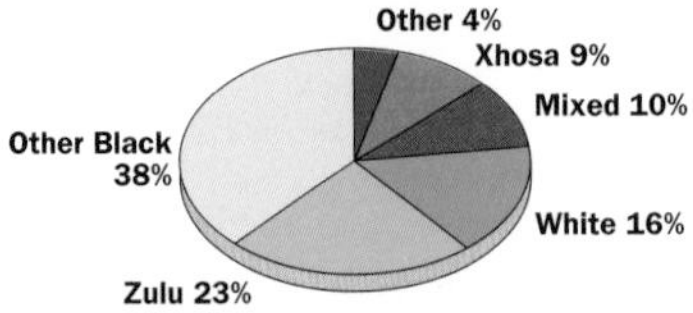
Other 4%
Xhosa 9%
Mixed 10%
Other Black 38%
White 16%
Zulu 23%

Under apartheid, South Africans were divided into racial categories: whites (Afrikaners and English-speakers), and three black groups (Coloreds, people whose descent was deemed mixed; Asians, mainly Indians; and Africans). Each category had different political, economic, and social rights, with whites enjoying the most privileges and Africans the fewest. While blacks now dominate politics, English-speaking whites continue to control the economy.

The extended family has been undermined by regulations forcing men to migrate for work, leaving their wives and children in the rural areas. A small black middle class has developed, but most black South Africans are underemployed.

The expected postapartheid ethnic conflict failed to materialize, although Inkatha has exploited feelings of Zulu identity in its quest for greater political power. An area of the Kalahari Desert was returned to a Khomani San (Bushmen) tribe in 1999.

Many women are now prominent in public life. The new constitution guarantees equality of the sexes.

POPULATION AGE BREAKDOWN

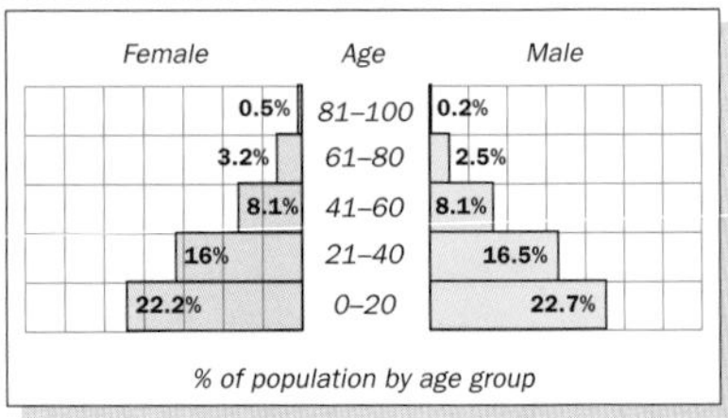
Female
Age
Male
0.5%
81–100
0.2%
3.2%
61–80
2.5%
8.1%
41–60
8.1%
16%
21–40
16.5%
22.2%
0–20
22.7%
% of population by age group

S

POLITICS

Multiparty elections

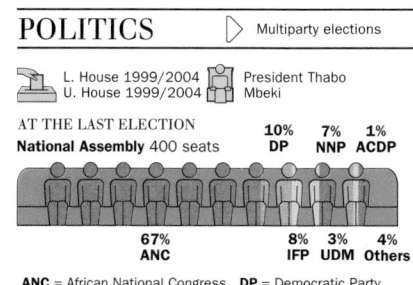

L. House 1999/2004 President Thabo
U. House 1999/2004 Mbeki

AT THE LAST ELECTION

National Assembly 400 seats

10% DP
7% NNP
1% ACDP
67% ANC
8% IFP
3% UDM
4% Others

ANC = African National Congress **DP** = Democratic Party **IFP** = Inkatha Freedom Party **NNP** = New National Party **UDM** = United Democratic Movement **ACDP** = African Christian Democratic Party

National Council of Provinces 90 seats

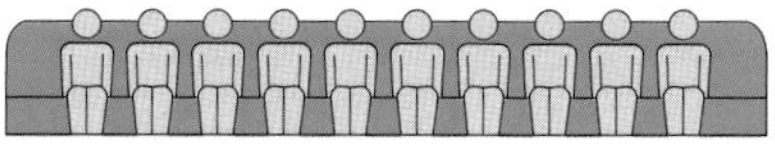

10 members are elected to the National Council of Provinces by each of the nine provincial legislatures.

South Africa became a multiracial democracy following elections in 1994.

MAIN POLITICAL ISSUES

Maintaining unity

In April 1994, South Africa confounded the proponents of violence and ethnic division by holding peaceful elections. The ANC-dominated government, while heeding the aspirations of the black majority, has tried to avoid marginalizing minorities. To deal with the apartheid past, it mandated an innovative Truth and Reconciliation Commission (TRC). Two years of painful and sometimes controversial hearings culminated in a final report in 1998, which won praise for addressing wrongdoings on all sides.

Reconstruction and development

The government's costly Reconstruction and Development Program (RDP) aims at improving health, housing, and education, and boosting employment. Implementation is too slow for many blacks, who had hoped for immediate benefits from democratic rule, while some members of the minorities see the RDP's affirmative action as reverse discrimination.

PROFILE

The 1994 elections ended 45 years of apartheid. A new liberal constitution was adopted in 1996. The 1999 elections saw the ANC slightly increase its majority; Thabo Mbeki succeeded Nelson Mandela as president. The DP overtook the strife-ridden NNP to become the official opposition, and in 2000 the two organizations merged to form an opposition Democratic Alliance (DA). The DA took 25% of votes in local elections in December 2000, prompting predictions that South Africa is on the road to becoming a two-party state for the first time.

WORLD AFFAIRS

Joined UN in 1945

Comm | WTO | G24 | OAU | SADC

After several decades of political isolation and economic sanctions, South Africa has been welcomed back to the international fold, and rejoined the UN and the Commonwealth. It now hopes to attract international investors and to encourage the return of those who stopped investing during the 1980s. Improved relations with neighboring states and non-aligned countries are also important. South Africa joined the SADC and led continental opinion on Congo (former Zaire), Angola, and Nigeria. Former President Mandela often intervened to help resolve foreign conflicts. However, some saw his dispatch of troops to Lesotho in 1998 as bungling, unwarranted interference. Likewise, Western powers were wary of Mandela's loyalty to ANC allies during the apartheid period, such as Libya and Cuba.

SOUTH AFRICA

Total Land Area : 1 221 040 sq. km (471 443 sq. miles)

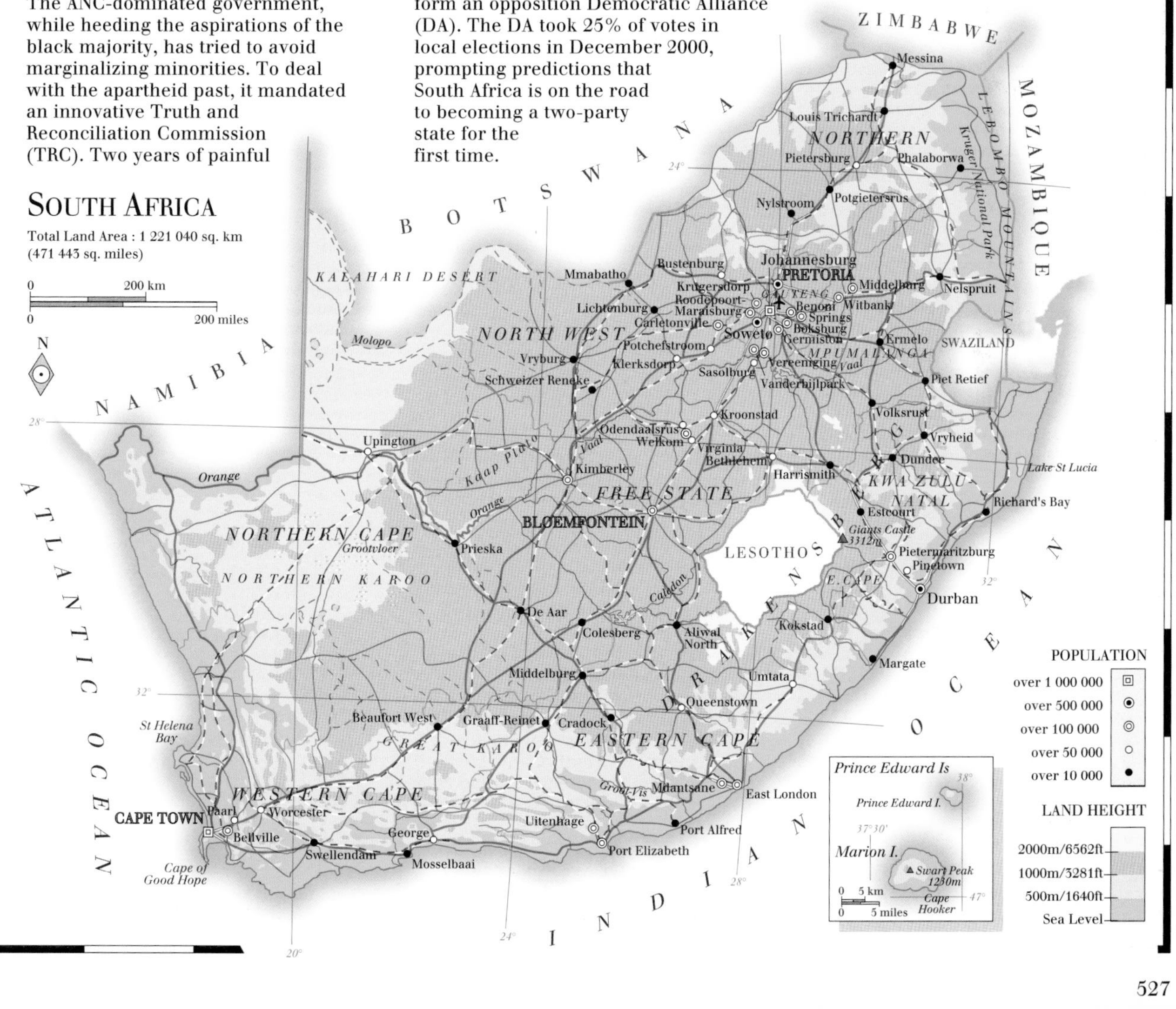
0 200 km
0 200 miles
N
ZIMBABWE
MOZAMBIQUE
BOTSWANA
NAMIBIA
ATLANTIC OCEAN
INDIAN OCEAN
LESOTHO
SWAZILAND
KALAHARI DESERT
NORTHERN
NORTH WEST
MPUMALANGA
FREE STATE
KWA ZULU-NATAL
NORTHERN CAPE
NORTHERN KAROO
EASTERN CAPE
WESTERN CAPE
GREAT KAROO
DRAKENSBERG
LEBOMBO MOUNTAINS
Kruger National Park
Messina
Louis Trichardt
Pietersburg
Phalaborwa
Potgietersrus
Nylstroom
Johannesburg
PRETORIA
Middelburg
Nelspruit
Witbank
Benoni
Springs
Boksburg
Germiston
Krugersdorp
Roodepoort-Maraisburg
Carletonville
Soweto
Vereeniging
Vanderbijlpark
Sasolburg
Rustenburg
Mmabatho
Lichtenburg
Potchefstroom
Klerksdorp
Vryburg
Schweizer Reneke
Ermelo
Piet Retief
Volksrust
Vryheid
Dundee
Kroonstad
Odendaalsrus
Welkom
Virginia
Bethlehem
Harrismith
Kimberley
BLOEMFONTEIN
Upington
Prieska
De Aar
Colesberg
Aliwal North
Kokstad
Estcourt
Giants Castle 3312m
Pietermaritzburg
Pinetown
Durban
Richard's Bay
Lake St Lucia
Margate
Umtata
Queenstown
Middelburg
Cradock
Graaff-Reinet
Beaufort West
East London
Mdantsane
Port Alfred
Port Elizabeth
Uitenhage
George
Mosselbaai
Swellendam
Worcester
Paarl
Bellville
CAPE TOWN
Cape of Good Hope
St Helena Bay
Molopo
Orange
Vaal
Kaap Plato
Caledon
Grootvloer
Groot-Vis
E. CAPE
Prince Edward Is
Prince Edward I.
Marion I.
Swart Peak 1230m
Cape Hooker
0 5 km
0 5 miles
POPULATION
over 1 000 000
over 500 000
over 100 000
over 50 000
over 10 000
LAND HEIGHT
2000m/6562ft
1000m/3281ft
500m/1640ft
Sea Level

S

AID

Recipient

$539m (receipts) | Up 5% in 1999

South Africa was denied aid during the apartheid years, particularly from the World Bank and the IMF. It now seeks financial assistance for massive reconstruction programs. In 1998 the UK pledged up to 275 million rand annually to fund customs, training, policing, and environmental measures.

CHRONOLOGY

Until 1652, what is now South Africa was peopled by Bantu-speaking groups and Bushmen. Then Dutch settlers arrived. British colonizers followed in the 18th century.

- **1910** Union of South Africa set up as British dominion; white monopoly of power formalized.
- **1912** ANC formed.
- **1934** Independence.
- **1948** NP takes power; apartheid segregationist policy introduced.
- **1958–1966** Hendrik Verwoerd prime minister. "Grand Apartheid" policy implemented.
- **1959** Pan African Congress (PAC) formed.
- **1960** Sharpeville massacre. ANC, PAC banned.
- **1961** South Africa becomes republic; leaves Commonwealth.
- **1964** Senior ANC leader Nelson Mandela jailed.
- **1976** Soweto uprisings by black students; hundreds killed.
- **1978** P. W. Botha in office.
- **1984** New constitution: Indians and Coloreds get some representation. Growing black opposition.
- **1985** State of emergency introduced. International sanctions.
- **1989** F. W. De Klerk replaces Botha as president. Elections underline white conservative hostility to change.
- **1990** De Klerk legalizes ANC and PAC; frees Nelson Mandela.
- **1990–1993** International sanctions gradually withdrawn.
- **1991** Convention for a Democratic South Africa (CODESA) starts work.
- **1992** De Klerk wins whites-only referendum.
- **1993** Mandela and De Klerk win Nobel Peace Prize.
- **1994** Multiracial elections won by ANC; Mandela president.
- **1996** TRC begins work.
- **1997** New constitution takes effect.
- **1998** TRC report condemns both apartheid crimes and ANC excesses.
- **1999** ANC election victory; Thabo Mbeki succeeds Mandela as president.
- **2000** DA wins nearly 25% of votes in local elections.

DEFENSE

No compulsory military service

$1.76bn | Down 8% in 1999

SOUTH AFRICAN ARMED FORCES

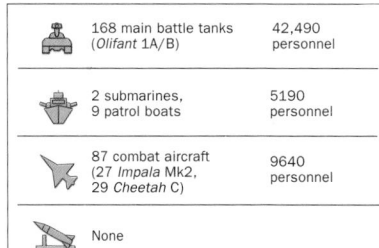

168 main battle tanks (*Olifant* 1A/B)	42,490 personnel
2 submarines, 9 patrol boats	5190 personnel
87 combat aircraft (27 *Impala* Mk2, 29 *Cheetah* C)	9640 personnel
None	

Post-apartheid South Africa's creation of a truly national defense force seems almost miraculous, as it fuses together once bitter enemies: soldiers from the old white-run army, and guerrillas from the liberation groups.

However, swingeing cuts in defense spending were allegedly hampering the army's ability to defend the nation's borders. Cuts particularly damaged the navy. A 29 billion rand arms procurement program, announced in late 1998 satisfied some critics, but others chastised the government for its "unwise" spending priorities.

In 1998 South African troops (controversially) helped quell unrest in neighboring Lesotho.

Sanctions encouraged a major arms industry, making South Africa the world's 12th-largest arms exporter.

ECONOMICS

Inflation 10.2% p.a. (1990–1999)

$134bn | 6.158–7.570 rand

SCORE CARD

World GNP Ranking	28th
GNP per Capita	$3170
Balance of Payments	$-464m
Inflation	5.2%
Unemployment	30%

EXPORTS

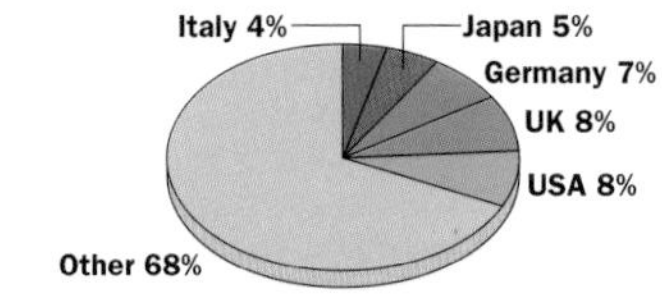

Italy 4%
Japan 5%
Germany 7%
UK 8%
USA 8%
Other 68%

IMPORTS

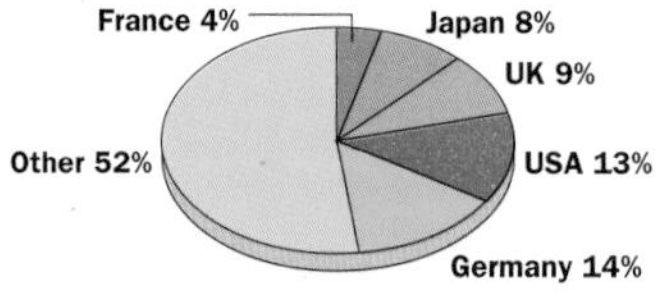

France 4%
Japan 8%
UK 9%
USA 13%
Germany 14%
Other 52%

Strengths

Africa's largest and most developed economy; highly diversified with modern infrastructure. Strong financial sector for mobilizing investment. Growing manufacturing sector. Varied resource base, particularly of strategically important minerals.

Weaknesses

Political fears deter foreign investment. Growth too low to overcome deprivation among black majority. Black unemployment growing by 2.5% a year. Emigration of skilled workers. Population boom. Falling gold price undermines many sectors.

Profile

South Africa has a large and diverse private sector, much of it controlled by multinationals. International sanctions forced the government to play a central economic role through state corporations in the 1980s. This is now being reduced in a series of privatizations. The ANC has declared its intention to work with big business in order to revivify the economy and develop the townships.

ECONOMIC PERFORMANCE INDICATOR

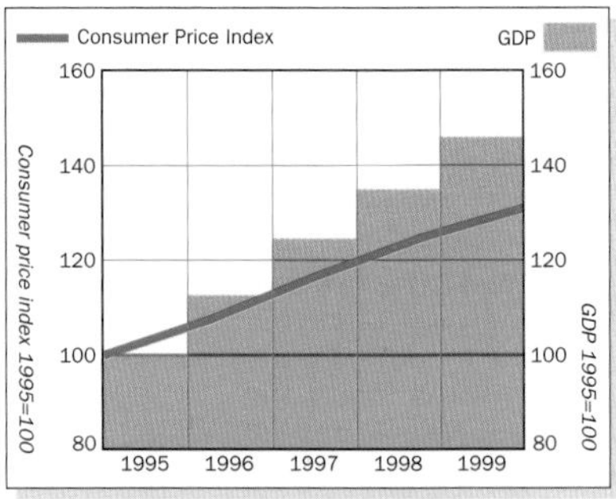

Consumer Price Index
GDP
160
140
120
100
80
Consumer price index 1995=100
GDP 1995=100
1995
1996
1997
1998
1999

SOUTH AFRICA : MAJOR BUSINESSES

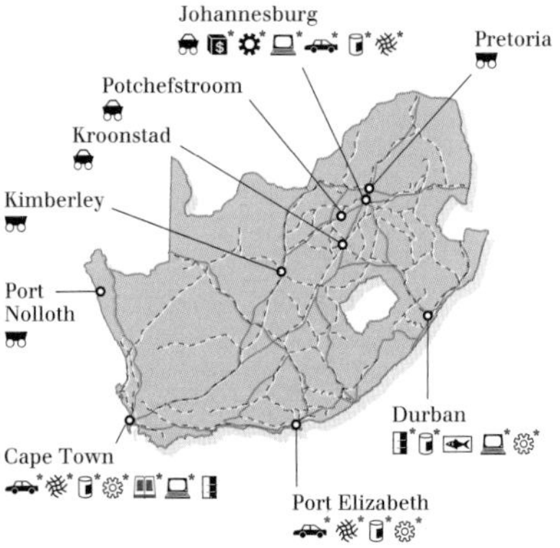

Johannesburg
Pretoria
Potchefstroom
Kroonstad
Kimberley
Port Nolloth
Durban
Cape Town
Port Elizabeth

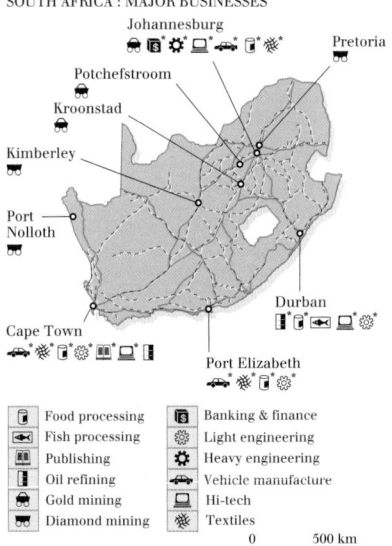

Food processing	Banking & finance
Fish processing	Light engineering
Publishing	Heavy engineering
Oil refining	Vehicle manufacture
Gold mining	Hi-tech
Diamond mining	Textiles

0 500 km / 0 500 miles

* significant multinational ownership

S

RESOURCES

Electric power 35.9m kw

513,586 tonnes

148,370 b/d (reserves 54,168,000 bbl)

28.7m sheep, 13.7m cattle, 61m chickens

Gold, coal, vanadium, vermiciline, diamonds, chromium, manganese, uranium, nickel

ELECTRICITY GENERATION

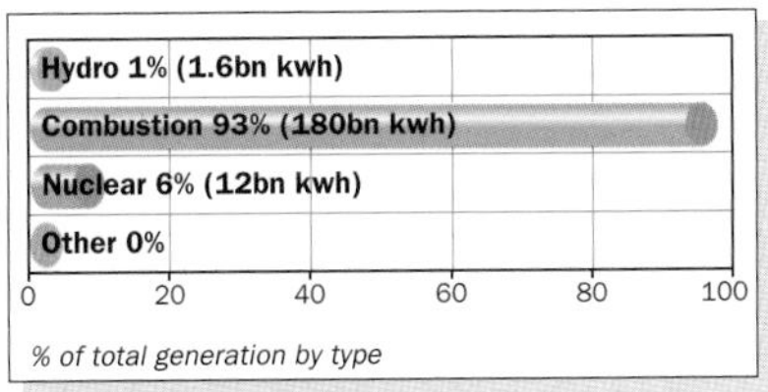
Hydro 1% (1.6bn kwh)
Combustion 93% (180bn kwh)
Nuclear 6% (12bn kwh)
Other 0%
0
20
40
60
80
100
% of total generation by type

South Africa has some of the continent's richest natural resources, in particular minerals. Its dominance of the world market in gold and diamonds helped it survive sanctions during apartheid. The falling price of gold in 2000 meant that for the first time sales of platinum group metals outstripped those of gold. South Africa is the largest single producer of manganese, chrome ore, vanadium, and vermiciline. It also produces uranium.

With no oil, South Africa pioneered the transformation of coal into oil, and otherwise uses its huge coal reserves to generate electricity. About 80% of black homes lack electricity, and the government is considering non-grid options. Agriculture is varied and provides lucrative export earnings.

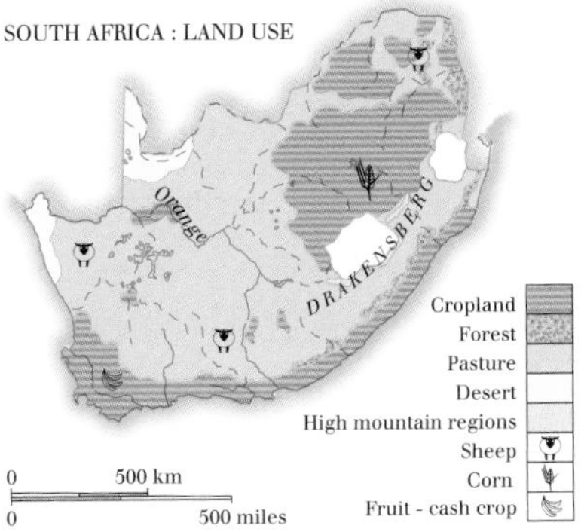
SOUTH AFRICA : LAND USE
Orange
DRAKENSBERG
Cropland
Forest
Pasture
Desert
High mountain regions
Sheep
Corn
Fruit - cash crop
0
500 km
0
500 miles

ENVIRONMENT

Sustainability rank: 45th

5% (4% partially protected)

7.9 tonnes per capita

ENVIRONMENTAL TREATIES

Yes — Yes — Yes

Yes — Yes — No

Floods and drought are familiar hazards. The main concern is protecting animal species. A plan to create the world's largest game park, with the governments of Zimbabwe and Mozambique, was announced in 2000.

MEDIA

TV ownership medium

Daily newspaper circulation 34 per 1000 people

PUBLISHING AND BROADCAST MEDIA

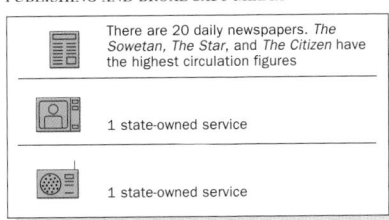

There are 20 daily newspapers. *The Sowetan, The Star,* and *The Citizen* have the highest circulation figures

1 state-owned service

1 state-owned service

A drive to combat racial stereotyping in the media was launched following a report on the subject to the Human Rights Commission in early 2000.

CRIME

Death penalty not used

160,000 prisoners

Rapid rise in violent crime

CRIME RATES

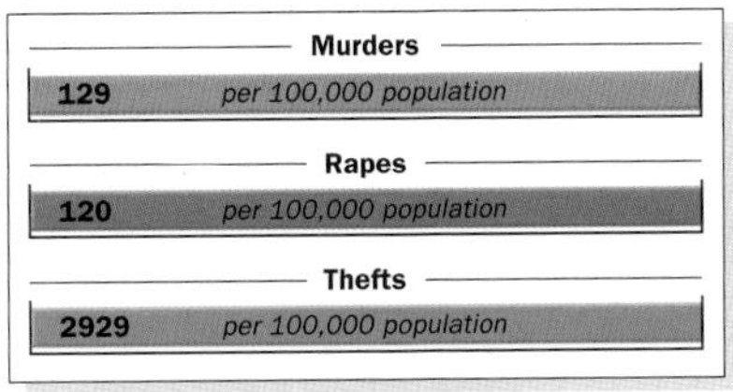
Murders
129 per 100,000 population
Rapes
120 per 100,000 population
Thefts
2929 per 100,000 population

South Africa is a dangerous country: murders occur with extreme frequency, and rape, armed robberies, and muggings are rife. Vigilanteism is a huge problem in the Cape. New gun laws were introduced in 2000. The death penalty was abolished in 1997.

EDUCATION

School leaving age: 16

85%

617,897 students

THE EDUCATION SYSTEM

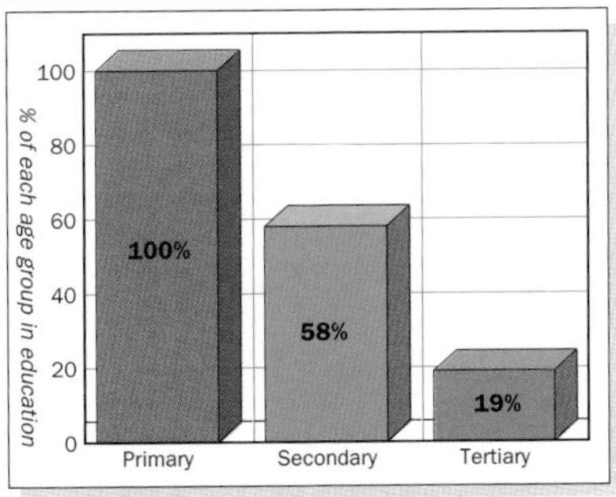
% of each age group in education
100
80
60
40
20
0
100%
58%
19%
Primary
Secondary
Tertiary

Society has to overcome the effects of school boycotts by blacks and closures during the apartheid era. In 1999, the new education minister promised to address persistent illiteracy, violence, and unequal resources. Government/ NGO cooperation provides worksite training programs and technology in schools.

HEALTH

Welfare state health benefits

1 per 1667 people

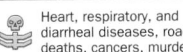

Heart, respiratory, and diarrheal diseases, road deaths, cancers, murder

Health services were formally desegregated in 1990, but equal access to care is still a distant goal. Statistics on medical provision hide a strong bias toward whites and urban areas, where 80% of doctors work. Poor provision for rural areas may explain why one in five children there die before the age of five – a rate considerably higher than the sub-Saharan average. The incidence of tuberculosis is 60 times higher than in the USA; nearly 20% of adults were carriers of HIV/AIDS in 2001. The government has won the right to buy cheaper generic drugs for AIDS sufferers.

SPENDING

GDP/cap. increase

CONSUMPTION AND SPENDING

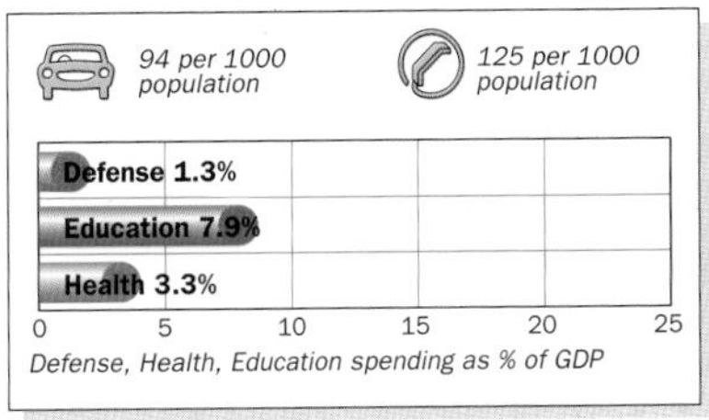
94 per 1000 population
125 per 1000 population
Defense 1.3%
Education 7.9%
Health 3.3%
0
5
10
15
20
25
Defense, Health, Education spending as % of GDP

In South Africa, the black majority forms the poorest group in society. Wealth disparities are marked. At the top, the white elite enjoys living standards similar to those of Californians. In contrast, black living conditions are among Africa's poorest. Nearly half of black adults are unemployed. In between are the mixed race and Asian communities, who enjoyed more privileges under apartheid's strict racial hierarchy. However, a small black middle class is growing slowly, with some black-owned firms doing well on the stock market.

WORLD RANKING

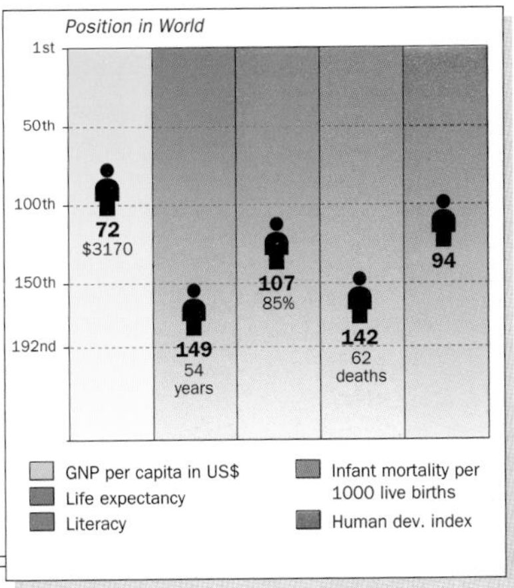
Position in World
1st
50th
100th
150th
192nd
72
$3170
149
54
years
107
85%
142
62
deaths
94
GNP per capita in US$
Life expectancy
Literacy
Infant mortality per 1000 live births
Human dev. index

S

SPAIN

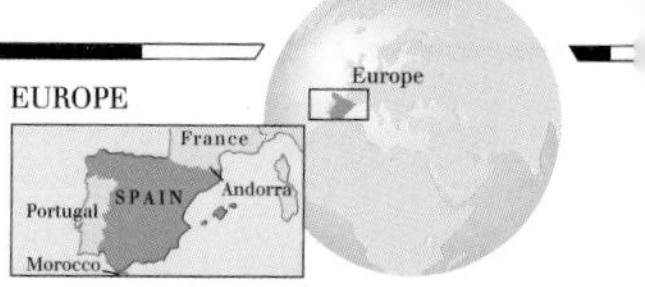
EUROPE
Europe
France
Andorra
SPAIN
Portugal
Morocco

OFFICIAL NAME: Kingdom of Spain **CAPITAL:** Madrid **POPULATION:** 39.6 million
CURRENCY: Euro (Spanish peseta until 2002) **OFFICIAL LANGUAGES:** Spanish, Galician, Basque, and Catalan

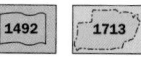

1492 | 1713 | Oct 12 | E | +1 | +34 | .es

Alcaudete, Jaén Province, in the Andalusian mountains between Granada and the River Guadalquivir. The ruined castle is Moorish.

OCCUPYING THE MAJOR PART of the Iberian peninsula in southwest Europe, Spain has both an Atlantic and a Mediterranean coast, and is dominated by a central plateau. After the death of General Franco in 1975, Spain managed a rapid and relatively peaceful transition to democracy under the supervision of King Juan Carlos I. Since EU membership in 1986, there has been an increasing devolution of power to the regions. For just over 13 years from 1982, Spain had a center-left government, but the right-of-center Popular Party has dominated since 1996.

CLIMATE

Medterranean/ maritime/mountain

WEATHER CHART

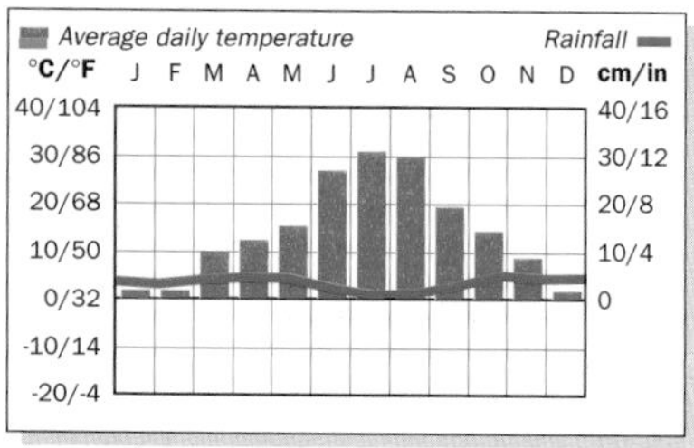
Average daily temperature
Rainfall
°C/°F
J F M A M J J A S O N D
cm/in
40/104
30/86
20/68
10/50
0/32
-10/14
-20/-4
40/16
30/12
20/8
10/4
0

The central plateau, or *meseta*, endures an extreme climate. Coastal areas are milder, and wetter in the north than in the south.

TRANSPORTATION

Drive on right

Barajas, Madrid 28m passengers

1570 ships 1.8m grt

THE TRANSPORTATION NETWORK

343,389 km (213,372 miles)

9063 km (5631 miles)

13,878 km (8624 miles)

1045 km (649 miles)

Modern communications include the AVE, a high-speed train linking Madrid and Seville. Significant expressway construction is under way in Galicia.

PEOPLE

Pop. density medium

Spanish, Catalan, Galician, Basque

79/km² (205/mi²)

THE URBAN/RURAL POPULATION SPLIT

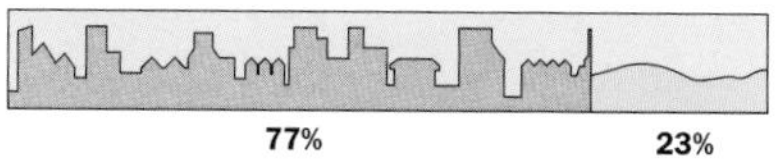
77%
23%

RELIGIOUS PERSUASION

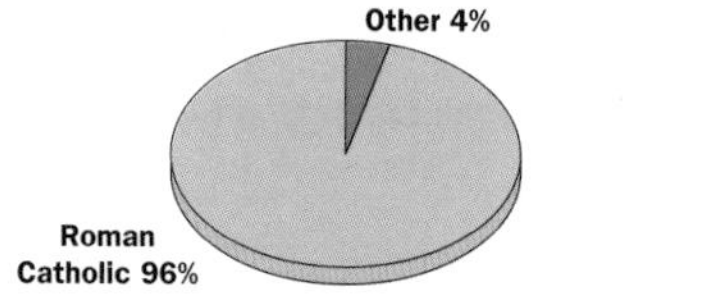
Other 4%
Roman Catholic 96%

ETHNIC MAKEUP

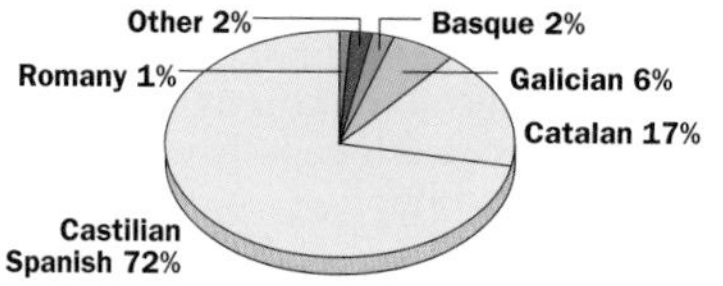
Other 2%
Basque 2%
Romany 1%
Galician 6%
Catalan 17%
Castilian Spanish 72%

POPULATION AGE BREAKDOWN

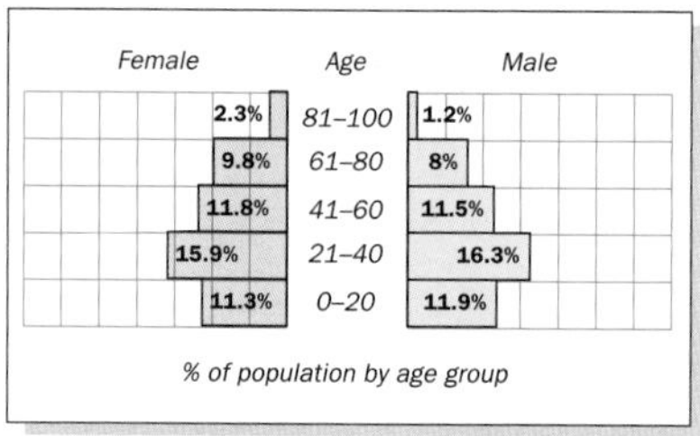
Female
Age
Male
2.3%
81–100
1.2%
9.8%
61–80
8%
11.8%
41–60
11.5%
15.9%
21–40
16.3%
11.3%
0–20
11.9%
% of population by age group

A vigorous regionalism, suppressed under Franco, now flourishes. Catalonia is an example, with Barcelona its vibrant capital. In the Basque region, the ETA separatists who fight for independence by waging a high-profile terror campaign remain in a minority.

Spain today has one of the lowest birthrates in Europe, just half that of 1975. The influence of the Roman Catholic Church on personal behavior has declined, and attitudes to sexuality are now relaxed. The divorce rate is very low, and family ties remain strong; men often live at home until their late 20s.

Economic growth from the 1970s led to a change in the composition of society. Migration from poor rural regions to the coast was associated with the arrival of job-seeking immigrants from Latin America and – especially – north Africa. A rise in racial tensions and racism has resulted from the subsequent economic downturn and competition for scarce jobs.

Spanish women are increasingly emancipated and more influential in public life, making up 27% of the deputies and senators in the Spanish parliament, and heading 30% of businesses.

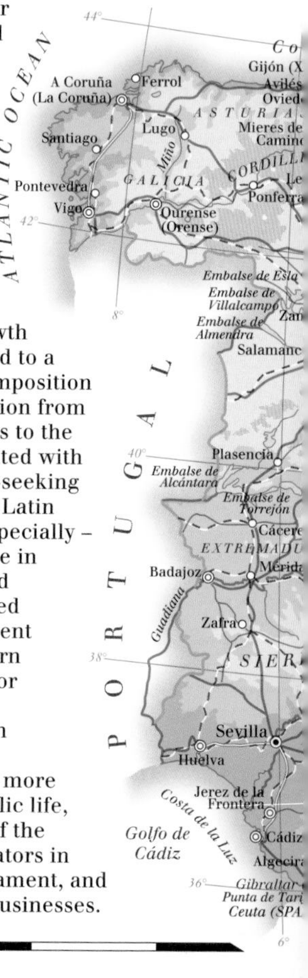
ATLANTIC OCEAN
A Coruña (La Coruña)
Ferrol
Gijón
Avilés
Oviedo
ASTURIAS
Mieres de Camino
Santiago
Lugo
Miño
GALICIA
Pontevedra
Vigo
Ourense (Orense)
Ponferrada
Embalse de Esla
Embalse de Villalcampo
Embalse de Almendra
Salamanca
PORTUGAL
Plasencia
Embalse de Alcántara
Embalse de Torrejón
Cáceres
EXTREMADURA
Badajoz
Mérida
Guadiana
Zafra
SIERRA
Sevilla
Huelva
Jerez de la Frontera
Costa de la Luz
Golfo de Cádiz
Cádiz
Algeciras
Gibraltar
Punta de Tarifa
Ceuta (SPAIN)

TOURISM

Visitors : Population 1.2:1

48.2m visitors

Up 3% in 2000

MAIN TOURIST ARRIVALS

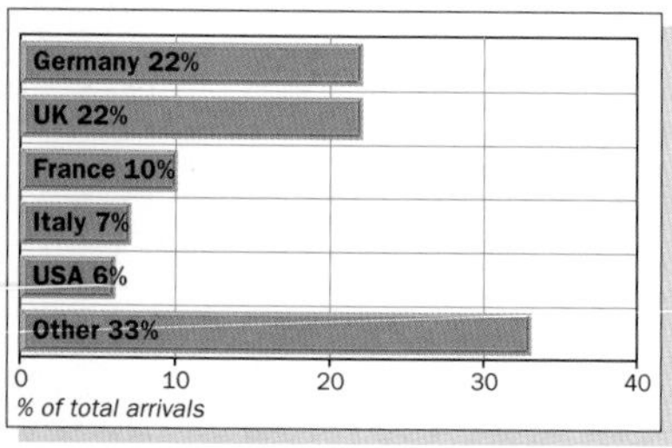
Germany 22%
UK 22%
France 10%
Italy 7%
USA 6%
Other 33%
0
10
20
30
40
% of total arrivals

Tourism earnings in 2000 topped $31 billion, with Germany and the UK still accounting for almost 50% of all arrivals. Long dominant in the vacation package sector, Spain has recently adopted marketing strategies to boost additional cultural, historical, and environmental tourism. Several areas began levying an environmental tax on tourist arrivals in 2001. The cut-price package industry has benefited from political turbulence in potential competitor countries in the Mediterranean.

POLITICS

Multiparty elections

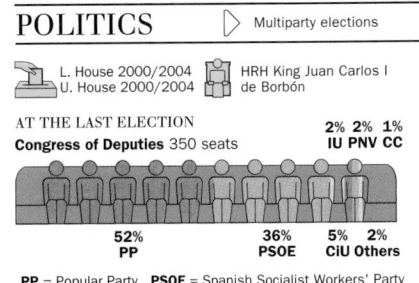

L. House 2000/2004
U. House 2000/2004

HRH King Juan Carlos I de Borbón

AT THE LAST ELECTION

Congress of Deputies 350 seats

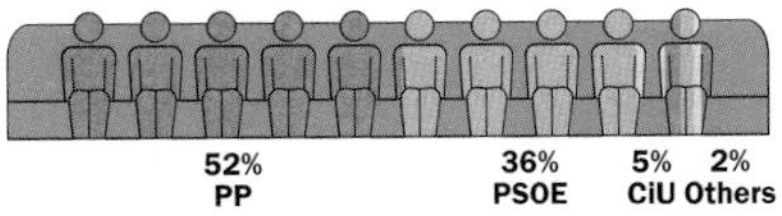
2% IU
2% PNV
1% CC
52% PP
36% PSOE
5% CiU
2% Others

PP = Popular Party **PSOE** = Spanish Socialist Workers' Party **CiU** = Convergence and Union **IU** = United Left **PNV** = Basque Nationalist Party **CC** = Canary Islands Coalition **App** = Appointed

Senate 259 seats

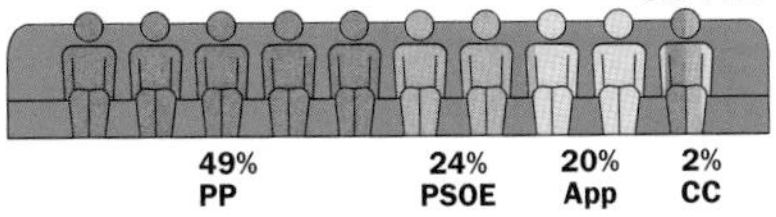
3% CiU
2% PNV
49% PP
24% PSOE
20% App
2% CC

208 members are directly elected to the Senate, and 51 appointed by autonomous communities.

Since 1978, Spain has been a semifederal multiparty parliamentary monarchy. Each region has a legislative assembly.

Main Political Issues

Increasing regionalism

Spain's 17 autonomous regions all vie for greater funds or independence from Madrid. Many have bypassed central government to borrow funds on the international money markets, and have come close to breaching their legal debt limits. In 1996 the PP government approved a new model of financing for the regions which gave them new powers for raising tax revenue. The Basque separatist movement ETA has waged a protracted violent struggle for independence, with intermittent cease-fire announcements. Renewed bomb attacks after the ending of one such cease-fire in December 1999 prompted large-scale demonstrations calling for a halt to violence.

Clean government

The PP government has suffered less from the corruption scandals which dogged the last years of its PSOE predecessor led by Felipe González. Allegations of a "dirty war" against ETA led to the PSOE interior minister later receiving a ten-year prison sentence.

Profile

The PSOE's long period in power blurred the boundaries between party and state. The *Cortes* (parliament) failed to check executive power, and political disputes were often left to the judiciary, while political corruption undermined voters' faith in Spain's political system. The PP government led by José María Aznar from 1996 benefited from being seen as a fresh start. Its relative success in running the economy helped it win a second term in 2000, despite an electoral pact between the PSOE and the United Left. Ideological issues no longer sharply divide the main parties, which hold similar views on economic policy and EU membership.

King Juan Carlos, *who became head of state on the death of Franco in 1975.*

José María Aznar, *who became prime minister in 1996.*

WORLD AFFAIRS

Joined UN in 1955

CE | NATO | OECD | OSCE | EU

Spain remains an enthusiastic member of the EU, but has been chary of enlarging the union to include central Europe, which it sees as a threat to its direct financial benefit. Elsewhere, Spain has sponsored an Ibero-American Community of Nations (a Hispanic Commonwealth). Spain is anxious to establish itself as a major international player. Former Spanish defense minister Javier Solana served a term as NATO secretary-general before being chosen in 1999 to head a new EU common foreign and security policy office in Brussels. Spain's first troop contribution to a UN peacekeeping force was for operations in the former Yugoslavia.

SPAIN
Total Land Area : 499 440 sq. km (192 834 sq. miles)
POPULATION
over 1 000 000
over 500 000
over 100 000
over 50 000
over 10 000
LAND HEIGHT
3000m/9843ft
2000m/6562ft
1000m/3281ft
500m/1640ft
Sea Level
N
0 100 km
0 100 miles
Bay of Biscay
FRANCE
PYRENEES
ANDORRA
MEDITERRANEAN SEA
Islas Baleares
Golfo de Valencia
Santander
Bilbao
Baracaldo
Irún
Donostia-San Sebastian
Pamplona (Iruña)
Vitoria
Miranda de Ebro
Burgos
Logroño
Huesca
Soria
Zaragoza
Lleida
Valladolid
Figueres
Girona (Gerona)
Terrassa
Sabadell
Mataró
Badalona
Barcelona
Tarragona
Reus
Tortosa
Segovia
MADRID
Alcalá de Henares
Leganés
Getafe
Cuenca
Teruel
Toledo
Castellón de la Plana
Paterna
Valencia
Ciudad Real
Albacete
Gandia
Benidorm
Alicante
Elda
Elche
Cieza
Murcia
Cartagena
Lorca
Linares
Andújar
Jaén
Alcaudete
Granada
Cerro de Mulhacén 3481m
Almería
Málaga
Motril
Costa del Sol
Costa Brava
Costa Daurada
Costa del Azahar
Costa Blanca
Costa Calida
Menorca
Mallorca
Palma
Eivissa
Formentera
Melilla (SPAIN)
MOROCCO
Islas Canarias
La Palma
Santa Cruz de Tenerife
La Laguna
Las Palmas
Lanzarote
Fuerteventura
Gomera
Tenerife
Hierro
Gran Canaria
0 100 km
0 100 miles

CHRONOLOGY

United under Ferdinand and Isabella in 1492, Spain became a dominant force. A long period of economic and political decline followed, however, and by the mid-19th century, Spain lagged behind many other European countries in stability and prosperity.

- ❏ **1874** Constitutional monarchy restored under Alfonso XII.
- ❏ **1879** PSOE founded.
- ❏ **1881** Trade unions legalized.
- ❏ **1885** Death of Alfonso XII.
- ❏ **1898** Defeat in war with USA results in loss of Cuba, Puerto Rico, and the Philippines.
- ❏ **1914–1918** Spain neutral in World War I.
- ❏ **1921** Spanish army routed by Berbers in Spanish Morocco.
- ❏ **1923** Coup by General Primo de Rivera accepted by King Alfonso XIII. Military dictatorship.
- ❏ **1930** Primo de Rivera dismissed by monarchy.
- ❏ **1931** Second Republic proclaimed. Alfonso XIII flees Spain.
- ❏ **1933** Center-right coalition wins general election.

S

CHRONOLOGY *continued*

- ❏ **1934** Asturias uprising quashed by army. Failure of attempt to form Catalan state.
- ❏ **1936** Popular Front wins elections. Right-wing military uprising against Republic. General Francisco Franco subsequently appointed leader.
- ❏ **1939** Franco wins civil war which claims 300,000 lives.
- ❏ **1940** Franco meets Hitler, but does not enter World War II.
- ❏ **1946** UN condemns Franco regime.
- ❏ **1948** Spain excluded from the Marshall Plan.
- ❏ **1950** UN lifts veto.
- ❏ **1953** Concordat with Vatican. Spain grants USA military bases.
- ❏ **1955** Spain joins UN.
- ❏ **1959** Stabilization Plan is basis for 1960s rapid economic growth.
- ❏ **1962** Franco government applies for eventual membership of EEC.
- ❏ **1969** Gen. Franco names Juan Carlos, grandson of Alfonso XIII, his successor.
- ❏ **1970** Spain signs preferential trade agreement with EEC.
- ❏ **1973** Basque separatists assassinate Prime Minister Carrero Blanco; replaced by Arias Navarro.
- ❏ **1975** Death of Franco. Proclamation of King Juan Carlos I.
- ❏ **1976** King appoints Adolfo Suárez as prime minister.
- ❏ **1977** First democratic elections since 1936 won by Suárez's Democratic Center Union.
- ❏ **1978** New constitution declares Spain a parliamentary monarchy.
- ❏ **1981** Leopoldo Calvo Sotelo replaces Suárez. King foils military coup. Calvo takes Spain into NATO.
- ❏ **1982** Felipe González wins landslide victory for PSOE.
- ❏ **1986** Joins European Communities. González wins referendum on keeping Spain in NATO.
- ❏ **1992** Olympic Games held in Barcelona, Expo '92 in Seville.
- ❏ **1996** PSOE loses election; José María Aznar of PP prime minister.
- ❏ **1998** Former PSOE minister and two others found guilty of involvement in Basque kidnappings.
- ❏ **1999** Introduction of euro. December, ETA ends cease-fire.
- ❏ **2000** Aznar and PP win elections.

AID

▷ Donor

$1.36bn (donations)

Down 1% in 1999

Spain has taken steps to increase grant aid after criticism that Spanish aid was of poor quality and tied to the acquisition of goods and services. Aid in 1999 represented 0.23% of GNP.

DEFENSE

▷ No compulsory military service

$7.26bn

Down 3% in 1999

A substantial, largely state-owned and commercially nonviable defense industry is subsidized for strategic reasons. Full integration of NATO military structures was approved in 1997. Defense spending has fallen in recent years, and is now well below the NATO average. National service has been abolished, with the last conscripts working out their terms of duty in the course of 2002.

SPANISH ARMED FORCES

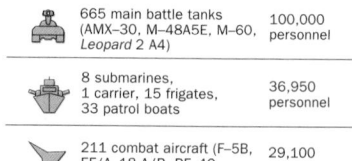

665 main battle tanks (AMX-30, M-48A5E, M-60, *Leopard* 2 A4)	100,000 personnel
8 submarines, 1 carrier, 15 frigates, 33 patrol boats	36,950 personnel
211 combat aircraft (F-5B, EF/A-18 A/B, RF-4C, *Mirage* F-1CF/BE/EE)	29,100 personnel
None	

ECONOMICS

▷ Inflation 4.1% p.a. (1990–1999)

$583.1bn

166.0–177.2 pesetas

SCORE CARD

❏ World GNP Ranking	10th
❏ GNP per Capita	$14,800
❏ Balance of Payments	$–12.62bn
❏ Inflation	2.3%
❏ Unemployment	9%

EXPORTS

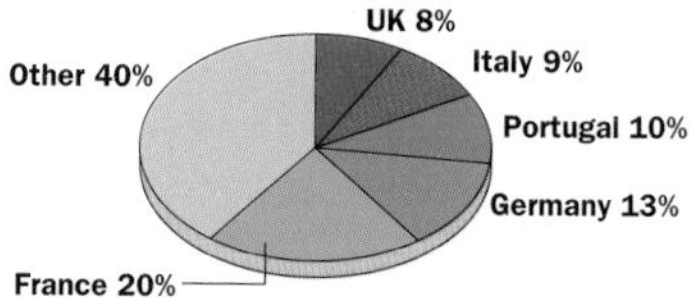

UK 8%
Italy 9%
Portugal 10%
Germany 13%
France 20%
Other 40%

IMPORTS

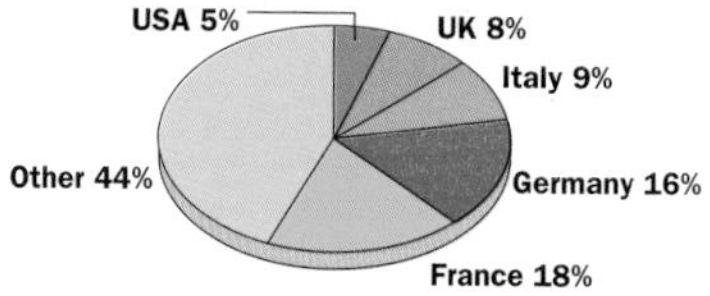

USA 5%
UK 8%
Italy 9%
Germany 16%
France 18%
Other 44%

Strengths

Spain has one of the fastest-growing OECD economies. Well-qualified labor force with relatively low labor costs. Privatization has introduced greater competition into the gas, oil refining, electricity, and telecommunications sectors.

Weaknesses

Massive foreign penetration of economy and absence of Spanish multinationals. Low investment in research and development, concentration in declining industries, and low productivity – notably in agriculture. Persistent high unemployment, although the official rate dipped below 9% in 2000 for the first time in 20 years.

Profile

Real convergence with the major European economies first became a realistic objective in the late 1980s, as Spain posted the highest investment-led output growth in the OECD. By 1991, GDP per capita stood at almost 80% of the EU average. The recession which set in in 1992 was turned around in mid-decade – accompanied by three devaluations of the peseta by a total of 18% – and strong growth has since been maintained. Spain succeeded in meeting the economic convergence criteria necessary for economic and monetary union and was among the 11 EU countries to introduce the euro from January 1999. This in turn encouraged continuing growth and high domestic demand. The government has adopted the goal of full employment by 2010.

ECONOMIC PERFORMANCE INDICATOR

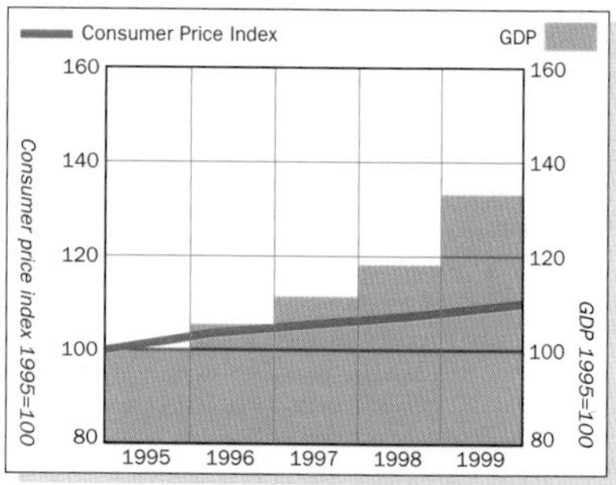

Consumer Price Index
GDP
160
140
120
100
80
Consumer price index 1995=100
GDP 1995=100
1995
1996
1997
1998
1999

SPAIN : MAJOR BUSINESSES

La Coruña
Bilbao
Zaragoza
Barcelona
Vigo
Madrid
Huelva
Valencia
Sevilla
Málaga
Cartagena
Textiles
Agribusiness
Chemicals
Shipbuilding
Vehicle manufacture
Heavy engineering
Light engineering
Fish processing
0 200 km
0 200 miles
* significant multinational ownership

S

RESOURCES

Electric power 48.7m kw

1.34m tonnes

7439 b/d (reserves 5,431,440 bbl)

23.7m sheep, 23.7m pigs, 128m chickens

Coal, oil, iron, uranium, mercury, fluorite, gypsum

ELECTRICITY GENERATION

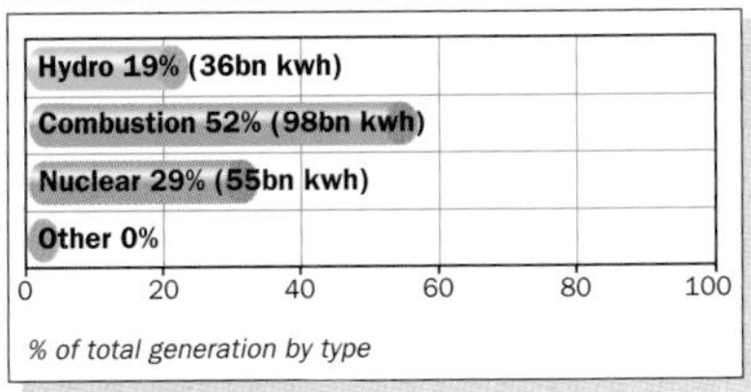
Hydro 19% (36bn kwh)
Combustion 52% (98bn kwh)
Nuclear 29% (55bn kwh)
Other 0%
0
20
40
60
80
100
% of total generation by type

Spain lacks natural resources, especially water, and is heavily dependent on imported oil and gas. Coal, mined mainly to generate industry, is a declining but still subsidized sector, concentrated in the Asturias region. Spain has one of the world's largest fishing fleets, but EU restrictions have forced cuts in catches since the 1990s.

SPAIN : LAND USE

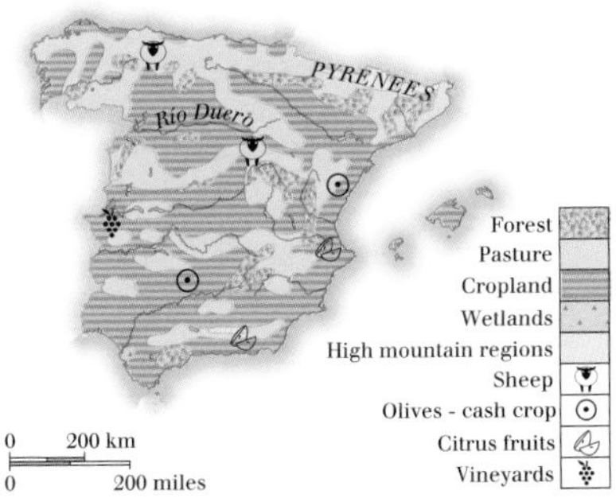
PYRENEES
Río Duero
Forest
Pasture
Cropland
Wetlands
High mountain regions
Sheep
Olives - cash crop
Citrus fruits
Vineyards
0 200 km
0 200 miles

ENVIRONMENT

Sustainability rank: 25th

8%

6.6 tonnes per capita

ENVIRONMENTAL TREATIES

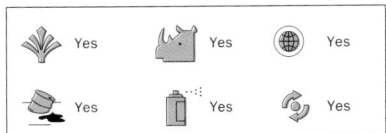

Yes · Yes · Yes

Yes · Yes · Yes

Until very recently environmental matters had little significance, but public opinion is becoming increasingly vocal. Renewable energy, although still tiny in extent, is becoming more visible, particularly with the growth of wind farms. The benefits of a national tree-planting scheme to reduce soil erosion have been offset by increasingly frequent intentional forest fires. More land has national park status than any other country in Europe. The 1998 toxic waste spill which threatened the Coto de Doñana wetlands, Europe's largest bird reserve, caused headlines worldwide. A large new dam project is threatening the habitat, and hence the survival, of Spain's last brown bears.

MEDIA

TV ownership high

Daily newspaper circulation 99 per 1000 people

PUBLISHING AND BROADCAST MEDIA

There are 87 daily newspapers. *ABC*, *El País*, *Marca*, and *El Mundo* are national.

16 state-owned services, also independent services

363 services: 13 state-owned, 350 independent

Despite the large number of daily newspapers, readership is among the lowest in Europe. Both public and private TV are popular. Radio is of a generally high standard.

CRIME

Death penalty not used

40,157 prisoners

Down 2% 1996–1998

CRIME RATES

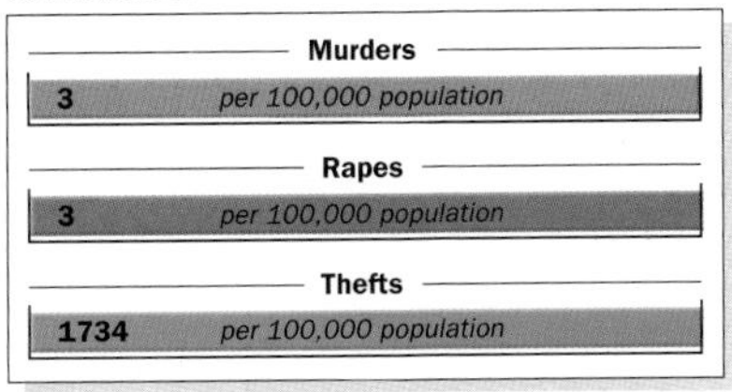
Murders
3 per 100,000 population
Rapes
3 per 100,000 population
Thefts
1734 per 100,000 population

Spain is a major crossroads in the world narcotics trade, and drugs-related crime is rising. Illegal immigration soared in 2000, with authorities in the south unable to cope with the influx.

EDUCATION

School leaving age: 16

98%

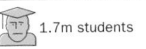

1.7m students

THE EDUCATION SYSTEM

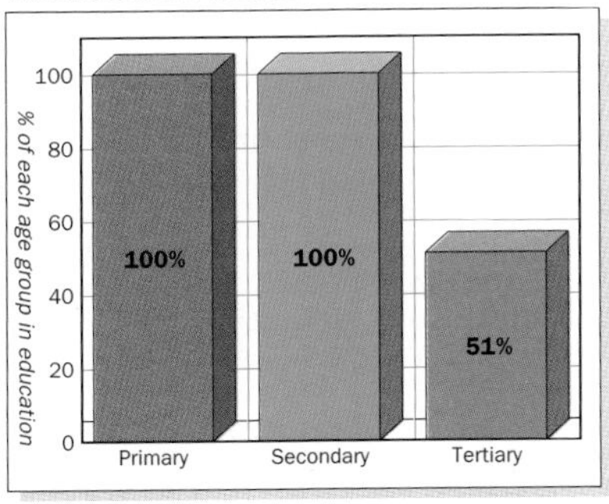
100
80
60
40
20
0
% of each age group in education
100%
100%
51%
Primary
Secondary
Tertiary

The school leaving age has increased gradually from 14 to 16 since 1990. The latest secondary education reforms, announced in 2000, offer a number of additional subjects, improvements in mathematics, philosophy, and languages, and increasing attention to information technology. Autonomous regions regulate by decree the teaching of languages other than Spanish, such as Basque or Catalan.

HEALTH

Welfare state health benefits

1 per 238 people

Heart and circulatory diseases, cancers, accidents

Public health care is of high quality and readily available. Public hospitals, although widely considered to be superior, are outnumbered by private ones. In spite of very high tobacco and alcohol consumption, Spain has a healthy population, possibly due to its Mediterranean diet. The incidence of AIDS has risen alarmingly, however, to become the highest in western Europe and higher than that in the USA.

SPENDING

GDP/cap. increase

CONSUMPTION AND SPENDING

389 per 1000 population

410 per 1000 population

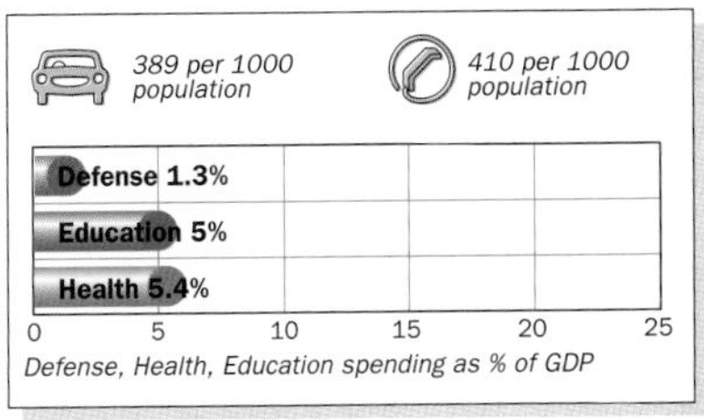
Defense 1.3%
Education 5%
Health 5.4%
0
5
10
15
20
25
Defense, Health, Education spending as % of GDP

In the late 1980s, it became fashionable in Spain to compete openly, make money, and acquire consumer goods. Rapid economic growth at this time greatly enriched the professional and managerial classes. The latter became the best-paid, in real terms, in Europe. Some media celebrities, such as the now disgraced banker Mario Conde of Banesto, rivaled soccer players in popularity. In spite of high taxes, the rich became richer and more ostentatious. Spain quickly became an important market for luxury cars and yachts; a personal bodyguard was also a status symbol. The recession of the early 1990s changed attitudes, as the unemployment rate soared to become one of the highest in Europe, although it has now begun to fall as growth has resumed.

WORLD RANKING

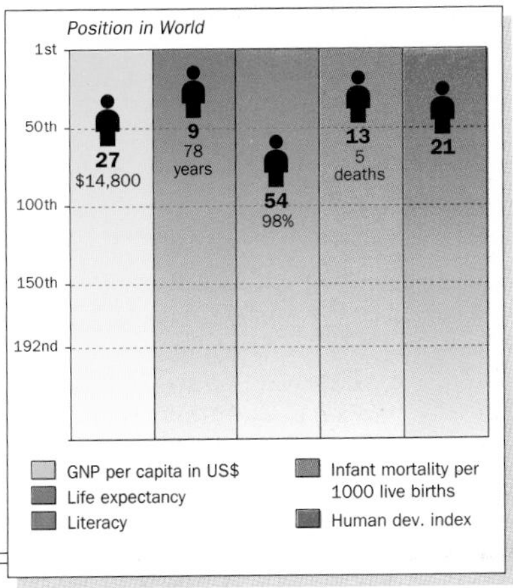
Position in World
1st
50th
100th
150th
192nd
27
$14,800
9
78
years
54
98%
13
5
deaths
21
GNP per capita in US$
Life expectancy
Literacy
Infant mortality per 1000 live births
Human dev. index

S

Sri Lanka

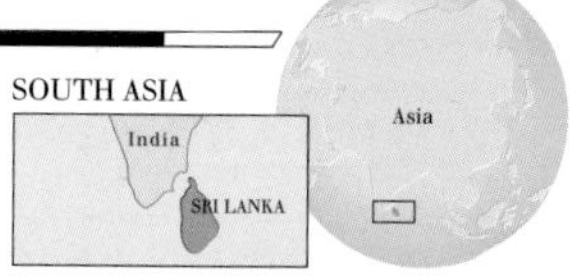
SOUTH ASIA
India
SRI LANKA
Asia

Official Name: Democratic Socialist Republic of Sri Lanka **Capital:** Colombo
Population: 18.8 million **Currency:** Sri Lanka rupee **Official Languages:** Sinhala, Tamil, and English

1948 | 1948 | Feb 4 | CL | +5.5 | +94 | .lk

SEPARATED FROM INDIA by the Palk Strait, Sri Lanka comprises one large island and several coral islets to the northwest in the Palk Strait. The main island is dominated by rugged central uplands. The fertile plains to the north are crisscrossed by rivers and bordered to the southeast by the Mahaweli River. Sri Lankan affairs are dominated by the long-standing conflict between the government and the Tamils, who are fighting for an independent state.

CLIMATE

Tropical monsoon/ equatorial

WEATHER CHART

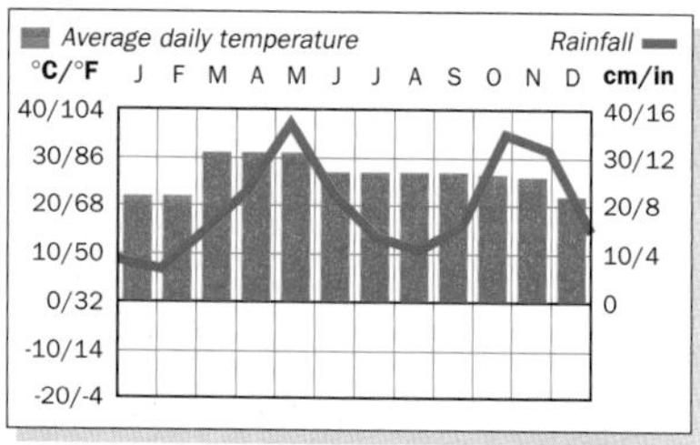
Average daily temperature
Rainfall
°C/°F
J F M A M J J A S O N D
cm/in
40/104
30/86
20/68
10/50
0/32
-10/14
-20/-4
40/16
30/12
20/8
10/4
0

The climate is tropical, with afternoon breezes on the coast and cooler air in the highlands. The northeast is driest.

TRANSPORTATION

Drive on left

Bandaranaike, Colombo 2.65m passengers

60 ships 189,200 grt

THE TRANSPORTATION NETWORK

10,721 km (6662 miles)	None
1463 km (909 miles)	430 km (267 miles)

Main roads are crowded and slow, but those to resorts are being improved. Air Lanka now flies nonstop to Europe.

TOURISM

Visitors : Population 1:47

400,000 visitors

Down 8% in 2000

MAIN TOURIST ARRIVALS

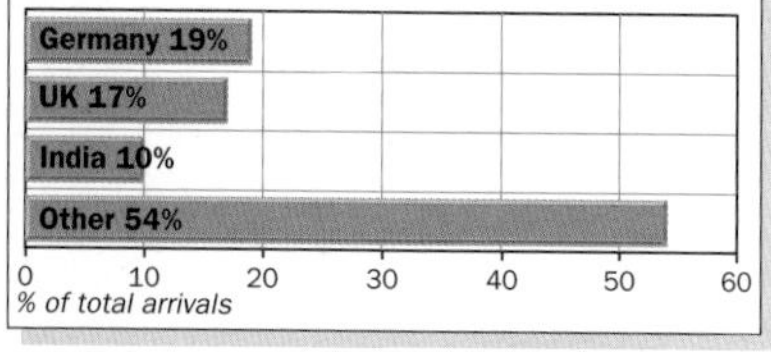
Germany 19%
UK 17%
India 10%
Other 54%
0
10
20
30
40
50
60
% of total arrivals

Sri Lanka remains a popular destination, despite the civil war. A Tamil attack in July 2001 on the military air base next to Colombo's Bandaranaike international airport threatened the lives of dozens of tourists.

PEOPLE

Pop. density high

Sinhalese, Tamil, Sinhalese-Tamil, English

290/km² (752/mi²)

THE URBAN/RURAL POPULATION SPLIT

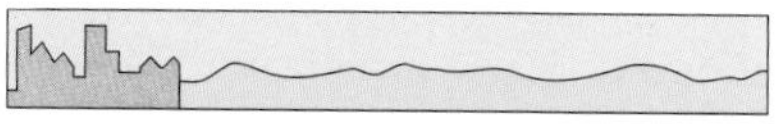
23%
77%

ETHNIC MAKEUP

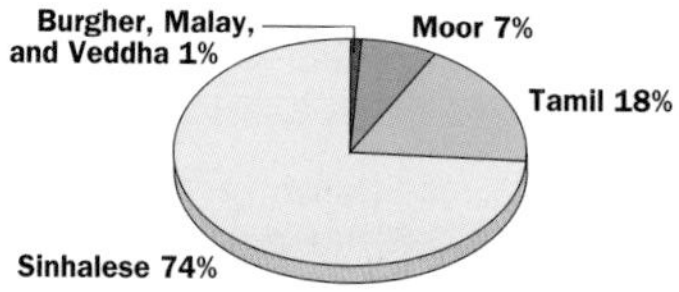
Burgher, Malay, and Veddha 1%
Moor 7%
Tamil 18%
Sinhalese 74%

Ethnic tensions between the minority Tamils and majority Sinhalese erupted into civil war in 1983. The Tamils were the minority group favored by the British colonists. When the British left, laws were passed to redress the balance by favoring the Sinhalese. The effect was to make Tamils feel sidelined, and support for secession grew. The conflict also has a religious dimension. Most Sinhalese are Buddhist, while Tamils are mainly Hindu or Muslim.

POLITICS

Multiparty elections

2000/2006

President Chandrika Bandaranaike Kumaratunga

AT THE LAST ELECTION

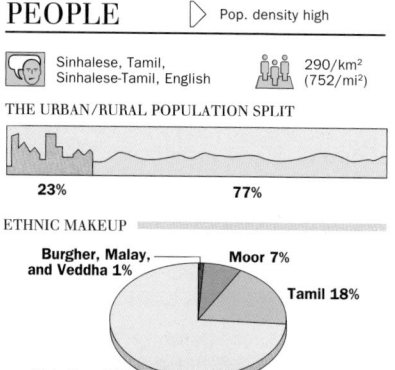

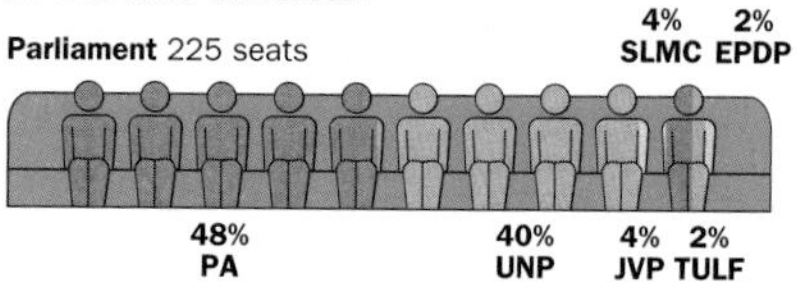
Parliament 225 seats
4% SLMC
2% EPDP
48% PA
40% UNP
4% JVP
2% TULF

PA = People's Alliance, dominated by the Sri Lanka Freedom Party (SLFP) UNP = United National Party JVP = People's Liberation Front SLMC = Sri Lanka Muslim Congress TULF = Tamil United Liberation Front EPDP = Eelam People's Democratic Party

The Tamil–Sinhalese conflict colors all political debate; a civil war in the north and east has raged since 1983. The Liberation Tigers of Tamil Eelam (LTTE or Tamil Tigers) are fighting for an independent state. Despite massive army operations, government victory remains elusive. The Tamil Tigers also pursue bombing campaigns outside the conflict area. A left-wing People's Alliance formed by Chandrika Kumaratunga has held power since 1994, despite failing to produce the promised peace. The Buddhist clergy are a powerful influence, helping to preserve Sinhalese nationalism, and opposing any federalist compromise.

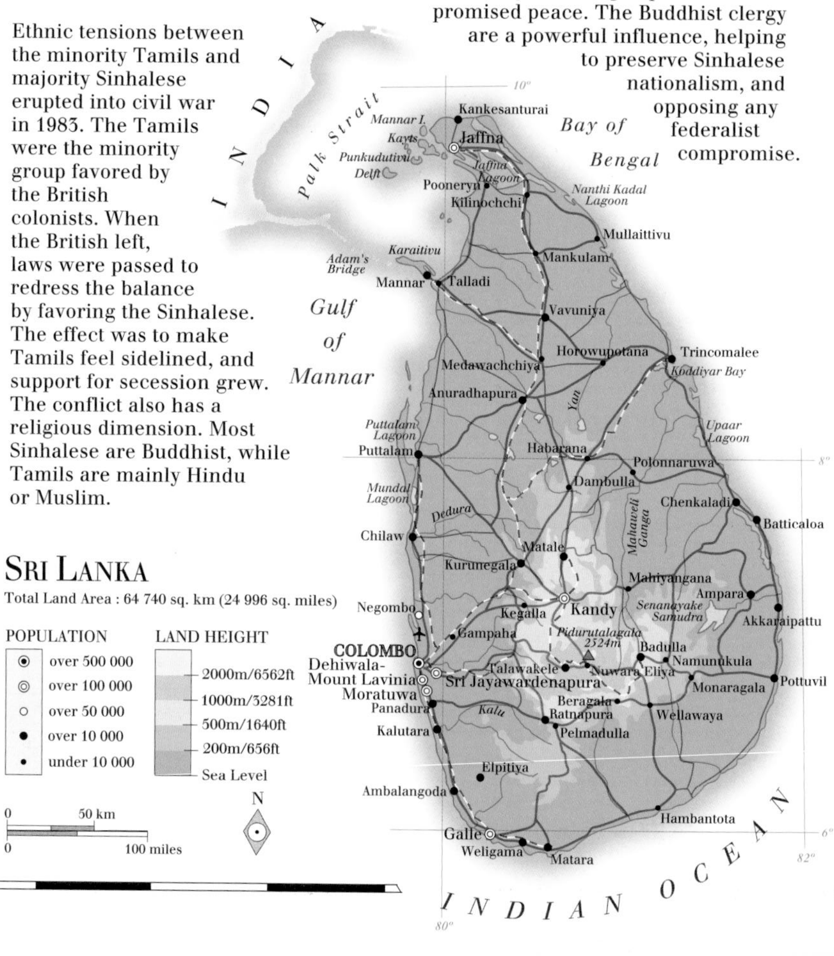
INDIA
Palk Strait
Mannar I.
Kayts
Punkudutivu
Delft
Kankesanturai
Jaffna
Jaffna Lagoon
Pooneryn
Kilinochchi
Nanthi Kadal Lagoon
Mullaittivu
Karaitivu
Adam's Bridge
Mannar
Talladi
Mankulam
Vavuniya
Gulf of Mannar
Bay of Bengal
Medawachchiya
Horowupotana
Trincomalee
Koddiyar Bay
Anuradhapura
Yan
Puttalam Lagoon
Puttalam
Upaar Lagoon
Habarana
Polonnaruwa
Dambulla
Mundal Lagoon
Chenkaladi
Dedura
Batticaloa
Chilaw
Matale
Mahaweli Ganga
Kurunegala
Mahiyangana
Ampara
Negombo
Kegalla
Kandy
Senanayake Samudra
Akkaraipattu
Gampaha
Pidurutalagala 2524m
Badulla
COLOMBO
Dehiwala-Mount Lavinia
Moratuwa
Talawakele
Sri Jayawardenapura
Nuwara Eliya
Namunukula
Monaragala
Pottuvil
Panadura
Kalu
Beragala
Ratnapura
Wellawaya
Kalutara
Pelmadulla
Elpitiya
Ambalangoda
Hambantota
Galle
Weligama
Matara
INDIAN OCEAN
10°
8°
6°
80°
82°
SRI LANKA
Total Land Area : 64 740 sq. km (24 996 sq. miles)
POPULATION
over 500 000
over 100 000
over 50 000
over 10 000
under 10 000
LAND HEIGHT
2000m/6562ft
1000m/3281ft
500m/1640ft
200m/656ft
Sea Level
0
50 km
0
100 miles
N

WORLD AFFAIRS

Joined UN in 1955

Comm | G24 | NAM | SAARC | WTO

Relations with India are paramount. However, India's role as peacemaker under the 1987 Indo-Sri Lankan accords was fiercely resisted by the LTTE, and India was forced to withdraw its peacekeeping troops. In 1992 LTTE militants assassinated the then Indian prime minister Rajiv Gandhi.

AID

Recipient

$251m (receipts)

Down 49% in 1999

The president has responded positively to Western aid donors seeking improvements in Sri Lanka's human rights record.

DEFENSE

No compulsory military service

$807m

Up 40% in 2000

Defense spending increased by over 40% in 2000, and a recruitment drive aimed for 10,000 new troops. Defeating the LTTE is the overwhelming concern.

ECONOMICS

Inflation 9.4% p.a. (1990–1999)

$15.6bn

71.2–82.7 Sri Lanka rupees

SCORE CARD

❑ World GNP Ranking	76th
❑ GNP per Capita	$820
❑ Balance of Payments	$-288m
❑ Inflation	4.7%
❑ Unemployment	11%

Strengths

World's largest tea exporter. Export processing zones and state privatization programs attracting foreign investment. The left-wing government of President Kumaratunga has continued the sale of state assets.

Weaknesses

Civil war is a drain on government funds, and deters investors and many tourists.

EXPORTS

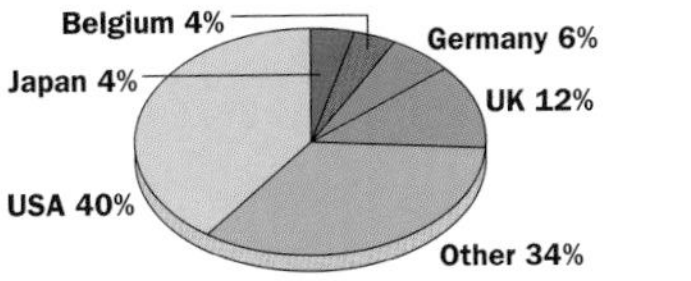
Belgium 4%
Germany 6%
Japan 4%
UK 12%
USA 40%
Other 34%

IMPORTS

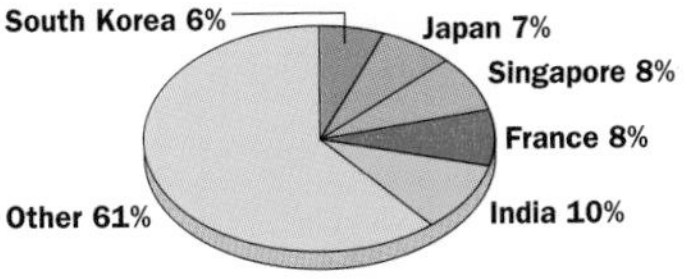
South Korea 6%
Japan 7%
Singapore 8%
France 8%
Other 61%
India 10%

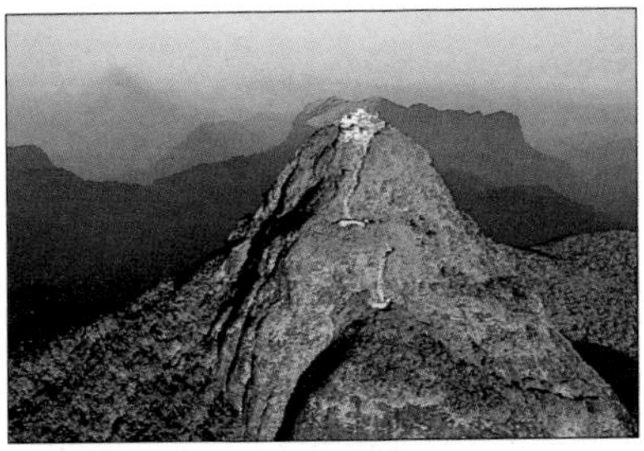

***Adam's peak in mountainous** central Sri Lanka is a famous religious site with a Buddhist shrine at the summit.*

RESOURCES

Electric power 1.7m kw

247,000 tonnes

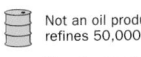

Not an oil producer; refines 50,000 b/d

1.62m cattle, 727,700 buffaloes, 9.92m chickens

Gemstones, graphite, iron, monazite, uranium, ilmenite, clay

Sri Lanka has to import all its oil. Hydropower supplies 75% of electricity; droughts are frequent and supplies can be erratic. Sri Lanka is keen to diversify power sources and is turning to coal-powered generation.

ENVIRONMENT

Sustainability rank: 51st

13% (4% partially protected)

0.4 tonnes per capita

Sri Lanka has successfully promoted national parks. Their development is opposed by the Veddha people, who have traditionally occupied such land.

MEDIA

TV ownership medium

Daily newspaper circulation 29 per 1000 people

PUBLISHING AND BROADCAST MEDIA

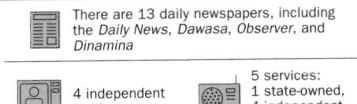

There are 13 daily newspapers, including the *Daily News, Dawasa, Observer*, and *Dinamina*

4 independent services

5 services: 1 state-owned, 4 independent

Press censorship was imposed in 1995 to control war reporting by local news agencies. Since 1998 foreign journalists have faced similar restrictions.

CRIME

Death penalty not used

14,128 prisoners

Up 52% 1992–1996

Both the army and the LTTE have been accused of human rights abuses. The civil war has claimed at least 30,000 lives since 1983. LTTE members carry cyanide capsules in case of arrest.

EDUCATION

School leaving age: 14

92%

63,660 students

Sri Lanka has the highest literacy rate of any developing nation. Many Sri Lankans attend US universities.

CHRONOLOGY

Sri Lanka has been inhabited by the Tamils and Sinhalese since before the 6th century. Named Ceylon under the British Empire, the island became independent in 1948.

- ❑ **1948** Indian Tamil workers stripped of suffrage and citizenship rights.
- ❑ **1956** SLFP wins election, promotes Sinhalese language.
- ❑ **1972** Name changed to Sri Lanka.
- ❑ **1983** Tamil Tigers begin civil war.
- ❑ **1993** President Premadasa killed.
- ❑ **1994** Left-wing PA wins election; Chandrika Kumaratunga president.
- ❑ **1995–1996** Collapse of peace talks, civil war resumes.
- ❑ **1999** Kumaratunga survives assassination attempt; reelected.
- ❑ **2000** Sirimavo Bandaranaike, world's first woman prime minister, dies.

HEALTH

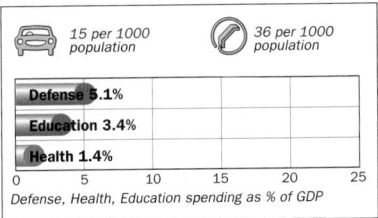

Welfare state health benefits

1 per 5000 people

Heart attacks, cancers, pneumonia, strokes

Years of high spending on health have resulted in an accessible, fee-free system. Ayurvedic medicine is popular.

SPENDING

GDP/cap. increase

CONSUMPTION AND SPENDING

15 per 1000 population

36 per 1000 population

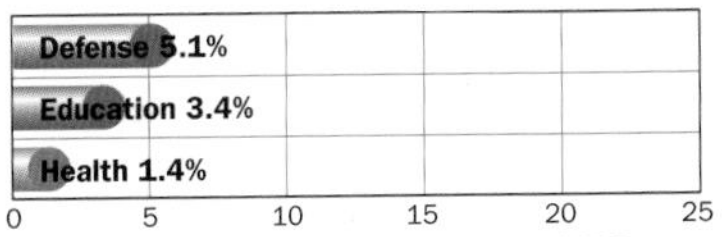
Defense 5.1%
Education 3.4%
Health 1.4%
0
5
10
15
20
25

Defense, Health, Education spending as % of GDP

Economic growth has created a new class of wealthy Sinhalese. Tamil tea workers are the poorest group.

WORLD RANKING

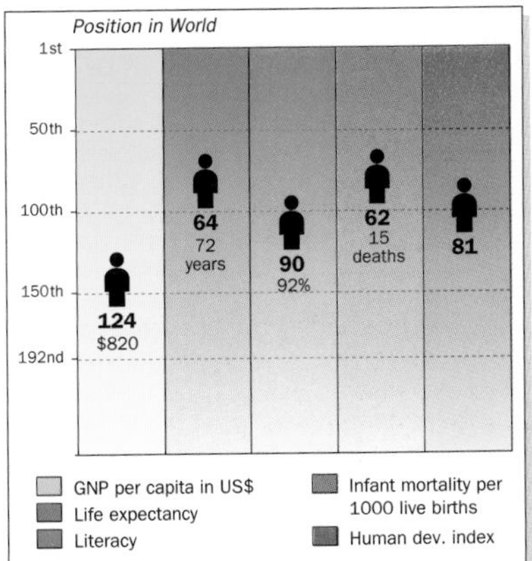
Position in World
1st
50th
100th
150th
192nd
124
$820
64
72 years
90
92%
62
15 deaths
81
GNP per capita in US$
Life expectancy
Literacy
Infant mortality per 1000 live births
Human dev. index

S

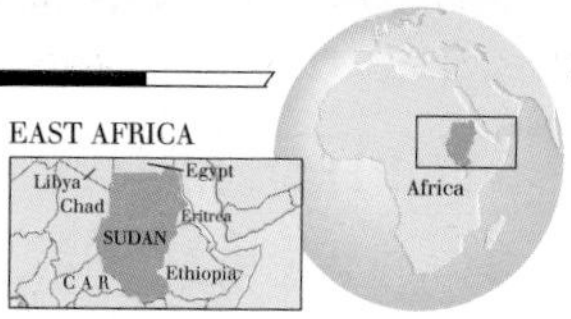
EAST AFRICA
Libya
Egypt
Chad
Eritrea
SUDAN
C.A.R.
Ethiopia
Africa

SUDAN

OFFICIAL NAME: Republic of Sudan **CAPITAL:** Khartoum **POPULATION:** 29.5 million
CURRENCY: Sudanese pound or dinar **OFFICIAL LANGUAGE:** Arabic

1956 | 1956 | Jan 1 | SUD | +2 | +249 | .sd

BORDERED BY THE RED SEA, Sudan is the largest country in Africa. Its landscape changes from desert in the north to lush tropical in the south, with grassy plains and swamps in the center. Tensions between the Arab north and African south have led to two civil wars since independence from British and Egyptian rule in 1956. The second of these conflicts remains unresolved. In 1989, an army coup installed a military Islamic fundamentalist regime.

Camel caravan in the dry north. *Periodic drought coupled with war disruption mean that Sudan requires large amounts of food aid.*

CLIMATE

Hot desert/steppe/ tropical

WEATHER CHART

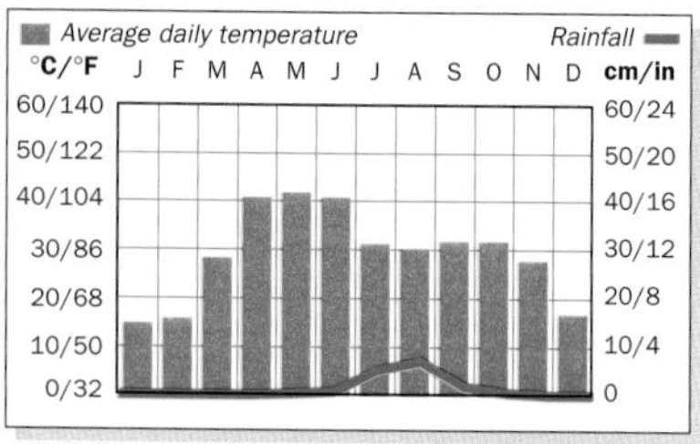
Average daily temperature
Rainfall
°C/°F
J F M A M J J A S O N D
cm/in
60/140
50/122
40/104
30/86
20/68
10/50
0/32
60/24
50/20
40/16
30/12
20/8
10/4
0

Sudan's northern half is hot arid desert with constant dry winds. The rest has a rainy season varying from two months in the center to eight in the south.

TRANSPORTATION

Drive on right

Khartoum International

19 ships 43,078 grt

THE TRANSPORTATION NETWORK

4320 km (2684 miles)	None
4595 km (2855 miles)	5310 km (3299 miles)

The Port Sudan–Khartoum railroad and road are Sudan's most important links. There are few other roads, but Iran is financing a north–southl highway. Civil war has stopped all Nile shipping.

TOURISM

Visitors : Population 1:590

50,000 visitors

Up 28% in 2000

MAIN TOURIST ARRIVALS

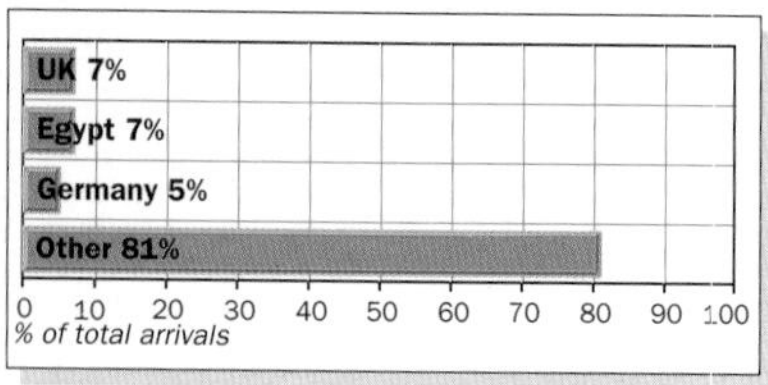
UK 7%
Egypt 7%
Germany 5%
Other 81%
0 10 20 30 40 50 60 70 80 90 100
% of total arrivals

The civil war means that Sudan has very few tourists. Visitors are mostly aid workers or on business.

PEOPLE

Pop. density low

Arabic, Dinka, Nuer, Nubian, Beja, Zande, Bari, Fur, Shilluk, Lotuko

12/km² (32/mi²)

THE URBAN/RURAL POPULATION SPLIT

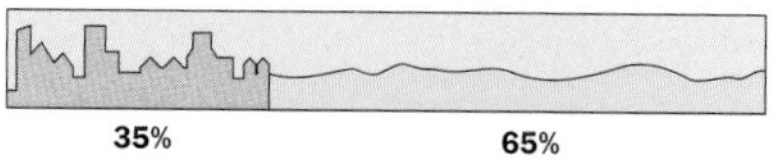
35%
65%

RELIGIOUS PERSUASION

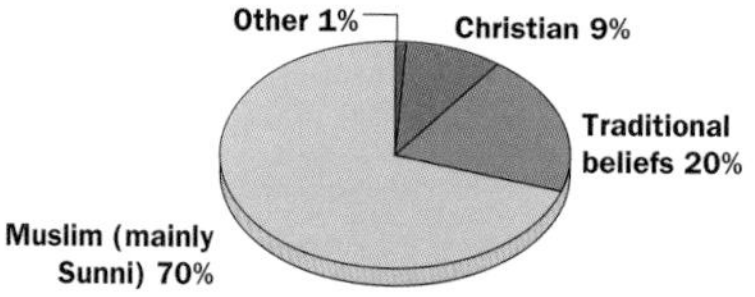
Other 1%
Christian 9%
Traditional beliefs 20%
Muslim (mainly Sunni) 70%

Sudan has a large number of ethnic and linguistic groups. About two million Sudanese are nomads. The major social division, however, is between the Arabized Muslims in the north and the mostly African, largely animist or Christian population in the south. Attempts to impose Arab and Islamic values throughout Sudan have been the root cause of the civil war that has ravaged the south since 1983. However, the rebels have now split into two factions, pitting southern Sudan's small ethnic groups against the Dinka, the south's largest tribe. There are some non-Arab groups in the north and the densely populated Darfur region. Women not wearing Islamic dress can suffer harassment or even public flogging.

POLITICS

No multiparty elections

2000/2004

President Omar Hassan Ahmad al-Bashir

AT THE LAST ELECTION

National Assembly 400 seats

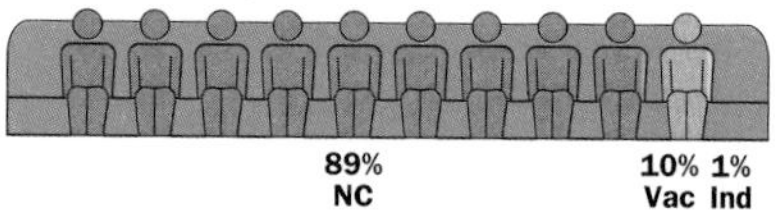
89% NC
10% Vac
1% Ind

NC = National Congress supporters Vac = Vacant
Ind = Independents

Having sidelined his main Islamist political rival, former NC leader Hassan al-Turabi, General Omar Bashir called a national reconciliation conference in mid-2000. Elections in December, under the 1999 constitution allowing "political associations," were boycotted by the opposition, and returned Bashir and his NC bloc to power. The willingness of the Sudanese People's Liberation Army (SPLA) to enter peace talks raised the possibility of an end to nearly 20 years of civil conflict between Muslim north and Christian south.

SUDAN

Total Land Area : 2 376 000 sq. km (917 374 sq. miles)

0 400 km
0 400 miles

LAND HEIGHT

- 2000m/6562ft
- 1000m/3281ft
- 500m/1640ft
- 200m/656ft
- Sea Level

POPULATION

- over 500 000
- over 100 000
- over 50 000
- over 10 000
- under 10 000

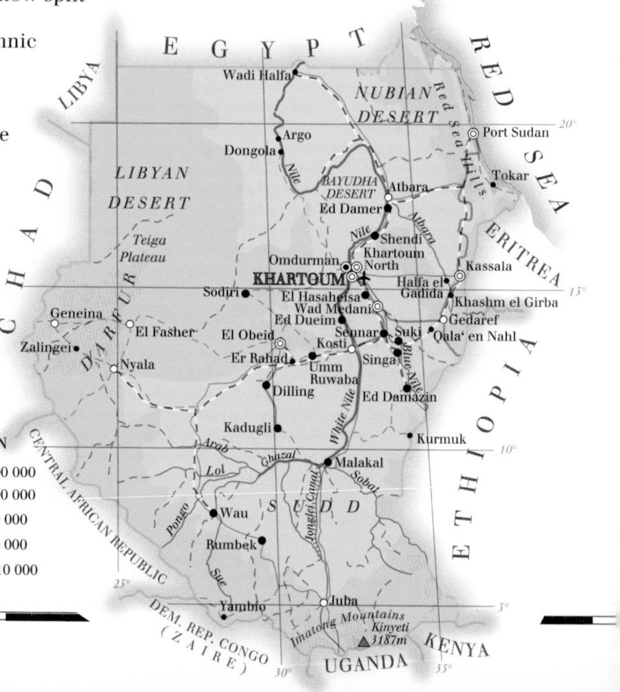
EGYPT
LIBYA
RED SEA
Wadi Halfa
NUBIAN DESERT
Port Sudan
Argo
Dongola
Tokar
LIBYAN DESERT
BAYUDHA DESERT
Atbara
Ed Damer
ERITREA
Teiga Plateau
Shendi
Khartoum North
Omdurman
KHARTOUM
Kassala
CHAD
DARFUR
Sodiri
Halfa el Gadida
El Hasaheisa
Wad Medani
Khashm el Girba
Gedaref
Geneina
El Fasher
El Obeid
Ed Dueim
Sennar
Suki
Qala' en Nahl
Zalingei
Nyala
Er Rahad
Kosti
Umm Ruwaba
Singa
Dilling
Ed Damazin
Kadugli
Kurmuk
ETHIOPIA
Malakal
Lol
Wau
SUDD
Rumbek
CENTRAL AFRICAN REPUBLIC
Yambio
Juba
Imatong Mountains
Kinyeti 3187m
DEM. REP. CONGO (ZAIRE)
UGANDA
KENYA
White Nile
Blue Nile
Nile
Atbara
Sobat
Jonglei Canal
Pongo
Sue

S

WORLD AFFAIRS

Joined UN in 1956

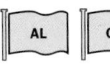

AL | OIC | COMESA | IGAD | OAU

Sudan's support for Iraq in the Gulf War and suspicion that it sponsors terrorism have led to its increasing isolation from the West and the Arab world. Only Iran, Yemen, and Libya maintain friendly relations.

AID

Recipient

$243m (receipts)

Up 16% in 1999

The only substantial bilateral aid comes from Iran. IMF funding ceased in 1990. Sudan depends on food aid.

DEFENSE

Compulsory military service

$424m

Up 11% in 1999

The NC controls the military and police and has its own paramilitary militia. Sudan's 100,000-strong army is engaged in fighting the two factions of the southern Sudanese People's Liberation Army, which number a similar size.

ECONOMICS

Inflation 80.4% p.a. (1990–1999)

$9.4bn

256.00–258.70 Sudanese dinars

SCORE CARD

❑ World GNP Ranking	86th
❑ GNP per Capita	$330
❑ Balance of Payments	$-465m
❑ Inflation	16%
❑ Unemployment	30%

Strengths
Oil, gas, cotton, gum arabic, sesame, sugar. Some gold mining.

Weaknesses
Low industrialization. Lack of foreign exchange for importing energy and spare parts for industry. Drought. Little transportation infrastructure. Huge distances between towns. Civil war delayed the exploitation of oil reserves. Alienation of Arab donors and investors.

EXPORTS

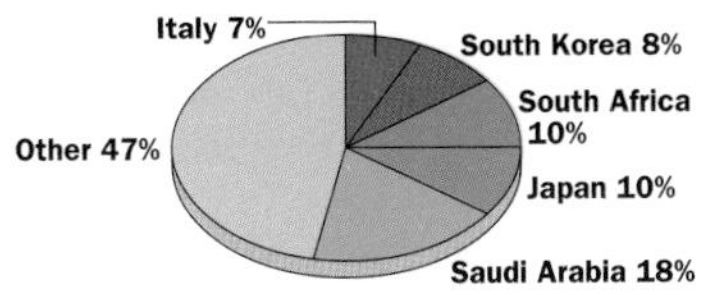
Italy 7%
South Korea 8%
South Africa 10%
Japan 10%
Saudi Arabia 18%
Other 47%

IMPORTS

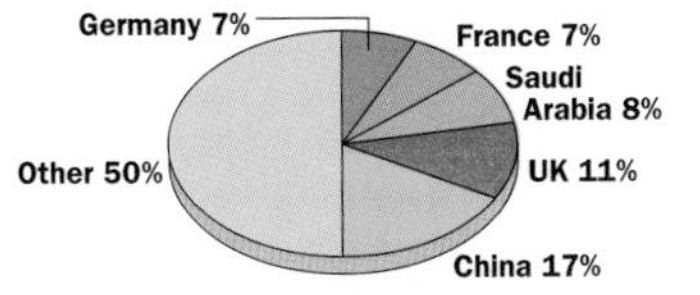
Germany 7%
France 7%
Saudi Arabia 8%
UK 11%
China 17%
Other 50%

RESOURCES

Electric power 500,000 kw

48,072 tonnes

Reserves of 300,000,000 bbl

42.8m sheep, 37.8m goats, 41.5m chickens

Oil, gas, gold, copper, gypsum, marble, mica, silver, chromium, zinc

Large oil and gas reserves were found in the south in the 1980s; oil exports started in 1999. The half-thermal, half-hydroelectric generating capacity is insufficient, and week-long power cuts are frequent. Gold mining has the potential for expansion.

ENVIRONMENT

Sustainability rank: 107th

4% (0.3% partially protected)

0.1 tonnes per capita

Flooding from the White Nile into the Sudd, the world's largest swamp and a rich wetland habitat, would have been affected by the Jonglei canal irrigation scheme, halted in 1986.

MEDIA

TV ownership medium

Daily newspaper circulation 27 per 1000 people

PUBLISHING AND BROADCAST MEDIA

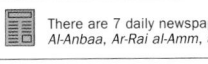

There are 7 daily newspapers, including *Al-Anbaa*, *Ar-Rai al-Amm*, and *Al-Nasr*

1 state-controlled service

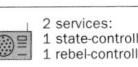

2 services: 1 state-controlled, 1 rebel-controlled

The media are controlled either by the government or the army, and are heavily censored.

CRIME

Death penalty used

6603 prisoners

Down 7% 1992–1994

Antigovernment dissent is often suppressed by violence, and torture by the security forces is widespread. The UN has condemned Sudan's poor human rights record.

EDUCATION

School leaving age: 13

58%

59,824 students

In 1991, measures were introduced to Islamicize education. Primary school children must have two years of Islamic religious instruction, and men wishing to enter university must first serve for a year in the People's Militia.

HEALTH

Welfare state health benefits

1 per 10,000 people

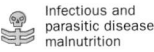

Infectious and parasitic diseases, malnutrition

Health service standards in rural areas are basic. The civil war has led to an increase in communicable diseases, especially the parasitic infection leishmaniasis.

CHRONOLOGY

Northern Sudan was taken by Egypt in 1821, the south by Britain in 1877.

- ❑ **1882** British invade Egypt.
- ❑ **1883** Muslim revolt in Sudan led by Muhammad Ahmed, the Mahdi.
- ❑ **1898** Mahdists defeated. Anglo-Egyptian condominium set up.
- ❑ **1954** Becomes self-governing.
- ❑ **1955** Rebellion in south starts 17 years of civil war.
- ❑ **1956** Independence as republic.
- ❑ **1958–1964** Military rule.
- ❑ **1965** Civilian revolution, elections.
- ❑ **1969** Coup led by Col. Jaafar Nimeiri.
- ❑ **1972** South gets limited autonomy.
- ❑ **1973** Sudanese Socialist Union is sole party.
- ❑ **1983** Southern rebellion resumes. *Sharia* law imposed.
- ❑ **1984** Devastating drought.
- ❑ **1986** Army coup.
- ❑ **1989** Gen. Omar Bashir takes over.
- ❑ **1991** *Sharia* penal code instituted. Pro-Iraq stance in Gulf War.
- ❑ **2000** Bashir ousts fundamentalist al-Turabi from leadership of NC. New attempts to make peace with southern rebels.

SPENDING

GDP/cap. increase

CONSUMPTION AND SPENDING

10 per 1000 population

9 per 1000 population

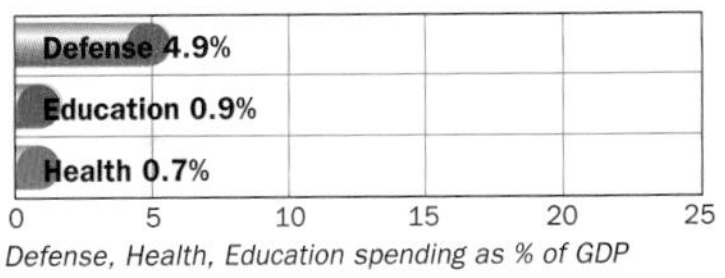
Defense 4.9%
Education 0.9%
Health 0.7%
0
5
10
15
20
25

Defense, Health, Education spending as % of GDP

Wealth is limited to the NC and southern rebel elites. Most of the population struggles to survive.

WORLD RANKING

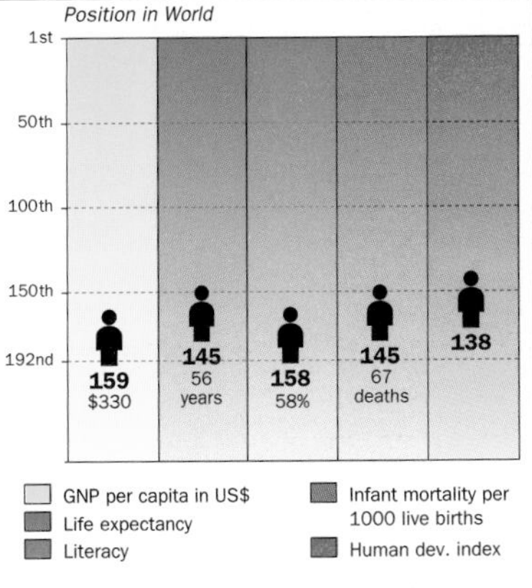
Position in World
1st
50th
100th
150th
192nd
159 $330
145 56 years
158 58%
145 67 deaths
138
GNP per capita in US$
Life expectancy
Literacy
Infant mortality per 1000 live births
Human dev. index

S

SURINAME

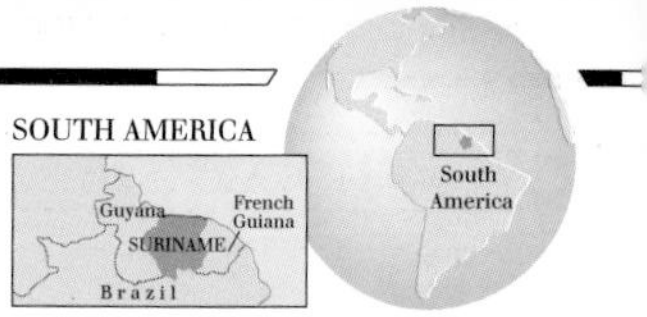
SOUTH AMERICA
Guyana
SURINAME
French Guiana
Brazil
South America

OFFICIAL NAME: Republic of Suriname **CAPITAL:** Paramaribo
POPULATION: 417,000 **CURRENCY:** Suriname guilder or florin **OFFICIAL LANGUAGE:** Dutch

1975 | 1975 | Nov 25 | SME | -3 | +597 | .sr

LOCATED ON THE NORTH COAST of South America, Suriname is bordered by Guyana, French Guiana, and Brazil. The interior is rainforested highlands; most people live near the coast. In 1975, after almost 300 years of Dutch rule, Suriname became independent. The Netherlands is still its main aid supplier, and is home to one-third of Surinamese. Democracy was restored in 1991, after almost 11 years of military rule.

Congested street in Paramaribo. *It boasts 18th and 19th century Dutch architecture and the Caribbean's largest mosque.*

CLIMATE

Tropical equatorial

WEATHER CHART

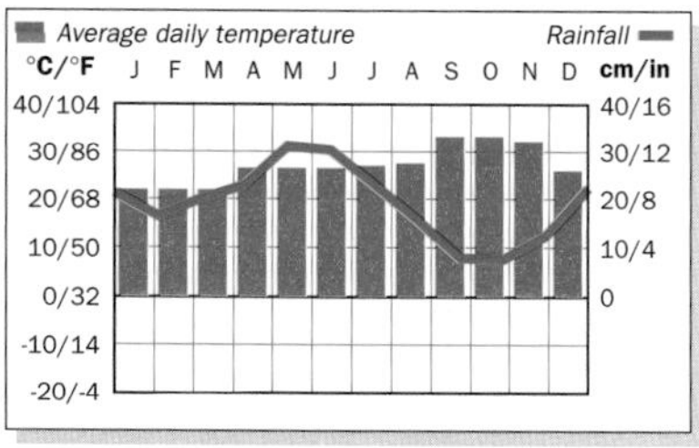
Average daily temperature
Rainfall
°C/°F
J F M A M J J A S O N D
cm/in
40/104
30/86
20/68
10/50
0/32
-10/14
-20/-4
40/16
30/12
20/8
10/4
0

Suriname's tropical climate is cooled by the trade winds. Rainfall varies from 150 to 300 cm (59 to 118 in) between coast and interior.

TRANSPORTATION

Drive on left

Johann Pengel International, Paramaribo 175,000 passengers

17 ships 6154 grt

THE TRANSPORTATION NETWORK

1178 km (732 miles)

None

157 km (98 miles)

1200 km (746 miles)

Rivers provide the main north–south links, and the vast interior relies on water or air transportation. The road network runs east–west and focuses on the coast and its immediate hinterland.

TOURISM

Visitors : Population 1:7.3

57,000 visitors

Up 4% in 1999

MAIN TOURIST ARRIVALS

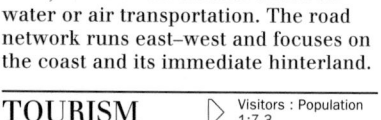

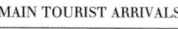

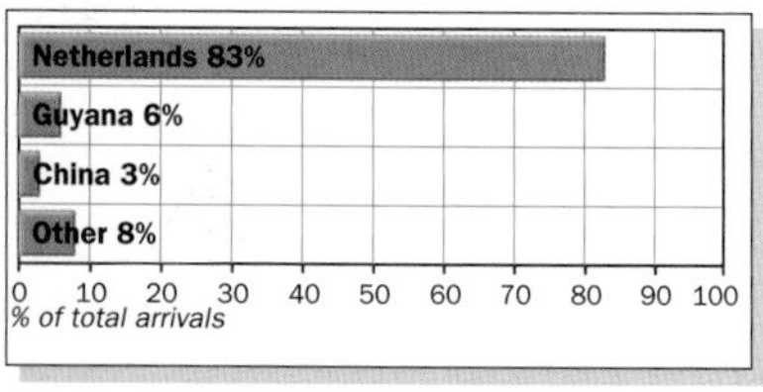
Netherlands 83%
Guyana 6%
China 3%
Other 8%
0 10 20 30 40 50 60 70 80 90 100
% of total arrivals

Tourism is undeveloped. Travelers outside Paramaribo are advised to carry their own hammock and food.

PEOPLE

Pop. density low

Sranan, Dutch, Javanese, Sarnami Hindi, Saramaccan, Chinese, Carib

3/km² (7/mi²)

THE URBAN/RURAL POPULATION SPLIT

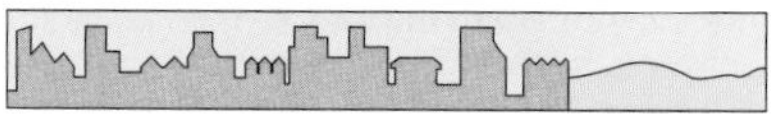
74%
26%

ETHNIC MAKEUP

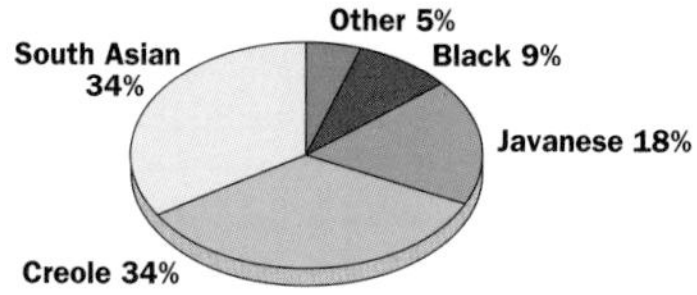
Other 5%
Black 9%
South Asian 34%
Javanese 18%
Creole 34%

About 250,000 Surinamese have emigrated since 1975. Of those who remain, 90% live near the coast, while the rest live in scattered rainforest communities. Tension between the Creole-dominated government, *bosnegers* (the descendants of runaway slaves), and Amerindians spilled over into armed rebellion in the 1980s. Many South Asians and Javanese work in farming. Christianity, Hinduism, and Islam are the dominant religions.

POLITICS

Multiparty elections

2000/2005

President Ronald Venetiaan

AT THE LAST ELECTION

National Assembly 51 seats

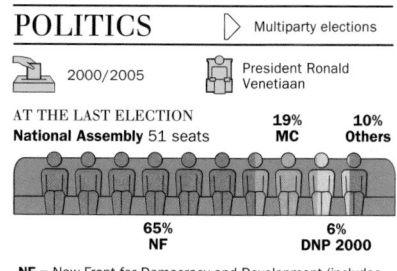

19% MC
10% Others
65% NF
6% DNP 2000

NF = New Front for Democracy and Development (includes the Suriname National Party, the Progressive Reform Party, the Suriname Labor Party, and Pertjajah Luhur)
MC = Millennium Combination (includes the National Democratic Party (**NDP**), the Democratic Alternative, and the Party for Unity and Harmony)
DNP 2000 = Democratic National Platform 2000

A coalition government representing Creoles, South Asians, and Javanese took power in 1991, but it lost power in 1996 to the NDP, controlled by Desi Bouterse, the military dictator from 1980 to 1988. Bouterse was behind the 1990 coup which ended Suriname's first attempt to return to democracy. In mid-1999 President Jules Wijdenbosch of the NDP faced a second attempt by opponents in the National Assembly to replace him. He held on to office, but was massively defeated by the opposition NF in legislative elections in May 2000. The new Assembly elected NF leader Ronald Venetiaan as president in August.

ATLANTIC OCEAN
GUYANA
FRENCH GUIANA
BRAZIL
PARAMARIBO
Nieuw Nickerie
Totness
Groningen
Calcutta
Boskamp
Wageningen
Jenny
Nieuw Amsterdam
Galibi
Moengo
Albina
Lelydorp
Onverwacht
Paranam
Republiek
Pilgrimkondre
Jóden Savanne
Kwakoegron
Zanderij
Apoera
Bitagron
Kaaimanston
Berg en Dal
Brokopondo
Brownsweg
Afobaka
Njoeng
Jacobkondre
Langatabbetje
W.J. van Blommesteinmeer
Pokigron
Stoelmanseiland
Boti-Pasi
Ladoewani
Poeketi
Asidonhopo
Cottica
Juliana Top 1230m
Teboe Top
Intelewa
Appikalo
Nickerie
Coppename
Marowijne
Corantijn
Kabalebo
Lucie
Gran
Tapanahony
Zuid
Coeroeni
Sipaliwini
Litani
Lawa
0 50 km
0 50 miles

SURINAME

Total Land Area : 161 470 sq. km (62 344 sq. miles)

LAND HEIGHT
1000m/3281ft
500m/1640ft
200m/1640ft
Sea Level

POPULATION
over 100 000
over 10 000
under 10 000

S

WORLD AFFAIRS

Joined UN in 1975

ACS | AmCC | Caricom | OAS | OIC

Relations with the Netherlands and the USA, Suriname's key aid and trading partners, have been weakened over charges of official connivance in narcotics trafficking. The Dutch have tried *in absentia* the former dictator Desi Bouterse on drug charges. Greater integration with the Caribbean is a priority.

AID

Recipient

$36m (receipts) | Down 39% in 1999

The Netherlands was the largest donor until deteriorating relations saw aid suspended in 1998. The IDB and European Investment Bank granted loans, also in 1998, for agricultural and industrial development.

DEFENSE

No compulsory military service

$22m | Up 47% in 1999

The army was politically dominant in the 1980s under Lt.-Col. Desi Bouterse, who resigned as army chief in 1992. President Wijdenbosch was his right-hand man. A six-year civil war against *bosneger* rebels ended in 1992.

ECONOMICS

Inflation 90% p.a. (1990–1999)

$684m | 809.5–981.0 Suriname guilders

SCORE CARD

- ❑ WORLD GNP RANKING........................161st
- ❑ GNP PER CAPITA $1660
- ❑ BALANCE OF PAYMENTS $73m
- ❑ INFLATION 98.9%
- ❑ UNEMPLOYMENT.................................20%

STRENGTHS

Bauxite. Gold. Timber potential. Oil. Agricultural exports: rice, bananas, citrus fruits. Shrimp exports.

WEAKNESSES

Overdependence on declining bauxite reserves and decreased foreign aid. Weak currency. Severe shortage of foreign exchange. Vulnerability to falls in world commodity prices. Net food importer.

EXPORTS

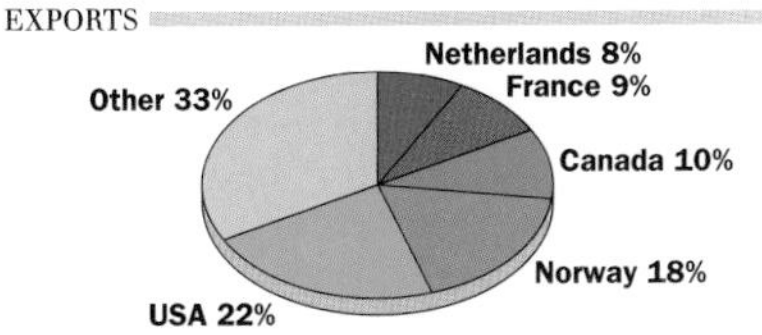
Netherlands 8%
France 9%
Other 33%
Canada 10%
Norway 18%
USA 22%

IMPORTS

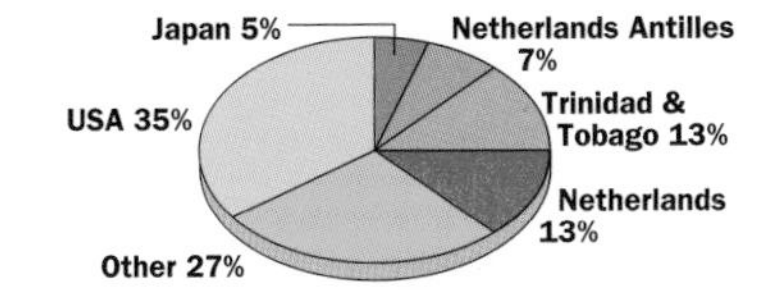
Japan 5%
Netherlands Antilles 7%
USA 35%
Trinidad & Tobago 13%
Netherlands 13%
Other 27%

RESOURCES

Electric power 425,000 kw

13,001 tonnes | 4932 b/d (reserves 88,235,280 bbl)

106,000 cattle, 66,000 ducks, 2.2m chickens | Bauxite, iron, gold, manganese, copper, nickel, platinum, oil

Suriname is a major exporter of aluminum and bauxite, but the minerals sector is affected by poor world prices, as is raw gold production. Oil consumption is almost double the level of oil production. Exploitation of the rainforests has begun. Rice and fruit are Suriname's key agricultural products.

ENVIRONMENT

Not available

10% partially protected | 5.2 tonnes per capita

In 1998 the government declared some 16,000 sq km (6150 sq miles) of rainforest – almost one-tenth of the country – to be a natural reserve barred to logging. The organization Conservation International gave US$1 million in support.

MEDIA

TV ownership medium

Daily newspaper circulation 122 per 1000 people

PUBLISHING AND BROADCAST MEDIA

There are 2 daily newspapers, *De Ware Tijd* and *De West*

2 state-owned services | 10 services: 1 state-owned, 9 independent

There are radio broadcasts in a number of languages. Dutch is used by the daily newspapers and for most TV programs.

CRIME

Death penalty not used

Suriname does not publish prison figures | Relatively high crime levels

Human rights abuses associated with the former military regime have largely ended. Rival armed factions remain in some interior regions. Drug trafficking and money laundering are a problem, as is urban street crime.

EDUCATION

School leaving age: 12

94% | 4319 students

Education is free and includes adult literacy programs. There is a long tradition of higher education, but most graduates now live in the Netherlands.

CHRONOLOGY

Dutch rule began in 1667, after an Anglo-Dutch treaty whose terms included Britain ceding its colony in Suriname to the Dutch but gaining Nieuw Amsterdam (New York).

- ❑ **1975** Independence.
- ❑ **1980** Coup. Rule by Lieutenant Colonel Desi Bouterse.
- ❑ **1982** Opponents executed. Dutch suspend aid for six years.
- ❑ **1986–1992** *Bosneger* rebel war.
- ❑ **1988–1991** Elections, coup, and new elections.
- ❑ **1992** Bouterse quits as army head.
- ❑ **1998–1999** President Wijdenbosch refuses to extradite Bouterse to the Netherlands on drug charges.
- ❑ **2000** Opposition NF wins elections.

HEALTH

Welfare state health benefits

1 per 2500 people | Heart attacks, cancers, malaria, malnutrition, tuberculosis

Urban medical facilities are relatively good; Paramaribo has several hospitals. Provision in the interior is basic.

SPENDING

GDP/cap. increase

CONSUMPTION AND SPENDING

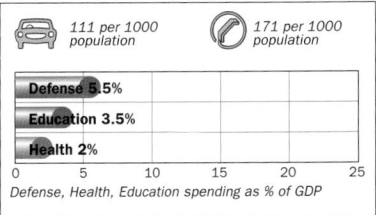

111 per 1000 population | *171 per 1000 population*

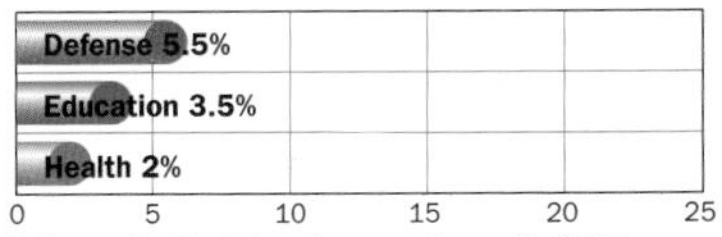
Defense 5.5%
Education 3.5%
Health 2%
0
5
10
15
20
25

Defense, Health, Education spending as % of GDP

Living standards have fallen since 1982, due to the effects of civil war and to aid and loan suspension. Urban Creoles dominate the rich elite. Amerindians and *bosnegers* are the poorest groups.

WORLD RANKING

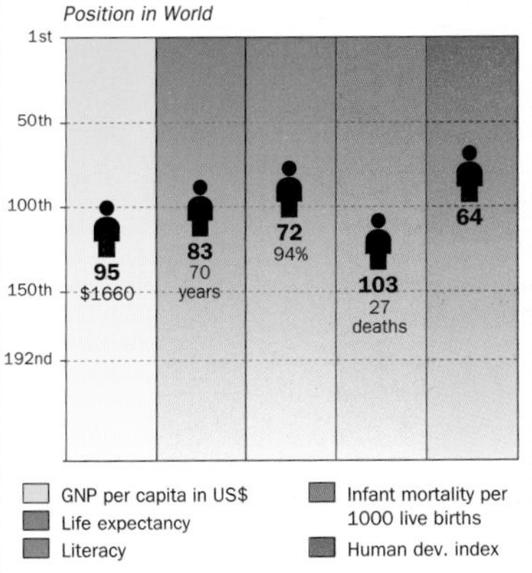
Position in World
1st
50th
100th
150th
192nd
95
$1660
83
70
years
72
94%
103
27
deaths
64
GNP per capita in US$
Life expectancy
Literacy
Infant mortality per 1000 live births
Human dev. index

S

SWAZILAND

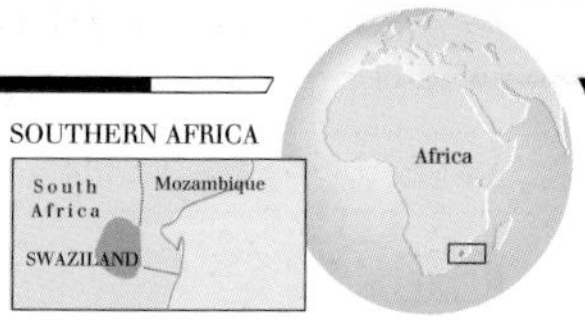
SOUTHERN AFRICA
South Africa
Mozambique
SWAZILAND
Africa

OFFICIAL NAME: Kingdom of Swaziland **CAPITAL:** Mbabane
POPULATION: 1 million **CURRENCY:** Lilangeni **OFFICIAL LANGUAGES:** English and siSwati

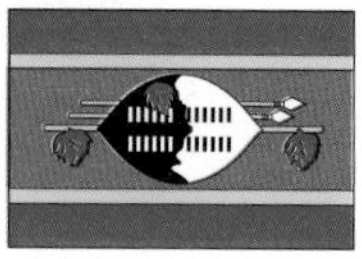

1968 | 1968 | Sept 6 | SD | +2 | +268 | .sz

THE TINY SOUTHERN African kingdom of Swaziland, bordered on three sides by South Africa and to the east by Mozambique, comprises mainly upland plateaus and mountains. Governed by a strong hereditary monarchy, Swaziland is a country in which tradition is being challenged by demands for modern multiparty government. King Mswati III, crowned in 1986, has overhauled the electoral process, but has still to legalize party politics.

CLIMATE

Subtropical

WEATHER CHART

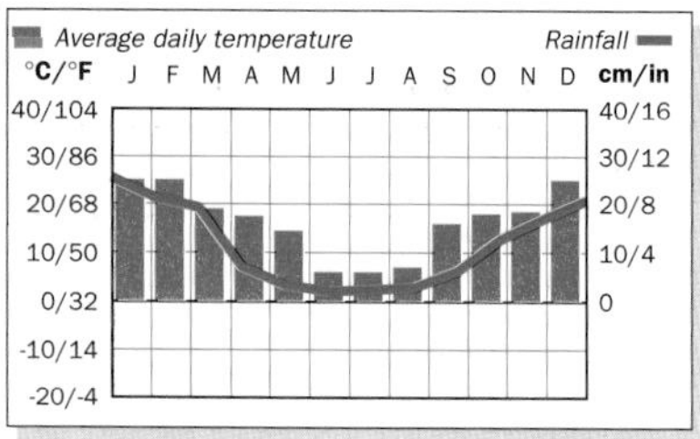
Average daily temperature
Rainfall
°C/°F
J F M A M J J A S O N D
cm/in
40/104
30/86
20/68
10/50
0/32
-10/14
-20/-4
40/16
30/12
20/8
10/4
0

Swaziland is temperate. Temperatures rise and rainfall declines as the land descends eastward, from high to low *veld*. The Low Veld is prone to drought.

TRANSPORTATION

Drive on left

Matsapha, Manzini 93,000 passengers | Has no fleet

THE TRANSPORTATION NETWORK

814 km (506 miles)	None
297 km (185 miles)	None

A sharp rise in road traffic has necessitated road improvements. The railroad, running to Mozambique and South Africa, mainly carries exports.

TOURISM

Visitors : Population 1:3.2

319,000 visitors | Down 1% in 1998

MAIN TOURIST ARRIVALS

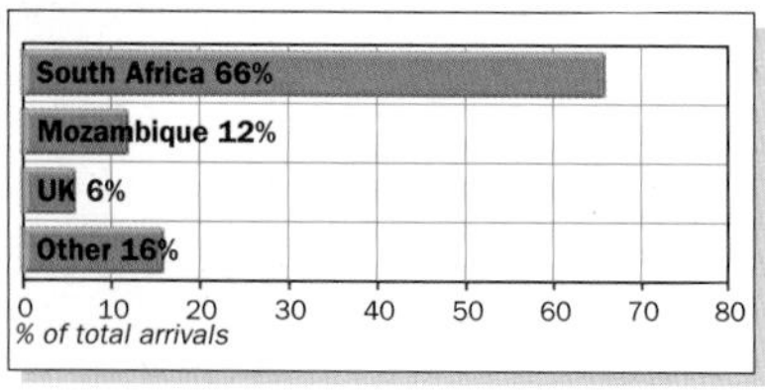
South Africa 66%
Mozambique 12%
UK 6%
Other 16%
0 10 20 30 40 50 60 70 80
% of total arrivals

Swaziland's attractions are its game reserves, mountain scenery, and, for the South Africans who make up two-thirds of tourists, its casinos.

The outskirts of Mbabane. *It lies on the High Veld, where traditional cattle farming has become more difficult owing to overgrazing.*

PEOPLE

Pop. density medium

English, siSwati, Zulu, Tsonga | 59/km² (152/mi²)

THE URBAN/RURAL POPULATION SPLIT

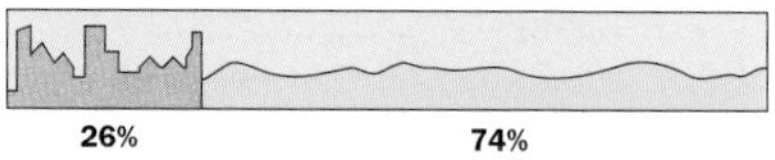
26%
74%

RELIGIOUS PERSUASION

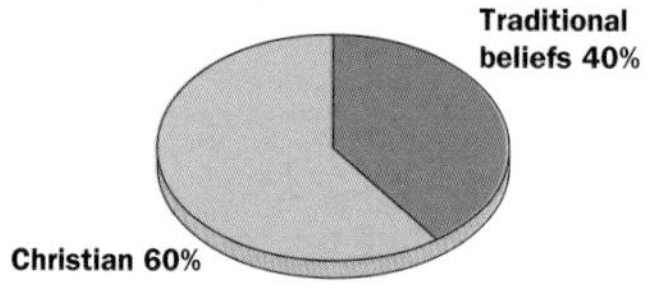
Traditional beliefs 40%
Christian 60%

Over 95% of the population belong to the Swazi ethnic group, making Swaziland one of Africa's most homogeneous states. It is also very conservative, but is now facing pressure from urban-based modernizers. The powerful monarchy dominates politics. Ancient traditions, such as *incwala*, the rainy season's annual movable feast, remain popular. Society is patriarchal and focused around the clan. Chiefs own much "national land," and wield authority through local consultations, called *tindkhundla*. Polygamy is tolerated. Women farm and may vote, but lack economic or political power. The exception is the Queen Mother, the "Great She Elephant," whose power as regent was clear during the mid-1980s.

POLITICS

No multiparty elections

L. House 1998/2003
U. House 1998/2003

HM King Mswati III

AT THE LAST ELECTION

House of Assembly 65 seats

There are no political parties. 10 members of the House of Assembly are appointed by the king

Senate 30 seats

20 members of the Senate are appointed by the king and 10 elected by the House of Assembly

Politics is dominated by a strong executive monarchy and rivalries within the ruling Dlamini clan. Royal advisers complement a nominated cabinet. Direct elections were held in 1993, but parties remain banned. Responding to mounting popular unrest, in 1996 the king appointed Sibusiso Dlamini as prime minister and set up a commission to review the political system. Pro-democracy activists staged mass protests against the government in 2000.

SWAZILAND

Total Land Area : 17 200 sq. km (6641 sq. miles)

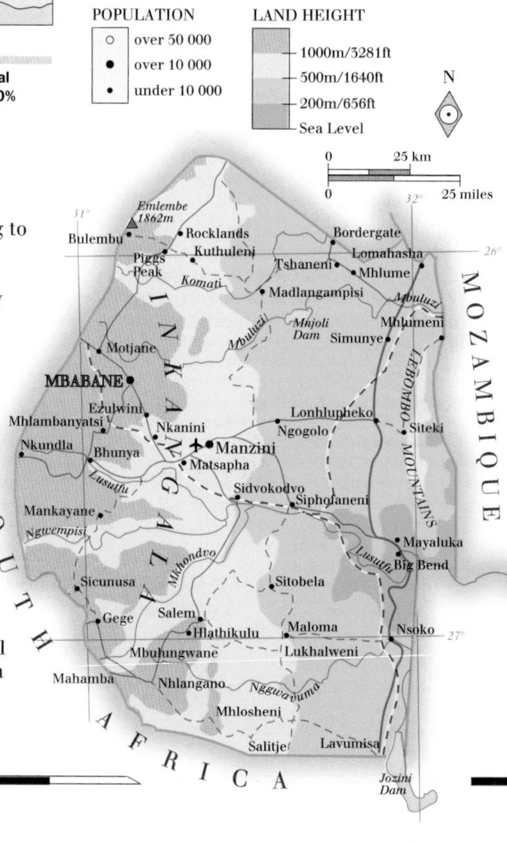
POPULATION
over 50 000
over 10 000
under 10 000
LAND HEIGHT
1000m/3281ft
500m/1640ft
200m/656ft
Sea Level
N
0 25 km
0 25 miles
MOZAMBIQUE
SOUTH AFRICA
INKANGALA
LEBOMBO MOUNTAINS
Emlembe 1862m
Bulembu
Rocklands
Piggs Peak
Kuthuleni
Komati
Bordergate
Tshaneni
Lomahasha
Mhlume
Madlangampisi
Mbuluzi
Mjoli Dam
Simunye
Mhlumeni
Motjane
MBABANE
Ezulwini
Mhlambanyatsi
Nkanini
Nkundla
Bhunya
Manzini
Matsapha
Lonhlupheko
Ngogolo
Siteki
Lusutfu
Sidvokodvo
Siphofaneni
Mankayane
Ngwempisi
Mkhondvo
Mayaluka
Big Bend
Sicunusa
Sitobela
Gege
Salem
Hlathikulu
Maloma
Nsoko
Mbulungwane
Lukhalweni
Mahamba
Nhlangano
Ngwavuma
Mhlosheni
Salitje
Lavumisa
Jozini Dam

S

WORLD AFFAIRS

Joined UN in 1968

ACP | Comm | NAM | OAU | SADC

Swaziland's membership of the SACU reinforces its traditional economic dependence on its giant neighbor. While welcoming the election of an ANC-led government in Pretoria, King Mswati has expressed concern over their support for Swazi prodemocracy campaigners. Peace in Mozambique has meant the return there of 134,000 Mozambican refugees.

AID

Recipient

$29m (receipts)

Down 3% in 1999

Aid helps the balance of payments, and funds the development of the Matsapha industrial estate, roads, and social projects. Donors include Germany, the USA, the UK, and the World Bank. EU aid mainly targets "microprojects," such as schools, and supports constitutional reform.

DEFENSE

No compulsory military service

$20m

No significant change

The Swaziland Defense Force numbers just 3000 troops. Although it does not play an overt political role, its loyalty is to the monarch and the status quo.

ECONOMICS

Inflation 12.1% p.a. (1990–1999)

$1.4bn

6.158–7.570 emalangeni

SCORE CARD

❑ World GNP Ranking	150th
❑ GNP per Capita	$1350
❑ Balance of Payments	$17m
❑ Inflation	6.1%
❑ Unemployment	22%

Strengths

Economy quite diversified and buoyant. Manufacturing 32% of GDP. Investment rules attractive. Sugar 33% of export earnings. Wood pulp. Debt service low: only 3.8% of export earnings in 1993. Renewed regional stability has reduced risk to exports.

Weaknesses

Sugar is vulnerable to world price fluctuations. Dependence on South Africa for jobs, revenue, investment, electricity, and imported goods. Small plots of land and lack of land title hinder farm modernization. High population growth.

EXPORTS

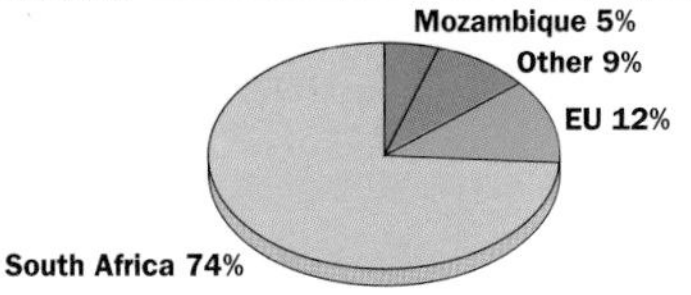
Mozambique 5%
Other 9%
EU 12%
South Africa 74%

IMPORTS

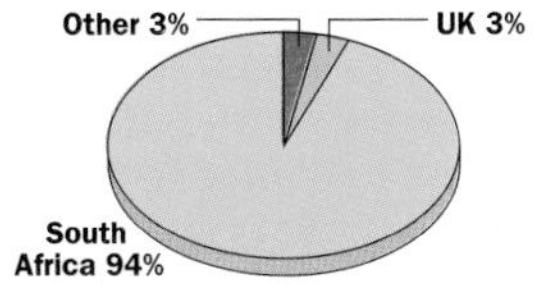
Other 3%
UK 3%
South Africa 94%

RESOURCES

Not available

131 tonnes

Not an oil producer

665,000 cattle, 440,000 goats, 3m chickens

Coal, diamonds, gold, asbestos, cassiterite, iron, tin

Swaziland's main export is sugar cane, followed by wood pulp, coal, and asbestos. The development of hydroelectric power stations has cut energy imports from South Africa.

ENVIRONMENT

Not available

3% partially protected

0.4 tonnes per capita

In 1998 Swaziland, Mozambique, and South Africa began an ecological project on the world's largest wetlands – the foothills of the Lebombo mountains.

MEDIA

TV ownership low

Daily newspaper circulation 27 per 1000 people

PUBLISHING AND BROADCAST MEDIA

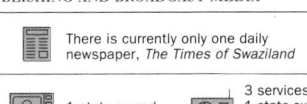

There is currently only one daily newspaper, *The Times of Swaziland*

1 state-owned service

3 services: 1 state-owned, 2 independent

The king, responding to pressure, rapidly reversed his 2001 decree which had ensured the continued closure of the independent *Swaziland Observer*.

CRIME

Death penalty used

Swaziland does not publish prison figures

Down 20% 1992–1998

The crime rate is low. The numbers of illegal weapons brought in by refugees have boosted armed crime.

EDUCATION

School leaving age: 13

80%

5658 students

Education is compulsory. Parents pay fees at all levels; even so, primary enrollment is about 93%. Drop-out rates at secondary level are high.

CHRONOLOGY

Swaziland became a British protectorate in 1903.

- ❑ **1968** Independence.
- ❑ **1973** King bans political activity, repeals constitution.
- ❑ **1978** New constitution confirms king's executive, legislative control.
- ❑ **1982** King Sobhuza dies. Queen Mother becomes regent for Prince Makhosetive. Power struggle between modernists and traditionalists in royal Dlamini clan.
- ❑ **1986** Makhosetive crowned King Mswati III at the age of 18.
- ❑ **1992** Limited electoral reforms; parties still banned.
- ❑ **1993** Elections under new system.
- ❑ **1996** Review of political system.
- ❑ **1998** Poor turnout at elections.
- ❑ **2000** Mass prodemocracy protests.

HEALTH

No welfare state health benefits

1 per 6700 people

Diarrheal and respiratory diseases

Health facilities are rudimentary. About a quarter of the population aged 15 to 49 is said to carry HIV/AIDS.

SPENDING

GDP/cap. increase

CONSUMPTION AND SPENDING

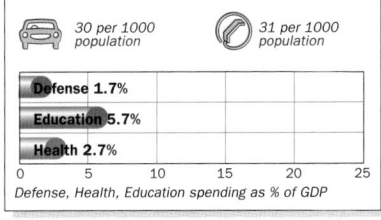

30 per 1000 population

31 per 1000 population

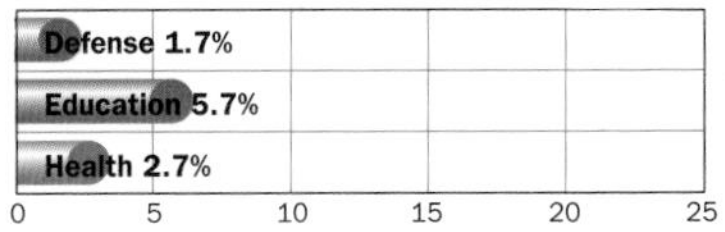
Defense 1.7%
Education 5.7%
Health 2.7%
0
5
10
15
20
25

Defense, Health, Education spending as % of GDP

About 50% of Swazis live below the UN poverty line. The royal Dlamini clan enjoys Western luxuries and travel.

WORLD RANKING

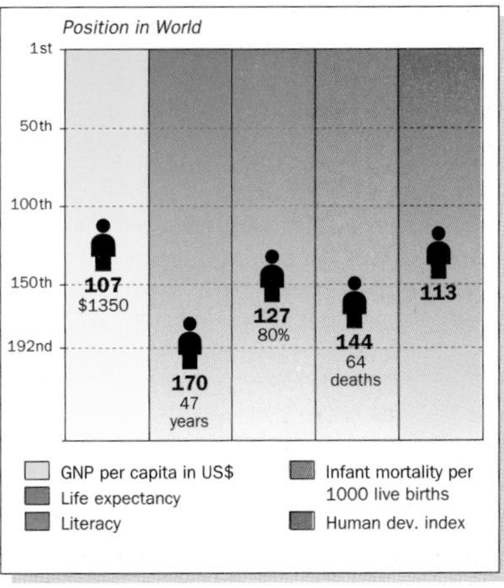
Position in World
1st
50th
100th
150th
192nd
107
$1350
170
47
years
127
80%
144
64
deaths
113
GNP per capita in US$
Life expectancy
Literacy
Infant mortality per 1000 live births
Human dev. index

S

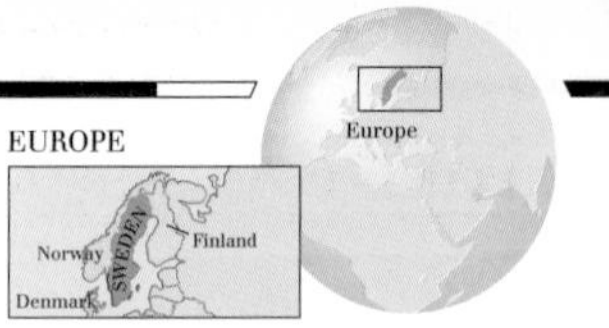
EUROPE
Europe
Norway
SWEDEN
Finland
Denmark

SWEDEN

OFFICIAL NAME: Kingdom of Sweden **CAPITAL:** Stockholm
POPULATION: 8.9 million **CURRENCY:** Swedish krona **OFFICIAL LANGUAGE:** Swedish

1523 | 1905 | June 6 | S | +1 | +46 | .se

SITUATED ON THE SCANDINAVIAN peninsula with Norway to its west, Sweden is a densely forested country with numerous lakes. The north of Sweden falls within the Arctic Circle; much of the south is fertile and widely cultivated. Sweden has one of the most extensive welfare systems in the world, and is among the world's leading proponents of equal rights for women. Its economic strengths include high-tech industries, such as Ericsson, and car production, most notably Volvo and Saab. Unlike neighboring Norway, it joined the EU in January 1995.

CLIMATE

Subarctic/continental

WEATHER CHART

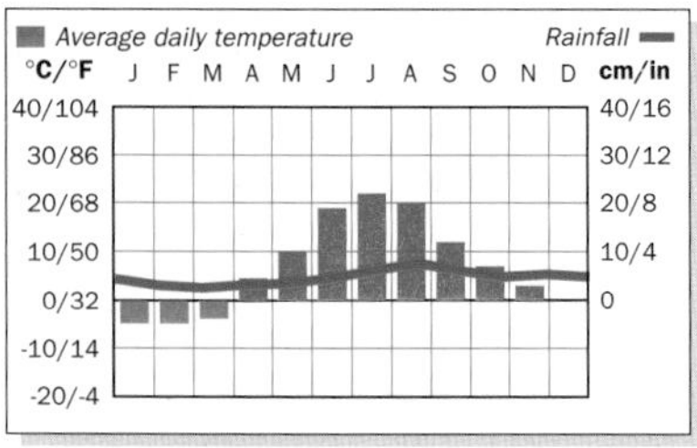
Average daily temperature
Rainfall
°C/°F J F M A M J J A S O N D cm/in
40/104
30/86
20/68
10/50
0/32
-10/14
-20/-4
40/16
30/12
20/8
10/4
0

Sweden has a largely continental climate. The Baltic Sea often freezes in winter, making the east coast much colder than western regions. Summers are mild everywhere, with temperatures varying surprisingly little between northern and southern regions.

TRANSPORTATION

Drive on right

Arlanda, Stockholm
17.4m passengers

412 ships
2.9m grt

THE TRANSPORTATION NETWORK

163,453 km (101,565 miles)

1439 km (894 miles)

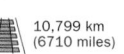

10,799 km (6710 miles)

2052 km (1275 miles)

Maintaining and improving transportation links are of prime concern in what is Europe's fourth-largest country. Swedish governments have traditionally spent large sums on infrastructure. Transportation spending is also seen as a way of boosting the economy as a whole.

A 16-km (10-mile) Øresund road and rail link by bridge and tunnel connecting Malmö with Copenhagen opened in 2000, providing Sweden with a new road and rail link with Denmark and the rest of Europe. A new rail link between Arlanda airport and Stockholm is also planned. By law, cars must travel with their headlights on at all times.

TOURISM

Visitors : Population 1:3.4

2.6m visitors

Up 1% in 1999

MAIN TOURIST ARRIVALS

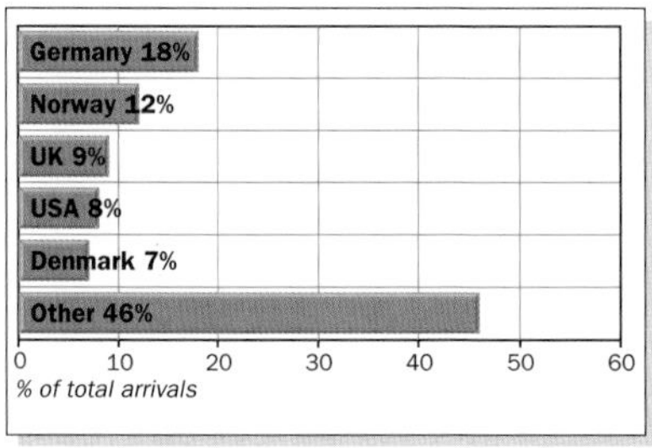
Germany 18%
Norway 12%
UK 9%
USA 8%
Denmark 7%
Other 46%
0 10 20 30 40 50 60
% of total arrivals

Sweden expanded rapidly as a tourist destination in the 1970s and 1980s. Stockholm is renowned for its palaces, while the international success of the pop group Abba in the 1970s boosted its vibrant nightlife. Visitors to the capital are typically young and affluent.

Sweden has fewer lakes than Finland, and lacks Norway's dramatic scenery, but it has many natural attractions. The mountains of the "Midnight Sun" lie north of the Arctic Circle, while the southern coast has many white sandy beaches. The vast tracts of deserted landscape and the simple country communal living also attract visitors, but the cost of travel to Sweden means that most visitors come from other Scandinavian countries and Germany.

***A crofter's holding in Dalarna,** central Sweden, an area which is still mainly forested. The timber and paper industries play a major role in Sweden's economy.*

PEOPLE

Pop. density low

Swedish, Finnish, Sami

22/km² (56/mi²)

THE URBAN/RURAL POPULATION SPLIT

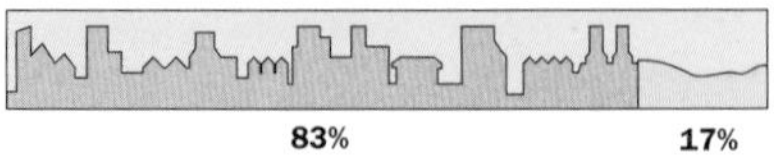
83%
17%

RELIGIOUS PERSUASION

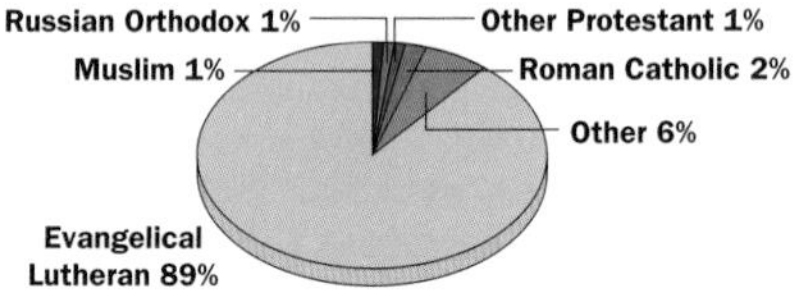
Russian Orthodox 1%
Other Protestant 1%
Muslim 1%
Roman Catholic 2%
Other 6%
Evangelical Lutheran 89%

ETHNIC MAKEUP

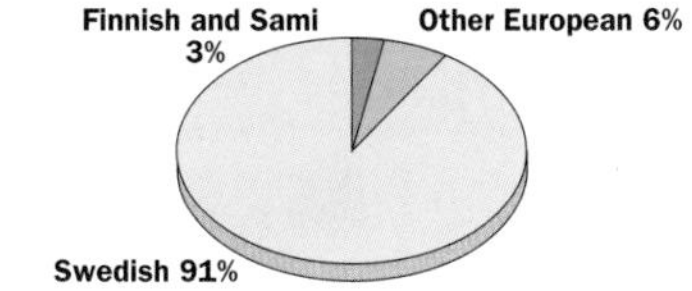
Finnish and Sami 3%
Other European 6%
Swedish 91%

As in all of Scandinavia, the nuclear family forms the basis of society. The birthrate is low with, on average, fewer than two children per family. Marriage is declining, and cohabitation outside marriage is common.

Swedish society has an egalitarian tradition. The role of the state is seen as providing conditions allowing each person to gain economic independence through employment. The welfare system is one of the most extensive in the world. However, in the early 1990s, recession reduced benefits; mothers in particular face problems with the closure of childcare facilities. Women make up nearly half the workforce. Over 40% of MPs are women, the highest percentage in the world. In 1999 the Swedish cabinet became the first in the world to have a majority of women ministers.

Swedish has generous asylum laws, but immigration is tightly controlled. A 17,000-strong minority of Sami live in northern Sweden. Their traditional way of life is protected.

The Evangelical Lutheran church was disestablished in 2000.

POPULATION AGE BREAKDOWN

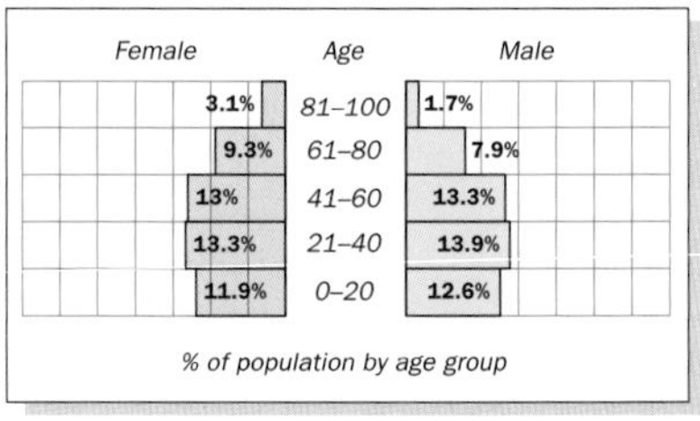
Female
Age
Male
3.1%
81–100
1.7%
9.3%
61–80
7.9%
13%
41–60
13.3%
13.3%
21–40
13.9%
11.9%
0–20
12.6%
% of population by age group

S

POLITICS

Multiparty elections

1998/2002 | King Carl XVI Gustaf

AT THE LAST ELECTION

Parliament (Riksdag) 349 seats

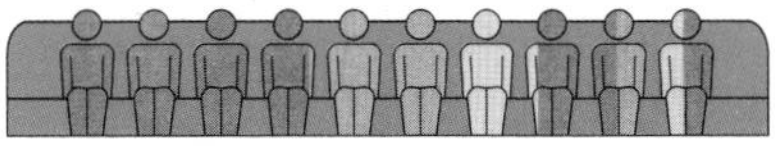
12% KdS
5% CP
38% SAP
23% MS
12% VP
5% FP
5% MpG

SAP = Social Democratic Labor Party **MS** = Moderate Party
VP = Left Party **KdS** = Christian Democratic Party
CP = Center Party **FP** = Liberal Party **MpG** = Green Party

Sweden is a constitutional monarchy with an elected parliament under the leadership of the prime minister.

Main Political Issues

EU membership

Sweden joined the EU in 1995 with Austria and Finland, but, like the UK and Denmark, opted out of introducing the euro from 1999. It supports EU membership for central European states.

High cost of the welfare state

The cost of the welfare system contributed to enormous budget deficits in the late 1980s and early 1990s. While this has been brought under control, social security pressures remain from the relatively high level of unemployment and the growing number of pensioners.

Profile

Politics have traditionally been split between the SAP and trade unions on the left, and a host of moderate center and right-wing parties. Since the 1930s, the SAP has governed every term, except in 1976–1982 and 1991–1994. A shift to the right in 1991 was reversed in the 1994 elections, but the SAP failed to gain an absolute majority of seats. Ingvar Carlsson, SAP leader, formed a minority government but resigned in 1996 and was replaced by Göran Persson. The SAP lost ground in elections in 1998, leaving Persson more heavily dependent on support from the Left and Green parties.

Carl XVI Gustaf, *ascended the throne in 1973. His role is purely ceremonial.*

Göran Persson *became prime minister in 1996.*

WORLD AFFAIRS

Joined UN in 1946

EU | CE | NC | OECD | OSCE

Sweden's main recent foreign policy concern has been adjustment to EU membership, which it achieved in 1995. In 1998 parliament voted to join the Schengen passport-free zone linking nine EU states. Since the collapse of the Soviet Union, Sweden has altered its traditionally neutral stance and now has WEU observer status. This contrasts sharply with Prime Minister Olof Palme's period in office in the 1980s, when Sweden was a vociferous critic of the USA's antagonistic policy towards the USSR. Sweden participates in several UN peacekeeping operations.

AID

Donor

$1.63bn (donations) | Up 4% in 1999

Sweden is one of the few countries to exceed the UN target of allocating 0.7% of GNP to development aid. Most bilateral aid goes to African countries.

SWEDEN

Total Land Area : 411 620 sq. km (158 926 sq. miles)

POPULATION
- over 1 000 000
- over 100 000
- over 50 000
- over 10 000

LAND HEIGHT
- 1000m/3281ft
- 500m/1640ft
- 200m/656ft
- Sea Level

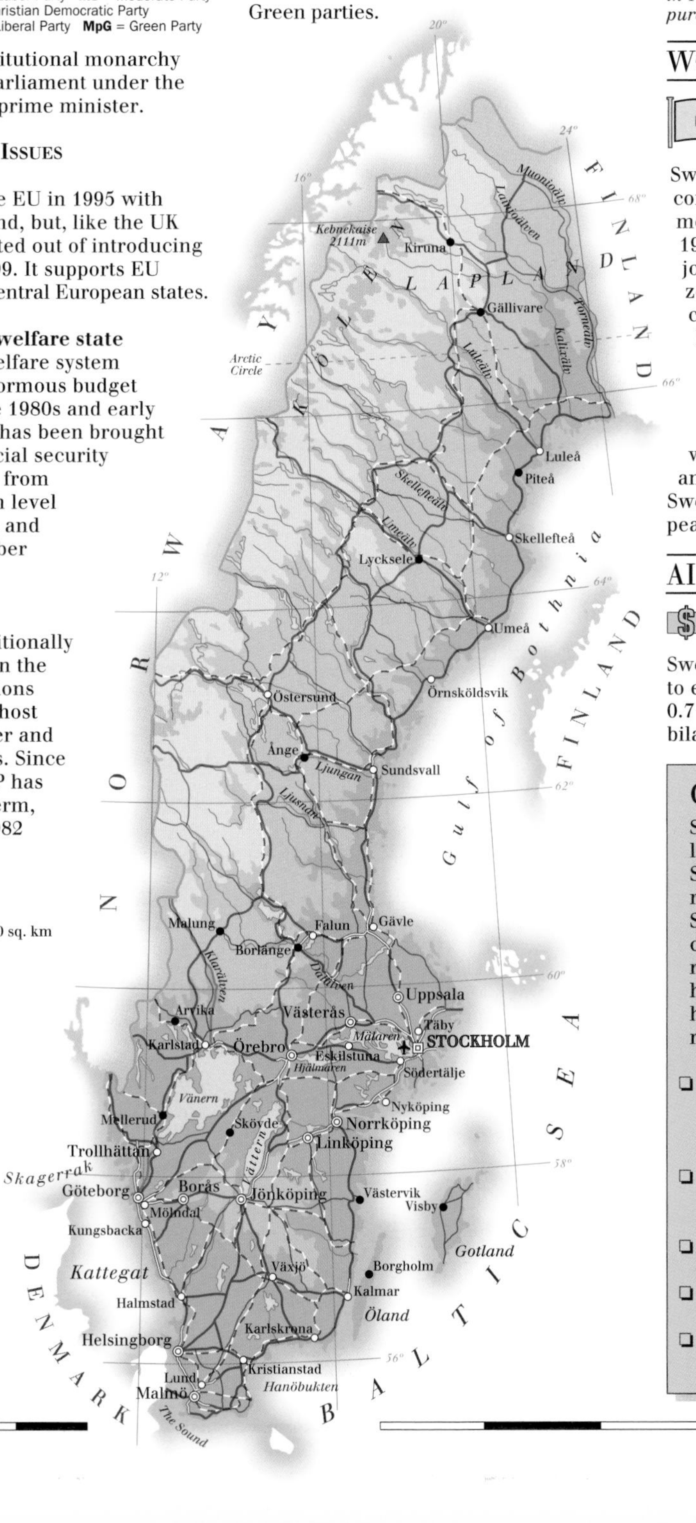
N
0 100 km
0 100 miles
NORWAY
LAPLAND
FINLAND
Kebnekaise 2111m
Kiruna
Gällivare
Arctic Circle
Luleå
Piteå
Skellefteå
Lycksele
Umeå
Gulf of Bothnia
Örnsköldsvik
Östersund
Ånge
Ljungan
Sundsvall
Ljusnan
Malung
Falun
Gävle
Borlänge
Dalälven
Uppsala
Arvika
Västerås
Täby
STOCKHOLM
Karlstad
Örebro
Eskilstuna
Mälaren
Hjälmaren
Södertälje
Vänern
Nyköping
Mellerud
Skövde
Norrköping
Trollhättan
Linköping
Vättern
Skagerrak
Göteborg
Borås
Jönköping
Västervik
Visby
Mölndal
Kungsbacka
Gotland
Kattegat
Växjö
Borgholm
Kalmar
Halmstad
Öland
Karlskrona
Helsingborg
Kristianstad
Hanöbukten
Lund
Malmö
The Sound
DENMARK
BALTIC SEA
FINLAND
Muonioälv
Lainioälven
Torneälv
Kalixälv
Luleälv
Skellefteälv
Umeälv
Klarälven
16°
20°
24°
12°
68°
66°
64°
62°
60°
58°
56°

CHRONOLOGY

Sweden's history has been closely linked to the control of the Baltic Sea and its highly profitable trade routes. Under the house of Vasa, Sweden became a major power, controlling much of the Baltic region. By the 18th century, however, Sweden's position had been eroded by its regional rivals, particularly Russia.

- **1814–1815** Congress of Vienna. Sweden cedes territory to Russia and Denmark. Period of unbroken peace begins.
- **1865–1866** Riksdag (parliament) reformed into a bicameral structure.
- **1905** Norway gains independence from Sweden.
- **1911** First Liberal government comes to power.
- **1914** Government resigns over defense policy.

S

CHRONOLOGY *continued*

- **1914–1917** Sweden remains neutral during WWI but supplies Germany. Allied blockade.
- **1917** Food shortages. Conservative government falls. Nils Edén forms a Liberal government: limits exports contributing to German war effort.
- **1919** Universal adult suffrage.
- **1921** Finland gains Åland Islands as retribution for Sweden's war role.
- **1932** Severe recession. Social Democrat government under Per Albin Hansson elected.
- **1939–1945** Sweden neutral. Grants transit rights to German forces.
- **1945–1976** Continuing Social Democratic rule under Tage Erlander establishes Sweden as world's most advanced welfare state, and one of the most affluent.
- **1950** Gustav VI Adolf becomes king.
- **1953** Nordic Council member.
- **1959** Founder member of EFTA.
- **1969** Erlander succeeded by Olof Palme as prime minister.
- **1973** Carl XVI Gustaf on throne.
- **1975** Major constitutional reform. Riksdag (parliament) becomes unicameral with a three-year term. Role of monarchy reduced to ceremonial functions.
- **1976** SAP loses power. Nonsocialist coalition led by Thorbjörn Fälldin in government.
- **1978** Fälldin resigns over issue of nuclear power. Ola Ullsten prime minister.
- **1979** Fälldin prime minister again.
- **1982** Elections. SAP forms minority government. Palme returns as prime minister.
- **1986** Palme shot dead. His deputy, Ingvar Carlsson, succeeds him as prime minister. Police fail to find the killer.
- **1990** Carlsson introduces moderate austerity package, cuts government spending, raises indirect taxes.
- **1991** Sweden applies to join EU. SAP remains largest party after general election but is unable to form government; Carlsson resigns. Carl Bildt, leader of Moderate Party (MS), forms coalition of nonsocialist parties in middle of serious recession.
- **1992** Austerity measures succeed in reducing inflation but SAP refuses to support further spending cuts.
- **1994** Terms of EU membership settled. Elections return SAP to power. Referendum favors joining EU.
- **1995** Joins EU.
- **1996** Carlsson resigns; replaced by Göran Persson.
- **1998** Persson remains in office, despite SAP losses in elections; dependent on Left and Greens for parliamentary majority.

S

DEFENSE

Compulsory military service

$5.25bn

Down 9% in 1999

SWEDISH ARMED FORCES

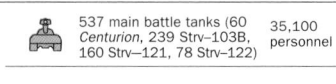

537 main battle tanks (60 *Centurion*, 239 Strv–103B, 160 Strv–121, 78 Strv–122)	35,100 personnel
9 submarines, 45 patrol boats	9200 personnel
250 combat aircraft (30 SAAB AJS–37, 90 SAAB JAS–39, 130 SAAB JA–37)	8400 personnel
None	

Sweden's sophisticated and powerful military force is supplied with weaponry manufactured by its advanced home defense industry, including Saab fighter jets and Bofor antiaircraft guns. However, with the end of the Cold War, strategic priorities have changed. Sweden feels less bound to its neutral stance; it has participated in NATO's Partnerships for Peace program since 1994 and has WEU observer status. In 1999 spending cuts were announced, foreshadowing halving the size of the armed forces, because of the reduced military threat in the Scandinavian and Baltic region. A ten-year reform program began in 2001, bringing personnel onto regular office hours and canceling large-scale exercises.

ECONOMICS

Inflation 2.2% p.a. (1990–1999)

$236.9bn

8.543–9.436 Swedish kronor

SCORE CARD

World GNP Ranking	21st
GNP per Capita	$26,750
Balance of Payments	$4.64bn
Inflation	0.5%
Unemployment	6%

EXPORTS

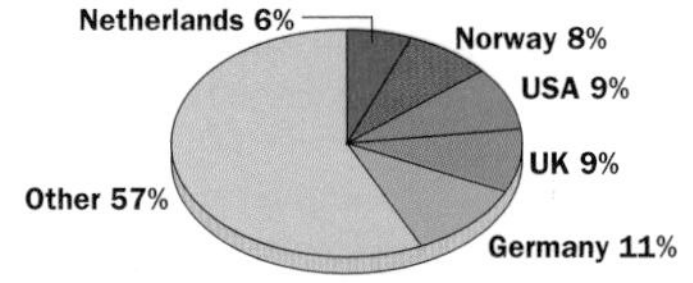
Netherlands 6%
Norway 8%
USA 9%
UK 9%
Germany 11%
Other 57%

IMPORTS

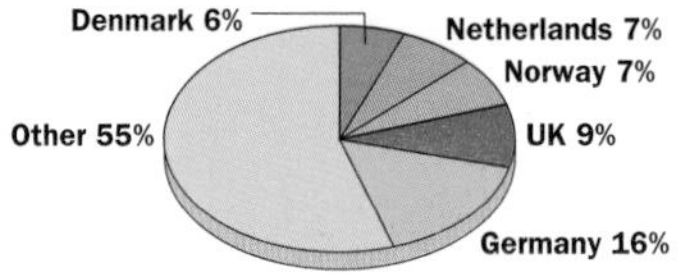
Denmark 6%
Netherlands 7%
Norway 7%
UK 9%
Germany 16%
Other 55%

ECONOMIC PERFORMANCE INDICATOR

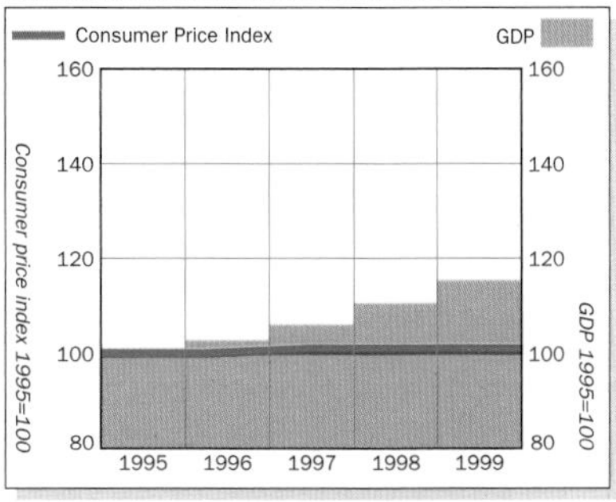
Consumer Price Index
GDP
160
140
120
100
80
Consumer price index 1995=100
GDP 1995=100
1995
1996
1997
1998
1999

Strengths
Companies of global importance, including Saab, Volvo, Electrolux and SKF, the world's biggest roller bearing manufacturer. Highly developed and constantly updated infrastructure. Sophisticated technology. Skilled labor force virtually bilingual in English.

Weaknesses
Labor costs remain uncompetitive. Highest taxation in the OECD, accounting for over 60% of GDP. Peripheral location, raising costs for producers and exporters.

Profile
The state plays a significant role in the economy, but tends to restrict its role to services and infrastructure. Sweden's industrial giants have mostly been private-sector companies. The early 1990s saw a shift in economic policy. Perceptions of the social role of government were modified to favor business. However, greater growth did not follow, and unemployment and the overall cost of welfare drove up the budget deficit to one of the OECD's highest in 1994. Growth has now resumed and the deficit has been cut back, but unemployment remains relatively high. Sweden opted not to introduce the euro from 1999, but the ruling Social Democrats adopted a pro-euro stance in March 2000; the issue is to be decided by national referendum.

SWEDEN : MAJOR BUSINESSES

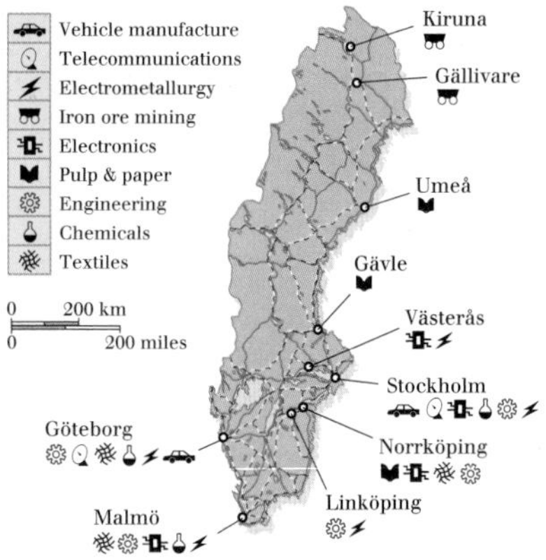
Vehicle manufacture
Telecommunications
Electrometallurgy
Iron ore mining
Electronics
Pulp & paper
Engineering
Chemicals
Textiles
0 200 km
0 200 miles
Kiruna
Gällivare
Umeå
Gävle
Västerås
Stockholm
Norrköping
Linköping
Göteborg
Malmö

RESOURCES

Electric power 35.5m kw

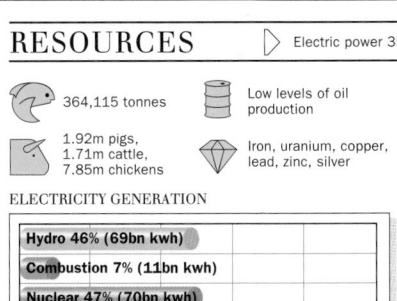

364,115 tonnes

Low levels of oil production

1.92m pigs, 1.71m cattle, 7.85m chickens

Iron, uranium, copper, lead, zinc, silver

ELECTRICITY GENERATION

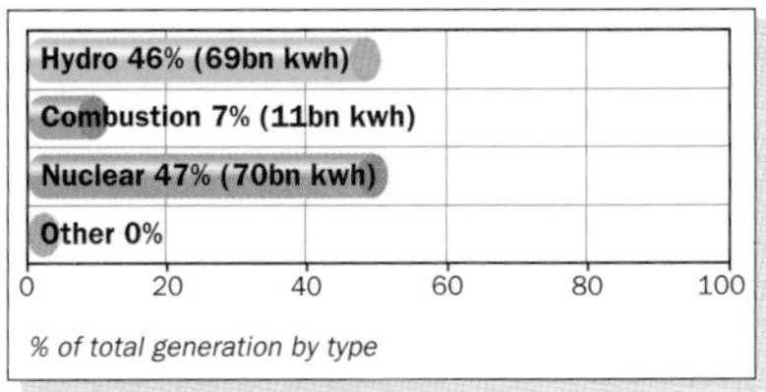

Hydro 46% (69bn kwh)
Combustion 7% (11bn kwh)
Nuclear 47% (70bn kwh)
Other 0%
0
20
40
60
80
100
% of total generation by type

Sweden is rich in minerals, including iron, copper, and silver. While mining and quarrying account for only 0.3% of GDP, they underpin other industrial sectors. In a referendum in 1980 Sweden decided, on environmental grounds, to abandon nuclear power – which in the 1990s accounted for about half of electricity generation – by the year 2010. However, problems in securing sufficient new energy supplies and in reducing consumption meant that, by the end of 2000, only one of the country's four nuclear reactors had been closed down.

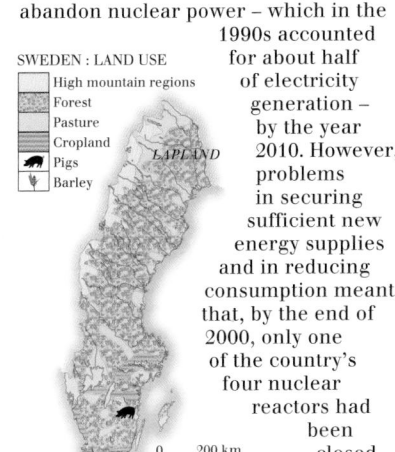

SWEDEN : LAND USE

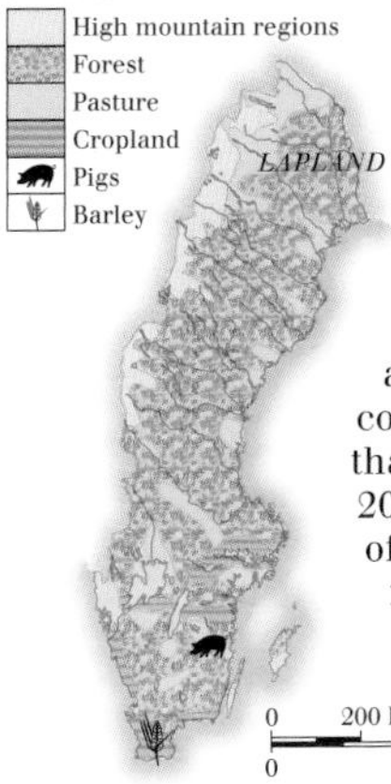

High mountain regions
Forest
Pasture
Cropland
Pigs
Barley
LAPLAND
0 200 km
0 200 miles

ENVIRONMENT

Sustainability rank: 4th

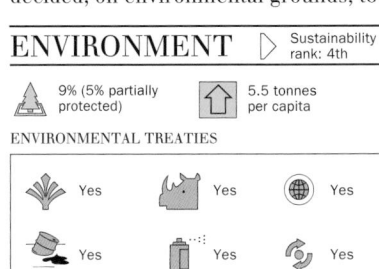

9% (5% partially protected)

5.5 tonnes per capita

ENVIRONMENTAL TREATIES

Yes Yes Yes

Yes Yes Yes

Since its pioneering Environment Protection Act in 1969, Sweden has invested heavily in environmental protection measures. It has blamed the considerable acid rain damage to forests and lakes on airborne sulfur dioxide from factories in western Europe. Swedish nuclear reactors are said to be very safe, with filtered venting systems designed to retain 90% of all radioactivity released in the event of a core meltdown.

MEDIA

TV ownership high

Daily newspaper circulation 445 per 1000 people

PUBLISHING AND BROADCAST MEDIA

There are over 100 dailies; the most influential are *Expressen*, *Dagens Nyheter*, *Aftonbladet*, and *Svenska Dagbladet*

6 services: 2 state-owned, 4 independent

3 services: 2 state-controlled, 1 private

Press freedom is strongly entrenched, although radical views are rarely expressed in the Swedish press. The major daily newspapers' influence is largely confined to Stockholm, since the provinces have their own strong press. Six companies control most of Sweden's magazines.

CRIME

Death penalty not used

5767 prisoners

Down 2% 1992–1996

CRIME RATES

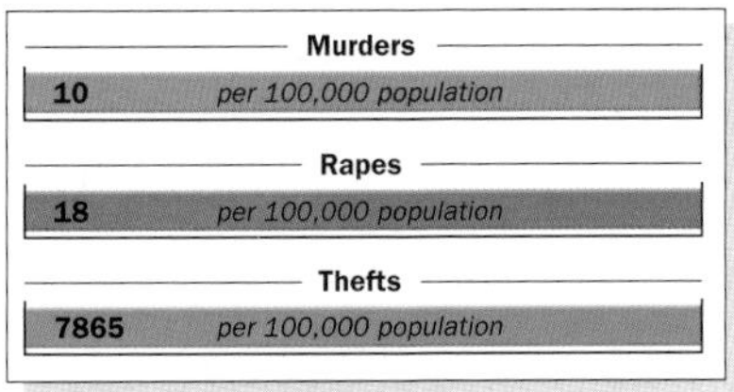

Murders
10 per 100,000 population
Rapes
18 per 100,000 population
Thefts
7865 per 100,000 population

Crime rates are below the European average, although they are the highest among Scandinavian countries. Assault, rape, and theft are growing problems, especially in the cities.

EDUCATION

School leaving age: 15

99%

275,217 students

THE EDUCATION SYSTEM

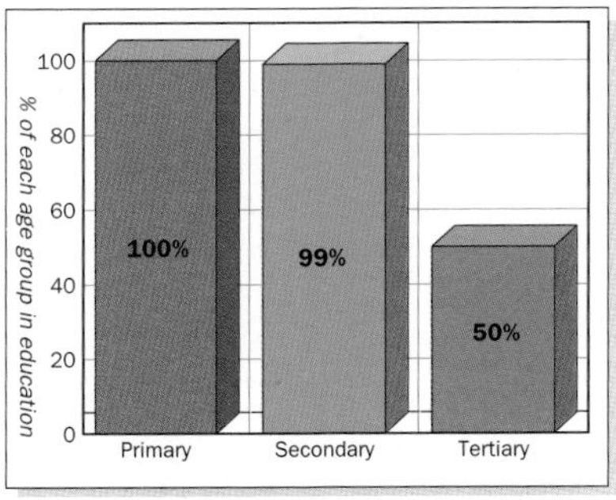

100
80
60
40
20
0
% of each age group in education
100%
99%
50%
Primary
Secondary
Tertiary

Education spending (public and private) is among the OECD's highest as a percentage of GDP.

Coeducational comprehensive schools are the norm. The higher education system is freely available to most of the population, and many adults return to college to do further courses.

HEALTH

Welfare state health benefits

1 per 323 people

Heart and cerebrovascular diseases, cancers, accidents

Sweden's health care system is comprehensive and of a universally high standard. Spending fell by an average of 2% in real terms in the 1990s, but the trend is now being reversed. Savings have been made by increasing outpatient care, reducing hospital beds, and cutting jobs. Since 1994 individuals have had the right to choose their own doctor, while doctors and specialists can now set up private practices. In 1999 the government agreed to compensate more than 60,000 people subjected to enforced sterilization in 1935–1975.

SPENDING

GDP/cap. increase

CONSUMPTION AND SPENDING

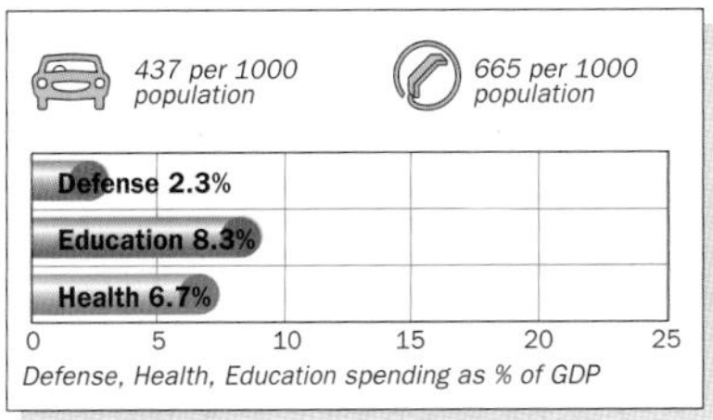

437 per 1000 population
665 per 1000 population
Defense 2.3%
Education 8.3%
Health 6.7%
0
5
10
15
20
25
Defense, Health, Education spending as % of GDP

Sweden has small income differentials, and Swedish executives are paid less than some of their European counterparts. Social competition and a sense of hierarchy are limited compared with other European states or the USA. Despite some cuts in services, the welfare system still offers some of the best provisions in Europe.

Swedes are keen overseas property buyers, particularly of villas in Italy and the south of France. Net overseas per capita investment remains among the highest in the world. PC ownership is high, and nearly 60% of Swedes had used the Internet by 2001.

WORLD RANKING

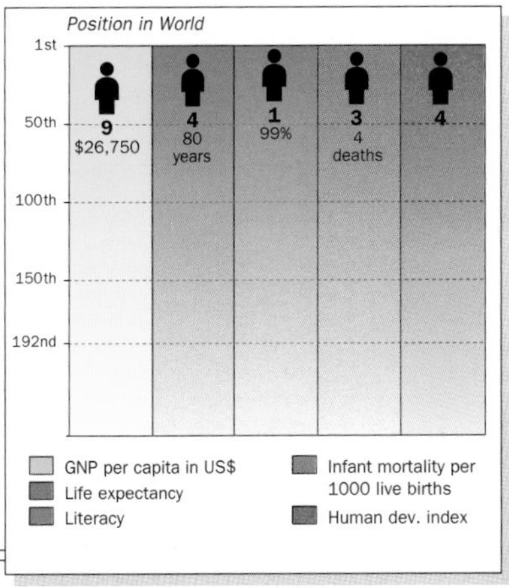

Position in World
1st
50th
100th
150th
192nd
9
$26,750
4
80 years
1
99%
3
4 deaths
4
GNP per capita in US$
Life expectancy
Literacy
Infant mortality per 1000 live births
Human dev. index

S

SWITZERLAND

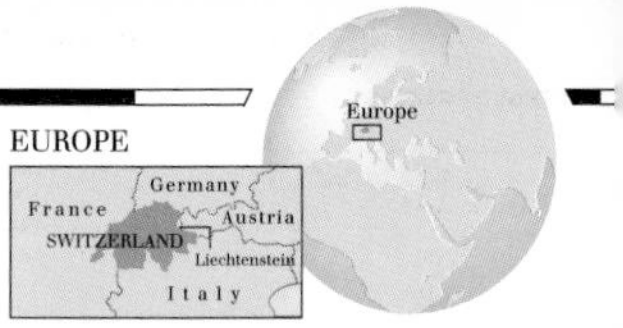
Europe
EUROPE
Germany
France
Austria
SWITZERLAND
Liechtenstein
Italy

OFFICIAL NAME: Swiss Confederation **CAPITAL:** Berne (Bern)
POPULATION: 7.4 million **CURRENCY:** Swiss franc **OFFICIAL LANGUAGES:** French, German, and Italian

1291 | 1857 | Aug 1 | CH | +1 | +41 | .ch

SWITZERLAND LIES at the center of western Europe geographically, but outside it politically. Sometimes called Europe's water tower, it is the source of all four of the region's major river systems: the Po, the Rhine, the Rhône, and the Inn–Danube. Switzerland has built one of the world's most prosperous economies, aided by the fact that it has retained its neutral status through every major European conflict since 1815. The process of European integration has been the latest and strongest challenge to Swiss neutralism, but it remains outside the EU.

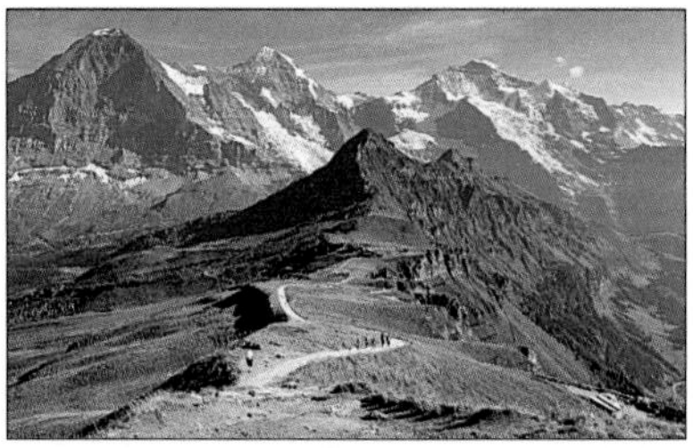

***The Eiger in the Berner Oberland.** In 1994, a referendum voted to ban all lorry transit traffic from the Swiss Alps from 2004.*

CLIMATE

Mountain/continental

WEATHER CHART

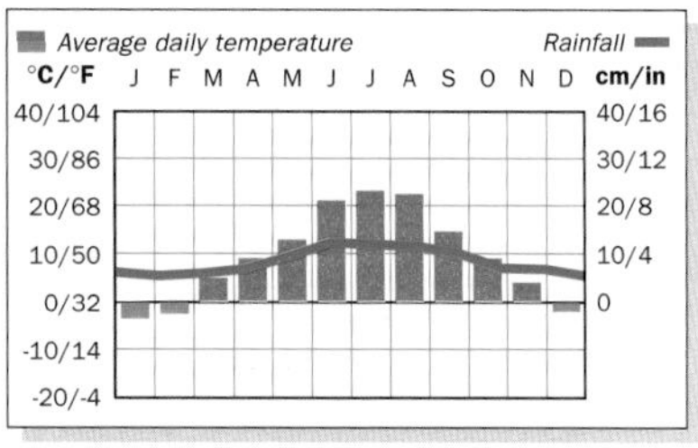
Average daily temperature
Rainfall
°C/°F
J F M A M J J A S O N D
cm/in
40/104
30/86
20/68
10/50
0/32
-10/14
-20/-4
40/16
30/12
20/8
10/4
0

Temperature and weather fluctuate enormously, not only seasonally but because of the huge variations in altitude and the country's location in the center of Europe. On the plateau north of the Alps, where most of the population lives, summers are warm and winters dry, cool, and often foggy. South of the Alps, it is warmer and sunnier. Strong southerly winds, or *föhn*, can bring summerlike weather even in winter. Avalanches have been a problem in recent years.

TRANSPORTATION

Drive on right

Kloten, Zürich
20.9m passengers

16 ships
368,000 grt

THE TRANSPORTATION NETWORK

71,059 km (44,154 miles)	1638 km (1018 miles)
3143 km (1953 miles)	1208 km (751 miles)

Switzerland is a major European freight transit route. Pollution from trucks is a major concern, as is safety, after a major fire in the Mont Blanc tunnel in 1999. The NEAT project, inaugurated in 1996, will provide two new high-speed rail lines through two tunnels, one of 57 km and one of 33 km, linking Basel and Milan, whose trains will carry trucks.

TOURISM

Visitors : Population 1.5:1

11.4m visitors

Up 7% in 2000

MAIN TOURIST ARRIVALS

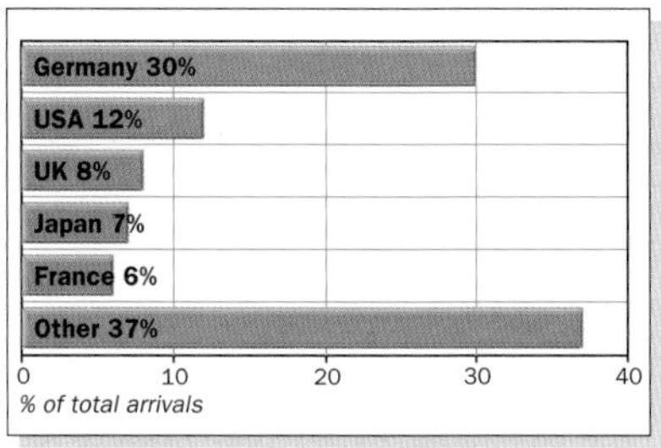
Germany 30%
USA 12%
UK 8%
Japan 7%
France 6%
Other 37%
0
10
20
30
40
% of total arrivals

Tourism is Switzerland's third-largest industry. About 350,000 Swiss earn their living from it, and tourism accounts for around 3% of GDP. The Alps are the main attraction, drawing winter and summer tourists from around the world. However, several factors have led to the recent downturn in the industry: warmer winters have resulted in a shorter skiing season; the rise in value of the Swiss franc has made Switzerland an expensive destination; and Austria is offering tough competition.

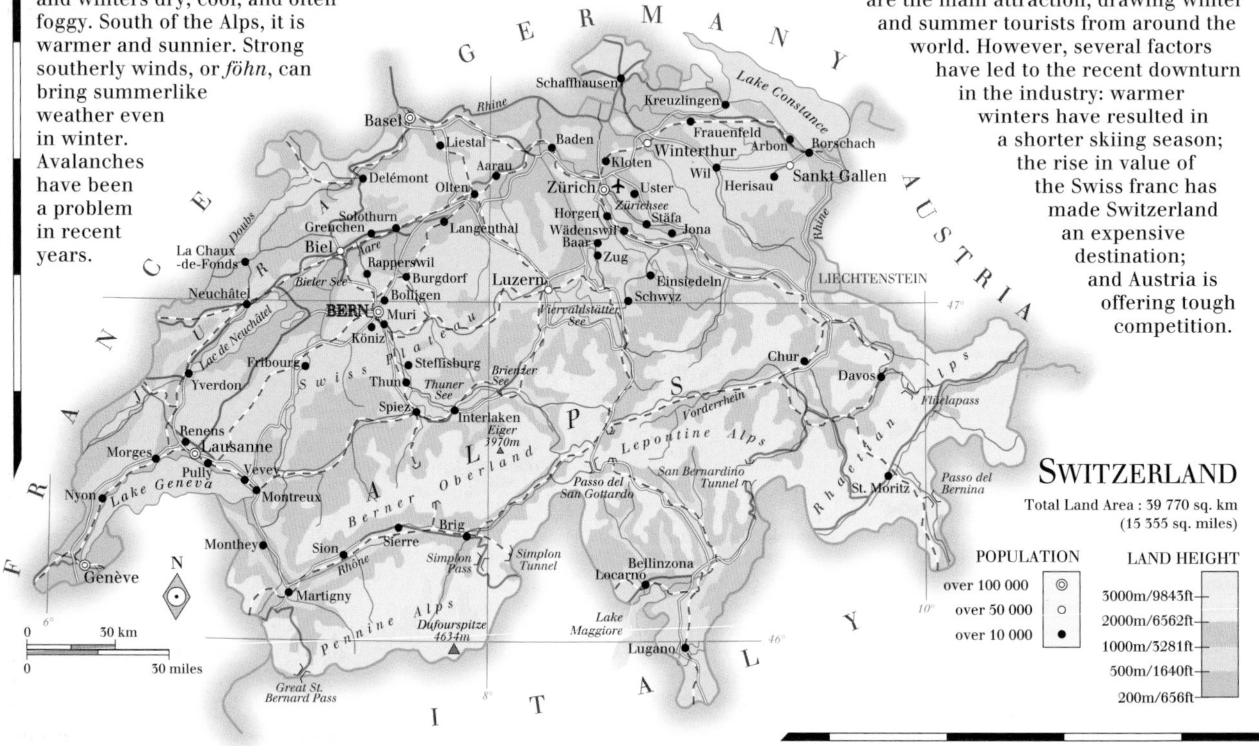
GERMANY
FRANCE
AUSTRIA
ITALY
LIECHTENSTEIN
Schaffhausen
Basel
Rhine
Kreuzlingen
Lake Constance
Liestal
Baden
Frauenfeld
Arbon
Rorschach
Winterthur
Kloten
Wil
Herisau
Sankt Gallen
Delémont
Aarau
Olten
Zürich
Uster
Zürichsee
Horgen
Stäfa
Jona
Wädenswil
Baar
Zug
Solothurn
Grenchen
Langenthal
Biel
Aare
Rapperswil
La Chaux-de-Fonds
Doubs
Burgdorf
Bieler See
Luzern
Einsiedeln
Schwyz
Neuchâtel
Bolligen
BERN
Muri
Vierwaldstätter See
Köniz
Lac de Neuchâtel
Fribourg
Steffisburg
Swiss Plateau
Brienzer See
Yverdon
Thun
Thuner See
Spiez
Interlaken
Chur
Davos
Flüelapass
Vorderrhein
Renens
Lausanne
Morges
Pully
Vevey
Montreux
Lake Geneva
Nyon
Eiger 3970m
Berner Oberland
Lepontine Alps
Rhaetian Alps
San Bernardino Tunnel
Passo del San Gottardo
St. Moritz
Passo del Bernina
Brig
Sion
Sierre
Monthey
Rhône
Simplon Pass
Simplon Tunnel
Bellinzona
Locarno
Genève
Martigny
Pennine Alps
Dufourspitze 4634m
Lake Maggiore
Lugano
Great St. Bernard Pass
Jura
N
0 30 km
0 30 miles
47°
46°
6°
8°
10°
SWITZERLAND
Total Land Area : 39 770 sq. km (15 355 sq. miles)
POPULATION
over 100 000
over 50 000
over 10 000
LAND HEIGHT
3000m/9843ft
2000m/6562ft
1000m/3281ft
500m/1640ft
200m/656ft

S

PEOPLE

Pop. density medium

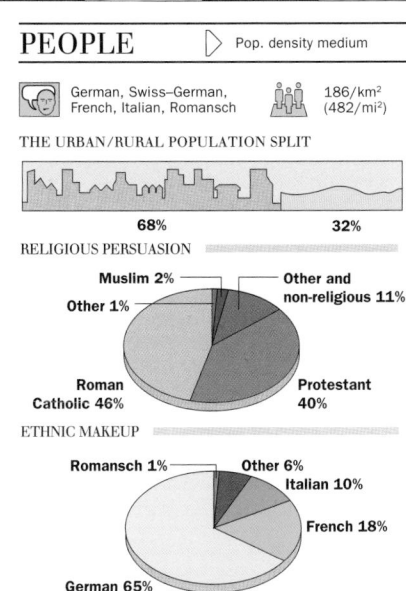

German, Swiss-German, French, Italian, Romansch

186/km² (482/mi²)

THE URBAN/RURAL POPULATION SPLIT

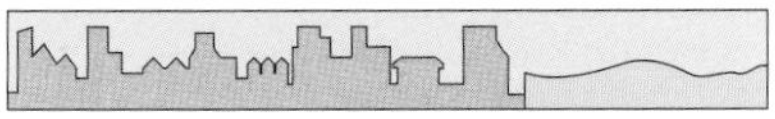
68%
32%

RELIGIOUS PERSUASION

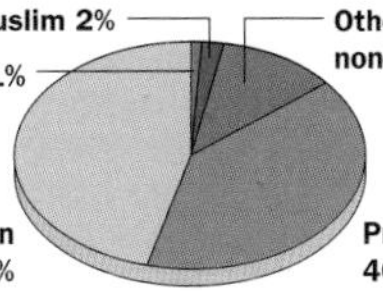
Muslim 2%
Other and non-religious 11%
Other 1%
Roman Catholic 46%
Protestant 40%

ETHNIC MAKEUP

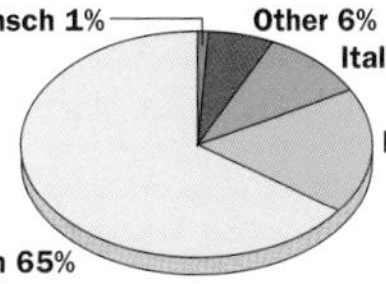
Romansch 1%
Other 6%
Italian 10%
French 18%
German 65%

Switzerland is composed of distinct German-Swiss, French-Swiss, and Italian-Swiss linguistic groups. About 40,000 in the eastern canton of Grisons speak Romansch. The German-Swiss, in the majority, are a tightly knit community, with a dialect that is impenetrable to most outsiders. In recent years, the three groups have grown further apart. The French-Swiss, in favor of joining the EU, are opposed by the German-Swiss. In Italian-speaking Ticino, a political party has emerged to champion Italian-Swiss interests. Tension between Swiss and immigrant workers gave rise to vocal support for strict limits on the number of foreigners, but in 2000 this was heavily defeated as a referendum proposal.

Society retains strong conservative elements. Two half-cantons granted women the vote at regional level only in 1989 and 1990. Marriage rates are high and divorce is less common than in most other European states.

POPULATION AGE BREAKDOWN

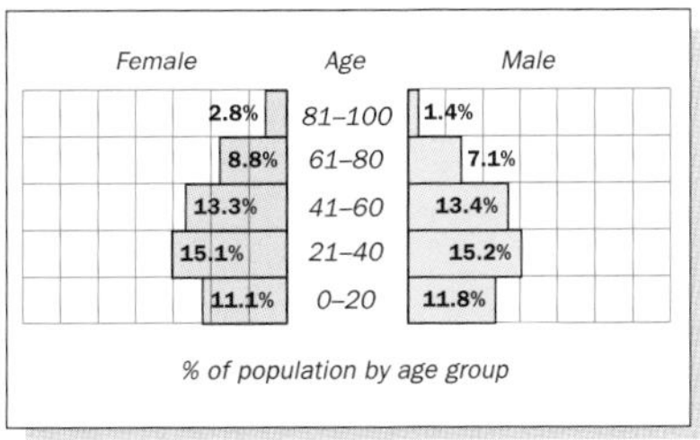
Female
Age
Male
2.8% 81–100 1.4%
8.8% 61–80 7.1%
13.3% 41–60 13.4%
15.1% 21–40 15.2%
11.1% 0–20 11.8%
% of population by age group

WORLD AFFAIRS

Not a member of the UN

CE | G10 | OECD | OSCE | PfP

The basis of Switzerland's foreign policy remains its neutrality. Geneva has retained its position as a center for many international organizations. The UN has its European headquarters there, and it is home to the ICRC. The city has often hosted diplomatic negotiations: those for the START nuclear reduction treaties, and attempts to resolve the conflict in the former Yugoslavia took place there.

Switzerland has so far not joined the process of closer European integration. In 1992 voters rejected membership of the EEA, widely seen as the first step toward membership of the EU. Many advocates of joining the EU believe that the economy will suffer without closer integration. Opponents argue that Switzerland's seeming isolation will enhance its role as an international tax haven. In 2000 voters approved a series of bilateral agreements with the EU on specific issues, but in 2001 they overwhelmingly rejected a proposal that Switzerland should apply for EU membership.

POLITICS

Multiparty elections

L. House 1999/2003
U. House 1999/2003

President Moritz Leuenberger

AT THE LAST ELECTION

National Council 200 seats

9% Others
26% SP/PS
22% SVP/UDC
21% FDP/PRD
17% CVP/PDC
5% GPS/PES

SP/PS = Social Democratic Party **SVP/UDC** = Swiss People's Party **FDP/PRD** = Radical Democratic Party **CVP/PDC** = Christian Democratic People's Party **GPS/PES** = Green Party of Switzerland

Council of States 46 seats

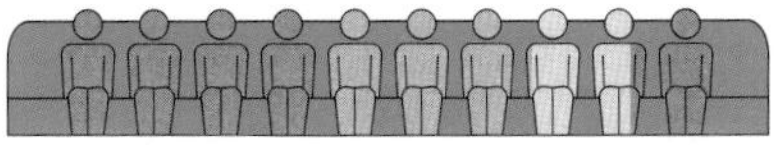
39% FDP/PRD
33% CVP/PDC
15% SVP/UDC
13% SP/PS

Switzerland is a federal democratic republic with 26 autonomous cantons. The presidency rotates every year.

MAIN POLITICAL ISSUES

European integration

Almost all politicians and business leaders favor joining the EU, or at least the European Economic Area (EEA), but voters remain sharply divided. The Swiss are strongly attached to their decentralized style of government and fear that this would be lost within the EU. There are also worries that in a barrier-free Europe, Switzerland's high standards of living would fall because of a large influx of immigrants.

Swiss banks and Holocaust victims' funds

The banks have faced criticism for failing to help return deposited funds to the relatives of victims of the Nazi Holocaust. In 1997 Swiss banks agreed to establish a Holocaust fund, while the government formed a new Fund for Needy Holocaust Victims. In 1998 the two largest Swiss banks agreed a $1.25 billion settlement with 31,500 Holocaust victims and their families in return for agreement that there would be no future claims against Swiss banks or the government.

PROFILE

The same four-party coalition has been in power in Switzerland since 1959. Domestic and foreign policies have changed little. Politics has recently become more contentious, however, with voting patterns becoming more polarized. Divisive issues are those of drugs and of membership of the EU. Both right-wing and green minority parties have recently gained more seats in parliament. The right-wing SVP/UDC in particular capitalized on growing hostility to immigration to perform strongly in the 1999 elections.

Switzerland's political system is unique in Europe, in that taking important decisions depends on the results of referenda. A petition of more than 100,000 signatures can force a referendum on any issue.

***Ruth Dreifuss,** of the CVP, first woman president, held office in 1999.*

***Vice President Kaspar Villiger,** set to be president in 2002.*

CHRONOLOGY

The autonomy of the Swiss cantons was curtailed by the Habsburg Empire in the 11th century. In 1291, the three cantons of Unterwalden, Schwyz, and Uri set up the Perpetual League to pursue Swiss liberty. Joined by other cantons, they succeeded in 1499 in gaining virtual independence. The Habsburgs retained a titular role.

- **1648** Peace of Westphalia ending Thirty Years' War, in which Switzerland played no active part, recognizes full Swiss independence.
- **1798** Invaded by French.
- **1815** Congress of Vienna after Napoleon's defeat confirms Swiss independence and establishes its neutrality. Geneva and Valais join Swiss Confederation.

S

CHRONOLOGY *continued*

- **1848** New constitution – central government given more powers, but cantons' powers guaranteed.
- **1857** Neuchâtel joins confederation.
- **1863** Henri Dunant founds ICRC in Geneva.
- **1874** Referendum established as important decision-making tool.
- **1914–1918** Plays humanitarian role in World War I.
- **1919** Proportional representation ensures future political stability.
- **1920** Joins League of Nations.
- **1939–1945** Neutral again. Refuses to join UN in 1945.
- **1959** Founder member of EFTA. Present four-party coalition comes to power, taking over FDP/PRD dominance of government.
- **1967** Right-wing groups make electoral gains, campaigning to restrict entry of foreign workers.
- **1971** Most women granted right to vote in federal elections.
- **1984** Parliament approves application for UN membership. Elisabeth Kopp is first woman minister (justice minister).
- **1986** Referendum opposes joining UN. Immigrant numbers restricted.
- **1988** Kopp resigns over allegedly violating secrecy of information laws.
- **1990** Kopp acquitted. Case revealed Public Prosecutor's office held secret files on 200,000 people. Violent protests. State security laws amended.
- **1991** Large increase in attacks on asylum-seekers' hostels.
- **1992** Joins IMF and World Bank. Referendum vetoes joining EEA.
- **1994** Referendum approves new antiracism law and tighter laws against narcotics traffickers and illegal immigrants.
- **1998** $1.25 billion compensation for Holocaust victims whose funds were deposited in Swiss banks.
- **1999** Ruth Dreifuss first woman president.
- **2000** Referendum endorses close trade links with EU.
- **2001** EU membership again rejected in referendum.

AID

Donor

$969m (donations) — Up 8% in 1999

With total disbursements amounting to 0.35% of GNP in 1999, Switzerland ranks above the (OECD) average of 0.24% as an aid donor. Good governance and promoting investment are current priorities. Yugoslavia (including Kosovo) currently receives most, followed by Bangladesh and Mozambique.

DEFENSE

Compulsory military service

$3.11bn — Down 16% in 1999

SWISS ARMED FORCES

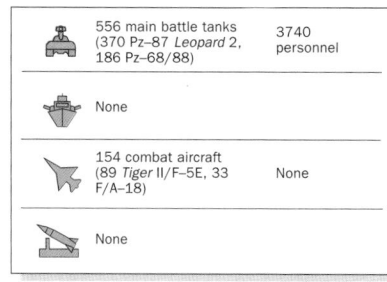

Army	556 main battle tanks (370 Pz–87 *Leopard* 2, 186 Pz–68/88)	3740 personnel
Navy	None	
Air force	154 combat aircraft (89 *Tiger* II/F–5E, 33 F/A–18)	None
Missiles	None	

The army is, in one sense, among the largest in Europe. It is organized so that almost 400,000 conscripts can be called up and armed in a few hours; it still uses skis, bicycles, and horses to protect the Alps. Bridges and tunnels are mined in accordance with a defense strategy drafted in the early 1900s. Military service and further training at intervals is compulsory for males, up to the age of 50.

As in the rest of Europe, force numbers are being cut in response to the end of the Cold War. In 1995, legislation allowing civilian service in place of military service was passed. Voters approved in 2001 a referendum proposal allowing Swiss soldiers to bear arms when on international peacekeeping operations.

ECONOMICS

Inflation 1.4% p.a. (1990–1999)

$273.9bn — 1.6007–1.6205 Swiss francs

SCORE CARD

World GNP Ranking	19th
GNP per Capita	$38,380
Balance of Payments	$24.5bn
Inflation	0.8%
Unemployment	3%

EXPORTS

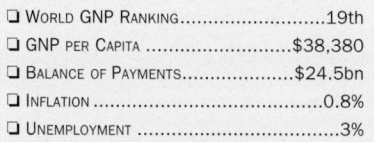

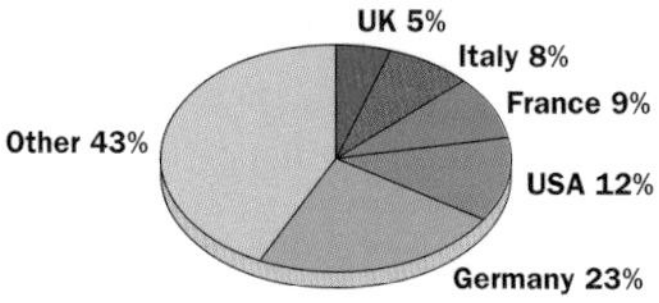
UK 5%
Italy 8%
France 9%
USA 12%
Germany 23%
Other 43%

IMPORTS

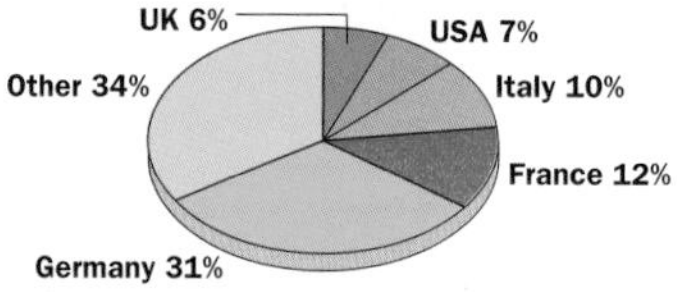
UK 6%
USA 7%
Italy 10%
France 12%
Germany 31%
Other 34%

Strengths

Highly skilled workforce. Reliable service provider. Major machine tool and precision engineering industries. Powerful chemical, pharmaceutical, and banking multinationals. Banking secrecy laws attract foreign capital; banking sector contributes 9% of GNP. Ability to innovate to capture mass markets, typified by Swatch watch and Swatch car.

Weaknesses

Protected cartels result in many overpriced goods. Highly subsidized agricultural sector.

Profile

The economy is widely diversified, with 62% of GDP coming from services and 34% from industry. There are several large multinational enterprises and, notably, a highly successful banking sector managing around one-third of the world's offshore private wealth. In the 1990s, bank accounts belonging to Nazi Holocaust victims were uncovered. In 1997 a Holocaust fund was established, and in 1998 the three largest Swiss banks offered $1.25 billion to settle Holocaust victims' claims.

ECONOMIC PERFORMANCE INDICATOR

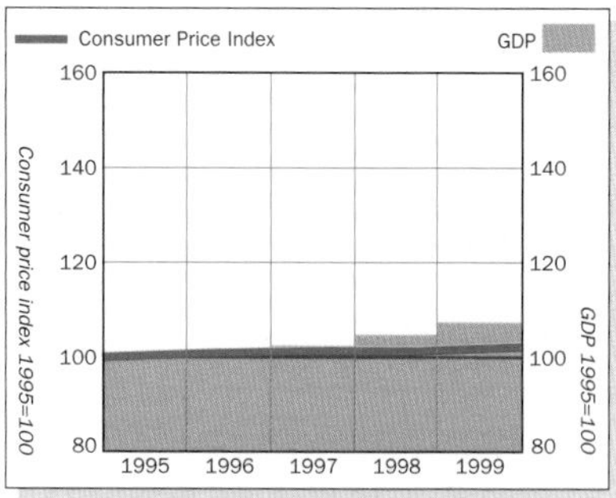
Consumer Price Index
GDP
160
140
120
100
80
Consumer price index 1995=100
GDP 1995=100
1995
1996
1997
1998
1999

SWITZERLAND : MAJOR BUSINESSES

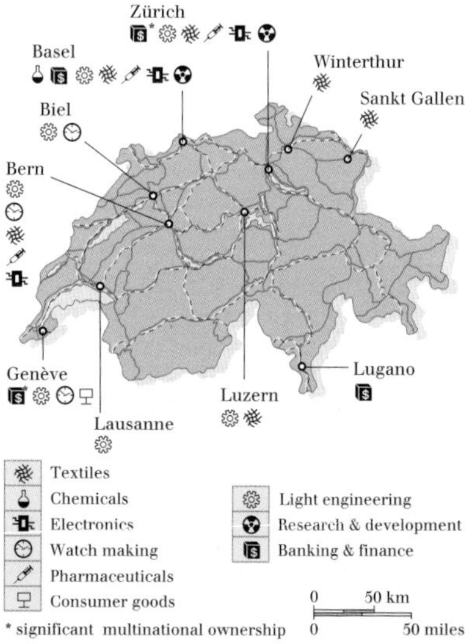
Zürich
Basel
Winterthur
Sankt Gallen
Biel
Bern
Genève
Lausanne
Luzern
Lugano
Textiles
Chemicals
Electronics
Watch making
Pharmaceuticals
Consumer goods
Light engineering
Research & development
Banking & finance
* significant multinational ownership
0 50 km
0 50 miles

RESOURCES

Electric power 16.7m kw

3009 tonnes

Not an oil producer; refines 132,000 b/d

1.6m cattle, 1.4m pigs, 6.7m chickens

Rock salt, marble, gypsum

ELECTRICITY GENERATION

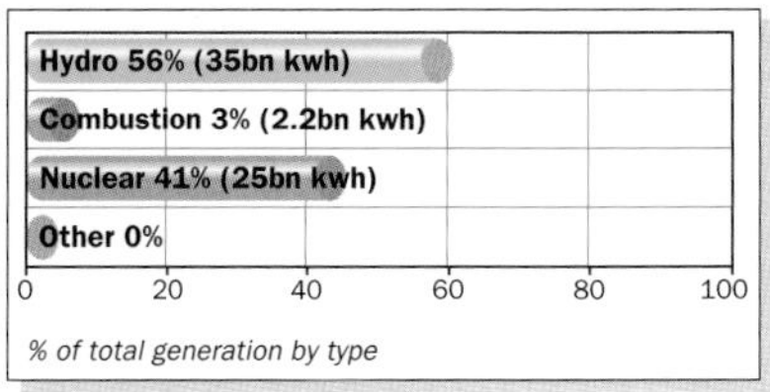
Hydro 56% (35bn kwh)
Combustion 3% (2.2bn kwh)
Nuclear 41% (25bn kwh)
Other 0%
0
20
40
60
80
100
% of total generation by type

Switzerland is poor in natural resources, having no valuable minerals in commercially exploitable quantities. Over half of its electricity comes from hydropower, while five nuclear plants supply most of the rest, so that spending on imported oil and coal is kept to a minimum – they account for less than 4% of the total import bill. The 1986 Chernobyl accident inspired large-scale antinuclear-power demonstrations and a sixth plant was canceled. However, a referendum approved continued use of existing plants.

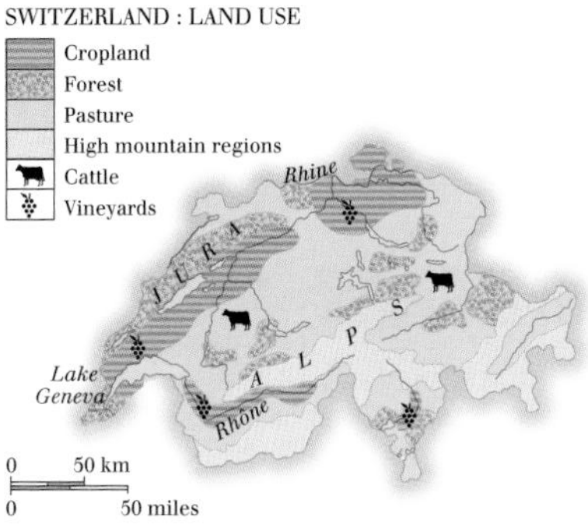
SWITZERLAND : LAND USE
Cropland
Forest
Pasture
High mountain regions
Cattle
Vineyards
Rhine
JURA
ALPS
Lake Geneva
Rhône
0
50 km
0
50 miles

ENVIRONMENT

Sustainability rank: 5th

18%

6 tonnes per capita

ENVIRONMENTAL TREATIES

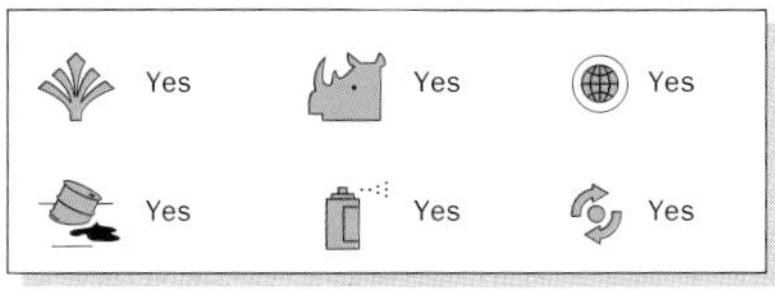
Yes
Yes
Yes
Yes
Yes
Yes

The Swiss are among the most environmentally conscious people in the world and are willing to back their convictions with money: the Basel–Milan tunnel plan was approved by referendum, despite the estimated $13.3bn cost. The planners aim to achieve a total ban on truck traffic through Switzerland by 2004, although some argue that a ban will not be necessary, since by traveling on trains trucks will cut two hours off the Basel–Milan journey. The Swiss are keen recyclers and taxation is used to encourage this.

MEDIA

TV ownership high

Daily newspaper circulation 331 per 1000 people

PUBLISHING AND BROADCAST MEDIA

There are 84 daily newspapers. The largest circulations are held by *Tages Anzeiger* and the Zürich-based tabloid *Blick*

3 independent services broadcasting in German, Romansch, French, and Italian

3 independent services broadcasting in German, Romansch, French, and Italian

The Swiss media are organized broadly along regional lines, and reflect the country's linguistic divisions. The German-, Romansch-, French-, and Italian-language TV and radio stations tend to focus on the interests of their specific communities. German, Italian, and French satellite TV is widely available. Few newspapers are distributed throughout the country. *Tribune de Genève* and *Neue Zürcher Zeitung* are exceptions.

CRIME

Death penalty not used

5655 prisoners

Up 6% 1996–1998

CRIME RATES

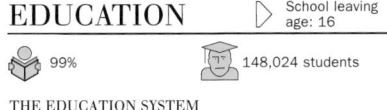

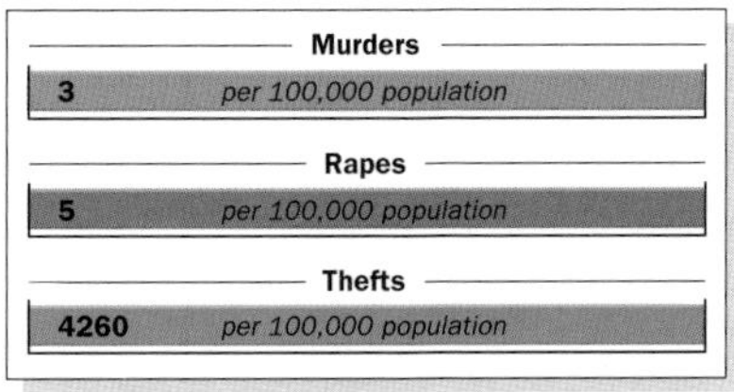
Murders
3
per 100,000 population
Rapes
5
per 100,000 population
Thefts
4260
per 100,000 population

Crime rates are low by international standards. Muggings and burglaries are on the increase and are often related to narcotics. More cases of banking secrecy laws attracting laundered funds are coming to light.

EDUCATION

School leaving age: 16

99%

148,024 students

THE EDUCATION SYSTEM

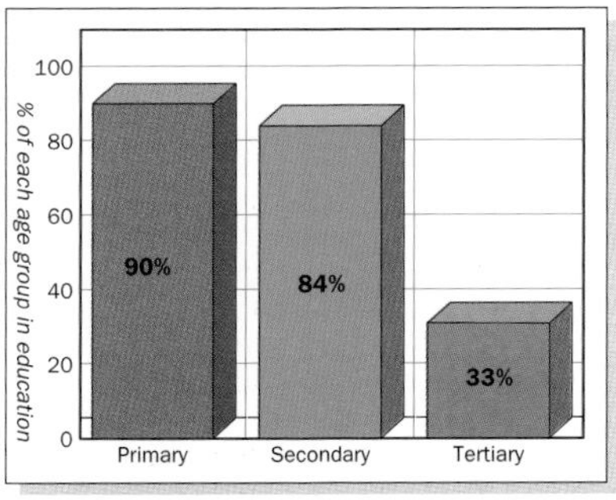
100
80
60
40
20
0
% of each age group in education
90%
84%
33%
Primary
Secondary
Tertiary

Of total government expenditure, around 16% is spent on education. Primary and secondary education are controlled by the cantons, so that there are 26 different sytems in operation. Most students after the age of 16 are encouraged to take up vocational studies. Training is thorough and is usually combined with three or four years' apprenticeship in the student's chosen field. The Federal Technological Institute in Zürich has gained an international reputation for its computer programming research.

HEALTH

Welfare state health benefits

1 per 526 people

Heart and cerebrovascular diseases, cancers, accidents

The health system is among the most efficient and pioneering in the world, and is ranked second, after Japan, by the WHO for attainment. Health costs are covered by compulsory insurance schemes.

SPENDING

GDP/cap. increase

CONSUMPTION AND SPENDING

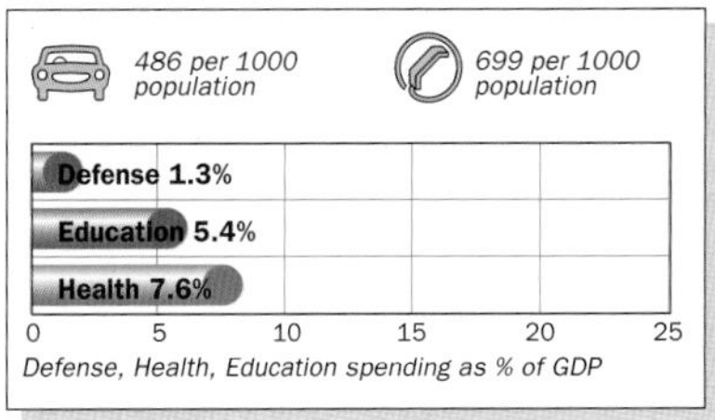
486 per 1000 population
699 per 1000 population
Defense 1.3%
Education 5.4%
Health 7.6%
0
5
10
15
20
25
Defense, Health, Education spending as % of GDP

Immigrant workers do most low-paid and menial jobs. Wages in office jobs are relatively high, although the cost of living is also well above the European average. Many workers choose to live in France and commute across the border. The land market is highly regulated.

WORLD RANKING

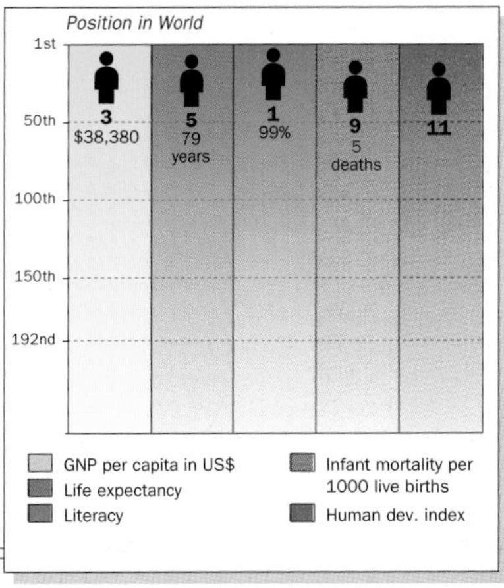
Position in World
1st
50th
100th
150th
192nd
3
$38,380
5
79
years
1
99%
9
5
deaths
11
GNP per capita in US$
Life expectancy
Literacy
Infant mortality per 1000 live births
Human dev. index

S

SYRIA

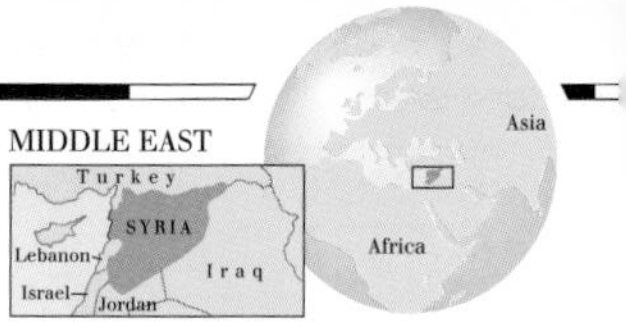
MIDDLE EAST
Turkey
SYRIA
Lebanon
Israel
Jordan
Iraq
Asia
Africa

OFFICIAL NAME: Syrian Arab Republic **CAPITAL:** Damascus
POPULATION: 16.1 million **CURRENCY:** Syrian pound **OFFICIAL LANGUAGE:** Arabic

1941 | 1967 | April 17 | SYR | +2 | +963 | .sy

SYRIA SHARES BORDERS with Lebanon, Israel, Jordan, Iraq, and Turkey. Many Syrians regard their country as an artificial creation of French mandated rule, which lasted from 1920 to independence. They identify instead with a Greater Syria encompassing Lebanon, Jordan, and Palestine. Since independence, Syria's foreign relations have been turbulent, although President Hafez al-Assad's authoritarian Ba'athist regime brought a measure of internal stability.

CLIMATE

Steppe/hot desert/ Mediterranean

WEATHER CHART

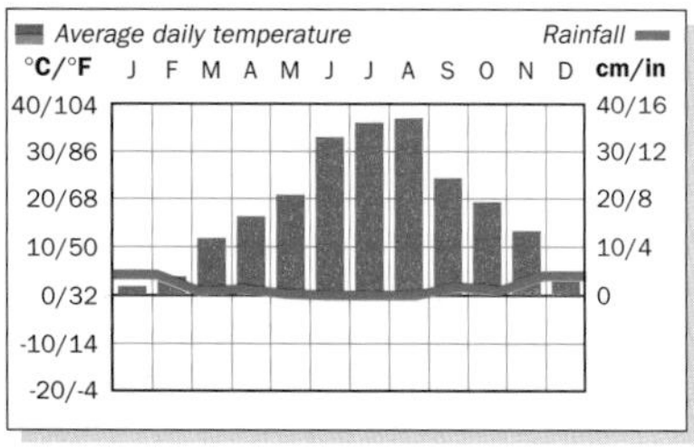
Average daily temperature
Rainfall
°C/°F
J F M A M J J A S O N D
cm/in
40/104
30/86
20/68
10/50
0/32
-10/14
-20/-4
40/16
30/12
20/8
10/4
0

The coastal climate is Mediterranean, with mild, wet winters and dry, hot summers. Away from the coast, the country is increasingly arid, with some desert areas. In the mountains, snow is common in winter. Most of the country receives less than 25 cm (10 in) of rainfall a year and, away from the coast, rainfall is very unpredictable.

TRANSPORTATION

Drive on right

Damascus International 1.5m passengers

220 ships 427,500 grt

THE TRANSPORTATION NETWORK

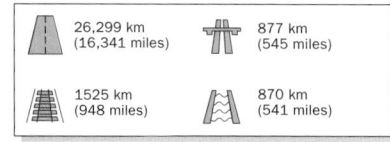

26,299 km (16,341 miles)

877 km (545 miles)

1525 km (948 miles)

870 km (541 miles)

The road network is unreliable in rural areas, especially during the winter after rain. Bus services operate to most towns from Damascus and Aleppo. Roads are integrated with the railroads, which carry over four million passengers a year and are vital to freight transportation. The rail link from Aleppo to Al' Mawsil, Iraq, reopened in mid-2000. Damascus is the main international airport and Latakia the main port.

TOURISM

Visitors : Population 1:12

1.4m visitors

Up 9% in 1999

MAIN TOURIST ARRIVALS

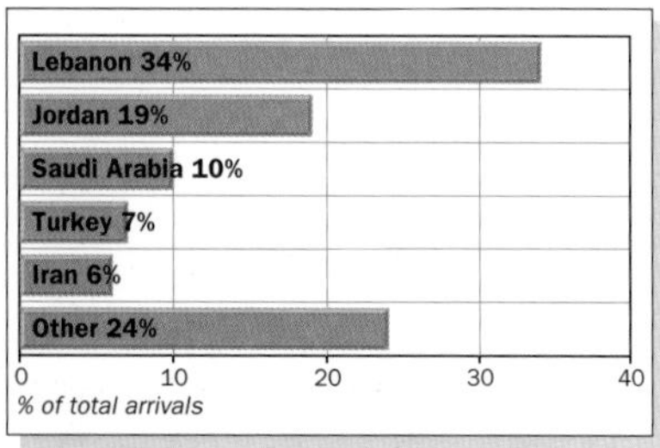
Lebanon 34%
Jordan 19%
Saudi Arabia 10%
Turkey 7%
Iran 6%
Other 24%
0
10
20
30
40
% of total arrivals

Years of political turbulence, allegations of human rights abuses committed under Hafez al-Assad's regime, and strict, complex travel regulations retarded the development of tourism. However, just before the 1990–1991 Gulf War, Syria began to compete with other Middle Eastern states as a holiday destination. Modern hotels were built in most cities and facilities improved to cater for growing numbers of Western visitors. Following the war, tourist numbers dropped sharply, but are now gradually recovering. Syria's main attractions are its antiquities and historic cities, with their covered markets (*soukhs*), baths, and mosques – Damascus, said to be the oldest inhabited city in the world; the ruined desert city of Palmyra; and Aleppo, with its citadel. Syria has a wealth of castles dating back to the Crusades and sites associated with the advent of Islam. In addition, there are as many as 3500 as yet unexcavated archaeological sites. Syria's coastline on the Mediterranean has fine beaches, and there are mountain resorts in Latakia.

The ancient city of Palmyra, *in Syria's central region, was once the capital of the kingdom of Queen Zenobia.*

PEOPLE

Pop. density medium

Arabic, French, Kurdish, Armenian, Circassian, Turkmen, Assyrian, Aramaic

87/km² (227/mi²)

THE URBAN/RURAL POPULATION SPLIT

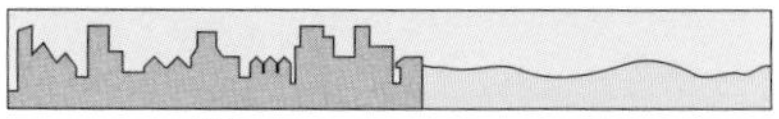
54%
46%

RELIGIOUS PERSUASION

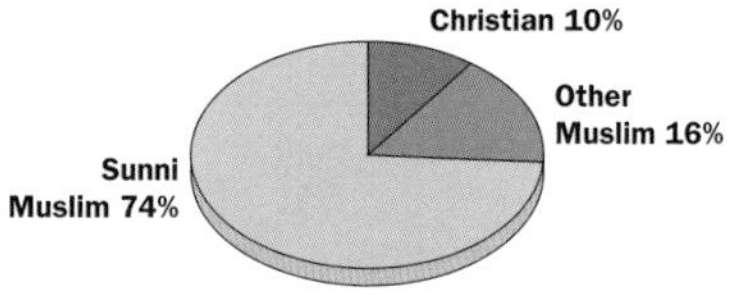
Christian 10%
Other Muslim 16%
Sunni Muslim 74%

ETHNIC MAKEUP

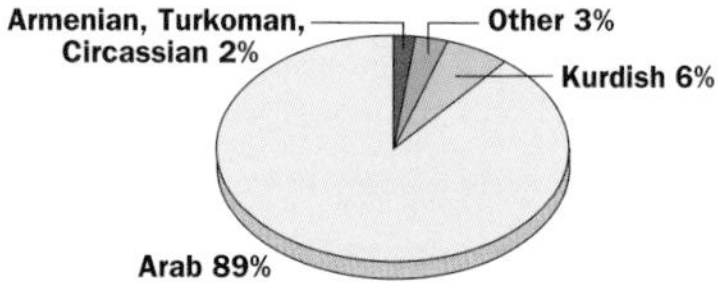
Armenian, Turkoman, Circassian 2%
Other 3%
Kurdish 6%
Arab 89%

Most Syrians live near the coast, where the largest cities are sited. About 90% are Muslim. They include the politically dominant Alawis, a heterodox offshoot of Shi'a, representing 12% of the population, based in Latakia and Tartous provinces. There is also a sizable Christian minority. In the west and north a mosaic of groups exists, including Kurds, Turkic-speakers, and Armenians, the latter based in cities. Damascus, Al Qamishli, and Aleppo have small Jewish communities, and there are three villages where Aramaic is spoken. In addition, some 300,000 Palestinian refugees have settled in Syria. Minorities were initially attracted to the ruling Ba'ath Party because of its emphasis on the state over sectarian interests. However, disputes between factions led to the Alawis taking control, fostering resentment among the Sunni Muslim majority.

The emancipation of women, promoted initially in the late 1960s, was carried forward under President Hafez al-Assad. His first woman cabinet minister was appointed in 1976.

POPULATION AGE BREAKDOWN

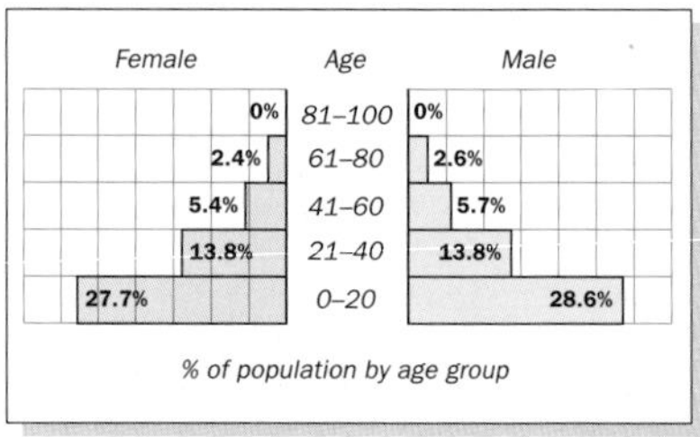
Female
Age
Male
0% 81–100 0%
2.4% 61–80 2.6%
5.4% 41–60 5.7%
13.8% 21–40 13.8%
27.7% 0–20 28.6%
% of population by age group

S

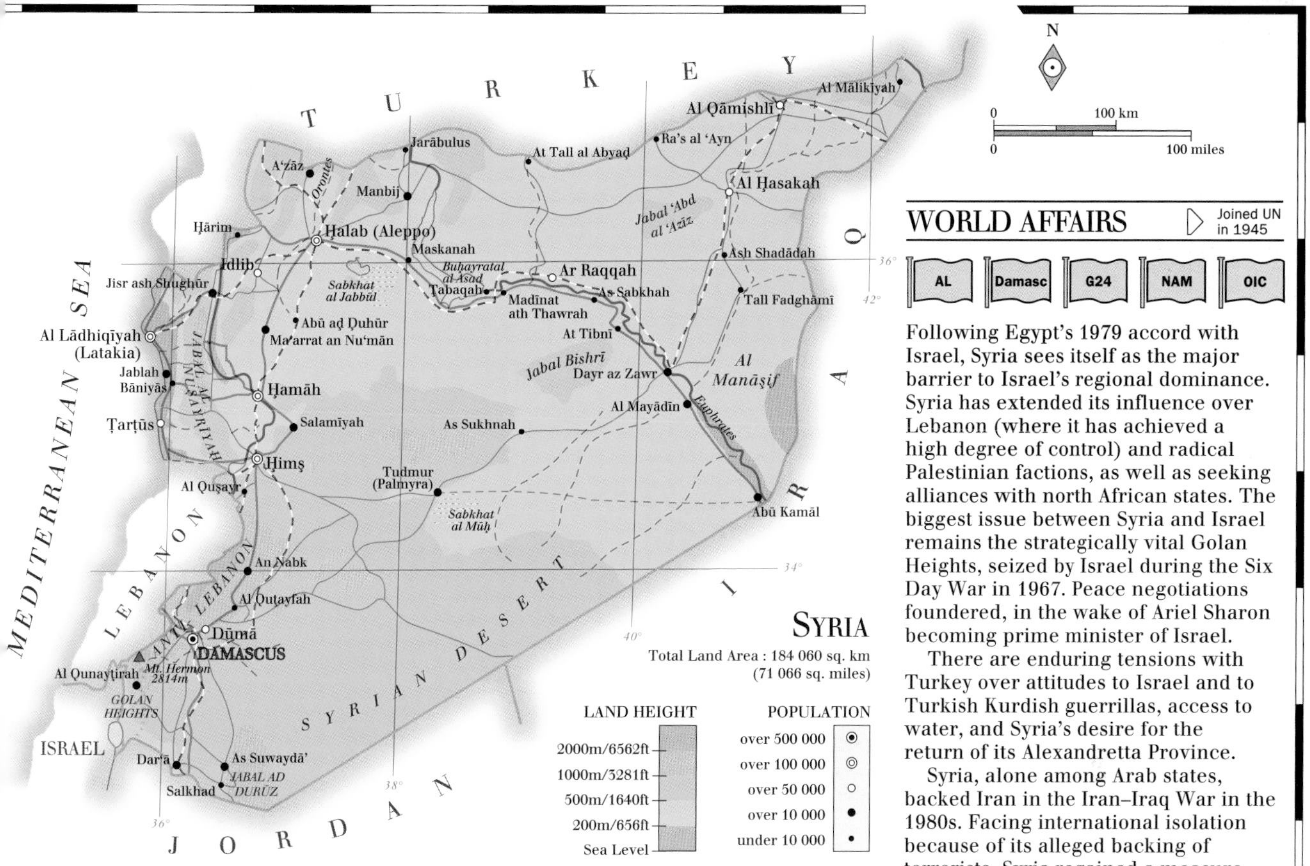
T U R K E Y
Al Mālikīyah
Al Qāmishlī
Ra's al 'Ayn
At Tall al Abyad
Jarābulus
A'zāz
Manbij
Orontes
Ḩārim
Ḩalab (Aleppo)
Maskanah
Idlib
Jisr ash Shughūr
Sabkhat al Jabbūl
Buḩayrat al Asad
Ţabaqah
Ar Raqqah
As Sabkhah
Madīnat ath Thawrah
Jabal 'Abd al 'Azīz
Al Ḩasakah
Ash Shadādah
Tall Fadghāmī
Abū aḑ Ḑuhūr
Ma'arrat an Nu'mān
Al Lādhiqīyah (Latakia)
Jablah
Bāniyās
Ţarţūs
JABAL AN NUŞAYRĪYAH
Ḩamāh
Salamīyah
Ḩimş
Al Quşayr
At Tibnī
Jabal Bishrī
Dayr az Zawr
Al Manāşif
Al Mayādīn
Euphrates
As Sukhnah
Tudmur (Palmyra)
Sabkhat al Mūḩ
Abū Kamāl
I R A Q
MEDITERRANEAN SEA
LEBANON
ANTI-LEBANON
An Nabk
Al Quţayfah
Dūmā
DAMASCUS
Mt. Hermon 2814m
Al Qunayţirah
GOLAN HEIGHTS
ISRAEL
Dar'ā
As Suwaydā'
JABAL AD DURŪZ
Salkhad
SYRIAN DESERT
J O R D A N
N
0 100 km
0 100 miles
SYRIA
Total Land Area : 184 060 sq. km (71 066 sq. miles)
LAND HEIGHT
2000m/6562ft
1000m/3281ft
500m/1640ft
200m/656ft
Sea Level
POPULATION
over 500 000
over 100 000
over 50 000
over 10 000
under 10 000

WORLD AFFAIRS

Joined UN in 1945

AL | Damasc | G24 | NAM | OIC

Following Egypt's 1979 accord with Israel, Syria sees itself as the major barrier to Israel's regional dominance. Syria has extended its influence over Lebanon (where it has achieved a high degree of control) and radical Palestinian factions, as well as seeking alliances with north African states. The biggest issue between Syria and Israel remains the strategically vital Golan Heights, seized by Israel during the Six Day War in 1967. Peace negotiations foundered, in the wake of Ariel Sharon becoming prime minister of Israel.

There are enduring tensions with Turkey over attitudes to Israel and to Turkish Kurdish guerrillas, access to water, and Syria's desire for the return of its Alexandretta Province.

Syria, alone among Arab states, backed Iran in the Iran–Iraq War in the 1980s. Facing international isolation because of its alleged backing of terrorists, Syria regained a measure of respect by securing the release of Western hostages in Lebanon by Shi'a militants. Assad backed the US-led Western allies in the 1990–1991 Gulf War, and by contributing troops legitimized the action in the eyes of the Arab world. In 2000, however, Syria sent humanitarian aid to Iraq, in defiance of the UN blockade.

POLITICS

No multiparty elections

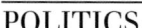

1998/2002

President Bashar al-Assad

AT THE LAST ELECTION

People's Assembly 250 seats

67% **Ba'ath Party**   **33%** **Other Ba'ath**

Ba'ath Party = Members of the National Progressive Front (allies of the Ba'ath Party) **Other Ba'ath** = Parties allied to the Ba'ath Party

Syria is in effect a single-party state. Its military-backed leader from 1970 to 2000 was Hafez al-Assad, a lifelong Ba'ath Party militant. His personal dominance ensured the succession of his son Bashar after his death in June 2000.

Main Political Issues

Human rights

Martial law has not been rescinded since 1963, but the regime has improved its human rights record in recent years. Political prisoners are released under frequent amnesties, and in 1994 all members of the Jewish minority were granted exit visas to travel abroad.

Political pluralism

President Assad dominated Syrian politics for 30 years. His military-backed regime, drawn mainly from his own Alawi minority grouping, kept a tight hold on power, although in his last decade Sunnis gained high political posts. Despite promises made under heavy international pressure Assad never permitted genuine multipartyism. Shortly before Assad's death, the long-serving prime minister Mahmoud az-Zoubi, was forced from office and replace by the modernizing Mohammed Miro. However, Assad's death was immediately followed by his son's election to the party leadership, which was overwhelmingly approved by referendum.

Profile

The Ba'athist military swept to power in 1963 with a vision of uniting all Arab nations under a single Syrian-dominated socialist system. The coup ended the power of city elites and promoted citizens from rural areas. The state became the main employer.

When Assad came to power in 1971, he consolidated the Ba'ath Party as the major political force. Unrest among Islamic militants was crushed, and Assad focused on foreign affairs in a bid to make Syria a major power. Plans in 1978 to unite with fellow Ba'athist Iraq fell apart, however, amid mutual recriminations.

AID

Recipient

$228m (receipts)   Up 46% in 1999

Syria has historically received little aid owing to its human rights record and substantial oil income. It received one-off payments totaling $2 billion in 1992 and $1.2 billion in 1993 after the Gulf War, mainly from Saudi Arabia and the Gulf states, but with contributions from the West and Japan.

Hafez al-Assad, *ruled for three decades until his death in 2000.*

Bashar al-Assad, *succeeded his father as president.*

S

CHRONOLOGY

Under French mandate from 1920, Syria declared independence in 1941, and achieved full autonomy in 1946. From 1958 to 1961 Syria merged with Egypt to form the United Arab Republic.

- ❑ **1963** Ba'athist military junta seizes power. Major General Amin al-Hafez president.
- ❑ **1966** Hafez ousted by military coup supported by radical Ba'ath Party members.
- ❑ **1967** Israel overruns Syrian positions above Lake Tiberias, seizes Golan Heights, and occupies Quneitra. Syria boycotts Arab summit and rejects compromise with Israel.
- ❑ **1970** Hafez al-Assad seizes power in "corrective coup."
- ❑ **1971** Assad elected president for a seven-year term.
- ❑ **1973** New constitution approved by plebiscite confirming Ba'ath Party as dominant force. War launched with Egypt against Israel to regain territory lost in 1967. Further territory temporarily lost to Israel.
- ❑ **1976** With peacekeeping mandate from Arab League, Syria intervenes to quell fighting in Lebanon.
- ❑ **1977** Relations broken off with Egypt after President Sadat's visit to Jerusalem.
- ❑ **1978** National charter signed with Iraq for union. Assad returned for second term.
- ❑ **1980** Membership of Muslim Brotherhood made capital offense. Treaty of Friendship with USSR.
- ❑ **1981** Israel formally annexes Golan Heights. Charter with Iraq collapses.
- ❑ **1982** Islamic extremist uprising in Hama crushed; thousands killed. Israel invades Lebanon; Syrian missiles in Bekaa Valley destroyed.
- ❑ **1985** Assad reelected president. USA claims Syrian links to airport bombings at Rome and Vienna.
- ❑ **1986** Syrian complicity alleged in planting of bomb aboard Israeli airliner in London. EU states, with exception of Greece, impose sanctions.
- ❑ **1989** Diplomatic relations reestablished with Egypt.
- ❑ **1991** Troops take part in Operation Desert Storm. Damascus Declaration aid and defense pact signed with Egypt, Saudi Arabia, Kuwait, UAE, Qatar, Bahrain, and Oman.
- ❑ **1992, 1999** Assad reconfirmed as president.
- ❑ **2000** Forced resignation after 13 years and subsequent suicide of prime minister, Mahmoud az-Zoubi. Death of Hafez al-Assad. Succession of his son Bashar.

DEFENSE

Compulsory military service

$989m

Up 1% in 1999

Syria sees its extensive military capability as a significant deterrent to Israel's territorial expansion. It has fought four wars against Israel since 1948, and is the Arab world's strongest military power after Egypt. Much of its military equipment has been obtained from the former Soviet Union.

During the 1980s, Syrian forces fought off a series of Israeli encroachments in the region, and also foiled Israeli attempts to control Lebanon. Syria remains the power Israel fears most. Throughout 2000, increasing numbers of Lebanese protested against the presence of Syrian troops on their soil – in apparent contravention of the 1989 Taif Accords – and in 2001, Syrian troops were withdrawn from Beirut.

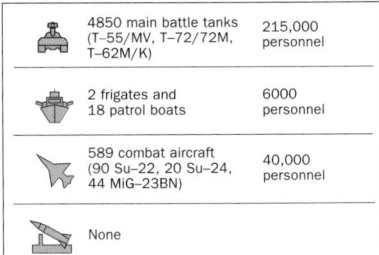

SYRIAN ARMED FORCES

4850 main battle tanks (T-55/MV, T-72/72M, T-62M/K)	215,000 personnel
2 frigates and 18 patrol boats	6000 personnel
589 combat aircraft (90 Su-22, 20 Su-24, 44 MiG-23BN)	40,000 personnel
None	

ECONOMICS

Inflation 8.7% p.a. (1990–1999)

$15.2bn

45.00–53.50 Syrian pounds

SCORE CARD

❑ World GNP Ranking	77th
❑ GNP per Capita	$970
❑ Balance of Payments	$59m
❑ Inflation	–0.5%
❑ Unemployment	15%

EXPORTS

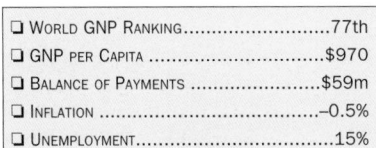

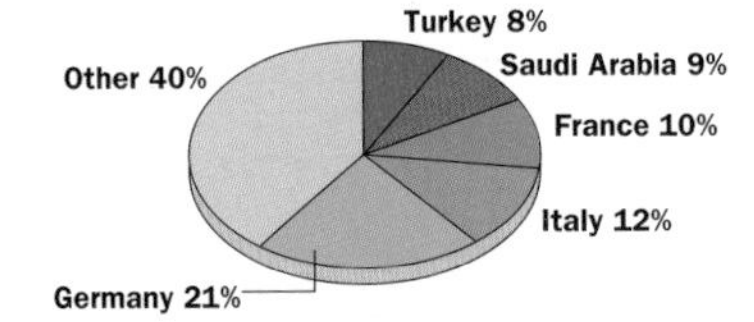
Turkey 8%
Saudi Arabia 9%
France 10%
Italy 12%
Germany 21%
Other 40%

IMPORTS

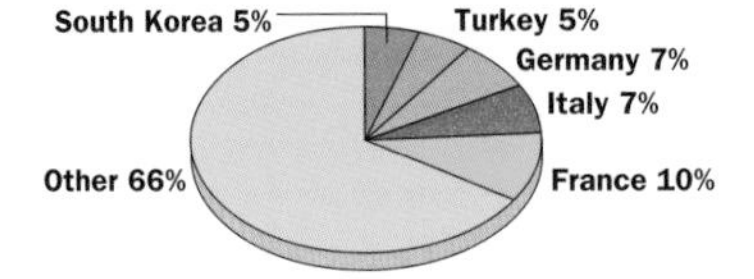
South Korea 5%
Turkey 5%
Germany 7%
Italy 7%
France 10%
Other 66%

Strengths

Exporter of crude oil – production increasing as a result of new oil strikes. Manufacturing base has grown. Thriving agricultural sector.

Weaknesses

High defense spending a major drain on economy. Large black market. Domination of inefficient state-run companies. Lack of foreign investment; foreign currency accounts banned. High population growth. Vulnerable water supply.

Profile

Billions of dollars flowed into the economy from the USA, Japan, the EU, and Saudi Arabia and other Gulf states after the 1990–1991 Gulf War. This cash injection, along with increased oil revenue, led to rapid growth. Diversion of water from the river Euphrates toward fertile plains, rather than poorer land, led to a rise in agricultural output. However, long-term economic prospects remain uncertain. The public sector employs 20% of the workforce, and state controls inhibit private enterprise and investment, and have created a booming black market. Businessmen often channel funds through the freer Lebanese economy. An economic reform package in 2000 created a stock exchange and permitted private banks.

ECONOMIC PERFORMANCE INDICATOR

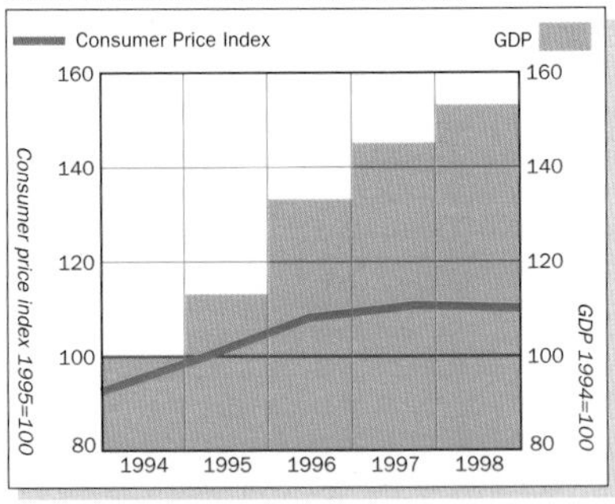
Consumer Price Index
GDP
Consumer price index 1995=100
GDP 1994=100
160
140
120
100
80
1994
1995
1996
1997
1998

SYRIA : MAJOR BUSINESSES

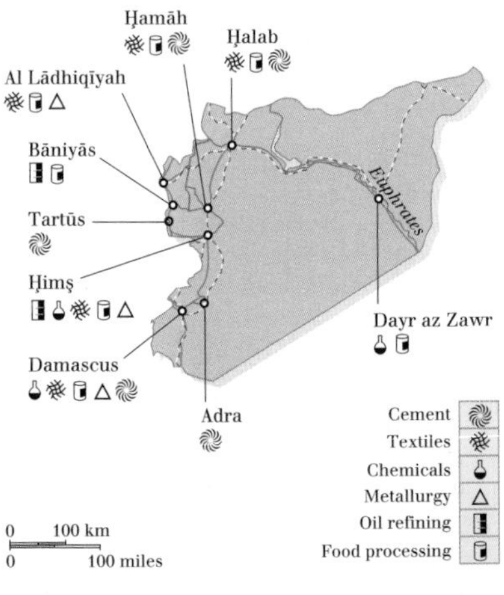
Ḩamāh
Ḩalab
Al Lādhiqīyah
Bāniyās
Tartūs
Ḩimş
Damascus
Adra
Dayr az Zawr
Euphrates
Cement
Textiles
Chemicals
Metallurgy
Oil refining
Food processing
0 100 km
0 100 miles

S

RESOURCES

Electric power 4.5m kw

7721 tonnes

540,000 b/d (reserves 2,500,000,000 bbl)

14.5m sheep, 1.1m goats, 920,000 cattle, 22m chickens

Phosphates, oil, natural gas, iron

ELECTRICITY GENERATION

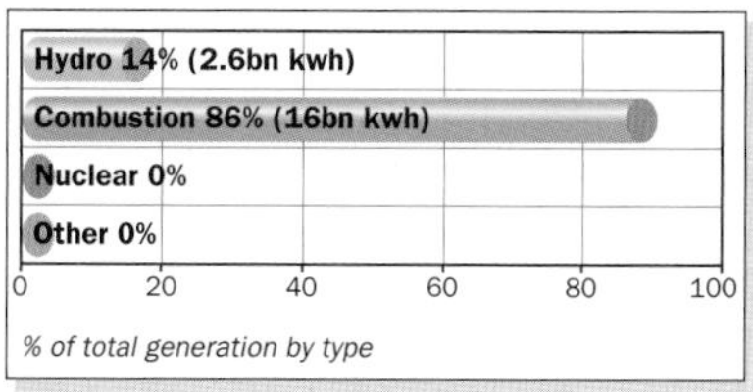
Hydro 14% (2.6bn kwh)
Combustion 86% (16bn kwh)
Nuclear 0%
Other 0%
0
20
40
60
80
100
% of total generation by type

Syria has large supplies of oil, mostly good-quality light crude, which was discovered along the Euphrates in the 1980s. Gas was found in substantial quantities near Palmyra. Syria's other important minerals are phosphates and iron ore. Hydroelectric power satisfies most other energy requirements. The manufacturing base is largely made up of oil-derived industries, including plastics and chemicals, textiles, and food products. Cotton is the main cash crop, but fruit and vegetables are also grown. Livestock, especially sheep and goats, supports the rural economy.

SYRIA : LAND USE

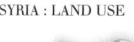

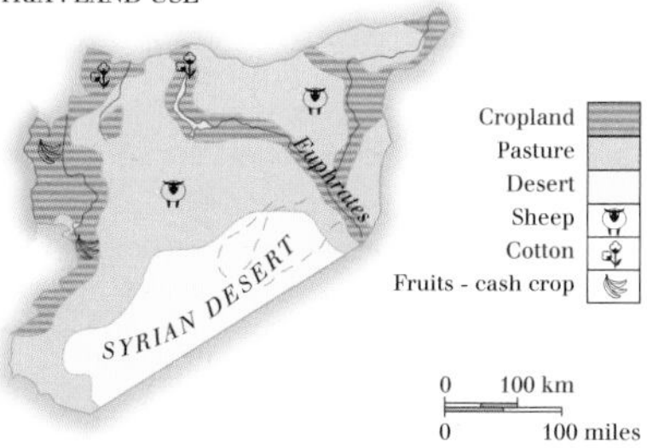
Euphrates
SYRIAN DESERT
Cropland
Pasture
Desert
Sheep
Cotton
Fruits - cash crop
0 100 km
0 100 miles

ENVIRONMENT

Sustainability rank: 106th

None

3.3 tonnes per capita

ENVIRONMENTAL TREATIES

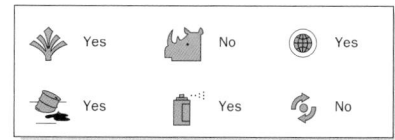

Yes	No	Yes
Yes	Yes	No

The Assad regime's most expensive and controversial environmental project has been the Euphrates dam, power station, and irrigation network at Tabaqah. The dam's vast man-made reservoir, Lake Buhayratal al Asad, engulfed some 300 villages and destroyed 25,000 hectares (62,000 acres) of fertile farmland. A giant cement factory, built by former East Germany at Tartus in the mid-1970s, has been responsible for polluting a stretch of Syria's Mediterranean coastline.

MEDIA

TV ownership medium

Daily newspaper circulation 20 per 1000 people

Virtually all media outlets are controlled by the regime. However, information is becoming freer after Jordanian papers were again allowed into Syria in 1999, and with the advent of satellite TV, which is widely watched. Bashar al-Assad has personally encouraged the use of the Internet.

PUBLISHING AND BROADCAST MEDIA

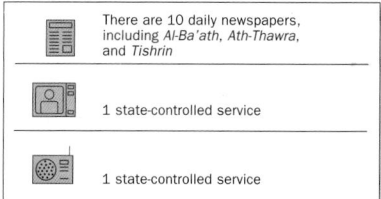

There are 10 daily newspapers, including *Al-Ba'ath*, *Ath-Thawra*, and *Tishrin*

1 state-controlled service

1 state-controlled service

CRIME

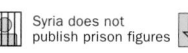

Death penalty used

Syria does not publish prison figures

Down 82% 1992–1994

CRIME RATES

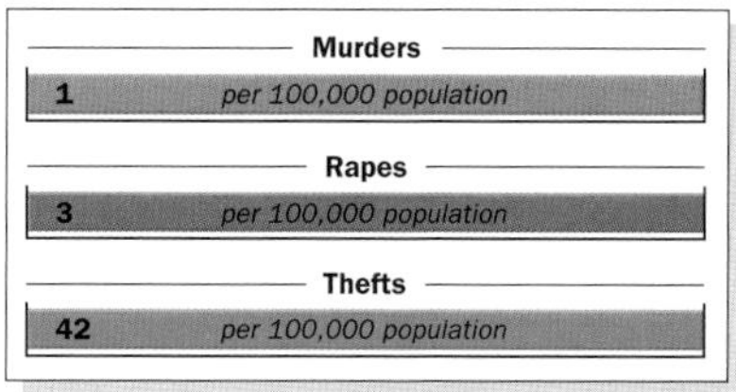
Murders
1 per 100,000 population
Rapes
3 per 100,000 population
Thefts
42 per 100,000 population

There is no truly independent judiciary. The powerful security services exercise arbitrary powers of arrest and detention. There are widespread reports of torture in custody. Most politicians overthrown by President Hafez al-Assad in the 1970s have recently been released from prison in Damascus.

EDUCATION

School leaving age: 12

75%

215,734 students

THE EDUCATION SYSTEM

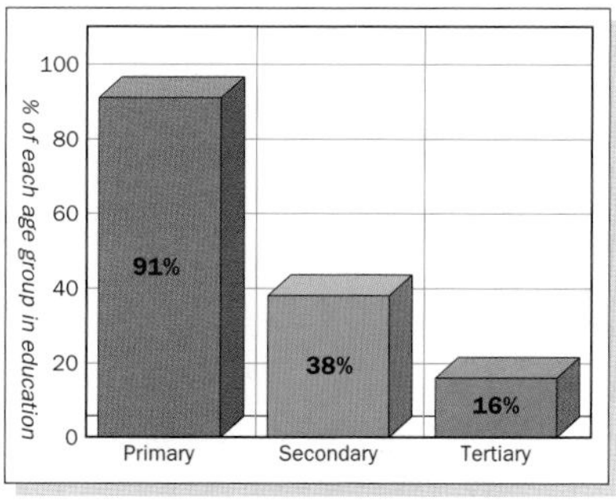
100
80
60
40
20
0
% of each age group in education
91%
38%
16%
Primary
Secondary
Tertiary

The development of a modern and universally accessible system of education remains an important objective. A free and compulsory system of primary education for all was a priority of the Ba'ath Party when it came to power. Coeducation for boys and girls began in the cities and spread to rural areas under the Assad regime. Higher education is provided by seven state universities, notably at Damascus, Aleppo, Tishrin, and Homs. Private universities were allowed from 2001. Education ranks second, though is far behind defense, in government expenditure.

HEALTH

Welfare state health benefits

1 per 769 people

Heart, respiratory, digestive, infectious, and parasitic diseases

An adequate system of primary health care has been set up since the Ba'ath Party came to power. Treatment is free for those unable to pay. However, hospitals often lack modern equipment and medical services are in need of further investment. Rural areas in particular need assistance to combat the spread of heart, respiratory, and infectious diseases.

SPENDING

GDP/cap. increase

CONSUMPTION AND SPENDING

9 per 1000 population

99 per 1000 population

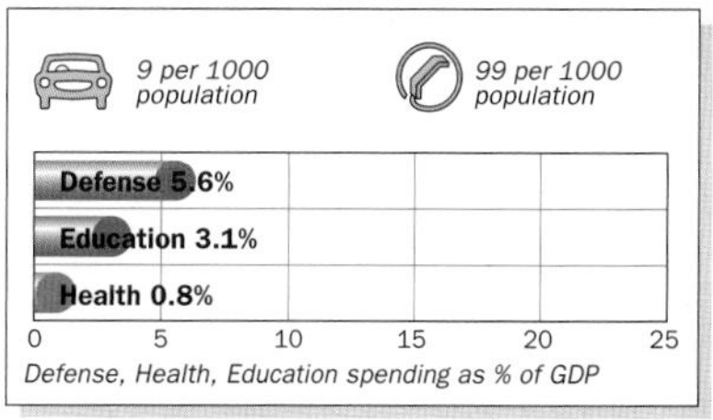
Defense 5.6%
Education 3.1%
Health 0.8%
0
5
10
15
20
25
Defense, Health, Education spending as % of GDP

Syria is far from the equitable society that early Ba'ath Party thinkers envisioned. The gulf between Syria's rich and poor is widening. The political elite, many of whom live in the West Malki suburb of Damascus, is more numerous and richer than ever before. Palestinian refugees and the urban unemployed make up the poorest groups.

WORLD RANKING

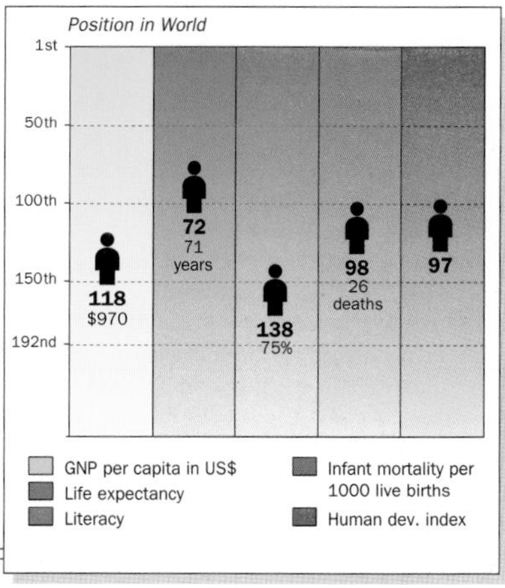
Position in World
1st
50th
100th
150th
192nd
118
$970
72
71 years
138
75%
98
26 deaths
97
GNP per capita in US$
Life expectancy
Literacy
Infant mortality per 1000 live births
Human dev. index

S

TAIWAN

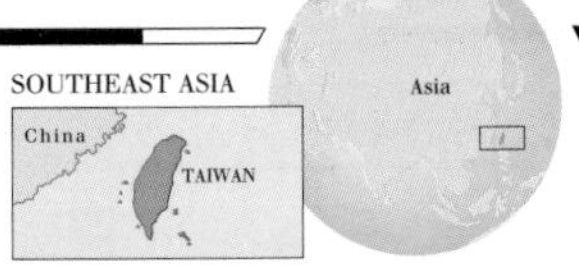
SOUTHEAST ASIA
China
TAIWAN
Asia

OFFICIAL NAME: Republic of China (Taiwan) **CAPITAL:** T'aipei
POPULATION: 22.2 million **CURRENCY:** Taiwan dollar **OFFICIAL LANGUAGE:** Mandarin Chinese

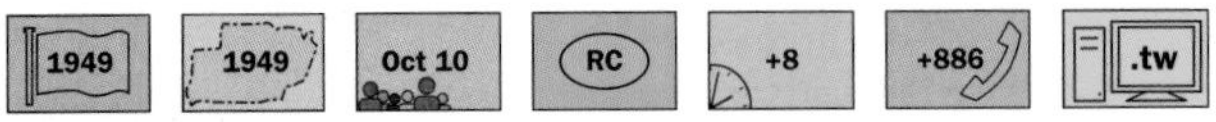
1949
1949
Oct 10
RC
+8
+886
.tw

THE ISLAND OF TAIWAN, formerly known as Formosa, lies off the southeast coast of mainland China. Mountains run north to south, covering two-thirds of the island. The lowlands are highly fertile, cultivated mostly with rice, and densely populated. In 1949, when the Chinese communists ousted Chiang Kai-shek's Kuomintang (KMT) from power on the mainland, he established the Republic of China government on the island. *De facto* military rule has been democratized progressively since 1986. The KMT's grip on power was shaken by defeat in the 2000 presidential election. Mainland China still considers Taiwan a renegade province, and only a few countries now give official recognition to the regime there.

Wen Wu Temple, *on the shores of Sun Moon Lake in the mountains of central Taiwan – a region famous for its many temples. Nearly the whole population are Buddhists.*

CLIMATE

Tropical monsoon

WEATHER CHART

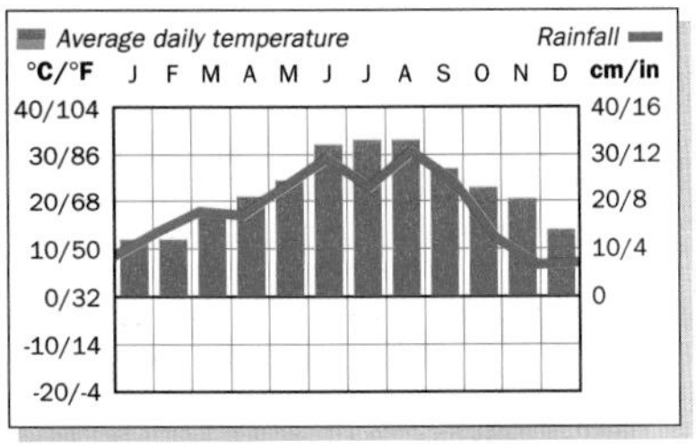
Average daily temperature
Rainfall
°C/°F
J F M A M J J A S O N D
cm/in
40/104
30/86
20/68
10/50
0/32
-10/14
-20/-4
40/16
30/12
20/8
10/4
0

Taiwan has a tropical monsoon climate similar to that of the southern Chinese mainland. Typhoons from the South China Sea between June and October bring the heaviest rains.

TRANSPORTATION

Drive on right

Chiang Kai-shek International, Taoyuan
16.4m passengers

686 ships
5.5m grt

THE TRANSPORTATION NETWORK

31,271 km (19,431 miles)	Sun Yatsen highway: 538 km (334 miles)
1104 km (686 miles)	None

Taiwan has launched several major new transportation infrastructure projects as part of the latest six-year economic plan. Subway and rapid transit systems are being built in Taipei and Kaohsiung. Several new roads are in progress, including an extension of the north–south Sun Yatsen highway to Pingtung. The plan is motivated by the fear that congestion will restrain future growth. Most urban Taiwanese currently ride motor scooters, but transportation planners anticipate a sharp increase in car ownership over the next decade. The bicycle is not as popular in Taiwan as in mainland China. However, Taiwan is the world's biggest bicycle producer, exporting mostly to Europe and the USA.

TOURISM

Visitors : Population 1:8.5

2.6m visitors

Up 9% in 2000

MAIN TOURIST ARRIVALS

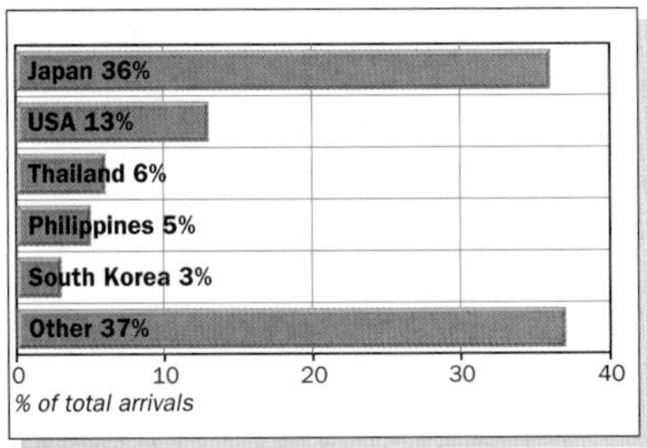
Japan 36%
USA 13%
Thailand 6%
Philippines 5%
South Korea 3%
Other 37%
0
10
20
30
40
% of total arrivals

Taiwan is not a major tourist destination, and it has only recently begun to target tourists in the USA and Japan. As part of the most recent Six-Year Plan, hotels are being upgraded and tourist facilities at international airports are being improved. The major attraction is the Palace Museum in Taipei, which includes the massive treasure looted by the Nationalists from Beijing. Only 5% can be shown at any one time. Sex tourism is an important business in Taipei. Sex establishments often masquerade as barbershops.

PEOPLE

Pop. density high

Amoy Chinese, Mandarin Chinese, Hakka Chinese

688/km² (1782/mi²)

THE URBAN/RURAL POPULATION SPLIT

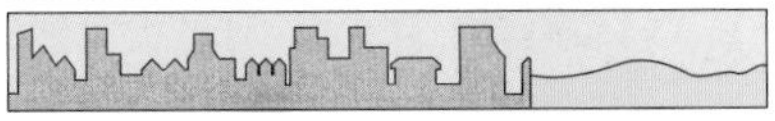
69%
31%

RELIGIOUS PERSUASION

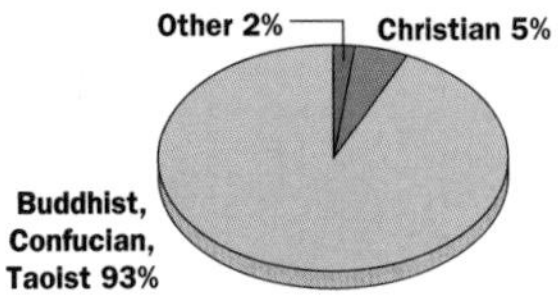
Other 2%
Christian 5%
Buddhist, Confucian, Taoist 93%

ETHNIC MAKEUP

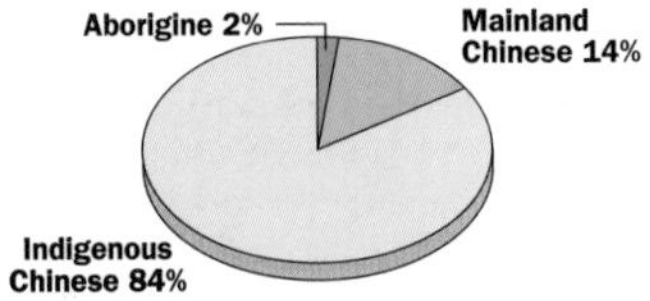
Aborigine 2%
Mainland Chinese 14%
Indigenous Chinese 84%

Most Taiwanese are Han Chinese, descendants of the 1644 migration of the Ming dynasty from mainland China. The 100,000 Nationalists who arrived in 1949 established themselves as a ruling class and monopolized the most prestigious jobs in the civil service. This caused resentment among the local inhabitants, but as the generation elected on the mainland in 1947 have aged, so local Taiwanese have entered the political process.

There is little ethnic tension in Taiwan, although the indigenous minorities who live in the eastern hills do suffer considerable discrimination.

As in the rest of southeast Asia, the extended family is still important and provides a social security net for the elderly. However, the trend is toward European-style nuclear families. Housing shortages are a major issue.

Women are not well represented in the political process, but are prominent in business and the civil service.

POPULATION AGE BREAKDOWN

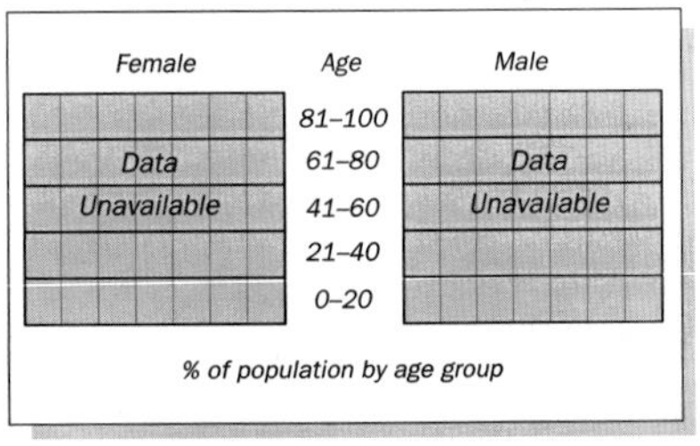
Female
Age
Male
81–100
61–80
41–60
21–40
0–20
Data Unavailable
Data Unavailable
% of population by age group

T

POLITICS

Multiparty elections

1998/2001

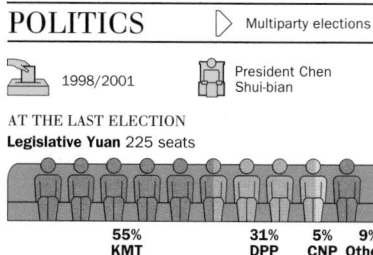

President Chen Shui-bian

AT THE LAST ELECTION

Legislative Yuan 225 seats

55% KMT
31% DPP
5% CNP
9% Others

KMT = National Party of China (Kuomintang) **DPP** = Democratic Progressive Party **CNP** = Chinese New Party

From 1986 Taiwan has been a multiparty democracy, though electoral domination by the KMT only ended in 2000. The government is headed by the president, who is answerable to the National Assembly, an additional body elected when constitutional affairs arise.

MAIN POLITICAL ISSUES

Relations with China

The DPP, in opposition in parliament but boosted by victory in the 2000 presidential election, has advocated independence from China, despite Chinese threats of military action. Adopting a more prudent stance since his poll victory, Chen Shui-bian promised to make no independence declaration during his term of office. The KMT, officially committed to eventual reunification with China, now favors a more flexible arrangement that presupposes the recognition of a separate Taiwanese national identity.

Political stability

In the 1998 legislative elections, the ruling KMT, which had posted its worst-ever result in 1995, secured an absolute majority. The proindependence opposition DPP also performed impressively, but the CNP, with its emphasis on reunification with China, won little support. The outcome strengthened the moderate wing of the KMT under the then President Lee Teng-hui, who increasingly favored the development of a "new Taiwanese" identity that blurs the division between native Taiwanese and Chinese from the mainland. The preservation of political and economic stability, however, remains essential as China intensifies its sovereignty claims on Taiwan after the return of Hong Kong in 1997.

Chiang Kai-shek, who established Taiwan in 1949.

Chen Shui-bian, the first non-KMT president since 1949.

PROFILE

Between 1949 and 1986, Chiang Kai-shek's KMT monopolized political power and ruled by strict martial law. In 1986, General Chiang Ching-kuo, Chiang Kai-shek's son and successor, decided to pave the way for democracy. Free multiparty elections were first held in 1986. In March 1996 Lee Teng-hui became the country's first directly elected president.

The KMT's 50-year political monopoly came to an end with the presidential elections in March 2000 which saw the KMT candidate coming a poor third. Chen Shui-bian of the DPP took office in May 2000.

WORLD AFFAIRS

Not a member of the UN

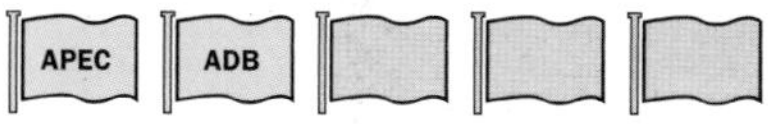
APEC
ADB

China rejects Taiwan's sovereignty claims and regards it as a renegade province, so Taiwan conducts overseas relations via trade delegations. Since losing its seat on the Security Council in 1971, it has been unable to rejoin the UN. The handover to China of Hong Kong in July 1997 deepened fears that China would intensify pressure on countries to sever links with Taiwan. China mounted military exercises in 1999 after President Lee spoke of Taiwan as a separate state. In 2000 China sought unsuccessfully to frighten Taiwanese voters away from backing pro-independence candidate Chen Shui-bian. However, each depends on the other economically; Taiwan is a major foreign investor in China. After US rapprochement with China in 1972, Taiwan effectively ceased to be a US client state. US security guarantees are vague, but in practice there are strong bilateral ties with the USA and Japan.

TAIWAN

Total Land Area : 32 260 sq. km (12 456 sq. miles)

POPULATION

- over 1 000 000
- over 500 000
- over 100 000
- over 50 000
- over 10 000
- under 10 000

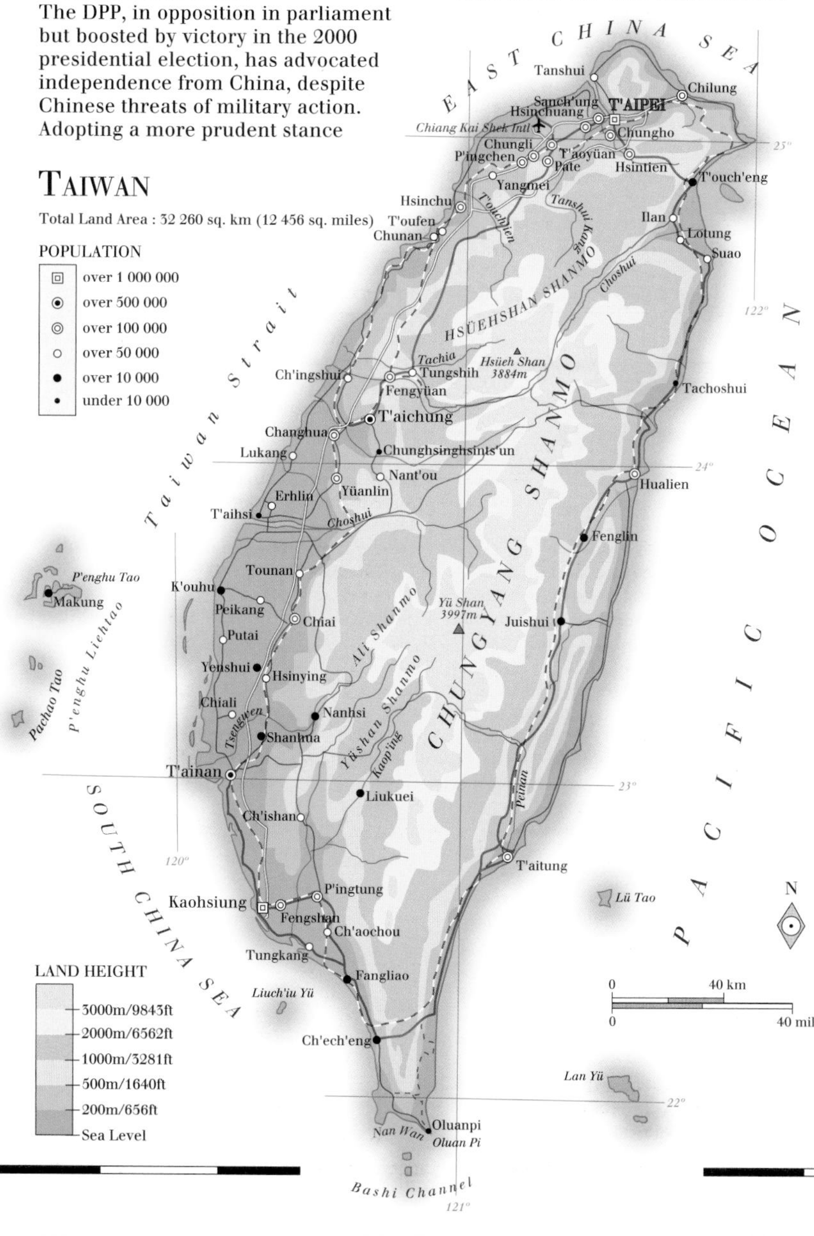
EAST CHINA SEA
Tanshui
Chilung
Sanch'ung
Hsinchuang
T'AIPEI
Chiang Kai Shek Intl
Chungho
Chungli
P'ingchen
T'aoyüan
Pate
Hsintien
Yangmei
T'ouch'eng
Hsinchu
T'oufen
Chunan
Ilan
Lotung
Suao
HSÜEHSHAN SHANMO
Tachia
Hsüeh Shan 3884m
Tungshih
Fengyüan
Ch'ingshui
T'aichung
Tachoshui
Changhua
Lukang
Chunghsingshints'un
Nant'ou
Hualien
Erhlin
Yüanlin
T'aihsi
Choshui
Taiwan Strait
Fenglin
P'enghu Tao
Makung
P'enghu Liehtao
Pachao Tao
Tounan
K'ouhu
Peikang
Chiai
Putai
Yü Shan 3997m
Juishui
Ali Shanmo
CHUNGYANG SHANMO
Yenshui
Hsinying
Chiali
Nanhsi
Shanhua
Yüshan Shanmo
T'ainan
Liukuei
Peinan
Ch'ishan
SOUTH CHINA SEA
T'aitung
PACIFIC OCEAN
P'ingtung
Kaohsiung
Fengshan
Ch'aochou
Lü Tao
Tungkang
Fangliao
Liuch'iu Yü
Ch'ech'eng
Lan Yü
Nan Wan
Oluanpi
Oluan Pi
Bashi Channel
N
0 40 km
0 40 miles
25°
24°
23°
22°
120°
121°
122°
LAND HEIGHT
3000m/9843ft
2000m/6562ft
1000m/3281ft
500m/1640ft
200m/656ft
Sea Level

T

AID

Donor

US$92m (donations)

Up 16% in 1995

Taiwan has a large aid fund devoted to states which have granted it diplomatic recognition. These include the Pacific states of Kiribati and Tonga, which have looked out for Taiwan's interests in the UN since 1971, when it lost its seat to the People's Republic of China. In 1998 Taiwan donated more than US$2 million to seven Central American supporters, including Panama, to promote literacy.

CHRONOLOGY

Following the 1949 Communist revolution in China, General Chiang Kai-shek's nationalist KMT party sought refuge in the island province of Taiwan. The KMT saw the revolution as illegal and itself as the sole rightful Chinese government.

- ❑ **1971** People's Republic of China replaces Taiwan at UN and on UN Security Council.
- ❑ **1973** Taipei's KMT regime rejects Beijing's offer of secret talks on reunification of China.
- ❑ **1975** President Chiang Kai-shek dies. His son General Chiang Ching-kuo becomes KMT leader. Yen Chia-kan succeeds as president.
- ❑ **1978** Chiang Ching-kuo elected president.
- ❑ **1979** USA severs relations with Taiwan and formally recognizes People's Republic of China.
- ❑ **1984** President Chiang reelected.
- ❑ **1986** Political reforms: KMT allows multiparty democracy, ends martial law, and permits visits to Chinese mainland for "humanitarian" purposes for first time in 38 years. In 1988, mainland Chinese are allowed to visit Taiwan on same basis.
- ❑ **1988** Lee Teng-hui president.
- ❑ **1990** KMT formally ends state of war with People's Republic of China.
- ❑ **1991** DPP draft constitution for Taiwan independence opposed by ruling KMT and Beijing. KMT reelected with large majority.
- ❑ **1995–1996** Legislative elections. KMT majority reduced.
- ❑ **1996** Lee Teng-hui wins first direct presidential elections.
- ❑ **1998** KMT secures absolute majority in elections to Legislative *Yuan.*
- ❑ **1999** Chinese threats over reference to "separate states" status. September, thousands die in earthquake.
- ❑ **2000** March, Chen Shui-bian of DPP wins presidency; overturns KMT dominance.

DEFENSE

Compulsory military service

US$14.96bn

Up 4% in 1999

China remains the main defense threat, given the recurring tensions over the issue of independence or reunification. Taiwan has the fifth-largest army in the world, in order to face a possible Chinese invasion. There are over one-and-a-half million reservists, and military service lasts for two years. Worries about US loyalty have resulted in the purchase of French *Mirage* fighters in addition to US F-16s.

TAIWANESE ARMED FORCES

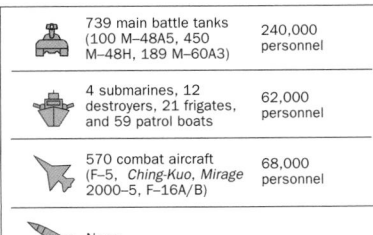

739 main battle tanks (100 M–48A5, 450 M–48H, 189 M–60A3)	240,000 personnel
4 submarines, 12 destroyers, 21 frigates, and 59 patrol boats	62,000 personnel
570 combat aircraft (F–5, *Ching-Kuo, Mirage* 2000–5, F–16A/B)	68,000 personnel
None	

ECONOMICS

Inflation 5% p.a. (1985–1996)

US$283.5bn

31.35–33.08 Taiwan dollars

SCORE CARD

❑ World GNP Ranking	17th
❑ GNP per Capita	US$13,450
❑ Balance of Payments	US$3.73bn
❑ Inflation	1.5%
❑ Unemployment	3%

EXPORTS

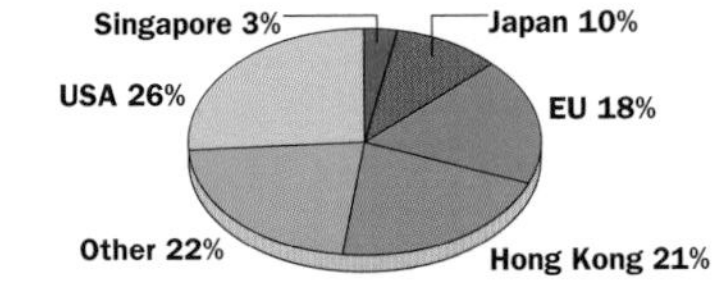
Singapore 3%
Japan 10%
USA 26%
EU 18%
Other 22%
Hong Kong 21%

IMPORTS

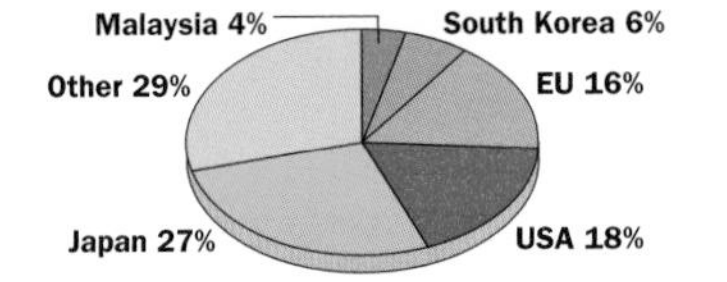
Malaysia 4%
South Korea 6%
Other 29%
EU 16%
Japan 27%
USA 18%

ECONOMIC PERFORMANCE INDICATOR

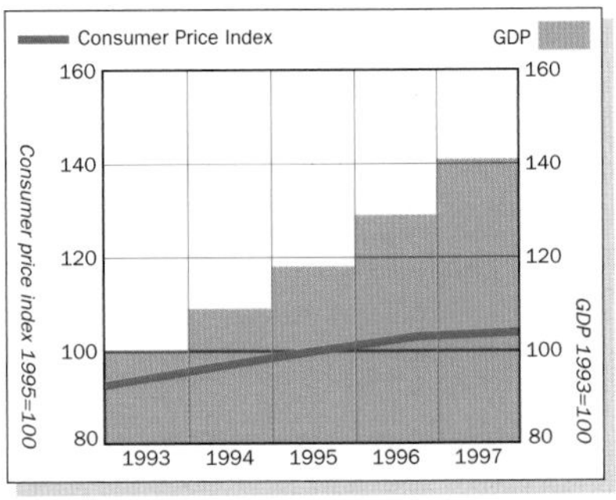
Consumer Price Index
GDP
160
140
120
100
80
Consumer price index 1995=100
GDP 1993=100
1993
1994
1995
1996
1997

Strengths

Highly educated and ambitious workforce, many US-trained and educated, with an inside knowledge of the US market. Manufacturing economy based on small companies which have proved extremely adaptable to changing market conditions. Track record of capturing major markets. Taiwan was successively the world's biggest TV producer, watch producer, PC producer, and track shoe manufacturer. Economy in strong surplus, allowing it to invest in other southeast Asian economies.

Weaknesses

Small economic units lack the muscle of Western multinationals, and are unable to follow predatory pricing policies. Weak research and development: economy has no tradition of generating new products or creating new markets. Unresponsive banking system.

Profile

One of the world's most successful economies. Although double-digit growth is now over, Taiwan emerged relatively unscathed from the financial crisis that engulfed most Asian economies in 1997–1998. Competition from underdeveloped countries with low production costs is dictating a difficult transition toward service industries. This will entail moving from labor-intensive to capital- and technology-intensive industries. Comprehensive Six-Year Plans reflect a strong element of state direction. Heavy investment abroad includes over 60% of inward investment into China since 1990.

TAIWAN : MAJOR BUSINESSES

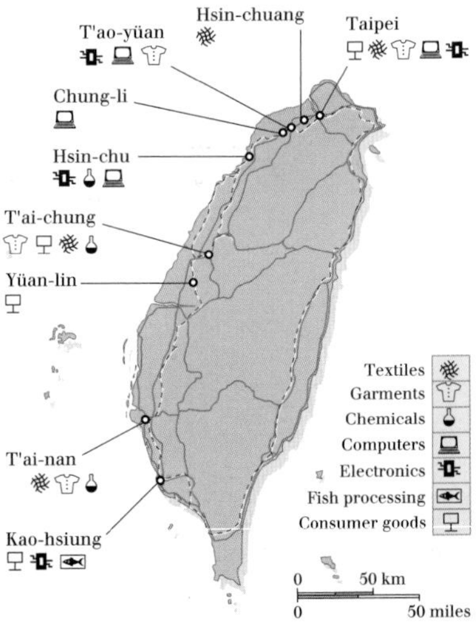
Hsin-chuang
T'ao-yüan
Taipei
Chung-li
Hsin-chu
T'ai-chung
Yüan-lin
T'ai-nan
Kao-hsiung
Textiles
Garments
Chemicals
Computers
Electronics
Fish processing
Consumer goods
0
50 km
0
50 miles

T

RESOURCES

Not available

1.29m tonnes

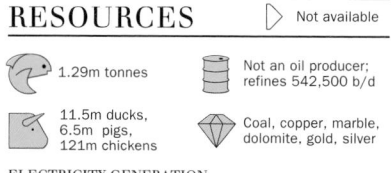

Not an oil producer; refines 542,500 b/d

11.5m ducks, 6.5m pigs, 121m chickens

Coal, copper, marble, dolomite, gold, silver

ELECTRICITY GENERATION

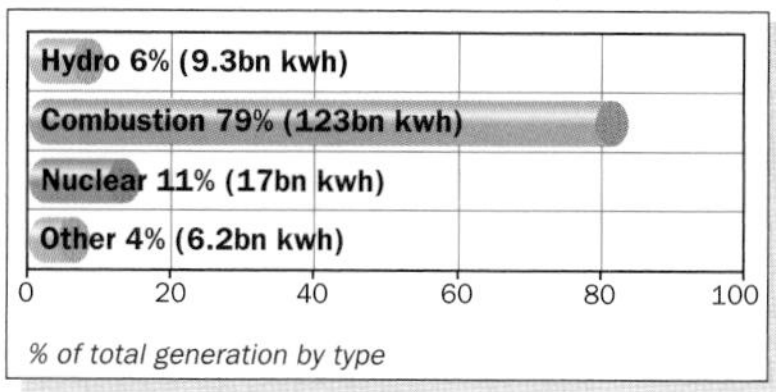
Hydro 6% (9.3bn kwh)
Combustion 79% (123bn kwh)
Nuclear 11% (17bn kwh)
Other 4% (6.2bn kwh)
0
20
40
60
80
100
% of total generation by type

Taiwan has few strategic resources and its minerals industry is not a significant foreign exchange earner. Oil is imported. Taiwan is a major buyer of South African uranium, but heavy reliance on nuclear power is now politically unfeasible due to serious safety and waste disposal problems. Hydroelectric power has been largely exploited and thermal power remains a controversial option. Fishing is highly successful, and Taiwan is a major supplier to the huge Japanese market. The fleet is often accused of plundering Atlantic stocks.

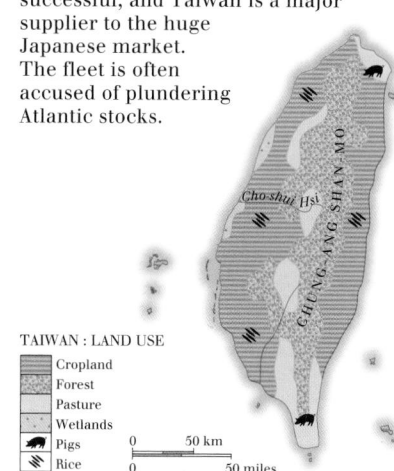

Cho-shui Hsi
CHUNG-YANG SHAN MO
0
50 km
0
50 miles

TAIWAN : LAND USE

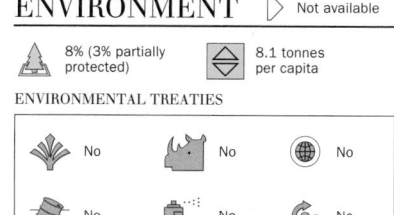

- Cropland
- Forest
- Pasture
- Wetlands
- Pigs
- Rice

ENVIRONMENT

Not available

8% (3% partially protected)

8.1 tonnes per capita

ENVIRONMENTAL TREATIES

No	No	No
No	No	No

The dash for growth meant the absence of city planning or pollution laws. An increasingly aware public now opposes a fourth nuclear power station and is wary of coal-fired thermal power. Taiwan's fishing industry has been criticized for using long-line techniques which trap dolphins, and for plundering other countries' fishing grounds without regard to stock levels.

MEDIA

TV ownership medium

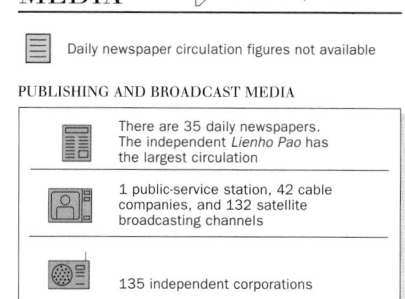

Daily newspaper circulation figures not available

PUBLISHING AND BROADCAST MEDIA

There are 35 daily newspapers. The independent *Lienho Pao* has the largest circulation

1 public-service station, 42 cable companies, and 132 satellite broadcasting channels

135 independent corporations

The rigid state control which used to exist over the media has been relaxed. Opposition parties now have access to the state media. Before the 1990s, press with simplified Chinese characters was banned, thus excluding all publications from the mainland. Taiwan has a large domestic TV and film industry.

CRIME

Death penalty used

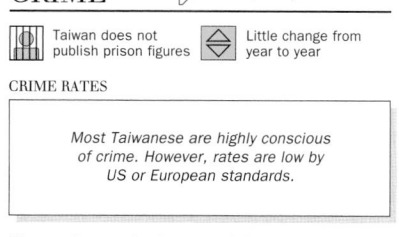

Taiwan does not publish prison figures

Little change from year to year

CRIME RATES

Most Taiwanese are highly conscious of crime. However, rates are low by US or European standards.

Since the end of martial law in 1986, most political prisoners have been released. Taiwan does not suffer from organized crime to the extent found in Hong Kong or Japan. Multimedia pirating is a major problem.

EDUCATION

School leaving age: 15

94%

795,547 students

THE EDUCATION SYSTEM

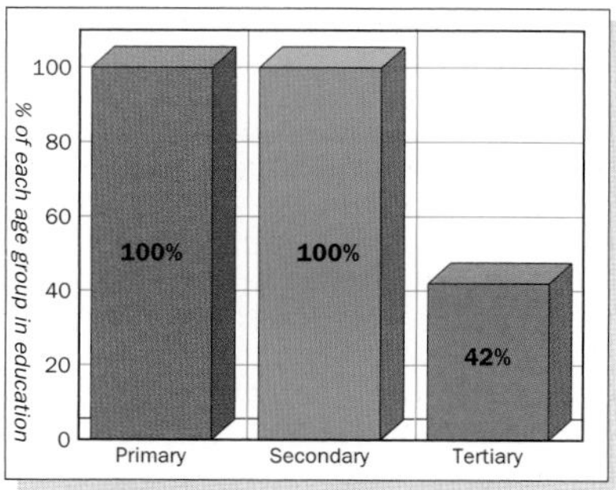
100
80
60
40
20
0
% of each age group in education
100%
100%
42%
Primary
Secondary
Tertiary

The reform of Taiwan's antiquated education system, which is rigid and heavily exam-oriented, is a major government priority.

Free schooling is available to age 15 (junior high school level), and there are also a number of private schools. Attendance at tertiary level, at a variety of institutions, is one of the highest in the world. Many Taiwanese study in the USA.

HEALTH

No welfare state health benefits

1 per 894 people

Cerebrovascular and heart diseases, hypertension

Most health provision in Taiwan is in the private sector. Taiwanese take out elaborate health insurance schemes and it is essential to prove cover before treatment is provided. Health facilities are on a par with the best in the world, and the Taiwanese enjoy a high life expectancy, similar to that in Sweden or Japan. The incidence of AIDS is in line with the southeast Asian average. An enteroviral epidemic swept Taiwan in 1998, killing scores of babies and affecting thousands of young children.

SPENDING

GDP/cap. increase

CONSUMPTION AND SPENDING

205 per 1000 population

500 per 1000 population

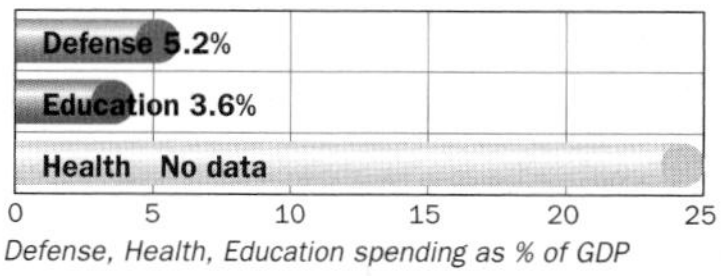
Defense 5.2%
Education 3.6%
Health No data
0
5
10
15
20
25
Defense, Health, Education spending as % of GDP

Until 1987, Taiwan had the largest cash reserves of any country in the world. This was a situation reflecting the closed nature of its markets and the success of the export economy. Taiwanese have shared in much of this wealth. Inequalities of income distribution are comparatively small, and a high degree of social cohesion has been achieved. In part, this is the result of the land reforms of the 1950s, which gave agricultural workers control of the land while compensating landowners and encouraging them to set up business in the cities. Today, the great majority of Taiwanese would describe themselves as middle class. Consumer goods are widely available, and conspicuous consumption is celebrated.

WORLD RANKING

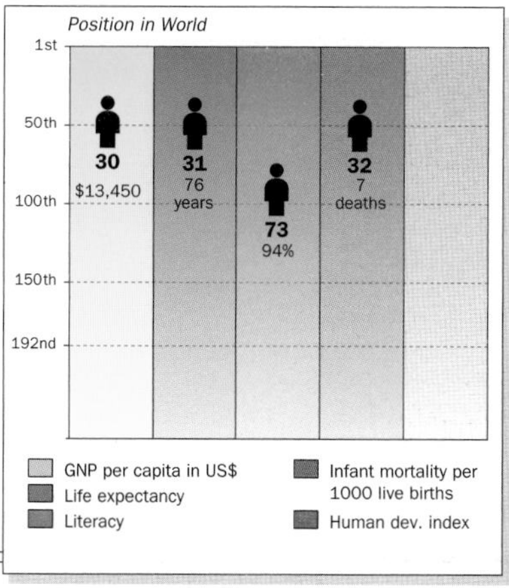
Position in World
1st
50th
100th
150th
192nd
30
$13,450
31
76 years
73
94%
32
7 deaths
GNP per capita in US$
Life expectancy
Literacy
Infant mortality per 1000 live births
Human dev. index

T

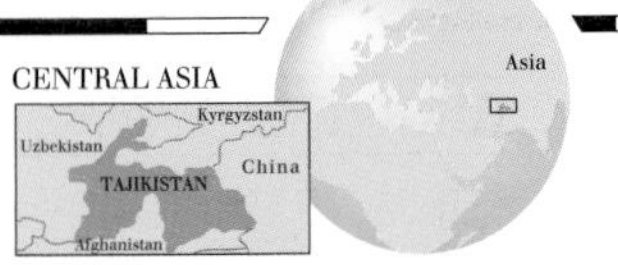
CENTRAL ASIA
Asia
Uzbekistan
Kyrgyzstan
TAJIKISTAN
China
Afghanistan

TAJIKISTAN

OFFICIAL NAME: Republic of Tajikistan **CAPITAL:** Dushanbe
POPULATION: 6.2 million **CURRENCY:** Somoni **OFFICIAL LANGUAGE:** Tajik

1991 | 1991 | Sept 9 | TJ | +5 | +992 | .tj

TAJIKISTAN LIES ON the western slopes of the Pamirs in central Asia. Language and traditions are similar to those of Iran rather than those of Turkic Uzbekistan. Tajikistan decided on independence only when neighboring Soviet republics declared theirs in late 1991. Fighting between communist government forces and Islamist rebels, which erupted shortly afterwards, has been contained since 1997 by a tenuous peace agreement.

Goat herd in the Varzob Gorge, north of Dushanbe. Livestock drives the rural economy.

CLIMATE

Mountain

WEATHER CHART

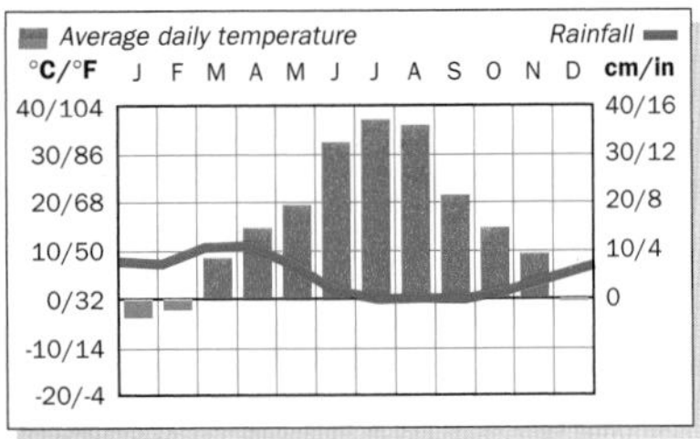
Average daily temperature
Rainfall
°C/°F
J F M A M J J A S O N D
cm/in
40/104
30/86
20/68
10/50
0/32
-10/14
-20/-4
40/16
30/12
20/8
10/4
0

Rainfall is low in the valleys. Winter temperatures can fall below –45°C (–49°F) in mountainous areas.

TRANSPORTATION

Drive on right

Dushanbe International

Has no fleet

THE TRANSPORTATION NETWORK

11,330 km (7040 miles)	None
547 km (340 miles)	200 km (124 miles)

Tajikistan has good cross-border roads and well-maintained airfields, the result of its use as a staging post by Soviet forces during the Afghan war. The best way to visit the mountainous interior is by air.

TOURISM

Visitors : Population 1:12

511,000 visitors

Increasing slowly

MAIN TOURIST ARRIVALS

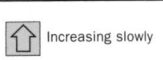

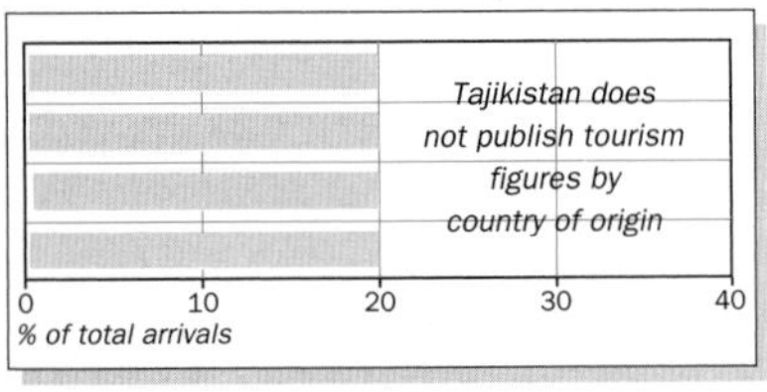
Tajikistan does not publish tourism figures by country of origin
0
10
20
30
40
% of total arrivals

Tensions in Tajikistan make travel almost impossible. Journalists from the West are often attacked.

PEOPLE

Pop. density low

Tajik, Russian

43/km² (112/mi²)

THE URBAN/RURAL POPULATION SPLIT

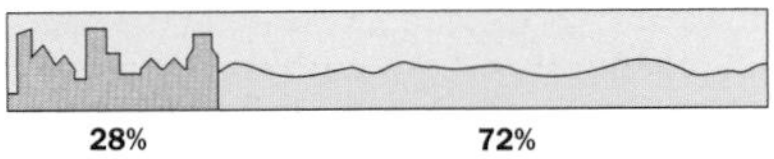
28%
72%

RELIGIOUS PERSUASION

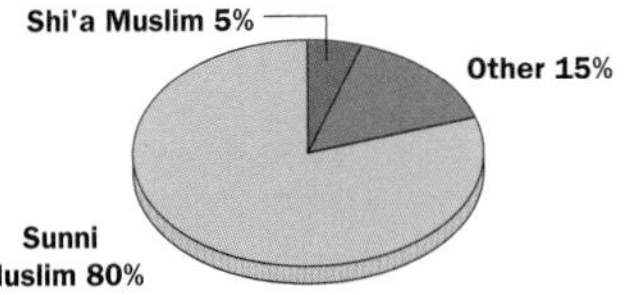
Shi'a Muslim 5%
Other 15%
Sunni Muslim 80%

The main ethnic conflict in Tajikistan is between the Tajiks and Uzbeks, of Persian and Turkic origin respectively. As in neighboring Uzbekistan, however, Russians are discriminated against, and their population has thinned from 400,000 in 1989 to fewer than 200,000. By 1990, the 35,000-strong German minority had left. The struggle between Dushanbe-based communists and the Islamist militants in the central and eastern regions displaced more than 50,000 refugees into Afghanistan, whose own Tajik population numbers over a million. It is estimated that about 20,000 refugees remain in Afghanistan.

POLITICS

Multiparty elections

L. House 2000/2005
U. House 2000/2005

President Imomali Rakhmanov

AT THE LAST ELECTION

Assembly of Representatives 63 seats

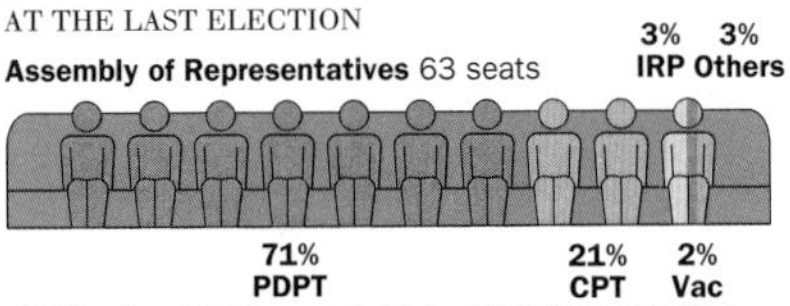
3% IRP
3% Others
71% PDPT
21% CPT
2% Vac

PDPT = People's Democratic Party of Tajikistan and allies
CPT = Communist Party of Tajikistan IRP = Islamic Revival Party Vac = Vacant

National Assembly 33 seats

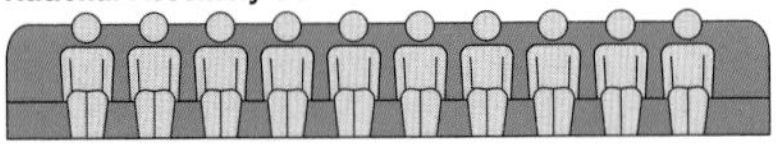

Five deputies are elected by each regional assembly, and a further eight deputies are appointed by the president.

The lull in fighting between government forces and Islamist rebels, aided by a 1997 peace accord, has consolidated the regime of former communists led by President Rakhmanov. In 1998, the Islamist United Tajik Opposition (UTO) joined the government in accordance with the accord, which provided for a National Reconciliation Commission along with parliamentary elections. In the 2000 elections the pro-Rakhmanov PDPT, which headed the poll, claimed some support from former UTO members.

TAJIKISTAN

Total Land Area : 143 100 sq. km (55 251 sq. miles)

POPULATION

- over 500 000
- over 100 000
- over 50 000
- over 10 000
- under 10 000

LAND HEIGHT

- 4000m/13 124ft
- 3000m/9843ft
- 2000m/6562ft
- 1000m/3281ft
- 500m/1640ft
- 200m/656ft

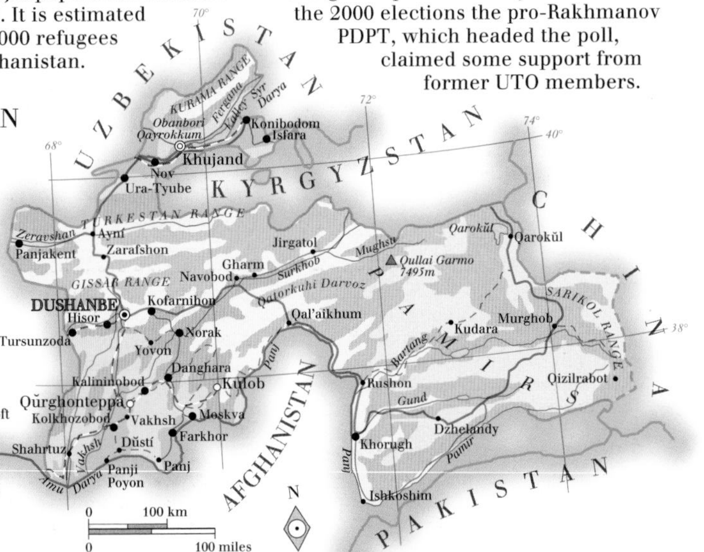
UZBEKISTAN
KYRGYZSTAN
CHINA
AFGHANISTAN
PAKISTAN
KURAMA RANGE
Fergana Valley
Syr Darya
Obanbori Qayrokkum
Konibodom
Isfara
Khujand
Nov
Ura-Tyube
TURKESTAN RANGE
Zeravshan
Panjakent
Ayni
Zarafshon
GISSAR RANGE
DUSHANBE
Hisor
Tursunzoda
Kofarnihon
Norak
Yovon
Gharm
Navobod
Jirgatol
Surkhob
Mughsu
Qatorkuhi Darvoz
Qal'aikhum
Qarokŭl
Qullai Garmo 7495m
SARIKOL RANGE
Murghob
Kudara
PAMIRS
Bartang
Rushon
Gund
Qizilrabot
Dzhelandy
Khorugh
Pamir
Panj
Ishkoshim
Danghara
Kulob
Kalininobod
Qŭrghonteppa
Kolkhozobod
Vakhsh
Moskva
Dŭsti
Farkhor
Shahrtuz
Panji Poyon
Amu Darya
68°
70°
72°
74°
40°
38°
0
100 km
100 miles

WORLD AFFAIRS

Joined UN in 1992

CIS | SCO | EAPC | OIC | OSCE

Tajikistan remains heavily dependent on Russia for economic and military assistance. In 1995, Tajikistan accepted Russia's conditions for joining the rouble zone, thereby ceding considerable economic autonomy to Russia. This was partially reversed with the introduction in 1995 of Tajikistan's own currency. Russia lends military support to further the Tajik government's aim of limiting the influence of Islamic fundamentalism. A joint operation with Uzbekistan and Kyrgyzstan began in 2000 to combat the Islamic Movement of Uzbekistan, based in northern Tajikistan.

AID

Recipient

$122m (receipts) — Up 16% in 1999

Russia and Uzbekistan provide military aid. Food aid was required in 2000 and 2001 after severe droughts.

DEFENSE

Compulsory military service

$92m — Down 10% in 1999

The Tajik armed forces depend on CIS peacekeeping forces to contain Tajik rebels active in the Gorno Badakhshan region bordering Afghanistan. They are kept at bay by government forces assisted by Russian border guards.

ECONOMICS

Not available

$1.7bn — 2.40 somoni

SCORE CARD

- World GNP Ranking 143rd
- GNP per Capita $280
- Balance of Payments $67m
- Inflation 49.9%
- Unemployment 6%

Strengths

Few, though Tajikistan has 14% of known world uranium reserves. Hydroelectric power has considerable potential. Carpet-making.

Weaknesses

Formal economy precarious. Dependence on barter economy. No central planning. Little diversification in agriculture; only 6% of land is arable. Exodus of skilled Russians. Production in all sectors in decline.

EXPORTS

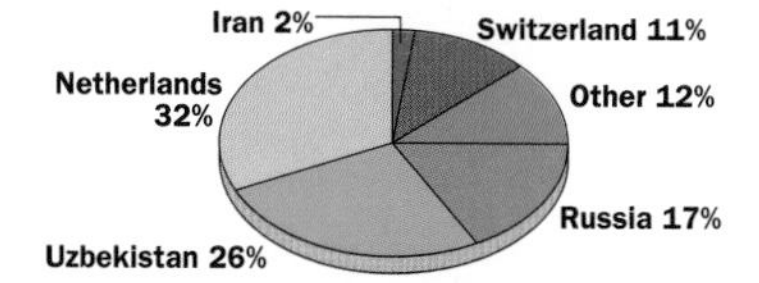
Iran 2%
Switzerland 11%
Netherlands 32%
Other 12%
Russia 17%
Uzbekistan 26%

IMPORTS

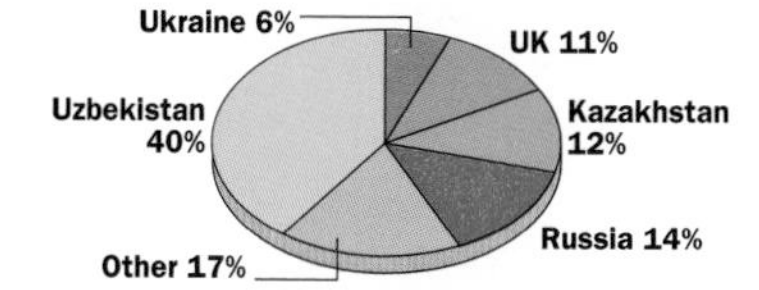
Ukraine 6%
UK 11%
Uzbekistan 40%
Kazakhstan 12%
Russia 14%
Other 17%

RESOURCES

Electric power 4.4m kw

285 tonnes — 501 b/d (reserves 14,640,000 bbl)

1.6m sheep, 1m cattle, 800,000 chickens — Uranium, gold, iron, coal, lead, mercury, tin

Tajikistan has one key resource – uranium – which accounted for 30% of the USSR's total production before 1990. The end of the nuclear arms race has reduced its value, however. Most of Tajikistan is bare mountain and just 6% of the land can be used for agriculture. Industry is concentrated in the Fergana Valley, close to the Uzbek border.

ENVIRONMENT

Not available

4% — 0.9 tonnes per capita

Landslides are a problem which in 1998 caused the country's worst natural disaster in 30 years. Excessive irrigation for cotton production has increased salination of the soil.

MEDIA

TV ownership high

Daily newspaper circulation 21 per 1000 people

PUBLISHING AND BROADCAST MEDIA

There are 3 daily newspapers, but the weeklies *Djavononi Todjikiston* and *Tochikiston ovozi* are more influential

3 state-controlled services — 1 state-controlled service

Communist control over the media was tightened in early 1994 with the takeover by President Rakhmanov of the press and broadcast media.

CRIME

Death penalty used

Tajikistan does not publish prison figures — Crime has been rising dramatically

Only remote areas escape the violence perpetrated by armed gangs. Narcotics smuggling along the border with Afghanistan is on the increase.

EDUCATION

School leaving age: 17

99% — 108,203 students

The university at Dushanbe has been weakened by the departure of its Russian academics.

CHRONOLOGY

In the 19th century, Tajikistan was a collection of semi-independent principalities, some under Russian control, others under the influence of the Emirate of Bukhara.

- **1925** Soviets take over Tajikistan.
- **1940** Cyrillic script introduced.
- **1989** Tajik becomes official language.
- **1991** Independence from Moscow.
- **1994, 1999** Imomali Rakhmanov reelected president.
- **1995** Legislative elections. Tajik currency introduced.
- **1997–1998** Peace accord with rebels; UTO joins government.
- **2000** Pro-Rakhmanov PDPT wins legislative elections.

HEALTH

No welfare state health benefits

1 per 476 people — Heart, cerebrovascular, respiratory, infectious, and parasitic diseases

Tajikistan's health service has always been poor. The infant mortality rate before 1990 was one of the highest in the USSR.

SPENDING

GDP/cap. decrease

CONSUMPTION AND SPENDING

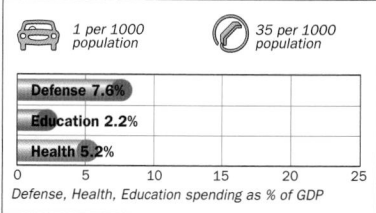

1 per 1000 population — *35 per 1000 population*

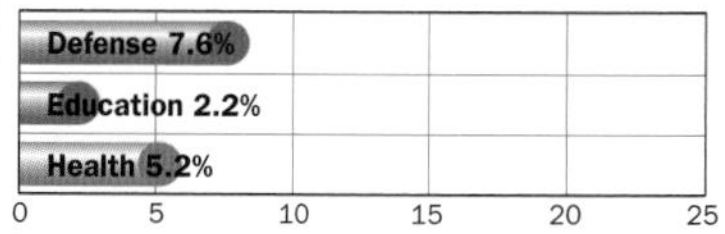
Defense 7.6%
Education 2.2%
Health 5.2%
0
5
10
15
20
25

Defense, Health, Education spending as % of GDP

More than 80% of Tajik people live below the UN-defined poverty line; the war against the Islamist rebels worsened conditions. The former communist bureaucrats continue to be the wealthiest group.

WORLD RANKING

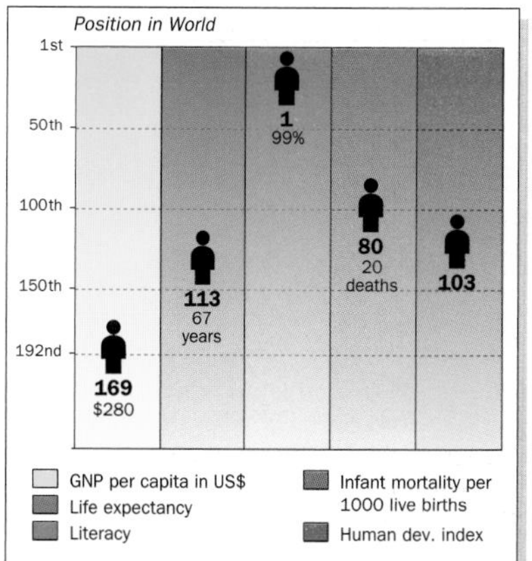
Position in World
1st
50th
100th
150th
192nd
169
$280
113
67
years
1
99%
80
20
deaths
103
GNP per capita in US$
Life expectancy
Literacy
Infant mortality per 1000 live births
Human dev. index

T

TANZANIA

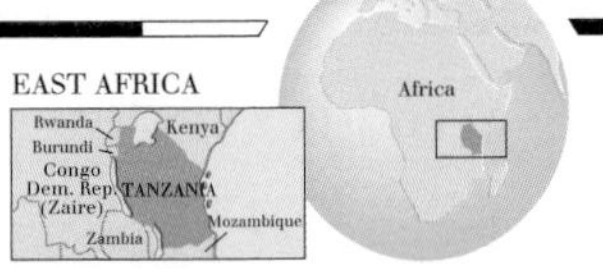
EAST AFRICA
Rwanda
Burundi
Kenya
Congo
Dem. Rep. (Zaire)
TANZANIA
Zambia
Mozambique
Africa

OFFICIAL NAME: United Republic of Tanzania **CAPITAL:** Dodoma
POPULATION: 33.5 million **CURRENCY:** Tanzanian shilling **OFFICIAL LANGUAGES:** English and Swahili

1961 | 1964 | April 26 | EAT | +3 | +255 | .tz

Arusha National Park. *Lying within the Ngurdoto volcanic crater, the park has herds of buffalo, rhinos, elephants, and giraffes.*

TANZANIA LIES BETWEEN Kenya and Mozambique on the east African coast. Formed by the union of Tanganyika and Zanzibar and other islands, Tanzania comprises a coastal lowland, volcanic highlands, and the Great Rift Valley. It includes Mount Kilimanjaro, Africa's highest peak. Tanzania was led by the socialist Julius Nyerere from 1962 until 1985. His Revolutionary Party of Tanzania (CCM) has won multiparty elections held in 1995 and 2000.

CLIMATE

Tropical/mountain

WEATHER CHART

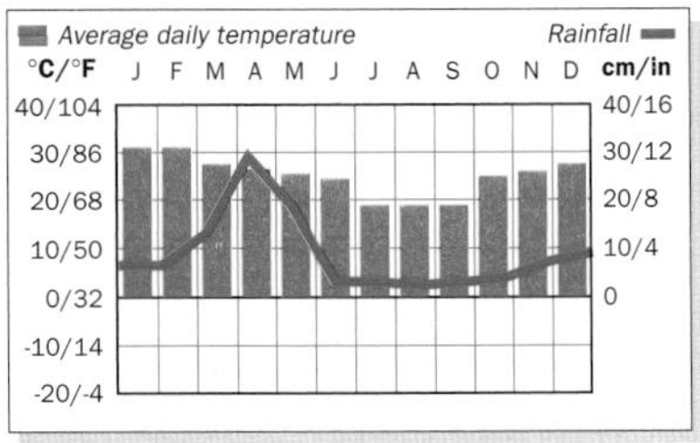
Average daily temperature
Rainfall
°C/°F
J F M A M J J A S O N D
cm/in
40/104
30/86
20/68
10/50
0/32
-10/14
-20/-4
40/16
30/12
20/8
10/4
0

The coast and Zanzibar are tropical. The central plateau is semiarid and the highlands are semitemperate.

TRANSPORTATION

Drive on left

Dar es Salaam International 582,166 passengers

53 ships 35,500 grt

THE TRANSPORTATION NETWORK

3704 km (2302 miles)

None

2721 km (1691 miles)

Lakes Tanganyika, Victoria, and Nyasa are navigable

The roads, railroads, and ports are being upgraded, notably by an $870 million program to improve 70% of Tanzania's trunk roads.

TOURISM

Visitors : Population 1:74

450,000 visitors

Up 29% in 1998

MAIN TOURIST ARRIVALS

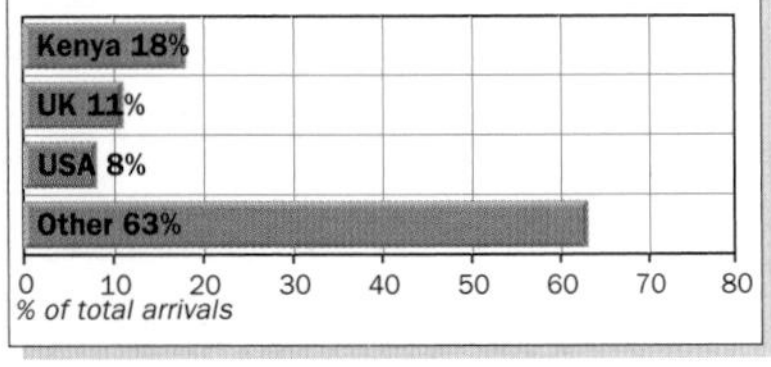
Kenya 18%
UK 11%
USA 8%
Other 63%
0 10 20 30 40 50 60 70 80
% of total arrivals

One-third of Tanzania is national park or game reserve. The Ngorongoro Crater and the Serengeti Plain are top attractions. Tourist numbers have risen sharply since 1990.

PEOPLE

Pop. density low

Swahili, Sukuma, Chagga, Nyamwezi, Hehe, Makonde, Yao, Sandawe, English

38/km² (98/mi²)

THE URBAN/RURAL POPULATION SPLIT

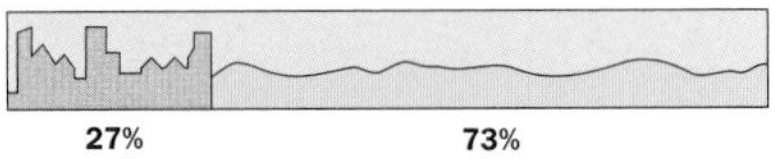
27%
73%

RELIGIOUS PERSUASION

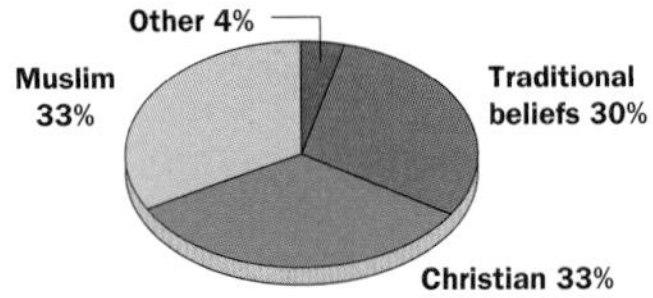
Other 4%
Muslim 33%
Traditional beliefs 30%
Christian 33%

For many Tanzanians the family is the focus of traditional rural life. About 99% belong to one of 120 small ethnic Bantu groups. The remainder comprise Arab, Asian, and European minorities. The use of Swahili as a *lingua franca* has helped make ethnic rivalries almost nonexistent.

POLITICS

Multiparty elections

2000/2005

President Benjamin Mkapa

AT THE LAST ELECTION

National Assembly 296 seats

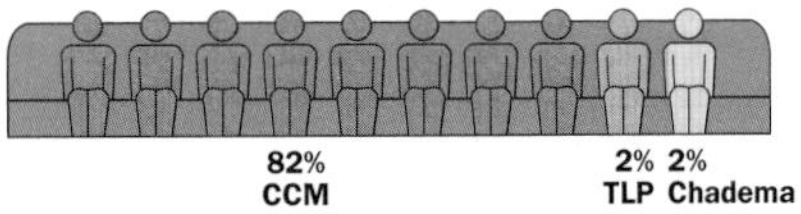
7% CUF
7% Others
82% CCM
2% TLP
2% Chadema

CCM = Revolutionary Party of Tanzania **CUF** = Civic United Front **TLP** = Tanzania Labor Party **Chadema** = Party for Democracy and Progress
Others include 5 members chosen by the Zanzibar House of Representatives, 10 appointed by the president, and the attorney general who has a seat ex-officio

Julius Nyerere was the dominant force in Tanzanian politics for 21 years. He founded the ruling party, the CCM, and his philosophy of African socialism guided Tanzania's development. Ali Hassan Mwinyi succeeded Nyerere as president in 1985, introducing a transition to multiparty democracy. Mwinyi stood down in 1995, when Benjamin Mkapa was elected president. Separatism in Zanzibar is a key issue, flaring into violent protests in 2001.

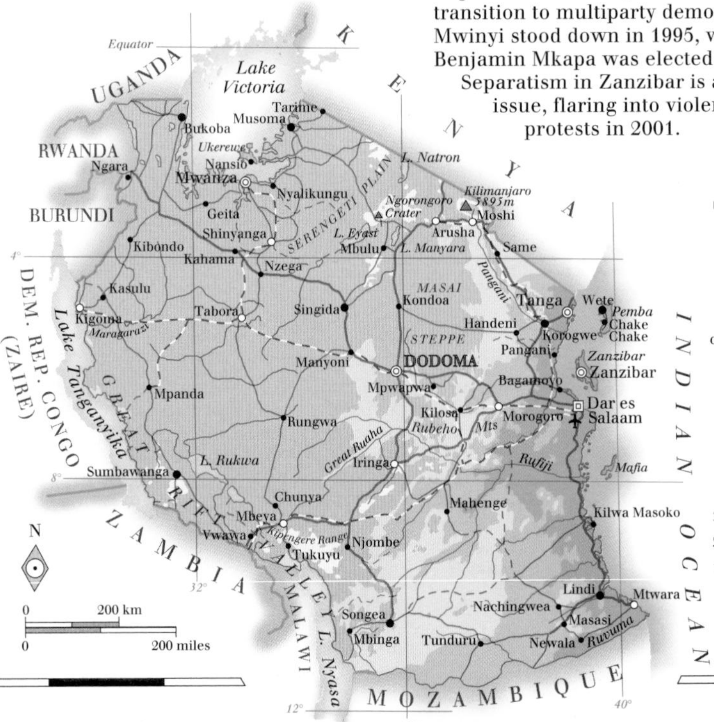
Equator
UGANDA
KENYA
Lake Victoria
RWANDA
BURUNDI
DEM. REP. CONGO (ZAIRE)
Lake Tanganyika
ZAMBIA
MALAWI
L. Nyasa
MOZAMBIQUE
INDIAN OCEAN
Bukoba
Musoma
Tarime
Ukerewe
Nansio
Mwanza
Ngara
Geita
Nyalikungu
SERENGETI PLAIN
L. Natron
Ngorongoro Crater
Kilimanjaro 5895m
Moshi
Arusha
Shinyanga
L. Eyasi
Mbulu
L. Manyara
Same
Kibondo
Kahama
Nzega
MASAI STEPPE
Kasulu
Kigoma
Malagarasi
Tabora
Singida
Kondoa
Tanga
Wete
Pemba
Chake Chake
Korogwe
Handeni
Pangani
Zanzibar
Manyoni
DODOMA
Bagamoyo
Mpwapwa
Dar es Salaam
Mpanda
Kilosa
Rubeho Mts
Morogoro
Rungwa
Great Ruaha
Rufiji
Mafia
L. Rukwa
Iringa
Sumbawanga
GREAT RIFT VALLEY
Chunya
Mahenge
Kilwa Masoko
Mbeya
Vwawa
Kipengere Range
Njombe
Tukuyu
Lindi
Mtwara
Nachingwea
Masasi
Songea
Mbinga
Tunduru
Newala
Ruvuma
N
0 200 km
0 200 miles
4°
8°
12°
32°
36°
40°

TANZANIA

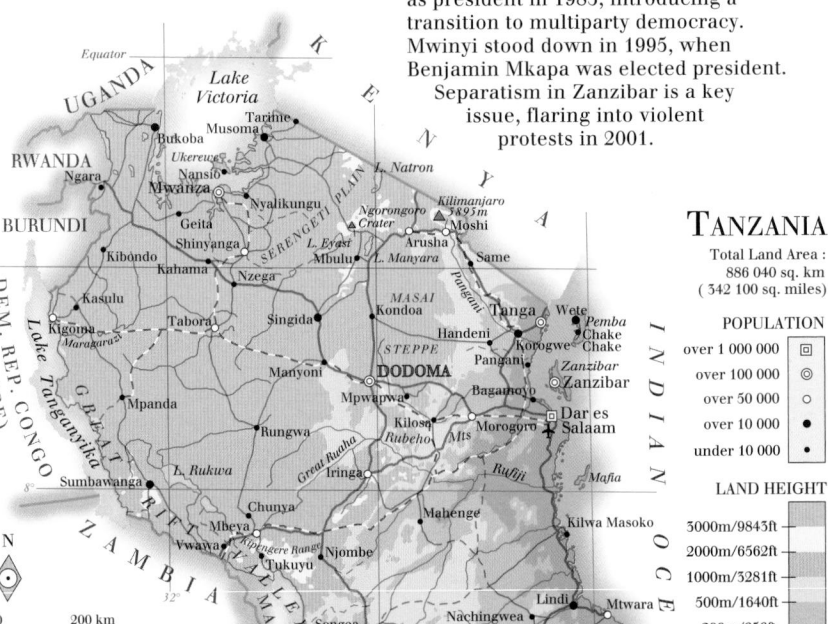

Total Land Area : 886 040 sq. km (342 100 sq. miles)

POPULATION

over 1 000 000
over 100 000
over 50 000
over 10 000
under 10 000

LAND HEIGHT

3000m/9843ft
2000m/6562ft
1000m/3281ft
500m/1640ft
200m/656ft
Sea Level

WORLD AFFAIRS

Joined UN in 1961

Comm · ACP · EAC · OAU · SADC

The instability of Tanzania's central African neighbors is a concern. It accepted over half a million Rwandan and Burundian refugees in the 1990s, but instigated mass repatriations in 1996. Improved relations with Uganda and Kenya since 1985 have led to the rebirth in 2001 of the East African Community.

AID

Recipient

$990m (receipts)

Down 1% in 1999

Tanzania is heavily dependent on aid to help offset a severe balance of payments deficit. Most aid is now linked to an IMF-backed economic reform program. Net aid receipts constituted over 25% of GNP in 1990, but had fallen to barely 10% by 1999.

DEFENSE

Compulsory military service

$141m

Down 3% in 1999

Defense accounts for 3.5% of budget spending. The armed forces are closely linked with the ruling CCM. There is an 80,000-strong citizens' reserve force.

ECONOMICS

Inflation 23.1% p.a. (1990–1999)

$8.5bn

797.0–805.0 Tanzanian shillings

SCORE CARD

WORLD GNP RANKING	91st
GNP PER CAPITA	$260
BALANCE OF PAYMENTS	$-956m
INFLATION	7.9%
UNEMPLOYMENT	Not available

STRENGTHS

Coffee, cotton, sisal, tea, cashew nuts. Zanzibar a major producer of cloves. Diamonds. Expansion in non-traditional exports. State commitment to effective reforms. Rise in inward investment. Return to positive growth.

WEAKNESSES

Growth still too low to increase per capita income. Shortage of foreign exchange. Poor credit and equipment limit agricultural development.

EXPORTS

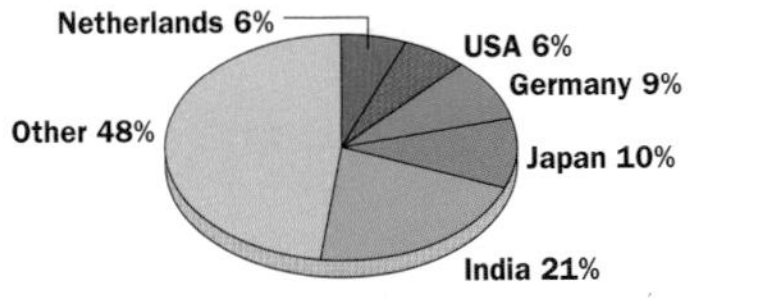
Netherlands 6%
USA 6%
Germany 9%
Other 48%
Japan 10%
India 21%

IMPORTS

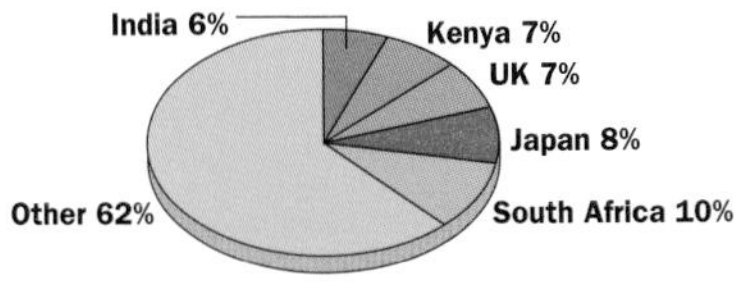
India 6%
Kenya 7%
UK 7%
Japan 8%
Other 62%
South Africa 10%

RESOURCES

Electric power 543,000 kw

357,210 tonnes

Not an oil producer

14.4m cattle, 10m goats, 4.2m sheep, 29m chickens

Natural gas, oil, iron, diamonds, gold, salt, phosphates, coal

Agriculture, including livestock and forestry, is the key economic resource. It accounts for half of GDP and 80% of employment and exports. Forests cover 50% of Tanzania. More than 90% of energy demand is met from wood and charcoal. Hydropower provides 70% of electricity and is being expanded. To reduce oil imports, which take 40% of export earnings, Tanzania is starting to exploit offshore gas at Songo Songo. Oil has been discovered off Pemba Island.

ENVIRONMENT

Sustainability rank: 94th

16%

0.1 tonnes per capita

The demand for fuelwood is a threat to forests. Tourism's demands have to be carefully balanced with those of fragile wildlife environments such as the Ngorongoro Crater and the Serengeti.

MEDIA

TV ownership low

Daily newspaper circulation 4 per 1000 people

PUBLISHING AND BROADCAST MEDIA

There are 9 daily newspapers, including the *Daily News, Uhuru,* and *Kipanga*

3 independent services

5 services: 2 state-owned, 3 independent

The daily press is mainly state-owned. There are some privately owned Swahili papers, and independent TV stations.

CRIME

Death penalty used

Tanzania does not publish prison figures

Up 2% 1996–1998

Crime levels are low, although theft in Dar es Salaam has risen. Tanzania's human rights record is good.

EDUCATION

School leaving age: 14

76%

17,812 students

Primary education, which begins at seven and lasts for seven years, is free; secondary students pay fees. In 1999, enrollment was 75% at primary level, but only 6% for secondary education.

CHRONOLOGY

The mainland became the German colony of Tanganyika in 1884. The Sultanate of Zanzibar became a British protectorate in 1890.

- **1918** Tanganyika British mandate.
- **1961** Tanganyika independent.
- **1962** Nyerere becomes president.
- **1963** Zanzibar independent.
- **1964** Zanzibar signs union with Tanganyika to form Tanzania.
- **1985** President Mwinyi begins relaxation of socialist policies.
- **1992** Political parties allowed.
- **1995** Multiparty elections. Benjamin Mkapa becomes president.
- **1999** Death of Nyerere.
- **2000** Mkapa elected for second term.
- **2001** Increasing unrest among Zanzibar separatists.

HEALTH

Welfare state health benefits

1 per 20,000 people

Diarrheal and respiratory diseases, malaria

Basic care is provided by the state and Christian missions. The AIDS epidemic is causing appalling damage.

SPENDING

GDP/cap. increase

CONSUMPTION AND SPENDING

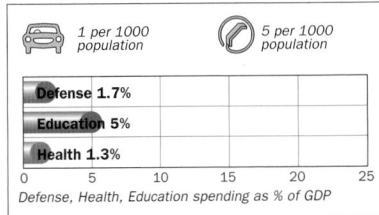

1 per 1000 population

5 per 1000 population

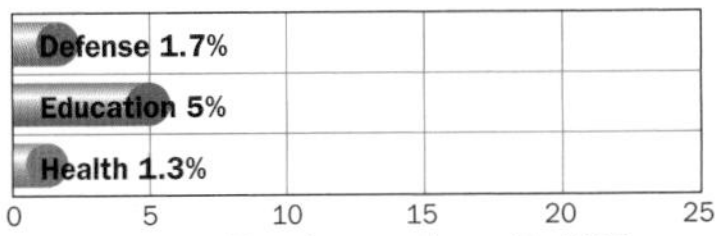
Defense 1.7%
Education 5%
Health 1.3%
0
5
10
15
20
25

Defense, Health, Education spending as % of GDP

The majority of Tanzanians are subsistence farmers. The country's wealthy elite is small, and is composed mainly of Asian and Arab business families.

WORLD RANKING

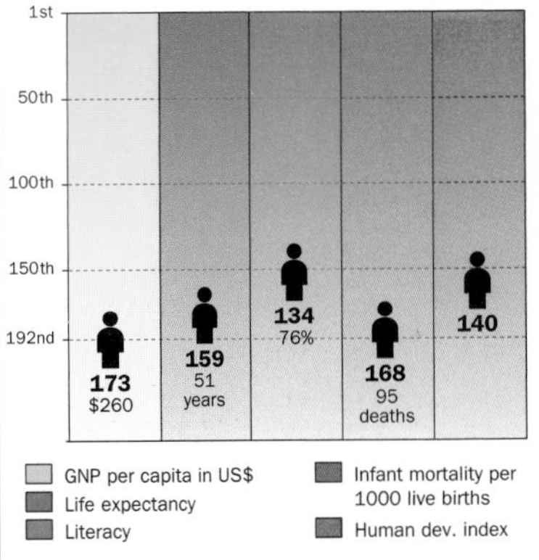
Position in World
1st
50th
100th
150th
192nd
173
$260
159
51 years
134
76%
168
95 deaths
140
GNP per capita in US$
Life expectancy
Literacy
Infant mortality per 1000 live births
Human dev. index

T

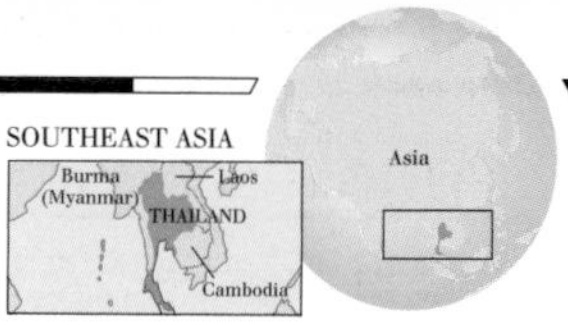
SOUTHEAST ASIA
Burma (Myanmar)
Laos
THAILAND
Cambodia
Asia

THAILAND

OFFICIAL NAME: Kingdom of Thailand **CAPITAL:** Bangkok
POPULATION: 61.4 million **CURRENCY:** Baht **OFFICIAL LANGUAGE:** Thai

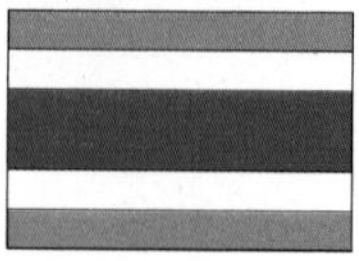

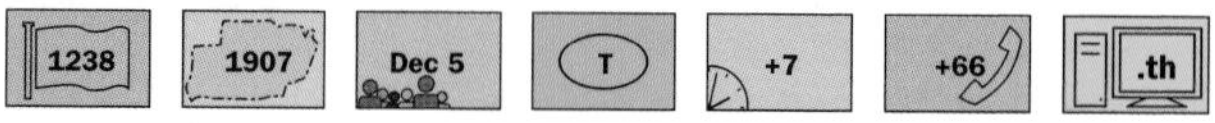
1238
1907
Dec 5
T
+7
+66
.th

THAILAND LIES IN SOUTHEAST ASIA, between the Indian and Pacific Oceans. The north, the western border with Burma, and the long Isthmus of Kra are mountainous. The central plain is the most fertile and densely populated area, while the low northeastern plateau is the poorest region. Thailand has been an independent kingdom for most of its history and, since 1932, a constitutional monarchy with alternating military and civilian governments. Continuing rapid industrialization is resulting in massive congestion in Bangkok and a serious depletion of natural resources.

CLIMATE

Tropical equatorial/ monsoon

WEATHER CHART

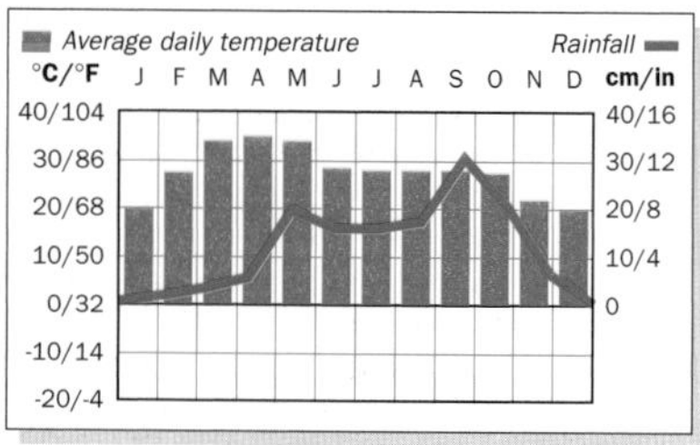
Average daily temperature
Rainfall
°C/°F
J F M A M J J A S O N D
cm/in
40/104
30/86
20/68
10/50
0/32
-10/14
-20/-4
40/16
30/12
20/8
10/4
0

Thailand's tropical monsoon climate has three seasons – a hot sultry period, rains from May to October, and a dry, cooler season from November to March.

TRANSPORTATION

Drive on left

Don Muang International, Bangkok
27.3m passengers

552 ships
2m grt

THE TRANSPORTATION NETWORK

62,985 km (39,137 miles)	None
4623 km (2873 miles)	3701 km (2300 miles)

Bangkok suffers from huge traffic jams. Its first mass transit system – an elevated railroad – became partially operational in 1999. Good US-built roads run to the north and east. The Chao Phraya river carries most freight.

Island in the Andaman Sea. *The over-development of Thailand's best-known resorts is pushing tourism into new, remoter locations.*

TOURISM

Visitors : Population 1:6.5

9.5m visitors

Up 10% in 2000

MAIN TOURIST ARRIVALS

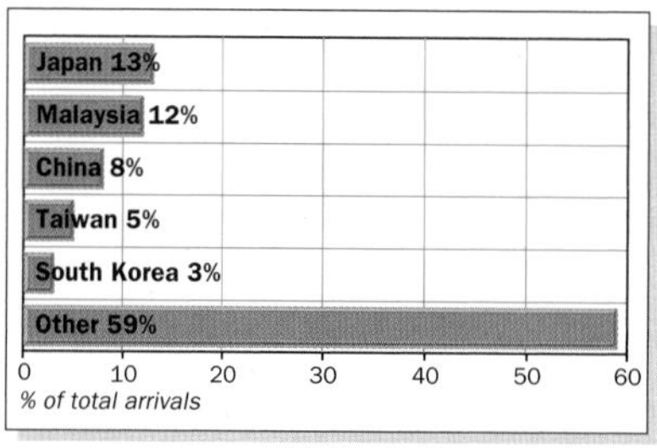
Japan 13%
Malaysia 12%
China 8%
Taiwan 5%
South Korea 3%
Other 59%
0
10
20
30
40
50
60
% of total arrivals

Tourism is an important contributor to the Thai economy. Tourist numbers fell in the early 1990s as a result of both the worldwide recession and local overdevelopment during the 1980s boom. Although the number of arrivals has since recovered, visitors are tending to seek the less developed resorts. Bangkok's hotel occupancy rates are still falling as yet more hotels are built. Pattaya beach resort, opposite Phetchaburi, has seen such uncontrolled development that sea pollution is now a serious problem, while opposition to the intrusion of large numbers of tourists is growing among northern hill tribes.

Although prostitution is illegal, Bangkok and Pattaya are centers for sex tourism, which thrives despite the state's embarrassment at its effect on Thailand's image. Japanese and German men are among the main clients, while Burmese girls are increasingly recruited as prostitutes. Child prostitution is also a major problem.

There has been a boom in golf tourism, especially among the Japanese. The large number of new golf courses which are under construction will make Thailand the largest golf destination in Asia. The vast amounts of water needed to maintain the courses is aggravating Thailand's serious water shortage.

PEOPLE

Pop. density medium

Thai, Chinese, Malay, Khmer, Mon, Karen, Miao

120/km² (311/mi²)

THE URBAN/RURAL POPULATION SPLIT

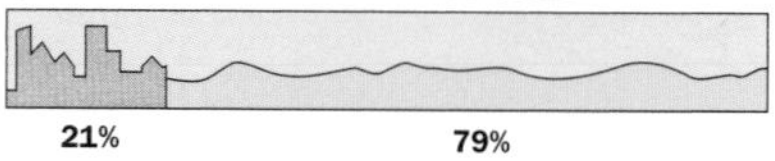
21%
79%

RELIGIOUS PERSUASION

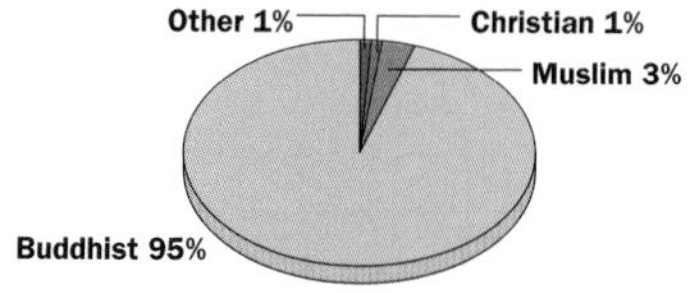
Other 1%
Christian 1%
Muslim 3%
Buddhist 95%

ETHNIC MAKEUP

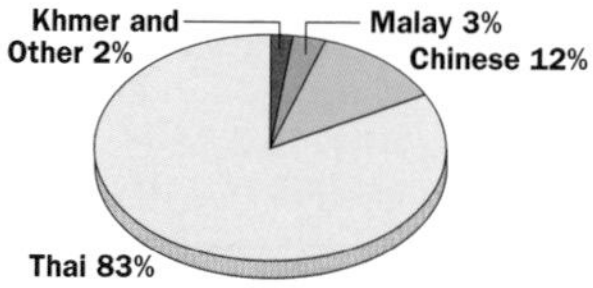
Khmer and Other 2%
Malay 3%
Chinese 12%
Thai 83%

There is little ethnic tension in Thailand, and Buddhism is a great binding force. The majority of Thais follow Theravada Buddhism, although the reformist Asoke Santi Buddhist sect, which advocates a new moral austerity, is gaining influence. Its principles have been espoused in particular by the Palang Dharma (PD), which seeks to clean up politics.

The far north and northeast hills are home to about 600,000 tribespeople with their own languages, and to permanently settled refugees from Laos, mostly of the Hmong tribal group.

The large Chinese community is the most assimilated in southeast Asia. Sino-Thais are particularly dominant in agricultural marketing. Most of Thailand's one million Muslim Malays live in southern Thailand, bordering Malaysia. They feel stronger affinity with Muslims in Malaysia than with Thai culture, and this has given rise to a secessionist movement.

Women are important in business, but their involvement in national politics is limited.

POPULATION AGE BREAKDOWN

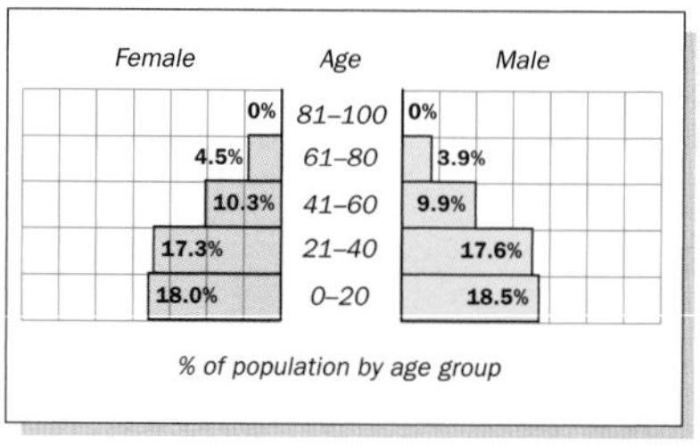
Female
Age
Male
0%
81–100
0%
4.5%
61–80
3.9%
10.3%
41–60
9.9%
17.3%
21–40
17.6%
18.0%
0–20
18.5%
% of population by age group

T

POLITICS

Multiparty elections

L. House 2001/2005
U. House 2000/2006

HM King Bhumibol Adulyadej (Rama IX)

House of Representatives 500 seats

8% CT | 6% CP

49% TRT | 26% DP | 7% NAP | 4% Others

TRT = Thai Rak Thai **DP** = Democrat Party **CT** = Chart Thai (Thai Nation) **NAP** = New Aspiration Party **CP** = Chart Patthana (National Development)

Senate 200 seats

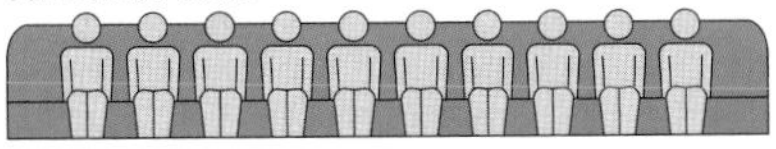

Under the 1997 constitution, the members of the Senate are directly elected on a non-party basis.

Thailand is a parliamentary democracy. The king is the head of state. Despite his position as a constitutional monarch, he has immense personal prestige. Criticism of the king is not tolerated.

MAIN POLITICAL ISSUES

The military–democratic cycle

Thailand has been ruled by alternating military and civilian governments since 1932. In 1992 promilitary parties chose an unelected army general as prime minister. Violent demonstrations erupted which forced the resignation of the prime minister and precipitated a constitutional amendment obliging future prime ministers to be elected members of the legislature. The military has since maintained a low profile during general elections, and refrained from interfering in government changes.

Congestion in Bangkok

A major issue is the concentration of industry and commerce in the Bangkok area. Uncontrolled development has left it with traffic congestion which not only is among the world's worst but is also a serious hindrance to economic activity. In December 1999 the first stage of a mass transit system – an elevated railroad – was formally opened.

In 1993, the government began offering incentives for relocating industry to the provinces. This is also intended to help distribute wealth more evenly – up to 60% of GDP is generated in the Bangkok area.

Water

The national water shortage, caused by rapid industrialization, is so acute that it is affecting farm and industrial output.

King Bhumibol. *On the throne since 1946, he is the world's longest-serving ruler.*

Thaksin Shinawatra, *a controversial billionaire, elected premier in 2001.*

PROFILE

The Thai political process is highly personalized and parties seldom have strong ideologies. Coalitions are often unstable, while the lack of coordination between coalition partners is a recurring problem. A political stalemate in 1996 was resolved only by calling a fresh general election, from which the NAP emerged as the largest party and its leader Chaovalit Yongchaiyuth as prime minister. This government fell in 1997, blamed for mismanaging the economic crisis. It was replaced by another coalition under Chuan Leekpai of the DP. He succeeded in retaining office despite the volatility of coalition politics. However, in the 2001 elections the new populist TRT triumphed, winning just short of a majority of seats. TRT leader and former deputy prime minister Thaksin Shinawatra formed a three-party government, despite an indictment for corruption against him.

WORLD AFFAIRS

Joined UN in 1946

APEC | ASEAN | Mekong River | NAM | WTO

Thailand has friendly relations with China. However, relations with neighboring Burma have been strained over Burma's alleged support for Thai ethnic guerrillas operating along the Thai–Burmese border. Many Thai logging concerns, often run by the military, have been active in Burma since Thailand's 1988 logging ban at home. Relations with Vietnam are cordial, despite Thailand's opposition to the Vietnamese regime in Cambodia in the 1980s.

Thailand, Indonesia, and Malaysia have liberalized trade to promote development in each country in regions which are distant from their respective capitals.

Thailand maintains close relations with the USA, despite some tension over intellectual property rights and minor trade issues, but no longer has any US military bases on its territory.

LAOS
BURMA (MYANMAR)
ANDAMAN SEA
CAMBODIA
MALAYSIA
Gulf of Thailand
Chiang Mai
Doi Inthanon 2594m
Nan
Lampang
Phrae
Uttaradit
Loei
Udon Thani
Nong Khai
Nakhon Phanom
Sakon Nakhon
Tak
Phitsanulok
Lom Sak
Kalasin
Khon Kaen
Maha Sarakham
Roi Et
KORAT PLATEAU
Ubon Ratchathani
Mekong
Nakhon Sawan
Chaiyaphum
Buriram
Nakhon Ratchasima
Surin
Phanom Dang Raek
Chao Phraya
Lop Buri
Sara Buri
Ayutthaya
Thon Buri
BANGKOK
Nakhon Pathom
Samut Sakhon
Samut Prakan
Chachoengsao
Ratchaburi
Phetchaburi
Chon Buri
Ao Krung Thep
Ban Hua Hin
Rayong
Chanthaburi
Ko Chang
TANEN RANGE
Mae Nam Ping
Chumphon
Isthmus Of Kra
Ko Phangan
Ko Samui
Surat Thani
Nakhon Si Thammarat
Ko Phuket
Phuket
Trang
MALAY PENINSULA
Songkhla
Hat Yai
Pattani
Yala
Narathiwat
N
0 200 km
0 200 miles

THAILAND

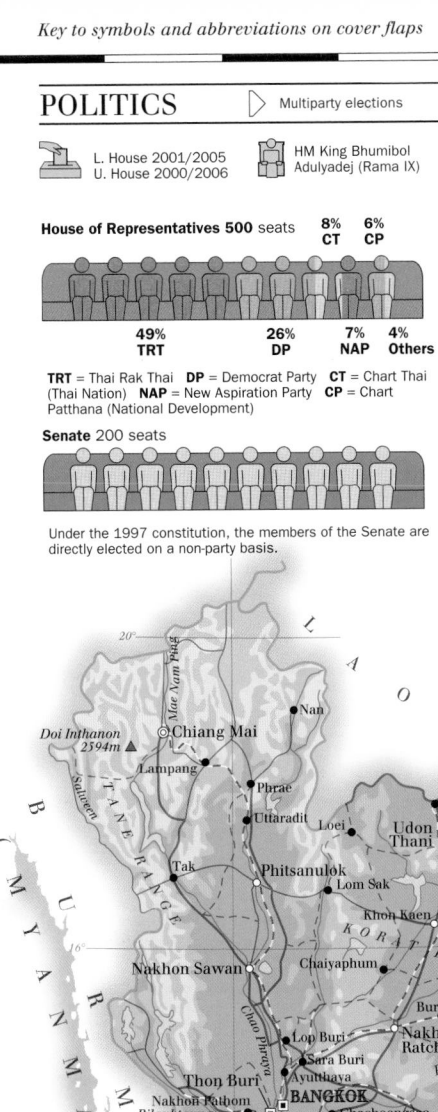

Total Land Area : 510 890 sq. km (197 255 sq. miles)

LAND HEIGHT: 2000m/6562ft, 1000m/3281ft, 500m/1640ft, 200m/656ft, Sea Level

POPULATION: over 5 000 000, over 1 000 000, over 100 000, over 50 000, over 10 000

AID

▷ Recipient

$1bn (receipts) — Up 45% in 1999

The World Bank and Japan are the largest aid donors. Thailand has imposed a ceiling on foreign borrowing to keep its debt stable.

CHRONOLOGY

Thailand emerged as a kingdom in the 13th century, and by the late 17th century its then capital, Ayutthya, was the largest city in southeast Asia. In 1782, the present Chakri dynasty and a new capital, Bangkok, were founded.

- ❑ **1855** King Mongut signs Bowring trade treaty with British – Thailand never colonized by Europeans.
- ❑ **1868–1910** King Chulalongkorn westernizes Thailand.
- ❑ **1907** Thailand cedes western Khmer (Cambodia) to France.
- ❑ **1925** King Prajadhipok begins absolute rule.
- ❑ **1932** Bloodless military–civilian coup. Constitutional monarchy.
- ❑ **1933** Military takes control.
- ❑ **1941** Japanese invade. Government collaborates.
- ❑ **1944** Pro-Japanese prime minister and prewar military dictator Phibun voted out of office.
- ❑ **1945** Exiled King Ananda returns.
- ❑ **1946** Ananda assassinated. King Bhumibol accedes.
- ❑ **1947** Military coup. Phibun back.
- ❑ **1957** Military coup. Constitution abolished.
- ❑ **1965** Thailand allows USA to use Thai bases in Vietnam War.
- ❑ **1969** New constitution endorses elected parliament.
- ❑ **1971** Army suspends constitution.
- ❑ **1973–1976** Student riots lead to interlude of democracy.
- ❑ **1976** Military takeover.
- ❑ **1980–1988** General Prem Tinsulanond prime minister. Partial democracy.
- ❑ **1988** Elections. General Chatichai Choonhaven, right-wing CT leader, named prime minister.
- ❑ **1991** Military coup. Civilian Anand Panyarachun caretaker premier.
- ❑ **1992** Elections. General Suchinda named premier. Demonstrations. King forces Suchinda to step down and reinstalls Anand. Moderates win new elections.
- ❑ **1995** CT wins general election.
- ❑ **1996** Early elections; Chaovalit Yongchaiyuth of NAP becomes prime minister.
- ❑ **1997** Financial and economic crisis; Chaovalit government falls; DP's Chuan Leekpai prime minister.
- ❑ **2001** TRT, led by Thaksin Shinawatra, wins elections.

T

DEFENSE

▷ No compulsory military service

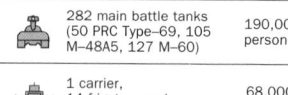

$2.64bn — Up 24% in 1999

THAI ARMED FORCES

282 main battle tanks (50 PRC Type–69, 105 M–48A5, 127 M–60)	190,000 personnel
1 carrier, 14 frigates, and 88 patrol boats	68,000 personnel
153 combat aircraft (14 F–5A/B, 34 F–16A/B, 33 F–5E/F)	43,000 personnel
None	

The military has either ruled Thailand, or played a prominent role in politics, since 1932. It last intervened by taking power in 1991. In 1996, its role in the appointed Senate – hitherto a military stronghold – was reduced. Retired military figures are, however, prominent in the major political parties.

Since 1986, spending has focused on the navy and air force. China, Germany, and Spain are supplying naval vessels, the UK, the USA, and Russia, aircraft.

The main defense concerns are border disputes with Cambodia, Burma, and Laos; the Muslim secessionist movement in the south; and piracy and fishing disputes in the South China Sea.

ECONOMICS

▷ Inflation 4.6% p.a. (1990–1999)

$121.1bn — 37.58–43.38 baht

SCORE CARD

❑ World GNP Ranking	32nd
❑ GNP per capita	$2010
❑ Balance of Payments	$11bn
❑ Inflation	0.3%
❑ Unemployment	3%

EXPORTS

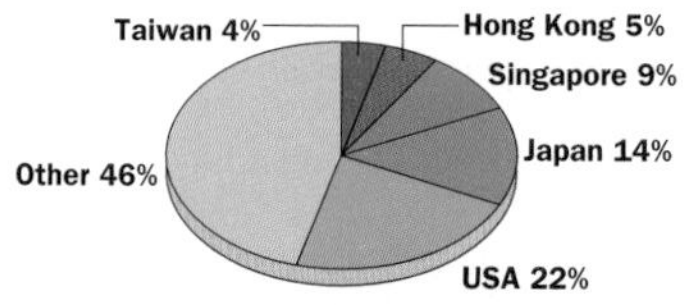
Taiwan 4%
Hong Kong 5%
Singapore 9%
Japan 14%
USA 22%
Other 46%

IMPORTS

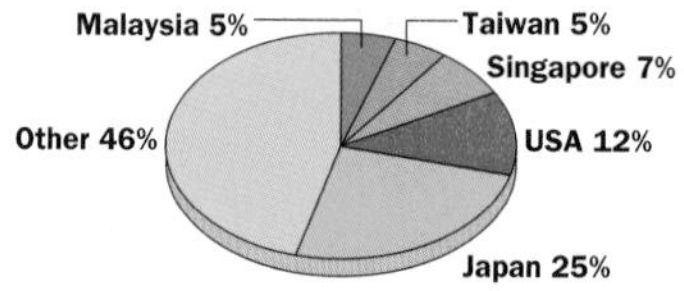
Malaysia 5%
Taiwan 5%
Singapore 7%
USA 12%
Japan 25%
Other 46%

Strengths

Success of export-based and import-substituting manufacturing. Rapid economic growth. Natural gas. Tourism. Chief world exporter of rice and rubber.

Weaknesses

Concentration of economic activity in congested Bangkok area. Inadequate water storage facilities. Rapid growth of foreign debt. 60% of population in low-profit farming.

Profile

Until the late 1990s, the economy grew at over 9% a year for a decade, driven by a rise in manufacturing and huge overseas investments, especially from Japan. However, as domestic wages rose, Thailand faced stiff competition from China and Vietnam. Thailand also lacked a skilled labor force to develop high-tech production, though it is a big producer of electronics goods.

In 1997 mounting foreign debt and the sharp depreciation of the baht made necessary an IMF-led rescue package. Massive retrenchment and stringent austerity measures followed. By mid-2000 the IMF had ended its direct involvement and was optimistic for future expansion, predicting GDP growth of 4.5% in the following year.

ECONOMIC PERFORMANCE INDICATOR

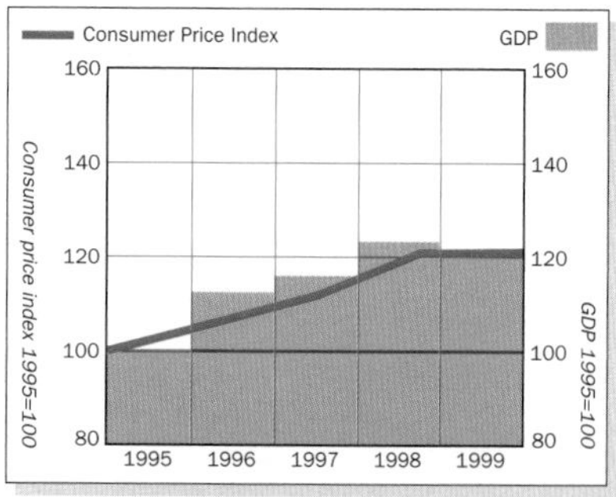
Consumer Price Index
GDP
160
140
120
100
80
Consumer price index 1995=100
GDP 1995=100
1995
1996
1997
1998
1999

THAILAND : MAJOR BUSINESSES

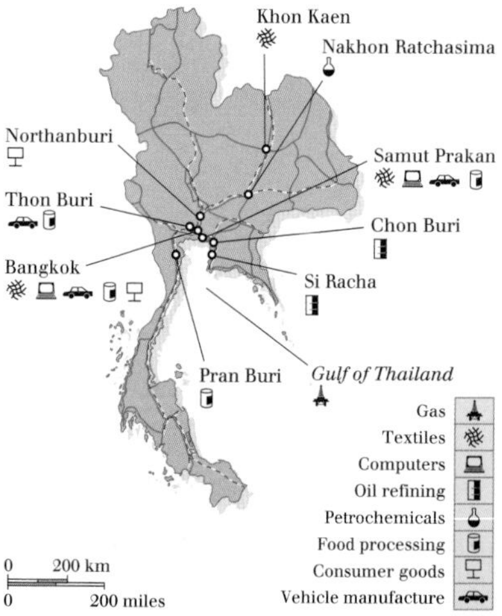
Khon Kaen
Nakhon Ratchasima
Northanburi
Samut Prakan
Thon Buri
Chon Buri
Bangkok
Si Racha
Pran Buri
Gulf of Thailand
Gas
Textiles
Computers
Oil refining
Petrochemicals
Food processing
Consumer goods
Vehicle manufacture
0 200 km
0 200 miles

RESOURCES

Electric power 20.4m kw

3.49m tonnes

165,000 b/d (reserves 400,000,000 bbl)

22m ducks, 7.68m pigs, 6.1m cattle, 172m chickens

Tin, lignite, gas, gems, oil, tungsten, lead, gold, zinc, antimony, copper

ELECTRICITY GENERATION

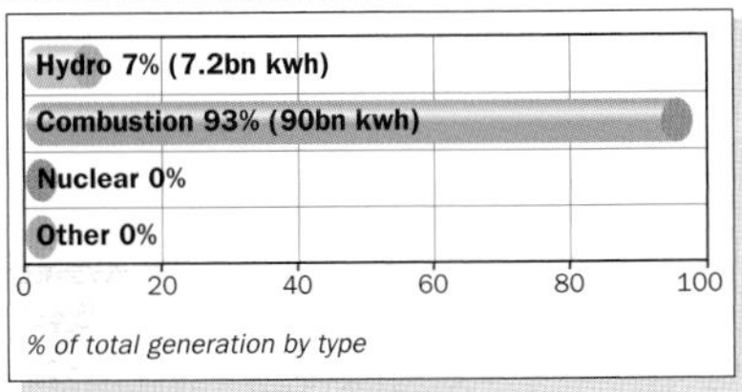
Hydro 7% (7.2bn kwh)
Combustion 93% (90bn kwh)
Nuclear 0%
Other 0%
0
20
40
60
80
100
% of total generation by type

Thailand has minimal crude oil and has rejected the nuclear option in favor of speeding up development of its large natural gas fields. It also has significant lignite deposits for power generation. World demand for Thailand's tin has declined, but recent gold and copper finds offer new potential. Thailand has valuable gemstone deposits. It is also the world's biggest shrimp producer.

THAILAND : LAND USE

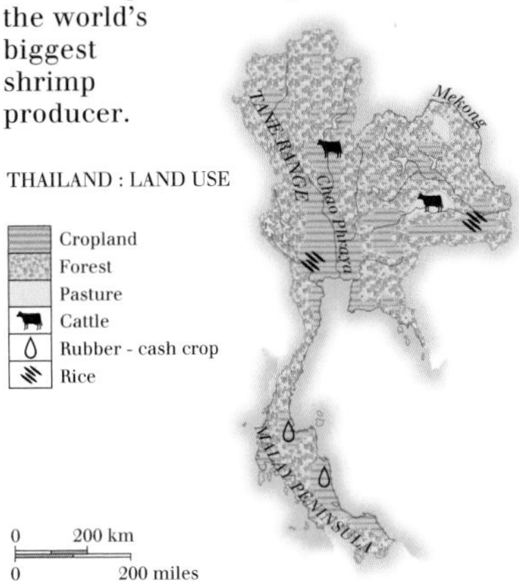
Cropland
Forest
Pasture
Cattle
Rubber - cash crop
Rice
TANEN RANGE
Chao Phraya
Mekong
MALAY PENINSULA
0 200 km
0 200 miles

ENVIRONMENT

Sustainability rank: 74th

14%

3.8 tonnes per capita

ENVIRONMENTAL TREATIES

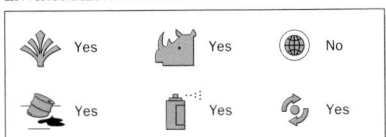

Yes	Yes	No
Yes	Yes	Yes

Deforestation, especially of the watersheds in the north, has led to the increasing severity of both floods and droughts. Particularly serious flooding in the south resulted in a total logging ban in 1988. Illegal logging continues, however. Reforestation projects, some criticized for using single quick-growing species, will not solve the national water shortage. There is evidence of growing official concern at pollution levels. The worst-polluting factories are being forced to move out of Bangkok and no new factories may use CFCs.

MEDIA

TV ownership high

Daily newspaper circulation 64 per 1000 people

PUBLISHING AND BROADCAST MEDIA

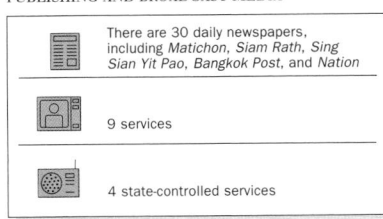

There are 30 daily newspapers, including *Matichon, Siam Rath, Sing Sian Yit Pao, Bangkok Post*, and *Nation*

9 services

4 state-controlled services

Newspapers enjoy a high level of freedom in political reporting. Two of the TV stations are run by the military. There are 60 radio stations around Bangkok, mainly state-run.

CRIME

Death penalty used

106,676 prisoners

Up 95% 1992–1996

CRIME RATES

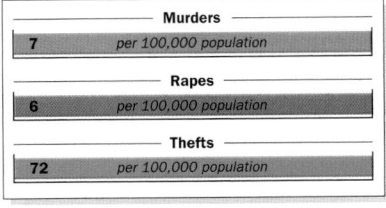

Murders: 7 per 100,000 population

Rapes: 6 per 100,000 population

Thefts: 72 per 100,000 population

Political imprisonment is now extremely rare. There is some police involvement in crime, and extrajudicial killings and ill-treatment of prisoners in police detention are quite common. The king has inspired an opium-substitution crop program. In the south, drug addiction is a major problem. The government has cracked down on music, software, and video piracy.

EDUCATION

School leaving age: 15

96%

1.5m students

THE EDUCATION SYSTEM

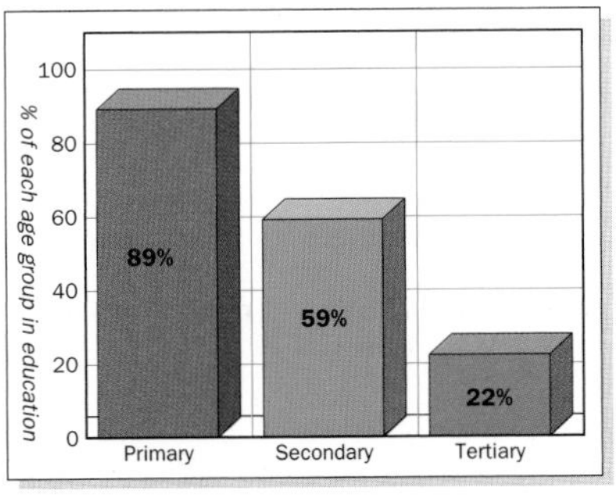
% of each age group in education
100
80
60
40
20
0
89%
59%
22%
Primary
Secondary
Tertiary

A poorly developed education system has led to a shortage of skills needed for the expansion of high-tech industries.

In 1993, the first steps were taken to make schooling compulsory for nine years instead of six.

HEALTH

Welfare state health benefits

1 per 2500 people

Heart diseases, gastroenteritis

High-quality health care is heavily concentrated in Bangkok. Most of the 75% of the population who live in rural areas have access to primary health care. Trained personnel are aided by village health volunteers, monks, teachers, and traditional healers. In 1993 the decision was taken to improve the skills of primary health workers, as a means to improve rural health care. However, estimates suggest that only 30% of users can afford to pay. The poor can apply annually for a certificate entitling them to free health care.

High-profile family planning programs are slowing population growth. An effective AIDS prevention campaign has helped reduce the number of new infections, although the government has been in conflict with international drug companies over its right to produce cheaper generic drugs for AIDS sufferers. Prostitutes have benefited from an extensive sex education program.

SPENDING

GDP/cap. increase

CONSUMPTION AND SPENDING

28 per 1000 population

86 per 1000 population

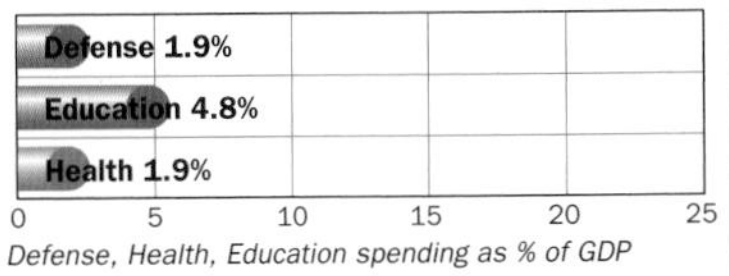
Defense 1.9%
Education 4.8%
Health 1.9%
0
5
10
15
20
25
Defense, Health, Education spending as % of GDP

The government is trying to diffuse to the provinces the people and wealth currently concentrated to a very great extent in Bangkok. The northeast in particular is very poor. The gap between rich and poor is greater in Thailand than in other industrializing southeast Asian states.

WORLD RANKING

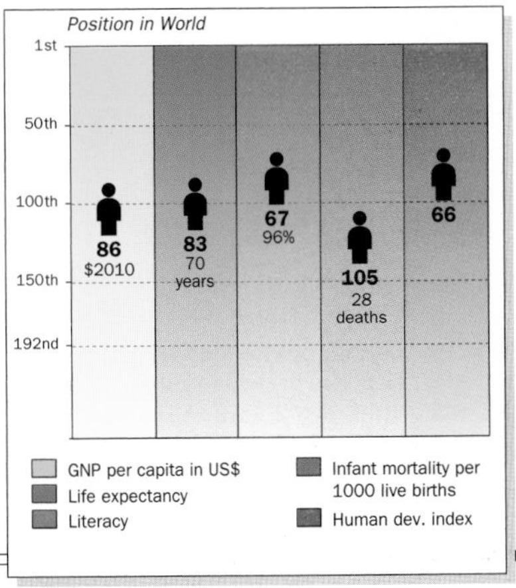
Position in World
1st
50th
100th
150th
192nd
86
$2010
83
70
years
67
96%
105
28
deaths
66
GNP per capita in US$
Life expectancy
Literacy
Infant mortality per 1000 live births
Human dev. index

T

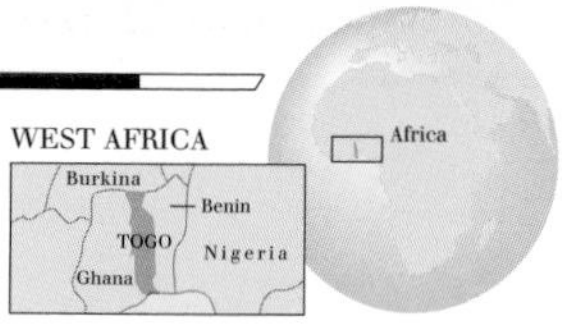
WEST AFRICA
Burkina
Benin
TOGO
Nigeria
Ghana
Africa

TOGO

OFFICIAL NAME: Togolese Republic **CAPITAL:** Lomé
POPULATION: 4.6 million **CURRENCY:** CFA franc **OFFICIAL LANGUAGE:** French

1960 | 1960 | April 27 | TG | 0 | +228 | .tg

TOGO IS SANDWICHED between Ghana and Benin in west Africa. A central forested region is bounded by savanna lands to the north and south. The port of Lomé is an important entrepôt for west African trade. The president, General Gnassingbé Eyadéma, has been in power since 1967.

CLIMATE

Tropical equatorial/ wet and dry

WEATHER CHART

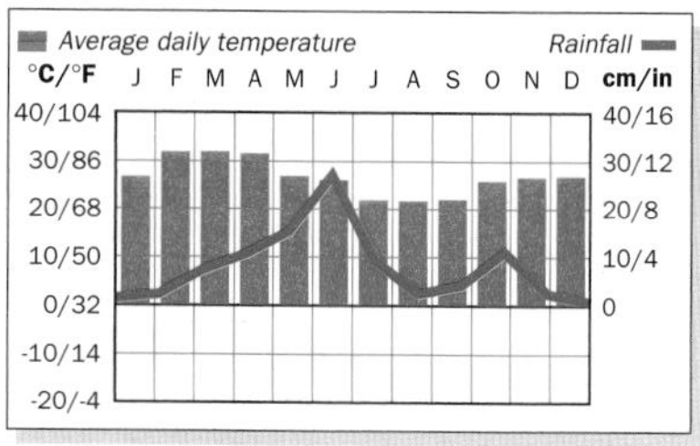
Average daily temperature
Rainfall
°C/°F
J F M A M J J A S O N D
cm/in
40/104
30/86
20/68
10/50
0/32
-10/14
-20/-4
40/16
30/12
20/8
10/4
0

Togo has a typical Gulf of Guinea climate – very hot and humid on the coast, and drier inland.

TRANSPORTATION

Drive on right

Tokoin, Lomé
219,444 passengers

9 ships
1608 grt

THE TRANSPORTATION NETWORK

2376 km (1476 miles)

None

517 km (321 miles)

50 km (31 miles)

Improving the already good road network and Lomé's port facilities are priorities, given Togo's role as an entrepôt. Air and rail links to the interior, however, are limited.

TOURISM

Visitors : Population 1:77

60,000 visitors

Down 14% in 2000

MAIN TOURIST ARRIVALS

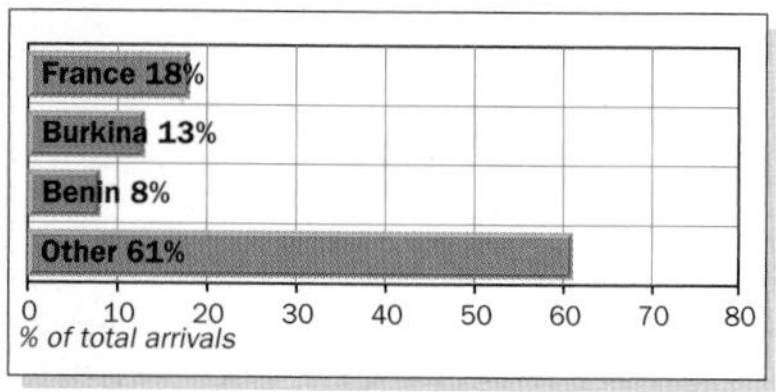
France 18%
Burkina 13%
Benin 8%
Other 61%
0 10 20 30 40 50 60 70 80
% of total arrivals

There is some package tourism, mainly French and German, to coastal tourist villages and hotels built during the expansion program of the 1980s. Tourists have been deterred by the political uncertainty since 1990.

PEOPLE

Pop. density medium

Ewe, Kabye, Gurma, French

85/km² (219/mi²)

THE URBAN/RURAL POPULATION SPLIT

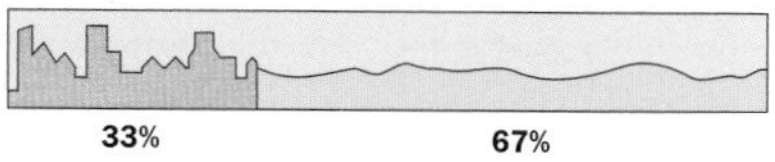
33%
67%

RELIGIOUS PERSUASION

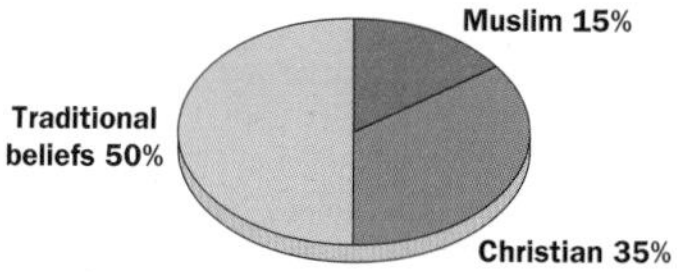
Muslim 15%
Traditional beliefs 50%
Christian 35%

A bitter divide has existed between north and south since before independence. Most southern resentment is directed toward a northern minority, the Kabye people from the Kabye plateau, because of their domination of the military. The Kabye and other northerners in turn resent their own underdevelopment in contrast to the high development, especially educationally, of all southerners. The dominant southern group is the Ewe, who make up more than 40% of the population.

As elsewhere in Africa, the extended family is important and tribalism and nepotism are key factors in everyday life. Some Togolese ethnic groups, such as the Mina, have matriarchal societies. The "Nana Benz," the market-women of Lomé, control the retail trade and have considerable private money. Politics, however, remains a male preserve.

Kabye cultivations near Kara, *in northern Togo. The main food crops grown are cassava, yams, and maize.*

POLITICS

Multiparty elections

1999/2002

President Gnassingbé Eyadéma

AT THE LAST ELECTION

National Assembly 81 seats

95%
RPT
3%
Ind
2%
Vac

RPT = Rally of the Togolese People
Ind = Independents
Vac = Vacant: results of two seats were annulled

Politics has been dominated for two decades by General Gnassingbé Eyadéma, who took power at the head of a military government in 1967, and is Africa's longest-serving leader.

A democracy movement has been gathering momentum since 1990, when serious rioting occurred in Lomé. Multiparty presidential elections held in 1993 confirmed Eyadéma in power, but were boycotted by some opposition candidates in protest at the exclusion from the elections of Gilchrist Olympio, the son of a former president. Eyadéma claimed victory over Olympio once again in presidential elections in 1998, amid accusations of malpractice and of the killing of hundreds of opposition supporters immediately afterwards in the runup to the 1999 Assembly election. During subsequent negotiations, the opposition accepted the election results, and Eyadéma stated that he would not stand for reelection in 2003. The resulting 1999 accord provided for a new independent electoral body and a political code of conduct. A UN/OAU report in February 2001 confirmed there had been serious human rights violations during 1998.

WORLD AFFAIRS

Joined UN in 1960

OIC | ECOWAS | FZ | OAU | UEMOA

The priority is maintaining traditional links, especially with France. President Eyadéma became chairman in 1998 of ECOWAS, in which capacity he acted as mediator in the Guinea-Bissau conflict and hosted talks in Sierra Leone. He was president of the OAU for 2000/2001.

AID

Recipient

$71m (receipts)

Down 45% in 1999

Development projects and the health of the economy overall have suffered from aid suspensions in 1998 by donors including the USA and the EU.

T

TOGO

Total Land Area : 54 390 sq. km (21 000 sq. miles)

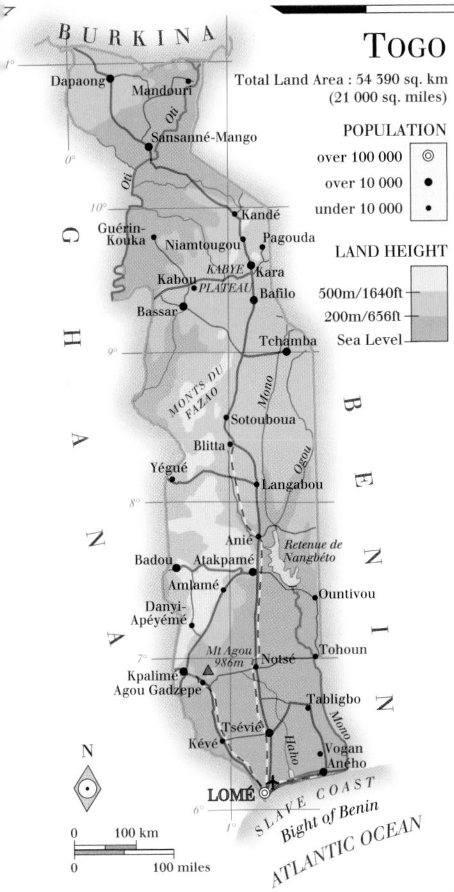
BURKINA
GHANA
BENIN
Dapaong
Mandouri
Oti
Sansanné-Mango
Kandé
Guérin-Kouka
Niamtougou
Pagouda
KABYE
Kara
Kabou
PLATEAU
Bafilo
Bassar
Tchamba
MONTS DU FAZAO
Mono
Sotouboua
Blitta
Ogou
Yégué
Langabou
Anié
Retenue de Nangbéto
Badou
Atakpamé
Amlamé
Ountivou
Danyi-Apéyémé
Mt Agou 986m
Notsé
Tohoun
Kpalimé
Agou Gadzepe
Tabligbo
Tsévié
Haho
Kévé
Vogan
Aného
LOMÉ
SLAVE COAST
Bight of Benin
ATLANTIC OCEAN
N
0 100 km
0 100 miles
POPULATION
over 100 000
over 10 000
under 10 000
LAND HEIGHT
500m/1640ft
200m/656ft
Sea Level

DEFENSE

Compulsory military service

$34m

Down 3% in 1999

The military has an important role in Togo, and spending on defense is high. The army's senior ranks are dominated by loyalists from President Eyadéma's northern Kabré tribe. France guarantees Togo's security through a defense accord, and supplies most military equipment and training.

RESOURCES

Electric power 34,000 kw

14,310 tonnes

Not an oil producer

1.11m goats, 850,000 pigs, 7.5m chickens

Phosphates, iron, chromite, bauxite, marble, dolomite

Phosphates are Togo's most important resource. Offshore oil and gas deposits were found in 1999. The Nangbeto dam, constructed jointly with Benin and opened in 1988, has reduced dependence on Ghana for energy.

ENVIRONMENT

Sustainability rank: 101st

8%

0.2 tonnes per capita

Ecologists have been critical of the transformation of nature reserves into hunting grounds for the military elite. Other problems include coastal erosion around Aneho and desertification.

MEDIA

TV ownership low

Daily newspaper circulation 4 per 1000 people

PUBLISHING AND BROADCAST MEDIA

There are 2 daily newspapers, *Togo-Presse*, published by the government, and *Les Echos du Demain*

1 state-owned service

3 services: 1 state-owned, 2 independent

Opposition papers now challenge the government daily *Togo-Presse*, despite some official harassment.

CRIME

Death penalty not used

Togo does not publish prison figures

Theft on increase in the capital

Togo is normally relatively peaceable, but urban crime generally increased during the 1990s, particularly during periods of political unrest in the capital.

CHRONOLOGY

After colonization by Germany in 1894, Togoland was divided between France and the UK in 1922.

- **1960** French sector independent as Togo (UK part joined to Ghana).
- **1967** Eyadéma takes power.
- **1991–1992** General strike; repression.
- **1993** Eyadéma elected president.
- **1998** Eyadéma claims victory in disputed election.

EDUCATION

School leaving age: 12

57%

13,124 students

Schooling is based on the French model. The University of Bénin in Lomé has more than 4000 students.

HEALTH

No welfare state health benefits

1 per 10,000 people

Malaria, diarrheal, infectious, and parasitic diseases

Health care suffers from a lack of resources. Over 50% of qualified medical staff are based in Lomé.

SPENDING

GDP/cap. increase

CONSUMPTION AND SPENDING

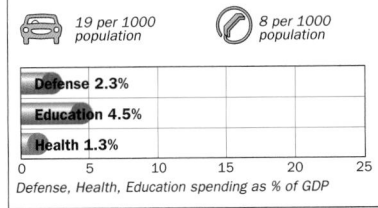

19 per 1000 population

8 per 1000 population

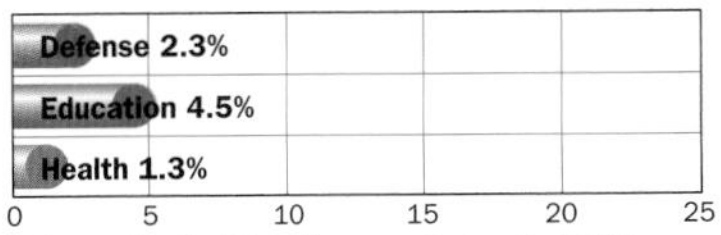
Defense 2.3%
Education 4.5%
Health 1.3%
0
5
10
15
20
25

Defense, Health, Education spending as % of GDP

Considerable wealth disparities exist between those who work the land and the country's political and business classes. The urban class has been hit by an economic downturn in the late 1990s.

ECONOMICS

Inflation 7.6% p.a. (1990–1999)

$1.4bn

654.42–698.69 CFA francs

SCORE CARD

- World GNP Ranking........................149th
- GNP per Capita $310
- Balance of Payments...................$–140m
- Inflation ....–0.1%
- Unemployment ....Not available

EXPORTS

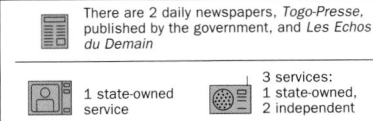

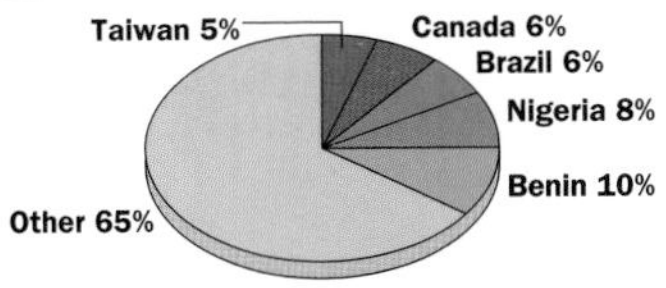
Taiwan 5%
Canada 6%
Brazil 6%
Nigeria 8%
Benin 10%
Other 65%

IMPORTS

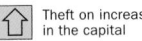

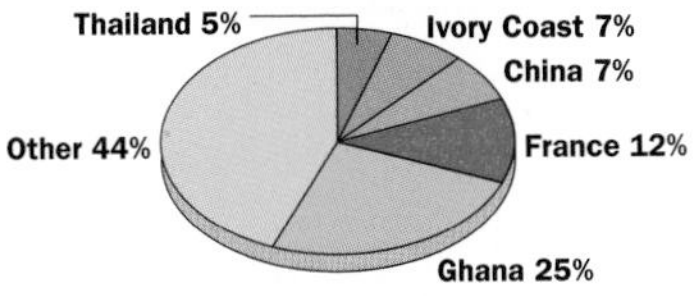
Thailand 5%
Ivory Coast 7%
China 7%
France 12%
Other 44%
Ghana 25%

STRENGTHS

Efficient civil service. Ideal location for role as entrepôt, based on Lomé port. Resourceful entrepreneurs, notably market-women. Proceeds of widespread smuggling. Phosphate deposits have the world's highest mineral content. Self-sufficient in basic foodstuffs.

WEAKNESSES

Political pariah status led to aid reductions in the 1990s. Low world prices for phosphates. Hydropower generation is vulnerable to drought.

WORLD RANKING

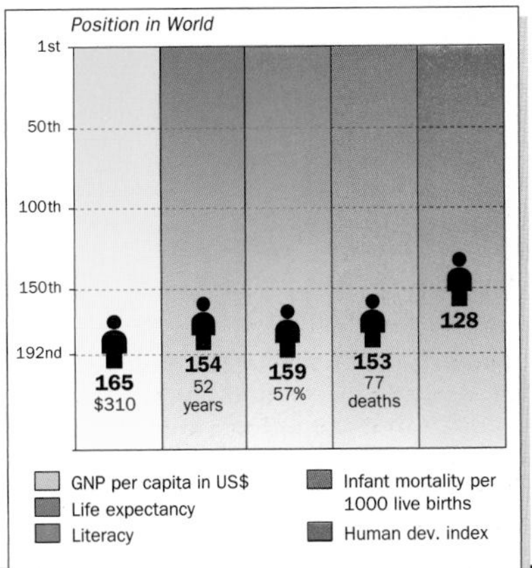
Position in World
1st
50th
100th
150th
192nd
165
$310
154
52 years
159
57%
153
77 deaths
128
GNP per capita in US$
Life expectancy
Literacy
Infant mortality per 1000 live births
Human dev. index

T

TONGA

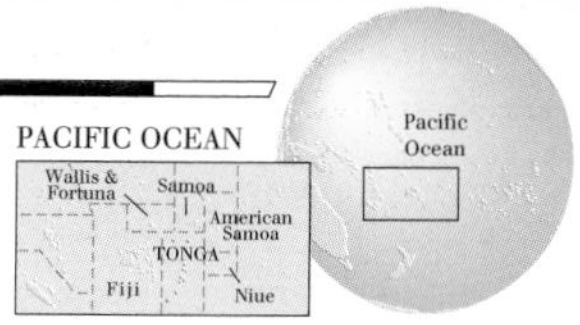
PACIFIC OCEAN
Pacific Ocean
Wallis & Fortuna
Samoa
American Samoa
TONGA
Fiji
Niue

OFFICIAL NAME: Kingdom of Tonga **CAPITAL:** Nuku'alofa **POPULATION:** 102,200
CURRENCY: Pa'anga (Tongan dollar) **OFFICIAL LANGUAGES:** English and Tongan

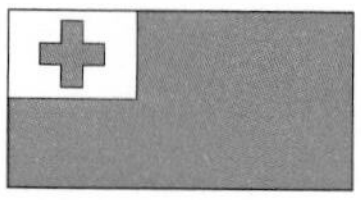

1970
1970
June 4
TO
+13
+676
.to

LOCATED IN THE SOUTH PACIFIC northeast of New Zealand, Tonga is an archipelago of 170 islands. These are divided into three main groups, Vava'u, Ha'apai, and Tongatapu. Tonga's easterly islands are generally low and fertile. Those in the west are higher and volcanic in origin. Tonga's economy is based on agriculture, especially coconut, cassava, and passion fruit production. Politics is effectively controlled by the king.

CLIMATE

Tropical oceanic

WEATHER CHART

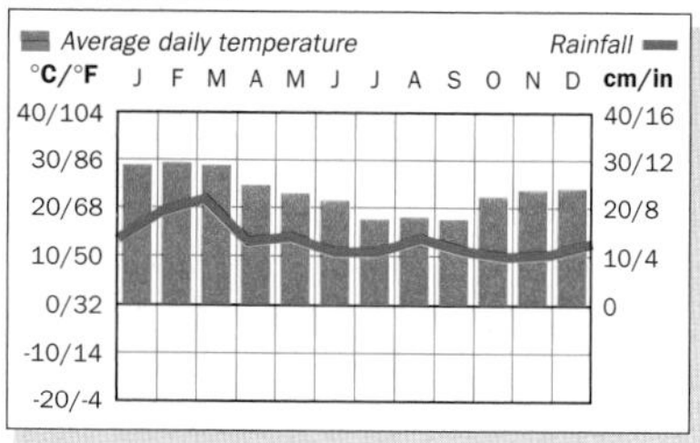
Average daily temperature
Rainfall
°C/°F
J F M A M J J A S O N D
cm/in
40/104
30/86
20/68
10/50
0/32
-10/14
-20/-4
40/16
30/12
20/8
10/4
0

Tonga has a tropical oceanic climate, with year-round temperatures ranging between 17°C (63°F) and 30°C (86°F).

TRANSPORTATION

Drive on left

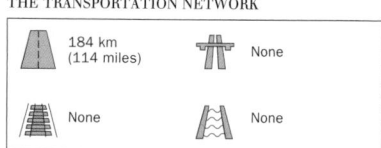

Fua'amotu International, Tongatabu
67,000 passengers

18 ships
22,200 grt

THE TRANSPORTATION NETWORK

184 km (114 miles)

None

None

None

Improvements at Fua'amotu Airport have led to an increase in flights to and from Tonga.

TOURISM

Visitors : Population 1:2.9

35,000 visitors

Up 13% in 2000

MAIN TOURIST ARRIVALS

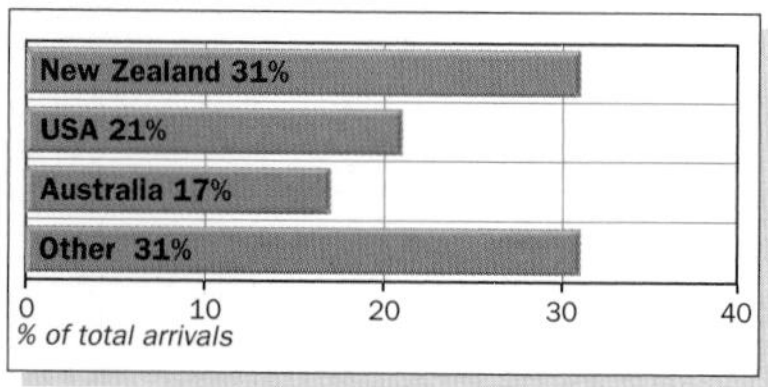
New Zealand 31%
USA 21%
Australia 17%
Other 31%
0
10
20
30
40
% of total arrivals

Tonga's main attractions are its tropical beaches. Flagging tourism was boosted in 2000 by the political insecurity in the Solomon Islands and Fiji. Fears have been expressed that too many visitors may erode traditional Tongan culture.

Mountainous scenery typical of Tonga's westerly islands. Tonga's 170 islands are scattered over a wide expanse of the South Pacific. Only 45 are inhabited.

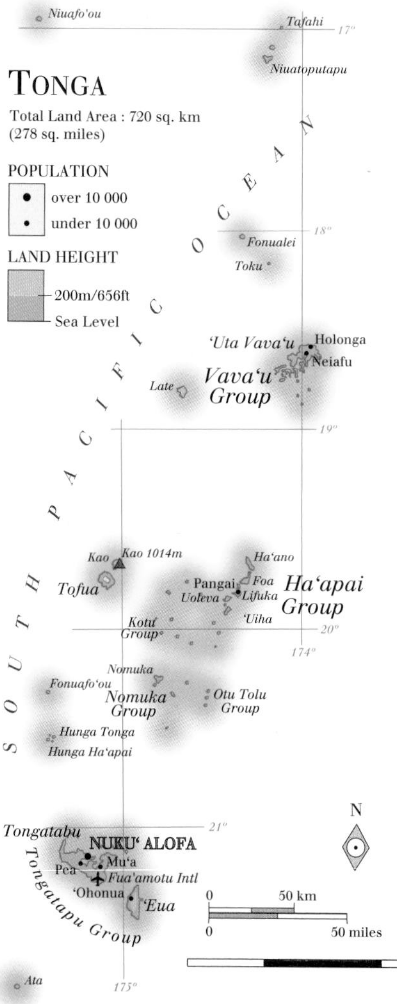
TONGA
Total Land Area : 720 sq. km (278 sq. miles)
POPULATION
over 10 000
under 10 000
LAND HEIGHT
200m/656ft
Sea Level
Niuafo'ou
Tafahi
Niuatoputapu
SOUTH PACIFIC OCEAN
Fonualei
Toku
'Uta Vava'u
Holonga
Neiafu
Vava'u Group
Late
Kao
Kao 1014m
Tofua
Ha'ano
Pangai
Foa
Uoleva
Lifuka
Ha'apai Group
Kotu Group
'Uiha
Nomuka
Fonuafo'ou
Nomuka Group
Otu Tolu Group
Hunga Tonga
Hunga Ha'apai
Tongatabu
NUKU'ALOFA
Pea
Mu'a
Fua'amotu Intl
'Ohonua
'Eua
Tongatapu Group
Ata
N
0
50 km
50 miles
17°
18°
19°
20°
21°
174°
175°

PEOPLE

Pop. density medium

English, Tongan

142/km² (368/mi²)

THE URBAN/RURAL POPULATION SPLIT

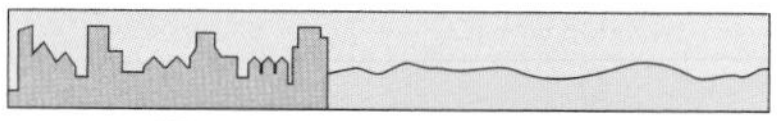
42%
58%

RELIGIOUS PERSUASION

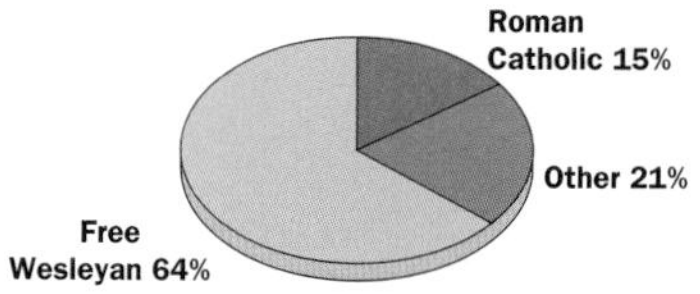
Roman Catholic 15%
Other 21%
Free Wesleyan 64%

Tonga has strong ethnic ties with eastern Fiji and there has traditionally been considerable population movement between the two states. Tongans tend to see themselves as unique among Pacific islanders, as retaining their monarchy and never having been fully colonized.

Respect for traditional values and institutions remains high. Tongans are strong churchgoers; the Wesleyan, Roman Catholic, and Mormon churches are influential and often fund education. A new generation of Western-educated Tongans is querying some traditional attitudes.

POLITICS

No multiparty elections

1999/2002

HM King Taufa'ahau Tupou IV

AT THE LAST ELECTION

Legislative Assembly 30 seats

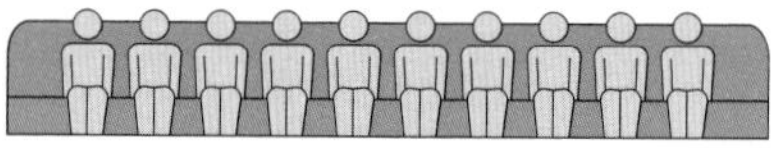

The Legislative Assembly comprises the king, the 11 members of the Privy Council, 9 directly elected members, and 9 members indirectly elected by nobles

The main power brokers in Tongan politics are the king, the noble establishment, and the landowners. King Taufa'ahau, who succeeded his mother Queen Salote in 1965, effectively heads his government, frequently exercising kingly powers. The Legislative Assembly defers to his judgment and the king has instigated several development projects which have been undertaken without reference to the government.

The king's resistance to growing calls for greater democracy was highlighted in 2000, when he passed over his reformist eldest son and appointed his conservative third son, Prince Ulukalala Lavaka Ata, as premier for life.

T

WORLD AFFAIRS

Joined UN in 1999

ACP | Comm | PC | PIF | ADB

In 1996, after accepting the Pacific nuclear interests of the USA and France in the preceding decade, Tonga finally acceded to the South Pacific Nuclear-free Zone Treaty. It broke its ties with Taiwan in 1998 in return for closer relations with China.

AID

Recipient

$21m (receipts)

Down 16% in 1999

Aid finances major infrastructure projects; Australia, the USA, New Zealand, the EU, and the ADB are primary donors. Since losing aid in 1997, Tonga fought to reclaim its "least developed country" status.

DEFENSE

No compulsory military service

$2m (est.)

No significant change

Tonga has a small defense force, which includes both regulars and reserves. Tongan police assisted in security efforts in the Solomon Islands in 2000.

ECONOMICS

Inflation 4.1% p.a. (1990–1999)

$172m

1.5282–1.7997 pa'anga

SCORE CARD

World GNP Ranking	185th
GNP per Capita	$1730
Balance of Payments	$–6m
Inflation	4.5%
Unemployment	13%

Strengths

Agriculture contributes largest percentage of GDP. Tourism main source of hard currency earnings.

Weaknesses

Off main shipping routes. Heavily dependent on aid. Large importer of food. Many educated Tongans live abroad.

EXPORTS

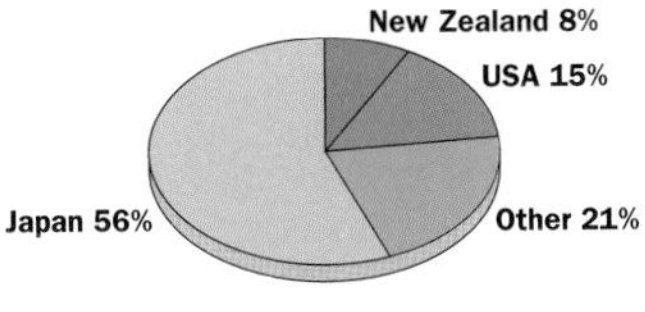
New Zealand 8%
USA 15%
Japan 56%
Other 21%

IMPORTS

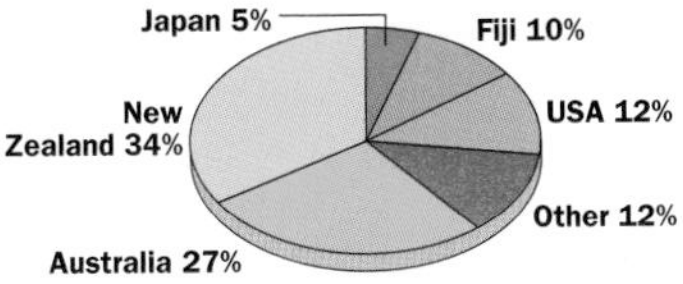
Japan 5%
Fiji 10%
New Zealand 34%
USA 12%
Other 12%
Australia 27%

RESOURCES

Electric power 7000 kw

2739 tonnes

Not an oil producer

80,853 pigs, 13,939 goats, 266,000 chickens

None

Tonga has no strategic or mineral resources. Electricity is generated from imported fuel. Recent exploration has failed to identify any oil reserves. Tongan waters contain large numbers of tuna.

ENVIRONMENT

Not available

None

1.2 tonnes per capita

Tonga does not suffer from serious environmental problems, although it is occasionally afflicted by natural disasters, such as the 1997–1998 El Niño effect. Commercial activity has made little impact on the environment.

MEDIA

TV ownership low

Daily newspaper circulation 72 per 1000 people

PUBLISHING AND BROADCAST MEDIA

There is 1 daily newspaper. Weeklies include the *Conch Shell* and the *Tonga Chronicle*

1 service relaying US programs

4 independent services

In 2000 Cable and Wireless relinquished control of Tonga's telecommunications services, which it had run since 1978, to a local company.

CRIME

Death penalty not used

58 prisoners

Rising levels of theft

Crime rates are generally low, partly due to the strong influence of the family. However, offenses such as breaking and entering have increased, along with rising unemployment levels, among young Tongans.

EDUCATION

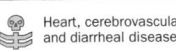

School leaving age: 14

98%

705 students

Church participation in schools is high. Plans for a new national university were approved in 2000 following violence in Fiji, where Tongan students attend the University of the South Pacific.

HEALTH

No welfare state health benefits

1 per 2176 people

Heart, cerebrovascular, and diarrheal diseases

Tonga has some modern health care facilities. However, patients have to be flown out to Australia or New Zealand for sophisticated surgery.

CHRONOLOGY

Originally discovered by the Polynesians, Tonga was visited by the Dutch in the 17th century and Captain Cook in the 18th century. In the latter half of the 19th century, during the reign of King George Tupou I, the islands became a unified state after a period of civil war.

- **1875** First constitution established.
- **1900** Concern over German ambitions in region; Treaty of Friendship and Protection with UK.
- **1918–1965** Reign of Queen Salote Tupou III.
- **1958** Greater autonomy from UK enshrined in Friendship Treaty.
- **1965** King Taufa'ahau Tupou IV accedes on his mother's death.
- **1970** Full independence within British Commonwealth.
- **1988** Treaty allowing US nuclear warships right of transit through Tongan waters signed.
- **1996, 1999** General election sees strong showing by prodemocracy candidates for the few directly elected seats.
- **2000** King appoints third son as prime minister.

SPENDING

GDP/cap. increase

CONSUMPTION AND SPENDING

12 per 1000 population

93 per 1000 population

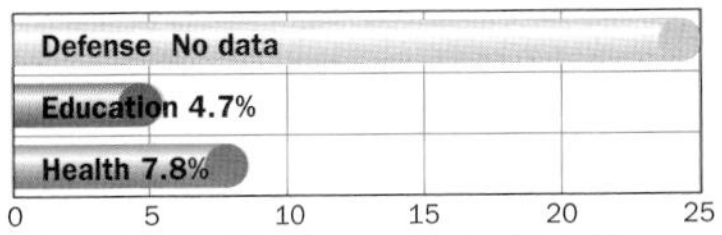
Defense No data
Education 4.7%
Health 7.8%
0
5
10
15
20
25

Defense, Health, Education spending as % of GDP

Tongans indulge in few ostentatious displays of wealth. The well-off provide financial support for relatives.

WORLD RANKING

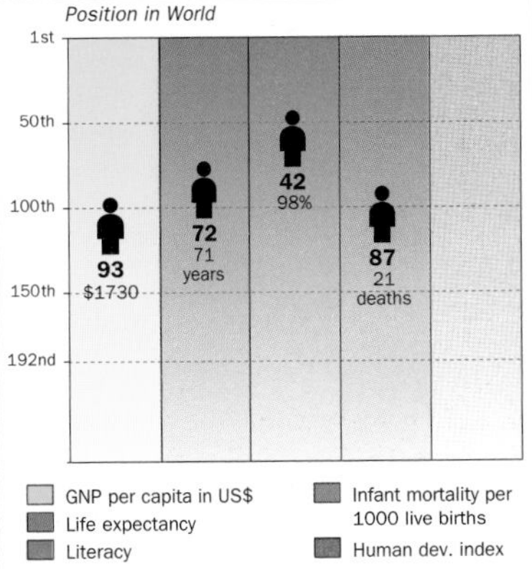
Position in World
1st
50th
100th
150th
192nd
93
$1730
72
71
years
42
98%
87
21
deaths
GNP per capita in US$
Life expectancy
Literacy
Infant mortality per 1000 live births
Human dev. index

T

Trinidad & Tobago

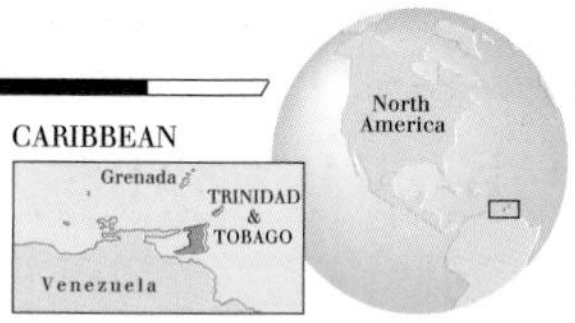

CARIBBEAN
Grenada
TRINIDAD & TOBAGO
Venezuela
North America

Official Name: Republic of Trinidad and Tobago **Capital:** Port-of-Spain
Population: 1.3 million **Currency:** Trinidad and Tobago dollar **Official Language:** English

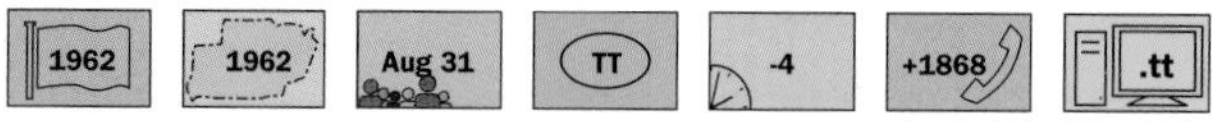

1962
1962
Aug 31
TT
-4
+1868
.tt

The two islands of Trinidad and Tobago are the most southerly of the Caribbean Windward Islands and lie just 15 km (9 miles) off the Venezuelan coast. They gained joint independence from Britain in 1962, and Tobago was given internal autonomy in 1987. The spectacular mountain ranges and large swamps are rich in tropical flora and fauna. Pitch Lake in Trinidad is the world's largest natural reservoir of asphalt.

CLIMATE

Tropical oceanic

WEATHER CHART

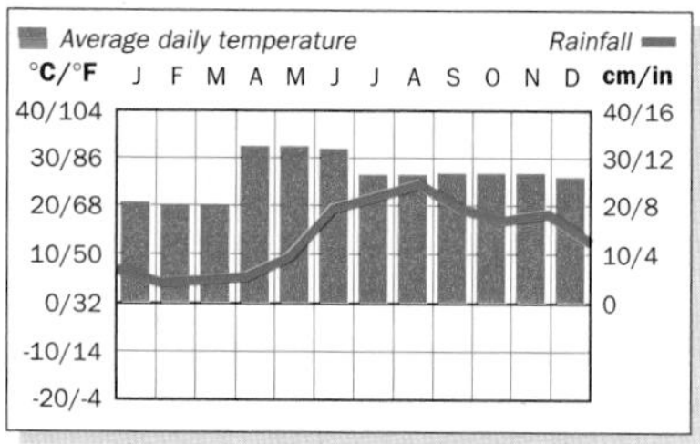

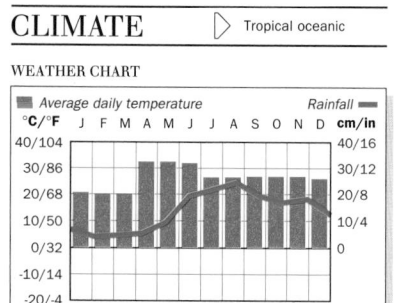

Average daily temperature
Rainfall
°C/°F
J F M A M J J A S O N D
cm/in
40/104
30/86
20/68
10/50
0/32
-10/14
-20/-4
40/16
30/12
20/8
10/4
0

The islands are a little warmer than others in the Caribbean and escape the hurricanes, which pass by to the north.

TRANSPORTATION

Drive on left

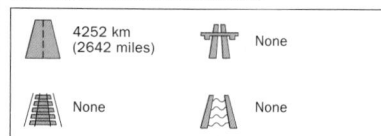

Piarco International, Port-of-Spain 1.77m passengers

50 ships 18,600 grt

THE TRANSPORTATION NETWORK

4252 km (2642 miles)

None

None

None

The road network is well developed; there are taxis or minibuses for set routes. National carrier BWIA and Air Caribbean operate Trinidad–Tobago routes. BWIA flies to the USA.

TOURISM

Visitors : Population 1:3.9

336,000 visitors

Down 3% in 1999

MAIN TOURIST ARRIVALS

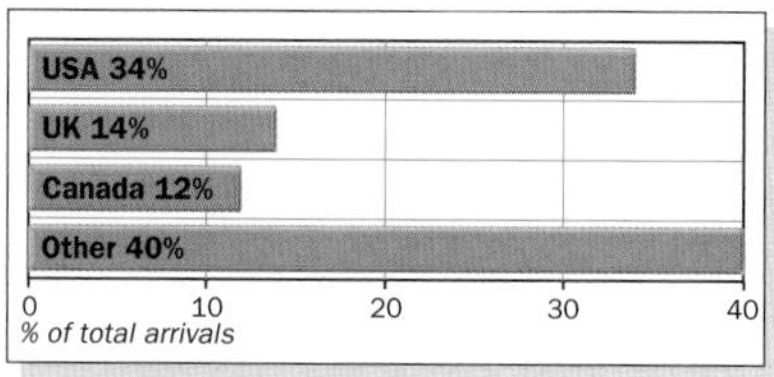

USA 34%
UK 14%
Canada 12%
Other 40%
0
10
20
30
40
% of total arrivals

Concentration on oil meant that Trinidad was one of the last Caribbean states to develop tourism. Most is centered on Tobago (said to be the model for the island in *Robinson Crusoe*), famous for its enormous variety of South American wildlife, including 210 species of tropical birds.

Trinidad & Tobago

Total Land Area : 5130 sq. km (1981 sq. miles)

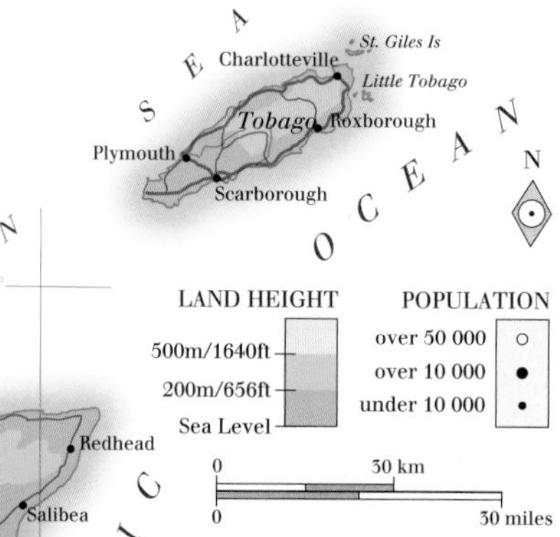

SEA
St. Giles Is
Charlotteville
Little Tobago
Tobago
Roxborough
Plymouth
Scarborough
OCEAN
N
LAND HEIGHT
500m/1640ft
200m/656ft
Sea Level
POPULATION
over 50 000
over 10 000
under 10 000
0
30 km
0
30 miles

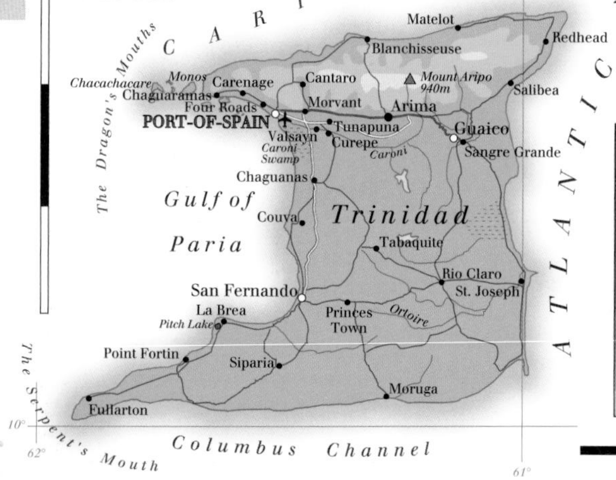

CARIBBEAN
Matelot
Redhead
Blanchisseuse
Chacachacare
Monos
Carenage
Cantaro
Mount Aripo 940m
Salibea
Chaguaramas
Four Roads
Morvant
Arima
PORT-OF-SPAIN
Tunapuna
Valsayn
Curepe
Guaico
Caroni Swamp
Caroni
Sangre Grande
Chaguanas
The Dragon's Mouths
Gulf of Paria
Couva
Trinidad
Tabaquite
ATLANTIC
Rio Claro
St. Joseph
San Fernando
La Brea
Pitch Lake
Princes Town
Ortoire
Point Fortin
Siparia
Moruga
Fullarton
The Serpent's Mouth
Columbus Channel

PEOPLE

Pop. density high

English Creole, English, Hindi, French, Spanish

253/km² (656/mi²)

THE URBAN/RURAL POPULATION SPLIT

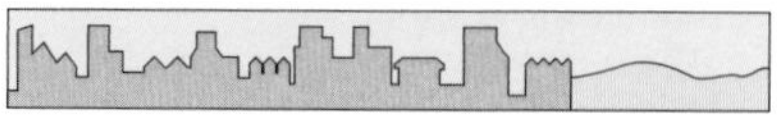

74%
26%

ETHNIC MAKEUP

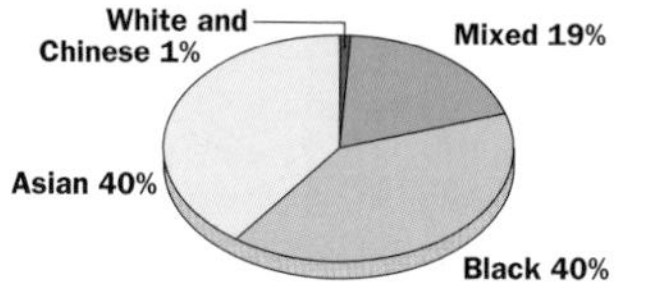

White and Chinese 1%
Mixed 19%
Asian 40%
Black 40%

Trinidad's south Asian community is the largest in the Caribbean, and holds on to its Muslim and Hindu inheritance. The open discussion of racial issues in Trinidad goes some way to dissipating latent tensions between black and south Asian Trinidadians.

POLITICS

Multiparty elections

L. House 2000/2005
U. House 2001/2006

President Arthur N. Robinson

AT THE LAST ELECTION

House of Representatives 36 seats

50% UNC	47% PNM	3% NAR

UNC = United National Congress **PNM** = People's National Movement **NAR** = National Alliance for Reconstruction

Senate 31 seats

Senators are appointed by the president, including 16 nominated by the prime minister and 6 by the leader of the opposition

The increasingly right-wing PNM dominated politics from independence in 1962 to the 1990s, leading to political fragmentation and an attempted coup by Muslim extremists in 1990. The UNC's Basdeo Panday, the first ethnic Asian prime minister, was elected in 1995. He pledged his coalition government to reducing unemployment, crime, and racial discrimination. The UNC's outright majority in the 2000 elections was disputed by the PNM. Panday has asserted that an arms cache discovered in Florida in June 2001 was destined for a coup attempt by oppostion forces in Trinidad.

***Tobago's white sand beaches,** verdant landscape, and natural anchorages have enabled it to develop a thriving tourist industry.*

T

WORLD AFFAIRS

Joined UN in 1962

ACS | Caricom | Comm | NAM | OAS

Trinidad withdrew in 1998 and 1999 from the Inter-American and UN Commissions on Human Rights respectively, over appeals against death sentences. New trade agreements include those with Costa Rica, Panama, Dominican Republic, and Mexico. Sea border disputes with Venezuela relate to fishing and marine oil rights.

AID

Recipient

US$26m (receipts) | Up 86% in 1999

Aid is modest: China provided an interest-free loan of US$20 million in 2000 to help small businesses.

DEFENSE

No compulsory military service

US$62m | Up 40% in 1999

Defense forces comprise a land army, a small air force, and coastguard. This last is used to patrol fishing grounds.

ECONOMICS

Inflation 5.8% p.a. (1990–1999)

US$6.1bn | 6.2436–6.2400 Trinidad and Tobago dollars

SCORE CARD

❑ World GNP Ranking	103rd
❑ GNP per Capita	US$4750
❑ Balance of Payments	US$–644m
❑ Inflation	3.4%
❑ Unemployment	14%

Strengths

Oil, which accounts for 70% of export earnings. Gas increasingly exploited to support new industries. Oil methanol, ammonia, iron, and steel exports. Tourism, especially on Tobago.

Weaknesses

Insufficiently diversified economy. Reliance on oil – highly sensitive to world price movements. High unemployment.

EXPORTS

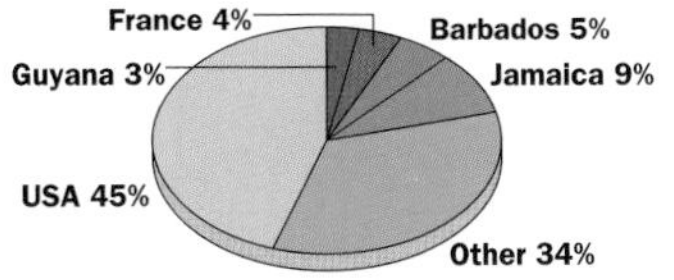
France 4%
Barbados 5%
Guyana 3%
Jamaica 9%
USA 45%
Other 34%

IMPORTS

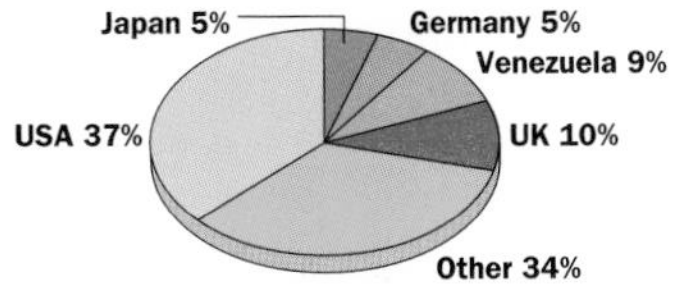
Japan 5%
Germany 5%
Venezuela 9%
USA 37%
UK 10%
Other 34%

RESOURCES

Electric power 1.2m kw

15,012 tonnes | 170,000 b/d (reserves 700,000,000 bbl)

59,000 goats, 41,000 pigs, 10m chickens | Oil, natural gas, asphalt, iron

Oil and gas are major resources. In 1998 big offshore gas and oil finds were made, including the largest discovery of crude oil in 25 years.

ENVIRONMENT

Sustainability rank: 68th

4% | 17.4 tonnes per capita

Spillages from oil tankers threaten coastal conservation areas such as the Caroni Swamp, with its many species of butterflies. Forest fires due to periodic drought, and traffic-related pollution and congestion are serious concerns.

MEDIA

TV ownership high

Daily newspaper circulation 123 per 1000 people

PUBLISHING AND BROADCAST MEDIA

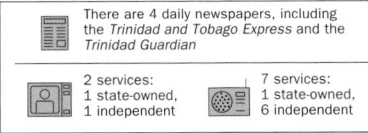

There are 4 daily newspapers, including the *Trinidad and Tobago Express* and the *Trinidad Guardian*

2 services: 1 state-owned, 1 independent | 7 services: 1 state-owned, 6 independent

Television schedules are dominated by US programs, while around carnival time radio stations play little but calypso.

CRIME

Death penalty used

2387 prisoners | Down 63% 1992–1998

Narcotics-related crime boosts the murder rate. The country was party to the decision taken in 2001 to replace the authority of the UK's Privy Council with a Caribbean Court of Justice.

EDUCATION

School leaving age: 12

94% | 8170 students

Education is based on the former British 11-plus system. Most students go on to the University of the West Indies; Trinidad hosts the St. Augustine campus. Wealthy Trinidadians, however, go to universities in the USA.

HEALTH

Welfare state health benefits

1 per 1250 people | Heart disease, cancers, diabetes, accidents, violence

Oil wealth has given Trinidad a better public health service than most Caribbean states, and more private clinics, mainly serving the expatriate community. However, treatment delays are a problem. 98% of the population have safe water.

CHRONOLOGY

Britain seized Trinidad from Spain in 1797 and Tobago from France in 1802. They were unified in 1888.

- ❑ **1956** Eric Williams founds PNM and wins general election: main support from blacks. Asian population supports opposition.
- ❑ **1958–1961** Member of West Indian Federation.
- ❑ **1962** Independence.
- ❑ **1970** Black Power demonstrations.
- ❑ **1980** Tobago gets own House of Assembly; internal autonomy 1987.
- ❑ **1990–1991** Premier taken hostage in failed fundamentalist coup. PNM returned to power.
- ❑ **1995** UNC's Basdeo Panday is first Asian-origin prime minister.
- ❑ **1998–1999** Trinidad withdraws from international human rights bodies over death sentences.
- ❑ **2001** UNC reelected.

SPENDING

GDP/cap. increase

CONSUMPTION AND SPENDING

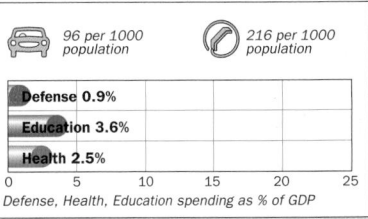

96 per 1000 population | *216 per 1000 population*

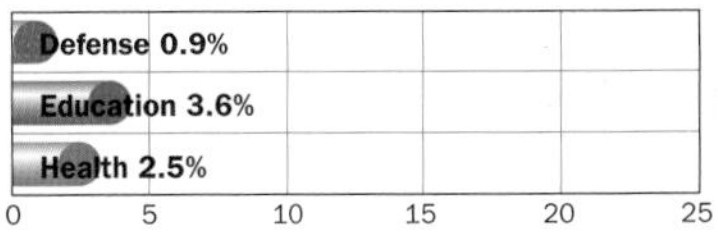
Defense 0.9%
Education 3.6%
Health 2.5%
0
5
10
15
20
25

Defense, Health, Education spending as % of GDP

In Trinidad wealth disparities between the affluent oil-rich business elite, many of whom are expatriate, and farm laborers are particularly marked. Service workers in Tobago's high-value tourism sector are poorly paid. Rural poverty in the interior, particularly among south Asian Trinidadian farmers, is a serious problem.

WORLD RANKING

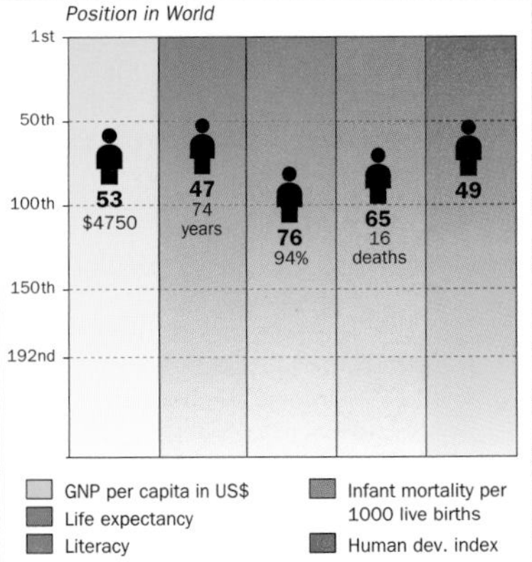
Position in World
1st
50th
100th
150th
192nd
53
$4750
47
74
years
76
94%
65
16
deaths
49
GNP per capita in US$
Life expectancy
Literacy
Infant mortality per 1000 live births
Human dev. index

T

TUNISIA

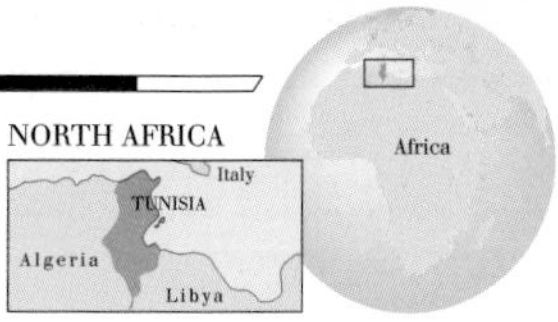
NORTH AFRICA
Africa
Italy
TUNISIA
Algeria
Libya

OFFICIAL NAME: Republic of Tunisia **CAPITAL:** Tunis
POPULATION: 9.6 million **CURRENCY:** Tunisian dinar **OFFICIAL LANGUAGE:** Arabic

1956 | 1956 | March 20 | TN | +1 | +216 | .tn

NORTH AFRICA'S SMALLEST country, Tunisia lies sandwiched between Libya and Algeria. The populous north is mountainous, fertile in places and has a long Mediterranean coastline. The south is largely desert. Habib Bourguiba ruled the country from independence in 1956 until a bloodless coup in 1987. Under President Ben Ali, the government has slowly moved toward multiparty democracy, but faces a challenge from Islamic fundamentalists. Closer ties with the EU, Tunisia's main trading partner, were strengthened through the first Euro-Mediterranean conference held in 1995. Manufacturing and tourism are expanding.

CLIMATE

Mediterranean/ hot desert

WEATHER CHART

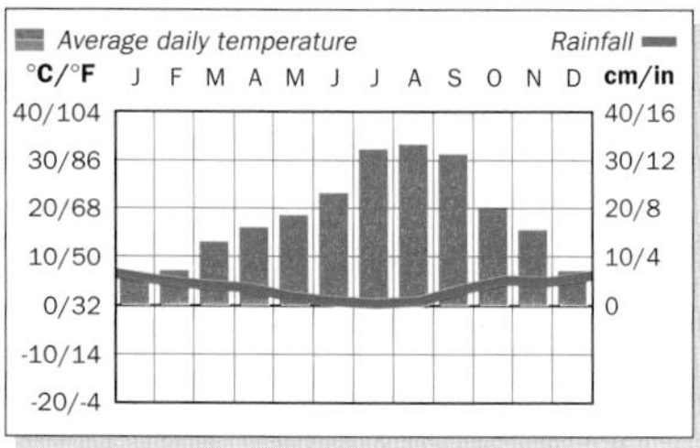
Average daily temperature
Rainfall
°C/°F
J F M A M J J A S O N D
cm/in
40/104
30/86
20/68
10/50
0/32
-10/14
-20/-4
40/16
30/12
20/8
10/4
0

Tunisia is hot in summer. The north is often wet and windy in winter. The far south is arid. The spring brings the dry, dusty *chili* wind from the Sahara.

TRANSPORTATION

Drive on right

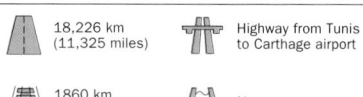

Skanes Airport, Monastir 3.61m passengers

78 ships 193,500 grt

THE TRANSPORTATION NETWORK

18,226 km (11,325 miles)	Highway from Tunis to Carthage airport
1860 km (1156 miles)	None

Tunisia has six international airports. A highway from Tunis to Carthage airport opened in 1993. A light metro in Tunis and a rail link from Gafsa to Gabès are being built. The southern third of the country has few roads.

TOURISM

Visitors : Population 1:1.9

5.1m visitors

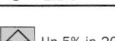

Up 5% in 2000

MAIN TOURIST ARRIVALS

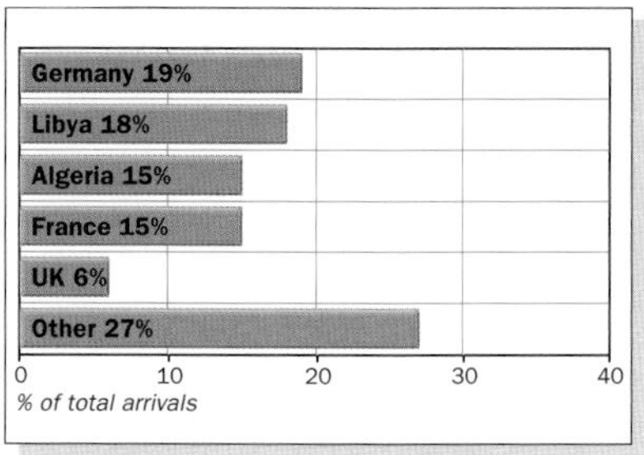
Germany 19%
Libya 18%
Algeria 15%
France 15%
UK 6%
Other 27%
0
10
20
30
40
% of total arrivals

Tourists have flocked to Tunisia since the 1960s, attracted by its winter sunshine, beaches, desert, and archaeological remains. One of the Mediterranean's cheapest package destinations, Tunisia attracts more than two million European visitors a year. However, numbers were hit in 1990–1991 by the Gulf War and the fear of attacks by Islamists. Tourism employs more than 200,000 people and is a focus of investment. Capacity was set to top 200,000 beds in 2001. However, concern about the environmental impact is growing.

PEOPLE

Pop. density medium

Arabic, French

62/km² (160/mi²)

THE URBAN/RURAL POPULATION SPLIT

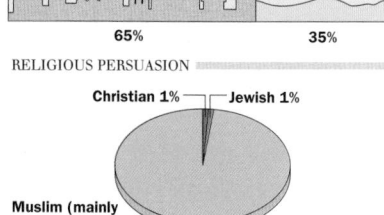

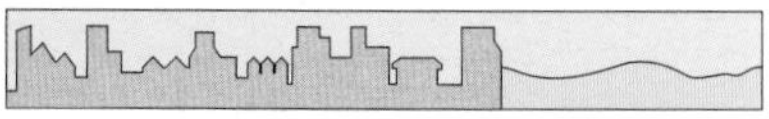
65%
35%

RELIGIOUS PERSUASION

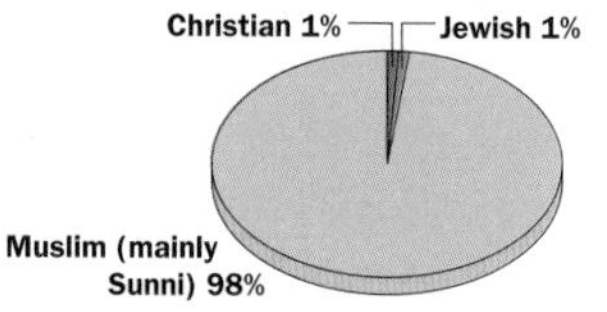
Christian 1%
Jewish 1%
Muslim (mainly Sunni) 98%

ETHNIC MAKEUP

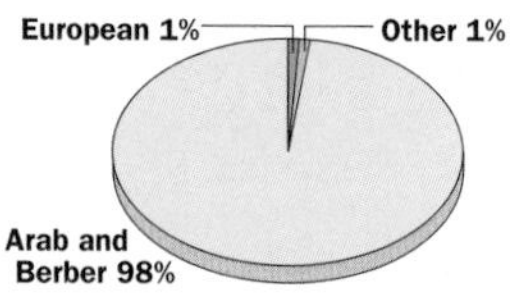
European 1%
Other 1%
Arab and Berber 98%

The population is almost entirely Muslim, of Arab and Berber descent, although there are Jewish and Christian minorities. Many Tunisians still live in extended family groups, in which three or four generations are represented.

Tunisia has traditionally been one of the most liberal Arab states. The 1956 Personal Statutes Code of President Bourguiba gave women fuller rights than in any other Arab country. Further legislation has since given women the right to custody of children in divorce cases, made family violence against women punishable by law, and helped divorced women to get alimony. Family planning and contraception have been freely available since the early 1960s. Tunisia's population growth rate has halved since the 1980s. Women make up 31% of the total workforce and 35% of the industrial workforce. Company ownership by women is steadily increasing; politics, however, remains an exclusively male preserve.

These freedoms are threatened by the growth in recent years of Islamic fundamentalism, which also worries the mainly French-speaking political and business elite who wish to strengthen links with Europe.

The Ben Ali regime, although not as repressive as its predecessor, has been criticized for its actions against Islamic activists, in particular the banned *Al-Nahda* party. Amnesty International has detailed a number of human rights abuses, mainly against female members of *Al-Nahda*.

POPULATION AGE BREAKDOWN

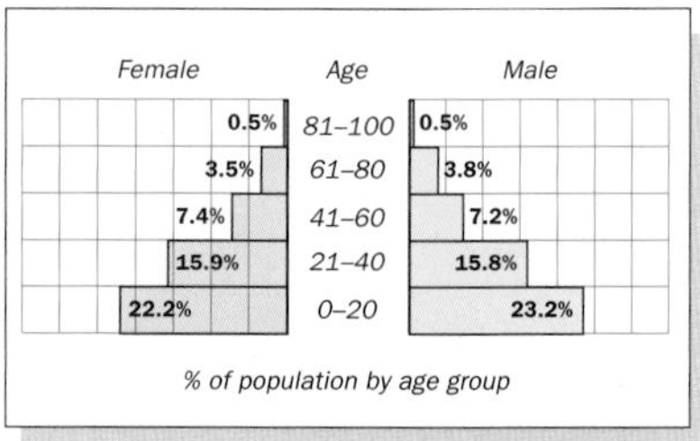
Female
Age
Male
0.5%
81–100
0.5%
3.5%
61–80
3.8%
7.4%
41–60
7.2%
15.9%
21–40
15.8%
22.2%
0–20
23.2%
% of population by age group

Roman remains *in the western Tozeur region. Diverse archaeological remains can be found throughout Tunisia.*

T

POLITICS

Multiparty elections

1999/2004

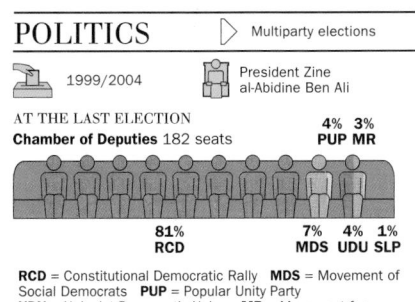

President Zine al-Abidine Ben Ali

AT THE LAST ELECTION
Chamber of Deputies 182 seats

4% PUP
3% MR
81% RCD
7% MDS
4% UDU
1% SLP

RCD = Constitutional Democratic Rally **MDS** = Movement of Social Democrats **PUP** = Popular Unity Party **UDU** = Unionist Democratic Union **MR** = Movement for Renewal **SLP** = Social Liberal Party

President Ben Ali *became head of state in 1987.*

Mohammed Ghannouchi, *prime minister since 1999.*

Formally a multiparty democracy since 1988, Tunisia is still dominated by the RCD and President Ben Ali.

Main Political Issues

Fundamentalism
The RCD has clamped down on Islamic fundamentalists, particularly the outlawed *Al-Nahda*, or Renewal Party. In 1991, 500 *Al-Nahda* members were arrested following a failed coup, thought to be inspired by fundamentalists. Its leader, Rachid Ghannouchi, is in exile.

Human rights
The RCD has been under increasing attack over its human rights record. The Tunisia League of Human Rights' activities was suspended in January 2001. The RCD is committed to promoting women's rights.

Profile

President Ben Ali has made some effort to liberalize the political system. The life presidency has been abolished, and political parties and press freedom are encouraged. While allowing for a degree of political plurality, a complex proportional representation system ensured that there was an overwhelming victory for the RCD in the 1994 general election. This situation was confirmed in 1999 by the result of the next elections. Since 1994, there has been evidence of a renewed crackdown against the left-wing opposition. In 2000, more measures were announced with the aim of furthering democratization and promoting human rights.

TUNISIA

Total Land Area : 155 360 sq. km (59 984 sq. miles)

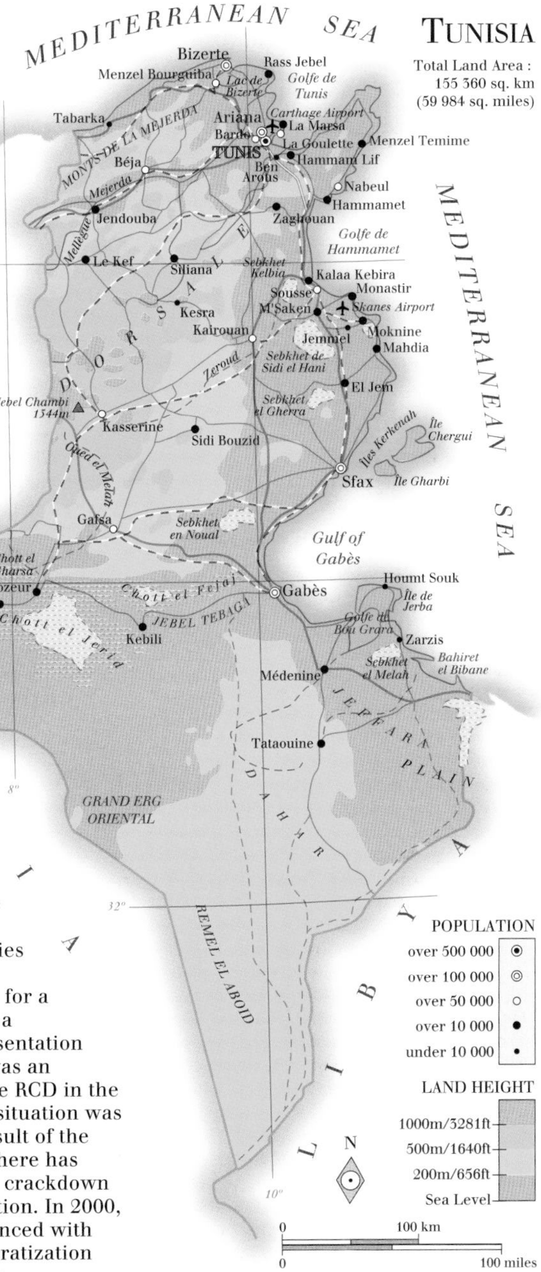

MEDITERRANEAN SEA
Bizerte
Rass Jebel
Menzel Bourguiba
Lac de Bizerte
Golfe de Tunis
Tabarka
Carthage Airport
Ariana
La Marsa
Bardo
TUNIS
La Goulette
Menzel Temime
Hammam Lif
Ben Arous
Béja
MONTS DE LA MEJERDA
Mejerda
Nabeul
Hammamet
Jendouba
Zaghouan
Golfe de Hammamet
Mellègue
Le Kef
Siliana
Sebkhet Kelbia
Kalaa Kebira
Sousse
Monastir
Kesra
M'Saken
Skanes Airport
Kairouan
Jemmel
Moknine
Mahdia
DORSALE
Zeroud
Sebkhet de Sidi el Hani
El Jem
Jebel Chambi 1544m
Sebkhet el Gherra
Kasserine
Sidi Bouzid
Iles Kerkenah
Ile Chergui
Oued el Melah
Sfax
Ile Gharbi
Gafsa
Sebkhet en Noual
Gulf of Gabès
Chott el Gharsa
Houmt Souk
Tozeur
Chott el Fejaj
Gabès
Nefta
Ile de Jerba
Chott el Jerid
JEBEL TEBAGA
Kebili
Golfe de Bou Grara
Zarzis
Sebkhet el Melah
Bahiret el Bibane
Médenine
JEFFARA PLAIN
Tataouine
GRAND ERG ORIENTAL
DAHAR
REMEL EL ABOID
ALGERIA
LIBYA
MEDITERRANEAN SEA
POPULATION
over 500 000
over 100 000
over 50 000
over 10 000
under 10 000
LAND HEIGHT
1000m/3281ft
500m/1640ft
200m/656ft
Sea Level
N
0
100 km
100 miles

WORLD AFFAIRS

Joined UN in 1956

AL | AMU | OIF | NAM | OIC

A foreign policy priority is to strengthen contacts with the West, which have generally been good because of Tunisia's liberal economic and social policies. Attention is focused on the EU, Tunisia's main export market, with Tunisia playing an important role in the run-up to the first Euro-Mediterranean conference, which was held in 1995.

Tunis was host to the PLO after that organization was expelled from Lebanon. Relations with other Arab states, particularly Kuwait and Saudi Arabia, were soured by Tunisia's support for Iraq in the Gulf War. The government regards the political success of Islamic fundamentalism in neighboring Algeria with concern. Relations with Libya are improving, helped by the fact that Tunisia turned a blind eye to sanctions-busters operating through its territory.

CHRONOLOGY

Tunisia has been home to the Zenata Berbers since earliest times and its history is linked to the rise and fall of the Mediterranean-centered empires. Carthage (near present-day Tunis), founded in the 9th century BCE, became the hub of a 1000-year Phoenician trading empire which linked European and African trading networks. Tunisia was then incorporated into the Roman, Byzantine, Arab, Ottoman, and, finally, French empires.

- ❑ **1883** La Marsa Treaty makes Tunisia a French protectorate, ending its semi-independence. Bey of Tunis remains monarch.
- ❑ **1900** Influx of French and Italians.
- ❑ **1920** Destour (Constitution) Party formed; calls for self-government.
- ❑ **1935** Habib Bourguiba forms Neo-Destour (New Constitution) Party.
- ❑ **1943** Defeat of Axis powers by British troops restores French rule.
- ❑ **1955** Internal autonomy. Bourguiba returns from exile.
- ❑ **1956** Independence. Bourguiba elected prime minister. Personal Statutes Code gives rights to women. Family planning introduced.
- ❑ **1957** Bey is deposed. Tunisia becomes republic with Bourguiba as first president.
- ❑ **1964** Neo-Destour made sole legal party; renamed Destour Socialist Party (PSD). Moderate socialist economic program is introduced.
- ❑ **1969** Agricultural collectivization program, begun 1964, abandoned. ➪

T

CHRONOLOGY *continued*

- **1974** Bourguiba elected president-for-life by National Assembly.
- **1974–1976** Hundreds imprisoned for belonging to "illegal organizations."
- **1978** Trade union movement, UGTT, holds 24-hour general strike; more than 50 killed in clashes. UGTT leadership replaced with PSD loyalists.
- **1980** New prime minister Muhammed Mazli ushers in greater political tolerance.
- **1981** Elections. Opposition groups allege electoral malpractice.
- **1984** Widespread riots after food price increases.
- **1986** Gen. Zine al-Abidine Ben Ali becomes interior minister. Four Muslim fundamentalists sentenced to death.
- **1987** Fundamentalist leader Rachid Ghannouchi arrested. Ben Ali becomes prime minister; takes over presidency after doctors certify Bourguiba senile. PSD renamed RCD.
- **1988** Most political prisoners released. Constitutional reforms introduce multiparty system and abolish life presidency. Two opposition parties legalized.
- **1989** Elections: RCD wins all seats, Ben Ali president. Fundamentalists take 13% of vote.
- **1990** Tunisia backs Iraq in Gulf War. Clampdown on fundamentalists intensifies.
- **1991** Abortive coup blamed on *Al-Nahda*; over 500 arrests.
- **1993** Multiparty agreement on electoral reform.
- **1994** Presidential and legislative elections. Ben Ali, sole candidate, is reelected. Ruling RCD wins all elected seats; opposition parties gain 19 reserved seats.
- **1996** Opposition MDS leader Mohammed Moada imprisoned for dealings with foreign agents.
- **1999** Ben Ali and RCD again dominate elections.

T

AID

Recipient

$244m (receipts) | Up 66% in 1999

France is the largest single donor, providing more than one-third of bilateral aid. Italy, Germany, the World Bank, and the African Development Bank are other important sources of assistance. Oil-rich Arab states, including Saudi Arabia and Kuwait, suspended their aid programs to Tunisia after 1990 because of its pro-Iraq stance in the Gulf War. Tunisia's total external debt is estimated at over half of GNP.

DEFENSE

Compulsory military service

$348m | Down 4% in 1999

Despite its small size – 35,000 troops, of which around two-thirds are conscripts – the military is an important political force, armed mainly with US weapons. Officer training is carried out in the USA and France, as well as in Tunisia. Border security with Algeria was tightened in 1995 after Algerian Islamists attacked Tunisian border guards in protest against Tunisian support for Algerian security forces.

TUNISIAN ARMED FORCES

84 main battle tanks (54 M–60A3, 30 M–60A1)	27,000 personnel
19 patrol boats	4500 personnel
44 combat aircraft (15 F–5E/F)	3500 personnel
None	

ECONOMICS

Inflation 4.6% p.a. (1990–1999)

$19.8bn | 1.2607–1.3844 dinars

SCORE CARD

World GNP Ranking	67th
GNP per Capita	$2090
Balance of Payments	$-503m
Inflation	2.7%
Unemployment	17%

EXPORTS

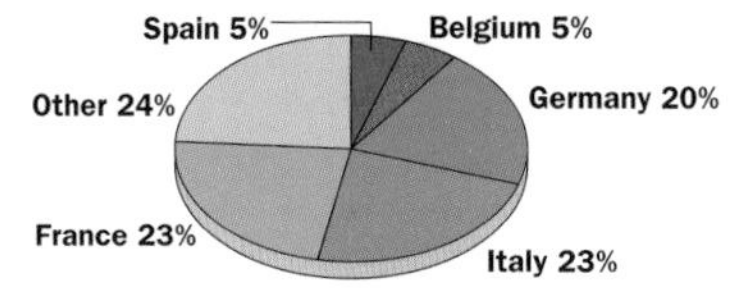
Spain 5%
Belgium 5%
Other 24%
Germany 20%
France 23%
Italy 23%

IMPORTS

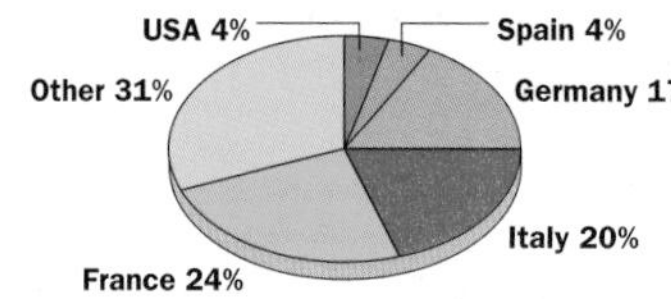
USA 4%
Spain 4%
Other 31%
Germany 17%
Italy 20%
France 24%

Strengths

A well-diversified economy, despite limited resources. Tourism. Oil and gas exports, also agricultural exports: olive oil, olives, citrus fruit, dates. Expanding manufacturing sector, average annual increase was 5.4% in 1990–1998; important sectors are textiles, construction materials, machinery, chemicals. European investment. Ranked as the most competitive economy in Africa by the World Economic Forum in 2000.

Weaknesses

Dependence on growth of drought-prone agricultural sector. Growing domestic energy demand on oil and gas resources.

Profile

Since it began a process of structural adjustment in 1988, supported by the IMF and the World Bank, Tunisia has become an increasingly open, market-oriented economy. Real GDP growth has averaged 5% since 1987, rising to 6% in 2001. Annual inflation remained stable, at just below 3% in 2000, despite higher food and energy prices. Prices have been freed, most state companies privatized, and import barriers reduced.

The balance of payments relies on fluctuating tourism receipts to offset a trade deficit. The government must also balance growth with better social provisions. The member states of the EU are Tunisia's main trading partners, accounting for well over 70% of its imports and nearly 80% of its exports; trade has increased significantly since 1999.

ECONOMIC PERFORMANCE INDICATOR

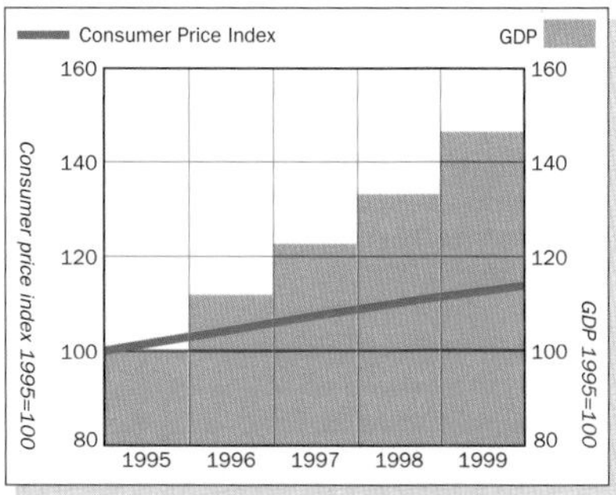
Consumer Price Index
GDP
160
140
120
100
80
1995
1996
1997
1998
1999
Consumer price index 1995=100
GDP 1995=100

TUNISIA : MAJOR BUSINESSES

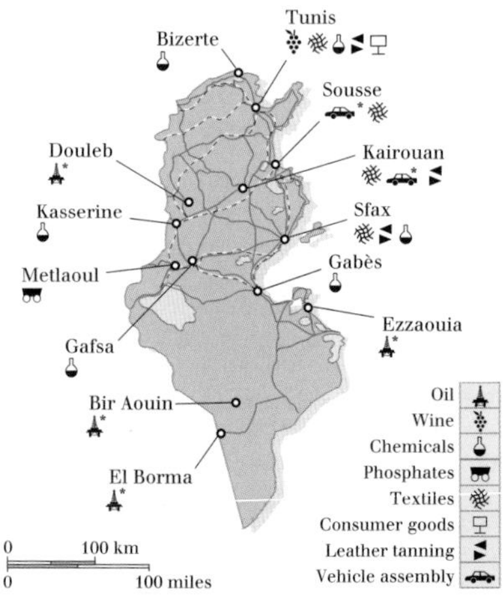
Tunis
Bizerte
Sousse
Douleb
Kairouan
Kasserine
Sfax
Metlaoul
Gabès
Ezzaouia
Gafsa
Bir Aouin
El Borma
Oil
Wine
Chemicals
Phosphates
Textiles
Consumer goods
Leather tanning
Vehicle assembly
0 100 km
0 100 miles
* significant multinational ownership

RESOURCES

Electric power 2m kw

89,027 tonnes

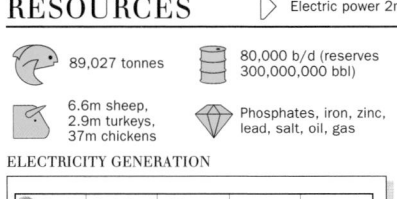

80,000 b/d (reserves 300,000,000 bbl)

6.6m sheep, 2.9m turkeys, 37m chickens

Phosphates, iron, zinc, lead, salt, oil, gas

ELECTRICITY GENERATION

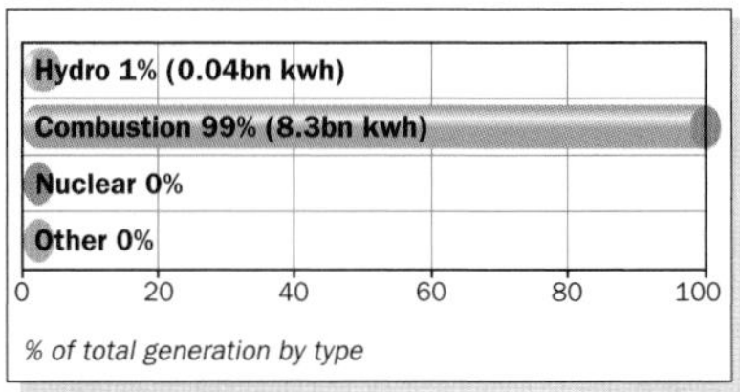
Hydro 1% (0.04bn kwh)
Combustion 99% (8.3bn kwh)
Nuclear 0%
Other 0%
0
20
40
60
80
100
% of total generation by type

TUNISIA : LAND USE

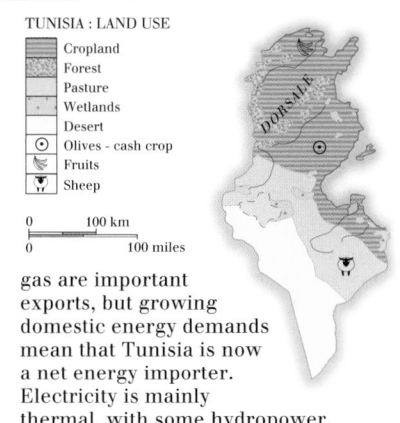

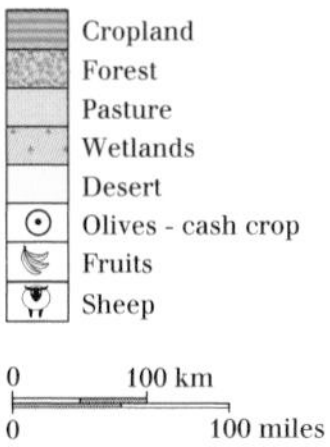
Cropland
Forest
Pasture
Wetlands
Desert
Olives - cash crop
Fruits
Sheep
0
100 km
0
100 miles

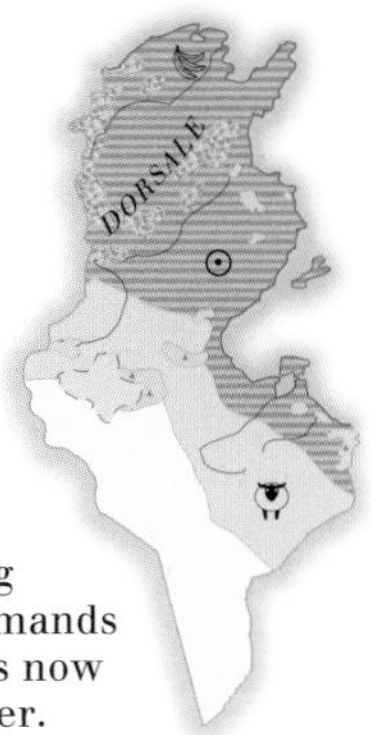
DORSALE

Tunisia is one of the world's leading producers of phosphates for fertilizers, mainly from mines near Gafsa. Oil and gas are important exports, but growing domestic energy demands mean that Tunisia is now a net energy importer. Electricity is mainly thermal, with some hydropower.

HEALTH

Welfare state health benefits

1 per 1429 people

Heart and cerebrovascular diseases

Well-developed family planning facilities have almost halved Tunisia's birthrate over the past 30 years. The population growth rate has dropped from 3.2% to 1.9% – the lowest in the region. The mortality rate has been halved, to 5.7 per 1000 population a year, reflecting the extension of free medical services to over 70% of the population. While services lack sophistication, an umbrella of primary care facilities covers all but the most isolated rural communities. Regional committees care for the old, needy, and orphaned.

ENVIRONMENT

Sustainability rank: 83rd

1%

2 tonnes per capita

ENVIRONMENTAL TREATIES

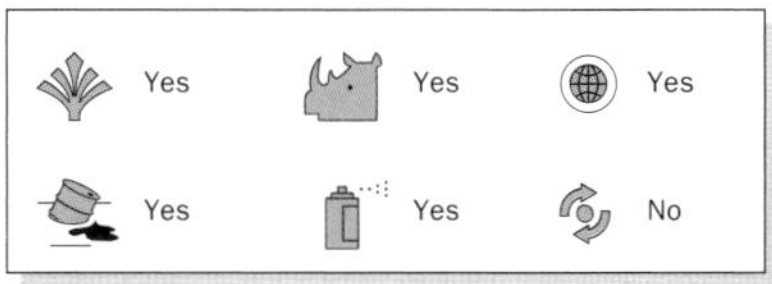
Yes
Yes
Yes
Yes
Yes
No

Desertification is a serious problem in the largely arid central and southern regions. However, the dominant environmental issue is the rapid expansion of tourism since the 1980s. Large, insensitively designed hotel and resort developments, which do not fit in with the local architecture, are spoiling coastal areas such as the Isle of Jerba and Hammamet (although building height restrictions are applied here). Tourism is also making an impact on the fragile desert ecology of the south.

MEDIA

TV ownership medium

Daily newspaper circulation 31 per 1000 people

PUBLISHING AND BROADCAST MEDIA

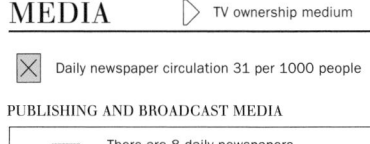

There are 8 daily newspapers, including *al-Amal*, *La Presse de Tunisie*, and *As-Sabah*

2 state-owned services

1 state-owned service

Reforms since the late 1980s have in theory increased press freedom in Tunisia, traditionally considered a source of liberal ideas in the Arab world. In practice, government restrictions remain. The foreign press is also occasionally banned, but the arrival of satellite TV from Europe has enabled people to receive a wide range of programs. The Internet is heavily censored.

CRIME

Death penalty used

Tunisia does not publish prison figures

Up 4% 1996–1998

CRIME RATES

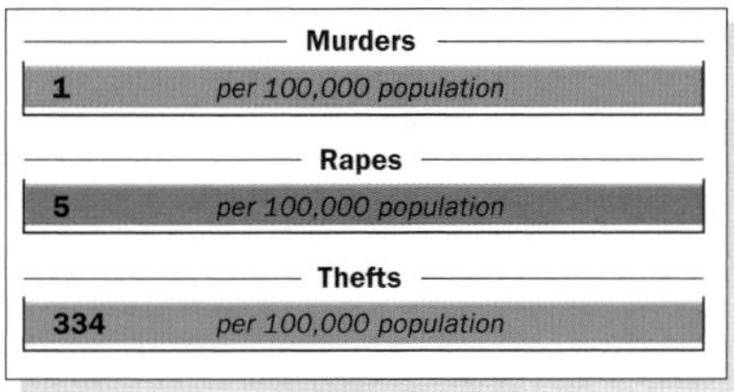
Murders
1
per 100,000 population
Rapes
5
per 100,000 population
Thefts
334
per 100,000 population

Street crime is unusual. However, Tunisia's poor human rights record has prompted criticism of its maltreatment of political and other detainees. Arbitrary arrests and torture while in police custody, especially of suspected Islamist activists, are routine.

EDUCATION

School leaving age: 16

71%

121,787 students

THE EDUCATION SYSTEM

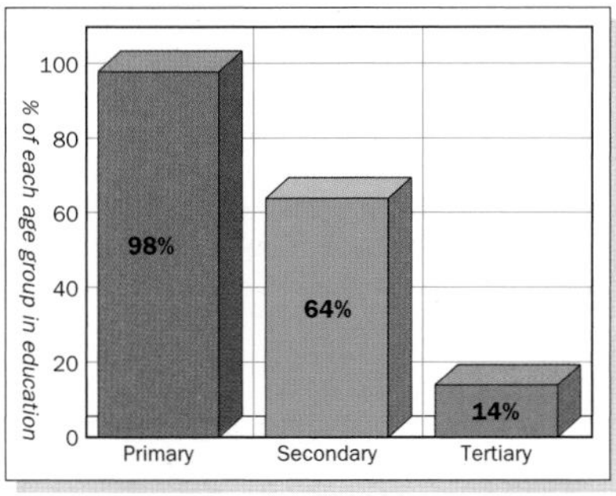
100
80
60
40
20
0
% of each age group in education
98%
64%
14%
Primary
Secondary
Tertiary

Education is compulsory for nine years between the ages of six and 16, with secondary education beginning at the age of 12. Arabic is the first language in schools, but French is also taught, and is used almost exclusively in higher education. There are seven universities; student enrollment has doubled since 1995.

SPENDING

GDP/cap. increase

CONSUMPTION AND SPENDING

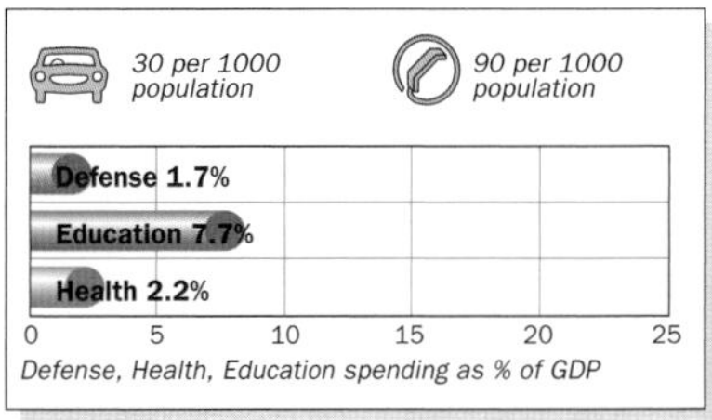
30 per 1000 population
90 per 1000 population
Defense 1.7%
Education 7.7%
Health 2.2%
0
5
10
15
20
25
Defense, Health, Education spending as % of GDP

Today 6% of Tunisians are estimated to live in absolute poverty. In 1970, the figure was 30%. The poorest in the community tend to live in the urban shanty towns, or *bidonvilles*. The Western-oriented elite has links with government or business. Social security covers sickness, old age and maternity, but not unemployment. The government is concerned that the lack of jobs is encouraging the spread of Islamic fundamentalism; economic growth is its medium-term solution to the problem. Special projects are being set up in the most deprived urban areas to offset the worst effects of poverty.

WORLD RANKING

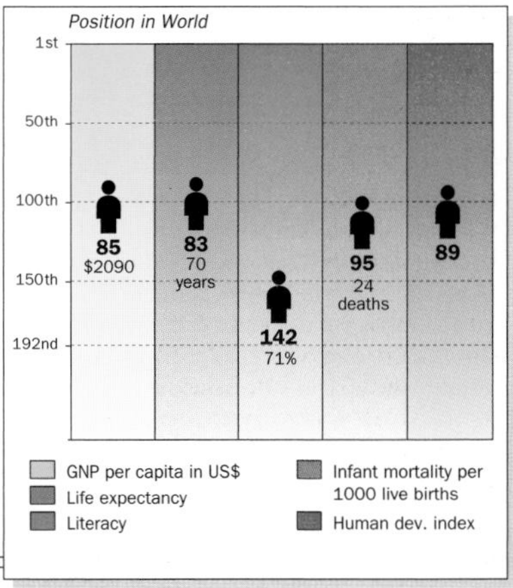
Position in World
1st
50th
100th
150th
192nd
85
$2090
83
70
years
142
71%
95
24
deaths
89
GNP per capita in US$
Life expectancy
Literacy
Infant mortality per 1000 live births
Human dev. index

T

TURKEY

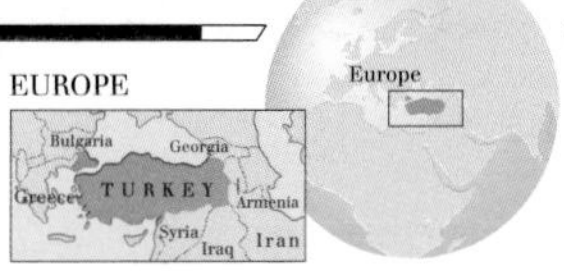
EUROPE
Europe
Bulgaria
Georgia
TURKEY
Greece
Armenia
Syria
Iraq
Iran

OFFICIAL NAME: Republic of Turkey **CAPITAL:** Ankara
POPULATION: 66.6 million **CURRENCY:** Turkish lira **OFFICIAL LANGUAGE:** Turkish

1923 | 1939 | Oct 29 | TR | +2 | +90 | .tr

TURKEY, MAINLY IN WESTERN ASIA, also includes the region of Eastern Thrace in Europe. It thus controls the entrance to the Black Sea, which is straddled by Turkey's largest city, Istanbul. Most Turks live in the western half of the country. The eastern and southeastern reaches of the Anatolia Plateau are Kurdish regions. Turkey's strategic location gives it great influence in the Black Sea, the Mediterranean, and the Middle East. Lying on a major earthquake fault line, many Turkish towns are vulnerable to earthquakes such as the one which devastated Izmit in 1999.

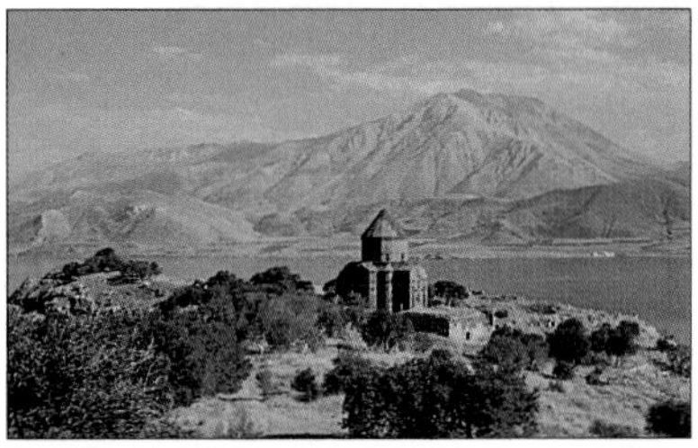

The Church of the Holy Cross, *on Akdamar Island in Lake Van, was built in the 10th-century when Christianity was dominant in the region.*

CLIMATE

Mountain/ Mediterranean

WEATHER CHART

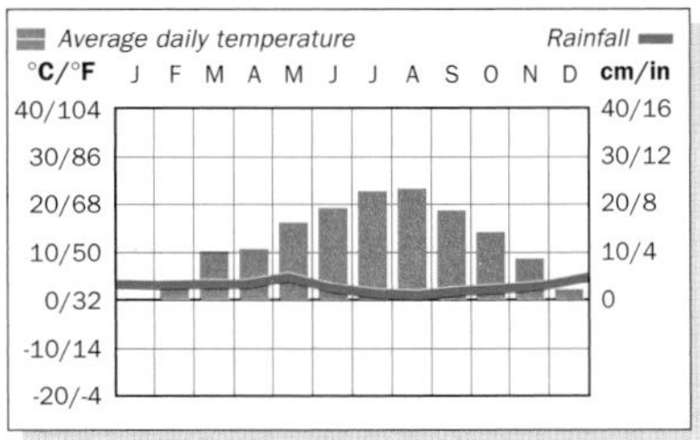
Average daily temperature
Rainfall
°C/°F J F M A M J J A S O N D cm/in
40/104
30/86
20/68
10/50
0/32
-10/14
-20/-4
40/16
30/12
20/8
10/4
0

Coastal regions have a Mediterranean climate. The interior has cold, snowy winters and hot, dry summers.

TRANSPORTATION

Drive on right

Atatürk International, Istanbul
13.2m passengers

1135 ships
6.3m grt

THE TRANSPORTATION NETWORK

95,599 km (59,402 miles)

1726 km (1072 miles)

8682 km (5395 miles)

1200 km (746 miles)

Plans are under way for a high-speed rail link between Istanbul and Ankara. Shipping forms a high proportion of transportation traffic, handled by an extensive network of ports and harbors, including Istanbul and Izmir.

PEOPLE

Pop. density medium

Turkish, Kurdish, Arabic, Circassian, Armenian, Greek, Georgian, Ladino

87/km² (224/mi²)

THE URBAN/RURAL POPULATION SPLIT

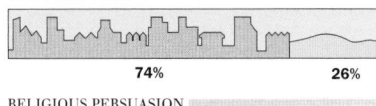

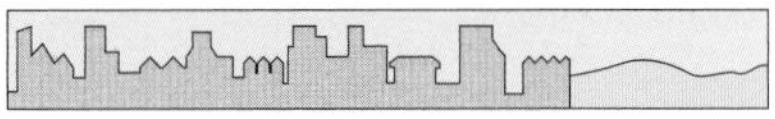
74%
26%

RELIGIOUS PERSUASION

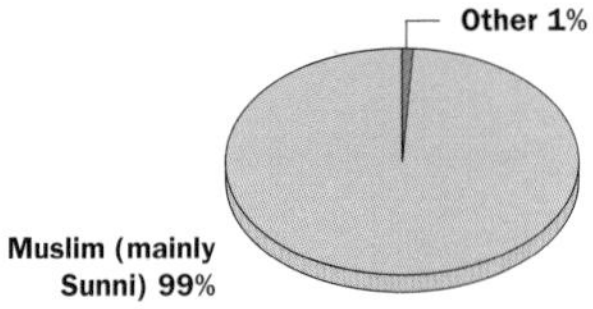
Other 1%
Muslim (mainly Sunni) 99%

ETHNIC MAKEUP

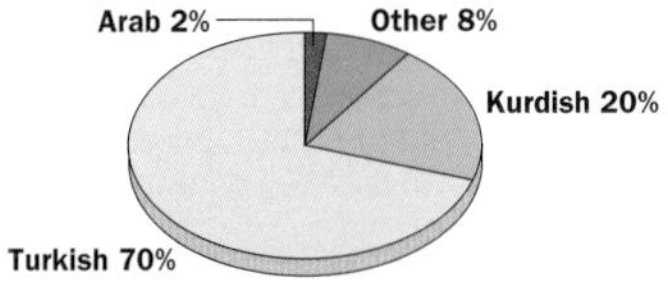
Arab 2%
Other 8%
Kurdish 20%
Turkish 70%

The Turks are racially diverse. Many are the descendants of refugees, often from the Balkans, but a strong sense of national identity is rooted in a shared language and religion. Most are Sunni Muslim, although a Shi'a community is growing fast, including the heterodox Alawite sect. The largest minority are the Kurds, while there are some 500,000 Arabic speakers. While women have equal rights in law, men dominate political and even family life. There is controversy over the right of women to wear Islamic headscarves, which are banned in state universities. Tansu Çiller was Turkey's first woman prime minister, in 1993–1996.

POPULATION AGE BREAKDOWN

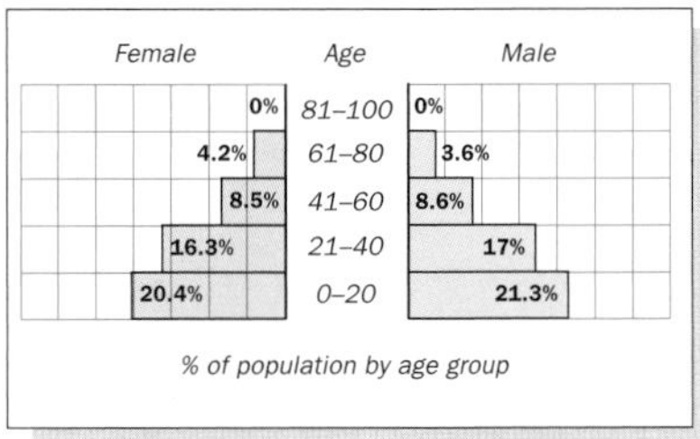
Female
Age
Male
0%
81–100
0%
4.2%
61–80
3.6%
8.5%
41–60
8.6%
16.3%
21–40
17%
20.4%
0–20
21.3%
% of population by age group

TOURISM

Visitors : Population 1:6.9

9.6m visitors

Up 39% in 2000

Visitors are attracted by fine beaches, classical sites such as Ephesus and Troy, and antiquities from the prehistoric to the Ottoman periods. Attacks on foreigners by Kurdish militants in 1994 hit the tourist trade, but business then recovered, and in 1997 tourists spent $7 billion. Visitor numbers dropped in 1999, however, the year of the Izmit earthquake.

MAIN TOURIST ARRIVALS

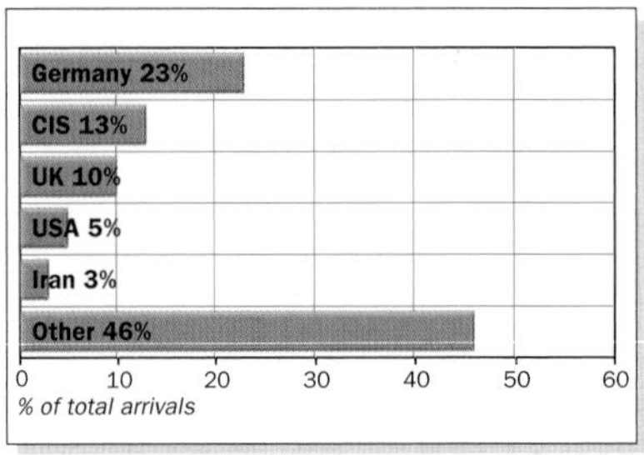
Germany 23%
CIS 13%
UK 10%
USA 5%
Iran 3%
Other 46%
0 10 20 30 40 50 60
% of total arrivals

BULGARIA
GREECE
Edirne
Kırklareli
Tekirdağ
Kâğıthane
İstanbul Boğazi
İstanbul
Marmara Denizi
Yalova
İzmit
Adapazar
Zong
Bolu
Bandırma
Çanakkale
Dardenelles
Bursa
Bilecik
Sakarya
Balıkesir
Eskişehir
Kütahya
AEGEAN SEA
Manisa
Akhisar
İzmir
Afyon
Uşak
Turgutlu
Aydın
Nazilli
Söke
Büyükmenderes
Denizli
Burdur
Isparta
Milas
Bodrum
Muğla
Marmaris
Fethiye
Antalya
Finike
Kaş
Antalya Körfe
MEDITERRANE
40°
36°
28°

T

POLITICS

Multiparty elections

1999/2004

President Ahmet Necdet Sezer

AT THE LAST ELECTION

Turkish Grand National Assembly 550 seats

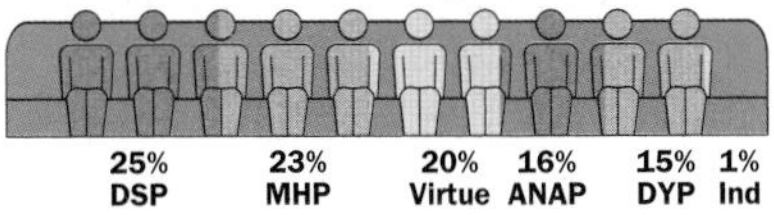

25% DSP
23% MHP
20% Virtue
16% ANAP
15% DYP
1% Ind

DSP = Democratic Left Party **MHP** = Nationalist Action Party **Virtue** = Virtue Party **ANAP** = Motherland Party **DYP** = True Path Party **Ind** = Independents

Under its 1982 constitution, Turkey is a multiparty republic with a national assembly elected every five years. The president, who serves a seven-year term, appoints the prime minister.

MAIN POLITICAL ISSUES

Islamic fundamentalism

Modern Turkey's identity as a secular state was profoundly challenged in the mid-1990s by the Islamist agenda of the Welfare Party (RP) – the largest parliamentary party after the 1995 election. A secular coalition to keep the RP out of power disintegrated in mid-1996, when RP leader Necmettin Erbakan formed a coalition with the True Path Party. Ousted in mid-1997, the RP was banned in 1998. Many RP MPs allied themselves with the Virtue Party, which in turn was banned in 2001.

Kurdish separatists

Thousands have been killed since 1984 in a bitter civil war in southeast Turkey. The secessionist Kurdistan Workers' Party (PKK) has proclaimed three cease-fires since 1992 and now professes simply to favor recognition of Kurdish rights within Turkey. In 1999 its leader Abdullah Ocalan was captured abroad, tried, and sentenced to death. He has not yet been executed and, from prison, has urged his supporters to abandon armed struggle.

Human rights

Turkey's human rights record has been subject to intense international criticism. Reforms in 1995 lifted a number of civil liberty restrictions written into the 1982 constitution, but concerns remain over illegal executions and the treatment of Kurds. A hunger strike campaign against conditions in high-security prisons gained worldwide attention in early 2001.

PROFILE

Aside from the Islamic–secular division, politics is divided by personalities rather than ideologies. The military-dominated National Security Council also retains political influence.

Bulent Ecevit became prime minister in 1999 after the strong showing of the DSP in the election. Ecevit formed a new coalition with the far-right MHP, and with ANAP (backed by Istanbul's metropolitan interests). He staked his government's future on the reelection of President Süleyman Demirel, but the Assembly failed to vote through the required constitutional changes in April 2000. The coalition remained in power, however, and Demirel was replaced in May by a non-party candidate, Ahmet Necdet Sezer.

***Bulent Ecevit,** prime minister since 1999. He ordered the invasion of Cyprus in 1974.*

***President Ahmet Necdet Sezer,** has frequently clashed with Ecevit.*

WORLD AFFAIRS

Joined UN in 1945

CE | NATO | OECD | OIC | OSCE

Turkey had great strategic significance as NATO's first Western line of defense during the Cold War. It now has closer ties with former communist neighbors, particularly Bulgaria and Georgia, and with Turkic-speaking central Asian states. It has joined the Black Sea Economic Cooperation Project, and has tried to mediate in the war between Armenia and Azerbaijan. In 2000 Turkey agreed to send arms to Uzbekistan to contain Islamic rebels – its first such military involvement in central Asia since the collapse of the Soviet Union in 1991. Turkey's pro-Islamic government in 1996–1997 sought briefly to strengthen ties with Arab states.

Negotiations on joining the EU opened in 1999, and are aided by a recent improvement in Turkey's relations with Greece, although the Turkish-backed *de facto* partition of Cyprus remains an obstacle, as are the EU's concerns over human rights.

AID

Recipient

$14m (receipts)

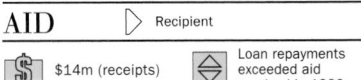

Loan repayments exceeded aid received in 1999

Turkey was a net recipient of aid (especially from the Gulf War allies) until 1997, despite US suspension of aid in 1994 in protest at the treatment of Kurds. The acute economic crisis in 2000–2001 prompted a $10 billion loan from the IMF. Greece, a traditional adversary, offered humanitarian aid after the 1999 Izmit earthquake.

TURKEY

Total Land Area : 769 630 sq. km (297 154 sq. miles)

LAND HEIGHT	POPULATION
3000m/9843ft	over 5 000 000
2000m/6562ft	over 1 000 000
1000m/3281ft	over 500 000
500m/1640ft	over 100 000
200m/656ft	over 50 000
Sea Level	over 10 000
	under 10 000

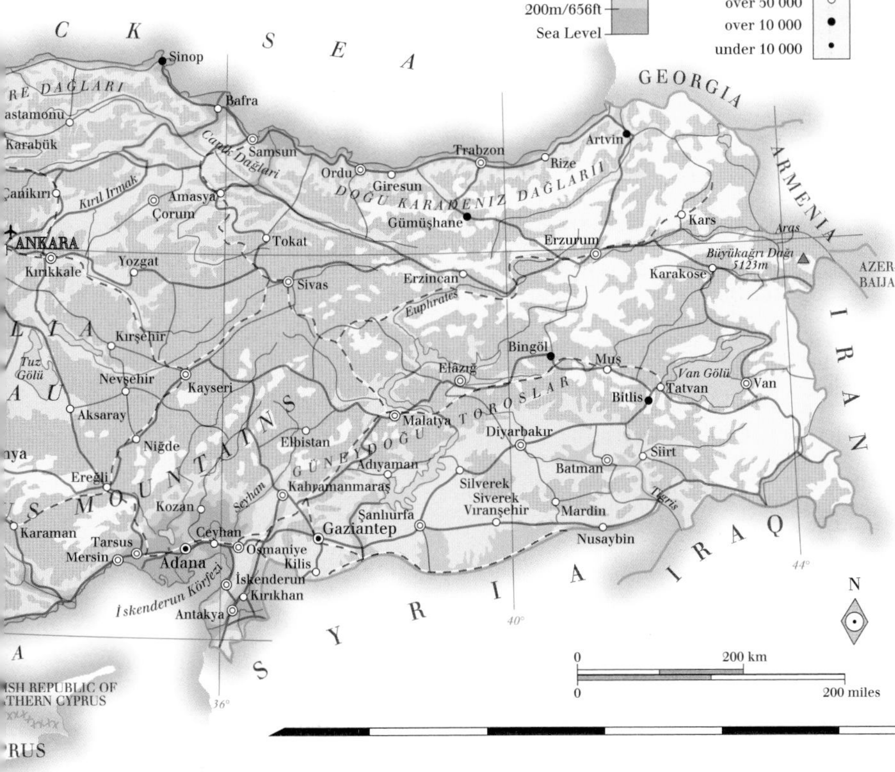

Sinop
Bafra
Samsun
Canik Dağları
Kastamonu
Karabük
Çankırı
ANKARA
Kırıkkale
Yozgat
Amasya
Çorum
Kızıl Irmak
Tokat
Ordu
Giresun
Trabzon
Rize
Artvin
DOĞU KARADENIZ DAĞLARI
Gümüşhane
Kars
Erzurum
Aras
Büyükağrı Dağı 5123m
Karakose
AZER-BAIJAN
Sivas
Erzincan
Euphrates
Kırşehir
Tuz Gölü
Nevşehir
Kayseri
Aksaray
Niğde
Elbistan
Malatya
Elâzığ
Bingöl
Muş
Van Gölü
Tatvan
Van
Bitlis
Diyarbakır
Batman
Siirt
Adıyaman
Kahramanmaraş
Şanlıurfa
Gaziantep
Siverek
Viranşehir
Mardin
Nusaybin
Tigris
Ereğli
Karaman
Kozan
Ceyhan
Seyhan
Tarsus
Mersin
Adana
Osmaniye
Kilis
İskenderun
İskenderun Körfezi
Kırıkhan
Antakya
TOROS
GÜNEYDOĞU TOROSLAR
GEORGIA
ARMENIA
IRAN
IRAQ
SYRIA
BLACK SEA
TAURUS MOUNTAINS
ANATOLIA
N
0 200 km
0 200 miles
40°
44°
36°

T

CHRONOLOGY

Following the collapse of the Ottoman Empire and Turkey's defeat in World War I, nationalist Mustafa Kemal Ataturk deposed the ruling sultan in 1922, declaring Turkey a republic in 1923.

- ❑ **1924** Religious courts abolished.
- ❑ **1928** Islam no longer state religion.
- ❑ **1934** Women given the vote.
- ❑ **1938** President Ataturk dies. Succeeded by Ismet Inonu.
- ❑ **1945** Turkey declares war on Germany. Joins UN.
- ❑ **1952** Joins CE and NATO.
- ❑ **1960** Army stages coup against ruling Democratic Party and suspends National Assembly.
- ❑ **1961** New constitution.
- ❑ **1963** Association agreement with European Economic Community.
- ❑ **1974** Invades northern Cyprus.
- ❑ **1980** Military coup; martial law.
- ❑ **1982** New constitution.
- ❑ **1983** General election won by Turgut Özal's ANAP.
- ❑ **1984** Turkey recognizes "Turkish Republic of Northern Cyprus." Kurdish separatist PKK launches guerrilla war in southeast.
- ❑ **1987** Applies to join European Communities.
- ❑ **1990** US-led coalition launches air strikes on Iraq from Turkish bases.
- ❑ **1991** Elections won by DYP. Süleyman Demirel premier.
- ❑ **1992** Joins Black Sea alliance.
- ❑ **1993** Demirel elected president. Tansu Çiller becomes DYP leader and heads coalition.
- ❑ **1995** Major anti-Kurdish offensive. Reforms lower voting age to 18. Çiller coalition collapses. Pro-Islamic RP wins election, but center-right DYP–ANAP coalition takes office. Customs union with EU.
- ❑ **1996–1997** RP leader Necmettin Erbakan heads first pro-Islamic government since the 1923 creation of a secular republic.
- ❑ **1997** Mesut Yilmaz reappointed to head minority ANAP government.
- ❑ **1998** RP banned; many of its MPs join Virtue Party. Yilmaz resigns amid corruption allegations; replaced by Bulent Ecevit of DSP.
- ❑ **1999** DSP wins most seats in general election; Ecevit heads right-wing coalition. Captured Kurdish leader Abdullah Ocalan sentenced to death. Izmit earthquake kills 14,000.
- ❑ **2000** National Assembly refuses to endorse Demirel's reelection. He is replaced by Ahmet Necdet Sezer.
- ❑ **2001** Acute financial crisis. Prisoners and their relatives die staging hunger strikes against conditions and discrimination in high-security prisons. June, Virtue Party banned.

DEFENSE

▷ Compulsory military service

$10.2bn — Up 5% in 1999

TURKISH ARMED FORCES

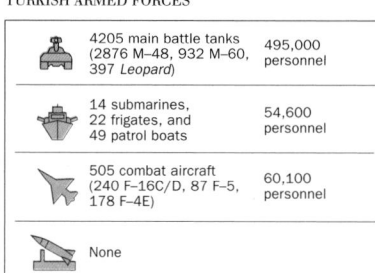

4205 main battle tanks (2876 M–48, 932 M–60, 397 *Leopard*)	495,000 personnel
14 submarines, 22 frigates, and 49 patrol boats	54,600 personnel
505 combat aircraft (240 F–16C/D, 87 F–5, 178 F–4E)	60,100 personnel
None	

Turkey's armed forces are the second-largest in NATO, which it joined in 1952. Turkey is a sizable military power, and it spends a higher percentage of GDP on defense than any other NATO country except Greece. The great majority of its personnel are conscripts; 18 months' service is compulsory for all males at the age of 20. NATO membership gives Turkey easy access to Western arms suppliers, although in 1994 Germany threatened a ban on arms sales, claiming that they were being used to suppress the Kurdish minority. Offensives against Kurdish separatists in northern Iraq and in Turkey's own southeastern provinces have involved over 50,000 troops and repeated incursions into Iraqi territory.

ECONOMICS

▷ Inflation 78.3% p.a. (1990–1999)

$186bn — 542,400–670,300 Turkish lira

SCORE CARD

❑ World GNP Ranking	23rd
❑ GNP per Capita	$2900
❑ Balance of Payments	$1.87bn
❑ Inflation	64.9%
❑ Unemployment	7%

EXPORTS

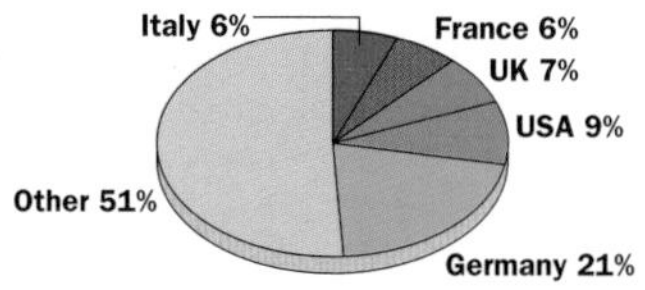
Italy 6%
France 6%
UK 7%
USA 9%
Other 51%
Germany 21%

IMPORTS

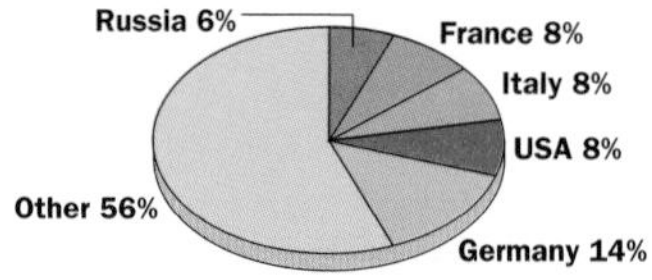
Russia 6%
France 8%
Italy 8%
USA 8%
Other 56%
Germany 14%

Strengths

Liberalized economy resulted in strong growth in the 1990s. Self-sufficient in agriculture. Textiles, manufacturing, and construction sectors competitive on world markets. Tourism industry. Dynamic private sector economy. Skilled labor force. Customs union with EU since 1995.

Weaknesses

Persistently high inflation. Unsound public finances. Large government bureaucracy. Uneven privatization program. Ailing banking sector. Influence of organized crime. High cost of military action against Kurds.

Profile

Turkey has one of the oldest and most advanced emerging market economies. In the 1990s it grew strongly, but continued to suffer from persistently high inflation. In 1997–1998, the government introduced new tax laws to improve tax collection, and embarked on structural reforms. These were threatened by a serious financial crisis in 2000–2001, which necessitated rescue packages by the IMF in February and May 2001, in return for radical laws reforming the banking sector and privatizing debt-laden state companies.

ECONOMIC PERFORMANCE INDICATOR

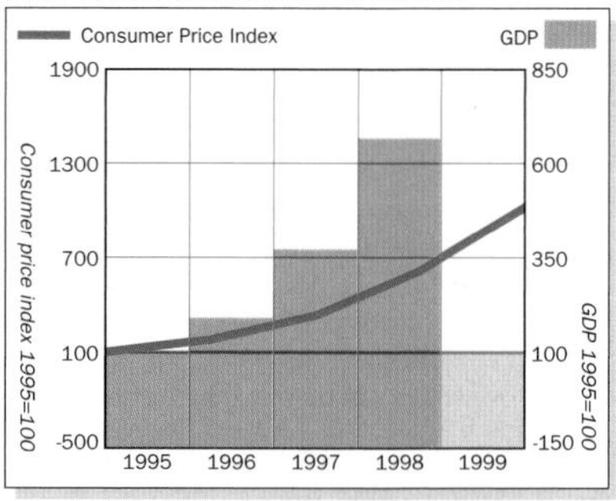
Consumer Price Index
GDP
1900
1300
700
100
-500
850
600
350
100
-150
1995
1996
1997
1998
1999
Consumer price index 1995=100
GDP 1995=100

TURKEY : MAJOR BUSINESSES

Istanbul
Ankara
Bursa
İzmit
Kırıkkale
Erzurum
Sivas
İsparta
Adana
Diyarbakır
İzmir
Mersin
Cement
Oil refining
Textiles
Iron & steel
Chemicals
Food processing
Electronics
Vehicle manufacture
* significant multinational ownership
0
200 km
0
200 miles

RESOURCES

Electric power 21.9m kw

500,260 tonnes

69,152 b/d (reserves 252,466,800 bbl)

30.2m sheep, 11.2m cattle, 8.4m goats, 237m chickens

Chromium, oil, copper, borax, coal, gas, bauxite, iron

ELECTRICITY GENERATION

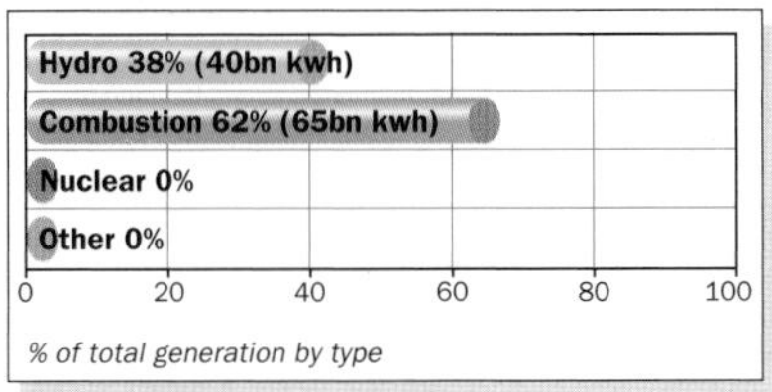
Hydro 38% (40bn kwh)
Combustion 62% (65bn kwh)
Nuclear 0%
Other 0%
0
20
40
60
80
100
% of total generation by type

Under the controversial Southeastern Anatolian Project (GAP) launched in the mid-1980s, Turkey is building 22 dams on the Tigris and Euphrates rivers. In 1999 controversy focused on the Ilisu dam on the Tigris, which will flood 15 towns and 52 villages, and in 2001 on the Birecik dam on the Euphrates, which threatens the ancient Roman town of Zengma. Turkey produces oil around Raman, on the north of the Tigris. Eastern provinces are rich in minerals, such as chromium, of which Turkey is the world's largest producer.

TURKEY : LAND USE

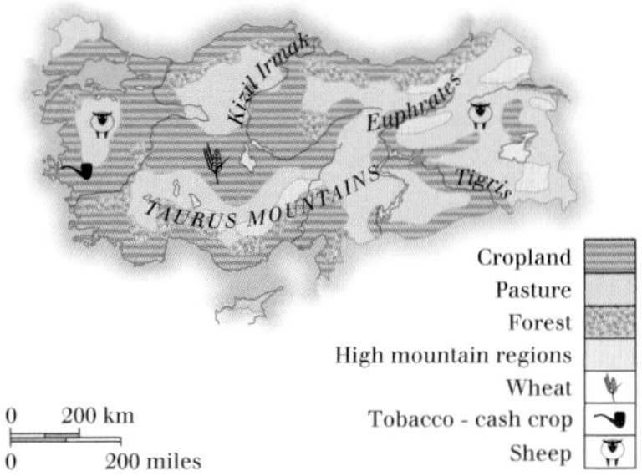
Kizil Irmak
Euphrates
TAURUS MOUNTAINS
Tigris
Cropland
Pasture
Forest
High mountain regions
Wheat
Tobacco - cash crop
Sheep
0 200 km
0 200 miles

ENVIRONMENT

Sustainability rank: 70th

1%

3.5 tonnes per capita

ENVIRONMENTAL TREATIES

Yes	Yes	Yes
Yes	Yes	No

Turkey's program of dam-building on the Tigris and Euphrates has met with international condemnation, particularly from Syria and Iraq, whose rivers will suffer reduced flow rates as a result. Concern has also been expressed at plans to build a nuclear power plant. Much of the western coast has been spoilt by lack of planning and by uncontrolled tourist developments.

MEDIA

TV ownership high

Daily newspaper circulation 110 per 1000 people

PUBLISHING AND BROADCAST MEDIA

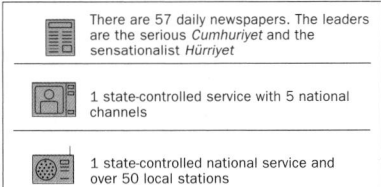

There are 57 daily newspapers. The leaders are the serious *Cumhuriyet* and the sensationalist *Hürriyet*

1 state-controlled service with 5 national channels

1 state-controlled national service and over 50 local stations

The Turkish press is diverse, vigorous, and largely privately owned. In 1995, the National Assembly amended censorship laws dating back to 1980, to ease restrictions on the propagation of Kurdish rights. A particularly high number of journalists are, however, imprisoned in Turkey. Islam is the dominant religion, but the media are not subject to the moral censorship found in the Gulf states. Almost all Istanbul newspapers are printed in Ankara and Izmir on the same day. Foreign satellite or cable broadcasts are available, as well as the five national channels of the state Turkish Radio and Television Corporation.

CRIME

Death penalty not used

44,342 prisoners

Down 15% 1996–1998

CRIME RATES

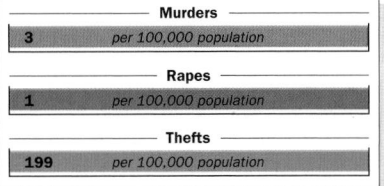

Crime	Rate	
Murders	3	per 100,000 population
Rapes	1	per 100,000 population
Thefts	199	per 100,000 population

Mafia activities and narcotics-related crime are continuing to increase, especially in the southeast. Routine torture and rape by the police, and the deaths of prisoners in custody, cause concern among human rights groups worldwide.

EDUCATION

School leaving age: 14

85%

1.43m students

THE EDUCATION SYSTEM

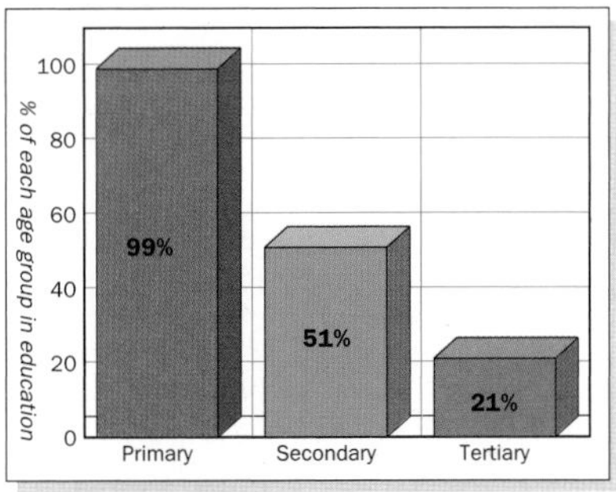
100
80
60
40
20
0
% of each age group in education
99%
51%
21%
Primary
Secondary
Tertiary

After 1923, educational establishments were nationalized. In 1928, a Turkish alphabet with Latin characters was introduced.

In 1997, compulsory education was extended from five to eight years, raising the age for entry into Islamic schools from 11 to 14, in a move seen as designed to reduce attendance at such schools. State schools are coeducational and free. Engineering is usually the strongest faculty in Turkey's many universities.

HEALTH

Welfare state health benefits

1 per 833 people

Heart, cerebrovascular, respiratory, and digestive diseases

Turkey possesses an adequate national system of primary health care. By Western standards, however, hospitals are under-equipped. There are fewer doctors per head than in any western European country.

SPENDING

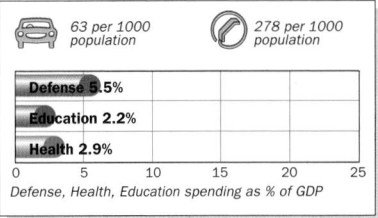

GDP/cap. increase

CONSUMPTION AND SPENDING

63 per 1000 population

278 per 1000 population

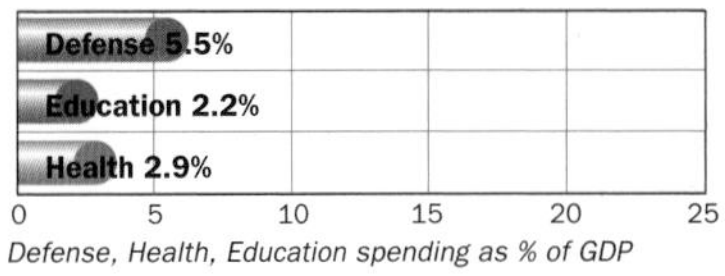
Defense 5.5%
Education 2.2%
Health 2.9%
0
5
10
15
20
25
Defense, Health, Education spending as % of GDP

The economic expansion of the 1980s has created a new class of wealthy entrepreneurs. Urban/rural differences remain pronounced. High inflation in the 1990s eroded earnings of those on fixed incomes, and income inequality has grown. Many Turks take jobs as *Gastarbeiter* (guest workers) in Germany and the Netherlands.

WORLD RANKING

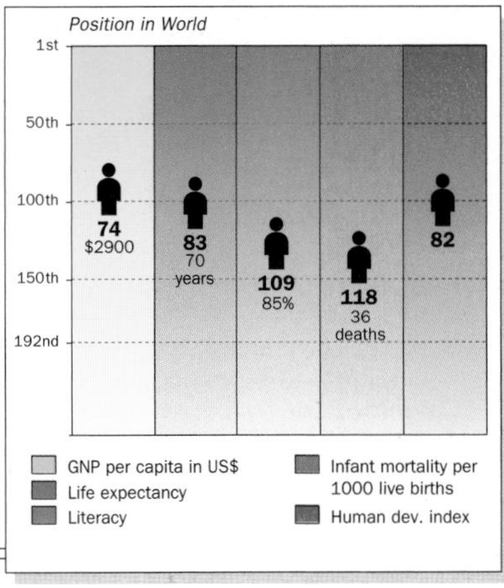
Position in World
1st
50th
100th
150th
192nd
74
$2900
83
70
years
109
85%
118
36
deaths
82
GNP per capita in US$
Life expectancy
Literacy
Infant mortality per 1000 live births
Human dev. index

T

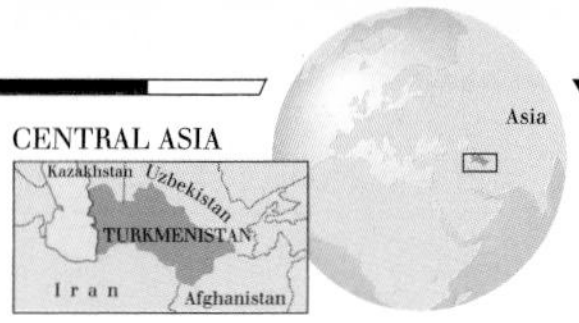
CENTRAL ASIA
Asia
Kazakhstan
Uzbekistan
TURKMENISTAN
Iran
Afghanistan

TURKMENISTAN

OFFICIAL NAME: Turkmenistan **CAPITAL:** Ashgabat
POPULATION: 4.5 million **CURRENCY:** Manat **OFFICIAL LANGUAGE:** Turkmen

1991 | 1991 | Oct 27 | TM | +5 | +993 | .tm

ORIGINALLY THE POOREST state among the former Soviet republics, Turkmenistan has adjusted better than most to independence, exploiting the market value of its abundant natural gas supplies. A largely Sunni Muslim area, Turkmenistan is part of the former Turkestan, the last expanse of central Asia incorporated into czarist Russia. Much of life is still based on tribal relationships. Turkmenistan is isolated – telephones are rare and other communications limited.

CLIMATE

Desert/steppe

WEATHER CHART

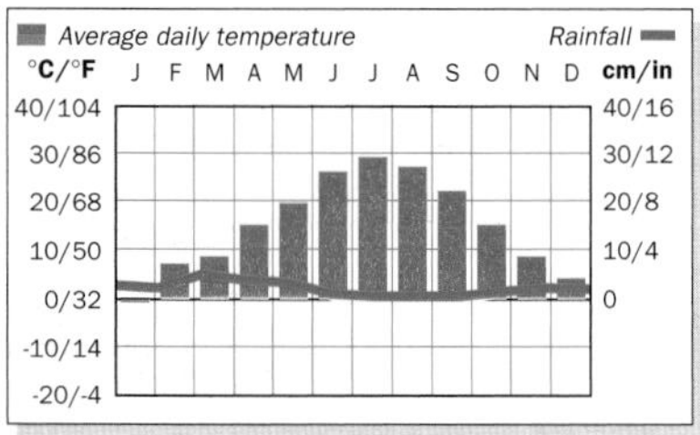
Average daily temperature
Rainfall
°C/°F
J F M A M J J A S O N D
cm/in
40/104
30/86
20/68
10/50
0/32
-10/14
-20/-4
40/16
30/12
20/8
10/4
0

Most of Turkmenistan is arid desert, so that only 2% of the total land area is suitable for agriculture.

TRANSPORTATION

Drive on right

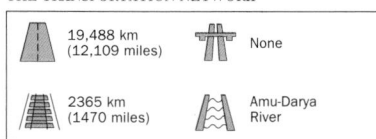

Turkmenistan International, Ashgabat

38 ships
38,400 grt

THE TRANSPORTATION NETWORK

19,488 km (12,109 miles)

None

2365 km (1470 miles)

Amu-Darya River

Road and railroad links to Tehran are being upgraded. The modernization of Ashgabat airport is under way.

TOURISM

Visitors : Population 1:15

300,000 visitors

Up 26% in 1998

MAIN TOURIST ARRIVALS

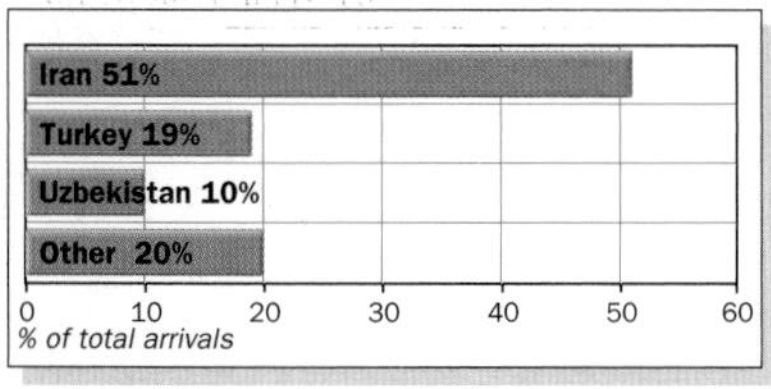
Iran 51%
Turkey 19%
Uzbekistan 10%
Other 20%
0
10
20
30
40
50
60
% of total arrivals

Most visitors are businessmen attracted by Turkmenistan's stability under President Niyazov. Turkmenistan may become a popular tourist destination in future; traditional Turkmen Muslim monuments are slowly being restored.

***Kara Kum Canal zone:** salt flats and the Kopetdag mountains on the Iranian border. The Kara Kum is Turkmenistan's largest desert.*

PEOPLE

Pop. density low

Turkmen, Uzbek, Russian

9/km² (24/mi²)

THE URBAN/RURAL POPULATION SPLIT

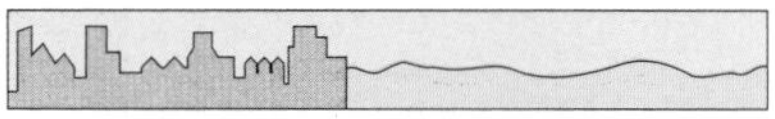
45%
55%

RELIGIOUS PERSUASION

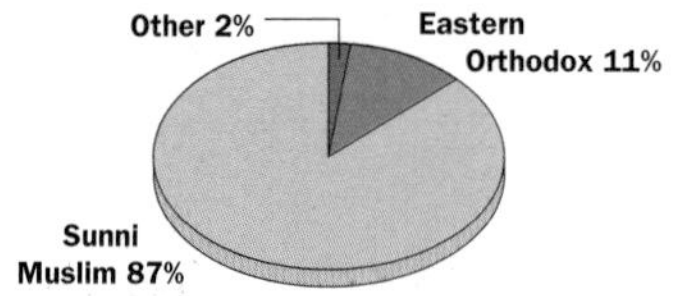
Other 2%
Eastern Orthodox 11%
Sunni Muslim 87%

Before czarist Russia annexed Turkmenistan in 1884, the Turkmen were a largely nomadic tribal people. The tribal unit remains strong – the largest tribes are the Tekke in the center, the Ersary on the eastern Afghan border, and the Yomud in the west. Tribal conflicts among the Turkmen, rather than tensions with the two main minorities – Russians and Uzbeks – are a source of strife. Paradoxically, this has meant that since independence from Moscow there has been less virulent nationalism than in other former Soviet republics. Since 1989, Turkmenistan has been rehabilitating its traditional language and culture, as well as reassessing its history. Islam is again central to the Turkmen, although few perform the *haj* (pilgrimage) to Mecca and many continue to maintain a cult of ancestors.

POLITICS

No multiparty elections

L. House 1999/2004
U. House 1998/2003

President Saparmurad Niyazov

AT THE LAST ELECTION

Parliament 50 seats

In elections to the Parliament in 1999 all of the seats were won by supporters of the ruling Democratic Party of Turkmenistan (**DPT**) – the only registered party.

People's Council 110 seats

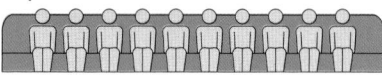

The People's Council has 50 directly elected members, the 50 members of the Parliament, 10 appointed regional members and a varying number of ex-officio members.

Officially, Turkmenistan became a multiparty democracy at independence, although President Niyazov has banned the formation of new parties. As in other ex-Soviet states, former communists, regrouped as the Democratic Party of Turkmenistan, still dominate the political process. The DPT harbors the traditional communist suspicion of Islamic fundamentalism. President Niyazov has encouraged a personality cult, exemplified by the observance since 1995 of an official holiday to mark his birthday and the unveiling of a 12-meter high gold-plated statue of himself in the center of Ashgabat in 1998. He sustains his popularity through the provision of free electricity and water.

Turkmenistan's main concern is to prevent the social and nationalistic conflicts that have blighted other CIS republics. Russian remains the bureaucratic language.

WORLD AFFAIRS

Joined UN in 1992

CIS | ECO | EAPC | OIC | OSCE

Turkmenistan is concentrating on establishing good relations with Iran and Turkey. It needs investment from both countries, but is wary of Islamic fundamentalism. President Niyazov opposes economic union with the CIS, and has also expressed caution about closer political union with other Turkic-speaking central Asian states.

AID

Recipient

$21m (receipts)

Up 24% in 1999

Aid is mostly concentrated in the oil and gas industries and comes from Turkey, Iran, Switzerland, and Germany.

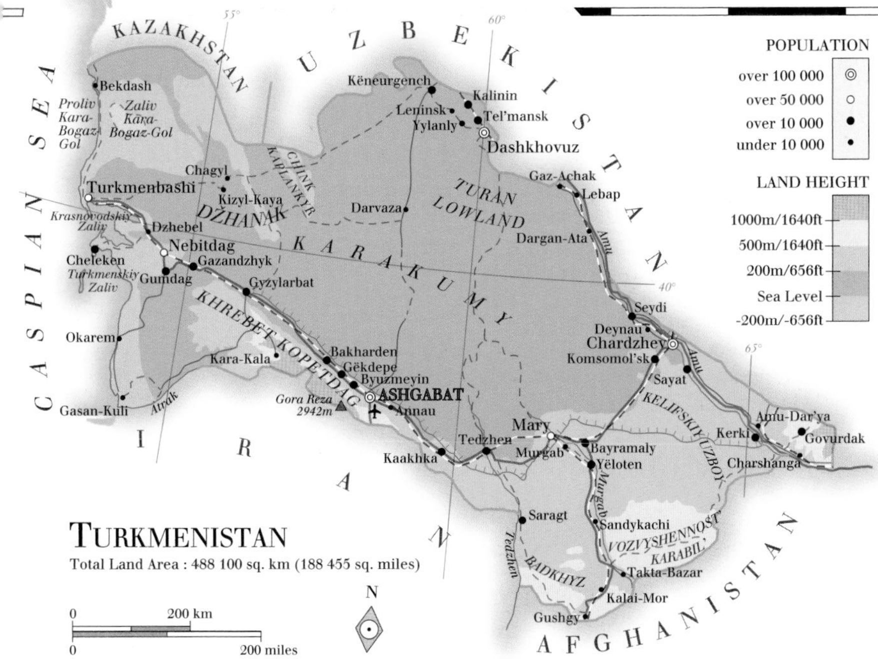
KAZAKHSTAN
UZBEKISTAN
CASPIAN SEA
IRAN
AFGHANISTAN
Bekdash
Proliv Kara-Bogaz Gol
Zaliv Kara-Bogaz-Gol
Këneurgench
Kalinin
Leninsk
Tel'mansk
Ylanly
Dashkhovuz
Chagyl
Turkmenbashi
Kizyl-Kaya
CHINK KAPLANKYR
DZHANAK
Darvaza
TURAN LOWLAND
Gaz-Achak
Lebap
Krasnovodskiy Zaliv
Dzhebel
Nebitdag
Gazandzhyk
Dargan-Ata
Amu
Cheleken
Turkmenskiy Zaliv
Gumdag
Gyzylarbat
KARAKUM
Seydi
Okarem
KHREBET KOPETDAG
Deynau
Chardzhev
Komsomol'sk
Bakharden
Gëkdepe
Kara-Kala
Byuzmeyin
ASHGABAT
Gora Reza 2942m
Annau
Gasan-Kuli
Atrak
Sayat
KELIFSKIY UZBOY
Amu-Dar'ya
Govurdak
Kerki
Mary
Tedzhen
Murgab
Bayramaly
Yëloten
Charshanga
Kaakhka
Saragt
Sandykachi
VOZVYSHENNOST KARABIL
BADKHYZ
Takhta-Bazar
Kalai-Mor
Gushgy
POPULATION
over 100 000
over 50 000
over 10 000
under 10 000
LAND HEIGHT
1000m/1640ft
500m/1640ft
200m/656ft
Sea Level
-200m/-656ft
0 200 km
0 200 miles
N

TURKMENISTAN

Total Land Area : 488 100 sq. km (188 455 sq. miles)

CHRONOLOGY

The nomadic peoples of western Turkestan came under Russian imperial control from the 1850s.

- ❑ **1924** Creation of Turkmenistan.
- ❑ **1991** Independence from USSR. Niyazov retains power, becoming president.
- ❑ **1994** Former communists win first elections.
- ❑ **1999** Niyazov's term extended indefinitely by parliament.

DEFENSE

Compulsory military sevice

$112m

Up 30% in 1999

Turkmenistan depends on Russia for defense. Its army is under joint control.

ECONOMICS

Inflation 516.9% p.a. (1990–1999)

$3.2bn

5200 manats

SCORE CARD

❑ World GNP Ranking	130th
❑ GNP per Capita	$670
❑ Balance of Payments	$-571m
❑ Inflation	13.5%
❑ Unemployment	2%

Strengths

Cotton and gas. Decision to abolish collective farms gradually encouraging private initiative and enterprise.

Weaknesses

Cotton monoculture has forced rising food imports. Thriving black market all but wiped out value of manat in 1995.

EXPORTS

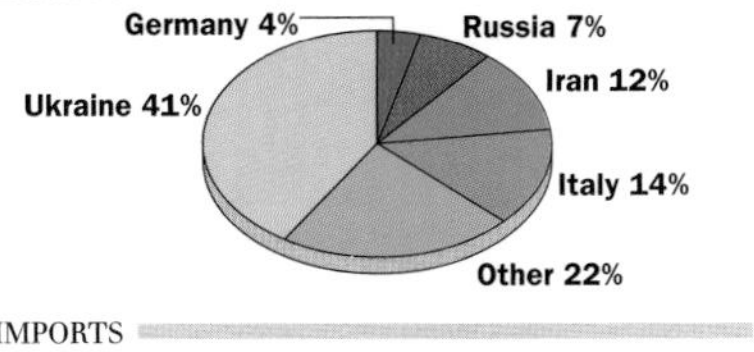
Germany 4%
Russia 7%
Iran 12%
Ukraine 41%
Italy 14%
Other 22%

IMPORTS

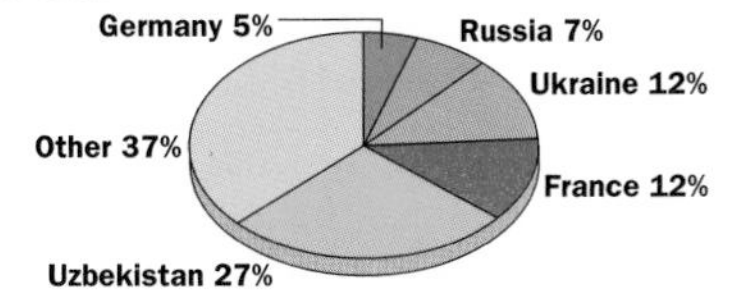
Germany 5%
Russia 7%
Ukraine 12%
Other 37%
France 12%
Uzbekistan 27%

RESOURCES

Electric power 3.9m kw

8828 tonnes

150,000 b/d (reserves 500,000,000 bbl)

5.6m sheep, 850,000 cattle, 4.4m chickens

Oil, natural gas, potassium, sulfur, sodium sulfate

During the Soviet years most Turkmen agriculture was turned over to cotton – seen by Moscow as a strategic crop.

ENVIRONMENT

Not available

4%

6.7 tonnes per capita

The building of the Kara Kum canal has reduced the flow of water to the Aral Sea by 35%. Plans were announced in 2000 for the construction of a large artificial lake in the Kara Kum Desert.

MEDIA

TV ownership medium

Daily newspaper circulation figures are not available

PUBLISHING AND BROADCAST MEDIA

There are 2 daily newspapers, *Neitralnyi Turkmenistan* and *Turkmenistan*, both published in Turkmen

1 state-controlled service

1 state-controlled service

Iranian and Afghan radio stations, beaming in Islamic programs, are popular. TV is only available in cities.

CRIME

Death penalty not used

Turkmenistan does not publish prison figures

Increasing levels of theft

Levels of crime are generally low. The death penalty was finally abolished in December 1999.

EDUCATION

School leaving age: 17

98%

76,000 students

The Turkmen language and literature (banned until 1987) are now on the syllabus. However, Russian schools continue to have higher standards.

HEALTH

Welfare state health benefits

1 per 5000 people

Cerebrovascular, heart, and respiratory diseases

Highly polluted water is a major health hazard; less than 40% of the population have treated mains supply.

SPENDING

GDP/cap. decrease

CONSUMPTION AND SPENDING

No data

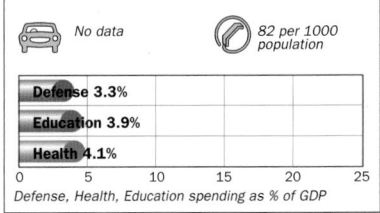

82 per 1000 population

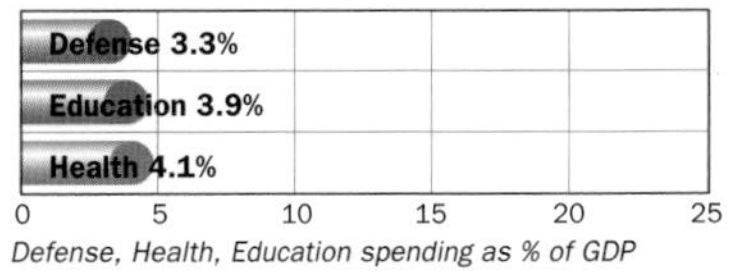
Defense 3.3%
Education 3.9%
Health 4.1%
0
5
10
15
20
25
Defense, Health, Education spending as % of GDP

The ex-communist bureaucrats are still the richest group. They favor Japanese and Korean luxury goods.

WORLD RANKING

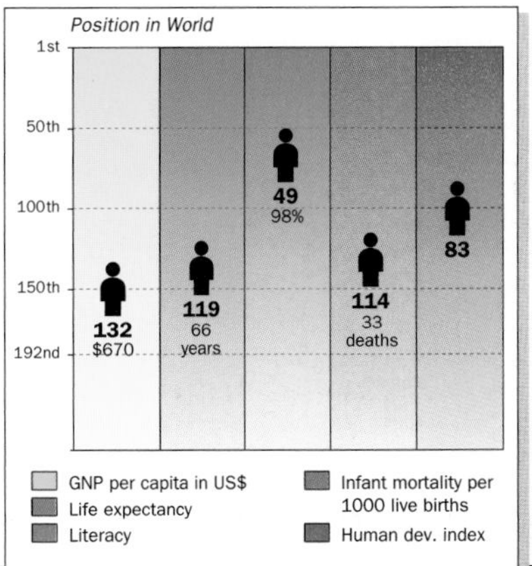
Position in World
1st
50th
100th
150th
192nd
132
$670
119
66 years
49
98%
114
33 deaths
83
GNP per capita in US$
Life expectancy
Literacy
Infant mortality per 1000 live births
Human dev. index

T

TUVALU

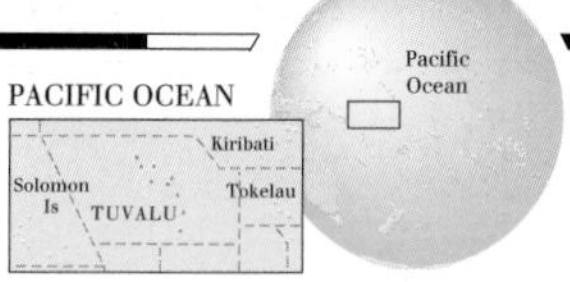
PACIFIC OCEAN
Pacific Ocean
Kiribati
Solomon Is
TUVALU
Tokelau

OFFICIAL NAME: Tuvalu **CAPITAL:** Fongafale, on Funafuti Atoll **POPULATION:** 10,800
CURRENCY: Australian dollar and Tuvaluan dollar **OFFICIAL LANGUAGE:** English

1978 | 1978 | Oct 1 | TUV | +12 | +688 | .tv

ONE OF THE WORLD'S smallest, most isolated states, Tuvalu lies 1050 km (650 miles) north of Fiji in the central Pacific. A chain of nine coral atolls, it has a land area of just 26 square km (10 sq miles). As the Ellice Islands, it was linked to the Gilbert Islands as a British colony until independence in 1978. Politically and socially conservative, Tuvaluans live by subsistence farming and fishing.

CLIMATE
Tropical oceanic

WEATHER CHART

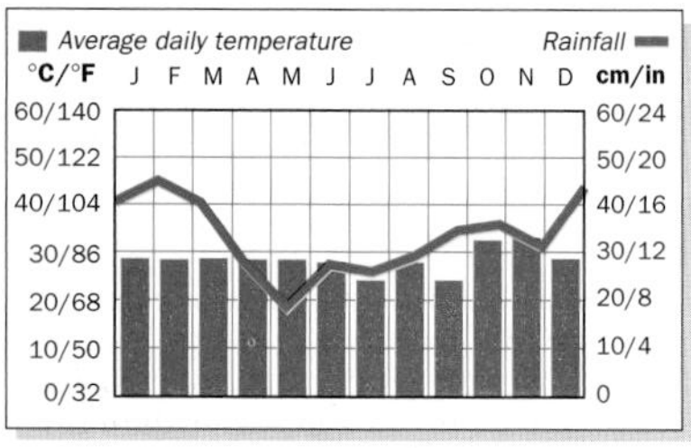
Average daily temperature
Rainfall
°C/°F
J F M A M J J A S O N D
cm/in
60/140
50/122
40/104
30/86
20/68
10/50
0/32
60/24
50/20
40/16
30/12
20/8
10/4
0

Although average humidity exceeds 90%, the climate is pleasantly warm. The mean annual temperature is 29°C (84°F). The October–March hurricane season brings many violent storms.

TRANSPORTATION
Drive on right

There is an airstrip on Funafuti atoll

1 ship 57,000 grt

THE TRANSPORTATION NETWORK

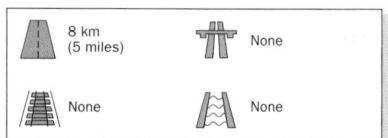

Roads	8 km (5 miles)	Highways	None
Railways	None	Waterways	None

A ferry links the atolls. There are air links with Kiribati and Fiji. Funafuti and Nukufetau have deep-water berths.

TOURISM
Visitors : Population 1:11

1000 visitors

No change in 2000

MAIN TOURIST ARRIVALS

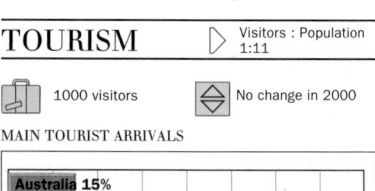

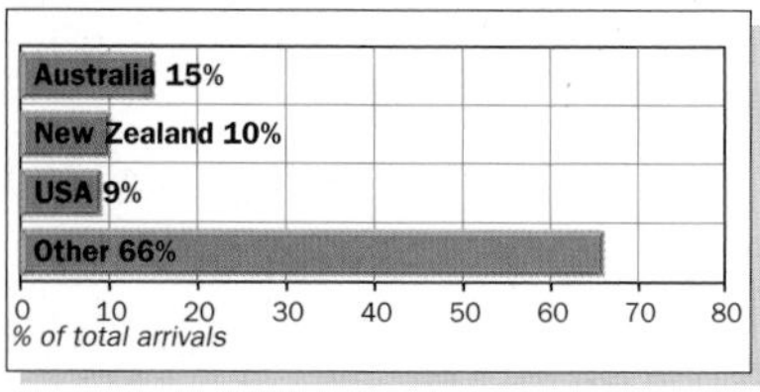
Australia 15%
New Zealand 10%
USA 9%
Other 66%
0 10 20 30 40 50 60 70 80
% of total arrivals

Unspoiled and lapped by some of the world's warmest waters, these remote coral atolls have few visitors. Tourism plans focus on the only paved airstrip, and on Taiwanese investment in Tuvalu's sole hotel, on Funafuti.

PEOPLE
Pop. density high

Tuvaluan, Kiribati, English

417/km² (1080/mi²)

THE URBAN/RURAL POPULATION SPLIT

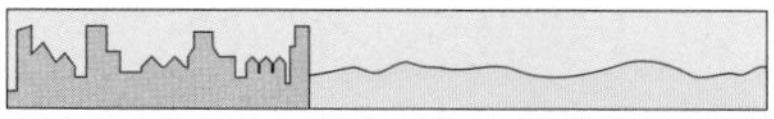
40%
60%

RELIGIOUS PERSUASION

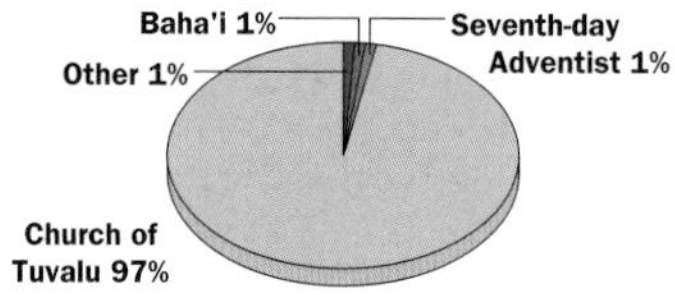
Baha'i 1%
Seventh-day Adventist 1%
Other 1%
Church of Tuvalu 97%

Around 95% of Tuvaluans are ethnically Polynesian. Their ancestors came from Tonga and Samoa 2000 years ago. Nui atoll has Micronesian influences. There is an I-Kiribati community on Funafuti; many Tuvaluans who worked in Kiribati took local wives. Over 40% of the population now live on Funafuti, pushing its population density to almost 1600 per square km (4000 per square mile). Life is still communal, traditional, and hard. Droughts are common and fresh water is precious. About 80% of people depend on subsistence farming, digging special pits out of the coral to grow most of the islands' limited range of crops. Fishing is also important, and Tuvaluans have a reputation as excellent sailors. Some 1000 Tuvaluans work overseas, many in Nauru's phosphate mines, others as merchant seamen.

***Tuvalu's soil** is porous, but sufficiently fertile to support coconut palms, pandanus, and salt-tolerant plants. Fresh water supply is limited.*

POLITICS
Multiparty elections

1998/2002

HM Queen Elizabeth II

AT THE LAST ELECTION

Parliament of Tuvalu 13 seats

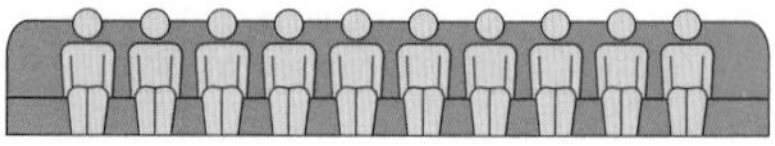

There are no political parties. All members are independent candidates

The 13 MPs, elected every four years, are independents who work in loose political associations. The prime minister, an MP elected by Parliament, works with a cabinet of up to four other MPs. Politics was dominated from independence until 1998 by two men, Tomasi Puapua (now governor-general) and Bikenibeu Paeniu. Faimalaga Luka became prime minister in 2001, after the sudden death of Ionatana Ionatana in December 2000. Day-to-day administration lies in the hands of an elected council on each of Tuvalu's islands.

WORLD AFFAIRS
Joined UN in 2000

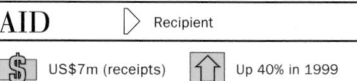

ACP | Comm | PC | PIF | ADB

Tuvalu's admission to the UN was approved by the UN Security Council in 2000. Agreements exist with Taiwan, Korea, and the USA, whose vessels may exploit Tuvalu's fish-rich territorial waters, which extend for 3.2 million square miles. To reflect Tuvalu's growing involvement in world affairs, the Commonwealth admitted it as a full member in mid-2000.

AID
Recipient

US$7m (receipts)

Up 40% in 1999

With a visible trade deficit, aid is crucial to Tuvalu. Most importantly, in 1987 a trust fund was set up, with A$41 million in grants from Australia, New Zealand, and the UK. While support from the UK has reduced, aid from Taiwan and Japan grows. Tuvalu is planning to reduce its reliance on aid through public-sector reform and privatization.

DEFENSE
No compulsory military service

There are no armed forces

Not applicable

Tuvalu has no military. Internal security is the responsibility of the small police force.

T

ECONOMICS

Not available

US$3m

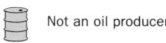

1.5282–1.7997 Australian dollars

SCORE CARD

- WORLD GNP RANKING 191st
- GNP PER CAPITA .... US$330
- BALANCE OF PAYMENTS .... Not available
- INFLATION 3.9%
- UNEMPLOYMENT .... Low

STRENGTHS

Sustainable subsistence economy. EEZ: source of jobs and income. Income from trust fund. US$175 million a year from Internet deal for use of .tv suffix.

WEAKNESSES

World's smallest economy. Physical isolation. Few exports: copra, stamps, garments. Dependence on imports and aid. Remittances from overseas workers set to fall, as Nauru phosphate mines nearly worked out.

EXPORTS

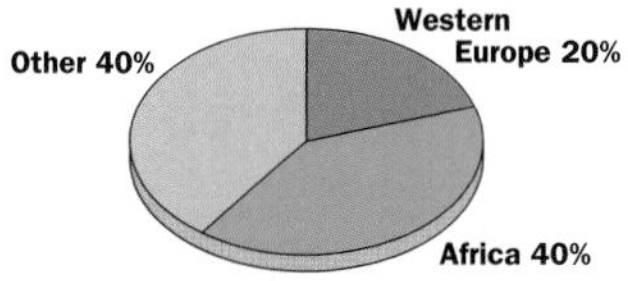
Western Europe 20%
Other 40%
Africa 40%

IMPORTS

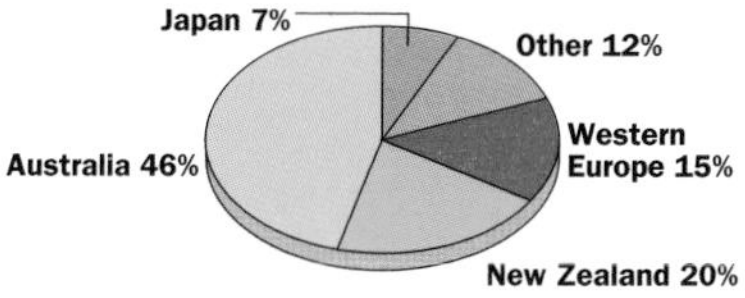
Japan 7%
Other 12%
Western Europe 15%
Australia 46%
New Zealand 20%

RESOURCES

Not available

400 tonnes

Not an oil producer

12,600 pigs, 7000 ducks, 27,000 chickens

None

Tuvalu's resource potential lies in the waters of its 3.2 million-square mile EEZ. Its rich fish stocks are being exploited mainly by foreign boats in return for licensing fees. Hopes of valuable mineral reserves have been raised by the discovery of an undersea mountain in the EEZ. Solar energy is being developed to cut the use of gasoline for power generation. Fuel accounts for about 14% of import costs. The rights to Tuvalu's Internet suffix have been sold to a Canadian media company for up to US$175 million a year.

TUVALU

Total Land Area : 26 sq. km (10 sq. miles)

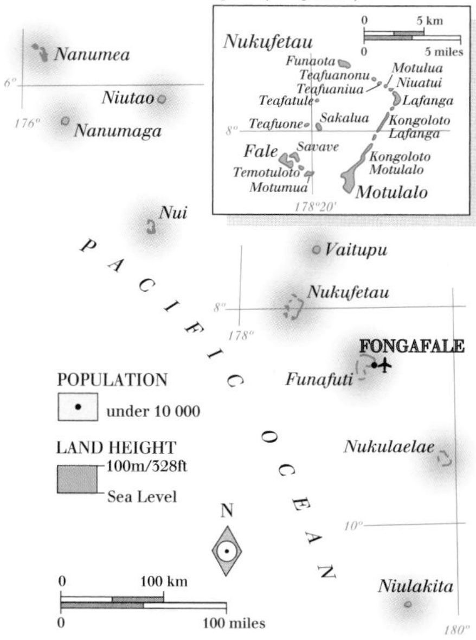
Nanumea
Niutao
Nanumaga
Nui
Vaitupu
Nukufetau
FONGAFALE
Funafuti
Nukulaelae
Niulakita
PACIFIC OCEAN
Nukufetau
Funaota
Teafuanonu
Teafuaniua
Teafatule
Teafuone
Sakalua
Fale
Savave
Temotuloto
Motumua
Motulua
Niuatui
Lafanga
Kongoloto
Lafanga
Kongoloto
Motulalo
Motulalo
0 5 km
0 5 miles
178°20'
6°
176°
8°
178°
10°
180°
N
0 100 km
0 100 miles

POPULATION

under 10 000

LAND HEIGHT

100m/328ft

Sea Level

ENVIRONMENT

Not available

None

Not available

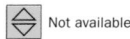

Efforts to protect the environmentally fragile atolls include reafforestation and solar energy projects. On Funafuti, population pressure is leading to overfishing in the atoll lagoon. The "greenhouse effect" is a major concern, since climate changes attributed to it are blamed for a steep rise in cyclone frequency. Any rise in sea levels induced by global warming would quickly submerge the atolls.

MEDIA

TV ownership low

There are no daily newspapers

PUBLISHING AND BROADCAST MEDIA

There are no daily newspapers. The English-language *Tuvalu Echoes* is published fortnightly

No TV service

1 state-owned service

Two bimonthly papers and a religious monthly, *Te Lama*, are the only publications.

CRIME

Death penalty not used

Tuvalu does not publish prison figures

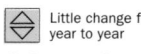

Little change from year to year

Crime is minimal and the result mainly of alcohol-related violence, particularly at the weekends.

EDUCATION

School leaving age: 14

95%

Not available

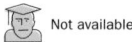

Each island has a primary school. A secondary school and a marine training school are based on Funafuti. Students who attend the University of the South Pacific in Fiji are state-funded.

CHRONOLOGY

The former Ellice Islands, together with the Gilbert Islands, were annexed by the UK in 1892.

- **1974** Ellice Islanders vote to separate from Gilbertese.
- **1978** Independence as Tuvalu.
- **1987** Tuvalu Trust Fund set up.
- **1996–1998** Bikenibeu Paeniu prime minister.
- **2000** Joins UN as 189th member. December, sudden death of Prime Minister Ionatana.

HEALTH

No welfare state health benefits

1 per 1125 people

Malaria, diarrheal, infectious and parasitic diseases

Concerted efforts since independence to improve health care facilities and programs have cut the incidence of communicable diseases. Average life expectancy is higher than other Pacific Island states, but is still lower than the regional mean of 71 years.

SPENDING

GDP/cap. increase

CONSUMPTION AND SPENDING

No data

50 per 1000 population

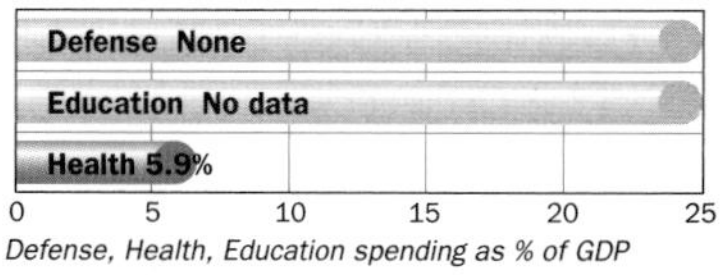
Defense None
Education No data
Health 5.9%
0
5
10
15
20
25

Defense, Health, Education spending as % of GDP

Although living standards are very low, traditional social support systems mean that extreme poverty is rare. Most people rely on fishing and subsistence agriculture, supplemented by remittances from expatriate Tuvaluans.

WORLD RANKING

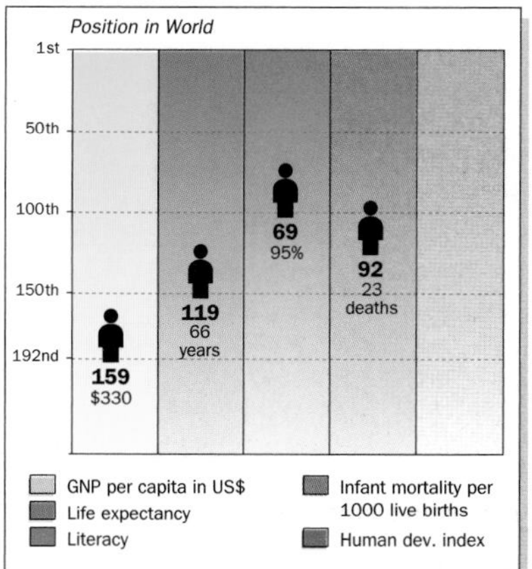
Position in World
1st
50th
100th
150th
192nd
159
$330
119
66
years
69
95%
92
23
deaths
GNP per capita in US$
Life expectancy
Literacy
Infant mortality per 1000 live births
Human dev. index

T

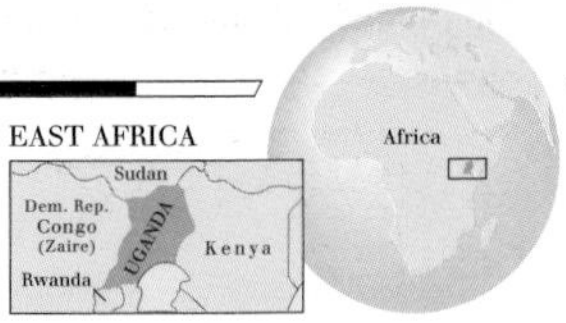
EAST AFRICA
Sudan
Dem. Rep. Congo (Zaire)
UGANDA
Kenya
Rwanda
Africa

UGANDA

OFFICIAL NAME: Republic of Uganda **CAPITAL:** Kampala **POPULATION:** 21.8 million
CURRENCY: New Uganda shilling **OFFICIAL LANGUAGE:** English and Swahili

1962 | 1962 | Oct 9 | EAU | +3 | +256 | .ug

AN EAST AFRICAN COUNTRY of fertile upland plateaus and mountains, Uganda has outlets to the sea through Kenya and Tanzania. Its history from independence in 1962 until 1986 was one of ethnic strife. Since 1986, under President Museveni, peace has been restored and steps have been taken to rebuild the economy and democracy.

Kampala, Uganda's capital. *It has 774,000 inhabitants, but only 25,000 of the city's households are supplied with running water.*

CLIMATE

Tropical wet & dry

WEATHER CHART

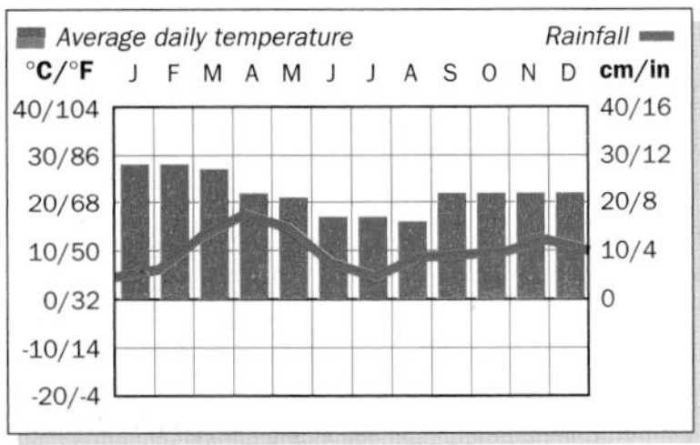
Average daily temperature
Rainfall
°C/°F
J F M A M J J A S O N D
cm/in
40/104
30/86
20/68
10/50
0/32
-10/14
-20/-4
40/16
30/12
20/8
10/4
0

Altitude and the influence of Lake Victoria moderate Uganda's climate. March–May is the wettest period.

TRANSPORTATION

Drive on left

Entebbe International 448,528 passengers

2 ships 5900 dwt

THE TRANSPORTATION NETWORK

1800 km (1118 miles)

None

261 km (162 miles)

Lake Victoria and other lakes are navigable

The government is rebuilding the transportation infrastructure with the help of international aid.

TOURISM

Visitors : Population 1:92

238,000 visitors

Up 5% in 1998

MAIN TOURIST ARRIVALS

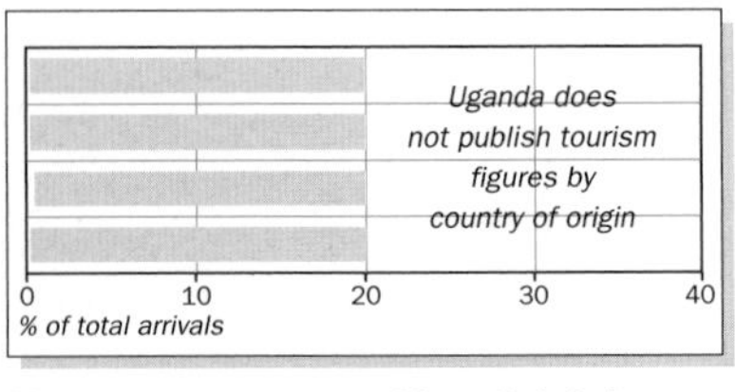
Uganda does not publish tourism figures by country of origin
0
10
20
30
40
% of total arrivals

Major attractions are Uganda's lakes and mountains, notably the rugged Ruwenzori range – the Mountains of the Moon. The brutal murder of eight foreign tourists by Rwandan fighters at the Bwindi national park in March 1999 was a severe setback for Uganda's recovery as a tourist destination.

PEOPLE

Pop. density medium

Luganda, Nkole, Chiga, Lango, Acholi, Teso, Lugbara, English

109/km² (283/mi²)

THE URBAN/RURAL POPULATION SPLIT

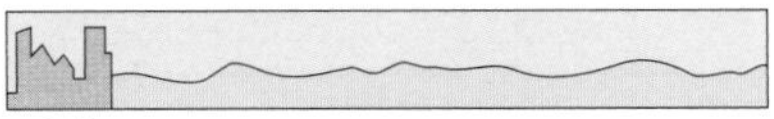
14%
86%

RELIGIOUS PERSUASION

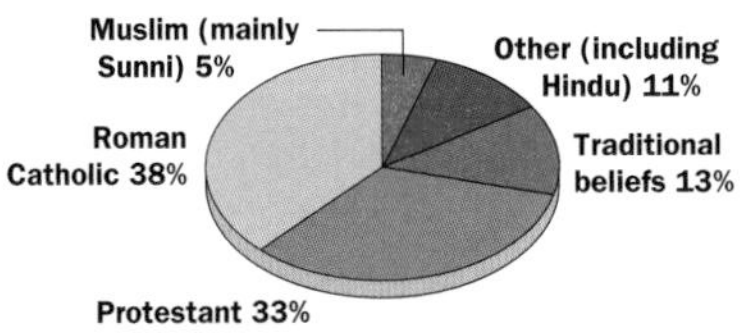
Muslim (mainly Sunni) 5%
Other (including Hindu) 11%
Traditional beliefs 13%
Roman Catholic 38%
Protestant 33%

The predominantly rural population consists of 13 main ethnic groups. Traditional animosities were manipulated by ex-rulers Amin and Obote. Since 1986 President Museveni has worked hard for reconciliation, in 1993 allowing the restoration of the four historical monarchies. Uganda now has one of the best human rights records in Africa.

POLITICS

No multiparty elections

2001/2006

President Yoweri Kaguta Museveni

AT THE LAST ELECTION

Parliament 276 members

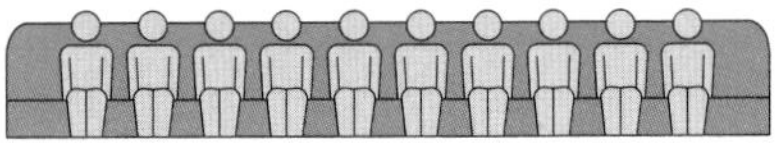

Elections to the Parliament took place on a "no-party" basis in June 2001

Since 1986, President Museveni has run a "no-party democracy," with political parties represented in a broadly based government, but banned from campaigning. Continuing to overcome ethnic tension is the main issue after its catastrophic effect in the 1970s and 1980s. Rebel insurgencies in the north and west led to the deaths, kidnapping, and displacement of tens of thousands of people, and destroyed Uganda's economy. A referendum in June 2000 on a return to full multipartyism resulted in an overwhelming vote of support for the "no-party" system. In 2001, Museveni won another term in office, taking 69% of the vote, and his supporters maintained a clear majority in the legislative elections.

UGANDA

Total Land Area : 199 550 sq. km (77 046 sq. miles)

SUDAN
KENYA
DEM. REP. CONGO (ZAIRE)
TANZANIA
RWANDA
Moyo
Yumbe
Atiak
Kitgum
Kaabong
Loyoro
Kotido
Pager
Arua
Rhino Camp
Albert Nile
Gulu
Achwa
Moroto
Lira
Pakwach
Amudat
Lake Kwania
Kaberamaido
Lake Albert
Butiaba
Masindi
Hoima
Soroti
Lake Bisina
Lake Kyoga
Kafu
Nakasongola
Kapchorwa
Mt Elgon 4321m
Mbale
Nkusi
Victoria Nile
Kaliro
Semliki
Iganga
Tororo
Kabarole
Mubende
Bombo
Owen Falls Dam
Jinja
Margherita Peak 5110m
RUWENZORI
Kasese
Mpigi
KAMPALA
Equator
Katonga
Ntusi
Entebbe
Buvuma I.
Lake George
Kome I.
Lake Edward
Masaka
Bukakata
Bukasa I.
Mbarara
Bugala I.
Rukungiri
Sese Islands
Kagera
Lake Victoria
Kisoro
Kabale
4°
2°
30°
32°
34°

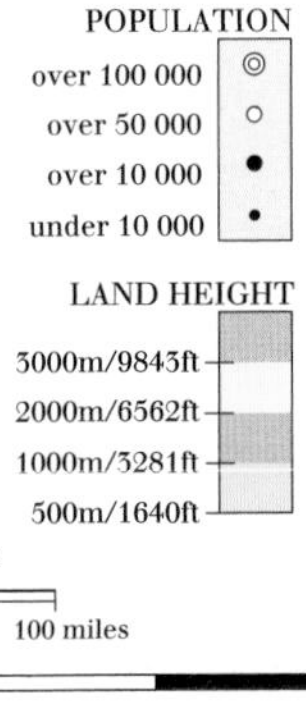
POPULATION
over 100 000
over 50 000
over 10 000
under 10 000
LAND HEIGHT
3000m/9843ft
2000m/6562ft
1000m/3281ft
500m/1640ft
N
0
100 km
0
100 miles

WORLD AFFAIRS

Joined UN in 1962

Comm | COMESA | IGAD | EAC | OIC

Relations with Sudan and Congo (former Zaire) are strained. Conflicts in these countries and in Rwanda have caused a large influx of refugees into Uganda. Uganda's support for anti-government rebels in Sudan appeared to end during 1999. Ugandan forces embroiled in the fighting in Congo (former Zaire) were withdrawn from the front line in 2001.

AID

Recipient

$590m (receipts)

Up 25% in 1999

Aid has risen, mainly from the World Bank and the IMF, encouraged by Uganda's adoption of economic liberalization and private-sector investment policies. Aid has focused on balance of payments support, the rehabilitation of the key transportation sector, and the fight against AIDS.

DEFENSE

No compulsory military service

$199m

Down 13% in 1999

The pre-1986 army was responsible for many atrocities under Amin's rule. During the 1990s, Uganda was preoccupied with conflicts in neighboring countries, particularly Congo (former Zaire), where it supported anti-government rebels. The army has also been deployed to suppress internal rebellions.

ECONOMICS

Inflation 13.8% p.a. (1990–1999)

$6.8bn

1505.0–1767.5 new Uganda shillings

SCORE CARD

- ❑ WORLD GNP RANKING 99th
- ❑ GNP PER CAPITA $320
- ❑ BALANCE OF PAYMENTS .... $–746m
- ❑ INFLATION 6.4%
- ❑ UNEMPLOYMENT .... Widespread

STRENGTHS

Agriculture. Coffee brings in 93% of export earnings. Potential for more export crops. Road system is being repaired. Proinvestment policies.

WEAKNESSES

Lack of skilled workforce. Instability in the subregion affects confidence. World coffee price fluctuations. High transportation costs.

EXPORTS

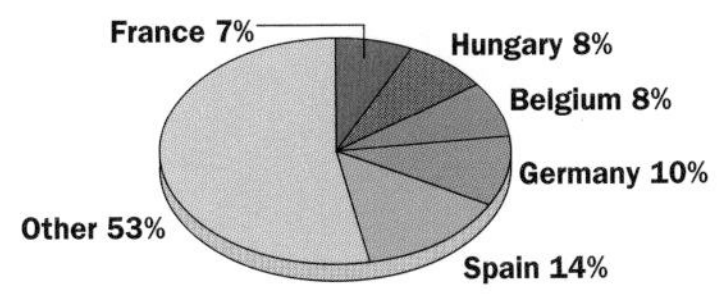
France 7%
Hungary 8%
Belgium 8%
Germany 10%
Spain 14%
Other 53%

IMPORTS

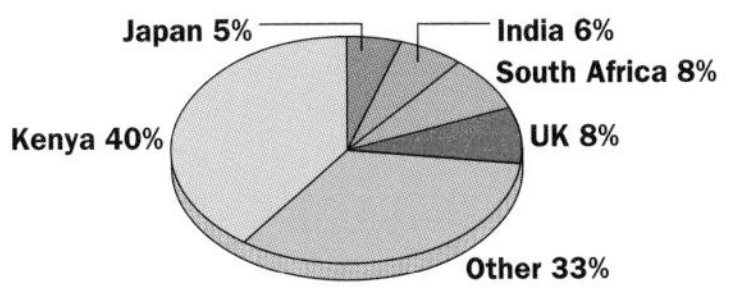
Japan 5%
India 6%
South Africa 8%
UK 8%
Other 33%
Kenya 40%

RESOURCES

Electric power 162,000 kw

218,236 tonnes

Not an oil producer

5.9m cattle, 3.7m goats, 2m sheep, 25m chickens

Copper, cobalt, tin, apatite, magnetite, tungsten, gold

Mineral resources are varied but barely exploited. Uganda has sizable copper deposits. The mines, closed under Obote, are now being reopened. Gold and cobalt mining are also due to resume and oil exploration is under way. Hydroelectric output is being expanded, notably at Owen Falls, with the aim of replacing 50% of oil imports.

ENVIRONMENT

Sustainability rank: 81st

10% (4% partially protected)

0.1 tonnes per capita

Uganda's priority is economic reconstruction, but ecological issues are not ignored. The construction of a huge hydroelectric power station at the Kabalega (Murchison) Falls, above Lake Albert, was canceled, following widespread environmental objections.

MEDIA

TV ownership low

Daily newspaper circulation 2 per 1000 people

PUBLISHING AND BROADCAST MEDIA

There are 5 daily newspapers, *New Vision, The Star, The Monitor, Ngabo,* and *Taifa Uganda Empya*

2 services: 1 state-controlled, 1 independent

4 services: 1 state-controlled, 3 independent

The 13 daily and weekly papers cover the political and religious spectrum; eight are published in English. Only *New Vision* is government-controlled.

CRIME

Death penalty used

10,445 prisoners

Up 12% 1996–1998

Crime levels are low, though theft in Kampala is a growing problem. In 2000, the remains were discovered of 780 followers of the cult of the Restoration of the Ten Commandments of God.

CHRONOLOGY

Uganda's ancient kingdoms were ruled under a British protectorate from 1893 until independence in 1962.

- ❑ **1962–1971** Milton Obote in power.
- ❑ **1971–1986** Ethnic strife, economic collapse under Idi Amin and Obote.
- ❑ **1986** President Museveni in power.
- ❑ **1996** Museveni wins first presidential elections.
- ❑ **2000** Referendum endorses "no-party" system.

EDUCATION

Schooling is not compulsory

67%

34,773 students

All schools charge fees. Enrollment in primary schools is 94%, but only 11% of pupils go on to secondary school.

HEALTH

Welfare state health benefits

1 per 20,000 people

Malaria, respiratory, and diarrheal diseases, measles

A successful education and prevention campaign has reduced the prevalence of HIV/AIDS to about 8%, from a peak of 14% in the early 1990s.

SPENDING

GDP/cap. increase

CONSUMPTION AND SPENDING

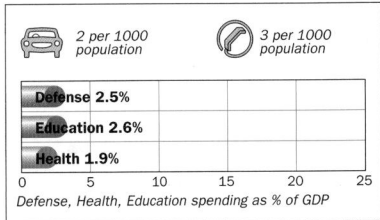

2 per 1000 population

3 per 1000 population

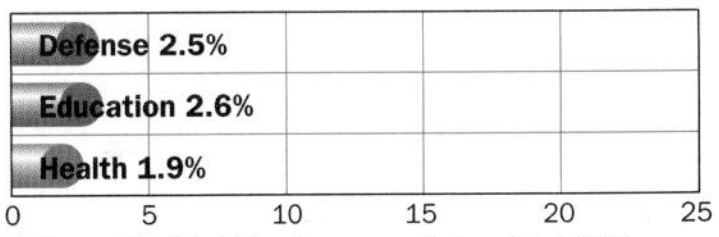
Defense 2.5%
Education 2.6%
Health 1.9%
0
5
10
15
20
25

Defense, Health, Education spending as % of GDP

Uganda has a small but growing middle class. Those close to the government form the wealthiest group. 44% of the population live below the poverty line.

WORLD RANKING

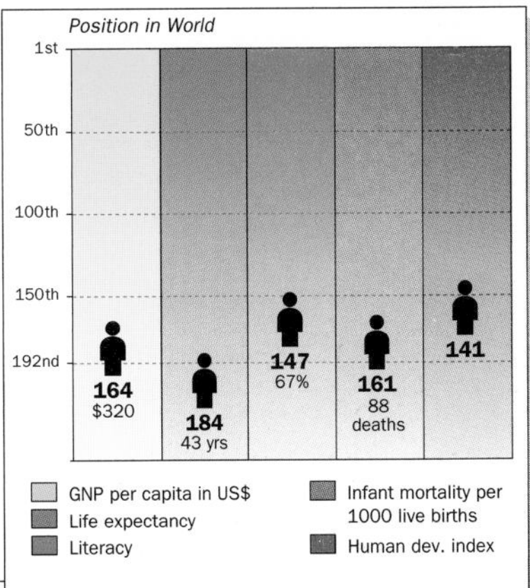
Position in World
1st
50th
100th
150th
192nd
164
$320
184
43 yrs
147
67%
161
88 deaths
141
GNP per capita in US$
Life expectancy
Literacy
Infant mortality per 1000 live births
Human dev. index

U

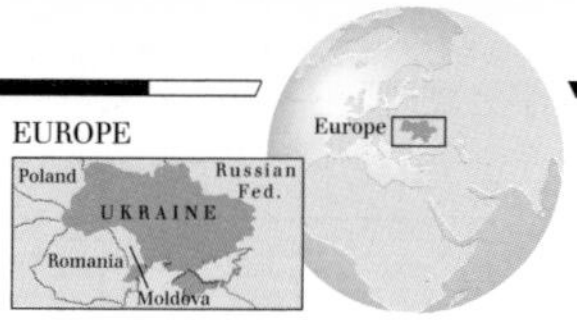
EUROPE
Europe
Poland
Russian Fed.
UKRAINE
Romania
Moldova

UKRAINE

OFFICIAL NAME: Ukraine **CAPITAL:** Kiev
POPULATION: 50.5 million **CURRENCY:** Hryvna **OFFICIAL LANGUAGE:** Ukrainian

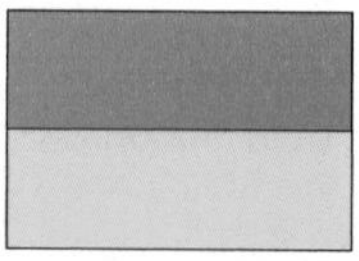

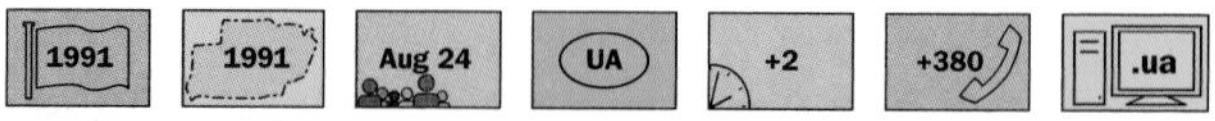
1991
1991
Aug 24
UA
+2
+380
.ua

UKRAINE IS BORDERED by seven states; to the south it lies on the Black Sea and the Sea of Azov. An independent Ukrainian state was established in 1918, but was overrun in the same year by Soviet forces from the east and Polish forces from the west. In 1991, Ukraine again became an independent state. The country has historically been divided between the nationally conscious and Ukrainian-speaking west (including areas which were part of Poland until World War II) and the east, which has a large ethnic Russian population.

***View toward the Cathedral** of the Assumption in Kharkiv. Many Ukrainian cities are equipped with elaborate trolley networks.*

CLIMATE

Continental/steppe/Mediterranean

WEATHER CHART

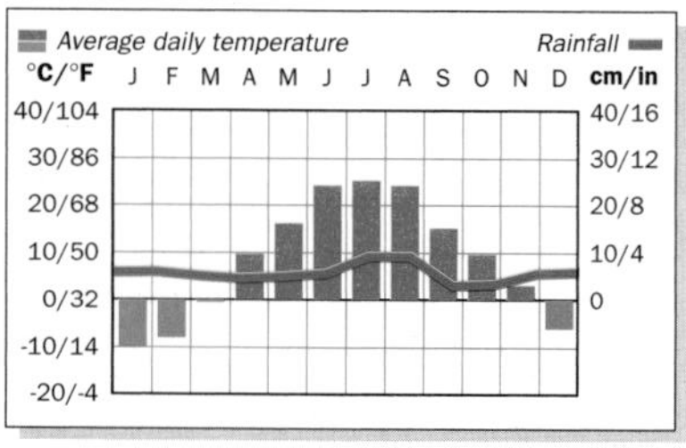
Average daily temperature
Rainfall
°C/°F
J F M A M J J A S O N D
cm/in
40/104
30/86
20/68
10/50
0/32
-10/14
-20/-4
40/16
30/12
20/8
10/4
0

Ukraine has a continental climate, with the exception of the southern coast of Crimea, which has a Mediterranean climate. There are four distinct seasons.

TRANSPORTATION

Drive on right

Boryspiel International, Kiev
1.33m passengers

966 ships
2m grt

THE TRANSPORTATION NETWORK

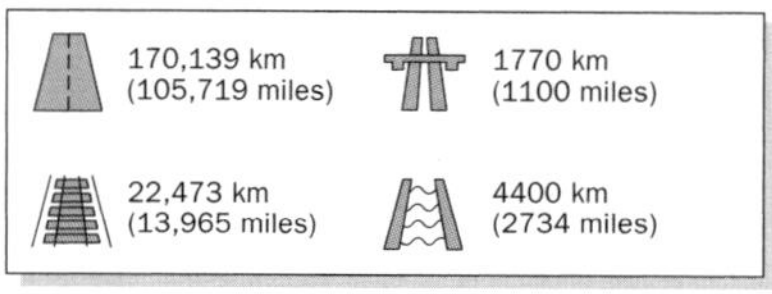
170,139 km
(105,719 miles)
1770 km
(1100 miles)
22,473 km
(13,965 miles)
4400 km
(2734 miles)

There are Soviet-style subways and trolley networks in the major cities. The rail system and the main highway linking Kiev and Lviv are being upgraded. Part of a former submarine port at Sevastopol has been opened to commercial shipping.

TOURISM

Visitors : Population 1:12

4.2m visitors

Down 32% in 1999

MAIN TOURIST ARRIVALS

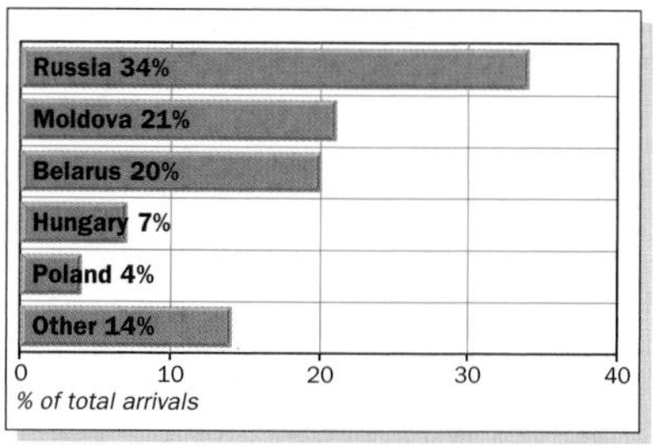
Russia 34%
Moldova 21%
Belarus 20%
Hungary 7%
Poland 4%
Other 14%
0
10
20
30
40
% of total arrivals

Among potential tourist attractions are warm resort areas in Crimea and the south, and the Carpathian Mountains. The government has maintained a highly regulated system of managing tourism, and bureaucratic hurdles have held up the development of Western-style hotels.

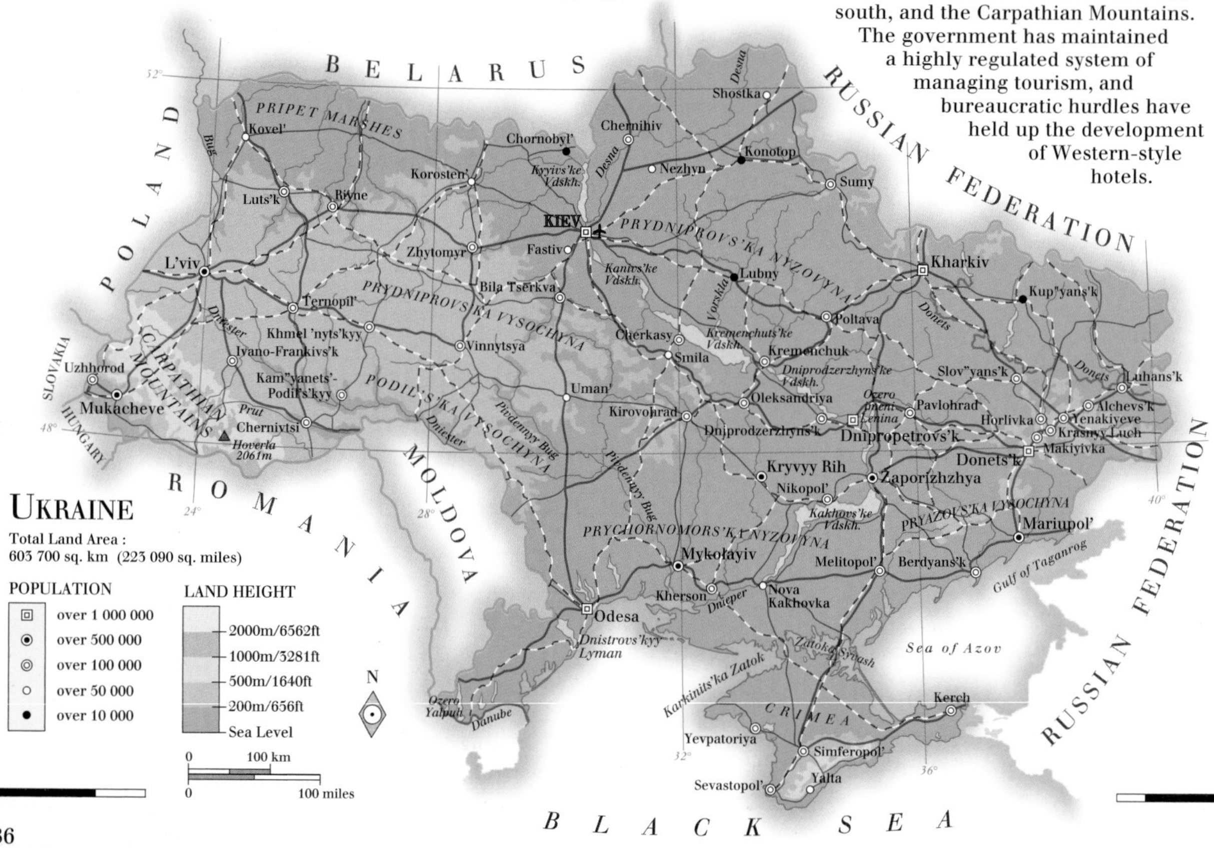
BELARUS
RUSSIAN FEDERATION
POLAND
ROMANIA
MOLDOVA
SLOVAKIA
HUNGARY
BLACK SEA
Sea of Azov
Gulf of Taganrog
PRIPET MARSHES
PRYDNIPROVS'KA NYZOVYNA
PRYDNIPROVS'KA VYSOCHYNA
PODIL'S'KA VYSOCHYNA
PRYCHORNOMORS'KA NYZOVYNA
PRYAZOVS'KA VYSOCHYNA
CARPATHIAN MOUNTAINS
CRIMEA
KIEV
Kharkiv
Dnipropetrovs'k
Donets'k
Odesa
Zaporizhzhya
L'viv
Kryvyy Rih
Mykolayiv
Mariupol'
Luhans'k
Sevastopol'
Simferopol'
Kherson
Chernihiv
Chornobyl'
Shostka
Konotop
Nezhyn
Sumy
Kovel'
Luts'k
Rivne
Korosten'
Zhytomyr
Fastiv
Bila Tserkva
Ternopil'
Khmel 'nyts'kyy
Ivano-Frankivs'k
Uzhhorod
Mukacheve
Kam"yanets'-Podil's'kyy
Chernivtsi
Hoverla 2061m
Vinnytsya
Uman'
Cherkasy
Smila
Kirovohrad
Kremenchuk
Lubny
Poltava
Kup"yans'k
Slov"yans'k
Horlivka
Alchevs'k
Yenakiyeve
Krasnyy Luch
Makiyivka
Pavlohrad
Oleksandriya
Dniprodzerzhyns'k
Nikopol'
Melitopol'
Berdyans'k
Nova Kakhovka
Yevpatoriya
Yalta
Kerch
Kakhovs'ke Vdskh.
Kremenchuts'ke Vdskh.
Kanivs'ke Vdskh.
Kyyivs'ke Vdskh.
Dniprodzerzhyns'ke Vdskh.
Ozero Lenina
Dnistrovs'kyy Lyman
Ozero Yalpuh
Karkinits'ka Zatoka
Zatoka Syvash
Desna
Bug
Dniester
Prut
Vorskla
Donets
Pivdennyy Bug
Dnieper
Danube
52°
48°
24°
28°
32°
36°
40°
UKRAINE
Total Land Area :
603 700 sq. km (223 090 sq. miles)
POPULATION
over 1 000 000
over 500 000
over 100 000
over 50 000
over 10 000
LAND HEIGHT
2000m/6562ft
1000m/3281ft
500m/1640ft
200m/656ft
Sea Level
0
100 km
0
100 miles
N

PEOPLE

Population density medium

Ukrainian, Russian, Tatar

84/km² (217/mi²)

THE URBAN/RURAL POPULATION SPLIT

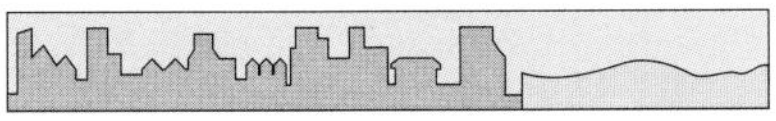

68% 32%

RELIGIOUS PERSUASION

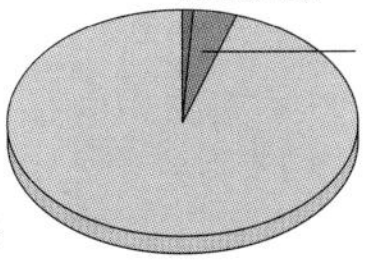
Jewish 1%
Other 4%
Christian (mainly Ukrainian Orthodox) 95%

ETHNIC MAKEUP

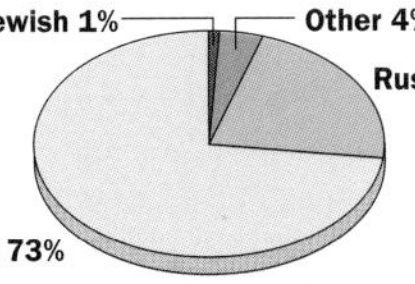
Jewish 1%
Other 4%
Russian 22%
Ukrainian 73%

In the cities and countryside of western Ukraine, Ukrainians make up the vast majority of the population. Russian is spoken by 60% of the people, and in several of the large cities of the east and south, ethnic Russians form a majority, a legacy of 19th-century industrialization, and of more recent migration in the Soviet-era. At independence, most Russians accepted Ukrainian sovereignty, though tensions remain.

In Crimea, however, where Russians make up two-thirds of the population, the central government is wary of separatist tendencies. The Crimea's other main minority, besides ethnic Ukrainians, is the Turkic-speaking Tatar people. Deported en masse to the eastern USSR in 1944 under Stalin, the Tatars have been returning to the Crimea since 1990 and now make up 12% of its population. There is a Romanian-speaking minority in the Odessa region.

POPULATION AGE BREAKDOWN

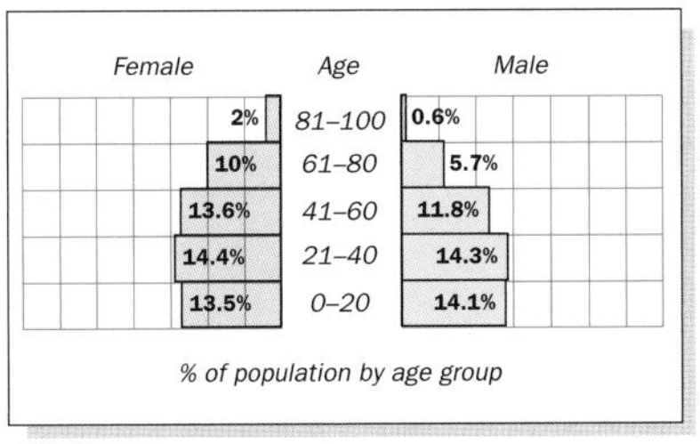
Female
Age
Male
2%
81–100
0.6%
10%
61–80
5.7%
13.6%
41–60
11.8%
14.4%
21–40
14.3%
13.5%
0–20
14.1%
% of population by age group

POLITICS

Multiparty elections

1998/2002

President Leonid Kuchma

AT THE LAST ELECTION

Parliament 450 seats

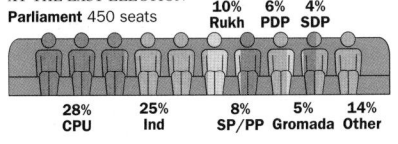

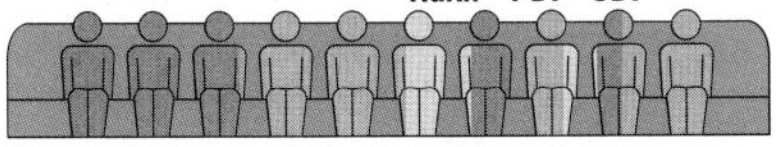
10% Rukh
6% PDP
4% SDP
28% CPU
25% Ind
8% SP/PP
5% Gromada
14% Other

CPU = Communist Party **Ind** = Independents
Rukh = Ukrainian People's Movement
SP/PP = Socialist–Peasants Alliance **PDP** = People's Democratic Party **SDP** = Social Democratic Party
Other includes the Green Party and the Progressive Socialist Party

Ukraine introduced a multiparty system in 1991.

MAIN POLITICAL ISSUES

Economic reform and corruption

There is generally more support for economic reform in western and central Ukraine than in eastern regions. There have been spasmodic efforts to promote the transition to a market economy, notably during 2000 under the then prime minister Yuri Yushchenko. Such radicalism has foundered on opposition in parliament, lack of sufficient backing from Kuchma, and problems of high-level corruption as powerful business and political factions vie to gain advantage.

Separatism among ethnic Russians

The Crimean parliament's declaration of independence in 1994 has been the strongest threat so far to Ukraine's integrity. It was resisted and later rescinded, although Kiev reaffirmed Crimea's status as an autonomous republic. A new Crimean constitution was approved in 1999. Donbass has also pressed for more autonomy, and the Donetsk region has voted to make Russian a joint official language.

PROFILE

Ex-premier Leonid Kuchma, who had defeated Ukrainian nationalist Leonid Kravchuk in the 1994 presidential elections, gained increased powers after 1996 constitutional changes. Multiparty legislative elections were first held in 1994, and the strong position of the communists and allied pro-Kuchma groups was confirmed four years later. Kuchma's own reelection in 1999 was fiercely contested, however, with opponents claiming fraud. and violent confrontations taking place in parliament and on the streets. The boost which Kuchma gained in early 2000 from a referendum backing electoral changes, and Western enthusiasm for his new pro-reform government, was dissipated by a scandal linking him with the murder of a journalist later that year, and the uncovering of massive financial frauds. By mid-2001 Kuchma had replaced Prime Minister Yushchenko after his parliamentary defeat, but the ranks of his opponents included growing numbers of discarded former ministers.

Leonid Kuchma, who became president in 1994.

Yulia Timoshenko, once deputy premier, became a figurehead of the opposition.

WORLD AFFAIRS

Joined UN in 1945

BSEC | CE | CIS | IAEA | OSCE

In the immediate post-independence period, Russia was seen as the major threat. Ukrainians feared that if the pro-Russian regions in Ukraine demanded unification with Russia, it could spark a civil war and encourage Russian intervention. The USA and some European states, on the other hand, regarded Ukraine as a buffer to Russia. Western backing for Ukraine, however, has not made it strong enough to offset its economic dependence on Russia, especially for fuel. Ties with Russia have been strengthened under Kuchma, with a friendship treaty in 1997, a ten-year economic cooperation accord in 1998, and a warm welcome for visiting Russian president Vladimir Putin in early 2001. Ukraine signed a trade agreement with the EU in 1995 and was admitted to the Council of Europe in the same year. Despite an ongoing territorial dispute with Romania, a friendship and cooperation treaty was signed in 1997.

CHRONOLOGY

In 1240, Kiev was conquered by the Mongols. The Ukrainian Cossacks later came under the domination of Lithuania, Poland, and Russia.

- **1918** Independent Ukrainian state after collapse of Russian and Austrian empires. Brest-Litovsk Treaty signed with Germany.
- **1919** Red Army invades. Ukrainian Soviet Socialist Republic proclaimed.
- **1920** Poland invades; western Ukraine under Polish occupation.
- **1922** USSR founded; Ukrainian SSR is one of founder members.
- **1922–1930** Cultural revival under Lenin's "Ukrainianization" policy to pacify national sentiment.
- **1932–1933** "Ukrainianization" policy reversed. Stalin induces famine to eliminate Ukraine as source of opposition; seven million die.

U

CHRONOLOGY *continued*

- **1939** Soviet Union invades Poland and incorporates its ethnic Ukrainian territories into the Ukrainian SSR.
- **1941** Germany invades USSR. 7.5 million Ukrainians die by 1945.
- **1942** Nationalists form Ukrainian Insurgent Army, which wages war against both Germans and Soviets.
- **1954** Crimea ceded to Ukrainian SSR.
- **1972** Widespread arrests of intellectuals and dissidents by Soviet state. Vladimir Shcherbitsky, a Brezhnevite, replaces moderate reformer Petr Shelest as head of Communist Party of Ukraine (CPU).
- **1986** World's worst nuclear disaster at Chernobyl power station.
- **1989** First major coalminers' strike in Donbass. Pro-Gorbachev Volodymyr Ivashko heads CPU.
- **1990** Ukrainian parliament declares Ukrainian SSR a sovereign state. Leonid Kravchuk replaces Ivashko.
- **1991** Government declares full independence, conditional on approval by referendum, supported by 90% of voters. CPU banned. Crimea declared an autonomous republic within Ukrainian SSR.
- **1993** Major strike in Donbass results in costly settlement, which exacerbates budget deficit and stimulates hyperinflation. CPU reestablished at Donetsk congress.
- **1994** Crimea elects Yuri Meshkov as its first president. Leonid Kuchma defeats Kravchuk to become first democratically elected president of Ukraine.
- **1996** Hryvna replaces karbovanets as national currency. New constitution comes into force.
- **1997** Friendship treaty signed with Russia. Accord on Black Sea fleet.
- **1998** Ten-year cooperation agreement with Russia. CPU secures largest number of seats in general election.
- **1999** Reelection of Kuchma. Opposition claims of fraud. Kuchma appoints pro-reform government.
- **2000** Chernobyl site closed.
- **2001** Growing protests linking Kuchma with murder of journalist. May, Kuchma replaces reformist premier after parliamentary defeat.

AID

Recipient

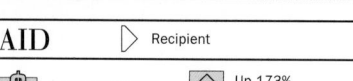

$480m (receipts) — Up 173% 1997–1999

US assistance in the 1990s was the world's fourth-largest aid program, while EU assistance totaled $3.5 billion in 1991–1999. In 2000 lenders pressed for better controls on fund allocations.

DEFENSE

Compulsory military service

$1.44bn — Up 2% in 1999

UKRAINIAN ARMED FORCES

3895 main battle tanks (145 T–55, 2250 T–64, 1230 T–72, 270 T–80)	151,200 personnel
Black Sea fleet: 1 submarine, 1 cruiser, 3 frigates, 10 patrol boats	13,000 personnel
911 combat aircraft (MiG–23, MiG–29, Su–27, Su–25, Su–24)	96,000 personnel
27 ICBM	

Ukraine was a center for arms manufacture under the old Soviet system, and now has a major weapons export trade. A member of the CIS, Ukraine finally resolved in 1997 its long-smoldering dispute with Russia over control of the Black Sea fleet, with agreement on the division of the fleet and a 20-year Russian lease on port facilities in Sevastopol. Meanwhile, the Ukrainian parliament had ratified the START-I nuclear disarmament treaty, and Ukraine's nuclear warheads were transferred to Russia under a trilateral weapons dismantling accord also involving substantial US aid.

In 2000 it was decided that compulsory military service, which lasts 18 months, should be ended by 2015. The armed forces have been slimmed down, with further cuts planned to result in a total strength of 285,000 (including central and administrative staff) by 2005.

Ukraine joined NATO's Partnership for Peace in 1995 and signed a security pact with NATO in 1997, when joint maneuvers were held with NATO forces in the Crimea.

ECONOMICS

Inflation 339.1% p.a. (1990–1999)

$42bn — 5.215–5.435 hryvnas

SCORE CARD

World GNP Ranking	53rd
GNP per Capita	$840
Balance of Payments	$834m
Inflation	15.9%
Unemployment	4%

EXPORTS

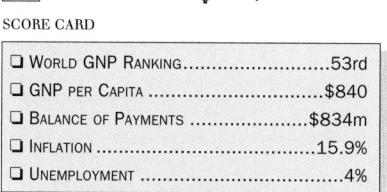

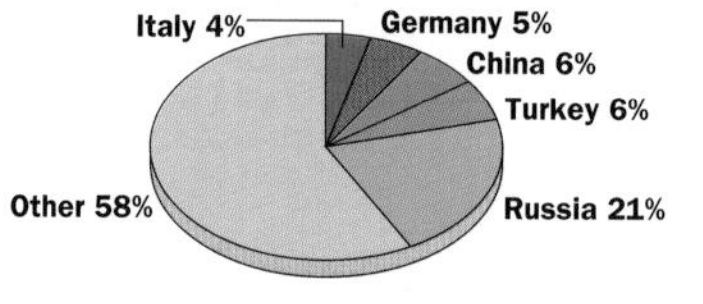
Italy 4%
Germany 5%
China 6%
Turkey 6%
Other 58%
Russia 21%

IMPORTS

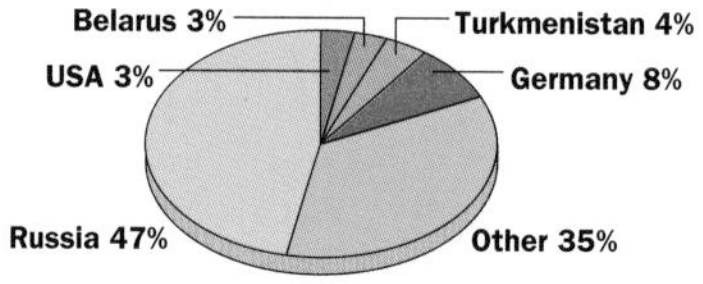
Belarus 3%
Turkmenistan 4%
USA 3%
Germany 8%
Russia 47%
Other 35%

Strengths

Well-educated workforce. Good urban transportation infrastructure. Potential for grain and food export. Mineral reserves. Technological potential, especially in aerospace and computers; many research institutes in these areas.

Weaknesses

Failure to reform centrally planned economy. High inflation. Weak currency. Huge debt. Anti-reform political elites. Inefficient, subsidized manufacturing industries. Corruption.

Profile

For ten years the economy contracted by over half, until real growth was at last recorded in 2000. Privatization of large enterprises has barely begun. There are many traders and street vendors, but bureaucracy stifles private enterprise and investment. Lack of land reform holds back agriculture in the "bread basket" of Europe.

ECONOMIC PERFORMANCE INDICATOR

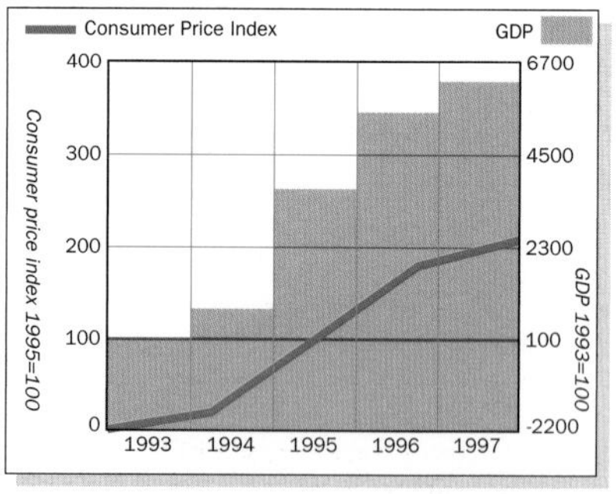
Consumer Price Index
GDP
400
300
200
100
0
6700
4500
2300
100
-2200
Consumer price index 1995=100
GDP 1993=100
1993
1994
1995
1996
1997

UKRAINE : MAJOR BUSINESSES

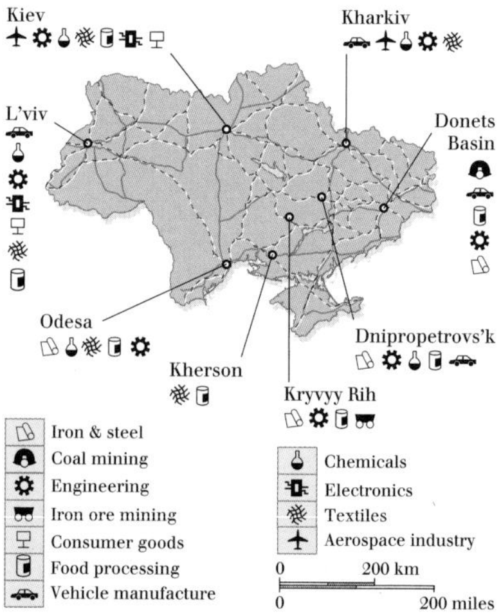
Kiev
Kharkiv
L'viv
Donets Basin
Odesa
Dnipropetrovs'k
Kherson
Kryvyy Rih
Iron & steel
Coal mining
Engineering
Iron ore mining
Consumer goods
Food processing
Vehicle manufacture
Chemicals
Electronics
Textiles
Aerospace industry
0 200 km
0 200 miles

RESOURCES

Electric power 53.8m kw

403,005 tonnes

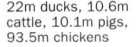

82,766 b/d (reserves 1,601,498,800 bbl)

22m ducks, 10.6m cattle, 10.1m pigs, 93.5m chickens

Coal, iron, oil, natural gas, manganese, lignite, peat, mercury

ELECTRICITY GENERATION

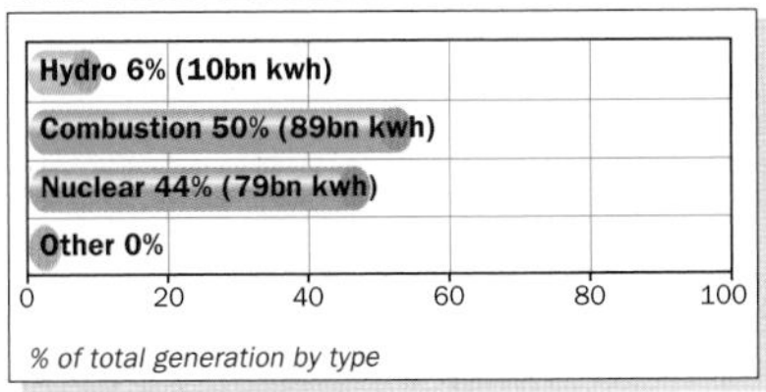

Hydro 6% (10bn kwh)
Combustion 50% (89bn kwh)
Nuclear 44% (79bn kwh)
Other 0%
0
20
40
60
80
100
% of total generation by type

Ukraine imports 80% of its oil and gas (its main source of energy), mostly from Russia. Some gas is instead of transit fees for pipelines carrying Russian gas, but it repeatedly fails to keep up payments for the rest. Yet Ukraine has oil and gas reserves of its own. Just under half of electricity is nuclear-generated. Coal is mined, in appalling safety conditions, mainly in the Donbass–Donetsk region.

Ukraine has 5% of global mineral reserves, including the largest titanium reserves, the third-largest deposits of iron ore, and 30% of global manganese ore. There is also mercury, uranium, nickel, and some gold. The metal industry accounted for nearly 20% of GDP in 1997 and 28% of exports. The steel industry has now begun to grow again after seven years of decline.

UKRAINE : LAND USE

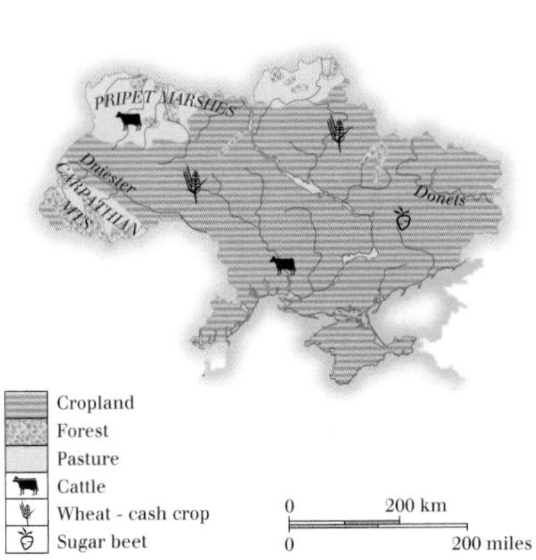

PRIPET MARSHES
Dniester
CARPATHIAN MTS
Donets
Cropland
Forest
Pasture
Cattle
Wheat - cash crop
Sugar beet
0
200 km
0
200 miles

ENVIRONMENT

Sustainability rank: 110th

2%

7.3 tonnes per capita

ENVIRONMENTAL TREATIES

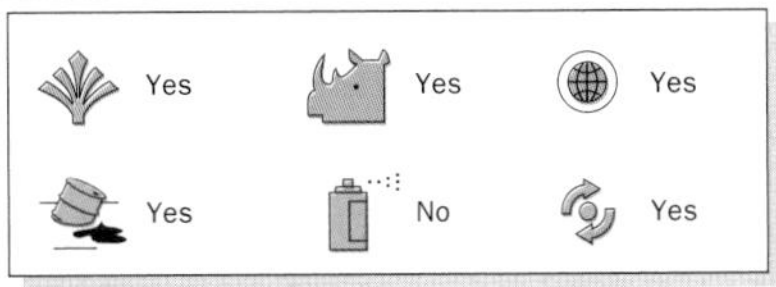

Yes
Yes
Yes
Yes
No
Yes

As a result of the Chernobyl nuclear disaster in 1986 – the world's worst nuclear accident – over three million Ukrainians live in dangerously radioactive areas and 12% of arable land is contaminated. The last working reactor at Chernobyl closed at the end of 2000, under agreements in which Western countries provided large-scale financial assistance. However, nuclear production continues elsewhere because of the cost of Russian oil and gas imports. Coal-fired power stations are old-fashioned, highly polluting, and inefficient. Industrial pollution is widespread, especially from steel and chemical works in the Donbass region, contributing to the acute problem of low air quality in eight major cities.

MEDIA

TV ownership high

Daily newspaper circulation 54 per 1000 people

PUBLISHING AND BROADCAST MEDIA

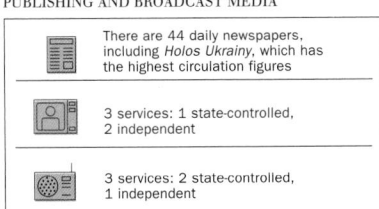

There are 44 daily newspapers, including *Holos Ukrainy*, which has the highest circulation figures

3 services: 1 state-controlled, 2 independent

3 services: 2 state-controlled, 1 independent

Independent, mass-circulation newspapers are published, mainly in Russian. Local TV stations reflect regional political differences.

CRIME

Death penalty not used

203,988 prisoners

Down 4% 1996–1998

CRIME RATES

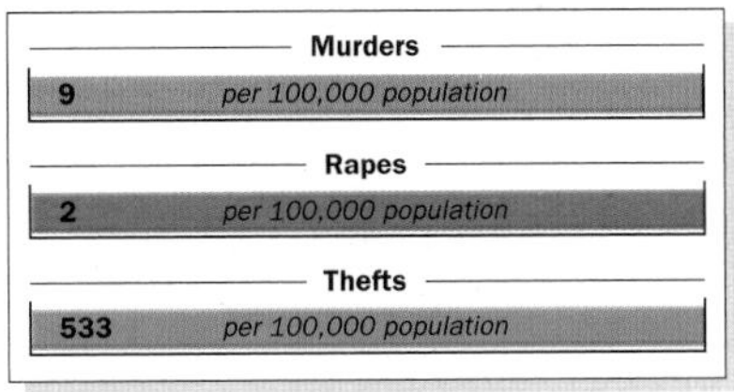

Murders
9
per 100,000 population
Rapes
2
per 100,000 population
Thefts
533
per 100,000 population

Street crime, robberies, violence, and carjackings have increased sharply. Corruption is rampant across the economy. Political killings made headlines, as did the murder in 2000 of journalist Gyorgy Gongadze. In 1999 Anatoliy Onopriyenko was sentenced to death for murdering 52 people. The death penalty was later abolished.

EDUCATION

School leaving age: 15

99%

1.54m students

THE EDUCATION SYSTEM

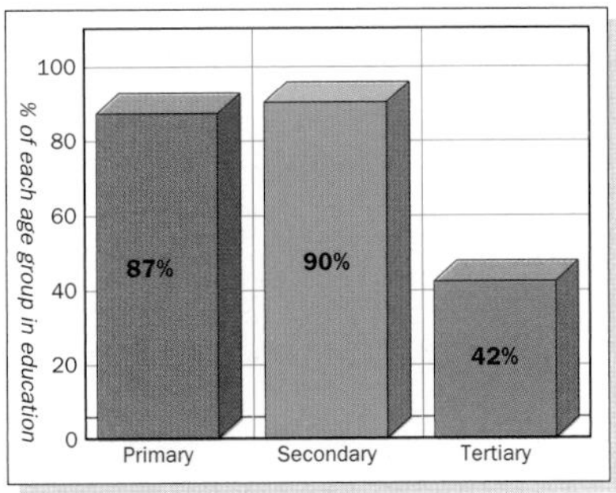

100
80
60
40
20
0
% of each age group in education
87%
90%
42%
Primary
Secondary
Tertiary

Using Ukrainian in schools is the main element in the drive to promote the once-banned language. Some schools in the west no longer teach Russian. Most university teaching is in Russian in eastern regions, and in Ukrainian in those in the west.

HEALTH

Welfare state health benefits

1 per 222 people

Heart disease, cancers, accidents, violence, tuberculosis

Health care, supposedly free to all, has declined significantly in the post-Soviet period. Even basic medical supplies are inadequate. A $2 million UN program provides treatment and preventive care for the 350,000 people who dealt with the Chernobyl disaster.

SPENDING

GDP/cap. decrease

CONSUMPTION AND SPENDING

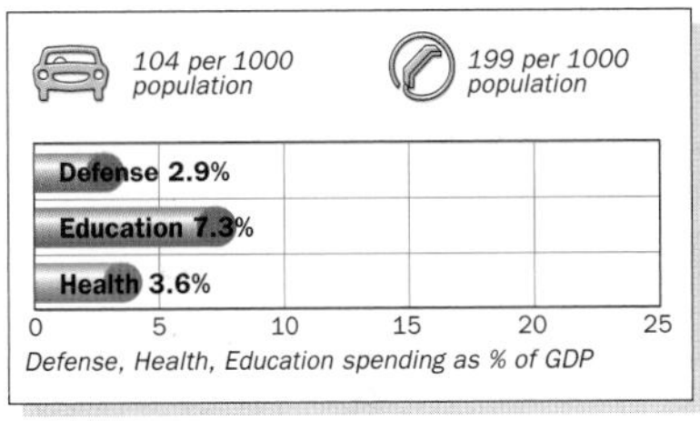

104 per 1000 population
199 per 1000 population
Defense 2.9%
Education 7.3%
Health 3.6%
0
5
10
15
20
25
Defense, Health, Education spending as % of GDP

The gap between rich and poor has widened significantly. Wage arrears – and massive hidden unemployment – are major problems.

WORLD RANKING

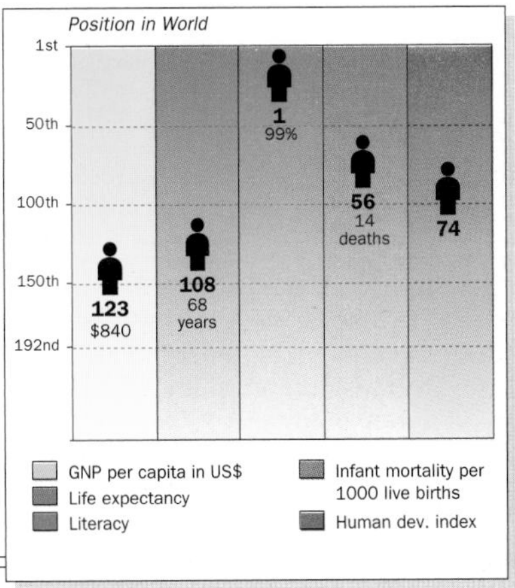

Position in World
1st
50th
100th
150th
192nd
123
$840
108
68
years
1
99%
56
14
deaths
74
GNP per capita in US$
Life expectancy
Literacy
Infant mortality per 1000 live births
Human dev. index

U

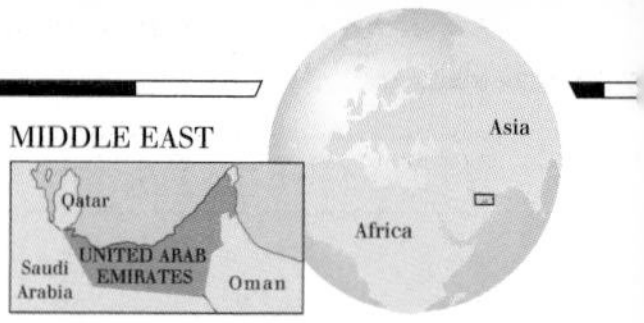
MIDDLE EAST
Asia
Africa
Qatar
Saudi Arabia
UNITED ARAB EMIRATES
Oman

UNITED ARAB EMIRATES

OFFICIAL NAME: United Arab Emirates **CAPITAL:** Abu Dhabi
POPULATION: 2.4 million **CURRENCY:** UAE dirham **OFFICIAL LANGUAGE:** Arabic

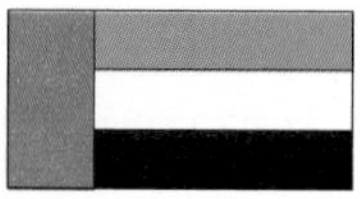

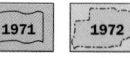

1971 | 1972 | Dec 2 | UAE | +4 | +971 | .ae

THE ARAB WORLD'S only working federation, the United Arab Emirates (UAE) shares borders with Oman, Saudi Arabia, and Qatar, as well as a disputed maritime boundary with Iran. The UAE is mostly semiarid desert relieved by occasional oases. The cities, watered by extensive irrigation systems, have lavish greenery. The UAE's economic prosperity once relied on pearls, but it is now a sizable gas and oil exporter, and has a growing services sector.

CLIMATE

Hot desert

WEATHER CHART

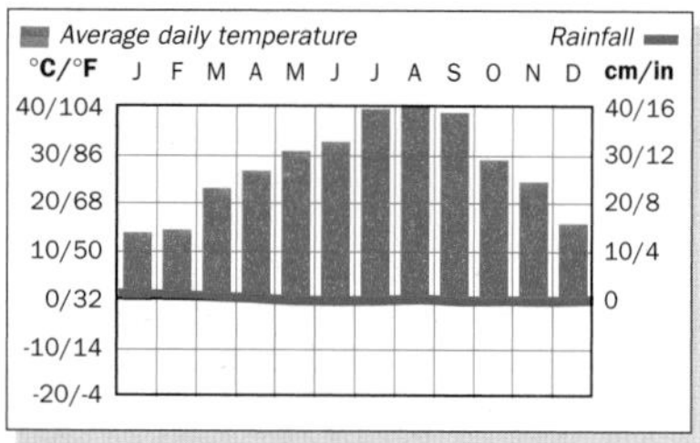
Average daily temperature
Rainfall
°C/°F
J F M A M J J A S O N D
cm/in
40/104
30/86
20/68
10/50
0/32
-10/14
-20/-4
40/16
30/12
20/8
10/4
0

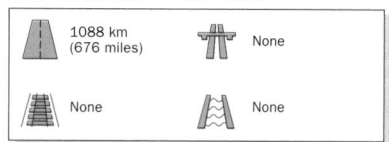

Although rainfall is minimal, summers are humid. Sand-laden *shamal* winds often blow in winter and spring.

TRANSPORTATION

Drive on right

Dubai International 10.75m passengers

332 ships 933,000 grt

THE TRANSPORTATION NETWORK

1088 km (676 miles)

None

None

None

The roads are good. Five of the seven emirates have international airports, of which the busiest is Dubai International.

TOURISM

Visitors : Population 1:1

2.5m visitors

Up 14% in 1999

MAIN TOURIST ARRIVALS

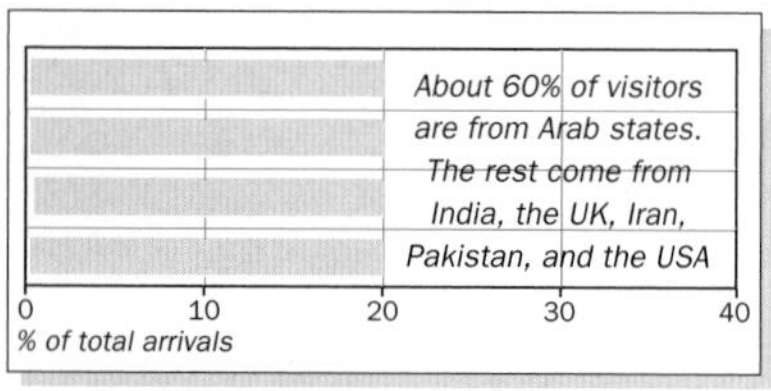
About 60% of visitors are from Arab states. The rest come from India, the UK, Iran, Pakistan, and the USA
0
10
20
30
40
% of total arrivals

Until the mid-1980s, tourism was minimal. Led by Dubai, the UAE has now launched initiatives to attract visitors during the Western winter for sunshine, heritage, water sports, desert safaris, and duty-free shopping.

PEOPLE

Pop. density low

Arabic, Persian, Indian and Pakistani languages, English

29/km² (74/mi²)

THE URBAN/RURAL POPULATION SPLIT

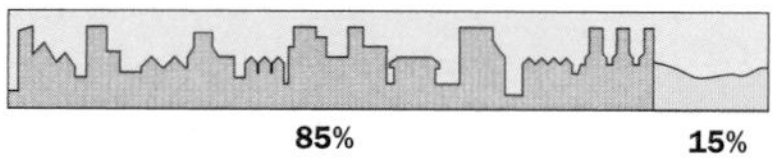
85%
15%

ETHNIC MAKEUP

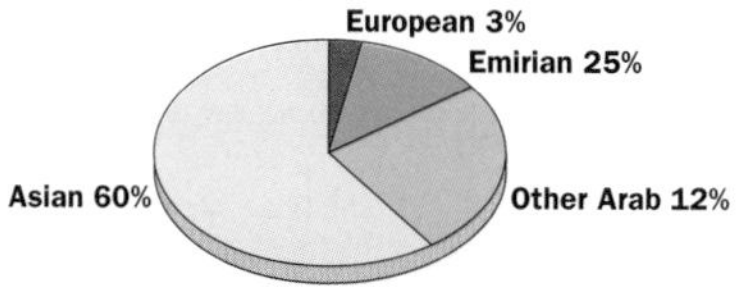
European 3%
Emirian 25%
Asian 60%
Other Arab 12%

UAE nationals are largely city dwellers, with Abu Dhabi and Dubai the dominant centers. They are mostly conservative Sunni Muslims of Bedouin descent. They are greatly outnumbered by expatriates who arrived in the 1970s during the oil boom.

There is a Shi'a community in Dubai with links to Iran. The Western expatriate community is permitted a virtually unrestricted lifestyle. Islamic fundamentalism, however, is a growing force among the young.

Poverty is rare in the UAE. The government remains the biggest employer. Women in theory enjoy equal rights with men. A Presidential Marriage Fund discourages UAE men from taking foreign wives.

POLITICS

No multiparty elections

Not applicable

President Shaikh Zayed bin Sultan al-Nahyan

LEGISLATIVE OR ADVISORY BODIES

Federal National Council 40 seats

There are no political parties. The method of appointment of members of the Federal National Council is determined individually by each of the seven members of the Federation.

The UAE's seven emirates – Abu Dhabi, Dubai, Sharjah, Ras al Khaimah, Ajman, Umm al Qaiwain, and Fujairah – are dominated by their ruling families. The main personalities are the ruler of Abu Dhabi, Shaikh Zayed, who holds the UAE presidency, and the four al-Maktoum brothers who control Dubai. The eldest, Shaikh Maktoum al-Maktoum, is ruler of Dubai and vice president and prime minister of the UAE.

President Zayed has relaunched the advisory Federal National Council in response to criticism of the lack of democracy. The growth of Islamic fundamentalism is also a concern. The freedoms granted to Westerners have aroused some anger but, for economic reasons, they are unlikely to be withdrawn.

UNITED ARAB EMIRATES

Total Land Area : 83 600 sq. km (32 278 sq. miles)

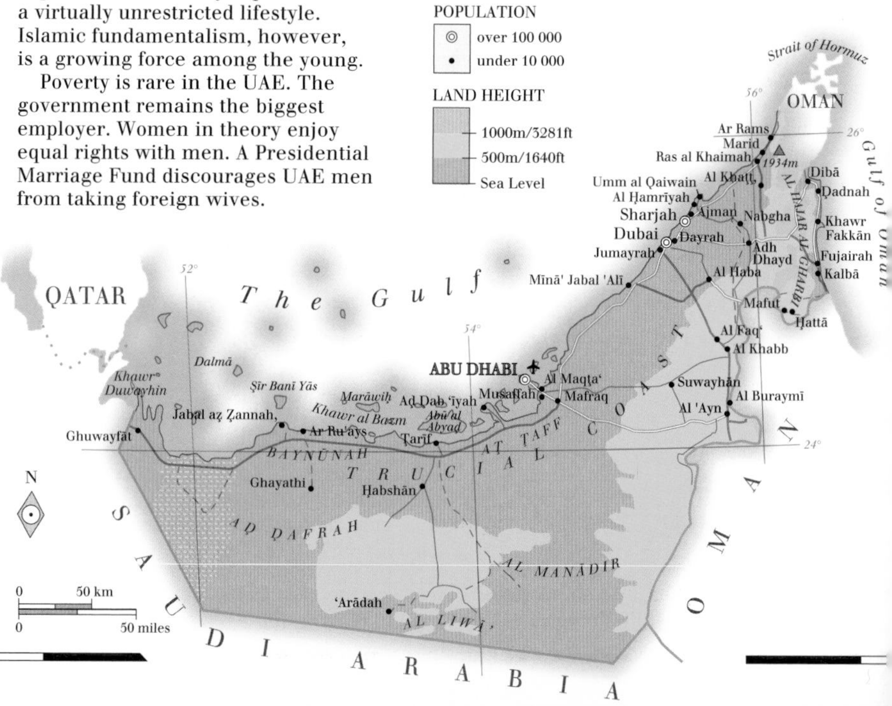
POPULATION
over 100 000
under 10 000
LAND HEIGHT
1000m/3281ft
500m/1640ft
Sea Level
Strait of Hormuz
OMAN
Ar Rams
Marid
Ras al Khaimah
1934m
Umm al Qaiwain
Al Ḩamrīyah
Sharjah
Ajman
Dubai
Dayrah
Jumayrah
Dibā
Dadnah
Masāfi
Khawr Fakkān
Fujairah
Kalbā
Al Ḩaba
Adh Dhayd
Mīnā' Jabal 'Alī
Mafut
Ḩattā
Al Faqa'
Al Khabb
QATAR
The Gulf
Dalmā
Khawr Duwayhin
Şīr Banī Yās
Jabal az Zannah
Marāwiḩ
Khawr al Bazm
Ad Dab'iyah
Abū al Abyaḑ
ABU DHABI
Al Maqta'
Musaffah
Mafraq
Suwayhān
Al Buraymī
Al 'Ayn
Ghuwayfāt
Ar Ru'ays
Tarif
BAYNŪNAH
Ghayathi
Ḩabshān
TRUCIAL COAST
AḐ DAFRAH
AL MANĀDIR
'Arādah
AL LIWĀ
SAUDI ARABIA
OMAN
Gulf of Oman
N
0
50 km
50 miles

WORLD AFFAIRS

Joined UN in 1971

AL | OIC | GCC | OAPEC | OPEC

The UAE is well known as an advocate of moderation within the Arab world. It maintains close links with most OECD states, especially the UK and the USA. In 1992, conflict flared when Iran seized control of three islands in the Strait of Hormuz. Attempts are being made to settle the dispute through diplomacy.

AID

Donor

$92m (donations) — Up 46% in 1999

Once a generous donor to developing countries, the UAE's contributions have fluctuated with energy prices.

DEFENSE

No compulsory military sevice

$3.19bn — Up 4% in 1999

Training of UAE forces is limited, and personnel are mainly drawn from other Arab states and the Indian subcontinent. During the 1991 Gulf War, UAE air bases were used by Western forces for strikes against Iraq. There were military defense agreements with the USA in 1994, and France in 1995, and a $8 billion purchase of jets and missiles from Lockheed Martin in 2000.

ECONOMICS

Inflation 2.4% p.a. (1990–1998)

$48.7bn — 3.6729–3.6730 UAE dirhams

SCORE CARD

❑ World GNP Ranking	49th
❑ GNP per Capita	$17,870
❑ Balance of Payments	$24.3bn
❑ Inflation	1.6%
❑ Unemployment	None

STRENGTHS

Oil and gas reserves are the fourth-biggest in OPEC. Soaring oil prices in 2000. Development of service industries and manufacturing sector. Since 2000, regional tax-free base for e-commerce.

WEAKNESSES

Lack of skilled manpower. Most raw materials and foodstuffs have to be imported. Water resources scarce.

EXPORTS

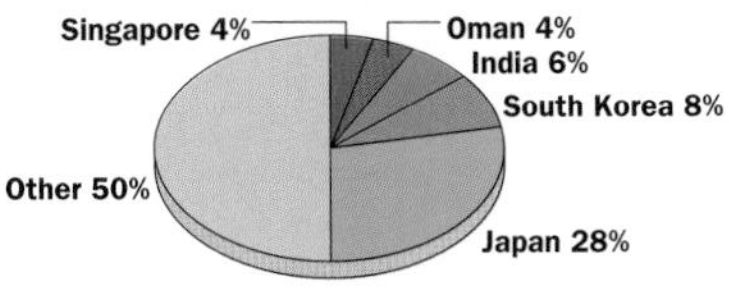
Singapore 4%
Oman 4%
India 6%
South Korea 8%
Other 50%
Japan 28%

IMPORTS

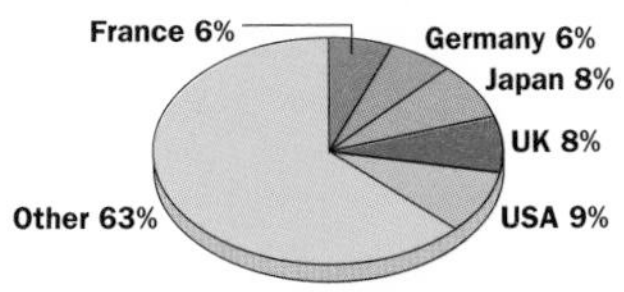
France 6%
Germany 6%
Japan 8%
UK 8%
Other 63%
USA 9%

RESOURCES

Electric power 5.6m kw

114,358 tonnes — 2.5m b/d (reserves 97,800,000,000 bbl)

1.05m goats, 440,000 sheep, 195,000 camels — Oil, natural gas

The UAE is a major exporter of crude oil and natural gas. Oil production accounts for a great part of export revenue. Mina Jabal Ali in Dubai is the world's largest man-made port and has attracted companies from more than 50 countries. Saadiyat Island off Abu Dhabi is being developed as a financial resort.

ENVIRONMENT

Not available

None — 32 tonnes per capita

Despite its harsh desert climate, there is a rich variety of plants and animals. Shaikh Zayed champions conservation parks to avert the threat from hunting.

MEDIA

TV ownership high

Daily newspaper circulation 170 per 1000 people

PUBLISHING AND BROADCAST MEDIA

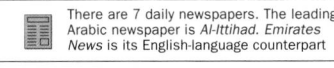

There are 7 daily newspapers. The leading Arabic newspaper is *Al-Ittihad. Emirates News* is its English-language counterpart

4 state-owned services — 7 state-owned services

Satellite TV is unrestricted. Dubai Media City, opened in 2001, promotes greater press freedoms.

CRIME

Death penalty used

The UAE does not publish prison figures — Down 76% 1996–1998

Street crime and muggings are rare. However, Dubai has a reputation as a transit point for narcotics.

***An oasis village**, inland from Fujairah, now accessible through a well-developed network of new roads.*

CHRONOLOGY

The UAE was influenced by the Portuguese and the Ottomans, but British control became dominant in the 19th century.

- ❑ **1971** The UK withdraws as protecting power and the UAE federation is formed.
- ❑ **1991** UAE offers bases to Western forces after Kuwait is invaded.

EDUCATION

School leaving age: 12

76% — 16,213 students

UAE citizens enjoy completely free education. Zayed University was set up in three emirates in 1998.

HEALTH

Welfare state health benefits

1 per 556 people — Circulatory and respiratory diseases, cancers

A high-quality system of primary health care is in place for all UAE citizens, with hospitals able to carry out most operations.

SPENDING

GDP/cap. increase

CONSUMPTION AND SPENDING

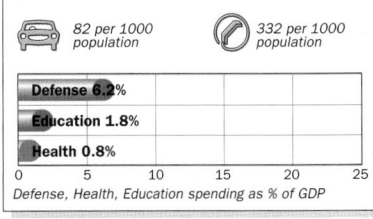

82 per 1000 population — *332 per 1000 population*

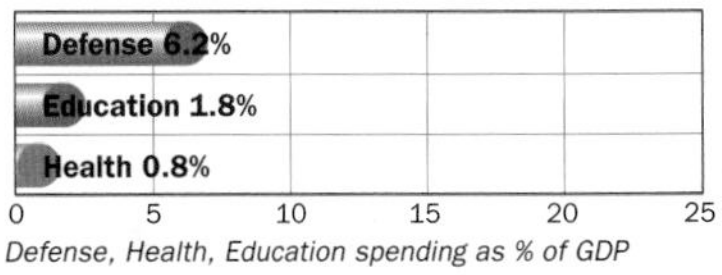
Defense 6.2%
Education 1.8%
Health 0.8%
0
5
10
15
20
25
Defense, Health, Education spending as % of GDP

UAE nationals have the highest per capita income in the Arab world. There is no income tax and oil revenues subsidize public services. Government policies encourage entrepreneurs.

WORLD RANKING

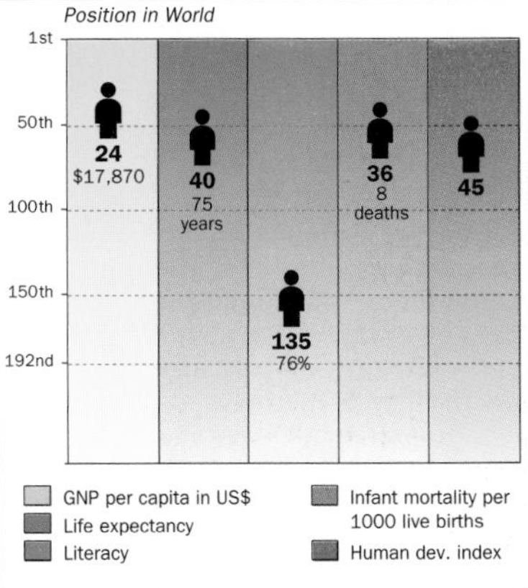
Position in World
1st
50th
100th
150th
192nd
24
$17,870
40
75
years
135
76%
36
8
deaths
45
GNP per capita in US$
Life expectancy
Literacy
Infant mortality per 1000 live births
Human dev. index

U

UNITED KINGDOM

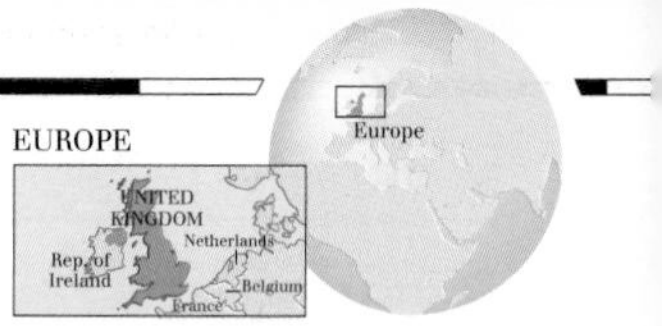
EUROPE
UNITED KINGDOM
Netherlands
Rep. of Ireland
Belgium
France
Europe

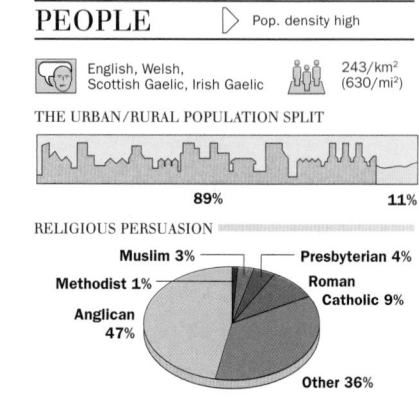

OFFICIAL NAME: United Kingdom of Great Britain and Northern Ireland **CAPITAL:** London
POPULATION: 58.8 million **CURRENCY:** Pound sterling **OFFICIAL LANGUAGES:** English, Welsh (in Wales)

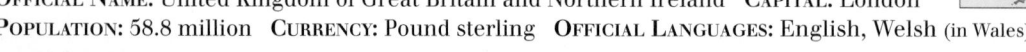

1707
1922
None
GB
0
+44
.uk

LYING IN NORTHWESTERN Europe, the United Kingdom (UK) occupies the major portion of the British Isles. It includes the countries of England, Scotland, and Wales, the constitutionally distinct region of Northern Ireland, and several outlying islands. Its only land border is with the Republic of Ireland. The UK is separated from the European mainland by the English Channel and the North Sea. To the west lies the Atlantic Ocean. Most of the population live in towns and cities and, in England, is fairly well scattered. The most densely populated region is the southeast. Scotland is the wildest region, with the Highlands less populated today than in the 18th century. The UK joined the European Communities (EC – later the EU) in 1973, and most of its trade is now with its European partners. Membership of the UN Security Council also gives the UK a prominent role in international diplomacy.

CLIMATE

Maritime

WEATHER CHART

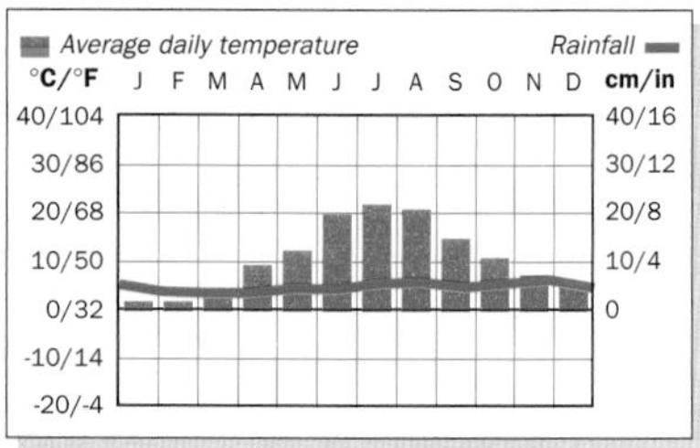
Average daily temperature
Rainfall
°C/°F
J F M A M J J A S O N D
cm/in
40/104
30/86
20/68
10/50
0/32
-10/14
-20/-4
40/16
30/12
20/8
10/4
0

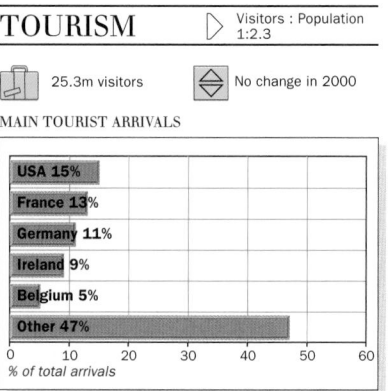

The UK has a generally mild, temperate, and highly changeable climate. Rain, regarded as synonymous with Britain's weather, is fairly well distributed throughout the year, but recently unusually long dry or wet spells have caused water shortages in some areas, and flooding in others. The west is generally wetter than the east, and the south warmer than the north.

TRANSPORTATION

Drive on left

Heathrow, London
62.3m passengers

1421 ships
4.1m grt

THE TRANSPORTATION NETWORK

371,603 km (230,903 miles)

3303 km (2052 miles)

17,064 km (10,604 miles)

5700 km (3542 miles)

The government has not fulfilled its 1997 campaign promise of a more integrated policy, faced with congestion, pollution, and motorists' resentment of high fuel taxes. The rail services, after the rushed privatization of the 1990s, suffer from underinvestment, maintenance problems, and fragmented services. Britain still has no high-speed rail link to the Channel Tunnel, which opened in 1994.

TOURISM

Visitors : Population 1:2.3

25.3m visitors

No change in 2000

MAIN TOURIST ARRIVALS

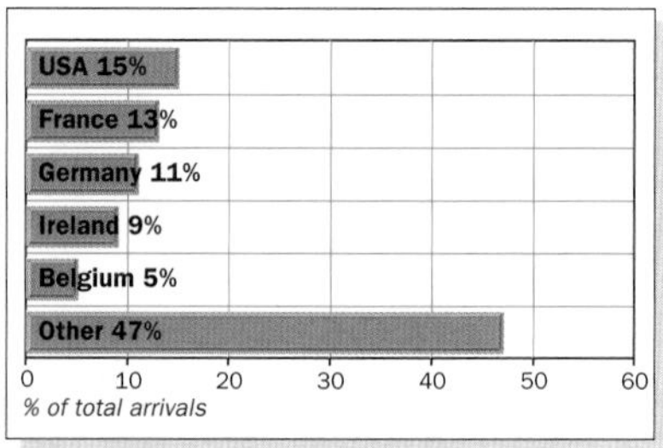
USA 15%
France 13%
Germany 11%
Ireland 9%
Belgium 5%
Other 47%
0
10
20
30
40
50
60
% of total arrivals

The UK ranks fifth in the world as a tourist destination. Tourism is among the country's most important industries and a growing source of employment. Heritage is the principal selling point, North Americans, French, and Germans are the main visitors, and London, with its art galleries, theaters, and historic buildings, remains the major destination. Visitors also head for the Roman splendors of Bath, the Shakespearean associations of Stratford-upon-Avon, the medieval buildings of Oxford and York, and Scotland, where the Highlands are a particular attraction.

***Oxford,** home to the oldest university in the UK. Teaching began in 1096; the first college was founded in 1249. One of the city's finest buildings is the 17th-century semi-oval Sheldonian Theatre.*

PEOPLE

Pop. density high

English, Welsh, Scottish Gaelic, Irish Gaelic

243/km² (630/mi²)

THE URBAN/RURAL POPULATION SPLIT

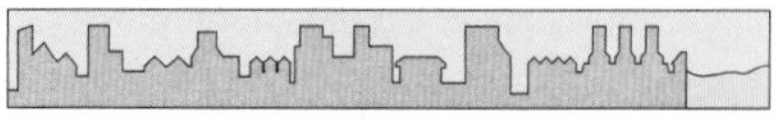
89%
11%

RELIGIOUS PERSUASION

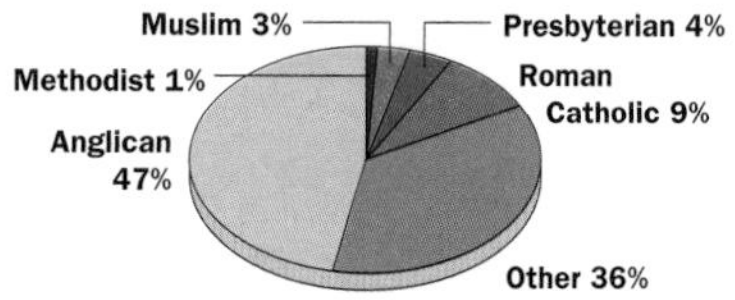
Muslim 3%
Presbyterian 4%
Methodist 1%
Roman Catholic 9%
Anglican 47%
Other 36%

ETHNIC MAKEUP

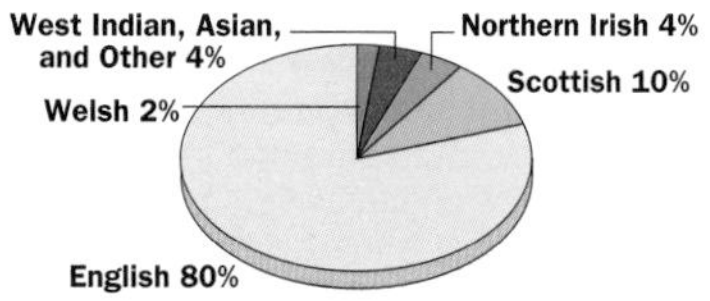
West Indian, Asian, and Other 4%
Northern Irish 4%
Scottish 10%
Welsh 2%
English 80%

The UK ranks 21st for population size but sixth for density. The Scottish and Welsh nations remain recognizably distinct, government has recently become more devolved, and Scots also retain their own legal and educational systems.

Britain's ethnic minorities account for less than 5% of the total population. Over 50% were born in Britain. Ethnic minority communities are generally concentrated in the inner cities, where they face problems of deprivation and social stress, and may also suffer from isolation, particularly among women. Although there is little support for overt racist politics, multi-ethnic recruitment has made little progress in key areas such as policing, and prejudices persist. The level of institutionalized racism was criticized by the UN in 2000.

One-third of all births occur outside marriage, compared with 12% in 1980, but most of these are to cohabiting couples. Single-parent households account for one-fifth of all families with children under 18.

POPULATION AGE BREAKDOWN

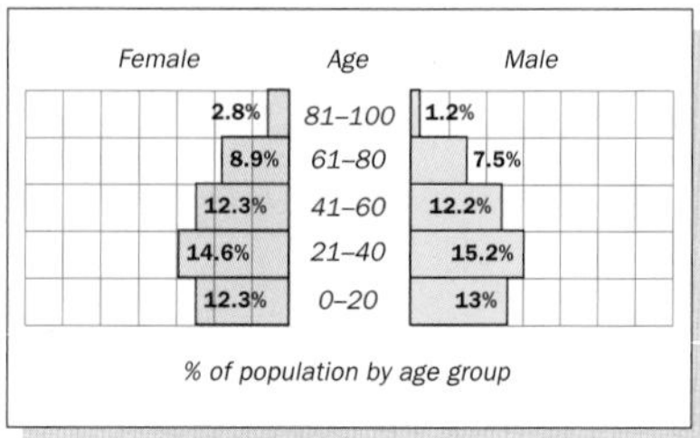
Female
Age
Male
2.8%
81–100
1.2%
8.9%
61–80
7.5%
12.3%
41–60
12.2%
14.6%
21–40
15.2%
12.3%
0–20
13%
% of population by age group

***Black Mount, Rannoch Moor,** in the Scottish Highlands. The Highlands are one of the UK's wildest regions.*

CHRONOLOGY

Great Britain began the 20th century as one of the world's most advanced economies, backed by a massive trading empire.

- ❑ **1906** Reformist Liberal government.
- ❑ **1914** World War I begins.
- ❑ **1918** Armistice signals end of war. Cost to Britain: 750,000 dead.
- ❑ **1921** Irish Free State agreed.
- ❑ **1926** General Strike.
- ❑ **1929** World stock market crash. Widespread unemployment.
- ❑ **1931** UK leaves gold standard and devalues pound.
- ❑ **1936** Edward VIII abdicates over marriage to Mrs. Simpson.
- ❑ **1938** Prime Minister Neville Chamberlain meets Hitler in Munich over Czech crisis, says threat of war with Germany averted.
- ❑ **1939** Germany invades Poland. UK declares war on Germany. Start of World War II.
- ❑ **1940** Winston Churchill prime minister. Battle of Britain.
- ❑ **1944** 6 June, D-Day invasion of German-occupied France.
- ❑ **1945** End of World War II. War costs 330,000 British lives. Labour government comes to power on social welfare platform.
- ❑ **1946** Nationalization of Bank of England, railroads, coal, utilities.
- ❑ **1947** Indian independence.

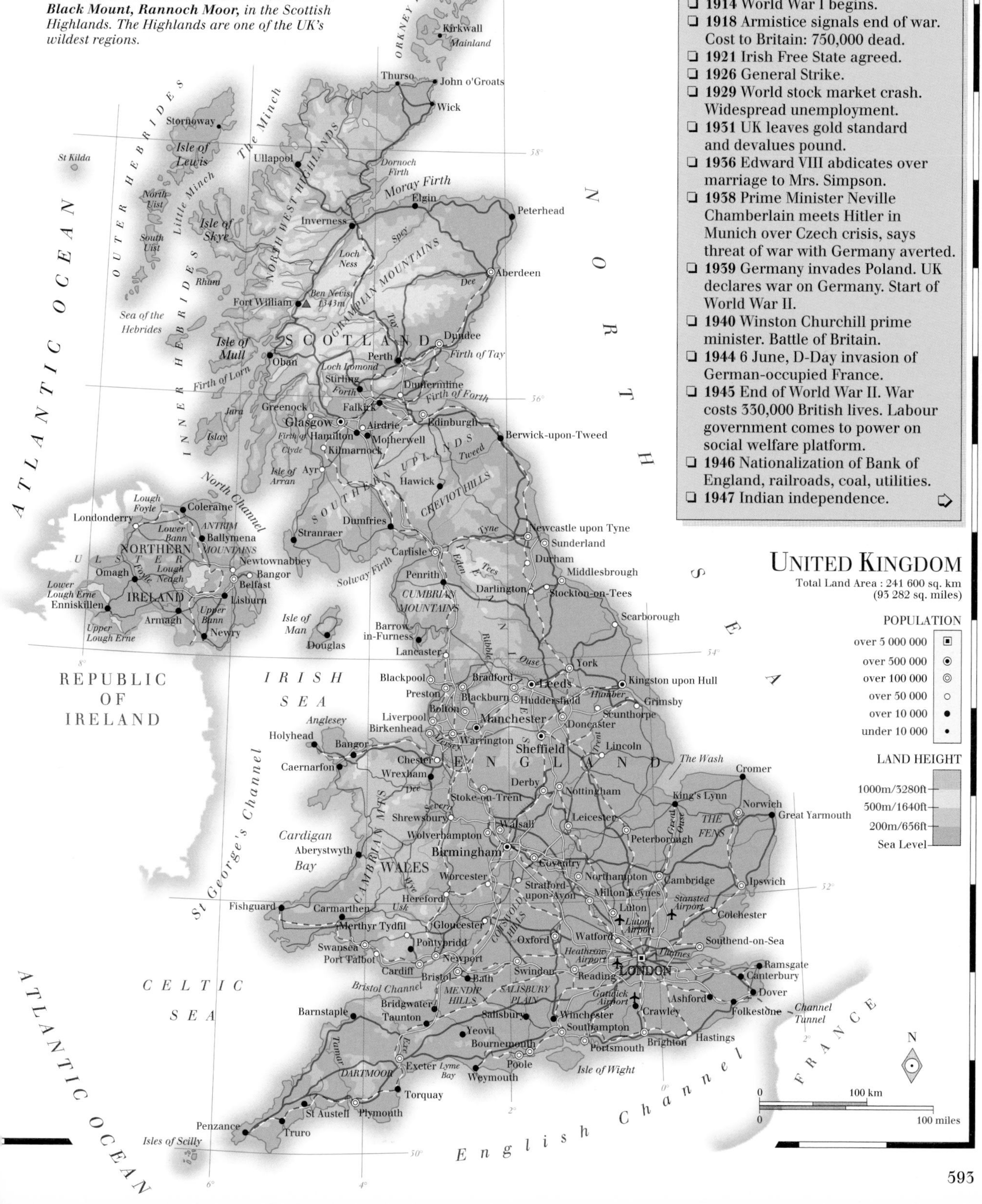

UNITED KINGDOM
Total Land Area : 241 600 sq. km (93 282 sq. miles)
POPULATION
over 5 000 000
over 500 000
over 100 000
over 50 000
over 10 000
under 10 000
LAND HEIGHT
1000m/3280ft
500m/1640ft
200m/656ft
Sea Level
100 km
100 miles
N
SHETLAND ISLANDS
Mainland
Lerwick
Fair I.
ORKNEY ISLANDS
Kirkwall
Mainland
Thurso
John o'Groats
Wick
OUTER HEBRIDES
Stornoway
Isle of Lewis
St Kilda
North Uist
South Uist
Little Minch
The Minch
Ullapool
NORTH WEST HIGHLANDS
Dornoch Firth
Moray Firth
Elgin
Peterhead
Inverness
Isle of Skye
Loch Ness
Spey
GRAMPIAN MOUNTAINS
Aberdeen
Dee
Rhum
Fort William
Ben Nevis 1343m
Sea of the Hebrides
INNER HEBRIDES
SCOTLAND
Dundee
Isle of Mull
Oban
Perth
Firth of Tay
Tay
Firth of Lorn
Loch Lomond
Stirling
Forth
Dunfermline
Firth of Forth
Jura
Greenock
Falkirk
Glasgow
Airdrie
Edinburgh
Islay
Firth of Clyde
Hamilton
Motherwell
Berwick-upon-Tweed
Kilmarnock
SOUTHERN UPLANDS
Tweed
Isle of Arran
Ayr
Hawick
CHEVIOT HILLS
North Channel
Lough Foyle
Coleraine
Londonderry
Lower Bann
ANTRIM MOUNTAINS
Ballymena
NORTHERN IRELAND
ULSTER
Omagh
Foyle
Lough Neagh
Newtownabbey
Bangor
Belfast
Lower Lough Erne
Enniskillen
Lisburn
Armagh
Upper Bann
Upper Lough Erne
Newry
Dumfries
Stranraer
Carlisle
Solway Firth
Eden
Tyne
Newcastle upon Tyne
Sunderland
Durham
Tees
Middlesbrough
Darlington
Stockton-on-Tees
Penrith
CUMBRIAN MOUNTAINS
PENNINES
Scarborough
Isle of Man
Douglas
Barrow-in-Furness
Ribble
Ouse
Lancaster
York
REPUBLIC OF IRELAND
IRISH SEA
Blackpool
Bradford
Leeds
Kingston upon Hull
Preston
Blackburn
Huddersfield
Humber
Grimsby
Bolton
Liverpool
Manchester
Scunthorpe
Anglesey
Birkenhead
Doncaster
Holyhead
Warrington
Sheffield
Mersey
Trent
Lincoln
Bangor
Caernarfon
Chester
ENGLAND
The Wash
Wrexham
Cromer
Dee
Derby
Nottingham
King's Lynn
Norwich
Stoke-on-Trent
Great Yarmouth
Severn
Shrewsbury
Great Ouse
THE FENS
Leicester
Wolverhampton
Walsall
Peterborough
Cardigan Bay
Aberystwyth
CAMBRIAN MTS
Birmingham
WALES
Coventry
Northampton
Cambridge
Ipswich
Worcester
Stratford-upon-Avon
Milton Keynes
Stansted Airport
Wye
Hereford
COTSWOLD HILLS
Luton
Luton Airport
Colchester
Fishguard
Carmarthen
Usk
Merthyr Tydfil
Gloucester
St George's Channel
Watford
Oxford
Southend-on-Sea
Swansea
Pontypridd
Thames
Port Talbot
Newport
Heathrow Airport
LONDON
Ramsgate
Cardiff
Bristol
Bath
Swindon
Reading
Canterbury
CELTIC SEA
Bristol Channel
MENDIP HILLS
SALISBURY PLAIN
Gatwick Airport
Dover
Ashford
Bridgwater
Barnstaple
Taunton
Salisbury
Winchester
Crawley
Folkestone
Channel Tunnel
Southampton
Yeovil
Tamar
Exe
Bournemouth
Portsmouth
Brighton
Hastings
FRANCE
Poole
Exeter
Lyme Bay
Isle of Wight
DARTMOOR
Weymouth
Torquay
St Austell
Plymouth
Penzance
Truro
Isles of Scilly
English Channel
NORTH SEA
ATLANTIC OCEAN

CHRONOLOGY *continued*

- **1948** National Health Service established.
- **1949** Founder member of NATO.
- **1956** Suez crisis. UK intervenes in Canal Zone. Withdraws under US pressure.
- **1957** US nuclear missiles accepted on UK soil.
- **1961** UK application to EC rejected by French President de Gaulle.
- **1968** Abortion and homosexuality are legalized.
- **1969** British troops sent into Northern Ireland.
- **1970** Conservatives in power under Edward Heath.
- **1973** Joins EC. Oil crisis. Industry on three-day week following strikes by power workers and miners.
- **1974** Labour government, under Harold Wilson, concedes miners' demands; strikes end. High inflation.
- **1975** Margaret Thatcher leader of Conservatives. Referendum ratifies EC membership. First North Sea oil pipeline in operation.
- **1979–1997** Conservative rule.
- **1980** Anti-US Cruise missiles protests. Rising unemployment. Inner-city riots.
- **1981** Privatization program begun.
- **1982** Argentina invades Falklands. Islands retaken by UK task force.
- **1983** Tax-cutting policies.
- **1986** Financial services market deregularized ("Big Bang").
- **1990** John Major Conservative leader. UK joins Gulf War.
- **1992** Conservatives win fourth consecutive election.
- **1994** Tony Blair Labour leader.
- **1996** Dunblane primary school massacre; tightening of gun control laws. Health crisis linking "mad cow" disease (BSE) with fatal variant Creutzfeldt-Jakob disease (vCJD).
- **1997** 1 May, landslide election victory for Labour. August, Diana, Princess of Wales, killed in car crash in Paris. September, Scottish and Welsh referendums approve creation of own assemblies.
- **1998–1999** "Good Friday" agreement on political settlement in Northern Ireland, endorsed by referendum but held up by disputes over decommissioning weapons.
- **1999** March–June, involvement in NATO air war with Yugoslavia over Kosovo crisis. May, Scottish Parliament and Welsh Assembly elected, inaugurated. December, devolution to power-sharing executive in Northern Ireland.
- **2001** Foot-and-mouth epidemic and mass livestock culling. June, Labour wins second term in office with huge majority.

POLITICS

Multiparty elections

2001/2006

HM Queen Elizabeth II

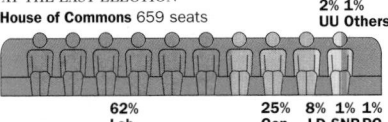

AT THE LAST ELECTION

House of Commons 659 seats

2% 1%
UU Others
62%
Lab
25%
Con
8% 1% 1%
LD SNP PC

Lab = Labour Party **Con** = Conservative and Unionist Party **LD** = Liberal Democrats **UU** = Ulster Unionist parties – (official) Ulster Unionist Party, Democratic Unionist Party, UK Unionist **SNP** = Scottish National Party **PC** = Plaid Cymru

House of Lords 679 seats

The House of Lords is an unelected body of just under 100 hereditary peers, 26 spiritual peers (bishops), and over 500 life peers (including lords of appeal – judges), appointed by the monarch

Queen Elizabeth II, *head of state since 1952 and head of the Commonwealth.*

Tony Blair, *prime minister since 1997, and leader of the Labour Party.*

Chancellor of the Exchequer Gordon Brown, *known as the "Iron Chancellor."*

Baroness Thatcher, *the country's only female prime minister (1979–1990).*

The UK is a multiparty democracy. The monarch's power is largely ceremonial.

Main Political Issues

Europe

Labour plans a referendum on joining the euro single currency. The Conservatives, in opposition, have become increasingly "Eurosceptic," considering that membership of the EU erodes national sovereignty.

Constitutional change

Major changes were made to the UK's system of government in the late 1990s. A separate Scottish Parliament, with substantial devolved powers, was approved by referendum and elected in May 1999, as was a new Welsh Assembly. The House of Lords was substantially changed by the abolition of voting rights for all but 75 hereditary peers, pending its complete overhaul; 15 "people's peers" were chosen in 2001. London gained greater autonomy in 2000 with the election both of its own assembly and of a mayor.

In Northern Ireland, the 1998 Good Friday agreement provided for a power-sharing framework to include unionists and Irish republicans. However, progress has stalled over decommissioning the weapons of the paramilitaries. A joint executive formed in late 1999 has on occasion been suspended, and direct rule reimposed by the British government, with each side blaming the other for deadlock. In August 2001 the IRA withdrew its latest offer on putting their weapons "beyond use," blaming the lack of positive response.

The economy

Fundamental alternatives on running the economy are no longer argued within mainstream politics. Labour no longer believes in renationalizing privatized industries, and is wary of increasing taxes. Its belief in using private finance and management within publicly owned services, such as health and education, has alienated some traditional Labour supporters, and the financial benefits of this policy are questioned by others.

Profile

Margaret Thatcher's 1979 election victory ushered in almost 18 years of Conservative rule, and monetarist and privatization policies. The Labour Party won back power in 1997 as the Conservatives lost impetus and popularity. Tony Blair's "New Labour" government, occupying the political center, retained a massive majority in the June 2001 election. The low turnout, however, reflected a growing perception that it had become arrogant and "out of touch." The Conservative Party has so far failed to build a credible challenge around pledges to reduce taxes and opposition to the euro.

Canary Wharf, *the centerpiece of the London Docklands development.*

U

WORLD AFFAIRS

Joined UN in 1945

Comm | EU | G7 | NATO | OECD

The UK, historically a "great power" in world affairs, still holds a permanent seat on the UN Security Council and was the third country to achieve nuclear weapons status. A founder member of NATO, it joined the EC only in 1973, and remains suspicious of full integration in Europe. Generally following a pro-US line during and since the Cold War, the UK has supported US-led action against Iraq, and NATO's 1999 air war to compel Yugoslav forces to pull out of Kosovo. The question of participation in a new US missile defense system promised to be a key test of the UK–US relationship, but in September 2001 both gave top priority to waging a "war" against terrorism worldwide.

AID

Donor

$3.4bn (donations) | Down 12% in 1999

UK foreign aid fell between 1980 and 1997 to below the European average, and well below the nominal target of 0.7% of GNP for industrialized countries. After 1997 the government moved to end the decline, although the figure in 1999 was only 0.24% of GNP. More significant was its concentration on the poorest countries and on partnership with NGOs, building on a change of emphasis already introduced in 1996, when 85% of bilateral aid was directed at 20 states in sub-Saharan Africa and south Asia. The "trade for aid" provision, by which much of the aid budget was tied to contracts for British firms, has been abolished. The program's aims include encouraging good government, widening opportunities for women, and protecting the environment.

DEFENSE

No compulsory military service

$36.9bn | Down 3% in 1999

BRITISH ARMED FORCES

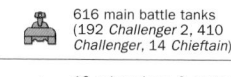

616 main battle tanks (192 *Challenger* 2, 410 *Challenger*, 14 *Chieftain*)	113,950 personnel
16 submarines, 3 carriers, 11 destroyers, 20 frigates, and 23 patrol boats	43,700 personnel
566 combat aircraft (214 *Tornado*, 79 *Jaguar*, 86 *Harrier*, 182 F–3)	54,730 personnel
58 SLBM in 4 SSBN	

The post-Cold War program Options for Change, implemented in 1993, made significant cuts in army and navy personnel and equipment orders. The UK's independent nuclear deterrent was scaled down. Despite such cuts, defense spending is high. Troops remain stationed in Northern Ireland, but the strategic emphasis has increasingly been on developing military capabilities relevant for rapid reaction. UK forces have been prominent in peacekeeping in the former Yugoslavia (Bosnia, Kosovo, and, in 2001, Macedonia) and elsewhere, such as Sierra Leone.

The UK is one of the world's leading arms exporters. Major buyers include Middle Eastern and southeast Asian countries.

ECONOMICS

Inflation 3% p.a. (1990–1999)

$1404bn

0.6205–0.6694 pounds sterling

SCORE CARD

- ❏ WORLD GNP RANKING............................5th
- ❏ GNP PER CAPITA..........................$23,590
- ❏ BALANCE OF PAYMENTS ....$-20.6bn
- ❏ INFLATION 1.6%
- ❏ UNEMPLOYMENT....................................6%

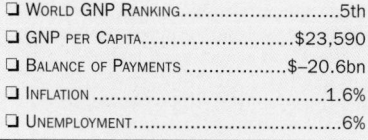

EXPORTS

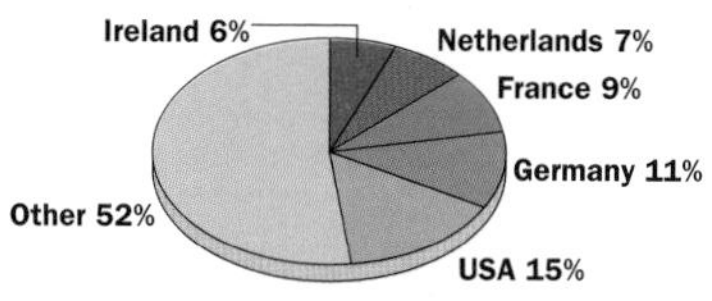
Ireland 6%
Netherlands 7%
France 9%
Germany 11%
USA 15%
Other 52%

IMPORTS

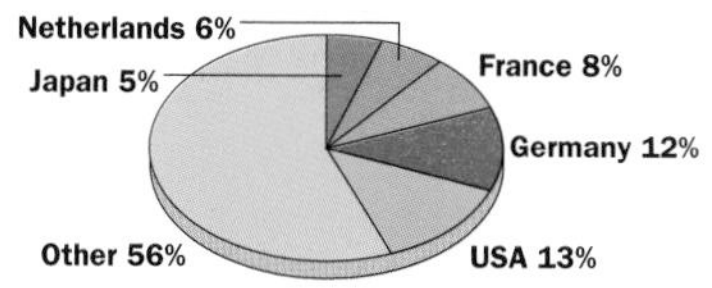
Netherlands 6%
Japan 5%
France 8%
Germany 12%
USA 13%
Other 56%

STRENGTHS

World leader in financial services, pharmaceuticals, and defense industries. Strong multinationals. Precision engineering and high-tech industries, including telecommunications and biotechnology. Energy sector based on North Sea oil and gas production. Innovative in computer software development. Flexible working practices. Success in controlling inflationary tendencies.

WEAKNESSES

Decline of manufacturing sector since 1970s, particularly heavy industries, car manufacturing. Quick-return mentality of many investment decisions. Non-participation in euro threatens former status as EU's largest recipient of inward investment, and has prompted some major investors to close UK factories.

PROFILE

Manufacturing has been in long-term decline, particularly since the 1980s, when sectors such as financial services expanded rapidly. After sharp recession in 1991, revival was sluggish, but by the latter half of the 1990s growth was faster than in European competitors. Exporters remained concerned that sterling was overvalued. In 2000 the government received a £22 billion windfall from the sale of "third generation" mobile phone operators' licenses. The US economic downturn and the collapse of the Internet "dot.com" boom brought back fears of possible recession; interest rate cuts in 2001 aimed to boost domestic demand. The rural economy was hit hard by a serious epidemic of foot-and-mouth disease in livestock in 2001.

ECONOMIC PERFORMANCE INDICATOR

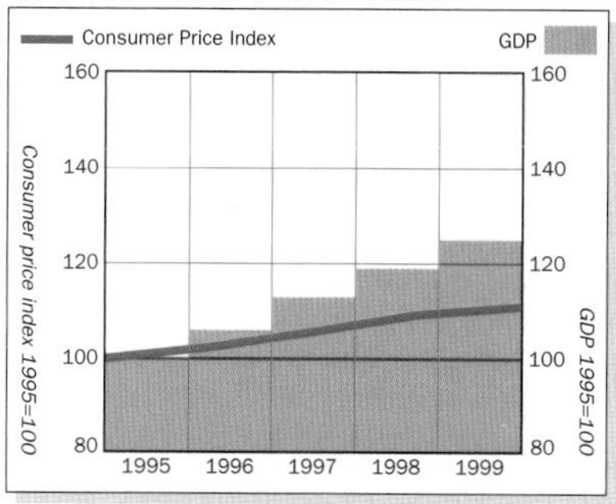
Consumer Price Index
GDP
160
140
120
100
80
1995
1996
1997
1998
1999
Consumer price index 1995=100
GDP 1995=100

UNITED KINGDOM : MAJOR BUSINESSES

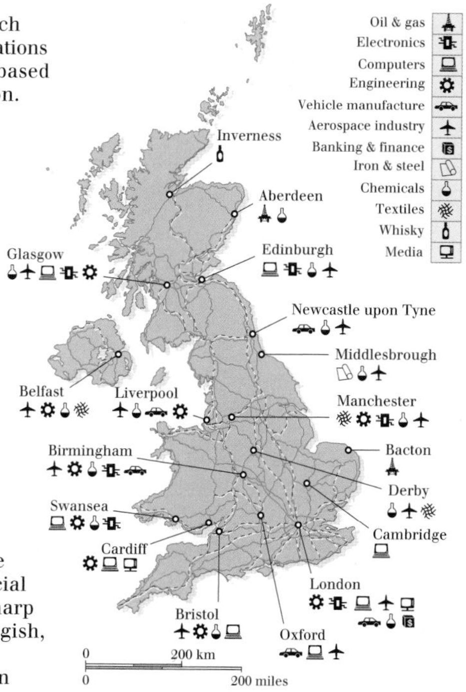
Oil & gas
Electronics
Computers
Engineering
Vehicle manufacture
Aerospace industry
Banking & finance
Iron & steel
Chemicals
Textiles
Whisky
Media
Inverness
Aberdeen
Glasgow
Edinburgh
Newcastle upon Tyne
Middlesbrough
Belfast
Liverpool
Manchester
Bacton
Birmingham
Derby
Swansea
Cambridge
Cardiff
London
Bristol
Oxford
0
200 km
0
200 miles

RESOURCES

Electric power 72.6m kw

1.03m tonnes

2.7m b/d (reserves 5,000,000,000 bbl)

45m sheep, 12m turkeys, 11m cattle, 154m chickens

Coal, oil, limestone, natural gas

ELECTRICITY GENERATION

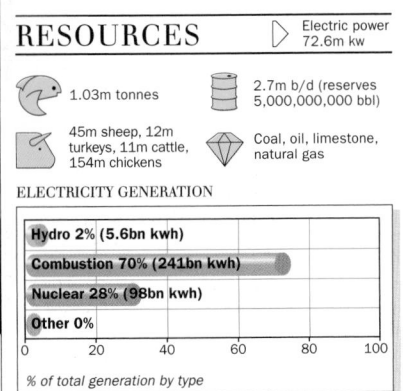

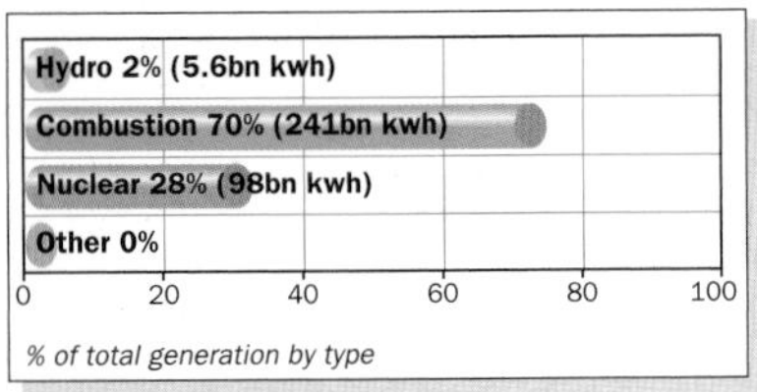
Hydro 2% (5.6bn kwh)
Combustion 70% (241bn kwh)
Nuclear 28% (98bn kwh)
Other 0%
0
20
40
60
80
100
% of total generation by type

The UK has the largest energy resources of any EU state, with substantial oil and gas reserves offshore on the continental shelf in the North Sea, and fresh fields in the north Atlantic. Drilled under difficult conditions, North Sea oil is of a high grade. Revenues from taxes on oil companies have been a major contributor to government finances, averaging around $12 billion a year.

Coal reserves are also sizable, but all but a handful of pits have closed, faced with cheap imports and falling demand. Privatization of the electricity industry, and pressure to cut pollution, encouraged the switch from coal to gas-fired power plants, prompting emergency government measures in the late 1990s and efforts to boost the role of "cleaner coal" technology.

The UK produces few other minerals in significant quantities. Cornwall's last tin mines teeter between closure and rescue. Some very small-scale gold mining survives in Wales and Scotland.

UNITED KINGDOM : LAND USE

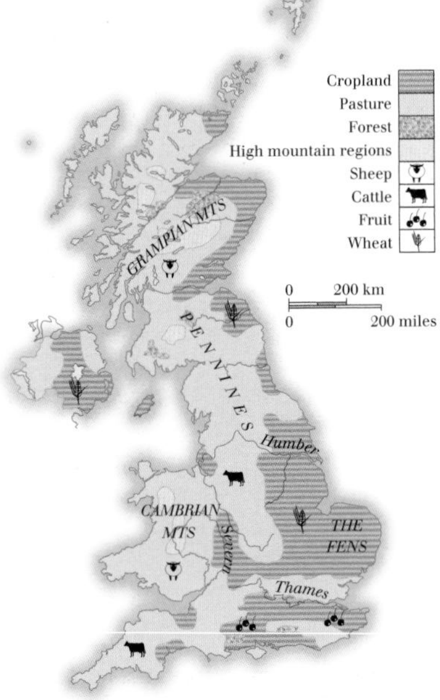
Cropland
Pasture
Forest
High mountain regions
Sheep
Cattle
Fruit
Wheat
0 200 km
0 200 miles
GRAMPIAN MTS
PENNINES
Humber
CAMBRIAN MTS
Severn
THE FENS
Thames

ENVIRONMENT

Sustainability rank: 16th

21%

8.9 tonnes per capita

ENVIRONMENTAL TREATIES

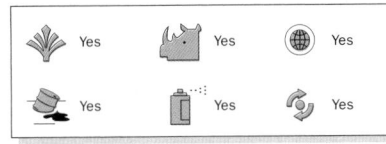

Yes Yes Yes

Yes Yes Yes

Apart from destruction of rural environments by road building and sprawling development, the most important issues are health-related. Urban air pollution from traffic is a major focus, as are nuclear safety issues. Food scares have gripped the public since BSE ("mad cow disease") was linked in the mid-1990s with human deaths. Opposition to genetically modified (GM) foods is widespread and GM crop trials have been disrupted, for fear that modified genes contaminate other species.

MEDIA

TV ownership high

Daily newspaper circulation 331 per 1000 people

PUBLISHING AND BROADCAST MEDIA

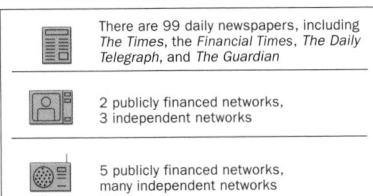

There are 99 daily newspapers, including *The Times*, the *Financial Times*, *The Daily Telegraph*, and *The Guardian*

2 publicly financed networks, 3 independent networks

5 publicly financed networks, many independent networks

Newspapers are owned mostly by large media corporations. Many publish Internet editions. Criticized for invasions of privacy, the press presents self-regulation as preferable to legislation. Publication deemed contrary to "national interests" may be banned. Satellite TV and digital terrestrial broadcasting have increased competition with the BBC. The BBC's World Service, despite cutbacks, remains an influential international news source.

***The Welsh coal industry** has virtually disappeared. Wales now has the highest percentage of small business start-ups, relative to the population, of any part of the UK.*

CRIME

Death penalty not used

58,702 prisoners

Up 34% 1996–1998

CRIME RATES

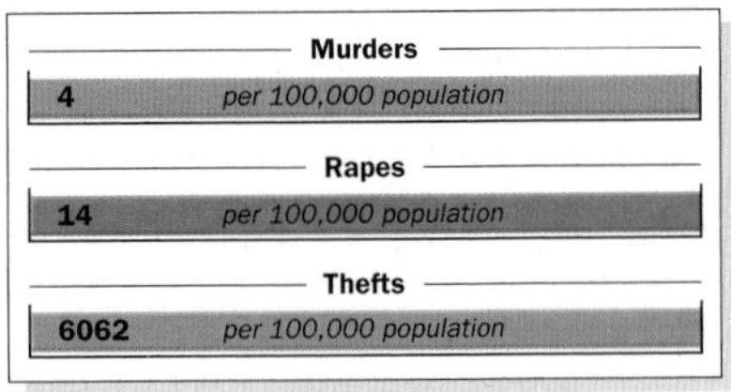
Murders
4 per 100,000 population
Rapes
14 per 100,000 population
Thefts
6062 per 100,000 population

Burglary and car theft peaked in the early 1990s. Violent crime and domestic abuse are growing problems. Inner-city violence is partly fueled by drug dependency and trafficking. Gun controls were tightened after a shocking massacre at Dunblane primary school in Scotland in 1996. The Labour government since 1997 has retained a "tough on crime" stance, but sentencing policies place the penal system under serious strain.

EDUCATION

School leaving age: 16

99%

1.8m students

THE EDUCATION SYSTEM

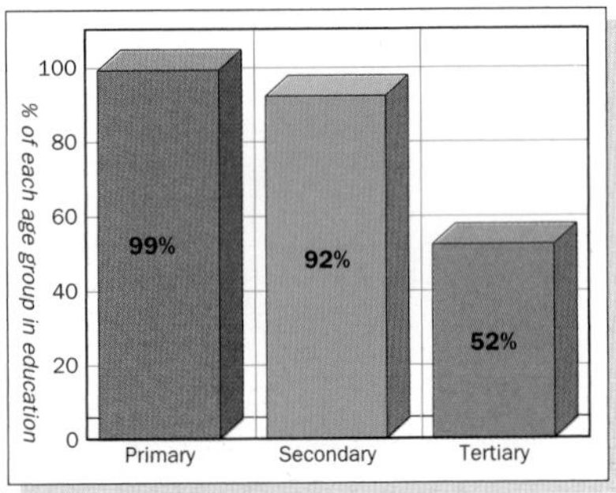
100
80
60
40
20
0
% of each age group in education
99%
92%
52%
Primary
Secondary
Tertiary

The state system is used by 94% of children. Others attend fee-paying private schools, including the traditional elite establishments confusingly known as public schools. Catholic schools are particularly significant in Northern Ireland, but there is now a new enthusiasm in government for "faith-based" schools.

From the 1960s onwards, a two-tier state school system based on academic selection at age 11 was replaced to a great extent by mixed ability comprehensive schools. The 1988 education reforms introduced a national curriculum and weakened the role of local education authorities. The post-1997 Labour government has focused on testing, assessing teaching standards, and tackling "failing" schools.

More colleges were given university status in the 1990s but established centers, particularly Oxford and Cambridge, are the most prestigious and best resourced.

U

REPRESENTATION AND DEVOLUTION

The United Kingdom dates from 1801 and the Act of Union joining Ireland with Great Britain – partly undone when Ireland (except Northern Ireland) became independent in 1922. The English and Scottish crowns had been united in 1603 (James VI of Scotland becoming James I of England) and their parliaments in 1707, also by an Act of Union, although Scotland's legal system remained separate. The principality of Wales had lost its separate status and been joined with England in 1536.

The rise of Welsh and particularly Scottish nationalism prompted an abortive initiative in the 1970s to devolve powers to regional governments. The post-1997 Labour government gave fresh impetus to devolution, created new assemblies in Northern Ireland, Scotland, and Wales, and also raised the idea of English regional assemblies.

SCOTLAND
Glasgow
Edinburgh
NORTHERN IRELAND
Belfast
Newcastle upon Tyne
Leeds
Liverpool
Manchester
ENGLAND
Birmingham
WALES
Cardiff
Bristol
LONDON

NORTHERN IRELAND

In Northern Ireland (population 1.65 million, area 14,120 sq km /5450 sq miles, capital Belfast) the majority Protestant community dominated a "home rule" parliament at Stormont throughout its 50-year existence, until 1972. After that the troubled province was mainly under direct rule from London, interspersed with attempts to create power-sharing institutions, until the 1998 Good Friday agreement. This created a 108-member Northern Ireland Assembly, elected that June by proportional representation, and a 12-member power-sharing executive. However, implementation of the agreement stalled amid disputes mainly about disarming rival Irish republican and unionist "loyalist" paramilitaries.

***The Scottish Parliament** building, Edinburgh.*

SCOTLAND AND WALES

The Scottish National Party's electoral breakthrough in 1974 was fueled by the perception that independence could be viable, if Scotland controlled the oil wealth of the North Sea. The UK government offered devolution to both Scotland and Wales, but in referendums in 1979 the majority in Scotland was insufficient to carry the proposals, while Wales actually voted no. The devolution proposals of 1997, on the other hand, won endorsement both in Scotland and (narrowly) in Wales.

Scotland (pop. 5.13 million, area 78,742 sq km/30,394 sq miles, capital Edinburgh) now has a Scottish Parliament of 129 MSPs, elected in 1999. The Scottish Executive, consisting of a First Minister and an 11-member cabinet, is responsible to the parliament. The Parliament's powers notably cover education, and changing tax rates to generate revenue for Scottish expenditure. One of its first distinctive initiatives was to reject the imposition of university tuition fees, so controversial elsewhere in the UK.

In Wales (pop. 2.9 million, area 20,761 sq km/8041 sq miles, capital Cardiff), a 60-member Welsh Assembly was also elected in 1999. It has fewer powers, not including tax-raising, exercised by an eight-member administration also headed by a First Minister.

***The extensive upland areas** of both Scotland and Wales are used extensively for sheep farming and forestry.*

HEALTH

Welfare state health benefits

1 per 588 people

Heart, cerebrovascular, and respiratory diseases, cancers

The National Health Service (NHS) offers universal free health care, but financial pressures have led to shortages and hospital closures, and charges in some areas. In response, the 2000 budget promised major investment. Private health care has grown rapidly since the 1970s. Recent crises have focused on food safety, from cases of salmonella poisoning to fatal brain disease attributed to eating beef from cattle with "mad cow" disease. Rates of obesity have tripled since 1980.

SPENDING

GDP/cap. increase

CONSUMPTION AND SPENDING

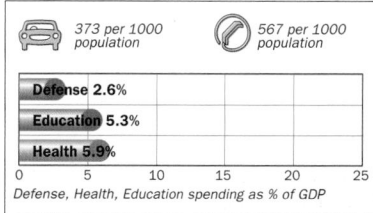

373 per 1000 population

567 per 1000 population

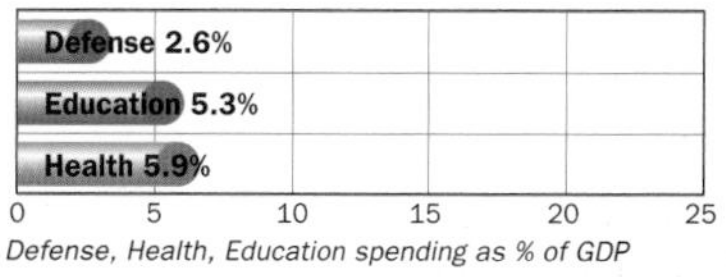
Defense 2.6%
Education 5.3%
Health 5.9%
0
5
10
15
20
25
Defense, Health, Education spending as % of GDP

Income inequality in the UK is greater than in 1884, when records first began. Average wages for manufacturing workers in 2001 were $29,000 a year, only 4% of the average received by chief executives in large companies. Under Conservative governments in the 1980s and early 1990s, taxation for higher earners was cut, whereas the value of state benefits and pensions fell. Since the mid-1990s, economic growth has helped to bring unemployment down. Labour's 1997 election promises precluded raising income tax. This limited any scope for redistributive action, leaving anti-poverty strategies dependent on better targeting of welfare benefits.

Almost 40% of the population had used the Internet by 2001, with ten million households connected.

WORLD RANKING

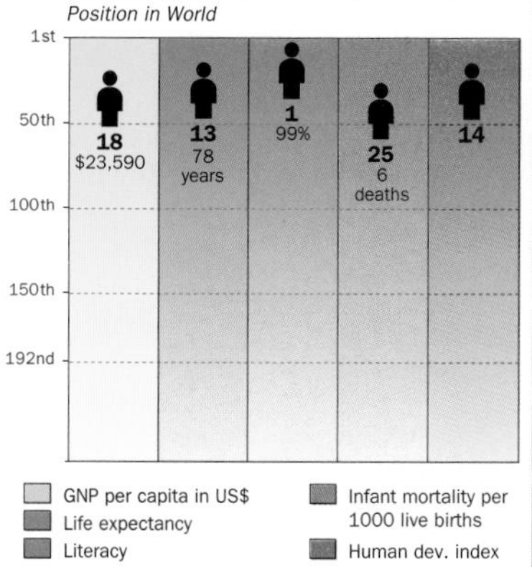
Position in World
1st
50th
100th
150th
192nd
18
$23,590
13
78
years
1
99%
25
6
deaths
14
GNP per capita in US$
Life expectancy
Literacy
Infant mortality per 1000 live births
Human dev. index

U

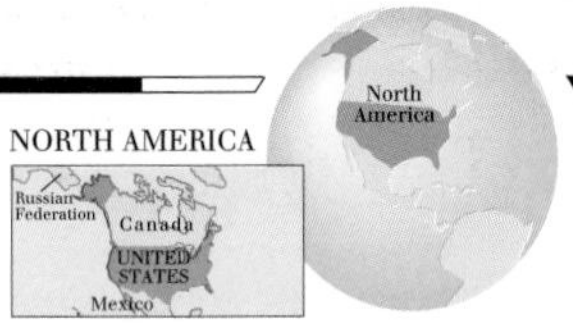
NORTH AMERICA
North America
Russian Federation
Canada
UNITED STATES
Mexico

UNITED STATES

OFFICIAL NAME: United States of America **CAPITAL:** Washington D.C.
POPULATION: 281.4 million **CURRENCY:** US dollar **OFFICIAL LANGUAGE:** English

1776
1959
July 4
USA
-5 to -11
+1
n/a

THE WORLD'S FOURTH-LARGEST country, the United States is neither overpopulated (like China) nor in the main subject to extremes of climate (like much of Russia and Canada). Its main landmass, bounded by Canada and Mexico, contains 48 of its 50 states. The two others, Alaska at the northwest tip of the Americas and Hawaii in the Pacific, became states in 1959. The USA was not built on ethnic identity but on a concept of nationhood intimately bound up with the 18th-century founding fathers' ideas of democracy and liberty – still powerful touchstones in both a political and an economic sense. Since the breakup of the Soviet Union, the USA holds a unique position – but arouses extreme hatreds – as the sole global superpower.

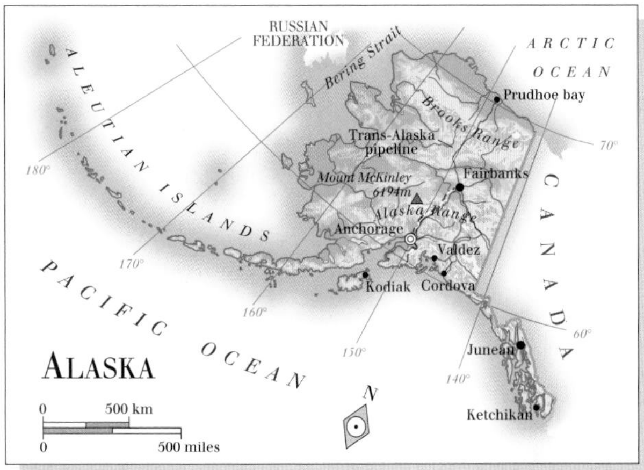
RUSSIAN FEDERATION
Bering Strait
ARCTIC OCEAN
Prudhoe bay
Brooks Range
Trans-Alaska pipeline
Mount McKinley 6194m
Fairbanks
Alaska Range
Anchorage
Valdez
Kodiak
Cordova
ALEUTIAN ISLANDS
PACIFIC OCEAN
CANADA
Juneau
Ketchikan
ALASKA
0 500 km
0 500 miles
N

CLIMATE

Continental/subtropical/mountain/desert/maritime

WEATHER CHART

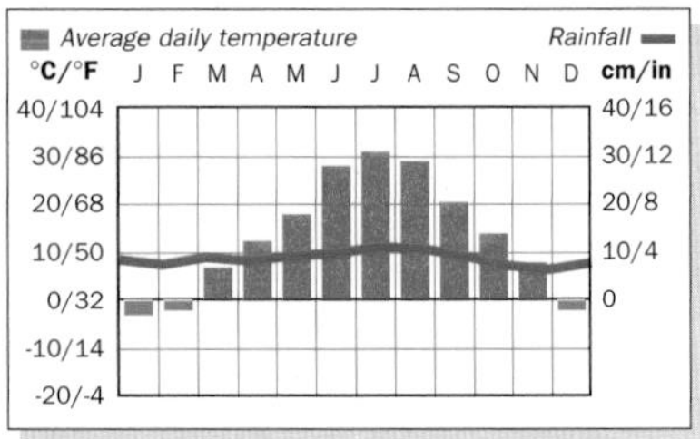
Average daily temperature
Rainfall
°C/°F
J F M A M J J A S O N D
cm/in
40/104
30/86
20/68
10/50
0/32
-10/14
-20/-4
40/16
30/12
20/8
10/4
0

Spanning a continent and extending far into the Pacific Ocean, the USA displays a wide range of climatic conditions. Mean annual temperatures range from 29°C (84°F) in Florida to –13°C (9°F) in Alaska. Except for New England, Alaska, and the Pacific northwest, summer temperatures are higher than in Europe. Southern summers are humid; in the southwest they are dry. Winters are particularly severe in the western mountains and plains and in the Midwest – where the Great Lakes can freeze. The northeast can have heavy snow from November to April. The weather is frequently dramatic, with tornadoes, cyclones, thunderstorms, hurricanes, floods, and droughts. Weather-related damage has risen since 1990, a trend linked with global climate change.

The Chippendale Block, New York, a notable example of postmodern architecture by the influential US architect Philip Johnson.

PACIFIC OCEAN
Seattle
Tacoma
Olympia
WASHINGTON
Spokane
Columbia
Portland
Salem
Corvallis
Eugene
Lewiston
Missoula
Great Falls
Helena
OREGON
IDAHO
Medford
Nampa
Boise
Idaho Falls
Pocatello
Twin Falls
Great Salt Lake
Ogden
Salt Lake City
Orem
Provo
Reno
Carson City
GREAT BASIN
NEVADA
Sacramento
Oakland
San Francisco
Mount Whitney 4418m
UTAH
Grand Junction
Lake Powell
Las Vegas
Lake Mead
Grand Canyon
CALIFORNIA
Los Angeles
San Diego
ARIZONA
Phoenix
Tucson
Albuquerque
Las Cruces
El Paso
ROCKY MOUNTAINS
CASCADE RANGE
COAST RANGES
SIERRA NEVADA
Snake
Colorado
Rock S
Billin
Sher
Farmi
Santa
C
M E X

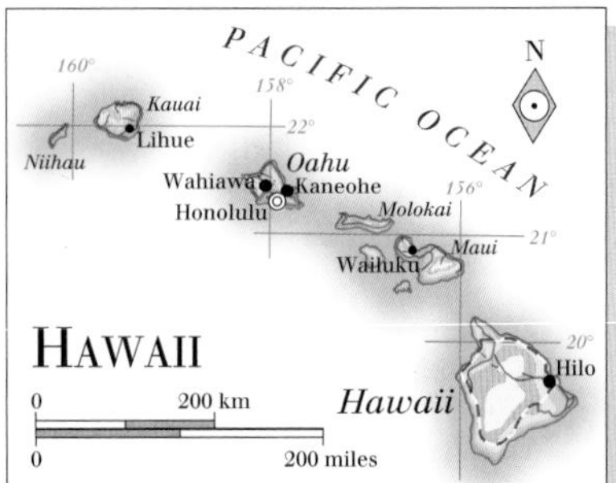
PACIFIC OCEAN
N
Kauai
Lihue
Niihau
Oahu
Wahiawa
Kaneohe
Honolulu
Molokai
Maui
Wailuku
Hilo
Hawaii
HAWAII
0 200 km
0 200 miles

U

TRANSPORTATION

Drive on right

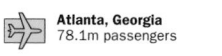

Atlanta, Georgia
78.1m passengers

330 ships
10.3m dwt

THE TRANSPORTATION NETWORK

3.73m km (2.32m miles)	88,727 km (55,132 miles)
234,131 km (145,489 miles)	41,009 km (25,482 miles)

The Mississippi–Missouri river system provided the USA's first transportation network. Today, the USA has the world's cheapest, most extensive internal air network and a good system of interstate highways. Railroads, comparatively neglected for years, mainly carry freight, although modern high-speed trains are starting to attract passengers back. Americans have been wedded to the car since Henry Ford began mass production 90 years ago. By 1919 there were nine million cars in the USA. Today the total tops 210 million, including pickups and the ubiquitous "sports utes" (SUVs). Americans make more than half of the world's car journeys. Cheap gasoline underpinned the rise of the car, but problems of congestion and pollution, and the environmental costs of ever more oil production, mean that its role in society needs reviewing.

The Mittens, Monument Valley, Arizona. *These striking natural rock formations are created by erosion of red sandstone. The Valley is home to the Navajo people.*

NORTH DAKOTA
SOUTH DAKOTA
MINNESOTA
WISCONSIN
MICHIGAN
IOWA
NEBRASKA
KANSAS
MISSOURI
OKLAHOMA
ARKANSAS
TEXAS
LOUISIANA
MISSISSIPPI
ALABAMA
GEORGIA
FLORIDA
TENNESSEE
KENTUCKY
ILLINOIS
INDIANA
OHIO
WEST VIRGINIA
VIRGINIA
NORTH CAROLINA
SOUTH CAROLINA
PENNSYLVANIA
NEW YORK
NEW JERSEY
MARYLAND
DEL.
CONN.
RHODE I.
MASS.
VERM.
NEW HAMP.
MAINE
GREAT PLAINS
APPALACHIAN MTS
Lake Superior
Lake Michigan
Lake Huron
L. Erie
L. Ontario
St Lawrence
Hudson
Missouri
Mississippi
Ohio
Arkansas
Red
Canadian
N. Platte
Colorado
Pecos
Rio Grande
L. Okeechobee
ATLANTIC OCEAN
GULF OF MEXICO
BAHAMAS
Minot
Grand Forks
Bismarck
Fargo
Duluth
Aberdeen
Pierre
Rapid City
Minneapolis
St Paul
Rochester
Sioux Falls
Sioux City
Green Bay
Milwaukee
Madison
Grand Rapids
Flint
Lansing
Detroit
Ann Arbor
Racine
Chicago
Rockford
Cedar Rapids
Des Moines
Davenport
Omaha
Lincoln
Grand Island
Gary
South Bend
Toledo
Cleveland
Akron
Fort Wayne
Peoria
Springfield
Indianapolis
Columbus
Dayton
Cincinnati
Topeka
Kansas City
Jefferson City
St Louis
Louisville
Frankfort
Lexington
Evansville
Huntington
Charleston
Wichita
Springfield
Tulsa
Oklahoma City
Norman
Lawton
Fort Smith
Fayetteville
Little Rock
Hot Springs
Pine Bluff
Memphis
Nashville
Knoxville
Huntsville
Chattanooga
Birmingham
Tuscaloosa
Greenville
Columbus
Jackson
Meridian
Montgomery
Hattiesburg
Shreveport
Dallas
Fort Worth
Austin
San Antonio
Houston
Baton Rouge
New Orleans
Biloxi
Mobile
Tallahassee
Jacksonville
Tampa
St Petersburg
Fort Lauderdale
Miami
Atlanta
Macon
Columbia
Savannah
Charleston
Greenville
Spartanburg
Charlotte
Winston-Salem
Greensboro
Raleigh
Richmond
Newport News
Norfolk
Washington DC
Annapolis
Baltimore
Dover
Wilmington
Philadelphia
Trenton
Harrisburg
Pittsburgh
Allentown
Erie
Buffalo
Rochester
Syracuse
Albany
New York
JFK
Hartford
New Haven
Springfield
Providence
Worcester
Boston
Lowell
Manchester
Concord
Portland
Lewiston
Augusta
Bangor
Burlington
Montpelier
Cheyenne
Denver
Colorado Springs
Pueblo
UNITED STATES
Total Land Area : 9 166 600 sq. km
(3 539 224 sq. miles)
POPULATION
over 5 000 000
over 1 000 000
over 500 000
over 100 000
over 50 000
over 10 000
under 10 000
LAND HEIGHT
3000m/9843ft
2000m/6562ft
1000m/3281ft
500m/1640ft
200m/656ft
Sea Level
0
400 km
400 miles
N

U

TOURISM

Visitors : Population 1:5.5

50.9m visitors

Up 5% in 2000

MAIN TOURIST ARRIVALS

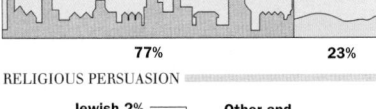

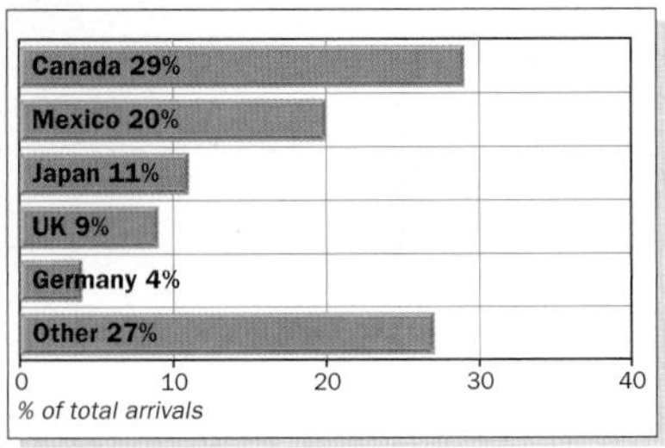
Canada 29%
Mexico 20%
Japan 11%
UK 9%
Germany 4%
Other 27%
0
10
20
30
40
% of total arrivals

Tourism caters to ever-growing demand from both Americans themselves and overseas visitors, and brought in over $85 billion in 2000 in receipts from foreign tourists. The number of foreign visitors has been boosted especially by the deregulation of air fares. Domestic tourism has expanded just as rapidly, along with the rise in real incomes.

Tourism is a major generator of jobs, especially in areas of industrial decline, such as the northeast. All the states have their attractions, and most court tourists. Top tourist destinations include Florida's Disney World and Disneyland in California, Niagara Falls, Las Vegas, New York, San Francisco, Los Angeles and Hollywood, the Grand Canyon, Death Valley, New Orleans, Atlantic City, and Washington D.C.

Tourism's rapid expansion has also brought some problems. The parks and sites run by the National Parks Service (NPS) have been particular casualties; visitor numbers have rocketed in the three decades since 1970. To try and reduce pressure on the most popular areas, there has been a significant expansion in the area of protected land under NPS management since the mid-1970s. Even so, Yellowstone Park has a continuing traffic management crisis, bumper-to-bumper cars plague other high-profile attractions, and those wanting to take a raft ride down the Grand Canyon are likely to spend many months on a waiting list.

PEOPLE

Pop. density low

English, Spanish, Italian, French, German, Polish, Chinese, Greek, Indic, Tagalog, Korean, Japanese

31/km² (80/mi²)

THE URBAN/RURAL POPULATION SPLIT

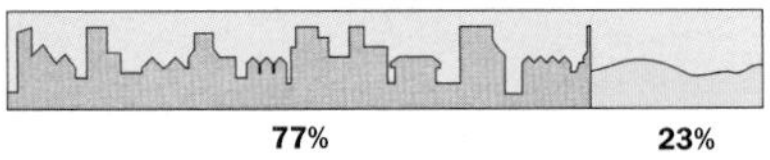
77%
23%

RELIGIOUS PERSUASION

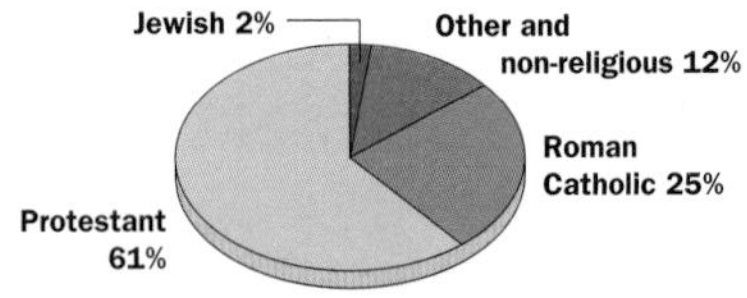
Jewish 2%
Other and non-religious 12%
Roman Catholic 25%
Protestant 61%

ETHNIC MAKEUP

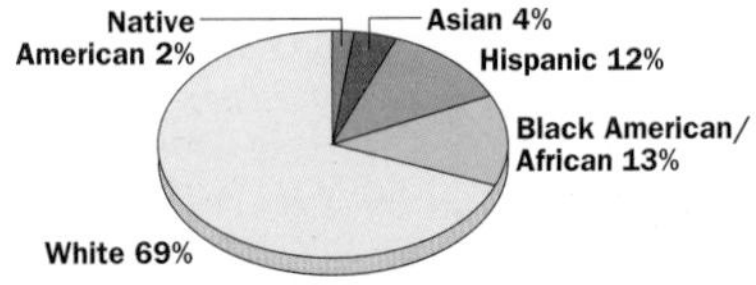
Native American 2%
Asian 4%
Hispanic 12%
Black American/ African 13%
White 69%

Native Americans, the sole inhabitants before white settlers arrived, were dispossessed in the 19th century and now make up under 3% of the total population. In their reservations, some of the USA's worst poverty and deprivation can be found.

The USA's population increased by some 25 million residents during the 1990s. An immigration boom peaked in the late 1980s and early 1990s, but since then numbers have fallen below a million a year. The new immigrants are disproportionately drawn from Asia and Latin America, with more than two million from Mexico alone in the 1980s.

Census Bureau projections for the year 2050 suggest that 53% of the population will be white non-Hispanics, and just under 14% black, while Asians (and Pacific islanders) will total nearly 9% and as many as a quarter of the population will be Hispanics. There is already concern about the position of American blacks, who increasingly find they have to compete politically and economically with the newer immigrants. In some communities, such as Los Angeles, this has been a source of tension leading to inner-city riots.

Despite the growth of a black business leadership class, only two black people – television personality Oprah Winfrey and Black Entertainment Television founder Robert L. Johnson – make the list of the 400 richest Americans. The 1995 acquittal of O. J. Simpson, tried for murdering his white estranged wife, exposed how far the country was divided by race in its perceptions of the justice system. The Nation of Islam, led by Louis Farrakhan, is prominent in emphasizing self-discipline, self-improvement, and community in the quest for empowerment among African-Americans.

POPULATION AGE BREAKDOWN

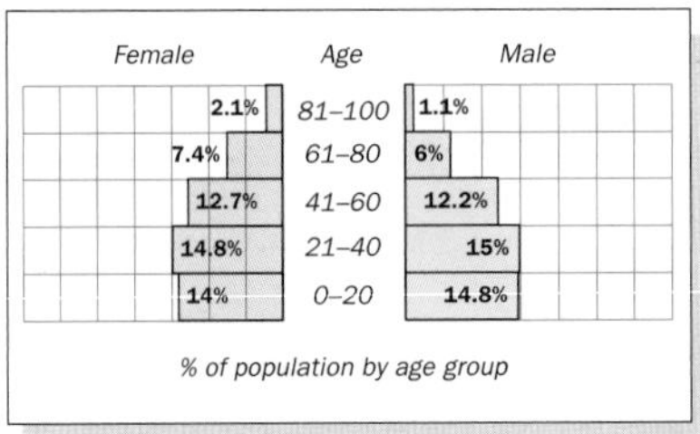
Female
Age
Male
2.1%
81–100
1.1%
7.4%
61–80
6%
12.7%
41–60
12.2%
14.8%
21–40
15%
14%
0–20
14.8%
% of population by age group

POLITICS

Multiparty elections

U. House 2000/2002
L. House 2000/2002

President George W. Bush

AT THE LAST ELECTION

House of Representatives 435 seats

51% **Rep** **48%** **Dem** **1%** **Ind**

Rep = Republican Party **Dem** = Democratic Party **Ind** = Independents

Senate 100 seats

50% **Rep** **50%** **Dem**

Presidential elections take place every 4 years, House elections every 2 years. One-third of the senators are elected every 2 years for six-year terms.

The USA is a democracy with a federal system of government. Many issues are dealt with by the 50 individual states.

Main Political Issues

The limits of government

The USA has a strong tradition of resisting the extension of government powers. The vigorous defense of constitutional liberties and the rights of citizens, such as freedom of speech or the right to bear arms, is sometimes taken to lengths which appear extreme to other societies. States similarly resist the arrogation of powers by the federal authorities. In areas such as health care and education, conservatives oppose as interference what others see as the proper concern of government with social welfare. "Big government" is also denounced in the economic sphere. Opponents of environmental controls, for example, portray them as an obstruction of free enterprise and wealth creation.

The prestige of the presidency

When George W. Bush took office in January 2001, the presidency faced a threefold challenge. The tendentious manner of his election, with fewer votes nationwide than his Democrat rival Al Gore, left questions as to the legitimacy of his victory. The narrow Republican majority in the House of Representatives, and a "hung" Senate, with an effective Democrat majority

***George W. Bush**, took office in 2001 after a controversial presidential election.*

***Gen. Colin Powell**, who became the first African-American Secretary of State.*

U

POLITICS *continued*

after one elected Republican switched to independent, promised problems. Thirdly, the moral authority of the office of president had suffered serious damage under the outgoing administration of Bill Clinton, beset by personal, financial, and political scandals, and hamstrung toward the end by impeachment proceedings. The emergence of sordid details of Clinton's affair with White House intern Monica Lewinsky, and his lack of candor, discredited and isolated the presidency to such an extent that almost all Democrats seeking election in 2000 distanced themselves from his administration.

Energy and the environment

Controversial energy policies introduced by Bush in 2001, at the height of a crisis over Californian electricity shortages, offered much freer rein for the US oil industry to exploit reserves in Alaska. Wilderness conservation activists were appalled. The expansion of nuclear power was also revived as an issue under the Bush energy plan, while the USA, alone, chose to repudiate an international agreement on cutting carbon dioxide emissions.

Crime, race and poverty

Efforts to regenerate depressed urban areas have relied on new economic opportunities and programs that empower the poor (such as self-management of public housing projects). Both rates of criminality and crime victims are higher in the black community than in any other. Tough anti-crime policies in cities such as New York have had a real impact in reducing the level of violence, but have also been accused of unfairly targeting minority ethnic groups; there remains the prospect of a permanently disaffected urban underclass.

PROFILE

New Republican president George W. Bush was denied, by the narrowest of margins in the Senate, the rare opportunity of working with a congressional majority from his own party. His predecessors, whether Democrat (Clinton, elected in 1992) or Republican, had struggled to get major initiatives enacted by a hostile Congress. There was unprecedented legal wrangling to determine the outcome of the 2000 presidential elections, before the decisive Florida votes were awarded to Bush. In September 2001 a wave of patriotic emotion rallied the nation behind Bush following the world's worst ever terrorist atrocities, when two hijacked aircraft were flown into the twin World Trade Center towers in New York, killing thousands, and a third into the Pentagon.

***Hillary Clinton,** senator for New York and wife of former president Bill Clinton.*

***Alan Greenspan,** chairman of the Federal Reserve since 1987.*

WORLD AFFAIRS

Joined UN in 1945

G7 | NATO | NAFTA | OAS | OECD

Isolated by two great oceans, the USA has for much of its history been able to choose the extent of its involvement in the affairs of others. Only reluctantly involved in the two world wars, after 1945 it swapped isolationism for involvement. The USA took its seat on the Security Council of the UN, based in New York. It helped to set up NATO, although for the USA the Cold War was most immediate – and costly – in the Korean and Vietnam wars. The death toll and shock of defeat in Vietnam in the 1970s kept the USA out of military involvement overseas for over a decade. Instead, it focused on diplomacy – particularly with China and in the Middle East – and on supporting the opponents of left-wing regimes in developing countries including Nicaragua, Cuba, and Angola.

The collapse of the Eastern bloc after 1989 meant that the USA had to redetermine the scope of its foreign responsibilities as the only remaining superpower. It led the intervention in the 1991 Gulf War, but a fiasco in Somalia and a lack of clear policy on Bosnia and Haiti showed its uncertainty about a role as world policeman. Increasingly isolated in actions against Iraq, the USA again showed a preference for air power – and aversion to committing ground forces – in the 1999 bombardment of Yugoslavia over the Kosovo crisis. The new administration's highly controversial missile defense "shield" project alarmed Russia and China in 2001, and risked upsetting treaties regulating strategic nuclear missile numbers. The US stance toward China under Bush is notably more confrontational than previously.

Even before the 2001 World Trade Center attack, the USA had used air strikes to hit back at anti-US terrorism and its alleged sponsors. The September 2001 atrocities, however, spurred Bush to prioritize the "war on terrorism," with Islamic extremists its primary focus.

***Manhattan Island,** bounded by the Hudson and East Rivers. The twin towers of the World Trade Center, destroyed by terrorists in 2001, stood at the heart of the financial district.*

AID

Donor

$9.15bn (donations)

Up 4% in 1999

The USA gives proportionately little foreign aid, only 0.1% of GNP, and aid allocations are often held hostage to special pleading in Congress. Most went to Israel and Egypt until the 1990s, and Egypt is still the largest single recipient. The USA has objected to funding some UN agencies.

DEFENSE

No compulsory military service

$283bn

Up 1% in 1999

AMERICAN ARMED FORCES

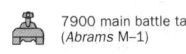

7900 main battle tanks (*Abrams* M-1)	471,700 personnel
74 submarines, 12 carriers, 27 cruisers, 52 destroyers, 35 frigates, & 21 patrol boats	370,700 personnel
3533 combat aircraft (F-4, F-15, F-16, A-10A, F-117, OA-10A)	353,600 personnel
432 SLBM in 18 SSBN, 550 ICBM	

Emphasis has shifted from strategic nuclear deterrence and large warships to "smart" missile systems and "long-range power projection," with rapid intervention capabilities built around air power. Despite setbacks in early tests, a project to create a missile defense "shield" system was taken up enthusiastically by the incoming Bush administration in 2001. In mid-2000 IBM unveiled the ASCI White computer, whose processing speed made "virtual" tests of nuclear weapons possible.

The enormous US military–industrial complex dates only from the close of World War II. In the 1990s a combination of the end of the Cold War and the need to cut the budget deficit meant that, in real terms, the defense budget fell to its lowest level since 1945. The 2000/2001 budget, however, was up by almost 5% to $310.5 billion, amounting to one-third of all military spending worldwide.

THE IMPACT OF INFORMATION TECHNOLOGY

THE UNITED STATES has been, and remains, at the forefront of the so-called information revolution. US society is undergoing profound changes at the beginning of the 21st century as a result of the spread of the personal computer and connectivity through access to electronic mail (e-mail) and the World Wide Web. The Web itself first emerged as a phenomenon of the 1990s, though the Internet on which it is based originated in the 1960s. The Net, developed to allow vital defense communications to be maintained in the event of an attack on a central control site, was first popularized as a medium for exchange within and between universities.

Access to virtual space

Mass ownership of the motor car and cheap fuel had conditioned the attitudes of previous generations of Americans to distance, and helped determine the pattern of development of the cities and towns in which the majority of them live. Information technology, the concept of "cyberspace," and the availability of instant "virtual" interaction, are now sometimes described as having abolished distance.

High-speed connections to the Internet are becoming increasingly popular, but for most individual users the link is at present still by dial-up on an ordinary telephone line to the local number of their Internet service provider. One consequence has been an explosion in phone line use, particularly because the recently deregulated telephone industry offers most Americans the chance to pay for their local calls on a single flat rate rather than by the minute. Computer modems can thus be left connected for long periods.

As with the automobile, part of society is excluded. In 1998, PC ownership stood at some 43 per cent of the population, of whom half were online (connected to

***Access to the Internet** remains out of reach to those who cannot afford a personal computer, such as residents of some of the USA's poverty-stricken inner city areas like the Bronx in New York.*

***The Microsoft Campus** in Redmond, Washington State. Microsoft is the world's biggest computer software manufacturer; its founder, Bill Gates, is the world's richest man.*

the Internet). By 2001, 60% had used the Internet, more than half of them female. Special initiatives to spread access among disadvantaged groups have had only limited impact, however.

Impact on the political process

The US administration and Congress now publish huge amounts of information of all kinds via the Internet. Citizens can also use the Net interactively to lodge requests and file the returns required of them, among other things for income tax purposes. The technology has greatly reinforced the impact of laws ensuring freedom of information, as well as exposing its users to the problems of information overload and a deluge of unsolicited communication. The notion of a "wired" democracy has taken hold to the extent that most politicians have their own website and many use them extensively to publicize their activities. The 2000 presidential election was somewhat fancifully heralded as the first "Internet election," just as the campaign in which John F. Kennedy defeated Richard Nixon 40 years previously was regarded as marking the ascendancy of television in the US political process.

Security

Activists of different kinds have made increasing use of the Internet to spread their views and maintain contact among their supporters. There are serious security concerns about the use of this tool not only by mainstream political organizations and lobbyists but by fringe groups, terrorists, and the pornography and sex industries. Such concerns underlay the battle in the late 1990s about the use of encryption software to ensure the privacy of electronic communications. The Federal Bureau of Investigation (FBI) and the Central Intelligence Agency (CIA) fought to ensure that all such software should have a key allowing the security authorities to decipher messages. Unfortunately for them, it is notoriously difficult to prevent the rapid spread of software which is made available on the Internet, and impossible to pin down the location of such programs in the usual geographical sense. The policing of a national jurisdiction is compromised by a communications network which recognizes no national boundaries. The same is true with computer viruses, which can infect the programs running on computers that come into contact with them and affect the way they function, in some cases very destructively.

***Shopping malls** are a typical feature of the urban and suburban landscape of the USA. Online "virtual malls" are spreading fast.*

Commerce

The shopping mall, which has had a major influence in reshaping consumer shopping habits since the 1960s, and the mail-order catalog on which many American households rely so heavily for clothes and similar purchases, are now under challenge from the online "virtual mall." The online shopping landscape is only now really taking shape, with many companies having to take a trial-and-error approach to developing e-commerce. Initial predictions about its rapid growth have proved overstated. However, it is thought that the number of people in the USA who regularly buy necessities such as groceries and related goods online will reach 20 million by 2007. Completing business transactions via the Internet became more feasible with legislation making "e-signatures" legally binding, with effect from October 2000.

TRAFFIC AND MOBILITY

The take-up of e-commerce on this scale would replace at least half of Americans' average 17 monthly shopping trips made to grocery stores and related outlets. It has the added attraction of shielding shoppers from the perceived dangers of being assaulted or robbed when venturing outside their homes. This is an area where the out-of-town shopping mall itself, complete with security guards and closed circuit television monitoring, had hitherto prospered as a more attractive option than shopping downtown.

Information technology is affecting patterns of personal transportation and mobility in other ways too. At one level, online information services and selling techniques make using the Net a more convenient and efficient way of booking airline tickets. At the same time, improvements in communications make it increasingly possible and productive for people to work at home or in decentralized facilities away from company headquarters. So-called "knowledge workers" in particular have had to learn new ways of networking electronically to replace the face-to-face contact of the office environment, and the use of special-interest discussion facilities and so-called newsgroups on the Internet has mushroomed accordingly. "Telecommuters" continue to form only a small fraction of the total US working population, but their number is nevertheless becoming significant in terms of managing peak-time commuter traffic. However, videoconferencing is struggling to make headway as an alternative to traveling long distances to hold business meetings, despite the active encouragement of some gurus of the environmental lobby.

The rise of the electronic superhighway is changing the way in which US citizens both shop and work. Home working is set to rise in the next decade, minimizing the need for the daily commute to work.

ECONOMICS

Inflation 2.1% p.a. (1990–1999)

$8880bn

Currency is US dollar

SCORE CARD

❑ WORLD GNP RANKING	1st
❑ GNP PER CAPITA	$31,910
❑ BALANCE OF PAYMENTS	$-339bn
❑ INFLATION	2.2%
❑ UNEMPLOYMENT	4%

EXPORTS

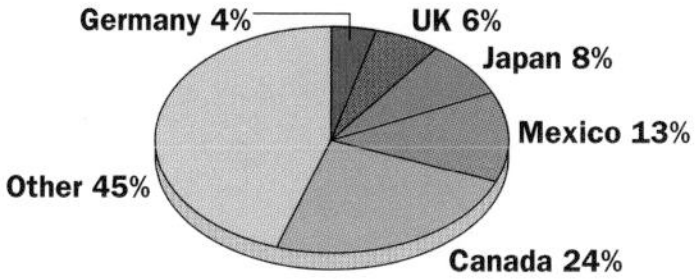
Germany 4%
UK 6%
Japan 8%
Mexico 13%
Other 45%
Canada 24%

IMPORTS

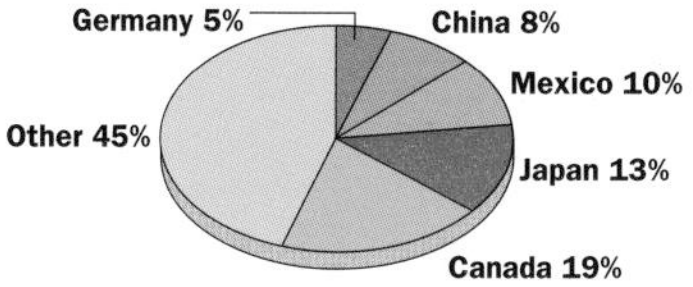
Germany 5%
China 8%
Mexico 10%
Other 45%
Japan 13%
Canada 19%

STRENGTHS

The world's largest economy. Wealth of natural resources, including energy, raw materials, and food. Strong high-tech base and world-leading research and development. Sophisticated service sector, as well as advanced and competitive manufacturing industry. World-class multinationals such as Ford, GM, Exxon. Global leader in computer software. Entrepreneurial business ethic. High quality of postgraduate education, especially related to application of high-tech to business. Global dominance of US culture a major boost to US manufacturers.

UNITED STATES : MAJOR BUSINESSES

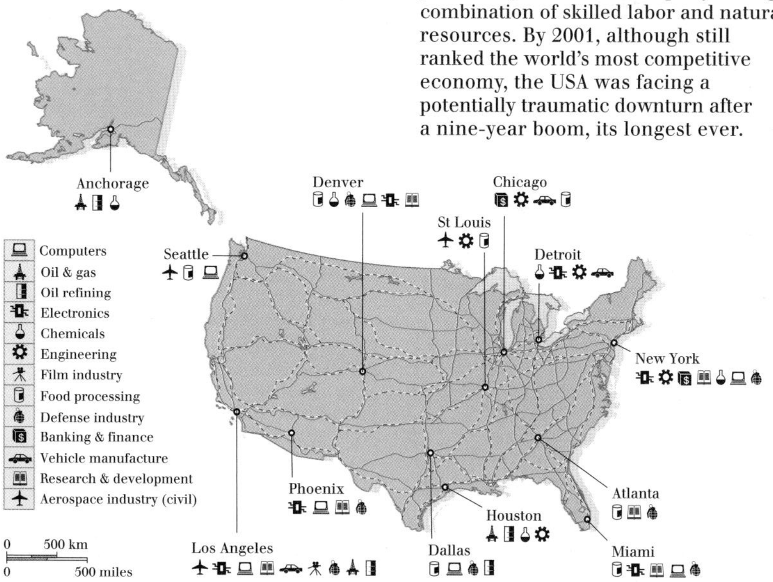
Anchorage
Denver
Chicago
St Louis
Seattle
Detroit
New York
Phoenix
Atlanta
Houston
Los Angeles
Dallas
Miami
Computers
Oil & gas
Oil refining
Electronics
Chemicals
Engineering
Film industry
Food processing
Defense industry
Banking & finance
Vehicle manufacture
Research & development
Aerospace industry (civil)
0 500 km
0 500 miles

ECONOMIC PERFORMANCE INDICATOR

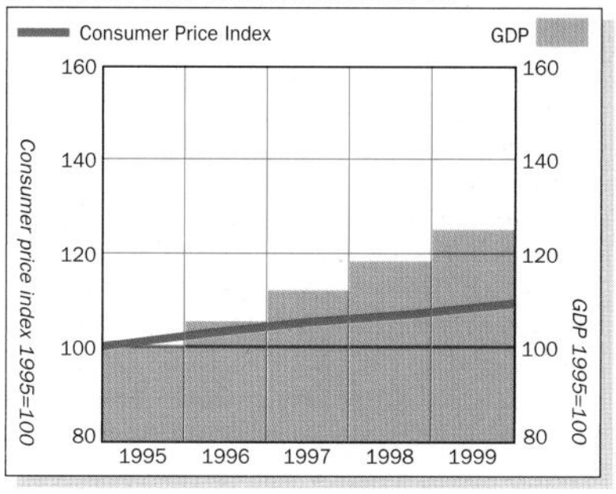
Consumer Price Index
GDP
160
140
120
100
80
Consumer price index 1995=100
GDP 1995=100
1995
1996
1997
1998
1999

WEAKNESSES

Dramatic fall in manufacturing employment over recent decades, although still 15% of workforce, contributing 17% of GDP. Postwar economic boom was built on low-skilled, high-waged employment in areas such as car industry. Globalization, problem of job losses to lower-wage economies. Tough competition from Asia and EU in leading-edge technologies. Lower savings rate than many competitors. World's largest debtor country despite reducing public debt via recent budget surpluses.

PROFILE

In 1945, the USA accounted for about 50% of world output; by the 1990s its share was down to about 25%. That is not, as Americans often think, a sign of failure, but a clear indication that the 1940s and 1950s were unusual periods. The current total of 25% is about the same share of the world market that the USA claimed in 1914, when it was already the world's greatest economy.

The USA has become a great exporter, and continues to have both a stable political system and a uniquely strong combination of skilled labor and natural resources. By 2001, although still ranked the world's most competitive economy, the USA was facing a potentially traumatic downturn after a nine-year boom, its longest ever.

U

CHRONOLOGY

The original 13 colonies, first established by British settlers on the eastern seaboard in the 17th century, joined to wage a war for independence, 1775–1781, which Britain recognized in 1783. The 1776 Declaration of Independence was followed by the writing of the world's first constitution. A century of westward expansion began. Following the victory of the northern states in the 1861–1865 Civil War, slavery was abolished throughout the USA, but native Americans were dispossessed of their land in a series of conflicts.

- **1917** Enters World War I.
- **1929** New York stock market collapse; economic depression.
- **1941** Japanese attack on Pearl Harbor; USA enters World War II.
- **1950–1953** Korean War.
- **1954** Supreme Court rules racial segregation in schools is unconstitutional. Blacks, seeking constitutional rights, start campaign of civil disobedience.
- **1959** Alaska, Hawaii become states.
- **1961** John F. Kennedy president. Promises aid to South Vietnam. US-backed invasion of Cuba defeated at Bay of Pigs.
- **1962** Soviet missile bases found on Cuba; threat of nuclear war averted.
- **1963** November, Kennedy assassinated. Lyndon Baines Johnson president.
- **1964** US involvement in Vietnam stepped up. Civil Rights Act gives blacks constitutional equality.
- **1968** Martin Luther King is assassinated.
- **1969** Republican Richard Nixon takes office as president. Growing public opposition to Vietnam War.
- **1972** Nixon reelected. Makes historic visit to China.
- **1973** Withdrawal of US troops from Vietnam; 58,000 US troops dead by end of war.
- **1974** August, Nixon resigns following "Watergate" scandal over break-in to Democrat headquarters. Gerald Ford president.
- **1976** Democrat Jimmy Carter elected president.
- **1978** US-sponsored "Camp David" accord between Egypt and Israel.
- **1979** Seizure of US hostages in Tehran, Iran.
- **1980** Ronald Reagan wins elections for Republicans. Adopts tough anticommunist foreign policy.
- **1983** Military invasion of Grenada.
- **1985** Air strikes against Libyan cities. Relations with USSR improve; first of three summits held.
- **1986** Iran-Contra affair revealed. ⇨

RESOURCES

Electric power 792m kw

5.45m tonnes

7.7m b/d (reserves 29,700,000,000 bbl)

98m cattle, 86m turkeys, 59.3m pigs, 1.72bn chickens

Phosphates, gypsum, oil, coal, sulfur, lead, zinc, copper, gold

ELECTRICITY GENERATION

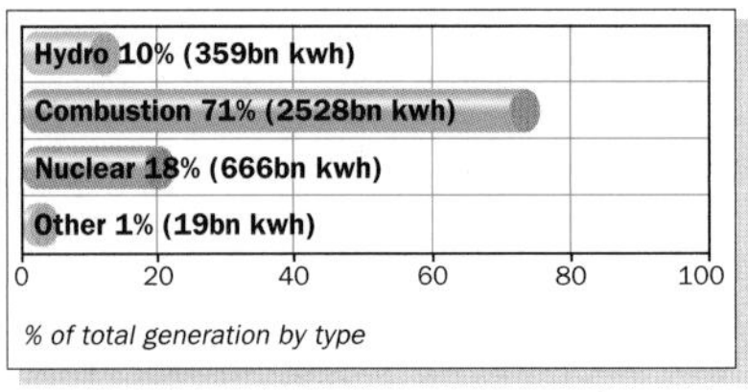
Hydro 10% (359bn kwh)
Combustion 71% (2528bn kwh)
Nuclear 18% (666bn kwh)
Other 1% (19bn kwh)
0 20 40 60 80 100
% of total generation by type

The USA has an abundance of natural resources, including oil. The 2001 energy plan aims to step up oil exploration and output, reducing the need for imports. There are massive deposits of coal in the western states – where almost all mining is open-cast – and substantial mineral deposits in the mountains and intramontane basins.

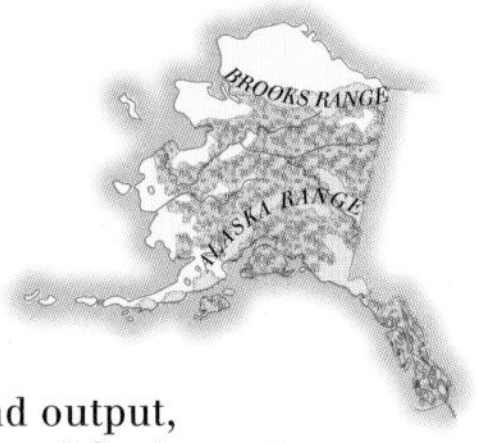
BROOKS RANGE
ALASKA RANGE

Environmental concerns halted the development of nuclear power after the 1979 accident at Three Mile Island, but expansion is now being considered.

The timber industry, forced to retreat by conservationists in the Pacific northwest, especially Washington State, has moved to the south, where great stands of pine are harvested as if they were fields of wheat. The USA has harnessed hydroelectric power in the past; today, imports of hydropower from Canada are commonplace.

By comparison with western Europe, the USA is not intensively farmed. The huge size of farms in the Midwest and west has allowed both arable and livestock farming to be based on a low-input for low-output model.

UNITED STATES : LAND USE

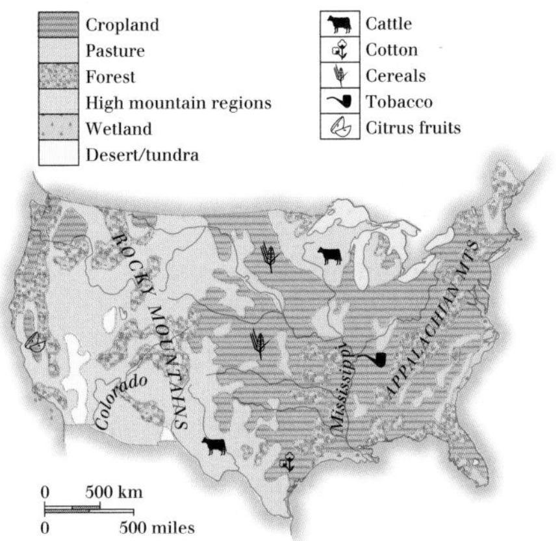
Cropland
Pasture
Forest
High mountain regions
Wetland
Desert/tundra
Cattle
Cotton
Cereals
Tobacco
Citrus fruits
ROCKY MOUNTAINS
APPALACHIAN MTS
Mississippi
Colorado
0 500 km
0 500 miles

ENVIRONMENT

Sustainability rank: 11th

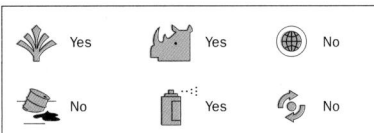

13% (6% partially protected)

20.1 tonnes per capita

ENVIRONMENTAL TREATIES

Yes	Yes	No
No	Yes	No

Although teaching is strong in schools, the USA lags far behind other Western countries on environmental issues. The international commitment made at the 1997 Kyoto conference on cutting carbon dioxide emissions was scrapped by new Republican president George Bush in 2001. The intramontane west is a battleground between those who want to maintain its beauty, and those who advocate "wise use" – in practice this often means giving ranchers and miners free rein. Similar issues surround the arguments over extending oil drilling in the Alaskan wilderness. The USA is the home of genetically modified (GM) food. Huge acreages have been planted to GM cereals, and over 60% of soybean production had gone GM by 2001. A consumer backlash, especially in Europe, has worried many farmers.

MEDIA

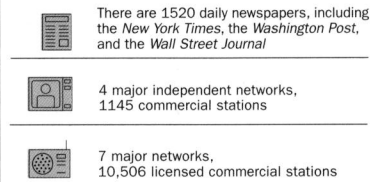

TV ownership high

Daily newspaper circulation 212 per 1000 people

PUBLISHING AND BROADCAST MEDIA

There are 1520 daily newspapers, including the *New York Times*, the *Washington Post*, and the *Wall Street Journal*

4 major independent networks, 1145 commercial stations

7 major networks, 10,506 licensed commercial stations

Mass media as a phenomenon was born in the USA, where the Internet is the most recent of a series of nationwide communication revolutions. No other society has ever had anything quite like US network TV, and no other society has so easily moved into the world of multichannel TV; homes with 50 or more channels are commonplace. Newspapers, however, which are mostly local rather than national, with very low cover prices, and gaining most of their revenue from advertising, are under increasing threat from cable TV and other outlets. Companies exploring multimedia and investing in ways of providing online news, information, and other services were hit hard by a crash in stock values in 2000.

U

CHRONOLOGY *continued*

- ❑ **1987** Intermediate Nuclear Forces Treaty signed by USA and USSR.
- ❑ **1988** Vice President George Bush Sr. wins presidency.
- ❑ **1989** US overthrows General Noriega of Panama, arrested on drug charges.
- ❑ **1991** January–February, Gulf War against Iraq. USA and USSR sign START arms reduction treaty.
- ❑ **1992** Black youths riot in Los Angeles and other cities. Bush–Yeltsin summit agrees further arms reductions. Democrat Bill Clinton defeats Bush in election.
- ❑ **1994** Health care reform legislation defeated in Congress. Special counsel investigation of Whitewater scandal begins, over Clintons' financial dealings in Arkansas. Sexual harassment charges filed against Clinton. Midterm elections, Republican majorities in both houses of Congress.
- ❑ **1995** Oklahoma bombing by Timothy McVeigh, over 160 die. Clinton in conflict with Congress over budget.
- ❑ **1996** Bomb kills two in Atlanta while hosting Olympic Games. President Clinton reelected.
- ❑ **1997** Madeleine Albright first woman to head State Department.
- ❑ **1998** Scandal over Clinton's affair with White House intern leads to impeachment proceedings. August, bombing of US embassies in Kenya and Tanzania; revenge air strikes on Sudan and Afghanistan. December, air strikes against Iraq.
- ❑ **1999** February, Clinton acquitted in Senate impeachment trial. April, Columbine High School shootings by two students. March–June, NATO involvement to end Kosovo conflict, bombardment of Yugoslavia.
- ❑ **2000** November–December, Al Gore concedes tightest presidential election ever to George W. Bush.
- ❑ **2001** January, President Bush takes office. September, world's worst terrorist attack kills thousands as hijacked planes destroy World Trade Center, damage Pentagon.

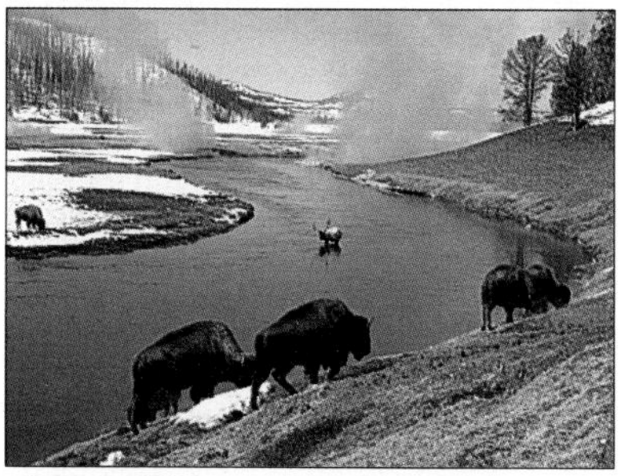

Bison in Yellowstone National Park. *The park's ecosystem is under severe strain due to the number of visitors it attracts.*

CRIME

▷ Death penalty used

2m prisoners

Down 10% 1992–1996

CRIME RATES

Murders
6 per 100,000 population

Rapes
36 per 100,000 population

Thefts
1145 per 100,000 population

Violent crime – especially murder – is much more common than in other developed countries, even in relatively well-off areas. However, the murder rate has fallen; six deaths per 100,000 people in 2000 was the lowest for over 30 years. Mass shootings have made gun control a major issue, but a powerful lobby opposes restrictions, basing its arguments on the constitution and the defense of individual liberties.

Imprisonment for narcotics crimes in the USA is much more widespread than in most Western countries. Capital punishment has increased since the 1980s, especially in the south. Texas carries out most executions. There are two million people in prison in the USA, a quarter of the world total.

EDUCATION

▷ School leaving age: 16

99%

14.3m students

THE EDUCATION SYSTEM

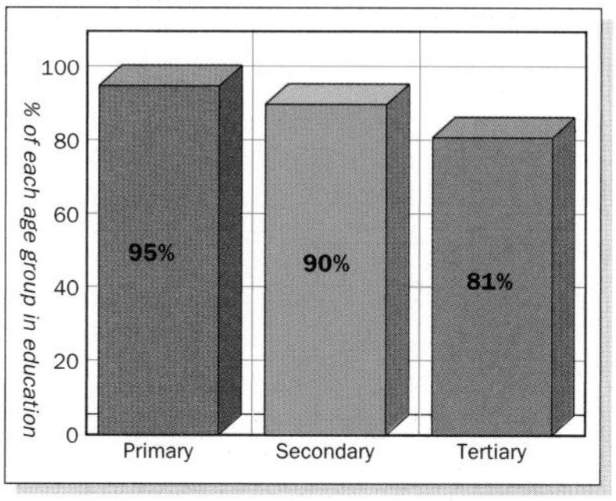

100
80
60
40
20
0
% of each age group in education
95%
90%
81%
Primary
Secondary
Tertiary

Education in the USA is primarily the responsibility of the state governments.

Recent reports critical of standards in US high schools cite problems of discipline, poor structural maintenance, and lack of resources in many areas as driving people away from the public education sector. Private education at secondary level continues to develop rapidly. While the number of Catholic private schools has shrunk, more nondenominational fee-paying schools have been founded.

Four out of every five high school students now go on to some form of tertiary college. The leading US universities are internationally recognized as being of world class.

HEALTH

▷ Limited welfare state health benefits

1 per 370 people

Heart and cerebro-vascular diseases, cancers, accidents

There are enormous disparities in US health provision, but a proposed reform of the health care system, high on the Democrats' political agenda in the early 1990s, was blocked by Congress. Sophisticated techniques are available to those with insurance (which they typically receive from their employer); the Texas Medical Center, in Houston, for example, has a budget equivalent to that of some small countries. On the other hand, costs have skyrocketed, and facilities for those dependent on state medical care and aid are woefully underfunded. Preventive care fails to reach all sections of society, and infant mortality statistics in some areas are at near-African levels.

Nearly one in five of the population is clinically obese, and one in every two adults is overweight.

SPENDING

▷ GDP/cap. increase

CONSUMPTION AND SPENDING

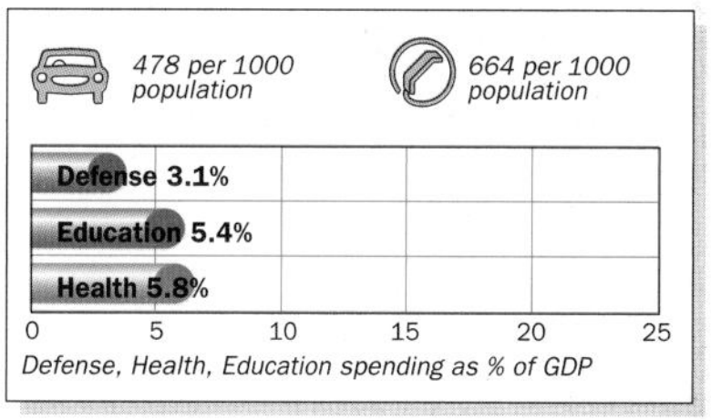

478 per 1000 population
664 per 1000 population
Defense 3.1%
Education 5.4%
Health 5.8%
0
5
10
15
20
25
Defense, Health, Education spending as % of GDP

Between 1945 and 1973, most Americans got richer. Since then, however, living standards have gone on rising only among those who finish high school. This "education effect" has led to noticeable class divisions, despite the long economic boom of the 1990s. The top 20% had average household incomes of $137,500 by 2000, whereas the incomes of the poorest 20% averaged only $13,000 – and were lower in real terms than in 1980.

WORLD RANKING

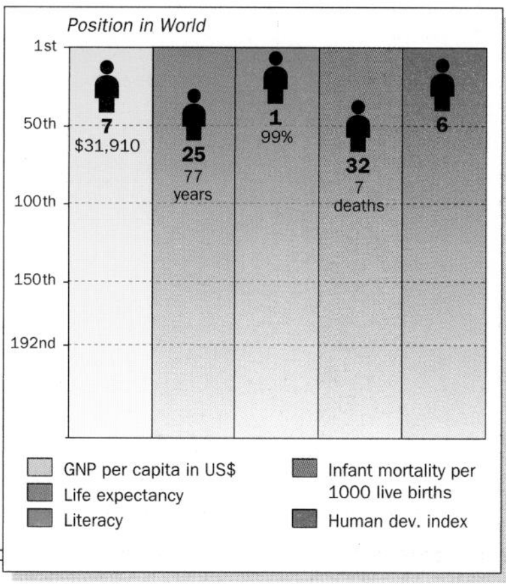

Position in World
1st
50th
100th
150th
192nd
7
$31,910
25
77
years
1
99%
32
7
deaths
6
GNP per capita in US$
Life expectancy
Literacy
Infant mortality per 1000 live births
Human dev. index

U

See also OVERSEAS TERRITORIES *p.640*

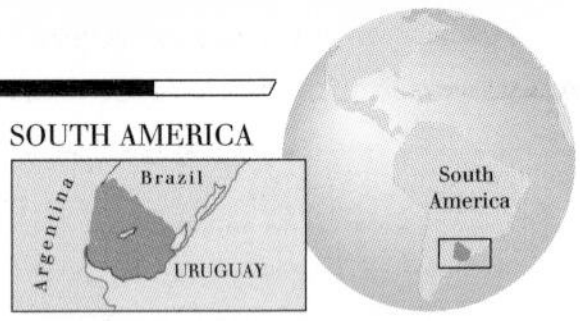
SOUTH AMERICA
Brazil
Argentina
URUGUAY
South America

URUGUAY

OFFICIAL NAME: Eastern Republic of Uruguay **CAPITAL:** Montevideo
POPULATION: 3.3 million **CURRENCY:** Uruguayan peso **OFFICIAL LANGUAGE:** Spanish

1828 | 1828 | Aug 25 | ROU | -3 | +598 | .uy

URUGUAY IS SITUATED IN southeastern South America. Its capital, Montevideo, is an Atlantic port on the River Plate, lying across the river from Buenos Aires, Argentina's capital. Uruguay became independent in 1828, after nearly 150 years of Spanish and Portuguese control. Decades of liberal government ended in 1973 with a military coup that was to result in 12 years of dictatorship, during which 400,000 people emigrated. Most have since returned. Almost the entire low-lying landscape is devoted to the rearing of livestock, especially cattle and sheep. Uruguay is the world's second-largest wool exporter. Tourism and offshore banking now bring in substantial foreign earnings.

Uruguayan grasslands. *Rich pasture covers three-quarters of the country, ideal for cattle and sheep. Animals and animal products account for over one-third of export earnings.*

CLIMATE

Subtropical

WEATHER CHART

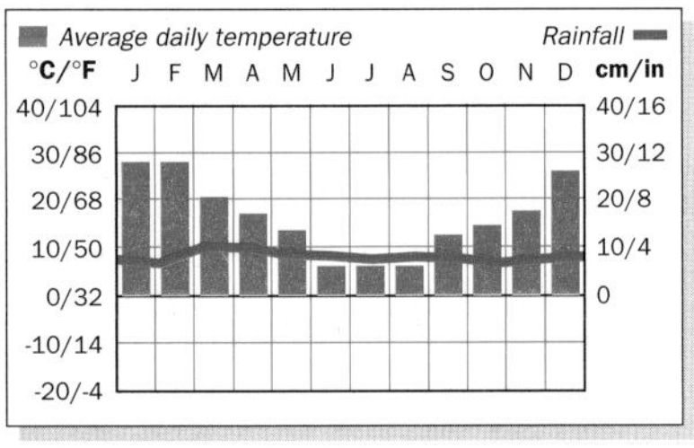
Average daily temperature
Rainfall
°C/°F
J F M A M J J A S O N D
cm/in
40/104
30/86
20/68
10/50
0/32
-10/14
-20/-4
40/16
30/12
20/8
10/4
0

Uruguay has one of the most benign climates in the world. It is uniformly temperate over the whole country. Winters are mild, frost is rare, and it never snows. Summers are generally cool for these latitudes and rarely tropically hot. The moderate rainfall tends to fall in heavy showers, leaving most days sunny.

TRANSPORTATION

Drive on right

Carrasco, Montevideo
1.17m passengers

91 ships
106,900 grt

THE TRANSPORTATION NETWORK

8085 km (5024 miles)

8683 km (5395 miles)

3002 km (1865 miles)

1600 km (994 miles)

The government has sold off its share in the national bus industry – there are extensive internal and international coach and bus services – and has closed down all passenger railroad services. In 1998 the Senate gave the go-ahead for a $1 billion, 45-km (30-mile) road bridge across the River Plate from Colonia to Buenos Aires. Raising international finance for the project will be difficult.

TOURISM

Visitors : Population 1:1.7

2m visitors

Down 5% in 2000

MAIN TOURIST ARRIVALS

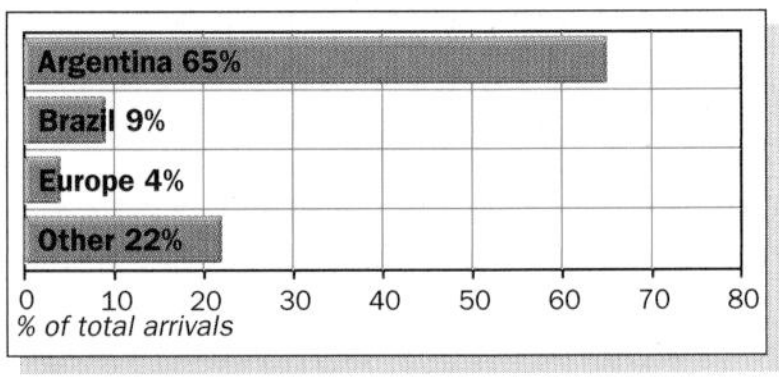
Argentina 65%
Brazil 9%
Europe 4%
Other 22%
0
10
20
30
40
50
60
70
80
% of total arrivals

Sandy beaches near the River Plate estuary are a major attraction. The old Spanish fortifications of Montevideo have been destroyed, but the city retains a colonial atmosphere. Punta del Este, 138 km (86 miles) east of the capital, is the main beach resort. Argentines account for the majority of visitors.

PEOPLE

Population density low

Spanish

19/km² (49/mi²)

THE URBAN/RURAL POPULATION SPLIT

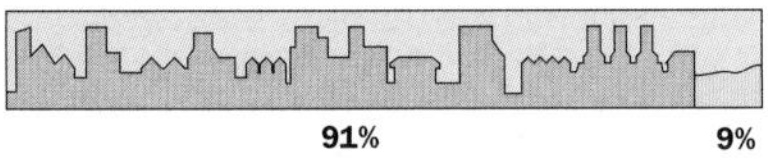
91%
9%

RELIGIOUS PERSUASION

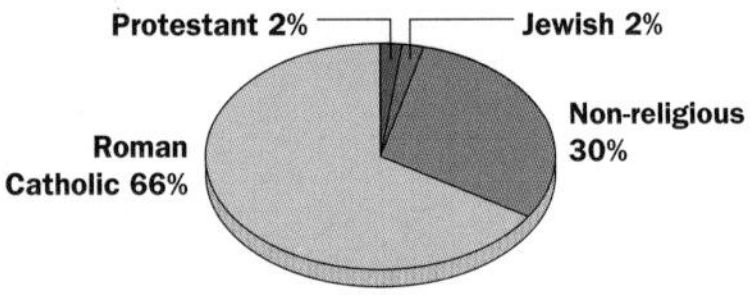
Protestant 2%
Jewish 2%
Non-religious 30%
Roman Catholic 66%

ETHNIC MAKEUP

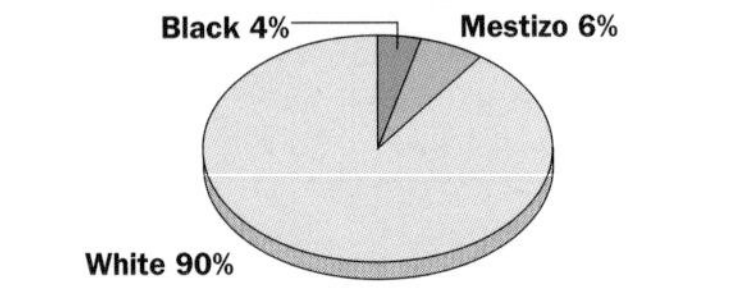
Black 4%
Mestizo 6%
White 90%

Most Uruguayans are second- or third-generation European, mostly of Spanish or Italian descent. There are also some *mestizos* and a small minority of people descended from Africans or immigrants from Brazil, who live in or around Montevideo or near the Brazilian border. All indigenous Amerindian groups became integrated in the *mestizo* population by the mid-19th century. More recent immigrants include Jews, Armenians, and Lebanese. Historically, ethnic tensions have been few. The birthrate is low for Latin America.

The considerable prosperity derived from cattle ranching allowed Uruguay to become a welfare state long before any other Latin American country. In spite of Uruguay's serious economic decline since the end of the 1950s, there is still a sizable, if less prosperous, middle class. A clear sign of the country's economic and social deterioration during the years of military dictatorship was the unprecedented growth of shanty towns around Montevideo.

Although Uruguay is a Roman Catholic country, it is liberal in its attitude to religion, and all forms are tolerated. Divorce is legal. Women, who gained the vote in 1932, are regarded as equal to men.

POPULATION AGE BREAKDOWN

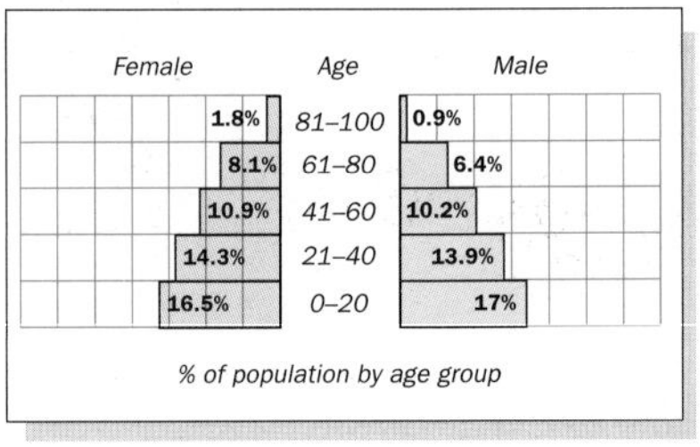
Female
Age
Male
1.8%
81–100
0.9%
8.1%
61–80
6.4%
10.9%
41–60
10.2%
14.3%
21–40
13.9%
16.5%
0–20
17%
% of population by age group

U

POLITICS

Multiparty elections

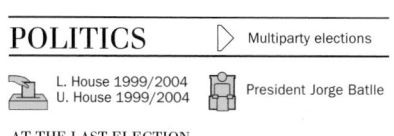

L. House 1999/2004
U. House 1999/2004

President Jorge Batlle

AT THE LAST ELECTION

Chamber of Representatives 99 seats

41% EPFA	33% PC	22% PN	4% NE

EPFA = Progressive Broad Front **PC** = Colorado Party (Colorados) **PN** = National Party (Blancos) **NE** = New Space **Res** = Reserved for the vice president

Senate 31 seats

39% EPFA	32% PC	23% PN	3% NE	3% Res

Uruguay is a presidential multiparty democracy.

MAIN POLITICAL ISSUES

Major privatizations

Faced with a struggling economy, President Batlle needs to make progress on structural reforms. Public opinion, however, is hostile to a program of major privatizations.

The disappeared

President Batlle has established an official inquiry into the fate of 160 people who "disappeared" under military rule (1973–1985), stating that its aim is to give Uruguay a "moral and ethical answer."

PROFILE

The elections of 1984 marked Uruguay's return to democracy. Since then the main *Colorado* (PC) and *Blanco* (PN) parties have monopolized power, either alone or in coalitions, despite being traditional opponents. The left-wing Broad Front has been the effective opposition, frequently in alliance with trade unions fighting austerity measures and reform of the social security system. Despite the crowded electoral calendar in 1999, and in-fighting among *Blanco* factions, there was broad political consensus on the need for continuing economic reform. In the 1999 elections, Jorge Batlle, the *Colorado* candidate, won the presidency in the face of an unusually strong left-wing challenge.

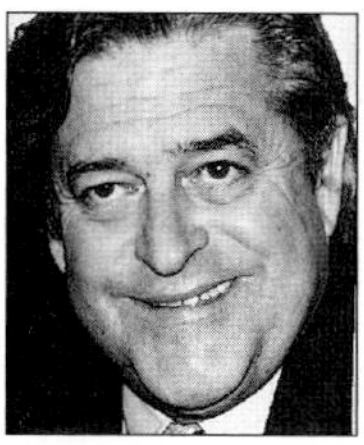

Luis Alberto Lacalle Herrera, *president from 1990–1995.*

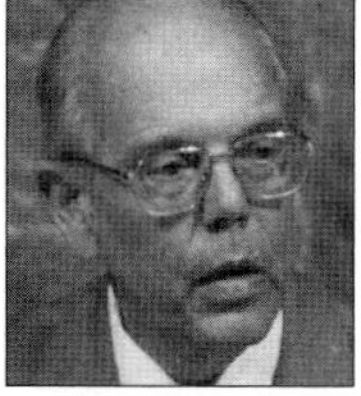

Jorge Batlle Ibáñez, *who took office as president in 2000.*

URUGUAY

Total Land Area : 174 810 sq. km (67 494 sq. miles)

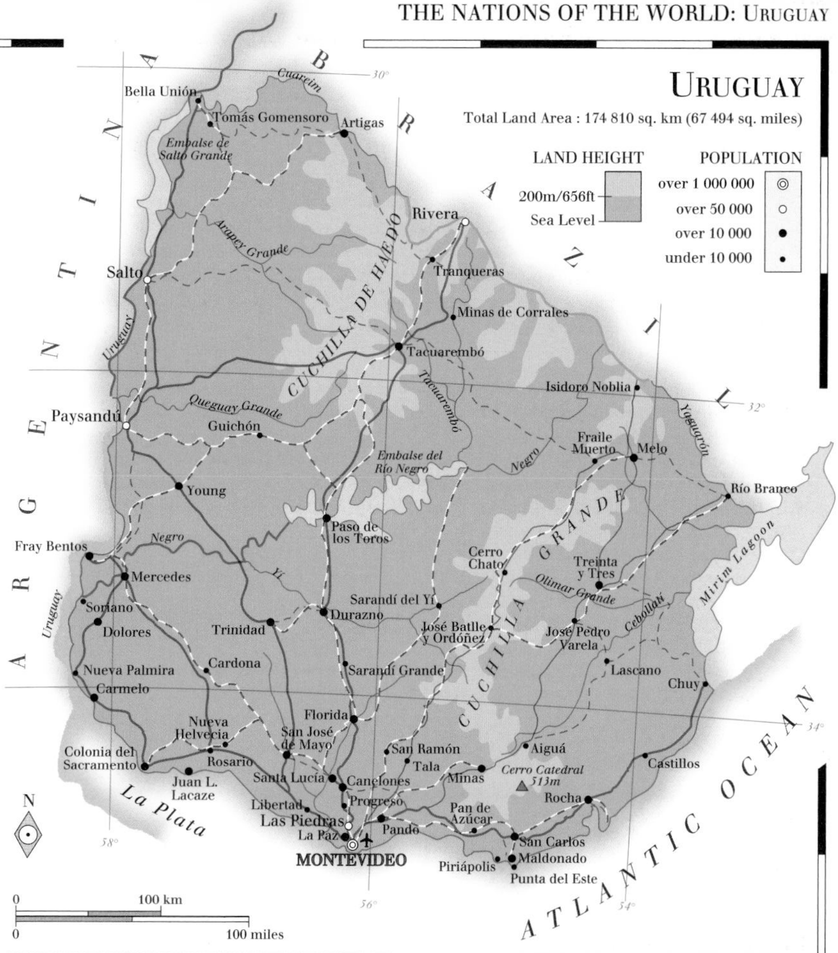
LAND HEIGHT
200m/656ft
Sea Level
POPULATION
over 1 000 000
over 50 000
over 10 000
under 10 000
BRAZIL
ARGENTINA
ATLANTIC OCEAN
Bella Unión
Tomás Gomensoro
Artigas
Cuareim
Embalse de Salto Grande
Rivera
Tranqueras
Salto
Arapey Grande
CUCHILLA DE HAEDO
Minas de Corrales
Tacuarembó
Uruguay
Isidoro Noblia
Yaguarón
Paysandú
Queguay Grande
Guichón
Embalse del Río Negro
Negro
Fraile Muerto
Melo
Río Branco
Young
Mirim Lagoon
Paso de los Toros
Fray Bentos
Cerro Chato
CUCHILLA GRANDE
Treinta y Tres
Mercedes
Olimar Grande
Sarandí del Yí
Soriano
Durazno
José Batlle y Ordóñez
José Pedro Varela
Cebollatí
Dolores
Trinidad
Yí
Nueva Palmira
Cardona
Sarandí Grande
Lascano
Carmelo
Chuy
Florida
Nueva Helvecia
San José de Mayo
San Ramón
Aiguá
Colonia del Sacramento
Rosario
Tala
Cerro Catedral 513m
Castillos
Juan L. Lacaze
Santa Lucía
Canelones
Minas
La Plata
Libertad
Progreso
Pan de Azúcar
Rocha
Las Piedras
Pando
La Paz
San Carlos
MONTEVIDEO
Piriápolis
Maldonado
Punta del Este
N
0 100 km
0 100 miles

WORLD AFFAIRS

Joined UN in 1945

Geplac | Mercsr | IBRD | OAS | RG

Uruguay's chief foreign policy aim is that of achieving full regional integration, with Argentina, Brazil, and Paraguay, in MERCOSUR, the common market of southern South America. It considers that its role has been reduced to being a buffer country between Brazil and Argentina. Uruguay is part of a continental defense alliance with other Latin American countries and the USA. Ongoing border problems exist with Brazil. Uruguay allowed the UK to use its ports during the Falklands conflict.

Uruguay and the USA have signed a legal assistance treaty to allow easier access to the bank accounts of those suspected of laundering the proceeds from narcotics trafficking. This has increasingly been carried out through Montevideo's liberal banking sector.

AID

Recipient

$22m (receipts) Down 8% in 1999

Uruguay received IMF-supported debt reduction loans in the early 1990s, but aid remains modest.

CHRONOLOGY

The Spaniards were the first to colonize the area north of the River Plate. In 1680, the Portuguese also founded a colony there, at Colonia del Sacramento, so starting 150 years of rivalry between the colonial powers for control of the territory.

- **1726** Spaniards found Montevideo. By end of the century, whole country is divided into large cattle ranches.
- **1808** Montevideo declares independence from Buenos Aires.
- **1811** Patriotic rancher and local caudillo, José Gervasio Artigas, fends off Brazilian attack.
- **1812–1820** Uruguayans, known as *Orientales* ("Easterners," from the eastern side of the River Plate), fight wars against Argentinian and Brazilian invaders. Brazil finally takes Montevideo.
- **1827** General Lavalleja defeats Brazilians with Argentine help.
- **1828** Seeing trade benefits that an independent Uruguay would bring as a buffer state between Argentina and Brazil, Britain mediates and secures Uruguayan independence.
- **1836** Start of large-scale European immigration.

U

CHRONOLOGY *continued*

- **1838–1865** La Guerra Grande civil war between *Blancos* (Whites, future conservative party) and *Colorados* (Reds, future liberals).
- **1865–1870** *Colorado* president, General Venancio Flores, takes Uruguay into War of the Triple Alliance against Paraguay.
- **1872** Peace under military rule. *Blancos* strong in country, *Colorados* in cities.
- **1890s** Violent strikes by immigrant trade unionists against landed elite enriched by massive European investment in ranching.
- **1903–1907** Reformist *Colorado*, José Batllé y Ordóñez, president.
- **1911–1915** Batllé serves second term in office. *Batllismo* creates the only welfare state in Latin America with pensions, social security, and free education and health service; also nationalizations, disestablishment of Church, abolition of death penalty.
- **1933** Military coup. Opposition groups excluded from politics.
- **1942** President Alfredo Baldomir dismisses government and tries to bring back proper representation.
- **1939–1945** Neutral in World War II.
- **1951** New constitution replaces president with nine-member council. Decade of great prosperity follows until world agricultural prices plummet. Sharp drop in foreign investment.
- **1958** *Blancos* win elections for first time in 93 years.
- **1962** Tupamaros urban guerrillas founded. Its guerrilla campaign lasts until 1973.
- **1966** Presidency reinstated. *Colorados* back in power.
- **1967** Jorge Pacheco president. Tries to stifle opposition to tough anti-inflation policies.
- **1973** Military coup. Promises to encourage foreign investment counteracted by denial of political freedom and brutal repression of the left; 400,000 emigrate.
- **1984–1985** Military step down. Elections. Julio Sanguinetti (*Colorado*) president.
- **1986** Those guilty of human rights abuse granted amnesty.
- **1989** Referendum endorses amnesty in interests of stability. Elections won by Lacalle Herrera and *Blancos*.
- **1994–1995** Sanguinetti reelected, forms coalition government. MERCOSUR membership.
- **1999** October, presidential election won by *Colorado* Jorge Batlle.
- **2000** Foot-and-mouth disease forces temporary suspension of beef exports.

DEFENSE

No compulsory military service

$317m

Down 1% in 1999

The military withdrew from power in 1985 and has since respected civilian rule. "Lodges" operate within the army to promote officers' interests and have displayed opposition to the government's replacements and promotions within the military hierarchy. A 1986 law virtually blocked investigations into killings, torture, and "disappearances" during the dictatorship, but there is still pressure to bring guilty officers to justice. A presidential decree in 1997 granted amnesty to officers punished for political offenses under military rule.

URUGUAYAN ARMED FORCES

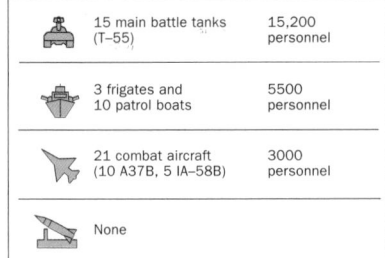

15 main battle tanks (T-55)	15,200 personnel
3 frigates and 10 patrol boats	5500 personnel
21 combat aircraft (10 A37B, 5 IA-58B)	3000 personnel
None	

The defense budget is modest; most equipment is bought from the USA.

ECONOMICS

Inflation 35.2% p.a. (1990–1999)

$20.6bn

11.63–12.51 Uruguayan pesos

SCORE CARD

World GNP Ranking	61st
GNP per Capita	$6220
Balance of Payments	$-605m
Inflation	5.7%
Unemployment	12%

EXPORTS

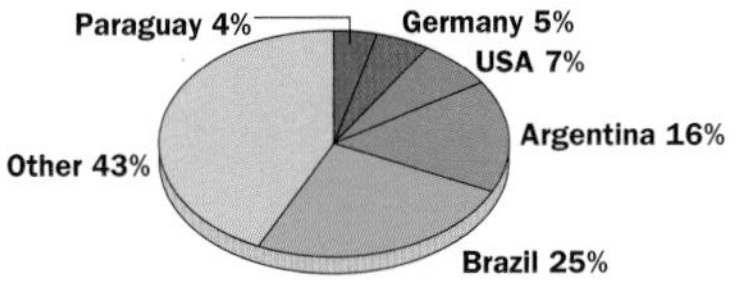
Paraguay 4%
Germany 5%
USA 7%
Argentina 16%
Other 43%
Brazil 25%

IMPORTS

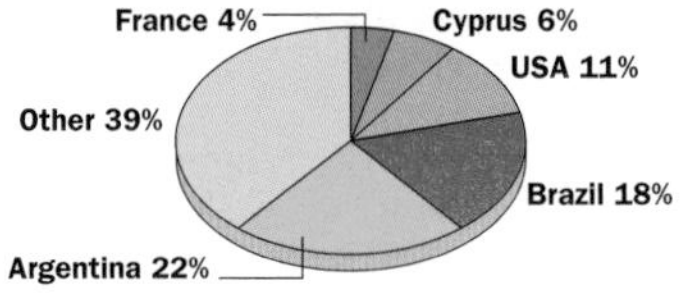
France 4%
Cyprus 6%
USA 11%
Other 39%
Brazil 18%
Argentina 22%

Strengths

Substantial earnings from offshore banking. Buoyant tourism. Fertile grasslands. World's second-largest wool exporter.

Weaknesses

Few natural resources. Dependence on Brazil and Argentine markets. Modest industry. Large public sector deficit. Sluggish economic growth. Potential threat to investment grade status.

Profile

Traditionally an agricultural economy, three-quarters of the country is rich pasture, supporting livestock. Much of the rest is given over to crops. Farming, which formerly brought great wealth, still employs about 15% of the labor force, accounting for some 19% of GDP. Livestock and animal products, especially meat and wool, account for over one-third of export earnings. Manufacturing, accounting for some 18% of GDP, is farm-based. Tourism is increasingly important. Most economic activity – and half the population – is concentrated in Montevideo. Recently growth has been sluggish, making it difficult to achieve GDP and fiscal targets agreed with the IMF. Unions resist spending cuts, and, with public opinion hostile to major privatizations, there has been little progress in necessary structural reforms.

ECONOMIC PERFORMANCE INDICATOR

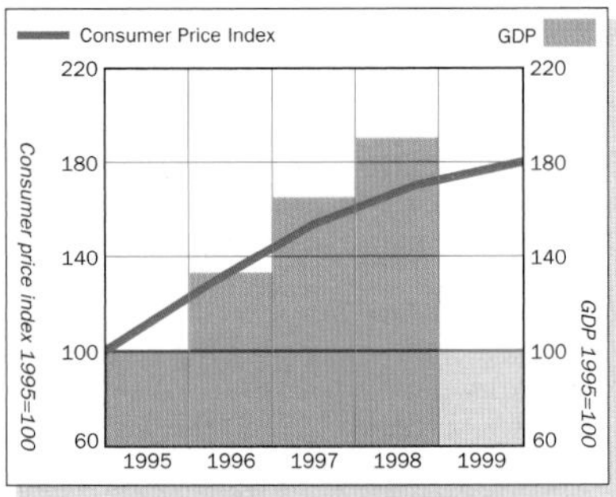
Consumer Price Index
GDP
220
180
140
100
60
1995
1996
1997
1998
1999
Consumer price index 1995=100
GDP 1995=100

URUGUAY : MAJOR BUSINESSES

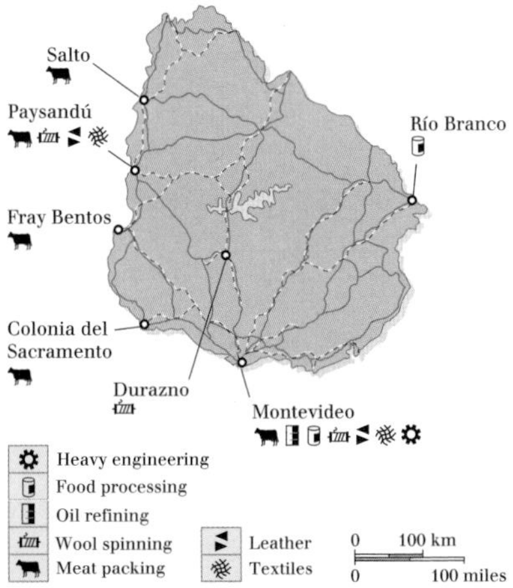
Salto
Paysandú
Río Branco
Fray Bentos
Colonia del Sacramento
Durazno
Montevideo
Heavy engineering
Food processing
Oil refining
Wool spinning
Meat packing
Leather
Textiles
0 100 km
0 100 miles

RESOURCES

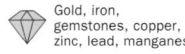

Electric power 2.2m kw

136,912 tonnes

Not an oil producer

15.2m sheep, 10.8m cattle, 13m chickens

Gold, iron, gemstones, copper, zinc, lead, manganese

Most of Uruguay is farmland, much of it given over to cattle and sheep. Rice is the country's only other significant export. There are no known oil or natural gas resources. Considerable potential is believed to exist for the mining sector, but only small quantities of building materials and jewelry-quality agate and amethysts are so far extracted. Gold deposits are currently being developed. Hydroelectric power generates most of the electricity.

ELECTRICITY GENERATION

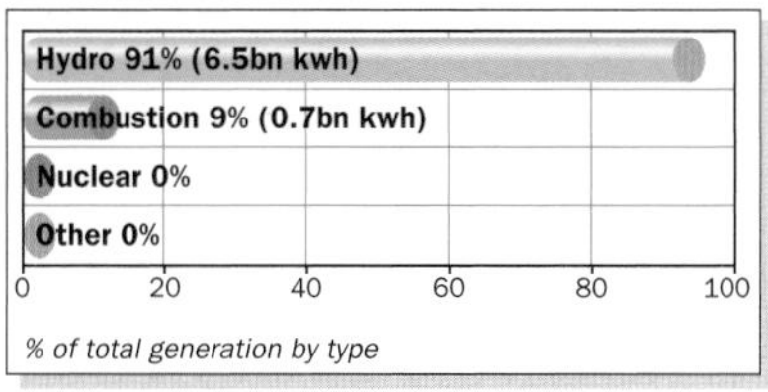
Hydro 91% (6.5bn kwh)
Combustion 9% (0.7bn kwh)
Nuclear 0%
Other 0%
0
20
40
60
80
100
% of total generation by type

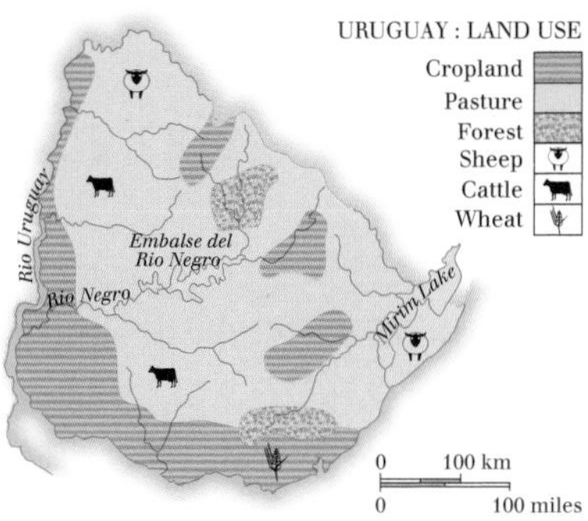
URUGUAY : LAND USE
Cropland
Pasture
Forest
Sheep
Cattle
Wheat
Río Uruguay
Embalse del Río Negro
Río Negro
Mirim Lake
0
100 km
0
100 miles

ENVIRONMENT

Sustainability rank: 14th

1% (0.1% partially protected)

1.8 tonnes per capita

ENVIRONMENTAL TREATIES

Yes

Yes

Yes

Yes

Yes

Yes

Pollution of the main Uruguay and Plate rivers is a concern, as is traffic density in Montevideo.

MEDIA

TV ownership high

Daily newspaper circulation 293 per 1000 people

PUBLISHING AND BROADCAST MEDIA

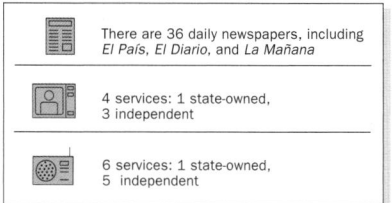

There are 36 daily newspapers, including *El País*, *El Diario*, and *La Mañana*

4 services: 1 state-owned, 3 independent

6 services: 1 state-owned, 5 independent

The press is relatively free. *El País* supports the *Blancos* (PN), while *La Mañana* backs the *Colorados* (PC).

CRIME

Death penalty not used

3159 prisoners

Crime is rising

CRIME RATES

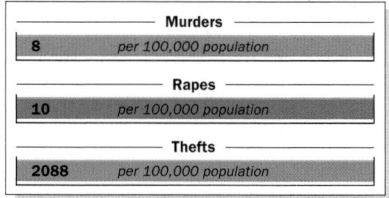

Crime	Rate
Murders	8 per 100,000 population
Rapes	10 per 100,000 population
Thefts	2088 per 100,000 population

Crime levels in Uruguay are low, particularly compared with its neighbors Brazil and Argentina. Domestic theft is the main problem. Bribery is not common.

EDUCATION

School leaving age: 14

98%

79,691 students

THE EDUCATION SYSTEM

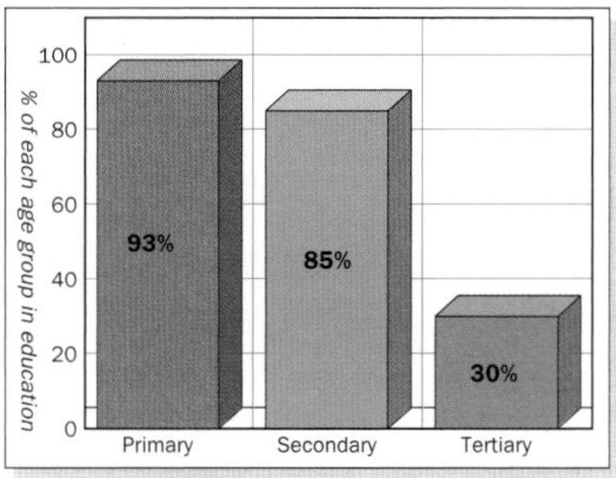
100
80
60
40
20
0
% of each age group in education
93%
85%
30%
Primary
Secondary
Tertiary

Education, inspired by the French *lycée* system, is state-funded for 12 years up to secondary level and is compulsory for all children between the ages of six and fourteen. Both state and private schools follow the same curriculum; private schools are monitored by the government. Facilities are rudimentary in rural areas. Uruguay has two state-funded universities. The children of wealthy Uruguayans tend to complete their studies in the USA. Resistance to tax increases and pressure to reduce the fiscal deficit have both placed serious constraints on spending on education. Secondary school students staged protests in 2000 against the resulting effects on the system.

HEALTH

Welfare state health benefits

1 per 270 people

Cerebrovascular and heart diseases, cancers, accidents

Most Uruguayans have easy access to health services. Average life expectancy is high. Public services provide for 40% of the population, while the private sector caters for the remaining 60%. Despite opposition, the government has privatized some of the state medical establishments.

Health spending has in recent years been a victim of the budget cuts and social welfare reforms aimed at controlling the fiscal deficit.

SPENDING

GDP/cap. increase

CONSUMPTION AND SPENDING

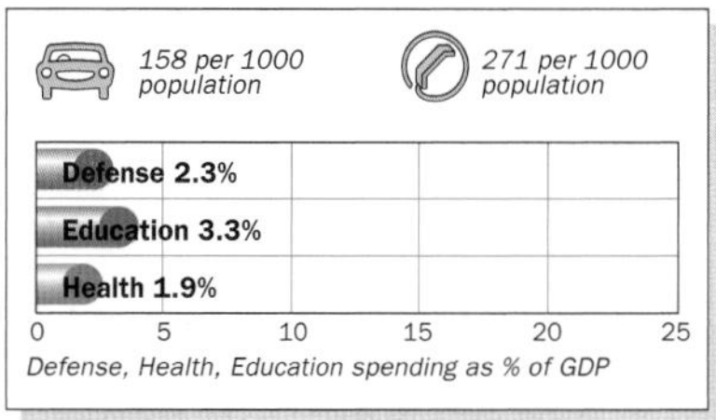
158 per 1000 population
271 per 1000 population
Defense 2.3%
Education 3.3%
Health 1.9%
0
5
10
15
20
25
Defense, Health, Education spending as % of GDP

Uruguay possesses the social mobility which is typical of countries created through decades of large-scale immigration. Many professionals come from modest backgrounds. A 1999 report by the IDB exempted Uruguay (along with Costa Rica and Jamaica) from the regional trend of serious income inequality.

The wealthy tend either to be landowners or are employed in the financial sector. They have traditionally looked toward Europe, rather than the USA, for luxury goods.

The most deprived sections of Uruguayan society are the urban poor of Montevideo, a large proportion of whom are of mixed African and European descent, and the rural poor, who own little or no land.

WORLD RANKING

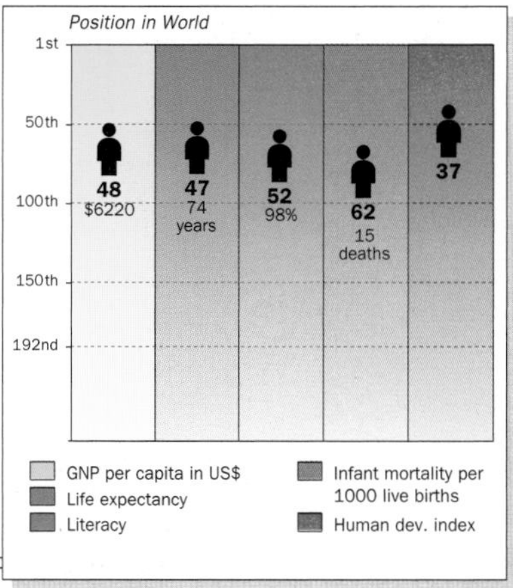
Position in World
1st
50th
100th
150th
192nd
48
$6220
47
74 years
52
98%
62
15 deaths
37
GNP per capita in US$
Life expectancy
Literacy
Infant mortality per 1000 live births
Human dev. index

U

UZBEKISTAN

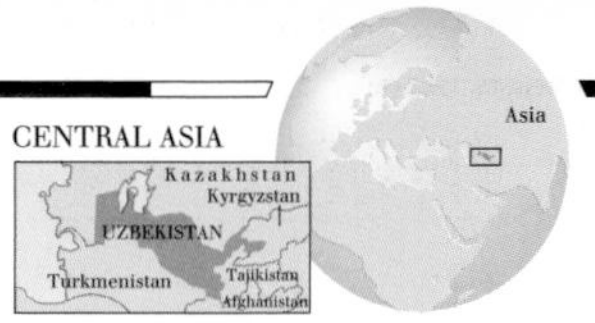
CENTRAL ASIA
Asia
Kazakhstan
Kyrgyzstan
UZBEKISTAN
Turkmenistan
Tajikistan
Afghanistan

OFFICIAL NAME: Republic of Uzbekistan **CAPITAL:** Tashkent
POPULATION: 24.3 million **CURRENCY:** Som **OFFICIAL LANGUAGE:** Uzbek

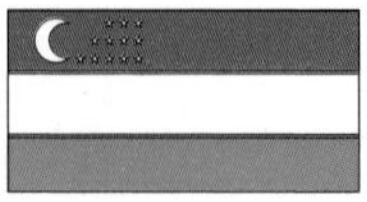

1991
1991
Sept 1
UZ
+5 to +6
+998
.uz

SHARING THE ARAL SEA coastline with its northern neighbor, Kazakhstan, Uzbekistan has common borders with five countries, including Afghanistan to the south. It is the most populous central Asian republic and has considerable natural resources. Uzbekistan contains the ancient cities of Samarqand, Bukhara (Bukhoro), Khiva, and Tashkent. The dictatorship of President Karimov has prevented the spread of Islamic fundamentalism.

CLIMATE

Desert/mountain

WEATHER CHART

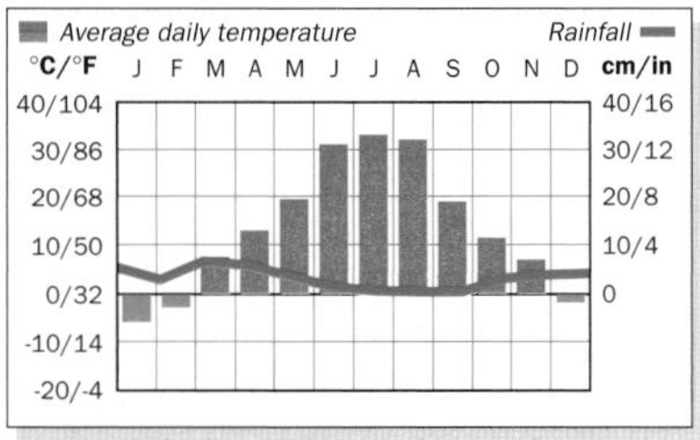
Average daily temperature
Rainfall
°C/°F
J F M A M J J A S O N D
cm/in
40/104
30/86
20/68
10/50
0/32
-10/14
-20/-4
40/16
30/12
20/8
10/4
0

Uzbekistan has a harsh continental climate. Summers can be extremely hot and dry. Large areas of the country are desert.

TRANSPORTATION

Drive on right

Tashkent International 1.85m passengers

Has no fleet

THE TRANSPORTATION NETWORK

71,237 km (44,265 miles)	None
3645 km (2265 miles)	1100 km (684 miles)

Uzbekistan has a well-developed transportation system. An extensive network of buses serves country areas, while good Soviet-style systems of trolley buses and trolleys operate in the major cities. Road and rail networks have deteriorated since 1991, however, and are concentrated in the south and east. The national airline is Uzbek Khavo Yullari (Uzbekistan Airways).

TOURISM

Visitors : Population 1:89

272,000 visitors

Up 196% 1995–1998

MAIN TOURIST ARRIVALS

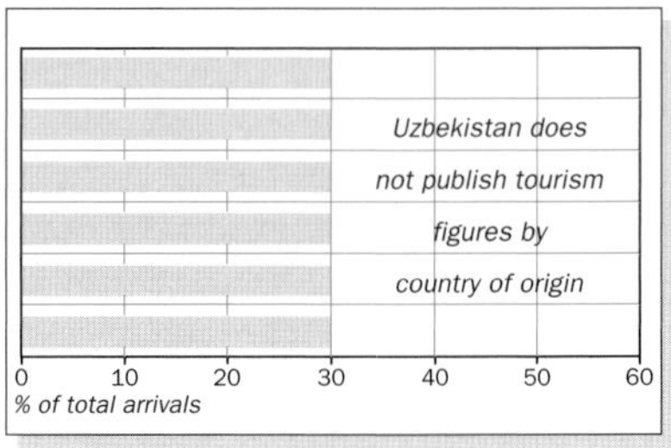
Uzbekistan does not publish tourism figures by country of origin
0
10
20
30
40
50
60
% of total arrivals

Uzbekistan has considerable tourist potential. Bukhara, once a trading center on the silk route, is famous worldwide for its architecture and carpet-making. It has great religious significance for Muslims, who are encouraged to make at least one pilgrimage to its holy shrines. Bukhara's Kalyan Mosque is famous for its minaret built of unbaked bricks. The city of Samarkand was expanded in the 14th century by Timur, and contains the monumental gateway of the Shir Dar Madrasa, which vies with India's Taj Mahal as one of the most beautiful buildings in the Islamic world.

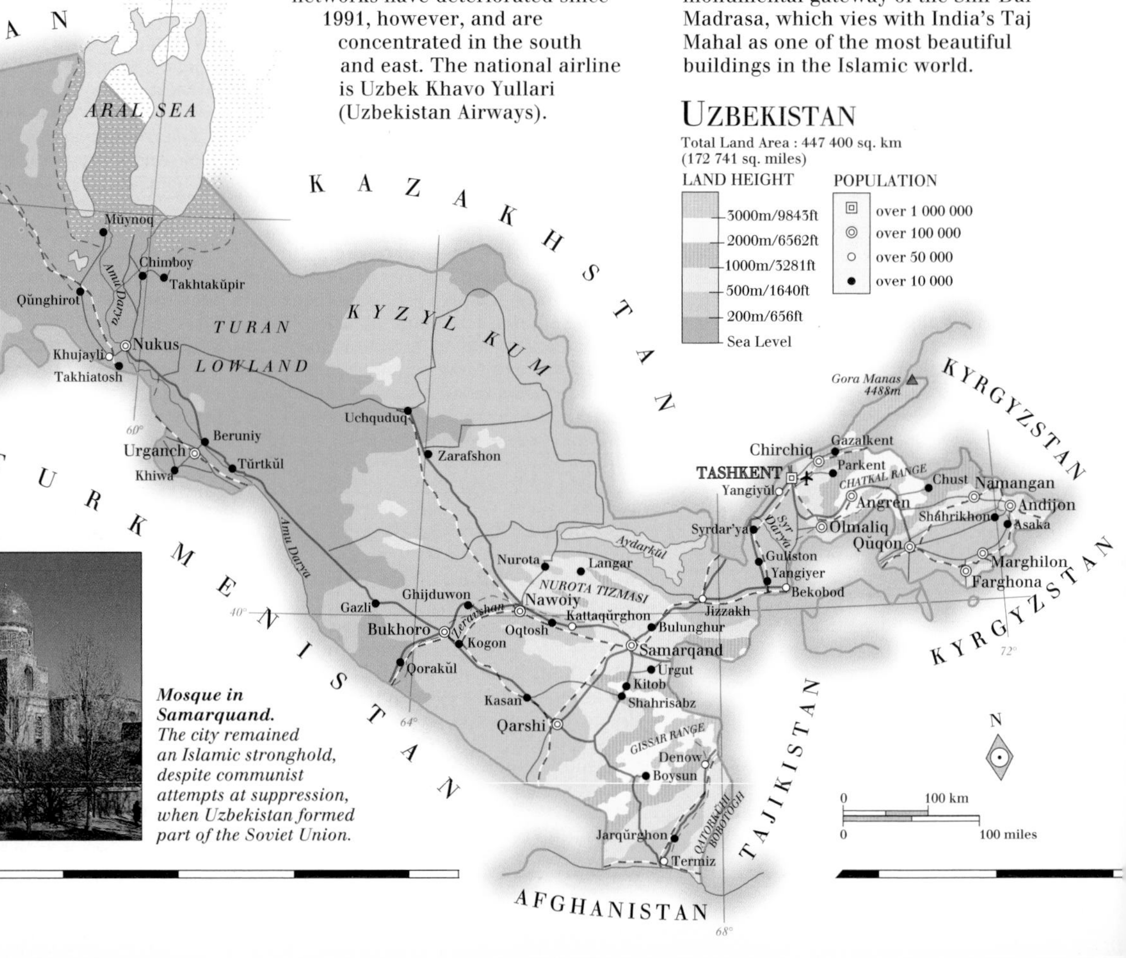
UZBEKISTAN
Total Land Area : 447 400 sq. km
(172 741 sq. miles)
LAND HEIGHT
3000m/9843ft
2000m/6562ft
1000m/3281ft
500m/1640ft
200m/656ft
Sea Level
POPULATION
over 1 000 000
over 100 000
over 50 000
over 10 000
KAZAKHSTAN
KAZAKHSTAN
KAZAKHSTAN
ARAL SEA
USTYURT PLATEAU
TURAN LOWLAND
KYZYL KUM
TURKMENISTAN
KYRGYZSTAN
KYRGYZSTAN
TAJIKISTAN
AFGHANISTAN
Mŭynoq
Chimboy
Takhtakŭpir
Qŭnghirot
Amu Darya
Nukus
Khujayli
Takhiatosh
Uchquduq
Zarafshon
Beruniy
Urganch
Khiwa
Tŭrtkŭl
Gora Manas 4488m
Chirchiq
Gazalkent
Parkent
TASHKENT
Yangiyŭl
CHATKAL RANGE
Chust
Namangan
Angren
Andijon
Shahrikhon
Asaka
Syrdar'ya
Syr Darya
Olmaliq
Qŭqon
Marghilon
Farghona
Gulistan
Yangiyer
Bekobod
Aydarkŭl
Nurota
Langar
NUROTA TIZMASI
Nawoiy
Ghijduwon
Gazli
Bukhoro
Zeravshan
Kogon
Oqtosh
Kattaqŭrghon
Jizzakh
Bulunghur
Samarqand
Urgut
Qorakŭl
Kitob
Shahrisabz
Kasan
Qarshi
GISSAR RANGE
Denow
Boysun
Jarqŭrghon
Termiz
44°
40°
36°
60°
64°
68°
72°
N
0
100 km
0
100 miles

Mosque in Samarquand. *The city remained an Islamic stronghold, despite communist attempts at suppression, when Uzbekistan formed part of the Soviet Union.*

PEOPLE

Pop. density medium

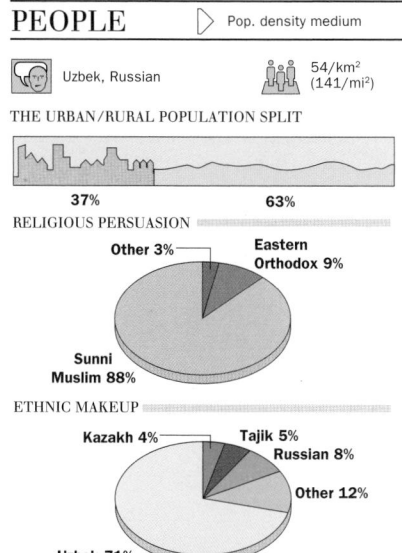

Uzbek, Russian

54/km² (141/mi²)

THE URBAN/RURAL POPULATION SPLIT

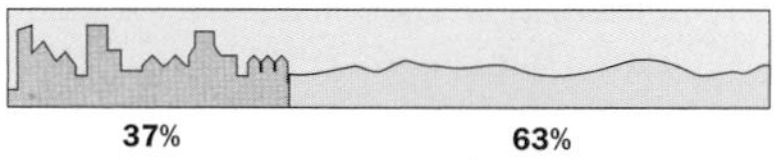
37%
63%

RELIGIOUS PERSUASION

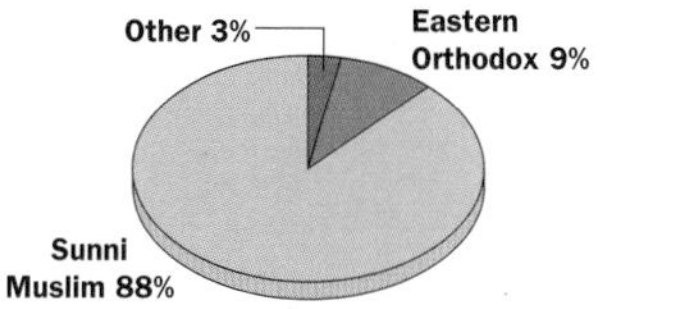
Other 3%
Eastern Orthodox 9%
Sunni Muslim 88%

ETHNIC MAKEUP

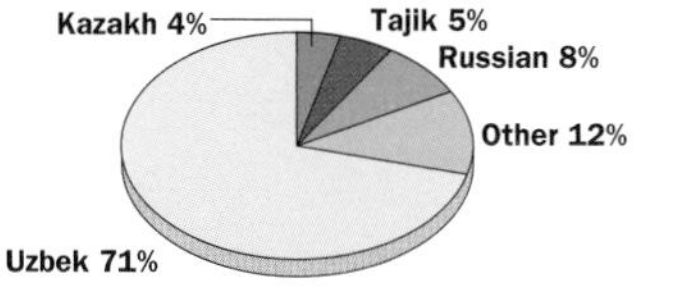
Kazakh 4%
Tajik 5%
Russian 8%
Other 12%
Uzbek 71%

Among the former Soviet republics, Uzbekistan has a relatively complex makeup. In addition to the Uzbeks, Russians, Tajiks, and Kazakhs, there are small minorities of Tatars and Karakalpaks. The proportion of Russians has been declining since the 1970s, when net emigration of Russians began. Tensions among ethnic groups have the potential to create regional and racial conflict. The authoritarian nature of the Karimov leadership has so far prevented these antagonisms from becoming violent. Incidents such as the 1989 and 1990 clashes between Meskhetian Turks and Uzbeks are rare. The removal of the dominance of the Communist Party has meant that Uzbek society has reverted to traditional social patterns based on family, religion, clan, and region, rather than on membership of the party. Independence has done little to alter the minor role of women in politics. Arranged marriages are still the custom in the countryside.

POPULATION AGE BREAKDOWN

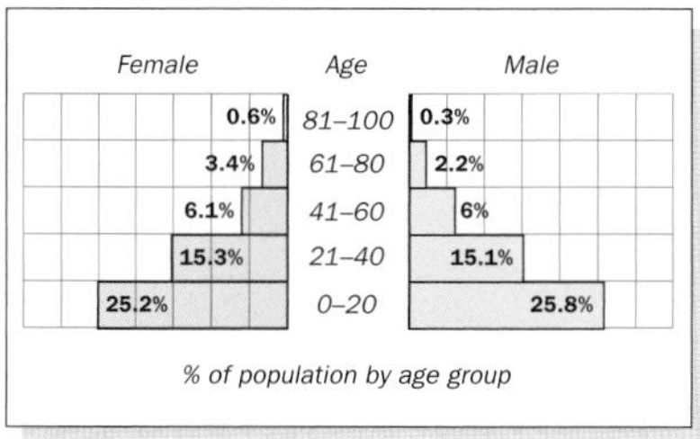
Female
Age
Male
0.6%
81–100
0.3%
3.4%
61–80
2.2%
6.1%
41–60
6%
15.3%
21–40
15.1%
25.2%
0–20
25.8%
% of population by age group

POLITICS

Multiparty elections

1999/2004

President Islam Karimov

AT THE LAST ELECTION

National Parliament 250 seats

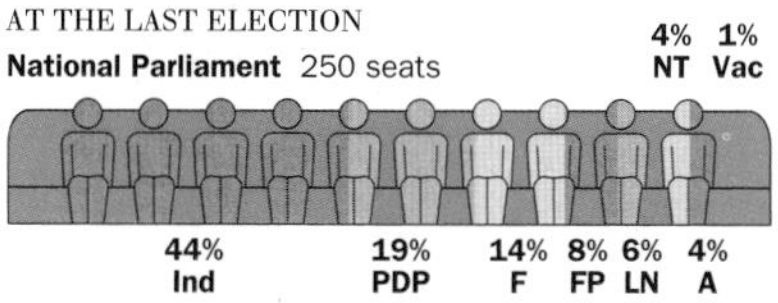
4% NT
1% Vac
44% Ind
19% PDP
14% F
8% FP
6% LN
4% A

Ind = Independents **PDP** = People's Democratic Party
F = Fidorkorlar **FP** = Fatherland Progress Party
LN = Local nominees **A** = Adolat
NT = National Renaissance **Vac** = Vacant

Uzbekistan is effectively run by a presidential dictatorship.

MAIN POLITICAL ISSUES

Islamic fundamentalism

The civil war in neighboring Tajikistan made the Karimov leadership wary of Islamic fundamentalism taking hold in Uzbekistan. The Uzbek constitution stipulates the separation of Islam and the state, and Islam has been carefully kept out of politics. A joint operation with Kyrgyzstan and Tajikistan against the pan-regional Islamic Movement of Uzbekistan began in mid-2000, as cross-border attacks increased.

Regionalism

Uzbekistan's high birthrate is putting pressure on limited agricultural resources. There have been calls for secession from some regions wishing to stop large numbers of people moving from poorer areas. In the eastern Fergana Valley, one of the most densely populated regions, there has been a number of violent incidents.

PROFILE

President Karimov's PDP has not been willing to devolve or share power. A constitution adopted in December 1992 appeared to endorse multiparty politics along Western lines. However, Karimov took advantage of greater powers granted to his office by banning a number of opposition parties, including the nationalist *Birlik* (Unity) movement and the Islamic Renaissance Party. The only legal opposition party, *Erk* (Will), was proscribed in 1993, and in 1995 incurred the wrath of the government when a group of activists received stiff prison sentences after being found guilty of political subversion.

Opposition is now entirely underground. The intimidation and arbitrary imprisonment of political dissidents are common. Karimov has kept the support of the Russian minority by avoiding nationalist rhetoric.

Islam Karimov, *first elected president in 1990 and Uzbekistan's sole leader since independence.*

WORLD AFFAIRS

Joined UN in 1992

CIS | SCO | OIC | NAM | OSCE

Unlike neighboring Turkmenistan, Kyrgyzstan, and Tajikistan, Uzbekistan has the resources to allow it to follow a relatively independent foreign policy. The Karimov leadership has used this to promote Uzbekistan as the leading central Asian state. It has established itself as the CIS regional power base, and was a key player in the formation of a central Asian common market (with Kazakhstan and Kyrgyzstan) in 1994. In 1995, Karimov called for a common "Turkestan" republic comprising the five former Soviet central Asian republics, and later that year endorsed plans for a common central Asian defense council.

Relations with Turkey are also developing. While Western companies have difficulty in sealing contracts in Uzbekistan, Turkish companies have been commissioned to build vital installations such as telecommunications.

The crucial relationship, however, remains that with Russia, which has 100,000 troops stationed in the country. In 1994 a bilateral treaty envisaged Uzbekistan's economic integration with Russia. Karimov's antinationalist approach to domestic politics has Russian support.

CHRONOLOGY

Part of the great Mongol empire, present-day Uzbekistan was incorporated into the Russian Empire between 1865 and 1876. Russification of the area was superficial, and it was not until Soviet rule that significant Slav immigration occurred. A further influx of Slavs occurred during Stalin's program of forced collectivization.

- **1917** Soviet power established in Tashkent.
- **1918** Turkestan Autonomous Soviet Socialist Republic (ASSR), incorporating present-day Uzbekistan, proclaimed.
- **1923–1941** Language changed repeatedly: from Arabic alphabet to Latin, then based on Iranized Tashkent, and finally replaced by Cyrillic.
- **1924** Basmachi rebels who resisted Soviet rule crushed. Uzbek SSR founded (which, until 1929, included the Tajik ASSR).
- **1925** Anti-Islamic campaign bans schools and closes mosques.
- **1936** Karakalpak ASSR (formerly part of the Russian Soviet Federative Socialist Republic) incorporated into the Uzbek SSR.

U

CHRONOLOGY *continued*

- **1937** Uzbek communist leadership is purged by Stalin.
- **1941–1945** Industrial boom.
- **1959** Sharaf Rashidov becomes first secretary of Communist Party of Uzbekistan (CPUz). Retains position until 1983.
- **1982–1983** Yuri Andropov becomes leader in Moscow. His anticorruption purge results in emergence of a new generation of central Asian officials.
- **1989** First noncommunist political movement, Unity Party (*Birlik*), formed but not officially registered. June, clashes erupt between Meskhetian Turks and indigenous Uzbek population of Fergana Valley resulting in more than 100 deaths. October, *Birlik* campaign leads to Uzbek being declared the official language.
- **1990** Islam Karimov becomes executive president of the new Uzbek Supreme Soviet. Further interethnic fighting in Fergana Valley; 320 killed.
- **1991** August, independence is proclaimed and Republic of Uzbekistan is adopted as official name. October, Uzbekistan signs treaty establishing economic community with seven other former Soviet republics. November, CPUz restructured as the People's Democratic Party of Uzbekistan (PDP); Karimov remains its leader. December, Karimov confirmed in post of president. Uzbekistan joins the CIS.
- **1992** Price liberalization provokes student riots in Tashkent. New post-Soviet constitution adopted along Western democratic lines. All religious parties banned. September, Uzbekistan sends troops to Tajikistan to suppress violence and strengthen border controls.
- **1993** Growing harassment of opposition political parties, *Erk* and *Birlik*.
- **1994** March, signing of integration treaty with Russia. July, introduction of new currency, the som, which becomes sole legal tender in October.
- **1995** January, Karimov's PDP wins legislative elections. March, referendum extends Karimov's presidential term until 2000. December, Utkur Sultanov replaces Abdulashim Mutalov as prime minister.
- **1999** Bomb attacks by Islamic terrorists lead to crackdown and arrests of hundreds of opposition activists. Legislative elections.
- **2000** Karimov reelected as president.

U

AID

Recipient

$134m (receipts)

Down 8% in 1999

A lack of commitment to economic stabilization and allegations of human rights violations have generally deterred bilateral aid donors. The World Bank is the largest donor, allocating millions of dollars to support economic reform and a range of agricultural, financial, and social projects.

DEFENSE

Compulsory military service

$615m

Down 8% in 1999

Uzbekistan has a 1000-strong National Guard, which generally acts as the personal army of Karimov. Russian troops are still based on Uzbek territory to protect the Russian minority. In 1995, Uzbekistan approved a joint central Asian regional defense council with Kazakhstan and Kyrgyzstan.

President Karimov is a strong advocate of a nuclear-free zone in central Asia.

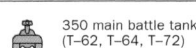

UZBEK ARMED FORCES

350 main battle tanks (T-62, T-64, T-72)	50,000 personnel
None	
135 combat aircraft (Su-17, Su-24, Su-25, Su-27, MiG-29)	9100 personnel
None	

ECONOMICS

Inflation 293% p.a. (1990–1999)

$17.6bn

650.0–322.8 som

SCORE CARD

- WORLD GNP RANKING 72nd
- GNP PER CAPITA $720
- BALANCE OF PAYMENTS ....$-39m
- INFLATION ....-24.6%
- UNEMPLOYMENT 1%

EXPORTS

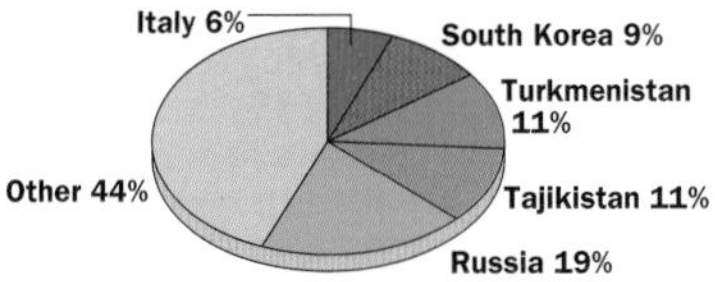
Italy 6%
South Korea 9%
Turkmenistan 11%
Tajikistan 11%
Russia 19%
Other 44%

IMPORTS

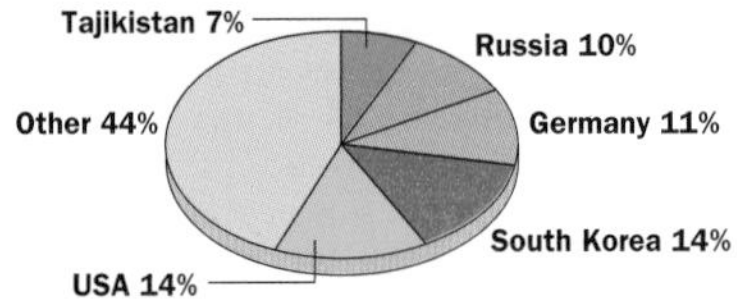
Tajikistan 7%
Russia 10%
Germany 11%
South Korea 14%
USA 14%
Other 44%

ECONOMIC PERFORMANCE INDICATOR

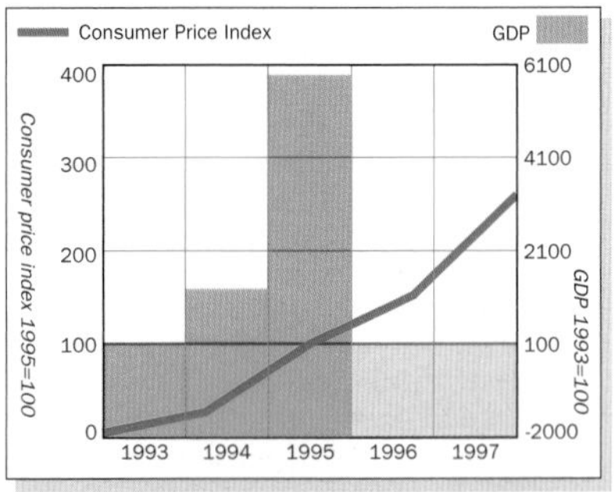
Consumer Price Index
GDP
Consumer price index 1995=100
GDP 1993=100
400
300
200
100
0
6100
4100
2100
100
-2000
1993
1994
1995
1996
1997

STRENGTHS
Gold. Well-developed cotton market. Considerable unexploited deposits of oil and natural gas. Current production of natural gas makes significant contribution to electricity generation. Manufacturing tradition includes agricultural machinery and central Asia's only aviation factory.

WEAKNESSES
Dependent on grain imports, as domestic production meets only 25% of needs. Very limited economic reform. High inflation. Environmentally damaging irrigation scheme for cotton production.

PROFILE
Uzbekistan's economy is predominantly agricultural with the exception of Tashkent, which became an industrial area during World War II. Pro-market reforms have been slow, despite fresh assistance from the World Bank to raise the efficiency of privatized companies. Rocketing food prices fueled by a 1500% inflation rate led to food rationing in 1995. The gold sector has attracted investment by US companies. Energy resources are still to be fully exploited.

UZBEKISTAN : MAJOR BUSINESSES

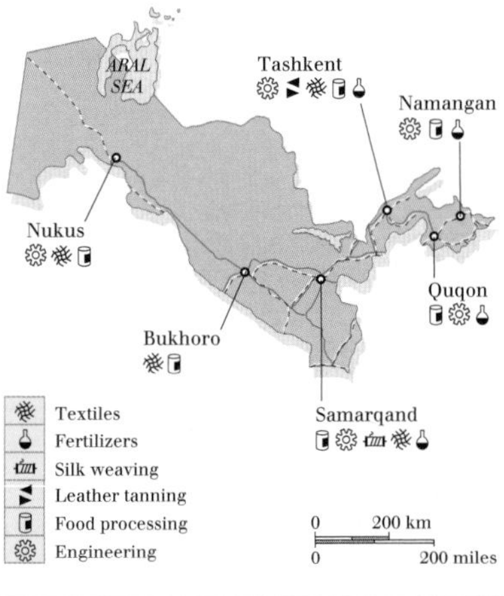
ARAL SEA
Tashkent
Namangan
Nukus
Quqon
Bukhoro
Samarqand
Textiles
Fertilizers
Silk weaving
Leather tanning
Food processing
Engineering
0
200 km
0
200 miles

RESOURCES

Electric power 11.7m kw

10,565 tonnes

175,000 b/d (reserves 600,000,000 bbl)

8.92m sheep, 5.27m cattle, 14.4m chickens

Natural gas, coal, oil, gold, uranium, copper, tungsten, aluminum

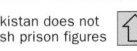

ELECTRICITY GENERATION

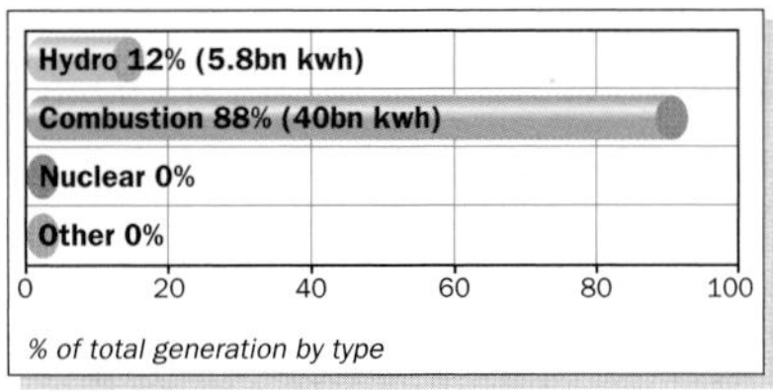

Hydro 12% (5.8bn kwh)
Combustion 88% (40bn kwh)
Nuclear 0%
Other 0%
0
20
40
60
80
100
% of total generation by type

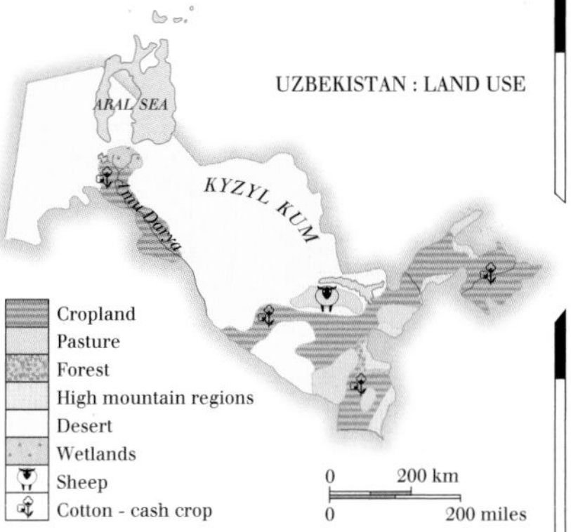

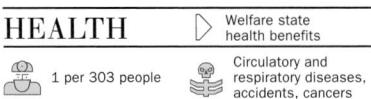

UZBEKISTAN : LAND USE
ARAL SEA
KYZYL KUM
Cropland
Pasture
Forest
High mountain regions
Desert
Wetlands
Sheep
Cotton - cash crop
0
200 km
0
200 miles

Uzbekistan has the world's largest gold mine, at Murantau in the Kyzyl Kum desert, and also large deposits of natural gas, petroleum, coal, and uranium. An important oilfield was discovered in 1992 in the Namangan region and production will rise with further investment. Most gas produced is currently used domestically, but it could also become a strong export.

Cotton is the main focus of agriculture: Uzbekistan is the world's fourth-largest producer. A decision after independence to diversify was reversed when the value of cotton as a commodity on the world market became clear. Fruit, silk cocoons, and vegetables for Moscow's markets are also of rising importance.

ENVIRONMENT

Sustainability rank: 90th

2%

4.4 tonnes per capita

ENVIRONMENTAL TREATIES

Yes	Yes	Yes
Yes	Yes	Yes

The irrigation schemes required to sustain the cotton industry have wreaked considerable environmental damage. Soil salination is now a major problem. The Aral Sea has also been seriously depleted. From 61,836 sq km (23,875 sq miles) in 1974, it had shrunk to less than half that area by 1997. In 1998 the World Bank approved more than $11 million to save the Aral Sea region. The indiscriminate use of fertilizers and pesticides to raise production has polluted many rivers.

MEDIA

TV ownership high

Daily newspaper circulation 3 per 1000 people

PUBLISHING AND BROADCAST MEDIA

There are 3 daily newspapers, including the Uzbek *Khalk suzi* and the Russian *Pravda Vostoka*

2 state-controlled services

1 state-controlled service broadcasting in many languages

Restrictions on independent publications, designed to encourage the promotion of the personality cult and policies of Karimov, were eased in mid-1998 with the publication of the first private newspaper. However, the opposition press is still closely monitored and the expression of Islamic and nationalist opinion is forbidden.

CRIME

Death penalty used

Uzbekistan does not publish prison figures

Up 5% 1996–1998

CRIME RATES

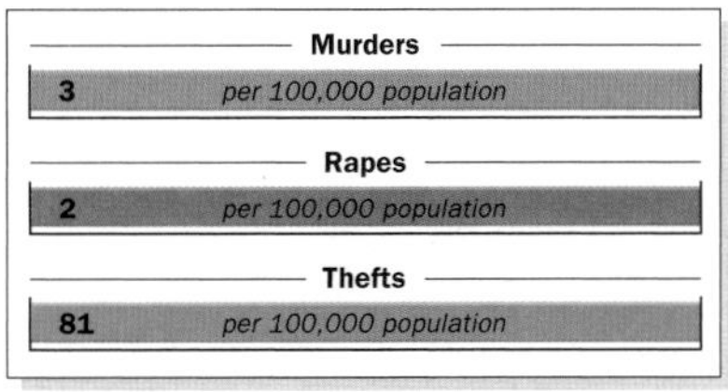

Murders
3
per 100,000 population
Rapes
2
per 100,000 population
Thefts
81
per 100,000 population

Crime has risen as living standards have declined. In rural areas, drug-producing plants, particularly poppies, are grown to boost falling incomes. Unofficial Islamic courts in the Fergana Valley are a sign of opposition to the government.

EDUCATION

School leaving age: 17

89%

638,200 students

THE EDUCATION SYSTEM

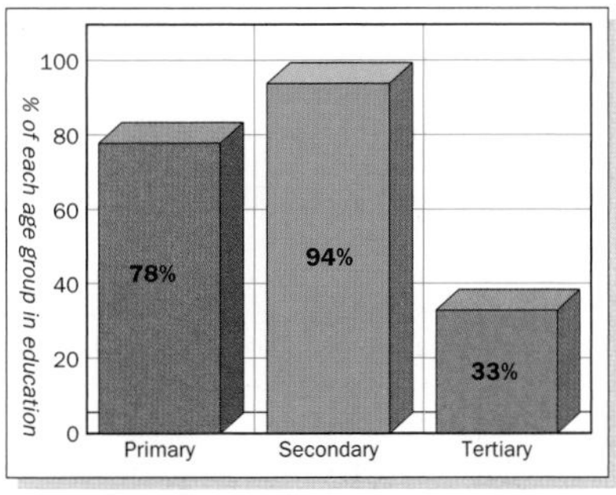

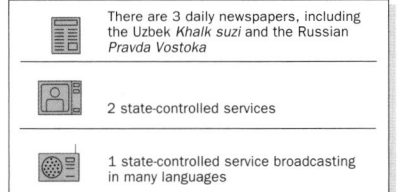

100
80
60
40
20
0
% of each age group in education
78%
94%
33%
Primary
Secondary
Tertiary

The state system still follows the Soviet model, though some instruction is in Uzbek. In the late 1980s, there were a few ethnic Tajik schools and a university in Samarkand. These were closed down in 1992 as relations deteriorated between Uzbekistan and Tajikistan. The rise in Islamic consciousness has led to a growing number of *madrasas*, schools attached to mosques. In 1999 the establishment of Tashkent Islamic University was agreed.

HEALTH

Welfare state health benefits

1 per 303 people

Circulatory and respiratory diseases, accidents, cancers

The health service has been in decline since the dissolution of the USSR. Some rural areas are not served at all. In 1998 a $69.7 million project to improve health services was announced, with the World Bank providing a loan of some $30 million. Serious respiratory diseases among cotton growers are increasing.

SPENDING

GDP/cap. decrease

CONSUMPTION AND SPENDING

No data

66 per 1000 population

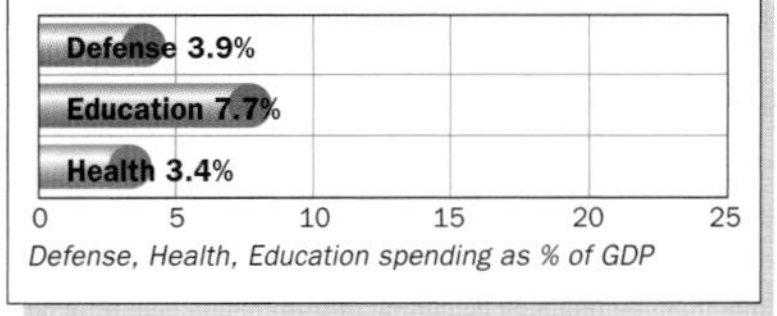

Defense 3.9%
Education 7.7%
Health 3.4%
0
5
10
15
20
25
Defense, Health, Education spending as % of GDP

Former communists are still the wealthiest group, since they retain control of the economy. Many rural poor live below the poverty line.

WORLD RANKING

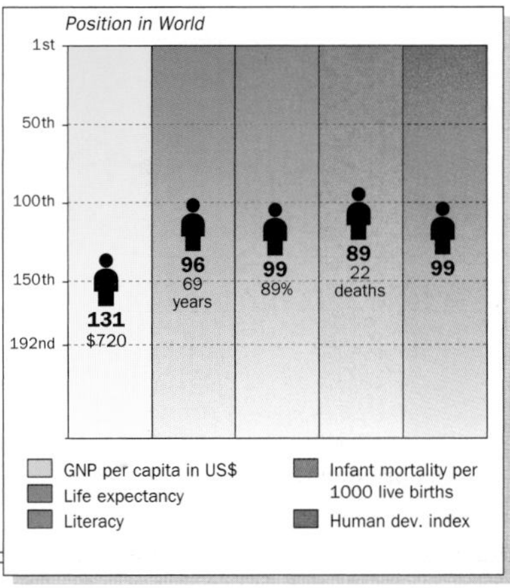

Position in World
1st
50th
100th
150th
192nd
131
$720
96
69
years
99
89%
89
22
deaths
99
GNP per capita in US$
Life expectancy
Literacy
Infant mortality per 1000 live births
Human dev. index

U

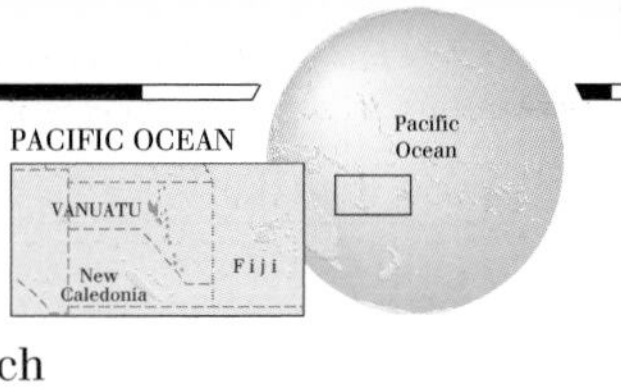
PACIFIC OCEAN
VANUATU
New Caledonia
Fiji
Pacific Ocean

VANUATU

OFFICIAL NAME: Republic of Vanuatu **CAPITAL:** Port-Vila
POPULATION: 200,000 **CURRENCY:** Vatu **OFFICIAL LANGUAGES:** Bislama, English, and French

1980 | 1980 | July 30 | VU | +11 | +678 | .vu

AN ARCHIPELAGO strung out over 1300 km (800 miles) of the South Pacific, Vanuatu lies 1000 km (620 miles) west of Fiji. Mountainous and volcanic in origin, only 12 of the 82 islands are of significant size – Espiritu Santo and Malekula are the largest. Formerly the New Hebrides – ruled jointly by France and Britain from 1906 – Vanuatu became independent in 1980. Politics since independence have been democratic but volatile.

CLIMATE

Tropical oceanic

WEATHER CHART

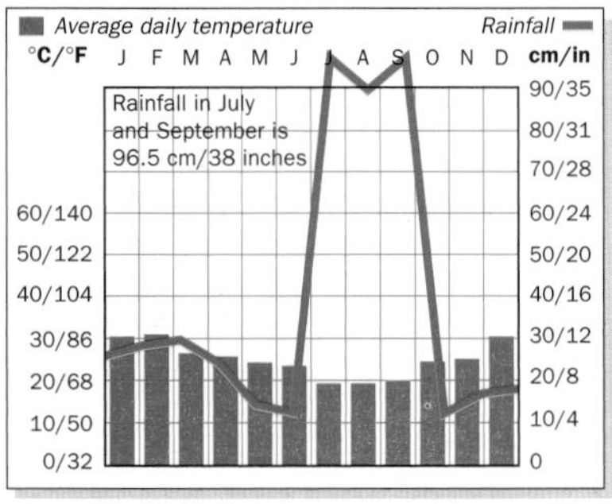
Average daily temperature
Rainfall
°C/°F
J F M A M J J A S O N D
cm/in
Rainfall in July and September is 96.5 cm/38 inches
60/140
50/122
40/104
30/86
20/68
10/50
0/32
90/35
80/31
70/28
60/24
50/20
40/16
30/12
20/8
10/4
0

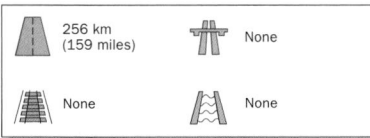

The climate is tropical and hot. Rainfall and temperatures decrease north to south. Cyclones occur November–April.

TRANSPORTATION

Drive on right

Bauerfield, Port-Vila | 293 ships 1.6m grt

THE TRANSPORTATION NETWORK

256 km (159 miles)	None
None	None

International carrier Air Vanuatu merged with the domestic carrier Vanair in March 2001.

TOURISM

Visitors : Population 1:3.5

57,000 visitors | Up 14% in 2000

MAIN TOURIST ARRIVALS

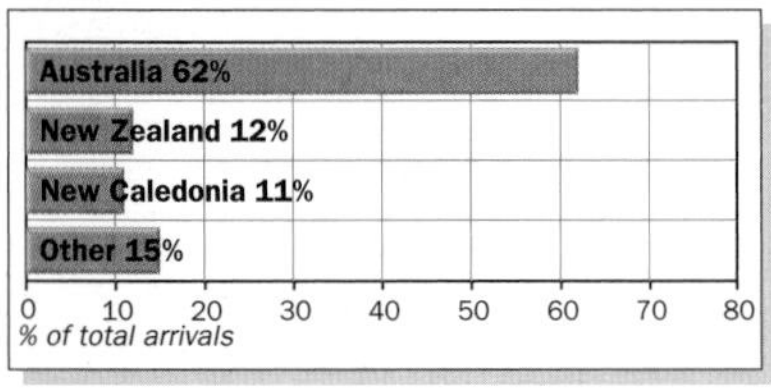
Australia 62%
New Zealand 12%
New Caledonia 11%
Other 15%
0 10 20 30 40 50 60 70 80
% of total arrivals

Tourism is the fastest-growing sector of the economy. Organized tours include sea fishing, sailing, kayaking, and diving.

PEOPLE

Pop. density low

Bislama (Melanesian pidgin), English, French | 16/km² (42/mi²)

THE URBAN/RURAL POPULATION SPLIT

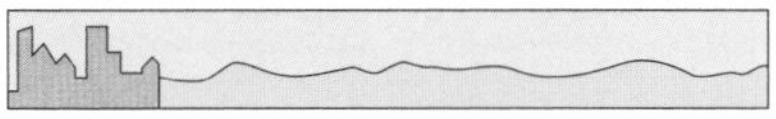
20%
80%

RELIGIOUS PERSUASION

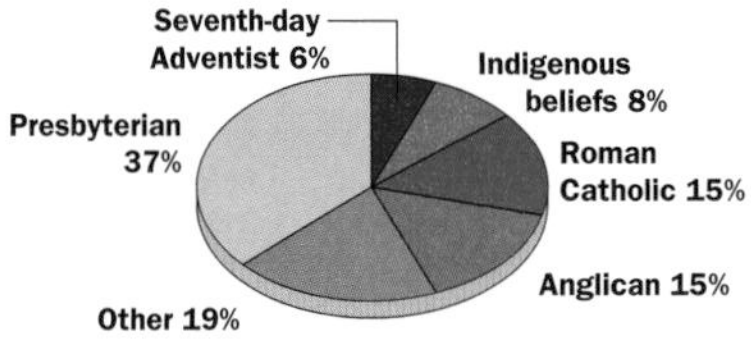
Seventh-day Adventist 6%
Indigenous beliefs 8%
Roman Catholic 15%
Anglican 15%
Other 19%
Presbyterian 37%

Indigenous Melanesians, ni-Vanuatu, comprise 94% of the population. Of Vanuatu's 82 islands, 67 are inhabited, but 80% of people live on 12 main islands. The population is becoming more urbanized as one in eight ni-Vanuatu now lives in Port-Vila. However, 75% of the population still live by subsistence agriculture.

Vanuatu is home to some of the Pacific's most traditional peoples, and local social and religious customs are strong. With 105 indigenous languages, Vanuatu boasts the world's highest per capita density of languages. Bislama pidgin is the lingua franca.

Women have lower social status than men, and bride price is still commonly paid. Many educated women refuse to marry because of loss of property rights. To boost equality, primary schools must now take 50% girls.

***Vanuatu's unspoilt beaches** are one of the reasons for the upsurge in the tourist industry.*

POLITICS

Multiparty elections

1998/2002 | President Fr. John Bani

AT THE LAST ELECTION

Parliament 52 seats

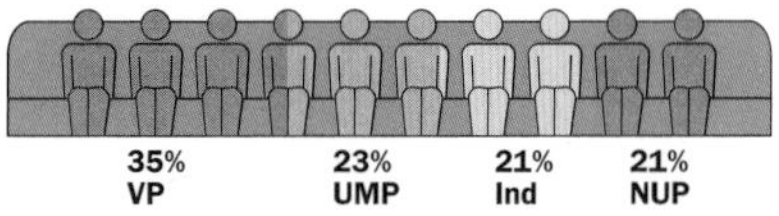
35% VP
23% UMP
21% Ind
21% NUP

VP = Vanua'aku Pati **UMP** = Union of Moderate Parties
Ind = Independents **NUP** = National United Party

Vanuatu politics are best described as anarchic. Political allegiances are swiftly changed and governments often toppled. Instability was behind the reluctance of France – not shared by Britain – to grant independence in 1980, and led to French support, reinforced by the anti-French stance of the VP, for an abortive bid for independence by Espiritu Santo that year.

The VP has dominated the political scene, ruling unbroken under the charismatic Fr. Walter Lini from 1980 to 1991. Although Lini was dismissed as premier in 1991 and defected from the VP, he continued to be a dominant political figure until his death in 1999. The VP had returned to power in 1998, leading a government based on patched-up relations with Lini and his supporters, but by the end of the year, unable to command a stable majority, the VP had gone into opposition. One of Lini's major opponents and fellow VP founder, Barak Sope, was elected in 1999 to head a broad-based anti-VP coalition, only to be ousted in a vote of no confidence in April 2001, when the VP again returned to power.

WORLD AFFAIRS

Joined UN in 1981

OIF | Comm | NAM | PC | PIF

Vanuatu was the first South Pacific nation to gain full membership of the Non-Aligned Movement. Relations with France have improved since the 1993 bilateral cooperation agreement.

AID

Recipient

$37m (receipts) | Down 10% in 1999

Vanuatu is Melanesia's most aid-dependent state. Leading donors are Australia, New Zealand, the UK, Japan, and France. Classed as a "least developed country" by the UN, Vanuatu receives guaranteed aid support.

V

DEFENSE

No compulsory military service

There is no army | Not applicable

There is a small paramilitary force, which receives training from the USA. Papua New Guinea troops helped to end the 1980 secessionist movement on Espiritu Santo.

ECONOMICS

Inflation 3.9% p.a. (1990–1999)

$227m | 129.07–143.01 vatu

SCORE CARD

❑ WORLD GNP RANKING	179th
❑ GNP PER CAPITA	$1180
❑ BALANCE OF PAYMENTS	$5m
❑ INFLATION	3.3%
❑ UNEMPLOYMENT	Low

STRENGTHS

Expanding services sector, including tourism and offshore finance. Major economic reforms recently instituted, including the introduction of a 12.5% value-added tax and resizing of the public service in return for assistance from the ADB.

WEAKNESSES

Large trade and budget deficits. Rate of growth has stagnated in recent years, contracting in 1999. Dependence on agricultural sector, vulnerable to adverse weather and fluctuating market prices. Shortage of skilled indigenous labor.

EXPORTS

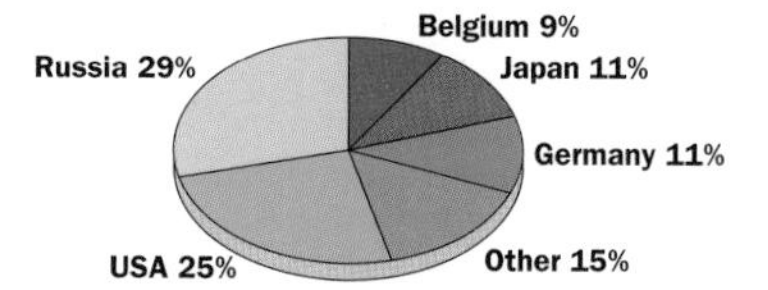
Belgium 9%
Russia 29%
Japan 11%
Germany 11%
USA 25%
Other 15%

IMPORTS

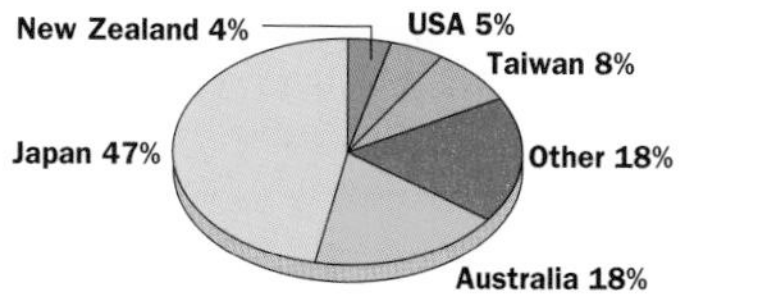
New Zealand 4%
USA 5%
Taiwan 8%
Japan 47%
Other 18%
Australia 18%

RESOURCES

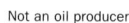

Electric power 11,000 kw

2589 tonnes | Not an oil producer

152,000 cattle, 62,000 pigs, 320,000 chickens | None

Vanuatu's main resources are its arable land – only partly utilized – and its forests and waters. These could be exploited by the tourist, timber, and fishing industries. New export crops are being explored to offset declining copra and cocoa exports. Beef is of growing importance. Nuclear power development was banned under 1983 legislation.

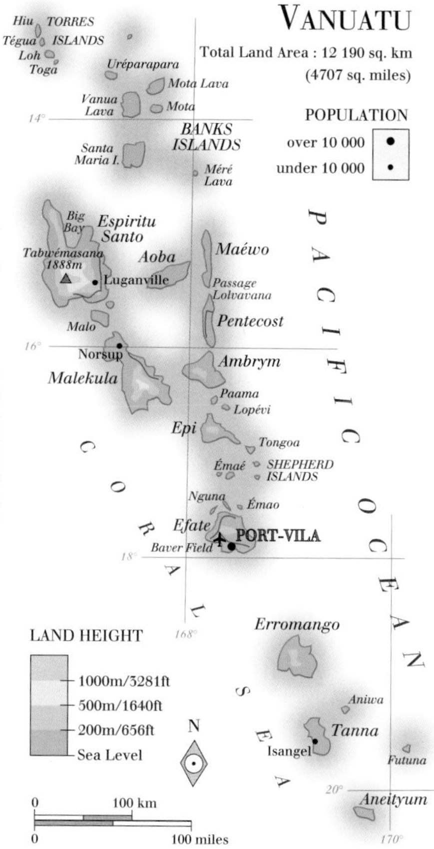
VANUATU
Total Land Area : 12 190 sq. km (4707 sq. miles)
POPULATION
over 10 000
under 10 000
Hiu
TORRES ISLANDS
Tégua
Loh
Toga
Uréparapara
Mota Lava
Vanua Lava
Mota
BANKS ISLANDS
Santa Maria I.
Méré Lava
Big Bay
Espiritu Santo
Tabwémasana 1888m
Luganville
Aoba
Maéwo
Passage Lolvavana
Pentecost
Malo
Norsup
Malekula
Ambrym
Paama
Lopévi
Epi
Tongoa
Émaé
SHEPHERD ISLANDS
Nguna
Émao
Efate
PORT-VILA
Baver Field
PACIFIC OCEAN
CORAL SEA
Erromango
Aniwa
Tanna
Isangel
Futuna
Aneityum
LAND HEIGHT
1000m/3281ft
500m/1640ft
200m/656ft
Sea Level
N
0 100 km
0 100 miles

ENVIRONMENT

Not available

None | 0.3 tonnes per capita

Logging is increasing, but most of the rainforest remains, and round log exports are banned. Population growth is high, at nearly 3% a year, but not yet a major problem. A majority of the population does not have access to a potable and reliable water supply.

MEDIA

TV ownership low

Daily newspaper circulation is very low

PUBLISHING AND BROADCAST MEDIA

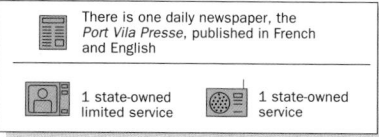

There is one daily newspaper, the *Port Vila Presse*, published in French and English

1 state-owned limited service | 1 state-owned service

The *Vanuatu Weekly* appears in each official language. Television Blong Vanuatu broadcasts four hours a day.

CRIME

Death penalty not used

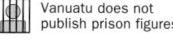

Vanuatu does not publish prison figures | Little change from year to year

Domestic violence apart, Vanuatu is almost crime-free, with little alcohol-related violence.

CHRONOLOGY

In 1906, Britain and France set up the New Hebrides under joint rule.

- ❑ **1980** Independence; Walter Lini of VP prime minister. Secession bid by Espiritu Santo.
- ❑ **1991** UMP coalition with NUP set up by Lini after his expulsion from VP.
- ❑ **1999** Tidal wave causes extensive damage.
- ❑ **2001** Prime Minister Sope ousted in no-confidence vote.

EDUCATION

School leaving age: 12

64% | Not available

The abolition of fees has helped to boost primary enrollment. Illiteracy is a major concern.

HEALTH

Welfare state health benefits

1 per 14,100 people | Heart diseases, cancers, malaria

A network of rural clinics and village health workers has helped to improve health levels. Nominal fees are charged.

SPENDING

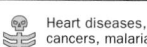

GDP/cap. decrease

CONSUMPTION AND SPENDING

44 per 1000 population | *28 per 1000 population*

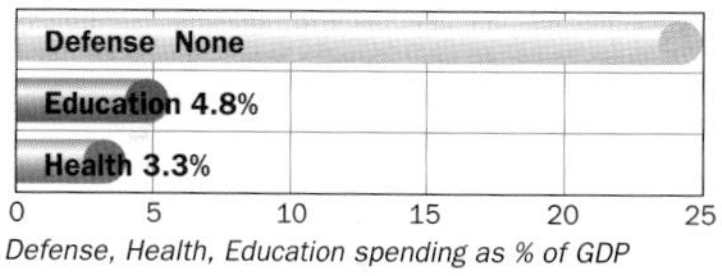
Defense None
Education 4.8%
Health 3.3%
0
5
10
15
20
25
Defense, Health, Education spending as % of GDP

The dominance of subsistence farming and small-scale cash cropping has helped to prevent extreme poverty. Most of the rich are not ni-Vanuatu.

WORLD RANKING

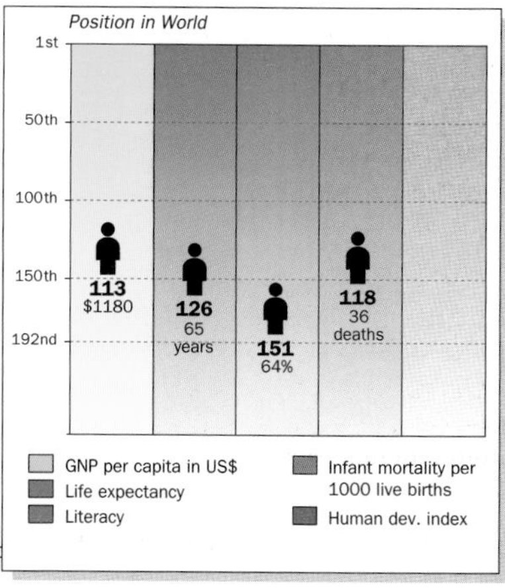
Position in World
1st
50th
100th
150th
192nd
113 $1180
126 65 years
151 64%
118 36 deaths
GNP per capita in US$
Life expectancy
Literacy
Infant mortality per 1000 live births
Human dev. index

V

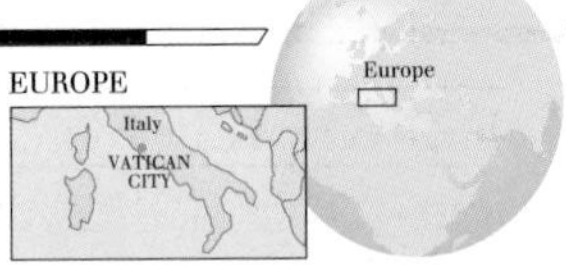
EUROPE
Europe
Italy
VATICAN CITY

VATICAN CITY

OFFICIAL NAME: State of the Vatican City **CAPITAL:** Vatican City **POPULATION:** 1000
CURRENCY: Euro (lira until 2002) **OFFICIAL LANGUAGES:** Italian and Latin

1929 | 1929 | Oct 22 | V | +1 | +39 | .va

THE VATICAN CITY lies close to the Tiber in central Rome and is the world's smallest independent state. It also includes ten other buildings in Rome and the pope's residence at Castel Gandolfo. As the Holy See it is the seat of the Roman Catholic Church, deriving its income from investments and voluntary contributions known as Peter's Pence.

***The buildings and gardens** of the Vatican City. St. Peter's Basilica was built from 1506–1626 on the traditional site of St. Peter's tomb.*

CLIMATE

Mediterranean

WEATHER CHART

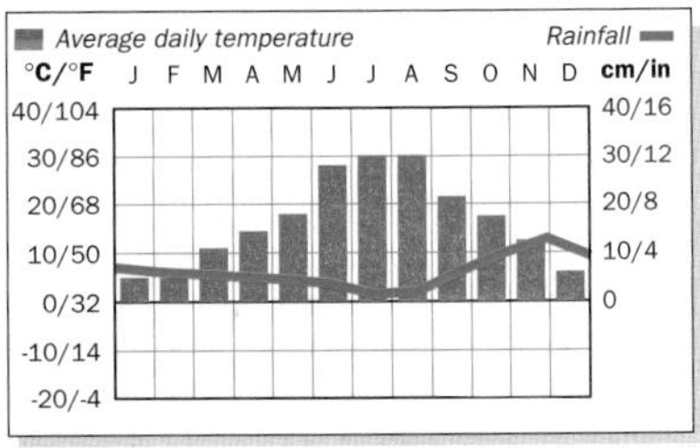
Average daily temperature
Rainfall
°C/°F
J F M A M J J A S O N D
cm/in
40/104
30/86
20/68
10/50
0/32
-10/14
-20/-4
40/16
30/12
20/8
10/4
0

Winters are mild, though November is particularly gray, and summers are hot.

TRANSPORTATION

Drive on right

Heliport for official visitors

Has no fleet

THE TRANSPORTATION NETWORK

None	None
1 km (0.6 miles)	None

The railroad is only used for carrying freight. Official visitors are transferred from Rome airport by helicopter.

TOURISM

Not available

The Vatican museums can accommodate 20,000 visitors daily

Little change from year to year

MAIN TOURIST ARRIVALS

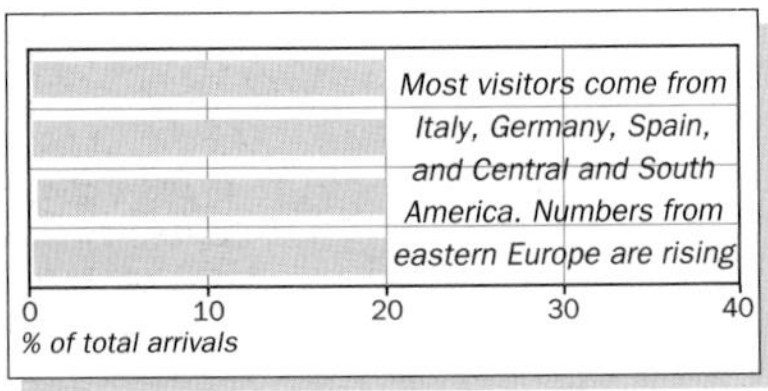
Most visitors come from Italy, Germany, Spain, and Central and South America. Numbers from eastern Europe are rising
0
10
20
30
40
% of total arrivals

Almost all tourists who visit Rome visit the Vatican, while others come as pilgrims. Up to 100,000 hear the pope's annual Easter Message in St. Peter's Square. The Vatican's art collections are among the greatest in the world. Years of restoration work on the Sistine Chapel frescoes were completed in 1994.

PEOPLE

Pop. density high

Italian, Latin

2273/km² (5886/mi²)

THE URBAN/RURAL POPULATION SPLIT

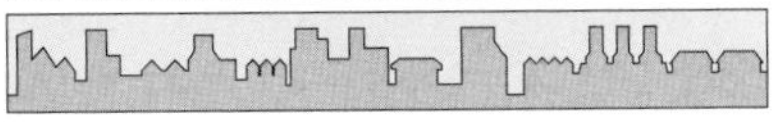
100%

RELIGIOUS PERSUASION

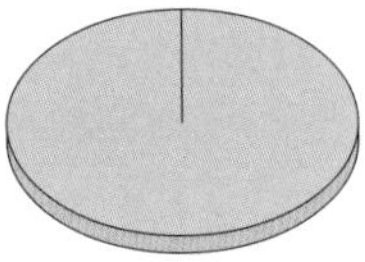
Roman Catholic 100%

The Vatican has about 1000 permanent inhabitants, including several hundred lay persons, and employs a further 3400 lay staff. Citizenship can be acquired through stable residence and holding an office or job within the City. A citizen's family can gain residence only by authorization.

The pope is the spiritual leader of almost 18% of the world's population. The countries with the largest number of Roman Catholics are Brazil, Mexico, Italy, the USA, and the Philippines.

POLITICS

No multiparty elections

On death of reigning pope

His Holiness Pope John Paul II

LEGISLATIVE OR ADVISORY BODIES

College of Cardinals 120 seats

Cardinals under the age of 80 are eligible to elect a new pope. There are no political parties.

The Vatican City operates in the manner of an elected monarchy, as the reigning pope has supreme executive, legislative, and judicial powers, and holds office for life. He is elected by the College of Cardinals, who vote until one candidate for the position of Supreme Pontiff achieves a two-thirds majority.

The administration of the Vatican City State, of which the pope is temporal head, is conducted by the Pontifical Commission. The Holy See, which is the governing body of the Roman Catholic Church worldwide and of which the pope is spiritual head, is governed by the Roman Curia, the Church's administrative network. It is the Holy See that maintains diplomatic relations abroad. Pope John Paul II, elected in 1978, was the first non-Italian pope since 1523. Now in his 80s, he continues to fulfill his duties despite suffering from Parkinson's disease.

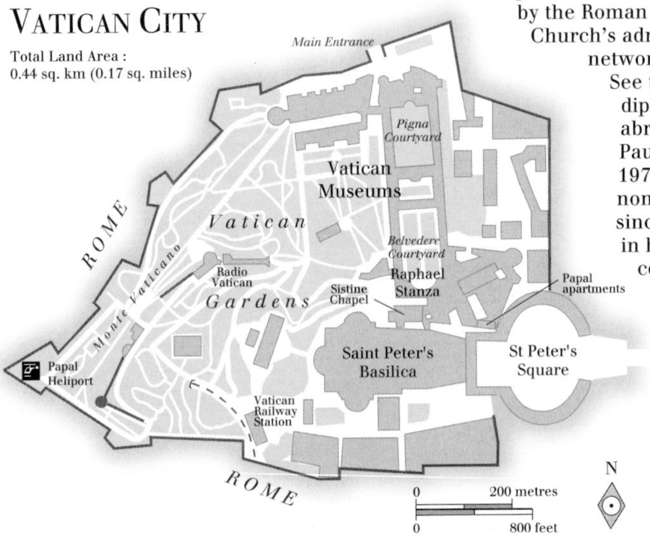
VATICAN CITY
Total Land Area :
0.44 sq. km (0.17 sq. miles)
Main Entrance
Pigna Courtyard
Vatican Museums
ROME
Vatican
Monte Vaticano
Radio Vatican
Belvedere Courtyard
Raphael Stanza
Sistine Chapel
Gardens
Papal apartments
Saint Peter's Basilica
St Peter's Square
Papal Heliport
Vatican Railway Station
ROME
0
200 metres
0
800 feet
N

V

WORLD AFFAIRS

Not a member of the UN

OSCE | IAEA

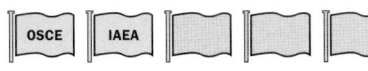

The Vatican maintains a neutral stance in world affairs and has observer status in many international organizations. It has mediated in many conflicts, notably achieving the 1993 peace agreement in Mozambique. Pope John Paul II has traveled more extensively than any other pope. His main aims have been to promote political dialogue and bridge religious divides, both within and outside the Catholic Church. In 2000, while on a major tour of the Holy Land, he made an unprecedented apology for the Church's 2000 years of anti-Judaism. In May 2001 he became the first pope to enter (and pray in) a mosque – in Syria – and the first to visit Orthodox Greece.

AID

Donor

Undisclosed | Undisclosed

Aid is donated through the pope's charities (such as the Holy Childhood Association, which distributes around $15 million a year to children's causes), through funds donated for use at the pope's discretion, and through religious orders acting under papal charter.

DEFENSE

No compulsory military service

Ceremonial Swiss Guard only | Not applicable

The Vatican is strictly neutral territory. Under the 1954 Hague Convention, it is recognized as "a moral, artistic, and cultural patrimony worthy of being respected as a treasure for all mankind."

ECONOMICS

Not applicable

Not applicable | 1932–2062 lire

SCORE CARD

- WORLD GNP RANKING .... *The Vatican*
- GNP PER CAPITA .... *does not have*
- BALANCE OF PAYMENTS .... *a national*
- INFLATION .... *economy in the*
- UNEMPLOYMENT .... *usual sense*

STRENGTHS

Istituto per le Opere di Religione has assets of $3–$4 billion. Voluntary contributions from thousands of Catholics worldwide (Peter's Pence). Interest on investments. Gold reserves in Fort Knox, USA. Stamp and coin issues. Budgetary deficit of 23 years reversed to modest surplus in 1993.

WEAKNESSES

Losses incurred by Vatican radio and newspaper, cost of foreign papal visits, buildings maintenance, and diplomatic missions. Repayment of creditors from Banco Ambrosiano bankruptcy in 1982.

EXPORTS/IMPORTS

The Vatican produces no goods for export. All commodities are imported, mainly from Italy.

RESOURCES

Not applicable

None | None

None | None

The Vatican imports all its energy. It has no farmland; its area is restricted to buildings and their formal gardens.

ENVIRONMENT

Not available

None | Not available

The Vatican is increasingly concerned about the need to balance development and conservation. In 1993, the pope urged a gathering of scientists to press colleagues worldwide to inform people on the need to protect the environment.

MEDIA

TV ownership medium

Daily newspaper circulation figures not available

PUBLISHING AND BROADCAST MEDIA

There is one daily newspaper, *L'Osservatore Romano*, which is also published weekly in 5 European languages, and monthly in Polish

1 state-owned service | 1 state-owned service

Radio Vatican's longwave transmissions were found to breach permitted radiation levels and were stopped in 2001.

CRIME

Death penalty not used

There are no prisons in the Vatican City | Minimal crime levels

The reputation of the 105-strong Swiss Guard was shaken in 1998, when a young guard shot dead his commandant and the latter's wife and then committed suicide. Three Vatican Bank officials were earlier alleged to have been involved in the Banco Ambrosiano affair.

EDUCATION

Not applicable

99% | 14,403 students

The university, founded by Gregory XIII, is renowned for its theological and philosophical learning. There are more than 110,000 primary and secondary Catholic schools around the world.

CHRONOLOGY

The Vatican is located in Rome because tradition held that St. Peter was buried on the site of the Church of Constantine, which was pulled down in the Renaissance to make way for the building of St. Peter's Basilica. The Vatican has been the pope's usual residence since 1417, when the pontiffs returned from Avignon in France at the end of the 39 years of Great Schism.

- **1870** Italy annexes Papal States in central Italy.
- **1929** Lateran Treaty – Italy accepts Vatican City as independent state.
- **1978** Cardinal Karol Wojtyla pope.
- **1981–1982** Attempts on pope's life.
- **1984** Catholicism disestablished as Italian state religion.
- **1985** Catholic Catechism revised for first time since 1566.
- **1994–1995** Opposition to abortion and contraception reiterated at UN conferences in Cairo and Beijing.
- **1998** Statement repenting Catholic passivity during Nazi Holocaust.
- **2000** Jubilee Year. Papal apology for Catholic violence and oppression over two millennia.
- **2001** John Paul II becomes first pope to enter a mosque.

HEALTH

Welfare state health benefits

Pope's own doctor is in permanent residence at Vatican | Heart and cardiovascular diseases, cancers

Pope John Paul II's strong opposition to abortion and contraception has prompted criticism from around the world, and from within the Church.

SPENDING

Not available

CONSUMPTION AND SPENDING

No data | *No data*

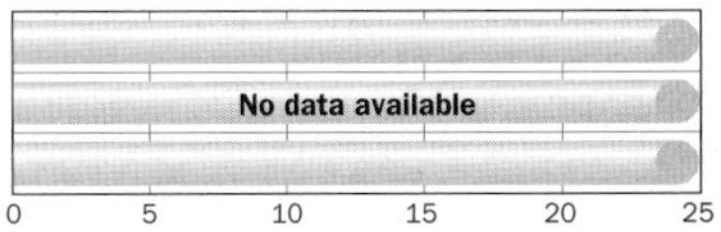
No data available
0
5
10
15
20
25

Defense, Health, Education spending as % of GDP

The wealth of the Vatican is primarily that of the Catholic Church. Its art treasures may not be sold. It is not known how much personal wealth its citizens have.

WORLD RANKING

The Pope and his Vatican staff enjoy one of the highest standards of living in the world.

V

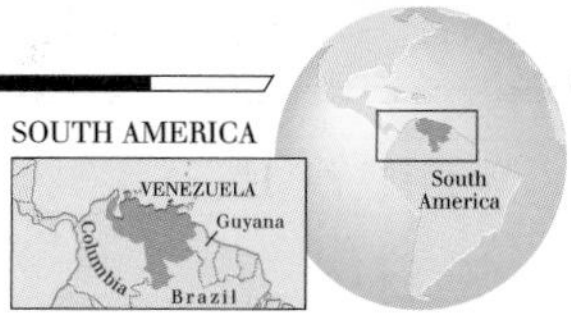
SOUTH AMERICA
VENEZUELA
Guyana
Colombia
Brazil
South America

VENEZUELA

OFFICIAL NAME: Bolivarian Republic of Venezuela **CAPITAL:** Caracas
POPULATION: 24.2 million **CURRENCY:** Bolívar **OFFICIAL LANGUAGES:** Spanish and Amerindian languages

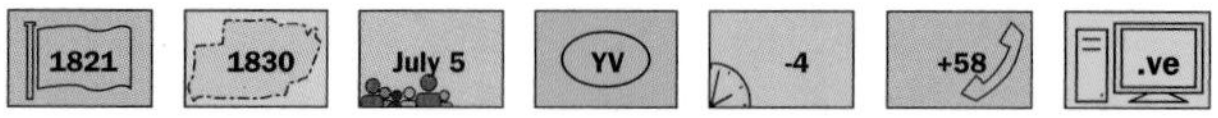
1821
1830
July 5
YV
-4
+58
.ve

LOCATED ON THE NORTHERN COAST of South America, Venezuela's vast central plain is drained by the Orinoco, while the Guiana Highlands dominate the southwest of the country. A Spanish colony until 1811, Venezuela was lauded as Latin America's most stable democracy. Recent political upheavals have, however, led to fears of instability. Despite having one of the largest known oil deposits outside the Middle East, much of Venezuela's population still lives in shanty-town squalor.

***President Hugo Chávez,** renamed the country as part of his Bolivarian Revolution.*

***Adina Bastidas,** who was appointed vice president in December 2000.*

CLIMATE

Tropical wet & dry/ equatorial

WEATHER CHART

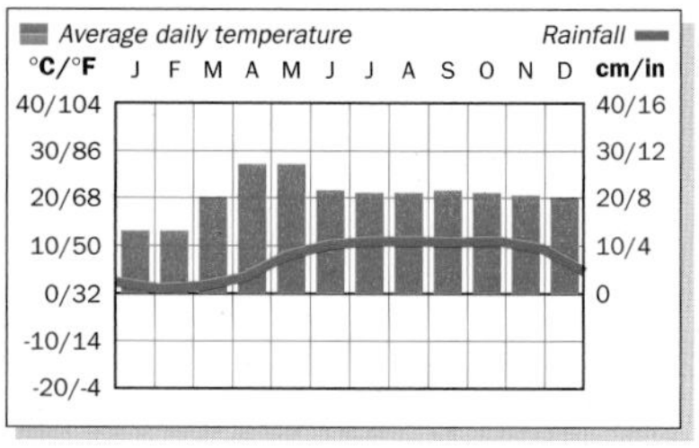
Average daily temperature
Rainfall
°C/°F
J F M A M J J A S O N D
cm/in
40/104
30/86
20/68
10/50
0/32
-10/14
-20/-4
40/16
30/12
20/8
10/4
0

The hot Maracaibo coast is surprisingly dry; the Orinoco *Llanos* are alternately parched or flooded. Uplands are cold.

TOURISM

Visitors : Population 1:41

587,000 visitors

Down 14% in 1999

MAIN TOURIST ARRIVALS

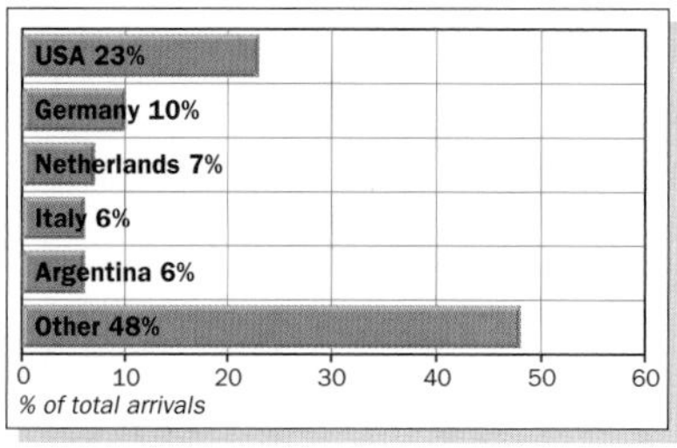
USA 23%
Germany 10%
Netherlands 7%
Italy 6%
Argentina 6%
Other 48%
0
10
20
30
40
50
60
% of total arrivals

Tourism is still a relatively minor industry in Venezuela, but one with enormous potential. Venezuela has many beaches that are the equal of any Caribbean island's, and a fascinating jungle interior which is a target for tourists. For many years, the high value of the bolívar made Venezuela an expensive destination, but, after recent devaluations, it has become one of the cheapest in the Caribbean. Privatizing state-run hotels was part of a drive to attract foreign investment.

TRANSPORTATION

Drive on right

Simón Bolívar International, Caracas
6.81m passengers

246 ships
665,300 grt

THE TRANSPORTATION NETWORK

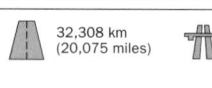

32,308 km (20,075 miles)

2690 km (1671 miles)

336 km (209 miles)

7100 km (4412 miles)

Massive road building from the 1960s onwards has benefited the oil and aluminum industries.The French-designed Caracas subway was completed in 1995. Work on the Centro-Occidental highway and other major roads is ongoing, as is rail development.

***The Orinoco.** Its huge* Llanos *(plains) are grazed by five million cattle, which are herded down close to the river in the dry season.*

PEOPLE

Pop. density low

Spanish, Amerindian languages

27/km² (71/mi²)

THE URBAN/RURAL POPULATION SPLIT

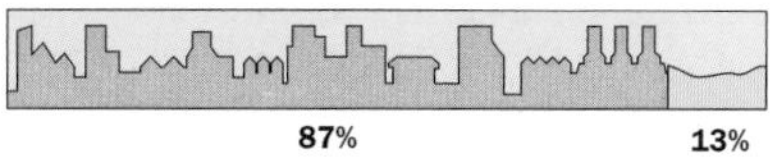
87%
13%

RELIGIOUS PERSUASION

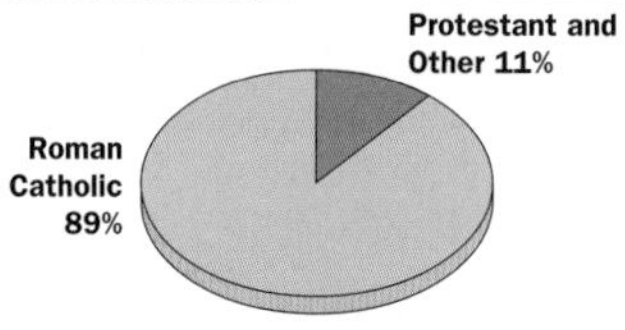
Protestant and Other 11%
Roman Catholic 89%

ETHNIC MAKEUP

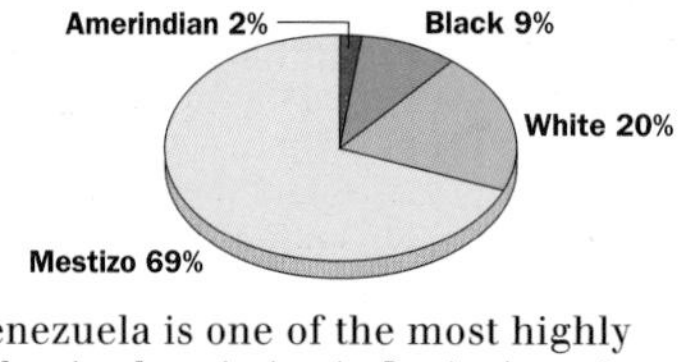
Amerindian 2%
Black 9%
White 20%
Mestizo 69%

Venezuela is one of the most highly urbanized societies in Latin America, with most of its population living in cities, mainly in the north. A historic "melting pot," it has experienced large-scale immigration from Italy, Portugal, Spain, and all over Latin America. There remains little of the white Hispanic aristocracy that survives in Colombia and Ecuador. The small number of native Amerindians, such as the Yanomami and Pemón, live in remote regions now threatened by illegal settlers. Most of the black population, who are descended from Africans brought over to work in the cacao industry in the 19th century, live along the Caribbean coast.

Oil wealth has brought comparative prosperity, but life in the *barrios* (shanty towns) which sprawl over the hillsides around Caracas is one of extreme poverty. Discontent peaked in the food riots of 1989 and 1991, which left scores dead along with the country's reputation for being a model democracy. The oil boom accelerated change for women, who today are to be found in all the professions. Politics, however, remains a largely masculine preserve. Oil wealth has also brought a measure of Americanization – boxing and baseball are among the most popular sports.

POPULATION AGE BREAKDOWN

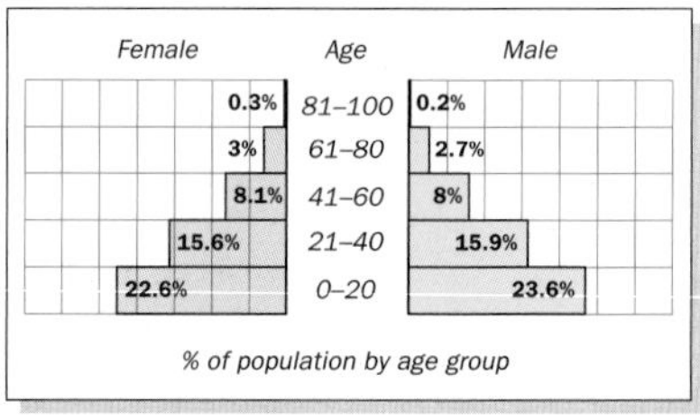
Female
Age
Male
0.3%
81–100
0.2%
3%
61–80
2.7%
8.1%
41–60
8%
15.6%
21–40
15.9%
22.6%
0–20
23.6%
% of population by age group

Key to symbols and abbreviations on cover flaps

VENEZUELA

Total Land Area : 882 050 sq. km
(340 560 sq. miles)

POPULATION

- over 1 000 000
- over 500 000
- over 100 000
- over 50 000
- over 10 000

LAND HEIGHT

- 3000m/9843ft
- 2000m/6562ft
- 1000m/3281ft
- 500m/1640ft
- Sea Level

Projected Railway

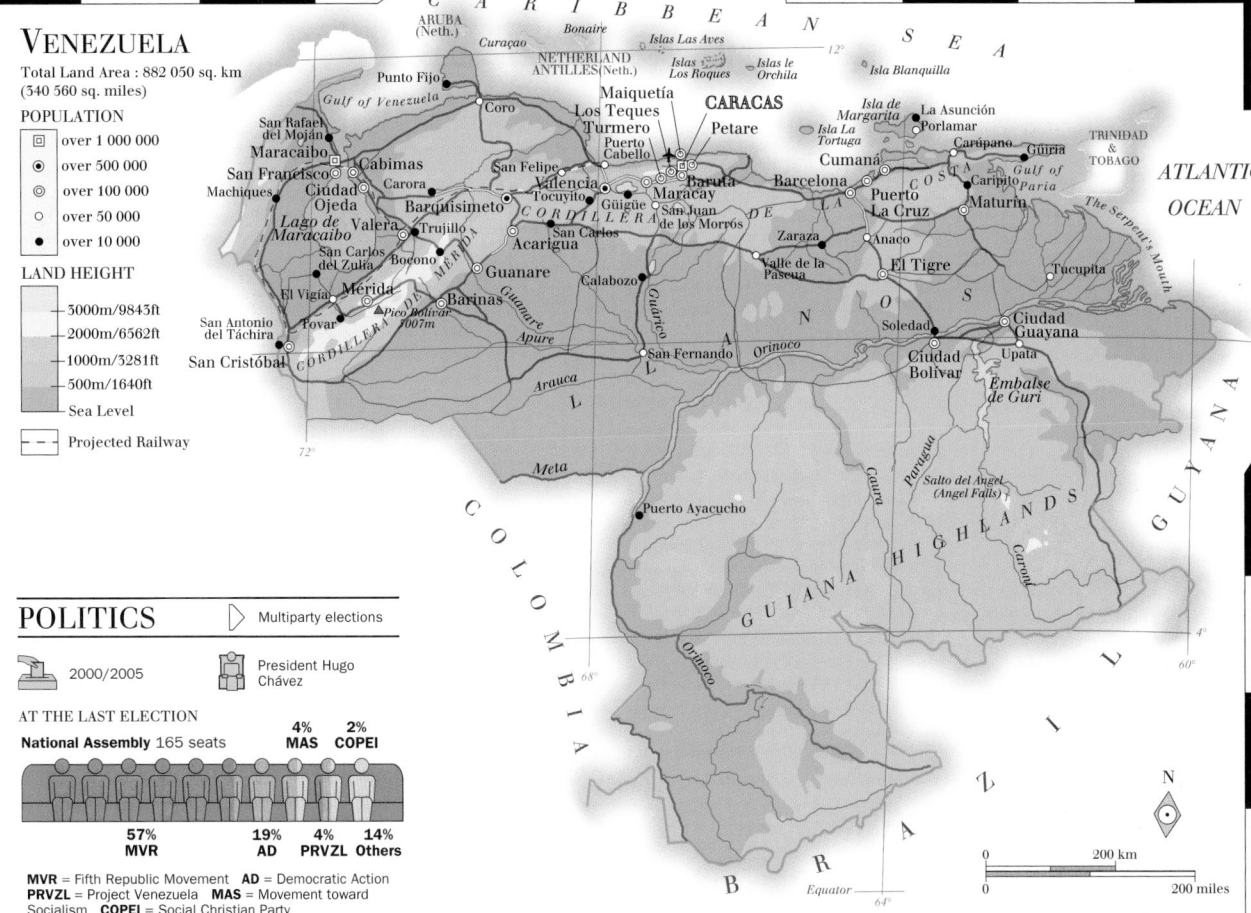

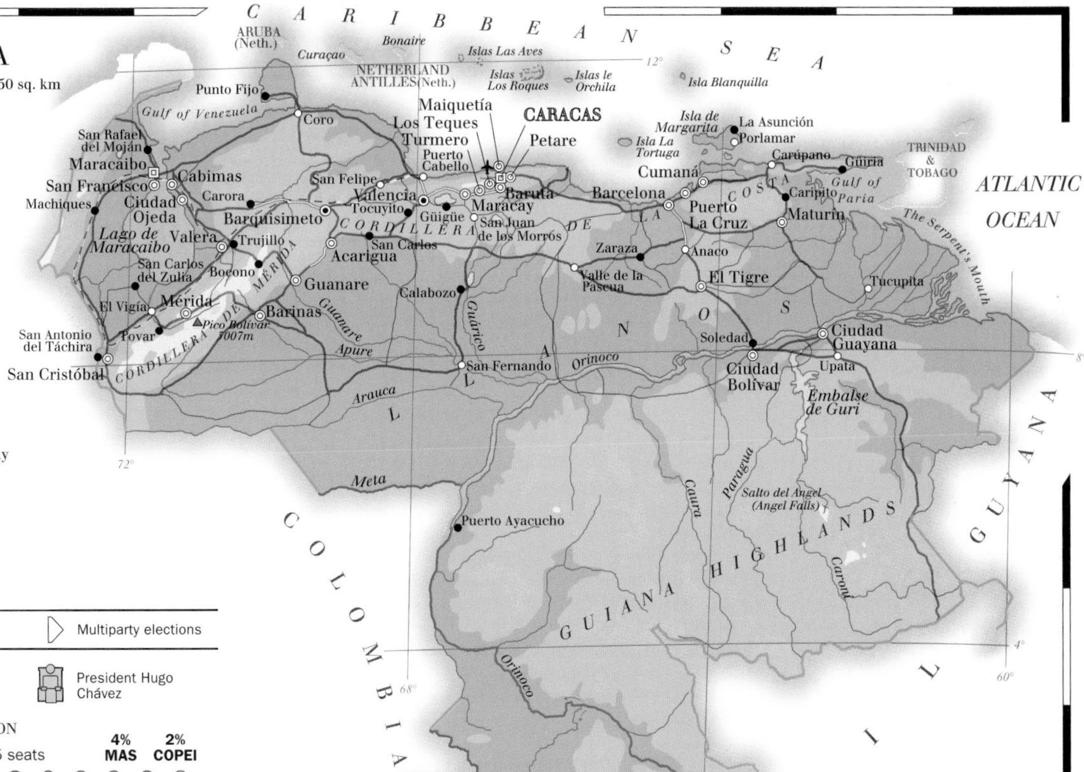

C A R I B B E A N S E A
ARUBA (Neth.)
Curaçao
Bonaire
NETHERLAND ANTILLES (Neth.)
Islas Las Aves
Islas Los Roques
Islas le Orchila
Isla Blanquilla
Punto Fijo
Gulf of Venezuela
Coro
Maiquetía
Los Teques
Turmero
CARACAS
Petare
Isla de Margarita
La Asunción
Porlamar
Isla La Tortuga
Carúpano
Güiria
TRINIDAD & TOBAGO
ATLANTIC OCEAN
San Rafael del Moján
Maracaibo
Cabimas
San Francisco
Machiques
Ciudad Ojeda
Lago de Maracaibo
Carora
San Felipe
Puerto Cabello
Valencia
Tocuyito
Maracay
Baruta
Güigüe
San Juan de los Morros
Barcelona
Cumaná
Puerto La Cruz
Caripito
Gulf of Paria
Maturín
The Serpent's Mouth
Barquisimeto
Valera
Trujillo
San Carlos del Zulia
Boconó
Acarigua
San Carlos
Zaraza
Anaco
El Tigre
Valle de la Pascua
Tucupita
Mérida
El Vigía
Guanare
Calabozo
Barinas
Pico Bolívar 5007m
Tovar
San Antonio del Táchira
San Cristóbal
Apure
Guárico
San Fernando
Orinoco
Soledad
Ciudad Guayana
Ciudad Bolívar
Upata
Embalse de Guri
Arauca
Meta
Puerto Ayacucho
Caura
Paragua
Salto del Angel (Angel Falls)
Caroní
GUIANA HIGHLANDS
COLOMBIA
BRAZIL
GUYANA
Equator
N
0 200 km
0 200 miles

POLITICS

Multiparty elections

2000/2005

President Hugo Chávez

AT THE LAST ELECTION

National Assembly 165 seats

4% MAS
2% COPEI
57% MVR
19% AD
4% PRVZL
14% Others

MVR = Fifth Republic Movement **AD** = Democratic Action **PRVZL** = Project Venezuela **MAS** = Movement toward Socialism **COPEI** = Social Christian Party
The Patriotic Front (**PP**) comprises the MVR, the MAS, and some smaller parties

Venezuela is a democracy, with multiparty elections.

Main Political Issues

Political and judicial reform

President Chávez's fiery rhetoric and populist stance won him the presidency in 1998, with strong support among the poor. He set out to reform the Congress and the judiciary and to rewrite the constitution, calling elections to a new Constituent Assembly, which convened in 1999. It temporarily took over many of the powers of the existing Congress, provoking protests from Chávez's opponents, who called it an effective coup d'état. Under a new "Bolivarian" constitution approved by referendum in 1999, presidential and legislative elections were held in 2000, giving Chávez a renewed mandate. Of concern are a "nominating committee," to choose candidates for key government posts, and an enabling law allowing Chávez to approve a broad range of legislation by executive decree.

Overdependence on oil

Chávez's populist policies mean that he needs the kind of revenue stream which Venezuela gets only in periods when world oil prices are high.

Profile

Official corruption, austerity, rising poverty, and anti-price-rise riots in Caracas were the backdrop for two coup attempts in 1992. One of these was led by Chávez, whose election as president in 1998 broke the stranglehold on power of the traditional parties. He raised high expectations among the poor, but his increasingly autocratic style has attracted growing opposition.

WORLD AFFAIRS

Joined UN in 1945

ACS | AP | OAS | OPEC | RG

Venezuela has traditionally favored the USA, as the destination of most of its oil exports and the source of its imports. President Chávez wants to steer a more independent line, especially in relation to Cuba. Ongoing objectives are support of oil prices and quotas within OPEC, economic integration with the Caribbean region, and a free-trade agreement with MERCOSUR. Oil-sector marketing and technology cooperation has been agreed with Brazil. The Caracas accord in 2000 guaranteed the provision of subsidized oil to 11 Central American and Caribbean countries.

Border disputes continue with Colombia and Guyana.

CHRONOLOGY

Venezuela was the first of the Spanish imperial colonies to repudiate Madrid's authority under the guidance of the revolutionary, Simón Bolívar, in 1811.

- **1821** Battle of Carabobo finally overthrows Spanish rule and leads to consolidation of independence within Gran Colombia (Venezuela, Colombia, and Ecuador).
- **1830** Gran Colombia collapses. José Antonio Páez rules Venezuela; coffee planters effectively in control.
- **1870** Guzmán Blanco in power. Rail system constructed.
- **1908** General Juan Vicente Gómez dictator; oil industry developed.
- **1935** Gómez falls from power. Increasing mass participation in political process.
- **1945** Military coup. Rómulo Betancourt of AD takes power as leader of a civilian–military junta.
- **1948** AD wins elections, with novelist Rómulo Gallegos as presidential candidate. Military coup. Marcos Pérez Jiménez forms government, with US and military backing.

V

CHRONOLOGY *continued*

- ❑ **1958** General strike. Admiral Larrázabal leads military coup. Free elections. Betancourt, newly returned from exile, wins presidential election for AD. Anticommunist campaign mounted. A few state welfare programs introduced.
- ❑ **1960** Movement of the Revolutionary Left (MIR) splits from AD, begins antigovernment activities.
- ❑ **1961** Founder member of OPEC.
- ❑ **1962** Communist-backed guerrilla warfare attempts repetition of Cuban revolution in Venezuela; fails to gain popular support.
- ❑ **1963** Raúl Leoni (AD) elected president – first democratic transference of power. Antiguerrilla campaign continues.
- ❑ **1966** Unsuccessful coup attempt by supporters of former president, Pérez Jiménez.
- ❑ **1969** Rafael Caldera Rodríguez of COPEI becomes president. Continues Leoni policies.
- ❑ **1973** Oil and steel industries nationalized. World oil crisis. Venezuelan currency peaks in value against the US dollar.
- ❑ **1978** Elections won by COPEI's Luis Herrera Campíns. Disastrous economic programs.
- ❑ **1983** AD election victory under Jaime Lusinchi. Fall in world oil prices leads to unrest and cuts in state welfare.
- ❑ **1988–1989** Carlos Andrés Pérez wins elections for AD. Caracas food riots; 1500 dead.
- ❑ **1993–1995** Andrés Pérez ousted on charges of corruption; Caldera Rodríguez reelected. More social unrest.
- ❑ **1998–1999** Hugo Chávez's Patriotic Front coalition defeats COPEI-led coalition in elections; Chávez embarks on political reform.
- ❑ **1999** August, controversial Constituent Assembly elected, assumes far-reaching powers. November, Assembly approves new constitution, subsequently endorsed by referendum. December, thousands killed in floods and mud slides.
- ❑ **2000** Chávez's mandate confirmed by presidential elections. New National Assembly convenes.

AID

▷ Recipient

$44m (receipts) — Up 19% in 1999

The IDB is supporting the long-term reform of Venezuela's social security system.

DEFENSE

▷ Compulsory military service

$1.33bn — Down 1% in 1999

Young officers, opposed to austerity and corruption, staged coup attempts in 1992. One of them, Hugo Chávez, later became president. He deployed army personnel as the "spearhead of development" and appointed military officers to run key ministries. The first civilian defense minister was appointed in 2001, but exercises little direct power over the armed forces.

VENEZUELAN ARMED FORCES

81 main battle tanks (AMX–30)	34,000 personnel
2 submarines, 6 frigates, and 6 patrol boats	15,000 personnel
124 combat aircraft (CF–5A/B, NF–5A/B, F–16A/B, *Mirage* 50EV/DV)	7000 personnel
None	

ECONOMICS

▷ Inflation 47.5% p.a. (1990–1999)

$87.3bn — 648.75–699.75 bolívares

SCORE CARD

❑ World GNP Ranking	38th
❑ GNP per Capita	$3680
❑ Balance of Payments	$–2.56bn
❑ Inflation	23.6%
❑ Unemployment	18%

EXPORTS

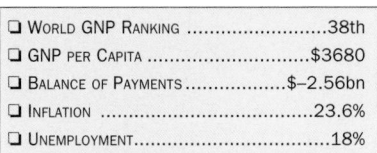

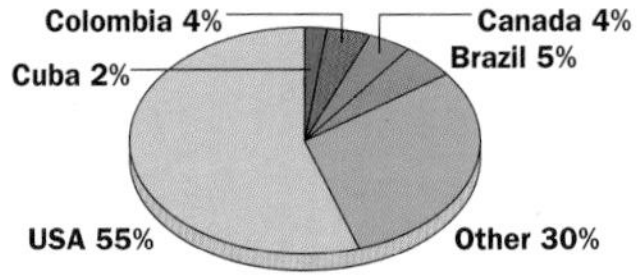
Colombia 4%
Canada 4%
Brazil 5%
Cuba 2%
USA 55%
Other 30%

IMPORTS

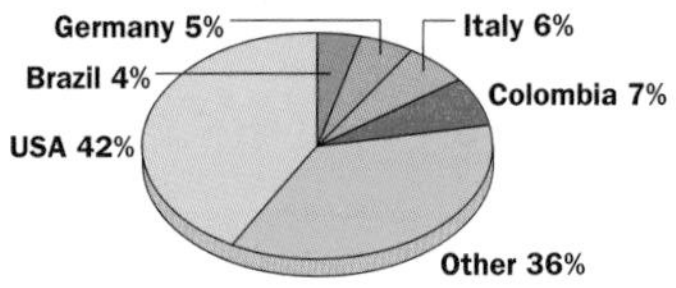
Germany 5%
Italy 6%
Brazil 4%
Colombia 7%
USA 42%
Other 36%

Strengths

The largest proven oil deposits outside the Middle East and the CIS. World oil prices soared in 2000, signifying recovery from the 1986 collapse. Massive reserves of coal, bauxite, iron, and gold, and successful development of new bitumen fuel which has attracted considerable foreign investment. New foreign investment, including banking, telecoms, iron, and steel. Producer of high-grade aluminum. More flexible labor market.

Weaknesses

Huge, cumbersome state sector; despite some privatization, large areas of the state sector are still overmanned and inefficient and subject to widespread corruption. Poor public services which, despite Venezuela's wealth during the oil-boom years, have been badly maintained. Major infrastructure renewal is now long overdue. Widespread tax evasion. Weak currency.

ECONOMIC PERFORMANCE INDICATOR

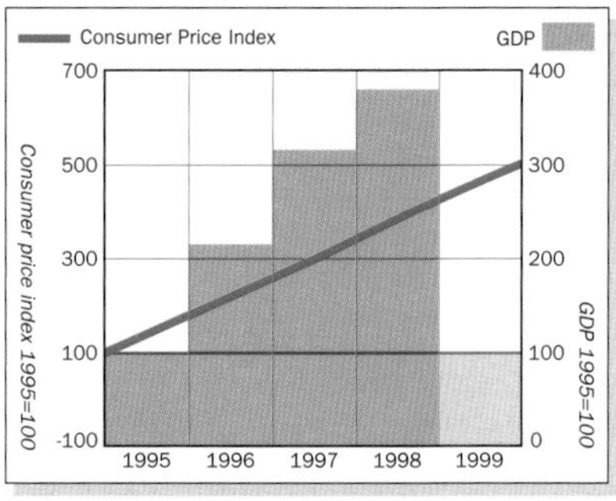
Consumer Price Index
GDP
700
500
300
100
-100
400
300
200
100
0
1995
1996
1997
1998
1999
Consumer price index 1995=100
GDP 1995=100

Profile

Venezuela is an economic paradox. While it has one of the strongest economies in Latin America, its government finances have habitually been in crisis due to a culture of non-accountability and politically motivated patronage in state-owned industries and government bureaucracies. To date, privatizations and government cuts have failed to solve the problem. Promises by President Chávez to deal with excesses and diversify the economy, by lowering dependence on crude oil exports and promoting domestic processing industries, have received a mixed response from investors who favor more market-oriented reforms.

VENEZUELA : MAJOR BUSINESSES

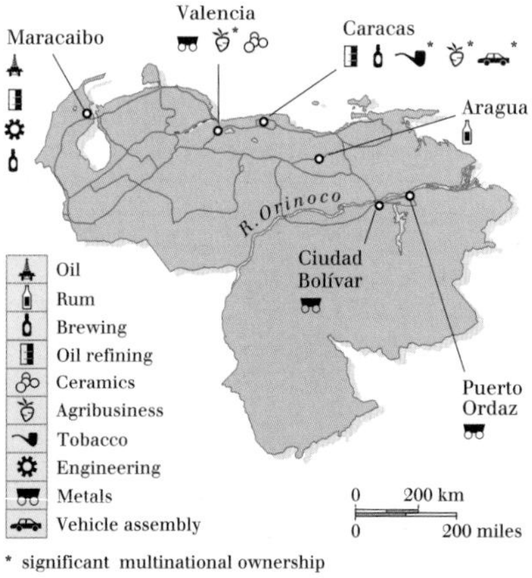
Maracaibo
Valencia
Caracas
Aragua
R. Orinoco
Ciudad Bolívar
Puerto Ordaz
Oil
Rum
Brewing
Oil refining
Ceramics
Agribusiness
Tobacco
Engineering
Metals
Vehicle assembly
0 200 km
0 200 miles

* significant multinational ownership

RESOURCES

Electric power 21.3m kw

502,728 tonnes

3.2m b/d (reserves 76,900,000,000 bbl)

15.8m cattle, 4.5m pigs, 4m goats, 110m chickens

Oil, bauxite, iron, natural gas, coal, gold, diamonds, aluminum

ELECTRICITY GENERATION

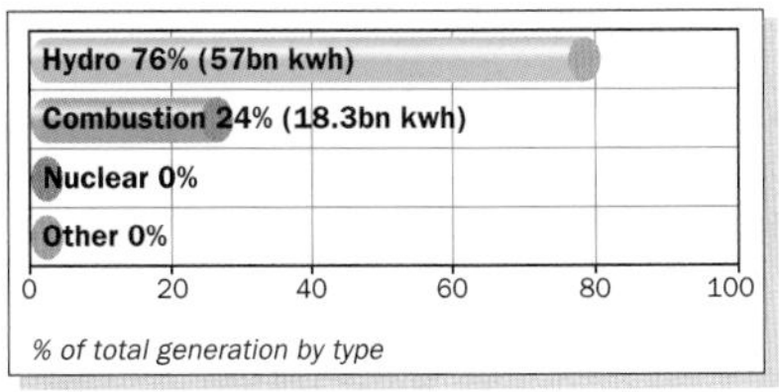

Hydro 76% (57bn kwh)
Combustion 24% (18.3bn kwh)
Nuclear 0%
Other 0%
0
20
40
60
80
100
% of total generation by type

Venezuela has a remarkable diversity of resources. It has proven oil reserves of 77 billion barrels, vast quantities of coal, iron ore, bauxite, and gold, and cheap hydroelectric power. Huge investment programs are currently under way to raise production in all these sectors as well as in oil refining capacity. However, the Chávez government wants to cut the investment budget of the state oil company, PDVSA, reduce its output, and increase its contributions to the exchequer. Such uncertainty could unsettle private investors.

Venezuela has begun exploitation of Orimulsion, a new bitumen-based fuel from the Orinoco; commercially exploitable reserves are estimated at 270 billion barrels. Venezuela's aim to be the world's largest aluminum producer is threatened after difficulties associated with privatizing the sector.

VENEZUELA : LAND USE

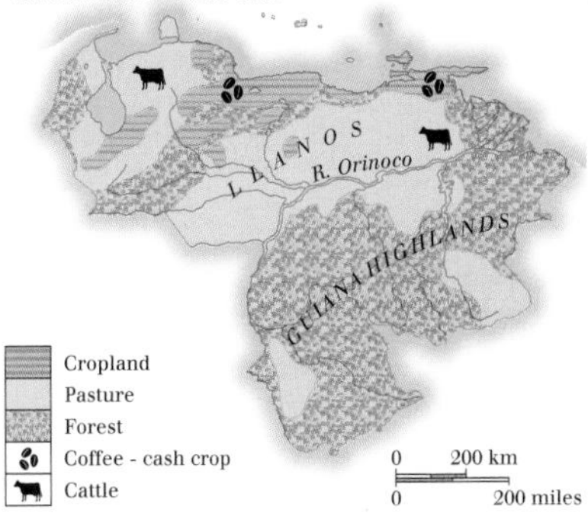

LLANOS
R. Orinoco
GUIANA HIGHLANDS
Cropland
Pasture
Forest
Coffee - cash crop
Cattle
0
200 km
0
200 miles

ENVIRONMENT

Sustainability rank: 47th

36%

8.4 tonnes per capita

ENVIRONMENTAL TREATIES

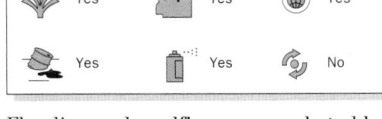

Yes

Yes

Yes

Yes

Yes

No

Flooding and mudflows, exacerbated by overdevelopment of the coastal strip, caused thousands of deaths in late 1999.

MEDIA

TV ownership medium

Daily newspaper circulation 206 per 1000 people

PUBLISHING AND BROADCAST MEDIA

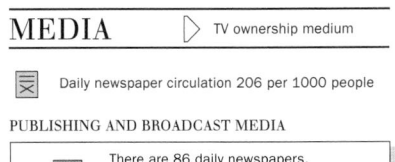

There are 86 daily newspapers. *El Universal* and *El Nacional* are the most prominent

8 services: 2 state-owned, 6 independent

1 state-owned service, 500 independent stations

Most of the press is independent of the main political parties. Venezuelan soap operas vie for dominance with Mexican rivals.

EDUCATION

School leaving age: 15

93%

550,783 students

THE EDUCATION SYSTEM

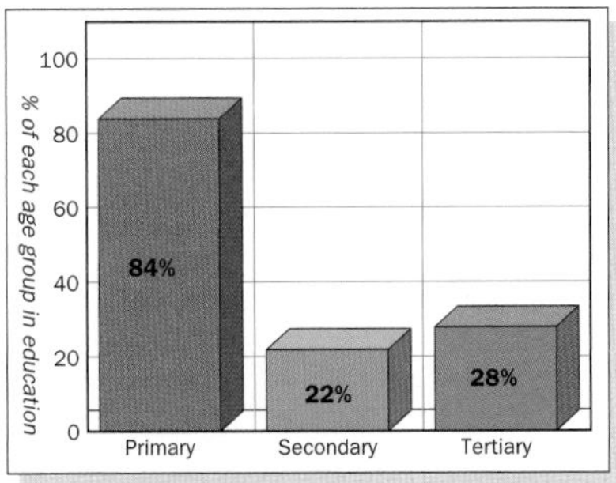

100
80
60
40
20
0
% of each age group in education
84%
22%
28%
Primary
Secondary
Tertiary

An extra $1 billion in social spending approved in 2000 includes raising entitlement in the state sector. Education is characterized by teacher shortages and a high drop-out rate; the quality of education at state universities is low. The private sector is growing.

SPENDING

GDP/cap. increase

CONSUMPTION AND SPENDING

68 per 1000 population

109 per 1000 population

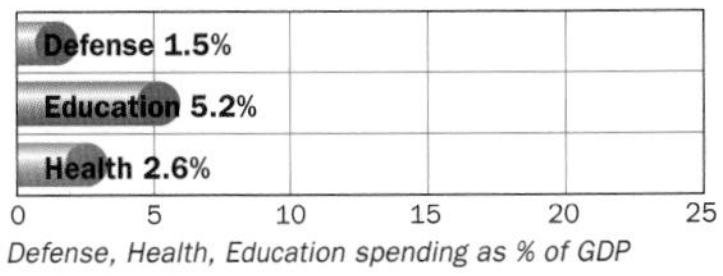

Defense 1.5%
Education 5.2%
Health 2.6%
0
5
10
15
20
25
Defense, Health, Education spending as % of GDP

The oil boom years of the 1970s largely benefited those already rich, with middle-income consumers doing well out of government-sponsored improvements in health and education and subsidized goods, largely at the expense of the poor.

The collapse of world oil prices, economic austerity measures, high inflation, and the devaluation of the bolívar in the 1980s and 1990s has squeezed the middle class and in addition seriously eroded the living standards of working-class households. A 2001 report by Ocei, the official central information office, stated that 20.7% of Venezuelans live in extreme poverty, representing a three-point increase on 1999.

CRIME

Death penalty not used

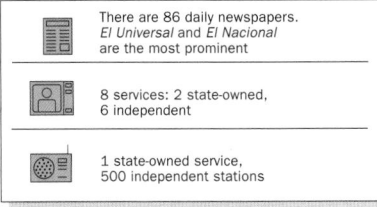

32,000 prisoners

Little change 1992–1996

CRIME RATES

Murders

23 *per 100,000 population*

Rapes

16 *per 100,000 population*

Thefts

173 *per 100,000 population*

Urban robberies and violence involving young delinquents are major problems, as is narcotics-related crime. Cattle-smuggling to Colombia is rife.

HEALTH

Welfare state health benefits

1 per 417 people

Heart disease, accidents, violence, cancers

The health service suffered along with other public services from poor management in the 1970s and severe cuts in the 1980s and 1990s. Most health care is concentrated in the towns, and people from indigenous communities often have to travel long distances to receive treatment. Medicines, which have to be paid for, are expensive and preventable diseases are recurring. Hospitals need modernization.

An additional $1 billion in social spending approved in 2000 includes spending on health.

WORLD RANKING

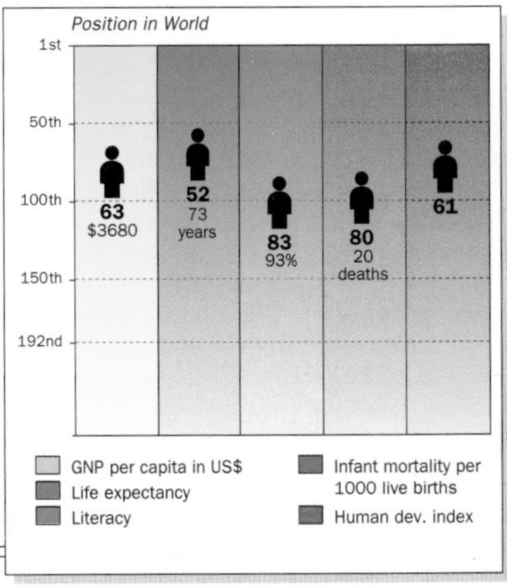

Position in World
1st
50th
100th
150th
192nd
63
$3680
52
73
years
83
93%
80
20
deaths
61
GNP per capita in US$
Life expectancy
Literacy
Infant mortality per 1000 live births
Human dev. index

V

VIETNAM

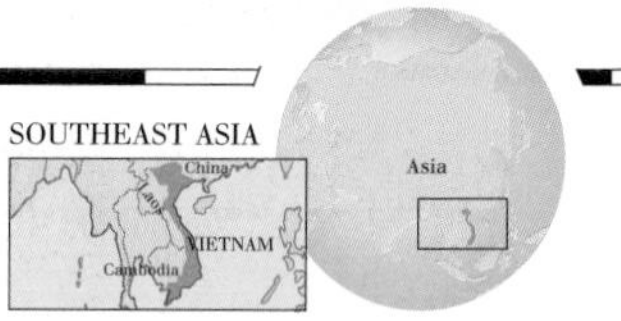
SOUTHEAST ASIA
China
VIETNAM
Cambodia
Asia

OFFICIAL NAME: Socialist Republic of Vietnam **CAPITAL:** Hanoi
POPULATION: 79.8 million **CURRENCY:** Dông **OFFICIAL LANGUAGE:** Vietnamese

1954 | 1976 | Sept 2 | VN | +7 | +84 | .vn

LOCATED ON THE EASTERN coast of the Indochinese peninsula, over half of Vietnam is dominated by the heavily forested mountain range, the Chaîne Annamitique. The most populated areas, which are also the most intensively cultivated, are along the Red and Mekong rivers. Partitioned after World War II, the country was reunited when the communist north won the world's longest modern-day conflict, the 1962–1975 Vietnam War. Vietnam is now a single-party state ruled by the Communist Party. Since 1986, the regime has pursued a liberal economic policy known as *doi moi* (renovation).

CLIMATE

Tropical monsoon

WEATHER CHART

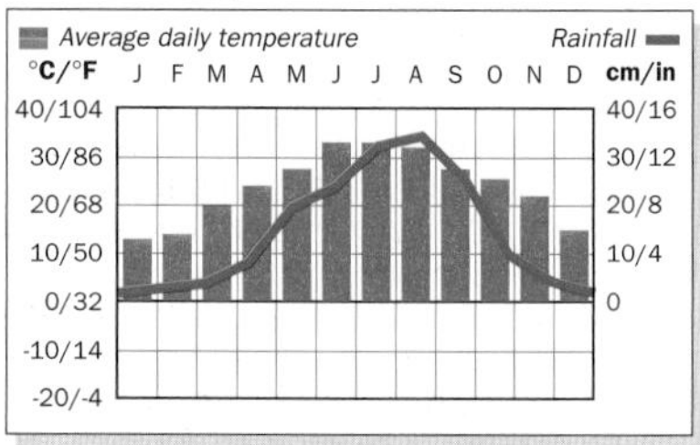
Average daily temperature
Rainfall
°C/°F
J F M A M J J A S O N D
cm/in
40/104
30/86
20/68
10/50
0/32
-10/14
-20/-4
40/16
30/12
20/8
10/4
0

Vietnam has a sharply contrasting climate. The north has cool winters, while the south is tropical, with even temperatures all year round. The central provinces are affected by typhoons. The intensively cultivated northern Red River delta is subject to drought, while the Mekong delta in the south, also intensively cultivated, suffers heavy flooding.

TRANSPORTATION

Drive on right

Tan Son Naht International, Ho Chi Minh City

629 ships
784,000 grt

THE TRANSPORTATION NETWORK

23,418 km (14,551 miles)

430 km (267 miles)

2632 km (1636 miles)

17,702 km (10,999 miles)

Rebuilding infrastructure is still a priority. The flagship project, the four-lane Ho Chi Minh Highway linking Hanoi and the south, is unlikely to meet the target of completion by 2003. A major port development plan is under way. Trains travel slowly, with an average speed of around 15 km/h (9 mph), and take three days from Hanoi to Ho Chi Minh City. The bus network is extensive but journeys are also time-consuming. Taxis and cycles provide cheap local transportation. Hanoi has plans for an elevated metro line.

TOURISM

Visitors : Population 1:37

2.1m visitors

Up 20% in 2000

MAIN TOURIST ARRIVALS

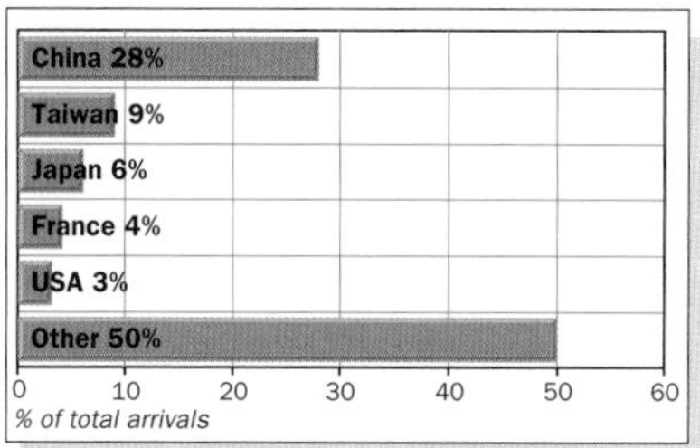
China 28%
Taiwan 9%
Japan 6%
France 4%
USA 3%
Other 50%
0
10
20
30
40
50
60
% of total arrivals

Until the government opened the way to large-scale tourism in the 1990s, Russians, eastern Europeans, and backpackers from the West made up the bulk of visitors. Other travelers were either on business, or overseas Vietnamese, *Viet Kie*, who were visiting relatives.

Under a "master plan" adopted in 1995, massive investment was channeled into hotels, but an official target of three million tourists a year by the year 2000 proved about a million too high. Poor transportation infrastructure remains a problem. Vietnam's appeal rests on its unspoiled Asian way of life and areas of spectacular natural beauty such as Ha Long Bay on the Red River delta.

Boats moored near Nha Trang. *With 3444 km (2140 miles) of coastline, use of the sea, for transportation and fishing, is vital to Vietnam.*

PEOPLE

Pop. density high

Vietnamese, Chinese, Thai, Khmer, Muong, Nung, Miao, Yao, Jarai

245/km² (635/mi²)

THE URBAN/RURAL POPULATION SPLIT

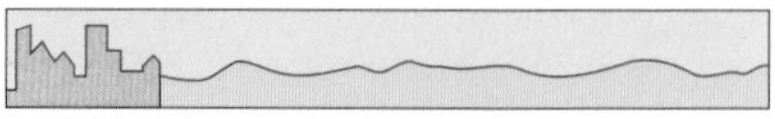
20%
80%

RELIGIOUS PERSUASION

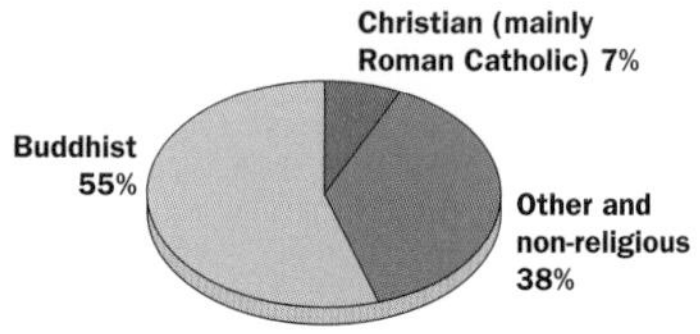
Christian (mainly Roman Catholic) 7%
Buddhist 55%
Other and non-religious 38%

ETHNIC MAKEUP

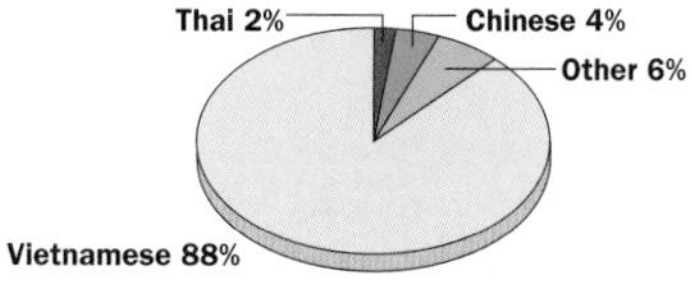
Thai 2%
Chinese 4%
Other 6%
Vietnamese 88%

Family life is strong and is based on kinship groups within village clans. A pronounced north–south cultural split remains evident in the cities. Chinese are the largest minority group. When the victorious communists reunited north and south Vietnam in 1976, they viewed the Saigon Chinese (in what was renamed Ho Chi Minh city), with their Taiwanese links, as a corrupt bourgeoisie. The northern Mountain Chinese were also suspect as a possible fifth column for China's ambitions in Vietnam. Various other mountain minorities (*Montagnards*), with a history of collaboration with the French and Americans, were also sidelined by the regime in Hanoi. *Montagnard* resentment over the resettling of lowlanders in mountain regions sparked violent protests in early 2001.

In the older generations, women outnumber men, largely because of war deaths. They form a high proportion of the industrial workforce, and are starting to get greater political representation, most notably Vice President Nguyen Thi Binh.

POPULATION AGE BREAKDOWN

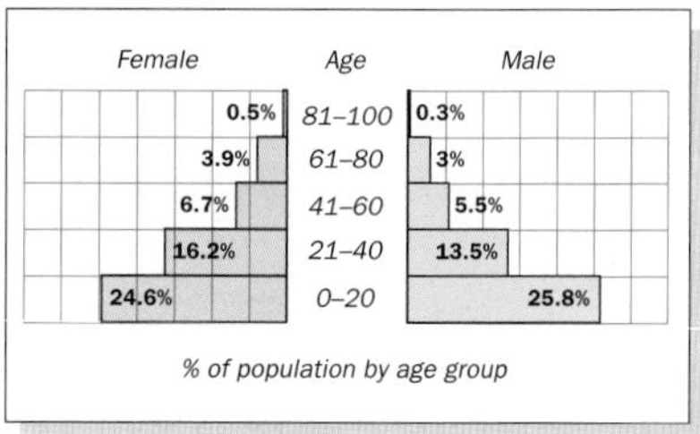
Female
Age
Male
0.5%
81–100
0.3%
3.9%
61–80
3%
6.7%
41–60
5.5%
16.2%
21–40
13.5%
24.6%
0–20
25.8%
% of population by age group

Tran Duc Luong, *president since 1997.*

Nong Duc Manh, *powerful general secretary of the CPV.*

POLITICS

No multiparty elections

1997/2002

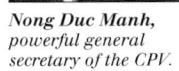

President Tran Duc Luong

AT THE LAST ELECTION

National Assembly 450 seats

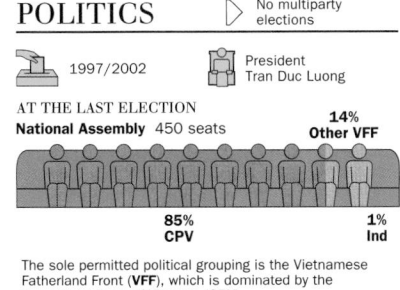

14%
Other VFF
85%
CPV
1%
Ind

The sole permitted political grouping is the Vietnamese Fatherland Front (**VFF**), which is dominated by the Communist Party of Vietnam (**CPV**)
Other VFF = Socialist Party and Democratic Party
Ind = Independents

Vietnam is effectively a single-party communist state.

Main Political Issue
Economic reform

Vietnam is attempting to move to a market economy without political liberalization. The veteran CPV leaders of the 1950s–1970s were slow to transfer power and resisted democratizing the political process. Changes in senior posts in 1997 left reformers such as new prime minister Phan Van Khai still outnumbered by conservatives. The 2001 party congress balanced the theme of greater democracy with a renewed commitment to socialism.

Profile

A traditional communist system is still in place, with a powerful politburo elected by the party central committee. Heading the secretariat and politburo, the party general secretary wields much power, alongside the prime minister and president. The hand of the economic reformers was strengthened by Nong Duc Manh's elevation to the party leadership at the April 2001 congress, but there remains real concern that opening collective farming and state enterprises to competition will undermine stability, encourage "individualism," and weaken the party's monopoly on power.

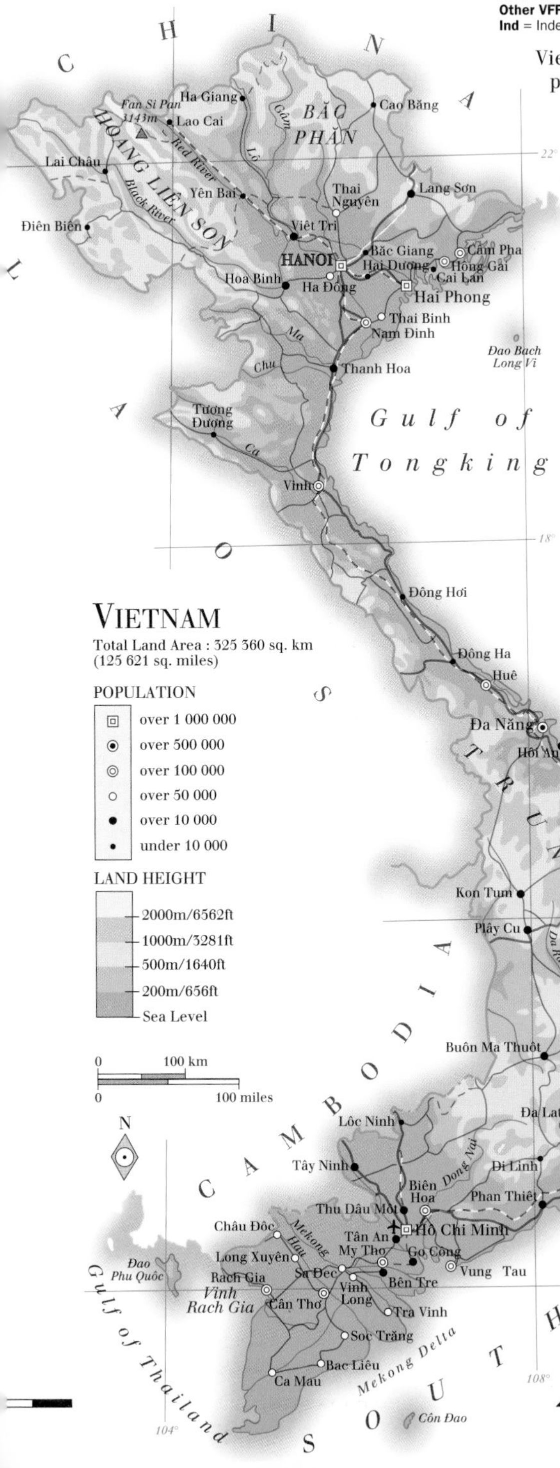
VIETNAM
Total Land Area : 325 360 sq. km (125 621 sq. miles)
POPULATION
over 1 000 000
over 500 000
over 100 000
over 50 000
over 10 000
under 10 000
LAND HEIGHT
2000m/6562ft
1000m/3281ft
500m/1640ft
200m/656ft
Sea Level
0 100 km
0 100 miles
N
CHINA
LAOS
CAMBODIA
SOUTH CHINA SEA
Gulf of Tongking
Gulf of Thailand
HOANG LIEN SON
BĂC PHĂN
TRUNG PHAN
Fan Si Pan 3143m
Ha Giang
Lao Cai
Cao Băng
Lai Châu
Yên Bai
Lang Sơn
Thai Nguyên
Điên Biên
Viêt Tri
HANOI
Băc Giang
Cẩm Pha
Hai Dương
Hông Gai
Cai Lan
Hoa Binh
Ha Đông
Hai Phong
Thai Binh
Nam Đinh
Dao Bach Long Vi
Thanh Hoa
Tương Dương
Vinh
Đông Hơi
Đông Ha
Huê
Đa Năng
Hôi An
Tam Ky
Quang Ngai
Kon Tum
Plây Cu
Qui Nhơn
Tuy Hoa
Buôn Ma Thuôt
Nha Trang
Đa Lat
Cam Ranh
Phan Rang-Thap Cham
Lôc Ninh
Tây Ninh
Di Linh
Biên Hoa
Phan Thiêt
Thu Dâu Môt
Hô Chi Minh
Châu Đôc
Tân An
My Tho
Go Công
Vung Tau
Long Xuyên
Dao Phu Quôc
Rach Gia
Sa Đec
Bên Tre
Vinh Long
Vinh Rach Gia
Cân Thơ
Tra Vinh
Soc Trăng
Bac Liêu
Ca Mau
Mekong Delta
Côn Đao
Red River
Black River
Mekong
Dong Nai
22°
18°
14°
10°
104°
108°

WORLD AFFAIRS

Joined UN in 1977

ASEAN | IAEA | OIF | Mekong River | NAM

Economic liberalization has improved relations with the USA, with lifting of the aid and trade embargo in 1993, full diplomatic relations in 1995, and a landmark bilateral trade agreement in 2000, ahead of a visit by US President Bill Clinton that November.

Vietnam joined ASEAN in 1995, in the wake of the Cambodia settlement. Trade and economic cooperation links with Japan were strengthened in 1999–2000. Agreement in 1999 over the land border reduced tension with China, although competing claims to the Spratly Islands remain a source of friction.

AID

Recipient

$1.42bn (receipts) | Up 22% in 1999

Vietnam's invasion of Cambodia in 1978 halted all aid from China, Japan, and the West (except for Scandinavian countries), leaving it mostly dependent on the USSR. Western donors resumed assistance in the early 1990s. Their aid rapidly became the main source of capital for improving infrastructure, although foreign investment fell away significantly in the late 1990s.

CHRONOLOGY

From 1825, the brutal persecution of the Catholic community, originally converted by French priests in the 17th century, gave France the excuse to colonize Cochin-China, Annam, and Tonkin, and then merge them with Laos and Cambodia.

- **1920** *Quoc ngu* (Roman script) replaces Chinese script.
- **1930** Ho Chi Minh founds Indo-china Communist Party.
- **1940** Japanese invasion.
- **1941** Viet Minh resistance founded in exile in China.
- **1945** Viet Minh take Saigon and Hanoi. Emperor abdicates. Republic proclaimed with Ho Chi Minh as president.
- **1946** French reenter. First Indo-China War.
- **1954** French defeated at Dien Bien Phu. Vietnam divided at 17°N. USSR supports North; USA arms South.
- **1960** Groups opposed to Diem's regime in South unite as Viet Cong.
- **1961** USA pours in military advisers.
- **1964** US Congress approves war.
- **1965** Gen. Nguyen Van Thieu takes over military government of South. First US combat troops arrive.
- **1965–1968** Operation Rolling ⇨

V

CHRONOLOGY *continued*

Thunder – intense bombing of North by South and USA.

- **1967** Antiwar protests start in USA and elsewhere.
- **1968** *Tet* (New Year) Offensive – 105 towns attacked simultaneously in South with infiltrated arms. Viet Cong suffer serious losses. Peace talks begin. USA eases bombing and starts withdrawing troops.
- **1969** Ho Chi Minh dies. Succeeded by Le Duan. War intensifies in spite of talks.
- **1970** USA begins secret attacks in Laos and Cambodia and new mass bombing of North to try to stop arms reaching Viet Cong.
- **1972** 11-day Christmas Campaign is heaviest US bombing of war.
- **1973** Paris Peace Agreements signed, but fighting continues.
- **1975** Fall of Saigon to combined forces of North and Provisional Revolutionary (Viet Cong) Government of South. One million flee after end of war.
- **1976** Vietnam united as Socialist Republic of Vietnam. Saigon renamed Ho Chi Minh City.
- **1978** Invasion of Cambodia to oust Pol Pot regime (by January 1979).
- **1979** Nine-Day War with China. Chinese troops pushed back after destroying everything for 40 km (25 miles) inside Vietnam. "Boat people" crisis. At UN conference, Vietnam agrees to allow legal emigration, but exodus continues.
- **1986** Death of Le Duan. Nguyen Van Linh, new Communist Party general secretary, initiates liberal economic policy of *doi moi* (renovation).
- **1987** Fighting in Thailand as Vietnam pursues Kampuchean resistance fighters across border.
- **1989** Troops leave Cambodia.
- **1991** Open anticommunist dissent made a criminal offense.
- **1992** Revised constitution allows foreign investment, but essential role of Communist Party is unchanged.
- **1995** US-Vietnamese relations normalized. Vietnam joins ASEAN.
- **1996** Eighth Communist Party congress.
- **1997** Legislative elections. Tran Duc Luong president, Phan Van Khai prime minister.
- **1998** Asian financial crisis dampens economic boom.
- **1999** Signing of border treaty with China.
- **2000** Visit by US president Clinton.
- **2001** March, visit by Russian president Putin. April, ninth party congress. Nong Duc Manh becomes general secretary.

DEFENSE

Compulsory military service

$890m

Down 6% in 1999

Vietnam has large and well-equipped armed forces, notably the world's ninth-largest army. Military service is compulsory, with conscripts serving a two-year term. The army's role in preserving both stability and socialism was reaffirmed in 2001. Increased defense spending on the navy reflects the rising tensions in the South China Sea, where there are disputed claims to the Spratly and Paracel Islands.

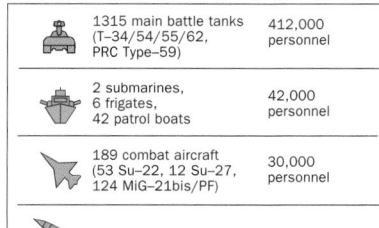

VIETNAMESE ARMED FORCES

1315 main battle tanks (T-34/54/55/62, PRC Type-59)	412,000 personnel
2 submarines, 6 frigates, 42 patrol boats	42,000 personnel
189 combat aircraft (53 Su-22, 12 Su-27, 124 MiG-21bis/PF)	30,000 personnel
None	

ECONOMICS

Inflation 16.8% p.a. (1990–1999)

$28.7bn

14,029–14,514 đông

SCORE CARD

World GNP Ranking	59th
GNP per Capita	$370
Balance of Payments	$-64m
Inflation	7.7%
Unemployment	25%

EXPORTS

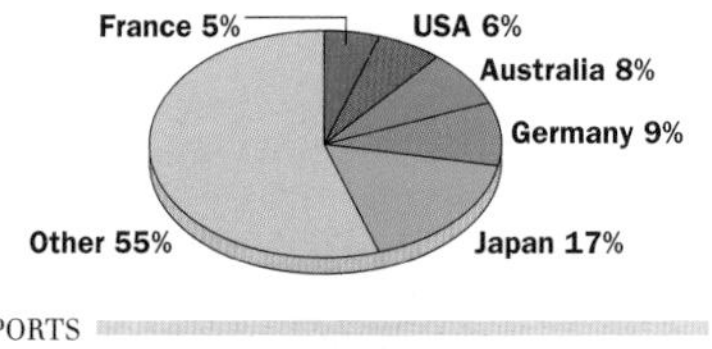
France 5%
USA 6%
Australia 8%
Germany 9%
Japan 17%
Other 55%

IMPORTS

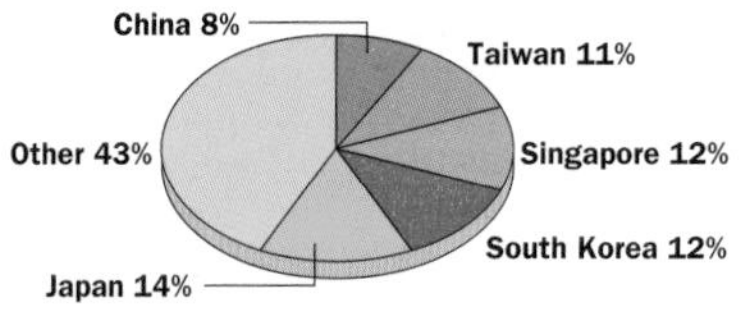
China 8%
Taiwan 11%
Singapore 12%
South Korea 12%
Japan 14%
Other 43%

Strengths

Diverse resource base. Young, literate, low-cost labor force. Strong light industrial and handicraft export industries.

Weaknesses

Weak economic institutions. Weight of bureaucracy. Heavy dependence on aid for reconstruction. Enduring suspicion of entrepreneurial southern attitudes and "individualism." Corruption.

Profile

The encouragement of private enterprise began in 1988. Touted by some commentators in the mid-1990s as the next Asian "tiger," Vietnam has aimed at more moderate growth since the Asian crisis of 1997–1998. Annual GDP increases, over 5% again by 2000 and predicted to reach 7% by 2003, are impressive, but much depends on the courage of the reformists and attracting sufficient foreign investment. In mid-2000 the country's first stock exchange opened. The government has set a target of doubling GDP in the next decade. The potential certainly exists, based on an educated and highly motivated young labor force and mineral resources, located mostly in the north. Increased rice production has boosted incomes, and domestic demand helped the post-1998 upswing. Inflation, once a huge problem, was held down in the 1990s, and is now under firm control. A three-year reform plan for state-owned enterprises promises more scope for joint ventures, and new laws on trade-licensing and investment, passed in 2000, opened the way for a more attractive regime for foreign capital.

ECONOMIC PERFORMANCE INDICATOR

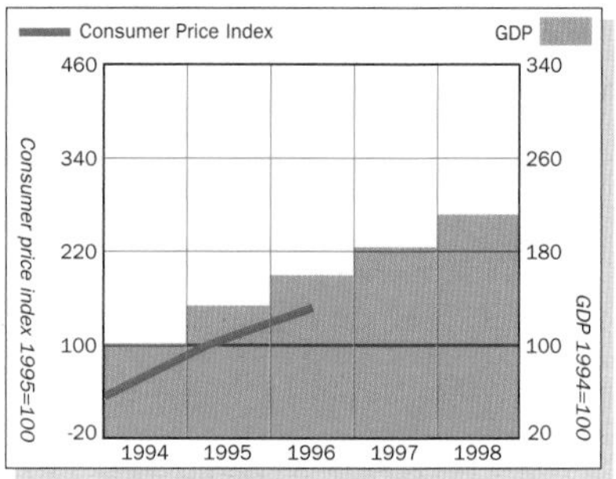
Consumer Price Index
GDP
460
340
220
100
-20
340
260
180
100
20
Consumer price index 1995=100
GDP 1994=100
1994
1995
1996
1997
1998

VIETNAM : MAJOR BUSINESSES

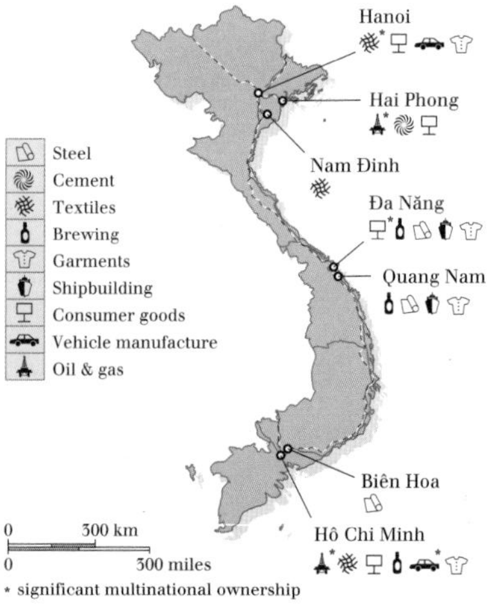
Hanoi
Hai Phong
Nam Đinh
Đa Năng
Quang Nam
Biên Hoa
Hô Chi Minh
Steel
Cement
Textiles
Brewing
Garments
Shipbuilding
Consumer goods
Vehicle manufacture
Oil & gas
0 300 km
0 300 miles
* significant multinational ownership

RESOURCES

Electric power 4.6m kw

1.55m tonnes

320,000 b/d (reserves 600,000,000 bbl)

50m ducks, 19.6m pigs, 4.1m cattle, 190m chickens

Coal, oil, tin, zinc, iron, antimony, apatite, salt, bauxite

ELECTRICITY GENERATION

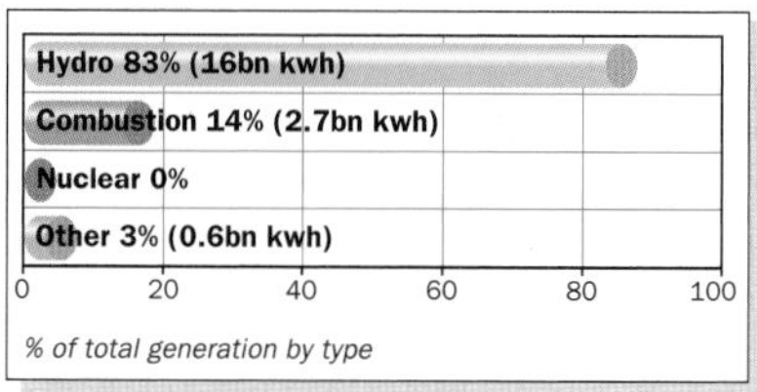

Hydro 83% (16bn kwh)
Combustion 14% (2.7bn kwh)
Nuclear 0%
Other 3% (0.6bn kwh)
0
20
40
60
80
100
% of total generation by type

Vietnam is the world's third-largest exporter of rice and the second-largest coffee producer.

Oil production, small by world standards, is sufficient to make it Vietnam's biggest export earner. The Oil and Gas Corporation of Vietnam (PetroVietnam) is involved in joint ventures with international oil firms. Vietnam has unexploited gas reserves in the South China Sea; gas from the only producing field has to be flared off.

Timber exports have been banned since 1997 to preserve forests.

Northern Vietnam has a surplus of electricity, mainly from hydroelectric schemes.

VIETNAM : LAND USE

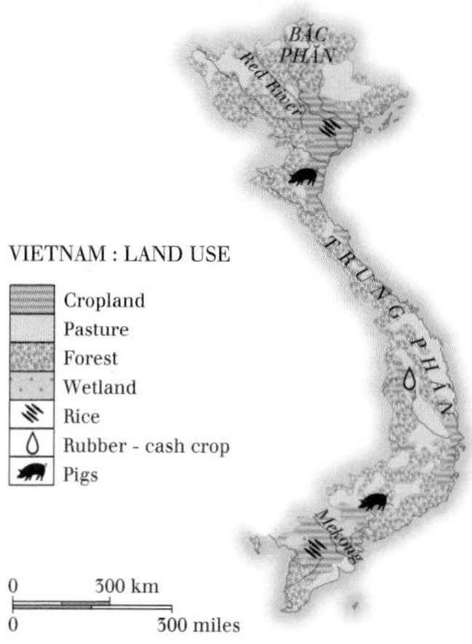

BAC PHAN
Red River
TRUNG PHAN
Mekong
Cropland
Pasture
Forest
Wetland
Rice
Rubber - cash crop
Pigs
0
300 km
0
300 miles

ENVIRONMENT

Sustainability rank: 114th

3%

0.6 tonnes per capita

ENVIRONMENTAL TREATIES

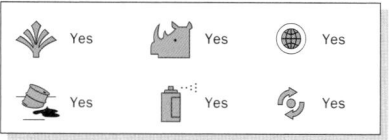

Yes	Yes	Yes
Yes	Yes	Yes

In the Vietnam War, seven million tonnes of bombs were dropped, and the defoliant chemical Agent Orange was sprayed over vast areas; a "census" of the continuing health impact was announced in 1999. 50% of Vietnam's forests were seriously damaged and some 5% destroyed. Deforestation continued into the 1990s due to logging and expansion of coffee-growing, causing soil erosion and flooding. Floods along the Mekong in 2000 were the worst for 40 years.

CRIME

Death penalty used

Vietnam does not publish prison figures

Increase in petty theft

CRIME RATES

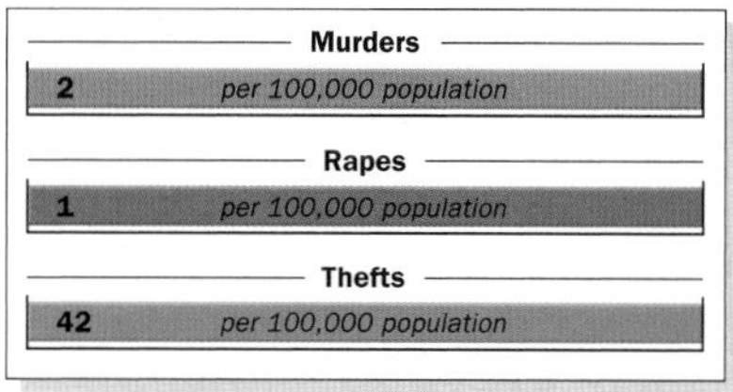

Murders
2 per 100,000 population
Rapes
1 per 100,000 population
Thefts
42 per 100,000 population

The judicial system is based on the Soviet model. The education camps established after liberation have now closed, but religious and political dissidents are still held without trial.

Corruption has risen sharply since economic liberalization, as has the illegal drift of young people to urban areas, where they are blamed for increasing petty crime and "social evils" such as begging, prostitution, and drug-taking. Theft from foreigners is a problem in major cities.

HEALTH

Welfare state health benefits

1 per 1667 people

Heart disease, cancers, malaria

Vietnam's medical achievements include developing a vaccine for hepatitis B, and extracting artemisinin (an anti-malarial drug) from the thanh hao tree. An extensive campaign is under way to combat the spread of AIDS.

SPENDING

GDP/cap. increase

CONSUMPTION AND SPENDING

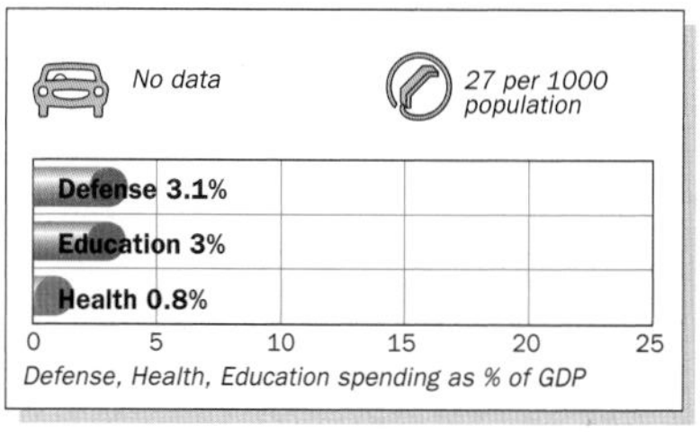

No data
27 per 1000 population
Defense 3.1%
Education 3%
Health 0.8%
0
5
10
15
20
25
Defense, Health, Education spending as % of GDP

Ostentatious consumerism is rising despite official disapproval, but is beyond most people's reach. Good rice harvests have helped to double incomes since 1993.

MEDIA

TV ownership medium

Daily newspaper circulation 4 per 1000 people

PUBLISHING AND BROADCAST MEDIA

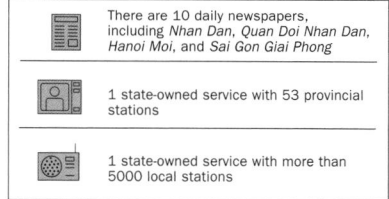

There are 10 daily newspapers, including *Nhan Dan*, *Quan Doi Nhan Dan*, *Hanoi Moi*, and *Sai Gon Giai Phong*

1 state-owned service with 53 provincial stations

1 state-owned service with more than 5000 local stations

The media are tightly regulated and all editors have to be Party members, but criticism of the authorities is still possible. The weekly *Tuoi Tre* is known for its investigative reporting, and even *Nhan Dan*, the Party newspaper, has been known to expose laxity in the system, especially in the judiciary. The army daily, *Quan Doi Nhan Dan*, is the most hard-line paper.

EDUCATION

School leaving age: 11

93%

509,300 students

THE EDUCATION SYSTEM

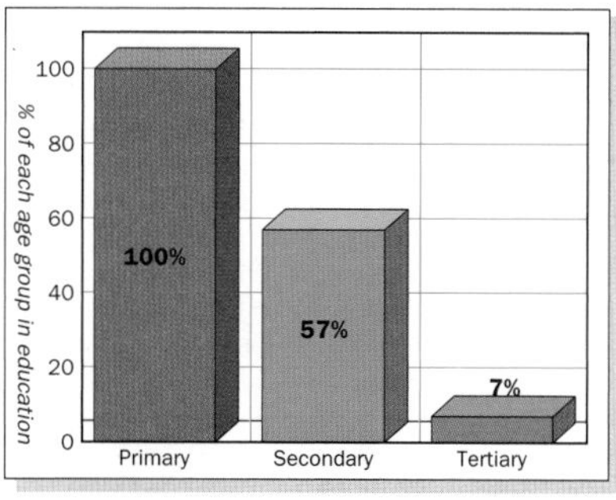

100
80
60
40
20
0
% of each age group in education
100%
57%
7%
Primary
Secondary
Tertiary

A law approved in 1998 encourages private sponsorship of education by individuals and businesses.

Students have to pay fees for higher education. Vietnamese universities have a strong liberal arts tradition.

WORLD RANKING

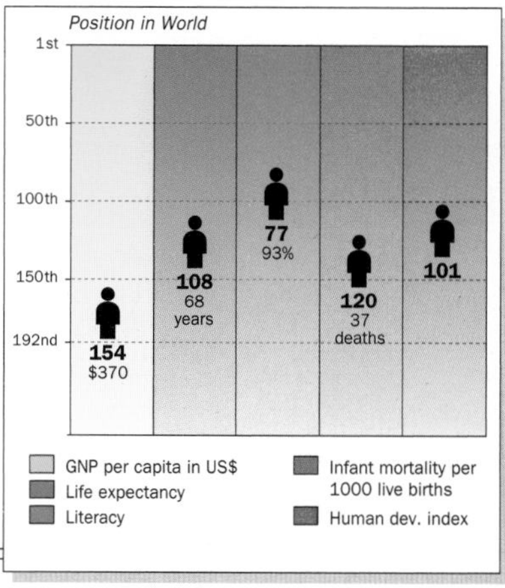

Position in World
1st
50th
100th
150th
192nd
154
$370
108
68
years
77
93%
120
37
deaths
101
GNP per capita in US$
Life expectancy
Literacy
Infant mortality per 1000 live births
Human dev. index

V

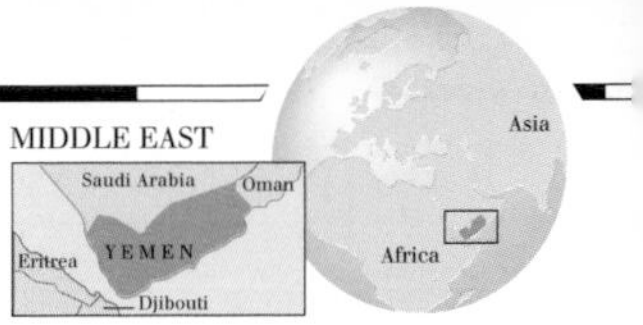
MIDDLE EAST
Saudi Arabia
Oman
YEMEN
Eritrea
Djibouti
Asia
Africa

YEMEN

OFFICIAL NAME: Republic of Yemen **CAPITAL:** Sana
POPULATION: 18.1 million **CURRENCY:** Rial **OFFICIAL LANGUAGE:** Arabic

1990
1990
May 22
ADN
+3
+967
.ye

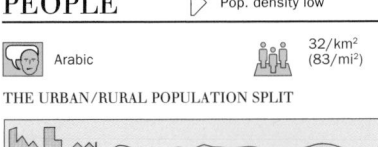

YEMEN IS LOCATED in southern Arabia neighboring Saudi Arabia and Oman. The north is mountainous, with a fertile strip along the Red Sea. The south is largely arid mountains and desert. Until 1990 Yemen was two countries, the Yemen Arab Republic in the north and the People's Democratic Republic of Yemen in the south. The north was run by successive military regimes; the poorer south was the Arab world's only Marxist state. Postunification conflict between the two ruling hierarchies, nominally in coalition, led to full-scale civil war in 1994 and the ousting of the southern-based former Marxists.

CLIMATE

Hot desert/mountain

WEATHER CHART

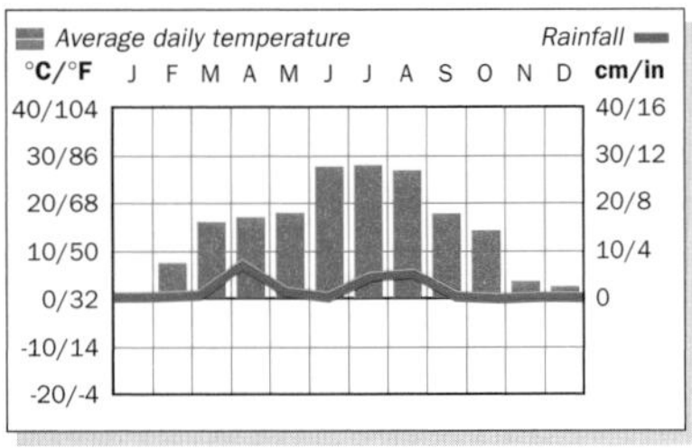
Average daily temperature
Rainfall
°C/°F
J F M A M J J A S O N D
cm/in
40/104
30/86
20/68
10/50
0/32
-10/14
-20/-4
40/16
30/12
20/8
10/4
0

The desert climate is modified by altitude, which affects temperatures by as much as 12°C (54°F). Rainfall increases in northwest and central Yemen.

TRANSPORTATION

Drive on right

Sana International 624,000 passengers

45 ships 25,300 grt

THE TRANSPORTATION NETWORK

7700 km (4785 miles)

None

None

None

Aden's key position at the entrance to the Red Sea makes it a significant port. The main cities are linked by adequate roads, but many rural areas are inaccessible. Sana and Aden are served by international airlines.

***Hilltop village** in northern Yemen, showing traditionally decorated, multistorey houses built from mud bricks.*

TOURISM

Visitors : Population 1:206

88,000 visitors

Up 5% in 1998

MAIN TOURIST ARRIVALS

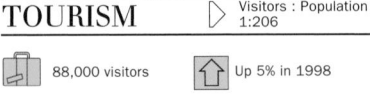

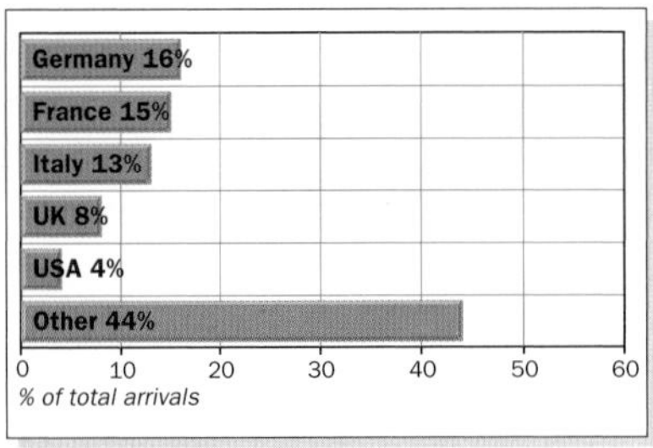
Germany 16%
France 15%
Italy 13%
UK 8%
USA 4%
Other 44%
0 10 20 30 40 50 60
% of total arrivals

Believed to be the home of the legendary Queen of Sheba, Yemen attracts tourists interested in Arab society, architecture, archeology, and historical remains. The Romans called Yemen *Arabia Felix* because of its fertile farmlands and dominance in the frankincense trade. Yemen was the second country, after Saudi Arabia, to convert to Islam.

Southern Yemen has been open to Western visitors only since 1990. Its run-down infrastructure and lack of hotels, especially on the coast, have hindered tourism. Sana, a walled medieval city, is the more interesting center for tourists. It has impressive architecture, particularly tall stone and mud brick Arab houses, and the palaces of the former imamate. Despite being over 100 km (62 miles) from the capital, the Marib Dam, built in ancient times, is another major attraction.

German and French tourists were the first to travel to North Yemen during the 1980s. Hopes of a major rise in tourism following the end of the 1994 civil war were dashed in 1998 after tribesmen kidnapped and killed four tourists.

Tourists are subject to a ban on the consumption of alcohol, except in five-star hotels. Whisky and beer are available on the black market, which operates out of Djibouti.

PEOPLE

Pop. density low

Arabic

32/km² (83/mi²)

THE URBAN/RURAL POPULATION SPLIT

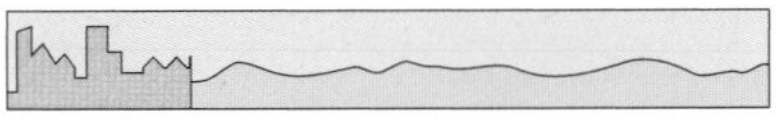
24%
76%

RELIGIOUS PERSUASION

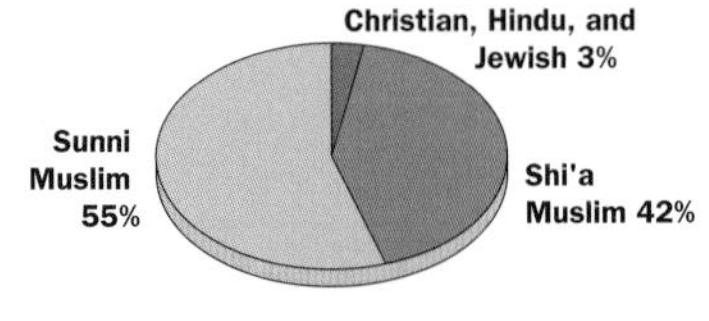
Christian, Hindu, and Jewish 3%
Sunni Muslim 55%
Shi'a Muslim 42%

ETHNIC MAKEUP

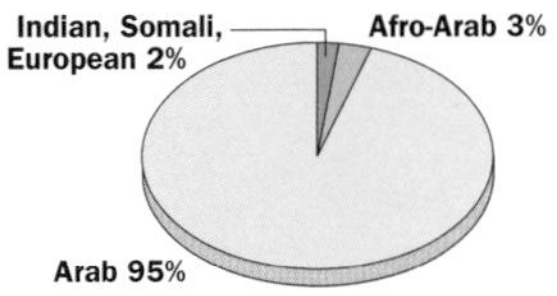
Indian, Somali, European 2%
Afro-Arab 3%
Arab 95%

Yemenis are almost entirely of Arab and Bedouin descent, though there is a small, dwindling, Jewish minority and people of mixed African and Arab descent along the south coast. The majority are Sunni Muslims, of the Shafi sect. However, Zaydi Shi'ites are strong in the north, where many people have close family in Saudi Arabia. Many Yemenis consider Saudi Arabia's Asir province to be part of Yemen.

Agriculture supports more than half the population. Many Yemenis went to work in Saudi Arabia and the Gulf states during the 1970s oil boom. More than a million worked in Saudi Arabia, and their expulsion, due to Yemen's support for Iraq's invasion of Kuwait in 1990, has increased domestic unemployment.

In rural areas and in the north, Islamic orthodoxy is strong and most women wear the veil. In the south, however, women still claim the freedoms they had under the Marxist regime, especially in urban areas.

Tension continues to exist between the south, led by cosmopolitan Aden, and the more conservative north, leading in 1994 to civil war.

POPULATION AGE BREAKDOWN

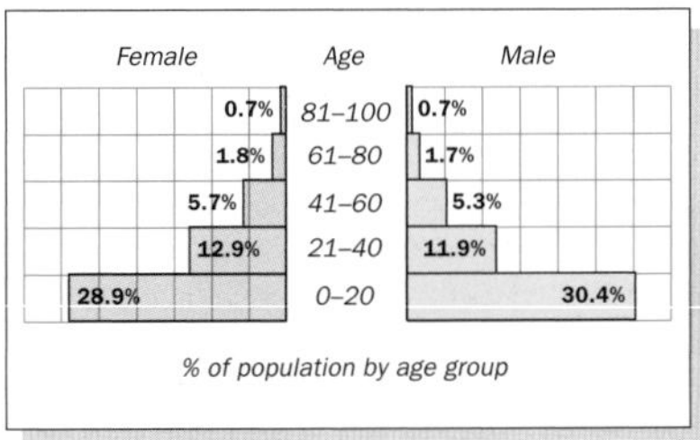
Female
Age
Male
0.7% 81–100 0.7%
1.8% 61–80 1.7%
5.7% 41–60 5.3%
12.9% 21–40 11.9%
28.9% 0–20 30.4%
% of population by age group

Y

YEMEN

Total Land Area : 562 970 sq. km
(217 362 sq. miles)

SAUDI ARABIA
OMAN
RUB AL KHALI
RED SEA
GULF OF ADEN
RAMLAT DAHM
RAMLAT AS SAB'ATAYAN
HADRAMAWT
AL KATHIR
Sa'dah
Midi
Harad
Huth
Khamir
'Abs
Wadi Mawr
Hajjah
'Amran
Al Luhayyah
Kamaran
Az Zaydiyah
Jabal an Nabi Shu'ayb 3760m
SANA
Ma'rib
Harib
Bajil
Al Hudaydah
Bayt al Faqih
Dhamar
Rada'
Wadi Zabid
Yarim
Ibb
Zabid
Al Bayda'
Lawdar
Ramadah
Ta'izz
Wadi Tuban
Al Mukha
At Turbah
Lahij
Madinat ash Sha'b
Shaykh 'Uthman
Zinjibar
'Adan (Aden)
Barim
Bab el Mandeb
Shuqrah
Ahwar
Nisab
Ar Rawdah
Al Hawrah
'Irqah
Balhaf
As Sufal
Burum
Al Mukalla
Ar Riyan
Ash Shihr
Harrah
Al Fardah
Al Khuraybah
'Amd
Al Hajarayn
Shibam
Hawra'
Tarim
Say'un
Layjun
Minwakh
Wadi Arwat as Sayar
Wadi Abrad
Wadi al Masilah
Wadi al Jiz'
Sanaw
Al Buzun
Sayhut
Qishn
Al Ghaydah
Ghubbat al Qamar
Damqawt
Qalansiyah
Hadiboh
Suqutra
Abd-Al-Kuri
0 100 km
0 100 miles
POPULATION
over 500 000
over 100 000
over 10 000
under 10 000
LAND HEIGHT
3000m/9843ft
2000m/6562ft
1000m/3281ft
500m/1640ft
200m/656ft
Sea Level

POLITICS

Multiparty elections

1997/2003

President Ali Abdullah Saleh

AT THE LAST ELECTION

House of Representatives 301 seats

1% Ba'ath
62% GPC
18% Ind
18% YAR
1% NUPO

GPC = General People's Congress **Ind** = Independents
YAR = Yemeni Alliance for Reform (al-Islah)
NUPO = Nasserite Unionist Popular Organization
Ba'ath = Arab Socialist Ba'ath Party

Yemen is a multiparty democracy. The president retains executive power.

MAIN POLITICAL ISSUES

Instability

Since the ending of the civil war, a vicious border dispute with Saudi Arabia, growing tribal insurgency, and mounting popular discontent with President Saleh's government have threatened stability.

Saudi interference

Relations with Saudi Arabia have long been strained – over oil exploration rights and accusations that Riyadh is funding insurgent tribesmen. In early 1995 a memorandum of understanding on border issues was signed, but the two sides clashed violently in 1998 over the 1600 km (1000 miles) in question. In early 2001, both sides withdrew border troops in accordance with a pact reached the previous June.

PROFILE

The merger of North and South Yemen in 1990 united Yemenis under one ruler for the first time since 1735. At first, President Ali Saleh skillfully maintained unity. Then, in 1994, a bloody civil war erupted, fueling a secessionist movement in the south. By mid-1994, the fighting had subsided and the southerners were crushed. In legislative elections held in 1997 President Saleh's GPC won an absolute majority of seats, in part due to a boycott by the former southern-ruling Yemen Socialist Party, and in 1999 he won the region's first ever direct election of a head of state. However, Saleh's regime still faces threats from disgruntled southern tribesmen angry at levels of poverty in their oil-rich country. Since 1992, tribesmen have kidnapped more than 100 foreigners, including diplomats and tourists.

Ali Abdullah Saleh, *former North Yemen president, now leader of the unified Yemen.*

Ali Salem al-Baidh, *former vice-president, ousted when south resecession failed.*

CHRONOLOGY

From the 9th century, the Zaydi dynasty ruled Yemen until their defeat by the Ottoman Turks in 1517. The Turks were expelled by the Zaydi imams in 1636.

- **1839** Britain occupies Aden.
- **1918** Yemen gains independence.
- **1937** Aden made a Crown Colony, hinterland a Protectorate.
- **1962** Army coup. Imam deposed, Yemen Arab Republic (YAR) declared in north.
- **1962–1970** Northern civil war between royalists and republicans.
- **1963** Aden and Protectorate united to form Federation of South Arabia.
- **1967** British troops leave Aden.
- **1970** South Yemen renamed People's Democratic Republic of Yemen (PDRY). Republicans victorious in the north.
- **1971** Civilian elections in YAR.
- **1972** War between YAR and PDRY ends in peace settlement.
- **1974** Army coup in YAR.
- **1975** Sultan of Oman defeats revolt backed by PDRY in Dhofar province.
- **1978** Lieutenant-Colonel Ali Saleh YAR president. Coup in PDRY. Radical Abdalfattah Ismail in power.
- **1979** PDRY 20-year treaty with USSR.
- **1980** Ismail replaced by moderate Ali Muhammed.
- **1982** PDRY signs peace treaty with Sultan of Oman.

Y

CHRONOLOGY *continued*

- **1984** YAR signs 20-year cooperation treaty with USSR.
- **1986** Coup attempt in PDRY leads to civil war. Rebels take control of Aden. New PDRY president meets YAR counterpart.
- **1987** Oil production starts in YAR.
- **1988** YAR holds elections for consultative council; Muslim brotherhood gains influence.
- **1989** Speeding-up of unification process. PDRY publishes a program of free-market reforms. YAR and PDRY sign unification agreement. Constitution of unified Yemen published.
- **1990** January, restrictions on travel between YAR and PDRY lifted. May, formal unification amid protests from pro-Islamic groups opposed to secular constitution. Ali Saleh becomes president of Republic of Yemen.
- **1991** Yemeni guest workers expelled by Saudi Arabia in retaliation for Yemen's position over the Iraqi invasion of Kuwait. Arab states boycott independence celebrations.
- **1992** Assassinations and political unrest delay elections.
- **1994** Southern secessionists defeated in civil war.
- **1997** President Saleh's GPC wins an absolute majority of seats in general election.
- **1998–1999** Violent border dispute with Saudi Arabia. Kidnapping of tourists, four killed; three members of Islamic Army of Aden (IAA) sentenced to death.
- **1999** Saleh reelected.
- **2000** Yemen agrees border with Saudi Arabia after 66-year dispute.
- **2001** Referendum approves extension of presidential term to seven years.

WORLD AFFAIRS

Joined UN in 1947/1967

AL | AMF | IBRD | NAM | OIC

Agreement in 2000 with Saudi Arabia over their disputed border resolved what had been the main foreign policy issue. Yemen remains relatively isolated internationally after supporting Iraq in the 1991 Gulf War.

AID

Recipient

$456m (receipts) — Up 47% in 1999

In early 1996, Yemen received some $700 million from the IMF and donor countries in support of its economic reform program.

DEFENSE

Compulsory military service

$429m — Up 6% in 1999

The control of insurgent tribesmen is the main internal security concern. Internationally, fears of terrorism were exacerbated by the sinking of USS *Cole* off Aden in late 2000.

Following unification in 1990, mutual suspicion hampered the integration of the defense forces of former North and South Yemen. Sporadic, bitter clashes have taken place, most notably in 1994.

YEMENI ARMED FORCES

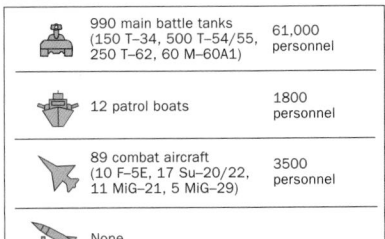

990 main battle tanks (150 T-34, 500 T-54/55, 250 T-62, 60 M-60A1)	61,000 personnel
12 patrol boats	1800 personnel
89 combat aircraft (10 F-5E, 17 Su-20/22, 11 MiG-21, 5 MiG-29)	3500 personnel
None	

ECONOMICS

Inflation 26.1% p.a. (1990–1999)

$6.1bn — 159.73–164.39 Yemeni rials

SCORE CARD

World GNP Ranking	104th
GNP per Capita	$360
Balance of Payments	$-228m
Inflation	8%
Unemployment	30%

EXPORTS

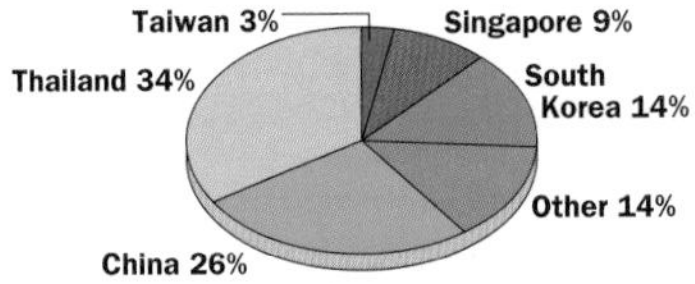

Taiwan 3%
Singapore 9%
Thailand 34%
South Korea 14%
Other 14%
China 26%

IMPORTS

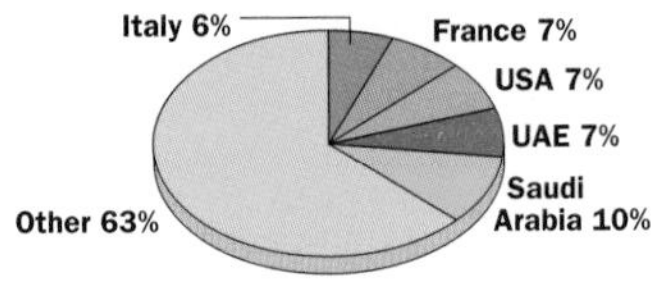

Italy 6%
France 7%
USA 7%
UAE 7%
Saudi Arabia 10%
Other 63%

Strengths

Rising oil production. Salt mining. Deposits of copper, gold, lead, zinc, and molybdenum. Industries include oil refining, chemicals, food products, cement, and leather.

Weaknesses

Political instability deters foreign investment. Well-organized black market undermines tax base. Large balance of payments deficit. Dependence on subsistence agriculture. Burden of high population growth.

Profile

Unification in 1990 aimed to transform the economy. High expectations were placed on the exploitation of large oil and natural gas reserves, discovered in 1984; exports of oil began in 1987. Plans were also made to encourage industrial investment around the port of Aden. These policies for regeneration suffered severe setbacks as a result of the 1990–1991 Gulf War. In addition, the expulsion of over one million Yemeni guest

ECONOMIC PERFORMANCE INDICATOR

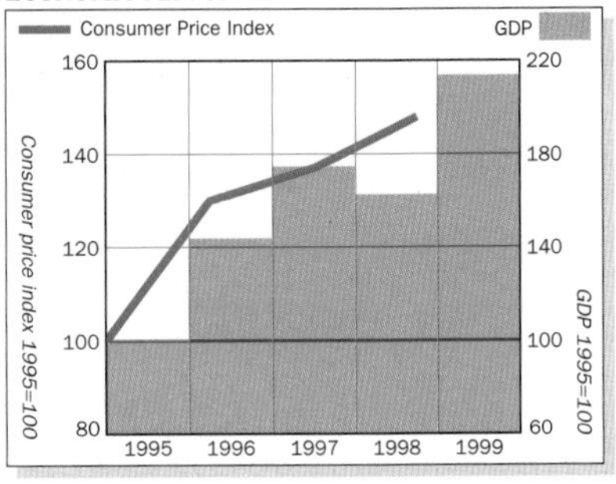

Consumer Price Index
GDP
160
140
120
100
80
220
180
140
100
60
1995
1996
1997
1998
1999
Consumer price index 1995=100
GDP 1995=100

workers from Saudi Arabia imposed a huge burden on the economy and ended the flow of workers' remittances.

The ensuing economic crisis forced the government to reduce expenditure and subsidies on certain staple foods. This provoked widespread civil unrest and encouraged many farmers to switch from food crops, such as wheat, to growing the more profitable narcotic plant *qat*. As a result, Yemen has increasingly had to import foodstuffs.

The 1994 civil war seriously damaged the economy – oil refineries, water systems, and communications centers were destroyed. In 1995, the government embarked on an IMF-backed reform program aimed at stabilizing the economy. A 1998 decision to remove subsidies on staple foods led to violent demonstrations.

YEMEN : MAJOR BUSINESSES

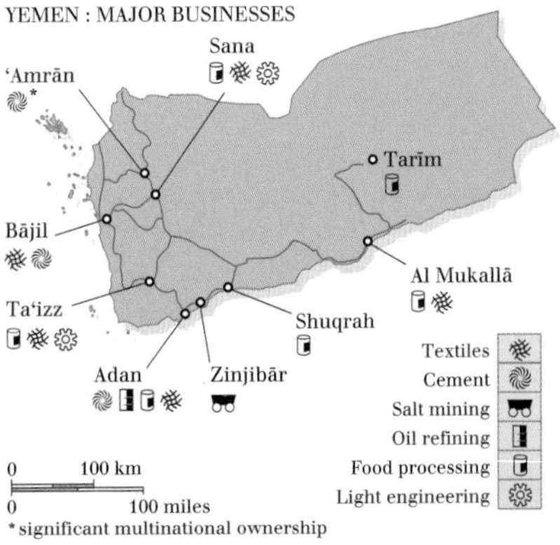

Sana
'Amrān
Tarīm
Bājil
Al Mukallā
Ta'izz
Shuqrah
Adan
Zinjibār
Textiles
Cement
Salt mining
Oil refining
Food processing
Light engineering
0 100 km
0 100 miles
* significant multinational ownership

Y

RESOURCES

Electric power 810,000 kw

115,654 tonnes

440,000 b/d (reserves 4,000,000,000

4.6m sheep, 4.2m goats, 1.3m cattle, 27.3m chickens

Oil, natural gas, salt, gold, copper, lead, zinc, molybdenum

ELECTRICITY GENERATION

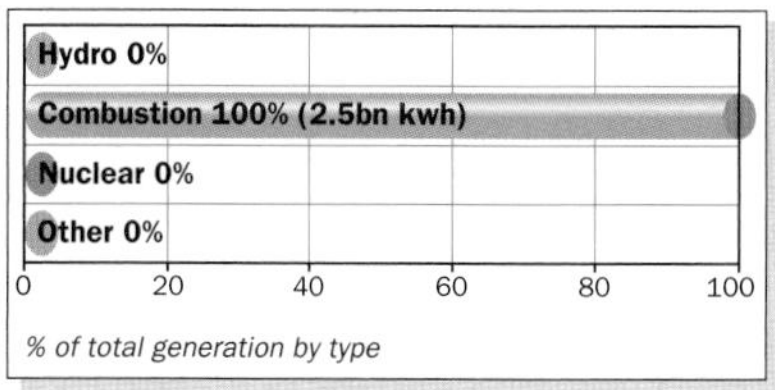
Hydro 0%
Combustion 100% (2.5bn kwh)
Nuclear 0%
Other 0%
0
20
40
60
80
100
% of total generation by type

There are considerable reserves of oil and gas. Crude oil production and refining has been held back by Western companies' reluctance to offend Saudi Arabia. Despite attacks by bandits, exploration is continuing in many areas. The 2000 border agreement with Saudi Arabia promises better Yemeni access to rich oilfields. Salt is the only other mineral commercially exploited at present, and its production continues to grow steadily.

The agricultural sector employs 55% of the working population and accounts for more than 20% of GDP. Cotton is grown as a cash crop. There is also some forestry and hunting for animal skins. Livestock and livestock products, including dairy produce and hides, are the economic mainstays of the north. Yemen's rich fishing grounds in the Arabian Sea now provide a major source of earnings, despite poor equipment.

YEMEN : LAND USE

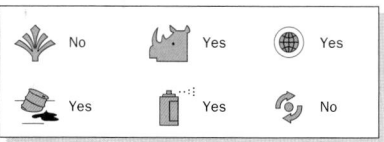

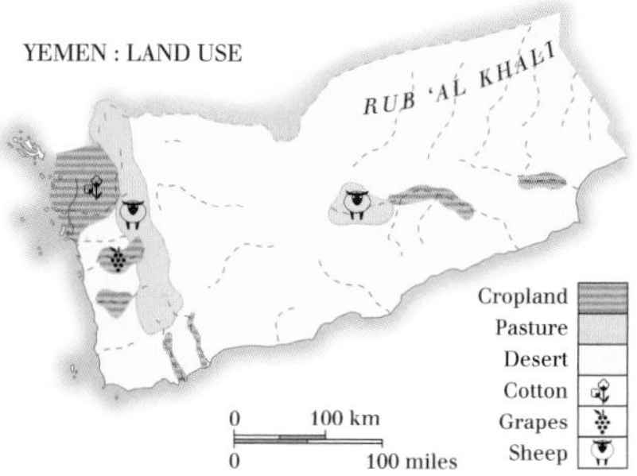
RUB 'AL KHALI
Cropland
Pasture
Desert
Cotton
Grapes
Sheep
0 100 km
0 100 miles

ENVIRONMENT

Not available

None

1 tonne per capita

ENVIRONMENTAL TREATIES

No

Yes

Yes

Yes

Yes

No

Limited economic development has left much land untouched. Problems include desertification, water scarcity, overgrazing, and soil erosion.

MEDIA

TV ownership low

Daily newspaper circulation 15 per 1000 people

PUBLISHING AND BROADCAST MEDIA

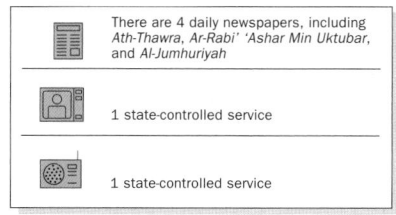

There are 4 daily newspapers, including *Ath-Thawra, Ar-Rabi' 'Ashar Min Uktubar,* and *Al-Jumhuriyah*

1 state-controlled service

1 state-controlled service

CRIME

Death penalty used

Yemen does not publish prison figures

Down 51% 1991–1996

CRIME RATES

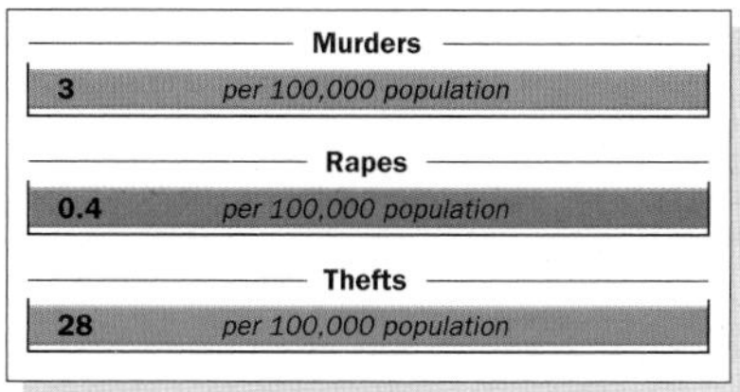
Murders
3
per 100,000 population
Rapes
0.4
per 100,000 population
Thefts
28
per 100,000 population

Political assassinations continue to threaten political stability. There is little formal law enforcement outside the main cities; foreign companies risk kidnappings and theft by Bedouin raiders. There is a proliferation of illicit weapons; the number of firearms has been estimated at 50 million – three times the population. Some blame lawlessness on the narcotic, *qat*.

EDUCATION

School leaving age: 15

46%

65,675 students

THE EDUCATION SYSTEM

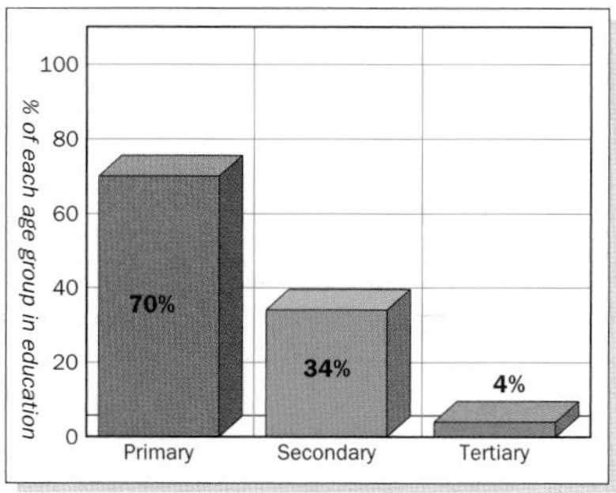
100
80
60
40
20
0
% of each age group in education
70%
34%
4%
Primary
Secondary
Tertiary

Some 80% of the population have no formal classroom education. Schooling barely extends into the rural areas. Illiteracy is especially high among women: 74% cannot read or write. Only 13% of students at Yemen's two universities – Sana and Aden – are female. Yemen also has some technical colleges. The government's unpopular economic policies have encouraged student activism.

Yemen has a long, distinguished tradition of intellectual debate, and legislation in 1990 embodied freedom of the press, which, however, is poorly developed. The government keeps a tight control on the media and vets the entry of foreign journalists. TV and radio are state-controlled and have a limited range around the principal cities. Satellite TV is not generally available. Ownership of radio and TV receivers is low, with only a tiny minority owning a television set.

HEALTH

No welfare state health benefits

1 per 5000 people

Diarrheal diseases, tuberculosis, malaria, bilharzia

The major cities have an adequate primary health care system. A new 300-bed hospital in Sana is due to be completed in 2004. Rural areas are less well served. Health services are under threat from tribal gangs. In 1998 three nuns working as health volunteers at the Dar al-Salam Hospital in the western city of Hudaydah were shot dead by a tribal gunman.

SPENDING

GDP/cap. increase

CONSUMPTION AND SPENDING

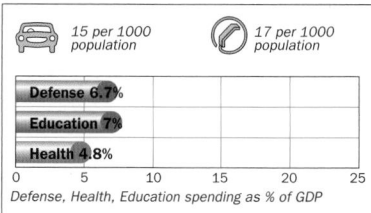

15 per 1000 population

17 per 1000 population

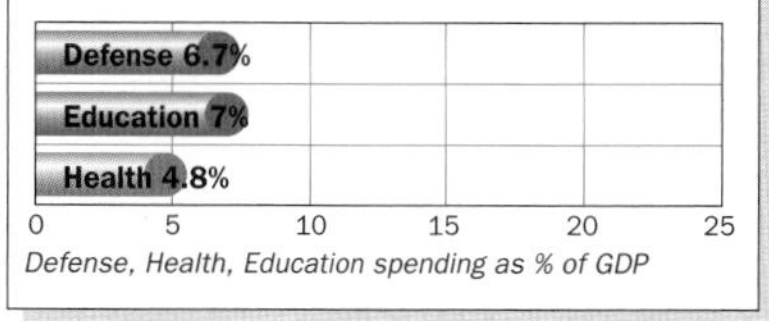
Defense 6.7%
Education 7%
Health 4.8%
0
5
10
15
20
25
Defense, Health, Education spending as % of GDP

Most Yemenis suffered a fall in living standards after Saudi Arabia expelled its Yemeni workers. A lack of jobs in other Gulf states has fueled unemployment, estimated at around 30%. Except for a small elite, the ownership of consumer goods is low.

WORLD RANKING

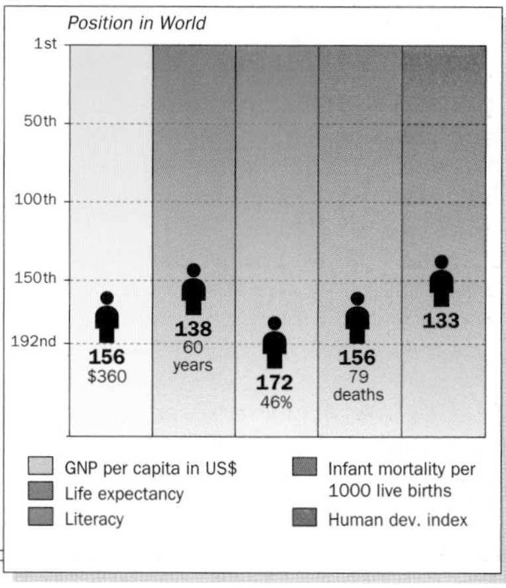
Position in World
1st
50th
100th
150th
192nd
156
$360
138
60 years
172
46%
156
79 deaths
133
GNP per capita in US$
Life expectancy
Literacy
Infant mortality per 1000 live births
Human dev. index

Y

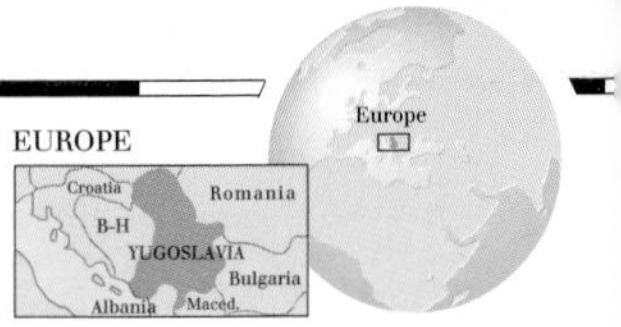
Europe
EUROPE
Croatia
B-H
Romania
YUGOSLAVIA
Bulgaria
Albania
Maced.

YUGOSLAVIA (SERBIA & MONTENEGRO)

OFFICIAL NAME: Federal Republic of Yugoslavia **CAPITAL:** Belgrade
POPULATION: 10.6 million **CURRENCY:** Yugoslav dinar **OFFICIAL LANGUAGE:** Serbo-croat

1992 | 1992 | Nov 29 | YU | +1 | +381 | .yu

THE FEDERAL REPUBLIC of Yugoslavia (FRY) consists of Serbia and Montenegro, two of the six republics of pre-1991 Yugoslavia. Slobodan Milošević whipped up Serbian nationalist feeling in rising to power as the socialist federation disintegrated. His regime was condemned internationally over the Bosnian war (1992–1995), and for backing "ethnic cleansing" in the majority-Albanian province of Kosovo, until NATO bombing in 1999 forced it to withdraw. Within two years of this debacle, Milošević was ousted and handed over to face trial in The Hague for war crimes.

CLIMATE

Continental

WEATHER CHART

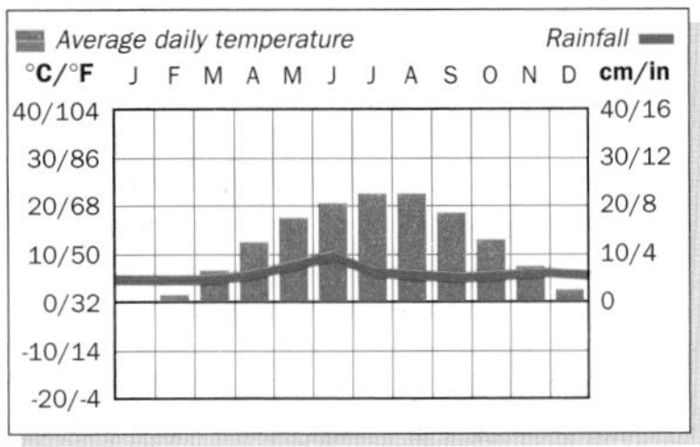
Average daily temperature
Rainfall
°C/°F
J F M A M J J A S O N D
cm/in
40/104
30/86
20/68
10/50
0/32
-10/14
-20/-4
40/16
30/12
20/8
10/4
0

The climate is continental inland and Mediterranean along the Montenegrin coast. Summers are hot and springs rainy. Winters are cold, with heavy snowfalls. In July and August, the average maximum in Belgrade is 23°C (73°F), while in January it is 3°C (37°F).

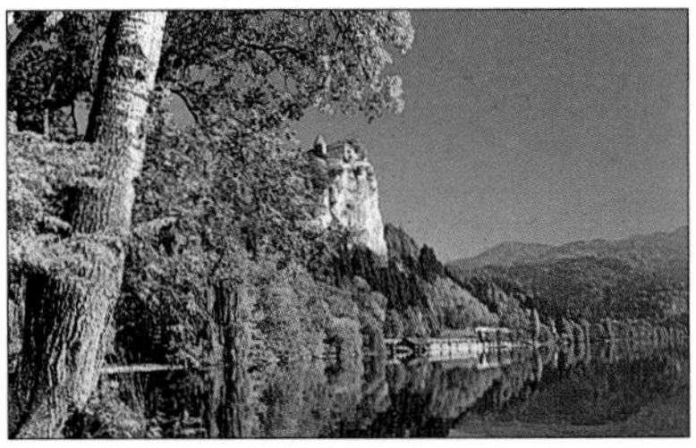

Yugoslavia's stunning scenery is a potential draw for tourists. Before the 1990s it attracted millions every year.

TOURISM

Visitors : Population 1:70

152,000 visitors

Down 46% in 1999

MAIN TOURIST ARRIVALS

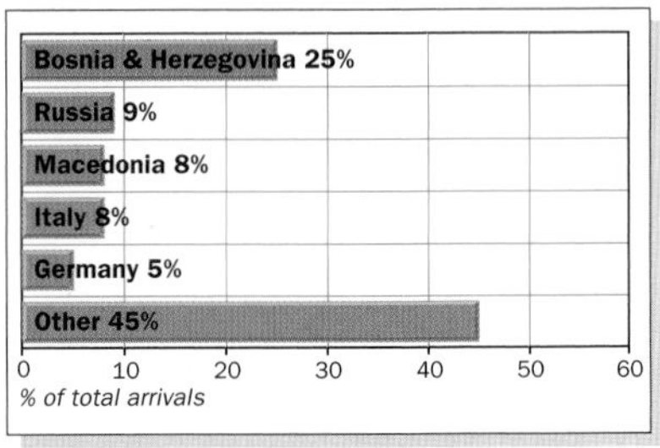
Bosnia & Herzegovina 25%
Russia 9%
Macedonia 8%
Italy 8%
Germany 5%
Other 45%
0
10
20
30
40
50
60
% of total arrivals

Serbia has never been a center of tourism. The Montenegrin coast, however, has renowned beaches. Before 1999 they were monopolized by Serbians, particularly by political and criminal elements of the Serbian elite. Hyperinflation and recession kept the average Yugoslav vacationer away. The impact of UN sanctions and the conflict over Kosovo meant that foreign tourism ceased in the 1990s.

TRANSPORTATION

Drive on right

Surcin, Belgrade
544,509 passengers

9 ships
4700 grt

THE TRANSPORTATION NETWORK

28,822 km (17,909 miles)	560 km (348 miles)
4059 km (2522 miles)	587 km (365 miles)

About one-third of railroads in the FRY are electrified. The rail link to Greece is one of Serbia's main trading routes, and lines through Serbia remain the best link between Budapest and Sofia. Many foreign travelers choose longer routes through neighboring countries, although transit visas have always been issued relatively freely.

Bridges and railroads were specifically targeted during the NATO bombing in 1999. The bombing of the bridge over the Danube at Novi Sad closed the river as a major regional trading artery, and its reopening was made a priority for international assistance once the Milošević regime had fallen.

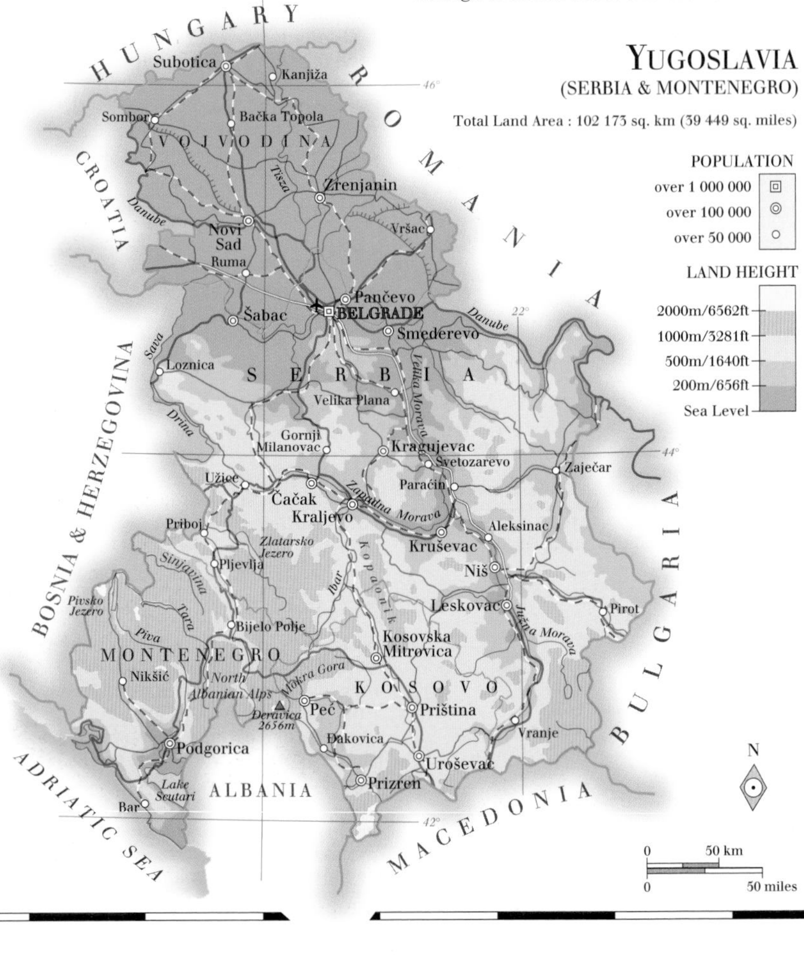
YUGOSLAVIA
(SERBIA & MONTENEGRO)
Total Land Area : 102 173 sq. km (39 449 sq. miles)
POPULATION
over 1 000 000
over 100 000
over 50 000
LAND HEIGHT
2000m/6562ft
1000m/3281ft
500m/1640ft
200m/656ft
Sea Level
HUNGARY
ROMANIA
CROATIA
BOSNIA & HERZEGOVINA
BULGARIA
MACEDONIA
ALBANIA
ADRIATIC SEA
VOJVODINA
SERBIA
MONTENEGRO
KOSOVO
Subotica
Kanjiža
Sombor
Bačka Topola
Zrenjanin
Novi Sad
Ruma
Vršac
Pančevo
BELGRADE
Šabac
Smederevo
Loznica
Velika Plana
Gornji Milanovac
Kragujevac
Svetozarevo
Zaječar
Užice
Čačak
Kraljevo
Paraćin
Priboj
Aleksinac
Kruševac
Pljevlja
Niš
Leskovac
Pirot
Bijelo Polje
Kosovska Mitrovica
Nikšić
Peč
Priština
Đakovica
Vranje
Podgorica
Uroševac
Prizren
Bar
Danube
Tisza
Sava
Drina
Velika Morava
Zapadna Morava
Južna Morava
Ibar
Tara
Piva
Sinjavina
Zlatarsko Jezero
Pivsko Jezero
Kopaonik
North Albanian Alps
Mokra Gora
Đeravica 2656m
Lake Scutari
20°
22°
46°
44°
42°
N
0
50 km
0
50 miles

PEOPLE

Pop. density medium

Serbo-Croat, Albanian, Hungarian

104/km² (269/mi²)

THE URBAN/RURAL POPULATION SPLIT

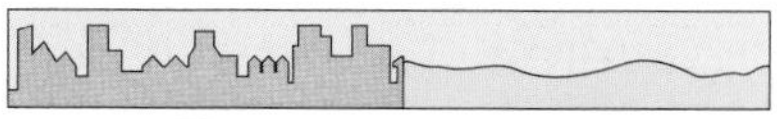
52%
48%

RELIGIOUS PERSUASION

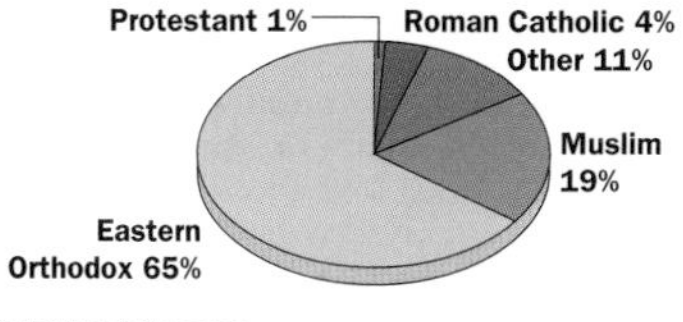
Protestant 1%
Roman Catholic 4%
Other 11%
Muslim 19%
Eastern Orthodox 65%

ETHNIC MAKEUP

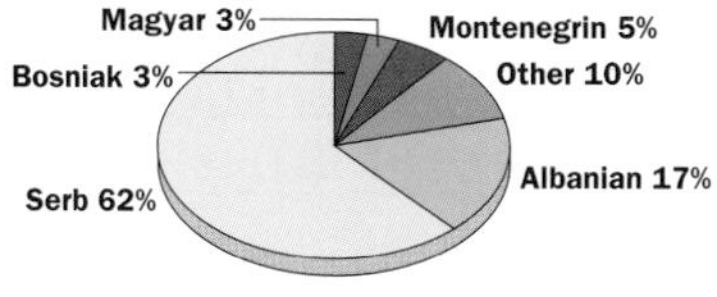
Magyar 3%
Montenegrin 5%
Bosniak 3%
Other 10%
Albanian 17%
Serb 62%

The social order in the FRY has been devastated by the last decade of conflict in the region. The professional classes have effectively been driven out. There is a depressingly high suicide rate among the old living in cities. In Kosovo, 900,000 ethnic Albanians fled (mainly to Albania and Macedonia) during the 1999 conflict. The June 1999 agreement opened the way for most to return, since which time many of the province's embattled Serb minority have gone (or been driven out) themselves, fearing both vengeance and the longer-term prospect of Kosovan independence.

The Hungarian (and mainly Roman Catholic) minority is concentrated in the northern Serbian province of Vojvodina, where pressure for greater autonomy is mainly for economic reasons to limit the draining of local resources to fund the Serbian budget. Orthodox Serbs who converted to Islam during Ottoman rule are considered to be an ethnically separate group.

POPULATION AGE BREAKDOWN

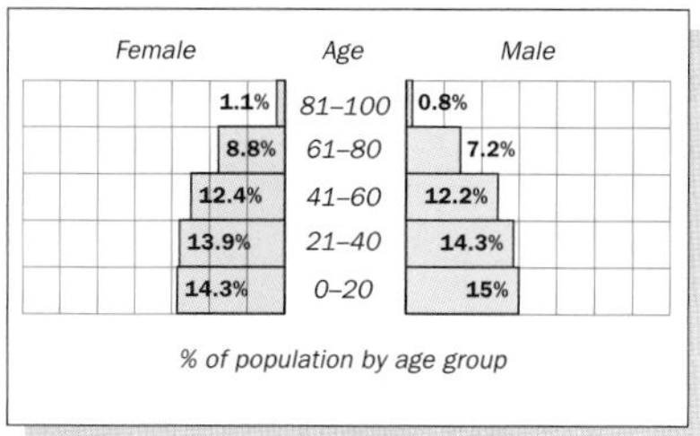
Female
Age
Male
1.1%
81–100
0.8%
8.8%
61–80
7.2%
12.4%
41–60
12.2%
13.9%
21–40
14.3%
14.3%
0–20
15%
% of population by age group

WORLD AFFAIRS

Joined UN in 1945

CEI IAEA EBRD IMF OSCE

The pariah status of the Milošević regime in the late 1990s was underlined by his indictment by the International Criminal Tribunal for the former Yugoslavia in 1999, and the military action by NATO forces over the situation in Kosovo. Russia, long an ally of Serbia, shares its Orthodox Christianity and its Slavic ethnicity, and strongly opposed the NATO military action over Kosovo, but backed the settlement proposals which Yugoslavia accepted to end it. The inauguration of the Kostunica government in 2000 was welcomed enthusiastically by the West and Russia. The new regime was quickly invited to take up its vacant seat in the UN.

Five years previously, mutual recognition among the countries which had constituted the Socialist Federal Republic of Yugoslavia had paved the way for the normalization of relations between them following the Bosnian peace accord.

AID

Recipient

$638m (receipts) Up 496% in 1999

Milošević's removal was an explicit condition of large-scale Western aid, urgently needed to rebuild the damaged economy. Yugoslavia rejoined the World Bank in May 2001 and received pledges of $1.3 billion in aid immediately upon the extradition of Milošević.

POLITICS

Multiparty elections

L. House 2000/2004
U. House 2000/2004

President Vojislav Kostunica

AT THE LAST ELECTION

Chamber of Citizens 138 seats

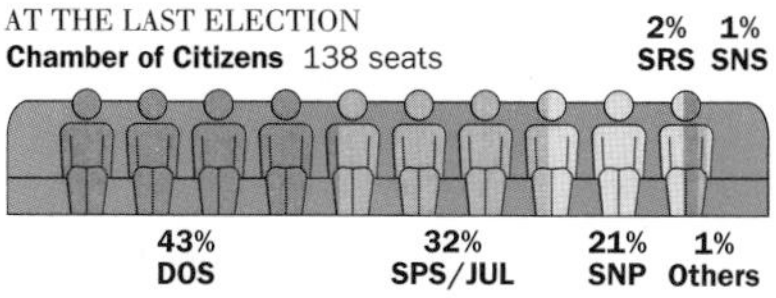
2% SRS
1% SNS
43% DOS
32% SPS/JUL
21% SNP
1% Others

DOS = Democratic Opposition of Serbia
SPS/JUL = Socialist Party of Serbia/Yugoslav Left
SNP = Socialist People's Party **SRS** = Serbian Radical Party
SNS = Serbian People's Party
SPO = Serbian Renewal Movement

Chamber of Republics 40 seats

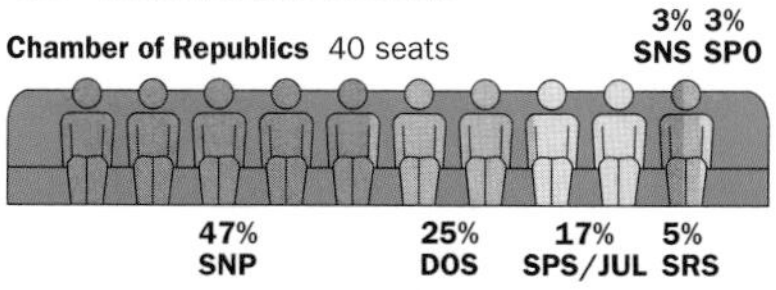
3% SNS
3% SPO
47% SNP
25% DOS
17% SPS/JUL
5% SRS

20 delegates are elected to the Chamber of Republics by each of the two republics of Serbia and Montenegro

Serbia and Montenegro, each with a separate parliament and president, are represented in the bicameral Federal Assembly.

MAIN POLITICAL ISSUES

Kosovo

FRY troops had to withdraw from Kosovo to end NATO bombing in 1999. The ethnic Albanian majority awaits a promised referendum on its future. International administrators have announced elections for November 2001 to a Kosovo assembly. Local Serbs see even this as a step too far. Violent clashes continue sporadically.

Montenegro

Although less subservient to Serbia after Milo Djukanović became its president in 1997, the smaller FRY republic backed away from holding a referendum on secession in mid-2001.

PROFILE

Milošević, Serbian president from 1989, dominated Yugoslavia for a decade. Conflict from 1991 to 1995, then again over Kosovo, created a permanent sense of siege. It was the tightening of UN sanctions in 1999, more than the NATO bombing, that sealed Milošević's fate. After he was ousted in the October 2000 popular uprising, the reformists consolidated their position, dominating elections in December. The ruling DOS contains disparate elements, however, and nationalists, including President Vojislav Kostunica, were affronted by Milošević's extradition in June 2001.

Vojislav Kostunica, *federal president since the ousting of Milošević in 2000.*

Slobodan Milošević, *disgraced former president charged with war crimes.*

CHRONOLOGY

The Serbs were defeated by the Turks at the Battle of Kosovo in 1389. Parts of the region were later ruled by the Austrian Habsburg empire.

- **1878** Independence gained by Serbia and Montenegro at Congress of Berlin.
- **1918** Joint Kingdom of Serbs, Croats, and Slovenes created.
- **1929** King Alexander of Serbia assumes absolute powers over state; changes name to Yugoslavia.
- **1941** Germans launch surprise attack. Rival resistance groups: Chetniks (Serb royalist) and Partisans (communist, under Tito).
- **1945** Federal People's Republic of Yugoslavia founded with Tito as prime minister (and president from 1953).
- **1948** Tito breaks with Stalin.
- **1951** Farmers permitted to sell produce on free market.
- **1955** Yugoslav–Soviet détente.

Y

CHRONOLOGY *continued*

- **1963** Third postwar constitution adopts name Socialist Federal Republic of Yugoslavia (SFRY).
- **1973** Economic cooperation agreement with West Germany. Agreement of noninterference signed with USSR. Croat nationalists purged from party leadership and government.
- **1974** New constitution decentralizes government. Vojvodina and Kosovo given greater autonomy.
- **1980** Tito dies. Succeeded by collective presidency.
- **1981** Unrest among Kosovo Albanians; state of emergency.
- **1985** Serbian intellectuals publish memorandum listing Serb grievances within Yugoslavia.
- **1986** Slobodan Milošević becomes leader of Communist (later Socialist) Party of Serbia.
- **1987** Wage freeze to combat inflation. Banking system crisis.
- **1988** Belgrade protests against economic austerity. Government brought down over budget failure.
- **1989** 600th anniversary of Battle of Kosovo. Kosovo Albanians protest against Serb police unit; crackdown ends Kosovo's autonomy.
- **1990** Milošević and Socialist Party victorious in elections in Serbia. Communists win presidency and dominate Montenegro elections.
- **1992** EU recognizes breakaway republics of Croatia, Slovenia, and Bosnia and Herzegovina. Bosnian war begins. UN sanctions imposed. Ibrahim Rugova elected president of self-declared republic of Kosovo. Milošević reelected president of Serbia, but SPS loses majority.
- **1995** Milošević signs Bosnian peace accord.
- **1996** UN sanctions formally lifted.
- **1997** Concessions after big protests, acknowledging malpractice in municipal elections. Milošević becomes federal president.
- **1998** Conflict in Kosovo escalates.
- **1999** March, Kosovo talks break down; "ethnic cleansing" precipitates mass exodus. NATO aerial bombing of FRY. June, withdrawal of Serbian forces and police from Kosovo, and entry of international force, KFOR.
- **2000** September, defeat of Milošević in first round of presidential election. October, opposition candidate Vojislav Kostunica swept to power by massive anti-Milošević protests. December, Democratic Opposition dominates Serbian elections.
- **2001** April, arrest of Milošević. June, Milošević extradited to face war crimes tribunal in The Hague.

DEFENSE

Compulsory military service

$1.65bn — Up 4% in 1999

YUGOSLAVIAN ARMED FORCES

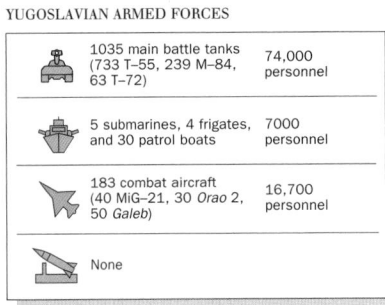

1035 main battle tanks (733 T–55, 239 M–84, 63 T–72)	74,000 personnel
5 submarines, 4 frigates, and 30 patrol boats	7000 personnel
183 combat aircraft (40 MiG–21, 30 *Orao* 2, 50 *Galeb*)	16,700 personnel
None	

The FRY's military capability was specifically targeted for "degrading" by the NATO air strikes in 1999. The impact on anti-aircraft defenses, heavy weaponry, logistics capacity, and infrastructure was less severe than first claimed, however.

The Serbian military had previously played a major role in the conflicts in the former Yugoslavia in the early 1990s. Traditionally the center of Yugoslav armaments manufacture, Serbia was able to arm itself – although the need to create money to pay for domestically produced weapons was a major factor in the crippling hyperinflation of that era.

Compulsory military service is for a period of 12–15 months. There are 50,000 NATO-led troops in the Kosovo force (KFOR).

ECONOMICS

Not available

$9.5bn — 11.61–13.65 dinars

SCORE CARD

World GNP Ranking	85th
GNP per Capita	$900
Balance of Payments	$–1.16bn
Inflation	42%
Unemployment	30%

EXPORTS

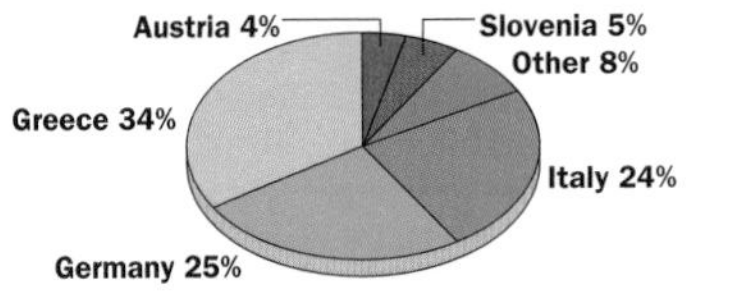
Austria 4%
Slovenia 5%
Other 8%
Greece 34%
Italy 24%
Germany 25%

IMPORTS

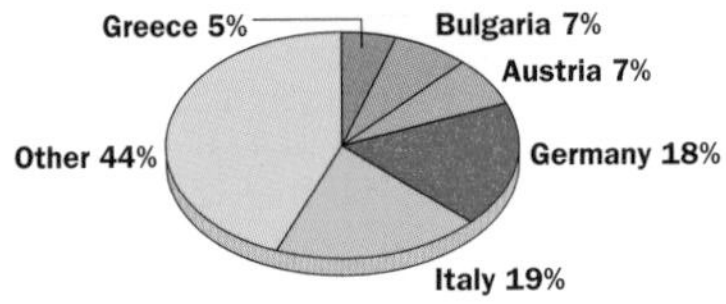
Greece 5%
Bulgaria 7%
Austria 7%
Other 44%
Germany 18%
Italy 19%

STRENGTHS

Return of international aid and investment in 2000–2001. Economic potential of the Danube.

WEAKNESSES

Severe damage caused by sanctions and 1999 bombings. Low hard-currency reserves.

PROFILE

The former Yugoslavia was among the most advanced of the socialist countries in terms of its living standards. Since then it has all but collapsed, although as much as 50% of all activity goes on within the resilient informal sector. The conflicts of the early 1990s effectively stalled much-needed economic reform. Sanctions maintained until after the end of the Bosnian war in 1996, and reimposed more fully in 1999, stifled trade and decimated both the emerging private and the state sectors. Hyperinflation had already pushed the economy to virtual collapse. Damage to infrastructure caused by NATO bombing in 1999 was extensive; the EBRD estimated reconstruction costs at $20 billion over three years. Sanctions were lifted shortly after Milošević's downfall, and prospects for investment boosted by his extradition.

ECONOMIC PERFORMANCE INDICATOR

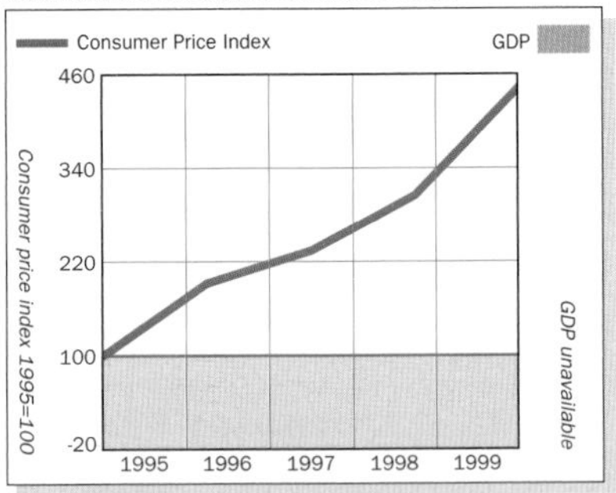
Consumer Price Index
GDP
460
340
220
100
-20
1995
1996
1997
1998
1999
Consumer price index 1995=100
GDP unavailable

YUGOSLAVIA : MAJOR BUSINESSES

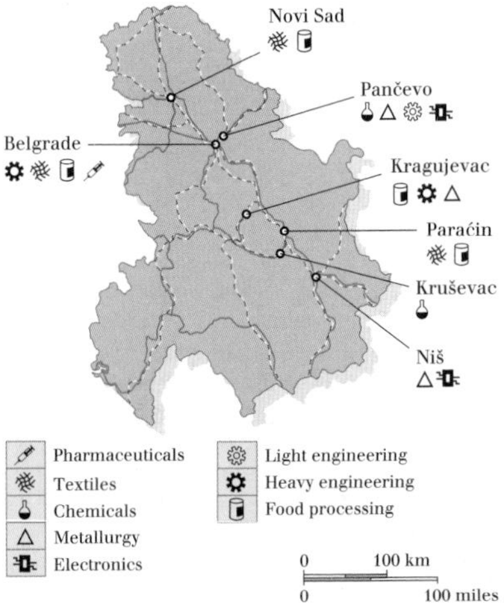
Novi Sad
Pančevo
Belgrade
Kragujevac
Paraćin
Kruševac
Niš
Pharmaceuticals
Textiles
Chemicals
Metallurgy
Electronics
Light engineering
Heavy engineering
Food processing
0
100 km
0
100 miles

Y

RESOURCES

Electric power 11.8m kw

7366 tonnes

19,629 b/d (reserves 78,829,080 bbl)

4.37m pigs, 2.39m sheep, 1.83m cattle, 24.3m chickens

Coal, bauxite, iron, lead, copper, zinc

ELECTRICITY GENERATION

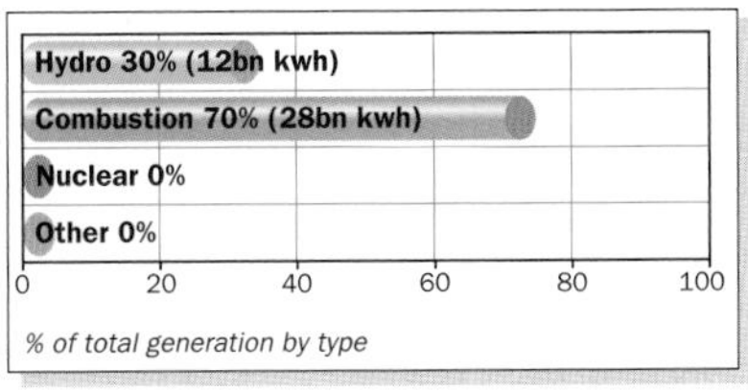
Hydro 30% (12bn kwh)
Combustion 70% (28bn kwh)
Nuclear 0%
Other 0%
0
20
40
60
80
100
% of total generation by type

The FRY is self-sufficient in coal and electricity production. Vojvodina's oil industry could cater for one-third of the FRY's needs, but was badly hit by NATO bombing in March–June 1999.

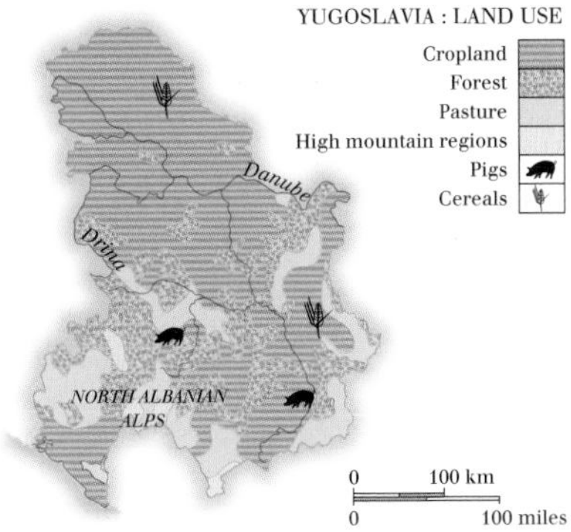
YUGOSLAVIA : LAND USE
Cropland
Forest
Pasture
High mountain regions
Pigs
Cereals
Danube
Drina
NORTH ALBANIAN ALPS
0
100 km
0
100 miles

ENVIRONMENT

Not available

None

4.7 tonnes per capita

ENVIRONMENTAL TREATIES

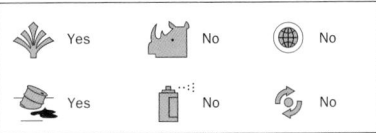

Yes	No	No
Yes	No	No

In Serbia, ecological awareness peaked in the late 1980s when the Ecological Forum was active. NATO bombing of Serbia in 1999 caused extensive pollution of the Danube and raised fears of contamination from dioxins. Depleted uranium from NATO munitions has also aroused serious concerns both in Serbia proper and in Kosovo.

MEDIA

TV ownership high

Daily newspaper circulation 106 per 1000 people

PUBLISHING AND BROADCAST MEDIA

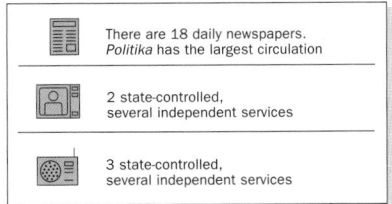

There are 18 daily newspapers. *Politika* has the largest circulation

2 state-controlled, several independent services

3 state-controlled, several independent services

The state broadcasting center was a prime target in the October 2000 popular uprising against the Milošević regime; it had used the broadcast media to control public opinion, while the press was held in check by government control of newsprint. Many journalists supported the opposition. The B92 radio station, when not forced off air, was a beacon of independent reporting. The Serbian opposition-controlled Studio B television station was targeted in a clampdown in May 2000.

CRIME

Death penalty used

Yugoslavia does not publish prison figures

High crime levels

CRIME RATES

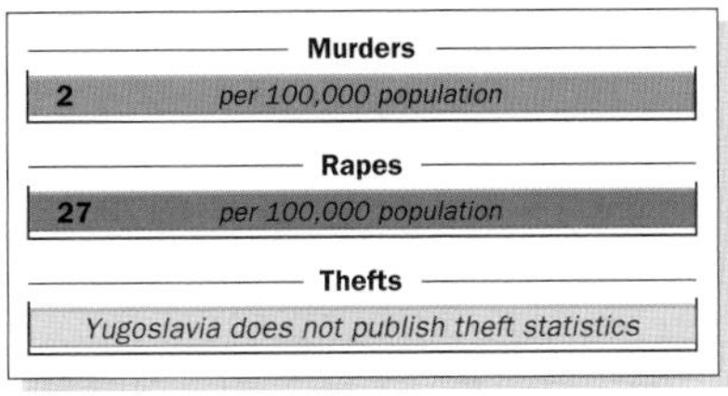
Murders
2
per 100,000 population
Rapes
27
per 100,000 population
Thefts
Yugoslavia does not publish theft statistics

Crime was rife under Milošević – from currency trading and black marketeering to narcotics and extortion. Yugoslavia began cooperating with the International Criminal Tribunal for the Former Yugoslavia by arresting and handing over indicted suspects in 2001.

EDUCATION

School leaving age: 15

93%

172,313 students

THE EDUCATION SYSTEM

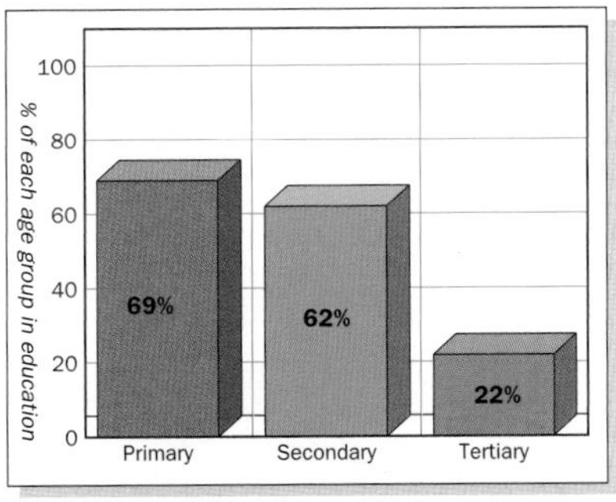
100
80
60
40
20
0
% of each age group in education
69%
62%
22%
Primary
Secondary
Tertiary

Schooling was totally disrupted by the Kosovo conflict in 1999, leaving the education system in crisis; the wealthy go abroad for their education. Literacy rates in Kosovo, where ethnic Albanian schools were closed in 1990, were below the FRY average even before the conflict. Rebuilding the education system is key to reconstruction and reconciliation.

HEALTH

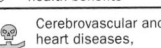

Welfare state health benefits

1 per 500 people

Cerebrovascular and heart diseases, cancers, accidents

Isolation from former trading partners has affected the quality of the health service, despite the exemption of medicines and medical supplies from sanctions. Social insurance is obligatory for those in employment, but medicines are scarce and costly, and death rates among infants and the elderly have risen dramatically. With many suffering malnutrition, health problems are aggravated by bitingly cold winters.

SPENDING

GDP/cap. decrease

CONSUMPTION AND SPENDING

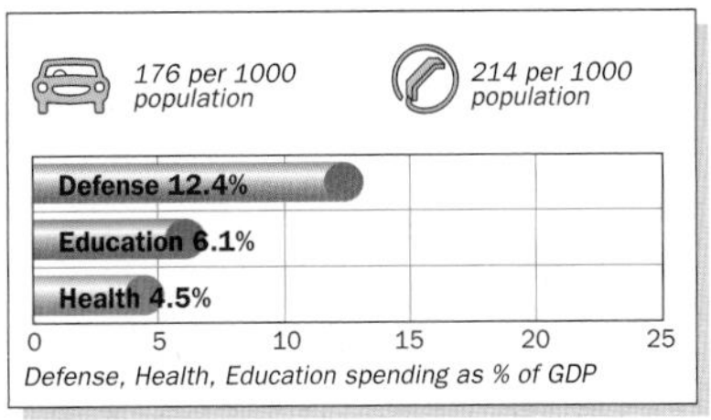
176 per 1000 population
214 per 1000 population
Defense 12.4%
Education 6.1%
Health 4.5%
0
5
10
15
20
25
Defense, Health, Education spending as % of GDP

The country as a whole was seriously impoverished by sanctions; real incomes fell dramatically, yet food prices remained higher than in much of western Europe. Bank collapses in 1992 and continuing hyperinflation in 1992–1994 wiped out dinar savings. One business that did expand was the illegal import of sanctions-busting goods for the few who could afford them – black marketeers and those close to Milošević.

The lifting of sanctions in 1995–1996 had hardly begun to be reflected in improvements in living conditions when the Kosovo conflict brought further dislocation and hardship in 1999. Even before it erupted, an estimated two-thirds of the population were living below subsistence level. Apart from the desperate situation of refugees and internally displaced families, unsupported pensioners fare worst.

WORLD RANKING

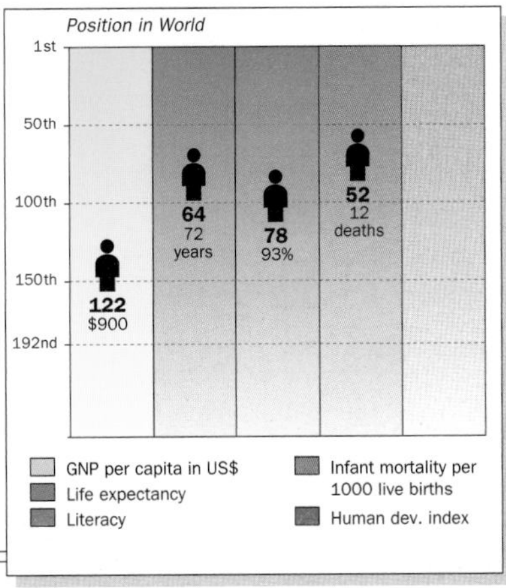
Position in World
1st
50th
100th
150th
192nd
122
$900
64
72
years
78
93%
52
12
deaths
GNP per capita in US$
Life expectancy
Literacy
Infant mortality per 1000 live births
Human dev. index

Y

ZAMBIA

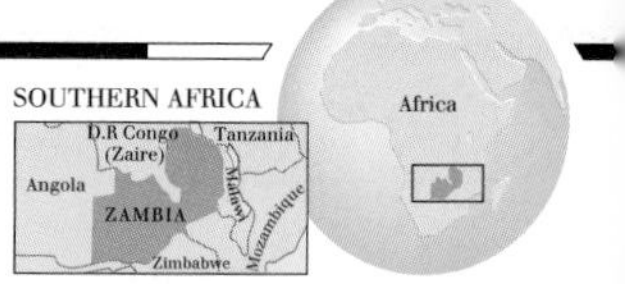
SOUTHERN AFRICA
D.R Congo (Zaire)
Tanzania
Angola
ZAMBIA
Malawi
Mozambique
Zimbabwe
Africa

OFFICIAL NAME: Republic of Zambia **CAPITAL:** Lusaka
POPULATION: 9.2 million **CURRENCY:** Zambian kwacha **OFFICIAL LANGUAGE:** English

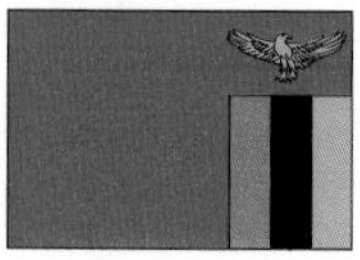

1964 | 1964 | Oct 24 | Z | +2 | +260 | .zm

LYING IN THE HEART of southern Africa, Zambia is a country of upland plateaus, bordered to the south by the Zambezi river. Its economic fortunes are tied to the copper industry. Falling copper prices in the late 1970s, and then the growing inaccessibility of remaining reserves, have led to a severe decline in the economy. In 1991, Zambia achieved a peaceful transition from single-party rule to multiparty democracy.

CLIMATE

Tropical wet & dry

WEATHER CHART

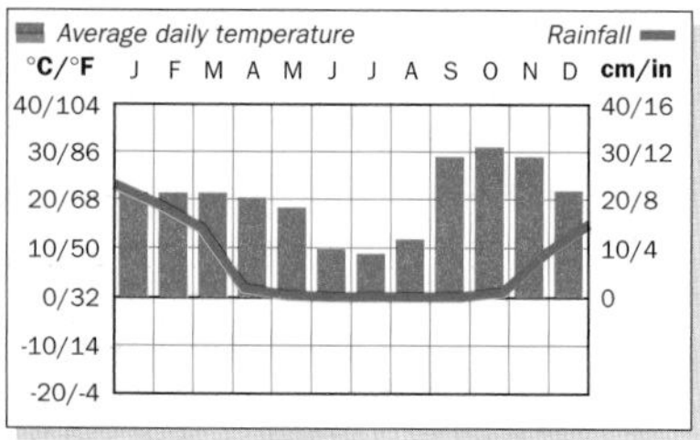
Average daily temperature
Rainfall
°C/°F
J F M A M J J A S O N D
cm/in
40/104
30/86
20/68
10/50
0/32
-10/14
-20/-4
40/16
30/12
20/8
10/4
0

Zambia has a tropical climate, with rains from November to April. The southwest is prone to drought.

TRANSPORTATION

Drive on left

Lusaka International 341,361 passengers

Has no fleet

THE TRANSPORTATION NETWORK

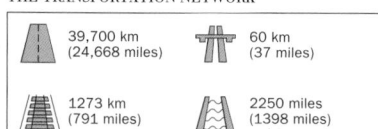

39,700 km (24,668 miles)

60 km (37 miles)

1273 km (791 miles)

2250 miles (1398 miles)

The poor rail and road networks, in need of urgent rehabilitation, could sabotage economic recovery. Zambian Airways was liquidated in 1994, and private airlines are now in operation.

TOURISM

Visitors : Population 1:16

574,000 visitors

Up 26% in 2000

MAIN TOURIST ARRIVALS

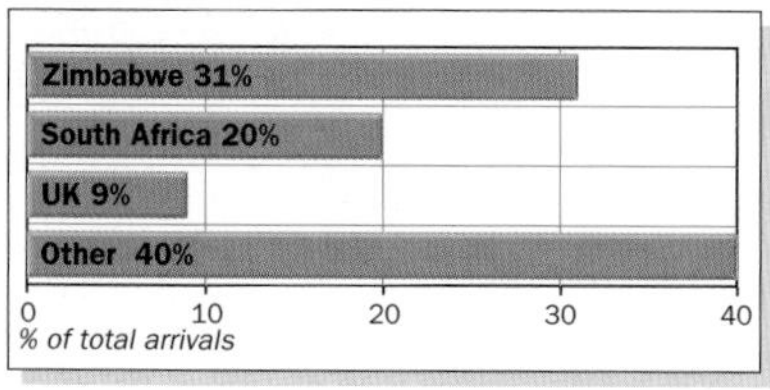
Zimbabwe 31%
South Africa 20%
UK 9%
Other 40%
0
10
20
30
40
% of total arrivals

Wildlife, the Victoria Falls, and white-water rafting are major attractions. Recent increases in tourism have been at the expense of neighboring Zimbabwe.

PEOPLE

Pop. density low

Bemba, Nyanja, Tonga, Kaonde, Lunda, Luvale, Lozi, English

12/km² (32/mi²)

THE URBAN/RURAL POPULATION SPLIT

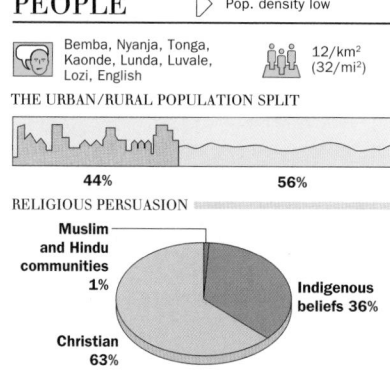

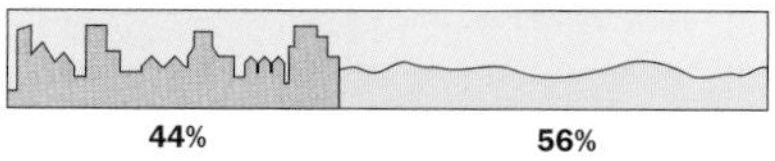
44%
56%

RELIGIOUS PERSUASION

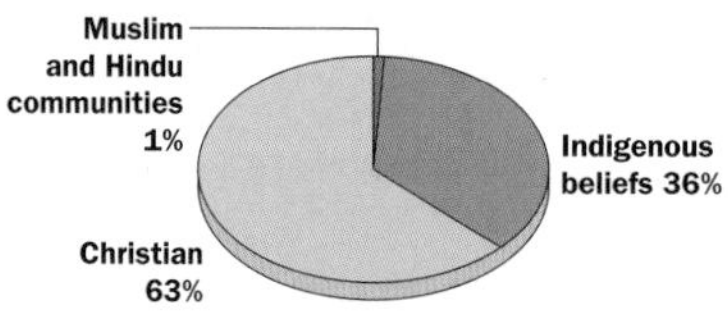
Muslim and Hindu communities 1%
Indigenous beliefs 36%
Christian 63%

Although ethnically heterogeneous, with more than 70 different groups, Zambia has been less affected by ethnic tension than many African states. The largest ethnic group, about 34% of the population, is the Bemba, who live in the northeast and predominate in the central Copperbelt. Other major groups are the southern Tonga people, the eastern Nyanja, and the Lozi, who live to the west. Zambia is also home to some 225,000 refugees, mainly from Angola.

Zambia is one of Africa's most urbanized countries, with many third- and fourth-generation town-dwellers in the Copperbelt, the main urban area. The rural population live mainly by subsistence farming. A National Gender Policy was issued in October 2000 to redress inequalities between the sexes, women having traditionally played a subordinate role.

Musi-o-Tunya (The Smoke That Thunders), known in English as Victoria Falls. Spray from the falls can be seen 30 km (12 miles) away.

POLITICS

Multiparty elections

1996/2001

President Frederick Chiluba

AT THE LAST ELECTION

National Assembly 158 seats

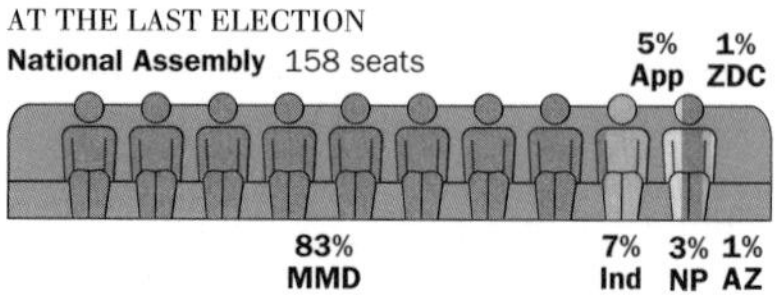
5% App
1% ZDC
83% MMD
7% Ind
3% NP
1% AZ

MMD = Movement for Multiparty Democracy **Ind** = Independents **App** = Appointed **NP** = National Party **AZ** = Agenda for Zambia **ZDC** = Zambia Democratic Congress

Up to eight members are appointed by the president, and the speaker is also a member

The 1991 defeat of Kenneth Kaunda, in the first multiparty elections for 19 years, expressed popular discontent with the ailing economy and official corruption. President Frederick Chiluba and the MMD government have since made little headway in revitalizing the economy, despite socially painful reforms. Chiluba himself, once widely respected as a rallying-point for the democratic opposition to Kaunda, is now much criticized for arbitrary and authoritarian rule, and for failing to address poverty and HIV/AIDS. The 1996 elections were boycotted by the opposition. In 2001 Chiluba purged the MMD of key opponents, prompting the formation of new opposition parties.

WORLD AFFAIRS

Joined UN in 1964

Comm | ACP | NAM | OAU | SADC

Under Kuanda, Zambia led Africa's opposition to apartheid South Africa and now enjoys close links with Pretoria. It also has a significant role as a mediator in neighboring conflicts.

AID

Recipient

$623m (receipts)

Up 79% in 1999

International aid has recommenced after a freeze in 1997 on donations of nearly $1.5 billion a year, prompted by state corruption. The IMF granted a $349 million three-year loan in 1999, and agreed a $3.8 billion debt service relief package in 2000.

DEFENSE

No compulsory military service

$88m

Up 33% in 1999

Despite the relatively small budget, the 21,600-strong armed forces are well equipped. Security along the Angolan border is a main concern.

ECONOMICS

Inflation 57.4% p.a. (1990–1999)

$3.2bn

2805-4500 Zambian kwacha

SCORE CARD

- ❑ WORLD GNP RANKING........................128th
- ❑ GNP PER CAPITA...............................$330
- ❑ BALANCE OF PAYMENTS....................$–306m
- ❑ INFLATION......................................23.2%
- ❑ UNEMPLOYMENT.................................25%

STRENGTHS

Potential for self-sufficiency in food. Boom in new export crops, such as cotton and flowers. Minerals, notably copper, cobalt, and coal. Market-oriented reforms and privatization drive attracting foreign private investors.

WEAKNESSES

Dependence on copper for 90% of export earnings, as its price plummets. Domestic reserves declining. Shortage of finance for restructuring, exacerbated by aid donors' boycott. High inflation, negative growth, and serious drought in 1998. Arable land underutilized. Delays in privatizing state-owned copper consortium.

EXPORTS

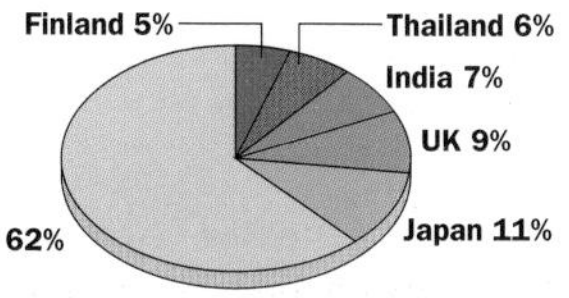
Finland 5%
Thailand 6%
India 7%
UK 9%
Japan 11%
Other 62%

IMPORTS

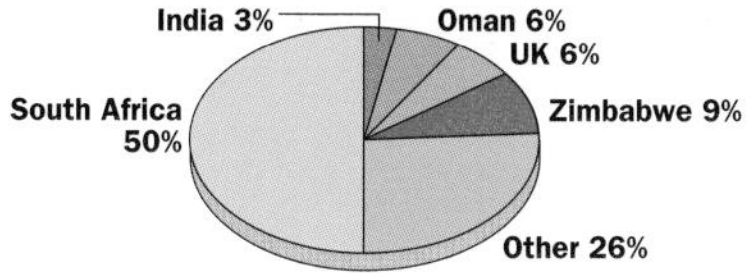
India 3%
Oman 6%
UK 6%
Zimbabwe 9%
South Africa 50%
Other 26%

RESOURCES

Electric power 2.4m kw

70,702 tonnes

Not an oil producer

2.37m cattle, 1.25m goats, 29m chickens

Copper, cobalt, coal, zinc, lead, gold, emeralds, amethyst

Despite declining reserves, copper is still the key resource; Zambia is the world's sixth-largest producer. It also has rich hydropower potential.

ENVIRONMENT

Sustainability rank: 97th

9%

0.3 tonnes per capita

Drought is a recurrent hazard. Rhinos are almost extinct as a result of poaching. Revenues from legal hunting are being channeled into villages to encourage support for conservation.

MEDIA

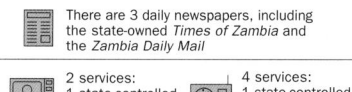

TV ownership medium

Daily newspaper circulation 14 per 1000 people

PUBLISHING AND BROADCAST MEDIA

There are 3 daily newspapers, including the state-owned *Times of Zambia* and the *Zambia Daily Mail*

2 services: 1 state-controlled, 1 educational

4 services: 1 state-controlled, 3 independent

Dailies face competition from privately owned weeklies. Opposition journalists have been accused of treason.

CRIME

Death penalty used

26,175 prisoners

Up 17% 1992–1994

Cases of violent crime, burglary, and rape are rising rapidly. In 1998 Zambia promised to overhaul its prison and police services.

CHRONOLOGY

Northern Rhodesia was developed by Britain solely for its copper. The United National Independence Party (UNIP), led by Kaunda, took power at Zambian independence in 1964.

- ❑ **1972** UNIP one-party government.
- ❑ **1982–1991** Austerity measures and corruption: pressure for democracy.
- ❑ **1991** MMD government elected; Frederick Chiluba defeats Kaunda.
- ❑ **1996** Controversial elections return Chiluba and MMD to power.

EDUCATION

School leaving age: 14

78%

10,489 students

Primary education is compulsory. Fees for secondary students have affected the already very low attendance rate.

HEALTH

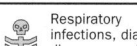

No welfare state health benefits

1 per 10,000 people

Respiratory infections, diarrheal diseases, malaria

An HIV prevention program is reducing rates of infection in Lusaka. More than 25% of town-dwellers are HIV-positive.

SPENDING

GDP/cap. increase

CONSUMPTION AND SPENDING

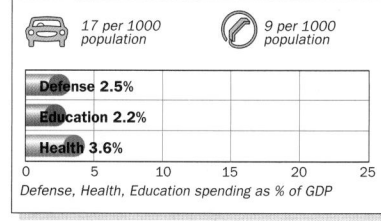

17 per 1000 population

9 per 1000 population

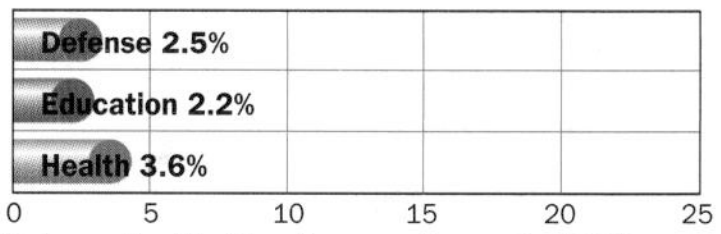
Defense 2.5%
Education 2.2%
Health 3.6%
0
5
10
15
20
25

Defense, Health, Education spending as % of GDP

Standards of living for most Zambians are now lower in real terms than at independence in 1964. Many people lack basic nutrition.

WORLD RANKING

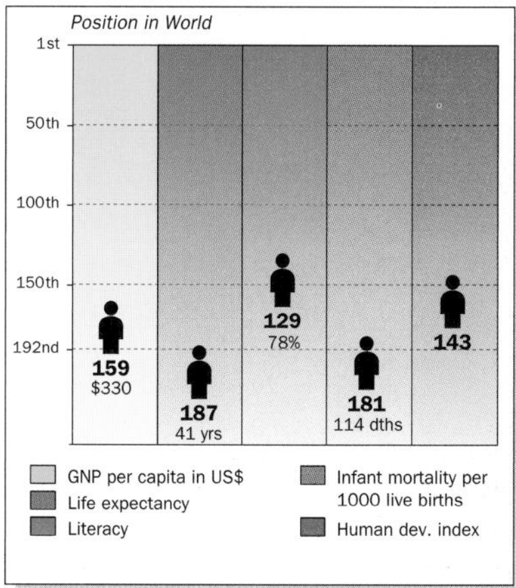
Position in World
1st
50th
100th
150th
192nd
159
$330
187
41 yrs
129
78%
181
114 dths
143
GNP per capita in US$
Life expectancy
Literacy
Infant mortality per 1000 live births
Human dev. index

ZAMBIA

Total Land Area : 740 720 sq. km (285 992 sq. miles)

POPULATION

◉	over 500 000
◎	over 100 000
○	over 50 000
●	over 10 000
•	under 10 000

DEM. REP. CONGO (ZAIRE)
TANZANIA
MALAWI
MOZAMBIQUE
ZIMBABWE
ANGOLA
NAMIBIA
BOTSWANA
Lake Mweru Wantipa
Lake Tanganyika
Lake Mweru
Mpulungu
Mbala
Sunzu 2067m
Mporokoso
Nchelenge
Kawambwa
Kasama
Mungwi
Isoka
Mwenda
Lake Bangweulu
Mansa
Samfya
Mpika
Solwezi
Chililabombwe
Mufulira
Chingola
Kitwe
Kalulushi
Ndola
Luanshya
Serenje
Chipata
Zambezi
Kabompo
Kapiri Mposhi
Kabwe
Petauke
Katete
Kaoma
Kalabo
Limulunga
Mumbwa
Mongu
Chongwe
Chilanga
LUSAKA
Mazabuka
Kafue
Monze
Senanga
Choma
Kalomo
Lake Kariba
Sinazongwe
Livingstone
Victoria Falls
Luapula
Chambeshi
Luangwa
Kafue
Lunga
Lungwebungu
Machile
Kwando
West Lunga
Lunsemfwa
Lukusashi
12°
16°
24°
28°
32°
N
LAND HEIGHT
1000m/3281ft
500m/1640ft
200m/656ft
200 km
200 miles
0

ZIMBABWE

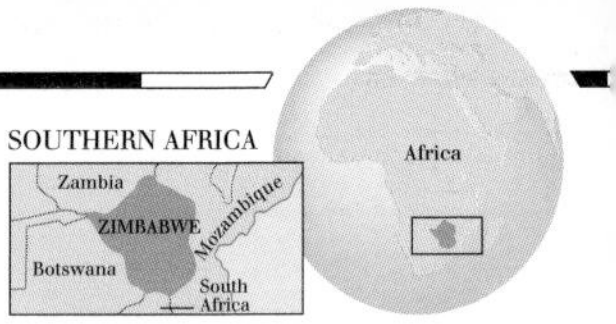
SOUTHERN AFRICA
Africa
Zambia
ZIMBABWE
Mozambique
Botswana
South Africa

OFFICIAL NAME: Republic of Zimbabwe **CAPITAL:** Harare
POPULATION: 11.7 million **CURRENCY:** Zimbabwe dollar **OFFICIAL LANGUAGE:** English

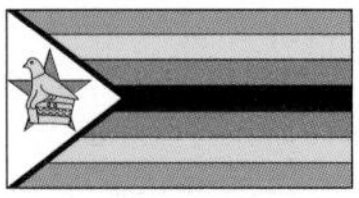

1980 | 1980 | April 18 | ZW | +2 | +263 | .zw

SITUATED IN SOUTHERN AFRICA, Zimbabwe is bordered by South Africa, Botswana, Zambia, and Mozambique. The upland center is crisscrossed by rivers, which flow into Lake Kariba and the Zambezi River. The Zambezi possesses Zimbabwe's most spectacular natural feature, the Victoria Falls. Formerly the British colony of Southern Rhodesia, Zimbabwe achieved independence in 1980, after a struggle between the white minority, led by the prime minister, Ian Smith, and the black majority, represented by Robert Mugabe and Joshua Nkomo's Patriotic Front (PF).

__The Kariba Dam__, which has created the vast Lake Kariba on the Zambezi River, lies on Zimbabwe's northwest border with Zambia.

CLIMATE

Tropical wet & dry/ steppe

WEATHER CHART

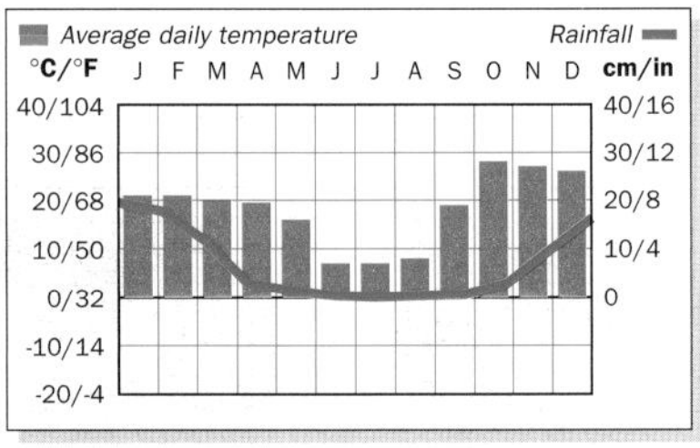
Average daily temperature
Rainfall
°C/°F
J F M A M J J A S O N D
cm/in
40/104
30/86
20/68
10/50
0/32
-10/14
-20/4
40/16
30/12
20/8
10/4
0

Because of its altitude, Zimbabwe is comparatively temperate for a country in the tropics; humidity is also low. The rainy season occurs between November and March but, with the exception of the eastern highlands, rainfall is erratic and drought is common. Annual rainfall ranges from 140 cm (55 in) in the eastern highlands to 40 cm (16 in) in the Limpopo valley.

TRANSPORTATION

Drive on left

Harare International 1.02m passengers

Has no fleet

THE TRANSPORTATION NETWORK

8692 km (5401 miles)	None
2592 km (1611 miles)	Lake Kariba

The number of international air links is being increased. Zimbabwe's rail network, among the densest in sub-Saharan Africa, is being updated.

TOURISM

Visitors : Population 1:6.3

1.9m visitors

Down 11% in 2000

MAIN TOURIST ARRIVALS

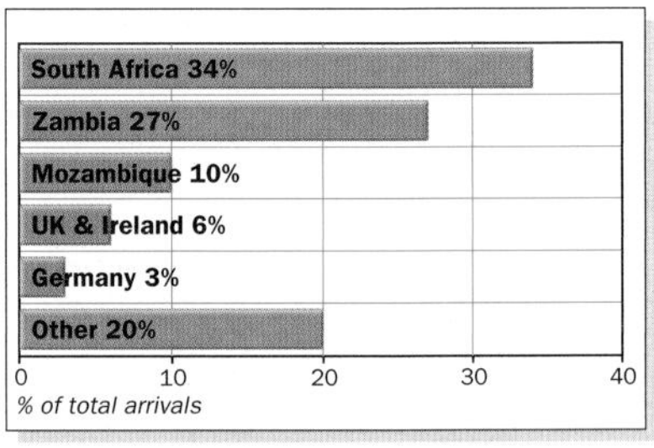
South Africa 34%
Zambia 27%
Mozambique 10%
UK & Ireland 6%
Germany 3%
Other 20%
0
10
20
30
40
% of total arrivals

Zimbabwe's principal attractions are the Victoria Falls, the Kariba dam, numerous national parks, the Great Zimbabwe ruins near Masvingo, and World's View in the Matopo Hills. Invasions of commercial farms led by "war veterans" and the violence in the run-up to the 2000 elections have put Zimbabwe on the list of unsafe destinations for visitors. Fuel and foreign currency shortages have further undermined the tourism sector.

In addition, Zimbabwe is wary of a glut of mass-market tourists which might seriously damage the environment. However, the lure of foreign exchange has encouraged the development of conference facilities in Harare and vacation complexes around Victoria Falls, such as Elephant Hills. State law requires that there be 30% local ownership of tourist ventures.

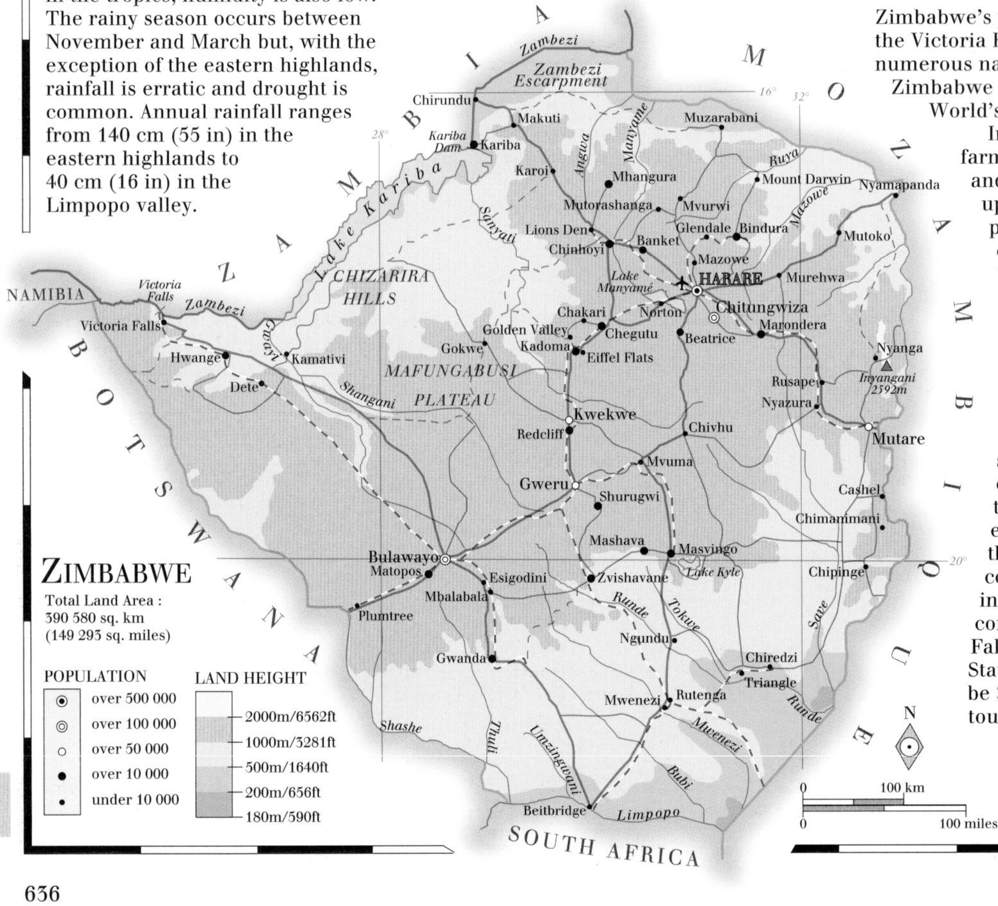
ZAMBIA
MOZAMBIQUE
BOTSWANA
SOUTH AFRICA
NAMIBIA
Zambezi
Zambezi Escarpment
Chirundu
Makuti
Muzarabani
Kariba Dam
Kariba
Karoi
Mhangura
Ruya
Mount Darwin
Nyamapanda
Mutorashanga
Mvurwi
Lions Den
Glendale
Bindura
Mutoko
Chinhoyi
Banket
Mazowe
Lake Kariba
CHIZARIRA HILLS
Lake Manyame
HARARE
Murehwa
Victoria Falls
Chakari
Norton
Chitungwiza
Golden Valley
Chegutu
Marondera
Gokwe
Kadoma
Beatrice
Hwange
Kamativi
Eiffel Flats
Nyanga
Inyangani 2592m
Dete
MAFUNGABUSI PLATEAU
Shangani
Rusape
Nyazura
Kwekwe
Chivhu
Redcliff
Mutare
Mvuma
Gweru
Shurugwi
Cashel
Chimanimani
Mashava
Masvingo
Bulawayo
Matopos
Esigodini
Zvishavane
Lake Kyle
Chipinge
Mbalabala
Plumtree
Runde
Tokwe
Save
Ngundu
Gwanda
Chiredzi
Triangle
Mwenezi
Rutenga
Shashe
Thuli
Umzingwani
Mwenezi
Bubi
Beitbridge
Limpopo
ZIMBABWE
Total Land Area : 390 580 sq. km (149 293 sq. miles)
POPULATION
over 500 000
over 100 000
over 50 000
over 10 000
under 10 000
LAND HEIGHT
2000m/6562ft
1000m/3281ft
500m/1640ft
200m/656ft
180m/590ft
N
0
100 km
100 miles

Z

PEOPLE

Pop. density low

Shona, Ndebele, English

30/km² (78/mi²)

THE URBAN/RURAL POPULATION SPLIT

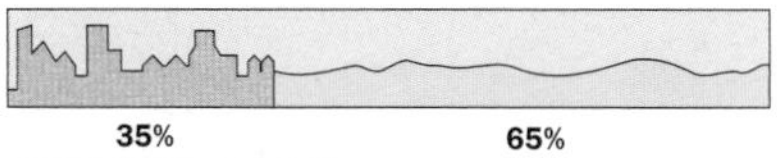
35%
65%

RELIGIOUS PERSUASION

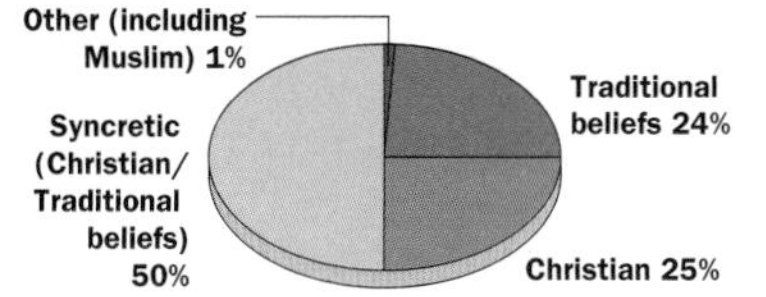
Other (including Muslim) 1%
Traditional beliefs 24%
Syncretic (Christian/ Traditional beliefs) 50%
Christian 25%

ETHNIC MAKEUP

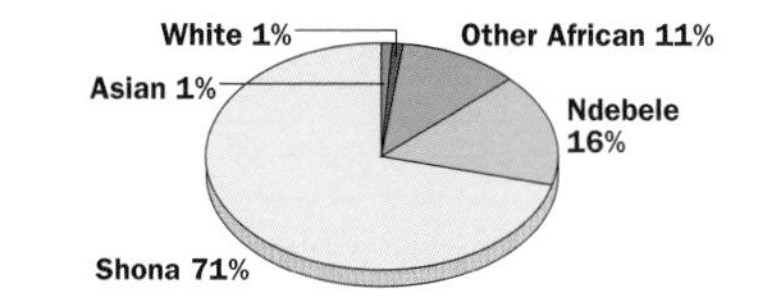
White 1%
Other African 11%
Asian 1%
Ndebele 16%
Shona 71%

There are two main ethnic groups, the majority Shona in the north and the Ndebele in the south. Europeans and Asians comprise 2% of the population.

Ethnic tensions plagued the 1980s. 1500 Ndebele were massacred by the army in 1983 alone as the ruling, Shona-dominated, ZANU–PF attempted to suppress the predominantly Ndebele Zimbabwe African People's Union (PF–ZAPU). A Unity Accord in 1987 eased the conflict, and ZAPU leader Joshua Nkomo was appointed vice president in 1990.

As a legacy of colonial rule, whites remain generally far more affluent than blacks. This imbalance has been redressed in part by policies to improve black education and increase office employment. Land redistribution, which was previously slow and dogged by accusations of corruption, was stepped up in 2000, when the government

POPULATION AGE BREAKDOWN

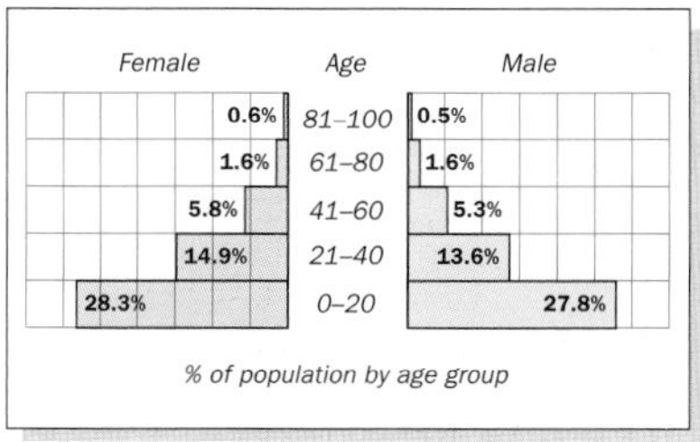
Female
Age
Male
0.6%
81–100
0.5%
1.6%
61–80
1.6%
5.8%
41–60
5.3%
14.9%
21–40
13.6%
28.3%
0–20
27.8%
% of population by age group

backed a movement to seize white-owned farms, prompting tensions between blacks and whites.

Families are large, and almost half the population is under 15. Zimbabwean society is traditionally patriarchal. In 1999 a Supreme Court ruling provoked protest by according only "junior male" status to black women, especially those marrying under traditional law.

POLITICS

Multiparty elections

2000/2005

President Robert Gabriel Mugabe

AT THE LAST ELECTION

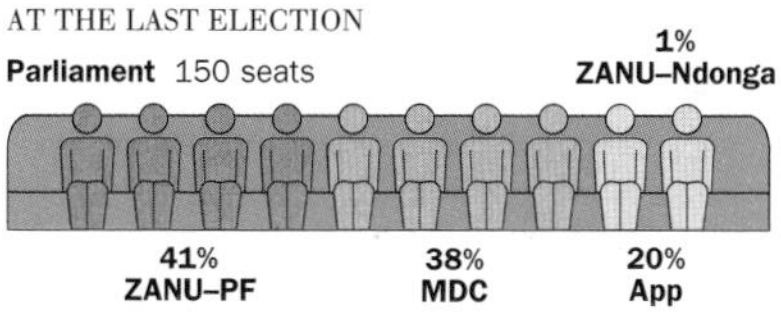
Parliament 150 seats
1% ZANU–Ndonga
41% ZANU–PF
38% MDC
20% App

ZANU–PF = Zimbabwe African National Union
MDC = Movement for Democratic Change **App** = Appointed
ZANU–Ndonga = Zimbabwe African National Union – Ndonga

30 seats are set aside for presidential appointments and traditional chiefs

Of the 150 MPs, 80% are elected for a five-year term. The president is selected by Parliament every six years.

Main Political Issues

The rule of President Mugabe

Robert Mugabe was appointed president in 1987. His attempts to create a one-party socialist state were called off in 1991 as opposition to white South Africa and support for the Soviet bloc became meaningless. His ZANU–PF has since lost support in the face of economic collapse and a reinvigorated opposition led by the Movement for Democratic Change (MDC). Mugabe's plans to strengthen his position through a referendum were defeated and ZANU–PF only just held on to power in elections in 2000, making his position increasingly precarious.

Land redistribution

Though all are agreed that the distribution of farmland unfairly favors the white minority, the speed and method of belated land redistribution has provoked protest. Mugabe drew up plans in 2000 to confiscate white-owned farms without compensation and backed the violent occupation led by "war veterans." The MDC has conversely backed calls to slow the process and compensate the farmers.

Profile

ZANU–PF emerged victorious in 1980 from the long struggle with the white-supremacist government of Ian Smith. Rivalries with ZAPU were resolved in 1987 and Mugabe led the country in his socialist experiment. In reality repression flourished and the civil service is closed to non ZANU–PF members.

The influence of ZANU–PF was rocked in 2000 when the electorate turned their backs on the ruling party and the MDC won a convincing share of votes despite widespread pre-electoral intimidation.

Robert Mugabe, elected prime minister in 1980 and president in 1987.

Morgan Tsvangirai, leader of the opposition MDC.

AID

Recipient

US$244m (receipts)

Down 13% in 1999

In 1992 the IMF promised Zimbabwe US$484 million to support its economic and financial reform program. The EU pledged somewhat less. Bilateral aid fell by a third between 1994 and 1996, after donors including the UK, Denmark, the USA, France, and Germany learned that aid intended for small farmers and indigenous enterprises was siphoned off to large industrial projects. In 1998 the IMF approved US$175 million in standby credit. Political violence in 2000 prompted the UK, the EU, and the IMF to suspend financial support.

WORLD AFFAIRS

Joined UN in 1980

Comm | G15 | NAM | OAU | SADC

Zimbabwe cooperates with its neighbors through the SADC and the Preferential Trade Area for East and South Africa. It actively opposed apartheid; since 1990, when Nelson Mandela was freed, relations with Pretoria have improved.

For ideological reasons, and to maintain access to the sea, Zimbabwe's military supported the Mozambican government against RENAMO guerrillas, and Mugabe helped to mediate the Mozambican peace accord of August 1992. In 1993, he sent troops to Somalia, and in 1998 a much larger contingent supported the then president of Congo (former Zaire), Laurent Kabila. Mugabe also defied sanctions on Libya, accused the UK of hostile propaganda, and promised to back the Angolan government against UNITA rebels. He has been strongly backed by other African leaders over his support for recent moves, ruled illegal and including violence, in carrying out the land redistribution program.

CHRONOLOGY

In 1953, the British colony of Southern Rhodesia became part of the Federation of Rhodesia and Nyasaland with Northern Rhodesia (now Zambia) and Nyasaland (now Malawi).

- ❑ **1961** Joshua Nkomo forms ZAPU.
- ❑ **1962** ZAPU banned. Segregationist Rhodesian Front (RF) wins elections.
- ❑ **1963** African nationalists in Northern Rhodesia and Nyasaland demand dissolution of Federation. ZANU, offshoot of ZAPU, formed by Rev. Sithole and Robert Mugabe.
- ❑ **1964** New RF prime minister Ian Smith rejects British demands for majority rule. ZANU banned.
- ❑ **1965** May, RF reelected. November, state of emergency declared (renewed until 1990). Smith's unilateral declaration of independence. UK imposes economic sanctions. ANC, ZANU, and ZAPU begin guerrilla war.
- ❑ **1974** RF regime agrees cease-fire terms with African nationalists.
- ❑ **1976** ZANU and ZAPU unite as Patriotic Front (PF).
- ❑ **1977** PF backed by "frontline" African states: Mozambique, Tanzania, Botswana, and Zambia.
- ❑ **1979** After four years, eventual agreement on constitution.
- ❑ **1980** Independence as Zimbabwe. Following violent election campaign, Mugabe becomes prime minister of ZANU–PF/ ZAPU–PF coalition. Relations severed with South Africa.
- ❑ **1983–1984** Unrest in Matabeleland, ZAPU–PF's power base.
- ❑ **1985** Elections return ZANU–PF, with manifesto to create one-party state. Many ZAPU–PF members arrested.
- ❑ **1987** June, ZAPU–PF banned. September, provision for white seats in parliament abolished. December, ZANU–PF and ZAPU–PF sign unity agreement (merge in 1989). Mugabe elected president.
- ❑ **1990** Elections won by ZANU–PF. Mugabe reelected president.
- ❑ **1991** Mugabe abandons plan for one-party state.
- ❑ **1998** Nationwide strikes, student protests and talk of attempted military coup.
- ❑ **1999** Death of Vice President Nkomo. Opposition forms MDC.
- ❑ **2000** February, referendum on new constitution: government defeated. Expropriations of white-owned farmland by squatters. June, strong MDC performance in general election. ZANU–PF accused of using intimidation to retain majority.

DEFENSE

No compulsory military service

US$418m

Up 25% in 1999

Nationalist guerrillas were the heroes of independence in 1980. By the late 1990s, however, resentment grew when ex-combatants demanded enormous pensions.

In the early 1980s, some soldiers deserted to fight government forces in the Matabele bush. Dissidents plagued the regime until the Unity Accord of 1987. Zimbabwe has received military aid and training from the UK and South Korea. Although formally non-aligned, Zimbabwe supported the Mozambican regime against RENAMO guerrillas and backed the US-led operation in Somalia in 1992–1995.

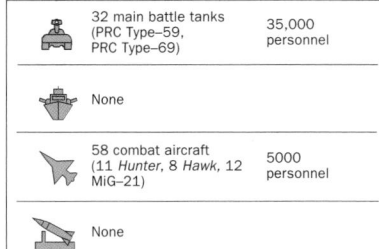

ZIMBABWEAN ARMED FORCES

32 main battle tanks (PRC Type–59, PRC Type–69)	35,000 personnel
None	
58 combat aircraft (11 *Hunter*, 8 *Hawk*, 12 MiG–21)	5000 personnel
None	

The withdrawal of troops from Congo (former Zaire), dispatched there in 1998 to help President Kabila fight rebels, began in April 2001, following the Lusaka peace accord.

ECONOMICS

Inflation 23.6% p.a. (1990–1999)

US$6.3bn

37.95–55.10 Zimbabwe dollars

SCORE CARD

❑ World GNP Ranking	102nd
❑ GNP per Capita	US$530
❑ Balance of Payments	US$–425m
❑ Inflation	31.8%
❑ Unemployment	50%

EXPORTS

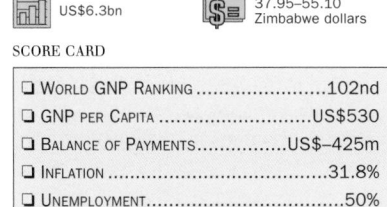

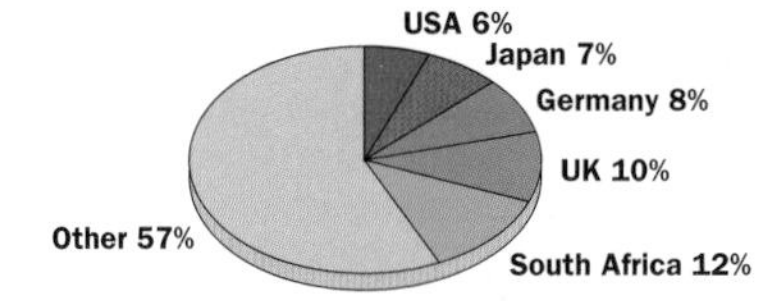
USA 6%
Japan 7%
Germany 8%
UK 10%
South Africa 12%
Other 57%

IMPORTS

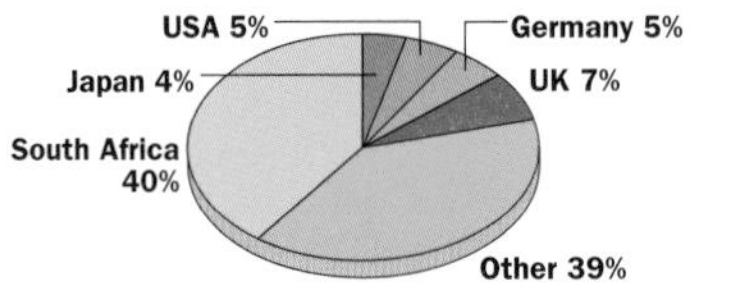
USA 5%
Germany 5%
Japan 4%
UK 7%
South Africa 40%
Other 39%

Strengths

Most broadly based African economy after South Africa. Sound infrastructure. Virtual self-sufficiency in food and energy. Founder member of regional free trade area. Gold, coal, tobacco, horticulture.

Weaknesses

Agricultural and hydroelectric output affected by drought. Large budget deficits. High unemployment and inflation. Labor unrest, bank collapses, food price riots. Currency value halved in 1998; devalued again in 2000. Cheap imports damage local industries. Political violence and economic collapse in 2000 scared off investors.

Profile

The socialist policies of the 1980s were superseded by a more market-oriented economy, introduced in 1991, which increased unemployment and inflation. Prospects for the mining industry appear particularly bleak: privatization of state copper interests was repeatedly delayed, while collapsing mineral prices have forced the closure of diamond, gold, platinum, and chromium mines. The cost of living and inflation soared during the economic chaos of 2000. Land acquisition is a perennial issue.

ECONOMIC PERFORMANCE INDICATOR

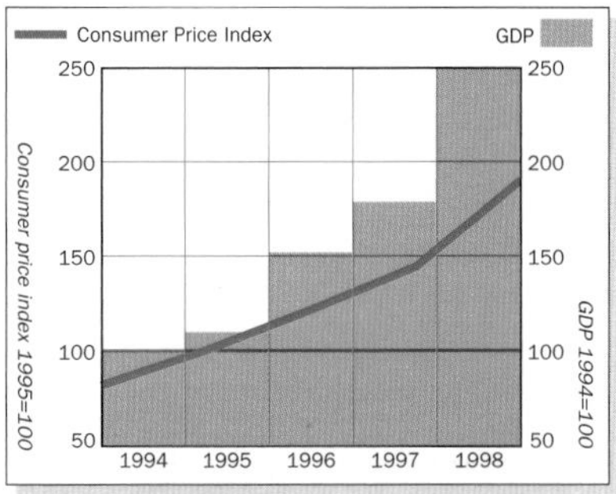
Consumer Price Index
GDP
250
200
150
100
50
1994
1995
1996
1997
1998
Consumer price index 1995=100
GDP 1994=100

ZIMBABWE : MAJOR BUSINESSES

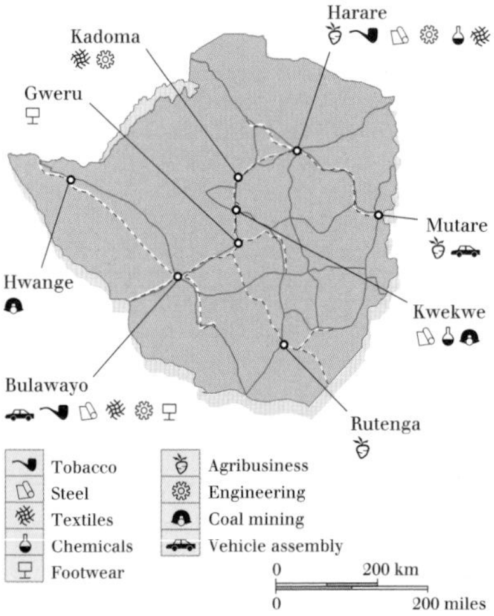
Harare
Kadoma
Gweru
Mutare
Hwange
Kwekwe
Bulawayo
Rutenga
Tobacco
Steel
Textiles
Chemicals
Footwear
Agribusiness
Engineering
Coal mining
Vehicle assembly
0
200 km
0
200 miles

Z

RESOURCES

Electric power 2.1m kw

18,241 tonnes

Not an oil producer

5.6m cattle, 2.8m goats, 16m chickens

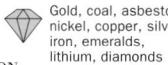

Gold, coal, asbestos, nickel, copper, silver, iron, emeralds, lithium, diamonds

ELECTRICITY GENERATION

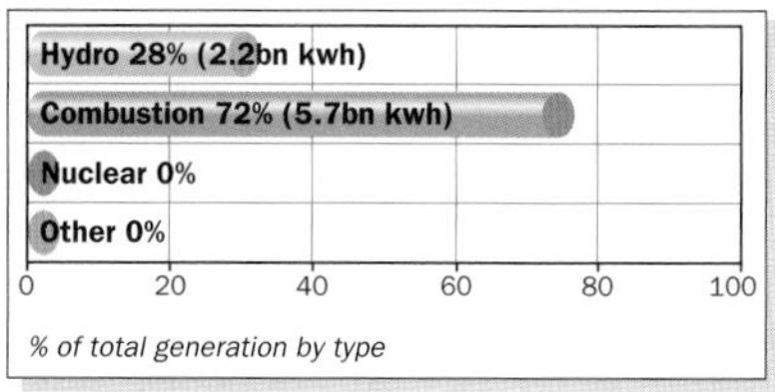

Hydro 28% (2.2bn kwh)
Combustion 72% (5.7bn kwh)
Nuclear 0%
Other 0%
0
20
40
60
80
100
% of total generation by type

Almost 30% of Zimbabwe's electricity needs are met by hydropower, notably from the Kariba dam, jointly owned with Zambia. The state power company is seeking to maximize capacity. In 1991, the government agreed to build an extension facility at Kariba South, and with Zambia a joint HEP station at Bartoka Gorge. An oil pipeline from Beira, Mozambique, to Mutare is being extended to Harare. Coal mining is expanding at Hwange, where Malaysian investments are helping to exploit deposits of 400 million tonnes.

ZIMBABWE : LAND USE

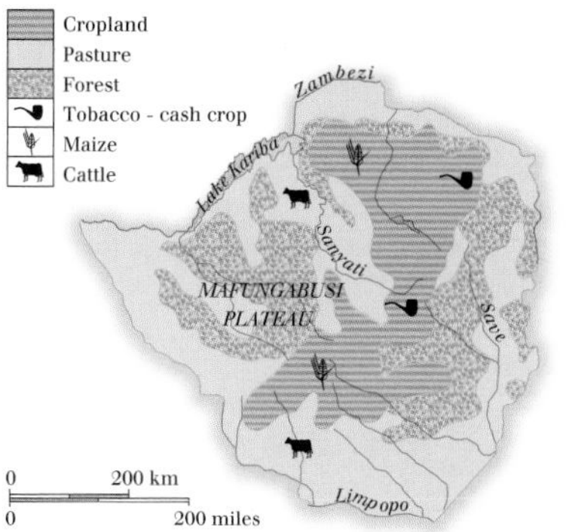

Cropland
Pasture
Forest
Tobacco - cash crop
Maize
Cattle
Zambezi
Lake Kariba
Sanyati
MAFUNGABUSI PLATEAU
Save
Limpopo
0 200 km
0 200 miles

ENVIRONMENT

Sustainability rank: 42nd

8% (1% partially protected)

1.6 tonnes per capita

ENVIRONMENTAL TREATIES

No	Yes	Yes
No	Yes	No

The 1991–1992 drought left half the population in need of drought relief, and used up 20% of public spending.

In communal areas, the land is suffering from overpopulation and overstocking. Deforestation, soil erosion, and deterioration of wildlife and water resources are widespread.

Measures have been taken to protect the black rhinoceros, including moving animals to safer areas and combating poaching – patrols have killed 150 poachers since 1986. The government also supports a scheme for dehorning rhinos – the horn is the poachers' main target. In 1997 Zimbabwe led the move at the Convention on International Trade in Endangered Species to allow a limited resumption of international trade in ivory. An increase in ivory poaching since 1999 has led to calls for more protection for elephants.

MEDIA

TV ownership medium

Daily newspaper circulation 19 per 1000 people

PUBLISHING AND BROADCAST MEDIA

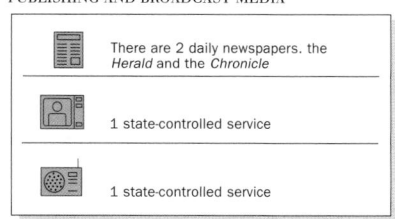

There are 2 daily newspapers. the *Herald* and the *Chronicle*

1 state-controlled service

1 state-controlled service

The state has a controlling interest in the two main newspapers. Other editors have been persecuted by security forces. Rigid guidelines are laid down for broadcasting stations.

CRIME

Death penalty used

21,000 prisoners

Up 4% 1996–1998

CRIME RATES

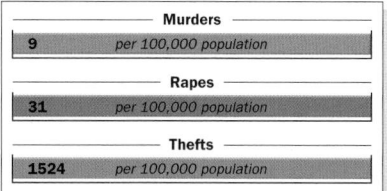

Crime	Rate
Murders	9 per 100,000 population
Rapes	31 per 100,000 population
Thefts	1524 per 100,000 population

Murder and narcotics-related offenses are rife in urban areas. The illegal occupation of white-owned farms, supported by the government, and electoral violence led to many deaths in 2000. The secret service and the army have been criticized for human rights abuses.

EDUCATION

School leaving age: 15

89%

46,673 students

THE EDUCATION SYSTEM

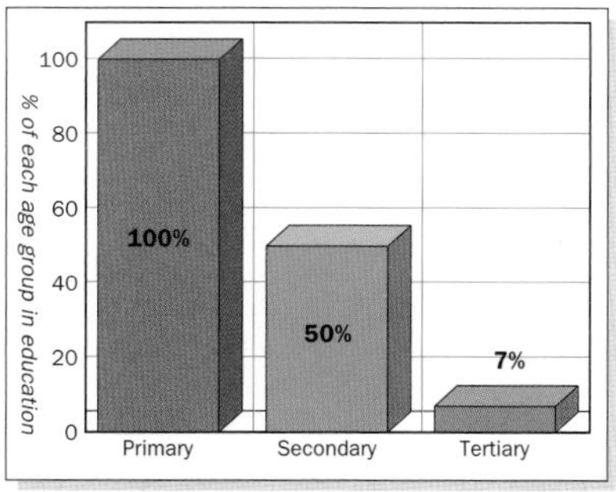

100
80
60
40
20
0
% of each age group in education
100%
50%
7%
Primary
Secondary
Tertiary

Improving education has been one of ZANU–PF's great successes. In barely ten years, primary school attendance rose from 820,000 to some 2.3 million. Education is compulsory and instruction is in English. Fees were introduced after 1992. The government built two new universities, at Bulawayo and Mutare; it encourages vocational training to create a workforce with skills in agriculture, medicine, and engineering.

HEALTH

No welfare state health benefits

1 per 10,000 people

AIDS, tuberculosis, accidents, malaria, heart disease, cancers

The largest single threat to health is AIDS. It has reduced life expectancy to just 43 years, created some 800,000 orphans, and kills 700 people a week. A belated AIDS awareness program is now in place. Malaria and tuberculosis account for many other deaths. The beleaguered health system is free for the poor, but short of expertise and staff.

SPENDING

GDP/cap. increase

CONSUMPTION AND SPENDING

29 per 1000 population

21 per 1000 population

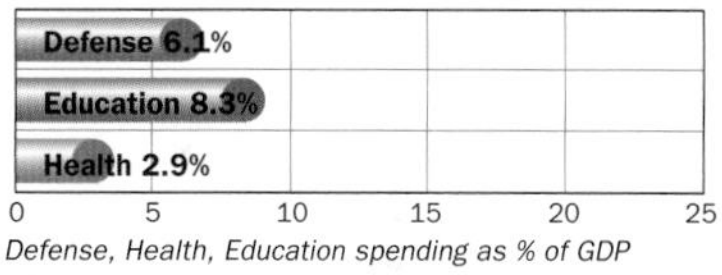

Defense 6.1%
Education 8.3%
Health 2.9%
0
5
10
15
20
25
Defense, Health, Education spending as % of GDP

Socialist policies in the 1980s lessened the gap between blacks and whites. But currency depreciation and inflation have since greatly reduced real wages.

WORLD RANKING

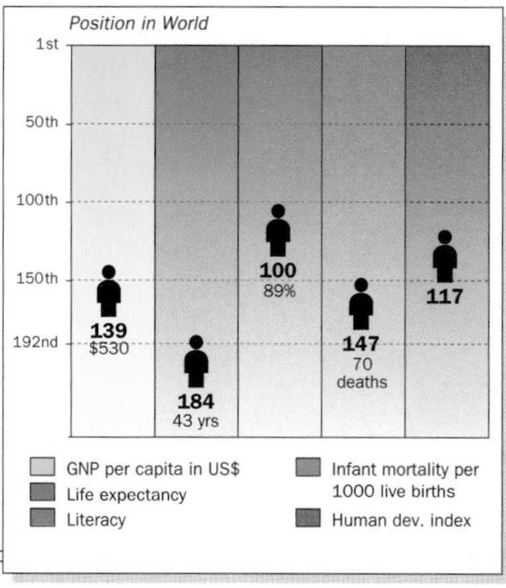

Position in World
1st
50th
100th
150th
192nd
139 $530
184 43 yrs
100 89%
147 70 deaths
117
GNP per capita in US$
Life expectancy
Literacy
Infant mortality per 1000 live births
Human dev. index

Z

OVERSEAS TERRITORIES & DEPENDENCIES

DESPITE THE RAPID process of decolonization since 1945 (pages 52–55), roughly seven million people around the world still live in non-sovereign territories under the protection of the UK, USA, France, Netherlands, Denmark, Norway, Australia, or New Zealand. These remnants of former colonial empires may have persisted for economic, strategic, or political reasons. Hong Kong and Macao reverted to Chinese control in the late 1990s. Others await political developments, such as referenda, which will determine their future status. Finally, a large group of territories are considered too small, remote, or weak to be able to survive as independent nations.

Svalbard
(to Norway)
BARENTS SEA
Jan Mayen
(to Norway)
Faeroe Islands
(to Denmark)
NORWAY
BALTIC SEA
NORTH SEA
Isle of Man
(to UK)
UNITED KINGDOM
DENMARK
NETHERLANDS
Channel Islands:
Guernsey and Jersey
(to UK)
FRANCE
EUROPE
PORTUGAL
Gibraltar
(to UK)
MEDITERRANEAN SEA
ASIA
SEA OF JAPAN
YELLOW SEA
EAST CHINA SEA
AFRICA
ARABIAN SEA
Paracel Islands
(Disputed)
SOUTH CHINA SEA
Spratly Islands
(Disputed)
Northern Mariana Islands (to US)
Guam (to US)
British Indian Ocean Territory
(to UK)
Cocos (Keeling) Islands
(to Australia)
JAVA SEA
ARAFURA SEA
Ascension
(Administered by St Helena)
Mayotte (to France)
Christmas Island
(to Australia)
Ashmore & Cartier Islands
(to Australia)
St Helena
(to UK)
ATLANTIC OCEAN
Réunion (to France)
Europa
(Administered by Réunion)
Bassas da India
(Administered by Réunion)
INDIAN OCEAN
AUSTRALIA
Amsterdam Island
St. Paul Island
French Southern & Antarctic Territories
(France)
Tristan da Cunha
(Administered by St Helena)
Gough Island
(Administered by St Helena)
Crozet Islands
Kerguelen
Heard & McDonald Islands
(to Australia)
Bouvet Island
(to Norway)
French Southern and Antarctic territories are not included in the following section. Any territories which involve an Antarctic claim are not shown.

UNITED KINGDOM

THE UK STILL HAS THE LARGEST number of overseas territories in the world. They are split into Crown colonies, Crown dependencies, and dependent territories. The distinction between each is largely constitutional, since most sustain a large degree of local autonomy, and the terminology and the nature of citizenship are now under review. Britain generally operates a policy of non-interference. If a territory expresses a constitutional desire for formal independence then it may have it, as long as it can form a viable independent country.

NEW ZEALAND

NEW ZEALAND'S GOVERNMENT has no desire to retain any overseas territories. However, the economic weakness of its dependent territory Tokelau and its freely associated states, Niue and the Cook Islands, has forced New Zealand to remain responsible for their foreign policy and defense.

UNITED STATES OF AMERICA

THE USA'S OVERSEAS TERRITORIES have been seen as strategically useful, if expensive, links with its "backyards." The USA has, in most cases, given the local population a say in deciding their own status. Thus, three former US-administered UN Trust Territories have been granted full sovereignty. A US Commonwealth territory, such as Puerto Rico, has a greater level of independence than that of a US unincorporated or external territory.

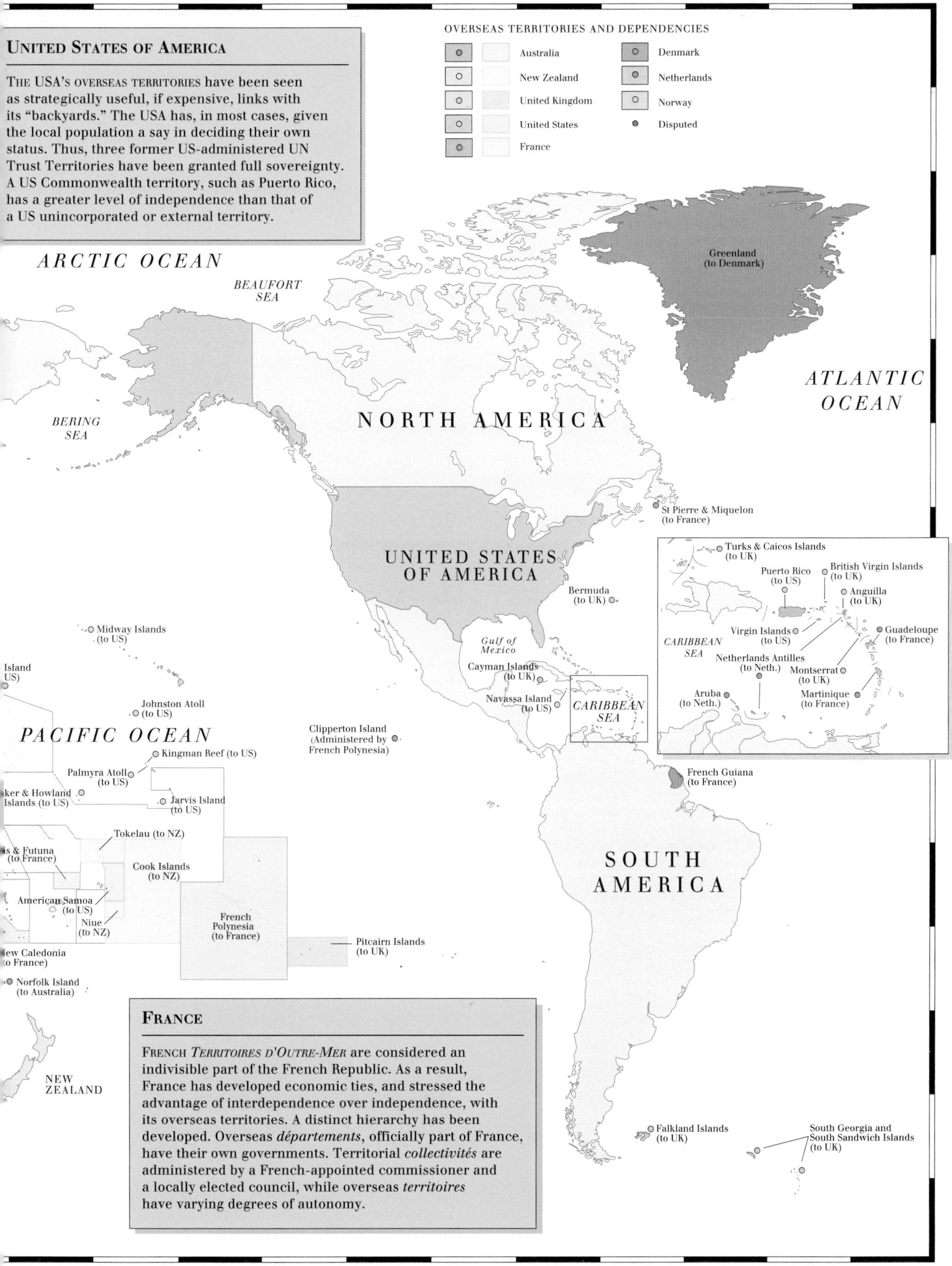
OVERSEAS TERRITORIES AND DEPENDENCIES
Australia
New Zealand
United Kingdom
United States
France
Denmark
Netherlands
Norway
Disputed
ARCTIC OCEAN
BEAUFORT SEA
Greenland (to Denmark)
ATLANTIC OCEAN
BERING SEA
NORTH AMERICA
St Pierre & Miquelon (to France)
UNITED STATES OF AMERICA
Bermuda (to UK)
Turks & Caicos Islands (to UK)
Puerto Rico (to US)
British Virgin Islands (to UK)
Anguilla (to UK)
Virgin Islands (to US)
Guadeloupe (to France)
CARIBBEAN SEA
Netherlands Antilles (to Neth.)
Montserrat (to UK)
Aruba (to Neth.)
Martinique (to France)
Midway Islands (to US)
Gulf of Mexico
Cayman Islands (to UK)
Navassa Island (to US)
CARIBBEAN SEA
Island US)
Johnston Atoll (to US)
PACIFIC OCEAN
Clipperton Island (Administered by French Polynesia)
Kingman Reef (to US)
Palmyra Atoll (to US)
ker & Howland Islands (to US)
Jarvis Island (to US)
French Guiana (to France)
Tokelau (to NZ)
s & Futuna (to France)
Cook Islands (to NZ)
SOUTH AMERICA
American Samoa (to US)
Niue (to NZ)
French Polynesia (to France)
Pitcairn Islands (to UK)
ew Caledonia o France)
Norfolk Island (to Australia)
NEW ZEALAND
Falkland Islands (to UK)
South Georgia and South Sandwich Islands (to UK)

FRANCE

FRENCH *TERRITOIRES D'OUTRE-MER* are considered an indivisible part of the French Republic. As a result, France has developed economic ties, and stressed the advantage of interdependence over independence, with its overseas territories. A distinct hierarchy has been developed. Overseas *départements*, officially part of France, have their own governments. Territorial *collectivités* are administered by a French-appointed commissioner and a locally elected council, while overseas *territoires* have varying degrees of autonomy.

American Samoa

Status: Unincorporated territory of the USA **Claimed:** 1900
Capital: Pago Pago **Pop.:** 63,781 **Density:** 327/km² (850/mi²)

AMERICAN SAMOA CONSISTS of five volcanic islands and two coral atolls in the southern Pacific Ocean. It has a tropical climate with an average annual rainfall of 500 cm (200 in). Typhoons and tropical storms are common from December to March. *Fa'a Samoa* – "the Samoan way of life" – still directs Samoan society, with the extended family, the *aiga*, at its base; traditional chiefs retain their central role in government. However, younger generations are attracted by *fa'a Amerika*. Tuna processed by Pago Pago's canneries represent 95% of the territory's exports, and in an effort at diversification, the government has encouraged the development of other light industries and tourism, helped by the designation of a national park to protect a large area of native forest and coral reef. The islands were shocked in 2000 when working conditions were exposed at the Daewoosa Samoa garment factory, and hundreds of Vietnamese workers were repatriated.

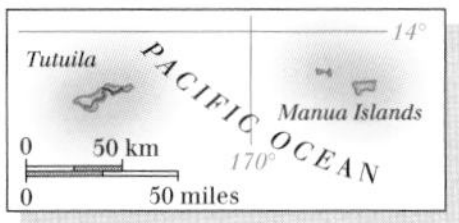
Tutuila
PACIFIC OCEAN
Manua Islands
14°
170°
0 50 km
0 50 miles

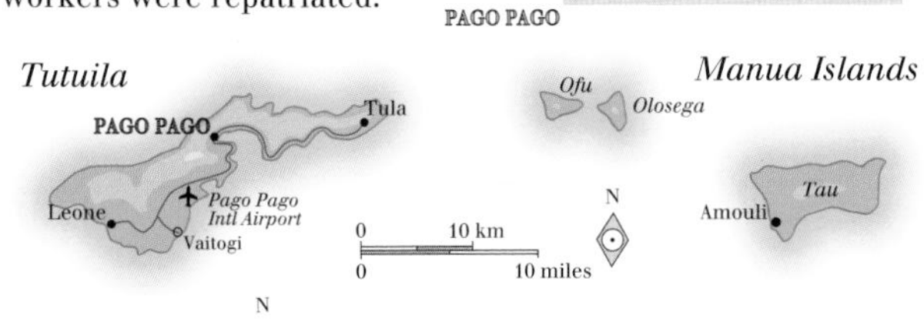
PAGO PAGO
Tutuila
Manua Islands
PAGO PAGO
Tula
Ofu
Olosega
Pago Pago Intl Airport
Leone
Vaitogi
Tau
Amouli
N
0 10 km
0 10 miles
N

Anguilla

Status: British dependent territory **Claimed:** 1650
Capital: The Valley **Pop.:** 11,407 **Density:** 119/km² (308/mi²)

ANGUILLA IS SITUATED at the northern end of the Leeward Islands, in the Caribbean. It has a subtropical climate, the heat and humidity being tempered by trade winds. In 1967, Anguillans refused to follow St. Kitts and Nevis into independence, preferring instead to retain the economic stability that came with dependent status. The People's Progressive Party, renamed the Anguilla National Alliance in 1980, dominated politics until ousted by an opposition coalition in 1994, but returned to power six years later in coalition with the Anguilla Democratic Party. New Chief Minister Osbourne Fleming inherited a policy of developing the tourist sector and expanding offshore banking. Economic growth has been due largely to tourism. Visitor numbers dropped after the devastating hurricane of 1995, but quickly recovered.

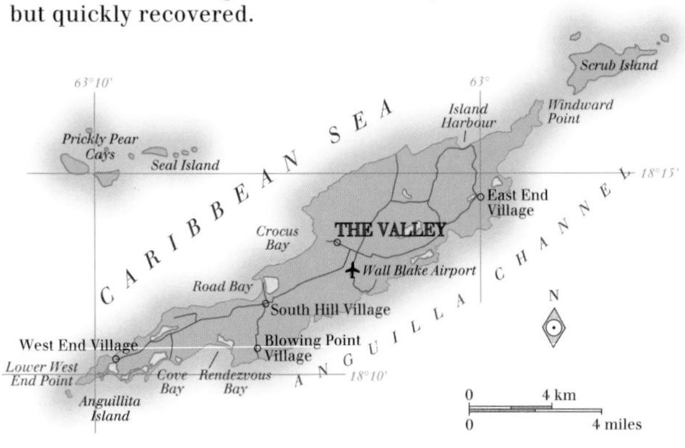
Scrub Island
63°10'
63°
Island Harbour
Windward Point
CARIBBEAN SEA
Prickly Pear Cays
Seal Island
18°15'
East End Village
Crocus Bay
THE VALLEY
Wall Blake Airport
Road Bay
South Hill Village
ANGUILLA CHANNEL
N
West End Village
Blowing Point Village
Lower West End Point
Cove Bay
Rendezvous Bay
18°10'
Anguillita Island
0 4 km
0 4 miles

Aruba

Status: Autonomous part of the Netherlands **Claimed:** 1643
Capital: Oranjestad **Pop.:** 95,201 **Density:** 493/km² (1269/mi²)

ONE OF THE SMALLEST islands in the Dutch Caribbean, Aruba lies 25 km (16 miles) off the coast of Venezuela. It has a tropical climate moderated by constant trade winds sweeping in from the Atlantic. Formerly the richest island in the Netherlands Antilles, Aruba became a separate dependency of the Netherlands in 1986. Transition to full independence, expected in 1996, was halted in 1994, by agreement between the governments of the Netherlands, Aruba, and the Netherlands Antilles. The Netherlands voiced concern over the island's security and the danger of it becoming a base for narcotics trafficking, and the Aruban government, led by Hendrik Eman, questioned the desirability of full independence, citing high unemployment and economic instability.

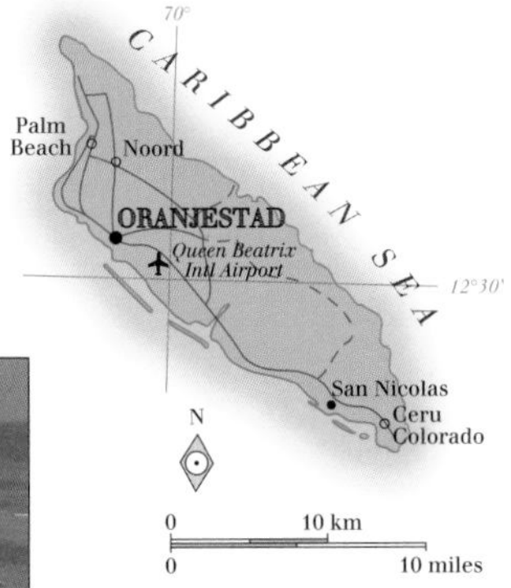
70°
CARIBBEAN SEA
Palm Beach
Noord
ORANJESTAD
Queen Beatrix Intl Airport
12°30'
San Nicolas
Ceru Colorado
N
0 10 km
0 10 miles

The economy of Aruba, formerly dependent on oil refining, has diversified since 1986. Tourism and offshore finance have become the most important sectors of the economy, and there are now more than 700,000 visitors annually; nearly 60% of them come from the USA. However, the rapid expansion of tourism has put considerable strain on Aruba's infrastructure, and some attempt has been made to restrict the number of visitors. At the same time facilities have been improved to encourage the growth of a data-processing industry.

***Palm Beach, Aruba,** also known as the Turquoise Coast, lies on the western side of the island. The beach stretches for 10 km (6 miles) and is the site of a low-rise beach resort.*

***Oranjestad,** Aruba's capital, contains many Dutch colonial-style buildings. Although first claimed by the Spanish in 1499, Aruba was colonized by the Dutch in the 17th century.*

Aruba's cooperation with the USA in the region includes support for its actions against narcotics trafficking from South America, and since the closure of the US base in Panama in 1999, US aircraft have used bases on the island to launch reconnaissance flights. Those who oppose this cooperation fear that it could drag Aruba unnecessarily into the civil conflict in Colombia.

LAND HEIGHT above Sea Level 200m/656ft 500m/1640ft 1000m/3281ft 1500m/4572ft above 2000m/6562ft

BERMUDA

STATUS: British Crown colony **CLAIMED:** 1612
CAPITAL: Hamilton **POP.:** 64,000 **DENSITY:** 1208/km² (3200/mi²)

SITUATED MORE THAN 900 km (558 miles) off the coast of South Carolina, USA, Bermuda consists of a chain of over 150 coral islands. The Gulf Stream, flowing between Bermuda and the USA's eastern seaboard, keeps the climate mild and humid. Bermuda is racially mixed; some 60% of the population are of mostly European extraction. Racial tension has declined since the 1960s and 1970s. A more representative electoral system was established after a Royal Commission visited Bermuda in 1978.

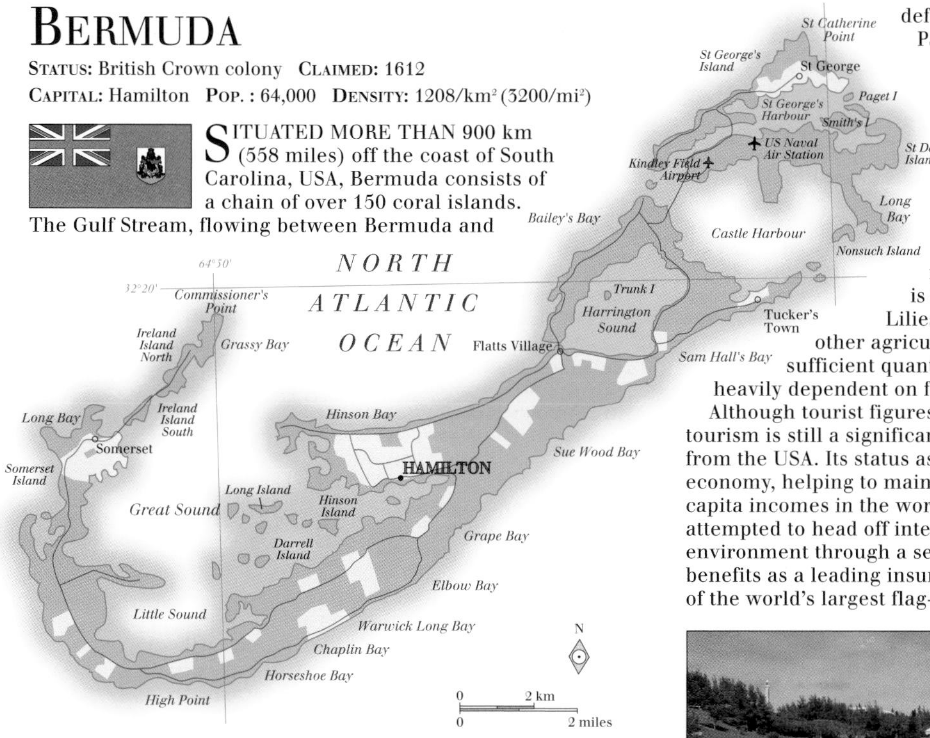
St Catherine Point
St George's Island
St George
St George's Harbour
Paget I
Smith's I
US Naval Air Station
St David's Island
Kindley Field Airport
Long Bay
Bailey's Bay
Castle Harbour
Nonsuch Island
NORTH ATLANTIC OCEAN
64°50'
32°20'
Commissioner's Point
Trunk I
Harrington Sound
Ireland Island North
Grassy Bay
Flatts Village
Tucker's Town
Sam Hall's Bay
Hinson Bay
Long Bay
Ireland Island South
Somerset
Somerset Island
Sue Wood Bay
HAMILTON
Long Island
Great Sound
Hinson Island
Darrell Island
Grape Bay
Elbow Bay
Little Sound
Warwick Long Bay
Chaplin Bay
Horseshoe Bay
High Point
N
0 2 km
0 2 miles

For 30 years after the first general election, held in 1968, Bermuda was ruled by the conservative United Bermuda Party (UBP). Its veteran leader Sir John Swan, resigned as prime minister and party leader in 1995, when a referendum decisively rejected his campaign for independence from the UK. In a general election in November 1998 the UBP, now under the leadership of Pamela Gordon, was decisively defeated by the Progressive Labour Party, led by Jennifer Smith, who said that she had no plans to pursue her party's own pro-independence aspirations.

Major issues are the social and economic challenges posed by the withdrawal in 1995 of both the US naval base and the British military base, environmental issues, and narcotics trafficking. Bermuda is overwhelmingly a service economy. Lilies are grown for export, but few other agricultural products are grown in sufficient quantity, and the islands are heavily dependent on food imports.

Although tourist figures have been falling steadily, tourism is still a significant industry, most visitors coming from the USA. Its status as a tax haven has boosted the economy, helping to maintain one of the highest per capita incomes in the world. However, the government has attempted to head off international criticism of its financial environment through a series of reforms. Bermuda also benefits as a leading insurance market and operates one of the world's largest flag-of-convenience shipping fleets.

***Bermuda** has one of the highest densities of golf courses in the world. Eight courses have now been developed.*

BRITISH INDIAN OCEAN TERRITORY

STATUS: British dependent territory **CLAIMED:** 1814
CAPITAL: Diego Garcia **POP.:** 3100 **DENSITY:** 52/km² (135/mi²)

THE BRITISH Indian Ocean Territory, or Chagos Islands, lies in the middle of the Indian Ocean. The coral atolls are uninhabited, except for the US–UK military base on Diego Garcia, and the UK has undertaken to cede the islands to Mauritius when they are no longer required. In 2000 the Ilois people, evicted by the UK from the islands in 1968, won the right in the UK High Court to return, but face strong resistance from the USA.

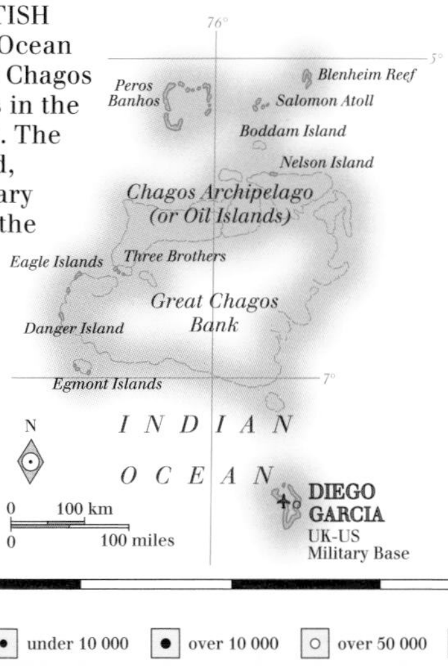
76°
5°
Peros Banhos
Blenheim Reef
Salomon Atoll
Boddam Island
Nelson Island
Chagos Archipelago (or Oil Islands)
Eagle Islands
Three Brothers
Great Chagos Bank
Danger Island
Egmont Islands
7°
INDIAN OCEAN
N
0 100 km
0 100 miles
DIEGO GARCIA
UK-US Military Base

BRITISH VIRGIN ISLANDS

STATUS: British dependent territory **CLAIMED:** 1672
CAPITAL: Road Town **POP.:** 19,864 **DENSITY:** 130/km² (337/mi²)

AN ARCHIPELAGO of 60 Caribbean islands, 15 of them inhabited, the British Virgin Islands lie at the eastern end of the Greater Antilles. Tourism, now a major economic activity, is suited to the tropical climate, but there is concern about its effect on the environment. There are also fears that traditional place names are being altered to be more tourist-friendly. The offshore finance sector is important, and has been more tightly regulated since 1990, following scandals involving foreign companies registered in the islands.

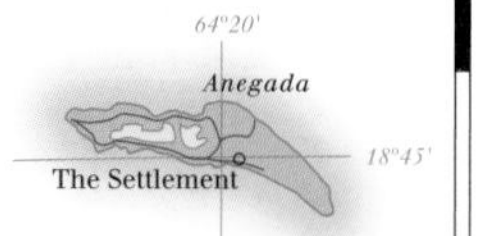
64°20'
Anegada
The Settlement
18°45'

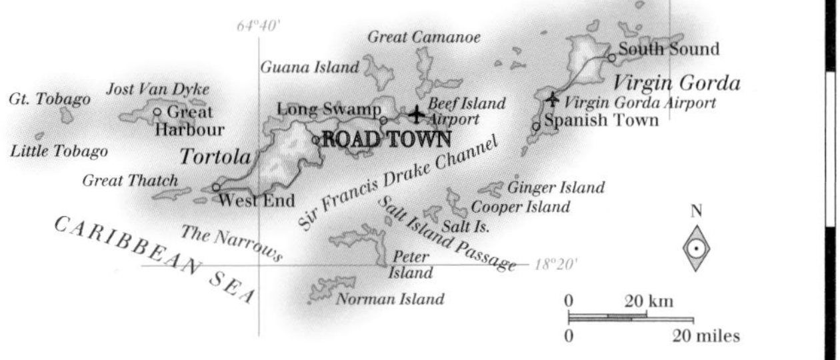
ATLANTIC OCEAN
64°40'
Great Camanoe
South Sound
Guana Island
Virgin Gorda
Gt. Tobago
Jost Van Dyke
Great Harbour
Long Swamp
Beef Island Airport
Virgin Gorda Airport
Spanish Town
ROAD TOWN
Little Tobago
Tortola
Sir Francis Drake Channel
Great Thatch
West End
Ginger Island
Cooper Island
Salt Island Passage
Salt Is.
CARIBBEAN SEA
The Narrows
Peter Island
18°20'
Norman Island
N
0 20 km
0 20 miles

Cayman Islands

Status: British dependent territory **Claimed:** 1670
Capital: George Town **Pop.:** 39,000 **Density:** 151/km² (390/mi²)

THE LARGEST OF Britain's territories in the Caribbean, the Cayman Islands lie 225 km (140 miles) west of Jamaica and south of Cuba. The abundance of exotic wildlife, especially marine life, is a powerful draw for tourists. Grand Cayman is credited as the home of modern scuba diving, the first ever specialist shop opening there in 1957. The islanders rejected greater autonomy, persuaded that their economic stability is linked to their dependent territory status. Thanks to the absence of tax and foreign-exchange controls, the islands are one of the world's largest offshore financial centers, but tourism continues to underpin the economy.

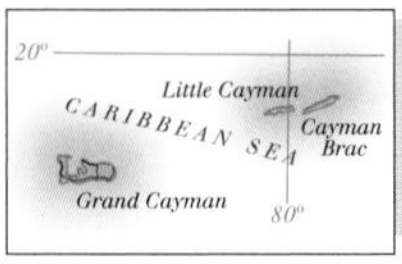
20°
Little Cayman
CARIBBEAN SEA
Cayman Brac
Grand Cayman
80°

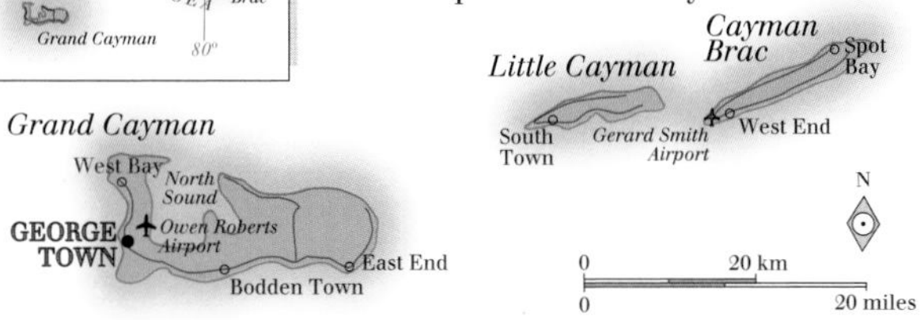
Cayman Brac
Spot Bay
Little Cayman
South Town
Gerard Smith Airport
West End
Grand Cayman
West Bay
North Sound
GEORGE TOWN
Owen Roberts Airport
East End
Bodden Town
N
0 20 km
0 20 miles

Christmas Island

Status: Australian external territory **Claimed:** 1958
Capital: Flying Fish Cove **Pop.:** 1906 **Density:** 14/km² (37/mi²)

SO NAMED because it was sighted on Christmas Day in 1643, the island lies in the Indian Ocean, 360 km (225 miles) south of Java. The population is mostly Malay and Chinese, descended from laborers imported to mine rich phosphate deposits. A national park covers some 70% of the island. In 2001 the Australian government agreed with Russia to begin construction of a rocket-launching site on the island.

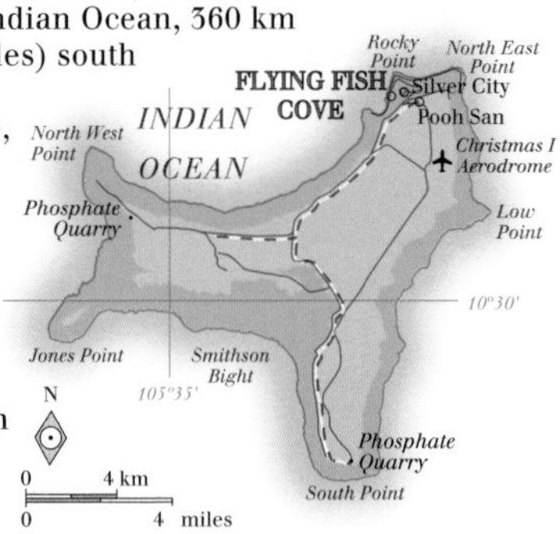
Rocky Point
North East Point
FLYING FISH COVE
Silver City
Poon San
INDIAN OCEAN
North West Point
Christmas I Aerodrome
Phosphate Quarry
Low Point
10°30'
Jones Point
Smithson Bight
105°35'
Phosphate Quarry
South Point
N
0 4 km
0 4 miles

Cocos (Keeling) Islands

Status: Australian external territory **Claimed:** 1955
Capital: West Island **Pop.:** 621 **Density:** 44/km² (124/mi²)

IN ALL, 27 coral atolls make up the Cocos (Keeling) Islands. Situated in the Indian Ocean, roughly halfway between Australia and Sri Lanka, they have been part of the Northern Territory electoral district since 1992. The inhabited islands are the European-dominated West Island and Home Island, with a mainly Cocos Malay community. Coconuts are the sole cash crop.

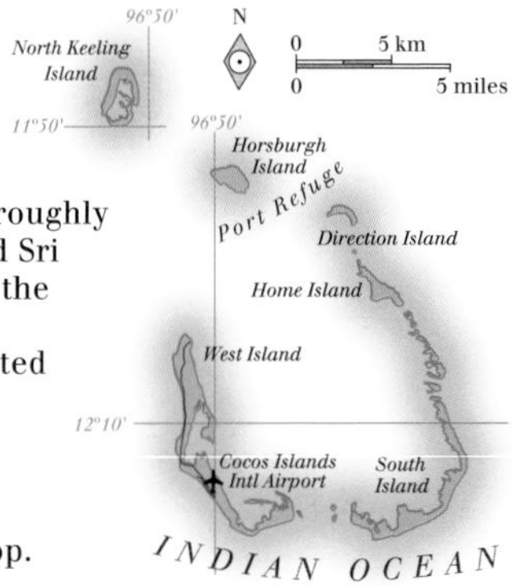
96°50'
N
0 5 km
0 5 miles
North Keeling Island
11°50'
96°50'
Horsburgh Island
Port Refuge
Direction Island
Home Island
West Island
12°10'
Cocos Islands Intl Airport
South Island
INDIAN OCEAN

Cook Islands

Status: Territory in free association with New Zealand **Claimed:** 1901
Capital: Avarua **Pop.:** 14,300 **Density:** 60/km² (155/mi²)

LYING IN THE MIDDLE of the South Pacific 3013 km (1883 miles) from New Zealand, the Cook Islands are a combination of 24 coral atolls and volcanic islands. They achieved self-government in 1965 and have adopted a diversified economy. As well as tourism and banking, giant clam and pearl farming have been developed. There are also significant mineral deposits on the surrounding seabed.

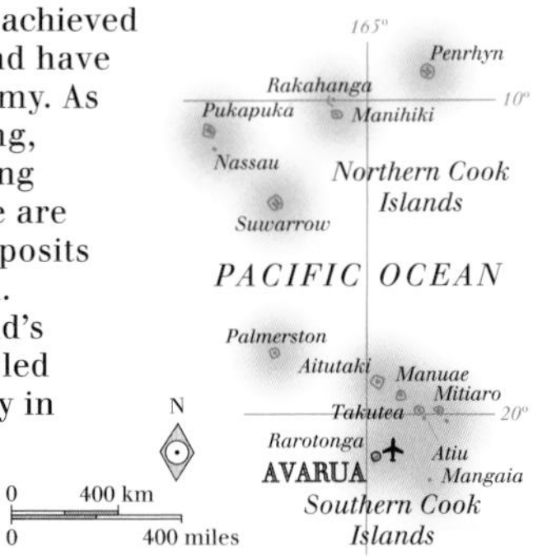
165°
Penrhyn
Rakahanga
10°
Pukapuka
Manihiki
Nassau
Northern Cook Islands
Suwarrow
PACIFIC OCEAN
Palmerston
Aitutaki
Manuae
Mitiaro
Takutea
20°
N
Rarotonga
Atiu
AVARUA
Mangaia
0 400 km
0 400 miles
Southern Cook Islands

Doubts over New Zealand's ability to defend the islands led to a declaration of neutrality in 1986. In 1991, a friendship treaty was signed with France, covering economic development, trade, and French surveillance of the Cook Islands exclusive economic zone (EEZ). Relations with France deteriorated, however, when the latter went ahead with six nuclear-weapons tests in the Pacific at Mururoa Atoll.

Controversial plans to develop the environmentally important Suwarrow atoll for pearl farming were dropped in 2001, after public outrage.

Faeroe Islands

Status: Self-governing territory of Denmark **Claimed:** 1380
Capital: Tórshavn **Pop.:** 46,122 **Density:** 33/km² (85/mi²)

Midway between Scotland and Iceland in the North Atlantic, the Faeroe Islands have a moderate climate for their latitude – a result of the warm Gulf Stream current. Home rule since 1948 has given the Faeroese a strong sense of national identity – they voted against joining the European Communities with Denmark in 1973, but now have favorable terms of trade with most EU members. Fishing is the dominant industry, providing over 90% of exports. In the face of international criticism, the Faeroese have also continued their traditional cull of pilot whales and bottle-nosed dolphins. Sheep farming is important, and there is a small textile industry which exports traditional woolens, and puffin and eider-duck feathers.

Denmark's moves toward ever closer European integration has strengthened calls in the Faeroes for full independence. Negotiations to establish a "sovereign nation" under the Danish monarchy began in 1998. However, the Danish government's threat to suspend subsidies to the islands in 2001 quashed calls for a referendum.

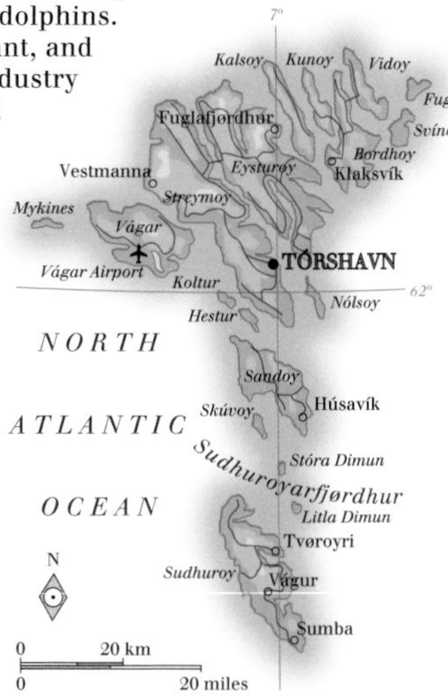
7°
Kalsoy
Kunoy
Vidoy
Fugloy
Svínoy
Fuglafjørdhur
Bordhoy
Klaksvík
Vestmanna
Eysturoy
Streymoy
Mykines
Vágar
TÓRSHAVN
Vágar Airport
Koltur
62°
Nólsoy
Hestur
NORTH
Sandoy
Skúvoy
Húsavík
ATLANTIC
Sudhuroyarfjørdhur
Stóra Dimun
Litla Dimun
OCEAN
Tvøroyri
N
Sudhuroy
Vágur
Sumba
0 20 km
0 20 miles

LAND HEIGHT above Sea Level 200m/656ft 500m/1640ft 1000m/3281ft 1500m/4572ft above 2000m/6562ft

FALKLAND ISLANDS

STATUS: British dependent territory **CLAIMED:** 1832

CAPITAL: Stanley **POP.:** 2826 **DENSITY:** 0.23/km² (0.6/mi²)

SITUATED IN the South Atlantic Ocean, over 12,000 km (7440 miles) from Britain, the Falkland Islands are influenced by the cold Antarctic current. The main islands of East and West Falkland and the hundreds of outlying islands have a cool, temperate climate with frequent strong winds.

The islands gained international attention with the Argentine invasion, and subsequent British recapture, in 1982. Since then, the British government has invested heavily in a "Fortress Falklands" policy. A new runway and military base were built at Mount Pleasant to house an enlarged garrison. The islanders, for their part, are determined to maintain the political *status quo*, but in 1999 improving relations led to the restoration of scheduled air connections with Argentina (via Chile). Since the Falklands War, the economy of the islands has prospered. Falklanders invested heavily in schools, roads, and tourism in a fresh drive for a strong identity. By 1987, the Falklands had become financially solvent through the sale of fishing licenses. Although sales of cheaper, less restrictive licenses by Argentina forced a slump in fishing revenues, fishing is still the major source of income and employment. Depressed wool prices have affected the living standards of the predominantly sheep-farming community. The UK and Argentina reached agreement in 1995 on oil exploration, and the discovery of oil reserves in the Falklands' territorial waters is revolutionizing prospects for the economy. Tourism, attracting birdwatchers, photographers, and military historians, is steadily growing.

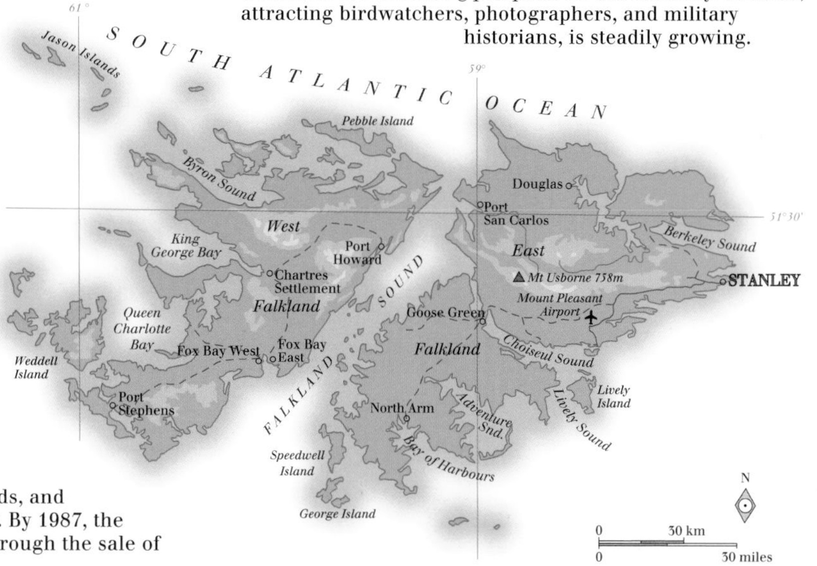
SOUTH ATLANTIC OCEAN
61°
59°
51°30'
Jason Islands
Pebble Island
Byron Sound
West
Falkland
King George Bay
Port Howard
Chartres Settlement
Queen Charlotte Bay
Weddell Island
Fox Bay West
Fox Bay East
Port Stephens
FALKLAND SOUND
Speedwell Island
George Island
Douglas
Port San Carlos
East
Falkland
Berkeley Sound
Mt Usborne 738m
STANLEY
Mount Pleasant Airport
Goose Green
Choiseul Sound
North Arm
Adventure Snd.
Bay of Harbours
Lively Island
Lively Sound
N
0 30 km
0 30 miles

FRENCH GUIANA

STATUS: French overseas department **CLAIMED:** 1817

CAPITAL: Cayenne **POP.:** 157,213 **DENSITY:** 2/km² (4/mi²)

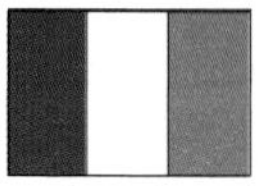

SANDWICHED BETWEEN Brazil and Suriname, French Guiana is the only remaining colony in South America. A belt of coastal marsh, and an interior of equatorial jungle, combine in a location which was, for years, notorious for the offshore penal colony, Devil's Island. The rainforest, which covers 90% of the territory, is particularly rich in flora and fauna. It harbors over 400,000 species, including more different kinds of birds than in the whole of Europe.

Concentrated near the coast, the population is ethnically mixed. While 40% are creoles, there are some 20,000 Amerindians and a village of 1000 Hmong who fled civil war in Laos in the 1980s.

Kourou was selected for the launch of the Ariane rocket because of its equatorial site. The town has grown from 800 to 13,000 people.

A campaign for greater autonomy in the late 1970s and early 1980s led to limited decentralization of power to a regional council. The previous grip on local power by the Guianese Socialist Party (PSG) has been threatened since 1993 by a more unified opposition, but it is still the largest party in the regional council.

During the 1990s the people have become increasingly vocal in their condemnation of the French government's perceived indifference to their country's problems, and there were riots in 1996 and 1997 over the education system. The PSG has accordingly campaigned for greater autonomy. As an overseas *département* of metropolitan France, French Guiana is also a region of the EU, but it is heavily dependent on France itself for aid, food, and manufactured goods. It has a number of valuable natural resources, including gold, fishing, and forestry, and also has potential for increased tourism, but these are yet to be fully exploited because of a lack of skilled labor and investment and an underdeveloped infrastructure. The Guiana Space Center, which is situated on the coast at Kourou, has been operational since 1964. From there the Ariane rockets of the European Space Agency (ESA) are launched.

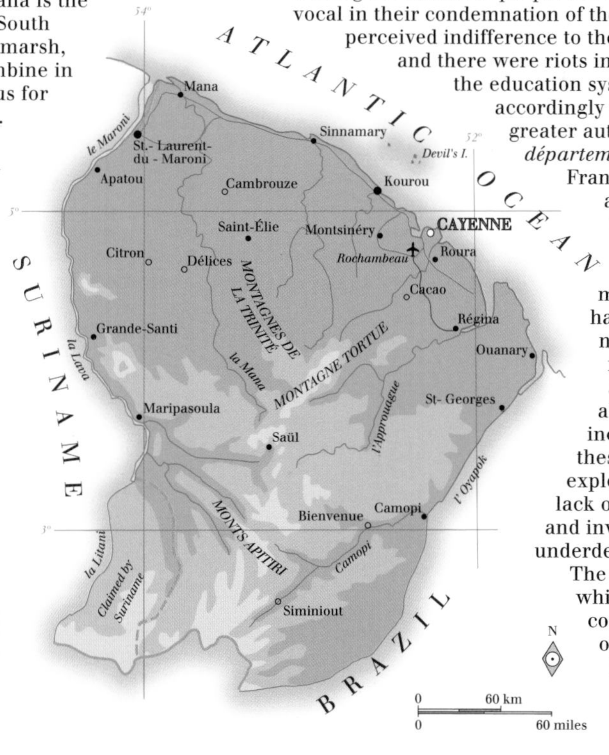
ATLANTIC OCEAN
SURINAME
BRAZIL
54°
52°
5°
3°
Mana
le Maroni
St.-Laurent-du-Maroni
Apatou
Sinnamary
Devil's I.
Cambrouze
Kourou
Saint-Élie
Montsinéry
CAYENNE
Rochambeau
Roura
Citron
Délices
MONTAGNES DE LA TRINITÉ
Cacao
Grande-Santi
Régina
la Lawa
Ouanary
la Mana
MONTAGNE TORTUE
Maripasoula
St-Georges
l'Approuague
Saül
l'Oyapok
Camopi
Bienvenue
MONTS APITIRI
la Litani
Claimed by Suriname
Camopi
Siminiout
N
0 60 km
0 60 miles

French Polynesia

Status: French overseas possession **Claimed:** 1843

Capital: Papeete **Pop.:** 231,500 **Density:** 66/km² (170/mi²)

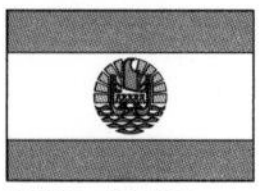

A SCATTER OF 130 South Pacific islands and coral atolls combine to form French Polynesia, in an area the size of Europe. The average annual temperature varies between 20°C (68°F) and 29°C (84°F), with rainfall of over 150 cm (58 in). Nearly 75% of the population live on the main island of Tahiti. The French administration has developed the islands with little regard for local wishes, and the 70% West Polynesian (Mahoi) majority have seen their simple, self-sufficient economy transformed into one dependent on the French military and tourism. Nuclear testing on Mururoa atoll created many jobs, but there was growing opposition, and a final series of tests, held in 1995–1996 despite widespread international protests, provoked local demonstrations and riots in Papeete.

The Polynesian majority has called increasingly for more autonomy, reduced tourism, and the rebuilding of indigenous trade. future hopes rest largely on new tuna fishing ventures.

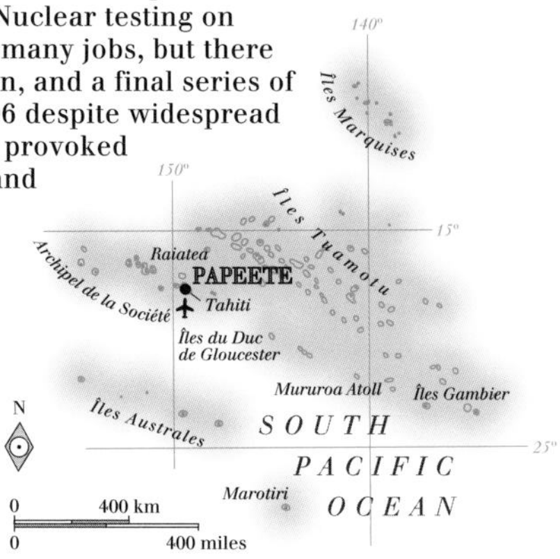

140°
Îles Marquises
150°
Îles Tuamotu
15°
Archipel de la Société
Raiatea
PAPEETE
Tahiti
Îles du Duc de Gloucester
Mururoa Atoll
Îles Gambier
Îles Australes
SOUTH
PACIFIC
OCEAN
25°
Marotiri
N
0 400 km
0 400 miles

Greenland

Status: Self governing territory of Denmark **Claimed:** 1380

Capital: Nuuk **Pop.:** 56,307 **Density:** 0.03/km² (0.07/mi²)

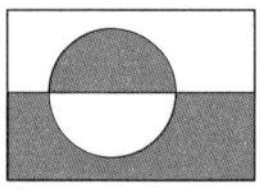

THE WORLD'S LARGEST island after Australia, Greenland is situated in the North Atlantic and surrounded by seas that are either frozen or cooled by cold Arctic currents. With an Arctic climate, much of its land is permanently ice-covered. Granted home rule in 1979, Greenlanders are of mixed Inuit and European origin. Younger islanders increasingly reject the traditional, fishing-based, subsistence lifestyle by moving to towns, placing a heavy burden on the advanced welfare system. Proposals to develop the mining of ice for drinking water could create vast revenues, even raising the possibility of economic independence.

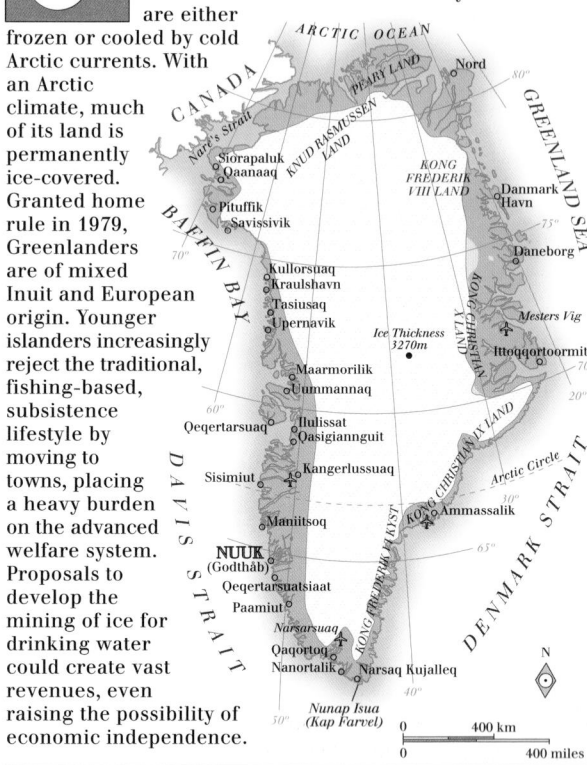

ARCTIC OCEAN
CANADA
PEARY LAND
Nord
80°
GREENLAND SEA
Nares Strait
KNUD RASMUSSEN LAND
Siorapaluk
Qaanaaq
KONG FREDERIK VIII LAND
Danmark Havn
Pituffik
Savissivik
75°
BAFFIN BAY
Daneborg
70°
Kullorsuaq
Kraulshavn
Tasiusaq
Upernavik
KONG CHRISTIAN X LAND
Mesters Vig
Ice Thickness 3270m
Ittoqqortoormit
Maarmorilik
Uummannaq
70°
20°
60°
Ilulissat
Qasigiannguit
Qeqertarsuaq
KONG CHRISTIAN IX LAND
DAVIS STRAIT
Sisimiut
Kangerlussuaq
Arctic Circle
Ammassalik
Maniitsoq
DENMARK STRAIT
65°
NUUK (Godthåb)
Qeqertarsuatsiaat
KONG FREDERIK VI KYST
Paamiut
Narsarsuaq
Qaqortoq
Nanortalik
Narsaq
Kujalleq
N
40°
Nunap Isua (Kap Farvel)
50°
0 400 km
0 400 miles

Gibraltar

Status: British Crown colony **Claimed:** 1713

Capital: Gibraltar **Pop.:** 27,025 **Density:** 3861/km² (9008/mi²)

GUARDING THE western entrance to the Mediterranean, Gibraltar has survived on military and marine revenues. However, as Britain has cut defense spending, so its military presence on the Rock has declined. In response Gibraltarians have developed a vibrant offshore banking industry. Strict antismuggling legislation, in force since 1995, has curbed extensive smuggling from north Africa into Spain. Gibraltar's relationship with Britain and Spain remains contentious. The Social Democrats under Peter Caruana favor closer ties with the UK, while Spain continues to press for control over the Rock. The border with Spain is frequently obstructed.

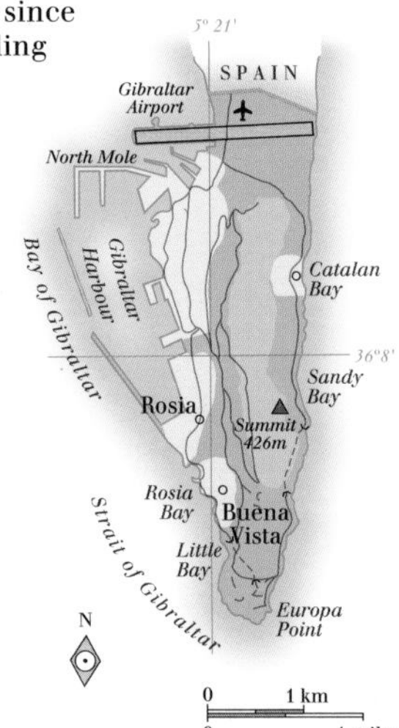

5° 21'
SPAIN
Gibraltar Airport
North Mole
Bay of Gibraltar
Gibraltar Harbour
Catalan Bay
36°8'
Sandy Bay
Rosia
Summit 426m
Rosia Bay
Buena Vista
Little Bay
Strait of Gibraltar
Europa Point
N
0 1 km
0 1 mile

***The Rock of Gibraltar.** The British built 143 caves, 50 km of roads and as many km of tunnels for defensive purposes.*

Guadeloupe

Status: French overseas department **Claimed:** 1635

Capital: Basse-Terre **Pop.:** 422,496 **Density:** 237/km² (615/mi²)

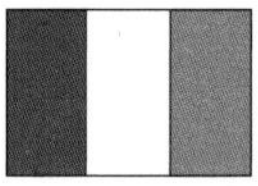

GUADELOUPE lies at the northern end of the Windward Islands in the Caribbean. The movement for independence from France has been pronounced and intermittently violent since the 1960s. The economy is largely based on agriculture and tourism, with sugar, rum, and bananas the main exports, but the islands are dependent on French and EU regional aid. The vulnerability of the banana industry to hurricanes and world market prices has led the local government to seek to expand sugar production and develop tourism.

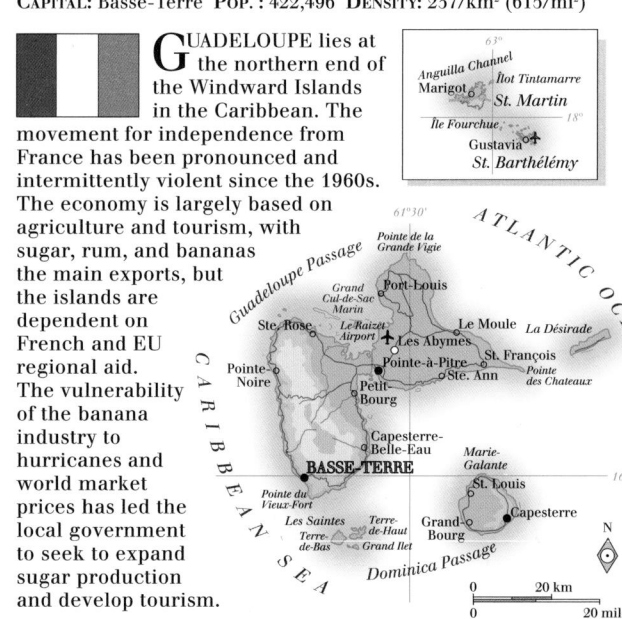

63°
Anguilla Channel
Îlot Tintamarre
Marigot
St. Martin
18°
Île Fourchue
Gustavia
St. Barthélémy

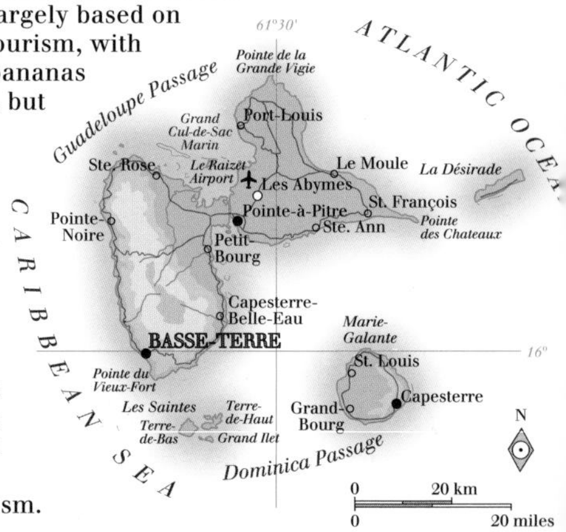

61°30'
ATLANTIC OCEAN
Pointe de la Grande Vigie
Guadeloupe Passage
Grand Cul-de-Sac Marin
Port-Louis
Ste. Rose
Le Raizet Airport
Le Moule
La Désirade
Les Abymes
St. François
Pointe-Noire
Pointe-à-Pitre
Ste. Ann
Pointe des Chateaux
Petit-Bourg
CARIBBEAN SEA
Capesterre-Belle-Eau
Marie-Galante
BASSE-TERRE
16°
St. Louis
Pointe du Vieux-Fort
Capesterre
Les Saintes
Terre-de-Haut
Grand-Bourg
Terre-de-Bas
Grand Ilet
Dominica Passage
N
0 20 km
0 20 miles

GUERNSEY

STATUS: British Crown dependency **CLAIMED:** 1066
CAPITAL: St. Peter Port **POP.:** 58,681 **DENSITY:** 903/km² (2347/mi²)

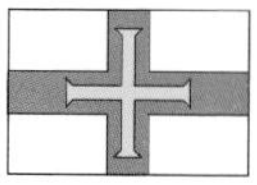

LYING 47 KM (29 miles) off the coast of France, Guernsey and its dependencies form the northwestern part of the Channel Islands, historically part of the Duchy of Normandy. English is the language most commonly used, but the Norman *patois* is spoken in some villages, and French is used in some formalities of the legislature. Travel to France is easier than to the UK; Alderney is only 13 km (8 miles) from the French mainland. Residents on the smaller islands have no need for cars, and life continues in an unhurried manner that has changed little through the centuries. The islanders guard this lifestyle with strict residence laws. Guernsey's mild climate has encouraged the development of tourism and market gardening as major industries. Tomatoes and flowers are produced mainly for the UK market. The low tax system, independent of the UK, has led to a substantial and profitable financial services industry. Many international banks have Guernsey subsidiaries.

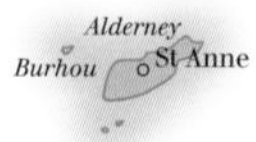
Alderney
Burhou
St Anne

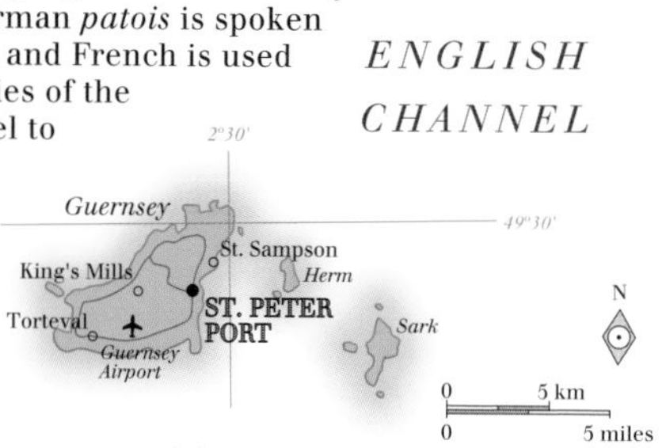
ENGLISH CHANNEL
2°30'
49°30'
Guernsey
King's Mills
St. Sampson
Herm
ST. PETER PORT
Torteval
Guernsey Airport
Sark
0 5 km
0 5 miles

Tomato packaging. *Tomatoes and flowers ripening early in Guernsey's mild climate, are despatched to mainland Britain.*

GUAM

STATUS: Unincorporated territory of the USA **CLAIMED:** 1898
CAPITAL: Hågatña **POP.:** 154,805 **DENSITY:** 282/km² (730/mi²)

THE VOLCANIC island of Guam lies at the southern end of the Mariana Archipelago in the Pacific. Its tropical climate has encouraged tourism, although it lies in a region where typhoons are common. Guam's indigenous Chamorro people, who comprise just under half the population, dominate the island's political and social life. They are famous for a set of facial expressions, called "eyebrow," which virtually constitutes a language of its own. Although English is the official language, Chamorro is commonly spoken, and in 1998 the spelling of the capital was changed from Agaña to the Chamorran Hågatña. The US military base, covering one-third of the island, has made Guam strategically important to the USA. Military spending and tourism revenues have given islanders a high living standard. The influx of US culture has, however, threatened to upset Guam's social stability. Greater independence has been an issue since the early 1980s, with a series of referenda since 1982. In 2001 a draft Commonwealth Act was still awaiting a full hearing in the US Congress.

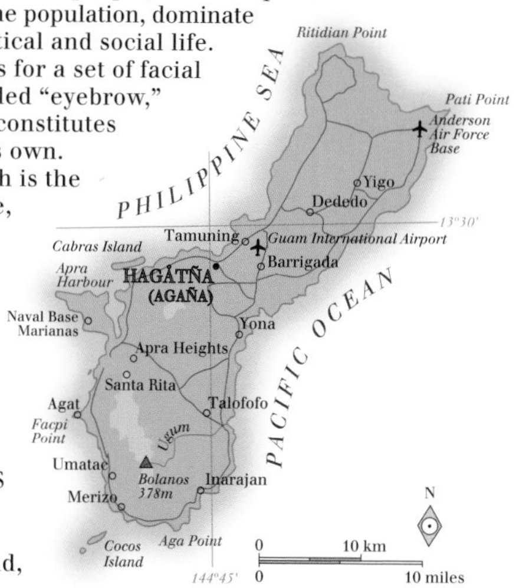
Ritidian Point
PHILIPPINE SEA
Pati Point
Anderson Air Force Base
Yigo
Dededo
13°30'
Tamuning
Guam International Airport
Cabras Island
Apra Harbour
HAGÅTÑA (AGAÑA)
Barrigada
Naval Base Marianas
Yona
PACIFIC OCEAN
Apra Heights
Santa Rita
Agat
Talofofo
Facpi Point
Ugum
Umatac
Bolanos 378m
Inarajan
Merizo
Cocos Island
Aga Point
144°45'
0 10 km
0 10 miles

ISLE OF MAN

STATUS: British Crown dependency **CLAIMED:** 1765
CAPITAL: Douglas **POP.:** 71,714 **DENSITY:** 125/km² (324/mi²)

LYING HALFWAY BETWEEN England and Northern Ireland in the Irish Sea, the Isle of Man has been inhabited for centuries by the Celtic Manx people. Established by the Vikings in the ninth century, the Manx parliament, the Tynwold, has autonomy from the UK in a number of matters, including taxation, and the death penalty was only officially abolished in 1993. The islanders have used this independence to establish a thriving financial and business sector, which has aided employment as the traditional industries of agriculture and fishing decline. There is still a shellfishing industry, specializing in scallops. Tourism is also important; there are more than 200,000 visitors each year. The Manx culture received a boost in 1993, when the local language, which was in danger of dying out, once more began to be taught in the island's schools. The Calf of Man, which is a small uninhabited island, is administered as a nature reserve.

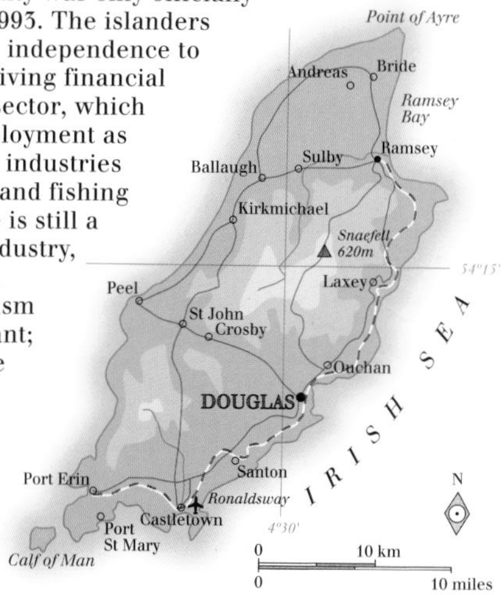
Point of Ayre
Andreas
Bride
Ramsey Bay
Ballaugh
Sulby
Ramsey
Kirkmichael
Snaefell 620m
54°15'
Peel
Laxey
St John
Crosby
IRISH SEA
Onchan
DOUGLAS
Port Erin
Santon
Ronaldsway
Castletown
Port St Mary
Calf of Man
4°30'
0 10 km
0 10 miles

The annual TT motorbike race *on the Isle of Man. Thousands of people come each year to watch the island's famous Touring Trophy race. It is run on a 61-km circuit of the island.*

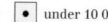

Jersey

Status: British Crown dependency **Claimed:** 1066
Capital: St. Helier **Pop.:** 85,150 **Density:** 734/km² (1892/mi²)

THE BAILIWICK OF JERSEY, the largest of the Channel Islands, lies some 22 km (14 miles) from the coast of Normandy in France. The official language (since 1960) is English, but French is still used in the courts. The island has a mild climate owing to the Gulf Stream, fine beaches, and more sunshine than anywhere in the British Isles. Jersey has its own legislative and taxation systems which are a blend of the French and British versions. The Jersey States Assembly is one of the oldest legislative bodies in the world. Members stand as independents, rather than for political parties. It is considered a "Peculiar" of the UK monarchy, and has the right to reject "unacceptable" UK laws.

Historically, agriculture has been Jersey's most important industry, with dairy cows its most famous export, closely followed by early-harvested potatoes, tomatoes, and flowers. By the end of the twentieth century, however, farming had been eclipsed by the rise of offshore finance and tourism. The growth of these sectors, and rigid controls on the rights of residence, have ensured high living standards for most of the inhabitants. Jersey is also host to a large Portuguese community which works in the island's tourist industry.

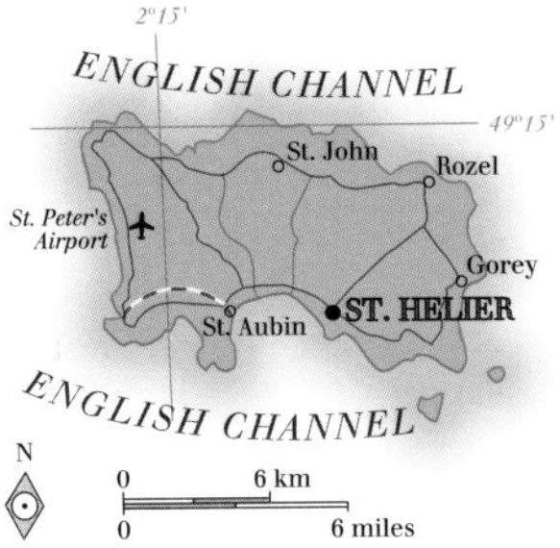
2°15'
ENGLISH CHANNEL
49°15'
St. John
Rozel
St. Peter's Airport
Gorey
St. Aubin
ST. HELIER
ENGLISH CHANNEL
N
0 6 km
0 6 miles

Johnston Atoll

Status: Unincorporated territory of the USA **Claimed:** 1858
Capital: *Not applicable* **Pop.:** 173 **Density:** 67/km² (173/mi²)

JOHNSTON ATOLL LIES 1150 km (714 miles) southwest of Hawaii. The atoll consists of a coral reef, two highly modified natural islands, Johnston and Sand, and two completely man-made islands, Akau (North) and Hikina (East). The islands, which were used by the USA for nuclear weapons tests, were seriously contaminated with plutonium in 1962, when a nuclear missile exploded during testing. Regular tests began in 1971, and until 2000 the islands were also used for the storage of nuclear material and the destruction of chemical and biological weapons, including sarin nerve gas and the defoliant Agent Orange. Cleanup operations began in 2000. The only inhabitants left are US government personnel and civilian contractors who maintain the plant. The islands have also been designated by the USA as a wildlife refuge, a breeding place for seabirds and green turtles. The US army intends to evacuate the base entirely by 2003.

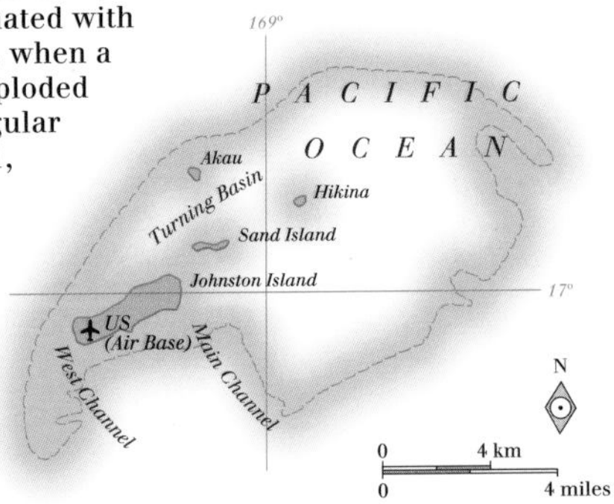
169°
PACIFIC
OCEAN
Akau
Turning Basin
Hikina
Sand Island
Johnston Island
17°
US (Air Base)
West Channel
Main Channel
N
0 4 km
0 4 miles

Martinique

Status: French overseas department **Claimed:** 1635
Capital: Fort-de-France **Pop.:** 381,427 **Density:** 338/km² (875/mi²)

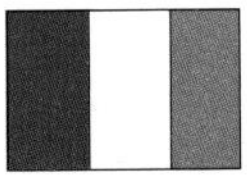

CHRISTOPHER COLUMBUS described Martinique as "the most beautiful country in the world." It lies in the eastern Caribbean and is dominated by the now dormant volcano Montagne Pelée, whose eruption in 1902 engulfed the old capital, St. Pierre. The island is also situated in the Caribbean's hurricane belt, and suffers an average of one natural disaster every five years. Nearly 90% of the population are of African or mixed ethnicity. However, economic power remains in the hands of the *Bekes* (descendants of white colonial settlers), who own most of the agricultural land, and the bureaucracy is largely staffed by expatriates. This situation has led to outbreaks of violence and increased popular demands for more autonomy. However, the islanders are aware that their good living standards, despite high unemployment rates, depend on French subsidies, which support a French-style social welfare system.

The economy traditionally relied on agriculture, particularly sugar cane and bananas, but tourism has become the biggest source of income, and the largest provider of employment, as EU subsidy reductions have forced the island to diversify its economy. Martinique has been successful in appealing to the upper end of the tourist market. Almost 80% of the half-million annual visitors come from France. Despite lower productivity, wage levels have officially been linked to those in metropolitan France; despite this, protests over low salaries in 1998 led to nearly 400 people at a holiday village being held hostage by staff. Emigration and nemployment have been high since the late 1980s, with the result that over 30% of Martiniquais nationals are resident in metropolitan France.

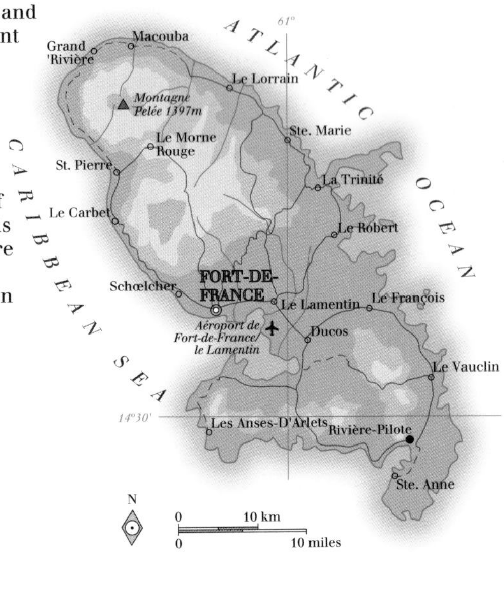
61°
ATLANTIC OCEAN
CARIBBEAN SEA
Grand 'Rivière
Macouba
Le Lorrain
Montagne Pelée 1397m
Ste. Marie
Le Morne Rouge
St. Pierre
La Trinité
Le Carbet
Le Robert
Schœlcher
FORT-DE-FRANCE
Le Lamentin
Le François
Aéroport de Fort-de-France/ le Lamentin
Ducos
Le Vauclin
14°30'
Les Anses-D'Arlets
Rivière-Pilote
Ste. Anne
N
0 10 km
0 10 miles

***Martinique.** Tourists are attracted to the island's beaches, its mountainous interior, and the historic towns of Fort-de-France and Saint Pierre.*

LAND HEIGHT: above Sea Level | 200m/656ft | 500m/1640ft | 1000m/3281ft | 1500m/4572ft | above 2000m/6562ft

MAYOTTE

STATUS: French territorial collectivity **CLAIMED:** 1843
CAPITAL: Mamoudzou **POP.:** 142,000 **DENSITY:** 380/km² (986/mi²)

PART OF THE COMOROS archipelago, Mayotte lies about 8000 km (5000 miles) from France between Madagascar and the east African coast. It was the only island in the archipelago to vote against independence from France in a 1974 referendum. The other islands declared unilateral independence in 1975 and laid claim to Mayotte. Despite widespread poverty, endemic unemployment, and a cost of living twice that of France, the Mahorais voted again in 1976 to maintain the link. The main political movement has since unsuccessfully demanded that Mayotte be given the status of a French *département*, hoping that this would bring more aid to develop their largely agricultural economy. France opposes this idea because of the expense involved, but did grant the island *département*-style autonomy in July 2000.

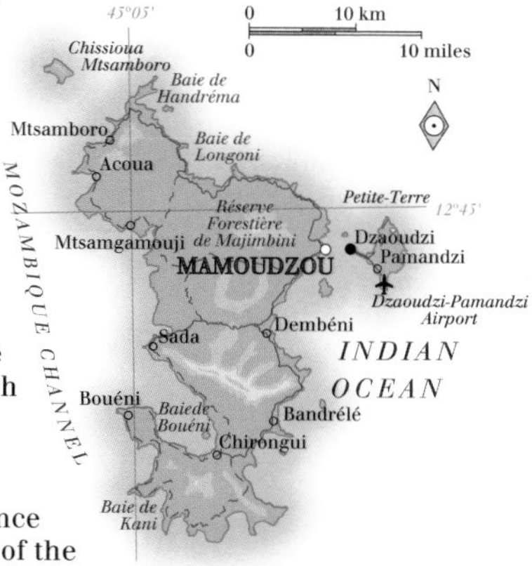
45°05'
0 10 km
0 10 miles
N
Chissioua Mtsamboro
Baie de Handréma
Mtsamboro
Baie de Longoni
Acoua
MOZAMBIQUE CHANNEL
Petite-Terre
12°45'
Réserve Forestière de Majimbini
Dzaoudzi
Mtsamgamouji
Pamandzi
MAMOUDZOU
Dzaoudzi-Pamandzi Airport
Sada
Dembéni
INDIAN OCEAN
Bouéni
Baie de Bouéni
Bandrélé
Chirongui
Baie de Kani

The economy is still largely agricultural, producing crops both for internal consumption and for export. However, large quantities of foodstuffs are also imported. France has invested in an airport and port, but the tourism industry has been slow to develop. Nevertheless, the relative prosperity of Mayotte has encouraged separatist movements on the two other small Comoros islands to seek closer relations with France.

MIDWAY ISLANDS

STATUS: Unincorporated territory of the USA **CLAIMED:** 1867
CAPITAL: *Not applicable* **POP.:** 453 **DENSITY:** 91/km² (235/mi²)

NAMED BECAUSE of its position between California and Japan, Midway is a coral atoll at the western end of the Hawaiian islands; there have been moves to make it part of Hawaii. The site of a major World War II battle, the atoll comprises two large islands, totaling over 4 sq km (1.5 sq miles), and several smaller ones. It functions as a naval air base and wildlife refuge. The population is limited to military personnel and civilian contractors, but some tourism is permitted, mainly connected with the wildlife.

MONTSERRAT

STATUS: British dependent territory **CLAIMED:** 1632
CAPITAL: Plymouth **POP.:** 5000 **DENSITY:** 49/km² (128/mi²)

MONTSERRAT IS ONE of the Leeward Islands chain in the eastern Caribbean. It was devastated by volcanic eruptions which began in 1995 and culminated in massive explosions of the Soufrière Hills volcano in 1997 and 1998. As a result, the southern two-thirds of the island, where Plymouth and Blackburne airport are located, have become uninhabitable and it is illegal to enter the volcano "exclusion zone." Over half of the 10,000 population left permanently for neighboring islands or the UK. Calls for independence, based on a tourist boom in the 1980s, have been largely dropped, as the island is now dependent on UK aid. However, the disaster soured relations, setting off a bitter dispute over the cost of resettlement and reconstruction. A new capital, tentatively named Port Diana, is planned for the "safe" northern coast. The tourism industry is struggling to rebuild itself, but is hindered by the closure of both the airport and seaport by the eruption. Montserrat can now only be reached via neighboring Antigua.

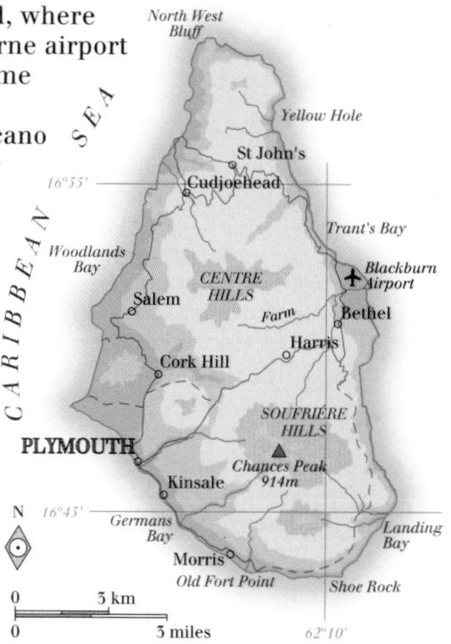
North West Bluff
Yellow Hole
St John's
Cudjoehead
16°55'
CARIBBEAN SEA
Trant's Bay
Woodlands Bay
Blackburn Airport
CENTRE HILLS
Salem
Farm
Bethel
Harris
Cork Hill
SOUFRIÈRE HILLS
PLYMOUTH
Chances Peak 914m
Kinsale
N
16°45'
Germans Bay
Landing Bay
Morris
Old Fort Point
Shoe Rock
0 3 km
0 3 miles
62°10'

Montserrat. *Known as the Caribbean's "emerald isle" because of its luxuriant flora and Irish heritage.*

NETHERLANDS ANTILLES

STATUS: Autonomous part of the Netherlands **CLAIMED:** 1816
CAPITAL: Willemstad **POP.:** 207,175 **DENSITY:** 259/km² (670/mi²)

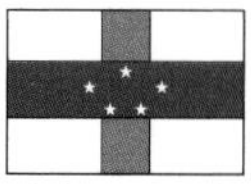

THE NETHERLANDS Antilles are composed of two Caribbean island groups. Curaçao – the richest and wealthiest island – and Bonaire lie just off the Venezuelan coast, while Saba, St. Eustatius, and Sint Maarten – whose northern half is part of Guadeloupe – lie 800 km (500 miles) to the north. Financial scandals, political instability, and the issue of the federation's future, among other things, have strained relations with the Dutch government, the major aid provider. Refining petroleum using oil from Venezuela is the islands' principal industrial activity.

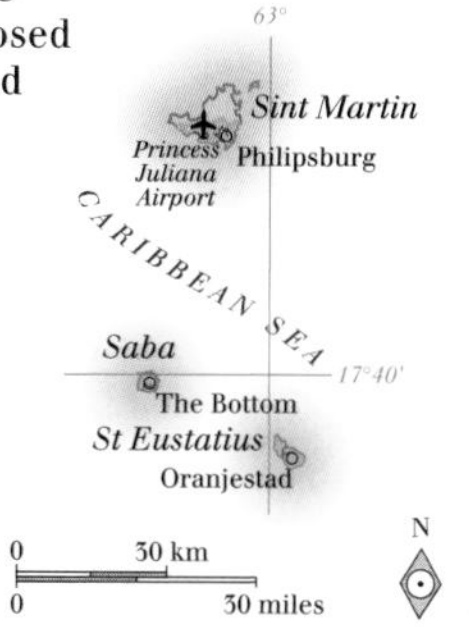
63°
Sint Martin
Princess Juliana Airport
Philipsburg
CARIBBEAN SEA
Saba
17°40'
The Bottom
St Eustatius
Oranjestad
0 30 km
0 30 miles
N

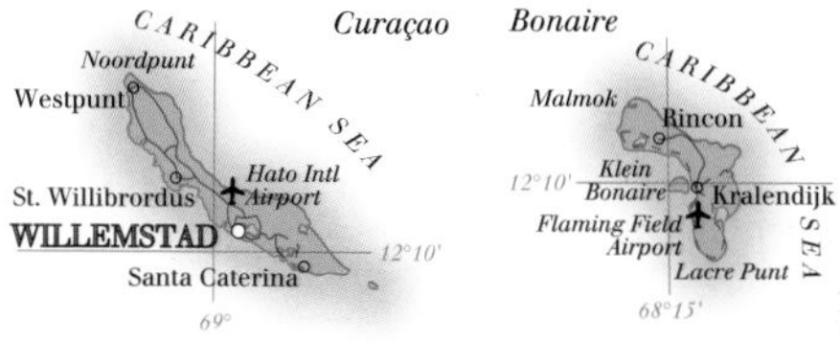
Curaçao
Bonaire
CARIBBEAN SEA
Noordpunt
Westpunt
St. Willibrordus
Hato Intl Airport
WILLEMSTAD
Santa Caterina
12°10'
69°
Malmok
Rincon
Klein Bonaire
Kralendijk
Flaming Field Airport
Lacre Punt
68°15'

POPULATION ○ under 5000 • under 10 000 ● over 10 000 ○ over 50 000 ◎ over 100 000 ☐ Urban areas AIRPORTS ✈ International ✈ Local

New Caledonia

Status: French overseas territory **Claimed:** 1853
Capital: Nouméa **Pop.:** 209,222 **Density:** 11/km² (28/mi²)

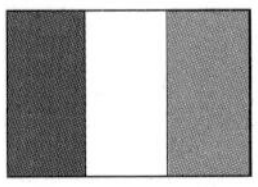

NEW CALEDONIA, or as the indigenous Kanaks call it, Kanaky, is an island group 1350 km (840 miles) off the northeast coast of Australia. Tension over socioeconomic inequalities and independence between the Melanesian Kanaks, who form over half of the population, and the Caldoches, the pro-French expatriate population who are a large and influential minority, have resulted in a long history of political violence. Under the 1988 Matignon Accord, France imposed a year of direct rule as the prelude to a new constitutional structure which attempted to address Kanak grievances by providing greater provincial autonomy. The Nouméa accord, signed in April 1998, set out a 15-year program of gradual autonomy ending in an eventual vote on self-determination. Although some racial violence continued after 1988, it has not again reached the same level.

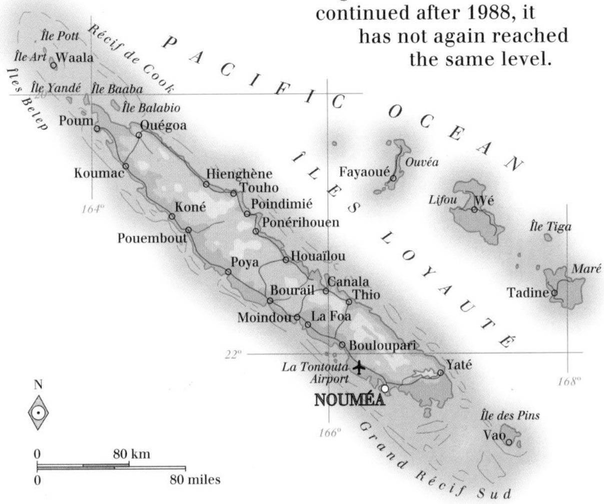
PACIFIC OCEAN
Île Pott
Île Art
Waala
Récif de Cook
Îles Belep
Île Yandé
Île Baaba
Île Balabio
Poum
Ouégoa
Koumac
Hienghène
Touho
Poindimié
Ponérihouen
Koné
Pouembout
Houaïlou
Poya
Bourail
Canala
Thio
Moindou
La Foa
Boulouparì
La Tontouta Airport
Yaté
NOUMÉA
Fayaoué
Ouvéa
Lifou
Wé
Île Tiga
Maré
Tadine
ÎLES LOYAUTÉ
Île des Pins
Vao
Grand Récif Sud
164°
166°
168°
22°
N
0 80 km
0 80 miles

Nickel mining is the territory's most valuable export industry, at over 90% of export income. New Caledonia has 30% of world reserves, and is the largest producer in the world, but the industry employs relatively few people, and is vulnerable to fluctuations in the world price. It was seriously affected by the Asian financial crisis of 1997–1998, when 300 jobs were lost. Tourism and agriculture are bigger employers, although less than 1% of total land area is cultivated. Corn, yams, sweet potatoes, and coconuts have traditionally been the main crops, and since the 1990s large numbers of melons have been exported to Japan. Fishing is important, the main products being tuna and shrimps, most of which are also exported to Japan. A project for the production of giant clams started in 1996. Unemployment nevertheless remains high among young Kanaks.

A nickel mine, *New Caledonia. The importance of the nickel industry to the territory's economy has made the control of reserves a dominant issue in politics, and in negotiations over the island's independence from France.*

Niue

Status: Territory in free association with New Zealand **Claimed:** 1901
Capital: Alofi **Pop.:** 1857 **Density:** 7/km² (18/mi²)

THE WORLD'S LARGEST coral island, Niue lies 2400 km (1500 miles) northeast of New Zealand. The subsistence economy produces tropical fruits, while tourism and the sale of postage stamps provide foreign currency. Despite the island's paradise image, nearly 10,000 Niueans, frustrated by the lack of job prospects, live in New Zealand. In the hope of stopping further emigration, New Zealand has invested heavily in the economy. However, cyclone damage and the inefficient use of aid have held back growth.

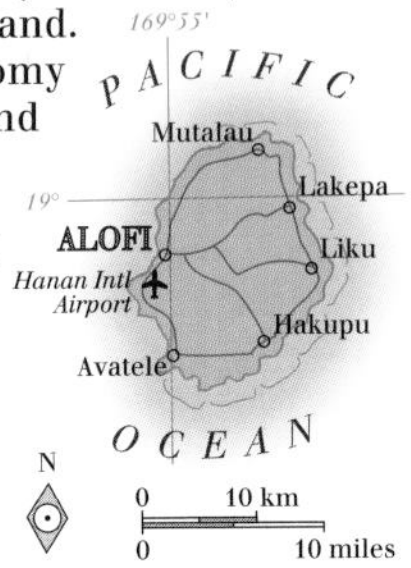
169°55'
PACIFIC OCEAN
Mutalau
Lakepa
Liku
ALOFI
Hanan Intl Airport
Hakupu
Avatele
19°
N
0 10 km
0 10 miles

Norfolk Island

Status: Australian external territory **Claimed:** 1774
Capital: Kingston **Pop.:** 2181 **Density:** 62/km² (168/mi²)

INHABITED by Australian migrants and descendants of the mutineers of HMS *Bounty*, Norfolk Island lies 1400 km (869 miles) east of Australia. Islanders speak a hybrid language, mixing Westcountry English, Gaelic, and ancient Tahitian. They enjoy substantial autonomy, and in 1991 rejected a plan to become part of the Australian federal state. Tourists, attracted by the climate and unique flora, have brought islanders a relatively high standard of living.

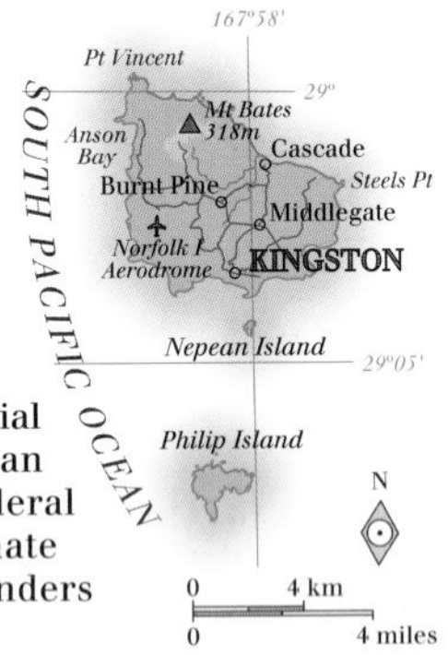
167°58'
Pt Vincent
29°
Mt Bates 318m
Anson Bay
Cascade
Steels Pt
Burnt Pine
Middlegate
Norfolk I Aerodrome
KINGSTON
SOUTH PACIFIC OCEAN
Nepean Island
29°05'
Philip Island
N
0 4 km
0 4 miles

Northern Mariana Is.

Status: Commonwealth territory of the USA **Claimed:** 1947
Capital: Saipan **Pop.:** 69,221 **Density:** 151/km² (393/mi²)

A FORMER UN trust territory, the Northern Marianas preferred in 1987 to retain links with the USA rather than opt for independence. However, local politicians have questioned their current status. US aid fueled a boom during the 1980s, but it depended on immigrant workers who by the early 1990s outnumbered the local Chamorro population. In addition, tourism has speeded the decline of the traditional subsistence economy.

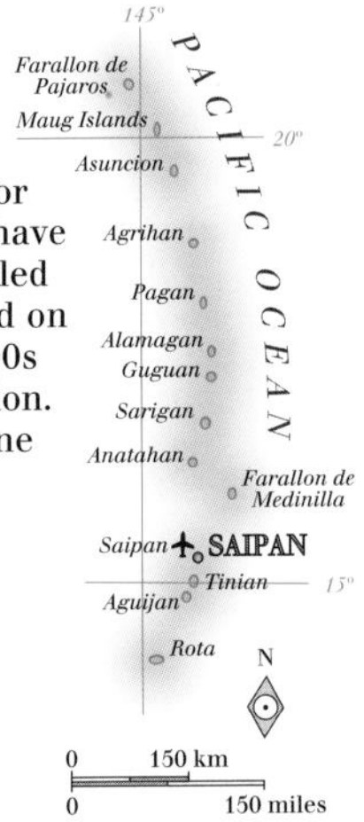
145°
PACIFIC OCEAN
Farallon de Pajaros
Maug Islands
20°
Asuncion
Agrihan
Pagan
Alamagan
Guguan
Sarigan
Anatahan
Farallon de Medinilla
Saipan
SAIPAN
Tinian
15°
Aguijan
Rota
N
0 150 km
0 150 miles

Rota, Northern Marianas. *The limestone outcrop of Wedding Cake Mountain overlooks the small village of Songsong.*

LAND HEIGHT: above Sea Level | 200m/656ft | 500m/1640ft | 1000m/3281ft | 1500m/4572ft | above 2000m/6562ft

PARACEL ISLANDS

STATUS: *Disputed* **CLAIMED:** *Not applicable*
CAPITAL: Woody Island **POPULATION:** *Unknown*

OCCUPIED BY CHINESE FORCES (who call them the Xisha islands), but also claimed by Taiwan and Vietnam, the Paracel Islands are a small collection of coral atolls situated some 325 km (200 miles) east of Vietnam, in the South China Sea. Subject to frequent typhoons and with a tropical climate, the Paracels are at the center of a regional dispute over the vast reserves of oil and natural gas which are believed to lie beneath their territorial waters. China has built port facilities and an airport on Woody Island to support its claim.

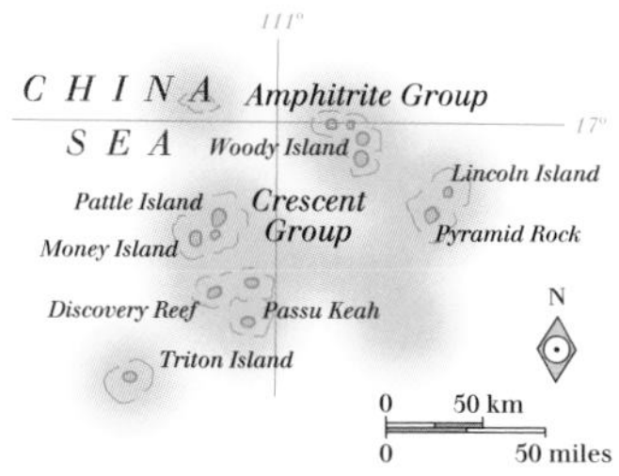
C H I N A
S E A
Amphitrite Group
Woody Island
Lincoln Island
Pattle Island
Crescent Group
Pyramid Rock
Money Island
Discovery Reef
Passu Keah
Triton Island
N
0 50 km
0 50 miles

PITCAIRN ISLANDS

STATUS: British dependent territory **CLAIMED:** 1887
CAPITAL: Adamstown **POP.:** 44 **DENSITY:** 1.2/km² (3/mi²)

A GROUP OF VOLCANIC South Pacific islands, Pitcairn is Britain's most isolated dependency. Pitcairn Island was the last refuge for the mutineers from HMS *Bounty*. Emigration has greatly reduced the number of Pitcairners, who depend on regular airdrops from New Zealand and periodic visits by supply vessels. The economy operates by barter, fishing, and subsistence farming. Postage stamp sales provide foreign currency earnings.

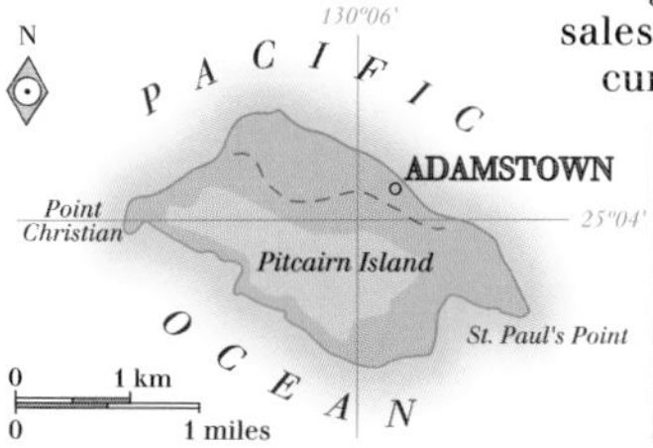
N
P A C I F I C
O C E A N
ADAMSTOWN
Point Christian
Pitcairn Island
St. Paul's Point
0 1 km
0 1 miles

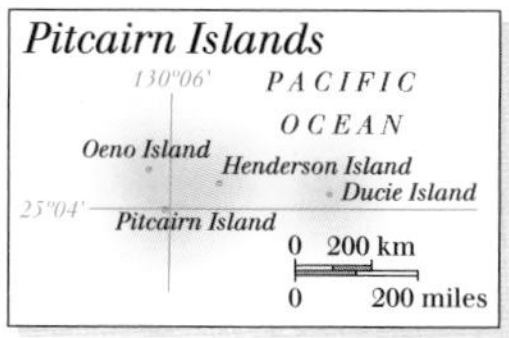
Pitcairn Islands
P A C I F I C
O C E A N
Oeno Island
Henderson Island
Ducie Island
Pitcairn Island
0 200 km
0 200 miles

PUERTO RICO

STATUS: Commonwealth territory of the USA **CLAIMED:** 1898
CAPITAL: San Juan **POP.:** 3.8 million **DENSITY:** 425/km² (1101/mi²)

PUERTO RICO, a US territory since its invasion in 1898, is by far the most populous non-independent territory. It is the easternmost of the Greater Antilles chain in the Caribbean. The population density, highest around San Juan, is comparable with the Netherlands and is higher than in any US state. The tropical climate attracts growing numbers of tourists, 80% from the USA, and there have been major efforts to expand hotel and resort facilities.

Puerto Rico was granted its current commonwealth status in 1952, four years after an abortive pro-independence uprising. The inhabitants have US citizenship but only limited self-government. In three plebiscites, in 1967, 1993, and 1998, the islanders endorsed continued commonwealth status rather than opting for either US statehood or independence. The most recent of these votes was extremely close, but the pro-statehood governor who called the 1993 and 1998 votes, Pedro Rossello, was replaced by the anti-statehood Sila Calderón – the first female governor of Puerto Rico – in 2001.

Although thousands of the mostly Spanish-speaking Puerto Ricans have migrated to the US mainland in search of higher wages, the islanders have one of the highest living standards in the region. Tax relief, cheap labor, and the island's role as an export-processing zone, mainly for the US market, attracted many businesses. Clothing, electronics, petrochemical, and pharmaceutical industries traditionally dominated, but the decision to phase out tax exemptions for companies reinvesting in the island caused a slump in 1996, and more emphasis is now being placed on the service sector. New industries include health care and clinical testing, biotechnology, and other knowledge-based areas.

Governor Calderón spearheaded the campaign to stop the US navy from using the populated eastern island of Vieques for bombing practice. In 2000 an invasion of the bombing range by protestors led to some high-profile arrests, including that of Robert Kennedy Jr. A year later newly elected US president George W. Bush announced that the navy would not use the island after 2003.

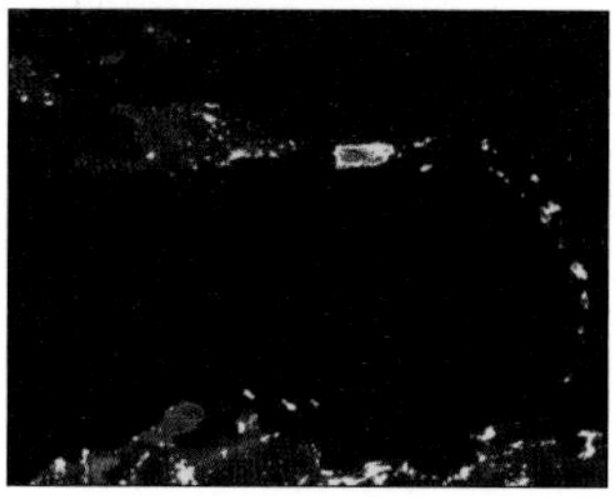

At night, the bright lights of Puerto Rico's well developed roads, settlements and busy ports are in sharp contrast to the rest of the Caribbean – notably the dark outline of Haiti, just to the west.

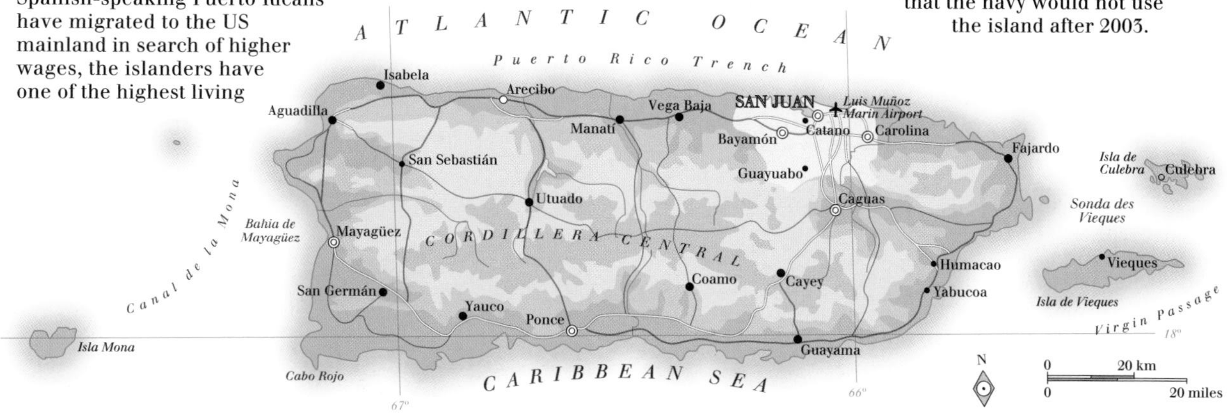
A T L A N T I C O C E A N
Puerto Rico Trench
Isabela
Arecibo
Aguadilla
Vega Baja
SAN JUAN
Luis Muñoz Marín Airport
Manatí
Bayamón
Cataño
Carolina
San Sebastián
Guayuabo
Fajardo
Isla de Culebra
Culebra
Utuado
Caguas
Sonda des Vieques
Bahía de Mayagüez
Mayagüez
C O R D I L L E R A C E N T R A L
Canal de la Mona
Humacao
Vieques
Coamo
Cayey
San Germán
Yabucoa
Isla de Vieques
Yauco
Virgin Passage
Ponce
Isla Mona
Guayama
Cabo Rojo
C A R I B B E A N S E A
N
0 20 km
0 20 miles

POPULATION ○ under 5000 • under 10 000 ● over 10 000 ○ over 50 000 ◎ over 100 000 ▢ Urban areas AIRPORTS ✈ International ✈ Local

Réunion

Status: French overseas department **Claimed:** 1638
Capital: Saint-Denis **Pop.:** 706,300 **Density:** 281/km² (728/mi²)

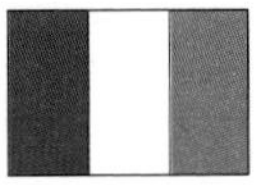

THE LARGE VOLCANIC ISLAND of Réunion, 800 km (500 miles) east of Madagascar, provides France with an important strategic presence – and a large military base – in the Indian Ocean. Its mountainous interior has forced the majority of the population to live along the coast. Socioeconomic differences between the poorer black community and the wealthier Indian and European groups have increased ethnic tensions, which were the cause of severe rioting in 1991. The French government responded with a series of measures, applicable to all overseas *départements*, to improve economic and social conditions to the level of those of France itself. Réunion's main crop is sugarcane.

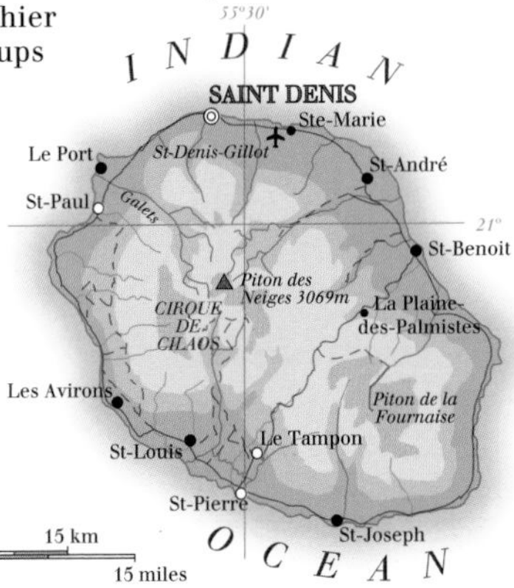
INDIAN OCEAN
SAINT DENIS
Ste-Marie
St-Denis-Gillot
Le Port
St-André
St-Paul
Galets
St-Benoit
Piton des Neiges 3069m
CIRQUE DE CHAOS
La Plaine-des-Palmistes
Les Avirons
Piton de la Fournaise
Le Tampon
St-Louis
St-Pierre
St-Joseph
0 15 km
0 15 miles

St. Pierre & Miquelon

Status: French territorial collectivity **Claimed:** 1604
Capital: St. Pierre **Pop.:** 6316 **Density:** 26/km² (68/mi²)

ST. PIERRE & Miquelon is a group of barren islands lying just off the south coast of Newfoundland, Canada. The islands are surrounded by some of the world's richest fishing grounds. Their inhabitants have traditionally earned a living from fishing, and from servicing foreign trawler fleets off the coast. A long-running and sometimes bitter dispute between Canada and France over fishing and mineral rights was settled in 1992. The ruling, which was generally deemed to be in Canada's favor, has led the French authorities to diversify the economy by developing port facilities and encouraging tourism.

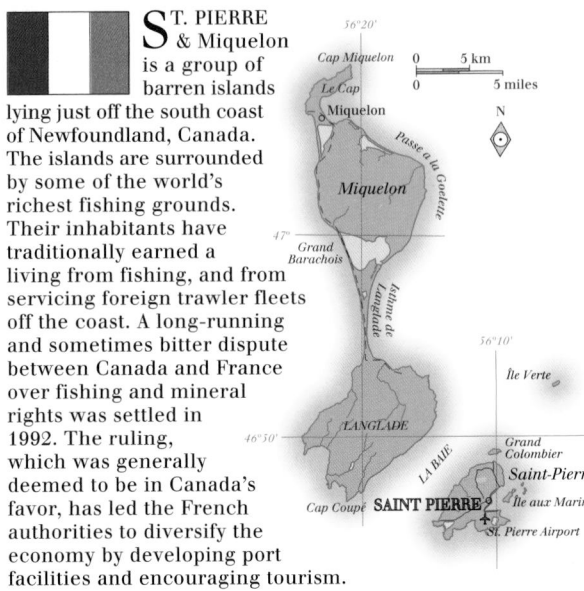

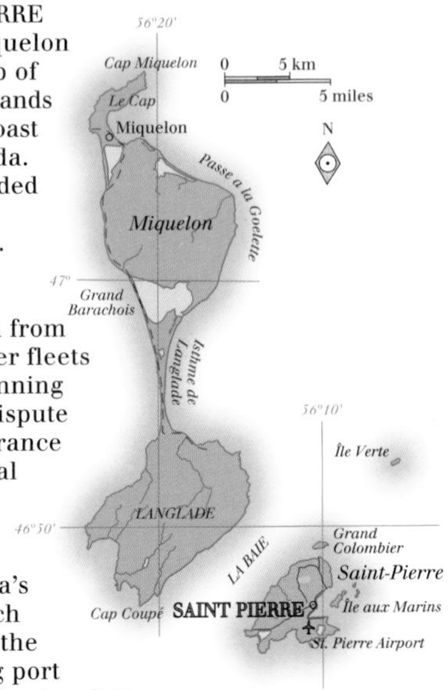
Cap Miquelon
Le Cap
Miquelon
Passe a la Goelette
Miquelon
Grand Barachois
Isthme de Langlade
Île Verte
LANGLADE
LA BAIE
Grand Colombier
Saint-Pierre
Île aux Marins
Cap Coupé
SAINT PIERRE
St. Pierre Airport
0 5 km
0 5 miles

St. Helena & Dependencies

Status: British dependent territory **Claimed:** 1673
Capital: Jamestown **Pop.:** 6472 **Density:** 53/km² (138/mi²)

TOGETHER, the islands of St. Helena, Tristan da Cunha, and Ascension form Britain's main dependency in the south Atlantic. St. Helena is famed for being the final place of exile for Napoleon. Its main economic activities – fishing, livestock farming, and the sale of handicrafts – are unable to support the population; as a result, underemployment on the island is a major problem. Many St. Helenians have been forced to seek work on Ascension Island, which has no resident population and is operated as a military base and communications center, although civilian flights have been permitted since 1998. Tristan da Cunha, a volcanic island 2000 km (1240 miles) south of St. Helena, is inhabited by a small, closely knit farming community. It was badly hit by severe winter storms in 2001. The removal in 1981 of the islanders' right to residence in the UK provoked calls for a renegotiation of their constitutional status.

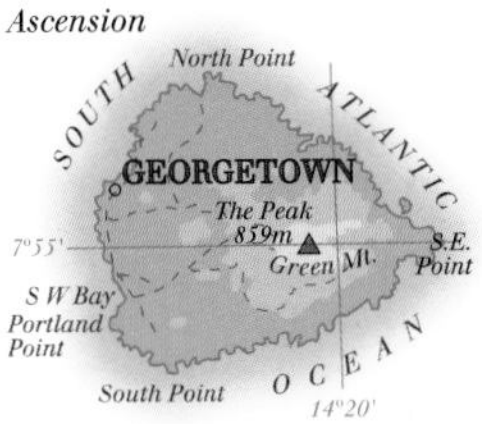
Ascension
North Point
SOUTH ATLANTIC OCEAN
GEORGETOWN
The Peak 859m
Green Mt.
S.E. Point
S W Bay
Portland Point
South Point

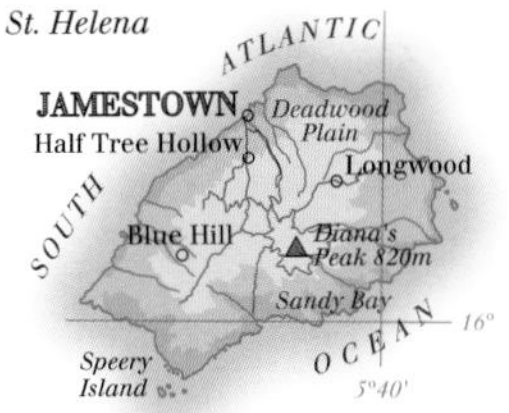
St. Helena
SOUTH ATLANTIC OCEAN
JAMESTOWN
Deadwood Plain
Half Tree Hollow
Longwood
Blue Hill
Diana's Peak 820m
Sandy Bay
Speery Island

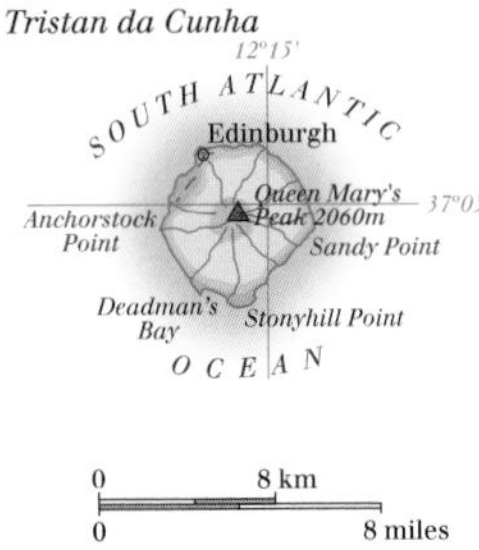
Tristan da Cunha
SOUTH ATLANTIC OCEAN
Edinburgh
Queen Mary's Peak 2060m
Anchorstock Point
Sandy Point
Deadman's Bay
Stonyhill Point
0 8 km
0 8 miles

Spratly Islands

Status: *Disputed* **Claimed:** *Not applicable*
Capital: *Not applicable* **Population:** *Unknown*

SCATTERED ACROSS a large area of the South China Sea, the reefs, islands, and atolls that make up the Spratly Islands have become one of South Asia's most serious security issues. Claimed, all or in part, by China, Taiwan, Vietnam, Brunei, Malaysia, and the Philippines, more than 40 of the larger islands now have garrisons from some of the claimant states. The reasons for this interest, and the occasional skirmish, are twofold. Strategically, the islands control some of the world's most important shipping lanes. In addition, surveys suggest that some of the largest oil and gas reserves yet found lie in the Spratlys' territorial waters.

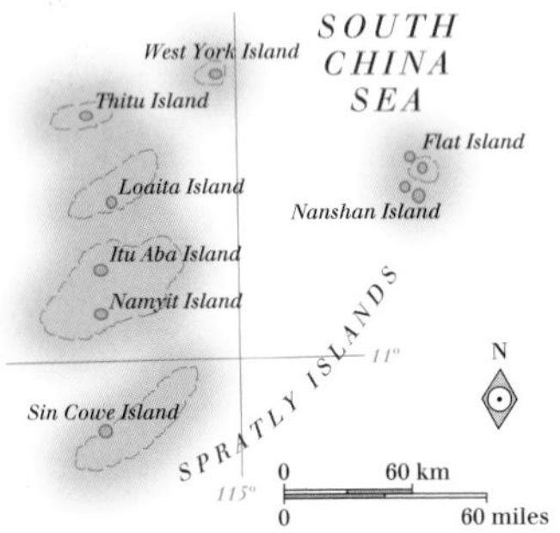
SOUTH CHINA SEA
West York Island
Thitu Island
Flat Island
Loaita Island
Nanshan Island
Itu Aba Island
Namyit Island
Sin Cowe Island
SPRATLY ISLANDS
0 60 km
0 60 miles

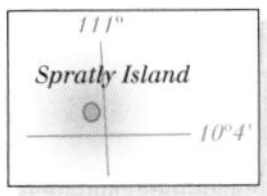
Spratly Island

The isolated Chinese occupying force on one of the Spratly Islands.

LAND HEIGHT: above Sea Level; 200m/656ft; 500m/1640ft; 1000m/3281ft; 1500m/4572ft; above 2000m/6562ft

SVALBARD

STATUS: Norwegian dependency **CLAIMED:** 1920
CAPITAL: Longyearbyen **POP.:** 2591 **DENSITY:** 0.04/km² (0.1/mi²)

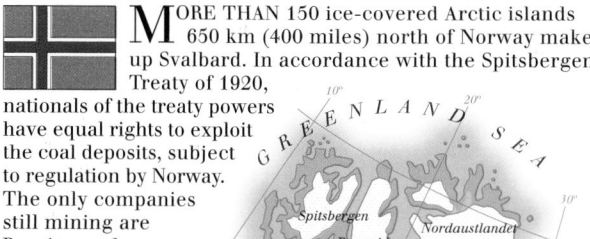

MORE THAN 150 ice-covered Arctic islands 650 km (400 miles) north of Norway make up Svalbard. In accordance with the Spitsbergen Treaty of 1920, nationals of the treaty powers have equal rights to exploit the coal deposits, subject to regulation by Norway. The only companies still mining are Russian and Norwegian. There has been conflict with Iceland over fishing rights. Over half of the area of the islands is designated as environmentally protected.

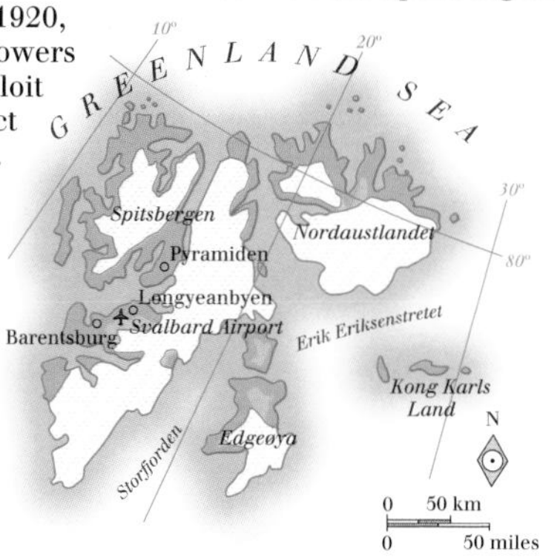
GREENLAND SEA
Spitsbergen
Pyramiden
Nordaustlandet
Longyearbyen
Svalbard Airport
Barentsburg
Erik Eriksenstretet
Kong Karls Land
Edgeøya
Storfjorden
10°
20°
30°
80°
N
0 50 km
0 50 miles

TOKELAU

STATUS: New Zealand dependent territory **CLAIMED:** 1926
CAPITAL: *Not applicable* **POP.:** 1487 **DENSITY:** 149/km² (372/mi²)

A 1989 UN REPORT states that in the 21st century this island in the South Pacific will disappear under the sea, unless action is taken to stop global warming. The economy depends on a tuna cannery and the sale of fishing licenses, postage stamps, and coins; a catamaran link between the atolls has increased tourist potential. Its small size and economic fragility make independence unlikely, but in May 1996 it gained the right to enact its own internal legislation, and since July 2001 the local authorities have had full control of the island's public services. Nearly 3000 Tokelauans live in New Zealand.

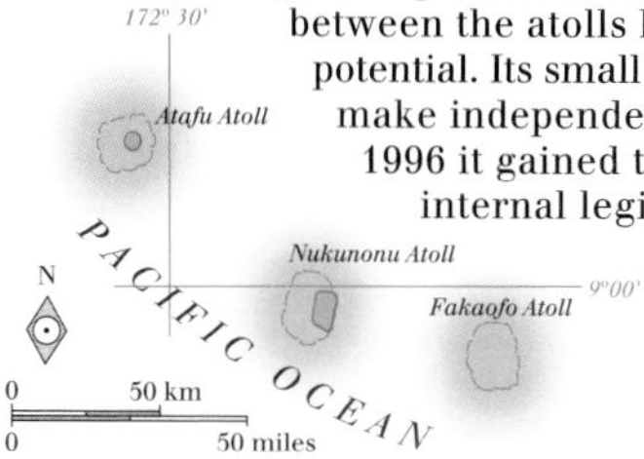
172° 30'
Atafu Atoll
Nukunonu Atoll
Fakaofo Atoll
9°00'
PACIFIC OCEAN
N
0 50 km
0 50 miles

TURKS & CAICOS ISLANDS

STATUS: British dependent territory **CLAIMED:** 1766
CAPITAL: Cockburn Town **POP.:** 16,863 **DENSITY:** 39/km² (102/mi²)

SITUATED 40 km (25 miles) south of the Bahamas, the Turks and Caicos Islands is a group of 30 low-lying islands, eight of which are inhabited. A traditional salt-based economy was exhausted in 1964, leading to two decades of stagnation. Since the 1980s, however, tourism and offshore banking, have led a dramatic turnaround in the islands' fortunes.

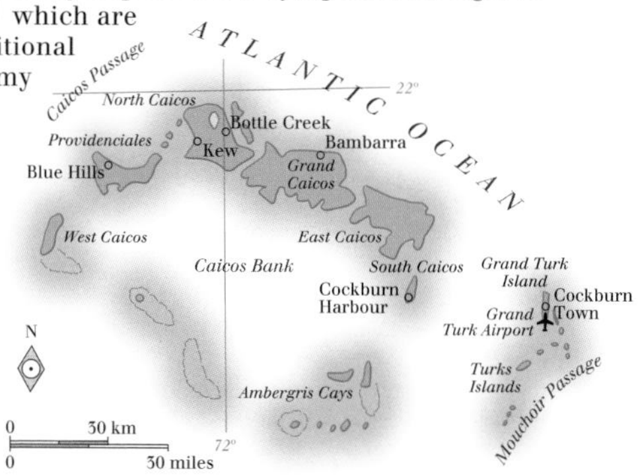
ATLANTIC OCEAN
Caicos Passage
North Caicos
Providenciales
Bottle Creek
Kew
Bambarra
Blue Hills
Grand Caicos
West Caicos
East Caicos
Caicos Bank
South Caicos
Cockburn Harbour
Grand Turk Island
Cockburn Town
Grand Turk Airport
Turks Islands
Ambergris Cays
Mouchoir Passage
22°
72°
N
0 30 km
0 30 miles

VIRGIN ISLANDS (US)

STATUS: Unincorporated territory of the USA **CLAIMED:** 1917
CAPITAL: Charlotte Amalie **POP.:** 101,809 **DENS.:** 293/km² (760/mi²)

THE US VIRGIN ISLANDS are a collection of 53 volcanic islands, just to the east of Puerto Rico. Most of the population – a mix of African and European ethnic groups – live on the main islands of St. John, St. Thomas, and St. Croix. Tourism is the principal activity, although St. Croix has also used federal aid to develop industry. It has one of the world's largest oil refineries.

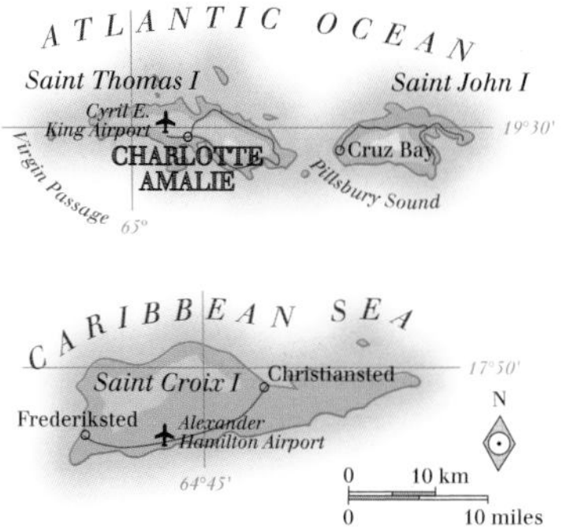
ATLANTIC OCEAN
Saint Thomas I
Saint John I
Cyril E. King Airport
CHARLOTTE AMALIE
Cruz Bay
Virgin Passage
Pillsbury Sound
19°30'
65°
CARIBBEAN SEA
Saint Croix I
Christiansted
Frederiksted
Alexander Hamilton Airport
17°50'
64°45'
N
0 10 km
0 10 miles

St. Thomas, US Virgin Islands, is a major stop-off for Caribbean cruise ships. Tourists are attracted by the island's duty-free shopping.

WAKE ISLAND

STATUS: Unincorporated territory of the USA **CLAIMED:** 1898
CAPITAL: Not applicable **POP.:** 302 **DENSITY:** 38/km² (101/mi²)

FORMED BY the rim of an extinct volcano, Wake Island has a US air base, whose airstrip can be used in emergencies by trans-Pacific flights. A proposal in 1998 to store nuclear waste was dropped after widespread condemnation. The three islands are claimed by the Marshall Islands.

WALLIS & FUTUNA

STATUS: French overseas territory **CLAIMED:** 1842
CAPITAL: Matá'Utu **POP.:** 14,375 **DENSITY:** 52/km² (136/mi²)

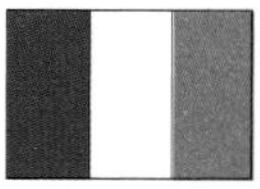

UNLIKE FRANCE'S other South Pacific overseas territories, the inhabitants of Wallis and Futuna have little desire for greater autonomy. The islands' subsistence economy produces a variety of tropical crops, while expatriate remittances and the sale of licenses to Japanese and South Korean fishing fleets provide foreign exchange. Deforestation, leading to soil erosion, is of great concern.

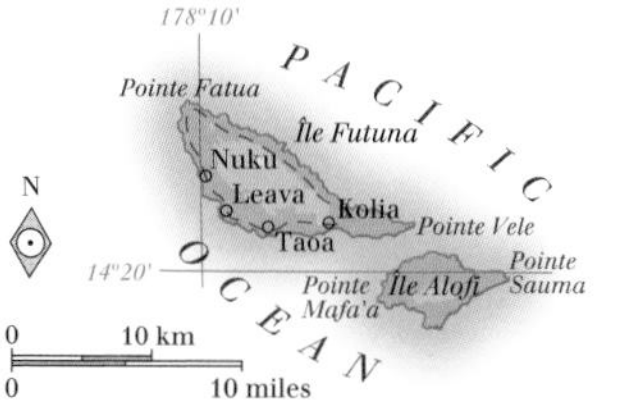
178°10'
PACIFIC OCEAN
Pointe Fatua
Île Futuna
Nuku
Leava
Kolia
Taoa
Pointe Vele
Pointe Mafa'a
Île Alofi
Pointe Sauma
14°20'
N
0 10 km
0 10 miles

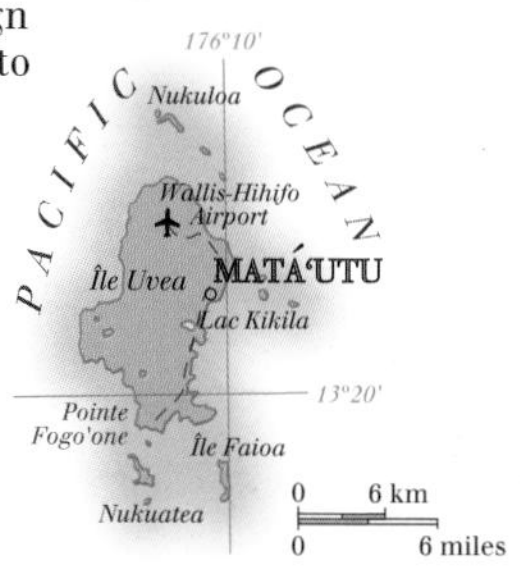
176°10'
PACIFIC OCEAN
Nukuloa
Wallis-Hihifo Airport
Île Uvea
MATÁ'UTU
Lac Kikila
13°20'
Pointe Fogo'one
Île Faioa
Nukuatea
0 6 km
0 6 miles

Glossary of Geographical Terms

The glossary following lists all geographical terms occurring on the maps and in main-entry names in the Index~Gazetteer. These terms may precede, follow or be run together with the proper element of the name; where they precede it the term is reversed for indexing purposes - thus Poluostrov Yamal is indexed as Yamal, Poluostrov.

KEY
Geographical term *Language,* Term

A
Å *Danish, Norwegian,* River
Alpen *German,* Alps
Altiplanicie *Spanish,* Plateau
Älv(en) *Swedish,* River
Anse *French,* Bay
Archipiélago *Spanish,* Archipelago
Arcipelago *Italian,* Archipelago
Arquipélago *Portuguese,* Archipelago
Aukštuma *Lithuanian,* Upland

B
Bahía *Spanish,* Bay
Baía *Portuguese,* Bay
Baḩr *Arabic,* River
Baie *French,* Bay
Bandao *Chinese,* Peninsula
Banjaran *Malay,* Mountain range
Batang *Malay,* Stream
-berg *Afrikaans, Norwegian,* Mountain
Birket *Arabic* , Lake
Boğazı *Turkish,* Lake
Bucht *German,* Bay
Bugten *Danish,* Bay
Buḩayrat *Arabic,* Lake, reservoir
Buḩeiret *Arabic,* Lake
Bukit *Malay,* Mountain
-bukta *Norwegian,* Bay
bukten *Swedish,* Bay
Burnu *Turkish,* Cape, point
Buuraha *Somali,* Mountains

C
Cabo *Portuguese,* Cape
Cap *French,* Cape
Cascada *Portuguese,* Waterfall
Cerro *Spanish,* Mountain
Chaîne *French,* Mountain range
Chau *Cantonese,* Island
Chāy *Turkish,* River
Chhâk *Cambodian,* Bay
Chhu *Tibetan,* River
-chŏsuji *Korean,* Reservoir
Chott *Arabic,* Salt lake, depression
Ch'ün-tao *Chinese,* Island group
Chuôr Phnum *Cambodian,* Mountains
Cordillera *Spanish,* Mountain range
Costa *Spanish,* Coast
Côte *French,* Coast
Cuchilla *Spanish,* Mountains

D
Dağı *Azerbaijani, Turkish,* Mountain
Dağları *Azerbaijani, Turkish,* Mountains
-dake *Japanese,* Peak
Danau *Indonesian,* Lake
Đao *Vietnamese,* Island
Daryā *Persian,* River
Daryācheh *Persian,* Lake
Dasht *Persian,* Plain, desert
Dawḩat *Arabic,* Bay
Dere *Turkish,* Stream
Dili *Azerbaijani,* Spit
-do *Korean,* Island
Dooxo *Somali,* Valley
Düzü *Azerbaijani,* Steppe
-dwīp *Bengali,* Island

E
Embalse *Spanish,* Reservoir
Erg *Arabic,* Dunes
Estany *Catalan,* Lake
Estrecho *Spanish,* Strait
-ey *Icelandic,* Island
Ezero *Bulgarian, Macedonian,* Lake

F
Fjord *Danish,* Fjord
-fjorden *Norwegian,* Fjord
-fjørdhur *Faeroese,* Fjord
Fleuve *French,* River
Fliegu *Maltese,* Channel
-fljór *Icelandic,* River

G
-gang *Korean,* River
Ganga *Nepali, Sinhala,* River
Gaoyuan *Chinese,* Plateau
-gawa *Japanese,* River
Gebel *Arabic,* Mountain
-gebirge *German,* Mountains
Ghubbat *Arabic,* Bay
Gjiri *Albanian,* Bay
Gol *Mongolian,* River
Golfe *French,* Gulf
Golfo *Italian, Spanish,* Gulf
Gora *Russian, Serbian,* Mountain
Gory *Russian,* Mountains
Guba *Russian,* Bay
Gunung *Malay,* Mountain

H
Ḩadd *Arabic,* Spit
-haehyŏp *Korean,* Strait
Haff *German,* Lagoon
Hai *Chinese,* Sea, bay
Ḩammādat *Arabic,* Plateau
Hāmūn *Persian,* Lake
Hawr *Arabic,* Lake
Hāyk' *Amharic,* Lake
He *Chinese,* River
Helodrano *Malagasy,* Bay
-hegység *Hungarian,* Mountain range
Hka *Burmese,* River
-ho *Korean,* Lake
Hô *Korean,* Reservoir
Ḫolot *Hebrew,* Dunes
Hora *Belarussian,* Mountain
Hrada *Belarussian,* Mountains, ridge
Hsi *Chinese,* River
Hu *Chinese,* Lake

I
Île(s) *French,* Island(s)
Ilha(s) *Portuguese,* Island(s)
Ilhéu(s) *Portuguese,* Islet(s)
Irmak *Turkish,* River
Isla(s) *Spanish,* Island(s)
Isola (Isole) *Italian,* Island(s)

J
Jabal *Arabic,* Mountain
Jāl *Arabic,* Ridge
-järvi *Finnish,* Lake
Jazīrat *Arabic,* Island
Jazīreh *Persian,* Island
Jebel *Arabic,* Mountain
Jezero *Serbo-Croat,* Lake
Jiang *Chinese,* River
-joki *Finnish,* River
-jökull *Icelandic,* Glacier
Juzur *Arabic,* Islands

K
Kaikyō *Japanese,* Strait
-kaise *Lappish,* Mountain
Kali *Nepali,* River
Kalnas *Lithuanian,* Mountain
Kalns *Latvian,* Mountain
Kang *Chinese,* Harbor
Kangri *Tibetan,* Mountain(s)
Kaôh *Cambodian,* Island
Kapp *Norwegian,* Cape
Kavīr *Persian,* Desert
K'edi *Georgian,* Mountain range
Kediet *Arabic,* Mountain
Kepulauan *Indonesian, Malay,* Island group
Khalîg, Khalīj *Arabic,* Gulf
Khawr *Arabic,* Inlet
Khola *Nepali,* River
Khrebet *Russian,* Mountain range
Ko *Thai,* Island
Kolpos *Greek,* Bay
-kopf *German,* Peak
Körfäzi *Azerbaijani,* Bay
Körfezi *Turkish,* Bay

Kõrgustik *Estonian,* Upland
Koshi *Nepali,* River
Kowtal *Persian,* Pass
Kūh(hā) *Persian,* Mountain(s)
-kundo *Korean,* Island group
-kysten *Norwegian,* Coast
Kyun *Burmese,* Island

L

Laaq *Somali,* Watercourse
Lac *French,* Lake
Lacul *Romanian,* Lake
Lago *Italian, Portuguese, Spanish,* Lake
Laguna *Spanish,* Lagoon, Lake
Laht *Estonian,* Bay
Laut *Indonesian,* Sea
Lembalemba *Malagasy,* Plateau
Lerr *Armenian,* Mountain
Lerrnashght'a *Armenian,* Mountain range
Les *Czech,* Forest
Lich *Armenian,* Lake
Liqeni *Albanian,* Lake
Lumi *Albanian,* River
Lyman *Ukrainian,* Estuary

M

Mae Nam *Thai,* River
-mägi *Estonian,* Hill
Maja *Albanian,* Mountain
-man *Korean,* Bay
Marios *Lithuanian,* Lake
-meer *Dutch,* Lake
Melkosopochnik *Russian,* Plain
-meri *Estonian,* Sea
Mifraẕ *Hebrew,* Bay
Monkhafad *Arabic,* Depression
Mont(s) *French,* Mountain(s)
Monte *Italian, Portuguese,* Mountain
More *Russian,* Sea
Mörön *Mongolian,* River

N

Nagor'ye *Russian,* Upland
Naẖal *Hebrew,* River
Nahr *Arabic,* River
Nam *Laotian,* River
Nehri *Turkish,* River
Nevado *Spanish,* Mountain (snow-capped)
Nisoi *Greek,* Islands
Nizmennost' *Russian,* Lowland, plain
Nosy *Malagasy,* Island
Nur *Mongolian,* Lake
Nuruu *Mongolian,* Mountains
Nuur *Mongolian,* Lake
Nyzovyna *Ukrainian,* Lowland, plain

O

Ostrov(a) *Russian,* Island(s)
Oued *Arabic,* Watercourse
-oy *Faeroese,* Island
-øy(a) *Norwegian,* Island
Oya *Sinhala,* River
Ozero *Russian, Ukrainian,* Lake

P

Passo *Italian,* Pass
Pegunungan *Indonesian, Malay,* Mountain range
Pelagos *Greek,* Sea
Penisola *Italian,* Peninsula
Peski *Russian,* Sands
Phanom *Thai,* Mountain
Phou *Laotian,* Mountain
Pi *Chinese,* Point
Pic *Catalan,* Peak
Pico *Portuguese, Spanish,* Peak
Pik *Russian,* Peak
Planalto *Portuguese,* Plateau
Planina, Planini *Bulgarian, Macedonian, Serbo-Croat,* Mountain range
Ploskogor'ye *Russian,* Upland
Poluostrov *Russian,* Peninsula
Potamos *Greek,* River
Proliv *Russian,* Strait
Pulau *Indonesian, Malay,* Island
Pulu *Malay,* Island
Punta *Portuguese, Spanish,* Point

Q

Qā' *Arabic,* Depression
Qolleh *Persian,* Mountain

R

Raas *Somali,* Cape
-rags *Latvian,* Cape
Ramlat *Arabic,* Sands
Ra's *Arabic,* Cape, point, headland
Ravnina *Bulgarian, Russian,* Plain
Récif *French,* Reef
Represa (Rep.) *Spanish, Portuguese,* Reservoir
-rettō *Japanese,* Island chain
Riacho *Spanish,* Stream
Riban' *Malagasy,* Mountains
Rio *Portuguese,* River
Río *Spanish,* River
Riu *Catalan,* River
Rivier *Dutch,* River
Rivière *French,* River
Rowd *Pashtu,* River
Rūd *Persian,* River
Rudohorie *Slovak,* Mountains
Ruisseau *French,* Stream

S

Sabkhat *Arabic,* Salt marsh
Şaḩrā' *Arabic,* Desert
Samudra *Sinhala,* Reservoir
-san *Japanese, Korean,* Mountain
-sanchi *Japanese,* Mountains
-sanmaek *Korean,*
Sarīr *Arabic,* Desert
Sebkha, Sebkhet *Arabic,* Salt marsh, depression
See *German,* Lake
Selat *Indonesian,* Strait
-selkä *Finnish,* Ridge
Selseleh *Persian,* Mountain range
Serra *Portuguese,* Mountain
Serranía *Spanish,* Mountain
Sha'īb *Arabic,* Watercourse
Shamo *Chinese,* Desert
Shan *Chinese,* Mountain(s)
Shan-mo *Chinese,* Mountain range
Shaţţ *Arabic,* Distributary
-shima *Japanese,* Island
Shiqqat *Arabic,* Depression
Shui-tao *Chinese,* Channel
Sierra *Spanish,* Mountains
Sơn *Vietnamese,* Mountain
Sông *Vietnamese,* River
-spitze *German,* Peak
Štít *Slovak,* Peak
Stoeng *Cambodian,* River
Stretto *Italian,* Strait
Su Anbarı *Azerbaijani,* Reservoir
Sungai *Indonesian, Malay,* River
Suu *Turkish,* River

T

Tal *Mongolian,* Plain
Tandavan' *Malagasy,* Mountain range
Tangorombohitr' *Malagasy,* Mountain massif
Tao *Chinese,* Island
Tassili *Berber,* Plateau, mountain
Tau *Russian,* Mountain(s)
Taungdan *Burmese,* Mountain range
Teluk *Indonesian, Malay,* Bay
Terara *Amharic,* Mountain
Tog *Somali,* Valley
Tônlé *Cambodian,* Lake
Top *Dutch,* Peak
-tunturi *Finnish,* Mountain
Tur'at *Arabic,* Channel

V

Väin *Estonian,* Strait
-vatn *Icelandic,* Lake
-vesi *Finnish,* Lake
Vinh *Vietnamese,* Bay
Vodokhranilishche (Vdkhr.) *Russian,* Reservoir
Vodoskhovyshche (Vdskh.) *Ukrainian,* Reservoir
Volcán *Spanish,* Volcano
Vozvyshennost' *Russian,* Upland, plateau
Vrh *Macedonian,* Peak
Vysochyna *Ukrainian,* Upland
Vysočina *Czech,* Upland

W

Waadi *Somali,* Watercourse
Wādī *Arabic,* Watercourse
Wāḩat, Wâhat *Arabic,* Oasis
Wald *German,* Forest
Wan *Chinese,* Bay
Wyżyna *Polish,* Upland

X

Xé *Laotian,* River

Y

Yarımadası *Azerbaijani,* Peninsula
Yazovir *Bulgarian,* Reservoir
Yoma *Burmese,* Mountains
Yü *Chinese,* Island

Z

Zaliv *Bulgarian, Russian,* Bay
Zatoka *Ukrainian,* Bay
Zemlya *Russian,* Bay

Glossary of Abbreviations

This glossary provides a comprehensive guide to the abbreviations used.

A

abbrev. abbreviated
ABM anti-ballistic missile(s)
Afr. Afrikaans
AIDS acquired immunodeficiency syndrome
Alb. Albanian
ALCM air-launched Cruise missile(s)
Amh. Amharic
ANC African National Congress
anc. ancient
APC armored personnel carrier(s)
approx. approximately
Ar. Arabic
Arm. Armenian
ASSR Autonomous Soviet Socialist Republic
Aust. Australian
Az. Azerbaijani
Azerb. Azerbaijan

B

bbl barrels
Basq. Basque
BBC British Broadcasting Corporation
BCE Before Common Era
b/d barrels per day
Bel. Belarussian
Ben. Bengali
Ber. Berber
B-H Bosnia and Herzegovina
bn billion (1000 million)
BP British Petroleum
Bret. Breton
Brig. Brigadier
Brit. British
BSE bovine spongiform encephalopathy
Bul. Bulgarian
Bur. Burmese

C

C central
C. Cape
°C degrees (Centigrade)
Cam. Cambodian
Cant. Cantonese
Capt. Captain
CAR Central African Republic
Cast. Castilian
Cat. Catalan
CE Common Era
Chin. Chinese
CIA Central Intelligence Agency
cm centimeter(s)
Cmdr. Commander
CNN Cable News Network
Col. Colonel
Cro. Croat
Cz. Czech
Czech Rep. Czech Republic

D E

Dan. Danish
dept. department
dev. development
Dom. Rep. Dominican Republic
Dr. Doctor
DRC Democratic Republic of Congo
Dut. Dutch
dwt dead weight tonnage
E east
EEC/EC European Community
EEZ Exclusive Economic Zone
ECU European Currency Unit
EMS European Monetary System
Eng. English
est. estimated
Est. Estonian

F G

°F degrees (Fahrenheit)
Faer. Faeroese
Fij. Fijian
Fin. Finnish
Fr. Father
Fr. French
Franc Francophone
Fris. Frisian
ft foot/feet
FYRM Former Yugoslav Republic of Macedonia
FZ Franc Zone
g gram(s)
Gael. Gaelic
Gal. Galician
GATT General Agreement on Tariffs and Trade
GDP Gross Domestic Product (the total value of goods and services produced by a country excluding income from foreign countries)
Gen. General
Geor. Georgian
Ger. German
Gk Greek
GNP Gross National Product (the total value of goods and services produced by a country)

H I

Heb. Hebrew
HEP hydroelectric power
HH His/Her Highness
Hind. Hindi
HIPC heavily indebted poor country(ies)
hist. historical
HIV human immunodeficiency virus
HM His/Her Majesty
HMS His/Her Majesty's ship
HRH His/Her Royal Highness
HSH His/Her Serene Highness
Hung. Hungarian
I. Island
ICBM intercontinental ballistic missile(s)
Icel. Icelandic
in inch(es)
In. Inuit (Eskimo)
Ind. Indonesian
Intl International
Ir. Irish
IRBM intermediate-range ballistic missile(s)
Is Islands
It. Italian

J K L

Jap. Japanese
Kaz. Kazakh
kg kilogram(s)
Kir. Kirghiz
km kilometer(s)
km² square kilometer (singular)
Kor. Korean
Kurd. Kurdish
kw kilowatt(s)
kwh kilowatt hour(s)
L. Lake
Lao. Laotian
Lat. Latin
Latv. Latvian
Liech. Liechtenstein
Lith. Lithuanian
LNG liquefied natural gas
Lt. Lieutenant
Lusoph Lusophone
Lux. Luxembourg

M N

m million/meter(s)
Mac. Macedonian
Maced. Macedonia
Maj. Major
Mal. Malay
Malg. Malagasy
Malt. Maltese
MBA Master of Business Administration
mi. mile(s)
mi² square mile(s)
Mong. Mongolian
MP Member of Parliament
Mt. Mountain/Mount
Mts Mountains
MW megawatt(s)
N north
NASA National Aeronautics and Space Administration
Nep. Nepali
Neth. Netherlands
NGO Non-Governmental Organization
NIC Newly Industrialized Country
Nic. Nicaraguan
Nor. Norwegian
NPT Non-Proliferation Treaty
NZ New Zealand

P Q R

Pash. Pashtu
PC personal computer
Per. Persian
PLO Palestine Liberation Organization
PNG Papua New Guinea
Pol. Polish
Poly. Polynesian
Port. Portuguese
POW prisoner of war
prev. previously
Rep. Represa (Spanish, Portuguese for reservoir)
Rep. Republic
Res. Reservoir
Rev Reverend
Rmsch. Romansch
Rom. Romanian
Rus. Russian
Russ. Fed. Russian Federation

S

S south
SALT Strategic Arms Limitation Treaty
SCr. Serbo-Croatian
Serb. Serbian
Sinh. Sinhala
SLBM submarine-launched ballistic missile(s)
Slvk. Slovak
Slvn. Slovene
Som. Somali
Sp. Spanish
sq square
SSBN nuclear-fuelled ballistic-missile submarine(s)
SSM surface-to-surface missile(s)
St. Saint
START Strategic Arms Reduction Treaty
Strs. Straits
Swa. Swahili
Swe. Swedish
Switz. Switzerland

T U

Taj. Tajik
TGV *train à grande vitesse*
Th. Thai
Thai. Thailand
Tib. Tibetan
Turk. Turkish
Turkm. Turkmenistan
TV television
UAE United Arab Emirates
Uigh. Uighur
UK United Kingdom
Ukr. Ukrainian
UN United Nations
Urd. Urdu
US/USA United States of America
USS United States ship
USSR Union of Soviet Socialist Republics
Uzb. Uzbek

V W X Y

var. variant
VCR video cassette recorder
Vdkhr. Vodokhranilishche (Russian for reservoir)
Vdskh. Vodoskhovyshche (Ukrainian for reservoir)
Vtn. Vietnamese
W west
Wel. Welsh
Yugo. Yugoslavia

GEOGRAPHICAL PLACE-NAMES

THE CHOICES confronting a map-maker when deciding which place-name style to use on a map are surprisingly varied. The criteria adopted may be affected by a range of factors: the existence of foreign and native language forms of a place name (London, Londres, Londra), variant spellings used within the country itself (Gent, Gand), and the existence of completely different language forms for international features (the English Channel, La Manche).

In addition to these, political expedience, simple clarity, and the use to which the published map may be put are all factors that need consideration.

The revision of place-name forms and spellings, which is a continuing administrative activity worldwide, adds a further dimension of complexity to the subject. Since the collapse of Soviet communism, for instance, place-names in Russia have been altered to expunge traces of communist ideology (the most famous being the 1991 reversion of Leningrad to its pre-1914 name, St. Petersburg). In many former Soviet republics, Russian names have been replaced with native language forms (notably in Ukraine, Belarus, Georgia, and Armenia).

Standardized Arabic names have been hindered by the persistent use of French forms in practice.

THE MAPS

The maps in the Nations of the World section of this book have used the most up-to-date reference sources available to provide local name forms and spellings, that is to say those used within the country. In an age when international travel, on holiday or on business, is commonplace, this criterion seems the most appropriate.

English conventional forms have been used for all international features (such as sea areas between countries, and cross-border mountain ranges); for all country names (the Index-Gazetteer provides local forms and spellings, while commonly used alternative names, such as Burma/Myanmar are also made clear in the national A–Z entry); and for all capital cities. The Index-Gazetteer provides a fully cross-referenced system that will guide the reader the short distance from the English conventional "Florence" to the local "Firenze," as used on the maps.

English conventional forms also appear on all the maps in the World Factfile. These maps have not been indexed, as all contemporary places featured are most usefully and accurately identified on the national maps.

THE INDEX-GAZETTEER

The Index-Gazetteer lists all names that appear on the maps in the Nations of the World section of the book. Physical features are defined as such, as are countries and those administrative or regional names included on the maps; all other names are those of population centers. Location is given by page number, then country, and is narrowed down by positional reference as N(orth), S(outh), E(ast), W(est), or C(entral), or combinations of these as appropriate.

Following each main entry name are given: variant spellings of the name most commonly found; its previous name or names; and such foreign-language forms of the name as are pertinent to modern history since 1940. This is the cut-off date generally adopted, permitting the inclusion of all place-name changes made during or after World War II. Exceptionally, name changes made in Russia and other countries of the former Soviet Union before 1940 are given, since many old names in these countries are now being restored.

INDEX

PAGE NUMBERS SHOWN IN ITALICS

Geographical Terms and Abbreviations on pages 654-657 / ❖ = *capital*

A

Aa *see* Gauja
Aabenraa *see* Åbenrå
Aachen *264 Fr.* Aix-la-Chapelle, *Dut.* Aken. W Germany
Aalborg *see* Ålborg
Aalesund *see* Ålesund
Aaley *364 var.* Ālayh, Aley. C Lebanon
Aalsmeer *429* W Netherlands
Aalst *127 Fr.* Alost. C Belgium
Aanaarjärvi *see* Inarijärvi
Aanjar *364* C Lebanon
Aarau *546* N Switzerland
Aare *546 var.* Aar. River of W Switzerland
Aarhus *see* Århus
Aarlen *see* Arlon
Aarschot *127* C Belgium
Aassi, Nahr el *see* Orantes
Aba *440* S Nigeria
Abaco Island *112* island of N Bahamas
Ābādān *307* W Iran
Abai *see* Blue Nile
Abaiang *346* island of the Gilbert Is, W Kiribati
Abakan *485 prev.* Khakassk, Ust'-Abakanskoye. C Russian Federation
Abancay *463* SE Peru
Abariringa *see* Kanton
Ābaya Hāyk' *243 It.* Abbaia, *Eng.* Lake Margherita. Lake of SW Ethiopia
Abay Wenz *see* Blue Nile
Abbeville *253* N France
'Abd al 'Azīz, Jabal *551* mountains of NE Syria
'Abdalī *354* S Kuwait
Abd-Al-Kuri *627* island of SE Yemen, off the Horn of Africa
Abéché *180 var.* Abécher. E Chad
Abemama *346* island of the Gilbert Is, W Kiribati
Abengourou *326* E Ivory Coast
Åbenrå *218 var.* Aabenraa, *Ger.* Apenrade. Jylland, SW Denmark
Abeokuta *440* SW Nigeria
Abercorn *see* Mbala
Aberdeen *593* NE Scotland, UK
Aberdeen *599* South Dakota, NC USA
Abergwaun *see* Fishguard
Abersee *see* Wolfgangsee
Abertawe *see* Swansea
Aberystwyth *593* W Wales, UK
Abhā *506* S Saudi Arabia
Abhe, Lake *222, 243 Amh.* Ābhē Bid Hāyk'. Lake of Djibouti and Ethiopia
Abidjan *326* S Ivory Coast
Åbo *see* Turku
Aboisso *326* SE Ivory Coast
Abo, Massif d' *180* mountain range of N Chad
Abomey *132* S Benin
Abong Mbang *168* SE Cameroon
Abou-Déïa *180* S Chad
Aboudouhour *see* Abū aḍ Ḍuhūr
Abou Kémal *see* Abū Kamāl
Aboumi *258* E Gabon
Abovyan *98 var.* Abovjan. C Armenia
Abra *466* river of Luzon, N Philippines
Abrād, Wādī *627* seasonal river of NW Yemen
Abraham Bay *see* Carlton, The
Abruzzese, Appennino *321* mountain range of C Italy
'Abs *627 var.* Sūq 'Abs. W Yemen
Abşeron Yarımadası *110 Rus.* Apsheronskiy Poluostrov. Oil-rich peninsula of E Azerbaijan
Abū aḍ Ḍuhūr *551 Fr.* Aboudouhour. NW Syria
Abū al Abyaḍ *590* island of N United Arab Emirates
Abū al Jirfān, Sha'īb *354 var.* Sh'ib Abu Jarfan. Dry watercourse of N Kuwait
Abū al Khaṣīb *310 var.* Abul Khasib. SE Iraq
Abu al Mawj, Ra's *115* cape of W Bahrain
Abu Dhabi *590 Ar.* Abū Ẓaby, *var.* Abū Ẓabī. ❖ of United Arab Emirates
Abuja *440* ❖ of Nigeria, C Nigeria
Abū Jarjūr, Ra's *115* cape of E Bahrain
Abū Kamāl *551 Fr.* Abou Kémal. E Syria
Abul Khasib *see* Abū al Khaṣīb
Abuná *136* river of Bolivia and Brazil
Abū Thaylah *479* NE Qatar
Abū Ẓabī *see* Abu Dhabi
Abū Ẓaby *see* Abu Dhabi
Abyaḍ, Baḥr al *see* White Nile
Åbybro *218* N Denmark
Abyssinia *see* Ethiopia
Acaill *see* Achill Island
Acajutla *235* W El Salvador
Acapulco *403 var.* Acapulco de Juárez. S Mexico
Acaraí, Serra *144 Eng.* Acarai Mountains. Mountain range of Brazil and Guyana
Acarigua *619* NW Venezuela
Accra *270* ❖ of Ghana, SE Ghana
Achacachi *136* W Bolivia
Acharnés *273 prev.* Akharnaí. SE Greece
Acheloos *273 var.* Aspropotamos, *prev.* Akhelóös. River of W Greece
Achénouma *439* NE Niger
Achill Island *314 Ir.* Acaill. Island of W Ireland
Achna *see* Athna
Achorstock Point *652* headland of W Tristan da Cunha
Achwa *584 var.* Aswa. River of N Uganda
Acireale *321* Sicilia, S Italy
Acklins Island *112* island of S Bahamas
Aconcagua, Cerro *95* mountain of W Argentina
Açores *see* Azores
Açores, Arquipélago dos *see* Azores
A Coruña *530 Cast.* La Coruña. NW Spain
Acoua *649* NW Mayotte
Acquaviva *502* NW San Marino
Acre *see* 'Akko
Acurnam *236 var.* Acurenan, Akurenan. S Río Muni, Equatorial Guinea
Adalia *see* Antalya
Adalia, Gulf of *see* Antalya Körfezi
Adam *448* N Oman
Adama *see* Nazrēt
Adamaoua, Massif d' *168 Eng.* Adamawa. Plateau of West Africa
Adam-jo-Tando *see* Tando Ādam
Adam's Bridge *534* chain of shoals to the NW of Sri Lanka
Adamstown *651* ❖ of Pitcairn Islands, NE Pitcairn Island, Pitcairn Islands
'Adan *627 Eng.* Aden. SW Yemen
Adana *577 var.* Seyhan. S Turkey
Adapazarı *576 var.* Sakarya. NW Turkey
Aḍ Ḍab 'īyah *590* C United Arab Emirates
Aḍ Ḍafrah *590* desert region of W United Arab Emirates
Ad Dahnā' *506* N Saudi Arabia
Ad Dakhla *414* W Western Sahara
Ad Dalanj *see* Dilling
Ad Dammām *506* desert region of NE Saudi Arabia
Ad Dawḥah *see* Doha
Ad Dibdibah *354* mountain of W Kuwait
Addīgrat *243* N Ethiopia
Ad Dirāz *115* NW Bahrain
Addis Ababa *243 Amh.* Ādīs Ābeba. ❖ of Ethiopia, C Ethiopia
Ad Dīwānīyah *310 var.* Diwaniya. C Iraq
Addu Atoll *390* atoll of S Maldives
Adelaide *101* S Australia
Adelphi *498* E St Vincent, St Vincent & the Grenadines
Adelsberg *see* Postojna
Aden *see* 'Adan
Aden, Gulf of *222, 524, 627 var.* Badyarada 'Adméd. Gulf connecting the Indian Ocean and Red Sea
Adh Dhayd *590 var.* Deira. NE United Arab Emirates
Adh Dhirā' *336* W Jordan
Ādī Ārk'ay *243 var.* Addi Arkay. N Ethiopia
Adige *321 Ger.* Etsch. River of N Italy
Adi Keyih *238 var.* Adi Keyah. SE Eritrea
Adi Kwala *238* S Eritrea
Ādīs Ābeba *see* Addis Ababa
Ādīs Zemen *243* NW Ethiopia
Adi Tekelezan *238* C Eritrea
Adıyaman *577* SE Turkey
Admiralty Islands *458* island group of N Papua New Guinea
Ado-Ekiti *440* SW Nigeria
Adola *see* Kibre Mengist
Ado-Odo *440 var.* Ado. SW Nigeria
Adour *253* river of SW France
Adrar des Iforas *392* mountainous region of C Sahara, NE Mali
Adriatic Sea *321, 630 It.* Mare Adriatico, *Slvn.* Jadransko Morje, *SCr.* Jadransko More, *Alb.* Deti Adriatik. Area of the Mediterranean Sea, between Italy and SE Europe
Adriatik, Deti *see* Adriatic Sea
Adventure Sound *645* bay of the South Atlantic Ocean, E Falkland Islands
Ādwa *243 var.* Adowa, *It.* Adua. N Ethiopia
Adygeya, Respublika *484* autonomous republic of SW Russian Federation
Adzopé *326* SE Ivory Coast
Aeankan District *396* district of Majuro, SE Marshall Islands
Aegean Sea *273, 576 Gk* Aigaío Pélagos, *Turk.* Ege Denizi. Area of the Mediterranean Sea
Aeolian Islands *see* Eolie, Isole
Ærø *218 Ger.* Arrö. Island of S Denmark
Afadjado *270 var.* Afadjato, Afadjoto. Mountain of SE Ghana
'Afak *310* C Iraq
Afar Depression *see* Danakil Desert
Afghanistan *76-79* officially Islamic State of Afghanistan, *prev.* Republic of Afghanistan. Country of C Asia divided into 30 admin. units (velayats). ❖ Kābul
Afgooye *524 It.* Afgoi. S Somalia
Afikpo *440* S Nigeria
Afobaka *538* NE Suriname
'Afula *317* N Israel
Afyon *576 prev.* Afyonkarahisar. W Turkey
Agadez *439 prev.* Agadès. C Niger
Agadir *414* SW Morocco
Agaña *see* Hagåtña
Aga Point *647* headland on the S coast of Guam
Āgaro *243* W Ethiopia
Agat *647* W Guam
Agboville *326* SE Ivory Coast
Ağcabädi *110 Rus.* Agdzhabedi, *var.* Agdžabedi. C Azerbaijan
Agdam *110* SW Azerbaijan
Agedabia *see* Ajdābiyā
Agen *253* SW France
Agere Hiywet *see* Hāgere Hiywet
Agia Napa *see* Ayia Napa
Agigialousa *see* Yenierenköy
Agios Ioannis *see* Ayios Ioannis
Agona Swedru *270 var.* Swedru. SE Ghana
Agordat *see* Akordat
Agou Gadzepe *567* SW Togo
Agou, Mont *567 prev.* Pic Baumann. Mountain of SW Togo
Āgra *296* N India
Agram *see* Zagreb
Agrigento *321 prev.* Girgenti. Sicilia, S Italy
Agrihan *650* island of N Northern Mariana Islands
Agrínio *273 prev.* Agrínion. W Greece
Aguachica *195* N Colombia
Aguadilla *651* NW Puerto Rico
Aguadulce *456* S Panama
Aguán *288* river of N Honduras
Aguarico *228* river of Ecuador and Peru
Aguascalientes *403* C Mexico
Aguijan *650* island of S Northern Mariana Islands
Agusan *466* river of Mindanao, S Philippines
Ahaggar *83 var.* Hoggar. Mountain range of SE Algeria
Ahja *240 var.* Ahja Jõgi. River of SE Estonia
Ahmadābād *296 var.* Ahmedabad. W India
Ahmadpur East *451* E Pakistan
Ahuachapán *235* W El Salvador
Ahvāz *307 var.* Ahwāz. W Iran
Ahvenanmaa *see* Åland
Aḥwar *627* SW Yemen
Aibak *see* Āybak
Aigaío Pélagos *see* Aegean Sea
Aiguá *607* S Uruguay
Ai-hun *see* Heihe
Ailigandí *456* E Panama
Ailinginae *396* island of NW Marshall Islands
Ailinglaplap *396 prev.* Ailinglapalap. Island of S Marshall Islands
Ailuk *396* island of NE Marshall Islands
'Aïn Ben Tili *398* N Mauritania
Aïn Oussera *83 var.* Aïn Wessara. N Algeria
Aintab *see* Gaziantep
Aïoun el Atroûss *see* 'Ayoûn el 'Atroûs
Aiquile *136* C Bolivia
Airai *455* C Palau
Airdrie *170* SW Canada
Airdrie *593* C Scotland, UK
Airlalang *see* Rokan
Aitape *458 var.* Eitape. NW Papua New Guinea
Aitos *see* Aytos
Aitutaki *644* island of Southern Cook Islands, S Cook Islands
Aix-en-Provence *253* SE France
Aix-la-Chapelle *see* Aachen
Aizu-Wakamatsu *330* Honshū, N Japan
Ajaccio *253* Corse, SE France
Ajdābiyā *371 var.* Ajdābiyah, Agedabia. NE Libya
Ajeltake District *396* district of Majuro, SE Marshall Islands
Ajjinena *see* Geneina
Ajka *290* W Hungary
Ajman *590 Ar.* 'Ajmān, *var.* 'Ujmān. NE United Arab Emirates
Ajtos *see* Aytos
Akaba *see* Al 'Aqabah
Akagera *162, 492, 584 var.* Kagera. River of E Africa

Āk'akī Besek'a *243 var.* Akaki. C Ethiopia
Akan *466* river of Mindanao, S Philippines
Akanthou *see* Tatlisu
Akanyaru *162, 492 var.* Kanyaru. River of Burundi and Rwanda
Akashi *330* Honshū, C Japan
Akau *648* island of NW Johnston Atoll
Akdogan *see* Lysi
Aken *see* Aachen
Akhalts'ikhe *262* SW Georgia
Akharnaí *see* Acharnés
Akhisar *576* W Turkey
Akhmîm *230 var.* Akhmīm. E Egypt
Akhna *see* Athna
Akhuryan *98* NW Armenia
Akiéni *258* E Gabon
Akita *330* Honshū, N Japan
Akjoujt *398 prev.* Fort-Repoux. W Mauritania
Akkaraipattu *534* E Sri Lanka
'Akko *317 Eng.* Acre. N Israel
Akmola *see* Astana
Akobo *243* river of Ethiopia and Sudan
Akonolinga *168* S Cameroon
Akordat *238 var.* Agordat. C Eritrea
Akosombo Dam *270* dam of SE Ghana
Akranes *294* W Iceland
Åkrehamn *444* SW Norway
Akron *599* Ohio, NE USA
Akrotiri *215* UK air base in S Cyprus
Akrotiri Bay *215* bay of the Mediterranean Sea, to the S of Cyprus
Aksai Chin *186, 296* disputed territory of China and India
Aksaray *577* C Turkey
Aksay *338* NW Kazakhstan
Āksum *243* N Ethiopia
Aktash *see* Oqtosh
Aktau *338 prev.* Shevchenko, *Kaz.* Aqtaū. W Kazakhstan
Aktí *273* peninsula of NE Greece
Aktyubinsk *338 Kaz.* Aqtöbe. NW Kazakhstan
Akure *440* SW Nigeria
Akurenan *see* Acurnam
Akureyri *294* N Iceland
Akyab *see* Sittwe
Alabama *599* state of SE USA
Alacant *see* Alicante
Alah *466* river of Mindanao, S Philippines
Al Aḩmadī *354* E Kuwait
Alaïli Ḏaḏḏa' *222* N Djibouti
Alai Range *357 Rus.* Alayskiy Khrebet. Mountain range of SW Kyrgyzstan
Alajuela *206* C Costa Rica
Alakol', Ozero *338 Kaz.* Alaköl. Lake of E Kazakhstan
Al 'Āl *336* NW Jordan
Alamagan *650* island of C Northern Mariana Islands
Al 'Amārah *310 var.* Amara. E Iraq
Alamikamba *436* E Nicaragua
Åland *249 Fin.* Ahvenanmaa. Island group of SW Finland
Alaotra, Farihy *382 var.* Farihin Alaotra, Lac Alaotra. Lake of E Madagascar
Al 'Aqabah *336 var.* Aqaba, Akaba. SW Jordan
Al Arish *see* El 'Arîsh
Al Ashkharah *448* NE Oman
Alaska *598* non-contiguous state of USA, NW North America
Alaska Range *598* mountain range of Alaska, USA, NW North America
Älät *110 Rus.* Alyat, Aljat, *prev.* Alyaty-Pristan'. SE Azerbaijan
Alausí *228* C Ecuador
Alaverdi *98* N Armenia
Ālayh *see* Aaley
Alaykel' *see* Këk-Art
Al 'Ayn *590 var.* Al Ain. E United Arab Emirates
Alayskiy Khrebet *see* Alai Range
Alazani *262* river of Azerbaijan and Georgia
Al Azimiyah *354* N Kuwait
Al 'Azīzīyah *371* NW Libya
Albacete *531* C Spain
Al Baḩrah *354* NE Kuwait
Al Baḩr al Mayyit *see* Dead Sea
Al Baḩrayn *see* Bahrain
Alba Iulia *480 Ger.* Karlsburg, *prev.* Weissenburg, *Hung.* Gyulafehérvár. W Romania
Albania *80-81* officially Republic of Albania, *prev.* People's Socialist Republic of Albania, *Alb.* Shqipni. Country of S Europe divided into 26 admin. units. (districts). ❖ Tirana
Albany *100* SW Australia
Albany *171* river of S Canada
Albany *599* New York, NE USA
Al Başrah *310 var.* Basra. SE Iraq
Al Bāţinah *448 var.* Batinah. Coastal region of Oman
Al Batrūn *see* Batroûn
Al Baydā' *371 var.* Beida. NE Libya
Al Bayḑā' *627 var.* Al Beida. SW Yemen
Alberdi *460* S Paraguay
Alberta *170* province of W Canada
Albert Edward Nyanza *see* Edward, Lake
Albert, Lake *584, 203 var.* Albert Nyanza, Lac Mobutu Sese Seko. Lake of Uganda and Dem. Rep. Congo (Zaire)
Albert Nile *584* river of NW Uganda
Albertville *see* Kalemie
Albi *253* S France
Albina *538* NE Suriname
Al Biqā' *see* El Beqaa
Al Birk *506* SW Saudi Arabia
Ålborg *218 var.* Aalborg. Jylland, N Denmark
Alborz, Reshteh-ye Kuhhā-ye *307 Eng.* Elburz Mountains. Mountains of N Iran
Ålborg Bugt *218* bay to the N of Jylland, Denmark
Al Budayyi' *115* NW Bahrain
Albuquerque *598* New Mexico, SW USA
Al Buraymī *448 var.* Al Buraimi, Buraimi. NW Oman
Al Buraymī *590 var.* Buraimi. Oasis of Oman and United Arab Emirates
Al Burayqah *371 var.* Marsá al Burayqah. N Libya
Albury *101* SE Australia
Al Busaytīn *115* Jazirat al Muharraq, Bahrain
Al Buşayyir *479 var.* Al Busayer. NW Qatar
Al Buzūn *627* E Yemen
Alcácer do Sal *474* W Portugal
Alcalá de Henares *530* C Spain
Alcalde Díaz *456* C Panama
Alcamo *321* Sicilia, S Italy
Alcántara, Embalse de *531* reservoir of W Spain
Alcaudete *531* S Spain
Alchevs'k *586 prev.* Kommunarsk, Voroshilovsk. E Ukraine
Aldabra Atoll *512* Atoll of the Aldabra Group, SW Seychelles
Aldabra Group *512* island group of SW Seychelles
Aldan *485* river of E Russian Federation
Aldanskoye Nagor'ye *485 Eng.* Aldan Plateau. Highland plateau of E Russian Federation
Alderney *647* island of N Guernsey
Al Djem *see* El Jem
Aleg *398* SW Mauritania
Alejandro Selkirk, Isla *183* island of Juan Fernández Islands, W Chile
Aleksandriya *see* Oleksandriya
Aleksandropol' *see* Gyumri
Aleksandrovsk *see* Zaporizhzhya
Aleksandrovsk-Sakhalinskiy *485* SE Russian Federation
Aleksinac *630* SE Serbia, Yugoslavia
Alençon *253* NW France
Alep *see* Ḩalab
Aleppo *see* Ḩalab
Alert *171* Ellesmere Island, N Canada
Alessandria *320 Fr.* Alexandrie. N Italy
Ålesund *444 var.* Aalesund. SW Norway
A-le-t'ai *see* Altay
Aleutian Islands *598* island group of Alaska, USA
Alexander Range *see* Kirghiz Range
Alexandra *433* SW South Island, New Zealand
Alexandretta *see* İskenderun
Alexandretta, Gulf of *see* İskenderun Körfezi
Alexandria *230 Ar.* Al Iskandarīya, El Iskandarîyah. N Egypt
Alexandria *480* S Romania
Alexandrie *see* Alessandria
Alexandroúpoli *273 Turk.* Dedeagaç, Dedeagach. NE Greece
Al Fallūjah *310 var.* Falluja. C Iraq
Al Faq' *590 var.* Al Faqa. E United Arab Emirates
Al Farḑah *627* C Yemen
Al Fāshir *see* El Fasher
Al Fayyūm *see* El Faiyûm
Alfeiós *273 prev.* Alfiós. River of S Greece
Alföld *290 Eng.* Great Hungarian Plain. Plain of SE Hungary
Al Fuḩayḩīl *354 var.* Fahaheel. E Kuwait
Al Fujayrah *see* Fujairah
Al Fuqahā *371* C Libya
Al Fuwayriţ *479 var.* Fuwairet. NE Qatar
Alga *338* NW Kazakhstan
Algeciras *530* SW Spain
Algena *238* N Eritrea
Alger *see* Algiers
Algeria *82-83* officially Democratic and Popular Republic of Algeria. Country of N Africa divided into 48 admin. units (wilayat). ❖ Algiers
Al Ghārīyah *479 var.* Al Ghariyeh. NE Qatar
Al Gharrāfah *479* E Qatar
Al Ghayḑah *627* E Yemen
Alghero *321* Sardegna, W Italy
Al Ghuwayrīyah *479* N Qatar
Algiers *83 var.* El Djazaïr, *Fr.* Alger. ❖ of Algeria, N Algeria
Al Haba *590* NE United Arab Emirates
Al Ḩabbānīyah *310* C Iraq
Al Ḩadd *448 var.* Ras al Hadd. NE Oman
Al Ḩadd *see* Al Ḩidd
Al Haggounia *414* N Western Sahara
Al Ḩajarah *310* desert of S Iraq
Al Hajarayn *627* C Yemen
Al Hamalah *115* NW Bahrain
Al Ḩammādah al Ḩamrā *371* desert region of NW Libya
Al Ḩamrīyah *590 var.* Hamriya. NE United Arab Emirates
Al Harūj al Aswad *371* desert region of C Libya
Al Hasahisa *see* El Hasaheisa
Al Ḩasakah *551 var.* El Haseke, *Fr.* Hassetché. NE Syria
Al Ḩawrah *627* S Yemen
Al Ḩidd *115 var.* Al Ḩadd. Jazirat al Muharraq, Bahrain
Al Ḩijāz *506* coastal and highland region of NW Saudi Arabia
Al Ḩillah *310 var.* Hilla. C Iraq
Al Hindīyah *310 var.* Hindiya. C Iraq
Al Hoceima *414 var.* Al Hoceïma, Alhucemas, *prev.* Villa Sanjurjo. N Morocco
Alhucemas *see* Al Hoceima
Al Ḩudaydah *627 Eng.* Hodeida. W Yemen
Al Hufūf *506 var.* Hofuf. NE Saudi Arabia
Al Ḩuşayḩişah *see* El Hasaheisa
'Ālī *115* NW Bahrain
'Ali 'Aḍdé *222* SE Djibouti
Aliákmonas *273 prev.* Aliákmon. River of NW Greece
'Alī al Gharbī *310* E Iraq
Äli-Bayramlı *110 Rus.* Ali-Bayramly, *var.* Ali Bajramly. SE Azerbaijan
Alibori *132* river of N Benin
Alicante *531 Cat.* Alacant. SE Spain
Alice Springs *101* C Australia
Alima *200* river of C Congo
Alindao *179* S Central African Republic
'Ali Sabieh *222* S Djibouti
Ali Shanmo *555* mountain range of C Taiwan
Al Iskandarīya *see* Alexandria
Al Ismā'īlīyah *see* Ismâ'ilîya
Al Ittiḩād *see* Madīnat ash Sha'b
Ali Wahībah, Ramlat *448* N Oman
Aliwal North *527 Afr.* Aliwal-Noord. Eastern Cape, C South Africa
Al Jabal al Akhḑar *371* mountain range of NE Libya
Al Jabal al Akhḑar *448 var.* Jabal Akhdar. Mountain range of NW Oman
Al Jabal ash Sharqi *see* Anti-Lebanon
Al Jafr *336* SW Jordan
Al Jaghbūb *371* NE Libya
Al Jahrah *354 var.* Jahra, Al Jahrā'. C Kuwait
Al Jamīl *see* Al Jumayl
Al Jamm *see* El Jem
Al Jasrah *115* NW Bahrain
Aljat *see* Älät
Al Jawārah *448* E Oman
Al Jawf *506 var.* Jauf. N Saudi Arabia
Al Jazīrah *310* physical region of Iraq and Syria
Al Jifārah *see* Jeffara Plain
Al Jīzah *see* El Gîza
Al Jubayl *506 var.* Al Jubail. NE Saudi Arabia
Al Jufayr *115 var.* Al Juffair. NE Bahrain
Al Jumayl *371 var.* Al Jamīl. NW Libya
Al Jumaylīyah *479* N Qatar
Al Junaynah *see* Geneina
Al Ka'aban *see* Madīnat al Ka'bān
Al Kahlil *see* Hebron
Al Kāmil *448* NE Oman
Al Karak *336* W Jordan
Al Khabb *590* E United Arab Emirates
Al Khābūrah *448 var.* Khabura. N Oman
Al Khalīj al 'Arabī *see* The Gulf
Al Khāliş *310* C Iraq
Al Khaluf *see* Khalūf
Al Khārijah *see* El Khârga
Al Khārijīyah *115* NE Bahrain
Al Kharrārah *479* S Qatar
Al Khaşab *448 var.* Khasab. Musandam Peninsula, N Oman
Al Khatt *590 var.* Khatt. NE United Arab Emirates
Al Khaţţ *414* seasonal river of N Western Sahara
Al Khawr *479 var.* Al Khaur, Al Khor. NE Qatar
Al Khīrān *354* SE Kuwait
Al Khubar *506 var.* Al-Khobar. NE Saudi Arabia
Al Khums *371 var.* Khoms, Homs. N Libya
Al Khuraybah *627* C Yemen
Al Khurţūm *see* Khartoum
Al Khuwayr *479 var.* Al Khuwair. N Qatar
Al Kir'ānah *479 var.* Kharanah. SW Qatar
Alkmaar *429* NW Netherlands
Al Kūfah *310* S Iraq
Al Kufrah *371 It.* Cufra. Oasis of SE Libya
Al Kūt *310 var.* Kūt al 'Amārah, Kut al Imara. E Iraq
Al Kuwayt *see* Kuwait City
Allada *132* S Benin
Al Lādhiqīyah *551 Eng.* Latakia. W Syria
Allahābād *296* NE India
Allanmyo *159* W Burma
'Allâqi, Wâdi el *230 var.* Wādī al 'Allāqi. Dry watercourse of SE Egypt
All Awash Island *498* island of E St Vincent & the Grenadines
Allenstein *see* Olsztyn
Allentown *599* Pennsylvania, NE USA

Al Liwā' *590* oasis region of SW United Arab Emirates
All Saints *92* C Antigua, Antigua & Barbuda
Al Lubnān *see* Lebanon
Al Luḩayyah *627* W Yemen
Al Ma'āmīr *115* NE Bahrain
Alma-Ata *see* Almaty
Almada *474* W Portugal
Al Madīnah *506 Eng.* Medina. W Saudi Arabia
Al Mafraq *336 var.* Mafraq. N Jordan
Al Mahdīyah *see* Mahdia
Al Maḩmūdīyah *310 var.* Mahmudiya. C Iraq
Al Mahrah *627* mountains of E Yemen
Al Majma'ah *506* C Saudi Arabia
Al Mālikīyah *115* W Bahrain
Al Mālikīyah *551 var.* Dayrīk. NE Syria
Almalyk *see* Olmaliq
Al Mamlakah *see* Morocco
Al Manādir *590 var.* Al Manadir. Desert region of Oman and United Arab Emirates
Al Manāmah *see* Manama
Al Manāşif *551* mountains of E Syria
Al Manşūrah *see* El Manşûra
Al Maqta' *590* C United Arab Emirates
Al Marj *371 var.* Barka, *It.* Barce. NE Libya
Al Marsá *see* La Marsa
Almaty *338 var.* Alma-Ata. SE Kazakhstan
Al Mawşil *310 Eng.* Mosul. N Iraq
Al Mayādīn *551 Fr.* Meyadine. E Syria
Al Mazra'ah *336* W Jordan
Almelo *429* E Netherlands
Almendra, Embalse de *531* reservoir of NW Spain
Almere *429* C Netherlands
Almería *531* S Spain
Al Mīnā' *see* El Mina
Al Minyā *see* El Minya
Al Miqdādīyah *see* Al Muqdādīyah
Almirante *456* W Panama
Al Mubarraz *506* NE Saudi Arabia
Al Mudawwarah *336* SW Jordan
Al Muḩammadīyah *115 var.* Umm aş Şabbān. Island of NW Bahrain
Al Muḩarraq *115 var.* Moharek, Muharraq, Jazirat al Muharraq. Bahrain
Al Mukallā *627 var.* Mukalla. SE Yemen
Al Mukhā *627 Eng.* Mocha. SW Yemen
Al Muknīn *see* Moknine
Al Munastīr *see* Monastir
Al Muqdādīyah *310 var.* Al Miqdādīyah. C Iraq
Al Mussayyib *310* C Iraq
Al Obayyid *see* El Obeid
Alofi *650* ❖ of Niue, W Niue
Alofi, Île *653* island of Île Futuna, N Wallis & Futuna
Alohungari *261* E Gambia
Alor, Kepulauan *302* island group of E Indonesia
Alor, Pulau *302* island of E Indonesia
Alor Setar *386 var.* Alur Setar, Alor Star. NW Peninsular Malaysia
Alost *see* Aalst
Alotau *458* SE Papua New Guinea
Aloupos *215 var.* Çiftlik Dere. River of NW Cyprus
Alpen *see* Alps
Alpes *see* Alps
Alphen aan de Rijn *429* W Netherlands
Alphonse Group *512* island group of C Seychelles
Alpi *see* Alps
Alps *106, 253, 320, 546 It.* Alpi, *Fr.* Alpes, *Ger.* Alpen. Mountain range of C Europe
Al Qābil *448 var.* Qabil. NW Oman
Al Qaḑārif *see* Gedaref
Al Qāhirah *see* Cairo
Al Qal'ah al Kubrá *see* Kalaa Kebira
Al Qāmishlī *551 var.* Kamishli. NE Syria
Al Qaryah *115* NE Bahrain
Al Qaryāt *371* NW Libya
Al Qaşr *336* W Jordan
Al-Qaşrayn *see* Kasserine
Al Qayrawān *see* Kairouan
Al Qubayyāt *see* Qoubaïyât
Al Qubbah *371* NE Libya
Al Quds *see* Jerusalem
Al Qunayţirah *551 var.* El Quneitra, Kuneitra. SW Syria
Al Quşayr *551 var.* El Quseir, *Fr.* Kousseir. W Syria
Al Quţayfah *551 var.* Quţayfah, Quteife, *Fr.* Kouteifé. SW Syria
Al Quwayrah *336 var.* Makhfar al Quwayrah, El Quweira. SW Jordan
Als *218 Ger.* Alsen. Island of S Denmark
Alsace *253* cultural region of NE France
Alsen *see* Als
Al Shahaniyah *see* Ash Shaḩanīyah
Alt *see* Olt
Alta *444* NE Norway
Altai Mountains *412* mountain range of C Asia
Altay *186 Chin.* A-le-t'ai, *prev.* Ch'eng-hua, *var.* Chenghwa, *Mong.* Sharasume. Xinjiang Uygur Zizhiqu, NW China
Altay *412* W Mongolia
Altay, Respublika *485* autonomous republic of C Russian Federation
Alt de la Coma Pedrosa, Pic *86* mountain of NW Andorra
Altkanischa *see* Kanjiža
Alto Molócuè *419* C Mozambique
Alto Paraná *see* Paraná
Alt-Schwanenburg *see* Gulbene
Altsohl *see* Zvolen
Altun Shan *186 var.* Altyn Tagh. Mountain range of Xinjiang Uygur Zizhiqu, NW China
Altyn Tagh *see* Altun Shan
Alu *see* Shortland Island
Al Ubayyiḑ *see* El Obeid
Alūksne *362 Ger.* Marienburg. NE Latvia
Al 'Ulā *506* NW Saudi Arabia
Al 'Umarī *336* C Jordan
Al Uqşur *see* Luxor
Al Wafrā' *354* SE Kuwait
Al Wāḩāt al Khārijah *see* El Wâhât el Khârga
Al Wajh *506* NW Saudi Arabia
Al Wakrah *479 var.* Wakra. E Qatar
Al Wukayr *479 var.* Al Wukair. E Qatar
Alyat *see* Älät
Alyaty-Pristan' *see* Älät
Alytus *376 Pol.* Olita. S Lithuania
Al Zubair *see* Az Zubayr
Amadora *474* W Portugal
Amakusa-shotō *330* island group to the W of Kyūshū, SW Japan
Amala *342* river of SW Kenya
Amami-Ō-shima *330* island of Amami-shotō, SW Japan
Amami-shotō *330* island group of Nansei-shotō, SW Japan
Amara *see* Al 'Amārah
Amarapura *159* C Burma
Amasia *98 Rus.* Amasiya, *var.* Amasija. NW Armenia
Amasya *577* N Turkey
Amatique, Bahía de, *278* bay of the Gulf of Honduras
Amaury *400* NE Mauritius
Amazon *145, 195, 463 Sp.* Amazonas. River of South America
Amazon Basin *144* physical region of C South America
Ambalangoda *534* SW Sri Lanka
Ambalavao *382* S Madagascar
Ambam *168* S Cameroon
Ambanja *382* N Madagascar
Ambato *228* C Ecuador
Ambatondrazaka *382* E Madagascar
Ambergris Cay *130* island of NE Belize
Ambergris Cays *653* island group of S Turks and Caicos Islands
Ambilobe *382* N Madagascar
Amblève *127* river of E Belgium
Ambo *see* Hāgere Hiywet
Amboasary *382* S Madagascar
Ambohidratrimo *382* C Madagascar
Ambon *302 prev.* Amboina. Ambon, C Indonesia
Ambositra *382* C Madagascar
Ambre, Ile d' *400* Island of NE Mauritius
Ambriz *88* NW Angola
Ambrym *615 var.* Ambrim. Island of E Vanuatu
'Amd *627* C Yemen
Ameland *429* island of Waddeneilanden, N Netherlands
American Samoa *642* unincorporated territory of the USA, Pacific Ocean. ❖ Pago Pago
Amersfoort *429* C Netherlands
Amherst *see* Kyaikkami
Amiens *253* N France
Amilḩayt, Wādī *448 var.* Wādī Umml Ḩayt. Seasonal watercourse of SW Oman
Amīndīvi Islands *296* island group of Lakshadweep, SW India
Amioun *364 var.* Amyūn. N Lebanon
Amirante Islands *512 var.* Amirantes Group. Island of C Seychelles
Amlamé *567* C Togo
Amman *336 Ar.* 'Ammān. ❖ of Jordan, NW Jordan
Ammassalik *646 var.* Angmagssalik. SE Greenland
Ammochostos *see* Gazimağusa
Ammochostos Bay *see* Famagusta Bay
Amnok *see* Yalu
Āmol *307 var.* Amul. N Iran
Amorgós *273* island of SE Greece
Amouli *642 var.* Tau. Tau, E American Samoa
Amourj *398* SE Mauritania
Ampara *534* E Sri Lanka
Amphitrite Group *651* island group of N Paracel Islands
'Amrān *627* W Yemen
Amrāvati *296 prev.* Amraoti. C India
Amritsar *296* N India
Amstelveen *429* W Netherlands
Amsterdam *429* ❖ of the Netherlands, C Netherlands
Amstetten *106* N Austria
Am Timan *180* SE Chad
Amu Darya *77, 558, 581, 610 Turkm.* Amyderya, *Uzb.* Amudaryo. River of C Asia
Amudat *584* E Uganda
Amul *see* Āmol
Amund Ringnes Island *170* island of Sverdrup Islands, N Canada
Amundsen Gulf *170* gulf of the Beaufort Sea, on the NW coast of Canada
Amundsen-Scott *90* US research station at the South Pole, Greater Antarctica, Antarctica
Amundsen Sea *90* sea of the Pacific Ocean, off Antarctica
Amur *187, 485 Chin.* Heilong Jiang. River of China and Russian Federation
Amyderya *see* Amu Darya
Amyūn *see* Amioun
An Abhainn Mhór *see* Blackwater
Anaco *619* NE Venezuela
Anadolu Dağları *see* Doğu Karadeniz Dağlarıı
Anadyr' *485* NE Russian Federation
Anadyr, Gulf of *see* Anadyrskiy Zaliv
Anadyrskiy Zaliv *485 Eng.* Gulf of Anadyr. Gulf of Bering Sea, bordering NE Russian Federation
Anáfi *273* island of SE Greece
Anaiza *see* 'Unayzah
Analalava *382* N Madagascar
Analamaitsa Plateau *382* plateau of NE Madagascar
Anambas, Kepulauan *302* island group to the NW of Borneo, W Indonesia
Anan *330* Shikoku, SW Japan
Anantapur *296* S India
Anápolis *145* S Brazil
Anarjokka *see* Inarijoki
Anatahan *650* island of C Northern Mariana Islands
Anatolia Plateau *576* plateau of C Turkey
Anatom *see* Aneityum
An Bhearú *see* Barrow
An Bhóinn *see* Boyne
Anchorage *598* Alaska, USA
Ancona *321* C Italy
Andalucia *530-531* autonomous community of S Spain
Andaman Islands *296* island group of SE India
Andaman Sea *159, 302, 563* sea of Indian Ocean, to the SW of Burma and Thailand
'Andām, Wadi *448* seasonal desert watercourse of E Oman
Andapa *382* NE Madagascar
Andaung Pech *see* Bâ Kêv
Andenne *127* SE Belgium
Andersen Air Force Base *647* NE Guam
Andes *95, 136, 183, 195, 463* mountain range of South America, running the entire length of the west coast
Andfjorden *444* fjord of NE Norway
Andijon *610 Rus.* Andizhan. E Uzbekistan
Andizhan *see* Andijon
Andkhvoy *101* N Afghanistan
Andoany *382 prev.* Hell-Ville. N Madagascar
Andong *350 Jap.* Antō. E South Korea
Andong-ho *350* reservoir of E South Korea
Andorra *86-87* officially Principality of Andorra. Country of SW Europe divided into 7 admin. units (parishes). ❖ Andorra la Vella
Andorra la Vella *86* ❖ of Andorra, W Andorra
Andreas *647* N Isle of Man
Andreas, Cape *see* Apostolos Andreas, Cape
Andria *321* S Italy
Androna, Lembalemba Ambanin' *382 var.* Plateau de l'Androna. Plateau of N Madagascar
Ándros *273* island of SE Greece
Andros Island *112* island of W Bahamas
Andros Town *112* Andros Island, Bahamas
Andújar *531* SW Spain
Anegada *643* island of NE British Virgin Islands
Aného *567 var.* Anécho, *prev.* Petit-Popo. S Togo
Aneityum *615 var.* Anatom, *prev.* Kéamu. Island of S Vanuatu
Änew *see* Annau
An Fheoir *see* Nore
Anfile Bay *238* bay of the Red Sea to the E of Eritrea
Angara *485* river of C Russian Federation
Angarsk *485* C Russian Federation
Angaur *455* island of S Palau
Ånge *543* C Sweden
Angel *see* Úhlava
Ángel de la Guarda, Isla *403* island of NW Mexico
Angeles *466* Luzon, N Philippines
Angers *253* NW France
Ângk Tasaôm *165 prev.* Angtassom. S Cambodia
Anglesey *593 Wel.* Môn. Island of NW Wales, UK
Angmagssalik *see* Ammassalik
Angoche *419* E Mozambique
Angola *88-89* officially Republic of Angola, *prev.* People's Republic of Angola. Country of Central Africa divided into 18 admin. units (provinces). ❖ Luanda
Angora *see* Ankara
Angoram *458* N Papua New Guinea
Angoulême *253* W France
Angra Pequena *see* Lüderitz
Angren *610* E Uzbekistan
Angtassom *see* Ângk Tasaôm
Anguilla *642* British dependent territory of the Caribbean Sea. ❖ The Valley.

Anguilla Cays *112* islets of W Bahamas
Anguilla Channel *642, 646* channel of the Caribbean Sea between Anguilla and St-Martin
Anguilles, Rivière des *400* river of S Mauritius
Anguillita Island *642* island of S Anguilla
Angwa *636* river of Mozambique and Zimbabwe
Anhui *187 var.* Anhwei. Province of E China
Anhwei *see* Anhui
Anié *567* C Togo
Añisoc *236 var.* Añisok. NE Río Muni, Equatorial Guinea
Añisok *see* Añisoc
Aniwa *615* island of S Vanuatu
Anjou *252-253* cultural region of NW France
Anju *349* W North Korea
Ankara *577 prev.* Angora. ❖ of Turkey, C Turkey
Ankaratra, Tangorombohitr' *382 var.* Ankaratra Range. Mountains of C Madagascar
An Laoi *see* Lee
Ânlong Vêng *165* NW Cambodia
An Mhuir Cheilteach *see* Celtic Sea
Annaba *83 prev.* Bône. NE Algeria
An Nabk *551 var.* Nebk, El Nebk, *Fr.* Nébeck. SW Syria
An Nafūd *506* desert region of N Saudi Arabia
Annai *284* SW Guyana
An Najaf *310 var.* Najaf. C Iraq
Annam *see* Trung Phân
Annapolis *599* Maryland, E USA
Anna, Pulo *455* island of S Palau
Annapurna *427* mountain massif of C Nepal
An Nāqūrah *see* En Nâqoûra
Ann Arbor *599* Michigan, NC USA
An Nás *see* Naas
An Nāşirīyah *310 var.* Nasiriya. SE Iraq
Annau *581 Turkm.* Änew. S Turkmenistan
Annecy *253* E France
An Nīl al Abyaḑ *see* White Nile
An Nīl al Azraq *see* Blue Nile
Annotto Bay *329* E Jamaica
An Nuwaydirāt *115* NE Bahrain
Anşāb *see* Nişāb
Anse-à-Galets *286* Île de la Gonâve, Haiti
Anseba *238* seasonal river of W Eritrea
Anse Boileau *512* Mahé, Seychelles
Anse-d'Hainault *286* SW Haiti
Anse Étoile *512* Mahé, Seychelles
Anse Ger *497* SE St Lucia
Anse La Raye *497* NW St Lucia
Anse-Rouge *286* NW Haiti
Anse Royale *512 var.* Anse Royal. Mahé, Seychelles
Anshan *187 var.* An-shan. Liaoning, NE China
Anson Bay *650* bay of the South Pacific Ocean, NW Norfolk Island
Ansongo *392* E Mali
Antakya *577 var.* Hatay. S Turkey
Antalaha *382* NE Madagascar
Antalya *576 prev.* Adalia. SW Turkey
Antalya Körfezi *576 var.* Gulf of Adalia, *Eng.* Gulf of Antalya. Gulf of the Mediterranean Sea
Antananarivo *382 prev.* Tananarive. ❖ of Madagascar, C Madagascar
Antarctica *90-91* largely ice-covered continent centred on the South Pole. Though not internationally recognized, the following territorial claims have been made: Argentine Antarctica Sector, Australian Antarctic Territory, British Antarctic Territory, Chilean Antarctic Territory, Queen Maud Land (*Nor.*) Dronning Maud Land, Ross Dependency (*NZ*), Terre Adélie (*Fr.*)
Antequera *531* S Spain
Antibes *253* SE France
Antigua *see* Antigua Guatemala
Antigua *92* island of Lesser Antilles which, with Barbuda, forms Antigua & Barbuda
Antigua and Barbuda *92-93* island state of the West Indies, divided into 6 admin. units (parishes). ❖ St John's
Anti-Atlas *414* mountain range of SW Morocco
Antigua Guatemala *278 var.* Antigua. SW Guatemala
Antikýthira *273* island of S Greece
Anti-Lebanon Mountains *364, 551 Fr.* Anti-Liban, *Ar.* Al Jabal ash Sharqī, *var.* Jebel esh Sharqi. Mountain range of Lebanon and Syria
Anti-Liban *see* Anti-Lebanon
Antípsara *273* island of E Greece
Antivari *see* Bar
Antō *see* Andong
Antofagasta *183* N Chile
Antongila, Helodrano *382 var.* Baie d'Antongil, Antongil Bay. Bay to the NE of Madagascar
Antrim Mountains *593* mountain range of NE Northern Ireland, UK
Antseranana *see* Antsirañana
An tSionainn *see* Shannon
Antsirabe *382* C Madagascar
Antsirañana *382 var.* Antseranana, Antsirane, *prev.* Diégo-Suarez. N Madagascar
An tSiúir *see* Suir
Antsla *240 Ger.* Anzen. SE Estonia
An tSláine *see* Slaney
Antsohihy *382* N Madagascar
An-tung *see* Dandong
Antwerp *see* Antwerpen
Antwerpen *127 Eng.* Antwerp, *Fr.* Anvers. N Belgium
Anuradhapura *534* N Sri Lanka
Anuta *522 var.* Cherry I. Island of E Solomon Islands
Anvers *see* Antwerpen
Anyang *350* NW South Korea
Anzen *see* Antsla
Aoba *615 var.* Omba, Ambae. Island of C Vanuatu
Aola *522* NE Guadalcanal, Solomon Is
Aomen *see* Macao
Aomori *330* Honshū, N Japan
Ā'opo *500* Sauai'i, Samoa
Aorangi *see* Mount Cook
Aosta *320* N Italy
Ao Thai *see* Thailand, Gulf of
Aouk *179, 180* river of Central African Republic and Chad
Aozou *180* N Chad
Apaporis *195* river of Brazil and Colombia
Aparan *98* C Armenia
Apartadó *195* NW Colombia
Apatity *484* NW Russian Federation
Apatou *645* NW French Guiana
Ape *362* NE Latvia
Apeldoorn *429* C Netherlands
Apennines *320, 502 It.* Appennino. Mountain range of C Italy
Apenrade *see* Åbenrå
Apéyémé *see* Danyi-Apéyémé
Āpia *500* ❖ of Samoa, Upolu, Samoa
Apitiri, Monts *645* mountain range of S French Guiana
Apoera *538* NW Suriname
Apolima *500* Upolu, Samoa
Apolima Strait *500* strait between Savai'i and Upolu, Samoa
Apo, Mount *466* mountain of Mindanao, S Philippines
Apopa *235* C El Salvador
Apostolos Andreas, Cape *215 var.* Cape Andreas, Zafer Burnu. Cape of Cyprus
Apoteri *284* C Guyana
Appalachian Mountains *599* mountain range of E USA
Appennino *see* Apennines
Appikalo *538* S Suriname
Approuague, l' *645* river of E French Guiana
Apra Harbour *647* harbour of W Guam
Apra Heights *647* W Guam
Apsheronskiy Poluostrov *see* Abşeron Yarımadası
Apure *619* river of W Venezuela
Apurímac *463* river of S Peru
Aqaba *see* Al 'Aqabah
Aqaba, Gulf of *230, 317, 336 var.* Gulf of 'Aqabah, Gulf of Elat, *Ar.* Khalīj al 'Aqabah. Gulf of Red Sea between Egypt and Jordan
'Aqabah, Gulf of *see* Aqaba, Gulf of
Āqchah *77 var.* Āqcheh. N Afghanistan
Aqmola *see* Akmola
Aqtaū *see* Aktau
Aqtöbe *see* Aktyubinsk
Aquila *see* L'Aquila
Aquila degli Abruzzi *see* L'Aquila
Aquin *286* SW Haiti
'Arabah, Wādī al *317, 336 Heb.* Ha'Arava. Dry watercourse of Israel and Jordan
Arabian Gulf *see* The Gulf
Arabian Sea *448, 420-451* sea of the Indian Ocean between Arabia and India
'Arab, Baḩr al *see* Arab, Bahr el
Arab, Bahr el *536 var.* Baḩr al 'Arab. River of S Sudan
'Arabī, Khalīj al *see* The Gulf
Arab Sahara *see* Sahara
'Arab, Shaţţ al *310 Per.* Arvand Rūd. River of Iran and Iraq
Aracaju *145* E Brazil
Árachthos *273 prev.* Árakhthos. River of W Greece
Arad *480* W Romania
'Arad *317* S Israel
'Arād *115* NE Bahrain
'Arādah *590* SW United Arab Emirates
Aradhippou *215 var.* Aradippou. SE Cyprus
Arafura Sea *101, 302* sea of the Indian Ocean between Australia and New Guinea
Aragac *see* Aragats Lerr
Aragats Lerr *98 var.* Aragac. Mountain of W Armenia
Aragón *531* autonomous community of E Spain
Araguaia *145 var.* Araguaya. River of C Brazil
Araguaya *see* Araguaia
Aragvi *262* river of C Georgia
Arai *330* Honshū, C Japan
Arainn Mhór *see* Aran Island
Arāk *307* NW Iran
Arakan Yoma *159* mountain range of W Burma
Araks *see* Aras
Aral Sea *338, 610 Kaz.* Aral Tengizi, *Rus.* Aral'skoye More, *Uzb.* Orol Dengizi. Inland sea of Kazakhstan and Uzbekistan
Aral'sk *338 var.* Aral. SW Kazakhstan
Aral Tengizi *see* Aral Sea
Aran Island *314 Ir.* Arainn Mhór. Island of NW Ireland
Aran Islands *314* island group of W Ireland
Aranos *423* SE Namibia
Aranuka *346* island of the Gilbert Is, W Kiribati
Aranyosmarót *see* Zlaté Moravce
Arao *330* Kyūshū, SW Japan
Araouane *392* N Mali
Arapey Grande *607* river of N Uruguay
Ararat *98* S Armenia
Ararat, Mount *see* Büyükağrı Dağı
Aras *98, 110, 307, 577 Arm.* Arak's, *Per.* Rūd-e Aras, *Rus.* Araks, *Turk.* Aras Nehri. River of SW Asia
Arauca *195* NE Colombia
Arauca *619* river of Colombia and Venezuela
Arawa *458* Bougainville I, Papua New Guinea
Ārba Minch' *243* SW Ethiopia
Arbatax *320* Sardegna, W Italy
Arbīl *310 var.* Irbīl, Erbil, *Kurd.* Hawlēr. N Iraq
Arbon *546* NE Switzerland
Arcalis *86* NW Andorra
Archangel *see* Arkhangel'sk
Arctic Bay *170* N Canada
Arctic Ocean *170, 444, 485 Nor.* Nordishavet, *Rus.* Severnyy Ledovityy Okean. Ocean surrounding North Pole, between N America, N Europe and N Asia
Arctowski *90* Polish research station of South Shetland Islands, Antarctica
Arda *152* river of Bulgaria and Geece
Ardabīl *307 var.* Ardebil. NW Iran
Arḑ aş Şawwān *336 var.* Ardh es Suwwān. ain of C Jordan
Ardennes *127, 378* plateau of W Europe
Arecibo *651* N Puerto Rico
Arel *see* Arlon
Arenal, Laguna *206* lake of NW Costa Rica
Arenas *456* SW Panama
Arendal *444* S Norway
Arensburg *see* Kuressaare
Arequipa *463* SE Peru
Arezzo *321* C Italy
Argentina *94-97* officially Argentine Republic. Country of S South America divided into 23 admin. units (22 provinces, 1 district). ❖ Buenos Aires
Arghandāb, Daryā-ye *77* river of S Afghanistan
Argirocastro *see* Gjirokastër
Argo *536* N Sudan
Argoub *414* W Western Sahara
Argun' *485* river of China and Russian Federation
Argungu *440* NW Nigeria
Argyle, Lake *101* salt lake of NW Australia
Argyrokastron *see* Gjirokastër
Århus *218 var.* Aarhus. C Denmark
Ariamsvlei *423* S Namibia
Ariana *573 var.* Aryānah, L'Ariana. N Tunisia
Ari Atoll *390* atoll of C Maldives
Arica *183* N Chile
Aride, Île *512* island of the Inner Islands, NE Seychelles
Arīḩā *see* Jericho
Arima *570* N Trinidad, Trinidad & Tobago
Arinsal *86* NW Andorra
Arinsal, Riu d' *86* river of NW Andorra
Aripo, Mount *570 var.* El Cerro del Aripo. Mountain of N Trinidad & Tobago
Aripuanã *144* river of W Brazil
Arizona *598* state of SW USA
Arkalyk *338 Kaz.* Arqalyk. C Kazakhstan
Arkansas *599* river of SC USA
Arkansas *599* state of SC USA
Arkhangel'sk *484 Eng.* Archangel. NW Russian Federation
Arklow *314 Ir.* Inbhear Mór. E Ireland
Arles *253* SE France
Arlon *127 Dut.* Aarlen, *Ger.* Arel. SE Belgium
Armagh *593* Northern Ireland, UK
Armathia *273* island of SE Greece
Armenia *195* W Colombia
Armenia *98-99* officially Republic of Armenia *prev.* Armenian Soviet Socialist Republic. Country of SW Asia divided into 39 admin. units (shrjaner). ❖ Yerevan
Armidale *101* E Australia
Arnaouti, Cape *215* cape of W Cyprus
Arnhem *429* SE Netherlands
Arnhem Land *101* region of N Australia
Arno *320* river C of Italy
Arno *396* island of SE Marshall Islands
Aroab *423* SE Namibia
Aroe Islands *see* Aru, Kepulauan
Arop Island *458 var.* Long I. Island of E Papua New Guinea
Arorae *346* island of the Gilbert Is, W Kiribati
Arp'a *98* river of Armenia and Azerbaijan
Arqalyk *see* Arkalyk
Ar Rahad *see* Er Rahad

Arraiján 456 C Panama
Arrak District 396 district of Majuro, SE Marshall Islands
Ar Ramādī 310 C Iraq
Ar Rams 590 NE United Arab Emirates
Ar Ramthā 336 N Jordan
Arran, Isle of 593 island of W Scotland, UK
Ar Raqqah 551 *Fr.* Rakka. N Syria
Arras 253 N France
Ar Rawḑah 627 S Yemen
Ar Rawḑatayn 354 N Kuwait
Ar Rayyān 479 *var.* Al Rayyan. E Qatar
Ar Rifā' al Gharbī 115 N Bahrain
Ar Rifā' ash Sharqī 115 NE Bahrain
Ar Riyāḑ *see* Riyadh
Ar Riyān 627 S Yemen
Arrö *see* Ærø
Ar Ru'ays 479 *var.* Ar Ruways, Al Ruweis, Ruwais. N Qatar
Ar Ru'ays 590 *var.* Ruwaisv, Ar Ruways. W United Arab Emirates
Ar Rufayq 479 *var.* Al Rufaig. NW Qatar
Ar Rustāq 448 *var.* Rostak. N Oman
Ar Ruwayshid 336 NE Jordan
Ar Safad *see* Ẕefat
'Arta 222 SE Djibouti
Artashat 98 *var.* Artašat. S Armenia
Artemisa 210 NW Cuba
Artëm-Ostrov *see* Artyom
Artibonite 286 river of Haiti
Artigas 607 *prev.* San Eugenio, *var.* San Eugenio del Cuareim. N Uruguay
Art'ik 98 W Armenia
Art, Île 650 island of Îles Belep, W New Caledonia
Artois 253 cultural region of N France
Artsvashen 98 *var.* Bashkend. NE Armenia
Artvin 577 NE Turkey
Artyom 110 *Rus.* Artëm-Ostrov. E Azerbaijan
Arua 584 NW Uganda
Aruângua *see* Luangwa
Aruba 642 autonomous part of the Netherlands, Caribbean Sea. ❖ Oranjestad
Aru, Kepulauan 302-303 *prev.* Aroe Islands. Island group to the SW of Irian Jaya, W Indonesia
Aruliho 522 NW Guadalcanal, Solomon Is
Årup 218 Fyn, SW Denmark
Arusha 560 N Tanzania
Aruwimi 203 river of NE Dem. Rep. Congo (Zaire)
Arvand Rūd *see* 'Arab, Shaṭṭ al
Arvayheer 412 C Mongolia
Arvika 543 SW Sweden
Aryānah *see* Ariana
Asadābād 77 E Afghanistan
Asad, Buḩayrat al 551 reservoir of Syria
Asahi-dake 331 mountain of Hokkaidō, N Japan
Asahikawa 331 Hokkaidō, N Japan
Asaka 610 *Rus.* Assake, *prev.* Leninsk. E Uzbekistan
Asamankese 270 SE Ghana
Āsau 500 Savai'i, Samoa
Āsbe Teferī 243 *var.* Asba Tafari. C Ethiopia
Ascension 652 dependent territory of St Helena, South Atlantic Ocean
Ascension *see* Pohnpei
Ascoli Piceno 321 C Italy
Aseb 238 *var.* Assab, *Amh.* Āseb. SE Eritrea
'As 'Êla 222 SW Djibouti
Āsela 243 *var.* Aselle, Asella, Asselle. C Ethiopia
Asenovgrad 152 S Bulgaria
Aseri 240 *Ger.* Asserin. NE Estonia
Ashburton 433 C South Island, New Zealand
Ashdod 317 C Israel
Ashford 593 SE England, UK
Ashgabat 581 *prev.* Ashkhabad, Poltoratsk. ❖ of Turkmenistan, S Turkmenistan
Ashikaya 330 Honshū, SE Japan
Ashkhabad *see* Ashgabat
Ashmyany 122 NW Belarus
Ashots'k 98 *prev.* Ghukasyan, *Rus.* Gukasyan. NW Armenia
Ashqelon 317 C Israel
Ash Shadādah 551 *var.* Ash Shaddādah, Shaddādī, Shedadi, Tell Shedadi. NE ria
Ash Shaḩanīyah 479 *var.* Al Shahaniyah. C Qatar
Ash Shāmīyah 310 C Iraq
Ash Sharāh 336 *var.* Esh Sharā. Mountains of W Jordan
Ash Shaṭrah 310 SE Iraq
Ash Shawbak 336 *var.* Ash Shawbak an Nijil. W Jordan
Ash Shiḩr 627 SE Yemen
Ash Shiṣar 448 SW Oman
Ash Shuqayq 354 *var.* As Shageeg. Desert region of S Kuwait
Ashtarak 98 *var.* Aštarak. W Armenia
Ashton 498 Union I, St Vincent & the Grenadines
Asidonhopo 538 C Suriname
'Asi, Nahr al *see* Orantes
'Asi Oronte, Nahr al *see* Orantes
Asipovichy 122 *Rus.* Osipovichi. C Belarus
'Askar 115 E Bahrain
Asmara 238 *Amh.* Asmera. ❖ of Eritrea, C Eritrea
Aspinwall *see* Colón
Aspropotamos *see* Acheloos
Assab *see* Aseb
Aş Şabirīyah 354 NE Kuwait
Aş Şabīyah 354 *var.* Sabyah. NE Kuwait
As Sabkhah 551 *var.* Sabkha. NE Syria
Aş Şafāwī 336 N Jordan
Aş Şafī 336 *var.* Safi. W Jordan
'Assa Gaïla 222 N Djibouti
As Sahlat al Ḩadrīyah 115 N Bahrain
Aş Şaḩrā' *see* Sahara
Aş Şaḩrā' al Gharbīyah *see* Sahara el Gharqîya
Aş Şaḩrā' al Lībīyah *see* Libyan Desrt
Aş Şaḩrā' ash Sharqīyah *see* Sahara el Sharqîya
Assake *see* Asaka
As Salimi 354 *var.* Salemy. W Kuwait
As Salīmīyah 354 E Kuwait
'Assal, Lac 222 lake of C Djibouti
As Salṭ 336 *var.* Salt. NW Jordan
As Salwá 479 *var.* Salwah, Salwa. SW Qatar
Assamaka 439 *var.* Assamakka. NW Niger
As Samāwah 310 *var.* Samawa. S Iraq
'Assâmo 222 S Djibouti
Aş Şarīḩ 336 NW Jordan
Assen 429 NE Netherlands
Asserin *see* Aseri
As Shageeg *see* Ash Shuqayq
As Sīb 448 N Oman
Assiout *see* Asyût
Assisi 321 C Italy
Assling *see* Jesenice
Assomption 512 island of the Aldabra Group, SW Seychelles
Aş Şubayḩīyah 354 S Kuwait
As Sufāl 627 S Yemen
As Sukhnah 551 *var.* Sukhne, *Fr.* Soukhné. C Syria
As Sulaymānīyah 310 *var.* Sulaimaniya, *Kurd.* Slēmānī. NE Iraq
As Sulayyil 506 C Saudi Arabia
As Suwaydā' 551 *var.* El Suweida, *Fr.* Soueida. SW Syria
As Suwayq 448 *var.* Suwaik. N Oman
As Suways *see* Suez
Astana 338 *prev* Akmola ❖ of Kazakhstan, N Kazakhstan
Astara 110 S Azerbaijan
Aštarak *see* Ashtarak
Asti 320 N Italy
Astipálaia 273 island of SE Greece
Astove 512 island of the Aldabra Group, SW Seychelles
Astrakhan' 484 SW Russian Federation
Astrakhan-Bazar *see* Cälilabad
Astrida *see* Butare
Asturias 530 autonomous community of NW Spain
Asuka 90 Japanese research station of Greater Antarctica, Antarctica
Āsuisui, Cape 500 cape on the coast of Savai'i, Samoa
Asuncion 650 island of N Northern Mariana Islands
Asunción 460 ❖ of Paraguay, S Paraguay
Asunción Mita 278 SE Guatemala
Aswa *see* Achwa
Aswân 230 *var.* Aswān. SE Egypt
Aswân High Dam 230 dam of SE Egypt
Asyût 230 *var.* Assiout. C Egypt
Ata 568 island of SW Tonga
Atacama Desert 183 desert of N Chile
Atafu Atoll 653 island of NW Tokelau
Atakora, Chaîne de l' 132 *var.* Atakora Mountains. Mountain range of N Benin
Atakpamé 567 C Togo
Aṭâr 398 C Mauritania
Atas, Pulu *see* South Island
Atbara 536 *var.* Nahr 'Aṭbarah. River of NE Sudan
Atbara 536 *var.* 'Aṭbarah. NE Sudan
'Aṭbarah, Nahr *see* Atbara
Atbasar 338 N Kazakhstan
At-Bashy 357 *var.* At-Bashi, At-Baši. C Kyrgyzstan
Athabasca 170 *var.* Athabaska. River of W Canada
Athabasca, Lake 170 lake of W Canada
Athabaska *see* Athabasca
Athens 273 *Gk* Athína, *prev.* Athínai. ❖ of Greece, SE mainland Greece
Athi 342 river of S Kenya
Athienou 215 SE Cyprus
Athína *see* Athens
Athínai *see* Athens
Athlone 314 *Ir.* Áth Luain. C Ireland
Áth Luain *see* Athlone
Athna 215 *var.* Achna, Akhna, *Turk.* Düzce. E Cyprus
Ati 180 C Chad
Atiak 584 NW Uganda
Atitlán, Lago de 278 lake of W Guatemala
Atiu 644 island of Southern Cook Islands, S Cook Islands
Atlanta 599 Georgia, SE USA
Atlantic Ocean 90, 294, 593, 643 *var.* Atlantshaf. Ocean bounded to the W by the Americas, to the E by Europe and Africa and to the S by Antarctica
Atlantshaf *see* Atlantic Ocean
Atlas Mountains 414 mountain range of C Morocco
Atlas Saharien 83 mountain range of N Algeria
Atrak 307, 581 *Rus.* Atrek, *Turkm.* Etrek. River of Iran and Turkmenistan
Atrato 195 river of NW Colombia
Atrek *see* Atrak
Aṭ Ṭaff 590 desert region of C United Arab Emirates
Aṭ Ṭafīlah 336 W Jordan
Aṭ Ṭā'if 506 W Saudi Arabia
At Tall al Abyaḑ 551 *Fr.* Tell Abaid. N Syria
Attapu 359 *var.* Attopeu. SE Laos
Attersee 106 *var.* Kammersee. Lake of N Austria
At Tibnī 551 NE Syria
Attopeu *see* Attapu
At Turbah 627 SW Yemen
Atyrau 338 *prev.* Gur'yev. W Kazakhstan
Auch 253 SW France
Auckland 433 N North Island, New Zealand
Augier 497 S St Lucia
Augila *see* Awjilah
Augsburg 265 S Germany
Augusta 321 Sicilia, S Italy
Augusta 599 Maine, NE USA
Aujā et Taḩtā 318 E West Bank
Auki 522 NW Malaita, Solomon Is
Auliye-Ata *see* Taraz
Aur 396 island of E Marshall Islands
Aurich 264 NW Germany
Aurillac 253 S France
Aurine, Alpi *see* Zillertaler Alpen
Aurora 284 NW Guyana
Aurora *see* Maéwo
Aus 423 SW Namibia
Aussig *see* Ústí nad Labem
Austin 599 Texas, SC USA
Australes, Îles 646 island group of SW French Polynesia
Australia 100-105 officially Commonwealth of Australia. Country situated between the Indian and Pacific Oceans, divided into 8 admin. units (6 states and 2 territories). ❖ Canberra
Australian Alps 101 mountain range of SE Australia
Australian Capital Territory 101 territory of SE Australia
Austria 106-107 officially Republic of Austria, *Ger.* Österreich. Country of C Europe divided into 9 admin. units (states). ❖ Vienna
Ausuitoq *see* Grise Fiord
Auvergne 253 cultural region of SE France
Auxerre 253 N France
Avarua 644 ❖ of Cook Islands, Rarotonga, S Cook Islands
Avatele 650 S Niue
Aveiro 474 W Portugal
Avellino 321 S Italy
Aves, Islas les 619 island group of N Venezuela
Aveyron 253 river of S France
Avezzano 321 C Italy
Avignon 253 SE France
Avila 531 C Spain
Avilés 530 NW Spain
Avranches 252 NW France
Avuavu 522 SE Guadalcanal, Solomon Is
Awaaso 270 *var.* Awaso. SW Ghana
'Awālī 115 C Bahrain
Awara Plain 342 plain of NE Kenya
Awash 243 *var.* Hawash. River of C Ethiopia
Awbārī 371 W Libya
Awbārī, Şaḩrā' 371 desert of W Libya
Awjilah 371 *It.* Augila. NE Libya
Awled Djellal *see* Ouled Djellal
Axarfjördhur *see* Öxarfjördhur
Axel Heiberg Island 170 *var.* Axel Heiburg. Island of Sverdrup Islands, N Canada
Axim 270 S Ghana
Axios *see* Vadar
Ayabe 330 Honshū, C Japan
Ayacucho 463 S Peru
Ayaguz 338 *Kaz.* Ayaköz. E Kazakhstan
Ayaköz *see* Ayaguz
Ayamé Reservoir 326 reservoir of E Ivory Coast
Ayamiken 236 NW Río Muni, Equatorial Guinea
Āybak 77 *var.* Aibak, Haibak. NE Afghanistan
Aydarkŭl 610 *Rus.* Ozero Aydarkul'. River of E Uzbekistan
Aydın 576 SW Turkey
Ayer Chawan, Pulau 517 island of SW Singapore
Ayer Hitam 386 S Peninsular Malaysia
Ayer Merbau, Pulau 517 island of SW Singapore
Ayers Rock *see* Uluru
Ayeyarwady *see* Irrawaddy
Ayia Napa 215 *var.* Agia Napa. E Cyprus
Ayios Amvrosios *see* Esentepe
Áyios Eustratios 273 island of E Greece
Ayios Ioannis 215 *var.* Agios Ioannis. SW Cyprus
Ayios Seryios *see* Yeniboğaziçi

Ayios Theodhoros *see* Çayirova
'Ayn al Ghazāl *371* SE Libya
'Ayn ath Tha'lab *371* C Libya
Ayní *558* W Tajikistan
Ayorou *439* W Niger
'Ayoûn el 'Atroûs *398 var.* Aïoun el Atroûss. SE Mauritania
Ayr *593* W Scotland, UK
Ayre, Point of *647* headland on the N coast of Isle of Man
Ayrs' *338* S Kazakhstan
Āysha *243* NE Ethiopia
Aytos *152 var.* Aitos, Ajtos. E Bulgaria
Ayutthaya *563 var.* Phra Nakhon Si Ayutthaya. C Thailand
Aywat aş Şay'ar, Wādī *627* seasonal river of N Yemen
Azaha, Costa del *531* coastal region of E Spain
Azaouagh, Vallée de l' *439 var.* Azaouak. Seasonal river of W Niger
Azaouak *see* Azaouagh, Vallée de l'
Azärbaycan *see* Azerbaijan
A'zāz *551* NW Syria
Azbine *see* Aïr
Azerbaijan *110-111* officially Republic of Azerbaijan, *Az.* Azärbaycan, *prev.* Azerbaijan SSR. Country of SE Caucasus divided into 90 admin. units (rayons). ❖ Baku
Āzezo *243* NW Ethiopia
Azimabad *see* Patna
Azizbekov *see* Vayk'
Azogues *228* S Ecuador
Azores *474 Port.* Arquipélago dos Açores, *var.* Açores. Island group of W Portugal
Azoum *180* river of SE Chad
Azov, Sea of *484, 586 Ukr.* Azovs'ke More, *Rus.* Azovskoye More. Area of Black Sea between Russian Federation and Ukraine
Azovs'ke More *see* Azov, Sea of
Azovskoye More *see* Azov, Sea of
Azraq, Bahr el *see* Blue Nile
Azraq, Wāḩat al *336* oasis of N Jordan
Azrou *414* C Morocco
Azua *226* SE Dominican Republic
Azuero, Península de *456* peninsula of S Panama
Azul *95* E Argentina
Azur, Côte d' *253* coastal region of SE France
'Azza *see* Gaza
Az Zāb al Kabīr *see* Great Zab
Az Zāb aş Şaghīr *see* Little Zab
Az Zahrān *506 Eng.* Dhahran. NE Saudi Arabia
Az Zallāq *115* W Bahrain
Az Zarqā' *336* NW Jordan
Az Zāwiyah *371* NW Libya
Azzel Matti, Sebkha *83 var.* Sebkra Azz el Matti. Salt flat of C Algeria
Az Zaydīyah *627* W Yemen
Az Zilfī *506* C Saudi Arabia
Az Zubayr *310 var.* Al Zubair. SE Iraq

B

Ba *see* Sông Da Rang
Ba *246 prev.* Mba. Viti Levu, W Fiji
Baa Atoll *see* South Maalhosmadulu Atoll
Baaba, Île *650* island of Îles Belep, W New Caledonia
Baabda *364 var.* B'abdā. C Lebanon
Baalbek *364 var.* Ba'labakk. E Lebanon
Baar *546* N Switzerland
Baardheere *524 var.* Bardere, *It.* Bardera. SW Somalia
Baarle-Hertog *127* exclave of N Belgium
Baba *381 var.* Buševa Planina. Mountain range of Greece and FYR Macedonia
Bababé *398* SW Mauritania
Babahoyo *228 prev.* Bodegas. C Ecuador
Bābā, Kūh-e *77* mountain range of C Afghanistan
Bāb al Mandab *see* Bab el Mandeb
Babatag, Khrebet *see* Bobotogh, Qatorkūhi
Bab el Mandeb *222, 627 Ar.* Bāb al Māndab. Strait connecting the Gulf of Aden and Red Sea, between Djibouti and Yemen
Babelthuap *455* island of E Palau
Babian Jiang *see* Black River
Babonneau *497* N St Lucia
Babruysk *122 Rus.* Bobruysk. E Belarus
Babuyan Channel *466* channel connecting South China Sea and Pacific Ocean
Babuyan Islands *466* island of N Philippines
Bacan, Pulau *302 prev.* Batjan. Island of Maluku, E Indonesia
Bacău *480* NE Romania
Băc Bô, Vinh *see* Tongking, Gulf of
Băc Giang *623* N Vietnam
Bach Long Vi, Đao *623* island of N Vietnam
Bačka Topola *630 Hung.* Topolya, *prev.* Bácstopolya. N Serbia, Yugoslavia
Bac Liêu *623 var.* Vinh Loi. S Vietnam
Bacolod *466* Negros, C Philippines
Bac Phân *623 var.* Tonkin, Tongking. Cultural region of N Vietnam
Bácstopolya *see* Bačka Topola
Badajoz *530* W Spain
Badalona *531* E Spain
Badas *150* W Brunei
Baden *106 var.* Baden bei Wien. NE Austria J678
Baden *546* N Switzerland
Bad Ischl *106* C Austria
Bādiyat ash Badkhyz *581 var.* Badhyz, *Turkm.* Bathyz. Region of S Turkmenistan
Bādiyat ash Shām *see* Syrian Desert
Badkhyz ash Shām *see* Syrian Desert
Badou *567* W Togo
Badulla *534* C Sri Lanka
Badyarada 'Adméd *see* Aden, Gulf of
Baetic Mountains *see* Penibético, Sistema
Bafang *168* W Cameroon
Bafatá *282* C Guinea-Bissau
Baffin Bay *171, 646* bay of the Atlantic Ocean, between Baffin Island, NE Canada and Greenland
Baffin Island *171* island of NE Canada
Bafia *168* C Cameroon
Bafilo *567* NE Togo
Bafing *281, 392* headstream of the Senegal river, Guinea and Mali
Bafoussam *168* W Cameroon
Bafra *577* N Turkey
Baga *441* NE Nigeria
Bagaces *206* NW Costa Rica
Bagamoyo *560* E Tanzania
Baganuur *412* C Mongolia
Baghdad *310 var.* Bagdad, *Ar.* Baghdād. ❖ of Iraq, C Iraq
Bāgherhat *117* SW Bangladesh
Baghlān *77* NE Afghanistan
Baghramyan *98 var.* Bagramyan. W Armenia
Baglung *427* C Nepal
Bago *466 var.* Bago City. Negros, C Philippines
Bago *see* Pegu
Bagoé *392* river of Ivory Coast and Mali
Bagramyan *see* Baghramyan
Baguio *466* Luzon, N Philippines
Bagzane, Monts *439* mountain of N Niger
Bahamas *112-113* officially The Commonwealth of the Bahamas. Island state of the W Atlantic Ocean. ❖ Nassau
Bahāwalpur *451 var.* Bhawalpur. E Pakistan
Bäherden *see* Bakharden
Bahía Blanca *95* E Argentina
Bahía de Caráquez *see* Caráquez
Bahía, Islas de la *288* island group to the N of Honduras
Bahir Dar *243 var.* Bahr Dar. NW Ethiopia
Bahlah *448 var.* Bahla. N Oman
Bahrain *114-115* officially State of Bahrain, *Ar.* Al Baḩrayn, *prev.* Bahrein. Country of the The Gulf divided into 9 admin. units (municipalities and regions). ❖ Manama
Bahrain, Gulf of *115, 479 var.* Khalīj al Baḩrayn. Area of the The Gulf, off the E coast of Arabian Peninsula
Bahrām Chāh *77* SW Afghanistan
Bahr Dar *see* Bahir Dar
Bahrein *see* Bahrain
Baia Mare *480 Hung.* Nagybánya, *Ger.* Neustadt. N Romania
Baïbokoum *180* S Chad
Baicheng *187 var.* Pai-ch'eng, *prev.* T'aon-an. Jilin. NE China
Baidoa *see* Baydhabo
Baikal, Lake *see* Baykal, Ozero
Baile Átha Cliath *see* Dublin
Bailey's Bay *643* bay of the North Atlantic Ocean, N Bermuda
Bailundo *88 Port.* Vila Teixeira da Silva. C Angola
Bainet *286* S Haiti
Bā'ir *see* Bāyir
Bairiki *346* S Tarawa, Kiribati
Baitadi *427* W Nepal
Baitou Shan *see* Paektu-san
Baiyuda *see* Bayudha Desert
Baja *290* S Hungary
Baja California *403 Eng.* Lower California. Peninsula of NW Mexico
Bājil *627* W Yemen
Bajo Boquete *see* Boquete
Bajos de Haina *226* S Dominican Republic
Bajram Curri *81* N Albania
Bajura *see* Martadi
Bakala *179* C Central African Republic
Bakau *261* W Gambia
Bakel *510* E Senegal
Bâ Kêv *165 var.* Bo Kheo, *prev.* Andaung Pech. NE Cambodia
Bakharden *581 prev.* Bakherden, *Turkm.* Bäherden. SW Turkmenistan
Bākhtarān *307 prev.* Kermānshāh, Qahremānshahr. W Iran
Bakı *see* Baku
Bakı Komissarı *110 Rus.* Imeni 26 Bakinskikh Komissarov. SE Azerbaijan
Bakkaflói *294* area of the Norwegian Sea
Bakony *290 Eng.* Bakony Mountains. Mountain range of W Hungary
Bakoumba *258* SE Gabon
Bakoy *392* headstream of the Senegal river, W Mali
Baku *110 Az.* Bakı, *var.* Baky. ❖ of Azerbaijan, E Azerbaijan
Bakwanga *see* Mbuji-Mayi
Balabac Island *466* island of W Philippines
Balabac Strait *387, 466* strait connecting the South China Sea and Sulu Sea
Balabio, Île *650* island of W New Caledonia
Balaka *385* S Malawi
Balakovo *484* W Russian Federation
Bal'amā *336* NW Jordan
Bālā Morghāb *77* NW Afghanistan
Balata *497* N St Lucia
Balaton *290 var.* Lake Balaton, *Ger.* Plattensee. Lake of W Hungary
Balbina, Represa *144* reservoir of NW Brazil
Balboa *456* C Panama
Balcarce *95* E Argentina
Balclutha *433* S South Island, New Zealand
Bâle *see* Basel
Baleares, Islas *531 Eng.* Balearic Islands. Island group of E Spain
Balearic Islands *see* Islas Baleares
Balḩāf *627* S Yemen
Balho *222* NW Djibouti
Bali *303* island of C Indonesia
Baliceaux *498* island of C St Vincent & the Grenadines
Balıkesir *576* W Turkey
Balikpapan *302* Borneo, C Indonesia
Balimo *458* SW Papua New Guinea
Balkan Mountains *152 Bul.* Stara Planina. Mountain range of Bulgaria and Yugoslavia
Balkh *77* N Afghanistan
Balkhash *338 Kaz.* Balqash. SE Kazakhstan
Balkhash, Ozero *338 Eng.* Lake Balkhash, *Kaz.* Balqash Köl. Lake of SE Kazakhstan
Balla Balla *see* Mbalabala
Ballarat *101* SE Australia
Ballari *see* Bellary
Ballaugh *647* NW Isle of Man
Balleny Islands *90* island group to the N of Victoria Land, Antarctica
Ballina *314* NW Ireland
Ballymena *593* Northern Ireland, UK
Balqash *see* Balkhash
Balqash Köl *see* Balkhash, Ozero
Balsas *403 var.* Mexcala. River of S Mexico
Balsas *456* river of SE Panama
Bălţi *408 Rus.* Bel'tsy. N Moldova
Baltic Port *see* Paldiski
Baltic Sea *240, 249, 265, 362, 376 Ger.* Ostee. Sea of the Atlantic Ocean between Scandinavia and NE Europe
Baltimore *599* Maryland, E USA
Baltischport *see* Paldiski
Baltiski *see* Paldiski
Baluchistan *420-451* administrative region of SW Pakistan
Balykchy *357 prev.* Issyk-Kul', Rybach'ye, *Kir.* Ysyk-Köl. NE Kyrgyzstan
Balzar *228* W Ecuador
Balzers *374* S Liechtenstein
Bamako *392* ❖ of Mali, SW Mali
Bambadinca *282* C Guinea-Bissau
Bambama *200* SW Congo
Bambari *179* C Central African Republic
Bambarra *653* Grand Caicos, N Turks and Caicos Islands
Bamberg *265* S Germany
Bambey *510* W Senegal
Bamenda *168* W Cameroon
Bāmīān *77* NE Afghanistan
Bamingui *179* river of N Central African Republic
Banaba *346* island of W Kiribati
Banamba *392* W Mali
Banana *346 prev.* Main Camp. Kiritimati, E Kiribati
Banana Islands *514* island group of W Sierra Leone
Bananal, Ilha do *145* island between the two branches of the river Araguaia, C Brazil
Banda, Laut *302 Eng.* Banda Sea. Sea of the Pacific Ocean, E Indonesia
Bandama *326* river of S Ivory Coast
Bandama Blanc *326* river of C Ivory Coast
Bandama Rouge *326 var.* Marahoué. River of C Ivory Coast
Bandar-e 'Abbās *307* SE Iran
Bandar-e Būshehr *307 var.* Būshehr, *Eng.* Bushire. SW Iran
Bandar Maharani *see* Muar
Bandar Penggaram *see* Batu Pahat
Bandar Seri Begawan *150 prev.* Brunei Town. ❖ of Brunei, N Brunei
Bandar Sri Aman *386 prev.* Simanggang. SW Borneo, Malaysia
Banda Sea *see* Banda, Laut
Band-e Torkestān *77* NW Afghanistan
Bandiagara *392* C Mali
Bandırma *576* NW Turkey
Bandoeng *see* Bandung
Bandrélé *649* SE Mayotte
Bandundu *203 prev.* Banningville. W Dem. Rep. Congo (Zaire)
Bandung *302 prev.* Bandoeng. Java, C Indonesia
Banes *211* SE Cuba
Baney *236* N Bioko, Equatorial Guinea
Banfora *157* SW Burkina

Bangalore *296, 301* S India
Bangangté *168* W Cameroon
Bangar *150* NE Brunei
Bangassou *179* SE Central African Republic
Bangfai *359* river of S Laos
Banggai, Kepulauan *302* island group to the E of Celebes, C Indonesia
Banggi, Pulau *387* *var.* Banggi. Island of NE Borneo, Malaysia
Banghāzī *371* *Eng.* Benghazi, *It.* Bengasi. N Libya
Banghiang *359* *var.* Bang Hieng. River of S Laos
Bangka, Pulau *302* island to the SE of Sumatra, W Indonesia
Bangkok *563* *Th.* Krung Thep. ❖ of Thailand, C Thailand
Bangladesh *116-119* officially People's Republic of Bangladesh, *prev.* East Pakistan. Country of S Asia divided into 4 admin. units (divisions). ❖ Dhaka
Bangor *593* Northern Ireland, UK
Bangor *593* N Wales, UK
Bangor *599* Maine, NE USA
Bangui *179* ❖ of Central African Republic, SW Central African Republic
Bangweulu, Lake *635* *var.* Lake Bengweulu. Lake of N Zambia
Banhā *see* Benha
Ban Hat Yai *see* Hat Yai
Ban Hin Heup *359* C Laos
Ban Houayxay *359* *var.* Ban Houei Sai. NW Sai Laos
Ban Hua Hin *563* C Thailand
Baní *226* S Dominican Republic
Bani *392* river of S Mali
Banias *see* Bāniyās
Banī Jamrah *115* NW Bahrain
Banikoara *132* N Benin
Banī Suwayf *see* Beni Suef
Banī Walīd *371* NW Libya
Bāniyās *551* *var.* Banias. W Syria
Banja Luka *140* NW Bosnia & Herzegovina
Banjarmasin *302* *prev.* Bandjarmasin. Borneo, C Indonesia
Banjës, Liqeni i *81* lake of C Albania
Banjul *261* *prev.* Bathurst. ❖ of Gambia, W Gambia
Ban Kenggnang *359* SE Laos
Ban Kengkabao *359* S Laos
Banket *636* N Zimbabwe
Banks, Îles *see* Banks Islands
Banks Island *170* island of NW Canada
Banks Islands *615* *Fr.* Îles Banks. Island group of N Vanuatu
Banks Peninsula *433* peninsula of E South Island, New Zealand
Ban Lakxao *359* *var.* Lak Sao. E Laos
Banmo *see* Bhamo
Ban Mun-Houamuang *359* SE Laos
Ban Nadou *359* S Laos
Ban Nakha *359* C Laos
Ban Na Kout *359* C Laos
Ban Na Môn *359* NE Laos
Ban Nanai *359* S Laos
Ban Nangeo *359* S Laos
Ban Napha *359* C Laos
Ban Nasi *359* E Laos
Ban Naxon *359* C Laos
Banningville *see* Bandundu
Ban Nongkeun *359* C Laos
Ban Nongsim *359* S Laos
Baños *228* C Ecuador
Bánovce nad Bebravou *519* *var.* Bánovce. W Slovakia
Ban Phon *359* *var.* Ban Phone. SE Laos
Ban Phone *see* Ban Phon
Ban Phou A Douk *359* E Laos
Ban Saka *359* C Laos
Bansang *261* E Gambia
Ban Set *359* S Laos
Banská Bystrica *519* *Ger.* Neusohl, *Hung.* Besztercebánya. C Slovakia
Ban Talak *359* E Laos
Bantè *132* W Benin
Ban Thabôk *359* C Laos
Bantry *314* SW Ireland
Bantry Bay *314* *Ir.* Bá Bheanntrai. Area of the Celtic Sea, SW Ireland
Ban Xot *359* S Laos
Banyak, Kepulauan *302* island group to the NW of Sumatra, W Indonesia
Banyo *168* N Cameroon
Banzart *see* Bizerte
Baoding *187* *var.* Pao-ting, *prev.* Tsingyuan. Hebei, NE China
Baoji *187* *var.* Pao-chi, Paoki. Shaanxi, C China
Baoro *179* W Central African Republic
Baoshan *186* *var.* Pao-shan. Yunnan, SW China
Baotou *187* *var.* Pao-t'ou, Paotow. Nei Mongol Zizhiqu, N China
Ba'qūbah *310* C Iraq
Bar *630* *It.* Antivari. S Montenegro, Yugoslavia
Baraawe *524* *It.* Brava. S Somalia
Baracaldo *531* N Spain
Baracoa *211* SE Cuba
Barahona *226* SW Dominican Republic
Baraka *238* seasonal river of Eritrea and Sudan
Barakī Barak *77* E Afghanistan
Baram *387* *var.* Barram. River of C Borneo, Malaysia
Barama *284* river of N Guyana
Baramanni *284* N Guyana
Baramita *284* NW Guyana
Baranavichy *122* *Rus.* Baranovichi, *Pol.* Baranowicze. W Belarus
Barbados *120-121* island state of the Lesser Antilles, Caribbean Sea divided into 11 admin. units (districts or parishes). ❖ Bridgetown
Bārbār *115* NW Bahrain
Barbuda *92* island of Lesser Antilles which, with Antigua, forms Antigua & Barbuda
Barce *see* Al Marj
Barcellona *321* Sicilia, S Italy
Barcelona *531* E Spain
Barcelona *619* NE Venezuela
Barclayville *368* SW Liberia
Barcoo *see* Cooper Creek
Bärdä *110* C Azerbaijan
Bardaï *180* N Chad
Bardejov *519* *Hung.* Bártfa, *Ger.* Bartfeld. NE Slovakia
Bardera *see* Baardheere
Bardo *573* *var.* Bārdaw, Le Bardo. N Tunisia
Bareilly *296* *Hind.* Bareli. N India
Bareli *see* Bareilly
Barentsburg *653* Spitsbergen, W Svalbard
Barents Sea *444, 484* *Nor.* Barentshavet, *Rus.* Barentsevo More. Sea of Arctic Ocean bordering N Europe
Barentu *238* W Eritrea
Bargny *510* W Senegal
Bari *321* *var.* Bari delle Puglie. S Italy
Bari delle Puglie *see* Bari
Barika *83* N Algeria
Barīkowṭ *77* *var.* Barikot. NE Afghanistan
Barillas *278* NW Guatemala
Barīm *627* *Eng.* Perim. Island of SW Yemen
Barinas *619* W Venezuela
Baringo, Lake *342* lake of W Kenya
Barisāl *117* S Bangladesh
Barisan, Pegunungan *302* mountain range of Sumatra, W Indonesia
Barito *302* river of Borneo, C Indonesia
Barkā' *448* *var.* Birka. N Oman
Barka *see* Al Marj
Barkly Tableland *101* plateau of N Australia
Bârlad *480* E Romania
Barlavento, Ilhas de *176* northernmost of the two main island groups comprising Cape Verde
Bar-le-Duc *253* NE France
Barletta *321* S Italy
Barnaul *485* C Russian Federation
Barnes Hill *92* N Antigua, Antigua & Barbuda
Barneveld *429* C Netherlands
Barnstaple *593* SW England, UK
Baroda *see* Vadodara
Barouk, Nahr el *364* river of C Lebanon
Baroul *see* Salisbury
Barqah *371* *Eng.* Cyrenaica. Cultural region of NE Libya
Barquisimeto *619* NW Venezuela
Barrage de Nzilo *see* Nzilo, Lac
Barrancabermeja *195* NW Colombia
Barranquilla *195* N Colombia
Barreiro *474* W Portugal
Barrier Reef *130* coral reef E of Belize
Barrigada *647* C Guam
Barril *176* São Nicolau, N Cape Verde
Barrouallie *498* W St Vincent, St Vincent & the Grenadines
Barrow *314* *Ir.* An Bhearú. River of SE Ireland
Barrow-in-Furness *593* NW England, UK
Barr, Ra's al *115* cape of S Bahrain
Barsalogo *157* *var.* Barsalogho. N Burkina
Bartang *558* river of SE Tajikistan
Bártfa *see* Bardejov
Bartfeld *see* Bardejov
Bartica *284* NE Guyana
Bartolomé Masó *210* SE Cuba
Baruta *619* N Venezuela
Baruun-Urt *412* E Mongolia
Barú, Volcán *456* *var.* Volcán de Chiriquí. Volcanic peak of W Panama
Barxudarli *110* W Azerbaijan
Barysaw *122* *Rus.* Borisov. NE Belarus
Basăk *165* river of Cambodia and Vietnam
Basarabeasca *408* *Rus.* Bessarabka. SE Moldova
Basel *546* *Eng.* Basle, *Fr.* Bâle. NW Switzerland
Bashi Channel *555* *Chin.* Pa-shih Hai-hsia. Channel connecting the South China Sea and Pacific Ocean
Bashkend *see* Artsvashen
Bashkortostan, Respublika *484* autonomous republic of W Russian Federation
Basilan Island *466* island of SW Philippines
Basilé, Pico de *236* *var.* Pico de Santa Isabel. Mountain of C Bioko, Equatorial Guinea
Basle *see* Basel
Basra *see* Al Baṣrah
Bassam *see* Grand-Bassam
Bassar *567* *var.* Bassari. NW Togo
Bassein *159* *var.* Pathein. SW Burma
Basse Santa Su *261* E Gambia
Basse-Terre *646* ❖ of Guadeloupe, SW Guadeloupe
Basseterre *494* ❖ of St Kitts & Nevis, S St Kitts
Bassikounou *398* SE Mauritania
Bassila *132* W Benin
Bass Strait *101* SE strait connecting South Pacific Ocean and Southern Ocean, between Australia and Tasmania
Bastia *253* Corse, SE France
Bastogne *127* SE Belgium
Basutoland *see* Lesotho
Bata *236* NW Río Muni, Equatorial Guinea
Batabanó, Golfo de *210* gulf of the Caribbean Sea, on the S coast of Cuba
Bataka *224* NE Dominica
Batak, Yazovir *152* reservoir of SW Bulgaria
Batangafo *179* NW Central African Republic
Batangas *466* Luzon, N Philippines
Batan Islands *466* island group of N Philippines
Batavia *see* Jakarta
Bătdâmbâng *165* *prev.* Battambang. W Cambodia
Batéké, Plateaux *200* plateau of Congo
Bates, Mount *650* mountain of N Norfolk Island
Bath *593* SW England, UK
Bath *329* E Jamaica
Bath *494* SW Nevis, St Kitts & Nevis
Batha *180* seasonal river of S Chad
Bathsheba *121* E Barbados
Bathurst *101* SE Australia
Bathurst *see* Banjul
Bathurst Island *101* island of N Australia
Bathurst Island *170* island of Parry Islands, N Canada
Bathyz *see* Badkhyz
Batī *243* NE Ethiopia
Batiki *246* *prev.* Mbatiki. Island to the E of Viti Levu, C Fiji
Bāṭin, Wādī al *354, 506* dry watercourse of SW Asia
Batjan *see* Bacan, Pulau
Batman *577* *var.* Īluh. SE Turkey
Batna *83* NE Algeria
Batoe *see* Batu, Kepulauan
Baton Rouge *599* Louisiana, SC USA
Batouri *168* E Cameroon
Batroûn *364* *var.* Al Batrūn. N Lebanon
Battambang *see* Bătdâmbâng
Batticaloa *534* E Sri Lanka
Battowia *498* island of C St Vincent & the Grenadines
Batu Gajah *386* W Peninsular Malaysia
Batu, Kepulauan *302* *prev.* Batoe. Island group to the W of Sumatra, W Indonesia
Bat'umi *262* W Georgia
Batu Pahat *386* *prev.* Bandar Penggaram. S Peninsular Malaysia
Bat Yam *317* C Israel
Bauchi *440* NE Nigeria
Baumann, Pic *see* Agou, Mont
Baures *136* river of NE Bolivia
Bauru *145* S Brazil
Bauska *362* *Ger.* Bauske. S Latvia
Bautzen *265* E Germany
Bavarian Alps *106, 265* *Ger.* Bayerische Alpen. Mountain range of Austria and Germany
Bawku *270* N Ghana
Baxoi *186* Xizang Zizhiqu, W China
Bayamo *210* SE Cuba
Bayamón *651* NE Puerto Rico
Bayanhongor *412* C Mongolia
Bayano, Lago *456* lake of E Panama
Baydhabo *524* *var.* Isha Baydhabo, *It.* Baidoa. SW Somalia
Bayerische Alpen *see* Bavarian Alps
Bāyir *336* *var.* Bā'ir. C Jordan
Bāyir, Wādī *336* *var.* Wādī Bā'ir. Dry watercourse of C Jordan
Baykal, Ozero *485* *Eng.* Lake Baikal. Lake of S Russian Federation
Bay, Laguna de *466* lake of Luzon, N Philippines
Baynūnah *590* desert region of W United Arab Emirates
Bayonne *252* SW France
Bayram-Ali *see* Bayramaly
Bayramaly *581* *prev.* Bayram-Ali, *var.* Bajram-Ali. SE Turkmenistan
Bayrūt *see* Beirut
Baysun *see* Boysun
Bayt al Faqīh *627* W Yemen
Bayt Lahm *see* Bethlehem
Bayudha Desert *536* *var.* Baiyuda, Ṣaḥrā' Bayyūḍah. Desert NE Sudan
Bayy al Kabīr, Wādī *371* dry watercourse of NW Libya
Bayyūḍah, Ṣaḥrā' *see* Bayudha Desert
Bazardüzü Dağ *110* *Rus.* Gora Bazardyuzyu. Mountain of N Azerbaijan
Bazargic *see* Dobrich
Bazgrad *152* NE Bulgaria
Bazin *see* Pezinok
Bcharré *364* *var.* Bsharrī. NE Lebanon
Beagle Channel *183* channel connecting Pacific Ocean and Atlantic Ocean

Beata, Isla *226* island of SW Dominican Republic
Beatrice *636* NE Zimbabwe
Beau Bassin *400* W Mauritius
Beaufort Sea *170* sea of the Arctic Ocean to the N of North America
Beaufort West *527* *Afr.* Beaufort-Wes. Western Cape, SW South Africa
Beauvais *253* N France
Béchar *83* *prev.* Colomb-Béchar. W Algeria
Bécs *see* Vienna
Bedanda *282* S Guinea-Bissau
Bedok Reservoir *517* E Singapore
Be'ér Sheva' *317* S Israel
Begamganj *117* SE Bangladesh
Begna *444* river of S Norway
Begovat *see* Bekobod
Behagle *see* Laï
Beibu Wan *see* Tongking, Gulf of
Beida *see* Al Baydā'
Beijing *187, 190* *Eng.* Peking, *var.* Pei-ching, *prev.* Pei-ping. ❖ and municipaltiy of China
Beira *419* C Mozambique
Beirut *364* *var.* Beyrouth, Bayrūt. ❖ of Lebanon, W Lebanon
Beitbridge *636* S Zimbabwe
Beit Lahiya *317, 318* NE Gaza Strip
Beja *474* SE Portugal
Béja *573* *var.* Bājah. N Tunisia
Béjaïa *83* *prev.* Bougie. N Algeria
Bejhi *451* *var.* Beji. River of W Pakistan
Bekaa Valley *see* El Beqaa
Bek-Budi *see* Qarshi
Bekdash *581* *var.* Bekdaš. NW Turkmenistan
Békéscsaba *290* SE Hungary
Bekobod *610* *prev.* Begovat, *Rus.* Bekabad. SE Uzbekistan
Bekwai *270* C Ghana
Bélabo *168* C Cameroon
Belait, Sungai *150* river of C Brunei
Belarus *see* Belarus
Bela Vista *419* S Mozambique
Belaya Tserkov' *see* Bila Tserkva
Belbeis *see* Bilbeis
Belcher Is *171* island group in Hudson Bay, C Canada
Beledweyne *524* *var.* Belet Huen, *It.* Belet Uen. C Somalia
Belém *145* *prev.* Pará. N Brazil
Belep, Îles *650* island group of W New Caledonia
Belfast *593* Northern Ireland, UK
Belfort *253* NE France
Belgium *126-129* officially Kingdom of Belgium. Country of W Europe divided into 9 admin. units (provinces). ❖ Brussels
Belgian Congo *see* Dem. Rep. Congo (Zaire)
Belgorod *484* W Russian Federation
Belgrade *630* *SCr.* Beograd. ❖ of Yugoslavia, N Serbia, Yugoslavia
Belgrano II *90* Argentinian research station of Greater Antarctica, Antarctica
Belice *see* Belize City
Beligrad *see* Berat
Beli Manastir *209* *Hung.* Pélmonostor. NE Croatia
Belitoeng *see* Belitung, Pulau
Belitung, Pulau *302* *prev.* Belitoeng, Billiton. Island to the SE of Sumatra, W Indonesia
Belize *130* river of Belize and Guatemala
Belize *130-131* Country of Central America divided into 6 admin units (districts). ❖ Belmopan
Belize City *130* *Sp.* Belice. E Belize
Beljak *see* Villach
Bellary *296* *Hind.* Ballari. S India
Bella Unión *607* N Uruguay
Belle-Anse *286* S Haiti
Belle Île *252* island of NW France
Bellenz *see* Bellinzona
Belleplaine *121* N Barbados
Belle Vue *497* S St Lucia
Bellevue Chopin *224* S Dominica
Belle Vue Maurel *400* NE Mauritius
Bellingshausen *90* CIS research station of South Shetland Islands, Antarctica
Bellinzona *546* *Ger.* Bellenz. S Switzerland
Bello *195* NW Colombia
Bello Horizonte *see* Belo Horizonte
Belluno *321* N Italy
Bellville *527* Western Cape, SW South Africa
Belmanier *224* N Dominica
Belmopan *130* ❖ of Belize, C Belize
Belmullet *314* NW Ireland
Belo Horizonte *145* *prev.* Bello Horizonte. SE Brazil
Bel Ombre *400* SW Mauritius
Bel Ombre *512* Mahé, Seychelles
Belarus *122-125* officially Republic of Belarus, *var.* Belarus, *prev.* Belorussian SSR, *Rus.* Belorusskaya SSR. Country of Europe divided into 6 admin. units (oblasts). ❖ Minsk
Belorusskaya Gryada *see* Byelruskaya Hrada
Beloshchel'ye *see* Nar'yan-Mar
Belostok *see* Białystok
Belo Tsiribihina *382* *var.* Belo-Tsiribihina, Belo-sur-Tsiribihina. W Madagascar
Belovár *see* Bjelovar
Beloye More *249, 484* *Eng.* White Sea. Sea of Arctic Ocean, bordering NW Russian Federation
Bel'tsy *see* Bălţi
Belukha, Gora *338* mountain of E Kazakhstan and Russian Federation
Bembèrèkè *132* *var.* Bembéréké. N Benin
Benaco *see* Garda, Lago di
Benares *see* Vārānasi
Ben Arous *573* *var.* Bin Arūs. N Tunisia
Bender Beyla *524* *var.* Bandarbeyla, Bender Beila. NE Somalia
Bender Cassim *see* Boosaaso
Bendern *374* NW Liechtenstein
Bendery *see* Tighina
Bendigo *101* SE Australia
Bendugu *514* N Sierra Leone
Benduma *368* NW Liberia
Benemérita de San Cristóbal *see* San Cristóbal
Beneški Zaliv *see* Gulf of Venice
Benešov *216* W Czech Republic
Benevento *321* S Italy
Bengal, Bay of *117, 159, 297, 534* bay of the Indian Ocean
Bengasi *see* Banghāzī
Bengbu *187* *var.* Peng-pu. Anhui, E China
Benghazi *see* Banghāzī
Benguela *88* *var.* Benguella. W Angola
Bengweulu *see* Bangweulu, Lake
Benha *230* *var.* Banhā. N Egypt
Beni *136* river of N Bolivia
Beni *203* NE Dem. Rep. Congo (Zaire)
Benidorm *531* SE Spain
Beni Mellal *414* C Morocco
Benin *132-133* officially Republic of Benin, *prev.* Dahomey. Country of W Africa divided into 6 admin. units (departments). ❖ Porto-Novo
Benin, Bight of *132, 440, 567* area of the Gulf of Guinea
Benin City *440* SW Nigeria
Beni Suef *230* *var.* Banī Suwayf. N Egypt
Bénitiers, Ile aux *400* island of SW Mauritius
Ben Nevis *593* mountain of C Scotland, UK
Benoni *527* Pretoria-Witwatersrand-Vereeniging, NE South Africa
Be, Nosy *382* *var.* Nossi-Bé. Island of N Madagascar
Bénoué *see* Benue
Bénoy *180* S Chad
Benque Viejo del Carmen *130* *var.* Benque Viejo. W Belize
Bense *224* N Dominica
Bensheim *264* SW Germany
Bensonville *368* *prev.* Bentol. W Liberia
Bent Jbaïl *364* *var.* Bint Jubayl. S Lebanon
Bentol *see* Bensonville
Bentong *386* *var.* Bentung. C Peninsular Malaysia
Bên Tre *623* *var.* Truc Giang. S Vietnam
Benue *168, 440* *Fr.* Bénoué. River of Cameroon and Nigeria
Benxi *187* *var.* Pen-ch'i, Penki. Liaoning, NE China
Beograd *see* Belgrade
Beqa *246* *prev.* Mbengga. Island to the S of Viti Levu, W Fiji
Bequia *498* island of C St Vincent & the Grenadines
Beragala *534* SE Sri Lanka
Berat *81* *var.* Berati, *SCr.* Beligrad. C Albania
Beraun *see* Berounka
Berbera *524* NW Somalia
Berbérati *179* SW Central African Republic
Berbice *284* river of NE Guyana
Berd *98* NE Armenia
Berdyans'k *586* *Rus.* Berdyansk, *prev.* Osipenko. SE Ukraine
Bereeda *524* *var.* Bareeda, *It.* Bereda. NE Somalia
Berekua *224* S Dominica
Berekum *270* W Ghana
Berettyó *290* river of Hungary and Romania
Berezina *see* Byerazino
Berezino *see* Byerazino
Berezniki *484* W Russian Federation
Bergamo *320* N Italy
Bergen *444* SW Norway
Bergen *see* Mons
Berg en Dal *538* NE Suriname
Bergen op Zoom *429* SW Netherlands
Bergisch Gladbach *264* W Germany
Beringen *127* NE Belgium
Bering Sea *485* *Rus.* Beringovo More. Sea of Pacific Ocean between NE Asia and NW North America
Bering Strait *485, 598* *Rus.* Beringov Proliv. Strait connecting Bering Sea and Chukchi Sea, between NE Russian Federation and Alaska, USA
Berkane *414* NE Morocco
Berkeley Sound *645* area of the South Atlantic Ocean, NE Falkland Islands
Berlin *265, 269* ❖ of Germany, NE Germany
Bermuda *643* British Crown colony of the North Atlantic Ocean. ❖ Hamilton.
Bermudian Landing *130* C Belize
Bern *546* *Fr.* Berne. ❖ of Switzerland, W Switzerland
Bernal *463* NW Peru
Bernberg *265* C Germany
Berner Oberland *546* *Eng.* Bernese Oberland. Mountain range of SW Switzerland
Bernina, Passo del *546* mountain pass of SE Switzerland
Béroubouay *see* Gbéroubouè
Beroun *216* W Czech Republic
Berounka *216* *Ger.* Beraun. River of W Czech Republic
Berovo *381* E FYR Macedonia
Berry Islands *112* island group of N Bahamas
Bertoua *168* E Cameroon
Beru *346* island of the Gilbert Is, W Kiribati
Beruniy *610* *var.* Biruni, *Rus.* Beruni. W Uzbekistan
Berwick-upon-Tweed *593* NE England, UK
Besalampy *382* NW Madagascar
Besançon *253* E France
Beskiden *see* Beskid Mountains
Beskid Mountains *519* *var.* Beskids, *Slvk.* Beskydy, *Ger.* Beskiden, *Pol.* Beskidy. Mountain range of C Europe
Beskra *see* Biskra
Bessarabka *see* Basarabeasca
Beszterce *see* Bistriţa
Besztercebánya *see* Banská Bystrica
Betanzos *136* S Bolivia
Bétérou *132* *var.* Betérou. C Benin
Bethanien *423* *var.* Bethanie, Bethany. S Namibia
Bethel *649* E Montserrat
Bethesda *92* SE Antigua, Antigua & Barbuda
Bethlehem *527* Orange Free State, C South Africa
Bethlehem *317, 318* *Heb.* Bet Leḥem, *Ar.* Bayt Lahm. C West Bank
Betio *346* Tarawa, W Kiribati
Bétou *200* N Congo
Bet Shemesh *317* C Israel
Betsiboka *382* river of C Madagascar
Bette, Pic *371* *It.* Picco Bette. Mountain peak of Chad and Libya
Bettembourg *378* S Luxembourg
Beuthen *see* Bytom
Beveren *127* N Belgium
Beverwijk *429* W Netherlands
Bexon *497* C St Lucia
Beyla *281* SE Guinea
Beylul *238* SE Eritrea
Beyneu *338* W Kazakhstan
Beyrouth *see* Beirut
Béziers *253* S France
Bezmein *see* Byuzmeyin
Bezwada *see* Vijayawāda
Bhāgalpur *297* NE India
Bhairab Bāzār *117* *var.* Bhairab. C Bangladesh
Bhairahawa *427* C Nepal
Bhaktapur *427* C Nepal
Bhamdoun *364* *var.* Bḥamdūn. C Lebanon
Bhamo *159* *var.* Banmo. N Burma
Bhangtar *134* SE Bhutan
Bharat *see* India
Bhawalpur *see* Bahāwalpur
Bheanntrai, Bá *see* Bantry Bay
Bheri *427* river of W Nepal
Bhimphedi *427* C Nepal
Bhojpur *427* E Nepal
Bhōpal *296* C India
Bhunya *540* *var.* Bunya. W Swaziland
Bhutan *134-135* officially Kingdom of Bhutan. Country of S Asia divided into 18 admin. units (districts). ❖ Thimpu
Biabou *498* E St Vincent, St Vincent & the Grenadines
Biafra, Bight of *236, 440* *var.* Bight of Bonny. Bay of the Gulf of Guinea, on the coast of W Africa
Biak, Pulau *303* island to the NW of Irian Jaya, E Indonesia
Białystok *471* *Rus.* Belostok. E Poland
Biankouma *326* W Ivory Coast
Biarritz *252* SW France
Bibane, Bahiret el *573* lagoon of the Mediterranean Sea on the E coast of Tunisia
Bida *440* C Nigeria
Biel *546* *Fr.* Bienne. W Switzerland
Bielefeld *264* NW Germany
Bieler See *546* *Fr.* Lac de Bienne. Lake of W Switzerland
Bielitz-Biala *see* Bielsko-Biała
Biella *320* N Italy
Bielsko-Biała *471* *Ger.* Bielitz-Biala. S Poland
Biên Đông *see* South China Sea
Biên Hoa *623* S Vietnam
Bienne, Lac de *see* Bieler See
Bienvenue *645* SE French Guiana
Bíe, Planalto do *88* *var.* Bié Plateau. Plateau of C Angola
Bié Plateau *see* Planalto do Bíe
Big Bay *615* bay of the Pacific Ocean, off Espiritu Santo, C Vanuatu
Big Bend *540* SE Swaziland
Bigene *282* NW Guinea-Bissau
Bight, The *112* Cat I, Bahamas
Bignona *510* SW Senegal
Bihać *140* NW Bosnia & Herzegovina
Bijagós, Arquipélago dos *282* *var.* Bijagos Archipelago. Island group of W Guinea-Bissau
Bijeljina *140* NE Bosnia & Herzegovina

Bijelo Polje *630* E Montenegro, Yugoslavia
Bikaner *296* NW India
Bikar *396* island of N Marshall Islands
Bikini *396* island of NW Marshall Islands
Bilād Manaḩ *see* Manaḩ
Bilāspur *296* NE India
Biläsuvar *110* *Rus.* Bilyasuvar, *prev.* Pushkino, *var.* Puškino. S Azerbaijan
Bila Tserkva *586* *Rus.* Belaya Tserkov'. NW Ukraine
Bilauktaung Range *159, 563* *var.* Thanintari Taungdan. Mountain range of Burma and Thailand
Bilbao *531* *var.* Bilbo. N Spain
Bilbeis *230* *var.* Belbeis, Bilbays. N Egypt
Bilecik *576* NW Turkey
Biliran Island *466* island of E Philippines
Bilisht *81* *var.* Bilishti. SE Albania
Billings *598* Montana, NW USA
Billiton *see* Belitung, Pulau
Bilo Gora *209* mountains of N Croatia
Biloku *284* S Guyana
Biloxi *599* Mississippi, SE USA
Biltine *180* E Chad
Bilwi *see* Puerto Cabezas
Bilyasuvar *see* Biläsuvar
Bimbo *179* SW Central African Republic
Bimini Islands *112* *var.* Biminis. Island group of N Bahamas
Biminis *see* Bimini Islands
Binche *127* SW Belgium
Bindura *636* NE Zimbabwe
Binga, Monte *419* mountain of C Mozambique
Bingerville *326* SE Ivory Coast
Bin Ghalfān, Jazā'ir *see* Ḩalānīyāt, Juzur al
Bin Ghanīmah, Jabal *371* *var.* Jabal Bin Ghunaymah. Mountain range of C Libya
Bin Ghashīr *371* NW Libya
Bingol *577* E Turkey
Binkolo *514* C Sierra Leone
Bintang *261* river of Gambia and Senegal
Bintang *261* SW Gambia
Bintimani *514* mountain of NE Sierra Leone
Bint Jubayl *see* Bent Jbaïl
Bintulu *386* W Borneo, Malaysia
Bío Bío *183* river of C Chile
Bioko *168, 236* *prev.* Macías Nguema Biyogo, *Eng.* Fernando Po, *Sp.* Fernando Póo. Island of NW Equatorial Guinea
Birāk *371* W Libya
Birambo *492* W Rwanda
Birao *179* N Central African Republic
Biratnagar *427* E Nepal
Birch Grove *276* C Grenada island, Grenada
Bird Island *see* Vaches, Île aux
Bird Island *276* island to the NE of Grenada island, Grenada
Bird of Paradise Island *see* Little Tobago
Birdsville *101* C Australia
Birendranagar *427* *var.* Surkhet. W Nepal
Birgu *see* Vittoriosa
Birkenhead *593* NW England, UK
Birket Qârûn *230* *var.* Birkat Qārūn. N Egypt
Birkirkara *395* C Malta
Birmingham *593* C England, UK
Birmingham *599* Alabama, SE USA
Bîr Mogreïn *398* *var.* Bir Moghrein, *prev.* Fort-Trinquet. N Mauritania
Birnie Island *346* island of the Phoenix Is, C Kiribati
Birni Graouré *439* *var.* Birni-Ngaouré. SW Niger
Birnin Konni *439* *var.* Birni-Nkonni. SW Niger
Birobidzhan *485* SE Russian Federation
Birsen *see* Biržai
Biruni *see* Beruniy
Biržai *376* *Ger.* Birsen. NE Lithuania
Birżebbuġa *395* SE Malta
Biscay, Bay of *252, 531* *Fr.* Golfe de Gascogne, *Sp.* Golfo de Vizcaya. Bay of the Atlantic Ocean between W France and N Spain
Biscoftù *see* Debre Zeyit
Bīshah, Wādī *506* dry watercourse of SW Saudi Arabia
Bishkek *357* *prev.* Frunze, Pishpek. ❖ of Kyrgyzstan, N Kyrgyzstan
Bishoftu *see* Debre Zeyit
Bishrī, Jabal *551* mountains of C Syria
Bisina, Lake *584* *prev.* Lake Salisbury. Lake of E Uganda
Biskra *83* *var.* Beskra. NE Algeria
Bismarck *599* North Dakota, NC USA
Bismarck Archipelago *458* island group of NE Papua New Guinea
Bismarck Sea *458* sea of the Pacific Ocean to the NE of Papua New Guinea
Bissagos Islands *see* Bijagós, Arquipélago dos
Bissau *282* ❖ of Guinea-Bissau, W Guinea-Bissau
Bissîdiro *222* N Djibouti
Bissorã *282* W Guinea-Bissau
Bistriţa *480* *Ger.* Bistritz, *Hung.* Beszterce, *prev.* Nösen. N Romania
Bitagron *538* NW Suriname
Bitam *258* N Gabon
Bitlis *577* SE Turkey
Bitola *381* *prev.* Bitolj, *Turk.* Monastir. S FYR Macedonia
Bitter Lakes *230* lakes of NE Egypt
Biu *441* E Nigeria
Biumba *see* Byumba
Biwa-ko *330* lake of Honshū, C Japan
Biyagundi *238* SW Eritrea
Bizerte *573* *Eng.* Bizerta, *Ar.* Banzart. N Tunisia
Bizerte, Lac de *573* *Eng.* Lake Bizerta, *Ar.* Buḩayrat Banzart. Lake of N Tunisia
Bjala Slatina *see* Byala Slatina
Bjelovar *209* *Hung.* Belovár. N Croatia
Bjeshkët e Nemuna *see* North Albanian Alps
Björneborg *see* Pori
Blackburn *593* N England, UK
Black Drin *see* Drinit të Zi
Black Forest *264* *Ger.* Schwarzwald. Forested mountain range of SW Germany
Blackpool *593* NW England, UK
Black River *623* *var.* Sông Đa, *Chin.* Babian Jiang, *Fr.* Rivière Noire. River of China and Vietnam
Black River *329* SW Jamaica
Black Rock *121* W Barbados
Black Rocks *100* NW Australia
Black Sea *152, 576, 586* *Bul.* Cherno More, *Rom.* Marea Neagră, *Rus.* Chernoye More, *Turk.* Karadeniz, *Ukr.* Chorne More, *Eng.* Euxine Sea. Area of the Mediterranean Seatween W Asia and E Europe
Black Umbeluzi *see* Mubuluzi
Black Volta *157, 270, 326* *Fr.* Volta Noire, *var.* Borongo, Moun Hou. River of Burkina, Ghana and Ivory Coast
Blackwater *314* *Ir.* An Abhainn Mhór. River of S Ireland
Blagoevgrad *152* *prev.* Gorna Dzhumaya. W Bulgaria
Blagoveshchensk *485* SE Russian Federation
Blama *514* S Sierra Leone
Blanca, Bahía *95* bay of the Atlantic Ocean, to the E of Argentina
Blanca, Costa *531* coastal region of SE Spain
Blanchard *497* SE St Lucia
Blanchisseuse *570* N Trinidad, Trinidad & Tobago
Blanquilla, Isla *619* island of N Venezuela
Blantyre *385* SW Malawi
Blenheim *433* NE South Island, New Zealand
Blenheim Reef *643* reef of the Indian Ocean, N British Indian Ocean Territory
Bleus, Monts *203* mountains of Uganda and Dem. Rep. Congo (Zaire)
Blida *83* *var.* El Boulaida. N Algeria
Bligh Water *246* area of water to the N of Viti Levu, N Fiji
Blitta *567* C Togo
Bloemfontein *527* Judicial capital of South Africa, Orange Free State, C South Africa
Blois *253* NW France
Blönduós *294* N Iceland
Blowing Point Village *642* SE Anguilla
Bludenz *106* W Austria
Bluefields *436* SE Nicaragua
Blue Hill *652* W St Helena
Blue Hills *653* Providenciales, NW Turks and Caicos Islands
Blue Mountain Peak *329* mountain of E Jamaica
Blue Nile *243, 536* *var.* Bahr el Azraq, *Ar.* An Nīl al Azraq, *Amh.* Abay Wenz, *var.* Abai. River of Ethiopia and Sudan
Blumenau *145* S Brazil
Bo *514* S Sierra Leone
Boaco *436* C Nicaragua
Boa Esperança, Represa *145* NE Brazil
Boajibu *514* C Sierra Leone
Boali *179* SW Central African Republic
Boa Vista *144* NW Brazil
Boa Vista *176* island of E Cape Verde
Bobigny *253* N France
Bobo-Dioulasso *157* SW Burkina
Bobonong *142* E Botswana
Bobotogh, Qatorkŭhi *610* *Rus.* Khrebet Babatag. Mountains of Tajikistan and Uzbekistan
Bobruysk *see* Babruysk
Boca de la Serpiente *see* Serpent's Mouth, The
Boca de Yuma *226* SE Dominican Republic
Bocage *497* NW St Lucia
Bocas del Dragón *see* Dragon's Mouths, The
Bocas del Toro *456* W Panama
Bochum *264* W Germany
Bococo *236* SW Bioko, Equatorial Guinea
Bocono *619* W Venezuela
Boda *179* SW Central African Republic
Bodaybo *485* E Russian Federation
Boddam Island *643* island of N British Indian Ocean Territory
Bodden Town *644* Grand Cayman, W Cayman Islands
Bodegas *see* Babahoyo
Bodensee *see* Constance, Lake
Bodø *444* NE Norway
Bodrum *576* SW Turkey
Bodza *see* Buzău
Boé *282* *var.* Madina do Boé. SE Guinea-Bissau
Boende *203* NW Dem. Rep. Congo (Zaire)
Boeroe *see* Buru
Boetica *224* SE Dominica
Boetoeng *see* Butung, Pulau
Boffa *281* W Guinea
Bogale *159* S Burma
Bogal, Lagh *342* *var.* Lak Boggal. Dry watercourse of N Kenya
Bogandé *157* C Burkina
Bogarfjördhur *294* E Iceland
Bogdanovka *see* Ninotsminda
Bogd Khan *412* national park of C Mongolia
Boggy Peak *92* mountain SW of Antigua, Antigua & Barbuda
Boghotu *see* Santa Isabel
Bogor *302* *Dut.* Buitenzorg. Java, C Indonesia
Bogotá *195* ❖ of Colombia, C Colombia
Bogra *117* N Bangladesh
Bogué *398* SW Mauritania
Bo Hai *187* *var.* Gulf of Chihli. Gulf of Yellow Sea, off NE China
Bohemia *216* historical and cultural region, W Czech Republic
Bohemian Forest *216, 265* *Ger.* Böhmerwald, *Cz.* Česky Les, Šumava. Forested mountain range of Czech Republic and Germany
Bohemian-Moravian Highlands *see* Českomoravská Vrchovina
Bohicon *132* S Benin
Böhmisch-Mährische Höhe *see* Českomoravská Vrchovina
Bohol *466* island of C Philippines
Bohol Sea *466* *var.* Mindanao Sea. Sea of the Pacific Ocean
Boise *598* Idaho, NW USA
Bois, Lac des *see* Woods, Lake of the
Bois-le-Duc *see* 's-Hertogenbosch
Boji Plain *342* plain of E Kenya
Bokak *396* island of N Marshall Islands
Boké *281* W Guinea
Bo Kheo *see* Bâ Kêv
Bokhol Plain *342* plain of NE Kenya
Bokiba *see* Lengoué
Boknafjorden *444* fjord of SW Norway
Boko *200* S Congo
Boksburg *527* Pretoria-Witwatersrand-Vereeniging, NE South Africa
Bol *180* W Chad
Bolama *282* SW Guinea-Bissau
Bolama, Ilha de *282* island of Arquipélago dos Bijagós, SW Guinea-Bissau
Bolanos *647* mountain peak of S Guam
Bolans *92* SW Antigua, Antigua & Barbuda
Bolgatanga *270* N Ghana
Bolívar, Pico *619* mountain peak of the Cordillera de Mérida, W Venezuela
Bolivia *136-139* officially Republic of Bolivia. Country of South America divided into 9 admin. units (departments). ❖ La Paz, Sucre
Bolligen *546* W Switzerland
Bologna *321* N Italy
Bol'shevik, Ostrov *485* island of Severnaya Zemlya, N Russian Federation
Bol'shoy Kavkaz *see* Greater Caucasus
Bol'shoy Lyakhovskiy, Ostrov *485* island of Novosibirskiye Ostrovo, N Russian Federation
Bolsón de Mapimí *403* mountain range of N Mexico
Bolton *593* N England, UK
Bolu *576* NW Turkey
Bolungarvík *294* NW Iceland
Bolzano *321* *Ger.* Bozen. N Italy
Boma *203* W Dem. Rep. Congo (Zaire)
Bomassa *200* NW Congo
Bombay *see* Mumbai
Bomberai, Jazirah *302* peninsula of Irian Jaya, E Indonesia
Bombo *584* S Uganda
Bombom, Ilha *505* island to the N of Príncipe, Sao Tome & Principe
Bomi *368* W Liberia
Bomu *179, 203* *Fr.* Mbomou, *var.* M'Bomu, Mbomu. River of Central African Republic and Dem. Rep. Congo (Zaire)
Bonaire *619, 650* island of the Netherland Antilles, Caribbean Sea
Bonao *226* C Dominican Republic
Bonaparte Archipelago *100* island group of NW Australia
Bondoukou *326* E Ivory Coast
Bône *see* Annaba
Bone, Teluk *302* bay of Laut Flores on the S coast of Celebes, E Indonesia
Bonga *243* SW Ethiopia
Bongolava *382* mountains of W Madagascar
Bongo, Massif des *179* *var.* Chaîne des Mongos. Mountainous region of Central African Republic

Bongor *180* SW Chad
Bongouanou *326* E Ivory Coast
Bongoville *258* E Gabon
Bon Grara, Golfe de *573* inlet of the Gulf of Gabès on the E coast of Tunisia
Bonifacio, Strait of *253* *Fr.* Bouches de Bonifacio, *It.* Bocche de Bonifacio. Strait of the Mediterranean Sea between the islands of Corse, France and Sardegna, Italy
Bonn *264* W Germany
Bonny, Bight of *see* Biafra, Bight of
Bonriki *346* Tarawa, W Kiribati
Bonthe *514* Sherbro I, Sierra Leone
Boosaaso *524* *var.* Bosaso, Bender Qaasim, *It.* Bender Cassim. N Somalia
Boothia Felix *see* Boothia Peninsula
Boothia, Gulf of *170* gulf of the Arctic Ocean between the Boothia Peninsula and Melville Peninsula, N Canada
Boothia Peninsula *170* *prev.* Boothia Felix. Peninsula of N Canada
Booué *258* NE Gabon
Bophuthatswana Bantustan 'self-governing homeland'; abolished in 1994
Bopolu *368* NW Liberia
Boquete *456* *var.* Bajo Boquete. W Panama
Boraha, Nosy *see* Sainte Marie, Nosy
Borås *543* SW Sweden
Borborema, Planalto da *145* plateau of NE Brazil
Bordeaux *253* SW France
Borden Peninsula *171* peninsula of Baffin Island, N Canada
Bordergate *540* NE Swaziland
Bordhoy *644* *var.* Bordø. Island of NE Faeroe Islands
Bordj Bou Arreridj *83* N Algeria
Borgarnes *294* W Iceland
Borgholm *543* Öland, S Sweden
Borgo Maggiore *502* NW San Marino
Borikhan *359* *var.* Borikhane. C Laos
Borisov *see* Barysaw
Bor, Lagh *342* *var.* Lak Bor. Dry watercourse of NE Kenya
Borlänge *543* C Sweden
Borneo *302, 386-387* island of SE Asia divided between Brunei, two Malaysian states and part of Indonesia
Bornholm *218* island of E Denmark
Boromo *157* SW Burkina
Borongo *see* Black Volta
Borovo *209* NE Croatia
Borujerd *307* *var.* Burujird. W Iran
Börzsöny *290* mountain range of N Hungary
Bosanska Gradiška *140* N Bosnia & Herzegovina
Bosanski Brod *140* N Bosnia & Herzegovina
Bosanski Šamac *140* N Bosnia & Herzegovina
Boscobelle *121* NE Barbados
Bösing *see* Pezinok
Boskamp *538* N Suriname
Boskovice *216* SE Czech Republic
Bosna *140* river of N Bosnia & Herzegovina
Bosna I Hercegovina, Federacija *140* *republic* Bosnia & Herzegovina
Bosnia & Herzegovina *140-141* officially The Republic of Bosnia and Herzegovina. Country of SE Europe. ❖ Sarajevo
Bosporus *see* İstanbul Boğazi
Bossangoa *179* C Central African Republic
Bossembélé *179* C Central African Republic
Boston *599* Massachusetts, NE USA
Boteti *142* *var.* Botletle. River of C Botswana
Botevgrad *152* *prev.* Orkhanie, Orkhaniye. W Bulgaria
Bothnia, Gulf of *249, 543* *Fin.* Pohjanlahti, *Swe.* Bottniska Viken. Gulf of the Baltic Sea, between Finland and Sweden
Boti-Pasi *538* C Suriname
Botna *408* river of E Moldova
Botoşani *480* NE Romania
Botrange *127* mountain of E Belgium
Botswana *142-143* officially Republic of Botswana. Country of southern Africa divided into 10 admin. units (districts). ❖ Gaborone
Bottle Creek *653* North Caicos, N Turks and Caicos Islands
Bottniska Viken *see* Bothnia, Gulf of
Bottom, The *650* Saba, N Netherlands Antilles
Bouaflé *326* C Ivory Coast
Bouaké *326* *var.* Bwake. C Ivory Coast
Bouar *179* W Central African Republic
Bouca *179* C Central African Republic
Bouéni *649* SW Mayotte
Bouéni, Baie de *649* *var.* Bonéni Bay. Bay of the Mozambique Channel on the SW coast of Mayotte
Bouenza *200* river of S Congo
Boufarik *83* N Algeria
Bougainville Island *458* island of E Papua New Guinea
Bougie *see* Béjaïa
Bougouni *392* SW Mali
Bougouriba *157* river of SW Burkina
Boujdour *414* W Western Sahara
Boukoumbé *132* *var.* Boukombé. NW Benin
Boukra *414* C Western Sahara
Boulder *599* Colorado, SW USA
Boulogne-sur-Mer *253* *var.* Boulogne. N France
Bouloupari *650* S New Caledonia
Bouma *246* Taveuni, N Fiji
Boumango *258* SE Gabon
Boumba *168* river of SE Cameroon
Boumbé II *179* river of Cameroon and Central African Republic
Boûmdeïd *398* S Mauritania
Bouna *326* NE Ivory Coast
Boundiali *326* N Ivory Coast
Boungou *179* river of C Central African Republic
Bourail *650* C New Caledonia
Bourgas *see* Burgas
Bourg-en-Bresse *253* E France
Bourges *253* C France
Bourgogne *253* *Eng.* Burgundy. Cultural region of E France
Bourke *101* E Australia
Bournemouth *593* S England, UK
Boussé *157* C Burkina
Boussouma *157* C Burkina
Boutilimit *398* SW Mauritania
Bouton *497* W St Lucia
Bovec *520* *Ger.* Flitsch, *It.* Plezzo. NW Slovenia
Boven Kapuas, Pegunungan *386* mountain range of SW Borneo, Malaysia
Boyd's *494* S St Kitts, St Kitts & Nevis
Boyne *314* *Ir.* An Bhóinn. River of E Ireland
Boysun *610* *Rus.* Baysun. SE Uzbekistan
Bozen *see* Bolzano
Bozoum *179* W Central African Republic
Brač *209* *var.* Brach, *It.* Brazza. Island of S Croatia
Bradford *593* N England, UK
Braga *474* NW Portugal
Bragado *95* E Argentina
Bragança *474* *Eng.* Braganza. NE Portugal
Braganza *see* Bragança
Brahestad *see* Raahe
Brāhmanbāria *117* E Bangladesh
Brahmaputra *117, 186, 297* *var.* Tsangpo, *Ben.* Jamuna. River of S Asia
Brăila *480* E Romania
Braine-l'Alleud *127* C Belgium
Branco *144* river of NW Brazil
Branco, Ilhéu *176* island of N Cape Verde
Brandberg *423* mountain of NW Namibia
Brande *218* Jylland, W Denmark
Brandenburg *265* C Germany
Brandon *170* S Canada
Brani, Pulau *517* island of S Singapore
Brasília *145* ❖ of Brazil, C Brazil
Braslaw *122* N Belarus
Braşov *480* *prev.* Stalin, *Ger.* Kronstadt, *Hung.* Brassó. C Romania
Brasschaat *127* N Belgium
Brassey, Banjaran *387* *var.* Brassey Range. Mountain range of E Borneo, Malaysia
Brassey Range *see* Brassey, Banjaran
Bratislava *519* *Ger.* Pressburg, *Hung.* Pozsony. ❖ of Slovakia, SW Slovakia
Bratsk *485* C Russian Federation
Bratskoye Vodokhranilishche *485* *Eng.* Bratsk Reservoir. C Russian Federation
Braunau am Inn *106* *var.* Braunau. N Austria
Braunschweig *265* *Eng.* Brunswick. N Germany
Brava *see* Baraawe
Brava *176* island of SW Cape Verde
Brava, Costa *531* coastal region of E Spain
Bravo Del Norte *see* Grande, Río
Bray *314* *Ir.* Bri Chuallan. E Ireland
Brazil *146-149* officially Federative Republic of Brazil. Country of South America divided into 28 admin. units (26 states, 1 territory, 1 federal district). ❖ Brasília
Brazos *599* river of SW USA
Brazza *see* Brač
Brazzaville *200* ❖ of Congo, S Congo
Brčko *140* NE Bosnia & Herzegovina
Breda *429* SW Netherlands
Bregalnica *381* river of E FYR Macedonia
Bregenz *106* W Austria
Breidhafjördhur *294* bay of the Denmark Strait, on the coast of W Iceland
Bremen *264* NW Germany
Bremerhaven *264* NW Germany
Bremersdorp *see* Manzini
Brennero, Passo del *see* Brenner Pass
Brenner Pass *106, 321* *It.* Passo del Brennero, *Ger.* Brennerpass, *var.* Brenner Sattel. Mountain pass of Austria and Italy
Brerton *121* C Barbados
Brescia *320* N Italy
Breslau *see* Wrocław
Brest *122* *Pol.* Brześć nad Bugiem, *prev.* Brześć Litewski, *Rus.* Brest-Litovsk. SW Belarus
Brest *252* NW France
Bretagne *252* *Eng.* Brittany. Cultural region of NW France
Brewerville *368* W Liberia
Brezhnev *see* Naberezhnyye
Brežice *520* *Ger.* Rann. E Slovenia
Brezno *519* *prev.* Brezno nad Hronom, *Ger.* Bries, *var.* Briesen, *Hung.* Breznóbánya. C Slovakia
Bria *179* C Central African Republic
Bribrí *206* E Costa Rica
Bri Chuallan *see* Bray
Bride *647* N Isle of Man
Bridgetown *100* SW Australia
Bridgetown *121* ❖ of Barbados, SW Barbados
Bridgwater *593* SW England, UK
Brienzer See *546* lake of SW Switzerland
Brig *546* SW Switzerland
Brighton *593* SE England, UK
Brikama *261* W Gambia
Brindisi *321* S Italy
Brinstone Hill *494* NW St Kitts, St Kitts & Nevis
Brisbane *101* E Australia
Bristol *593* SW England, UK
Bristol Channel *593* inlet of the Atlantic Ocean, SW England, UK
British Columbia *170* province of SW Canada
British Guiana *see* Guyana
British Indian Ocean Territory *643* British dependent territory of the Indian Ocean. ❖ Diego Garcia
British North America *see* Canada
British Virgin Islands *643* British dependent territory of the Caribbean Sea. ❖ Road Town.
Brittany *see* Bretagne
Brizan *276* W Grenada island, Grenada
Brno *216* *Ger.* Brünn. SE Czech Republic
Bród *see* Slavonski Brod
Brodeur Peninsula *170* peninsula of Baffin Island, N Canada
Broken Hill *101* S Australia
Brokopondo *538* NE Suriname
Bromberg *see* Bydgoszcz
Brønderslev *218* Jylland, N Denmark
Brooks Range *598* mountain range of Alaska, USA
Broome *100* NW Australia
Brorup *218* Jylland, W Denmark
Broughton Bay *see* Tongjosŏn-man
Brown Hill *494* S Nevis, St Kitts & Nevis
Browns Town *329* N Jamaica
Brownsweg *538* C Suriname
Bruck an der Mur *106* *var.* Bruck. C Austria
Brufut *261* W Gambia
Brugge *127* *Fr.* Bruges. NW Belgium
Bruit, Pulau *386* island of W Borneo, Malaysia
Brunei *150-151, 386* officially Sultanate of Brunei, *Mal.* Negara Brunei Darussalam. Country on island of Borneo, SE Asia, divided into 4 admin. units (districts). ❖ Bandar Seri Begawan
Brunei Bay *386* *var.* Teluk Brunei. Bay of the South China Sea
Brunei Town *see* Bandar Seri Begawan
Brünn *see* Brno
Brunswick *see* Braunschweig
Brusa *see* Bursa
Brussels *127* *Fr.* Bruxelles, *Dut.* Brussel, *Ger.* Brüssel. ❖ of Belgium, C Belgium
Brüx *see* Most
Bryansk *484* W Russian Federation
Brześć Litewski *see* Brest
Brześć nad Bugiem *see* Brest
Bsharrī *see* Bcharré
Bua *385* river of C Malawi
Bu'aale *524* SW Somalia
Buada Lagoon *424* lagoon on the coast of Nauru
Buala *522* SE Santa Isabel, Solomon Islands
Bū al Ḩīdān, Wādī *371* dry watercourse of C Libya
Buba *282* S Guinea-Bissau
Bubanza *162* NW Burundi
Bubaque *282* Ilha de Bubaque, Guinea-Bissau
Bubaque, Ilha de *282* island of SW Guinea-Bissau
Bubi *636* *var.* Bubye. River of S Zimbabwe
Būbīyan, Jazirat *354* island of NE Kuwait
Buca *246* *prev.* Mbutha. Vanua Levu, N Fiji
Bucaramanga *195* N Colombia
Buchanan *368* *prev.* Grand Bassa. SW Liberia
Bucharest *480* *Rom.* Bucureşti. ❖ of Romania, S Romania
Budapest *290* ❖ of Hungary, N Hungary
Búdhardalur *294* W Iceland
Budweis *see* České Budějovice
Buea *168* SW Cameroon
Buenaventura *195* W Colombia
Buena Vista *130* N Belize
Buena Vista *136* C Bolivia
Buena Vista *646* S Gibraltar
Buenos Aires *95* ❖ of Argentina, E Argentina
Buenos Aires *206* SE Costa Rica
Buenos Aires, Lago *95, 183* *Sp.* Lago General Carrera. Lake of Argentina and Chile
Buffalo *599* New York, NE USA
Buff Bay *329* E Jamaica

Bug *471, 586 Ukr.* Zakhidnyy Buh, *Rus.* Zapadnyy Bug. River of E Europe
Buga *195* W Colombia
Bugala Island *584* island of Sese Islands, S Uganda
Buganda *162* NW Burundi
Bugarama *492* SW Rwanda
Bughotu *see* Santa Isabel
Buġibba *395* N Malta
Bugojno *140* C Bosnia & Herzegovina
Bugumya *492* SW Rwanda
Buin *458* Bougainville I, Papua New Guinea
Buitenzorg *see* Bogor
Bujumbura *162 prev.* Usumbura. ❖ of Burundi, W Burundi
Buka Island *458* island of E Papua New Guinea
Bukakata *584* S Uganda
Bukasa Island *584* island of Sese Islands, S Uganda
Bukavu *203 prev.* Costermansville. E Dem. Rep. Congo (Zaire)
Bukeye *162 var.* Bukaye. C Burundi
Bukhoro *610 var.* Bokhara, *Rus.* Bukhara. S Uzbekistan
Bukit Mertajam *386* NW Peninsular Malaysia
Bukit Panjang *517* area of C Singapore
Bukit Timah *517* area of C Singapore
Bükk *290* mountain range of NE Hungary
Bukoba *560* NW Tanzania
Bukum Kechil, Pulau *517* island of SW Singapore
Bukum, Pulau *517* island of S Singapore
Bula *282* W Guinea-Bissau
Bulawayo *636 var.* Buluwayo. SW Zimbabwe
Bulembu *540* NW Swaziland
Bulgan *412* N Mongolia
Bulgaria *152-155* officially Republic of Bulgaria, *prev.* People's Republic of Bulgaria. Country of E Europe divided into 8 admin. units (regions). ❖ Sofia
Buller *433* river of N South Island, New Zealand
Bulolo *458* SE Papua New Guinea
Bulunghur *610 prev.* Krasnogvardeysk, *Rus.* Bulungur. SE Uzbekistan
Bumba *203* N Dem. Rep. Congo (Zaire)
Bumbah, Khalīj *371 var.* Kalīj Bumbah. Gulf of the Mediterranean Sea, on the N coast of Libya
Bumbuna *514* C Sierra Leone
Bunbury *100* SW Australia
Bundaberg *101* E Australia
Bundoran *314* N Ireland
Bungoma *342* W Kenya
Bunia *203* NE Dem. Rep. Congo (Zaire)
Bunya *see* Bhunya
Buôn Ma Thuôt *623 var.* Lac Giao. S Vietnam
Bur Acaba *see* Buurhakaba
Buraimi *see* Al Buraymī
Buraydah *506 var.* Buraida. C Saudi Arabia
Burco *524 var.* Burao, Bur'o. NW Somalia
Burdur *576* SW Turkey
Burē *243* NW Ethiopia
Burera, Lac *492* lake of N Rwanda
Būrewāla *see* Mandi Būrewāla
Burgas *152 var.* Bourgas. E Bulgaria
Burgaski Zaliv *152* bay of the Black Sea on the E coast of Bulgaria
Burgdorf *546* NW Switzerland
Burgos *531* N Spain
Burgundy *see* Bourgogne
Burhou *647* island of N Guernsey
Burias Island *466* island of C Philippines
Buriram *563* E Thailand
Burkina *156-157* officially Burkina Faso, *prev.* Upper Volta. Country of West Africa divided into 30 admin. units (provinces). ❖ Ouagadougou
Burlington *599* Vermont, NE USA
Burma *158-161* officially Union of Myanmar, *var.* Myanmar. Country of SE Asia divided into 14 admin. units (7 states, 7 divisions). ❖ Rangoon
Burnie *101* Tasmania, SE Australia
Burnt Pine *650* C Norfolk Island
Burrel *81 var.* Burreli. C Albania
Burrell Boom *130* E Belize
Bursa *576 prev.* Brusa, *var.* Brusa. NW Turkey
Būr Sa'īd *see* Port Said
Būr Sūdān *see* Port Sudan
Burtnieku Ezers *362* lake of N Latvia
Buru *302 prev.* Boeroe. Island of Maluku, E Indonesia
Burujird *see* Borujerd
Burūm *627* SE Yemen
Burundi *162-163* officially Republic of Burundi, *prev.* Kingdom of Burundi. Country of Central Africa divided into 15 admin. units (provinces). ❖ Bujumbura
Bururi *162* SW Burundi
Buryatiya, Respublika *485* autonomous republic of C Russian Federation
Busan *see* Pusan
Busengo *492* NW Rwanda
Buševa Planina *see* Baba
Bushire *see* Bandar-e Bushehr
Busia *342* W Kenya
Busing, Pulau *517* island of SW Singapore
Busira *203* river of NW Dem. Rep. Congo (Zaire)
Busoro *492* S Rwanda
Busuanga Island *466* island of W Philippines
Buta *203* N Dem. Rep. Congo (Zaire)
Butare *492 prev.* Astrida. S Rwanda
Butaritari *346* island of the Gilbert Is, W Kiribati
Butawal *see* Butwal
Butembo *203* NE Dem. Rep. Congo (Zaire)
Butha Buthe *366* N Lesotho
Butiaba *584* NW Uganda
Butterworth *386* NW Peninsular Malaysia
Butuan *466* Mindanao, S Philippines
Butung, Pulau *302 var.* Buton, *prev.* Boetoeng. Island to the SE of Celebes, C Indonesia
Butwal *427 var.* Butawal. C Nepal
Buurgplaatz *378* mountain of N Luxembourg
Buurhakaba *524 var.* Bur Hakkaba, *It.* Bur Acaba. SW Somalia
Buvuma Island *584* island of S Uganda
Büyükağrı Dağı *577 Eng.* Mount Ararat, *var.* Great Ararat. Mountain of E Turkey
Büyükmenderes *576* river of SW Turkey
Büyükzap Suyu *see* Great Zab
Buzău *480 Hung.* Bodza. SE Romania
Buzi *419* river of C Mozambique
Bwake *see* Bouaké
Bwiam *261* SW Gambia
Byahoml' *122* N Belarus
Byala Slatina *152 var.* Bjala Slatina. NW Bulgaria
Byaroza *122* SW Belarus
Bydgoszcz *471 Ger.* Bromberg. N Poland
Byelruskaya Hrada *122 Rus.* Belorusskaya Gryada. Hilly region of N Belarus
Byerazino *122 Rus.* Berezina. River of C Belarus
Byerazino *122 Rus.* Berezino. C Belarus
Bykhaw *122 Rus.* Bykhov. E Belarus
Byron Sound *645* area of the South Atlantic Ocean, NW Falkland Islands
Byrranga, Gory *485* mountain range of N Russian Federation
Bystrovka *see* Kemin
Bytom *471 Ger.* Beuthen. S Poland
Byumba *492 var.* Biumba. N Rwanda
Byuzmeyin *581 prev.* Bezmein. S Turkmenistan

C

Caacupé *460* S Paraguay
Caaguazú *460* SE Paraguay
Caála *88 var.* Kaala, *Port.* Vila Robert Williams. C Angola
Caatinga, Serra da *145* mountain range of E Brazil
Caazapá *460* S Paraguay
Cabaiguán *210* C Cuba
Cabanatuan City *466* Luzon, Philippines
Cabháin *see* Cavan
Cabimas *619* NW Venezuela
Cabinda *88 var.* Kabinda. Non-contiguous region, NW Angola
Cabinda *88 var.* Kabinda. NW Angola
Cabora Bassa, Lake *see* Cahora Bassa, Lago de
Cabot Strait *171* strait connecting the Atlantic Ocean and Gulf of St. Lawrence, between Newfoundland and Nova Scotia
Cape Verde, Ilhas de *see* Cape Verde
Cabras, Ilha das *505* island to the N of São Tomé, Sao Tome & Principe
Cabras Island *647* island, W Guam
Čačak *630* C Serbia, Yugoslavia
Cacao *645* NE French Guiana
Cáceres *531* W Spain
Cachacrou *see* Scotts Head Village
Cacheu *282 var.* Cacheo. W Guinea-Bissau
Cacheu *282* river of NW Guinea-Bissau
Cachimbo, Serra do *145* mountain range of C Brazil
Cacine *282* S Guinea-Bissau
Cacine *282* river of S Guinea-Bissau
Caconda *88* C Angola
Čadca *519 Hung.* Csaca. N Slovakia
Cadiz *466* Negros, Philippines
Cádiz *530* SW Spain
Cádiz, Golfo de *474, 531* area of the Atlantic Ocean, on the SW coast of Spain
Caen *253* NW France
Caerdydd *see* Cardiff
Caerfyrddin *see* Carmarthen
Caergybi *see* Holyhead
Caernarfon *593 var.* Caernarvon. N Wales, UK
Cagayan *466* river of Luzon, Philippines
Cagayan de Oro *466* Mindanao, Philippines
Cagayan Islands *466* island group of C Philippines
Cagliari *320* Sardegna, W Italy
Caguas *651* E Puerto Rico
Cahabón *278* river of C Guatemala
Cahora Bassa Dam *419* dam of NW Mozambique
Cahora Bassa, Lago de *419 var.* Lake Cabora Bassa. Reservoir of NW Mozambique
Cahors *253* S France
Cahul *408 Rus.* Kagul. S Moldova
Caia *419* C Mozambique
Caibarién *210* C Cuba
Caicos Bank *653* undersea feature of the Atlantic Ocean
Caicos Passage *112, 653* strait of the Atlantic Ocean, between the Bahamas and Caicos Islands
Cai Lan *623* N Vietnam
Caille Island *276* island to the N of Grenada island, Grenada
Cailungo *502* N San Marino
Caió *282* W Guinea-Bissau
Cairns *101* NE Australia
Cairo *230 Ar.* Al Qāhirah, *var.* El Qâhira. N Egypt
Cajamarca *463 prev.* Caxamarca. NW Peru
Cajón, Represa el *288* reservoir of W Honduras
Çakilli Dere *see* Yialias
Čakovec *209 Hung.* Csáktornya, *Ger.* Csakathurn, *prev.* Tschakathurn. N Croatia
Calabar *440* S Nigeria
Calabozo *619* C Venezuela
Calabrai *325.* S Italy
Calagua Islands *466* island group of N Philippines
Calais *253* N France
Calama *183* N Chile
Calamian Group *466* island group of W Philippines
Calandula *88 var.* Kalandula. NW Angola
Calanscio Sand Sea *see* Kalanshiyū, Sarīr
Călăraşi 480 *SE Romania*
Călăraşi 408 var. *Călăras,* Kalarash. C Moldova
Calbayog *466* Samar, W Philippines
Calceta *228* W Ecuador
Calcutta *130* N Belize
Calcutta *297 var.* Kolkata. E India
Calcutta *538* N Suriname
Caldas da Rainha *474* W Portugal
Caledon *366, 527* river of Lesotho and South Africa
Caleta Olivia *95* SE Argentina
Calf of Man *647* island of S Isle of Man
Calgary *170* SW Canada
Calhau *176* São Vincente, N Cape Verde
Cali *195* W Colombia
Calibishie *224* N Dominica
Calicut *296 var.* Kozhikode. S India
Calida, Costa *531* coastal region of SE Spain
California *598* state of W USA
California, Golfo de *403* gulf of the Pacific Ocean
Cälilabad *110 Rus.* Dzhalilabad, *var.* Džalilabad, *prev.* Astrakhan-Bazar. S Azerbaijan
Callao *463* W Peru
Calliaqua *498* S St Vincent, St Vincent & the Grenadines
Caltagirone *321* Sicilia, S Italy
Caltanissetta *321* Sicilia, S Italy
Camá *226* river of C Dominican Republic
Camabatela *88* NW Angola
Camacupa *88 Port.* General Machado. C Angola
Camagüey *210 prev.* Puerto Príncipe. C Cuba
Camagüey, Archipiélago de *210* island group of N Cuba
Ca Mau *623 var.* Quan Long. S Vietnam
Cambay, Gulf of *see* Khambhat, Gulf of
Cambodia *164-167* officially State of Cambodia, *Cam.* Kampuchea, *prev.* People's Democratic Republic of Kampuchea. Country of SE Asia divided into 20 admin. units (provinces). ❖ Phnom Penh
Cambrian Mountains *593* mountain range of Wales, UK
Cambridge *329* NW Jamaica
Cambridge *433* C North Island, New Zealand
Cambridge *593* E England, UK
Cambridge Bay *170* Victoria Island, NW Canada
Cambrouze *645* N French Guiana
Cambulo *88* NE Angola
Camden Park *498* SW St Vincent, St Vincent & the Grenadines
Cameron Highlands *386* highlands of C Peninsular Malaysia
Cameroon *168-169* officially Republic of Cameroon, *Fr.* Cameroun. Country of W Africa divided into 10 admin. units (provinces). ❖ Yaoundé
Camiri *136* S Bolivia
Camopi *645* river of SE French Guiana
Camopi *645* E French Guiana
Camotes Islands *466* island group of E Philippines
Campana *95* E Argentina
Campbell River *170* Vancouver Island, SW Canada
Campeche *403* SE Mexico
Campeche, Bahía de *403 var.* Gulf of Campeche. Bay of the Gulf of Mexico

Campeche, Gulf of *see* Campeche, Bahía de
Câm Pha *623* N Vietnam
Campina Grande *145* E Brazil
Campinas *145* S Brazil
Campine *see* Kempen
Campobasso *321* S Italy
Campo Grande *145* SW Brazil
Campos *145* *var.* Campo dos Goitacazes. SE Brazil
Campossa *282* river of E Guinea-Bissau
Cam Ranh *623* SE Vietnam
Camrose *170* SW Canada
Canada *170-175* *prev.* British North America. Country of North America, divided into 12 admin. units (10 provinces, 2 territories). ❖ Ottawa
Cañada de Gómez *95* C Argentina
Canadian *599* river of SW USA
Çanakkale *576* W Turkey
Canakkale Boğazi *576* *Eng.* Dardanelles. Strait connecting Marmara Denizi and Aegean Sea
Canala *650* C New Caledonia
Canarias, Islas *531* *Eng.* Canary Islands. Islands of the Atlantic Ocean, part of Spain.
Canaries *497* W St Lucia
Canarreos, Archipiélago de los *210* island group of W Cuba
Canary Islands *see* Canarias, Islas
Cañas *206* NW Costa Rica
Canberra *101* ❖ of Australia, SE Australia
Canchungo *282* *prev.* Teixeira Pinto. W Guinea-Bissau
Cancuén *see* Santa Isabel
Candia *see* Irákleio
Canea *see* Chaniá
Canelones *607* *var.* Guadalupe. S Uruguay
Canguzo *see* Cankuzo
Canik Dağları *577* mountain range of N Turkey
Canillo *86* C Andorra
Canjambari *282* river of N Guinea-Bissau
Çankırı *577* N Turkey
Cankuzo *162* *var.* Canguzo. E Burundi
Cannes *253* SE France
Canoas *145* S Brazil
Cano, Pico do *176* mountain of Fogo, S Cape Verde
Canot, Rivière *286* river of C Haiti
Canouan *498* island of S St Vincent & the Grenadines
Cantabria *531* autonomous community of N Spain
Cantábrica, Cordillera *530-531* mountains of N Spain
Cantaro *570* N Trinidad, Trinidad & Tobago
Canterbury *593* SE England, UK
Canterbury Bight *433* area of the Pacific Ocean, SE New Zealand
Canterbury Plains *433* plain of C South Island, New Zealand
Cân Thơ *623* S Vietnam
Canton *see* Guangzhou
Canton Island *see* Kanton
Cao Băng *623* N Vietnam
Cape Breton Island *171* *Fr.* Île du Cap-Breton. Island of SE Canada
Cape Coast *270* *prev.* Cape Coast Castle. S Ghana
Cape Domesnes *see* Kolkasrags
Capellen *378* SW Luxembourg
Cape Palmas *see* Harper
Capesterre *646* Marie-Galante, S Guadeloupe
Capesterre-Belle-Eau *646* S Guadeloupe
Cape Town *527* *Afr.* Kaapstad. Legislative capital of South Africa, Western Cape, SW South Africa
Cape Verde *176-177* officially Republic of Cape Verde, *Port.* Ilhas do Cabo Verde. Country of volcanic islands in the Atlantic Ocean divided into 14 admin. units (districts). ❖ Cidade de Praia
Cape York *101* N Australia
Cape York Peninsula *101* peninsula of N Australia
Cap-Haïtien *286* *var.* Le Cap. N Haiti
Capitán Arturo Prat *90* Chilian research station of South Shetland Islands, Antarctica
Capitán Bado *460* E Paraguay
Capitán Pablo Lagerenza *460* *var.* Mayor Pablo Lagerenza. N Paraguay
Capodistria *see* Koper
Capri, Isola di *321* island of S Italy
Caprivi Concession *see* Caprivi Strip
Caprivi Strip *142, 423* *prev.* Caprivi Concession, *Ger.* Caprivizipfel. Finger of territory of NE Namibia
Caprivizipfel *see* Caprivi Strip
Cap Saint-Jacques *see* Vung Tau
Caquetá *195* river of S Colombia
CAR *see* Central African Republic
Caracal *480* S Romania
Caracas *619* ❖ of Venezuela, N Venezuela
Carache, Ilha de *282* island of W Guinea-Bissau
Caracollo *136* W Bolivia
Caransebes *480* W Romania
Caráquez *228* *prev.* Bahía de Caráquez. W Ecuador
Caratasca, Laguna de *288* lagoon on the E coast of Honduras
Caravela *282* Ilha Caravela, Guinea-Bissau
Caravela, Ilha *282* island of Arquipélago dos Bijagós, W Guinea-Bissau
Carbonia *320* SW Sardegna, Italy
Carcassonne *253* S France
Cardamom, Chaîne des *see* Krâvanh, Chuŏr Phmun
Cardamom Mountains *see* Krâvanh, Chuŏr Phmun
Cárdenas *210* NW Cuba
Cardiff *593* *Wel.* Caerdydd. S Wales, UK
Cardigan Bay *593* bay of W Wales, UK
Cardona *607* SW Uruguay
Cardonagh *314* N Ireland
Čardžou *see* Chardzhev
Carenage *570* NW Trinidad, Trinidad & Tobago
Caribbean Sea *206, 286, 642, 643* arm of the Atlantic Ocean, Central America
Caripito *619* NE Venezuela
Carlton, The *112* *var.* Abraham Bay. Mayaguana, Bahamas
Carletonville *527* North West, N South Africa
Carlisle *593* NW England, UK
Carlow *314* SE Ireland
Carlsruhe *see* Karlsruhe
Carmarthen *593* *Wel.* Caerfyrddin. W Wales, UK
Carmelo *607* *var.* Carmelo del Este. SW Uruguay
Carmona *206* W Costa Rica
Carmona *see* Uíge
Carnavon *100* W Australia
Carnegie, Lake *100* salt lake of W Australia
Carnot *179* W Central African Republic
Caroço, Ilha *505* island to the S of Príncipe, Sao Tome & Principe
Carolina *651* NE Puerto Rico
Caroline Island *see* Millennium island
Caroline Islands *406* island group of Micronesia
Caroni *570* river of N Trinidad, Trinidad & Tobago
Caroní *619* river of E Venezuela
Carora *619* NW Venezuela
Carpathian Mountains *216, 471, 480, 586* *var.* Carpathians, *Ger.* Karpaten, *Cz./Pol.* Karpaty. Mountain range of E Europe
Carpaţii Meridionali *480* *var.* South Carpathians, *Eng.* Transylvanian Alps. Mountain range of C Romania
Carpaţii Occidentali *480* mountain range of W Romania
Carpentaria, Gulf of *101* gulf of the Arafura Sea, on the coast of N Australia
Carrantual *see* Carrauntoohill
Carrara *320* N Italy
Carrauntoohill *314* *var.* Carrauntohil, *Ir.* Carrantual. Mountain of SW Ireland
Carriacou *276* island to the north of Grenada, Grenada
Carrick on Shannon *314* N Ireland
Carson City *598* Nevada, W USA
Carstensz, Puntjak *see* Jaya, Puncak
Cartagena *195* NW Colombia
Cartagena *531* SE Spain
Cartago *195* W Colombia
Cartago *206* C Costa Rica
Carúpano *619* NE Venezuela
Casablanca *414* *Ar.* Dar el Beida. NW Morocco
Casamance *510* cultural region of SW Senegal
Casamance *510* river of SW Senegal
Cascade *650* NE Norfolk Island
Cascade *512* Mahé, Seychelles
Cascade Range *598* mountain range of Canada and USA
Casey *90* Australian research station of Greater Antarctica, Antarctica
Caseyr, Raas *524* *var.* Ras Aser, *prev.* Cape Guardafui. Cape on the NE coast of Somalia
Cashel *636* E Zimbabwe
Casilda *95* C Argentina
Ca *623* river of Laos and Vietnam
Casper *599* Wyoming, NW USA
Caspian Sea *110* *Az.* Xäzär Dänizi, *Rus.* Kaspiyskoye More, *Per.* Daryā-ye Khazar, Baḩr-e Khazar, *Kaz.* Kaspiy Tengizi. Shallow inland sea tween W Asia and E Europe
Cassacatiza *419* NW Mozambique
Cassai *see* Kasai
Cassel *see* Kassel
Cassiar Mountains *170* mountain range of W Canada
Castellamare di Stabia *321* S Italy
Castellón de la Plana *531* *Cat.* Castelló de la Plana. E Spain
Castelo Branco *474* C Portugal
Castelvetrano *321* Sicilia, S Italy
Castilhiano *176* São Nicolau, N Cape Verde
Castilla *463* NW Peru
Castilla-La Mancha *531* autonomous community of NE Spain
Castillos *607* SE Uruguay
Castlebar *314* W Ireland
Castle Bruce *224* NE Dominica
Castle Harbour *643* inlet of the North Atlantic Ocean, E Bermuda
Castletown *647* SE Isle of Man
Castries *497* ❖ of St Lucia, N St Lucia
Castro *183* Isla de Chiloé, W Chile
Castrovillari *321* SE Italy
Catacamas *288* C Honduras
Catacaos *463* NW Peru
Catalan Bay *646* *var.* Caleta. Bay of the Mediterranean Sea on the E coast of Gibraltar
Cataluña *531* autonomous community of N Spain
Catamarca *see* San Fernando del Valle de Catamarca
Catanduanes Island *466* island of E Philippines
Catania *321* Sicilia, S Italy
Catano *651* NE Puerto Rico
Catanzaro *321* SE Italy
Catedral, Cerro *607* mountain of S Uruguay
Catherine, Mount *see* Katherina, Gebel
Catholic Island *498* island of SW St Vincent & the Grenadines
Catió *282* S Guinea-Bissau
Cat Island *112* island of C Bahamas
Catuane *419* S Mozambique
Catumbela *88* W Angola
Cauca *195* river of N Colombia
Caucasia *195* NW Colombia
Caucasus *262, 484* *Rus.* Kavkaz. Mountain range of SE Europe and SW Asia, commonly taken as the boundary between Asia and Europe
Caura *619* river of E Venezuela
Căuşeni *408* *Rus.* Kaushany. E Moldova
Causse du Kelifely *see* Kôsin' i Kelifely
Cauto *210* river of SE Cuba
Cavaia *see* Kavajë
Cavalla *see* Cavally
Cavally *326, 368* *var.* Cavalla. River of Ivory Coast and Liberia
Cavan *314* *Ir.* Cabháin. NE Ireland
Cave Hill *121* W Barbados
Caviana de Fora, Ilha *145* *var.* Ilha Cavinana. Island of N Brazil
Cawnpore *see* Kānpur
Caxamarca *see* Cajamarca
Caxias do Sul *145* S Brazil
Caxito *88* NW Angola
Cayambe *228* N Ecuador
Cayenne *645* ❖ of French Guiana, NE French Guiana
Cayey *651* SE Puerto Rico
Çayırova *215* *var.* Ayios Theodhoros. NE Cyprus
Cayman Brac *644* island, E Cayman Islands
Cayman Islands *644* British dependent territory of the Caribbean Sea. ❖ George Town.
Cayo *see* San Ignacio
Cayon *494* E St Kitts, St Kitts & Nevis
Cayes *286* *var.* Les Cayes. SW Haiti
Cay Sal *112* islet of W Bahamas
Cazin *140* NW Bosnia & Herzegovina
Ceadâr-Lunga *see* Ciadîr-Lunga
Ceanannus Mór *314* NE Ireland
Ceará *see* Fortaleza
Cébaco, Isla *456* island of SW Panama
Cebollatí *607* river of E Uruguay
Cebu *466* Cebu, C Philippines
Cebu *466* island of C Philippines
Cedar Grove *92* N Antigua, Antigua & Barbuda
Cedar Rapids *599* Iowa, C USA
Cedros, Isla *403* island of NW Mexico
Ceelbuur *524* *It.* El Bur. C Somalia
Ceeldheere *524* *var.* Ceel Dheere, *It.* El Dere. E Somalia
Ceel Gaal *524* *var.* El Gal. NW Somalia
Ceel Xamurre *see* Jirriiban
Ceerigaabo *524* *var.* Erigabo, Erigavo. N Somalia
Cegléd *290* *prev.* Czegléd. C Hungary
Celaya *403* C Mexico
Celebes *302* *Ind.* Sulawesi. Island of C Indonesia
Celebes Sea *302, 387, 466* *Ind.* Laut Sulawesi. Sea of the Pacific Ocean, between N Indonesia and S Philippines
Čeleken *see* Cheleken
Celje *520* *Ger.* Cilli. C Slovenia
Celtic Sea *314, 593* *Ir.* An Mhuir Cheilteach. Sea of the Atlantic Ocean, between S Ireland and SW England, UK
Cenderawasih, Teluk *303* bay of the Pacific Ocean on the NW coast of Irian Jaya, E Indonesia
Central African Republic *178-179* abbrev. CAR. Country of Central Africa divided into 16 admin. units (prefectures). ❖ Bangui
Central Brāhui Range *451* mountain range of W Pakistan
Central China *191*
Central, Cordillera *195* range of the Andes in W Colombia
Central, Cordillera *226* mountain range of C Dominican Republic
Central, Cordillera *466* mountain range of Luzon, N Philippines
Central, Cordillera *651* mountain range of C Puerto Rico
Central Group *see* Inner Islands
Central Island *342* island in Lake Rudolf, NW Kenya
Central Makrān Range *450* mountain range of W Pakistan
Central Range *458* mountain range of C Papua New Guinea

Central Siberian Plateau *see* Srednesibirskoye Ploskogor'ye
Centre de Flacq *400* E Mauritius
Centre Hills *649* mountain range, C Montserrat
Cephalonia *see* Kefallinía
Ceram *see* Seram
Ceram Sea *see* Seram, Laut
Cerfs, Ile aux *400 var.* Isle aux Cerfs. Island of E Mauritius
Cernăuţi *see* Chernivtsi
Cërrik *81 var.* Cerriku. C Albania
Cerro Chato *607* C Uruguay
Cerro de Pasco *463* C Peru
Cerrón Grande, Embalse *235* reservoir of N El Salvador
Ceru Colorado *642* S Aruba
Červen brjag *see* Cherven-Bryag
Cesena *321* N Italy
Cēsis *362 Ger.* Wenden. NE Latvia
České Budějovice *216 Ger.* Budweis. SW Czech Republic
Českomoravská Vrchovina *216 var.* Bohemian-Moravian Highlands, Ceskomoravská Vrchovina, *Ger.* Böhmisch-Mährische Höhe. Mountain range of S Czech Republic
Český Krumlov *216* SW Czech Republic
Český Les *see* Bohemian Forest
Céspedes *210* SE Cuba
Cess *368 var.* Rivercess. S Liberia
Cestos *368 var.* Cess. River of Liberia
Ceuta *414, 531* exclave of Spain, N Morocco
Cévennes *253* mountain range of SE France
Ceylon *see* Sri Lanka
Ceyhan *577* S Turkey
Chacachacare *570* island to the NW of Trinidad, Trinidad & Tobago
Chachapoyas *463* NW Peru
Chachoengsao *563* C Thailand
Chaclacayo *463* W Peru
Chaco *see* Gran Chaco
Chad *180-181* officially Republic of Chad, *Fr.* Tchad. Country of Equatorial Africa divided into 14 admin. units (prefectures). ❖ N'Djamena
Chã da Igreja *176* Santo Antão, N Cape Verde
Chad, Lake *168, 180, 439, 441 Fr.* Lac Tchad. Lake of C Africa
Chadyr-Lunga *see* Ciadîr-Lunga
Chaeryŏng *349* SW North Korea
Chāgai Hills *450* mountain range of Afghanistan and Pakistan
Chaghcharān *77* C Afghanistan
Chagos Archipelago *643 var.* Oil Islands. Island group of C British Indian Ocean Territory
Chaguanas *570* W Trinidad, Trinidad & Tobago
Chaguaramas *570* NW Trinidad, Trinidad & Tobago
Chagyl *581* NW Turkmenistan
Chahārborjak *77* SW Afghanistan
Chaillu, Massif du *258* C Gabon
Mongos, Chaîne des *see* Bongo, Massif des
Chainpur *427* W Nepal
Chaiyaphum *563* N Thailand
Chakari *636* N Zimbabwe
Chake Chake *360* Pemba, E Tanzania
Chakwāl *451* NE Pakistan
Chalándri *273 prev.* Khalándrion. SE Greece
Chalap Dalam *77* mountain range of W Afghanistan
Chalatenango *235* N El Salvador
Chalbi Desert *342* desert region of N Kenya
Chalchuapa *235* W El Salvador
Chalkída *273 Eng.* Chalcis, *prev.* Khalkís. Evvoia, E Greece
Chalkidikí *273 prev.* Khalkidhikí, *Eng.* Chalcidice. Peninsula of NE Greece
Challapata *136* SW Bolivia
Challengers *494* S St Kitts, St Kitts & Nevis
Châlons-en-Champagne *253 prev.* Châlons-sur-Marne. NE France
Chaman *451* NW Pakistan
Chambas *210* C Cuba
Chambéry *253* E France
Chambeshi *635* river of NE Zambia
Chambi, Jebel *573* mountain of W Tunisia
Chamelecón, Río *288* river of NW Honduras
Chamouny *400* S Mauritius
Champagne *253* cultural region of NE France
Champasak *359* S Laos
Chañaral *183* N Chile
Chances Peak *649* mountain peak of S Montserrat
Chan Chen *130* N Belize
Chan-chiang *see* Zhanjiang
Chandīgarh *296* N India
Chandlers Falls *342 var.* Chanlers Falls. Waterfall of C Kenya
Chāndpur *117* E Bangladesh
Changane *419* river of S Mozambique
Changara *419* W Mozambique
Changchun *187 prev.* Hsinking. Jilin, NE China
Changhua *555 Jap.* Shōka. W Taiwan
Changi *517* area of E Singapore
Chang Jiang *187 var.* Yangtze Kiang. River of C China
Changkiakow *see* Zhangjiakou
Chang, Ko *563* island of C Thailand
Changsha *187* Hunan, S China
Chang-tien *see* Zibo
Changuinola *456* W Panama
Ch'angwŏn *350* S South Korea
Changyŏn *349* SW North Korea
Chaniá *273 Eng.* Canea, *prev.* Khaniá. Crete, S Greece
Channel Islands *252* island group to the NW of France *see* Jersey, Guernsey, Alderney, Sark
Channel, The *see* English Channel
Channel Tunnel *593* tunnel between France and SE England, UK
Chanthaburi *563* C Thailand
Ch'aochou *555 var.* Chaochow, *Jap.* Chōshū. SW Taiwan
Chao Phraya *563* river of C Thailand
Chaouèn *414 var.* Chechaouèn, Chefchaouèn, *Sp.* Xauen. N Morocco
Chapada Diamantina *145* plateau of E Brazil
Chapala, Lago de *403* lake of SW Mexico
Chapelton *329* C Jamaica
Chaplin Bay *643* bay of the North Atlantic Ocean, W Bermuda
Chardonnières *286* SW Haiti
Chardzhev *581 prev.* Chardzhou, *var.* Čardžou, *prev.* Leninsk, *Turkm.* Chärjew. E Turkmenistan
Chardzhou *see* Chardzhev
Ch'arents'avan *98 var.* Čarencaven. C Armenia
Chari *180 var.* Shari. River of C Africa
Chārīkār *77* NE Afghanistan
Charity *284* NE Guyana
Chärjew *see* Chardzhev
Charkhliq *see* Ruoqiang
Charleroi *127* S Belgium
Charleston *599* South Carolina, SE USA
Charleston *599* West Virginia, E USA
Charlestown *494* SW Nevis, St Kitts & Nevis
Charlestown *498* Canouan, St Vincent & the Grenadines
Charleville *101* E Australia
Charleville-Mézieres *253* NE France
Charlotte *599* North Carolina, SE USA
Charlotte Amalie *653* ❖ of Virgin Islands (US), S Saint Thomas Island
Charlotte Town *see* Gouyave
Charlottetown *171* Prince Edward Island, SE Canada
Charlotte Ville *224* SW Dominica
Charlotteville *570* N Tobago, Trinidad & Tobago
Charshanga *581 prev.* Charshangy, *Turkm.* Charshangngy. SE Turkmenistan
Charsk *see* Shar
Chartres *253* N France
Chartres Settlement *645* West Falkland, W Falkland Islands
Chateaubelair *498* NW St Vincent, St Vincent & the Grenadines
Châteauroux *253* C France
Chateaux, Pointe des *646* headland of E Guadeloupe
Châtelet *127* S Belgium
Chatham Island *433* island of Chatham Islands, E New Zealand
Chatham Islands *433* islands of E New Zealand
Chatkal Range *357, 610 Rus.* Chatkal'skiy Khrebet. Mountain range of Kyrgyzstan and Uzbekistan
Chăttagām *see* Chittagong
Chattanooga *599* Tennessee, SE USA
Chatyr-Tash *357* E Kyrgyzstan
Châu Đôc *623 var.* Chau Phu. SW Vietnam
Chauk *159* W Burma
Chaumont *252* NE France
Chau Phu *see* Châu Đôc
Chautara *427* C Nepal
Chaves *474* N Portugal
Chbar *165* E Cambodia
Cheb *216 Ger.* Eger. W Czech Republic
Chechaouèn *see* Chaouèn
Ch'ech'eng *555* S Taiwan
Che-chiang *see* Zhejiang
Chechenskaya, Respublika *484, 488* autonomous republic of SW Russian Federation
Chech'ŏn *350 Jap.* Teisen. N South Korea
Checker Hall *121* N Barbados
Cheduba Island *159* island of W Burma
Chefoo *see* Yantai
Chegutu *636 prev.* Hartley. N Zimbabwe
Cheju *350 Jap.* Saishū. Cheju-do, South Korea
Cheju-do *350 prev.* Quelpart, *Jap.* Saishu. Island of S South Korea
Cheju Strait *350 var.* Chejuhaehyop, Cheju-Haehyop. Strait connecting the Korea Strait and Yellow Sea
Chekiang *see* Zhejiang
Cheleken *581 var.* Čeleken. W Turkmenistan
Chelkar *338* W Kazakhstan
Chelyabinsk *484* C Russian Federation
Chemin Grenier *400* S Mauritius
Chemnitz *265 prev.* Karl-Marx-Stadt. E Germany
Chemulpo *see* Inch'ŏn
Ch'eng-chou *see* Zhengzhou
Chengchow *see* Zhengzhou
Chengdu *187 var.* Chengtu. Sichuan, SW China
Chenghsien *see* Zhengzhou
Ch'eng-hua *see* Altay
Chenghwa *see* Altay
Chenkaladi *534* E Sri Lanka
Chennai *296 var.* Madras. S India
Cheom Ksan *see* Chŏâm Khsant
Chepo *456* NE Panama
Cher *253* river of C France
Cherbourg *253* NW France
Cheren *see* Keren
Cherepovets *484* W Russian Federation
Chergui, Chott ech *83* salt lake of NW Algeria
Chergui, Île *573 Ar.* Jazirat ash Sharqi. Island of E Tunisia
Cherikaw *122* E Belarus
Cherkasy *586 Rus.* Cherkassy. C Ukraine
Cherne More *see* Black Sea
Chernivtsi *586 Rus.* Chernovtsy, *Rom.* Cernăuţi, *Ger.* Czernowitz. W Ukraine
Chernobyl' *see* Chornobyl'
Cherno More *see* Black Sea
Cherry Island *see* Anuta
Cherskiy *485* NE Russian Federation
Cherskogo, Khrebet *485* mountain range of NE Russian Federation
Cherso *see* Cres
Cherson *see* Kherson
Cherven-Bryag *152 var.* Červen brjag. NW Bulgaria
Chester *593* NW England, UK
Chetumal, Bahia *130 var.* Chetumal Bay. Bay of the Caribbean Sea
Chetumal Bay *see* Chetumal, Bahia
Cheviot Hills *593* hills of England and Scotland, UK
Ch'ew Bahir *243 var.* Lake Stefanie. Lake of SW Ethiopia
Cheyenne *599* Wyoming, NW USA
Chhlong *see* Phumĭ Chhlong
Chhuk *see* Phumĭ Chhuk
Chhukha *134* SW Bhutan
Chiai *555 var.* Chiayi, Kiayi, *Jap.* Kagi. W Taiwan
Chiali *555 var.* Kiali, *Jap.* Kari. W Taiwan
Chia-mu-ssu *see* Jiamusi
Chiang-hsi *see* Jiangxi
Chiang Mai *563 var.* Chiengmai. NW Thailand
Chiang-su *see* Jiangsu
Chiat'ura *262* C Georgia
Chiba *330* Honshū, SE Japan
Chibuto *419* S Mozambique
Chicago *599* Illinois, C USA
Chīchāwatni *451* E Pakistan
Chichicastenango *278* W Guatemala
Chichigalpa *436* W Nicaragua
Ch'i-ch'i-ha-erh *see* Qiqihar
Chiclayo *463* NW Peru
Chicoutimi *171* SE Canada
Chicualacuala *419* SW Mozambique
Chiemsee *265* lake of SE Germany
Chiesanuova *502* SW San Marino
Chih-fu *see* Yantai
Chihli *see* Hebei
Chihli, Gulf of *see* Bo Hai
Chi-hsi *see* Jixi
Chihuahua *403* NW Mexico
Ch'ikhareshi *262* N Georgia
Chikwawa *385* SW Malawi
Chilanga *635* S Zambia
Chilaw *534* W Sri Lanka
Chile *182-185* officially Republic of Chile. Country of South America divided into 13 admin. units (12 regions and 1 metropolitan area). ❖ Santiago
Chile Chico *183* W Chile
Chilika Lake *296* lake of E India
Chililabombwe *635* C Zambia
Chi-lin *see* Jilin
Chillán *183* C Chile
Chilliwack *170* SW Canada
Chiloé, Isla de *183 var.* Isla Grande de Chiloé. Island of W Chile
Chilumba *385 prev.* Deep Bay. N Malawi
Chilung *555 var.* Keelung, *Jap.* Kirun. N Taiwan
Chilwa, Lake *385 var.* Lake Shirwa, *Port.* Lago Chirua. Lake of SE Malawi
Chimaltenango *278* W Guatemala
Chimanimani *636 prev.* Mandidzudzure, *prev.* Melsetter. E Zimbabwe
Chimbay *see* Chimboy
Chimborazo *228* mountain of C Ecuador
Chimbote *463* W Peru
Chimboy *610 Rus.* Chimbay. NW Uzbekistan
Chimishliya *see* Cimişlia
Chimkent *see* Shymkent
Chimoio *419* C Mozambique
China *186-193* officially People's Republic of China, *Chin.* Zhonghua Renmin Gonghe Guo, *var.* Chung-hua Jen-min Kung-ho-kuo, *prev.* Chinese Empire (until January 1912). Country of E Asia divided into 30 admin. units (22 ovinces, 5 autonomous regions, 3 province-level municipalities). ❖ Beijing
Chinan *see* Jinan
Chinandega *436* W Nicaragua
Chincha Alta *463* SW Peru
Chin-chiang *see* Quanzhou
Chin-chou *see* Jinzhou
Chinchow *see* Jinzhou
Chin-do *350 Jap.* Chin-tō. Island of SW South Korea
Chindwin *159* river of NW Burma
Ch'ing Hai *see* Qinghai Hu
Chinghai *see* Qinghai
Chingola *635* C Zambia

Ch'ingshui *555 var.* Tsingshui, *Jap.* Kiyomizu. W Taiwan
Ching-Tao *see* Qingdao
Chinguetti *398* C Mauritania
Chinhae *350 Jap.* Chinkai. S South Korea
Chinhoyi *636 var.* Sinoia. N Zimbabwe
Chinhsien *see* Jinzhou
Chiniot *451* NE Pakistan
Chinit *165 var.* Chinit. River of C Cambodia
Chinju *350 Jap.* Shinshū. S South Korea
Chinkai *see* Chinhae
Chink Kaplankyr *581* ridge of NW Turkmenistan
Chinko *179* river of E Central African Republic
Chintheche *385 var.* Chinteche. N Malawi
Chin-tō *see* Chin-do
Chios *273 prev.* Khíos. Island of E Greece
Chíos *273 prev.* Khíos, *It.* Scio, *Turk.* Sakis-Adasi. Chios, E Greece
Chipata *635 prev.* Fort Jameson. E Zambia
Chipinge *636 prev.* Chipinga. E Zimbabwe
Chiponde *385* SE Malawi
Chiquimula *278* SE Guatemala
Chiquimulilla *278* S Guatemala
Chiradzulu *385* S Malawi
Chirang *134* S Bhutan
Chirchik *610 Rus.* Chirchik. E Uzbekistan
Chire *see* Shire
Chiredzi *636* SE Zimbabwe
Chirilagua *235* SE El Salvador
Chiriquí, Golfo de *456* gulf of the Pacific Ocean to the SW of Panama
Chiriquí Grande *456* W Panama
Chiriquí, Laguna de *456* lagoon of W Panama
Chiromo *385* S Malawi
Chirongui *649* S Mayotte
Chirripó Grande, Cerro *206* mountain of E Costa Rica
Chirua, Lago *see* Chilwa, Lake
Chirundu *636* N Zimbabwe
Chisenga *385* NW Malawi
Ch'ishan *555 var.* Kishan, *Jap.* Kizan. SW Taiwan
Chishtiān Mandi *451* E Pakistan
Chisimaio *see* Kismaayo
Chişinău *408 var.* Kishinev. ❖ of Moldova, C Moldova
Chissioua Mtsamboro *649* island of NW Mayotte
Chita *485* C Russian Federation
Chitipa *385 prev.* Fort Hill. NW Malawi
Chitose *331* Hokkaidō, N Japan
Chitré *456* S Panama
Chittagong *117 Ben.* Chāttagām. SE Bangladesh
Chittagong Hills *117* hilly region of S Asia
Chitungwiza *636 prev.* Chitangwiza. NE Zimbabwe
Chiuta, Lake *385* lake of SE Malawi
Chivhu *636 prev.* Enkeldoorn. C Zimbabwe
Chixoy *278 var.* Río Negro, Salinas. River of Guatemala and Mexico
Chizarira Hills *636* hilly region of NW Zimbabwe
Chizumulu Island *385 var.* Chisumulu Island. Island of Lake Nyasa, E Malawi
Chkalov *see* Orenburg
Chlef *83 prev.* El Asnam, Orléansville, *var.* Ech Cheliff, Ech Chleff. NW Algeria
Choa Chu Kang *517* area of W Singapore
Chŏâm Khsant *165 prev.* Cheom Ksan. N Cambodia
Choiseul *497* SW St Lucia
Choiseul *522 var.* Lauru. Island of the W Solomon Islands
Choiseul Sound *645* area of the South Atlantic Ocean, E Falkland Islands
Cholo *see* Thyolo
Choluteca *288* S Honduras
Choluteca *288* river of S Honduras
Choma *635* S Zambia
Chomo Lhari *134* mountain of NW Bhutan
Chomutov *216 Ger.* Komotau. NW Czech Republic
Ch'ŏnan *350 Jap.* Tenan. W South Korea
Chon Buri *563* C Thailand
Chone *228* W Ecuador
Ch'ŏngch'ŏn *349* river of W North Korea
Ch'ŏngjin *349* NE North Korea
Chŏngju *349* W North Korea
Chŏngju *350 prev.* Chŏngup, *Jap.* Seiyu. SW South Korea
Ch'ŏngju *350 var.* Chŏngju. C South Korea
Chongqing *187 var.* Chungking, Ch'ung-ching, Yuzhou. Sichuan, SW China
Chongwe *635* E Zambia
Chŏnju *350 Jap.* Zenshū. SW South Korea
Chorne More *see* Black Sea
Chornobyl' *586 Rus.* Chernobyl'. N Ukraine
Chorzów *471 Ger.* Königshütte. S Poland
Chōsen-kaikyō *see* Korea Strait
Chōshū *see* Ch'aochou
Choshui Hsi *555* river of W and NE Taiwan
Chota Nagpur Plateau *296* plateau of NE India
Choybalsan *412* E Mongolia
Christchurch *433* E South Island, New Zealand
Christiana *329* C Jamaica
Christiania *see* Oslo
Christian, Point *651* headland of Pitcairn Island, S Pitcairn Islands
Christiansand *see* Kristiansand
Christianshåb *see* Qasigiannguit
Christiansted *653* Saint Croix, S Virgin Islands (US)
Christiansund *see* Kristiansund
Christmas Island *644* Australian external territory of the Indian Ocean. ❖ Flying Fish Cove.
Christmas Island *see* Kiritimati
Chrysochou Bay *see* Khrysokhou Bay
Chu *see* Shū
Chu *357 var.* Ču, *Kir.* Chüy. River of Kazakhstan and Kyrgyzstan
Chu *623* river of Laos and Vietnam
Chuādānga *117* W Bangladesh
Ch'uan-chou *see* Quanzhou
Chubek *see* Moskva
Ch'u-chiang *see* Shaoguan
Chucunaque *456* river of E Panama
Chudskoye Ozero *see* Peipus, Lake
Chūgoku-sanchi *330* mountain range of Honshū, W Japan
Chuí *see* Chuy
Chukai *386 var.* Cukai. E Peninsular Malaysia
Chukchi Sea *485 Rus.* Chukotskoye More. Sea of Arctic Ocean between NE Asia and NW N America
Chukotskiy Poluostrov *485 Eng.* Chukchi Peninsula. Peninsula of NE Russian Federation
Chulucanas *463* NW Peru
Chumphon *563* S Thailand
Chunan *555* NW Taiwan
Ch'unch'ŏn *350 Jap.* Shunsen. N South Korea
Chungyang Shanmo *555* mountain range of C Taiwan
Ch'ung-ching *see* Chongqing
Chungho *555* N Taiwan
Chunghsinghsints'un *555* W Taiwan
Chung-hua Jen-min Kung-ho-kuo *see* China
Ch'ungju *350 Jap.* Chūshū. C South Korea
Ch'ungju-ho *350* reservoir of C South Korea
Chungking *see* Chongqing
Chungli *555 Jap.* Chūreki. N Taiwan
Ch'ungmu *350* S South Korea
Chunya *560* SW Tanzania
Chuquicamata *183* N Chile
Chur *546 It.* Coira, *Rmsch.* Cuera, *Fr.* Coire. E Switzerland
Church Cay *498* cay of E St Vincent & the Grenadines
Churchill *170* C Canada
Church Village *121* SE Barbados
Chūreki *see* Chungli
Chūshū *see* Ch'ungju
Chust *610 var.* Čust. E Uzbekistan
Chuuk Islands *406 var.* Hogoley Islands. Island group of C Micronesia
Chuvashskaya *484* autonomous republic of W Russian Federation
Chuy *607 var.* Chuí. SE Uruguay
Chykotskoye Nagor'ye *485* mountain range of NE Russian Federation
Ciadîr-Lunga *408 var.* Ceadâr-Lunga, *Rus.* Chadyr-Lunga. S Moldova
Cibitoke *162* NW Burundi
Ciceron *497* NW St Lucia
Cicia *246 prev.* Thithia. Island of the Lau Group, E Fiji
Cidade Velha *176* Santiago, S Cape Verde
Ciego de Ávila *210* C Cuba
Ciénaga *195* N Colombia
Cienfuegos *210* C Cuba
Cieza *531* SE Spain
Çiftlik Dere *see* Aloupos
Cifuentes *210* C Cuba
Cikobia *246 prev.* Thikombia. Island to the N of Vanua Levu, N Fiji
Cilacap *302 prev.* Tjilatjap. Java, C Indonesia
Cill Airne *see* Killarney
Cill Choinnigh *see* Kilkenny
Cilli *see* Celje
Cill Mhantáin *see* Wicklow
Cimişlia *408 Rus.* Chimishliya. S Moldova
Cina Selatan, Laut *see* South China Sea
Cincinnati *599* Ohio, NE USA
Ciney *127* SE Belgium
Ciotat *253* SE France
Cirebon *302 prev.* Tjirebon. Java, C Indonesia
Cirque de Cilaos *652* mountain range of W Réunion
Cirquenizza *see* Crikvenica
Ciskei Bantustan 'self-governing homeland' comprising 2 non-contiguous territories of E Cape Province, South Africa; created in 1981, abolished in 1994
Citlaltépetl *see* Orizaba, Volcán Pico de
Citron *645* NW French Guiana
Citron, River *400* river of NW Mauritius
Ciudad Arce *235* W El Salvador
Ciudad Bolívar *619* E Venezuela
Ciudad de Guatemala *see* Guatemala City
Ciudad del Este *460 prev.* Puerto Presidente Stroessner. SE Paraguay
Ciudad de México *see* Mexico City
Ciudad de Panama *see* Panama City
Ciudad Guayana *619* E Venezuela
Ciudad Juárez *403* NW Mexico
Ciudad Obregón *403* NW Mexico
Ciudad Ojeda *619* NW Venezuela
Ciudad Real *531* C Spain
Ciudad Trujillo *see* Santo Domingo
Ciudad Victoria *403* C Mexico
Civitavecchia *321* C Italy
Clarence *433* river of NE South Island, New Zealand
Clarence Island *90* island of South Shetland Islands, Antarctica
Clarence Town *112* Long Island, Bahamas
Clermont-Ferrand *253* C France
Clervaux *378* N Luxembourg
Cleveland *599* Ohio, NE USA
Clifden *314* W Ireland
Clifton *224* NW Dominica
Clifton *498* Union I, St Vincent & the Grenadines
Cloncurry *101* NE Australia
Clonmel *314 Ir.* Cluain Meala. S Ireland
Cluj-Napoca *480 prev.* Cluj, *Hung.* Kolozsvár, *Ger.* Klausenburg. NW Romania
Clutha *433* river of SW South Island, New Zealand
Clyde, Firth of *593* estuary of the river Clyde, SW Scotland, UK
Coamo *651* S Puerto Rico
Coast Mountains *170 Fr.* Chaîne Côtière. Mountain range of Canada and USA
Coast Ranges *598* mountain range of W USA
Coatepeque *278* W Guatemala
Coatepeque, Lago de *235* lake of W El Salvador
Coatzacoalcos *403 prev.* Puerto México. SE Mexico
Cobán *278* C Guatemala
Cobija *136* NW Bolivia
Cochabamba *136* C Bolivia
Cochin *296 var.* Kochi. S India
Cocibolca *see* Nicaragua, Lago de
Cockburn Harbour *653* South Caicos, E Turks and Caicos Islands
Cockburn Town *112* Great Exuma I, Bahamas
Cockburn Town *653* ❖ Turks and Caicos Islands, Grand Turk Island, SE Turks and Caicos Islands
Cockpit Country, The *329* physical region of NW Jamaica
Coco *288, 436 var.* Wangkí, Segovia. River of Honduras and Nicaragua
Cocobeach *258* NW Gabon
Coco, Isla del *206* island of SW Costa Rica
Cocoli *see* Corubal
Cocos (Keeling) Islands *644* Australian external territory of the Indian Ocean. ❖ West Island
Cocos Island *647* island group of S Guam
Codrington *92* C Barbuda, Antigua & Barbuda
Codrington Lagoon *92* W Barbuda, Antigua & Barbuda
Coeroeni *see* Corantijn
Coëtivy *512* island of E Seychelles
Coffs Harbour *101* E Australia
Cogîlnic *408 var.* Cogâlnic, *Rus.* Kogil'nik. River of SE Moldova
Cognac *253* W France
Cogo *236 var.* Kogo, *prev.* Puerto Iradier. SW Equatorial Guinea
Cohoha *see* Cyohoha-Sud Lac
Coiba, Isla de *456* island of SW Panama
Coihaique *183 var.* Coyhaique. S Chile
Coimbatore *296* S India
Coimbra *474* W Portugal
Coin de Mire *see* Gunners Quoin
Coira *see* Chur
Coire *see* Chur
Coi, Sông *see* Red River
Cojutepeque *235* C El Salvador
Colchester *593* E England, UK
Coleraine *593* Northern Ireland, UK
Colesberg *527* Northern Cape, C South Africa
Colihaut *224 var.* Kulihao. W Dominica
Collie *100* SW Australia
Collingwood Bay *458* bay of the Solomon Sea to the E of Papua New Guinea
Colmar *253 Ger.* Kolmar. NE France
Cöln *see* Köln
Cologne *see* Köln
Colomb-Béchar *see* Béchar
Colombia *194-197* officially Republic of Colombia. Country of South America divided into 32 admin. units (departments). ❖ Bogotá
Colombo *534* ❖ of Sri Lanka, W Sri Lanka
Colón *210* NW Cuba
Colón *456 prev.* Aspinwall. N Panama
Colón, Archipiélago de *see* Galapagos Islands
Colonia *see* Kolonia

Colonia del Sacramento *607* SW Uruguay
Colorado *206* river of NE Costa Rica
Colorado *599* river of Texas, SC USA
Colorado *599* river of SW USA
Colorado *598-599* state of SW USA
Colorados, Archipiélago de los *210* island group of NW Cuba
Colorado Springs *599* Colorado, SW USA
Columbia *598* river of NW USA
Columbia *599* South Carolina, SE USA
Columbia, District of *599* federal district of NE USA
Columbus *599* Georgia, SE USA
Columbus *599* Ohio, NE USA
Columbus Channel *570* channel connecting the Atlantic Ocean and Gulf of Paria
Colville Channel *433* channel linking the Bay of Plenty and Hauraki Gulf, N of North Island, New Zealand
Comandante Ferraz *90* Brazilian research station of Antarctic Peninsula, Antarctica
Comarapa *136* C Bolivia
Comas *463* W Peru
Comayagua *288* W Honduras
Comendador *226 prev.* Elías Piña. W Dominican Republic
Comer *see* Como, Lago di
Comilla *117 Ben.* Kumillā. E Bangladesh
Commissioner's Point *643* headland of Ireland Island North, W Bermuda
Communism Peak *see* Garmo, Qullai
Como *320* N Italy
Comodoro Rivadavia *95* SE Argentina
Como, Lago di *320 var.* Lario, *Eng.* Lake Como, *Ger.* Comer See. Lake of N Italy
Comoros *198-199* officially Federal Islamic Republic of the Comoros. Island group of the Indian Ocean, between Madagascar and the African mainland, divided into 3 admin. units (districts). ❖ Moroni
Comrat *408 Rus.* Komrat. S Moldova
Conakry *281* ❖ of Guinea, SW Guinea
Concepción *136* E Bolivia
[illegible]
Concepción de La Vega *see* La Vega
Conchos *403* river of NW Mexico
Concord *276* W Grenada island, Grenada
Concord *599* New Hampshire, NE USA
Concordia *95* E Argentina
Condado *210* C Cuba
Côn Dao *623 var.* Con Son. Island of S Vietnam
Condroz *127* physical region of SE Belgium
Congo *88, 200, 203 var.* Zaire, Kongo, Lualaba. River of C Africa
Congo *200-201* officially The Republic of the Congo. Country of C Africa divided into 9 admin. units (regions). ❖ Brazzaville
Congo Basin *203* drainage basin of C Africa
Congo, Democratic Republic of (Zaire) *202-205* officially Democratic Republic of Congo (Zaire), *prev.* Congo (Kinshasa), Belgian Congo, Zaire. Country of C Africa divided into 11 admin. units (10 provinces, 1 city). ❖ Kinshasa
Con, Loch *see* Conn, Lough
Connaught *314* province of W Ireland
Connecticut *599* state of NE USA
Conn, Lough *314 Ir.* Loch Con. Lake of NW Ireland
Consolación del Sur *210* W Cuba
Constance, Lake *106, 264, 346 Ger.* Bodensee. Lake of C Europe
Constanţa *480 Ger.* Konstantza, *Turk.* Köstence, *var.* Küstendje, *Eng.* Constanza. SE Romania
Constantine *83 Ar.* Qoussantina, *var.* Qacentina, NE Algeria
Constantine *276* SW Grenada island, Grenada
Constantinople *see* İstanbul
Constant Spring *329* SE Jamaica
Constanza *226* C Dominican Republic
Contagem *145* SE Brazil
Contuboel *282* NE Guinea-Bissau
Cook Islands *644* territory in free association with New Zealand, Pacific Ocean. ❖ Avarua.
Cook, Mount *433 prev.* Aorangi. Mountain of W South Island, New Zealand
Cook, Récif de *650* reef of the Pacific Ocean, N New Caledonia
Cook Strait *433 var.* Raukawa. Strait between North and South Islands of New Zealand, connecting the South Pacific Ocean and Tasman Sea
Cooktown *101* NE Australia
Cooper Creek *101 var.* Barcoo, Cooper's Creek. River of C Australia
Cooper Island *643* island of SE British Virgin Islands
Copacabana *136* W Bolivia
Copenhagen *218 Dan.* København. ❖ of Denmark, Sjælland, E Denmark
Copiapó *183* N Chile
Coppename *538 var.* Koppename. River of C Suriname
Coppermine *see* Kugluktuk
Coquilhatville *see* Mbandaka
Coquimbo *183* N Chile
Corail *286* SW Haiti
Coral Harbour *171* Southampton Island, NE Canada
Coral Sea *101, 615, 458* sea of the Pacific Ocean between Australia and Papua New Guinea
Corantijn *284, 538 var.* Coeroeni, Corentyne, Courantyne. River of Guyana and Suriname
Córdoba *95* C Argentina
Córdoba *531 var.* Cordoba, *Eng.* Cordova. SW Spain
Cordova *598* Alaska, USA
Corentyne *see* Corantijn
Corfu *see* Kérkyra
Corinth *see* Kórinthos
Corinth *276* SE Grenada island, Grenada
Corinth, Gulf of *see* Korinthiakós Kólpos
Corinth, Isthmus of *see* Korínthou, Isthmós
Corinto *436* W Nicaragua
Coriole *see* Qoryooley
Corisco, Isla de *236* Island of SW Equatorial Guinea
Cork *314 Ir.* Corcaigh. S Ireland
Cork Hill *649* W Montserrat
Corleone *321* Sicilia, S Italy
Corner Brook *171* Newfoundland, E Canada
Corn Exchange *366* NW Lesotho
Corn Islands *see* Maíz, Islas
Cornwallis Island *170* island of Parry Islands, N Canada
Coro *619 var.* Santa Ana de Coro. NW Venezuela
Corocoro *136* W Bolivia
Coromandel Peninsula *433* peninsula of NE North Island, New Zealand
Coronel Bogado *460* S Paraguay
Coronel Oviedo *460* SE Paraguay
Çorovodë *81 var.* Çorovoda, Corovoda. SE Albania
Corozal *130* N Belize
Corrib, Lough *314 Ir.* Loch Corrib. Lake of W Ireland
Corrientes *95* NE Argentina
Corriverton *284* E Guyana
Corriza *see* Korçë
Corse *253 Eng.* Corsica. Island of SE France
Corsica *see* Corse
Cortés *206* SE Costa Rica
Corubal *282 var.* Cocoli, Rio Grande. River of W Africa
Çorum *577* N Turkey
Corvallis *598* Oregon, NW USA
Corvo *474 var.* Ilha do Corvo. Island of the Azores, Portugal
Cosenza *321* S Italy
Cosmolédo Atoll *512* atoll of the Aldabra Group, SW Seychelles
Cospicua *395* E Malta
Costa, Cordillera de la *619 var.* Cordillera de Venezuela. Mountain range of N Venezuela
Costa Rica *206-207* officially Republic of Costa Rica. Country of Central America divided into 7 admin. units (provinces). ❖ San José
Costermansville *see* Bukavu
Cotagaita *136* S Bolivia
Côte d'Ivoire *see* Ivory Coast
Côtière, Chaîne *see* Coast Mountains
Cotonou *132 var.* Kotonu. S Benin
Cotopaxi *228* active volcano of N Ecuador
Cotswold Hills *593* hills of W England, UK
Cottbus *265 prev.* Kottbus. E Germany
Cottica *538* E Suriname
Cotton Ground *494* NW Nevis, St Kitts & Nevis
Cotuí *226* C Dominican Republic
Coulibistri *224* W Dominica
Coupe, Cap *652* cape of the Atlantic Ocean on the coast of Miquelon, S Saint Pierre and Miquelon
Courantyne *see* Corantijn
Courcelles *127* S Belgium
Courland *see* Kurzeme
Courtrai *see* Kortrijk
Couva *570* W Trinidad, Trinidad & Tobago
Couvin *127* S Belgium
Cova Figueira *176* Fogo, S Cape Verde
Cove Bay *642* bay of the Caribbean Sea on the S coast of Anguilla
Coventry *593* C England, UK
Covilhã *474* E Portugal
Cox's Bāzār *117* S Bangladesh
Coyah *281* SW Guinea
Coyhaique *see* Coihaique
Cozumel, Isla de *403* island of SE Mexico
Cracow *see* Kraków
Cradock *527* Eastern Cape, S South Africa
Craiova *480* SW Romania
Cranbrook *170* SW Canada
Crane, The *121* SE Barbados
Crawley *593* SE England, UK
Créoles, River des *400* river of SE Mauritius
Cres *209 It.* Cherso. Island of W Croatia
Crescent Group *651* island group of C Paracel Islands
Crete *see* Kríti
Créteil *253* N France
Crete, Sea of *273 Gk* Kritikó Pélagos. Area of the Mediterranean Sea, SE Greece
Creuse *253* river of C France
Crikvenica *209 It.* Cirquenizza. NW Croatia
Crimea *see* Krym
Cristóbal *456* N Panama
Cristóbal Colón, Pico *195* peak of N Colombia
Crna Gora *see* Montenegro
Crna reka *381* river of S FYR Macedonia
Crni Drim *see* Drinit të Zi
Črnomelj *520 Ger.* Tschernembl. S Slovenia
Croatia *236 -209* officially Republic of Croatia, *SCr.* Hrvatska. Country of S Europe divided into 21 admin. units (provinces). ❖ Zagreb
Crochu *276* SE Grenada island, Grenada
Crocker, Banjaran *387 var.* Crocker Range. Mountain range of C Borneo, Malaysia
Crocodile *see* Limpopo
Crocus Bay *642* bay of the Caribbean Sea on the W coast of Anguilla
Croia *see* Krujë
Cromer *593* E England, UK
Crooked Island *112* island of the E Bahamas
Crooked Island Passage *112* passage of the Atlantic Ocean between Crooked Island and Long Island, Bahamas
Crooked Tree *130* NE Belize
Crosby *647* C Isle of Man
Cross *440* river of Cameroon and Nigeria
Crossroads *314* N Ireland
Crotone *321* S Italy
Crucero Contramaestre *210* S Cuba
Cruz Bay *653* Saint John, E Virgin Islands (US)
Cruz del Eje *95* C Argentina
Csaca *see* Čadca
Csakathurn *see* Čakovec
Csáktornya *see* Čakovec
Csíkszereda *see* Miercurea-Ciuc
Cuamba *419* N Mozambique
Cuan Dhun Dealgan *see* Dundalk Bay
Cuando *88, 635 var.* Kwando. River of southern Africa
Cuango *see* Kwango
Cuan na Gaillimhe *see* Galway Bay
Cuanza *88 var.* Kwanza. River of Angola
Cuareim *607 Port.* Quaraí. River of Brazil and Uruguay
Cuba *210-213* officially Republic of Cuba. Country of the West Indies divided into 15 admin. units (14 provinces and 1 special municipality). ❖ Havana
Cubal *88* W Angola
Cubango *88 var.* Kuvango, *Port.* Vila Artuur de Paiva, Vila da Ponte. C Angola
Cubango *88, 142, 423 var.* Kavango, Kavengo, Kubango, Okavango, Okavanggo. River of Southern Africa
Cúcuta *195 var.* San José de Cúcuta. N Colombia
Cuddapah *296* S India
Cudjoehead *649* NW Montserrat
Cuenca *228* S Ecuador
Cuenca *531* C Spain
Cueno *320* N Italy
Cuera *see* Chur
Cuernavaca *403* S Mexico
Cueto *210* SE Cuba
Cufra *see* Al Kufrah
Cuiabá *145 prev.* Cuyabá. SW Brazil
Cuilapa *278* S Guatemala
Cuito *88 var.* Kwito. River of Angola
Cuito Cuanquale *88* S Angola
Culebra *651* Isla de Culebra, NE Puerto Rico
Culebra, Isla de *651* island of NE Puerto Rico
Culiacán *403* W Mexico
Culion Island *466* island of Calamian Group, W Philippines
Cumaná *619* NE Venezuela
Cumberland *498* river of W St Vincent, St Vincent & the Grenadines
Cumberland Peninsula *171* peninsula of Baffin Island, NE Canada
Cumbrian Mountains *593 var.* Lake District. Mountain range of NW England, UK
Cunene *88, 423 var.* Kunene. River of Angola and Namibia
Cunnamulla *101* E Australia
Curaçao *619, 650* island of the Netherland Antilles, Caribbean Sea
Curanilahue *183* C Chile
Curaray *228* river of Ecuador and Peru
Curepe *570* NW Trinidad, Trinidad & Tobago
Curepipe *400* C Mauritius
Curicó *183* C Chile
Curitiba *145 prev.* Curytiba. S Brazil
Curral Velho *176* Boa Vista, Cape Verde
Current *112* Eleuthera Island, Bahamas
Curuguaty *460* E Paraguay
Curzola *see* Korčula
Cusco *463 var.* Cuzco. SE Peru
Čust *see* Chust
Cutch, Gulf of *see* Kachch, Gulf of
Cuttack *296* E India
Cutting Camp *366* SW Lesotho

Cuxhaven *264* NW Germany
Cuyabá *see* Cuiabá
Cuyo East Passage *466* passage of the Sulu Sea between Cuyo Islands and Panay, Philippines
Cuyo Islands *466* islands of C Philippines
Cuyo West Passage *466* passage of the Sulu Sea between Cuyo Islands and Palawan, Philippines
Cuyuni *284* river of Guyana and Venezuela
Cuzco *see* Cusco
Čvrsnica *140* mountain range of SW Bosnia & Herzegovina
Cyambwe, Lac *492* lake of E Rwanda
Cyangugu *492* SW Rwanda
Cyclades *see* Kyklades
Cymru *see* Wales
Cyohoha Sud, Lac *162, 492* *var.* Cohoha, Lac Tshohoha Sud. Lake of Burundi and Rwanda
Cyprus *214-215* officially Republic of Cyprus, *Gk* Kypros, *Turk.* Kıbrıs, Kıbrıs Cumhuriyeti. Country of E Mediterranean divided into 5 admin. units (districts). ❖ Nicosia. Following Turkish invasion of 1974, northern sector became self-proclaimed state, officially Turkish Republic of Northern Cyprus (TRNC). ❖ Nicosia
Cyrenaica *see* Barqah
Czechoslovakia *see* Czech Republic and Slovakia
Czech Republic *216-217* *Cz.* Česká Republika, *prev.* constituent republic of Czechoslovakia. Country of C Europe divided into 7 admin. units (regions). ❖ Prague
Czegléd *see* Cegléd
Czernowitz *see* Chernivtsi
Częstochowa *471* *Ger.* Tschenstochau. S Poland

D

Dabakala *326* NE Ivory Coast
Dabola *281* C Guinea
Dabou *326* S Ivory Coast
Dąbrowa Górnicza *471* S Poland
Dacca *see* Dhaka
Dachau *265* S Germany
Dadanawa *284* SW Guyana
Dadda 'to *222* N Djibouti
Dadeldhura *427* *var.* Dandeldhura. W Nepal
Ḑadnah *590* *var.* Dhadnah. NE United Arab Emirates
Daegu *see* Taegu
Daga *134* S Bhutan
Dagana *510* N Senegal
Dagden *see* Hiiumaa
Dagestan, Respublika *484* autonomous republic of SW Russian Federation
Dagö *see* Hiiumaa
Dagupan *466* Luzon, N Philippines
Dahar *573* physical region of S Tunisia
Da Hinggan Ling *187* *Eng.* Great Khingan Range. Mountain range of Nei Mongol Zizhiqu, NE China
Dahlak Archipelago *238* island group of E Eritrea
Dahlak Island *238* island of Dahlak Archipelago, E Eritrea
Dahm, Ramlat *627* desert region of NW Yemen
Dahomey *see* Benin
Dahra *see* Dara
Dahūk *310* *var.* Dohuk, *Kurd.* Dihōk. N Iraq
Dai Island *522* island of E Solomon Is
Dailekh *427* W Nepal
Daingin, Bá an *see* Dingle Bay
Dajabón *226* NW Dominican Republic
Dakar *510* ❖ of Senegal, W Senegal
Dakoro *439* SW Niger
Đakovica *630* *var.* Djakovica, *Alb.* Gjakovë. S Serbia, Yugoslavia
Đakovo *209* *var.* Djakovo, *Hung.* Diakovár. NE Croatia
Dakshin *see* Deccan
Dalaba *281* W Guinea
Dalai Nor *see* Hulun Nur
Dalälven *543* river of SE Sweden
Dalandzadgad *412* S Mongolia
Dalap District *396* district of Majuro, SE Marshall Islands
Đa Lat *623* S Vietnam
Dali *see* Dhali
Dalian *187* *var.* Jay Dairen, Ta-lien, *Rus.* Dalny. Liaoning, NE China
Dallas *599* Texas, SC USA
Dallol Bosso *439* seasonal watercourse of W Niger
Dalmā *590* island of W United Arab Emirates
Dalmacija *209* *Eng.* Dalmatia. Cultural region of S Croatia
Dalmatia *see* Dalmacija
Dalny *see* Dalian
Daloa *326* C Ivory Coast
Dalvík *294* N Iceland
Damanhûr *230* *var.* Damanhūr. N Egypt
Damar, Kepulauan *302* *var.* Kepulauan Barat Daya. Island group to the E of Nusa Tenggara, C Indonesia
Damara *179* S Central African Republic
Damasak *441* NE Nigeria
Damascus *551* *var.* Esh Sham, *Fr.* Damas, *Ar.* Dimashq. ❖ of Syria, SW Syria
Damāvand, Qolleh-ye *307* mountain of N Iran
Dambulla *534* C Sri Lanka
Dame-Marie *286* SW Haiti
Damêrdjôg *222* E Djibouti
Damietta *see* Dumyât
Damongo *270* NW Ghana
Damoûr *364* *var.* Ad Dāmūr. W Lebanon
Damphu *134* S Bhutan
Damqawt *627* *var.* Damqut. E Yemen
Dâmrei, Chuŏr Phmun *165* *Fr.* Chaîne de l'Éléphant. Mountain range of SW Cambodia
Danakil Desert *238, 243* *var.* Danakil Plain, Afar Depression. Desert region of Eritrea and Ethiopia
Danané *326* W Ivory Coast
Đă Nâng *623* *prev.* Tourane. C Vietnam
Dandeldhura *see* Dadeldhura
Dandong *187* *var.* Tan-tung, *prev.* An-tung. Liaoning, NE China
Daneborg *646* *var.* Danborg. E Greenland
Dänew *see* Deynau
Dangal *238* SE Eritrea
Dangara *see* Danghara
Danger Island *643* island of W British Indian Ocean Territory
Danghara *558* *Rus.* Dangara. W Tajikistan
Dānglā *243* *var.* Dangila. NW Ethiopia
Dangme *134* river of S Bhutan
Dang Raek, Phanom *165, 563* *var.* Phanom Dong Rak, *Cam.* Chuor Phmum Dângrêk, *Fr.* Chaîne des Dangrek. Mountain range of Cambodia and Thailand
Dangrak, Chaîne des *see* Dang Raek, Phanom
Dângrêk, Chuŏr Phmun *see* Dang Raek, Phanom
Dangriga *130* *var.* Stann Creek. SE Belize
Ḑank *448* *var.* Dhank. NW Oman
Danlí *288* S Honduras
Danmark *see* Denmark
Danmark Havn *646* E Greenland
Danmarksstraedet *see* Denmark Strait
Danube *106, 152, 209, 265*, *Bul.* Danav, *Hung.* Duna, *Cz.* Dunaj, *Ger.* Donau, *Rom.* Dunărea. River of C Europe
Danube, Mouths of the *480* *Rom.* Delta Dunării. Delta of Romania and Ukraine
Danubian Plain *see* Dunavska Ravnina
Danyi-Apéyémé *567* *prev.* Apéyémé. W Togo
Danzig *see* Gdańsk
Danzig, Gulf of *471* *var.* Gulf of Gdańsk,*Gk* Danziger Bucht, *Pol.* Zatoka Gdańska, *Rus.* Gdan'skaya Bukhta. Gulf of the Baltic Sea, N Pola
Dapaong *567* N Togo
Dara *510* *var.* Dahra. NW Senegal
Dar'ā *551* *var.* Der'a, *Fr.* Déraa. SW Syria
Da Rang *623* *var.* Ba. River of S Vietnam
Dardanelles *see* Canakkale Boğazi
Dar el Beida *see* Casablanca
Dar es Salaam *560* E Tanzania
Darfur *536* *var.* Darfur Massif. Mountain range of W Sudan
Dargan-Ata *581* *var.* Darganata. E Turkmenistan
Dargaville *433* NW North Island, New Zealand
Dargol *439* W Niger
Darhan *412* N Mongolia
Darien, Isthmus of *see* Panamá, Istmo de
Darién, Serranía del *456* mountain range of Colombia and Panama
Darjiling *297* *prev.* Darjeeling. NE India
Darling *101* river of E Australia
Darling Range *100* mountain range of SW Australia
Darlington *593* N England, UK
Darmstadt *264* SW Germany
Darnah *371* *var.* Derna. NE Libya
Daroot-Korgon *357* *var.* Daraut-Kurgan. SW Kyrgyzstan
Darou Mousti *510* NW Senegal
Darrell Island *643* island of W Bermuda
Dartmoor *593* moorland of SW England, UK
Dartmouth *171* SE Canada
Daru *458* SW Papua New Guinea
Daru *514* SE Sierra Leone
Darvaza *581* *Turkm.* Derweze. C Turkmenistan
Darvel Bay *see* Lahad Datu, Telukan
Darvel, Teluk *see* Lahad Datu, Telukan
Darvos, Qatorkŭhi *558* *Rus.* Darvazskiy Khrebet. Mountain range of C Tajikistan
Darwin *101* N Australia
Darwin, Isla *228* island of the NW Galapagos Is, Ecuador
Dashkhovuz *581* *prev.* Tashauz, *var.* Tašauz, *Turkm.* Dashhowuz. N Turkmenistan
Dasht Kaur *450* river of SW Pakistan
Daska *451* NE Pakistan
Da, Sông *see* Black River
Dassa *132* *var.* Dassa-Zoumé. S Benin
Datong *187* *var.* Ta-t'ung. Shanxi, N China
Datu, Teluk *386* bay of the South China Sea, on the coast of Borneo, E Malaysia
Daua *342* *Amh.* Dawa Wenz. River of E Africa
Daugava *see* Western Dvina
Daugavpils *362* *Ger.* Dünaburg, *Rus.* Dvinsk. SE Latvia
Daule *228* W Ecuador
Daule *228* river of W Ecuador
Daurada, Costa *530* *var.* Costa Dorada. Coastal region of E Spain
Davao *466* Mindanao, S Philippines
Davao Gulf *466* gulf of the Pacific Ocean
Davenport *599* Iowa, C USA
David *456* W Panama
Davis *90* Australian research station of Greater Antarctica, Antarctica
Davis Strait *171, 646* strait connecting the Atlantic Ocean and Baffin Bay, NE Canada between Baffin Island and Greenland
Davos *546* E Switzerland
Davyd-Haradok *122* *Rus.* David Gorodok, *Pol.* Dawidgródek. S Belarus
Dawa Wenz *see* Daua
Dawei *see* Tavoy
Dawidgródek *see* Davyd-Haradok
Dawra *414* NW Western Sahara
Dawson *170* NW Canada
Dawwah *448* *var.* Dauwa. E Oman
Dayrah *590* *var.* Deira. NE United Arab Emirates
Dayr az Zawr *551* *var.* Deir ez Zor. E Syria
Dayrīk *see* Al Mālikīyah
Dayton *599* Ohio, NE USA
De Aar *527* Northern Cape, C South Africa
Deadman's Bay *652* bay of the South Atlantic Ocean on the SW coast of Tristan da Cunha
Dead Sea *317, 318, 336* *Ar.* Al Baḩr al Mayyit, Baḩrat Lūt, *Heb.* Yam HaMelah̲ Salt lake of SW Asia
Deadwood Plain *652* plain of N St Helena
Debar *381* W FYR Macedonia
Débo, Lac *392* lake of C Mali
Debre Birhan *243* *var.* Debra Birhan. C Ethiopia
Debrecen *290* *prev.* Debreczen, *Ger.* Debreczin. E Hungary
Debre Mark'os *243* NW Ethiopia
Debre Tabor *243* NW Ethiopia
Debre Zebīt *243* N Ethiopia
Debre Zeyit *243* *var.* Debre Zeyt, *prev.* Bishoftu, *It.* Biscoftù. C Ethiopia
Deccan *296* *Hind.* Dakshin. Plateau of C India
Děčín *216* *Ger.* Tetschen. NW Czech Republic
Dedeagach *see* Alexandroúpoli
Dededo *647* N Guam
Dedegaç *see* Alexandroúpoli
Dedoplistsqaro *262* *Rus.* Dedoplis-Tskaro, *prev.* Tsiteli-Tskaro. SE Georgia
Dédougou *157* W Burkina
Deduru Oya *534* C Sri Lanka
Dedza *385* SW Malawi
Dee *593* river of NE Scotland, UK
Dee *593* *Wel.* Dyfrdwy. River of N Wales, UK
Deep Bay *see* Chilumba
Deep Water Bay *see* Hau Hoi Wan
Değirmenlik *215* *var.* Kythrea. N Cyprus
Dehiwala-Mount Lavinia *534* SW Sri Lanka
Deinze *127* W Belgium
Deira *see* Adh Dhayd
Deir el Balaḩ *317, 318* C Gaza Strip
Deir el-Bahri *230* E Egypt
Deir ez Zo *see* Dayr az Zawr
Deirgeirt, Loch *see* Derg, Lough
Dej *480* NW Romania
Dekemhare *238* S Eritrea
Dékoa *179* C Central African Republic
Delagoa Bay *see* Maputo, Baía de
Delārām *77* SW Afghanistan
Delaware *599* state of E USA
Delčevo *381* NE FYR Macedonia
Delcommune, Lac *see* Nzilo, Lac
Delémont *546* *Ger.* Delsberg. NW Switzerland
Delft *429* W Netherlands
Delft *534* island of NW Sri Lanka
Delfzijl *429* NE Netherlands
Delhi *296* *Hind.* Dilli. N India
Délices *224* SE Dominica
Délices *645* C French Guiana
Delsberg *see* Delémont
Delvinë *81* *var.* Delvina, *It.* Delvino. S Albania
Delvino *see* Delvinë
Demba *203* C Dem. Rep. Congo (Zaire)
Dembéni *649* E Mayotte
Dembéni *198* S Grande Comore, Comoros
Dembī Dolo *243* *var.* Dembidollo. W Ethiopia
Demerara *284* river of N Guyana
Denau *see* Denow
Dender *127* *Fr.* Dendre. River of W Belgium
Dendre *see* Dender
Den Haag *see* 's-Gravenhage

Den Helder *429* NW Netherlands
Denis, Île *512* island of the Inner Islands, NE Seychelles
Denizli *576* SW Turkey
Denmark *218-221* officially Kingdom of Denmark, *Dan.* Danmark. Country of W Europe, divided into 14 admin. units (counties). ❖ Copenhagen
Denmark Strait *294, 646* *var.* Danmarksstraedet. Strait between Greenland and Iceland
Dennery *497* E St Lucia
Denow *610* *Rus.* Denau. SE Uzbekistan
Denpasar *302* *prev.* Paloe. Bali, C Indonesia
D'Entrecasteaux Islands *458* island group of SE Papua New Guinea
Denver *599* Colorado, SW USA
Der'a *see* Dar'ā
Deraa *see* Dar'ā
Dera Ghāzi Khān *451* C Pakistan
Dera Ismāīl Khān *451* N Pakistan*
Đeravica *630* *var.* Durmitor. Mountain of S Yugoslavia
Derby *593* C England, UK
Derg, Lough *314* *Ir.* Loch Deirgeirt. Lake of C Ireland
Dernière Rivière *497* NE St Lucia
Derrick *498* Bequia, St Vincent & the Grenadines
Derrière Morne *497* S St Lucia
Derrubado *176* N Boa Vista, E Cape Verde
Derry *see* Londonderry
Derventa *140* N Bosnia & Herzegovina
Derweze *see* Darvaza
Deryneia *see* Dherinia
Desaguadero *136* river of Bolivia and Peru
Desbarra *497* NE St Lucia
Desdunes *286* W Haiti
Desē *243* *var.* Desse, *It.* Dessie. N Ethiopia
Desertas, Ilhas *474* island group of the Madeira Is, Portugal
Des Moines *599* Iowa, C USA
Desna *586* river of N Ukraine
Despoto Planina *see* Rhodope Mountains
Desroches, Île *512* *var.* Desroches. Island of the Amirante Islands, C Seychelles
Desruisseaux *497* SE St Lucia
Dessau *265* C Germany
Dessie *see* Desē
Destêrro *see* Florianópolis
Dete *636* *prev.* Dett. W Zimbabwe
Detroit *599* Michigan, NC USA
Deutsch-Brod *see* Havlíčkův Brod
Deutsche Bucht *see* German Bight
Deutschendorf *see* Poprad
Deutschland *see* Germany
Deva *480* *Ger.* Diemrich, *Hung.* Déva. W Romania
Đevđelija *see* Gevgelija
Deventer *429* E Netherlands
Devil's Island *645* island of N French Guiana
Devollit *81* *var.* Devoll. River of SE Albania
Devon Island *170-171* *prev.* North Devon Island. Island of Parry Islands, N Canada
Devonport *101* Tasmania, Australia
Deynau *581* *var.* Dyanev, *Turkm.* Dänew. E Turkmenistan
Dezfūl *307* *var.* Dizful. W Iran
Dhaalu Atoll *see* South Nilandhe Atoll
Dhahran *see* Aẓ Ẓahrān
Dhaka *117* *var.* Dacca. ❖ of Bangladesh, C Bangladesh
Dhali *215* *var.* Dali. C Cyprus
Dhamar *627* W Yemen
Dhanbād *296* NE India
Dhankuta *427* E Nepal
Dharan *427* *var.* Dharan Bazar. E Nepal
Dheere Laaq *524* *It.* Lach Dera. Seasonal river of SW Somalia
Dhekelia *215* *var.* Dekeleia. UK Air base, SE Cyprus
Dherinia *215* *var.* Deryneia. E Cyprus
Dhiarizos *215* *var.* Diarizos. River of SW Cyprus
Dhībān *336* NW Jordan
Dhofar *see* Ẓufār
Dhráma *see* Dráma
Dhún na nGall, Bá *see* Donegal Bay
Dhuudo *524* *It.* Uadi Dudo. Seasonal river of NE Somalia
Dhuusa Marreeb *524* *var.* Dusa Marreb, *It.* Dusa Mareb. C Somalia
Diafarabé *392* C Mali
Diakovár *see* Đakovo
Diamond Island *276* island to the N of Grenada island, Grenada
Diana's Peak *652* mountain of C St Helena
Diangounté-Kamara *392* W Mali
Diapaga *157* E Burkina
Diarizos *see* Dhiarizos
Dibā *590* *var.* Dibā al Ḩişn, Dibba. NE United Arab Emirates
Dicle *see* Tigris
Diébougou *157* SW Burkina
Diego Garcia *643* island of S British Indian Ocean Territory
Diego Garcia *643* ❖ of British Indian Ocean Territory, Diego Garcia, S British Indian Ocean Territory
Diégo-Suarez *see* Antsirañana
Diekirch *378* C Luxembourg
Diéma *392* W Mali
Diemrich *see* Deva
Điên Biên *623* *var.* Dien Bien Phu. NW Vietnam
Dieppe *253* N France
Dieppe Bay Town *494* N St Kitts, St Kitts & Nevis
Diffa *439* SE Niger
Differdange *378* SW Luxembourg
Digne *253* SE France
Digoin *253* C France
Digul *303* *prev.* Digoel. River of Irian Jaya, E Indonesia
Dihōk *see* Dahūk
Dijlah *see* Tigris
Dijon *253* NE France
Dikhil *222* SW Djibouti
Dīla *243* *var.* Dilla. S Ethiopia
Dilbeek *127* C Belgium
Dili *305* ❖ of East Timor, N East Timor
Dilia *439* *var.* Dillia. Seasonal river of SE Niger
Dilijan *98* *Rus.* Dilizhan, *var.* Diližan. NE Armenia
Di Linh *623* S Vietnam
Dilli *see* Delhi
Dillia *see* Dilia
Dillikot *427* W Nepal
Dilling *536* *var.* Ad Dalanj. C Sudan
Dilolo *203* S Dem. Rep. Congo (Zaire)
Dimashq *see* Damascus
Dimbokro *326* E Ivory Coast
Dimitrovgrad *152* S Bulgaria
Dimitrovo *see* Pernik
Dimlang *440* *var.* Vogel Peak. Mountain of E Nigeria
Dimona *317* S Israel
Dinagat Island *466* island of E Philippines
Dinājpur *117* NW Bangladesh
Dinan *252* NW France
Dinant *127* S Belgium
Dinara *209* mountain of S Croatia
Dinara *140, 209* mountain range of Bosnia & Herzegovina and Croatia
Dinaric Alps *209* mountain range of Bosnia & Herzegovina and Croatia
Dindigal *296* S India
Dingle Bay *314* *Ir.* Bá an Daingin. Bay of the Atlantic Ocean, SW Ireland
Dingli *395* SW Malta
Dingli Cliffs *395* cliffs of SW Malta
Dinguiraye *281* C Guinea
Dion *281* river of S Guinea
Dioro *392* *var.* Dyero. SW Mali
Diourbel *510* W Senegal
Dipayal *427* W Nepal
Dipkarpaz *215* *var.* Rizokarpaso. NE Cyprus
Direction Island *644* *var.* Pulu Tikus. Island of E Cocos Islands
Dirē Dawa *243* E Ethiopia
Diriamba *436* SW Nicaragua
Dirj *371* NW Libya
Dirk Hartog Island *100* island of W Australia
Disappointment, Lake *100* salt lake of W Australia
Discovery Reef *651* reef of the China Sea, W Paracel Islands
Disna *see* Drysa
Disûq *230* *var.* Disūq. N Egypt
Diu *296* W India
Diuata Mountains *466* mountain range of Mindanao, S Philippines
Diva *see* Piva
Divinópolis *145* SE Brazil
Divisa *456* S Panama
Divo *326* S Ivory Coast
Diwaniya *see* Ad Dīwanīyah
Diyālā *310* *Per.* Rūdkhāneh-ye Sīrvān,irwan. River of Iran and Iraq
Diyarbakır *577* SE Turkey
Dizful *see* Dezfūl
Dja *168* river of SE Cameroon
Djailolo *see* Halmahera
Djakarta *see* Jakarta
Djakovica *see* Đakovica
Djakovo *see* Đakovo
Djamâa *83* NE Algeria
Djambala *200* W Congo
Djambi *see* Hari
Djambi *see* Jambi
Djanet *83* *prev.* Fort Charlet. SE Algeria
Djawa *see* Java
Djéblé *see* Jablah
Djelfa *83* *var.* El Djelfa. N Algeria
Djéma *179* E Central African Republic
Djember *see* Jember
Djénné *392* *var.* Jenné. C Mali
Djérablous *see* Jarābulus
Djerba *see* Jerba, Île de
Djerba *see* Houmt Souk
Djerem *168* *var.* Djérem. River of C Cameroon
Djevdjelija *see* Gevgelija
Djibo *157* N Burkina
Djibouti *222* *var.* Jibuti. ❖ of Djibouti, E Djibouti
Djibouti *222-223* officially Republic of Djibouti, *var.* Jibuti, *prev.* French Territory of the Afars and Issas 1967-77, French Somaliland -1967. Country of East Africa divided into 5 admin. units (districts). ❖ Djibouti
Djidjel *see* Jijel
Djidjelli *see* Jijel
Djiguéni *398* SE Mauritania
Djirataoua *439* S Niger
Djisr el Choghour *see* Jisr ashShughúr
Djoua *200* river of Congo and Gabon
Djoué *200* river of S Congo
Djougou *132* W Benin
Djúpivogur *294* SE Iceland
Dmitriyevsk *see* Makiyivka
Dnieper *586* *Bel.* Dnyapro, *Ukr.* Dnipro, *Rus.* Dnepr. River of E Europe
Dniester *408, 586* *Rom.* Nistru, *Rus.* Dnestr, *Ukr.* Dnister. River of Moldova and Ukraine
Dniprodzerzhyns'k *586* *Rus.* Dneprodzerzhinsk, *prev.* Kamenskoye. E Ukraine
Dniprodzerzhyns'ke Vodoskhovyshche *586* *Rus.* Dneprodzerzhinskoye Vodokhranilische. Reservoir of C Ukraine
Dnipropetrovs'k *586* *Rus.* Dnepropetrovsk, *prev.* Ekaterinoslav. E Ukraine
Dnistrovs'kyy Lyman *586* *Rus.* Dnestrovskiy Liman. Inlet of the Black Sea, SW Ukraine
Dnyapro *see* Dnieper
Doba *180* S Chad
Dobele *362* *Ger.* Doblen. W Latvia
Doberai, Jazirah *302* *Dut.* Vogelkop. Region of Irian Jaya, E Indonesia
Doboj *140* N Bosnia & Herzegovina
Dobrich *152* *var.* Dobrič, *prev.* Tolbukhin, *Rom.* Bazargic. NE Bulgaria
Dobrush *122* SE Belarus
Doctor Pedro P. Peña *460* W Paraguay
Dodekánisos *273* *prev.* Dhodhekánisos, *var.* Noties Sporádes, *Eng.* Dodecanese. Island group of SE Greece
Dodoma *560* ❖ of Tanzania, C Tanzania
Dodona *273* site of ancient city, N Greece
Dodwekon *368* *var.* Dudwiokahn. SE Liberia
Doetinchem *429* SE Netherlands
Dogana *502* NE San Marino
Dogondoutchi *439* SW Niger
Doğu Karadeniz Dağlarıı *577* *var.* Anadolu Dağları. Mountain range of NE Turkey
Doha *479* *Ar.* Ad Dawḩah. ❖ of Qatar, E Qatar
Dohuk *see* Dahuk
Doko *281* NE Guinea
Dolisie *see* Loubomo
Dolobil *368* C Liberia
Dolomites *see* Dolomitiche, Alpi
Dolomitiche, Alpi *321* *var.* Dolomiti, *Eng.* Dolomites. Mountain range of N Italy
Dolo Odo *243* *var.* Dollo Odo, Dolo. S Ethiopia
Dolores *278* N Guatemala
Dolores *607* W Uruguay
Domagnano *502* NE San Marino
Domel Island *see* Letsok-aw I
Dominica *224-225* officially Commonwealth of Dominica. Country of the West Indies divided into 10 admin. units (parishes). ❖ Roseau
Dominica Channel *see* Martinique Passage
Dominican Republic *226-227* Country of the West Indies divided into 30 admin. units (1 national district and 29 provinces). ❖ Santo Domingo
Dominica Passage *646* passage of the Caribbean Sea, N Guadeloupe
Domoni *198* SE Anjouan, Comoros
Don *484* river of W Russian Federation
Donau *see* Danube
Doncaster *593* N England, UK
Dondo *88* NW Angola
Dondo *419* C Mozambique
Donegal *314* N Ireland
Donegal Bay *314* *Ir.* Bá Dhún na nGall. Bay of the Atlantic Ocean, to the N of Ireland
Donets *586* *Rus.* Severskiy Donets, *Ukr.* Sivers'kyy Donets'. River of E Ukraine
Donets'k *586* *prev.* Stalino, *Rus.* Donetsk. E Ukraine
Donga *168* river of Cameroon and Nigeria
Đông Ha *623* C Vietnam
Đông Hơi *623* C Vietnam
Dong Nai *623* *var.* Donnai, Dong-nai, Dong Noi. River of S Vietnam
Dongola *536* *var.* Dunqulah, Donqola N Sudan
Dongou *200* NE Congo
Dong Rak, Phanom *see* Dang Rak, Phanom
Dongting Hu *187* *var.* Tung-t'ing Hu. Lake of SE China
Donostia-San Sebastián *531* N Spai
Doornik *see* Tournai
Dorada, Costa *see* Daurada, Costa
Dordogne *253* river of SW France
Dordrecht *429* SW Netherlands
Dori *157* N Burkina
Dornbirn *106* W Austria
Dornoch Firth *593* estuary of the river Dornoch, NE Scotland, UK
Dorpat *see* Tartu
Dorra *222* NW Djibouti
Dorsale *573* mountain range of N Tunisia
Dortmund *264* W Germany
Dos D'Âne *224* N Dominica
Dospad Dagh *see* Rhodope Mountains
Dos Puntas, Cabo *236* cape on the W coast of Río Muni, Equatorial Guinea

Dosso *439* SW Niger
Dostuk *357* C Kyrgyzstan
Douai *253* N France
Douala *168 var.* Duala. SW Cameroon
Double Headed Shot Cays *112* islets of W Bahamas
Doubs *546 var.* Le Doubs. River of France and Switzerland
Doudoub Bololé *222* S Djibouti
Doué *510* river of N Senegal
Douglas *645* East Falkland, NE Falkland Islands
Douglas *593, 647* ❖ of Isle of Man, SE Isle of Man
Douma *see* Dūmā
Douro *see* Duero
Dover *593 Fr.* Douvres.SE England,UK
Dover *599* Delaware, E USA
Dover, Strait of *253 var.* Straits of Dover, *Fr.* Pas de Calais. Strait connecting the English Channel and North Sea between England and France
Dovrefjell *444* mountain of SW Norway
Dowa *385* C Malawi
Dōzen *330* island to the N of Honshū, W Japan
Drâa *414* seasonal river of S Morocco
Drac *see* Durrës
Draç *see* Durrës
Dragon's Mouths, The *570 Sp.* Bocas del Dragón. Strait connecting the Caribbean Sea and Gulf of Paria
Dra, Hamada du *83 var.* Haut Plateau du Dra, Hammada du Drâa. Desert region of W Algeria
Drakensberg *366, 527* mountain range of Lesotho and South Africa
Drake Passage *183* passage connecting Pacific Ocean and Atlantic Ocean between South America and Antarctica
Dráma *273 var.* Dhráma. NE Greece
Drammen *444* S Norway
Drangajökull *294* glacier of NW Iceland
Drava *106, 209, 290, 520 Eng.* Drave, *Hung.* Dráva, *Ger.* Drau, *SCr.* Drava. River of C Europe
Dresden *265* E Germany
Drina *140, 630* river of Bosnia & Herzegovina and Yugoslavia
Drin Gulf *see* Drinit, Gjiri i
Drinit *81 var.* Drin. River of NW Albania
Drinit, Gjiri i *81 var.* Pellg i Drinit, Drin Gulf. Gulf of the Adriatic Sea, NW Albania
Drinit të Zi *81, 381 var.* Drin i Zi, *Eng.* Black Drin, *SCr.* Crni Drim. River of Albania and FYR Macedonia
Drin i Zi *see* Drinit të Zi
Drinos *81* river of S Albania
Drissa *122* river of Belarus and Russian Federation
Drobeta-Turnu Severin *480 prev.* Turnu Severin. SW Romania
Drochia *408 Rus.* Drokiya. N Moldova
Drogheda *314 Ir.* Droichead Átha. E Ireland
Drontheim *see* Trondheim
Druskininkai *376 Pol.* Druskienniki. S Lithuania
Drysa *122 Rus.* Disna. River of Belarus and Lithuania
Dschang *168* W Cameroon
Duala *see* Douala
Duarte, Pico *226* mountain of C Dominican Republic
Dubai *590 Ar.* Dubayy. NE United Arab Emirates
Dubăsari *408 Rus.* Dubossary. NE Moldova
Dubăsari Reservoir *408* reservoir of NE Moldova
Dubawnt *170* river of C Canada
Dubbo *101* E Australia
Dublanc *224* NW Dominica
Dublin *314 Ir.* Baile Átha Cliath. ❖ of Ireland, E Ireland
Dubnica nad Váhom *519 Hung.* Máriatölgyes, *prev.* Dubnicz. NW Slovakia
Dubnicz *see* Dubnica nad Váhom
Dubossary *see* Dubăsari
Dubréka *281* SW Guinea
Dubrovnik *209 It.* Ragusa. SE Croatia
Duc de Gloucester, Îles du *646* island group of C French Polynesia
Ducie Island *651* island of E Pitcairn Islands
Ducos *649* C Martinique
Dudelange *378* S Luxembourg
Dudo, Uadi *see* Dhuudo
Dudwiokahn *see* Dodwekon
Duékoué *326* W Ivory Coast
Duero *474, 530-531 Port.* Douro. River of Portugal and Spain
Duesseldorf *see* Düsseldorf
Duff Islands *522* small island group within Santa Cruz Is, Solomon Is
Dufourspitze *546* mountain of S Switzerland
Dugi Otok *209 It.* Isola Lunga. Island of W Croatia
Duinkerden *see* Dunkerque
Duisburg *264* W Germany
Duitama *195* C Colombia
Duitse Bocht *see* German Bight
Dukhān *479* W Qatar
Dukhan Heights *see* Dukhān, Jabal
Dukhān, Jabal *479 var.* Dukhan Heights. Hilly region of SW Qatar
Dukhan, Jabal *see* Dukhān, Jabal ad
Dukhān, Jabal ad *115 var.* Dukhan Heights, Jabal Dukhan. Mountain of C Bahrain
Dukou *see* Panzhihua
Dulce, Golfo *see* Izabal, Lago de
Dulce Nombre de Culmí *288* Honduras
Dulit, Banjaran *386 var.* Dulit Range. Mountain range of W Borneo, Malaysia
Duluth *599* Minnesota, NC USA
Dūmā *551 Fr.* Douma. SW Syria
Dumfries *593* SW Scotland, UK
Dumistān *115* NW Bahrain
Dumont d'Urville *90* French research station of Greater Antarctica, Antarctica
Dumyât *230 Eng.* Damietta. N Egypt
Düna *see* Western Dvina
Dünaburg *see* Daugavpils
Dunai *427* W Nepal
Dunaj *see* Danube
Dunaj *see* Vienna
Dunajská Streda *519 Hung.* Dunaszerdahely. SW Slovakia
Dunapentele *see* Dunaújváros
Dunărea *see* Danube
Dunării, Delta *see* Danube, Mouths of the
Dunaszerdahely *see* Dunajská Streda
Dunaújváros *290 prev.* Sztálinváros, *prev.* Dunapentele. C Hungary
Dunav *see* Danube
Dunavska Ravnina *152 Eng.* Danubian Plain. Lowland region of N Bulgaria
Dundalk *314 Ir.* Dún Dealgan. NE Ireland
Dundalk Bay *314 Ir.* Cuan Dhun Dealgan. Bay of the Irish Sea, to the NE of Ireland
Dundas *see* Pituffik
Dundee *527* Kwazulu Natal, E South Africa
Dundee *593* E Scotland, UK
Dunedin *433* S South Island, New Zealand
Dunfermline *593* E Scotland, UK
Dungarvan *314 Ir.* Dun Garbhain. S Ireland
Dunkerque *253 Eng.* Dunkirk, *Dut.* Duinkerken. N France
Dunkirk *see* Dunkerque
Dunkwa *270* SW Ghana
Dún Laoghaire *314 prev.* Kingstown. E Ireland
Dunqulah *see* Dongola
Dupnitsa *152 prev.* Stanke Dimitrov, *prev.* Marek. W Bulgaria
Duqm *448 var.* Daqm. E Oman
Duque de Caxias *145* SE Brazil
Durán *see* Eloy Alfaro
Durance *253* river of SE France
Durango *403* W Mexico
Durazno *607 var.* San Pedro del Durazno. C Uruguay
Durazzo *see* Durrës
Durazzo, Gulf of *see* Durrësit, Gjiri i
Durban *527* Kwazulu Natal, E South Africa
Durbe *362 Ger.* Durben. W Latvia
Durben *see* Durbe
Durdur *524* seasonal river of NW Somalia
Durham *593* NE England, UK
Durmitor *see* Đeravica
Durrës *81 var.* Durrësi, Dursi, *It.* Durazzo, *SCr.* Drač, *Turk.* Draç. W Albania
Durrësit, Gjiri i *81 var.* Gulf of Durazzo. Gulf of the Adriatic Sea, W Albania
Durūz, Jabal ad *551* mountain range of SW Syria
D'Urville Island *433* island to the NE of South Island, New Zealand
Dusa Mareb *see* Dhuusa Marreeb
Dushanbe *558 var.* Dušanbe, Dyushambe, *prev.* Stalinabad. ❖ of Tajikistan, W Tajikistan
Düsseldorf *264 var.* Duesseldorf. W Germany
Dŭstí *558* SW Tajikistan
Dutch New Guinea *see* Irian Jaya
Dutch East Indies *see* Indonesia
Dutch West Indies *see* Netherlands Antilles
Düzce *see* Athna
Dvinsk *see* Daugavpils
Dyanev *see* Deynau
Dyero *see* Dioro
Dyfrdwy *see* Dee
Dyushambe *see* Dushanbe
Džalilabad *see* Cälilabad
Dzaoudzi *649* Petite-Terre, E Mayotte
Džarkurgan *see* Dzharkurgan
Dzaudzhikau *see* Vladikavkaz
Dzavhan *412* river of W Mongolia
Džebel *see* Dzhebel
Dzerzhinskiy *see* Nar'yan-Mar
Dzhalal-Abad *357 var.* Džalal-Abad, *Kir.* Jalal-Abad. SW Kyrgyzstan
Dzhalilabad *see* Cälilabad
Dzhambul *see* Taraz
Džhanak *581* region of W Turkmenistan
Dzharkurgan *see* Jarqŭrghon
Dzhebel *581 var.* Džebel, *Turkm.* Jebel. W Turkmenistan
Dzhelandy *558* SE Tajikistan
Dzhergalan *357 var.* Džergalan, *Kir.* Jyrgalan. NE Kyrgyzstan
Dzhermuk *see* Jermuk
Dzhetygara *338 Kaz.* Zhetiqara. NW Kazakhstan
Dzhezkazgan *see* Zhezkazgan
Dzhirgatal' *see* Jirgatol
Dzhizak *see* Jizzakh
Dzhugdzhur, Khrebet *485* mountain range of E Russian Federation
Dzhusaly *338* SW Kazakhstan
Dzongsa *134* SW Bhutan
Dzunnmod *412* C Mongolia
Dzüünharaa *412* N Mongolia
Dzvina *see* Western Dvina
Dzyarzhynskaya, Hora *122* mountain of C Belarus

E

Eagle Islands *643* island group of W British Indian Ocean Territory
Eagle Passage *645* passage connecting Falkland Sound and Atlantic Ocean, S Falkland Islands
East Caicos *653* island of N Turks and Caicos Islands
East China Sea *555 Chin.* Nan Hai. Sea of Pacific Ocean, off E Asia
East End *644* Grand Cayman, W Cayman Islands
East End Village *642* E Anguilla
Easter Island *183* Pacific island of Chile
Eastern Cape *527* province of SE South Africa
Eastern Desert *see* Sharqîya, Sahara el
Eastern Ghats *296* mountains of SE India
Eastern Sayans *see* Vostochnyy Sayan
Eastern Scheldt *see* Oosterschelde
Eastern Sierra Madre *see* Sierra Madre Oriental
Eastern Transvaal *see* Mpumalanga
East Falkland *645* island of E Falkland Islands
East Fayu Island *406* island of C Micronesia
East Frisian Islands *see* Ostfriesische Inseln
East London *527 Afr.* Oos-Londen. Eastern Cape, S South Africa
East Pakistan *see* Bangladesh
East Malaysia *386-387* eastern part of Malaysia situated on N Borneo
East Siberian Sea *see* Vostochno-Sibirskoye More
East Timor *305* Country of SE Asia, under UN Transitional Authority from Feburary 2000. ❖ Dili
Eauripik *406* atoll of C Micronesia
Ebebiyin *236* NE Río Muni, Equatorial Guinea
Ebeltoft *218* Jylland, C Denmark
Ebetsu *331* Hokkaidō, N Japan
Ebinayon *see* Evinayong
Eblana *see* Dublin
Ebolowa *168* S Cameroon
Ebon *396* island of S Marshall Islands
Ébrié, Lagune *326* lake of SW Ivory Coast
Ebro *531* river of NE Spain
Ech Cheliff *see* Chlef
Echmiadzin *see* Ejmiadzin
Echternach *378* E Luxembourg
Écija *531* SW Spain
Ečmiadzin *see* Ejmiadzin
Ecuador *228-229* officially Republic of Ecuador. Country of NW South America divided into 20 admin. units (provinces). ❖ Quito
Ed *238* SE Eritrea
Ed Damazin *536 var.* Ad Damazīn. E Sudan
Ed Damer *536 var.* Ad Dāmir, Ad Damar. NE Sudan
Ed Dueim *536 var.* Ad Duwaym, Ad Duwēm. C Sudan
Ede *429* C Netherlands
Ede *440* W Nigeria
Edéa *168* SW Cameroon
Eden *593* river of NW England, UK
Edfu *see* Idfu
Edgeøya *653* island of S Svalbard
Edina *368* SW Liberia
Edinburgh *652* N Tristan da Cunha
Edinburgh *593* E Scotland, UK
Edineţ *408 var.* Edineţi, *Rus.* Yedintsy. NW Moldova
Edirne *576* NW Turkey
Edmonton *170* SW Canada
Edward, Lake *584, 203 var.* Lake Rutanzige, Edward Nyanza, Albert Edward Nyanza, Lac Idi Amin. Lake of Uganda and Dem. Rep. Congo (Zaire)
Eems *see* Ems
Eesti Vabariik *see* Estonia
Efate *615 Fr.* Vaté, *prev.* Sandwich Islands. Island group of C Vanuatu
Egadi, Isole *321* island group to the W of Sicilia, S Italy
Ege Denizi *see* Aegean Sea
Eger *290 Ger.* Erlau. NE Hungary
Eger *see* Cheb
Eger *see* Ohře
Egersund *444* SW Norway
Egilsstadhir *294* E Iceland
Egmont, Cape *433* cape of SW North Island, New Zealand
Egmont Islands *643* island group of W British Indian Ocean Territory
Egmont, Mount *see* Taranaki, Mount
Egypt *230-233* officially Arab Republic of Egypt, *prev.* United Arab Republic. Country of NE Africa divided into 26 admin. units (governorates). ❖ Cairo
Eidsvoll *444* S Norway

Eifel *264* plateau of W Germany
Eiffel Flats *636* C Zimbabwe
Eight Degree Channel *390* channel of the Indian Ocean between N Maldives and Lakshadweep, SW India
Eil *see* Eyl
Eilat *see* Elat
Eil Malk *455* island of S Palau
Eindhoven *429* S Netherlands
Einsiedeln *546* NE Switzerland
Eipel *see* Ipeľ, Ipoly
Eire *see* Ireland, Republic of
Eisen *see* Yŏngch'ŏn
Eisenstadt *106* E Austria
Eishū *see* Yŏngju
Eitape *see* Aitape
Eivissa *531* *Cast.* Ibiza, *var.* Iviza. Island of the Islas Baleares, E Spain
Ejmiadzin *98* *Rus.* Echmiadzin, Ečmiadzin, Etchmiadzin. W Armenia
Ekaterinoslav *see* Dnipropetrovs'k
Ekerem *see* Okarem
Ekeren *127* N Belgium
Ekibastuz *338* NE Kazakhstan
El Alto *136* W Bolivia
El Araïche *see* Larache
El 'Arîsh *230* *var.* Al Arīsh. NE Egypt
El Asnam *see* Chlef
Elat *317* *var.* Elath, Eilat. S Israel
Elat, Gulf of *see* Aqaba, Gulf of,
Elato *406* atoll of C Micronesia
Elâzığ *577* *var.* Elâziz, Elâziğ. E Turkey
Elba, Isola d' *320* island of C Italy
Elbasan *81* *var.* Elbasani. C Albania
Elbe *216, 265* *Cz.* Labe. River of Czech Republic and Germany
El Beqaa *364* *var.* Al Biqā', Bekaa Valley. Valley of E Lebanon
Elbing *see* Elbląg
Elbistan *577* S Turkey
Elbląg *471* *Ger.* Elbing. N Poland
El Boulaida *see* Blida
Elbow Bay *643* bay of the North Atlantic Ocean, C Bermuda
El Bur *see* Ceelbuur
Elburgon *342* W Kenya
Elburz Mountains *see* Alborz, Reshteh-ye Kuhhā-ye
El Carmen de Bolívar *195* NW Colombia
El Cayo *see* San Ignacio
El Cerro del Aripo *see* Aripo, Mount
Elche *531* *Cat.* Elx. SE Spain
El Congo *235* W El Salvador
El Copé *456* C Panama
Elda *531* SE Spain
El Dere *see* Ceeldheere
El Djazaïr *see* Algiers
El Djelfa *see* Djelfa
Eldoret *342* W Kenya
Eleja *362* C Latvia
Elemi Triangle *243, 342* disputed region of Kenya and Sudan
Éléphant, Chaîne de l' *see* Dâmrei, Chuŏr Phmun
Elephant Island *90* island of South Shetland Islands, Antarctica
Eleuthera Island *112* island of C Bahamas
El Faiyûm *230* *var.* Al Fayyūm. N Egypt
El Fasher *536* *var.* Al Fāshir. W Sudan
El Ferrol del Caudillo *see* Ferrol
El Gal *see* Ceel Gaal
El Gedaref *see* Gedaref
Elgin *593* NE Scotland, UK
El Gîza *230* *var.* Gîza, Al Jīzah. N Egypt
El Goléa *83* C Algeria
Elgon, Mount *584* mountain of E Uganda
El Hasaheisa *536* *var.* Al Ḩuşayḩişah, Al Hasahisa, Hasaheisa. C Sudan
El Haseke *see* Al Ḩasakah
Elías Piña *see* Comendador
Elimina *270* S Ghana
Élisabethville *see* Lubumbashi
El Iskandarîyah *see* Alexandria
Elizabeth *101* S Australia
El Jadida *414* *prev.* Mazagan. W Morocco
El Jafr *see* Qā' al Jafr
El Jem *573* *var.* Al Djem, Al Jamm. NE Tunisia
El Kef *see* Le Kef
El Kelâa des Srarhna *414* C Morocco
El Khârga *230* *var.* Al Khārijah. C Egypt
El Khiyam *364* *var.* Khiam. S Lebanon
Elkhovo *152* *var.* Elhovo. SE Bulgaria
Ellás *see* Greece
Ellef Ringnes Island *170* island of Sverdrup Islands, N Canada
Ellerton *121* C Barbados
Ellesmere Island *170* island of Queen Elizabeth Islands, N Canada
Ellice Islands *see* Tuvalu
Ellsworth Land *90* physical region of Lesser Antarctica, Antarctica
El Mahalla el Kubra *230* *var.* Maḩallah al Kubrá. N Egypt
El Manşûra *230* *var.* Al Manşūrah. N Egypt
El Mediyya *see* Médéa
El Mina *364* *var.* Al Mīnā'. N Lebanon
El Minya *230* *var.* Al Minyā. C Egypt
El Mohammaidia *see* Mohammadia
Elmshorn *264* N Germany
El Nebk *see* An Nabk
El Obeid *536* *var.* Al Ubayyiḑ, Al Obayyid. C Sudan
El Oued *83* *var.* El Ouâdi, El Wad. NE Algeria
Eloy Alfaro *228* *var.* Durán. SW Ecuador
El Palmar *136* E Bolivia
El Paraíso *288* S Honduras
el Pas de las Casa *86* E Andorra
El Paso *598* Texas, SC USA
Elpitiya *534* S Sri Lanka
El Porvenir *456* NE Panama
El Progreso *278* *var.* Guastatoya. C Guatemala
El Progreso *288* NW Honduras
El Qâhira *see* Cairo
Elqui *183* river of N Chile
El Quneitra *see* Al Qunayţirah
El Quseir *see* Al Quşayr
El Quweira *see* Al Quwayrah
El Rama *436* SE Nicaragua
El Salvador *211* SE Cuba
El Salvador *234-235* officially Republic of El Salvador. Country of Central America divided into 14 admin. units (13 departments, 1 metropolitan area). ❖ San Salvador
El Seibo *226* *var.* Santa Cruz de El Seibo. E Dominican Republic
el Serrat *86* N Andorra
Elsinore *see* Helsingør
El Suweida *see* As Suwaydā'
el Tarter *86* NE Andorra
El Tigre *619* NE Venezuela
El Tigre de San Lorenzo *456* SW Panama
El Triunfo *235* SE El Salvador
Elva *240* *Ger.* Elwa. SE Estonia
Elvas *474* C Portugal
Elverum *444* S Norway
El Vigía *619* W Venezuela
El Wad *see* El Oued
El Wâhât el Khârga *230* *var.* Al Wāḩāt al Khārijah. S Egypt
Elx *see* Elche
Émaé *615* island of C Vanuatu
Emajõgi *240* *var.* Emajygi, Ema Jõgi. River of SE Estonia
Emao *615* island of C Vanuatu
Emba *338* W Kazakhstan
Emba *338* river of W Kazakhstan
Embangweni *385* *var.* Ephangweni. NW Malawi
Emborcação, Represa da *145* reservoir of S Brazil
Embu *342* C Kenya
Emden *264* NW Germany
Emerald *101* E Australia
Emi Koussi *180* mountain of N Chad
Emlembe *540* mountain of South Africa and Swaziland
Emmen *429* NE Netherlands
Empada *282* SW Guinea-Bissau
Empty Quarter *see* Rub'al Khali
Ems *264, 429* *Dut.* Eems. River of Germany and Netherlands
Enareträsk *see* Inarijärvi
Encamp *86* C Andorra
Encarnación *460* S Paraguay
Enchi *270* SW Ghana
Endeavour *121* NW Barbados
Endelave *218* island of C Denmark
Enderbury Island *346* island of the Phoenix Is, C Kiribati
Enderby Land *90* physical region of Greater Antarctica, Antarctica
Enewetak *396* *var.* Eniwetok. Atoll of W Marshall Islands
Enghershatu *238* mountain of N Eritrea
England *593* national region of UK
English Channel *253, 593, 647* *var.* The Channel, *Fr.* La Manche. Channel connecting the North Sea and Atlantic Ocean between England and France
English Harbour Town *92* S Antigua, Antigua & Barbuda
Engordany *86* C Andorra
Engures Ezers *362* lake of NW Latvia
Enguri *262* *Rus.* Inguri. River of NW Georgia
Eniwetok *see* Enewetak
Enkeldoorn *see* Chivhu
Enkhuizen *429* NW Netherlands
Enna *321* Sicilia, S Italy
En Nâqaoûra *364* *var.* An Nāqūrah. SW Lebanon
Ennedi *180* plateau of E Chad
Ennis *314* *Ir.* Inis. W Ireland
Enniscorthy *314* E Ireland
Enniskillen *593* Northern Ireland, UK
Enns *106* river of C Austria
Enriquillo, Lago *226* lake of SW Dominican Republic
Enschede *429* E Netherlands
Ensenada *403* NW Mexico
Entebbe *584* S Uganda
Enugu *440* S Nigeria
Enu, Ilha de *282* island of SW Guinea-Bissau
Eolie, Isole *321* *var.* Isole Lipari, *Eng.* Lipari Islands, *var.* Aeolian Islands. Island group of S Italy
Epéna *200* NE Congo
Eperies *see* Prešov
Eperjes *see* Prešov
Ephangweni *see* Embangweni
Epi *615* island of C Vanuatu
Épinal *253* NE France
Epira *284* E Guyana
Episkopi *215* SW Cyprus
Episkopi Bay *215* bay of the Mediterranean Sea, on the SE coast of Cyprus
Epping Forest *276* S Grenada island, Grenada
Equatorial Channel *390* channel of the Indian Ocean between the atolls of Fuammulah and South Huvadhu Atoll, S Maldives
Equatorial Guinea *236-237* officially Republic of Equatorial Guinea. Country of W Africa divided into 7 admin. units (provinces). ❖ Malabo
Erbil *see* Arbīl
Erdenet *412* N Mongolia
Erdi Ma *180* desert region of NE Chad
Ereğli *577* S Turkey
Erenköy *see* Kokkina
Erenköy *215* W Cyprus
Erevan *see* Yerevan
Erfurt *265* C Germany
Erg Chech *83* desert region of SW Algeria
Erg du Djourab *180* desert region of C Chad
Erguig *180* river of SW Chad
Erhlin *555* *Jap.* Nirin. W Taiwan
Erie *599* Pennsylvania, NE USA
Erie, Lake *171, 599* *Fr.* Lac Érié. Lake of Canada and USA
Erigabo *see* Ceerigaabo
Erik Erikenstretet *653* strait of the Arctic Ocean, E Svalbard
Erikub *396* island of C Marshall Islands
Eritrea *238-239* officially State of Eritrea. Country of E Africa divided into 10 admin. units (regions). ❖ Asmara
Erivan *see* Yerevan
Erlangen *265* S Germany
Erlau *see* Eger
Ermak *see* Yermak
Ermelo *527* Eastern Transvaal, NE South Africa
Er Rachidia *414* E Morocco
Er Rahad *536* *var.* Ar Rahad. C Sudan
Er Rif *see* Rif
Erromango *615* island of S Vanuatu
Ersekë *81* *var.* Erseka, Kolonjë. SE Albania
Érsekújvár *see* Nové Zámky
Ertis *see* Irtysh
Erzenit *81* *var.* Erzen. River of C Albania
Erzgebirge *216, 265* *Cz.* Krušné Hory, *Eng.* Ore Mountains. Mountain range of Czech Republic and Germany
Erzincan *577* E Turkey
Erzurum *577* *prev.* Erzerum. NE Turkey
Esa'ala *458* Normanby I, Papua New Guinea
Esbjerg *218* Jylland, W Denmark
Esbo *see* Espoo
Escaut *see* Scheldt
Eschen *374* NW Liechtenstein
Esch-sur-Alzette *378* S Luxembourg
Escuintla *278* S Guatemala
Eséka *168* SW Cameroon
Esenguly *see* Gasan-Kuli
Esentepe *215* *var.* Ayios Amvrosios. N Cyprus
Eşfahān *307* *var.* Ispahan. W Iran
Esh Sham *see* Damascus
Esh Sharā *see* Ash Sharāh
Esigodini *636* *prev.* Essexvale. SW Zimbabwe
Esil *see* Ishim
Eski Dzhumaya *see* Turgovishte
Eskifjördhur *294* E Iceland
Eskije *see* Xánthi
Eskilstuna *543* S Sweden
Eskişehir *576* W Turkey
Esla, Embalse de *531* *var.* Embalse de Elsa. Reservoir of NW Spain
Esmeralda *210* E Cuba
Esmeraldas *228* N Ecuador
Esna *see* Isna
Esneux *127* E Belgium
España *see* Spain
Española, Isla *228* island of SE Galapagos Is, Ecuador
Esparta *288* NW Honduras
Esperance *100* SW Australia
Esperanza *90* Argentinian research station of Antarctic Peninsula, Antarctica
Esperanza *226* N Dominican Republic
Espinal *195* C Colombia
Espinhaço, Serra do *145* mountain range of SE Brazil
Espiritu Santo *615* *var.* Santo. Island of C Vanuatu
Espoo *249* *Swe.* Esbo. SW Finland
Espungabera *419* SW Mozambique
Esquel *95* SW Argentina
Esquipulas *278* SE Guatemala
Êssalou *222* river of N Djibouti
Essaouira *414* *prev.* Mogador. W Morocco
Essau *261* W Gambia
Esseg *see* Osijek
Essen *264* W Germany
Essequibo *284* river of Guyana
Essequibo Islands *284* islands of N Guyana
Essexvale *see* Esigodini
Estados, Isla de los *95* *Eng.* Staten Island. Island to the E of Tierra del Fuego, Argentina
Estanyó, Pic de l' *86* mountain of N Andorra
Estcourt *527* Kwazulu Natal, E South Africa
Estelí *436* W Nicaragua
Estevan *170* S Canada

Est, Ile de l' *400* E Mauritius
Estonia *240-241* officially Republic of Estonia, *Est.* Eesti Vabariik, *prev.* Estonian SSR, *Rus.* Estonskaya SSR. Country of E Europe divided into 15 admin. units (counties). ❖ Tallinn
Estoril *474* W Portugal
Estrela *474* mountain of C Portugal
Estrela, Serra de *474* mountain range of C Portugal
Eszék *see* Osijek
Esztergom *290* *Ger.* Gran. N Hungary
Etchmiadzin *see* Ejmiadzin
Etembue *236* SW Río Muni, Equatorial Guinea
Ethiopia *242-245* *prev.* Abyssinia. Country of E Africa divided into 14 admin. units (regions). ❖ Addis Ababa
Ethiopian Plateau *243* plateau of W Ethiopia
Etna, Mount *321* volcano of Sicilia, S Italy
Etosha Pan *423* salt basin of N Namibia
Etoumbi *200* NW Congo
Etrek *see* Atrak
Etsch *see* Adige
Ettelbrück *378* C Luxembourg
'Eua *568* *prev.* Middleburg Island. Island of Tongatapu Group, Tonga
Eugene *598* Oregon, NW USA
Euphrates *310, 551, 576* River of SW Asia
Eureka *170* Ellesmere Island, N Canada
Europa Point *646* headland on the S coast of Gibraltar
Euthini *385* *var.* Eutini. NW Malawi
Euxine Sea *see* Black Sea
Evansville *599* Indiana, C USA
Everest, Mount *186, 427* *Chin.* Qomolangma Feng, *Nep.* Sagarmatha. Mountain of China and Nepal
Evesham *498* SE St Vincent, St Vincent & the Grenadines
Evinayong *236* *var.* Evinayoung, Ebinayon. S Río Muni, Equatorial Guinea
Évora *474* C Portugal
Évreux *253* N France
Évry *253* N France
Evrykhou *215* *var.* Evrychou. W Cyprus
Évvoia *273* Island of E Greece
Ewarton *329* C Jamaica
Ewaso Ngiro *342* river of C Kenya
Ewo *200* W Congo
Exe *593* river of SW England, UK
Exeter *593* SW England, UK
Exuma Cays *112* islets of C Bahamas
Exuma Sound *112* stretch of water between Cat I and Exuma Cays, Bahamas
Eyasi, Lake *560* lake of N Tanzania
Eyl *524* *It.* Eil. E Somalia
Eyre North, Lake *101* salt lake of C Australia
Eyre Peninsula *101* peninsula of S Australia
Eyre South, Lake *101* salt lake of C Australia
Eysturoy *644* *var.* Østerø. Island of N Faeroe Islands
Extremadura *530* autonomous community of W Spain
Ezulwini *540* W Swaziland

F

Faadhippolhu Atoll *390* *var.* Fadiffolu, Lhaviyani Atoll. Atoll of N Maldives
Faafu Atoll *see* North Nilandhe Atoll
Fåborg *218* Fyn, S Denmark
Fabriano *321* C Italy
Facpi Point *647* headland on the SW coast of Guam
Fada *180* E Chad
Fada-N'gourma *157* *var.* Fadan-Gourma. E Burkina
Fadghāmī *see* Tall Fadghāmī
Fadiffolu *see* Faadhippolhu Atoll
Fadugu *514* N Sierra Leone
Færingehavn *646* *var.* Kangerluarsoruseq, S Greenland
Faeroe Islands *644* *Faer.* Fóroyar, *Dan.* Færøerne. Self-governing territory of Denmark, North Atlantic Ocean. ❖ Tórshavn
Faetano *502* E San Marino
Fagaloa Bay *500* bay of the Pacific Ocean on Upolu, SE Samoa
Fagamālo *500* Savai'i, Samoa
Făgăraş *480* C Romania
Faguibine, Lac *392* *var.* Lake Fagibina. Lake of NW Mali
Fahaheel *see* Al Fuḩayḩīl
Faial *474* *var.* Ilha do Faial. Island of the Azores, Portugal
Faifo *see* Hôi An
Failaka Island *see* Faylakah
Faioa, Île *653* island of Île Uvea, S Wallis & Futuna
Fairbanks *598* Alaska, USA
Fair Isle *593* island of N Scotland, UK
Fais *406* island of W Micronesia
Faisalābād *451* *prev.* Lyallpur. NE Pakistan
Faizabad *see* Feyzābād
Fajã *176* Brava, S Cape Verde
Fajara *261* W Gambia
Fajardo *651* NE Puerto Rico
Fajãzinha *176* Fogo, S Cape Verde
Fakaofo Atoll *653* island of SE Tokelau
Fako *168* active volcano of W Cameroon
Falaba *514* N Sierra Leone
Falam *159* NW Burma
Falciano *502* NE San Marino
Fale *583* islet of Nukufetau, Tuvalu
Faleālupo *500* Savai'i, Samoa
Falelima *500* Savai'i, Samoa
Falémé *392, 510* river of W Africa
Faleshty *see* Făleşti
Făleşti *408* *Rus.* Faleshty. NW Moldova
Falkat *238* seasonal river of N Eritrea
Falkirk *593* C Scotland, UK
Falkland Islands *95, 645* *Sp.* Islas Malvinas. British dependent territory of the South Atlantic Ocean. ❖ Stanley.
Falkland Sound *645* strait of the South Atlantic Ocean between East Falkland and West Falkland, Falkland Islands
Falluja *see* Al Fallūjah
Falmouth *92* S Antigua, Antigua & Barbuda
Falmouth *329* NW Jamaica
Falster *218* island of SE Denmark
Falun *543* C Sweden
Famagusta *see* Gazimağusa
Famagusta Bay *215* *var.* Ammochostos Bay, Gazimağusa Körfezi. Bay of the Mediterranean Sea, on the E coast of Cyprus
Fandriana *382* C Madagascar
Fangliao *555* SW Taiwan
Fanning Island *see* Tabuaeran
Fano *321* N Italy
Fan Si Pan *623* mountain of NW Vietnam
Faraday *90* UK research station of Antarctic Peninsula, Antarctica
Faradofay *see* Tôlañaro
Farafangana *382* SE Madagascar
Farafenni *261* NW Gambia
Farāh *77* W Afghanistan
Farāh Rūd *77* river of W Afghanistan
Farallon de Medinilla *650* island of C Northern Mariana Islands
Farallon de Pajaros *650* island of N Northern Mariana Islands
Faranah *281* S Guinea
Faraulep *406* atoll of C Micronesia
Farghona *610* *Rus.* Fergana, *prev.* Novyy Margilan. E Uzbekistan
Fargo *599* North Dakota, NC USA
Farīdābād *296* N India
Farīdpur *117* C Bangladesh
Farim *282* NW Guinea-Bissau
Farkhor *558* *Rus.* Parkhar. SW Tajikistan
Farm *649* river of E Montserrat
Farmington *598* New Mexico, SW USA
Faro *168* river of Cameroon and Nigeria
Faro *474* S Portugal
Farquhar Atoll *512* atoll of the Farquhar Group, S Seychelles
Farquhar Group *512* island group of S Seychelles
Fars, Khalīj-e *see* The Gulf
Farvel, Kap *see* Nunap Isua
Fass *261* W Gambia
Fastiv *586* NW Ukraine
Fatala *281* river of W Guinea
Fatick *510* W Senegal
Fátima *474* W Portugal
Fatoto *261* E Gambia
Fatua, Pointe *653* *var.* Pointe Nord. Headland of Île Futuna, N Wallis & Futuna
Fatutaka *522* *var.* Mitre I. Island of E Solomon Islands
Faxaflói *294* bay of North Atlantic Ocean, on SW coast of Iceland
Faya *180* N Chad
Fayaoué *650* Ouvéa, Îles Loyauté, N New Caledonia
Fayetteville *599* Arkansas, SC USA
Faylakah *354* *var.* Failaka Island. Island of E Kuwait
Fazao, Monts du *567* mountain range of W Togo
Fazzān *371* *Eng.* Fezzan. Cultural region of W Libya
Fdérik *398* *prev.* Fort-Gouraud. NW Mauritania
Feabhai, Loch *see* Foyle, Lough
Fédala *see* Mohammedia
Fehmarn *265* island of N Germany
Fehmarnbelt *265* strait connecting Kieler Bucht and Mecklenburger Bucht, between Denmark and Germany
Feira de Santana *145* *prev.* Feira. E Brazil
Feistritz *106* river of SE Austria
Fejaj, Chott el *573* salt lake of C Tunisia
Feldkirch *106* W Austria
Félegyháza *see* Kiskunfélegyháza
Felidhu Atoll *390* atoll of C Maldives
Fénérive *see* Fenoarivo Atsinanana
Fenglin *555* *Jap.* Hōrin. E Taiwan
Fengshan *555* *Jap.* Hōzan. SW Taiwan
Fengtien *see* Shenyang
Fengtien *see* Liaoning
Fengyüan *555* *var.* Toyohara, *Jap.* Hōgen. W Taiwan
Feni *117* E Bangladesh
Fennern *see* Vändra
Fenoarivo Atsinanana *382* *prev.* Fénérive. NE Madagascar
Fens, The *593* wetlands of E England, UK
Ferdinand *see* Montana
Fergana *see* Farghona
Fergana Valley *558* physical region of C Asia
Fergusson Island *458* *var.* Kaluwawa. Island of SE Papua New Guinea
Ferizaj *see* Uroševac
Ferkessédougou *326* N Ivory Coast
Ferlo *see* Vallée du Ferlo
Fernandina, Isla *228* island of W Galapagos Is, Ecuador
Fernando de la Mora *460* S Paraguay
Fernando de Noronha *145* island of E Brazil
Fernando Po *see* Bioko
Ferrara *321* N Italy
Ferrol *530* *prev.* El Ferrol del Caudillo. NW Spain
Ferryville *see* Menzel Bourguiba
Ferto-tó *see* Neusiedler See
Fès *414* *Eng.* Fez. N Morocco
Fethiye *576* SW Turkey
Feyzābād *77* *var.* Faizabad. NE Afghanistan
Fezzan *see* Fazzān
Fianarantsoa *382* C Madagascar
Fianga *180* SW Chad
Fichē *243* *It.* Ficce. C Ethiopia
Fielding *433* S North Island, New Zealand
Fier *81* *var.* Fieri. SW Albania
Fierzës, Liqeni i *81* lake of N Albania
Fig Tree *494* S Nevis, St Kitts & Nevis
Figueira da Foz *474* W Portugal
Figueres *531* E Spain
Figuig *414* *var.* Figig. E Morocco
Fiji *246-247* officially Republic of Fiji, *Fij.* Viti. Country of the Pacific Ocean divided into 4 admin. units (divisions). ❖ Suva
Filadelfia *206* W Costa Rica
Filingué *439* W Niger
Fimi *203* river of W Dem. Rep. Congo (Zaire)
Finike *576* SW Turkey
Finland *248-251* officially Republic of Finland, *Fin.* Suomen Tasavalta. Country of N Europe divided into 12 admin. units (11 provinces and 1 autonomous region). ❖ Helsinki
Finland, Gulf of *240, 249, 484* *Fin.* Suomenlahti, *Swe.* Finska Viken, *Est.* Soome Laht, *Rus.* Finskiy Zaliv. Gulf of the Baltic Sea, NE Europe
Finnmarksvidda *444* physical region of NE Norway
Fins *448* NE Oman
Finskiy Zaliv *see* Finland, Gulf of
Fiorina *502* NE San Marino
Firenze *320* *Eng.* Florence. NW Italy
Fischbacher Alpen *106* mountain range of E Austria
Fish *423* *Afr.* Vis. River of S Namibia
Fishguard *593* *Wel.* Abergwaun. W Wales, UK
Fiskeræsset *646* *var.* Qeqertarsuatsiaat, S Greenland
Fiume *see* Rijeka
Five Islands Village *92* W Antigua, Antigua & Barbuda
Fizuli *see* Füzuli
Fjerritslev *218* Jylland, NW Denmark
Fläming *265* hill region of NE Germany
Flanders *127* *Dut.* Vlaanderen, *Fr.* Flandres. Cultural region of W Belgium
Flat Island *400* *var.* Île Plate. Island of N Mauritius
Flat Island *652* island of NE Spratly Islands
Flatts Village *643* C Bermuda
Flensburg *264* N Germany
Flessingue *see* Vlissingen
Flinders *101* river of N Australia
Flinders Island *101* island of SE Australia
Flinders Ranges *101* mountain range of S Australia
Flin Flon *170* SW Canada
Flint *599* Michigan, NC USA
Flint Island *346* island of the Line Is, E Kiribati
Flitsch *see* Bovec
Floréal *400* C Mauritius
Florence *see* Firenze
Florencia *195* SW Colombia
Flores *278* N Guatemala
Flores *302* island of Nusa Tenggara, C Indonesia
Flores *474* island of the Azores, Portugal
Flores, Lago de *see* Petén Itza, Lago
Flores, Laut *302* *Eng.* Flores Sea. Sea of the Pacific Ocean, C Indonesia
Floreşti *408* *Rus.* Floreshty. N Moldova
Florianópolis *145* *prev.* Destêrro. S Brazil
Florida *210* SE Cuba
Florida *288* W Honduras
Florida *599, 603* state of SE USA
Florida *607* S Uruguay
Floridablanca *195* NE Colombia
Florida Islands *522* group of islands of C Solomon Is
Florida, Straits of *112, 210* strait connecting the Atlantic Ocean and Gulf of Mexico
Flórina *273* *var.* Phlórina. N Greece
Flüelapass *546* mountain pass of E Switzerland

Flushing *see* Vlissingen
Fly *458* river of Indonesia and Papua New Guinea
Flying Fish Cove *644* ❖ of Christmas Island
Fnjóská *294* river of C Iceland
Foa *568* island of Ha'apai Group, Tonga
Foča *140* SE Bosnia & Herzegovina
Focşani *480* E Romania
Foggia *321* S Italy
Fogo *176* island of SW Cape Verde
Fogo'one, Pointe *653* headland of Île Uvea, S Wallis & Futuna
Foix *253* S France
Folkestone *593* SE England, UK
Fomboni *198* N Mohéli, Comoros
Fon *281* mountainous region of E Guinea
Fond St. Jean *224* S Dominica
Fongafale *583* *var.* Funafuti. ❖ of Tuvalu, Funafuti, Tuvalu
Fonseca, Gulf of *235, 288, 436* gulf of the Pacific Ocean, on the W coast of Central America
Fontvieille *410* SW Monaco
Fonuafo'ou *568* island of Nomuka Group, W Tonga
Fonualei *568* island of N Tonga
Foochow *see* Fuzhou
Forécariah *281* SW Guinea
Forestière *497* N St Lucia
Forlì *321* N Italy
Formentera *531* island of the Islas Baleares, E Spain
Formosa *95* NE Argentina
Formosa Bay *see* Ungama Bay
Formosa, Ilha *282* island of Arquipélago dos Bijagós, SW Guinea-Bissau
Formosa, Serra *145* mountains of C Brazil
Formosa Strait *see* Taiwan Strait
Forssa *249* SW Finland
Fortaleza *136* N Bolivia
Fortaleza *145* *prev.* Ceará. NE Brazil
Fort-Archambault *see* Sarh
Fort-Bayard *see* Zhanjiang
Fort-Cappolani *see* Tidjikja
Fort Charlet *see* Djanet
Fort Collins *599* Colorado, SW USA
Fort-Crampel *see* Kaga Bandoro
Fort-Dauphin *see* Tôlañaro
Fort-de-France *649* ❖ of Martinique, W Martinique
Fort-Foureau *see* Kousséri
Fort George *see* Grande Rivière, La
Fort-Gouraud *see* Fdérik
Forth *593* river of C Scotland, UK
Fort Hall *see* Murang'a
Forth, Firth of *593* estuary of the river Forth, E Scotland, UK
Fort Hill *see* Chitipa
Fortín General Diaz *460* W Paraguay
Fortín General Eugenio Garay *see* General Eugenio A. Garay
Fort Jameson *see* Chipata
Fort Johnson *see* Mangochi
Fort-Lamy *see* N'Djamena
Fort Lauderdale *599* Florida, SE USA
Fort-Liberté *286* N Haiti
Fort Manning *see* Mchinji
Fort McMurray *170* W Canada
Fort-Repoux *see* Akjoujt
Fort Rosebery *see* Mansa
Fort Saint John *170* W Canada
Fort Saskatchewan *170* SW Canada
Fort-Shevchenko *338* W Kazakhstan
Fort-Sibut *see* Sibut
Fort Smith *170* W Canada
Fort Smith *599* Arkansas, SC USA
Fort-Trinquet *see* Bîr Mogreïn
Fort Victoria *see* Masvingo
Fort Wayne *599* Indiana, C USA
Fort William *593* W Scotland, UK
Fort Worth *599* Texas, SC USA
Fougamou *258* C Gabon
Foulenzem *258* NW Gabon
Foumban *168* NW Cameroon
Foumbouni *198* S Grande Comore, Comoros
Fourchue, Île *646* island of N Guadeloupe
Fournaise, Piton de la *652* mountain of SE Réunion
Four Roads *570* NW Trinidad, Trinidad & Tobago
Fouta Djallon *281* *var.* Futa Jallon. Mountainous region of W Guinea
Foveaux Strait *433* strait between South Island and Stewart Island, New Zealand
Fox Bay East *645* West Falkland, W Falkland Islands
Fox Bay West *645* West Falkland, W Falkland Islands
Foxe Peninsula *171* peninsula of Baffin Island, NE Canada
Foyle *593* river of Ireland and UK
Foyle, Lough *314, 593* *Ir.* Loch Feabhai. Inlet of the Atlantic Ocean, Ireland and UK
Fraile Muerto *607* E Uruguay
Frakštát *see* Hlohovec
France *252-257* officially The French Republic. Country of Europe divided into 22 admin. units (regions, comprising 96 departments). ❖ Paris
Franceville *see* Massoukou
Francistown *142* NE Botswana
Franconian Jura *see* Fränkische Alb
Frankfort *599* Kentucky, C USA
Frankfurt am Main *264* *Eng.* Frankfort on the Main, Frankfurt. SW Germany
Frankfurt an der Oder *265* E Germany
Fränkische Alb *265* *Eng.* Franconian Jura. Mountain range of S Germany
Frantsa-Iosifa, Zemlya *454-485* *Eng.* Franz Josef Land. Island group of N Russian Federation
Fraser *170* river of SW Canada
Fraser Island *101* *var.* Great Sandy Island. Island of E Australia
Frauenburg *see* Saldus
Frauenfeld *546* NE Switzerland
Fray Bentos *607* W Uruguay
Fredericia *218* Jylland, SW Denmark
Fredericton *171* SE Canada
Frederiksdal *see* Narsaq Kujalleq
Frederikshåb *see* Paamiut
Frederikshavn *218* Jylland, N Denmark
Frederiksted *653* Saint Croix, S Virgin Islands
Fredrikshald *see* Halden
Fredrikstad *444* S Norway
Freemans *92* C Antigua, Antigua & Barbuda
Freeport *112* *var.* Freeport-Lucaya. Bahamas
Freetown *92* SE Antigua, Antigua & Barbuda
Free State *527* *prev.* Orange Free State. Province of C South Africa
Freetown *514* ❖ of Sierra Leone, W Sierra Leone
Frégate *512* island of the Inner Islands, NE Seychelles
Freiburg *see* Fribourg
Freiburg im Breisgau *264* *var.* Freiburg. SW Germany
Freistadtl *see* Hlohovec
Fremantle *100* SW Australia
French Guiana *645* *var.* Guyane. French overseas department of N South America. ❖ Cayenne.
French Polynesia *646* French overseas possession of the Pacific Ocean.❖ Papeete.
French Somaliland *see* Djibouti
French Sudan *see* Mali
French Territory of the Afars and Issas *see* Djibouti
French Togoland *see* Togo
Fria *281* W Guinea
Fribourg *546* *Ger.* Freiburg. W Switzerland
Friedek-Mistek *see* Frýdek-Místek
Friedrichshafen *264* S Germany
Friendly Islands *see* Tonga
Frigate Island *276* island to the S of Carriacou, Grenada
Frigate Island *498* island of SW St Vincent & the Grenadines
Frisches Haff *see* Vistula Lagoon
Frobisher Bay *see* Iqaluit
Frome, Lake *101* salt lake of S Australia
Front Range *see* Maluti
Frunze *see* Bishkek
Frýdek - Místek *216* *Ger.* Friedek - Mistek. SE Czech Republic
Fuammulah *390* *var.* Gnaviyani Atoll. Atoll of S Maldives
Fu-chien *see* Fujian
Fu-chou *see* Fuzhou
Fucht *414* W Western Sahara
Fuenlabrada *531* C Spain
Fuerte Olimpo *460* NE Paraguay
Fuerteventura *531* island of Islas Canarias, SW Spain
Fuglafjørdhur *644* *var.* Fuglefjord. Eysturoy, N Faeroe Islands
Fugloy *644* *var.* Fuglø. Island of NE Faeroe Islands
Fu-hsin *see* Fuxin
Fujairah *590* *Ar.* Al Fujayrah. NE United Arab Emirates
Fuji *330* Honshū, SE Japan
Fujian *187* *var.* Fukien, Fu-chien. Province of SE China
Fuji-san *330* mountain of Honshū, SE Japan
Fujisawa *330* Honshū, SE Japan
Fukuchiyama *330* Honshū, C Japan
Fukue *330* island of Gotō-rettō, SW Japan
Fukue *330* Gotō-rettō, SW Japan
Fukui *330* Honshū, C Japan
Fukuoka *330* Kyūshū, SW Japan
Fukushima *330* Honshū, N Japan
Fukuyama *330* Honshū, W Japan
Fulacunda *282* C Guinea-Bissau
Fulaga *246* island of the Lau Group, E Fiji
Fulda *264* C Germany
Fullarton *570* SW Trinidad, Trinidad & Tobago
Funabashi *330* Honshū, SE Japan
Funafuti *see* Fongafale
Funafuti *583* coral atoll of C Tuvalu
Funaota *583* islet of Nukufetau, Tuvalu
Funchal *474* Madeira, Madeira Islands, Portugal
Fünen *see* Fyn
Fünfkirchen *see* Pécs
Funhalouro *419* SE Mozambique
Furna *176* Brava, S Cape Verde
Furnas, Represa de *145* reservoir of SE Brazil
Furneaux Group *101* island group of SE Australia
Furstenwald *265* NE Germany
Fusan *see* Pusan
Fushun *187* Liaoning, NE China
Futa Jallon *see* Fouta Djallon
Futuna *615* island of S Vanuatu
Futuna, Île *653* island of N Wallis & Futuna
Fuwairet *see* Al Fuwayriţ
Fuxin *187* *var.* Fu-hsin, Fusin. Liaoning, NE China
Fuzhou *187* *var.* Foochow, Fu-chou. Fujian, SE China
Füzuli *110* *Rus.* Fizuli SW Azerbaijan
Fyn *218* *Ger.* Fünen. Island of C Denmark

G

Gaafu Alifu Atoll *see* North Huvadhu Atoll
Gaafu Dhaalu Atoll *see* South Huvadhu Atoll
Gaalkacyo *524* *var.* Galka'yo, *It.* Galcaio. C Somalia
Gabela *88* W Angola
Gabès *573* *var.* Qābis. C Tunisia
Gabès, Gulf of *573* gulf of the Mediterranean Sea to the E of Tunisia
Gablonz an der Neisse *see* Jablonec nad Nisou
Gabon *258-259* officially The Gabonese Republic. Country of West Africa divided into 9 admin. units (provinces). ❖ Libreville
Gaborone *142* *prev.* Gaberones. ❖ of Botswana, SE Botswana
Gabriel, Ilot *400* *Eng.* Gabriel Island. Island of N Mauritius
Gabrovo *152* C Bulgaria
Gabú *282* *prev.* Nova Lamego. E Guinea-Bissau
Gaeta, Golfo di *321* *var.* Gulf of Gaeta. Gulf of the Tyrrhenian Sea, on the W coast of Italy
Gaferut *406* island of C Micronesia
Gafsa *573* *var.* Qafşah. W Tunisia
Gagnoa *326* C Ivory Coast
Gagra *262* NW Georgia
Gaherré *222* NE Djibouti
Gahnpa *see* Ganta
Gaibānda *117* NW Bangladesh
Gaillimh *see* Galway
Gailtaler Alpen *106* mountain range of S Austria
Gairdner, Lake *101* salt lake of S Australia
Gaiziņ *see* Gaizina Kalns
Gaizina Kalns *362* *var.* Gaiziņ. Mountain of E Latvia
Gâlâfi *222* W Djibouti
Galana *342* river of SE Kenya
Galapagos Islands *228* *var.* Tortoise Islands, *Sp.* Archipiélago de Colón. Island group of W Ecuador in the Pacific Ocean
Galaţi *480* *Ger.* Galatz. E Romania
Galaymor *see* Kalai-Mor
Galcaio *see* Gaalkacyo
Gales Point *130* E Belize
Galets *652* river of NW Réunion
Galgóc *see* Hlohovec
Galibi *538* NE Suriname
Galicia *531* NW Spain
Galilee, Sea of *see* Tiberias, Lake
Galle *534* *prev.* Point de Galle. SW Sri Lanka
Gällivare *543* N Sweden
Gâlma *see* Guelma
Galomaro *282* C Guinea-Bissau
Galway *314* *Ir.* Gaillimh. W Ireland
Galway Bay *314* *Ir.* Cuan na Gaillimhe. Bay of the Atlantic Ocean, to the W of Ireland
Gamamudo *282* NE Guinea-Bissau
Gamba *258* SW Gabon
Gambia *260-261* officially Republic of the Gambia. Country of W Africa divided into 6 admin. units (divisions). ❖ Banjul
Gambia *261, 281, 510* *Fr.* Gambie. River of W Africa
Gambier, Îles *646* island group of E French Polynesia
Gambissara *261* E Gambia
Gamboma *200* E Congo
Gamboula *179* SW Central African Republic
Gamgadhi *427* *var.* Gum. W Nepal
Gamlakarleby *see* Kokkola
Gammouda *see* Sidi Bouzid
Gampaha *534* W Sri Lanka
Gamprin *374* NW Liechtenstein
Gâm *623* river of N Vietnam
Gan *390* C Maldives
Ganaane *see* Juba
Gäncä *110* *Rus.* Gyandzha, *prev.* Kirovabad, Yelisavetpol. W Azerbaijan
Gand *see* Gent
Gandajika *203* S Dem. Rep. Congo (Zaire)
Gandía *531* E Spain
Ganges *117, 296-297* *Ben.* Padma, *Hind.* Ganga. River of S Asia
Ganges, Mouths of the *117, 297* large delta area of Bangladesh and India
Gansu *187* *var.* Kansu. Province of NW China
Ganta *368* *var.* Gahnpa. NE Liberia
Gao *392* E Mali
Gaoua *157* SW Burkina
Gaoual *281* N Guinea
Gap *253* E France

Garabogazköl Bogazy *see* Kara-Bogaz-Gol, Proliv
Garagum *see* Karakumy
Garagum Kanaly *see* Karakumskiy Kanal
Garam *see* Hron
Garamszentkereszt *see* Žiar nad Hronom
Garango *157* C Burkina
Garbahaarrey *524 It.* Garba Harre. SW Somalia
Garda, Lago di *320 var.* Benaco, *Eng.* Lake Garda. Lake of N Italy
Gardēz *77 var.* Gardeyz. E Afghanistan
Gardner Island *see* Nikumaroro
Gardo *see* Qardho
Garissa *342* E Kenya
Garm *see* Gharm
Garmo, Qullai *558 Eng.* Communism Peak, *Rus.* Kommunizma Pik, *prev.* Stalin Peak. Mounain of E Tajikistan
Garonne *253* river of SW France
Garoowe *524 var.* Garoe. N Somalia
Garoua *168 var.* Garua. N Cameroon
Garowal *261* E Gambia
Garrygala *see* Kara-Kala
Garsen *342* SE Kenya
Gary *599* Indiana, C USA
Garyllis *215* river of S Cyprus
Garzón *195* SW Colombia
Gasan-Kuli *581 var.* Esenguly. W Turkmenistan
Gasa Tashi Thongmen *134* NW Bhutan
Gascogne *252-253 Eng.* Gascony. Cultural region of SW France
Gascogne, Golfe de *see* Biscay, Bay of
Gascony *see* Gascogne
Gaspé, Péninsule de *171 var.* Péninsule de la Gaspésie. Peninsula of SE Canada
Gasteiz *see* Vitoria
Gat *see* Ghat
Gata *176* Boa Vista, E Cape Verde
Gata, Cape *215* cape of S Cyprus
Gatooma *see* Kadoma
Gatún, Lago *456* reservoir of C Panama
Gau *246 prev.* Ngau. Island to the E of Viti Levu, C Fiji
Gauhāti *see* Guwāhāti
Gauja *362 Ger.* Aa. River of N Latvia
Gaulette *224* E Dominica
Gauteng *527 prev.* Pretoria-Whitwatersrand-Vereeniging. Province of NE South Africa
Gävle *543* E Sweden
Gaya *439* SW Niger
Gaza *317, 318 Heb.* ‘Azza, *Ar.* Ghazzah. NE Gaza Strip
Gaz-Achak *581 Turkm.* Gazojak. NE Turkmenistan
Ghazāl, Baḩr al *see* Ghazal, Bahr el
Ghazal, Bahr el *536 var.* Baḩr al Ghazāl. River of S Sudan
Gazalkent *see* Ghazalkent
Gazandzhyk *581 var.* Kazandzhik, *Turkm.* Gazanjyk. W Turkmenistan
Gaza Strip *317, 318 Ar.* Qita Ghazzah. Disputed territory of SW Asia
Gaziantep *577 prev.* Aintab. S Turkey
Gazimağusa *215 var.* Famagusta *Gk* Ammochostos. E Cyprus
Gazimağusa Körfezi *see* Famagusta Bay
Gazli *610* S Uzbekistan
Gbangbatok *514* SW Sierra Leone
Gbarnga *368* C Liberia
Gbéroubouè *132 var.* Béroubouay. N Benin
Gdańsk *471 Ger.* Danzig. N Poland
Gdan'skaya Bukhta *see* Danzig, Gulf of
Gdańsk, Gulf of *see* Danzig, Gulf of
Gdańska, Zatoka *see* Danzig, Gulf of
Gdynia *471 Ger.* Gdingen. N Poland
Gêba *282* river of W Africa
Gêba, Canal do *282* canal of W Guinea-Bissau
Geçitkale *215 var.* Lefkoniko. NE Cyprus
Gedaref *536 var.* Al Qaḑārif, El Gedaref. E Sudan
Gedser *218* Falster, SE Denmark
Geel *127* NE Belgium
Geelong *101* SE Australia
Gege *540* SW Swaziland
Gefara *see* Jeffara Plain
Geghama Lernnashght'a *98 Rus.* Gegamskiy Khrebet. Mountain range of C Armenia
Geita *560* NW Tanzania
Gëkdepe *581 prev.* Geok-Tepe, *Turkm.* Gökdepe. SW Turkmenistan
Gela *321* Sicilia, S Italy
Gelang *see* Geylang
Geleen *429* S Netherlands
Gelib *see* Jilib
Gelsenkirchen *264* W Germany
Gemena *203* NW Dem. Rep. Congo (Zaire)
Genalē Wenz *see* Juba
Geneina *536 var.* Al Junaynah, Ajjinena. W Sudan
General Bernardo O'Higgins *90* Chilean research station of Antarctic Peninsula, Antarctica
General Carrera, Lago *see* Buenos Aires, Lago
General Eugenio A. Garay *460 var.* Fortín General Eugenio Garay, *prev.* Yrendagüé. NW Paraguay
General J.F. Uriburu *see* Zárate
General Machado *see* Camacupa
General Santos *466* Mindanao, S Philippines
Gênes *see* Genova
Geneva, Lake *253, 546 Fr.* Lac Léman, *var.* Le Léman, Lac de Genève, *Ger.* Genfer See. Lake of France and Switzerland
Genève *546 Eng.* Geneva, *Ger.* Genf, *It.* Ginevra. SW Switzerland
Genk *127 var.* Genck. NE Belgium
Gennargentu, Monti del *321* mountain of Sardegna, W Italy
Genova *320 Eng.* Genoa, *Fr.* Gênes. N Italy
Genova, Golfo di *320 Eng.* Gulf of Genoa. Gulf of the Ligurian Sea, on the W coast of Italy
Genovesa, Isla *228* island of N Galapagos Is, Ecuador
Genshū *see* Wŏnju
Gent *127 Eng.* Ghent, *Fr.* Gand. NW Belgium
Geokchay *see* Göyçay
Geok-Tepe *see* Gëkdepe
Georga, Zemlya *484 Eng.* George Land. Island of Zemlya Frantsa-Iosifa, N Russian Federation
George *527* Western Cape, S South Africa
George Island *645* island of S Falkland Islands
George, Lake *584* lake of SW Uganda
George Land *see* Zemlya Georga
Georgenburg *see* Jurbarkas
George Town *112* San Salvador, Bahamas
George Town *386 var.* Penang, Pinang. NW Peninsular Malaysia
George Town *644* ❖ of Cayman Islands, Grand Cayman, W Cayman Islands
Georgetown *652* ❖ of Ascension Island, W Ascension Island
Georgetown *261* E Gambia
Georgetown *284* ❖ of Guyana, NE Guyana
Georgetown *498* NE St Vincent & the Grenadines
Georgeville *130* W Belize
Georgia *599* state of SE USA
Georgia *262-263* officially Republic of Georgia, *Geor.* Sak'art'velo, *Rus.* Gruziya, *prev.* Georgian SSR, *Rus.* Gruzinskaya SSR. Country of E Europe divided into 65 admin units (raioni). ❖ Tbilisi
Georgi Dimitrov, Yazovir *152* reservoir of C Bulgaria
Georg von Neumayer *90* German research station of Greater Antarctica, Antarctica
Gera *265* C Germany
Geral de Goiás, Serra *145* mountain range of E Brazil
Geraldton *100* W Australia
Gereshk *77* SW Afghanistan
Gerlachovský Štít *519 var.* Gerlachovka, *Ger.* Gerlsdorfer Spitze. Peak of Slovakia
German Bight *264 Ger.* Deutsche Bucht, *Dut.* Duitse Bocht. Bay of the North Sea
German East Africa *see* Tanzania
German Southwest Africa *see* Namibia
German Ocean *see* North Sea
Germans Bay *649* bay of the Caribbean Sea on the SW coast of Montserrat
Germany *264-269* officially Federal Republic of Germany, *Ger.* Deutschland. Country of Western Europe divided into 16 admin. units (Länder). ❖ Berlin
Germering *265* S Germany
Germiston *527 var.* Pretoria-Witwatersrand-Vereeniging, NE South Africa
Gerona *see* Girona
Getafe *531* C Spain
Gevgelija *381 var.* Đevđelija, Djevdjelija, *Turk.* Gevgeli. SE FYR Macedonia
Geylang *517 var.* Gelang. River of SE Singapore
Geylegphug *134* S Bhutan
Ghadāmis *371 var.* Rhadames. NW Libya
Ghana *270-371* officially Republic of Ghana. Country of W. Africa divided into 10 admin. units (regions). ❖ Accra
Ghanongga *see* Ranongga
Ghanzi *142* W Botswana
Ghap'an *see* Kapan
Gharbi, Île *573 Ar.* Jazirat al Gharbi. Island of E Tunisia
Ghardaïa *83* N Algeria
Gharm *558 Rus.* Garm. C Tajikistan
Gharsa, Chott el *573 var.* Shaţţ al Gharsah. Salt lake of W Tunisia
Gharyān *371* NW Libya
Ghāt *371 var.* Gat. W Libya
Ghawdex *see* Gozo
Ghawdex, Il-Fliegu ta' *395 Eng.* North Comino Channel. Strait of Mediterranean Sea between Gozo and Kemmuna, NW Malta
Ghayathi *590* W United Arab Emirates
Ghazal *180 var.* Soro. Seasonal river of C Chad
Ghazalkent *610 Rus.* Gazalkent. E Uzbekistan
Ghaznī *77* E Afghanistan
Ghazzah *see* Gaza
Ghelîzâne *see* Relizane
Ghent *see* Gent
Gherra, Sebkhet el *573* salt flat of NE Tunisia
Ghijduwon *610 Rus.* Gizhduvan. S Uzbekistan
Ghilizane *see* Relizane
Ghimbi *see* Gīmbī
Ghochas *see* Gochas
Ghûdara *558 var.* Gudara, *Rus.* Kudara. E Tajikistan
Ghukasyan *see* Ashots'k
Ghūriān *77* W Afghanistan
Ghuwayfāt *590 var.* Gheweifat. W United Arab Emirates
Giahel, Uadi *see* Jaceel
Giamame *see* Jamaame
Giants Castle *527* mountain of Lesotho and South Africa.
Gibeon *423* S Namibia
Gibraltar *531, 646* British Crown Colony, to the S of Spain
Gibraltar, Bay of *646 var.* Bahía de Algeciras. Bay of the Atlantic Ocean on the W coast of Gibraltar
Gibraltar Harbour *646* W Gibraltar
Gibraltar, Strait of *414, 531, 646 Sp.* Estrecho de Gibraltar. Strait connecting the Atlantic Ocean and Mediterranean Sea, between Gibraltar and Morocco
Gibson Desert *100-101* desert of W Australia
Gifu *330* Honshū, C Japan
Giggiga *see* Jijiga
Gihanga *162* NW Burundi
Gijón *531 var.* Xixón. NW Spain
Gikongoro *492* SW Rwanda
Gilbert Islands *346* island group of W Kiribati
Gilf Kebir Plateau *230 Ar.* Haḑabat al Jilf al Kabīr. Plateau of SW Egypt
Gilgit *451* river of N Pakistan
Gilolo *see* Halmahera
Gīmbī *243 It.* Ghimbi. W Ethiopia
Gimie, Mount *497* mountain of C St Lucia
Gimma *see* Jīma
Ginda *238* C Eritrea
Ginevra *see* Genève
Ginger Island *643* island of SE British Virgin Islands
Giohar *see* Jawhar
Giran *see* Ilan
Girardot *195* C Colombia
Giraudel *224* S Dominica
Girba, Khashm el *536 var.* Khashm al Qirbah, Khashim Al Qirba. E Sudan
Girgenti *see* Agrigento
Girne *215 var.* Keryneia, Kyrenia. N Cyprus
Girón *195* N Colombia
Girona *531 var.* Gerona. E Spain
Girsun *577* NE Turkey
Gisagara *492* S Rwanda
Gisborne *433* E North Island, New Zealand
Giseifu *see* Ŭijŏngbu
Gisenyi *492 var.* Gisenye.NW Rwanda
Gishyita *492* W Rwanda
Gissar *see* Hisor
Gissar Range *558, 610 Rus.* Gissarskiy Khrebet. Mountains of Tajikistan and Uzbekistan
Gissarskiy Khrebet *see* Gissar Range
Gisuru *162 prev.* Kisuru. E Burundi
Gitarama *492* C Rwanda
Gitega *162 prev.* Kitega. C Burundi
Giteranyi *162* NW Burundi
Giulie, Alpi *see* Julian Alps
Giurgiu *480* S Romania
Give *218* Jylland, W Denmark
Giyon *243 var.* Wehso. C Ethiopia
Gîza *see* El Gîza
Gizhduvan *see* Ghijduwon
Gizo *522* New Georgia Is, Solomon Is
Gjakovë *see* Đakovica
Gjirokastër *81 var.* Gjirokastra, *prev.* Gjinokastër, Gjinokastra, *It.* Argirocastro, *Gk* Argyrokastron. S Albania
Gjoa Haven *170* King William Island, N Canada
Gjøvik *444* S Norway
Gkreko, Cape *see* Greco, Cape
Glåma *see* Glomma
Glanvilles *92* E Antigua, Antigua & Barbuda
Glanvillia *224* NW Dominica
Glasgow *593* W Scotland, UK
Glazoué *132* S Benin
Glendale *636* NE Zimbabwe
Glenties *314* N Ireland
Glina *209* NE Croatia
Glittertind *444 var.* Glittertinden. Mountain of S Norway
Gliwice *471 Ger.* Gleiwitz. S Poland
Głogów *471 Ger.* Glogau. W Poland
Glomma *444 var.* Glommen, Glåma. River of S Norway
Gloucester *593* C England, UK
Glover Island *276 var.* Ramier I. Island to the S of Grenada island, Grenada
Glubokoye *see* Hlybokaye
Gmünd *106* N Austria
Gmundner See *see* Traunsee
Gnaviyani Atoll *see* Fuammulah

Goascorán *235* river of El Salvador and Honduras
Goascorán *288* river of SW Honduras
Goat Island *92* island to the N of Barbuda, Antigua & Barbuda
Goba *243 var.* Gobba. S Ethiopia
Gobabis *423* E Namibia
Gobi *187, 412* desert of China and Mongolia
Goce Delčev *see* Gorna Oryakhovitsa
Gochas *423 var.* Ghochas. SE Namibia
Go Công *623* S Vietnam
Godāveri *296* river of C India
Godhavn *646 var.* Qeqertarsuaq, W Greenland
Göding *see* Hodonín
Gödöllő *290* N Hungary
Godoy Cruz *95* W Argentina
Godthåb *see* Nuuk
Godwin Austen, Mount *see* K2
Goedgegun *see* Nhlangano
Goelette, Passe a la *652* channel of the Atlantic Ocean, to the E of Miquelon, Saint Pierre and Miquelon
Goeree *429* island of SW Netherlands
Goes *429* SW Netherlands
Goettingen *see* Göttingen
Gogounou *132* N Benin
Goiânia *145 prev.* Goyania. S Brazil
Gökdepe *see* Gëkdepe
Gokwe *636* NW Zimbabwe
Gol *444* S Norway
Golan Heights *317* disputed territory of SW Syria
Gold Coast *101* coastal region of E Australia
Gold Coast *270* coastal region of W Africa
Golden Bay *433* bay on the coast of N South Island, New Zealand
Golden Valley *636* N Zimbabwe
Goldingen *see* Kuldīga
Golfito *206* SE Costa Rica
Gollel *see* Lavumisa
Golmud *186 var.* Golmo, *Chin.* Ko-erh-mu. Qinghai, W China
Golungo Alto *88* NW Angola
Goma *203* NE Dem. Rep. Congo (Zaire)
Gombe *440* E Nigeria
Gomel' *see* Homyel'
Gomera *531* island of Islas Canarias, SW Spain
Gómez Palacio *403* NW Mexico
Gonaïves *286* W Haiti
Gonâve, Canal de la *286 var.* Canal de Sud. Channel of the Caribbean Sea between Île de la Gonâve and Haiti
Gonâve, Golfe de la *286* gulf of the Caribbean Sea to the W of Haiti
Gonâve, Île de la *286* island of W Haiti
Gonder *243 var.* Gondar. NW Ethiopia
Gondomar *474* NW Portugal
Goodenough Island *458 var.* Morata. Island of SE Papua New Guinea
Good Hope *224* E Dominica
Good Hope, Cape of *527* *Afr.* Kaap die Gooie Hoop. Coastal feature of SW South Africa
Goodlands *400* NE Mauritius
Goose Bay *see* Happy Valley-Goose Bay
Goose Green *645* East Falkland, C Falkland Islands
Gopālpur *117* N Bangladesh
Gorakhpur *296* NE India
Gorce Island *510* island of W Senegal
Gore *433* S South Island,New Zealand
Goré *180* S Chad
Gorē *243* W Ethiopia
Gorey *648* E Jersey
Gorgān *307 var.* Gurgan. N Iran
Gori *262* C Georgia
Goris *98* SE Armenia
Gorki *see* Horki
Gor'kiy *see* Nizhniy Novgorod
Görlitz *265* E Germany
Gorlovka *see* Horlivka
Gorna Dzhumaya *see* Blagoevgrad
Gorna Oryakhovitsa *152* *var.* Gorna Orjahovica. N Bulgaria
Gornji Milanovac *630* C Serbia, Yugoslavia
Gorno Altaysk *485* S Russian Federation
Goroka *458* C Papua New Guinea
Gorontalo, Teluk *see* Tomini, Teluk
Gorzów Wielkopolski *471* *Ger.* Landsberg. W Poland
Gosford *101* E Australia
Goshogawara *330* Honshū, N Japan
Gospić *209* C Croatia
Gostivar *381* W FYR Macedonia
Göteborg *543 Eng.* Gothenburg. SW Sweden
Gotland *543* island of SE Sweden
Gotō-rettō *330* island group to the W of Kyūshū, SW Japan
Gotse-Delchev *152 var.* Goce Delčev. SW Bulgaria
Gottardo, San Passo del *546* *Eng.* St. Gotthard Pass. Mountain pass of S Switzerland
Göttingen *265 var.* Goettingen. C Germany
Gottschee *see* Kočevje
Gottwaldov *see* Zlín
Goubétto *222* SE Djibouti
Gouda *429* SW Netherlands
Goulburn *101* SE Australia
Goundam *392* NW Mali
Gourcy *157* NW Burkina
Gouré *439* SE Niger
Gourma *157* cultural region of E Burkina
Gouyave *276 var.* Charlotte Town. W Grenada island, Grenada
Goverla, Gora *see* Hoverla
Governador Valadares *145* SE Brazil
Governor's Harbour *112* Eleuthera Island, Bahamas
Govurdak *581 prev.* Guardak, *Turkm.* Gowurdak. SE Turkmenistan
Goya *95* NE Argentina
Goyania *see* Goiânia
Göyçay *110 Rus.* Geokchay. C Azerbaijan
Goz-Beïda *180* SE Chad
Gozo *395 var.* Għawdex. Island of NW Malta
Graaff-Reinet *527* Eastern Cape, S South Africa
Gračanica *140* NE Bosnia & Herzegovina
Gracias *288* W Honduras
Graciosa *474 var.* Ilha Graciosa. Island of the Azores, Portugal
Gradačac *140* N Bosnia & Herzegovina
Gradaús, Serra dos *145* mountain range of C Brazil
Gradsko *381* C FYR Macedonia
Grafton *101* E Australia
Graham Bell Island *see* Greem Bell, Ostrov
Grain Coast *368* coastal region of Liberia
Grampian Mountains *593* mountain range of C Scotland, UK
Gramsh *81 var.* Gramshi. C Albania
Gran *see* Hron
Gran *see* Esztergom
Gran *538* river of C Suriname
Granada *436* S Nicaragua
Granada *531* S Spain
Gran Canaria *531 Eng.* Grand Canary. Island of Islas Canarias, SW Spain
Gran Chaco *95, 136, 460 var.* Chaco. Lowland plain of C South America
Grand Anse *276* SW Grenada island, Grenada
Grand'Anse *512* Praslin, Seychelles
Grand Bahama Island *112* island of N Bahamas
Grand Baie *400 var.* Grande Baie. NW Mauritius
Grand Barachois *652* inlet of the Atlantic Ocean on the coast of Miquelon, N Saint Pierre and Miquelon
Grand Bassa *see* Buchanan
Grand-Bassam *326 var.* Bassam. SE Ivory Coast
Grand Bay *276* E Carriacou, Grenada
Grand Bourg *646* Marie-Galante, S Guadeloupe
Grand Caicos *653 var.* Middle Caicos. Island of N Turks and Caicos Islands
Grand Canary *see* Gran Canaria
Grand Canyon *598* canyon of SW USA
Grand Cayman *644* island of W Cayman Islands
Grand Cess *368* SE Liberia
Grand Colombier *652* island of SE Saint Pierre and Miquelon
Grand Cul-de-Sac Marin *646* bay of the Caribbean Sea, N Guadeloupe
Grande-Anse *see* Portsmouth
Grande, Bahía *95* bay of the Atlantic Ocean, to the SE of Argentina
Grande Comore *198 var.* Njazidja. Island of Comoros
Grande, Cuchilla *607* mountain range of E Uruguay
Grande de Buba, Rio *282* river of S Guinea-Bissau
Grande de Chiloé, Isla *see* Chiloé, Isla de
Grande de Gurupá, Ilha *145* island of N Brazil
Grande de Matagalpa, Río *436* river of C Nicaragua
Grande de Santiago, Río *403* *var.* Santiago. River of SW Mexico
Grande de Tárcoles, Río *206* river of C Costa Rica
Grande de Térraba, Río *206* river of SE Costa Rica
Grande Prairie *170* W Canada
Grand Erg Occidental *83* desert region of W Algeria
Grand Erg Oriental *83, 573* desert region of Algeria and Tunisia
Grande, Río *403, 598-599 Sp.* Bravo Del Norte. River of Mexico and USA
Grande Rivière *497* N St Lucia
Grande Rivière *497* C St Lucia
Grande-Rivière-du-Nord *286* N Haiti
Grande Rivière, La *171* *var.* Fort George River. River of SE Canada
Grande-Saline *286* W Haiti
Grande-Santi *645* W French Guiana
Grande Terre *512* island of the Aldabra Group, SW Seychelles
Grande Vigie, Pointe de la *646* headland of N Guadeloupe
Grand Falls *342* waterfall of C Kenya
Grand Forks *599* North Dakota, NC USA
Grand Goâve *286* S Haiti
Grand Harbour *395* port of Valletta, E Malta
Grand Ilet *646* bay of the Caribbean Sea, S Guadeloupe
Grand Island *599* Nebraska, C USA
Grand Junction *598* Colorado, SW USA
Grand Lac de l'Ours *see* Great Bear Lake
Grand Lac des Esclaves *see* Great Slave Lake
Grand Montagne *400* Rodrigues, Mauritius
Grand Paradis *see* Gran Paradiso
Grand-Popo *132* S Benin
Grand Rapids *599* Michigan, NC USA
Grand Récif Sud *650* reef of the Pacific Ocean, S New Caledonia
Grand River South East *400* river of E Mauritius
Grand 'Rivière *649* N Martinique
Grand Roy *276* W Grenada island, Grenada
Grand Turk Island *653* island of SE Turks and Caicos Islands
Granges *see* Grenchen
Gran Lago *see* Nicaragua, Lago de
Gran Paradiso *320 Fr.* Grand Paradis. Mountain of NW Italy
Gran San Bernardo, Passo di *see* Great St Bernard Pass
Grape Bay *643* bay of the North Atlantic Ocean, E Bermuda
Grassy Bay *643* bay of the North Atlantic Ocean, W Bermuda
Gråsten *218* Jylland, SW Denmark
Graudenz *see* Grudziądz
Grau Roig *86* E Andorra
Graz *106* SE Austria
Great Abaco *112* island of N Bahamas
Great Admiralty Island *see* Manus Island
Great Ararat *see* Büyükağrı Dağı
Great Artesian Basin *101* lowlands of C Australia
Great Australian Bight *101* large bay of the Indian Ocean, S Australia
Great Barrier Island *433* island to the NE of North Island, New Zealand
Great Barrier Reef *101, 458* coral reef to the NE of Australia, and the largest in the world
Great Basin *598* physical region of W USA
Great Bear Lake *170* *Fr.* Grand Lac de l'Ours. Lake of NW Canada
Great Belt *see* Storebælt
Great Camanoe *643* island of N British Virgin Islands
Great Chagos Bank *643* undersea feature of the Indian Ocean, C British Indian Ocean Territory
Great Coco Island *159* island of SW Burma
Great Dividing Range *101* mountain range of E Australia
Greater Antarctica *90* physical region of Antarctica
Greater Caucasus *110* *Rus.* Bol'shoy Kavkaz. Mountain range of SW Asia and SE Europe
Great Exhibition Bay *433* inlet of the Pacific Ocean, on the NE coast of North Island, New Zealand
Great Exuma Island *112* island of C Bahamas
Great Falls *598* Montana, NW USA
Great Fish *see* Groot-Vis
Great Harbour *643* Jost Van Dyke, W British Virgin Islands
Great Hungarian Plain *see* Alföld
Great Inagua *112* island of S Bahamas
Great Indian Desert *see* Thar Desert
Great Karoo *527 var.* Great Karroo, *Afr.* Groot Karoo. Plateau region of S South Africa
Great Khingan Range *see* Da Hinggan Ling
Great Lake *see* Tônlé Sap
Great Lakes, the *602 see* also Erie, Huron, Michigan, Ontario, Superior
Great Mercury Island *433* island to the NE of North Island, New Zealand
Great Nicobar *296* island of Nicobar Islands, to the SE of India
Great Ouse *593 var.* Ouse. River of E England, UK
Great Plains *599* plains of Canada and USA
Great Rift Valley *243, 342, 385, 560* *var.* Rift Valley. Depression of E Africa and SW Asia
Great Ruaha *560* river of C Tanzania
Great Saint Bernard Pass *546* *Fr.* Col du Grand-Saint-Bernard, *It.* Passo di Gran San Bernardo. Mountain pass of SW Switzerland
Great Salt Lake *598* salt lake of SW USA
Great Salt Pond *494* SE St Kitts, St Kitts & Nevis
Great Sand Sea. *230, 371* desert of Egypt and Libya
Great Sandy Desert *100* desert region of W Australia
Great Sandy Desert *see* Rub 'al Khali
Great Sandy Island *see* Fraser Island
Great Slave Lake *170* *Fr.* Grand Lac des Esclaves. Lake of W Canada
Great Sound *643* bay of W Bermuda
Great Thatch *643* island of W British Virgin Islands
Great Tobago *643* island of W British Virgin Islands
Great Usutu *see* Lusutfu
Great Victoria Desert *100 -101* desert region of S Australia
Great Wall *90* Chinese research station of South Shetland Islands, Antarctica

Great Zab *310* *Ar.* Az Zāb Al Kabīr, *Turk.* Büyükzap Suyu, *Kurd.* Zē-i Bādīnān. River of Iraq and Turkey
Greco, Cape *215* *var.* Cape Gkreko. Cape of E Cyprus
Greece *272-275* officially Hellenic Republic, *Gk* Ellás. Country of SE Europe divided into 51 admin. units (nomos). ❖ Athens
Greeley *599* Colorado, SW USA
Greem Bell, Ostrov *485* *Eng.* Graham Bell Island. Island of Zemlya Frantsa-Iosifa, N Russian Federation
Green Bay *599* Wisconsin, NC USA
Green Island *92* island to the E of Antigua, Antigua & Barbuda
Green Island *276* island to the N of Grenada island, Grenada
Green Islands *458* *var.* Nissan Is. Island group of E Papua New Guinea
Greenland *646* *var.* Grønland. Self governing territory of Denmark, North Atlantic Ocean. ❖ Nuuk.
Greenland Sea *646* sea of the Arctic Ocean, NE Greenland
Green Mountain *652* mountain of C Ascension Island
Greenock *593* W Scotland, UK
Greensboro *599* North Carolina, SE USA
Greenville *368* *var.* Sino, Sinoe. SE Liberia
Greenville *599* Mississippi, SE USA
Greenville *599* South Carolina, SE USA
Greifswald *265* NE Germany
Grenå *218* NJylland, Denmark
Grenada *276* island which, with the southern Grenadines, comprises the independent state of Grenada
Grenada *276-277* island state of the West Indies, comprising of Grenada island and the southern Grenadine islands to the north. Divided into 6 admin. units (parishes). ❖ St George's
Grenadines *276, 498* group of over 500 small islands between Grenada and St Vincent in the Caribbean Sea. The southern islands are administered by Grenada, while the northern islands form, with St Vincent, the independent state of St Vincent the Grenadines
Grenchen *546* *Fr.* Granges. NW Switzerland
Grenoble *253* E France
Grenville *276* E Grenada island, Grenada
Grevelingen *429* inlet of the North Sea, on the coast of SW Netherlands
Grevenmacher *378* E Luxembourg
Greymouth *433* W South Island, New Zealand
Grey Range *101* mountain range of E Australia
Gribingui *see* Nana-Grébizi
Griffith *101* SE Australia
Grijalva *403* *var.* Tabasco. River of SE Mexico
Grimari *179* C Central African Republic
Grimbergen *127* C Belgium
Grimsby *593* NE England, UK
Grímsey Island *294* *var.* Grimsey. Island of N Iceland
Grímsstadhir *294* E Iceland
Grindavík *294* W Iceland
Grindsted *218* Jylland, W Denmark
Grise Fiord *170* *var.* Ausuitoq. Ellesmere Island, N Canada
Grmeč *140* mountain range of NW Bosnia & Herzegovina
Grobiņa *362* W Latvia
Grodno *see* Hrodna
Groningen *429* NE Netherlands
Groningen *538* N Suriname
Groote Eylandt *101* island of N Australia
Grootfontein *423* N Namibia
Groot Karoo *see* Great Karoo
Groot-Vis *527* *Eng.* Great Fish. River of S South Africa
Grootvloer *527* salt flat of Northern Cape, W South Africa
Gros Islet *497* N St Lucia
Gros-Morne *286* N Haiti
Gros Piton *497* mountain of SW St Lucia
Grossbetschkerek *see* Zrenjanin
Grosseto *320* NW Italy
Grossglockner *106* mountain of W Austria
Grosskanizsa *see* Nagykanizsa
Grossmichel *see* Michalovce
Gross-Sankt-Johannis *see* Suure-Jaani
Gross-Steffelsdorf *see* Rimavská Sobota
Grosswardein *see* Oradea
Groznyy *484* SW Russian Federation
Grudziądz *471* *Ger.* Graudenz. N Poland
Grünau *423* S Namibia
Grünberg in Schlesien *see* Zielona Góra
Gruziya *see* Georgia
Guabalá *456* SW Panama
Guacanayabo, Golfo de *210* gulf of the Caribbean Sea, on the S coast of Cuba
Guácimo *206* NE Costa Rica
Guadalajara *403* SW Mexico
Guadalcanal *522* island of C Solomon Is
Guadalquivir *530-531* river of W Spain
Guadalupe *456* C Panama
Guadalupe *see* Canelones
Guadeloupe *646* French overseas department of the Caribbean Sea. ❖ Basse-Terre
Guadeloupe Passage *92, 224* passage connecting the Atlantic Ocean and Caribbean Sea between Guadeloupe and Dominica
Guadiana *474, 530-531* river of Portugal and Spain
Guaico *570* NE Trinidad, Trinidad & Tobago
Guáimero *210* S Cuba
Gualaco *288* C Honduras
Gualán *278* C Guatemala
Gualdicciolo *502* NW San Marino
Gualeguaychú *95* E Argentina
Guam *647* unincorporated territory of the USA, Pacific Ocean. ❖ Hagåtña
Guanabacoa *210* NW Cuba
Guanabo *210* NW Cuba
Guana Island *643* island of N British Virgin Islands
Guanaja *288* Islas de la Bahía, Honduras
Guanajay *210* NW Cuba
Guanajuato *403* C Mexico
Guanare *619* NW Venezuela
Guanare *619* river of W Venezuela
Guangdong *187* *var.* Kwangtung, Kuang-tung. Province of SE China
Guangju *see* Kwangju
Guangxi *187* *Chin.* Guangxi Zhuangzu Zizhiqu, *Eng.* Kwangsi Chuang Autonomous Region, *var.* Kuang-hsi. Autonomous region of S China
Guangyuan *187* *var.* Kuang-yuan, Kwangyuan. Sichuan, SW China
Guangzhou *187* *var.* Kwangchow, Kuang-chou, *Eng.* Canton. Guangdong, SE China
Guantánamo *211* SE Cuba
Guantanamo Bay *211* US military base, E Cuba
Guaporé *136, 144* *var.* Iténez. River of Bolivia and Brazil
Guaranda *228* C Ecuador
Guardafui, Cape *see* Caseyr, Raas
Guardak *see* Govurdak
Guárico *619* river of C Venezuela
Guasave *403* W Mexico
Guastatoya *see* El Progreso
Guatemala *278-279* officially Republic of Guatemala. Country of Central America divided into 22 admin. units (departments). ❖ Guatemala City
Guatemala City *278* *Sp.* Ciudad de Guatemala. ❖ of Guatemala, C Guatemala
Guaviare *195* river of E Colombia
Guayama *651* SE Puerto Rico
Guayaquil *228* *var.* Santiago de Guayaquil. SW Ecuador
Guayaquil, Gulf of *228, 463* gulf of the Pacific Ocean to the W of Ecuador and Peru
Guayaramerín *136* N Bolivia
Guayuabo *651* N Puerto Rico
Gudara *see* Ghŭdara
Gudenå *218* river of Jylland, NW Denmark
Guékédou *281* *var.* Guéckédou. S Guinea
Guélîlé *222* S Djibouti
Guelma *83* *var.* Gâlma. NE Algeria
Guelta Zemmur *414* E Western Sahara
Guéné *132* NE Benin
Güera *see* Guérou
Guéret *253* C France
Guerguerat *414* SW Western Sahara
Guérin-Kouka *567* NW Togo
Guernsey *252, 647* *var.* Bailiwick of Guernsey. British Crown dependency, Channel Islands, English Channel. ❖ St Peter Port.
Guérou *398* *var.* Güera. S Mauritania
Guesneau *497* N St Lucia
Guguan *650* island of C Northern Mariana Islands
Guiana Highlands *144-145, 284, 145, 284, 619* *Port.* Planalto das Guianas. Mountain range of N South America
Guiana Island *92* island to the NE of Antigua, Antigua & Barbuda
Guiba *see* Juba
Guichón *607* NW Uruguay
Guider *168* *var.* Guidder. N Cameroon
Guidimouni *439* S Niger
Guier, Lac de *510* *var.* Lac de Guiers. Lake of N Senegal
Guietsou *258* SW Gabon
Guiglo *326* W Ivory Coast
Güigüe *619* N Venezuela
Güija, Lago de *235* lake of El Salvador and Guatemala
Guillet *224* NW Dominica
Guimarães *474* N Portugal
Guinea *280-281* officially Republic of Guinea, *prev.* People's Revolutionary Republic of Guinea. Country of West Africa divided into 4 admin. units (regions). ❖ Conakry
Guinea-Bissau *282-283* officially Republic of Guinea-Bissau, *Port.* Guiné-Bissau. Independent state of West Africa divided into 8 admin. units (regions). ❖ Bissau
Guinea, Gulf of *168, 236, 270, 326* *Fr.* Golfe de Guinée. Gulf of the Atlantic Ocean, on the W coast of Africa
Guinguinéo *510* W Senegal
Güiria *619* NE Venezuela
Guiyang *187* *var.* Kuei-Yang, Kweiyang. Guizhou, S China
Guizhou *187* *var.* Kweichow, Kuei-chou. Province of S China
Gujrānwāla *451* NE Pakistan
Gujrāt *451* NE Pakistan
Gukasyan *see* Ashots'k
Gulariya *427* *var.* Gularia. W Nepal
Gulbene *362* *Ger.* Alt-Schwanenburg. NE Latvia
Gul'cha *357* *var.* Gul'ča, *Kir.* Gülchö. SW Kyrgyzstan
Gülchö *see* Gul'cha
Gulf, The *115, 310, 354, 479, 506* *var.* Persian Gulf, *Ar.* Khalīj al 'Arabī, *Per.* Khalīj-e Fars. Gulf of the Arabian Sea between the Arabian Peninsula and Iran
Guliston *610* *Rus.* Gulistan. E Uzbekistan
Gulja *see* Yining
Gulu *584* N Uganda
Gum *see* Gamgadhi
Gumal *451* river of Afghanistan and Pakistan
Gumdag *581* *prev.* Kum-Dag. W Turkmenistan
Gümülcine *see* Komotiní
Gümüljina *see* Komotiní
Gümüşhane *577* NE Turkey
Gund *558* *Rus.* Gunt. River of S Tajikistan
Güneydoğu Toroslar *577* mountain range of SE Turkey
Gunjur *261* W Gambia
Gunner's Quoin *400* *var.* Coin de Mire. Island of N Mauritius
Gunsan *see* Kunsan
Guntūr *296* SE India
Gunzan *see* Kunsan
Gurgan *see* Gorgān
Guri, Embalse de *619* reservoir of E Venezuela
Gurjaani *262* *Rus.* Gurdzhaani. E Georgia
Gurk *106* river of S Austria
Gurkfeld *see* Krško
Gurktaler Alpen *106* mountain range of S Austria
Gur'yev *see* Atyrau
Gusau *440* N Nigeria
Gushgy *581* *prev.* Kushka. S Turkmenistan
Gustavia *646* St. Barthélémy, N Guadeloupe
Gutenstein *see* Ravne na Koroškem
Gutland *378* physical region of S Luxembourg
Guwāhāti *297* *prev.* Gauhāti. NE India
Guyana *284-285* officially Co-operative Republic of Guyana, *prev.* British Guiana. Country of Central America divided into 10 admin. units (regions). ❖ Georgetown
Guyane *see* French Guiana
Güzelyurt *215* *var.* Morfou, Morphou. W Cyprus
Güzelyurt Körfezi *see* Morphou Bay
Gwādar *450* SW Pakistan
Gwalior *296* N India
Gwanda *636* SW Zimbabwe
Gwayi *636* river of W Zimbabwe
Gweru *636* *prev.* Gwelo. C Zimbabwe
Gwy *see* Wye
Gyandzha *see* Gäncä
Gydanskiy Poluostrov *484* *Eng.* Gyda Peninsula. Peninsula of N Russian Federation
Gympie *101* E Australia
Gyöngyös *290* NE Hungary
Győr *290* *Ger.* Raab. NW Hungary
Gyula *290* SE Hungary
Gyulafehérvár *see* Alba Iulia
Gyumri *98* *Rus.* Kumayri, *prev.* Leninakan, Aleksandropol'. W Armenia
Gyzylarbat *581* *prev.* Kizyl-Arvat. W Turkmenistan
Gyzylgaya *see* Kizyl-Kaya
Ġzira *395* N Malta

H

Ha *134* W Bhutan
Ha'ano *568* island of the Ha'apai Group, Tonga
Ha'apai Group *568* *var.* Haabai. Island group of C Tonga
Haapsalu *240* *Ger.* Hapsal. W Estonia
Haarlem *429* W Netherlands
Hab *451* river of S Pakistan
Habarana *534* C Sri Lanka
Ḩabbānīyah, Buḩhayrat al *310* *var.* Hawr al Ḩabbānīyah. Lake of C Iraq
Habiganj *117* NE Bangladesh
Habomai Islands *331* disputed island group of SE Russian Federation
Ḩabshān *590* SW United Arab Emirates
Hachijō-jima *330* island to the SE of Honshū, SE Japan
Hachinohe *330* Honshū, N Japan
Hačmas *see* Xaçmaz
Hadama *see* Nazrēt
Ḩadd al Jamal *115* *var.* Ra's al Yaman. Cape of E Bahrain
Haddummati Atoll *see* Hadhdhunmathi Atoll
Hadejia *440* N Nigeria

Hadejia *440* river of N Nigeria
Hadera *317* C Israel
Haderslev *218* *Ger.* Hadersleben. Jylland, SW Denmark
Hadhdhunmathi Atoll *390* *var.* Haddummati Atoll, Laamu Atoll. Atoll of S Maldives
Hadhramaut *see* Ḩaḑramawt
Hadíboh *627* NE Suqutra, Yemen
Ha Đông *623* N Vietnam
Ḩaḑramawt *627* *Eng.* Hadhramaut. Mountain range of S Yemen
Haedo, Cuchilla de *607* mountain range of NW Uruguay
Haeju *349* S North Korea
Ha-erh-pin *see* Harbin
Ḩafar al Bāţin *506* N Saudi Arabia
Hafnarfjördhur *294* W Iceland
Hafnarhreppur *294* S Iceland
Hafren *see* Severn
Hagar Nish Plateau *238* plateau of N Eritrea
Hagåtña *647* *var.* Agaña. ❖ of Guam, NW Guam
Hagen *264* W Germany
Hägere Hiywet *243* *var.* Agere Hiywet, Ambo. C Ethiopia
Hagi *330* Honshū, SW Japan
Ha Giang *623* NW Vietnam
Hago, Lac *492* lake of NE Rwanda
Hague, The *see* 's-Gravenhage
Haibak *see* Āybak
Haidarabad *see* Hyderābād
Hai Dương *623* N Vietnam
Haifa, Bay of *see* Mifraz Hefa
Haikou *187* *var.* Hoihow. Hainan, S China
Ḩā'il *506* N Saudi Arabia
Hailuoto *249* *Swe.* Karlö. Island of W Finland
Hainan *187* province of S China
Hainan Dao *187* island of S China
Hai Phong *623* *var.* Haiphong. N Vietnam
Haiti *286-287* officially Republic of Haiti. Country of the West Indies divided into 9 admin. units (departments). ❖ Port-au-Prince
Hajdarken *see* Khaydarkan
Hajdúböszörmény *290* NE Hungary
Ḩājī Ebrāhīm, Kūh-e *310* mountain of Iran and Iraq
Ḩajjah *627* W Yemen
Hakodate *330* Hokkaidō, N Japan
Hakupu *650* E Niue
Ḩalab *551* *Eng.* Aleppo, *Fr.* Alep. NW Syria
Ḩalabja *310* NE Iraq
Ḩalānīyāt, Juzur al *448* *var.* Jazā'iBin Ghalfān, Jazā'ir Khurīyā Murīyā, *Eng.* Kuria Maria Islands. Island group of S Oman
Ḩalānīyāt, Khalīj al *448* *Eng.* Kuria Mur Bay. Bay of the Arabian Sea, S Oman
Halas *see* Kiskunhalas
Haldefjäll *see* Haltiatunturi
Halden *444* *prev.* Fredrikshald. S Norway
Halditjåkko *see* Haltiatunturi
Halfa el Gadida *536* *var.* New Halfa, Halfa Al Jadida. E Sudan
Halfmoon Bay *433* Stewart Island, SW New Zealand
Half Tree Hollow *652* N St Helena
Halifax *171* SE Canada
Halīl Rūd *307* river of SE Iran
Halla-san *350* *Jap.* Kanra-san. Mountain of Cheju-do, S South Korea
Halle *265* C Germany
Hallein *106* N Austria
Halley *90* UK research station of Greater Antarctica, Antarctica
Hall Islands *406* island group of C Micronesia
Hall Peninsula *171* peninsula of Baffin Island, NE Canada
Halls Creek *101* NW Australia
Halmahera *302* *prev.* Djailolo, Jailolo, Gilolo. Island of Maluku, E Indonesia
Halmahera, Laut *302* sea of the Pacific Ocean, E Indonesia
Halmstad *543* SW Sweden
Ḩalq al Wādī *see* La Goulette
Hälsingborg *see* Helsingborg
Haltiatunturi *249* *Swe.* Haldefjäll, *prev.* Halditjåkko, *Nor.* Reisduoddarhalde. Mountain of Finland and Norway
Ḩamad *see* Madīnat Ḩamad
Hamada *330* Honshū, W Japan
Hamadān *307* NW Iran
Hamada Town *see* Madīnat Ḩamad
Ḩamāh *551* W Syria
Hamamatsu *330* Honshū, C Japan
Hamar *444* S Norway
Hambantota *534* SE Sri Lanka
Hamburg *265* N Germany
Ḩamḑ, Wādī al *506* dry watercourse of W Saudi Arabia
Hämeenlinna *249* *Swe.* Tavastehus. SW Finland
Hamersley Range *100* mountain range to the W of Australia
Hamgyŏng-sanmaek *349* mountain range of N North Korea
Hamhŭng *349* C North Korea
Hami *186* *Uigh.* Kumul, *var.* Qomul. Xinjiang Uygur Zizhiqu. NW China
Hamilton *643* ❖ Bermuda, C Bermuda
Hamilton *171* S Canada
Hamilton *433* C North Island, New Zealand
Hamilton *593* C Scotland, UK
Ḩamīm, Wādī al *371* dry watercourse of NE Libya
Hamm *264* W Germany
Hammamet *573* *var.* Ḩammāmāt. N Tunisia
Hammamet, Golfe de *573* gulf of the Mediterranean Sea to the E of Tunisia
Hammam Lif *573* *var.* Ḩammām al Anf. N Tunisia
Ḩammār, Hawr al *310* lake of SE Iraq
Hammerfest *444* NE Norway
Ḩamrīn, Jabal *310* mountain range of N Iraq
Hamriya *see* Al Ḩamrīyah
Hamrun *395* C Malta
Hāmūn, Daryācheh-ye *see* Sīstān, Daryācheh-ye
Han *350* *Jap.* Kan-kō. River of N South Korea
Hanábana *210* river of C Cuba
Hânceşti *see* Hînceşti
Handan *187* *var.* Han-tan. Hebei, NE China
Handeni *560* E Tanzania
Handréma, Baie de *649* *var.* Mandréma Bay. Bay of the Indian Ocean on the N coast of Mayotte
HaNegev *317* *Eng.* Negev. Desert of S Israel
Hanga Roa *183* Easter I, W Chile
Hangayn Nuruu *412* mountain range of W Mongolia
Hangzhou *187* *var.* Hangchow, Hang-chou. Zhejiang, E China
Hanka, Lake *see* Khanka, Lake
Hanko *249* *Swe.* Hangö. SW Finland
Hankow *see* Wuhan
Hannover *264* *Eng.* Hanover. NW Germany
Hanöbukten *543* bay of the Baltic Sea to the S of Sweden
Hanoi *623* *Vtn.* Ha Nôi. ❖ of Vietnam, N Vietnam
Hanover *see* Hannover
Hanstholm *218* Jylland, NW Denmark
Han-tan *see* Handan
Hantu, Pulau *517* island of SW Singapore
Hāora *297* *prev.* Howrah. E India
Haouach, Ouadi *180* dry watercourse of E Chad
Happy Valley-Goose Bay *171* *prev.* Goose Bay. E Canada
Hapsal *see* Haapsalu
Ḩaraḑ *506* *var.* Haradh. E Saudi Arabia
Ḩaraḑ *627* N Yemen
Hara Laht *240* bay of the Gulf of Finland, on the coast of N Estonia
Harare *636* *prev.* Salisbury. ❖ of Zimbabwe, NE Zimbabwe
Haraze-Mangueigne *180* SE Chad
Harbel *368* W Liberia
Harbin *187* *var.* Ha-erh-pin, *prev.* Pinkiang. Heilongjiang, NE China
Harbours, Bay of *645* bay of the South Atlantic Ocean, SE Falkland Islands
Harbour View *329* E Jamaica
Hardangerfjorden *444* fjord of SW Norway
Hardap Dam *423* dam of C Namibia
Haré Meron *317* Mountain of N Israel
Hārer *243* E Ethiopia
Hargeysa *524* NW Somalia
Hari *302* *var.* Batang Hari, *prev.* Djambi. River of Sumatra, W Indonesia
Ḩarīb *627* W Yemen
Hari Kurk *240* channel of Baltic Sea, between the island of Hiiumaa and Estonia mainland
Ḩārim *551* NW Syria
Ḩarīmā *336* N Jordan
Haringhat *117* river of SW Bangladesh
Harīrūd *77* river of C Asia
Harīrūd *see* Tedzhen
Harlingen *429* *Fris.* Harns. N Netherlands
Harmanli *see* Kharmanli
Harns *see* Harlingen
Harper *368* *var.* Cape Palmas. S Liberia
Ḩarrah *627* SE Yemen
Harrington Sound *643* bay of the North Atlantic Ocean, N Bermuda
Harris *649* E Montserrat
Harrisburg *599* Pennsylvania, NE USA
Harrismith *527* Orange Free State, E South Africa
Harstad *444* NE Norway
Hartford *368* SW Liberia
Hartford *599* Connecticut, NE USA
Hartley *see* Chegutu
Harz *265* *var.* Harz Mountains. Mountain range of C Germany
HaSharon *317* *Eng.* Plain of Sharon. Plain of C Israel
Haskovo *see* Khaskovo
Haspengouw *see* Hesbaye
Hasselt *127* NE Belgium
Hassetché *see* Al Ḩasakah
Hastings *121* SW Barbados
Hastings *433* SE North Island, New Zealand
Hastings *514* W Sierra Leone
Hastings *593* SE England, UK
Hatay *see* Antakya
Hātia *117* river and one of the main mouths of the Ganges, S Bangladesh
Hato Mayor *226* E Dominican Republic
Ḩattā *590* E United Arab Emirates
Hattiesburg *599* Mississippi, SE USA
Hattieville *130* E Belize
Hat Yai *563* *var.* Ban Hat Yai. S Thailand
Haud *243* *var.* Hawd. Plateau of Somalia and Ethiopia.
Haugesund *444* SW Norway
Haukeligrand *444* SW Norway
Haukivesi *249* lake of SE Finland
Hauraki Gulf *433* gulf on the N coast of North Island, New Zealand
Hau *623* river of SW Vietnam
Haut Atlas *414* *Eng.* High Atlas. Mountain range of C Morocco
Haute-Sangha *see* Mambéré-Kadéi
Hautes Fagnes *127* *Ger.* Hohes Venn. Mountain range of Belgium
Haute Sûre, Lac de la *378* reservoir of NW Luxembourg
Haut Plateau du Dra *see* Dra, Hamada du
Hauts Plateaux *83* plateau of NW Algeria
Havana *210* *var.* La Habana. ❖ of Cuba, NW Cuba
Havířov *216* E Czech Republic
Havlíčkův Brod *216* *prev.* Německý Brod, *Ger.* Deutsch-Brod. S Czech Republic
Hawaii *598* island of Hawaiian group, Hawaii, USA, C Pacific
Hawaii *598* non-contiguous state of USA, C Pacific
Ḩawallī *354* E Kuwait
Hawar Islands *115* islands of SE Bahrain
Hawash *see* Awash
Hawea, Lake *433* W South Island, New Zealand
Hawera *433* SW North Island, New Zealand
Hawick *593* S Scotland, UK
Hawke Bay *433* bay of the South Pacific Ocean, on the SE coast of North Island, New Zealand
Hawlēr *see* Arbīl
Ḩawmat as Sūq *see* Houmt Souk
Ḩawrā' *627* C Yemen
Ḩawrān, Wādī *310* dry watercourse of W Iraq
Hawwārah *336* *var.* Huwwāra. N Jordan
HaYarden *see* Jordan
Hay River *170* W Canada
Ḩayyān, Ra's *115* *var.* Ra's Ḩayyān. Cape of E Bahrain
Hebei *187* *var.* Hopei. Province of NE China
Hebrides, Sea of the *593* sea of the Atlantic Ocean to the NW of UK
Hebron *317, 318* *Ar.* Al Khalil. S West Bank
Heerenveen *429* NE Netherlands
Heerlen *429* S Netherlands
Hefa *317* N Israel
Hefa, Mifraz *317* *Eng.* Bay of Haifa. Bay of the Mediterranean Sea
Hefei *187* *var.* Hofei, *hist.* Luchow. Anhui, E China
Heichin *see* P'ingchen
Heidelberg *264* SW Germany
Heihe *187* *prev.* Ai-hun. Heilongjiang, NE China
Hei-ho *see* Nagqu
Heilbronn *264* SW Germany
Heiligenkreuz *see* Žiar nad Hronom
Heilong Jiang *see* Amur
Heilongjiang *187* *var.* Heilungkiang, Hei-lung-chiang. Province of NE China
Heimaey Island *294* *var.* Heimaey, Heimaæy. Island of S Iceland
Heitō *see* P'ingtung
Helen *455* island of S Palau
Helena *598* Montana, NW USA
Helgoland *264* *Eng.* Heligoland. Island of NW Germany
Helgoländer Bucht *264* *var.* Helgoland Bay, Heligoland Bight. Bay of the North Sea
Hell-Ville *see* Andoany
Helmand, Daryā-ye *77* river of Afghanistan and Iran
Helmond *429* S Netherlands
Helsingborg *543* *prev.* Hälsingborg. S Sweden
Helsingør *218* *Eng.* Elsinore. Sjælland, E Denmark
Helsinki *249* *Swe.* Helsingfors. ❖ of Finland, S Finland
Ḩelwân *230* *var.* Ḩulwān, Ḩilwān. N Egypt
Henan *187* *var.* Honan. Province of C China
Henderson Island *651* island of N Pitcairn Islands
Hendū Kosh *see* Hindu Kush
Hengduan Shan *186* mountain range of SW China
Hengelo *429* E Netherlands
Hengyang *187* Hunan, S China
Hentiesbaai *423* W Namibia
Henzada *159* SW Burma
Heradhsvötn *294* river of C Iceland
Herāt *77* W Afghanistan
Heredia *206* C Costa Rica
Hereford *593* C England, UK
Herisau *546* *Fr.* Hérisau. NE Switzerland
Héristal *see* Herstal
Herm *647* island of S Guernsey
Hermannstadt *see* Sibiu
Hermansverk *444* SW Norway
Hermel *364* *var.* Hirmil. NE Lebanon

Hermitage *276* C Grenada island, Grenada
Hermon, Mount *551 Ar.* Jabal ash Shaykh. Mountain of SW Syria
Hermosillo *403* NW Mexico
Hernád *see* Hornád
Hernandarias *460 prev.* Tacurupucú. SE Paraguay
Herne *264* W Germany
Herning *218* Jylland, W Denmark
Herstal *127 Fr.* Héristal. E Belgium
Herzliyya *317* C Israel
Herzogenbusch *see* 's-Hertogenbosch
Hesbaye *127 Dut.* Haspengouw. Physical region of C Belgium
Hesperange *378* SE Luxembourg
Hestur *644* island of C Faeroe Islands
Hetauda *427* C Nepal
Hida-sammyaku *330* mountain range of Honshū, C Japan
Hienghène *650* W New Caledonia
Hierro *531 var.* Ferro. Island of Islas Canarias, SW Spain
High Atlas *see* Haut Atlas
Highgate *329* NE Jamaica
Highlands, The *92* highlands of Barbuda, Antigua & Barbuda
High Point *643* headland of W Bermuda
High Veld *see* Northern Karoo
Higüey *226 var.* Salvaleon de Higüey. E Dominican Republic
Hiiumaa *240 var.* Hiuma, *Ger.* Dagden, Swed. Dagö. Island of W Estonia
Hikina *648* island, NE Johnston Atoll
Hildesheim *264* NW Germany
Hilla *see* Al Ḩillah
Hillaby, Mount *121* mountain of Barbados
Hillerød *218* Sjælland, E Denmark
Hillsborough *276* W Carriacou, Grenada
Hilo *598* Hawaii, USA
Hilversum *429* C Netherlands
Ḩilwan *see* Ḩelwân
Himachal Pradesh *296* state of N India
Himalayas *134, 186, 296, 427* mountain range of S Asia
Himeji *330* Honshū, C Japan
Himora *243 var.* Humera. NW Ethiopia
Ḩimş *551 var.* Homs. W Syria
Hînceşti *408 var.* Hânceşti, *prev.* Kotovsk. C Moldova
Hinche *286* C Haiti
Hindenburg *see* Zabrze
Hindiya *see* Al Hindīyah
Hindu Kush *77, 451 Per.* Hendū Kosh. Mountain range of C Asia
Hingol *450* river of SW Pakistan
Hinson Island *643* island of W Bermuda
Hirmil *see* Hermel
Hirosaki *330* Honshū, N Japan
Hiroshima *330* Honshū, W Japan
Hirschberg in Riesengebirge *see* Jelenia Góra
Hirtshals *218* Jylland, N Denmark
Ḩisbān *336* NW Jordan
Ḩisb, Sha'īb *310 var.* Sha'ib Hasb. Dry watercourse of S Iraq
Hisor *558 Rus.* Gissar. W Tajikistan
Hitachi *330* Honshū, SE Japan
Hitra *444 prev.* Hitteren. Island of W Norway
Hitteren *see* Hitra
Hiu *615* Torres Islands, N Vanuatu
Hjälmaren *543 Eng.* Lake Hjalmar. Lake of S Sweden
Hjalmar, Lake *see* Hjälmaren
Hjørring *218* Jylland, N Denmark
Hkakabo Razi *159* mountain of Burma and China
Hlathikulu *540 var.* Hlatikulu. S Swaziland
Hlohovec *519 prev.* Frakštát, *Ger.* Freistadtl, *Hung.* Galgóc. W Slovakia
Hlotse *366 var.* Leribe. NW Lesotho
Hlybokaye *122 Rus.* Glubokoye. N Belarus
Ho *270* SE Ghana
Hoa Binh *623* N Vietnam
Hoang Liên Sơn *623* mountain range of China and Vietnam
Hoani *198* NW Mohéli, Comoros
Hobart *101* Tasmania, Australia
Hobro *218* Jylland, NW Denmark
Hobyo *524 It.* Obbia. E Somalia
Hô Chi Minh *623 var.* Ho Chi Minh City, *prev.* Saigon. S Vietnam
Hodeida *see* Al Ḩudaydah
Hódmezővásárhely *290* SE Hungary
Hodonín *216 Ger.* Göding. SE Czech Republic
Hoë Karoo *see* Northern Karoo
Hoeryŏng *349* NE North Korea
Höfdhakaupstadhur *see* Skagaströnd
Hofei *see* Hefei
Hofsá *294* river of E Iceland
Hofsjökull *294* glacier of C Iceland
Hofuf *see* Al Hufuf
Högen *see* Fengyüan
Hoggar *see* Ahaggar
Hogoley Islands *see* Chuuk Islands
Hohenems *106* W Austria
Hohes Venn *see* Hautes Fagnes
Hohe Tauern *106* mountain range of W Austria
Hohhot *187 var.* Huhehot, *prev.* Kweisui. Nei Mongol Zizhiqu, N China
Hôi An *623 prev.* Faifo. C Vietnam
Hoihow *see* Haikou
Hoima *584* W Uganda
Hojancha *206* W Costa Rica
Hokitika *433* W South Island, New Zealand
Hokkaidō *331, 335* island of N Japan
Hokkō *see* Peikang
Hokō *see* P'ohang
Hoktemberyan *98 Rus.* Oktemberyan. SW Armenia
Holbæk *218* Sjælland, E Denmark
Holetown *121 prev.* Jamestown. W Barbados
Holguín *210* SE Cuba
Holhol *222* SE Djibouti
Holland *see* Netherlands
Hollandia *see* Jayapura
Hólmavík *294* NW Iceland
Holmsland Klit *218* fjord of Jylland, W Denmark
Ḥolon *317* C Israel
Holonga *568* Uta Vava'u, Tonga
Ḥolot Ḥaluẓa *317* historic site of S Israel
Holstebro *218* Jylland, W Denmark
Holsteinsborg *see* Sisimiut
Holyhead *593* N Wales, UK
Homa Bay *342* W Kenya
Homāyūnshahr *see* Khomeynīshahr
Hombori Tondo *392* mountain of E Mali
Home Island *644* island of C Cocos Islands
Homenau *see* Humenné
Homonna *see* Humenné
Homs *see* Ḩimş
Homs *see* Al Khums
Homyel' *122 Rus.* Gomel'. SE Belarus
Honan *see* Henan
Hondo *130, 403* river of Central America
Honduras *288-289* officially Republic of Honduras. Country of C America divided into 18 admin. units (departments). ❖ Tegucigalpa
Honduras, Gulf of *130, 278* gulf of the Caribbean Sea to the E of Central America
Hønefoss *444* S Norway
Hông Gai *623 var.* Hongay. N Vietnam
Hong Kong *187 var.* Xianggang. S China
Hongwŏn *349* E North Korea
Hongze Hu *187 var.* Hung-tse Hu. Lake of E China
Honiara *522* ❖ of the Solomon Islands, N Guadalcanal, Solomon Islands
Honolulu *598* Oahu, Hawaii, USA
Honshū *330* island of C Japan
Honte *see* Westerschelde
Hoogeveen *429* NE Netherlands
Hoogezand *429* NE Netherlands
Hooker, Cape *527* cape of Marion Island, S South Africa
Hoorn *429* NW Netherlands
Hopei *see* Hebei
Hope Town *112* Great Abaco, Bahamas
Horgen *546* N Switzerland
Hōrin *see* Fenglin
Horki *122 Rus.* Gorki. NE Belarus
Horlivka *586 Rus.* Gorlovka. E Ukraine
Hormuz, Strait of *307, 448, 590 var.* Strait of Ormuz, *Per.* Tangeh-ye Hormoz. Strait connecting the The Gulf and Arabian Sea
Hornád *519 Ger.* Hernad, *Hung.* Hernád. River of Hungary and Slovakia
Horn, Cape *183* cape of S Chile
Horog *see* Khorugh
Horoshiri-dake *331* mountain of Hokkaidō, N Japan
Horowupotana *534* NE Sri Lanka
Horqueta *460* C Paraguay
Horsburgh Atoll *390* atoll of N Maldives
Horsburgh Island *644 var.* Pulu Luar. Island of C Cocos Islands
Horsens *218* Jylland, C Denmark
Horseshoe Bay *643* bay of the North Atlantic Ocean, W Bermuda
Horsham *101* SE Australia
Hørsholm *218* Sjælland, E Denmark
Hortabágny-Berettyó *290* river of E Hungary
Horten *444* S Norway
Horug *see* Khorugh
Hosa'ina *243 var.* Hosseina, *It.* Hosanna. SW Ethiopia
Hose, Penunungan *386 var.* Hose Mountains. Mountain range of Borneo, E Malaysia
Hotan *186 var.* Khotan, *Chin.* Ho-t'ien. Xinjiang Uygur Zizhiqu. NW China
Hot Springs *599* Arkansas, SC USA
Hotte, Massif de la *286* highlands of SW Haiti
Houaïlou *650* C New Caledonia
Houmt Souk *573 var.* Djerba, Ḩawmat as Sūd, Jerba. Île de Jerba, Tunisia
Houndé *157* SW Burkina
Houston *599* Texas, SC USA
Hovd *412* W Mongolia
Hoverla *586 Rus.* Gora Goverla. Mountain of W Ukraine
Hövsgöl Nuur *412* lake of N Mongolia
Howe, Cape *101* cape on the SE coast of Australia
Howakil Bay *238* bay of the Red Sea to the E of Eritrea
Howrah *see* Hāora
Hōzan *see* Fengshan
Hradec Králové *216 Ger.* Königgrätz. E Czech Republic
Hrazdan *98 Rus.* Razdan. C Armenia
Hrazdan *98 Rus.* Razdan, Zanga. River of C Armenia
Hrodna *122 Rus.* Grodno. W Belarus
Hron *519 Ger.* Gran, *Hung.* Garam. River of C Slovakia
Hsüeh Shan *555* mountain of N Taiwan
Hsi-an *see* Xi'an
Hsiang-t'an *see* Xiangtan
Hsi Chiang *see* Xi Jiang
Hsinchu *555* NW Taiwan
Hsinchuang *555 var.* Sinchwang, *Jap.* Shinshō. N Taiwan
Hsing-K'ai Hu *see* Khanka, Lake
Hsi-ning *see* Xining
Hsinking *see* Changchun
Hsintien *555 var.* Sintien, *Jap.* Shinten. N Taiwan
Hsin-yang *see* Xinyang
Hsinying *555 var.* Sinying, *Jap.* Shinei. W Taiwan
Hsu-chou *see* Xuzhou
Hsüehshan Shanmo *555* mountain range of N Taiwan
Huacho *463* W Peru
Huainan *187 var.* Hwainan. Anhui, E China
Hualien *555 var.* Hwalien, *Jap.* Karen. E Taiwan
Huallaga *463* river of N Peru
Huambo *88 Port.* Nova Lisboa. C Angola
Huancavelica *463* SW Peru
Huancayo *463* C Peru
Huang Hai *see* Yellow Sea
Huang He *187 Eng.* Yellow River. River of C China
Huánuco *463* C Peru
Huanuni *136* W Bolivia
Huaral *463* W Peru
Huascarán, Nevado *463* mountain of W Peru
Huaraz *463 var.* Huaráz. W Peru
Hubei *187 var.* Hupei. Province of C China
Hubli *296* SW India
Huddersfield *593* N England, UK
Hudson *599* river of NE USA
Hudson Bay *171* bay of the Atlantic Ocean, NE Canada
Hudson Strait *171* strait connecting the Atlantic Ocean and Hudson Bay
Huê *623* C Vietnam
Huehuetenango *278* W Guatemala
Huelva *530* SW Spain
Huesca *531* NE Spain
Hughenden *101* NE Australia
Huhehot *see* Hohhot
Hŭich'ŏn *349* C North Korea
Huizen *429* C Netherlands
Huksan-kundo *350 var.* Huksan-chedo. Island group of SW South Korea
Hull *see* Kingston-upon-Hull
Hull *171* SE Canada
Hullo *240* Vormsi, Estonia
Hulun Nur *187 Chin.* Hu-lun Ch'ih, *prev.* Dalai Nor. Lake of Nei Mongol Zizhiqu, NE China
Ḩulwan *see* Ḩelwân
Humacao *651* E Puerto Rico
Humaitá *460* S Paraguay
Humber *593* river of NE England, UK
Humenné *519 Ger.* Homenau, *Hung.* Homonna. E Slovakia
Humera *see* Himora
Húnaflói *294* bay of the Norwegian Sea on the N coast of Iceland
Hunan *187* province of S China
Hundested *218* Sjælland, E Denmark
Hunga Ha'apai *568* island of the Nomuka Group, W Tonga
Hungary *290-293* officially Republic of Hungary, *Hung.* Magyarország, *prev.* Hungarian People's Republic. Country of C Europe divided into 19 admin. units (counties). ❖ Budapest
Hunga Tonga *568* island of the Nomuka Group, W Tonga
Hŭngnam *349* E North Korea
Hung-tse Hu *see* Hongze Hu
Huntington *599* West Virginia, E USA
Huntsville *599* Alabama, SE USA
Hunyani *see* Manyame
Huon Gulf *458* gulf of the Solomon Sea, to the E of Papua New Guinea
Huo-shao Tao *see* Lan Yü
Hupei *see* Hubei
Hurghada *230* E Egypt
Huron, Lake *171, 599* lake of Canada and USA
Hurunui *433* river of NE South Island, New Zealand
Húsavík *644* Sandoy, C Faeroe Islands
Húsavík *294* NE Iceland
Ḩuşayn, Dawḩat al *479 var.* Dauhat al Husein. Inlet of the Gulf of Bahrain on the NW coast of Qatar
Hūth *627* NW Yemen
Huwwāra *see* Hawwārah
Hvammstangi *294* N Iceland
Hvannadalshnúkur *294* mountain of S Iceland
Hvar *209 It.* Lesina. Island of S Croatia
Hvítá *294* river of W Iceland

Hvolsvöllur *294* SW Iceland
Hwach'ŏn-chŏsuji *see* P'aro-ho
Hwainan *see* Huainan
Hwange *636 prev.* Wankie. W Zimbabwe
Hwang-Hae *see* Yellow Sea
Hyargas Nuur *412* lake of W Mongolia
Hyderābād *296 Hind.* Hyderābad. C India
Hyderābād *451 var.* Haidarabad. S Pakistan
Hyères *253* SE France
Hyères, Îles d' *253* island group of SE France
Hyesan *349* NE North Korea
Hyvinge *see* Hyvinkää
Hyvinkää *249 Swe.* Hyvinge. S Finland

I

Ialomiţa *480* river of SE Romania
Ialpug *408 Rus.* Yalpug. River of S Moldova
Iaşi *480 Ger.* Jassy. NE Romania
Ibadan *440* SW Nigeria
Ibagué *195* C Colombia
Ibar *630* river of SW Serbia, Yugoslavia
Ibarra *228 var.* San Miguel de Ibarra. N Ecuador
Ibb *627* W Yemen
Ibbenbüren *264* NW Germany
Ibenga *200* river of N Congo
Ibérico, Sistema *531 var.* Cordillera Ibérica, *Eng.* Iberian Mountains. Mountains of NE Spain
Ibiza *see* Eivissa
Ibo *see* Sassandra
Iboundji *258* C Gabon
Ibrā' *448* N Oman
Ibrī *448* NW Oman
Irbīl *see* Arbīl
Ibusuki *330* Kyūshū, SW Japan
Içá *144* river of NW Brazil
Ica *463* SW Peru
Iceflavik *see* Keflavík
İçel *see* Mersin
Iceland *294-295* officially Republic of Iceland, *Icel.* Ísland. Country of the North Atlantic Ocean divided into 8 admin. units (regions). ❖ Reykjavík
Ichinomiya *330* Honshū, C Japan
Ichinoseki *330* Honshū, N Japan
Idah *440* S Nigeria
Idaho *598* state of NW USA
Idaho Falls *598* Idaho, NW USA
Idensalmi *see* Iisalmi
Idfu *230 var.* Idfū, Edfu. SE Egypt
Idi Amin, Lac *see* Edward, Lake
Idlib *551* NW Syria
Idrija *520 It.* Idria. W Slovenia
Idzhevan *see* Ijevan
Iecava *362* C Latvia
Ieper *127 Fr.* Ypres. W Belgium
Ifalik *406* atoll of C Micronesia
Ife *440* SW Nigeria
Iferouâne *439* N Niger
Iferten *see* Yverdon
Iganga *584* SE Uganda
Igarka *485* N Russian Federation
Igatimí *see* Ygatimí
Iglau *see* Jihlava
Iglesias *320* Sardegna, W Italy
Igló *see* Spišská Nová Ves
Ignalina *376* E Lithuania
Iguaçu, Salto do *145 Sp.* Cataratas del Iguazú, *prev.* Victoria Falls. Waterfall of Argentina and Brazil
Iguetti, Sebkhet *398* salt lake of N Mauritania
Ihavandippolhu Atoll *390 var.* Ihavandiffulu Atoll. Atoll of N Maldives
Ihema, Lac *492* lake of Burundi and Rwanda
Ihosy *382* S Madagascar
Iida *330* Honshū, C Japan
Iijoki *249* river of C Finland
Irbīl *see* Arbīl
Iisalmi *249 Swe.* Idensalmi. C Finland
Ijebu-Ode *440* SW Nigeria
Ijevan *98 Rus.* Idzhevan, *var.* Idževan. N Armenia
IJssel *429 var.* Yssel. River of C Netherlands
IJsselmeer *429 prev.* Zuider Zee. Lake of N Netherlands
Ikare *440* SW Nigeria
Ikaría *273* island of SE Greece
Ikast *218* Jylland, W Denmark
Ikeja *440* SW Nigeria
Ikerre *440 var.* Ikerre-Ekiti. SW Nigeria
Iki *330* island to the NW of Kyūshū, SW Japan
Ikom *440* S Nigeria
Ikopa *382* river of N Madagascar
Ila *440* W Nigeria
Ilam *427* W Nepal
Ilan *555 Jap.* Giran. NE Taiwan
Ile *see* Ili
Ilebo *203 prev.* Port Francqui. W Dem. Rep. Congo (Zaire)
Ilesha *440* SW Nigeria
Ilha Solteira, Represa de *145* reservoir of S Brazil
Ili *338 Kaz.* Ile. River of China and Kazakhstan
Iligan *466* Mindanao, S Philippines
Ilirska Bistrica *520* SW Slovenia
Il'jaly *see* Ylanly
Illapel *183* C Chile
Illiassa *261* NW Gambia
Illinois *599* state of C USA
Ilobasco *235* C El Salvador
Ilobu *440* W Nigeria
Iloilo *466* Panay, C Philippines
Ilopango, Lago de *235* volcanic lake of C El Salvador
Ilorin *440* W Nigeria
Īluh *see* Batman
Ilulissat *646 Dan.* Jakobshavn. W Greenland
Il'yaly *see* Ylanly
Imatong Mountains *536* mountains of S Sudan
Imatra *249* SE Finland
Imeni 26 Bakinskikh Komissarov *see* Bakı Komissarı
Imilili *414* W Western Sahara
İmişli *110 Rus.* Imishli, Imišli. C Azerbaijan
Imja-do *350* island of SW South Korea
Imola *321* N Italy
Imperatriz *145* NE Brazil
Imperia *320* N Italy
Impfondo *200* NE Congo
Imphāl *297* E India
Ina *330* Honshū, C Japan
Inakona *522* S Guadalcanal, Solomon Is
In Aménas *83 var.* I-n-Amenas, In Amnas. E Algeria
Inárajan *647* SE Guam
Inarijärvi *249 Swe.* Enareträsk, *Lapp.* Aanaarjävri. Lake of N Finland
Inarijoki *249 Nor.* Anarjokka. River of Finland and Norway
Inawashiro-ko *330* lake of Honshū, N Japan
Inbhear Mór *see* Arklow
Inch'ŏn *350 prev.* Chemulpo, *Jap.* Jinsen. NW South Korea
Inchope *419* C Mozambique
Incles *86* river of NE Andorra
Independence *130* SE Belize
Inderagiri *see* Indragiri
India *296-301* officially Republic of India, *Hind.* Bharat. Country divided into 32 admin. units (25 states and 7 union territories). ❖ New Delhi
Indiana *599* state of C USA
Indianapolis *599* Indiana, C USA
Indian Desert *see* Thar Desert
Indian Ocean *90, 644* ocean bounded to the W by Africa, to the E by Australia and to the S by Antarctica
Indigirka *485* River of NE Russian Federation
Indonesia *302-305* officially Republic of Indonesia, *Ind.* Republik Indonesia, *prev.* United States of Indonesia, Dutch East Indies, Netherlands East Indies. Country of SE Asia divided into 25 admin. units (24 provinces and 1 autonous district). ❖ Jakarta
Indonesian Borneo *see* Kalimantan
Indore *296* NW India
Indragiri *302 var.* Inderagiri. River of Sumatra, W Indonesia
Indre *253* river of C France
Indus *296, 451* river of S Asia
Indus, Mouths of the *451* river delta of S Pakistan
Infante Dom Henrique *505* SE Príncipe, Sao Tome & Principe
Ingolstadt *265* S Germany
Inguri *see* Enguri
Ingushetiya, Respublika *484* autonomous republic of SW Russian Federation
Ingushskaya, Respublika *484* autonomous republic of SW Russian Federation
Ingwavuma *see* Nggwavuma
Inhambane *419* S Mozambique
I-ning *see* Yining
Inírida *195* river of E Colombia
Inis *see* Ennis
Inland Sea *330 var.* Seto Naikai. Sea of the Pacific Ocean between Honshū and Shikoku,W Japan
Inn *106, 265* river of C Europe
Inner Channel *130 var.* Main Channel. Inlet of W Caribbean Sea
Inner Hebrides *593* island group of NW Scotland, UK
Inner Islands *512 var.* Central Group. Island group of NE Seychelles
Inner Mongolian Autonomous Region *see* Nei Mongol Zizhiqu
Innsbruck *106* W Austria
Inrin *see* Yüanlin
In Salah *83 var.* I-n-Salah. C Algeria
Insein *159* S Burma
Intelewa *538* S Suriname
Interlaken *546* SW Switzerland
Inthanon, Doi *563* mountain of NW Thailand
Intipucá *235* SE El Salvador
Inuvik *170* NW Canada
Invercargill *433* SW South Island, New Zealand
Inverness *593* N Scotland, UK
Inyanga *see* Nyanga
Inyangani *636* mountain of E Zimbabwe
Inyazura *see* Nyazura
Ioánnina *273 var.* Janina, Yannina. W Greece
Iolotan' *see* Yëloten
Ionian Islands *see* Iónioi Nísoi
Ionian Sea *81, 273, 321 Gk* Iónio Pélagos, *It.* Mar Ionio. Area of the Mediterranean Sea, between Italy and SE Europe
Ionio, Mar *see* Ionian Sea
Iónioi Nísoi *273 Eng.* Ionian Islands. Island group of W Greece
Iori *262* river of Azerbaijan and Georgia
Íos *273* island of SE Greece
Iowa *599* state of C USA
Ipeľ *see* Ipoly
Ipiales *195* SW Colombia
Ipoh *386* W Peninsular Malaysia
Ipoly *290, 519 Slvk.* Ipeľ, *Ger.* Eipel. River of Hungary and Slovakia
Ippy *179* C Central African Republic
Ipswich *101* E Australia
Ipswich *593* E England, UK
Iqaluit *171 prev.* Frobisher Bay. Baffin Island, NE Canada
Iquique *183* N Chile
Iquitos *463* N Peru
Irákleio *273 Eng.* Candia, *prev.* Iráklion. Crete, S Greece
Iran *306-309* officially Islamic Republic of Iran, *prev.* Persia. Country of SW Asia divided into 24 admin. units (provinces). ❖ Tehrān
Iran, Pegunungan *387 var.* Iran Mountains. Mountain range of Borneo, Indonesia and Malaysia
Iran, Plateau of *307* plateau of C Iran
Irapuato *403* C Mexico
Iraq *310-313* officially Republic of Iraq, *Ar.* 'Irāq. Country of SW Asia divided into 18 admin. units (governorates). ❖ Baghdad
Irbe Strait *240 Est.* Kura Kurk, *prev.* Irbe Väin, *Latv.* Irbes Šaurums. Strait connecting the Baltic Sea and Gulf of Riga
Irbid *336* N Jordan
Ireland Island North *643* island of W Bermuda
Ireland Island South *643* island of W Bermuda
Ireland, Northern *see* Northern Ireland
Ireland, Republic of *314-315* officially Republic of Ireland, Éire. Country of W Europe divided into 26 admin. units (counties). ❖ Dublin
Ireng *284 var.* Maú. River of Brazil and Guyana
Irgalem *see* Yirga 'Alem
Iri *350 Jap.* Riri. W South Korea
Irian *see* New Guinea
Irian Jaya *302-303 Eng.* West Irian, *prev.* Dutch New Guinea. Province of W Indonesia
Iringa *560* C Tanzania
Iriomote-jima *330* island of Sakishima-shotō, SW Japan
Iriri *145* river of N Brazil
Irish Sea *314, 593, 647 Ir.* Muir Eireann. Sea of the Atlantic Ocean between Ireland and UK
Irkeshtam *357 var.* Irkeštam. SW Kyrgyzstan
Irkutsk *485* C Russian Federation
Irmak *577* river of N Turkey
Iroise *252* area of the Atlantic Ocean to the NW of France
'Irqah *627* SW Yemen
Irrawaddy *159 var.* Ayeyarwady. River of C Burma
Irrawaddy, Mouths of the *159* delta area of SW Burma
Irrsee *106* lake of N Austria
Irtysh *338, 484 Kaz.* Ertis. River of Kazakhstan and Russian Federation
Irun *531* N Spain
Iruña *see* Pamplona
Isabela *651* NW Puerto Rico
Isabela, Isla *228* island of SW Galapagos Is, Ecuador
Isachsen *170* Ellef Ringnes Island, N Canada
Ísafdhardjúp *294* inlet of the Atlantic Ocean, NW Iceland
Isangel *615* Tanna, Vanuatu
Isa Town *see* Madīnat 'Īsá
Isalo, Tangorombohitr' *382* mountains of SW Madagascar
Ischia, Isola d' *321* island of S Italy
Ise *330* Honshū, C Japan
Isefjord *218* fjord of Sjælland, E Denmark
Isére *253* river of SE France
Iseyin *440* W Nigeria
Isfara *558* N Tajikistan
Ísfjördhur *294* NW Iceland
Isha Baydhabo *see* Baydhabo
Isherton *284* S Guyana
Ishigaki-jima *330* island of Sakishima-shotō, SW Japan
Ishikari *331* river of Hokkaidō, N Japan
Ishim *338 Kaz.* Esil. River of Kazakhstan and Russian Federation
Ishinomaki *330* Honshū, N Japan
Ishkoshim *558 Rus.* Ishkashim. S Tajikistan
Ishurdi *117* W Bangladesh
Isidoro Noblia *607* NE Uruguay
Isiolo *342* C Kenya
Isiro *203* NE Dem. Rep. Congo (Zaire)
Iskeçe *see* Xánthi
İskele *215 var.* Trikomo. E Cyprus

İskenderun *577 Eng.* Alexandretta. S Turkey
İskenderun Körfezi *577 Eng.* Gulf of Alexandretta. Gulf of the Mediterranean Sea
Iskŭr *152* river of NW Bulgaria
Iskŭr, Yazovir *152* reservoir of W Bulgaria
Islāmābād *451* ❖ of Pakistan, NE Pakistan
Island Harbour *642* bay of the Caribbean Sea on the N coast of Anguilla
Islay *593* island of Inner Hebrides, W Scotland, UK
Isle *253* river of SW France
Ismâ'ilîya *230 var.* Al Ismā'īlīyah, *Eng.* Ismaila. N Egypt
Isna *230 var.* Isnā, Esna. SE Egypt
Isoka *635* NE Zambia
Isonzo *see* Soča.
Ispahan *see* Eşfahān
İsparta *577* SW Turkey
Israel *316-319* officially State of Israel, *Heb.* Yisra'el. Country of SW Asia divided into 6 admin. units (districts). ❖ Jerusalem
Issano *284* C Guyana
Issia *326* SW Ivory Coast
Issyk-Kul' *see* Balykchy
Issyk-Kul', Ozero *357 var.* Issiq Köl. Lake of NE Kyrgyzstan
İstanbul *577 prev.* Constantinople, *Bul.* Tsarigrad. NW Turkey
İstanbul Boğazi *577* Karadeniz Boğazi, *Eng.* Bosporus. Strait connecting rmara Denizi and Black Sea
Istra *209 Eng.* Istria. Peninsula of SE Europe
Istria *see* Istra
Itabuna *145* E Brazil
Itagüí *195* NW Colombia
Itaipú, Represa de *145, 460* reservoir of Brazil and Paraguay
Italy *320-325* officially Italian Republic, *It.* Italia, Repubblica Italiana. Country of S Europe divided into 20 admin. units (regions). ❖ Rome
Itany *see* Litani
Itassi *see* Vieille Case
Iténez *see* Guaporé
Itonamas *136* river of NE Bolivia
Itremo *382 var.* Massif de l'Itremo. Mountain range of C Madagascar
Itsamia *198* S Mohéli, Comoros
Itsandra *198* W Grande Comore, Comoros
Ittoqqortoormiit *646 Dan.* Scoresbysund. E Greenland
Itu Aba Island *652* island of W Spratly Islands
Ituni *284* C Guyana
Iturup *331* disputed island of Kurile Islands, SE Russian Federation
Ivakoany *382 var.* Massif de l'Ivakoany. Mountain range of SE Madagascar
Ivalojoki *249* river of N Finland
Ivano-Frankivs'k *586 Rus.* Ivano-Frankovsk, *prev.* Stanislav, *Pol.* Stanisławów, *Ger.* Stanislau. W Ukraine
Ivanovo *484* W Russian Federation
Ivatsevichy *122* SW Belarus
Ivindo *258* river of C Africa
Iviza *see* Eivissa
Ivoire, Côte d' *see* Ivory Coast
Ivory Coast *326 Fr.* Côte d'Ivoire. Coastal region of S Ivory Coast
Ivory Coast *326-327* officially Republic of the Côte d'Ivoire, *Fr.* Côte d'Ivoire. Country of W Africa divided into 34 admin. units (departments). ❖ Yamoussoukro
Ivujivik *171* NE Canada
Iwakuni *330* Honshū, W Japan
Iwaki *330* Honshū, N Japan
Iwo *440* SW Nigeria
Iwŏn *349* E North Korea
Ixcán *278* river of Guatemala and Mexico
Izabal, Lago de *278 prev.* Golfo Dulce. Lake of E Guatemala
Izhevsk *484 prev.* Ustinov. W Russian Federation
Izkī *448* N Oman
İzmir *577 prev.* Smyrna. W Turkey
İzmit *577 var.* Kocaeli. NW Turkey
Izuhara *330* Tsushima, W Japan
Izumo *330* Honshū, W Japan
Izu-shotō *330* island group to the SE of Honshū, SE Japan

J

Jabal aẓ Ẓannah *590 var.* Jebel Dhanna, W United Arab Emirates
Jabāliya *317, 318* NE Gaza Strip
Jabalpur *296 prev.* Jubbulpore. C India
Jabat *396 var.* Jabwot Island. island of S Marshall Islands
Jabbul, Sabkhat al *551* salt-flat of NW Syria
Jablah *551 var.* Jeble, *Fr.* Djéblé. W Syria
Jablanica *81* mountain range of E Albania
Jablonec nad Nisou *216 Ger.* Gablonz an der Neisse. N Czech Republic
Jaboatão *145* E Brazil
Jabwot Island *see* Jabat
Jaceel *524 It.* Uadi Giahel. Seasonal river of NE Somalia
Jackson *599* Mississippi, SE USA
Jacksonville *599* Florida, SE USA
Jacmel *286 var.* Jaquemel. S Haiti
Jacó *206* SW Costa Rica
Jacob *see* Nkayi
Jacobābād *451* SW Pakistan
Jadotville *see* Likasi
Jadransko More *see* Adriatic Sea
Jādū *371* NW Libya
Jaén *531* SW Spain
Jaffna *534* N Sri Lanka
Jaffna Lagoon *534* lagoon of N Sri Lanka
Jafr, Qā' al *336 var.* El Jafr. Salt pan of S Jordan
Jägala *240 var.* Jägala Jõgi. River of N Estonia
Jägerndorf *see* Krnov
Jagodina *see* Svetozarevo
Jaguarão *see* Yaguarón
Jailolo *see* Halmahera
Jaipur *296 prev.* Jeypore. N India
Jaipur Hāt *117* NW Bangladesh
Jajce *140* W Bosnia & Herzegovina
Jakar *134* C Bhutan
Jakarta *302 prev.* Djakarta, *Dut.* Batavia. ❖ of Indonesia, Java, C Indonesia
Jakobshavn *see* Ilulissat
Jakobstad *see* Pietersaari. W Finland
Jakobstadt *see* Jēkabpils
Jalal-Abad *see* Dzhalal-Abad
Jalālābād *77* E Afghanistan
Jalandhar *296 prev.* Jullundur. N India
Jalapa *403 var.* Jalapa Enríquez, *prev.* Xalapa. SE Mexico
Jalapa *278* C Guatemala
Jalousie *497* SW St Lucia
Jālū *371* NE Libya
Jaluit *396* island of S Marshall Islands
Jamaame *524 It.* Giamame. S Somalia
Jamaare *440* river of NE Nigeria
Jamaica *328-329* island state of the West Indies, divided into 14 admin. units (parishes). ❖ Kingston
Jamaica Channel *286, 329* channel of the Caribbean Sea between Haiti and Jamaica
Jamālpur *117* N Bangladesh
Jambi *302 prev.* Djambi, *var.* Telanaipura. Sumatra, W Indonesia
Jambol *see* Yambol
Jamdena *see* Yamdena, Pulau
James Bay *171* inlet of Hudson Bay, C Canada
Jamestown *652* ❖ of St Helena, N St Helena
Jamestown *see* Holetown
Jammāl *see* Jemmel
Jammerbugten *218* bay to the NW of Denmark
Jammu *296* N India
Jāmnagar *296 prev.* Navangar. W India
Jämsä *249* S Finland
Jamshedpur *296* E India
Jamuna *117* lower course of the Brahmaputra, N Bangladesh
Jamundá *see* Nhamundá
Janakpur *427* E Nepal
Janela *176* Santo Antão, N Cape Verde
Jangijul *see* Yangiyŭl
Janīn *see* Jenin
Janina *see* Ioánnina
Janow *see* Jonava
Jantra *see* Yambol
Janzūr *371* NW Libya
Japan *330-335* country of E Asia, divided into 47 admin. units (prefectures). ❖ Tokyo
Japan, Sea of *330, 349, 485, 350 Rus.* Yapanskoye More. Sea of Pacific Ocean, between E Asia and Japan
Jappeni *261* C Gambia
Japurá *144 var.* Yapurá. River of Brazil
Jaquemel *see* Jacmel
Jarabacoa *226* C Dominican Republic
Jarābulus *551 var.* Jerablus, *Fr.* Djérablous. N Syria
Jarash *336 var.* Jerash. NW Jordan
Jarbah, Jazīrat *see* Jerba, Île de
Jardines de la Reina, Archipiélago de los *210* island group of S Cuba
Jarej District *396* district of Majuro, SE Marshall Islands
Jari *145 var.* Jary. River of N Brazil
Jarīd, Shaṭṭ al *see* Jerid, Chott el
Jaroměř *216* NE Czech Republic
Jarqŭrghon *610 Rus.* Dzharkurgan. SE Uzbekistan
Jars, Plain of *see* Xiangkhoang, Plateau de
Järvenpää *249 Swe.* Träskända. S Finland
Jason Islands *645* island group of NW Falkland Islands
Jassy *see* Iaşi
Jastrzębie Zdrój *471* S Poland
Jászberény *290* NE Hungary
Jauf *see* Al Jawf
Jaunpiebalga *362* NE Latvia
Java *302 var.* Jawa, *prev.* Djawa. Island of C Indonesia
Javari *144-145 var.* Yavarí. River of Brazil and Peru
Java Sea *see* Jawa, Laut
Jawa *see* Java
Jawa, Laut *302 Eng.* Java Sea. Sea of the Pacific Ocean, C Indonesia
Jawhar *524 var.* Jowhar, *It.* Giohar. S Somalia
Jayapura *303 prev.* Sukarnapura, *Dut.* Hollandia. Irian Jaya, E Indonesia
Jay Dairen *see* Dalian
Jaya, Puncak *303 prev.* Puntjak Sukarno, Puntjak Carstensz. Mountain of Irian Jaya, E Indonesia
Jazā'ir, Ra's al *115* cape of SW Bahrain
Jaz Murian, Hamun-e *307* lake of SE Iran
Jazzīn *see* Jezzine
Jbaïl *364 var.* Jubayl. W Lebanon
Jdiriya *414* NE Western Sahara
Jebba *440* W Nigeria
Jebel *see* Dzhebel
Jebel, Bahr el *see* White Nile
Jebel Dhanna *see* Jabal aẓ Ẓannah
Jeble *see* Jablah
Jedda *see* Jiddah
Jeffara Plain *371, 573 var.* Gefara, Al Jifārah. Plain of Libya and Tunisia
Jefferson City *599* Missouri, C USA
Jega *440* NW Nigeria
Jehegnadzor *see* Yeghegnadzor
Jēkabpils *362 Ger.* Jakobstadt. SE Latvia
Jelenia Góra *471 Ger.* Hirschberg in Riesengebirge. SW Poland
Jelgava *362 Ger.* Mitau. C Latvia
Jember *302 prev.* Djember. Java, C Indonesia
Jemmel *573 var.* Jammāl. N Tunisia
Jemo *396* island of C Marshall Islands
Jena *265* C Germany
Jendouba *573 var.* Jundūbah. NW Tunisia
Jenin *317, 318 var.* Janīn, *Ar.* Jinīn. N West Bank
Jenné *see* Djenné
Jennings *92* W Antigua, Antigua & Barbuda
Jenny *538* N Suriname
Jequitinhonha *145* river of E Brazil
Jerablus *see* Jarābulus
Jerada *414* NE Morocco
Jerash *see* Jarash
Jerba *see* Houmt Souk
Jerba, Île de *573 var.* Djerba, Jazīrat Jarbah. Island of E Tunisia
Jérémie *286* SW Haiti
Jerevan *see* Yerevan
Jerez de la Frontera *530* SW Spain
Jericho *317, 318 Heb.* Yeriḥo, *Ar.* Arīḥā. E West Bank
Jerid, Chott el *573 var.* Shaṭṭ al Jarīd. Salt lake of SW Tunisia
Jermuk *98 Rus.* Dzhermuk. SE Armenia
Jersey *252, 648* British Crown dependency of the English Channel. ❖ St Helier.
Jerusalem *317, 318 Ar.* Al Quds, *Heb.* Yerushalayim. ❖ of Israel, Israel and West Bank
Jesenice *520 Ger.* Assling. NW Slovenia
Jesselton *see* Kota Kinabalu
Jessore *117* W Bangladesh
Jesús Menéndez *210* SE Cuba
Jeta, Ilha de *282* island of W Guinea-Bissau
Jevlah *see* Yevlax
Jeypore *see* Jaipur
Jezercës, Maja e *81 var.* Jezerce. Mountain of N Albania
Jezzine *364 var.* Jazzīn. S Lebanon
Jhālakāti *117* S Bangladesh
Jhang *451 var.* Jhang Sadar, Jhang Sadr. NE Pakistan
Jhelum *451* NE Pakistan
Jhelum *451* river of India and Pakistan
Jhenida *117* W Bangladesh
Jiamusi *187 var.* Chia-mu-ssu, Kiamusze. Heilongjiang, NE China
Jiangsu *187 var.* Kiangsu, Chiang-su. Province of E China
Jiangxi *187 var.* Kiangsi, Chiang-hsi. Province of SE China
Jibuti *see* Djibouti
Jičín *216* N Czech Republic
Jiddah *506 Eng.* Jedda. W Saudi Arabia
Jiddah *115* island of NW Bahrain
Jidd Ḩafş *115 var.* Judd Ḩafş. N Bahrain
Jiftilik Post *318* E West Bank
Jiguaní *210* SE Cuba
Jihlava *216 Ger.* Iglau. S Czech Republic
Jijel *83 var.* Djidjel, *prev.* Djidjelli. NE Algeria
Jijiga *243 It.* Giggiga. E Ethiopia
Jilf al Kabīr, Haḑabat al *see* Gilf Kebir Plateau
Jilib *524 It.* Gelib. S Somalia
Jilin *187 var.* Kirin, Chi-lin, *prev.* Yungki. Jilin, NE China
Jilin *187 var.* Kirin, Chi-lin. Province of NE China
Jīma *243 var.* Jimma, Ft. Gimma. SW Ethiopia
Jimaní *226* W Dominican Republic
Jinan *187 var.* Chinan, Tsinan. Shandong, E China
Jinīn *see* Jenin
Jinja *584* S Uganda
Jinotega *436* C Nicaragua
Jinotepe *436* S Nicaragua
Jinsen *see* Inch'ŏn
Jintotlolo Channel *466* channel connecting Mindoro Strait and Visayan Sea
Jinzhou *187 var.* Chin-chou, Chinchow, *prev.* Chinhsien. Liaoning, NE China
Jipijapa *228* W Ecuador

Jiquilisco *235* S El Salvador
Jiquilisco, Bahia de *235* bay of the Pacific Ocean to the S of El Salvador
Jirgatol *558 Rus.* Dzhirgatal'. C Tajikistan
Jirriiban *524 prev.* Ceel Xamurre, *It.* El Hamurre. E Somalia
Jisr ash Shughūr *551* *var.* Djisr el Choghour. NW Syria
Jiu *480 Ger.* Schyl, *Hung.* Zsily. River of S Romania
Jiulong *see* Kowloon
Jixi *187 var.* Chi-hsi. Heilongjiang, NE China
Jīzān *506 var.* Qīzān. S Saudi Arabia
Jizuka *330* Kyūshū, SW Japan
Jiz', Wādī al *627* dry watercourse of E Yemen
Jizzakh *610 Rus.* Dzhizak. SE Uzbekistan
Jleeb, Shagat Al *see* Qalīb, Shiqqat al
Jleeb al Shuyoukh *see* Qalīb ash Shuyūkh
Joal-Fadiout *510 prev.* Joal. W Senegal
João Barrosa *176* Boa Vista, E Cape Verde
João Pessoa *145 prev.* Paraíba. E Brazil
Jo-ch'iang *see* Ruoqiang
Joden Savanne *538* NE Suriname
Jodhpur *296* NW India
Joel's Drift *366* N Lesotho
Joensuu *249* SE Finland
Jõgeva *240 Ger.* Laisholm. C Estonia
Jogjakarta *see* Yogyakarta
Johannesburg *527* Pretoria-Witwatersrand-Vereeniging, NE South Africa
John o'Groats *593* N Scotland, UK
Johnsons Point *92* SW Antigua, Antigua & Barbuda
Johnson, Rapides *203* rapids of Dem. Rep. Congo (Zaire) and Zambia
Johnston Atoll *648* unincorporated territory of the USA, Pacific Ocean
Johnston Island *648* island of S Johnston Atoll
Johor Bahru *386* SE Peninsular Malaysia
Johore Strait *517* strait connecting Strait of Malacca and South China Sea
Joinville *145 var.* Joinvile. S Brazil
Jolo Group *466* island group of Sulu Archipelago, SW Philippines
Jolo Island *466* island of Jolo Group, SW Philippines
Jomsom *427* W Nepal
Jona *546* NE Switzerland
Jonava *376 Ger.* Janow. C Lithuania
Jones Point *644* headland on the W coast of Christmas Island
Jonglei Canal *536* canal of S Sudan
Jönköping *543* S Sweden
Jonquière *171* SE Canada
Jordan *317, 318, 336 Ar.* Urdunn, *Heb.* HaYarden. River of SW Asia
Jordan *336-337* officially Hashemite Kingdom of Jordan, *Ar.* Al Urdunn. Country of SW Asia divided into 8 admin. units (governorates). ❖ Amman
Jos *440* C Nigeria
José Batlle y Ordóñez *607* C Uruguay
José E. Bisanó *226* N Dominican Republic
José Pedro Varela *607* SE Uruguay
Joseph Bonaparte Gulf *101* gulf of Timor Sea on the coast of NW Australia
Jos Plateau *440* plateau of C Nigeria
Jos Sudarso *see* Yos Sudarso, Pulau
Jost Van Dyke *643* island of W British Virgin Islands
Jotunheimen *444* mountains of SW Norway
Joûnié *364 var.* Jūniyah, Juniye. W Lebanon
Jovellanos *210* NW Cuba
Jozini Dam *540* reservoir of South Africa and Swaziland
Jsahaya *330* Kyūshū, SW Japan
Juan Fernández Islands *183* island group of W Chile
Juan L. Lacaze *607 prev.* Sauce. SW Uruguay
Juarzon *368 var.* Juazohn. SE Liberia
Juazeiro do Norte *145* E Brazil
Juazohn *see* Juarzon
Juba *243, 524 Som.* Jubba, *var.* Ganaane, *Amh.* Genale Wenz, *It.* Guiba. River of Ethiopia and Somalia
Juba *536 var.* Jūbā. S Sudan
Jubany *90* Argentinian research station of Antarctic Peninsula, Antarctica
Jubba *see* Juba
Jubbulpore *see* Jabalpur
Júcar *531* river of C Spain
Juclà, Estany de *86* lake of NE Andorra
Judd Ḩafş *see* Jidd Ḩafş
Judenburg *106* C Austria
Juigalpa *436* S Nicaragua
Juishui *555* E Taiwan
Juiz de Fora *145* SE Brazil
Jujuy *see* San Salvador de Jujuy
Juliaca *463* SE Peru
Julian Alps *520 Ger.* Julische Alpen, *It.* Alpi Giulie, *Slvn.* Julijske Alpe. Mountains of NW Slovenia
Juliana Top *538* mountain of C Suriname
Julianehåb *see* Qaqortoq
Jullundur *see* Jalandhar
Jumayrah *590 var.* Jumeirah. NE United Arab Emirates
Jumla *427* E Nepal
Jumna *see* Yamuna
Jundūbah *see* Jendouba
Juneau *598* Alaska, USA
Jungbunzlau *see* Mladá Boleslav
Junín *95* E Argentina
Junk Bay *see* Tseung Kwan O
Juntas *206* W Costa Rica
Junten *see* Sunch'ŏn
Juozapinės Kalnas *376* mountain of SE Lithuania
Jupiá, Represa de *145* reservoir of S Brazil
Jura *593* island of Inner Hebrides, W Scotland, UK
Jura *253, 546 var.* Jura Mountains. Mountain range of France and Switzerland
Juraguá *210* C Cuba
Jura Mountains *see* Jura
Jurbarkas *376 Ger.* Jurburg, *var.* Georgenburg. W Lithuania
Jūrmala *362* NW Latvia
Jurong Lake *517* lake of W Singapore
Jurong Town *517* W Singapore
Juruá *144* river of Brazil and Peru
Juruena *144* river of W Brazil
Jutiapa *278* S Guatemala
Juticalpa *288* C Honduras
Jutland *see* Jylland
Juventud, Isla de la *210* *var.* Isla de Pinos, *Eng.* Isle of Pines. Island of W Cuba
Južna Morava *630* river of SE Serbia, Yugoslavia
Jwaneng *142* S Botswana
Jylland *218 Eng.* Jutland. Island of W Denmark
Jyrgalan *see* Dzhergalan
Jyväskylä *249* S Finland

K

K2 *451 Eng.* Mount Godwin Austen. Mountain of China and Pakistan
Kaabong *584* NE Uganda
Kaafu Atoll *see* Male' Atoll
Kaaimanston *538* NW Suriname
Kaakhka *581 var.* Kaachka, Kaka. S Turkmenistan
Kaala *see* Caála
Kaapstad *see* Cape Town
Kaba *514 var.* Little Scarcies. River of Guinea and Sierra Leone
Kabakama *261* E Gambia
Kabala *514* N Sierra Leone
Kabale *584* SW Uganda
Kabalega Falls *see* Murchison Falls
Kabara *246 prev.* Kambara. Island of the Lau Group, E Fiji
Kabardino-Balkarskaya, Respublika *484* autonomous republic of SW Russian Federation
Kabarnet *342* W Kenya
Kabarole *584* W Uganda
Kabaya *492* NW Rwanda
Kaberamaido *584* C Uganda
Kabinda *203* SE Dem. Rep. Congo (Zaire)
Kabinda *see* Cabinda
Kābol *see* Kābul
Kabompo *635* W Zambia
Kabompo *635* river of W Zambia
Kabou *567* N Togo
Kābul *77 Per.* Kābol. ❖ of Afghanistan, E Afghanistan
Kabul *77, 451* river of Afghanistan and Pakistan
Kabwe *635* C Zambia
Kabye Plateau *567* plateau of E Togo
Kachch, Gulf of *296 var.* Gulf of Cutch, Gulf of Kutch. Gulf of Arabian Sea to the W of India
Kachhi *451* lowland region of C Pakistan
Kadan Island *159 prev.* King I. Island of S Burma
Kadavu *246 prev.* Kandavu. Island to the S of Viti Levu, SW Fiji
Kadavu Passage *246* channel of the Pacific Ocean between Kadavu and Vitu Levu, Fiji
Kadéï *168, 179* river of Cameroon and Central African Republic
Kadoma *636 prev.* Gatooma. C Zimbabwe
Kadugli *536 var.* Kāduqlī. S Sudan
Kaduha *492* SW Rwanda
Kaduna *440* C Nigeria
Kaduna *440* river of N Nigeria
Kadzharan *see* K'ajaran
Kadzhi-Say *357 Kir.* Kajisay. NE Kyrgyzstan
Kaédi *398* S Mauritania
Kaélé *168* N Cameroon
Kaesŏng *349* S North Korea
Kaewieng *see* Kavieng
Kafan *see* Kapan
Kāfar Jar Ghar *77* mountain range of C Afghanistan
Kaffrine *510* C Senegal
Kafr el Dauwâr *230 var.* Kafr ad Dawwār. N Egypt
Kafr el Sheikh *230* *var.* Kafr ash Shaykh. N Egypt
Kafu *584 var.* Kafo. River of W Uganda
Kafue *635* river of C Zambia
Kafue *635* SE Zambia
Kaga Bandoro *179 prev.* Fort-Crampel. C Central African Republic
Kagan *see* Kogon
Kaganovichabad *see* Kolkhozobod
Kagera *see* Akagera
Kagi *see* Chiai
Kâgıthane *577* NW Turkey
Kagoshima *330* Kyūshū, SW Japan
Kagul *see* Cahul
Kahama *560* NW Tanzania
Kahayan *302* river of Borneo, C Indonesia
Kahnple *368* NE Liberia
Kahnwia *368* SE Liberia
Kahramanmaraş *577 var.* Marash, Maraş. S Turkey
Kaiaf *261* S Gambia
Kaieteur Falls *284* waterfall of C Guyana
Kaifeng *187* Henan, C China
Kai, Kepulauan *302 prev.* Kei Islands. Island group of Maluku, E Indonesia
Kaikoura *433* NE South Island, New Zealand
Kailahun *514* E Sierra Leone
Kainan *330* Honshū, C Japan
Kainji Reservoir *440* reservoir of W Nigeria
Kaipara Harbour *433* harbour of NW North Island, New Zealand
Kairouan *573 var.* Al Qayrawān. N Tunisia
Kaiserslautern *264* SW Germany
Kaitaia *433* NW North Island, New Zealand
Kajaani *249 Swe.* Kajana. C Finland
Kajana *see* Kajaani
Kajang *386* W Peninsular Malaysia
K'ajaran *98 Rus.* Kadzharan, *var.* Kadžaran. SE Armenia
Kajisay *see* Kadzhi-Say
Kaka *see* Kaakhaa
Kakamega *342* W Kenya
Kakata *368* C Liberia
Kakhovs'ke Vodokhovyshche *586 Rus.* Kakhovskoye Vodokhranilische. Reservoir of SE Ukraine
Kakia *see* Khakhea
Kakogawa *330* Honshū, C Japan
Kakshaal-Too, Khrebet *see* Kokshaal-Tau
Kalaa Kebira *573 var.* Al Qal'ah al Kubrá. N Tunisia
Kalabo *635* W Zambia
Kalahari Desert *142, 423, 527* desert region of southern Africa
Kalaikhum *see* Qal'aikhum
Kalai-Mor *581 Turkm.* Galaymor. SE Turkmenistan
Kalamáki *273 prev.* Kalmákion. SE Greece
Kalamariá *273 prev.* Kalamaria. N Greece
Kalámata *273 prev.* Kalámai. S Greece
Kalandula *see* Calandula
Kalang *see* Kallang
Kalanshiyū, Sarīr *371* *var.* Calanscio Sand Sea. Desert region of E Libya
Kalarash *see* Călăraşi
Kalasin *563 var.* Muang Kalasin. NE Thailand
Kalāt *77 var.* Qalāt. S Afghanistan
Kālat *451 var.* Kelat. W Pakistan
Kalbā *590 var.* Kalba, NE United Arab Emirates
Kaldakvísl *294* river of C Iceland
Kalemie *203 prev.* Albertville. SE Dem. Rep. Congo (Zaire)
Kalgan *see* Zhangjiakou
Kalgoorlie *100* SW Australia
Kali Gandaki *427* river of C Nepal
Kalima *203* E Dem. Rep. Congo (Zaire)
Kalimantan *302 Eng.* Indonesian Borneo. Region of Borneo, administered by Indonesia
Kalinin *581* N Turkmenistan
Kalininabad *see* Kalininobod
Kaliningrad *484* W Russian Federation
Kalinino *see* Tashir
Kalininobod *558 Rus.* Kalininabad. SW Tajikistan
Kalinkavichy *122 Rus.* Kalinkovichi. SE Belarus
Kaliro *584* SE Uganda
Kalisz *471 Ger.* Kalisch. C Poland
Kalixälv *543* river of NE Sweden
Kalkandelen *see* Tetovo
Kalkfeld *423* NW Namibia
Kallang *517 var.* Kalang. River of C Singapore
Kallaste *240 Ger.* Krasnogor. E Estonia
Kallavesi *249* lake of SE Finland
Kalmar *543* S Sweden
Kalmykiya, Respublika *484* autonomous republic of SW Russian Federation
Kalomo *635* S Zambia
Kalpeni Island *296* island of Lakshadweep, SW India
Kalsoy *644 var.* Kalsø. Island of N Faeroe Islands
Kalu Ganga *534* river of S Sri Lanka
Kalulushi *635* C Zambia
Kalundborg *218* Sjælland, C Denmark
Kalungwishi *635* river of N Zambia
Kalutara *534* SW Sri Lanka
Kaluwawa *see* Fergusson Island
Kalyān *296* W India
Kálymnas *273* island of SE Greece
Kama *203* E Dem. Rep. Congo (Zaire)
Kamai *180* N Chad
Kamaishi *331* Honshū, N Japan
Kamakwie *514* NW Sierra Leone
Kamālia *451* NE Pakistan

Kamanjab *423* NW Namibia
Kamarān *627* island of W Yemen
Kamarang *284* W Guyana
Kamativi *636* W Zimbabwe
Kambar *451* *var.* Qambar. SW Pakistan
Kambing, Pulau *305* island of E Timor
Kambara *see* Kabara
Kamchatka, Poluostrov *485* *Eng.* Kamchatka Peninsula. Peninsula of NE Russian Federation
Kamchiya *152* *var.* Kamčija. River of E Bulgaria
Kamenets-Podol'sk *see* Kam"yanets'-Podil's'kyy
Kamenets-Podol'skiy *see* Kam"yanets'-Podil's'kyy
Kamenica *381* NE FYR Macedonia
Kamenskoye *see* Dniprodzerzhyns'k
Kamina *203* S Dem. Rep. Congo (Zaire)
Kamishli *see* Al Qāmishlī
Kamloops *170* SW Canada
Kammersee *see* Attersee
Kamnik *520* *Ger.* Stein. C Slovenia
Kamo *98* C Armenia
Kamp *106* river of N Austria
Kampala *584* ❖ of Uganda, S Uganda
Kampar *386* W Peninsular Malaysia
Kampar *302* river of Sumatra, W Indonesia
Kampo *see* Ntem
Kampong Batang Duri *150* NE Brunei
Kampong Benutan *150* C Brunei
Kampong Bukit Sawat *150* C Brunei
Kampong Bunut *150* N Brunei
Kâmpóng Cham *165* *prev.* Kompong Cham. S Cambodia
Kâmpóng Chhnăng *165* C Cambodia
Kampong Jerudong *150* N Brunei
Kâmpóng Khleăng *165* *prev.* Kompong Kleang. NW Cambodia
Kampong Kuala Abang *150* C Brunei
Kampong Kuala Balai *150* SW Brunei
Kampong Labi *150* S Brunei
Kampong Labu *150* NE Brunei
Kampong Lumut *150* W Brunei
Kampong Paring *150* N Brunei
Kampong Parit *150* N Brunei
Kâmpóng Saôm *165* *var.* Kompong Som, *prev.* Sihanoukville. SW Cambodia
Kâmpóng Saôm, Chhâk *165* *Fr.* Baie de Kompong Som. Bay of the Gulf of Thailand on the SW coast of Cambodia
Kâmpóng Spoe *165* *prev.* Kompong Speu. S Cambodia
Kampong Sukang *150* S Brunei
Kampong Tanajor *150* C Brunei
Kampong Teraja *150* S Brunei
Kâmpóng Thum *165* *prev.* Kompong Thom. C Cambodia
Kâmpôt *165* S Cambodia
Kampuchea *see* Cambodia
Kamsar *281* W Guinea
Kam"yanets'-Podil's'kyy *586* *Rus.* Kamenets-Podol'skiy, *prev.* Kamenets-Podol'sk. W Ukraine
Kanacea *246* *prev.* Kanathea. Taveuni, N Fiji
Kanacea *246* island of the Lau Group, E Fiji
Kananga *203* *prev.* Luluabourg. SW Dem. Rep. Congo (Zaire)
Kanazawa *330* Honshū, C Japan
Kanazi *492* SE Rwanda
Kandahār *77* *var.* Qandahār. S Afghanistan
Kandavu *see* Kadavu
Kandé *567* NE Togo
Kandi *132* N Benin
Kandrian *458* New Britain, E Papua New Guinea
Kandy *534* C Sri Lanka
Kaneohe *598* Oahu, Hawaii, USA
Kanevskoye Vodokhranilische *see* Kanivs'ke Vodoskhovyshche
Kang *142* C Botswana
Kangar *386* NW Peninsular Malaysia
Kangaroo Island *101* island of S Australia
Kangaruma *284* C Guyana
Kangchenjunga *297* *var.* Kanchenjunga. Mountain of NE India
Kangerlussuaq *646* *Dan.* Søndre Strømfjord. SW Greenland
Kanggye *349* N North Korea
Kanghwa-do *350* *Jap.* Kōka-tō. Island of NW South Korea
Kangnŭng *350* *Jap.* Kōryō. NE South Korea
Kango *258* NW Gabon
Kanibadam *558* N Tajikistan
Kani, Baie de *649* *var.* Kani Bay. Bay of the Mozambique Channel on the SW coast of Mayotte
Kanivs'ke Vodoskhovyshche *586* *Rus.* Kanevskoye Vodokhranilische. Reservoir of C Ukraine
Kanjiža *630* *prev.* Stara Kanjiža, *Ger.* Altkanischa, *Hung.* Magyarkanizsa, Ókanizsa. N Serbia, Yugoslavia
Kankan *281* E Guinea
Kankesanturai *534* N Sri Lanka
Kan-kō *see* Han
Kankossa *398* S Mauritania
Kanli Dere *see* Pedhieos
Kanmaw Island *159* *var.* Kettharin I, Kisseraing. Island of S Burma
Kano *440* N Nigeria
Kanombe *492* C Rwanda
Kanoya *330* Kyūshū, SW Japan
Kānpur *296* *prev.* Cawnpore. N India
Kanra-san *see* Halla-san
Kansas *599* state of C USA
Kansas City *599* Kansas, C USA
Kant *357* C Kyrgyzstan
Kantipur *see* Kathmandu
Kanton *346* *var.* Abariringa, Canton I, *prev.* Mary I. Island of the Phoenix Is, C Kiribati
Kanyaru *see* Akanyaru
Kanye *142* S Botswana
Kao *568* island of W Tonga
Kao *568* mountain of Kao, Tonga
Kaôh Nhêk *165* E Cambodia
Kaohsiung *555* *var.* Kaohiung, *Jap.* Takao. SW Taiwan
Kaolack *510* *var.* Kaolak. W Senegal
Kaolak *see* Kaolack
Kaolan *see* Lanzhou
Kaoma *635* W Zambia
Kaop'ing Hsi *555* river of C Taiwan
Kapan *98* *var.* Ghap'an. *Rus.* Kafan. SE Armenia
Kapchorwa *584* E Uganda
Kapenguria *342* W Kenya
Kapfenberg *106* C Austria
Kapingamarangi *406* atoll of S Micronesia
Kapiri Mposhi *635* C Zambia
Kapiti Island *433* island to the S of North Island, New Zealand
Kapka, Massif du *180* mountains of E Chad
Kaposvár *290* SW Hungary
Kaproncza *see* Koprivnica
Kapsabet *342* W Kenya
Kapsukas *see* Marijampolė
Kapuas *302* *prev.* Kapoeas. River of Borneo, C Indonesia
Kapuas Mountains *302, 386* *Ind.* Pegunungan Kapuas Hulu. Mountain range of Indonesia and Malaysia
Kara *567* *var.* Lama-Kara. NE Togo
Karaba *492* SW Rwanda
Kara-Balta *357* NW Kyrgyzstan
Karabil', Vozvyshennost' *581* region of SE Turkmenistan
Kara-Bogaz-Gol, Zaliv *581* NW Turkmenistan
Kara-Bogaz-Gol, Proliv *581* *Turkm.* Garabogazköl Bogazy. Strait of the Caspian Sea, on the NW coast of Turkmenistan
Karabük *577* N Turkey
Karachayevo-Cherkesskaya SSR *484* autonomous republic of SW Russian Federation
Karāchi *451* S Pakistan
Karadeniz *see* Black Sea
Karadeniz Boğazi *see* İstanbul Boğazi
Karaferiye *see* Véroia
Karaganda *338* *Kaz.* Qaraghandy. C Kazakhstan
Karaitivu *534* N Sri Lanka
Karaj *307* NW Iran
Karak *see* Al Karak
Kara-Kala *581* *var.* Garrygala. SW Turkmenistan
Karaklin *see* Vanadzar
Karakol *357* *var.* Karakolka. E Kyrgyzstan
Karakol *357* *prev.* Przheval'sk, *var.* Prževalsk. NE Kyrgyzstan
Karakoram Range *296, 451* mountain range of C Asia
Karakose *577* NE Turkey
Kara-Kul' *357* *Kir.* Kara-Köl. W Kyrgyzstan
Karakul' *see* Qorakŭl
Karakul' *see* Qarokŭl
Karakul', Ozero *see* Qarokŭl
Karakumskiy Kanal *581* *Turkm.* Garagum Kanaly. Canal of SE Turkmenistan
Karakumy *581* *Eng.* Kara Kum, *Turkm.* Garagum, *var.* Qara Qum. Desert region of C Turkmenistan
Karaman *577* S Turkey
Karamay *186* *var.* Karamai, *Chin.* K'o-la-ma-i. Xinjiang Uygur Zizhiqu, NW China
Karamea Bight *433* area of the Tasman Sea, on the NW coast of South Island, New Zealand
Kara-Say *357* E Kyrgyzstan
Karasburg *423* S Namibia
Kara Sea *see* Karskoye More
Karasjok *444* NE Norway
Kara Su *see* Mesta, Néstos
Karatau *338* *Kaz.* Qarataū. S Kazakhstan
Karatsu *330* Kyūshū, SW Japan
Karavastasë, Laguna e *81* *var.* Kënet' e Karavastas, Kravasta Lagoon. Lagoon of W Albania
Karawang *302* *prev.* Krawang. Java, C Indonesia
Karawanken *106* *Slvn.* Karavanke. Mountain range of C Europe
Karbalā' *310* *var.* Kerbala. C Iraq
Kardítsa *273* C Greece
Kärdla *240* *Ger.* Kertel. Hiiumaa, Estonia
Kareliya, Respublika *484* autonomous republic of NW Russian Federation
Karen *see* Hualien
Kari *see* Chiali
Kariba *636* N Zimbabwe
Kariba Dam *636* dam at NE end of Lake Kariba, on Zambezi river, NW Zimbabwe
Kariba, Lake *635, 636* reservoir of Zambia and Zimbabwe
Karibib *423* C Namibia
Karimama *132* N Benin
Karimata, Selat *302* strait connecting Laut Jawa and the South China Sea, E Indonesia
Karisimbi, Volcan *492* *var.* Mount Karisimbi. Mountain of Rwanda and Dem. Rep. Congo (Zaire)
Karkaralinsk *338* E Kazakhstan
Karkar Island *458* island of NE Papua New Guinea
Karkinits'ka Zatoka *586* *Rus.* Karkinitskiy Zaliv. Gulf of the Black Sea, S Ukraine
Karleby *see* Kokkola
Karl-Marx-Stadt *see* Chemnitz
Karlö *see* Hailuoto
Karlovac *209* *Ger.* Karlstadt, *Hung.* Károlyváros. N Croatia
Karlovo *152* *prev.* Levskigrad. C Bulgaria
Karlovy Vary *216* *Ger.* Karlsbad, *var.* Carlsbad. W Czech Republic
Karlsbad *see* Karlovy Vary
Karlskrona *543* S Sweden
Karlsruhe *264* *var.* Carlsruhe. SW Germany
Karlstad *543* SW Sweden
Karlstadt *see* Karlovac
Karmi 'él *317* N Israel
Karnali *427* *var.* Kauriala. River of W Nepal
Karnobat *152* E Bulgaria
Karoi *636* N Zimbabwe
Károlyváros *see* Karlovac
Karonga *385* N Malawi
Karonje, Mount *162* mountain of W Burundi
Karpasia *215* *var.* Karpas Peninsula. Peninsular of NE Cyprus
Karpaten *see* Carpathian Mountains
Kárpathos *273* island of SE Greece
Karpaty *see* Carpathian Mountains
Karrānah *115* N Bahrain
Kars *577* NE Turkey
Karshi *see* Qarshi
Karskoye More *485* *Eng.* Kara Sea. Sea of Arctic Ocean, bordering N Russian Federation
Karumba *101* NE Australia
Kartung *261* W Gambia
Kārūn *307* river of W Iran
Karungu Bay *342* bay of Lake Victoria, to the SW of Kenya
Karuzi *162* C Burundi
Karviná *216* *Ger.* Karwin. E Czech Republic
Karzakkān *115* NW Bahrain
Kas *577* SW Turkey
Kasai *88, 203* *var.* Kassai, Cassai. River of Angola and Dem. Rep. Congo (Zaire)
Kasama *635* N Zambia
Kasan *see* Koson
Kasane *142* N Botswana
Kasari *240* river of W Estonia
Kasbegi *see* Qazbegi
Kaschau *see* Koṛice
Kasese *584* SW Uganda
Kashaf Rūd *307* river of NE Iran
Kāshān *307* NW Iran
Kashgar *see* Kashi
Kashi *186* *Uigh.* Kashgar. Xinjiang Uygur Zizhiqu, NW China
Kashiwa *330* Honshū, SE Japan
Kashiwazaki *330* Honshū, N Japan
Käsmark *see* Kežmarok
Kasongo *203* E Dem. Rep. Congo (Zaire)
Kaspi *262* C Georgia
Kaspiyskoye More *see* Caspian Sea
Kaspiy Tengizi *see* Caspian Sea
Kassa *see* Košice
Kassai *see* Kasai
Kassala *536* *var.* Kassalā, Kasala. E Sudan
Kassándra *273* peninsula of NE Greece
Kassel *264* *prev.* Cassel. C Germany
Kasserine *573* *var.* Al-Qaşrayn. W Tunisia
Kassikaityu *284* river of S Guyana
Kastamonu *577* N Turkey
Kastsyukovichy *122* E Belarus
Kasugai *330* Honshū, C Japan
Kasulu *560* W Tanzania
Kasumiga-ura *330* lake of Honshū, SE Japan
Kasungu *385* C Malawi
Kasupe *see* Machinga
Katchang *261* C Gambia
Kateríni *273* N Greece
Katete *635* E Zambia
Katha *159* N Burma
Katherina, Gebel *230* *var.* Jabal Katrīnah, *Eng.* Mt. Catherine. Mountain of NE Egypt
Katherine *101* N Australia
Kathmandu *427* *prev.* Kantipur. ❖ of Nepal, C Nepal
Kati *392* SW Mali
Katima Mulilo *423* *var.* Ngweze. NE Namibia
Katiola *326* C Ivory Coast
Katonga *584* river of SW Uganda
Katowice *471* *Ger.* Kattowitz. S Poland
Katrīnah, Jabal *see* Katherina, Gebel
Katsina *440* N Nigeria
Kattaqŭrghon *610* *Rus.* Kattakurgan. SE Uzbekistan
Kattegat *218, 543* strait between Denmark and Sweden

Katumbi 385 NW Malawi
Katwijk aan Zee 429 W Netherlands
Kauai 598 island of Hawaii, USA, C Pacific
Kaufbeuren 265 S Germany
Kaunas 376 *Ger.* Kauen, *Pol.* Kowno, *Rus.* Kovno. C Lithuania
Kauno Marios 376 reservoir of S Lithuania
Kauriala *see* Karnali
Kaushany *see* Căuşeni
Kau-Ur 261 N Gambia
Kavadarci 381 S FYR Macedonia
Kavajë 81 *It.* Cavaia. W Albania
Kavála 273 *prev.* Kaválla. NE Greece
Kavango *see* Cubango
Kavaratti Island 296 island of Lakshadweep, SW India
Kavengo *see* Cubango
Kavieng 458 *var.* Kaewieng. New Ireland I, Papua New Guinea
Kavīr, Dasht-e 307 desert region of N Iran
Kavirondo Gulf *see* Winam Gulf
Kavkaz *see* Caucasus
Kawagoe 330 Honshū, SE Japan
Kawambwa 635 N Zambia
Kawasaki 330 Honshū, SE Japan
Kaya 157 C Burkina
Kayagangiri, Mont 179 mountain of W Central African Republic
Kayan 302 river of Borneo, C Indonesia
Kayan 159 S Burma
Kayangel Islands 455 island group of N Palau
Kayanza 162 N Burundi
Kayes 392 W Mali
Kayl 378 S Luxembourg
Kayogoro 162 S Burundi
Kayokwe 162 C Burundi
Kayrakkumskoye Vodokhranilishche *see* Qayrokkum, Obanbori
Kayseri 577 C Turkey
Kayts 534 island of N Sri Lanka
Kazakh *see* Qazax
Kazakhskiy Melkosopochnik 338 *Eng.* Kazakh Uplands. Uplands of C Kazakhstan
Kazakhstan 338-341 officially Republic of Kazakhstan, *Kaz.* Qazaqstan, *prev.* Kazakh SSR. *Rus.* Kazakhskay SSR. Country of C Asia divided into 19 admin. units (provinces). ❖ Astana
Kazakh Uplands *see* Kazakhskiy Melkosopochnik
Kazan' 484 W Russian Federation
Kazandzhik *see* Gazandzhyk
Kazanlŭk 152 *var.* Kazanlăk, Kazanlik. C Bulgaria
Kazan-rettō 330 *Eng.* Volcano Islands. Island group to the SE of Honshū, SE Japan
Kazarman 357 C Kyrgyzstan
Kazbek 262 mountain of N Georgia
Kazi Magomed *see* Qazimämmäd
Kazincbarcika 290 NE Hungary
Kazvin *see* Qazvin
Kéa 273 island of SE Greece
Kéamu *see* Aneityum
Kebili 573 *var.* Qibilī. C Tunisia
Kebnekaise 543 mountain of N Sweden
Kecskemét 290 C Hungary
Kėdainiai 376 C Lithuania
Kediet ej Jill 398 *var.* Kediet Ijill, Kédia d'Idjil. Mountain of NW Mauritania
Kediri 302 Java, C Indonesia
Kédougou 510 SE Senegal
Keeling Islands *see* Cocos Islands
Keelung *see* Chilung
Keetmanshoop 423 S Namibia
Kefallinía 273 *Eng.* Cephalonia. Island of W Greece
Kefar Sava 317 C Israel
Keflavík 294 *var.* Iceflavik. W Iceland
Kegalla 534 *var.* Kegalle. C Sri Lanka
Kegel *see* Keila
Kei Islands *see* Kai, Kepulauan
Keijō *see* Seoul
Keila 240 *Ger.* Kegel. NW Estonia
Keila 240 *var.* Keila Jōgi. River of NW Estonia
Keishū *see* Kyŏngju
Kéita 180 *var.* Doka. River of S Chad
Keïta 439 SW Niger
Keitele 249 lake of C Finland
Këk-Art 357 *prev.* Alaykel'. SW Kyrgyzstan
Kékes 290 mountain of N Hungary
Kelang 386 *var.* Klang, *prev.* Port Swettenham. W Peninsular Malaysia
Kelantan 386 river of N Peninsular Malaysia
Kelbia, Sebkhet 573 *var.* Sabkhat Kalbīyah. Salt flat of NE Tunisia
Këlcyrë 81 *var.* Këlcyra. S Albania
Kelifskiy Uzboy 581 region of SE Turkmenistan
Kéllé 200 W Congo
Kelmė 376 NW Lithuania
Kélo 180 SW Chad
Kelowna 170 SW Canada
Keluang 386 *var.* Kluang. SE Peninsular Malaysia
Kembolcha 243 *var.* Kombolcha. N Ethiopia
Kemerovo 485 *prev.* Shcheglovsk. C Russian Federation
Kemi 249 NW Finland
Kemijärvi 249 N Finland
Kemijoki 249 river of NW Finland
Kemin 357 *prev.* Bystrovka. N Kyrgyzstan
Kemiö *see* Kimito
Kemmuna 395 island of NW Malta
Kemmunett 395 island of NW Malta
Kempen 127 *Fr.* Campine, *Ger.* Kempenland. Heathland of NE Belgium
Kempten 265 S Germany
Kenema 514 SE Sierra Leone
Këneurgench 581 *prev.* Kunya-Urgench, Kunja-Urgenč, *Turkm.* Köneür gench. N Turkmenistan
Kénitra 414 *prev.* Port Lyautey. NW Morocco
Kenmare 314 SW Ireland
Kentau 338 S Kazakhstan
Kentucky 599 state of C USA
Kenya 342-345 officially Republic of Kenya. Country of E Africa divided into 7 admin. units (provinces). ❖ Nairobi
Kenya, Mount *see* Kirinyaga
Keppel Harbour 517 harbour, S Singapore
Keppel Island *see* Niuatoputapu
Kerava 249 *Swe.* Kervo. S Finland
Kerch 586 *Rus.* Kerch'. SE Ukraine
Kerema 458 S Papua New Guinea
Keren 238 *var.* Cheren. C Eritrea
Kerewan 261 W Gambia
Kericho 342 W Kenya
Kerio 342 river of W Kenya
Kerkenah, Îles 573 *var.* Kerkenna Islands, *Ar.* Juzur Qarqannah. Island group of E Tunisia
Kerki 581 SE Turkmenistan
Kerkrade 429 S Netherlands
Kérkyra 273 *prev.* Kérkira, *Eng.* Corfu. Island of W Greece
Kérkyra 273 *Eng.* Corfu, *prev.* Kérkira. W Greece
Kermān 307 *var.* Kirman. SE Iran
Kermānshāh *see* Bākhtarān
Kerora 238 N Eritrea
Kérouané 281 SE Guinea
Kertel *see* Kärdla
Kerulen 412 *var.* Herlen Gol. River of China and Mongolia
Kervo *see* Kerava
Keryneia *see* Girne
Kesen'-numa 331 Honshū, N Japan
Késmárk *see* Kežmarok
Kesra 573 *var.* Kisrah. NW Tunisia
Keta 270 SE Ghana
Ketchikan 598 Alaska, USA
Kete-Krachi 270 *var.* Kete Krakye. E Ghana
Kétou 132 SE Benin
Kettharin Island *see* Kanmaw Island
Keur Massène 398 SW Mauritania
Kévé 567 SW Togo
Kew 653 North Caicos, NW Turks and Caicos Islands
Kežmarok 519 *Ger.* Käsmark, *Hung.* Késmárk. NE Slovakia
Khabarovsk 485 SE Russian Federation
Khabura *see* Al Khaburah
Khachmas *see* Xaçmaz
Khairpur 451 S Pakistan
Khakasiya, Respublika 485 autonomous republic of C Russian Federation
Khakassk *see* Abakan
Khakhea 142 *var.* Kakia. S Botswana
Khalándrion *see* Chalándri
Khalkidhikí *see* Chalkidikí
Khalkís *see* Chalkída
Khalūf 448 *var.* Al Khaluf. S Oman
Khambhat, Gulf of 296 *Eng.* Gulf of Cambay. Gulf of Arabian Sea to the W of India
Khamir 627 *var.* Khamr. W Yemen
Khamīs Mushayṭ 506 S Saudi Arabia
Khānābād 77 NE Afghanistan
Khānaqīn 310 E Iraq
Khānewāl 451 NE Pakistan
Khanh Hung *see* Soc Trăng
Khanka, Lake 187, 485 *var.* Lake Hanka, *Rus.* Ozero Khanka, *Chin.* Xingkai Hu, Hsing-K'ai Hu. Lake of China and Russian Federation
Khanka, Ozero *see* Khanka, Lake
Khankendy *see* Xankändi
Khānpur 451 SE Pakistan
Khanty-Mansiysk 484 *prev.* Ostyako-Voguls'k. C Russian Federation
Khān Yūnis 317, 318 *Ar.* Khan Yunus. Gaza Strip
Kharâb, Ghoubbet el 222 bay at the head of Golfe de Tadjoura, E of Djibouti
Kharanah *see* Al Kir'ānah
Khāriān 451 NE Pakistan
Kharît, Wâdi el 230 *var.* Wādī al Kharīṭ. Dry watercoursef SE Egypt
Kharkiv 586 *Rus.* Khar'kov. NE Ukraine
Kharmanli 152 *var.* Harmanli. S Bulgaria
Khartoum 536 *var.* Al Khurṭūm. ❖ of Sudan, C Sudan
Khartoum North 536 *var.* Al Khurṭūm al Baḥrī. E Sudan
Khasab *see* Al Khaṣab
Khāsh Rūd 77 river of W Afghanistan
Khashuri 262 C Georgia
Khaskovo 152 *var.* Haskovo. S Bulgaria
Khatt *see* Al Khaṭṭ
Khawr al Bazm 590 *var.* Khor al Bizm. Inlet of the The Gulf, on the coast of United Arab Emirates
Khawr al 'Udayd 479 *var.* Khor al Udeid. Inlet of the The Gulf on the coast of SE Qatar
Duwayhin, Khawr 590 inlet of the The Gulf, on the coast of United Arab Emirates
Khawr Fakkān 590 *var.* Khor Fakkan. NE United Arab Emirates
Khaydarkan 357 *var.* Khaydarken, Hajdarken. SW Kyrgyzstan
Khazar, Baḥr-e *see* Caspian Sea
Khazar, Daryā-ye *see* Caspian Sea
Khenchela 83 *var.* Khenchla. NE Algeria
Khénifra 414 C Morocco
Kherson 586 *var.* Cherson. S Ukraine
Khezqazghan *see* Zhezkazgan
Khíos *see* Chíos
Khiwa 610 *Uzb.* Khiwa. W Uzbekistan
Khmel 'nyts'kyy 586 *Rus.* Khmel'nitskiy, *prev.* Proskurov. W Ukraine
Khodzhent *see* Khujand
Khodzheyli *see* Khujayli
Khoi *see* Khvoy
Khojend *see* Khujand
Kholm 77 N Afghanistan
Khomeynīshahr 307 *prev.* Homāyūnshahr. W Iran
Khoms *see* Al Khums
Khong Sedone *see* Muang Khôngxédôn
Khon Kaen 563 *var.* Muang Khon Kaen. N Thailand
Khor al Udeid *see* Khawr al 'Udayd
Khôr 'Angar 222 NE Djibouti
Khorixas 423 NW Namibia
Khorramābād 307 W Iran
Khorramshahr 307 *prev.* Khūnīnshahr. W Iran
Khorugh 558 *var.* Horug, *Rus.* Khorog. S Tajikistan
Khotan *see* Hotan
Khouribga 414 C Morocco
Khowst 77 E Afghanistan
Khoyniki 122 SE Belarus
Khrysokhou Bay 215 *var.* Chrysochou Bay. Bay of the Mediterranean Sea, on the NW coast of Cyprus
Khujand 558 *prev.* Leninabad, Khodzhent, Khojend. NW Tajikistan
Khujayli 610 *Rus.* Khodzheyli. W Uzbekistan
Khulna 117 SW Bangladesh
Khūnīnshahr *see* Khorramshahr
Khurīyā Murīyā, Jazā'ir *see* Ḥalānīyāt, Juzur al
Khurramshahr *see* Khorramshahr
Khushāb 451 NE Pakistan
Khvoy 307 *var.* Khoi. NW Iran
Khyber Pass 77, 451 mountain pass connecting Afghanistan with Pakistan
Kia 522 SW Santa Isabel, Solomon Is
Kiamusze *see* Jiamusi
Kiangsi *see* Jiangxi
Kiangsu *see* Jiangsu
Kiayi *see* Chiai
Kibondo 560 NW Tanzania
Kibre Mengist 243 *var.* Adola. S Ethiopia
Kibungo 492 *var.* Kibungu. SE Rwanda
Kibuye 492 W Rwanda
Kičevo 381 W FYR Macedonia
Kidaho 492 NW Rwanda
Kiel 265 N Germany
Kiel Bay 218, 265 *Ger.* Kieler Bucht. Bay of the Baltic Sea
Kielce 471 S Poland
Kieler Bucht *see* Kiel Bay
Kieta 458 Bougainville I, Papua New Guinea
Kiev 586 *Ukr.* Kyyiv, *Rus.* Kiyev. ❖ of Ukraine, N Ukraine
Kiffa 398 S Mauritania
Kigali 492 ❖ of Rwanda, C Rwanda
Kigembe 492 S Rwanda
Kigoma 560 W Tanzania
Kigwena 162 SW Burundi
Kikila, Lac 653 lake of Île Uvea, S Wallis & Futuna
Kihnu 240 island of SW Estonia
Kikládhes *see* Kyklades
Kikori 458 river of C Papua New Guinea
Kikwit 203 W Dem. Rep. Congo(Zaire)
Kilchu 349 NE North Korea
Kili 396 island of S Marshall Islands
Kilien Mountains *see* Qilian Shan
Kilifi 342 SE Kenya
Kilimanjaro 560 mountain of NE Tanzania
Kilingi-Nõmme 240 *Ger.* Kurkund. S Estonia
Kilinochchi 534 N Sri Lanka
Kilis 577 S Turkey
Kilkee 314 W Ireland
Kilkenny 314 *Ir.* Cill Choinnigh. SE Ireland
Kilkís 273 N Greece
Kilkoch 314 E Ireland
Killarney 314 *Ir.* Cill Airne. SW Ireland
Kilmarnock 593 W Scotland, UK
Kilosa 560 C Tanzania
Kilwa Masoko 560 SE Tanzania
Kimbe 458 New Britain, Papua New Guinea
Kimberley 527 Northern Cape, C South Africa

Kimberley Plateau 100 plateau of NW Australia
Kimch'aek 349 prev. Sŏngjin. E North Korea
Kimch'ŏn 350 C South Korea
Kimhae 350 SE South Korea
Kimito 249 Swe. Kemiö. Island of SW Finland
Kimje 350 SW South Korea
Kinabatangan 386 river of NE Borneo, Malaysia
Kinabalu, Gunung 386 mountain of N Borneo, Malaysia
Kindamba 200 S Congo
Kindia 281 SW Guinea
Kindu 203 C Dem. Rep. Congo (Zaire)
King George Bay 645 bay of the South Atlantic Ocean, W Falkland Islands
King George Land 90 island of South Shetland Islands, Antarctica
King Island 101 island of SE Australia
King Island see Kadan I
Kingissepp see Kuressaare
King Sejong 90 South Korea research station of Antarctic Peninsula, Antarctica
King's Lynn 593 E England, UK
King's Mills 647 SW Guernsey
Kingston 171 SE Canada
Kingston 329 ❖ of Jamaica, E Jamaica
Kingston 650 ❖ of Norfolk Island, S Norfolk Island
Kingston upon Hull 593 var. Hull. NE England, UK
Kingstown 498 ❖ of St Vincent & the Grenadines, SW St Vincent
King William Island 170 var. King William. Island of N Canada
Kinihira 492 N Rwanda
Kinkala 200 S Congo
Kinneret-Negev Conduit 317 canal of S Israel
Kinsale 649 SW Montserrat
Kinshasa 203 prev. Léopoldville. ❖ of Dem. Rep. Congo (Zaire), W Dem. Rep. Congo (Zaire)
Kintampo 270 C Ghana
Kinyeti 536 mountain of S Sudan
Kinyinya 162 SE Burundi
Kioa 246 island to the E of Vanua Levu, N Fiji
Kipengere Range 560 SW Tanzania
Kipushi 203 SE Dem. Rep. Congo (Zaire)
Kirakira 522 San Cristobal I, Solomon Islands
Kirambo 492 N Rwanda
Kirdzhali see Kŭrdzhali
Kirehe 492 SE Rwanda
Kirghizia see Kyrgyzstan
Kirghiz Range 357 Rus. Kirgizskiy Khrebet, prev. Alexander Range. Mountain range of Kazakhstan and Kyrgyzstan
Kirghiz Steppe 338 plain of W Kazakhstan
Kiribati 346-347 officially Republic of Kiribati, prev. Gilbert Islands, Phoenix Islands, Line Islands. Country of the SC Pacific Ocean. ❖ Bairiki
Kırıkhan 577 S Turkey
Kırıkkale 577 C Turkey
Kirin see Jilin
Kirinyaga 342 var. Mount Kenya. Extinct volcano of C Kenya
Kiritimati 346 var. Christmas I. Island of the Line Is, E Kiribati
Kiriwina Islands 458 var. Trobriand Is. Island group of SE Papua New Guinea
Kirkenes 444 NE Norway
Kirklareli 577 NW Turkey
Kirkmichael 647 W Isle of Man
Kirkpatrick, Mount 90 mountain of Greater Antarctica, Antarctica
Kirkūk 310 var. Karkūk. N Iraq
Kirkwall 593 Orkney Islands, N Scotland, UK
Kirman see Kermān
Kirov 484 prev. Vyatka. W Russian Federation
Kirovabad see Gäncä
Kirovakan see Vanadzor
Kirovohrad 586 prev. Kirovo, Zinov'yevsk, Yelizavetgrad. C Ukraine
Kirşehir 577 C Turkey
Kīrthar Range 451 mountain range of S Pakistan
Kirun see Chi-lung
Kiruna 543 N Sweden
Kirundo 162 var. Kirundu. N Burundi
Kiryū 330 Honshū, SE Japan
Kisangani 203 prev. Stanleyville. NE Dem. Rep. Congo (Zaire)
Kishan see Ch'ishan
Kishinev see Chişinău
Kishiwada 330 Honshū, C Japan
Kishorganj 117 NE Bangladesh
Kisii 342 SW Kenya
Kiskörei-víztároló 290 reservoir of E Hungary
Kiskunfélegyháza 290 prev. Félegyháza. C Hungary
Kiskunhalas 290 prev. Halas. S Hungary
Kismaayo 524 var. Kismayu, Chisimayu, It. Chisimaio. S Somalia
Kisoro 584 SW Uganda
Kisseraing see Kanmaw Island
Kissidougou 281 S Guinea
Kistna see Krishna
Kisumu 342 prev. Port Florence. W Kenya
Kisuru see Gisuru
Kita 392 W Mali
Kitakami 330 Honshū, N Japan
Kitakyūshū 330 Kyūshū, SW Japan
Kitale 342 W Kenya
Kitami 331 Hokkaidō, N Japan
Kitchener 171 S Canada
Kitega see Gitega
Kitgum 584 N Uganda
Kitinen 249 river of N Finland
Kitob 610 Rus. Kitab. SE Uzbekistan
Kit Stoddart's 494 SE St Kitts, St Kitts & Nevis
Kittitian Village 494 SE St Kitts, St Kitts & Nevis
Kitui 342 S Kenya
Kitwe 635 var. Kitwe-Nkana. C Zambia
Kitzbühler Alpen 106 mountain range of W Austria
Kiunga 458 W Papua New Guinea
Kivalo 249 ridge of C Finland
Kiviõli 240 NE Estonia
Kivu, Lac see Kivu, Lake
Kivu, Lake 492, 203 Fr. Lac Kivu. Lake of Rwanda and Dem. Rep. Congo (Zaire)
Kivumba, Lac 492 lake of E Rwanda
Kiyev see Kiev
Kiyevskoy Vodokhranilische see Kyyivs'ke Vodoskhovyshche
Kiyomizu see Ch'ing-shui
Kiyumba 492 C Rwanda
Kizan see Ch'ishan
Kizyl-Arvat see Gyzylarbat
Kizyl-Kaya 581 var. Kizyl-Kaja, Gyzylgaya. NW Turkmenistan
Kjølen see Kölen
Kladno 216 NW Czech Republic
Klagenfurt 106 S Austria
Klaipėda 376 Ger. Memel. NW Lithuania
Klaksvík 644 Bordhoy, N Faeroe Islands
Klang see Kelang
Klarälven 543 river of SW Sweden
Klatovy 216 W Czech Republic
Klausenburg see Cluj-Napoca
Klein Bonaire 650 island to the W of Bonaire, S Netherlands Antilles
Klerksdorp 527 North West, N South Africa
Klirou 215 W Cyprus
Ključ 140 NW Bosnia & Herzegovina
Klosterneuburg 106 NE Austria
Kloten 546 N Switzerland
Kluang see Keluang
Klyuchevskaya Sopka 485 Mountain of NE Russian Federation
Knezha 152 var. Kneža. NW Bulgaria
Knin 209 S Croatia
Knittelfeld 106 C Austria
Knox Atoll see Narikrik
Knoxville 599 Tennessee, SE USA
Knud Rasmussen Land 646 physical region of N Greenland
Kōbe 330 Honshū, C Japan
København see Copenhagen
Kobenni 398 S Mauritania
Koblenz 264 W Germany
Kobryn 122 Rus. Kobrin. SW Belarus
Kocaeli see İzmit
Kočani 381 NE FYR Macedonia
Kočevje 520 Ger. Gottschee. S Slovenia
Kōchi see Cochin
Kochi 330 Shikoku, SW Japan
Kochkor see Kochkorka
Kochkorka 357 Kir. Kochkor. NE Kyrgyzstan
Koddiyar Bay 534 bay of the Indian Ocean, on the NE coast of Sri Lanka
Kodiak 598 Alaska, USA
Koedoes see Kudus
Koeln see Köln
Ko-erh-mu see Golmud
Koes 423 SE Namibia
Koetai see Mahakam
Kofarnihon 558 prev. Ordzhonikidzeabad. W Tajikistan
Kofinou see Kouklia
Koforidua 270 SE Ghana
Køge 218 Sjælland, E Denmark
Kogil'nik see Cogîlnic
Kogo see Cogo
Kogon 281 river of W Guinea
Kogon 610 Rus. Kagan. S Uzbekistan
Kŏgŭm-do 350 island of S South Korea
Kohāt 451 N Pakistan
Kohtla-Järve 240 NE Estonia
Kohŭng 350 S South Korea
Koilabas 427 W Nepal
Koimbani 198 E Grande Comore, Comoros
Koindu 514 E Sierra Leone
Koi Sanjaq 310 var. Kūysanjaq, Koysanjaq. N Iraq
Kŏje-do 350 Jap. Kyōsai-tō. Island of S South Korea
Kokand see Qŭqon
Kōka-tō see Kanghwa-do
Kokemäenjoki 249 river of SW Finland
Kök-Janggak see Kok-Yangak
Kokkina 215 var. Erenköy. W Cyprus
Kokkola 249 Swe. Karleby, prev. Gamlakarleby. W Finland
Koko Nor see Qinghai Hu
Kokshaal-Tau 357 Rus. Khrebet Kakshaal-Too. Mountain range of China and Kyrgyzstan
Kokshetau 338 N Kazakhstan
Kokstad 527 Kwazulu Natal, E South Africa
Kok-Yangak 357 var. Kok-Jangak, Kir. Kök-Janggak. SW Kyrgyzstan
Kolahun 368 N Liberia
K'o-la-ma-i see Karamay
Kola Peninsula see Kol'skiy Poluostrov
Kolda 510 S Senegal
Kolding 218 Jylland, W Denmark
Kölen 543 Nor. Kjølen. Mountains of N Sweden
Kolenté 281 river of Guinea and Sierra Leone
Kolga Laht 240 bay of the Gulf of Finland, on the coast of N Estonia
Kolguyev, Ostrov 484 Island of NW Russian Federation
Kolhāpur 296 SW India
Kolhumadulu Atoll 390 var. Kolumadulu Atoll, Thaa Atoll. Atoll of S Maldives
Kolia 653 Île Futuna, N Wallis & Futuna
Koliba 281 river of NW Guinea
Kolín 216 Ger. Kolin. C Czech Republic
Kolkasrags 362 prev. Cape Domesnes. Cape of NW Latvia
Kolkata see Calcutta
Kolkhozobod 558 var. Kaganovichabad, Tugalan; Rus. Kolkhozabad. SW Tajikistan
Kolmar see Colmar
Köln 264 var. Koeln, prev. Cöln, Eng. Cologne. W Germany
Kolokani 392 W Mali
Kolombangara 522 var. Nduke. New Georgia Is, Solomon Islands
Kolomskoye Nagor'ye 485 Eng. Kolyma Range. Mountain range of NE Russian Federation
Kolonia 406 var. Colonia. Pohnpei, Micronesia
Kolonjë see Ersekë
Kolonyama 366 NW Lesotho
Kolozsvár see Cluj-Napoca
Kolpa 520 SCr. Kupa, Ger. Kulpa. River of S Slovenia
Kol'skiy Poluostrov 484 Eng. Kola Peninsula. Peninsula of NW Russian Federation
Koltur 644 island of C Faeroe Islands
Kolumadulu Atoll see Kolhumadulu Atoll
Kolwezi 203 S Dem. Rep. Congo (Zaire)
Kolyma 485 river of NE Russian Federation
Kolyma Lowland see Kolymskaya Nizmennost'
Kolymskaya Nizmennost' 485 Eng. Kolyma Lowland. Lowland region of NE Russian Federation
Komanit, Liqeni i 81 lake of N Albania
Komárno 519 Ger. Komorn, Hung. Komárom. SW Slovakia
Komárom see Komárno
Komati 540 river of SE Africa
Komatsu 330 Honshū, C Japan
Kombissiri 157 var. Kombissiguiri. C Burkina
Kome Island 584 island of S Uganda
Komi, Respublika 484 autonomous republic of NW Russian Federation
Komló 290 SW Hungary
Kommunarsk see Alchevs'k
Komoé 326 river of E Ivory Coast
Komono 200 SW Congo
Komorn see Komárno
Komotau see Chomutov
Komotiní 273 Turk. Gümülcine, Gümüljina. NE Greece
Kompong Kleang see Kâmpóng Khleang
Kompong Som see Kâmpóng Saôm
Kompong Speu see Kâmpóng Spoe
Kompong Thom see Kâmpóng Thum
Komsomol see Komsomol'sk
Komsomolets, Ostrov 485 island of Severnaya Zemlya, N Russian Federation
Komsomol'sk 581 Turkm. Komsomol. SE Turkmenistan
Komsomol'sk-na-Amure 485 SE Russian Federation
Komusan 349 NE North Korea
Kondoa 560 C Tanzania
Koné 650 W New Caledonia
Köneürgench see Këneurgench
Kŏng 165, 359 river of Cambodia and Laos
Kŏng, Kaôh 165 prev. Kas Kong. Island of SW Cambodia
Kong Christian IX Land 646 physical region of SE Greenland
Kong Christian X Land 646 physical region of E Greenland
Kong Frederik VIII Land 646 physical region of NE Greenland
Kong Frederik VI Kyst 646 physical region of SE Greenland
Kongju 350 Jap. Kōshū. W South Korea
Kong Karls Land 653 island group of SE Svalbard
Kongo see Congo
Kongoloto Lafanga 583 islet of Nukufetau, Tuvalu
Kongoloto Motulalo 583 islet of Nukufetau, Tuvalu
Kongoussi 157 N Burkina
Kongsberg 444 S Norway
Kongsvinger 444 S Norway
Königgrätz see Hradec Králové

Königshütte *see* Chorzów
Konispol *81 var.* Konispoli. S Albania
Köniz *546* W Switzerland
Konjic *140* S Bosnia & Herzegovina
Konkämäälv *see* Konkämäeno
Konkämäeno *249 Swe.* Konkämäälv. River of N Europe
Konkouré *281* river of W Guinea
Konotop *586* NE Ukraine
Konrei *455* N Palau
Konsankoro *281* SE Guinea
Konstantza *see* Constanţa
Konstanz *264* S Germany
Kontagora *440* NW Nigeria
Kon Tum *623 var.* Kontum. S Vietnam
Konya *577 prev.* Konia. C Turkey
Kopaonik *630* mountain range of C Serbia, Yugoslavia
Kópavogur *294* W Iceland
Köpenick *265* NE Germany
Koper *520 It.* Capodistria. SW Slovenia
Kopetdag, Khrebet *581 Turkm.* Kopetdag Gershi, *Per.* Koppeh Dāgh. Mountain range of W Turkmenistan
Kophinou *215* S Cyprus
Kophinou *see* Kouklia
Koplik *81* N Albania
Koppeh Dāgh *see* Kopetdag Khrebet
Koppename *see* Coppename
Koprivnica *209 Ger.* Kopreinitz, *Hung.* Kapronсza. NE Croatia
Köprülü *see* Titov Veles
Köprülü Rezevuar *see* Kouklia Reservoir
Korat *see* Nakhon Ratchasima
Korat Plateau *563* plateau of NE Thailand
Korçë *81 var.* Korça, *prev.* Koritsa, *It.* Corriza, *Gk* Korytsa. SE Albania
Korčula *209 It.* Curzola. Island of S Croatia
Korea *see* North Korea, South Korea
Korea Bay *187, 349* bay of Yellow Sea, off the coast of E Asia
Korea Strait *350 Kor.* Taehan-haehyŏp, *Jap.* Chōsen-kaikyō. Channel connecting the East China Sea and e Sea of Japan, E Asia
Korhogo *326* N Ivory Coast
Koribundu *514* S Sierra Leone
Korinthiakós Kólpos *273 Eng.* Gulf of Corinth. Gulf of the Ionian Sea, C Greece
Kórinthos *273 Eng.* Corinth. S Greece
Korínthou, Isthmós *273 Eng.* Isthmus of Corinth. Narrow strip of land joining Pelepónnisos and SE Greece
Koritsa *see* Korçë
Kōriyama *330* Honshū, N Japan
Korla *186 Chin.* K'u-erh-lo. Xinjiang Uygur Zizhiqu, NW China
Kormakiti, Cape *215 var.* Korucam Burnu. Cape of NW Cyprus
Koro *246* island to the SE of Vanua Levu, C Fiji
Korogwe *560* E Tanzania
Korolevu *246* Viti Levu, W Fiji
Koror *455* ❖ of Palau, C Palau
Kőrös *see* Križevci
Körös *290* river of E Hungary
Koro Sea *246* sea of the Pacific Ocean, C Fiji
Korosten' *586* NW Ukraine
Koro Toro *180* C Chad
Korovou *246* Viti Levu, W Fiji
Korsør *218* Sjælland, S Denmark
Kortrijk *127 Fr.* Courtrai. W Belgium
Korucam Burnu *see* Kormakiti, Cape
Koryakskoye Nagor'ye *485 Eng.* Koryak Range. Mountain range of NE Russian Federation
Kōryō *see* Kangnŭng
Kos *273* island of SE Greece
Kosan *349* SE North Korea
Kosciuszko, Mount *101* mountain of SE Australia
Koshikijima-rettō *330* island group to the W of Kyūshū, SW Japan
Kōshū *see* Kongju
Košice *519 Ger.* Kaschau, *Hung.* Kassa. E Slovakia
Kôsin' i Kelifely *382 var.* Causse du Kelifely. NW Madagascar
Koson *610* Rus. Kasan. S Uzbekistan
Kosŏng *349* SE North Korea
Kosovo *630 prev.* Autonomous Province of Kosovo and Metohija. Region of S Serbia, Yugoslavia
Kosovska Mitrovica *630 prev.* Titova Mitrovica, *prev.* Mitrovica, *Alb.* Mitrovicë. S Serbia, Yugoslavia
Kosrae *406 prev.* Kusaie. Island of E Micronesia
Kostanay *338 var.* Kustanay, *Kaz.* Qostanay. N Kazakhstan
Köstence *see* Constanţa
Kosti *536 var.* Kūstī. C Sudan
Kostroma *484* NW Russian Federation
Koszalin *471 Ger.* Köslin. NW Poland
Kota *296 prev.* Kotah. NW India
Kota Bharu *386* N Peninsular Malaysia
Kota Kinabalu *387 prev.* Jesselton. N Borneo, Malaysia
Kota Kota *see* Nkhotakota
Kotel'nyy, Ostrov *485* island of Novosibirskiye Ostrovo, N Russian Federation
Kotido *584* NE Uganda
Kotka *249* S Finland
Kotlas *484* NW Russian Federation
Kotonu *see* Cotonou
Kotovsk *see* Hînceşti
Kottbus *see* Cottbus
Kotte *see* Sri Jayawardenapura
Kotto *179* river of C Africa
Kotu Group *568* island group of W Tonga
Kouandé *132* NW Benin
Kouango *179* S Central African Republic
Koubia *281* NW Guinea
Koudougou *157* C Burkina
Kouffo *132* river of S Benin
K'ouhu *555* W Taiwan
Kouilou *200* river of S Congo
Kouklia *215 var.* Kophinou, Kofinou. SW Cyprus
Kouklia Reservoir *215 var.* Köprülü Rezevuar. Reservoir of E Cyprus
Koulamoutou *258* C Gabon
Koulikoro *392* SW Mali
Koulountou *281, 510* river of Guinea and Senegal
Koumac *650* W New Caledonia
Koumandou *281* SE Guinea
Koumra *180* S Chad
Koundâra *281* NW Guinea
Koungheul *510* C Senegal
Koupéla *157* C Burkina
Kouri *215* river of S Cyprus
Kourou *645* N French Guiana
Kouroussa *281* C Guinea
Kousseir *see* Al Quşayr
Kousséri *168 prev.* Fort-Foureau. NE Cameroon
Koûta Boûyya *222* SW Djibouti
Kouteifé *see* Al Quţayfah
Koutiala *392* S Mali
Kouvola *249* S Finland
Kouyou *200* river of C Congo
Kovel' *586* NW Ukraine
Kovno *see* Kaunas
Kowkcheh *77* seasonal river of NE Afghanistan
Kowno *see* Kaunas
Kowŏn *349* E North Korea
Kowtal-e Khaybar *see* Vākhān, Kūh-e
Kowt-e 'Ashrow *77* E Afghanistan
Kōya, Zē-i *see* Little Zab
Koysanjaq *see* Koi Sanjaq
Kozan *577* S Turkey
Kozáni *273* N Greece
Kozara *140* mountain range of NW Bosnia & Herzegovina
Kozhikode *see* Calicut
Kpagouda *see* Pagouda
Kpalimé *567 var.* Palimé. SW Togo
Kpandu *270* E Ghana
Krâchéh *165 prev.* Kratie. E Cambodia
Kragujevac *630* C Serbia, Yugoslavia
Krainburg *see* Kranj
Kra, Isthmus of *159, 563* strip of land joining Malay Peninsula to Thailand, and separating the Andaman Sea and Gulf of Thailand
Kraków *471 Eng.* Cracow, *Ger.* Krakau. S Poland
Krâlănh *165* NW Cambodia
Kralendijk *650* Bonaire, S Netherlands Antilles
Kraljevo *630 prev.* Rankovićevo. C Serbia, Yugoslavia
Kranj *520 Ger.* Krainburg. NW Slovenia
Kranji Reservoir *517* reservoir of W Singapore
Krapina *209* river of N Croatia
Krasnodar *484 prev.* Yekaterinodar. SW Russian Federation
Krasnogor *see* Kallaste
Krasnogvardeysk *see* Bulunghur
Krasnovodsk *see* Turkmenbashi
Krasnovodskiy Zaliv *581 Turkm.* Krasnowodsk Aylagy. Gulf of the Caspian Sea, on the W coast of Turkmenistan
Krasnoyarsk *485* C Russian Federation
Krasnoyarsk Kray *489* administrative region of C Russian Federation
Krasnyy Luch *586 prev.* Krindachevka. E Ukraine
Kraszna *290* river of Hungary and Romania
Kratie *see* Krâchéh
Kratovo *381* NE FYR Macedonia
Kraulshavn *646 var.* Nuussuaq. NW Greenland
Krâvanh, Chuŏr Phmun *165 Eng.* Cardamom Mountains, *Fr.* Chaîne des Cardamomes. Mountain range of SW Cambodia
Kravasta Lagoon *see* Karavastasë, Laguna e
Krawang *see* Karawang
Kremenchuk *586 Rus.* Kremenchug. C Ukraine
Kremenchuts'ke Vodokhovyshche *586 Rus.* Kremenchugskoye Vodokhranilische. Reservoir of C Ukraine
Krems an der Donau *106* N Austria
Kretinga *376 Ger.* Krottingen. NW Lithuania
Kreuz *see* Križevci
Kreuzlingen *546* NE Switzerland
Kribi *168* SW Cameroon
Krichev *see* Krychaw
Krindachevka *see* Krasnyy Luch
Krishna *296 prev.* Kistna. River of C India
Kristiansand *444 prev.* Christiansand. SW Norway
Kristianstad *543* S Sweden
Kristiansund *444 prev.* Christiansund. SW Norway
Kríti *273 Eng.* Crete. Island of S Greece
Kritikó Pélagos *see* Sea of Crete
Kriva Palanka *381* NE FYR Macedonia
Krivoy Rog *see* Kryvyy Rih
Križevci *209 Ger.* Kreuz, *Hung.* Kőrös. NE Croatia
Krk *209 It.* Veglia. Island of NW Croatia
Krnov *216 Ger.* Jägerndorf. E Czech Republic
Krŏng Kaôh Kŏng *165* SW Cambodia
Kronstadt *see* Braşov
Kroonstad *527* Orange Free State, C South Africa
Krottingen *see* Kretinga
Krško *520 prev.* Videm-Krško, *Ger.* Gurkfeld. E Slovenia
Kruševac *630* C Serbia, Yugoslavia
Krugersdorp *527* Pretoria-Witwatersrand-Vereeniging, NE South Africa
Krujë *81 var.* Kruja, *It.* Croia. C Albania
Krung Thep *see* Bangkok
Krung Thep, Ao *563* bay within Gulf of Thailand
Kruševo *381* SW FYR Macedonia
Krušné Hory *see* Erzgebirge
Krychaw *122 Rus.* Krichev. E Belarus
Krym *586 var.* Crimes. Peninsula and region of SE Ukraine
Kryvyy Rih *586 Rus.* Krivoy Rog. SE Ukraine
Ksar el Kebir *414* NW Morocco
Kuala Belait *150* W Brunei
Kuala Dungun *386 var.* Dungun. E Peninsular Malaysia
Kuala Kangsar *386* W Peninsular Malaysia
Kuala Lumpur *386* ❖ of Malaysia, W Peninsular Malaysia
Kuala Pilah *386* SW Peninsular Malaysia
Kuala Terengganu *386 var.* Kuala Trengganu. NE Peninsular Malaysia
Kuang-chou *see* Guangzhou
Kuang-hsi *see* Guangxi
Kuang-tung *see* Guangdong
Kuang-yuan *see* Guangyuan
Kuantan *386* E Peninsular Malaysia
Kuba *see* Quba
Kubango *see* Cubango
Kuching *386* W Borneo, Malaysia
Kūchnay Darvīshān *77* SW Afghanistan
Kuçovë *81 var.* Kuçova, *prev.* Qyteti Stalin. C Albania
Kudara Ghŭdara
Kudat *387* NE Borneo, Malaysia
Kudus *302 prev.* Koedoes. Java, C Indonesia
Kuei-chou *see* Guizhou
Kuei-Yang *see* Guiyang
K'u-erh-lo *see* Korla
Kufranja *see* Kufrinjah
Kufrinjah *336 var.* Kufranja. NW Jordan
Kugluktuk *170 var.* Qurlurtuuq, *prev.* Coppermine. NW Canada
Kuhmo *249* E Finland
Kuito *88 Port.* Silva Porto. C Angola
Kuivastu *240 Ger.* Kuiwast. Muhu, Estonia
Kujang *349* W North Korea
Kujū-san *330* mountain of Kyūshū, SW Japan
Kukës *81 var.* Kuksi, Kukësi. NE Albania
Kukong *see* Shaoguan
Kulai *386* SE Peninsular Malaysia
Kula Kangri *134* mountain of N Bhutan
Kuldīga *362 Ger.* Goldingen. W Latvia
Kuldja *see* Yining
Kulihao *see* Colihaut
Kulim *386* NW Peninsular Malaysia
Kullorsuaq *646* NW Greenland
Kŭlob *558 Rus.* Kulyab. SW Tajikistan
Kulyab *see* Kŭlob
Kum *see* Qom
Kŭm *350 Jap.* Kin-kō. River of W South Korea
Kumagaya *330* Honshū, SE Japan
Kumaka *284* SE Guyana
Kumamoto *330* Kyūshū, SW Japan
Kumanovo *381* N FYR Macedonia
Kumasi *270* C Ghana
Kumayri *see* Gyumri
Kumba *168* W Cameroon
Kumbo *168* NW Cameroon
Kŭmch'ŏn *349* S North Korea
Kum-Dag *see* Gumdag
Kumho *350* river of SE South Korea
Kumi *350* C South Korea
Kumillā *see* Comilla
Kumo *440* E Nigeria
Kŭmsong *350 prev.* Naju *Jap.* Rashū. SW South Korea
Kumul *see* Hami
Kunashir *331* disputed island of Kurile Islands, SE Russian Federation
Kunda *240* N Estonia
Kunda *240 var.* Kunda Jõgi. River of NE Estonia
Kundiawa *458* C Papua New Guinea
Kunduz *77 var.* Kondūz, Qondūz, Kondoz. NE Afghanistan
Kuneitra *see* Al Qunayţirah
Kunene *see* Cunene

Kungei Ala-Tau *357* *Rus.* Khrebet Kyungëy Ala-Too, *Kir.* Küngöy Ala-Too. Mountain range of Kazakhstan and Kyrgyzstan
Kungrad Qŭnghirot
Kungsbacka *543* SW Sweden
Kunlun Shan *186* mountain range of W China
Kunming *187* *var.* K'un-ming.Yunnan, SW China
K'un-ming *see* Kunming
Kunoy *644* *var.* Kunøisland. Island of N Faeroe Islands
Kunsan *350* *var.* Gunsan, *Jap.* Gunzan. W South Korea
Kuntaur *261* NE Gambia
Kunu *349* W North Korea
Kunya-Urgench *see* Këneurgench
Kuop *406* atoll of C Micronesia
Kuopio *249* C Finland
Kupa *see* Kolpa
Kupang *302* *prev.* Koepang. Timor, C Indonesia
Kupiano *458* SE Papua New Guinea
Kup'yans'k *586* E Ukraine
Kura *110, 262* *Az.* Kür. River of Azerbaijan and Georgia
Kura Kurk *see* Irbe Strait
Kurama Range *558* *Rus.* Kuraminskiy Khrebet. Mountain range of C Asia
Kurashiki *330* Honshū, W Japan
Kürdämir *110* *Rus.* Kyurdamir. C Azerbaijan
Kŭrdzhali *152* *var.* Kirdzhali. S Bulgaria
Kure *330* Honshū, W Japan
Küre Dağları *576* mountain range of N Turkey
Kuressaare *240* *prev.* Kingissepp, *Ger.* Arensburg. SW Estonia
Kurgan *484* C Russian Federation
Kurgan-Tyube *see* Qŭrghonteppa
Kuria Maria Islands *see* Ḩalānīyāt, Juzur al
Kuria Muria Bay *see* Ḩalānīyāt, Khalī al
Kurīgrām *117* N Bangladesh
Kurile Islands *see* Kuril'skiye Ostrova
Kuril'sk *331* Kurile Islands, SE Russian Federation
Kuril'skiye Ostrova *331, 485* *Eng.* Kurile Islands. Partially disputed island group of E Russian Federation
Kurkund *see* Kilingi-Nõmme
Kurmuk *536* SE Sudan
Kurnool *296* S India
Kurram *451* river of Afghanistan and Pakistan
Kuršėnai *376* *var.* Kuršenaj, Kuršenai. NW Lithuania
Kursk *484* W Russian Federation
Kuru *134* river of E Bhutan
Kurubonla *514* NE Sierra Leone
Kurume *330* Kyūshū, SW Japan
Kurunegala *534* C Sri Lanka
Kurupukari *284* C Guyana
Kurzeme *362* *Eng.* Courland. Region of W Latvia
Kusaie *see* Kosrae
Kushiro *331* Hokkaidō, N Japan
Kushiro *331* river of Hokkaidō, N Japan
Kushka *see* Gushgy
Kushmurun *338* N Kazakhstan
Kusho *see* Kwangju
Kushtia *117* W Bangladesh
Kusŏng *349* W North Korea
Kussharo-ko *330* lake of Hokkaidō, N Japan
Kustanay *see* Kostanay
Küstendje *see* Constanţa
Kusu Island *see* Tembakul, Pulau
Kütahya *577* *prev.* Kutaiah. W Turkey
Kutai *see* Mahakam
K'ut'aisi *262* W Georgia
Kūt al 'Amārah *see* Al Kūt
Kut al Imara *see* Al Kūt
Kutch, Gulf of *see* Kachch, Gulf of
Kuthuleni *540* NW Swaziland
Kutina *209* NE Croatia
Kuŭm *349* SE North Korea
Kuusamo *249* E Finland
Kuusankoski *249* S Finland
Kuwait *354-355* officially State of Kuwait. Country of SW Asia divided into 5 admin units (governorates). ❖ Kuwait City
Kuwait Bay *354* bay of the The Gulf, on the coast of E Kuwait
Kuwait City *354* *var.* Al Kuwayt. ❖ of Kuwait, E Kuwait
Kuybyshev *see* Samara
Kuybyshevskoye Vodokhranilishche *484* *Eng.* Kuybyshev Reservoir. W Russian Federation
Kūysanjaq *see* Koi Sanjaq
Kuyuwini *284* river of S Guyana
Kværndrup *218* Fyn, S Denmark
Kvaløya *444* island of NE Norway
Kvareli *see* Qvareli
Kvarner *209* *It.* Quarnero. Gulf of the Adriatic Sea, to the W of Croatia
K'vemo K'edi *262* SE Georgia
Kwa *203* river of W Dem. Rep. Congo (Zaire)
Kwahu Plateau *270* plateau of Ghana
Kwajalein *396* island of C Marshall Islands
Kwakoegron *538* N Suriname
Kwakwani *284* E Guyana
Kwale *342* S Kenya
Kwando *see* Cuando
Kwangchow *see* Guangzhou
Kwangju *350* *var.* Kwangchu, Guangju *Jap.* Kōshū. SW South Korea
Kwango *88, 203* *Port.* Cuango. River of Angola and Dem. Rep. Congo (Zaire)
Kwangsi Chuang Autonomous Region *see* Guangxi
Kwangtung *see* Guangdong
Kwangyuan *see* Guangyuan
Kwania, Lake *584* lake of C Uganda
Kwanza *see* Cuanza
Kwazulu Natal *527* province of E South Africa
Kweichow *see* Guizhou
Kweisui *see* Hohhot
Kweiyang *see* Guiyang
Kwekwe *636* *prev.* Que Que. C Zimbabwe
Kwenge *203* river of Angola and Dem. Rep. Congo (Zaire)
Kwitaro *284* River of C Guyana
Kwito *see* Cuito
Kyabé *180* S Chad
Kyaikkami *159* *var.* Amherst. SE Burma
Kyaiklat *159* S Burma
Kyaikto *159* S Burma
Kyaukpyu *159* W Burma
Kyaukse *159* C Burma
Kyklades *273* *prev.* Kikládhes, *Eng.* Cyclades. Island group of SE Greece
Kyle, Lake *636* reservoir of SE Zimbabwe
Kymijoki *249* river of S Finland
Kyoga, Lake *584* *var.* Lake Kioga. Lake of C Uganda
Kyŏnggi-man *349, 350* bay of the Yellow Sea off NW South Korea
Kyŏnghŭng *349* NE North Korea
Kyŏngju *350* *Jap.* Keishū. SE South Korea
Kyŏngsŏng *see* Seoul
Kyŏsai-tō *see* Kŏje-do
Kyōto *330* Honshū, C Japan
Kyperounda *215* *var.* Kyperounta. C Cyprus
Kypros *see* Cyprus
Kyrenia *see* Girne
Kyrgyzstan *356-357* officially Kyrgyz Republic, *var.* Kirghizia, *prev.* Republic of Kyrgyzstan, *prev.* Kirghiz SSR, Kirgizskaya SSR. Country of C Asia divided into 6 admin. units (oblasts). ❖ Bishkek
Kýthira *273* island of S Greece
Kýthnos *273* island of SE Greece
Kythrea *see* Degirmenlik
Kyungëy Ala-Too, Khrebet *see* Kungei Ala-Tau
Kyurdamir *see* Kürdämir
Kyūshū *330* island of SW Japan
Kyustendil *152* W Bulgaria
Kyyiv *see* Kiev
Kyyivs'le Vodoskhovyshche *586* *Rus.* Kiyevskoy Vodokhranilische. Reservoir of NW Ukraine
Kyzyl *485* C Russian Federation
Kyzyl-Kiya *357* *var.* Kyzyl-Kija, *Kir.* Kyzyl-Kyya. SW Kyrgyzstan
Kyzyl Kum *610* *var.* Kizil Kum, *Uzb.* Qizilqum. Desert region of Kazakhstan and Uzbekistan
Kyzylorda *338* *Kaz.* Qyzylorda. SW Kazakhstan
Kyzylrabot *see* Qizilrabot
Kyzyl-Suu *357* *prev.* Pokrovka. NE Kyrgyzstan
Kyzyl-Suu *357* *var.* Kyzylsu. River of Kyrgyzstan and Tajikistan

L

Laagen *see* Lågen
Laaland *see* Lolland
Laamu Atoll *see* Hadhdhunmathi Atoll
Laas Dawaco *524* *var.* Las Dawa'o, Laz Daua. N Somalia
Lâ'assa *222* NE Djibouti
La Asunción *619* Isla de Margarita, Venezuela
Laâyoune *414* NW Western Sahara
La Baie *652* channel of the Atlantic Ocean between Saint Pierre and Miquelon, S Saint Pierre and Miquelon
Labasa *246* *prev.* Lambasa. Vanua Levu, N Fiji
Labe *see* Elbe
Labé *281* NW Guinea
Laborec *519* *Hung.* Laborca. River of E Slovakia
Laborie *497* S St Lucia
Labrador *171* cultural region of E Canada
Labrador City *171* E Canada
Labrador Sea *171* area of the Atlantic Ocean, off E Canada
La Brea *570* SW Trinidad, Trinidad & Tobago
Labuan *see* Victoria
Labuan, Pulau *387* island of N Borneo, Malaysia
Labuk *387* river of NE Borneo, Malaysia
Labuk, Telukan *387* *var.* Labuk Bay. Bay of the Sulu Sea, on the NE coast of Borneo, Malaysia
Labutta *159* SW Burma
La Caye *497* E St Lucia
Laccadive Islands *see* Lakshadweep
La Ceiba *288* N Honduras
Lacepede Bay *101* bay on the coast of SE Australia
Lac Giao *see* Buôn Ma Thuôt
La Chaux-de-Fonds *546* W Switzerland
La Chaux, River *400* river of SE Mauritius
Lachlan *101* river of SE Australia
La Chorrera *456* C Panama
La Concepción *456* W Panama
La Condamine *410* W Monaco
la Cortinada *86* NW Andorra
La Coruña *see* A Coruña
Lacre Punt *650* headland of Bonaire, S Netherlands Antilles
La Croix Maingot *497* NW St Lucia
La Cruz *206* NW Costa Rica
La Désirade *646* island of E Guadeloupe
La Digue *512* island of the Inner Islands, NE Seychelles
Ladoewani *538* C Suriname
Ladoga, Lake *see* Ladozhskoye Ozero
Ladozhskoye Ozero *249, 484* *Eng.* Lake Ladoga. Lake of NW Russian Federation
Lae *396* island of W Marshall Islands
Lae *458* E Papua New Guinea
Læsø *218* island of N Denmark
La Esperanza *288* *var.* La Esperanza Intibucá. SW Honduras
Lafanga *583* islet of Nukufetau, Tuvalu
La Fe *see* Santa Fé
La Fé *210* W Cuba
Lafia *440* C Nigeria
Lafiagi *440* W Nigeria
La Foa *650* S New Caledonia
Lagarfljót *see* Lögurinn
Lagdo, Lac de *168* lake of N Cameroon
Lågen *444* *var.* Laagen. River of S Norway
Laghouat *83* N Algeria
Lagone *see* Logone
Lagos *440* SW Nigeria
Lagos *474* S Portugal
La Goulette *573* *var.* Ḩalq al Wādī. N Tunisia
Lagunillas *136* SE Bolivia
La Habana *see* Havana
Lahad Datu, Telukan *387* *var.* Teluk Darvel, Darvel Bay. Bay of the Celebes Sea, on the NE coast of Borneo, Malaysia
La Haye *see* 's-Gravenhage
Laḩij *627* *var.* Laḩj, *Eng.* Lahej. SW Yemen
Lahore *451* NE Pakistan
Lahti *249* *Swe.* Lahtis. S Finland
Laï *180* *var.* Behagle. S Chad
Laibach *see* Ljubljana
Lai Châu *623* NW Vietnam
Lainioälven *543* river of N Sweden
Laisholm *see* Jõgeva
Laitokitok *see* Oloitokitok
Lajes *145* S Brazil
Lakamti *see* Nek'emtē
Lakeba *246* *prev.* Lakemba. Island of the Lau Group, E Fiji
Lakeba Passage *246* channel of the Pacific Ocean E Fiji
Lake District *see* Cumbrian Mountains
Lakepa *650* NE Niue
Lakhnau *see* Lucknow
Lakota *326* S Ivory Coast
Lak Sao *see* Ban Lakxao
Lakshadweep *296* *Eng.* Laccadive Islands. Island group to the SW of India
Lakshām *117* E Bangladesh
Lakshmipur *117* S Bangladesh
La Laguna *531* Islas Canarias, SW Spain
Lāla Mūsa *451* NE Pakistan
Lalëzit, Gjiri i *81* *var.* Gji i Lalzës. Gulf of the Adriatic Sea, SW Albania
La Libertad *278* N Guatemala
La Libertad *235* SW El Salvador
La Libertad *228* W Ecuador
Lalitpur *427* C Nepal
Lālmanir Hāt *117* N Bangladesh
La Louvière *127* SW Belgium
la Maçana *86* W Andorra
Lama-Kara *see* Kara
La Manche *see* English Channel
La Marsa *573* *var.* Al Marsá. N Tunisia
La Matepec *see* Santa Ana, Volcan de
Lambaré *460* S Paraguay
Lambaréné *258* W Gabon
Lambi *522* W Guadalcanal, Solomon Islands
Lami *246* Viti Levu, W Fiji
Lamía *273* C Greece
Lamin *261* W Gambia
Lamiti *246* Gau, C Fiji
Lamotrek *406* atoll of C Micronesia
Lampang *563* *var.* Muang Lampang. NW Thailand
Lamu *342* SE Kenya
Lanao, Lake *466* *var.* Lake Sultan Alonto. Lake of Mindanao, S Philippines
Lanbi Island *159* *prev.* Sullivan I. Island of S Burma
Lancang Jiang *see* Mekong
Lancaster *593* NW England, UK
Lancaster Sound *171* stretch of water between Baffin Island and Devon Island, NE Canada
Lance aux Epines *276* *S* Grenada island, Grenada

Lanchow *see* Lanzhou
Landes *252* cultural region of SW France
Landing Bay *649* bay of the Caribbean Sea on the SE coast of Montserrat
Landsberg *see* Gorzów Wielkopolski
Landshut *265* SE Germany
Langabou *567* C Togo
Langar *610 Rus.* Lyangar. SE Uzbekistan
Langatabbetje *538* E Suriname
Langeland *218* island of S Denmark
Langenthal *546* NW Switzerland
Langjökull *294* glacier of C Iceland
Langkawi, Pulau *386* island to the NW of Peninsular Malaysia
Langlade *652* physical region of Miquelon, S Saint Pierre and Miquelon
Langlade, Isthme de *652* isthmus of Miquelon, C Saint Pierre and Miquelon
Lang Sơn *623* N Vietnam
Languedoc *253, 256* cultural region of SE France
Länkäran *110 Rus.* Lenkoran'. S Azerbaijan
Lansing *599* Michigan, NC USA
Lan Yü *555 var.* Huo-shao Tao, *Eng.* Orchid Island. Island of SE Taiwan
Lanzarote *531* island of Islas Canarias, SW Spain
Lanzhou *187 var.* Lanchow, *prev.* Kaolan. Gansu province, C China
Lao Cai *623* NW Vietnam
Laojunmiao *see* Yumen
Laon *253* N France
La Oroya *463* C Peru
Laos *358-361* officially Lao People's Democratic Republic. Country of SE Asia divided into 16 admin. units (provinces, khouèng). ❖ Vientiane
La Palma *531* island of Islas Canarias, SW Spain
La Palma *456* E Panama
La Palma *235* N El Salvador
La Paz *288* SW Honduras
La Paz *136 var.* La Paz de Ayacucho. ❖ of Bolivia, W Bolivia
La Paz *607* S Uruguay
La-Perouse Strait *331* strait connecting the Sea of Japan and Pacific Ocean between Sakhalia, SE Russian Federationand Hokkaidō, N Japan
Lapithos *see* Lapta
La Plaine *224* SE Dominica
La Plaine-des-Palmistes *652* E Réunion
Lapland *249, 444, 543 var.* Lappland, *Fin.* Lappi. Cultural region of N Europe, extending over the N of Finland, Norway and Sweden, and the Kola Peninsula of NW Russian Federation
La Plata *607* estuary of Argentina and Uruguay
La Plata *95* E Argentina
La Pointe *see* Pointe Michel
La Pointe *497* E St Lucia
Lappeenranta *249 Swe.* Villmanstrand. SE Finland
Lappland *see* Lapland
Lapta *215 var.* Lapithos. NW Cyprus
Laptev Sea *see* Laptevykh, More
Laptevykh, More *485 Eng.* Laptev Sea. Sea of Arctic Ocean, bordering N Russian Federation
L'Aquila *321 var.* Aquila, Aquila degli Abruzzi. C Italy
Larache *414 prev.* El Araïche. NW Morocco
La Resource *497* S St Lucia
La Ressource *497* NE St Lucia
Large Island *276* island to the S of Carriacou, Grenada
Largo, Cayo *210* island of SW Cuba
L'Ariana *see* Ariana
Larieu *224* N Dominica
Lario *see* Como, Lago di
La Rioja *95* NW Argentina
La Rioja *531* autonomous community of N Spain
Lárisa *273 var.* Larissa. E Greece
Lārkāna *451* SW Pakistan
Larnaca *215 var.* Larnaka, Larnax. SE Cyprus
Larnaca Bay *215 var.* Larnaka Gulf. Bay of the Mediterranean Sea, to the SE of Cyprus
la Rochelle *252* W France
la Roche-sur-Yon *252* W France
La Romana *226* SE Dominican Republic
Larvik *444* S Norway
Larvotto *410* N Monaco
La-sa *see* Lhasa
Lascahobas *286* SE Haiti
Lascano *607* SE Uruguay
Las Cruces *598* New Mexico, SW USA
La Selle *see* Selle, Pic la
La Serena *183* N Chile
la Seyne-sur-Mer *253* SE France
Las Heras *95* W Argentina
Lashio *159* NE Burma
Lashkar Gāh *77* SW Afghanistan
La Sila *321* mountain range of S Italy
Las Minas, Cerro *288* mountain of W Honduras
La Soie *see* Wesley
La Soufrière *498* mountain of N St Vincent, St Vincent & the Grenadines
Las Palmas *531 var.* Las Palmas de Gran Canaria. Islas Canarias, SW Spain
La Spezia *320* N Italy
Las Piedras *607* S Uruguay
Las Tablas *456* S Panama
La Tapoa *439* SW Niger
Lastoursville *258* E Gabon
Las Tunas *210* SE Cuba
Las Vegas *598* Nevada, W USA
Lata *522* E Nendö, Solomon Islands
Latacunga *228* C Ecuador
Latagle *362 Eng.* Latgalia. Region of SE Latvia
Latakia *see* Al Lādhiqīyah
Late *568* island of the Vava'u Group, Tonga
Latina *321* S Italy
La Tortuga, Isla *619* island of N Venezuela
La Trinité *649* E Martinique
Latvia *362-363* officially Republic of Latvia, *Latv.* Latvija, Latvijas Republika, *Ger.* Lettland, *prev.* Latvian SSR, *Rus.* Latviyskaya SSR. Country of NE Europe divided into 26 admin. units (rajons). ❖ Riga
Laudat *224* S Dominica
Lau Group *246* island group of E Fiji
Lauis *see* Lugano
Launceston *101* Tasmania, SE Australia
La Unión *183* C Chile
La Unión *235* SE El Salvador
Laurentian Mountains *171* mountains of E Canada
Lauru *see* Choiseul
Lausanne *546* SW Switzerland
Lautaro *183* C Chile
Lautoka *246* Viti Levu, W Fiji
Laut, Pulau *302 var.* Laoet. Island to the SE of Borneo, C Indonesia
Laval *171* SE Canada
Laval *252* NW France
Lava, la *645* river of French Guiana and Suriname
Lavant *106* river of S Austria
La Vega *226 var.* Concepción de La Vega. C Dominican Republic
Laventure *400* NE Mauritius
Lavumisa *540 prev.* Gollel. S Swaziland
Lawa *538* river of French Guiana and Suriname
Lawdar *627* SW Yemen
Lawton *599* Oklahoma, SC USA
Laxey *647* E Isle of Man
Layjūn *627* C Yemen
Laylá *506 var.* Laila. C Saudi Arabia
Layou *224* river of W Dominica
Layou *498* W St Vincent, St Vincent & the Grenadines
Lazarus Island *see* Sakijang Pelepah, Pulau
Laz Daua *see* Laas Dawaco
Lazovsk *see* Sîngerei
Leal *see* Lihula
Leamhcán *see* Lucan
Leava *653* Île Futuna, N Wallis & Futuna
Lébamba *258* S Gabon
Lebanon *364-365* officially Republic of Lebanon, *Ar.* Al Lubnān. Country of SW Asia divided into 5 admin. units (governorates). ❖ Beirut
Lebap *581* NE Turkmenistan
Lebombo Mountains *527, 540* mountain range of southern Africa
Le Cap *652* peninsula of N Saint Pierre and Miquelon
Le Cap *see* Cap-Haïtien
Le Carbet *649* NW Martinique
Lecce *321* S Italy
Lecco *320* N Italy
Lech *106* river of Austria and Germany
Leduc *170* SW Canada
Lee *314 Ir.* An Laoi. River of S Ireland
Leeds *593* N England, UK
Leeuwarden *429 Fris.* Ljouwert. N Netherlands
Leeuwin, Cape *100* cape on the SW coast of Australia
Léfini *200* river of SE Congo
Lefka *215 var.* Lefke. W Cyprus
Lefkada *273 prev.* Levkás, *var.* Leucas, *It.* Santa Maura. Island of W Greece
Lefke *see* Lefka
Lefkoniko *see* Geçitkale
Lefkoşa *see* Nicosia
Lefkosia *see* Nicosia
Le François *649* E Martinique
Leganés *531* C Spain
Legaspi *466 var.* Legzpi. Luzon, N Philippines
Leghorn *see* Livorno
Legnica *471 Ger.* Liegnitz. W Poland
le Havre *253* N France
Leiah *451* NE Pakistan
Leicester *593* C England, UK
Leiden *429 prev.* Leyden. W Netherlands
Leie *127 Fr.* Lys. River of Belgium and France
Léim an Bhradáin *see* Leixlip
Leinster *314* province of E Ireland
Leipzig *265 Pol.* Lipsk. C Germany
Leivádia *273 prev.* Levádhia. SE Greece
Leixlip *314 Ir.* Léim an Bhradáin. E Ireland
Leizhou Bandao *187 var.* Luichow Peninsula. Peninsula of S China
Lejone *366* N Lesotho
Lek *429* river of SW Netherlands
Lékana *200* W Congo
Le Kartala *198* mountain of Grande Comore, Comoros
Le Kef *573 var.* Al Kāf, El Kef. NW Tunisia
Lékéti *200* river of W Congo
Lékéti, Monts de la *200 var.* Monts de la Leketi, Mont de la Lékéti. Mountain range of W Congo
Lékila *258* E Gabon
Lékoni *258* E Gabon
Le Lamentin *649* C Martinique
Le Lorrain *649* NE Martinique
Lélouma *281* W Guinea
Lelydorp *538* N Suriname
Lelystad *429* C Netherlands
le Mans *253* NW France
Lemberg *see* L'viv
Lemdiyya *see* Médéa
Lemesos *see* Limassol
Le Morne Rouge *649* N Martinique
Le Moule *646* NE Guadeloupe
Lempa *235* river of El Salvador and Honduras
Lemsid *414* NW Western Sahara
Le Murge *321* mountain range of S Italy
Lemvig *218* Jylland, W Denmark
Lena *485* River of E Russian Federation
Lengoué *200 var.* Bokiba. River of C Congo
Lenin *see* Leninsk
Lenina, Ozero imeni *586* lake of E Ukraine
Leninabad *see* Khujand
Leninakan *see* Gyumri
Leningrad *see* St. Petersburg
Leningradskaya *90* CIS research station of Greater Antarctica, Antarctica
Leninogorsk *338* E Kazakhstan
Leninpol' *357* NW Kyrgyzstan
Leninsk *see* Asaka
Leninsk *581 Turkm.* Lenin. N Turkmenistan
Leninsk *see* Chardzhev
Lenkoran' *see* Länkäran
Lennox, Isla *183* S Chile
Lens *253* N France
Léo *157* SW Burkina
Leoben *106* C Austria
Léogâne *286* S Haiti
León *403 var.* León de los Aldamas. C Mexico
León *531* NW Spain
León *436* W Nicaragua
Leonardville *423* E Namibia
Leonarisso *see* Ziyamet
León, Cerro *460* mountain of NW Paraguay
Leonding *106* N Austria
Leone *642* Tutuila, W American Samoa
Léopold II, Lac *see* Mai-Ndombe, Lac
Léopoldville *see* Kinshasa
Leova *408 Rus.* Leovo. SW Moldova
Lepā *500* Upolu, Samoa
Lepel' *see* Lyepyel'
Lépontiennes, Alpes *see* Lepontine Alps
Lepontine, Alpi *see* Lepontine Alps
Lepontine Alps *546 Fr.* Alpes Lépontiennes, *It.* Alpi Lepontine. Mountain range of SE Switzerland
Le Port *652* NW Réunion
le Puy *253* SE France
Léraba *157, 326* river of Burkina and Ivory Coast
Léré *180* SW Chad
Leribe *see* Hlotse
Lérida *see* Lleida
Le Robert *649* E Martinique
Lerwick *593* Mainland, Shetland Islands, NE Scotland, UK
Les Abymes *646* C Guadeloupe
Les Anses-D'Arlets *649* SW Martinique
Les Avirons *652* W Réunion
Lesbos *see* Lésvos
les Escaldes *86* C Andorra
Les Gonaïves *see* Gonaïves
Lesh *see* Lezhë
Lesina *see* Hvar
Leskovac *630* SE Serbia, Yugoslavia
Lesotho *366-367* officially Kingdom of Lesotho, *prev.* Basutoland. Country of Africa divided into 10 admin. units (districts). ❖ Maseru
Les Saintes *646* island group of S Guadeloupe
Lesser Antarctica *90* physical region of Antarctica
Lesser Caucasus *110, 262 Rus.* Malyy Kavkaz. Mountain range of SW Asia
Lesser Khingan Range *see* Xiao Hinggan Ling
Lesser Sunda Islands *see* Nusa Tenggara
Les Tantes *276* islands to the N of Grenada island, Grenada
L'Esterre *276* SW Carriacou, Grenada
Lésvos *273 var.* Lesbos. Island of E Greece
Le Tampon *652* SW Réunion
Lethbridge *170* SW Canada
Lethem *284 prev.* Rupununi. SW Guyana
Leticia *195* S Colombia
Leti, Kepulauan *302* island group of Maluku, E Indonesia

Letir Ceanainn *see* Letterkenny
Letpadan *159* SW Burma
Letsok-aw Island *159 var.* Letsutan Island, *prev.* Domel Island. Island of S Burma
Letsutan Island *see* Letsok-aw Island
Letterkenny *314 Ir.* Letir Ceanainn. N Ireland
Lettland *see* Latvia
Lëtzebuerg *see* Luxembourg
Leucas *see* Lefkada
Leulumoega *500* Upolu, Samoa
Leuven *127 Fr.* Louvain, *Ger.* Löwen. C Belgium
Léva *see* Levice
Le Vauclin *649* SE Martinique
Levera Island *see* Sugar Loaf
Leverkusen *264* W Germany
Levice *519 Ger.* Lewenz, Hung. Léva. SW Slovakia
Levin *433* S North Island, New Zealand
Levkás *see* Lefkada
Levoča *519 Ger.* Leutschau, Hung. Lőcse. NE Slovakia
Levskigrad *see* Karlovo
Levuka *246* Ovalau, C Fiji
Lewenz *see* Levice
Lewis, Isle of *593* island of Outer Hebrides, NW Scotland, UK
Lewiston *598* Idaho, NW USA
Lewiston *599* Maine, NE USA
Lexington *599* Kentucky, C USA
Leyte *466* island of E Philippines
Leyte Gulf *466* gulf of the Pacific Ocean, E Philippines
Lezhë *81 var.* Lezha, *prev.* Lesh, Leshi. NW Albania
Lhasa *186 var.* La-sa. Xizang Zizhiqu, W China
Lhaviyani Atoll *see* Faadhippolhu Atoll
Lhuntshi *134* E Bhutan
Lhut, Uadi *see* Luud, Waadi
Liamuiga, Mount *494 var.* Mount Misery. Mountain of C St Kitts, St Kitts & Nevis
Liangyungang *187 var.* Xinpu, Lien-yun. Jiangsu, E China
Liaodong Bandao *187 var.* Liaotung Peninsula. Peninsula of NE China
Liaoning *187 hist.* Shenking, Fengtien. Province of NE China
Lib *396* island of C Marshall Islands
Liban, Jebel *364 Eng.* Lebanon, Mount Lebanon, *Ar.* Jabal Lubnān. Mountain range of C Lebanon
Libau *see* Liepāja
Liberec *216 Ger.* Reichenberg. N Czech Republic
Liberia *206* NW Costa Rica
Liberia *368-369* officially The Republic of Liberia. Country of West Africa, divided into 9 admin. units (counties). ❖ Monrovia
Liberta *92* S Antigua, Antigua & Barbuda
Libertad *607* S Uruguay
Libertad *130 prev.* Pembroke Hall. N Belize
Librazhd *81 var.* Librazhdi. E Albania
Libreville *258* ❖ of Gabon, NW Gabon
Libya *370-373* officially The Great Socialist People's Libyan Arab Jamahiriya, *prev.* Libyan Arab Republic. Country of N Africa, the current administrative structure is not clear. ❖ Tripoli
Libyan Desert *230, 371, 536 Ar.* Aş Şahrā' al Lībīyah. Desert of N Africa
Libyan Plateau *230, 371 Ar.* Aḍ Diffah. Plateau of Egypt and Libya
Licata *321* Sicilia, S Italy
Lichinga *419* N Mozambique
Lichtenburg *527* North West, N South Africa
Lida *122* W Belarus
Lido di Ostia *321* C Italy
Liechtenstein *374-375* officially Principality of Liechtenstein. Country of C Europe divided into 11 admin. units (communes). ❖ Vaduz
Liège *127 Dut.* Luik, *Ger.* Lüttich. E Belgium
Liegnitz *see* Legnica
Lieksa *249* E Finland
Lien-yun *see* Liangyungang
Lienz *106* W Austria
Liepāja *362 Ger.* Libau. W Latvia
Lier *127 Fr.* Lierre. N Belgium
Liestal *546* N Switzerland
Lievenhof *see* Līvāni
Liezen *106* C Austria
Lifford *314* N Ireland
Lifou *650* island, Îles Loyauté, E New Caledonia
Lifuka *568* island of Ha'apai Group, Tonga
Līgatne *362* NE Latvia
Ligure, Appennino *320* mountain range of N Italy
Ligure, Mar *see* Ligurian Sea
Ligurian Sea *253, 320 It.* Mar Ligure, *Fr.* Mer Ligurienne. Area of the Mediterranean Sea, between France and Italy
Lihue *598* Kauai, Hawaii, USA
Lihula *240 Ger.* Leal. W Estonia
Liivi Laht *see* Riga, Gulf of
Likasi *203 prev.* Jadotville. SE Dem. Rep. Congo (Zaire)
Likiep *396* island of C Marshall Islands
Likouala *200* river of NW Congo
Likouala aux Herbes *200* river of E Congo
Liku *650* E Niue
Lille *253 Dut.* Rijssel. N France
Lillebælt *218 Eng.* Little Belt, *var.* Lille Bælt. Straits between Fyn and Jylland, SW Denmark
Lillehammer *444* S Norway
Lillestrøm *444* S Norway
Lilongwe *385* ❖ of Malawi, W Malawi
Lilongwe *385* river of W Malawi
Lima *463* ❖ of Peru, W Peru
Limassol *215 var.* Lemesos. SW Cyprus
Limbe *385* S Malawi
Limbe *168 prev.* Victoria. SW Cameroon
Limbé *286* N Haiti
Lim Chu Kang *517* area of NW Singapore
Limerick *314 Ir.* Luimneach. SW Ireland
Limfjorden *218* fjord of Jylland, NW Denmark
Límni Megáli Préspa *see* Prespa, Lake
Limni Prespa *see* Prespa, Lake
Límnos *273 var.* Lemnos. Island of E Greece
Limoges *253* C France
Limón *206* E Costa Rica
Limón *288* NE Honduras
Limon, Mont *400* mountain of Rodrigues, Mauritius
Limousin *253* cultural region of C France
Limpopo *142, 419, 423, 636 var.* Crocodile. River of southern Africa
Limulunga *635* W Zambia
Linakeng *366* E Lesotho
Linares *183* C Chile
Linares *531* S Spain
Lincoln *593* E England, UK
Lincoln *599* Nebraska, C USA
Lincoln Island *651* island of E Paracel Islands
Linden *284* E Guyana
Lindi *203* river of NE Dem. Rep. Congo (Zaire)
Lindi *560* SE Tanzania
Line Islands *346* island group of E Kiribati
Lingayen Gulf *466* gulf of the South China Sea, N Philippines
Lingga, Kepulauan *302* island group to the E of Sumatra, W Indonesia
Linguère *510* N Senegal
Linköping *543* S Sweden
Linyanti *142* river of Botswana and Namibia
Linz *106* N Austria
Lion, Golfe du *253 Eng.* Gulf of Lions. Gulf of the Mediterranean Sea to the S of France
Lions Den *636* N Zimbabwe
Lipa *466* Luzon, N Philippines
Lipari Islands *see* Eolie, Isole
Lipari, Isola *321* island of S Italy
Lipari, Isole *see* Eolie, Isole
Lipetsk *484* W Russian Federation
Lippstadt *264* W Germany
Lipsk *see* Leipzig
Liptovský Mikuláš *519 Ger.* Liptau-Sankt-Nikolaus, *Hung.* Liptószentmiklós. C Slovakia
Lira *584* N Uganda
Liranga *200* E Congo
Liri *321* river of C Italy
Lisala *203* N Dem. Rep. Congo (Zaire)
Lisbon *474 Port.* Lisboa. ❖ of Portugal, W Portugal
Lisburn *593* Northern Ireland, UK
Lisieux *253* NW France
Lismore *101* E Australia
Lissa *see* Vis
Litani *538, 645 var.* Itany. River of French Guiana and Suriname
Litani *364* river of C Lebanon
Litaven *see* Lithuania
Litavra *see* Lithuania
Lithgow *101* SE Australia
Lithuania *376-377* officially Republic of Lithuania, *Lith.* Lietuva, *Ger.* Litauen, *Pol.* Litwa, *Rus.* Litva, *prev.* Lithuanian SSR, *Rus.* Litovskaya SSR. Country of E Europe divided into 44 admin. units (disicts). ❖ Vilnius
Litla Dimun *644* island of S Faeroe Islands
Little Abaco *112* island of N Bahamas
Little Alföld *290* plain of Hungary and Slovakia
Little Andaman *296* island of Andaman Islands to the SE of India
Little Barrier Island *433* island to the N of North Island, New Zealand
Little Belt *see* Lillebælt
Little Cayman *644* island of C Cayman Islands
Little Coco Island *159* island of SW Burma
Little Inagua *112* island of S Bahamas
Little Minch *593* strait of the Atlantic Ocean, NW Scotland, UK
Little Rock *599* Arkansas, SC USA
Little Scarcies *see* Kaba
Little Sound *643* bay of the North Atlantic Ocean, W Bermuda
Little Tobago *643* island of W British Virgin Islands
Little Tobago *570 var.* Bird of Paradise Island. Island to the E of Tobago, Trinidad & Tobago
Little Zab *310 Ar.* Zāb aş Şaghīr, *Kurd.* Zē-i Kya. River of Iran and Iraq
Litva *see* Lithuania
Litwa *see* Lithuania
Liuch'iu Yü *555* island of SW Taiwan
Liukuei *555* S Taiwan
Liuzhou *187 var.* Liu-chou, Liuchow. Guangxi, S China
Livadhi *215 var.* Leivadi. River of W Cyprus
Līvāni *362 Ger.* Lievenhof. SE Latvia
Lively Island *645* island of E Falkland Islands
Lively Sound *645* area of the South Atlantic Ocean, E Falkland Islands
Liverpool *593* NW England, UK
Lívingston *278* E Guatemala
Livingstone *635 var.* Maramba. S Zambia
Livingstonia *385* N Malawi
Livno *140* SW Bosnia & Herzegovina
Livojoki *249* river of C Finland
Livonia *see* Vidzeme
Livorno *320 Eng.* Leghorn. C Italy
Liwonde *385* S Malawi
Liyāḩ, Jāl al *354* ridge of NW Kuwait
Ljouwert *see* Leeuwarden
Ljubelj *see* Loibl Pass
Ljubljana *520 var.* Lyublyana, *Ger.* Laibach, *It.* Lubiana. ❖ of Slovenia, C Slovenia
Ljubrlj *see* Loibl Pass
Ljungan *543* river of C Sweden
Ljusnan *543* river of C Sweden
Llallagua *136* SW Bolivia
Lleida *531 Cast.* Lérida. NE Spain
Llolleo *183* C Chile
Lloydminster *170* SW Canada
Lô *623* river of China and Vietnam
Loaita Island *652* island of W Spratly Islands
Loangwa *see* Luangwa
Lobatse *142 var.* Lobatsi. S Botswana
Lobaye *179* river of SW Central African Republic
Lobito *88* W Angola
Lob Nor *see* Lop Nur
Locarno *546 Ger.* Luggarus. S Switzerland
Lôc Ninh *623* SW Vietnam
Locri *321* S Italy
Lőcse *see* Levoča
Lod *317 var.* Lydda. C Israel
Lodge *494* NE St Kitts, St Kitts & Nevis
Lodja *203* C Dem. Rep. Congo (Zaire)
Lodwar *342* NW Kenya
Łódź *471 Rus.* Lodz. C Poland
Loei *563 var.* Muang Loei. N Thailand
Lofa *368 var.* Loffa. River of Guinea and Liberia
Lofoten *444 var.* Lofoten Islands. Islands of NE Norway
Loga *439* W Niger
Logan, Mount *170* mountain of NW Canada
Logone *168, 180 var.* Lagone. River of Cameroon and Chad
Logroño *531* N Spain
Lögurinn *294 var.* Lagarfljót. Lake of E Iceland
Loh *615* Torres Islands, N Vanuatu
Loibl Pass *106 var.* Ljubelj, *Ger.* Loiblpass, *Slvn.* Ljubrlj. Mountain pass of Austria and Slovenia
Loikaw *159* E Burma
Loir *253* river of NW France
Loire *253* river of C France
Loita Hills *342* hilly region of SW Kenya
Loja *228* S Ecuador
Lökbatan *110 Rus.* Lokbatan. E Azerbaijan
Lokeren *127* NW Belgium
Lokitaung *342* NW Kenya
Løkken *218* Jylland, NW Denmark
Lokoja *440* C Nigeria
Lokossa *132* S Benin
Loksa *240 Ger.* Loxa. N Estonia
Lol *536* river of S Sudan
Lola *281* SE Guinea
Lolland *218 prev.* Laaland. Island of S Denmark
Lolotique *235* SE El Salvador
Lolvavana, Passage *615* strait between Maewo and Pentecost, C Seychelles
Lom *152 prev.* Lom-Palanka. NW Bulgaria
Lom *168* river of Cameroon and Central African Republic
Lomahasha *540* NE Swaziland
Lomami *203* river of C Dem. Rep. Congo (Zaire)
Lomas de Zamora *95* E Argentina
Lombok *302* island of Nusa Tenggara, C Indonesia
Lomé *567* ❖ of Togo, S Togo
Lomond, Loch *593* lake of C Scotland, UK
Lom Sak *563 var.* Muang Lom Sak. N Thailand
Londiani *342* W Kenya
London *593, 597* ❖ of United Kingdom
London *171* S Canada
London *346* Kiritimati, E Kiribati
London Bridge *276* island to the N of Grenada island, Grenada
Londonderry *593 var.* Derry. Northern Ireland, UK
Londrina *145* S Brazil
Longa, Proliv *485 Eng.* Long Strait. Strait connecting Chukchi Sea and East Siberian Sea, between NE Asia and NW North America
Long Bay *643* bay of the North Atlantic Ocean, E Bermuda

Long Bay 643 bay of the North Atlantic Ocean, W Bermuda
Longford 314 Ir. Longphort. C Ireland
Long Island 643 island of W Bermuda
Long Island see Arop Island
Long Island 112 island of C Bahamas
Long Island 92 island to the N of Antigua, Antigua & Barbuda
Longmont 599 Colorado, SW USA
Longoni, Baie de 649 var. Longoni Bay. Bay of the Indian Ocean on the N coast of Mayotte
Longphort see Longford
Longreach 101 E Australia
Long Strait see Longa, Proliv
Long Swamp 643 Tortola, C British Virgin Islands
Longwood 652 E St Helena
Long Xuyên 623 SW Vietnam
Longyearbyen 653 ❖ of Svalbard, Spitsbergen, W Svalbard
Lonhlupheko 540 E Swaziland
Lons-le-Saunier 253 E France
Loop Head 314 promontory on the W coast of Ireland
Lop Buri 563 C Thailand
Lopévi 615 island of C Vanuatu
Lopez, Cap 258 W Gabon
Lop Nur 186 var. Lop Nor, Lob Nor, Chin. Lo-pu Po. Lake of Xinjiang Uygur Zizhiqu, NW China
Lo-pu Po see Lop Nur
Lora, Hāmūn-i- 450 salt marsh of W Pakistan
Lord Howe Island island of E Australia
Lord Howe Island see Ontong Java Atoll
Lorca 531 S Spain
Lorengau 458 var. Lorungau, Manus I, Papua New Guinea
Lorentz 303 river of Irian Jaya, E Indonesia
Loreto 460 C Paraguay
Lorian Swamp 342 swamp E Kenya
Lorient 252 W France
Lorn, Firth of 593 inlet of Atlantic Ocean, W Scotland, UK
Lorraine 253 cultural region of NE France
Los Amates 278 E Guatemala
Los Andes 183 C Chile
Los Angeles 598 California, W USA
Los Ángeles 183 C Chile
Losap 406 atoll of C Micronesia
Los Chiles 206 NW Costa Rica
Los, Îles de 281 Island group to the SW of Guinea
Lošinj 209 It. Lussino. Island of W Croatia
Loslau see Wodzisław Śląski
Los Mochis 403 W Mexico
Losonc see Lučenec
Losontz see Lučenec
Lospalos 305 E East Timor
Los Roques, Islas 619 island group of N Venezuela
Los Teques 619 N Venezuela
Lot 253 river of S France
Lotofaga 500 Upolu, Samoa
Lo-tung 555 Jap. Ratō. NE Taiwan
Louang Namtha 359 var. Luong Nam Tha. N Laos
Louangphrabang 359 var. Luang Prabang. C Laos
Loubiere 224 SW Dominica
Loubomo 200 prev. Dolisie. S Congo
Loudima 200 S Congo
Louéssé 200 river of SW Congo
Louga 510 NW Senegal
Loughrea 314 W Ireland
Louis Gentil see Youssoufia
Louisiade Archipelago 458 island group of SE Papua New Guinea
Louisiana 599 state of SC USA
Louis Trichardt 527 Northern Transvaal, NE South Africa
Louisville 599 Kentucky, C USA
Louisville 130 N Belize
Loukoléla 200 E Congo
Loum 168 W Cameroon
Louna 200 river of SE Congo
Louny 216 NW Czech Republic
Lourenço Marques see Maputo
Lourenço Marques, Baía de see Maputo, Baía de
Louvain see Leuven
Lovech 152 var. Loveč. NW Bulgaria
Lovell Village 498 Mustique, St Vincent & the Grenadines
Lóvua 88 N Angola
Lowell 599 Massachusetts, NE USA
Löwen see Leuven
Lower Bann 593 river of Northern Ireland, UK
Lower California see Baja California
Lower Carlton 121 NW Barbados
Lower Hutt 433 S North Island, New Zealand
Lower Lough Erne 593 lake of Northern Ireland, UK
Lower Mortlocks 406 island group of C Micronesia
Lower Rhine see Neder-Rijn
Lower Tunguska see Nizhnyaya Tunguska
Lower West End Point 642 headland on the SW coast of Anguilla
Low Point 644 headland on the E coast of Christmas Island
Loyada 222 E Djibouti
l'Oyapok see Oiapoque
Loyauté, Îles 650 island group of E New Caledonia
Loyoro 584 NE Uganda
Loznica 630 W Serbia, Yugoslavia
Lualaba 203 var. Zaire, Fr. Loualaba. River of Dem. Rep. Congo (Zaire)
Luampa 635 river of W Zambia
Luanda 88 ❖ of Angola, NW Angola
Luang Prabang see Louangphrabang
Luang Prabang Range 359 mountain range of W Laos
Luangwa 635 Port. Aruângua. River of Mozambique and Zambia
Luanshya 635 C Zambia
Luapula 203, 635 river of Dem. Rep. Congo (Zaire) and Zambia
Luar, Pulu see Horsburgh Island
Luba 236 prev. San Carlos. W Bioko, Equatorial Guinea
Lubānas Ezers 362 lake of E Latvia
Lubang Island 466 island of N Philippines
Lubango 88 Port. Sá da Bandeira. SW Angola
Lubao 203 SE Dem. Rep. Congo (Zaire)
Lübeck 265 N Germany
Lubelska, Wyżyna 471 plateau of SE Poland
Lubiana see Ljubljana
Lublin 471 Rus. Lyublin. E Poland
Lubnān, Jabal see Liban, Jebel
Lubny 586 C Ukraine
Lubumbashi 203 prev. Élisabethville. SE Dem. Rep. Congo (Zaire)
Luca 136 SW Bolivia
Lucala 88 NW Angola
Lucan 314 Ir. Leamhcán. E Ireland
Lucano, Appennino 321 mountain range of S Italy
Lucapa 88 var. Lukapa. NE Angola
Lucea 329 NW Jamaica
Lucena 466 Luzon, N Philippines
Lučenec 519 Hung. Losonc, Ger. Losontz. C Slovakia
Lucerne see Luzern
Lucerne, Lake of see Vierwaldstätter See
Luchow see Hefei
Lucie 538 Suriname
Łuck see Luts'k
Lucknow 296 Hind. Lakhnau. N India
Lüderitz 423 prev. Angra Pequena. SW Namibia
Ludhiāna 296 N India
Ludwigshafen 264 var. Ludwigshafen am Rhein. SW Germany
Luebo 203 SW Dem. Rep. Congo (Zaire)
Luena 88 Port. Luso. E Angola
Lufira, Lac de Retenue de la 203 var. Lac Tshangalele. Lake of SE Dem. Rep. Congo (Zaire)
Lugano 546 Ger. Lauis. S Switzerland
Luganville 615 Espiritu Santo, Vanuatu
Lugards Falls 342 waterfall of SE Kenya
Lugenda 419 river of N Mozambique
Luggarus see Locarno
Lugh Ganana see Luuq
Lugo 531 NW Spain
Lugoj 480 W Romania
Lugusi see Rugusye
Luhans'k 586 Rus. Lugansk, prev. Voroshilovgrad. E Ukraine
Luiana 88 river of SE Angola
Luichow Peninsula see Leizhou Bandao
Luik see Liège
Luimneach see Limerick
Luján 95 C Argentina
Lukang 555 var. Lu-chiang, Jap. Rokkō. W Taiwan
Lukapa see Lucapa
Lukenie 203 river of C Dem. Rep. Congo (Zaire)
Lukhalweni 540 S Swaziland
Lukusashi 635 river of C Zambia
Luleå 543 NE Sweden
Luleälv 543 river of NE Sweden
Lulonga 203 river of NW Dem. Rep. Congo (Zaire)
Lulua 203 river of S Dem. Rep. Congo (Zaire)
Luluabourg see Kananga
Lumbo 419 NE Mozambique
Lumi 458 NW Papua New Guinea
Lumphăt 165 prev. Lomphat. NE Cambodia
Lumpungu see Rumpungwe
Lund 543 S Sweden
Lunga 635 river of Zambia
Lunga, Isola see Dugi Otok
Lungi 514 W Sierra Leone
Lungkiang see Qiqihar
Lungwebungu 635 river of Angola and Zambia
Luninyets 122 Rus. Luninets. SW Belarus
Lunsar 514 W Sierra Leone
Lunsemfwa 635 river C Zambia
Luong Nam Tha see Louang Namtha
Luoyang 187 Henan, C China
Luque 460 S Paraguay
Lúrio 419 NE Mozambique
Lúrio 419 river of NE Mozambique
Lusaka 635 ❖ of Zambia, SE Zambia
Lushnjë 81 var. Lushnja. C Albania
Luso see Luena
Lussino see Lošinj
Lustenau 106 W Austria
Lusutfu 540 var. Usutu, Great Usutu. River of southern Africa
Lü Tao 555 island of SE Taiwan
Lūt, Baḩrat see Dead Sea
Lūt, Dasht-e 307 var. Kavīr-e Lūt. Desert region of E Iran
Luton 593 C England, UK
Luts'k 586 Rus. Lutsk, Pol. Łuck. NW Ukraine
Lüttich see Liège
Luud, Waadi 524 It. Uadi Lhut. Seasonal river of N Somalia
Luuq 524 It. Lugh Ganana. SW Somalia
Luvironza see Ruvyironza
Luxembourg 378 ❖ of Luxembourg
Luxembourg 378-379 officially Grand Duchy of Luxembourg, var. Lëtzebuerg. Country of W Europe divided into 3 admin. units (districts). ❖ Luxembourg
Luxor 230 Ar. Al Uqşur. E Egypt
Luz, Costa de la 531 coastal region of SW Spain
Luzern 546 Fr. Lucerne. C Switzerland
Luzon 466 island of N Philippines
L'viv 586 Rus. L'vov, Pol. Lwów, Ger. Lemberg. W Ukraine
Lyallpur see Faisalābād
Lyangar see Langar
Lycksele 543 N Sweden
Lydda see Lod
Lyepyel' 122 Rus. Lepel'. N Belarus
Lyme Bay 593 bay of S England, UK
Lyon 253 Eng. Lyons E France
Lys see Leie
Lysi 215 var. Akdoğan. C Cyprus
Lyublin see Lublin
Lyublyana see Ljubljana

M

Ma'ān 336 SW Jordan
Maanselkä 249 mountain range of NE Finland
Maardu 240 Ger. Maart. N Estonia
Maarianhamina see Mariehamn
Maarmorilik 646 W Greenland
Ma'arrat an Nu'mān 551 NW Syria
Maarssen 429 C Netherlands
Maart see Maardu
Maas see Meuse
Maasmechelen 127 NE Belgium
Maastricht 429 S Netherlands
Maaza Plateau 230 plateau of NE Egypt
Mabalane 419 S Mozambique
Mabanda 258 S Gabon
Mabayi 162 NW Burundi
Mabouya Island 276 island to the W of Carriacou, Grenada
Macao 187 Chin. Aomen. SE China
Macapá 145 N Brazil
Macará 228 S Ecuador
Macarsca see Makarska
MacArthur see Ormoc
Macas 228 SE Ecuador
Macassar see Ujungpandang
Macdonnell Ranges 101 mountain range of C Australia
Macedonia 380-381 officially the Former Yugoslav Republic of Macedonia, abbrev. FYR Macedonia, FYROM, Mac. Makedonija. Country of SE Europe divided into 34 admin. units (opcine). ❖ Skopje
Maceió 145 E Brazil
Macenta 281 SE Guinea
Macgillicuddy's Reeks 314 var. Macgillicuddy's Reeks Mountains, Ir. Na Cruacha Dubha. Mountain range of SW Ireland
Machakos 342 S Kenya
Machala 228 SW Ecuador
Machaneng 142 SE Botswana
Machanga 419 SE Mozambique
Machaze 419 SW Mozambique
Machile 635 var. Machili. River of SW Zambia
Machinga 385 var. Kasupe, Kasupi. S Malawi
Machiques 619 NW Venezuela
Machu Picchu 463 S Peru
Macia 419 var. Vila de Macia. S Mozambique
Macías Nguema Biyogo see Bioko
Mackay 101 NE Australia
Mackay, Lake 101 salt lake of C Australia
Mackenzie 170 river of NW Canada
Mackenzie Mountains 170 mountain range of NW Canada
Macleod, Lake 100 lake of W Australia
Macomer 320 Sardegna, S Italy
Macon 599 Georgia, SE USA
Mâcon 253 E France
Macouba 649 N Martinique
MacRitchie Reservoir 517 reservoir of C Singapore
Macroom 314 SW Ireland
Macuelizo 288 W Honduras
Ma'dabā 336 var. Mādabā. NW Jordan
Madagascar 382-383 officially Democratic Republic of Madagascar, Malg. Madagasikara, prev. Malagasy Republic. Country of SE Africa divided into 6 admin. units (provinces). ❖ Antananarivo
Madan 152 S Bulgaria
Madang 458 E Papua New Guinea
Madanīyīn see Médenine
Mādārīpur 117 S Bangladesh
Madeira 474 var. Ilha de Madeira. Madeira Is, Portugal
Madeira 144 river of Bolivia and Brazil

Madeira, Arquipélago da *see* Madeira Islands
Madeira Islands *474 Port.* Arquipélago da Madeira. Island group to the SW of Portugal
Madina do Boé *see* Boé
Madīnat al Abyār *371* NE Libya
Madīnat al Ka'bān *479 var.* Al Ka'aban. N Qatar
Madīnat ash Sha'b *627 prev.* Al Ittiḥād. SW Yemen
Madīnat ash Shamāl *479 var.* Madinat el Shamal. N Qatar
Madīnat ath Thawrah *551* N Syria
Madinat el Shamal *see* Madīnat ash Shamāl
Madīnat Ḥamad *115 var.* Hamada Town, Hamad. W Bahrain
Madīnat 'Isá *115 var.* Isa Town. N Bahrain
Madīnat Khalīfa *479* E Qatar
Madingo-Kayes *200* S Congo
Madingou *200* S Congo
Madison *599* Wisconsin, NC USA
Madiun *302 prev.* Madioen. Java, C Indonesia
Madlangampisi *540* N Swaziland
Madona *362 Ger.* Modohn. E Latvia
Madras *see* Chennai
Madre de Dios *136, 463* river of Bolivia and Peru
Madrid *531* ❖ of Spain, C Spain
Madriu, Riu *86* river of S Andorra
Madura *302 prev.* Madoera. Island to NE of Java, C Indonesia
Madurai *296 prev.* Madura. S India
Maebashi *330* Honshū, SE Japan
Mae Name Khong *see* Mekong
Mae Nam Khong *see* Mekong
Mae Nam Moi *see* Thaungyin
Mae Nam Ping *563* river of NW Thailand
Maéwo *615 prev.* Aurora. Island of C Vanuatu
Mafa'a, Pointe *653* headland of Île Alofi, N Wallis & Futuna
Mafeteng *366* W Lesotho
Mafia *560* island of E Tanzania
Mafou *281* river of C Guinea
Mafraq *see* Al Mafraq
Mafraq *590* C United Arab Emirates
Mafungabusi Plateau *636* plateau of C Zimbabwe
Mafut *590* NE United Arab Emirates
Magadan *485* NE Russian Federation
Magadi *342* SW Kenya
Magadi, Lake *342* lake of SW Kenya
Magallanes *see* Punta Arenas
Magallanes, Estrecho *see* Magellan, Strait of
Magangué *195* N Colombia
Magaria *439* S Niger
Magat *466* river of Luzon, N Philippines
Magburaka *514* C Sierra Leone
Magdalena *195* river of C Colombia
Magdalena *136* N Bolivia
Magdeburg *265* C Germany
Magelang *302* Java, C Indonesia
Magellan, Strait of *95, 183 Sp.* Estrecho de Magallanes. Strait connecting the S Atlantic and S Pacific Oceans between Tierra del Fuego and mainland South America
Magerøya *444 var.* Magerøy. Island of NE Norway
Maggiore, Lake *320, 346 It.* Lago Maggiore. Lake of Italy and Switzerland
Magh Ealla *see* Mallow
Maglaj *140* N Bosnia & Herzegovina
Magnitogorsk *484* C Russian Federation
Mago *246 prev.* Mango. Island of the Lau Group, E Fiji
Magta' Lahjar *398* SW Mauritania
Māgura *117* W Bangladesh
Magwe *159 var.* Magway. W Burma
Magyarkanizsa *see* Kanjiža
Magyarország *see* Hungary
Magyaróvár *see* Mosonmagyaróvár
Mahafaly, Lembalemban' *382 var.*Plateau Mahafaly. Plateau of SW Madagascar
Mahaicony Village *284* E Guyana
Mahajamba *382* seasonal river of N Madagascar
Mahajanga *382 prev.* Majunga. N Madagascar
Mahajilo *382* seasonal river of C Madagascar
Mahakali *427* river of India and Nepal
Mahakam *302 var.* Kutai, Koetai. River of Borneo, C Indonesia
Mahalapye *142 var.* Mahalatswe. SE Botswana
Maḥallah al Kubrá *see* El Mahalla el Kubra
Mahamba *540* SW Swaziland
Mahanādi *296* river of E India
Mahanoro *382* E Madagascar
Maha Sarakham *563* NE Thailand
Mahaut *224* W Dominica
Mahavavy *382* seasonal river of N Madagascar
Mahaweli Ganga *534* river of C Sri Lanka
Mahdia *573 var.* Al Mahdīyah, Mehdia. NE Tunisia
Mahdia *284* C Guyana
Mahé *512* island of NE Seychelles
Mahebourg *400* SE Mauritius
Mahenge *560* SE Tanzania
Mahia Peninsula *433* peninsula of E North Island, New Zealand
Mahilyow *122 Rus.* Mogilëv. E Belarus
Mahina *392* W Mali
Mahiyangana *534* E Sri Lanka
Maḥmūd-e Rāqī *77* NE Afghanistan
Mahmudiya *see* Al Maḥmūdīyah
Mahou *392* S Mali
Mährisch-Ostrau *see* Ostrava
Mährisch-Schönberg *see* Šumperk
Maiana *346* island of the Gilbert Is, W Kiribati
Maicao *195* N Colombia
Mai Ceu *see* Maych'ew
Mai Chio *see* Maych'ew
Maiduguri *441* NE Nigeria
Mailand *see* Milano
Maimāna *see* Meymaneh
Main *264* river of C Germany
Main Camp *see* Banana
Main Channel *648* channel of the Pacific Ocean, S Johnston Atoll
Main Channel *see* Inner Channel
Mai-Ndombe, Lac *203 prev.* Lac Léopold II. Lake of W Dem. Rep. Congo (Zaire)
Maine *599* state of NE USA
Maine *253* cultural region of NW France
Maïné-Soroa *439* SE Niger
Mainland *593* Shetland, NE UK
Mainland *593* Orkney, NE UK
Maintirano *382* W Madagascar
Mainz *264 Fr.* Mayence. SW Germany
Maio *176 var.* Vila de Maio. Maio, S Cape Verde
Maio *176* island of SE Cape Verde
Maiquetía *619* N Venezuela
Maissade *286* C Haiti
Maisur *see* Mysore
Maitland *101* E Australia
Maitri *90* Indian research station of Greater Antarctica, Antarctica
Maíz, Islas *436 var.* Corn Islands. Island group of E Nicaragua
Maizuru *330* Honshū, C Japan
Majardah, Wādī *see* Mejerda, Oued
Majimbini, Réserve Forestière de *649* forest reserve of C Mayotte
Majorca *see* Mallorca
Majunga *see* Mahajanga
Majuro *396* atoll of SE Marshall Islands
Majuro District *396* district of Majuro, SE Marshall Islands
Makamba *162* S Burundi
Makarska *209 It.* Macarsca. SE Croatia
Makasar *see* Ujungpandang
Makasar, Selat *302 Eng.* Makassar Strait. Strait connecting the Celebes Sea and Laut Flores, C Indonesia
Makassar Strait *see* Makasar, Selat
Makay, Tangorombohitr' i *382 var.* Massif du Makay. Mountains of SW Madagascar
Makebuko *162* C Burundi
Makeni *514* C Sierra Leone
Makgadikgadi *142 var.* Makarikari Pans. Saltpans of NE Botswana
Makhachkala *484 prev.* Petrovsk-Port. SW Russian Federation
Makharadze *see* Ozurget'i
Makhfar al Quwayrah *see* Al Quwayrah
Makin *346* island of the Gilbert Is, W Kiribati
Makira *see* San Cristobal
Makiyivka *586 Rus.* Makeyevka, *prev.* Dmitriyevsk. E Ukraine
Makkah *506 Eng.* Mecca. W Saudi Arabia
Makō *see* MaKung
Makó *290* SE Hungary
Makogai *246* island to the NE of Viti Levu, C Fiji
Makokou *258* NE Gabon
Makona *281* river of S Guinea
Makoua *200* C Congo
Makran Coast *307* coastal region of SE Iran
MaKung *555 Jap.* Makō. P'eng-hu Tao, W Taiwan
Makunudhoo Atoll *390 var.* Makunudu Atoll. Atoll of N Maldives
Makurazaki *330* Kyūshū, SW Japan
Makurdi *440* C Nigeria
Makuti *636* N Zimbabwe
Makwate *142* SE Botswana
Mala *see* Malaita
Malabo *236 prev.* Santa Isabel. ❖ of Equatorial Guinea, N Bioko
Malacca *see* Melaka
Malacca, Strait of *302* strait connecting the Andaman Sea and South China Sea between Malay Peninsula and Sumatra, SE Asia
Malacka *see* Malacky
Malacky *519 Hung.* Malacka. W Slovakia
Maladzyechna *122 Rus.* Molodechno, *Pol.* Molodeczno. NW Belarus
Málaga *531* S Spain
Malagasy Republic *see* Madagascar
Malaita *522 var.* Mala, Island of C Solomon Islands
Malakal *536 var.* Malakāl. S Sudan
Malambo *195* N Colombia
Malang *302* SE Java, Indonesia
Malange *see* Malanje
Malanje *88 var.* Malange. NW Angola
Malanville *132* NE Benin
Mälaren *543* lake of SE Sweden
Malatya *576* SE Turkey
Malawi *384-385* officially Republic of Malawi, *prev.* Nyasaland, Nyasaland Protectorate. Country of S Africa divided into 3 admin. units (regions). ❖ Lilongwe
Malawi, Lake *see* Nyasa, Lake
Malaya *see* Peninsular Malaysia
Malāyer *307* NW Iran
Malay Peninsula *563* peninsula of Malaysia and Thailand
Malaysia *386-389* officially Republic of Maldives, *prev.* the separate territories of Federation of Malaya, Singapore (left 1965), Sarawak and Sabah (North Borneo). Country of SE Asia divided into 15 admin. units (13 states, 2 federal territories). ❖ Kuala Lumpur
Maldegem *127* NW Belgium
Malden Island *346* island of the Line Is, E Kiribati
Maldives *390-391* Officially Republic of Maldives, Maldivian Divehi. Country of the Indian Ocean divided into 19 admin. units (districts). ❖ Male'
Maldonado *607* S Uruguay
Male' *390 var.* Male. ❖ of Maldives, Male' Atoll, C Maldives
Male *see* Male'
Male' Atoll *390 var.* Kaafu Atoll. Atoll of C Maldives
Malebo Pool *see* Stanley Pool
Malékoula *see* Malekula
Malekula *615 var.* Malakula, *prev.* Mallicolo. Island of W Vanuatu
Mali *392-393* officially Republic of Mali, *prev.* Sudanese Republic, French Sudan. Country divided into 8 admin. units (7 regions and 1 capital district). ❖ Bamako
Maliana *305* W East Timor
Malibamatso *366* river of C Lesotho
Mali Hka *159* river of N Burma forming a headstream of the Irrawaddy river
Malindi *342* SE Kenya
Malines *see* Mechelen
Malinga *258* SE Gabon
Malin Head *314* headland on the N coast of Ireland
Mallāq, Wādī *see* Mellègue, Oued
Mallawi *230 var.* Mallawī. C Egypt
Mallicolo *see* Malekula
Mallorca *531 Eng.* Majorca. Island of the Islas Baleares, E Spain
Mallow *314 Ir.* Magh Ealla. SW Ireland
Malmédy *127* E Belgium
Malmö *543* S Sweden
Malmok *650* headland of Bonaire, S Netherlands Antilles
Malo *615* island of W Vanuatu
Maloelap *396* island of E Marshall Islands
Malolo *246* island of the Mamanuca-i-ra Group, W Fiji
Malolos *466* Luzon, N Philippines
Maloma *540* S Swaziland
Malombe, Lake *385* lake of SE Malawi
Małopolska *471* plateau of S Poland
Maloti Mountains *see* Maluti
Malpasso *226* SW Dominican Republic
Mäls *374* S Liechtenstein
Malta *395* island of the Mediterranean Sea, with Gozo and Kemmuna forms the state of Malta
Malta *394-395* officially Republic of Malta. Country of the Mediterranean Sea. ❖ Valletta
Malta Channel *395 It.* Canale di Malta. Strait of Mediterranean Sea between Malta and Sicily
Maltahöhe *423* S Namibia
Malta, Il-Fliegu ta' *395 Eng.* South Comino Channel. Strait of Mediterranean Sea between Kemmuna and Malta islands, NW Malta
Maluku *302 prev.* Spice Islands, *Eng.* Moluccas. Island group of E Indonesia
Maluku, Laut *302 Eng.* Molucca Sea. Sea of the Pacific Ocean, E Indonesia
Malung *543* C Sweden
Maluti *366 var.* Maluti Mountains, Maloti Mountains, Front Range. Mountain range of C Lesotho
Malvinas, Islas *see* Falkland Islands
Malyy Kavkaz *see* Lesser Caucasus
Mamanuca-i-ra Group *246* islands of W Fiji
Mamates *366* NW Lesotho
Mambéré *179* river of SW Central African Republic
Mambili *200* river of W Congo
Mamer *378* SW Luxembourg
Mamfe *168* W Cameroon
Mamiku *497* E St Lucia
Mamoré *136* river of Bolivia and Brazil
Mamou *281* W Guinea
Mamoudzou *649* ❖ of Mayotte, N Mayotte
Mampong *270* C Ghana
Mamṭalah, Ra's al *see* Mummaṭalah, Ra's al
Mamuno *142* W Botswana
Man *326* W Ivory Coast
Mana *645* NW French Guiana
Manado *302 prev.* Menado. Celebes, C Indonesia
Managua *436* ❖ of Nicaragua, W Nicaragua
Managua, Lago de *436 var.* Xolotlán. Lake of W Nicaragua

Manaḩ *448 var.* Bilād Manaḩ. N Oman
Manakara *382* SE Madagascar
Mana *645* river of C French Guiana
Manama *115 Ar.* Al Manāmah. ❖ of Bahrain, NE Bahrain
Manambaho *382* seasonal river of NW Madagascar
Manambolo *382* river of W Madagascar
Mananjary *382* SE Madagascar
Manantali, Lac de *392* reservoir of W Mali
Manāqīsh *354 var.* Manageesh. S Kuwait
Manas, Gora *610* mountain of NE Uzbekistan
Manatí *651* N Puerto Rico
Manatuto *305* N East Timor
Manaus *144 prev.* Manáos. NW Brazil
Manbij *551 Fr.* Membidj. N Syria
Manchester *593* N England, UK
Manchester *599* New Hampshire, NE USA
Man-chou-li *see* Manzhouli
Manda Island *342* island of SE Kenya
Mandal *444* SW Norway
Mandalay *159* N Burma
Mandalgovĭ *412* S Mongolia
Mandali *310* E Iraq
Mandaue *466* Cebu, C Philippines
Mandera *342* NE Kenya
Mandeville *329* SW Jamaica
Mandiana *281* E Guinea
Mandi Būrewāla *451 var.* Būrewāla. E Pakistan
Mandidzudzure *see* Chimanimani
Mandié *419* NW Mozambique
Mandimba *419* N Mozambique
Mandji *258* C Gabon
Mandouri *567* N Togo
Manfredonia *321* S Italy
Manga *157* C Burkina
Mangai *203* W Dem. Rep. Congo (Zaire)
Mangaia *644* island of Southern Cook Islands, S Cook Islands
Mangalia *480* SE Romania
Mangalmé *180* SE Chad
Mangalore *296* SW India
Mangde *134* river of S Bhutan
Mange *514* NW Sierra Leone
Mango *see* Sansanné-Mango
Mango *see* Mago
Mangoche *see* Mangochi
Mangochi *385 var.* Mangoche, *prev.* Fort Johnson. SE Malawi
Mangoky *382* river of SW Madagascar
Mangula *see* Mhangura
Mania *382* river of C Madagascar
Manica *419 var.* Vila de Manica. W Mozambique
Manihiki *644* island of Northern Cook Islands, N Cook Islands
Maniitsoq *646 Dan.* Sukkertoppen. SW Greenland
Manikaraku *522* E Guadalcanal, Solomon Is
Manikganj *117* C Bangladesh
Manila *466 var.* Manila City. ❖ of the Philippines, Luzon, N Philippines
Manisa *576 prev.* Saruhan. W Turkey
Man, Isle of *593, 647* British Crown dependency of the Irish Sea. ❖ Douglas
Manitoba *170* province of S Canada
Manizales *195* W Colombia
Manjimup *100* SW Australia
Mankayane *540 var.* Mankaiana. W Swaziland
Mankono *326* C Ivory Coast
Mankulam *534* N Sri Lanka
Mannar *534 var.* Manar. NW Sri Lanka
Mannar, Gulf of *296, 534* gulf of Indian Ocean, to the S of India
Mannar Island *534* island to the N of Sri Lanka
Mannheim *264* SW Germany
Mano *514* SW Sierra Leone
Mano *514* river of Liberia and Sierra Leone
Manombo Atsimo *382 var.* Manombo. SW Madagascar
Manono *500* Upolu, Samoa
Manono *203* SE Dem. Rep. Congo (Zaire)
Manorhamilton *314* N Ireland
Manp'o *349 var.* Manp'ojin. NW North Korea
Manra *346 var.* Sydney I. Island of the Phoenix Is, C Kiribati
Mansa *635 prev.* Fort Rosebery. N Zambia
Mansabá *282* NW Guinea-Bissau
Mansajang Kunda *261* E Gambia
Mansa Konko *261* C Gambia
Mansion *494* NE St Kitts, St Kitts & Nevis
Mansôa *282* W Guinea-Bissau
Mansôa *282* river of W Guinea-Bissau
Manta *228* W Ecuador
Mantes-la-Jolie *253 prev.* Mantes-sur-Seine, Mantes-Gassicourt. N France
Mantova *320 Eng.* Mantua, *Fr.* Mantoue. N Italy
Mantsonyane *366* C Lesotho
Manuae *644* island of Southern Cook Islands, S Cook Islands
Manua Islands *642* island group of E American Samoa
Manukau Harbour *433* harbour of W North Island, New Zealand
Manurewa *433* N North Island, New Zealand
Manus Island *458 var.* Great Admiralty I. Island of NE Papua New Guinea
Manyame *636 var.* Panhame, *prev.* Hunyani. River of Mozambique and Zimbabwe
Manyame, Lake *636 prev.* Robertson, Lake. Reservoir of N Zimbabwe
Manyara, Lake *560* lake of NE Tanzania
Manyoni *560* C Tanzania
Manzanillo *210* SE Cuba
Manzhouli *187 var.* Man-chou-li. Nei Mongol Zizhiqu, NE China
Manzil Bū Ruqaybah *see* Menzel Bourguiba
Manzil Tamīm *see* Menzel Temime
Manzini *540 prev.* Bremersdorp. C Swaziland
Mao *180* W Chad
Mao *226* NW Dominican Republic
Maoke, Pegunungan *303 Dut.* Sneeuw-gebergte, *Eng.* Snow Mountains. Mountain range of Irian Jaya, E Indonesia
Mapoteng *366* NW Lesotho
Mapou *400* N Mauritius
Maputo *419 prev.* Lourenço Marques. ❖ of Mozambique, S Mozambique
Maputo, Baía de *419 var.* Baía de Lourenço Marques, *Eng.* Delagoa Bay. Bay on the coast of Mozambique
Mara *284* E Guyana
Marabá *145* NE Brazil
Maracaibo *619* NW Venezuela
Maracaibo, Lago de *619* inlet of Caribbean Sea, NW Venezuela
Maracay *619* N Venezuela
Marada *371* N Libya
Maradi *439* S Niger
Maragarazi *162, 560 var.* Muragarazi. River of Burundi and Tanzania
Marāgheh *307 var.* Maragha. NW Iran
Marahoué *see* Bandama Rouge
Marajó, Baía de *145* N Brazil
Marajó, Ilha de *145* island of N Brazil
Marakabei *366 var.* Marakabeis. C Lesotho
Marakei *346* island of the Gilbert Is, W Kiribati
Maralal *342* C Kenya
Maralik *98* W Armenia
Maramasike *522* island of E Solomon Is
Maramba *see* Livingstone
Marambio *90* Argentinian research station near Antarctic Peninsula, Antarctica
Maramvya *162* SW Burundi
Marandellas *see* Marondera
Marañón *463* river of N Peru
Marash *see* Kahramanmaraş
Maravovo *522* W Guadalcanal, Solomon Is
Marāwiḩ *590 var.* Merawwah. Island of W United Arab Emirates
Marbella *531* S Spain
Marburg *see* Maribor
Marburg an der Lahn *264* W Germany
Marcal *290* river of W Hungary
Marche *253* cultural region of C France
Marche-en-Famenne *127* SE Belgium
Marchena, Isla *228* island of N Galapagos Is, Ecuador
Marchfield *121* SE Barbados
Mar Chiquita, Lago *95* lake of C Argentina
Marcounda *see* Markounda
Marcovia *288* S Honduras
Mardān *451* N Pakistan
Mar del Plata *95* E Argentina
Mardin *577* SE Turkey
Maré *650* island, Îles Loyauté, E New Caledonia
Mareeq *524 var.* Mereeg, *It.* Meregh. E Somalia
Marek *see* Dupnitsa
Marfa Ridge *395* ridge of NW Malta
Margarita, Isla de *619* island of N Venezuela
Margate *527* Kwazulu Natal, SE South Africa
Margherita, Lake *see* Ābaya Hāyk'
Margherita Peak *584, 203* mountain of Uganda and Dem. Rep. Congo (Zaire)
Marghilon *610 var.* Margelan, *Rus.* Margilan. E Uzbekistan
Māragow, Dasht-e- *77* desert of SW Afghanistan
Mari *215* S Cyprus
Marianao *210* NW Cuba
Marías, Islas *403* Island of W Mexico
Maria-Theresiopel *see* Subotica
Máriatölgyes *see* Dubnica nad Váhom
Mar'ib *627* W Yemen
Maribo *218* Lolland, S Denmark
Maribor *520 Ger.* Marburg. NE Slovenia
Marid *590* NE United Arab Emirates
Marie Byrd Land *90* physical region of Greater Antarctica, Antarctica
Marie-Galante *646* island of SE Guadeloupe
Mariehamn *249 var.* Maarianhamina. Aland, Finland
Mariel *210* NW Cuba
Marienburg *see* Alūksne
Mariental *423* S Namibia
Marigot *646* St. Martin, N Guadeloupe
Marigot *224* NE Dominica
Marigot de Baïla *510* river of SW Senegal
Mariguana *see* Mayaguana
Marijampolė *376 prev.* Kapsukas. S Lithuania
Marília *145* S Brazil
Marinduque Island *466* island of C Philippines
Maringá *145* S Brazil
Marins, Île aux *652* island of SE Saint Pierre and Miquelon
Marion Island *527* island of Prince Edward Islands, S South Africa
Ionio, Mar *see* Ionian Sea
Maripasoula *645* W French Guiana
Mariscal Estigarribia *460* NW Paraguay
Marisule Estate *497* N St Lucia
Maritsa *152, 273 var.* Marica, *Gk* Évros, *Turk.* Meriç. River of SE Europe
Mariupol' *586 prev.* Zhdanov. SE Ukraine
Mariy El, Respublika *484* autonomous republic of W Russian Federation
Märjamaa *240 Ger.* Merjama. W Estonia
Marjayoun *364 var.* Marj 'Uyūn. S Lebanon
Marka *524 var.* Merca. S Somalia
Marka *385* S Malawi
Market Shop *494* SE Nevis, St Kitts & Nevis
Markounda *179 var.* Marcounda. NW Central African Republic
Marlánské Lázně *216* W Czech Republic
Marmara Denizi *576 Eng.* Sea of Marmara. Sea to the NW of Turkey
Marmaris *576* SW Turkey
Marne *253* river of NE France
Marneuli *262* S Georgia
Maro *180* S Chad
Maroantsetra *382* NE Madagascar
Maromokotro *382* mountain of N Madagascar
Marondera *636 var.* Marandellas. NE Zimbabwe
Maroni *538, 645 Dut.* Marowijne. River of French Guiana and Suriname
Maros *see* Mureş
Marosvásárhely *see* Târgu Mureş
Marotiri *646* island group of S French Polynesia
Maroua *168* N Cameroon
Marovoay *382* NW Madagascar
Marowijne *see* Maroni
Marqūbān *115* NE Bahrain
Marquises, Îles *646* island group of N French Polynesia
Marrakech *414 var.* Marakesh, *Eng.* Marrakesh, *prev.* Morocco. W Morocco
Marrupa *419* N Mozambique
Marsa *395* C Malta
Marsá al Burayqah *see* Al Burayqah
Marsabit *342* N Kenya
Marsala *321* Sicilia, S Italy
Marsaxlokk *395* SE Malta
Marsaxlokk Bay *395* inlet on the SW coast of Malta
Marseille *253 prev. Eng.* Marseilles. SE France
Marshall *368* W Liberia
Marshall Islands *396-397* officially Republic of the Marshall Islands. Country of the Pacific Ocean divided into 33 admin. units (districts). ❖ Majuro
Marsh Harbour *112* Great Abaco, Bahamas
Martaban *159* SE Burma
Martadi *427 var.* Bajura. W Nepal
Martigny *546* SW Switzerland
Martigues *253* SE France
Martin *519 prev.* Turčianský Svätý Martin, *Ger.* Sankt Martin, *Hung.* Turócszentmárton. NW Slovakia
Martinique *649* French overseas department of the Caribbean Sea. ❖ Fort-de-France.
Martinique Passage *224 var.* Dominica Channel, Martinique Channel. Passage connecting the Atlantic Ocean and Caribbean Sea between Dominica and Martinique
Martuni *98* E Armenia
Marungu *203* mountain range of SE Dem. Rep. Congo (Zaire)
Mary *581 prev.* Merv. SE Turkmenistan
Maryborough *101* E Australia
Mary Island *see* Kanton
Maryland *599* state of E USA
Marzūq *see* Murzuq
Masai Steppe *560* grassland of NW Tanzania
Masaka *584* SW Uganda
Masākin *see* M'saken
Masally *see* Massılı
Masampo *see* Masan
Masan *350 prev.* Masampo. S South Korea
Masasi *560* SE Tanzania
Masatepe *436* SW Nicaragua
Masaya *436* S Nicaragua
Masbate *466* island of C Philippines
Mascara *83 var.* Mouaskar. NW Algeria
Maseru *366* ❖ of Lesotho, W Lesotho
Mas-ha *318* W West Bank
Mashava *636 prev.* Mashaba. SE Zimbabwe
Mashhad *307 var.* Meshed. NE Iran
Māshkel *307, 450 var.* Rūd-i Māshkel, Māshkīd. River of Iran and Pakistan

Māshkel, Hāmūn-i *450* salt marsh of Iran and Pakistan
Māshkīd *see* Māshkel
Mashtagi *see* Mastaği
Masīlah, Wādī al *627* dry watercourse of E Yemen
Masindi *584* W Uganda
Masinga Reservoir *342* reservoir of C Kenya
Masirah, Gulf of *see* Maşīrah, Khalīj
Maşīrah, Jazīrat *448* *var.* Masirah, Masira. Island of E Oman
Maşīrah, Khalīj *448* *var.* Gulf of Masirah. Bay of the Arabian Sea, E Oman
Masis *98* SW Armenia
Masjed Soleymān *307* *var.* Masjed-e Soleymān, Masjid-i Sulaiman. W Iran
Maskall *130* NE Belize
Maskanah *551* *var.* Meskene. N Syria
Maskin *448* *var.* Miskin. N Oman
Mask, Lough *314* *Ir.* Loch Measca. Lake of W Ireland
Ma *623* river of Laos and Vietnam
Massa *320* N Italy
Massachusetts *599* state of NE USA
Massacre *224* W Dominica
Massawa *238* *Amh.* Mits'iwa. E Eritrea
Massawa Channel *238* channel of the Red Sea between Dahlak Archipelago and mainland Eritrea
Massenya *180* SW Chad
Massif Central *253* plateau region of C France
Massilı *110* *Rus.* Masally. S Azerbaijan
Massoukou *258* *var.* Masuku, *prev.* Franceville. E Gabon
Maştağa *110* *Rus.* Mastaga, *var.* Maštaga, Mashtagi. E Azerbaijan
Masterton *433* S North Island, New Zealand
Masuda *330* Honshū, W Japan
Masunga *142* NE Botswana
Masvingo *636* *prev.* Nyanda, *prev.* Fort Victoria. SE Zimbabwe
Mât *652* river of NE Réunion
Matacawa Levu *246* island of the Yasawa Group, NW Fiji
Matadi *203* W Dem. Rep. Congo (Zaire)
Matagalpa *436* C Nicaragua
Matale *534* C Sri Lanka
Matam *510* NE Senegal
Matamoros *403* E Mexico
Matana *162* C Burundi
Matanzas *210* NW Cuba
Matara *534* S Sri Lanka
Mataró *531* E Spain
Mataura *433* river of SW South Island, New Zealand
Matautu *500* Upolu, Samoa
Matā 'Utu *653* *var.* Mata Uta. ❖ of Wallis & Futuna, Île Uvea, S Wallis & Futuna
Matela's *366* W Lesotho
Matelot *570* NE Trinidad, Trinidad & Tobago
Matiguás *436* C Nicaragua
Matina *206* E Costa Rica
Matit *81* *var.* Mat. River of C Albania
Mato Grosso, Planalto de *145* plateau of C Brazil
Matopos *636* SW Zimbabwe
Matosinhos *474* *prev.* Matozinhos. NW Portugal
Mátra *290* mountain range of N Hungary
Maţraḩ *448* *var.* Mutrah. NE Oman
Matrûh *230* *var.* Maţrūḩ. NW Egypt
Matsapha *540* *var.* Matsapal, Mtsapa. C Swaziland
Matsieng *366* W Lesotho
Matsue *330* Honshū, W Japan
Matsumato *330* Honshū, C Japan
Matsusaka *330* Honshū, C Japan
Matsuyama *330* Shikoku, SW Japan
Matthews Ridge *284* N Guyana
Matthew Town *112* Great Inagua, Bahamas
Mattsee *106* lake of N Austria
Matuku *246* island to the SE of Viti Levu, S Fiji
Maturín *619* NE Venezuela
Mauga Silisili *see* Silisili, Mount
Maug Islands *650* island group of N Northern Mariana Islands
Maui *598* island of Hawaii, USA, C Pacific
Maun *142* C Botswana
Mauren *374* NE Liechtenstein
Maurice *see* Mauritius
Maú *see* Ireng
Mauritania *398-399* officially Islamic Republic of Mauritania, *Ar.* Mūrītānīyah. Country of W Africa divided into 12 admin. units (regions). ❖ Nouakchott
Mauritius *400-401* *Fr.* Maurice. Country of Indian Ocean divided into 9 admin. units (districts). ❖ Port Louis
Mavrovsko Ezero *381* lake of W FYR Macedonia
Mawlaik *159* NW Burma
Mawlamyine *see* Moulmein
Mawr, Wādī *627* dry watercourse of NW Yemen
Mawson *90* Australian research station of Greater Antarctica, Antarctica
Mayaguana *112* Island of S Bahamas
Mayaguana Passage *112* passage between Crooked I and Mayaguana, Bahamas
Mayagüez *651* W Puerto Rico
Mayagüez, Bahia *651* bay of the Caribbean Sea on the W coast of Puerto Rico
Mayaluka *540* SE Swaziland
Maya Mts *130* mountain range of Belize and Guatemala
Mayarí *211* SE Cuba
Maych'ew *243* *var.* Mai Chio, *It.* Mai Ceu. N Ethiopia
Maydī *see* Midī
Mayence *see* Mainz
Mayenne *253* river of NW France
Maykop 484 SW Russian Federation
Mayli-Say *357* *Kir.* Mayly-Say. W Kyrgyzstan
Mayly-Say *see* Mayli-Say
Maymyo *159* N Burma
Mayoko *200* SW Congo
Mayor Pablo Lagerenza *see* Capitán Pablo Lagerenza
Mayotte *649* French territorial collectivity of the Indian Ocean. ❖ Mamoudzou.
May Pen *329* S Jamaica
Mayreau *498* island of SW St Vincent & the Grenadines
Mayumba *258* S Gabon
Mazabuka *635* S Zambia
Mazagan *see* El Jadida
Mazār-e Sharīf *77* N Afghanistan
Mazaruni *284* river of N Guyana
Mazatenango *278* SW Guatemala
Mazatlán *403* W Mexico
Mažeikiai *376* NW Lithuania
Mazirbe *362* NW Latvia
Mazowe *636* *prev.* Mazoe. NE Zimbabwe
Mazowe *636* *var.* Mazoe. River of Mozambique and Zimbabwe
Mazra'at Turaynā *479* *var.* Traina Garden. S Qatar
Mazury *471* region of NE Poland
Mazyr *122* *Rus.* Mozyr'. SE Belarus
Mba *see* Ba
Mbabane *540* ❖ of Swaziland, NW Swaziland
Mbacké *see* Mbaké
Mbagne *398* SW Mauritania
Mbaïki *179* *var.* M'Baiki. SW Central African Republic
Mbakaou, Lac de *168* lake of C Cameroon
Mbaké *510* *var.* Mbacké. W Senegal
Mbala *635* *prev.* Abercorn. NE Zambia
Mbalabala *636* *prev.* Balla Balla. SW Zimbabwe
Mbale *584* E Uganda
Mbalmayo *168* *var.* M'Balmayo. S Cameroon
Mbalo *522* SE Guadalcanal, Solomon Is
Mbam *168* river of NW Cameroon
Mbanda *162* S Burundi
Mbandaka *203* *prev.* Coquilhatville. NW Dem. Rep. Congo (Zaire)
Mbanga *168* W Cameroon
M'Banza Congo *88* *Port.* São Salvador do Congo. NW Angola
Mbanza-Ngungu *203* W Dem. Rep. Congo (Zaire)
Mbarara *584* SW Uganda
Mbatiki *see* Batiki
Mbé *168* N Cameroon
Mbengga *see* Beqa
Mbéni *198* NE Grande Comore, Comoros
Mbeya *560* SW Tanzania
Mbigou *258* C Gabon
Mbilua *see* Vella Lavella
Mbinga *560* S Tanzania
Mbini *236* W Río Muni, Equatorial Guinea
Mbini *see* Uolo, Río
Mbomo *200* NW Congo
Mbomou *see* Bomu
Mbour *510* W Senegal
M'Bout *see* Mbout
Mbout *398* *var.* M'Bout. S Mauritania
Mbrès *179* C Central African Republic
Mbuji-Mayi *203* *prev.* Bakwanga. S Dem. Rep. Congo (Zaire)
Mbulu *560* N Tanzania
Mbulungwane *540* S Swaziland
Mbuluzi *540* *var.* Black Umbeluzi. River of Mozambique and Swaziland
Mbutha *see* Buca
Mbuye *162* C Burundi
Mchinji *385* *prev.* Fort Manning. W Malawi
McKean Island *346* island of the Phoenix Is, C Kiribati
M'Clintock Channel *170* *var.* McClintock Channel. Channel between Prince of Wales Island and Victoria Island, N Canada
McMurdo *90* US research station near Ross Shelf, Antarctica
Mdantsane *527* Eastern Cape, SE South Africa
Mdina *395* W Malta
Mead, Lake *598* reservoir of SW USA
Measca, Loch *see* Mask, Lough
Mecca *see* Makkah
Mechelen *127* *Fr.* Malines. C Belgium
Mecheria *83* *var.* Mechriyya. NW Algeria
Mecklenburger Bucht *265* bay of the Baltic Sea, on the N coast of Germany
Mecsek *290* mountain range of SW Hungary
Medan *302* Sumatra, E Indonesia
Medawachchiya *534* N Sri Lanka
Médéa *83* *var.* Lemdiyya, El Mediyya. N Algeria
Medellín *195* NW Colombia
Médenine *573* *var.* Madanīyīn. SE Tunisia
Medford *598* Oregon, NW USA
Medicine Hat *170* SW Canada
Medina *see* Al Madīnah
Médina Gonassé *see* Médina Gounas
Médina Gounas *510* *var.* Médina Gonassé. S Senegal
Medina Seringe Mass *261* W Gambia
Mediterranean Sea *253, 317, 576* *Fr.* Mer Méditerranée. Sea of the Atlantic Ocean, enclosed by N Africa, SW Asia and S Europe
Medjerda *see* Mejerda, Oued
Medoc *252* cultural region of SW France
Médouneu *258* N Gabon
Meekatharra *100* W Australia
Meemu Atoll *see* Mulaku Atoll
Meenen *see* Menen
Meerut *296* N India
Meghna *117* river of S Bangladesh
Meghri *98* *var.* Megri. SE Armenia
Mehdia *see* Mahdia
Meherpur *117* W Bangladesh
Meheso *see* Mī'ēso
Me Hka *see* Nmai Hka
Mehtarlām *77* *var.* Methariam, Meterlam. E Afghanistan
Meiganga *168* NE Cameroon
Meiktila *159* C Burma
Meissen *265* E Germany
Mejerda, Monts de la *573* *var.* Monts de la Medjerda, Monts de la Majardah. Mountain range of Algeria and Tunisia
Mejerda, Oued *573* *var.* Medjerda, Wādī Majardah. River of Algeria and Tunisia
Méjico *see* Mexico
Mejit *396* island of NE Marshall Islands
Mékambo *258* NE Gabon
Mek'elē *243* *var.* Makale. N Ethiopia
Mekerrhane, Sebkha *83* *var.* Sebkra Mekerrhane, Sebkha Meqerghane. Salt flat of C Algeria
Mékhé *510* NW Senegal
Meknès *414* N Morocco
Mekong *159, 165, 186, 359, 563, 623* *Chin.* Lancang Jiang, *var.* Lan-ts'ang Chiang, *Cam.* Mékôngk, *Lao.* Mènam Khong, *Th.* Mae Name Khong, *Vtn.* Sông Tiên Giang, *Tib.* Za Qu, *var.* Dza Chu. River of SE Asia
Mekong Delta *623* delta of S Vietnam
Mékrou *132, 157* river of W Africa
Melah, Oued el *573* *var.* Wādī al Milḩ. Dry watercourse of W Tunisia
Melah, Sebkhet el *573* *var.* Sabkhat al Milḩ. Salt flat of SE Tunisia
Melaka *386* *var.* Malacca. SW Peninsular Malaysia
Melbourne *101* SE Australia
Meleda *see* Mljet
Melekeiok *455* C Palau
Melfi *180* S Chad
Melilla *414, 531* enclave of Spain, NE Morocco
Melitopol' *586* SE Ukraine
Melle *264* NW Germany
Mellègue, Oued *573* *var.* Wādī Mallāq. River of Algeria and Tunisia
Mellerud *543* SW Sweden
Mellieħa *395* NW Malta
Mellieħa Ridge *395* ridge of Malta island, Malta
Mělnik *216* NW Czech Republic
Melo *607* E Uruguay
Melo, Ilha de *282* *var.* Melho Island. Island of S Guinea-Bissau
Melsetter *see* Chimanimani
Melun *253* N France
Melville Hall *224* river of N Dominica
Melville Island *101* island of N Australia
Melville Island *170* island of Parry Islands, N Canada
Melville Islands *see* St. Giles Islands
Melville Peninsula *171* peninsula of N Canada
Melville Sound *see* Viscount Melville Sound
Memel *see* Neman
Memel *see* Klaipėda
Memphis *599* Tennessee, SE USA
Menabe *382* physical region of W Madagascar
Menado *see* Manado
Ménaka *392* E Mali
Mènam Khong *see* Mekong
Menbij *see* Manbij
Mendawai *302* river of Borneo, C Indonesia
Mende *253* S France
Mendefera *238* S Eritrea
Mendi *458* C Papua New Guinea
Mendip Hills *593* hills of W England, UK
Mendoza *95* W Argentina
Menen *127* *prev.* Meenen, *Fr.* Menin. W Belgium
Menongue *88* *Port.* Serpa Pinto. C Angola
Menorca *531* *Eng.* Minorca. Island of the Islas Baleares, E Spain
Mentakap *386* *var.* Mentakab. C Peninsular Malaysia
Mentawai, Kepulauan *302* island group to the W of Sumatra, Indonesia
Mentawai, Selat *302* strait of the Indian Ocean between Pulau Siberut and Sumatra, W Indonesia
Menzel Bourguiba *573* *prev.* Ferryville, *var.* Manzil Bū Ruqaybah. N Tunisia

Menzel Temime *573 var.* Manzil Tamīm. N Tunisia
Meppel *429* NE Netherlands
Merawwah *see* Marāwiḥ
Merca *see* Marka
Mercedes *see* Villa Mercedes
Mercedes *95* NE Argentina
Mercedes *95* E Argentina
Mercedes *607* W Uruguay
Mercedes Umaña *235* SE El Salvador
Meregh *see* Mareeq
Méré Lava *615* Banks Islands, N Vanuatu
Mergui *159* SE Burma
Mergui Archipelago *159* island group of S Burma
Meriç *see* Maritsa
Mérida *403* E Mexico
Mérida *531* W Spain
Mérida *619* W Venezuela
Mérida, Cordillera de *619 var.* Sierra Nevada de Mérida. Mountain range of W Venezuela
Meridian *599* Mississippi, SE USA
Merir *455* island of S Palau
Merizo *647* SW Guam
Merjama *see* Märjamaa
Melrhir, Chott *83 var.* Chott Melghir. Salt lake of E Algeria
Merlimau, Pulau *517* island of SW Singapore
Merredin *100* SW Australia
Mersa Fatma *238* E Eritrea
Mersa Teklay *238* N Eritrea
Mersch *378* C Luxembourg
Mersey *593* river of NW England, UK
Mersin *577 var.* İçel. S Turkey
Mersing *386* SE Peninsular Malaysia
Merthyr Tydfil *593* S Wales, UK
Meru *342* C Kenya
Merv *see* Mary
Meshed *see* Mashhad
Meskene *see* Maskanah
Mesopotamia *310* historical region of SW Asia
Mesopotamia *498* SE St Vincent, St Vincent & the Grenadines
Messalo *419 var.* Mualo. River of NE Mozambique
Messina *321 var.* Messana. Sicilia, S Italy
Messina *527* Northern Transvaal, NE South Africa
Messina, Stretto di *321 Eng.* Strait of Messina. Strait connecting the Ionian Sea and Tyrrhenian Sea, between mainland Italy and Sicilia
Mesta *see* Néstos
Mestghanem *see* Mostaganem
Mestia *262 var.* Mestiya. N Georgia
Meta *195, 619* river of Colombia and Venezuela
Meta Incognita Peninsula *171* peninsula of Baffin Island, NE Canada
Metangula *419* N Mozambique
Metapán *235* NW El Salvador
Metema *243* NW Ethiopia
Meterlam *see* Mehtarlām
Methariam *see* Mehtarlām
Metković *209* SE Croatia
Metu *243 var.* Mattu, Mettu. W Ethiopia
Metz *253* NE France
Meuse *127, 253, 429 var.* Maas. River of W Europe
Mexcala *see* Balsas
Mexiana, Ilha *145* island of N Brazil
Mexicali *403* NW Mexico
Mexicana, Altiplanicie *403 Eng.* Plateau of Mexico, Mexican Plateau. Plateau of N Mexico
Mexico *402-405* officially United States of Mexico, *Sp.* Estados Unidos Mexicanos, Méjico. Country of North or Central America divided into 31 admin. units (states). ❖ Mexico City
Mexico City *403 Sp.* Ciudad de México. of Mexico, C Mexico
Mexico, Gulf of *210, 403 Sp.* Golfo de México. Gulf of the Atlantic Ocean, on the SE coast of North America
Mexico, Plateau of *see* Mexicana, Altiplanicie
Meyadine *see* Al Mayādīn
Meymaneh *77 var.* Maimana. NW Afghanistan
Mezdra *152* NW Bulgaria
Mfanganu Island *342 var.* Mfangano Island. Island of Lake Victoria, SW Kenya
Mfouati *200* S Congo
Mhangura *636 var.* Mangula. N Zimbabwe
Mhlambanyatsi *540* W Swaziland
Mhlosheni *540* S Swaziland
Mhlume *540* NE Swaziland
Mhlumeni *540* NE Swaziland
Miami *599* Florida, SE USA
Miānwāli *451* NE Pakistan
Michalovce *519 Ger.* Grossmichel, *Hung.* Nagymihály. E Slovakia
Michigan *599* state of NC USA
Michigan, Lake *171, 599* Lake of NC USA
Micomeseng *see* Mikomeseng
Micoud *497* SE St Lucia
Micronesia *406-407* officially Federated States of Micronesia, *prev.* Caroline Islands. Country of the Pacific Ocean divided into 4 admin. units (states). ❖ Palikir
Middelburg *429* SW Netherlands
Middelburg *527* Eastern Cape, S South Africa
Middelburg *527* Eastern Transvaal, NE South Africa
Middelfart *218* Fyn, SW Denmark
Middle Andaman *296* island of Andaman Islands to the SE of India
Middle Atlas *see* Moyen Atlas
Middlegate *650* C Norfolk Island
Middle Island *494* W St Kitts, St Kitts & Nevis
Middlesbrough *593* NE England, UK
Middlesex *130* E Belize
Mīdī *627 var.* Maydī. NW Yemen
Miercurea-Ciuc *480 Hung.* Csíkszereda. C Romania
Mieres del Camino *531* NW Spain
Mi'eso *243 var.* Miesso, Meheso. C Ethiopia
Mikhaylovgrad *see* Montana
Mikhaylovka *484* W Russian Federation
Mikkeli *249 Swe.* Sankt Michel. S Finland
Mikomeseng *236 var.* Micomeseng. NE Río Muni, Equatorial Guinea
Mikuni-sammyaku *330* mountain range of Honshū, N Japan
Milagro *228* SW Ecuador
Milange *419* N Mozambique
Milano *320, 325. Eng.* Milan, *Ger.* Mailand. N Italy
Milas *576* SW Turkey
Mildura *101* SE Australia
Mil Düzü *110 Rus.* Mil'skaya Step'. Physical region of C Azerbaijan
Milgis *342 var.* Malgis. River of C Kenya
Mili *396* island of SE Marshall Islands
Milḥ, Baḥr al *see* Razāzah, Buḥayrat ar
Milḥ, Wādī al *see* Melah, Oued el
Millennium Island *346 prev.* Caroline Island. Island of the Line Is, E Kiribati
Millet *497* C St Lucia
Millstätter See *106* lake of S Austria
Milo *281* river of E Guinea
Milondo, Mont *258* mountain of C Gabon
Mílos *273* island of SE Greece
Mil'skaya Step' *see* Mil Düzü
Milton Keynes *593* C England, UK
Milwaukee *599* Wisconsin, NC USA
Milyang *see* Miryang
Mimongo *258* C Gabon
Mīnā' 'Abd Allāh *354 var.* Mina Abdulla. E Kuwait
Mīnā' al Aḥmadī *354 var.* Mina Ahmadi. E Kuwait
Mīnā' Jabal 'Alī *590* NE United Arab Emirates
Minas *607* S Uruguay
Mīnā' Sa'ūd *354 var.* Mīnā' Su'ūd. SE Kuwait
Minas de Corrales *607* N Uruguay
Minas de Matahambre *210* W Cuba
Minatitlán *403* SE Mexico
Minbu *159* W Burma
Minch, The *593* strait of the Atlantic Ocean, between Outer Hebrides and Scotland
Mincivan *110 Rus.* Mindzhivan. SW Azerbaijan
Mindanao *466* island of S Philippines
Mindanao Sea *see* Bohol Sea
Mindelo *176 var.* Porto Grande. São Vincente, N Cape Verde
Mindoro *466* island of C Philippines
Mindoro Strait *466* strait connecting South China Sea and Sulu Sea
Mindouli *200* S Congo
Mindživan *see* Mincivan
Mingäçevir *110 Rus.* Mingechaur *var.* Mingečaur. C Azerbaijan
Mingäçevir Su Anbarı *110 Rus.* Mingechaurskoye Vodokhranilishche. Reservoir of NW Azerbaijan
Mingala *179* SE Central African Republic
Mingāora *451 var.* Mingora, Mongora. N Pakistan
Mingechaurskoye Vodokhranilishche *see* Mingäçevir Su Anbarı
Ming-Kush *see* Min-Kush
Minho *see* Miño
Minicoy Island *296* island of Lakshadweep, SW India
Min-Kush *357 Kir.* Ming-Kush. C Kyrgyzstan
Minna *440* C Nigeria
Minneapolis *599* Minnesota, NC USA
Minnesota *599* state of NC USA
Miño *474, 530 Port.* Minho. River of Portugal and Spain
Minorca *see* Menorca
Minot *599* North Dakota, NC USA
Minsk *122* ❖ of Belarus, C Belarus
Minto Reef *406* atoll of C Micronesia
Minvoul *258* N Gabon
Minwakh *627* N Yemen
Miquelon *652* N Saint Pierre and Miquelon
Miquelon *652* island of N Saint Pierre and Miquelon
Miquelon, Cap *652* cape of the Atlantic Ocean on the coast of Miquelon, N Saint Pierre and Miquelon
Miragoâne *286* SW Haiti
Miranda de Ebro *531* N Spain
Mirbāṭ *448 var.* Marbat. SW Oman
Mirebalais *286* C Haiti
Miri *386* NW Borneo, Malaysia
Mirim Lagoon *145, 607 var.* Lake Mirim. Lagoon of Brazil and Uruguay
Mirim, Lake *see* Mirim Lagoon
Mirny *90* CIS research station of Greater Antarctica, Antarctica
Mirnyy *485* C Russian Federation
Mīrpur *see* New Mīrpur
Mirtóo Pelagos *273 Eng.* Mirtoan Sea. Area of the Mediterranean Sea, S Greece
Miryang *350 var.* Milyang *Jap.* Mitsuō. SE South Korea
Misery, Mount *see* Liamuiga, Mount
Miskito Coast *see* Mosquito Coast
Miskitos, Cayos *436* island group of NE Nicaragua
Miskolc *290* NE Hungary
Misool, Pulau *302* island of Maluku, E Indonesia
Miṣrātah *371 var.* Misurata. N Libya
Mississippi *599* river of C USA
Mississippi *599* state of SE USA
Missoula *598* Montana, NW USA
Missouri *599* river of NC USA
Missouri *599* state of C USA
Misurata *see* Miṣrātah
Mitau *see* Jelgava
Mitchell *101* river of NE Australia
Mitèmboni *see* Mitemele, Río
Mitemele, Río *236 var.* Mitèmboni, Temboni, Utamboni. River of Equatorial Guinea and Gabon
Mitiaro *644* island of Southern Cook Islands, S Cook Islands
Mito *330* Honshū, SE Japan
Mitre Island *see* Fatutaka
Mitrovica *see* Kosovska Mitrovica
Mitrovicë *see* Kosovska Mitrovica
Mitsamiouli *198* N Grande Comore, Comoros
Mits'iwa *see* Massawa
Mitsoudjé *198* SW Grande Comore, Comoros
Mitsuyō *see* Miryang
Mitú *195* SE Colombia
Mitumba, Monts *203 var.* Chaîne des Mitumba, Mitumba Range. Mountain range of E Dem. Rep. Congo (Zaire)
Mitzic *258* N Gabon
Miyako *331* Honshū, N Japan
Miyako-jima *330* island of Sakishima-shotō, SW Japan
Miyakonojō *330* Kyūshū, SW Japan
Miyazaki *330* Kyūshū, SW Japan
Miyoshi *330* Honshū, W Japan
Mizdah *371 var.* Mizda. NW Libya
Mjøsa *444 var.* Mjøsen. Lake of SE Norway
Mkhondvo *540 var.* Mkondo. River of South Africa and Swaziland
Mladá Boleslav *216 Ger.* Jungbunzlau. N Czech Republic
Mlanje *see* Mulanje
Mljet *209 It.* Meleda. Island of S Croatia
Mmabatho *527* North West, N South Africa
Mmathethe *142* S Botswana
Mnjoli Dam *540* reservoir of NE Swaziland
Mo *444* NE Norway
Moa *514* river of W Africa
Moa *211* SE Cuba
Moabi *258* SW Gabon
Moala *246* island to the SE of Viti Levu, S Fiji
Moamba *419* SW Mozambique
Moanda *258* SE Gabon
Moba *203* E Dem. Rep. Congo (Zaire)
Mobaye *179* S Central African Republic
Mobile *599* Alabama, SE USA
Moca *226* N Dominican Republic
Moçambique *419* island and settlement of NE Mozambique
Moçâmedes *see* Namibe
Moce *246* island of the Lau Group, E Fiji
Mocha *see* Al Mukhā
Mochudi *142* S Botswana
Mocímboa da Praia *419 var.* Vila de Mocímboa da Praia. N Mozambique
Môco *88 var.* Serra Môco, Morro de Môco. Mountain of W Angola
Mocoa *195* SW Colombia
Mocuba *419* E Mozambique
Modena *320* NW Italy
Mödling *106* NE Austria
Modohn *see* Madona
Modriča *140* N Bosnia & Herzegovina
Moe *101* SE Australia
Moen *see* Weno
Möen *see* Møn
Moena *see* Muna, Pulau
Moengo *538* NE Suriname
Moers *264* W Germany
Moesi *see* Musi
Moeskroen *see* Mouscron
Mogadishu *524 Som.* Muqdisho, *It.* Mogadiscio. ❖ of Somalia, S Somalia
Mogador *see* Essaouira
Mogilëv *see* Mahilyow
Mogotón, Pico *436* mountain of NW Nicaragua
Mohales Hoek *366* SW Lesotho
Mohammadia *83 var.* El Mohammaidia. NW Algeria
Mohammedia *414 prev.* Fédala. NW Morocco
Moharek *see* Al Muḥarraq
Mohéli *198 var.* Mwali. Island of Comoros
Mohn *see* Muhu
Moindou *650* C New Caledonia
Mõisaküla *240 Ger.* Moiseküll. S Estonia

Moïssala *180* S Chad
Mokhotlong *366* NE Lesotho
Mokil *406* atoll of E Micronesia
Moknine *573* *var.* Al Muknīn. NE Tunisia
Mokp'o *350* *Jap.* Moppo. SW South Korea
Mokra Gora *630* mountain range of SW Serbia, Yugoslavia
Mokwa *440* W Nigeria
Moldau *see* Vltava
Moldova *408-409* officially Republic of Moldova, *var.* Moldova, *prev.* Moldavian SSR, *Rus.* Moldavskaya SSR. Country of E Europe divided into 40 admin. units (districts). ❖ Chişinău
Molde *444* SW Norway
Moldo-Too, Khrebet *357* mountain range of C Kyrgyzstan
Moldova *see* Moldova
Molepolole *142* S Botswana
Môle-St-Nicolas *286* NW Haiti
Molineux *494* NE St Kitts, St Kitts & Nevis
Möll *106* river of S Austria
Mölndal *543* SW Sweden
Molodechno *see* Maladzyechna
Molodeczno *see* Maladzyechna
Molodezhnaya *90* CIS research station of Greater Antarctica, Antarctica
Molokai *598* island of Hawaii, USA, C Pacific
Molopo *142, 527* seasonal river of southern Africa
Molotov *see* Severodvinsk
Molotov *see* Perm'
Moloundou *168* SE Cameroon
Moluccas *see* Maluku
Molucca Sea *see* Maluku, Laut
Mombasa *342* SE Kenya
Môn *see* Anglesey
Møn *218* *prev.* Möen. Island of SE Denmark
Mona, Canal de la *226, 651* channel connecting the Atlantic Ocean and Caribbean Sea, between Dominican Republica and Puerto Rico
Monaco *410-411* officially Principality of Monaco. Country of W Europe divided into 4 admin. units (quarters). ❖ Monaco
Monaco *see* München
Monaghan *314* *Ir.* Muineachán. NE Ireland
Monagrillo *456* S Panama
Mona, Isla *651* island of SW Puerto Rico
Monapo *419* NE Mozambique
Monaragala *534* SE Sri Lanka
Monastir *573* *var.* Al Munastīr. NE Tunisia
Monastir *see* Bitola
Mönchengladbach *264* *prev.* München-Gladbach. W Germany
Monchy *497* N St Lucia
Monclova *403* N Mexico
Moncton *171* SE Canada
Mondego *474* river of N Portugal
Mondsee *106* lake of N Austria
Money Island *651* island of W Paracel Islands
Monfalcone *321* N Italy
Mongar *134* E Bhutan
Mongo *180* C Chad
Mongolia *412-413* country of NE Asia divided into 21 admin. units (18 provinces, 3 cities). ❖ Ulan Bator
Mongomo *236* E Río Muni, Equatorial Guinea
Mongora *see* Mingāora
Mongos, Chaîne des *see* Bongo, Massif des
Mongouge *497* SW St Lucia
Mongoumba *179* SW Central African Republic
Mongu *635* W Zambia
Mönh Hayrhan Uul *412* mountain of W Mongolia
Moni *215* S Cyprus
Monkey Bay *385* SE Malawi
Monkey River Town *130* SE Belize
Mono *132, 567* river of Benin and Togo
Monopoi *321* E Italy
Monos *570* island to the NW of Trinidad, Trinidad & Tobago
Mon Repos *497* E St Lucia
Monrovia *368* ❖ of Liberia, W Liberia
Mons *127* *Dut.* Bergen. SW Belgium
Montana *598-599* state of NW USA
Montana *152* *prev.* Mikhaylovgrad, *var.* Mihajlovgrad, Mikhailovgrad, *prev.* Ferdinand. NW Bulgaria
Montauban *253* S France
Montbéliard *253* NE France
Mont Blanc *253, 320* *It.* Monte Bianco. Mountain of France and Italy
Mont-de-Marsan *253* SW France
Monteagudo *136* S Bolivia
Monte-Carlo *410* NE Monaco
Monte Cristi *226* NW Dominican Republic
Monte Croce Carnico, Passo di *see* Plöcken
Montegiardino *502* SE San Marino
Montego Bay *329* NW Jamaica
Montelindo *460* river of C Paraguay
Montenegro *630* *Serb.* Crna Gora. Republic of Yugoslavia
Monte Plata *226* C Dominican Republic
Montepuez *419* N Mozambique
Montería *195* NW Colombia
Montero *136* C Bolivia
Monterrey *403* N Mexico
Montes Claros *145* SE Brazil
Montevideo *607* ❖ of Uruguay, S Uruguay
Montgomery *599* Alabama, SE USA
Montgomery *see* Sāhīwāl
Monthey *546* SW Switzerland
Montijo *474* W Portugal
Montpelier *599* Vermont, NE USA
Montpellier *253* S France
Montréal *171* *Eng.* Montreal. SE Canada
Montreux *546* SW Switzerland
Montserrat *649* British dependent territory of the Caribbean Sea. ❖ Plymouth
Montsinéry *645* NE French Guiana
Monywa *159* NW Burma
Monza *320* N Italy
Monze *635* S Zambia
Moora *100* W Australia
Moose Jaw *170* SW Canada
Moosonee *171* SE Canada
Moppo *see* Mokp'o
Mopti *392* C Mali
Moqor *77* SE Afghanistan
Moquegua *463* SE Peru
Morales *278* E Guatemala
Moramanga *382* E Madagascar
Morant Bay *329* E Jamaica
Morata *see* Goodenough Island
Moratuwa *534* SW Sri Lanka
Morava *see* Velika Morava
Morava *216, 519* *Ger.* March. River of C Europe
Moravia *216* cultural region of E Czech Republic
Moravská Ostrava *see* Ostrava
Morawhanna *284* N Guyana
Moray Firth *593* inlet of Atlantic Ocean, NE Scotland, UK
Mordoviya SSR *484* autonomous republic of W Russian Federation
Moree *101* E Australia
Morehead *458* SW Papua New Guinea
Morelia *403* C Mexico
Moreno *136* N Bolivia
Morfou *see* Güzelyurt
Morfou Bay *see* Morphou Bay
Morges *546* SW Switzerland
Morghāb, Daryā-ye *77* river of Afghanistan and Turkmenistan
Morija *366* W Lesotho
Morioka *330* Honshū, N Japan
Morne Aux Frégates *224* E Dominica
Morne Diablotins *224* mountain of N Dominica
Morne Raquette *224* W Dominica
Morne Seychellois *512* mountain of Mahé, NE Seychelles
Morne Trois Pitons *224* mountain of C Dominica
Morocco *see* Marrakech
Morocco *414-417* officially Kingdom of Morocco, *Ar.* Al Mamlakah. Country of N Africa divided into 37 admin. units (provinces and prefectures). ❖ Rabat
Morogoro *560* E Tanzania
Moro Gulf *466* area of the Sulu Sea
Morombe *382* SW Madagascar
Morón *210* C Cuba
Morón *95* E Argentina
Mörön *412* N Mongolia
Morondava *382* W Madagascar
Moroni *198* ❖ of Comoros, W Grande Comore, Comoros
Morotai, Pulau *302* island of Maluku, E Indonesia
Moroto *584* NE Uganda
Morphou *see* Güzelyurt
Morphou Bay *215* *var.* Morfou Bay, Güzelyurt Körfezi. Bay of the Mediterranean Sea, on the NW coast of Cyprus
Morris *649* S Montserrat
Morro de Môco *see* Môco
Mors *218* island of NW Denmark
Moruga *570* S Trinidad, Trinidad & Tobago
Morvan *253* physical region of NE France
Morvant *570* NW Trinidad, Trinidad & Tobago
Morwell *101* SE Australia
Moscow *484, 488* *Rus.* Moskva. ❖ of Russia, W Russian Federation
Mosel *253, 264, 378* *Fr.* Moselle. River of W Europe
Moselle *see* Mosel
Moshi *560* NE Tanzania
Mosjøen *444* C Norway
Moskva *558* *prev.* Chubek; *Rus.* Moskovskiy. SW Tajikistan
Moson *see* Mosonmagyaróvár
Mosoni-Duna *290* river of NW Hungary
Mosonmagyaróvár *290* *prev.* Moson, Magyaróvár, *Ger.* Wieselburg. NW Hungary
Mosquito Coast *288, 436* *var.* Miskito Coast, *Sp.* La Mosquitia. Coastal region of E Central America
Mosquitos, Golfo de *456* gulf of the Caribbean Sea to the N of Panama
Moss *444* S Norway
Mossâmedes *see* Namibe
Mosselbaai *527* *Eng.* Mossel Bay. Western Cape S South Africa
Mossendjo *200* SW Congo
Mossoró *145* NE Brazil
Most *216* *Ger.* Brüx. NW Czech Republic
Mosta *395* *var.* Musta. C Malta
Mostaganem *83* *var.* Mestghanem. NW Algeria
Mostar *140* S Bosnia & Herzegovina
Mosul *see* Al Mawşil
Mota *615* Banks Islands, N Vanuatu
Motaba *200* river of N Congo
Motagua *278* river of Guatemala and Honduras
Mota Lava *615* Banks Islands, N Vanuatu
Mothae *366* NE Lesotho
Motherwell *593* C Scotland, UK
Motjane *540* NW Swaziland
Motril *531* S Spain
Motueka *433* river of NE of South Island, New Zealand
Motulalo *583* islet of Nukufetau, Tuvalu
Motulua *583* islet of Nukufetau, Tuvalu
Motumua *583* islet of Nukufetau, Tuvalu
Mouaskar *see* Mascara
Moucha, Îles *222* islands in the Gulf of Aden, of E Djibouti
Mouchoir Passage *653* passage of the Pacific Ocean, SE Turks and Caicos Islands
Moudjéria *398* SW Mauritania
Mouila *258* C Gabon
Mould Bay *170* Prince Patrick Island, N Canada
Moulèngui Binza *258* S Gabon
Moulhoulé *222* N Djibouti
Moulins *253* C France
Moulmein *159* *var.* Mawlamyine. SE Burma
Moulmeingyun *159* SW Burma
Mouloud *222* SW Djibouti
Moulouya *414* seasonal river of NE Morocco
Moun Hou *see* Black Volta
Mounana *258* S Gabon
Moundou *180* SW Chad
Moŭng Roessi *165* *var.* Moung. W Cambodia
Mount Barclay *368* W Liberia
Mount Darwin *636* NE Zimbabwe
Mount Friendship *121* SW Barbados
Mount Gambier *101* SE Australia
Mount Hagen *458* C Papua New Guinea
Mount Isa *101* C Australia
Mount Lebanon *see* Liban, Jebel
Mount Magnet *100* W Australia
Mount Maunganui *433* C North Island, New Zealand
Mount Moorosi *366* SW Lesotho
Mount Moritz *276* SW Grenada island, Grenada
Mount Rose *276* NE Grenada island, Grenada
Mourdi, Dépression de *180* desert lowland of E Chad
Mouscron *127* *Dut.* Moeskroen. W Belgium
Moussa 'Ali *222* mountain of NW Djibouti
Moussoro *180* W Chad
Moutsamoudou *198* NW Anjouan, Comoros
Moya *198* SW Anjouan Comoros
Moyale *243* S Ethiopia
Moyale *342* N Kenya
Moyamba *514* W Sierra Leone
Moyen Atlas *414* *Eng.* Middle Atlas. Mountain range of N Morocco
Moyeni *366* *var.* Quthing. SW Lesotho
Moyo *584* NW Uganda
Moyobamba *463* NW Peru
Moyuta *278* S Guatemala
Mozambique *418-421* officially Republic of Mozambique, *prev.* People's Republic of Mozambique, Portuguese East Africa. Country of East Africa divided into 10 admin. units (provinces). ❖ Maputo
Mozambique Channel *198, 382* *var.* Canal de Mozambique, Canal de Moçambique, Lakandranon' i Mozambika. Strait of the Indian Ocean, between Mozambique and Madagascar
Mozambique Island *see* Moçambique
Mozyr' *see* Mazyr
Mpama *200* river of C Congo
Mpanda *560* W Tanzania
Mpanga, Lac *492* lake of E Rwanda
Mphaki *366* S Lesotho
Mpigi *584* S Uganda
Mpika *635* NE Zambia
Mporokoso *635* N Zambia
Mpulungu *635* N Zambia
Mpumalanga *527* *prev.* Eastern Transvaal. Province of NE South Africa
Mpwapwa *560* C Tanzania
Mqocha *385* NW Malawi
Mrémani *198* S Anjouan, Comoros
M'Saken *573* *var.* Masakin. N Tunisia
Msida *395* C Malta
M 'Sila *83* N Algeria
Mtoko *see* Mutoko
Mtsamboro *649* N Mayotte
Mtsamgamouji *649* W Mayotte
Mtsapa *see* Matsapha
Mtwara *560* SE Tanzania
Mu'a *568* Tongatabu, Tongatapu Group, Tonga
Mualama *419* E Mozambique
Mualo *see* Messalo
Muang Ham *359* NE Laos
Muang Hinboun *359* S Laos

Muang Kalasin *see* Kalasin
Muang Kap *359* S Laos
Muang Khammouan *359* *var.* Thakhek. S Laos
Muang Không *359* S Laos
Muang Khôngxédôn *359* *var.* Khong Sedone. S Laos
Muang Khon Kaen *see* Khon Kaen
Muang Lampang *see* Lampang
Muang Loei *see* Loei
Muang Lom Sak *see* Lom Sak
Muang Nakhon Sawan *see* Nakhon Sawan
Muang Namo *359* N Laos
Muang Nan *see* Nan
Muang Pakxan *359* *var.* Pak Sane. C Laos
Muang Phalan *359* S Laos
Muang Phin *359* S Laos
Muang Phitsanulok *see* Phitsanulok
Muang Phôn-Hông *359* C Laos
Muang Phrae *see* Phrae
Muang Roi Et *see* Roi Et
Muang Samut Prakan *see* Samut Prakan
Muang Sing *359* NW Laos
Muang Vangviang *359* C Laos
Muang Xaignabouri *359* *var.* Sayaboury. W Laos
Muang Xay *359* *var.* Muong Sai. N Laos
Muang Xépôn *359* *var.* Sepone. SE Laos
Muar *386* river of S Peninsular Malaysia
Muar *386* *prev.* Bandar Maharani. S Peninsular Malaysia
Muara Besar, Pulau *150* island of N Brunei
Mubende *584* SW Uganda
Mucojo *419* N Mozambique
Mudanjiang *187* *var.* Mu-tan-chiang. Heliongjiang, NE China
Mudon *159* SE Burma
Mueda *419* NE Mozambique
Muenster *see* Münster
Mufulira *635* C Zambia
Muğan Düzü *110* *Rus.* Muganskaya Step'. Physical region of S Azerbaijan
Mugera *162* C Burundi
Mugesera, Lac *492* lake of E Rwanda
Mughsu *558* *Rus.* Muksu. River of NE Tajikistan
Mugi *330* Shikoku, SW Japan
Mugla *576* SW Turkey
Muharraq *see* Al Muḩarraq
Muḩarraq, Jazīrat al *115* island of N Bahrain
Muhazi, Lac *492* lake of E Rwanda
Muhinga *see* Muyinga
Muh, Sabkhat al *551* salt-flat of S Syria
Muhu *240* *Ger.* Mohn, Moon. Island of W Estonia
Muhu Väin *see* Väinameri
Muineachán *see* Monaghan
Muir Bhreatan *see* St. George's Channel
Muir Eireann *see* Irish Sea
Mukacheve *586* W Ukraine
Mukalla *see* Al Mukallā
Mukden *see* Shenyang
Muksu *558* river of NE Tajikistan
Mukungwa *492* river of NW Rwanda
Mulaku Atoll *390* *var.* Meemu Atoll. Atoll of C Maldives
Mulanje *385* *var.* Mlanje. S Malawi
Mulhacén, Cerro de *531* mountain of SE Spain
Mulchén *183* C Chile
Mülheim *264* *var.* Mulheim an der Ruhr. W Germany
Mulhouse *253* *Ger.* Mülhausen. NE France
Mulifanua *500* Upolu, Samoa
Mulinu'ū, Cape *500* cape of Savai'i, Samoa
Mullaittivu *534* *var.* Mullaitivu. NE Sri Lanka
Muller, Pegunungan *302* *Dut.* Müller-gerbergte. Mountain range of Borneo, C Indonesia
Mullingar *314* C Ireland
Mull, Isle of *593* island of Inner Hebrides, W Scotland, UK
Multān *451* E Pakistan
Mumbai *296, 301* *Eng.* Bombay. W India
Mumbwa *635* C Zambia
Mummatalah, Ra's al *115* *var.* Ra's al Mamtalah. Cape of SW Bahrain
Munamägi *see* Suur Munamägi
Muna, Pulau *302* *prev.* Moena. Island to the SE of Celebes, C Indonesia
München *265, 269* *Eng.* Munich, *It.* Monaco. S Germany
Munch'ŏn *349* SE North Korea
Munda *522* New Georgia, C Solomon Islands
Mundal Lagooon *534* lagoon of W Sri Lanka
Mu Nggava *see* Rennell
Mungla *117* S Bangladesh
Mungwi *635* NE Zambia
Munia *246* island of the Lau Group, E Fiji
Munich *see* München
Munini *492* SW Rwanda
Munshiganj *117* C Bangladesh
Munster *314* province of S Ireland
Münster *264* *var.* Muenster. NW Germany
Muntinglupa *466* Luzon, N Philippines
Muong Sai *see* Muang Xay
Muonioälv *see* Muoniojoki
Muoniojoki *249, 543* *Swe.* Muonioälv. River of Finland and Sweden
Muqdisho *see* Mogadishu
Mur *106, 520* *SCr.* Mura. River of C Europe
Mura *see* Mur
Muragarazi *see* Maragarazi
Murai Reservoir *517* reservoir of NW Singapore
Murambi *492* C Rwanda
Muramvya *162* C Burundi
Murang'a *342* *prev.* Fort Hall. SW Kenya
Murata *502* S San Marino
Murchison Falls *584* *var.* Kabalega Falls. Waterfall of NW Uganda
Murcia *531* autonomous community of SE Spain
Mureş *480* *var.* Mureşul, *Hung.* Maros, *Ger.* Muresch. River of Hungary and Romania
Murehwa *636* *var.* Murewa. NE Zimbabwe
Muresch *see* Mureş
Murgab *581* *prev.* Murgap. SE Turkmenistan
Murgab *581* *var.* Murghab. River of SE Turkmenistan
Murgab *see* Murghob
Murghob *558* *Rus.* Murgab. E Tajikistan
Muri *546* *var.* Muri bei Bern. W Switzerland
Murilo *406* atoll of N Micronesia
Mūrītānīyah *see* Mauritania
Müritz *265* *var.* Müritzee. Lake of NE Germany
Murmansk *484* NW Russian Federation
Muroran *330* Hokkaidō, N Japan
Muroto *330* Shikoku, SW Japan
Murray *101* river of SE Australia
Murray, Lake *458* lake in swamp region of W Papua New Guinea
Murrumbidgee *101* river of SE Australia
Murska Sobota *520* *Ger.* Olsnitz. NE Slovenia
Murua Island *458* *var.* Woodlark I. Island of SE Papua New Guinea
Murupara *433* SE North Island, New Zealand
Mururoa Atoll *646* var. Moruroa. Atoll of French Polynesia
Murzuq *371* *var.* Marzūq, Murzuk. W Libya
Murzuq, Ḩammādat *371* plateau of W Libya
Muş *577* E Turkey
Mūša *376* river of N Lithuania
Musaffah *590* C United Arab Emirates
Musā'id *371* NE Libya
Musala *152* *prev.* Stalin Peak. Mountain of W Bulgaria
Musan *349* NE North Korea
Musandam Peninsula *448* *Ar.* Ra's Musandam, *var.* Ras Masandam. Peninsular of N Oman
Musay'īd *479* *var.* Umm Sa'īd. SE Qatar
Muscat *448* *Ar.* Masqaţ. ❖ of Oman, N Oman
Muscat and Oman *see* Oman
Mushin *440* SW Nigeria
Musi *302* *prev.* Moesi. River of Sumatra, W Indonesia
Musoma *560* N Tanzania
Mussau Island *458* island of NE Papua New Guinea
Mustafa-Pasha *see* Svilengrad
Mustique *498* island of C St Vincent & the Grenadines
Mustvee *240* *Ger.* Tschorna. E Estonia
Mutalau *650* N Niue
Mu-tan-chiang *see* Mudanjiang
Mutare *636* *prev.* Umtali. E Zimbabwe
Mutoko *636* *prev.* Mtoko. NE Zimbabwe
Mutorashanga *636* *prev.* Mtorashanga. N Zimbabwe
Muyaga *162* E Burundi
Muyinga *162* *var.* Muhinga. NE Burundi
Muy Muy *436* C Nicaragua
Mŭynoq *610* *Rus.* Muynak. NW Uzbekistan
Muyunkum, Peski *338* desert region of S Kazakhstan
Muzaffargarh *451* E Pakistan
Muzarabani *636* N Zimbabwe
Mvuma *636* *prev.* Umvuma. C Zimbabwe
Mvurwi *636* *prev.* Umvukwes. N Zimbabwe
Mwali *see* Mohéli
Mwanza *560* NW Tanzania
Mwanza *385* SW Malawi
Mweka *203* C Dem. Rep. Congo (Zaire)
Mwenda *635* N Zambia
Mwene-Ditu *203* S Dem. Rep. Congo (Zaire)
Mwenezi *636* river of S Zimbabwe
Mwenezi *636* *prev.* Nuanetsi. S Zimbabwe
Mweru, Lake *203, 635* *Fr.* Lac Moero. Lake of Dem. Rep. Congo (Zaire) and Zambia
Mweru Wantipa, Lake *635* lake of N Zambia
Mwombezhi *635* river of W Zambia
Myanaung *159* SW Burma
Myanmar *see* Burma
Myaungmya *159* SW Burma
Myingyan *159* C Burma
Myitkyina *159* N Burma
Myitnge *159* river of NE Burma
Mykines *644* island of W Faeroe Islands
Mykolayiv *586* *Rus.* Nikolayev. S Ukraine
Mýkonos *273* island of SE Greece
Mymensingh *117* *prev.* Nasirābād. N Bangladesh
Myŏngch'ŏn *349* NE North Korea
Mýrdalsjökull *294* glacier of S Iceland
Mysore *296* *var.* Maisur. S India
My Tho *623* S Vietnam
Mytilíni *273* Lésvos, E Greece
Mývatn *294* lake of C Iceland
Mzimba *385* NW Malawi
Mzuzu *385* N Malawi

N

Naas *314* *Ir.* Nás Na Riogh, An Nás. E Ireland
Nabatîyé *364* *var.* Nabatiyet et Tahta, An Nabatīyah at Taḩtā. SW Lebanon
Nabavatu *246* Vanua Levu, N Fiji
Naberezhnyye Chelny *484* *prev.* Brezhnev. W Russian Federation
Nabeul *573* *var.* Nābul. N Tunisia
Nabgha *590* NE United Arab Emirates
Nabīh aş Şalīḩ, Jazīrat an *115* *var.* Nabih Saleh, Nabīh Salīh. Island of NE Bahrain
Nabī Shu'ayb, Jabal an *627* mountain of W Yemen
Nāblus *317, 318* *Heb.* Shekhem. N West Bank
Nabouwalu *246* Vanua Levu, N Fiji
Nacala *419* NE Mozambique
Nacaome *288* S Honduras
Na-Chii *see* Nagqu
Nachingwea *560* SE Tanzania
Na Cruacha Dubha *see* Macgillicuddy's Reeks
Nacula *246* *prev.* Nathula. Island of the Yasawa Group, NW Fiji
Nadi *246* *prev.* Nandi. Viti Levu, W Fiji
Nador *414* *prev.* Villa Nador. NE Morocco
Nadur *395* Gozo, Malta
Naduri *246* *prev.* Nanduri. Vanua Levu, N Fiji
Nadym *484* N Russian Federation
Næstved *218* Sjælland, SE Denmark
Nafūsah, Jabal *371* mountain range of NW Libya
Naga *466* *prev.* Nueva Caceres. Luzon, N Philippines
Nagano *330* Honshū, C Japan
Nagaoka *330* Honshū, N Japan
Nagarote *436* SW Nicaragua
Nagasaki *330* Kyūshū, SW Japan
Nāgercoil *296* S India
Nagorno-Karabakh *110* former autonomous region of SW Azerbaijan
Nagoya *330* Honshū, C Japan
Nāgpur *296* C India
Nagqu *186* *Chin.* Na-Ch'ii, *prev.* Hei-ho. Xizang Zizhiqu, W China
Nagua *226* N Dominican Republic
Nagybánya *see* Baia Mare
Nagybecskerek *see* Zrenjanin
Nagykanizsa *290* *Ger.* Grosskanizsa. SW Hungary
Nagykőrös *290* C Hungary
Nagymihály *see* Michalovce
Nagysurány *see* Šurany
Nagyszeben *see* Sibiu
Nagyszombat *see* Trnava
Nagytapolcsány *see* Topoľčany
Nagyvárad *see* Oradea
Naha *330* Nansei-shotō, SW Japan
Nahariyya *317* N Israel
Nahiçevan' *see* Naxçıvan
Nairai *246* island to the E of Viti Levu, C Fiji
Nairobi *342* ❖ of Kenya, S Kenya
Naitaba *246* *prev.* Naitamba. Island of the Lau Group, E Fiji
Naitamba *see* Naitaba
Naivasha *342* SW Kenya
Naivasha, Lake *342* lake of SW Kenya
Najaf *see* An Najaf
Najafābād *307* W Iran
Najd *506* *var.* Nejd. Region of C Saudi Arabia
Najin *349* NE North Korea
Najrān *506* S Saudi Arabia
Naju *see* Kumsong
Nakadōri-jima *330* island of Gotō-rettō, SW Japan
Nakamura *330* Shikoku, SW Japan
Nakasongola *584* W Uganda
Nakatsu *330* Kyūshū, SW Japan
Nakatsugawa *330* Honshū, C Japan
Nakfa *238* N Eritrea
Nakhichevan' *see* Naxcivan
Nakhodka *485* SE Russian Federation
Nakhon Pathom *563* C Thailand
Nakhon Phanom *563* NE Thailand
Nakhon Ratchasima *563* *var.* Korat. E Thailand
Nakhon Sawan *563* *var.* Muang Nakhon Sawan. W Thailand
Nakhon Si Thammarat *563* S Thailand

Nakskov *218* Lolland, S Denmark
Naktong *350 var.* Nakdong, *Jap.* Rakutō-kō. River of South Korea
Nakuru *342* W Kenya
Nāl *451* river of W Pakistan
Nalayh *412* C Mongolia
Nal'chik *484* SW Russian Federation
Nālūt *371* NW Libya
Nam *349* river of C North Korea
Nam *350* river of S South Korea
Namaacha *419* S Mozambique
Namacurra *419* E Mozambique
Namak, Daryācheh-ye *307* lake of W Iran
Namak, Kavīr-e *307* desert region of NE Iran
Namanga *342* S Kenya
Namangan *610* E Uzbekistan
Namatanai *458* New Ireland, Papua New Guinea
Nam Đinh *623* N Vietnam
Namen *see* Namur
Namhae-do *350 Jap.* Nankai-tō. Island of S South Korea
Namib Desert *423* coastal desert region of W Namibia
Namibe *88 Port.* Moçâmedes, *var.* Mossâmedes. SW Angola
Namibia *422-423* officially The Republic of Namibia, *prev.* South-West Africa, German Southwest Africa. Country of Southern Africa divided into 13 admin. units (districts). ❖ Windhoek
Namoluk *406* island of SE Micronesia
Namonuito *406* atoll of NW Micronesia
Namorik *396* island of S Marshall Islands
Nampa *598* Idaho, NW USA
Namp'o *349* SW North Korea
Nampula *419* NE Mozambique
Namsos *444* C Norway
Namu *396* island of C Marshall Islands
Namuka-i-lau *246* island of the Lau Group, E Fiji
Namunukula *534* SE Sri Lanka
Namur *127 Dut.* Namen. SE Belgium
Namutoni *423* N Namibia
Namwŏn *350 Jap.* Nangen. S South Korea
Namyit Island *652* island of S Spratly Islands
Nan *563 var.* Muang Nan. N Thailand
Nanaimo *170* Vancouver Island, SW Canada
Nanao *330* Honshū, C Japan
Nanchang *187* Jianxi, SE China
Nan-ching *see* Nanjing
Nancy *253* NE France
Nanda Devi *296* mountain of N India
Nandaime *436* S Nicaragua
Nandi *see* Nadi
Nanduri *see* Naduri
Nanga Eboko *168* C Cameroon
Nangbéto, Retenue de *567* reservoir of C Togo
Nangen *see* Namwŏn
Nan Hai *see* East China Sea and South China Sea
Nanhsi *555* SW Taiwan
Nanjing *187 var.* Nanking, Nan-ching. Jiangsu, E China
Nankai-tō *see* Namhae-do
Nanning *187 prev.* Yung-ning. Guangxi, S China
Nanortalik *646* S Greenland
Nansei-shotō *330* island group to the SW of Kyūshū, SW Japan
Nanshan Island *652* island of E Spratly Islands
Nansio *560* NW Tanzania
Nanterre *253* N France
Nantes *252* W France
Nanthi Kadal Lagoon *534* lagoon of N Sri Lanka
Nant'ou *555* W Taiwan
Nanuku Passage *246* channel of the Pacific Ocean between the Lau Group and Taveuni, NE Fiji
Nanumaga *583 prev.* Nanumanga. Coral atoll of NW Tuvalu
Nanumea *583* coral atoll of NW Tuvalu
Nan Wan *555* bay of the South China Sea, S Taiwan
Nanyang *187* Henan, C China
Nanyuki *342* C Kenya
Naogaon *117* NW Bangladesh
Napier *433* SE North Island, New Zealand
Naples *see* Napoli
Napo *228, 463* river of Ecuador and Peru
Napoli *321 Eng.* Naples, *Ger.* Neapel. S Italy
Nāra *451* irrigation canal of S Pakistan
Nara *330* Honshū, C Japan
Narathiwat *563* S Thailand
Narayani *427* river of C Nepal
Narbada *see* Narmada
Narbonne *253* S France
Nare's Strait *646* strait of NW Greenland
Narew *471* river of E Poland
Narganá *456* NE Panama
Narikrik *396 prev.* Knox Atoll. Atoll of SE Marshall Islands
Narmada *296 var.* Narbada. River of C India
Narok *342* SW Kenya
Närpes *249 Swe.* Närpiö. SW Finland
Narrows, The *494* channel connecting the Atlantic Ocean and Caribbean Sea, between Nevis and St Kitts
Narsaq Kujalleq *646 Dan.* Frederiksdal. S Greenland
Narsingdi *117* C Bangladesh
Nartës, Gjol i *see* Nartës, Liqeni i
Nartës, Liqeni i *81 var.* Gjol i Nartës. Lake of SW Albania
Naruto *330* Shikoku, SW Japan
Narva *240 prev.* Narova. River of Estonia and Russian Federation
Narva *240* NE Estonia
Narva Bay *240 Est.* Narva Laht, *Rus.* Narviskiy Zaliv. Bay of the Gulf of Finland
Narva Reservoir *240 Est.* Narva Veehoidla. Reservoir of Estonia and Russian Federation
Narvik *444* NE Norway
Nar'yan-Mar *484 prev.* Dzerzhinskiy, *prev.* Beloshchel'ye. NW Russian Federation
Naryn *357* E Kyrgyzstan
Naryn *357* river of Kyrgyzstan and Uzbekistan
Nasau *246* Koro, C Fiji
Nāshik *296 prev.* Nāsik. W India
Nasho, Lac *492* lake of E Rwanda
Nashville *599* Tennessee, SE USA
Näsijärvi *249* lake of SW Finland
Nasirābād *see* Mymensingh
Nâşir, Buḩeiret *230 var.* Buḩayrat Nāşir, *Eng.* Lake Nser. Lake of Egypt and Sudan
Nasiriya *see* An Nāşirīyah
Nás Na Riogh *see* Naas
Nassau *112* ❖ of Bahamas, New Providence, Bahamas
Nassau *644* island of Northern Cook Islands, N Cook Islands
Nasser, Lake *see* Nâsir, Buheiret
Nata *142* NE Botswana
Natal *145* E Brazil
Nathula *see* Nacula
Natitingou *132* NW Benin
Natl *336 var.* Nitil. NW Jordan
Nator *117* W Bangladesh
Natron, Lake *560* lake of Kenya and Tanzania
Natuna Besar, Pulau *302* island of Kepulauan Natuna, W Indonesia
Natuna, Kepulauan *302* island group to the NW of Borneo, W Indonesia
Nau *see* Nov
Naujoji Akmenė *376* NW Lithuania
Nā'ūr *336* NW Jordan
Nauru *424-425* officially The Republic of Nauru, *prev.* Pleasant Island. Island country of the Pacific Ocean divided into 14 admin. units (districts)
Naushahra *see* Nowshera
Nausori *246* Viti Levu, Fiji
Navabad *see* Navobod
Navaga *246* W Koro, W Fiji
Navahrudak *122 Rus.* Novogrudok, *Pol.* Nowogródek. W Belarus
Navangar *see* Jāmnagar
Navapolatsk *122 Rus.* Novopolotsk. N Belarus
Navarra *531* autonomous community of N Spain
Naviti *246* island of the Yasawa Group, NW Fiji
Navoalevu *246* NE Vanua Levu, N Fiji
Navobod *558 Rus.* Navabad. W Tajikistan
Navoi *see.* Nawoiy
Navua *246* Viti Levu, W Fiji
Nawābganj *117* NW Bangladesh
Nawābshāh *451* S Pakistan
Nawmah, Ra's *115 var.* Ra's Noma. Cape of SW Bahrain
Nawoiy *610 Rus.* Navoi. S Uzbekistan
Naxçıvan *110 Rus.* Nakhichevan', *var.* Nahičevan'. SW Azerbaijan
Náxos *273* island of SE Greece
Nayau *246* island of the Lau Group, E Fiji
Nazareth *see* Naẕerat
Nazca *463* S Peru
Naze *330* Nansei-shotō, SW Japan
Naẕerat *317 Eng.* Nazareth. N Israel
Naẕerat 'Illit *317* N Israel
Nazilli *576* SW Turkey
Nazran' *484* SW Russian Federation
Nazrēt *243 var.* Adama, Hadama. C Ethiopia
Nazwá *448* N Oman
Nchelenge *635* N Zambia
Ncheu *see* Ntcheu
Nchisi *see* Ntchisi
Ncue *236* N Río Muni, EquatorialGuinea
Ndaghamcha, Sebkra de *see* Te-n-Dghâmcha, Sebkhet
N'Dalatando *88 Port.* Vila Salazar. NW Angola
Ndali *132* C Benin
Ndélé *179* N Central African Republic
Ndendé *258* S Gabon
Ndeni *see* Nendö
Ndindi *258* S Gabon
N'Djamena *180 var.* Njamena, *prev.* Fort-Lamy. ❖ of Chad, W Chad
Ndjolé *258* C Gabon
Ndoki *200* river of N Congo
Ndola *635* C Zambia
Ndora *162* NW Burundi
Ndréméani *198* S Mohéli, Comoros
Ndrhamcha, Sebkha de *see* Te-n-Dghâmcha, Sebkhet
Nduindui *522* S Guadalcanal, Solomon Is
Nduke *see* Kolombangara
Neagh, Lough *593* lake of Northern Ireland, UK
Neapel *see* Napoli
Nébeck *see* An Nabk
Nebitdag *581* W Turkmenistan
Nebk *see* An Nabk
Neblina, Pico da *144* mountain of NW Brazil
Nebraska *599* state of C USA
Neckar *264* river of SW Germany
Necochea *95* E Argentina
Nederland *see* Netherlands
Neder-Rijn *429 Eng.* Lower Rhine. River of C Netherlands
Nefasit *238* C Eritrea
Nefta *573 var.* Naftah. W Tunisia
Neftezavodsk *see* Seydi
Negara Brunei Darussalam *see* Brunei
Negēlē *243 var.* Negelli, *It.* Neghelli. S Ethiopia
Negev *see* HaNegev
Neghelli *see* Negēlē
Negomane *419 var.* Negomano. N Mozambique
Negombo *534* SW Sri Lanka
Negotino *381* C FYR Macedonia
Negril *329* W Jamaica
Negro, Rio *144, 195* river of N South America
Negro, Río *see* Sico
Negro, Río *607* river of Brazil and Uruguay
Negro, Río *see* Chixoy
Negros *466* island of C Philippines
Neiafu *568* Uta Vava'u, Vava'u Group, Tonga
Neiba *226* SW Dominican Republic
Neiges, Piton des *652* mountain of C Réunion
Neily *206* SE Costa Rica
Nei Mongol Zizhiqu *187 Eng.* Inner Mongolian Autonomous Region, *prev.* Nei Monggol Zizhiqu. Autonomous region of N China
Neiva *195* W Colombia
Nek'emtē *243 var.* Nakamti, Lakamti, Lekemti. W Ethiopia
Nelson *170* river of C Canada
Nelson *433* N South Island, New Zealand
Nelson Island *643* island of N British Indian Ocean Territory
Nelspruit *527* Eastern Transvaal, NE South Africa
Néma *398* SE Mauritania
Neman *122, 376 Bel.* Nyoman, *Lith.* Nemunas, *Ger.* Memel, *Pol.* Niemen. River of NE Europe
Německý Brod *see* Havlíčkův Brod
Nemunas *see* Neman
Nenagh *314* S Ireland
Nendeln *374* C Liechtenstein
Nendö *522 var.* Ndeni. Santa Cruz Is, Solomon Islands
Nepal *426-427* officially Kingdom of Nepal. Country of Asia divided into 5 admin. units (regions). ❖ kathmandu
Nepalganj *427* W Nepal
Nepean Island *650* island of C Norfolk Island
Neretva *140* river of S Bosnia & Herzegovina
Neris *376 Bel.* Viliya, *Pol.* Wilja. River of Belarus and Lithuania
Neskaupstadhur *294* E Iceland
Ness, Loch *593* lake of N Scotland, UK
Néstos *152, 273 Turk.* Kara Su, *Bul.* Mesta. River of Bulgaria and Greece
Netanya *317* C Israel
Netherlands *430-431* officially Kingdom of the Netherlands, *var.* Holland, *Dut.* Nederland. Country of W Europe divided into 12 admin. units (provinces). ❖ Amsterdam, The Hague
Netherlands Antilles *619, 650 prev.* Dutch West Indies. Autonomous part of the Netherlands, Caribbean Sea. ❖ Willemstad
Netherlands East Indies *see* Indonesia
Netrakona *117* N Bangladesh
Netze *see* Noteć
Neubrandenburg *265* NE Germany
Neuchâtel *546 Ger.* Neuenburg. W Switzerland
Neuchâtel, Lac de *546 Ger.* Neuenburger See. Lake of W Switzerland
Neuenburger See *see* Neuchâtel, Lac de
Neugradiska *see* Nova Gradiška
Neuhäusl *see* Nové Zámky
Neumarkt *see* Târgu Mures
Neumarktl *see* Tržič
Neumünster *265* N Germany
Neunkirchen *106* E Austria
Neuquén *95* SE Argentina
Neusatz *see* Novi Sad
Neusiedler See *106, 290 Hung.* Fertő-tó. Lake of Austria and Hungary
Neusohl *see* Banská Bystrica
Neustadt *see* Baia Mare
Neustadtl *see* Novo Mesto
Neutra *see* Nitra
Neu-Ulm *265* S Germany
Nevada *598* state of W USA
Nevers *253* C France
Nevis *494* island of the Lesser Antilles which, with St Kitts, forms the independent state of St Kitts & Nevis
Nevis Peak *494* mountain peak of C Nevis, St Kitts & Nevis
Nevşehir *577* C Turkey
Newala *560* SE Tanzania
New Amsterdam *284* E Guyana

New Britain *458* island of E Papua New Guinea
New Brunswick *171* province of SE Canada
New Bussa *440* W Nigeria
New Caledonia *650* French overseas territory of the Pacific Ocean ❖ Nouméa
Newcastle *101* E Australia
Newcastle *494* N Nevis, St Kitts & Nevis
Newcastle upon Tyne *593* NE England, UK
New Delhi *296* ❖ of India, N India
Newfield *92* SE Antigua, Antigua & Barbuda
Newfoundland *171* *Fr.* Terre-Neuve. Island of S E Canada
Newfoundland *171* province of E Canada
New Georgia *522* island of the New Georgia Is, W Solomon Is
New Georgia Islands *522* island group of W Solomon Is
New Guinea *303, 458* *Dut.* Nieuw Guinea, *Ind.* Irian. Large island of W Pacific Ocean, divided administratively into the Indonesian state of Irian Jaya and the independent country of Papua New Guinea
New Halfa *see* Halfa el Gadida
New Hampshire *599* state of NE USA
New Haven *599* Connecticut, NE USA
New Hebrides *see* Vanuatu
New Ireland *458* island of NE Papua New Guinea
New Jersey *599* state of E USA
Newman *100* W Australia
New Mexico *598-599* state of SW USA
New Mīrpur *451* *prev.* Mīrpur. NE Pakistan
New Orleans *599* Louisiana, SC USA
New Plymouth *433* SW North Island, New Zealand
Newport *593* S Wales, UK
Newport News *599* Virginia, E USA
New Providence *112* island of C Bahamas
New River *284* river of SE Guyana
New River *130* river of N Belize
New Ross *314* SE Ireland
Newry *593* Northern Ireland, UK
New Sandy Bay Village *498* N St Vincent, St Vincent & the Grenadines
New Siberian Islands *see* Novosibirskiye Ostrova
New South Wales *101* state of SE Australia
Newton Ground *494* NW St Kitts, St Kitts & Nevis
Newtownabbey *593* Northern Ireland, UK
New Winthorpes *92* N Antigua, Antigua & Barbuda
New York *599* state of NE USA
New York *599, 603* New York, NE USA
New Zealand *432-435* officially The Dominion of New Zealand. Country of the Pacific Ocean, divided into 14 admin. units (regions). ❖ Wellington
Nezhyn *586* N Ukraine
Ngabé *200* SE Congo
Ngadda *441* river of NE Nigeria
Ngala *441* NE Nigeria
Ngangerabeli Plain *342* plain of SE Kenya
Ngaoundéré *168* *var.* N'Gaoundéré, N'Gaundere. N Cameroon
Ngara *560* NW Tanzania
Ngarama *492* N Rwanda
Ngardmau *455* C Palau
Ngaruangl *455* island of N Palau
Ngatik *406* atoll of E Micronesia
Ngau *see* Gau
N'Gaundere *see* Ngaoundéré
Nggamea *see* Qamea
Nggatokae *522* island of the New Georgia Islands, W Solomon Islands
Nggwavuma *540* *var.* Ingwavuma. River of South Africa and Swaziland
N'Giva *88* *var.* Ondjiva *Port.* Vila Pereira de Eça. S Angola
Ngo *200* SE Congo
Ngogolo *540* C Swaziland
Ngoko *168, 200* river of Cameroon and Congo
Ngorongoro Crater *560* crater and conservation area of N Tanzania
Ngororero *492* W Rwanda
Ngounié *258* river of Congo and Gabon
Ngouoni *258* E Gabon
Ngourti *439* E Niger
Ngozi *162* N Burundi
Nguigmi *439* SE Niger
Ngulu *406* atoll of W Micronesia
Ngum *359* river of C Laos
Nguna *615* island of C Vanuatu
Ngundu *636* S Zimbabwe
N'Gunza *see* Sumbe
Nguru *440* NE Nigeria
Ngwempisi *540* river of South Africa and Swaziland
Ngweze *see* Katima Mulilo
Nhacra *282* W Guinea-Bissau
Nhamundá *144* *var.* Yamundá, Jamundá. River of NW Brazil
Nha Trang *623* SE Vietnam
Nhlangano *540* *prev.* Goedgegun. SW Swaziland
Niagara Falls *171* SE Canada
Niagassola *281* *var.* Nyagassola. NE Guinea
Niamey *439* ❖ of Niger, SW Niger
Niamtougou *567* N Togo
Niandan *281* river of E Guinea
Niangay, Lac *392* lake of E Mali
Nianija Bolon *261* river of Gambia and Senegal
Niantanina *281* E Guinea
Niari *200* river of S Congo
Nias, Pulau *302* island to the W of Sumatra, W Indonesia
Niassa, Lago *see* Nyasa, Lake
Nicaragua *436-437* officially Republic of Nicaragua. Country of Central America divided into 16 admin. units (departments). ❖ Managua
Nicaragua, Lago de *436* *var.* Cocibolca, Gran Lago. Lake of S Nicaragua
Nicastro *321* S Italy
Nice *253* *It.* Nizza. SE France
Nicholls Town *112* Andros I, Bahamas
Nickerie *538* river of NW Suriname
Nicobar Islands *296* island group to the SE of India
Nicosia *215* *var.* Lefkosia, *Turk.* Lefkoşa. ❖ of Cyprus, C Cyprus
Nicoya *206* W Costa Rica
Nicoya, Península de *206* peninsula of W Costa Rica
Nictheroy *see* Niterói
Nidaros *see* Trondheim
Niedere Tauern *106* mountain range of C Austria
Niefang *236* *var.* Sevilla de Niefang. NW Río Muni, Equatorial Guinea
Niemen *see* Neman
Niéri Ko *510* river of SE Senegal
Nieuw Amsterdam *538* N Suriname
Nieuwegein *429* C Netherlands
Nieuwkoop *429* W Netherlands
Nieuw Nickerie *538* NW Suriname
Niğde *577* C Turkey
Niger *132, 281, 392, 439* river of W Africa
Niger *438-439* officially Republic of Niger. Country of West Africa divided into 7 admin. units (departments). ❖ Niamey
Nigeria *440-441* officially Federal Republic of Nigeria. Country of West Africa divided into 20 admin. units (19 states and 1 federal capital Territory). ❖ Abuja
Niger, Mouths of the *440* delta of the river Niger, on the S coast of Nigeria
Niigata *330* Honshū, N Japan
Niihama *330* Shikoku, SW Japan
Niihau *598* island of Hawaii, USA, C Pacific
Niimi *330* Honshū, W Japan
Nijmegen *429* *Ger.* Nimwegen. SE Netherlands
Nikki *132* E Benin
Nikolainkaupunki *see* Vaasa
Nikolayev *see* Mykolayiv
Nikol'skiy *338* C Kazakhstan
Nikol'sk-Ussuriyskiy *see* Ussuriysk
Nikopol' *586* SE Ukraine
Nikšić *630* W Montenegro, Yugoslavia
Nikumaroro *346* *var.* Gardner I. Island of the Phoenix Is, C Kiribati
Nikunau *346* island of the Gilbert Is, W Kiribati
Nile *230, 536* *Ar.* Nahr an Nīl. River of N Africa
Nile Delta *230* delta of N Egypt
Nīl, Nahr an *see* Nile
Nilphāmāri *117* NW Bangladesh
Nimba, Monts *281* *var.* Nimba Mountains. Mountain range of W Africa
Nimba, Mount *326, 368* mountain of W Africa
Nimba Mountains *see* Nimba, Monts
Nîmes *253* SE France
Nimwegen *see* Nijmegen
Ningbo *187* *var.* Ning-po, *prev.* Ninghsien. Zhejiang, E China
Ning-hsia *see* Ningxia
Ninghsien *see* Ningbo
Ning-po *see* Ningbo
Ningxia *187* *Chin.* Ningxia Huizu Zizhiqu, *Eng.* Ningsia Hui Autonomous Region, *var.* Ning-hsia. Autonomous region of N China
Ninotsminda *262* *prev.* Bogdanovka. S Georgia
Ninove *127* C Belgium
Niokolo Koba *510* river of SE Senegal
Niono *392* C Mali
Nioro *392* *var.* Nioro du Sahel. W Mali
Nioro du Rip *510* SW Senegal
Niort *253* W France
Nippon-kai *see* Japan, Sea of
Niquero *210* S Cuba
Nirin *see* Erhlin
Niš *630* *Eng.* Nish. E Serbia, Yugoslavia
Nişāb *627* *var.* Anşāb. SW Yemen
Nisporeni *408* *Rus.* Nisporeny. W Moldova
Nissan Islands *see* Green Islands
Nissum Bredning *218* inlet of North Sea on the NW coast of Denmark
Nistru *see* Dniester
Niterói *145* *prev.* Nictheroy. SE Brazil
Nitil *see* Natl
Nitra *519* *Ger.* Neutra, *Hung.* Nyitra. River of SW Slovakia
Nitra *519* *Ger.* Neutra, *Hung.* Nyitra. SW Slovakia
Niuafo'ou *568* *var.* Niuafoo. Island of NW Tonga
Niuatoputapu *568* *var.* Niuatobutabu, *prev.* Keppel Island. Island of N Tonga
Niuatui *583* islet of Nukufetau, Tuvalu
Niue *650* territory in free association with New Zealand, Pacific Ocean. ❖ Alofi
Niulakita *583* *var.* Nurakita. Coral atoll of S Tuvalu
Niutao *583* coral atoll of NW Tuvalu
Nizāmābād *296* C India
Nizhnevartovsk *484* C Russian Federation
Nizhniy Novgorod *484* *prev.* Gor'kiy. W Russian Federation
Nizhniy Pyandzh *see* Panji Poyon
Nizhnyaya Tunguska *485* *Eng.* Lower Tunguska. River of C Russian Federation
Nizza *see* Nice
Njaba *see* Nja Kunda
Njaiama *514* E Sierra Leone
Nja Kunda *261* *var.* Njaba. NW Gambia
Njamena *see* N'Djamena
Njardhvík *294* SW Iceland
Njazidja *see* Grande Comore
Njoeng Jacobkondre *538* C Suriname
Njombe *560* S Tanzania
Njoro *342* W Kenya
Nkanini *540* W Swaziland
Nkata Bay *see* Nkhata Bay
Nkayi *200* *var.* N'Kayi, *prev.* Jacob. S Congo
Nkhata Bay *385* *var.* Nkata Bay. N Malawi
Nkhotakota *385* *var.* Kota Kota, Nkota Kota. C Malawi
Nkonfap *440* S Nigeria
Nkongsamba *168* *var.* N'Kongsamba. W Cameroon
Nkumekie *236* C Río Muni, Equatorial Guinea
Nkundla *540* W Swaziland
Nkusi *584* river of W Uganda
Nmai Hka *159* *var.* Me Hka. River of N Burma forming a headstream of the Irrawaddy river
Noākhāli *117* *prev.* Sudharam. S Bangladesh
Nobeoka *330* Kyūshū, W Japan
Noboribetsu *330* Hokkaidō, N Japan
Nogal, Uadi *see* Nugaal
Noire, Rivière *400* river of SW Mauritius
Noire, Rivière *see* Black River
Noirmoutier, Île de *252* island of W France
Nokia *249* SW Finland
Nokou *180* W Chad
Nokoué, Lac *132* lake of S Benin
Nola *179* SW Central African Republic
Nólsoy *644* island of E Faeroe Islands
Noma, Ra's *see* Nawmah, Ra's
Nomuka *568* island of the Nomuka Group, Tonga
Nomuka Group *568* island group of W Tonga
Nomwin *406* atoll of C Micronesia
Nông Hèt *359* E Laos
Nong Khai *563* NE Thailand
Nonouti *346* island of the Gilbert Is, W Kiribati
Nonsan *350* *Jap.* Ronzan. W South Korea
Nonsuch Island *643* island of E Bermuda
Noord *642* N Aruba
Noord-Beveland *429* island of SW Netherlands
Noordoewer *423* S Namibia
Noordpunt *650* headland of Curaçao, W Netherlands Antilles
Noordzee *see* North Sea
Nor Achin *see* Nor Hachn
Nor Ačin *see* Nor Hachn
Norak *558* *Rus.* Nurek. W Tajikistan
Nord *646* N Greenland
Nordaustlandet *653* island of NE Svalbard
Norddeutsches Tiefland *264-265* *Eng.* North German Plain. Plain of N Germany
Nordfriesische Inseln *264* *Eng.* North Frisian Islands. Island group of NW Germany
Nordhausen *265* C Germany
Nordishavet *see* Arctic Ocean
Nord, Massif du *286* mountainous region of Haiti
Nord, Mer du *see* North Sea
Nord-Pas de Calais *256* administrative region of N France
Nordsee *see* North Sea
Nordsjøen *see* North Sea
Nordsøen *see* North Sea
Nordtiroler Kalkalpen *106* mountain range of W Austria
Nore *314* *Ir.* An Fheoir. River of SE Ireland
Norfolk *599* Virginia, E USA
Norfolk Island *650* Australian external territory of the South Pacific Ocean. ❖ Kingston
Norge *see* Norway
Nor Hachn *98* *var.* Nor Hachyn, *Rus.* Nor Achin, *var.* Nor Ačcin. C Armenia
Nor Hachyn *see* Nor Hachn
Noril'sk *485* N Russian Federation
Norman *599* Oklahoma, SC USA
Normanby Island *458* island of SE Papua New Guinea
Normandie *253* *Eng.* Normandy. Cultural region of N France
Normandie, Collines de *253* hilly region of NW France
Norman Island *643* island of S British Virgin Islands

Norrköping *543* S Sweden
Norseman *100* SW Australia
Norskehavet *see* Norwegian Sea
Norsup *615* Malekula, Vanuatu
North Albanian Alps *81, 630* *SCr.* Prokletije, *Alb.* Bjeshkët e Nemuna. Mountain range of Albania and Yugoslavia
Northam *100* SW Australia
Northampton *593* C England, UK
North Andaman *159, 296* island of the Andaman Is, E India
North Battleford *170* SW Canada
North Bay *171* SE Canada
North Caicos *653* island of NW Turks and Caicos Islands
North Carolina *599* state of SE USA
North Channel *593* strait of Atlantic Ocean, between Northern Ireland and Scotland, UK
North Comino Channel *see* Ghawdex, Il-Fliegu ta'
North Dakota *599* state of NC USA
North Devon Island *see* Devon Island
Northern Territory *101* territory of N Australia
North East China *191*
North East Point *644* headland on the NE coast of Christmas Island
Northeast Providence Channel *112* channel between Eleuthera I and Great Abaco I, Bahamas
Northern *527* *prev.* Northern Transvaal. Province of NE South Africa
Northern Cape *527* province of W South Africa
Northern Cook Islands *644* island group of N Cook Islands
Northern Cyprus, Republic of *see* Cyprus
Northern Dvina *see* Severnaya Dvina
Northern Forest Reserve *224* nature reserve of N Dominica
Northern Ireland *593* *var.* the Six Counties. Political division of UK
Northern Karoo *527* *var.* High Veld, *Afr.* Hoë Karoo. Plateau region of W South Africa
Northern Mariana Islands *650* Commonwealth territory of the USA, Pacific Ocean. ❖ Saipan
Northern Rhodesia *see* Zambia
Northern Sporades *see* Vor eioi Sporades
Northern Transvaal *see* Northern
North Frisian Islands *see* Nordfriesische Inseln
North German Plain *see* Norddeutsches Tiefland
North Huvadhu Atoll *390* *var.* Gaafu Alifu Atoll. Atoll of S Maldives
North Island *433* northernmost of the two main islands that comprise New Zealand
North Keeling Island *644* island of NW Cocos Islands
North Korea *348-349* officially Democratic People's Republic of Korea. Country of E Asia divided into 12 admin. units (9 provinces, 3 independent municipalities). ❖ Pyongyang
North Maalhosmadulu Atoll *390* *var.* North Malosmadulu Atoll, Raa Atoll. Atoll of N Maldives
North Miladummadulu Atoll *390* atoll of N Maldives
North Nilandhe Atoll *390* *var.* Faafu Atoll. Atoll of C Maldives
North Point *652* headland on the N coast of Ascension Island
North Saskatchewan *170* river of SW Canada
North Sea *264, 593* *Dan.* Nordsøen, *Nor.* Nordsjøen, *Fr.* Mer du Nord, Dut. Noordzee, *Ger.* Nordsee, *prev.* German Ocean. Sea of the Atlantic Ocean, between mainland Europe and Britain
North Siberian Lowland *see* Severo-Sibirskaya Nizmennost'
North Siberian Plain *see* Severo-Sibirskaya Nizmennost'
North Sound *644* area of the Caribbean Sea, Grand Cayman, W Cayman Islands
North Taranaki Bight *433* area of the Tasman Sea, to the W of North Island, New Zealand
North Uist *593* island of Outer Hebrides, NW Scotland, UK
North Union *498* E St Vincent, St Vincent & the Grenadines
North West *527* province of N South Africa
North West Bluff *649* headland on the N coast of Montserrat
North West Highlands *593* mountain range of N Scotland, UK
North West Point *644* headland on the NW coast of Christmas Island
Northwest Providence Channel *112* channel of Atlantic Ocean, between Grand Bahama Island and Bimini Islands, Bahamas
Northwest Territories *170 -171, 175* territory of N Canada
Norton *636* NE Zimbabwe
Norway *444-447* officially Kingdom of Norway, *Nor.* Norge. Country of N Europe divided into 19 admin. units (counties). ❖ Oslo
Norwegian Sea *294, 444* *var.* Norske Havet, Norskehavet. Area of Arctic Ocean between Iceland, Greenland and Norway
Norwich *593* E England, UK
Nösen *see* Bistriţa
Noshiro *330* Honshū, N Japan
Nosop *142, 423* *var.* Nossob, Nossop. River of southern Africa
Nossob *see* Nosop
Nossop *see* Nosop
Noteć *471* *Ger.* Netze. River of NW Poland
Noties Sporádes *see* Dodekánisos
Notodden *444* S Norway
Notsé *567* S Togo
Nottingham *593* C England, UK
Nouâdhibou *398* *prev.* Port Étienne. W Mauritania
Nouakchott *398* ❖ of Mauritania, SW Mauritania
Noual, Sebkhet en *573* *var.* Sabkhat an Nawāl. Salt flat of C Tunisia
Nouméa *650* ❖ of New Caledonia, S New Caledonia
Nouna *157* W Burkina
Nouvelle France *400* S Mauritius
Nov *558* *Rus.* Nau. NW Tajikistan
Nová Dubnica *519* W Slovakia
Nova Gorica *520* W Slovenia
Nova Gradiška *209* *Ger.* Neugradiska, *Hung.* Újgradiska. NE Croatia
Nova Iguaçu *145* SE Brazil
Nova Kakhovka *586* SE Ukraine
Nova Lamego *see* Gabú
Nova Lisboa *see* Huambo
Novara *320* N Italy
Nova Scotia *171* province of SE Canada
Novaya Sibir', Ostrov *485* island of Novosibirskiye Ostrovo, N Russian Federation
Novaya Zemlya *484* island group of N Russian Federation
Nova Zagora *152* C Bulgaria
Nové Mesto nad Váhom *519* *Ger.* Waagneustadtl, *Hung.* Vágújhely. W Slovakia
Nové Zámky *519* *Ger.* Neuhäusl, *Hung.* Érsekújvár. SW Slovakia
Novgorod *484* NW Russian Federation
Novi Sad *630* *Ger.* Neusatz, *Hung.* Újvidék. N Serbia, Yugoslavia
Novogrudok *see* Navahrudak
Novokazalinsk *338* *Kaz.* Zhangaqazaly. SW Kazakhstan
Novokuznetsk *485* *prev.* Stalinsk. C Russian Federation
Novolazarevskaya *90* CIS research station of Greater Antarctica, Antarctica
Novo Mesto *520* *Ger.* Rudolfswert, *prev.* Neustadtl. SE Slovenia
Novopolotsk *see* Navapolatsk
Novo Redondo *see* Sumbe
Novosibirsk *485* C Russian Federation
Novosibirskiye Ostrova *485* *Eng.* New Siberian Islands. Island Group of N Russian Federation
Novo Urgench *see* Urganch
Nový Jičín *216* SE Czech Republic
Novyy Margilan *see* Farghona
Novyy Uzen' *see* Zhanaozen
Nowogródek *see* Navahrudak
Nowshera *451* *var.* Naushahra. NE Pakistan
Nowy Sącz *471* S Poland
Noyemberyan *98* N Armenia
Nsanje *385* S Malawi
Nsawam *270* SE Ghana
Nsoc *236* *var.* Nsork. SE Río Muni, Equatorial Guinea
Nsoc-Nsomo *236* E Río Muni, Equatorial Guinea
Nsoko *540* SE Swaziland
Nsuta *270* SW Ghana
Ntcheu *385* *var.* Ncheu. S Malawi
Ntchisi *385* *var.* Nchisi. C Malawi
Ntega *162* N Burundi
Ntem *168, 236* *prev.* Campo, *var.* Kampo. River of Cameroon and Equatorial Guinea
Ntomba, Lac *203* *var.* Lac Tumba. Lake of NW Dem. Rep. Congo (Zaire)
Ntoum *258* NW Gabon
NTsaouéni *198* NW Grande Comore, Comoros
Ntusi *584* SW Uganda
Nuanetsi *see* Mwenezi
Nubian Desert *536* desert of NE Sudan
Nu Chiang *see* Salween
Nu'eima *318* E West Bank
Nueva Caceres *see* Naga
Nueva Concepción *278* SW Guatemala
Nueva Gerona *210* Isla de la Juventud, Cuba
Nueva Helvecia *607* SW Uruguay
Nueva Loja *228* NE Ecuador
Nueva Ocotepeque *288* W Honduras
Nueva Palmira *607* SW Uruguay
Nueva San Salvador *235* *prev.* Santa Tecla. SW El Salvador
Nuevitas *210* E Cuba
Nuevo Laredo *403* N Mexico
Nuevo Rocafuerte *228* E Ecuador
Nugaal *524* *It.* Uadi Nogal. Seasonal river of N Somalia
Nui *583* coral atoll of W Tuvalu
Nu Jiang *see* Salween
Nukha *see* Şäki
Nuku *653* Île Futuna, N Wallis & Futuna
Nuku' alofa *568* ❖ of Tonga, Tongatabu, Tongatapu Group, Tonga
Nukuatea *653* island of Île Uvea, S Wallis & Futuna
Nukufetau *583* coral atoll of C Tuvalu
Nukulaelae *583* *var.* Nukulailai. Coral atoll of E Tuvalu
Nukuloa *653* island of Île Uvea, S Wallis & Futuna
Nukunonu Atoll *653* island of C Tokelau
Nukuoro *406* atoll of SE Micronesia
Nukus *610* W Uzbekistan
Nullarbor Plain *100 -101* plateau of S Australia
Numan *441* E Nigeria
Numazu *330* Honshū, SE Japan
Nunap Isua *646* *var.* Uummannarsuaq. *Dan.* Kap Farvel, *Eng.* Cape Farewell. Cape on the S coast of Greenland
Nunavut *170 -171, 175* territory of N Canada
Nuoro *320* Sardegna, W Italy
Nupani *522* Santa Cruz Is, Solomon Is
Nuquí *195* W Colombia
Nurakita *see* Niulakita
Nurata *see* Nurota
Nuratau, Khrebet *see* Nurota Tizmasi
Nurek *see* Norak
Nurmes *249* E Finland
Nürnberg *265* *Eng.* Nuremberg. S Germany
Nurota *610* *Rus.* Nurata. SE Uzbekistan
Nurota Tizmasi *610* *Rus.* Khrebet Muratau. Mountains of E Uzbekistan
Nusa Tenggara *302* *Eng.* Lesser Sunda Islands. Island group of C Indonesia
Nusaybin *577* SE Turkey
Nuşayrīyah, Jabal al *551* mountains of W Syria
Nuuk *646* *Dan.* Godthåb. ❖ Greenland, SW Greenland
Nuwara Eliya *534* S Sri Lanka
Nyaake *368* SE Liberia
Nyabarongo *492* river of W Rwanda
Nyabisindu *492* SW Rwanda
Nyabugogo *492* river of C Rwanda
Nyagassola *see* Niagassola
Nyahururu *342* W Kenya
Nyainqêntanglha Shan *186* mountain range of Xizang Zizhiqu, W China
Nyala *536* W Sudan
Nyalikungu *560* N Tanzania
Nyamapanda *636* NE Zimbabwe
Nyanda *see* Masvingo
Nyanga *636* *var.* Inyanga. E Zimbabwe
Nyanga *200, 258* river of Congo and Gabon
Nyanza-Lac *162* S Burundi
Nyarutovu *492* NW Rwanda
Nyasa, Lake *385, 419, 560* *var.* Lake Malawi, *Port.* Lago Niassa, *prev.* Lago Nyassa. Great lake of E Africa
Nyasaland *see* Malawi
Nyasvizh *122* W Belarus
Nyaunglebin *159* S Burma
Nyazura *636* *prev.* Inyazura. E Zimbabwe
Nyenyen *368* C Liberia
Nyeri *342* C Kenya
Nyika *342* plain of SE Kenya
Nyika Plateau *385* *var.* Nyika Uplands. Plateau of N Malawi
Nyíregyháza *290* NE Hungary
Nyiri Desert *342* desert region of SE Kenya
Nyitra *see* Nitra
Nykøbing *218* Sjælland, E Denmark
Nykøbing-Falster *218* *var.* Nykøbing. Falster, S Denmark
Nyköping *543* SE Sweden
Nylstroom *527* Northern Transvaal, NE South Africa
Nyoman *see* Neman
Nyon *546* SW Switzerland
Nyong *168* river of SW Cameroon
Nyslott *see* Savonlinna
Nzambi *200* S Congo
Nzega *560* NW Tanzania
Nzérékoré *281* SE Guinea
Nzi *326* river of C Ivory Coast
Nzilo, Lac *203* *var.* Barrage de Nzilo, *prev.* Lac Delcommune. Lake of SE Dem. Rep. Congo (Zaire)
Nzwani *see* Anjouan

O

Oahu *598* island of Hawaii, USA, C Pacific
Oakland *598* California, W USA
Oamaru *433* S South Island, New Zealand
Oaxaca *403* *var.* Oaxaca de Juárez. S Mexico
Ob' *454-485* river of C Russian Federation
Oban *593* W Scotland, UK
Obando *see* Puerto Inírida
Obbia *see* Hobyo
Obdorsk *see* Salekhard
Oberhausen *264* W Germany
Oberpahlen *see* Põltsamaa
Obihiro *331* Hokkaidō, N Japan
Obo *179* E Central African Republic
Obock *222* E Djibouti

Obskaya Guba *485* bay of Karskoye More, N Russian Federation
Obuasi *270* C Ghana
Ocaña *195* N Colombia
Occidental, Cordillera *136* range of the Andes in Bolivia and Chile
Occidental, Cordillera *195* range of the Andes in W Colombia
Occidental, Cordillera *463* range of the Andes in W Peru
Ocean Falls *170* W Canada
Ocean Island *see* Banaba
Och'amch'ire *262* *Rus.* Ochamchira. W Georgia
Ocho Rios *329* N Jamaica
Ocotal *436* NW Nicaragua
October Revolution Island *see* Oktyabr'skoy Revolyutsii, Ostrov
Oda *270* SE Ghana
Ōdate *330* Honshū, N Japan
Odawara *330* Honshū, SE Japan
Oddur *see* Xuddur
Ödenburg *see* Sopron
Odendaalsrus *527* Orange Free State, C South Africa
Odenpäh *see* Otepää
Odense *218* Fyn, S Denmark
Oder *216, 265, 471* *Cz./Pol.* Odra. River of C Europe
Oderhaff *265, 471* *var.* Stettiner Haff, *Pol.* Zalew Szczeciński. Bay of the Baltic Sea, on the N coast of Germany and Poland
Odesa *586* *Rus.* Odessa. S Ukraine
Odienné *326* NW Ivory Coast
Ôdôngk *165* S Cambodia
Oeno Island *651* island of NW Pitcairn Islands
Ofanto *321* river of S Italy
Offa *440* W Nigeria
Offenbach *264* *var.* Offenbach am Main. SW Germany
Offenbach am Main *see* Offenbach
Offenburg *264* SW Germany
Ofu *642* island of Manua Islands, E American Samoa
Ogaden *243* arid plateau of SE Ethiopia
Ōgaki *330* Honshū, C Japan
Ogasawara-shotō *330* *Eng.* Bonin Islands. Island group to the SE of Honshū, SE Japan
Ogbomosho *440* W Nigeria
Ogden *598* Utah, SW USA
Ogea Driki *246* island of the Lau Group, E Fiji
Ogea Levu *246* island of the Lau Group, E Fiji
Ogooué *200, 258* river of Congo and Gabon
Ogou *567* river of E Togo
Ogražden *381* mountain range of Bulgaria and FYR Macedonia
Ogre *362* *Ger.* Oger. C Latvia
Ogulin *209* N Croatia
Ohau, Lake *433* W South Island, New Zealand
Ohio *599* river of NC USA
Ohio *599* state of NE USA
Ohobela *366* N Lesotho
'Ohonua *568* 'Eua, Tongatapu Group, Tonga
Ohře *216* *Ger.* Eger. River of Czech Republic and Germany
Ohrid *381* *var.* Ochrida. SW FYR Macedonia
Ohrid, Lake *81, 381* *var.* Lake Ochrida, *Alb.* Liqeni i Ohrit, *Maced.* Ohridsko Ezero. Lake of Albania and Macedonia
Oiapoque *145, 645* *var.* l'Oyapok. River of Brazil and French Guiana
Oil Islands *see* Chagos Archipelago
Oise *253* river of N France
Oistins *121* S Barbados
Ōita *330* Kyūshū, SW Japan
Ojos del Salado, Nevado *183* mountain of N Chile
Okahandja *423* C Namibia
Okakarara *423* N Namibia
Ókanizsa *see* Kanjiža
Okāra *451* E Pakistan
Okarem *581* *Turkm.* Ekerem. W Turkmenistan
Okavango *see* Cubango
Okavango Delta *142* large wetland area of N Botswana
Okaya *330* Honshū, C Japan
Okayama *330* Honshū, W Japan
Okazaki *330* Honshū, C Japan
Okeechobee, Lake *599* lake of Florida, SE USA
Okhotsk, Sea of *485* *Rus.* Okhotskoye More. Sea of Pacific Ocean, bordering E Russian Federation
Oki *330* island to the N of Honshū, W Japan
Okinawa-shotō *330* island group of Nansei-shotō, SW Japan
Oklahoma *599* state of SC USA
Oklahoma City *599* Oklahoma, SC USA
Okondja *258* E Gabon
Okovanggo *see* Cubango
Okoyo *200* W Congo
Okpara *132* river of Benin and Nigeria
Oktemberyan *see* Hoktemberyan
Oktyabr'skoy Revolyutsii, Ostrov *485* *Eng.* October Revolution Island. Island of Severnaya Zemlya, N Russian Federation
Okushiri-tō *330* island to the W of Hokkaidō, N Japan
Ólafsfjördhur *294* N Iceland
Ólafsvík *294* W Iceland
Olaine *362* C Latvia
Olanchito *288* C Honduras
Öland *543* island of S Sweden
Olavarría *95* E Argentina
Olbia *320* Sardegna, W Italy
Oldenburg *264* NW Germany
Old Fort Point *649* headland on the S coast of Montserrat
Old Harbour *329* S Jamaica
Old Road *92* SW Antigua, Antigua & Barbuda
Old Road Town *494* W St Kitts, St Kitts & Nevis
Olëkminsk *485* C Russian Federation
Oleksandriya *586* *Rus.* Aleksandriya. C Ukraine
Olenëk *485* *var.* Olenyok. N Russian Federation
Oléron, Île d' *252* island of W France
Ölgiy *412* W Mongolia
Olhão *474* S Portugal
Olimarao *406* atoll of C Micronesia
Olimar Grande *607* *var.* Olimar. River of E Uruguay
Ólimbos *see* Ólympos
Olinda *145* E Brazil
Olita *see* Alytus
Olmaliq *610* *Rus.* Almalyk. E Uzbekistan
Olmütz *see* Olomouc
Olocuilta *235* SW El Salvador
Oloitokitok *342* *var.* Laitokitok. S Kenya
Olomouc *216* *Ger.* Olmütz. SE Czech Republic
Olongapo *466* Luzon, N Philippines
Olosega *642* island of Manua Islands, E American Samoa
Olsnitz *see* Murska Sobota
Olsztyn *471* *Ger.* Allenstein. N Poland
Olt *480* *Ger.* Alt. River of S Romania
Olten *546* NW Switzerland
O-luan Pi *555* *var.* Cape Olwanpi. Cape on the S coast of Taiwan
Oluanpi *555* S Taiwan
Olympia *598* Washington, NW USA
Ólympos *273* *Eng.* Mount Olympus, *prev.* Ólimbos. Mountain of N Greece
Olympus, Mount *215* *var.* Troodos, Olympos. Mountain of C Cyprus
Olympus, Mount *see* Ólympos
Omagh *593* Northern Ireland, UK
Omaha *599* Nebraska, C USA
Oman *448-449* officially Sultanate of Oman, *prev.* Muscat & Oman. Country of SW Asia divided into 5 admin. units (governorates). ❖ Muscat
Oman, Gulf of *307, 448, 590* *Ar.* Khalīj 'Umān. Gulf of the Arabian Sea
Omaruru *423* C Namibia
Omba *see* Aoba
Omboué *258* W Gabon
Omdurman *536* *var.* Umm Durmān. C Sudan
Ometepe, Isla de *436* island on Lago de Nicaragua, S Nicaragua
Om Hajer *238* SW Eritrea
Ōmiya *330* Honshū, SE Japan
Omo Wenz *243* river of SW Ethiopia
Omsk *484* C Russian Federation
Ōmuta *330* Kyūshū, SW Japan
Ondangwa *423* *var.* Ondangua. N Namibia
Ondava *519* river of NE Slovakia
Ondjiva *see* N'Giva
Ondo *440* SW Nigeria
Öndörhaan *412* E Mongolia
One and Half Degree Channel *390* channel of the Indian Ocean, S Maldives
Oneata *246* island of the Lau Group, E Fiji
Onega, Lake *see* Onezhskoye Ozero
Onezhskoye Ozero *484* *Eng.* Lake Onega. Lake of NW Russian Federation
Onga *258* E Gabon
Ongjin *349* SW North Korea
Oni *262* N Georgia
Onilahy *382* river of SW Madagascar
Onitsha *440* S Nigeria
Ono *246* island to the S of Viti Levu, SW Fiji
Ono-i-lau *246* island to the S of the Lau Group, SW Fiji
Onomichi *330* Honshū, W Japan
Ononte *see* Orantes
Onotoa *346* island of the Gilbert Is, W Kiribati
Onslow *100* W Australia
Onsŏng *349* NE North Korea
Ontario *170-171* province of S Canada
Ontario, Lake *171, 599* lake of Canada and USA
Ontong Java Atoll *522* *prev.* Lord Howe Island. Atoll of N Solomon Is
Onverwacht *538* N Suriname
Ooma *346* Banaba, W Kiribati
Oos-Londen *see* East London
Oostende *127* *Fr.* Ostende, *Eng.* Ostend. NW Belgium
Oosterhout *429* SW Netherlands
Oosterschelde *429* *Eng.* Eastern Scheldt. Inlet of the North Sea, on the coast of SW Netherlands
Opava *216* *Ger.* Troppau. E Czech Republic
Opole *471* *Ger.* Oppeln. SW Poland
Oporto *see* Porto
Oppdal *444* S Norway
Oppeln *see* Opole
Opuwo *423* NW Namibia
Oqtosh *610* *Rus.* Aktash. S Uzbekistan
Oradea *480* *prev.* Oradea Mare, *Ger.* Grosswardein, *Hung.* Nagyvárad. NW Romania
Oral *see* Ural'sk
Oran *83* *var.* Ouahran, Wahran. NW Algeria
Orange *101* SE Australia
Orange Free State *see* Free State
Orange Mouth *see* Oranjemund
Orangemund *see* Oranjemund
Orange River *366, 423, 527* *Afr.* Oranjerivier. River of southern Africa
Orange Walk *130* N Belize
Orango, Ilha de *282* island of Arquipélago dos Bijagós, SW Guinea-Bissau
Orangozinho, Ilha de *282* island of SW Guinea-Bissau
Oranjemund *423* *var.* Orangemund, *Eng.* Orange Mouth. S Namibia
Oranjestad *650* St Eustatius, N Netherlands Antilles
Oranjestad *642* ❖ of Aruba, W Aruba
Orantes *364, 551* *var.* Ononte, Orontes, *Ar.* Nahr al 'Aṣī, *var.* Nahr al 'Āsī Oronte, Nr el Aassi. River of SW Asia
Orany *see* Varėna
Orapa *142* C Botswana
Orcadas *90* Argentinian research station of Greater Antarctica, Antarctica
Orchid Island *see* Lan Yü
Orchila, Isla le *619* island of N Venezuela
Ordino *86* NW Andorra
Ordu *577* N Turkey
Ordubad *110* SW Azerbaijan
Ordzhonikidze *see* Yenakiyeve
Ordzhonikidze *see* Vladikavkaz
Ordzhonikidzeabad *see* Kofarnihon
Orealla *284* E Guyana
Örebro *543* S Sweden
Oregon *598* state of NW USA
Orël *484* W Russian Federation
Orem *598* Utah, SW USA
Orenburg *484* *prev.* Chkalov. W Russian Federation
Orense *see* Ourense
Orestiáda *273* *prev.* Orestiás. NE Greece
Öresund *see* Sound, The
Øresund *see* Sound, The
Oreti *433* river of S South Island, New Zealand
Orgeyev *see* Orhei
Orhei *408* *var.* Orheiu, *Rus.* Orgeyev. N Moldova
Orhon Gol *412* river of N Mongolia
Oriental, Cordillera *136* range of the Andes in C Bolivia
Oriental, Cordillera *195* range of the Andes in C Colombia
Oriental, Cordillera *463* range of the Andes of C Peru
Orikum *81* *var.* Oriku. SW Albania
Orinoco *195, 619* river of Colombia and Venezuela
Oristano *320* Sardegna, W Italy
Orizaba, Volcán Pico de *403* *var.* Citlaltépetl. Mountain of SE Mexico
Orkhanie *see* Botevgrad
Orkney *593* islands of NE UK
Orlau *see* Orlová
Orléanais *253* cultural region of N France
Orléans *253* N France
Orléansville *see* Chlef
Orlová *216* *Ger.* Orlau, *Pol.* Orlowa. SE Czech Republic
Ormoc *466* *var.* MacArthur. Leyte, E Philippines
Ormsö *see* Vormsi
Ormuz, Strait of *see* Hormuz, Strait of
Örnsköldsvik *543* NE Sweden
Oro *349* E North Korea
Orodara *157* SW Burkina
Orol Dengizi *see* Aral Sea
Oroluk *406* atoll of C Micronesia
Oron *440* S Nigeria
Orona *346* *var.* Hull I. Island of the Phoenix Is, C Kiribati
Oronoque *284* river of SE Guyana
Orontes *see* Orantes
Orosháza *290* SE Hungary
Orotina *206* W Costa Rica
Orsha *122* NE Belarus
Orsk *484* C Russian Federation
Ørsta *444* SW Norway
Ortoire *570* river of S Trinidad, Trinidad & Tobago
Orto-Tokoy *357* *var.* Orto Tokoj. N Kyrgyzstan
Orūmīyeh *307* *prev.* Reẕā'īyeh, Urmia. NW Iran
Orūmīyeh, Daryācheh-ye *307* *prev.* Daryācheh-ye Reẕā'īyeh, *Eng.* Lake Urmia. Lake of NW Iran
Oruro *136* W Bolivia
Orvieto *321* C Italy
Oryakhovo *152* *var.* Orjahovo. NW Bulgaria
Oryokko *see* Yalu
Ōsaka *330, 335* Honshū, C Japan
Osa, Península de *206* peninsula of S Costa Rica
Ösel *see* Saaremaa
Osh *357* *var.* Oš. SW Kyrgyzstan
Oshakati *423* N Namibia
Oshawa *171* SE Canada
Oshikango *423* N Namibia
Oshogbo *440* W Nigeria
Osijek *209* *Hung.* Eszék, *Ger.* Esseg. NE Croatia

Osipenko *see* Berdyans'k
Osipovichi *see* Asipovichy
Öskemen *see* Ust'-Kamenogorsk
Ösling *378* physical region of N Luxembourg
Oslo *444* *prev.* Christiania. ❖ of Norway, S Norway
Oslofjorden *444* fjord of S Norway
Osmaniye *577* S Turkey
Osnabrück *264* NW Germany
Osogovski Planini *381* *var.* Osogovske Planine. Mountain range of Bulgaria and FYR Macedonia
Oss *429* S Netherlands
Ossa, Serra de *474* mountain range of SE Portugal
Ostee *see* Baltic Sea
Ostend *see* Oostende
Ostende *see* Oostende
Österbotten *see* Pohjanmaa
Östermyra *see* Seinäjoki
Österreich *see* Austria
Östersund *543* C Sweden
Ostfriesische Inseln *264* *Eng.* East Frisian Islands. Island group of NW Germany
Ostrava *216* *Ger.* Mährisch-Ostrau, *prev.* Moravská Ostrava. E Czech Republic
Ostrobothnia *see* Pohjanmaa
Ostrov *216* NW Czech Republic
Ostrowiec Świętokrzyski *471* E Poland
Ostyako-Voguls'k *see* Khanty-Mansiysk
Ōsumi-shotō *330* island group of Nansei-shotō, SW Japan
Osumit *81* *var.* Osum. River of SE Albania
Otago Peninsula *433* peninsula of SE South Island, New Zealand
Otaru *330* Hokkaidō, N Japan
Otavalo *228* N Ecuador
Otavi *423* N Namibia
Otepää *240* *Ger.* Odenpäh. SE Estonia
Oti *132, 270, 567* river of W Africa
Otjinene *423* NE Namibia
Otjiwarongo *423* N Namibia
Otra *444* river of SW Norway
Otranto, Strait of *81, 321* *It.* Canale d'Otranto. Strait connecting the Adriatic Sea and Ionian Sea, between Albania and Italy
Otrokovice *216* SE Czech Republic
Ōtsu *330* Honshū, C Japan
Ottawa *171* ❖ of Canada, SE Canada
Ottawa *170* *Fr.* Outaouais. River of SE Canada
Otterup *218* Fyn, C Denmark
Otu Tolu Group *568* island group of SE Tonga
Ötztaler Alpen *106* *It.* Alpi Venoste. Mountain range of Austria and Italy
Ou *359* river of N Laos
Ouaddi *222* NE Djibouti
Ouâd Nâga *398* SW Mauritania
Ouagadougou *157* *var.* Wagadugu. ❖ of Burkina, C Burkina
Ouâhayyi *222* river of Djibouti and Somalia
Ouahigouya *157* NW Burkina
Ouahran *see* Oran
Ouaka *179* river of C Central African Republic
Oualâta *398* SE Mauritania
Ouallam *439* *var.* Oualam. W Niger
Ouanary *645* E French Guiana
Ouanda Djallé *179* NE Central African Republic
Ouani *198* N Anjouan, Comoros
Ouara *179* river of E Central African Republic
Ouargla *83* *var.* Wargla. NE Algeria
Ouarkziz *414* seasonal river of SW Morocco
Ouarzazate *414* S Morocco
Ouazzane *414* N Morocco
Oubangui *see* Ubangi
Ouchan *647* E Isle of Man
Oued Zem *414* C Morocco
Ouégoa *650* N New Caledonia
Ouéléssébougou *392* *var.* Ouolossébougou. SW Mali
Ouémé *132* river of C Benin
Ouessant, Île d' *252* *Eng.* Ushant. Island of NW France
Ouèssè *132* *var.* Ouéssé. E Benin
Ouésso *200* NW Congo
Ouham *179, 180* river of Central African Republic and Chad
Ouidah *132* *Eng.* Whydah, *var.* Wida. S Benin
Oujda *414* NE Morocco
Oujeft *398* C Mauritania
Ould Yenjé *398* S Mauritania
Ouled Djellal *83* *var.* Awled Djellal. N Algeria
Oulu *249* *Swe.* Uleåborg. C Finland
Oulujärvi *249* *Swe.* Uleträsk. Lake of C Finland
Oulujoki *249* *Swe.* Uleälv. River of C Finland
Oumé *326* C Ivory Coast
Oum er Rbia *414* river of C Morocco
Oumm ed Droûs Telli, Sebkhet *398* salt lake of N Mauritania
Ounasjoki *249* river of N Finland
Ounianga Kébir *180* NE Chad
Ountivou *567* E Togo
Ouolossébougou *see* Ouéléssébougou
Our *378* river of W Europe
Ourense *530* *Cast.* Orense. NW Spain
Ourthe *127* river of E Belgium
Ouse *see* Great Ouse
Ouse *593* river of N England, UK
Outaouais *see* Ottawa
Outer Hebrides *593* *var.* Western Isles. Island group of NW Scotland, UK
Outer Islands *512* island group of C and SW Seychelles
Outjo *423* N Namibia
Ouvéa *650* island of Îles Loyauté, NE New Caledonia
Ovalau *246* island to the NE of Viti Levu, C Fiji
Ovalle *183* N Chile
Ovan *258* NE Gabon
Overflakkee *429* island of SW Netherlands
Overhalla *444* C Norway
Ovgos *215* river of NW Cyprus
Oviedo *530* NW Spain
Owando *200* C Congo
Owen Falls Dam *584* dam of S Uganda
Owen Stanley Range *458* mountain range of SE Papua New Guinea
Owerri *440* S Nigeria
Owia *498* N St Vincent, St Vincent & the Grenadines
Owo *440* SW Nigeria
Öxarfjördhur *294* *var.* Axarfjördhur. Fjord of NE Iceland
Oxbow *366* N Lesotho
Oxford *593* C England, UK
Oyama *330* Honshū, N Japan
Oyem *258* N Gabon
Oyo *440* W Nigeria
Oyo *200* C Congo
Oyster Island *159* island of W Burma
Ozama *226* river of S Dominican Republic
Ózd *290* NE Hungary
Özgön *see* Uzgen
Ozurget'i *262* *prev.* Makharadze. W Georgia

P

Paama *615* island of C Vanuatu
Paamiut *646* *Dan.* Frederikshåb. SW Greenland
Paarl *527* Western Cape, SW South Africa
Pābna *117* W Bangladesh
Pacaraima, Serra *145, 284* *var.* Pakaraima Mountains. Mountain range of N South America
Pachao Tao *555* island group of W Taiwan
Pachna *see* Pakhna
Pachuca *403* *var.* Pachuca de Soto. C Mexico
Pacific Ocean *90, 281, 330-331, 642, 647* world's largest ocean bounded by Asia and Australia to the W, the Americas to the E and Antarctica to the S
Padang *302* Sumatra, W Indonesia
Paderborn *264* NW Germany
Padma *117* name of the Ganges in Bangladesh, *see* Ganges
Padova *321* *Eng.* Padua. N Italy
Paektu-san *349* *Chin.* Baitou Shan. Mountain of China and North Korea
Pafos *see* Paphos
Pag *209* *It.* Pago. Island of C Croatia
Pagan *650* island of C Northern Mariana Islands
Pager *584* river of NE Uganda
Paget Island *643* island of E Bermuda
Pago *see* Pag
Pagon, Bukit *150* mountain of SE Brunei
Pago Pago *642* ❖ of American Samoa, Tutuila, W American Samoa
Pagouda *567* *var.* Kpagouda. NE Togo
Pahang *386* *var.* Syngei Pahang. River of C Peninsular Malaysia
Pai-ch'eng *see* Baicheng
Paide *240* *Ger.* Weissenstein. C Estonia
Päijänne *249* lake of S Finland
Pailĭn *165* W Cambodia
Paine, Cerro *183* mountain of S Chile
Paisance *see* Piacenza
País Valenciano *531* *Cat.* València, *Eng.* Valencia. Autonomous community of NE Spain
País Vasco *531* autonomous community of N Spain
Pakambaru *302* Sumatra, W Indonesia
Pakaraima Mountains *see* Pacaraima, Serra
Pakch'ŏn *349* W North Korea
Pakhna *215* *var.* Pachna. SW Cyprus
Pakin *406* atoll of E Micronesia
Pakistan *450-453* officially Islamic Republic of Pakistan. Country of Asia divided into 4 admin. units (provinces). v Islāmābād
Pak Lay *359* W Laos
Pakokku *159* W Burma
Pākpattan *451* E Pakistan
Pak Sane *see* Muang Pakxan
Pāksey *117* W Bangladesh
Pakwach *584* NW Uganda
Pakxé *359* *var.* Pakse. S Laos
Pal *86* W Andorra
Pala *180* SW Chad
Palapye *142* SE Botswana
Palau *454-455* *var.* Belau. Country of the Pacific Ocean. ❖ Koror
Palauli Bay *500* bay of Pacific Ocean off Sava'i, SW Samoa
Palawan *466* island of W Philippines
Palawan Passage *466* passage of the South China Sea, between Spratly Islands and Palawan, Philippines
Paldiski *240* *prev.* Baltiski, *Eng.* Baltic Port, *Ger.* Baltischport. NW Estonia
Palembang *302* Sumatra, W Indonesia
Palencia *531* NW Spain
Palermo *321* *Fr.* Palerme. Sicilia, S Italy
Palikir *406* ❖ of Micronesia, Pohnpei, Micronesia
Palimé *see* Kpalimé
Palk Strait *296, 534* strait connecting the Bay of Bengal and Gulf of Mannar, between India and Sri Lanka
Palma *531* *var.* Palma de Mallorca. Mallorca, E Spain
Palma *419* N Mozambique
Palmar Norte *206* SE Costa Rica
Palma Soriano *210* SE Cuba
Palm Beach *642* NW Aruba
Palmeira *176* Sal, NE Cape Verde
Palmer *90* US research station of Antarctic Peninsula, Antarctica
Palmerston *644* island of Southern Cook Islands, S Cook Islands
Palmerston North *433* S North Island, New Zealand
Palmetto Point *92* SW Barbuda, Antigua & Barbuda
Palmira *195* W Colombia
Palmyra *see* Tudmur
Paloe *see* Denpasar
Palu *302* Celebes, C Indonesia
Pamandzi *649* Petite-Terre, E Mayotte
Pamir *558* river of Afghanistan, Pakistan and Tajikistan
Pamirs *558* mountain range of E Tajikistan
Pampa Aullagas, Lago *see* Poopó, Lago
Pampas *95* flatlands of South America
Pampeluna *see* Pamplona
Pamplemousses *400* NW Mauritius
Pamplona *531* *var.* Pampeluna, *Basq.* Iruña. N Spain
Pamplona *195* NE Colombia
Pana *258* S Gabon
Panadura *534* SW Sri Lanka
Panagyurishte *152* *var.* Panagjurište. W Bulgaria
Panama *456-457* officially Republic of Panama. Country of Central America divided into 10 admin. units (9 provinces, and 1 special territory). ❖ Panama City
Panamá, Bahía de *456* bay to the S of Panama
Panama Canal *456* shipping canal linking the Caribbean Sea to the Pacific Ocean, passing through C Panama
Panama City *456* *Sp.* Panamá, *var.* Ciudad de Panama. ❖ of Panama, C Panama
Panamá, Golfo de *456* gulf of the Pacific Ocean to the S of Panama
Panamá, Istmo de *456* *prev.* Isthmus of Darien, *Eng.* Isthmus of Panama. Narrow strip of land, between North America and South America
Panay *466* island of C Philippines
Panay Gulf *466* gulf of the Sulu Sea
Pančevo *630* *Ger.* Pantschowa, *Hung.* Pancsova. N Serbia, Yugoslavia
Panda *419* S Mozambique
Pandan, Selat *517* strait connecting Strait of Malacca and South China Sea
Pandan Reservoir *517* reservoir of SW Singapore
Pandaruan *150* river of NE Brunei
Pan de Azúcar *607* S Uruguay
Pandėlys *376* *var.* Pandelis. NE Lithuania
Pandivere Kõrgustik *240* *var.* Pandivere Kõrgendik. Plateau of NW and NE Estonia
Pando *607* S Uruguay
Panevėžys *376* NE Lithuania
Panfilov *338* SE Kazakhstan
Pangai *568* Lifuka, Hai'pai Group, Tonga
Pangani *560* E Tanzania
Pangani *560* river of NE Tanzania
Pangar *168* river of C Cameroon
Pangkalpinang *302* Pulau Bangka, W Indonesia
Panguma *514* E Sierra Leone
Panguna *458* Bougainville I, Papua New Guinea
Pangutaran Group *466* island group of Sulu Archipelago, SW Philippines
Panhame *see* Manyame
Paniai, Danau *302* lake of Irian Jaya, E Indonesia
Panj *558* *Rus.* Pyandzh. SW Tajikistan
Panj *77, 558* *Rus.* Pyandzh. River of Afghanistan and Tajikistan
Panjakent *558* *Rus.* Pendzhikent. W Tajikistan
Panjang, Pulu *see* West Island
Pānji *296* SW India
Panji Poyon *558* *Rus.* Nizhniy Pyandzh. SW Tajikistan
Pano Lefkara *215* S Cyprus
Pano Panayia *215* *var.* Pano Panagia. W Cyprus
Pano Platres *215* SW Cyprus
Pantanal *144, 149* swamp region of SW Brazil

Pantelleria *321* island to the SW of Sicilia, S Italy
Pante Makasar *305* W East Timor
Pantschowa *see* Pančevo
Pánuco *403* river of C Mexico
Panzhihua *187* *prev.* Dukou *var.* Tu-k'ou. Sichuan, SW China
Panzós *278* E Guatemala
Pao-chi *see* Baoji
Paoki *see* Baoji
Paola *395* E Malta
Paola *321* S Italy
Pao-shan *see* Baoshan
Pao-ting *see* Baoding
Pao-t'ou *see* Baotou
Paotow *see* Baotou
Pápa *290* W Hungary
Papakura *433* N North Island, New Zealand
Papatoetoe *433* NW North Island, New Zealand
Papayes, River *400* river of W Mauritius
Papeete *646* ❖ of French Polynesia, Tahiti, W French Polynesia
Paphos *215* *var.* Pafos. W Cyprus
Papua, Gulf of *458* gulf of the Coral Sea, to the S of Papua New Guinea
Papua New Guinea *458-459* officially Independent State of Papua New Guinea, *prev.* Territory of Papua and New Guinea. Country of the SW Pacific divided into 19 admin. units (provinces). ❖ Port Moresby
Papuk *209* mountain range of NE Croatia
Paquera *206* W Costa Rica
Pará *see* Belém
Paraburdoo *100* W Australia
Paracel Islands *651* disputed island group of the South China Sea. ❖ Woody Island
Paraćin *630* C Serbia, Yugoslavia
Paradise *276* E Grenada island, Grenada
Paraguá *136* river of NE Bolivia
Paragua *619* river of SE Venezuela
Paraguaçu *145* *var.* Paraguassú. River of E Brazil
Paraguai *see* Paraguay
Paraguarí *460* S Paraguay
Paraguassú *see* Paraguaçu
Paraguay *95, 144, 460* *Port.* Paraguai. River of C South America
Paraguay *460-461* officially Republic of Paraguay. Country of South America divided into 20 admin. units (19 departments and 1 province). ❖ Asunción
Paraíba *see* Joao Pessoa
Paraíso *206* C Costa Rica
Parakou *132* C Benin
Paralimni *215* E Cyprus
Paramaribo *538* ❖ of Suriname, N Suriname
Paraná *95* E Argentina
Paraná *95, 145, 460* *var.* Alto Paraná. River of C South America
Paranam *538* N Suriname
Paraparaumu *433* S North Island, New Zealand
Pardubice *216* *Ger.* Pardubitz, C Czech Republic
Pardubitz *see* Pardubice
Parecis, Chapada dos *144* *var.* Serra dos Parecis. Mountain range of W Brazil
Pares *92* E Antigua, Antigua & Barbuda
Parham *92* NE Antigua, Antigua & Barbuda
Paria, Gulf of *570, 619* gulf of the Atlantic Ocean, between Trinidad and Venezuela
Parika *284* NE Guyana
Parima, Serra *144* mountain range of Brazil and Venezuela
Paris *253, 256* ❖ of France, N France
Paris *346* Kiritimati, E Kiribati
Parita, Bahía de *456* bay of the Gulf of Panama
Parkan *see* Štúrovo
Párkány *see* Štúrovo
Parkent *610* E Uzbekistan
Parkhar *see* Farkhor
Parma *320* N Italy
Parnaíba *145* river of NE Brazil
Pärnu *240* *Rus.* Pyarnu, *prev.* Pernov, *Ger.* Pernau. SW Estonia
Pärnu *240* *var.* Pärnu Jõgi, *Ger.* Pernau. River of SW Estonia
Pärnu Laht *240* bay of the Gulf of Riga, on the SW coast of Estonia
Paro *134* W Bhutan
P'aro-ho *350* *var.* Hwach'ŏn-chŏsuji. Reservoir of N South Korea
Páros *273* island of SE Greece
Parral *183* C Chile
Parrita *206* S Costa Rica
Parry Islands *170* island group of N Canada
Parry's *494* SE St Kitts, St Kitts & Nevis
Parson's Ground *494* N St Kitts, St Kitts & Nevis
Partizánske *519* *prev.* Šimonovany, *Hung.* Simony. W Slovakia
Pasaje *228* SW Ecuador
Pasaquina *235* E El Salvador
Pas de Calais *see* Dover, Strait of
Pa-shih Hai-hsia *see* Bashi Channel
Pashmakli *see* Smolyan
Pasión *278* river of N Guatemala
Pasir Mas *386* N Peninsular Malaysia
Pasir Panjang *517* reservoir of SW Singapore
Paso de los Toros *607* C Uruguay
Passau *265* SE Germany
Passo Fundo *145* S Brazil
Passu Keah *651* island of S Paracel Islands
Pastavy *122* *Rus.* Postavy, *Pol.* Postawy. NW Belarus
Pastaza *228, 463* river of Ecuador and Peru
Pasto *195* SW Colombia
Patagonia *95* semi-arid region of S South America
Patchchacan *130* N Belize
Pate *555* N Taiwan
Pate Island *342* *var.* Patta Island. Island of SE Kenya
Paterna *531* E Spain
Pathein *see* Bassein
Patía *195* river of SW Colombia
Patience *497* E St Lucia
Pati Point *647* headland on the NE coast of Guam
Patlong *366* S Lesotho
Patna *296* *var.* Azimabad. NE India
Patos *81* *var.* Patosi. SW Albania
Patos, Lagoa dos *145* lagoon of S Brazil
Pátra *273* *var.* Patras, *prev.* Pátrai. S Greece
Patta Island *see* Pate Island
Pattani *563* S Thailand
Pattle Island *651* island of W Paracel Islands
Patuākhāli *117* S Bangladesh
Patuca *288* river of E Honduras
Pau *253* SW France
Paungde *159* SW Burma
Pāvilosta *362* W Latvia
Pavlodar *338* NE Kazakhstan
Pavlohrad *586* *Rus.* Pavlograd. E Ukraine
Pavuvu *522* island of C Solomon Islands
Pawai, Pulau *517* island of SW Singapore
Paysandú *607* NW Uruguay
Paz *235* river of Guatemala and El Salvador
Pazardzhik *152* *var.* Pazardžik, *prev.* Tatar Pazardzhik. SW Bulgaria
Pazin *209* NW Croatia
Pčinja *381* river of N FYR Macedonia
Pea *568* Tongatabu, Tongatapu Group, Tonga
Peace *170* river of W Canada
Peak, The *652* mountain of C Ascension Island
Pearl Islands *see* Perlas, Archipiélago de las
Pearl Lagoon *see* Perlas, Laguna de
Peary Land *646* physical region of N Greenland
Pebble Island *645* island of N Falkland Islands
Peć *630* S Serbia, Yugoslavia
Pechora *484* River of NW Russian Federation
Pecixe, Ilha de *282* island of W Guinea-Bissau
Pecos *599* river of SW USA
Pécs *290* *Ger.* Fünfkirchen. SW Hungary
Pedernales *226* SW Dominican Republic
Pedhieos *215* *var.* Kanli Dere. River of NE Cyprus
Pedhoulas *215* W Cyprus
Pedja *240* *var.* Pedja Jõgi. River of C Estonia
Pedoulas *see* Pedhoulas
Pedra Lume *176* Sal, NE Cape Verde
Pedregal *456* W Panama
Pedro Juan Caballero *456* E Paraguay
Pedro Santana *226* W Dominican Republic
Peel *647* W Isle of Man
Pegasus Bay *433* bay of the South Pacific Ocean, on the E coast of South Island, New Zealand
Pegeia *see* Peyia
Pegu *159* *var.* Bago. S Burma
Péhonko *132* NW Benin
Pei-ching *see* Beijing
Peikang *555* *var.* Pei-chiang, *Jap.* Hokkō. W Taiwan
Peinan Hsi *555* river of C Taiwan
Peineville *224* N Dominica
Peipsi Järv *see* Peipus, Lake
Peipus, Lake *240* *Est.* Peipsi Järv, *Rus.* Chudskoye Ozero. Lake of Estonia and Russian Federation
Peiraías *273* *prev.* Piraiévs, *Eng.* Piraeus. SE Greece
Peka *366* NW Lesotho
Pekalongan *302* Java, C Indonesia
Pekan Muara *150* N Brunei
Pekan Seria *150* W Brunei
Peking *see* Beijing
Pelée, Montagne *649* mountain of N Martinique
Peleliu *455* island of S Palau
Péligre, Lac de *286* C Haiti
Pelly Bay *170* N Canada
Pelmadulla *534* S Sri Lanka
Pélmonostor *see* Beli Manastir
Pelopónnisos *273* *Eng.* Peloponnese. Peninsula of S Greece
Pelotas *145* S Brazil
Pemagatsel *134* SE Bhutan
Pematangsiantar *302* Sumatra, W Indonesia
Pemba *560* island of E Tanzania
Pemba *419* *prev.* Porto Amélia. NE Mozambique
Pembroke *498* SW St Vincent, St Vincent & the Grenadines
Pembroke Hall *see* Libertad
Penambo, Banjaran *387* *var.* Penambo Range, Banjaran Tama Abu. Mountain range of Borneo, Malaysia and Indonesia
Penambo Range *see* Penambo, Banjaran
Penang *see* George Town
Peñas Blancas *436* S Nicaragua
Pen-ch'i *see* Benxi
Pendé *179* river of Central African Republic and Chad
Pendembu *514* E Sierra Leone
Pendjari *132, 157* river of Benin and Burkina
Pendzhikent *see* Panjakent
P'enghu Liehtao *555* *Eng.*Pescadores Islands. Island group of W Taiwan
P'eng-hu Shui-tao *555* *Eng.* Pescadores Channel. Channel connecting South China Sea and Taiwan Strait
P'enghu Tao *555* island of W Taiwan
Peng-pu *see* Bengbu
Penibético, Sistema *531* *Eng.* Baetic Cordillera, Baetic Mountains. Mountain range of S Spain
Peniche *474* W Portugal
Peninsular Malaysia *386* *var.* Malaya, *prev.* West Malaysia. Western part of Malaysia situated on S Malay Peninsula
Penki *see* Benxi
Pennine Alps *546* *var.* Alpes Penninae, *Fr.* Alpes Pennines, *It.* Alpi Pennine. Mountain range of SW Switzerland
Pennines *593* *var.* Pennine Chain. Mountain range of N England, UK
Pennsylvania *599* state of NE USA
Penong *101* S Australia
Penonomé *456* C Panama
Penrhyn *644* island of Northern Cook Islands, N Cook Islands
Penrith *593* NW England, UK
Pentaschoinos *see* Yermasoyia
Pentecost *615* *Fr.* Pentecôte. Island of C Vanuatu
Penticton *170* SW Canada
Penza *484* W Russian Federation
Penzance *593* SW England, UK
Peoria *599* Illinois, C USA
Pepel *514* W Sierra Leone
Pereira *195* W Colombia
Pergamino *95* E Argentina
Perico *210* NW Cuba
Périgueux *253* SW France
Perim *see* Barīm
Peringat *386* N Peninsular Malaysia
Perkhemahan Berakas *150* N Brunei
Perlas, Archipiélago de las *456* *var.* Pearl Islands. Island group of SE Panama
Perlas, Laguna de *436* *var.* Pearl Lagoon. Lagoon of the Caribbean Sea on the E coast of Nicaragua
Perlepe *see* Prilep
Perm' *484* *prev.* Molotov. W Russian Federation
Përmet *81* *var.* Permeti, Premet. S Albania
Pernambuco *see* Recife
Pernau *see* Pärnu
Pernik *152* *prev.* Dimitrovo. W Bulgaria
Pernov *see* Pärnu
Peros Banhos *643* island of N British Indian Ocean Territory
Pérouse *see* Perugia
Perpignan *253* S France
Perquín *235* E El Salvador
Përrenjas *81* *var.* Prenjasi, Prenjas. E Albania
Persian Gulf *see* The Gulf
Persia *see* Iran
Perth *100* SW Australia
Perth *593* N Scotland, UK
Peru *462-465* officially Republic of Peru. Country of South America divided into 25 admin. units (24 departments and 1 constitutional province). ❖ Lima
Perugia *321* *Fr.* Pérouse. C Italy
Perugia, Lake of *see* Trasimeno, Lago
Pesaro *321* N Italy
Pescadores Channel *see* P'enghu Liehtao
Pescadores Islands *see* P'eng-hu Ch'ü-tao
Pescara *321* C Italy
Pesek Kechil, Pulau *517* island of SW Singapore
Pesek, Pulau *517* island of SW Singapore
Peshāwar *451* N Pakistan
Peshkopi *81* *var.* Peshkopia, Peshkopija. NE Albania
Pessons, Pic dels *86* mountain of SE Andorra
Petah Tiqwa *317* C Israel
Petaling Jaya *386* W Peninsular Malaysia
Pétange *378* SW Luxembourg
Petani *386* *var.* Patani. NW Peninsular Malaysia
Petare *619* N Venezuela
Petauke *635* E Zambia
Petén Itzá, Lago *278* *var.* Lago de Flores. Lake of N Guatemala
Peterborough *593* E England, UK
Peterborough *171* SE Canada

Peterhead *593* NE Scotland, UK
Peter Island *643* island of S British Virgin Islands
Peters Mine *284* NW Guyana
Pétionville *286* S Haiti
Petit-Bourg *646* C Guadeloupe
Petit Canouan *498* island of S St Vincent & the Grenadines
Petite Butte *400* Rodrigues, Mauritius
Petite Côte *510* coastal region of W Senegal
Petite Dominique *276* island to the NE of Carriacou, Grenada
Petite Martinique *276* island to the NE of Carriacou, Grenada
Petite-Rivière-de-l'Artibonite *286* C Haiti
Petite-Rivière Noire, Piton de la *400* mountain range of SW Mauritius
Petite Savane *224* S Dominica
Petite Soufrière *224* E Dominica
Petite-Terre *649* island, E Mayotte
Petit-Goâve *286* S Haiti
Petitjean *see* Sidi Kacem
Petit Mustique *498* island of C St Vincent & the Grenadines
Petit Piton *497* mountain of SW St Lucia
Petit-Popo *see* Aného
Petit St. Vincent Island *276* island to the NE of Carriacou, Grenada
Petra *336* archaeological site of W Jordan
Petre Bay *433* bay of the South Pacific Ocean, on the coast of Chatham Island, New Zealand
Petrich *152 var.* Petrič. SW Bulgaria
Petrinja *209* N Croatia
Petroaleksandrovsk *see* Tŭrtkŭl
Petropavlovsk *338* N Kazakhstan
Petropavlovsk-Kamchatskiy *485* NE Russian Federation
Petrópolis *145* SE Brazil
Petrosani *480* W Romania
Petrovgrad *see* Zrenjanin
Petrovsk-Port *see* Makhachkala
Petrozavodsk *484 Fin.* Petroskoi. NW Russian Federation
Pettau *see* Ptuj
Pevek *485* NE Russian Federation
Peyia *215 var.* Pegeia. SW Cyprus
Pezinok *519 Ger.* Bösing, *Hung.* Bazin. SW Slovakia
Pforzheim *264* SW Germany
Phalaborwa *527* Northern Transvaal, NE South Africa
Phangan, Ko *563* island of S Thailand
Phan Rang-Thap Cham *623* SE Vietnam
Phan Thiêt *623* S Vietnam
Phet Buri *see* Phetchaburi
Phetchaburi *563 var.* Phet Buri. C Thailand
Philadelphia *599* Pennsylvania, NE USA
Philip Island *650* island of S Norfolk Island
Philippeville *see* Skikda
Philippines *466-469* officially Republic of the Philippines. Country of SE Asia divided into 14 admin. units (regions). ❖ Manila
Philippine Sea *406, 466* sea of the Pacific Ocean to the E of the Philippines
Philipsburg *650* St Martin, N Netherlands Antilles
Phillips *494* NE St Kitts, St Kitts & Nevis
Phitsanulok *563 var.* Muang Phitsanulok. N Thailand
Phlórina *see* Flórina
Phnom Penh *165 Cam.* Phnum Pénh. ❖ of Cambodia, S Cambodia
Phnum Aôral *165 prev.* Phnom Aural. Mountain of W Cambodia
Phoenix *598* Arizona, SW USA
Phoenix *400* C Mauritius
Phoenix Island *see* Rawaki
Phoenix Islands *346* island group of C Kiribati
Phôngsali *359 var.* Phong Saly. N Laos
Phong Saly *see* Phôngsali
Phou Bia *359 var.* Pou Bia. Mountain of C Laos
Phrae *563 var.* Muang Phrae. N Thailand
Phra Nakhon Si Ayutthaya *see* Ayutthaya
Phu Cuong *see* Thu Dâu Môt
Phuket *563 Mal.* Ujung Salang. S Thailand
Phuket, Ko *563* island of S Thailand
Phumĭ Chhlong *165* S Cambodia
Phumĭ Chhuk *165* S Cambodia
Phumĭ Chŏăm *165* SW Cambodia
Phumĭ Kâmpóng Trâbék *165 prev.* Phum Kompong Trabek. C Cambodia
Phumĭ Koŭk Kdoŭch *165* NW Cambodia
Phumĭ Krêk *165* SE Cambodia
Phumĭ Labăng Siĕk *165* NE Cambodia
Phumĭ Mlu Prey *165* N Cambodia
Phumĭ Sâmraông *165 var.* Phumĭ Sâmroŭng, *prev.* Phum Samrong. NW Cambodia
Phumĭ Spoe Tbong *165* C Cambodia
Phumĭ Thmâ Pôk *165* NW Cambodia
Phumĭ Véal Rénh *165* SW Cambodia
Phuntsholing *134* SW Bhutan
Phu Quôc, Đao *623* island of SW Vietnam
Piacenza *320 Fr.* Paisance. N Italy
Piatra-Neamţ *480* NE Romania
Piave *321* river of N Italy
Piaye *497* S St Lucia
Pibor *243* river of Ethiopia and Sudan
Picardie *253 Eng.* Picardy. Cultural region of N France
Pichelin *224* S Dominica
Pico *474 var.* Ilha do Pico. Island of the Azores, Portugal
Picton, Isla *183* island of S Chile
Pidjani *198* SE Grande Comore, Comoros
Pidurutalagala *534* mountain of S Sri Lanka
Piedras *463* river of E Peru
Pielinen *249 var.* Pielisjärvi. Lake of E Finland
Pierre *599* South Dakota, NC USA
Piešťany *519 Ger.* Pistyan, *Hung.* Pöstyén. W Slovakia
Pietermaritzburg *527* Kwazulu Natal, E South Africa
Pietersaari *see* Jakobstad
Pietersburg *527* Northern Transvaal, NE South Africa
Piet Retief *527* Eastern Transvaal, E South Africa
Piggs Peak *540* NW Swaziland
Pigs, Bay of *210* bay of the Caribbean Sea, on southern coast of C Cuba
Pihkva Järv *see* Pskov, Lake
Pikelot *406* island of C Micronesia
Pikine *510* W Senegal
Pikounda *200* C Congo
Piła *471 Ger.* Schneidemühl. NW Poland
Pilar *460 var.* Villa del Pilar. S Paraguay
Pilas Group *466* island group of Sulu Archipelago, SW Philippines
Pilcomayo *95, 136, 460* river of C South America
Pilgrimkondre *538* NE Suriname
Pilis *290 var.* Philis. Mountain range of N Hungary
Pillories, The *498* islands of C St Vincent & the Grenadines
Pillsbury Sound *653* strait of the Caribbean Sea, C Virgin Islands
Pilsen *see* Plzeň
Pimpri *296* W India
Pinang *see* George Town
Pinang, Pulau *386 prev.* Prince of Wales Island. Island of NW Peninsular Malaysia
Pinar del Río *210* W Cuba
Píndos *273 prev.* Píndhos, *Eng.* Pindus Mountains, *var.* Píndhos Óros. Mountain range of C Greece
Pine Bluff *599* Arkansas, SC USA
Pinciós *273 prev.* Piniós. River of C Greece
Pines, Isle of *see* Juventud, Isla de la
Pinetown *527* Kwazulu Natal, E South Africa
P'ingchen *555 Jap.* Heichin. N Taiwan
Pingelap *406* atoll of E Micronesia
P'ingtung *555 Jap.* Heitō. SW Taiwan
Pinkiang *see* Harbin
Pinos, Isla de *see* Juventud, Isla de la
Pins, Île des *650 var.* Kunyé. Island of S New Caledonia
Pinsk *122 Pol.* Pińsk. SW Belarus
Pinta, Isla *228* island of N Galapagos Is, Ecuador
Piracicaba *145* S Brazil
Pirada *282* NE Guinea-Bissau
Piran *520 It.* Pirano. SW Slovenia
Piriápolis *607* S Uruguay
Pirita *240* river of N Estonia
Pirna *265* E Germany
Pirojpur *117* SW Bangladesh
Pirot *630* SE Serbia, Yugoslavia
Pisa *320* N Italy
Pisco *463* SW Peru
Písek *216* SW Czech Republic
Pishpek *see* Bishkek
Pissila *157* C Burkina
Pistoia *320* N Italy
Pistyan *see* Piešťany
Pita *281* NW Guinea
Pitalito *195* SW Colombia
Pitcairn Island *651* island of S Pitcairn Islands
Pitcairn Islands *651* British dependent territory of the Pacific Ocean. ❖ Adamstown
Pitche *282* E Guinea-Bissau
Piteå *543* NE Sweden
Piteşti *480* S Romania
Pitseng *366* N Lesotho
Pitt Island *433* island of Chatham Islands, New Zealand
Pittsburgh *599* Pennsylvania, NE USA
Pitt Strait *433* strait of Pacific Ocean, between Chatham Island and Pitt Island, New Zealand
Pituffik *646 prev.* Dundas. NW Greenland
Piura *463* NW Peru
Piva *630 var.* Diva. River of C Montenegro, Yugoslavia
Pivdennyy Bug *586 Rus.* Yuzhnyy Bug. River of W and S Ukraine
Pivsko Jezero *630* lake of NW Montenegro, Yugoslavia
Pjandž *see* Pyandzh
Placetas *210* C Cuba
Plačkovica *381* mountain range of E FYR Macedonia
Plaisance *286* N Haiti
Plakenska Planina *381* mountain range of SW FYR Macedonia
Plana Cays *112* islets of S Bahamas
Planken *374* C Liechtenstein
Plasencia *531* W Spain
Plate, Île *see* Flat Island
Platte *598-599* river of C USA
Platte, Île *512* Island of E Seychelles
Plattensee *see* Balaton
Plauer See *265* lake of NE Germany
Plây Cu *623 var.* Pleiku. S Vietnam
Pleasant Island *see* Nauru
Pleebo *see* Plibo
Pleiku *see* Plây Cu
Plenty, Bay of *433* inlet of the Pacific Ocean, on the coast of NE North Island, New Zealand
Pleskau *see* Pskov
Pleven *152 prev.* Plevna. N Bulgaria
Plezzo *see* Bovec
Plibo *368 var.* Pleebo. SE Liberia
Pljevlja *630 prev.* Plevlje. W Serbia, Yugoslavia
Płock *471* C Poland
Plöcken *106 It.* Passo di Monte Croce Carnico, *var.* Plöcken Pass, *Ger.* Plöckenpass. Mountain pass of SW Austria
Pločno *140* mountain of SW Bosnia & Herzegovina
Ploieşti *480 prev.* Ploeşti. SE Romania
Plovdiv *152 Gk* Philippopolisanc, *prev.* Eumolpias. SW Bulgaria
Plumtree *636* SW Zimbabwe
Plungė *376* NW Lithuania
Plyeshchanitsy *122* N Belarus
Plymouth *649* ❖ of Montserrat, SW Montserrat
Plymouth *593* SW England, UK
Plymouth *570* SW Tobago, Trinidad & Tobago
Plzeň *216 Ger.* Pilsen. W Czech Republic
Po *321* river of N Italy
Pô *157* S Burkina
Poabil *368* E Liberia
Pobè *132 var.* Pobé. S Benin
Pobedy, Pik *357 var.* Pobeda Peak, *Chin.* Tomur Feng. Mountain of China and Kyrgyzstan
Pocatello *598* Idaho, NW USA
Pocrí *456* S Panama
Podgorica *630 prev.* Titograd. S Montenegro, Yugoslavia
Podil's'ka Vysochyna *586* mountain range of SW Ukraine
Podkamennaya Tunguska *485 Eng.* Stony Tunguska. River of C Russian Federation
Podravska Slatina *see* Slatina
Poeketi *538* E Suriname
Pogradec *81 var.* Pogradeci. SE Albania
P'ohang *350 Jap.* Hokō. E South Korea
Pohjanlahti *see* Bothnia, Gulf of
Pohjanmaa *249 Swe.* Österbotten, *Eng.* Ostrobothnia. Physical region of W Finland
Pohnpei *406 prev.* Ascension, Ponape. Island of E Micronesia
Pohnpei Islands *406* island group E Micronesia
Poindimié *650* C New Caledonia
Point de Galle *see* Galle
Pointe-à-Pitre *646* C Guadeloupe
Pointe-à-Raquette *286* Île de la Gonâve, Haiti
Pointe Michel *224 var.* La Pointe. SW Dominica
Pointe-Noire *646* W Guadeloupe
Pointe-Noire *200* S Congo
Point Fortin *570* SW Trinidad, Trinidad & Tobago
Poitiers *253* C France
Poitou *252-253* cultural region of W France
Poivre Atoll *512* atoll of the Amirante Islands, C Seychelles
Pokhara *427* C Nepal
Pokigron *538* C Suriname
Pokrovka *see* Kyzyl-Suu
Pola *see* Pula
Poland *470-473* officially Republic of Poland, *Pol.* Polska. Country of E Europe divided into 49 admin. units (województwo). ❖ Warsaw
Polatli *576* C Turkey
Polatsk *122 Rus.* Polotsk. N Belarus
Pol-e Khomrī *77 var.* Pul-i-Khumri. NE Afghanistan
Poliçan *81 var.* Poliçani. S Albania
Polillo Islands *466* island group of N Philippines
Polis *215 var.* Poli. W Cyprus
Polochic *278* river of C Guatemala
Polonnaruwa *534* C Sri Lanka
Poltava *586* NE Ukraine
Poltoratsk *see* Ashgabat
Põltsamaa *240 Ger.* Oberpahlen. C Estonia
Põltsamaa *240 var.* Pyltsamaa. River of C Estonia
Põlva *240 Ger.* Pölwe. SE Estonia
Pomeranian Bay *265, 471 Pol.* Zatoka Pomorska, *Ger.* Pommersche Bucht. Bay of the Baltic Sea, on the coasts of Germany and Poland
Pomio *458* New Britain, Papua New Guinea
Pommersche Bucht *see* Pomeranian Bay
Pomona *130* E Belize
Pomorie *152 var.* Pomoriye. E Bulgaria
Pomorska, Zatoka *see* Pomeranian Bay
Ponape *see* Pohnpei
Ponce *651* S Puerto Rico
Pondicherry *296* S India
Ponérihouen *650* C New Caledonia
Ponferrada *531* NW Spain

Pongo *536* river of S Sudan
Ponta Delgada *474* São Miguel, Azores, Portugal
Ponta Grossa *145* S Brazil
Pontevedra *531* NW Spain
Pontianak *302* Borneo, C Indonesia
Pontian Kechil *386* *var.* Puntian Kecil, Pontian Kecil. S Peninsular Malaysia
Pontoise *253* N France
Pontypridd *593* S Wales, UK
Ponziane, Isole *321* island of C Italy
Pooh San *644* NE Christmas Island
Poole *593* S England, UK
Poona *see* Pune
Pooneryn *534* N Sri Lanka
Poopó, Lago *136* *var.* Lago Pampa Aullagas. Lake of W Bolivia
Popayán *195* SW Colombia
Popomanaseu, Mount *522* mountain of S Guadalcanal, Solomon Islands
Popondetta *458* SE Papua New Guinea
Popovo *152* N Bulgaria
Poprad *519* *Ger.* Deutschendorf, *Hung.* Poprád. NE Slovakia
Poprad *519* *Ger.* Popper, *Hung.*Poprád. River of Poland and Slovakia
Pori *249* *Swe.* Björneborg. SW Finland
Porirua *433* S North Island, New Zealand
Porlamar *619* Isla de Margarita, Venezuela
Porsangen *444* fjord of N Norway
Porsgrunn *444* S Norway
Portachuelo *136* C Bolivia
Portage la Prairie *170* S Canada
Portalegre *474* E Portugal
Port Alfred *527* Eastern Cape, S South Africa
Port Antonio *329* E Jamaica
Port Augusta *101* S Australia
Port-au-Prince *286* ❖ of Haiti, S Haiti
Port Blair *296* S Andaman, SE India
Port-Bouët *326* SE Ivory Coast
Port d'Envalira *86* zigzag pass of E Andorra
Port-de-Paix *286* N Haiti
Port Dickson *386* SW Peninsular Malaysia
Port Elizabeth *498* Bequia, St Vincent & the Grenadines
Port Elizabeth *527* Eastern Cape, S South Africa
Port Erin *647* SW Isle of Man
Port Étienne *see* Nouâdhibou
Port Florence *see* Kisumu
Port Francqui *see* Ilebo
Port-Gentil *258* W Gabon
Port Harcourt *440* S Nigeria
Port Hedland *100* NW Australia
Port Howard *645* West Falkland, C Falkland Islands
Portimão *474* *var.* Vila Nova de Portimão. S Portugal
Port Láirge *see* Waterford
Portland *599* Maine, NE USA
Portland *598* Oregon, NW USA
Portland Bight *329* bay of Caribbean Sea
Portland Point *652* headland on the SW coast of Ascension Island
Port Laoise *314* *Ir.* Portlaoighise, Portlaoise, *prev.* Maryborough. C Ireland
Port Lincoln *101* S Australia
Port Loko *514* W Sierra Leone
Port-Louis *646* N Guadeloupe
Port Louis *400* *var.* Port-Louis. ❖ of Mauritius, NW Mauritius
Port Lyautey *see* Kénitra
Port Macquarie *101* E Australia
Port Maria *329* N Jamaica
Port Mathurin *400* Rodrigues, Mauritius
Port Morant *329* E Jamaica
Portmore *329* SE Jamaica
Port Moresby *458* ❖ of Papua New Guinea, SE Papua New Guinea
Porto *474* *Eng.* Oporto. NW Portugal
Porto Alegre *145* *prev.* Pôrto Alegre. S Brazil
Porto Alegre *505* S São Tomé, Sao Tome & Principe
Porto Alexandre *see* Tombua
Porto Amélia *see* Pemba
Portobelo *456* *var.* Porto Bello, Puerto Bello. N Panama
Porto Edda *see* Sarandë
Port-of-Spain *570* ❖ of Trinidad & Tobago, NW Trinidad, Trinidad & Tobago
Porto Gole *282* C Guinea-Bissau
Porto Grande *see* Mindelo
Porto-Novo *132* ❖ of Benin, S Benin
Porto Santo *474* *var.* Ilha do Porto Santo. Island of the Madeira Is, Portugal
Porto Torres *321* Sardegna, W Italy
Porto Velho *144* *prev.* Pôrto Velho. W Brazil
Portoviejo *228* *var.* Puertoviejo. W Ecuador
Port Pirie *101* S Australia
Port Refuge *644* strait of the Indian Ocean between Horsburgh Island and Direction Island, C Cocos Islands
Port Royal *329* SE Jamaica
Port Said *230* *Ar.* Bur Sa'íd. N Egypt
Port St Mary *647* S Isle of Man
Portsmouth *593* S England, UK
Portsmouth *224* *var.* Grande-Anse. NW Dominica
Port Stanley *see* Stanley
Port Stephens *645* West Falkland, W Falkland Islands
Port Sudan *536* *var.* Būr Sūdān. NE Sudan
Port Swettenham *see* Kelang
Port Talbot *593* S Wales, UK
Portugal *474-477* officially Republic of Portugal. Country of W Europe divided into 18 admin. units (districts). ❖ Lisbon
Portuguese East Africa *see* Mozambique
Port-Vila *615* *var.* Vila. ❖ of Vanuatu, Éfate, Vanuatu
Porvenir *183* Tierra del Fuego, Chile
Porvenir *136* NW Bolivia
Posadas *95* NE Argentina
Posen *see* Poznań
Posŏng *350* river of S South Korea
Postojna *520* *Ger.* Adelsberg, *It.* Postumia. SW Slovenia
Pöstyén *see* Piešťany
Potaro *284* river of C Guyana
Potchefstroom *527* North West, N South Africa
Potenza *321* S Italy
Potgietersrus *527* Northern Transvaal, NE South Africa
Pot House *121* E Barbados
P'ot'i *262* W Georgia
Potiskum *440* NE Nigeria
Potoru *514* S Sierra Leone
Potosí *136* S Bolivia
Potsdam *265* NE Germany
Potters Village *92* C Antigua, Antigua & Barbuda
Pott, Île *650* island of Îles Belep, W New Caledonia
Pottuvil *534* SE Sri Lanka
Potwar Plateau *450* plateau of NE Pakistan
Poudre d'Or *400* NE Mauritius
Pouembout *653* W New Caledonia
Poum *650* W New Caledonia
Pout *510* W Senegal
Poutasi *500* Upolu, Samoa
Poŭthĭsăt *165* *var.* Pursat. River of W Cambodia
Poŭthĭsăt *165* *prev.* Pursat. W Cambodia
Po Valley *320* valley of N Italy
Považská Bystrica *519* *Ger.* Waagbistritz, *Hung.* Vágbeszterce. NW Slovakia
Póvoa de Varzim *474* NW Portugal
Powell, Lake *598* reservoir of SW USA
Poya *650* C New Caledonia
Poyang Hu *187* lake of E China
Poyan Reservoir *517* reservoir of W Singapore
Poza Rica *403* *var.* Poza Rica de Hidalgo. C Mexico
Poznań *471* *Ger.* Posen. W Poland
Pozo Colorado *460* C Paraguay
Pozsega *see* Slavonska Požega
Pozsony *see* Bratislava
Prábis *282* W Guinea-Bissau
Præstø *218* Sjælland, SE Denmark
Prague *216* *Cz.* Praha, *Ger.* Prag. ❖ of Czech Republic, NW Czech Republic
Praia *176* ❖ of Cape Verde, Santiago, S Cape Verde
Praslin *512* island of the Inner Islands, NE Seychelles
Praslin *497* E St Lucia
Prato *320* N Italy
Preguiça *176* São Nicolau, N Cape Verde
Prenjas *see* Përrenjas
Preparis Island *159* island of SW Burma
Přerov *216* *Ger.* Prerau. SE Czech Republic
Presidente Prudente *145* S Brazil
Prešov *519* *Ger.* Eperies, *var.* Preschau, *Hung.* Eperjes. NE Slovakia
Prespa, Lake *81, 273, 381* *Alb.* Liqen i Prespës, *Mac.* Prespansko Ezero, *Gk* Límni Megáli Préspa, *var.* Limni Prespa. Lake of SE Europe
Prespës, Liqen i *see* Prespa, Lake
Pressburg *see* Bratislava
Prestea *270* SW Ghana
Preston *593* NW England, UK
Pretoria *527* ❖ of South Africa. Pretoria-Witwatersrand-Vereeniging, NE South Africa
Pretoria-Witwatersrand-Vereeniging *527* province of NE South Africa
Préveza *273* W Greece
Prey Vêng *165* S Cambodia
Priboj *630* W Serbia, Yugoslavia
Příbram *216* W Czech Republic
Prickly Pear Cays *642* island group of NW Anguilla
Prieska *527* Northern Cape, C South Africa
Prievidza *519* C Slovakia
Prijedor *140* NW Bosnia & Herzegovina
Prilep *381* *Turk.* Perlepe. S FYR Macedonia
Prince Albert *170* SW Canada
Prince Edward Island *171* province and island of SE Canada
Prince Edward Island *527* island of the Prince Edward Islands, S South Africa
Prince Edward Islands *527* island group of S South Africa
Prince George *170* W Canada
Prince Island *see* Príncipe
Prince of Wales Island *see* Pinang, Pulau
Prince of Wales Island *170* island of N Canada
Prince Patrick Island *170* island of Parry Islands, N Canada
Prince Rupert *170* W Canada
Prince Rupert Bay *224* bay of the Caribbean Sea, to the NW of Dominica
Princes Town *570* SW Trinidad, Trinidad & Tobago
Príncipe *505* *var.* Príncipe Island, *Eng.* Prince Island. Island to the N of São Tomé, Sao Tome & Principe
Pripet *122* river of S Belarus
Pripet Marshes *122, 586* forested and swampy region of Belarus and Ukraine
Priština *630* S Serbia, Yugoslavia
Privas *253* SE France
Privigye *see* Prievidza
Priwitz *see* Prievidza
Prizren *630* *Alb.* Prizreni. S Serbia, Yugoslavia
Probištip *381* N FYR Macedonia
Probolinggo *302* Java, C Indonesia
Progreso *607* S Uruguay
Prome *159* *var.* Pyè. SW Burma
Promissão, Represa de *145* reservoir of S Brazil
Proskurov *see* Khmel 'nyts'kyy
Prostějov *216* *Ger.* Prossnitz. SE Czech Republic
Provadiya *152* *var.* Provadija. E Bulgaria
Provence *253* cultural region of SE France
Providence *599* Rhode Island, NE USA
Providence *121* S Barbados
Providence Atoll *512* *var.* Providence. Atoll of the Farquhar Group, S Seychelles
Providenciales *653* island of NW Turks and Caicos Islands
Provo *598* Utah, SW USA
Prudhoe Bay *598* Alaska, USA
Prune Island *498* island of SW St Vincent & the Grenadines
Prut *408, 480, 586* *Ger.* Pruth. River of E Europe
Pruth *see* Prut
Pruzhany *122* SW Belarus
Pryazova'ks Vysochyna *586* mountain range of SE Ukraine
Prychornomors'ka Nyzovyna *586* mountain range of S Ukraine
Prydniprovs'ka Nyzovyna *586* mountain range of NE Ukraine
Prydniprovs'ka Vysochnya *586* mountain range of NW Ukraine
Przemyśl *471* SE Poland
Przheval'sk *see* Karakol
Pskov *484* *Ger.* Pleskau. W Russian Federation
Pskov, Lake *240* *Est.* Pihkva Järv, *Rus.* Pskovskoye Ozero. Lake of Estonia and Russian Federation
Ptsich *122* *Rus.* Ptich'. River of C Belarus
Ptuj *520* *Ger.* Pettau. NE Slovenia
Pua'a, Cape *500* cape on the coast of Savai'i, NW Samoa
Pu'apu'a *500* Savali'i, Samoa
Pucallpa *463* C Peru
Puch'ŏn *350* *prev.* Punwŏn. NW South Korea
Pudasjärvi *249* C Finland
Puebla *403* *var.* Puebla de Zaragoza. S Mexico
Pueblo *599* Colorado, SW USA
Pueblo Nuevo Tiquisate *278* *var.* Tiquisate. SW Guatemala
Puente Alto *183* C Chile
Puerto Acosta *136* W Bolivia
Puerto Aisén *183* S Chile
Puerto Armuelles *456* W Panama
Puerto Ayacucho *619* SW Venezuela
Puerto Bahía Negra *460* N Paraguay
Puerto Baquerizo Moreno *228* San Cristobal I, Galapagos Is.
Puerto Barrios *278* E Guatemala
Puerto Bello *see* Portobelo
Puerto Berrío *195* N Colombia
Puerto Busch *136* *var.* Puerto General Busch. SE Bolivia
Puerto Cabello *619* N Venezuela
Puerto Cabezas *436* *var.* Bilwi. NE Nicaragua
Puerto Carreño *195* E Colombia
Puerto Casado *460* C Paraguay
Puerto Cooper *460* C Paraguay
Puerto Cortés *288* NW Honduras
Puerto El Carmen de Putumayo *228* *var.* Putumayo. NW Ecuador
Puerto el Triunfo *235* S El Salvador
Puerto Inírida *195* *var.* Obando. E Colombia
Puerto Iradier *see* Cogo
Puerto La Cruz *619* NE Venezuela
Puerto Lempira *288* E Honduras
Puertolland *531* SW Spain
Puerto Maldonado *463* E Peru
Puerto México *see* Coatzacoalcos
Puerto Montt *183* C Chile
Puerto Natales *183* S Chile
Puerto Padre *210* SE Cuba
Puerto Pinasco *460* C Paraguay
Puerto Plata *226* *var.* San Felipe de Puerto Plata. N Dominican Republic
Puerto Presidente Stroessner *see* Ciudad del Este
Puerto Princesa *466* Palawan, W Philippines
Puerto Príncipe *see* Camagüey
Puerto Rico *651* Commonwealth territory of the USA, Caribbean Sea. ❖ San Juan

Puerto Rico Trench *651* undersea feature of the Caribbean Sea, N Puerto Rico
Puerto San José *278 var.* San José. S Guatemala
Puerto Suárez *136* E Bolivia
Puerto Vallarta *403* W Mexico
Puerto Varas *183* C Chile
Puerto Viejo *206* NE Costa Rica
Puertoviejo *see* Portoviejo
Pujehun *514* S Sierra Leone
Pukaki, Lake *433* lake of C South Island, New Zealand
Pukapuka *644* island of Northern Cook Islands, N Cook Islands
Pukch'ŏng *349* E North Korea
Pukë *81 var.* Puka. N Albania
Pukekohe *433* NW North Island, New Zealand
Pukhan *350* river of North Korea and South Korea
Pula *209 prev.* Pulj, *It.* Pola. W Croatia
Pulangi *466* river of Mindanao, S Philippines
Pulap *406* atoll of C Micronesia
Pulau *303* river of Irian Jaya, E Indonesia
Pulau Tekong Reservoir *517* reservoir of E Singapore
Pul-i-Khumri *see* Pol-e Khomrī
Pully *546* SW Switzerland
Pulusuk *406* island of C Micronesia
Puluwat *406* atoll of C Micronesia
Puná, Isla *228* island to the SW of Ecuador, in the Gulf of Guayaquil
Punakha *134* C Bhutan
Punata *136* C Bolivia
Pune *296 prev.* Poona. W India
Punggol *517* area of NE Singapore
Púngoè *419 var.* Pungue, Pungwe. River of C Mozambique
Punkudutivu *534* island of N Sri Lanka
Puno *463* SE Peru
Punta Arenas *183 prev.* Magallanes. S Chile
Punta Chame *456* C Panama
Punta del Este *607* S Uruguay
Punta Gorda *130* S Belize
Puntarenas *206* W Costa Rica
Punta Santiago *236* S Bioko, Equatorial Guinea
Punto Fijo *619* NW Venezuela
Punwŏn *see* Puch'ŏn
Purari *458* river of C Papua New Guinea
Puri *296* E India
Purmerend *429* NW Netherlands
Pursat *see* Poŭthĭsăt
Purus *144* river of Brazil and Peru
Pusan *350 var.* Busan, *Jap.* Fusan. SE South Korea
Pusat Gayo, Pegunungan *302* mountain range of Sumatra, W Indonesia
Pushkino *see* Biläsuvar
Putai *555* W Taiwan
Putorana, Plato *485* mountain range of N Russian Federation
Puttalam *534* W Sri Lanka
Puttalam Lagoon *534* lagoon of W Sri Lanka
Putumayo *195, 463* river of NW South America
Putumayo *see* Puerto El Carmen de Putumayo
Puyo *228* C Ecuador
Pyandzh *see* Panj
Pyapon *159* S Burma
Pyarnu *see* Pärnu
Pyinmana *159* C Burma
Pyltsamaa *see* Põltsamaa
P'yŏngt'aek *350* NW South Korea
Pyongyang *349 Kor.* P'yŏngyang. ❖ of North Korea, SW North Korea
Pyramiden *653* Spitsbergen, W Svalbard
Pyramid Rock *651* island of E Paracel Islands
Pyrenees *86, 252-253, 531 Sp.* Pirineos, *Fr.* Pyrénées. Mountain range of SW Europe
Pyu *159* S Burma
Pyuntaza *159* S Burma
Pyuthan *427* W Nepal

Q

Qaanaaq *646 Dan.* Thule. NW Greenland
Qabātiya *318* N West Bank
Qābis *see* Gabès
Qacentina *see* Constantine
Qafṣah *see* Gafsa
Qahremānshahr *see* Bākhtarān
Qala' en Nahl *536 var.* Qala' an Naḥl. E Sudan
Qal'aikhum *558 Rus.* Kalaikhum. C Tajikistan
Qalali *115* Jazirat al Muharraq, Bahrain
Qalansīyah *627* NW Suqutra, Yemen
Qalāt *see* Kalāt
Qal 'at Bīshah *506* SW Saudi Arabia
Qal'eh-ye Now *77 var.* Qala Nau. NW Afghanistan
Qalīb ash Shuyūkh *354 var.* Jleeb al Shuyoukh. C Kuwait
Qalīb, Shiqqat al *354 var.* Shagat Al Jleeb. Desert region of NW Kuwait
Qalqīlya *318* NW West Bank
Qamar, Ghubbat al *627* bay of Arabian Sea, E Yemen
Qamar, Jabal al *448* mountain range of SW Oman
Qambar *see* Kambar
Qamea *246 prev.* Nggamea. Island to the E of Taveuni, N Fiji
Qandahār *see* Kandahār
Qaqortoq *646 Dan.* Julianehåb. S Greenland
Qaraghandy *see* Karaganda
Qaraoun, Lac de *364 var.* Buḩayrat al Qir'awn. Lake of S Lebanon
Qara Qum *see* Karakumy
Qarataū *see* Karatau
Qardho *524 It.* Gardo. N Somalia
Qareh Chāy *307* river of NW Iran
Qarkilik *see* Ruoqiang
Qarokŭl *558 Rus.* Karakul'. E Tajikistan
Qarokŭl *558 Rus.* Ozero Karakul'. Lake of E Tajikistan
Qarshi *610 Rus.* Karshi, *prev.* Bek-Budi. S Uzbekistan
Qartaba *364 var.* Qarṭabā. N Lebanon
Qasigianguit *646 Dan.* Christianshåb. W Greenland
Qatar *478-479* officially State of Qatar. Country of SW Asia divided into 9 admin. units (municipalities). ❖ Doha
Qaṭṭâra, Monkhafad el *230 var.* Munkhafaḍ al Qaṭṭārah, *Eng.* Qattara Depression. Arid desert bin of NW Egypt
Qayrokkum, Obanbori *558 Rus.* Kayrakkumskoye Vodolkhranilishche. Reservoir of NW Tajikistan
Qazaqstan *see* Kazakhstan
Qazax *110 Rus.* Kazakh. W Azerbaijan
Qazbegi *262 Rus.* Kazbegi. NE Georgia
Qazimämmäd *110 Rus.* Kazi-Magomed. SE Azerbaijan
Qazvīn *307 var.* Kazvin. NW Iran
Qena *230 var.* Qina. E Egypt
Qena, Wâdi *230 var.* Wādī Qinā. Seasonal river of E Egypt
Qeqertarsuaq *646 Dan.* Godhavn. W Greenland
Qeqertarsuatsiaat *646 Dan.* Fiskenæsset. SW Greenland
Qeshm *307 var.* Jazīreh-ye Qeshm, Qeshm Island. Island of S Iran
Qezel Owzan *307* river of NW Iran
Qibili *see* Kebili
Qilian Shan *186 var.* Kilien Mountains. Mountain range of W China
Qingdao *187 var.* Tsintao, Ching-Tao, Ch'ing-tao. Shandong, E China
Qinghai *186 var.* Chinghai, Tsinghai. Province of W China
Qinghai Hu *186 var.* Ch'ing Hai *Mong.* Koko Nor. Lake of W China
Qing-Zang Gaoyuan *186 Eng.* Plateau of Tibet. Plateau of Xizang Zizhiqu, W China
Qiqihar *187 prev.* Lungkiang, *var.* Tsitsihar, Ch'i-ch'i-ha-erh. Heilongjiang, NE China
Qir'awn, Buḩayrat al *see* Qaraoun, Lac de
Qirba, Khashim Al *see* Girba, Khashm el
Qiryat Ata *317* N Israel
Qiryat Gat *317* C Israel
Qiryat Motzkin *317* N Israel
Qiryat Shemona *317* N Israel
Qishn *627* SE Yemen
Qishon, Naḥal *317* river of N Israel
Qīzān *see* Jīzān
Qizilqum *see* Kyzyl Kum
Qizilrabot *558 Rus.* Kyzylrabot. E Tajikistan
Qom *307 var.* Qum, Kum. NW Iran
Qomolangma Feng *see* Everest, Mount
Qomul *see* Hami
Qondūz *see* Kunduz
Qondūz, Daryā-ye *77* seasonal river of NE Afghanistan
Qorakŭl *610 Rus.* Karakul'. S Uzbekistan
Qormi *395* C Malta
Qornet es Saouda *364* mountain of NE Lebanon
Qoryooley *524 It.* Coriole. SW Somalia
Qostanay *see* Kostanay
Qoubaïyât *364 var.* Al Qubayyāt. NE Lebanon
Qoussantîna *see* Constantine
Quang Ngai *623* E Vietnam
Quan Long *see* Ca Mau
Quanzhou *187 var.* Ch'uan-chou, *prev.* Chin-chiang, *var.* Tsinkiang. Fujian, SE China
Quaraí *see* Cuareim
Quarles, Pegunungan *302* mountain range of Celebes, W Indonesia
Quarnero *see* Kvarner
Quartier Militaire *400* C Mauritius
Quatre Bornes *400* W Mauritius
Quatre Bornes *512* Mahé, Seychelles
Quatre, Isle à *498* island of C St Vincent & the Grenadines
Quba *110 Rus.* Kuba. N Azerbaijan
Queanbeyan *101* SE Australia
Québec *171* SE Canada
Quebec *171, 175* province of SE Canada
Quebo *282* S Guinea-Bissau
Queen Charlotte Bay *645* bay of the South Atlantic Ocean, W Falkland Islands
Queen Charlotte Islands *170 Fr.* Îles de la Reine-Charlotte. Island group of SW Canada
Queen Charlotte Sound *170* area of the Pacific Ocean between the Queen Charlotte Islands and Vancouver Island, SW Canada
Queen Elizabeth Islands *170 Fr.* Îles de la Reine-Élisabeth. Island group of N Canada
Queen Mary's Peak *652* mountain of C Tristan da Cunha
Queen Maud Gulf *170* gulf of the Arctic Ocean on the coast of N Canada
Queen Maud Land *90* physical region of Greater Antarctica, Antarctica
Queensland *101, 105* state of N Australia
Queenstown *433* S South Island, New Zealand
Queenstown *517* area of S Singapore
Queenstown *527* Eastern Cape, S South Africa
Queguay Grande *607* river of W Uruguay
Quelimane *419* E Mozambique
Quelpart *see* Cheju-do
Queluz *474* W Portugal
Quepos *206* S Costa Rica
Que Que *see* Kwekwe
Querétaro *403* C Mexico
Quesada *206* N Costa Rica
Questelles *498* SW St Vincent, St Vincent & the Grenadines
Quetta *451* NW Pakistan
Quezaltenango *278 var.* Quetzaltenango. W Guatemala
Quezaltepeque *235* C El Salvador
Quibdó *195* W Colombia
Quillacollo *136* C Bolivia
Quilpué *183* C Chile
Quimper *252* W France
Quinhámel *282* W Guinea-Bissau
Quiniluban Group *466* island group of C Philippines
Quissico *419* S Mozambique
Quito *228* ❖ of Ecuador, N Ecuador
Qum *see* Qom
Qŭnghirot *610 Rus.* Kungrad. NW Uzbekistan
Qŭqon *610 var.* Khokand, *Rus.* Kokand. E Uzbekistan
Qurayn, Ra's al *115* cape of SE Bahrain
Qurayyāt *448 var.* Qurayat, Quraiyat. NE Oman
Qŭrghonteppa *558 Rus.* Kurgan-Tyube. W Tajikistan
Qurlurtuuq *see* Kugluktuk
Qus *230 var.* Qûş. E Egypt
Quthing *see* Moyeni
Quy Nhơn *623 var.* Qui Nhon, Quinhon. SE Vietnam
Qvareli *262 Rus.* Kvareli. E Georgia
Qyteti Stalin *see* Kuçovë
Qyzylorda *see* Kyzylorda

R

Raab *see* Rába
Raab *see* Győr
Raahe *249 Swe.* Brahestad. W Finland
Ra'ananna *317* C Israel
Raas Xaatuun *524 It.* Ras Hafun. NE Somalia
Rába *106, 290 Ger.* Raab. River of Austria and Hungary
Rabat *395* W Malta
Rabat *414* ❖ of Morocco, NW Morocco
Rabaul *458* New Britain, NE Papua New Guinea
Rabbit Island *498* island of SE St Vincent & the Grenadines
Rábca *290* river of NW Hungary
Rabi *246 prev.* Rambi. Island to the E of Vanua Levu, N Fiji
Rābigh *506* W Saudi Arabia
Rabinal *278* C Guatemala
Râbniţa *see* Rîbniţa
Rabyānah, Ramlat *371 var.* Şaḩrā' Rabyāh. Desert of SE Libya
Rachaïya *364 var.* Rāshayyā. S Lebanon
Rach Gia *623* SW Vietnam
Rach Gia, Vinh *623* bay of the Gulf of Thailand on the SW coast of Vietnam
Racine *599* Wisconsin, NC USA
Radā *627 var.* Ridā. W Yemen
Radom *471* C Poland
Radoviš *381 var.* Radovište. E FYR Macedonia
Radviliškis *376* N Lithuania
Rafaela *95* E Argentina
Rafah *317, 318 Heb.* Rafiaḥ. SW Gaza Strip
Rafḩā' *506* N Saudi Arabia
Ragged Island Range *112* island group of S Bahamas
Ragusa *321* Sicilia, S Italy
Ragusa *see* Dubrovnik
Rahachow *122 Rus.* Rogachëv. E Belarus
Rahaeng *see* Tak
Rahīmyār Khān *451* SE Pakistan
Raiatea *646* island of W French Polynesia
Raipur *296* C India
Rairok District *396* district of Majuro, SE Marshall Islands
Rājahmundry *296* SE India
Rajang *386* river of SW Borneo, Malaysia
Rājbāri *117* C Bangladesh
Rajbiraj *427* E Nepal
Rājkot *296* W India
Rājshāhi *117 prev.* Rampur Boalia. W Bangladesh
Rakahanga *644* island of Northern Cook Islands, N Cook Islands

Rakaia 433 river of C South Island, New Zealand
Rakhshān 450 river of W Pakistan
Rakiraki 246 N Viti Levu, W Fiji
Rakka see Ar Raqqah
Rakutō-kō see Naktong
Rakvere 240 Ger. Wesenberg. N Estonia
Raleigh 599 North Carolina, SE USA
Ralik Chain 396 island group of W Marshall Islands
Ramādah 627 W Yemen
Ramallah 317, 318 C West Bank
Ramat Gan 317 C Israel
Ramatlabama 142 S Botswana
Rambi see Rabi
Ramechhap 427 C Nepal
Ramier Island see Glover Island
Ramla 317 C Israel
Ramm, Jabal 336 mountain of SW Jordan
Râmnicu Sarat 480 E Romania
Râmnicu Vâlcea 480 prev. Rîmnicu-Vîlcea. C Romania
Ramotswa 142 S Botswana
Rampur Boalia see Rajshahi
Ramree Island 159 island of W Burma
Ramsey 647 NE Isle of Man
Ramsey Bay 647 bay of the Irish Sea on the NE coast of Isle of Man
Ramsgate 593 SE England, UK
Ramu 458 river of NE Papua New Guinea
Rancagua 183 C Chile
Rānchi 296 E India
Randa 222 C Djibouti
Randers 218 Jylland, N Denmark
Rāngāmāti 117 SE Bangladesh
Rangiora 433 E South Island, New Zealand
Rangitaiki 433 river of E North Island, New Zealand
Rangitata 433 river of C South Island, New Zealand
Rangitikei 433 river of S North Island, New Zealand
Rangoon 159 var. Yangon. ❖ of Burma, S Burma
Rangpur 117 N Bangladesh
Rankin Inlet 170 C Canada
Rankovićevo see Kraljevo
Rann see Brežice
Rann of Kachch 296 var. Rann of Cutch, Rann of Kutch. Salt marsh of India and Pakistan
Ranongga 522 var. Ghanongga. New Georgia Is, Solomon Islands
Rantau, Puala see Tebingtinggi, Pulau
Rapallo 320 N Italy
Rapid City 599 South Dakota, NC USA
Räpina 240 Ger. Rappin. SE Estonia
Rapla 240 Ger. Rappel. NW Estonia
Rapperswil 546 NW Switzerland
Rappin see Räpina
Rarotonga 644 island of Southern Cook Islands, S Cook Islands
Ra's al 'Ayn 551 N Syria
Ras al Hadd see Al Ḩadd
Ras al Khaimah 590 NE United Arab Emirates
Ra's an Naqb 336 SW Jordan
Ras Dashen Terara 243 mountain of N Ethiopia
Rasdu Atoll 390 atoll of C Maldives
Raseiniai 376 W Lithuania
Rashîd 230 Eng. Rosetta. N Egypt
Rasht 307 var. Resht. NW Iran
Rashū see Kŭmsong
Raso, Ilhéu 176 island of NW Cape Verde
Rass Jebel 573 var. Ra's al Jabal. N Tunisia
Rastalt 264 SW Germany
Ras Tannūrah 506 E Saudi Arabia
Ratak Chain 396 island group of E Marshall Islands
Ratchaburi 563 var. Rat Buri. C Thailand
Rathkeale 314 SW Ireland
Rätische Alpen see Rhaetian Alps
Ratnapura 534 S Sri Lanka
Ratō see Lotung
Raub 386 C Peninsular Malaysia
Raufarhöfn 294 NE Iceland
Raukawa see Cook Strait
Rauma 249 Swe. Raumo. SW Finland
Rauna 362 NE Latvia
Răuţel 408 var. Reuţel. River of N Moldova
Ravenna 321 N Italy
Ravensthorpe 100 SW Australia
Rāvi 451 river of India and Pakistan
Ravne na Koroškem 520 Ger. Gutenstein. N Slovenia
Rawaki 346 var. Phoenix Island. Island of Phoenix Islands, C Kiribati
Rāwalpindi 451 NE Pakistan
Rawson 95 SE Argentina
Rayak 364 var. Riyāq. E Lebanon
Rayong 563 C Thailand
Raysūt 448 SW Oman
Razāzah, Buḩayrat ar 310 var. Baḩr al Milḩ. Lake of C Iraq
Razdan see Hrazdan
Razim, Lacul 480 prev. Lacul Rezelm. Lagoon of E Romania
Reading 593 SE England, UK
Reăng Kései 165 W Cambodia
Rebun-tō 330 island to the NW of Hokkaidō, N Japan
Rechytsa 122 Rus. Rechitsa. SE Belarus
Recife 145 prev. Pernambuco. E Brazil
Recklinghausen 264 W Germany
Reconquista 95 NE Argentina
Redange 378 W Luxembourg
Redcliff 636 C Zimbabwe
Red Deer 170 SW Canada
Redhead 570 NE Trinidad, Trinidad & Tobago
Redon 252 NW France
Red River 170 river of Canada and USA
Red River 599 river of SC USA
Red River 623 var. Sông Coi, Chin. Yuan Jiang. River of China and Vietnam
Red Sea 238, 627 sea of Indian Ocean, between the Arabian Peninsula and NE Africa
Red Sea Hills 536 hilly region of NE Sudan
Red Volta 157 Fr. Volta Rouge. River of Burkina and Ghana
Ree, Lough 314 Ir. Loch Ri. Lake of C Ireland
Reefton 433 N South Island, New Zealand
Regar see Tursunzode
Regensburg 265 SE Germany
Reggane 83 C Algeria
Reggio di Calabria 321 var. Reggio Calabria. S Italy
Reggio nell' Emilia 320 var. Reggio Emilia. N Italy
Reghin 480 N Romania
Regina 170 S Canada
Régina 645 E French Guiana
Rehoboth 423 C Namibia
Reḩovot 317 C Israel
Reichenberg see Liberec
Reifnitz see Ribnica
Ré, Île de 252 island of W France
Reims 253 Eng. Rheims. NE France
Reine-Charlotte, Îles de la see Queen Charlotte Islands
Reine-Élisabeth, Îles de la see Queen Elizabeth Islands
Reisduoddarhalde see Haltiatunturi
Reisui see Yŏsu
Reka see Rijeka
Relizane 83 var. Ghilizane, Ghelîzâne. NW Algeria
Remel el Abiod 573 desert region of S Tunisia
Remich 378 SE Luxembourg
Remscheid 264 W Germany
Rendezvous Bay 642 bay of the Caribbean Sea on the S coast of Anguilla
Rendova 522 island of the New Georgia Is, W Solomon Is
Renens 546 SW Switzerland
Rengo 183 C Chile
Rennell 522 var. Mu Nggava. Island of S Solomon Islands
Rennes 252 Bret. Roazon. NW France
Reno 598 Nevada, W USA
Réo 157 W Burkina
Republiek 538 N Suriname
Rere 522 E Guadalcanal, Solomon Is
Resen 381 SW FYR Macedonia
Resistencia 95 NE Argentina
Reşiţa 480 Hung. Resicabánya, Ger. Reschiza. W Romania
Resolute 170 Cornwallis Island, N Canada
Resolution Island 433 island to the SW of South Island, New Zealand
Retalhuleu 278 SW Guatemala
Retan Laut, Pulau 517 island SW Singapore
Retiche, Alpi see Rhaetian Alps
Réunion 652 French overseas department of the Indian Ocean. ❖ St Denis
Reus 531 E Spain
Reutlingen 264 S Germany
Reval see Tallinn
Rewa 284 river of S Guyana
Rey 307 var. Shahr Rey. NW Iran
Reyes 136 NW Bolivia
Rey, Isla del 456 island of SE Panama
Reykjahlídh 294 NE Iceland
Reykjavík 294 ❖ of Iceland, W Iceland
Reynosa 403 N Mexico
Reza, Gora 581 var. Gora Riza. Mountain of SW Turkmenistan
Reẕā 'īyeh see Orūmīyeh
Reẕā'īyeh, Daryācheh-ye see Orūmīeh, Daryācheh-ye
Rēzekne 362 Ger. Rositten, Rus. Rezhitsa. E Latvia
Rezina 408 NE Moldova
Rēznas Ezers 362 lake of SE Latvia
Rhadames see Ghadamis
Rhaetian Alps 546 Ger. Rätische Alpen, Fr. Alpes Rhétiques, It. Alpi Retiche. Mountain range of E Switzerland
Rheden 429 SE Netherlands
Rhein see Rhine
Rheine 264 NW Germany
Rheinisches Schiefergebirge 264 Eng. Rhenish Slate Mountains. Mountains of W Germany
Rhenish Slate Mountains see Rheinisches Schiefergebirge
Rhétiques, Alpes see Rhaetian Alps
Rhine 253, 264, 374, 546 Ger. Rhein, Fr. Rhin, Dut. Rijn. River of W Europe
Rhino Camp 584 NW Uganda
Rhode Island 599 state of NE USA
Rhodes see Rodos
Rhodesia see Zimbabwe
Rhodope Mountains 152, 273 Gk Orosirá Rodópis, Bul. Despoto Planina, Turk. Dospad Dagh. Mountain range of Bulgaria and Greece
Rhône 253, 546 river of France and Switzerland
Rhum 593 var. Rum. Island of Inner Hebrides, W Scotland, UK
Riaba 236 prev. Concepción. S Bioko, Equatorial Guinea
Riau, Kepulauan 302 var. Riau Archipelago, Dut. Riouw Archipel. Island group to the E of Sumatra, W Indonesia
Riban i Manamby 382 S Madagascar
Ribáuè 419 NE Mozambique
Ribble 593 river of NW England, UK
Ribe 218 Jylland, SW Denmark
Ribeira da Barça 176 Santiago, S Cape Verde
Ribeira Funda 176 São Nicolau, N Cape Verde
Ribeira Grande 176 Santo Antão, N Cape Verde
Ribeirão Preto 145 S Brazil
Riberalta 136 N Bolivia
Ribnica 520 Ger. Reifnitz. S Slovenia
Rîbniţa 408 var. Râbniţa, Rus. Rybnitsa. NE Moldova
Richard's Bay 527 Kwazulu Natal, E South Africa
Richard Toll 510 N Senegal
Riche Fond 497 E St Lucia
Richmond 599 Virginia, E USA
Richmond Vale 498 NW St Vincent, St Vincent & the Grenadines
Ridā see Radāa
Ridderkerk 429 SW Netherlands
Rif 414 var. Riff, Er Rif. Mountain range of N Morocco
Rift Valley see Great Rift Valley
Riga 362 Latv. Rīga. ❖ of Latvia, C Latvia
Riga, Gulf of 240, 362 Est. Liivi Laht, prev. Riia Laht, Rus. Rizhskiy Zaliv, Latv. Rīgas Jūras Līci Gulf of the Baltic Sea, on the coasts of Estonia and Latvia
Rīgestān 77 var. Registan. Desert region of S Afghanistan
Riihimäki 249 SW Finland
Rijeka 209 Slvn. Reka, Ger. Sankt Veit am Flaum, It. Fiume. NW Croatia
Rijn see Rhine
Rijssel see Lille
Ri, Loch see Ree, Lough
Rimah, Wādī ar 506 dry watercourse of C Saudi Arabia
Rimaszombat see Rimavská Sobota
Rimavská Sobota 519 Ger. Gross-Steffelsdorf, Hung. Rimaszombat. SE Slovakia
Rimini 321 N Italy
Rincon 650 Bonaire, S Netherlands Antilles
Ringe 218 Fyn, S Denmark
Ringkøbing 218 Jylland, W Denmark
Ringkøbing Fjord 218 fjord of Jylland, W Denmark
Ringsted 218 Sjælland, SE Denmark
Ringvassøya 444 island of NE Norway
Riobamba 228 C Ecuador
Rio Branco 144 W Brazil
Río Branco 607 E Uruguay
Rio Claro 570 SE Trinidad, Trinidad & Tobago
Río Cuarto 95 C Argentina
Rio de Janeiro 145 SE Brazil
Río Gallegos 95 var. Puerto Gallegos, Gallegos. S Argentina
Rio Grande 145 var. São Pedro do Rio Grande do Sul. S Brazil
Ríohacha 195 N Colombia
Río Muni 236 mainland region of Equatorial Guinea
Río Negro, Embalse del 607 var. Lago Artificial de Rincón del Bonete. Reservoir of C Uruguay
Rioni 262 river of W Georgia
Río Sereno 456 W Panama
Riouw Archipel see Riau, Kepulauan
Riri see Iri
Rîşcani 408 var. Râşcani. NW Moldova
Rishiri-tō 330 island to the NW of Hokkaidō, N Japan
Rishon Le Ẕiyyon 317 C Israel
Ritidian Point 647 headland on the N coast of Guam
Rivadavia 95 W Argentina
Rivas 436 S Nicaragua
Rivera 607 N Uruguay
Rivercess see Cess
River Sallee 276 NE Grenada island, Grenada
Rivière des Anguilles 400 S Mauritius
Rivière-Pilote 649 SE Martinique
Rivne 586 Pol. Równe, Rus. Rovno. NW Ukraine
Riyadh 506 var. Ar Riyāḑ. ❖ of Saudi Arabia, C Saudi Arabia
Riyāq see Rayak
Rize 577 NE Turkey
Rizhskiy Zaliv see Riga, Gulf of
Rizokarpaso see Dipkarpaz
Rkîz, Lac 398 lake of SW Mauritania
Road Bay 642 bay of the Caribbean Sea on the W coast of Anguilla
Road Town 643 ❖ of British Virgin Islands, Tortola, C British Virgin Islands
Roanne 253 E France
Roaring Creek 130 C Belize
Roatán 288 Islas de la Bahía, Honduras
Roazon see Rennes
Robertson, Lake see Manyame, Lake
Robertsport 368 W Liberia
Robinson Crusoe, Isla 183 island of Juan Fernández Islands, W Chile

Rocas, Atol das *145* island of E Brazil
Rocha *607* SE Uruguay
Rochambeau *645* NE French Guiana
Rochester *599* Minnesota, NC USA
Rochester *599* New York, NE USA
Rocheuses, Montagnes *see* Rocky Mountains
Rock, The *646* E Gibraltar
Rockford *599* Illinois, C USA
Rockhampton *101* E Australia
Rockies *see* Rocky Mountains
Rockingham *100* SW Australia
Rocklands *540* NW Swaziland
Rock Sound *112* Eleuthera I, Bahamas
Rock Springs *598* Wyoming, NW USA
Rockstone *284* E Guyana
Rocky Mountains *170, 598* *var.* Rockies, *Fr.* Montagnes Rocheuses. Mountain range of NW America
Rocky Point *644* headland on the N coast of Christmas Island
Rodez *253* S France
Ródhos *see* Rodos
Rodi *see* Rodos
Rodi Garganico *321* C Italy
Rodonit, Gjiri i *81* gulf of the Adriatic Sea, NW Albania
Rodópis, Orosirá *see* Rhodope Mountains
Rodos *273* *Eng.* Rhodes, *It.* Rodi, *prev.* Ródhos. Island of SE Greece
Ródos *273* *Eng.* Rhodes, *It.* Rodi, *prev.* Ródhos. Ródos, SE Greece
Rodosto *see* Tekirdağ
Rodrigues *400* *var.* Rodriquez. Island of E Mauritius
Roermond *429* S Netherlands
Roeselare *127* *Fr.* Roulers, *prev.* Rousselaere. W Belgium
Rogachëv *see* Rahachow
Rogaška Slatina *520* *prev.* Rogatec-Slatina, *Ger.* Rohitsch-Sauerbrunn. E Slovenia
Rogatec-Slatina *see* Rogaška Slatina
Roger *224* W Dominica
Rogozhina *see* Rrogozhinë
Rohitsch-Sauerbrunn *see* Rogaška Slatina
Roi Et *563* *var.* Muang Roi Et. NE Thailand
Roja *362* NW Latvia
Rojo, Cabo *651* cape on the SW coast of Puerto Rico
Rokan *302* *var.* Airlalang. River of Sumatra, W Indonesia
Rokel *514* *var.* Seli. River of C Sierra Leone
Rokkō *see* Lukang
Rôlas, Ilha das *505* island to the S of São Tomé, Sao Tome & Principe
Roma *see* Rome
Roma *366* W Lesotho
Romang Strait *302* strait connecting the Arafura Sea and Laut Banda, E Indonesia
Romania *480-483* *prev.* Socialist Republic of Romania, *var.* Rumania. Country of SE Europe, divided into 40 admin. units (judeţ). ❖ Bucharest
Romano, Cayo *210* island of NE Cuba
Rombo, Ilhéus do *176* *var.* Ilhéus Secos. Island of S Cape Verde
Rome *321* *It.* Roma. ❖ of Italy, C Italy
Rømø *218* island of SW Denmark
Ronde, Île *see* Round Island
Ronde Island *276* island to the N of Grenada island, Grenada
Rongelap *396* island of NW Marshall Islands
Rongerik *396* island of N Marshall Islands
Rong, Kas *see* Rung, Kaôh
Rongrong District *396* district of Majuro, SE Marshall Islands
Rønne *218* Bornholm, E Denmark
Ronne Ice Shelf *90* ice shelf of Antarctica, over Atlantic Ocean
Ronzan *see* Nonsan
Roodepoort-Maraisburg *527* Pretoria-Witwatersrand-Vereeniging, NE South Africa
Rooke Island *see* Umboi
Roosendaal *429* SW Netherlands
Roosevelt *144* river of W Brazil
Roraima, Mount *284* mountain of N South America
Røros *444* S Norway
Rorschach *546* NE Switzerland
Rosa, Lake *112* lake of Great Inagua, Bahamas
Rosalie *224* E Dominica
Rosario *95* E Argentina
Rosario *460* C Paraguay
Rosario *607* SW Uruguay
Roscommon *314* C Ireland
Roscrea *314* C Ireland
Roseau *224* ❖ of Dominica, SW Dominica
Roseau *497* river of NW St Lucia
Roseaux *286* SW Haiti
Rose Bank *498* NW St Vincent, St Vincent & the Grenadines
Rose Belle *400* SE Mauritius
Rose Hall *284* E Guyana
Rose Hill *121* N Barbados
Rose Hill *400* W Mauritius
Rosenau *see* Rožňava
Rosenberg *see* Ružomberok
Rosenheim *265* S Germany
Rosenhof *see* Zilupe
Rosetta *see* Rashîd
Rosh Pinah *423* S Namibia
Rosia *646* W Gibraltar
Rosia Bay *646* bay of the Atlantic Ocean on the SW coast of Gibraltar
Rosignol *284* E Guyana
Rosiori de Vede *480* S Romania
Rosita *436* NE Nicaragua
Rositten *see* Rēzekne
Roskilde *218* Sjælland, E Denmark
Rossano *321* S Italy
Ross Ice Shelf *90* ice shelf of Antarctica, over Pacific Ocean
Rosso *398* SW Mauritania
Ross Sea *90* sea of the Pacific Ocean, off Antarctica
Rostak *see* Ar Rustāq
Rostock *265* N Germany
Rostov-na-Donu *484* *var.* Rostov, *Eng.* Rostov-on-Don. SW Russian Federation
Roswell *599* New Mexico, SW USA
Rota *650* island of S Northern Mariana Islands
Rothera *90* UK research station of Antarctic Peninsula, Antarctica
Roti, Pulau *302* island to the SW of Timor, C Indonesia
Rotifunk *514* W Sierra Leone
Rotorua *433* C North Island, New Zealand
Rotorua, Lake *433* lake of C North Island, New Zealand
Rotterdam *429* SW Netherlands
Rotuma *246* island to the W of Vanua Levu, NW Fiji
Rouen *253* N France
Round Island *400* *var.* Île Ronde. Island of N Mauritius
Roulers *see* Roeselare
Roura *645* NE French Guiana
Rousselaere *see* Roeselare
Rovaniemi *249* N Finland
Rovigno *see* Rovinj
Rovigo *321* N Italy
Rovinj *209* *It.* Rovigno. W Croatia
Rovno *see* Rivne
Rovuma *see* Ruvuma
Rowd-e Lūrah *77* river of S Afghanistan
Równe *see* Rivne
Roxa, Ilha *282* island of SW Guinea-Bissau
Roxborough *570* E Tobago, Trinidad & Tobago
Roxo, Cap *510* cape on the SW coast of Senegal
Rozel *648* N Jersey
Rožňava *519* *Ger.* Rosenau, *Hung.* Rozsnyó. E Slovakia
Rózsahegy *see* Ružomberok
Rrëshen *81* *var.* Rresheni, Rrshen. N Albania
Rrogozhinë *81* *var.* Rrogozhina, Rogozhina, Rogozhinë. W Albania
Ruacana *423* NW Namibia
Ruanda *see* Rwanda
Ruapehu, Mount *433* mountain of C North Island, New Zealand
Ruatoria *433* E North Island, New Zealand
Ruavatu *522* NE Guadalcanal, Solomon Is
Ru'ays, Wādī ar *371* dry watercourse of C Libya
Rub 'al Khali *448, 506, 627* *Eng.* Great Sandy Desert, Empty Quarter. Desert region of SW Asia
Rubeho Mountains *560* mountain range of C Tanzania
Rubtsovsk *484* C Russian Federation
Rucava *362* SW Latvia
Ruda Śląska *471* S Poland
Rūd-i Māshkel *see* Māshkel
Rudnyy *338* N Kazakhstan
Rudolf, Lake *see* Turkana, Lake
Rudolfswert *see* Novo Mesto
Rufiji *560* river of E Tanzania
Rufisque *510* W Senegal
Ruggell *374* N Liechtenstein
Rugombo *162* NW Burundi
Rugusye *162* *var.* Lugusi. River of E Burundi
Rugwero, Lac *see* Rweru
Ruhango *492* SW Rwanda
Ruhengeri *492* NW Rwanda
Ruhnu *240* island of SW Estonia
Ruhondo, Lac *492* lake of N Rwanda
Ruhr Valley *264* industrial region of W Germany
Ruhwa *492* river of Burundi and Rwanda
Ruki *203* river of W Dem. Rep. Congo (Zaire)
Rukungiri *584* SW Uganda
Rukwa, Lake *560* shallow lake of W Tanzania
Ruma *630* NW Serbia, Yugoslavia
Rumania *see* Romania
Rumbek *536* S Sudan
Rum Cay *112* island of S Bahamas
Rumphi *385* N Malawi
Rumpi, Monts *168* *var.* Rumpi Hills. Hilly region of W Cameroon
Rumpungwe *162* *var.* Lumpungu. River of E Burundi
Runde *636* river of SE Zimbabwe
Rundu *423* *var.* Runtu. N Namibia
Rŭng, Kaôh *165* *prev.* Kas Kong. Island of SW Cambodia
Rŭng Sâmlŏem, Kaôh *165* *prev.* Kas Rong Sam Lem. Island of SW Cambodia
Rungwa *560* C Tanzania
Runway Bay *329* N Jamaica
Ruo *385* river of S Malawi
Ruoqiang *186* *var.* Jo-ch'iang, *Uigh.* Qarkilik, *var.* Charkhlik, Charkhliq. Xinjiang Uygur Zizhiqu, NW China
Rupat, Pulau *302* *prev.* Roepat. Island to the E of Sumatra, W Indonesia
Rupel *127* river of N Belgium
Rupununi *284* river of SW Guyana
Rušan *see* Rushon
Rusape *636* E Zimbabwe
Ruse *152* *Turk.* Rusçuk, *var.* Ruschuk, Rustchuk. N Bulgaria
Rusengo *162* C Burundi
Rushashi *492* NW Rwanda
Rushon *558* *var.* Rušan, *Rus.* Rushan. SE Tajikistan
Rusinga Island *342* island of Lake Victoria, SW Kenya
Rusizi *162* *var.* Ruzizi. River of E Africa
Russell Islands *522* island group of C Solomon Is
Russia *see* Russian Federation
Russian Federation *484-491* officially Russian Federation, *var.* Russia. Country of E Europe and N Asia, divided into 77 admin. units (21 autonomous republics, 1 autonomous oblast, 49 oblasts and 6 kraj). ❖ Moscow
Russkaya *90* CIS research station of Lesser Antarctica, Antarctica
Rust'avi *262* SE Georgia
Rustenburg *527* North West, N South Africa
Rusumo *492* E Rwanda
Rutana *162* C Burundi
Rutanzige, Lac *see* Edward, Lake
Rutovu *162* S Burundi
Ru'ūs al Jibāl *448* mountain range of Oman and United Arab Emirates
Ruvubu *162* *var.* Ruvuvu. River of C Burundi
Ruvuma *419, 560* *Port.* Rovuma. River of Mozambique and Tanzania
Ruvyironza *162* *var.* Luvironza. River of C Burundi
Ruwais *see* Ar Ru'ays
Ruwaisv *see* Ar Ru'ays
Ruwenzori *584* mountains of Uganda and Dem. Rep. Congo (Zaire)
Ruya *636* river of Mozambique and Zimbabwe
Ruyigi *162* C Burundi
Ružomberok *519* *Hung.* Rózsahegy, *Ger.* Rosenberg. N Slovakia
Rwamagana *492* E Rwanda
Rwamatamu *492* W Rwanda
Rwanda *492-493* officially Republic of Rwanda, *prev.* Ruanda. Country of Central Africa divided into 10 admin. units (prefectures). ❖ Kigali
Rwanyakizinga, Lac *492* lake of NE Rwanda
Rweru *162, 162* *var.* Lac Rugwero. Lake of Burundi and Rwanda
Rwesero *492* SW Rwanda
Ryazan' *484* W Russian Federation
Rybinskoye Vodokhranilishche *484* *Eng.* Rybinsk Reservoir. Reservoir of W Russian Federation
Rybnik *471* S Poland
Rybnitsa *see* Rîbniţa
Rykovo *see* Yenakiyeve
Rysy *471* mountain of S Poland
Rzeszów *471* SE Poland

S

Saale *265* river of C Germany
Saarbrücken *264* *Fr.* Sarrebruck. SW Germany
Sääre *240* Saaremaa, Estonia
Saaremaa *240* *var.* Saare, Sarema, *Ger.* Ösel, *var.* Oesel. Island of W Estonia
Saaristomeri *249* sea area of Baltic Sea
Saartuz *558* W Tajikistan
Saati *238* E Eritrea
Saatlı *110* *Rus.* Saatly. C Azerbaijan
Saatta *238* NW Eritrea
Sab *165* river of S Cambodia
Saba *650* island of N Netherlands Antilles
Šabac *630* NW Serbia, Yugoslavia
Sabadell *531* E Spain
Sabana, Archipiélago de *210* island group of N Cuba
Sabana de la Mar *226* E Dominican Republic
Sabanalarga *195* N Colombia
Sabaneta *226* NW Dominican Republic
Sab'atayn, Ramlat as *627* desert region of C Yemen
Sabaya *136* S Bolivia
Şāberī, Hāmūn-e *77* *var.* Sīstān, Daryācheh-ye. Lake of Afghanistan and Iran
Sabhā *371* W Libya
Sabi *261* E Gambia
Sabi *see* Save
Sabinal, Cayo *210* island of NE Cuba
Sabirabad *110* C Azerbaijan
Sabkha *see* As Sabkhah
Sabkhat al Mūh *551* river of S Syria
Sabyah *see* Aş Şabīyah
Sabzevār *307* NE Iran
Sacavém *474* W Portugal
Sachs Harbour *170* Banks Island, NW Canada
Sacramento *598* California, W USA
Sada *649* W Mayotte
Sá da Bandeira *see* Lubango
Şa'dah *627* NW Yemen
Sadaï *222* river of NE Djibouti

Sa Đec *623* S Vietnam
Sādiqābād *451* SE Pakistan
Sa'dīyah, Hawr as *310* lake of E Iraq
Sadlers *494* N St Kitts, St Kitts & Nevis
Sado *330* island to the W of Honshū, N Japan
Safāqis *see* Sfax
Safi *414* W Morocco
Safi *see* Aş Şafī
Safīd Khers, Kūh-e *77* mountain range of NE Afghanistan
Safīd Kūh *77* mountain range of NW Afghanistan
Safim *282* W Guinea-Bissau
Saga *330* Kyūshū, SW Japan
Sagaing *159* C Burma
Saganthit Island *159* *var.* Sakanthit, *prev.* Sellore I. Island of S Burma
Sagarmatha *see* Everest, Mount
Sagay *466* Negros, C Philippines
Sagua la Grande *210* C Cuba
Saguia al Hamra *414* river of N Western Sahara
Saḩam *336* *var.* Sahm. N Jordan
Sahara *180, 371, 392, 398* *Ar.* Aş Şaḩrā'. Vast desert area of N Africa
Sahara el Gharqîya *230* *var.* Aş Şaḩrā' al Gharbīyah, *Eng.* Western Desert. Desert of C Egypt
Sahara el Sharqîya *230* *var.* Aş Şaḩrā' ash Sharqīyah, *Eng.* Eastern Dest. Desert of E Egypt
Sāhīwāl *451* *prev.* Montgomery. E Pakistan
Saïda *364* *var.* Şaydā. W Lebanon
Saïda *83* NW Algeria
Saidpur *117* NW Bangladesh
Saigon *see* Hô Chi Minh
Saiki *330* Kyūshū, SW Japan
Sail Rock *498* islet of S St Vincent & the Grenadines
Saimaa *249* lake of SE Finland
Saint Albert *170* SW Canada
St-André *652* NE Réunion
St. Anne *647* Alderney, N Guernsey
St. Ann's Bay *329* N Jamaica
St Aubin *648* S Jersey
St Austell *593* SW England, UK
St. Barthélémy *646* island of N Guadeloupe
St-Benoit *652* E Réunion
St-Brieuc *252* NW France
St. Catherine, Mt *276* mountain C Grenada island, Grenada
St. Catherine Point *643* headland of E Bermuda
Saint Catherines *171* SE Canada
St-Chamond *253* E France
Saint Croix *653* island of S Virgin Islands
St. David's *276* SE Grenada island, Grenada
St. David's Island *643* island of E Bermuda
St-Denis *652* ❖ of Réunion, N Réunion
Ste Anne *649* SE Martinique
Ste. Anne *646* E Guadeloupe
Saint-Élie *645* N French Guiana
Ste. Rose *646* W Guadeloupe
Saintes *253* W France
St-Étienne *253* E France
St Eustatius *650* island of C Netherlands Antilles
St. François *646* E Guadeloupe
Saint-Gall *see* Sankt Gallen
St-Georges *645* E French Guiana
St. George *643* St. George's Island, N Bermuda
St. George's *276* ❖ of Grenada, SW Grenada
St. George's Channel *314, 593* *Ir.* Muir Bhreatan. Channel connecting the Celtic Sea and Irish Sea
St. George's Harbour *643* bay of E Bermuda
St. George's Island *643* island of E Bermuda
St. Giles Islands *570* *prev.* Melville Islands. Islands to the NE of Tobago, Trinidad & Tobago
St Helena *652* British dependent territory of the South Atlantic Ocean ❖ Jamestown
St. Helena Bay *527* bay of Atlantic Ocean, of coast of W South Africa
St Helier *648* ❖ of Jersey, S Jersey
St John *648* N Jersey
St John *647* C Isle of Man
Saint John *171* SE Canada
St. John *368* river of Guinea and Liberia
Saint John Island *653* island of NE Virgin Islands
St John's *649* N Montserrat
Saint John's *171* Newfoundland, E Canada
St. John's *92* ❖ of Antigua & Barbuda, NW Antigua
St. John's Island *see* Sakijang Bendera, Pulau
St. Johnston Village *92* C Antigua, Antigua & Barbuda
St-Joseph *652* S Réunion
St Joseph *224* W Dominica
St. Joseph *570* SE Trinidad, Trinidad & Tobago
St Julian's *395* N Malta
St Kilda *593* island of NW Scotland, UK
Saint Kitts *494* island of the Lesser Antilles, which, with Nevis, forms the independent state of St Kitts & Nevis
Saint Kitts and Nevis *494-495* officially Federation of Saint Christopher and Nevis. Country of the West Indies. ❖ Basseterre
Saint-Laurent, Golfe du *see* Saint Lawrence, Gulf of
St-Laurent-du-Maroni *645* NW French Guiana
Saint Lawrence *171* *Fr.* Fleuve Saint-Laurent. River of SE Canada
Saint Lawrence, Gulf of *170* Gulf of of the Atlantic Ocean, SE Canada
St-Lô *252* NW France
St-Louis *652* SW Réunion
St Louis *646* Marie-Galante, S Guadeloupe
St Louis *599* Missouri, C USA
Saint-Louis *510* NW Senegal
St-Louis-du-Nord *286* *var.* St-Luis du Nord. N Haiti
Saint Lucia *496-497* independent island state of the Caribbean. ❖ Castries
Saint Lucia Channel *497* channel connecting the Atlantic Ocean and Caribbean Sea
St. Lucia, Lake *527* lake of Kwazulu Natal, E South Africa
St-Malo *252* NW France
St-Malo, Golfe de *252* gulf of the English Channel to the NW of France
St-Marc *286* W Haiti
St-Marc, Canal de *286* channel of the Caribbean Sea between Île de la Gonâve and W Haiti
Sainte Marie, Nosy *382* *var.* Nosy Boraha. Island of NE Madagascar
Ste. Marie *649* NE Martinique
Ste-Marie *652* NE Réunion
St Martin *650* island of N Netherlands Antilles
St. Martin *646* island of N Guadeloupe
St. Martins *121* SE Barbados
St.Moritz *546* *Ger.* Sankt Mortiz, *Rmsch.* San Murezzan. SE Switzerland
St-Nazaire *252* W France
St-Nicolas *see* Sint-Niklaas
St. Patricks *121* S Barbados
St-Paul *652* NW Réunion
St Paul *599* Minnesota, NC USA
St. Paul *368* river of Guinea and Liberia
St. Paul's *494* NW St Kitts, St Kitts & Nevis
Saint Paul's Bay *see* San Pawl il Baħar
St Paul's Point *651* headland of Pitcairn Island, S Pitcairn Islands
St Peter Port *647* ❖ of Guernsey, C Guernsey
St Peters *494* SE St Kitts, St Kitts & Nevis
St Petersburg *599* Florida, SE USA
Saint Petersburg *484, 488* *var.* Sankt-Peterburg, *prev.* Leningrad, Petrograd. NW Russian Federation
St. Philips *92* SE Antigua, Antigua & Barbuda
Saint-Pierre *652* ❖ of Saint Pierre and Miquelon, SE Saint Pierre
Saint Pierre *652* island of SE Saint Pierre and Miquelon
St-Pierre *652* SW Réunion
St Pierre *649* NW Martinique
St. Pierre *512* island of the Farquhar Group, Seychelles
St. Pierre and Miquelon *652* French territorial collectivity of the Atlantic Ocean ❖ Saint-Pierre
St. Sampson *647* S Guernsey
Saint Sauveur *224* E Dominica
Saint Thomas Island *653* island of W Virgin Islands
Saint Thomas Island *see* São Tomé
St-Trond *see* Sint-Truiden
Saint Vincent *498* island of the Lesser Antilles which, with the Northern Grenadines forms the independent state of St Vincent & the Grenadines
Saint Vincent and the Grenadines *498-499* country of the West Indies. ❖ Kingstown
St Willibrordus *650* Curaçao, S Netherlands Antilles
Saipan *650* island of S Northern Mariana Islands
Saipan *650* ❖ of Northern Mariana Islands, Saipan, S Northern Mariana Islands
Saishū *see* Cheju
Sajama, Nevado *136* mountain of W Bolivia
Sakaide *330* Shikoku, SW Japan
Sakākah *506* N Saudi Arabia
Sakalua *583* islet of Nukufetau, Tuvalu
Sakanthit *see* Saganthit Island
Sakarya *see* Adapazarı
Sakarya *576* river of NW Turkey
Sakata *330* Honshū, N Japan
Sakchu *349* W North Korea
Sakété *132* S Benin
Sakhalin, Ostrov *485* island of SE Russian Federation
Sakha, Respublika *484* *var.* Respublika Yakutiya. Autonomous republic of E Russian Federation
Şäki *110* *Rus.* Sheki, *var.* Šeki, *prev.* Nukha. NW Azerbaijan
Sakijang Bendera, Pulau *517* *prev.* St. John's Island S Singapore
Sakijang Pelepah, Pulau *517* *prev.* Lazarus Island S Singapore
Sakis-Adasi *see* Chíos
Sakishima-shotō *330* island group of Nansei-shotō, SW Japan
Sakon Nakhon *563* NE Thailand
Sakra, Pulau *517* island of SW Singapore
Sakskøbing *218* Lolland, SE Denmark
Sal *176* island of NE Cape Verde
Šaľa *519* *Hung.* Sellye. SW Slovakia
Sala Ban Thin *359* C Laos
Salacgrīva *362* N Latvia
Salado *210* river of SE Cuba
Salaga *270* C Ghana
Sala'ilua *500* Savai'i, Samoa
Salala *368* C Liberia
Şalalah *448* SW Oman
Salamá *278* C Guatemala
Salamanca *403* C Mexico
Salamanca *530* NW Spain
Salamat *180* river of S Chad
Salamīyah *551* *var.* Selemia. W Syria
Salani *500* Upolu, Samoa
Salcedo *226* N Dominican Republic
Šalčininkai *376* SE Lithuania
Saldus *362* *Ger.* Frauenburg. W Latvia
Sale *101* SE Australia
Salé *414* NW Morocco
Sale'imou *500* Upolu, Samoa
Salekhard *484* *prev.* Obdorsk. N Russian Federation
Salelologa *500* Savai'i, Samoa
Salem *649* W Montserrat
Salem *296* S India
Salem *540* S Swaziland
Salem *598* Oregon, NW USA
Salemy *see* As Salimi
Salentina, Penisola *321* peninsula of S Italy
Salerno *321* S Italy
Salerno, Golfo di *321* gulf of the Tyrrhenian Sea, on the W coast of Italy
Salgótarján *290* N Hungary
Salibea *570* NE Trinidad, Trinidad & Tobago
Salibia *224* NE Dominica
Salihorsk *122* *Rus.* Soligorsk. S Belarus
Salikene *261* W Gambia
Salima *385* C Malawi
Salinas *see* Chixoy
Salinas *228* W Ecuador
Saline Island *276* island to the S of Carriacou, Grenada
Salisbury *593* S England, UK
Salisbury *224* *var.* Baroui. W Dominica
Salisbury *see* Harare
Salisbury, Lake *see* Bisina, Lake
Salisbury Plain *593* plain of S England, UK
Salitje *540* S Swaziland
Saljani *see* Salyan
Salkhad *551* SW Syria
Salla *249* NE Finland
Sallūm, Khalīj as *see* Sollum, Gulf of
Sallyana *see* Salyan
Salomon Atoll *643* atoll of N British Indian Ocean Territory
Salona *see* Solin
Salon-de-Provence *253* SE France
Salonica *see* Thessaloníki
Saloum *510* river of C Senegal
Salpausselkä *249* physical region of S Finland
Sal Rei *176* *var.* Vila de Sal Rei. Boa Vista, E Cape Verde
Salt *see* As Salţ
Salta *95* N Argentina
Saltholm *218* island of E Denmark
Saltibus *497* S St Lucia
Saltillo *403* N Mexico
Salt Island *643* island of SE British Virgin Islands
Salt Island Passage *643* passage of the Caribbean Sea between Peter Island and Salt Island, S British Virgin Islands
Salt Lake City *598* Utah, SW USA
Salto *607* NW Uruguay
Salto del Guairá *460* E Paraguay
Salto Grande, Embalse de *607* reservoir of Argentina and Uruguay
Saltpond *270* SE Ghana
Salvador *145* *prev.* São Salvador. E Brazil
Salvaleón de Higüey *see* Higüey
Salwa *see* As Salwá
Salwá, Dawḩat as *479* *var.* Dawḩat Salwah. Inlet of the Gulf of Bahrain on the coast of SW Qatar
Salwah *see* As Salwá
Salween *159, 186, 563* *Chin.* Nu Chiang, *var.* Nu Jiang, *Bur.* Thanlwin. River of SE Asia
Salyan *110* *Rus.* Sal'yany, *var.* Saljani. SE Azerbaijan
Salyan *427* *var.* Sallyana. W Nepal
Salzburg *106* N Austria
Salzburg Alps *106* *Ger.* Salzburger Kalkalpen. Mountain range of C Austria
Salzgitter *265* *prev.* Watenstedt-Salzgitter. C Germany
Samāhīj *115* Jazirat al Muharraq, Bahrain
Samā'il *448* *var.* Sumail. NE Oman
Samales Group *466* island group of Sulu Archipelago, SW Philippines

Samaná *226* NE Dominican Republic
Samana Cay *112* island of SE Bahamas
Samar *466* island of E Philippines
Samar *336* NW Jordan
Samara *484* *prev.* Kuybyshev. W Russian Federation
Samarai *458* SE Papua New Guinea
Samarinda *302* Borneo, C Indonesia
Samarkandski *see* Temirtau
Samarqand *610* *Rus.* Samarkand. SE Uzbekistan
Sāmarrā' *310* C Iraq
Samawa *see* As Samāwah
Şamaxı *110* *Rus.* Shemakha. C Azerbaijan
Sambava *382* NE Madagascar
Sambre *127* river of Belgium and France
Samchi *134* SW Bhutan
Samch'ŏk *350* *Jap.* Sanchoku. NE South Korea
Samch'ŏnpŏ *350* *Jap.* Sansenhō. S South Korea
Samdrup Jongkhar *134* SE Bhutan
Same *560* NE Tanzania
Samfya *635* *var.* Samfya Mission. N Zambia
Sam Hall's Bay *643* bay of the North Atlantic Ocean, E Bermuda
Samina *374* river of Austria and Liechtenstein
Saminatal Valley *374* valley of Austria and Liechtenstein
Sam Neua *see* Xam Nua
Samoa *500-501* officially Independent State of Samoa, Sam. Samoa i Sisfo. Country of the Pacific Ocean divided into 11 admin. units (districts). ❖ Apia
Samobor *209* N Croatia
Samokov *152* W Bulgaria
Sámos *273* island of SE Greece
Samosch *see* Someş
Samothráki *273* *Eng.* Samothrace. Island of NE Greece
Samsø *218* island of C Denmark
Samsun *577* N Turkey
Samtredia *262* W Georgia
Samui, Ko *563* island of S Thailand
Samur *110* river of Azerbaijan and Russian Federation
Samut Prakan *563* *var.* Muang Samut Prakan. C Thailand
Samut Sakhon *563* C Thailand
San *165* *var.* Se San. River of Cambodia and Vietnam
San *392* C Mali
San *471* river of SE Poland
Sana *140* river of NW Bosnia & Herzegovina
Sana *627* *Ar.* Şan'ā'. ❖ of Yemen, W Yemen
Saña *463* NW Peru
Sanābis *115* N Bahrain
Sanae *90* South African research station of Greater Antarctica, Antarctica
Sanaga *168* river of C Cameroon
Sanandaj *307* NW Iran
San Antonio *130* SW Belize
San Antonio *599* Texas, SC USA
San Antonio, Cabo *210* cape of W Cuba
San Antonio de Cortés *288* W Honduras
San Antonio del Táchira *619* W Venezuela
San Antonio de Ureca *see* Ureca
Sanāw *627* *var.* Sanaw. NE Yemen
San Bernardo *183* C Chile
San Blas, Cordillera de *456* mountain range of NE Panama
San Carlos *645* East Falkland, N Falkland Islands
San Carlos *183* C Chile
San Carlos *466* Luzon, N Philippines
San Carlos *206* river of N Costa Rica
San Carlos *619* C Venezuela
San Carlos *see* Luba
San Carlos *460* river of C Paraguay
San Carlos *607* S Uruguay
San Carlos *436* S Nicaragua
San Carlos City *466* Negros, C Philippines
San Carlos de Bariloche *95* SW Argentina
San Carlos del Zulia *619* W Venezuela
Sanchoku *see* Samch'ŏk
San-ch'ung *555* N Taiwan
San Cristobal *522* *var.* Makira. Island of the E Solomon Islands
San Cristóbal *210* W Cuba
San Cristóbal *619* W Venezuela
San Cristóbal *226* *var.* Benemérita de San Cristóbal. S Dominican Republic
San Cristóbal, Isla *228* island of SE Galapagos Is, Ecuador
Sancti Spíritus *210* C Cuba
Sandakan *387* NE Borneo, Malaysia
Sandalwood Island *see* Sumba
Sandefjord *444* S Norway
San Diego *598* California, W USA
Sand Island *648* island of C Johnston Atoll
Sandnes *444* SW Norway
Sandoway *159* W Burma
Sandoy *644* island of C Faeroe Islands
Sandwich Islands *see* Efate
Sandwīp Channel *117* river of S Bangladesh
Sandy Bay *652* bay of the South Atlantic Ocean on the S coast of St Helena
Sandy Desert *450* desert region of W Pakistan
Sandy Island *276* island to the N of Grenada island, Grenada
Sandykachi *581* *var.* Sandykači, *Turkm.* Sandykgachy. SE Turkmenistan
Sandy Point *652* headland on the E coast of Tristan da Cunha
Sandy Point Town *494* W St Kitts, St Kitts & Nevis
Sanem *378* S Luxembourg
San Estanislao *460* C Paraguay
San Eugenio *see* Artigas
San Eugenio del Cuareim *see* Artigas
San Felipe *619* NW Venezuela
San Felipe de Puerto Plata *see* Puerto Plata
San Fernando *466* Luzon, N Philippines
San Fernando *619* *var.* San Fernando de Apure. C Venezuela
San Fernando *570* SW Trinidad & Tobago, Trinidad & Tobago
San Fernando del Valle de Catamarca *95* *var.* Catamarca. NW Argentina
San Francisco *598* California, W USA
San Francisco *619* NW Venezuela
San Francisco *235* *var.* San Francisco Gotera. E El Salvador
San Francisco *95* C Argentina
San Francisco de la Paz *288* C Honduras
San Francisco de Macorís *226* NE Dominican Republic
Sângerei *see* Sîngerei
San Germán *651* W Puerto Rico
Sangha *200* river of N Congo
Sangihe, Kepulauan *302* island group to the NE of Celebes, C Indonesia
Sangju *350* *Jap.* Shōshū. C South Korea
Sângkê *165* *prev.* Sangker. River of W Cambodia
Sangmélima *168* S Cameroon
Sangre Grande *570* NE Trinidad, Trinidad & Tobago
San Ignacio *460* S Paraguay
San Ignacio *136* E Bolivia
San Ignacio *136* N Bolivia
San Ignacio *235* N El Salvador
San Ignacio *130* *prev.* El Cayo, Cayo. W Belize
Saniquellie *see* Sanniquellie
San Isidro *206* SE Costa Rica
San Javier *183* C Chile
San Jorge *522* island to the SE of Santa Isabel, Solomon Is
San Jorge, Golfo *95* gulf of the Atlantic Ocean, to the SE of Argentina
San José *206* ❖ of Costa Rica, C Costa Rica
San José *136* *var.* San José de Chiquitos. E Bolivia
San José *see* Puerto San José
San José de Cúcuta *see* Cúcuta
San José de Bocay *436* N Nicaragua
San José del Guaviare *195* SE Colombia
San José de Mayo *607* S Uruguay
San José de Ocoa *226* S Dominican Republic
San Juan *651* ❖ of Puerto Rico, N Puerto Rico
San Juan *206* river of Costa Rica and Nicaragua
San Juan *226* W Dominican Republic
San Juan *95* W Argentina
San Juan, Cabo *236* cape on the W coast of Río Muni, Equatorial Guinea
San Juan *436* river of S Nicaragua
San Juan Bautista *183* Isla Robinson Crusoe, W Chile
San Juan Bautista *460* S Paraguay
San Juan del Monte *466* Luzon, N Philippines
San Juan de los Morros *619* N Venezuela
Sankal *222* border crossing point, SW Djibouti
Sankarani *281* river of NE Guinea
Sankosh *134* river of S Bhutan
Sankt Anton am Arlberg *106* W Austria
Sankt Gallen *546* *Fr.* Saint-Gall, *Eng.* Saint Gall. NE Switzerland
Sankt Martin *see* Martin
Sankt Michel *see* Mikkeli
Sankt-Peterburg *see* St. Petersburg
Sankt Pölten *106* N Austria
Sankt Veit am Flaum *see* Rijeka
Sankt Veit an der Glan *106* S Austria
Sankt Wolfgangsee *see* Wolfgangsee
Sankuru *203* river of C Dem. Rep. Congo (Zaire)
San Lázaro *460* NE Paraguay
Şanlıurfa *577* *prev.* Urfa. S Turkey
San Lorenzo *288* S Honduras
San Lorenzo *136* S Bolivia
San Lorenzo *228* N Ecuador
San Lorenzo *436* S Nicaragua
San Lucas *130* S Belize
San Luis *210* SE Cuba
San Luis *278* NE Guatemala
San Luis *235* S El Salvador
San Luis *95* C Argentina
San Luis Potosí *403* C Mexico
San Marcos *206* C Costa Rica
San Marcos *278* W Guatemala
San Marino *502* ❖ of San Marino, C San Marino
San Marino *321, 502-503* officially Republic of San Marino. Country of S Europe divided into 9 admin. units (districts). ❖ San Marino
San Martín *90* Argentinian research station of Antarctic Peninsula, Antarctica
San Martín *235* C El Salvador
San Matías *136* E Bolivia
San Matías, Golfo *95* gulf of the Atlantic Ocean, on the E coast of Argentina
San Miguel *456* Isla del Rey, Panama
San Miguel *235* SE El Salvador
San Miguel *228* river of Colombia and Ecuador
San Miguel de Ibarra *see* Ibarra
San Miguel de Tucumán *95* *var.* Tucumán. N Argentina
San Miguel, Golfo de *456* inlet of the Gulf of Panama to the S of Panama
San Miguelito *456* C Panama
San Murezzan *see* St.Moritz
Sannār *see* Senna
San Nicolas *642* S Aruba
San Nicolás de los Arroyos *95* E Argentina
Sanniquellie *368* NE Liberia
San Pablo *466* Luzon, N Philippines
San Pablo *456* river of SW Panama
San Pablo *136* S Bolivia
San Pablo *130* N Belize
San Pawl il Baħar *395* *Eng.* Saint Paul's Bay. NW Malta
San Pedro *460* SE Paraguay
San Pedro *278* river of Guatemala and Mexico
San Pedro *130* NE Belize
San-Pédro *326* S Ivory Coast
San Pedro Carchá *278* C Guatemala
San Pedro del Durazno *see* Durazno
San Pedro de Lloc *463* NW Peru
San Pedro de Macorís *226* SE Dominican Republic
San Pedro Sula *288* NW Honduras
San Rafael *206* NW Costa Rica
San Rafael *235* C El Salvador
San Rafael *95* W Argentina
San Rafael del Moján *619* NW Venezuela
San Rafael del Sur *436* SW Nicaragua
San Ramón *206* C Costa Rica
San Ramón *607* S Uruguay
San Remo *320* N Italy
San Salvador *235* ❖ of El Salvador, SW El Salvador
San Salvador *112* *prev.* Watlings I. Island of E Bahamas
San Salvador, Isla *see* Santiago, Isla
San Salvador de Jujuy *95* *var.* Jujuy. N Argentina
Sansanné-Mango *567* *var.* Mango. N Togo
San Sebastián *651* NW Puerto Rico
Sansenhō *see* Samch'ŏnpŏ
San Severo *321* S Italy
Santa Ana *235* NW El Salvador
Santa Ana, Volcan de *235* *var.* La Matepec. Volcanic peak of W El Salvador
Santa Ana de Coro *see* Coro
Santa Bárbara *288* W Honduras
Santa Caterina *650* Curaçao, S Netherlands Antilles
Santa Clara *210* C Cuba
Santa Coloma *86* SW Andorra
Santa Comba *see* Uaco Cungo
Santa Cruz *206* W Costa Rica
Santa Cruz *505* SE São Tomé, Sao Tome & Principe
Santa Cruz *136* *var.* Santa Cruz de la Sierra. C Bolivia
Santa Cruz *329* SW Jamaica
Santa Cruz, Isla *228* island of C Galapagos Is, Ecuador
Santa Cruz de El Seibo *see* El Seibo
Santa Cruz del Sur *210* S Cuba
Santa Cruz de Tenerife *531* Islas Canarias, SW Spain
Santa Cruz Islands *522* island group of E Solomon Is
Santa Elena *130* W Belize
Santa Fe *95* NE Argentina
Santa Fé *210* *var.* La Fe. Isla de la Juventud, Cuba
Santa Fé *456* W Panama
Santa Fe *598* New Mexico, SW USA
Santa Isabel *see* Malabo
Santa Isabel *522* *Poly.* Boghotu. Island of the C Solomon Islands
Santa Isabel *278* *var.* Cancuén. River of N Guatemala
Santa Isabel, Pico de *see* Basilé, Pico de
Santa Lucía *607* S Uruguay
Santa Lucía Cotzumalguapa *278* SW Guatemala
Santa Luzia *176* island of N Cape Verde
Santa Maria *474* island of the Azores, Portugal
Santa Maria *206* S Costa Rica
Santa Maria *145* S Brazil
Santa Maria *176* Sal, NE Cape Verde
Santa María, Isla *228* island of S Galapagos Is, Ecuador
Santa Maria Island *615* Banks Islands, N Vanuatu
Santa Marta *195* N Colombia
Santa Maura *see* Lefkada
Santana *505* NE São Tomé, Sao Tome & Principe
Santander *531* N Spain
Sant' Antioco *320* Sardegna, W Italy
Santarém *474* W Portugal
Santarém *145* N Brazil

Santa Rita *647* SW Guam
Santa Rosa *228* SW Ecuador
Santa Rosa *95* C Argentina
Santa Rosa de Copán *288* W Honduras
Santa Rosa de Lima *235* E El Salvador
Santa Tecla *see* Nueva San Salvador
Santiago *see* Grande de Santiago
Santiago *183* ❖ of Chile, C Chile
Santiago *530* *var.* Santiago de Compostela. NW Spain
Santiago *226* *var.* Santiago de los Caballeros. NW Dominican Republic
Santiago *176* *var.* São Tiago. Island of S Cape Verde
Santiago *456* SW Panama
Santiago de Cuba *210* SE Cuba
Santiago de Guayaquil *see* Guayaquil
Santiago del Estero *95* C Argentina
Santiago, Isla *228* *var.* Isla San Salvador. Island of C Galapagos Is, Ecuador
Santiago Maior *176* Santiago, S Cape Verde
Santi Quaranta *see* Sarandë
Sant Joan de Caselles *86* NE Andorra
Sant Julià de Lòria *86* SW Andorra
Sant Miguel d'Engolasters *86* C Andorra
Santo *see* Espiritu Santo
Santo André *145* S Brazil
Santo Antão *176* island of N Cape Verde
Santo António *176* Maio, S Cape Verde
Santo António *505* *var.* São António. N Príncipe, Sao Tome & Principe
Santo Domingo *210* C Cuba
Santo Domingo *226* *prev.* Ciudad Trujillo. ❖ of Dominican Republic, S Dominican Republic
Santo Domingo de los Colorados *228* NW Ecuador
Santon *647* SE Isle of Man
Santos *145* S Brazil
Santo Tomás *235* SW El Salvador
Santo Tomás de Castilla *278* E Guatemala
Santuari de Méritxell *86* C Andorra
San Vicente *235* C El Salvador
San Vito *206* SE Costa Rica
Sanyati *636* river of N Zimbabwe
São Bernardo do Campo *145* S Brazil
São Domingos *282* W Guinea-Bissau
São Filipe *176* Fogo island, S Cape Verde
São Francisco *145* river of E Brazil
São Jorge *474* island of the Azores, Portugal
São José do Rio Preto *145* S Brazil
São José dos Campos *145* S Brazil
São Luís *145* NE Brazil
São Manuel *144-145* *var.* Teles Piras. River of W Brazil
São Marcos, Baía de *145* bay of the Atlantic Ocean, on the coast of N Brazil
São Miguel *474* island of the Azores, Portugal
Saona, Isla *226* island of SE Dominican Republic
Saône *253* river of E France
São Nicolau *176* island of N Cape Verde
São Paulo *145, 149* S Brazil
São Pedro *176* São Vincente, N Cape Verde
São Pedro do Rio Grande do Sul *see* Rio Grande
São Salvador *see* Salvador
São Salvador do Congo *see* M'Banza Congo
São Simão, Represa de *145* reservoir of S Brazil
São Tiago *see* Santiago
São Tomé *505* *Eng.* Saint Thomas. Island of S Sao Tome & Principe
São Tomé *505* ❖ of Sao Tome & Principe, NE São Tomé
Sao Tome & Principe *504-505* officially Democratic Republic of Sao Tome and Principe, *Port.* São Tomé e Príncipe. Country of W Africa divided into 7 admin. units (districts). ❖ São Tomé
São Tomé, Pico de *505* mountain of São Tomé, Sao Tome & Principe
São Vicente *145* S Brazil
São Vicente *176* island of N Cape Verde
Sapele *440* S Nigeria
Sapitwa *385* mountain of S Malawi
Saponé *157* C Burkina
Sappemeer *429* NE Netherlands
Sapporo *330* Hokkaidō, N Japan
Sapta Koshi *427* river of India and Nepal
Sār *115* NW Bahrain
Šara *381* mountain range of FYR Macedonia and Yugoslavia
Sara Buri *563* C Thailand
Saragossa *see* Zaragoza
Saragt *581* *prev.* Serakhs, *var.* Serahs. S Turkmenistan
Sarajevo *140* ❖ of Bosnia & Herzegovina, SE Bosnia & Herzegovina
Saran' *338* C Kazakhstan
Sarandë *81* *var.* Saranda, *It.* Porto Edda, *prev.* Santi Quaranta. S Albania
Sarandí del Yí *607* C Uruguay
Sarandí Grande *607* S Uruguay
Sarangani Islands *466* island group of SE Philippines
Saratov *484* W Russian Federation
Saravan *359* *var.* Saravane. SE Laos
Sarbhang *134* S Bhutan
Sardegna *320* *Eng.* Sardinia. Island of W Italy
Sardinia *see* Sardegna
Sargodha *451* NE Pakistan
Sarh *180* *prev.* Fort-Archambault. S Chad
Sārī *307* N Iran
Sarigan *650* island of C Northern Mariana Islands
Sarikol Range *558* *Rus.* Sarykol'skiy Khrebet. Mountain range of China and Tajikistan
Sarimbun Reservoir *517* NW Singapore
Sariwŏn *349* SW North Korea
Sark *647* island of SE Guernsey
Sarpsborg *444* S Norway
Sarrebruck *see* Saarbrücken
Sarstoon *130, 278* *var.* Sarstún. River of Belize and Guatemala
Sarstún *see* Sarstoon
Sarthe *253* river of NW France
Saruhan *see* Manisa
Sarykol'skiy Khrebet *see* Sarikol Range
Sary-Tash *357* *var.* Sary-Ta#. SW Kyrgyzstan
Sasebo *330* Kyūshū, SW Japan
Saseno *see* Sazan
Saskatchewan *170* river of C Canada
Saskatchewan *170* province of C Canada
Saskatoon *170* SW Canada
Sasolburg *527* Orange Free State, C South Africa
Sassandra *326* S Ivory Coast
Sassandra *326* *var.* Ibo. River of S Ivory Coast
Sassari *320* Sardegna, W Italy
Sassnitz *265* NE Germany
Sasstown *368* SE Liberia
Sataua *500* Savai'i, Samoa
Satawal *406* island of C Micronesia
Satawan *406* atoll of C Micronesia
Sātkhira *117* SW Bangladesh
Satpura Range *296* mountains of C India
Satu Mare *480* *Hung.* Szatmárnémeti. NW Romania
Satunan-shotō *330* island group of Nansei-shotō, SW Japan
Sau *see* Sava
Sauce *see* Juan L. Lacaze
Saudhárkrókur *294* N Iceland
Saudi Arabia *506-509* officially Kingdom of Saudi Arabia. Country of SW Asia divided into 13 admin. units (provinces). ❖ Riyadh
Saül *645* C French Guiana
Saulkrasti *362* N Latvia
Sault Sainte Marie *171* S Canada
Sauma, Pointe *653* headland of Île Alofi, N Wallis & Futuna
Saûmâtre, Étang *286* lake of SE Haiti
Saurimo *88* *Port.* Vila Henrique de Carvalho. NE Angola
Sauteurs *276* N Grenada island, Grenada
Sava *140, 209, 520, 630* *Eng.* Save, *Hung.* Száva, *Ger.* Sau. River of SE Europe
Savai'i *500* island of NW Samoa
Savalou *132* S Benin
Savan Island *498* island of S St Vincent & the Grenadines
Savannah *599* Georgia, SE USA
Savannakhét *359* S Laos
Savanna-La-Mar *329* W Jamaica
Savave *583* islet of Nukufetau, Tuvalu
Save *419, 636* *var.* Sabi. River of Mozambique and Zimbabwe
Savè *132* SE Benin
Savissivik *646* NW Greenland
Savona *320* N Italy
Savonlinna *249* *Swe.* Nyslott. SE Finland
Savusavu *246* Vanua Levu, N Fiji
Savu Sea *see* Sawu, Laut
Savute *142* river of N Botswana
Sawdā', Jabal *506* mountain of SW Saudi Arabia
Sawdā, Jabal as *371* mountain range of C Libya
Sawdirī *see* Sodiri
Sawhaj *see* Sohâg
Şawqirah *448* SE Oman
Şawqirah, Ghubbat *see* Suqrah Bay
Sawu, Laut *302* *Eng.* Savu Sea. Sea of the Indian Ocean, C Indonesia
Say *439* SW Niger
Sayaboury *see* Muang Xaignabouri
Sayat *581* E Turkmenistan
Sayhūt *627* E Yemen
Saylac *524* *var.* Zeila. NW Somalia
Saynshand *412* S Mongolia
Say 'ūn *627* *var.* Saywūn. C Yemen
Sazan *81* *It.* Saseno. Island of SW Albania
Scaldis *see* Scheldt
Scarborough *593* NE England, UK
Scarborough *570* S Tobago, Trinidad & Tobago
Scarborough *121* S Barbados
Scebeli *see* Shebeli
Schaan *374* W Liechtenstein
Schaanwald *374* NE Liechtenstein
Schaffhausen *546* N Switzerland
Schaulen *see* Šiauliai
Schefferville *171* E Canada
Scheldt *127* *Dut.* Schelde, *Fr.* Escaut. River of W Europe
Schellenberg *374* N Liechtenstein
Schiedam *429* SW Netherlands
Schiermonnikoog *429* island of Waddeneilanden, N Netherlands
Schifflange *378* S Luxembourg
Schneekoppe *see* Sněžka
Schneidemühl *see* Pila
Schœlcher *649* W Martinique
Schoten *127* N Belgium
Schouwen *429* island of SW Netherlands
Schwäbische Alb *264* *Eng.* Swabian Jura. Mountain range of SW Germany
Schwarzwald *see* Black Forest
Schwaz *106* W Austria
Schweizer Mittelland *see* Swiss Plateau
Schweizer Reneke *527* North West, N South Africa
Schwerin *265* N Germany
Schweriner See *264* lake of N Germany
Schwyz *546* C Switzerland
Schyl *see* Jiu
Sciacca *321* Sicilia, S Italy
Sciasciamana *see* Shashemenee
Scio *see* Chíos
Scoresbysund *see* Ittoqqortoormiit
Scotland *593, 597* national region of UK divided into 12 admin. units (9 regions, 3 island authorities)
Scott Base *90* New Zealand research station near Ross Shelf, Antarctica
Scott Island *90* island to the N of Ross Ice Shelf, Antarctica
Scotts Head Village *224* *var.* Cachacrou. S Dominica
Scrub Island *642* island of NE Anguilla
Scunthorpe *593* NE England, UK
Scutari *see* Shkodër
Scutari, Lake *81, 630* *Alb.* Liqeni i Shkodrës, *SCr.* Skadarsko Jezero. Lake of Albania and Yugoslavia
Seal Island *642* island of NW Anguilla
Seatons *92* E Antigua, Antigua & Barbuda
Seattle *598, 603* Washington, NW USA
Sébaco *436* C Nicaragua
Sebaiera *414* C Western Sahara
Sebapala *366* SW Lesotho
Sebarok, Pulau *517* island S Singapore
Sebastían Vizcaíno, Bahía *403* bay of the Pacific Ocean, on the NW coast of Mexico
Sebastopol *see* Sevastopol'
Sebenico *see* Šibenik
Sébikhoutane *510* W Senegal
Sebou *414* river of N Morocco
Secos, Ilhéus *see* Rombo, Ilhéus de
Sedberat *238* W Eritrea
Sédhiou *510* SW Senegal
Seeheim Noord *423* S Namibia
Seeland *see* Sjælland
Sefadu *514* E Sierra Leone
Sefrou *414* N Morocco
Segamat *386* S of Peninsular Malaysia
Ségbana *132* NE Benin
Segewold *see* Sigulda
Segna *see* Senj
Ségou *392* *var.* Segu C Mali
Segovia *531* C Spain
Segovia *see* Coco
Segu *see* Ségou
Séguédine *439* NE Niger
Séguéla *326* W Ivory Coast
Séguénéga *157* NW Burkina
Segura *531* river of S Spain
Sehlabathebe *366* E Lesotho
Seinäjoki *249* *Swe.* Östermyra. SW Finland
Seine *253* river of N France
Seine, Baie de la *252-253* bay of the English Channel to the NW of France
Seiyū *see* Chŏngju
Sejerø *218* island of C Denmark
Šeki *see* Şäki
Sekoma *142* S Botswana
Sekondi-Takoradi *270* S Ghana
Selânik *see* Thessaloníki
Selemia *see* Salamīyah
Selenge *412* river of Mongolia and Russian Federation
Seletar Reservoir *517* reservoir of C Singapore
Selfoss *294* SW Iceland
Seli *see* Rokel
Sélibabi *398* S Mauritania
Selibi Phikwe *142* E Botswana
Sélingué, Lac de *392* reservoir of S Mali
Selle, Massif de la *286* mountain range of S Haiti
Selle, Pic la *286* *var.* La Selle. Mountain of S Haiti
Sellore Island *see* Saganthit Island
Sellye *see* Skalica
Sellye *see* Šaľa
Sélouma *281* C Guinea
Selukwe *see* Shurugwi
Selvagens, Ilhas *474* island group of the Madeira Is, Portugal
Semakau, Pulau *517* island S Singapore
Semanit *81* *var.* Seman. River of W Albania
Semara *414* N Western Sahara
Semarang *302* Java, C Indonesia
Sembawang *517* area of N Singapore
Sembé *200* NW Congo
Sembehun *514* SW Sierra Leone
Semberong *386* river of SE Peninsular Malaysia

Semendria *see* Smederevo
Semipalatinsk *338 Kaz.* Semey. E Kazakhstan
Semirara Islands *466* island group of C Philippines
Semliki *584* river of W Uganda
Sên *165 var.* Sen. River of C Cambodia
Sena *see* Vila de Sena
Senafe *238* SE Eritrea
Senanayake Samudra *534* lake of E Sri Lanka
Senanga *635* SW Zambia
Senang, Pulau *517* island of S Singapore
Sendai *330* Kyūshū, SW Japan
Sendai *330* Honshū, N Japan
Senegal *510-511* officially Republic of Senegal. *Fr.* Sénégal. Country of West Africa divided into 10 admin. units (regions). ❖ Dakar
Senegal *398, 392, 510 Fr.* Sénégal. River of W Africa
Senica *519 Ger.* Senitz, *Hung.* Szenice. W Slovakia
Senigallia *321* C Italy
Senj *209 Ger.* Zengg, Ital. Segna. NW Croatia
Senja *444 prev.* Senjen. Island of NW Norway
Senkaku-shotō *330* island group of Nansei-shotō, SW Japan
Senmonorom *165* E Cambodia
Sennar *536 var.* Sannār. C Sudan
Senne *127 Dut.* Zenne. River of C Belgium
Senqunyane *366* river of C Lesotho
Senshin-kō *see* Sŏmjin
Sensuntepeque *235* NE El Salvador
Sentery *203* SE Dem. Rep. Congo (Zaire)
Sentosa *517* island S Singapore
Senye *236* W Río Muni, Equatorial Guinea
Seongnam *see* Sŏngnam
Seoul *350 Kor.* Sŏul, *prev.* Kyŏngsŏng, *Jap.* Keijō. of South Kore NW South Korea
Sepik *458* river of Indonesia and Papua New Guinea
Sepone *see* Muang Xéphôn
Sept-Iles *170* E Canada
Serahs *see* Saragt
Seraing *127* E Belgium
Serakhis *see* Serrakhis
Serakhs *see* Saragt
Seram *302 var.* Serang, *Eng.* Ceram. Island of Maluku, E Indonesia
Seram, Laut *302 Eng.* Ceram Sea. Sea of the Pacific Ocean, E Indonesia
Serang *302* Java, C Indonesia
Serangoon Harbour *517* harbour, E Singapore
Serasan, Selat *302, 386* strait of the South China Sea between Borneo and Kepulauan Natuna, W Indonesia
Seraya, Pulau *517* island of SW Singapore
Serbia *630 Serb.* Srbija. Republic of Yugoslavia
Sereď *519 Hung.* Szered. SW Slovakia
Serekunda *261* W Gambia
Seremban *386* W Peninsular Malaysia
Serengeti Plain *560* plain of N Tanzania
Serenje *635* E Zambia
Sereth *see* Siret
Sérifos *273* island of SE Greece
Serov *484* C Russian Federation
Serowe *142* SE Botswana
Serpa Pinto *see* Menongue
Serpent's Mouth, The *570 Sp.* Boca de la Serpiente. Strait connecting the Colombus Channel and the Gulf of Paria
Serrakhis *215 var.* Serrachis, Serakhis. River of NW Cyprus
Serravalle *502* N San Marino
Sérres *273 prev.* Sérrai. NE Greece
Serule *142* E Botswana
Se San *see* Tônlé San
Sesana *see* Sežana
Sese Islands *584* island group of S Uganda
Sesvete *209* N Croatia
Seti *427* river of W Nepal
Sétif *83 var.* Stif. N Algeria
Settat *414* W Morocco
Setté Cama *258* SW Gabon
Settlement, The *643* Anegada, N British Virgin Islands
Setúbal *474* W Portugal
Setúbal, Baía de *474* bay of the Atlantic Ocean, to the SW of Portugal
Sevan *98* C Armenia
Sevana Lich *98 Eng.* Lake Sevan. Lake of E Armenia
Sevani Lerrnashght'a *see* Shakh-Dag
Sevan, Lake *see* Sevana Lich
Sévaré *392* C Mali
Sevastopol' *586 Eng.* Sebastopol. S Ukraine
Severn *593 Wel.* Hafren. River of England and Wales, UK
Severn *170* river of S Canada
Severnaya Dvina *484 Eng.* Northern Dvina. River of NW Russian Federation
Severnaya Osetiya-Alaniya *484* autonomous republic of SW Russian Federation
Severnaya Zemlya *485* island group of N Russian Federation
Severnyy Ledovityy Okean *see* Arctic Ocean
Severodvinsk *484 prev.* Molotov, *prev.* Sudostroy. NW Russian Federation
Severo-Sibirskaya Nizmennost' *485 Eng.* North Siberian Lowland, *var.* North Siberian Plain. Lowland region of N Russian Federation
Severskiy Donets *see* Donets
Sevilla *530 Eng.* Seville. SW Spain
Sevilla de Niefang *see* Niefang
Sevlievo *152* C Bulgaria
Sewa *514* river E Sierra Leone
Seychelles *512-513* officially Republic of the Seychelles. Country of the Indian Ocean divided into 23 admin. units (districts). ❖ Victoria
Seydhisfjördhur *294* E Iceland
Seydi *581 prev.* Neftezavodsk. E Turkmenistan
Seyhan *577* river of S Turkey
Seyhan *see* Adana
Sežana *520 It.* Sesana. SW Slovenia
Sfântu Gheorghe *480 prev.* Sfintu Gheorghe. C Romania
Sfax *573 var.* Safāqis. E Tunisia
's-Gravenhage *429 var.* Den Haag, *Eng.* The Hague, *Fr.* La Haye. Seat of government, W Netherlands
Shaanxi *187 var.* Shensi, Shan-hsi. Province of C China
Shabani *see* Zvishavane
Shabeelle, Webi *see* Shebeli
Shaddādī *see* Ash Shadādah
Shah Alam *386* W Peninsular Malaysia
Shāhbāzpur *117* river of S Bangladesh
Shāhdādkot *451* SW Pakistan
Shaḥḥāt *371* NE Libya
Shahrikhon *610 Rus.* Shakhrikhan. E Uzbekistan
Shahrisabz *610 Rus.* Shakhrisabz. SE Uzbekistan
Shahr Rey *see* Rey
Shahrtuz *558 Rus.* Shaartuz. W Tajikistan
Shahzadpur *117* W Bangladesh
Shakawe *142* NW Botswana
Shakh-Dag *98 Arm.* Sevani Lerrnashght'a, *Rus.* Shakhdagskiy Khrebet. Mountain range of Armenia and Azerbaijan
Shakhdagskiy Khrebet *see* Shakh-Dag
Shakhrisabz *see* Shahrisabz
Shakhtinsk *338* C Kazakhstan
Shaki *440* W Nigeria
Shām, Bādiyat ash *see* Syrian Desert
Shām, Jabal ash *448 var.* Jebel Sham. Mountain of N Oman
Shandī *see* Shendi
Shandong *187 var.* Shantung. Province of E China
Shandong Bandao *187 var.* Shantung Peninsula. Peninsula of E China
Shangani *636* river of W Zimbabwe
Shanghai *187, 190* city and municipality of E China
Shan-hsi *see* Shaanxi
Shan-hsi *see* Shanxi
Shanhua *555* SW Taiwan
Shannon *314 Ir.* An tSionainn. River of C Ireland
Shansi *see* Shanxi
Shantar Islands *see* Shantarskiye Ostrova
Shantarskiye Ostrova *485 Eng.* Shantar Islands. Island group of SE Russian Federation
Shantou *187 var.* Swatow. Guangdong, SE China
Shantung *see* Shandong
Shantung Peninsula *see* Shandong Bandao
Shanxi *187 var.* Shansi, Shan-hsi. Province of NE China
Shaoguan *187 var.* Shao-kuan, *prev.* Ch'u-chiang, *Cant.* Kukong. Guangdong, SE China
Shao-kuan *see* Shaoguan
Shaqrā' *506* C Saudi Arabia
Shaqrā *see* Shuqrah
Shar *338 var.* Charsk. E Kazakhstan
Sharasume *see* Altay
Shari *see* Chari
Sharïn Gol *412* N Mongolia
Sharjah *590* NE United Arab Emirates
Shark Bay *100* bay to the W of Australia
Sharon, Plain of *see* HaSharon
Sharqī, Jabal ash *see* Anti-Lebanon
Sharqī, Jazīrat ash *see* Chergui, Île
Sharqī, Jebel esh *see* Anti-Lebanon
Shashe *142, 636 var.* Shashi. River of Botswana and Zimbabwe
Shashemenē *243 var.* Shashemenne, Shashhamana, *It.* Sciasciamana. S Ethiopia
Shashi *187 var.* Sha-shih, Shasi. Hubei, C China
Shāṭi', Wādī ash *371* dry watercourse of W Libya
Shaykh, Jabal ash *see* Hermon, Mount
Shaykh 'Uthmān *627* SW Yemen
Shcheglovsk *see* Kemerovo
Shchuchinsk *338* N Kazakhstan
Shea *284* S Guyana
Shebeli *524 Som.* Webi Shabeelle, *Amh.* Shebele Wenz, *It.* Scebeli. River of Ethiopia and Somalia
Sheberghān *77 var.* Shibarghan. N Afghanistan
Shedadi *see* Ash Shadādah
Shefar 'am *317* N Israel
Sheffield *593* N England, UK
Shekhem *see* Náblus
Shekhūpura *451* NE Pakistan
Sheki *see* Şäki
Shelikhova, Zaliv *485 Eng.* Shelekhov Gulf. Gulf of Sea of Okhotsk, bordering NE Russian Federation
Shemakha *see* Şamaxı
Shemgang *134* C Bhutan
Shendi *536 var.* Shandī. NE Sudan
Shengking *see* Liaoning
Shensi *see* Shaanxi
Shenyang *187 prev.* Fengtien, *Eng.* Mukden. Liaoning, NE China
Shepherd Islands *615* islands to the C of Vanuatu
Shepparton *101* SE Australia
Sherbro Island *514* island of SW Sierra Leone
Sherbrooke *171* SE Canada
Sheridan *598* Wyoming, NW USA
Sherpur *117* N Bangladesh
's-Hertogenbosch *429 Ger.* Herzogenbusch, *Fr.* Bois-le-Duc. S Netherlands
Sherwood Ranch *142* SE Botswana
Shetland *593* islands of NE Scotland,UK
Shevchenko *see* Aktau
Shibām *627* C Yemen
Shibarghan *see* Sheberghān
Shibata *330* Honshū, N Japan
Shibh Jazīrat Sīnā' *see* Sinai
Shibīn el Kôm *230 var.* Shibīn al Kawm. N Egypt
Shihmen *see* Shijiazhuang
Shijak *81 var.* Shijaku. W Albania
Shijiazhuang *187 var.* Shihkiaehwang, Shih-chia-chuang, *prev.* Shihmen. Hebei, NE China
Shikārpur *451* S Pakistan
Shikoku *330* island of SW Japan
Shiliguri *296 prev.* Siliguri. NE India
Shimbiris *524 var.* Shimbir Berris. Mountain of N Somalia
Shimizu *330* Honshū, SE Japan
Shimonoseki *330* Honshū, W Japan
Shimonoseki-kaikyō *330* strait connecting the Sea of Japan and Inland Sea, between Honshū and Kyūsh ū, W Japan
Shinano *330* river of Honshū, N Japan
Shināş *448* NW Oman
Shīndand *77* W Afghanistan
Shinei *see* Hsinying
Shinshō *see* Hsinchuang
Shinshū *see* Chinju
Shinten *see* Hsintien
Shinyanga *560* NW Tanzania
Shiogama *330* Honshū, N Japan
Shīrāz *307* SW Iran
Shire *385 Port.* Chire. River of Malawi and Mozambique
Shire Highlands *385* hilly region of S Malawi
Shirvanskaya Step' *see* Şirvan Düzü
Shirwa, Lake *see* Chilwa, Lake
Shizuoka *330* Honshū, SE Japan
Shkodër *81 var.* Shkodra, *It.* Scutari, *SCr.* Skadar. NW Albania
Shkodrës, Liqeni i *see* Scutari, Lake
Shkubinit *81 var.* Shkumbî, Shkumbin. River of C Albania
Shoe Rock *649* headland on the S coast of Montserrat
Shōka *see* Changhua
Sholāpur *see* Solāpur
Shorkot *451* NE Pakistan
Shortland Island *522 var.* Alu. Island of the Shortland Is, W Solomon Islands
Shortland Islands *522* island group of the W Solomon Islands
Shostka *586* N Ukraine
Shreveport *599* Louisiana, SC USA
Shrewsbury *593* C England, UK
Shū *338 var.* Chu. SE Kazakhstan
Shu'aybah *354 var.* Shuaiba. E Kuwait
Shubrâ el Kheima *230 var.* Shubrā al Khaymah. N Egypt
Shūlgareh *77* N Afghanistan
Shumen *152 var.* Šumen. E Bulgaria
Shunsen *see* Ch'unch'ŏn
Shuqrah *627 var.* Shaqrā. SW Yemen
Shurugwi *636 prev.* Selukwe. C Zimbabwe
Shwebo *159* N Burma
Shweli *159* river of Burma and China
Shymkent *338 prev.* Chimkent. S Kazakhstan
Shyashchytsy *122* C Belarus
Siāhān Range *450* mountain range of W Pakistan
Sīāh Kūh *77* mountain range of W Afghanistan
Siālkot *451* NE Pakistan
Siam *see* Thailand
Siam, Gulf of *see* Thailand, Gulf of
Sian *see* Xi'an
Siangtan *see* Xiangtan
Siargao Island *466* island of E Philippines
Šiauliai *376 Ger.* Schaulen. NW Lithuania
Siazan' *see* Siyäzän
Šibenik *209 It.* Sebenico. S Croatia
Siberut, Pulau *302* island of Kepulauan Mentawai, W Indonesia
Sibi *451* C Pakistan
Sibiti *200* S Congo
Sibiu *480 Ger.* Hermannstadt, *Hung.* Nagyszeben. C Romania
Sibu *386* W Borneo, Malaysia
Sibut *179 prev.* Fort-Sibut. C Central African Republic
Sibutu Passage *386* passage connecting Celebes Sea and Sulu Sea

Sibuyan Island *466* island of C Philippines
Sibuyan Sea *466* sea of the Pacific Ocean
Sichuan *187* *var.* Szechuan, Ssu-ch'uan. Province of SW China
Sicilia *321* *Eng.* Sicily. Island of S Italy
Sicily *see* Sicilia
Sico *288* *var.* Tinto, Río Negro. River of NE Honduras
Sicunusa *540* SW Swaziland
Siders *see* Sierre
Sidi Bel Abbès *83* NW Algeria
Sidi Bouzid *573* *var.* Sīdī bū Zayd, Gammouda. C Tunisia
Sidi el Hani, Sebkhet de *573* *var.* Sabkhat Sīd' al Hānī'. Salt flat of NE Tunisia
Sidi Kacem *414* *prev.* Petitjean. N Morocco
Sidra *see* Surt
Sidra, Gulf of *see* Surt, Khalīj
Sidvokodvo *540* C Swaziland
Siegen *264* W Germany
Sielo *368* N Liberia
Siĕmréab *165* *prev.* Siem Reap. NW Cambodia
Siena *321* *Fr.* Sienne. C Italy
Sienne *see* Siena
Sierra de Guadarrama *531* mountains of C Spain
Sierra Leone *514-515* officially Republic of Sierra Leone. Country of W Africa divided into 4 admin. units (provinces). ❖ Freetown
Sierra Madre *466* mountain range of Luzon, N Philippines
Sierra Madre *278, 403* mountain range of Guatemala and Mexico
Sierra Madre del Sur *403* mountain range of S Mexico
Sierra Madre Occidental *403* *var.* Western Sierra Madre. Mountain range of NW Mexico
Sierra Madre Oriental *403* *var.* Eastern Sierra Madre. Mountain range of N Mexico
Sierra Maestra *210* mountain range of SE Cuba
Sierra Morena *530-531* mountain range of SW Spain
Sierra Nevada *598* mountain range of W USA
Sierra Nevada de Mérida *see* Mérida, Cordillera de
Sierre *546* *Ger.* Siders. SW Switzerland
Sigatoka *246* *prev.* Singatoka. Viti Levu, W Fiji
Siġġiewi *395* S Malta
Sighişoara *480* C Romania
Siglufjördhur *294* N Iceland
Signy *90* UK research station of South Orkney Islands, Antarctica
Sigsig *228* S Ecuador
Siguatepeque *288* W Honduras
Siguiri *281* NE Guinea
Sigulda *362* *Ger.* Segewold. NE Latvia
Sihanoukville *see* Kâmpóng Saôm
Siirt *577* SE Turkey
Sikasso *392* S Mali
Sikwane *142* S Botswana
Silay *466* Negros, C Philippines
Silesia *471* region of SW Poland
Silgadhi *427* *var.* Silgarhi. W Nepal
Silhouette *512* island of the Inner Islands, SE Seychelles
Siliana *573* *var.* Silyānah. NW Tunisia
Silicon Valley *602* business region of SW USA
Siliguri *see* Shiliguri
Silil *524* *var.* Silel. Seasonal river of NW Somalia
Silinhot *see* Xilinhot
Silisili, Mount *500* *var.* Mauga Silisili. Mountain of NW Samoa
Silistra *152* *var.* Silistria. NE Bulgaria
Silkeborg *218* Jylland, W Denmark
Sillamäe *240* *Ger.* Sillamäggi. NE Estonia
Sillein *see* Žilina
Šilutė *376* *var.* Šilute. W Lithuania
Silva Porto *see* Kuito
Silver City *644* NE Christmas Island
Silverek *577* SE Turkey
Sima *198* W Anjouan, Comoros
Simanggang *see* Bandar Sri Aman
Simbirsk *see* Ul'yanovsk
Simeto *321* river of Sicilia, S Italy
Simeulue, Pulau *302* island to the NW of Sumatra, W Indonesia
Simferopol *586* S Ukraine
Simikot *427* W Nepal
Siminiout *645* S French Guiana
Šimonovany *see* Partizánske
Simony *see* Partizánske
Simplon Pass *546* mountain pass of S Switzerland
Simplon Tunnel *546* tunnel of Italy and Switzerland
Simpson Desert *101* desert region of C Australia
Simunye *540* NE Swaziland
Sinai *230* *Ar.* Shibh Jazīrat Sīnā'. Desert region of NE Egypt
Sinazongwe *635* S Zambia
Sincelejo *195* NW Colombia
Sinchwang *see* Hsinchuang
Sin Cowe Island *652* island of SW Spratly Islands
Sindh *451* administrative region of SE Pakistan
Sindhulimadi *427* C Nepal
Sindi *240* SW Estonia
Sine *510* river of W Senegal
Sinendé *132* N Benin
Sines *474* S Portugal
Sinfra *326* C Ivory Coast
Singa *536* *var.* Sinjah, Sinja. E Sudan
Singapore *517* river of S Singapore
Singapore *516-517* officially Republic of Singapore. Country of SE Asia divided into 5 admin. units (districts). ❖ Singapore City
Singapore Strait *386, 517* *var.* Strait of Singapore. Strait connecting Strait of Malacca and South China Sea
Singatoka *see* Sigatoka
Sîngerei *408* *var.* Sângerei, *prev.* Lazovsk. N Moldova
Singida *560* C Tanzania
Singora *see* Songkhla
Sining *see* Xining
Sinj *209* SE Croatia
Sinjavina *630* *var.* Sinjajevina. Mountain range of N Montenegro, Yugoslavia
Sinkiang Uighur Autonomous Region *see* Xinjiang Uygur Zizhiqu
Sinnamary *645* N French Guiana
Sinnûris *230* *var.* Sinnūris. N Egypt
Sino *see* Greenville
Sinoe *see* Greenville
Sinoia *see* Chinhoyi
Sinoie, Lacul *480* *prev.* Lacul Sinoe. Lagoon of E Romania
Sinop *577* N Turkey
Sinp'o *349* E North Korea
Sintien *see* Hsintien
Sint-Niklaas *127* *Fr.* St.-Nicolas. N Belgium
Sintra *474* *prev.* Cintra. W Portugal
Sint-Truiden *127* *Fr.* St.-Trond. E Belgium
Sinŭiju *349* W North Korea
Sinyang *see* Xinyang
Sió *290* river of W Hungary
Sion *546* *Ger.* Sitten. SW Switzerland
Siorapaluk *646* NW Greenland
Sioux City *599* Iowa, C USA
Sioux Falls *599* South Dakota, NC USA
Sipaliwini *538* river of S Suriname
Siparia *570* SW Trinidad, Trinidad & Tobago
Siphofaneni *540* *var.* Sipofaneni. C Swaziland
Siping *187* *var.* Ssu-p'ing, Szeping, *prev.* Ssu-p'ing-chieh. Jilin, NE China
Siple *90* US research station of South Orkney Islands, Antarctica
Siput *386* *var.* Sungei Siput. NW Peninsular Malaysia
Siquirres *206* E Costa Rica
Siracusa *321* *Eng.* Syracuse. Sicilia, S Italy
Sirājganj *117* N Bangladesh
Şīr Banī Yās *590* island of W United Arab Emirates
Sirdaryo *see* Syr Darya
Sir Edward Pellew Group *101* island group of N Australia
Siret *480* *var.* Siretul, *Ger.* Sereth. River of Romania and Ukraine
Sir Francis Drake Channel *643* channel connecting the Atlantic Ocean and Caribbean Sea, C British Virgin Islands
Sirte *see* Surt
Sirte, Gulf of *see* Surt, Khalīj
Şirvan Düzü *110* *Rus.* Shirvanskaya Step'. Mountain range of C Azerbaijan
Sirwan *see* Diyālá
Sisak *209* *Hung.* Sziszek, *Ger.* Sissek. N Croatia
Sisian *98* SE Armenia
Sisimiut *646* *var.* Holsteinsborg. SW Greenland
Sisŏphŏn *165* NW Cambodia
Sissek *see* Sisak
Sīstān, Daryācheh-ye *307* *var.* HāmūŞāberī, Daryācheh-ye Hāmūn. Lake of E Iran
Sisters, The *276* islands N of Grenada island, Grenada
Siteki *540* *var.* Stegi. E Swaziland
Sithoniá *273* peninsula of NE Greece
Sitobela *540* S Swaziland
Sitona *238* SW Eritrea
Sitrah *115* *var.* Sitra. Island of NE Bahrain
Sittang *159* *var.* Sittoung. River of C Burma
Sittard *429* S Netherlands
Sitten *see* Sion
Sittwe *159* *prev.* Akyab. W Burma
Siuna *436* NE Nicaragua
Sivas *577* C Turkey
Sivers'kyy Donets' *see* Donets
Six Counties, the *see* Northern Ireland
Siyäzän *110* *Rus.* Siazan'. NE Azerbaijan
Sjælland *218* *Ger.* Seeland, *Eng.* Zealand. Island of E Denmark
Skadar *see* Shkodër
Skadarsko Jezero *see* Scutari, Lake
Skagaströnd *294* *prev.* Höfdhakaupstadhur. N Iceland
Skagen *218* Jylland, N Denmark
Skagerrak *218, 444, 543* *var.* Skagerak. Area of the Baltic Sea
Skalica *519* *Hung.* Sellye. W Slovakia
Skeleton Coast *423* coastal region of NW Namibia
Skellefteå *543* NE Sweden
Skellefteälv *543* river of N Sweden
Skien *444* S Norway
Skikda *83* *prev.* Philippeville. NE Algeria
Skive *218* Jylland, NW Denmark
Skjálfandafljót *294* river of C Iceland
Skjern *218* Jylland, W Denmark
Skjern Å *218* river of W Denmark
Skon *165* S Cambodia
Skopje *381* *prev.* Skoplje, *Turk.* Üsküb. ❖ of FYR Macedonia, N FYR Macedonia
Skoplje *see* Skopje
Skövde *543* S Sweden
Skrunda *362* W Latvia
Skúvoy *644* island of C Faeroe Islands
Skye, Isle of *593* island of W Scotland, UK
Skýros *273* island of E Greece
Slagelse *218* Sjælland, SE Denmark
Slaney *314* *Ir.* An tSláine. River of SE Ireland
Slatina *209* *prev.* Podravska Slatina, *Hung.* Szlatina. NE Croatia
Slatina *480* S Romania
Slave Coast *567* coastal region of W Africa, Atlantic Ocean
Slavonska Požega *209* *prev.* Požega, *Hung.* Pozsega. NE Croatia
Slavonski Brod *209* *prev.* Brod, *Hung.* Bród. E Croatia
Slavyansk *see* Slov"yans'k
Sléibhte Chill Mhantáin *see* Wicklow Mountains
Slēmānī *see* As Sulaymānīyah
Sliema *395* N Malta
Sligo *314* *Ir.* Sligeach. N Ireland
Sliven *152* *var.* Slivno. E Bulgaria
Slobozia *480* SE Romania
Slobozia *408* *Rus.* Slobodzeya. E Moldova
Slonim *122* *Rus.* Slonin. W Belarus
Slovakia *518-519* officially Slovak Republika, *prev.* constituent republic of Czechoslovakia. Country of C Europe divided into 4 admin. regions (kraj). ❖ Bratislava
Slovenia *520-521* officially Republic of Slovenia, *Slvn.* Slovenija. Country divided into 86 admin. units (občina). ❖ Ljubljana
Slovenské Rudohorie *519* *Ger.* Slowakisches Erzgebirge, *var.* Ungarisches Erzgebirge. Mountain range of C Slovakia
Slov'yans'k *586* *Rus.* Slavyansk. E Ukraine
Słupsk *471* *Ger.* Stolp. N Poland
Slutsk *122* C Belarus
Smallwood Reservoir *171* lake of S Canada
Smarhon' *122* NW Belarus
Smederevo *630* *Ger.* Semendria. N Serbia, Yugoslavia
Smila *586* C Ukraine
Smith's Island *643* island of E Bermuda
Smithson Bight *644* bay of the Indian Ocean on the S coast of Christmas Island
Smolensk *484* W Russian Federation
Smolyan *152* *var.* Smoljan, *prev.* Pashmakli. SW Bulgaria
Smyrna *see* İzmir
Snaefell *647* mountain of C Isle of Man
Snake *598* river of NW USA
Sneeuw-gebergte *see* Maoke, Pegunungan
Sněžka *216* *Ger.* Schneekoppe. Mountain of N Czech Republic
Snow Mountains *see* Maoke, Pegunungan
Snug Corner *276* SW Grenada island, Grenada
Snuŏl *165* E Cambodia
Soacha *195* C Colombia
Sobaek-sanmaek *350* mountain range of S South Korea
Sobat *536* river of Ethiopia and Sudan
Sobradinho, Represa de *145* *var.* Barragem de Sobradinho. Reservoir of E Brazil
Soča *321, 520* *It.* Isonzo. River of Italy and Slovenia
Socabaya *463* SE Peru
Sochi *484* SW Russian Federation
Société, Archipel de la *646* island group of W French Polynesia
Socotra *see* Suquţrá
Soc Trăng *623* *var.* Khanh, *Hung.* S Vietnam
Sodankylä *249* N Finland
Södertälje *543* SE Sweden
Sodiri *536* *var.* Sawdirī, Sodari. C Sudan
Sodo *243* *var.* Soddo, Soddu. SW Ethiopia
Soekaboemi *see* Sukabumi
Soela Väin *240* strait of Baltic Sea, between the islands of Hiiumaa and Saaremaa, W Estonia
Soembawa *see* Sumbawa
Soerabaja *see* Surabaya
Soerakarta *see* Surakarta
Sofala, Baía de *419* Bay of Indian Ocean, off Mozambique
Sofia *382* seasonal river of NW Madagascar
Sofia *152* *var.* Sofija, *Bul.* Sofiya. ❖ of Bulgaria, W Bulgaria
Sogamoso *195* C Colombia
Sognefjorden *444* fjord of SW Norway
Sohâg *230* *var.* Sawhaj. C Egypt
Sŏjosŏn-man *349* inlet of Korea Bay, on W coast of N Korea
Sokch'o *350* N South Korea
Söke *577* SW Turkey
Sokhumi *262* *Rus.* Sukhumi. NW Georgia

Sokodé *567* C Togo
Sokolov *216* NW Czech Republic
Sokoto *440* NW Nigeria
Sokoto *440* river of NW Nigeria
Sola *444* SW Norway
Solapur *296* *var.* Sholapur. SW India
Sol, Costa del *531* coastal region of S Spain
Soldeu *86* NE Andorra
Soledad *619* E Venezuela
Soledad *195* N Colombia
Soleure *see* Solothurn
Soligorsk *see* Salihorsk
Solimões *145* local name for a stretch of the Amazon river, NW Brazil
Solin *209* *It.* Salona. S Croatia
Solingen *264* W Germany
Sollum, Gulf of *230* *Ar.* Khalīj as Sallūm. Gulf of the Mediterranean Sea, NW Egypt
Sololá *278* W Guatemala
Solomon Islands *522-523* *prev.* British Solomon Islands Protectorate. Country of the South Pacific Ocean divided into 7 admin. units (provinces). ❖ Honiara
Solomon Sea *458, 522* sea of the Pacific Ocean, to the E of Papua New Guinea
Solothurn *546* *Fr.* Soleure. NW Switzerland
Solun *see* Thessaloníki
Solway Firth *593* arm of the Irish Sea, W UK
Solwezi *635* NW Zambia
Soma *261* C Gambia
Somalia *524-525* officially Somali Democratic Republic, *prev.* Somaliland Protectorate, Italian Somaliland. Country of E Africa divided into 16 admin. units (regions). ❖ Mogadishu
Sombor *630* *Hung.* Zombor. NW Serbia, Yugoslavia
Somerset *643* Somerset Island, W Bermuda
Somerset Island *643* island of W Bermuda
Somerset Island *170* island of N Canada
Somerset Nile *see* Victoria Nile
Someş *290, 480* *Hung.* Szamos, *Ger.* Samosch. River of Hungary and Romania
Sŏmjin *350* *Jap.* Senshin-kō. River of S South Korea
Somme *253* river of N France
Somosomo *246* Taveuni, N Fiji
Somotillo *436* W Nicaragua
Somoto *436* NW Nicaragua
Soná *456* SW Panama
Sonaco *282* NE Guinea-Bissau
Sonda des Vieques *651* bay of the Caribbean Sea, E Puerto Rico
Sønderborg *218* *Ger.* Sonderburg. Als, S Denmark
Søndre Strømfjord *see* Kangerlussuaq
Songea *560* S Tanzania
Songhua Jiang *see* Sungari
Sŏngjin *see* Kimch'aek
Songkhla *563* *Mal.* Singora. S Thailand
Sŏngnam *350* *var.* Seongnam. NW South Korea
Songnim *349* SW North Korea
Songo *419* NW Mozambique
Sông Tiên Giang *see* Mekong
Songwe *385* river of Malawi and Tanzania
Sonmiāni Bay *451* bay of the Arabian Sea, on the S coast of Pakistan
Sonoran Desert *10* desert Mexico/USA
Sonsonate *235* W El Salvador
Sonsorol Islands *455* island group of Palau
Soochow *see* Suzhou
Soomaaliya *see* Somalia
Soome Laht *see* Finland, Gulf of
Sop Hao *359* NE Laos
Sopron *290* *Ger.* Ödenburg. NW Hungary
Sôp Xai *359* NE Laos
Sórd Choluim Chille *see* Swords
Soria *531* N Spain
Soriano *607* W Uruguay
Soro *see* Ghazal
Sorø *218* Sjælland, SE Denmark
Soroca *408* *Rus.* Soroki. N Moldova
Sorocaba *145* S Brazil
Sorol *406* atoll of W Micronesia
Soroti *584* C Uganda
Sørøya *444* *var.* Sørøy. Island of N Norway
Sŏsan *350* *Jap.* Zuisan. W South Korea
Sosnowiec *471* *Ger.* Sosnowitz. S Poland
Sota *132* river of NE Benin
Sotavento, Ilhas de *176* southernmost of the two main island groups comprising Cape Verde
Sotouboua *567* C Togo
Souanké *200* NW Congo
Soubré *326* S Ivory Coast
Soueida *see* As Suwaydā'
Soufrière *224* S Dominica
Soufrière *497* W St Lucia
Soufrière Hills *649* mountain range, E Montserrat
Souillac *400* S Mauritius
Souk Ahras *83* NE Algeria
Soukhné *see* As Sukhnah
Sŏul *see* Seoul
Sound, The *543* *Swe.* Öresund, *Nor.* Øresund. Strait between Denmark and Sweden, connecting the Baltic Sea and Kattegat
Soûr *364* *var.* Şūr. SW Lebanon
Sousse *573* *var.* Sūsah. N Tunisia
South Africa *526-529* officially Republic of South Africa. Country of southern Africa, divided into 9 admin. units (provinces). ❖ Pretoria, Cape Town, Bloemfontein
Southampton *593* S England, UK
Southampton Island *171* island of N Canada
South Andaman *296* island of the Andaman Islands, SE India
South Australia *101* state of S Australia
South Bend *599* Indiana, C USA
South Caicos *653* island of C Turks and Caicos Islands
South Carolina *599* state of SE USA
South Carpathians *see* Carpaţii Meridionali
South China Sea *386, 466, 517, 555* *Ind.* Laut Cina Selatan, *Chin.* Nan Hai, *Vtn.* Biển Đông. Sea of the Pacific Ocean
South Comino Channel *see* Malta, Il-Fliegu ta'
South Dakota *599* state of NC USA
South East China *190* region of SE China
Southeast Island *see* Tagula Island
South East Point *652* headland on the E coast of Ascension Island
Southend-on-Sea *593* SE England, UK
Southern Alps *433* mountains of N South Island, New Zealand
Southern Cook Islands *644* island group of S Cook Islands
Southern Uplands *593* mountain range of S Scotland, UK
South Hill Village *642* C Anguilla
South Huvadhu Atoll *390* *var.* Gaafu Dhaalu Atoll. Atoll of S Maldives
South Island *644* *var.* Pulu Atas. Island of SE Cocos Islands
South Island *433* southernmost of the two main islands that comprise New Zealand
South Island *342* NW Kenya
South Korea *350-353* officially Republic of South Korea, *Kor.* Taehan. Country of E Asia divided into 9 admin. units (provinces). ❖ Seoul
South Maalhosmadulu Atoll *390* *var.* Baa Atoll. Atoll of N Maldives
South Miladummadulu Atoll *390* atoll of N Maldives
South Nilandhe Atoll *390* *var.* Dhaalu Atoll. Atoll of C Maldives
South Orkney Islands *90* island group to the NE of Antarctic Peninsula, Antarctica
South Point *652* headland on the S coast of Ascension Island
South Point *644* headland on the S coast of Christmas Island
South Rukuru *385* river of NW Malawi
South Saskatchewan *170* river of SW Canada
South Shetland Islands *90* island group to the W of Antarctic Peninsula, Antarctica
South Sound *643* Virgin Gorda, E British Virgin Islands
South Taranaki Bight *433* area of the Tasman Sea, SW of North Island, New Zealand
South Town *644* Little Cayman, C Cayman Islands
South Uist *593* island of Outer Hebrides, NW Scotland, UK
South West Bay *652* bay of the South Atlantic Ocean on the SW coast of Ascension Island
Sowa *142* *var.* Sua. NE Botswana
Soweto *527* Pretoria-Witwatersrand-Vereeniging, NE South Africa
Soyang-ho *350* reservoir of N South Korea
Sozh *122* river of NE Europe
Spain *530-533* officially Kingdom of Spain, *Sp.* España. Country of SW Europe divided into 18 admin. units (autonomous communities, comprised of 50 provinces). ❖ Madrid
Spalato *see* Split
Spaldings *329* C Jamaica
Spanish Point *92* S Barbuda, Antigua & Barbuda
Spanish Town *643* Virgin Gorda, E British Virgin Islands
Spanish Town *329* SE Jamaica
Spanish Wells *112* Eleuthera I, Bahamas
Spartanburg *599* South Carolina, SE USA
Spárti *273* *Eng.* Sparta. S Greece
Speedwell Island *645* island of S Falkland Islands
Speery Island *652* island of SW St Helena
Speightstown *121* N Barbados
Spence Bay *170* N Canada
Spencer Gulf *101* gulf of S Australia
Spey *593* river of NE Scotland, UK
Spice Islands *see* Maluku
Spiez *546* W Switzerland
Spijkenisse *429* SW Netherlands
Spīn Būldak *77* S Afghanistan
Spišská Nová Ves *519* *Ger.* Zipser Neudorf, *Hung.* Igló. E Slovakia
Spitak *98* NW Armenia
Spitsbergen *653* island of NW Svalbard
Spittal an der Drau *106* *var.* Spittal. S Austria
Split *209* *It.* Spalato. S Croatia
Spokane *598* Washington, NW USA
Spot Bay *644* Cayman Brac, NE Cayman Islands
Spratly Island *652* island of Spratly Islands
Spratly Islands *652* Disputed island group of the South China Sea
Spree *265* river of E Germany
Springfield *599* Illinois, C USA
Springfield *599* Massachusetts, NE USA
Springfield *599* Missouri, C USA
Spring Garden *284* NE Guyana
Springs *527* Pretoria-Witwatersrand-Vereeniging, NE South Africa
Springs *276* SW Grenada island, Grenada
Srbija *see* Serbia, Yugoslavia
Srê Âmběl *165* SW Cambodia
Srebrenica *140* E Bosnia & Herzegovina
Sredna Gora *152* mountain range of Bulgaria
Srednesibirskoye Ploskogor'ye *485* *Eng.* Central Siberian Plateau, *var.* Central Siberian Uplands. Large upland area of C Russian Federation
Sreng *165* river of NW Cambodia
Srêpôk *165* river of Cambodia and Vietnam
Sri Jayawardenapura *534* *prev.* Kotte. Suburb of Colombo and admin. ❖ of Sri Lanka, W Sri Lanka
Sri Lanka *534-535* officially Democratic Socialist Republic of Sri Lanka, *prev.* Ceylon. Country of South Asia divided into 25 admin. units (districts). ❖ Colombo
Srimongal *117* E Bangladesh
Srīnagar *296* N India
Srpska, Republika *140* *republic* Bosnia & Herzegovina
Ssu-ch'uan *see* Sichuan
Ssu-p'ing *see* Siping
Ssu-p'ing-chieh *see* Siping
Stacklen *see* Strenči
Stadskanaal *429* NE Netherlands
Stäfa *546* NE Switzerland
Stalin *see* Braşov
Stalin *see* Varna
Stalinabad *see* Dushanbe
Stalingrad *see* Volgograd
Stalino *see* Donets'k
Stalin Peak *see* Garmo, Qullai
Stalin Peak *see* Musala
Stalinsk *see* Novokuznetsk
Stampriet *423* S Namibia
Stamsund *444* NE Norway
Stange *444* S Norway
Stanislav *see* Ivano-Frankivs'k
Stanke Dimitrov *see* Dupnitsa
Stanley *645* *var.* Port Stanley. ❖ of Falkland Islands, East Falkland, Falkland Islands
Stanley *see* Chek Chue
Stanley Pool *200, 203* *var.* Pool Malebo. Expanded section of the Congo river between Congo and Dem. Rep. Congo (Zaire)
Stanleyville *see* Kisangani
Stann Creek *see* Dangriga
Stanovoye Nagor'ye *485* mountain range of E Russian Federation
Stara Kanjiža *see* Kanjiža
Stara Planina *see* Balkan Mountains
Stara Zagora *152* C Bulgaria
Starbuck Island *346* island of the Line Is, E Kiribati
Staten Island *see* Estados, Isla de los
Station Hill *121* SW Barbados
Stavanger *444* SW Norway
Stavropol' *484* *prev.* Voroshilovsk. SW Russian Federation
Stavropol' *see* Tol'yatti
Stavropol'sky Kray *484* administrative region of SW Russian Federation
Steels Point *650* headland of E Norfolk Island
Stefanie, Lake *see* Ch'ew Bahir
Steffisburg *546* W Switzerland
Stegi *see* Siteki
Stein *see* Kamnik
Steinamanger *see* Szombathely
Steinkjer *444* C Norway
Steirisch *106* mountain range of C Austria
Stendal *265* C Germany
Stende *362* NW Latvia
Stepanakert *see* Xankändi
Step'anavan *98* N Armenia
Sterlitamak *484* W Russian Federation
Stettin *see* Szczecin
Stettiner Haff *see* Oderhaff
Stewart Island *433* island to the S of South Island, New Zealand
Steyr *106* N Austria
Stif *see* Sétif
Štip *381* E FYR Macedonia
Stirling *593* C Scotland, UK
Stjørdal *444* C Norway
Stockerau *106* NE Austria
Stockholm *543* ❖ of Sweden, SE Sweden
Stockton-on-Tees *593* NE England, UK
Stoelmanseiland *538* E Suriname
Stoke-on-Trent *593* C England, UK
Stolp *see* Słupsk

Stonyhill Point *652* headland on the S coast of Tristan da Cunha
Stony Tunguska *see* Podkamennaya Tunguska
Stóra Dimun *644* island of S Faeroe Islands
Storebælt *218* *Eng.* Great Belt, *var.* Store Bælt. Channel between Fyn and Sjælland Denmark
Store Heddinge *218* Sjælland, E Denmark
Støren *444* C Norway
Storfjorden *653* area of the Greenland Sea, S Svalbard
Stornoway *593* Isle of Lewis, Outer Hebrides, NW Scotland, UK
Strakonice *216* SW Czech Republic
Stralsund *265* N Germany
Stranraer *593* SW Scotland, UK
Strasbourg *253* *Ger.* Strassburg. NE France
Strășeni *408* *var.* Strasheny.C Moldova
Strassburg *see* Strasbourg
Stratford-upon-Avon *593* C England, UK
Strenči *362* *Ger.* Stacklen. NE Latvia
Streymoy *644* *var.* Strømø. Island of N Faeroe Islands
Strickland *458* river of W Papua New Guinea
Strimón *273* *Bul.* Struma. River of Bulgaria and Greece
Struer *218* Jylland, W Denmark
Struga *381* SW FYR Macedonia
Struma *152* *Gk* Strimón. River of Bulgaria and Greece
Strumeshnitsa *see* Strumica
Strumica *381* E FYR Macedonia
Strumica *381* *var.* Strumitsa, *Bul.* Strumeshnitsa. River of Bulgaria and FYR Macedonia
Strumitsa *see* Strumica
Stuart Peak *527* mountain of Central Marion Island, South Africa
Stubbs *498* SE St Vincent, St Vincent & the Grenadines
Studen Kladenets, Yazovir *152* reservoir of Bulgaria
Stuhlweissenburg *see* Székesfehérvár
Štúrovo *519* *prev.* Parkan, *Hung.* Párkány. S Slovakia
Stuttgart *264, 269* SW Germany
Stykkishólmur *294* W Iceland
Sua *see* Sowa
Suai *305* W East Timor
Suao *555* *Jap.* Suō. NE Taiwan
Subic Bay *466* bay of South China Sea, Luzon, N Philippines
Subotica *630* *Hung.* Szabadka, *Ger.* Maria-Theresiopel. N Serbia, Yugoslavia
Suceava *480* *Ger.* Suczawa. NE Romania
Suchow *see* Suzhou
Sucre *136* ❖ (judicial & legal) of Bolivia, S Bolivia
Suczawa *see* Suceava
Sudan *536-537* officially Republic of Sudan, *prev.* Anglo-Egyptian Sudan. Country of NE Africa divided into 9 admin. units (states). ❖ Khartoum
Sudan *157* physical region of C Africa, composed of desert region, plains and grassy steppes
Sudbury *171* S Canada
Sudd *536* swamp region of S Sudan
Suddie *284* NE Guyana
Sudeten *216, 471* *var.* Sudetenland, Sudetes, Sudetic Mountains, *Cz./Pol.* Sudety. Mountain range of Czech Republic and Poland
Sudharam *see* Noākhāli
Sudhuroy *644* *var.* Suderø. Island of S Faeroe Islands
Sudhuroyarfjørdhur *644* strait between Sudhuroy and Sandoy, C Faeroe Islands
Sudong, Pulau *517* island of SW Singapore
Sudostroy *see* Severodvinsk
Sue *536* river of S Sudan
Sue Wood Bay *643* bay of the North Atlantic Ocean, C Bermuda
Suez *230* *Ar.* As Suways, *var.* El Suweis. NE Egypt
Suez Canal *230* *Ar.* Qanāt as Suways. Canal of NE Egypt
Suez, Gulf of *230* *Ar.* Khalīj al 'Aqabah. Gulf of the Red Sea, to the NE of Egypt
Sūf *336* NW Jordan
Sugar Loaf *276* *var.* Levera Island. N of Grenada island, Grenada
Şuḥār *448* *var.* Sohar. NW Oman
Sühbaatar *412* N Mongolia
Suigen *see* Suwŏn
Suir *314* *Ir.* An tSiúir. River of S Ireland
Sukabumi *302* *prev.* Soekaboemi. Java, C Indonesia
Sukagawa *330* Honshū, N Japan
Sukarnapura *see* Jayapura
Sukarno, Puntjak *see* Jaya, Puncak
Sukhne *see* As Sukhnah
Sukhumi *see* Sokhumi
Suki *536* E Sudan
Sukkertoppen *see* Maniitsoq
Sukkur *451* S Pakistan
Sukuta *261* W Gambia
Sulaimaniya *see* As Sulaymānīyah
Sulaimān Range *451* mountain range of C Pakistan
Sula, Kepulauan *302* *prev.* Xulla Islands, Soela. Island group to the E of Celebes, E Indonesia
Sulawesi *see* Celebes
Sulawesi, Laut *see* Celebes Sea
Sulby *647* N Isle of Man
Sullana *463* NW Peru
Sullivan Island *see* Lanbi Island
Sultan Alonto, Lake *see* Lanao, Lake
Sulu Archipelago *466* island group of SW Philippines
Sulu Sea *387, 466* sea of the Pacific Ocean, to the NE of Borneo, Malaysia
Sulyukta *357* *Kir.* Sülüktü. SW Kyrgyzstan
Sumatera *see* Sumatra
Sumatra *302* *var.* Sumatera. Island of W Indonesia
Šumava *see* Bohemian Forest
Sumba *644* Sudhuroy, S Faeroe Islands
Sumba *302* *prev.* Soemba, *Eng.* Sandalwood Island. Island of Nusa Tenggara, C Indonesia
Sumba, Selat *302* strait of the Indian Ocean between Sumba and Sumbawa, C Indonesia
Sumbawa *302* *prev.* Soembawa. Island of Nusa Tenggara, C Indonesia
Sumbawanga *560* W Tanzania
Sumbe *88* *Port.* Novo Redondo. W Angola
Sumbuya *514* S Sierra Leone
Šumen *see* Shumen
Sumisu-jima *330* island to the SE of Honshū, SE Japan
Šumperk *216* *Ger.* Mährisch-Schönberg. E Czech Republic
Sumpul *235* river of Honduras and El Salvador
Sumqayıt *110* *Rus.* Sumgait. E Azerbaijan
Sumy *586* NE Ukraine
Sunan *349* SW North Korea
Sunch'ŏn *349* SW North Korea
Sunch'ŏn *350* *Jap.* Junten. S South Korea
Sunda, Selat *302* strait connecting Indian Ocean and Laut Jawa between Java and Sumatra, W Indonesia
Sunderland *593* NE England, UK
Sundsvall *543* C Sweden
Sungai Seletar Reservoir *517* reservoir of N Singapore
Sungari *187* *Chin.* Songhua Jiang. River of NE China
Sun Koshi *427* river of E Nepal
Suntar-Khayata, Khrebet *485* mountain range of NE Russian Federation
Sunyani *270* W Ghana
Sunzu *635* mountain NE Zambia
Suō *see* Suao
Suomenlahti *see* Finland, Gulf of
Suomenselkä *249* physical region of C Finland
Suŏng *165* SE Cambodia
Superior de Tristaina, Estany *86* lake of NW Andorra
Superior, Lake *171, 599* *Fr.* Lac Supérieur. Lake of Canada and USA
Sup'ung-ho *349* reservoir of China and North Korea
Sūq 'Abs *see* 'Abs
Sūq ash Shuyūkh *310* SE Iraq
Suqrah Bay *448* Bay of the Arabian Sea, SE Oman
Suquṭrá *627* *Eng.* Socotra. Island of SE Yemen, off the Horn of Africa
Şūr *448* NE Oman
Surabaya *302* *prev.* Surabaja, Soerabaja. Java, C Indonesia
Surakarta *302* *prev.* Soerakarta. Java, C Indonesia
Šurany *519* *Hung.* Nagysurány. SW Slovakia
Sūrat *296* W India
Surat Thani *563* S Thailand
Sûre *378* river of W Europe
Sure, Lagh *342* dry watercourse of NE Kenya
Surfers Paradise *101* Queensland, E Australia
Surin *563* E Thailand
Surinam *400* S Mauritius
Suriname *538-539* officially Republic of Suriname, *var.* Surinam. Country of Central America divided into 8 admin. units (provinces). ❖ Paramaribo
Surinam *121* E Barbados
Surkhet *see* Birendranagar
Surkhob *558* river of C Tajikistan
Şurmān *371* NW Libya
Surt *371* *var.* Sidra, Sirte. N Libya
Surt, Khalīj *371* *var.* Gulf of Sirte, Gulf of Sidra. Gulf of the Mediterranean Sea, off N coast of Libya
Sūsah *see* Sousse
Susana *282* W Guinea-Bissau
Susuman *485* Ostrov Sakhalin, E Russian Federation
Sutlej *451* river of India and Pakistan
Suure-Jaani *240* *Ger.* Gross-Sankt-Johannis. C Estonia
Suur Munamägi *240* *var.* Munamägi. Mountain of SE Estonia
Suur Väin *240* strait of the Baltic Sea, between the mainland and the island of Muhu, W Estonia
Suva *246* ❖ of Fiji, Viti Levu, W Fiji
Suwa *238* SE Eritrea
Suwarrow *644* island of Northern Cook Islands, N Cook Islands
Suwayhān *590* E United Arab Emirates
Suways, Qanāt as *see* Suez Canal
Suwŏn *350* *var.* Suweon, *Jap.* Suigen. NW South Korea
Suzhou *187* *var.* Soochow, Su-chou, Suchow, *prev.* Wuhsien. Jiangsu, E China
Suzuka *330* Honshū, C Japan
Svalbard *653* Norwegian dependency of the Greenland Sea
Sväty Kríž nad Hronom *see* Žiar nad Hronom
Svay Chék *165* river of Cambodia and Thailand
Svay Riĕng *165* SE Cambodia
Svendborg *218* Fyn, S Denmark
Sverdlovsk *see* Yekaterinburg
Sverdrup Islands *170* island group of N Canada
Sveti Nikole *381* *prev.* Sveti Nikola. C FYR Macedonia
Svetlogorsk *see* Svyetlahorsk
Svetozarevo *630* *prev.* Jagodina. C Serbia, Yugoslavia
Svilengrad *152* *prev.* Mustafa-Pasha. SE Bulgaria
Svínoy *644* *var.* Svinø. Island of NE Faeroe Islands
Svishtov *152* *var.* Svištov. N Bulgaria
Svitavy *216* E Czech Republic
Svyetlahorsk *122* *Rus.* Svetlogorsk. SE Belarus
Swabian Jura *see* Schwäbische Alb
Swakopmund *423* W Namibia
Swallow Islands *522* small island group within Santa Cruz Is, E Solomon Is
Swan *100* river of SW Australia
Swansea *593* *Wel.* Abertawe. S Wales, UK
Swatow *see* Shantou
Swaziland *540-541* officially Kingdom of Swaziland. Country of southern Africa divided into 4 admin. units (districts).❖ Mbabane
Sweden *542-545* officially Kingdom of Sweden, *Swe.* Sverige. Country of Scandinavia divided into 24 admin. units (läns).❖ Stockholm
Swedru *see* Agona Swedru
Swellendam *527* Western Cape, S South Africa
Swetes *92* S Antigua, Antigua & Barbuda
Swift Current *170* SW Canada
Swindon *593* C England, UK
Swiss Plateau *546* *Ger.* Schweizer Mittelland. Plateau of W Switzerland
Switzerland *546-549* officially Swiss Confederation, *Ger.* Schweiz, *It.* Svizzera. Country of C Europe divided into 26 admin. units (cantons). ❖ Bern
Swords *314* *Ir.* Sórd Choluim Chille. E Ireland
Syaphrubesi *427* *var.* Syabrubensi. C Nepal
Sydney *101, 105* SE Australia
Sydney *171* Cape Breton Island, SE Canada
Sydney Island *see* Manra
Syktyvkar *484* *prev.* Ust'-Sisol'sk. NW Russian Federation
Sylhet *117* NE Bangladesh
Syowa *90* Japanese research station of Greater Antarctica, Antarctica
Syracuse *599* New York, NE USA
Syracuse *see* Siracusa
Syr Darya *338, 558, 610* *Rus.* Syrdar'ya, *Kaz.* Syrdariya, *Uzb.* Sirdaryo. River of C Asia
Syrdar'ya *610* E Uzbekistan
Syria *550-553* officially Syrian Arab Republic, *Ar.* Suriyah. Country divided into 13 admin. units (governorates).❖ Damascus
Syriam *159* S Burma
Syrian Desert *310, 336, 551* *Ar.* Bādiyat ash Shām. Desert of SW Asia
Syvash, Zatoka *586* inlet of the Sea of Azov
Szabadka *see* Subotica
Szamos *see* Someş
Szatmárnémeti *see* Satu Mare
Szczecin *471* *Ger.* Stettin. NW Poland
Szczeciński, Zalew *see* Oderhaff
Szechuan *see* Sichuan
Szeged *290* *Ger.* Szegedin.SE Hungary
Székesfehérvár *290* *Ger.* Stuhlweissenburg. W Hungary
Szekszárd *290* S Hungary
Szenice *see* Senica
Szentes *290* SE Hungary
Szeping *see* Siping
Szered *see* Sereď
Sziszek *see* Sisak
Szlatina *see* Podravska Slatina
Szolnok *290* C Hungary
Szombathely *290* *Ger.* Steinamanger. W Hungary
Sztálinváros *see* Dunaújváros

T

Tabac, River *400* river of S Mauritius
Ṭabaqah *551* N Syria
Tabaquite *570* C Trinidad, Trinidad & Tobago
Tabarka *573* *var.* Ṭabarqah. NW Tunisia
Tabasará, Serranía de *456* mountain range of W Panama

Tabasco *see* Grijalva
Tabernacle *494* NE St Kitts, St Kitts & Nevis
Tabiteuea *346* island of the Gilbert Is, W Kiribati
Tablas Island *466* island of C Philippines
Table Hill Gordon *92* SE Antigua, Antigua & Barbuda
Tabligbo *567* SE Togo
Tábor *216* SW Czech Republic
Tabora *560* W Tanzania
Tabou *326* *var.* Tabu. S Ivory Coast
Tabrīz *307* NW Iran
Tabuaeran *346* *var.* Fanning Island. Island of the Line Is, E Kiribati
Tabūk *506* NW Saudi Arabia
Tabwémasana *615* mountain of Espiritu Santo, W Vanuatu
Täby *543* SE Sweden
Tachia Hsi *555* river of W Taiwan
Tachoshui *555* E Taiwan
Tacloban *466* Leyte, E Philippines
Tacna *463* SE Peru
Tacoma *598* Washington, NW USA
Tacuarembó *607* N Uruguay
Tacuarembó *607* river of C Uruguay
Tacurupucú *see* Hernandarias
Tademaït, Plateau du *83* plateau of C Algeria
Tadine *650* Maré, Îles Loyauté, E New Caledonia
Tadjoura *222* E Djibouti
Tadjoura, Golfe de *222* inlet of the Gulf of Aden, E of Djibouti
T'aebaek-sanmaek *350* mountain range of South Korea
Taedong *349* river of C North Korea
Taegu *350* *var.* Daegu, *Jap.* Taikyū. SE South Korea
Taehan-haehyŏp *see* Korea Strait
Taejŏn *350* *Jap.* Taiden. C South Korea
Tafahi *568* island of N Tonga
Tafí Viejo *95* NW Argentina
Taftlund *218* Jylland, SW Denmark
Taga *500* Savai'i, Samoa
Taganrog, Gulf of *586* *Ukr.* Tahanroz'ka Zatoka, *Rus.* Taganrogskiy Zaliv. Gulf of the Sea of Azov, SE Ukraine
Tagarzimat *414* W Western Sahara
Tagiura *see* Tājūrā'
Tagliamento *321* river of N Italy
Tagtabazar *see* Takhta-Bazar
Taguasco *210* C Cuba
Taguatinga *145* C Brazil
Tagula Island *458* *prev.* Southeast I. Island of SE Papua New Guinea
Tagum *466* river of Mindanao, S Philippines
Tahanroz'ka Zatoka *see* Taganrog, Gulf of
Tahat *83* mountain of SE Algeria
Tahiti *646* island of W French Polynesia
Tahoua *439* W Niger
Taia *514* river of C Sierra Leone
Taiama *514* C Sierra Leone
T'aichung *555* *Jap.* Taichū. W Taiwan
Taiden *see* Taejŏn
Taieri *433* river of S South Island, New Zealand
Taihoku *see* Taipei
T'aihsi *555* W Taiwan
Tai Hu *187* lake of E China
Taikyū *see* Taegu
T'ainan *555* *Jap.* Tainan. SW Taiwan
Tai Pang Wan *see* Mirs Bay
T"aipei *555* *var.* Taipei, *Jap.* Taihoku. ❖ of Taiwan, N Taiwan
Taiping *386* NW Peninsular Malaysia
T'aitung *555* *Jap.* Taitō. SE Taiwan
Taiwan *554-557* officially Republic of China (Taiwan). Country of E Asia divided into 16 admin. units (counties). ❖ Taipei
Taiwan Strait *187, 555* *var.* Formosa Strait, *Chin.* T'ai-wan Hai-hsia. Strait connecting East China Sea and South China Sea, between Taiwan and China
Taiyuan *187* *var.* T'ai-yuan *prev.* Yangku. Shanxi, N China
Ta'izz *627* SW Yemen
Tajarhī *371* SW Libya
Tajikistan *558-559* officially Republic of Tajikistan, *Rus.* Tadzhikistan, *Taj.* Jumhurii Tojikiston *prev.* Tajik S.S.R. Country of C Asia divided into 3 admin. units (2 oblasts, 1 autonomous region). ❖ Dushanbe
Tajo *see* Tagus
Tajrīsh *307* NW Iran
Tajumulco, Volcán *278* mountain of W Guatemala
Tājūrā' *371* *var.* Tagiura, NW Libya
Tak *563* *var.* Rahaeng. W Thailand
Taka *396* island of N Marshall Islands
Takamaka *512* Mahé, Seychelles
Takamatsu *330* Shikoku, SW Japan
Takao *see* Kaohsiung
Takaoka *330* Honshū, C Japan
Takapuna *433* NW North Island, New Zealand
Takasaki *330* Honshū, SE Japan
Takefu *330* Honshū, C Japan
Takêv *165* S Cambodia
Takhiatosh *610* *Rus.* Takhiatash. W Uzbekistan
Ta Khmau *165* S Cambodia
Takhta-Bazar *581* *var* Tagtabazar. SE Turkmenistan
Takhtakŭpir *610* *Rus.* Takhtakupyr. NW Uzbekistan
Takikawa *331* Hokkaidō, N Japan
Taklimakan Shamo *186* Desert of Xinjiang Uygur Zizhiqu, NW China
Takutea *644* island of Southern Cook Islands, S Cook Islands
Tala *607* S Uruguay
Talamanca, Cordillera de *206* mountain range of Costa Rica
Talara *463* NW Peru
Talas *357* NW Kyrgyzstan
Talaud, Kepulauan *302* island group to the NE of Celebes, E Indonesia
Talawakele *534* S Sri Lanka
Talca *183* C Chile
Talcahuano *183* C Chile
Taldykorgan *338* *prev.* Taldy-Kurgan, *Kaz.* Taldyqorghan. SE Kazakhstan
Taldy-Kurgan *see* Taldykorgan
Taldyqorghan *see* Taldykorgan
Ta-lien *see* Dalian
T'alin *98* *prev.* Verin T'alin. W Armenia
Talish Mountains *110* *Az.* Taliş Dagları, *Rus.* Talyshskiye Gory, *Per.* Kūhhā-ye Ţavālesh. Mountain range of S Azerbaijan and Iran
Talladi *534* NW Sri Lanka
Tall 'Afar *310* N Iraq
Tallahassee *599* Florida, SE USA
Tall Fadghāmī *551* *var.* Fadghāmī. NE Syria
Tallinn *240* *prev.* Revel, *Ger.* Reval, *Rus.* Tallin. ❖ of Estonia, NW Estonia
Talofofo *647* SE Guam
Tāloqān *77* NE Afghanistan
Talsi *362* *Ger.* Talsen. NW Latvia
Talyshskiye Gory *see* Talish Mountains
Tama Abu, Banjaran *see* Penambo, Banjaran
Tamabo, Banjaran *387* mountain range of Borneo, E Malaysia
Tamale *270* C Ghana
Tamana *346* island of the Gilbert Is, W Kiribati
Tamanrasset *83* SE Algeria
Tamar *593* river of SW England, UK
Tamarin *400* E Mauritius
Tamatave *see* Toamasina
Tambach *342* W Kenya
Tambacounda *510* SE Senegal
Tambov *484* W Russian Federation
Tâmchekkeţ *398* *var.* Tamchaket. S Mauritania
Tamiš *see* Timiş
Tam Ky *623* E Vietnam
Tammerfors *see* Tampere
Tampa *599* Florida, SE USA
Tampere *249* *Swe.* Tammerfors. SW Finland
Tampico *403* C Mexico
Tamuning *647* NW Guam
Tamworth *101* E Australia
Tana *249, 444* *Fin.* Teno. River of Finland and Norway
Tana *444* NE Norway
Tana *342* river of SE Kenya
Tanabe *330* Honshū, C Japan
T'ana Hāyk' *243* *var.* Lake Tana. Lake of NW Ethiopia
Tanami Desert *101* desert region of N Australia
Tân An *623* S Vietnam
Tananarive *see* Antananarivo
Tanaro *320* river of N Italy
Tanārūt, Wādī *371* dry watercourse of NW Libya
Tanch'ŏn *349* E North Korea
Tandil *95* E Argentina
Tando Ādam *451* *var.* Adam-jo-Tando. S Pakistan
Tane Range *563* *Bur.* Tanen Taunggy. Mountain range of N Thailand
Tanezrouft *83* desert region of Algeria and Mali
Tanga *560* E Tanzania
Tangail *117* C Bangladesh
Tanganyika, Lake *162, 560, 203, 635* lake of E Africa
Tangarare *522* W Guadalcanal, Solomon Is
Tanger *414* *var.* Tangiers, *Sp.* Tánger, *Fr/Ger.* Tanger. NW Morocco
Tanggula Shan *186* *var.* Tanglha Range. Mountain range of Xizang Zizhiqu, W China
Tangiers *see* Tanger
Tangkak *386* S Peninsular Malaysia
Tangshan *187* Hebei, NE China
Tanguiéta *132* NW Benin
Tanimbar, Kepulauan *302* island group of Maluku, E Indonesia
Tanjungkarang *302* *var.* Tanjungkarang-Telukbetung. Sumatra, W Indonesia
Tanna *615* island of S Vanuatu
Tansen *427* C Nepal
Tanshui *555* *Jap.* Tansui. N Taiwan
Tanshui Kang *555* river of N Taiwan
Ţanţâ *230* N Egypt
Tan-Tan *414* SW Morocco
Tan-tung *see* Dandong
Tanzania *560-561* officially United Republic of Tanzania, *Swa.* Jamhuri ya Muungano wa Tanzania, *prev.* Tanganyika and Zanzibar, earlier German East Africa. Country of E Africa divided into 21 admin. units (districts). ❖ Dodoma
Taoa *653* Île Futuna, N Wallis & Futuna
T'aon-an *see* Baicheng
Taormina *321* Sicilia, S Italy
Taoudenni *392* *var.* Taoudenit. N Mali
Taourirt *414* NE Morocco
T'aoyüan *555* *Jap.* Tōen. N Taiwan
Tapa *240* *Ger.* Taps. N Estonia
Tapachula *403* SE Mexico
Tāpaga, Cape *500* *var.* Tapaga Point. Cape on the SE coast of Upolu, Samoa
Tapajós *145* *var.* Tapajóz. River of NW Brazil
Tapanahony *538* *var.* Tapanahoni. River of E Suriname
Tapeta *368* C Liberia
Tāpi *296* *prev.* Tāpti. River of W India
Tapiantana Group *466* island group of Sulu Archipelago, SW Philippines
Tapiwa *346* Banaba, W Kiribati
Tapoa *157* river of E Burkina
Taps *see* Tapa
Tapul Group *466* island group of Sulu Archipelago, SW Philippines
Ţarābulus al-Gharb *see* Tripoli
Taraclia *408* *Rus.* Tarakilya. S Moldova
Taranaki, Mount *433* *var.* Mount Egmont. Mountain of SW North Island, New Zealand
Taranto *321* S Italy
Taranto, Golfo di *321* *Eng.* Gulf of Taranto. Gulf of the Mediterranean Sea, on the S coast of Italy
Tarapoto *463* N Peru
Tarawa *346* island of the Gilbert Is, W Kiribati
Taraz *338* *prev.* Zhambyl, Dzhambul, Auliye-Ata. S Kazakhstan
Tarbela Reservoir *451* reservoir of N Pakistan
Tarbes *253* SW France
Tarca *see* Torysa
Taree *101* E Australia
Tărgovište *see* Tŭrgovishte
Târgovişte *480* Tîrgovişte. S Romania
Târgu-Jiu *480* *prev.* Tîrgu Jiu. W Romania
Târgu Mureş *480* *Hung.* Marosvásárhely, *prev.* Tirgu Mures, *Ger.* Neumarkt. C Romania
Tarhūnah *371* NW Libya
Ţarīf *590* W United Arab Emirates
Tarifa, Punta de *530* cape to the SW of Spain
Tarija *136* S Bolivia
Tarīm *627* C Yemen
Tarime *560* N Tanzania
Tarim He *186* river of Xinjiang Uygur Zizhiqu, NW China
Tarīn Kowt *77* C Afghanistan
Tarkwa *270* S Ghana
Tarlac *466* Luzon, N Philippines
Tarma *463* C Peru
Tarn *253* river of S France
Tarnopol *see* Ternopil'
Tarnów *471* S Poland
Tarrafal *176* Santiago, S Cape Verde
Tarrafal *176* Santo Antão, N Cape Verde
Tarragona *531* E Spain
Tarrasa *see* Terrassa
Tarsus *577* S Turkey
Tärtär *110* *Rus.* Terter. River of SW Azerbaijan
Tartu *240* *prev.* Yu'rev, *var.* Yurev, *Ger.* Dorpat. SE Estonia
Ţarţus *551* W Syria
Tarxien *395* E Malta
Tašauz *see* Dashkhovuz
Tasek Kenyir *386* region of NE Peninsular Malaysia
Tashauz *see* Dashkhovuz
Tashigang *134* E Bhutan
Tashir *98* *prev.* Kalinino. N Armenia
Tashi Yangtsi *134* E Bhutan
Tashkent *see.* Toshkent
Tash-Kumyr *357* *Kir.* Tash-Kömür. W Kyrgyzstan
Tasikmalaya *302* *prev.* Tasikmalaja. Java, C Indonesia
Tasiusaq *646* W Greenland
Tasman Bay *433* inlet of the Tasman Sea, on the N coast of South Island, New Zealand
Tasman Sea *101, 433* sea of the Pacific Ocean, to the of SE Australia
Tassili N'Ajjer *83* *var.* Hamada du Tinghert. Desert plateau of SE Algeria
Tassili ta-n-Ahaggar *83* *var.* Tassili du Hoggar. Desert plateau of S Algeria
Tastrup *218* Sjælland, E Denmark
Tatabánya *290* NW Hungary
Tataouine *573* *var.* Ţātawīn. SE Tunisia
Tatar Pazardzhik *see* Pazardzhik
Tatarskiy Provliv *485* *Eng.* Tatar Strait. Strait connecting Sea of Okhotsk and Sea of Japan, between Ostrov Sakhalin and the coast of SE Russian Federation
Tatarstan, Respublika *484* autonomous republic of W Russian Federation
Tathlīth *506* S Saudi Arabia
Tatlisu *215* *var.* Akanthou. NE Cyprus
Tatra Mountains *471, 519* *var.* High Tatra, *Slvk.* Tatry, *var.* Vysoké Tatry, *Ger.* Tatra, *var.* Hohe Tatra, *Hung.* Magas Tátra, *Pol.* Tatry. Mountains of Poland and Slovakia
Ta-t'ung *see* Datong
Tatvin *577* E Turkey
Tau *see* Amouli

Tau *642* island of Manua Islands, E American Samoa
Taubaté *145* S Brazil
Taumarunui *433* S North Island, New Zealand
Taungdwingyi *159* W Burma
Taunggyi *159* C Burma
Taunton *593* SW England, UK
Taupo *433* S North Island, New Zealand
Taupo, Lake *433* lake of C North Island, New Zealand
Tauragė *376* W Lithuania
Tauranga *433* C North Island, New Zealand
Taurus Mountains *576* *Turk.* Toros Dağları. Mountain range of S Turkey
Tauz *see* Tovuz
Ţavālesh, Kūhhā-ye *see* Talish Mountains
Tavastehus *see* Hämeenlinna
Taveta *342* S Kenya
Taveuni *246* island of N Fiji
Tavoy *159* *var.* Dawei. SE Burma
Tavua *246* Viti Levu, W Fiji
Tavuki *246* Kadavu, SW Fiji
Tawau *387* E Borneo, Malaysia
Tawi-Tawi *466* island of Tawi-Tawi Group, Philippines
Tawi-Tawi Group *466* island group of Sulu Archipelago, SW Philippines
Ţawkar *see* Tokar
Tawzar *see* Tozeur
Tay *593* river of C Scotland, UK
Tay, Firth of *593* estuary of the Tay, E Scotland, UK
Taymā' *506* NW Saudi Arabia
Taymyr, Ozero *485* Lake of N Russian Federation
Taymyr, Poluostrov *485* Peninsula of N Russian Federation
Tây Ninh *623* SW Vietnam
Taza *414* N Morocco
Tbilisi *262* *Geor.* T'bilisi, *prev.* Tiflis. ❖ of Georgia, SE Georgia
Tchad, Lac *see* Chad, Lake
Tchamba *567* E Togo
Tchaourou *132* E Benin
Tchetti *132* SW Benin
Tchibanga *258* S Gabon
Tchibenda, Lac *200* lake of S Congo
Teafatule *583* islet of Nukufetau, Tuvalu
Teafuaniua *583* islet of Nukufetau, Tuvalu
Teafuanonu *583* islet of Nukufetau, Tuvalu
Teafuone *583* islet of Nukufetau, Tuvalu
Te Anau *433* SW South Island, New Zealand
Te Anau, Lake *433* lake of W South Island, New Zealand
Tebaga, Jebel *573* mountain range of C Tunisia
Tébessa *83* NE Algeria
Tebicuary *460* river of S Paraguay
Tebingtinggi *302* NE Sumatra, W Indonesia
Tebingtinggi, Pulau *302* *var.* Pulau Rantau. Island to the E of Sumatra, W Indonesia
Teboe Top *538* SE Suriname
Tecuci *480* E Romania
Tedzhen *581* *Turkm.* Tejen. S Turkmenistan
Tedzhen *581* *Turkm.* Tejen, *Per.* Harīrūd. River of Turkmenistan and Iran
Tees *593* river of NE England, UK
Tegal *302* Java, C Indonesia
Tégua *615* Torres Islands, N Vanuatu
Tegucigalpa *288* ❖ of Honduras, SW Honduras
Tehrān *307* *var.* Teheran. ❖ of Iran, NW Iran
Tehuantepec, Golfo de *403* gulf of the Pacific Ocean
Tehuantepec, Istmo de *403* *var.* Isthmus of Tehuantepec. Narrowest part of Mexico, between the Bahía de Campeche and Golfo de Tehuantepec
Teiga Plateau *536* plateau of W Sudan
Teisen *see* Chech'ŏn
Teixeira Pinto *see* Canchungo
Tejo *see* Tagus
Tekapo, Lake *433* lake of C South Island, New Zealand
Tekeli *338* SE Kazakhstan
Tekeze *238, 243* *var.* Takkaze. River of Eritrea and Ethiopia
Tekirdağ *576* *It.* Rodosto. NW Turkey
Tekong, Pulau *517* island of E Singapore
Tekong Kechil, Pulau *517* island of E Singapore
Tela *288* NW Honduras
Telanaipura *see* Jambi
T'elavi *262* E Georgia
Tel Aviv-Yafo *317* C Israel
Teles Piras *see* São Manuel
Telica *436* W Nicaragua
Télimélé *281* W Guinea
Telire *206* river of E Costa Rica
Tell Abaid *see* At Tall al Abyaḑ
Tell Shedadi *see* Ash Shadādah
Tel'mansk *581* *Turkm.* Tel'man. N Turkmenistan
Telok Blangah *517* area of S Singapore
Telšiai *376* *Ger.* Telschen. NW Lithuania
Teluk Intan *386* *prev.* Teluk Anson. W Peninsular Malaysia
Tema *270* SE Ghana
Tembakul, Pulau *517* *prev.* Kusu Island. S Singapore
Temboni *see* Mitemele, Río
Temburong, Sungai *150* river of NE Brunei
Temelín *216* SW Czech Republic
Temerluh *386* *var.* Temerloh. SE Peninsular Malaysia
Temes *see* Timiş
Temesch *see* Timiş
Temeschwar *see* Timişoara
Temesvár *see* Timişoara
Temir *338* W Kazakhstan
Temirtau *338* *prev.* Samarkandski. C Kazakhstan
Temotuloto *583* islet of Nukufetau, Tuvalu
Tempisque *206* river of NW Costa Rica
Temuco *183* C Chile
Tena *228* C Ecuador
Ténado *157* W Burkina
Téna Kourou *157* mountain of SW Burkina
Tenan *see* Ch'ŏnan
Tenavatu *522* N Guadalcanal, Solomon Is
Tendaho *243* NE Ethiopia
Te-n-Dghâmcha, Sebkhet *398* *var.* Sebkha de Ndrhamcha, Sebkra de Ndaghamcha. Salt lake of W Mauritania
Tendō *330* Honshū, N Japan
Ténenkou *392* C Mali
Tenerife *531* island of Islas Canarias, SW Spain
Tengeh Reservoir *517* reservoir of W Singapore
Tengiz, Ozero *338* *Kaz.* Tengiz Köl. Salt lake of C Kazakhstan
Tengréla *326* *var.* Tingréla. N Ivory Coast
Teniente Rodolfo Marsh *90* Chilean research station of South Shetland Islands, Antarctica
Tenkodogo *157* S Burkina
Tennant Creek *101* C Australia
Tennessee *599* state of SE USA
Teno *see* Tana
Tenryū *330* river of Honshū, C Japan
Tensift *414* seasonal river of W Morocco
Tepelenë *81* *var.* Tepelena, *It.* Tepeleni. S Albania
Tepic *403* W Mexico
Teniente Rodolfo Marsh *90* Chilean research station of Antarctic Peninsula, Antarctica
Teplice *216* *Ger.* Teplitz, *prev.* Teplice-Šanov, *Ger.* Teplitz-Schönau. NW Czech Republic
Téra *439* W Niger
Teracina *321* S Italy
Teraina *346* *var.* Washington Island. Island of the Line Is, E Kiribati
Teramo *321* C Italy
Terceira *474* *var.* Ilha Terceira. Island of the Azores, Portugal
Terek-Say *357* *var.* Terek-Saj. W Kyrgyzstan
Teresina *145* *var.* Therezina. NE Brazil
Terevaka *183* mountain of Easter Island, W Chile
Terhathum *427* E Nepal
Termiz *610* *Rus.* Termez. SE Uzbekistan
Terneuzen *429* SW Netherlands
Terni *321* C Italy
Ternitz *106* E Austria
Ternopil' *586* *Rus.* Ternopol', *Pol.* Tarnopol. W Ukraine
Terrassa *531* *Cast.* Tarrasa. E Spain
Terre-de-Bas *646* island of S Guadeloupe
Terre-de-Haut *646* island of S Guadeloupe
Terre-Neuve *see* Newfoundland
Terschelling *429* island of Waddeneilanden, N Netherlands
Terter *see* Tärtär
Teruel *531* E Spain
Teseney *238* W Eritrea
Teslić *140* N Bosnia & Herzegovina
Tessalit *392* NE Mali
Tessaoua *439* S Niger
Tete *419* NW Mozambique
Tête Morne *224* S Dominica
Tetepare *522* island of the New Georgia Is, C Solomon Is
Tétouan *414* *Sp.* Tetuán. N Morocco
Tetovo *381* *Turk.* Kalkandelen, *Alb.* Tetovë, Tetova. NW FYR Macedonia
Tetschen *see* Děčín
Tetulia *117* river and W outlet of Ganges, S Bangladesh
Teupasenti *288* S Honduras
Tevere *321* river of C Italy
Teverya *317* *Eng.* Tiberias. N Israel
Texas *599* state of SC USA
Texel *429* island of Waddeneilanden, NW Netherlands
Teyateyaneng *366* NW Lesotho
Tha *359* river of NW Laos
Thaa Atoll *see* Kolhumadulu Atoll
Thabana Ntlenyana *366* *var.* Thabantshonyana. Mountain of E Lesotho
Thaba Tseka *366* C Lesotho
Thai, Ao *see* Thailand, Gulf of
Thai Binh *623* N Vietnam
Thailand *562-565* officially Kingdom of Thailand, *prev.* Siam. Country of SE Asia divided into 95 admin. units (provinces). ❖ Bangkok
Thailand, Gulf of *165, 563, 623* *var.* Gulf of Siam, *Th.* Ao Thai, *Vtn.* Vinh Thai Lan. Gulf of the South China Sea on the SW coast of SE Asia
Thai Nguyên *623* N Vietnam
Thakhek *see* Muang Khammouan
Thākurgaon *117* NW Bangladesh
Thamaga *142* S Botswana
Thames *593* river of S England, UK
Thāne *296* *prev.* Thana. W India
Thanh Hoa *623* N Vietnam
Thanintari Taungdan *see* Bilauktaung Range
Thanlwin *see* Salween
Thar Desert *296, 451* *var.* Great Indian Desert, Indian Desert. Desert region of India and Pakistan
Tharrawaddy *159* SW Burma
Tharthār, Buḩayrat ath *310* lake of C Iraq
Thásos *273* island of NE Greece
Thaton *159* SE Burma
Thaungyin *159* *Th.* Mae Nam Moi. River of Burma and Thailand
Thayetmyo *159* W Burma
Thebaide *276* SE Grenada island, Grenada
Therezina *see* Teresina
Thermaïkós Kólpos *273* *Eng.* Thermaic Gulf. Gulf of the Aegean Sea, N Greece
Thessaloníki *273* *Eng.* Salonica, *var.* Salonika, *SCr.* Solun, *Turk.* Selânik. N Greece
Thibaud *224* N Dominica
Thiès *510* W Senegal
Thika *342* S Kenya
Thikombia *see* Cikobia
Thiladhunmathi Atoll *390* *var.* Tiladummati Atoll. Atoll of N Maldives
Thimphu *134* ❖ of Bhutan, W Bhutan
Thio *650* C New Caledonia
Thionville *253* NE France
Thíra *273* island of SE Greece
Thiruvanathapuram *see* Trivandrum
Thisted *218* Jylland, NW Denmark
Thistilfjördhur *294* *var.* Thistil Fjord. Fjord of NE Iceland
Thithia *see* Cicia
Thitu Island *652* island of NW Spratly Islands
Thjórsá *294* river of C Iceland
Tholen *429* island to the SW of Netherlands
Thompson *170* C Canada
Thon Buri *563* C Thailand
Thonze *159* SW Burma
Thórisvatn *294* lake of C Iceland
Thorlákshöfn *294* SW Iceland
Thorn *see* Toruń
Thórshöfn *294* NE Iceland
Thoune *see* Thun
Thracian Sea *273* *Gk* Thrakikó Pélagos. Area of the Mediterranean Sea, NE Greece
Three Brothers *643* island group of C British Indian Ocean Territory
Thu Dâu Môt *623* *var.* Phu Cuong. S Vietnam
Thule *see* Qaanaaq
Thuli *636* *var.* Tuli. River of S Zimbabwe
Thun *546* *Fr.* Thoune. W Switzerland
Thunder Bay *171* formed 1970 by amalgamation of Fort William and Port Arthur. S Canada
Thuner See *546* lake of C Switzerland
Thüringer Wald *265* *Eng.* Thuringian Forest. Forested mountain range of C Germany
Thurso *593* N Scotland, UK
Thyolo *385* *var.* Cholo. S Malawi
Tianjin *187* *var.* T'ien-ching, Tientsin. City and municipality of NE China
Tiaret *83* *var.* Tihert. N Algeria
Tiaroye *510* W Senegal
Ti'avea *500* Upolu, Samoa
Tibastī, Sarīr *371* desert of Chad and Libya
Tibati *168* N Cameroon
Tiberias *see* Teverya
Tiberias, Lake *317* *var.* Sea of Galilee, *Heb.* Yam Kinneret, *Ar.* Bahrat Tabariya. Lake of N Israel
Tibesti *180, 371* *var.* Tibesti Massif. Mountain range of Chad and Libya
Tibet *191* cultural region of W China
Tibetan Autonomous Region *see* Xizang Zizhiqu
Tibet, Plateau of *see* Qing-Zang Gaoyuan
Tibnine *364* *var.* Tibnīn. S Lebanon
Tiburón, Isla del *403* *var.* Isla Tiburón. Island of NW Mexico
Tichau *see* Tychy
Tîchît *398* C Mauritania
Tichla *414* SW Western Sahara
Ticino *320* river of N Italy
Tidjikja *398* *prev.* Fort-Cappolani C Mauritania
Tîdra, Et *398* island to the W of Mauritania
Tiébélé *157* S Burkina
Tiel *429* S Netherlands
T'ien-ching *see* Tianjin
Tienen *127* *Fr.* Tirlemont. C Belgium
Tien Shan *186, 357* *Chin.* Tian Shan, *Rus.* Tyan'-Shan'. Mountain range of C Asia
Tientsin *see* Tianjin

Tierra del Fuego *95* island of Argentina and Chile
Tiflis *see* Tbilisi
Tiga, Île *650* island of Îles Loyauté, W New Caledonia
Tighina *408* *prev.* Bendery. E Moldova
Tigray *243* cultural region of N Ethiopia
Tigre *463* river of N Peru
Tigris *310, 577* *Ar.* Dijlah, *Turk.* Dicle. River of SW Asia
Tihert *see* Tiaret
Ti-hua *see* Ürümqi
Tijuana *403* NW Mexico
Tikinsso *281* river of C Guinea
Tiko *168* SW Cameroon
Tikopia *522* island of E Solomon Is
Tikus, Pulu *see* Direction Island
Tiladummati Atoll *see* Thiladhunmathi Atoll
Tilarán *206* NW Costa Rica
Tilburg *429* S Netherlands
Tilimsen *see* Tlemcen
Tillabéri *439* *var.* Tillabéry. W Niger
Timah, Bukit *517* hill of C Singapore
Timaru *433* C South Island, New Zealand
Timbedgha *398* *var.* Timbédra. SE Mauritania
Timbuktu *see* Tombouctou
Timiş *480* *Hung.* Temes, *Ger.* Temesch, *SCr.* Tamiš. River of Romania and Yugoslavia
Timişoara *480* *Hung.* Temesvár, *Ger.* Temeschwar. W Romania
Timmins *171* S Canada
Timor *302* island of Nusa Tenggara, C Indonesia
Timor Sea *100, 302* area of the Indian Ocean between Australia and Indonesia
Tindouf *83* W Algeria
Tingréla *see* Tengréla
Tinguilinta *281* river of W Guinea
Tinhosa Grande *505* island to the S of Príncipe, Sao Tome & Principe
Tinhosa Pequena *505* island to the S of Príncipe, Sao Tome & Principe
Tinian *650* island of S Northern Mariana Islands
Tínos *273* island of SE Greece
Tintamarre, Îlot *646* island of N Guadeloupe
Ţînţâne *398* S Mauritania
Tinto *see* Sico
Tiobraid Árainn *see* Tipperary
Tioman, Pulau *386* *var.* Tioman Island. Island of SE Peninsular Malaysia
Tipitapa *436* SW Nicaragua
Tipperary *314* *Ir.* Tiobraid Árainn. S Ireland
Tiquisate *see* Pueblo Nuevo Tiquisate
Tiranë *81* *Alb.* Tirana. ❖ of Albania, C Albania
Tiraspol *408* *Rus.* Tiraspol'. E Moldova
Tirlemont *see* Tienen
Tirol *106* *var.* Tyrol, *It.* Tirolo. Cultural region of W Austria
Tirreno, Mare *see* Tyrrhenian Sea
Tirso *320* river of Sardegna, W Italy
Tiruchchirāppalli *296* *prev.* Trichinopoly. S India
Tisa *see* Tisza
Tisza *290, 630* *Ger.* Theiss, *Cz/Rom/SCr.* Tisa. River of E Europe
Titano, Monte *502* mountain of C San Marino
Titao *157* NW Burkina
Tite *282* SW Guinea-Bissau
Titicaca, Lake *136, 463* lake of Bolivia and Peru
Titograd *see* Podgorica
Titova Mitrovica *see* Kosovska Mitrovica
Titovo Užice *see* Užice
Titov Veles *381* *prev.* Veles, *Turk.* Köprülü. C FYR Macedonia
Titov Vrh *381* mountain of NW FYR Macedonia
Tivaouane *510* W Senegal
Tivoli *276* NE Grenada island, Grenada
Tivoli *321* C Italy
Ţīwī *448* NE Oman
Tizi Ouzou *83* N Algeria
Tiznit *414* SW Morocco
Tjilatjap *see* Cilacap
Tjirebon *see* Cirebon
Tkibuli *see* Tqibuli
Tkvarcheli *see* Tqvarch'eli
Tlemcen *83* *var.* Tilimsen. NW Algeria
Tlokoeng *366* NE Lesotho
Tlokweng *142* S Botswana
Tmassah *371* C Libya
Toamasina *382* *prev.* Tamatave. E Madagascar
Toba, Danau *302* lake of Sumatra, W Indonesia
Tobago *570* island of the West Indies which, with Trinidad, forms Trinidad & Tobago
Tobago Cays *498* cays of SW St Vincent & the Grenadines
Toba Kākar Range *451* mountain range of NW Pakistan
Tobi *455* island of S Palau
Tobol'sk *484* C Russian Federation
Tobruch *see* Ţubruq
Tobruk *see* Ţubruq
Tocantins *145* river of N Brazil
Tocumen *456* C Panama
Tocuyito *619* NW Venezuela
Todos os Santos, Baía de *145* bay of the Atlantic Ocean, on the E coast of Brazil
Tōen *see* T'aoyüan
Tofua *568* island of Ha'apai Group, Tonga
Toga *615* Torres Islands, N Vanuatu
Togo *566-567* officially Togolese Republic of Togo, *prev.* French Togoland. Country of West Africa divided into 5 admin. units (regions). ❖ Lomé
Tohoun *567* SE Togo
Tokar *536* *var.* Ţawkar. NE Sudan
Tokat *577* N Turkey
Tŏkchŏk-kundo *350* island group of NW South Korea
Tŏkch'ŏn *349* C North Korea
Tokelau *653* New Zealand dependent territory of the Pacific Ocean
Tőketerebes *see* Trebišov
Tokmak *357* *Kir.* Tokmok. N Kyrgyzstan
Tōkō *see* Tungkang
Tokoroa *433* C North Island, New Zealand
Toktogul *357* W Kyrgyzstan
Toku *568* island of N Tonga
Tokuno-shima *330* island of Amami-shotō, SW Japan
Tokushima *330* Shikoku, SW Japan
Tokuyama *330* Honshū, W Japan
Tokwe *636* river of SE Zimbabwe
Tokyo *330, 335* *var.* Tōkyō. ❖ of Japan, Honshū, SE Japan
Tôlañaro *382* *prev.* Faradofay, Fort-Dauphin. S Madagascar
Tolbukhin *see* Dobrich
Toledo *136* W Bolivia
Toledo *466* *var.* Toledo City. Cebu, Philippines
Toledo *531* C Spain
Toledo *599* Ohio, NE USA
Toledo Settlement *130* SE Belize
Toliara *382* *var.* Toliary, *prev.* Tuléar. SW Madagascar
Tolmin *520* *Ger.* Tolmein. W Slovenia
Tolo, Teluk *302* bay of Laut Banda on the E coast of Celebes, C Indonesia
Tolsan-do *350* island of S South Korea
Toluca *403* *var.* Toluca de Lerdo. C Mexico
Toluca de Lerdo *see* Toluca
Tol'yatti *484* *prev.* Stavropol'. W Russian Federation
Toma *157* W Burkina
Tomakomai *331* Hokkaidō, N Japan
Tomar *474* W Portugal
Tomanivi *246* *var.* Mount Victoria. Mountain of Viti Levu, W Fiji
Tomás Gomensoro *607* N Uruguay
Tombali *282* river of SW Guinea-Bissau
Tombeau, River du *400* river of NW Mauritius
Tombouctou *392* *Eng.* Timbuktu. N Mali
Tombua *88* *Port.* Porto Alexandre. SW Angola
Tominé *281* river of W Guinea
Tomini, Teluk *302* *prev.* Teluk Gorontalo. Bay of Laut Maluku on the E coast of Celebes, C Indonesia
Tomsk *485* C Russian Federation
Tomur Feng *see* Pobedy, Pik
Tönder *218* Jylland, SW Denmark
Tonga *568-569* officially Kingdom of Tonga, Friendly Islands. Country of the Pacific Ocean divided into 5 admin units. ❖ Nuku'Alofa
Tongatapu *568* island of Tongatapu Group, Tonga
Tongatapu Group *568* island group of S Tonga
Tonghae *350* NE South Korea
Tong-hae *see* Japan, Sea of
Tonghua *187* Jilin, NE China
Tongjosŏn-man *349* *prev.* Broughton Bay. Bay of the Sea of Japan on the E coast of North Korea
Tongking, Gulf of *187, 623* *Chin.* Beibu Wan, *Vtn.* Vinh Bắc Bô. Gulf of the South China Sea, SE Asia
Tongsa *134* C Bhutan
Tongue of the Ocean *112* strait between Exuma Cays and Andros I, Bahamas
Tônlé Sap *165* *Eng.* Great Lake. Lake of W Cambodia
Tonosí *456* S Panama
Tønsberg *444* S Norway
Toowoomba *101* E Australia
Topeka *599* Kansas, C USA
Topľa *519* *Hung.* Toplya. River of NE Slovakia
Toplya *see* Topľa
Topoľčany *519* *Hung.* Nagytapolcsány. W Slovakia
Topolya *see* Bačka Topola
Toraigh *see* Tory Island
Torbeck *286* SW Haiti
Torghay *338* W Kazakhstan
Torino *320* *Eng.* Turin. N Italy
Torneälv *543* river of NE Sweden
Tornio *249* *Swe.* Torneå. NW Finland
Tornionjoki *249* *Swe.* Torneälven. River of Finland and Sweden
Torola *235* river of El Salvador and Honduras
Toronto *171, 175* S Canada
Tororo *584* E Uganda
Toros Dağları *see* Taurus Mountains
Torquay *593* SW England, UK
Torre del Greco *321* S Italy
Torrejón, Embalse de *531* reservoir of W Spain
Torrelevega *531* N Spain
Torrens, Lake *101* salt lake of S Australia
Torreón *403* N Mexico
Torres Islands *615* *Fr.* Îles Torrès. Island group of N Vanuatu
Torres Strait *101, 458* strait connecting the Arafura Sea and Coral Sea, between Australia and the island of New Guinea
Torsa *134* river of SW Bhutan
Tórshavn *644* *var.* Thorshavn. ❖ of Faeroe Islands, Streymoy, N Faeroe Islands
Torteval *647* SW Guernsey
Tortoise Islands *see* Galapagos Islands
Tortola *643* island of C British Virgin Islands
Tortosa *531* E Spain
Tortue, Île de la *286* *var.* Tortuga I. Island of N Haiti
Tortue, Montagne *645* mountain range of C French Guiana
Toruń *471* *Ger.* Thorn. C Poland
Tõrva *240* *Ger.* Törwa. S Estonia
Tory Island *314* *Ir.* Toraigh. Island of N Ireland
Torysa *519* *Hung.* Tarca. River of NE Slovakia
Toscano, Archipelago *320* *var.* Tuscan Archipelago. Island group of C Italy
Tosco-Emiliano, Appennino *320* mountain range of C Italy
Tōsei *see* Tungshih
Toshkent *610* *Rus.* Tashkent. ❖ of Uzbekistan, E Uzbekistan
Toteng *142* C Botswana
Totness *538* N Suriname
Totonicapán *278* W Guatemala
Totota *368* C Liberia
Totoya *246* island to the SE of Viti Levu, S Fiji
Tottori *330* Honshū, W Japan
Touba *326* W Ivory Coast
Touba *510* W Senegal
Touboro *168* NE Cameroon
Toubkal, Jebel *414* mountain of W Morocco
T'ouch'eng *555* NE Taiwan
T'ouch'ien Hsi *555* river of NW Taiwan
T'oufen *555* NW Taiwan
Tougan *157* W Burkina
Tougana *439* SW Niger
Touggourt *83* NE Algeria
Tougué *281* NW Guinea
Touho *650* Île Balabio, E New Caledonia
Toukoto *392* W Mali
Toulon *253* SE France
Toulouse *253* S France
Toumodi *326* C Ivory Coast
Tounan *555* W Taiwan
Toungoo *159* S Burma
Tourane *see* Đà Nẵng
Tournai *127* *Dut.* Doornik. W Belgium
Tours *253* NW France
Tovar *619* W Venezuela
Tovuz *110* *Rus.* Tauz. W Azerbaijan
Towada *330* Honshū, N Japan
Townsville *101* NE Australia
Towraghondī *101* NW Afghanistan
Towuti, Danau *302* lake of Celebes, C Indonesia
Toyama *330* Honshū, C Japan
Toyohara *see* Fengyüan
Toyohara *see* Yuzhno-Sakhalinsk
Toyohashi *330* Honshū, C Japan
Toyonaka *330* Honshū, C Japan
Toyota *330* Honshū, C Japan
Tozeur *573* *var.* Tawzar. W Tunisia
Tqibuli *262* *Rus.* Tkibuli. W Georgia
Tqvarch'eli *262* *Rus.* Tkvarcheli. NW Georgia
Trabzon *577* *Eng.* Trebizond. NE Turkey
Trafalgar *224* S Dominica
Tráighlí *see* Tralee
Traiguén *183* C Chile
Traina Garden *see* Mazra'at Turaynā
Traisen *106* river of NE Austria
Trakai *376* SE Lithuania
Tralee *314* *Ir.* Tráighlí. SW Ireland
Trang *563* S Thailand
Tranqueras *607* N Uruguay
Trans-Alaska pipeline *598* oil pipeline of Alaska, USA
Transantarctic Mountains *90* mountain range of Antarctica
Transkei Bantustan 'self-governing homeland' of E Cape Province, South Africa; created in 1963, abolished in 1994
Transylvania *480* cultural region of NW Romania
Transylvanian Alps *see* Carpaţii Meridionali
Trant's Bay *649* bay of the Caribbean Sea on the E coast of Montserrat
Trapani *321* Sicilia, S Italy
Trâpeăng Vêng *165* C Cambodia
Traralgon *101* SE Australia
Trasimeno, Lago *321* *var.* Lake of Perugia, *Ger.* Trasimenischersee. Lake of C Italy
Träskända *see* Järvenpää
Traù *see* Trogir
Traun *106* river of N Austria
Traun *106* N Austria
Traunsee *106* *var.* Gmundner See, *Eng.* Lake Traun. Lake of N Austria

Trautenau *see* Trutnov
Tra Vinh *623 var.* Phu Vinh. S Vietnam
Travnik *140* C Bosnia & Herzegovina
Trbovlje *520 Ger.* Trifail. C Slovenia
Treasury Islands *522* island group of W Solomon Is
Třebíč *216 Ger.* Trebitsch. S Czech Republic
Trebinje *140* S Bosnia & Herzegovina
Trebišov *519 Hung.* Tőketerebes. E Slovakia
Trebizond *see* Trabzon
Trebnje *520* SE Slovenia
Treinta y Tres *607* E Uruguay
Trelew *95* SE Argentina
Trenčín *519 Ger.* Trentschin, *Hung.* Trencsén. W Slovakia
Treng *165 prev.* Treng. NE Cambodia
Trent *593* river of C England, UK
Trento *320 Eng.* Trent, *Ger.* Trient. N Italy
Trenton *599* New Jersey, E USA
Tres Arroyos *95* E Argentina
Treskavica *140* mountain range of SE Bosnia & Herzegovina
Três Marias, Represa *145* reservoir of SE Brazil
Treviso *321* N Italy
Trial Farm *130* N Belize
Triangle *636* SE Zimbabwe
Tricaorno *see* Triglav
Trichinopoly *see* Tiruchchirāppalli
Trichūr *296* S India
Trient *see* Trento
Trier *264* W Germany
Triesen *374* SW Liechtenstein
Triesenberg *374* SW Liechtenstein
Trieste *321 Slvn.* Trst. N Italy
Trieste, Gulf of *520 It.* Golfo di Trieste, *Slvn.* Tržaški Zaliv, *Croat.* Tršćanski Zaljev. Gulf to the SW of Slonia
Trifail *see* Trbovlje
Triglav *520 It.* Tricaorno. Mountain of NW Slovenia
Tríkala *273 prev.* Trikkala. C Greece
Trikomo *see* Iskele
Trincomalee *534* NE Sri Lanka
Třinec *216 Ger.* Trzynietz. SE Czech Republic
Trinidad *136* N Bolivia
Trinidad *570* island of the West Indies which, with Tobago, forms Trinidad & Tobago
Trinidad *607* SW Uruguay
Trinidad and Tobago *570-571* officially Republic of Trinidad and Tobago. Country of the West Indies divided into 6 admin. units (counties). ❖ Port-of-Spain
Trinité, Montagnes de la *645* mountain range of C French Guiana
Triolet *400* NW Mauritius
Trípoli *273 prev.* Trípolis. S Greece
Tripoli *364 var.* Trâblous, Ţarābulus. N Lebanon
Tripoli *371 Ar.* Ţarābulus al-Gharb. ❖ of Libya, NW Libya
Tristan da Cunha *652* dependent territory of St Helena, South Atlantic Ocean
Tristao, Îles *281* islands to the W of Guinea
Triton Island *651* island of S Paracel Islands
Trivandrum *296 var.* Thiruvanathapuram. S India
Trnava *519 Ger.* Tyrnau, *Hung.* Nagyszombat. W Slovakia
Trobriand Islands *see* Kiriwina Islands
Trogir *209 It.* Traù. S Croatia
Troía Peninsula *474* peninsula of W Portugal
Trois-Rivières *171* SE Canada
Trojan *see* Troyan
Trollhättan *543* SW Sweden
Tromsø *444* NE Norway
Trondheim *444 prev.* Nidaros, Trondhjem, *Ger.* Drontheim. C Norway
Trondheimsfjorden *444* fjord of SW Norway
Troodos *see* Olympus, Mount
Troodos Mountains *215 var.* Troödos. Mountain range of C Cyprus
Troppau *see* Opava
Trou-du-Nord *286* N Haiti
Troumaka *498* NW St Vincent, St Vincent & the Grenadines
Troyan *152 var.* Trojan. NW Bulgaria
Troyes *253* NE France
Tršćanski Zaljev *see* Trieste, Gulf of
Trst *see* Trieste
Truc Giang *see* Bên Tre
Trucial Coast *590* coastal region of the United Arab Emirates
Trucial States *see* United Arab Emirates
Trujillo *288* N Honduras
Trujillo *463* NW Peru
Trujillo *619* NW Venezuela
Trung Phân *623 prev.* Annam. Cultural region of Vietnam
Trunk Island *643* island of C Bermuda
Truro *593* SW England, UK
Trutnov *216 Ger.* Trautenau. NE Czech Republic
Tržaški Zaliv *see* Trieste, Gulf of
Tržič *520 Ger.* Neumarktl. NW Slovenia
Trzynietz *see* Třinec
Tsabong *see* Tshabong
Tsaghkahovit *98* W Armenia
Tsamkong *see* Zhanjiang
Tsangpo *see* Brahmaputra
Tsaratanana, Tangorombohitr' i *382 var.* Massif du Tsaratanana. Mountains of N Madagascar
Tsarigrad *see* İstanbul
Tsaritsyn *see* Volgograd
Tschakathurn *see* Čakovec
Tschenstochau *see* Częstochowa
Tschernembl *see* Črnomelj
Tschorna *see* Mustvee
Tselinograd *see* Akmola
Tsengwen Hsi *555* river of SW Taiwan
Tsetserleg *412* W Mongolia
Tsévié *567* S Togo
Tshabong *142 var.* Tsabong. SW Botswana
Tshane *142* C Botswana
Tshaneni *540* NE Swaziland
Tshangalele, Lac *see* Lufira, Lac de Retenue de la
Tshela *203* W Dem. Rep. Congo (Zaire)
Tshikapa *203* SW Dem. Rep. Congo (Zaire)
Tshohoha Sud, Lac *see* Cyohoha Sud, Lac
Tshuapa *203* river of C Dem. Rep. Congo (Zaire)
Tsinan *see* Jinan
Tsing Hai *see* Qinghai Hu
Tsinghai *see* Qinghai
Tsingtao *see* Qingdao
Tsingyuan *see* Baoding
Tsinkiang *see* Quanzhou
Tsiroanomandidy *382* C Madagascar
Tsiteli-Tskaro *see* Dedoplistsqaro
Tsitsihar *see* Qiqihar
Tskhinvall *262* C Georgia
Tsna *122* river of S Belarus
Tsodilo Hills *142* mountain range of NW Botswana
Tsoelike *366* SE Lesotho
Tsu *330* Honshū, C Japan
Tsuchiura *330* Honshū, SE Japan
Tsugara-kaikyō *330* strait connecting the Sea of Japan and Pacific Ocean, between Hokkaidō and Honshū, N Japan
Tsumeb *423* N Namibia
Tsumkwe *423* NE Namibia
Tsuruga *330* Honshū, C Japan
Tsuruoka *330* Honshū, N Japan
Tsushima *330* island group to the W of Honshū, W Japan
Tsushima Strait *330 var.* Korea Strait. Strait connecting the Sea of Japan and East China Sea, between South Korea and Japan
Tsuyama *330* Honshū, W Japan
Tuamotu, Îles *646* island group of N French Polynesia
Tuasivi *500* Savai'i, Samoa
Tuban, Wādī *627* dry watercourse of S Yemen
Tubmanburg *368* NW Liberia
Ţubruq *371 Eng.* Tobruk, *It.* Tobruch. NE Libya
Tucker's Town *643* E Bermuda
Tuckum *see* Tukums
Tucson *598* Arizona, SW USA
Tucumán *see* San Miguel de Tucumán
Tucupita *619* E Venezuela
Tucuruí, Represa de *145* reservoir of N Brazil
Tudmur *551 var.* Tadmur, *Eng.* Palmyra. C Syria
Tugalan *see* Kolkhozobod
Tuira *456* river of SE Panama
Tukangbesi, Kepulauan *302* island group to the SE of Celebes, C Indonesia
Tu-k'ou *see* Panzhihua
Tūkrah *371* NE Libya
Tukums *362 Ger.* Tuckum. W Latvia
Tukuyu *560* S Tanzania
Tula *642* Tutuila, W American Samoa
Tula *484* W Russian Federation
Tulaghi *522* Florida I. Solomon Islands
Tulcán *228* N Ecuador
Tulcea *480* E Romania
Tuléar *see* Toliara
Tuli *see* Thuli
Tūlkarm *317, 318* NW West Bank
Tulle *253* S France
Tulsa *599* Oklahoma, SC USA
Tulsipur *427* W Nepal
Tuluá *195* W Colombia
Tumaco *195* SW Colombia
Tumareng *284* NW Guyana
Tumba, Lac *see* Ntomba, Lac
Tumbes *463* NW Peru
Tumen *349 Rus.* Tumyntszyan. River of China and North Korea
Tumpat *386* N Peninsular Malaysia
Tumuc-Humac Mountains *145 Port.* Serra Tumuc-Humac. Mountain range of N South America
Tumuc-Humac, Serra *see* Tumuc-Humac Mountains
Tunapuna *570* N Trinidad, Trinidad & Tobago
Tunduru *560* S Tanzania
Tundzha *152 var.* Tundža. River of Bulgaria and Turkey
Tungabhadra *296* river of S India
Tungaru *346 prev.* Gilbert Islands. Island group of W Kiribati
Tungkang *555 var.* Tung-chiang, *Jap.* Tōkō. SW Taiwan
T'ung-shan *see* Xuzhou
Tungshih *555 Jap.* Tōsei. W Taiwan
Tung-t'ing Hu *see* Dongting Hu
Tunis *573 var.* Tūnis. of Tunisia, NE Tunisia
Tunis, Golfe de *573* gulf of the Mediterranean Sea on the NE coast of Tunisia
Tunisia *572-575* officially Republic of Tunisia. Country of North Africa divided into 23 admin. units (governorates). ❖ Tunis
Tunja *195* C Colombia
Tương Đương *623* NW Vietnam
Tupiza *136* S Bolivia
Turan Lowland *581, 610 var.* Turan Plain, *Rus.* Turanskaya Nizmennost'. Plain of Turkmenistan and Uzbekistan
Ţurayf *506* N Saudi Arabia
Turbat *450* W Pakistan
Turčianský Svätý Martin *see* Martin
Turda *480* NW Romania
Turgel *see* Türi
Tŭrgovishte *152 var.* Tărgovište, *prev.* Eski Dzhumaya. NE Bulgaria
Turgutlu *576* W Turkey
Türi *240 Ger.* Turgel. C Estonia
Turin *see* Torino
Turkana, Lake *243, 342 Eng.* Lake Rudolf. Lake of E Africa
Turkestan *338 Kaz.* Türkistan. S Kazakhstan
Turkestan Range *558 Rus.* Turkestanskiy Khrebet. Mountain range of NW Tajikistan
Turkestanskiy Khrebet *see* Turkestan Range
Turkey *576-577* officially Republic of Turkey, *Turk.* Türkiye Cumhuriyeti. Country of W Asia divided into 73 admin. units. ❖ Ankara
Turkish Republic of Northern Cyprus *see* Cyprus
Turkmenbashi *581 prev.* Krasnovodsk. W Turkmenistan
Turkmenistan *580-581* officially Republic of Turkmenistan, *prev.* Turkmenskaya Soviet Socialist Republic. Country divided into 4 admin. units (oblasts). ❖ Ashgabat
Turkmenskiy Zaliv *581 Turkm.* Türkmen Aylagy. Inlet of the Caspian Sea, on the W coast of Turkmenistan
Turks and Caicos Islands *653* British dependent territory of the Atlantic Ocean
Turks Islands *653* island group of SE Turks and Caicos Islands
Turku *249 Swe.* Åbo. SW Finland
Turkwel *342* seasonal river of NW Kenya
Turmero *619* N Venezuela
Turneffe Islands *130* islands of E Belize
Turnhout *127* NE Belgium
Turning Basin *648* undersea feature of the Pacific Ocean, NW Johnston Atoll
Turnov *216* N Czech Republic
Turnu Severin *see* Drobeta-Turnu Severin
Turócszentmárton *see* Martin
Turquino, Pico *210* mountain of SE Cuba
Turrialba *206* E Costa Rica
Tursunzode *558 prev.* Regar. W Tajikistan
Tŭrtkŭl' *610 prev.* Petroaleksandrovsk, *Rus.* Turtkul. W Uzbekistan
Turtle Islands *514* island group of SW Sierra Leone
Tuscaloosa *599* Alabama, SE USA
Tuscan Archipelago *see* Toscano, Arcipelago
Tuscany *325.* region of Italy
Tuticorin *296* S India
Tutong *150* NW Brunei
Tutong *150* river of C Brunei
Tutrakan *152* N Bulgaria
Tutuala *305* W East Timor
Tutuila *642* island of W American Samoa
Tutume *142* E Botswana
Tuvalu *582-583 prev.* The Ellice Islands. Country of the Pacific Ocean. ❖ Fongafale
Tuvana-i-colo *246* island to the S of the Lau Group, SE Fiji
Tuvana-i-ra *246* island to the S of the Lau Group, SE Fiji
Tuvuca *246 prev.* Tuvutha. Island of the Lau Group, E Fiji
Ţuwayq, Jabal *506* mountain range of C Saudi Arabia
Tuxtla Gutiérrez *403 var.* Tuxtla. SE Mexico
Tuy Hoa *623* SE Vietnam
Tuz Gölü *577 Eng.* Lake Tuz. Lake of C Turkey
Tuz Khurmātū *310* N Iraq
Tuzla *140* NE Bosnia & Herzegovina
Tver' *484* W Russian Federation
Tvøroyri *644 var.* Tverå. Sudhuroy, S Faeroe Islands
Twante *159* S Burma
Tweed *593* river of SE Scotland, UK
Twin Falls *598* Idaho, NW USA
Twizel *433* C South Island, New Zealand

Tychy 471 Ger. Tichau. S Poland
Tynda 485 E Russian Federation
Tyne 593 river of NE England, UK
Tyneside 569
Tyrnau see Trnava
Tyrol see Tirol
Tyrrhenian Sea 321 It. Mare Tirreno. Area of the Mediterranean Sea
Tyumen' 484, 489 C Russian Federation
Tyup 357 var. Tjup. NE Kyrgyzstan
Tyva, Respublika 484 autonomous republic of C Russian Federation
Tzekung see Zigong

U

Uaco Cungo 88 var. Waku Kungo, Port. Santa Comba. C Angola
UAE see United Arab Emirates
Uamba see Wamba
Uanle Uen see Wanlaweyn
Ubangi 179, 200, 203 Fr. Oubangui. River of C Africa
Ubarts' 122 river of Belarus and Ukraine
Ubayyiḑ, Wādī al 310 dry watercourse of SW Iraq
Ube 330 Honshū, W Japan
Uberaba 145 S Brazil
Uberlândia 145 S Brazil
Ubin, Pulau 517 island of NE Singapore
Ubon Ratchathani 563 E Thailand
Ucar 110 Rus. Udzhary. C Azerbaijan
Ucayali 463 river of C Peru
Uchquduq 610 Rus. Uchkuduk. C Uzbekistan
Udine 321 N Italy
Udmurtskya Respublika 484 autonomous republic of W Russian Federation
Udon Thani 563 N Thailand
Udzhary see Ucar
Ueda 330 Honshū, C Japan
Uele 203 var. Welle. River of N Dem. Rep. Congo (Zaire)
Ufa 484 W Russian Federation
Ugāle 362 NW Latvia
Uganda 584-585 officially Republic of Uganda. Country of E Africa divided into 39 admin. units (districts). ❖ Kampala
Ugum 647 river, S Guam
Uherské Hradiště 216 Ger. Ungarisch-Hradisch. SE Czech Republic
Úhlava 216 Ger. Angel. River of W Czech Republic
Uíge 88 Port. Vila Marechal Carmona, Carmona. NW Angola
'Uiha 568 var. Uiha. Island of the Ha'apai Group, Tonga
Ŭijŏngbu 350 Jap. Giseifu. NW South Korea
Uis 423 NW Namibia
Uitenhage 527 Eastern Cape, S South Africa
Ujae 396 island of W Marshall Islands
Ujelang 396 island of W Marshall Islands
Újgradiska see Nova Gradiška
'Ujman see Ajman
Ujungpandang 302 prev. Makasar, Macassar. Celebes, C Indonesia
Ujung Salang see Phuket
Újvidék see Novi Sad
UK see United Kingdom
Ukerewe 560 island of NW Tanzania, situated at the S of Lake Victoria
Uki Island 522 island of E Solomon Islands
Ukmergė 376 E Lithuania
Ukraine 586-589 officially Republic of Ukraine, Ukr. Ukrayina, Rus. Ukraina, prev. Ukrainian Soviet Socialist Republic, Ukrainskaya S.S.R. Country of E Europe divided into 25 admin. units (24 regions and 1 republic). ❖ Kiev
Uku-jima 330 island of Gotō-rettō, SW Japan
Ula 122 Rus. Ulla. River of N Belarus
Ulaangom 412 NW Mongolia
Ulan Bator 412 var. Ulaanbaatar. ❖ of Mongolia, C Mongolia
Ulan-Ude 485 prev. Verkhneudinsk. C Russian Federation
Ulawa Island 522 island of E Solomon Is
Uleåborg see Oulu
Uleälv see Oulujoki
Uleträsk see Oulujärvi
Uli 338 NW Kazakhstan
Uliastay 412 W Mongolia
Ulithi 406 atoll of W Micronesia
Ulla see Ula
Ullapool 593 N Scotland, UK
Ulm 265 S Germany
Ulonguè 419 var. Ulongwé. NW Mozambique
Ulsan 350 Jap. Urusan. SE South Korea
Ulster 593 province of Ireland, mostly included within Northern Ireland, UK
Ulúa 288 river of NW Honduras
Uluru 101 var. Ayers Rock. Rocky outcrop of C Australia
Ulverstone 101 Tasmania, Australia
Ul'yanovsk 484 prev. Simbirsk. W Russian Federation
Uman' 586 C Ukraine
'Umān, Khalīj see Gulf of Oman
Umatac 647 SW Guam
Umboi 458 var. Rooke I. Island of E Papua New Guinea
Umbro-Marchigiano, Appennino 321 mountains of C Italy
Umeå 543 NE Sweden
Umeälv 543 river of NE Sweden
Umm al Ḩayt, Wādī see Amilḩayt, Wādī
Umm al Qaiwain 590 Ar. Umm al Qaywayn. NE United Arab Emirates
Umm an Na'sān 115 island of W Bahrain
Umm aş Şabbān see Al Muḩammadīyah
Umm as Samin 448 seasonal desert lake of W Oman
Umm Bāb 479 W Qatar
Umm Durmān see Omdurman
Umm Ruwaba 536 var. Umm Ruwābah, Um Ruwāba. C Sudan
Umm Sa'īd see Musay'īd
Umm Şalāl 'Alī 479 var. Umm Silal Ali. NE Qatar
Umm Şalāl Muḩammad 479 var. Umm Silal Mohammed. E Qatar
Umtali see Mutare
Umtata 527 Eastern Cape, SE South Africa
Umvukwes see Mvurwi
Umvuma see Mvuma
Umzingwani 636 river of S Zimbabwe
Una 140, 209 river of Bosnia & Herzegovina and Croatia
'Unayzah 506 var. Anaiza. C Saudi Arabia
Ungama Bay 342 var. Formosa Bay. Bay of the Indian Ocean to the SE of Kenya
Ungarisches Erzgebirge see Slovenské Rudohorie
Ungarisch-Hradisch see Uherské Hradiště
Ungava Bay 171 bay of the Labrador Sea, E Canada
Ungava, Péninsule d' 171 peninsula of E Canada
Ungheni 408 Rus. Ungeny. W Moldova
Ungvár see Uzhhorod
Union 276 NW Grenada island, Grenada
Union Island 498 island of SW St Vincent & the Grenadines
United Arab Emirates 590-591 prev. Trucial States, abbrev. U.A.E. Country of SW Asia comprised of 7 admin units (states). ❖ Abu Dhabi
United Kingdom 592-597 officially United Kingdom of Great Britain and Northern Ireland, abbrev. UK. Country of NW Europe comprising from 1st April 1998, England (149 admin. units -35 counties, 45 unitary authorities, 36 metropolitan boroughs, 32 London boroughs and the City of London), Wales (22 admin. units - unitary authorities), Scotland (22 admin. units - local authorities) and Northern Ireland (26 admin. units - districts). ❖ London
United States of America 598-605 officially United States of America, abbrev. USA. Country of North America divided into 51 admin. units (50 states, 1 federal district). ❖ Washington DC
Uno 282 Ilha de Uno, Guinea-Bissau
Uno, Ilha de 282 island of SW Guinea-Bissau
Uoleva 568 island of the Ha'apai Group, Tonga
Uolo, Río 236 var. Mbini, Woleu. River of Equatorial Guinea and Gabon
Uozu 330 Honshū, C Japan
Upaar Lagoon 534 lagoon of E Sri Lanka
Upala 206 NW Costa Rica
Upata 619 E Venezuela
Upernavik 646 W Greenland
Upington 527 Northern Cape, W South Africa
'Upolu 500 island of SE Samoa
Upper Bann 593 river of Northern Ireland, UK
Upper Conaree 494 E St Kitts, St Kitts & Nevis
Upper Hutt 433 S North Island, New Zealand
Upper Lough Erne 593 lake of Northern Ireland, UK
Upper Mortlocks 406 island group of C Micronesia
Upper Peirce Reservoir 517 reservoir of C Singapore
Upper Volta see Burkina
Uppsala 543 SE Sweden
Ural 338, 484 Kaz. Zayyq. River of Kazakhstan and Russian Federation
Ural Mountains 484 var. Ural'skiy Khrebet, Ural'skiye Gory. Mountain range of W Russian Federation
Ural'sk 338 Kaz. Oral. NW Kazakhstan
Ura-Tyube 558 NW Tajikistan
Ureca 236 prev. San Antonio de Ureca. S Bioko, Equatorial Guinea
Uréparapara 615 Banks Islands, N Vanuatu
Urfa see Şanlıurfa
Urganch 610 Rus. Urgench, prev. Novo-Urgench. W Uzbekistan
Urgench see Urganch
Urgut 610 SE Uzbekistan
Urlings 92 SW Antigua, Antigua & Barbuda
Urmia see Orūmīyeh
Urmia, Lake see Orūmīyeh, Daryācheh-ye
Uroševac 630 Alb. Ferizaj. S Serbia, Yugoslavia
Uruapan 403 var. Uruapan del Progreso. SW Mexico
Uruguaiana 144 S Brazil
Urubamba 463 river of C Peru
Uruguay 95, 145, 607 Port. Uruguai. River of S South America
Uruguay 606-609 officially Eastern Republic of Uruguay. Country of South America divided into 19 admin. units (departments). ❖ Montevideo
Urukthapel 455 island of C Palau
Ürümqi 186 var. Urumchi, Wu-lu-mu-ch'i, prev. Ti-hua. Xinjiang Uygur Zizhiqu, NW China
Urusan see Ulsan
USA see United States of America
Uşak 576 prev. Ushak. W Turkey
Usakos 423 C Namibia
Usborne, Mount 645 mountain of East Falkland, E Falkland Islands
Ushant see Ouessant, Île d'
Ushuaia 95 S Tierra del Fuego, Argentina
Usk 593 Wel. Wysg. River of S Wales,UK
Üsküb see Skopje
Usmas Ezers 362 lake of W Latvia
Usol'ye-Sibirskoye 485 C Russian Federation
Ussuriysk 485 prev. Voroshilov, Nikol'sk-Ussuriyskiy. SE Russian Federation
Ust'-Abakanskoye see Abakan
Uster 546 NE Switzerland
Ustica, Isola de 321 island of S Italy
Ústí nad Labem 216 Ger. Aussig. NW Czech Republic
Ustinov see Izhevsk
Ust'-Kamchatsk 485 NE Russian Federation
Ust'-Kamenogorsk 338 Kaz. Öskemen. E Kazakhstan
Ust'-Sisol'sk see Syktyvkar
Ustyurt Plateau 338, 610 Uzb. Ustyurt Platosi. Plateau of Kazakhstan and Uzbekistan
Usulután 235 SE El Salvador
Usumacinta 278, 403 river of Guatemala and Mexico
Usumbura see Bujumbura
Usutu see Lusutfu
Utah 598 state of SW USA
Utamboni see Mitemele, Río
'Uta Vava'u 568 island of the Vava'u Group, Tonga
Utena 376 E Lithuania
Utirik 396 island of N Marshall Islands
Utrecht 429 C Netherlands
Utsunomiya 330 Honshū, SE Japan
Uttaradit 563 var. Utaradit. N Thailand
Utuado 651 C Puerto Rico
Utupua 522 island of the Santa Cruz Is, E Solomon Is
Uummannaq 646 W Greenland
Uummannarsuaq see Nunap Isua
Uvea, Île 653 island of S Wallis & Futuna
Uvs Nuur 412 lake of NW Mongolia
Uwajima 330 Shikoku, SW Japan
Uyo 440 S Nigeria
Uyuni 136 W Bolivia
Uzbekistan 610-613 officially Republic of Uzbekistan. Country of C Asia divided into 12 admin. units (oblastey). ❖ Tashkent
Uzgen 357 Kir. Özgön. W Kyrgyzstan
Uzhhorod 586 Rus. Uzhgorod, Cz. Užhorod, Hung. Ungvár. W Ukraine
Užice 630 var. Titovo Užice. W Serbia, Yugoslavia

V

Vaal 527 river of C South Africa
Vaasa 249 prev. Nikolainkaupunki, Swe. Vasa. W Finland
Vác 290 Ger. Waitzen. N Hungary
Vaches, Île aux 512 var. Bird Island. Island group of the Inner Islands, N Seychelles
Vacoas 400 W Mauritius
Vadar 273 prev. Axios. River of Greece and FYR Macedonia
Vadile see Vatili
Vadodara 296 prev. Baroda. W India
Vaduz 374 ❖ of Liechtenstein, W Liechtenstein
Vágar 644 var. Vågø. Island of W Faeroe Islands
Vágbeszterce see Považská Bystrica
Vágújhely see Nové Mesto nad Váhom
Vágur 644 var. Våg. Sudhuroy, S Faeroe Islands
Váh 519 Ger. Waag, Hung. Vág. River of W Slovakia
Väike-Emajõgi 240 river of S Estonia
Väinameri 240 prev. Muhu Väin. Area of Baltic Sea, off the coast of W Estonia
Vaitogi 642 Tutuila, W American Samoa

Vaitupu *583* coral atoll of C Tuvalu
Vakhah *558 var.* Vahš. SW Tajikistan
Vākhān, Kūh-e *77 Per.* Kowtal-e Khaybar. Mountain range of C Asia
Vakhsh *558 var.* Vahš. River of SW Tajikistan
Valdecañas, Embalse de *531* reservoir of W Spain
Valdez *598* Alaska, USA
Valdia *see* Weldiya
Valdivia *183* C Chile
Valence *253* SE France
Valencia *531 Cat.* València. Autonomous community of NE Spain
Valencia *619* NW Venezuela
Valencia, Golfo de *531* area of the Mediterranean Sea, E of Spain
Valera *619* W Venezuela
Valga *240 Ger.* Walk. S Estonia
Valira *86* river of Andorra and Spain
Valira del Nord *86* river of NW Andorra
Valira d'Orient *86* river of C Andorra
Valkeakoski *249* SW Finland
Valladolid *531* NW Spain
Valle de la Pascua *619* C Venezuela
Valledupar *195* N Colombia
Vallée de Mboun *510* river of C Senegal
Vallée du Ferlo *510 var.* Ferlo. River of N Senegal
Vallegrande *136* C Bolivia
Vallenar *183* N Chile
Valletta *395 prev.* Valetta. ❖ of Malta, E Malta
Valley *121* C Barbados
Valley, The *642* ❖ of Anguilla, E Anguilla
Vallgrund *249* island of W Finland
Valmiera *362 Ger.* Wolmar. NE Latvia
Valona *see* Vlorë
Valona, Bay of *see* Vlorës, Gjiri i
Valparaíso *183* C Chile
Valsayn *570* NW Trinidad, Trinidad & Tobago
Van *577* E Turkey
Vanadzor *98 prev.* Kirovakan. N Armenia
Vanard *497* NW St Lucia
Vana-Vändra *see* Vändra
Vancouver *170* SW Canada
Vancouver Island *170* island of SW Canada
Vanda *see* Vantaa
Vanderbijlpark *527* Pretoria-Witwatersrand-Vereeniging, NE South Africa
Vändra *240 prev.* Vana-Vändra, *Ger.* Fennern. C Estonia
Vaner, Lake *see* Vänern
Vänern *543 Eng.* Lake Vaner, *prev.* Lake Vener. Lake of SW Sweden
Vangaindrano *382* S Madagascar
Van Gölü *576 Eng.* Lake Van. Lake of E Turkey
Vangunu *522* island of the New Georgia Is, Solomon Is
Vanikolo *522 var.* Vanikoro. Island of the Santa Cruz Is, E Solomon Islands
Vanimo *458* NW Papua New Guinea
Van, Lake *see* Van Gölü
Vannes *252* W France
Vantaa *249 Swe.* Vanda. SW Finland
Vanua Balavu *246 prev.* Vanua Mbalavu. Island of the Lau Group, E Fiji
Vanua Lava *615* Banks Islands, N Vanuatu
Vanua Levu *246* island of N Fiji
Vanuatu, Republic of *614-615* officially Republic of Vanuatu, *prev.* New Hebrides. Country of the Pacific Ocean divided into 11 admin. units (districts). ❖ Port-Vila
Vanua Vatu *246* island of the Lau Group, E Fiji
Vao *650* Île des Pins, S New Caledonia
Varadero *210* NW Cuba
Vārānasi *296 prev.* Benares. NE India
Varangerfjorden *444* fjord of NE Norway
Varannó *see* Vranov nad Topľou
Varaždin *209 Hung.* Varasd, *Ger.* Warasdin. N Croatia
Vardar *381* river of Greece and FYR Macedonia
Varde *218* Jylland, W Denmark
Vardenis *98* E Armenia
Varėna *376 Pol.* Orany. S Lithuania
Varesa *320* N Italy
Vârful Moldoveanu *480 prev.* Vîrful Moldoveanu. Mountain of C Romania
Varkaus *249* SE Finland
Varna *152 prev.* Stalin. E Bulgaria
Varnenski Zaliv *152 prev.* Stalinski Zaliv. Bay of the Black Sea to the E of Bulgaria
Varnensko Ezero *152* lake of E Bulgaria
Vasa *see* Vaasa
Vaslui *480* E Romania
Västerås *543* S Sweden
Västervik *543* S Sweden
Vasto *321* C Italy
Vaté *see* Efate
Vatican City *321, 616-617* officially Vatican City State. City state at the C of Rome, C Italy
Vatili *215 var.* Vadili. C Cyprus
Vatnajökull *294* glacier of SE Iceland
Vatneyri *294* NW Iceland
Vatoa *246* island to the S of the Lau Group, SE Fiji
Vättern *543 Eng.* Lake Vatter, *prev.* Lake Vetter. Lake of S Sweden
Vatukoula *246* Viti Levu, W Fiji
Vatulele *246* island to the S of Viti Levu, SW Fiji
Vatu Vara *246* island of the Lau Group, E Fiji
Vaupés *195* river of Brazil and Colombia
Vava'u Group *568* island group of N Tonga
Vavuniya *534* N Sri Lanka
Vawkavysk *122 Rus.* Volkovysk, *Pol.* Wołkowysk. W Belarus
Växjö *543* S Sweden
Vaygach, Ostrov *484* island of NW Russian Federation
Vayk' *98 prev.* Azizbekov. SE Armenia
Vedi *98* S Armenia
Vega Baja *651* N Puerto Rico
Veglia *see* Krk
Vejle *218* Jylland, W Denmark
Velasco Ibarra *228* W Ecuador
Velebit *209* mountain range of C Croatia
Velenje *520 Ger.* Wöllan. NE Slovenia
Vele, Pointe *653* headland of Île Futuna, N Wallis & Futuna
Veles *see* Titov Veles
Velika Gorica *209* N Croatia
Velika Morava *630 var.* Morava, Glavn'a Morava, *Ger.* Grosse Morava. River of C Serbia, Yugoslavia
Velika Plana *630* C Serbia, Yugoslavia
Veliki Bečkerek *see* Zrenjanin
Veliko Tŭrnovo *152 prev.* Tŭrnovo. C Bulgaria
Vélingara *510* S Senegal
Velingrad *152* W Bulgaria
Velké Meziříčí *216* SE Czech Republic
Vella Lavella *522 var.* Mbilua. New Georgia Is, Solomon Islands
Vellore *296* S India
Velsen *429* W Netherlands
Venda Bantustan 'self-governing homeland' comprising 2 non-contiguous territories of NE Transvaal, South Africa; created in 1979, abolished in 1994
Venedig *see* Venezia
Vener, Lake *see* Vänern
Venezia *321 Eng.* Venice, *Ger.* Venedig, *Fr.* Venise. N Italy
Venezuela *618-621* officially Republic of Venezuela, *prev.* United States of Venezuela. Country of South America divided into 24 admin. units (20 states and 4 federal entities). ❖ Caracas
Venezuela, Cordillera de *see* Costa, Cordillera de la
Venezuela, Gulf of *619* gulf of the Caribbean Sea, on the N coast of Venezuela
Venice *see* Venezia
Venice, Gulf of *209, 321, 520 It.* Golfo di Venezia, *Slvn.* Beneški Zaliv. Gulf of the Adriatic Sea
Venise *see* Venezia
Venlo *429* SE Netherlands
Vennesla *444* SW Norway
Venoste, Alpi *see* Ötztaler Alpen
Venta *362, 376 Ger.* Windau. River of Latvia and Lithuania
Ventoso *502* N San Marino
Ventspils *362 Ger.* Windau. NW Latvia
Veracruz *403 var.* Veracruz Llave. SE Mexico
Vercelli *320* N Italy
Verdal *444* C Norway
Verde *136* river of Bolivia and Brazil
Verde, Costa *530-531* coastal region of N Spain
Verdun *171* SE Canada
Vereeniging *527* Pretoria-Witwatersrand-Vereeniging, NE South Africa
Verin T'alin *see* T'alin
Verkhneudinsk *see* Ulan-Ude
Verkhoyanskiy Khrebet *485* Mountain range of E Russian Federation
Vermont *599* state of NE USA
Vernon *170* SW Canada
Verőcze *see* Virovitica
Véroia *273 Turk.* Karaferiye. N Greece
Verona *320* N Italy
Versailles *253* N France
Versecz *see* Vršac
Vert, Cap *510* cape of W Senegal
Verte, Île *652* island of E Saint Pierre and Miquelon
Vértes *290* mountain range of NW Hungary
Vertientes *210* S Cuba
Verviers *127* E Belgium
Vesoul *253* NE France
Vesterålen *444 var.* Vesteraalen. Island group of NW Norway
Vestfjorden *444* fjord of NW Norway
Vestmanna *644 var.* Vestmanhavn. Streymoy, N Faeroe Islands
Vestmannaeyjar *294* Heimaey I, S Iceland
Vesuvio *321* volcano of S Italy
Veszprém *290 Ger.* Veszprim. W Hungary
Vetter, Lake *see* Vättern
Vevey *546 Ger.* Vivis. SW Switzerland
Viacha *136* W Bolivia
Viana *88* NW Angola
Viana do Castelo *474* NW Portugal
Vianden *378* NE Luxembourg
Viangchan *see* Vientiane
Viangphoukha *359 var.* Vieng Pou Kha. NW Laos
Viareggio *320* N Italy
Viborg *218* Jylland, NW Denmark
Vicente Noble *226* SW Dominican Republic
Vicenza *321* N Italy
Vichada *195* river of C and E Colombia
Vichy *253* C France
Victoria *101* state of SE Australia
Victoria *170* Vancouver Island, SW Canada
Victoria *183* C Chile
Victoria *276* NW Grenada island, Grenada
Victoria *387 var.* Labuan. Pulau Labuan, NW Malaysia
Victoria *395* Gozo, NW Malta
Victoria *512* ❖ of Seychelles, Mahé Island, Seychelles
Victoria *see* Limbe
Victoria, Mount *see* Tomanivi
Victoria Falls *636* W Zimbabwe
Victoria Falls *635, 636* falls of the Zambezi river, Zambia and Zimbabwe
Victoria Falls *see* Iguaçu, Salto do
Victoria Island *170* island of N Canada
Victoria, Lake *342, 560, 584 var.* Victoria Nyanza. Lake of E Africa
Victoria Land *90* physical region of Greater Antarctica, Antarctica
Victoria Nile *584 var.* Somerset Nile. River of C Uganda
Victoria Peak *130* mountain of C Belize
Videm-Krško *see* Krško
Vidin *152* NW Bulgaria
Vidoy *644* island of N Faeroe Islands
Vidzeme *362 Eng.* Livonia. Cultural region of NE Latvia
Viedma *95* E Argentina
Vieille Case *224 var.* Itassi. N Dominica
Viekšniai *376* NW Lithuania
Vienna *106 Ger.* Wien, *Hung.* Bécs, *Slvn.* Dunaj. ❖ of Austria, NE Austria
Vienne *253* river of C France
Vientiane *359 Lao.* Viangchan. ❖ of Laos, C Laos
Vieques *651* Isla de Vieques, SE Puerto Rico
Vieques, Isla de *651* island of SE Puerto Rico
Vierwaldstätter See *546 Eng.* Lake of Lucerne, Lake of C Switzerland
Vietnam *622-625* officially Socialist Republic of Viet-nam, *Vtn.* Công Hoa Xa Hôi Chu Nghia Viêt Nam. Country of SE Asia divided into 53 admin. units (50 provinces, 3 municipalities). ❖ Hanoi
Viêt Tri *623* N Vietnam
Vieux Fort *497* S St Lucia
Vieux-Fort, Pointe du *646* headland of S Guadeloupe
Vigo *530* NW Spain
Vijayawāda *296 prev.* Bezwada. SE India
Vila Artuur de Paiva *see* Cubango
Vila da Ponte *see* Cubango
Vila de Brava *176* São Nicolau, N Cape Verde
Vila de João Belo *see* Xai-Xai
Vila de Macia *see* Macia
Vila de Maio *see* Maio
Vila de Manica *see* Manica
Vila de Mocímboa da Praia *see* Mocímboa da Praia
Vila de Sal Rei *see* Sal Rei
Vila de Sena *419 var.* Sena. C Mozambique
Vila do Conde *474* NW Portugal
Vila do Zumbo *419 prev.* Vila do Zumbu, *var.* Zumbo. NW Mozambique
Vila Henrique de Carvalho *see* Saurimo
Vila Marechal Carmona *see* Uíge
Vila Maria Pia *176* Santo Antão. N Cape Verde
Vila Nova de Gaia *474* NW Portugal
Vila Nova de Portimão *see* Portimão
Vila Pereira de Eça *see* N'Giva
Vila Real *474* N Portugal
Vila Robert Williams *see* Caála
Vila Salazar *see* N'Dalatando
Vila Teixeira da Silva *see* Bailundo
Vil'cheka, Zemlya *485 Eng.* Wilczek Land. Island of Zemlya Frantsa-Iosifa, N Russian Federation
Viliya *see* Neris
Viljandi *240 Ger.* Fellin. S Estonia
Villa Altagracia *226* C Dominican Republic
Villach *106 Slvn.* Beljak. S Austria
Villa Concepción *see* Concepción
Villa del Pilar *see* Pilar
Villa Dolores *95* C Argentina
Villa Hayes *460* S Paraguay
Villahermosa *403* SE Mexico
Villalcampo, Embalse de *531* reservoir of NW Spain
Villa Martín *136* SW Bolivia
Villa Mercedes *95 var.* Mercedes C Argentina
Villa Nador *see* Nador
Villa Nueva *95* W Argentina
Villanueva *288* NW Honduras
Villa Rosario *195* NE Colombia
Villarrica *460* SE Paraguay

Villa Sandino *436* S Nicaragua
Villa Sanjurjo *see* Al Hoceima
Villavicencio *195* C Colombia
Villazón *136* S Bolivia
Villmanstrand *see* Lappeenranta
Vilnius *376* *Pol.* Wilno, *Ger.* Wilna, *prev. Rus.* Vilna. ❖ of Lithuania, SE Lithuania
Vilvoorde *127* *Fr.* Vilvorde. C Belgium
Vilyeyka *122* NW Belarus
Vina *168* river of Cameroon and Chad
Viña del Mar *183* C Chile
Vincent, Point *650* headland of N Norfolk Island
Vinces *228* C Ecuador
Vindeby *218* S Denmark
Vindhya Range *296* *var.* Vindhya Mountains. Mountains of C India
Vinh *623* NE Vietnam
Vinh Loi *see* Bac Liêu
Vinh Long *623* S Vietnam
Vinica *381* NE FYR Macedonia
Vinkovci *209* *Ger.* Winkowitz, *Hung.* Vinkovce. NE Croatia
Vinnitsa *see* Vinnytsya
Vinnytsya *586* *Rus.* Vinnitsa. W Ukraine
Viranşehir *577* SE Turkey
Virgin Gorda *643* island of E British Virgin Islands
Virginia *527* Orange Free State, C South Africa
Virginia *599* state of E USA
Virgin Islands (US) *653* Unincorporated territory of the USA, Caribbean Sea. ❖ Charlotte Amalie.
Virgin Passage *651, 653* passage of the Caribbean Sea, between Puerto Rico and the Virgin Islands (US)
Virôchey *165* NE Cambodia
Virovitica *209* *Ger.* Virovititz, *prev.* Werowitz, *Hung.* Verőcze. NE Croatia
Virtsu *240* *Ger.* Werder. W Estonia
Vis *209* *It.* Lissa. Island of S Croatia
Vis *see* Fish
Visākhapatnam *296* SE India
Visale *522* NW Guadalcanal, Solomon Is
Visayan Sea *466* sea of the Pacific Ocean
Visby *543* *Ger.* Wisby. SE Sweden
Viscount Melville Sound *170* *prev.* Melville Sound. Area of the Arctic Ocean between Melville Island and Victoria Island, N Canada
Viseu *474* *prev.* Vizeu. N Portugal
Vistula *see* Wisła
Vistula Lagoon *471* *Pol.* Zalew Wiślany, *Rus.* Vislinskiy Zaliv, *Ger.* Frisches Haff. Lagoon of N Poland.
Viterbo *321* C Italy
Vitiaz Strait *458* strait connecting the Bismarck Sea and Solomon Sea
Vitim *485* river of C Russian Federation
Vitória *145* SE Brazil
Vitoria *531* *Cast.* Gasteiz, N Spain
Vitória da Conquista *145* E Brazil
Vitsyebsk *122* *Rus.* Vitebsk. NE Belarus
Vittoria *321* Sicilia, S Italy
Vittoriosa *395* *Malt.* Birgu. E Malta
Vitu Levu *246* island of W Fiji
Vivis *see* Vevey
Viwa *246* island to the W of Yasawa Group, NW Fiji
Vizcaya, Golfo de *see* Biscay, Bay of
Vjosës *81* *var.* Vijosë. River of Albania and Greece
Vlaanderen *see* Flanders
Vlaardingen *429* SW Netherlands
Vladikavkaz *484* *prev.* Ordzhonikidze, *prev.* Dzaudzhikau. SW Russian Federation
Vladimir *484* W Russian Federation
Vladimirovka *see* Yuzhno-Sakhalinsk
Vladivostok *485* SE Russian Federation
Vlasenica *140* E Bosnia & Herzegovina
Vlieland *429* island of Waddeneilanden, N Netherlands
Vlissingen *429* *Fr.* Flessingue, *Eng.* Flushing. SW Netherlands
Vlorë *81* *prev.* Vlonë, *It.* Valona. SW Albania
Vlorës, Gjiri i *81* *var.* Bay of Valona. Bay of the Adriatic Sea, SW Albania
Vltava *216* *Ger.* Moldau. River of W Czech Republic
Vogan *567* S Togo
Vogelkop *see* Doberai, Jazirah
Vogel Peak *see* Dimlang
Võhandu *240* *var.* Võhandu Jõgi. River of SE Estonia
Voi *342* S Kenya
Voinjama *368* N Liberia
Vojvodina *630* *Ger.* Wojwodina. Region of N Serbia, Yugoslavia
Volcán *456* W Panama
Volga *484* river of W Russian Federation
Volgograd *484* *prev.* Stalingrad, *prev.* Tsaritsyn. SW Russian Federation
Volkovysk *see* Vawkavysk
Volksrust *527* Eastern Transvaal, E South Africa
Vologda *484* W Russian Federation
Vólos *273* E Greece
Volta *270* river of SE Ghana
Volta, Lake *270* reservoir of SE Ghana
Volta Redonda *145* S Brazil
Volta Rouge *see* Red Volta
Volturno *321* river of C Italy
Vopnafjördhur *294* E Iceland
Vorder Grauspitz *374* mountain of Liechtenstein and Switzerland
Vorderrhein *546* river of SE Switzerland
Vordingborg *218* Sjælland, SE Denmark
Vor eioi Sporades *273* *prev.* Vórioi Sporádhes, *Eng.* Northern Sporades. Island group of E Greece
Vorkuta *484* NW Russian Federation
Vormsi *240* *Ger.* Worms, Swed. Ormsö. Island of W Estonia
Voronezh *484* SW Russian Federation
Voroshilov *see* Ussuriysk
Voroshilovgrad *see* Luhans'k
Voroshilovsk *see* Alchevs'k
Voroshilovsk *see* Stavropol'
Vorotan *98* river of Armenia and Azerbaijan
Vorskla *586* river of C Ukraine
Võrtsjärv *240* lake of S Estonia
Võru *240* *Ger.* Werro. SE Estonia
Vosges *253* mountain range of NE France
Voss *444* SW Norway
Vostochno-Sibirskoye More *485* *Eng.* East Siberian Sea. Sea of Arctic Ocean, bordering NE Russian Federation
Vostochnyy Sayan *485* *Eng.* Eastern Sayans. Mountain range of Mongolia and Russian Federation
Vostok *90* CIS research station of Greater Antarctica, Antarctica
Vostok Island *346* island of the Line Is, E Kiribati
Vrangelya, Ostrov *485* *Eng.* Wrangel Island. Island of NE Russian Federation
Vranje *630* SE Serbia, Yugoslavia
Vranov nad Topľou *519* *Hung.* Varannó. E Slovakia
Vratsa *152* *var.* Vraca. NW Bulgaria
Vrbas *140* river of N Bosnia & Herzegovina
Vršac *630* *Ger.* Werschetz, *Hung.* Versecz. N Serbia, Yugoslavia
Vryburg *527* North West, N South Africa
Vryheid *527* Kwazulu Natal, E South Africa
Vsetín *216* SE Czech Republic
Vuaqava *246* *prev.* Vuanggava. Island of the Lau Group, SE Fiji
Vukovar *209* NE Croatia
Vulcăneşti *408* *Rus.* Vulkaneshty. S Moldova
Vulcano *321* island of S Italy
Vulkaneshty *see* Vulcăneşti
Vumbi *162* N Burundi
Vung Tau *623* *prev.* Cap Saint-Jacques. S Vietnam
Vunisea *246* Kadavu, Fiji
Vwawa *560* SW Tanzania
Vyatka *see* Kirov
Vyškov *216* SE Czech Republic
Vysoké Tatry *see* Tatra Mountains

W

Wa *270* NW Ghana
Waag *see* Váh
Waagbistritz *see* Považská Bystrica
Waagneustadtl *see* Nové Mesto nad Váhom
Waal *429* river of SW Netherlands
Waala *650* Île Art, Îles Belep, W New Caledonia
Wabag *458* C Papua New Guinea
Waddān *371* NW Libya
Waddeneilanden *429* *Eng.* West Frisian Islands. Islands of N Netherlands
Waddenzee *429* N Netherlands
Wädenswil *546* N Switzerland
Wādī as Sīr *336* *var.* Wadi es Sir. NW Jordan
Wadi es Sir *see* Wādī as Sīr
Wadi Halfa *536* *var.* Wādī Ḥalfā'. N Sudan
Wādī Mūsa' *336* *var.* Wādī Músá, Wādī Mūsā. W Jordan
Wādiyān *115* NE Bahrain
Wad Medani *536* *var.* Wad Madanī. C Sudan
Wagadugu *see* Ouagadougou
Wageningen *538* NW Suriname
Wagga Wagga *101* SE Australia
Wagin *100* SW Australia
Wāh *451* NE Pakistan
Wahiawa *598* Oahu, Hawaii, USA
Wahran *see* Oran
Waiau *433* river of SW South Island, New Zealand
Waigeo, Pulau *302* island of Maluku, E Indonesia
Waiheke Island *433* island to the N of North Island, New Zealand
Waikaremoana, Lake *433* lake of SE North Island, New Zealand
Waikato *433* river of C North Island, New Zealand
Wailuku *598* Maui, Hawaii, USA
Waimakariri *433* river of C South Island, New Zealand
Waini *284* river of N Guyana
Wairarapa, Lake *433* lake of S North Island, New Zealand
Wairau *433* river of NE South Island, New Zealand
Wairoa *433* SE North Island, New Zealand
Waitaki *433* river of C South Island, New Zealand
Waitangi *433* Chatham Islands, New Zealand
Waitzen *see* Vác
Wajir *342* NE Kenya
Wakatipu, Lake *433* W South Island, New Zealand
Wakaya *246* island to the NE of Viti Levu, C Fiji
Wakayama *330* Honshū, C Japan
Wakkanai *331* Hokkaidō, N Japan
Wakra *see* Al Wakrah
Waku Kungo *see* Uaco Cungo
Walachia *480* cultural region of S Romania
Wałbrzych *471* *Ger.* Waldenburg. SW Poland
Walcheren *429* island of SW Netherlands
Walcourt *127* S Belgium
Waldenburg *see* Wałbrzych
Wales *593* *Wel.* Cymru. National region of UK divided into 8 admin. units (counties)
Walferdange *378* C Luxembourg
Walk *see* Valga
Wallersee *106* lake of N Austria
Wallis & Futuna *653* *Fr.* Wallis et Futuna. French overseas territory of t he Pacific Ocean. ❖ Matā 'Utu
Walsall *593* C England, UK
Walvisbaai *see* Walvis Bay
Walvis Bay *423* *Afr.* Walvisbaai. W Namibia
Walvis Bay *423* bay of the Atlantic Ocean
Wamba *203* *var.* Uamba. River of SW Dem. Rep. Congo (Zaire)
Wanaka *433* W South Island, New Zealand
Wanaka, Lake *433* lake of W South Island, New Zealand
Wanchuan *see* Zhangjiakou
Wang *134* river of SW Bhutan
Wanganui *433* S North Island, New Zealand
Wanganui *433* river of S North Island, New Zealand
Wangaratta *101* SE Australia
Wangdi Phodrang *134* C Bhutan
Wangkí *see* Coco
Wankie *see* Hwange
Wanlaweyn *524* *var.* Wanle Weyn, *It.* Uanle Uen. SW Somalia
Warangal *296* C India
Warasdin *see* Varaždin
Warbah, Jazīrat *354* island of NE Kuwait
Wardija Ridge *395* ridge of NW Malta
Waregem *127* W Belgium
Wargla *see* Ouargla
Warmbad *423* S Namibia
Warnes *136* C Bolivia
Warri *440* S Nigeria
Warrington *593* N England, UK
Warrnambool *101* SE Australia
Warsaw *471* *Pol.* Warszawa, *Ger.* Warschau. ❖ of Poland, C Poland
Warta *471* *Ger.* Warthe. River of W Poland
Warwick Long Bay *643* bay of the North Atlantic Ocean, W Bermuda
Washington *598* state of NW USA
Washington DC *599* federal district and ❖ of USA, E USA
Washington Island *see* Teraina
Wash, The *593* estuarine inlet of the North Sea, E England, UK
Waspam *436* NE Nicaragua
Wasserbillig *378* E Luxembourg
Watenstedt-Salzgitter *see* Salzgitter
Waterford *314* *Ir.* Port Láirge. SE Ireland
Waterloo *514* W Sierra Leone
Watford *593* SE England, UK
Watlings I *see* San Salvador
Watsa *203* NE Dem. Rep. Congo (Zaire)
Watson Lake *170* W Canada
Wau *536* *var.* Wāw. S Sudan
Wau *458* C Papua New Guinea
Wawa *171* S Canada
Wāw al Kabīr *371* C Libya
Waya *246* island of the Yasawa Group, NW Fiji
Wazīrābād *451* NE Pakistan
Wé *650* Lifou, Îles Loyauté, E New Caledonia
Weddell Island *645* island of SW Falkland Islands
Weddell Sea *90* sea of the Atlantic Ocean, off Antarctica
Wehso *see* Giyon
Weichsel *see* Wisła
Weiden *265* SE Germany
Weifang *187* *prev.* Weihsien. Shandong, E China
Weiselburg *see* Mosonmagyaróvár
Weissenburg *see* Alba Iulia
Weissenstein *see* Paide
Welchman Hall *121* C Barbados
Weldiya *243* *var.* Waldia, *It.* Valdia. N Ethiopia
Weligama *534* S Sri Lanka
Welkom *527* Orange Free State, C South Africa
Wellawaya *534* SE Sri Lanka

Welle *see* Uele
Wellesley Islands *101* island group of N Australia
Wellhouse *121* SE Barbados
Wellington *433* ❖ of New Zealand, S North Island, New Zealand
Wellington *514* W Sierra Leone
Wellington, Isla *183* *var.* Wellington. Island of S Chile
Wels *106* N Austria
Wenchi *270* W Ghana
Wen-chou *see* Wenzhou
Wenden *see* Cēsis
Wendo *243* S Ethiopia
Weno *406* *prev.* Moen. Kuop, C Micronesia
Wenzhou *187* *var.* Wen-chou. Zhejiang, E China
Werda *142* S Botswana
Werdēr *243* SE Ethiopia
Werder *see* Virtsu
Werowitz *see* Virovitica
Werro *see* Võru
Werschetz *see* Vrsac
Wesenberg *see* Rakvere
Weser *265* river of NW Germany
Wesley *224* *var.* La Soie. N Dominica
Wessel Islands *101* island group of N Australia
West Bank *317, 318* disputed territory of SW Asia
West Bay *644* Grand Cayman, W Cayman Islands
West Bengal *301* region of NE India
West Caicos *653* island of W Turks and Caicos Islands
West Channel *648* channel of the Pacific Ocean, S Johnston Atoll
West End *112* Grand Bahama, Bahamas
West End *643* Tortola, W British Virgin Islands
West End *644* Cayman Brac, NE Cayman Islands
West End Village *642* SW Anguilla
Westerhall Point *276* S Grenada island, Grenada
Western Australia *100, 105* state of W Australia
Western Cape *527* province of SW South Africa
Western Desert *see* Gharqîya, Sahara el
Western Dvina *122, 362* *Bel.* Dzvina, *Ger.* Düna, *Latv.* Daugava, *Rus.* Zapadnaya Dvina. River of C Latvia
Western Ghats *296* mountains of SW India
Western Isles *see* Outer Hebrides
Western Sahara *414* disputed territory of N Africa, administered by Morocco
Western Sayans *see* Zapadnyy Sayan
Western Sierra Madre *see* Sierra Madre Occidental
Westerschelde *429* *Eng.* Western Scheldt, *prev.* Honte. Inlet of the North Sea, on the coast of SW Netherlands
West Falkland *645* island of W Falkland Islands
West Fayu *406* island of C Micronesia
West Frisian Islands *see* Waddeneilanden
West Irian *see* Irian Jaya
West Island *644* *var.* Pulu Panjang. ❖ of W Cocos Islands
West Lunga *635* river of W Zambia
West Malaysia *see* Peninsular Malaysia
Westport *314* W Ireland
Westport *433* N South Island, New Zealand
Westpunt *650* Curaçao, S Netherlands Antilles
West River *see* Xi Jiang
West Siberian Plain *see* Zapadno-Sibirskaya Ravnina
West Virginia *599* state of E USA
Westwood *498* NW St Vincent, St Vincent & the Grenadines
West York Island *652* island of N Spratly Islands
Wetar, Pulau *302* island to the E of Nusa Tenggara, E Indonesia
Wetaskiwin *170* SW Canada
Wete *560* *var.* Weti. Pemba, Tanzania
Weti *see* Wete
Wetzlar *264* W Germany
Wewak *458* N Papua New Guinea
Wexford *314* SE Ireland
Weyburn *170* SW Canada
Weymouth *593* S England, UK
Whakatane *433* E North Island, New Zealand
Whangarei *433* NW North Island, New Zealand
Whitehorse *170* W Canada
White Island *276* S of Carriacou, Grenada
White Island *433* island to the N of North Island, New Zealand
White Nile *536* *Ar.* An Nīl al Abyaḑ, *var.* Baḩr al Abyaḑ, Bahr el Jebel. Riv of SE Sudan
White Sea *see* Beloye More
White Volta *157, 270* *Fr.* Volta Blanche. River of Burkina and Ghana
Whitney, Mount *598* mountain of S Rocky Mts, W USA
Whyalla *101* S Australia
Whydah *see* Ouidah
Wichita *599* Kansas, C USA
Wick *593* NE Scotland, UK
Wicklow *314* *Ir.* Cill Mhantáin. E Ireland
Wicklow Mountains *314* *Ir.* Sléibhte Chill Mhantáin. Mountain range of E Ireland
Wida *see* Ouidah
Wien *see* Vienna
Wiener Neustadt *106* E Austria
Wiesbaden *264* SW Germany
Wight, Isle of *593* island of S England, UK
Wil *546* NE Switzerland
Wilczek Land *see* Vil'cheka, Zemlya
Wilhelm, Mount *458* mountain of C Papua New Guinea
Wilhemshaven *264* NW Germany
Wilja *see* Neris
Wilkes Land *90* physical region of Greater Antarctica, Antarctica
Willemstad *650* ❖ Netherlands Antilles, Curaçao, S Netherlands Antilles
Willikies *92* E Antigua, Antigua & Barbuda
Willis *276* SW Grenada island, Grenada
Wilmington *599* Delaware, E USA
Wilna *see* Vilnius
Wilno *see* Vilnius
Wiltz *378* NW Luxembourg
Winam Gulf *342* *var.* Kavirondo Gulf. Gulf of Lake Victoria to the SW of Kenya
Winchester *593* S England, UK
Windau *see* Ventspils
Windhoek *423* *Ger.* Windhuk. ❖ of Namibia, C Namibia
Windsor *171* S Canada
Windward *276* N Carriacou, Grenada
Windward Passage *210, 286* channel connecting the Atlantic Ocean and the Caribbean Sea between Cuba and Haiti
Windward Point *642* headland on the NE coast of Anguilla
Winisk *171* C Canada
Winkowitz *see* Vinkovci
Winneba *270* SE Ghana
Winnipeg *170* S Canada
Winnipeg, Lake *170* lake of S Canada
Winnipegosis, Lake *170* lake of S Canada
Winston-Salem *599* North Carolina, SE USA
Winterthur *546* NE Switzerland
Winton *101* E Australia
Wisby *see* Visby
Wisconsin *599* state of NC USA
Wisła *471* *Ger.* Weichsel, *Eng.* Vistula. River of C Poland
Wiślany, Zalew *see* Vistula Lagoon
Wismar *264* N Germany
Witbank *527* Eastern Transvaal, NE South Africa
Witten *264* W Germany
Witti, Banjaran *386* *var.* Witti Range. Mountain range of NE Borneo, Malaysia
W.J. van Blommesteinmeer *538* reservoir of NE Suriname
Włocławek *471* C Poland
Wodzisław Śląski *471* *Ger.* Loslau. S Poland
Woja District *396* district of Majuro, SE Marshall Islands
Wojwodina *see* Vojvodina
Woleai *406* atoll of C Micronesia
Woleu *see* Uolo, Río
Wolfgangsee *106* *var.* St Wolfgangsee, Abersee. Lake of N Austria
Wolf, Isla *228* island of NW Galapagos Is, Ecuador
Wolfsberg *106* SE Austria
Wolfsburg *265* N Germany
Wołkowysk *see* Vawkavysk
Wöllan *see* Velenje
Wollaston Peninsula *170* peninsula of Victoria Island, NW Canada
Wollongong *101* SE Australia
Wolmar *see* Valmiera
Wolverhampton *593* C England, UK
Wŏnju *350* *Jap.* Genshū. N South Korea
Wŏnsan *349* SE North Korea
Woodlands Bay *649* bay of the Caribbean Sea on the W coast of Montserrat
Woodlark Island *see* Murua Island
Woods, Lake of the *170* *Fr.* Lac des Bois. Lake of Canada and USA
Woody Island *651* island of Amphitrite Group, N Paracel Islands
Worcester *527* Western Cape, SW South Africa
Worcester *593* C England, UK
Worcester *599* Massachusetts, NE USA
Worms *see* Vormsi
Worthing *121* SW Barbados
Wotho *396* island of W Marshall Islands
Wotje *396* island of E Marshall Islands
Wrangel Island *see* Vrangelya, Ostrov
Wrexham *593* N Wales, UK
Wrocław *471* *Ger.* Breslau. SW Poland
Wu-chou *see* Wuzhou
Wuday 'ah *506* S Saudi Arabia
Wuhan *187* *prev.* Hankow, *var.* Han-k'ou, Hanyang, Wuchang. Hubei, C China
Wu-hsi *see* Wuxi
Wuhsien *see* Suzhou
Wuhu *187* *var.* Wu-na-mu. Anhui, E China
Wukari *440* E Nigeria
Wu-lu-mu-ch'i *see* Ürümqi
Wum *168* W Cameroon
Wu-na-mu *see* Wuhu
Wuppertal *264* W Germany
Würzburg *265* SW Germany
Wusih *see* Wuxi
Wuxi *187* *var.* Wu-hsi, Wusih. Jiangsu, E China
Wuzhou *187* *var.* Wu-chou, Wuchow. Guangxi, S China
Wye *593* *Wel.* Gwy. River of England and Wales, UK
Wyndham *101* N Australia
Wyoming *598-599* state of NW USA
Wysg *see* Usk

X

Xaçmaz *110* *Rus.* Khachmas, *var.* Hačmas. N Azerbaijan
Xagħra *395* Gozo, Malta
Xai-Xai *419* *prev.* Vila de João Belo, *var.* João Belo S Mozambique
Xam Nua *359* *var.* Sam Neua. NE Laos
Xankändi *110* *Rus.* Khankendy, *prev.* Stepanakert. SW Azerbaijan
Xánthi *273* *var.* Eskije, *Turk.* Iskeçe. NE Greece
Xauen *see* Chaouèn
Xäzär Dänizi *see* Caspian Sea
Xi'an *187* *var.* Hsi-an Sian. Shaanxi, C China
Xianggang *see* Hong Kong
Xiangkhoang *359* *var.* Xieng Khouang. E Laos
Xiangkhoang, Plateau de *359* *var.* Plain of Jars. Plateau of C Laos
Xiang Ngeun *359* C Laos
Xiangtan *187* *var.* Hsiang-t'an, Siangtan. Hunan, S China
Xiao Hinggan Ling *187* *Eng.* Lesser Khingan Range. Mountain range of NE China
Xieng Khouang *see* Xiangkhoang
Xi Jiang *187* *var.* Hsi Chiang. *Eng.* West River. River of S China
Xilinhot *187* *var.* Silinhot. Nei Mongol Zizhiqu, NE China
Xingkai Hu *see* Khanka, Lake
Xingu *145* river of C Brazil
Xining *187* *var.* Sining, Hsi-ning. Qinghai province, W China
Xinjiang Uygur Zizhiqu *186* *Eng.* Sinkiang Uighur Autonomous Region. Autonomous region of NW China
Xinpu *see* Liangyungang
Xinyang *187* *var.* Hsin-yang, Sinyang. Henan, C China
Xitole *282* SE Guinea-Bissau
Xixón *see* Gijón.
Xizang Zizhiqu *186* *Eng.* Tibetan Autonomous Region. Autonomous region of W China
Xolotlán *see* Managua, Lago de
Xuddur *524* *It.* Oddur. SW Somalia
Xulla Islands *see* Sula, Kepulauan
Xuzhou *187* *var.* Hsu-chou, Suchow, *prev.* T'ung-shan. Jiangsu, E China
Xylophaghou *215* *var.* Xylofagou. SE Cyprus

Y

Yabassi *168* W Cameroon
Yabēlo *243* S Ethiopia
Yablonovyy Khrebet *485* mountain range of C Russian Federation
Yabucoa *651* SE Puerto Rico
Yacata *246* island of the Lau Group, E Fiji
Yacuiba *136* S Bolivia
Yadua *246* *prev.* Yandua. Island to the W of Vanua Levu, NW Fiji
Yafran *371* NW Libya
Yagasa Cluster *246* islands of the Lau Group, E Fiji
Yagoua *168* NE Cameroon
Yaguarón *607* *var.* Jaguarão. River of Brazil and Uruguay
Yakhegnadzor *see* Yeghegnadzor
Yako *157* W Burkina
Yakutiya, Respublika *see* Sakha, Respublika
Yakutsk *485* E Russian Federation
Yala *563* S Thailand
Yalala, Chute *203* waterfall of W Dem. Rep. Congo (Zaire)
Yalinga *179* C Central African Republic
Yalova *576* NW Turkey
Yalpug *see* Ialpug
Yalpuh, Ozero *586* *Rus.* Ozero Yalpug. Lake of SW Ukraine
Yalta *586* S Ukraine
Yalu *349* *var.* Yalü, Amnok, *Jap.* Oryokko. River of China and North Korea
Yamagata *330* Honshū, N Japan
Yamaguchi *330* Honshū, W Japan
Yamal, Poluostrov *484* Peninsula of N Russian Federation
Yaman, Ra's al *see* Ḩadd al Jamal
Yambio *536* *var.* Yambiyo. S Sudan
Yambol *152* *var.* Jambol, *Turk.* Yanboli. E Bulgaria
Yamdena, Pulau *302* *prev.* Jamdena. Island of Kepulauan Tanimbar, Indonesia

Yamethin *159* C Burma
Yam HaMelaḥ *see* Dead Sea
Yamoussoukro *326* ❖ of Ivory Coast, C Ivory Coast
Yamuna *296 prev.* Jumna. River of N India
Yamundá *see* Nhamundá
Yanboli *see* Yambol
Yanbu' al Baḥr *506* W Saudi Arabia
Yandé, Île *650* island of Îles Belep, W New Caledonia
Yandua *see* Yadua
Yangambi *203* N Dem. Rep. Congo (Zaire)
Yangdŏk *349* S North Korea
Yanggeta *see* Yaqeta
Yangiyer *610* E Uzbekistan
Yangiyŭl *610 var.* Jangijul. E Uzbekistan
Yangku *see* Taiyuan
Yangmei *555* N Taiwan
Yangon *see* Rangoon
Yangtze Kiang *see* Chang Jiang
Yannina *see* Ioánnina
Yan Oya *534* river of N Sri Lanka
Yantai *187 var.* Yan-t'ai, *prev.* Chih-fu, *var.* Chefoo. Shandong, E China
Yantra *152 var.* Jantra. N Bulgaria
Yaoundé *168 var.* Yaunde. ❖ of Cameroon, S Cameroon
Yap *406* island of W Micronesia
Yapanskoye More *see* Japan, Sea of
Yapen, Pulau *303* island to the N of Irian Jaya, E Indonesia
Yapurá *see* Japurá
Yaqaga *246* island to the W of Vanua Levu, N Fiji
Yaqeta *246 prev.* Yanggeta. Island of the Yasawa Group, NW Fiji
Yaque del Norte *226* river of NW Dominican Republic
Yaque del Sur *226* river of SW Dominican Republic
Yaqui *403* river of NW Mexico
Yarīm *627* W Yemen
Yarlung Zangbo Jiang *see* Brahmaputra
Yarmouth *171* SE Canada
Yaroslavl' *484* W Russian Federation
Yarumal *195* NW Colombia
Yasawa *246* island of the Yasawa Group, NW Fiji
Yasawa Group *246* island group of NW Fiji
Yasyel'da *122* river of SW Belarus
Yaté *650* S New Caledonia
Yatsushiro *330* Kyūshū, SW Japan
Yatta Plateau *342* plateau of SE Kenya
Yauco *651* SW Puerto Rico
Yaunde *see* Yaoundé
Yavan *see* Javan
Yavarí *see* Javari
Yaviza *456* SE Panama
Yawatahama *330* Shikoku, SW Japan
Yazd *307 var.* Yezd. C Iran
Ybbs *106* river of C Austria
Yding Skovhøj *218* hill of Jylland, C Denmark
Ye *159* SE Burma
Yedintsy *see* Edineţ
Yedseram *441* river of E Nigeria
Yeghegnadzor *98 Rus.* Yakhegnadzor, *var.* Jehegnadzor. SE Armenia
Yégué *567* W Togo
Yekaterinburg *484 prev.* Sverdlovsk. C Russian Federation
Yekaterinodar *see* Krasnodar
Yekepa *368* NE Liberia
Yele *514* C Sierra Leone
Yelisavetpol *see* Gäncä
Yelizavetgrad *see* Kirovohrad
Yellow Hole *649* bay of the Caribbean Sea on the NE coast of Montserrat
Yellowknife *170* W Canada
Yellow River *see* Huang He
Yellow Sea *350 Kor.* Hwang-Hae, *Chin.* Huang Hai. Sea of the Pacific Ocean between China and Korea
Yellowstone *598-599* river of NW USA
Yëloteu *581 prev.* Iolotan, *Turkm.* Yolöten. SE Turkmenistan
Yel'sk *122* SE Belarus
Yelwa *440* E Nigeria
Yelwa *440* W Nigeria
Yemen *626-629* officially Republic of Yemen, *Ar.* Al Yaman, Al Jumhuriyah al Yamaniyah, *prev.* divided into South Yemen and Yemen Arab Republic (North Yemen) *prev.* Federation of South Arabia, Aden Protectorate. Country dividednto 17 admin. units (governorates). ❖ Sana
Yenakiyeve *586 Rus.* Yenakiyevo, *prev.* Ordzhonikidze, Rykovo. E Ukraine
Yenangyaung *159* W Burma
Yên Bai *623* NW Vietnam
Yendi *270* NE Ghana
Yeniboğaziçi *215 var.* Ayios Seryios. E Cyprus
Yenierenköy *215 var.* Agigialousa, Yialousa. NE Cyprus
Yenisey *485* river of C Russian Federation
Yenshui *555* W Taiwan
Yeovil *593* S England, UK
Yerevan *98 var.* Erevan, Jerevan, *Eng.* Erivan. ❖ of Armenia, C Armenia
Yeriḥo *see* Jericho
Yermak *338 Kaz.* Ermak. NE Kazakhstan
Yermasoyia *215 var.* Pentaschoinos. River of S Cyprus
Yerushalayim *see* Jerusalem
Yeu, Île d' *252* island of W France
Yevlax *110 Rus.* Yevlakh, *var.* Jevlah. C Azerbaijan
Yevpatoriya *586* S Ukraine
Yerreyskiya *485 Eng.* Jewish Autonomous Oblast. Autonomous region of SE Russian Federation
Yezd *see* Yazd
Ygatimí *460 var.* Igatimí. E Paraguay
Yí *607* river of C Uruguay
Yialias *215 var.* Yalyas, Çakilli Dere. River of C Cyprus
Yialousa *see* Yenierenköy
Yigo *647* NE Guam
Yinchuan *187 var.* Yinchwan. Ningxia, C China
Yining *186 var.* I-ning, *Uigh.* Gulja, *var.* Kuldja. Xinjiang Uygur Zizhiqu, NW China
Yirga 'Alem *243 It.* Irgalem. S Ethiopia
Yisra'el *see* Israel
Yoboki *222* C Djibouti
Yof *510* W Senegal
Yogyakarta *302 prev.* Jogjakarta. Java, C Indonesia
Yojoa, Lago de *288* lake of W Honduras
Yokkaichi *330* Honshū, C Japan
Yokohama *330* Honshū, SE Japan
Yokosuka *330* Honshū, SE Japan
Yola *441* E Nigeria
Yolöten *see* Yëloten
Yomou *281* SE Guinea
Yona *647* E Guam
Yonago *330* Honshū, W Japan
Yonezawa *330* Honshū, N Japan
Yŏngch'ŏn *350 Jap.* Eisen. SE South Korea
Yŏngju *350 Jap.* Eishū. C South Korea
Yongnŭng *349* E North Korea
Yonibana *514* W Sierra Leone
Yonne *253* river of C France
Yopal *195 var.* El Yopal. C Colombia
York *593* N England, UK
York Factory *170* C Canada
Yorkton *170* S Canada
Yoro *288* C Honduras
Yorosso *392* S Mali
Yoshino
Yos Sudarso, Pulau *303 prev.* Jos Sudarso. Island to the SW of Irian Jaya, E Indonesia
Yŏsu *350 Jap.* Reisui. S South Korea
Youghal *314* S Ireland
Young *607* W Uruguay
Youssoufia *414 prev.* Louis Gentil. W Morocco
Yovon *558 Rus.* Yavan. W Tajikistan
Yozgat *577* C Turkey
Ypres *see* Ieper
Yrendagüé *see* General Eugenio A. Garay
Ysabel Channel *458* channel connecting Pacific Ocean with Bismarck Sea
Yssel *see* IJssel
Ysyk-Köl *see* Balykchy
Yuan Jiang *see* Red River
Yüanlin *555 Jap.* Inrin.W Taiwan
Yucatan Channel *210, 403 Sp.* Canal de Yucatán. Channel connecting the Gulf of Mexico and Caribbean Sea
Yucatán, Península de *403 Eng.* Yucatan Peninsula. Peninsula of SE Mexico
Yugoslavia *630-633* officially Federal Republic of Yugoslavia, *SCr.* Jugoslavija, Savenzna Republika Jugoslavija. Country of S Europe comprising former Yugoslav republics of Serbia and Montenegro, divided into 210 admin. units (dtricts, opstina). ❖ Belgrade
Yukon *170* river of Canada and USA
Yukon Territory *170* territory of NW Canada
Yumbe *584* NW Uganda
Yumen *186 var.* Yu-men, Laojunmiao. Gansu, C China
Yuna *226* river of E Dominican Republic
Yundum *261* W Gambia
Yungki *see* Jilin
Yung-ning *see* Nanning
Yunnan *187 var.* Yun-nan. Province of SW China
Yurev *see* Tartu
Yuscarán *288* S Honduras
Yü Shan *555* mountain of C Taiwan
YüShan Shanmo *555* mountain range of C Taiwan
Yuty *460* S Paraguay
Yuxari Äskipara *110* W Azerbaijan
Yuzhno-Sakhalinsk *485 prev.* Vladimirovka, *Jap.* Toyohara. Ostrov Sakhalin, SE Russian Federation
Yuzhnyy Bug *see* Pivdennyy Bug
Yuzhou *see* Chongqing
Yverdon *546 var.* Yverdon-les-Bains, *Ger.* Iferten. W Switzerland
Yylanly *581 prev.* Il'yaly, *var.* Il'jaly. N Turkmenistan

Z

Zaandam *429* C Netherlands
Żabbar *395* SE Malta
Zabīd *627* W Yemen
Zabid, Wādī *627* dry watercourse of W Yemen
Zabré *157 var.* Zabéré. S Burkina
Zabrze *471 Ger.* Hindenburg. S Poland
Zacapa *278* E Guatemala
Zacatecas *403* C Mexico
Zacatecoluca *235* S El Salvador
Zadar *209 It.* Zara. W Croatia
Zafer Burnu *see* Apostolos Andreas, Cape
Zafra *530* SW Spain
Zagazig *230 var.* Az Zaqāzīq. N Egypt
Zaghouan *573 var.* Zaghwān. N Tunisia
Zagny *290* river of N Hungary
Zagreb *209 Ger.* Agram, *Hung.* Zágráb. ❖ of Croatia, N Croatia
Zāgros, Kuhhā-ye *307 Eng.* Zagros Mountains. Mountains of Iran
Zagros Mountains *see* Zāgros, Kuhhā-ye
Zāhedān *307 var.* Zahidan. E Iran
Zahlé *364 var.* Zaḥlah. C Lebanon
Ẓahrān *506* S Saudi Arabia
Zaire *see* Congo River
Zaječar *630* E Serbia, Yugoslavia
Zakataly *see* Zaqatala
Zakhidnyy Buh *see* Bug
Zākhō *310 var.* Zākhū. N Iraq
Zákynthos *273 It.* Zante, *prev.* Zákinthos. Island of W Greece
Zalaegerszeg *290* W Hungary
Zalău *480 Ger.* Zillenmarkt, *Hung.* Zilah. NW Romania
Ẓalim *506* C Saudi Arabia
Zalingei *536 var.* Zalinje. W Sudan
Zambezi *635* W Zambia
Zambezi *88, 419, 423, 423, 635 var.* Zambesi, *Port.* Zambeze. River of southern Africa
Zambezi Escarpment *636* slopes of N Zimbabwe
Zambia *634-635* officially Republic of Zambia, *prev.* Northern Rhodesia. Country of Central Africa divided into 9 admin. units (provinces). ❖ Lusaka
Zamboanga *466* Mindanao, S Philippines
Zamora *228* S Ecuador
Zamora *531* NW Spain
Zamzam, Wādī *371* dry watercourse of NW Libya
Zanderij *538* NE Suriname
Zanga *see* Hrazdan
Zangezur Range *98, 110 Arm.* Zangezuri Lerrnashght'a, *Az.* Zängäzur Silsiläsi, *Rus.* Zangezurskiy Khrebet. Mountain range of Armenia and Azerbaijan
Zanjān *307 var.* Zenjan, Zinjan. NW Iran
Zante *see* Zákynthos
Zanzibar *560* Zanzibar, Tanzania
Zanzibar *560* island of E Tanzania
Zapadna Morava *630* river of C Serbia, Yugoslavia
Zapadno-Sibirskaya Ravnina *484 Eng.* West Siberian Plain. Large plain of C Russian Federation
Zapadnyy Bug *see* Bug
Zapadnyy Sayan *485 Eng.* Western Sayans. Mountain range of C Russian Federation
Zapátoca *195* N Colombia
Zaporizhzhya *586 Rus.* Zaporozh'ye, *prev.* Aleksandrovsk. SE Ukraine
Zaqatala *110 Rus.* Zakataly. NW Azerbaijan
Za Qu *see* Mekong
Zara *see* Zadar
Zarafshon *610 Rus.* Zarafshan. C Uzbekistan
Zarafshon *558 Rus.* Zeravshan. W Tajikistan
Zaragoza *531 Eng.* Saragossa. NE Spain
Zaranj *77* SW Afghanistan
Zárate *95 prev.* General J.F. Uriburu. E Argentina
Zaraza *619* NE Venezuela
Zarcero *206* C Costa Rica
Zarghūn Shahr *77* SE Afghanistan
Zaria *440* C Nigeria
Zarzis *573 var.* Jarjīs. SE Tunisia
Žatec *216* NW Czech Republic
Zawīlah *see* Zuwaylah
Zāwiyat al Mukhaylá *371* NE Libya
Zawr, Jāl az *354 var.* Jal az-Zor. Ridge of NE Kuwait
Zaysan, Ozero *338 Kaz.* Zaysan Köl. Lake of E Kazakhstan
Zayyq *see* Ural
Zealand *see* Sjælland
Żebbuġ *395* C Malta
Zeebrugge *127* NW Belgium
Ẕefat *317 Ar.* Safad. N Israel
Zē-i Bādīnān *see* Great Zab
Zeila *see* Saylac
Zeist *429* C Netherlands
Żejtun *395* E Malta
Zelimai *368* N Liberia
Žemaičių Aukštumas *376* physical region of NW Lithuania
Zémio *179* E Central African Republic
Zempléni-hegység *290* mountain range of NE Hungary
Zengg *see* Senj
Zenica *140* C Bosnia & Herzegovina
Zenjan *see* Zanjān
Zenne *see* Senne
Zenshū *see* Chŏnju
Zeravshan *558, 610 Uzb.* Zarafshon. River of Tajikistan and Uzbekistan
Zeravshan *see* Zarafshon
Zeroud, Oued *573 var.* Zeroud, Wādī Zurūd. Dry watercourse of N Tunisia
Zêzere *474* river of C Portugal

Zgharta *364* N Lebanon
Zhambyl *see* Taraz
Zhanaozen *338* *Rus.* Novyy Uzen'. *Kaz.* Zhangaözen. W Kazakhstan
Zhangaözen *see* Zhanaozen
Zhangaqazaly *see* Novokazalinsk
Zhangdian *see* Zibo
Zhangjiakou *187* *var.* Zhang-chia-k'ou, Changkiakow, *prev.* Wanchuan, *Eng.* Kalgan. Hebei, NE China
Zhanjiang *187* *var.* Chan-chiang, *Cant.* Tsamkong, *Fr.* Fort-Bayard. Guangxi, S China
Zhdanov *see* Mariupol'
Zhejiang *187* *var.* Chekiang, Che-chiang. Province of E China
Zhengzhou *187* *var.* Ch'eng-chou, Chengchow, *prev.* Chenghsien. Henan, C China
Zhetiqara *see* Dzhetygara
Zhezkazgan *338* *prev.* Dzhezkazgan, *Kaz.* Khezqazghan. C Kazakhstan
Zhitomir *see* Zhytomyr
Zhlobin *122* E Belarus
Zhob *451* river of C Pakistan
Zhodino *see* Zhodzina
Zhodzina *122* *Rus.* Zhodino. N Belarus
Zhongshan *90* Chinese research station of Greater Antarctica, Antarctica
Zhytkavichy *122* SE Belarus
Zhytomyr *586* *Rus.* Zhitomir. NW Ukraine
Žiar nad Hronom *519* *var.* Sväty Kríž nad Hronom, *Ger.* Heiligenkreuz, *Hung.* Garamszentkereszt. W Slovakia
Zia Town *368* E Liberia
Zībāk *77* NE Afghanistan
Zibo *187* *var.* Zhangdian, Chang-tien. Shandong, E China
Zielona Góra *471* *Ger.* Grünberg in Schlesien. W Poland
Zienzu *368* C Liberia
Zigong *187* Tzekung. Sichuan, SW China
Ziguinchor *510* SW Senegal
Zilah *see* Zalău
Žilina *519* *Hung.* Zsolna, *Ger.* Sillein. NW Slovakia
Zillah *371* C Libya
Zillenmarkt *see* Zalău
Ziller *106* river of W Austria
Zillertaler Alpen *106* *It.* Alpi Aurine, Zillertal Alps. Mountain range of Austria and Italy
Zilupe *362* *Ger.* Rosenhof. E Latvia
Zimbabwe *636-639* officially Republic of Zimbabwe, *prev.* Rhodesia (1964-1979) part of Central African Federation (1953-1963). Country of Africa divided into 8 admin. units (provinces). ❖ Harare
Zimmi *514* S Sierra Leone
Zinder *439* S Niger
Ziniaré *157* C Burkina
Zinjibār *627* SW Yemen
Zinov'yevsk *see* Kirovohrad
Zion *494* E Nevis, St Kitts & Nevis
Zipaquirá *195* C Colombia
Zipser Neudorf *see* Spišská Nová Ves
Zitundo *419* S Mozambique
Ziway Hāyk' *243* *var.* Lake Zway. Lake of C Ethiopia
Ziyamet *215* *var.* Leonarisso. NE Cyprus
Zlatarsko Jezero *630* lake of SW Serbia, Yugoslavia
Zlaté Moravce *519* *Hung.* Aranyosmarót. SW Slovakia
Zletovo *381* NE FYR Macedonia
Zlín *216* *prev.* Gottwaldov. SE Czech Republic
Zlīṭan *371* *var.* Zliṭān. N Libya
Znaim *see* Znojmo
Znojmo *216* *Ger.* Znaim, S Czech Republic
Zóbuè *419* NW Mozambique
Zoetermeer *429* W Netherlands
Zólyom *see* Zvolen
Zomba *385* S Malawi
Zombor *see* Sombor
Zongo *203* N Dem. Rep. Congo (Zaire)
Zonguldak *576* NW Turkey
Zorzor *368* N Liberia
Zou *132* river of S Benin
Zouar *180* N Chad
Zouérat *398* *var.* Zouérate, Zouîrât. N Mauritania
Zrenjanin *630* *prev.* Petrovgrad, Veliki Bečkerek, *Ger.* Grossbetschkerek, *Hung.* Nagybecskerek. N Serbia, Yugoslavia
Zsily *see* Jiu
Zsolna *see* Žilina
Zsupanya *see* Županja
Zueila *see* Zuwaylah
Zuénoula *326* C Ivory Coast
Ẓufār *448* *Eng.* Dhofar. Administrative region of SW Oman
Zug *546* C Switzerland
Zugdidi *262* W Georgia
Zugspitze *265* mountain of Austria and Germany
Zuid *538* river of SW Suriname
Zuid-Beveland *429* island of SW Netherlands
Zuider Zee *see* IJsselmeer
Zuisan *see* Sŏsan
Zumbo *see* Vila do Zumbo
Županja *209* *Hung.* Zsupanya. NE Croatia
Zürich *546* *Eng.* Zurich. N Switzerland
Zürichsee *546* *Eng.* Lake Zurich. Lake of NE Switzerland
Żurrieq *395* S Malta
Zurūd, Wādī *see* Zeroud, Oued
Zuwārah *371* NW Libya
Zuwaylah *371* *var.* Zawīlah, *It.* Zueila. SW Libya
Zvishavane *636* *prev.* Shabani. S Zimbabwe
Zvolen *519* *Ger.* Altsohl, *Hung.* Zólyom. C Slovakia
Zvornik *140* E Bosnia & Herzegovina
Zway, Lake *see* Ziway Hāyk'
Zwedru *368* E Liberia
Zwettl *106* N Austria
Zwickau *265* SE Germany
Zwijndrecht *429* SW Netherlands
Zwolle *429* NE Netherlands
Zyryanovsk *338* E Kazakhstan

Acknowledgments

Dorling Kindersley would like to express their thanks to the following individuals, companies and institutions for their help in preparing this atlas:

Additional Cartography
Advanced Illustration (Congleton, UK)
Andrew Bright
Cosmographics (Watford, UK)
Malcolm Porter
Swanston Publishing (Derby, UK)
Andrew Thompson

Design
Boyd Annison, Icon Solutions (Chesham, UK) *for Macintosh consultancy and chart templates*
Bruno Maag, Dalton Maag (London, UK) *for font consultancy and production*

Research and Reference
Dr D Alkhateeb, Organization of Petroleum Exporting Countries (OPEC, Vienna, Austria)
Amnesty International (London, UK)
Caroline Blunden
CNN International (New York, USA)
Dataquest Europe SA (Paris, France)
CSL Davies
Department of Trade and Industry Export Market Information Centre (London, UK)
The Flag Institute (Chester, UK)
Foreign and Commonwealth Office (London, UK)
Alexander Fyges-Walker
Christel Heideloff, Institute of Shipping Economics and Logistics (Bremen, Germany)
International Bank for Reconstruction and Development (World Bank, Washington, DC, USA)
International Committee of the Red Cross (ICRC, Geneva, Switzerland)
International Civil Aviation Organization (ICAO, Montreal, Canada)
International Criminal Police Organization (INTERPOL, Lyon, France)
International Institute for Strategic Studies, for information from *The Military Balance* (London, UK)
International Boundaries Research Unit, University of Durham
Institute of Latin American Studies, University of London (London, UK)
Intermediate Technology Development Group (Rugby, UK)
Chris Joseph, United States Travel and Tourism Administration (USTTA, London, UK)
Latin American Bureau (London, UK)
Patrick Mahaffey, Ohio European Office (Brussels, Belgium)
Peter Mansfield
Robert Minton-Taylor
National Meteorological Library and Archive (Bracknell, UK)
Oil and Gas Journal (Houston, Texas)
Organization for Economic Cooperation and Development (OECD, Paris, France)
Penal Reform International (London, UK)
Matt Ridley
Screen Digest (London, UK)
William Smith, Chicago Sun-Times (Chicago, USA)
Tourism Concern (London, UK)
United Nations Crime Prevention and Criminal Justice Branch (UNCPC, Vienna, Austria)
United Nations Development Programme (UNDP, New York, USA)
United Nations Environment Programme (UNEP, Nairobi, Kenya)
United Nations Food and Agriculture Organization (UNFAO, Rome, Italy)
United Nations International Labour Organization (UNILO, Geneva, Switzerland)
United Nations Population Fund (UNFPA, New York, USA)
Westminster Reference Library (London, UK)
World Conservation Monitoring Centre (Cambridge, UK)
World Health Organization (WHO, Geneva, Switzerland)
World Tourism Organization (Madrid, Spain)

The many embassies, High Commissions, airports, national information and tourist offices in London and around the world.

Picture Credits

t=top, b=below, a=above, l=left, r=right, c=center

Agence France Presse: Victor Drachev 123bcr; Hoang Dinh Nam 358bcr; **Ancient Art & Architecture Collection:** 44bcr; 45bl; 45cr; 47tc; G Tortoli 45tcb; **Arcaid:** P Mauss Esto 598bc; **Art Archive:** 44bl; 49bl; 49cr; 51tcl; **Aspect Picture Library:** 202tr; Brian Seed 418c; D Bayes 370bl; Fiona Nichols 302tr; **Associated Press AP:** 243bcr; AFP 415bcr; Aaron Favila 467crl; Guilherme Venancio 475bcr; Hans Edinger 267br; Michel Spingler 254bcr; Humberto Pradera/Agencia Estado 149cb; Bullit Marquez 191bl; Jan Bauer 269cb Alexander Zemlianichenko 488cb; **Bridgeman Art Library, London/New York:** Hermitage, St Petersburg 46bc; Lauros - Giraudon / Château de Malmaison 48bcr; National Maritime Museum, London 47br; Private Collection 48bcl; **D Donne Bryant Stock Picture Agency:** 461tc; Byron Augustin 436tr; **Dale Buckton:** 594br; **Camera Press:** A Pucciano 95cr; F Goodman 649bca; H Andrews 627bcr; S Smith 243bcl; T Charlier 607bl; **The J Allan Cash Photolibrary:** 55tl; 106c; 116bc; 146br; 149tl; 168tr; 171tr; 239tr; 289tc; 306tr; 318br, 337cr; 342bl; 383tc; 386c; 438bc; 440tr; 451bc; 474tr; 566bc; **Bruce Coleman Ltd:** 498bl; B&C Calhoun 174bc; Dr MP Kahl 94tr; F Prenzel 104tc; Gerald Cubitt 88tr; Gerald Cubitt 242bc; Gordon Langsbury 260bc; J Fry 511tc; J Jurka 542bc; K. Maj 470c; Kim Taylor 515tr; L Lee Rue 91tl; LC Marigo 279tc; M Berge 396tr; MPL Fogden 462ca; O Langrand 370tr; P Davey 214bc; S Prato 272bc; **Colorific:** J Polleross / JB Pictures 78br; M Kreiner 54cl; M Rogers 536tr; Sandro Tucci 159bl; **Comstock:** 194bc, 24tl, 535tc; Tor Eigeland 399tc; **Corbis UK Ltd:** AFP 387bcl; Bettmann 146car, 231bcr, 555tcr; Bob Krist 642br; Francoise de Mulder 141bc; Jack Fields 648bl; Jack Fields 650bl; James L Amos 647tr; Miki Kratsman 486br; Nik Wheeler 175tc; Franz-Marc Frei 259cb; Peter Wilson 325cb; Joseph Sohm 603bl; **James Davis Travel Photography:** 144bl; 145tl; 218c; 248bc; 328bc; 379tl; 390tr; 401tc; 411tl; 428bc; 432bc; 493tc; 494bl; 496bl; 502tr; 550bc; 558tr; 586tr; 601tr; 626bl; 643cr; Prisma 86cla; Prisma / Schwarz 226tr; S Begawan 151tl; S Thingeyjar 295tc; World View - Fototheek Amsterdam 177tc; **Mary Evans Picture Library:** 47bl, 47trb; **Chris Fairclough Colour Library:** 51cr; 375tl; 572br; **Robert Harding Picture Library:** 76tr; 180c; 225tl; 271tc; 280bl; 291tr; 310tr; 334bl; 356bc; 449tc; 466tr; 480tr; 484tr; 501tc; 513tc; A Woolfitt 114bc; C Martin 264bc; C Rennie 580ca; D Hughes 257bc; Explorer 377tc; Explorer / Roy 110tr; F Dubes 148bl; Frerck / Odyssey 402tr; G Hellier 217tr; G Hellier 518tr; G Roli 444tr; Gascoine 610bl; P Craven 252tr; Photri 222ca; R Rainford 593tl; Rosehaven Management Ltd 653cr; Sassoon 134cb; Sassoon 262cl; **Paul Harris Photography:** Paul Harris Photography 491bl; **Hulton Getty:** 50bcr; 51br; 53br; **Robert Hunt Library:** 53tc; **Hutchison Library:** 136bl; 369tc; 596bc; 636tr; Andrew Hill 634bc; Bernard Gérard 259bc; Christine Pemberton 210tr; J Henderson 284ca; JG Fuller 650bcr; L Taylor 484bl; M Macintyre 568ca; Robert Francis 560tr; Trevor Page 524ca; **Image Bank:** 394bl; A Rippy 186tr; G Jung 576tr; GA Rossi 646bl; M Beebe 209cl; ME Newman 322tr; P Trummer 230tr; T Madison 187br; **Images Colour Library:** 426bl; **Image Select:** Ann Ronan 42bc; **Impact Photos:** A le Garsmeur 412ca; Alain leGarsmeur 175bl; Ben Edwards 450tr; C Penn 584tr; G-J Norman 354tr; J Arthur 526tcr; Mark Henley 188tr; Robin Lubbock 234tr; Ben Edwards 301bl; Lionel Derimais 335bl; B Babarov/Vika 489bl; **David King Collection:** 55tcb **Magnum:** H Cartier-Bresson 53tcb; **Panos Pictures:** B Tobiasson 327bc; Chris Stowers 331bl; D Hulcher 358tr; Jeremy Hartley 156bc; Marc French 287tc; Morris Carpenter 365bc; Neil Cooper 130tr; R Giling 538tr; S Sprague 160tr; Sean Sprague 136c; Penny Tweedie 105tc; Michael Harvey 149cl; John Miles 190tr;.JC Tordai 318cl; 335tc; 488tr; 597cb; 602bl; **Pa News Photo Library:** 445cr; AFP 419cbl; **Popperfoto:** 51trb; 52br; 55bl; AFP / Armand 54br; David Mercado / Reuters 137crl; Will Burgess / Reuters 105bl; Reuters 269cl; Sunil Malhorta / Reuters 301tc; Jeremy Piper / Reuters 102bcr; John Cobb / Reuters 343tr; Kamal Kishore / Reuters 298crb; Official U.S. Air Force Photo 55cr; Oleg Popov / Reuters 153bcr; **Popperfoto / Reuters**: Toshiyuki Aizawa 332bc; Peter Andrews 637cr; Simon Baker 433tlb; Denis Balibouse 203cl; Russell Boyce 594cra; Andreas Comas 95cbr, 415bcl; Bogdan Cristel 481cr; Jack Dabaghian 551br; Dimitar Dilkoff 153bcl; Larry Downing 601bl; Gleb Garanich 587tr; Marcus Gyger 107bcl; Mohamed Hammi 573tcr; HO 618tr; Lee Jae-Won 351bcr; Hyungwon Kang 601bcr; Sergei Karpukhin 487bcl; Kamal Kishore 298cbr; John Lehmann 172crb; Francois Lenoir 127bcr; Havakuk Levison 316bcr; David Loh 623tcl; Christinne Muschi 172cbr; Alexander Natruskin 487bl; Patrick de Noirmont 159bcl; Enny Nuraheni 303bcr; Pilar Olivares 463tcl; V Hugo Ordonez 137cr; Charles Platiau 254crb; Hrvoje Polan 291bcr; Romero Ranoco 467cr; Molly Riley 266bcr; Oswaldo Rivas 555tr; Henry Romero 403bcl; Jayanta Shaw 623tl; Ruben Sprich 547cr; STR 451tr, 577car; Ray Stubblebine 249tcr, 291bcl, 577trb, 607bcl; Eriko Sugita 332cbr; Sukree Sukplang 563tr; Supri 303bcl; Susumu Takahashi 332cbl; Martin Thomas 182tr; Goran Tomasevic 631bcl; Pierre Virot 476bcl; Haydn West 594tcr; Kimberly White 618tcr; Darren Whiteside 165tcr; Rick Wilking 600bcr, 600br; Shamil Zhumatov 339bcr; **Reuters:** 123bcl, 146tcr; 507br; **Rex Features:** 116tcbr; 172bcr; 188br; 249tr; 254cb; 273tcr; 273tr; 339bcl; 481cbr; 486bcr; 516bl; 526tr; 543tcl; 587tcr; 594tr; 594trb; 611bc; 627bcl; Andy Hernandez 488cl, J Sutton Hibbert 597ct; Paul Brown 602cr; David Hartley 219tr; F Stevens 211bcl; Farnood 307tcr; Ken McKay 531tr; Sipa-Press 77tcr; Sipa-Press 83bcl; Sipa-Press 127bcl; Sipa-Press 188bcr; Sipa-Press 311c; Sipa-Press 316br; Sipa-Press 429tcl; Sipa-Press 445c; Sipa-Press 563tcr; Sipa-Press 631bcr; Sipa-Press 645bl; Tony Kyriacou 351bcl; Torregano 419cl; **Harry Smith Collection:** 46clb; **South American Pictures:** Jevan Berrange 206br; P Dixon 456tr; T Morrison 606tr; **Sovfoto/Eastfoto:** 652br; **Frank Spooner Pictures:** 53bl; 83bl; 322bc;343tcr; 543tr; A Denize 371tcr; A Sassaku 146tr; Alain Morvan / Gamma 547c; Alexis Duclos 182tcr; Bob Stern / Liason 241tr; C Hires 551bcr; C Poulet 647cr; Eric Vandeville 195tr; Tim Crosby / Gamma - Liaison 602ct; Gamma 195tcr; Gamma 471tr; Gamma / B Iverson 231bcl; Gamma / E de Keerle 471tcr; Gamma / F Apesteguy 507bcr; Gamma / Iliona - Figaro Magazine 113tc; Gamma / K Al Arab 573tcl; Gamma / L Chaperon 266cbr; Gamma / N Jallot 408tr; Gamma / Najer 387bcr; Gamma / Xinhua 188bcl; Georges Merillon 441bcl; KJ Eddy 107bcl; L Anticoli 322cbr; Liason / Peterson 441bcr; Liason / Markel 637c; N Sagansky 203cr; P Perrin 311cr; Patrick Piel 266bra; Reglain 165tr; Victoria Brynner 451tcr; **Tony Stone Images:** 179bc; 198tr; 352bl; 444br; A Cassidy 300br; Alan Kearney 182bc; Alan Smith 362c; C Waite 592bc; D Armand 172tr; D Hanson 562bl; D Schultz 50bl; Dennis Stone 342tr; G Allison 605bl; H Kurihara 268bc; J Pragen 616tr; Joe Cornish 315bc; Marcus Brooke 158tr; O Benn 93tc; 277tr; P Chesley 406ca; Penny Tweedie 384bc; R Evans 152tr; R. Everts 415tr; R Smith 102tr; R Smith 229tl; S Egan 530tr; S Egan 546tr; Steven Rothfeld 393tc; **Sygma:** Baldev 348ca; R Reuter 502bl; **Telegraph Colour Library:** 100tr; Ford Motor Company Ltd 52clb; **Topham Picturepoint:** 133tc; 236tr; 318br; 325cl; 371tr; 433cal; 478bc; 487tr; 504bc; 642c; Keystone 322cbl; **Trip:** 506bl; G Spenceley 380tr; T Goodman 283tc; V Shuba 122c; V Sidoropolev 338tr; **World Pictures:** 83cla; 320bl; 422ca; 554tr; **Zefa Picture Library**: 80bc; 120bl; 200ca; 526bl; 570bc; 618bl; Everts 630ca; F Lanting 142tr; Streichan 266bl.

NOTES

This book has its own website. For the very latest information, visit
www.dk.com/world-desk-reference

NOTES

This book has its own website. For the very latest information, visit
www.dk.com/world-desk-reference

NOTES

This book has its own website. For the very latest information, visit
www.dk.com/world-desk-reference

NOTES

This book has its own website. For the very latest information, visit
www.dk.com/world-desk-reference